U0063101

80000词
英汉英英汉英词典

ENGLISH-CHINESE ENGLISH-ENGLISH
CHINESE-ENGLISH
DICTIONARY OF 80000 WORDS

李德芳　姜兰　主编

·全新版·

NEW EDITION

四川辞书出版社

图书在版编目(CIP)数据

80000 词英汉英英汉英词典：全新版 / 李德芳，姜兰主编. —成都：四川辞书出版社，2024.1

ISBN 978-7-5579-1414-1

Ⅰ.①8… Ⅱ.①李…②姜… Ⅲ.①英语－词典②词典—英、汉 Ⅳ.①H316

中国国家版本馆 CIP 数据核字(2023)第 218153 号

80000 词英汉英英汉英词典 全新版

80000 CI YINGHAN YINGYING HANYING CIDIAN QUANXINBAN

李德芳　姜　兰　**主编**

责任编辑 / 李薇薇　雷　敏　袁一丹
封面设计 / 成都编悦文化传播有限公司
责任印制 / 肖　鹏
出版发行 / 四川辞书出版社
地　　址 / 成都市锦江区三色路 238 号
邮政编码 / 610023
印　　刷 / 成都国图广告印务有限公司
开　　本 / 850 mm×1168 mm　1/32
印　　张 / 42
版　　次 / 2024 年 1 月第 1 版
印　　次 / 2024 年 1 月第 1 次印刷
书　　号 / ISBN 978-7-5579-1414-1
定　　价 / 59.80 元

出版说明

Preface

本词典是一部内容丰富的英汉英英汉英词典，适合大、中学生及具有中级或中级以上英语水平的各类读者使用，既可以用作查阅的工具，也可以作为翻译或写作的帮手。

本词典的英汉部分收录词汇丰富，基本上涵盖了我国教育部颁布的《初中英语新课程标准》词汇表、《高中英语新课程标准》词汇表和《大学英语教学大纲》词汇表中所列词汇。本词典还针对英语学习和英语教学的实际需要，列举了实用的短语和派生词，有助于读者从多层次、多角度学习、掌握和运用英语词语。

本词典的英英部分用英语解释英语单词，不仅可以让读者正确地理解每个单词和词组的含义，同时又能让读者准确恰当地进行运用，为其在英语写作或会话时选择更为贴切、精当的词语提供诸多可能。

本词典的汉英部分，除一般词和大量新词外，还收入一些常见的方言、成语、谚语及自然科学的常用词语。词条的选择注重科学性和规范性，英语释义地道准确，原汁原味，简明易懂。所收词条涵盖面广，在日常学习、生活与社交活动中使用频率高，搭配能力强，可供读者口头交际和书面表达时使用。

随着时代的发展，人们使用的语言中不断涌现出反映时代面貌的新词语或新义项。因此在本词典编纂过程中，编纂人员选收了部分在报刊、影视、网络等媒体上使用频率较高的新词语，使本词典具有鲜明的时代特色。

参加本词典编纂工作的人员，既有权威的语言学专家，又有长期在英语教学第一线工作的经验丰富的教师，这为本词典的高质量提供了可靠的保障。然而，由于时间所限，词典中也难免会存在疏漏或不足。我们欢迎广大读者不吝赐教，以便使本词典更加完善。

编　者

目　录

Contents

凡 例

Guide to the Use of the Dictionary

本词典由英汉、英英和汉英三部分组成。

英汉部分

1. 词条：单词用黑正体按字母顺序突出两个字母排列。拼写相近、词义相同的单词列为一条，如：analyze(-se)或 colo(u)r；拼写相同、词源和词义不同者，原则上另列词条，并在右上角标以1,2……数码。例中出现词条词用"～"代替，但词尾有变化的或词头大写的，则全词写出。
2. 注音：采用新版国际音标。主重音注在左上方，次重音注在左下方，单词的同一词性有不同发音的，同时放入斜括号内，用逗号分开，如：always /ˈɒlweɪz, ˈɔːlweɪz/。
3. 词性：用白斜体缩写形式表示，一个词的不同词性前冠罗马数字Ⅰ,Ⅱ,Ⅲ等。动词只写 *v.*，表示既可作及物也可作不及物动词；若写明 *vt.*，表示只作及物动词；写明 *vi.*，表明只作不及物动词。名词只写 *n.*，表示既可作可数也可作不可数名词，标有[C]表示只作可数名词，标有[U]表示只作不可数名词。
4. 屈折变化：不规则的动词和形容词、副词分别按过去式、过去分词、现在分词(如有不规则的)和比较级、最高级的顺序，注上音标，放入圆括号中；名词复数不规则的注明 *pl.* 后标出不规则形式，放入圆括号中。
5. 词义：多义词的不同义项用 ❶,❷,❸……排列。同一义项如有两个或两个以上的汉语释义时，意思相近的用逗号隔开，否则用分号隔开。

6. 派生词和短语：本词典的派生词用白正体，短语用黑体，短语有多义的分别用①，②，③……区别。短语中出现词条词用“～”代替。

英英部分

1. 词条：单词用黑正体按字母顺序排列。拼写相近、词义相同的单词列为一条，如 catalog(ue)或 neighbo(u)r；拼写相同、词源和词义不同者，原则上另列词条，并在右上角标以1，2……数码。例中出现词条词用“～”代替。
2. 词性：用白斜体缩写形式表示，一个词的不同词性前冠罗马数字Ⅰ，Ⅱ，Ⅲ等。动词写作 *v.*，名词写作 *n.*。
3. 词义：多义词的不同义项用❶，❷，❸……排列。同一义项如有两个或两个以上释义时，用分号隔开。

汉英部分

1. 所收条目分单字条目和多字条目，并按汉语拼音字母顺序排列。
2. 单字条目及多字条目若有多个义项，用❶，❷，❸……标注顺序，并在序号后先提供用法提示，再提供英文译文。
3. 某些单字条目为多音字时，在单字条目的下方，以“另见……”标示其另外的读音。
4. 例证中出现词条词用“～”代替。可用作替换或省略的词则放在圆括号之内。
5. 条目的释义与例证之间加冒号“：”；例证如有不同的英文译文，则用分号“；”隔开；例证与例证之间用分号“；”隔开。

略 语 表

Abbreviations Used in the Dictionary

adj. adjective 形容词

art. article 冠词

[C] countable noun 可数名词

int. interjection 感叹词

num. number 数词

prep. preposition 介词

sb. somebody 某人

[U] uncountable noun 不可数名词

vi. intransitive verb 不及物动词

adv. adverb 副词

aux. *v*. auxiliary verb 助动词

conj. conjunction 连词

n. noun 名词

pl. plural 复数

pron. pronoun 代词

sth. something 某事物

v. verb 动词

vt. transitive verb 及物动词

英汉词典

English-Chinese Dictionary

ENGLISH-CHINESE DICTIONARY

A

A a

a / eɪ,ə / ,**an** / æn,ən / *art*. ❶一(个、本、件、把……) ❷某个:A Mr Smith came to see you this morning. 今天早上有一位史密斯先生来看你。❸任何一个:A dog is a faithful animal. 狗是忠实的动物。

aback / əˈbæk / *adv*. 向后,朝后:be taken ~(被……) 吓了一跳;大吃一惊

abacus / ˈæbəkəs / *n*. [C] (*pl*. abaci / ˈæbəsaɪ /或 abacuses / ˈæbəkəsɪz /)算盘:use (operate) an ~ 打算盘

abandon / əˈbændən / *vt*. 抛弃;遗弃:~ one's family (one's country,one's post,a ship) 抛弃家人(背弃祖国,放弃职位,弃船)

abate / əˈbeɪt / *vt*. 减少,减弱;减轻,减退:~ sb. 's enthusiasm 挫伤某人的热情/drugs to ~ pain 镇痛药 —*vi*. 减小,减弱;减轻,减退:The wind ~d in fury. 风力减弱了。

abbey / ˈæbi / *n*. [C]大修道院;大寺院

abbreviation / əˌbriːvɪˈeɪʃn / *n*. ❶[U]缩写;简略 ❷[C] 缩写词

abdomen / ˈæbdəmən / *n*. [C]腹(部)

abduct / æbˈdʌkt / *vt*. 诱拐;绑架;劫持:~ a child for ransom 诱拐儿童以勒索赎金 派 abduction *n*.

abhor / əbˈhɔː(r) / *vt*. (-horred;-horring)憎恶;厌恶;痛恨:We all ~ cruelty to animals. 我们都憎恨虐待动物。

abide / əˈbaɪd / (abode 或 abided) *vi*. ❶遵守(法律、诺言、决定等):~ disciplines 遵守纪律 ❷坚持(意见等) —*vt*. 忍受,容忍;顶住:Nobody can ~ such a cruel person. 没有人能够容忍这种残忍的人。派 abidance *n*.

ability / əˈbɪləti / *n*. ❶[U] 能力:the ~ to speak English 说英语的能力/One's writing ~ grows by practice. 一个人的写作能力靠实践来提高。❷才干;才智;本事:He is a man of abilities. 他是一位有才干的人。

abject / ˈæbdʒekt, æbˈdʒekt/ *adj*. ❶凄惨的;绝望的:an ~ failure (frustration) 惨败(痛创) / a beggar so ~ that he plucks at the sleeves of passers-by 可怜巴巴地拉过路人衣袖的乞丐 ❷卑鄙的,可鄙的;卑劣的;卑怯的:an ~ coward (liar) 可鄙的懦夫(说谎者) / What an ~ performance! 多么卑劣的行为! 派 abjectly *adv*. ;abjectness *n*.

ablaze / əˈbleɪz / *adj*. &*adv*. 着火(的);熊熊燃烧的:set the logs ~点燃木柴

able / ˈeɪbl / *adj*. ❶有能力的:an ~ man 有才干的人/ **be ~ to do sth.** 有能力(办法、机会)做某事:She was ~ to catch an early bus. 她能赶上早班公共汽车。❷有才干的;聪明的;能干的:The woman is particularly ~. 那个女子

A

特别能干。

abnormal /æbˈnɔːml/ *adj.* 不正常的;反常的:It is absolutely ~ behavior. 这完全是反常的行为。派 abnormally *adv.*

aboard /əˈbɔːd/ *adv.* & *prep.* 在(车、船、飞机)上;上(车、船、飞机):The captain is ~. 船长在船上。/Welcome ~! 请上船(上车,上飞机)!

abolish /əˈbɒlɪʃ/ *vt.* 废除(法律、旧风俗、旧习惯);消灭(战争等):The bad customs have been ~ed. 这些不良风俗业已废除。派 abolition *n.*

abominable /əˈbɒmɪnəbl/ *adj.* ❶讨厌的;可恶的,可憎的:Shall we pass by this ~ practice? 难道我们能对此卑劣的行为置之不理吗? / Any food that savours of onions is ~ to me. 我对任何带洋葱味儿的食品都感到厌恶。❷(天气、食物等)糟糕透顶的,极坏的:The weather was ~. 天气糟透了。/ the ~ food in this hotel 这家饭店里难以下咽的饭菜 ❸粗劣的,低劣的:They used to live in ~ conditions. 他们以前住在恶劣的环境里。派 abominably *adv.*

aboriginal /ˌæbəˈrɪdʒɪnəl/ Ⅰ *adj.* ❶土著居民的,具有土著人特征的:~ customs in Australia 澳大利亚土著风俗 ❷土著的;最初的,原始的:The Indians are the ~ inhabitants of America. 印第安人是美洲的土著居民。Ⅱ *n.* [C]土著居民;(常作 **A-**)澳大利亚土著居民派 aboriginally *adv.*

aborigine /ˌæbəˈrɪdʒɪni/ *n.* [C] ❶土著居民:The Inuit are among the ~s of North America. 因纽特人属北美土著居民。❷(常作 **A-**)澳大利亚土著居民

abort /əˈbɔːt/ Ⅰ *vi.* ❶流产,小产:She ~ed when she was four months pregnant. 她怀孕 4 个月后流产了。❷(计划等)中途失败,夭折;中辍:Without their help all further plans must inevitably ~. 没有他们的鼎力相助,所有进一步的计划都必然夭折。/ The fighter ~ed from its mission. 战斗机中途取消了飞行任务。Ⅱ *n.* [C]中途失败;中止;(飞行任务等的)中辍:Any malfunction of the power plant will cause an ~ and loss of the missile. 导弹的动力设备发生任何故障,都会导致其中途失败并损毁。

abortion /əˈbɔːʃn/ *n.* 流产;堕胎:Her mother asked her to have an ~ at once. 她母亲要求她立即做人工流产。

abound /əˈbaʊnd/ *vi.* ❶大量存在:a stream in which trout ~ 一条多鳟鱼的溪流 / Rock ~s under the soil. 土壤下面多岩石。❷富于;盛产;多:~ in opportunities 有很多机会/ ~ with rain 多雨

about /əˈbaʊt/ Ⅰ *prep.* 关于;在周围:What do you know ~ him? 关于他,你知道些什么? / He was tired of walking ~ the street. 他讨厌在街上走来走去。Ⅱ *adv.* 周围;到处;大约:She must be somewhere ~. 她一定在附近某处。/ **be ~ to** 正要;将要:She is ~ to start. 她正要动身。

above /əˈbʌv/ Ⅰ *prep.* 在……之上;超过:~ sea level 高出海平面;海拔/ We flew ~ the clouds. 我们在云层之上飞行。/~ **all** 首先;尤其是:And ~ all, don't tell him about it. 最重要的是不要将此事告诉他。Ⅱ *adv.* 在上面:Her bedroom is just ~. 她的卧室就在上面。

aboveboard /əˌbʌvˈbɔːd/ *adj.* & *adv.* 公开的(地),光明正大的(地),坦率的(地):Their actions are open and ~. 他

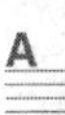

们的行为是光明正大的。/ Be open and ~ with me. 对我要坦诚相见。

abrade /əˈbreɪd/ *vt.* 磨损，磨蚀；擦毛……的表面：Glaciers ~ rocks. 冰川磨蚀岩石。/ The skin on Tom's knee was ~d by his fall. 汤姆膝盖上的皮跌跤时擦破了。

abrasion /əˈbreɪʒən/ *n.* ❶[U]磨损；磨耗；刮擦：All coins will, by wear or ~, become thinner. 所有的硬币因磨损都会变薄。❷[C]擦伤处；磨损处：The least ~ of the skin is likely to result in an ulcer. 皮肤稍有擦伤很可能导致溃疡。

abreast /əˈbrest/ *adv.* & *adj.* ❶(同方向)并排(的)；并肩(的)：The soldiers marched three ~. 士兵们三人一排并肩前进。/ The street is so narrow that two can barely walk ~. 这条街很窄，两人很难并排行走。❷保持与……并列；了解……的最新情况：be (keep) ~ of recent scientific developments 跟上科学的最新发展

abridge /əˈbrɪdʒ/ *vt.* (在保留主要内容的同时)精简……的篇幅，删节，节略：~ a novel 缩写一部小说

abroad /əˈbrɔːd/ *adv.* 在国外；到国外：at home and ~ 国内外/ study ~ 留学/ His brother went ~ last year. 他的兄弟去年出国了。/ Her father has returned from ~. 她父亲已从国外回来。

abrupt /əˈbrʌpt/ *adj.* ❶突然的；出其不意的：~ departure 突然的离去 ❷陡峭的；险峻的：~ slope 陡峭的山坡 ❸粗鲁的；无礼的：~ manner 粗鲁的态度；唐突的举止 ❹(讲话、文章等)不连贯的；支离破碎的

absence /ˈæbsəns/ *n.* 缺席；不在：an ~ of two years 离开两年/ I didn't notice his ~. 我没注意到他缺席。

absent Ⅰ/ˈæbsənt/ *adj.* ❶缺席的；不在的：Three members of the class are ~ today. 班上今天有三人缺席。/ He's been ~ from work all week. 他整整一个星期没有上班。❷不存在的；缺乏的：Snow is ~ in some countries. 有些国家从不下雪。❸心不在焉的；茫然的；恍惚的；走神的：an ~ stare 茫然的凝视 / His look had grown ~, as if he were calling up memories. 他脸上一副心不在焉的神情，好像想起了什么往事似的。Ⅱ/əbˈsent/ *vt.* 缺席；退出：~ **oneself** 使缺席；使退出：She had ~ herself for an entire day. 她一整天都没有露面。/ The club attempted to induce its members to ~ themselves from the bar. 俱乐部极力鼓励成员不要涉足酒吧。派 absently *adv.*

absolute /ˈæbsəluːt/ *adj.* 绝对的；完全的：~ majority 绝对多数/~ truth 绝对真理/ A child has ~ trust in his mother. 孩子绝对信赖母亲。

absolutely /ˈæbsəˌluːtli/ *adv.* ❶完全地；彻底地；非常，极其：an ~ fascinating piece of work 一部绝妙的作品 / You're ~ right. 你完全正确。❷(口语)一点不错，完全正确；当然，对极了：—I trust that we are still brothers-in-arms. —Absolutely! —我想我们仍然是战友吧？—那当然！

absolve /əbˈzɒlv/ *vt.* ❶赦免，宽恕；使免受惩罚：~ sb. from (any) blame 使某人免受责备 ❷解除……的责任(或义务、履行诺言等)

absorb /əbˈsɔːb/ *vt.* ❶吸收(水、热、光等)：Plants ~ energy from the sun. 植物从太阳吸取能量。❷吸引；使全神贯注于：**be ~ed in** 被……迷住；专心于：

A

He is ~ed in study. 他专注于学习。

absorbent /əbˈsɔːbənt/ Ⅰ *adj.* 能吸收(水、光、热等)的：~ paper towels 吸水纸巾 Ⅱ *n.* [C]吸收剂；吸收物：Tons of high-powered ~ are needed to clean up the oil spill. 需用数吨吸收剂才能将这溢出的油污收拾干净。派 absorbency *n.*

abstain /əbˈsteɪn/ *vi.* ❶(自制地)戒除，戒绝；有意回避(与 from 连用)：When the cigarettes were passed, he ~. 香烟递来时，他谢绝了。/I ~ from all alcohol. 凡是含酒精的饮料，我一概不喝。❷弃权(不投票)：He ~ed (from voting) in the election. 选举中他弃权了。/ There were six votes in favour, two against, and two ~ing. 有 6 票赞成，2 票反对，2 票弃权。派 abstainer *n.*

abstract Ⅰ/ˈæbstrækt/ *adj.* 理论上的；抽象的；深奥的：~ art 抽象艺术/ ~ concept 抽象概念/ His plan was too ~ to put into operation. 他的计划太抽象，无法付诸实施。Ⅱ/ˈæbstrækt/ *n.* ❶摘要；概括：~s information 文摘信息/ ~s paper 文摘报 ❷抽象；抽象概念 Ⅲ/æbˈstrækt/ *vt.* ❶提取；抽取：~ metal from ore 从矿石中提取金属 ❷摘录……的要点：write an ~ of ... 写……的摘要 派 abstraction *n.*

abstraction /æbˈstrækʃən/ *n.* ❶[C]抽象概念：Good and evil are ~s. “好”和“坏”都是抽象概念。❷[U]出神；心不在焉，分心：wear a look of ~ 脸上一副心不在焉的神情 / He pretended to be listening to me but his ~ was obvious. 他装作专心听我讲，不过一眼就可以看出他走神儿了。

abstruse /æbˈstruːs/ *adj.* 难懂的；深奥的；晦涩的：~ legal documents 深奥的法律文件 / His theories are always considered ~ by beginners. 对初学者来说，他的学说总是非常玄奥，难以理解。派 abstrusely *adv.* ；abstruseness *n.*

absurd /əbˈsɜːd/ *adj.* 不合理的；荒唐可笑的；愚蠢的：an ~ idea 荒谬的想法/ an ~ novel 荒诞小说/ an ~ suggestion 荒谬的建议 派 absurdity *n.*

abundance /əˈbʌndəns/ *n.* [U]丰富；充裕；大量：live in ~生活富裕/ year of ~ 丰年

abundant /əˈbʌndənt/ *adj.* 丰富的；充裕的：China is ~ in (with) natural resources. 中国的自然资源丰富。派 abundantly *adv.*

abuse /əˈbjuːs/ Ⅰ *vt.* ❶滥用；虐待：Don't ~ your power. 不要滥用你的权力。❷辱骂 Ⅱ *n.* ❶滥用；虐待：~ of children 虐待儿童 ❷辱骂：personal ~人身攻击

abysmal /əˈbɪzməl/ *adj.* ❶深渊(似)的；无底的；深不可测的：an ~precipice 万丈峭壁 ❷极坏的，糟糕透顶的：work in ~ conditions 在极其恶劣的条件下工作 派 abysmally *adv.*

academic /ˌækəˈdemɪk/ Ⅰ *adj.* 大学的；高等教育的；学术的：~ authority 学术权威/ ~ circles (world)学术界/ ~ degree 学位/ ~ exchange 学术交流/ ~ paper 学术论文/ ~ research 学术研究 Ⅱ *n.* [C]大学学生；大学教师；学究式人物

academician /əˌkædəˈmɪʃən/ *n.* [C] 院士

academy /əˈkædəmi/ *n.* [C] 高等专科学校；研究院；学院；学会：a military ~ 陆军军官学校/ an ~ of fine arts 美术学院/an ~ of music 音乐学院/ the Chinese ~ of Sciences 中国科学院

accede /ækˈsiːd/ *vi.* ❶答应，同意；应

允，依从(与 to 连用)：~ to a demand 答应要求❷就职，就任；即位；继承(与 to 连用)：~ to an office 就职

accelerate /əkˈseləˌreɪt/ *vt.* ❶使加快，使加速：the open door policy intended to ~ economic development 旨在加速经济发展的开放政策 ❷促进：~ world peace 促进世界和平 —*vi.* ❶加快，增速：This building's decay has ~d due to neglect. 由于无人看管，这座楼房破败得更快了。❷增长，增加：Stock prices surged yesterday as volume ~d sharply. 昨天随着交易额的急剧上升，股票价格猛涨。派 acceleration *n.*

accelerator /ækˈseləˌreɪtə(r)/ *n.* [C] (汽车等的)加速踏板，油门踏板，油门

accent /ˈæksent/ *n.* [C] ❶口音；腔调：He speaks English with an American ~. 他讲英语带有美国口音。❷重音；重读：In the word "begin", the ~ is on the second syllable. "begin"这个词的重音在第二个音节上。

accept /əkˈsept/ *vt.* 接受；承认；答应：I ~ed his presents. 我接受了他送的礼物。/ The boy ~ed full responsibility for breaking the window. 这男孩对打坏窗户之事负全责。

acceptable /əkˈseptəbəl/ *adj.* ❶值得接受的；可以接受的：Is this ~ to you? 这一点你能接受吗？/ No compromise would be ~. 绝不能接受任何妥协。❷勉强够格的；差强人意的，尚可的：Performances varied from excellent to ~. 演出从出类拔萃到差强人意不等。❸可忍受的；可容许的；承受得住的：behaviour that is not socially ~ 为社会所不容的行为 派 acceptability *n.*；acceptably *adv.*

acceptance /əkˈseptəns/ *n.* ❶接受，接收；领受；验收：~ a test 对一项试验进行验收 ❷承认；认可：meet with general ~ 得到广泛的承认

access /ˈækses/ *n.* [U] ❶通路；入口：This is the only ~ to the library. 这是到图书馆的唯一通路。❷有进入(接触、接近、会面的)机会(或权利)/**gain** (**get**, **have**) ~ **to** 有……机会(或权利)：Students must gain ~ to books. 学生们必须有读书的机会。

accessible /əkˈsesəbəl/ *adj.* ❶可接近的；可进入的：This desert island is ~ only by helicopter. 这座荒岛只有乘直升机方可抵达。❷可使用(或得到)的：Computers will be cheap enough to be ~ to virtually everyone. 计算机将会便宜到几乎人人都买得起。派 accessibility *n.* ；accessibly *adv.*

accessory /əkˈsesəri/ Ⅰ *n.* [C] ❶附件；附属品：auto (car) accessories 汽车配件 ❷同谋；帮凶：an ~ to a crime 从犯 Ⅱ *adj.* ❶附属的；附加的：an ~ school 附属学校 ❷同谋的

accident /ˈæksɪdənt/ *n.* [C] 意外事故；偶发事件：a traffic ~ 交通事故/ an unfortunate ~不幸事故/ He had a bad ~. 他出了大事故。/**by** ~偶然；意外地：I met him in the street by ~. 我偶然在街上遇见了他。**without** ~安全地：The night passed without ~. 一夜平安无事。派 accidental *adj.*

acclaim /əˈkleɪm/ Ⅰ *v.* 欢呼；喝彩：warmly ~ the success 热烈欢呼取得成功 Ⅱ *n.* [U]欢呼；喝彩；称赞

accommodate /əˈkɒmədeɪt/ *v.* ❶容纳；接纳；提供；供给，供应：~ sb. with lodging 给某人提供住宿 ❷适应；迁就；调节：~ oneself to new conditions 适应新情况

A

accommodation /əˌkɒməˈdeɪʃn/ *n.* ❶招待设备;膳宿;住宿: seek ~s 寻找住处 ❷适应;调节: the ~ of a man to his surroundings 人对环境的适应

accompany /əˈkʌmpəni/ *vt.* ❶陪伴: He always accompanied his mother wherever she went. 他母亲走到哪里,他就陪伴到哪里。❷为……伴奏: The pianist accompanied her singing. 她唱歌,钢琴家为她伴奏。

accomplice /əˈkɒmplɪs, əˈkʌmplɪs/ *n.* [C]共犯,同案犯: an ~ in (to) a crime 一桩罪行的同案犯 / He was an ~ with (of) Bugotu in the bank robbery. 在抢劫银行一案中他是布戈图的共犯。

accomplish /əˈkʌmplɪʃ/ *vt.* 完成;达到;实现: ~ one's purpose 达到某人的目的 / The task will not be ~ed in one generation. 这任务不是一代人所能完成的。派 accomplishment *n.*

accomplished /əˈkʌmplɪʃt/ *adj.* 熟练的;精通的;有造诣的;有才艺的: an ~ surgeon (scholar) 技术精湛的外科医生(造诣颇深的学者) / be ~ at (in) dancing and singing 能歌善舞

accord /əˈkɔːd/ *n.* [U] ❶一致;协调/**in ~ with** 与……一致: His words are in complete ~ with his thoughts. 他心口如一。❷自愿;主动: I did it of my own ~. 我是自愿做这件事的。

accordance /əˈkɔːdəns/ *n.* 依照,依据/ **in ~ with (to)** 根据,依照;与……一致: The order will be executed in ~ with the terms agreed. 订单将按商定的条款执行。/ I am in ~ with him in this matter. 在这件事情上,我和他的意见是一致的。

according /əˈkɔːdɪŋ/ *adv.* 按照;根据/ ~ **to** 根据……: from each ~ to his ability 各尽所能/ The books are placed on the shelves ~ to authors. 这些书是按作者姓名排序摆在书架上的。

accordingly /əˈkɔːdɪŋli/ *adv.* ❶(通常用于句首或句中)因此,所以;于是: I was told to hurry; ~, I came by train. 叫我要快点来,所以,我乘火车赶来了。❷(通常用于句末)照着;相应: These are the rules, act ~. 这些都是规定,照着办就是了。

accordion /əˈkɔːdiən/ *n.* [C]手风琴: play the ~ 拉手风琴

accost /əˈkɒst/ *vt.* (尤指贸然地)上前跟……攀谈(或搭讪): A stranger ~ed him, asking for directions. 一位陌生人走上来向他问路。

account /əˈkaʊnt/ Ⅰ *v.* ❶说明原因;解释: ~ **for** 解释: He could not ~ for his absence from school. 他无法解释他缺课的原因。❷以为;认为: He ~s himself lucky to be alive after that accident. 他认为在那次事故中能活下来是他的幸运。Ⅱ *n.* [C] ❶账户;账目: examine an ~ 检查账目/ hand in one's ~ 交账/ open an ~ 开账户/ settle the ~ 结账/ current ~ 活期存款账户/ fixed ~ 定期存款账户 ❷描写,叙述;报道: a false ~ 虚假报道/ a trustworthy ~ 一篇内容可靠的报道 ❸重要性;价值: **take sth. into ~** 考虑;重视: You must take this into ~. 你必须考虑到这一点。**on ~ of** 因为;由于;归于: She could not come on ~ of her illness. 她因病不能来。**on no (not on any) ~** 决不;毫不;无论如何不: I will not do such a thing on any ~. 无论如何我也不会做这样的事。

accountable /əˈkaʊntəbl/ *adj.* ❶负有责任的;应做解释(或说明)的: Each person is ~ for his own work. 人人都

应该对自己的工作负责。/ I am ~ to my superiors for my actions. 我应该为自己的行为对上司负责。❷可解释(或说明)的;可理解的:It is a very ~ obstinacy. 这是一种完全可以理解的固执态度。派 accountability *n.* ; accountably *adv.*

accountant / əˈkaʊntənt / *n.* [C]会计;会计师:certified public ~ 持证会计师/ work as ~ 做会计师

accounting / əˈkaʊntɪŋ / *n.* [U]会计学;清算账目:~ control 会计监督/ the public ~ firm 会计事务所/ ~ statement 会计报表

accumulate / əˈkjuːmjʊleɪt / *v.* 积累;积聚;堆积:~ a fortune 积累财富/~ funds for ... 为……积累资金 派 accumulator *n.*

accumulation / əˌkjuːmjʊˈleɪʃn / *n.* [U]积累;积蓄:~ of knowledge 知识积累

accuracy / ˈækjərəsi / *n.* [C]精确;精确度:test the ~ of ...检测……的精确度/ with ~ 精确地

accurate / ˈækjərət / *adj.* 精确的;准确的:His information is quite ~. 他的消息相当准确。派 accurately *adv.*

accusation / ˌækjʊˈzeɪʃn / *n.* [U]指控,控告;指责,谴责:by false ~根据诬告/ eyes full of ~满是指责的目光

accuse / əˈkjuːz / *vt.* 控告;指责:falsely ~ sb. 诬告某人/ ~ **sb. of sth.** 就某事控告某人:We ~d him of his immoral conduct toward her. 我们指责他对她的不道德行为。

accustom / əˈkʌstəm / *vt.* 使习惯:~ sb. to (doing) sth. 使某人习惯于……/~ oneself to the environment 适应环境

accustomed / əˈkʌstəmd / *adj.* ❶通常的,惯常的;Pauline went to her ~ restaurant for lunch. 波林到她常去的那家餐馆里吃午饭。❷习惯了的;适应了的(与 to 连用):She is ~ to working late. 她习惯于工作到深夜。/The boy was ~ to have his own way. 这男孩子任性惯了。

ace /eɪs / *n.* [C] ❶(纸牌、骰子的)一点;A 牌:~ of spades (hearts, diamonds, clubs) 黑桃(红桃、红方、梅花)A 牌 ❷(开赛车或飞机的)王牌驾驶员;空中英雄;能手;专家:football ~ 足球球王

ache / eɪk / Ⅰ *n.* [C]疼痛:She had ~s and pains all over. 她感到周身疼痛。Ⅱ *vi.* 痛:My head ~s badly. 我头痛得厉害。

achieve / əˈtʃiːv / *vt.* 实现;完成;达到:~ success 成功/ ~ one's purpose 达到目的/All this cannot be ~d overnight. 所有这一切不是一夜之间就能实现的。

achievement / əˈtʃiːvmənt / *n.* ❶[U]完成;达到 ❷[C]成就;成绩;功绩:His ~s are worthy of record. 他的功绩值得记载。/ heroic ~s 英雄业绩/ scholarly ~s 学术成就/ scientific and technological ~s科技成果

acid / ˈæsɪd / Ⅰ *adj.* ❶酸性的:an ~ solution 酸溶液/ ~ rain 酸雨 ❷酸的,酸味的:Lemons are an ~ fruit. 柠檬是一种酸味水果。Ⅱ *n.* 酸

acknowledge / əkˈnɒlɪdʒ / *v.* ❶承认:~ defeat 认输/ He openly ~d his fault. 他公开承认了他的过失。❷致谢:~ with thanks 感激;答谢

acknowledgement / əkˌnɒˈlɪdʒmənt / *n.* ❶承认:make an ~ of ... 承认…… ❷感谢:in ~ of one's help 为答谢某人的帮助

acorn / ˈeɪkɔːn / *n.* [C]橡子;橡树果实

acquaint /əˈkweɪnt/ *vt.* 使熟悉；使了解：I ~ed him with my intention. 我让他了解我的意图。/**be (get) ~ed with** 对……熟悉：I am not personally ~ed with him. 我个人和他并不熟悉。

acquaintance /əˈkweɪntəns/ *n.* 相识，熟悉；熟人：make the ~ of sb. 结识某人 / I have a nodding ~ with her. 我和她是点头之交。

acquire /əˈkwaɪə(r)/ *v.* 学得（知识、技术）；获得（财产、权利）：~ a knowledge of 学到（获得）……的知识 派 acquirement *n.*

acquisition /ˌækwɪˈzɪʃn/ *n.* ❶[U]获得，取得；占有：The ~ of knowledge is a social process. 知识的获取是一种社会性的活动。❷[C]获得物；增添的人（或物）：Our museum's latest ~ is a Picasso. 我们博物馆最近增添了一幅毕加索的画。/He is a valuable ~ to the team. 他是该球队不可多得的新队员。

acquit /əˈkwɪt/ *vt.* (-quitted; -quitting) ❶宣告……无罪；无罪释放：John Campell was ~ted on all charges. 约翰·坎贝尔被宣告在所控罪行上是无辜的。❷使（自己）做出某种表现；使（自己）履行（或完成）：He ~ted himself well at the interview. 面试时，他表现得不错。

acre /ˈeɪkə(r)/ *n.* [C] 英亩（合 4046.86 平方米）

acrid /ˈækrɪd/ *adj.* ❶（气味等）辛辣的，苦的；刺激的，呛人的：~ smoke from burning rubber 橡胶燃烧的呛鼻烟雾 ❷（言辞、性格等）刻薄的；讥讽的：an ~ disposition 刻薄的性格

acrimonious /ˌækrɪˈməʊnɪəs/ *adj.* （脾气、言辞、态度等）尖酸刻薄的；讽刺的；激烈的：an ~dispute 激烈的争论 / the ~struggle in the Senate to pass a budget resolution 为预算案在参议院得以通过而进行的一场激烈斗争

acrimony /ˈækrɪməni/ *n.* [U]（脾气、言辞、态度等的）尖刻；严厉；辛辣：attack sb. with great ~ 以极其激烈的言辞攻击某人

acrobat /ˈækrəbæt/ *n.* [C]杂技演员

acrobatics /ˌækrəˈbætɪks/ *n.* [U]（*pl.*）❶杂技；杂技表演：perform (do) ~ 表演杂技 ❷（用作单数）杂技技艺，杂技艺术：Her ~ is of Olympic standard. 她的杂技技艺是奥林匹克级的。❸（处理复杂或微妙事情的）巧妙手法；技巧

across /əˈkrɒs/ Ⅰ *prep.* ❶横过；穿过：~ the country 全国各地 ❷在……的另一边：There is a forest ~ the rive. 河对岸有一片森林。Ⅱ *adv.* 横过，穿过；从一边到另一边：I'll row you ~. 我将把你渡到河对岸去。

act /ækt/ Ⅰ *v.* 做；表演；起作用：His son ~ed badly in school. 他儿子在学校表现不好。/ She ~ed in this play. 她演过此戏。/ **~ as** 担任；扮演；充当：He ~ed as conductor. 他担任指挥。**~(up) on** 对……起作用；按照……行动：This medicine ~s on the heart. 这种药对心脏病有效。/ You should ~ on others' advice. 你应该按照别人的建议去做。**~ out** 表演；比画着表达：He tried to ~ out a story he had read. 他试图把读过的故事表演出来。Ⅱ *n.* [C] ❶举动；行为：He did another noble ~. 他又做了一件高尚的事。❷法令；条例

action /ˈækʃn/ *n.* [U] ❶行动；行为；活动：go into ~ 开始行动 / take ~ 采取行动 / in ~ 在活动；在运转 ❷作用：put out of ~ 使失去作用

activate / ˈæktɪveɪt / *vt.* 使活动;使激活:~ public opinion 活跃舆论 / be ~d by economic interests 为经济利益所驱使

active / ˈæktɪv / *adj.* ❶主动的;积极的;活跃的:~ defense 积极防御 / ~ remedy 速效药物 ❷在活动中的;现行的;现役的:~ volcano 活火山/ ~ capital 流动资本 / ~ military unit 现役军队

activist / ˈæktɪvɪst / *n.* [C] 积极分子

activity / ækˈtɪvəti / *n.* [C] 活动;所做的事情:reading activities 读书活动 / social activities 社会活动;社交活动 / terrorist activities 恐怖活动 / take part in an ~ 参加活动

actor / ˈæktə(r) / *n.* [C] 男演员:a celebrated ~ 名演员 / the best ~ 最佳男主角 / the best supporting ~ 最佳男配角

actress / ˈæktrəs / *n.* [C] 女演员:the best ~ 最佳女主角/ the best supporting ~ 最佳女配角

actual / ˈæktʃuəl / *adj.* 实际的;现实的:~ state 现状 / This is an ~ step. 这是一个实际的步骤。派 actually *adv.*

acupuncture / ˈækjupʌŋktʃə(r) / *n.* [U] 针刺;针刺疗法

acute / əˈkjuːt / *adj.* ❶尖锐的;敏锐的:~ angle 锐角 / ~ eyesight 敏锐的眼光 ❷剧烈的;严重的:~ pain 剧痛

ad / æd / *n.* (= advertisement)[C]广告

AD, A. D. (拉丁文 Anno Domini 的缩写)公元(放在年代之前或之后)

adage / ˈædɪdʒ / *n.* [C]谚语;格言

adapt / əˈdæpt / *v.* ❶使适应;使适合:She lacks the ability to ~ easily. 她的适应能力不太强。/ ~ **oneself to** 适应:Can you ~ yourself to the new job? 你能适应新工作吗? ❷改编;改写:~ a film from a novel 把小说改编成电影 派 adapter *n.*

add / æd / *v.* 加;添加;增加:Add five to nine. 把5与9相加。/~ **to** 补充;增添:That will only ~ to our difficulties. 那只会给我们增加困难。~ **up to** 总计达:The costs ~ed up to 20 million American dollars. 费用总计达2 000万美元。

addict Ⅰ / əˈdɪkt / *vt.* ❶使沉溺于:be ~ed to work 工作入迷 ❷使成瘾:be ~ed to smoking 吸烟成瘾 Ⅱ / ˈædɪkt /*n.* [C] 有瘾的人:a drug ~ 吸毒上瘾的人

addiction / əˈdɪkʃən/ *n.* ❶[U]瘾:helpless victims to drug ~ 无可救药的毒瘾受害者 ❷沉溺,入迷;嗜好,癖好(与 to 连用):overcome one's ~ to alcohol 克服贪杯的癖好

addition / əˈdɪʃn / *n.* [U]加法;增加/ **in ~ to** 除……之外:In ~ to English, he has to study a second foreign language. 除英语外,他还得学第二门外语。

additional / əˈdɪʃən(ə)l / *adj.* 附加的;追加的;另外的:~ investment 追加投资/ ~ tax 附加税

additive / ˈædətɪv / Ⅰ *n.* [C]添加剂;添加物;加法:food ~ 食品添加剂/ free from chemical ~ 无化学添加剂 Ⅱ *adj.* 添加的;附加的

address / əˈdres / Ⅰ *n.* [C] ❶住处;通信处:Can you tell me your ~? 你能告诉我你的住址吗? ❷演讲:The president made an ~ over the radio. 总统发表了广播演讲。Ⅱ *v.* ❶写地址:This letter was wrongly ~ed. 这封信的地址写错了。❷讲话;演讲

adept / ˈædept, əˈdept/ Ⅰ *adj.* ❶巧妙的;灵巧的:the ~ touch of the artist 那位画家巧妙的手法 ❷娴熟的,擅长的,内行的:an ~ table-tennis player 乒乓球

好手/ She is ~ in music. 她擅长音乐。Ⅱ*n*. [C]能手,内行,行家:an ~ in (at) philosophy 哲学大师 派 adeptly *adv*.; adeptness *n*.

adequacy /ˈædɪkwəsi/ *n*. [U]充分;足够;适合

adequate /ˈædɪkwət/ *adj*. ❶充分的;足够的;适当的:His wages are ~ to support four people. 他的工资足够养活四口人。/ take ~ measures 采取适当措施 ❷胜任的:Though a bit too old, he is ~ to the work. 虽然他年龄大了一点,但仍能胜任这份工作。派 adequately *adv*.

adhere /ədˈhɪə(r)/ *v*. ❶黏附:Wax ~s to the fingers. 蜡粘在手指上。❷坚持(与 to 连用):~ to one's ideas 坚持自己的观点/ He said he should ~ to the original plan. 他说他应该坚持原计划。

adherent /ədˈhɪərent/ *n*. [C]追随者,支持者,拥护者;信徒

adhesive /ədˈhiːsɪv/ Ⅰ*adj*. ❶黏性的;可黏着的:~ tape 黏胶带 ❷涂有黏性物质(如胶水等)的:an ~ label 带胶标签 / an ~ envelope 胶口信封 Ⅱ*n*. 黏合剂,黏结剂

adjacent /əˈdʒeɪs(ə)nt/ *adj*. ❶邻近的,毗连的(与 to 连用):the city square and the ~ streets 都市广场及其邻近街道/The house ~ to yours has been sold. 与你家毗邻的房子已经被卖掉了。❷紧接着的,相接触的:a map on an ~ page 紧接在前面(或后面)一页的地图

adjective /ˈædʒɪktɪv/ *n*. [C] 形容词

adjoin /əˈdʒɔɪn/ *vt*. 贴近,紧靠,与……毗连:Canada ~s the United States. 加拿大与美国接壤。/ a field ~ing to the highway 紧靠公路旁的田野 —*vi*. 毗连,邻近:The two lots ~. 两块土地相互毗连。派 adjoining *adj*.

adjourn /əˈdʒɜːn/ *v*. ❶暂停;休会:~ for an hour 休会一小时 ❷推迟;推算:~ a decision 推迟做出决定 派 adjournment *n*.

adjust /əˈdʒʌst/ *vt*. 调整;使适合:I must ~ my watch. 我必须将手表调一下。派 adjustable *adj*.; adjustor, adjuster *n*.

adjustment /əˈdʒʌstmənt/ *n*. [U]调整;调节;校准;校正:~ of exchange rate 汇率调整/~ of salary 工资调整/ ~ tax 调节税/ make a price ~ 调整价格

administer /ədˈmɪnɪstə(r)/ *v*. ❶管理;支配:~ a government department 管理一个政府部门 ❷执行;施行;实施:~ justice (laws)执法 派 administrator *n*.

administration /ədˌmɪnɪˈstreɪʃn/ *n*. [U] ❶管理;经营:have experience in ~ 有行政管理经验/ a master of business ~ (MBA)工商管理硕士 ❷管理部门;行政机关;政府

administrative /ədˈmɪnɪstrətɪv/ *adj*. 行政的;管理的:simplify the ~ structure 精简机构/ ~ objective management 行政目标管理/ ~ interference 行政干预

admirable /ˈædmərəbl/ *adj*. 可钦佩的;令人羡慕的;极好的:His honesty is ~. 他的诚实令人钦佩。

admiration /ˌædməˈreɪʃn/ *n*. [U]羡慕,赞赏;钦佩:win a high ~ 享有盛誉/ I was struck with ~. 我十分佩服。

admire /ədˈmaɪə(r)/ *vt*. 钦佩;赞美,夸奖:I ~ your frankness. 我钦佩你的坦率。/ We ~ him for his bravery. 我们佩服他的勇敢。

admission /ədˈmɪʃn/ *n*. ❶[U](进入、入学、入会的)许可:~ line 录取分数线/ ~ notice 录取通知书/ ~ office 招生办公室/~ quote 录取名额/ ~ ticket

入场券/ ~ by ticket 凭票入场/ An ~ is limited to the invited guests. 入场仅限于应邀来宾。❷[C]承认;自白:by one's own ~ 据某人自己承认

admit /ədˈmɪt/ *vt.* (-mitted;-mitting) ❶允许进入:He opened the door and ~ted me into the room. 他打开门让我进屋。❷承认:He finally ~ted himself beaten. 他终于认输了。

admittance /ədˈmɪt(ə)ns/ *n.* [U]准许进入(或加入);进入(或加入)权:She had ~ to all the theatres free of charge. 她享有免费进入各剧场的权利。

admonish /ədˈmɒnɪʃ/ *vt.* ❶警告:The policeman ~ed him not to drive so fast. 警察警告他不要把车开得太快。/ He ~ed her of obligation. 他提醒她应尽的义务。❷责怪;告诫:~ sb. about excessive noise 责怪某人太吵 / ~ sb. for being lazy 告诫某人不要偷懒 派 admonishment *n.*

adolescence /ˌædəˈles(ə)ns/ *n.* [U]青少年时期;青春期:Adolescence is a beautiful time in one's life. 青少年时期是人生的美好时期。

adolescent /ˌædəˈles(ə)nt/ Ⅰ *adj.* 青春期的 Ⅱ *n.* [C]青少年:~ psychology (psychology of the ~) 青春期心理

adopt /əˈdɒpt/ *vt.* ❶采纳;采取;采用:~ a bill 通过议案/ ~ a measure 采取措施 / I'll ~ your teaching method in my school. 我将在我校采用你的教学方法。❷收养:one's ~ed son (daughter) 某人的养子(养女)/ ~ a child 收养孩子

adoption /əˈdɒpʃn/ *n.* ❶采纳;采取:move the ~ of the bill 提议;通过议案 ❷收养:put a child up for ~ 把孩子送给人抚养

adore /əˈdɔː(r)/ *v.* ❶崇拜(上帝);敬慕:~ sb. for ... 因为……而崇拜某人 ❷很喜欢:~ one's wife (parents) 疼爱妻子(父母) 派 adoration *n.*; adoringly *adv.*

adorn /əˈdɔːn/ *vt.* 装饰,装点;佩带;装扮:They ~ed their hair with garlands of flowers. 她们头上戴着花环。/a book ~ed with numerous excellent illustrations 配有大量精美插图的书籍

adult /ˈædʌlt,əˈdʌlt/ Ⅰ *n.* [C]成年人:He is an ~ now. 他现在已是一个成年人了。Ⅱ *adj.* 成年的;成熟的:~ education 成人教育/ ~ examination for higher education 成人高考

adulthood /ˈædʌlthʊd/ *n.* [U]成年:enter one's ~ 进入成年期 / in one's ~ 在成年时期

advance /ədˈvɑːns/ Ⅰ *v.* 推进;进展:They ~d toward the castle. 他们朝着城堡前进。Ⅱ *n.* 前进;增长:You can't stop the ~ of aging. 人总是要老的。/ **in ~** 预先,事先;在前面:Everything has been fixed in ~. 一切都预先安排好了。

advanced /ədˈvɑːnst/ *adj.* 先进的;高级的:~ English 高级英语/Shanghai is an technologically ~ city in China. 上海是中国一个技术先进的城市。

advancement /ədˈvɑːnsmənt/ *n.* ❶[U]前进;进展;促进:for the ~ of peace 为了促进和平 / further (speed) one's professional ~ 加快业务上的成长 / gain ~ in one's work 在工作方面取得进展 ❷[C]提高;增加:a rapid (slow) ~ in pay 工资的迅速(缓慢)增长

advantage /ədˈvɑːntɪdʒ/ *n.* ❶[C]益处;优点,优势:Each has his ~s. 各有各的优点。❷[U]利益;好处:It has no ~ to me at all. 这对我没有任何好处。/**take ~ of** 利用;乘机:I can't take ~ of your

A

good nature. 我不能因你性情善良而占你的便宜。派 advantageous *adj.*

advent / ˈædvent, ˈædv(ə)nt / *n.* ❶[C](重要人物或事物的)出现;来临,到来:the ~ of a new era 新时代的来临/at the ~ of spring 在春天到来时 ❷(常作 A-)基督降临节(圣诞节前包括四个星期日的节期)

adventure / ədˈventʃə(r) / *n.* [U]冒险;奇遇:I've read the novel *The Life and Strange Adventures of Robinson Crusoe.* 我已读过小说《鲁滨孙漂流记》。派 adventurous *adj.*

adverb / ˈædvɜːb / *n.* [C] 副词

adverbial /ædvɜːbɪəl/ Ⅰ *adj.* 副词的;状语的 Ⅱ *n.* 状语

adversary / ˈædvəsəri / *n.* [C]敌手;对手:a worthy (well-matched) ~ 劲敌

adverse / ˈædvɜːs / *adj.* ❶逆的;相反的;敌对的:~ circumstances 逆境/ ~ current 逆流/ ~ psychology 逆反心理 ❷不利的;有害的:be ~ to sb. 不利于某人

adversity / ədˈvɜːsɪti/ *n.* ❶[U]逆境;厄运;(尤指经济方面的)窘境:A friend will show his true colors in times of ~. 患难见真情。/ They continued to fight in the face of ~. 面对困境,他们继续战斗。❷[C](常作复数)灾祸;危难;不幸遭遇:the prosperities and adversities of the life 人生的盛衰荣枯 / the adversities of old age 老年的种种苦楚

advertise(-ze) / ˈædvətaɪz / *v.* 登广告,为……做广告

advertisement / ədˈvɜːtɪsmənt, ˌædvəˈtaɪzmənt/ *n.* [C]广告;公告;启示:If you want a job, put an ~ in the newspaper. 如果你想找工作,在报上登一则广告好了。

advertising(-zing) / ˈædvətaɪzɪŋ / Ⅰ *n.* [U]广告业;(总称)广告;登广告;广告宣传:outdoor ~ 户外(室外)广告 / TV ~ 电视广告 Ⅱ *adj.* 广告的:~ affairs 广告业务

advice / ədˈvaɪs / *n.* [U] 劝告,忠告;意见:seek ~ from sb. 向某人请教 / If you take his ~ and study harder, you'll pass the examination. 要是你听他的劝告,更加努力学习,你就会通过考试。

advisable / ədˈvaɪzəbəl/ *adj.* 适当的;合理的,明智的:The doctor does not think it ~ for you to drink. 医生认为你不宜饮酒。/ It's undoubtedly ~ to ring up first to make an appointment. 先打电话预约无疑是明智的。派 advisability *n.* ; advisably *adv.*

advise / ədˈvaɪz / *v.* 劝告,忠告;建议:Which book would you ~ me to buy? 你建议我买哪本书?

adviser(-or) / ədˈvaɪzə(r) / *n.* [C] 劝告者;顾问:~ on economic policy 经济政策顾问 / technical ~ 技术顾问

advocate / ˈædvəkeɪt / Ⅰ *n.* [C]提倡者;辩护者;鼓吹者:consumer ~ 消费者权益维护者 Ⅱ *vt.* 提倡;拥护;主张;鼓吹:firmly ~ social security 坚决提倡社会保障

advocator / ˈædvəkeɪtə / *n.* [C]提倡者;拥护者

aerial / ˈeərɪəl / Ⅰ *adj.* 空中的;空气的;航空的:~ chart 航空图/ ~ attack 空袭/ ~ transportation 空运 Ⅱ *n.* [C](=antenna)(无线电的)天线

aerobics / eəˈrəʊbɪks / *n.* [U]健身操;健美操;韵律操

aeroplane / ˈeərəpleɪn / *n.* (=airplane)[C]

(英)飞机

aerosol / ˈeərəsɒl / *n.* [C]烟;雾;烟雾剂

aerospace / ˈeərəˌspeɪs / Ⅰ *n.* [U]航空航天空间,宇宙空间 Ⅱ *adj.* 航空航天(空间)的;航空航天器的;航空航天器制造的:~ research 航空航天研究

aesthetic(al) / iːsˈθetɪk(əl) / *adj.* 美学的;审美的;艺术的:~ education 美育(美学教育)/ ~ value 审美价值

aesthetics / iːsˈθetɪks / *n.* [U]美学

afar / əˈfɑː(r) / *adv.* 在远处;从远处;到远处;遥远地:roam ~远游/Explorers went ~ in search of new lands. 探险家们去遥远的地方探寻新大陆。/**from** ~ 自远方,从远方:She grinned at me from ~. 她老远就冲我咧嘴一笑。

affair / əˈfeə(r) / *n.* [C]事情:It's an ~ of great importance. 这是一件很重要的事情。/ ~s of state 国家大事/ foreign ~s 外交事务/ home ~s 内政 / public ~s 公事/ private ~s 私事/ ~s review 时事评论

affect / əˈfekt / *v.* ❶影响:Whatever she says will not ~ my decision. 无论她说什么都不会影响我的决定。❷感动;打动:His speech ~ed the audience deeply. 他的讲话深深地打动了听众。/ All the people in the room were ~ed to tears. 屋里所有的人都感动得流下了眼泪。

affection / əˈfekʃn / *n.* 爱;感情:the ~ of parents for their children 父母对儿女的爱

affectionate / əˈfekʃənɪt/ *adj.* 慈爱的;充满深情的;温柔亲切的:~ kisses 深情的吻/ A child needs ~ parents. 孩子需要慈爱的双亲。/ She is very ~ to (towards) her children. 她很爱自己的孩子。/ They are ~ to (with) each other. 他们相互爱慕。派 affectionately *adv.*

affiliate Ⅰ /əˈfɪlɪˌeɪt/ *vt.* ❶使紧密联系:The two clubs were ~d with each other. 这两个俱乐部联系密切。❷使隶属(或附属)于;使成为……的分支机构;使成为会员:The parent company ~d a new store. 母公司又接纳了一家商店为其附属机构。/~ oneself with (to) a political party 加入某一政党 —*vi.* 发生联系;参加(与 with 连用):refuse to ~ with an organization 拒绝加入某个组织 Ⅱ /əˈfɪlɪət/ *n.* [C]成员;附属(或隶属)机构,分支机构:the establishment of bank ~ 银行分行的设立 派 affiliation *n.*

affirm / əˈfɜːm / *vt.* 断言;肯定;证实:~ one's judgement 证实某人的判断

affirmation / ˌæfəˈmeɪʃən/ *n.* ❶断言;肯定;确认:~ of human rights 对人权的确认 / A single nod implies an ~. 点一点头暗示肯定。❷[U]证实;批准 ❸[C](不经宣誓而做的)证词

affirmative / əˈfɜːmətɪv / *adj.* 肯定的:an ~ answer 肯定的答复

afflict / əˈflɪkt / *vt.* 折磨;使苦恼,使痛苦:The pangs of conscience ~ed him. 一阵阵良心的责备使他痛苦不已。/ She is continually ~ed by headaches. 她经常为头痛病所苦。

affluence / ˈæfluəns / *n.* [U]❶富裕;富足:live in ~生活优裕❷大量;丰富;充裕:~ of rain 大量的雨水

affluent / ˈæfluənt / *adj.* ❶富裕的;富足的:an ~ family 富裕的家庭/live in ~ times 生活在富足的年代 ❷大量的,充裕的,丰富的;富饶的:florid and ~ fancy 丰富多彩的想象力/a land ~ in natural resources 自然资源丰富的地区

afford / əˈfɔːd / *vt.* ❶买得起;负担得起:

A

He said he couldn't ~ a car. 他说他买不起汽车。❷提供；给予：I can hardly ~ the time for I'm very busy. 我很忙，抽不出时间。

afraid /əˈfreɪd/ *adj.* ❶害怕的：Don't be ~. 别害怕。/ She is ~ of dogs. 她怕狗。❷担心；唯恐：She was weak and ~ that she could not do the job. 她体弱，担心干不了这活儿。

Africa /ˈæfrɪkə/ *n.* 非洲

African /ˈæfrɪkən/ Ⅰ *adj.* 非洲的 Ⅱ *n.* [C] 非洲人

after /ˈɑːftə(r)/ Ⅰ *prep.* 在……之后；在后面：We shall leave ~ breakfast. 我们吃完早饭就走。/~ **a while** 过一会儿；不久；即刻：He will be here ~ a while. 他即刻就到。~ **all** 毕竟；到底；终归：After all, he is a boy of five. 毕竟，他只是一个五岁的孩子。Ⅱ *conj.* 在……以后：After his father died, he lived with his aunt. 他父亲死后，他就和婶婶住在一起。

afternoon /ˌɑːftəˈnuːn/ *n.* 下午；午后：this ~ 今天下午/ on Monday ~ 星期一下午 / have ~ tea 喝下午茶

afterward(s) /ˈɑːftəwəd(z)/ *adv.* 后来；以后：He told me ~that he had not enjoyed the film. 他事后告诉我，他并不喜欢那部影片。/ I decided to run away and explain ~. 我决定先离开，以后再解释理由。

again /əˈgeɪn/ *adv.* 又；再：Please say it ~. 请再说一遍。/ ~ **and** ~ 再三地；反复地：I warned him ~ and ~. 我一再警告他。**now and** ~ 时时：The couple quarreled now and ~. 这对夫妇时时吵架。**once** ~ 再一次：You may try it once ~. 你可再试一次。

against /əˈgeɪnst/ *prep.* 对着；紧靠着；逆；反对：The house is ~ the hospital. 房子在医院对面。/ He always advances ~ difficulties. 他总是迎着困难前进。/ They are ~ the plan. 他们反对这个计划。

age /eɪdʒ/ Ⅰ *n.* 年龄；岁数；时代：~ ago 很久以前 / for ~s 很长时间；长期/ over ~ 超龄/ under ~ 未成年/ What's your ~? 你多大年龄？/ **at the** ~ **of** 在……岁时：He went abroad at the ~ of eighteen. 他 18 岁出国。Ⅱ *v.* 变老；老化；成熟

aged /eɪdʒd/ *adj.* ❶年老的：an association of ~ people 老年人协会/ a society of the ~ 老年型社会 ❷(用作表语)……岁的：six students ~ 13 to 16 (years) 年龄从 13 到 16 岁的 6 名学生 ❸(酒、食品等)陈的，熟化的：~ whiskey 陈年威士忌

ag(e)ing /ˈeɪdʒɪŋ/ *n.* [U]变陈；成熟；老化：the ~ of the population 人口老化

agency /ˈeɪdʒənsi/ *n.* [C]经办；代办(处)；代理(处)：travel ~ 旅行社/ sales ~ 销售代理

agenda /əˈdʒendə/ *n.* (agendum 的单数)[C]议事日程；记事本：put (place) sth. on the ~ 把某事列入议事日程 /draw (make) up an ~ 制定议事日程

agent /ˈeɪdʒənt/ *n.* [C]代言人；代理人：the right of ~ 代理权/ the sole ~ 独家代理

aggravate /ˈægrəˌveɪt/ *vt.* ❶加重，加剧；使恶化，使更坏：~ an illness 使病情加重/A lie will only ~ you guilt. 撒谎只会使你错上加错。❷使恼火；激怒：The whispering in class ~s our teacher. 课堂上的窃窃私语使我们的老师很恼火。

aggregate Ⅰ /ˈægrɪgət/ *adj.* 聚合的；总

的,合计的:the rate of growth of ~ demand 总需求量的增长率/newspapers with an ~ circulation of 6 million 总发行量为 600 万份的报纸 Ⅱ/ 'ægrɪgət / *n.*[C]合计:He spent an ~ of fifteen years in various jails. 他在不同的监狱里总共待了 15 年。/**on** ~总共;作为整体:take things on ~从整体上把握事物 Ⅲ/ 'ægrɪˌgeɪt / *vt.* ❶总计达:The money collected will ~ $1,000. 募集到的款项总额达 1 000 美元。❷使聚集,使积聚:~ riches 积聚财富

aggression / ə'greʃn / *n.* [U] 侵略;侵犯:a war of ~ 侵略战争

aggressive / ə'gresɪv / *adj.* ❶攻击性的,侵略的;好与人争吵的:an ~ war 侵略战争 / an ~ weapon 进攻性武器 ❷有进取心的;积极的:an ~ salesman 有干劲的推销员

aggressor / ə'gresə(r) / *n.* [C] 侵略者;侵略国

aghast / ə'gæst, ə'gɑːst / *adj.* 惊呆的;惊骇的;惊愕的 He stood, with his mouth wide open, ~ with wonder. 他吓得目瞪口呆,站在那里摸不着头脑。

agile / 'ædʒaɪl / *adj.* ❶敏捷的;灵活的;活泼的:An acrobat has to be ~. 杂技演员必须身手敏捷。❷机敏的,头脑灵敏的:You need an ~ mind to solve puzzles. 破解谜语脑子要灵敏。

agitate / 'ædʒɪˌteɪt / *vt.* ❶搅动,搅拌;摇动,拨动:A mixer ~s the cement until it is ready to pour. 搅拌器搅拌水泥,直至可以用来灌注。/The hurricane winds ~d the sea. 阵阵飓风掀起惊涛骇浪。❷鼓动;煽动:~ strongly for a piece of legislation 极力鼓动支持一项法律

agony / 'ægəni / *n.* (肉体或心灵上极度的)痛苦;创痛:The accident victim spent hours in mortal ~ before dying. 事故的受害者临死前几个小时一直处于极度的痛苦之中。/The loss of her husband filled her with ~. 失去了丈夫,她痛不欲生。

ago / ə'gəʊ / *adv.* 以前:He left five minutes ~. 他五分钟前离开的。/ long, long ~ 很久以前

agree / ə'griː / *vi.* 同意;赞同;应允:I don't ~ with you on this point. 在这一点上,我不同意你的意见。/ Everybody ~ d to the plan at the meeting. 在会上,所有的人都同意这个计划。

agreeable / ə'griːəbl / *adj.* 同意的,欣然同意的;惬意的,令人愉快的:~ voice 悦耳的声音/ ~ weather 舒适的天气

agreement / ə'griːmənt / *n.* ❶[U]一致;同意:The two sides reached ~ at once. 双方马上达成了一致协议。❷[C] 协定;协议;契约:an ~ concerning sci-tech 科技合作协定 / arrive at (come to, make, reach) an ~ 达成协议/ a verbal ~ 口头协定/ violate an ~ 违反协议

agricultural / ˌægrɪ'kʌltʃərəl / *adj.* 农业的;农艺的:~ tax 农业税/ ~ ecological environment 农业生态环境/ ~ modernization 农业现代化

agriculture / 'ægrɪkʌltʃə(r) / *n.* [U] 农业;农艺:distribution of ~ 农业布局/ go in for ~ 务农

ahead / ə'hed / *adv.* 在前面;在前头:Walk ~ of me. 走我前面。/ go ~ 前进;干吧/ ~ of time 提前

aid / eɪd / Ⅰ *vt.* 帮助;援助:I will ~ him in the matter. 我愿意帮助他处理这件事。/ ~ the poor 扶贫 Ⅱ *n.* [U]帮助;援助;救助:first ~ 急救/ provide ~ 提供援助

AIDS / eɪdz / *n.* [U]艾滋病:get ~ 患艾滋病

A

/ the World ~ Day 世界艾滋病日

ailment / ˈeɪlmənt / *n*. [C]疾病(常指小病);病痛(尤指慢性疾病):a skin ~皮肤病/Children often have minor ~. 小孩子常常闹些小病小灾的。

aim / eɪm / Ⅰ *v*. ❶对准;瞄准:He ~ed the gun at the target. 他举枪瞄准目标。❷立志:He ~s to be a scientist. 他立志当一名科学家。Ⅱ *n*. [C]目的;目标;愿望:He does everything without ~. 他做事毫无目标。/ accomplish (realize) one's ~ 实现目标/achieve one's ~ 达到目标

aimless / ˈeɪmlɪs/ *adj*. 漫无目的的,无目标的:~ wanderings 漫无目的的游荡/ lead an ~ life (existence) 过一种浑浑噩噩的生活 派 aimlessly *adv*.; aimlessness *n*.

air / eə(r) / *n*. [U] ❶天空;空气;大气:~disaster 空难/ ~ fare 机票(价)/ ~ pollution 空气污染 / **by** ~ 乘飞机:Are you going to travel by ~? 你打算乘飞机旅行吗? **in the** ~ 在空中;悬而未决 **on the** ~ 广播;播音 ❷外观;神态;样子:put on ~s 摆架子;装腔作势 / with the ~ of ... 带着……神情

aircraft / ˈeəkrɑːft / *n*. [C]飞机;航空器;飞艇:an ~ carrier 航空母舰 / pilot (fly) an ~ 驾驶飞机

airline / ˈeəlaɪn / *n*. [C]航空公司;航线:domestic ~ 国内航线 / overseas ~ 国外航线

airmail / ˈeəmeɪl / *n*. [U]航空邮寄件;航空邮政

airplane / ˈeəpleɪn / *n*. [C](美)飞机

airport / ˈeəpɔːt / *n*. [C]机场;航空站:I'll meet him at the ~ this afternoon. 今天下午我去机场接他。

airtight / ˈeəˌtaɪt/ *adj*. ❶不透气的,气密的,密封的:Keep food in ~ tins. 用密封的罐头盒保存食物。❷(论点、契约等的)无漏洞的;(防守等)严密的:an ~ contract 字斟句酌的合同 / an ~ argument 天衣无缝的论据

airy / ˈeəri / *adj*. ❶通风的;通气的:an ~ room 通风的房间 ❷不切实际的,虚幻的;无实际内容的,空洞的;出于空想的:~ dreams 梦幻/an ~ title 虚衔/an ~ plan 不切实际的计划

aisle / aɪl / *n*. [C]走廊;通道;走道:an ~ seat 靠过道的座位 / clear an ~ 疏通走道

alarm / əˈlɑːm / Ⅰ *n*. [U]警报;惊慌:sound the ~ 发警报 / His condition gave his friends the deepest ~. 他目前的状况使他的朋友们极为惊慌。/ ~ bell 警钟/ ~ clock 闹钟/ air-raid ~ 空袭警报 / in ~ 惊慌地 Ⅱ *vt*. ❶ 恐吓,使害怕:She was terribly ~ed. 她极度惊恐。❷向……报警

alas / əˈlæs / *int*. 唉;哎呀(表示悲哀或惋惜)

album / ˈælbəm / *n*. [C] 相册;集邮册;专辑

alcohol / ˈælkəhɒl / *n*. [U]酒;酒精;含酒精的饮料:abstain from ~ 戒酒

alcoholic / ˌælkəˈhɒlɪk / Ⅰ *adj*. (含有)酒精的 Ⅱ *n*. [C]酗酒者;酒鬼

alcoholism / ˈælkəhɒlɪzəm / *n*. [U]酒精中毒;酗酒

alert / əˈlɜːt / Ⅰ *adj*. 警惕的;警觉的:be ~ to ... 对……警觉;对……敏感 Ⅱ *n*. [C]警报;警戒:sound out an air ~ 发出空袭警报

algebra / ˈældʒɪbrə / *n*. [U]代数(学):do ~ 做代数题

alien / ˈeɪlɪən / Ⅰ*adj.* ❶外国的；外国人的；陌生的 ❷异己的；相异的 Ⅱ*n.* [C] 外侨；外国人

alienate / ˈeɪlɪəneɪt / *vt.* 使疏远；离间：~ oneself from one's friends 疏远朋友

align / əˈlaɪn / *vt.* ❶使成一直线；使排成一行；使排齐；对准，校直：His books were neatly ~ed in two rows on the shelf. 他的书整整齐齐地在书架上排成两行。❷校正，调准；调整：~ the lenses of a telescope 调准望远镜的镜头 ❸使结盟：~ nations against warfare 联合各国一致反对战争 派 alignment *n.*

alike / əˈlaɪk / *adj.* 相同的；相像的：He and his brother are very much ~. 他和他哥哥长得很像。

alive / əˈlaɪv / *adj.* 活着的；有活力的：I fear the dog is no longer ~. 恐怕那只狗已经死了。/ He is very much ~. 他充满活力。

all / ɔːl / Ⅰ*adj.* 所有的；整个的；全部的：All the children will be asleep before nine o'clock. 所有孩子9点钟前都会入睡。Ⅱ*pron.* 所有一切；全体：Is that ~ you can carry? 你就能提那么多吗？/ All of us are here except John. 除约翰外，我们全都在这儿。Ⅲ*adv.* 完全地；彻底地：This shirt is ~ worn out. 这件衬衣全破了。/~ **along** 一直，自始至终：I know that ~ along. 自始至终我都知道那事。~ **alone** 独自：She is ~ alone in the house. 她独自一人在家。~ **at once** 突然：The storm broke out ~ at once. 暴风雨突然来临。~ **but** 差不多；除了……全：We found them ~ but two. 除两个外，其他的我们全找到了。~ **in** 疲乏到极点（多用于口语）：I am ~ in. 我累得要死。~ **over** 到处，遍布：He has traveled ~ over the country. 他周游过全国。~ **right** 好，行：Everything is ~ right. 一切正常。

allegation / ˌælɪˈgeɪʃn / *n.* [C] 断言；宣称，声称：He made an ~ that Jon has stolen ＄300. 他声称乔恩偷了300美元。/I thought their ~s but reasonable. 我认为他们的断言毫无道理。

allege / əˈledʒ / *vt.* 断言；宣称，声称；（无证据地或未经证实地）硬说：Jack ~d that she stole the money. 杰克声称她偷了钱。/Nothing particular could be ~d against him. 他的为人无懈可击。

allegory / ˈælɪgəri/ *n.* ❶[C]寓言；讽喻：George Orwell's *Animal Farm* is an ~. 乔治·奥威尔的《兽园》是一则寓言故事。❷[U]（说话或写作时采用的）讽喻法；讽喻体 派 allegoric(al) *adj.*；allegorically *adv.*

allergic / əˈlɜːdʒɪk / *adj.* 过敏性的；变应性的；对……过敏的：have an ~ to milk 对牛奶过敏

alleviate / əˈliːvɪˌeɪt/ *vt.* 使（痛苦、忧愁等）易于忍受；减轻，缓解，缓和：apply acupuncture to ~ post-operation pain 运用针灸减轻手术后的疼痛 / ~ severe economic downturn 使严重的经济滑坡缓和下来 派 alleviation *n.*

alley / ˈæli / *n.* [C]小路；巷

alliance / əˈlaɪəns / *n.* [C]结盟；同盟；联盟：in ~ with 与……结盟 / offensive and defensive ~ 攻守同盟

allied / ˈælaɪd / *adj.* ❶联合的，结盟的，联盟的；联姻的：China, France, Great Britain, Russia and the United States were ~ nations during World War II. 在第二次世界大战期间，中国、法国、英国、苏联及美国为同盟国。❷相连的；有亲缘关系的，同源的：~ banks 联号银行/nationalize the aircraft and ~ indus-

A

tries 使飞机以及与此相关的工业国有化

allocate /ˈæləkeɪt/ *vt.* ❶分配；分派；派给：~ funds to schools 把经费分给各校 ❷把(物资、资金等)划归：~ money for research 拨款进行研究

allocation /ˌæləˈkeɪʃn/ *n.* ❶[U]分配；分派；拨给：~ of communication and transportation 交通布局 / fixed direction ~ 定向分配 ❷[C]分配物；配给物

allot /əˈlɒt/ (-lotted；-lotting) *vt.* ❶分配；配给：~ a task to sb. 给某人分配一项任务 ❷拨给：~ money for a park 拨款修公园

allow /əˈlaʊ/ *v.* 允许；给；让……得到：Smoking is not ~ed in the cinema. 不准在电影院内吸烟。/ I can't ~ you to go out. 我不允许你出去。

allowance /əˈlaʊəns/ *n.* [C] ❶容许；准许 ❷津贴；补贴；补助(费)：government ~ 政府津贴 / traffic ~ 交通费

alloy /ˈælɔɪ/ *n.* 合金

allure /əˈl(j)ʊə(r)/ *n.* [U]吸引力；魅力；诱惑力：the ~ of fame 名望的诱惑力/The cottage's ~ was its isolation. 这间小屋的魅力就在于它远离尘嚣。

ally Ⅰ/ˈælaɪ/ *n.* [C]同盟者；同盟国 Ⅱ/əˈlaɪ/ *vt.* 使结盟

almighty /ɔːlmaɪti/ *adj.* ❶有无限权力的；有强大力量的；万能的：the ~ press 有强大影响力的新闻界/Love of the ~ dollar has ruined many people. 对万能的金钱贪婪断送了许多人。❷(口语)极其的，非常的：There is an ~ argument going on next door. 隔壁那一家子正吵得天翻地覆哩。

almost /ˈɔːlməʊst/ *adv.* 差不多；几乎：It's ~ eleven o'clock. 差不多快 11 点钟了。

aloe /ˈæləʊ/ *n.* [C]芦荟

aloft /əˈlɒft/ *adv.* & *adj.* ❶在上方(的)，在高处(的)；在空中(的)：Some birds fly thousands of feet ~. 有些鸟能在离地数千英尺的高空中飞翔 ❷向上(的)，向高处(的)；向空中(的)：soar ~ like a kite 风筝似的向空中飞升

alone /əˈləʊn/ Ⅰ*adj.* 单独的：She was ~ in the room. 她一个人待在屋子里。Ⅱ*adv.* 单独地；独自地：He went to cinema ~. 他独自去看电影。

along /əˈlɒŋ/ Ⅰ*prep.* 沿着：There are many new houses and shops ~ the street. 沿街有许多新房子和商店。Ⅱ*adv.* 向前；一道：Come ~！来吧！/ ~ **with** 偕同：She will go ~ with her dog. 她将带狗一同去。**get ~ with** 相处；进展：These boys get ~ with each other quite well. 这些男孩子彼此相处得很好。

alongside /əˌlɒŋˈsaɪd/ Ⅰ*prep.* 在……旁边；与……并肩：~ a river 在河边 Ⅱ*adv.* 并排地；并肩地

aloud /əˈlaʊd/ *adv.* 大声地；高声地：I asked her to read the text ~. 我要她朗读课文。

alphabet /ˈælfəbet/ *n.* [C]字母表

already /ɔːlˈredi/ *adv.* 已经；早已：They had ~ arrived home when I called. 我打电话时他们已经到家了。

also /ˈɔːlsəʊ/ *adv.* 也；同样；还：She likes swimming, and I ~. 她喜欢游泳，我也喜欢。/ **not only ... but ~...** 不但……而且……：I not only saw him but ~ had supper with him. 我不但见到他了，还和他一起共进晚餐。

alter /ˈɔːltə(r)/ *vt.* 改变；变更：~ for

the better (worse)变好(坏)

alteration / ˌɔːltəˈreɪʃn / *n.* ❶[U]改动;更改:This green coat needs ~. 这件绿色的外套需要改一下。❷[C]变化;调整;变动:There have been a few ~s to the winter courses. 冬季的课程有一些变动。

alternate Ⅰ/ ɔːlˈtɜːneɪt / *v.* 交替;轮流 Ⅱ/ ɔːlˈtɜːnɪt /*adj.* ❶交替的;轮流的;间隔的;交错的:~ current 交流电/ write in ~ lines 隔行书写 ❷供选择的;供替换的;预备的;候补的:~ routes 可供选择的路线/ ~ sources of energy 替代能源

alternation / ˌɔːltəˈneɪʃn / *n.* 变更;改变;改动

alternative / ɔːlˈtɜːnətɪv/ Ⅰ*n.* [C] ❶两者(或在两者以上之间)择一;取舍;抉择:face the ~ of dismissal or resignation 面临要么被解雇要么提出辞呈的抉择 ❷可供选择的事物;供替代的抉择;替代品:The only ~ is to wait and see. 除了观望,别无选择。/ Resignation is the only ~ to being fired. 除被解雇以外,唯一的可能就是辞职。❸选择的自由(或余地):They had therefore no ~ but to pack up. 于是,他们没有选择余地,只得卷起铺盖走人。Ⅱ*adj.* ❶供选择的;供替代的;另一个的:an ~ proposition 供选择的建议 / We returned by the ~ road. 我们从另一条路返回。派 alternatively *adv.*

although / ɔːlˈðəʊ / *conj.* 虽然;尽管;纵使:Although he is very old, he tries his best in building socialism. 他虽然老了,但仍在为建设社会主义尽心竭力。

altitude / ˈæltɪtjuːd / *n.* [C] ❶高;高度;海拔:at an ~ 在某一高度/ reach an ~ of ... 达到……的高度 ❷(*pl.*)高地;高处

altogether / ˌɔːltəˈgeðə(r) / *adv.* 总共;完全;总之:There are ten computers in our classroom ~. 我们教室里总共有10台计算机。

aluminium / ˌæljəˈmɪnɪəm / *n.* [U]铝

always / ˈɒlweɪz, ˈɔːlweɪz / *adv.* 无例外地;总是:I ~ work hard at English. 我一直努力学英语。

AM, a. m. (拉丁文 ante meridiem 的缩写)午前;上午

am / æm, əm / *v.* (我)是

amass / əˈmæs / *vt.* ❶积聚(尤指财富);积累;聚集:During the past two years alone, be ~ed a staggering $ 1.5 billion in profits for himself. 单单在过去的两年里,他就为自己聚集到15亿元之巨的利润。/~ political power 积聚政治权力 ❷堆积,把……聚成堆:He ~ed his papers for his memories. 他把文件汇集起来,准备写回忆录。

amateur / ˈæmətə(r) / Ⅰ*adj.* 业余的;外行的 Ⅱ*n.* [C]业余爱好者:music ~ 业余音乐爱好者

amaze / əˈmeɪz / *vt.* 使惊奇:I was ~d at his conduct. 我对他的行为感到惊奇。

amazement / əˈmeɪzmənt / *n.* [U]惊奇;诧异:to one's ~ 使某人感到吃惊的是/ He looked at us in ~. 他惊奇地看着我们。

amazing / əˈmeɪzɪŋ / *adj.* 令人惊奇的:The story is very ~. 这故事令人感到惊奇。

ambassador / æmˈbæsədə(r) / *n.* [C]大使;使节:exchange ~s 互换大使/American ~ to China (Beijing)美国驻华(北京)大使/ appoint an ~ 任命大使/ recall an ~ 召回大使

A

ambiguous /æmˈbɪɡjʊəs/ *adj*. 模棱两可的;含糊不清的:~ answer 含糊的答复

ambition /æmˈbɪʃn/ *n*. 雄心;野心;抱负;志向:have a high ~ 胸怀大志;怀有野心/ realize one's ~ 实现某人的抱负/ She is clever but lacks ~. 她很聪明,但胸无大志。

ambitious /æmˈbɪʃəs/ *adj*. 有雄(野)心的

amble /ˈæmbl/ *vt*. 悠闲地走;从容漫步;缓行:We were ambling along enjoying the scenery. 我们一边缓步前行,一边观赏着景色。/~ up and down the room 在房间里来回踱步

ambulance /ˈæmbjələns/ *n*. [C]救护车:call an ~ 叫救护车

ambush /ˈæmbʊʃ/ Ⅰ *n*. 埋伏;伏击:lay an ~ for sb. 设埋伏以待某人/The enemy fell into the ~. 敌人中了埋伏。Ⅱ *vt*. 伏击:An entire platoon was ~ed during a patrol and wiped out. 整整一个排在巡逻中遭到伏击,并被歼灭。

amend /əˈmend/ *vt*. ❶修改,修订(法律、议案等):~ the constitution 修改宪法 ❷改进;改善;改良:~ conditions in the slums 改善贫民窟的境况/~ one's life 革心洗面

amendment /əˈmendmənt/ *n*. ❶[U]改进;改善;改良:the promise of reform and ~ 改过自新的诺言 ❷[C]修改,修订;修正案,修正条款:an ~ to a law 法律的修正条款 / put forward an ~ 提出修正案

America /əˈmerɪkə/ *n*. 美洲;美国:the United States of ~ (U. S. A. ; USA) 美利坚合众国/ Central ~ 中美洲/ Latin ~ 拉丁美洲/ North ~ 北美洲/ South ~南美洲

American /əˈmerɪkən/ Ⅰ *adj*. ❶美洲的;美国的 ❷美国人的 Ⅱ *n*. [C]美国人

amiable /ˈeɪmɪəbl/ *adj*. 和蔼可亲的;亲切友好的;悦人的:an ~ tone of voice 悦耳的语调/an ~ greeting 亲切的问候/She has an ~ disposition. 她性情温柔。派 amiability *n*. ; amiably *adv*.

amid /əˈmɪd/ *prep*. 在……中;在……当中

amidst /əˈmɪdst/ *prep*. (= amid) 在……中;在……当中

amiss /əˈmɪs/ Ⅰ *adv*. ❶不正确地;错误地:If you think he is guilty, you judge ~. 如果你认为他有罪,那就判断错了。❷不顺利;出差错;有缺陷地:Something went ~ with the arrangements. 安排上出了些差错。Ⅱ *adj*. ❶不正确的;错误的;有缺陷的:I think something is ~ in your calculations. 我认为你的计算有错误。❷出差错的;有毛病的:What's ~ with that machine today? 今天这部机器是怎么啦?

ammonia /əˈməʊnɪə/ *n*. [U]氨;氨水

ammunition /ˌæmjʊˈnɪʃn/ *n*. [U] ❶弹药;军火:live ~真枪实弹 ❷子弹,炮弹(指可用来攻击别人或为自己辩护的材料、证据等):The scandal provided ~ for press attacks against the government. 这起丑闻向新闻界提供了攻击政府的炮弹。

among /əˈmʌŋ/ *prep*. 在中间;在……之中:She is sitting ~ the children. 她坐在孩子们中间。

amongst /əˈmʌŋst/ *prep*. (=among)在……之中;在……中间

amoral /əˈmɒrəl/ *adj*. ❶与道德无关的;不属道德范畴的:Science as such is completely ~. 科学本身完全是无所谓

道德或不道德的。❷没有道德意识的；无从区分是非的：Young children and animals are ~. 幼童和动物是没有道德意识的。

amorous /ˈæmərəs/ *adj*.（有关）爱情的；求爱的；示爱的：~ songs 情歌/He gave the blonde an ~glance. 他朝那个金发碧眼女郎投去情意脉脉的一瞥。

amount /əˈmaʊnt/ Ⅰ *n*. [C] ❶总额；总数 ❷数量；数额：We only want a small ~. 我们只要少许。/**a large ~ of** 大量的：He has spent a large ~ of money on books. 他花了很多钱买书。**in (great, large) ~s** 大量地 Ⅱ *vi*. 总共；总计：What you have spent ~s to more than fifty yuan. 你花的钱总共有 50 多元。

ampere /ˈæmpeə(r)/ *n*. [C]安培：~-hour 安培小时 / ~-meter 安培计

amphibian /æmˈfɪbɪən/ *n*. [C]两栖动物；水陆两用飞机

ample /ˈæmpl/ *adj*. ❶大量的；充裕的；富裕的：a man of ~ means 富裕阔绰的人/Stocks are ~. 存货充足。❷面积(或空间)大的；宽敞的：an ~ lawn 大草坪/The flat's ~ for a family of five. 这个单元住五口之家还是宽宽绰绰的。

amplify /ˈæmplɪfaɪ/ *vt*. 放大；扩大；增强：~ on (upon)引申；进一步阐述/ ~ radio signals 增强无线电信号

amplitude /ˈæmplɪtjuːd/ *n*. [U] ❶广大；广阔：an island of some ~颇为广阔的岛屿 ❷丰富；充裕；充足：an ~ of money 巨额钱财

amuse /əˈmjuːz/ *vt*. 娱乐；使感到有趣：His answer ~d me very much. 他的回答使我觉得很好笑。/~ **oneself by doing sth.** 做某事以自娱：The boys ~d themselves by drawing. 男孩子们以画画取乐。

amusement /əˈmjuːzmənt/ *n*. 娱乐；消遣；乐趣；娱乐活动：a ~ park (grounds)游乐场 / to one's ~ 令……感到有趣

analog(ue) /ˈænəlɒg/ *n*. [C] ❶类似物；模拟：~ pattern 模拟系统/ ~ simulation 模拟仿真/ be ~ to (with)类似于 ❷同源语

analogous /əˈnæləgəs/ *adj*. 类似的；相似的：~ with each other 两者相似

analogy /əˈnælədʒi/ *n*. 相似；类似；类推：by ~ 照此类推 / on the ~ of ... 根据……类推

analyse(-ze) /ˈænəlaɪz/ *vt*. 分析；分解：We ~d the causes of our failure. 我们分析了失败的原因。

analysis /əˈnæləsɪs/ *n*. (*pl*. analyses /əˈnæləsiːz/)分析；分解：We made a careful ~ of the problem. 我们仔细分析了那个问题。

anarchy /ˈænəki/ *n*. [U] ❶无政府(状态)；政治混乱：After its defeat in war the country was in a state of ~. 战败之后，该国处于无政府动乱状态。❷混乱，无秩序：Intellectual and moral ~ followed the loss of faith. 信仰的失落导致思想和道德的混乱。

anatomy /əˈnætəmi/ *n*. [U]分解；解剖(学)

ancestor /ˈænsestə(r)/ *n*. [C]祖先；祖宗

ancestry /ˈænsestri/ *n*. ❶祖先；列祖：trace one's ~ (to)... 追溯祖先(到……) ❷世系；血统：be born of good ~ 出身名门

anchor /ˈæŋkə(r)/ Ⅰ *n*. [C]锚：raise (weigh) the ~ 起锚；起航 Ⅱ *v*. 抛锚；停泊：~ one's hope on sb. 把希望寄托在

A

某人身上

ancient / ˈeɪnʃənt / *adj*. 古代的；古老的：~ Rome 古罗马 / ~ times 古代

and / ænd，ənd / *conj*. ❶和，又（表示并列关系）：a book ~ a pen 一本书和一支笔 / read ~ write 读和写 / my father ~ I 我和我父亲 / ~ **so on** 等等；诸如此类 ❷于是；而且

anecdote / ˈænɪkdəʊt / *n*. 轶事：amusing (funny) ~ 趣闻轶事 / literary ~ 文坛轶事

anew / əˈnjuː / *adv*. 重新；再：repent and start ~ 悔过自新

angel / ˈeɪndʒəl/ *n*. ［C］❶（侍奉上帝的）天使；神的使者 ❷（可代表善或恶的）精灵；保护神：The nurse was like a ministering ~ to him. 对他来说，这位护士像一位救死扶伤的看护神。❸安琪儿（尤指女人或小孩）；心上人，爱人；（有时也用作称呼语）亲爱的 派 angelic *adj*. ；angelically *adv*.

anger / ˈæŋgə(r) / *n*. ［U］生气；愤怒：He was filled with ~. 他满腔怒火。

angina / ænˈdʒaɪnə / *n*. ［U］心绞痛

angle / ˈæŋgl / *n*. ［C］❶角；角的度数：external (internal) ~ 外（内）角 ❷角度：view sth. from a different ~ 从不同的角度看问题

angry / ˈæŋgri / *adj*. 发怒的；生气的；狂暴的：They were very ~ at what she had done. 他们对她所做之事很生气。/ He was very ~ with me when I was late. 我迟到了，他对我大发脾气。/ ~ winds 狂风 派 angrily *adv*.

anguish / ˈæŋgwɪʃ / *n*. ［U］（身体上的）剧痛；（尤指精神上的）极度痛苦：the ~ of grief 悲痛欲绝/The parents were in deep mental ~ at what might have happened. 想到可能发生的事儿，做父母的精神上痛苦不已。

angular / ˈæŋgjələ(r) / *adj*. 有角的；尖的

animal / ˈænɪməl / *n*. ［C］动物；牲畜：wild ~s 野生动物/ domestic ~s 家畜

animate Ⅰ / ˈænɪˌmeɪt / *vt*. ❶使有生命，赋予……以生命：the mysterious force that ~s the cells of the body 使身体细胞具有生命的神奇力量 ❷激励；鼓舞；使活泼；使有生气：He was able to ~ a lecture on a dull subject with witty remarks. 他妙语连珠，能把一个枯涩的题目讲得妙趣横生。❸把……摄制（或绘制）成动画片：~ a film sequence 制作系列动画片 Ⅱ / ˈænɪmɪt / *adj*. ❶活着的；有生命的：Plants are part of ~ nature. 植物是生物界的组成部分。❷活泼的；有活力的；生气勃勃的：an ~ expression of joy 喜笑颜开

animation / ˌænɪˈmeɪʃən/ *n*. ❶生气；活力；热情；激动，兴奋：the ~ of eyes 炯炯有神的目光 / They were full of ~ as they talked of their holiday plans. 他们谈论假日计划时个个都显得格外兴奋。❷动画片制作技术

ankle / ˈæŋkl / *n*. ［C］踝

annex / əˈneks / *vt*. ❶附加，追加；附带：~ a codicil to a will 对遗嘱增补内容/ To each establishment is ~ed a cookshop. 每设一个机构均附设一家小饭馆。❷并吞，兼并，霸占（领土等）：The United States ~ed Texas in 1845. 1845 年，美国兼并了得克萨斯。

annihilate / əˈnaɪəˌleɪt / *vt*. 消灭；歼灭；毁灭：The epidemic ~d the population of the town. 这场流行病夺去了全镇人的生命。/The invasion force was ~d to the last man. 入侵者被一个不剩地歼

灭了。

anniversary /ˌænɪˈvɜːsəri/ *n.* [C]周年；周年纪念日：celebrate the 10th ~ of ... 庆祝……的 10 周年纪念日

annotate /ˈænəʊˌteɪt/ *vt.* 给……注释(或评注)：This new edition has been elaborately ~d by the author. 作者对这本新版书做了详尽的注解 派 annotation *n.*

announce /əˈnaʊns/ *vt.* 宣告；宣布；发表：It has been ~d that the meeting will be held next week. 下周开会的事已经宣布了。派 announcer *n.*

announcement /əˈnaʊnsmənt/ *n.* [C]宣布；通知；告示：make (issue) a public ~ 发布公告 / An ~ will be made next Monday. 通告将在下星期一发出。

annoy /əˈnɒɪ/ *vt.* 使人烦恼：She was ~ed because she missed the bus. 她因没赶上公共汽车而感到烦恼。

annoyance /əˈnɒɪəns/ *n.* ❶[C]令人烦恼的人(或事)：That brat is a real ~. 那个小鬼简直让人伤透脑筋。/ Low-flying planes are an ~ in the area. 在这一带，低飞的飞机吵得人心烦。❷[U]烦恼；恼怒；气恼：Much to my ~, the train had just left when I got to the station. 我赶到车站时，列车刚开走，真让人恼火。

annual /ˈænjʊəl/ *adj.* 每年的；一年一度的：~ budget 年度预算/ ~ income 年收入/ ~ pay (salary) 年薪/ ~ output 年产量/~ ring 年轮 派 annually *adv.*

anonymous /əˈnɒnɪməs/ *adj.* ❶匿名的；无名的；姓氏不明的：an ~ letter phone (call) 匿名信(电话)/The giver of the prizes wished to remain ~. 奖金设立者不希望自己的姓名被披露。❷出自无名氏之手的；来源不明的：This book was written by an ~ author. 这本书出自无名氏作者之手。

another /əˈnʌðə(r)/ *adj. & pron.* 又一(个)；再一(个)：one ~ 相互/Will you have ~ cup of tea? 再来一杯茶，好吗？

answer /ˈɑːnsə(r)/ Ⅰ *vt.* 回答；答复：We must ~ his letter right away. 我们必须立即给他回信。/~ **for** ① 负责：We must ~ for her safety. 我们必须对她的安全负责。②接受处罚：You'll ~ for your wrong doing one day. 总有一天你会为所做的错事受到惩罚。Ⅱ *n.* [C]回答；答复；答案：find an ~ to the question 找出问题的答案/ His ~ to the question is correct. 他对这个问题的回答正确。

answerable /ˈɑːnsərəbəl/ *adj.* ❶有责任的；应承担责任的：be ~ for sb.'s safety 对某人的安全负责 / She is ~ for the whole project. 她对整个工程负有责任。❷可回答的；可答复的；可驳斥的：a question ~ by mail 可通过信件回答的问题 / That question is easily ~. 那个问题很容易回答。

ant /ænt/ *n.* [C] 蚂蚁

antagonist /ænˈtægənɪst/ *n.* [C] ❶对抗者；对手：His ~ in the debate was smarter than he. 他的辩论对手比他精明。❷(戏剧、小说等中主角的)对立面；反面人物：Iago is the ~ of Othello. 伊阿古是奥赛罗的对立面。

Antarctic /ænˈtɑːktɪk/ Ⅰ *adj.* 南极的；南极区的：the ~ Circle 南极圈/ the ~ Zone 南极地带 Ⅱ *n.* 南极(地区)；南极圈

Antarctica /ænˈtɑːktɪkə/ *n.* 南极洲

antenna /ænˈtenə/ *n.* [C](*pl.* antennae 或 antennas)(＝aerial)天线：communi-

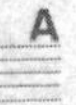

ty ~ 共用天线/ internal ~ 室内天线/ master ~ TV system 共用天线电视系统

anthem / ˈænθəm / *n.* [C] ❶赞美诗;颂歌 ❷国歌

anthropologist / ˌænθrəˈpɒlədʒɪst / *n.* [C] 人类学家

anthropology / ˌænθrəˈpɒlədʒi / *n.* [U]人类学

anti- / ˈæntɪ / (前缀)(放在名词或形容词之前)表示"反""抗""阻""排斥"等: anti-dumping policy 反倾销政策 / anti-dumping duty 反倾销税 / anti-riot police 防暴警察 /anti-unfair-competition 反不正当竞争 / anti-corruption 反腐败

antibiotics / ˌæntɪbaɪɒˈtɪks / *n.* 抗生素

anticipate / ænˈtɪsɪpeɪt / *vt.* 预料;预先;预期:~ one's wages 提前使用工资 / ~ the rival 抢在对手之前 / ~ doing sth. 期望做某事

anticipation / ænˌtɪsɪˈpeɪʃn / *n.* [U]预料;预期:in ~ of 预先;预料;期待

antipathy / ænˈtɪpəθi / *n.* [U](尤指出自本性且根深蒂固的)反感,厌恶,憎恶: There is a great deal of ~ between them. 他们之间的嫌隙甚深。/I can't overcome my ~ for hypocrisy. 我无法克制自己对虚伪的厌憎。

antique / ænˈtiːk / Ⅰ *adj.* 古时的;古代的;旧式的:an ~ shop 古玩店 Ⅱ *n.* [C] 古物;古器;古玩:a genuine ~ 一件珍稀古董

antisocial / ˌæntɪˈsəʊʃl / *adj.* ❶讨厌社交的;不善交际的:an ~ life 离群索居的隐退生活/He's not ~, but shy. 他并非厌恶社交,只是生性腼腆。❷反社会的;妨害公众利益的:~ acts 反社会行为/It is ~ to spit and litter in public places. 在公共场地随地吐痰和乱扔杂物是妨害公益的。

antonym / ˈæntənɪm / *n.* [C]反义词

anxiety / æŋˈzaɪəti / *n.* [U] ❶忧虑;担心:I feel great ~ about the boy's safety. 我对男孩的安危感到非常担忧。❷渴望

anxious / ˈæŋkʃəs / *adj.* 焦急的;急切的;渴望的:He is ~ to know the exam result. 他急着想知道考试结果。/ **be ~ for** 渴望:I am ~ for a change. 我渴望换个环境。**be ~ about** 担心;担忧:He is ~ about her health. 他担心她的健康。

派 anxiously *adv.*

any / ˈeni / Ⅰ *adj.* 任何的;无论什么: Any book will do. 任何一本书都行。/ If you see ~ interesting book, please buy a copy for me. 如果你看到有趣的书,请帮我买一本。Ⅱ *pron.* 一个;无论哪个;一些:Have you ~ books? 你有书吗?

anybody / ˈenibɒdi / *pron.* 任何人;无论谁

anyhow / ˈenihaʊ / *adv.* 无论如何

anymore / ˈeniˈmɔː(r) / *adv.* 而今再也: Sally doesn't work here ~. 萨莉不再在这儿工作了。/Do you play tennis ~? 你还打网球吗?

anyone / ˈeniwʌn / *pron.* 任何人

anything / ˈeniθɪŋ / *pron.* 任何事物;任何事情;一切:I don't find ~ in the room. 在房间里我什么也没找到。/ He is ~ but a good teacher. 他根本不是一位好老师。

anyway / ˈeniweɪ / *adv.* (=anyhow)无论如何;不管怎样:Anyway, I finished the job. 不管怎样,我把那事做完了。

anywhere / ˈeniweə(r) / *adv.* 任何地方;无论何处:You may go ~ you want. 你

想去哪儿就去哪儿。

apart /əˈpɑːt/ *adv.* 分别；相距：~ from 除了/ He stood far ~ from me. 他远离我站着。

apartment /əˈpɑːtmənt/ *n.* [C]公寓；住宅

apathy /ˈæpəθi/ *n.* [U] 无兴趣；冷漠；无动于衷：His ~ towards his work was annoying. 他对工作所持的冷漠态度叫人生气。

ape /eɪp/ *n.* [C]猿：~man 猿人

apex /ˈeɪpeks/ *n.* [U]（*pl.* apexes 或 apices /ˈeɪpɪˌsiːz/）❶顶；顶点；最高点：the ~ of a triangle 三角形的顶点/at the ~ of a mountain 在山顶/the ~ of a career 事业的顶点 ❷（心、肺、树叶等的）尖端：the ~ of a leaf 树叶的尖端/the ~ of the tongue 舌尖

apologise(-ze) /əˈpɒlədʒaɪz/ *vi.* 道歉；认错：~ **to sb. for sth.** 因某事向某人道歉：She ~d to her teacher for coming to school late. 她因上学迟到向老师道歉。

apology /əˈpɒlədʒi/ *n.* [C]道歉；谢罪：**make an ~ to sb.** 向某人道歉：You should make an ~ to her. 你应该向她道歉。

apostrophe /əˈpɒstrəfi/ *n.* [C]撇号；省字号

appal(l) /əˈpɔːl/ *vt.* (-palled; -palling) 使惊骇；使胆寒：I was ~ed at how ill he looked. 见他一脸的病容，我不觉惊呆了。/We are ~ed to see the misery around us. 我们看到周围一片凄惨的景象，不觉大为愕然。

apparatus /ˌæpəˈreɪtəs/ *n.* [C]（*pl.* apparatus 或 apparatuses /ˌæpəˈreɪtəsɪz/）仪器；装置；器官：chemical ~ 化学仪器/ digestive ~ 消化器官

apparent /əˈpærənt/ *adj.* 明显的；外表的

apparently /əˈpærəntli/ *adv.* 显然

appeal /əˈpiːl/ *vi.* & *n.* 恳求；呼吁；上诉：~ to arms 诉诸武力 / reject an ~ 驳回上诉/~ **to sb. to do (for) sth.** 恳求某人做某事：The old man ~ed to us for help. 这位老人恳求我们帮助他.

appealing /əˈpiːlɪŋ/ *adj.* 有感染力的；吸引人的；动人的；媚人的：an ~ sense of humor 极富感染力的幽默感/What an ~ little baby! 好一个逗人喜爱的小宝宝！

appear /əˈpɪə(r)/ *vi.* ❶ 出现；显得；好像：She ~s older than she is. 她看起来比她实际年龄大。❷来到；露面：~ in person 亲自到场

appearance /əˈpɪərəns/ *n.* [C] ❶出现；显露；来到；露面：to all ~s 显然 / enter an ~ 到场 ❷外貌；外观；外表：in ~ 表面上；在外表上 / Never judge by ~. 不可以貌取人。

appease /əˈpiːz/ *vt.* ❶使平静；平息（怒气、争吵等）；（用满足要求等方式）抚慰：She tried to ~ the crying baby by giving him the breast. 她给啼哭的婴儿喂奶使他不哭。/~ sb.'s anger 使某人息怒 ❷解（渴）；充（饥）；满足（欲望、好奇心等）：~ one's thirst with a watermelon 吃西瓜解渴/He ~d his curiosity by asking a few questions. 他问了几个问题，满足了自己的好奇心。❸安抚；绥靖；姑息；对……做出让步：The boy ~d his father and got up from television to finish his homework. 那男孩听从父亲的劝说，离开电视机做作业去了。

append /əˈpend/ *vt.* 附加；增补：~ a note to a letter 在信上加注/a chart ~ed to statement 附在文字说明上的图表

appendix /ə'pendɪks/ *n.* [C]（*pl.* appendices 或 appendix）❶附录；附录；附属物：consult the ～ 查阅附录 ❷阑尾：remove the ～ 切除阑尾

appetite /'æpɪtaɪt/ *n.* ❶食欲；胃口：He has a good ～. 他胃口好。/ She lost her ～. 她食欲不振。❷欲望；兴趣；爱好：It is to my ～. 这很合我的胃口。

applaud /ə'plɔːd/ *v.* 鼓掌；赞许：When he finished his speech, the audience warmly ～ed. 他演讲完毕时，观众热烈鼓掌。

applause /ə'plɔːz/ *n.* [U]掌声；热烈鼓掌；喝彩；称赞；赞成：greet sb. with warm ～ 热烈鼓掌欢迎某人/ win the ～ of ...得到……的赞扬

apple /'æpl/ *n.* [C] 苹果

appliance /ə'plaɪəns/ *n.* [C] ❶用具；器具；器械；装置：household electrical ～ 家用器具/ medical ～ 医疗器械 / office ～ 办公用具 ❷应用；适用

applicable /'æplɪkəbl/ *adj.* 能应用的；可适用的；合适的：The treaty will be ～ from Oct. 1. 条约从 10 月 1 日起生效。/ ～ **to** ...可适用于……

applicant /'æplɪkənt/ *n.* [C]申请人：an ～ for a scholarship 奖学金申请人

application /ˌæplɪ'keɪʃn/ *n.* [C] ❶申请；申请书；申请表：an ～ form 一份申请表 / an ～ for employment 求职申请书 ❷应用；适用；运用 ❸（计算机）应用程序

apply /ə'plaɪ/ *v.* 应用；申请：～ for a visa 申请护照 / ～ a theory to practice 把理论运用于实践 /～ **to sb. for sth.** 向某人申请某样东西：He applied to the shop for a job. 他向商店求职。～ **oneself to** 致力于；专心于：She applied herself to English teaching. 她致力于英语教学。

appoint /ə'pɔɪnt/ *v.* 指定；任命；委派：～sb. to a post 委派某人任某职/ He was ～ed mayor of the city. 他被任命为该市市长。

appointment /ə'pɔɪntmənt/ *n.* ❶任命；选派；职位：a letter of ～ 聘书 /accept an ～ 接受任命 / take up an ～ 就任 ❷约定；约会：make an ～ with sb. 与某人约会/ keep (break) an ～ 守(违)约

apportion /ə'pɔːʃn/ *vt.* 分派；分摊；按比例分配：The execution of the will ～ed the property equally to each heir. 遗嘱执行是将财产平分给每个继承人。/ ～ expenses among the three men 三个人分担费用

apposition /æpə'zɪʃən/ *n.* [C]同位语

appraisal /ə'preɪzəl/ *n.* ❶评价；鉴定：The venture passed national ～. 该企业通过了国家级评估。❷[C]估计；估价：an objective ～ of the facts 对事实做客观的估计 / give (make) an ～ of $15,000 on the new barn 对新谷仓做 15 000美元的估价

appraise /ə'preɪz/ *vt.* ❶评价；鉴定：～ ability and achievement in students 对学生的能力和成绩做评估 ❷估计；估价：Property is ～d for taxation. 为报税而估价财产。/a painting ～d at $1 million 一幅估价 100 万美元的画

appreciate /ə'priːʃɪeɪt/ *vt.* 感激；欣赏；鉴赏：～ **sb. for sth.** 为某事感激某人：I ～ you for your timely help. 真感谢你的及时帮助。

appreciation /əˌpriːʃɪ'eɪʃn/ *n.* [U]❶欣赏；鉴赏；赏识：have an ～ for 有鉴赏力 ❷评价；估价；鉴别 ❸感谢；感激：show (express) one's ～ for... 对……表示

感谢

apprehend /ˌæprɪˈhend/ *vt.* ❶逮捕;拘押:The thief was ~ed and put in jail. 小偷被逮捕,并被关进监狱。❷理解;领会;领悟;明白;懂得:I can ~ the meaning of your words. 我能懂你说的话的意思。/It was ~ed at a glance by everyone. 大家对它一目了然。

apprehension /ˌæprɪˈhenʃən/ *n.* ❶[C]畏惧;恐惧;担心;忧虑;挂念:I feel a certain ~ about my interview tomorrow. 我对明天的面试感到有些担心。/ I have so many ~s about his future. 我对他的未来忧心忡忡。❷[U]理解(力);领会;领悟:a man of weak ~ 理解力差的人 / He had no clear ~ of the situation. 他对时局认识不清。❸[U]逮捕;拘押;拿获:cooperate in the ~ of the gangsters 联手捉拿歹徒

apprentice /əˈprentɪs/ *n.* [C]学徒;初学者;生手:take an ~ 收徒弟

approach /əˈprəʊtʃ/ Ⅰ *v.* 临近;逼近:Christmas is ~ing. 圣诞节即将来临。Ⅱ *n.* [C]途径;方法;通路:This is the ~ to the cinema. 这是去电影院的路。/ When you are learning a foreign language, the effective ~ is to study the spoken language. 学习外语的有效方法是学口语。

appropriate /əˈprəʊprɪət/ *adj.* 适当的;恰如其分的:at an ~ time 在适当的时间 / take ~ measures 采取恰当的措施

approval /əˈpruːv(ə)l/ *n.* [U]赞成;认可:The manager gave his ~ for my plan. 经理同意了我的计划。

approve /əˈpruːv/ *v.* 赞同;允许(与 of 连用):We ~ of your choice. 我们赞同你的选择。

approximate Ⅰ /əˈprɒksɪmɪt/ *adj.* 大概的;大约的;约莫的:The ~time of our arrival will be two o'clock. 我们大约 2 点钟抵达。/ Her ~ age is thirty. 她约莫 30 岁光景。Ⅱ /əˈprɒksɪˌmeɪt/ *vt.* 接近,近似;与……几乎一样:Your account of what happened ~s the truth. 你对所发生的情况的叙述接近于事实真相。/ The crowd ~ three hundred people. 人群约有 300 人之众。—*vi.* 接近:His account of the incident ~s to that of the other witness. 他对事故的描述与其他目击者的大致相仿。/ The cost of the project will ~ to £10,000. 这项工程的成本约需 10 000 英镑。派 approximately *adv.*

April /ˈeɪprəl/ *n.* 四月(略作 Apr.)

apron /ˈeɪprən/ *n.* [C] 围裙

apt /æpt/ *adj.* ❶有……倾向的;易于……的:He was ~ to behave impulsively. 他好感情用事。/When one is tired one is ~ to make mistakes. 人疲倦时容易出差错。❷适当的;恰当的:an ~ observation 中肯的意见/an ~ metaphor 贴切的比喻

aptitude /ˈæptɪtjuːd/ *n.* ❶自然倾向 ❷能力;才能:develop one's ~ to negotiate 培养谈判才能/ special (peculiar) ~ 特长

Arab /ˈærəb/ *n.* [C] 阿拉伯人

Arabian /əˈreɪbɪən/ Ⅰ *adj.* 阿拉伯的;阿拉伯人的:the ~ Desert 阿拉伯沙漠/ *The ~ Nights*《天方夜谭》Ⅱ *n.* [C]阿拉伯人

Arabic /ˈærəbɪk/ *adj.* 阿拉伯的;阿拉伯人的;阿拉伯语的

arbitrary /ˈɑːbɪtrəri/ *adj.* 专断的;专横的;任意的:an ~ decision 武断的决定

A

arbitrator /ˈɑːbɪtreɪtə(r)/ *n.* [C]仲裁人

arc /ɑːk/ *n.* [C] ❶弧；弓形；拱 ❷弧光：～ light 弧光；弧光灯

arch /ɑːtʃ/ Ⅰ *n.* [C]弓形；拱门；桥洞：～ bridge 拱桥 Ⅱ *v.* 拱；成弓形

archaeologist /ˌɑːkɪˈɒlədʒɪst/ *n.* [C]考古学家；考古学者

archaeology /ˌɑːkɪˈɒlədʒi/ *n.* [U]考古学

archetype /ˈɑːkɪˌtaɪp/ *n.* [C] ❶原型：That little engine is the ～ of huge modern locomotives. 那台小发动机是现代大机车的原型。❷典型；范例：an ～ of the American rags-to-riches dream 典型的从一贫如洗到万贯家财的美国梦

architect /ˈɑːkɪtekt/ *n.* [C]建筑师；缔造者

architecture /ˈɑːkɪtektʃə(r)/ *n.* [U] 建筑；建筑学

Arctic /ˈɑːktɪk/ Ⅰ *n.* 北极；北极圈；北极区 Ⅱ *adj.* 北极的；北极区的：the ～ Circle 北极圈/ the ～ Ocean 北冰洋 / the ～ Regions 北极地区

ardent /ˈɑːdənt/ *adj.* ❶热烈的；强烈的；激动的：one's ～ desire for freedom 某人对自由的热望 ❷热情的；热切的；忠诚的：an ～ theatre-goer 戏迷/ an ～ longing 热切的企盼

are /ɑː(r)/ *v.* (你，你们，我们，他们，她们，它们)是

area /ˈeərɪə/ *n.* ❶[C]地区；地域；范围：high and new tech ～ 高新技术开发区/ ～ code (电话)区号 ❷面积：coverage ～ 覆盖面积

argue /ˈɑːgjuː/ *v.* 辩论；争论/ ～ **with sb. about (on, over, upon) sth.** 与某人辩论某事：It is no use arguing with him about the matter. 和他辩论此事是徒劳。～ **sb. into (out of) doing sth.** 劝某人做(不做)某事：Do you want to ～ me into agreeing to your plan? 你想说服我同意你的计划吗？

argument /ˈɑːgjʊmənt/ *n.* 辩论；争论；论战；论点：get into an ～ 卷入一场争论/ beyond ～ 无可争辩/ put forward an ～ 提出一个论点

arise /əˈraɪz/ *v.* (arose /əˈrəʊz/, arisen /əˈrɪzn/) 出现；起来；升起：Problems have ～n. 问题出现了。/ The children arose from their seats. 孩子们从座位上站了起来。

aristocrat /əˈrɪstəˌkræt/ *n.* [C](一个)贵族 派 aristocratic *adj.*

arithmetic /əˈrɪθmətɪk/ *n.* [U] 算术：do ～ 做算术题

arm /ɑːm/ Ⅰ *n.* [C] ❶手臂；胳膊/～ **in** ～ 肩并肩；手挽手：The two children are walking ～ in ～. 这两个孩子挽臂而行。/ look with folded ～s 袖手旁观 ❷(*pl.*)武器：～s race 军备竞赛 Ⅱ *v.* 武装；装备：～ed forces 武装部队/They have been ～ed with new weapons. 他们已经配备了新武器。

armo(u)r /ˈɑːmə(r)/ *n.* [C] ❶装甲兵；装甲兵部队 ❷盔甲

army /ˈɑːmi/ *n.* ❶军；军队：join the ～ 参军/ serve in the ～ 服兵役/ ～ construction 军队建设/ the Army Day (August 1)(中国人民解放军)八一建军节 ❷大群；大批：an ～ of ... 一群……

aroma /əˈrəʊmə/ *n.* [C](植物、菜肴等的)芳香；香味；香气：The ～ of cooking made me hungry. 烧菜时的香味使我觉得饥肠辘辘。/ coffee with a fine ～香味纯正的咖啡

around /əˈraʊnd/ Ⅰ *prep.* 在……周围；环绕着；到处；整整一圈：all ～ 周围；到

处 / the world ~ 遍及全世界 / all the year ~ 一年到头 / ~ the clock 日夜；24 小时 / There are many trees ~ the building. 大楼周围有很多树。Ⅱ *adv.* 四处；周围；大约：~ ten o'clock 十点钟左右 / We looked ~ but saw nothing. 我们环顾四周，什么也没看见。

arouse /əˈraʊz/ *vt.* 唤醒；引起；激起：Don't ~ my anger. 不要惹我生气。/ His words ~d our suspicion. 他的话引起了我们的怀疑。

arrange /əˈreɪndʒ/ *vt.* 整理；安排：It is all ~d. 这事全都安排好了。/ ~ **for** 预先准备：The room has been ~d for the evening party. 开晚会的房间已安排妥当。

arrangement /əˈreɪndʒmənt/ *n.* ❶整理；排列；布置：by ~ 安排次序 ❷安排；准备：make ~s for ... 为……做准备

array /əˈreɪ/ *n.* ❶队列；排列：in battle ~ 成战斗队形 / an ~ of 一批；一列 ❷衣服；盛装：in holiday ~ 穿着节日盛装

arrest /əˈrest/ *vt.* & *n.* ❶逮捕；扣留：house ~ 软禁 / resist ~ 拒捕 ❷停止；阻止

arrival /əˈraɪv(ə)l/ *n.* 到达；到来；到达者：a new ~ 新来的人；新到的货 / an ~ form 来客登记表 / on one's ~ ……一到达；……到达时

arrive /əˈraɪv/ *vi.* 到达；达到 / ~ **at (in)** 到达某地：They ~d in Beijing yesterday. 他们昨日到达北京。/ It was about 12 o'clock when they ~d at the village. 他们到达村里时大约 12 点钟。/ ~ **at a conclusion** 得出结论：They can't ~ at a conclusion at this meeting. 在这次会议上他们不可能得出结论。

arrogance /ˈærəgəns/ *n.* [U]骄傲自大；傲慢：We should guard against ~ at any time. 任何时候我们都要力戒骄傲自大。派 arrogant *adj.*；arrogantly *adv.*

arrow /ˈærəʊ/ *n.* [C] 箭

arson /ˈɑːsn/ *n.* [U]放火；纵火：It was a young man who committed ~ last night. 是一个年轻人在昨晚放火。

art /ɑːt/ *n.* ❶美术；艺术：~ gallery 美术馆 / ~ show 美术展览 / fine ~s 美术 ❷技术；技艺：martial ~s 武术 ❸(*pl.*) 人文学科：Bachelor of Arts 文学士 / Master of Arts 文学硕士 / liberal ~s 人文学科

artery /ˈɑːtəri/ *n.* [C] ❶干线：economic arteries 经济命脉 / traffic ~ 交通干线 ❷动脉

article /ˈɑːtɪkl/ *n.* [C] ❶文章；论文：He published an ~ on space travel last month. 上个月他发表了一篇有关太空旅行的文章。❷冠词 ❸物品；商品：household ~s 家庭用品 / toilet ~ 盥洗用品

artificial /ˌɑːtɪˈfɪʃl/ *adj.* 人造的；人工的：~ flower 人造花 / ~ silk 人造丝 / ~ rainfall 人工降雨

artist /ˈɑːtɪst/ *n.* [C] 艺术家；艺人；能手

artistic(al) /ɑːˈtɪstɪk(əl)/ *adj.* ❶艺术的；美术的：~ creation 艺术创作 / ~ criticism 艺术批评 / ~ effect 艺术效果 ❷艺术家的；美术家的

as /æz, əz/ Ⅰ *conj.* 当……时；因为，由于；如，像：She sang ~ she worked. 她一边工作，一边唱歌。/ As you are tired, you'd better rest. 你已疲倦，最好休息一下。/ He does not speak ~ other people do. 他说起话来不像其他人。/ ~ **if** 好像：She spoke ~ if she had known everything. 听她说起来就好像她什么都知道。~ **it were** 似乎；可以说：You are，~ it were，a naughty boy. 可以说你是个很调皮的孩子。~ **long** ~ 只要：You may go ~ long ~ you have finished your job. 只要任务完成了，你就可以走。~ **soon** ~ 一……就……：Call to me ~ soon ~ you get home. 一到家就给我来电话。Ⅱ *prep*. 作为：~ **a result** 因此；结果：Tom didn't work hard enough and he failed the exam ~ a result. 汤姆努力不够，因此考试没及格。~ **a rule** 通常：He comes on Sunday ~ a rule. 他通常星期天来。Ⅲ *adv*. 同样地：He is ~ interested ~ you are in the matter. 他和你一样关心此事。/ ~ **usual** 通常；照常：The shops are open ~ usual. 商店照常营业。~ **well** 也：Please take this ~ well. 这个也请拿去。

ascend /əˈsend/ *v*. ❶攀登；登上；升高：~ a hill 登山/ ~ the throne 登上王位 ❷追溯（到某个时间）

ascent /əˈsent/ *n*.［C］登高；上升；斜坡：his first ~ of Mount Tai 他的首次登泰山/ rapid ~ 急坡；陡坡/ We saw the ~ of a balloon in the air. 我们看到了一只气球升上空。

ascribe /əˈskraɪb/ *vt*. ❶把……归因（于）（与 to 连用）：~ one's wealth to hard work 认为其财富乃是勤劳所得/ He ~s beauty to that which is simple. 他认为，美自质朴出。❷认为……属（于）；认为……源（自）（与 to 连用）：For many years these poems were wrongly ~d to Marlowe. 多少年来这些诗曾被误认为是马洛的作品。

ash /æʃ/ *n*. ❶灰，灰烬（不与数字连用）：Don't drop cigarette ~ on the floor. 不要让烟灰落在地板上。❷（*pl.*）骨灰

ashamed /əˈʃeɪmd/ *adj*.（表语形容词）羞愧的；耻辱的：You should be ~ of what you have done. 你应该为你的所作所为感到羞愧。

ashore /əˈʃɔː(r)/ *adv*. 向岸；向陆地；上岸；上陆地：The sailor went ~. 那水手离船上岸。/The schooner was driven ~. 那条帆船被冲上了岸。/This ship got ~ on a rock. 那条船碰在礁石上搁浅了。/They swam ~. 他们向岸边游去。

Asia /ˈeɪʃə/ *n*. 亚洲：Southeast ~ 东南亚

Asian /ˈeɪʃn, ˈeɪʒn/ Ⅰ *adj*. 亚洲的 Ⅱ *n*.［C］亚洲人

aside /əˈsaɪd/ *adv*. 在一边；向一边：move ~ 移开

ask /ɑːsk/ *v*. 问；请；要：May I ~ you a question? 我可以问你一个问题吗？/ He ~ed me to come on time. 他叫我准时来。/ ~ for leave 请假/ ~ the way 问路/ ~ for trouble 自寻烦恼 /~ **after** 询问；问候：They ~ed after their sick classmate. 他们问候生病的同学。~ **for** 要：The girl ~ed for some new books. 这个女孩要几本新书。

asleep /əˈsliːp/ *adj*.（表语形容词）睡着的：fall ~ 入睡/ fast ~ 熟睡/ He is not ~ yet. 他还没有睡着。

aspect /ˈæspekt/ *n*. 局面；看法；样子；方面：from an ~ 从一个方面/You've only considered one ~ of the problem. 你只考虑到这问题的一个方面。/ Our maths teacher is a man with a serious ~. 我们的数学老师是一个外貌严肃的人。

aspiration /ˌæspəˈreɪʃn/ *n*. 志气；抱负；

渴望：noble (lofty) ~ 崇高的志向 / cherish (have) high ~ 胸怀大志 / He realized his ~ at last. 他终于实现了他的抱负。

aspire /əˈspaɪə(r)/ *vi.* 渴求；追求（知识、名誉等）：~ for knowledge 渴求知识/ ~ for truth 追求真理/ ~ after independence 渴望独立

aspirin /ˈæspərɪn/ *n.* 阿司匹林（药片）

ass /æs/ *n.* [C] 驴子

assassination /əˌsæsɪˈneɪʃn/ *n.* ❶暗杀；行刺 ❷恶意中伤；破坏（名誉等）

assault /əˈsɔːlt/ Ⅰ *n.* [C]（武力或口头上的）攻击；袭击；突击：They carried out an ~ against the fortress. 他们向那座堡垒发动攻击。Ⅱ *vt.* 攻击；袭击；突击：Two lads of nine were accused of ~ing a boy of there. 有人告状说两个9岁的孩子殴打一个3岁的小孩。/A crowd of critics ~ed his verse. 一批评论家群起攻击他的诗歌。

assemble /əˈsembl/ *v.* ❶聚集；会集；集合：~ forces 调集兵力 / The pupils ~d on the field. 学生们聚集在运动场上。❷装配；组装：~ a machine 组装一台机器/assembling workshop 装配车间

assembly /əˈsembli/ *n.* [C] ❶（特殊目的的）集会，会议：an ~ hall 会议厅/ freedom of speech and ~ 言论和集会自由/ hold an ~ 举行集会 ❷（机械的）装配；配件：配件：~ line 装配线，生产线

assent /əˈsent/ Ⅰ *vi.* 同意；赞成；赞同：Everyone ~ed to the plans for the dance. 大家都同意对舞会的安排。Ⅱ *n.* [U]同意；赞成；赞同：a nod of ~点头表示同意/by common ~一致同意

assert /əˈsɜːt/ *vt.* ❶（坚决）主张；坚持；维护：The dominant American ideology ~ed a faith in individual advancement. 美国的主导思想主张个体的发展。❷坚称；力陈；断言：We encouraged him to ~ his own view of the matter. 我们鼓励他明确地说出自己对此事的看法。/~ **oneself** 坚持自己的权利（或意见）：A leader must ~ himself sometimes in order to be followed. 领袖有时必须坚持自己的主张才能赢得民众。

assess /əˈses/ *vt.* ❶评价；估价：They ~ed the house at a million dollars. 他们估价那房屋值100万美元。❷征收（税款、罚款等）：~ a fine against (upon) sb. 对某人进行罚款 派 assessor *n.*

assessment /əˈsesmənt/ *n.* [U]估价；评价；（价格的）评定

asset /ˈæset/ *n.* [C] ❶财产；资产：~s revaluation 资产重估/current ~s 流动资产/ fixed ~s 固定资产/ the loss of state-owned ~s 国有资产流失 ❷宝贵的人（或物）

assign /əˈsaɪn/ *vt.* 指定；分配：These rooms have been ~ed to them. 这些房间已分配给他们。

assignment /əˈsaɪnmənt/ *n.* 分配（任务、作业、工作等）：What's today's ~ in English? 今天的英语作业是什么？

assimilate /əˈsɪmɪˌleɪt/ *vt.* 吸收；吸取：The mind ~s knowledge 大脑吸收知识。/Plants ~ food from the earth. 植物土壤中吸收养分。

assist /əˈsɪst/ *v.* 帮助；协助：I'll ~ her in this task. 我要协助她完成这项任务。

assistance /əˈsɪstəns/ *n.* [U]帮助；援助：be of ~ to sb. 有助于某人/give ~ to sb. 给某人以帮助

assistant /əˈsɪstənt/ Ⅰ *n.* [C]助手；助理：He is ~ manager of our company. 他

A

是我们公司的副经理。Ⅱ *adj*. 助理的；辅助的：~ professor 助理教授/ ~ manager 副经理/ special ~ 特别助理/ shop ~ 营业员

associate Ⅰ/ əˈsəʊʃɪeɪt / *v*. 联系；联合；联想：The little girl always ~s cake with her birthday. 小女孩总是把蛋糕和她的生日联想在一起。Ⅱ / əˈsəʊʃɪət / *n*.[C]伙伴；合伙人；同事：business ~ 合伙经商人 / ~ in crime 同案犯 Ⅲ/ əˈsəʊʃɪət / *adj*. 副的：~ professor 副教授

association / əˌsəʊsɪˈeɪʃn / *n*. ❶[U]联合；联系；交往：bring up ~ 引起联想 ❷[C]协会；社团：establish an ~ 建立协会

associative / əˈsəʊʃɪətɪv / *adj*. 联合的；联想的：~ memory 联想记忆/ ~ thinking 联想思维/ ~ Chinese Character Cards 联想式汉字卡

assume / əˈsjuːm / *v*. ❶假装；假定；设想：Let's ~ the young man to be innocent. 让我们设想这年轻人是无罪的吧。❷担任；承担：You should ~ the responsibility. 你应当承担这个责任。

assumption / əˈsʌmpʃn / *n*. 假定；设想

assurance / əˈʃʊərəns / *n*. ❶保证；担保 ❷保险

assure / əˈʃʊə(r) / *vt*. ❶使确信；使放心：He checked the machine carefully to ~ that it was in good condition. 他仔细检查了机器，直到确信一切正常为止。❷对……进行保险

astonish / əˈstɒnɪʃ / *vt*. 使吃惊；使惊讶：I was ~ed at the news. 听到这个消息，我感到震惊。

astonishment / əˈstɒnɪʃmənt / *n*. [U] 惊讶：she watched the boy with ~. 她吃惊地望着那男孩。

astound / əˈstaʊnd / *vt*. 使震惊；使惊骇；使大吃一惊：She was ~ed at (by) the news that she had won the contest. 她听到自己在竞赛中获胜的消息后感到吃惊。/I was ~ing that he was prepared to give me a job. 他准备给我一份工作。这使我大吃一惊。

astride / əˈstraɪd / *prep*. 跨在……上：The naughty boy sat ~ his grandpa's cane. 那个小淘气把他祖父的拐杖当马骑。

astronaut / ˈæstrənɔːt / *n*.[C]太空人；宇航员

astronomy / əˈstrɒnəmi / *n*. [U]天文学

astronomer / əˈstrɒnəmə(r) / *n*. [C]天文学家

at / æt, ət / *prep*. 在，于(表示时间或空间的一点)：She is an English teacher ~ a middle school. 她在一所中学当英语教师。/ At that time she was in Shanghai. 那时她在上海。

athlete / ˈæθliːt / *n*. [C]运动员：track and field ~s田径运动员/ all-round ~ 全能运动员

athletic / æθˈletɪk / *adj*. 运动的；体育的：~ sports 体育运动；竞技

athletics / æθˈletɪks / *n*. [U](*pl*.)体育运动；竞技

Atlantic / ətˈlæntɪk / Ⅰ *adj*. 大西洋的 Ⅱ *n*. (the Atlantic)大西洋

atlas / ˈætləs/ *n*. [C] ❶地图册；地图集 ❷图表集：an ~of human anatomy 人体解剖图表(集)

atmosphere / ˈætməsfɪə(r) / *n*.[U] 空气；大气：~ pollution 大气污染/ ~ pressure 大气压力

atmospheric / ˌætməsˈferɪk / *adj*. 大气

的;大气层的;空气的:~ pollution 大气污染

atom /ˈætəm/ *n.* [C]原子:~bomb 原子弹

atomic /əˈtɒmɪk/ *adj.* 原子的;原子能的:~ age 原子时代/ ~ reactor原子反应堆/ ~ power station 原子能发电站

attach /əˈtætʃ/ *v.* 系;附上;使隶属于:He ~ed his horse to a tree. 他把马拴在一棵树上。/ This hospital is ~ed to the college. 这医院附属于那所学院。

attachment /əˈtætʃmənt/ *n.* [C] ❶依附;(计算机的)附件:~s of a contract 合同附件 ❷依恋:feel ~ to one's parents 依恋父母

attack /əˈtæk/ Ⅰ *v.* 进攻;攻击:The village was ~ed by the enemy. 这个村子遭到敌人的袭击。Ⅱ *n.* 进攻;攻击;(疾病)侵袭:a surprise ~ 突袭 / a heart ~ 犯心脏病

attain /əˈteɪn/ *v.* 达到;获得:He ~ed success through hard work. 他经过艰苦努力获得了成功。/ I can never hope to ~ to his height. 我从不敢企望达到他的高度。

attempt /əˈtempt/ Ⅰ *vt.* 试做;企图:They are ~ing a difficult task. 他们正在试干一项艰难的工作。Ⅱ *n.* [C]企图;努力:The young man made an ~ at saving this child. 这位青年人试图拯救这小孩。/ **make an ~ on** 向某人进攻;夺取:The thief made an ~ on the old woman's life. 盗贼想杀死这位老太太。

attend /əˈtend/ *v.* ❶照顾;照料:The nurses ~ed to the wounded day and night. 护士们日夜护理伤员。❷出席;参加:We'll ~ the meeting. 我们将出席这次会议。/ Children should ~ school. 孩子们应该上学。❸注意;留心:Are you ~ing to what is being said? 你在注意听人家说话吗?

attendance /əˈtendəns/ *n.* ❶到场;出席:~ book 签到簿 ❷出席人数;出勤率:check the ~ 检查出席人数 ❸护理;照顾:a doctor in ~ 护理医生

attendant /əˈtendənt/ *n.* [C] ❶出席者;侍者;服务员:lift ~ 电梯服务员 ❷随从:an~to an ambassador 大使随员

attention /əˈtenʃn/ *n.* [U]专心;注意;注意力:A good teacher must know how to secure the ~ of his pupils. 一个好教师必须懂得如何吸引学生的注意力。

attentive /əˈtentɪv/ *adj.* 注意的;周到的:The pupils are very ~ to their teacher's. 学生们很注意听老师讲课。派 attentively *adv.*

attitude /ˈætɪtjuːd/ *n.* [C]态度;看法:a matter-of-fact ~ 求实精神/ We should take an active ~ to it. 对这事我们应采取积极的态度。

attract /əˈtrækt/ *vt.* 吸引;引诱:Bees are ~ed by flowers. 蜜蜂为花所吸引。

attraction /əˈtrækʃn/ *n.* 吸引;吸引力;诱惑力:personal ~s 个人魅力

attractive /əˈtræktɪv/ *adj.* 有吸引力的;有迷惑力的:goods ~ in price 价格诱人的货物

attribute /əˈtrɪbjuːt/ *vt.* 把……归因于;把……归咎于:~... **to** ... 把……归因于……:He ~d his failure to bad luck. 他把失败归因于运气不好。

auction /ˈɔːkʃn/ Ⅰ *n.* 拍卖:~ shop 拍卖行/sell a curiosity by ~拍卖一件古董 Ⅱ *vt.* 拍卖:~ off a building 拍卖掉一栋楼房

audible /ˈɔːdɪbl/ *adj.* ❶可听见的:~

A

whisper 听得见的低语 ❷音响的:~ signal 音响信号

audience / ˈɔːdiəns / *n.* [C]听众;观众:television ~ 电视观众/ There was a large (small)~. 听众(观众)很多(少)。

audio / ˈɔːdiəʊ / *adj.* 听觉的;声音的;音频的:~ frequency 音频/~ system 组合音响

audio-visual / ˌɔːdiəʊˈvɪʒʊəl / *adj.* 视听的;~ education 视听教育/ ~ center 视听中心/ ~ equipment 视听设备/ ~ teaching materials 视听教材

audit / ˈɔːdɪt / Ⅰ *v.* 审计;查账 Ⅱ *n.* 审计;查账:~ program 审计程序/ an ~ report 审计报告

auditor / ˈɔːdɪtə(r)/ *n.* [C] ❶审计员;查账员 ❷(大学)旁听生

auditorium / ˌɔːdɪˈtɔːrɪəm / *n.* (*pl.* auditoria)[C]大会堂;礼堂:lecture ~ 演讲大厅/ main ~ 大礼堂

August / ˈɔːgəst / *n.* (略作 Aug.)八月

aunt / ɑːnt / *n.* [C]伯母;婶;舅母;姑;姨

aural / ˈɔːrəl / *adj.* 听觉的;耳的:~ comprehension 听力理解/ ~ surgeon 耳科大夫

authentic / ɔːˈθentɪk / *adj.* ❶真的;真正的;真实的;名副其实的:Are your documents ~ or faked? 你的这些文件是真的还是仿造的? ❷可靠的;可信的;确实的;来源可靠的:an ~ news report 可靠的新闻报道/give ~ oral testimony 拿出过硬的口头证据

author / ˈɔːθə(r) / *n.* [C] ❶作者:a contemporary ~ 当代作家❷网页制作人

authoritative / ɔːˈθɒrətətɪv / *adj.* 有权威的;官方的:~ information 官方消息/ an ~ person 权威人士

authorize(-se) / ˈɔːθəraɪz / *vt.* 授权;委托;允许:~ an agent 指定代理人/ ~d by usage 约定俗成 / be ~d to do sth. 被允许做某事

authority / ɔːˈθɒrəti / *n.* ❶权威;权限;职权;专家:academic ~ 学术权威 /abuse one's ~滥用职权 ❷(常用 *pl.*)当局,官方;有关方面:authorities concerned 有关当局

auto / ˈɔːtəʊ / *n.* (=automobile)[C](*pl.* autos)汽车;机动车

autobiography / ˌɔːtəbaɪˈɒgrəfi / *n.* [C] 自传 派 autobiographic(al) *adj.*

autograph / ˈɔːtəʊˌgrɑːf / *n.* [C]亲笔;(尤指名人的)亲笔签名:Many people collect the ~s of celebrities. 许多人收藏名人的亲笔签名。

automate / ˈɔːtəmeɪt / *vt.* 使自动化:~ the procedures 使程序自动化

automatic / ˌɔːtəˈmætɪk / *adj.* ❶自动的;自动装置的:~ control system 自动控制系统 ❷机械的;无意识的;习惯性的

automation / ˌɔːtəˈmeɪʃn / *n.* [U]自动控制;自动化:office ~ system(OAS)办公室自动化系统

automobile / ˈɔːtəməbiːl / *n.* (=auto)[C]汽车(主要用在美国英语中,英国英语中多用 motorcar,意义上相当于 car):~ industry 汽车工业

autonomous / ɔːˈtɒnəməs / *adj.* [U]自治的;自治权的:an ~ region 自治区/ ~ investment 自主投资/ an ~ port 自由港

autonomy / ɔːˈtɒnəmi / *n.* [U]自治;自治权;自主

autumn / ˈɔːtəm / *n.* (=fall)秋季;秋天

auxiliary / ɔːgˈzɪljəri / *adj.* ❶附属的;从属的:several ~ branches of the library

该图书馆的几个分馆 ❷辅助的；当助手的：Some sailboats have ~ engines. 有些帆船装有辅助发动机。/an ~ nurse 助理护士 ❸备用的；后备的：The hospital has an ~ power system in case of blackout. 这家医院装有备用发电系统以防停电。/an ~ police force 后备警力

avail /əˈveɪl/ Ⅰ *v.* 有用；有益；有助：This proud tradition now ~s them well in their present struggles. 这一光荣传统在他们目前的斗争中起着很大作用。/ ~(**oneself**) **of** 利用：There's moral in everything, if we would only ~ ourselves of it . 只要我们善于吸取，从每件事中都可以吸取教训。Ⅱ *n.* [U] 效用，用途；好处，利益；帮助：His efforts were of little ~. 他的种种努力不起作用。/He tried to revive her but to no ~. 他极力想让她苏醒过来，但是没有成功。

available /əˈveɪləbl/ *adj.* 可利用的；可得到的；有效的：Can this kind of washing machine ~ in this shop? 在这家商店能买到这种型号的洗衣机吗？/ The ticket is ~ only today. 此票只有今天有效。

avenge /əˈvendʒ/ *vt.* 复仇；报仇；报复：He said he would ~ his parents. 他说他定要为他的父母报仇。

avenue /ˈævənjuː/ *n.* [C]大街；林荫大道；途径；手段：That is a good ~ to success. 那是通往成功的佳径。

average /ˈævərɪdʒ/ Ⅰ *n.* 平均；平均数：above(below)~ 超过(低于)平均数/ on an ~ 平均起来；一般说来 Ⅱ *adj.* 平均的；一般的：the ~ age 平均年龄/ the ~ rate of growth 平均增长率 Ⅲ *v.* 均分

avert /əˈvɜːt/ *vt.* ❶转移(目光、注意力等)：She ~ed her eyes from the wreck. 她转移目光不再看失事飞机的残骸。❷防止，防范，避免，消除(灾难、危险等)：The driver ~ed an accident by a quick turn of the steering wheel. 司机急忙掉转方向盘，从而避免了一起车祸。

avoid /əˈvɒɪd/ *vt.* 避免；逃避；回避：She told her child to ~ talking with a stranger. 她告诉孩子不要和陌生人讲话。

await /əˈweɪt/ *vt.* 等候；期待：He has ~ed your coming for a week. 他等候你的到来已有一周了。

awake /əˈweɪk/ Ⅰ *vt.* (awoke /əˈwəuk/, awoke 或 awaked) 醒来；叫醒，唤醒：I awoke with a start. 我从梦中惊醒。Ⅱ *adj.* 醒着的：She is ~ now. 她现在是醒着的。

awaken /əˈweɪkən/ *vt.* 使醒；使觉醒：Please ~ me at six. 请6点钟叫醒我。/ His honesty ~ed my sympathy. 他的诚实唤起了我的同情。

award /əˈwɔːd/ Ⅰ *n.* [C]奖；奖金；奖学金：grant an ~授奖/ receive an ~获奖/ sci-tech results ~s 科技成果奖 Ⅱ *vt.* 授予；奖给

aware /əˈweə/ *adj.* 知道的；意识到的：Are you ~ that you have hurt her feelings? 你有没有觉察到你已经伤害了她的感情？/ I became ~ how he might feel. 我意识到他会有怎样的感受。/ **be ~ of** 觉察到；意识到：He wasn't ~ of the dan ger. 他没意识到有危险。

away /əˈweɪ/ *adv.* 远离；离开；走开：do ~ with 废除；去掉/ She went ~. 她走开了。

awe /ɔː/ *n.* [U](对神等的)敬畏；(对崇高品质等的)敬佩：Deep ~ fell upon them all. 众人不禁凛然敬畏。/The

A

book is worth our ~. 这是一本值得我们肃然起敬的书。/**in ~ of** 敬畏：They rather stand in ~ of Charles. 他们非常敬畏查尔斯。

awful /ˈɔːfl/ *adj*. 非常的；极坏的：A million dollars is an ~ lot of money. 100 万美元是非常大的一笔钱。派 awfully *adv*.

awkward /ˈɔːkwəd/ *adj*. 笨拙的；为难的；尴尬的：in an ~ situation 处境尴尬/an ~ problem 棘手的问题

ax(e) /æks/ *n*. [C] ❶斧头 ❷(经费、人员等的)削减：give sb. the ~解雇某人/His father got the ~ last month. 上月他的父亲被解雇了。

axis /ˈæksɪs/ *n*. [C](*pl*. exes)轴；轴线；中心线：on an ~在轴心上/~ of communication 交通干线

axle /ˈæksl/ *n*. [C]车轴；轮轴

B

B b

baby /ˈbeɪbi/ *n.* [C] ❶婴儿：a newborn ~新生儿/a ~ boy(girl)男婴(女婴) ❷幼畜

baby-sit /ˈbeɪbɪˌsɪt/ *vt.* (-sat; -sitting) 代人临时照看小孩：~ with sb.'s children during church service 教堂做礼拜时为某人照看孩子

bachelor /ˈbætʃələ(r)/ *n.* [C] ❶学士；学士学位：~'s degree 学士学位/Bachelor of Arts 文学士(简作 BA)/ Bachelor of Science 理学士(简作 BS) ❷未婚男子；单身汉

back /bæk/ Ⅰ *adv.* 回；向后：Please put the book ~ on the shelf. 请把书放回书架上。Ⅱ *n.* 背，脊背；后面：If you lie on your ~, you can see the sky. 你若仰卧，就能望见天空。/~ **and forth** 来回：She walked ~ and forth along the shore. 她在岸边来回走动。Ⅲ *adj.* 后面的；背面的：Please go out through the ~ door. 请从后门出去。Ⅳ *v.* 支持：Many of his friends ~ed his plan. 他的很多朋友支持他的计划。/~ **up** 支持：Don't worry. They will ~ us up. 别着急，他们会支持我们的。

backache /ˈbækeɪk/ *n.* 背痛

backbone /ˈbækˌbəʊn/ *n.* ❶[C](人或动物的)脊，脊骨，脊柱 ❷[U]骨气；勇气；毅力：He showed real ~ in the crisis period. 在危急时期他表现出真正的骨气。❸[C]骨干；中坚；栋梁；支柱；基础：Agriculture is the ~ of the economy. 农业是经济的基础。

background /ˈbækgraʊnd/ *n.* [C]背景；经历：in the ~暗中；幕后

backing /ˈbækɪŋ/ *n.* [U]支持；后盾；帮助；资助：financial ~财政上的支持

backspace /ˈbækspeɪs/ Ⅰ *vt.* 退后一格 Ⅱ *n.* 退格：~ key (计算机的)退格键

backtrack /ˈbækˌtræk/ *vi.* ❶走原路返回；走回头路：~ to camp 顺原路返回营地 ❷变卦；出尔反尔；取消诺言：He ~ed on the promise be made last week. 他背弃了上星期所做的许诺。

backward /ˈbækwəd/ Ⅰ *adj.* ❶向后的 ❷倒的；相反的 ❸落后的；(进展)缓慢的 Ⅱ *adv.* ❶向后：He looked ~ to see if his mother was following him. 他向后看看是不是妈妈跟在后面。❷倒；逆：go ~ 倒退；退步

backyard /ˌbækˈjɑːd/ *n.* [C]庭院；后院

bacon /ˈbeɪkən/ *n.* [U]咸猪肉；熏猪肉

bacteria /bækˈtɪərɪə/ *n.* (bacterium 的复数) 细菌：harmful ~有害细菌/ destroy(kill) ~ 消灭细菌

bacteriology /bækˌtɪərɪˈɒlədʒi/ *n.* [U] 细菌学

bacterial /bækˈtɪərɪə/ *adj.* 细菌的；细菌引起的：~ infection 细菌感染

bad /bæd/ (worse, worst) *adj.* ❶坏的;恶劣的;不道德的: We hate ~ people and things. 我们讨厌不道德的人和事。❷(价值、质量等)低劣的: This kind of tea is very ~. 这种茶质量极差。❸有害的;不利的: Smoking is ~ for health. 吸烟有害健康。❹严重的;厉害的: She had a ~ cold yesterday. 昨天她患了重感冒。❺病的;痛的;不舒服的: He had a ~ nose. 他鼻子疼。❻(食物等)腐败的: ~ egg 坏蛋/ The food went ~. 食物坏了。❼错误的;不适当的: It's a ~ idea. 这主意不好。❽使人不愉快的;讨厌的: ~ manners 没有礼貌

badge /bædʒ/ *n.* [C]徽章;像章: a school ~ 校徽/ a police ~ 警徽

badly /ˈbædli/ (worse, worst) *adv.* ❶坏;恶劣地 ❷有缺点地;拙劣地: He writes ~. 他书写很糟。❸严重地;非常: She is ~ ill. 她病得厉害。

badminton /ˈbædmɪntən/ *n.* [U]羽毛球;羽毛球运动

baffle /ˈbæfl/ *vt.* 使困惑,使迷惑;使为难;难倒: It ~d me that they rejected our offer. 他们居然拒绝我们的建议,我百思不得其解。/Her disease had long ~d the skill of her physicians. 她的病早就使她的医生感到束手无策。

bag /bæg/ *n.* [C]提包;口袋;书包: a travelling ~ 旅行袋 / a money ~ 钱袋

baggage /ˈbægɪdʒ/ *n.* [U] ❶[=(英) luggage](美)行李: ~ train 行李车/ ~ office 行李房/ claim one's ~ 认领行李 ❷包袱;束缚;负担: emotional ~感情负担

bail /beɪl/ Ⅰ *vt.* 准许保释: ~sb. out of prison 保释某人出狱 Ⅱ *n.* 保释;保释人;保释金: He said that he would go ~ for Tom. 他说他要保释汤姆。

bait /beɪt/ Ⅰ *n.* 饵;引诱物;诱惑: Little boys are easy to take (swallow, rise to) the ~. 小男孩很容易上当。Ⅱ *vt.* 引诱;诱惑

bake /beɪk/ *vt.* 烘,焙(面包等): The cook ~s bread and cake in the oven. 厨师用烤箱烤面包和饼。

bakery /ˈbeɪkəri/ *n.* [C]面包(或糕饼)烘房;面包(或糕饼)店: buy a cake at the ~ for dessert 在面包店买块蛋糕作甜点

balance /ˈbæləns/ Ⅰ *n.* ❶ 天平;秤 ❷平衡;均衡: ~ beam 平衡木/ ~ development 均衡发展 Ⅱ *v.* 用天平称;权衡,对比

balcony /ˈbælkəni/ *n.* [C] 阳台;露台

bald /bɔːld/ *adj.* ❶(头)秃的;秃头的: He went ~ very young. 他很年轻时就秃顶了。❷无毛的;无树的;光秃的: The hill became ~ only within three years. 仅仅三年时间,那小山就变得光秃秃的了。❸ 毫不掩饰的;赤裸裸的: It is just a ~ lie. 这简直是赤裸裸的谎言。

bale /beɪl/ *n.* [C](货物捆扎成的)大包,大捆: a ~ of cotton 一大包棉花/a ~ of hay 一大捆干草

ball /bɔːl/ *n.* [C] ❶ 球: a ~ game (match)一场球赛 ❷ 舞会: They had a ~ after work. 下班后他们举行了一场舞会。

ballet /ˈbæleɪ/ *n.* 芭蕾(舞);芭蕾舞剧团: dance a ~ 跳芭蕾舞/ a ~dancer 芭蕾舞演员/ water ~ 水上芭蕾

balloon /bəˈluːn/ *n.* [C]气球: an ad. ~ 广告气球

ballot /ˈbælət/ Ⅰ *n.* 投票表决(法);投票选举(法);无记名投票: vote by secret not open ～进行非公开的秘密选票选举 Ⅱ*vi.* 投票：～ for president of the club 投票选举俱乐部主席/～ for a candidate 对某候选人投赞成票

ball(-)point /ˈbɔːlˌpɒɪnt/ *n.* [C]圆珠笔，原子笔

bamboo /ˌbæmˈbuː/ *n.* [U]竹

ban /bæn/ Ⅰ*n.* [C]禁止；禁令：There is a ～ on shouting here. 禁止在此高声喧哗。Ⅱ(banned; banning) *vt.* 禁止；取缔：He ～ned the workers from smoking in the workshop. 他禁止工人们在车间里吸烟。

banana /bəˈnɑːnə/ *n.* [C]香蕉：a hand of ～s 一串香蕉

band[1] /bænd/ *n.* [C] ❶管乐队：string～ 管弦乐队/ military～ 军乐队/ rock～ 摇滚乐队/ jazz ～ 爵士乐队/ form a school ～ 组成校乐队 ❷一帮；一伙：a ～ of robbers 一帮(伙)土匪 ❸(收音机)波段

band[2] /bænd/ Ⅰ*n.* [C]带；带状物：He always wears a ～ round his head. 他总是在头上扎一根带子。Ⅱ *vt.* (用带子)绑，扎

bandage /ˈbændɪdʒ/ Ⅰ*n.* [C]绷带：put on a ～ 包扎 Ⅱ*vt.* 用绷带包扎

bang /bæŋ/ Ⅰ*v.* ❶猛敲；猛撞；猛地关上：Don't ～ at (on) the door. 不要砰砰打门。❷ 砰砰作响 Ⅱ*n.* 猛敲；猛撞；砰砰的声音：with a ～ 砰的一声

bandit /ˈbændɪt/ *n.* [C]土匪；强盗：～ and tyrant on road 车匪路霸

banish /ˈbænɪʃ/ *vt.* ❶流放；放逐：～ sb. from a country 驱逐某人出境 ❷消除；排除(顾虑、恐惧等)：～ worries from heart 排除心中的忧虑 派 banishment *n.*

bank[1] /bæŋk/ *n.* [C] ❶(河、海、湖的)岸；堤：construct a ～ 修筑河堤/ His company is on the south ～ of the river. 他的公司在河的南岸。/ I often take a walk along the ～ after supper. 晚饭后我常沿着河岸散步。❷埂；垄；堆：a ～ of snow 一堆雪

bank[2] /bæŋk/ *n.* [C] ❶银行：a ～ account 银行账户/ a ～ book 银行存折/ ～ deposit 银行存款/ a～draft 银行汇票/ ～ one's money 把钱存入银行/ an investment ～ 投资银行/ a commercial ～商业银行/ a nation development ～ 国家开发银行 ❷库：a talents ～ 人才库/ a blood ～ 血库/ a gene ～ 基因库/ a data ～ 信息库/ a question ～ 试题库

banker /ˈbæŋkə(r)/ *n.* [C]银行家

banking /ˈbæŋkɪŋ/ *n.* [U]银行业；银行学；金融：～ hours 银行营业时间/ ～ service 银行服务

banknote /ˈbæŋknəʊt/ *n.* [C]纸币；钞票

bankrupt /ˈbæŋkrʌpt/ Ⅰ*n.* [C]破产者 Ⅱ*adj.* 破产的；无力偿还的：go ～破产/ The company is to be declared ～. 那家公司即将宣告破产。

bankruptcy /ˈbæŋkrʌptsi/ *n.* 破产；倒闭：～ law 破产法 / file for (declare) ～ 申请(宣布)破产

banner /ˈbænə(r)/ *n.* [C]旗，旗帜；横幅：welcoming ～ 欢迎条幅

banquet /ˈbæŋkwɪt/ *n.* [C]宴会；盛宴：state ～ 国宴/ wedding ～婚宴/ ～hall 宴会厅/ farewell (welcome) ～ 告别(欢迎)宴会

bar /bɑː(r)/ Ⅰ*n.* [C] ❶小酒店；酒吧：They went to the ～ together. 他们一道去了酒吧。❷条；杆；棒：～ code 条码；条形码/ There are seven iron ～s across his window. 他的窗户上钉有七根铁条。❸栏；栅；障碍物：It is the ~ to success. 这就是成功的障碍。Ⅱ *vt.* (barred; barring) 闩上；阻挡：Please ~ the door after you. 请把门闩上。

barbarian /bɑːˈbeərɪən/ Ⅰ *n.* [C] ❶野蛮人；未开化的人；原始人：He is a ~ in the arts of the table. 他对烹调艺术一窍不通。❷无教养的人；粗野的人；残暴的人：He has the manners of a ~. 他举止粗鲁。Ⅱ *adj.* ❶未开化的；原始的；野蛮人(似)的：~ tribes 原始部族 / ~ customs 野蛮人的习俗 ❷不文明的；粗鲁的；残暴的：The children of warring countries are often victims of ~ treatment. 交战国儿童经常是遭到残暴虐待的受害者。

barbarity /bɑːˈbærɪti/ *n.* ❶[U]野蛮；残暴；人性泯灭：treat the captives with ~ 虐待俘虏 ❷[C]暴行：commit the barbarities of warfare 犯下战争暴行

barbarous /ˈbɑːbərəs/ *adj.* 野蛮的；残暴的；未开化的

barbecue /ˈbɑːbɪkjuː/ *n.* [C]烧烤：have a ~ 举行烧烤野餐

barber /ˈbɑːbə(r)/ *n.* [C]理发师：I had a haircut at the ~'s yesterday. 我昨天在理发店理了发。

bare /beə(r)/ *adj.* 赤裸的；光秃秃的：The hill is ~ of trees. 这座山上没有树。/ The poor match girl stood ~foot in the snow. 可怜的卖火柴的小女孩赤着脚站在雪地里。

barely /ˈbeəli/ *adv.* 好容易才；几乎不能；勉强：He ~ has money to support his family. 他几乎没钱养活家人。

bargain /ˈbɑːgən/ Ⅰ *n.* [C] ❶合同；买卖契约；交易：black market ~s 黑市交易 / We made a ~ at last. 我们终于达成交易。❷廉价品；特价品 Ⅱ *v.* 谈判；订合同；讨价还价：He doesn't know how to ~ in the market. 他不知道在市场上买东西如何讨价还价。

barge /bɑːdʒ/ *n.* [C]驳船；游艇

barium /ˈbeərɪəm/ *n.* [U]钡

bark[1] /bɑːk/ *n.* 树皮

bark[2] /bɑːk/ Ⅰ *vi.* (狗)吠，叫：The dog ~s at him. 这狗对着他叫。Ⅱ *n.* 狗或狐狸的叫声：She cannot endure the ~ of that dog. 她不能忍受那条狗的叫声。

barley /ˈbɑːli/ *n.* [U]大麦

barn /bɑːn/ *n.* [C] ❶谷仓 ❷(美)马房；牛舍

barometer /bəˈrɒmɪtə(r)/ *n.* [C]晴雨表；气压表

baron /ˈbærən/ *n.* [C] ❶男爵；贵族 ❷巨商：a ~ of industry 工业巨子 / an oil ~ 石油大王 / a coal ~ 煤炭大王

baroque /bəˈrəuk/ *adj.* ❶巴罗克风格风靡时期(约 1600~1750)的；巴罗克后期的；洛可可式的 ❷巴罗克风格的

barracks /ˈbærəks/ *n.* (单复数同形)兵营；营房

barrel /ˈbærəl/ *n.* [C]大桶

barren /ˈbærən/ *adj.* ❶不结果实的；不结籽的：Exposure to radioactivity may make animals and plants ~. 放射线的照射会使动物丧失生育能力，使植物不结果实。❷(土地等)贫瘠的；不毛的；荒芜的：a ~ desert 荒漠

barrier /ˈbærɪə(r)/ *n.* [C]障碍；阻碍；关卡：set up ~s on the road 设立路障 / overcome language ~s 克服语言障碍

base /beɪs/ Ⅰ *n.* [C]底部；基础；基地：a ~ for export and foreign exchange earning 出口创汇基地 / Shanghai is one of the most important industrial ~s in China. 上海是中国最重要的工业基地之一。Ⅱ*v.* 基于：~ **on** 基于；以……作为根据：Socialism ~s itself on materialism. 社会主义以唯物论为基础。

baseball /ˈbeɪsbɔːl/ *n.* 棒球；棒球运动

basement /ˈbeɪsmənt/ *n.* [C]地下室；底层；基部

bash /bæʃ/ Ⅰ *vt.* 猛击；猛撞：~ a door in 把门撞开/ ~ one's head on the wall 用头猛撞墙 Ⅱ *n.* [C]猛击；重击；猛撞：a ~ in the face 脸上重重地挨了一拳

bashful /ˈbæʃful/ *adj.* 局促不安的；腼腆的；忸怩的；羞怯的：The little girl was too ~ to greet us. 那小姑娘过于羞怯，不敢跟我们打招呼。/She is ~ in doing anything. 她做什么事都是忸忸怩怩的。

basic /ˈbeɪsɪk/ *adj.* 基本的；基础的：a ~ principle 基本原则/a ~ problem 基本问题/ the ~ vocabulary 基本词汇/ ~ state policy 基本国策/ ~ subject 基础学科 派 basically *adv.*

basin /ˈbeɪsn/ *n.* [C] ❶水盆；面盆 ❷盆地；流域：the Mississippi ~ 密西西比河流域

basis /ˈbeɪsɪs/ *n.* [C](*pl.* bases /ˈbeɪsiːz/) 基础；根据：economic ~ 经济基础/ theoretical ~理论依据

basket /ˈbɑːskɪt/ *n.* [C]篮子；筐：a ~ of fruit 一篮水果

basketball /ˈbɑːskɪtbɔːl/ *n.* 篮球：篮球运动：play ~ 打篮球

bass[1] /beɪs/ Ⅰ *n.* 男低音：sing ~ 唱男低音/ sing in ~ 用男低音唱 Ⅱ *adj.* 低音的

bass[2] /bæs/ *n.* 鲈鱼

bastard /ˈbæstəd/ *n.* [C]私生子

bat[1] /bæt/ Ⅰ *n.* [C]球拍 Ⅱ *v.* 击球

bat[2] /bæt/ *n.* [C]蝙蝠：as blind as a ~ 和蝙蝠一样瞎的；有眼无珠

batch /bætʃ/ *n.* [C]批；批次；整批(货)：~ number 批号/ in ~es 成批；分批

bath /bɑːθ/ *n.* [C]洗澡：Have a hot ~. 洗一个热水澡吧！

bathe /beɪð/ *vi.* 洗澡：~ in cold water 洗冷水浴/ ~ in sweat 汗流浃背/ ~ in tears 泪流满面/ I often ~ in the river in summer. 我夏天常去河里洗澡。

bathing /ˈbeɪðɪŋ/ *n.* [U]洗澡；游泳；沐浴：Water used for ~ is also to be used for flashing toilets. 洗澡用过的水也可用来冲马桶。/ The chief attraction of the resort is ~. 该胜地吸引人的地方是游泳。

bathroom /ˈbæθˌruːm/ *n.* [C] ❶浴室；盥洗室 ❷卫生间；厕所：Is there a ~ in this restaurant? 这饭馆里有卫生间吗？/go to (use) the ~上卫生间，上厕所

baton /ˈbætən, bəˈtɒn/ *n.* [C] ❶(乐队、歌唱队指挥用的)指挥棒 ❷短棍；短棒；警棍 ❸(接力赛跑用的)接力棒

batter /ˈbætə(r)/ *v.* 持续打击；捣毁，砸烂；重创；(用炮火)轰击：Blizzards ~ed Britain for the third day. 暴风雨连续三天袭击英国。/They have been known to ~ their children. 大家都知道，他们经常殴打孩子。

battery /ˈbætəri/ *n.* [C]电池(组)：dry ~ 干电池/ charge a ~ 给电池充电

battle /ˈbætl/ *n.* [C]战役；战斗；会战：We should fight a ~ against pollution. 我们应当与环境污染做斗争。

bawl /bɔːl/ *v.* ❶ 恸哭；号啕大哭：~ like a baby 孩子般地号啕大哭 ❷大叫；

B

大喊：Trains ~ed and hurtled by. 一列列火车呼啸疾驰而过。/~ one's dissatisfaction 大声发泄不满情绪

bay /beɪ/ *n.* [C]海湾

bayonet /ˈbeɪənət/ *n.* [C](枪上的)刺刀

BC, B. C. (=Before Christ)公元前(写在年代之后)

be /biː, bɪ/ *v.* (现在式 am, is, are; 过去式 was, were; 过去分词 been; 现在分词 being) ❶*vi.* 是；成为；存在；有：Horses are animals. 马是动物。/ Knowledge is power. 知识就是力量。/ Has the postman been here yet? 邮递员已来过了吗？/ He was a doctor. 他当过医生。❷ *aux. v.* (助动词，帮助构成时态、语态)：English is taught in our school. 我们学校教英语。/ I was lying in bed when the teacher came. 老师来时，我正躺在床上。

beach /biːtʃ/ *n.* [C]海滩；海滨：bathing ~ 海滨浴场

beacon /ˈbiːkən/ *n.* [C]灯塔

bead /biːd/ *n.* [C] ❶(有孔的)小珠：the ~s of a necklace 项链上的珠子 ❷(汗、血等的)小滴；水珠：~s of sweat 滴滴汗珠/~s of dew 露珠/ **draw a ~ on** 瞄准：The marksman drew a ~ on his garget. 神枪手瞄准了靶子。

beak /biːk/ *n.* [C](鸟的)嘴；喙

beam /biːm/ *n.* [C] ❶(光线的)束，柱：a ~ of hope 一线希望/ a laster ~ 一束激光 ❷梁；横梁；横木：The ~s can bear the weight of the roof. 横梁能够承受屋顶的重量。

bean /biːn/ *n.* [C]豆

bear[1] /beə(r)/ *n.* [C]熊

bear[2] /beə(r)/ *vt.* (bore /bɔː/, borne 或 born /bɔːn/) ❶忍受；支持；负担：I cannot ~ wet weather. 我受不了潮湿的天气。❷ 生(孩子)：She was born in 1958. 她生于 1958 年。❸怀有；抱有：I'll ~ your advice in mind. 我将记住你的忠告。

bearable /ˈbeərəbl/ *adj.* 可忍受的；可容忍的；忍耐得住的：With a headache the noise was not ~. 头一痛起来，那吵闹声就无法忍受。/ Without their help, this work could not have been completed in a ~ time. 如果没有他们的帮助，这项工作完成起来就会拖拖拉拉，叫人难以忍受。

beard /bɪəd/ *n.* [C] 胡子；须

bearing /ˈbeərɪŋ/ *n.* ❶[C]轴承；承座 ❷[U]关系，联系；影响：His foolish question has no ~ on the problem. 他提的那个愚蠢的问题与本题无关。/ What he says has some ~ on what we're talking about. 他说的与我们现在谈的有点关系。❸[U]举止；姿态；气质；风度：a man of dignified ~ 举止端庄的人 / In his ~ was something of majesty. 在他言谈举止间有一种威严。❹[U]忍耐；忍受；容忍：Your conduct is past ~. 你的行为让人忍无可忍。

beast /biːst/ *n.* [C]兽：wild ~ 野兽

beastly /ˈbiːstli/ Ⅰ *adj.* ❶(口语)令人不快的；令人厌恶的：The ~ stench almost made him faint. 恶臭几乎把他熏得晕倒。❷野兽(般)的；野蛮的，凶残的：~ behaviour of the savages 野蛮人的残暴行为 Ⅱ *adv.* (口语)很，非常，极其：It's ~ hard to please him. 要讨他好比登天还难。派 beastliness *n.*

beat /biːt/ *v.* (beat, beaten /ˈbiːtn/) 打，敲；(心脏)跳动：Stop ~ing him. 不要打他了！/ Her heart ~ madly with fright. 由于惊吓她的心狂跳不已。/ ~

the record 打破纪录

beating /ˈbiːtɪŋ/ *n.* ❶打，敲，击；拍打；锤打：give sb. a good ~ 狠揍某人 / get a brutal ~ at the hands of thugs 遭暴徒一顿毒打 ❷[C]（尤指在比赛中）失败，败北：get a merciless (good) ~ in the finals 在决赛中遭到惨败 ❸[U]跳动；震动：Can you feel the ~ of my heart? 你能感觉到我的心跳吗？

beautiful /ˈbjuːtɪfl/ *adj.* 美丽的；优美的：the true, the good, the ~ 真善美/ The girl is ~. 这女孩真美。派 beautifully *adv.*

beautify /ˈbjuːtɪfaɪ/ *v.* 使美丽；美化；装饰：~ our life 美化生活/ ~ the environment 美化环境

beauty /ˈbjuːti/ *n.* ❶[U]美；美丽：wholesome ~ 健康美/ ~ culture 美容术(业) ❷[C]美人；美的东西：choose the ~；a ~ pageant 选美比赛

because /bɪˈkɒz/ *conj.* 因为：He didn't come ~ he was ill. 他病了，所以没来。/~ **of** 由于；因为：He didn't attend the meeting ~ of his illness. 他因病没来开会。

beckon /ˈbekən/ *v.* (以招手、点头等)示意；召唤：The guide ~ed us to follow him. 导游示意我们跟着他。/He ~ed and the girl came over. 他招了招手，那姑娘就走了过来。

become /bɪˈkʌm/ *vi.* (became /bɪˈkeɪm/, become) 变成；成为：China will ~ a modern and strong socialist country. 中国将成为现代化的社会主义强国。

bed /bed/ *n.* [C] ❶床；床位：go to ~ 睡觉；就寝/ make the ~ 整理床铺/ double (single) ~ 双(单)人床 ❷苗床；苗圃：seed ~ 苗圃/ a flower ~ 花坛 ❸河床；海底；湖底：You can see the river ~ under the water there. 在那里你可以看到水下的河床。

bedclothes /ˈbedkləʊðz/ *n.* 床上用品；被褥：Do you need any ~? 你还需要什么床上用的东西吗？

bedding /ˈbedɪŋ/ *n.* [U]被褥；卧具

bedroom /ˈbedruːm/ *n.* [C]寝室；卧室：His ~ is under mine. 他的寝室就在我楼下。

bedtime /ˈbedtaɪm/ *n.* [U]就寝时间；睡觉时间：My ~ is about eleven o'clock. 我就寝的时间大约是 11 点。

bee /biː/ *n.* [C]蜜蜂

beef /biːf/ *n.* [C](*pl.* beeves /biːvz/) 牛肉；菜牛：~-steak 牛排

beehive /ˈbiːhaɪv/ *n.* [C]蜂箱：Bees live in the ~. 蜜蜂住在蜂箱里。

beep /biːp/ Ⅰ *n.* [C](汽车喇叭等发出的)短促刺耳的嘟嘟声；(电台、无线电装置等发出的)短促尖厉的信号声：Please give your message when you hear the ~. 听见嘟嘟响就请你讲话。Ⅱ *vi.* ❶按响喇叭：The cars ~ed and ~ed, but no one moved. 汽车喇叭响了又响，但是谁也没动。❷发出短促尖厉的声音：When the timer ~s, take the cake out of the oven. 定时器嘟嘟一响，就把炉子里的蛋糕取出。

beeper /ˈbiːpə(r)/ *n.* [C]BP 机；寻呼机

beer /bɪə(r)/ *n.* [U]啤酒

beet /biːt/ *n.* 甜菜；糖萝卜

beetle /ˈbiːtl/ *n.* [C] ❶甲虫 ❷眼睛近视的人

befall /bɪˈfɔːl/ *vt.* (-fell/-ˈfel/, -fallen /-ˈfɔːlən/)(通常指不幸的事)发生于；降临于：Bad luck and ill health befell him throughout his life. 他一生都不走运，而且病魔缠身。

B

before /bɪˈfɔː(r)/ Ⅰ *prep.* 在……以前：Must I be home ~ eight o'clock? 我 8 点钟前必须在家吗？Ⅱ *conj.* 在……以前：Think well ~ you decide. 决定之前应好好想想。Ⅲ *adv.* 以前：I haven't seen her ~. 我以前没有见过她。/ ~ **long** 不久：I'll get the dictionary ~ long. 我不久就会得到这本词典。**long** ~ 很久以前：I saw her long ~. 我很久以前看见过她。

beforehand /bɪˈfɔːhænd/ *adv.* 预先；事先；提前地：You should tell me the news ~. 你应当事先把那个消息告诉我。

befriend /bɪˈfrend/ *vt.* 友好对待；亲近；与……交朋友：The children ~ed the lost dog. 孩子们亲近迷了路的狗。/She ~ed the new girl in class. 她与班上新来的女同学交上了朋友。

beg /beg/ *v.* (begged; begging) 请求；乞求/~ **one's pardon** 请某人再说一遍 ~ **sb. to do sth.** 请求某人做某事：I ~ged him to excuse me for doing such a foolish thing. 我请求他原谅我做的蠢事。~ **for sth.** 请求得到某物：He ~ged for my help. 他恳求我的帮助。

beggar /ˈbegə(r)/ *n.* [C]乞丐；叫花子

begin /bɪˈgɪn/ *v.* (began/bɪgæn/, begun/bɪˈgʌn/; beginning) 开始：Classes ~ at eight in the morning. 早上 8 点钟开始上课。/ When did you ~ to study English? 你什么时候开始学英语的？

beginner /bɪˈgɪnə(r)/ *n.* [C] ❶初学者；生手：This is a book for ~. 这是一本初学者的入门书。❷创始人：They said that he was the ~ of the impressionist. 他们说他是印象派的创始人。

beginning /bɪˈgɪnɪŋ/ *n.* 开始；开端；起源：at the ~ (of)在开始时；起初/ from the ~ to the end 自始至终；从头到尾/ I'll read the book from the very ~ to see if I can find something useful for me. 我要从头读读这本书，看看能否找到有用的东西。

begrudge /bɪˈgrʌdʒ/ *vt.* ❶对……表示不满；对……发怨言：He ~s every penny he pays in tax. 他每缴一分钱税都要发牢骚。❷嫉妒；羡慕：Let's not ~ (him) his good fortune. 咱们可别嫉妒他的好运。

behalf /bɪˈhɑːf/ *n.* 为帮助某人；支持 / **on** ~ **of** 代表；为了：The lawyer spoke on ~ of his client convincingly. 那位律师代表他的当事人所说的话令人信服。

behave /bɪˈheɪv/ *v.* ❶表现；以某种态度对待(与 to, towards 连用)：teach a child to ~s well 教孩子举止端正 / He ~s like a gentleman. 他的一举一动像个绅士。/ How did they ~ towards you? 他们对你怎么样？❷行为规矩；举止良好；听话：Children are taught to ~. 要教孩子们听话。/~ **oneself** 使(自己)表现良好：The little boy ~d himself in school. 小男孩在学校里表现良好。❸(机器、轮船、汽车等)运行，运转：The ship ~s well even in rough water. 即使遇到风浪，船的航行情况仍然良好。/ How's your watch behaving? 你的手表走得怎么样？

behavio(u)r /bɪˈheɪvjə(r)/ *n.* [U]行为；举止；表现：Her good ~ deserves praise. 她的良好表现值得称赞。

behind /bɪˈhaɪnd/ Ⅰ *prep.* 在……后面：The clock is a little ~ time. 这钟走得稍微慢了一点。Ⅱ *adv.* 在后；向后：Please look ~. 请向后看。

being /ˈbiːɪŋ/ *n.* ❶[U]存在；生存/**come into** ~ 形成；产生：We do not know when the world came into ~. 我们不知道世界是何时产生。❷[C]生物;存在物:a human ~人/ living ~ s 生物

belch / beltʃ / Ⅰ *v.* ❶打嗝,暖气:He ~ed after eating too much. 他暴食之后打起嗝来。❷喷发,喷射;大量冒出(烟等):factory chimneys ~ing smoke 一座座冒着烟的工厂烟囱 Ⅱ *n.* [C]打嗝,暖气

belief / bɪˈliːf / *n.* (*pl.* beliefs)信心;信念;信仰:religious ~ 宗教信仰/ I don't think it is right to laugh at other's ~. 我认为嘲笑别人的信仰是不对的。

believe / bɪˈliːv / *v.* 相信;认为:I ~ what you said. 我相信你说的话。/~ **in** 相信;信任;信仰:I ~ in his honesty. 我相信他的诚实。

belittle / bɪˈlɪtl / *vt.* 轻视;小看;贬低:~ sb. 's merits 贬低某人的优点/~ sb. 's achievements 贬低某人的成就

bell / bel / *n.* [C]钟;铃:door~ 门铃/ sound the ~ 敲钟/ The ~ rings. 铃声响了。

bellicose / ˈbelɪkəʊs / *adj.* 好战的;好争斗的;好吵架的:a ~ people 好战的民族/His facial expression was unpleasantly ~. 他脸上露出一副气势汹汹的样子,令人讨厌。

bellow / ˈbeləʊ / Ⅰ *v.* 怒吼;吼叫:Don't ~ at little children. 别对小孩大吼大叫。Ⅱ *n.* [C]怒吼声;吼叫声

belly / ˈbeli / *n.* [C]腹部;肚子;胃:have a large ~ 大腹便便

belong / bɪˈlɒŋ / *vi.* 属于:~ **to** 属于:That dictionary ~s to her. 那本词典是她的。/ Li Ning ~s to our team. 李宁是我们队的队员。

belongings / bɪˈlɒŋɪŋz / *n.* 附属物;所属物;财产:personal ~个人财产/ After they packed up their ~, they left the room. 收拾好自己的东西后,他们便离开了房间。

beloved / bɪˈlʌvd / *adj.* 敬爱的;受到爱戴的:The teacher is ~ by all. 这位老师受到大家的爱戴。

below / bɪˈləʊ / Ⅰ *adv.* 在下方:Is it above or ~? 它在上面还是在下面? Ⅱ *prep.* 在……下面:The Dead Sea is ~ sea level. 死海的海面低于海平面。

belt / belt / *n.* [C]带子;皮带:life ~ 安全带;救生带

bench / bentʃ / *n.* [C]长凳:warm on the ~(体育比赛中)当替补队员/ work ~ 工作台

bend / bend / *v.* (bent/bent/, bent)弯曲;弄弯;屈身:His head was bent so low. 他的头垂得很低。

beneath / bɪˈniːθ / Ⅰ *prep.* 在……之下:~ the average 在平均值以下 Ⅱ *adv.* 在下方

beneficial / ˌbenɪˈfɪʃl / *adj.* 有益的;有利的;有助的:Eating apples is ~ to health. 吃苹果有益于健康。

benefit / ˈbenɪfɪt / Ⅰ *n.* 利益;好处:Your advice is of good ~ to me. 你的劝告对我很有益。Ⅱ *v.* 得益;有益于:We ~ed greatly by this frank talk. 我们从这次坦率的谈话中获益匪浅。

benevolence / bəˈnevələns / *n.* [U] ❶仁慈;善行:He gave the little girl 10 dollars out of ~. 出于仁慈之心,他给了那小女孩 10 美元。❷捐助物;捐款:A lot of people contributed ~ after the tsunami. 海啸发生后,很多人都去捐款。

benevolent / bəˈnevələnt / *adj.* 仁慈的;

慈善的：~society 慈善团体

benign /bɪˈnaɪn/ *adj.* ❶善良的；和蔼的；亲切的：a ~ old man 和蔼的老人/the ~ features of Mr. Potts 波茨先生慈祥的面容 ❷(疾病)对生命不构成危险的；(肿瘤等)良性的：a ~ illness 不危及生命的疾病/a ~ tumour 良性肿瘤

bent /bent/ *adj.* 弯曲的；曲背的：The old farmer's back was ~ from years of toil. 这位老农因长年劳累而驼了背。

benumbed /bɪˈnʌmd/ *adj.* 僵冷的；僵硬的；失去知觉的：fingers ~ with the cold 冻僵的手指

berry /ˈberi/ *n.* [C]浆果；莓

berth /bɜːθ/ *n.* [C] ❶(船、车、飞机上的)卧铺，铺位；座位：Have you booked a ~ on the ship? 你预订船上的铺位了吗？❷锚地；泊位；船台

beside /bɪˈsaɪd/ *prep.* 在……旁；在……附近；在……之外：~ the point 离题/ The young man is ~ the bus. 那位年轻人站在汽车旁。

besides /bɪˈsaɪdz/ Ⅰ *prep.* 除……之外，还有：There are many other places to visit in China ~ Suzhou. 除苏州外，中国还有许多地方可游览。Ⅱ *adv.* 而且；此外：She doesn't like it. Besides, she can't afford it. 她不喜欢也买不起它。

besiege /bɪˈsiːdʒ/ *vt.* ❶包围；围攻；围困：They were ~d for six months but refused to surrender. 他们已被围困了6个月，但仍拒绝投降。❷挤在……的周围；围住：Employment agencies were ~d by the jobless. 职业介绍所被失业者围了个水泄不通。

best /best/ Ⅰ *adj.* (good 的最高级形式)最好的：She is my ~ friend at school. 她是我学生时代最好的朋友。Ⅱ *adv.* (well 的最高级形式)最：Which book do you like ~? 你最喜欢哪本书？Ⅲ *n.* 最佳；全力 / **do one's** ~ 尽力；努力：I'll do my ~ to study English well. 我将尽全力把英语学好。**make the ~ of** 充分利用：You should make the ~ of this valuable opportunity. 你应该充分利用这个宝贵的机会。

bestow /bɪˈstəʊ/ *vt.* 把……赠予；把……给予：~ a doctorate on sb. 给某人授博士学位/Several gifts were ~ed on the royal visitors. 谒见国王的人被赠予一些礼物。派 bestowal *n.*

best-seller /ˈbestˈselə/ *n.* [C]畅销书；畅销唱片；畅销商品：His new book became the ~ that year. 他的新书成了那年的畅销书。

bet /bet/ Ⅰ *n.* [C]打赌；赌金；赌注：Let's make a ~. 让我们打个赌。Ⅱ *v.* (bet 或 betted; betting)赌；打赌；敢断定：I ~ she will come. 我敢断定她会来的。

betray /bɪˈtreɪ/ *vt.* ❶不忠：She ~ed her promises. 她未遵守诺言。❷出卖：They ~ed their country. 他们出卖了自己的国家。❸显露；暴露：What you said ~ed your ignorance. 你所说的话暴露出了你的无知。派 betrayal *n.*

better /ˈbetə(r)/ Ⅰ *adj.* (good 的比较级形式)较好的；更好的：Milk is ~ for babies than soybean milk. 对婴儿来说，牛奶比豆奶好。Ⅱ *adv.* (well 的比较级形式)较好地；更好地：She swims ~ than her brother does. 她游泳比她弟弟游得好。Ⅲ *v.* 改善：They tried to ~ their living conditions. 他们努力改善生活条件。/ **had** ~最好(后接动词原形)：You'd ~ put on your coat. 你最好穿上外衣。

between / bɪˈtwiːn / *prep.* 在……之间(一般指两者之间):~ the lines 在字里行间(体会言外之意)/ What's the difference ~ this and that? 这个和那个之间有什么区别?

beverage / ˈbevərɪdʒ / *n.* [U]饮料(如牛奶、茶、咖啡、啤酒等):alcoholic ~ 含酒精饮料/ cooling ~ 清凉饮料

beware / bɪˈweə(r) / *v.* 谨防;当心:~ of fire 当心火烛;当心失火

bewilder / bɪˈwɪldə(r) / *vt.* 迷惑;弄糊涂;使发愣;使为难:He was so ~ed that he didn't know what to do. 他茫然不知所措。

bewildered / bɪˈwɪldəd/ *adj.* 迷惑不解的;摸不着头脑的:a ~ look 一副迷惑不解的神情

bewitch / bɪˈwɪtʃ / *vt.* 使入迷;使陶醉:be ~ed by a glorious sunset 为壮丽的日落景象所陶醉/Shirley Temple ~ed a generation of moviegoers. 秀兰·邓波儿倾倒了一代电影观众。

beyond / bɪˈjɒnd / *prep.* 超出……(的范围):This is ~ my capacity. 这非我能力所及。

biannual / baɪˈænjuəl / *adj.* 一年两次的:~ congress 两年召开一次的大会

bias / ˈbaɪəs / Ⅰ *n.* [C] ❶ 斜线 ❷偏见;倾向性;癖好:He always has a ~ against his son. 他总是对自己的儿子有偏见。Ⅱ *vt.* 对……有偏见;有倾向性 派 biased *adj.*

Bible / ˈbaɪbl / *n.* (the Bible)《圣经》:swear on the ~手按《圣经》发誓

bibliography / ˌbɪblɪˈɒgrəfi / *n.* ❶[C]书目提要;文献目录 ❷[U]目录学;文献学

bicycle / ˈbaɪsɪkl / *n.* [C]自行车

bid / bɪd / Ⅰ *v.* (bade 或 bid, bidden 或 bid)❶报价;出价;投标:public ~ding 公开招标/ They bid against each other for the building of the main stadium of Beijing Olympic Games. 他们相互竞争投标北京奥运会主场馆的修建。❷(打桥牌时)叫牌 Ⅱ *n.* [C] ❶出价;投标:call for invite ~s 招标/make a ~ for 出价;投标 ❷叫牌

big / bɪg / (bigger, biggest) *adj.* 大的;重大的:Shanghai is a ~city. 上海是一座大城市。/The ~ news of today is the election of President. 今天的重大新闻是总统竞选。

bike /baɪk/ *n.* (=bicycle)[C]自行车

bikini / bɪˈkiːni / *n.* [C]比基尼(女式泳装)

bilateral / ˌbaɪˈlætərəl / *adj.* ❶两边的;双边的:~ talks 双边会谈 ❷互惠的;对等的:~ trade agreement 互惠贸易协定

bilingual / ˌbaɪˈlɪŋgwəl / Ⅰ *adj.* 熟悉两种语言的;使用两种语言的:a ~ dictionary 双语词典/ ~ education 双语教育 Ⅱ *n.* [C]能使用两种语言的人

bill / bɪl / *n.* [C] ❶账单:settle a ~ 结账/ pay a ~ 付账(单)/ Tom paid the ~ for repairing his car. 汤姆付了修车的账单。❷单子;清单:a ~ of fare 菜单;节目单 ❸ 招贴;广告;传单:post a ~ 张贴海报/ Post no ~s on the fence. 此栏杆上不准张贴广告。❹纸币;钞票:He found a dollar ~ under the desk. 他在桌下发现一张一美元的钞票。❺议案;法案:draft (pass) a ~ 草拟(通过)一项议案

billboard / ˈbɪlˌbɔːd / *n.* [C](户外)广告牌;告示牌;招贴板

B

billiards /ˈbɪlɪədz/ *n.* (*pl.*) 台球:play ~ 打台球/~table 台球桌

billion /ˈbɪljən/ *num.* (美)十亿;(英)万亿

billionaire /ˌbɪljəˈneə(r)/ *n.* [C]亿万富翁

billow /ˈbɪləʊ/ Ⅰ *vi.* (波浪)翻腾;波浪般起伏 Ⅱ *n.* 巨浪;波涛:~s of smoke 滚滚浓烟 派 billowy *adj.*

bin /bɪn/ *n.* [C]容器;箱子;垃圾箱:a grain ~ 粮仓/ a litter ~ 杂物箱/ a rubbish (dust) ~ 垃圾箱

bind /baɪnd/ *vt.* (bound,bound) ❶捆;扎;绑:He bound the girl with a piece of rope. 他用绳子捆住这个女孩。❷装订:The workers use machines to ~ the pages into books. 工人们用机器把书页装订成册。

binding /ˈbaɪndɪŋ/ Ⅰ *n.* ❶捆绑(物);束缚(物);黏合剂 ❷(书籍的)装订;装帧;封面 ❸镶边;滚条 Ⅱ *adj.* ❶紧身的;限制行动的:a shirt too ~ to wear 穿上太紧的衣服 ❷有约束力的;应履行的;必须遵守的:an agreement that is ~ on all parties 对各方面均有约束力的协定

biochemistry /ˌbaɪəʊˈkemɪstri/ *n.* [U] 生物化学

biography /baɪˈɒɡrəfi/ *n.* [C]传记;传记文学

biological /ˌbaɪəˈlɒdʒɪkl/ *adj.* 生物的;生物学的:~ clock 生物钟/ ~ chain 生物链/ ~ laboratory 生物学实验室/ ~ science 生物科学/ ~ technology industry 生物技术产业

biologist /baɪˈɒlədʒɪst/ *n.* [C]生物学家

biology /baɪˈɒlədʒi/ *n.* [U]生物学

biomedical /ˌbaɪəʊˈmedɪkl/ *adj.* 生物医学的

bionics /baɪˈɒnɪks/ *n.* 仿生学:~ techniques 仿生技术

biosphere /ˌbaɪəʊˈsfɪə(r)/ *n.* [C] ❶生物圈 ❷生命层

birch /bɜːtʃ/ *n.* 桦树

bird /bɜːd/ *n.* [C]鸟;禽:a flock of ~s 一群鸟/ migratory ~s 候鸟/ water ~s 水禽/ kill two ~s with one stone 一石二鸟;一举两得

bird's-eye /ˈbɜːdzˌaɪ/ *adj.* 俯视的,鸟瞰的;远眺的:From the plane we had a ~ view of London. 我们从飞机上俯瞰了伦敦的全景。

birth /bɜːθ/ *n.* [U] ❶诞生;出生:~ rate 出生率/ ~ control program 生育控制计划;计划生育/ The exact date of the ~ of Tom is January 1st. 汤姆出生的准确日子是1月1日。/ **give ~ to** 生产(婴儿);(喻)产生,造成:She gave ~ to twin girls. 她生了一对双胞胎女孩。❷起源;血统;出身:He is a man of noble ~. 他出身高贵。

birthday /ˈbɜːθdeɪ/ *n.* [C]生日:~ card 生日贺卡/ ~ party 生日聚会/ ~ present 生日礼物/ They celebrated Ann's ~ in the park. 他们在公园里庆祝安的生日。

birthplace /ˈbɜːθpleɪs/ *n.* 出生地;故乡:Tianjin is my ~. 天津是我的故乡。

biscuit /ˈbɪskɪt/ *n.* [C](英)饼干;(美)小面包,小点心

bisect /baɪˈsekt/ *v.* ❶把……二等分;把……一分为二:Bisect the apple as well as you can. 把这个苹果尽量对切分匀。❷和……相交;和……交叉;横穿:Highway 32 ~s highway 56 at this point. 32号公路和56号公路在这里相交。派 bisection *n.*

bishop / ˈbɪʃəp / *n.* [C](基督教)主教

bit / bɪt / *n.* 一点儿;少许:a ~ of meat 一小片肉 / ~ **by** ~ 一点一点地;渐次:Bit by ~ she understood his words. 她逐渐理解了他所说的话。**do one's** ~ 尽某人一份力量:We should do our ~ for our nation. 我们应该为国家尽一份力量。

bite / baɪt / *v.* (bit, bitten) 咬;叮:He was bitten by a snake. 他被蛇咬了。

biting / ˈbaɪtɪŋ / *adj.* ❶严寒的;刺痛的,刺骨的;凛冽的:~ winter 严冬/ a ~ east wind 凛冽的东风 ❷(言辞)刻薄的,尖刻的;讽刺的,挖苦的:a ~ comment 尖刻的评论

bitter / ˈbɪtə(r) / *adj.* ❶苦的;苦味的:Good medicine tastes ~. 良药苦口。❷难受的;令人悲伤的;痛苦的:Her failure to pass the examination was a ~ disappointment to her parents. 她考试失败是一件令她父母极为失望的事。派 bitterly *adv.*;bitterness *n.*

bitty / ˈbɪti / *adj.* ❶七零八碎的;东拼西凑的;无条理的;不连贯的:Conversation was ~ and irresolute. 谈话内容东拉西扯,而且口气也显得犹豫不决。❷细小的

bizarre / bɪˈzɑː(r) / *adj.* 奇形怪状的;古怪的;怪诞的;异乎寻常的:~ behaviour 古怪的行为/a ~ series of events 一连串的怪事

black / blæk / *adj.* 黑的;黑暗的:He was ~ in the face. 他脸色发紫。/ The sky grew ~ with clouds. 乌云使天空暗下来。/ ~ **and blue** 遍体鳞伤;青一块、紫一块:He was beaten ~ and blue. 他被打得遍体鳞伤。

blackboard / ˈblækbɔːd / *n.* [C]黑板:~ newspaper 黑板报/ A student cleaned off the ~ after class. 下课后一位学生把黑板擦干净了。

blacken / ˈblækən / *vt.* ❶使变黑;使变脏:Soot ~ed the snow. 煤灰将雪弄黑了。/Smoke ~ed the sky. 浓烟遮黑了天空。❷破坏,败坏(名誉等);诋毁:~ sb.'s reputation 败坏某人的声誉

blacklist / ˈblækˌlɪst / *n.* [C]黑名单:The police drew up a ~ for political reasons. 那个警察因政治原因而被列入黑名单。

blackmail / ˈblækmeɪl / *n.* [U]&*vt.* 敲诈;勒索;讹诈:The young man committed ~. 那年轻人犯了敲诈罪。

bladder / ˈblædə(r) / *n.* [C]膀胱

blade / bleɪd / *n.* [C]刀刃;刀片:sword with two ~s 双刃剑

blame / bleɪm / Ⅰ *vt.* 责备;责怪;埋怨:Bad workmen often ~ their tools. 拙匠常怪工具差。Ⅱ *n.* [U]责任;过失:He often throws ~s on his brother. 他常把过失推给他的兄弟。

blameless / ˈbleɪmlɪs/ *adj.* 无可指责的;无过错的,无过失的:Although the boy had not broken the window himself, he was not entirely ~. 尽管窗户不是那男孩打破的,但他也不是完全没有过错。

blank / blæŋk / Ⅰ *n.* [C]空白;空格;空白表格:an application ~ 申请表/ Please fill in the ~ with a proper word. 请用恰当的词填空。Ⅱ *adj.* 空白的,未写字的;无表情的:a ~ sheet of paper 一张白纸

blanket / ˈblæŋkɪt / Ⅰ *n.* [C]毯子;羊毛毯 Ⅱ *adj.* 综合的,总括的;一揽子的:a ~proposal(一揽子建议)

blast / blɑːst / *v.* 炸毁;摧毁;炸裂:The roof was ~ed off. 屋顶被炸毁了。

blaze /bleɪz/ Ⅰ*n.* [C]火焰；火光：He put some wood on the fire and it soon burst into a ~. 他放了些木柴在火上，木柴很快就燃起来了。Ⅱ*vi.* 发光；冒火焰：A fire was blazing well in the fireplace. 炉子中的火在熊熊燃烧。

bleach /bliːtʃ/ Ⅰ*vt.* 晒白；漂白；使脱色：~ the linen napkins in the wash 漂洗亚麻布餐巾 Ⅱ*n.* [U]漂白剂：a strong household ~高效家用漂白剂

bleak /bliːk/ *adj.* ❶光秃秃的；无遮蔽的；荒凉的：~ cliffs 光秃秃的悬崖峭壁 ❷无望的；黯淡的；惨淡的：Pandas are an endangered species with a ~ future. 大熊猫是一个前景不妙的濒危物种。派 bleakly *adv.*；bleakness *n.*

bleed /bliːd/ *v.* (bled/bled/, bled)流血；失血：His hand was ~ing. 他的手在淌血。

blemish /ˈblemɪʃ/ Ⅰ*n.* [C] ❶瑕疵；污点；缺点：leave a ~ on sb.'s reputation 给某人的名声染上污点 ❷(皮肤、水果等上的)斑；疤；痣：a ~ on a pear 梨上的斑点 Ⅱ*vt.* 使有疤；有损……的完美；玷污，使有缺点：One bad deed can ~ a good reputation. 做一次坏事就有可能使自己名誉扫地。

blend /blend/ Ⅰ*vt.* (blended 或 blent /blent/)使混合，使混杂；使交融；混合成：~ the eggs and milk (together) 把鸡蛋和牛奶拌和 Ⅱ*n.* [C] 混合物，混合体，混成品：This coffee is a ~ of three varieties. 这种咖啡是由三个品种混合配制而成的。

bless /bles/ *v.* (blessed 或 blest)祝福；保佑；保护……免于(灾祸等)：They married with their parents' ~ing. 他们结婚得到父母的祝福。

blind /blaɪnd/ *adj.* 瞎的；盲目的：~ import 盲目进口/ ~ investment 盲目投资/ ~ worship 盲目崇拜/ go ~失明/ He is ~ in the right eye. 他的右眼是瞎的。/ He is ~ to his own weakness. 他看不到自己的弱点。

blink /blɪŋk/ Ⅰ*v.* 眨眼睛；闪烁 Ⅱ*n.* ❶眨眼睛；闪光：You can see the ~ of the lighthouse along the riverside. 在河边你会看见灯塔的闪光。❷一瞬间：He ran out in a ~ of an eye. 一瞬间工夫他就跑了出去。

bliss /blɪs/ *n.* [U] ❶极乐，狂喜：David was swimming in wedded ~. 戴维沉浸在婚后的幸福之中。❷天堂之乐，天赐之福，洪福：There are times when ignorance is ~ indeed. 有的时候无知真是福气呐。

blizzard /ˈblɪzəd/ *n.* [C] ❶暴风雪，雪暴 ❷暴风雪似的一阵，猛烈的攻击：the ~ of mail at Christmas 圣诞节时雪片般的邮件

block /blɒk/ Ⅰ*n.* [C] ❶块；木块；石块：stumbling ~ 绊脚石/ wood ~木刻 ❷街区：Walk two ~s ahead and you'll find the hospital. 朝前走过两个街区，你就可以找到那家医院。❸阻塞；障碍物：traffic ~交通阻塞/ road~*n.* 路障 Ⅱ*v.* 堵塞；阻塞：A severe storm ~ed up the railways. 一场猛烈的暴风雨使铁路中断。

blockade /blɒˈkeɪd/ Ⅰ*n.* [C] 封锁：break (impose, lift, maintain) a ~ 突破(实施，解除，维持)封锁 Ⅱ*vt.* 封锁：The firemen ~d the area where the fire was raging. 消防人员封锁了大火蔓延地区。派 blockader *n.*

blockage /ˈblɒkɪdʒ/ *n.* [C] ❶封锁 ❷阻塞；堵塞：the ~ of the streets by heavy snows 大雪造成的街道交通堵塞

blond(e) /blɒnd/ *adj.* ❶亚麻色的；淡黄色的 ❷白肤金发碧眼的

blood /blʌd/ *n.* [U] ❶血；血液：~ pressure 血压/ ~ test 验血/ ~ transfusion 输血/ ~ type 血型/ ~ bank 血库/ ~vessels 血管/donate ~ 献血/ ~ donor 献血者 ❷血统；种族：flesh and ~ 血肉关系；亲骨肉 ❸血气；气质；脾气：He is a person of hot~. 他是个火暴脾气的人。派 bloodily *adj.*

bloodstream /ˈblʌdstriːm/ *n.* [U] ❶血流；体内循环的血液 ❷主流：the economic ~ of the society 社会经济的主流

bloody /ˈblʌdi/ *adj.* ❶出血的；流血的：It is a ~ fight. 这是一场流血的斗争。❷血腥的；残忍的：~ murder 血腥的谋杀

bloom /bluːm/ Ⅰ *vi.* 开花：The rose ~s beautifully. 开放的玫瑰花很漂亮。Ⅱ *n.* [C]花：The cherry trees have beautiful ~s. 樱花开得很美。/ **in ~** 在开花中：The tulips are in full ~ now. 郁金香花正盛开着。

blossom /ˈblɒsəm/ Ⅰ *vi.* 开花：The plum trees began to ~. 李子树开始开花。Ⅱ *n.* [C](尤指果树的)花：**in ~** 在开花中；开着花

blot /blɒt/ [C] Ⅰ *n.* ❶污渍；墨渍；(道德上的)污点：Don't make any ~ on the form. 别把墨水溅到表格上。Ⅱ *v.* (blotted; blotting)抹脏；弄上污渍

blouse /blaʊz/ *n.* [C](妇女或儿童穿的)短上衣；(宽大的)工作服

blow /bləʊ/ Ⅰ *vi.* (blew/bluː/, blown /bləʊn/) ❶吹：The papers were blown away by the wind. 报纸被风吹走了。❷爆炸：The ship blew up. 船爆炸了。Ⅱ *n.* [C]打；打击：This battle dealt the enemy hard ~s. 这一仗狠狠地打击了敌人。

blue /bluː/ Ⅰ *adj.* ❶蓝色的；青的：a ~ collar worker 蓝领工人/ His face was ~ from the cold. 他的脸冻得发紫。❷下流的：Children are not allowed to see ~ films. 小孩是不允许看黄色电影的。❸沮丧的；忧郁的：Her mother looks ~. 她妈妈神情忧郁。Ⅱ *n.* [U]蓝色：He was dressed in ~ yesterday. 昨天他穿的是蓝色衣服。

blueprint /ˈbluːprɪnt/ *n.* [C]蓝图；行动计划

bluff /blʌf/ *n.* 陡岸；悬崖；峭壁

blunder /ˈblʌndə(r)/ Ⅰ *n.* [C]大错，大娄子：Signing the agreement was a major ~ on the Prime Minister's part. 签订该条约是首相的一大失策。Ⅱ *vi.* 犯大错误，出大娄子：Just pray that he doesn't ~ again and get the names wrong. 但愿他别再出洋相，把名字又弄错了。

blunt /blʌnt/ *adj.* ❶(刀或刀口)不锋利的，钝的；(铅笔等)不尖的：sharpen a ~ knife 把钝刀磨快 ❷(人或态度)率直的，坦率的；生硬的；耿直的，欠圆通的：a ~ speech 没遮没拦的言辞

blur /blɜː(r)/ Ⅰ *v.* (blurred; blurring)使(视线、意识等)变得模糊不清；变得模糊：Tears ~red my eyes. 泪水模糊了我的双眼。/She cried and her eyes ~red with tears. 她哭得泪眼蒙眬。Ⅱ *n.* [C]模糊；模糊不清的事物：My memory of the accident is only a ~. 我对那场事故已经记不清楚了。

blush /blʌʃ/ Ⅰ *vi.* ❶(因害羞、窘迫、激动等)脸红；(脸)变红：Here comes the ~ing bride. 满脸羞红的新娘来了。❷羞愧，惭愧；感到难堪：He doesn't ~ at poverty. 他并不因贫穷而感到难为

情。Ⅱ *n.* (常用单数)脸红:His remark brought a ~ to (into) the young girl's cheeks. 少女听了他的话,双颊变得绯红。/**at (the) first** ~ 初看起来;乍一想:It seemed a good idea at first ~, but there were several drawbacks in it. 乍一想,那似乎是个好主意,可是其中却有好些缺点。

bluster /ˈblʌstə(r)/ Ⅰ *vi.* ❶咆哮,怒吼;气势汹汹地说话,逞威风:He ~s about revenge but does nothing. 他嚷着要报仇,却没采取任何行动。❷(风)狂吹,呼啸;(浪等)汹涌:The wind ~ed around the corner of the house. 大风呼啸着吹过屋角。Ⅱ *n.* [U]大声的恐吓;气势汹汹的大话;夸口:He impresses no one by his ~. 他大声恐吓,但没人把它当回事。

board /bɔːd/ Ⅰ *n.* [C] ❶木板;纸板;布告牌;甲板:I saw a note on the ~. 我看见布告牌上贴着通知。/ **on** ~ 在船上;在飞机上:The passenger has come on ~. 那位乘客已上船。❷委员会;董事会:He is a member of our school ~. 他是我们学校董事会的成员。Ⅱ *v.* 上船;上飞机:The passengers ~ed the plane at noon. 旅客们中午上的飞机。

boast /bəʊst/ *v.* 自夸;自吹;说大话:John ~s that he is the best man alive. 约翰自夸天下第一。/ He often ~s of his deeds, learning and cleverness. 他常夸耀自己的业绩、学识与智慧。

boat /bəʊt/ *n.* [C]小船;艇;小轮船:When we are in danger, we should be in the same~. 在危难中,我们应当同舟共济。

body /ˈbɒdi/ *n.* [C] ❶身体;躯体:We wear clothes to keep our bodies warm. 我们穿衣是为了保暖。❷团体:government ~行政机构 ❸尸体

boil /bɒɪl/ *v.* 沸腾;(液体)煮开:The water is ~ing. 水开了。/ She's ~ing the milk for her baby. 她正在给婴儿烧牛奶。

boiler /ˈbɔɪlə(r)/ *n.* [C] ❶锅炉;汽锅 ❷用来煮东西的器皿;(家用)烧水壶(或锅等);(供家庭集中取暖的)热水箱

boiling /ˈbɔɪlɪŋ/ Ⅰ *adj.* ❶达到沸点的,沸腾的:~ water 沸水 ❷炎热的,灼热的,极热的:It's ~ in here! 这儿热得像个蒸笼!❸翻腾的,汹涌的:the ~ seas 汹涌的海浪 ❹激昂的;(怒火等)强烈的,猛烈的:in a state of ~ indignation 处于极其愤怒的状态 Ⅱ *adv.* 极度地,非常地:It was ~ hot. 天气酷热难耐。

bold /bəʊld/ *adj.* ❶勇敢的;大胆的;冒失的:May I make so ~ as to ask your name? 我可以冒昧地问您的姓名吗?❷粗大的;醒目的:~ headlines 醒目的大标题 派 boldly *adv.*

bolster /ˈbəʊlstə(r)/ *vt.* ❶支持;加强;提高;充实:~ sb.'s hopes with false reports of outside assistance 拿有关外援的失实报道来支撑某人的希望 ❷(用支撑物)支撑,支承,加固

bolt /bəʊlt/ Ⅰ *n.* ❶[C]螺栓;插销;门闩 ❷闪电;霹雳:lightning ~s 一道道闪电/a ~from (out of) blue 晴天霹雳;突如其来的事情 Ⅱ *v.* 闩(门):Don't ~ a child alone in the room. 别把小孩一人关在屋子里。

bomb /bɒm/ *n.* [C]炸弹:atom ~ 原子弹/ nuclear ~ 核弹 / time ~定时炸弹

bomber /ˈbɒmə(r)/ *n.* [C] ❶轰炸机:a fighter ~ 战斗轰炸机 ❷(轰炸机上的)投弹手,炸弹员

bond /bɒnd/ Ⅰ *n.* [C] ❶ 联结;黏合

❷公债；债券：treasury ~s 国库债券/ issue a ~ 发行一种债券/ ~holder 债券持有者 Ⅱ *vt*. 结合；黏合：They ~ed the two different materials together. 他们把两种不同的材料黏合在一起。

bondage /ˈbɒndɪdʒ/ *n*. [U]奴役；束缚；羁绊：celebrate one's escape from ~庆祝自己摆脱了奴役苦

bone /bəʊn/ *n*. [C]骨骼；骨头：Dogs like ~s. 狗喜欢吃骨头。

bonfire /ˈbɒnfaɪə(r)/ *n*. [C]篝火；营火

bonus /ˈbəʊnəs/ *n*. [C]奖金；津贴；红利：annual ~ 年度奖金/distributing ~es improperly 滥发奖金/ wrapped ~ 红包/ ~ dividend 股息红利

bony /bəʊni/ *adj*. 多骨的；骨瘦如柴的

book /bʊk/ Ⅰ *n*. [C]书；书籍：E~s 电子图书/children's ~s 儿童读物/ reference ~s 参考书/ I can keep the ~ for two weeks. 这本书我可以借两周。Ⅱ *vt*. 预订：Tickets can be ~ed one week in advance. 票可以提前一周预订。

bookcase /ˈbʊkkeɪs/ *n*. [C]书橱；书柜：He has a big ~ in his room. 他房里有一个大书橱。

booking /ˈbʊkɪŋ/ *n*. 预约；预订；订货：a ~ note 订单/ make a ~ 预订/ a ~ clerk 售票员/a ~ office 售票处

booklet /ˈbʊklət/ *n*. [C]小册子

bookmark /ˈbʊkmɑːk/ *n*. [C]书签：I always use a piece of paper for my ~. 我常用一张小纸片做书签。

bookshelf /ˈbʊkʃelf/ *n*. [C]书架：He put a clock on his ~ . 他在书架上放了一只钟。

bookshop /ˈbʊkʃɒp/ *n*. [C]书店：There is a new ~ near our school. 我们学校附近有一家新书店。

bookworm /ˈbʊkˌstɔː(r)/ *n*. [C]极爱读书的人，终日埋头读书的人；书呆子

boom /buːm/ Ⅰ *vi*. 迅速发展；繁荣；兴旺 Ⅱ *n*. [C]繁荣；兴旺：business ~ 商业繁荣/population ~ 人口激增/ In recent years, there has been a travel ~ (tourist ~) throughout the country. 近年来全国掀起了一股旅游热。

boost /buːst/ Ⅰ *vt*. ❶推动，促进，激励；提高；增强：~ local business 促进当地商业的发展 ❷增加，使增长：help to ~ profits 有助于提高利润 Ⅱ *n*. [C] ❶推动，促进，激励：The promotion was a big ~ to his ego. 这一提升促使他更为自负。❷增加，增长，提高：receive a pay ~获得一次加薪/a ~ in exports 出口的增加

boot /buːt/ *n*. [C]长筒靴

booth /buːð/ *n*. [C]货摊；摊位；电话亭

border /ˈbɔːdə(r)/ *n*. [C]边缘；边界：~ trade 边境贸易/ You must go through the customs in order to pass across the ~. 你要过境就必须在海关办理手续。

borderline /ˈbɔːdəlaɪn/ Ⅰ *n*. [C] ❶边界(或边境)线；分界线：the ~ between France and Germany on the map 地图上法德两国的边界线 ❷模棱两可的状态：the ~ between friendship and love 介乎友情与爱情之间的情感 Ⅱ *adj*. ❶边界(或边境)线上的；靠近边界的：a ~ town 边境城镇 ❷不确定的，不明朗的：a ~ candidate 成败难卜的候选人

bore /bɔː(r)/ *vt*. 使厌烦；使厌倦：We were ~d by his talk. 他的讲话使我们感到厌烦。

boring /ˈbɔːrɪŋ/ *adj*. 令人厌烦的；枯燥乏味的；无聊的：The film is ~. Nobody likes to see it. 这部电影很无聊，没人爱看。

B

born / bɔːn / *adj*. 天生的，生来的：He said that the boy was a ~ athlete. 他说那小男孩是个天生的运动员。

borrow / ˈbɒrəʊ / *v*. 借；借用：a ~ed word 外来词/ May I ~ your Chinese-English dictionary? 我可以借用你的汉英词典吗？

bosom / ˈbʊzəm / *n*. 胸，胸部；胸怀；内心：take sb. to ~ 视某人为知己/ After that they made ~ friends with each other. 那以后他们就成了知心朋友。

boss / bɒs / *n*. [C]老板；上司；当家人：Who's the ~ in the house? 谁是这里的一家之主？/ She is the ~ of a clothing store. 她是一家服装店的老板。

botanical / bəˈtænɪkl / *adj*. 植物的；植物学的：There is a big ~ garden near our school. 我们学校附近有一个很大的植物园。

botany / ˈbɒtəni / *n*. [U]植物学

both / bəʊθ / Ⅰ *pron*. 两个；两者；双方：Both (of them) are teachers. 他们两人都是教师。Ⅱ *adv*. ~... **and** ... 两个都；既……又……：Both he and I are from Shanghai. 我和他都是上海人。

bother / ˈbɒðə(r) / *v*. 打扰；麻烦：He is always ~ing me. 他老是打扰我。/ It's not important. Don't ~ your head about it. 这并不重要，不要为它费心思。

bothersome / ˈbɒðəsəm/ *adj*. 麻烦的；烦人的，恼人的，讨厌的：~ demands 烦人的要求

bottle / ˈbɒtl / *n*. [C]瓶子：There is a ~ of ink on the desk. 桌子上有一瓶墨水。

bottom / ˈbɒtəm / *n*. [C]底部：at the ~ of the garden 在花园的尽头/ at the ~ of the mountain 在山脚下

bottomless / ˈbɒtəmlɪs / *adj*. ❶无限的，无穷无尽的：millionaires with ~ purses 财源滚滚的百万富翁 ❷不见底的，深不可测的，极深的：a ~ gorge 深不见底的峡谷

bough / baʊ / *n*. [C]树枝；(树的)主茎，主干：a slender ~细树枝

boulevard / ˈbuːləvɑːd/ *n*. [C] ❶林荫大道：Our address is 121 Granger Boulevard. 我们的地址是格兰居林荫大道121号。❷大街，主干道 ❸街心绿化带；(分隔马路车道的)街心岛

bounce / baʊns / *v*. 反弹；跳回：Striking a rock, the bullet ~d off. 子弹打在岩石上反弹开了。

bouncy / ˈbaʊnsi / *adj*. ❶(指球等)富有弹性的，弹性好的，弹力足的：An old tennis ball is not as ~ as a new ball. 旧网球的弹力没有新的足。❷生气勃勃的，精神饱满的；轻快活泼的：a ~ personality 活泼的个性 ❸跳跃的；颠弹的；颠跳的：Hard ground makes balls more ~. 坚硬的地面使球颠弹得更厉害。

bound[1] / baʊnd / Ⅰ *n*. [C]跳跃；弹跳：advance by leaps and ~s飞跃前进，突飞猛进 Ⅱ *vi*. 跳跃；弹回：Her heart ~ed with joy. 她高兴得心头怦怦直跳。

bound[2] / baʊnd / *adj*. 必定；一定/**be ~ to do** 一定，必然；负有义务，负有责任：Your plan is ~ to succeed. 你的计划一定会成功。/ We are ~ to obey the law. 我们有义务守法。

bound[3] / baʊnd / *adj*. 准备到…… 去的；开往(驶往)……的：He entered a train ~ for Beijing. 他登上一辆开往北京的火车。

bound[4] / baʊnd / *n*. (*pl*.)边界；界限；范

围：out of ~s 越界；禁止入内/ There are no ~s to her ambition. 她的野心是无止境的。

boundary /ˈbaʊndri/ *n.* [C]边界；分界线：beyond the ~ 超越界线/A river forms the ~ between the two countries. 一条河成了两国的分界线。

boundless /ˈbaʊndlɪs/ *adj.* ❶无边无际的，广阔的：Outer space is ~. 宇宙空间是无边无际的。❷无限的，无穷无尽的：be ~ in one's gratitude 感激不尽

bourgeois /ˈbʊəʒwɑː/ Ⅰ*adj.* 资产阶级的 Ⅱ*n.* [C]资产阶级分子

bow[1] /bəʊ/ *n.* [C](射箭用的)弓；弓形物：Draw not your ~ till your arrow is fixed. 箭没搭好别先拉弓(三思而后行)。

bow[2] /baʊ/ Ⅰ*v.* ❶鞠躬；点头：The host ~ed his guest in. 主人鞠躬迎接客人进屋。❷屈服；使弯曲：We shall never ~ down to our enemies. 我们决不向敌人屈服。/ The branches were ~ed down with the weight of the snow. 树枝被积雪压弯了。 Ⅱ*n.* [C]鞠躬；点头：He gave her a ~ for it. 他为此事向她鞠躬。

bowel /ˈbaʊəl/ *n.* (*pl.*)肠：The girl had loose ~s yesterday. 那女孩昨天腹泻。

bowl /bəʊl/ *n.* [C]碗；大杯；钵：He broke his ~. 他把碗打破了。/ She ate three ~s of rice. 她吃了三碗米饭。派 bowlful *n.*

bowling /ˈbəʊlɪŋ/ *n.* [U]保龄球：play ~ 打保龄球/ a ~ alley 保龄球场(馆)

box[1] /bɒks/ *n.* [C] ❶盒子；箱子：a ~ of matches 一盒火柴/ a tool ~ 工具箱/ black ~ 黑匣子 ❷包箱；专席：a press ~ 记者席/a witness ~ 证人席

box[2] /bɒks/ Ⅰ*v.* 拳击；打拳：They will ~ each other for the championship. 为争夺冠军他们将进行拳击比赛。Ⅱ*n.* [C]一拳；一巴掌

boxer /ˈbɒksə(r)/ *n.* [C] ❶拳击运动员，拳击手 ❷斗拳狗

boxing /ˈbɒksɪŋ/ *n.* [U]拳击(术)；拳击运动：They like to go in for ~ after work. 下班后他们爱去击拳。

box-office /ˈbɒksˌɒfɪs/ *adj.* ❶票房(收入)的：a ~ window 售票窗 / the ~ draw takings 票房收入 ❷叫座的，卖座的，受欢迎的：His latest movie was a ~ hit. 他的新影片非常叫座。/ This concert isn't ~. 这场音乐会不受欢迎。

boy /bɒɪ/ *n.* [C]男孩；少年：The ~ likes swimming. 那男孩很喜欢游泳。

boycott /ˈbɒɪkɒt/ Ⅰ*vt.* [C]联合抵制；拒绝参加：Products from that country are ~ed. 人们都抵制那个国家的产品。Ⅱ*n.* 联合抵制；拒绝参加：economic ~ 经济抵制/trade ~ 贸易抵制

boyish /ˈbɒɪɪʃ/ *adj.* 男孩子的；男孩子般的：~ ambitions 男孩子的志向

brace /breɪs/ *n.* [C]支架；支撑物

bracelet /ˈbreɪslət/ *n.* [C]手镯；手铐

bracket /ˈbrækɪt/ *n.* [C] ❶托架；支架 ❷(*pl.*)括号：Please put the words between the ~s. 请把单词写在括号里。

bract /brækt/ *n.* [C]苞叶，苞片，苞

brag /bræg/ *v.* (bragged; bragging)吹嘘，吹牛，夸口：He constantly ~s about how well he plays golf. 他老是吹嘘自己的高尔夫球打得多棒。/He ~s that he is the world's greatest boxer. 他吹嘘自己是世界上最伟大的拳击手。

braid /breɪd/ *n.* (*pl.*)辫子：She has beautiful ~s . 她的辫子很漂亮。

braille /breɪl/ *n.* [U](供盲人写作、阅

读、用手触摸的)点字法,布莱叶盲文

brain /breɪn/ *n.* [C] ❶头脑;脑子:He blew out his enemy's ~ with an axe. 他用斧头把敌人的脑袋砍开了花。❷(*pl.*)智慧;智力:beat one's ~s 绞尽脑汁/ Use your ~s before you act. 行动之前动动脑筋。

brainless /ˈbreɪnlɪs/ *adj.* 没有头脑的;傻头傻脑的:a ~ idiot 傻头傻脑的白痴

brainy /ˈbreɪni/ *adj.* 聪明的;有才智的;(头脑)机灵的:Mary was beautiful and ~. 玛丽才貌双全。

brake /breɪk/ Ⅰ *n.* [C]闸;刹车;制动器:hand ~ 手刹/ foot ~ 脚刹/ You should first learn how to apply the ~ suddenly to avoid an accident. 首先你得学会如何为避免意外事故而紧急刹车。Ⅱ *v.* 制动;刹车:The driver had to ~ hard when he saw a woman was in front of his car. 看到车前有一位妇女,司机不得不紧急刹车。

bran /bræn/ *n.* [U]麸子,糠

branch /brɑːntʃ/ *n.* [C] ❶枝条;树枝:He cut down all the ~es of that tree. 他把那棵树的枝条全都砍了下来。❷支流;部分;部门:English is a ~ of the Germanic language family. 英语是日耳曼语系中的一个分支。/ the Party ~ 党支部/ the League ~团支部/ open up a ~ 开分店(开分公司) 派 branchy *adj.*

brand /brænd/ Ⅰ *n.* [C]品牌;商标;烙印:~name 名牌 / ~name and quality products 名优产品/ ~name strategy 名牌战略/ This ~ of tinned beans is welcome by all. 这种品牌的青豆罐头受到大家的欢迎。Ⅱ *vt.* 打烙印;印商标

brand-new /ˈbrændˈnjuː/ *adj.* 崭新的,全新的;新制的:a ~ machine 崭新的机器 / The car is not ~ but it has only had one previous owner. 这辆汽车不算是全新的,不过它只转过一次手。

brandy /ˈbrændi/ *n.* [U]白兰地酒

brass /brɑːs/ *n.* [U]黄铜;铜器

brave /breɪv/ *adj.* 勇敢的:He is a ~ soldier. 他是个勇敢的士兵。派 bravely *adv.*

bravery /ˈbreɪvəri/ *n.* [U]勇敢;英勇:The policeman showed great ~ in saving the drowning child. 那位警察在抢救落水儿童时,表现极为勇敢。

brawl /brɔːl/ Ⅰ *n.* [C](大声)争吵;打架:The ~ between husband and wife kept the whole neighbourhood awake. 这场夫妻间的吵架扰得四邻五舍无法入睡。Ⅱ *v.* (激烈地)争吵;打架:Usually you could see them playing or ~ing in the street. 通常你能见到他们在大街上玩耍或打闹。

breach /briːtʃ/ Ⅰ *n.* ❶[C]裂口,豁口,缺口:A cannon ball made a ~ in the castle wall. 一发加农炮弹把城堡墙轰开一个缺口。/There's a ~ in our security. 我们的安全措施尚有罅隙。❷(对诺言、义务等的)违背;(对法律、协议等的)违反,违犯:serious ~es of discipline 种种严重违纪行为 ❸(友好关系的)破裂,疏远;裂痕:heal the ~ between the two parties 弥合两党间关系的裂痕 Ⅱ *vt.* 攻破,突破;打开缺口:~ the enemy barbed wire 突破敌人的铁丝网

bread /bred/ *n.* [U]面包:a loaf of ~ 一块面包/ buttered ~涂黄油的面包/ dry ~ 没涂黄油的面包/ He had to earn his ~ when he was very young. 他很小就不得不自己谋生。

breadth /bredθ/ *n.* ❶宽度;广度:Do you know the ~ of this room? 你知道这个房间有多宽吗? ❷(心胸等的)宽容;

大量：~ of mind 胸怀宽广 / We all admire his ~ of view. 我们都很羡慕他的见多识广。

break / breɪk / Ⅰ *v.* (broke/brəʊk/, broken /brəʊkn/) ❶打破；折断；破裂：Billy broke his colored pencil. 比利把他的彩色铅笔弄断了。/ Who broke the cup? 谁打烂了杯子？❷损坏；破坏：She broke her watch by winding it too tightly. 她把发条上得太紧，因而把表弄坏了。/~ **away**（**from**）逃脱；脱离：The prisoner broke away from his guards while being taken to another gaol. 那个囚犯在转狱途中挣脱看守逃走了。~ **down** ①（机器）损坏：The power generator broke down. 发电机坏了。②（健康或精神）垮掉：He has completely broke down in health. 他的身体彻底垮了。~ **in** ① 打断；插话：Don't ~ in while others are speaking. 别人说话时别插话。② 闯入；强行进入：The thief broke in. 贼破门而入。~ **into** 闯入；破门而入：The burglar broke into my house and stole my gold watch. 盗贼破门而入，盗走了我的金表。~ **off** ①突然中断；暂停：The conference broke off at noon. 会议中午暂停。② 折断：A branch of the tree broke off. 一根树枝断了。~ **out** 突然发生；爆发：When did the World War Ⅱ ~ out? 第二次世界大战什么时候爆发的？~ **through** 克服；制胜；冲破；突破：Our troops had little difficulty in ~ing through the enemy's line. 我们的军队毫不费力地突破了敌人的防线。~ **up** 拆散；打破；结束：When does your school ~ up for the summer holidays? 你们学校何时放暑假？Ⅱ *n.* ❶[C]破裂；决裂：How do you think about the ~ between the two countries? 你对两国的绝交有何看法？❷[U]破晓：They left the village at the ~ of day. 天破晓时他们离开了村子。❸[C]中止；停顿：He always writes in his study without a ~. 他总是不停地在书房里写作。❹[C]（课间或工间）休息时间：It's time for lunch. Let's take a ~ for twenty minutes. 该吃午饭了，我们休息 20 分钟吧。

breakable / ˈbreɪkəbəl/ *adj.* 易碎的：~ ornaments 易碎装饰品

breakage / ˈbreɪkɪdʒ/ *n.* ❶破碎；破裂；毁坏；损失：The ~ of the girder was due to a fault in the steel. 大梁毁损是因钢材有毛病所造成的。❷[C]（常用 *pl.*）破损物：All ~s have to be paid for. 所有破损的东西都必须赔偿。

breakdown / ˈbreɪkdaʊn / *n.* ❶崩溃；倒塌；（机器等的）损坏：~ in health 身体垮了 / have a ~ 出故障；（身体、精神）崩溃 ❷失败；挫折；停顿

breaker / ˈbreɪkə(r) / *n.* [C]破坏者；开拓者：a law ~ 不法分子

breakfast / ˈbrekfəst / *n.* 早饭；早餐

break-in / ˈbreɪkˌɪn / *n.* [C]（持不法动机）破门而入，非法闯入；盗窃（行为）：investigate a ~ at the local bank 调查一起闯入当地银行的盗窃案

breakthrough / ˈbreɪkθru: / *n.* [C]突破；突围；重大成就：They have made a great technological ~in recent years. 这些年以来，他们在技术上取得了重大的突破。

break-up / ˈbreɪkˌʌp / *n.* [C] ❶分散；分裂；分离：the ~ of a marriage 离婚 ❷解散，解体，瓦解，崩溃：They are on the brink of a ~ of the two party system. 他们处于两党制濒于崩溃的边缘。

breast / brest / *n.* [C]胸膛；胸部；乳房

B

breath / breθ / *n.* [U]呼吸/**out of** ~ 喘不过气；上气不接下气：He ran so fast that he was out of ~. 他跑得太快，以至于喘不过气来。**give out** (**take in**) ~ 吐气(吸气)；Taking in a deep ~, he dived into the water. 他深吸一口气潜入水里。

breathe / briːð / *v.* 呼吸：The doctor asked Mary to ~ deeply to check her health. 医生让玛丽做深呼吸以检查她的健康状况。

breathless / ˈbreθləs / *adj.* 无声息的；喘不过气来的：There was a ~ silence when the police came in. 警察进来时，房里安静得令人大气都不敢出。

breathtaking / ˈbreθteɪkɪŋ / *adj.* 惊人的；激动人心的：a ~ match 一场激动人心的比赛

breed / briːd / Ⅰ *n.* [C]品种；种类：fine ~ 优良品种 Ⅱ *vt.* (bred / bred /, bred) ❶饲养：They ~ cattle for market. 他们饲养牲口以供应市场。❷生育；繁殖：Rabbits ~ rapidly. 兔子繁殖迅速。❸教养；培养：He was born and bred in China. 他在中国土生土长。派 breeder *n.*

breeding / ˈbriːdɪŋ/ *n.* [U] ❶生育，生殖；繁殖：the process of ~ 繁殖过程 / ~ instincts 生殖本能 ❷(动植物良种的)培育；(动物的)饲养；(植物的)培植：keep horses for ~ purposes 为育种的需要而养马 ❸教养；教育，培养：a person of fine ~ 有良好教养的人/ She had her ~ at my father's charge. 她在我父亲的照管下受到了良好的教育。

breeze / briːz / *n.* [C]微风；和风：cool ~ 凉风/ on the ~ 迎风招展/ in the spring ~ 沐浴春风

brevity / ˈbrevɪti / *n.* [U](讲话、行文等的)简洁，简练，简短：send a telegram in its ~ 发一份文字简练的电报/essays written with clarity and ~文笔清晰简洁的散文

brew / bruː / Ⅰ *v.* 酿酒；酝酿：~ beer 酿造啤酒/ They are ~ing a plot. 他们正在酝酿一起阴谋。Ⅱ *n.* 酿造

brewery / ˈbruːəri / *n.* [C]酿造厂；酿酒厂：The ~ is famous all over the country. 那家酿酒厂全国有名。

bribe / braɪb / Ⅰ *v.* 贿赂；收买：He ~d himself into the committee. 他通过贿赂混进了委员会。Ⅱ *n.* [C] 贿赂；行贿物：He says that he will never take ~s. 他说他决不受贿。

brick / brɪk / *n.* [C]砖

bride / braɪd / *n.* [C]新娘

bridegroom / ˈbraɪdgruːm / *n.* [C]新郎

bridge / brɪdʒ / Ⅰ *n.* [C] ❶桥：an arched ~ 拱桥/ a cross-over ~ 天桥/ a draw (suspension)~吊桥/ a railway ~ 铁路桥/ a highway ~ 公路桥/ They are going to build (construct, lay, throw) a ~ across the river. 他们要在河上架桥。❷桥牌：He likes to play ~. 他喜欢打桥牌。Ⅱ *vt.* 联结；跨过(障碍)：The parents and children are trying hard to ~ their generation gap. 父母和子女都在尽力缩小他们之间的代沟。

brief / briːf / *adj.* 简短的；简洁的：He is ~ of speech. 他说话简洁。/ In ~, we should take action at once. 简而言之，我们必须马上采取行动。

bridle / ˈbraɪdl / *n.* [C]马勒；缰绳

briefcase / ˈbriːfkeɪs / *n.* [C]公文包

brigade / brɪˈgeɪd / *n.* [C]旅；队：a fire ~ 消防队/ a rescue ~ 急救队

bright / braɪt / *adj.* ❶明亮的；晴朗的；辉煌的：The garden is ~ with sunshine.

花园里阳光明媚。/ If you want to have a ~ future, you should work still harder. 想要有美好未来，你得更加努力地工作。❷聪明的：She is ~ beyond her years. 她年纪不大，人却很聪明。

brighten /ˈbraɪtn/ *v.* ❶发光；发亮：Her face ~ed up with joy. 她的脸上露出了兴奋的神情。❷使快活；使活跃：To be with their grandson ~ed up the old couple. 和孙子在一起使老两口非常快活。

brightness /ˈbraɪtnɪs/ *n.* [U] ❶明亮；亮度 ❷聪明；机灵：Not long after that I found her ~. 那以后不久我就发现她很聪明。

brilliant /ˈbrɪlɪənt/ *adj.* ❶光辉的；辉煌的：~ sunshine 灿烂的阳光/ The lights are far too ~. 灯光太耀眼了。❷卓越的；英明的；才华横溢的：His brother is a ~ student. 他的哥哥是一个很有才华的学生。/ We watched their ~ performance in the theatre. 我们在剧院里看了他们的卓越表演。派 brilliantly *adv.*

brim /brɪm/ Ⅰ *n.* [C] ❶(杯、碗等的)边，缘：be full to the ~ 满满当当 / on the ~ of a nervous breakdown 濒临精神崩溃的边缘 ❷帽檐 Ⅱ (brimmed; brimming) *vi.* 满，充盈，满溢(与 with 连用)：Her eyes ~med with tears. 她热泪盈眶。/ be ~ming with hope 满怀希望 —*vt.* 使满；装满，灌满，注满：~ a cup with wine 向杯中注满葡萄酒

bring /brɪŋ/ *vt.* (brought/brɔːt/, brought)带来；拿来：Please ~ a dictionary with you. 请随身带本词典来。/~ **about** 带来；造成：It may ~ about a good result. 这可能带来好的结果。~ **sb. around to (doing) sth.** 说服某人做某事：I'll try to ~ him around to your views. 我将努力劝说他同意你的观点。~ **forth** 提出；使产生；引起：He brought the plan forth to our consideration. 他提出计划让我们考虑。/ March winds and April showers ~ forth May flowers. 三月的春风、四月的阵雨催开五月的鲜花。~ **into** 使……进入(某种状态)：She brought me into touch with everything. 她使我接触到一切。~ **out** 使清楚；显示出来：He was so excited that he could hardly ~ out a "thank you". 他激动得连一声"谢谢"都说不出来。~ **to** 使……恢复知觉：She will soon be brought to. 她很快就会苏醒过来的。~ **to light** 发现；揭发：His enemies brought to light some foolish things he had done. 他的敌人揭穿了他干的一些蠢事。~ **to pass** 促成：By much planning, the mother brought the marriage to pass. 这位母亲花了很多心思促成这桩婚事。~ **up** ①抚养；养育；教养：He paid much attention to ~ing up his children. 他花了很多心思抚养孩子。②停止：Bill started to complain, but I brought him up short. 比尔开始抱怨，但我很快让他停止下来。③提出；谈及：At the meeting, he brought up the idea of a picnic. 在会上，他提出了野餐的事。

brink /brɪŋk/ *n.* [C] ❶(陡峭处的)边缘，边沿；(河、池等的)边，边沿；陡岸；滨：the ~ of the pond 池塘边 ❷顶点；始发点；边缘：beyond the ~ of sb.'s endurance 超出某人忍耐的限度/be on the ~ of war 处于战争边缘

brisk /brɪsk/ *adj.* ❶敏捷的；快的；轻快的；精力充沛的：She passed us at a ~ walk. 她步履轻捷地从我们身边走过。/a ~ old man 精神矍铄的老汉

B

❷(天气等)干冷的;清新的,令人爽快的:a ~ day 天气干冷的一天/The air was ~. 空气清新。

bristle / brɪsl / *n.* [C]硬毛;鬃毛

brittle / ˈbrɪtl / *adj.* 硬而脆的;易碎的,易损坏的:~ porcelain 易碎的瓷器

broad / brɔːd / *adj.* ❶宽的;宽阔的;广大的:The lake is a mile ~ here. 这里的湖面有一英里宽。/ We should serve the mass-es of the ~ people. 我们应该为广大人民群众服务。❷宽宏的:He is a man of ~ views. 他是一个宽宏大量的人。派 broadly *adv.*

broadcast / ˈbrɔːdkɑːst / Ⅰ *v.* (broadcast 或 broadcasted)广播;播音;传播:~ live 现场广播/ This station ~s sports news at seven. 这个台七点钟播体育新闻。/ You shouldn't ~ my secret to the whole class. 你不该向全班同学散布我的秘密。/ The news was ~ at eight o'clock last night. 这消息是昨天晚上八点钟播出的。Ⅱ *n.* ❶广播;播音:a ~ station 广播站/ the Central People's Broad-casting Station 中央人民广播电台 ❷播音节目:The blind girl listens to news ~ every evening. 那盲人女孩每天晚上收听新闻节目。

broaden / ˈbrɔːdn / *v.* 放宽;变阔;扩大:~ one's interests 拓宽兴趣/ The work-ers are ~ing the street. 工人们正在加宽街道。/ The stream ~s into a river here. 小溪流到这儿变宽了,成为一条河。

brochure / ˈbrəʊʃə(r) / *n.* [C]小册子:a holiday ~ 假日指南/ a sales ~ 商品推广手册

broil / brɔɪl / *vt.* ❶烤,炙,焙:~ a steak 烤牛排 ❷使灼热;把……烤煳,将……烧焦:We turned back, much ~ in the hot sun. 我们返回时,在烈日下被晒得灼热不堪。

broker / ˈbrəʊkə(r) / *n.* [C](股票、公债等的)经纪人;掮客;代理人;中间人:a ~ office, a ~ house 经纪人事务所/a real-estate ~ 地产经纪人/ He became an insurance ~ after graduation. 毕业后他当了保险经纪人。

bronze / brɒnz / *n.* 青铜,青铜制品;青铜色:He won a ~ medal at the sports. 在运动会上他获得一枚铜牌。/ They are setting up a ~ statue in the garden. 他们正在花园里竖一尊铜像。

brood / bruːd/ Ⅰ *n.* ❶[C](雏鸡或雏鸟等的)一窝;(昆虫、鱼等的)一次产出的卵:a ~ of chickens 一窝小鸡 ❷(一个家庭的)全体孩子:She stayed home with her ~. 她和她那群子女待在家里。Ⅱ *vi.* ❶孵蛋;孵出雏鸡(或雏鸟等):That hen is ~ing. 那只母鸡正在孵蛋。❷(不快或愤忿地)想;沉思,考虑;担忧:~ about the meaning of life 思索人生的意义

brook / brʊk / *n.* [C]小溪;小河

broom / bruːm / *n.* [C]扫帚

brother / ˈbrʌðə(r) / *n.* [C]兄弟:blood ~s 亲兄弟/ cousin ~s 堂兄弟;表兄弟/ elder ~ 哥哥 / younger ~ 弟弟 / half ~(异父或异母)弟兄/ twin ~s 孪生兄弟 派 brotherly *adj.*

brotherhood / ˈbrʌðəhʊd / *n.* 兄弟(般的)关系;兄弟情谊

brow / braʊ / *n.* [C](常用 *pl.*)眉毛:Knit the ~s and you will hit upon a stratagem. 眉头一皱,计上心来。

brown / braʊn / *adj.* 褐色的;棕色的:There is a room with ~ glass windows near my dormitory. 我的宿舍旁有一间

带褐色玻璃窗的房间。

browse /braʊz/ *v.* ❶随便翻阅；游览：~ through a market 逛市场/He spent the afternoon browsing in the bookstores. 他整个下午都泡在那些书店里翻阅书刊。❷看橱窗（里的商品）

bruise /bruːz/ Ⅰ *n.* [C] ❶青肿，挫伤，淤伤：His arms and backs were covered in ~s. 他的双臂和背部满是青肿块。❷（水果、植物等的）伤痕；（皮革等的）擦痕，磨损；（金属等的）凹痕 ❸（感情等方面的）挫折，伤害 Ⅱ *vt.* ❶使青肿，使受淤伤：be ~d from head to foot 从头到脚遍体鳞伤 ❷挫伤，伤害（感情等），使受到伤：He was apparently ~d by some personal experience. 他显然在个人经历上受过创伤。❷（感情等）易受伤害：Her feelings ~ easily. 她感情脆弱。

brush /brʌʃ/ Ⅰ *v.* 刷；擦；拂：The light wind gently ~ed his cheeks. 和风轻拂他的面颊。/ Please ~ your shoes. 请把鞋子擦一擦。Ⅱ *n.* [C]刷子；画笔：a Chinese ~ 毛笔/tooth~ 牙刷

brushup /ˈbrʌʃˌʌp/ *n.* [C]温习，复习；复习期：He gave his Spanish a ~ before his trip to Mexico. 去墨西哥之前，他温习了一下西班牙语。/The orchestra needed a good deal of ~ before the performance. 演出之前，这个管弦乐队需要进行大量的反复排练。

brutal /ˈbruːtl/ *adj.* 残忍的；野蛮的；严酷的：~ winter 严冬/ He is not accustomed to the ~ heat of Nanjing. 他很不适应南京的酷热天气。派 brutally *adv.*

brutality /bruːˈtæləti/ *n.* [U]残忍；残暴；暴行：In this film you can know about the concentration camp ~ at that time. 在这部电影里你可以了解到那时候集中营里的残暴行为。

brute /bruːt/ *n.* [C]禽兽；畜生；残忍的人

bubble /ˈbʌbl/ Ⅰ *n.* [C]水泡；气泡：soap ~s 肥皂泡 Ⅱ *v.* 吹泡；起泡

buck /bʌk/ *n.* [C](*pl.* buck 或 bucks) ❶雄鹿 ❷公羊

bucket /ˈbʌkɪt/ *n.* [C]桶；吊桶

buckle /ˈbʌkl/ Ⅰ *n.* [C]（皮带等的）扣子，搭扣，搭钩 Ⅱ *v.* ❶用搭扣把……扣上：~ one's shoes 扣上鞋带/He ~d on his revolver. 他用搭扣把左轮手枪扣紧。❷变形；弯曲；鼓起：Chopsticks of celluloid ~ easily in hot water. 赛璐珞筷子在热水中容易变形。/Her knees ~d with exhaustion. 她累得腿都直不起来。/ ~ **down** 倾全力（于）；专心致志（于）；开始认真从事（于）：~ down to writing a book 全力以赴地写书 ~ **up** 扣紧皮带（安全带，搭扣）：Please ~ up now, we're about to land. 请系好安全带，我们就要着陆了。

bud /bʌd/ *n.* [C]芽；花苞：Trees put forth ~s in spring. 树在春天发芽。

Buddhism /ˈbʊdɪzəm/ *n.* [U]佛教

Buddhist /ˈbʊdɪst/ Ⅰ *n.* [C]佛教徒 Ⅱ *adj.* 佛教的

budget /ˈbʌdʒɪt/ *n.* [C]预算；预算案：annual ~ 年度预算/ defence ~ 国防预算

buffalo /ˈbʌfələʊ/ *n.* [C] ❶水牛；野牛 ❷水陆坦克

buffet *n.* [C] ❶ /ˈbʌfeɪ/ 碗橱 ❷ /ˈbʊfeɪ/ 自助餐；快餐：He always goes to have a ~ after work. 下班后他总爱去吃自助餐。

bug /bʌg/ *n.* [C] ❶臭虫 ❷虫子（泛指某些昆虫）：You have to keep the millet free of ~s. 你得防止小米生虫。❸病菌;病毒:an intestinal ~s 肠道病毒 / There's a nasty ~s going around. 附近流行一种很厉害的病毒。❹(常用单数)(口语)浓烈的兴趣,迷恋,癖好;狂热:He's got (caught) the sports-car ~. 他迷上了赛车。/ I have rather a ~ about learning in class. 对于课堂学习,我有相当浓厚的兴趣。❺(常用单数)(口语)对某事有强烈兴趣者,迷,有癖好者:Someone who is interested in photography is called a camera ~ or a shutter ~. 对摄影着迷的人被称为摄影迷或快门迷。

bugle /ˈbjuːgl/ *n.* [C]号角;喇叭:blow the ~ 吹喇叭/ ~ born 号角

build /bɪld/ Ⅰ *v.* (built /bɪlt/, built)建立;创立;增强:The school was well built. 这所学校建造得很好。/ Sports and games ~ our bodies. 体育运动增强我们的体质。Ⅱ *n.* [U]构造;体格:He is a man of strong ~. 他是一个体格健壮的人。派 builder *n.*

building /ˈbɪldɪŋ/ *n.* [C] 建筑;建筑物;大楼:~ materials 建筑材料/ a public ~ 公共建筑/ a teaching ~ 教学楼/ Many of my classmates removed to new apartment ~s. 我的很多同学都搬进了新的公寓楼。

buildup /ˈbɪldˌʌp/ *n.* [C] ❶增长,增强,增进;发展:a ~ of pressure 压力的增大/The ~ of the national industry is vital. 发展民族工业至关重要。❷(尤指预先的)捧场;渲染,制造舆论;宣传攻势:She received a big ~ in the media. 她在传媒界大受好评。

built-in /ˌbɪltˈɪn/ *adj.* 内置的:My father's radio has a ~ aerial. 我父亲的收音机带内置天线。

bulb /bʌlb/ *n.* [C] ❶(植物的)球茎,鳞茎 ❷电灯泡;电灯;白炽灯,日光灯:Only a few of the ~s were working. 只有几只电灯泡还亮着。

bulge /bʌldʒ/ Ⅰ *n.* [C]膨胀,肿胀;鼓起,隆起,凸出:I could see the ~ of the body against the side of the tent. 我能看见帐篷边上鼓起的身体。Ⅱ *vi.* ❶鼓起,隆起,凸出;膨胀,肿胀:The wall buckled and ~d. 墙壁变形且向外凸出。❷装满,充满,塞满:The shelves were bulging with knick-knacks. 架子上放满了小装饰品。

bulk /bʌlk/ *n.* [U]大块;大批;大量:in ~ 大批;大量/ a man of large ~ 一个身材魁伟的人

bulky /ˈbʌlki/ *adj.* ❶巨大的,庞大的;粗壮的,肥硕的:Bulky shipments are often sent in freight cars. 体积大的货物常用货车运送。/ The males are bulkier than the females. 男性比女性身体粗壮。❷又大又笨的,不灵巧的:The equipment was so ~ that it had to be wheeled around on a large trolley. 设备这么笨重,所以人们只好使用大的架空滑轮将它运走。派 bulkiness *n.*

bull /bʊl/ *n.* [C]公牛:a ~ in a china shop 鲁莽闯祸的人/ ~fight 斗牛

bullet /ˈbʊlɪt/ *n.* [C]子弹:The soldier fired a ~ at the enemy. 战士向敌人开枪。

bulletin /ˈbʊlətɪn/ *n.* [C]公示;公告;新闻简报:a ~ board 布告牌/ news ~ 新闻简报

bullish /ˈbʊlɪʃ/ *adj.* ❶(像)公牛的;牛脾气的;执拗的 ❷(证券等行情)上涨的,看涨的:a ~ market 牛市/There was a ~ trend in the stock market. 股市行情看涨。

bully / ˈbʊli / *n.* [C]恶霸;暴徒:play the ~ 横行霸道

bump / bʌmp / Ⅰ *v.* 碰撞;击:The two cars ~ed together. 两辆车撞在一起了。/ ~ **into** 偶遇:We ~ed into an old friend yesterday. 昨天我们意外地遇到了一位老朋友。Ⅱ *n.* [C] ❶碰撞 ❷肿块

bumper / ˈbʌmpə(r) / Ⅰ *n.* [C] ❶满杯;丰盛 ❷(汽车等的)保险杠;减震物 Ⅱ *adj.* 丰盛的:a ~ harvest 大丰收/ They hope to have a ~ year. 他们希望迎来一个丰收年。

bumpy / ˈbʌmpi / *adj.* ❶高低不平的,崎岖的;隆起的:a ~ crust of rock and soil 由岩石和土壤形成的凹凸不平的地壳/~ muscles 隆起的肌肉 ❷颠簸的,不平稳的:The plane had a ~ flight in the storm. 飞机在风雨中颠簸着飞行。

bun / bʌn / *n.* [C]圆面包;馒头

bunch / bʌntʃ / *n.* [C]束;串:a ~ of flowers 一束花/ a ~ of keys 一串钥匙

bundle / ˈbʌndl / Ⅰ *n.* [C]包;捆;束:a ~ of clothes 一包衣服/ a ~ of banknotes 一扎钞票 Ⅱ *v.* 捆;包;把……乱塞入:He ~d everything into a drawer. 他把所有东西都塞进抽屉里。

bungalow / ˈbʌŋgələʊ / *n.* [C] 平房:Many old people like to live in ~. 许多老年人喜欢住平房。

bunk / bʌŋk / *n.* [C](车、船上的)床铺;铺位

buoy / bɔɪ / *n.* [C]浮标;航标;救生圈;救生衣:a life ~ 救生圈/ a light ~ 浮标灯

buoyancy / ˈbɒɪənsi/ *n.* [U] ❶浮力:A bladder provides ~ for fish. 气囊为鱼提供浮力。/ The ~ of water increases with density. 水的浮力随密度增长而加大。❷轻松愉快的心情;乐观情绪:take up one's task in ~ and hope 满怀希望地接受任务 / Her ~ kept us from being down-hearted. 她的乐观情绪使我们没有灰心丧气。

buoyant / ˈbɒɪənt / *adj.* ❶能浮起的,能漂起的;有浮力的:Cork is a very ~ material. 软木是一种浮力很大的材料。❷能使物体浮起的,有托浮力的:Balloons can float because air is ~. 气球能飘浮,是因为空气有托浮力。

burden / ˈbɜːdn / Ⅰ *n.* [C]担子;负担:His ~s have lightened a little. 他身上的负担已减轻了些。Ⅱ *v.* 使负重担;使劳累:They are not ~ed with families. 他们没有家庭拖累。/ Middle school teachers are so ~ed with teaching that they cannot engage themselves in research work. 中学教师教学负担太重,无暇顾及学术研究。

bureau / ˈbjʊərəʊ / *n.* [C](*pl.* bureaus 或 bureaux / ˈbjʊərəʊz /) 局;处;所:the Federal Bureau of Investigation (美)联邦调查局(缩写为 FBI)/ the Political Bureau of the Central Committee of the Communist Party of China 中国共产党中央委员会政治局/ the Public Security Bureau 公安局/ the Tax Bureau 税务局/ travel ~ 旅行社

bureaucracy / bjʊəˈrɒkrəsi / *n.* 官僚;官僚主义;官僚政治:overcome ~ 克服官僚主义

bureaucrat / ˈbjʊərəkræt / *n.* [C] ❶官员官僚 ❷官僚主义者

bureaucratic / ˌbjʊərəˈkrætɪk / *adj.* 官僚;专断的:~ government 官僚政府

burglar / ˈbɜːglə(r) / *n.* [C]窃贼;盗贼:The police caught a ~ last night. 昨夜

警察抓住了一个盗贼。

burglary /ˈbɜːgləri/ *n.* 盗窃(行为);盗窃罪:The young man committed (a) ~ and was sentenced to five years. 那年轻人犯了盗窃罪,被判刑五年。

burial /ˈberɪəl/ *n.* 安葬;埋葬;葬礼:His ~ will take place next Sunday. 他的葬礼下星期日举行。

burn /bɜːn/ *v.* (burnt /bɜːnt/ 或 burned /bɜːnd/)点燃;燃烧:Some materials do not ~. 有些物质不会燃烧。/ ~ daylight 白日点灯,徒劳无益/ ~ midnight oil 熬夜,开夜车/~ **up** 烧尽;烧毁:We shall ~ up all the garden rubbish. 我们要将花园里的垃圾全部焚烧掉。

burning /ˈbɜːnɪŋ/ *adj.* (常作定语) ❶燃烧的,着火的:~ coals 燃烧着的煤 ❷灼热的,滚烫的:~ sands 滚烫的沙子 / under a ~ sun 在毒热的阳光下 ❸火辣辣的;发热的:He had a ~ sensation in his throat. 他觉得喉咙里火辣辣的。❹强烈的;热烈的,激动人心的:a ~ interest in science 对科学的浓厚兴趣 / A ~ pain shot through his hands. 他双手突然感到一阵钻心的疼痛。❺紧急的,急迫的;关键的:a ~ situation 严峻的形势 派 burningly *adv.*

burrow /ˈbʌrəʊ, ˈbɜːrəʊ/ Ⅰ *n.* [C](兔、狐等动物刨的)地洞,洞穴;地道 Ⅱ *vi.* ❶掘地洞;挖地道:rats ~ing in the wall 在墙里打洞的老鼠 ❷钻进(钻入)某处;偷偷打入某组织:The train was ~ing through valleys. 火车在群山中穿行。派 burrower *n.*

burst /bɜːst/ Ⅰ *v.* (burst, burst) 冲破;破裂;爆炸:The sun ~ through the clouds and shone over the earth. 太阳冲破乌云,阳光普照大地。/~ into tears 突然大哭 /~ **forth (out)**爆发:A cry of horror ~ forth from the crowd. 人群中爆发出恐怖的叫声。/ "Don't hit me!" She ~ out. 她大声呼叫:"不要打我!" Ⅱ *n.* [C]爆发;迸发:a ~ of laughter 爆发出一阵笑声

bury /ˈberi/ *v.* 埋葬;掩盖:He was buried alive by the enemy. 他被敌人活埋了。

bus /bʌs/ *n.* [C]公共汽车:We missed the school ~ and had to take a taxi. 我们没有赶上校车,只好乘出租。/ **by** ~ 乘公共汽车:Shall we walk or go by ~? 我们是步行还是乘公共汽车去?

bush /bʊʃ/ *n.* [C]灌木;丛林:a clump of ~es 一片灌木林

bushy /ˈbʊʃi/ *adj.* ❶丛林密布的,灌木丛生的:a ~ garden 灌木丛生的花园 ❷茂密的,浓密的:a ~ beard 浓密的胡须/~ eyebrows 浓眉

business /ˈbɪznəs/ *n.* ❶[U]商业;业务,生意;事务:~ letters 商业信函 / E-~ 电子商务/ retail ~ 零售业/ wholesale ~ 批发业/ We do not do much ~ with them. 我们与他们没有多少生意上的往来。/ **on** ~ 因公;因事:He went to Shanghai on ~. 他因公去上海。**none of one's** ~ 与某人无关:Go on with your work. It is none of your ~. 继续干你的工作,那不关你的事。**have no ~ to do sth.** 无权做某事:You have no ~ to say things about me. 你无权谈论我的事。❷[C]商号;公司:He started a new ~ after he settled down in Guangzhou. 在广州定居下来后,他开办了一家新公司。

bust /bʌst/ *n.* [C]胸部;半身塑像:measure one's ~ 给某人量胸围/ In front of our teaching building there is a ~ of a poet. 我们教学楼前有一座诗人的半身塑像。

busy /ˈbɪzi/ *adj*.(-ier,-iest) ❶忙的:Autumn is a ~ season. 秋天是一个繁忙的季节。❷占用的;没空的:He can't see you right now. He is ~ with an important meeting. 他现在无法接见你。他正在开一个重要的会议。派 busily *adv*.

but /bʌt,bət/ Ⅰ *conj*. 可是;但是:She would like to go ~ she is too busy. 她想去,但太忙。/ It never rains, ~ it pours. 不雨则已,一雨倾盆。Ⅱ *adv*. 不过;只:She left ~ half an hour ago. 她离开不过才半小时。Ⅲ *prep*. 除了:There was nothing ~ water. 除了水以外,什么也没有。/~ **for** 要不是:But for your advice,I should have made a big mistake. 要是没有你的劝告,我已经犯大错了。

butcher /ˈbʊtʃə(r)/ *n*.[C]屠夫;卖肉者

butter /ˈbʌtə(r)/ *n*.[U]奶油;黄油

butterfly /ˈbʌtəflaɪ/ *n*.[C]蝴蝶

button /ˈbʌt(ə)n/ Ⅰ *n*.[C] ❶纽扣:You should sew on a ~ here. 你应该在这里缝上一个纽扣。❷按钮:a forward ~ 快进键/ a rewind ~ 倒退键/ a pause ~ 暂停键/ Press this ~ and you'll see the film. 按一下这个键,你就会看到那部电影。Ⅱ *v*. 钉扣子;扣扣子:Button (up) your coat. 把外衣纽扣扣上。

buy /baɪ/ *v*.(bought /bɔːt/,bought) 买;购买:I bought the tickets yesterday. 我昨天买的票。/ He will ~ his brother a new book. 他将给他兄弟买一本新书。

buzz /bʌz/ Ⅰ *v*.(蜂等)嗡嗡叫:The bees are ~ing among flowers. 蜜蜂在花丛中嗡嗡叫。Ⅱ *n*. 嗡嗡声;蜂鸣声

by /baɪ/ Ⅰ *prep*. ❶靠近;在……旁:There is a middle school ~ the church. 教堂旁有一所中学。❷不迟于;到……为止:Be back ~ ten o'clock. 十点钟以前回来。❸经过;由;沿:He walked right ~ me. 他正好从我身边走过。❹靠;用;通过;乘坐(交通工具):~ air (train,bus,spaceship,ship) 乘飞机(火车、汽车、宇宙飞船、轮船)/ He will go to Beijing ~ air (airplane). 他将乘飞机去北京。/~ **and** 不久:She will be here ~ and ~. 她很快就到这儿。~ **far** ……得多:This pen is better ~ far. 这支笔好得多。~ **hand** 用手:The letter was delivered ~ hand. 此信是靠人工递送的。~ **the end of** 到……为止:By the end of last term,we had learned 2,000 words. 到上学期末,我们已学了2 000个单词。Ⅱ *adv*. 在近旁;经过:A group of children passed ~. 一群孩子走过去了。/ The Smiths live close ~. 史密斯一家住得很近。

bye /baɪ/ *int*.(=goodbye)再见

byname /ˈbaɪneɪm/ *n*. 别名;绰号:Don't use your ~ in a formal meeting. 在正式会议上不要用别名。

bypass /ˈbaɪpɑːs/ Ⅰ *n*.[C]旁路;旁道 Ⅱ *vt*. 忽视;绕过:The bus ~ed the city and arrived at a small village. 汽车绕过城市开到一个小村子。

bystander /ˈbaɪˌstændə(r)/ *n*.[C]旁观者;局外人;看热闹的人:The police asked some of the ~s about the accident. 警方向一些旁观者了解出事的情况。

byte /baɪt/ *n*.[C](计算机)字节

C

C c

cab /kæb/ *n.* [C]出租汽车：call (hail) a ~(举手)叫出租车/You may take a ~to see your old friend. 你可以乘出租车去看你的老朋友。

cabbage /ˈkæbɪdʒ/ *n.* 白菜；卷心菜

cabin /ˈkæbɪn/ *n.* [C] ❶机舱；舰长室：a ~ boy 客舱服务员/ the ~ class (客轮)二等舱 ❷(简易的)小木屋；棚屋

cabinet /ˈkæbɪnət/ *n.* [C] ❶(有玻璃门的)橱柜，壁柜：a filing ~ 文件柜/ She put some bowls into the kitchen ~. 她把几只碗放进橱柜里。❷(the ~)内阁：The Cabinet Minister is having a meeting. 内阁部长正在开会。

cable /ˈkeɪbl/ *n.* [C]缆索；电缆；越洋电报：a ~car 缆车/ a ~way 索道/ a ~gram 越洋电报/ The workers are laying a ~. 工人们正在铺设电缆。

cactus /ˈkæktəs/ *n.* [C](*pl.* cacti /ˈkæktaɪ/ 或 cactuses)仙人掌

cadre /ˈkɑːdə(r)/ *n.* [C]干部；核心班子，骨干队伍：Cadres of all ranks should pay special attention to such problems. 各级干部都应特别重视这样的问题。

cafe /ˈkæfeɪ, kæˈfeɪ/ *n.* [C]咖啡馆；酒吧

cafeteria /ˌkæfəˈtɪərɪə/ *n.* [C]自助餐馆：Most students take meals in the school ~. 大多数学生在学生食堂就餐。

caffeine /ˈkæfiːn/ *n.* [U]咖啡因

cage /keɪdʒ/ *n.* [C]鸟笼；笼：A bird escaped from the ~. 有一只鸟从笼子里飞走了。

cake /keɪk/ *n.* [C]面包；蛋糕；饼：a piece of ~ 一块蛋糕/ She bought her son a birthday ~ this morning. 今天上午她为儿子买了一个生日蛋糕。

calamity /kəˈlæməti/ *n.* [C]灾难；不幸事件：A tsunami is a disastrous natural ~. 海啸是一种毁灭性的自然灾害。

calcify /ˈkælsɪˌfaɪ/ *v.* (使)石灰质化，(使)钙化；(使)骨化：Cartilage often calcifies in older people 老年人体内的软骨常常会钙化。/This calcium salts work to ~ the bones. 钙盐有使骨骼钙化的功效。

calcium /ˈkælsɪəm/ *n.* [U]钙

calculate /ˈkælkjuleɪt/ *v.* 计算：I must have ~d wrongly. 我一定算错了。/~ **on** 依赖；依靠；指望：We ~ on a hundred people attending the meeting. 我们指望有100人参加这个会议。

calculated /ˈkælkjʊˌleɪtɪd/ *adj.* ❶(只作定语)故意的，存心的；事先计划好的：a ~ attempt to deceive 精心策划的骗局 / That was a ~ threat：she meant to annoy you. 这是蓄意的威胁：她是有意让你不得安生。❷经过测算的，计算出来的 派 calculatedly *adv.*；calculated-ness *n.*

calculation / ˌkælkjʊˈleɪʃn / *n.* 计算;计算结果:The boy learned mathematical ~s at five. 那男孩五岁就学会了数学运算。/ My ~ is different from yours. 我的计算结果与你的不相同。

calculator / ˈkælkjuleɪtə(r) / *n.* [C]计算器;计算者:a pocket ~ 袖珍计算器/ You shouldn't take an electronic ~ to the examination. 考试时你不应该带计算器。

calculus / ˈkælkjʊləs / *n.* [U]微积分(学):differential ~微分(学)/integral ~积分(学)

calendar / ˈkælɪndə(r) / *n.* [C]日历;历书:a desk ~ 台历/a wall ~挂历 / a school ~ 校历

calf / kɑːf, kæf / *n.* [C](*pl.* calves /kɑːvz, kævz/) ❶小牛,牛犊 ❷(大型哺乳动物的)仔,幼兽:The children saw the new seal ~es at the zoo. 孩子们在动物园看到了新生的小海豹。

call / kɔːl / Ⅰ *v.* ❶喊;叫:When the teacher ~s you, please stand up. 老师叫你时,请站起来。❷命令;召集,召回:Call the children in for supper. 叫孩子们进来吃晚饭。❸打电话:I'll ~ you when I arrive in Beijing. 一到北京,我就打电话给你。❹命名;称呼:She is ~ed Lucy. 她叫露西。/~ **back** 使回想;召回;回电话:Please ask her to ~ back as soon as she comes. 她一来就请她回个电话。~ **down** 祈求;责骂,斥责:He was ~ed down by his mother for being late for class. 他因上课迟到而受到母亲的责骂。~ **for** ①来取;来接:I will ~ for you at your home. 我将去你家接你。②需要;需求:Success in school ~s for much hard study. 要想学习成绩好,需要多用功。~ **forth** 唤起;振作起;鼓起勇气(精神等):April showers ~ forth May flowers. 四月的阵雨浇出五月的鲜花。~ **off** 停止;取消:The basketball game was ~ed off because of rain. 篮球赛因雨取消。~ **on** (**upon**) ①恳求;请求;要求:We ~ed on our English teacher for a song. 我们请英语老师唱一首歌。②访问,拜访:She ~ed on an old friend when she was in the city. 她来该市时拜访了一位老朋友。~ **out** 大声叫喊:The old woman ~ed out with pain. 老太太痛得叫了起来。~ **up** ①提醒;使回忆起:The picture ~ed up memories of our class trip. 这张照片使我们回忆起班上旅行的事。②召唤,动员:He was ~ed up for military service. 他应征入伍。③打电话:She ~ed up a friend just for a chat. 她给朋友打电话聊天。Ⅱ *n.* [C]喊;信号;要求;通话;拜访:a dial-direct ~ 直拨电话/ a house ~ 上门出诊;上门维修/ a reporting ~ 举报电话 /**make** (**give**) **sb. a** ~ 打电话给某人:If I have something important, I'll make you a ~. 如有重要事情,我会打电话给你。**make** (**pay**) **a** ~ **on sb.** 访问某人:They said they were going to make a ~ on you the next day. 他们说第二天去拜访你。

caller / ˈkɔːlə(r) / *n.* [C] ❶(做短暂访问或探望的)来客,来访者:an unexpected ~不速之客/a regular ~常客 ❷打电话的人:an anonymous ~打匿名电话的人

calligraphy / kəˈlɪɡrəfi / *n.* [U](尤指好看的)字迹,笔迹;书法:practise ~ after a master sheet 临帖练习法

callow / ˈkæləʊ/ *adj.* 稚嫩的,幼稚的;没经验的:a ~ lad 乳臭未干的毛头小

伙儿 / It's so ~ of you! 你也太不懂事了!

calm / kɑːm / Ⅰ *adj.* 平静的;镇定的:The sea was ~. 海面平静。/ Though she was very frightened, she answered my question with a ~ voice. 尽管她很惊恐,但仍以平静的声音回答我的问题。Ⅱ *v.* 使平静;使镇定:Calm yourself! 请安静! / He stayed ~ at the meeting. 在会上他一直很镇定。派 calmly *adv.*

calorie / ˈkæləri / *n.* [C] 卡,卡路里(热量单位)

calorific / ˌkæləˈrɪfɪk / *adj.* 散热的,生热的,产热的:the ~ center 热中心/It is the ~ waves emitted by the sun which heat our air. 是太阳发出的热波使空气变热的。

camel / ˈkæməl / *n.* [C] 骆驼:Camels live in hot district. 骆驼生活在炎热地区。

camera / ˈkæmərə / *n.* [C]照相机;摄影机:an auto focus ~ 傻瓜相机/ I like a color digital ~. 我喜欢彩色数字摄像机。

cameraman / ˈkæmərəˌmæn / *n.* [C](尤指电影或电视的)(专业)摄影师,摄像师

camouflage / ˈkæməˌflɑːʒ / Ⅰ *n.* [U](出于军事目的的)伪装,掩饰;(动物的)(天然)保护色:natural ~天然保护色/ The soldiers covered their helmets with leaves as ~. 士兵用树叶遮盖钢盔作为伪装。Ⅱ *vt.* 伪装;掩饰:The boy ~d his embarrassment by laughing. 这男孩用大笑来掩饰他的窘态。

camp / kæmp / *n.* [C]野营地:They set up their ~ near the top of the mountain. 他们在靠近山顶的地方扎营。

campaign / kæmˈpeɪn / *n.* [C]战役;运动:a patriotic public health ~ 爱国卫生运动/ a ~ for contributions 募捐运动/ The students launched an anti-smoking ~ on campus. 学生们在校园里发起一场戒烟运动。

campus / ˈkæmpəs / *n.* [C] 校园:We have colorful ~ culture and life. 我们有丰富多彩的校园文化和校园生活。

can[1] / kæn, kən / *aux. v.* (could / kʊd /) ❶能,会:She ~ speak French. 她会说法语。❷可能:What he said couldn't be true. 他说的不可能是真的。❸(口语)可以(表示许可):The boy asked whether he could go for an outing. 小男孩问他是否可以去郊游。

can[2] / kæn / *n.* [C]罐头;听:a coffee ~ 咖啡罐头/ an oil ~ 油桶/ a water ~ 水桶/ an ash ~ (美)垃圾桶/ a ~ of beer 一听啤酒

canal / kəˈnæl / *n.* [C]运河;沟渠;水道:the Suez Canal 苏伊士运河/ China's Grand Canal 中国大运河/ The Panama Canal joins two oceans. 巴拿马运河连通两大洋。

cancel / ˈkænsl / *vt.* ❶取消;撤销:The teacher called to ~ tomorrow's class meeting. 老师打电话说取消明天的班会。❷删去;画掉:He ~ed an incorrect figure in his plan. 他把计划中的一个错误数字画掉。

cancellation / ˌkænsəˈleɪʃən/ *n.* ❶[U] 取消,撤销;废除;中止;删掉:~ of a baseball game 取消棒球赛 / ~ of the town ordinance 市镇法令的废止 / the ~ of the faulty passage 删去有错的一段 ❷[C]被取消(或拟出让)的事物;车(或船、飞机)的退票:Are there any ~s for this evening's performance? 有今晚演出的退票吗?

cancer /ˈkænsə(r)/ *n.* 癌：His grandfather died of lung ~. 他的祖父死于肺癌。

candid /ˈkændɪd/ *adj.* 直率的，坦诚的，直言不讳的：a ~ reply 坦诚的回答/a ~ excitement 毫不掩饰的兴奋/a ~ critic 直言不讳的评论家 派 candidly *adv.*

candidate /ˈkændɪdeɪt/ *n.* [C]候选人；应试者；应征者：There are eight ~s for president of the university. 有 8 名候选人竞选校长。/ The twenty ~s for the job all came from Shanghai. 20 名求职者都是上海人。

candle /ˈkændl/ *n.* [C]蜡烛：The old fisherman lit a ~ to see what was happening. 老渔夫点燃一支蜡烛看看发生什么事了。/ We seldom use ~s now. 现在我们很少使用蜡烛。

cando(u)r /ˈkændə(r)/ *n.* [U]直率；坦诚，诚恳：Her ~ was disarming. 她的坦率使人疑虑顿消。/The ~ of the speech impressed the audience. 讲话开诚布公，给听众留下了深刻的印象。

candy /ˈkændi/ *n.* (美)糖果

cane /keɪn/ *n.* [C]手杖；棍，棒；茎：sugar ~ 甘蔗/ The old man was walking with a ~. 老人拄着拐杖走路。

cannon /ˈkænən/ *n.* [C](*pl.* cannon 或 cannons)大炮；机关炮；火炮：The soldier fired a ~ at the enemy. 战士向敌人开炮。

canoe /kəˈnuː/ *n.* [C]独木舟

canon /ˈkænən/ *n.* [C] ❶教规：A priest is expressly forbidden by the ~s to enter a public inn. 教规明文禁止教士进酒吧。❷准则；规范；原则；标准：an official set of ~s of ethics 一套公认的伦理道德规范 / against the ~s of conduct 有违行为准则

canopy /ˈkænəpi/ *n.* [C]顶篷；(顶篷似的)遮盖物，笼罩物：a vast ~ of foliage 覆盖的绿荫

canteen /kænˈtiːn/ *n.* [C](工厂、公司、学校等的)食堂；小卖部：Most students have meals at the student ~. 多数学生在学生食堂用餐。

canvas /ˈkænvəs/ *n.* ❶[U]帆布 ❷[C]画布；油画

canyon /ˈkænjən/ *n.* [C]峡谷

cap /kæp/ *n.* [C]帽子；盖头：take off one's ~ 脱帽

capability /ˌkeɪpəˈbɪləti/ *n.* 能力；才能：Can you prove your ~ for the job? 你能证明你有能力胜任这项工作吗？/ It was beyond her capabilities. 那是她力所不能及的。

capable /ˈkeɪpəbl/ *adj.* 有能力的；有技能的：She is a ~ girl. 她是一个很能干的女孩。/ **be ~ of doing sth.** 有能力做某事：He is ~ of doing anything. 他什么事都能做。

capacious /kəˈpeɪʃəs/ *adj.* 宽敞的；容量大的：a ~ storage bin 大(容量)储藏柜/a man of ~ mind 心胸宽大的人

capacity /kəˈpæsəti/ *n.* ❶能力；才能：The boy has a great ~ for mathematics. 那男孩很有数学才能。❷容量；容积：The classroom has a seating ~ of 80 students. 这间教室可坐 80 名学生。

cape /keɪp/ *n.* [C]海角；岬：The Cape of Good Hope is in the south of Africa. 好望角在非洲南端。

capillary /kəˈpɪləri, ˈkæpɪləri/ *n.* [C]毛细(血)管

capital /ˈkæpɪtl/ *n.* [C] ❶首都；省会；

首府；都市；中心：Beijing is the ~ of China. 北京是中国的首都。❷资本；本钱：The company has a ~ of 3,000,000 dollars to improve its equipment. 这家公司用300万美元资金来改进设备。/ That is a special ~. 这是一笔专用资金。❸大写字母；(句子的)第一个字母：He wrote his name in ~s. 他用大写字母写名字。

capitalism /ˈkæpɪtəlɪzəm/ *n.* [U]资本主义

capitalist /ˈkæpɪtəlɪst/ Ⅰ *adj.* 资本主义的 Ⅱ *n.* [C]资本家

capitalize /ˈkæpɪtəˌlaɪz/ *vt.* ❶将……大写：Days of the week are usually ~d. 周日名称首字母通常都要大写。❷使资本化；使资金化：The company ~d its reserve funds. 公司将储备资金转为股本。❸为……提供资本，向……投资：~ a new business 向一家新公司投资 —*vi.* 利用，从中获利(与 on，by 连用)：She ~d on his mistake and won the game. 她利用他的失误而赢了这场比赛。

cappuccino /ˌkæpʊˈtʃiːnəʊ/ *n.* [U]卡布奇诺咖啡(一种加牛奶或奶油用蒸汽加热煮成的意大利浓咖啡)

caprice /kəˈpriːs/ *n.* ❶[C](行动或思想的)突变；怪念头；任性：He acted not from reason, but from ~. 他不是按理智行事，而是凭一时兴起想干什么就干什么。/ His lack of money was the result of ~ in spending on unnecessary things. 他缺钱是他任意挥霍买了许多不必要的东西的后果。❷[U]反复无常(的倾向)，多变(的倾向)：Public opinion has its ~s. 公众舆论变化无常。

capricious /kəˈprɪʃəs/ *adj.* ❶反复无常的，变幻莫测的：a ~ temper(性情多变而)喜怒无常的人 ❷不规则的，不定的，无法预见的 派 capriciously *adv.*

capsule /ˈkæpsjuːl/ *n.* [C] ❶胶囊：The patient must have three ~s at a time. 病人一次须服用三粒胶囊。❷密封舱；航天舱：a space ~ 航天舱；太空舱/ They recovered the ~ successfully. 他们成功地回收了太空舱。

captain /ˈkæptɪn/ *n.* [C]队长；长官：the ~ of a football team 足球队长/ the ~ of a ship 船长

caption /ˈkæpʃn/ *n.* [C]标题；说明；字幕：The film has a foreign language ~. 这部影片带外文字幕。/ He read the ~ under the photo carefully. 他仔细读了照片下面的说明。

captivate /ˈkæptɪˌveɪt/ *vt.* 使着迷；使倾倒；迷惑：The children were ~d by her story. 孩子们被她的故事迷住了。/The prima donna ~d the audience. 女主角使观众们着了迷。

captive /ˈkæptɪv/ *n.* [C]俘虏 ：They took 17 ~s in the battle. 战斗中他们活捉了17名俘虏。

capture /ˈkæptʃə(r)/ Ⅰ *vt.* 捕捉；捕获；俘虏：The police ~d the robber soon. 警察很快抓住了抢匪。Ⅱ *n.* [U]掳获，捕获；战利品；捕获物：With the ~ of the escaped criminal he was praised greatly. 由于捕获了逃犯，他受到高度赞扬。

car /kɑː(r)/ *n.* [C]小汽车；车；车厢：a baggage ~ 行李车/ a mail ~邮车/ a restaurant (dining) ~餐车/ a touring ~ 游览车/ a sleeping ~卧铺车厢/My colleagues bought a ~ one buy one recently. 最近我的同事们一个接一个地买了小汽车。

carapace /ˈkærəˌpeɪs/ *n.* [C](龟、蟹等的)硬壳，背甲

carat /ˈkærət/ *n.* [C] 克拉，公制克拉（钻石等珠宝的重量单位，等于 200 毫克；略作 c, ct）

carbohydrate /ˌkɑːbəʊˈhaɪdreɪt/ *n.* 碳水化合物：The food you eat everyday should have some ~ in. 你每天吃的食物中应当含有碳水化合物。

carbon /ˈkɑːbən/ *n.* [U] ❶碳：~ dioxide 二氧化碳/~ monooxide 一氧化碳 ❷[C]（一张）复写纸（= ~paper）

card /kɑːd/ *n.* [C] ❶卡片；名片：identification ~身份证/ a post ~ 明信片/ a calling ~ 名片/ a student ~ 学生证/ a greeting ~ 贺卡/a credit ~ 信用卡/ a boarding ~ 登机牌/He was given a red (yellow) ~ in the football match. 在这场足球赛中他得了一张得红（黄）牌。❷纸牌：They play ~s after work. 下班后他们打牌玩。

cardboard /ˈkɑːdbɔːd/ *n.* [U]纸板：He put his books in a ~box. 他把书放在一个厚纸盒里。

cardiac /ˈkɑːdɪˌæk/ *adj.* 心脏的；心脏病的；与心脏治疗有关的：~ disease 心脏病

cardinal /ˈkɑːdɪnl/ *adj.* 主要的；基本的：four ~ principles 四项基本原则/ Being kind to others is her ~ virtue. 对人友善是她的主要美德。

care /keə(r)/ Ⅰ *v.* ❶关心；担心：A good teacher always ~ s about his students. 一个好老师总是关心他的学生。❷关怀；照顾：She ~s a lot for children first. 她总是首先照顾孩子们。❸喜欢；愿意：I don't ~ to go shopping with you; I'd rather stay home reading. 我不愿意跟你去购物；我宁愿待在家里看书。❹介意；计较：I don't ~ what she said at the meeting. 我并不介意她在会上说了些什么。/ ~ **about**①喜欢，爱好；介意：I don't much ~ about going. 我并不很想去。/ She doesn't ~ about the matter. 她对此事毫不介意。②关心；重视：He often thinks only of himself. He doesn't ~ about other people. 他常常只想到自己，从不关心别人。~ **for** 喜爱；想；照料：Would you ~ for some tea? 你想喝点茶吗？Ⅱ *n.* 照管；关心；小心谨慎：You should drive with great ~in the town. 在市里开车你得十分小心。/ The little patient was left in my ~. 小病人留给我来照顾。/ **take ~ of** 照料，护理；看管：Let me take ~ of the cleaning. 让我来打扫吧。/ You should take good ~ of your books. 你应好好爱惜书。

career /kəˈrɪə(r)/ *n.* [C]职业；生涯；经历：She planned to make acting her ~. 她打算把表演作为她的职业。/ People are interested in his long diplomatic ~. 人们对他长期的外交官经历很感兴趣。

carefree /ˈkeəˌfriː/ *adj.* 无忧无虑的；轻松愉快的；无牵无挂的：lead a ~ life 过一种无忧无虑的生活

careful /ˈkeəfl/ *adj.* 小心的；细致的；关切的：She is ~ at her work. 她工作细心。/ Be ~ not to drive too fast. 小心别把车开得太快。派 carefully *adv.*

careless /ˈkeələs/ *adj.* 粗心的；漫不经心的：Don't be ~ with your pronunciation. 不要对你的发音不准漫不经心。

caretaker /ˈkeəˌteɪkə(r)/ *n.* [C]照看者；照看者；（大楼的）看管人；（学校等的）看门人

cargo /ˈkɑːgəʊ/ *n.* 货物：The workers are shipping the ~ at the part. 工人们在港口装货。

C

caricature /ˈkærɪkətjʊə(r)/ *n.* ❶[C]漫画,讽刺画;讽刺文章:Caricatures of celebrities appear daily in the newspaper. 报纸上每天都有讽刺名人的漫画。❷[C](滑稽可笑的)夸张性模仿(或表演);拙劣的模仿

caring /ˈkeərɪŋ/ *adj.* 有同情心的;(深表)同情的;一心一意的;为公民提供福利的:the ~ professions, such as nursing and social work 照料别人的职业,如看护和社区工作

carnation /kɑːˈneɪʃn/ *n.* [C](麝)香石竹,康乃馨

carnival /ˈkɑːnɪvəl/ *n.* ❶[U]狂欢节,嘉年华会 ❷[C](流动)游艺团,游艺场(有各种游戏、杂耍等)

carnivorous /kɑːˈnɪvərəs/ *adj.* 食肉的:Tigers and lions are ~ animals. 老虎和狮子都是食肉动物。

carol /ˈkærəl/ *n.* [C] ❶(尤指圣诞的)欢乐颂歌;(宗教的)祝颂歌,赞美诗:beautiful ~ music 优美的圣诞乐曲 ❷欢快的歌:the morning ~s of the birds 清晨鸟儿的欢啭

carp /kɑːp/ *n.* [C]鲤鱼

carpenter /ˈkɑːpəntə(r)/ *n.* [C]木工;木匠

carpet /ˈkɑːpɪt/ *n.* [C]地毯;地毡:The floor is covered with a ~. 地板上铺着地毯。

carriage /ˈkærɪdʒ/ *n.* [C]车;四轮马车;(铁路)客车厢

carrot /ˈkærət/ *n.* 胡萝卜

carry /ˈkæri/ *v.* 携带;运送;传送;支持:He carries his changes in his pocket. 他将零钱放在他口袋里。/ She was ~ing a box on her shoulder. 她肩上扛着一只箱子。/ These pillars ~ the weight of the roof. 这些柱子支撑着屋顶。/ The pipes ~ oil to cities. 这些管子把油送往城市。/~ **away** ①冲走;刮去:The bridge was carried away by the flood. 洪水冲走了桥。②使失去自制力;吸引住:The music carried her away. 这音乐吸引了她。~ **off** ①劫持,劫走:Cancer carried him off. 癌症夺走了他的生命。②意外成功:She carried off the palm in both tennis and swimming. 她在网球和游泳两项运动中获胜。~ **on** ①从事,进行:They carried on business for many years in Shanghai. 他们在上海经商多年。②继续:He carried on in spite of the difficult conditions. 尽管条件艰苦,他仍坚持下去。~ **out** 实施,执行;完成:We must ~ out reforms in education. 我们必须进行教育改革。/ We should ~ out the plan to the full. 我们应该不折不扣地执行计划。~ **through** 完成;结束:He carried his project through despite the opposition. 尽管有人反对,他还是完成了自己的项目。

carry-on /ˈkæriˌɒn/ Ⅰ *adj.* 可随身携带(上飞机)的:~ baggage 随身携带的行李 Ⅱ *n.* [C]一件随身携带的行李

carsick /ˈkɑːˌsɪk/ *adj.* 晕车的:They had to stop twice because Billy got ~. 因为比利晕车,他们不得不两次停车。

cart /kɑːt/ *n.* [C]大车;手推车:She put the goods she chose into the shopping ~. 她把选好的商品放进购物车里。

carton /ˈkɑːtən/ *n.* [C]纸(板)盒,纸(板)箱;(硬蜡纸或塑料制的)液体容器:a ~ of fruit juice 一盒果汁/Pack the books in a large ~. 把书装进一个大纸箱内。

cartoon /kɑːˈtuːn/ *n.* [C]卡通,动画片;漫画:The little boy draw ~s well. 小男

孩漫画画得很好。派 cartoonist *n*.

carve /kɑːv/ *vt*. ❶雕刻,刻;在……上雕刻(或刻);(用雕刻的图案)装饰:candles ~d in the shape of flowers 雕刻成花形的蜡烛 / ~ the wood into a figure 把木头刻成人像 / a figure ~d out of stone 用石头雕成的像 ❷切,切开;切碎;把……切成片;划分:~s the meat 切肉 / a state ~d into several districts 被划分为几个地区的州 —*vi*. ❶雕刻:They have been carving for years. 多少年来,他们一直在雕刻。❷切碎;切成片:Let me ~d this year. 今年让我来掌刀。/~ **out** (经过长期努力而)创出(事业);赢得(财富):She has ~d out a career for herself as a comic actress. 她为自己开创了一个做喜剧演员的前程。派 carver *n*.

case[1] / keɪs / *n*. [C] ❶情况;状况:Do you know what we should do in this ~? 你知道在这种情况下我们该做什么吗? ❷事实;实情:She thinks that her mother would be healthy forever but that is not the ~. 她认为她母亲会永远健康,但事实并非如此。❸事例;实例:a ~ in point 恰当的例子/ Please cite a ~ to explain the problem. 请举例解释这个问题。❹病症;病例;病人:He asked the doctor to explain his ~ to him carefully. 他要求大夫向他详细说明他的病情。/ The worst ~ was sent to hospital soon. 最严重的一个病人已被及时送进医院。❺诉讼;案件:This is a civil (criminal)~. 这是一桩民事(刑事)案件。/**in any** ~无论如何:In any ~ I shall return in a day or two. 总之,我一两天内就回来。**in** ~如果,万一:He doesn't dare to leave the room in ~ he should be recognized. 他不敢出门,生怕被人认出来。**in no** ~ 绝不,毫不:In no ~ can she go out. 她绝不能出去。

case[2] / keɪs / *n*. [C]箱(子);盒(子):a book ~书橱/ a brief ~ 公文包/ a note ~ 皮夹子/ a suit ~ 手提箱/ Please put it back in the ~. 用完请放回盒子里。

C

cash / kæʃ / Ⅰ*n*. [C]钱;现金;现款:She paid the TV set in ~. 买电视机她用现金付费。/ Cash or charge, please? 请问是付现金或是记账? / Sorry, I have no ~ with me. 很抱歉,我没带现金。Ⅱ *vt*. 把……兑现:You'd first ~ your check before you go to that small shop. 去那家小店之前,你得把支票兑换为现金。

cashier / kæ'ʃɪə(r) / *n*. [C]出纳员:A ~ should work very carefully. 出纳员应非常细心地工作。

casing / 'keɪsɪŋ / *n*. [C] ❶箱,盒;套,罩;壳:a shell ~炸弹壳 ❷(门、窗等的)框 ❸(做香肠等用的)肠衣

casino / kə'siːnəʊ / *n*. [C]赌场;夜总会;俱乐部

cassette / kə'set / *n*. [C]盒式录音带

cast / kɑːst / *v*. (cast,cast)投,掷,抛:~ a vote 投票/~ seeds 播种/~ a net 撒网/~ a glance (a look,an eye) at (over,on) sb. 向某人瞧了瞧 /~ **about** (**around**)①寻找:They are ~ing about for an experienced teacher to take Mr. Chen's place. 他们正在找寻一位有经验的老师代替陈先生。②思考,考虑:I am ~ing about how to get my bike back from John. 我正考虑怎样从约翰那里取回我的自行车。~ **aside** 抛弃:Cast your worries aside. 抛开你的顾虑吧! ~ **away** 抛弃;浪费:He will ~ away this money just as he has done in the past. 他会像以往一样把这笔钱浪费掉。~

out 赶走；驱逐：After the scandal, he was ~ out of the best society. 自那件丑闻后，他已被上流社会除名。

castle /ˈkɑːsl/ *n.* [C] 城堡：It is an ancient ~. 这是一座古城堡。

castor /ˈkɑːstə(r)/ *n.* [U] 蓖麻

casual /ˈkæʒuəl/ *adj.* ❶偶然的；碰巧的：I had a ~ meeting with Mr. Smith at the airport. 在机场我和史密斯先生不期而遇。❷随便的；非正式的；不拘礼的：You are not right to take a ~ attitude toward your teacher. 对老师态度随便是不对的。/ May I wear ~ clothes here? 在这里我可以穿便服吗？❸临时的；不定期的：The company employs him as a ~ laborer. 公司雇他为临时工。派 casually *adv.*

casualty /ˈkæʒjuəlti/ *n.* [C] 严重伤亡事故；(事故中的)伤亡人员；受害者：There were heavy casualties in the accident. 那场意外事故造成了惨重伤亡。

cat /kæt/ *n.* [C]猫

catalog(ue) /ˈkætəlɒg/ *n.* [C]目录；目录册：I looked up the author ~ and found the book I wanted. 我查作者目录找到了我要的书。

catalyst /ˈkætəlɪst/ *n.* [C] ❶催化剂：The enzyme was a ~ in that reaction. 酶是那个反应的催化剂。❷促进(或刺激)因素；起促进作用的人

catastrophe /kəˈtæstrəfi/ *n.* [C]大灾难；大祸；糟糕的结局：They survived a ~ in the tsunami. 他们逃脱了海啸这场大灾难。/ What caused the ~ of the party? 是什么使晚会的结局这么糟糕？

catastrophic /ˌkætəˈstrɒfɪk/ *adj.* ❶灾难性的：the ~ consequences of nuclear war 核战争的灾难性后果 ❷严重的；有害的：the high cost of treatments for the ~ illness 重病的高昂治疗费用 ❸极糟的；极坏的 派 catastrophically *adv.*

catch /kætʃ/ *v.* (caught /kɔːt/, caught) 捉；抓；捕；赶上；染上：He caught the ball. 他接住了球。/ They were caught in the rain last night. 昨晚他们被雨淋了。/~ (**a**) **cold** 感冒；伤风：Put on more clothes or you'll ~ (a) cold. 穿暖和些，否则你会着凉的。~ **fire** 着火：Paper ~es fire easily. 纸容易着火。~ **hold of** 抓住；握住：Please ~ hold of the rope. 请抓住绳子。~ **sight of** 一眼看见；突然看见：I suddenly caught sight of a thief behind the door. 我突然看见门后有个贼。~ **up with** 赶上；追上：You have to work hard in order to ~ up with the rest of the class. 你必须努力学习以赶上班里其他人。

catching /ˈkætʃɪŋ/ *adj.* ❶传染性的：Measles is very ~. 麻疹传染很快。❷有感染力的；迷人的，吸引人的：a ~ time 迷人的时刻/The singer has a ~ style. 那位歌手演唱的风格很吸引人。

catchword /ˈkætʃˌwɜːd/ *n.* [C]口头禅；标语，口号：His speech was full of ~s like "challenge" and "commitment". 他的演讲充满了"挑战"和"义务"之类的口号。

categorize /ˌkætɪgəˌraɪz/ *vt.* ❶将……分类，把……分类：We ~d the snowflakes into several shapes. 我们把雪花的形状分成几种。❷命名；描述：He was ~d as a slow reader. 他被认为是一个阅读慢的人。

category /ˈkætəgəri/ *n.* [C]种类；类目；类型：Does botany belong to the ~ of biology? 植物学属于生物学类吗？

cater /ˈkeɪtə(r)/ *vi.* 供应伙食；满足

(需要)；投合：A restaurant is difficult to ~ to all tastes. 一家餐馆很难满足所有人的口味。/ The hospital should ~ to the need of its patients. 医院应当满足病人的需要。

caterpillar /ˈkætəˌpɪlə(r)/ *n.* [C]毛虫；蠋(蝴蝶、蛾等鳞翅目昆虫的幼虫)

cathedral /kəˈθiːdrəl/ *n.* [C]大教堂

cathode /ˈkæθəʊd/ *n.* [C]阴极；负极

Catholic /ˈkæθlɪk/ Ⅰ *adj.* 天主教的 Ⅱ *n.* [C]天主教徒

catnap /ˈkætˌnæp/ Ⅰ *vi.* (-napped; -napping) 打瞌睡，打盹：He ~ped over his book. 他看书的时候打瞌睡。Ⅱ *n.* [C]瞌睡，盹儿：take a ~ on the couch 在长沙发上打盹

cattle /ˈkætl/ *n.* (总称)牛；家畜：The man raised ~ in the countryside. 那人在农村养牛。

cauliflower /ˈkɒlɪˌflaʊə(r)/ *n.* [C]花椰菜，花菜

cause /kɔːz/ Ⅰ *v.* 引起；给……带来：What ~d his failure? 什么致使他失败? / His carelessness ~d the accident. 他的粗心大意造成了这次意外事故。Ⅱ *n.* 原因，理由；目标；理想；事业：Don't stay away without good ~. 不要无故离开。/ We are engaged in a great and glorious ~. 我们正从事一项伟大而光荣的事业。

caustic /ˈkɔːstɪk/ *adj.* ❶(有)腐蚀性的：~ substances 有腐蚀性的物质 ❷讽刺的；尖利刻薄的，辛辣刺人的：a ~ smile 讥笑/~ remarks 刻薄话语

caution /ˈkɔːʃn/ *n.* ❶[U]小心；谨慎：He lifted the box with ~. 他小心地提起那只箱子。❷警告；告诫：The policeman gave the driver a ~ for illegal parking. 因违章停车警察警告了那位司机。

cautious /ˈkɔːʃəs/ *adj.* 小心的；谨慎的：She is ~ when riding across the street. 骑车过街时她非常小心。

cave /keɪv/ *n.* [C]岩洞；洞穴

cavity /ˈkævɪti/ *n.* [C] ❶洞，穴；凹处：a ~ in the earth 地洞 ❷腔，窝，盂：in chest ~ 在胸腔中 ❸(尤指因腐烂而形成的)牙洞，龋洞：My dentist said I have a ~ which will have to be filled. 我的牙医说我的牙齿有龋洞，得填上。

CD (=compact disk)激光唱片；光盘

cease /siːs/ *v.* 停止；中止；结束：The heart will ~ to beat when life ~s. 生命结束，心脏就会停止跳动。/ My joy shall never ~. 我的快乐永无休止。

ceaseless /ˈsiːslɪs/ *adj.* 不停的，不间断的；无休无止的：~ effort 不懈的努力/ the ~ stream 奔腾不息的溪流

cedar /ˈsiːdə(r)/ *n.* [C]雪松

cede /siːd/ *vt.* 放弃；割让；出让：~ territory to a country 把土地割让给某个国家/~ one's stance in debate 在辩论中放弃立场

ceiling /ˈsiːlɪŋ/ *n.* [C] ❶天花板；平顶：a lamp hanging from the ~ 天花板上的吊灯 ❷(开支等的)数额上限，最高限额：put (set, impose) a ~ on the military expenditure 给军事开支规定上限 / lift a farm-production ~ 取消农产品产量的最高限额

celebrate /ˈselɪbreɪt/ *vt.* 歌颂；庆祝：They warmly ~d this festival. 他们热烈地庆祝这个节日。/ His courage was ~d in all newspapers. 他的英勇行为赢得所有报纸的颂扬。

celebration /ˌselɪˈbreɪʃn/ *n.* 庆祝；庆祝

活动：We organized a ~ that evening. 那天晚上我们举行了庆祝会。/ The ~ lasted for a week. 庆祝活动持续了一个星期。

C

celebrity / səˈlebrəti / *n.* ❶[U]著名；名声：He teaches well and won ~ among students soon. 他教书教得好，很快在学生中赢得名声。❷[C]名人；著名人士：He often says that he knows many celebrities. 他常说他认识很多名人。

celery / ˈseləri / *n.* [U]芹菜

cell / sel / *n.* [C] ❶细胞：The doctor wrote an article on ~ division. 那位大夫写了一篇论细胞分裂的文章。❷小牢房：The criminal was shut in a jail ~. 罪犯被关在一间单人牢房里。❸电池：He put a dry ~ in the radio. 他在收音机里放进一只干电池。

cellar / ˈselə(r) / *n.* [C]地下室；地窖

cello / ˈtʃeləʊ / *n.* [C](*pl.* cellos)大提琴

cellular / ˈseljʊlə(r) / *adj.* 细胞的，由细胞组成的；细胞状的：~ structure 细胞结构

cement / sɪˈment/ Ⅰ *n.* ❶[U]水泥 ❷[U]胶接剂，胶结材料：a tube of paper ~ 一管黏纸用胶棒 ❸维系，纽带：Time is the ~ of friendship. 时间是巩固友谊的黏合剂。Ⅱ *vt.* ❶黏合，黏结，胶合：To finish the model，~ the wings onto the fuselage. 把机翼粘在机身上，模型就做好了。❷把水泥涂于：The workmen were ~ing the floors. 工人们正在地板上铺水泥。

cemetery / ˈsemətri / *n.* [C]公墓；墓地

censor / ˈsensə(r) / Ⅰ *n.* [C](书刊、报纸、新闻、电影、电视等的)审查员，检查员：military ~s 军事审查员 Ⅱ *vt.* ❶检查，审查；监察：a heavily ~ed editorial 一篇经过严格审查的社论/Mail from the troops was ~ed. 军队的邮件都受到检查。❷删除；修改：The figure has been ~ed from a report published today. 今天出版的报道中这个数字被删除了。

census / ˈsensəs / *n.* [C]人口普查；人口调查：They carry out a ~ every two years in this district. 在这个地区他们每两年进行一次人口普查。

cent / sent / *n.* ❶[C]分；分币：The color pencil cost sixty ~s. 这支彩色铅笔卖六角钱。❷[U]一百：five per ~ 百分之五，5%

centenarian / ˌsentɪˈneərɪən/ Ⅰ *n.* [C]百岁(或百岁以上的)老人 Ⅱ *adj.* (常作定语) ❶百岁(或百岁以上)的 ❷百年的；百年大庆的；一百周年的

centenary / senˈtiːnəri，senˈtenəri/ Ⅰ *n.* [C] ❶一百(周)年，一世纪：2011 is the first ~ of Xinhai Revolution. 2011 年是辛亥革命的第一个百年。❷一百周年庆典；一百周年纪念：The university is embracing its ~. 这所大学正在迎接它的百年华诞。Ⅱ *adj.* ❶一百年的，一世纪的；一百周年的：a ~ celebration 百周年庆典 ❷每逢百年的；百年一次的

centennial / senˈtenɪəl / Ⅰ *n.* [C]一百周年；一百周年纪念(日)：We celebrated the ~ of our teacher's birth last Saturday. 上星期六我们为老师庆祝了一百周年诞辰。Ⅱ *adj.* 一百年的；一百周年纪念的：This is a ~ tree. Let's take a picture in front of it . 这是一棵百年老树，我们在它前面照张相吧。

centigrade / ˈsentɪgreɪd / *adj.* 摄氏度的(略为℃)：The highest temperature here is thirty-five degrees ~. 这里的最高温度是 35 摄氏度(35℃)。

centigram(me) / ˈsentɪgræm / *n.* [C]厘克

centimeter / ˈsentɪmiːtə(r) / *n.* [C]厘米(略作 cm)

centipede / ˈsentɪˌpiːd / *n.* [C]蜈蚣;马陆

central / ˈsentrəl/*adj.* ❶中心的;中央的;中枢的:the ~ committee 中央委员会/ the ~ government 中央政府/ Their office building is in the ~ part of the city. 他们的办公大楼位于市中心。❷主要的;核心的:The ~ problem of today's discussion is how to reduce pollution. 今天讨论的主要问题是如何减少污染。派 centrally *adv.*

centralize / ˈsentrəˌlaɪz/ *vt.* ❶使集中:a ~d university catalog issued once a year 每年集中发布一次的大学名录❷使集权;使置于中央集权制下:~ the power of the monarchy 加强君主集权 派 centralization *n.*

centre(-er) / ˈsentə(r) / *n.* [C]中心;中央:a financial ~金融中心/ a shopping ~ 购物中心/a training ~ 培训中心/ The boys and girls often play around the fountain in the ~ of the park. 孩子们常在公园中央的喷水池四周玩耍。

century / ˈsentʃəri / *n.* [C]世纪;百年:The city changed a lot in the 90's of the 20th ~. 在 20 世纪 90 年代这座城市发生了很大的变化。/ He was a famous writer in the sixteenth ~. 他是 16 世纪的著名作家。

ceramics / sɪˈræmɪks / *n.* 陶瓷制品;陶瓷器;陶瓷艺术:pieces of smashed ~陶瓷品碎片

cereal / ˈsɪərɪəl / *n.* 谷类;五谷;谷类食物:I went to buy some breakfast ~ in the supermarket. 我去超市买了一些早餐吃的谷类食品。

ceremonial / ˌserɪˈməunjəl / *adj.* 礼仪的;典礼的;正式的;适于正式场合的:a ~ occasion 正式场合/~ dress 礼服

ceremony / ˈserəməni / *n.* [C]典礼;仪式:the flag-raising ~ 升旗仪式/ the ribbon-cutting ~ 剪彩仪式/ a wedding ~ 婚礼/the opening ~ 开幕式/ the closing ~ 闭幕式/ His father spoke at the graduation~. 他的父亲在毕业典礼上讲了话。

certain / ˈsɜːt(ə)n / *adj.* ❶(作表语)确定的,无疑的:It is ~ that this team will win the game. 可以肯定这个队会赢。❷(作表语)确信的,深信的:I am ~ that he won't come. 我确信他不会来。/ Are you ~ of that? 你对那事确信无疑吗? ❸(作定语)某一,某种:He did it for a ~ purpose. 他干此事是为了某种目的。

certainly / ˈsɜːtənli/ *adv.* ❶无疑地;确定;必定:I will ~ be at the party. 我一定会出席晚会的。/ Something was~ wrong with him. 他无疑是出了什么问题。❷(用于表达强烈的感情或热情)的确,确实:He ~ is successful. 无可否认,他获得了成功。/ She is ~ stupid. 她的确愚蠢。❸(用于回答)当然;行:Certainly, you may take the keys. 行,你拿着钥匙吧。/ —Shall I drive? —Certainly not! —我能开车吗? —当然不行!

certainty / ˈsɜːtənti/ *n.* ❶[U]确实;确信;确实性,确定性:know sth. with ~ 确知某事 / There was a lack of ~ about what to do next. 至于下面干什么事,我们没有把握。❷[C]必然的事;确定的事实;可靠的人(或事物):a dead (complete) ~ 确定无疑的事 / a ~ to win the match 肯定会赢得这场比赛/ **for a ~** 确定无疑地:I know for a ~

that the company has been bought up. 我确实知道那家公司已被收买了。

certificate /sə'tɪfɪkət/ *n.* [C]证(明)书;执照:a birth ~ 出生证明/ a death ~ 死亡证明/ a marriage ~ 结婚证书/ a medical ~ 诊断书/ They issued a ~ to him. 他们给他颁发了执照。

certification /ˌsɜːtɪfɪ'keɪʃn/ *n.* [C]证明;证明书

certify /'sɜːtɪfaɪ/ *vt.* 证明;发证书;发执照:The doctor certified the boy as healthy. 大夫证明小男孩身体健康。/ This is to ~ that he studied in our school five years ago. 兹证明他五年前在我校读书。

cessation /se'seɪʃən/ *n.* [C](常用单数)停止,休止;中断:a temporary ~ of breathing 呼吸的短暂停止 / a ~ of hostilities 敌对关系的结束/ a ~ from work 休息(或休假)

cession /'seʃən/ *n.* ❶[U](领土的)割让;(权利、财产等的)转让:the ~ of territories 放弃领土 ❷[C]割让的土地;转让的权利(或财产等)

chain /tʃeɪn/ *n.* [C] ❶链条;锁链:shake off ~s 摆脱枷锁/a watch ~表链/ Please don't keep the dog on a ~. 请别把狗拴在铁链上。❷一连串;一系列;连锁:He runs a ~ store near our school. 他在我们学校附近经营一家连锁店。/ After a ~ of events she knew a lot. 经过一连串的事件,她懂得了很多东西。

chair /tʃeə(r)/ *n.* [C]椅子

chairman /'tʃeəmən/ *n.* [C](*pl.* chairmen)主席;议长:He was elected ~ of the meeting. 他被选为会议主席。

chalk /tʃɔːk/ *n.* [U]粉笔:colored ~s 彩色粉笔/ a piece of ~ 一支粉笔

challenge /'tʃælɪndʒ/ Ⅰ *n.* [C]挑战;激励:give a ~ 提出挑战/accept a ~ 接受挑战/ a letter of ~ 挑战书 Ⅱ *v.* 向……挑战;要求:~ the limits 挑战极限/ He ~d me to play basketball. 他向我挑战比赛篮球。

chamber /'tʃeɪmbə(r)/ *n.* [C] ❶室,房间;(尤指)寝室:She retired to her ~. 她退进了她的卧室。❷(立法机关、地方长官、法官等的)会议厅;立法机关;司法机关:the council ~议事室 ❸(动植物体内的)室,腔:The heart has four ~s. 心脏有四室。

chameleon /kə'miːlɪən/ *n.* [C] ❶变色蜥蜴 ❷多变的人,变色龙:He is a ~ with no opinions of his own. 他是个反复无常的人,没有一点主见。派 chameleonlike *adj.*

champagne /ʃæm'peɪn/ *n.* [U]香槟酒:We always have ~ in our party. 我们总在聚会上喝香槟酒。

champion /'tʃæmpɪən/ *n.* [C]冠军;优胜者:He won the ~of the world cup. 他赢得了世界杯赛的冠军。

championship /'tʃæmpɪənˌʃɪp/ *n.* ❶[C](常作 *pl.*)锦标赛:the American national golf ~s 全美高尔夫球锦标赛 ❷[C]冠军身份(或地位);冠军称号:gain (lose, retain) a ~ 取得(失去,保持)冠军(称号) ❸[U]捍卫;拥护;支持:He undertook the ~ of our cause. 他支持我们的事业。

chance /tʃɑːns/ Ⅰ *n.* ❶[U]运气;偶然:take (stand, try) one's ~ 碰运气/It was pure ~ that I won the match. 我在那场比赛中获胜纯属偶然。❷机会;可能;侥幸:There is no ~ of his becoming a doctor. 他不可能成为医生。/ **by** ~ 偶然;意外地:I met him by ~. 我偶然

碰见了他。Ⅱ *v.* ❶碰巧;偶然发生:Perhaps you might ~ on (upon) the dictionary at some old bookstall. 或许你会碰巧在哪家旧书摊上买到这本字典。❷冒险;碰运气:It may be risky, but we'll ~ it. 这可能有风险,但我们要碰碰运气。

chancellor / ˈtʃɑːnsələ, ˈtʃænsələ / *n.* [C] ❶(奥地利、德国等的)总理,首相 ❷(大学的)名誉校长;(美国某些大学的)校长

change / tʃeɪndʒ / Ⅰ *v.* ❶改变;变化:She ~d her opinion. 她改变了看法。/ The city has ~d a great deal. 这座城市变化很大。❷更换;互换:Shall we ~ seats? 我们交换座位好吗? / ~... **into** ... 把……变成……:Water is ~d into steam by heat. 水加热变成蒸汽。Ⅱ *n.* ❶变化:Great ~s have taken place in our country. 我们国家发生了巨大的变化。❷[U]零钱,找头:I have no ~ for an ice-cream. 我没有零钱买冰激凌。

changeable / ˈtʃeɪndʒəbl/ *adj.* 多变的;易变的;不定的;难以揣摩的:a ~ temper 多变的脾气/ He was as ~ as the weather. 他像天气一样捉摸不透。派 changeability *n.*

changeover / ˈtʃeɪndʒˌəʊvə(r)/ *n.* (常用单数)(制度、方法、工艺、设备等的)彻底改变,重大变更;(人员的)更换;(情况等的)大转变:a ~ from a peacetime to a war economy 从和平时期的经济向战时经济的大转变

channel / ˈtʃæn(ə)l / *n.* [C] ❶海峡;水道,渠:They cut a ~ to bring water to their fields. 他们挖了一条水渠把水引入农田。❷频道;波段:He changed ~s to find the program he liked. 他不停地换频道找他喜欢的节目。

chant / tʃɑːnt / *n.* [C]歌;圣歌:赞美诗

chaos / ˈkeɪɒs / *n.* [U]混乱;无秩序的;混沌:The whole district was in ~ after the fire. 火灾后整个地区一片混乱。

chaotic / keɪˈɒtɪk / *adj.* 混乱的:The city traffic was ~. 城市交通乱糟糟的。

chapter / ˈtʃæptə(r) / *n.* [C]章;回:The sentence is at Chapter 4 . 那个句子在第四章。

character / ˈkærəktə(r) / *n.* ❶[U]特性,特征;品格:He has a noble ~. 他有高尚的品格。/ She is firm in ~. 她性格坚强。❷[C](小说、戏剧中的)角色,人物:He appears in the ~ of Hamlet. 他扮演哈姆雷特的角色。

characteristic / ˌkærəktəˈrɪstɪk / Ⅰ *adj.* 特有的;独特的 Ⅱ *n.* [C]特征;特性;特点:Everybody has his own individual ~. 每个人都有自己的个性。

characterize / ˈkærɪktəˌraɪz/ *vt.* ❶描述……的特征;描绘:~ a friend in a few words 用三言两语描绘朋友的特征❷成为……的特征,以……为特征:Rich metaphors ~ his poetry. 他的诗作的特征是采用丰富的暗喻。派 characterization *n.*

charcoal / ˈtʃɑːkəʊl / *n.* [U]木炭

charge / tʃɑːdʒ / Ⅰ *n.* ❶[C]费用;价钱:His ~s are not very high. 他收费不高。/ The tea in this hotel is free of ~ . 这个宾馆里的茶水是免费的。/ What is the ~ for renting the hall? 大厅的出租费是多少? ❷[U]管理;主管;看管:We let him ~ of our children. 我们请他照看我们的孩子。/ The museum is under the ~ of the city government. 这个博物馆由市政府主管。❸[C]控告;指控:She withdrew the ~ against her boss. 她撤回了对老板的指控。/**in ~ of** 主管:Who is in ~ of study? 谁管学习? **take ~ of** 负责;管理:It is he who takes ~ of the key to the classroom. 是他管教室的钥匙。Ⅱ *v.* ❶承担;使负荷:We ~d him with heavy responsibilities. 我们让他担当重任。❷控告;指控:The manager was ~d with bribery. 经理被控告受贿。/~ **sb. with sth.** 指控,控告:They ~d him with murder. 他们指控他犯了谋杀罪。❸充电

charity /ˈtʃærəti/ *n.* 慈善,仁慈;施舍;慈善团体:The poor here live on ~. 这里的穷人靠救济生活。

charm /tʃɑːm/ *n.* [U]魅力;妩媚:It shows the ~ of nature. 它显示了大自然的魅力。

charming /tʃɑːmɪŋ/ *adj.* 迷人的;可爱的;令人神往的:Her little stories are very ~ indeed. 她的小故事确实非常吸引人。

chart /tʃɑːt/ *n.* [C]图表:The expert is studying a weather ~. 专家正在研究一份天气图。

charter /ˈtʃɑːtə(r)/ Ⅰ *n.* ❶[U]包租(交通工具):We'll take a ~ flight to Hong Kong. 我们将乘包机去香港。❷[C]宪章:Have you ever read the Charter of the United Nations? 你读过《联合国宪章》吗? Ⅱ *vt.* 包租:You'd better ~ a bus to the airport. 你们最好包一辆车去机场。

chase /tʃeɪs/ *v.* 追逐;追求:Stop chasing about and sit down. 不要跑来跑去,坐下来! /~ **after** 跟踪;追逐:Chase after her and ask her to come earlier. 追上她,叫她早点来!

chasm /ˈkæzəm/ *n.* [C] ❶(地面的)裂缝;峡谷;缺口,裂口:a ~ in the earth 地面的裂隙 ❷(感情、兴趣等的)大分歧,大差异:a political ~ between the two countries 两个国家之间的政治纷争/bridge a ~弥合裂痕

chat /tʃæt/ Ⅰ *v.* (chatted; chatting) 闲谈;聊天:After supper we ~ted for an hour. 晚饭后我们闲聊了一个小时。Ⅱ *n.* 闲谈;聊天:I'd like to have a ~ with my parents. 我想和我父母聊聊天。

chatter /ˈtʃætə(r)/ *vi.* ❶喋喋不休,饶舌,唠叨:He was ~ing on about his new car. 他喋喋不休地谈论他的新车。/Off we set, with Bill ~ing a way all the time. 我们出发了,比尔一路上唠叨个没完 ❷(因寒冷或恐惧等而牙齿)打战:His teeth ~ed with cold. 他的牙齿因寒冷而直打战。

cheap /tʃiːp/ *adj.* 廉价的;便宜的:These books are ~. 这些书价格便宜。/ Things in a supermarket are ~. 超市里的东西很便宜。

cheat /tʃiːt/ Ⅰ *n.* 骗子;欺骗;欺诈:He is a ~. 他是一个骗子。Ⅱ *v.* 欺骗;骗取;行骗:She ~ed him of his money. 她骗了他的钱。/ He always ~s at examinations. 他考试总是作弊。

check /tʃek/ Ⅰ *vt.* ❶使突然停止;使减缓;中止;抑制;克制:~ one's anger 克制住自己的怒气 / A change of wind ~ed the fire. 风向的改变抑制了火势。/ She started to say something but ~ed herself. 她欲言又止。❷检查;核查,核实,核对:I'll just ~ (that) I've locked the door. 我就去查看一下我是否已锁上了门。/ She ~ed the copy against the original. 她对照原稿核对这份影印件。/ Check your answers with mine. 将你的答案和我的答案核对一下。❸在……上画"√"号,用"√"标出;(为表

示正误、取舍等）做标记于：Please ~ the correct answer. 请在正确的答案上画"√"号。Ⅱ *n.* ❶支票：pay by ~ 用支票付账 ❷[C]（餐馆的）账单：The waiter handed me a ~ for the meal. 服务员把餐费账单交给了我。❸[C]钩形符号，"√"号：❹[C]检查；核查，核对，核实：I don't think I've got a copy of the report，but I'll have a ~ through my files. 我想我没拿到那份报告的副本，不过先让我查一下我的卷宗再说。❺[C]检验；测试：a ~ on the quality of all goods leaving the factory 对所有出厂产品的质量进行的检验 / give the car a thorough ~ 对汽车做彻底的检修 /~ **in** （在旅馆）登记办理住宿手续；（在机场）办理登机手续：You must ~ in (at the airport) an hour before your plane leaves. 你必须在飞机起飞前一小时（到机场）办理登机手续。~ **on** 检查；调查：They decided to ~ on him. 他们决定对他进行调查。~ **out** ①（在旅店）办理退房手续；结账后离开（旅店）②得到证实：What he said ~ out. 他的话得到了证实。③查证；核实：The police are still ~ing out his story. 警察还在核实他交代的情况。④（机器等）已经接受检查；检查（机器等）的运行情况：The engine ~s out. 这部引擎已经检查过了。⑤办妥……的借出手续：~ out ten books at a time 一次借阅 10 本书

checked / tʃekt/ *adj.* 有方格图案的；有方格花纹的：a ~ blouse 方格女衬衫

checker / ˈtʃekə(r)/ *n.* [C] ❶审核员；检验员：a freight ~ in a shipping house 货运处的货物检验员 ❷（尤指超级市场、自助餐厅等的）收款员，收银员：a ~ at a supermarket counter 超级商场柜台的收银员 ❸（衣帽间的）服务员；（行李寄存处的）管理员

checkup / ˈtʃekˌʌp/ *n.* [C]体检：go for (have) an annual ~ 做每年一次的体检/ give sb. a thorough ~ 给某人做全面体检

cheek / tʃiːk / *n.* [C]脸颊：Before she left，she kissed her mother on the ~. 临走前她吻了吻母亲的脸颊。

cheer / tʃɪə(r) / *v.* 欢呼；使振奋：The students ~ed when they heard that there would be a party this weekend. 听说这个周末有聚会，学生们都欢呼起来。/ He was ~ed by the good news. 这个好消息使他感到振奋。/~ **up**（使）愉快起来：He ~ed up at the thought of seeing his old friend. 他一想到要见老朋友，心里就高兴。

cheerful / ˈtʃɪəful/ *adj.* ❶欢乐的，快乐的，高兴的，兴高采烈的：be in a ~ mood 情绪高昂 / She is ~ in spite of her misery. 她尽管不幸，但精神愉快。❷令人快乐的；给人愉悦感的：~ music 欢快的音乐 / a ~ atmosphere 轻松愉快的气氛 ❸愿意的，乐意的，情愿的：a ~ welcome 热忱的欢迎 / ~ help 乐意的帮助 派 cheerfully *adv.*；cheerfulness *n.*

cheers / tʃɪəz / *int.* 干杯；谢谢；再见

cheery / ˈtʃɪəri / *adj.* ❶高兴的，愉快的，兴高采烈的：He looked ~ that morning. 那天早晨他看上去很高兴。❷让人愉快的；令人振奋的：a ~ letter 一封让人振奋的信函

cheese / tʃiːz / *n.* [U]奶酪

chef / ʃef / *n.* [C]厨师：He is a famous ~ in France. 他是法国的著名厨师。

chemical / ˈkemɪkl / *adj.* 化学的：a ~ change 化学变化/~fertilizer 化肥/ a ~

formula 化学公式/ ~ reactions 化学反应

chemist / ˈkemɪst / *n.* [C]化学家；药剂师

chemistry / ˈkemɪstri / *n.* [U]化学：physical ~ 物理化学/warfare ~军事化学/ applied ~应用化学/ organic (inorganic) ~有机(无机)化学

cheque / tʃek / *n.* [C]支票

cherish / ˈtʃerɪʃ / *vt.* ❶爱护；珍视：Support the army and ~ the people. 拥军爱民。❷怀有(感情)；抱有(希望)：The old soldier ~s a deep love for his motherland. 老战士十分热爱自己的祖国。

cherry / ˈtʃeri / *n.* [C]樱桃；樱桃树

chess / tʃes / *n.* [U]棋；国际象棋：play ~ 下象棋/a ~ master 象棋大师/ I often have a ~game with my grandfather after dinner. 晚饭后我常和祖父下象棋。

chest / tʃest / *n.* [C] ❶柜子；箱子；橱：I put my ID card in the ~ but I didn't find it. 我把身份证放在柜子里了，但是我没有找到。❷胸；胸膛：The doctor said that she suffered from ~ disease. 大夫说她患了胸部疾病。

chestnut / ˈtʃesnʌt / *n.* ❶[C]栗子；栗树 ❷[U]栗色

chew / tʃuː / *v.* 咀嚼；咬碎：She told her son to ~ thoroughly when eating. 她告诉儿子吃东西要细嚼慢咽。/ ~ (**upon, over**) **sth.** 沉思，细想：Just ~ those facts over and let me know your opinion. 你细想一下这些事实，然后将你的意见告诉我。

chick / tʃɪk / *n.* [C]小鸡；小鸟；小孩

chicken / ˈtʃɪkɪn / *n.* 小鸡；鸡；鸡肉：They feed some ~s in the yard. 他们在院子里养了几只鸡。/ The ~ is delicious. 鸡肉美味可口。

chief / tʃiːf / Ⅰ *adj.* 主要的；首要的：The ~ news is printed on the front page of the newspaper. 主要新闻登在报纸的头版。Ⅱ *n.* [C]首领；领袖：a commander in ~总司令/ an editor in ~总编；主编/ the ~ of a police station 警察局局长/ the ~ of the delegates 首席代表/ the ~ of state 国家元首

chiefly / ˈtʃiːfli/ *adv.* ❶首先；首要：We visited Washington ~ to see the Capitol and the White House. 我们访问华盛顿首要的是为了参观国会大厦和白宫。/ Chiefly, he has to avoid fat. 首先他得少吃脂肪。❷主要地；大部分，大多：The accident happened ~ as a result of carelessness. 事故主要是因为疏忽造成的。/ He phoned ~ to let us know he was feeling better. 他打电话主要是告诉我们他感到好些了。

child / tʃaɪld / *n.* [C] (*pl.* children / ˈtʃɪldrən/)小孩；孩子：The ~ is interested in swimming. 那小孩对游泳很感兴趣。

childbirth / ˈtʃaɪldˌbɜːθ / *n.* 分娩，生产

childhood / ˈtʃaɪldhʊd / *n.* 童年，幼年；童年时期：My mother often recalls her happy ~ now. 现在我妈妈经常回忆她快乐的童年。/ He lived a poor life in his ~. 幼年时期他过着贫困的生活。

childish / ˈtʃaɪldɪʃ / *adj.* 孩子的；幼稚的：Looking at her ~face, I felt happy too. 看着她孩子气的脸蛋，我也高兴起来。/ I don't like such ~ games. 我不喜欢玩这种幼稚的游戏。

chill / tʃɪl / Ⅰ *n.* [C] ❶寒冷；寒气：the ~ of a fall day 秋日寒峭/She turned on the fire to take the ~ from the air. 她生火驱寒取暖。❷受凉；感冒；(由风寒引

起的)发烧:catch a ～着凉 Ⅱ *v.* (使)变冷;(使)觉得冷:The earth ～s when the sun sets. 太阳落山后地球温度就下降。/be ～ed to the bone 感到寒气彻骨

chili /ˈtʃɪli/ *n.* [U](干)辣椒:People in Sichuan and Hunan like ～ pepper very much. 四川人和湖南人都非常喜欢吃辣椒。

chilly /ˈtʃɪli/ *adj.* 寒冷的:I felt rather ～ outside the house. 在屋子外边我感到很冷。

chimney /ˈtʃɪmni/ *n.* [C]烟囱;烟道:You can see few big ～s in our city now. 现在你很难在我们这个城市里看到大烟囱了。/ He smokes like a ～. 他抽烟非常厉害。

chimpanzee /ˌtʃɪmpænˈziː/ *n.* [C]黑猩猩

chin /tʃɪn/ *n.* [C]下巴,颏:The man hit her on the ～. 那人打着她的下巴。

china /ˈtʃaɪnə/ *n.* [U]瓷器:She presented me a set of ～ as my birthday gift. 她送我一套瓷器做生日礼物。

chink /tʃɪŋk/ *n.* [C] ❶裂口,裂缝 ❷缝隙,(狭小的)空隙:a ～ between two buildings 两座建筑物之间的空隙

chip /tʃɪp/ Ⅰ *n.* [C]薄片;碎片;(*pl.*)炸土豆片:The girl likes potato ～s very much. 小女孩很喜欢吃炸土豆片。Ⅱ *vt.* (chipped;chipping)切成细条状

chisel /ˈtʃɪzəl/ Ⅰ *n.* [C]凿子,錾子 Ⅱ *vt.* 凿,刻,雕:～ a hole in the door to fit a new lock 在门上凿个新锁孔

chloride /ˈklɔːrɪd/ *n.* [U]氯化物

chlorine /ˈklɔːriːn/ *n.* [U]氯(符号 Cl)

chlorophyl(l) /ˈklɒrəfɪl/ *n.* [U]叶绿素

chock /tʃɒk/ Ⅰ *n.* [C](用以防滑等的)楔子,垫木,塞块 Ⅱ *vt.* 用楔子塞住,用垫块垫住(或固定住):～ the car before changing tires 在换轮胎前用垫木把汽车固定住

chocolate /ˈtʃɒklət/ *n.* [U]巧克力

choice /tʃɒɪs/ *n.* [C]选择;抉择:I found it difficult to make a correct ～. 我发现要做出正确的选择是很难的。

choir /ˈkwaɪə(r)/ *n.* [C]合唱团;(尤指教堂的)唱诗班;圣乐团

choke /tʃəʊk/ *v.* 窒息;哽噎;阻塞:She ～d up over the news. 听到这个消息,她哽得说不出话来。

cholera /ˈkɒlərə/ *n.* [U]霍乱

cholesterol /kəˈlestərɒl/ *n.* [U]胆固醇

choose /tʃuːz/ *v.* (chose/tʃəʊz/, chosen /ˈtʃəʊzn/) 挑选;选择:We chose her as our group leader. 我们选她当组长。/ She chose to be a teacher. 她选择了当教师。

chop /tʃɒp/ *vt.* (chopped;chopping)砍;劈;斩;剁:～ wood with an axe 用斧劈柴/～ down a tree 砍倒一棵树/～ **up** 剁碎,切细:～ up cabbage for coleslaw 为凉拌把卷心菜切成丝

chopstick /ˈtʃɒpstɪk/ *n.* [C]筷子:Mike uses ～s well. 迈克能很熟练地使用筷子。

chord /kɔːd/ *n.* [C] ❶和弦;和音 ❷心弦:His story struck a ～ of pity in the listeners. 他的遭遇触动了听众的怜悯心。❸(数学)弦

chore /ʃɔː(r)/ *n.* [C] ❶琐事;例行工作:the administrative ～s of the office 办公室的日常工作 ❷家庭杂务:the daily ～s of cleaning, cooking and shopping 打扫、做饭、购物这些日常家庭事务

chorus /ˈkɔːrəs/ Ⅰ *n.* [C] ❶合唱队;歌咏队;(教堂的)唱诗班:a huge ～ of 120 singers 一支拥有 120 人的大型歌唱队

❷合唱曲；合唱：a mixed ~ of male (female)男（女）声合唱 / The audience joined in the ~. 听众也加入了合唱。❸叠句，副歌；合唱部分 ❹齐声，同声：a ~ of boos 齐声喝倒彩/**in** ~ 齐声地，同声地；共同地：read in ~ 齐声朗读 Ⅱ *vt.* 齐声说出（或唱出），一起朗诵：The audience ~ed its approval by loud cheering. 听众一齐用欢呼声来表示赞同。

Christ / kraɪst / *n.* 救世主（特指耶稣基督）：before ~（略作 B.C.）公元前：That happened in 265 B.C. 那事发生在公元前 265 年。

Christian / ˈkrɪstsən / Ⅰ *n.* [C]基督教徒 Ⅱ *adj.* 基督教的

Christmas / ˈkrɪsməs / *n.* 圣诞节：~ Day 圣诞节/ a ~ card 圣诞卡/Father ~ 圣诞老人/ Merry ~ to you! 祝你圣诞快乐！

chromium / ˈkrəumɪəm / *n.* [U]铬

chromosome / ˈkrəuməsəum / *n.* [C]染色体：The scientists have won great achievements in studying ~. 在对染色体的研究中，科学家们取得了很大的成就。

chronic / ˈkrɒnɪk / *adj.* ❶（常作定语）长期的，一贯的：~ financial problems 长期的金融问题 ❷惯常的；恶习难改的：a ~ liar 一贯撒谎的人 ❸（疾病）慢性的，顽固的：~ hepatitis 慢性肝炎/ a ~ patient 慢性病患者

chronology / krəˈnɒlədʒi / *n.* [C]（大事）年表；（事件、资料等）按发生年月顺序的排列

chrysanthemum / krɪˈsænθəməm / *n.* [C]菊花

chuckle / ˈtʃʌkl / *vi.* 咯咯声；轻声笑；暗自笑：The little girl ~d happily over a cartoon. 小女孩边看动画片边高兴得咯咯笑。

chunk / tʃʌŋk / *n.* [C]厚片，大片，大块：a ~ of meat 一大块肉

church /tʃɜːtʃ/ *n.* [C]教堂：Jack and his family often go to ~. 杰克和家人常去教堂做礼拜。

cicada / sɪˈkeɪdə / *n.* [C]（*pl.* cicadas 或 cicadae/sɪˈkeɪdiː/）蝉，知了

cigar / sɪˈgɑː(r) / *n.* [C]雪茄烟

cigarette / ˌsɪgəˈret / *n.* [C] 香烟：a pack of ~s 一包香烟/ Cigarettes are not good for health. 香烟对健康无益。

cinema / ˈsɪnəmə / *n.* [C]电影院；电影：They met with an old friend in the ~. 在电影院他们遇到一位老朋友。/ Let's go to the ~. 咱们去看电影吧！

circle / ˈsɜːkl / Ⅰ *n.* [C] ❶圆；圆圈；环状物：Please draw a ~ with A for its centre. 以 A 为圆心画一个圆。❷圈子；集团：He is famous in academic ~. 在学术界他很有名。/**all ~s of life** 各行各业；各阶层人士 Ⅱ *v.* 环绕；盘绕：The fence ~s the yard. 院子四周围着篱笆。/ The good news soon ~d around. 喜讯很快就传开了。

circuit / ˈsɜːkɪt / *n.* [C] ❶电路；线路：closed ~ TV (CCTV) 闭路电视/ integrated ~集成电路 ❷环行；巡回：The moon takes a month to make its ~ around the earth. 月球绕地球一周要一个月时间。

circuitry / ˈsɜːkɪtri/ *n.* [U] ❶电路元件 ❷电路系统

circular / ˈsɜːkjələ(r) / *adj.* 圆形的；循环的

circulate / ˈsɜːkjəleɪt / *v.* 循环；流通：Blood ~s through the boy. 血液在体内循环。

circulation / ˌsɜːkjəˈleɪʃn / *n.* ❶[U]循环；血液循环；流通：The doctor said that the old man had a bad ~. 大夫说老人血液循环不好。/ The authority decided to put some new coins into~. 当局决定发行一些新硬币。❷[C]发行量；销售量：Her novels have a large ~. 她的小说发行量很大。

circumference / səˈkʌmfərəns / *n.* 圆周；周长：Do you know the ~ of the earth? 你知道地球的周长是多少吗？

circumstance / ˈsɜːkəmstəns / *n.* [C]事实；详情；环境：If ~s permit, I'll go abroad to study. 如果情况允许，我将要出国读书。/**in (under) no** ~ 决不：Under no ~ will I go with you. 无论怎样我也不跟你走。

circus / ˈsɜːkəs / *n.* [C]马戏；马戏团

cite / saɪt / *vt.* 引用；引证；举(例)：The judge ~d a few cases in the court. 法官在法庭上提出了几个案例。/ He often ~s Lu Xun in his articles. 他在文章中常常引用鲁迅的话。

citizen / ˈsɪtɪzn / *n.* [C]公民；市民；居民：The teacher asks us to be a law-abiding ~. 老师要求我们做一个守法的公民。/ He is an honorary ~ of our city. 他是我们市的荣誉市民。

city / ˈsɪtɪ / *n.* [C]城市；都市：an ancient ~古城/ the Forbidden City (北京的)紫禁城/ He spent half a month visiting a few coastal-line open cities. 他花半个月时间访问了几个沿海开放城市。

civic / ˈsɪvɪk / *adj.* ❶城市的，都市的：the new ~ centre 新的市中心 ❷公民的；市发的：~ duties 公民的义务 ❸民事的；平民的

civil / ˈsɪvl / *adj.* ❶公民的；市民的；民用的：We have not only ~ rights but also ~ duties. 我们不仅有公民权利，也有公民义务。❷国内的：The ~ war lasted for eight years. 那场内战持续了八年之久。❸文明的；有礼貌的：a ~ society 文明社会/ His father asks him to be a ~ person. 他父亲要求他做一个有礼貌的人。

civilian / səˈvɪlɪən / Ⅰ *n.* [C]平民；老百姓；非军事人员：~s and soldiers 军民 Ⅱ *adj.* 平民的；民间的；民用的：The Queen dreamed to live a ~life. 女王渴望过平民生活。

civilization(-sation) / ˌsɪvəlaɪˈzeɪʃn / *n.* 文明；文化：ancient ~古代文明/ modern ~现代文明/ materials~物质文明/ spiritual ~精神文明/ The ~ of China has a long history. 中国文化有悠久的历史。

civilize(-se) / ˈsɪvəlaɪz / *vt.* 使文明；使开化：a ~d neighborhood 文明街道/ a ~d school 文明学校/ a ~d unit 文明单位/ The development of education helped to ~ the people of that district. 教育的发展帮助那个地区的人文明起来。

claim / kleɪm / *v.* ❶声称，宣称：He ~ed to have finished his task without help. 他声称是在没有帮助的情况下完成任务的。❷要求，认领：Nobody come to ~ the luggage. 没有任何人来认领行李。

clamo(u)r / ˈklæmə(r) / Ⅰ *n.* ❶吵闹声，喧嚣声，喧嚷：He was interrupted in a speech by ~s of disapprobation. 他的演讲被人们大声的指责声打断了。❷吵嚷的要求(或抗议)；提出要求的呼声：a ~ against the new bill 反对新法案的呼声 Ⅱ *vi.* ❶吵嚷，吵闹，喧嚷 ❷嚷着要求(或反对)；大声疾呼：a crowd of demonstrators ~ing to see the minister 嚷着要

见部长的一群示威者

clamp / klæmp / Ⅰ *n.* [C]夹钳,钳;夹具:He used a ~ to hold the arm on the chair. 他用夹钳把扶手固定在椅子上。Ⅱ *vt.* 夹紧,紧紧抓住;固定:A picture frame must be ~ed together while the glue is drying. 照片镜框用胶接好后,胶水未干前必须用夹子夹紧。/He ~ed his hand over her mouth to stop her from screaming. 他用手紧紧捂住她的嘴,不让她发出尖叫声。/~ **down** (对……)实行限制;(对……)进行压制:The government has promised to ~ down on criminal activity. 政府已承诺要严厉打击犯罪活动。

clan /klæn/ *n.* [C]宗族;部族;家族:a Scottish ~ 苏格兰宗族 / a power struggle between two ~s 两个部族之间的权力之争 / Our whole ~ got together for Thanksgiving. 感恩节时我们家族大团圆。

clap / klæp / *v.* (clapped; clapping) 喝彩;拍(手):The audience ~ped the singer. 观众为歌唱家鼓掌。

clarify / ˈklærɪˌfaɪ / *vt.* ❶澄清,阐明,使清楚明了:The teacher's explanation clarified the difficult rules. 老师的解释阐明了难懂的规则。❷澄清(液体),消除(杂质);净化:~ syrup 使糖浆澄清 派 clarification *n.*

clash / klæʃ / Ⅰ *vi.* ❶(金属等)发出刺耳的碰撞声:The bell of St. Paul's ~ed out. 圣保罗教堂的钟叮当叮当地直响。❷发生冲突:The two factions ~ed over the seating arrangements. 两派为座位安排问题发生了冲突。/Her wedding ~ed with my exam so I couldn't go. 她的婚礼与我的考试时间冲突,所以我不能去参加。❸不协调;不相配,不一致:Those red shoes ~ violently with that orange dress and purple hat. 那双红鞋同橘色衣服、紫色帽子极不相配。Ⅱ *n.* [C] ❶(金属等的)刺耳的碰撞声 ❷冲突,矛盾;不协调,不一致:a verbal ~口角/a border ~ between two countries 两国边境冲突

clasp / klɑːsp / *v.* 紧握;扣住:She ~ed his hand tight in both of hers. 她紧紧握住他的双手。

class / klɑːs / *n.* ❶[C]种类;等级:These problems fell into three main ~es. 这些问题分成三大类。/ We have the first-~ equipment in our school lab. 我们学校实验室有一流的设备。❷[C]课;上课:She conducted an English ~ for Chinese students. 她给中国学生上英语课。❸[C]班;班级;年级:I am in Class Ⅲ. 我在 3 班。/ He is studying in a beginner's ~. 他正在初级班学习。❹[U]社会等级;阶级:He thinks that he belongs to the middle ~. 他认为他属于中产阶级。

classic / ˈklæsɪk / Ⅰ *n.* [C]名著;杰作;经典(著作):I like to read Chinese ~s after class. 课余我喜欢读中国名著。Ⅱ *adj.* (文学艺术等)第一流的;最优秀的;古典的:It is one of the greatest ~ myths. 这是最优秀的古希腊神话之一。

classical / ˈklæsɪkl / *adj.* 古典的;经典的:~ architecture 古典建筑/ Beethoven contributed greatly to the west ~ music. 贝多芬对西方古典音乐做出了极大贡献。

classification / ˌklæsɪfɪˈkeɪʃn / *n.* 分类;分级;类别;等级:job ~ 职业分类/ social ~ 社会等级

classified / ˈklæsɪfaɪd / *adj.* 分成类的:You'd better first look up the ~ catalog. 你最好先查一查分类目录。

classify /ˈklæsɪfaɪ/ *vt.* 把……分类；把……分级：Apples here are classified according to size. 这里的苹果依大小分等级。

classmate /ˈklɑːsmeɪt/ *n.* [C]同班同学：A ~ of mine won the first prize. 我的一位同班同学获得了一等奖。

classroom /ˈklɑːsrʊm/ *n.* [C]教室；课堂：She hurried out of the ~ with a book in her hand. 她手里拿着一本书匆匆忙忙地走出教室。

clause /klɔːz/ *n.* [C] ❶分句，从句，子句：a subordinate ~从句 ❷(正式文件或法律文件的)条款：a most-favoured nation ~最惠国待遇条款

claw /klɔː/ *n.* [C]脚爪：A hawk has sharp ~s. 鹰有锋利的爪子。

clay /kleɪ/ *n.* [U]黏土：Bricks are made from ~. 砖是泥做的。

clean /kliːn/ Ⅰ *adj.* 干净的；整洁的：The room is very ~. 房间很干净。/ Wash your hands ~ before dining. 吃饭前把手洗干净。Ⅱ *v.* 弄整洁；打扫；洗涤：She is ~ing the blackboard. 她正在擦黑板。/~ **out** 清扫；花光；抢光：The thieves ~ed out the store. 盗贼将商店洗劫一空。~ **up** 收拾；打扫；肃清：Can you ~ up the desks? 你能将这些书桌打扫干净吗？

cleanse /klenz/ *vt.* ❶使清洁；清洗：~ a wound before bandaging it 包扎前先清洗伤口 ❷使净化(与 of 连用)：~ one's thoughts of sin 清除邪念 / ~ the soul 净化心灵

cleanup /ˈkliːnˌʌp/ *n.* [C]打扫，扫除：give the house a good ~ 彻底打扫房子

clear /klɪə(r)/ *adj.* ❶明亮的；清澈的；明朗的：The day was beautifully ~. 那天碧空如洗。/ You can see the top of the mountain on a ~ day. 在晴朗的日子你可以看到山顶。❷清楚的；明白的：I am not ~ about what happened there. 我不清楚那里发生了什么事情。派 clearly *adv.*

clearance /ˈklɪərəns/ *n.* ❶[U]清除，除去；清空：The ~ of the room allowed them to decorate it more easily. 房间清空后，他们装饰起来要容易得多。❷空间；间隙，空隙：There was only a foot of ~ between the top of truck and the roof of the tunnel. 卡车顶部距隧道顶仅有一英尺的空间。❸批准，许可：apply for ~ to read sealed documents 申请查阅密封文件 ❹清仓大贱卖，大甩卖

cleavage /ˈkliːvɪdʒ/ *n.* [U]裂开；砍开；分开：a sharp ~ of fundamental interests 根本利益的尖锐分歧 / a growing ~ between the Conservative and Liberal wings of the party 该党保守派和自由派之间日益激化的分歧

cleave /kliːv/ *vt.* (cleft 或 cleaved 或 clove, cleft 或 cleaved 或 cloven) ❶砍开；使分开，使分裂：~ a tree down 砍倒一棵树 / ~ a branch from a tree 从树上砍下树枝 ❷掠过，穿过；游过：The airplane swept across the sky, cleaving the clouds. 飞机穿云破雾，掠过天空。—*vi.* (顺纹理或裂纹)裂开；被砍开：Pine fir wood ~s easily. 松科常绿树木容易裂开。

clench /klentʃ/ *v.* 咬紧牙关；握紧拳头：He ~ed his jaws and said not a single word. 他紧咬牙关，一声不吭。

clerk /klɑːk, klɜːk/ *n.* [C]办事员；职员：She is a bank ~. 她是银行职员。

clever /ˈklevə(r)/ *adj.* (-er, -est)聪明

的；灵巧的；机灵的：Tom was very ～ about such things. 汤姆在这类事情上挺精明。/ **be ～ at** 擅长于：He is ～ at writing comedies. 他擅长于写喜剧。

C

click /klɪk/ Ⅰ *n.* [C]咔嗒声 Ⅱ *v.* ❶(使)发出咔嗒声：The lock ～ed shut. 锁咔嗒一声锁上了。❷点击(鼠标)

client /ˈklaɪənt/ *n.* [C]客户；顾客；委托人：He serves the ～s wholeheartedly. 他全心全意为顾客服务。

cliff /klɪf/ *n.* [C]峭壁；悬崖：He was brave to stand on the edge of the ～ to overlook the beautiful scene. 他很勇敢，站在悬崖边上俯视下边的美景。

climate /ˈklaɪmət/ *n.* 气候：How do you like the ～ of Beijing? 你觉得北京的气候怎样？/ I like a mild ～. 我喜欢温和的气候。

climax /ˈklaɪmæks/ *n.* [C]高潮；顶点：She missed the ～ of the play. 她没有看到话剧的高潮部分。/ He is at the ～ of his business. 他正处于事业的顶峰。

climb /klaɪm/ *v.* 爬；攀登：They ～ed out through the window. 他们从窗子爬出去了。

cling /klɪŋ/ *v.* (clung/klʌŋ/, clung) 黏住；依附；坚持；抱住不放：The wet T-shirt clung to the boy's body. 湿湿的T恤衫紧紧地贴在小男孩身上。/ Don't always ～ to your own views. 别总是固执己见。

clinic /ˈklɪnɪk/ *n.* [C]诊所；门诊部

clinical /ˈklɪnɪkəl/ *adj.* ❶诊疗所的：～ treatment 门诊治疗 ❷临床实习的；临床教学的：～ medicine 临床医学/ a ～ diagnosis 临床诊断 ❸客观的；冷静的；超然的：cold ～ tone of voice 冷静淡然的语调

clip[1] /klɪp/ *n.* [C]夹；回形针

clip[2] /klɪp/ *vt.* 剪，剪短；修剪；剪辑：～ wool from a sheep 剪羊毛/～ one's hair short 剪短发/ He ～s some articles from the newspaper for his son. 他常常为儿子从报上剪下一些文章。

clipper /ˈklɪpə(r)/ *n.* [C] ❶修剪者，修剪物 ❷(常作 *pl.*)羊毛剪 ❸发剪；指甲剪：an electric hair ～ 电动理发剪 / a pair of nail ～s 一把指甲剪 ❹船

cloak /kləʊk/ *n.* [C]外套；斗篷

clock /klɒk/ *n.* [C]时钟：Please advance the ～ one hour. 请把时钟拨快1小时。/ The ～ struck eleven. 钟已敲过11点。/ **round the ～** 日夜：The workers often work round the ～. 工人们时常不分昼夜地工作。

clockwise /ˈklɒkˌwaɪz/ *adj.* & *adv.* 顺时针方向的(地)：You must turn the key ～ to unlock the door. 你必须按顺时针方向转动钥匙才能打开门。/ A ～ turn closes the water faucet. 按顺时针方向转动就会关掉水龙头。

clog /klɒg/ Ⅰ *v.* (clogged; clogging) ❶堵塞，阻挡；阻塞：Hair has ～ged the drain up again. 毛发又把排水管堵住了。/ The expressway always ～s during the rush hour. 这条高速公路一到交通高峰时间总是堵车。Ⅱ *n.* [C] ❶障碍物，堵塞物 ❷木屐；(跳舞用的)轻型木屐

clone /kləʊn/ *v.* 无性繁殖；克隆

cloning /ˈkləʊnɪŋ/ *n.* [U]无性繁殖；克隆技术

close /kləʊz/ Ⅰ *v.* 关，闭；封闭；结束：Please ～ the door. 请关门。/ The meeting ～d at half past eleven. 会议11:30结束。Ⅱ *adj.* 接近的；附近的；靠近的：

Winter is ~. 冬天已近。/ The store is ~ to the school. 商店在学校附近。Ⅲ *adv.* 接近;靠近:Come ~ so I can see you. 走近点,好让我看见你。派 closely *adv.*

closet / ˈklɒzɪt / *n.* [C]小房间;橱:a clothes ~衣橱/ a water ~ (WC)盥洗室

close-up / ˈkləusˌʌp / *n.* [C] ❶特写镜头;❷详尽的描写:a ~ of modern society 现代社会的详细写照

clot / klɒt / *n.* [C](液体、血等的)凝块;(粘在一起的)厚块:a ~ of soil 泥块/ She felt a ~ of emotion jammed in her throat. 她激动不已,喉头一阵哽咽。

cloth / klɒθ / *n.* [U]布;衣料:This ~ wears well. 这种布耐穿。/ Do you like this kind of ~? 你喜欢这种布料吗?

clothe / kləuð / *vt.* 给……穿衣;覆盖:He was thickly ~d. 他穿得很厚。/ The sun ~s the earth with light. 阳光普照大地。

clothes / kləuðz / *n.* (*pl.*)衣服;服装:holiday ~节日盛装/ night ~ 睡服;睡衣/ work (working) ~工作服/ sports ~ 运动服/ make ~ 做衣服/ mend (patch) ~ 补衣服/ put on ~ 穿衣服/ take off ~ 脱衣服

clothing / ˈkləuðɪŋ / *n.* [U](总称)衣服

cloud / klaud / *n.* 云;云状物:We watched a sea of ~s at the top of the mountain. 我们在山顶观看到了云海。

cloudy / ˈklaudi / *adj.* ❶多云的:It was ~ this morning but it turned out fine now. 今天早上天空多云,但是现在转晴了。❷模糊不清的;不明了的:I have only a ~idea about it. 对于这事我只有一个模糊的想法。

clown / klaun / *n.* [C]小丑;丑角:He plays the ~ in a circus. 他在一个马戏团里演小丑。

club / klʌb / *n.* [C]俱乐部:a book ~ 读书会/ a night~ 夜总会

clue / kluː / *n.* [C]线索;暗示:He said he could provide some ~s to help the police find the criminal. 他说他可以给警察提供一些线索帮助他们找到罪犯。

clump / klʌmp / *n.* [C] ❶一簇(树或灌木丛);一群;一束:a little ~ of buildings 一小群建筑物/The boy hid in the ~ of tress. 那男孩躲藏在树丛中。❷一团,一块:a ~ of muddy fur 一团脏兮兮的毛发

clumsy / ˈklʌmzi / *adj.* 笨拙的;愚蠢的:He is ~ in speaking. 他是个笨嘴拙舌的人。

cluster / ˈklʌstə(r) / Ⅰ *n.* [C] ❶一组,一丛,一束,一簇:~s of purple flowers 一束束紫色花 ❷(人或物的)一组,一批,一群:a ~ of stars 一组星星/ There was little ~ of admirers round the guest speaker. 只有寥寥几个仰慕者围在客座演讲人的四周。Ⅱ *v.* (使)聚集;(使)成簇;(使)成群:the jewels that are ~ed in one's bosom 堆簇在胸前的珠宝/ a hill where the white buildings ~ed together 一个白色建筑物聚集成群的小山丘

clutch / klʌtʃ / Ⅰ *vt.* 紧握;(急切地)抓住:She ~ed her handbag to stop the thieves stealing it. 她紧紧抓着手提包,不让小偷得手。Ⅱ *n.* [C] ❶手爪;控制,统治:Smith still has the press in his ~es. 史密斯仍控制着出版界。❷(机器、汽车等的)离合器踏板;离合器(杆)

coach / kəutʃ / *n.* [C] ❶客车;长途汽车:They traveled around by ~. 他们坐

长途客车四处旅行。❷教练;私人教师:He is our new football ~. 他是我们的新足球教练。

coagulate /kəʊˈægjʊˌleɪt/ *v.* (使)凝固;(使)凝结:Cooking ~s the white of egg. 烹煮能使蛋白凝固。/ Blood from a cut ~s. 伤口的血液会凝结。派 coagulation *n.*

coal /kəʊl/ *n.* [U] 煤:~ gas 煤气/ mine ~ 采煤/ a ~miner 煤矿工人

coarse /kɔːs/ *adj.* 粗糙的;粗鲁的:~ cloth 粗布/~ skin 粗糙的皮肤/~ manners 粗鲁的举止

coast /kəʊst/ *n.* [C]海岸:The city is on the south ~. 该城位于南岸。/ The ship sailed along the ~. 轮船沿海岸航行。

coastline /ˈkəʊstˌlaɪn/ *n.* [C] ❶海岸线:a rugged (rocky) ~ 多巉岩的海岸线 ❷沿岸地区;沿岸水域

coat /kəʊt/ *n.* [C]上衣;外套:She put on her ~ and went away. 她穿上外套走了。

coating /ˈkəʊtɪŋ/ *n.* [C]涂层,外膜,外层:electric wire with a plastic ~外包塑料皮的电线/a ~ of dust 一层灰

coax /kəʊks/ *vt.* 哄,哄劝;劝诱:~ and threaten sb. by turns 对某人软硬兼施/ The children had to be ~ed into going to school. 这些孩子得用好话哄着才去上学。

cocaine /kəʊˈkeɪn/ *n.* [U]可卡因

cock /kɒk/ *n.* [C] ❶公鸡:Cocks crow in the morning. 公鸡清晨打鸣。❷(水管、煤气管等的)旋塞;龙头:Please turn on (off) the ~. 请打开(关上)龙头。

cockroach /ˈkɒkˌrəʊtʃ/ *n.* [C]蟑螂

cocktail /ˈkɒkteɪl/ *n.* [C]鸡尾酒:make (prepare, mix) a ~ 调制鸡尾酒/ They held a ~ party in the hall. 他们在大厅举行鸡尾酒会。

cocky /ˈkɒki/ *adj.* 趾高气扬的,自鸣得意的,骄傲自大的:a ~ young fellow 自以为是的小伙子 / What makes you so ~? 是什么让你这样神气活现?派 cockily *adv.* ;cockiness *n.*

cocoa /ˈkəʊkəʊ/ *n.* [U]可可粉;可可茶

coconut /ˈkəʊkənʌt/ *n.* [C]椰子

cocoon /kəˈkuːn/ *n.* [C]茧

code /kəʊd/ *n.* [C] ❶代号;密码;电码:a bar ~ 条形码/ an area dialing ~电话区号/ a postal ~ 邮政编码 ❷法规,法典;准则:the civil ~ 民法/ the criminal ~ 刑法/ the moral ~ 道德准则

coexist /ˌkəʊɪgˈzɪst/ *vi.* ❶同时(或同地)存在,共存:Large number of species ~. 大量的物种同时存在。❷和平共处:Can the President ~ with a hostile Congress? 总统与一个怀有敌意的国会能和平共处吗?派 coexistence *n.*

coffee /ˈkɒfi/ *n.* [U]咖啡饮料;咖啡:black ~清咖啡/ white ~ 加奶咖啡

coffin /ˈkɒfɪn/ *n.* [C]棺材;灵柩

cognition /kɒgˌnɪʃn/ *n.* [U]认知,认识;理解;感知:in full ~ of the facts 充分认识事实/The brain waves fluctuate during ~. 脑电图在认知活动中会发生波动。

cohere /kəʊˈhɪə(r)/ *vi.* ❶黏合,附着;凝聚,团结:The two materials can ~ without special glue. 这两种材料不用特殊的胶水就可以黏合在一起。❷(论证、话语等)有条理,连贯,前后一致:Your arguments ~ nicely. 你的论点前后连贯。

coherent /kəʊˈhɪərənt/ *adj.* ❶连贯的,有条理的,前后呼应的:a ~ theory 脉络

清晰的理论 ❷(在说话、思路等方面)清晰的,明了的:When he went crazy he would be not ~. 他发疯时就会语无伦次。❸和谐的;融洽的:a ~ design 和谐的设计 派 coherently *adv.*

cohesion / kəʊˈhiːʒn / *n.* [U]黏合(性);聚合(性);凝聚力:The organization lacked ~. 这个组织缺乏凝聚力。

coil / kɒɪl / Ⅰ *vt.* ❶卷,缠,盘绕:She ~ed her scarf around her neck. 她把围巾缠在脖子上。/The dog ~ed round his legs. 狗盘缩着腿。/Thick smoke ~ up the chimney. 浓烟在烟囱上方升腾起来。Ⅱ *n.* [C](一)卷,(一)圈,(一)匝;盘状物:a ~ of rope 一卷绳子/~ of smoke rose from the accident site. 滚滚烟雾从出事地点上空盘旋着升起。

coin / kɒɪn / *n.* [C]硬币:~ phone 投币式电话/ toss a ~ 投币决定(某事)

coincide / ˌkəʊɪnˈsaɪd / *vi.* 同时发生;相符合;相一致:We didn't ~ in opinion. 我们的见解不同。

coincidence / kəʊˈɪnsɪdəns/ *n.* 巧合;巧事:Their meeting was pure ~. 他们的相遇纯属巧合。/ What a ~, seeing you in America! 在美国见到你真是太巧了! / By ~, we arrive at the same conclusion. 巧得很,我们俩的结论一致。/ ~ of events 事件的同时发生

coke / kəʊk / *n.* [U]焦炭:People there use ~ for fuel. 那里的人们用焦炭作燃料。

cold / kəʊld / Ⅰ *adj.* ❶ 冷的;寒冷的:Most children like ~ drink very much. 大多数孩子都喜欢喝冷饮。/ Yesterday was the ~est day of this winter. 昨天是今年冬天最冷的一天。❷冷淡的;不热情的:You shouldn't be so ~ toward others. 你不应该对他人这么冷淡。❸冷静的;冷酷的;无情的:He had to accept the ~ facts. 他不得不接受那严酷的事实。Ⅱ *n.* ❶[U]冷;寒冷:I really can't stand the ~here. 我真不能忍受这儿的寒冷气候。❷[C]伤风;感冒:She cannot come to the meeting because she caught (a) bad ~. 因患重感冒她不能来开会了。/**catch a** ~ 感冒:Most people ~ two or three ~s a year. 大多数人每年要患两三次感冒。**get (suffer) a bad (heavy, severe)** ~ 患重感冒:She was suffering a bad ~. 她患了重感冒。派 coldly *adv.*

cold-blooded / ˌkəʊldˈblʌdɪd/ *adj.* ❶冷血的:~ crocodiles 冷血的鳄鱼 ❷无情的;残忍的:a ~ serial killer 冷血的连环杀手 ❸害冷的,怕冷的:I'm ~ and need warm clothes in winter. 我这人怕冷,冬天需要穿暖和一些。派 cold-bloodedly *adv.* ;cold-bloodedness *n.*

collaborate / kəˈlæbəˌreɪt / *vi.* ❶(尤指在艺术创作上)合作;协作:The director has ~d with the playwright. 这位导演曾经和这位剧作家合作。❷ 勾结,通敌:~ with the enemy 与敌人狼狈为奸

collapse / kəˈlæps / Ⅰ *v.* 倒塌;崩溃;垮台:The hut ~d under the weight of snow. 小木屋因承受不了雪的重量而倒塌。Ⅱ *n.* 倒塌;崩溃;(价格)暴跌:We hope to see the ~ of the oil price. 我们希望看到油价暴跌的局面。

collar / ˈkɒlə(r) / *n.* [C]衣领

colleague / ˈkɒliːg / *n.* [C]同事;同僚:Uncle Li is my father's old ~. 李叔叔是我父亲的老同事。

collect / kəˈlekt / *v.* 搜集;聚集:A crowd of pupils ~ed at the school gate. 一群学生聚集在校门口。/ She ~ed all their exercise-books. 她将他们的练习本都收

C

了起来。

collection /kəˈlekʃn/ *n.* ❶收集;采集:The large ~ of coins took him about ten years. 他花大约十年时间收集了大量的钱币。❷[C]收藏品;收集物:This museum has a fine ~ of modern pictures. 这家博物馆收藏一些珍贵的现代绘画。❸[C]征收;收款;募捐:All students in his class made a ~ for the disabled child. 全班同学为那位残疾儿童募捐。

collective /kəˈlektɪv/ *adj.* 集体的;共同的;集体的:~ economy 集体经济/the ~ leadership 集体领导/the ~ ownership 共同所有权/ His father works in a ~-owned enterprise. 他父亲在一家集体企业上班。派 collectively *adv.*

collector /kəˈlektə(r)/ *n.* [C] ❶收集者,采集者;收藏家:an art ~ 艺术品收藏家 / an antique ~ 古玩收藏者 ❷收款人,收账人;收债人:a tax ~ 收税员/ a bill ~ 收账人

college /ˈkɒlɪdʒ/ *n.* [C]学院;专科学校:a junior ~专科学校/ a literature ~ 文学院/a naval ~ 海军学院/ a medical ~ 医学院/a normal training ~ 师范学院/ at (in) ~ 在大学/ go to ~ 上大学/ pass (go) through ~ 读完大学

collide /kəˈlaɪd/ *vi.* ❶碰撞,冲撞;相撞:The two cars ~d at a high speed. 这两辆汽车相撞时速度很高。❷冲突,抵触,不一致:Their views often ~d. 他们的观点经常相左。

collision /kəˈlɪʒn/ *n.* ❶碰撞;相撞;碰撞事件:a head-on ~ between a bus and a car 公共汽车和轿车之间的迎头相撞 ❷(利益、意见等的)冲突,抵触:a ~ of principles 原则上的冲突

collocate /ˈkɒləˌkeɪt/ *v.* ❶排列;并列,并置:~ the dishes on the table 将碟子并排放在饭桌上 ❷(词语)组合,组配,搭配:The word "see" ~s with "off" in the phrase "see off". "see"这个词同"off"在"see off"这个词组里搭配在一起。

colon /ˈkəʊlən/ *n.* [C]冒号(:):You should use a ~ here. 你该在这儿用一个冒号。

colonel /ˈkɜːnl/ *n.* [C](陆军、海军陆战队或美国空军)上校

colonial /kəˈləʊnɪəl/ *adj.* 殖民地的;殖民的

colonist /ˈkɒlənɪst/ *n.* [C]殖民者;移民

colony /ˈkɒləni/ *n.* [C]殖民地

colo(u)r /ˈkʌlə(r)/ *n.* 颜色;色彩:What ~ do you like best? 你最喜欢什么颜色? / Red, yellow and orange are called warm ~s. 红、黄、橙称为暖色。

colo(u)rful /ˈkʌləfl/ *adj.* 丰富多彩的;颜色鲜艳的:They are living a ~ life after retirement. 退休后他们过着多姿多彩的生活。/ Old foreign women like ~ dress-es. 外国老太太喜欢穿色彩鲜艳的衣服。

colo(u)ring /ˈkʌlərɪŋ/ *n.* [U] ❶气色,面色:a ruddy ~ 红光满面 / healthy ~ 健康的气色 ❷着色(法) ❸颜料;色素:food ~ 食品着色剂

column /ˈkɒləm/ *n.* [C] ❶柱;支柱;圆柱:The roof is supported by four ~s. 屋顶由四根圆柱支撑。❷(报刊的)专栏(文章):the advertising ~ 广告专栏/ the sports ~ 体育专栏/ the literary ~ 文学专栏/ He lives on writing ~s for the newspaper. 他靠给报纸撰写专栏文章为生。❸ 纵队;小分队:a tank ~ 坦克纵队

columnist /ˈkɒləmnɪst/ *n.* [C]报刊专栏

作者：The boy wants to become a sports ~. 那男孩想当一名体育专栏作家。

coma /ˈkəumə/ *n.* [C]昏迷：go into a ~ 昏迷过去 / in a ~ that lasted four months 处于持续四个月的昏迷状态之中

comb /kəum/ *n.* [C]梳子

combat /ˈkɒmbæt/ *n.* 战斗；斗争：Her son was killed in ~ many years ago. 许多年前她的儿子作战阵亡了。

combination /ˌkɒmbɪˈneɪʃn/ *n.* 结合；联合；化合

combine Ⅰ/kəmˈbaɪn/ *v.* 联合；结合；化合：We should ~ theory with practice. 我们应该把理论与实践结合起来。Ⅱ/ˈkɒmbaɪn/ *n.* [C]联合收割机；结合体

come /kʌm/ *vi.* (came /keɪm/, come) 来，到达；发生；出现；变成：Please ~ here. 请到这儿来。/ The hare came to a small tree. 兔子来到一棵小树前。/ May ~s between April and June. 5 月在 4 月与 6 月之间。/ Bad luck always ~s to me. 我总碰到倒霉的事。/~ **about** 发生；出现：Sometimes it is hard to tell how a quarrel ~s about. 有时很难说明争吵发生的原因。~ **across** 碰到；偶然见到：The other day I came across a book that you might like. 日前我偶然看到一本你可能喜欢的书。~ **along** 快点：Come along, it's nearly 12 o'clock. 快点，已经快 12 点了。~ **around** 复原；苏醒：You need not worry; this boy will ~ around very soon. 不必担心，这小孩不久即可痊愈。~ **back** 回来：When will you ~ back? 你什么时候回来？~ (**back**) **to life** 苏醒；复活：We thought he was drowned, but after an hour's artificial respiration he came (back) to life. 我们认为他已经淹死了，但经过一个小时的人工呼吸，他又活了。~ **by** ①经过：They came by three great cities on their journey. 旅途中，他们经过了三个大城市。②获得：He seemed to have ~ by a large fund of knowledge. 他似乎已获得丰富的知识。~ **down** 下降；下来：We saw them coming down the stairs. 我们看见他们下楼来。~ **in** 进入：That is where you ~ in. 那是你进来的地方。~ **into being** (事物、局面的)形成，产生：The committee came into being in 1969. 委员会于 1969 年成立。~ **into power** 当权；上台：Tom came again into power. 汤姆再度执政。~ **on** ①赶快；快点：Come on, or we'll be late. 赶快；不然我们就迟了。②出现；登台：He felt a cold coming on. 他觉得感冒了。~ **out** ①出现：The sun came out. 太阳出来了。②结果；结束，完成：How did the story ~ out？故事是怎样结束的？~ **over** 走过来：They came over. 他们走过来了。~ **to** ①复苏：She didn't ~ to until two days later. 她两天后才苏醒过来。②总计；达到：The expense ~s to a hundred dollars. 开支共计 100 美元。~ **to a conclusion** 得出结论；作决定：They have ~ to a conclusion upon this case. 关于这件案子，他们已得出结论。~ **to an agreement** 达成协议：We have ~ to an agreement with the workers in that factory. 我们已和那个工厂的工人达成了协议。~ **to an end** 结束：The story suddenly came to an end. 故事突然结束。~ **to one's rescue** 援救；营救：The dog was chasing our cat when Mary came to its rescue. 狗正在追我们的猫，这时玛丽跑去救猫。~ **true** 实现：His wish will ~ true. 他的愿望会实

现。~ **up** ①接近;走近:We saw a big black bear coming up. 我们看见一只大黑熊走过来。②发芽:The seeds haven't ~ up yet. 种子还未发芽。~ **up with** 赶上;追上:Let's go slowly so that the others may ~ up with us. 我们走慢些以便其他人能赶上来。

C

comedian /kəˈmiːdɪən/ *n.* [C]喜剧演员;喜剧作家

comedown /ˈkʌmˌdaʊn/ *n.* 落魄;潦倒,失势:It is quite a ~ for him as a college graduate to have to sweep streets. 像他这样一位大学毕业生不得不去扫大街,真是潦倒至极。

comedy /ˈkɒmədi/ *n.* [C] 喜剧;喜剧性事件:She is writing a ~. 她正在创作一部喜剧。

comet /ˈkɑːmət/ *n.* [C]彗星:Do you know anything about Halley's Comet? 你了解哈雷彗星吗?

comfort /ˈkʌmfət/ Ⅰ *vt.* 安慰;使舒适:Try to ~ him! 尽力安慰他吧! /He ~ed his back with soft cushions. 他放上软垫使背部舒适。Ⅱ *n.* [U]安慰,慰问;安逸,舒适:Her money and goods are not her only ~. 金钱与财产并不是她唯一的安慰。

comfortable /ˈkʌmftəbl/ *adj.* 舒适的;愉快的;自在的:The beds and chairs are fairly ~. 这些床和椅子让人觉得相当舒适。派 comfortably *adv.*

comic /ˈkɒmɪk/ Ⅰ *adj.* 喜剧的;滑稽的:The ~ performances of the comedians amused us greatly. 喜剧演员们的滑稽表演逗得我们十分开心。Ⅱ *n.* [C]喜剧演员;滑稽人物

coming /ˈkʌmɪŋ/ Ⅰ *n.* 来到,来临;到达:With the ~ of winter the days get shorter. 随着冬天的临近,白天也跟着变短了。/ ~**s and goings** 来来往往:all the ~s and goings of the train station 火车站里熙熙攘攘的人群 Ⅱ *adj.* (只作定语)(事件等)正在到来的,即将来临的;(月、年等)接着的,下一个的:this ~ summer 今年夏天 / the ~ weeks 今后几周 / this ~ Sunday 本周星期日

comma /ˈkɒmə/ *n.* [C]逗号;小停顿

command /kəˈmɑːnd/ *v.* 命令;指挥:If you ~ wisely, you'll be obeyed cheerfully. 指挥有方,人人乐从。

commander /kəˈmɑːndə(r)/ *n.* [C]司令官;指挥员:~ in chief 总司令

commemorate /kəˈmeməˌreɪt/ *vt.* ❶纪念:a festival ~ the 200th anniversary of the event 纪念这个事件发生 200 周年的节目 ❷庆祝,庆贺:~ the arrival of the new millennium 庆祝新千年的到来

commence /kəˈmens/ *v.* 开始发生;开始;着手:The meeting is scheduled to ~ at noon. 会议定于午间召开。

commend /kəˈmend/ *vt.* ❶表扬,称赞,嘉许;推崇:~ a soldier for bravery 嘉奖一位表现英勇的士兵/~ sb. upon his diligence 表扬某人勤奋 ❷推荐:~ an applicant to the company 向这家公司推荐一名申请人

comment /ˈkɒment/ Ⅰ *n.* 评论;意见:Have you any ~s to make on this problem? 你对此问题有何评论? / Her strange behaviour caused a good deal of ~s. 她的反常行为引得人们议论纷纷。Ⅱ *v.* 评论;评述:He often ~s on how different the two things are. 他常谈论这两件东西的不同之处。派 commentator *n.*

commentary /ˈkɒmənt(ə)ri/ *n.* ❶评论;(体育比赛的)现场解说,实况报道;(时事)述评:provide ~ on the players

对运动员进行评说 / a sports ~ on radio 电台体育述评 ❷[C]解释性论文;评介:write a ~ on the movie 撰写影评 ❸[C]说明,写照:The high inflation rate is a sad ~ on the financial system. 高通货膨胀率是对金融体制的可悲写照。

commerce /ˈkɒmɜːs/ *n.* [C]商业;贸易:He began to engage in ~ two years ago. 两年前他开始经商。

commercial /kəˈmɜːʃ(ə)l/ Ⅰ *adj.* 商业的;商务的:He graduated from a ~ college. 他毕业于一所商学院。/ This is a big ~ city. 这是一座大的商业城市。Ⅱ *n.* [C]商业广告:I don't like TV ~s. 我不喜欢电视广告节目。

commission /kəˈmɪʃn/ *n.* ❶委任;委托;代办:He is going to execute some ~s for his company in Hainan. 他将代公司在海南办几件事情。❷[C]任务;职权:He tried his best to carry out his ~. 他尽力完成了任务。❸[C]委员会:the Military Commission 军事委员会/ the Commission for Inspecting Discipline 纪律检查委员会 ❹[C]佣金;回扣:You can get a 15% ~ on the goods you sell. 你可以从你销售的商品中抽取20%的佣金。

commit /kəˈmɪt/ *vt.* (-mitted;-mitting) ❶犯罪;犯错:He was accused of ~ting robbery. 他被指控犯了抢劫罪。❷交付;托付:She ~ted her daughter to the care of her parents. 她把女儿托付给父母照顾。/~ **oneself to sth.** 答应对某事负责:I have ~ted myself to helping him. 我答应过帮助他。

commitment /kəˈmɪtmənt/ *n.* ❶承诺,允诺;保证;承担义务:fulfill one's ~s 履行承诺/They reaffirmed their ~ that they would help. 他们重申了他们将给予帮助的许诺。❷[U]致力;献身;投入:~ to a cause 为事业而献身/a professor with a real sense of ~ to his job 真正一心扑在工作上的教授

committee /kəˈmɪti/ *n.* [C]委员会;全体委员:The ~ is made up of nine members. 这个委员会由九人组成。/ The ~ are discussing a very important proposal. 委员们正讨论一份重要的提案。

commodity /kəˈmɒdəti/ *n.* [C]日用品;商品:She was angry that she bought some fake commodities. 买到假冒商品使她非常生气。

common /ˈkɒmən/ *adj.* 共同的;普通的,一般的:English is often used as the ~ language at international conferences. 在国际会议上英语常被当作通用语言使用。/ The boy has made a ~ mistake. 小男孩犯了一个常见的错误。/ **in** ~共有的;公用的:They had nothing in ~. 他们没什么共同之处。~ **sense** 常识:The old farmer had gotten along on a lot of ~ sense. 老农民凭着自己掌握的常识就这样一辈子。派 commonly *adv.*

commonplace /ˈkɒmənpleɪs/ *n.* [C]平凡的事;平常话:Traveling abroad has become a ~ for him. 出国旅游对他来说已是司空见惯的事情。

commonwealth /ˈkɒmənwelθ/ *n.* [C]共和国;联邦;共同体:Do you know when the Commonwealth of Independent Nations was founded? 你知道独联体(独立国家联合体)是哪年成立的吗?

communal /ˈkɒmjʊnəl/ *adj.* 共有的;集体的;公用的;公共的:a ~ television room in a hotel 旅馆里的公共电视室/ ~ property 公共财产

commune /ˈkɒmjuːn/ *n.* [C]公社

communicable /kəˈmjuːnɪkəbl/ *adj.* 可传播的；可传送的；（尤指疾病）可传染的，传染性的：a ~ disease 一种传染病/ Fear is a ~ emotion. 恐惧是一种可以传染给别人的情感。

communicate /kəˈmjuːnɪkeɪt/ *v.* 通信，通话；传递信息：The deaf ~ by the sign language. 耳聋的人靠手语进行交流。/ I immediately ~d with the police. 我立即与警方取得了联系。

communication /kəˌmjuːnɪˈkeɪʃn/ *n.* ❶[U]通信；信息；情报：Language is a major means of ~. 语言是主要的交流工具。/ He is studying the ~ of animals. 他正在研究动物的信息传递方式。❷[C]（*pl.*）通讯设施；交通设施：Our city has excellent ~s. 我们市里有完备的交通设施。

communism /ˈkɒmjʊnɪzəm/ *n.* [U]共产主义

communist /ˈkɒmjənɪst/ Ⅰ*adj.* 共产主义的：the Communist Party of China 中国共产党/ the Communist Youth League of China 中国共产主义青年团 Ⅱ*n.* [C]共产主义者

community /kəˈmjuːnəti/ *n.* 社会；社区；共同体：They have set up a new scientific ~ nearby. 他们在附近建起了一个新的科学园区。

compact[1] /kəmˈpækt/ Ⅰ*adj.* 紧密的；结实的：This is a ~ organization. 这是一个很严密的组织。Ⅱ*v.*（使）紧密；（使）简洁：a ~ed disk 压缩光盘/ He is ~ing the report for tomorrow. 他正在把明天的报告修改得更简洁。派 compactly *adv.*

compact[2] /ˈkɒmpækt/ *n.* [C]协定；合同；契约：a ~ among the great nations of the world 世界大国之间订立的协约/ They made (entered) into a ~ never to speak about that matter again. 他们达成协议，绝不再提那件事。

companion /kəmˈpænɪən/ *n.* [C]同事；朋友；伙伴；战友：Bad ~s on the Net led him astray. 在网上交的坏朋友使他误入歧途。/ The book is a ~ to the present volume. 那本书与现在的这一卷是姐妹篇。

companionship /kəmˈpænjənˌʃɪp/ *n.* [U]交情，有情，友谊；交往：He missed the ~ he'd enjoyed in the navy. 他非常想念他在海军服役时结下的友情。

company /ˈkʌmpəni/ *n.* ❶[C]公司：There are advantages in working for a large ~. 在大公司工作有很多好处。❷[U]陪同；同行：He keeps good (bad) ~. 他和好人（坏人）来往。/ I enjoyed his ~. 有他为伴，我觉得很愉快。/ **bear (keep) sb.** ~陪伴；陪同：I want somebody to bear me ~. 我想找一个人做伴。**in ~ with sb.** 与某人一起：He came in ~ with a group of girls. 他与一群女孩同来。

comparable /ˈkɒmpərəbl/ *adj.* ❶可比较的，有可比性的：His poetry isn't bad, but it's hardly ~ with Shakespeare's. 他的诗不错，但与莎士比亚不可同日而语。❷类似的：from approximately ~ social backgrounds 来自大致相仿的社会背景

comparative /kəmˈpærətɪv/ *adj.* 比较的；（语法）比较级的：She studies ~ literature. 她研究比较文学。/ You should use a ~ degree here. 这里你应该用比较级。

compare /kəmˈpeə(r)/ *v.* 比较；对比：

Read the two articles and ~ them. 读读这两篇文章，再将它们比较一下。/ ~ ... **with** ... 把……与……比较：He carefully ~d this book with that one. 他仔细地把这本书与那本书做了比较。/ My English cannot ~ with his. 我的英语不如他。~ ... **to** ... 把……比作……：Life is ~d to a voyage. 人生好比航海。

comparison / kəmˈpærɪsn / *n.* [U]比较；比喻：Please make a ~ between the two plans and choose the better. 请把这两个计划比较一下，选出好的一个。/ **in ~ with** 比较；相比：The advanced and the backward only exist in ~ with each other. 先进与落后只有相比较才存在。

compartment / kəmˈpɑːtmənt / *n.* [C]（列车车厢等的）分隔间：It is the luggage ~ of this train. 这是这趟火车的行李间。

compass / ˈkʌmpəs / *n.* [C]罗盘；指南针

compassion / kəmˈpæʃn / *n.* [U]同情，怜悯：fell great ~ for the starving children 对挨饿的孩子表示深切同情

compassionate / kəmˈpæʃən(ə)t/ *adj.* 有怜悯心的；(表示)同情的：the young policeman's ~ voice 那位年轻警察富于同情的语气 / a ~ letter 表示同情的信 ▒ compassionately *adv.*

compel / kəmˈpel / *v.* (-pelled; -pelling) 强迫；迫使：The boss ~led the workers to work 12 hours a day. 老板强迫工人们每天工作 12 小时。

compelling / kəmˈpelɪŋ/ *adj.* ❶强制性的：a ~ order 强制性命令 ❷激发兴趣的；极其吸引人的：a ~ adventure story 趣味盎然的探险故事 ❸令人信服的，有说服力的：provide a ~ justification in court 提供令人信服的呈堂证供 ▒ compellingly *adv.*

compendium / kəmˈpendɪəm/ *n.* [C]（*pl.* -diums或-dia /-dɪə/）梗概，概论；摘要，纲要；精编：comprise a veritable ~ of music of the day 编一本有关时下音乐的地道的精编集 / The city was the most complete ~ of the world. 这个城市是整个世界的完备浓缩。

compensate / ˈkɒmpenseɪt / *v.* 补偿；赔偿：The boss should ~ workers for their injuries during work. 工作期间工人受伤，老板应给予赔偿。

compensation / ˌkɒmpenˈseɪʃn / *n.* [U]补偿，赔偿；赔偿金，补偿金：He had to live on unemployment ~ then. 那时候他不得不靠失业补助金过日子。

compete / kəmˈpiːt / *vi.* 竞争；比赛：Whom are you competing against for the championship? 你将和谁争夺冠军？/ He is going to ~ against (with) his old rival in the second round. 第二回合时他将与老对手竞争。

competence / ˈkɒmpɪtəns / *n.* [U]能力；胜任，称职：The insane woman lacked the ~ to manage her own affairs. 那个神志不清的女人没有自理能力。/Dose she have the necessary ~ for the position? 她能胜任这项工作吗？

competent / ˈkɒmpɪtənt / *adj.* ❶有能力的；胜任的，称职的；合格的：be fully ~ at one's work 完全胜任工作/A doctor should be ~ to treat many diseases. 医生应有能力治疗多种疾病。❷有效的；足够的；恰当的：a ~ answer 有力的回答/a ~ salary 丰厚的薪金

competition / ˌkɒmpəˈtɪʃn / *n.* ❶[U]竞争；角逐：They were in ~ with each other for the prize. 他们为得奖而互相竞争。❷[C]比赛；竞赛：They held an open ~ last Friday. 上周五他们举行了

一场公开赛。

competitive /kəmˈpetɪtɪv/ *adj.* ❶竞争性的；靠竞争（或比赛）的：highly ~ spirit 昂扬的竞争斗志 / ~ sports 竞技体育 / a ~ examination 选拔考试 ❷好竞争的：a ~ personality 好与人一争高下的个性 ❸（价格等）有竞争力的：lose ~ edge 失去竞争优势 / Our price is ~ enough to induce business. 我们的价格有吸引业务的足够竞争力。派 competitively *adv.* ；competitiveness *n.*

competitor /kəmˈpetɪtə(r)/ *n.* [C]比赛者；竞争者；对手：Class Three is our strong ~ in the game. 三班是我们这次比赛的强大竞争对手。

compile /kəmˈpaɪl/ *vt.* 编辑；汇编：He is planning to ~ a new Chinese -English dictionary. 他正计划编写一本新的汉英词典。派 compiler *n.*

complain /kəmˈpleɪn/ *v.* 抱怨；诉苦；发牢骚；叫屈：They ~ed that there was not enough hot water. 他们抱怨热水不够。/ She is always ~ing about the weather. 她老是抱怨天气不好。

complaint /kəmˈpleɪnt/ *n.* 抱怨；不满：The manager seldom gets letters of ~ from the customers. 经理很少收到顾客的投诉信。/**make (lay, bring) a ~ against sb. of (about) sth.** 就某事对某人进行控告、控诉：A ~ was brought against him about the matter. 他因此事被控告了。

complement /ˈkɒmplɪmənt/ Ⅰ *n.* [C] ❶补充，补充物；互补物；配对物：A fine wine is a ~ to a good meal. 佳肴须得美酒配。/The lexicon is not a ~ of syntax. 词汇不是句法的补充。❷足数，全数；足额；全套：the aircraft's full ~ of crew 飞机的全体机组人员 ❸补（足）语 Ⅱ *vt.* 补足；补充；使完整：The two books ~ each other nicely. 这两本书互为补充，相得益彰。/The plot is ~ by a series of flashbacks. 这段情节用一系列的闪回作为补充。

complete /kəmˈpliːt/ Ⅰ *adj.* 完全的；全部的；彻底的：The year is now ~. 今年到此结束。/ This is the *Complete Works of Shakespeare*. 这是《莎士比亚全集》。Ⅱ *v.* 结束；完成：Complete a sentence with the correct word. 用正确的词完成句子。派 completely *adv.*

complex /ˈkɒmpleks/ Ⅰ *adj.* 合成的；复杂的；综合的：This is a ~ sentence. 这是一个复合句。/ I didn't understand the ~ argument. 我没有弄懂那个复杂的论点。Ⅱ *n.* [C]复合物；综合体

complexity /kəmˈpleksɪti/ *n.* ❶[U]复杂（性），错综（性）：the ~ of the human mind 人脑的复杂性 ❷[C]错综复杂的事物：the complexities of modern life 现代生活的复杂情况

complicated /ˈkɒmplɪkeɪtɪd/ *adj.* 复杂的；难懂的；错综的：This problem is too ~ to explain to a child. 这问题太复杂，难以向一个孩子讲清楚。

compliment /ˈkɒmplɪmənt/ Ⅰ *n.* [C] ❶称赞，恭维（话）；敬意：pay a ~ to sb. on sth. 为某事赞美（恭维）某人/ We did him the ~ of visiting him. 我们拜访他以示敬意。❷（*pl.*）问候，祝贺：exchange ~s互相问候（祝贺）/ Give my ~s to your parents. 代我向双亲问候。Ⅱ *v.* 夸奖，恭维；祝贺：~sb. on sth. 夸奖某人某事

complimentary /ˌkɒmplɪˈmentəri/ *adj.* ❶赞美的；恭维的；祝贺的；表示敬意的：a ~ remark 溢美之词 / a ~ address 贺词 / The guests were very ~ about the meal. 客人们对这顿饭赞不绝口。❷(通常作定语)赠送的:~ tickets 赠券 / The author received two ~ copies of his new book. 作者收到两册他刚出版的赠书。派 complimentarily *adv.* ;complimentariness *n.*

comply /kəm'plaɪ/ *vi.* 遵从,服从;顺从;听从:~ with the doctor's order/ With some reluctance he complied. 他有些不情愿地服从了。

component /kəm'pəunənt/ Ⅰ *n.* [C]组成部分;部件;元件:The engineer checked the ~s of the machine carefully. 工程师对机器的部件进行了仔细检查。Ⅱ *adj.* 组成的;成分的:He stopped his car by a shop and bought some ~ parts. 他把车停在一家商店旁,买了一些零部件。

compose /kəm'pəuz/ *v.* ❶构思;写作;构成;作曲:The music was ~d by Beethoven. 这首乐曲是贝多芬创作的。❷组成,构成:Water is ~d of hydrogen and oxygen. 水由氢和氧组成。

composed /kəm'pəuzd/ *adj.* 镇静的;沉着的:the doctor's ~ nature 医生的稳健性情/ a small, beautiful and ~ blonde 一位娇小、美丽又文静的金发女郎

composer /kəm'pəuzə(r)/ *n.* [C]作曲家;创作者;设计者:She became a popular ~ soon. 她很快成为一名受欢迎的作曲家。

composite /'kɒmpəzɪt, kəm'pɒzɪt/ Ⅰ *adj.* 混合的;合成的,集成的;拼凑的;复合的:make a ~ picture 制作合成照片 / a ~ drawing 拼图/ ~ material 复合材料 Ⅱ *n.* [C]合成物(如合成照片等):English is a ~ of many languages. 英语是多种语言的混合体。/ His character was a ~ of instinct and education. 他的性格是先天禀赋加上后天教育形成的。派 compositely *adv.*

composition /ˌkɒmpə'zɪʃn/ *n.* ❶组成;构成;成分:He is analysing the ~ of the soil. 他正在分析土壤成分。❷作文,文章;乐曲:We learn ~ at school. 我们在学校学习写作。/ She wrote a very good ~. 她写了一篇好作文。

compound Ⅰ/kɒm'paund/ *v.* 混合组成:The word is ~ed of a preposition and a verb. 这个词是由一个介词和一个动词合成的。Ⅱ/'kɒmpaund/ *adj.* 混合的:This is a ~ word. 这是一个复合词。

comprehend /ˌkɒmprɪ'hend/ *vt.* 理解,明白;领会,领悟:fully ~ the significance of the ambassador's remark 完全领会大使的讲话精神 / ~ the subtleties of a poem 领悟诗的微妙之处 / They did not ~ how hard he had struggled. 他们并不理解他付出过多么艰苦的努力。派 comprehensible *adj.*

comprehension /ˌkɒmprɪ'henʃn/ *n.* 理解;理解力:The teacher had no ~ of the boy's problem at home. 老师不了解这男孩在家里出现的问题。/ Reading ~ is very important in learning English. 阅读理解在学习英语中是很重要的。/ **above (beyond, past)** ~ 不可理解,难以理解:This is quite above (beyond, past) my ~. 这是我完全不能理解的。

comprehensive /ˌkɒmprɪ'hensɪv/ *adj.* 综合的;包含内容多的:a ~ development 综合发展/ a ~ planning 全面规划/a ~ university 综合大学/ At the end of the term he took a ~ view of his study. 学期末他对自己的学习进行了全面的检查。

compress /kəm'pres/ *vt.* ❶紧压,挤压:The fuel mixture is ~ed in the chamber by the piston. 活塞将混合燃料挤压在燃烧室。❷压缩：~ a story into a few short sentences 把故事浓缩成几个简单的句子

C

comprise / kəmˈpraɪz / *vt*. ❶包含，包括；由……构成，由……组成：The advisory board ~s six members. 咨询委员会由 6 名成员组成。/Cave art ~ed an astonishing variety and mastery of techniques. 洞穴艺术中表现出技巧的多样性及其运用的娴熟让人叹为观止。❷构成，组成：Seminars and lectures ~ed the day's activities. 专题讨论和讲座是这一天的全部活动内容。/The essays ~ed his total work. 这几篇文章就是他的全部著作。

compromise / ˈkɒmprəmaɪz / *vi*. 妥协；让步：We have to ~ with him on this point. 我们只好就这一点与他妥协。

compulsive / kəmˈpʌlsɪv/ *adj*. ❶(被)强制的；(被)强迫的；有强迫力(似)的：a ~ need to succeed 外因促使的成功的必要性 / ~ spending 强制消费 ❷有强烈诱惑力的；抵挡不住的：I found the movie ~ viewing . 我觉得这部电影值得一看再看。派 compulsively *adv*.

compulsory / kəmˈpʌlsəri / *adj*. 强制性的；义务的；(学科)必修的：~ education 义务教育/ We have five ~ subjects this term. 本学期我们上五门必修课。

compute / kəmˈpjuːt / *v*. 计算；估算：Their losses in the accident are ~d $500,000. 他们在这次意外事故中的损失估计达 50 万美元。

computer / kəmˈpjuːtə(r) / *n*. [C]计算机：a personal ~ (PC) 个人电脑/ a multi-media ~ 多媒体计算机/ The ~ communication is widely used now. 现在计算机通信得以广泛运用。派 computerize *vt*.

comrade / ˈkɒmreɪd / *n*. [C]同志；同事：He said he should stay with his ~ in time of danger. 他说危险时刻他应和自己的同志在一起。

concave / ˈkɒnˌkeɪv / Ⅰ *n*. 凹面；凹面体 Ⅱ *adj*. 凹的；凹面的：a ~ mirror 凹面镜

conceal / kənˈsiːl / *vt*. 隐藏；隐瞒：She ~ed her picture in an old dictionary. 她把照片藏在一本旧字典里。/~ **sth. from sb.** 向某人隐瞒某事：I didn't ~ anything from him. 我对他没隐瞒什么。

concede / kənˈsiːd / *vt*. ❶承认；宣布接受……为事实：~ defeat 承认失败/I'm willing to ~ that he's a good runner. 我愿意承认他是一名优秀的赛跑运动员。❷授予；给予；让与；放弃：The defeated nation ~d some of their territory to the enemy. 战败国把一部分领土割让给了敌国。派 conceded *adj*.

conceit / kənˈsiːt / *n*. [U]自负；自大；骄傲自满：He is full of ~. 他极其自负。/ Everybody should guard against ~. 每个人都应该防止骄傲自满。

conceive / kənˈsiːv / *v*. 想出；构思 /~ **of** 想象；设想，构想出：It is impossible to ~ of anything better than this. 想象不出比这更好的东西了。

concentrate / ˈkɒnsntreɪt / *v*. 集中；聚集：You'll solve the problem if you ~ on it. 要是全神贯注，你会解决这个问题的。

concentrated / ˈkɒnsnˌtreɪtɪd/ *adj*. ❶浓缩的；压缩的：~ orange juice 浓缩橙汁 / ~ feed 压缩饲料 ❷集中的；聚集的；集结的：a heavily ~ attack 炮火密集的进攻 ❸强烈的：a tone of ~ resolution 斩钉截铁的语气

concentration / ˌkɒnsənˈtreɪʃən/ *n.* ❶集中;汇集,聚集:a ~ of resources in the south of the country 国家南部地区资源的集中 / the massive ~ of forces 军队的大量集结 ❷[U](集中的)注意力;专心,专注;倾力:give the problem one's full ~ 专心致志地思考这个问题 / All demand great ~ from reader. 所有这一切都需要读者冥神凝想。

concentric / kənˈsentrɪk / *adj.* 同中心(或圆心)的;共轴的:a ~ circle 同心圆/ ~ annual rings 同心年轮 派 concentrically *adv.* ;concentricity *n.*

concept / ˈkɒnsept / *n.* [C]概念;观念;思想:You are late again. Do you have any ~ of what time it is? 又迟到了,你究竟有没有时间概念?

conception / kənˈsepʃən/ *n.* ❶[U]构想,设想;思想(或观念、概念)的形成:great powers of ~ 巨大的构想力 / The ~ of the book took five minutes, but writing it took a year. 这本书的构思花了五分钟,但写作却耗费了一年时间。❷[C]思想;观念;想法;概念:have a low ~ of sb. 对某人有着不屑的看法 / have no ~ of 完全不懂 派 conceptional, conceptive *adj.*

concern / kənˈsɜːn / *vt.* ❶与……有关;涉及:The event ~ed us greatly. 这事与我们关系极大。/~ **oneself with** 关心:Don't ~ yourself with other people's affairs. 少管别人的闲事。❷担心;忧虑:I'm ~ed at the condition of my sick friend. 我为朋友的病情担忧。派 concerned *adj.*

concerning / kənˈsɜːnɪŋ / *prep.* 关于:The officials are discussing problem ~ agriculture. 官员们正在讨论有关农业的问题。

concert / ˈkɒnsət / *n.* [C] 音乐会;演奏会:go to a ~去听音乐会/ attend a ~ 出席音乐会

concerto / kənˈtʃɜːtəʊ / *n.* [C] (*pl.* concerti 或 concertos)协奏曲:a piano ~ 钢琴协奏曲

concession / kənˈseʃn / *n.* 让步,退让;承认,认可(物);让予(物):pledge never to make ~s to terrorists 发誓绝不向恐怖主义者让步/make no ~ to caution 不听从告诫

concise / kənˈsaɪz / *adj.* 简洁明了的;扼要的:a ~ style 简洁的文体/a ~ panorama of the city 城市概貌

conclude / kənˈkluːd / *v.* ❶结束:The story ~d tragically. 这故事结局悲惨。❷下结论:The jury ~d from the evidence that the accused man was not guilty. 陪审团依据证据做出结论,认定被告无罪。❸缔结:~ a treaty (an agreement) with... 与……订立条约(协议)

conclusion / kənˈkluːʒn / *n.* [C]结尾;结局;结论:Please tell me the ~ of the movie. 请把电影的结局告诉我。/**come to a** ~ 得出结论:You should not come to ~s at once. 你不应立即下结论。

concord / ˈkɒŋkɔːd/ *n.* [U] ❶和睦;友好(关系):~ between friends 朋友之间的和睦 / These neighbouring states have lived in ~ for centuries. 这些邻国已和睦相处几个世纪了。❷(人称、性、数、格的)一致(关系):a subject-verb ~ rule 一条主语和动词一致关系的规则

concrete / ˈkɒŋkriːt / Ⅰ*adj.* 具体的;有形的;实在的 :You should make ~ analysis of ~ problems. 你应当具体问题具体分析。Ⅱ*n.* [U]混凝土

concur / kənˈkɜː(r) / *vi.* (-curred;-curring) ❶(碰巧)同时发生,His graduation day ~red with his birthday. 毕业典礼日适逢他的生日。❷ 同意;保持一致;赞同:The judges all ~red in giving me the prize. 裁判一致同意给我发奖。/We ~ with you in this respect. 在这方面,我们同意你们的意见。派 concurrence *n.*

condemn /kən'dem/ *vt.* ❶谴责;指责:He was ~ed smoking in public. 他在公共场所吸烟受到谴责。❷判……刑;宣告……有罪:The manager was ~ed for bribery and sent in prison. 他受贿被判刑入狱。

condense /kən'dens/ *vt.* ❶压缩;浓缩;使密集;使凝结:~ a gas into a liquid 把气体浓缩成液体/be ~ed into thick soup 熬成浓汤 ❷使紧凑;简缩;使简洁:a reworded, ~ed articles 重新措辞并简缩的文章/~ a paper into a few paragraphs 把一篇论文减缩成几个段落

condition /kən'dɪʃn/ *n.* [C]情况;状况;条件:The ~ is rapidly changing. 情况正在急速变化。/ That is China's actual ~. 这就是中国国情。/**on ~ that** 如果……;在……条件下:You may use my camera on ~ that you return it next saturday. 你可以用我的相机,条件是下周六必须归还。

conditioner /kən'dɪʃənə(r)/ *n.* 调节者;调节物;调节器;调节剂:dough ~ 酵母/ a soil ~ 土壤改良剂 / Apply ~ after shampooing. 洗完发后上护发素。

condole /kən'dəʊl/ *vi.* 吊唁;慰问,表示同情(与 with 连用):~ with sb. over the death of his (her) grandfather 向某人吊唁其祖父的逝世 / The widow's friends ~d with her at the funeral. 在葬礼上遗孀的朋友们都向她表示慰问。

condolence /kən'dəʊləns/ *n.* [U]吊唁,慰唁;慰问:a letter of ~吊唁信/I sent her an expression of ~ over the loss of her father. 我对她父亲的去世发了慰唁。

conduct Ⅰ/'kɒndʌkt/ *n.* [U]品行;行为:wrong ~ 错误行为/ dishonourable ~ 可耻行为/ violent ~ 暴行/ I'm glad to see your ~ at school has improved. 我很高兴看到你在学校的表现有所改进。Ⅱ/kən'dʌkt/ *v.* ❶引导;带领;指挥;指导:A girl ~ed him into the hall. 一位姑娘把他引入大厅。/ Though she is young, she is able to ~ an orchestra well. 尽管她很年轻,但她能把一支管弦乐队指挥得很好。❷实施;处理;经营:His father ~ed his company successfully. 他父亲经营公司很成功。❸传导;传(热、电):Most metals ~electricity well. 大多数金属都导电良好。

conductor /kən'dʌktə(r)/ *n.* [C] ❶导体;导线:A tall building needs a lightning ~. 高楼需要安装避雷针。❷售票员;列车员:a bus ~ 公共汽车售票员/ a train ~ 列车员 ❸(乐队、合唱队的)指挥

cone /kəʊn/ *n.* [C]圆锥;锥体

confederation /kənˌfedə'reɪʃn/ *n.* [C]联盟,同盟;政治联合体

conference /'kɒnfərəns/ *n.* [C]会议;讨论会:A news (press) ~ will be held next Monday. 下周一召开新闻发布会(记者招待会)。

confess /kən'fes/ *v.* 招认,供认;自白,坦白:At last he had to ~ himself to be guilty. 最终他不得不承认自己有罪。派 confession *n.*

confidence /'kɒnfɪdəns/ *n.* [U]信任;信

心：He had no ~ in himself. 他失去了信心。/ I have full ~ that I shall pass the exam. 我完全有把握通过这次考试。

confident /ˈkɒnfɪdənt/ *adj.* 确信的；有信心的：The little girl gave her mother a ~ smile. 那小女孩自信地对她母亲微笑。/ We are ~ of winning the game. 我们确信我们会赢得那场比赛。

confidential /ˌkɒnfɪˈdenʃəl/ *adj.* ❶秘密的；机密的：a ~ document 机密文件/ a strictly ~ letter 绝密信件 ❷负责秘密工作的，机要的：~ secretary 机要秘书 ❸信任的；知心的，亲密的，私密的：speak in low，~ tones 用低声的、十分信任的口吻说话 /~ remarks 悄悄话 派 confidentiality *n.* ；confidentially *adv.*

configuration /kənˌfɪgjʊˈreɪʃn/ *n.* [C] ❶结构，架构；构造：a ~ of small social units 小型社会单位的构成体 ❷外形，构形；轮廓：~ of mountains 群山的轮廓

confine /kənˈfaɪn/ *vt.* ❶限制，使局限：~ one's reading to biography 只读传记作品/Please ~ your remarks to the subject under discussion. 请把发言局限在讨论的问题上。❷控制，使不流传(或扩散)；使不外出，禁闭：be ~d to one's bed with illness 因病卧床/Efforts are made to ~ the epidemic to the farm where it has broken out. 做出努力将传染病控制在它所爆发的那个农场。

confinement /kənˈfaɪnmənt/ *n.* [U] ❶限制；约束；局限：My doctor recommended ~ to a bland diet. 医生建议我只吃些清淡食物。❷(被)关押，(被)监禁；(被)禁闭：pigs grown in ~ 圈养的猪 / They put him into solitary ~. 他们把他单独监禁。

confirm /kənˈfɜːm/ *vt.* 证实；确认；批准：You'd better phone the chairman to ~ the time and place of the meeting. 你最好给主席打个电话确认一下开会的时间和地点。派 confirmation *n.*

conflict Ⅰ/ˈkɒnflɪkt/ *n.* 斗争；争论；抵触；冲突 Ⅱ/kənˈflɪkt/ *vi.* 争执；相冲突；矛盾：Their stories ~ed with each other. 他们的说辞相互矛盾。

conform /kənˈfɔːm/ *vi.* ❶遵照；服从：~ to directions 遵照指示/Most of us tend to conceal our real selves by ~ing to the norm. 我们中的大部分人倾向于用遵循成规的方式来掩盖真实的自我。❷一致；相符；适合；适应：He ~s with my idea of a teacher. 他与我心目中的老师一样的。/Your design doesn't ~ with the regulations. 你们的设计不符合规定。

conformity /kənˈfɔːmɪti/ *n.* ❶[U]遵守；顺从，服从：in ~ to (with) the popular wish 顺应民意 ❷相似，相近：a face with a nice ~ of feature 五官端正的脸 / The stock market showed bearish trend，in ~ with the deteriorating economy. 股市呈现出熊市态势，与衰落的经济相一致。

confront /kənˈfrʌnt/ *vt.* ❶面对，正视；与……对峙：The two armies ~ed each other along the border. 两军在边界上相互对峙。/I don't understand your refusal to ~ reality. 我不明白你为什么不肯正视现实。❷面临；遭遇：The President ~s attacks from both reformers and conservatives. 总统面临来自改革派和保守派的双重抨击。

confrontation /ˌkɒnfrənˈteɪʃən/ *n.* 对抗，冲突：The use of ~ won't lead to peace. 对抗不能带来和平。

confucian /kənˈfjuːʃən/ Ⅰ*adj.* 孔子的；儒家的：The overseas students are visiting the ~temple. 留学生们正在参观孔庙。Ⅱ*n.* [C]孔子的门徒；儒家

C

confuse /kən'fjuːz/ *v.* 使混乱;使糊涂:He is always confusing sugar with salt. 他老是糖盐不分。/ We are always confusing the twin brothers. 我们总是辨认不清这对双胞胎兄弟谁是谁。/**be (become, get) ~d about (at, with) sth.** 混淆;搞糊涂:He was ~d at her sudden appearance. 她突然出现使他手足无措。

confusion /kən'fjuːʒn/ *n.* [U]混乱;慌乱:Everything was in ~. 一切都乱了套。

congratulate /kən'grætʃʊleɪt/ *vt.* 祝贺;庆贺:His colleagues came up to ~him. 他的同事们都过来向他表示祝贺。/ **~ sb. on (upon) sth.** 向某人祝贺某事:We ~d him on having passed the examination. 我们祝贺他通过了考试。

congratulation /kənˌgrætʃʊ'leɪʃn/ *n.* 祝贺;庆贺:Please accept my ~s. 请接受我的祝贺。

congregate /'kɒŋgrɪˌgeɪt/ *vi.* 聚集,集合;云集:The crowds ~d in the town square. 人群聚集在镇上的广场上。

congress /'kɒŋgres/ *n.* [C]代表大会;国会:an annual ~ 年会/ the National People's Congress 全国人民代表大会/ the United States Congress 美国国会

conjunction /kən'dʒʌŋkʃn/ *n.* ❶[U]结合;联合;联系 ❷[C]连接词

connect /kə'nekt/ *v.* 连接;联系:The two towns are ~ed by a railway. 两市由铁路相连。/ It is closely ~ed with this matter. 它与此事密切相关。派 connected *adj.*

connection /kə'nekʃn/ *n.* 连接;联系:Is there any ~ between the two cases? 这两件案子之间有联系吗?

connective /kə'nektɪv/ Ⅰ *adj.* 联结的,连接的:~ remarks between chapters 章节之间的过渡语 Ⅱ *n.* [C] ❶联结物,结合物 ❷连接词,关联词

connotation /ˌkɒnəʊ'teɪʃn/ *n.* [C]内涵义,隐含义;引申义:A possible ~ of "home" is a place of warmth, comfort and affection. "家"的一个可能的含义是温暖、舒适并且充满爱的地方。

conquer /'kɒŋkə(r)/ *v.* 征服;战胜;克服:We have never been ~ed by a foreign foe. 我们从未被外敌征服过。派 conqueror *n.*

conquest /'kɒŋkwest/ *n.* [U]征服;克服;获得:They made a ~ of the land by armed force. 他们以武装夺得了那块土地。

conscience /'kɒnʃəns/ *n.* 道德心;良心:He had a guilty ~. 他感到内疚。/ A guilty ~ is a thousand witnesses. 做贼心虚。

conscious /'kɒnʃəs/ *adj.* 有意识的;神志清醒的;自觉的:Is the patient ~ yet? 病人清醒了吗? / He was ~ that he had made a foolish mistake. 他意识到自己犯了一个愚蠢的错误。/ **be ~ of** 清楚知道:I'm quite ~ of my responsibility as a teacher. 我十分清楚作为一个教师的责任。

consciousness /'kɒnʃəsnəs/ *n.* [U]知觉;觉悟;意识:Man's social being determines his ~. 存在决定意识。/**lose (recover) one's ~** 失去(恢复)知觉:Jim recovered his ~ three hours later. 三个小时后吉米恢复了知觉。

consensus /kən'sensəs/ *n.* [C](意见等的)一致:by the ~s of expert opinion 根据专家一致意见

consent /kən'sent/ *vi.* 同意;允许:Her parents wouldn't ~ to her staying out at night. 她的父母不允许她在外过夜。

consequence /ˈkɒnsɪkwəns/ *n.* ❶[C]后果;结果:The boss had to fire him in ~ of his laziness. 由于他的懒惰,老板不得不把他解雇。❷[U]重要;重要性:The loss of his books is a matter of great ~ to a student. 书的遗失对学生来说是件大事。

consequently /ˈkɒnsɪkwəntli/ *adv.* 因此;必然地:She got up at nine and ~ she was late. 她九点钟才起床,因此迟到了。

conservation /ˌkɒnsəˈveɪʃn/ *n.* [U](尤指对自然资源等的)保护:measures for the ~ of mineral resources 矿产资源保护措施/~ area 自然(或历史)保护区

conservative /kənˈsɜːvətɪv/ *adj.* ❶保守的;保守主义的;守旧的:Are old people always more ~ than the young? 老年人总是比年轻人更保守吗? ❷保守的人;保守主义

conserve /kənˈsɜːv/ *vt.* 保存,保藏;保护:~ the energy for the last lap 为最后一圈保持体力/~ electricity 节电/We must ~ our forests and woodlands for future generations. 我们要为了孙后代保护好我们的森林和林地。

consider /kənˈsɪdə(r)/ *vt.* 思考,考虑;认为,把……看作:He always ~ed carefully before he acted. 他总是三思而后行。/~ **doing sth.** 考虑做某事:We are ~ing doing it. 我们正考虑做此事。~ **as ...** 把……当作(看作)……:We ~ed him as a fool. 我们认为他是一个傻瓜。

considerable /kənˈsɪdərəbl/ *adj.* 相当大的;相当或多的;重要的:The general manager has ~ income every year. 那位总经理每年的收入可观。/ The mayor is a ~ person in the city. 市长是一个城市中的重要人物。

considerate /kənˈsɪdərət/ *adj.* 体贴的;考虑周到的:She is ~ of (to, toward) old people. 她对老人很体贴。

considering /kənˈsɪdərɪŋ/ Ⅰ *prep.* 考虑到,鉴于:Considering the strength of the opposition, we did very well to score the goals. 考虑到对手的实力,我们能进这几个球已经很不错了。Ⅱ *conj.* 考虑到,鉴于:Considering that he received no help, his results are very good. 考虑到他没有任何帮助,结果可以说非常好。Ⅲ *adv.* (口语)考虑到所有情况;从各方面考虑起来:He paints very well, ~. 大体说来,他画得不错。

consign /kənˈsaɪn/ *vt.* ❶将……交付给,把……委托给(与 to 连用):The parents ~ed the child to its grandmother's care while they were away. 父母不在时把孩子托给祖母照料。❷发(货);托运;运送;寄售;寄存:We will ~ the goods to him by express. 我们将用快递把货发给他。/ The goods are to be ~ed to the order of Mr. Robert. 这批货将按罗伯特先生的订单交运。❸打发;消除:~ unpleasant thoughts to oblivion 将不愉快的想法彻底消除 派 consignable *adj.*

consist /kənˈsɪst/ *v.* ❶由……组成(与 of 连用):The paper ~s of eight pages. 该论文共有八页。❷在于;依赖于(与 in 连用):Happiness ~s in contentment. 知足常乐。❸与……一致;符合(与 with 连用):His actions do not ~ with his words. 他言行不一。

consistency /kənˈsɪstənsi/ *n.* ❶浓度,稠度:yogurts of varying ~不同稠度的酸乳 ❷[U]一致;符合;协调:~ and continuity in government policy 政府政策的一致性和连贯性/Your behaviour lacks ~—you say one thing and to another! 你言行不一,说一套,做一套。

consistent /kən'sɪstənt/ *adj.* ❶一贯的，始终如一的；坚持的：a ~ policy 一贯方针/The last five years have seen a ~ improvement in the country's economy. 近五年来，该国经济持续增长。❷和谐的；一致的；符合的，可共存的：a report that is not ~ with the facts 与事实不符的报告/Driving very fast on a rainy night is not ~ with safety. 雨夜高速开车不符合安全要求。/His words and actions are ~. 他言行一致。

console /kən'səʊl/ *vt.* 安慰，慰问：Only his children could ~ him when his wife died. 妻子死后，只有孩子们能够给他以安慰。派 consolation *n.*

consolidate /kən'sɒlɪˌdeɪt/ *vt.* 巩固，加强：The company has ~d its hold on the market. 公司巩固了自己对市场的控制。/The party ~d itself in a remote rural area. 该党在边远地区加强了自己的力量。派 consolidation *n.*

consonant /'kɒnsənənt/ *n.* [C]辅音；辅音字母(略作 cons)：a ~ cluster 辅音连缀

conspiracy /kən'spɪrəsi/ *n.* 阴谋；密谋

conspire /kən'spaɪə(r)/ *vi.* (共同)密谋，搞阴谋：~ against sb. 密谋反对某人/The two men ~d to steal the jewels. 那两个人密谋偷珠宝。

constant /'kɒnstənt/ *adj.* 不变的；永恒的；不断的；忠实的：He is ~ to the communist ideals. 他忠于共产主义理想。/ Three days of ~ rain made her depressed. 连续三天的阴雨使她很沮丧。派 constantly *adv.*

constellation /ˌkɒnstə'leɪʃən/ *n.* [C] ❶星座：The Big Dipper is the easiest ~ to locate. 北斗七星是最容易辨认的星座。❷星集，云集，群集；荟萃：a ~ of scholars at a convention 会上学者如云 / I was reluctant to do this, for a whole ~ of reasons. 由于诸多原因，我不愿做这事。

constitute /'kɒnstɪtjuːt/ *vt.* 组成；构成：Seven days ~ a week. 七天构成一个星期。/ **be ~d of** 由……组成：A baseball team is ~d of nine players. 棒球队由 9 名球员组成。

constitution /ˌkɒnstɪ'tjuːʃn/ *n.* ❶组成；构造：The scientist thinks that we should know more about the ~ of life. 科学家认为我们应当更多地了解生命的构造。❷[C]体格，体质：He is a good student with a strong ~. 他是一个体格强壮的好学生。❸[C]宪法；章程；法规：Presidential elections are held every four years according to the American ~. 按照美国宪法，总统每四年选举一次。

constrain /kən'streɪn/ *vt.* ❶强迫，迫使：be ~ed to admit the offense 被迫承认过错/I felt ~ed to do what he told me. 我照他的话去做是身不由己。❷关押，禁闭；限制；束缚：be ~ed in chains 身陷囹圄/Our research has been ~ed by lack of cash. 我们的研究苦于经费不足。

construct /kən'strʌkt/ *v.* 建造；构思；创立：The house was ~ed out of wood. 这房子是用木头建造的。/ The whole story is skilfully ~ed. 整个故事构思巧妙。派 constructor *n.*

construction /kən'strʌkʃn/ *n.* 建设，修建；建筑物：socialist ~ 社会主义建设/ a ~ site 建设工地/ capital ~ 基本建设/ The new railway is under construction. 新铁路正在修建中。

constructive /kən'strʌktɪv/ *adj.* 建设性的；有积极作用的：a very ~ attitude

非常积极的态度/During the experiment the teacher gave some ~ suggestions that prevented accidents. 试验中，老师提出了一些建议，防止了事故发生。

consul /ˈkɒnsl/ *n.* [C]领事：a ~ general 总领事

consulate /ˈkɒnsjələt/ *n.* [C]领事馆；领事职位

consult /kənˈsʌlt/ *v.* ❶请教；咨询；商量；协商：I ~ed my teacher on how to write English composition well. 我请教老师如何写好英语作文。/ They are ~ing about the way to solve the problem. 他们正商量解决问题的办法。❷查阅；查看：You can ~ the telephone book for her new address. 你可以查阅电话簿找她的新住址。派 consultation *n.*

consultant /kənˈsʌltənt/ *n.* [C]顾问；提供咨询的专家：You may go and ask your legal ~ on this problem. 就这个问题你可以去咨询你的法律顾问。/ Some experts set up a firm of ~s in the centre of the city. 几位专家在市中心成立了一家咨询公司。

consume /kənˈsjuːm/ *vt.* 消费；消耗；花费；耗尽：He ~d much time and energy in writing his thesis. 他花费了很多时间和精力写论文。/ His new refrigerator ~s a lot of electricity. 他的新冰箱很耗电。

consumer /kənˈsjuːmə(r)/ *n.* [C]消费者；用户：a ~ council 消费者委员会/ ~ goods 消费品 / A government should try hard to protect the legal rights of ~s. 政府应尽力保护消费者的合法权利。

consumption /kənˈsʌmpʃn/ *n.* [U]消耗；消费(量)：high-level ~ 高消费/~ ahead of time 超前消费/ We are glad to see that the ~ of wine is decreasing year by year. 我们很高兴看到酒的消费量正逐年减少。

contact /ˈkɒntækt/ Ⅰ *n.* 接触；联系；交往：Talking with young people, you can come into ~ with many new ideas. 与年轻人交谈，你能接触到许多新思想。/ I haven't been in ~ with my brother for a long time. 我好长时间没有和我哥哥保持联系了。Ⅱ *v.* 与……联系，与……接触：We ~ each other by telephone. 我们常通过电话相互联系。

contain /kənˈteɪn/ *v.* 容纳；包含：The suitcase ~ed nothing but dirty clothes. 箱子里除了脏衣服外，什么都没有。派 container *n.*

contemporary /kənˈtempərəri/ Ⅰ *adj.* 当代的；同时代的；同年龄的：He is a ~ outstanding poet. 他是当代著名诗人。Ⅱ *n.* [C]当代人；同龄人：He met with his contemporaries at college yesterday. 昨天他遇到了大学时代的几个同学。

contempt /kənˈtempt/ *n.* [U]鄙视；蔑视：~ for a traitor 对卖国贼的蔑视

contemptuous /kənˈtemptjuəs/ *adj.* 表示轻蔑的，鄙视的；无视的：~ remarks 侮慢的言语 / Contemptuous of danger, he rushed back into the burning building. 他置危险于不顾，又冲入燃烧着的房子。派 contemptuously *adv.* ; contemptuousness *n.*

content[1] /ˈkɒntent/ *n.* ❶容纳的东西；容量：The oxygen ~ of the air here is thin. 这里空气中的含氧量很少。❷内容，要旨；(*pl.*)(书籍)目录：I like both the style and the ~ of this book. 这本书的风格和内容我都喜欢。/ He read the ~s of the textbook first. 他先看了看教科书的目录。

content[2] /kənˈtent/ *adj.* 满意的；满足

的：The old lady is ~ to spend her weekends with her grandson. 老太太很乐意和孙子一起度周末。/~ **with** 满足于：She is ~ with the meal. 她对这顿饭感到满意。

C

contest Ⅰ/ ˈkɒntest / *n.* [C]竞赛；比赛：An English writing ~ was held in our school. 我们学校举行了英语写作比赛。Ⅱ/ kənˈtest / *v.* 争夺；角逐；比赛：She ~ed against the last opponent for the championship. 她和最后一个对手角逐冠军。

contestant / kənˈtestənt/ *n.* [C]竞争者；参赛者：The brothers were ~s in the race. 兄弟俩在赛跑中是对手。/ They may both be future ~s for the Labor leadership. 他们俩都有可能成为未来工党领袖的竞争者。

context / ˈkɒntekst / *n.* 上下文；前后关系：I always guess the meaning of an unknown word from the ~. 我总是从上下文猜一个不认识的词的意义。

continent / ˈkɒntɪnənt / *n.* 大陆；陆地；大洲：the ~ of Asia 亚洲大陆

continental / ˌkɒntɪˈnentl / *adj.* 大陆的；大陆性的：~ climate 大陆性气候

continual / kənˈtɪnjuəl / *adj.* ❶频繁的，反反复复的：~ bus departures 公共汽车频繁的发车 ❷不住的，从不间断的：Life is a ~ struggle. 人生即不断拼搏的过程。

continue / kənˈtɪnjuː / *v.* 持续；继续；依旧：The rain ~d for three days. 雨连续下了三天。/ She still ~s in low spirit. 她依然情绪低落。

continuous / kənˈtɪnjuəs / *adj.* 不断的；连续的：A man's brain needs a ~ supply of blood. 人的大脑需要不断的血液供给。派 continuously *adv.*

contort / kənˈtɔːt / *vt.* 扭曲，把……弄弯；歪曲：~ the truth 歪曲真相/Her face was ~ed with anger. 她的脸气得变了形。

contract Ⅰ/ ˈkɒntrækt / *n.* [C]合同；契约；承包：The clerk had a two-year ~ of employment with the company. 那位职员与公司签了两年的雇用合同。Ⅱ/ kɒnˈtrækt / *v.* 签合同；承包：The two countries ~ed a trade agreement three years ago. 两国在三年前签订了一项贸易协议。/ Do you know which firm did they ~ the project to? 你知道他们把这项工程承包给了哪家公司吗？派 contractor *n.*

contraction / kənˈtrækʃn / *n.* ❶收缩；缩小；缩短：Cold causes the ~ of liquids, gases, and solids. 冷却会使液体、气体和固体收缩。/The ~ of mercury by cold makes it go down in thermometers. 水银遇冷收缩，在温度计中下降。❷[C]缩约形式，缩约词；缩约："Can't" is a ~ of "cannot". "can't"是"cannot"的缩约形式。

contradict / ˌkɒntrəˈdɪkt / *vt.* 与……相矛盾；与……相反：His statements ~ with the facts. 他的话与事实相矛盾。

contradiction / ˌkɒntrəˈdɪkʃn / *n.* 矛盾：She fell into ~s. 她陷入矛盾之中。

contrary / ˈkɒntrəri / Ⅰ*n.* 相反；反面：He expected to pass the exam, but the result was the ~. 他希望能通过考试，但结果正相反。/**on the** ~反之，相反；另一方面：We thought the weather would be bad, but on the ~ we had fine sunshine. 我们原以为天气会很糟，但结果相反，那天阳光灿烂。Ⅱ *adj.* 相反的：His opinion is ~ to mine. 他的看法与我的相反。

contrast Ⅰ/ ˈkɒntrɑːst / *n.* 对立；对照；对

比：There is a great ~ between life of the present and the past. 现在的生活和过去的生活有天壤之别。Ⅱ/ kən'trɑːst / *v.* 对立，与……对照：It's very interesting to ~ birds and fishes. 把鸟和鱼进行对比是很有趣的。

contribute / kən'trɪbjuːt / *v.* ❶捐助；贡献：They ~d food and clothing to the orphans. 他们为孤儿捐献食物和衣服。❷投稿：My classmates often ~ articles to newspapers and magazines. 我的同学们经常向报刊投稿。❸有助于（与 to 连用）：Physical exercise ~s to good health. 身体锻炼有助于健康。

contribution / ˌkɒntrɪ'bjuːʃn / *n.* ❶捐助；贡献：They received a lot of charitable ~s. 他们收到大量慈善捐款。❷投稿：She sent a ~ to a magazine. 她向一家杂志社投稿。

contrive / kən'traɪv / *vt.* ❶发明，策划，设计；想出；造出：~ excuses on the spur of the moment 在一瞬间编出借口来/~ a new kind of engine with fewer moving parts 发明一种新的活动部件较少的发动机/I'm sure you'll ~ some way of dealings with the situation. 我相信你会想出应付这个局面的办法来的。❷设法做到；竟然弄到……的地步（与 to 连用）：I will ~ to be there by ten o'clock. 我设法 10 点钟赶到那儿。/Somehow we ~ to make a mess of it again. 不知怎么搞的，我们竟然又把事情弄得一团糟。

control / kən'trəʊl / Ⅰ *vt.* (-trolled; -trolling)控制；支配；克制：The machine is automatically ~led. 这台机器是自动控制的。Ⅱ *n.* 控制；支配；克制：He has good ~ of his class. 他对他的班级具有良好的控制能力。/**in** ~ 在控制之中；在掌握之中：The next moment he had himself in ~. 他很快就控制住自己。/ She is in ~ of the store. 这家商店由她管理。

controversy / 'kɒntrəˌvɜːsi，kən'trɒvəsi / *n.* 争论；辩论：a violent ~ over a commercial treaty 关于一项商业条约的激烈辩论

convenience / kən'viːnɪəns / *n.* 方便；便利设施：The apartment has all the modern ~s. 这套房子拥有一切现代化设施。/ **at your** ~在你方便的时候：Come to me at your earliest ~. 在你方便时及早来找我。**for ~'s sake** 为方便起见：I live near the school for ~'s sake. 为方便起见，我住在学校附近。

convenient / kən'viːnɪənt / *adj.* 方便的；合适的：Will it be ~ for you to start the work tomorrow? 明天开始工作你行吗？派 conveniently *adv.*

convention / kən'venʃn / *n.* ❶约定俗成；（正式的）习俗：~s of daily life 日常习俗/abandon the formal ~s of the past 摒弃旧日拘泥的习俗 ❷[C]（正式的）会议；（定期的）大会：a teachers' ~教师代表大会/a ~ on human rights for Africa 非洲人权问题大会 ❸常规，惯例；传统：the ~ of showing north at the top of a map 用地图上方表示北方的惯例/It is a matter of ~ that businessmen should wear suits. 商人穿西装是一种惯例。

conventional / kən'venʃənəl/ *adj.* ❶常规的，习惯（上）的：stray from the path of ~ behaviour 行为背离习俗 / "Good morning" is a ~ greeting. "早上好"是一句日常惯用问候语。❷按社会习俗行事的；因循守旧的：The people living next door are quiet，~ people. 隔壁邻居是一些不声不响的规矩人。派 conventionally *adv.*

conversation / ˌkɒnvə'seɪʃn / *n.* 谈话；会

话;会谈:We had several ~s with him. 我们已和他谈过几次。

converse /kən'vɜːs/ *v.* 交谈;谈话:My uncle who just came back from America often ~s in two languages with me. 我叔叔刚从美国回来,常常用两种语言和我交谈。

conversion /kən'vɜːʃən/ *n.* ❶变换,转换,转化,转变,改变:the ~ of steam into power 蒸汽转化为动力 / Heat causes the ~ of water into steam. 高温使水变成蒸汽。❷(信仰或立场、观点等的)改变;(宗教的)皈依:sb.'s ~ to Islam 某人皈依伊斯兰教

convert /kən'vɜːt/ *v.* ❶变换;转换;改变:These machines ~ cotton into cloth 这些机器将棉花加工成布。/a sofa that ~ s into abed一款可改变成床的沙发 ❷使改变信仰(或立场、观点等);使皈依,使归附

convex /'kɒnveks/ Ⅰ*n.* 凸面;凸面体 Ⅱ*adj.* 凸的;凸面的:a ~ mirror 凸面镜

convey /kən'veɪ/ *vt.* 运输,运送;传达:He ~ed the message to the premier. 他把信息呈送给总理了。/ Words failed to ~ my feeling. 用言语不能表达我的感情。

conveyance /kən'veɪəns/ *n.* ❶[U]输送,运送,转送:the ~ of goods by water 水路货物运输 ❷[C]运输工具,交通工具:Railroad trains and buses are public ~s. 火车和公共汽车是公共交通工具。❸[U]传送,传导;传播,传递,传达:the ~ of wishes 愿望的表达 / Books are for the ~ of ideas. 书籍是用来传播思想的。

convince /kən'vɪns/ *vt.* 使相信;说服:She tried to ~ me that she was innocent. 她尽力想让我相信她是无辜的。/ ~ **sb. of sth.** 说服某人相信某事:I couldn't ~ him of his mistake. 我无法说服他认识自己的错误。

coo /kuː/ *vi.* (鸽子)咕咕地叫

cook /kʊk/ Ⅰ*n.* [C]厨师:Too many ~s spoil the broth. 厨子多了煮坏汤。Ⅱ*v.* 烹调;煮:He ~ed his meals on a gas ring. 他在煤气灶上做饭。

cookery /'kʊkəri/ *n.* ❶[U]烹饪(术);烹饪业:~ lessons 烹饪课程 ❷[C]厨房

cookie /'kʊki/ *n.* [C] ❶(小)甜饼干:chocolate-chip ~s 巧克力饼干 ❷〈俚〉人,家伙:a smart ~机灵鬼/some tough ~s 一些难对付的家伙

cooking /'kʊkɪŋ/ Ⅰ*n.* [U] ❶烹饪,烹调 ❷烹饪术 Ⅱ*adj.* 烹饪用的:a ~ utensil 烹饪用具 / ~ sherry 烹调用雪利酒

cool /kuːl/ Ⅰ*adj.* 凉快的,凉爽的;冷静的:The evening is delightfully ~. 晚间凉爽宜人。/ He kept ~ in the face of danger. 面临危险他很镇静。Ⅱ*vt.* 使冷却;使凉快;使冷静下来:What he said ~ed her anger. 他的话使她不再生气。/ Some rain would ~ us off. 下点雨会使我们感到凉快。

cooperate /kəʊ'ɒpəreɪt/ *vi.* 合作;协作;配合:We are cooperating toward a common goal. 我们正为一个共同的目标而合作。/ He ~d with the company happily. 他与那家公司愉快地合作。

cooperation /kəʊˌɒpə'reɪʃn/ *n.* [U]合作;协作:technological ~ 技术合作/ international ~国际合作

cooperative /kəʊ'ɒpərətɪv/ Ⅰ*adj.* 合作的;协作的:~ development 合作开发/ We made a ~ effort to finish the task. 我们共同努力完成了任务。Ⅱ*n.* [C]合作社;合作团体 派 cooperatively *adv.*

coordinate Ⅰ/kəʊ'ɔːdɪˌneɪt/ *vt.* 整理;调

节;协调:A swimmer should ~ the movements of his arms and legs. 游泳者应该协调双臂和双腿的动作/We must ~ our operations with theirs. 我们必须使自己的行为和他们的行动协调一致。Ⅱ/kəʊˈɔːdɪnət/ *n.* [C]坐标

cop /kɒp/ *n.* [C](美俚)警察;警员

cope /kəʊp/ *vi.* 应付;对付(与 with 连用):I know how to ~ with a complicated situation. 我知道怎样对付复杂的局面。

copper /ˈkɒpə(r)/ *n.* 铜;铜币;铜制品

copy /ˈkɒpi/ Ⅰ *v.* 抄写;仿制;复印:He copied the passage in his notebook. 他把那段文字抄在笔记本上。/ Never ~ foreign things blindly. 绝不要盲目照搬外国的东西。Ⅱ *n.* [C]抄本;册,本;(电影)拷贝:I made two copies of this poem. 这首诗我抄了两份。/ How many copies of the book have you published? 这本书你们印制了多少册?

copyright /ˈkɒpɪraɪt/ *n.* 版权;著作权:The ~ law is to protect the right of the author. 版权法是保护作者著作权的法律。

coral /ˈkɒrəl/ *n.* [C]珊瑚:a ~ island 珊瑚岛

cord /kɔːd/ *n.* 绳;索;粗线:the electric ~ 电线/ the flexible ~ 花线;皮线

core /kɔː(r)/ *n.* [C]果实的核;核心;要点:The professor pointed out the ~ of the problem. 教授指出了问题的核心。

cork /kɔːk/ *n.* 软木;软木塞:I helped him to pull out the ~ of the bottle. 我帮他拔出了瓶子的软木塞。

corn /kɔːn/ *n.* [U]谷类;(美)玉蜀黍:Little children like pop ~. 小孩喜欢吃爆米花。

corner /ˈkɔːnə(r)/ *n.* [C]角落:The boy fell and hit his head against the ~ of a desk. 小男孩摔倒了,头撞上书桌角。/ Turn the ~, you'll find the hospital. 转过街角你就会找到那家医院。/**round the ~** 即将来临;靠近:Christmas is round the ~. 圣诞节即将来临。**from all ~s** 各地:People have come from all ~s of the country to watch the game. 人们从全国各地赶来观看比赛。

corporation /ˌkɔːpəˈreɪʃn/ *n.* [C](股份有限)公司,社团;法人,法人团体:a trading ~贸易公司/ a multinational ~ 跨国公司

corps /kɔː/ *n.* [C](*pl.* corps/kɔːz/) ❶(特殊兵种的)队,部队:the Marine ~ 海军陆战队/the dare-to-die ~敢死队 ❷(从同类专业工作的)一组:the diplomatic ~外交使团

corpse /kɔːps/ *n.* 尸体;(尤指人的)死尸,尸首

corpus /ˈkɔːpəs/ *n.* (书面或口语的)文集,文献,汇编;语料库:the whole ~ of Renaissance poetry 文艺复兴时期诗歌总汇

corpuscle /kɔːpʌsl/ *n.* (红或白)血球,血细胞

correct /kəˈrekt/ Ⅰ *vt.* 改正;校正;修改:Please ~ the mistakes in my exercises. 请把我练习中的错误改一下。Ⅱ *adj.* 正确的;恰当的:This sentence is ~. 这句话正确。※ correctly *adv.*

correction /kəˈrekʃn/ *n.* [U]改正;修改:The ~ of the essay took two hours. 修改论文花了两小时。

correspond /ˌkɒrəˈspɒnd/ *vi.* ❶相当于;一致:~ **to (with)...** 与……一致,相当于:The house ~s with my needs. 这房子符合我的要求。/ His expenses do not ~ to his income. 他的开支与他的收

人不相符。❷通信：They ~ every month. 他们每月都通信。/~ **with** 通信：I ~ed with her at that time. 那段时间我一直与她通信。

C

correspondence /ˌkɒrɪˈspɒndəns/ *n.* ❶符合；一致；类似；相当：~ between theory and practice 理论和实践相一致/ There is not much ~ between their ideals and ours. 他们的想法和我们的没有多少相似之处。❷[U]通信，信件联系：break off ~ 终止通信联系 ❸(总称)信件，函件：business (commercial) ~ 商业函件 / When I came home, I found a huge ~ waiting for me. 我回到家时，发现有大批信件等我阅后答复。

correspondent /ˌkɒrəˈspɒndənt/ *n.* [C] 通信员；记者：He is a ~for (on, of) *the People's Daily*. 他是《人民日报》的记者。

corridor /ˈkɒrɪdɔː(r)/ *n.* [C]走廊；过道

corrode /kəˈrəʊd/ *vt.* ❶腐蚀；侵蚀：Moist air ~s iron. 潮湿的空气使铁生锈腐蚀。/ Money sometimes ~s people's minds. 金钱有时会腐蚀人的灵魂。❷(渐渐)损害，损伤：It was sad to see him ~d with suspicion. 看到他因多疑而扭曲了性格，真让人伤心。—*vi.* 受腐蚀：This metal does not ~ easily. 这种金属不易腐蚀。

corrosive /kəˈrəʊsɪv/ *adj.* ❶腐蚀的；侵蚀(性)的：~ materials 腐蚀性的材料 / ~ action 腐蚀作用 ❷逐渐损害的，有害的：the ~ influence on society 对社会的有害影响

corrupt /kəˈrʌpt/ Ⅰ *adj.* 腐败的；贪污的；道德败坏的：It's not good for your health to work in the ~ air. 在污浊的空气中工作对你的身体健康不利。/ Honest people are disgusted with ~ officials. 正直的人们厌恶贪官污吏。Ⅱ *v.* 败坏；腐蚀；贿赂，收买：The businessman tried to ~ the tax official but was refused. 那商人企图贿赂税务官员但遭到拒绝。

corruption /kəˈrʌpʃn/ *n.* [U]腐坏；败坏；贿赂：Official ~ should be stopped. 官场腐败应当制止。

cosmetic /kɒzˈmetɪk/ Ⅰ *n.* [C]化妆品：Girls always like ~s. 女孩们总是喜欢化妆品的。Ⅱ *adj.* 化妆用的；整容的：~ surgery 整容手术

cosmos /ˈkɒzmɒs/ *n.* 宇宙：in the ~ 在宇宙中

cost /kɒst/ Ⅰ *v.* (cost, cost) 花费；消耗：This coat ~ me much money. 这件外套花了我很多钱。/ Careless driving may ~ you your life. 粗心驾车可能使你丧命。Ⅱ *n.* 价格，价值；费用；代价：The ~ of the used computer is only $50. 那台二手电脑的价格仅 50 美元。/ **at all ~s** 无论如何；不惜任何代价：We are determined to obtain our rights at all ~s. 我们决心不惜一切代价来取得我们的权利。**at the ~ of** 以……为代价，以……为牺牲：The young man saved the old man at the ~ of his own life. 那位年轻人以牺牲自己的生命为代价救了这位老人。

costly /ˈkɒstli/ *adj.* ❶昂贵的；豪华的：He bought a ~ fur coat to his wife as her birthday present. 他买了一件昂贵的毛皮大衣作为生日礼物送给妻子。❷牺牲重大的；代价高的：You have made a ~mistake. 你犯了一个代价极高的错误。

cosy(-zy) /ˈkəʊzi/ *adv.* 舒适的；安逸的：~ atmosphere 舒适的氛围

cottage /ˈkɒtɪdʒ/ *n.* [C]村舍，茅舍；别墅

cotton /ˈkɒtn/ *n.* [U]棉花;棉布:a ~ field 棉田/~ clothes 棉布衣

couch /kaʊtʃ/ *n.* [C]长沙发;睡椅

cough /kɒf/ Ⅰ*v.* 咳嗽:The old man ~ed badly at night. 老人晚上咳得厉害。Ⅱ*n.* [C]咳嗽:She was caught in the rain and had a bad ~. 她淋了雨,咳得厉害。

council /ˈkaʊnsl/ *n.* [C]大会;委员会;议事机构:an advisory ~ 顾问委员会/ a cabinet ~ 内阁会议/ a world ~ 国际会议/ the Security Council 联合国安全理事会/ the State Council (中国)国务院

council(l)or /ˈkaʊnsələ(r)/ *n.* [C]议员;顾问;评议员

counsel /ˈkaʊnsəl/ *n.* ❶商议;评议;审议:They took ~ with each other on the problem. 他们就那一问题共同商议。❷忠告;劝告:He followed his father's ~ to work as a lawyer. 他听从父亲的忠告,当了一名律师。❸律师;辩护人:He is ~ for the defense. 他是辩方律师。

count /kaʊnt/ *v.* 数;计算:Count from one to a hundred. 请从1数到100。/~ **in** 包括:Count me in. 算我一个。~ **on** 依靠;指望:Don't ~ on him to come. 别指望他会来。~ **...as...** 把……看作……:We ~ her as a friend. 我们把她看作朋友。~ **up to** 共计:It ~s up to more than fifty yuan. 共计50多元。

counter[1] /ˈkaʊntə(r)/ *n.* [C]柜台:After putting 100 yuan on the ~, she went out of the restaurant. 在柜台上放了100元钱后她离开了餐馆。/ The service ~ is inside the hall. 服务台设在大厅里。

counter[2] /ˈkaʊntə(r)/ Ⅰ*adj.* 相反的;对立的;反对的:Obviously your idea is ~ to mine. 很明显你的想法与我的正好相反。Ⅱ*adv.* 反方向地;相反地:What he did went ~ to what the teacher hoped for. 他所做的与老师所希望的背道而驰。

counteract /ˌkaʊntəˈrækt/ *vt.* 对……起反作用;对抗;抵消;中和:~ a fever with aspirin 用阿司匹林解热 / a drug that ~s the effects of the poison 能解这种毒的药物 派 counteractant *adj.*

counterclockwise /ˌkaʊntəˈklɒkwaɪz/ *adj.* & *adv.* 逆时针方向的(地)

counterfeit /ˈkaʊntəfɪt/ Ⅰ*n.* [C]冒牌货;赝品:The expert said that the oil painting was a ~. 专家说那幅油画是赝品。Ⅱ*adj.* 伪造的;仿造的;假冒的:a ~ trade-mark 冒牌商标/ ~ and shoddy commodities 假冒伪劣商品

country /ˈkʌntri/ *n.* ❶[C]国土,国家;领土;故土:Asian countries 亚洲国家 / One ~, two systems. 一国两制。/ The young man traveled all over the ~ by bicycle. 那年轻人骑车环游全国。❷乡间;田野:They are living in the ~. 他们住在乡下。

countryside /ˈkʌntrɪsaɪd/ *n.* [U]乡下;农村:I prefer to live in the ~ than (to) live in the city. 我宁愿住在农村而不愿住在城市。

county /ˈkaʊnti/ *n.* [C](美国的)县(州以下最大的行政区划);(英国的)郡(最大的地方行政区划,相当于中国的省);(中国等的)县:the local ~ government 地方县政府

couple /ˈkʌpl/ *n.* [C]一对,一双;夫妇;几个,几件事物:I found a ~ of socks in the bedroom, but they don't make a pair. 我在卧室里找到一双袜子,但不配对。/ a ~ of days (months, years) 几天(几月,几年)

coupon /ˈku:pɒn/ *n.* [C](附在货物上

的)赠券;(连在广告上的)礼券;购物优惠券

courage / ˈkʌrɪdʒ / *n.* [U] 勇敢;胆量:The boy had the ~ to jump down from the truck. 小男孩很勇敢,从卡车上跳下来。/ **lose** ~失去勇气,灰心:Cheer up! Don't lose ~. 振作起来,不要灰心丧气。**take** ~ 鼓起勇气:I took ~ to say "no". 我鼓起勇气说了声"不"。

courageous / kəˈreɪdʒəs / *adj.* 勇敢的;英勇的:You should be ~ enough to tell us the truth. 你应当勇敢地把真相告诉我们。

course / kɔːs / *n.* ❶[C]航线,路线:The ship is not on her right ~. 船未按正确航线航行。❷进程;过程:He knew something about the ~ of the event. 他了解一些这个事件的过程。❸[C]课程:elective ~s 选修课/ evening ~s 夜校课程/ self-teaching ~s 自修课/ short-term ~s 短训班/ **in the** ~ **of** 在……期间:in the ~ of discussion 在讨论过程中 **of** ~当然;一定:—May I use your dictionary? —Of ~. —我可以用一下你的字典吗? —当然可以。

court / kɔːt / *n.* ❶法院;法庭:He will be brought to ~ for trial. 他将被带进法庭接受审判。❷庭院;院子:There is a small ~ in front of her house. 她的房前有一个小院。❸场地;球场:Our school has two twins ~s. 我们学校有两个网球场。

countdown / ˈkaʊntˌdaʊn / *n.* [C]倒计数;倒计时(阶段):The (ten-second) ~ began at 16:00 hours. 16 时开始(10 秒钟的)倒计时。

courtesy / ˈkɜːtəsi / *n.* ❶[U]礼貌;谦恭有礼;殷勤周到:He could at least have had the ~ to say sorry. 他连起码说声对不起的礼貌都没有。❷[C]谦恭有礼的举止(或言辞):an exchange of ~相互致礼/**by** ~ **of** 蒙……的好意(或惠允);蒙……提供(或赠送):By ~ of the exhibitor, we have taken a number of photos of the art products on display. 承蒙展出者许可,我们拍摄了若干艺术陈列品的照片。

courtyard / ˈkɔːtjɑːd / *n.* [C]庭院;院子

cousin / ˈkʌzn / *n.* [C]堂兄弟,表兄弟;堂姐妹,表姐妹:I have three ~s on my father's (mother's) side. 我有三个堂(表)兄妹。

cover / ˈkʌvə(r) / Ⅰ *v.* ❶掩;盖:Dust ~ed your desk. 灰尘布满了你的书桌。/ **be** ~**ed with** 被……覆盖:The hills are ~ed with thick snow. 山上覆盖着厚厚的白雪。❷占用(时间、空间);包含,包括:His speach ~ed all aspects of the problem. 他的发言谈及了问题的各个方面。Ⅱ *n.* [C]封面;盖子;套子:The book needs a new ~. 需要给这本书换上新的封面。

covering / ˈkʌvərɪŋ / *n.* [C]覆盖物;套,罩

cow / kaʊ / *n.* [C] 母牛;乳牛

coward / ˈkaʊəd / *n.* [C] 懦夫

cowboy / ˈkaʊbɔɪ / *n.* [C] 牧童;牛仔:Young people like ~ suits. 年轻人喜欢穿牛仔服。

crab / kræb / *n.* 螃蟹;蟹肉

crack / kræk / Ⅰ *n.* [C]裂缝;裂纹;爆裂声:The ~s in the wall were caused by the earthquake. 墙上的裂缝是地震造成的。/I heard the ~ of fireworks outside. 我听到外边有鞭炮声。Ⅱ *v.* 爆裂;破裂;发出爆裂声:The glass bottle ~ed suddenly. 玻璃瓶突然裂了。

cracker / ˈkrækə(r) / *n.* [C]❶爆竹;鞭炮:The children are setting off ~s in the courtyard. 孩子们在院子里放鞭炮。❷薄脆饼干；饼干：a soda ~ 一块苏打饼干

cradle /ˈkreɪdl/ *n.* [C]摇篮；(喻)发源地，策源地：A man may meet with a lot of difficulties from the ~ to the grave. 人的一生会遇到许许多多的困难。/ The Jinggang Mountains are the ~ of the Chinese revolution. 井冈山是中国革命的摇篮(发源地)。

craft /krɑːft/ *n.* ❶工艺；手艺：She likes the making of potter's ~ very much. 她非常喜欢陶艺制作。❷[C]行业；职业；手工业：People seldom practise the carpenter's ~ now. 现在很少有人从事木匠业了。❸船；航空器

craftsman /ˈkrɑːftsmən/ *n.* [C](*pl.* craftsmen)手艺人；工匠：The factory needs master craftsmen. 工厂需要能工巧匠。

crane /kreɪn/ *n.* [C] ❶鹤 ❷起重机；吊车：She operates the ~ in the factory. 她在厂里开吊车。

crash /kræʃ/ Ⅰ *v.* ❶碰撞；坠落；坠毁：The truck ~ed into a wall. 卡车撞到一堵墙上。❷(计算机)死机：I don't know why the computer ~ed suddenly. 我不知道为什么计算机突然就死机了。Ⅱ *n.* [C] ❶碰撞；坠落；坠毁：The plane ~ caused the death of more than one hundred passengers. 飞机坠毁造成一百多人死亡。❷破裂声：The glass fell to the floor with a ~. 玻璃杯哗的一声摔到地上。❸(计算机)死机

crawl /krɔːl/ *v.* 爬；爬行；匍匐前进：The snake ~ed into a cave. 蛇爬进了洞里。

crayon /ˈkreɪən/ *n.* [C]蜡笔；颜色笔：colored ~s 彩色蜡笔/ a picture in ~ 蜡笔画

crazy /ˈkreɪzi/ *adj.* (-ier,-iest) ❶疯狂的，发疯的：The noise is driving me ~. 这声音吵得我快发疯了。❷热衷的，着迷的：He is ~ about football. 他对足球着了迷。❸愚蠢的，荒唐的：a ~ idea 荒唐的想法

creak /kriːk/ *vi.* 吱吱嘎嘎作响

cream /kriːm/ *n.* [U]奶油：Most children like icecream. 大多数孩子都喜欢吃冰激凌。

create /krɪˈeɪt/ *vt.* 创造；引起，造成；产生：Do you believe that God ~d the world? 你相信上帝创造了世界吗？/ We've ~d a beautiful new house out of an old ruin. 我们在废墟上建造了一栋漂亮的新屋。

creation /krɪˈeɪʃn/ *n.* 创造；创作；作品

creative /krɪˈeɪtɪv/ *adj.* 创造性的；有创造力的：That is a ~ idea. 那是一个很有创意的想法。

creature /ˈkriːtʃə(r)/ *n.* [C]动物；生物：the wild ~ 野生物/a good ~ 一个好人/ a poor ~ 一个可怜的人/ a weak ~ 一个软弱的人/ a human ~ 人

credential /krɪˈdenʃəl/ *n.* [C] ❶(学历、资历等的)证明，证书；文凭：Her ~s as a journalist were beyond dispute. 她作为新闻记者的资格无可置疑。/ No one is admitted without ~s. 没有身份证明任何人不得入内。❷(*pl.*)介绍材料；(大使递交的)国书

credible /ˈkredəbl/ *adj.* ❶(人或言论等)可信的；值得相信的：a ~ witness 可靠的证人/That boy's excuse for being absent was hardly ~. 那孩子缺席的理由几乎不可信。❷有效的；有威力的：They haven't produced any ~ policies for improving the situation. 他们尚未拿出改善局势的行之有效的对策。

credit / ˈkredɪt / *n.* [U] ❶信任,相信:The manager gave ~ to what he said. 经理相信了他说的话。❷信誉;声望;荣誉:Her success does her great ~. 她的成功给她带来极大的荣誉。/ Telling lies would hurt your ~. 说谎会使你的名声受到损害。❸信用;信贷:He drew some money with his ~ card. 他用信用卡取了一些钱。❹学分:English Ⅱ is a 4-~ course. 英语二级是四个学分的课程。

creek / kriːk / *n.* [C](河的)支流;小河溪

creep / kriːp / *vi.* (crept/ krept / ,crept)(身体贴着地面)爬行;悄悄地行进;(枝条)蔓生:The cat crept toward the mouse. 猫悄悄地靠近老鼠。/ The ivy crept up all over the wall. 常春藤爬满了墙壁。

crew / kruː / *n.* 全体乘务员:The ship has a ~ of twenty. 这艘船上有二十名船员。

cricket / ˈkrɪkɪt / *n.* ❶[C]蟋蟀 ❷[U]板球:play ~ 打板球

crime / kraɪm / *n.* 罪;犯罪:Crime is on the rise in many big cities. 在许多大城市里犯罪正在增加。/ He committed a ~ and was sent to prison. 他犯了罪被关进监狱。

criminal / ˈkrɪmɪn(ə)l / Ⅰ *adj.* 犯罪的;犯法的;刑事的:a ~ act 犯罪行为/ a ~ case 刑事案件 Ⅱ *n.* [C]犯人;刑事犯:The ~ was sentenced to five years' imprisonment. 犯人被判五年徒刑。

crinkle / ˈkrɪŋkl / *v.* (使)起皱;(使)起波纹:His face ~ into a smile 他满脸皱纹地笑了起来。/My clothes were all ~ when I got them out of the case. 我把衣服从箱子里拿出来时,它们全都起皱了。派 crinkly *adj.*

cripple / ˈkrɪpl / *n.* [C]跛子;伤残人:The ~ soldier was brave. 那位跛脚士兵很勇敢。

crisis / ˈkraɪsɪs / *n.* (*pl.* crises)危机;难关;危险期:The family united as one to ride out their economic ~ smoothly. 全家人团结一致顺利渡过了经济危机。

crisp / krɪsp / *adj.* 易碎的;脆的:The snow was ~ underfoot. 脚下的雪踩起来松脆。

criterion / kraɪˈtɪərɪən/ *n.* [C](*pl.* -ria /-rɪə/)(判断或评价的)标准;准则;尺度:a ~ of success 成功的标准 / meet (satisfy) criteria 符合标准 / a ~ for the examination 审查标准

critic / ˈkrɪtɪk / *n.* [C]批评家;评论家:a drama (literary, music) ~ 戏剧(文学、音乐)评论家

critical / ˈkrɪtɪkl / *adj.* ❶批评的;批判的:The editor is writing an important ~ essay. 编辑正在写一篇重要的评论文章。❷紧要的;关键性的;危急的:The wounded is now in ~ condition. 伤员现在情况危急。/ He is always the first to help others at ~ moment. 在危急关头他总是第一个出来帮助别人。派 critically *adv.*

criticism / ˈkrɪtɪsɪzəm / *n.* [U]评论;批评

criticize / ˈkrɪtɪsaɪz / *vt.* 批判;批评:The teacher ~d the student by name because of his lack of responsibility. 老师点名批评了那位学生的不负责任。/She's always criticizing her husband for being lazy. 她总是批评她丈夫懒惰。

crocodile / ˈkrɒkədaɪl / *n.* [C] 鳄鱼

crook / krʊk / *n.* [C] ❶(一头有弯钩的)手杖,曲柄杖 ❷臂弯:She held the baby in the ~ of her left arm. 她用左胳膊的臂弯抱着婴儿。❸弯曲物;弯曲部分;钩子:have a ~ in one's back 背驼/the ~ of a cane 手杖弯头

crooked / ˈkrʊkɪd/ *adj.* ❶歪的;弯曲的,不直的:a narrow,~ street 一条狭窄而弯弯曲曲的街道/ The picture seems to be ~. 那幅画看上去有点歪斜。❷扭曲的;弯腰驼背的:a ~ back 驼背 ❸不诚实的;狡诈的:a ~ scheme 骗局/ ~ profits 非法利润 ▩ crookedly *adv.* ;crookedness *n.*

crop / krɒp / *n.* [C]庄稼,作物;收成,收获:a big (rich, bumper, good)~ 丰收/ a bad (poor) ~ 歉收/ gather ~s 收庄稼/ raise ~s 种庄稼

cross / krɒs / Ⅰ *vt.* 穿越;横过:Be careful when ~ing the street. 过街时要小心。Ⅱ *n.* [C]十字架;十字形物品:the Red Cross (Society)红十字会 Ⅲ *adj.* 相反的:It was ~ to our design. 它与我们的计划相反。

crossing / ˈkrɒsɪŋ / *n.* [C] 交叉点;十字路口:The car stopped at the ~. 小车在交叉路口停下。

crossover / ˈkrɒsˌəʊvə(r) / *n.* [C]桥;跨路线桥;过道;渡口;人行横道:a ~ to the Classroom Building 通向教学大楼的横跨过道 / Take the exit just past the ~. 走贴近跨路线桥的出口。

crossroad / ˈkrɒsˌrəʊd / *n.* [C] ❶岔路,支路 ❷十字路口:a store at the ~在十字路口的商店/Traffic stalled at a ~. 交通在十字路口堵塞了。❸紧要关头,关键时刻:be at the ~s 面临重大抉择的关头

crow[1] / krəʊ / *n.* [C] 乌鸦

crow[2] / krəʊ / *vi.* ❶(雄鸡)啼 ❷(婴儿)欢叫 ❸自夸;洋洋自得,幸灾乐祸:~ over sb.'s failure 因某人遭失败而幸灾乐祸

crowd / kraʊd / Ⅰ *n.* [C]人群;大众:A big ~ gathered on the street. 街上聚集了一大群人。/ The writer often says that his books are for the ~. 那位作家常说他的书是为大众写的。Ⅱ *v.* 拥挤;挤满:The pupils ~ed round the teacher to ask questions. 学生们围着老师问问题。/ **be ~ed with** 挤满;充满;塞满:His mind is ~ed with whys. 他脑子里满是问号。

crown / kraʊn / Ⅰ *n.* ❶[C]王冠 ❷(the ~或 the Crown)王位,王权;君主,国王 Ⅱ *vt.* 为……加冕,立……为王;授予荣誉:He ~ed his son King. 他立他的儿子为国王。

crucial / ˈkruːʃ(ə)l / *adj.* 至关重要的;决定性的,关键的:a ~ moment 紧要关头/a ~ battle 决定性的战役

crude / kruːd / *adj.* ❶天然的;未加工的;未成熟的:That's only my ~ idea. 那只是我不成熟的想法。/ The price of ~ oil is on the rise. 原油价格不断上涨。❷粗糙的;粗鲁的:His ~ manners made me angry. 他的粗鲁态度使我很生气。

cruel / krʊəl / *adj.* 残酷的:She told the child not to be ~ to animals. 她告诉孩子不要虐待动物。▩ cruelly *adv.*

cruelty / ˈkruːəlti/ *n.* ❶[U]残忍;残暴;残酷:the ~ of fate 命运的残酷性 / It is ~ to the innocent not to punish the guilty. 对犯罪者的宽容,就是对无辜者的残忍。❷[C]残忍的行为(或言论):commit cruelties 犯下暴行

cruiser / ˈkruːzə(r) / *n.* [C] 巡洋舰;游艇

crumble / ˈkrʌmbl / *v.* ❶(使)成碎屑,弄碎:Do not ~ your bread on the table. 不要把面包搓碎在桌子上。/Acid rain has caused the stone facade to ~. 酸雨已经使这块石头的表面碎裂了。❷崩溃；分崩离析；瓦解：The empire ~d from the inside. 这个帝国是从内部土崩瓦解的。

crush /krʌʃ/ *vt.* 压，挤；压碎，粉碎：Be careful not to ~ the glass. 小心别压碎玻璃。/ They are trying to ~ into the front seats. 他们尽力想挤到前排的座位上去。

crust /krʌst/ *n.* 硬外皮；外壳：He knows little about the earth's ~. 他不了解地壳的情况。

crutch /krʌtʃ/ *n.* [C]拐杖；支柱：The patient can only walk on ~es. 那病人只能拄着拐杖走路。

cry /kraɪ/ Ⅰ *vi.* 哭；叫，喊：Little children always ~ when hurt. 小孩受伤时总是哭叫。/~ **down** 诋毁；看不起：He stood up to speak, but his audience cried him down. 他站起来说话，但听众把他轰了下去。~ **for** 迫切要求：The strikers cried for a raise of pay. 罢工者要求提高工资。~ **out** 大声叫喊：As soon as I went in, she cried out with pleasure. 我一进屋，她就高兴得叫了起来。Ⅱ *n.* [C]叫声；哭声：We heard a ~ of "Help!" 我们听到有人喊"救命！"

crystal /ˈkrɪstl/ Ⅰ *n.* 水晶；水晶制品 Ⅱ *adj.* 水晶般的；清澈的，透明的：It's wonderful to swim in a ~ stream. 在清澈见底的溪水里游泳真棒。

cube /kjuːb/ *n.* [C]立方体；立方形；立方；三次方

cubic /ˈkjuːbɪk/ *adj.* 立方体的；立方形的；立方的；三次方的

cuckoo /ˈkʊkuː/ *n.* [C] 杜鹃；布谷鸟

cucumber /ˈkjuːkʌmbə(r)/ *n.* 黄瓜

cue /kjuː/ *n.* [C] 提示；暗示：I don't know how to answer this question. Can you give me some ~s? 我不知道怎么回答这个问题。你能给我点提示吗？

cuff /kʌf/ *n.* [C] ❶袖口：Your ~ is dirty. 你的袖口脏了。❷(*pl.*)手铐：The criminal didn't wear ~s at the court. 罪犯在法庭上没有戴手铐。

cuisine /kwiːˈziːn/ *n.* [U] ❶烹调(术)，烹饪(术)：French Cuisine 法国烹调 ❷菜肴，饭菜：excellent ~美味佳肴

cultivate /ˈkʌltɪveɪt/ *vt.* ❶耕作；栽培；养殖：They ~d flowers and earned a lot of money. 他们种花挣了许多钱。❷培养；教养：He ~s the sort of people who can be useful to him in his business. 他培养对他的业务有用的人。

culture /ˈkʌltʃə(r)/ *n.* 文化；教养；修养：The doctor studies ancient Greek ~. 那位博士研究古希腊文化。/ Professor Li is a man of considerable ~. 李教授是一个文化修养很高的人。

cunning /ˈkʌnɪŋ/ Ⅰ *adj.* 狡猾的，狡诈的：a ~ thief 狡诈的窃贼/employ ~ means 使用狡诈的手段 Ⅱ *n.* [U]狡诈，狡猾：have a lot of ~诡计多端

cup /kʌp/ *n.* [C] 杯子；优胜杯；奖杯：a ~ of tea 一杯茶/a ~ of coffee 一杯咖啡/ They won the world cup. 他们赢得了世界杯。

cupboard /ˈkʌbəd/ *n.* [C] 碗橱

cure /kjʊə(r)/ *vt.* 医治；治愈：The medicine ~d my stomachache. 这药治好了我的胃痛。/ Time ~d him of his grief. 时光流逝消除了他的悲伤。

curiosity /ˌkjʊərɪˈɒsəti/ *n.* [U]好奇；好奇心：The crowd looked at them with great ~. 众人非常好奇地看着他们。/ To satisfy her ~, I told her the secret. 为满足她的好奇心，我把秘密告诉

了她。

curious /ˈkjʊərɪəs/ *adj.* 好奇的；稀奇的；奇妙的：Don't be too ~ about things you are not supposed to know. 对于你不应该知道的事别太好奇。

curl /kɜːl/ Ⅰ *n.* [C]卷毛；鬈发 Ⅱ *v.* (使)卷曲；蜷缩：Does her hair ~ naturally? 她的头发是天然鬈发吗？/ The frost ~ed up the leaves. 严霜使叶子卷起来。

currency /ˈkʌrənsi/ *n.* ❶通货；货币：The government issued some new ~. 政府发行了一些新货币。❷[U]通用；流通；流传：Very soon her novels got ~ among young students. 很快她的小说就在年轻学生中流传开来。

current /ˈkʌrənt/ Ⅰ *adj.* 通用的；流行的；当前的；现时的：The ~ situation is very complicated. 当前形势很复杂。Ⅱ *n.* [C]水流；电流；潮流；倾向：the cold (warm) ~ in the sea 寒(暖)流/ He turned off the ~ to check the machine. 他切断电流查看机器。/ Nothing can disturb the peaceful ~ of her life. 没有什么能扰乱她平静的生活。/ This type of mobile phones is no longer in ~. 这种型号的手机已不再流行了。

curriculum /kəˈrɪkjələm/ *n.* [C](*pl.* curriculums 或 curricula)(一门)课程；学校的全部课程：the new ~ standards 新课程标准/ The school designed the ~s according to students' need. 学校根据学生需求设置课程。

curry /ˈkʌri,ˈkɜːri/ *n.* 咖喱；咖喱饭；咖喱菜肴

curse /kɜːs/ Ⅰ *v.* 诅咒；咒骂：She ~d her neighbors with anger. 她生气地咒骂她的邻居。Ⅱ *n.* [C] ❶咒骂，诅咒之词：be under a ~被咒骂 ❷祸根，祸害；受诅咒的东西(人)

cursor /ˈkɜːsə(r)/ *n.* [C](计算尺)游标；(计算机)光标

curtain /ˈkɜːtn/ *n.* [C]窗帘；幕；幕布：raise the ~启幕/drop the ~ 落幕/ She opened the ~ to see if it was raining outside. 她拉开窗帘看看外边是不是在下雨。

curve /kɜːv/ *n.* [C]曲线；弯曲：Draw a ~ here. 在这里画条曲线。/ The automobile has to slow down to go around a sharp ~ in the road. 汽车急转弯时得减速。

cushion /ˈkʊʃn/ *n.* [C] 垫子；坐垫

custody /ˈkʌstədi/ *n.* [U]照看；监护；保管；监护权：The files are in the secretary's ~. 这些文件是由秘书保管的。/Parents have the ~ of their young children. 父母对自己年幼的儿女尽有监护义务。

custom /ˈkʌstəm/ *n.* ❶习惯；风俗；惯例：This ~ has been kept up for 2,000 years. 这一风俗已经保持了两千年。/ It is not my ~ to take off my shoes when I get into the hall. 我不习惯进入门厅脱鞋。❷(常用 Customs)海关；关税：It will take us over an hour to pass the Customs. 我们办完海关手续要一个多小时。

customer /ˈkʌstəmə/ *n.* [C]顾客；主顾：Customers First. 顾客第一。/ The old lady is a regular ~ of the shop. 老太太是这家商店的老主顾。

cut /kʌt/ *v.* (cut, cat; cutting) 切，割：Please ~ the bread into two. 请把面包一分为二。/~ **across** 走捷径：They ~ across an empty lot. 他们取捷径穿过一块空地。~ **away** 砍掉；剪掉：We should ~ away all the dead branches from the tree. 我们应该砍掉树上所有枯枝。~

down 减低，缩减；限制：The doctor told Mr. Wang to ~ down his consumption of cigarettes. 医生吩咐王先生少抽烟。~ **in** 插嘴；打断：While we were watching the show, a man ~ in to tell who won the election. 我们在看节目时，一个人突然插进来宣布谁竞选得胜。~ **off** 切断；割掉：The television show was ~ off by a special news report. 电视节目被特别新闻报道打断。~ **up**（口语）使伤心：She was ~ up at the news. 听到这个消息，她很伤心。

cutback /ˈkʌtˌbæk/ *n.* [C] ❶削减；缩减；裁减：a ~ in costs 成本的削减 / a ~ of military budget 军事预算的减少 ❷（小说、戏剧、电影等的）倒叙，回切：the boring ~s to the protagonist's childhood 回切到主人公儿提时代的情节

cute /kjuːt/ *adj.* ❶迷人的；娇小可爱的；小巧精致的：What a ~ baby! 多么漂亮的小宝贝啊！/ a pair of ~ glasses 一幅小巧的眼镜 / The hat looks ~ on her. 这帽子戴在她头上可爱极了。❷聪明伶俐的；精明的；狡猾的：That was a ~ move, getting the boss to back you. 这一招真刁钻，让你的老板给你撑腰。

派 cutely *adv.* cuteness *n.*

cutoff /ˈkʌtˌɒf/ Ⅰ *n.* [C] ❶近路，捷径：take the ~ from the main highway 走偏离大路的捷径 ❷最低限度，底线：We'll start the bargaining at 50%, but 35% is the ~; we won't go lower than that. 我们讨价还价的起价是原价的50%，但35%是底线，不能再低了。❸切断；截断 Ⅱ *adj.* 切断的；截止的：the ~ date for applications 申请的截止日期

cyber /ˈsaɪbə(r)/ Ⅰ *n.* 网络；网络空间 Ⅱ *adj.* 网络的；计算机的：~ affairs 网恋/ a ~ cafe 网络咖啡屋，网吧/ a ~ citizen (cult)网民（网虫）/ a ~ message board 网络浏览者

cycle /ˈsaɪkl/ *n.* ❶ [C]自行车：I saw him ride on a ~ at the corner of the street. 我在街角看见他骑着自行车。❷循环；周期：He is studying the life ~ of insects. 他在研究昆虫的生活周期。

cylinder /ˈsɪlɪndə(r)/ *n.* [C] ❶圆柱状物；圆柱体 ❷（发动机的）汽缸；泵体

cynical /ˈsɪnɪkl/ *adj.* 挖苦的；讽刺的；愤世嫉俗的

cynic /ˈsɪnɪk/ *n.* [C] ❶愤世嫉俗者；认为人皆自私（或利己）者 ❷好挖苦人者，冷嘲热讽的人

D d

dad / dæd / *n.* [C](口语)爸爸

daddy / ˈdædi / *n.* (＝dad)[C](口语)爸爸

dagger / ˈdægə(r) / *n.* [C] 匕首;短剑:The thief drew a ~ at a customer. 那小偷拔出匕首向一位顾客刺去。

daily / ˈdeɪli / Ⅰ *adj.* 每日的 Her ~ life is simply. 她的日常生活非常简朴。Ⅱ *n.* [C]日报:In order to improve his Chinese, Jim reads *the People's Daily* everyday. 为了提高汉语水平,杰米天天读《人民日报》。

dairy / ˈdeəri / *n.* [C]牛奶场;乳品店

dam / dæm / *n.* [C]堤;水闸;坝:There are several ~s across the Nile. 尼罗河上有好几个水坝。

damage / ˈdæmɪdʒ / Ⅰ *v.* 损害;毁坏:The crops were badly ~d this year. 今年庄稼遭损严重。Ⅱ *n.* ❶[U]损害;伤害:The snowstorm caused (did) heavy ~ to the crops. 那场暴风雪使农作物受损严重。❷(*pl.*)赔偿金:He claimed 50,000 dollar ~s from the company. 他向那家公司索要5万美元赔偿费。

damn / dæm / *vt.* 诅咒:Damn you! (God ~ you!)真该死! / Damn it (all)! (口)见鬼! 真糟糕!

damp / dæmp / Ⅰ *adj.* 潮湿的;有潮的:If you put on ~ clothes, you'll probably catch a cold. 要是穿湿衣服,你会着凉的。Ⅱ *n.* [U] 湿气;潮湿:There is too much ~ here. 这儿太潮湿。

dance / dɑːns / Ⅰ *vi.* 跳舞:The girl ~d with joy after she won the praise. 受到称赞,小女孩高兴得手舞足蹈。/ He ~s here every night. 他每晚都在这儿跳舞。Ⅱ *n.* 舞蹈;舞会:I like classical (modern, popular) ~. 我喜欢古典(现代,流行)舞。/ We'll hold a ~ next Saturday. 下周六我们将举行舞会。派 dancer *n.*

danger / ˈdeɪndʒə(r) / *n.* [U]危险;威胁:Smoking too much causes ~ to health. 吸烟过多威胁身体健康。/ **in** ~ 在危险中:The wounded soldier is in ~. 那位伤员有生命危险。**out of** ~ 脱险:The doctor said that his father was out of ~. 医生说他的父亲已脱离危险。

dangerous / ˈdeɪndʒərəs / *adj.* 危险的;不安全的:It's very ~ to do such a thing. 做这样的事很危险。派 dangerously *adv.*

dangle / ˈdæŋgl / *v.* (使)悬垂,(使)悬挂;悬荡;垂直摆动:a bunch of keys dangling at the end of a chain 悬挂在链端的一串钥匙/The children sat on the bridge dangling their feet in the water. 孩子们坐在桥上,把脚悬垂在河水中。

dare / deə(r) / Ⅰ *aux. v.* 敢,竟敢 Ⅱ *v.*

敢，敢于：~ hardships and danger 敢于面对艰险/ He ~d to tell the truth. 他敢于说出真相。

daring / ˈdeərɪŋ / *adj.* 大胆的；勇敢的：Be more ~！勇敢些！

dark / dɑːk / Ⅰ *adj.* ❶黑暗的；暗的：It was nearly ~ when we came home. 我们到家时，天已快黑了。❷黑色的；深色的：She colored the leaves ~ green. 她把树叶涂成深绿色。Ⅱ *n.* 黑夜；黑暗；暗处：She couldn't see anything clearly in the ~. 黑暗中她什么东西也看不清。

darling / ˈdɑːlɪŋ / *n.* [C]亲爱的人；宠儿：My ~！亲爱的！(夫妇、情人、父母与子女间使用的称呼) / Mary is her father's ~. 玛丽是她父亲的心肝宝贝。

darn / dɑːn / Ⅰ *vt.* 织补(织物、破洞等)：~ the holes in one's socks 织补袜子上的破洞 Ⅱ *n.* [C]织补处；补丁：an old sock full of ~s一只满是补丁的旧袜子

dart / dɑːt / *n.* [C] 标枪；飞镖；掷镖游戏：The boys are playing ~s. 男孩们在玩掷镖游戏。/ ~board (掷镖用的)标盘；标靶

dash / dæʃ / Ⅰ *v.* 猛冲；短跑；奔驰；突进：The horse ~ed away. 那匹马飞快地跑开了。Ⅱ *n.* [C] 急奔；猛冲；短跑：The cavalry rode off at a ~. 骑兵队急驰而去。

data / ˈdeɪtə / *n.* (datum 的复数) ❶资料；材料：We collected a lot of ~ for our research. 我们为研究工作收集了很多资料。/ Can you get the first-hand ~ for us? 你能为我们找到一些第一手资料吗？❷数据：~ analysis 数据分析/a ~ band(base) 数据库/a ~ processing system 数据处理系统/ Please give us some raw ~. 请给我们一些原始数据。

database / ˈdeɪtəbeɪs / *n.* [C] 资料库；(计算机)数据库：Very soon he set up a ~ for his own. 他很快建立起了自己的数据库。

date[1] / deɪt / *n.* [C] 枣

date[2] / deɪt / Ⅰ *n.* [C] ❶日期：What is the ~ today? 今天几月几日？/ Your application is out of ~. 你的申请已经过时。❷约会：She called off the ~ with her classmate because of her illness. 因为生病，她取消了与同学的约会。Ⅱ *v.* ❶(给……)注明日期；记日期：That would ~ back to ten years ago. 那事应当追溯到 10 年以前。/ The E-mail is ~d October 12. 那封电子邮件的日期是 10 月 12 日。❷(与……)约会；交往：The two have been dating each other for about half a year. 两人彼此交往已经半年左右。/ **out of** ~ 过时的；不时髦的：The fashion is getting out of ~. 这式样逐渐过时。**up to** ~ 现代的；最新式的；时兴的：You must have up-to-~ ideas. 你的思想必须跟上时代。

datum / ˈdeɪtəm / *n.* (*pl.* data) 资料；数据；情报

daughter / ˈdɔːtə(r) / *n.* [C]女儿：He brought up his ~s in great strictness. 他管教女儿们很严格。/ She is the only ~ of the family. 她是家里的独生女。

daughter-in-law / ˈdɔːtərɪnlɔː/ *n.* [C] (*pl.* daughters-in-law) (儿)媳妇

daunt / dɔːnt / *vt.* ❶威吓；吓倒：Danger did not ~ the hero. 危险并没有吓倒这位英雄。❷使气馁；使胆怯：We had been refused three times but nothing ~ us, we asked again. 我们遭到了三次拒绝，但我们并未灰心丧气，再次提出了要求。

dawdle / ˈdɔː(d)l / *vi.* 闲混，游荡；偷懒，浪费时间：Stop dawdling and help me with these packages! 别偷懒了，快来帮我拿包裹！/~ over breakfast 慢吞吞地吃着早餐

dawn /dɔːn/ *n.* 黎明；曙光；拂晓：Dawn shows a new day. 黎明预示着新的一天开始了。/ **at** ~黎明时：They get up at ~. 他们黎明时分起床。**from ~ till dusk** 从早到晚：They worked very hard from ~ till dusk. 他们从早到晚拼命工作。

day /deɪ/ *n.* ❶[C]一天，一日：What ~ is today? Today is Monday. 今天星期几？今天星期一。/ There are seven ~s in a week. 一个星期有七天。/ She goes to have dinner with her grandmother every other ~. 她每隔一天去陪她的祖母吃晚饭。❷白昼，白天：Most animals look for food in the ~. 大多数动物在白天觅食。❸(*pl.*)日子；时代：Today's children know little about the old ~s. 现在的孩子很少了解旧社会。/I was very happy in my school ~s. 在学生时代我非常快乐。❹节日；纪念日：All Fools' Day, April Fools' Day 愚人节/ Army Day 八一建军节/ Children's Day 儿童节/National Day 国庆节/ **all** ~全天：He worked all (the) ~ (long). 他全天工作。~ **and night** (**night and** ~)日日夜夜：He often works ~ and night. 他时常不分昼夜地工作。**all ~ and all night** 整日整夜 ~ **after** ~每天；一天又一天

daybreak /ˈdeɪbreɪk/ *n.* [U]拂晓，黎明：They started at ~. 他们天一亮就出发了。

daydream /ˈdeɪdriːm/ Ⅰ*n.* [C]白日梦，美梦，幻想；空想：be lost in ~s 想入非非 Ⅱ*vi.* (-dreamed 或-dreamt /-dremt/) 做白日梦，做美梦；幻想；空想：Stop ~ing and get on with your work. 别做白日梦了，快干活吧！/ She ~s about lottery wins. 她幻想着能中彩。

daylight /ˈdeɪlaɪt/ *n.* [U]白昼；日光；黎明：They started before ~. 他们黎明前出发。

daytime /ˈdeɪtaɪm/ Ⅰ*n.* [U]白天，白昼；日间：in the ~ 在白天 Ⅱ*adj.* (只作定语)白天(昼)的；日间的；白天发生的：~ classes 白天的课程

daze /deɪz/ Ⅰ*vt.* ❶使发昏，使呆住；使茫然：A blow on the head ~d him. 当头一击把他打晕了过去。❷使目眩，使眼花缭乱：The splendour of the palace ~d her. 这座富丽堂皇的宫殿使她眼花缭乱，目不暇接。Ⅱ*n.* [C]晕眩；恍惚；茫然，迷乱

dazzle /ˈdæzl/ Ⅰ*vt.* ❶(强光等)使目眩，使眼花；刺(目)，耀(眼)：The sun shone clear, and the reflection ~d our eyes. 那时烈日当空，反光使我们睁不开眼。/Don't drive with full headlights on a busy road or you'll ~ other drivers. 在繁忙的道路上开车不要打足车前灯光，不然会使其他开车的人眼发花的。❷使晕眩；使赞叹不已，使惊奇；使倾倒：He was ~d by the success of his first book. 他的处女作的成功冲昏了他的头脑。/She was ~d by his wit. 她为他的聪慧才智倾倒。Ⅱ*n.* [U] ❶耀眼的光，灿烂的光辉；耀眼物；令人赞叹的东西：the ~ of powerful electric lights 大功率电灯耀眼的光 ❷眩目，闪耀 ❸昏眩，迷乱：the ~ of fame 被名誉迷惑 派 dazzling *adj.*

dead /ded/ *adj.* 死的；无生命的：The cat has been ~ for 3 days. 那只猫已死三天了。/ This street is ~ at night. 这条街晚上寂静无声。

deadline /ˈdedlaɪn/ *n.* [C]最后期限；极限：I must finish the article within two days to meet the ~. 我必须在两天内写完这篇文章以赶上截止日期。

D

deadlock /ˈdedlɒk/ *n.* 僵持；僵局：The match was at a ~. 比赛处于僵持之中。/ In order to break the ~, he began to speak slowly. 为了打破僵局，他开始发言。

deadly /ˈdedli/ *adj.* 致命的：Fog is the sailor's deadly enemy. 雾是航海者致命的敌人。

deaf /def/ *adj.* 聋的；不愿听的：He is ~ in (of) one ear. 他一只耳朵聋了。/ He was ~ to any advice. 他听不进任何劝告。

deafen /ˈdef(ə)n/ *vt.* ❶使聋；使听不见：A hard blow on the ear ~ed him for life. 一记重重的耳光使他终生成了聋子。❷把……震聋；把……震昏：A sudden explosion ~ed us all for a moment. 突然的爆炸声令我们失聪了好一阵。❸淹没；压倒(声音)：The birds were often ~ed to silence with her song. 她的歌声一起，小鸟儿常常会悄无声息。派 deafening *adj.*

deal /diːl/ Ⅰ*v.* (dealt/delt/, dealt) ❶处理，应付(与 with 连用)：She can ~ properly with all kinds of complicated situations. 她能恰当地应付各种复杂的局面。❷分发；分配；发牌：The apples must be dealt out fairly. 这些苹果必须公平分配。❸做买卖：We've dealt with that firm for many years. 我们和那家公司做买卖多年了。Ⅱ*n.* ❶大量；许多：She spent a great ~ of money on clothes. 她把大量的钱花在买衣服上。❷交易；协议：He made a ~ with the company. 他和那家公司做生意。

dealer /ˈdiːlə(r)/ *n.* [C] 商人；贩子：a car ~ 汽车商/a real estate ~ 房地产商/ a special sales ~ 特约经销商/ In order to save money, he often buys goods from a wholesale ~. 为了省钱，他常常从批发商处购买商品。

dealing /ˈdiːlɪŋ/ *n.* [C]交易；商业往来：a ~ in stock and shares 股票交易/ a fair ~ 公平交易/ black-market ~s 黑市交易/ busi-ness (commercial) ~s 商业来往

dean /diːn/ *n.* [C](大学的)学院院长，教务长，系主任：His father is ~ of a university. 他父亲是一所大学的教务长。

dear /dɪə(r)/ Ⅰ*adj.* ❶亲爱的；可爱的：My ~ daughter is waiting for me at the gate. 我亲爱的女儿正在门口等我。❷昂贵的：This coat seems rather ~. 这件上衣看起来相当昂贵。Ⅱ*int.* 哎呀(表示焦急、伤心或惊奇) Ⅲ*adv.* 昂贵地；高价地：He sells his goods very ~. 他的货物卖得很贵。派 dearly *adv.*

death /deθ/ *n.* 死；死亡：Death comes to all men. 人皆有死。/ The criminal was shot to ~. 罪犯被击毙。

deathly /ˈdeθli/ Ⅰ*adj.* ❶极度的，大的；剧烈的，强烈的 ❷死一般的：a ~ silence 死寂 Ⅱ*adv.* ❶死一般地：The sick man grew ~ pale. 病人变得毫无血色，苍白得吓人。❷极其，非常；全然，完全，彻底：She felt ~ cold. 她觉得冷极了。

debase /dɪˈbeɪs/ *vt.* ❶降低(质量、价值等)；使(货币等)贬值：Money has been heavily ~d in the last ten years. 在过去的10年里，货币大大地贬值了。❷贬低(尊严、身份、人格等)：~ oneself for money 为金钱而卑躬屈膝

debate /dɪˈbeɪt/ Ⅰ*v.* 争论，辩论；讨论：The subject was hotly ~d. 这个问题曾

被激烈地辩论过。Ⅱ *n.* 争论；辩论；讨论：After a heated ～，they came to an agreement. 经过激烈辩论，他们达成了一致意见。

debit / ˈdebɪt / Ⅰ *n.* [C] ❶ 借方；借记；借人 ❷借项；借项总金额 Ⅱ *vt.* 把……记入账户的借方；记入(账户)的借方；记入(某人)账户的借方

debt / det / *n.* [C]债务；欠款：He spent little money until his ～s were paid off. 在债还完之前他很少花钱。/ **in** ～ 欠债：He is over head and ears in ～. 他债台高筑。**out of** ～ 不欠债：Out of ～，out of danger. 无债一身轻。**have (get into, run into, fall into)** ～ 借债，负债：It's easier to get into ～ than get out of it. 借债容易还债难。**pay (back) the** ～ 偿还债务：He was unable to pay his ～s. 他无力还债。

decade / ˈdekeɪd / *n.* [C]十年：Our school was founded there ～s ago. 我们学校是三十年前建立的。

decadent / ˈdekədənt / *adj.* 衰落的，衰败的，沦丧的；堕落的；颓废的：a ～ civilization 衰落的文明/That hat makes you look rather ～. 戴了那顶帽子使你显得非常萎靡不振。

decay / dɪˈkeɪ / *v.* 腐烂；腐朽；衰退：Too much sweet ～s children's teeth. 吃过多甜食会使小孩牙齿腐坏。/ The wooden door of his room began to ～. 他房间的木门开始腐烂了。派 decayed *adj.*

deceit / dɪˈsiːt / *n.* ❶[U]欺诈，欺骗：practice ～ against customers 对消费者行骗/She is incapable of ～. 她是绝不会骗人的。❷[C]欺骗行为；骗人的话；诡计，骗术：the con man's various ～s 那个骗子的种种诡计

deceive / dɪˈsiːv / *vt.* 欺骗；使弄错：He has entirely ～d us. 他完全欺骗了我们。/ ～**sb. into doing sth.** 骗某人做某事：We were ～d into buying that house. 我们受骗买下了那幢房子。

decelerate / diːˈseləˌreɪt / *vt.* 降低……的速度，使减速，使减缓：efforts to ～ inflation 降低通货膨胀的种种努力/He ～d the truck. 他使卡车减速。

December / dɪˈsembə(r) / *n.* 十二月(略作 Dec.)

decent / ˈdiːsnt / *adj.* 体面的；正派的；得体的；合乎礼仪的：She is always in ～ clothes. 她总是穿着得体。

decibel / ˈdesɪˌbel / *n.* [C]分贝(表示声音强度和功率比的单位，略作 dB，db)：Most people speak in a range between 45 and 75 ～. 大多数人讲话时的声音强度在 45 至 75 分贝之间。

decide / dɪˈsaɪd / *v.* 下决心；决定：She ～d to go. 她决定去。/ I ～ on having my holiday next month. 我决定下月休假。

decided / dɪˈsaɪdɪd/ *adj.* ❶明显的，明白的；明确的，确实的：a ～ change for the better 明显好转 / a ～ difference between black and white 黑白之间泾渭分明 ❷(人)下定决心的，坚决的；坚毅的，坚定的：a girl of ～ character 性格坚毅的女孩子/ I won't go; I'm quite ～ about it. 我可不去；对这事儿我是说一不二的。派 decidedly *adv.*

decimal / ˈdesɪməl / *adj.* 小数的；十进制的；以十为基础的：～ fraction 小数/ a ～ point 小数点/ a ～ system 十进制

decision / dɪˈsɪʒən / *n.* 决定；决议；决心：They passed the ～ at the meeting. 他们在会上通过了那项决议。/ **make(came to, arrive at) a** ～ 做出决定：I made (came to) a ～ to accept the job after the debate. 经过争论，我决定接受这项

D

工作。/ We'd better arrive at a ~ at once. 我们最好马上做出决定。

decisive /dɪˈsaɪsɪv/ *adj.* ❶决定性的:a ~ factor 决定性因素/ a ~ battle 决定性的战役 ❷果断的;明确的:Please give us a ~ reply as soon as possible. 请尽快给我们一个明确的答复。派 decisively *adv.*

deck /dek/ *n.* [C] 甲板

declaim /dɪˈkleɪm/ *vt.* 慷慨陈词;激辩:I wish you wouldn't ~ all the time. 我希望你说话不要总是这样慷慨激昂的样子。/Antony ~ed over the body of Caesar. 安东尼面对恺撒的遗体慷慨陈词。

declaration /ˌdekləˈreɪʃn/ *n.* ❶宣告,宣布;宣言 ❷(关税的)申报

declare /dɪˈkleə(r)/ *v.* ❶声称,声明;宣布,公布:He ~d that it was true. 他宣布这是真的。/ The war was ~d over. 战争宣告结束。❷(向税务机关、海关等)申报:Do you have anything to ~? 你有什么要报税的吗?

decline /dɪˈklaɪn/ *v.* ❶拒绝;谢绝:He ~d the invitation. 他辞谢了邀请。/ I invited her to dine, but she ~d. 我请她吃饭,可她婉言谢绝了。❷倾斜;衰落;下跌:The sun ~d toward the west. 太阳已西斜。/ His mother's health is declining. 他母亲的健康状况越来越差。/ The prices of daily necessities are declining. 日常用品的价格在下降。

decompose /ˌdiːkəmˈpəʊz/ *v.* ❶(使)分解;(使分离):~ a chemical compound 分解化合物 ❷(使)腐烂,(使)腐败:The old fruits and vegetables ~ quickly in the heat. 在热天,不新鲜的水果和蔬菜烂得快。

decorate /ˈdekəreɪt/ *vt.* 装饰,装潢;布置:The hall is ~d with colorful balloons. 礼堂装饰有五颜六色的气球。/ It cost him about 8,000 yuan to ~ his room. 他花了 8 000 元装修房间。

decoration /ˌdekəˈreɪʃn/ *n.* ❶装饰,装潢 ❷[C](常用 *pl.*)装饰物,装饰品

decrease Ⅰ /dɪˈkriːs/ *v.* 减少;减小:His interest in this subject gradually ~s. 他对这门学科的兴趣逐渐减弱。/ The number of traffic accidents has ~d greatly in this district. 这个地区的交通事故次数已极大减少。Ⅱ /ˈdiːkriːs/ *n.* 减少;降低:A big ~ in sales caused the store to close. 销售量大减使这家商店倒闭。

decree /dɪˈkriː/ *n.* [C] ❶法令,政令;敕令:issue a ~颁布法令/ignore a ~无视法令 ❷判决;裁定:a divorce ~ 离婚判决

decry /dɪˈkraɪ/ *vt.* (强烈)反对;(公开)批评,(公开)谴责:Nearly 50,000 people took to streets to ~ the resort to arms. 大约 5 万人走上街头,反对诉诸武力。

dedicate /ˈdedɪkeɪt/ *vt.* 奉献;献身:~ **oneself to** 献身于;致力于:They ~d themselves to the cause of scientific research. 他们献身于科研事业。

dedication /ˌdedɪˈkeɪʃən/ *n.* ❶[U]献身(精神);热衷;供奉;潜心:I admired her ~. 我仰慕她对事业的献身精神。/ He was given a medal for ~ to duty. 他因恪尽职守而被授予一枚奖章。❷[C](书籍等的)献词,题词:We can put the ~ at the top of the page. 我们可以在此页的上方题词。❸[C]奉献(典礼),供奉(典礼);落成典礼(仪式)

deduce /dɪˈdjuːs/ *vt.* 演绎,推断,推论:~ a conclusion from premises 从前提推

断出结论/From the height of the sun, I ~ that it was about ten o'clock. 我从太阳的高度推测出时间大约是 10 点钟。

deduct /dɪˈdʌkt/ *vt.* 减去，扣除：The teacher ~ed fifteen marks for his misspelling. 因拼法错误，老师扣了他 15 分。/Income tax is normally ~ed from a person's wages. 一般来说，所得税是从个人的工资收入中扣除。

deduction /dɪˈdʌkʃən/ *n.* ❶[U]减去，扣除：No ~ from one's pay is made for absence due to illness. 凡属病假一律不扣工资。❷[C]减免额，扣除数：a ~ of 50 dollars 扣除 50 美元 / What ~ will you give me if I pay cash? 如果我付现金，你给我打多少折扣？❸演绎(法)；推论，推断：His astute ~ was worthy of Sherlock Holmes. 他的推断精辟敏锐简直不亚于福尔摩斯。❹(用演绎法推得的)推理，结论：What ~s do you make from this evidence? 你从这个证词中可推断出哪些结论？

deed /diːd/ *n.* [C]行为；事迹：Their ~s did not agree with their words. 他们言行不一致。/ He did good ~s for passengers on the train. 他在火车上为乘客做好事。/ **in** ~ 事实上；真正地：A friend in need is a friend in ~. 患难之交是真交。

deep /diːp/ *adj.* ❶深的；深厚的：The well is ten feet ~. 这口井 10 英尺深。❷深情的；深切的：The teacher showed ~ concern for her pupils. 这位老师深切地关心自己的学生。/ **be ~ in** 专心于；全神贯注于：He is ~ in reading. 他正在专心读书。派 deeply *adv.*

deepen /ˈdiːpən/ *v.* ❶(使)变深；(使)深化：Do I need to ~ the hole any further? 我得把这个坑挖得更深些吗？❷(使)加深；(使)强烈；(使)变浓：Its failure would only ~ the diplomatic stalemate. 这次失败只会加深外交上的僵局。/ The color needs to be ~ed. 这颜色需要加浓。

D

deer /dɪə(r)/ *n.* [C](*pl.* deer)鹿

deface /dɪˈfeɪs/ *vt.* 毁坏……的容貌；毁坏，损害：His advertisements painted on rocks ~d the land scape. 他画在岩石上的广告画大煞风景。/He was arrested for defacing the War Memorial. 他因涂损战争纪念碑而被捕。

defame /dɪˈfeɪm/ *vt.* 破坏……的声誉；说……的坏语；诋毁，排谤，中伤：She accused him of defaming her good name. 她控告他诽谤她的好名声。

default /dɪˈfɔːlt/ Ⅰ *n.* [U] ❶(职责、义务等的)未履行：He lost his job by sheer ~ of duty. 他完全由于疏于职守而丢了工作。❷弃权：He progressed into the finals because of his opponent's ~. 由于对手的弃权，他进入了决赛。❸(计算机)系统设定(值)，系统预置；默认设定：~ program 系统设定程序 Ⅱ *vi.* ❶不履行义务；不履行债务，拖欠：~ on one's commitments 违背承诺/A party to the contract ~ed. 合同的一方没有履行合同。❷弃权，放弃比赛；因弃权而输掉：She ~ed in the tennis tournament. 她在网球锦标赛中弃权。

defeat /dɪˈfiːt/ Ⅰ *vt.* 击败；使受挫折：Our school team ~ed the team of the Second Middle School at football. 我校足球队在比赛中打败了二中的球队。Ⅱ *n.* 失败；击败：He is a man who knows no ~. 他是个不服输的人。

defect /dɪˈfekt/ *n.* [C]缺点；缺陷：The little girl has an inborn ~ in eyesight. 小女孩先天视力不足。

D

defective /dɪˈfektɪv/ *adj.* 有缺陷的,缺损的;有缺点的,有瑕疵的,有毛病的:a watch with ~ parts 一块许多零件有毛病的手表 / He has ~ hearing (vision). 他的听觉(视觉)有缺陷。/ He is mentally ~. 他心智不健全。派 defectively *adv.*;defectiveness *n.*

defence(-se) /dɪˈfens/ *n.* [U] 保卫;防御:The soldiers built up a strong ~. 战士们筑起了坚固的防御工事。

defend /dɪˈfend/ *vt.* 保卫;防守:The country is ~ed with a strong navy. 这个国家有强大的海军保卫。/~ **from** 保护,保卫;使不受……伤害:The bank was built to ~ the road from being washed away by the floods. 建造这座堤是为了保护这条路不被洪水冲垮。派 defender *n.*

defendant /dɪˈfendənt/ *n.* [C]被告:The ~ prevailed in the case. 被告在本案中胜诉。

defensive /dɪˈfensɪv/ *adj.* ❶防御(性)的;保卫(性)的:~ warfare 防御战/~ armament weapons 防御性武器/a ~ position 防御阵地 ❷防守的;(人的态度等)防备的,自卫的:a ~ attitude 守势/ The expression on his face was resentful and ~. 他的神色含着怨恨,如临大敌似的。

defer /dɪˈfɜː(r)/ *vt.* (-ferred;-ferring) 使推迟,使延期;拖延:As no one could agree, the decision was ~red. 由于大家都不同意,决定迟迟未能做出。

defiance /dɪˈfaɪəns/ *n.* [U] ❶蔑视,藐视;反抗,违抗:a ~ of regulations 违反规章制度/He shouted ~ at the policeman,他向警察大叫大嚷表示反抗。/ His refusal amounted to ~. 他的拒绝简直就是瞧不起人。❷挑战,挑衅:an action of ~ against nature 向大自然挑战的行动/ **in ~ of** 违抗;不顾,无视:He acted in ~ of public opinion. 他不顾公众舆论,仍旧我行我素。

deficiency /dɪˈfɪʃ(ə)nsi/ *n.* ❶缺少,短缺,匮乏,不足:deficiencies in personnel and equipment 人员和设备的匮乏/ She was vitamin ~. 她身体里缺乏维生素。❷[C]缺点;缺陷;毛病:His deficiencies for the job are only too clear. 对这项工作来说,他的不足之处是显而易见的。

deficient /dɪˈfɪʃ(ə)nt/ *adj.* ❶缺少的;缺乏的,匮乏的,不足的:a ~ supply of nutrients 营养供应不足 ❷有缺陷的,有缺点的:a mentally ~ person 心理(或智力)上有缺陷的人/Our knowledge of the subject is ~. 我们对该课题的了解是不全面的。

deficit /ˈdefɪsɪt,dɪˈfɪsɪt/ *n.* ❶[C]不足额;短缺额:a ~ of £250 250 英镑的缺额/trade ~s 贸易逆差 ❷赤字;逆差;亏空;亏损:The country has a ~ on its balance of payments. 该国收支上出现了赤字。

define /dɪˈfaɪn/ *vt.* ❶给……下定义,释(义);解释:The dictionary not only ~s words but also shows the user how to use them. 这部词典不但解释词义,而且告诉使用者如何使用词汇。❷详解,详述;使明确,使清楚:~s one's position on a subject 表明自己在某个问题上的立场/Please listen while I ~ your duties. 请听我详细说明你的任务。❸确定……的界线,限定:The boundary between the two countries still remains to be ~d. 这两个国家之间的边界尚待划定。

definite /ˈdefɪnət/ *adj.* 明确的;肯定的;限定的:His attitude was not very ~ at that time. 那时他的态度还不很明确。/ Please give me a ~ answer soon. 请尽快给我一个肯定的答复。派 definitely *adv.*

definition /ˌdefɪˈnɪʃn/ *n.* 定义；解释：He looked up the ~ of the difficult word in a dictionary. 他在字典里查那个难词的定义。

deflation /dɪˈfleɪʃən/ *n.* [U] ❶泄气，灰心丧气：I detected a slight air of ~ after the ceremony. 仪式后我觉察出有一丝灰心丧气的气氛。❷通货紧缩

deflect /dɪˈflekt/ *v.* ❶使偏斜；使弯曲：The ball hit one of the defenders and was ~ed into the net. 那球击中一名防守队员后被弹进了网。❷使偏离，使改道，使转向(与 from 连用)：~ a stream from its original course 使河流改道 / The wind ~ed the arrow's path. 风力使箭偏离了飞行方向。/The missile ~ed from its trajectory. 导弹偏离了它的弹道。

deflection /dɪˈflekʃn/ *n.* ❶偏斜；转向：Strong winds caused some ~ from the plane's charted course. 强烈的风使飞机偏离了原来规定的航线。❷转移；引开：scored on several ~s past the goalie 几次引开守门员而进球得分

deformity /dɪˈfɔːməti/ *n.* [U] 畸形；变形

defrost /dɪˈfrɒst/ *v.* 除霜；解冻：~ a refrigerator 给冰箱除霜/ Mother ~ed some meat for dinner. 妈妈把肉解冻了做晚饭。

deft /deft/ *adj.* 娴熟的；灵巧的；巧妙的：the ~ fingers of pianist 钢琴家灵巧的手指/a ~ performance 技艺娴熟的表演

defy /dɪˈfaɪ/ *vt.* ❶(公然)违抗，反抗；蔑视，藐视：~ public opinion 藐视社公众舆论/I felt Jimmy was waiting for an opportunity to ~ me. 我觉得吉米在等待时机跟我作对。❷激，挑：Defy you to prove that I cheated in the examination. 我倒要看看你能不能证明我考试作过弊。❸经受得起；顶得住：The problem defies all attempts to solve it. 这个难题怎么也解决不了。

D

degrade /dɪˈgreɪd/ *vt.* ❶降级，罢免，罢黜，谪贬：be ~d from public office 被解除公职 ❷使受侮辱；降低(身份等)：films that ~ women 糟践妇女的影片 ❸(化学)使降解

degree /dɪˈgriː/ *n.* ❶[U]程度：The two problems differ from each other in ~ and nature. 这两个问题在程度和性质上都不尽相同。❷[C]度，度数：The highest temperature here is only 28 ~s Centigrade (28℃) in summer. 这里夏天的最高温度只有 28 摄氏度。/ He drew an angle of 30 ~s. 他画了一个 30 度的角。❸[C]学位；学衔：a bachelor's ~ 学士学位/ a doctor's ~ 博士学位/ He received a master's ~ in London in 2006. 2006 年他在伦敦获得硕士学位。

dehydrate /diːˈhaɪdreɪt/ *vt.* 将(食品等)脱水，使干燥；使(身体等)失水(或缺水)；使极度口渴：Many vegetables are ~d in order to preserve. 许多蔬菜都做脱水处理以便保存。/ People can become ~d from not drinking enough fluid. 人们会因为饮水不足而变得极度口渴。

delay /dɪˈleɪ/ Ⅰ *v.* 推迟；延误：I ~ed answering you owing to pressure of work. 我因工作忙没有及时答复你。/ The train was ~ed by a heavy snow. 火车因大雪误点了。/ We will ~ the meeting for a week. 我们将把会议推迟一个星期。Ⅱ*n.* 耽搁；延误：After a ~ of one hour, we continued our journey. 耽搁一个小时之后，我们又继续旅行了。

D

delegate /ˈdelɪgət/ *n.* [C]代表；委员；特派员：a ~ to a conference 会议代表/ an official ~ 正式(官方)代表/ a chief ~ 首席代表/ a ~ without power to vote 列席代表/ They appointed a ~ to the congress. 他们派了一名代表参加大会。

delegation /ˌdelɪˈgeɪʃn/ *n.* 代表团：They sent a ~ to the United Nations. 他们向联合国派出自己的代表团。

delete /dɪˈliːt/ *vt.* 删掉；擦掉：He saw that the teacher ~d his name from the list. 他看到老师从名单上删掉了他的名字。

deliberate /dɪˈlɪbərət/ Ⅰ *adj.* ❶故意的，存心的，蓄意的：a ~ attempt to injure sb. 对某人的故意伤害/He wondered if her silence was ~. 他疑惑她是否故意缄默不语。❷从容的，慢条斯理的，悠闲的：Jane has a slow, ~ way of talking. 简讲起话来总是慢条斯理，不慌不忙。Ⅱ *v.* 仔细考虑，斟酌：They are deliberating what to do next. 他们正在考虑下一步做什么。/He is slow to answer, deliberating over each question. 他总是仔细考虑每一个问题，从不轻易作答。派 deliberately *adv.*

deliberation /dɪˌlɪbəˈreɪʃən/ *n.* ❶深思熟虑，斟酌，细想；研究：After long ~, I decided not to go. 考虑良久，我还是决定不去了。❷审议，评议；讨论，辩论：The board of directors held their ~ in the conference room. 董事会在会议室内开会审议。❸[U]谨慎，审慎；从容：The hunter aimed his gun with great ~. 猎人不慌不忙地用枪瞄准。

delicacy /ˈdelɪkəsi/ *n.* ❶[U]精致，精美；优雅，雅致：the ~ of lace 花边的精美 ❷[U]柔软；细嫩；娇美：the ~ of her features 她的绰约多姿 ❸[C]美味，佳肴：the delicacies of the season 时令珍馐美味 ❹[U]纤弱，娇弱：the ~ of her health 她身体的纤弱

delicate /ˈdelɪkət/ *adj.* ❶精致的，精美的；优雅的，雅致的：a ~ pattern on the wallpaper 壁纸上的精美图案 ❷(光、色等)柔和的；淡(雅)的：a ~ shade of pink 淡粉红色 ❸(食物)鲜美的，精淡可口的；(气味)清淡的：~ food 清淡可口的食物/Roses have a ~ fragrance. 玫瑰散发出一股幽幽的清香。❹脆的，易碎的；易损坏的；娇贵的：~ procelain 易碎的瓷器/~ flowers 娇嫩的鲜花 ❺灵敏的，敏锐的；敏感的；精密的：a ~ sense of hearing 灵敏的听觉/~ scientific instruments 精密的科学仪器 派 delicately *adv.*

delicious /dɪˈlɪʃəs/ *adj.* 美味的；可口的：Sichuan food is ~. 四川菜很好吃。

delight /dɪˈlaɪt/ Ⅰ *n.* [U] 欢喜；高兴：To the boy's ~, his father bought him a new computer. 令这男孩高兴的是，父亲给他买了一台新的计算机。/ **take ~ in** 喜爱，以……为乐：He takes much ~ in his studies. 他从学习中得到极大乐趣。Ⅱ *v.* 使高兴；感到高兴：He was ~ed at (by) the news. 听到这个消息他很高兴。/ I ~ed in doing good. 我以做好事为乐。派 delightful *adj.*

deliver /dɪˈlɪvə(r)/ *vt.* ❶递送；移交：表达，讲述：The thief was ~ed into the police. 小偷被交给了警察。❷表达；讲述：She ~ed herself well. 她表达能力不错。/He ~ed an address at the opening ceremony. 他在开幕式上致词。❸分

娩;接生:The young mother ~ed a boy. 这位年轻妈妈生了一个男孩。

delivery /dɪˈlɪvəri/ *n.* ❶投递,送交;分送;传送;运载:There are two parcel deliveries a week. 每周递送两次包裹。/ The next ~ is at 2 o'clock. 下次投递时间是 2 点。❷[C]投递的邮件;分送(或待送)的货物:We had a big ~ of mail today. 今天我们投递了大量邮件。❸(常用单数)讲话,演讲;演讲风格(或方式);表演,扮演:a speaker's excellent ~ 演讲者出色的演讲风格 / His ~ was clear and pleasant to listen to. 他的演说吐字清晰,悦耳动听。❹分娩,临盆:a natural ~ 自然分娩

delta /ˈdeltə/ *n.* [C](河流的)三角洲:the Yangtze (=Changjiang) Delta 长江三角洲

demand /dɪˈmɑːnd/ Ⅰ *v.* 要求;需要:He ~ed that he should be told everything. 他要求将一切都告诉他。/ Her aunt told her that the work ~ed care and patience. 婶婶告诉她做那项工作需要细心和耐心。Ⅱ *n.* 要求;需求:The supply of food does not meet the ~ in that district. 在那个地区食品供不应求。

demanding /dɪˈmɑːndɪŋ/ *adj.* 要求高的;需要技能的;费劲的:a ~ but worthwhile job 费力但值得一干的工作/The school is a ~ one. 那学校是所要求很严格的学校。

demean /dɪˈmiːn/ *vt.* 有损……的尊严,降低……的身份;有辱……的人格:Manual work ennobles rather than ~s us. 体力工作并不有损我们的尊严,反而会使我们的精神升华。

democracy /dɪˈmɒkrəsi/ *n.* [U] ❶民主:the sense of ~ 民主意识/ socialist ~ 社会主义民主 ❷民主国家;民主制:They are determined to establish a ~ for their own. 他们决心建立一个自己的民主国家。

democrat /ˈdeməkræt/ *n.* [C] 民主主义者;民主人士

democratic /ˌdeməˈkrætɪk/ *adj.* 民主的;民主政体的:~ election 民主选举 / ~ consultation 民主协商 / ~ parties 民主党派

democratize /dɪˈmɒkrətaɪz/ *v.* (使)民主化

demographer /dɪˈmɒgrəfə(r)/ *n.* [C]人口学家

demography /dɪˈmɒgrəfi/ *n.* [U]人口学;人口统计(学)

demolish /dɪˈmɒlɪʃ/ *vt.* ❶拆除(建筑物等);摧毁;爆破:The fire ~ed the area. 那场大火把这地区烧成一片废墟。❷终止,撤销(机构等);废除(制度等):~ a commission 撤销委员会/~ a feudal agrarian system 废除封建土地所有制 ❸推翻;驳倒(论点、理论等):~ a theory 推翻一种理论

demonstrate /ˈdemənstreɪt/ *v.* ❶表明;证明:He cited a lot of examples to ~ the truth of his theory. 他引用了大量事例证明他的理论是正确的。❷示范;演示:The salesman ~d the new washing-machine to the customer. 销售人员向顾客演示新型洗衣机如何使用。❸示威:The citizens ~d against the rising of taxes. 市民们示威游行反对提高税收。

demoralize /dɪˈmɒrəˌlaɪz/ *vt.* 使士气低落;使沮丧;使……失去勇气;使……丧失纪律:the political tactics to ~ or win over the enemy during fighting 在战争中瓦解或争取敌人的政治战术 / They were ~d by the completeness of their defeat. 这次彻底的失败把他们弄得意

志消沉。派 demoralization *n.*

den / den / *n.* [C] ❶兽穴(或窝);洞穴:The bear's ~ was in a cave. 那头熊的窝做在洞中。❷私室,密室;书斋

denial / dɪˈnaɪəl / *n.* ❶否认;反对:give a ~ to the rumour 辟谣/The colonel issued a ~ of any wrongdoing. 那位上校发表声明否认他干过任何坏事。❷[U]拒绝(给予),回绝:His ~ of petition caused the students to rebel. 他不准学生们请假,这激起了他们的反抗。

denizen / ˈdenɪzən/ *n.* [C](生活在特定地方的)栖息者,居民,居住者:~s of the forest 森林植物 / the finny ~s of the deep 深海鱼类 / the ~s of the inner cities 旧城区居民

denote / dɪˈnəʊt / *vt.* ❶预示,是……的征兆;标志着:A smile often ~s pleasure. 微笑常常表示愉悦。/Frost ~s the coming of winter. 霜冻现象预示冬季的来临。❷本义为,意思是:The word "stool"~s a small chair without a back. "凳子"一词的本义是没有靠背的小椅子。❸(符号等)代表,表示:In algebra, the sing "*x*" usually ~s an unknown quantity. 在代数里,符号 *x* 常常表示未知数。

denounce / dɪˈnaʊns / *vt.* (公开)谴责,斥责,指责:Smith ~s drug abuse roundly in his speeches. 史密斯在发言中痛斥滥用毒品的行为。/The new government ~d the old treaty as a mere scrap of paper. 新政府谴责旧条约不过是一纸空文而已。

demonstration / ˌdemənˈstreɪʃn / *n.* ❶证明;论证 ❷示范 ❸示威;游行

dense / dens / *adj.* 稠密的;密集的:The crowd was so ~ that we could hardly move. 人群密集,我们几乎不能动弹。

density / ˈdensəti / *n.* [U] 密集;浓密;密度:The population ~ of this area is great. 这个地区的人口密度很大。

dental / ˈdentəl/ *adj.* (只作定语) ❶牙(齿)的:~ bed (pad) 牙床 / ~ care 牙齿保健 / ~ health 口腔卫生 ❷牙科的,牙医的:undergo a ~ operation 做牙科手术 / ~ instruments 牙科医疗器械

dentist / ˈdentɪst / *n.* [C] 牙科医生;She went to see a ~ last Friday. 上周五她去看牙病。

deny / dɪˈnaɪ / *vt.* 否认;拒绝:The man denied knowing the truth. 那人不承认他知道事实的真相。/ She failed in the examination and denied herself to all visitors. 她考试失败,谢绝会见所有来客。

depart / dɪˈpɑːt/ *vi.* ❶出发,起程;离开,离去:As soon as he ~ed, I telephoned James. 他一出发,我就打电话告诉了詹姆斯。/ The flight ~s at 6 pm. 这次航班下午 6 点起飞。/ A number of us ~ for (on) an afternoon outing. 我们几个人下午出门作短途郊游。❷背离,违反(与 from 连用):~ from evil, and do good 改恶从善/ The new method ~s from the old in several respects. 这种新方法在好几个方面与原先的截然不同。❸去世:~ from life 去世

department / dɪˈpɑːtmənt / *n.* [C] 部;司;局;处;科;系:the Education Department 教育部/ the Health Department 卫生部/the Department of Agriculture 农业部/ the Department of the Treasury 财政部/ the Department of Foreign Languages 外语系/ the Chinese Department 中文系/ a ~ store 百货公司

departure / dɪˈpɑːtʃə(r) / *n.* 离开;出发;

起程：It suddenly rained at his ~. 他出发时突然下起雨来。

depend /dɪˈpend/ *vi.* 依靠；依赖；信任（与 on 连用）：A man's success ~s chiefly on himself. 一个人的成功主要靠自己。/ All ~s on the weather. 一切取决于天气。

dependant /dɪˈpendənt/ *n.* [C] ❶靠别人生活的人 ❷从属；侍从：army ~s 军属/ family ~s 家眷

dependence /dɪˈpendəns/ *n.* [U]依靠；依赖；信任：Young people should reduce economic ~ on their parents gradually. 年轻人应当逐渐减少对父母的经济依赖。

dependent /dɪˈpendənt/ Ⅰ *adj.* 依靠的；依赖的：Most college students are ~ on their parents in our country. 在我国多数大学生依靠父母生活。Ⅱ *n.* [C]受赡养者；从属

deploy /dɪˈplɒɪ/ *vt.* ❶部署，调遣：~ a battery of new missiles 部署一批新式导弹 ❷利用；调动；施展：~ one's resources as efficiently as possible 尽可能有效地利用自己的聪明才智/~ one's argument 施展自己的辩才 派 deployment *n.*

deposit /dɪˈpɒzɪt/ Ⅰ *vt.* ❶沉淀；沉积：The flood ~ed a layer of mud on the ground. 洪水过后地面沉积了一层泥土。❷存放；寄存：He ~ed his suitcase with me. 他把他的手提箱寄放在我处。/ People ~ their money in the bank. 人们把钱存在银行里。Ⅱ *n.* ❶沉积物；矿床 ❷存款：draw out one's ~ 提取存款/ make a large ~ 存入巨款/ a current (fixed) ~ 活期存款（定期存款）

depository /dɪˈpɒzɪt(ə)ri/ *n.* [C]仓库，储藏室，保管处：a ~ for secret government document 政府机要室 / a school board's textbook ~ 学校董事会的教材库

depress /dɪˈpres/ *vt.* ❶沮丧；消沉：The bad weather ~ed her. 坏天气使她情绪低落。❷使不景气：The market is ~ed. 市场萧条。

depressed /dɪˈprest/ *adj.* 压抑的；沮丧的；没精打采的：Don't be ~ about your failure. 别为失败而沮丧。/ She looks ~ because of headache. 因为头疼她看起来没精打采。

depression /dɪˈpreʃn/ *n.* [U]沮丧；消沉；萧条：He is in a state of deep ~ on account of his failure to pass the examination. 他因考试不及格深感沮丧。

deprive /dɪˈpraɪv/ *vt.* 剥夺；使丧失（与 of 连用）：The accident ~d him of his left arm. 那场意外事故使他失去了左臂。/ His death ~d China of one of its greatest poets. 他的逝世使中国失去了一位最伟大的诗人。

depth /depθ/ *n.* [U] 深；深度：An ancient tomb was found at a ~ of 50 feet. 古墓是在 50 英尺深处发现的。/ His thesis shows the ~ of the young scholar. 他的论文体现了年轻学者渊博的学识。

deputation /ˌdepjʊˈteɪʃən/ *n.* [C]代表团：Let us send a ~ to discuss the problem with the Council. 让我们派个代表团去和理事会商讨这个问题吧。

deputy /ˈdepjʊti/ *n.* [C] ❶代理人；代表：He was the ~ while our manager was on vacation. 我们经理休假时由他代理工作。❷副职：a ~ mayor 副市长

derive /dɪˈraɪv/ *v.* 得到；取得；追溯……起源：A lot of English words ~ from Latin. 很多英语词语来源于拉丁语。

descend /dɪ'send/ *vi*. 下降；下来；传给：The sun ~ed behind the hills. 太阳落到山后面去了。/ This house ~ed from my grandfather. 这房子是我祖父传下来的。

descendant(-ent) /dɪ'sendənt/ *n*. [C]子孙；后裔：We are all ~s of the Yellow Emperor. 我们都是炎黄子孙。

descended /dɪ'sendɪd/ *adj*. 为……的后裔，出身于(与 from 连用)：We are ~ from the kings of Ireland. 我们是爱尔兰王室的后裔。

descent /dɪ'sent/ *n*. ❶[C](常用单数)下降；下来；下倾：The plane began its ~ into Beijing. 飞机开始向北京降落。/ The ~ of the hill was quickly completed. 很快就从小山上下来。❷[C]斜坡；坡道：a steep ~ 陡坡 / a gradual ~ to the sea 通向海边的不陡的坡道 ❸[U]血统；世系：an American of Chinese ~ 华裔美国人/ Our boss was British by ~. 我们的上司祖籍英国。

describe /dɪ'skraɪb/ *vt*. 叙述；描述；形容：The landscape was vividly ~d in her composition. 她在作文中生动地描写了这一景色。

description /dɪ'skrɪpʃn/ *n*. 描写；叙述：Can you give me a ~ of your teacher? 你能给我描述一下你们老师的模样吗?

desert[1] /'dezət/ *n*. 荒地；沙漠：the Gobi Desert 戈壁滩/ the Desert of Sahara 撒哈拉沙漠

desert[2] /dɪ'zɜːt/ *vt*. 抛弃；丢弃：He was ~ed by his friends. 他遭朋友抛弃。/ How can a man ~ his wife and children? 一个男人怎么能抛妻离子呢?

deserve /dɪ'zɜːv/ *v*. 值得；应受：The place ~s a visit. 那地方值得一游。

deserved /dɪ'zɜːvd/ *adj*. 应得的，理所应当的：It was a well-~ victory. 那是一场理所应当的大胜仗。

deserving /dɪ'zɜːvɪŋ/ *adj*. ❶有功的，应赏的：A decoration of bravery was awarded to the ~ police officer. 那名立功的警官被授予一枚英勇勋章。❷值得的，该得的；理所应当的：He is ~ of the highest praise for his conduct. 他应该因其所作为而得到最高表彰。

design /dɪ'zaɪn/ Ⅰ*n*. [C] 图样；设计；计划：I think it necessary to carry out our ~ at once. 我认为必须马上执行我们的计划。/ These buildings are after his ~s. 这些大楼是照他的设计建造的。Ⅱ*v*. 计划；谋划；设计；预定：This is a book ~ed mainly for use in middle schools. 这是一本中学阶段使用的书。/ The room is ~ed as a children's playroom. 这房间计划用作儿童娱乐室。

designer /dɪ'zaɪnə(r)/ Ⅰ*n*. [C]设计者，设计师；构思者：a fashion ~ 时装设计师 / an interior ~ 室内装饰设计师 Ⅱ*adj*. (服装等)以设计师命名的；标有设计师姓名的

desirable /dɪ'zaɪərəbl/ *adj*. 合乎需要的；称心的；令人满意的：She wants to find a ~ job in the city. 她想在城里找一份满意的工作。

desire /dɪ'zaɪə(r)/ Ⅰ*v*. 向往；渴望；要求：The children ~d to visit the Summer Palace. 孩子们渴望参观颐和园。/ We ~ a room for the night. 我们希望有个房间过夜。Ⅱ*n*. 愿望；心愿：She has a strong ~ to travel the West Europe. 她极想去西欧旅游。

desk /desk/ *n*. [C]书桌；办公桌；工作台：an information ~ 问询处/ a reception ~ 服务台；接待处/ He was sitting at the ~ when I went in. 我进去时他正在办公。

desktop /ˈdesktɒp/ *adj.* (尤指微型计算机)适合书桌上用的,台式的:a ~ computer 台式计算机

desolate /ˈdesələt/ *adj.* ❶荒芜的;荒凉的;无人烟的:a ~ hillside 光秃秃的山坡/ a ~ industrial landscape 工业凋敝的景象 ❷孤苦无依的,孤凄的:a ~ life 孤独的一生/When her husband died, she was left ~. 丈夫去世后,她孤苦无依。

despair /dɪˈspeə(r)/ Ⅰ *n.* [U]失望;绝望:He gave up the attempt in ~. 他绝望地放弃了尝试。Ⅱ *vi.* 绝望;丧失信心:So long as you help me, I shall never ~. 只要你帮助我,我就不会绝望。

desperate /ˈdespərət/ *adj.* 令人绝望的;拼死的;不顾一切的:He became ~ after his wife's death. 妻子死后他非常绝望。

desperation /ˌdespəˈreɪʃn/ *n.* [U]绝望;冒险;自暴自弃:The death of her son drove her to ~. 失去儿子使她感到绝望。

despise /dɪˈspaɪz/ *vt.* 瞧不起;轻视;蔑视:Don't cheat at the examination, or you'll be ~d by your classmates. 考试不要作弊,否则你的同学会瞧不起你。

despite /dɪˈspaɪt/ *prep.* 不管;尽管:Despite their objections, I will do it just the same. 虽然他们反对,但我照样会去做。

despoil /dɪˈspɒɪl/ *vt.* 掠夺,抢劫;剥夺:The bandits ~ed the villages. 土匪们把一座座村庄洗劫一空。/She fell into evil company and was soon ~ed of her innocence. 她交上了坏朋友,很快她的纯洁天真就无迹可寻了。

dessert /dɪˈzɜːt/ *n.* 甜食,点心;尾餐:I like to have some icecream for ~. 我喜欢吃些冰激凌当作饭后的甜点。

destination /ˌdestɪˈneɪʃn/ *n.* [C]目的地;终点:Where is the ~ of your traveling? 你们旅行的目的地是哪儿?

destiny /ˈdestəni/ *n.* 命运:He believed that he could grasp his own ~. 他相信他能掌握自己的命运。

destroy /dɪˈstrɒɪ/ *vt.* 破坏;摧毁;消灭:The house was ~ed in the big fire. 房子在那场大火中给烧毁了。/ His hope to become a lawyer was ~ed. 他要当一名律师的希望破灭了。

destruction /dɪˈstrʌkʃn/ *n.* [U]破坏;毁灭;消灭:War usually means ~, not construction. 战争通常意味着破坏而不是建设。

detach /dɪˈtætʃ/ *vt.* 使分开,使分离:~ the key from the ring 从钥匙圈上取下钥匙/Please ~ the coupon and send it with your money to the following address. 请撕下购物优惠券,连同你的货款一起寄往下列地址。

detail /ˈdiːteɪl/ *n.* [C]细节;琐碎的事:Every ~ of the plan is important. 这份计划的每个细节都很重要。/ Don't omit a single ~. 不要漏掉任何一个细节。/ **in** ~ 详细地:Tell me what has happened in a few words, don't do in ~. 扼要地告诉我所发生的事,不要讲得过细。

detain /dɪˈteɪn/ *vt.* ❶耽搁,使滞留:contrive to ~ sb. 设法缠住某人 / We were ~ed at customs for two hours. 我们在海关滞留了两个小时。❷拘留,扣押:The police ~ed the suspected thief for questioning. 警察扣留了那个偷窃嫌疑人进行审问。/ He has been ~ed

indefinitely. 他被无限期地扣押起来。
派 detainment *n.*

detect /dɪˈtekt/ *vt.* ❶察觉；发觉：Two pupils helped the police ~ the robber. 两个小学生帮助警察发现了那个抢匪。❷侦察；探测：The machine can ~ the escape of gas. 这台机器可以测出天然气泄漏。

detection /dɪˈtekʃn/ *n.* [U]察觉；发觉；侦察；探测：The thief tried to escape ~ but failed. 小偷试图逃脱，但被发现了。

detective /dɪˈtektɪv/ *n.* [C]侦探；密探：a police ~ 警探/ The film star hired a private ~ to protect him. 那位影星雇了一名私人侦探保护自己。

detector /dɪˈtektə(r)/ *n.* [C]发觉者；探测器：Do you believe a lie ~? 你相信测谎仪吗？/ A smoke ~ is helpful. 烟雾探测器很有用。

determination /dɪˌtɜːmɪˈneɪʃn/ *n.* [U]决定；决心：You must carry out your plan with ~. 你必须坚定不移地实施你的计划。

determine /dɪˈtɜːmɪn/ *v.* 断定；决定；决心：Our plans must be ~d by circumstances. 我们的计划必须视情况而定。

determined /dɪˈtɜːmɪnd/ *adj.* 坚决的；有决心的：We are ~ to go and nothing will stop us. 我们决心去，什么也阻挡不了我们。

detest /dɪˈtest/ *vt.* 憎恶；讨厌：She ~ed having to get up early. 她讨厌早起而又不得不早起。

detour /ˈdiːtʊər/ *n.* [C]绕行的路，迂回路线：make a ~ through the mountains 绕道穿越群山/tread a wide ~ around sb. 对某人退避三舍/He took several ~s before getting the right answer. 他兜了好几个圈子才得到了正确答案。

devalue /diːˈvæljuː/ *vt.* ❶使(货币)贬值：The country ~ed its currency by 10%. 该国使其货币贬值10%。❷降低……的价值：criticism that ~s sb.'s works unjustly 不公正地贬低某人作品的评论 / Time has ~d his stature as a writer. 随着时光的流逝，作为一个作家他早已风光不再。

develop /dɪˈveləp/ *v.* ❶发展；开发：a ~ed country 发达国家/ a ~ing country 发展中国家/ The situation ~ed rapidly. 形势发展迅速。/ The new product they ~ed is welcome. 他们开发的新产品很受欢迎。❷发育；成长：He has ~ed into a strong man. 他长成一个健壮的人。❸显影；冲洗(胶片等)：He went to ~ some films in the darkroom. 他到暗室去冲洗胶卷去了。

development /dɪˈveləpmənt/ *n.* [U]进展；发展：The art received its greatest ~ in that period. 这种艺术在那段时期获得了最大的发展。

deviate /ˈdiːvɪˌeɪt/ *vi.* 偏离；背离(与from连用)：~ from the subject under discussion to minor issues 偏离主题而去讨论许多次要问题/~ from the course of routine 打破常规

device /dɪˈvaɪs/ *n.* [C]设计；装置，设置：They are setting up a new safety ~ in the workshop. 他们正在车间安装一种新的安全装置。

deviser /dɪˈvaɪzə/ *n.* [C]设计者；发明者

devil /ˈdevl/ *n.* [C] 魔鬼；恶人

devise /dɪˈvaɪz/ *vt.* ❶设计；发明：The boy often says that he will ~ a new TV set when he grows up. 小男孩常说他长大了要设计一种新的电视机。❷策划，(精心)设计；想出：The novelist ~d a number of incidents to illustrate the character he had created. 小说家炮制了若干故事来刻画其创造的人物。

devote /dɪˈvəʊt/ *vt*. 专心;献身 /~ **oneself to** 献身于;致力于;专心于:It is wrong to ~ yourself only to amusement. 你只专注于娱乐是不对的。

devoted /dɪˈvəʊtɪd/ *adj*. 热爱的;专心的;忠诚的;忠实的:a ~ friend 忠实的朋友 / **be ~ to** 忠实于;致力于;专心于:We are ~ to our country. 我们忠于我们的国家。/ She is ~ to her studies. 她专心于她的学业。

devotion /dɪˈvəʊʃn/ *n*. [U] 献身;忠诚,忠实:His ~ to the Party is unquestionable. 他对党的赤胆忠心不容置疑。

devout /dɪˈvaʊt/ *adj*. 虔诚的,虔敬的:a ~ Catholic 虔诚的天主教徒/She is sincere, loyal, ~ toward the body, the flesh. 她真挚、忠诚,守身如玉。派 devoutly *adv*.

dew /djuː/ *n*. [U] 露水

diabetes /daɪəˈbiːtiːz/ *n*. [U] 糖尿病

diagnose /ˈdaɪəgnəʊz/ *vt*. 诊断(疾病):The old doctor ~d his illness as flu. 老大夫诊断他患了流感。

diagnosis /ˌdaɪəgˈnəʊsɪs/ *n*. (*pl*. diagnoses) 诊断:I am afraid that the doctor has made an erroneous ~ of her disease. 我担心大夫误诊了她的病。

diagonal /daɪˈægən(ə)l/ Ⅰ *adj*. ❶对角(线)的:a ~ line 对角线/The path is ~ to the edge of the field. 这条小路与田边成对角。❷斜的:a ~ stripe in cloth 布上的一条斜条纹 Ⅱ *n*. [C] ❶对角线 ❷斜线:cut bread on a ~沿对角线切开面包

diagram /ˈdaɪəgræm/ *n*. [C]图解;图表;简图:The young engineer draws ~ well. 那位年轻的工程师绘图很好。

dial /ˈdaɪəl/ Ⅰ *n*. [C]钟(或表)面;标度盘;拨号盘:I cannot see the figures on the ~ clearly. 我看不清楚表面上的数字。Ⅱ *v*. (dialed 或 dialled;dialing 或 dialling) 拨(电话号码);打电话(给……):Mother taught her son how to ~ 110 in case of emergency. 妈妈教儿子如何在紧急时拨打110电话。

dialect /ˈdaɪəlekt/ *n*. [C]方言:The old lady speaks Shanghai ~. 那位老太太讲上海话。

dialog(ue) /ˈdaɪəlɒg/ *n*. 对话:Listen to the ~ and then fill in the blanks. 听对话填空。

diameter /daɪˈæmɪtə(r)/ *n*. [C] 直径

diamond /ˈdaɪəmənd/ *n*. 金刚石;钻石

diary /ˈdaɪəri/ *n*. [C]日记;日记簿:She often keeps a ~ in English. 她时常用英语写日记。/ His travel ~ is very interesting. 他的旅行日记写得很有趣。

dictate /dɪkˈteɪt/ *v*. 听写;口授;口述:Our teacher often ~s to us in class. 上课时老师经常让我们做听写练习。

dictation /dɪkˈteɪʃn/ *n*. 听写:How many mistakes are there in your ~? 你的听写中有多少错误?

dictator /dɪkˈteɪtə(r)/ *n*. [C] ❶独裁者;专制者 ❷口授者

dictatorship /ˌdɪkˈteɪtəʃɪp/ *n*. [U]专政:the people's democratic ~ 人民民主专政

dictionary /ˈdɪkʃənəri/ *n*. [C]字典;词典:look up a word in the ~ 查字典/We can buy convenient electronic dictionaries now. 现在我们能买到各种方便的电子词典了。

die / daɪ / *v.* 死；死亡；灭亡：Plants would ~ without water. 植物无水会枯死。/ ~ **away** 渐渐地消失：The color of the sunset ~d away. 落日的余晖渐渐消失了。~ **from** 因(疾病以外的原因而)死亡：He ~d from overwork (loss of blood, a wound, an accident, drinking too much). 他死于过度劳累(失血，外伤，事故，过量饮酒)。~ **of** 因(病、悲伤、饥饿、营养不良、焦虑、羞愧等)死亡：He ~d of cancer. 他死于癌症。~ **out** 逐渐消失：Many old customs are dying out. 许多旧习俗逐渐消失。

diesel / ˈdiːzl / *n.* [C] 柴油发动机；内燃机

diet / ˈdaɪət / *n.* 食物；饮食：She is on a low-fat ~. 她正在接受低脂肪饮食疗法。/ **go on a** ~节食

differ / ˈdɪfə(r) / *vi.* 不同；相异；有分歧：If you don't agree with me, I'm afraid we shall have to ~. 如果你不同意，恐怕我们只好保留不同的意见了。/ ~ **from** 不同于：I am sorry to ~ from you. 很遗憾，我的看法和你的不同。

difference / ˈdɪfrəns / *n.* 不同；差别；差异；差额：Please tell the ~ between the two. 请说出这两者的差异。/ The ~ between 9 and 4 is 5. 9 和 4 之差为 5。/ There are many ~s between them in character. 他们之间在性格上有很多差异。

different / ˈdɪfrənt / *adj.* 不同的；有差异的；各种的：They are studying in ~ classes. 他们在各自的班上学习。/ The two sisters are ~ in character. 两姐妹性格不同。/ ~ **from** (**to**) **...**与……不同：My house is ~ from yours. 我的房子与你的不同。

differential / ˌdɪfəˈrenʃəl/ Ⅰ *adj.* (只作定语)差别的；区别性的：have ~ taxes for different kinds of people 对不同类型的人征收不同的税额 / She complained of getting ~ treatment at work. 她抱怨在工作中受到歧视。Ⅱ *n.* [C]差别，差异；差额：wide ~s in values between China and the U.S. 中美两国之间价值观念的巨大差异/the price ~ 价格差额

difficult / ˈdɪfɪkəlt / *adj.* 困难的；艰难的；难对付的：~ days 艰难岁月/ He found it ~ to stop smoking. 他发觉戒烟很难。/ The place is ~ to find. 那个地方很难找。

difficulty / ˈdɪfɪkəlti / *n.* 困难；困境：avoid the ~ 回避困难/clear away the ~ 排除困难/They are trying hard to settle the ~. 他们正在竭力解决困难。/ **have much** (**great**) ~ **in doing sth.** 做某件事有困难：I have much ~ in falling to sleep. 我难以入睡。

diffuse[1] / dɪˈfjuːs / *v.* (光、热、气等)扩散，散发；传播：to ~ knowledge 传播知识

diffuse[2] / dɪˈfjuːs / *adj.* 扩散的；啰唆的；冗长的：His speech was too ~ for me to catch his point. 他的讲话冗长，我难以抓住要点。

dig / dɪg / *v.* (dug /dʌg/, dug; digging) ❶挖；掘：The fields need to be dug up. 这些田土需要翻挖。/ The workers dug a tunnel through the mountain. 工人们在山里挖了一条隧道。❷探究：He is ~ging away at his English. 他在刻苦钻研英语。派 digger *n.*

digest Ⅰ / daɪˈdʒest / *v.* 消化；领会，领悟：This food ~s ill (well). 这种食物难(易)消化。/ He read the report for the second time to ~ the important points of it better. 他又读了一遍那份报告，以便能更好地领会其中的要点。

Ⅱ/ ˈdaɪdʒest / *n.* 文摘；摘要：I like to read *Reader's Digest*. 我喜欢看《读者文摘》。

digestion / daɪˈdʒestʃən / *n.* [U]消化；消化力：Rice is easy of ～. 米饭很容易消化。/ Though the old man is over sixty, he has a good ～. 虽然老人六十多岁了，但他的消化力却很强。

digit / ˈdɪdʒɪt / *n.* [C] 阿拉伯数字：The number 2008 contains four ～s. 2008 是个四位数。

digital / ˈdɪdʒɪtl / *adj.* 数字的；数字显示的；记数的：a ～ camera 数码相机/～ display 数字显示/ ～ image processing 数字图像处理 / an optical ～ disk 数字光盘/ a ～ library 数字图书馆

dignified / ˈdɪgnɪˌfaɪd/ *adj.* 庄严的；有尊严的；端庄的；高贵的；高尚的：～ manners 落落大方的举止 / a white-haired ～ gentleman 一位满头白发的高贵绅士 / He is too ～ to do anything so silly. 他一向正经得很，不可能做出如此荒唐的事情来。

dignify / ˈdɪgnɪˌfaɪ / *vt.* 使有尊严；使变得庄严(或崇高)；为……增光，给……添彩：～ sb. 's departure with a ceremony 为某人举行仪式以壮行/The low farmhouse was dignified by the great elms around it. 那低矮的农舍四周有高大的榆树环绕，平添了几分庄严。

dignity / ˈdɪgnəti / *n.* [U]尊严；高贵：lose one's ～ 有失体面(掉价)/ pocket one's ～ 放下架子/ stand on one's ～ 摆架子

dilemma / dɪˈlemə / *n.* [C]困窘；困境；进退两难：To work or to retire put (placed, threw) him in a ～. 究竟是工作还是退休，这使他进退两难。

diligence / ˈdɪlɪdʒəns / *n.* [U]勤勉；勤奋：He succeeded in his studies by ～. 他通过勤奋获得了学习上的成功。

diligent / ˈdɪlɪdʒənt / *adj.* 勤奋的；刻苦的：**be ～ at (in)** 在某方面勤奋：He is ～ at (in) his lessons. 他学习勤奋。派 diligently *adv.*

dilute / dɪˈl(j)uːt, daɪˈl(j)uːt / *vt.* ❶使变稀；使变淡；稀释，冲淡：～ orange juice with 掺水冲淡橙汁/This dye must be ～d in a bowl of water. 这颜料必须放入一碗水中加以稀释。❷削弱；降低；减轻：～ sb. 's influence 削弱某人的影响力/The high price of a new car ～d our enthusiasm for buying one. 一辆新车的价格这么高，大大降低了人们的购买欲。Ⅱ*adj.* 稀释的，冲淡了的：～ whisky 掺水威士忌 派 dilution *n.*

dim / dɪm / *adj.* 昏暗的；暗淡的；朦胧的：The light is ～ here; I can't read anything. 这儿光线太暗，什么也无法读。

dimension / dɪˈmenʃn / *n.* [C]尺寸；长(宽、厚、深)度；大小：They measured the ～s of the room. 他们测出了屋子的大小。

dimensional / dɪˈmenʃənl / *adj.* ……维的；空间的；立体的：a three-～ film 立体电影

diminish / dɪˈmɪnɪʃ/ *vt.* ❶使变小，减小；使变少，减少，缩减；降低：Unforeseen expenses ～ed his savings. 一些始料未及的开销使他的存款锐减。/ Time will not ～ our friendship. 时间不会减弱我们间的友谊。❷降低……的声誉；贬低，贬损：～ sb.'s efforts (achievements) 贬低某人付出的努力(取得的成绩) —*vi.* 变小；变少，缩减；降低：As she turned the knob, the sound ～ed. 她转动旋钮，声音顿时变小了。/ The force of the wind gradually ～ed.

风力逐渐减弱了。派 diminished; diminishing *adj*.

dimple /ˈdɪmpl/ *n*. [C]酒窝,(笑)靥

dine /daɪn/ *vi*. 吃饭;进餐:He often ~s on fish. 他经常吃鱼。/~ **out** 外出吃饭:They decided to ~ out for a change. 他们决定外出吃饭换换口味。/ a dining-room 食堂;饭厅/ a dining car 餐车/ a dining table 餐桌

D

diner /ˈdaɪnə(r)/ *n*. [C] ❶(尤指餐馆里的)就餐者,食客 ❷(火车上的)餐车 ❸(廉价的)小餐馆,小饭店:We had ham and eggs at a roadside ~. 我们在一家路边小餐馆吃了火腿煎鸡蛋。

dingy /ˈdɪndʒi/ *adj*. (地方等)肮脏的,邋遢的;昏暗的:a ~ storeroom 阴暗肮脏的贮藏室/His clothes are getting dingier. 他的衣服越来越脏。

dinner /ˈdaɪnə(r)/ *n*. (一日间的)主餐;正餐:at ~ 在吃饭/ a nice ~ 美餐/ a plain ~ 家常便饭/ a state ~ 国宴/The engineer gave a ~ at a hotel in honor of his old friends. 工程师在宾馆设宴款待他的老朋友们。

dinosaur /ˈdaɪnəsɔː(r)/ *n*. [C]恐龙:Dinosaurs died out many years ago. 恐龙在许多年前就绝种了。

dioxide /daɪˈɒksaɪd/ *n*. 二氧化物:Do you know the difference between carbon ~ and carbon monoxide? 你知道二氧化碳和一氧化碳的区别吗?

dip /dɪp/ *v*. (dipped; dipping) 汲取;浸:The water is too cold to swim, so I'll just ~ a toe in. 水太冷,不能游泳,所以我只将脚打湿了一下。/ I can't give you any opinion because I only ~ped into the book. 我只是稍稍翻阅了一下这本书,不可能给你提供什么意见。

diploma /dɪˈpləʊmə/ *n*. [C](*pl*. diplomas 或 diplomata)毕业文凭;学位证书;执照:~ fad; ~-seeking spree 文凭热/ issue ~s recklessly 滥发文凭/ a ~ for prize 获奖证书/ He gained a ~ in history after four years' study. 在学习四年后他获得了历史学文凭。

diplomacy /dɪˈpləʊməsi/ *n*. [U]外交;交际手段:They settled the problem by using ~. 他们运用外交手段解决了问题。

diplomat /ˈdɪpləmæt/ *n*. [C]外交家;外交官 His father is a career (professional) ~. 他的父亲是一位职业外交官。

diplomatic /ˌdɪpləˈmætɪk/ *adj*. 外交的:The two countries resumed ~ relations three years ago. 三年前两国恢复了外交关系。

direct /dɪˈrekt/ Ⅰ *vt*. 管理;指导;指挥:One's thinking ~s one's actions. 思想指导行动。/ They ~ed me wrongly. 他们给我指错了方向。Ⅱ *adj*. 直接的;坦率的:Please give me a ~ answer. 请明确答复我。Ⅲ *adv*. 直接地:The train goes there ~. 火车直接去那里。

direction /dɪˈrekʃn/ *n*. [C]❶管理;指挥;指导:follow ~s 遵照指示/ obey ~s 服从指挥 ❷(*pl*.)用法说明:~s for use 使用说明 ❸方向;方位:in all ~s 四面八方

directly /dɪˈrektli/ Ⅰ *adv*. 立即;马上;直接:I'll be there ~. 我马上就去那里。Ⅱ *conj*. (=as soon as)(口语)一……就:We get up ~ the bell rings. 铃声一响我们就起床。

director /dɪˈrektə(r)/ *n*. [C] ❶指导者;主管:a music ~ 音乐指挥/ a factory ~ 厂长 ❷董事;理事:The board of ~s made a decision to hire a sales-manager at the meeting. 董事会在会议上决

定雇用一名销售部经理。❸导演：He became a film ~ after graduation. 毕业后他成为一名电影导演。

directory / dɪˈrektəri / *n.* [C]姓名地址录；(电话)号码簿：You can find his new number in the telephone ~. 你可以在电话号码簿上查到他新的电话号码。

dirt / dɜːt / *n.* [U]污物；灰尘：His clothes were covered with ~. 他衣服上满是脏东西。

dirty / ˈdɜːti / *adj.* 脏的；不干净的；下流的；不正当的：His face was ~. 他的脸很脏。/ Dirty books and magazines are not allowed in schools. 学校不允许兜售黄色书刊。

disability / ˌdɪsəˈbɪləti / *n.* ❶[U]无能力；无力；丧失能力：a learning ~学习困难/~ of raising one's head 抬头乏力 ❷[C]伤残，残废：physical ~生理残伤

disable / dɪsˈeɪbl / *vt.* 使丧失能力；使伤残：He was ~d in the war. 他在战争中受伤致残。/~ **sb. from doing sth.** 使某人丧失做某事的能力：An accident ~d him from walking. 一场事故使他再不能走路了。

disadvantage / ˌdɪsədˈvɑːntɪdʒ / *n.* [C]不利条件；损失；缺点：The ~s overweigh advantages. 不利条件超过有利条件。/ His poor English put him at a ~ at the international conference. 他的蹩脚英语使他在国际性会议上处于不利地位。

disagree / ˌdɪsəˈgriː / *vi.* 不同意；不一致；不适宜：Even friends sometimes ~. 即使是朋友，有时也会意见不合。/ I disagree with you about that. 在那个问题上我不同意你的看法。派 disagreement *n.*

disagreeable / ˌdɪsəˈgriːəbl / *adj.* ❶令人不愉快的；不合意的；讨厌的：a ~ job 不合意的工作/His remarks sound very ~ to the ear. 他的话不堪入耳。❷不友善的；脾气坏的，难相处的：be ~ towards sb. 对某人不友好/He gave his answers short and ~. 他只是爱理不理地答个三言两语。派 disagreeably *adv.*

disappear / ˌdɪsəˈpɪə(r) / *vi.* 消失；失踪：He ~ed into the night. 他消失在夜色之中。派 disappearance *n.*

disappoint / ˌdɪsəˈpɔɪnt / *vt.* 使……失望；使落空：What she said ~ed me greatly. 她说的话令我大失所望。/ The failure in the exam ~ed my hope. 考试失败令我的希望落空。/ **be ~ed at (in)** 对……感到失望：I was greatly ~ed in that affair. 那件事令我大失所望。

disappointed / ˌdɪs(ə)ˈpɔɪntɪd/ *adj.* 失望的；沮丧的：He is deeply ~ at (about, with) the result. 他对这一结果大失所望。/ He is bitterly ~ in (with) his son. 他对自己的儿子大为失望。/ Hunt was ~ to learn of ex-aide's underhanded activity. 亨特得知自己的前助手的勾当后很是沮丧。

disappointment / ˌdɪsəˈpɔɪntmənt / *n.* 失望；沮丧：She went home in ~ because she didn't find her lost son. 因为没有找到失踪的儿子，她失望地回到家里。

disapproval / ˌdɪsəˈpruːvl / *n.* [U]不赞成；不准许

disapprove / ˌdɪsəˈpruːv / *v.* 不赞成；不许可；不同意：I wholly ~ of what you say. 我完全不赞成你说的话。

disaster / dɪˈzɑːstə(r) / *n.* 灾难；大祸：an air ~ 空难/ a traffic ~ 车祸/ Only a six-year-old survived the ~. 只有一个六岁大的男孩从那场灾难中活了下来。

disastrous / dɪˈzɑːstrəs / *adj.* 灾难性的；不幸的：The ~ floods caused great losses. 那次特大洪水造成了极大的

损失。

disband / dɪsˈbænd / *vt.* 解散,散伙,解体;遣散:~ an organization 解散一个组织/~ an army 遣散一支军队/The group was ~ed after a few months. 几个月后该团体即被解散。

disc / dɪsk / *n.* (＝disk)[C] 圆盘;磁盘;唱片

discard / dɪsˈkɑːd / *vt.* 扔掉,丢弃,抛弃:~ an empty bottle 丢弃空瓶子/~ one's old friends 抛弃自己的老朋友

discharge Ⅰ/ dɪsˈtʃɑːdʒ / *vt.* ❶允许……离开;释放;解雇:The doctor ~d the patient from the hospital yesterday. 昨天大夫让病人出院了。/ They ~d the accused. 他们释放了那个被告。/ The young worker was ~d for his laziness. 那年轻工人因懒惰而被解雇。❷排出;放出:The big chimneys of the factory ~d thick smoke. 那家工厂的几个大烟囱排出浓烟。/ The stream in front of my home ~s into Changjiang River. 我家前面那条小溪流入长江。Ⅱ/ ˈdɪstʃɑːdʒ / *n.* [U] ❶获准离开;释放:He is over sixty and has got his ~ from the company. 他六十多了,已从公司离退。❷排出;流出:The ~ of dirty water from the factory ruined the crops. 从工厂排放的污水毁了庄稼。

disciple / dɪˈsaɪpl / *n.* [C] 门徒;信徒:a devoted ~ 忠实的信徒

discipline / ˈdɪsəplɪn / *n.* [U] ❶训练;锻炼:He was under perfect ~ when he was young. 他很小就受到良好的训练。❷纪律:the military ~ 军纪/ the Party ~ 党纪/ the school ~ 校纪/ The school is strict in ~. 这所学校纪律严明。

disclaim / dɪsˈkleɪm / *vt.* 否认;不承认:He ~ed all knowledge of the matter. 他矢口否认知道此事。/The planner ~ed responsibility for the consequences. 计划制定者拒绝对此后果承担责任。

disclose / dɪsˈkləʊz / *vt.* 揭发;揭开;泄露:She ~d the information to the press. 她把消息泄露给了新闻界。

disclosure / dɪsˈkləʊʒə(r)/ *n.* ❶[U]公开;透露,泄露;揭发:~ of a secret 泄密 / She made surprising ~s about his past life. 对他昔日的生活她做了多次令人吃惊的揭发。❷[C]揭发的事实;披露的秘闻:~s made in the media 传媒披露的事实/ He was distressed by the newspaper's ~s about his private life. 报纸对他私生活的披露使他忧心忡忡。

disco / ˈdɪskəʊ / *n.* [C] 迪斯科舞厅;迪斯科舞曲:The young couple often go to a ~ on weekends. 那对年轻夫妻常在周末去迪斯科舞厅跳舞。

discolo(u)r / dɪsˈkʌlə(r) / *vt.* & *vi.* (使)褪色;(使)变色;(被)玷污:The heat would ~ the paint. 高温会使油漆褪色。/Many materials fade and ~ of exposed to sunshine. 许多材料一旦暴露在阳光下就会褪色或变色。派 discolo(u)ration *n.*

discomfort / dɪsˈkʌmfət / *n.* [U]不舒适;不安;不自在:One has to bear a little ~ while travelling. 人旅行时总要忍受一点小小的不适。

disconnect / ˌdɪskəˈnekt / *vt.* ❶使断开;切断,割断:~ a television set 切断电视机的电源/If we don't pay the gas bill by Tuesday, we'll be ~ed. 我们如果到星期二还不付煤气费,将被切断煤气供应。❷使不连接,使分离:~ one freight car from another 使货车节节分开

discontent / ˌdɪskənˈtent / *n.* [U] ❶不满:bitter ~强烈的不满/They tried to stir up ~ among the employees. 他们企图在雇员中间挑起不满。❷不满意；不满足：Her ~ with her job is making her parents very unhappy. 她不满意自己的职业，这使她的父母极为不快。

discontinue /ˌdɪskənˈtɪnjuː/ *v.* 中断，终止；中止，停止：~ one's work 停止工作/This evening newspaper will ~ next month. 这份晚报将于下月停刊。

discontinuity /ˌdɪskəntɪˈnjuːɪti/ *n.* ❶[U]不连贯：~ of ideas 不连贯的想法 ❷[C]间断，中断：There has been a ~ in his education. 他曾经辍过学。

discord /ˈdɪskɔːd/ *n.* ❶[U]不一致，不协调：the glaring ~ between the architecture of the two buildings 那两幢大楼在建筑风格上明显的不协调 ❷不和；争吵，纷争：marital ~夫妻不和/stir up ~ in a community 在社区内挑起事端

discount Ⅰ /ˈdɪskaʊnt/ *n.* 折扣：They sold the goods at a ~ of ten percent. 他们打九折出售商品。Ⅱ /dɪsˈkaʊnt/ *vt.* 打折卖：The air tickets are ~ed at 20% now. 现在机票打八折出售。

discourage /dɪsˈkʌrɪdʒ/ *vt.* 阻止，劝阻；使气馁：Don't let one failure ~ you. 别因一次失败而气馁。/~ **sb. from doing sth.** 劝阻某人不做某事：We tried to ~ him from climbing the mountain without a guide. 我们试图劝他无向导不要爬山。

discouragement /dɪsˈkʌrɪdʒmənt/ *n.* ❶[U]泄气，灰心：Some ~ is natural after a defeat. 失败之后有些灰心是人之常情。❷[C]使人泄气的事情：She succeeded despite numerous ~s. 尽管遇到了众多的挫折，她还是成功了。

discover /dɪˈskʌvə(r)/ *vt.* 发现；找到；看出：We often ~ our mistakes when too late. 我们发现自己的错误时，往往为时已晚。派 discoverer *n.*

discovery /dɪˈskʌvəri/ *n.* 发现；发觉；被发现的事物：Man has made many new discoveries in science since 20th century. 20 世纪以来人类在科学上做出了许多新的发现。

discredit /dɪsˈkredɪt/ *vt.* ❶破坏……的名誉；使丢脸：Being caught cheating ~ed the boy among his classmates. 那位学生由于考试作弊被当场抓住而在同学们中间丢尽了脸。/She's been ~ed by the scandal. 她被这起丑闻弄得声誉扫地。❷使不可置信；使不可信赖：The insurance investigator ~ed his claim. 保险公司调查员证实他的索赔要求不可信。

discrepancy /dɪsˈkrepənsi/ *n.* [U]差异；不符，不一致：The ~ in their interests did not the least affect their friendship. 他们之间在兴趣爱好上的差异丝毫不影响他们的友谊。/There is (a) considerable ~ between the two accounts. 这两种说法有很大出入。

discriminate /dɪˈskrɪmɪneɪt/ *v.* ❶歧视；分别对待：Does this factory ~ between men and women? 这家工厂有性别歧视吗? ❷区别；辨别：Can't you ~ good from bad? 难道你不能分辨好坏吗?

discrimination /dɪˌskrɪmɪˈneɪʃn/ *n.* [U] ❶歧视：Sex ~ is not allowed. 性别歧视是不允许的。❷区别；辨别；识别力：He is a man of strong ~. 他是一个识别能力很强的人。

discus /ˈdɪskəs/ *n.* [C] 铁饼：throw the ~ 掷铁饼

discuss /dɪˈskʌs/ *vt.* 讨论；议论：~ a question with sb. 与某人讨论问题/ The students are ~ing how to protect our environment. 学生们正在讨论如何保护我们的自然环境。

discussion /dɪˈskʌʃn/ *n.* 讨论;议论:We had a long ~ about the question. 我们曾就此问题进行了长时间的讨论。

disdain /dɪsˈdeɪn/ Ⅰ *vt.* 蔑视,鄙视,鄙夷;不屑(做某事):The honest official ~ed the offer of a bribe. 那位正直的官员鄙夷对他的贿赂。/Now that she is rich, she ~s to speak to her old friends. 如今她有钱了,便不屑和她的老朋友搭腔了。Ⅱ *n.* [U]蔑视;鄙视;鄙夷

disease /dɪˈsiːz/ *n.* 病;疾病:Depression has become a common ~ among the group. 抑郁症已成为这群人中的一种常见病。/ Doctors are trying hard to bring his heart ~ under control. 大夫们正尽力控制他的心脏病。

disgrace /dɪsˈgreɪs/ *n.* [U]耻辱;丢脸:He who is sent to prison brings ~ on himself. 蹲监狱的人给他自己带来耻辱。

disguise /dɪsˈgaɪz/ *vt.* 伪装;假装;掩饰(事实、意图、感情等):John ~d himself as a policeman. 约翰把自己伪装成一名警察。

disgust /dɪsˈgʌst/ *vt.* 令人厌恶;令人作呕:We are ~ed at (by, with) what we heard and saw here. 我们对在这里的所见所闻感到厌恶。

dish /dɪʃ/ *n.* [C] 盘,碟;一道菜:I ate two ~es of ice-cream. 我吃了两份冰激凌。/ The cold ~ was delicious. 那道凉菜味道很好。

dishearten /dɪsˈhɑːtn/ *v.* 使沮丧;使泄气:She felt ~ed at her failure. 她因失败而感到沮丧。

dishonest /dɪsˈɒnɪst/ *adj.* 不老实的;不诚实的;不正直的:He doesn't want to make friends with a ~ man. 他不愿意和不诚实的人交朋友。

dishono(u)r /dɪsˈɒnə(r)/ *n.* 不光彩;丢脸;不名誉:They fired the man who brought ~ on their company. 他们解雇了败坏公司名誉的那个人。

disinfect /ˌdɪsɪnˈfekt/ *vt.* 为(伤口、房屋、衣物等)消毒(或杀菌):~ dental instruments 给牙科器械消毒/They had to ~ the soil before a new crop could be planted. 在种上新庄稼以前,他们必须先对土壤进行杀菌。

disinfectant /ˌdɪsɪnˈfektənt/ *n.* 消毒剂,杀菌剂

disinterested /dɪsˈɪntrɪstɪd/ *adj.* ❶公正的;无私的;不偏不倚的:make a ~ decision 做出公正的裁决/a ~ diplomatic observer 不带偏见的外交观察家 ❷不感兴趣的,漫不经心的,不关心的:discuss sth. in a ~ way 无动于衷地谈论某事

disk /dɪsk/ *n.* (=disc)[C] ❶圆盘:The moon is like a big bright ~. 月亮像一个明亮的大圆盘。❷唱片:The composer keeps a lot of old video ~s. 那位作曲家保留了很多旧唱片。❸磁盘:a floppy ~ 软盘/ a hard ~ 硬盘/ a back up ~ 备份盘

dislike /dɪsˈlaɪk/ Ⅰ *vt.* 不喜爱;厌恶:I ~ being interrupted at the meeting. 我讨厌在会上发言时被人打断。Ⅱ *n.* [C]不喜爱;厌恶:She shows a ~ for her job. 她不喜欢她的工作。

dislocate /ˈdɪsləʊˌkeɪt, ˌdɪsˈləʊkeɪt/ *vt.* ❶使(骨头)脱位,使脱臼:He ~d his shoulder. 他的肩胛骨脱臼了。❷扰乱,打乱,使混乱;使(机器)运转不正常:~ sb.'s mind 搅乱某人的心境 / Frequent strikes ~d the economy. 频繁的罢工扰乱了经济秩序。派 dislocation *n*.

dismal /ˈdɪzməl/ *adj*. ❶忧郁的；凄凉的：a ~ expression 忧郁的表情/Her voice sounds ~. 她的啜音听上去郁郁不乐。❷软弱无力的；沉闷无趣的；差劲的；乏味的：a ~ effort 软弱无力的尝试/a ~ performance 沉闷乏味的演出

dismantle /dɪsˈmæntl/ *vt*. 拆卸，拆开；解散：The machine had to be completely ~d to discover what was wrong with it. 为了发现毛病，只得把那台机器全部拆开。

dismay /dɪsˈmeɪ/ Ⅰ *vt*. 使失望；使气馁；使绝望：She was ~ed to learn of her husband's disloyalty. 她得知丈夫对她不忠，心里感到很失望。Ⅱ *n*. [U]失望，气馁；绝望：The results of exam filled us with ~. 这次考试成绩使我们感到气馁。

dismiss /dɪsˈmɪs/ *vt*. 开除；解雇；解散：The boy was ~ed from school. 那男孩被学校开除了。/ Our teacher always ~es the class ahead of time. 我们老师总是提前下课。/ He was ~ed for his stealing. 他因偷盗被解雇。派 dismissal *n*.

disobey /ˌdɪsəˈbeɪ/ *vt*. 不服从；违反：Don't ~ school discipline. 别违反学校纪律。

disorder /dɪsˈɔːdə(r)/ *n*. ❶[U] 无秩序；混乱，杂乱：Her room is always in ~. 她的房间总是乱糟糟的。/ Affairs in that district are in great ~. 那个地区的态势极端混乱。❷失调；紊乱；不适；小病：a bowel ~ 闹肚子/eating ~s 进食障碍

dispatch Ⅰ /dɪˈspætʃ/ *vt*. (迅速地)派遣；发送：~ a telegram 发电报/The captain ~ed a boat to bring a doctor on board ship. 船长调了一艘小艇去接医生上船。Ⅱ /dɪˈspætʃ, ˈdɪspætʃ/ *n*. ❶(部队、信使等的)派遣；(信件等的)发送：demand for the ~ of an envoy 要求派遣一名使节/the date of the ~ of the parcel 包裹寄出的日期 ❷ [C](公文)快信，急件；(记者等发往报社或电台的)快讯，(新闻)报道：send a ~ from New York to London 从纽约发往伦敦的急件

dispel /dɪˈspel/ *vt*. (-pelled;-pelling)驱散(云、雾等)；使消失，消除，消释：The sun soon ~led the mist. 太阳很快驱散了雾霭。/The fears were ~led. 这些忧虑烟消云散了。

dispense /dɪˈspens/ *vt*. ❶分发；分配；施与：~ a prize 分发奖品 / The Red Cross ~d food and clothing to the flood victims. 红十字会向水灾难民分发食品和衣物。❷实施；执行：~ the law without bias 公正无私地执法 ❸配(药)；发(药)：~ a prescription 配方 / Druggists must ~ medicines with the greatest care. 药剂师配药必须一丝不苟。/~ **with** 消除，去除；摒弃：Can we ~ with the formalities? 我们能摒弃这些繁文缛节吗？

disperse /dɪˈspɜːs/ *vt*. ❶使散开；赶散；疏散：A thunderstorm ~d the picnickers. 一场雷雨使得野炊的人们四散而去。❷消散；驱散：Building tall chimneys to ~ the smoke is no solution at all. 建造高耸入云的烟囱以消散烟雾的做法根本无济于事。/The chill night air was ~d with the dawn. 夜间的寒气随着黎明的到来消散了。

display /dɪˈspleɪ/ Ⅰ *vt*. 陈列；展出；显示：The oil painting which is ~ed in the museum is famous. 正在博物馆展出的

那幅油画非常著名。/ He ~ed no fear in front of the robber. 面对抢匪他显得毫无畏惧。Ⅱ *n.* [C] 显示；展示；(计算机) 显示屏，显示器：They went to watch a fashion ~ last Sunday. 上周日他们去观看了时装展。

D

displease /dɪsˈpliːz/ *vt.* 使不愉快；使生气：His rudeness ~d all the guests. 他的粗暴无礼令所有客人不快。派 displeased *adj.*

disposable /dɪˈspəuzəbl/ *adj.* 一次性(使用)的，用后即扔的：~ plastic spoons 一次性塑料勺

disposal /dɪˈspəuzəl/ *n.* [U] ❶排列；布置；配置；部署：the ~ of chessmen on a board (国际象棋) 棋子在棋盘上的排列 / the ~ of troops 军队的部署 ❷处理；处置；清除：waste ~ 垃圾处理 / a team of bomb ~ experts 一队排弹专家 ❸控制，管理，支配：I will use all the resources at my ~ to solve this problem. 我将运用我所有的聪明才智去解决这一难题。

dispose /dɪˈspəuz/ *vt.* ❶使愿意；使有意：These circumstances ~d me to sleep. 这些情形使我昏昏欲睡。/ More pay and shorter hours of work ~d him to take the new job. 较高的工资和较短的工作时间使他乐于接受新的工作。❷使有某种倾向；使易受感染：His temperament ~d him to argue readily with people. 他的性情使得他容易与人发生争论。❸安放；排列；布置；部署：~ one's feet on the table 把两只脚翘在桌子上 / The flags were ~d in a straight line for parade. 旗帜被排成一条直线供检阅。/~ **of** ①处理；处置；办妥；解决：The article ~d of the matter in two paragraphs. 该文用两段文字将此事论述一尽。/ This isn't something that can be ~d of with a smile. 这不是件可以一笑置之的小事。②去除；舍弃；消除；销毁：A driving rain brought the water in faster than the drain could be ~d of. 瓢泼大雨使排水沟里的水来不及排走。③卖掉；转让：She ~d of her shares a week ago. 她于一周前卖掉了自己的股份。

disposition /ˌdɪspəˈzɪʃn/ *n.* [C] ❶性情；性格：a cheerful ~开朗的性情/In this ~ of mind, I began my new life. 我以这种心情开始了新生活。❷排列；布置；配置：the ~ of furniture in a room 房间里家具的布置

disprove /dɪsˈpruːv/ *vt.* 证明……虚假(或不正确、不能成立)；反驳：They can neither prove nor ~ that it is genuine. 他们既不能证明也不能否认它的真实性。/ Yet all this was satisfactorily ~d. 可是这一切竟完全查无实据。派 disprovable *adj.*

dispute /dɪˈspjuːt/ *v.* 辩论；争吵；怀疑：They ~d with us for a prize. 他们为奖品和我们争论。

disqualify /dɪsˈkwɒlɪˌfaɪ/ *vt.* ❶取消……的资格；剥夺……的权利(与 from 连用)：be disqualified from driving for 12 months 被取消驾驶资格 12 个月/If the complaint is upheld he could be disqualified from election for three years. 控告一旦确认，他可能在三年内不得参加选举。❷使不能；使不合格；使不适合：His lame foot disqualified him for most sports. 他的跛脚使他不能参加大部分体育活动。/ Age disqualified him for the job. 他因年龄大而未能获得这份工作。派 disqualification *n.*

disregard /ˌdɪsrɪˈgɑːd/ *vt.* 不理；不顾；漠

视:It is not to be lightly ~ed. 这事不能等闲视之。

disrupt /dɪsˈrʌpt/ *vt.* ❶搅乱;扰乱:The news ~ed their conference. 这则消息搅乱了他们的会议。❷使中断;破坏……的完整性:Telephone service was ~ed for hours. 电话通信中断了数小时。

dissatisfy /dɪsˈsætɪsfaɪ/ *vi.* 使不满;使不平:We were dissatisfied with his impolite blame toward our teacher. 他对老师的无礼指责令我们感到不满。

dissertation /ˌdɪsəˈteɪʃn/ *n.* [C](研究)报告;(学术)论文:He finished his master's ~ a week ago. 一周前他写完了他的硕士论文。

dissolve /dɪˈzɒlv/ *v.* ❶分解;(使)溶解;(使)融化:Salt and sugar ~ easily in water. 盐和糖很容易溶于水。❷解散;取消(契约等);解除(婚约等):They ~d their business partnership because they couldn't agree with each other. 由于意见不合,他们解除了生意合伙关系。/ Jack and Marry have ~d their marriage. 杰克和玛丽已解除婚约。

distance /ˈdɪstəns/ *n.* 距离;远处:at a ~ 隔开一些/ from a ~ 从远处/in the ~ 在远处/ The ~ from my home to my school is not far. 从我家到学校的距离不远。

distant /ˈdɪstənt/ *adj.* 遥远的;远处的;疏远的:It is very ~ from the truth. 这与事实相差很远。/ Our school is three *li* ~ from the railway station. 我们学校离火车站有三里路。

distil(l) /dɪsˈtɪl/ *vt.* (-tilled;-tilling) ❶蒸馏;用蒸馏法提取(或提炼、生产):~ fresh water from sea water 从海水中蒸馏出新鲜淡水 ❷净化;提炼;浓缩;吸取……的精华:useful advice ~ed from a lifetime's experience 从一生经验中提炼出的有用的忠告/A proverb ~s the wisdom of the ages. 一则谚语浓缩了成百上千年的智慧。

distinct /dɪˈstɪŋkt/ *adj.* ❶不同的;有区别的:Beijing opera is ~ from our local drama. 京剧与我们的地方戏截然不同。❷清楚的;清晰的;明显的:They achieved a ~ improvement in their experiment. 他们的实验取得了明显的进展。派 distinctly *adv.*

distinction /dɪˈstɪŋkʃn/ *n.* ❶[U]差别;区别;区分;辨别:First we should draw a clear ~ between right and wrong. 首先我们应当分清是非。❷[C]荣誉;名声:The mayor is going to interview the scientist who won many ~s. 市长将接见那位获得过许多荣誉的科学家。

distinctive /dɪˈˈstɪŋktɪv/ *adj.* 有特色的;与众不同的:He comes from the south and has a ~ accent. 他来自南方,有着特别的口音。

distinguish /dɪˈstɪŋgwɪʃ/ *vt.* 区别;辨别;使杰出:He can readily ~ those two objects. 他能很容易地把那两个物体区别开来。/ The girl ~ed herself by winning the champion. 那姑娘因获得冠军而出名。/~ **... and ...** (**... from ...**, **between ...and ...**) 区别……和……:We must ~ friends from foes. 我们必须分清敌友。

distinguished /dɪˈstɪŋgwɪʃt/ *adj.* 著名的;杰出的:The Chinese nation is ~ for its diligence and courage. 中华民族以勤劳、勇敢著称。

distort /dɪˈstɔːt/ *vt.* 歪曲;曲解;扭曲:How can you ~ the facts in broad daylight? 在光天化日之下你怎么能歪曲

事实呢？派 distortion *n.*

distract /dɪˈstrækt/ *vt.* 分散(思想、注意力等)；使分心(与 from 连用)：Reading ~s the mind from grief. 读书能使人分心而减轻痛苦。

distress /dɪˈstres/ Ⅰ *n.* [U]苦恼；悲痛；危难；不幸：His death caused his relatives great ~. 他的去世令亲人们感到非常悲痛。Ⅱ *vt.* (多用被动语态)使苦恼，使痛苦：She was ~ed to find that her brother had got lung cancer. 她痛苦地发现她哥哥患了肺癌。

distribute /dɪˈstrɪbjuːt/ *vt.* 分配；分给；分发；分类：It is said that the professor's property was ~d among his students. 据说那位教授的财产分配给了他的学生们。/ The books in the library were ~d according to subjects. 图书馆里的书按科目分类。

distribution /ˌdɪstrɪˈbjuːʃn/ *n.* ❶分发；分配；发行：a ~ network 发行网/ Who has the ~ right of this film? 谁有这部电影的发行权？❷分布；散布：The population ~ in this district is wide. 这一地区的人口分布很广。

distributor /dɪˈstrɪbjətə(r)/ *n.* [C] 分发者；分配者；发行商

district /ˈdɪstrɪkt/ *n.* [C] 区；(行政)区域：He lives in different ~ from his mother. 他和母亲住在不同的地区。

distrust /dɪsˈtrʌst/ *vt.* 怀疑；不信任：I couldn't ~ my own eyes to face what he was doing. 面对他的所作所为，我简直不敢相信自己的眼睛。

disturb /dɪˈstɜːb/ *vt.* 打扰；扰乱：I am sorry to have ~ed you a lot. 对不起，太打扰你了。派 disturbance *n.*

disuse Ⅰ /dɪsˈjuːs/ *n.* [U](尤指逐渐的)废弃；不用：Many words common in Shakespeare's time have passed into (fell into) ~. 莎士比亚时代许多常用的词汇现已废弃不用。Ⅱ /dɪsˈjuːz/ *vt.* 将……废弃不用 派 disused *adj.*

ditch /dɪtʃ/ *n.* [C] 沟；渠：They are digging a drainage ~ to let dirty water out. 他们正挖一条排水沟把污水引出去。

dive /daɪv/ Ⅰ *v.* (dived 或 dove /dəʊv/, dived) 俯冲；跳水：~ into water 跳入水中/~ into books 埋头读书 Ⅱ *n.* [C]跳水；潜水：I like to watch fancy ~ game. 我喜欢观看花样跳水比赛。派 diver *n.*

diverge /daɪˈvɜːdʒ/ *vi.* ❶分岔；岔开：Their paths ~d at the fork in the road. 他们的路在道口分岔了。/ The path ~s from the main road. 这条小径岔离大路。❷(意见等)分歧，相左(与 from 连用)：I'm afraid our interests ~ from each other. 我们的兴趣恐怕各不相同。/ Our view of the cause of the accident ~s from theirs. 我们对事故的起因与他们意见不一。派 divergence *n.*

diverse /daɪˈvɜːs/ *adj.* ❶不同的，相异的：A great many ~ opinions were expressed at the meeting. 会议上众说纷纭，莫衷一是。❷ 多种多样的，种类繁多的：a culturally ~ population 文化多元的民族

diversion /daɪˈvɜːʃən/ *n.* ❶偏离；转向；转移：the ~ of an irrigation canal 灌溉渠的改道 / a ~ of industry into the war effort 将工业转入备战的做法 / create a ~ of attention 转移他人的注意力 ❷[C]消遣；娱乐：a popular ~ 大众化的消遣方式 / propose a new ~ 想出一个解闷的新法子

diversity /daɪˈvɜːsɪti/ *n.* ❶[U]差异(性)：~ of dispositions 禀性的差异/

There was considerable ~ in the style of the reports. 这几篇报道的文笔各不相同。❷多种多样；多样性：The ~ of food on the table made it hard for him to choose. 桌上菜肴品种多得让他不知道该吃哪种才好。

divert /daɪˈvɜːt/ *vt.* ❶使偏离，使转向：~ a stream from its natural course to a farm for irrigation 把小溪改道引进农场灌溉田地/~ the subject into a side issue 把话题扯向一个枝节问题 ❷转移；盗用，挪用（资金）❸转移（注意力等）：She pointed to the left to ~ the child's attention while she hid the cake. 她用手指向左边转移那孩子的注意力，同时把蛋糕藏了起来。

divide /dɪˈvaɪd/ *v.* 分，分开；除；分配；分摊：Ten ~d by two is five. 10 除以 2 等于 5。/~... **from** ... 把……和……分开：The Red Sea ~s Africa from Asia. 红海把非洲和亚洲分开来。~... **into** ... 把……分成……：Let's ~ ourselves into groups. 咱们分成几个小组吧。

dividend /ˈdɪvɪdend/ *n.* [C] ❶红利；股息：He pays a ~ of five percent each time. 他每次付 5%的股息。❷被除数

divider /dɪˈvaɪdə(r)/ *n.* [C] 除数

division /dɪˈvɪʒn/ *n.* [U]分割；分裂

divorce /dɪˈvɔːs/ Ⅰ *n.* [U]离婚；离异：He got a ~ from his wife three years ago. 三年前他和妻子离婚了。Ⅱ *v.* 离婚：The boy said that his parents were ~d last month. 小男孩说上个月他的父母离婚了。

dizzy /ˈdɪzi/ *adj.* 头晕眼花的；眩晕的：The smell made me ~. 那气味令我感到头晕。Don't be ~ with success. 别让胜利冲昏头脑。

do /duː/ *v.* (did/dɪd/, done /dʌn/；一般现在时第三人称单数 does/dʌz/) ❶助动词：①用于构成现在或过去时：Does he work in a middle school? 他在中学工作吗？/ I didn't go to see the film last night. 昨晚我没去看电影。②用以加强肯定句语气：But I ~ want to go. 可是真想去。③用于祈使句以加强语气：Do come on time. 务必准时来。❷代替动词：①用在肯定句中：She writes better than I ~. 她写得比我好。②用在问句和回答中：He loves his work, does he? Yes, he does. 他喜欢他的工作，是吗？是的。❸做；做完：She did all the work. 她做了全部工作。/~ a good deed 做好事~ / do harm to 对……有害/ ~ honour to sb. 向某人表示敬意；给某人带来荣誉 / ~ one's best 尽全力/ ~ **away with** 废除；消灭：The law did away with slavery. 这项法令废除了奴隶制。~ **by** (口语)对待：He did very well by me. 他待我很好。~ **for** 料理；挫败；毁灭；杀死：If Jim fails in that test, he is done for. 若吉姆考试不及格，他就完了。~ **in** 杀；谋害；毁灭；劳累：I felt done in after a long day's work. 苦干了一整天，我感到疲惫不堪。/ His business was done in by a big fire. 他的商行被一场大火烧毁了。~ **out** 扫除；整理；收拾：Do out the desk drawer. 把书桌抽屉整理一下。~ **up** 修整；恢复；筋疲力尽：Can you ~ up my shirt before tomorrow? 你能在明天以前把我的衬衫熨好吗？/ The house needs to be done up. 这房子需要重新装修。~ **with** 利用；处置；控制：It's difficult to ~ with her. 和她相处不易。/ The children didn't know what to ~ with themselves for joy. 孩子们高兴得难以控制自己。**can** (**could**) ~ **with** 可利用；满足

于;相处;忍受:I can't ~ with her insolence. 我不能容忍她的傲慢。/I could ~ with a cup of tea. 我喝杯茶就行了。**have something (much, nothing) to ~ with** 与……有(有很大,没有)关系:Hard work had much to ~ with his success. 工作努力与他的成功有很大的关系。~ **without** 将就;没有……也行:If there's no sugar, you'll have to ~ without it. 如果没有糖,你就只好将就了。

dock /dɒk/ Ⅰ *n*. [C] 码头;船坞;(*pl*.)港区:He worked at the ~s two years ago. 两年前他在港区工作。Ⅱ *v*. 停靠码头:The ship ~ed in Qingdao for repairs. 那艘船停靠在青岛码头维修。

doctor /ˈdɒktə(r)/ *n*. [C] ❶医生;大夫:She feels not well. You'd better send for a ~ soon. 她不舒服,你最好马上请大夫。/ Mother often sees a ~ on Monday morning. 妈妈常在星期一上午去看病。❷博士:Her son is a ~ of Philosophy (PhD). 她的儿子是哲学博士。

doctoral /ˈdɒktərəl/ *adj*. 博士的:He has finished his ~ dissertation. 他已经做完了他的博士论文。

doctrine /ˈdɒktrɪn/ *n*. 教条,教义;信条;主义:the Christian ~s 基督教教义/ strange and false ~s 异端邪说

document /ˈdɒkjʊmənt/ *n*. [C] 公文;文件;文献:a ~ center 文献中心/ official ~s 官方(正式)文件;公文/ He was drawing up a ~ when I came in. 我进去时他正在草拟一份文件。

documental /ˌdɒkjʊˈmentl/ *adj*. 公文的;文献的;纪实的:a ~ datum bank 文献数据库/ ~ information 文献信息/ a ~ film 纪录片

documentary /ˌdɒkjʊˈment(ə)ri/ Ⅰ *adj*. 记录的;纪实的;文献的;根据文件的:The ~ TV programs are moving. 纪实性电影节目很感人。/ I like ~ TV programs. 我喜欢看纪实性电视节目。Ⅱ *n*. [C] 纪录片,纪实片;纪实小说:a full-length ~ 大型纪录片

dog /dɒg/ *n*. [C] 狗;犬:The family keeps a guide ~. 这家人养了一只导盲犬。

doll /dɒl/ *n*. [C] 洋娃娃;玩具娃娃:The little girl sat on the floor playing with a ~. 小女孩坐在地板上玩洋娃娃。

dollar /ˈdɒlə(r)/ *n*. [C](货币单位)元;美元($):a Canadian ~ 加元/ a Hong Kong ~ 港元/ He exchanged five thousand American ~s for traveling abroad. 为出国旅游他兑换了5 000美元。

dolphin /ˈdɒlfɪn/ *n*. [C] 海豚:They are watching a school of ~s in the pool. 他们在观看水池里的一群海豚。

domestic /dəˈmestɪk/ *adj*. ❶本国的;国内的:gross ~ product (GDP) 国内生产总值 /He is especially interested in TV programs of ~ news. 他对国内新闻电视节目特别感兴趣。❷家(庭)的;家用的:She should be fully responsible for ~ troubles. 她应对这场家庭纷争负全责。❸ 驯养的;家养的:The farmer keeps some ~ animals. 那农夫养了一些家畜。

dominance /ˈdɒmɪnəns/ *n*. [U] ❶优势;支配(或统治)地位:Their ~ of the market is seriously threatened by this new product. 这种新产品严重威胁着他们在市场上的优势地位。/ Agriculture has lost its ~ in nation after nation. 农业已在一个又一个国家里失去其主导地位。❷最高权威;控制权:The treaty gave them ~ of the sea routes. 该条约赋予他们对这些海上航道的控

制权。

dominant /ˈdɒmɪnənt/ *adj.* ❶占优势的;支配的,处于统治地位的:the ~ force 起支配作用的力量 / The British were formerly ~ in India. 英国人曾统治过印度。/ a ~ figure 举足轻重的人物 ❷(在遗传上)优势的,显性的:Tallness is ~, dwarfness recessive. 高大是显性的,矮小则是隐性的。派 dominantly *adv.*

dominate /ˈdɒmɪneɪt/ *v.* 统治;支配:His new view is dominating over the academic circles. 他的新观点在学术界占领着支配地位。

Domino /ˈdɒmɪnəʊ/ *n.* [C](*pl.* dominoes 或 dominos)多米诺骨牌

donate /dəʊˈneɪt/ *vt.* 捐;捐赠;捐款:The old professor ~d a large sum of money to build a school for the children. 老教授捐了一大笔钱为孩子们修建学校。派 donator *n.*

donation /dəʊˈneɪʃn/ *n.* [C]捐赠;捐款;捐赠物;赠品:make financial ~s to help develop education 捐资助学/ Soon the people of the flooded area received a large ~ from all over the country. 很快灾区的人民就收到了来自全国各地大量的捐赠物。

donkey /ˈdɒŋki/ *n.* [C]❶驴:drive a ~ 赶驴子/ride a ~ 骑驴 ❷笨蛋:If a ~ brays at you, don't bray at him. 别和蠢人一般见识。

door /dɔː(r)/ *n.* [C] 门;门口:at the ~ 在门口/ knock at the ~ 敲门/ next ~ 隔壁/ from ~ to ~ 挨家挨户/ Please open the ~ to the visitor. 请为客人开门。

dormitory /ˈdɔːmətri/ *n.* [C](集体)宿舍(口语中亦可简称为 dorm):The boy students' ~ is on the hill. 男生宿舍在小山坡上。

dose /dəʊs/ *n.* [C] ❶(服药的)(一次)剂量;一剂,一服:take a ~ of cough medicine 服一剂咳嗽药/take medicine in small ~s 小剂量服药 ❷(不愉快经历的)一次,一份:a ~ of flattery 一通马屁

dot /dɒt/ Ⅰ *n.* [C] ❶点,小(圆)点:There is a ~ over the letter j. 字母"j"上面有一小点。/ A ~ on the chart marked the ship's position. 航图上的小圆点标示了该船所在的位置。/**on the ~** 准确地;准时地:She always arrives on the ~. 她总是准时到达。❷斑点,污点:Her blouse was black with white ~ on it. 她的衬衫是黑底白点。❸少量,微量,一点儿:a ~ of butter 一点儿黄油 / a mere ~ of a child 小不点儿(或小家伙) Ⅱ *vt.* (dotted; dotting) ❶加点于;用点在……上做标记:Dot your i's and j's. 写"i"和"j"时要打上上面的点。❷(星星点点地)布满,点缀:Fishing boats ~ the lake. 湖面上渔帆点点。/ You have ~ted my skirt with paint. 你在我的裙子上洒满了斑斑油漆。

dote /dəʊt/ *vi.* 溺爱;过分宠爱(与 on 连用):~ on classic music 特别喜爱古典音乐/They ~ on their youngest daughter. 他们溺爱小女儿。

double /ˈdʌbl/ *adj.* 两倍的;双的:He does ~ work to earn his tuition. 为挣学费他做两份工作。/ The students in this school are now ~ what they were five years ago. 这所学校现在的学生人数是五年前的两倍。

doubt /daʊt/ Ⅰ *v.* 怀疑;不相信:I ~ whether it is true. 我怀疑这是否真的。Ⅱ *n.* 怀疑;疑虑:arouse ~s 引起怀疑/

destroy ~s 消除疑虑/ There is not the least ~ that we shall win. 我们会取胜是毫无疑问的。/ **beyond** (**past**)~ 毫无疑问:Beyond ~, you'll recover soon. 你会很快恢复健康,这是毫无疑问的。**in** ~ 怀疑的;未确定的:The result of the election is still in ~. 选举结果尚未确定。**no** ~ 无疑地:You have no ~ heard the news. 你无疑已听到这消息了。**without** ~ 无疑地;毫无问题:Without ~ he is the best singer among us. 无疑他是我们中最好的歌手。

doubtful /ˈdaʊtfl/ *adj.* 令人怀疑的;可疑的:We are ~ about the weather for tomorrow. 我们说不准明天的天气会如何。/ He is ~ of the news. 他怀疑那条消息不可靠。

dove /dʌv/ *n.* [C]鸽子:The little girl draw ~s of peace well. 小女孩画和平鸽画得很好。

down /ˈdaʊn/ Ⅰ *adv.* 向下;下降:Put it ~, please . 请把它放下来。/ The oil price is ~. 油价降了。Ⅱ *prep.* 由上向下;沿着:The children ran ~ the hill. 孩子们跑下山。/ He was walking ~ the street. 他正沿着街道行走。Ⅲ *v.* 打倒;击落;放下:He is ~ed with flu. 他因患流感病倒了。

downfall /ˈdaʊnˌfɔːl/ *n.* [U]垮台;衰落;毁灭:the ~ of the government of this country 该国政府的倒台

download /ˌdaʊnˈləʊd/ *v.* (计算机)下载:He ~ed a great amount of information from the Internet. 他从因特网上下载了大量的资料。

downright /ˈdaʊnˌraɪt/ Ⅰ *adv.* 彻底地;完全地:She wasn't just unfriendly, she was ~ rude. 她不只是不客气,简直可说是无礼至极。Ⅱ *adj.* 彻底的,完全的,十足的:a ~ thief 地地道道的小偷/ a ~ falsehood 弥天大谎

downstairs /ˌdaʊnˈsteəz/ Ⅰ *adj.* 楼下的:The ~ room is empty. 楼下的房间是空着的。Ⅱ *adv.* 在楼下;往楼下:He didn't know who lives ~. 他不知道谁住在楼下。

down-to-earth /ˈdaʊntəˈɜːθ/ *adj.* 脚踏实地的;务实的;实际的:a ~ businessman 讲求实际的商人 / ~ advice 实实在在的忠告

downtown /ˌdaʊnˈtaʊn/ Ⅰ *adj.* (闹)市区的;商业区的:The ~ areas are developing rapidly. 城市商业区发展迅速。Ⅱ *adv.* 在市区;向市区:Generally speaking, old people don't like to live ~. 一般说来,老年人不喜欢住在闹市区。

downward /ˈdaʊnwəd/ Ⅰ *adj.* 向下的;下行的:There is a ~ slope in front of the house. 房屋前面有一个斜坡。Ⅱ *adv.* 向下;下行:He pulled the rope ~. 他把绳子往下拉。

downwind /ˈdaʊnˈwɪnd/ Ⅰ *adv.* ❶顺风地:The boat glided easily ~. 那条船顺风航行,毫不费力。❷在下风;向下风:The elephant stood ~ of us and caught our scent. 这头大象站在我们的下风,嗅到了我们的气味。Ⅱ *adj.* 顺风的:a ~ current 顺风的水流

doze /dəʊz/ Ⅰ *v.* 瞌睡;打盹:She was too tired and ~d off over reading. 她太疲倦,看书时都打瞌睡了。Ⅱ *n.* 瞌睡;打盹:You may have a ~ here. 你可以在这儿打打盹。

dozen /ˈdʌzn/ *n.* [C](一)打;十二个:Eggs are sold by the ~ in this district. 这个地区鸡蛋论打卖。/ A ~ of pencils is twelve. 一打铅笔是十二枝。/ ~**s of**

几十；许多：We need to choose ~s of excellent stamps more for the show. 我们还需要挑选几十张优秀邮票参展。

draft /drɑːft/ Ⅰ *n.* [C]草稿；草案；草图：The secretary was making a ~ of (for) a speech when I went in. 我进去时秘书正在起草一份讲话稿。Ⅱ *v.* 起草；草拟：He ~ed a letter to the president. 他草拟了一封给校长的信。

drag /dræg/ *v.* (dragged; dragging) 拉；拖：The horse was ~ging a heavy load. 马拖着重载。/ The workers ~ged the river for a sunken boat. 工人们在那条河里打捞沉船。

dragon /ˈdrægən/ *n.* [C] 龙：a ~ boat 龙船；龙舟/Dragon Well tea 龙井茶/ We are all successors of the Dragon. 我们都是龙的传人。

drain /dreɪn/ *n.* ❶[C]排水；下水道；排水系统：She asked the worker to clear the ~. 她请工人帮她疏通下水道。❷消耗；负担：Teaching his grandson English was a great ~ of his energy. 教孙子学英语消耗了他很大的精力。

drainage /ˈdreɪnɪdʒ/ *n.* [U] ❶排水；放水：areas with poor ~ 排水不畅的地区 ❷排水系统；排水装置：Massive big ~ ditches take the water away. 庞大的排水系统将水排走。❸排出的水；污水；污物：~ from the wound 从伤口排出的脓血

drama /ˈdrɑːmə/ *n.* 戏剧；剧本：They are students of ~. 他们是攻读戏剧的学生。/ The young man wrote a very good motion picture ~. 那年轻人写了一个很好的电影剧本。

dramatic /drəˈmætɪk/ *adj.* 戏剧的；戏剧性的：He told us that the whole event was really ~. 他告诉我们整个事件很富戏剧性。

dramatist /ˈdræmətɪst/ *n.* [C] 剧作家

draw /drɔː/ *v.* (drew/druː/, drawn /drɔːn/) 拉,拖；吸引；画：The boy is ~ing a plane. 男孩正在画飞机。/ The lecture drew a large audience. 那场讲座吸引了许多听众。/ She drew the curtain before she went to bed. 睡觉前她拉上窗帘。/~ **a conclusion** 得出结论：A conclusion has been ~n. 结论已得出。~ **a deep breath** 深深吸气：The doctor told him to ~ a deep breath. 医生要他深吸一口气。~ **back** 收回：He will not ~ back from what he has said. 他说过的话是不会收回的。~ **in** 引诱；缩短：She is ~n in to buy this coat. 她受骗去买这件外套。~ **near** 接近；临近：Christmas is ~ing near. 圣诞节即将来临。~ **off** 脱去；放掉：Please ~ off your socks. 请把袜子脱去。~ **on** 穿上；吸收：The man drew on his trousers hurriedly. 那个人匆匆穿上裤子。~ **out** 取出；引出；拉长：She drew two hundred dollars out of the bank to buy her mother a present. 她从银行取出 200 元钱给母亲买礼品。~ **up** 起草；草拟：The two countries drew up a peace treaty after the war ended. 两国在战争结束后草拟了和平条约。

drawback /ˈdrɔːbæk/ *n.* [C]不利；缺点；障碍：I think that watching TV has both benefits and ~s. 我认为看电视有利也有弊。/ He decided to remove the ~s on his way to success. 他决心要除掉通往成功道路上的各种障碍。

drawer /ˈdrɔː(r)/ *n.* [C]抽屉：She put her diary in the ~. 她把她的日记本放在抽屉里。

drawing /ˈdrɔːɪŋ/ *n.* [U] 绘画：Our monitor is good at ~. 我们班长擅长绘画。

dread /dred/ *v.* 害怕；恐惧；担心：Do you ~ a visit to the zoo? 你害怕去动物园吗？派 dreadful *adj.*

D

dream /driːm/ Ⅰ*v.* 梦想；想象：Do you ~ at night? 你晚上做梦吗？/ He ~ed a dreadful dream last night. 昨晚他做了一个噩梦。/~ **of** 想象；向往；渴望：Little did I ~ of succeeding so. 我做梦也想不到会这么成功。Ⅱ*n.* 梦；梦想；幻想：He has a beautiful ~ to sail around the world. 航海环游世界是他的美好梦想。派 dreamer *n.*

dreamy /ˈdriːmi/ *adj.* ❶朦胧的，模糊的：have only a ~ recollection of what had happened 依稀记得过去所发生的事 ❷轻柔的；安谧悦耳的：a ~ lullaby 温馨甜美的摇篮曲 / talk in gentle，~ voices 柔声细气地交谈 ❸爱空想的，好幻想的：a ~ girl 好幻想的女孩子 ❹绝妙的，妙不可言的：a ~ house 呱呱叫的房子 派 dreamily *adv.*

dress /dres/ Ⅰ*v.* 替……穿衣；打扮：She is ~ing her baby. 她正在给小孩穿衣。/ You are finely ~ed today. 你今天穿得真漂亮。Ⅱ*n.* 衣服；服装：evening ~ 晚礼服/ He is in informal ~ today. 今天他穿便服。

dressing /ˈdresɪŋ/ *n.* ❶（拌制色拉等的）调料：salad ~s 色拉调料 ❷[C]敷药；包扎：apply a ~ to a wound 对伤口敷药包扎

dribble /ˈdrɪbl/ *vi.* ❶一点一滴地落下；滴流；细流：That leaky faucet ~s. 那个漏水的龙头一直在滴滴答答地滴水。❷（婴儿等）流口水：The baby ~s on his bib. 婴儿的口水淌在围涎上面。❸（用手、脚或球棒等）带球；运球；盘球

drift /drɪft/ Ⅰ*v.*（使）漂流；漂泊：The boat was ~ing down the river. 小船顺着河流往下漂去。Ⅱ*n.* 漂流；漂泊：The ~ of this current is to the south. 这股水流向南方。

drill /drɪl/ *n.* ❶练习；操练：class ~s 课堂练习/ daily ~s 日常训练/ oral ~s 口头操练/ individual ~ 个别训练/ pattern ~ 句型练习/ They conducted a fire ~ last weekend. 上周末他们进行了消防演习。❷[C]钻头；钻床

drink /drɪŋk/ Ⅰ*v.*（drank/dræŋk/，drunk /drʌŋk/）喝，饮：~ a toast 祝酒/ Let's ~ to Mother's health. 让我们为妈妈的健康干杯。/~ **in** ❶吸收（水分）：The soil ~s in rain. 土壤吸收雨水。❷全神贯注地倾听：The girl drank in every word of the sailor's story of adventures. 这姑娘全神贯注地倾听水手所讲述的冒险故事，一个字也没漏掉。Ⅱ*n.* 饮料，酒：cold ~ 冷饮/ have a ~ 喝一杯 派 drinker *n.*

drip /drɪp/ Ⅰ*v.*（dripped；dripping）滴下；漏下：Sweat was ~ping down his face. 汗水从他脸上滴下来。Ⅱ*n.* [C]水滴；点滴：He is put on a ~ in the hospital. 他正在医院输液。

drive /draɪv/ *v.*（drove/drəuv/，driven /ˈdrɪvn/）驱赶；迫使；驾驶：Her husband ~s her to office everyday. 她丈夫每天开车送她上班。/~ **away** 驱逐；驱车离开：The enemies were driven away. 敌人被驱逐出去了。~ **off** 赶走：They drove the attackers off. 他们击退了进攻者。~ **sb. mad** 使某人发疯：What he said drove her mad. 他说的话使她发疯。

driver /ˈdraɪvə(r)/ *n.* [C] ❶驾驶员，司机：the ~ of a truck 卡车司机 / a bus ~ 公共汽车驾驶员 ❷传动器；驱动器；主

动轮 ❸磁盘(磁带)驱动器

droop /druːp/ *v.* 低垂,下垂;发蔫:The flowers were ~ing for want of water. 花因缺水而发蔫。

drop /drɒp/ Ⅰ *v.* (dropped; dropping) 掉下;滴下;下降;降落:The apple blossoms are beginning to ~. 苹果花开始掉了。/ His voice ~ped to a whisper. 他的声音降低成耳语。/ The price of eggs ~ped quickly. 鸡蛋的价格很快降下来了。/~ **in** 顺便拜访:Drop in some time tomorrow. 明天随便什么时候来玩一玩。~ **off** 散出;打盹儿;下车;降低:His friends ~ped off one by one. 他的朋友一个个走了。/ He ~ped off. 他打了个盹。~ **out** 退出:Three runners ~ped out. 三名赛跑运动员退出了比赛。Ⅱ *n.* [C] 水滴;水珠:The rain is falling in large ~s. 雨下得很大。/**at the ~ of a hat** 有机会就……;随时;马上:He used to blush at the ~ of a hat. 他以前动辄就脸红。~ **by** ~ 一点一点地;一滴一滴地:The water leaks from the tap ~ by ~. 水一滴一滴地从龙头里漏出来。

dropout /ˈdrɒpaʊt/ *n.* [C] 退学者:The school is trying hard to reduce its ~s. 学校正尽力减少流失生。

drought /draʊt/ *n.* 旱灾;长期干旱:The prolonged ~ brought difficulties to villagers. 持久的干旱给村民带来很多困难。

drown /draʊn/ *v.* 淹死;淹没:Do cats ~ easily? 猫容易被淹死吗? /My voice was ~ed by the noise of the machinery. 我的声音被机器声所淹没。

drowse /draʊz/ *vi.* 打盹,打瞌睡,假寐:She ~d in the garden. 她在花园里打起了瞌睡。/ He now and then ~d away into a half sleep. 他时而打盹假寐,似睡非睡。

drug /drʌg/ *n.* [C] 药;药物;(*pl.*)麻醉药:an acting ~ 速效药/ sleeping ~ 安眠药/ a ~ store 药房/ International Anti-Narcotic Drugs Day 国际禁毒品日/ He became a school dropout because of taking ~s. 由于吸毒他辍学了。

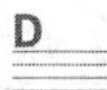

drum /drʌm/ Ⅰ *n.* [C] ❶鼓:beat the ~ 敲鼓 / roll (thump) a ~ 擂鼓/ **beat the ~ for** 鼓吹:The company beat the ~for their new product. 该公司在吹捧他们的新产品。❷鼓声;鼓乐:the roll of ~s 隆隆的鼓乐声 ❸(敲鼓似的)咚咚声,敲击声 Ⅱ *vi.* (drummed; drumming) ❶击鼓,打鼓,敲鼓:He ~s in the school dance band. 他在学校的伴舞乐队中打鼓。❷不停地敲打;有节奏地击打(或跳动):The rain started to ~ on the roof. 雨开始滴滴答答地落在屋顶上。

drunk /drʌŋk/ *adj.* 喝醉的;沉醉的;陶醉的:The little boy got ~ on excessive beer. 小男孩喝了过多的啤酒而醉了。/ They were ~ with joy after winning the champion. 他们陶醉在赢得冠军后的喜悦之中。

dry /draɪ/ Ⅰ *adj.* 干的;口干的;枯燥无味的:It's very ~ for this season of the year. 就这个季节来说,气候要算很干燥的了。/ These books are as ~ as dust. 这些书读起来枯燥无味。Ⅱ *v.* 晒干;弄干:She dried her hair. 她把头发弄干。

dual /ˈdjuːəl/ *adj.* ❶双的,两的;二元的:the ~ law which accounts for negative and positive electricity 解释正负电的二元法则 ❷双倍的;两重的:~ nationality 双重国籍/have a ~ function 具有双重作用

dubious / ˈdjuːbɪəs / *adj.* ❶怀疑的：I'm still ~ about the wisdom of that plan. 我对那个计划是否明智仍抱有怀疑。❷有问题的；靠不住的，不可靠的：a rather ~ character 可疑分子/a ~ account of what happened 对所发生的事情的不可靠说法 ❸疑惑的；犹豫的；迟疑的：She feels ~ as to what to do. 她犹豫不决，不知该怎么办。派 dubiously *adv.*

D

duck / dʌk / *n.* [C] 鸭子

duckling / ˈdʌklɪŋ / *n.* [C] 小鸭：Have you ever read *The Ugly Duckling* by Hans Andersen? 你读过安徒生写的《丑小鸭》吗？

due / djuː / *adj.* 合适的；应得的；预定的；约定的：The bus is ~ at nine. 公共汽车预定 9 点钟到。/~ **to** 因为；由于：The credit is ~ to you. 荣誉应该归你。

duke / djuːk / *n.* [C] 公爵；君主

dull / dʌl / *adj.* ❶钝的：a ~ knife 一把钝刀 ❷迟钝的；愚笨的：a ~ mind 愚钝的头脑 ❸(天气)阴沉的；阴暗的：~ color 暗淡的颜色/a ~ day 阴沉的天 ❹单调的；枯燥乏味的：a ~ story 一个乏味的故事

dumb / dʌm / *adj.* 哑的；无言的：He was born ~ but he is clever. 虽然他生下来就是哑巴，但他很聪明。

dumbfound / ˌdʌmˈfaʊnd/ *vt.* 使惊呆；使惊讶；使慌乱：She was utterly ~ed at (by) the news. 她完全被这消息惊呆了。/ He was ~ed to hear that he has been fired from his job. 他听说自己已被解雇，一下子给惊得慌了神儿。

dump / dʌmp / Ⅰ *n.* [C]垃圾堆；垃圾场 Ⅱ *v.* 倾倒；倾销：No ~ing. 禁止倒垃圾。/ They ~ed surplus goods abroad. 他们向国外倾销过剩货物。

dumpling / ˈdʌmplɪŋ / *n.* [C] 饺子：She treated us to ~s yesterday. 昨天她请我们吃饺子。

duplicate Ⅰ / ˈdjuːplɪkɪt / *n.* [C]副本，抄件；复制品：make a ~ of the original 做一份原件的副本 Ⅱ /ˈdjuːplɪˌkeɪt/ *vi.* ❶复制；复写；复印：Can you ~ the key for me? 你能帮我配一把这样的钥匙吗？❷重复；依样重做：He ~d his father's way of standing with his hands in his pockets. 他模仿其父两手插在口袋里站着的样子。

durable / ˈd(j)ʊərəbəl/ Ⅰ *adj.* ❶耐用的；坚固的：~ fabrics 耐穿的织物 ❷持久的，有永久性的：a ~ marriage 天长地久的婚姻 / a ~ peace 持久和平 Ⅱ*n.* (*pl.*)耐用品 派 durability *n.* ；durably *adv.*

duration / djʊəˈreɪʃn / *n.* [U]持续，延续；持续期间：a play of short ~ of life 寿命/ **for the** ~长期地，持续地：He was drafted for the ~ plus six. 他要再服六年兵役。

during / ˈdjʊərɪŋ / *prep.* 在……期间：I was in the army ~ the war. 战争期间我在部队当兵。

dusk / dʌsk / *n.* [U]黄昏；薄暮：They arrived home at ~. 黄昏时他们到家了。

dust / dʌst / Ⅰ *n.* [U]灰尘；屑，粉末：The ~ was blown about by the wind. 风吹得尘土到处飞扬。Ⅱ *vt.* 去掉灰尘：She ~ed the furniture. 她掸去家具上的灰尘。

dusty / ˈdʌsti/ *adj.* 多尘的；满是灰尘的：a ~ table 满是灰尘的桌子 / a ~ mountain track 尘土飞扬的山路 / The day was very hot and very ~. 那天天气酷热，而且灰尘弥漫。派 dustiness *n.*

dutiful / ˈdjuːtɪf(ʊ)l / *adj.* 尽职的，守本

分的,恭敬的,恭顺的;顺从的,服从的:~ citizen 本分公民/She is a ~ daughter to her parents. 她是父母的孝顺女儿。/He was ~ to his mother. 他对他母亲恪尽孝道。

duty / ˈdjuːti / *n.* ❶义务;责任;职责:It's my ~ to show respect to my teachers. 尊敬老师是我的本分。/ It is our ~ to obey the laws. 遵纪守法是我们的义务。/**on** ~ 值日:Who's on ~ today? 今天谁值日? ❷(*pl.*)税,关税:customs duties 海关关税/ import duties 进口税/Duties on cars are reducing. 小汽车的关税在下降。

dwarf / dwɔːf / *n.* [C] 矮子;侏儒

dwell / dwel / *vi.* (dwelt/dwelt/或dwelled,dwelt 或 dwelled) ❶居住;居留:The old couple have dwelt in the town for 25 years. 老两口在这个小镇上住了 25 年了。❷凝思;细想:He often ~s on his past. 他常常细想过去的事。

dwelling / ˈdwelɪŋ/ *n.* [C] ❶住处,住宅,寓所:You have changed your ~, haven't you? 你已搬了家,对吗? / cave ~ 窑洞 / lake ~ 湖上房屋 ❷常住处

dye / daɪ / Ⅰ *vt.* 染色;把……染上颜色:She ~d her curtain light blue. 她把窗帘染成淡蓝色。Ⅱ *n.* [U]染色;染料:This kind of cloth takes ~ well (badly). 这种布料(不)容易染上色。

dying / ˈdaɪɪŋ / *adj.* 垂死的;临终的:The patient told his doctor his ~ wish. 病人把临终心愿告诉了他的大夫。/ **be ~ for** 渴望:He said he was ~ for a hot bath. 他说他真渴望洗个热水澡。

dynamic(al) / daɪˈnæmɪk(əl) / *adj.* 动力的;动态的;有活力的:The housing market in our country is a ~ market. 我国的住房市场是一个很有活力的市场。

dynamics / daɪˈnæmɪks / *n.* [U]动力;动力学

dynamite / ˈdaɪnəmaɪt / *n.* [U] 甘油炸药

dynamo / ˈdaɪnəməʊ / *n.* [C] 电动机;发电机:an alternating current ~ 交流发电机/ a direct current ~ 直流发电机

dynasty / ˈdɪnəsti, ˈdaɪnəsti / *n.* [C] 王朝;朝代:the Ming Dynasty 明朝

E e

E

each /iːtʃ/ Ⅰ *adj*. 每;各;各自的:Each boy may try three times. 每个男孩可以试三次。Ⅱ *pron*. 各个;每个:Each of the students has a new book. 每个学生都有一本新书。~ **other** 彼此;互相:They often talk to ~ other in English. 他们常常用英语交谈。

eager /ˈiːɡə(r)/ *adj*. 热切的;渴望的:She was ~ to go abroad. 她渴望出国。/ **be** ~ **for** (**about**, **after**) 渴求某事:She is ~ for success. 她渴望成功。派 eagerly *adv*.

eagle /ˈiːɡl/ *n*. [C] 鹰

ear /ɪə(r)/ *n*. [C] ❶耳,耳朵/ **all** ~**s** 专心听:She was all ~s when the teacher spoke. 老师讲话时,她全神贯注地听。**give** ~**s to** 注意;留神:Please give ~s to his report. 请注意听他的报告。**go in** (**at**) **one** ~ **and out** (**at**) **the other** 左耳进,右耳出;当作耳边风:My repeated warning to her went in one ~ and out the other. 她把我的一再警告当作耳边风。❷听说;听力:The old woman is over sixty but has a keen ~. 尽管六十多岁了,老太太的听觉却很灵。❸(稻、麦等的)穗

eardrum /ˈɪəˌdrʌm/ *n*. (= drum) [C] ❶鼓膜,耳膜 ❷鼓室,中耳

early /ˈɜːli/ (-ier, -iest) Ⅰ *adj*. 早的;早期的:My grandfather is an ~ riser. 我爷爷是个早起的人。/ Mother likes to buy ~ vegetables. 妈妈喜欢购买时鲜蔬菜。Ⅱ *adv*. 早;在早期;在初期:Don't come too ~. 不要来得太早。

earn /ɜːn/ *vt*. 挣得;赢得;获得:How much did John ~ last month? 约翰上个月挣了多少钱? / He ~ed respect by his fair dealing. 他因行为公正而赢得了人们的尊敬。

earnest /ˈɜːnɪst/ *adj*. 热心的;热切的;认真的:Parents are always ~ about their children's education. 父母对孩子的教育总是非常热心。/ **be** ~ **for** 渴望:He is ~ for greater achievements. 他渴望取得更大的成就。派 earnestly *adv*.

earnings /ˈɜːnɪŋz/ *n*. ❶(*pl*.)工资;收入:The family live on his ~ only. 全家人仅靠他的工资过活。❷收益;利润:The total ~ of the factory will be about 30 million dollars a year. 这家工厂一年的总赢利将达到3 000万美元。

earphone /ˈɪəfəʊn/ *n*. [C] 耳机:The students put on their ~s and listened to the record attentively. 学生戴上耳机认真听录音。

earring /ˈɪəˌrɪŋ/ *n*. [C]耳环,耳坠子

earth /ɜːθ/ *n*. (the ~) 世界;地球:How far is the ~ from the sun? 地球离太阳

多远？/**on** ~ 究竟；到底：How on ~ did you know it? 你到底是怎么知道这事的？

earthen /ˈɜːθən/ *adj*. ❶泥土做的：an ~ dam 土坝 ❷陶制的：an ~ flowerpot 陶制花盆

earthly /ˈɜːθli/ *adj*. 尘世的，世俗的：~ passions 世俗的欲望/She believed that our ~ life is all that matters. 她认为我们的现世生活至关重要的。

earthquake /ˈɜːθkweɪk/ *n*. [C] 地震；大震荡：Many buildings collapsed in the devastating ~. 许多房屋在那次破坏性地震中倒塌了。

earthshaking /ˈɜːθˌʃeɪkɪŋ/ *adj*. 惊天动地的；极其重大的，影响深远的：an ~ event 石破天惊的重大事件 / be of ~ importance 极其重要的

earthworm /ˈɜːθˌwɜːm/ *n*. [C]蚯蚓，曲蟮，地龙

ease /iːz/ Ⅰ *n*. [U] 安逸；容易：They led a life of ~ in the countryside after they retired. 退休后他们在农村过着悠闲的生活。/**at** ~ 自由自在；悠闲，无拘束：His smile put us at ~. 他的微笑使我们感到无拘无束。**with** ~ 容易地：The soldiers marched twenty miles with ~. 士兵们轻而易举地行进了 20 英里。Ⅱ *v*. 使舒服；放松；减轻（疼痛）：This medicine will ~ the pain. 这药镇痛。/ The belt is too tight, ~ it a little. 皮带太紧，放松一点。

easel /ˈiːz(ə)l/ *n*. [C]画架；黑板架；图表架

easily /ˈiːzɪli/ *adv*. 容易地；不费力地：She finished the composition ~. 她轻松地写完了那篇作文。

east /iːst/ Ⅰ *n*. 东；东方：Japan is in the ~ of Asia. 日本位于亚洲的东部。Ⅱ *adj*. 东部的；来自东方的：They live in the ~ side of the city. 他们住在城市东区。Ⅲ *adv*. 在东方；向东方：My room faces ~. 我的房间朝东。

Easter /ˈiːstə(r)/ *n*. 复活节：An ~ egg is a very good gift. 复合节彩蛋是一份很好的礼物。

eastern /ˈiːstən/ Ⅰ *adj*. 东方的；东部的：He knows little about ~ provinces. 他对东部省份了解不多。Ⅱ *n*. [C]东方人

eastward /ˈiːstwəd/ Ⅰ *adj*. 向东的；朝东的：There is a temple on the ~ slope of the hill. 在小山上的东面斜坡上有一座庙宇。Ⅱ *adv*. (~s) 向东；朝东：They traveled ~s. 他们向东旅行。

easy /ˈiːzi/ *adj*. (-ier, -iest) ❶容易的；不费力的：It is not very ~ to write a diary in English. 用英语写日记不太容易。❷ 舒适的；安逸的：He is leading an ~ life. 他过着舒适的生活。❸ 随和的；易顺从的：He is ~ to get along with. 他平易近人。

eat /iːt/ *vt*. (ate/et/, eaten /ˈiːtn/)吃；吃饭：They are ~ing tomatoes. 他们在吃西红柿。/ The young couple often ~ out on weekends. 这对年轻夫妻周末常常去餐馆吃饭。/~ **one's words** 食言：She often ~s her words. 她经常食言。~ **one's heart out** 沮丧；悲伤：He ate his heart out over the defeat. 他因那次失败而感到沮丧。~ **up** 吃光；耗尽：He ate up his savings to buy a flat in the city. 他耗尽积蓄在市区买了一套房子。

eaves /iːvz/ *n*. 屋檐：Birds have nested under our ~. 鸟儿在我们家的屋檐下面筑巢。

eavesdrop /ˈiːvzdrɒp/ *v*. 偷听；窃听：~ in trains and hotels for political intelligence 在列车和旅馆里进行窃听以获取政治情报/I've just ~ped two demographers. 我刚刚偷听了两个人口学家的谈话。

ebb /eb/ Ⅰ *n.* [U]退潮；衰退：The tide is on the ~. 退潮了。Ⅱ *vi.* 退潮；退，落：The boys and girls were playing on the beach when the tide ~ed. 退潮时孩子们在海滩上玩耍。

E

eccentric /ɪkˈsentrɪk/ Ⅰ *adj.* (人或行为举止等)古怪的，怪僻的；不合常规的，异乎寻常的：an ~ conduct 古怪的行为/It's ~ to wear a mismatched pair of socks. 穿上一双不配对袜子真古怪。Ⅱ *n.* [C]古怪的人，怪僻的人：She was a mild ~. 她这个人有点儿怪。

echo /ˈekəʊ/ Ⅰ *n.* [C]回声：If you shout at the top of the mountain, you'll hear the ~ of your voices. 如果你在山顶上大声喊叫，你会听到你的声音回荡。Ⅱ *v.* 发回声；回响：His voices ~ed in the valley. 他的声音在山谷中回响。

eclipse /ɪˈklɪps/ *n.* [C] (日、月的)食：a solar (lunar) ~ 日食(月食)/a total ~ 全食

ecological /ˌiːkəˈlɒdʒɪkl/ *adj.* 生态的；生态学的：~ agriculture 生态农业/ ~ balance 生态平衡 / ~ environment 生态环境

ecology /ɪˈkɒlədʒi/ *n.* [U] 生态学

economic /ˌiːkəˈnɒmɪk/ *adj.* 经济学的；经济(上)的：the ~ base 经济基础/ the ~ aid 经济援助/the ~ policy 经济政策/a special ~ zone 经济特区

economical /ˌiːkəˈnɒmɪkl/ *adj.* 节省的；节俭的；经济的：an ~ person 一个节俭的人/ To buy a second-hand car is ~. 买二手车很合算。派 economically *adv.*

economics /ˌiːkəˈnɒmɪks/ *n.* [C]经济学：an expert in ~ 经济学专家/ a course in ~ 经济学课程/ He is majoring ~ in Britain. 他在英国主修经济学。

economist /ɪˈkɒnəmɪst/ *n.* [C] 经济学(专)家

economize /ɪˈkɒnəˌmaɪz/ *vt.* 节约，节省；充分利用：~ one's time 充分利用时间 —*vi.* 节约，节省；紧缩开支：I have to ~ where I can. 我能省的地方一定得省。/ ~ in food (time) 节约食物(时间) / We have to ~ on water during the dry season. 在干旱季节我们必须节约用水。

economy /ɪˈkɒnəmi/ *n.* 经济：domestic ~ 家庭经济/ national ~ 国民经济/ market ~ 市场经济

ecosystem /ˈiːkəʊsɪstəm/ *n.* [C] 生态系统：an agricultural ~ 农业生态系统

ecstasy /ˈekstəsi/ *n.* 狂喜：one's shrill cries of ~喜极而尖叫/They were in ~ at the thought of going home. 一想到回家，他们一个个欣喜若狂。派 ecstatic *adj.*

edge /edʒ/ *n.* [C] 边；边缘：Sitting on the ~ of the chair is not comfortable. 坐在椅子边上很不舒服。

edible /ˈedɪbl/ *adj.* 可以食用的，可以吃的：~ mushrooms 可食用的蘑菇/All parts of the plants are ~. 这些植物的所有部位均可食用。

edit /ˈedɪt/ Ⅰ *vt.* ❶编辑，编选，编校：~ the selected works of Shakespeare 编校莎士比亚作品选 ❷主编(报纸、杂志等)；担任(报纸、杂志、专栏等)的编辑：He used to ~ the *Washington Post*. 他曾任《华盛顿邮报》的主编。❸修改；改写：He carefully ~ed his speech after the fact. 他根据事实仔细修改自己的

讲稿。❹剪辑(影片、录音等) Ⅱ *n.* [C] 编辑;校订;剪辑;经编辑而改动的地方: He gave the book a final ~. 他对这本书做了最后一次校订。

edition / ɪˈdɪʃn / *n.* [C]版本: a pocket ~ 袖珍版/ They planned to publish a new ~ of the book. 他们计划出这本书的新版本。

editor / ˈedɪtə(r) / *n.* [C]编辑,编者: the ~ in chief 总编辑/a chief ~ 主编

editorial / ˌedɪˈtɔːrɪəl / Ⅰ *n.* [C]社论: publish an ~ 发表社论/ Have you read today's ~? 你读了今天的社论吗? Ⅱ *adj.* 编辑的;社论的: ~ staff 编辑人员

educate / ˈedʒʊkeɪt / *vt.* 教育;培养: She was ~d for the law. 她是学法律的。/ You should ~ your students to behave well. 你应教导你的学生们守规矩。

education / ˌedʒʊˈkeɪʃn / *n.* 教育;培养;训练: elementary (secondary, high) ~ 初等(中等,高等)教育 / nine-year compulsory ~ 九年制义务教育/ broadcasting (TV) ~ 广播(电视)教育/ legal ~ 法制教育/ Our country is reforming the management system of ~ . 我国正进行教育管理体制改革。/ She hopes that her daughter will have a college ~. 她希望她的女儿接受大学教育。

educational / ˌedʒʊˈkeɪʃənl / *adj.* 教育(性)的;有教育意义的: Educational Law 教育法/ ~ reform 教育改革

educator / ˈedʒukeɪtə(r) / *n.* [C] 教育家

effect / ɪˈfekt / *n.* 结果;影响: Did the medicine have any ~? 这药有效吗? / Our argument had no ~ on her. 我们的争论对她没有影响。/ **in** ~ 事实上;实际上: The two methods are in ~ identical. 这两个方法实际上是一样的。**of no** ~无效;不中用: The search has been of no ~. 这次搜查一无所获。**give** ~ **to** 实行;实施;使生效: We decided to give ~ to his plan. 我们决定实施他的计划。

effective / ɪˈfektɪv / *adj.* 有效的;生效的: This kind of medicine is ~ against TB. 这种药对治疗结核有效。/ The rule will be ~ from May 1. 这个规定将从5月1日起生效。派 effectively *adv.*

efficiency / ɪˈfɪʃnsi / *n.* [U]效率;功效;效能: The new machine will improve our ~ greatly. 这台新机器将极大地提高效率。

efficient / ɪˈfɪʃnt / *adj.* 效率高的;有能力的: With an ~ machine, one can do more work. 使用效率高的机器可以干更多的活。

effort / ˈefət / *n.* 努力;尽力;艰难的尝试: They finished the project in a common ~. 在共同的努力下,他们完成了那项工程。/ He carried the big box away with little ~. 他毫不费力地搬走了那个大箱子。

e. g. (=for example; for instance)例如

egg / eg / *n.* [C] 蛋;卵

eggplant / ˈegˌplɑːnt, ˈegˌplænt / *n.* [C] 茄;茄子

eggshell / ˈegˌʃel / *n.* [C]蛋壳

ego / ˈiːgəʊ, ˈegəʊ / *n.* [C](*pl.* egos) ❶自我,自己 ❷自尊(心);自我形象: boost sb.'s ~ 提升某人的形象/It was a blow to my ~. 这件事对我的自尊心是个打击。❸自我中心;自负: feed sb.'s ~满足某人的虚荣心

egoism / ˈiːgəʊˌɪz(ə)m/ *n.* [U] ❶自我中心;自私自利 ❷利己主义;自我主义;唯我主义

eight / eɪt / Ⅰ *num.* 八,8 Ⅱ *adj.* 八个

E

（的）

eighteen / ˌeɪˈtiːn / Ⅰ *num.* 十八，18 Ⅱ *adj.* 十八个(的)

eighth / eɪtθ / Ⅰ *num.* 第八；八分之一 Ⅱ *adj.* 第八的；八分之一的

eighty / ˈeɪti / Ⅰ *num.* 八十，80 Ⅱ *adj.* 八十个(的)

E

either / ˈaɪðə(r)，ˈiːðə(r) / Ⅰ *adj.*（两者之间）任何一个：Either of the girls is ready. 两个女孩都准备好了。/ He may go by ~ road. 两条路他随便走哪条都可以。Ⅱ *conj.* 或者；要么：**either ...or ...** 或者……或者……；不是……就是……：He must be ~ mad or drunk. 他不是疯了就是喝醉了。Ⅲ *adv.* 也(用于否定、疑问句中)：In the old days there were no factories in the town. There were no hospitals ~. 过去这座城镇既没有工厂，也没有医院。

elaborate Ⅰ / ɪˈlæbərət / *adj.* 精致的；详尽的；复杂的：with ~ care 无微不至地/Her skirt was decorated with ~ embroidery. 她的裙服绣有错落有致的花饰。Ⅱ / ɪˈlæbəreɪt/ *v.* ❶精心制作；详细搞出：He ~d his plans for the business. 他为这项业务悉心制订计划。❷详尽阐述：Just tell us the facts and don't ~ on them. 只需将事实见告，不必加以详述。派 elaborately *adv.*

elapse / ɪˈlæps / *vi.*（时间）流逝，消逝，过去：Thirty minutes ~d before the performance began. 过了 30 分钟演出才开始。/There months have ~d since he left home. 他离家已有三个月了。

elastic / ɪˈlæstɪk / Ⅰ *adj.* 弹性的；灵活的：an ~ waistband 弹力腰带 Ⅱ *n.*［C］松紧带；橡皮圈

elbow / ˈelbəʊ / *n.*［C］肘；弯头；弯管：He put his ~s on the desk while he was reading. 看书时他把双肘支在书桌上。

elder / ˈeldə(r) / Ⅰ *adj.* 年长的：~ brother 哥哥/~ sister 姐姐 Ⅱ *n.* 年龄较大者；(常用 *pl.*)年长者；长辈：She is my ~ by three years. 她比我大三岁。/ We should respect the ~s. 我们应当尊敬长辈。

elderly / ˈeldəli / *adj.* 上了年纪的；中年以上的：~ people 上年纪的人

elect / ɪˈlekt / *vt.* 选举；选择：He was ~ed. 他当选了。/ We ~ed him as team leader. 我们选他当队长。

election / ɪˈlekʃn / *n.* 选举；选举权：They will hold an ~ at the basic level first. 他们将首先举行基层选举。

elective / ɪˈlektɪv/ Ⅰ *adj.* ❶(官员、职位等)选任的；选举的，选举产生的：an ~ government (official) 选举产生的政府(官员) / the ~ post 选任的职位 ❷(机构)有选举权的：~ functions 选举的职能 / the ~ franchise 选举权 ❸(课程)选修的，可以选择的：an ~ course of study 选修课程 Ⅱ *n.*［C］选修科目，选修课程：Her major is biology, but she has room for two music ~s. 她的专业课是生物学，但她还可以再选两门音乐选修课。

electric / ɪˈlektrɪk / *adj.* 电的；电动的；带电的：an ~ automobile 电动汽车/ an ~ battery 蓄电池/ an ~ bell 电铃/ an ~ light 电灯/ ~ wave 电波/ ~ wire 电线

electrical / ɪˈlektrɪkl / *adj.* 与电有关的：an ~ engineer 电机工程师/ an ~ machine 电机

electrician / ɪˌlekˈtrɪʃn / *n.*［C］电工；电学家

electricity / ɪˌlekˈtrɪsəti / *n.*［U］电；电学；电力：a machine worked by ~ 用电

驱动的机器

electrify / ɪˈlektrɪfaɪ / *vt.* 使触电；使充电；使电气化

electro- / ɪˈlektrəʊ / （前缀）表示“电”“电的”“电解”：~lysis 电解 / ~plate 电镀 / ~therapy 电疗法

electrode / ɪˈlektrəʊd / *n.* [C] 电极

electron / ɪˈlektrɒn / *n.* [C] 电子：an ~ microscope 电子显微镜 / an ~ tube 电子管

electronic / ɪˌlekˈtrɒnɪk / *adj.* 电子的：~ books 电子图书/ an ~ dictionary 电子词典 / an ~ clock 电子钟/ ~ music 电子音乐 /Most little boys like ~ toys. 大多数小男孩都喜欢电子玩具。

electronics / ɪˌlekˈtrɒnɪks / *n.* [U] 电子学

elegant / ˈelɪgənt / *adj.* 优雅的；优美的；精致的：an ~ art 高雅的艺术/ Her husband is an ~ middle-aged gentleman. 她的丈夫是一位温文儒雅的中年绅士。派 elegantly *adv.*

element / ˈelɪmənt / *n.* 元素；要素；成分：The teacher asked his students to recite “the Periodic Table of the Elements”. 老师要求他的学生背诵元素周期表。/ Honesty is one of the main ~s of success. 诚实是成功的主要要素之一。

elementary / ˌelɪˈmentri / *adj.* 初等的；基本的：~ education 初等教育/a ~ school (美)小学

elephant / ˈelɪfənt / *n.* [C] 大象

elevate / ˈelɪˌveɪt / *vt.* ❶举起，提高；使上升；抬起，抬高：~ one's eyebrows 扬眉/~ a railway above ground level 架高铁路以高出地面 ❷提拔，提升……的职位；使晋级：be ~d to a higher rank for bravery 因勇敢而受提拔

elevation / ˌelɪˈveɪʃən/ *n.* ❶提高；抬升；架高；提升，晋级：sb.'s ~ to the presidency of the corporation 某人晋升为公司总裁 ❷高度；海拔：We were flying at an ~ of 20,000 m. 我们在海拔20 000米的高空中飞行。❸[C]高地；丘；(皮肤、地面等处的)隆起：I was on a slight ~ and could see the whole length of the gorge. 站在小丘之巅，我可以饱览峡谷的全貌。

elevator / ˈelɪveɪtə(r) / *n.* [C] ❶起重机，提升机 ❷[=(英)lift](美)电梯

eleven / ɪˈlevn / Ⅰ *num.* 十一，11 Ⅱ *adj.* 十一个(的)

eleventh / ɪˈlevnθ / Ⅰ *num.* 第十一；十一分之一 Ⅱ *adj.* 第十一的；十一分之一的

eliminate / ɪˈlɪmɪneɪt / *vt.* 消灭；排除；淘汰：This game will ~ the losing team. 这场比赛将淘汰输了的球队。/ You must ~ errors in your calculation. 你必须消灭计算中出现的差错。

elimination / ɪˌlɪmɪˈneɪʃn / *n.* [U]消灭；排除；淘汰：They will hold an ~ match next week. 下周他们举行预赛(淘汰赛)。

elite, élite / ɪˈliːt, eɪˈliːt / *n.* [C]出类拔萃的人(或物)；精英，尖子：a small intellectual ~寥若晨星的知识界精英/the ~ of teas 茶叶中的上品

ellipse / ɪˈlɪps / *n.* [C] 椭圆；椭圆形

ellipsis / ɪˈlɪpsɪs / *n.* 省略法；省略号

eloquence / ˈeləkwəns / *n.* [U] 雄辩；口才；修辞：He is matchless in ~. 他的口才无人匹敌。

eloquent / ˈeləkwənt / *adj.* 雄辩的；有说服力的：He is an ~ speaker. 他是一位雄辩的演说家。/ The lawyer produced ~ proof at the court. 在法庭上律师提

E

供了有力的证据。

else / els / *adj*. & *adv*. (常用在疑问代词、疑问副词、不定代词后)另外,其他:What ~ do you want? 你还想要什么?/ Is there anything ~ you want to say? 你还有什么话要说吗?

E

elsewhere / ˌelsˈweə(r) / *adv*. 在别处:We haven't the book you want; you may go ~ for it. 我们这儿没有你需要的那本书,你可以去别处看看。

elude / ɪˈljuːd / *vt*. ❶闪避,躲避(危险、追问等);逃避(责任、困难等),推托:~ capture by the police 逃避警方的追捕/ ~ observation 避人耳目/The sly fox ~d the dogs. 那只狡猾的狐狸机敏地避开了猎狗。❷使想不起;使不理解,使不懂:The cause of cancer has ~d all research. 癌症的病因还没有研究出来。/ I remember his face, but his name ~d me for the moment. 他的脸挺熟,但我一下子想不起他的名字来。

e-mail / ˈiːmeɪl / *n*. (= electronic mail) [C] 电子邮件:Please tell me your ~ address. 请把你的电子邮件地址告诉我。

emancipate / ɪˈmænsɪˌpeɪt / *vt*. 解除……的束缚;使从约束中解脱;释放,使自由;解放:Women have been ~d from many old restrictions. 妇女已从许许多多旧的束缚中解放出来。派 emancipation *n*.

embankment / ɪmˈbæŋkmənt/ *n*. [C] ❶(公路或铁路的)路堤;堤岸,堤围:a railway ~ 铁路路堤 ❷筑堤

embark / emˈbɑːk, ɪmˈbɑːk/ *v*. ❶上船,乘船;上飞机,登机;上车(与 for 连用):~ for Europe from Halifax 从哈利法克斯乘飞机去欧洲/The ship ~ed passengers and cargo at Australian port. 船在澳大利亚港载客装货。❷从事,着手,开始做(与 in, on, upon 连用):~ on a major programme of modernization 开始实施宏伟的现代化计划 / He is ~ing on a new career as an engineer. 他准备开始一种工程师的新生涯。派 embarkation *n*.

embarrass / ɪmˈbærəs / *vt*. 使窘迫;使为难:He felt ~ed about his foolish mistake. 他为所犯的愚蠢错误感到窘迫。/ Don't ~ her by asking her personal questions. 别提些个人隐私问题去为难她。派 embarrassment *n*.

embassy / ˈembəsi / *n*. [C]大使馆:He works in the Chinese Embassy in London. 他在中国驻伦敦大使馆工作。

embellish / ɪmˈbelɪʃ / *vt*. ❶美化;修饰,装饰:Hampton's office was already ~ed with masterly paintings. 汉普顿的办公室已经用许多幅名画布置了起来。❷添加(叙述)的细节;润色(文章),润饰;渲染:The events of his life were heavily ~ed by his biographers. 他的生平事迹已被传记作家们添油加醋地大加渲染。

embezzle / ɪmˈbezl / *vt*. 盗用,挪用;贪污(公款);霸占,侵吞(财物):He ~d all the old lady's money. 他侵吞了那个老太太的全部钱财。/An assistant manager was charged with embezzling 2 million from the bank. 一名助理经理被指控贪污了银行的 200 万美元。

emblem / ˈembləm/ *n*. [C](尤指抽象概念的)象征,标志,标记:The beaver and the maple leaf are both ~s of Canada. 海狸和枫叶都是加拿大的标志。/ Our child would be a dazzling ~ of our love. 我们的孩子将是我们令人称羡的爱情的象征。

embody / ɪmˈbɒdi / *vt*. ❶体现;使具体

化:The article embodies the author's ideas. 文章体现了作者的思想。❷包含;收录:The new machine embodies many improvements. 新机器有了不少改进。

embrace /ɪmˈbreɪs/ Ⅰ *vt.* ❶(拥)抱:The police came into the room embracing a baby in his arms. 警察走进房间,怀里抱着一个小婴儿。❷包括;包含:This passage ~s many new points. 这段文章包括许多新的要点。❸ 包围;环绕:The old lady lives in the house ~d by green trees. 老太太住在一座绿树环绕的房子里。Ⅱ *n.* [C]拥抱;怀抱:She gave her husband a tight ~ when she met him again. 再见面时,她紧紧拥抱自己的丈夫。

embroider /ɪmˈbrɒɪdə(r)/ *vt.* ❶刺绣;在……上绣(花样):~ a handkerchief with one's initials 在手绢上绣上自己姓名的首字母 ❷对(故事等)加以修饰,润色;对(叙述等)添枝加叶,渲染:He ~ed the account of the shipwreck to hold his listeners' interest. 为了吸引听众,他对那次海难事件大肆铺陈了一番。/He would take a theme and ~ upon it with drollery. 他会将一篇文章以调侃式的幽默笔调加以点染。

embryo /ˈembrɪəʊ/ *n.* [C] 胚胎:Do you know anything about the human ~? 你了解有关人类胚胎的知识吗?

emcee /ˈemˈsiː/ *n.* [C]司仪;(演出等的)节目主持人:Who was (the) ~ of the show last night? 昨晚那场演出的节目主持人是谁?

emend /ɪˈmend/ *vt.* 校订,校勘;修订(文稿等),修改(作品等):~ the text of a book 校订书中正文/The terms of the agreement should be ~ed to take the new conditions into account. 考虑到新的情况,协议书的条款应该修改。派 emendation *n.*

emerald /ˈem(ə)rəld/ Ⅰ *n.* ❶祖母绿,纯绿柱石 ❷[C]翡翠,绿宝石,绿刚玉:a ring set with ~s 一枚镶嵌绿宝石的戒指 Ⅱ *adj.* 绿宝石色的;翡翠绿的:~ green 翡翠绿

emerge /iˈmɜːdʒ/ *vi.* ❶(从液体中)浮现,浮出;出现;出来(与 from 连用):a ship emerging from the fog 从雾中驶出的船 / The chick ~d from its shell. 雏鸡钻出蛋壳。❷显现,暴露,为人所知:No new evidence ~d during the enquiry. 调查中没有发现新的证据。派 emergence

emergency /ɪˈmɜːdʒənsi/ *n.* 紧急情况;突发事件;非常时期:The state of ~ in that district has ended. 那个地区的紧急状态结束了。/ Please call an ~ ambulance to send her to hospital. 请叫一辆急救车送她去医院。

emigrate /ˈemɪgreɪt/ *v.* 移居国外:He and the whole family ~d from Japan to America three years ago. 三年前他和他的全家从日本移民到美国去了。

eminence /ˈemɪnəns/ *n.* ❶[U]卓越,杰出;著名,显赫:a woman of great ~ as a physicist 卓越的女物理学家 / achieve (win, attain) ~ as a painter 成为著名的画家 / have (occupy) a position of great ~ in the political world 在政界身居极显要的地位 ❷(**E-**)[C]阁下,大人(天主教中对红衣主教的尊称):Your Eminence 主教阁下

eminent /ˈemɪnənt/ *adj.* ❶卓越的,杰出的;著名的,有名的;显赫的:The committee has 10 members, each ~ in his or her particular field. 该委员会有10名成员,他们在各自的领域内都是

出类拔萃的。❷(品质)优秀的,突出的;非凡的;显著的:a man of ~ impartiality 大公无私的人

emit /ɪˈmɪt/ *vt.* (emitted; emitting) 散发;放射;发射:The dead fish ~ted a terrible smell. 死鱼发出可怕的臭味。/ To ~ black smoke into the sky is not allowed. 向天空排放浓烟是不允许的。

E

emotion /ɪˈməʊʃn/ *n.* [U] 感情;情绪;激动:deep ~ 深厚的感情/ mixed ~ 复杂的感情/ She was shaking with ~. 她激动得浑身发抖。派 emotional *adj.*

emperor /ˈempərə(r)/ *n.* [C] 皇帝

emphasis /ˈemfəsɪs/ *n.* 强调;重点:He spoke with ~ on the importance of learning English well. 他强调学好英语的重要性。/ **lay (place, put) ~ on** 强调:Some schools lay special ~ on improving the teaching conditions. 有些学校特别强调改善教学条件。

emphasize /ˈemfəsaɪz/ *vt.* 强调;着重:She ~d the importance of good health. 她强调身体健康的重要。

empire /ˈempaɪə(r)/ *n.* [C] 帝国:the Roman Empire 罗马帝国

employ /ɪmˈplɒɪ/ *vt.* 雇用;使用:She ~s her time wisely. 她善于利用时间。/ He was ~ed in a bank. 他受雇于一家银行。

employee /ˌemplɒɪˈiː, emˈplɒiː/ *n.* [C] 受雇者,雇工,雇员

employment /ɪmˈplɒɪmənt/ *n.* [U] 职业;工作:an ~ opportunity 就业机会 / the ~ rate 就业率 / a system of ~ under contract (合同)聘用制/ He has find ~. 他已找到工作。

empower /ɪmˈpaʊə(r)/ *vt.* 授权;准许:I ~ my agent to make the deal for me. 我授权我的代理人处理此项交易。/ His assistant will be ~ed to act on his behalf in less weighty matters. 他的助理被授权代表他处理那些次要事务。派 empowerment *n.*

empty /ˈempti/ Ⅰ *adj.* 空的;未占用的;空虚的:The box is ~. 箱子是空的。/ I found an ~ seat in the bus. 我在公共汽车上找到一个空座位。/ I don't want to hear your ~ talk. 我不想听你讲空话。Ⅱ *v.* 倒空;变空:The room emptied very quickly. 房子很快就腾空了。/ The dustbins haven't been emptied for two weeks. 垃圾箱已有两个星期没倒过了。

enable /ɪˈneɪbl/ *vt.* 使……能够 /~ **sb. to do sth.** 使某人能做某事:A fast car ~s them to reach Beijing before midnight. 高速汽车能使他们在午夜前赶到北京。

enchanted /ɪnˈtʃɑːntɪd/ *adj.* 着魔的;痴迷的;陶醉的:The little girl was ~ with her new dress. 那个小女孩对她那件新裙子着了迷了。

encircle /ɪnˈsɜːkl/ *vt.* 环绕;围绕;包围:The scientist was ~d by hundreds of young students. 科学家被几百名年轻学生围住了。

enclose /ɪnˈkləʊz/ *vt.* ❶围住;圈起:The teacher ~d the wrong words with a circle. 老师把错字圈起来。❷封入;附上:He ~d a check in the letter to his daughter. 他随信给女儿附寄了一张支票。

enclosure /ɪnˈkləʊʒə(r)/ *n.* ❶圈地;围场:the ~ of public land 围圈公地 / a fenced ~ 四周围有篱笆的场地 ❷[C] 装入物;(尤指信中的)附件:The letter said there was an ~, but they obviously forgot to put it in. 信中说内有附件,可

他们显然忘了把它装进信封。/ The envelope contained a letter and $5 as an ~. 信封内装有一封信,并附有5美元。

encounter / ɪnˈkaʊntə(r) / *v.* 遭遇;意外遇见:~ difficulties 遇到困难/ ~ an old friend 偶遇一位老朋友

encourage / ɪnˈkʌrɪdʒ / *vt.* 鼓励;促进:The good news of her success ~d me greatly. 她成功的喜讯极大地鼓励了我。/~ **sb. to do sth.** 鼓励某人做某事:He always ~s me to do the same. 他总是鼓励我做同样的事。

encyclopedia / ɪnˌsaɪkləˈpiːdɪə / *n.* [C] 百科全书:He needs an ~ of agriculture. 他需要一部农业百科全书。

end / end / Ⅰ *n.* [C] 端,尖;尽头;结束;目的,目标:I have read the book from beginning to ~. 我把那本书从头至尾读了一遍。/ They have traveled through the whole country by the ~ of the year. 到年底为止他们已游遍全国。/ In order to attain his ~, he worked very hard. 为了达到目的,他十分努力地工作。/ **in the** ~ 最后;终于:I am sure everything will turn out all right in the ~. 我确信最终一切都会好起来的。**no** ~ 无穷:That would help us no ~. 那对我们的帮助是无法估量的。**on** ~ 竖着;继续地:Place the box on ~. 把箱子竖起来放。/ We stood there for three hours on ~. 我们在那里一连站了三个小时。**put an** ~ **to** 终止;结束:We must put an ~ to this foolish behavior. 我们必须中止这种愚蠢的行为。Ⅱ *v.* 结束;终止:Wine ~ed him. 喝酒使他丧了命。/ He ~ed his speech with a proposal. 他以一个建议结束了讲话。

endanger / ɪnˈdeɪndʒə(r) / *vt.* 危及;危害;使危险:Smoking ~s man's health. 吸烟危害人类健康。

endeavo(u)r / ɪnˈdevə(r) / Ⅰ *vi.* 努力;尽力:He ~s to keep things nice about his place. 他努力把他周围的环境整理得很优雅。Ⅱ *n.* [C] 努力;尽力:Her ~s to persuade him to go with her but failed. 她尽力劝他同她一起去,但失败了。

endemic / enˈdemɪk/ *adj.* (疾病等)地方性的;区域性(或某人群中)流行的:Cholera is ~ in (to) India. 霍乱在印度很流行。/ an ~ disease among miners 矿工中流行的职业病

ending / ˈendɪŋ / *n.* [C] 结尾;结局:A good ~ is better than a good beginning. 好的结尾胜过好的开头。

endless / ˈendləs / *adj.* 无穷无尽的;没完没了的:~ discussion 无休止的讨论/ ~ talk 冗长的谈话

endow / ɪnˈdaʊ / *vt.* ❶向……捐钱(或物);捐赠;资助:~ a public institution 向某一公共机构捐赠基金 ❷给予,赋予;认为……具有某种物质:~ words with new significance 赋予词以新的含义/Nature ~ed her with beauty and wit. 她天生才貌双全。派 endowment *n.*

endurance / ɪnˈd(j)ʊərəns/ *n.* [U] ❶忍耐;忍耐力:The agony was beyond her ~. 这种痛苦她忍受不了。❷持久(性),耐久(性);强度,抗磨度;耐疲劳度:an athlete's powers of ~ 运动员的耐力 / You need great ~ to run a marathon. 跑马拉松需要巨大的耐久力。

endure / ɪnˈdjʊə(r) / *v.* 忍受;忍耐:I can't ~ her impoliteness. 我不能容忍她的无礼。

enduring / ɪnˈdjʊərɪŋ / *adj.* 持久的;不朽的:~ peace 永久和平

E

enemy / ˈenəmi / *n.* [C] 敌人；仇敌；敌军：The soldiers fired at the ~. 战士们向敌人开火。

energetic / ˌenəˈdʒetɪk / *adj.* 积极的；有力的；精力旺盛的：To play basketball needs ~ players. 打篮球需要精力旺盛的运动员。

energy / ˈenədʒi / *n.* 能量；精力；活力：mental and physical energies 脑力和体力/ solar ~ 太阳能/ youthful ~ 青春活力/ atomic ~ 原子能/ ~ sources 能源/ We welcome ~-saving products. 我们乐意接纳节能型产品。

enfold / ɪnˈfəʊld/ *vt.* ❶包，包起，包进；裹住：The lady was ~ed in a shawl. 那女士裹着一条围巾。❷抱，拥抱，怀抱：She ~ed the child lovingly in her arms. 她充满疼爱地将孩子抱在怀里。

enforce / ɪnˈfɔːs / *vt.* 实行；执行；强制：These rules should be ~d strictly. 这些规则应当严格执行。派 enforcement *n.*

engage / ɪnˈgeɪdʒ / *v.* ❶从事；忙于；参加：He has been ~d in foreign trade for eight years. 他从事外贸工作八年了。❷占用(时间等)：The line is ~d. 电话占线。/ Network games has ~d all his time. 玩网络游戏占去了他所有的时间。❸雇用；聘用：They broke a rule to ~ the young man as sales manager. 他们破格录用那年轻人当销售部经理。❹订婚：He is ~d to his secretary. 他和他的秘书订婚了。/~ **for** 担保，保证：That is more than I can ~ for. 我可负不了这么大的责任。

engagement / ɪnˈgeɪdʒmənt/ *n.* [C] ❶承诺，许诺，保证；契约；承担的义务：keep (break) an ~ 践约(违约) / fulfill all one's ~s 履行所有的承诺 ❷约会：enter into (make) an ~ with sb. 与某人约会 / have a dinner ~ with sb. 约某人吃饭 ❸订婚；婚约：announce (break off) one's ~ 宣布订婚(解除婚约) / a broken ~ 背弃的婚约 ❹雇，聘，约请；受雇(期)，受聘(期)：The actor had an ~ of three weeks in a play. 那位演员受聘参加该剧演出三周。

engine / ˈendʒɪn / *n.* [C] 发动机；引擎：There is something wrong with the fire ~. 消防车出了点毛病。

engineer / ˌendʒɪˈnɪə(r) / *n.* [C] 工程师；技师；火车司机：~s and technicians 工程技术人员/ a chief ~，an ~ in chief 总工程师

engineering / ˌendʒɪˈnɪərɪŋ / *n.* [U] 工程；工程学：space ~ 航天工程/ genetic ~遗传工程/ system ~ 系统工程/ My brother studies at an ~ college. 我哥哥在一所工学院上学。

English / ˈɪŋglɪʃ / Ⅰ *n.* [U]英语：He speaks ~ well. 他英语说得很好。/ I write diary in ~. 我用英语写日记。Ⅱ *adj.* 英国的；英语的：She made friends with an ~ girl. 她和一个英国女孩交朋友。/ I like to read ~ novels. 我喜欢读英语小说。

Englishman / ˈɪŋglɪʃmən / *n.* [C] (*pl.* Englishmen)英国人；英国男子

engrave / ɪnˈgreɪv / *vt.* ❶雕，雕刻，在……上雕刻：~ the ring in a floral pattern 把戒指刻成花卉图案 ❷使深深印入，铭刻；使铭记：childhood experiences ~d in our memory 深深印在我们记忆中的童年时代的往事

engross / ɪnˈgrəus/ *vt.* 使全神贯注，吸引(注意力)；占去(全部时间等)：~one's time 占去某人的全部时间 / She was ~ed by the interesting story. 她被那个有趣的故事迷住了。/ The artist was so

~ed in his painting that he didn't notice the people watching him. 画家全神贯注于作画,一点儿也没觉察到有人在瞧着他。派 engrossing *adj.*

engulf /ɪnˈɡʌlf/ *vt.* ❶吞没,淹没:A great wave ~ed the small boat. 巨浪把那条小船吞没了。/The house was ~ed in flames. 房子为大火所吞没。❷使沉浸在;使深陷于:be ~ed by debts 债台高筑/Vera was ~ed with a wave of terror. 维拉陷入了一阵恐怖之中。

enhance /ɪnˈhɑːns, ɪnˈhæns/ *vt.* 提高(质量、价值等);增加(魅力等),增大;增强,加强;使更好:~ one's image (beauty, prestige) 提升形象(使自己越发美丽,提高威望) / Rarity ~s the worth of things. 物以稀为贵。派 enhancement *n.*

enjoy /ɪnˈdʒɒɪ/ *vt.* 享受……的乐趣;喜爱;欣赏:Children ~ swimming in summer. 孩子们夏天喜爱游泳。/ We ~ sports very much. 我们非常喜爱运动。/ ~ **oneself** 过得快乐:Did you ~ yourselves during the winter vacation? 你们寒假过得愉快吗?

enjoyable /ɪnˈdʒɒɪəbəl/ *adj.* 可从中得到乐趣的,令人愉快的,使人快乐的:a very ~film 一部很有趣的影片 / have an ~day 度过愉快的一天

enjoyment /ɪnˈdʒɒɪmənt/ *n.* ❶[U]娱乐;欢乐:You can get much ~ out of that movie. 看了那部电影你会得到很多乐趣。❷[C]娱乐活动:Life has a lot of ~s. 生活中有很多乐趣。

enlarge /ɪnˈlɑːdʒ/ *vt.* 扩大;放大;增大:~ a photograph 放大照片/ ~ one's views 开阔视野 派 enlargement *n.*

enlighten /ɪnˈlaɪtn/ *vt.* 启发,启迪;指导,教育;使明白,使领悟:Radio should ~ the listener as well as entertain him. 无线电广播应该使听众既得到娱乐又受到教育。/Can you ~ me on the nature of your research project? 你能不能给我讲讲你的研究项目的性质? 派 enlightenment *n.*

enlist /ɪnˈlɪst/ *v.* ❶(尤指自愿地)从军;(使)入伍;征募:~ as a volunteer 作为志愿兵应征入伍/After graduation he was ~ed for (into) the army. 毕业后他应募入伍当了陆军。❷谋取……的赞助(或支持);赢得(支持、赞助等);争取:~ sb.'s support for the campaign to keep the hospital open 争取某人资助维持医院营业的运动 / ~ all the available resources 利用一切可以利用的资源

enmity /ˈenmɪti/ *n.* 敌意,憎恨,仇恨;敌对,不和:be at ~ with 与……不和/ have ~ against 对……怀有仇恨(或敌意)

enormous /ɪˈnɔːməs/ *adj.* 巨大的;庞大的:They held the meeting in an ~ hall. 他们在一个庞大的礼堂里开会。/ Where did you get such an ~ sum of money? 你从什么地方弄到了这么一大笔钱?

enough /ɪˈnʌf/ Ⅰ *adj.* 足够的;充足的:Five men will be quite ~. 五个人就足够了。/ Do you have ~ time to help me with my lessons? 你有时间帮助我复习功课吗? Ⅱ *pron.* 充足;足够:I have ~ to do. 我有好多事情要做。Ⅲ *adv.* 足够地;充分地:The children are old ~ to go to school. 孩子们已到上学的年龄了。

enquire /ɪnˈkwaɪə(r)/ *v.* (=inquire)询问;调查

enquiry /ɪnˈkwaɪəri/ *n.* (=inquiry)询问;调查

enrich / ɪnˈrɪtʃ / *vt.* ❶使富裕；使丰富：Our government has issued a lot of good policies to ~ the people. 我们的政府颁布了许多富民的好政策。/ She studied hard to ~ the mind with knowledge. 她努力学习知识以增长才智。❷使(土地)肥沃：They ~ed the soil with fertilizer. 他们施肥使土壤肥沃。派 enrichment *n.*

E

enrol(l) / ɪnˈrəʊl / (-rolled;-rolling) *vt.* 登记；招收：The school is going to ~ 300 new students this year. 今年学校要招收 300 名新生。—*vi.* 参军；注册；成为会员：Her son ~led himself in the army two years ago. 她儿子两年前参军了。/ I have ~led for three new courses. 本期我注册修三门新课。派 enrollment *n.*

enslave / ɪnˈsleɪv / *vt.* 使做奴隶；奴役：The captures there were ~d and ill-treated. 那里的战俘们受到奴役和虐待。派 enslavement *n.*

ensure / ɪnˈʃʊə(r) / *vt.* ❶保证；担保：The doctor often tells his patients that a good rest ~s quicker recovery. 大夫常常告诉病人好好休息能保证身体早日康复。❷保护；使安全：A teacher should have the responsibility to ~ his students against danger. 教师应当有责任保护学生免遭危险。

entangle / ɪnˈtæŋgl / *vt.* ❶缠绕，缠住；使纠缠：The bird got ~d in the net. 鸟给网圈套住了。❷使卷入；使陷入(困境等)；牵涉，牵连：He ~d himself in the activities of a group of criminals. 他卷入了一犯罪团伙的活动中。

enter / ˈentə(r) / *v.* 进入；参加；使加入：She ~ed the room. 她进了房间。/ My brother ~ed university two years ago. 两年前我哥哥上了大学。/ Their products have ~ed the international market. 他们的产品已跻身国际市场。

enterprise / ˈentəpraɪz / *n.* [C] 事业；企业

entertain / ˌentəˈteɪn / *v.* 使娱乐；使欢乐；使有兴趣；招待；款待：The Smiths ~ a great deal. 史密斯家常招待客人。/ The performance ~ed us very much. 我们饶有兴趣地看了那场演出。

entertainment / ˌentəˈteɪnmənt / *n.* ❶[U] 招待；款待：He is busy preparing for the ~ of his old friend. 他正忙着准备接待老朋友。❷[C]招待会：They will give a farewell ~ to the graduates next Monday. 他们下周一将为毕业生举行欢送会。❸表演会；文娱：Young people like ~ films. 年轻人喜欢看娱乐片。

enthusiasm / ɪnˈθjuːzɪæzəm / *n.* [U]热情；热心；热忱：The retired old man has a great ~ for fishing. 那位退休老人热衷于钓鱼。

enthusiastic / ɪnˌθjuːzɪˈæstɪk / *adj.* 热情的；热心的：My classmates are all ~ football fans. 我的同班同学都是热心的足球球迷。/ She is ~ over the part-time job. 她对那份兼职工作充满热情。派 enthusiastically *adv.*

entire / ɪnˈtaɪə(r) / *adj.* 全部的；整个的；完全的：She spent the ~ day reading the novel. 她花了一整天时间读那本小说。/ He has ~ confidence that his son will pass the college entrance examination. 他对儿子考上大学有完全的信心。派 entirety *n.*

entirely / ɪnˈtaɪəli / *adv.* 完全地；彻底地；全部地：I agree to your plan ~. 我完全同意你的计划。

entitle / ɪnˈtaɪtl / *vt.* ❶ 给……权利(或资格)：The disabled are still fully ~d to higher education. 残疾人也有充分的权利享受高等教育。❷给(书、文章)题名;给……称号:The writer ~d the book *Challenge*. 作者为那本书取名为《挑战》。

entrance /ˈentrəns/ *n.* ❶[C] 入口;门口:They are talking at the ~ to the building. 他们在大楼门口交谈。❷进入;入学;入会:No ~. 禁止入内。/ He didn't take the ~ examination because he was ill. 由于生病他没有参加入学考试。

entreat /ɪnˈtriːt/ *vt.* 恳求;乞求:He ~ed the judge for another chance. 他请求法官再给他一次机会。/I ~ your pardon. 请您原谅。

entrepreneur /ˌɒntrəprəˈnɜː(r)/ *n.* [C] 企业家:The report was made by a successful ~. 报告由一位成功的企业家所做。

entrust /ɪnˈtrʌst/ *vt.* 委托;信托;托管:Before leaving for London, she ~ed her house to her aunt. 去伦敦之前,她把房屋托付给她的婶婶代管。

entry /ˈentri/ *n.* ❶[C]入口处;门口;通道:Don't stop your car at the ~ of the teaching building. 别在教学楼的入口处停车。❷进入;入场;参赛:He is applying for the ~ to Harvard. 他正在申请进哈佛大学。/ Do you know when was China's first ~ into the Olympic Games? 你知道中国首次参加奥林匹克运动会是什么时候吗?

envelope /ˈenvələʊp/ *n.* [C]信封:a standardized ~ 标准信封/ a pay ~ 工资袋/ She forgot to address the ~. 她忘了在信封上写收信人的姓名地址了。

envious /ˈenvɪəs/ *adj.* 妒忌的;羡慕的:Don't be ~ of other's success. 不要妒忌他人的成功。/ I am ~ of his smartness. 我很羡慕他的精明机灵。

environment /ɪnˈvaɪrənmənt/ *n.* 环境;周围状况;外界:We should protect the ~ from pollution. 我们应当保护环境不遭受污染。/ He who pollutes the ~ should be punished severely. 污染环境的人应当受到严厉的惩罚。/ Everybody wants to have fine working ~. 所有人都希望有良好的工作环境。

environmental /ɪnˌvaɪrənˈmentəl/ *adj.* 环境的;环境产生的:~ monitoring 环境监测/ ~ program 环境规划/ ~ protection 环境保护

envy /ˈenvi/ Ⅰ *vt.* 羡慕;妒忌:How I ~ you! 我真羡慕你! /Don't ~ her good fortune. 不要羡慕她的好运气。Ⅱ *n.* [U]羡慕;妒忌:His success aroused her ~. 他的成功引起了她的妒忌(羡慕)。

enzyme /ˈenzaɪm/ *n.* [C]酶

epic /ˈepɪk/ Ⅰ *n.* [C] ❶史诗,叙事诗:a folk ~民间史诗 ❷史诗般的文艺作品;可歌可泣的事迹:film an ~ of ancient Egypt 拍一部关于古埃及的史诗影片/ the ~ of man's first journey to the moon 人类首次登月的可歌可颂的壮举 Ⅱ *adj.* ❶史诗的,叙事诗的;史诗般的:an ~ poem 史诗 ❷宏大的,巨大规模的:a banquet of ~ proportions 盛大宴会/see an ~ task through to the end 将这项艰巨的任务进行到底

epidemic /ˌepɪˈdemɪk/ *n.* [C] ❶(疾病的)流行,传播:an ~ of AIDS 艾滋病的蔓延 ❷流行病,传染病:Epidemics break out, spread, if they are not contained. 如不加以遏制,各种流行病就会爆发并传播开来。

episode /ˈepɪˌsəʊd/ *n.* [C] ❶(若干或一连串事件中的)一个事件;(人生的)一

段经历：an ~ of one's childhood 某人童年时代的一段经历/an important ~ in our own history 我们历史中的重要篇章 ❷(连载小说中的)一节；(戏剧、电影、电视等的)一出(或一集、一部分)：a TV drama serial of 20 ~s 一部 20 集的电视连续剧/Subsequent ~s will go out on Tuesday on TV. 续集将于星期二在电视上播放。

epoch /ˈiːpɒk/ *n.* [C]时代；纪元：The use of computers has marked an ~ in language teaching. 计算机的运用开创了语言教学的新纪元。

equal /ˈiːkwəl/ Ⅰ *adj.* 平等的；相等的：The women workers demanded ~ pay for ~ work. 女工们要求同工同酬。/ They are ~ in height. 他们身高相同。Ⅱ *n.* [C]相同的事物；对手：I am not her ~ in swimming. 我游泳不是她的对手。/~ **to** 等于：Twice two is ~ to four. 二二得四(2 乘以 2 等于 4)。派 equally *adv.*

equality /ɪˈkwɒləṭi/ *n.* [U]等同；相等；平等：Our society should ensure the ~ of opportunity between the sexes in obtaining employment. 我们的社会应当确保男女就业的机会均等。

equation /ɪˈkweɪʒn/ *n.* [C]方程式；等式：The chemical ~ is interesting. 这个化学方程式很有趣。

equator /ɪˈkweɪtə(r)/ *n.* (the ~) 赤道：The days and the nights are of equal length at the ~. 在赤道白天和夜晚的时间是相等的。

equidistant /ˌiːkwɪˈdɪstənt/ *adj.* 等距(离)的：Montreal and New York are ~ from Vancouver. 从温哥华到蒙特利尔和到纽约是等距离的。

equilateral /iːkwɪˈlætərəl/*adj.* 等边的：an ~ triangle 等边三角形

equilibrium /ˌiːkwɪˈlɪbrɪəm/ *n.* (*pl.* equilibrums 或 equilibria) ❶ 平衡；均衡：maintain ~ on a tight rope 在绷紧的绳索上保持平衡/find an ~ between work and play 在工作和玩乐之间寻求平衡/The scale is held in ~. 天平呈平衡状态。❷[U](心情的)平衡：preserve one's mind in a state of ~保持心境平和/David's ~ has been disturbed. 戴维心绪不宁。

equip /ɪˈkwɪp/ *vt.* (equipped; equipping)装备；配备：The students are fully ~ped for a long journey. 学生们装备齐全准备作一次长途旅行。/ Many offices are ~ped with computers and word processors now. 现在许多办公室都配有计算机和文字处理机。

equipment /ɪˈkwɪpmənt/ *n.* [U]装备；设备；器材：They installed the complete fire-fighting ~ for the factory. 他们为工厂安装了全套消防设备。

equivalent /ɪˈkwɪvələnt/ Ⅰ *adj.* 相等的；相当的；等量的；等值的：What is 100 dollars ~ to in RMB *yuan*? 100 美元相当于多少元人民币？/ The two sentences are ~ in meaning. 这两个句子意思相同。Ⅱ *n.* [C]相等物；等价物；对应物：Please tell the Chinese ~ of this English word. 请说出与这个英语单词相对应的汉语。

era /ˈɪərə/ *n.* [C] 时代；年代；纪元：We have entered an entire new ~. 我们已经进入一个全新的时期。

eradicate /ɪˈrædɪˌkeɪt/ *vt.* 根除；杜绝；消灭：~ crime 杜绝犯罪/~ illiteracy 扫除文盲

erase /ɪˈreɪs/ *vt.* 擦掉；删掉；除去：He ~d the wrong word with a rubber. 他用

橡皮把错字擦掉。/ The boy asked the teacher not to ~ his name from the list. 男孩请求老师不要把他的名字从名单上删掉。

erase /ɪˈreɪz/ *vt.* ❶擦掉,抹(擦)去:Erase the penciled notes in the margins. 把页边空白上的铅笔注解擦掉。❷消除,清除;使忘却:Time ~d grief. 悲伤随着时间的流逝逐渐淡化了。/ She couldn't ~ the tragic scene from her memory. 她无法将那悲惨的情景从记忆中抹去。派 erasable *adj.*

erect /ɪˈrekt/ Ⅰ *vt.* ❶使竖立;使起立:He ~ed a television antenna on the roof. 他在屋顶上架了一根电视接收天线。❷ 建造;建立:The statue was ~ed in 2001. 那座塑像是 2001 年建的。Ⅱ *adj.* 直立的;竖直的:He sat ~ to listen to the teacher. 他端坐着听老师讲课。派 erection *n.*

erode /ɪˈrəʊd/ *vt.* ❶腐蚀,侵蚀;蚀去:There cliffs have been ~d(away) by the sea. 这些峭壁已被海水侵蚀了。❷逐步毁坏;削弱:The scandal has ~d his reputation. 这起丑闻使他的名声不再。

erosion /ɪˈrəʊʒn/ *n.* 腐蚀;侵蚀;磨损;削弱:soil ~土壤的受蚀/wind ~风蚀(作用)/ the ~ of support for the party 对党支持的减少

error /ˈerə(r)/ *n.* [C] 过失;错误:The letter was sent to him in ~. 那封信错送给他了。/ The teacher pointed his ~s in spelling. 老师指出了他的拼写错误。

erupt /ɪˈrʌpt/ *vi.* 喷出;爆发:A glowing river of lava ~ed from the volcano. 炽热的熔岩浆从火山喷出。派 eruption *n.*

escalator /ˈeskəleɪtə(r)/ *n.* [C]自动扶梯:She took the ~ to the fifth floor. 她乘自动扶梯到五楼。

escape /ɪˈskeɪp/ *v.* 逃走;逃跑:He narrowly ~d with his life. 他死里逃生。/ ~ **from** 逃脱;漏出:Gas ~d from the pipe. 煤气从管子里漏出来了。

especial /ɪˈspeʃəl/ *adj.* 特别的;特殊的:They are discussing a question of ~ importance. 他们正在讨论一个特别重要的问题。/ The oil painting is of ~ value. 那幅油画具有特殊的价值。

especially /ɪˈspeʃəli/ *adj.* 特别;尤其;格外:It was ~ cold yesterday. 昨天天气特别冷。/ She writes well, ~ in English. 她的写作很好,特别是英语写作。

essay /ˈeseɪ/ *n.* [C] 议论文;散文,随笔:I wrote an ~ entitled *My Friends*. 我写了一篇题为《我的朋友》的散文。

essence /ˈesns/ *n.* [U] 精华;本质;核心:He didn't seize the ~ of the problem. 他没有抓住问题的本质。/**in** ~ 本质上:The two things are the same in outward form but different in ~. 这两样东西的外表相同,但本质不同。

essential /ɪˈsenʃ(ə)l/ Ⅰ *adj.* 基本的;必不可少的;必要的:Water is ~ to the growth of crops. 水对庄稼的生长是必不可少的。Ⅱ *n.* [C]本质;实质;要素:Diligence and patience are basic ~s to success. 勤奋和耐心是成功的基本要素。

establish /ɪˈstæblɪʃ/ *vt.* 创立;创办;建立:The building was ~ed on a solid base. 这幢大楼建立在坚实的基础上。/ The school ~ed a new course for students. 学校为学生开设了一门新课程。派 establishment *n.*

estate /ɪˈsteɪt/ *n.* [C]房地产;财产;产业:real ~ development 房地产开发 / a real ~ market 房地产交易市场 / He became an ~ agent three years ago. 三

年前他当了一名房地产经纪人。/ The young man inherited an ~ of 15 million dollars. 那年轻人继承了 150 万美元遗产。

esteem / ɪ'stiːm / Ⅰ *n.* [U] 尊敬;尊重:We have a great ~ for our English teacher. 我们对我们的英语老师非常敬重。Ⅱ *vt.* 尊敬;尊重:We ~ him for his great achievements in scientific research. 由于他在科研上获得巨大成就,我们非常尊重他。

esthetic / iːs'θetɪk / *adj.* (=aesthetic)审美的;美学的:According to my ~ standards, the room is decorated quite well. 依照我的审美标准看,这房间装饰得相当好。

estimate / 'estɪmeɪt / *vt.* 估价;估计:He cannot be too highly ~d. 对他的评价再高也不过分。

etc. / et'setərə / (拉丁文 et cetera 的缩写)等等

eternal / ɪ'tɜːnl / *adj.* 永久的;永恒的:Do you believe in ~ life? 你相信生命永恒(不朽)吗? 派 eternally *adv.*

ethical / 'eθɪkl / *adj.* 伦理的;道德的:~ education 伦理教育 / ~ principle 道德原则

ethics / 'eθɪks / *n.* [U]伦理(学);道德(学):professional ~ 职业道德/ A doctor should have medical ~. 一个医生应当有好的医德。

ethnic / 'eθnɪk/ *adj.* ❶种族(上)的;民族的;人种学的:an ~ group 族群 /~ conflicts 种族冲突 ❷有异国情调的,异域的:~ costume 富有异域特色的服饰

euro / 'jʊərəʊ / *n.* [C] 欧元:People use ~s in that country. 在那个国家人们使用欧元。

Europe / 'jʊərəp / *n.* 欧洲

European / ˌjʊərə'piːən / Ⅰ *adj.* 欧洲的 Ⅱ *n.* [C]欧洲人

euthanasia / ˌjuːθə'neɪzɪə / *n.* [U]安乐死

evade / ɪ'veɪd / *vt.* ❶(巧妙地)逃开,逃脱;躲开:~ the pursuit 逃脱追捕 ❷逃避(责任等);回避(问题等):He had found a loophole which allowed him to ~ responsibility. 他找到了逃避责任的可乘之隙。

evaluate / ɪ'væljʊeɪt / *v.* 评价;估价;把……定值:The manager ~s his ability through his work. 经理通过工作评价他的能力。/ Don't ~ people by clothes. 别以衣着论人。

evaluation / ɪˌvæljʊ'eɪʃn / *n.* [U]估计;评价;评估:an ~ system 评价体系/ the ~ of professional titles 职称评定/ job ~ 工作评估

evaporate / ɪ'væpəreɪt / *v.* 蒸发;挥发;脱水:The sun ~d the water on the road. 阳光把地上的水蒸发干了。/ They brought some ~d vegetables with them on their journey. 旅行中他们带了些脱水蔬菜。

eve / iːv / *n.* [C](节日的)前夜,前夕:on the ~ of 在……前夕/ New Year's Eve 除夕/ They had a big party on Christmas Eve. 在平安夜他们举行了一场盛大的晚会。

even1 / 'iːvn / *adv.* 甚至;还;更:Making model boats is ~ more difficult than making model planes. 做模型船比做模型飞机还要困难。/~ **if(though)** 即使:We'll go ~ if(though) he doesn't come. 即使他不来我们也要去。

even2 / 'iːvn / *adj.* ❶均匀的;平稳的;平坦的:She does an ~ work in the company. 她在那家公司干一份稳定的工作。/ They are going to build an airport on the ~ land. 他们将在那块平地上建造机场。❷相当的；均等的：My desk is ~ with the window. 我的书桌与窗户一般高。❸双数的；偶数的：Is 126 an ~ number or an odd number? 126是偶数还是奇数？派 evenly *adv.*

evening / ˈiːvnɪŋ / *n.* 晚上；傍晚；黄昏：The ~ draws on. 夜晚来临。/ He writes in the ~ . 他在晚上写作。

event / ɪˈvent / *n.* [C] ❶大事；事件；时事：current ~s 时事/ a national ~ 国内大事/ an ordinary ~ 平常事/ Marriage is quite an ~ to everybody. 对每个人来说婚姻都是一件大事。/**in any** ~ 不管怎样；反正：In any ~ I'll telephone you before I make a final decision. 不管怎样，我在做出最后决定前都会打电话给你。❷（运动的）比赛项目：field and truck ~s 田径赛/ a team ~ 团体赛

eventually / ɪˈventʃuəli / *adv.* 最后；终于：He worked day and night and ~ made himself ill. 他日夜不停地工作，终于病倒了。

ever / ˈevə(r) / *adv.* 任何时候；曾经：Have you ~ been to the Great Wall? 你去过长城吗？

evergreen / ˈevəˌgriːn / Ⅰ *adj.* 常绿的：~ foliage 常绿的树叶 Ⅱ *n.* [C]常绿植物；万年青：Most tropical plants are ~s. 大多数热带植物是常绿植物。

everlasting / ˌevəˈlɑːstɪŋ / *adj.* ❶永恒的，永存的，不朽的；无穷无尽的：the ~ beauty of the nature 大自然永恒的美 ❷持久的；不停的，不断的：the ~ snows of the mighty Himalayas 雄伟的喜马拉雅山脉的常年积雪

every / ˈevri / *adj.* 每个的；每一的；所有的：He goes to the school library ~ morning. 他每天上午都去学校图书馆。/~ **other** 每隔：I go to see my grandmother ~ other week. 每隔一周我都去看望我的祖母。

everybody / ˈevrɪbɒdi / *pron.* (= everyone)每人；人人：Everybody says it is a good film. 人人都说这是一部好影片。/ Not ~ likes to watch TV. 并不是每个人都喜欢看电视。

everyday / ˈevrɪdeɪ / *adj.* 每日的；日常的：~ life 日常生活/ She learned some ~ English. 她学会了一些日常英语。

everyone / ˈevrɪwʌn / *pron.* (= everybody) 每人；人人

everything / ˈevrɪθɪŋ / *pron.* 一切事物；每件事：I want to teach my students ~ I know. 我要把我所知道的一切都教给我的学生。/ She did ~ carefully. 她把每件事都仔细地做好。

everywhere / ˈevrɪweə(r) / *adv.* 处处；到处：Everywhere the delegation went, it was warmly welcomed. 代表团无论走到哪里，都受到热烈的欢迎。/ I looked ~ for my glasses but failed. 我到处找眼镜都没有找到。

evidence / ˈevɪdəns / *n.* [U]❶根据；证据：The corrupted official attempted to destroy the ~ of his guilt. 那贪官企图毁灭罪证。❷迹象；征兆：There is ~ that he has arrived at the remote village. 有迹象表明他已经到达那个边远的村庄。

evident / ˈevɪdənt / *adj.* 明显的；明白的：It is ~ that she didn't understand what the teacher meant. 很明显她并没有弄清楚老师的意思。派 evidently *adv.*

evil / ˈiːvl / Ⅰ *n.* 邪恶；罪恶；恶行：The teacher should often tell his students the ~s of smoking. 老师应当常给学生讲抽烟的坏处。/ Don't speak ~ of people behind their backs. 不要背后说人坏话。Ⅱ *adj*. 邪恶的;坏的;罪恶的:Everybody knows his ~ deeds in the village. 村里所有的人都知道他的罪恶行径。派 evilly *adv*.

evoke /ɪˈvəʊk/ *vt*. ❶使回忆起;使产生(共鸣、联想等):That old film ~d memories of my childhood. 那部老影片使我回忆起童年时代。❷ 引起,激起:~ reaction 引起反响/His words ~d an angry reply. 他的话引起了愤怒的反应。派 evo kation *n*.

evolution /ˌiːvəˈluːʃn/ *n*. [U]进化;发展;演变:The ~ of man took over millions of years. 人类的进化经历了数百万年时间。

evolve /ɪˈvɒlv/ *v*. ❶使逐步形成,设计出;发展,展开:He ~d a new theory after many years of research. 经过多年研究,他逐步发展出一种新学说。❷演化(成);逐步形成:I think that this policy must have ~d over many years. 这项政策想必是经过多年的努力才制定出来的。❸进化;成长;发育:The early fish have ~d into some 30,000 different species. 始初的鱼迄今已演化而繁衍为3万多个不同品种。

exact /ɪgˈzækt/ *adj*. 正确的;精密的;准确的:His translation is ~ to the letter. 他的翻译非常确切。

exactly /ɪgˈzæktli/ *adv*. 确切地;恰好;正是:That's ~ what I want. 这正是我想要的东西。

exaggerate /ɪgˈzædʒəreɪt/ *vt*. 夸张,夸大:It is ~d purposely. 这事被故意夸大了。

exam /ɪgˈzæm/ *n*. (examination 的缩写形式) [C]考试

examination /ɪgˌzæmɪˈneɪʃn/ *n*. ❶考试;考查:attend an ~参加考试/ fail in an ~ 考试不及格/ pass an ~ 考试合格/ get through an ~ 通过考试/ a final ~ 期终考试/ an ~ card (pass)准考证 ❷检查;调查:The doctor asked him to have a medical (physical) ~ every year. 大夫要求他每年进行一次体检。

examine /ɪgˈzæmɪn/ *vt*. ❶检查;仔细观察:The engineer is examining the machine to see if it has any defects. 那工程师正仔细检查机器是否有什么毛病。❷对……进行考试(考查):The teacher ~d his students in mathematics. 老师考查学生的数学学得如何。

example /ɪgˈzɑːmpl/ *n*. [C]例子;范例;榜样:A Party member should set a good ~ to others. 共产党员应当为他人树立好榜样。/ Please cite a few ~s to explain the problem. 请举几个例子来说明这个问题。/**for** ~ 例如:She likes sports, for ~, swimming and skiing. 她非常喜欢运动,比如游泳、滑雪。

exceed /ɪkˈsiːd/ *vt*. 超过;胜过;超出:A driver who ~s the speed limit of 120 miles in this road will be punished. 司机在这段路驾驶超过 120 英里的时速限制将会受到处罚。

exceedingly /ɪkˈsiːdɪŋli/ *adv*. 极度地;非常地;极大地:He is ~ generous toward his friends. 他对朋友极其慷慨大方。

excel /ɪkˈsel/ *v*. (-celled;-celling) ❶超过,胜过;优于:He ~s us all at cooking. 他的烹饪手艺胜过我们大家。❷擅长;(在……方面)突出:He ~s at tennis. 他擅长打网球。

Excellency /ˈeksələnsi/ *n*. [C]阁下(对首相、总督、主教、大使等的尊称):Your

~ 阁下(直接称呼时用) / Her (His) ~ 阁下(间接提到时用)

excellent / ˈeksələnt / *adj*. 优秀的;杰出的;极好的:He was ~ in English. 他英语极好。/ Her ~ composition received high praise. 她的优秀作文受到极大称赞。

except / ɪkˈsept / *prep*. 除……外:Everybody is ready ~ her. 除她以外人人都准备好了。/ ~ **for** 除……外;除……之外:The film is good ~ for the ending. 除了结尾之外,这部电影很好看。

exception / ɪkˈsepʃn / *n*. 例外;除外:Most boys like to play football, but Jimmy is an ~. 大多数男孩都喜欢踢足球,但吉米却是例外。/ Everyone went to swim that afternoon with the ~ of Mike. 除了迈克以外,那天下午大家都去游泳了。

exceptional / ɪkˈsepʃənəl/ *adj*. ❶例外的;特殊的;特别的,独特的;罕见的:an ~ use of a word 某词的特殊用法 / very ~ circumstances 在非常特殊的情形下/ It is quite ~ to have rain at this time of year. 一年中这个时候还下雨,实在罕见。❷卓越的,杰出的,出类拔萃的:an ~ violinist 卓越的小提琴演奏家 / This is an ~ opportunity. 这可是一个极好的机会。

excess / ɪkˈses / Ⅰ*n*. 超越;超过;过量;过度:The ~ of rain ruined the crops. 雨水过多毁坏了庄稼。Ⅱ*adj*. 过量的;额外的:A passenger must pay for his ~ luggage. 行李超重乘客须付钱。派 excessive *adj*. ;excessively *adv*.

exchange / ɪksˈtʃeɪndʒ / *v*. 交换;调换;交流;兑换:May I ~ seats with you? 我可以和你调换一下座位吗? / Our teacher often ~s ideas with us. 我们的老师经常和我们交流意见。/ He ~d Renminbi for foreign money before he went abroad. 出国前他把人民币兑换成外币。

excite / ɪkˈsaɪt / *vt*. 兴奋,激动:It's nothing to get ~d about. 这没有什么值得激动的。/ Don't get ~d over such a little matter. 不要为这样的小事情兴奋。

excitement / ɪkˈsaɪtmənt / *n*. [U] 兴奋;激动:They jumped in ~ when they knew that they won the champion. 得知赢得了冠军,他们兴奋得跳起来。

exciting / ɪkˈsaɪtɪŋ / *adj*. 令人兴奋的;使人激动的:We were glad when we heard the ~ news. 听到那振奋人心的消息,我们都非常高兴。

exclaim / ɪkˈskleɪm / *v*. 呼喊;惊叫;大声说:The passengers ~ed in despair when the bus was dropping down the bridge. 汽车掉下桥时乘客们都绝望地叫喊起来。

exclamation / ˌekskləˈmeɪʃn / *n*. ❶[U] 呼喊;惊叫;惊叹:She made an ~ of joy when she knew she had passed the examination. 知道考试及格了,她大声地欢呼起来。❷[C] 感叹词;惊叹语:He used an ~ mark at the end of the sentence. 他在句末用了一个惊叹号。

exclude / ɪkˈskluːd / *vt*. 把……排除在外;排斥;拒绝:Parents should ~ their children from watching such a horrible film. 父母应拒绝让孩子们看这种恐怖电影。

exclusive / ɪkˈskluːsɪv / *adj*. 除外的;排他的;专有的:The shop has the ~ right to sell the products of this factory. 该商店有出售这家工厂产品的专卖权。/ The card is ~ to members only. 这种卡只限会员使用。派 exclusively *adv*.

excursion /ɪkˈskɜːʃn/ *n.* [C]短途旅行；集体游览：The whole family made a day ~ to the suburb of London. 全家人到伦敦郊区一日游。

excuse Ⅰ/ɪkˈskjuːz/ *vt.* 原谅；宽恕；辩解：Excuse me, may I have a word with you again? 对不起，我可以再和你谈一谈吗？/ You can't ~ yourself for your mistake. 你不可以为自己的错误辩解。Ⅱ/ɪksˈkjuːs/ *n.* [C] 借口；托词：Some students found ~s for not being on time. 有些学生为他们迟到找借口。

execute /ˈeksɪkjuːt/ *vt.* ❶执行；实行：Your order will be ~d as speedily as possible. 你的命令将尽快被执行。❷处决；处死：He was ~d with fire. 他被处火刑。

execution /ˌeksɪˈkjuːʃn/ *n.* [U]执行；行刑：He was perfect in the ~ of his duties. 他执行任务丝毫不差。

executive /ɪgˈzekjətɪv/ *n.* [C]执行者；总经理；董事：a sales ~ 营业主管/ He is chief ~ officer (CEO) of the company. 他是公司的首席执行官。

exemplify /ɪgˈzemplɪˌfaɪ/ *vt.* ❶以示例说明；举例证明：He exemplifies the hopes and confidence we have in the future. 他举例说明了我们在未来所拥有的希望和信心。❷作为……的例证（或榜样、典型等）：The novel *Tom Sawyer* exemplifies 19-century life in the United States. 长篇小说《汤姆·索耶历险记》是美国 19 世纪生活的缩影。派 exemplification *n.*

exempt /ɪgˈzempt/ Ⅰ *adj.* 被免除（义务、责任、税收等）的；被豁免的：Charitable organizations are usually ~ from some taxes. 慈善机构一般免交一些税种。Ⅱ *vt.* 免除；豁免：No one is ~ed from paying taxes. 人人都必须纳税。

exercise /ˈeksəsaɪz/ *n.* [C]练习；锻炼：morning ~s 早操/ outdoor ~s 户外运动/ The doctor told him to take more ~. 医生告诉他要多运动。

exert /ɪgˈzɜːt/ *vt.* 运用，行使（权利等）；发挥（作用）；施加（影响）：~ authority 行使权利/~ pressure on sb. 对某人施加压力 / ~ **oneself** 使用力，使尽力：If you ~ yourself you can finish the task on time. 如果你加把劲，你就能按时完成任务。

exhaust /ɪgˈzɔːst/ *v.* 用尽；耗尽：~ one's strength 用尽了力气/Climbing up the mountain ~ed him. (=He was ~ed by climbing the mountain.) 爬山使他筋疲力尽。/**be ~ed with** 因……筋疲力尽：I am ~ed with toil. 我劳累不堪。

exhibit /ɪgˈzɪbɪt/ Ⅰ *v.* 陈列；展览；显示：The product was ~ed at a World Fair. 这种产品曾在世界博览会上展出。/ She ~ed great interest in pandas. 她对大熊猫表示出极大的兴趣。Ⅱ *n.* [C] 展品；陈列品：Do not touch the ~s. 请勿触摸展品。

exhibition /ˌeksɪˈbɪʃn/ *n.* [C] 展览；展览会：They will hold a sales ~ at the end of this month in our city. 本月底他们将在我市举办展销会。

exile /ˈeksaɪl/ Ⅰ *n.* ❶[U]放逐；流放：The court condemned the criminal to ~. 法庭判犯人流放刑。/ He wrote those poems in ~. 那些诗是他流放期间写的。❷[C] 被放逐者，流亡者：a political ~ 政治流亡者 Ⅱ *vt.* 放逐；使充军；支配

exist /ɪgˈzɪst/ *vi.* 存在；生存：We cannot ~ without air, food or water. 没有空气、食物和水，我们就不能生存。/~ **on**

靠……生存：She ~s on tea and bread. 她靠茶和面包维生。

existence /ɪgˈzɪstəns/ *n.* [U] 现实；存在；生存；生活：This is the largest ship in ~. 这是全世界现存的最大船只。

exit /ˈeksɪt/ *n.* [C] ❶出口；安全门；太平门：There are two emergency ~s in this theater. 这个剧场有两个紧急出口。❷退场；退出：The actors and actresses made their ~ from the door at the back of the stage. 男女演员们从舞台后面的门退场了。

exotic /ɪgˈzɒtɪk/ *adj.* ❶外(国)来的；外国产的，非本地产的：There are many restaurants with ~ foods in this city. 在这座城市里有很多外国风味的餐厅。❷(服饰等)奇异的，怪异的；异国情调的：He loves ~ clothes and travelling the ~ places. 他喜欢穿奇装异服，到充满异国情调的地方去旅游。

expand /ɪkˈspænd/ *v.* 扩大；扩充；膨胀：As the plant grew, its flowers and leaves gradually ~ed. 随着植物的生长，它的叶子和花朵也逐渐张开了。

expansion /ɪkˈspænʃn/ *n.* [U]扩充；膨胀：the ~ of gases 气体的膨胀/ the ~ of business 业务扩展

expect /ɪkˈspekt/ *vt.* 期待；指望；预料：The woman is ~ing a telephone call from her son. 那妇女正在等她儿子的电话。

expectation /ˌekspekˈteɪʃn/ *n.* [U] 期待；指望；预料：He has not much ~ of success. 他对成功不抱太大希望。

expedition /ˌekspɪˈdɪʃn/ *n.* [C](❶具有特定目的的)旅行，远征；探险；考察：go on an ~ to the South Pole 去南极探险 ❷远征队，探险队；考察队：a large ~ of scientists and millitary personnel 一支由科学家和军事队员组成的大型考察队

expel /ɪkˈspel/ *vt.* (-pelled;-pelling)开除；驱除：He was ~led from school. 他被学校开除了。

expend /ɪkˈspend/ *vt.* 花费，消耗，耗费(金钱、时间等)：~ much time and energy 耗去很多时间和精力 / He has ~ed half his income on housing. 他一半的收入花在了住房上。

expenditure /ɪkˈspendɪtʃə(r)/ *n.* ❶[U] 支出，花费；消耗，耗费：extraordinary (contingent) ~ 额外(临时性)支出 / A large project requires the ~ of money, time and effort. 一项大的工程往往需要耗费金钱、时间和精力。❷[C]支出额，消耗额；费用，经费：curb (curtail, cut down on, reduce) ~s 削减开支

expense /ɪkˈspens/ *n.* [U] 消费；费用；开支：We must keep down ~. 我们必须缩减开支。/**at the ~ of** 以……为代价：He became a brilliant scholar at the ~ of his health. 他成了知名学者，但牺牲了自己的健康。

expensive /ɪkˈspensɪv/ *adj.* 昂贵的；花钱多的：A flat is too ~ for me (to buy). 一套公寓房对我来说太贵了，我买不起。/ She bought her daughter an ~ necklace. 她给女儿买了一条昂贵的项链。派 expensively *adv.*

experience /ɪkˈspɪərɪəns/ *n.* ❶[U] 经验；体验：She has rich ~ in teaching English. 她教英语有丰富的经验。❷[C] 经历；阅历：an pleasant ~ 一次愉快的经历

experienced /ɪkˈspɪərɪənst/ *adj.* 有经验的；有阅历的；熟练的；老练的：an ~ doctor 有经验的医生 / have an ~ eye 有见识/ be well ~ in the world affairs

E

在处理国际事务上经验老到

experiment /ɪk'sperɪmənt/ Ⅰ *n.* [C]实验;试验:make an ~做实验/ An interesting ~ is being carried out by Prof. Wang. 王教授正在做一个有趣的实验。Ⅱ *vi.* 进行试验:They are ~ing with a new drug. 他们正在试验一种新药。派 experimental *adj.*

expert /'ekspɜːt/ Ⅰ *n.* [C]专家;内行;能手:Professor Li is an ~ in economics. 李教授是一位经济学专家。Ⅱ *adj.* 熟练的;老练的:He is an ~ driver. 他是一位老练的驾驶员。/**be ~ at (in)**熟练:He is ~ at figures. 他是计算的能手。

expertise /ˌekspɜː'tiːz/ *n.* [U]专门技能(或知识);专长:management ~管理技能/Landing a plane in fog takes a great deal of ~. 雾中降落飞机的技术含量很高。

expiration /ˌekspɪ'reɪʃən/ *n.* [U] ❶(气体等的)呼出;呼气,吐气:the ~ of air from the lungs 从肺里呼出的气体 ❷期满,届满;截止,告终:the ~ of a trade agreement between two countries 两国贸易协定的终止 / The mayor decided to run again at the ~ of his first term in office. 这位市长决定在第一个任期届满后再次参加竞选。

expire /ɪk'spaɪə(r),ek'spaɪ(r)/ *vi.* ❶期满,届满;(期限)终止;(合同、协议等)到期无效:The trade agreement will ~ at the end of this month. 贸易协定月底到期。❷呼气,吐气:The patient ~d irregularly. 病人的呼吸很不规则。

explain /ɪk'spleɪn/ *v.* 解释;说明:She ~ed why she was late. 她解释了她迟到的原因。

explanation /ˌeksplə'neɪʃn/ *n.* 解释;说明:I want to know the ~ for her being absent. 我想知道她缺席的理由是什么。

explicit /ɪk'splɪsɪt/ *adj.* ❶(解释说明)清楚的,明了的;明确的:a product with no ~ instruction 没有给出清楚的使用说明的产品 ❷坦率的,直言不讳的,毫无保留的:She was ~ with me about what she really felt. 她在我面前毫无保留地说出了她内心的真实感受。

explode /ɪk'spləʊd/ *v.* ❶爆炸;爆发:The country ~d another atom bomb. 那个国家又爆炸了一颗原子弹。❷(人的感情)发作:Hearing that he wanted to fly over the building, we ~d into laughter. 听说他想要从大楼上飞过去,我们哄然大笑起来。

exploit /ɪk'splɒɪt/ *vt.* ❶剥削:The boss ~ed child labor cruelly. 那老板残酷地剥削童工。❷利用:They ~ed every possibility to develop local agriculture. 他们利用一切可能性发展当地农业。❸开拓;开发;开采:The workers ~ed a new oil field. 工人们开采出一个新油田。

exploration /ˌeksplə'reɪʃn/ *n.* 考察;勘探;探查:He is interested in space ~. 他对太空探索很感兴趣。

explore /ɪk'splɔː(r)/ *v.* 探险;勘探;探索:The scientists ~d this district carefully. 科学家们对这一地区进行了仔细勘探。派 explorer *n.*

explosion /ɪk'spləʊʒn/ *n.* [C] 爆炸;爆发:The gas ~ caused twenty deaths. 瓦丝爆炸造成20人死亡。

explosive /ɪk'spləʊsɪv/ Ⅰ *adj.* ❶爆炸的;爆发的:an ~ device 爆炸装置 ❷易爆的,会(引起)爆炸的:an ~ chemical 易爆化学品 / Certain gases are highly ~ in hot weather. 有些气体在炎热天气中极易爆炸。❸激增的,剧增的;突然升级的:~ violence 急剧升级的暴力 /

the ~ growth in world population 世界人口的骤然猛增 ❹爆炸性的；一触即发的；极富争议的：a politically ~ issue 政治上具有爆炸性的问题 ❺(脾气)暴躁的，火暴的：an ~ temper 火暴脾气 Ⅱ*n.* [C]炸药，炸弹；易爆品 派 explosively *adv.*；explosiveness *n.*

export Ⅰ / ɪkˈspɔːt / *vt.* 输出；出口：The factory ~s toys to Africa. 这家工厂向非洲出口玩具。Ⅱ / ˈekspɔːt / *n.* 出口；输出；出口商品：The products of this factory are for ~. 这家工厂的产品供出口。

expose / ɪkˈspəʊz / *vt.* 暴露；揭露：The press ~d the truth of the whole event. 报纸揭露了整个事件的真相。/~ **to** 暴露：His foolish actions ~d him to ridicule. 他的愚蠢行为使他落为笑柄。

exposition / ˌekspəˈzɪʃən/ *n.* ❶(详细的)阐述；解释；评注：give a clear ~ of one's view 清晰地阐述自己的观点 ❷[C](公开的)展示；展览会，博览会：an automobile ~ 汽车博览会 / The diva gave a splendid ~ of vocal talent. 这名女歌剧演员展示了超凡的音乐天赋。

exposure / ɪkˈspəʊʒə(r) / *n.* 揭露；暴露

express / ɪkˈspres / Ⅰ *vt.* 表达：How can you ~ yourself in English? 你怎样用英语表达自己的想法呢？/ The film ~es the author's love of his motherland. 影片表达出作者对祖国的热爱。Ⅱ *adj.* 快的；快捷的：an ~ train 快车/ an ~ mail 邮政快件 Ⅲ *n.* 快车；快递；快运：He traveled by ~ around the country. 他乘快车游览全国。

expression / ɪkˈspreʃn / *n.* ❶ 表达；表现；表达方式：This gave ~ to the demands of the people. 这反映了人民的要求。/ Her smiling is an ~ of her pleasure. 她的微笑是她快乐的表现。❷ 表情；脸色：There is a happy ~ on her face. 她的脸上带着喜悦的表情。

expressive / ɪkˈspresɪv / *adj.* 富于表情的；富于表现力的；意味丰富的：an ~ voice 富于表现力的嗓音/The girl has large ~ eyes. 那姑娘有一双会说话的大眼睛。

expressway / ɪkˈspresˌweɪ / *n.* [C]高速公路；(部分立体交叉的)快速干道：a four-lane ~ 一条四车道高速公路

exquisite / ˈekskwɪzɪt，ekˈskwɪzɪt / *adj.* ❶精美的，精致的；制作精良的：an ~ design 精致的图案/~ foods 精美的食物 ❷精湛的；高雅的，雅致的：~ manners 优雅的风度/a ballet dancer of ~ skill 演技精湛的芭蕾舞演员 派 exquisitely *adv.*

extend / ɪkˈstend / *v.* 延长；延伸；扩大；扩充：The meeting ~ed late into the night. 会议一直开到深夜。/ The plains ~ far and wide. 平原向四面八方延伸。/ They ~ed the subway to the suburbs. 他们把地铁延伸到郊区。

extension / ɪkˈstenʃn / *n.* [C]❶伸展；扩大；延长；延长(扩大)部分：He asked a three-day ~ to his holidays. 他要求延长三天假期。❷(电话)分机：Could I have ~ 8，please? 请帮我接 8 号分机，好吗？

extensive / ɪkˈstensɪv / *adj.* 广阔的；广泛的：A lot of ~ reading improved her English comprehension. 大量的泛读提高了她的英语理解能力。

extent / ɪkˈstent / *n.* [U]区域；范围；长度；限度；程度：He has a farm of considerable ~. 他拥有一个相当大的农场。/ The worker is examining the ~ of damage to the machine. 工人在检查机器受损的程度。/**to a certain** ~ 部分地；有

些;在一定程度上:I agree with you to a certain ~. 我部分同意你的意见。**to what** ~ 到什么程度:To what ~ can he be trusted? 他可靠到什么程度?

exterior /ɪk'stɪərɪə(r)/ Ⅰ *adj.* ❶外部的;外表的:The ~ walls of the building are old now. 这栋大楼的外墙很旧了。❷对外的;外交的:The country insists on its own ~ policy. 该国坚持自己的对外政策。Ⅱ *n.* [C]外部;外表:The ~ of the car is beautiful. 这车的外观很好看。派 exteriorly *adv.*

exterminate /ɪk'stɜːmɪˌneɪt/ *vt.* 消灭,根除;使灭绝,使绝迹:~ insect pests 杀灭昆虫类害虫 / Has leprosy been completely ~d? 麻风病完全绝迹了吗? 派 extermination *n.*

external /ɪk'stɜːnl/ Ⅰ *adj.* 外部的;外面的;外用的:This is only the ~ cause of the accident. 这只是这次事故的外因。/ The medicine is for ~ use only. 这药仅供外用。Ⅱ *n.* [C]外部;外形:She is kind by ~s. 从外表看她很和蔼。派 externally *adv.*

extinct /ɪk'stɪŋkt/ *adj.* 绝种的;绝灭的;熄灭了的:Dinosaurs have become ~ for many years. 恐龙已经绝种许多年了。/ The scientists climbed up an ~ volcano. 科学家们爬上了一座死火山。派 extinction *n.*

extinguish /ɪk'stɪŋwɪʃ/ *vt.* 熄灭;扑灭;消灭:They were anxious that they hadn't enough water to ~ the fire. 他们担心没有足够的水灭火。

extort /ɪk'stɔːt/ *vt.* 敲诈,勒索;(利用人权)侵占,侵吞:~ money from a pedestrian 从一位行人那里勒索钱财 派 extortion *n.*

extra /'ekstrə/ Ⅰ *adj.* 额外的;外加的:I haven't any ~ time to go shopping with you today. 今天我没有多余的时间陪你去买东西。/ He took an ~ train to Tianjin. 他乘加班车去天津。Ⅱ *n.* [C] (*pl.*) ❶额外的人手;额外的事物 ❷附加费;另外的收费:The room service charges no ~s in this hotel. 在这家旅馆房间服务不额外收费。Ⅲ *adv.* 特别地;格外地;非常:He has been ~ busy with his thesis recently. 最近他做论文特别忙。

extract Ⅰ /ɪk'strækt/ *vt.* ❶拔出;抽出;取出:~ a bad tooth 拔掉坏牙 ❷提取;榨取:Mother ~ed some juice for the guests. 妈妈榨了一些果汁招待客人。❸摘要;摘录:He ~ed a good passage from the book as his opening speech. 他从那本书里摘取了一段好文章作为开幕词。Ⅱ /'ekstrækt/ *n.* [C] 摘录;选录;选段:She makes ~s from newspapers everyday. 她每天都摘录报纸。

extraction /ɪk'strækʃən/ *n.* ❶拔出;取出;榨取;提取,萃取:have eight ~s of teeth 拔了八次牙 / the ~ of money by extortion 用勒索的方式榨取钱财 ❷[U]血统,出身,家世:an American of Greek ~ 希腊裔美国人 ❸[C]提取物;萃取物

extradite /'ekstrədaɪt/ *vt.* 引渡:The police ~d the murderer back to his own country for trial. 警方把杀人犯引渡回国接受审判。

extraordinary /ɪk'strɔːdnəri/ *adj.* 非常的;非凡的;不寻常的:He is a man of ~ genius. 他是一个奇才。/ I don't like the ~ weather here. 我不喜欢这里反常的天气。

extravagance(-cy) /ɪk'strævəgəns(i)/ *n.* [U] 奢侈;浪费:We oppose ~ and waste. 我们反对铺张浪费。

extravagant /ɪkˈstrævəgənt/ *adj*. 奢侈的;浪费的;过分的:She is ~ in life. 她生活奢侈。派 extravagantly *adv*.

extreme /ɪkˈstriːm/ Ⅰ *adj*. 极端的;极度的;末端的;尽头的:That is an ~ case. 那是一个极罕见的例子。/ I have been to the ~ south of the island. 我曾去过这岛的最南端。Ⅱ *n*. [C]极端;极度:She is experiencing the ~ of joy in her life. 她正经历着一生最大的喜悦。/ **go to ~s** 走极端;采取极端手段:She goes to ~s in everything. 她凡事都走极端。**in the** (**an**) ~ 极端地;非常地:The building is magnificent in the ~. 那幢楼极为富丽堂皇。派 extremely *adv*.

extremity /ɪkˈstriːmɪti/ *n*. ❶[C]末端,端点;尽头:the peninsula's western ~ 半岛的西端 ❷[U]极端;极度;极点:the ~ of the violence 极端的暴力

extrude /ɪkˈstruːd/ *vt*. 挤出,压出:~ toothpaste from the tube 从管子里挤出牙膏/The machine ~s noodles through holes. 这台机器从孔中把面条挤压出来。

eye /aɪ/ *n*. [C] 眼睛;视力;视觉:The girl has beautiful blue ~s. 小女孩有一双漂亮的蓝眼睛。/ He has good (weak) ~s. 他的视力很好(差)。/**catch one's** ~ 引人注目:The schoolboy caught his master's ~s. 小学生引起了他老师的注意。**keep an** ~ **on** 照看;留意;照顾;监视:Please keep an ~ on my suitcase. 请照看一下我的箱子。

eyebrow /ˈaɪbraʊ/ *n*. [C] 眉毛:She has thick ~s. 她眉毛很浓。

eyesight /ˈaɪsaɪt/ *n*. [U] 视力;目力:I have good (bad) ~. 我的视力很好(不好)。

F f

fable / ˈfeɪbl / *n.* ❶[C] 寓言：*Aesop's Fables*《伊索寓言》❷[U]神话；传说：sort out facts from ~ 从传说中整理事实

fabric / ˈfæbrɪk / *n.* 织物；纺织品：woollen ~ 羊毛织品

fabricate / ˈfæbrɪˌkeɪt / *vt.* ❶制造，制作；建造；组装，装配：~ fine pottery 制造精美的陶器/ materials used to ~ electronic components 制造电子元件的材料 ❷捏造，伪造（文件等）；杜撰，编造：~ evidence against sb. 捏造不利于某人的证据/~ a diploma 伪造毕业文凭 派 fabrication *n.*

fabulous / ˈfæbjʊləs / *adj.* ❶惊人的，难以置信的；非常的；荒诞的：the ~ treasures of sunken ships 沉船上的稀世珍宝/ ~ rumors 无稽的谣言 ❷极好的，绝妙的：That's a ~ idea！这主意太妙了！/She's got a ~ figure. 她的身材妙不可言。派 fabulously *adv.*

face / feɪs / Ⅰ *n.* [C]面孔；脸；（表）面；外貌：The stone struck her on the ~. 石头击在她脸上。/ a care-worn ~ 饱经风霜的脸 / a fair (fine) ~ 漂亮的脸蛋 / a gloomy ~ 阴郁的脸 / a serious ~ 严肃的面孔 / a proud ~ 傲慢的表情 /~ **to** ~ 面对面：We sent for the man to accuse her ~ to ~. 我们叫那人来当面指控她。**in (the) ~ of** 面临：He remained calm even in the ~ of danger. 即使面临危险，他也镇定自若。**keep a straight ~** 板起面孔：He is so comical that no one can keep a straight ~. 他太滑稽了，人人都忍不住要笑。**make a ~ (faces) at** 向……做鬼脸：The children made ~s at one another. 孩子们互相做鬼脸玩。**put on (draw, pull, wear) a long ~** 愁眉苦脸；拉长了脸：I don't know why she is pulling a long ~ all day. 我不知道她为什么整天愁眉苦脸。**save one's ~** 保全面子：He didn't want to tell her about it in order to save his ~. 为了保全面子，他不想将此事告诉她。Ⅱ *v.* 面对；正视；朝；向：The house ~s the street. 这房子面朝街道。/**be ~d with** 面对；面临：He was ~d with two alternatives — death or submission. 他面临两种选择：死亡或者投降。We are ~d with the same problem. 我们遇到同样的问题。~ **up to** 勇敢面对：She won't ~ up to the fact that she is getting old. 她不肯承认她老了。

facet / ˈfæsɪt / *n.* [C] ❶（多面体的）面；（宝石等的）琢面：crystal ~水晶界面 ❷（问题、事物等的）一个方面：This case obviously has all sorts of ~ that will affect the trial. 很明显，这个案子牵涉到的方方面面，势必会对审判产生影响。

facial /ˈfeɪʃəl/ *adj.* 面部的：Did you notice her ~ expression when she came in? 你注意到她进来时的面部表情了吗?

facility /fəˈsɪləti/ *n.* ❶[C](常用 *pl.*)设施；设备：We have various transport facilities now. 现在我们有了各种各样的交通工具。❷[U]便利；熟练：She played the piano with ~. 她熟练地弹钢琴。

fact /fækt/ *n.* [C] 事实；实际；现实；真相：A ~ is something that we know to be true. 事实就是我们认知为真实的事情。/ It is important to distinguish ~ from fiction. 辨别现实与虚构是重要的。/**in** ~ 事实上；实际上：I saw him not long ago, in ~, I saw him yesterday. 我不久前见过他，实际上就是昨天见过他。

faction /ˈfækʃn/ *n.* [C](政党、组织等内部的)宗派、派别；(尤指持歧见的)小集团：A ~ in the club tried to make the president resign. 俱乐部内有一帮人想让董事长辞职。

factor /ˈfæktə(r)/ *n.* [C] 要素；因素：a positive ~ 积极因素 / a negative ~ 消极因素 / Diligence is the major ~ for his success. 勤奋是他获得成功的主要因素。

factory /ˈfæktəri/ *n.* [C] 工厂：He runs a ~ in the town. 他在镇上经营一家工厂。

factual /ˈfæktʃʊəl/ *adj.* ❶事实的；基于事实的：provide ~ material 提供事实材料 / They checked its ~ accuracy. 他们对其事实的精确性进行了核实。/ They properly have to be ~. 他们应该实事求是。❷真实的；确实的，确凿的；非虚构的：a ~ account of the war 关于战争的真实报道 / ~ information 凿凿有据的情报 派 factually *adv.*

faculty /ˈfækəlti/ *n.* [C] ❶才能；能力：The young girl has a ~ for painting. 那位年轻姑娘擅长绘画。❷(大学的)系；科；学院：He is working in the ~ of medicine. 他在医学系工作。❸全体教学人员：The teaching ~ are having a meeting in the hall. 全体教职人员正在大厅里开会。

fade /feɪd/ *v.* ❶(使)褪色；凋谢；枯萎：The wallpaper ~d. 墙纸褪色了。/ The newly planted trees ~d. 新栽的小树枯萎了。❷(声音等)逐渐减弱，消失：The sound of the motorcycle ~d away in the distance. 摩托车的声音渐渐消失在远处。

Fahrenheit /ˈfærənhaɪt/ *adj.* 华氏的：Water freezes at 32° ~. 水在华氏 32 度结冰。

fail /feɪl/ *vi.* 失败；不及格：He tried several times, but ~ed. 他试了几次，但都失败了。/ We're glad nobody ~ed in the exam this time. 让我们高兴的是，这次考试没有人不及格。

failure /ˈfeɪlɪə(r)/ *n.* 失败；失败者：Failure is the mother of success. 失败是成功之母。/ He was a ~ as a teacher. 他并不是一位成功的教师。

faint /feɪnt/ Ⅰ *adj.* 模糊的；虚弱的；微弱的；头昏目眩的：He was ~ with hunger. 他因饥饿而十分虚弱。Ⅱ *vi.* 昏；晕倒：The boy ~ed in the heat. 小男孩中暑晕倒了。

fair[1] /feə(r)/ Ⅰ *adj* ❶公平的；合理的；公正的：He is ~ to other people. 他对待他人很公正。/ We should be ~ in buying and selling. 我们应当买卖公平。❷相当的；尚可的：A ~ proportion of

F

the citizens voted against the proposal. 相当一部分市民投票反对那项提议。❸金发的；白皙的：The girl who has ~ hair is from Italy. 那位金发姑娘是意大利人。❹晴朗的：The ~ weather made her pleasant. 晴朗的天气让她心情愉快。❺美丽的：All the travelers were attracted by the ~ landscape there. 所有游客都被那儿的美景迷住了。Ⅱ *adv.* 明白地；公平地：If we play ~, I'm sure we will win the match. 如果公平地比赛，我肯定我们会赢。派 fairness *n.*

fair[2] / feə(r) / *n.* [C] ❶集市：The wife of our mayor often buys goods in the ~ trade market, too. 我们的市长夫人也常在集贸市场买东西。❷交易会；博览会：China's Spring (Autumn) Export Commodities Fair 中国春(秋)季商品出口交易会 / They planned to hold a trade ~ in the center of the city. 他们计划在市中心举行一次商品交易会。

fairly / ˈfeəli / *adv.* ❶公正地：He did not act ~ toward her. 他待她不公平。❷相当：She is a ~ good actress. 她是一位相当好的演员。

fairy / ˈfeəri / *n.* [C]仙女；神仙：Grandfather often told ~ tales to me when I was young. 小时候祖父常给我讲童话故事。

faith / feɪθ / *n.* [U]❶信任；信心；信念：The workers place (put) great ~ in their general manager. 工人们极其信任他们的总经理。/ We have firm ~ that our life will be better and better. 我们坚信我们的生活会越来越好。❷信仰：One should respect other's ~. 应当尊重他人的信仰。

faithful / ˈfeɪθfl / *adj.* 忠诚的；忠实的：Though he is young, he is ~ in his duties. 尽管年轻，他却忠于职守。派 faithfully *adv.*

fake / feɪk / Ⅰ *v.* 伪造；假装：Tell us the truth, don't ~ story. 告诉我们真相，不要编造故事。Ⅱ *n.* [C]冒牌货；赝品；骗子：The oil painting is a ~. 那幅油画是赝品。Ⅲ *adj.* 假的；伪造的；冒充的：Take care not to buy ~ and fault products. 小心别买到假冒伪劣产品。

fall / fɔːl / Ⅰ *vi.* (fell/fel/, fallen / ˈfɔːlən/) ❶落下；降落：The pen fell from the desk to the floor. 笔从书桌上掉落到地板上。/ The rain was ~ing steadily. 雨不停地下。❷跌倒；倒下；跌落：Babies often ~ when they are learning to walk. 小儿学步常跌倒。❸成为；变为：The child fell asleep. 小孩睡着了。He has ~en ill. 他生病了。/ Do not ~ into bad habits. 不要养成坏习惯。/ ~ **in love with** 爱上；喜爱：He fell in love with an actress. 他爱上了一名女演员。~ **back** 撤退；后退：Our attack was so vigorous that the enemy had to ~ back. 我们的攻势猛烈，敌人不得不撤退了。~ **behind** 落后：He always ~s behind when we are going uphill. 我们登山时他总是落在后面。~ **in** 塌陷；垮：The roof fell in. 屋顶塌陷了。~ **in with** ①偶遇：On my way home I fell in with our English teacher. 在回家的路上我偶然碰到了我们的英语老师。②同意：He fell in with my views at once. 他立刻同意了我的见解。~ **on one's knees** 跪下：She fell on her knees and thanked God for his mercy. 她跪下感谢上帝的仁慈。Ⅱ *n.* [C] ❶落下；跌落：He had a ~ from a horse. 他从马上跌下。❷(美)秋季：She was born in the ~ of 1992. 她是在1992年秋天出生的。

fallacy /ˈfæləsi/ *n.* ❶[C]谬论,谬见:It is a ~ to suppose that riches always bring happiness. 认为财富总能带来幸福,这是一种错误的见解。/ The belief that women are always weaker than men is just a ~. 妇女总是比男人弱的看法,只是一种偏见。❷错误推理;不可靠的论据:a statement based on ~ 基于谬误推理的陈述 / logical fallacies 逻辑推理错误

false /fɔːls/ *adj.* ❶假的;不真实的:His father has a set of ~ teeth. 他父亲戴一副假牙。❷仿造的:Using ~ coins is illegal. 使用伪币是违法的。❸ 错误的;谬误的:I think it is a ~ argument. 我认为这是一个错误的论点。

fame /feɪm/ *n.* [U]名声;名望:One cannot only go after (seek) ~ and money. 人不能只追求名利。/ **come to** ~ 成名;出名:She came to ~ in Beijing eight years ago. 八年前她在北京出了名。

familiar /fəˈmɪlɪə(r)/ *adj.* 熟悉的;通晓的:If you write things ~ to you, you'll get very good articles. 如果写熟悉的事物,你就会写出好文章。/ Her uncle has worked in France for twenty years;he is ~ with French. 她叔叔在法国工作了 20 年,法语相当好。/ **be on ~ terms with ...** 与……亲密;与……交情很好:He is on ~ terms with the old artist. 他和那位老艺术家交情很好。派 familiarity *n.* ;familiarize *vt.*

family /ˈfæməli/ *n.* [C] ❶家庭;家族;家庭成员:Every ~ in the village has a TV set. 这个村子里家家有电视机。/ Tom is the eldest of the ~. 汤姆是家中最大的孩子。❷(动植物的) 科;语系:animals of the cat ~ 猫科动物 / the Germanic ~ of languages 日耳曼语系

famine /ˈfæmɪn/ *n.* [U]饥荒:His grandfather die of ~ in 1927. 他的祖父于 1927 年死于饥荒。

famous /ˈfeɪməs/ *adj.* 著名的;驰名的:a ~ scientist 著名的科学家 / The town is ~ for its hot springs. 该城以温泉驰名。

fan /fæn/ *n.* [C] ❶扇子 ❷狂热爱好者;迷:He is not only a football ~,but also a film ~. 他不仅是一个足球迷,还是一个影迷。

fancier /ˈfænsɪə(r)/ *n.* [C]爱好者;迷恋者;迷:an art ~ 艺术爱好者 / a ~ of fine wines 迷恋美酒的人

fancy /ˈfænsi/ Ⅰ *n.* ❶[U]空想;幻想;幻想;幻想力:She has a lively ~ like a child. 她像小孩一样有丰富的幻想力。❷[C]爱好;喜爱;迷恋:She has a ~ for Internet shopping. 她热衷于网上购物。Ⅱ *adj.* 空想的;精美的,花式的:I don't like ~ ties. 我不喜欢太花哨的领带。/ I like to watch ~ diving. 我喜欢看花样跳水。

fantastic /fænˈtæstɪk/ *adj.* ❶(口语)极好的,很棒的:a ~ achievement 了不起的成就/You've got the job? Fantastic! 你得到那工作了?太好了!❷奇异的,怪诞的:~ dreams of forests 关于森林的怪梦 ❸很大的:The car costs a ~ amount of money. 这轿车的价钱贵得吓人。

fantasy /ˈfæntəsi/ *n.* 想象;幻想:make fantasies 胡思乱想/He indulges in fantasies but doesn't act them out. 他沉湎于奇思异想,却没有付诸行动。

far /fɑː(r)/ Ⅰ *adv.* (farther,farthest;further,furthest) ❶(用于疑问句和否定句)远,久远(指空间、时间):How ~ did you go? 你走了多远?❷(与介词、副

词连用)远,久远:~ back in the past 往昔 / ~ in the future 在遥远的未来 / ~ away (off, out, back, in) 遥远;深远 / He reviewed his lesson ~ into the night. 他复习功课直至深夜。/~ **from** 远非;绝非:You are ~ from well. 你一点也不健康。**go (carry) too** ~ 过分:Don't carry the joke too ~. 不要把玩笑开得过分了。~ **and near** (~ **and wide**) 到处:They searched ~ and wide for the missing child. 他们到处寻找那个走失的孩子。**so** ~ 到目前为止:So ~ the work has been easy. 到目前为止,这工作是容易的。**as (so)** ~ **as**:①到,直到:He walked as ~ as the post office. 他走到了邮局。②与……距离相等:We didn't go as (so) ~ as the others. 我们不如其他人走得那么远。③在……内;就……(的限度):So ~ as I know, he will be away for three months. 就我所知,他将外出三个月。❸(修饰形容词、副词的比较级)……得多:This is ~ better. 这个要好得多。Ⅱ *adj*. (farther, farthest; further, furthest) 远的;较远的:a ~ country 一个远方的国家 / at the ~ end of the street 在街的那一头 / on the ~ bank of the river 在河的彼岸

fare / feə(r) / *n*. [C]车船费;票价:A bus ~ is very cheap. 公共汽车票价很便宜。/ How much is the air ~ to Beijing? 去北京的飞机票要多少钱?

farewell / ˌfeəˈwel / Ⅰ *int*. 再见;告别 Ⅱ *n*. 再会:**make (bid) a** ~ **to sb.** 与某人告别:The visitors made their ~s and left. 访问者告别后离开了。

farm / fɑːm / *n*. [C]农场:He worked on a ~. 他在农场工作。派 farmer *n*.

far-reaching / ˌfɑːˈriːtʃɪŋ/ *adj*. (影响、效果等)深远的:~ changes 影响深远的变革 / be ~ in the consequences 具有深远的影响

far-sighted / ˌfɑːˈsaɪtɪd, ˈfɑːˌsaɪtɪd/ *adj*. ❶远视的;能看得很远的 ❷有远见的;深谋远虑的:a ~ man 远见卓识之士 / a ~ policy 一项具有前瞻性的政策 派 far-sightedness *n*.

fascinate / ˈfæsɪneɪt / *vt*. 迷住;强烈地吸引住:The children were ~d by the toys in the shop windows. 孩子们被商店橱窗里的玩具迷住了。

fascinating / ˈfæsɪneɪtɪŋ / *adj*. 迷人的;引人入胜的:What a ~ smile! 多么迷人的微笑啊!

fascination / ˌfæsɪˈneɪʃn / *n*. 入迷;着迷:English always has a ~ for me. 英语一向使我入迷。

fascism / ˈfæʃɪz(ə)m/ *n*. [U]法西斯主义

fashion / ˈfæʃn / *n*. 流行;式样;时尚:He walks in a peculiar ~. 他走路的样子很奇特。/ Short skirts are the ~ in 2007. 短裙是 2007 年的流行式样。派 fashionable *adj*.

fast / fɑːst / Ⅰ *adv*. ❶快;迅速地:He walks very ~. 他走路很快。❷紧紧地;牢固地;可靠地:He held the rope ~. 他紧紧地抓住绳子不放。Ⅱ *adj*. ❶快的;迅速的:My watch is ~. 我的表快了。❷紧的;牢固的;可靠的:He is my ~ friend. 他是我忠实可靠的朋友。

fasten / ˈfɑːsn / *v*. 系牢,束紧;闩上:Fasten your seat belt while you're driving. 开车时系紧安全带。

fat / fæt / Ⅰ *adj*. (fatter, fattest) 肥的;胖的:He is getting ~ter. 他长得更胖了。Ⅱ *n*. [U] 脂肪;肥肉:I do not like ~ (meat). 我不喜欢吃肥肉。

fatal / ˈfeɪtl / *adj*. 致命的;不幸的:a ~

wound 致命伤 / a ~ accident 不幸事件 / Cancer is a ~ disease. 癌症是一种致命的疾病。

fate / feɪt / *n.* [U] 命运：share the ~ with 与……共命运 / evil ~ 厄运/We should take our ~ into our own hands. 我们应当掌握自己的命运。

fateful / ˈfeɪtf(ʊ)l / *adj.* 决定性的，关键性的；(意义)重大的；影响深远的：a ~ decision 重大决定/a ~ meeting 具有深远影响的会议

father / ˈfɑːðə(r)/ Ⅰ *n.* [C] ❶父亲；岳父；公公 ❷(常用 *pl.*)(男性)祖宗，先人；前辈，长辈：the customs of one's ~s 祖先的遗风 / He went back to the home of his ~s. 他回到了祖辈们的故里。❸创始人，奠基人；鼻祖；缔造者：the ~ of the modern psychology 现代心理学之父 / George Washington is called the ~ of his country. 乔治·华盛顿被誉为美国国父。

father-in-law / ˈfɑːð(ə)rɪnˌlɔː/ *n.* [C] (*pl.* fathers-in-law 或 father-in-laws) 岳父；公公

fatigue / fəˈtiːg / *v.* 使疲劳；使劳累：He felt ~d with sitting up all night. 他因彻夜不眠而感到疲劳。

fatty / ˈfæti / *adj.* ❶脂肪的；似脂肪的：~ tissues 脂肪组织 ❷富含脂肪的；油腻的：~ foods 富含脂肪的食品

fault / fɔːlt / *n.* 缺点；错误；过失：This is not her ~. 这不是她的错。/ Parents should know the merits and ~s of their children well. 父母应当很好地了解自己孩子的优点和缺点。

faulty / ˈfɔːlti/ *adj.* 有缺点的，有缺陷的；有错误的，有过失的：a ~ design 不完美的设计 / ~ friends 有缺点的朋友 派 faultily *adv.* ；faultiness *n.*

favo(u)r / ˈfeɪvə(r) / *n.* [C] 好意；恩惠；帮助：May I ask a ~ of you? 请您帮个忙好吗？/**do sb. a ~** 帮助某人：Do me a ~ to come. 务请光临。/ Could you do me a ~? 你能帮我个忙吗？**in ~ of** 赞成；支持：The students are in ~ of reform. 学生们都赞成改革。**in sb.'s ~** 对某人有利：The situation both at home and abroad is in our ~. 国内外形势对我们有利。

favo(u)rable / ˈfeɪvərəbl / *adj.* 有利的；有帮助的：The wind is ~ for setting sail. 风向有利于起航。

favo(u)rite / ˈfeɪvərɪt / Ⅰ *n.* [C] 特别喜爱的人；特别喜爱的物：He is a ~ with everybody. 他是人人都喜欢的人。Ⅱ *adj.* 特别喜爱的：My ~ subject is English. 我最喜爱的科目是英语。

fax / fæks / *n.* 传真；传真机

fear / fɪə(r) / Ⅰ *v.* 害怕；恐惧：She always ~s mice. 她一向怕老鼠。/ I ~ for his safety. 我为他的安全担心。Ⅱ *n.* ❶害怕；恐惧：The boy didn't show any ~ in front of strangers. 在陌生人面前，这个小男孩一点也不害怕。/**for ~ of** 唯恐；为……担心；生怕：He is for ~ of failure. 他生怕失败。❷ 忧虑(与 of 连用)：He is in ~ of his living. 他为他的生计担忧。

fearful / ˈfɪəfl / *adj.* 担心的；可怕的；吓人的：She is ~ of wakening her baby. 她怕吵醒她的孩子。

fearless / ˈfɪələs / *adj.* 无畏的；大胆的：We are ~ of danger. 我们不怕危险。

feasible / ˈfiːzɪbl / *adj.* 可行的；行得通的；切合实际的：a ~ plan 可行的计划/ It is ~ to take his advice. 按他的建议行事是切实可行的。派 feasibility *n.*

feast / fiːst / *n.* [C] 宴会；酒席：a high ~

盛大宴会 / a noon ~ 午宴 / a festival ~ 节日宴会 / Mr. White makes a ~ tonight. 怀特先生今晚设宴款待。

feat / fiːt / *n.* [C]功绩;业绩;事迹:achieve a remarkable ~取得引人注目的业绩/a ~ of engineering 工程学上的壮举

F

feather / ˈfeðə(r) / *n.* [C]羽毛: as light as a ~ 轻如鸿毛

feature / ˈfiːtʃə(r) / *n.* [C] 面貌;特征;特点;特色:Her eyes are her best ~. 她的眼睛是长得最好的部分。/ The key ~ of the poem is simple. 这首诗的主要特点是简朴。

February / ˈfebruəri / *n.* 二月(略作 Feb.)

federal / ˈfedərəl / *adj.* ❶联盟的;联邦的 ❷联邦政府的

federation / ˌfedəˈreɪʃən/ *n.* ❶[U]结盟;联盟 ❷[C]联邦(政府):The United States is a ~. 美国是一个联邦制国家。❸[C]同盟;联盟;(社团等的)联合会;联合体:a ~ of students 学生联合会

fee / fiː / *n.* [C] 费;酬金:School ~s are high in England. 英国的学费很高。

feeble / ˈfiːbl / *adj.* 微弱的;虚弱的:a ~ old man 衰弱的老人/ a ~ mind 薄弱的意志 / a ~ cry 微弱的叫声 / a ~ attempt 没有成功的尝试

feed / fiːd / *v.* (fed /fed/,fed) 吃;喂;饲养;供给:The girl fed the chickens on corn. 小姑娘用玉米粒喂小鸡。/ Pandas ~ chiefly on bamboos. 熊猫主要以竹为食物。/ He fed the data into his computer. 他把那些数据输入计算机。/~ **on ...** 以……为食物;以……维持生命:What do you ~ your dog on? 你给狗喂什么食物? **be fed up with** 讨厌;厌恶:She is fed up with his grumbling. 她讨厌他老发牢骚。

feedback / ˈfiːdbæk / *n.* [U]反馈;反应:The shop welcomes the ~ from customers. 这家商店欢迎顾客反馈的信息。

feel / fiːl / *v.* (felt /felt/,felt) ❶感觉;感到:He felt his heart beating fast. 他感到他心跳得很快。/ I ~ as if it were going to rain. 我觉得好像要下雨了。❷触;摸:She felt the pot and found that it was hot. 她摸了摸那壶,发现壶是烫的。/~ **one's way** 摸索着走;谨慎处事:Since the staircase is rather dark, we must ~ our way carefully. 楼梯太黑暗,我们必须小心地摸着走。~ **about** 摸索:He was ~ing about in the dark. 他在黑暗中摸索。~ **for** 探索;摸索:He felt in his pocket for a penny. 他在口袋里摸到一便士。~ **like** 摸起来如同……;有……样的感觉;想要:I ~ like catching cold. 我感觉像是感冒了。/ She ~s like crying. 她真想哭。~ **up to** 能胜任;有能力做:He doesn't ~ up to a long walk. 他没有力气走远路。

feeler / ˈfiːlə(r)/ *n.* [C] ❶试探性的话语(或问题、暗示等): put out ~s to gauge people's reactions to the proposal 试探人们对这项建议的反应 ❷(动物或昆虫的)触角,触手,触毛,触须

feeling / ˈfiːlɪŋ / *n.* [C](常用 *pl.*)感情;感觉:What he said hurt her ~s. 他的话伤了她的感情。/ She suddenly had no ~ in her left hand. 她的左手突然没有了感觉。

fellow / ˈfeləʊ / Ⅰ *n.* [C] ❶人;家伙;小伙子:He is a good,honest ~. 他是一个诚实的好人。❷同伴;同辈:He always helps his ~s warm-heartedly. 他常常热心地帮助他的同伴们。Ⅱ *adj.* 同伴的;

同辈的：Her ~ workers didn't know that she was ill. 她的同事们不知道她生病了。

fellowship / ˈfeləʊˌʃɪp / *n.* ❶[U]伙伴关系；同志关系；交情：foster (promote) good ~ in the neighbourhood 增进睦邻友好关系 ❷[C](由志趣相同的人结成的)社团；协会；学会；联谊会：be admitted to the ~ 被接纳入会

female / ˈfiːmeɪl / Ⅰ *n.* [C]女子；雌性动物：Most teachers in the Primary schools are ~s. 这所小学的老师多数是女的。Ⅱ *adj.* 女性的；雌性的；母的：She raised a ~ cat. 她养了一只母猫。

feminine / ˈfemɪnɪn / *adj.* ❶女性特有的；女人味的；女性适用的：~ intuition 女性特有的直觉/If she puts on a little lipstick, she'll be more ~. 她如果抹点口红，就更有女人味。❷女性的；妇女的；女子的：~ staff members 女性职员 ❸(某些语言的语法中)阴性的：a ~ noun 阴性名词(如 queen, tigress)

fence[1] / fens / *n.* [C] 栅栏；围栏；篱笆：She looked out from the garden ~ and saw that her father was coming back. 从花园的栅栏望出去，她看到父亲正走回家。

fence[2] / fens / Ⅰ *v.* 练剑；习剑：~ with sb. 与某人练剑 Ⅱ *n.* [U]击剑；击剑术：Many young people like to watch a ~ game. 许多年轻人喜欢看击剑比赛。

ferment Ⅰ / ˈfɜːmənt / *n.* [U]骚扰；骚乱；激动：political ~ 政治动乱/She was thrown into a ~ by his unexpected arrival. 他不期而至，令她激动不已。Ⅱ /fəˈment/ *v.* (使)发酵：This enzyme ~s the wine faster. 这种酶能加快葡萄酒的发酵过程。

ferry / ˈferi / Ⅰ *n.* [C] 渡船；渡口：The pupils crossed the river by ~. 小学生们乘渡船过河。Ⅱ *vt.* 运送；摆渡；渡过：The old man ferries people to and fro everyday. 老人每天用渡船来摆渡行人过河。

fertile / ˈfɜːtaɪl / *adj.* ❶肥沃的；富饶的：The family has ~ fields and comfortable houses. 这家人有肥沃的田地和舒适的房屋。❷丰产的；丰富的：This district is ~ of fresh fruits. 这个地区盛产新鲜水果。

fertilizer / ˈfɜːtəlaɪzə(r) / *n.* [U]肥料：They are spreading chemical ~ in the fields. 他们正在田里施肥。

festival / ˈfestɪvl / *n.* [C] 节日；喜庆日子：a ~ of music 音乐节 / a film ~ 电影节 / the Spring Festival 春节/ the Lantern Festival 灯节；元宵节 / the Mid-autumn Festival 中秋节 / Dragon Festival 端午节(龙舟节) / Tomb-sweeping Festival 清明节

fetch / fetʃ / *v.* 去拿来；去取来：Please ~ me the dictionary. 请把词典给我拿来。

feudal / ˈfjuːdəl / *adj.* 封建的；封建制度的：a volume of ~ studies 一部研究封建制度的书/a ~ state 封建国家

feudalism / ˈfjuːdəˌlɪzəm / *n.* [U]封建主义；封建制度

fever / ˈfiːvə(r) / *n.* [U]发热，发烧；狂热：Her ~ has gone down. 她已经退烧了。/ They were in a ~ of joy when they won the champion. 赢得冠军时他们欣喜若狂。/**have a** ~ 发烧：She has a ~. 她发烧了。派 feverish *adj.*

few / fjuː / Ⅰ *adj.* 少数的，不多的；几乎没有的：Who made the ~est mistakes? 谁犯的错误最少？/ She is a girl of ~ words. 她是一个少言寡语的女孩。/ We stayed here only a ~ days. 我们在

F

此只待了几天。Ⅱ *pron.* 少数；几个：Few knew and ~ cared. 很少有人知道，也很少有人关心。/ I know a ~ of these people. 这些人中我认识几个。

fiancé / fɪˈɒnseɪ / *n.* [C]未婚夫

fiancée / fɪˈɒnseɪ / *n.* [C]未婚妻

fiber(-re) / ˈfaɪbə(r) / *n.* 纤维；纤维质：They use cotton ~s to spin into thread. 他们用棉纤维纺线。

F

fiction / ˈfɪkʃən / *n.* ❶[C] 小说：He is fond of reading detective ~s. 他喜欢读侦探小说。❷[U]虚构；捏造；编造：The whole story is pure ~. 整个故事纯属虚构。派 fictional *adj.*

fictionalize / ˈfɪkʃənəˌlaɪz/ *vt.* 把……编成小说；使小说化：~ a biography 使传记小说化

fictitious / fɪkˈtɪʃəs / *adj.* ❶假的；仿造的：The criminal used a ~ name. 罪犯用了假名。/a ~ bill 空头支票 ❷不真实的；想象的；虚构的：a ~ character in the novel 小说中一个虚构的人物/The characters in *Alice in Wonderland* are ~.《艾丽斯漫游奇境记》中的人物是虚构的。

fiddle / ˈfɪdl / *v.* ❶(手等)乱动；胡乱拨弄：~ at the hem of the skirt 用手摆弄裙边/Tom sat nervously, fiddling with a paperclip. 汤姆紧张地坐着，手里不停地拨弄着回形针。❷调节；修理：He cursed as he ~d with the volume control. 他一边骂着一边调节音量开关。

field / fiːld / *n.* [C] ❶田地，场地：The ~ must be manured. 田里必须施肥了。/ We found him in the football ~. 我们在足球场上找到了他。❷领域，界：Many great discoveries have been made in the ~ of science. 科学界已有许多伟大的发现。

fierce / fɪəs / *adj.* 凶猛的；猛烈的；激烈的：The dog is very ~. 那条狗极凶。/ A ~ storm hit the area. 一场狂风暴雨袭击了这个地区。

fifteen / ˌfɪfˈtiːn / Ⅰ *num.* 十五，15 Ⅱ *adj.* 十五个(的)

fifth / fɪfθ / Ⅰ *num.* 第五；五分之一 Ⅱ *adj.* 第五的；五分之一的

fiftieth / ˈfɪftɪəθ / Ⅰ *num.* 第五十；五十分之一 Ⅱ *adj.* 第五十的；五十分之一的

fifty / ˈfɪftɪ / Ⅰ *num.* 五十，50 Ⅱ *adj.* 五十个(的)

fight / faɪt / Ⅰ *v.* (fought /fɔːt /, fought) 战斗；斗争；打仗：They are ~ing for their freedom. 他们在为自由而战。/ England fought with France against Germany. 英法联合对德作战。Ⅱ *n.* [C] 战斗；斗争：It was a terrible ~. 那是一场可怕的战斗。

fighter / ˈfaɪtə(r)/ *n.* [C] ❶(职业)拳击手 ❷战斗机；歼击机 ❸战士；斗士：a tough ~ 顽强的战士

figment / ˈfɪgmənt / *n.* [C]编造(或想象)出的东西；虚幻的事物；稀奇古怪的念头：biographical and historical ~s 传记和历史方面的杜撰/The shrieks in the attic were just a ~ of his imagination. 楼阁上的尖叫声只是他想象的产物。

figurative / ˈfɪgjʊrətɪv, ˈfɪg(ə)ətɪv/ *adj.* ❶比喻的；借喻的(略作 fig.)：a ~ expression 比喻的说法 ❷象征(性)的：a ~ ceremony 象征性的仪式 ❸多比喻的；辞藻丰富的，有文采的：Elizabethan poetry is highly ~. 伊丽莎白时代的诗歌多用比喻。派 figuratively *adv.*

figure / ˈfɪgə(r) / Ⅰ *n.* [C] ❶数字：Are you good at ~? 你是否善于计算？❷体

形；外表：His ~ is small. 他身材矮小。/ This girl has a good ~. 这姑娘身材很好。/ Exercises improve a person's ~. 运动能改善人的体形。❸人物：a popular ~ 受众人欢迎的人物 / a great ~ in literature 大文豪 ❹图形；图表：The blackboard was covered with geometrical ~s. 黑板上画满了几何图形。Ⅱ *v.* 计算；估计：I ~ that she will win the first prize. 我估计她会得头等奖。/~ **on** 指望，依靠；料到：We ~ on your coming early. 我们指望你早些来。~ **out** 计算出；估计：Figure it out and see what it comes. 把它算出来，看结果得多少。/ I ~ out we shall reach Beijing on Friday. 我估计我们将在星期五到达北京。

file / faɪl / Ⅰ *n.* [C]档案；卷宗；(计算机)文件：Please put these documents in the ~. 请把这些文件放进卷宗里。/ He deleted some dated ~s. 他删除了一些过时的文件。Ⅱ *v.* ❶把……归档：He asked his secretary to ~ the letters in alphabetical order. 他要求秘书把信件按字母顺序归档。❷排成纵队行进：The children ~d into the hall. 孩子们排队进入大厅。

fill / fɪl / *vt.* 使……满，装满；占满：She is ~ed with boiling anger. 她满腔怒火。/ All the streets were ~ed with people. 所有街道都挤满了人。/~ **in** 填满；填充：Fill in the blanks with prepositions. 用介词填空。~ **out** 长得丰满，长胖；填充：When Jane was nineteen, she began to ~ out. 简 19 岁时开始长得丰满起来。/ Please ~ out a check. 请开张支票。~ **up** 装满：Fill up the bottle. 把瓶子装满。~... **with** ... 用……装满：Fill the glass with milk. 把杯子倒满牛奶。

film / fɪlm / *n.* [C]电影，影片；胶卷：Let's go to the ~s. 咱们去看电影吧。/ a black and white ~ 黑白片 / a color ~ 彩色影片 / a comic ~ 喜剧片 / a dramatic ~ 戏剧片 / a documentary ~ 纪录片

filter / ˈfɪltə(r) / *v.* 过滤；渗透：The water for drinking was ~ed. 饮用水是经过过滤的。

F

filth / fɪlθ / *n.* [U] ❶污(秽)物；(肮)脏物；污垢 ❷猥亵语；脏话；下流话

final / ˈfaɪnəl / *adj.* 最终的；最后的：the ~ examination 期末考试 / the ~ result 最后结果 / His ~ decision was to study abroad. 他的最后决定是去国外留学。派 finally *adv.*

finance / ˈfaɪnæns / Ⅰ *n.* 财政；金融；(*pl.*)资金：The bank needs an expert of ~. 那家银行需要一位金融专家。Ⅱ *vt.* 提供资金给……，融资：The company ~d ten students through college. 那家公司给 10 位学生提供读完大学的费用。

financial / faɪˈnænʃəl / *adj.* 财政上的；金融的：Do you know the ~ condition of the company? 你了解那家公司的财务状况吗？派 financially *adv.*

find / faɪnd / *vt.* (found /faʊnd/, found) ❶寻得；找到；发现：Did you ~ the pen you lost yesterday? 你找到昨天丢失的那支笔了吗？❷发觉，察觉；知道：I found it difficult to learn English well. 我觉得学好英语很困难。/ We found him dishonest. 我们发觉他不诚实。/~ **fault (with)** 抱怨，挑剔；对……吹毛求疵：That is the only fault to be found with him. 那是他身上挑出来的唯一毛病。~ **out** 发现；找出；查出：How can I ~ out who took my book? 我怎么能查出是谁把我的书拿走了？

finding / ˈfaɪndɪŋ / *n.* [C] 发现(物);(*pl.*)调查(或研究)结果:The scientist published his latest ~s in the newspaper. 科学家在报上发表了他的最新研究成果。

fine[1] / faɪn / Ⅰ *adj.* (天气)晴朗的;美好的;优秀的:It is ~ today. 今天天晴。/ What a ~ view! 多么美好的景色! / He is a ~ scholar. 他是一位优秀的学者。Ⅱ *adv.* (口语)很好,妙:—How are you? —Fine. Thank you. —你好吗? —好,谢谢。

fine[2] / faɪn / Ⅰ *n.* [C]罚金;罚款:He paid a $300 ~. 他交了 300 美元的罚款。Ⅱ *v.* 处……以罚款:The young man was ~d for speeding. 因超速行车那年轻人被处罚款。

finger / ˈfɪŋgə(r) / *n.* [C]手指:a fore ~ 食指/ a middle ~ 中指 / a ring ~ 无名指 / a little ~ 小指

fingerprint / ˈfɪŋgəˌprɪnt / *n.* [C]指纹;指纹印:Her ~s on the handle proved she'd been there. 她留在把手上的指纹证明她曾去过那里。

fingertip / ˈfɪŋgəˌtɪp/ *n.* [C]指尖;指头:I probed through his hair with my ~s and found a lump. 我的指尖探入他的头发摸到了一个肿块。/**have ... at one's ~s** 对……了如指掌;熟悉,精通:He has every stroke of the game at his ~s. 他对这个游戏的每一个动作都了如指掌。/ He has the whole answer at his ~s. 他熟知全部答案。**to one's ~s** 完全地;彻底地:He is pro-Western to his ~s. 他完全是亲西方的。

finish / ˈfɪnɪʃ / *vt.* 完成;结束:He said he had ~ed his homework. 他说他已完成家庭作业。

fire / ˈfaɪə(r) / Ⅰ *vt.* ❶开火;射击:We ~d our guns at the enemy. 我们向敌人开火。❷解雇:He was ~d by his boss. 他被老板解雇了。Ⅱ *n.* 火;火灾:He who plays with ~ gets burned. 玩火者自焚。/ a big (great) ~ 一场大火 / a blazing ~ 熊熊烈火

fireman / ˈfaɪəˌmən/ *n.* [C](*pl.* -men)消防队员

firework / ˈfaɪəˌwɜːk/ *n.* [C]爆竹,鞭炮;(*pl.*)烟花,焰火;烟火表演:A few loud ~s went off. 一些烟花带着响声绽放开来。/ Children are allowed, under proper supervision, to set off ~s. 孩子们在有人严格监督之下可以放鞭炮。

firm[1] / fɜːm / *adj.* 坚定的;牢固的;稳固的:I don't think that the chair is ~ enough to stand on. 我觉得这把椅子不够结实,不能站上去。/ as ~ as rock 坚如磐石 / a ~ faith 坚定的信仰 派 firmly *adv.*

firm[2] / fɜːm / *n.* [C] 公司;商行:He is thinking of starting another ~ in Hong Kong. 他正考虑在香港再开一家商行。/ a commercial ~ 贸易公司 / an engineering ~ 工程公司 / an exporting ~ 出口公司

first / fɜːst / Ⅰ *num.* 第一 Ⅱ *adj.* ❶第一的;最早的:January is the ~ month of the year. 一月是一年的第一个月。/ ~ floor (英)二楼;(美)一楼,底层 ❷第一流的;最重要的;主要的:He is the ~ violinist of the orchestra. 他是乐队的第一小提琴手。Ⅲ *adv.* 第一;最初(常用于强调):First, I'll tell you a good news. 首先,我要告诉你一个好消息。Ⅳ *n.* [C] 最初;第一名:She was the ~ to come to the office. 她是第一个到办公室的人。/**at** ~ 最初;当初:At ~ he didn't want to come. 他起初不想来。

from ~ to last 自始至终；始终；一直：He sat there thinking from ~ to last. 他始终坐在那儿沉思。

firsthand /ˌfɜːstˈhænd/ *adj.* (资料、经历、来源等)第一手的；亲身体验的；直接的：a ~ experience 亲身经历/book reviews based on ~ research 基于直接研究而写成的书评/Mary gave me a ~ account of the accident. 玛丽告诉我她所目睹的事故发生经过。

fish /fɪʃ/ *n.* ❶[C] (*pl.* fish 或 fishes) 鱼：catch a ~ 捉到一条鱼 ❷[U] 鱼肉：a ~ dinner 鱼餐

fisherman /ˈfɪʃəmən/ *n.* [C] (*pl.* fishermen)渔夫

fist /fɪst/ *n.* [C] 拳头

fishing /ˈfɪʃɪŋ/ *n.* [U]捕鱼；钓鱼：a small ~ boat 一艘小型捕鱼船 / We did a bit of ~ at the weekend. 周末我们钓了会儿鱼。

fission /ˈfɪʃən/ *n.* [U] ❶(核)裂变；(核)分裂：atomic (nuclear) ~ 核裂变 ❷分裂生殖，裂殖；细胞分裂：Many simple plants and animals reproduce by ~. 许多原始动植物通过分裂进行繁殖。

fit /fɪt/ Ⅰ *adj.* (fitter, fittest) ❶健康的：I am not feeling very ~ now. 眼下我觉得身体不大舒服。❷合适的；恰当的：The weather is not ~ to go out. 这天气不适合出去。Ⅱ *v.* (fit 或 fitted; fitting)适合；适应：That ~s you all right. 那对你很适合。/ ~ **in** 适应；配合：The house ~s in beautifully with its surroundings. 这座房子和周围的环境非常协调。~ **sb. (sth.) out** 供给必需品；装备；配备：The soldiers were ~ted out with guns and clothing. 士兵们配发了枪支和服装。~ **for** 使适合；使胜任：Military training ~s men for long marches. 军事训练使人能适应长途行军。~ **up** 装备；布置；安装：We ~ted up one of the bedrooms as a study. 我们把卧室中的一间改成了书房。Ⅲ *n.* [C] 疾病的突然发作；一股，一阵：a ~ of coughing 一阵咳嗽 / a ~ of pain 一阵痛 / a ~ of energy 一股劲 / a ~ of industry 一时的勤奋 / a ~ of weeping 一阵哭泣

fitting /ˈfɪtɪŋ/ *adj.* 合适的；恰当的；相称的：I do not have ~ words to express my satisfaction. 我无法用合适的词语来表达我的满意之情。/It is altogether ~ and proper that we should do this. 我们这样做，是理所当然的，恰如其分的。

five /faɪv/ Ⅰ *num.* 五，5 Ⅱ *adj.* 五个(的)

fix /fɪks/ *vt.* ❶使固定；钉牢：Please ~ the post in the ground. 请将柱子竖立在地上。❷确定；决定：They ~ed a date for the meeting. 他们已定好开会的日子。❸修理：This watch is easy to ~. 这块表好修。/~ **over** 修理：Can the old man ~ over the engine? 那位老人能把发动机修理一下吗? ~ **on (upon)** 选定：We've ~ed on the date to start. 我们选定了出发的日子。/ They ~ed upon me to do this work. 他们选定由我来做这项工作。~ **up** 安排；确定；安装：We've ~ed up a date for the dance. 我们已定好舞会的日期。

fixed /fɪkst/ *adj.* ❶固定的：a ~ seat 固定的座位 / a ~ deposit 定期存款 ❷(只作定语)不动的；集中的，专注的；僵硬的：a look of ~ attention 专注的神情 / a ~ smile 僵硬的笑容 ❸已确定的；已决定了的；不变的：a ~ price (rent) 定好的价格(租金) / The date's not completely ~ yet. 日期尚未完全敲定。

fizz /fɪz/ Ⅰ*vi.* ❶发嘶嘶声,发噼啪声:The firework ~ed for a while and went out. 花炮嘶嘶地响了一会儿就灭了。❷(饮料等)冒气泡,起泡沫:You can drink it while it ~es. 你可以趁冒气的时候喝。Ⅱ*n.* [U] ❶嘶嘶声,噼啪声:the ~ of soda water 汽水冒泡的响声 ❷(饮料等)冒气泡,起泡沫:This lemonade has lost its ~. 这杯柠檬水不冒泡了。

flag /flæg/ *n.* [C]国旗;旗帜:raise (fly) a ~ 升旗 / haul down (lower) a ~ 降旗 / the national ~ 国旗

flake /fleɪk/ *n.* [C] 薄片;(雪、羽毛等的)一片:snow ~ 雪片 / wheat ~s 麦片

flame /fleɪm/ *n.* 火焰;火苗:The red car burst into ~s suddenly. 那辆红色轿车突然起火燃烧。

flap /flæp/ Ⅰ(flapped; flapping) *vt.* ❶拍动;摆动;振(翅):A gust of wind ~ped the tents. 一阵风吹动帐篷。/ Grey pigeons ~ped up into the sky when frightened. 一群灰鸽受了惊,纷纷振翅飞向空中。❷(用扁平物)拍打,拍击:~ the flies away 赶走苍蝇 Ⅱ*n.* [C] ❶帽边;鞋舌;袋盖;(书的护封的)勒口;信封(或纸板箱)的口盖,折盖:the ~ of an envelope 信封的口盖 ❷摆动;飘动;(鸟翼等的)振动 ❸拍动;拍打;拍打声

flare /fleə(r)/ Ⅰ*n.* [U] 闪烁;闪光:We saw the ~ of a flashlight in the dark. 在黑暗中我们看到了手电筒的闪光。Ⅱ*vi.* 闪耀;发光:The torch ~s in the darkness. 火把在黑暗中闪亮。/~ **up** 突然发怒;激动:His anger ~d up when his motives were questioned. 有人对他的动机表示怀疑时,他勃然大怒。

flash /flæʃ/ Ⅰ*n.* [C] 闪烁;发光:a ~ of lightning 闪电 / **in a** ~即刻:I'll be here in a ~. 我即刻就到。Ⅱ*v.* 闪光;闪烁:Flash your light around to see if anyone is hiding here. 用你的灯四周照一照,看看有没有人藏在这里。/~ **across** 闪现;闪过:The lightning ~ed across the sky. 闪电从天空划过。

flashback /ˈflæʃˌbæk/ *n.* ❶(小说、戏剧等的)倒叙,倒叙情节;(电影、电视等的)闪回,闪回镜头:the ~ to the hero's school days 男主角学生时代的倒叙 ❷(往事在脑海中的)再现,重现;回忆,追忆:a sudden ~ of the accident 那次事件在脑海里的突然再现

flat[1] /flæt/ Ⅰ*adj.* ❶平坦的;平的:The floor is quite ~. 地很平。❷无味的;无聊的;枯燥的:The party was very ~. 那次聚会很乏味。/ **be** ~ **out** 精疲力竭:We are all ~ out after lifting the piano. 我们抬了那架钢琴后累得精疲力竭。Ⅱ*adv.* 平直地;断然地

flat[2] /flæt/ *n.* [C]一套房间;公寓:He bought a three-room ~ last year. 去年他买了一套有三个房间(一套三)的公寓。

flatten /ˈflætn/ *v.* 使平坦;使……平:The workers are ~ing the road. 工人们正在铺平道路。

flatter /ˈflætə(r)/ *v.* 奉承;阿谀;使某人高兴:I feel greatly ~ed by your invitation. 承蒙邀请,不胜荣幸。/ ~ **oneself** 自认为:She ~ed herself that she spoke English quite well. 她自认为英语说得相当好。

flattery /ˈflæt(ə)ri/ *n.* [U]❶谄媚;奉承;讨好;恭维:gain one's object by (means of) ~ 通过溜须拍马达到目的/ He is above (proof against) ~. 甜言蜜

语打动不了他。❷谄媚的话；恭维话；溢美之词：be hoodwinked by ~被甜言蜜语蒙蔽 / Those who like ~ but not criticism are bound to go astray. 只爱听恭维话而不爱听批评的人早晚要步入歧途。

flavo(u)r / ˈfleɪvə(r) / *n.* [C] ❶滋味；风味；情趣：I like icecream with different ~s. 我喜欢各种不同口味的冰激凌。/ The houses there have a strong local ~. 那儿的房屋具有很浓的地方韵味。❷香料；调味料

flaw / flɔː / *n.* [C] 瑕疵；缺点；缺陷：You can hardly find any ~ in the handicraft. 在这件手工艺品上你简直很难找出什么缺陷来。

flea / fliː / *n.* [C]蚤，跳蚤

flee / fliː / *v.* (fled /fled/, fled) 逃走；避开：He fled away at the first sight of danger. 他一见到危险就避开了。/ He killed his enemy and fled the country. 他杀死他的敌人后逃离了那个国家。

fleet / fliːt / *n.* [C] 舰队

flesh / fleʃ / *n.* [U] 肉；肌肉；肉体：Are lions and tigers ~-eating animals? 狮子和老虎是肉食动物吗？/**in the** ~ 本人；亲自：He's nicer in the ~ than in the photograph. 他本人比照片好看。

fleshy / ˈfleʃi/ *adj.* ❶多肉的；肥胖的；丰满的：a ~ woman 丰满的女子 ❷肉质的；多果肉的：a ~ peach 多肉的桃子

flex / fleks / *vt.* ❶弯曲，弯动(肢体、关节等)：stretch and ~ one's knees 伸屈膝关节 ❷使(肌肉)收缩，绷紧：~ one's biceps 收紧二头肌

flexible / ˈfleksəbl / *adj.* 柔韧的；易弯曲的；灵活的；可变通的：We should make a ~ plan. 我们应当制订一个灵活的计划。

flick / flɪk / *vt.* ❶轻打；轻拍；轻弹；拂；甩动：The driver ~ed the horse with his whip to make it go fast. 驾车人用鞭子轻轻抽打马儿，催它快走。/He ~ed an ash off his sleeve. 他轻轻拍掉衣袖上的烟灰。❷急速移动；按动；振动：He ~ed the switch. 他啪的一声打开开关。/A grasshopper ~ed its wings. 一只蚱蜢振翅欲飞。

flicker / ˈflɪkə(r) / Ⅰ *vi.* ❶(火、光等)摇曳，闪烁；忽隐忽现，闪现：The candle ~ed in the draught. 烛火在风中摇曳。/An idea ~ed through my brain. 一个主意掠过我的脑海。❷(旗等)飘动；(微微地)颤动，晃动，摆动；(急速地)来回转动：Her eyelids ~ed. 她眨了眨眼皮。Ⅱ *n.* [C] ❶摇曳(或闪动)的光(或火焰)：A faint ~ of lightning lit the room. 一道惨白的闪电照亮了房间。❷突然而短暂的动作，轻快的动作；闪现：a ~ of hope 一线希望/His face showed not a ~ of expression. 他的脸上声色不露。

flight / flaɪt / *n.* ❶[U] 飞行；飞翔：in the ~ 在飞行中 / A hen is incapable of ~. 母鸡不会飞。❷[C] 航空旅行；航程；航班：a lunar ~ 月球飞行 / the space ~ 宇宙飞行 / a round-the-world ~ 环球飞行 / We took Flight 3127 to London. 我们搭乘 3127 航班飞往伦敦。❸[C] 楼梯的一段：I climbed two ~s up to her room. 我上了两段楼梯去她的房间。❹[U]逃跑；溃退：The thief took to ~. 小偷逃跑了。/**in** ~ 逃走：They were in ~ from the flood. 他们避开洪水。**make (take) a** ~ 逃离：She took a ~ on hearing the terrible sound. 她一听到那可怕的声音就逃走了。

fling / flɪŋ / Ⅰ *vt.* (flung, flung) ❶(用

力地)扔,掷,抛,丢:~ out a ball 抛球/ They flung their hats in the air. 他们把帽子抛到空中。❷丢下;抛弃:~ aside all cares 丢开一切忧虑 /~ **oneself** 使冲向;使扑向;使投身;使用(精力等):~ himself into his work 全身心地投入工作 Ⅱ *n.* [C] ❶(用力的)扔,掷,抛,丢:An abrupt ~ of his hands threw her on the grass. 他双手突然一丢,使她摔倒在草坪上。❷一时的放纵;尽情欢乐的一阵

flip /flɪp/ (flipped; flipping) *vt.* ❶轻抛;使在空中翻转;扔;甩:Let's ~ a coin to decide who should go first. 我们抛硬币来决定谁先去吧。❷快速翻动;突然翻转:~ the fish on its back 将鱼翻个肚朝天/The years ~ped off the calendar like dry leaves from a lawn. 岁月催人,日历一张张撕掉,犹如落在草坪上的枯叶。❸浏览;(很快地)翻书:~ through a magazine 浏览杂志

float /fləʊt/ *v.* 漂浮;飘动:The boat ~ed down the river. 小船顺流而下。/ We saw a box ~ing on water. 我们看见一只箱子飘在水上。

flock /flɒk/ Ⅰ *n.* [C]一群;大量;众多:a ~ of geese (sheep, birds, pigeons, ducks, goats, sparrows, girls, visitors)一群鹅(羊、鸟、鸽子、鸭子、山羊、麻雀、少女、访问者)/ **in ~s** 成群:People came in ~s to see the new bridge. 人们成群结队前来参观这座新桥。Ⅱ *v.* 群集;成群地来:Sheep usually ~ together. 羊通常是成群生活的。

flood /flʌd/ Ⅰ *n.* [C] 洪水;水灾:The house of the peasant was washed away by the ~. 那个农民的房屋被洪水冲走了。Ⅱ *vt.* 淹没;使水泛滥:The river ~ed a lot of fields. 河水淹没了大量农田。

floor /flɔː(r)/ *n.* [C]地面;地板;楼层:The baby is sitting on the ~. 小婴孩坐在地板上。/ The old lady lives on the third ~. 老太太住在三楼。

floppy /ˈflɒpi/ *adj.* 松软的:a ~ disk 软磁盘

flora /ˈflɔːrə/ *n.* (*pl.* floras 或 florae /ˈflɔːriː/) ❶植物群;植物区系:~ and fauna 植物与动物/the ~s of the West Indies 西印度群岛各种植物群 ❷[U](人体内或肤表上的)细菌群:intestinal ~肠菌群

flour /ˈflaʊə(r)/ *n.* [U]面粉:We use ~ for making bread. 我们用面粉做面包。

flourish /ˈflʌrɪʃ/ *vi.* 繁荣;茂盛;兴旺:The young man runs a shop and his business is ~ing. 那年轻人开着一家商店,生意很兴隆。

flow /fləʊ/ *vi.* 淌;流动:Tears ~ed from her eyes. 眼泪从她眼里流了出来。/ The river ~s to south. 河水向南流去。

flower /ˈflaʊə(r)/ *n.* [C]花;花卉:The ~s bloom. 花开了。/ The ~s have faded. 花已凋谢。/ The roses are in full ~. 玫瑰花盛开。

flu /fluː/ *n.* [U](口语,influenza 的缩略形式)流行性感冒:She had caught ~, so she couldn't go to school. 她患了流感,不能上学。

fluctuate /ˈflʌktjʊˌeɪt/ *vi.* ❶(价格、数量等)涨落,波动;(意见、行为等)动摇,变化不定:The price of vegetables ~s according to the weather. 蔬菜的价格随天气变化而波动。/Her affections had been continually fluctuating. 她的感情常摇摆不定。❷(上下或来回)摆动,波动:The electric current ~s in the same manner. 电流以同样的方式波动。派

fluctuation *n.*

fluent / ˈfluːənt / *adj.* 流利的；流畅的：Our teacher speaks ～ English. 我们老师讲一口流利的英语。派 fluently *adv.*

fluid / ˈfluːɪd / *n.* 流体；液体：Water is a ～. 水是液体。

fluoride / ˈfluəˌraɪd / *n.* [U]氯化物：sodium ～氯化铵

fluorine / ˌfluəriː / *n.* [U]氯(符号 F)

flush / flʌʃ / *v.* (脸)变红，涨红：Her face ～ed with excitement. 她激动得满脸通红。

flute / fluːt / *n.* [C]长笛

flutter / ˈflʌtə(r) / *v.* 拍翅；飘动；颤动：A butterfly was ～ing in the sunshine. 一只蝴蝶在阳光下翩翩起舞。

fly[1] / flaɪ / Ⅰ *v.* (flew /fluː/, flown /fləʊn/) 飞；飞行；飘扬：On Sunday they often ～ their model planes in the fields. 星期天他们常常在田野里放模型飞机。/～ **by** 很快地飞过；(时间)飞逝：The summer flew by. 夏天很快就过去了。～ **into a great anger** (**rage**) 勃然大怒：She flew into rage at the news. 她一听到这消息就勃然大怒。Ⅱ *n.* 飞，飞行，飞行距离

fly[2] / flaɪ / *n.* [C]蝇；苍蝇

foam / fəʊm / *n.* [U]泡沫：The ～ of beer disappeared in a few moment. 不一会儿啤酒中的泡沫就消失了。

focus / ˈfəʊkəs / Ⅰ *n.* [C](*pl.* focuses 或 foci /ˈfəʊsaɪ/)焦点；中心：The problem of prices has become the ～ of argument. 价格问题已经成为人们议论的中心。Ⅱ *v.* 聚集；集中：He ～ed his attention on the improvement of his English reading comprehension. 他把注意力集中在提高英语阅读理解能力上。

fog / fɒg / *n.* [U]雾；浓雾：This city has a very bad ～ in winter. 这个城市冬季的雾很大。/ His mind is in a hazy ～. 他的思维如坠云雾中。

foil[1] / fɒɪl / *vt.* 阻挠，阻碍；挫败；击败：Quick thinking by the bank clerk ～ed the robbers. 银行职员的机智使抢劫犯没能得逞。/I was ～ed of my purpose. 我未能达到目的。

foil[2] / fɒɪl / [U]箔；金属薄片：aluminum ～铝箔

fold / fəʊld / *v.* 折叠，对折：If you ～ the letter into two, it will fit into the envelope. 你把信对折起来就能放进信封了。/ ～ **one's arms** 交臂；抱臂：When they sit, they often ～ their arms. 他们一坐下来，就常抱着手臂。

folder / ˈfəʊldə(r) / *n.* [C]文件夹；(存放散纸的)夹子

foliage / ˈfəʊlɪɪdʒ/ *n.* [U](绿)叶，叶子：dark green ～ 黑油油的绿叶 / These naked shoots shall put their graceful ～ on again. 这些光秃秃的嫩枝将会再次长出美丽的叶片。

folk / fəʊk / *n.* 人们；家人；亲属：Some ～s are never satisfied. 有些人永远不满足。/ old ～s 老乡

follow / ˈfɒləʊ / *vt.* ❶跟；随着：Tuesday ～s Monday. 星期二在星期一之后。/ Follow this road until you reach the church. 顺着这条路一直走到教堂。❷注视：We'll ～ closely the development of the situation. 我们将密切关注形势的发展。❸听从：Don't ～ other's advice blindly. 不要盲目听从别人的劝告。❹领会；了解：He spoke so fast that I couldn't ～ him. 他说得太快，我听不懂他的话。/～ **on** 随后到；继续：I'll be back soon. Meanwhile you ~ on. 我马上就回来,你继续干。~ **up** 跟踪;追查;继续:He thinks the story is worth ~ing up. 他认为这故事值得连载。~ **out** 贯彻;推行:We must ~ out this plan. 我们必须执行这个计划。

follower /ˈfɒləʊə(r)/ *n.* [C] ❶跟在后面的人(或物):He eluded his ~s by crossing the river. 他渡过那条河才摆脱了追踪者。❷追随者,拥护者;爱好者:a ~ of Marx 马克思的追随者 / Lloyd becomes a camp ~. 劳埃德成了一名野营爱好者。❸模仿者,仿效者:He was little more than a ~ of current modes. 他不过是个时尚的模仿者而已。

following /ˈfɒləʊɪŋ/ Ⅰ*n.* (集合名词)追随者;崇拜者:They have a ~ of their own. 他们有自己的一大批追随者。Ⅱ*adj.* 随后的;接着的:She stayed with us until the ~ afternoon. 她和我们一直待到第二天下午。

fond /fɒnd/ *adj.* 喜爱的;爱好的:He is very ~ of his mother. 他很爱他母亲。

food /fuːd/ *n.* [U](指某种特定的食物为可数名词) 食物;食品:Chinese ~ 中餐 / cooked ~ 熟食 / fast ~ 快餐 / mental ~ 精神食粮 / light ~ 清淡食物 / sweet ~ 甜食/ sea ~s 海味食品 / Our ~ is running short. 我们的食物快吃完了。

fool /fuːl/ Ⅰ*v.* 愚弄;欺骗;开玩笑:I was only ~ing. 我只是开开玩笑而已。/ You can't ~ me into doing that. 你不能骗我做那事。/ ~ **away** 虚度光阴:They ~ed the whole evening away. 他们把整个晚上的时间都给浪费了。Ⅱ*n.* [C] 笨人;傻瓜:All Fools' Day 愚人节/ Every man has a ~ in his sleeve. 人人都有糊涂的时候。/**make a ~ of sb.** 愚弄某人;让某人出丑:You are making a ~ of me. 你在愚弄我。**play the ~ with** 戏弄,愚弄;糟蹋,损坏:They warn you not to play the ~ with them. 他们警告你不要戏弄他们。

foolish /ˈfuːlɪʃ/ *adj.* 愚蠢的:It was very ~ of you to quarrel with a little girl. 你真傻,竟和一个小姑娘吵架。派 foolishly *adv.*

foolproof /ˈfuːlˌpruːf/ *adj.* ❶(操作等)极简单的;(机械等)极易操作的:a ~ automatic washer 操作简便的自动洗衣机 ❷不会出差错的,安全可靠的:a ~ scheme 万无一失的计划

foot /fʊt/ *n.* [C] (*pl.* feet /fiːt/) ❶脚;底部:He hurt his left ~. 他的左脚受伤了。/ There is a mistaken sentence at the ~ of Page 21. 在 21 页的下部有一个错句。/**on ~** 徒步;步行:I came on ~. 我是步行来的。**on one's feet** 站着:He is on his feet for sixteen hours a day. 他每天站 16 个小时。**under ~** 脚底下:It is very wet under ~. 脚底下很湿。**at the ~ of** 在……脚下:There is a hut at the ~ of the mountain. 山脚下有一间茅舍。**set sth. on ~** 发动;开始:He set the motor on ~. 他发动了汽车。**keep one's feet** 站稳:The boy stumbled on the stairs but was able to keep his feet. 这孩子在楼梯上绊了一下,但没有跌倒。**find one's feet** 学会走路:How old was the baby when it began to find its feet? 这孩子开始走路时多大? **put one's ~ down** 采取坚定的态度;坚决不退让:John didn't want to practise the piano, but his mother put his ~ down. 约翰不想练钢琴,但母亲坚持要他练。❷英尺:He is five ~ eight. 他 5 英尺 8

英寸高。

football /ˈfʊtˌbɔːl/ *n.* ❶[U]橄榄球运动：~ fans 橄榄球迷 / He knows a good bit about ~. 他挺懂橄榄球的。❷[C]橄榄球 ❸[U]（英）足球运动（= soccer）

foothold /ˈfʊtˌhəʊld/ *n.* [C] ❶（攀爬时的）立脚处，立足点：a pair of shallow foot-holds in the rock 岩石上浅浅的一对立脚处 ❶稳固的地位（或基础）；优势：chisel a ~ for oneself in the city 为自己在城里打稳基础/We need to get a ~ in the European market. 我们要在欧洲市场上找一个立足点。

footing /ˈfʊtɪŋ/ *n.* ❶[C]（常用单数）（企业等的）基础，根基：on a solid and durable ~ 在稳固长久的基础上 / They are on the same social ~. 他们处于同样的社会地位。❷[U]立脚点，立足处；稳固的地位 The steep cliff gave us no ~. 悬崖峭壁无处立足。/ She lost her ~ and fell. 她失足摔了下来。

footnote /ˈfʊtˌnəʊt/ *n.* [C]脚注；注解；补充说明：~s on the page 书页上的脚注 / the ~ to the exclusions 对例外情况的注释

footprint /ˈfʊtˌprɪnt/ *n.* [C] ❶脚印，足迹；痕迹：~s in the snow 雪地里的足印 / plant the first human ~ on the moon 首次在月球上留下了人类的足迹 ❷（计算机等占用的）台面，桌面

footstep /ˈfʊtstep/ *n.* [C] 脚步；脚步声；足迹：I heard ~s on the stairs. 我听到有人上楼的脚步声。

for /fɔː(r), fə(r)/ Ⅰ *prep.* ❶达，计（表时间、空间）：I haven't seen you ~ four years. 我有四年未见到你了。/ ~ **ever** 永远：I love the city ~ ever. 我永远爱这座城市。❷为了（表目的、意愿）：We study ~ the people. 我们为人民而学习。❸由于，因为（表原因）：For lack of money, he can't go abroad. 因为缺钱，他不能出国。❹赞成：Some people were ~ the plan and others were against it. 一些人赞成此计划，另一些人则反对。❺就……而言：The weather is rather cold ~ March. 就三月的天气而言，这算是很冷的了。Ⅱ *conj.* 因为：He felt no fear, ~ he was a brave man. 他无所畏惧，因为他是一位勇士。

forage /ˈfɒrɪdʒ/ Ⅰ *n.* [U]（马、牛等家畜的）草料，秣草；饲料：~ for the cattle 喂牛的饲料 Ⅱ *v.* 搜寻；翻查；搜寻食物（或供应物）：The boys ~d for old metal. 男孩子们在找寻废铜烂铁。

forbid /fəˈbɪd/ *vt.* （forbad /fəˈbæd/或 forbade /fəˈbeɪd/, forbidden /fəˈbɪdn/; -bidding) 禁止；不许：Smoking is strictly ~den here. 严禁吸烟。

force /fɔːs/ Ⅰ *vt.* 强迫；迫使；强制：The crowd were ~d back. 人群被迫后退。/ ~ **sb. to do sth.** 强迫某人做某事：The boss ~d him to work 13 hours a day. 老板强迫他一天工作 13 小时。~ **sb. into doing sth.** 被迫做某事：She was ~d into leaving her country. 她被迫离开了自己的国家。~ **through** 突破：He ~d his way through the crowd. 他从人群中挤了过去。Ⅱ *n.* ❶[U] 力量；气力；体力：The ~ of gravity makes things fall to the earth. 地球引力使物体向地面下落。/ Her physical ~ was weak, but her mental ~ was very great. 她体质弱，但她的精神力量却很强。❷[C]（有组织的）武装团体：an air ~ 空军 / The enemy ~s suffered severe death. 敌军伤亡惨重。/**by** ~ 强迫地；以武力：He took her money by ~. 他强行夺走了她

的钱。

forearm /ˈfɔːrɑːm/ *n.* [C]前臂

forebear /ˈfɔːbeə(r)/ *n.* [C]祖先;祖辈:the land from which one's ~s had been driven 其祖先被赶走的地方

forecast /ˈfɔːkɑːst/ Ⅰ *vt.* (forecast 或 forecasted) 预报;预测;预言:The station has ~ that it will rain tomorrow. 电视台预报明天有雨。Ⅱ *n.* [C]预测;预报:What is the ~ about the weather for today? 天气预报说今天天气怎么样?

F

forefinger /ˈfɔːfɪŋgə(r)/ *n.* [C] 食指

foreground /ˈfɔːgraʊnd/ *n.* [C] ❶(图画、景物等的)前景,近景:The ~ of the picture shows a cottage, while mountains loom in the background. 这张图片的前景是一间村舍小屋,背景是隐约可见的群山。❷最突出(或最重要)的位置:He likes to be in the ~ at very meeting. 每逢会议,他总爱出风头。

forehead /ˈfɒrɪd/ *n.* [C] 额;前部

foreign /ˈfɒrən/ *adj.* 外国的;在国外的:He's thinking of buying a new ~ car. 他想买一辆进口新车。/ They absorbed ~ capital to develop the local industry. 他们引进外资发展地方工业。

foreigner /ˈfɒrɪnə(r),ˈfɒrənə(r) *n.* [C] 外国人:We are all ~s in other countries. 在异国他乡我们都是外国人。

foreleg /ˈfɔːleg/ *n.* [C] (动物的)前腿

foremost /ˈfɔːməʊst/ *adj.* 首要的,最重要的;首位的;最杰出的,最著名的:A computer programmer is first and ~ an interpreter. 计算机程序编制者首先是一位解释者。/They have become ~ in nearly all the general lines of inland trade, commerce, and industry. 他们摇身一变成为几乎所有内陆贸易及工商业中的佼佼者。

foresee /fɔːˈsiː/ *vt.* (foresaw /fɔːˈsɔː/, foreseen /fɔːˈsiːn/) 预知,预见,预测:Can you ~ your future? 你能预知你的未来吗?

forest /ˈfɒrɪst/ *n.* 森林:preserve ~ 保护森林 / He got lost in the ~. 他在森林里迷路了。

forestall /fɔːˈstɔːl/ *vt.* (用先发制人的手段)预先阻止,抢先阻止:We ~ed them by taking advantage of their momentary discomfiture. 我们利用他们暂时失势的机会先发制人。

foretell /fɔːˈtel/ *vt.* (foretold, foretold) 预知;预见:Timely snow ~s a bumper harvest. 瑞雪兆丰年。

forever /fərˈevə(r)/ *adv.* (=for ever) 永远;常常:We love peace ~. 我们永远热爱和平。

foreword /ˈfɔːwɜːd/ *n.* [C] 序;序言;前言:His teacher wrote the ~ to his newly published book. 他的老师给他新出版的书写了序言。

forge /fɔːdʒ/ *vt.* 伪造;假造:~d bank notes 伪币;假钞 / He was sent to prison because he ~d passports. 他因伪造护照被关进监狱。

forgery /ˈfɔːdʒəri/ *n.* 伪造;伪造物;赝品:The police arrested the man for ~. 警察逮捕了伪造文件的人。/ This is a ~ painting. 这是一幅油画赝品。

forget /fəˈget/ *v.* (forgot /fəˈgɒt/, forgotten /fəˈgɒtn/或 forgot; forgetting)忘记;遗忘:They almost forgot what they went there for. 他们几乎忘了去那儿的目的。/ I forgot to give him the key to the door. 我忘了给他门钥匙。/ I shall never ~ hearing her singing that song.

我永远忘不了她唱那首歌的情景。

forgetful /fəˈgetfʊl/ *adj.* ❶健忘的；记忆力差的：a ~ person 忘性大的人 / She's become very ~ of things. 她变得很健忘。❷疏忽的；怠慢的（与 of 连用）：He worked demonically in his laboratory, ~ of the world outside. 他在实验室里潜心工作，完全忘却了外面的世界。/ Be not ~ to entertain guests. 千万别怠慢了客人。派 forgetfully *adv.*；forgetfulness *n.*

forgive /fəˈgɪv/ *vt.*（forgave /fəˈgeɪv/，forgiven /fəˈgɪvn/）原谅；饶恕：Forgive me for interrupting you. 请原谅我打扰了你。

forgiving /fəˈgɪvɪŋ/ *adj.* 宽容的；仁慈的：a ~ soul 宽厚的人/To be social is to be ~. 与人和谐相处就是要宽宏大量。

forgo /fɔːˈgəʊ/ *vt.*（forwent/-ˈwent/，forgone/-ˈgɒn/；forgoes）抛弃，弃绝；放弃；错过（机会、优势等）：Men are more likely to ~ a pleasant working environment for higher pay. 男人们多数会为了高薪而放弃舒适的工作条件。/The bank will ~ its fourth、quarter dividend. 这家银行将放弃第四季度的分红。

fork /fɔːk/ *n.*［C］叉；餐叉：She put a knife and ~ on the table . 她在桌上放了一副刀叉。

form /fɔːm/ Ⅰ *vt.* ❶形成；构成：Steam ~s when water boils. 水沸腾时产生水蒸气。❷建立；组成；养成：Three or four classes ~ a grade. 三四个班组成一个年级。/ She has ~ed a good habit to wash hands before meals. 她已经养成饭前洗手的好习惯。/ **be ~ed of** 由……组成：The country is ~ed of a few large islands. 这个国家由几个大的岛屿组成。Ⅱ *n.*［C］❶形式；方式：This English word has two ~s. 这个英语单词有两种形式。❷形状；形态：She has a tall graceful ~. 她有修长优美的体形。❸［C］表格：Please fill in the ~ with your name and address. 请在表上填写你的姓名和住址。

formal /ˈfɔːm(ə)l/ *adj.* ❶正式的；合乎格式的：A student's ~ education at college usually takes four years. 大学正规教育通常需要四年时间。/ This is a ~ contract. 这是一份正式合同。❷礼仪上的；合乎礼仪的：The prime minister paid a ~ call to his neighbor country last week. 上周首相对他的邻国进行了礼节性的拜访。派 formally *adv.*

formality /fɔːˈmælɪti/ *n.* ❶［U］拘泥形式；讲究礼节；拘谨：treat sb. with much ~ 对某人非常拘礼 / The host's kindness melt-ed his initial ~ quickly. 主人亲切的态度使他开始的拘谨很快消失了。❷［C］礼节；仪式；正式的手续；繁文缛节，俗套：go through the legal formalities 办理法律手续 / There are a certain formalities to attend to before we can give you a visa. 你要办好手续，我们才可以给你签证。

format /ˈfɔːmæt/ Ⅰ *n.*［C］❶（出版物的）版式，开本 ❷（程序、步骤等的）安排，计划；设计：The course will follow a seminar ~. 这门课将以讨论的形式进行。❸（计算机中资料存储的）格式 Ⅱ *vt.*（formatted；formatting）❶为……设计版式 ❷使（磁盘）格式化：The diskette must be ~ted for the computer being used. 磁盘必须格式化后才能使用。

formation /fɔːˈmeɪʃn/ *n.*［U］形成；构成；构成物：She paid great attention to the ~ of children's good habits. 她非常重视孩子们好习惯的养成。/ The ~ of the building is unique. 这幢建筑物的结构非常独特。

former / ˈfɔːmə(r) / Ⅰ *adj*. 以前的;从前的:He was the ~ manager of the department. 他是这个部门的前任经理。Ⅱ *pron*.(the ~) 前者

formula / ˈfɔːmjələ / *n*. [C](*pl*. formulas /ˈfɔːmjələz/ 或 formulae /ˈfɔːmjəliː/) ❶(数学) 公式;(化学)分子式 ❷处方;配方:Do you know the ~ of this pill? 你知道这种药丸的配方吗?

forsake / fəˈseɪk, fɔːˈseɪk / *vt*. (forsook /-ˈsʊk/, forsaken /-ˈseɪkən/) ❶遗弃;抛弃;摒弃:~ one's wicked habits 摒弃恶习/He forsook his wife and children and went off with another woman. 他遗弃妻儿,跟另一个女人私奔了。❷(永久地)离开:The artist forsook his country for an island in the South Pacific. 那位画家离开祖国来到了南太平洋的一个海岛上。

fort / fɔːt / *n*. [C] 要塞;堡垒:The soldiers took the enemy's ~ in two days. 战士们两天内攻下了敌人的堡垒。

forth / fɔːθ / *adv*. 向前;往前:He was anxious and walked back and ~ in the corridor. 他非常焦急,在走廊里走来走去。/**and so ~** (=**and so on**)等等

forthcoming / fɔːθˈkʌmɪŋ, ˈfɔːθˌkʌmɪŋ / *adj*. ❶即将到来的;即将出现的:Relief will be ~ for those left homeless by the flood. 救济的财物将要送到那些因洪水而无家可归的人手里。❷现成的,随时可提供的:She needed help, but none was ~. 她需要帮助,但没有人来帮忙。❸外向的,乐意结交人的;乐于助人的,友善的:They can afford to be ~ just as his attitude warrants. 正如他的态度所表明的,他们很乐意接待他。

fortieth / ˈfɔːtɪəθ / Ⅰ *num*. 第四十;四十分之一 Ⅱ *adj*. 第四十的;四十分之一的

fortress / ˈfɔːtrɪs/ *n*. [C]军事堡垒;防御堡垒;要塞:the capture of a ~ 攻陷要塞 / The town is under the shelter of a ~. 该城在要塞的保护之下。

fortunate / ˈfɔːtʃənət / *adj*. 幸运的;吉利的;带来好运的:That was ~ for you. 你真幸运。/ She was ~ to have passed the examination. 很幸运,她考试过关了。派 fortunately *adv*.

fortune / ˈfɔːtʃuːn / *n*. ❶[U]命运;运气:They had good ~ to win the game. 她非常幸运地在那场游戏中获胜。❷[C]财产;巨款:It was said that the boy inherited a large ~. 据说那小男孩继承了一大笔财产。

forty / ˈfɔːti / Ⅰ *num*. 四十,40 Ⅱ *adj*. 四十个(的)

forum / ˈfɔːrəm / *n*. [C] 公开讨论会;座谈会

forward / ˈfɔːwəd / *adv*. 向前方;前进:The teacher asked the students to move ~. 老师要求学生向前走。

fossil / ˈfɒsl / *n*. [C]化石:They are hunting for ~s of elephants. 他们正在寻找大象化石。

foster / ˈfɒstə(r) / *vt*. ❶培育,培养;鼓励,促进;(环境等)对……有利:provide opportunity to ~ productivity 创造机会促进生产/He ~ed a feeling of pride over his recent success. 他因最近的成功而变得心高气傲。❷养育,收养(常指非亲生的孩子):~ a homeless child 收养一个无家可归的孩子

found / faʊnd / *vt.* 建立；创办；成立：The college was ~ed in 1941. 这所学院是 1941 年创办的。/ This novel was ~ed on some facts. 这本小说是基于某些事实写成的。派 founder *n.*

foundation / faʊnˈdeɪʃn / *n.* ❶［U］成立；建立；创办：The ~ of a primary school in the mountain area is their common wish. 在山区创办一所小学是他们的共同愿望。❷［C］地基；基础；根据：He has laid a solid ~ for his future study. 他为未来的研究打下了坚实的基础。/ His report has no ~ of fact. 他的报告缺乏事实根据。❸［C］基金；基金会：We have a ~ for research in our college. 我们学院设有研究基金会。

fountain / ˈfaʊntən / *n.*［C］泉水；喷泉；源泉：This ~ is used to drink from. 这眼喷泉是用来提供饮水的。/ Knowledge is the ~ of wisdom. 知识是智慧的源泉。

four / fɔː(r) / Ⅰ *num.* 四，4 Ⅱ *adj.* 四个（的）

fourteen / fɔːˈtiːn/Ⅰ *num.* 十四，14 Ⅱ *adj.* 十四个（的）

fourteenth / ˌfɔːˈtiːnθ / Ⅰ *num.* 第十四；十四分之一 Ⅱ *adj.* 第十四的；十四分之一的

fourth / fɔːθ / Ⅰ *num.* 第四；四分之一 Ⅱ *adj.* 第四的；四分之一的

fowl / faʊl / *n.*［C］家禽；禽肉；飞禽

fox / fɒks / *n.*［C］狐狸

fraction / ˈfrækʃn / *n.*［C］❶碎片；片断；一小部分：She has finished only a ~ of the work . 她只完成了工作的一部分。❷（数学）分数

fracture / ˈfræktʃə(r) / Ⅰ *n.*［C］❶骨折；（软骨、软组织的）撕裂，挫伤：a ~ of the arm 臂部骨折/kidney ~肾破裂 ❷断裂；破裂；折断：a ~ of the ice 冰裂/a ~ of friendly relations 友好关系的破裂 Ⅱ *v.*（使）骨折；挫伤（软骨或软组织）：The boy fell from a tree and ~d his arm. 那个男孩从树上摔了下来，跌断了手臂。

fragile / ˈfrædʒaɪl / *adj.* 易碎的；脆的；体质弱的：We know that china is ~. 我们知道瓷器是易碎的。/ She looks very ~ but is still working. 她看起来身体虚弱，但她仍然在工作。

fragment Ⅰ / ˈfrægmənt / *n.*［C］❶碎片；小碎块，碎渣：burst into ~s 炸成碎片 ❷不完整（或未完成、不连贯）的部分；孤立的片断：I heard only a ~ of their conversation. 他们的对话，我只听了个只言片语。Ⅱ / frægˈment / *v.*（使）破碎，（使）成碎片；分裂：The vase was ~ed in shipment. 那个花瓶在运输中被打碎了。/The chair ~ed under his weight. 那张椅子在他身体的重压下散了架。派 fragmented *adj*，

fragrance / ˈfreɪgrəns / *n.*［C］❶芬芳，芳香；香气，香味：the ~ of flowers and the song of birds 花香鸟语/The air was heavy with the ~ of lush wild blooms and fruits. 空气中洋溢着茂盛的野生花草和果实的芳香。❷香料；香气

fragrant / ˈfreɪgrənt / *adj.* 香的；芬芳的；令人愉快的：~ memories of the party 对晚会的美好回忆 / She put fresh ~ flowers in the vase. 她在花瓶里插满芬芳的鲜花。

frame / freɪm / *n.*［C］框架；架子；结构：I broke the ~s of my glasses. 我把眼镜框打烂了。/ a door ~ 门框 / a ~ for a picture 画框 / the ~ of society 社会结构

framework /ˈfreɪmwɜːk/ *n.* [C]框架；结构；机构；组织：The bridge has a steel ~. 这座桥是钢结构的。

frank /fræŋk/ *adj.* 坦白的；直率的：Please give me a ~ reply soon. 请尽快给我一个坦率的答复。派 frankly *adv.*

fraud /frɔːd/ *n.* ❶[U]欺骗；诈骗；舞弊：obtain money by ~诈财 ❷[C]欺诈行为；不正当手段；谎言；骗局：The advertisement of a sale was a ~ to lure people into the store. 这则销售广告是骗人的把戏，目的是把人们引诱进商店。❸[C]骗子，说谎者；诈骗者；骗人的东西

F

free /friː/ Ⅰ*adj.* ❶自由的；无约束的：You are ~ to express yourself at today's meeting. 在今天的会上你可以畅所欲言。/ **set ~** 释放：The prisoners were set ~. 那些囚犯被释放了。**be ~ from** 不受……约束的：I am ~ from duty today. 今天我不当班。❷免费的；免税的：If your wages are small, they'll be ~ of income tax. 如果你工资低，你可免交所得税。❸有空的；未占据的：Her afternoons are usually ~. 她通常下午有空。/**make ~ with** 随意使用他人之物：They entered the house and made ~ with whatever they could lay their hands on. 他们进入屋子随便拿手能够着的东西。Ⅱ*vt.* 使自由；释放：You should ~ the bird from the cage. 你应当把鸟从笼中放出去。

freedom /ˈfriːdəm/ *n.* 自由；无拘束：~ of speech 言谈自由 / ~ of religion 宗教信仰自由 / He longed for ~. 他渴望自由。/**take (use) ~ with sb.** 对某人放肆；对某人无礼：Don't take ~ with her. 不许对她这么无礼。

freely /ˈfriːli/ *adv.* ❶自由地；不受操纵（或管制，监禁等）地：He's the country's first ~ elected president for 50 years. 他是50年来该国第一位经过自由选举而产生的总统。❷无阻碍地；自如地：The traffic on the motorway is flowing ~. 公路上交通畅通无阻。/ a glass gate swinging ~ 开关自如的玻璃门 ❸无拘束地；随便地：I fear I talk to you too ~. 我怕我对你讲的话太随便了。❹直爽地，坦率地：He ~ admitted that he made a mistake. 他痛快地承认犯了错。

freeway /ˈfriːˌweɪ/ *n.* [C] ❶高速公路 ❷免费高速干道

freewill /ˈfriːˌwɪl/ *adj.* 自愿的：a ~ choice 自由选择

freeze /friːz/ *v.* (froze /frəʊz/, frozen /ˈfrəʊzn/) ❶冻结；结冰：Fresh water ~s at 0℃. 淡水在零摄氏度结冰。❷令人愣住；呆住：The child froze at the sight of the snake. 那孩子一看见蛇就吓呆了。

freezer /ˈfriːzə(r)/ *n.* [C] ❶冷冻装置；制冷器；冷藏箱；冰箱，冰柜；（冰箱的）冷冻室 ❷冷藏室；冷库；冷藏车

freezing /ˈfriːzɪŋ/ *adj.* 极冷的；冻结的：What ~ weather it is! 今天天气真冷！

freight /freɪt/ *n.* [U]❶货运：the volume of ~货运量/Nowadays, the railways earn most of their profit from ~. 眼下，铁路的大部分赢利来自货运。❷（货运的）货物：Only 40% of ~ moves interstate by truck. 只有四成的货物用卡车在各州间运输。

French /frentʃ/ Ⅰ*adj.* 法国的；法国人的Ⅱ*n.* 法语：She became a teacher of ~ after graduation. 毕业后她成为一名法语教师。

Frenchman /ˈfrentʃmən/ *n.* [C]（*pl.*

Frenchmen)法国人，法兰西人；具法国血统的人

frequency / ˈfriːkwənsi / *n.* 频率；频繁：The ~ of traffic accidents in this road is high. 这段公路上交通事故的发生率高。

frequent / ˈfriːkwənt / *adj.* 频繁的；经常的；屡次的：He made ~ trips to Japan. 他经常去日本。/ Professor Li is a ~ visitor to the library. 李教授是图书馆的常客。派 frequently *adv.*

fresh / freʃ / *adj.* ❶新鲜的；新制的：The meat is not very ~. 这肉不是很新鲜。/ I like ~ bread. 我喜欢吃新烤的面包。❷不熟练的；无经验的：He is a ~ hand in this field. 在这一领域里他还是个新手。派 freshly *adv.*

freshman / ˈfreʃmən/ *n.* [C]（*pl.* freshmen）❶大学一年级新生；中学一年级学生：freshmen at the Constable School 警察学校的新生 ❷新手，没有经验的人

freshwater / ˈfreʃˌwɔːtə(r)/ *adj.* 淡水的；生长在淡水中的：a ~ fish (pearl) 淡水鱼(珍珠) / land and ~ habitats 陆地和淡水栖息地

friction / ˈfrɪkʃən / *n.* [U]摩擦；摩擦力：Oil reduces ~. 油能减少摩擦。

Friday / ˈfraɪdi / *n.* 星期五（略作 Fri.）

fridge / frɪdʒ / *n.* [C]电冰箱（＝refrigerator）

friend / frend / *n.* [C]朋友；友人：We have ~s all over the world. 我们的朋友遍世界。/**make ~s (with)**（与……）交朋友：Better not be so quick to make ~s. 交朋友最好不要太性急。

friendly / ˈfrendli / *adj.* 友好的；亲切的：He is very ~ to (towards) me. 他对我很友好。

friendship / ˈfrendʃɪp / *n.* 友爱；友情；友谊：He paid a ~ visit to Japan last month. 上个月他去日本进行友好访问。/I hope our ~ will last forever. 我希望我们的友谊长存。

fright / fraɪt / *n.* [U] 惊吓；恐怖：He gave me a great ~. 他使我大吃一惊。/ The boy shivered with ~. 那男孩吓得发抖。

frighten / ˈfraɪtn / *vt.* 吓唬；使害怕；使受惊吓：The child was badly ~ed. 那个小孩吓坏了。/~ **sb. into (out of) doing sth.** 恐吓某人做(不做)某事：He was ~ed into confessing. 他受恐吓后便招认了。

frightening / ˈfraɪtənɪŋ / *adj.* 令人惊恐的，骇人的：This is a ~ thought. 这个想法令人不寒而栗。/It was a ~ situation to be in. 当时的情景非常可怕。

frightful / ˈfraɪtful/ *adj.* ❶可怕的，可怖的，骇人的：a ~ accident 可怕的意外事故 /She let a ~ screech out of her. 她发出一种撕心裂肺的尖叫声。❷令人震惊的：The storm did ~ damage. 那场风暴所造成的损失令人震惊。❸糟糕的；讨厌的；令人十分不快的：a ~ poem 拙劣的诗 / The exam questions were ~. 考试题目简直难死人了！❹极度的；极大的：a ~ shock 巨大的打击 / We're in a ~ rush. 我们赶得急死了。派 frightfully *adv.*

frigid / ˈfrɪdʒɪd / *adj.* ❶寒冷的，酷寒的：The air on the mountaintop was ~. 山顶上的空气很寒冷。❷冷淡的，冷漠的；没有生气的；刻板的：a ~ reaction to the proposal 对提议做出的冷淡反应/a welcome that was polite but ~彬彬有礼但拘谨刻板的欢迎方式 派 frigidly *adv.*

fringe /frɪndʒ/ Ⅰ *n.* [C]❶穗，流苏；流苏饰边 ❷边缘；外围；界限：the outer ~s of Paris 巴黎的周边地区/water prints left across the ~s of the floor 留在地板边缘上的水印 ❸(头发的)刘海 Ⅱ *vt.* ❶加穗于；在……上加缘饰：The cloth of the tea table is ~d with elephants. 茶几桌布周边饰有大象图案。❷是(或作为)……的边缘：The lake was ~d with pine trees. 湖边种着松树。

frog /frɒg/ *n.* [C]青蛙

from /frɒm, frəm/ *prep.* ❶自；从(表示空间的距离)：~ door to door 挨家挨户 / ~ Beijing to London 从北京到伦敦 / ~ under the table 从桌子下 / ~ behind the door 从门后 ❷自，从(表示时间的起始)：~ the first of May 从五月一日起 / ~ one's childhood 自某人童年起 / ~ beginning to end 自始至终/ ~ then on 从那时起 / ~ time to time 不时地 / ~ three o'clock to five o'clock 从三点到五点 ❸由……发出；来自：He received a present ~ his friend. 他收到了他朋友给他的礼物。❹由，从，据(表示来源)：draw water ~ a well 由井里汲水 / Don't judge a person ~ his appearance. 不要以貌取人。

front /frʌnt/ Ⅰ *n.* [C]❶前面；正面：Please go in ~. 请前面走。/**in ~ of** 在……前面；当着……的面：There is a pond in ~ of the house. 房子前面有个池塘。**in the ~ of** 在……的前部：He is sitting in the ~ of the car with the driver. 他和驾驶员一起坐在汽车前面。❷前线；前方：go to the ~ 上前线 / on the production ~ 在生产前线 Ⅱ *adj.* 前面的；前部的；正面的：He sat in the ~ row. 他坐在前排。/ The news is in the ~ page of the newspaper. 这条消息登在报纸的头版。

frontier /ˈfrʌntɪə(r)/ *n.* [C] ❶边境；边界；国境；边疆：They drove across the ~ between Canada and the United States. 他们驾车驶过加美边界。/ He lives in a small town on the ~. 他住在一个边疆小城。❷ 新领域；尖端领域：The scientists are exploring the ~s of science. 科学家们正在探索新的科学领域。

frost /frɒst/ *n.* [U] 霜；霜冻；严寒：The roof was covered with ~ this morning. 今天早晨屋顶上覆盖着一层霜。/ The heavy ~ killed three sheep. 这场霜冻冻死了三只羊。

frostbite /ˈfrɒstˌbaɪt/ *n.* [U]冻伤；冻疮；霜害

frosty /ˈfrɒsti/ *adj.* ❶霜冻的；严寒的：a ~ night 寒夜 / ~ weather 霜冻天气 ❷结霜的，冰霜覆盖的；有霜的：The glass is ~. 玻璃上结满了霜。/ ~ designs on the windows (玻璃)窗户上的冰霜花纹 ❸冷淡的，冷漠的，冷若冰霜的：a ~ welcome 缺乏热情的欢迎/ get a ~ reception 受到冷遇 派 frostily *adv.*；frostiness *n.*

froth /frɒθ/ Ⅰ *n.* 泡，泡沫；白沫：a glass of beer with a lot of ~ on it 一杯泛起许多泡沫的啤酒/The ~ of the waves collected on the beach. 浪花泛起的白沫覆涌在海滩上。Ⅱ *vi.* 起泡沫；吐白沫：The beer ~ed and overflowed the glass. 啤酒泛起泡沫，溢出了杯子。

frown /fraʊn/ Ⅰ *vi.* ❶皱眉，蹙额：He sat at his desk, ~ing as he so often did. 他坐在办公桌前，像往常那样皱起眉头。❷表示不悦(或烦恼、不赞成)：He ~ed at my retort. 他见我顶嘴，脸显愠色。Ⅱ *n.* [C] ❶皱眉，蹙额：She read the letter quickly, a ~ on her face. 她很

快看了那封信，一边看一边皱起了眉头。❷不悦（或不赞成、严肃、沉思等）的表情：His smile turned into a ~ of dismay. 他先是笑容满面，不一会儿变得愁眉苦脸。

frozen /ˈfrəuzən/ *adj.* ❶结冰的，冰冻的；冻住的：a ~ river 结了冰的河流 ❷严寒的，极冷的：It's a beautiful day—~ and icy and clear. 天气很好，冰天冻地，晴朗晶莹。❸冻伤的，冻坏的；冻僵的：~ toes 冻伤的脚趾 ❹（行为、态度等）冷淡的，缺乏感情的：He kept chewing the inside of his lip a lot, ~ into complete silence. 他不停咬着内嘴唇，表情冷淡，默默无言。❺冷冻的，冷藏的：~ vegetables 冷冻的蔬菜

frugal /ˈfruːgəl/ *adj.* ❶节约的，节省的；生活俭朴的，省吃俭用的：a ~ housekeeper 节俭的家庭主妇/He is ~ with himself. 他自己花钱很节俭。❷廉价的，花钱少的；简陋的；少量的：a small and ~ apartment 狭小简陋的套房/a ~ diet 粗茶淡饭

fruit /fruːt/ *n.* ❶水果；果实：He eats much ~. 他吃很多水果。/ There are many ~s in the house. 屋子里有很多种水果。❷（常用 *pl.*）结果；成果：We are now enjoying the ~s of our hard work. 我们现在享受着辛勤劳动的成果。

fruitful /ˈfruːtfʊl/ *adj.* ❶富有成效的；成功的；有收益的；有利的：~ work 卓有成效的工作 / ~ areas of translation studies 硕果累累的翻译研究领域 / I hope the discussions prove ~. 我希望讨论会取得圆满成功。❷多产的：a ~ writer 多产的作家（作曲家）/ China is ~ in natural resources. 中国自然资源丰富。❸有助于多产的：~ soil 肥沃的土壤 派 fruitfully *adv.*；fruitfulness *n.*

fruitless /ˈfruːtlɪs/ *adj.* ❶不结果实的：a ~ tree 不结果实的树 ❷没有效果的；徒劳的；不成功的；无收益的：I don't think the African visit will be ~. 我认为非洲之行并非徒劳无益。/ Don't let more government money be spent on another ~ effort. 别再浪费国家的钱财了。派 fruitlessly *adv.*；fruitlessness *n.*

frustrate /frʌˈstreɪt, ˈfrʌstreɪt/ *vt.* ❶使（努力等）无用；使（计划，希望等）落空，使泡汤：The student's indifference ~d the teacher's efforts to help him. 这个学生无动于衷，老师对他的帮助都白费了。❷挫败，击败；使受挫折：~ an opponent 挫败对手 ❸使失望，使沮丧，使失意：The lack of money and facilities depressed and ~d him. 他因缺乏资金和设备而十分沮丧，一筹莫展。派 frustrated *adj.*；frustration *n.*

F

fry /fraɪ/ *v.* 油煎；油炸：Mother is ~ing fish in the kitchen. 妈妈正在厨房煎鱼。

fuel /ˈfjʊəl/ *n.* [U] 燃料：They have used up all their ~. 他们已经用完所有的燃料。

fugitive /ˈfjuːdʒɪtɪv/ *n.* [C] ❶逃亡者，亡命者；逃犯：a ~ from a dictatorial regime 逃脱独裁统治的亡命者/a jail ~越狱犯 ❷被放逐者；流亡国外的人；难民：~s from an invaded country 从被入侵国逃出来的难民

fulfil(l) /fʊlˈfɪl/ *vt.* (-filled;-filling) 履行；执行；完成：They have ~led their duties admirably. 他们出色地完成了任务。/ You must ~ your promise. 你必须履行你的诺言。派 fulfil(l)ment *n.*

full /fʊl/ *adj.* 满的；完全的；充满的：This bottle is ~. 这只瓶子是满的。/ The hall is ~ of teachers and students. 大厅里坐满了老师和学生。/**be ~ of** 充满：This bottle is ~ of water. 瓶子里装满了水。/ Our teacher's conversation is ~ of wits. 我们老师的谈话妙趣横生。派 fully *adv.*

full-scale / ˈfʊlˌskeɪl / *adj.* ❶(图画、模型等)与实体同样大小的,实比的:a ~ replica 与实物大小一致的复制品 ❷完全的;完整的;全面的:The police have started a ~ murder investigation. 警察已经对谋杀案展开了全面侦查。

F

full-time / ˈfʊlˌtaɪm / *adj.* &*adv.* 全部时间(的);专职(的);全日制(的):receive ~ education 获得全日制教育/a ~ domestic servant 全职保姆

fumble / ˈfʌmbl / *vi.* ❶瞎摸,乱摸;摸索:He was fumbling about for the bedside lamp in the dark. 他在黑暗里摸索着想打开床头灯。/She ~d through the hall and down the stairs to a landing below. 她跌跌撞撞地穿过大厅,走下楼梯来到下面的平台。❷笨拙地行事(或行进):~ with a kitchen knife 笨拙地使用菜刀

fume / fjuːm / Ⅰ *n.* (刺鼻、浓烈或有害的)烟,气,汽:be thick with the ~s of gunpowder 硝烟弥漫/He breathed whisky ~s all over my face. 他一嘴的酒气喷得我满脸都是。Ⅱ *vi.* ❶冒烟(或气、汽);(烟、气、汽等)冒出,散发:Staggering off ,he ~d with brandy. 他步履蹒跚地走了,身上散发出白兰地酒味。❷发怒,发火:I ~d at my own inability. 我深为自己的无能恼火。

fun / fʌn / *n.* [U]娱乐;有趣的事;乐趣:We had a lot of ~ at her birthday party. 在她的生日聚会上我们玩得很开心。/ What ~! 多么有趣! /**make ~ of** 嘲弄;取笑:Don't make ~ of the little girl. 不要取笑那个小女孩。

function / ˈfʌŋkʃn / Ⅰ *n.* [C] ❶功能;机能;作用:The ~ of this machine is to cut steel. 这台机器的功能是切割钢铁。/ What is the ~ of the English word in this sentence? 这个英语单词在句中起什么作用? ❷职务;职责:Her ~s are to take good care of the children. 她的职责是照管好这些孩子。❸函数:linear ~ 线性函数 Ⅱ *vi.* 运行;活动;起作用:The telephone in my office was not ~ing. 我办公室里的那部电话机坏了。/ This noun ~s as an adjective here. 这个名词在这里起形容词的作用。

fund / fʌnd / *n.* [C](*pl.*)资金;基金;专款:research ~s 科研经费 / welfare ~s 福利基金 / a relief ~ 救济款 / They decided to draw foreign ~s to build the expressway. 他们决定吸引外资来修建这条高速公路。

fundamental / ˌfʌndəˈmentl / Ⅰ *adj.* 基础的;基本的:He learned the ~ rules of English grammar first. 他首先学习了英语语法的基本规则。Ⅱ *n.* [C](*pl.*)基本原则;基本原理:A ~s of good behavior is honesty. 优良品行的一条基本原则就是诚实。

funeral / ˈfjuːnərəl / *n.* [C]葬礼:They held a state ~ for the dead president. 他们为去世的总统举行了国葬。

funnel / ˈfʌnəl / *n.* [C] ❶漏斗 ❷漏斗状物:a long ~of people 一长队排成扇形的人群 ❸(火车、轮船等的)烟囱;烟道,焰道

funny / ˈfʌni / *adj.* (-ier,-iest)滑稽可笑的;有趣的;稀奇的:He likes ~ movies. 他爱看滑稽电影。/ There is something ~ about the matter. 这事情有点稀奇古怪。

fur / fɜː(r) / *n.* [U]毛皮:He wore a pair of ~ gloves. 他戴着一双皮手套。

furious / ˈfjʊərɪəs / *adj.* ❶狂怒的,暴怒的:The ~ man pressed on. 那个怒火中烧的男子步步进逼。/be ~ with rage

火冒三丈 ❷狂暴的：a ~ sea 海怒/a ~ storm 狂风暴雨 ❸强烈的；猛烈的；激烈的；紧张的：a ~ argument 唇枪舌剑

furnace /ˈfɜːnɪs/ *n.* [C]火炉；熔炉

furnish /ˈfɜːnɪʃ/ *vt.* 装备；布置；提供：I want to ~ this room better. 我想把这房间好好布置一下。/ He ~ed me with the necessary information. 他向我提供了必要的信息。

furniture /ˈfɜːnɪtʃə(r)/ *n.* [U](集合名词)家具：They bought a piece (set) of ~. 他们买了一件(套)家具。

furrow /ˈfʌrəʊ/ *n.* [C] ❶犁沟：make ~s for sowing 耕地播种 ❷沟；车辙：deep ~s in the muddy road 泥泞路上的深深车辙 ❸褶皱；皱纹：Furrows of worry lined his faces. 他的脸上因忧愁而布满了皱纹。

further /ˈfɜːðə(r)/ Ⅰ *adj.* 更远的；更多的；进一步的：We should have a ~ discussion on the problem. 我们应当就此问题进行更深入的讨论。Ⅱ *adv.* 更远；而且；进一步：I can walk no ~. 我不能再往前走了。

furthermore /ˌfɜːðəˈmɔː(r)/ *adv.* 此外，另外；而且：Furthermore, she has successfully depicted the atmosphere of Edwardian India. 此外，她出色地描绘了爱德华时期的印度风情。

fury /ˈfjʊəri/ *n.* ❶狂怒，暴怒：drunken ~酒疯/Wilde was full of ~. 威尔德怒不可遏。❷[U]狂暴；激烈；猛烈；强烈；剧烈：the ~of a gathering storm 疾风骤雨的狂暴/She was paddling with a new ~. 她再次振臂奋力划动双桨。

fuse[1] /fjuːz/ *n.* [C] ❶导火索，导火线：He lit the ~ and waited for the explosion. 他点燃导火线后，在一旁等着爆炸。/ arm a ~装导火索 ❷引信，信管：a time ~定时引信 / **have a short** ~容易激动，动辄发怒：The manager has a rather short ~. 经理脾气暴躁，动不动就发火。

fuse[2] /fjuːz/ Ⅰ *n.* [C]保险丝，熔线：This plug uses a 5 amp ~. 这个插座要用一根 5 安培的保险丝。Ⅱ *v.* ❶(使)熔化：~ metals 熔融金属 ❷(使)熔合，(使)熔接：The intense heat ~d the rocks together. 高温将一块块岩石 熔合在一起。/zinc and copper fuse together to make brass 锌和铜熔合成黄铜 ❸融合：Sadness and joy are ~d in her poetry. 她的诗歌交织着悲和喜。/They disagreed at first but eventually their ideas ~d. 他们起先有分歧，但最终还是达成了一致意见。

fuss /fʌs/ *n.* 忙乱；大惊小怪：Don't make a ~ over such a small thing. 不要对这种小事大惊小怪。派 fussy *adj.*

futile /ˈfjuːtaɪl/ *adj.* ❶无用的，无效的，徒劳的，无益的：a ~ effort 徒劳/It is ~ to continue the investigation. 再继续调查就是白费心机。❷(话语等)不重要的；空洞的，无意义的：~ chatter 无聊的嗑牙扯淡 派 futility *n.*

future /ˈfjuːtʃə(r)/ *n.* 将来；未来；前途：The teacher often says that the boy has a bright ~. 老师常说这小孩前途无量。/ **in (the)** ~ 今后；将来：Try to live a better life in ~. 今后要努力过更好的生活。/ You should be confident in the ~. 你应对未来抱有信心。

F

G g

G

gain /ɡeɪn/ Ⅰ *v.* ❶获得;赢得;博得;挣得:~ experience 获得经验 / ~ the audience's attention 吸引观众的注意 / ~ a battle 打了胜仗 / ~ one's living 谋生 / ~ strength 恢复体力 ❷进步;改进;增加:~ in weight 增加重量 / ~ in health 更加健康 / The car is ~ing speed. 车子在加速。❸到达;抵达:After battling against the blizzard, we finally ~ed our destination. 在同暴风雪搏斗之后,我们终于到达了目的地。Ⅱ *n.* ❶[U](因贸易、工作)获得(利益、盈余):regardless of personal ~ or loss 不计个人得失 / be blinded by the love of gain 利令智昏/ Last year he got a clear gain of 1,000 *yuan*. 去年他获得净利润 1 000 元。❷[C]增加;增进:Increase of wealth is not always a gain to one's happiness. 财富的增加并非总是幸福的增进。

galaxy /ˈɡæləksi/ *n.* ❶[C]星系:the existence of galaxies beyond the Milky Way 银河外星系的存在 ❷(令人瞩目的人或东西等的)一群,一族:A ~ of fireworks went up. 焰火升空耀若群星。

gale /ɡeɪl/ *n.* [C]大风:It is blowing a ~. Let's close the windows. 刮大风了,我们把窗户关上吧。

gallery /ˈɡæləri/ *n.* [C] 画廊;美术馆;美术陈列馆:We visited the National ~ yesterday. 昨天我们参观了国家美术馆。

gallon /ˈɡælən/ *n.* [C]加仑(液体单位)

gallop /ˈɡæləp/ *vt.* ❶策马疾驰,着马飞奔:They ~ed after the hounds. 他们紧跟着猎狗策马飞驰。❷(马等)飞奔,疾驰:The wild house ~ed off. 那匹野马飞奔而去。❸飞奔,快跑:children ~ing over the dunes barefoot 赤足在沙滩上飞奔的孩子们

gamble /ˈɡæmbl/ Ⅰ *n.* [C]赌博;投机;冒险:Some people like ~ on horse races. 有些人喜欢赌马。/ Your new plan seems to be a ~. 你的新计划似乎是一次冒险。Ⅱ *vt.* 赌博;投机;冒险:He has ~d away all his money. 他赌博输光了所有的钱。派 gambler *n.*;gamblesome *adj.*

game /ɡeɪm/ *n.* [C]❶(有规则的)游戏;运动;比赛:play ~s 做游戏 / attend a ~ 参加游戏 / Boys always like football ~s. 男孩们总是喜欢足球比赛。❷(*pl.*)运动会;竞技赛:the Olympic ~s 奥林匹克运动会 ❸一次;一盘;一场:have a ~ at cards 打一局牌 / have a ~ of chess 下一盘象棋 / win four ~s in the first set 在第一回合中赢四局 / Our team won the first three ~s. 我队赢了前三局。

gang /ɡæŋ/ *n.* [C](一)帮;(一)伙;(一)

群：They formed two ～s and fought each other. 村里人结成两伙相互争斗。

gangster / ˈgæŋstə(r) / *n.* [C]匪徒；歹徒；暴徒：The police caught the ～ this morning. 今天上午警察抓住了那个歹徒。

gaol / dʒeɪl / *n.* [C]监狱；监禁：The young man has been sent to ～. 那年轻人已被送进监狱。

gap / gæp / *n.* [C]裂缝；缺口；空白；间隙；差距：bridge (fill up) a ～ 填补空白；弥合差距 / narrow the ～ 缩小差距 / a generation ～ 代沟 / a trade ～ 贸易差额 / a wide ～ 巨大分歧 / There is a great ～ between his idea and mine. 他的想法与我的大相径庭。

gape / geɪp / *v.* ❶好奇地凝视；茫然地瞪视；目瞪口呆地看：～ round-eyed at the distressing scene 睁大双眼望着那悲惨的情景 ❷张口，开口；绽裂：The curtains ～d when the wind blew. 窗帘让风刮得开了口。/Her lips ～d in laughter. 她开口大笑。

garage / ˈgærɑːʒ / *n.* [C]汽车库；汽车修理厂：He parked his car in the ～. 他把车停在车库里。/ My car is under repair in the ～. 我的车正在修车厂维修。

garbage / ˈgɑːbɪdʒ / *n.* [U]垃圾：Don't dump ～ anywhere. 不要把垃圾倒得到处都是。

garden / ˈgɑːdn / *n.* [C] ❶花园；果园；菜园：No ～ without its weeds. 没有不生杂草的花园。/ He is watering his vegetable ～. 他在给菜园浇水。❷公园：The old couple are having a walk in the public ～. 老两口正在公园散步。派 gardener *n.*

gardening / ˈgɑːdnɪŋ / *n.* [U]园艺：This book is about farming and ～. 这本书讲到农耕和园艺。

garlic / ˈgɑːlɪk / *n.* [U] 大蒜

garment / ˈgɑːmənt / *n.* [C] 衣服；外套：second-hand ～s 旧服装 / a sport ～ 运动服 / a woman's upper ～ 女上衣 / a working ～ 工作服 / ～s for outing 旅行装 / ～s for males 男士服装

garrison / ˈgærɪsn / *n.* [C]驻军；卫戍部队；警卫部队：the Beijing ～ 北京卫戍区 / the Shanghai ～ 上海警备区

gas / gæs / *n.* [U](与不定冠词连用指某一种气体，用复数指不同种类的气体) ❶气体：end ～ 尾气 / exhaust ～ 废气 / marsh ～ 沼气 / natural ～天然气 ❷煤气：burn ～烧煤气/ lay on ～安装煤气 / put out the ～ 把煤气关掉 / turn the ～ on 打开煤气 / His sister works in a ～ company. 他姐姐在一家煤气公司工作。

gash / gæʃ / Ⅰ*n.* [C]深长的切口(或伤口)；切痕，砍痕 Ⅱ*vt.* 在……上划开深长的口子；割开；划伤：She ～ed her arm on some broken glass. 她被一些碎玻璃划伤了胳膊。

gasolene(-ine) / ˈgæsəliːn / *n.* [U](美)汽油[＝(英)petrol，口语中简称 gas]：He stopped his car for ～. 他停下车来加油。

gasp / gɑːsp / *vi.* 喘息；喘气：She ～ed with rage. 她气得直喘气。

gastric / ˈgæstrɪk/ *adj.* 胃的，胃部的：～ juice 胃液

gate / geɪt / *n.* [C]大门：Who is the man at the ～? 在门口那里的人是谁？

gateway / ˈgeɪtˌweɪ/ *n.* [C] ❶门洞，门口，出入口；通道：an arched ～ 一座拱形门 ❷门框，门拱；门楼 ❸途径，方法，手段：A university degree is not necessarily a ～ to a good job. 大学学位并不

意味着能找到好工作。

gather /ˈɡæðə(r)/ *v.* 聚集;收集;采集:We must ~ the people to our side. 我们必须把人民团结到我们这一边。/ A crowd ~ed about the entrance. 一群人聚集在入口四周。/ The teacher asked a student to ~ the papers. 老师让一个学生收试卷。

gathering /ˈɡæðərɪŋ/ *n.* [C]集会;聚会;聚集:They said that they would have a ~ to celebrate their success. 他们说要举行一个集会来庆祝他们的胜利。

G

gay /ɡeɪ/ *adj.* 快乐的;高兴的:They were as ~ as little birds at the thought of the coming holiday. 想到假日就在眼前,他们快活得像小鸟一样。

gaze /ɡeɪz/ *vi.* 凝视;注视:For hours he sat gazing at the stars. 他坐在那里几个小时凝视天上的星星。

GDP (=gross domestic product)国内生产总值

gear /ɡɪə(r)/ Ⅰ *n.* 齿轮;传动装置;(汽车等的)排挡:The largest ~ was broken. 最大的那个齿轮断裂了。/ You should learn to use the reverse ~. 你应当学会使用倒车挡。Ⅱ *v.* 调整;(使)适合:I have to ~ myself to the new life here as soon as possible. 我得使自己尽快适应这里的新生活。

gel /dʒel/ *n.* ❶凝胶(体),冻胶;胶带体 ❷发胶

gem /dʒem/ *n.* [C] ❶(尤指经切割打磨用作首饰的)宝石 ❷珍品,精品;宝物:The ~ of his collection was a rare Italian stamp. 他藏品的精华是一枚罕见的意大利邮票。❸受人爱戴(或珍视)的人;尤物:a ~ like Barbara 像芭芭拉一样的尤物

gene /dʒiːn/ *n.* [C]遗传因子;基因:a ~ pool 基因库 / ~ engineering 基因工程 / The doctor says that he has good ~s. 大夫说他的遗传因子很好。

general /ˈdʒen(r)əl/ Ⅰ *adj.* ❶总的;全体的;大概的;笼统的:He is the ~ secretary of the conference. 他是大会的秘书长。/ I learned the ~ idea of the plan after talking with the ~ manager. 在与总经理交谈之后我了解了这个计划的大概内容。❷一般的;普通的;普遍的:Do you know the ~ attitude of the students towards this decision? 你知道学生对这个决定一般持什么态度吗? / The price of food is a matter of ~ anxiety. 食品的价格是人们普遍担忧的问题。Ⅱ *n.* [C]将军:The old ~ has a beautiful granddaughter. 老将军有一个漂亮的孙女。/ **in** ~一般说来;通常:In ~, your plan is good. 你们的方案总的来说是好的。

generalization /ˌdʒen(ə)r(ə)laɪˈzeɪʃn/ *n.* ❶概括,归纳,总结;普遍化:What we seek is valid ~ from an accumulation of examples. 我们需要的是从大量的例子中作出有价值的归纳。❷[C]普遍性概念,通则;概说,概论:a widely accepted ~ 公认的通则 / It is a ~ that the penguin originates in the Antarctic. 众所周知,企鹅产于南极。

generalize /ˈdʒen(ə)r(ə)ˌlaɪz/ *vi.* ❶概括,总结,归纳;得出一般性的结论:We can't ~ from so little evidence. 就这么点儿证据我们无法得出结论。❷笼统地说;含糊地说:You can't ~ about the incident. 你不能对这一事件一概而论。—*vt.* ❶归纳出,总结出;推断出,得出(一般性的结论):~ a conclusion 归纳出一个结论 / ~ one's ideas 概括自己

的思路 ❷推广,普及:~ a law 普及一部法律 /~ the use of the new product 推广使用这种新产品

generally / ˈdʒen(ə)rəli / *adv.* 一般;通常;大体上:It was once ~ believed that the earth was flat. 曾经人们一般都认为地球是平的。/ Generally speaking, she is friendly to us. 总的来说,她对我们很友好。

generate / ˈdʒen(ə)ˌreɪt/ *vt.* ❶引发,导致,招致;使发生:The new system has ~d some problems. 新的制度造成了一些问题。❷产生(电力、光、热等):~ power 发电 ❸萌生出,产生出(思想、感情等):~ a feeling of absolute isolation and loneliness 给人一种与世隔绝、孤立无援的感觉

generation / ˌdʒenəˈreɪʃn / *n.* ❶[C]一代:build up a new ~ 造就一代新人 / the future ~ 后代 / the last (past) ~ 上一代 / the older ~ 老一辈人 /~ after ~ 世世代代 ❷[U]产生;发生:This machine is used for the ~ of electricity. 这台机器是用来发电的。

generator / ˈdʒenəreɪtə(r) / *n.* [C]发电机

generosity / ˌdʒenəˈrɒsəti / *n.* [U]慷慨;大方;宽宏大量:Thank you for your ~. 感谢你的慷慨大方。

generous / ˈdʒenərəs / *adj.* 慷慨的;大方的;宽容的:He presented a ~ gift to her mother on her birthday. 妈妈生日他送了一份厚礼。/ We all like him because he has a ~ nature to others. 由于他对人宽宏大量,我们都很喜欢他。派 generously *adv.*

genetic / dʒəˈnetɪk / *adj.* 遗传的;遗传学的:~ code 遗传密码/ ~ engineering 遗传工程 派 genetically *adv.* ;geneticist *n.*

genetics / dʒəˈnetɪks / *n.* [U]遗传学

genius / ˈdʒiːnɪəs / *n.* ❶[U]天资;天赋:He has shown his wonderful creative ~. 他显示了惊人的创造天赋。/ The little girl has a ~ for languages. 那小女孩极具语言天赋。❷[C]天才;才子:a mathematical ~ 数学天才 / Einstein was a great scientific ~. 爱因斯坦是伟大的科学天才。

gentle / ˈdʒentl / *adj.* ❶温和的;有礼貌的;文雅的:~ nature 温和的性格 / ~ manners 文雅的举止 / The old lady has a ~ look. 老奶奶有一副和善的面容。❷轻柔的;徐缓的;不猛烈的:Her ~ voice made us comfortable. 她轻柔的嗓音让我们感到舒服。/ I saw the man went up the ~ slope slowly. 我看见那人慢慢地走上缓坡。

gentleman / ˈdʒentlmən / *n.* [C](*pl.* gentlemen) ❶绅士;有身份的人;有教养的人;彬彬有礼的人:A ~ cannot be so rude to a woman. 有教养的人不会这样粗鲁地对待妇女。❷ 先生:Ladies and ~! 女士们,先生们! / This ~ wishes to visit our school. 这位先生想参观我们的学校。

gentlewoman / ˈdʒentlwʊmən / *n.* [C] (*pl.* gentlewomen)女士;有身份的妇女

gently / ˈdʒentli / *adv.* 温柔地;轻柔地:The nurse said ~ to the patient that she was all right. 护士温柔地对病人说情况很好。/Speak ~ to the child. 对孩子说话应温和些。

genuine / ˈdʒenjʊɪn / *adj.* 真正的;真实的;真诚的:~ pearls 真珍珠 / a ~ signature 亲笔签名 / ~ sorrow 真实的伤感 / This is a ~ picture of Picasso. 这是一幅毕加索的真迹。

geography / dʒɪˈɒgrəfi / *n.* [U]地理学

geologist /dʒɪˈɒlədʒɪst/ *n.* [C] 地质学家;研究地质的学者

geology /dʒɪˈɒlədʒi/ *n.* [U]地质学

geometry /dʒɪˈɒmətri/ *n.* [U]几何学:plane ~ 平面几何学 / solid ~ 立体几何学

geophysics /ˌdʒiːəʊˈfɪzɪks/ *n.* [U]地球物理学

G

geophysicist /ˌdʒiːəʊˈfɪzɪsɪst/ *n.* [C]地球物理学家

germ /dʒɜːm/ *n.* [C]病菌;细菌:This disease is spread by ~s. 这种疾病是通过细菌传播的。/ A ~ warfare is disastrous. 细菌战是灾难性的战争。

germinate /ˈdʒɜːmɪˌneɪt/ *v.* ❶发芽;(使)抽芽;开始生长:Warmth, moisture, and oxygen ~s seeds. 种子发芽需要温度、湿度和氧气。❷萌发(观点、想法等);(使)产生;形成:The university presses ~d no ideas at all. 这些大学出版社没有拿出一点新的想法。/Some inventions ~ out of the experiences of daily life. 有些发明源于日常经验。派 germination *n.*

gesture /ˈdʒestʃə(r)/ *n.* [C]姿势;姿态;手势:a ~ language 手势语 / Her strange ~ made me puzzle. 她奇怪的手势让我感到困惑不解。

get /get/ *vt.* (got /gɒt/, got 或 gotten /ˈgɒtn/) 得到;获得,取;赢得:Where did you ~ the dictionary? 这本词典你在哪儿买的? / They've got five tickets. 他们买到了五张票。—*vi.* ❶变得;使:When spring comes, it ~s warmer and warmer. 春天到来了,天气越来越暖和。/ He got very angry. 他很气愤。/ She soon got well. 她不久便复原了。❷回到;走到;到达:Let's see who ~s there first. 让我们看看谁先到那里。/ They got to the factory at a quarter to nine. 他们是8:45到工厂的。/ He got home at nine last night. 他昨晚9:00回到家。❸达到(某种阶段):How did you ~ to know I was here? 你怎么知道我在这儿?❹使(成为某种状态):I must ~ (have) the breakfast ready. 我必须把早餐准备好。/ Can you ~ the clock going again? 你能为这钟上发条吗? / I must ~ (have) my hair cut. 我得去理发了。/~ **along** 过活;进展;进步;友善相处:How are you getting along? 你近况如何? / How is your son ~ing along with his school work? 你儿子的功课怎么样? ~ **away** 离去;去度假:The thief has got away. 那贼已逃之夭夭。/ She hopes to ~ away next Monday for a week. 她希望从下星期一起休假一周。~ **away from** 摆脱;回避:It is no use ~ting away from the facts. 这些事实是回避不了的。~ **sth. back** 回来;取回:I'll ~ the book back. 我要收回这本书。~ **down to** 认真着手处理;开始从事:You should ~ down to your work after the holiday. 假期后你应开始工作。~ **hold of** 抓住;握:He got hold of the tail of the dog. 他抓住狗的尾巴。~ **in**(使)进入;到达;收割;认识;插话;收集:He got in by the window. 他从窗口跳进去。/ The peasants are ~ting in the crops. 农民正在收割庄稼。/ I can't ~ him in at all. 我根本不能与他结识。/ May I ~ a word in? 我可以插一句话吗? ~ **into** 进入;陷入;穿上;升至:~ into trouble (difficulty) 陷入麻烦(困境) / She has got into bed. 她已上床。/ He got into his overcoat quickly. 他迅速穿上大衣。~ **off** 脱下;下车;走脱;离

开:The bus stopped and he got off. 公共汽车停了,他便下了车。/ Mother told him to ~ off his wet clothes. 母亲叫他脱下湿衣服。~ **on** 穿上;上车;使进步:~ on the train (a horse, a bike) 上火车(上马,骑上自行车)~ **out** 出去;传出去;拔出:The news has got out that you are leaving. 传闻你要走了。/ The dentist got her bad tooth out. 牙医帮她拔掉了虫牙。~ **over** 康复;克服;摆脱;越过:It took me a long time to ~ over my cold. 过了好久我的伤风才好。/ It is hard to ~ over the death of my father. 我很难从父亲去世的悲伤中恢复过来。~ **through** 通过;结束;完成;达到目的:Did you ~ through the exam? 你考试及格了吗? / I got through the book in one evening. 我一个晚上就看完了这本书。~ **to** 开始;到达:They will ~ to Beijing tomorrow. 他们明天到北京。/ He got to thinking that she wouldn't come after all. 他开始觉得她肯定不会来了。~ **to one's feet** 站起;站着:Sorry, you have to ~ to your feet. 对不起,你只好站着。~ **up** 起床:I like to ~ up early in the morning. 我喜欢早起。

ghastly /ˈgɑːstli, ˈgæstli/ *adj*. ❶可怕的,恐怖的,令人毛骨悚然的:The scene after the battle was ~. 战斗过后的场景惨不忍睹。❷极坏的,糟糕的;令人不快的:a ~ bowl of soup 一碗难喝的汤

ghost /gəʊst/ *n*. [C]鬼;幽灵;幻影般的东西:I don't believe in ~s. 我不相信有鬼存在。/ She came in like a ~. 她像幽灵一样进来。

giant /ˈdʒaɪənt/ Ⅰ *n*. [C] 巨人;巨物:He became a ~ in the field of finance when he was only thirty-eight. 他 38 岁就成了金融巨头。Ⅱ *adj*. 巨大的:We all like ~ pandas. 我们都喜欢大熊猫。/ China is taking ~ steps forward. 中国正以巨人般的步伐前进。

gift /gɪft/ *n*. [C] ❶礼物;礼品:I want to get some interesting ~s to take home. 我想买一些有趣的礼物带回家。❷天资;天赋;才能:She has a ~ for music. 她有音乐天赋。/ My uncle is a man of many ~s. 我的叔叔是一个多才多艺的人。

G

gifted /ˈgɪftɪd/ *adj*. 有天赋的;有天资的:He played piano well when he was only four. He is really a ~ musician. 他四岁时钢琴就弹得很好,真是一个有天赋的音乐家。

gigantic /dʒaɪˈgæntɪk/ *adj*. 巨大的:a ~ net 天罗地网

gill /gɪl/ *n*. [C]鳃

ginger /ˈdʒɪndʒə(r)/ *n*. [U] 生姜

ginseng /ˈdʒɪnseŋ/ *n*. [C]人参;(中国)人参;西洋参

giraffe /dʒəˈrɑːf/ *n*. [C]长颈鹿:A ~ may grow to 6 meters tall. 一只长颈鹿可以长到六米高。

girl /gɜːl/ *n*. [C] 女孩,少女,姑娘;女仆;女职员:an adult ~ 成年女子 / factory ~s 女工 / a modern ~ 摩登女郎 / the leading ~ 女主角/He sent his ~ to a ~'s school. 他把女儿送进一所女子学校读书。

give /gɪv/ *v*. (gave /geɪv/, given /ˈgɪvn/) ❶给,给予;赠给:I gave her a pen. 我给了她一支笔。/ Give one to me, please. 请给我一个。❷付出:I would ~ a lot to know where she is. 我愿出高价打听她的下落。❸供给;供应:The sun ~s us warmth and light. 太阳供给我们光和

热。❹致力于；献身于：He would rather die than ~ in. 他宁死不屈。/~ **off** 放出；流出；飞出：~ off vapor (smoke, light) 放出气(烟、光) / Rotten eggs ~ off a bad smell. 腐烂的鸡蛋发出一股臭味。~ **out** 发出；分发；分配；用尽：The cowboy ~ out a yell. 牛仔大叫一声。~ **up** ①放弃；屈服；投降：Jimmy is ~ing up his job as a newsboy when he goes back to school. 吉米回校后放弃了送报的工作。②戒除：The doctor told Tom to ~ up smoking. 医生叫汤姆戒烟。③放弃希望；放弃念头：You should ~ up the idea of going abroad. 你应放弃出国的念头。~ **rise to** 导致；招致：Such conduct might ~ rise to misunderstanding. 这种行为可能导致误解。~ **way (to)** ①退后；撤退：Our troops had to ~ way. 我们的部队只好撤退。②让出空间：Give way to traffic coming in from the right. 请让右边来的车先走。

given /ˈɡɪvn/ *adj*. 假设的；特定的；已知的：Given his support, I think we will finish the task on time. 如果得到他的支持，我想我们会按时完成任务的。/ You must reach there at a ~ time. 你得在指定的时间到达那儿。

glacier /ˈɡlæsɪə(r)/ *n*. [C]冰川；冰河

glad /ɡlæd/ (gladder, gladdest) *adj*. 高兴的；愉快的；情愿的；乐意的：I am very ~ to help you with your homework. 我很乐意帮助你完成家庭作业。/ We are ~ of your success. 我们为你的成功感到高兴。/ Her mother was very ~ about her arrival. 她的到来令她母亲感到很高兴。派 gladly *adv*.

gladden /ˈɡlædən/ *vt*. 使高兴；使快乐：In a little while, his heart would be ~ed. 不消说，他就会心花怒放。

glamour /ˈɡlæmə(r)/ *n*. [U] ❶(迷人的)美貌；妖艳：a girl with lots of ~性感十足的女孩 ❷魅力，诱惑力：Passenger business had the ~. 那时候搞客运业很吃香。❸冒险，刺激(性)：the ~ of the adventure 历险的乐趣

glance /ɡlɑːns/ Ⅰ *n*. [C]一瞥；一眼：They stole a ~ at John. 他们偷偷看了约翰一眼。Ⅱ *v*. 扫视；看一眼；瞧一下：I leaned back in my chair, glancing about the room. 我靠在椅子上，环视了一下房间。/~ **at** 瞥；扫视：She ~d at the sleeping boy and then hurried away. 她瞟了一眼熟睡的孩子，随即匆匆离去。

gland /ɡlænd/ *n*. [C]腺：adrenal ~肾上腺

glare /ɡleə(r)/ Ⅰ *n*. ❶[U] 强光：We could see nothing because of the ~ of the car's lights. 由于车灯刺眼，我们什么也看不见。❷[C]怒视；瞪：The boy gave his mother a ~. 那小男孩瞪了他母亲一眼。Ⅱ *v* ❶闪耀：The sunlight ~d on the ice. 阳光照在冰上反射出耀眼的光。❷怒目而视：They stood there glaring each other. 他们站在那儿怒目相视。

glaring /ˈɡleərɪŋ/ *adj*. ❶(光线等)刺眼的，炫目的，耀眼的：a ~ red 炫目的红色/It was a September day, hot and ~. 这是一个九月天，酷热难当，骄阳似火。❷显眼的，明显的，引人注目的：a ~ error in spelling 明显的拼写错误/a ~ lie 赤裸裸的谎言 派 glaringly *adv*.

glass /ɡlɑːs/ *n*. ❶[U]玻璃：a piece of ~ 一块玻璃 / broken ~ 碎玻璃 / cut ~ 刻花玻璃 / sheet ~ 平板玻璃 / Glass breaks easily. 玻璃易碎。❷[C]玻璃杯；玻璃制品：a ~ 玻璃杯 / a ~ of milk

一杯牛奶 / She put on her ~es to read the letter. 她戴上眼镜读信。

glassware /ˈglɑːsˌweə(r)/ *n.* [U]玻璃器皿,玻璃制品

gleam /gliːm/ *n.*[C] ❶微光;闪光:I saw the ~ from the window in the dark. 在黑暗中我看见了从窗户透进来的微光。❷闪现;出现:A ~ of hope came across her face. 她的脸上闪现出一线希望。

glide /glaɪd/ *v.* 滑动;滑行:Fishes were gliding about in the lake. 鱼儿在湖里轻快地游来游去。/ He ~d down from the slope. 他从坡上滑下去。

glimmer /ˈglɪmə(r)/ *n.* [C] ❶微光;闪烁(或摇曳)的光:in the ~ of the dawn 在晨光中 ❷(希望、理解等的)一点儿,一丝,些许(与 of 连用):a ~ of hope 一线希望/Some astute analysts saw ~s of the new mix of public attitudes. 有些目光敏锐的分析家已经看到了这种新的复杂的公众态度的苗头。

glimpse /glɪmps/ *n.* [C]一瞥;一看:He caught a ~ of the chairman after he came in. 他走进来以后看了主席一眼。

glitter /ˈglɪtə(r)/ *vi.* 闪耀,闪烁:Gold ~s brightly. 金子闪闪发光。

global /ˈgləʊbl/ *adj.* ❶球面的;球形的 ❷全球的;全世界的:a ~ flight 环球飞行 / on a ~ scale 在全球范围内/ We wish for ~ peace. 我们希望世界和平。/ Scientists of all countries are concerning the problem of ~ warming. 各国的科学家都在关注全球性变暖的问题。❸普遍的;综合的:派 globally *adv.*

globalism /ˈgləʊbəlɪz(ə)m/ *n.* [U]全球性,全球观念

globe /gləʊb/ *n.* [C] ❶地球;世界:He traveled around the ~ and learned a lot. 他环球旅行,学到了很多东西。❷球;球体;地球仪:The teacher rotated the ~ and found the location of the small island. 老师旋转地球仪找出了那个小岛的位置。

globular /ˈglɒbjʊlə(r)/ *adj.* ❶球状的;小球形的;圆的:a ~ container 一个圆形容器 ❷由小球组成的

gloom /gluːm/ *n.* [U] ❶黑暗;阴暗:He walked through the ~ of the thick forest. 他穿过茂密阴暗的森林。❷忧愁;沮丧:Don't let defeat fill you with ~. 别因失败而沮丧失望。

gloomy /ˈgluːmi/ *adj.* ❶黑暗的;昏暗的,幽暗的;阴暗的:a big ~ room 一间昏暗的大房间 / What a ~ day! 天色多么阴沉! ❷令人失望的,令人沮丧的,令人气馁的:a ~ situation 阴霾的局势 ❸情绪低落的;忧郁的,沮丧的;悲观的:a ~ mood 忧郁的心情 / She felt ~ about the future. 她对前途感到悲观。派 gloomily *adv.*

glorify /ˈglɔːrɪˌfaɪ/ *vt.* 给……荣耀,为……增光,使光荣:the names which ~ this country 为这个国家增光的人们 ❷使更美;美化;为……增色:Sunset glorified the valley. 落日的余晖使山谷更显得绚丽。❸称赞;赞美,颂扬:Her brave deeds were glorified in song and story. 她的英勇事迹被编成歌曲和故事广为传颂。

glorious /ˈglɔːrɪəs/ *adj.* ❶辉煌的;灿烂的;壮丽的:a ~ view 壮丽的景观 / a ~ time 一段愉快的时光 ❷ 光荣的:The town has a ~ history. 小镇有着光荣的历史。

glory /ˈglɔːri/ *n.* [U] ❶ 光荣;荣誉:He deserves his ~. 他无愧于所得的荣誉。/ They fight for ~, not for money. 他们

为荣誉而战,不是为金钱而战。❷壮丽;灿烂;辉煌:I like the ~ of the sunset very much. 我非常喜欢落日的壮观景象。

gloss /glɒs/ Ⅰ *n.* [U] ❶(表面的)光亮,光泽,色泽;光亮的表面:the ~ of metal 金属的光泽/This paint has a fine ~. 这种油漆光泽鲜亮。❷假象,虚饰;虚假的外表:a ~ of respectability 一副道貌岸然的样子 Ⅱ *v.* 掩饰,掩盖;敷衍(与 over 连用):You can't just ~ things over like that! 你可不能就那样敷衍了事。

G

glossary /ˈglɒsəri/ *n.* [C](附于书籍卷末的)词汇表;术语汇编:I haven't read the ~ of this book. 我还没看这本书的词汇表。

glove /glʌv/ *n.* [C]手套:draw (put on) one's ~s 戴手套/ put off (take off) one's ~s 脱手套/ a pair of ~s 一双手套

glow /gləʊ/ *vi.* 灼热;发光:The sunset ~s in the west. 日落西方,红霞满天。/ Her face ~ed with delight. 她满脸喜气。派 glowing *adj.*

glue /gluː/ Ⅰ *n.* [U]胶;胶水:This kind of ~ sticks fast. 这种胶水黏性强。Ⅱ *v.* 胶合;粘贴:He ~d two pieces of wood together. 他把两块木板粘在一起。

GMT, G. M. T. (= Greenwich Mean Time)格林尼治标准时间

gnaw /nɔː/ (gnawed, gnawed 或 gnawn /nɔːn/) *v.* ❶咬,啃,啮;咬成,啃成:~ the meat off a bone 啃掉骨头上的肉/~ into the board 咬穿木板 ❷磨损;消耗;侵蚀,腐蚀:The river continually ~s its banks. 河水不断地侵蚀着河岸。❸(使)痛苦,(使)烦恼;(受)折磨:~ sb.'s vanity 使某人的虚荣心受到伤害

GNP (=gross national product)国民生产总值

go /gəʊ/ *v.* (went /went/, gone /gɒn/) ❶去;动身;行走:Shall we ~ by bus or by train? 我们是坐汽车去还是坐火车去? / When did he ~ to Beijing? 他什么时候到北京去的? /~ bathing (shooting, hunting, fishing, mountain-climbing) 去沐浴(射击、狩猎、钓鱼、登山)/~ for a walk (ride, swim)去散步(骑马、游泳)/~ on a journey (a trip, a voyage, an outing) 去旅行(游览、航海、郊游)/~ to bed 上床睡觉/ ~ to college 上大学 ❷变得;变成:He went red with anger. 他因愤怒而脸红。❸(进行时与带 to 的不定式连用)打算;计划干(某事):I'm ~ing to do it in my own way. 我要按自己的方式去做。❹(进行时与带 to 的不定式连用)将要;即将:I am ~ing to tell you a story. 我这就给你们讲个故事。/ ~ **about** 四处走动;着手做:Go about your own business. 做你自己的事。~ **abroad** 出国:Many people can afford to ~ abroad now. 现在很多人都有钱出国了。~ **ahead** 有进展;先走一步:The work is ~ing ahead in good style. 这项工作进展顺利。~ **all out** 全力以赴;尽其所能:We should ~ all out to help him. 我们应尽全力帮助他。~ **along** 进行;继续:Things went along smoothly. 事情进展顺利。~ **along with** 陪伴:I'd like to have you ~ along with me. 我要你陪我一起去。~ **away** 离去:~ away from me. 给我走开。~ **back** 返回:He went back home last night. 昨晚他回了家。~ **by** 走过;(时间)流逝:Time ~es by quickly on vacation. 假期的时间过得很快。~ **down** (船只)下沉:The ship went down with all people on board. 那条船连同船上的

人都沉下去了。~ **down on one's knees** 跪下:Mother asked her son to ~ down on his knees. 母亲要儿子跪下。~ **forward** 前进;进行:If he thinks he is right, he ~es straight forward. 如果他认为他是正确的,他就勇往直前。~ **home** 回家;回国:When did you ~ home last night? 昨晚你什么时候回家的? ~ **in** 进入;参加:The thread will not ~ in. 线穿不进针孔。~ **in for** 从事,致力于;参加:What sport do you ~ in for? 你参加哪个体育项目? ~ **on** 继续,接着做;发生:He went on talking as though nothing had happened. 他若无其事地继续讲下去。/ I shall ~ on to deal with the gerund. 我现在接着讲动名词。/ Please ~ on with your work. 请继续做你的工作。~ **out** 出去;(灯)熄灭:He has ~ne out. 他已出去。/ The candlelight went out itself. 蜡烛自行熄灭了。~ **over** 复习;检查,核对:Let's ~ over this lesson. 咱们把这一课温习一下。/ The teacher is ~ing over the examination papers. 老师正在批阅考卷。~ **through** 通过;完成;检查:The proposal did not ~ through. 这项提议未被通过。~ **to pieces** 精神崩溃;身体衰弱;破碎;瓦解:At the news of her mother's death she went completely to pieces. 听到她母亲去世的消息,她的精神完全崩溃了。~ **up** 上升;升起:The path ~es up the hill. 小径通往山上。~ **with** 相配;配合;陪伴:Her coat doesn't ~ with her shoes. 她的外衣与鞋子不相配。

goal / gəʊl / *n.* [C] ❶目标;目的:We are fighting for one common ~. 我们正为着一个共同目标而奋斗。❷球门;得分:Team A won by two ~s. 甲队以两球获胜。/ My brother is the ~ keeper of the football team. 我哥哥是足球队的守门员。

goat / gəʊt / *n.* [C]山羊:He raises a lot of ~s. 他养了许多山羊。

god / gɒd / *n.* ❶ [C] 神 ❷上帝:God bless you. 愿上帝保佑你。/ God helps those who help themselves. (谚语)自助者天助。

goddess / ˈgɒdɪs/ *n.* [C] ❶女神:Aphrodite is the ~ of love. 阿芙罗狄蒂是爱情女神。❷极受崇拜(或仰慕)的女性:a business ~ 一位企业女明星 ❸美人,绝世佳人

gold / gəʊld / *n.* [U] 黄金;金子:a ~ watch 金表 / age of ~ 黄金时代 / All that glitters is not ~. 发光的东西不一定都是金子。/ He won a ~ medal in the match. 在比赛中他获得金奖。

golden / ˈgəʊldən / *adj.* 金色的;珍贵的;极好的:They walked in the field with ~ wheat. 他们行走在金黄色的麦田里。/ It is a ~ opportunity for you. 这是你的一个绝好机会。

goldfish / ˈgəʊldfɪʃ / *n.* [U]金鱼:Some ~ are swimming freely in the fish-tank. 几条金鱼在鱼缸里自由地游着。

golf / gɒlf / *n.* [U]高尔夫球运动:I like to play ~. 我喜欢打高尔夫球。派 golfer *n.*

good / gʊd / Ⅰ *adj.* (better /ˈbetə/, best /best/) ❶美好的;良好的;令人快乐的;令人满意的:~ news 好消息 / have a ~ time 过得很快乐 / have a ~ night 睡得好/This is a ~ tool. 这是一把好工具。❷善良的;有道德的:He is a very ~ man. 他是一个非常善良的人。/ It is ~ of you to tell me the news. 把这消息告诉我,你真好。❸能胜任的;有能力的:He is ~ at drawing. 他擅长绘画。❹相

当多的：a ~ deal of money 很多钱 / a ~ many people 很多人 / a ~ way 相当长的路程 / **as ... as** 实际上；几乎：His promise is as~ as gold. 他的保证很可靠。Ⅱ *n.* [U] ❶善；利益；好处：What's the ~ of doing that? 那样做有什么好处？/ We should do ~all our lives. 我们应一辈子做好事。/ I am telling you this for your ~. 我告诉你这个是为了你好。❷效用；用途；用处：A car is much ~ to him. 汽车对他很有用。It's no ~ doing that. 那样做是没有用的。/ **for** ~ 永久地：I have given up smoking for ~. 我永远不再抽烟了。**do sb.** ~ 对某人有益：Have a glass of beer, it will do you ~. 喝杯啤酒吧，对你有好处。

goodbye / ˌgʊdˈbaɪ / *int.* 再见；再会：She kissed her mother ~ at the airport. 在机场她和母亲吻别。/ They said ~ to each other after the conference. 会议结束后他们互相道别。

good-looking / ˌgʊdˈlʊkɪŋ/ *adj.* 好看的，漂亮的，英俊的：a ~ young lady 美貌的年轻女士 / a ~ hat 漂亮的帽子

good-natured / ˌgʊdˈneɪtʃəd/ *adj.* 性情温和的；和善的，和蔼的；脾气好的：a ~ old man 一位和蔼可亲的老人 / a ~ disposition 仁厚心肠/We must all keep ~. 我们大家都得心平气和。派 good-naturedly *adv.*

goodness / ˈgʊdnəs / *n.* [U]善良；善行；美德：He gave the boy some money out of the ~ of heart. 出自好心他给了小男孩一些钱。/ For ~' sake, I really don't know anything about it. 看在老天爷的分上，对这事我确实一无所知。

goodwill / ˌgʊdˈwɪl / *n.* [U]善意；友善；友好，亲善：return sb.'s ~报答某人的好心/The old man beamed with ~. 那老汉慈祥地笑了。

goods / gʊdz / *n.* (*pl.*)货物；商品：high-priced ~ 高档商品 / second-hand ~ 二手货 / defective ~ 次品(水货) / smuggled ~ 走私货/ They are sending some consumer ~ to the countryside. 他们正把消费品送往农村。/ This shop supplies easy-to-sell ~ only. 这家商店专供抢手货。

goose / guːs / *n.* [C] (*pl.* geese / giːs /) 鹅

gorge / ˈgɔːdʒ / *n.* [C]峡；峡谷；山峡：Three Gorges Project 三峡工程 / The foreigners are visiting the Three Gorges. 外宾正在参观三峡。

gorgeous / ˈgɔːdʒəs / *adj.* ❶(外观、色彩等)光彩夺目的，华丽的；豪华的，辉煌的：a ~ hall 金碧辉煌的大厅/trees in ~ fall colors 披上绚丽秋色的树木 ❷极好的；令人极其愉快的：This cake is ~. 这蛋糕好吃极了。

gorilla / gəˈrɪlə / *n.* [C]大猩猩

gossip / ˈgɒsɪp / *n.* ❶[U]闲话；聊天；流言蜚语：I was having a ~ with our teacher when you came. 你来时我正和老师聊天。/ Do you believe all the ~ you hear? 你会相信你听到的所有闲话吗？❷[C]爱说闲话的人；搬弄是非者：Don't be a dreadful ~. 别搬弄是非。

govern / ˈgʌvn / *v.* ❶管理；统治；支配：Who ~s the country? 谁统治这个国家？/ He has ~ed the country for more than 30 years. 他治理这个国家三十多年了。❷控制；抑制：You should ~ your temper. 你应该克制你的脾气。

government / ˈgʌvənmənt / *n.* ❶[C]政府；内阁：a central ~ 中央政府 / a special-zone ~ 特区政府 / People all over the country wish to build a clean and honest ~. 全国人民都希望建设一个廉洁的政府。❷[U]行政管理；治理；管理；支配：Our monitor is a member of the student ~. 我们班长是学生自治会成员。

governor /ˈgʌvənə(r)/ *n.* [C] ❶州长；地方长官；总督：He visited the ~ of Hawaii. 他拜访了夏威夷州的州长。❷主管；理事；董事

gown /gaʊn/ *n.* [C] 长袍；长外衣：He took a picture in an academic ~. 他穿着学位服照了张相。

grab /græb/ *v.* (grabbed; grabbing) 抢夺；抓牢；急抓：He ~bed me by the arm. 他抓住我的手臂。/ She ~bed at the opportunity of going abroad. 她抓住了出国的机会。

grace /greɪs/ *n.* ❶[U] 优美；优雅：She danced with ~. 她舞姿优美。❷[C] (*pl.*) 文雅；才艺：Speaking French and playing the piano are social ~s. 讲法语和弹钢琴是两大社交才艺。派 graceful *adj.*

gradation /grəˈdeɪʃən/ *n.* ❶[U](状态、性质、程度等的)渐变，递变；演进，演化：rise in dreadful ~ 急剧升级 / Perhaps the ~ of his copy rendered it not so readily perceptible. 大概是他潜移默化地学了些，大家才没一下子就看出来吧。❷[C](常用复数)(渐变过程中的)级次，阶段，程度；(颜色等的)层次：the subtle ~s of light in these paintings 这些绘画中细微的光度渐变

grade /greɪd/ *n.* [C] ❶班级；年级：An elementary school in America has eight ~s. 美国的小学有 8 个年级。/ He is a graduate of Grade 2006. 他是 2006 级毕业生。❷品位；级别；等级：Milk is sold in ~. 牛奶分等级售出。/ This kind of tea is of the highest ~. 这种茶叶是最上等的。❸成绩；分数：His ~ on history is "A". 他的历史成绩为"A"。

gradual /ˈgrædʒʊəl/ *adj.* 逐渐的；逐步的：The students are discussing the problem of the ~ increase in population of this district. 学生们正在讨论这一地区人口的逐步增长问题。

gradually /ˈgrædʒʊəli/ *adv.* 逐渐地；逐步地：After a month's rest his health ~ improved. 休息一个月之后他渐渐恢复了健康。/ Many people have noticed that prices are going up ~. 很多人都注意到物价在逐渐上涨。

graduate Ⅰ/ˈgrædʒʊeɪt/ *v.* 毕业：3,500 students ~d from this university last year. 该大学去年有 3 500 名学生毕业。Ⅱ/ˈgrædʒʊət/ *n.* [C]获学位者；毕业生：a ~ in philosophy 哲学专业毕业生 / Oxford ~s 牛津大学毕业生

graduation /ˌgrædʒʊˈeɪʃn/ *n.* ❶[U]毕业；大学毕业生：He was about twenty-two on his ~. 他毕业时大约 22 岁。/ The ~ found an ideal job in a big company. 那位大学毕业生在一家大公司找到了一份理想的工作。❷[C]毕业典礼：Will your parents come to attend the ~? 你父母会出席毕业典礼吗？

grain /greɪn/ *n.* 谷类；谷粒：We shouldn't waste a ~ of rice. 我们不应浪费一粒粮食。

gram(me) /græm/ *n.* [C]克(重量单位)：kilo gram 千克/ milli gram 毫克

grammar /ˈgræmə(r)/ *n.* [U] 语法；语法规则：a ~ book 语法书 / communication ~ 交际语法 / comparative ~ 比较语法 / functional ~ 功能语法 / general ~ 普通语法 / traditional ~ 传统语法 /

There is so much ~ to be learned in the first lesson. 第一课有许多语法知识要学。

grammatical /grəˈmætɪk(ə)l/ *adj.* ❶语法的;文法的:~ analysis 语法分析 ❷(句子)合乎语法的;遵从原则的,符合原理的:~ sentences 合乎语法规则的句子

gramophone /ˈgræməfəʊn/ *n.* [C]留声机:The old lady has an old ~ and some ~ records. 老太太有一台旧的留声机和一些唱片。

G

grand /grænd/ *adj.* 庄严的;伟大的;雄伟的;豪华的;华丽的:a ~ view 壮丽的景色 / a ~ air 宏伟的气派 / the ~ finale 大结局 / The King lived in a ~ palace. 国王住在宏伟的宫殿里。/ The famous film star lives in a ~ style. 那位著名影星过着奢华的生活。

grandchild /ˈgræntʃaɪld/ *n.* [C](*pl.* grandchildren)孙子(女);外孙(女)

granddaughter /ˈgrændɔːtə(r)/ *n.* [C]孙女;外孙女:great ~ 曾孙女;外曾孙女

grandfather /ˈgrænfɑːðə(r)/ *n.* [C]祖父;外祖父:great ~ 曾祖父;外曾祖父

grandma /ˈgrænmɑː/ *n.* [C]祖母;外祖母

grandmother /ˈgrænmʌðə(r)/ *n.* [C]祖母;外祖母:great ~ 曾祖母;外曾祖母

grandpa /ˈgrænpɑː/ *n.* [C]祖父;外祖父

grandparent /ˈgrænpeərənt/ *n.* [C]祖父或祖母;外祖父或外祖母:great ~s 曾祖父母;外曾祖父母

grandson /ˈgrænsʌn/ *n.* [C]孙子;外孙子:great ~ 曾孙;外曾孙

grandstand /ˈgræn(d)ˌstænd/ *n.* [C] ❶(体育场、足球场、赛马场等的)大看台,主看台 ❷大看台观众,主看台观众:The entire ~ cheered when our team won. 我队取胜时主看台上所有的观众都欢呼起来。

granite /ˈgrænɪt/ *n.* [U]花岗岩;花岗石

granny /ˈgræni/ *n.* [C]奶奶;姥姥;老奶奶

grant /grɑːnt/ *vt.* 答应;(姑且)承认;给予:I ~ that he has made a certain social success, but I still don't approve of his opinion. 我承认他取得了一定的社会成就,但我还是不赞同他的观点。/ He was ~ed the citizenship of that country. 他获得了那个国家的公民权。/ **take ... for ~ed** 视……为当然;认定:A teacher cannot take it for ~ed that students should completely obey him. 老师不能认为学生完全服从他是理所当然的。

grape /greɪp/ *n.* [C]葡萄:a bunch of ~s 一串葡萄

graph /grɑːf/ *n.* [C]曲线图;图表:The student is drawing a line ~. 学生正在画曲线图。

graphic /ˈgræfɪk/ Ⅰ *adj.* ❶(描写等)形象的;生动的,绘声绘色的:The soldier gave a ~ account of the battle. 那士兵把那场战斗讲得有声有色。❷(用图表、曲线图等)表示的;图示的;图解的:~ analysis 图表分析(法) ❸书写的;刻写的;写下的;记下的:Letters are ~ symbols. 字母是书写符号。Ⅱ *n.* [C] ❶书画刻印作品;版画作品 ❷(电脑制作的)图表(或图案、图形等) 派 graphical *adj.* ;graphically *adv.*

grasp /grɑːsp/ Ⅰ *v.* ❶抓住;握住:I ~ed his right hand firmly. 我紧紧抓住他的右手。❷领会;掌握;了解:It is not very easy for me to ~ his meaning. 对我来说,要领会他所说的意思没那么容易。

Ⅱ *n.* [U](常用单数)紧握;把握;理解:You seem to have a good ~ of English history. 你似乎对英国历史很了解。/ Success is within our ~ now. 现在我们已有取得成功的把握。

grass / grɑːs / *n.* [U] ❶草:green ~ 青草/ rank ~ 杂草/ withered ~ 枯草 ❷草原;草地:at ~ 在牧场上/ Keep off the ~! 勿踏草坪!

grasshopper / ˈgrɑːshɒpə(r) / *n.* [C]蚱蜢;蝗虫

grassy / ˈgrɑːsi, græsi / *adj.* 为草覆盖的;长满草的;草深的:a ~ mound 杂草丛生的土墩

grateful / ˈgreɪtfl / *adj.* 感激的;令人愉快的:I'm heartily ~ to you for what you have done for me. 我衷心感谢你为我做的一切。/ He has got a ~ letter. 他收到一封感谢信。

gratitude / ˈgrætɪtjuːd / *n.* [U]感谢;感激:I can hardly express my ~ to you. 我难以表达我对你的感激之情。/Her selfless help deserves our ~. 她无私的帮助值得我们感谢。

grave[1] / greɪv / *n.* [C] 坟墓;墓穴:dig one's own ~ 自掘坟墓 / a ~-digger 掘墓人 / a ~ yard 墓地 / The son set up a ~-stone for his parents. 儿子为父母竖了一块墓碑。

grave[2] / greɪv / *adj.* ❶严重的;重大的:He made a ~ mistake in the project. 在那项工程中他犯了一个严重的错误。/ Nobody knew the ~ consequence. 没有人知道那个严重的后果。❷严肃的;庄重的:a ~ face 庄重的面孔 / He was ~ as he told them about the accident. 在同他们谈到那次意外事故时,他非常严肃。

gravel / ˈgræv(ə)l / Ⅰ *n.* [U]沙砾,砾石;石碴 Ⅱ *vt.* 用石子铺盖;给……铺上石碴;铺沙砾子于:~ a road 在路上沙砾

gravity / ˈgrævəti / *n.* [U] ❶重力;重量:The stone rolled down the mountain by ~. 这块石头在重力作用下滚下山。❷严重性;重要性:He knew nothing about the ~ of the present situation. 他对目前形势的严重性一无所知。

gray / greɪ / (=grey) Ⅰ *adj.* 灰色的;灰白的:~ economy 灰色经济 / ~ expenditure 灰色消费 Ⅱ *n.* [U]灰色:dark ~ 深灰色 / light ~ 浅灰色 / Her grandmother likes to dress in ~. 她奶奶喜欢穿灰色衣服。

graze / greɪz / *v.* (牛、羊等)吃草;放牧:The cows were grazing on the hillside. 牛儿在山坡吃草。

grease / griːs / *n.* [U](动物的)油脂;(机械等的)润滑油

great / greɪt / *adj.* ❶伟大的;卓越的;优秀的:Mao Zedong was a ~ man. 毛泽东是一位伟人。❷重要的;重大的:That is a ~ discovery. 这是一个重大的发现。❸(与表示数量的词连用)很,非常:a ~ deal 很多/ a ~ number 很多 / a ~ while ago 很久以前/ a ~ majority 大多数 / We had a ~ time in the countryside. 在农村我们度过了非常愉快的时光。❹(口语) 善于;精通:He is ~ at chess. 他下象棋下得很好。❺(口语)极好的;极棒的:That's ~! 棒极了! 派 greatness *n.*

greatly / ˈgreɪtli/ *adv.* 非常,很,极度地,大大地:bother sb. ~ with questions 提些问题来给人平添许多麻烦 / The throat was ~ chafed. 喉部伤势严重。/ I was ~ impressed with his power over words. 我对他驾驭文字的能力佩服得

五体投地。

greed / griːd / *n.* [U] 贪心；贪婪：We hate his ~ for honors. 我们讨厌他爱慕虚荣。

greedy / ˈgriːdi / *adj.* 贪吃的；贪婪的；贪心的：The boy is ~ for more knowledge. 小男孩渴求学到更多的知识。/ Don't be ~ for power. You should serve for the people. 不要权欲熏心，要为人民服务。/**be ~ for (after, of)** 贪图：He is always ~ for something new. 他总是贪求新的东西。/ She is a woman ~ of money. 她是一个贪图金钱的人。

G

green / griːn / *adj.* ❶ 绿色的：a ~ coat 一件绿色上衣 / ~ food 绿色食品 / ~ product 环保型产品 / He is working in the ~ house. 他在温室里干活。❷未成熟的：~ banana 青香蕉 ❸无经验的；没经过训练的；幼稚的：The young man is still ~ to (at) his job. 这个年轻人尚无工作经验。/ Don't blame him. He is only a ~ hand. 不要责备他，他还只是一个新手。

greenery / ˈgriːn(ə)ri / *n.* [U] ❶绿色植物 ❷(装饰用的)青枝绿叶

greenhouse / ˈgriːnhaus / *n.* [C]温室；花房：the ~ effect 温室效应 / We can have various ~ vegetables in winter. 冬天我们能吃到各种各样的温室蔬菜。

greet / griːt / *vt.* 欢迎；致意：His speech was ~ed with loud cheers. 他的演说受到热烈欢迎。/ The students ~ed their teacher politely. 学生们很有礼貌地向老师打招呼。

greeting / ˈgriːtɪŋ / *n.* [C]欢迎；问候；致意：exchange ~s 互致问候 / wave a ~ 挥手致意 / New Year's ~s 新年祝贺 / the season's ~s 节日祝贺 / Give my ~s to your mother, please. 请代我向你母亲问好。

gregarious / grɪˈgeərəs / *adj.* ❶合群的；爱交际的：a ~ person 爱社交的人❷(动物、鸟类等)群居(性)的，共生的❸聚生的，簇生的

grenade / grɪˈneɪd / *n.* [C]手榴弹；枪榴弹

grey / greɪ / Ⅰ *adj.* 灰色的 Ⅱ *n.* [U]灰色

grief / griːf / *n.* [U] 忧伤；悲伤：We had much ~ at (for, over) that matter. 我们对那件事感到很悲伤。

grievance / ˈgriːv(ə)ns / *n.* ❶不平(之事)，不满(之事)；委屈；冤情：pour ~诉苦/settle ~ quickly 尽快处理冤情 ❷[C]抱怨；诉苦；申诉：A committee was set up to look into the workers' ~. 成立了一个委员会来调查工人们的申诉。

grieve / griːv / *v.* 悲痛；伤心；哀悼：We feel deeply ~d at your misfortune. 对你的不幸我们深感悲伤。

grill / grɪl / *n.* [C]烧烤架

grim / grɪm / *adj.* ❶表情严厉的；令人生畏的：a ~ man but a just one 一个严厉但正直的人 ❷严峻的；严酷的；无情的：an exam that was really ~一次真正严峻的考试/War is a ~ business. 战争是残酷的事情。❸可怕的，恐怖的；阴森的 ❹令人不愉快的；讨厌的；糟糕的：a ~ day 不愉快的一天 派 grimly *adv.*

grin / grɪn / Ⅰ *vi.* (grinned; grinning)咧嘴笑；露嘴笑；露齿笑：They ~ned with pleasure when I gave them the sweets. 我给他们糖果时，他们高兴得咧着嘴笑。Ⅱ *n.* [C]咧着嘴的笑，露齿的笑：He flashed a ~ of his white teeth. 他咧嘴一笑，露出洁白的牙齿。

grind /graɪnd/ *vt.* (ground /graʊnd/) ❶磨快；磨光；磨薄；把……磨成形：There was a knife being ground on a wheel. 砂轮上正磨着一把刀。❷用力擦(或压)：He ground his cigarette in the ashtray. 他把香烟掐在烟灰缸中。❸压迫；压榨；欺压：They were notorious for ~ing the poor. 他们因欺压穷人而声名狼藉。❹嘎吱嘎吱地摩擦；磨(牙)：Some people ~ their teeth while they're asleep. 有人睡觉时会磨牙。❺磨；磨碎，碾碎；咬碎，啃碎：~(up) the wheat to make flour 把小麦磨成面

grip /grɪp/ *v.* (gripped; gripping) 紧抓；紧握：Please ~ the stick tightly. 请牢牢抓住这根棍子。

groan /grəʊn/ *v.* & *n.* 呻吟：She was injured in the accident and ~ed with pain. 她在意外事故中受了伤，痛苦地呻吟着。

grocer /ˈgrəʊsə(r)/ *n.* [C] 杂货商；杂货店店主：I'll go to the ~'s (shop) to buy some food. 我要去杂货店买些食品。

grocery /ˈgrəʊsəri/ *n.* [C]❶杂货业；杂货店 ❷(*pl.*)食品杂货

groove /gruːv/ Ⅰ *n.* [C] ❶槽，沟：a steel plate with ~s cut in it 里面刻有凹槽的钢盘 ❷(唱片的)纹(道) ❸常规，成规；老一套：His mind works in a narrow ~. 他的思想囿于常规。Ⅱ *vt.* 在……上开槽(或沟等)：The sand on the shore has been ~d by the waves. 沙滩被海浪冲击出道道凹槽。

grope /grəʊp/ *vi.* ❶摸索；摸索着走：He ~d into the kitchen and switched on the light. 他摸索着走进厨房，打开电灯。❷探索，寻求：~ after the truth 探索真理/The two sides are groping towards an agreement. 双方正在寻求达成一项协议。

gross /grəʊs/ *adj.* 总计的；全部的：~ domestic product (GDP) 国内生产总值 / ~ weight 毛重 / ~ national product (GNP) 国民生产总值 / Her ~ income will very likely exceed 82,000 dollars this year. 她今年的总收入很可能超过8.2万美元。

ground /graʊnd/ *n.* ❶[U] 地；地面；土地：The ~ is covered with snow. 地上覆盖着雪。/ The boy was lying on the ~. 男孩躺在地上。❷[C](有特殊用途的)场地：a cricket ~ 板球场 / the sports ~ 运动场/ They built a new pleasure ~ near our school. 他们在我们学校附近修了一座新的游乐场。❸[C](*pl.*)(房屋四周的)土地；庭院：The cottage stands in lovely ~s. 小屋坐落在美丽的庭院中。❹[C]理由；根据：There is no ~ for anxiety. 没必要焦虑。/ You have no ~ for complaining of his conduct. 你没有理由控告他的行为。/**above (below)** ~ 活的(死的)：I am sure he is still above ~. 我相信他还活着。**gain** ~ 前进，进展；得势：The patient gained ~ daily. 病人日益恢复健康。**give (lose)** ~ 退却；让步；失利：Both of them would not give ~, so they quarrelled. 他们两人互不相让，于是吵了起来。**hold (stand, keep) one's** ~ 坚守；不让步：The referee held his ~ although his decision was hotly contested by the crowd. 尽管人们对裁判的决定提出了强烈抗议，但他仍然坚持他的立场。**shift one's** ~ 改变立场：He shifted his ~ whenever it was to his advantage. 只要对他有利，他就随时改变立场。

groundless /ˈgraʊndlɪs/ *adj.* 无理由

的，无根据的：a ~ fiction 毫无根据的杜撰/The fear fortunately proved to be ~. 幸而发现这只是一场虚惊。

groundwork /ˈgraʊndwɜːk/ *n.* [U]基础工作；基础根基：He completed the ~ for his thesis a year ago. 他一年前就完成了自己论文的前期工作。

group /gruːp/ *n.* [C]队，组，群；团体：a ~ of boys 一群男孩 / The children played in ~s. 孩子们分组游戏。/ We'll hold a ~ discussion on this problem. 对这个问题我们将进行小组讨论。

grow /grəʊ/ *v.* (grew/gruː/, grown /grəʊn/) ❶发育；生长；长大；增长：How quickly she is ~ing! 她长得多快呀！/ Cities grew rapidly. 城市发展迅速。/ The rice is ~ing fine. 水稻长势良好。/~ **out of** 长得穿不进；源于；由……而生：~ out of one's clothes 长得穿不下原来的衣服。/ The mistake grew out of his carelessness. 这错误是由于他粗心引起的。~ **up** 长大；成人：He was born in Beijing, but grew up in Shanghai. 他生在北京长在上海。❷(逐渐)变得：~ older 渐老 / ~ smaller 渐小 / It is ~ing dark. 天色渐晚。❸种植；使生长：We have ~n a lot of flowers this summer. 今年夏天我们种了很多花。

growl /graul/ Ⅰ *v.* ❶(狗等)发狺狺声；狂吠；嗥叫(at)：This dog ~s at anybody who comes close. 人一靠近，这条狗就对着他狂吠。❷低声怒吼；愤愤不平地抱怨(或嘟哝)(与 at 连用)：Dad's in a bad mood and he's ~ing at everybody today. 爸爸今天情绪不好，对谁都要吼一通。❸发轰隆声：My stomach started to ~ with hunger. 我肚子饿得咕咕直叫唤。Ⅱ *n.* [C] ❶低沉的怒声；狺狺声；轰隆声，辘辘声：the distant ~ of thunder 远处的轰隆雷声 / He answered with a ~ of anger. 他怒气冲冲地回答。❷愤愤不平的抱怨(或嘟哝)

grown /grəʊn/ *adj.* 成年的；长成的；成熟的：a ~ man 成年男子

grown-up /ˈgrəʊnʌp/ *n.* [C]成年人

growth /grəʊθ/ *n.*[U]增长；生长：The rapid ~ in economy of our country is inspiring. 我国经济的快速增长令人鼓舞。/ Her appearance changed a lot with ~. 随着年龄的增长她的外表发生了很大变化。

grudge /grʌdʒ/ Ⅰ *n.* [C]不满；嫌隙；积怨；恶意：a bitter ~深深的积怨 Ⅱ *vt.* ❶勉强地给；勉强地认可；不情愿地做：She will not ~ doing a bit extra unless it's really needed. 除非确实需要，否则她是不会加班加点的。❷怨恨，嫌恶；妒忌：He ~d me my success. 他嫉妒我的成功。

gruel /gruːəl/ *n.* [U]粥；稀饭：I have one bowl of ~ and an egg for breakfast. 我早餐吃一碗稀饭和一个鸡蛋。

grumble /ˈgrʌmb(ə)l/ *vi.* ❶抱怨，发牢骚；挑剔：When his boss would call on Sunday morning he would ~ but go to work. 每当星期天老板打来电话时他总是满肚子怨言，但还是去上班了。/ People ~d about inflation. 人们对通货膨胀牢骚满腹。❷咕哝，嘟囔；发哼声：Husbands ~ every summer as they dutifully pack the car for the family holiday. 每年夏天丈夫们一面嘟囔，一面却恪尽职守地把全家去度假要用的东西装到车里去。

grunt /grʌnt/ Ⅰ *n.* [C] ❶(猪等的)哼哼声，呼噜声，咕噜声：a pig's ~ 猪的哼哼声 ❷(表示厌恶、不满等的)哼声，嘟哝声，嘟囔声：answer the question with boorish ~s 粗鲁地嘟哝着回答问题 / utter a ~发出哼声 ❸步兵 Ⅱ *vi.* ❶(猪等)哼哼叫，发呼噜声 ❷(表示厌恶、不满、疲倦等)咕哝，嘟囔；发出哼哼声：He merely ~ed for a reply. 他哼哼唧唧地只求一个答复。

guarantee /ˌgærənˈtiː/ *n.* & *vt.* 保证；担保：the length of ~d service 保修期 / the quality ~ period 保质期 / Buying a train ticket doesn't ~ you a seat. 买到火车票并不保证你能有座位。/ This watch is ~d for two years. 这只表保修两年。

guaranty /ˈgær(ə)nti/ *n.* [C] ❶担保；担保书 ❷担保品，保证金，抵押品

guard /gɑːd/ Ⅰ *n.* [C]哨兵，警卫；警戒：mount ~ 放哨；站岗/**relieve** ~ 接班：The ~ is relieved at intervals. 卫兵每隔一段时间换一次班。**stand** ~ 站岗：The dog stood ~ over his wounded master. 这狗看守着它受伤的主人。**on** ~ 值班；当班：Get up. It's your turn to go on ~. 起来，该你值班了。Ⅱ *v.* 保卫；看管；防范：I'll ~ over the luggage while you get the ticket. 你去买票，我来看行李。/ The lunatic was carefully ~ed. 那个疯子被严加看管着。~ **against** 预防：He ~ed against repeating the mistake. 他警惕犯同样的错误。

guardian /ˈgɑːdɪən/ *n.* [C] ❶看守者，看护者；守护者；保卫者，捍卫者：the ~ of morals 伦理道德的捍卫者 ❷监护人 Ⅱ *adj.* 守护的：a ~ angel 守护者

guerrilla /gəˈrɪlə/ *n.* [C]游击战；游击队员：a ~ war (warfare) 游击战 / a ~ area 游击区 / ~ forces 游击队 / Her grandfather was a ~ during the anti-Japanese war. 在抗日战争期间她的祖父是一名游击队员。

guess /ges/ Ⅰ *v.* 猜测；猜中：~ a riddle 猜谜 / I ~ she'll be back in half an hour. 我猜她半小时后回来。/ If I ~, I often ~ most nearly. 我要是猜，常猜得八九不离十。Ⅱ *n.* [C] 猜测：make a ~ 猜测 / miss one's ~ 没猜中；猜错 / a wrong ~ 错误的推测。/ **at a** ~ 据猜测；凭估计：At a ~, I should say there were 50 people present. 依我估计有 50 人在场。**by** ~ 凭推测：Don't answer by ~, work the problem out. 不要凭猜想回答，把这道题算出来。

guest /gest/ *n.* [C] 客人；宾客；房客：We're expecting ~s to dinner. 我们在等候出席宴会的客人。/ This hotel can accommodate 300 ~s at the same time. 这家宾馆可以同时接待 300 位房客。

guidance /ˈgaɪdəns/ *n.* [U]指导，辅导；率领：The school provides occupation ~ for the students. 学校为学生提供就业指导。/ They are making an experiment under the ~ of the expert. 他们正在专家的指导下做实验。

guide /gaɪd/ Ⅰ *vt.* 引导；指导；指引：She ~d the child across the street. 她领着孩子过街。/The professor is guiding the postgraduates in research work. 教授在指导研究生进行科研。Ⅱ *n.* [C] ❶向导；导游：It would be safer to take a ~. 带个向导安全些。❷指南；手册：a study ~ 学习指南 / a traveller's ~ 旅游指南

guidebook /ˈgaɪdbʊk/ *n.* [C]手册；旅行指南：The eighteen- year-old girl traveled around the world with a ~. 那个十八岁的姑娘带着一本旅游指南环球旅行。

guideline /ˈgaɪdlaɪn/ *n.* [C]指导方针；

准则：~ on housing reform 住房改革的指导方针 / lay out economic ~s 制定经济方针

guidepost / ˈgaɪdpəʊst / *n.* [C]指标；路标；指导方针：The ~ shows the way to our school. 路标指着通往我们学校的路。

guilt / gɪlt / *n.* [U] ❶有罪；犯罪：The manage denied his ~. 经理否认自己有罪。❷内疚：She felt a good deal of ~ because she told a lie to her mother. 由于对母亲说谎，她感到非常内疚。

guilty / ˈgɪlti / *adj.* ❶有罪的：The man confessed himself ~ of theft. 那人承认自己犯了盗窃罪。❷内疚的：She felt ~ about being rude toward her parents. 对父母态度粗暴让她感到很内疚。

guise / gaɪz / *n.* [C]伪装；貌似，相似：in the ~ of a reporter 伪装成记者/ under the ~ of objective journalism 在标榜客观报道的幌子下

guitar / gɪˈtɑː(r) / *n.* [C]吉他：The boy plays the ~ very well. 这个男孩吉他弹得很好。

gulf / gʌlf / *n.* [C]海湾；深坑；深渊；鸿沟：the Persian Gulf 波斯湾/the Mexico Gulf 墨西哥湾/ This quarrel created a ~ between the old friends. 这次争吵使老朋友之间产生了隔阂。

gum / gʌm / *n.*[U]口香糖：Many young people like chewing ~. 许多年轻人都喜欢嚼口香糖。

gun / gʌn / *n.* [C]炮；枪：discharge a ~ 开炮 / fire a ~ 开枪/ an air ~ 气枪 / an antitank ~ 反坦克炮 / a machine ~ 机关枪 / a long-range ~ 远程炮

gunfight / ˈgʌnˌfaɪt/ *n.* [C]枪战；炮战

gunfire / ˈgʌnˌfaɪə(r)/ *n.* [U](尤指连续的)炮火：a barrage (burst，hail) of ~ 一阵枪林弹雨 / an exchange of ~ 交火

gunpowder / ˈgʌnpaʊdə(r) / *n.* [U]火药：Do you know who invented ~? 你知道是谁发明了火药吗?

gunpoint / ˈgʌnˌpɔɪnt/ *n.* [U]枪口：**at** ~ 在枪口的威胁下：hold sb. hostage at ~ 用枪把某人劫为人质

gunshot / ˈgʌnˌʃɒt/ *n.* ❶[C]枪炮射击；枪炮声：I heard a ~ and a man dropped dead. 我听到一声枪响，随即一个人应声倒毙。❷[U](射出的)枪弹；炮弹

gush / gʌʃ / Ⅰ *vi.* ❶喷；倾泻；涌流：The cool stream water ~ed over my hand. 清凉的溪水哗哗地从我手上流过。/Her heart was stricken, and the tears ~ed out like water from a rock. 她的心受到了伤害，眼泪犹如岩石上的水流一样哗哗地往下掉。❷说话滔滔不绝：Words ~ed out of him in an endless stream. 他口若悬河，滔滔不绝。Ⅱ *n.* [C]❶喷，涌出，倾泻：a ~ of tears 泪如泉涌/a ~ of congratulations 潮水般的祝贺 ❷迸发；(一阵)发作：a ~ of anger 发怒/a ~ of wind 一阵风

gust / gʌst / *n.* [C] ❶阵风；一阵狂风：A ~ of wind blew his hat off. 一阵狂风吹掉了他的帽子。❷(感情的)迸发；汹涌：He burst out a ~ of anger when he heard the news. 听到这则消息他勃然大怒。

guy / gaɪ / *n.* [C](美)人；家伙：He is a nice ~. 他是个好人。

gym / dʒɪm / *n.* [C] 体育馆；健身房(=gymnasium)

gymnasium / dʒɪmˈneɪzɪəm / *n.* [C](*pl.* gymnasia 或 gymnasiums)体育馆；健身房：She goes to the ~ every day. 她每天

都去健身房锻炼身体。

gymnast / ˈdʒɪmnæst / *n.* [C]体操家;体育家

gymnastic / dʒɪmˈnæstɪk / *adj.* 体操的;体育的:Our school bought some new ~ apparatus. 我们学校买了一些新的体育器械。/ He invited us to watch the ~ exhibition last Saturday. 上周六他邀请我们观看了体操表演。

gymnastics / dʒɪmˈnæstɪks / *n.* [U]体操;体育

H h

ha / hɑː / *int.* (表示惊奇、快乐、怀疑等)哈!嘿!

habit / ˈhæbɪt / *n.* ❶[C]习惯;惯常的行为:Many people say that smoking is a bad ~. 许多人都说抽烟是一种坏习惯。/ You should form the good ~ of getting up early. 你应该养成早起的好习惯。❷[U]脾性;习性:You'll not be afraid of snakes if you understand their ~. 如果了解蛇的习性,你就不会怕它们了。

habitat / ˈhæbɪtæt / *n.* [C](植物的)产地;(动物的)栖息地;住地:the giant panda ~ 熊猫栖息地 / the ginseng ~ 人参产地

habitation / ˌhæbɪˈteɪʃn / *n.* [U]居住;住处:The town is near the sea and is a place fit for ~. 小镇靠近海边,是一个适宜居住的地方。

habitual / həˈbɪtʃuəl / *adj.* 惯常的;通常的:He sat down in his ~ seat. 他坐在他常坐的座位上。

hack / hæk / *v.* ❶劈,砍;猛劈,乱砍:~ meat into bits 把肉剁碎/~ off the dead branches 砍下枯枝 ❷大砍大删,(大刀阔斧地)削减:~ a budget 大幅削减预算

hacker / ˈhækə(r) / *n.* [C](计算机)黑客:They think that ~s are often young people who are interested in computers. 他们认为"黑客"通常是一些对计算机很感兴趣的年轻人。

hail[1] / heɪl / *n.* [U]冰雹:The ~ stones are as big as peas. 冰雹像豌豆般大小。

hail[2] / heɪl / *vt.* ❶给……打招呼:~ an old friend 向老朋友打招呼 ❷向……欢呼,欢迎;热情赞扬;热情认可:Children ~ed the suggestion of a holiday with delight. 孩子们为放假这一提议而高兴得欢呼了起来。/ The old man is ~ed as the father of modern nuclear physics. 这位老人被誉为当代核物理学之父。❸招呼:~ a taxi 招呼出租车

hair / heə(r) / *n.* [U]毛发(尤指头发):brush (comb) one's ~ 梳头发 / do one's ~ 做头发 / dye ~ 染发 / have one's ~ cut 理发 / **make one's ~ stand on end** 使毛骨悚然:Her sudden scream made my ~ stand on end. 她突然尖叫,令我毛骨悚然。

haircut / ˈheəkʌt / *n.* [C]理发;发式:He had a ~ before the interview. 采访前他去理了发。/Girls like short ~ this year. 今年姑娘们都喜欢留短发。

hairdresser / ˈheədresə(r) / *n.* [C]理发师:Her ~ is a young fellow. 她的理发师是一个年轻的小伙子。

hair-raising / ˈheəreɪzɪŋ/ *adj.* 令人毛发竖起的,吓人的,恐怖的;惊险的:a ~ murder case 吓人的凶杀案 / ~ adventures 惊险的探险经历

hairstyle / ˈheəstaɪl/ *n.* [C]发式,发型:change one's ~ 改变发型

half / hɑːf / Ⅰ *n.* [C](*pl.* halves /hɑːvz/)一半;半个:the other ~ 另一半 / the return ~ of a return ticket 往返票的返程票 / the first ~ of a game 比赛的前半场 / Cut it in ~. 把它切成两半。/**by halves** 不完全地;不完善地:We do nothing by ~. 我们做事从不半途而废。Ⅱ *adv.* 一半;差不多;部分地:My work is not ~ done yet. 我的工作尚未完成一半。/ The beggar was ~ dead from hunger. 那乞丐已饿得半死。Ⅲ*adj*. 半个的;不完全的:A ~ truth is often no better than a lie. 半真半假的话不见得比谎话好。

half-time / ˈhɑːfˈtaɪm, ˈhæftaɪm / *n.* ❶[U](足球等比赛中的)半场休息,中场休息:The Rocket team was leading by two goals at ~. 中场休息时火箭队领先两个球。❷中场休息时间;半场休息时间:The coach made instructions to his men during ~. 中场休息时间里教练向他的队员部署打法。

halfway / ˌhɑːfˈweɪ, ˈhɑːfweɪ / Ⅰ *adv.* ❶在中途,半路上,半途地:We were ~ to Rome. 我们距罗马尚有一半路程。/ The project of the power plant stopped ~. 电厂项目中途搁浅了。❷几乎,大体上:These measures didn't go ~ towards solving our problems. 那些措施根本没能解决我们的问题。Ⅱ *adj.* ❶中途的;位于中途的:The runner reached the ~ mark in the Marathon race after 80 minutes. 马拉松比赛开始 80 分钟后,这位选手便跑到了中点线。❷部分的:~ measures 不彻底的措施 / **meet sb.** ~与某人妥协:If you can drop your price a little, I'll meet you ~. 你要是能减点价,我就愿意再让一步。

hall / hɔːl / *n.* [C]会堂;大厅;礼堂:the Great Hall of the People 人民大会堂 / an assembly ~ 会议厅 / a banquet ~ 宴会厅 / a concert ~ 音乐厅 / a dance ~ 舞厅 / a dining ~ 餐厅 / an entrance ~ 门厅 / the examination ~ 考场 / an exhibition ~ 展览厅 / the Hall of Justice 法院

halt / hɔːlt / Ⅰ *v.* 停止;休息:The soldiers ~ed for a short rest. 士兵们停下来休息一会儿。/ Nobody can ~ the advance of history. 没有人能阻挡历史的前进。Ⅱ *n.* 停止;(短暂的)休息:The car came to a sudden ~. 汽车突然停了下来。

ham / hæm / *n.* [C]火腿:a slice of ~ 一片火腿

hamburger / ˈhæmbɜːgə(r) / *n.* [C] 汉堡包;牛肉饼

hammer / ˈhæmə(r) / Ⅰ *n.* [C] 铁锤;木槌;榔头:strike with a ~ 用锤敲打 / a stone ~ 石锤 / wooden ~ 木榔头 Ⅱ *v.* 锤打:When you've packed the box, ~ the lid on. 箱子装好后,就把盖子钉上。

hamper / ˈhæmpə(r) / *vt.* ❶妨碍,使不能自由行动:The snow storm ~ed the efforts to rescue victims from the mountain. 暴风雪使营救山上遇险者的工作无法进行。❷阻碍,影响:Sales are ~ed by wide price fluctuations. 大幅度的价格波动妨碍了销售。

hand / hænd / Ⅰ *n.* [C] ❶手:It is a good habit to wash ~s before dinner. 饭前洗手是好习惯。/ **at** ~ 在近处;在手边:I haven't got my picture at ~, but I'll show it to you later. 我的照片没有

带在手边，以后再给你看吧。**at sb.'s ~** 出自某人之手：I did not expect such unkind treatment at your ~s. 我未料到你会如此刻薄。**by ~** 手工的：The box is made by ~. 这箱子是手工做的。**~ in ~** 手拉手；一起：They are walking ~ in ~. 他们手拉着手散步。**on (in) ~** 在手上；可用；握有：We have a large supply of goods on ~. 我们现有一大批货物。/ I still have some money in ~. 我手里还有些钱。**out of ~** 难以控制；不可收拾：His wrath got out of ~. 他怒不可遏。**lend a ~** 帮助：Please lend me a ~ to move the desk away. 请帮我把桌子搬走。**shake one's ~, shake ~s with sb.** 与某人握手：As soon as she saw me, she shoot my hand warmly. 她一见到我就和我热情地握手。❷人手；雇员：The com-pany is short of ~s. 这家公司缺人手。❸(钟表的)指针：the hour ~ 时针/ the minute ~ 分针/ the second ~ 秒针 Ⅱ *v.* 交给；传递：Please ~ me the pen. 请把钢笔递给我。/~ **in** 交上：Please ~ in your exercise books. 请把作业本交上来。~ **on** 依次传递：When you have read this, kindly ~ it on to your friends. 读完后，请将它传给你的朋友们。~ **out** 分发：They are ~ing out leaflets to people. 他们正在向人们散发传单。~ **over** 移交；交出：The offender was ~ed over to the police. 那个罪犯已经被送交警方。

handbag / ˈhændbæg / *n.* [C]手提包

handball / ˈhændbɔːl/ *n.* [U] ❶手球运动 ❷手球；(手球运动所使用的)球

handbook / ˈhændbʊk / *n.* [C]手册；指南：a ~ for teachers 教师手册 / a ~ to tourists 旅游指南

handcuff / hændkʌf/ Ⅰ *n.* [C] (*pl.*) 手铐：put ~s on a prisoner 给囚犯戴手铐 Ⅱ *vt.* ❶给……戴上手铐：The driver was robbed and ~ed to the steering wheel. 那位司机遭到抢劫，并且手也被铐在了方向盘上。❷束缚；限制：They feel ~ed by so many restrictions. 如此多的条条框框让他们感到处处受制。

handful / ˈhændfʊl / *n.* [C] 少数；一把；少量：She took a ~ of sand and played joyfully. 她抓起一把沙子快乐地玩着。

handicap / ˈhændɪkæp / *n.* [C]不利；妨碍；障碍：overcome a ~ 克服不利条件

handicraft / ˈhændɪkrɑːft / *n.* [C]手艺；手工艺品

handkerchief / ˈhæŋkətʃɪf / *n.* [C] (*pl.* handkerchiefs 或 handkerchieves) 手帕

handle / ˈhændl / Ⅰ *v.* ❶拿；摸：Wash your hands before you ~ my books. 请你在拿我的书以前先洗手。❷操纵；管理：An officer must know how to ~ sol-diers. 一个军官必须懂得怎样指挥士兵。❸对付；对待；经销：It should be cautiously ~d. 此事应审慎处理。/ This shop doesn't ~ foreign goods. 这个商店不经销外国货。Ⅱ *n.* [C](工具、杯、桶、门、抽屉等的)柄；把手；提手：The ~ is broken off. 门把手断了。

handmade / ˈhændˈmeɪd/ *adj.* 手工制作的：wonderful ~ cakes 绝妙的手工糕点

handout / ˈhændaʊt / *n.* [C] ❶施舍物；救济品：The old couple are living off ~s. 老两口靠救济生活。❷讲稿；传单；广告单：The students are reading the ~ carefully. 学生们仔细阅读散发的讲稿。

handrail / ˈhændreɪl / *n.* [C](楼梯的)扶手；(道路的)扶栏

handshake / ˈhændʃeɪk / *n.* [C] ❶握手：The manager welcomed him with a warm ~. 经理同他热情握手,欢迎他的到来。❷(计算机系统中的)信号交换

handsome /ˈhænsəm/ *adj.* 美观的;(男人)俊美的,英俊的;(女人)秀丽的,清秀的:What a ~ old building it is! 多么美观的一座古建筑!/ He's a ~ fellow. 他是一个很英俊的小伙子。

handwriting /ˈhændraɪtɪŋ/ *n.* [U]笔迹;笔法;书法:neat (poor) ~ 工整(蹩脚)的书法 / Not many people practise ~ now. 现在练书法的人很少。

handy /ˈhændi/ *adj.* ❶方便的;手边的;便于使用的:Put things you need ~. 把你需要的东西放在随手可取的地方。❷心灵手巧的:He is ~ at repairing computers. 他很擅长修计算机。

hang /hæŋ/ *v.* ❶(hung /hʌŋ/, hung) 悬;挂;吊;垂:The pictures are hung on the wall. 那些图画挂在墙上。/ Will you ~ a lamp from the ceiling? 将灯吊在天花板上好吗? / Don't ~ up. I'll tell you a secret. 别挂断电话,我要告诉你一个秘密。❷(hanged, hanged) 吊死,绞死(常用被动式):The murderer will be ~ed. 杀人凶手将被处以绞刑。

hanger /ˈhæŋə(r)/ *n.* [C]挂物的东西;衣架;(衣帽)挂钩

happen /ˈhæpən/ *vi.* ❶发生:He wondered what was going to ~. 他想知道下一步会发生什么事。❷碰巧:It ~ed to be a fine day. 那天恰巧是一个晴天。/ I ~ed to be out when he called. 他来访时,我正好出去了。❸偶然发现某物(与 on, upon 连用):He ~ed on the book in a small bookstore. 他在一家小书店偶然发现了这本书。

happy /ˈhæpi/ *adj.* (-ier, -iest) 幸福的;高兴的;快乐的:She is very ~. 她很幸福。/ That was the happiest day of my life. 那是我一生中最快乐的一天。
派 happily *adv.*; happiness *n.*

harass /ˈhærəs, həˈræs/ *vt.* ❶不断侵扰,骚扰:Several clubs were ~ed by the gang in the area. 几家俱乐部遭到地方上的流氓团伙的骚扰。❷不断打扰,烦扰;使苦恼:be ~ed by income tax 为所得税烦心 / She had been ~ed with anxieties since she was out of work. 失业以后她一直忧心忡忡。

harassment /ˈhærəsmənt/ *n.* [U]骚扰:sexual ~ 性骚扰/ She can't bear the noise ~. 她不能忍受噪声骚扰。

harbo(u)r /ˈhɑːbə(r)/ *n.* [C]港口:The ship entered a safe ~. 船只驶进了安全的港口。

hard /hɑːd/ Ⅰ *adv.* 努力地,费力地;剧烈地;艰苦地:He studies very ~. 他学习非常努力。/ It's raining ~. 雨下得很大。Ⅱ *adj.* ❶坚硬的;坚固的:~ currency 硬通货 / The ground is very ~. 地面很坚硬。❷强烈的;猛烈的:The ~ blow knocked the boxer down. 重重的一击使拳击手倒下了。❸艰难的;辛苦的;难以理解的;难以解释的:The teacher asked her a ~ question. 老师问了她一个很难的问题。❹严厉的;(天气)恶劣的:a ~ father 严父 / ~ words 严词 / ~ winter 严冬/ Don't be ~ on such a little boy. 别对这么小的孩子太严厉。

harden /ˈhɑːdən/ *v.* ❶(使)变得坚硬;(使)硬化:Steel can be ~ed through quench. 淬火可以使钢硬化。/This kind of chemical ~s as it cools. 这种化学品冷却后硬化。❷(使)变得冷酷无情(或麻木不仁):Her heart was ~ed by the rubs and worries of life. 生活的折磨与煎熬使她变得麻木不仁。/ She ~ed

H

her face against him. 她对他沉下了脸。❸使变得更坚强:Poverty ~ed his personality. 贫穷使他的性格变得更加坚强。

hard-hearted / ˌhɑːdˈhɑːtɪd / *adj.* 硬心肠的,无同情心的:Their anger had made them ~. 愤怒使他们的心肠变硬了。

hardly / ˈhɑːdli / *adv.* 几乎不;简直不:Her foot is hurt. She can ~ walk home. 她的脚受伤了,简直走不回家。

H

hardship / ˈhɑːdʃɪp / *n.* [U]艰难;困苦:bear ~ 吃苦 / suffer ~ 受苦 / His families endured great ~ during the war. 他的家人在战争中经受了巨大的苦难。

hardware / ˈhɑːdweə(r) / *n.* ❶[C](计算机)硬件 ❷[U]五金器具:The shop sells ~. 这商店出售五金用品。

hardy / ˈhɑːdi / *adj.* ❶强壮的;坚韧的;能吃苦耐劳的:a ~ constitution 强壮的体格/a ~ people 吃苦耐劳的民族 ❷需要耐力(或勇气)的:the hardiest sports 最能考验人耐力的体育运动 ❸(植物)耐寒的:a ~ perennial 一种耐寒的多年生植物 ❹勇敢的,大胆的;果敢的:the ~ explorers of the arctic 勇敢的北极探险者

hare / heə(r) / *n.* [C]野兔

harm / hɑːm / Ⅰ *vt.* 伤害;损害:The dog hasn't ~ed you, has it? 那条狗并没有伤害你,对吗? Ⅱ *n.* [U]损害;伤害;危害:It will do you no ~. 这对你无害。/ Please don't do any ~ to your pets. 请勿伤害宠物。派 harmful *adj.*

harmless / ˈhɑːmlɪs/ *adj.* ❶无害的;不致伤的:~ insects 不会伤人的昆虫 / Ozone is fairly ~ to people but it hurts plants. 臭氧对人没有什么危害,但对植物是有害的。❷无恶意的;无辜的:~ fun 没有恶意的玩笑 / ~ pedestrians 无辜的行人 派 harmlessly *adv.*

harmonious / hɑːˈməʊnɪəs / *adj.* 和谐的;和睦的;协调的:We are building up a ~ society. 我们正在建立一个和谐的社会。

harmonize / ˈhɑːməˌnaɪz/ *v.* ❶和谐;融洽;协调;一致(与 with 连用):~ in feelings 感情融洽 / These colors don't seem to ~ with each other. 这些颜色看上去并不协调。❷用和声演唱(或演奏);和谐地演唱(或演奏) 派 harmonization *n.*

harmony / ˈhɑːməni / *n.* 和谐;和睦:His idea is in ~ with mine. 他的想法与我的一致。

harness / ˈhɑːnɪs / Ⅰ *n.* [C] ❶马具;挽具:a set of ~一套马具 ❷挽具状物;吊带;背带:a safety ~安全带/a baby ~保护婴儿的系带 Ⅱ *vt.* ❶给……套上挽具:~ a horse to a cart 把马套到车上 ❷驾驭;控制;利用;治理:be ~ed to rules 照章办事/try to ~ wind and waves as new sources of power 设法利用风和海浪作为新动力源

harp / hɑːp / *n.* [C]竖琴:She played the ~ in the party. 在聚会上她演奏了竖琴。

harsh / hɑːʃ / *adj.* ❶残酷的;无情的:be ~ with others 无情地对待他人 ❷严厉的,苛刻的:a ~ master 严厉的主人/ The punishment was too ~ for such a minor offence. 对于这样的轻罪,这种惩罚过于严厉了。❸粗糙的;具刺激性的;(声音)刺耳的:His voice has grown ~. 他的声音变得很刺耳。/~ detergents 强刺激性洗涤剂 派 harshly *adv.* harshness *n.*

harvest / ˈhɑːvɪst / *n.* 收获;收成;成果:a

bad (poor) ~ 歉收/ a good (rich) ~ 丰收 / the summer ~ 夏收 / The rice crop bore a plentiful ~ last year. 去年水稻大丰收。

hassle /ˈhæsl/ Ⅰ *n.* [C] ❶激烈的争论;争吵:get into a ~ with sb. over sth. 为某事与某人争吵 ❷麻烦;困难 Ⅱ *v.* ❶激烈地争论;争吵:~ with sb. 与某人激烈争吵 ❷搅扰;烦扰,使烦恼:She'll ~ me until I agree to write the letter for her. 在我答应她帮忙写信前她会一直来烦我的。

haste /heɪst/ *n.* [U]急速;仓促:Haste makes waste. 忙中出错。/ More ~, less speed. 欲速则不达。/ He went off in great ~. 他匆匆离去。/**in** ~ 匆忙地;草率地:He packed his clothes into a trunk in ~ and went out of the room. 他匆匆地把衣服塞进箱子,走出房间。

hasten /ˈheɪsən/ *vi.* 赶快;赶紧;赶忙:He ~ed to the railway station. 他匆匆往火车站赶。/Don't ~ to a conclusion. 不要急于下结论。—*vt.* 促进;加速:~ one's pace (steps) 加快步伐

hasty /ˈheɪsti/ *adj.* 急速的;草率的:The ~ conclusion of the film made us very unhappy. 这部电影草率的结局令我们深感不快。

hat /hæt/ *n.* [C]帽子:a straw ~ 草帽 / wear a ~ 戴着帽子/ put off one's ~ 脱帽 / put on one's ~ 戴上帽子

hatch /hætʃ/ *v.* 孵化:Three chicks are ~ed today. 今天有三只小鸡孵出来了。

hate /heɪt/ *vt.* 憎恨;不愿;不喜欢:She ~s me for it. 她因此事而恨我。/ She ~s anyone listening while she's telephoning. 她打电话时讨厌别人听。

hateful /ˈheɪtfəl/ *adj.* ❶引起仇恨的;可恨的;可恶的:a bloody and ~ devil 一个嗜血成性、十恶不赦的魔鬼 ❷讨厌的;极不愉快的:That was a ~ thing to say. 那件事说起来令人生厌。❷显示仇恨的;充满敌意的;恶意的:~ eyes 充满仇恨的双眼 派 hatefully *adv.*

hatred /ˈheɪtrɪd/ *n.* [U]憎恨;怨恨:Do you know why he has a deep ~ for (of) English? 你知道他为什么痛恨英语吗?

haughty /ˈhɔːti/ *adj.* 傲慢的,趾高气扬的:~ aristocrats 傲慢的贵族们/carry a ~ air 摆出神气活现的架子

haul /hɔːl/ Ⅰ *vt.* ❶拖;拉;拽:~ the boat out of water 把船从水中拖上来/ His wife will ~ him to a highbrow play. 他妻子会强拽他去观看高雅的戏剧。❷(用车等)运送;拖运:~coal from the mines 从煤矿拖运煤 Ⅱ *n.* [C]❶拖;拉;拽:Give a ~ at the rope. 拉一下绳子。❷拖运;运送:long ~s by rail 长途铁路运输 ❸一次获得的量:a bumper ~ of fish 一大网鱼

haunting /ˈhɔːntɪŋ/ *adj.* 萦绕于心头的;难以忘怀的:a ~ melody 萦绕于脑际的乐曲/~ memories 难忘的记忆

have /hæv, həv, əv/ Ⅰ *vt.* (一般现在时第三人称单数为 has; 现在分词为 having; 过去式和过去分词为 had) ❶有,拥有(在美语中 have got 常代替 have,在否定句、疑问句中常用助动词 do):They ~ (got) a car. 他们有一辆汽车。/ Have you a Chinese-English dictionary? (= Do you ~ a Chinese-English dictionary?) 你有汉英词典吗? / She has many enemies. 她有很多敌人。/ I ~ only one sister. 我只有一个妹妹。/ The house has four rooms. 这房子有四个房间。❷进行;从事:~ a look (rest, match, swim, test, try, walk) 看一看(休息一会儿,举行一场比赛,游泳,进行测验,试一试,散散步):Let me ~ a try. 我来试试吧! ❸ 使;让:You'd better ~ your hair cut. 你最好把头发理了。❹经历:Did you ~ a good holiday? 你假日过得愉快吗? ❺吃;饮:~ breakfast 吃早饭/ ~ tea 喝茶/ What shall we ~ for breakfast? 我们早餐吃什么? ❻举行:When shall we ~ the meeting? 我们什么时候开会? ❼遭受:Do you often ~ colds? 你时常感冒吗? ❽必须;不得不(与不定式连用):I ~ to go now. 现在我得走了。/ The children don't ~ to go to school on weekends. 孩子们周末不必去上学。Ⅱ *aux. v.* 曾经;已经(加过去分词构成完成时态):I ~ seen the film before. 我以前看过这部电影。

hawk /hɔːk/ *n.* [C]鹰

hay /heɪ/ *n.* [U] 干草:a pile of ~ 一堆干草/ Make ~ while the sun shines. (谚语)晒草要趁太阳好。(做事要抓紧时机。)

hazard /ˈhæzəd/ *n.* [C]危险;冒险:The policeman put his life in ~ to help the drawn child. 警察冒着生命危险去救溺水儿童。

hazardous /ˈhæzədəs/ *adj.* 危险的;冒险的;危害的:~ chemicals 危险的化学品/~ road conditions 险象环生的路况

he /hiː, hɪ/ *pron.* 他(主格)

head /hed/ Ⅰ *n.* [C] ❶头;头部:My ~ aches. 我头痛。/ His ~ swims. 他头晕。/ **keep one's** ~ 保持镇静:Whatever happens, you should keep your ~. 无论出现什么情况,你都应该保持镇静。❷首脑;领头人:the family ~ of each household 户主/ a college (university) ~ 学院院长(大学校长) / a department ~ 部门主任/ the ~ of a factory 厂长 / the ~ waiter 领班 / the ~ of a school 校长 ❸(河流的)源头:~ of a lake 湖的源头 ❹上部;上方:the ~ of the page 该页的上方 Ⅱ *v.* ❶为……之首;率领:John's name ~ed the list. 约翰名列榜首。❷向……方向行进 /~ **for** 向……前进:They are ~ing straight for home. 他们径直向家走去。

headache /ˈhedeɪk/ *n.* [C]头痛;令人头痛的人(或事):The old lady constantly suffers from ~s. 老太太经常头痛。

headgear /ˈhedˌɡɪə(r)/ *n.* [U]头盔;安全帽

heading /ˈhedɪŋ/ *n.* [C]标题;题名:The ~ of the passage is in large letters. 这段文章的标题用的是大写字母。

headlight /ˈhedˌlait/ *n.* [C](汽车、火车头等的)前灯,头灯

headline /ˈhedlaɪn/ *n.* [C](*pl.*)新闻提要:Have you listened to today's ~s? 你听了今天的重要新闻吗? / Our manager is busy. He only has time to read the ~s. 我们经理很忙,只有时间读读新闻提要。

headmaster /ˌhedˈmɑːstə(r)/ *n.* [C](中小学校长)校长:Jack's father is a ~. 杰克的父亲是校长。

headmistress /ˌhedˈmɪstrəs/ *n.* [C]女校长

head-on /ˌhedˈɒn/ *adj.* ❶迎面的,正面的:a ~ collision 迎面相撞 ❷面对面的;直接的:a ~ attack on the government's new policies 正面攻击政府的新政策/a ~ confrontation 正面冲突

headphone /ˈhedˌfəun/ *n.* [C](常用 *pl.*)头戴式受话器(或听筒),耳机

headquarters /ˌhedˈkwɔːtəz/ *n.*(单数复

数同形)司令部;指挥部;总部:They set up their ~ at Tianjin. 他们在天津建立了总部。

headstrong /ˈhedˌstrɒŋ/ *adj*. 固执的,顽固的;一意孤行的:a ~ parliament 一意孤行的议会 / He's always so ~ and never takes others's advice. 他总是那么固执,听不得别人的意见。

heal /hiːl/ *v*. (伤口)愈合;痊愈;治愈:An old doctor ~ed her wound. 一位老医生治好了她的伤。

health /helθ/ *n*. [U]健康;健康状况:be in good (poor) ~ 身体好(不好) / be in broken ~ 体弱多病 / be in strong ~ 身体强壮 / be in weak ~ 身体虚弱/ favour one's ~ 恢复健康 / His ~ failed. 他的健康状况不好。/ She enjoys pretty good ~. 她的身体相当不错。

healthy /ˈhelθi/ *adj*. 健康的;健壮的:a ~ way of living 健康的生活方式/ He is a very ~ child. 他是一个很健康的孩子。

heap /hiːp/ *n*. [C]堆;大量;许多:a big ~ of books 一大堆书/ I have ~s of work to do. 我有很多工作要做。

hear /hɪə(r)/ *v*. (heard /hɜːd/, heard) ❶听见:We listened but could ~ nothing. 我们听了,可是什么也听不见。/ I ~ her singing in the next room. 我听见她在隔壁唱歌。❷听说;得知:I ~d that she was ill. 我听说她生病了。/~ **from** 收到信:How often do you ~ from your brother? 你多久能接到你哥哥一封信? ~ **of (about)** 听说,得知:I've never ~d of the girl. 我从未听说过这个女孩。

hearing /ˈhɪərɪŋ/ *n*. [U]听;听力:The blind man has sharp ~. 那盲人听觉灵敏。

heart /hɑːt/ *n*. [C] ❶心;心脏:Her ~ is beating violently. 她的心在剧烈地跳动。❷内心;心肠:She seems very hard, but has a kind ~. 她看起来很严厉,但却心地善良。❸勇气;精神:Don't lose ~ even if we fail the game. 即使输了比赛也不要丧失勇气。❹中心;实质;要点:Not many people prefer to live in the ~ of a city now. 现在不是许多人都愿意住在市中心。/ You'd better get to the ~ of the problem first. 你最好先谈谈问题的实质吧。/**at** ~ 在内心;在感情深处:He was sad at ~. 他很悲伤。**get (learn, know) sth. by** ~ 背出;记住:You should get the poem by ~. 你应背诵这首诗。**take** ~ 有信心;振作精神:He had taken fresh ~ at the little glimpse of hope. 他看到一线希望后重新振作了起来。

heartbeat /ˈhɑːtˌbiːt/ *n*. [C]心跳(声);心搏

heartbreak /ˈhɑːtˌbreɪk/ *n*. [U]心碎,伤心

heartbreaking /ˈhɑːtˌbreɪkɪŋ/ *adj*. 令人心碎的,让人悲痛欲绝的:a ~ news report 一则令人心碎的新闻报道 / a ~ loss 惨痛的损失

hearten /ˈhɑːtən/ *vt*. (常用被动语态)激励,鼓舞;使振作:We're all ~ed by the news. 这消息让我们大家感到振奋。/ His courage ~ed others. 他的勇气为其他人壮了胆。派 heartening *adj*.

heartless /ˈhɑːtlɪs/ *adj*. 无情的,狠心的,残忍的:a cold, ~ attitude 冷酷无情的态度 / How can you be so ~ to her? 你对她怎么能如此无情? 派 heartlessly *adv*. ;heartlessness *n*.

hearty /ˈhɑːti/ *adj*. ❶衷心的;热忱的:I'll give my ~ support to your proposal. 我会衷心支持你的提议。❷(饭菜)丰盛

的：a ~ meal 丰盛的一餐

heat /hiːt/ Ⅰ *v.* 使……热；变热：Water ~s slowly in winter. 冬天水热得慢。/ Please ~ up the cold soup. 请把冷汤热一热。Ⅱ *n.* [U]热；热度；热烈：body ~ 体温/ ~ energy 热能/ He felt the ~ of the fire on his face. 他感到脸上被火烤得热乎乎的。/ The students are discussing the problem with ~. 学生们正在热烈地讨论问题。

H

heated /ˈhiːtɪd/ *adj.* 激动的；愤怒的；(讨论等)热烈的；激烈的：a ~ discussion 一场热烈的讨论 / Why do you always get so ~ about politics? 你为什么一谈到政治总是那么激动？

heater /ˈhiːtə(r)/ *n.* [C]加热器，加热装置；发热器：an infrared ~ 红外线加热器 / the water ~ 热水器

heating /ˈhiːtɪŋ/ *n.* [U]供暖系统；暖气设备：central ~ 中央供暖设备

heatstroke /ˈhiːtˌstrəʊk/ *n.* [U]中暑

heave /hiːv/ Ⅰ *v.* (heaved 或 hove /həʊv/) ❶(用力)拉，提；举起：She ~d the pack up onto her back. 她用力背起背包。❷(使劲)投掷；抛出：His wife picked up a bulky dictionary and ~d it at him. 他妻子拿起一本厚词典，朝他掷过去。❸(使)起伏；(使)隆起：The wind ~s the waves. 风使水浪起伏。Ⅱ *n.* [C]拉，拖，拽；举：with a mighty ~ 使劲一拉/I gave the door a good ~. 我用力推了一下门。

heaven /ˈhevn/ *n.* ❶天堂，天国；天空：go to ~ 死去；上天堂 ❷上帝：Thank Heaven! 谢天谢地！/ Heaven knows! 天知道！/ Good Heavens! 天哪！/ It was the will of Heaven. 这是天意。

heavily /ˈhevɪli/ *adv.* 沉重地：The crime lies ~ on his conscience. 他的罪行使他良心极为不安。

heavy /ˈhevi/ *adj.* ❶重的；难以举起(携带、搬动)的：This suitcase is too ~ for me to carry. 这箱子太重，我提不动。❷超出一般大小(重量、力量)的：the ~ rain 大雨/ ~ work 繁重的工作/ a ~ blow 重击/ ~ heart 沉重的心情/ ~ food 难以消化的食物/ a ~ drinker (smoker) 酒鬼 (烟鬼)/ ~ traffic 流量大的交通

hectare /ˈhekteə(r)/ *n.* [C]公顷(略为 ha.)

hedge /hedʒ/ Ⅰ *n.* [C] ❶(灌木)树篱 ❷保护(手段)；防御(手段)：They bought gold as a ~ against inflation. 他们购买黄金作为抵御通货膨胀的手段。Ⅱ *v.* ❶用树篱围住(或隔开)：~ (in) a field 用树篱把场地围起来 ❷围住；设障碍于，阻碍：We've got the permission, but it's ~d in by many conditions. 我们获得了许可，但受到许多条件的限制。

hedgehog /ˈhedʒˌhɒg/ *n.* [C]刺猬

heed /hiːd/ Ⅰ *vt.* 留心；注意：~ sb.'s warning 理会某人的警告 / Heed what I say next. 留心我下面要说的话。Ⅱ *n.* [U]注意；留心：pay (give) no ~ to sb. (sth.) 不把某人(某事)当回事儿 / He took no ~ of other people while working. 他在工作时不去理会别人。派 heedful *adj.*

heel /hiːl/ *n.* [C]脚后跟；(鞋、袜等的)后跟：There is a hole in the ~ of his shoe. 他的鞋后跟上有一个洞。/**at sb.'s ~s** 紧跟在后面：The dog was snapping at his master's ~s. 狗紧紧跟在主人的后面。

height /haɪt/ *n.* ❶高度；身高：What's your ~? 你身高多少？/ He is six feet in ~. 他有六英尺高。❷(*pl.*)高地;高处:We stood on the ~s overlooking the valley. 我们站在高处俯瞰整个山谷。❸顶点;最高点:He retired at the ~ of his career. 他在事业的巅峰时退休了。

heighten /ˈhaɪt(ə)n/ *v.* ❶增强,加强;加剧:use lemon to ~ the flavour 用柠檬增味/~ the tension between the two countries 加剧两国间的紧张关系 ❷变强;变大:As she waited, her fears ~ed. 她越等就越感到恐惧。

heir /eə(r)/ *n.* [C]继承人;嗣子:He is the right ~ of the family. 他是这个家族的合法继承人。

heiress /ˈeərəs/ *n.* [C]女继承人

helicopter /ˈhelɪkɒptə(r)/ *n.* [C]直升机:Her uncle can fly a ~. 她的叔叔会驾驶直升机。

helix /ˈhiːlɪks/ *n.* [C](*pl.* helices 或 helixes)螺旋结构;螺旋形(物体)

hell /hel/ *n.* 地狱

hello /həˈləʊ/ *int.* (引起人注意或问候)喂!

helm /helm/ *n.* [C]舵;舵柄;舵轮:**at the ~** 掌权,处于领导地位:The present chairman has been at the ~ for 15 years. 现任总裁已掌权15年了。

helmet /ˈhelmɪt/ *n.* [C]头盔;钢盔:a safe ~ 安全帽/ a gas ~ 防毒面具

help /help/ Ⅰ *vt.* 帮助;援助;资助:This book will ~ you (to) improve your English. 这本书能帮助你提高英语水平。/ I can ~ you with your lessons. 我可以帮助你温习功课。/ My brother ~ed me through the university. 我哥哥资助我读完大学。/ **~ oneself to sth.** 自取;擅自取用:Please ~ yourself to the fruit. 请吃水果。/ Sometimes he ~s himself to my dictionary. 有时他擅自使用我的字典。**~ sb. with sth.** 帮助某人做某事:May I ~you with your luggage? 我帮你拿行李好吗? **can (could) not ~ doing sth.** 禁不住(忍不住)做某事:I couldn't ~ laughing when I heard such a story. 听到这个故事,我不禁大笑起来。Ⅱ *n.* 帮助;助手,帮手:Thank you for your ~. 谢谢你的帮助。/ The ~ hasn't come this morning. 助手今早还没来。/ With the ~ of the teacher, I've made great progress. 在老师的帮助下,我取得了很大的进步。

helpful /ˈhelpfəl/ *adj.* 有帮助的,有用的,有益的:a ~ person 帮手 / It is ~ of you to do that. 你那样做,真是太肯帮忙了。派 helpfully *adv.*;helpfulness *n.*

helpless /ˈhelplɪs/ *adj.* ❶不能自立的;无依无靠的;孤弱的:a ~ newborn baby 没有自理能力的新生儿 / a young ~ immigrant girl 一个举目无亲的移民姑娘 ❷无助的;无保护的:Without proper defences we'd be ~ against an enemy attack. 没有足够的防御,我们就不能抵御敌人的进攻。❸没有力量的;没有能力的:The kid was ~ with crying. 那小孩哭得全身无力。派 helplessly *adv.*;helplessness *n.*

hem /hem/ Ⅰ *vt.* (hemmed; hemming) ❶给……缝边;给……镶边:The skirt is ~med with golden fringe. 这条裙子镶上了金色滚边。❷包围,围绕:a yard ~med about by fences 用铁栅栏围起来的院子/~ the enemy troops in 将敌军包围起来 Ⅱ *n.* [C](衣服等的)褶边,贴边

hemisphere /ˈhemɪsfɪə(r)/ *n.* [C]半球:Asia is in the Northern Hemisphere. 亚洲位于北半球。

hen /hen/ *n.* [C]母鸡:Hens lay eggs.

母鸡生蛋。

hence / hens / *adv.* 因此,所以;今后:He said that he would be in London a month ~. 他说一个月后他会在伦敦。/ It is raining hard. Hence, I have to stay. 正在下大雨。因此,我不得不留下来。

henceforth / ˌhensˈfɔːθ, ˈhensfɔːθ / *adv.* 从今以后,从此以后:Henceforth, parties which fail to get 50% of the vote will not be represented in parliament. 从此,得票率不超过50%的党派在国会中不再有议席。

her / hɜː(r), hə(r) / *pron.* 她(she 的宾格);她的(形容词性物主代词)

herald / ˈherəld/ Ⅰ *n.* [C] ❶传令官;掌礼官 ❷先驱者;预报者;先兆:the ~ of a new age 新时代的前奏 / The swallows are ~s of spring. 燕子预示着春天的来临。Ⅱ *vt.* 预告,预示着……的来临:The singing of birds ~ (in) the day. 鸟儿的歌唱预示着一天的到来。

herb / hɜːb / *n.* [C]草本植物;药草:Chinese medical ~s 中草药

herbal / ˈhɜːbəl/ *adj.* (只作定语) ❶草本植物的 ❷药草的;用药草制的:~ medicine 草药

herd / hɜːd / *n.* [C]兽群:a ~ of elephants 一群大象

here / hɪə(r) / *adv.* 在这里;向这里:Come ~! 到这里来! Look ~! 看这里。/ Here comes the bus! 车来了。/ Here he comes. 他来了。/ Here you are. 这是你要的东西。/ ~ **and there** 到处:You can see new buildings ~ and there in this city. 在这座城市里,你四处可见新的楼房。

hereabout(s) / ˌhɪərəˈbaʊt(s) / *adv.* 在这一带,在附近:There is a post office somewhere ~. 这附近有个邮局。

hereby / hɪəˈbaɪ, ˈhɪəˌbaɪ / *adv.* (用于公文、布告等)以此方式,特此;兹:He is ~ licensed to drive motor vehicles of groups A and E. 他将有资格驾驶 A 照和 E 照的机动车辆,特发此证。/I ~ resign. 我特此请辞。

heritage / ˈherɪtɪdʒ / *n.* [C]遗产;继承物;传统:cultural ~ 文化遗产 / historical ~ 历史遗产 / We should preserve our national ~s well. 我们应当保护好我们的民族遗产。

hero / ˈhɪərəʊ / *n.* [C](*pl.* heroes) ❶英雄:He was an unknown ~. 他是一位无名英雄。❷男主人公:He is the ~ of the film. 他是这部电影的男主角。

heroic / həˈrəʊɪk / *adj.* 英勇的;英雄的:~ deeds 英雄行为 / ~ poems 英雄史诗

heroin / ˈherəʊɪn / *n.* [U]海洛因

heroine / ˈherəʊɪn / *n.* [C]女英雄;女主角

hers / hɜːz / *pron.* 她的(名词性物主代词):It's my pen; ~ is on the desk. 这是我的钢笔,她的在桌上。

herself / hɜːˈself / *pron.* 她自己(反身代词):She hurt ~. 她伤了自己。/ She ~ told me about the news. 她亲自把这个消息告诉了我。/ I saw Mary ~. 我看见玛丽本人。/ Can she do it by ~? 她自己能做吗?

hesitate / ˈhezɪteɪt / *vi.* 犹豫;踌躇:He ~d about what to do next. 他对下一步做什么犹豫不定。/ If you ~ too long, you'll miss the opportunity. 如果你老是犹豫不决,你就会错失良机。

hesitation / ˌhezɪˈteɪʃn / *n.* 犹豫;踌躇:He went to the front without any ~. 他毫不犹豫地走上前线。/ She had no ~

in making the decision. 她毫不迟疑地下了那个决定。

hey /heɪ/ *int*. (引起注意或表示惊讶)嘿!喂!

hibernate /ˈhaɪbəneɪt/ *vi*. (动物)冬眠:Snakes ~ in winter. 蛇在冬季冬眠。

hibernation /ˌhaɪbəˈneɪʃn/ *n*. [U]冬眠:Hibernation is a very deep sleep. 冬眠是一种深度的睡眠。

hiccup /ˈhɪkʌp/ *n*. [C]打嗝(声);呃逆:In the middle of the ceremony there was a loud ~ from his son. 在仪式进行中他的儿子打了个响嗝。

hide /haɪd/ *v*. (hid /hɪd/, hidden /ˈhɪdn/或 hid) ❶躲藏;隐藏:Where is he hiding? 他躲在哪里? / You'd better ~. 你最好躲起来。❷隐瞒;遮掩:She hid her face in her hands. 她用手遮住她的脸。/He hid this from his mother. 此事他瞒着他母亲。Ⅱ *n*. [C](观察动物的)隐藏之处

hide-and-seek /ˈhaɪdənˈsiːk/, *n*. [U]捉迷藏(游戏):play (at) ~ 玩捉迷藏游戏

high /haɪ/ Ⅰ *adj*. ❶高的:He is six feet ~. 他身高六英尺。❷高级的;主要的:~ education management 高等教育管理 / ~-priced goods 高档商品 / Last year she studied in a ~ school in America. 去年她在美国一所高中读书。❸高度的;强烈的:~ fidelity (Hi-Fi) music 高保真音乐 / in ~ spirits 高兴;兴高采烈;精神饱满 ❹高尚的;良好的:goods of ~ quality 高质量产品 / He is determined to be a man of ~ character. 他决心做一个品德高尚的人。Ⅱ *adv*. 高;高度地:pay ~ 付高价 /fly ~ (喻)有雄心

highland /ˈhaɪlənd/ Ⅰ *n*. [C](*pl*.)高地,高原;高原地区,丘陵地带 Ⅱ *adj*. (只作定语)高地的,高原的;高原地区的,丘陵地带的:~ sheep 高原绵羊 / the ~ landscape 高原地区的风景

highlight /ˈhaɪlaɪt/ *n*. [C]最精彩部分(场面):He went out for a while and missed the ~ of the competition. 他出去了一会儿,没有看到比赛最精彩的场面。

highly /ˈhaɪli/ *adv*. 高;高度地;高尚地;很,非常:They spoke ~ of him. 他们高度赞扬他。/ This is a ~ amusing film. 这是一部非常有趣的影片。

highway /ˈhaɪweɪ/ *n*. [C]公路;大路:Highways are built in the city. 这座城市正在修建许多公路。/ They met with an accident at 312 national ~. 他们在 312 国道上出了车祸。/ It is a ~ to fortune for peasants. 这是农民的一条致富之路。

hijack /ˈhaɪdʒæk/ *vt*. 劫持;劫机:~ a plane 劫持飞机

hike /haɪk/ *vi*. & *n*. [C]远足;徒步旅行:They decided to ~ to the country. 他们决定步行去乡下。派 hiker *n*.

hill /hɪl/ *n*. [C]丘陵,小山;斜坡;土堆:The sun was rising over the ~. 太阳正从山冈上升起。/ They arrived at the top of a ~ half an hour later,半小时后他们到达山顶。

hillside /ˈhɪlsaɪd/ *n*. [C](小山)山腰;山坡:There is a temple on the ~. 山腰上有一座寺庙。/ The child couldn't climb the steep ~. 小孩爬不上那个陡坡。

him /hɪm/ *pron*. 他(he 的宾格):I saw ~ yesterday. 我昨天看见他了。

himself /hɪmˈself/ *pron*. 他自己(反身代词):He cut ~. 他割伤了自己。/ He will go there by ~. 他亲自去那里。

hind /haɪnd/ *adj.* 在后的,后面的:the ~ legs of a horse 马的后腿/ the ~ wheels of a car 汽车的后轮

hinder /ˈhɪndə(r)/ *vt.* 妨碍;阻碍;阻止:Don't let me ~ you from going. 不要因为我而妨碍你去。/ Don't ~ him in his study. 不要妨碍他学习。/ She was ~ed by the heavy traffic. 拥挤的交通耽误了她的时间。

hint /hɪnt/ *n.* [C]提示;暗示:a broad ~ 明白的暗示/ a gentle ~ 委婉的暗示/ helpful (good) ~s 有益的提示/ ~s about letter-writing 写信须知/ ~s for beginners 初学者须知

hip /hɪp/ *n.* [C]臀部;髋

hire /ˈhaɪə(r)/ Ⅰ *vt.* 雇用;租:The girls are never ~d to do servant's work. 这些姑娘从不受雇去做服务员的工作。Ⅱ *n.* [U]租用;雇用;租金,工钱:Are there any bicycles for ~? 有供出租的自行车吗?/ He has horses on ~. 他有马匹出租。

his /hɪz/ *pron.* ❶他的(形容词性物主代词):His pen is on the desk. 他的笔放在桌上。❷ 他的东西(名词性物主代词):That book is ~, not yours. 那本书是他的,不是你的。

hiss /hɪs/ Ⅰ *vi.* ❶(蛇、鹅、沸水等)发出嘶嘶声:The snake raised its head and ~ed. 那条蛇昂起头,嘴里发出嘶嘶声。/ The water ~ed against the burning coal. 水洒在烧红的煤炭上嘶嘶直响。❷发出嘘声(以表示反对、鄙视、嘲笑等):Don't ~ at the speaker. 不要对发言者发嘘声。Ⅱ *n.* [C] ❶嘶嘶声:the ~ of rain in the pools 雨打池水的沙沙声 ❷(表示反对、鄙视、嘲笑等发出的)嘘声:She silenced him with a ~. 她朝他嘘了一声,使他不吱声。

historic /hɪˈstɒrɪk/ *adj.* 历史上著名的:a ~ spot (speech) 历史上著名的地点(演说)/ a ~ city of art and culture 文化艺术名城/ a ~ event 有历史意义的事件

historical /hɪˈstɒrɪkl/ *adj.* 历史上的;有关历史的:~ facts 历史事实/ ~ documents 历史文件/ ~ novels 历史小说/ a ~ play (film, painting) 历史题材的戏剧(影片、绘画)/ ~ events 历史事件/ ~ people 历史人物/~ studies 历史研究

history /ˈhɪst(ə)ri/ *n.* [U]历史学;历史:ancient ~ 古代史/contemporary ~ 现代史/world ~ 世界史/the science of ~ 史学/ People make their own ~. 人民创造自己的历史。

hit /hɪt/ *v.* (hit,hit) ❶击;打;碰;撞:I ~ my head against the wall. 我的头碰到了墙。/ The stone ~ the window. 石头击中了窗户。/ Mother ~ the child on the head. 母亲打孩子的头部。❷伤害……的感情;使受到打击:He was heavily ~ by his financial losses. 他因财产损失受到重大打击。

hitch[1] /hɪtʃ/ Ⅰ *vt.* ❶(用环、绳等)捆,系;拴;套:~ the horse to the post 把马拴到柱子上 ❷急拉,猛拽;(猛地)移动:~ up one's trouser legs 挽起裤管/He ~ed the pillow to a comfortable position. 他把枕头移到舒适的位置。Ⅱ *n.* [C] ❶捆,系;拴;套 ❷(向上的)急拉,猛拽;(猛的)移动:He gave his belt a ~. 他把皮带向上拉了一下。❸(临时)故障;突然停止;障碍:a ~ in the conversation 谈话中出现的小小问题

hitch[2] /hɪtʃ/ *v.* 免费搭乘(便车)旅行:~ a lift 搭便车旅行/They got there by ~ing. 他们是搭便车到那里的。

hitchhike /ˈhɪtʃhaɪk/ *v.* (免费)搭便车:The two students ~d from Beijing to Tianjin. 两个学生从北京搭便车到天津。派 hitchhiker *n.*

hitherto /ˌhɪðəˈtuː/ *adv.* 迄今,至今:No one ~ in this family had made any special mark. 这一家族至今还没有一个人有过什么特别大的名气。

hive /haɪv/ *n.* [C](木、草等制成的)蜂房;蜂箱

hoarse /hɔːs/ *adj.* (声音)嘶哑的:She had a ~ voice because she caught cold. 由于着凉她声音嘶哑。

hobble /ˈhɒbl/ *vi.* 跛行;蹒跚:He ~d along on crutches. 他拄着拐杖一瘸一拐地走路。/The old man was hobbling around with a stick. 老人正拄着手杖蹒跚而行。

hobby /ˈhɒbi/ *n.* [C]业余爱好:My ~ is collecting stamps. 我的业余爱好是集邮。

hockey /ˈhɒki/ *n.* [U]曲棍球:play ~ 打曲棍球

hoe /həʊ/ *n.* [C]锄头

hold /həʊld/ Ⅰ *vt.* (held/held/, held) ❶抓住;握住;拿住:She held her father's hands tightly. 她紧紧地抓住父亲的双手。/ The young woman held a little boy in her arms. 那年轻妇女怀里抱着一个小男孩。❷拥有;持有:Our manager ~s 50% share in the company. 我们经理在公司拥有 50%的股份。❸举行;主持:They'll ~ a poll to know the opinions of the masses. 他们将举行一次民意调查来了解群众的意见。/ When shall we ~ the meeting? 我们什么时候开会? / The Olympic Games was held in Beijing in 2008. 奥运会2008 年在北京举行。❹托住;支持:The roof was held up by four big pillars. 屋顶由四根大柱子支撑。❺容纳;装得下:The hall ~s 300 people at least. 这大厅至少容纳 300 人。/ Will this box ~ all your things? 这箱子装得下你所有的东西吗? Ⅱ *vi.* ❶持续;保持;坚持:How long will the fine weather ~? 好天气会持续多久? ❷有效;适用:The headmaster said that the rule would ~ in all cases. 校长说这条规定在任何情况下都有效。Ⅲ *n.* ❶抓住;握住:Please take a firm ~ of my hand. 请抓紧我的手。❷控制;掌握:Our monitor has got a good ~ of the subjects he is learning. 我们班长对所学学科都掌握得很好。/~ **back** 走开;退缩:No difficulty can ~ us back. 任何困难都不能阻挡我们前进。~ **off** 延期;迟滞:She held off from answering directly. 她迟迟不作直接回答。~ **out** 坚持,维持;伸出;提出:Hold out the hand of friendship. 伸出友谊之手。/ You should ~ out for a higher price. 你应坚持要更高的价格。~ **over** 延期(决定):The matter was held over until the next meeting. 此事拖延到下次会议解决。~ **together** 结合在一起:This old coat hardly ~s together now. 这件旧上衣几乎没连在一起了。~ **up** 举起;支持;停顿;延期:John held up his hand. 约翰举起手来。/ The government decided to ~ up the prices of farm produce. 政府决定维持农产品价格。/ They held up at the gate. 他们在大门口停了下来。

hold-up /ˈhəʊldˌʌp/ *n.* [C] ❶持枪抢劫 ❷延搁,耽搁,延迟:a ~ in the construction of the bridge 桥梁建设的耽搁

hole /həʊl/ *n.* [C] 洞;孔;坑:drill ~s

钻洞/ fill up a ~ 填洞/ There is a ~ in the tooth. 牙齿上有个洞。

holiday /ˈhɒlədeɪ/ *n.* [C]假日;节日:Our school had a half-day ~. 我们学校放了半天假。/ I plan to spend the summer ~s here. 我计划在这儿度暑假。/ Tom always takes a job in his ~s. 汤姆总是在他的假期里干零活。

hollow /ˈhɒləʊ/ *adj.* ❶空的;中空的:a ~ tree 空心树 ❷空洞的;空虚的;虚假的:What he said were only ~ words. 他说的只不过是些假话。

holly /ˈhɒli/ *n.* [U]冬青树

holy /ˈhəʊli/ *adj.* 神圣的;圣洁的;虔诚的

home /həʊm/ Ⅰ *n.* 家;家庭;家乡:He left ~ at the age of 13 他 13 岁离开家。/ They have a comfortable little ~. 他们有一个舒适的小家庭。/ **at** ~ 在家;在国内:She had to stay at ~ to care for her daughter. 她不得不待在家里照顾女儿。/ The next match will be held at ~. 下次比赛将在国内举行。**be (feel, make) oneself at** ~ 无拘束:Make yourself at ~. 请别拘束。Ⅱ *adv.* 在家,到家;在国内,到国内:I saw him on my way ~. 我在回家的路上看见了他。/ Her mother isn't ~ yet. 她的母亲还没回到家里。

homeland /ˈhəʊmˌlænd/ *n.* [C] ❶祖国;故乡 ❷(一个种族的)定居点,聚居地;家园

homeless /ˈhəʊmlɪs/ Ⅰ *adj.* 无家可归的;居无定所的:a ~ tramp 一位无家可归的流浪汉 Ⅱ *n.* 无家可归者,流浪者

homemade /ˈhəʊmˈmeɪd/ *adj.* ❶家里做的;自制的:~ bread 家制面包 / ~ apparatus 自制的设备 ❷本国制造的,国产的:a ~ car 国产车

homesick /ˈhəʊmˌsɪk/ *adj.* 想家的,思乡的;患思乡病的:write ~ letters 写信诉说思乡之情 / She is ~ for England. 她思念故乡英格兰。派 homesickness *n.*

homework /ˈhəʊmˌwɜːk/ *n.* [U] ❶(学生的)家庭作业,课外作业 ❷(会议、讨论等的)准备工作:He has done his ~ on the subject. 他已经就这个题目做了准备。

homogeneous /ˌhəʊməˈdʒiːnɪəs/ *adj.* ❶同种类的;同性质的;有相同特征的:~ cell population 同源细胞群体 ❷均匀的;均一的:a ~ distribution 均匀分布/ ~ light 单色光

honest /ˈɒnɪst/ *adj.* 诚实的;忠实的;坦白的:He has an ~ face. 他有一副诚实的面孔。/ I shall be quite ~ with you. 我会对你很坦白。/ To be ~, he is a good boy. 老实说,他确实是一个好孩子。派 honestly *adv.*

honesty /ˈɒnəsti/ *n.* [U] 老实,诚实;正直:Honesty is the best policy. 诚实才是上策。

honey /ˈhʌni/ *n.* [U] 蜂蜜;甜蜜:have ~ on one's lips and murder in one's heart 口蜜腹剑

honeymoon /ˈhʌnɪˌmuːn/ Ⅰ *n.* [C] ❶蜜月,蜜月假期;新婚旅行:go on (for) a ~蜜月旅行 ❷(新关系确立后出现的)和谐期 Ⅱ *vi.* 度蜜月:They ~ed in Europe last year. 去年他们去欧洲度蜜月了。

hono(u)r /ˈɒnə(r)/ *n.* [U] 光荣;荣幸;荣誉:I had the ~ of attending her evening party. 我有幸参加她的晚会。/**do ~ to sb.** 向某人表示敬意;给某人带来光荣:His contributions to science did ~ to our country. 他在科学上的贡献为我们国家增了光。/ Will you do me the ~ of dining with me this evening? 今晚你肯赏光与我共进晚餐吗? **in ~ of**, **in sb.'s(sth.'s)**~庆祝;纪念:We are planning a big birthday party in your ~. 我们正筹划为你举行一场盛大的生日晚会。

hono(u)rable /ˈɒnərəbl/ *adj.* 光荣的;尊敬的;高尚的:an ~ duty 荣誉职位/~ conduct 高尚行为 / The hospital gave the nurse an ~ task. 医院给了护士一个光荣的任务。

hoof /huːf/ *n.* [C](*pl.* hoofs 或 hooves)蹄;马蹄

hook /hʊk/ Ⅰ *n.* [C]钩;钩状物:Look! The fish has got ~ed. 看! 鱼上钩了。Ⅱ *vt.* 钩;钩住;引诱……上钩:The boy was glad that he ~ed a fish. 钓到一条鱼,小孩非常高兴。

hoop /huːp/ *n.* [C]箍;箍状物;篮圈:Hula ~ 呼啦圈

hooray /hʊˈreɪ/ *int.* (=hurrah)好哇!

hop /hɒp/ *v.* (hopped; hopping)单足跳;跳过;跳跃:He got hurt in the left leg and had to ~ along. 他的左腿受了伤,只得单脚跳着走。/ ~ **on** (**onto**) (口语)上车:He ~ped on a red car. 他跳上一辆红色小车。

hope /həʊp/ Ⅰ *v.* 希望;期望:I ~ to see you soon. 我希望很快见到你。/ Will it be fine tomorrow? I ~ so. 明天会晴吗?我希望会。/ It is ~d that he will come on time. 希望他能准时来。/ The teacher ~d that the students would learn English well. 老师希望学生们把英语学好。Ⅱ *n.* ❶希望;信心:There is a ray of ~. 有一线希望。/ He was disappointed in all ~s. 他完全失望了。/ We have a ~ of success. 我们有成功的希望。/ She has lost all ~s of victory. 她已失去取胜的信心。/ **past** (**beyond**) ~(成功、痊愈等)无望;不可救药:His little son seems past ~. 他的小儿子似乎是无救了。❷被寄托希望的人(或事):He was the ~ of the school. 他是学校的希望。/ You are my last ~. 你是我最后能指望的人。

hopeful /ˈhəʊpfəl/ *adj.* ❶(常作表语)抱有希望的;充满期望的;持乐观态度的:We were quite ~ of a successful agreement. 我们对成功签约抱有很大希望。/ He is ~ about getting into college. 他对上大学充满信心。❷给人以希望的,有希望的:a ~ pupil 前途无量的学生 派 hopefulness *n.*

hopeless /ˈhəʊplɪs/ *adj.* ❶不抱希望的,没指望的:a ~ sigh 失望的唉声叹气 ❷令人失望的,让人绝望的:at the ~ moment 在一筹莫展之际 / a ~ case 不治之症 ❸(人)没用的,无能的:She was ~ at tennis. 她怎么也学不会打网球。派 hopelessly *adv.*; hopelessness *n.*

horizon /həˈraɪzn/ *n.* [C]地平线;水平线:The sun was rising over the ~. 太阳从地平线上升起。

horizontal /ˌhɒrɪˈzɒnt(ə)l/ *adj.* ❶水平的,与地平线平行的;横(向)的:~ distance 水平距离 ❷平的,平坦的:~ surface 平坦的表面

hormone /ˈhɔːməʊn/ *n.* [C]激素;荷尔蒙

horn /hɒːn/ *n.* [C]❶(牛、鹿等动物的)角 ❷号角;喇叭:a motor ~ 汽车喇叭

horrible /ˈhɒrəbl/ *adj.* 可怕的;(口语)令人不愉快的;让人讨厌的:the ~ weather 让人讨厌的天气

horror /ˈhɒrə(r)/ *n.* [U]恐怖;极端厌恶:Little girls don't like ~ fiction or films. 小女孩不喜欢读恐怖小说和看恐怖电影。/ The girl has a ~ of spiders. 小女孩怕蜘蛛。

horse /hɔːs/ *n.* [C]马：a herd of ~s 一群马

horseman /ˈhɔːsmən/ *n.* [C](*pl.* horsemen) ❶牧马人；马夫 ❷骑手；马术师 ❸骑马的人

horsepower /ˈhɔːspauə(r)/ *n.* [C]马力

hospitable /ˈhɒspɪtəbl/ *adj.* ❶款待周到的；好客的；殷勤的：The villagers were ~ to every visitor. 乡亲们殷勤接待每一位客人。❷热情的，诚挚的：a ~ smile 热情的微笑 ❸(对新思想等)愿意接受的；思想开明的：He is ~ to new ideas. 他思想开明，愿意接受新观念。

hospital /ˈhɒspɪtl/ *n.* [C]医院：go to ~ 上医院/ enter (go into) (a) ~入院/ leave a ~ 出院/ He is still in ~. 他仍然在住院。/ This is a ~ of Chinese medicine. 这是一所中医医院。

hospitality /ˌhɒspɪˈtæləti/ *n.* [U]好客；殷勤：My sister is known for her ~. 我姐姐以好客著称。

host /həust/ *n.* [C] 主人；节目主持人；东道主：Beijing was the ~ city of the 2008 Olympic Games. 北京是2008年奥运会的主办城市。/ I don't know who is the ~ of the evening party. 我不知道晚会的主持人是谁。

hostage /ˈhɒstɪdʒ/ *n.* [C]人质；抵押品：In this event, five girl students were taken ~. 在这次事件中有五名女学生被扣作人质。/ The authority asked to free the ~s. 地方当局要求释放人质。

hostess /ˈhəustəs/ *n.* [C]女主人；女主持人；女东道主

hostile /ˈhɒstaɪl/ *adj.* 敌意的；敌对的；不友好的：a ~ country 敌国/Don't be ~ to your step mother. She is kind to you. 别对你的继母不友善，她对你很好。

hostility /hɒˈstɪləti/ *n.* ❶[U]敌意；敌视；敌对：arouse sb.'s ~ 激起某人的敌意 / feelings of ~ 敌对情绪 ❷[C]敌对行为；战争：Hostilities broke out between the two nations. 两国间爆发了战争。❸[U](对思想、计划等的)反对，抵制：The reform programme was greeted with much ~. 改革计划遭到了众人的反对。

hot /hɒt/ Ⅰ *adj.* (hotter, hottest)❶热的：a ~ well 温泉/ a ~ dog 热狗；红肠面包 / set up a ~ line 建立热线 / The weather here is not too ~ in summer. 这儿夏天不太热。/ You'd better have a ~ bath after running. 跑步后你最好洗个热水澡。❷辣的；刺激的：Most Sichuan people like ~ pepper very much. 多数四川人都非常喜欢吃辣椒。❸热衷的；热切的；热情的：The old professor is ~ on the research of archaeology. 老教授热衷于考古学的研究。❹激动的；急躁的：The doctors had a ~ debate on the special case. 大夫们就这个特殊的病例进行了激烈的争论。/ The young man has a ~ temper. 这年轻人性情急躁。Ⅱ *vt.* (hotted; hotting)变热；加温：Please ~ the rice up. 请把米饭加热一下。

hotbed /ˈhɒtˌbed/ *n.* [C] ❶(培育植物的)温床 ❷温床，(尤指坏事的)滋生地：a ~ of crime 滋生犯罪的温床

hotel /həuˈtel/ *n.* [C]旅馆：operate (run) a ~ 经营旅馆/ put up (stay) at a ~ 住旅馆/ They check out of the ~ at 10 o'clock. 十点钟他们结账离开了那家旅馆。

hothouse /ˈhɒtˌhaus/ Ⅰ *n.* [C]温室，暖房

Ⅱ*adj*.（只作定语）❶温室的；温室中生长的：~ tomatoes 生长于温室中的西红柿 ❷温室般的；过分保护的：a spoiled, ~child 一个被溺爱且备受呵护的孩子

hour /ˈaʊə(r)/ *n*. [C] ❶小时；钟头：two ~s' journey 两小时的旅行/ for an ~ or so 大约一小时/ in an ~ or two 过一两个小时/ a couple of ~s 两三个小时/ every ~ or two 每隔一两个小时 / Clocks call out the ~. 时钟报时。❷时刻；时间：office ~s 办公时间/ play ~s 娱乐时间/ rush (peak) ~s 交通高峰时间/ business ~s 营业时间/ the closing ~ 下班时间/ keep good ~s 按时作息/ We should keep early ~s . 我们应当早睡早起。

hourly /ˈaʊəli/ *adj*. ❶每小时(一次)的：an ~ news broadcasts 每小时一次的新闻广播 ❷按钟点计算的，以小时计算的：~ wages 计时工资

house /haʊs/ *n*. [C] ❶房屋；住宅：a hen ~ 鸡舍/ a cow ~ 牛栏/ a store ~ 仓库/ a bake ~ 面包厂/ I have bought a new ~. 我买了一幢新房子。❷议会；议会大楼：the House of Commons 下议院/ the House of Lords 上议院/ Lower House 下议院，众议院

household /ˈhaʊshəʊld/ Ⅰ*n*. [C]家庭；户；全家人：My father is head of my ~. 我父亲是我家的户主。Ⅱ*adj*. 家庭的；家常的；普通的：~ articles 家庭用品/ ~ expenses 家庭开支 / ~ duties 家务

housewife /ˈhaʊswaɪf/ *n*.[C]家庭主妇

housework /ˈhaʊswɜːk/ *n*. [C]家务事

housing /ˈhaʊzɪŋ/ *n*. [U]住房建设；(总称)房屋；住房：~ loan 住宅贷款 / ~ reform 住房改革 /Our ~ condition has been greatly improved. 我们的居住条件已得到极大的改善。

hover /ˈhɒvə(r)/ *vi*. (鸟、飞机等)盘旋：A hawk is ~ing over. 一只鹰在高空中盘旋。

how /haʊ/ *adv*. ❶怎样；如何：Please tell me ~ to spell the word. 告诉我怎样拼这个词。/ How are you? 你好吗？/ How do you do? 你好！/ How about going for a walk? 去散散步怎么样？❷多么；何等：How nice the picture is! 这幅画真美！

however /haʊˈevə(r)/ Ⅰ*conj*. 然而；可是：His wife asked him not to go out hunt-ing, ~, he insisted on going. 他妻子劝他别去打猎，然而他坚持要去。Ⅱ*adv*. 无论如何：He will never succeed ~ hard he tries. 无论如何努力，他也不会成功。

howl /haʊl/ *vi*. ❶(狼等)凄厉地长嚎，嗥叫；(狗)狂吠：The coyote was ~ing at the moon. 一只山狗对月狂叫。❷(因疼痛、悲伤等而)号哭；哀号；(因愤怒而)吼叫，咆哮，怒吼：She ~ed as the dentist began to pull the bad tooth. 牙科医生开始拔那颗蛀牙时，她直嚷嚷。❸(风等)呼啸，怒号：I lay in bed, lis-tening to the wind ~ing. 我躺在床上，听着风的呼啸声。

huddle /ˈhʌdl/ *vi*. ❶(因寒冷、恐惧等)挤成一团；聚集成群：~ together for warmth 挤在一起取暖 ❷(悄悄地)碰头；(秘密)开会：The leaders ~d to dis-cuss the matter. 首脑们暗中碰头讨论此事。

hue /hjuː/ *n*. [C] ❶色泽；色调；色度：a warm ~暖色调 ❷颜色，色彩：all the ~ of the rainbow 彩虹的七彩颜色
派 hued *adj*.

hug /hʌg/ *vt*. (hugged; hugging) 紧抱；搂抱：The child was ~ging her doll. 那小孩紧紧抱住她的洋娃娃。/ They ~ged each other when they met again.

再次见面,他们相互紧紧拥抱在一起。

huge / hjuːdʒ / *adj*. 巨大的;庞大的:There are many ~ ships on the river. 河上有许多大轮船。/ We have won ~ success. 我们获得了巨大的成功。派 hugely *adv*.

human / ˈhjuːmən / Ⅰ *adj*. 人的;人类的:a ~ being 人/ the ~ nature 人性/ ~ affairs 人事/ ~ race 人类 / ~ rights 人权/ She is not willing to talk about the ~ relationship in her company. 她不愿谈论她公司里的人际关系问题。Ⅱ *n*. [C](=human being)人

H

humane / hjuːˈmeɪn / *adj*. ❶仁慈的;仁爱的;人道的;富有同情心的:be ~ in the treatment of the prisoners 人道地对待囚犯/a more ~ world 一个更仁爱的世界 ❷人文(学科)的:~ studies(learning) 人文科学 派 humanely *adv*; humaneness *n*.

humanity / hjuːˈmænəti / *n*. [U]❶(统称)人类;人性 ❷(*pl*.)人文科学:departments in the humanities 文科各系

humble / ˈhʌmbl / *adj*. ❶谦逊的;谦恭的:In my ~ opinion, the machine should be improved. 依本人拙见,这台机器应当改进。/ He is ~ toward his superiors. 他对上司很谦恭。❷地位(或身份)低下的;卑贱的:There isn't any ~ occupation in our society. 在我们的社会中没有卑下的职业。/ He is a man of ~ birth but he has won great success through his hard work. 他出身卑微,但通过努力获得了巨大的成功。派 humbleness *n*. ; humbly *adv*.

humid / ˈhjuːmɪd / *adj*. 潮湿的:~ air 潮湿的空气

humidity / hjuːˈmɪdəti / *n*. [U]湿气;温度:They are measuring the ~ of the room. 他们在测房间的湿度。

humiliate / hjuːˈmɪlɪˌeɪt / *vt*. 使丢脸;羞辱,使蒙羞:She ~d me in front of my friends. 她当着我朋友的面羞辱我。

humorous / ˈhjuːmərəs / *adj*. 幽默的;可笑的:He is good at telling ~ stories. 他擅长讲幽默故事。派 humorously *adv*.

humo(u)r / ˈhjuːmə(r) / *n*. [U]幽默;可笑;滑稽:We like him because he is a man with a sense of ~. 我们喜欢他,因为他是一个有幽默感的人。

hump / hʌmp / *n*. [C]圆形隆起物;驼峰;驼背

hundred / ˈhʌndrəd / *num*. 百:two ~ and five boys 205 个男孩/ a few ~ people 几百人/~s of people 数以百计的人

hunger / ˈhʌŋgə(r) / *n*. [U] ❶饥饿;饿:suffer ~ 挨饿 / ~ strike 绝食 / satisfy one's ~ 充饥 / She is fainting with ~. Please give her something to eat. 她饿昏了,请拿点东西给她吃。❷渴望;欲望(与 for 连用):Children always have a ~ for knowledge. 小孩总是渴求知识的。

hungry / ˈhʌŋgri / *adj*. ❶饥饿的;感到饿的:I am ~. 我饿了。/ He felt ~ after a day's work. 一天工作之后,他感到很饿。❷渴望的(与 for 连用):Young people are ~ for truth. 年轻人渴求真理。派 hungrily *adv*.

hunt / hʌnt / *v*. 狩猎;搜寻;搜索:go out ~ing 去打猎/ ~ the big game 狩猎大猎物/~ **for** 寻找;搜索:~ for fame and game 追名逐利/ He is ~ing for a job. 他正在找工作。

hunter / ˈhʌntə(r)/ *n*. [C] ❶猎人,猎户,狩猎者 ❷搜寻者,搜索者,追逐者:a job ~ 求职者

hurl / hɜːl / *vt*. ❶猛投,用力掷:~ a pebble through the window 把小石子扔进窗子里/The boys ~ed themselves against the door. 男孩们用身体使劲撞门。❷大声地说出(或喊出):~ abuse at sb. 大声辱骂某人

hurrah /həˈrɑː/ *int.* 好哇;万岁

hurricane /ˈhʌrɪkən/ *n.* [C]飓风;十二级风:blow a ~ 刮飓风 / a ~ of applause 暴风雨般的掌声 / A ~ swept the whole district. 飓风横扫整个地区。

hurried /ˈhʌrɪd/ *adj.* 匆忙的;仓促的:have a ~ meal 急匆匆地吃饭

hurry /ˈhʌri/ Ⅰ *v.* 使匆忙;赶快:Let's ~ or we'll be late. 赶快,否则我们要迟到了。/~ **up** 赶快:Ask him to ~ up with those letters so that we can send them off today. 叫他们赶快把那些信写好,以便我们今天发出去。Ⅱ *n.* [U]匆忙(用于否定句、疑问句中):**in a ~** 匆忙地;仓促地:Nothing is ever done in a ~. 匆匆忙忙是办不好事的。

hurt /hɜːt/ *v.* (hurt,hurt) ❶使受伤;使疼痛;伤害:He ~ his shoulder when he fell. 他跌倒时伤了肩。❷使伤心;伤害感情:They will be ~ at our not going to pay a visit to them. 我们不去看他们,他们会难过的。

husband /ˈhʌzbənd/ *n.* [C]丈夫

hush /hʌʃ/ *int.* 嘘,别响;别作声

hustle /ˈhʌs(ə)l/ Ⅰ *vt.* ❶猛挤,猛推,推搡:The police ~d the protestors out. 警察把抗议者推了出去。❷催促;急匆匆地做(事):She ~d the children off to school. 她急急忙忙送孩子们去上学。—*vi.* ❶挤,推,搡:The woman accused the man of having ~d against her. 这位妇女指责那个男子挤了她。❷忙碌;奔忙:~ for wages 为挣工资而奔忙 Ⅱ *n.* ❶[U]挤;推 ❷[U]忙碌;奔忙:the ~ and bustle of the city 城市的熙熙攘攘

hut /hʌt/ *n.* [C](简陋的)小屋;棚屋:a bamboo ~ 小竹屋

hybrid /ˈhaɪbrɪd/ Ⅰ *n.* [C] ❶杂(交)种 ❷合成物,混合物:The cello is a kind of ~ between a violin and a double bass. 大提琴是将小提琴和低音提琴糅合在一起的一种乐器。Ⅱ *adj.* ❶杂交的;杂种的:a ~ rice 杂交水稻 ❷合成的;混合的 派 hybridism *n.*

hydrogen /ˈhaɪdrədʒən/ *n.* [U] 氢

hygiene /ˈhaɪdʒiːn/ *n.* [U]卫生;卫生学:Middle school students should learn about some knowledge of public and private ~. 中学生应当学习一点公共卫生和个人卫生知识。

hyphen /ˈhaɪfən/ *n.* [C]连字符

hypnosis /hɪpˈnəʊsɪs/ *n.* (*pl.* hypnoses /hɪpˈnəʊsiːz/) ❶催眠状态:be under deep ~处于催眠后的昏睡状态中 ❷催眠;催眠术

hypothesis /haɪˈpɒθəsɪs/ *n.* [C](*pl.* hypotheses /haɪˈpɒθəsiːz/)假设;假说

hysteria /hɪˈsterɪə/ *n.* [U]歇斯底里;过度的恐惧(或悲伤等)

hysterical /hɪˈsterɪkl/ *adj.* 歇斯底里的:I really don't know what caused her ~ laughter? 我真的不知道是什么引起了她歇斯底里的大笑?

I i

I /aɪ/ *pron.* 我(第一人称代词的主格)

ice /aɪs/ *n.* [U] 冰:In winter the lake is covered with ~. 冬天湖面上结了一层冰。a block of ~ 一块冰

iceberg /ˈaɪsbɜːg/ *n.* [C] ❶冰山;流冰:The ship struck an ~ and sank. 船撞到冰山上沉没了。❷略显端倪的事物:Such events are the tip of an ~ of repression. 此类事件使得镇压渐显端倪。❸冷漠的人,冷若冰霜的人

icebox /ˈaɪsˌbɒks/ *n.* [C]电冰箱(=refrigerator)

ice-cream /ˈaɪsˌkriːm/ *n.* 冰激凌

icon /ˈaɪkɒn/ *n.* [C](*pl.* icons 或 icones /-kəˌniːz/)❶圣像 ❷形象;图像,画像,雕像 ❸图标

icy /ˈaɪsi/ *adj.* ❶冰的;冰封的,结满冰的:He plunged into the ~ river. 他跳进结冰的河水中。❷冰冷的:As ~ winds howled through the canyon, people huddled beside their fires. 刺骨的寒风在峡谷中怒号,人们都缩在火炉旁取暖。❸缺乏热情的;冷淡的;不友好的:an ~ stare 不友好的目光 / There was an ~ note in his uncle's voice. 他叔叔说话的口气有些冷淡。派 iciness *n.*

idea /aɪˈdɪə/ *n.* [C] ❶思想;概念:We should fit our ~s to the new conditions. 我们应该使自己的思想适应新情况。/ I have no ~ (as to) what you mean. 我一点儿也不明白你的意思。❷意见;建议:He opposed the ~. 他反对这个意见。/ You shouldn't force your ~ on other people. 你不应把自己的意见强加给别人。❸计划;计策;主意:a fine (good) ~ 好主意/ a stupid ~ 笨主意 / a wise ~ 高见/ Then a bright ~ came to him. 然后他想到一个好主意。

ideal /aɪˈdɪəl/ Ⅰ *adj.* 理想的;完美的:an ~ society 理想社会/ an ~ state 理想的国家/ It was an ~ day for a picnic. 这是个外出野餐的好日子。Ⅱ *n.* [C] 理想的人或物:She is afraid that she will not realize her ~s. 她担心她实现不了自己的理想。/ He is determined to establish high ~s. 他决心树立崇高的理想。

idealism /aɪˈdɪəˌlɪz(ə)m/ *n.* [U]理想主义:ignite the public dormant ~ 激起大众潜在的理想主义

idealize /aɪˈdɪəˌlaɪz/ *v.* 理想化;把……视作理想的人(或物):They ~ their successful father. 他们把他们卓有成就的父亲理想化。/sb.'s tendency to ~ about retirement 某人将退休后的生活理想化的倾向 派 idealization *n.*

identical /aɪˈdentɪkl/ *adj.* 完全相同的;同一的:They have ~ views on this problem. 在这个问题上他们看法一致。

identification /aɪˌdentɪfɪˈkeɪʃn/ *n.* 辨认;鉴定;身份证明:a car ~ plate 汽车

牌照/He showed his ~ when the police came. 警察过来时，他出示了自己的身份证明。

identify /aɪˈdentɪfaɪ/ *vt.* ❶认出；鉴定；验明：The girl said that she couldn't ~ the man who robbed her. 女孩说她辨认不出那个抢劫她的人。❷等同；和……认同：You cannot ~ beauty with good manners. 你不能把漂亮等同于礼貌。

identity /aɪˈdentəti/ *n.* 身份；特征：an ~ card 身份证 / Are you certain of the murderer's ~? 你能确认那个杀人犯的身份吗？

ideology /ˌaɪdɪˈɒlədʒi/ *n.* 思想（体系）；思想意识；意识形态：socialist ~ 社会主义思想 / in the realm of ~ 在思想领域里

idiom /ˈɪdɪəm/ *n.* [C]成语；习惯用语：This expression is against ~. 这一表达方式不合乎语言习惯。

idiot /ˈɪdɪət/ *n.* [C]白痴，智力低下者

idle /ˈaɪdl/ Ⅰ *adj.* ❶ 懒散的；无所事事的：an ~ fellow 一个游手好闲的家伙/He is too ~ to do anything. 他太懒了，什么事也不干。❷闲着的；空闲的：~ machines 闲置的机器/ stand ~ 袖手旁观 Ⅱ *v.* 懒散；闲逛；无所事事：Don't ~ away your time. 不要虚度光阴。/ Don't ~. 不要闲逛。派 idleness *n.*

idol /ˈaɪdl/ *n.* [C]偶像；崇拜对象：Many young students like to worship singing ~s. 许多青年学生喜欢崇拜偶像歌星。

i. e. （拉丁语 id est 的缩写）（＝that is）即，那就是

if /ɪf/ *conj.* ❶假设；如果：If you can't finish the book in time, you may come and renew it. 假如你不能及时看完这本书，你可以来续借。/ If I were you, I would not go. 如果我是你，我就不去。❷是否（在口语中，if 可代替 whether）：Do you know ~ (whether) he is in the library? 你知道他是否在图书馆吗？/ **even** ~ 即使；纵然：Even ~ he did say that, I am sure he didn't intend to hurt your feelings. 即使他真的那么说，我也相信他无意伤你的感情。/ I'll do it even ~ it takes me all the afternoon. 虽然做这件事要花我整个下午的时间，但我还是要做。**as** ~ 好像；仿佛：He talks as ~ he knew all about it. 他谈起话来好像这事他全知道。~ **only** 要是……多好；但愿（常表示对现在或将来的期望）：If only he could dance. 要是他会跳舞该多好。

ignite /ɪgˈnaɪt/ *vt.* 点燃；燃烧，着火：He ~d the match by scratching it on the box. 他从盒子上划着了火柴。/Gasoline ~s easily. 汽油易燃。派 ignition *n.*

ignorance /ˈɪgnərəns/ *n.* [U]无知；愚昧：He committed a crime out of his ~ of the law. 他由于不懂法而犯罪。

ignorant /ˈɪgnərənt/ *adj.* ❶无知识的，无知的；愚昧的：If you don't want to be an ~ person, you must study hard. 如果你不想做一个愚昧无知的人，你就必须努力学习。❷不知道的：He is ~ of the whole thing. 对于整件事，他完全不知道。派 ignorantly *adv.*

ignore /ɪgˈnɔː(r)/ *vt.* 不理；不顾；忽视：He entirely ~d his personal danger. 他完全不顾自己的安危。

ill /ɪl/ Ⅰ *adj.* (worse/wɜːs/, worst /wɜːst/) ❶生病的；不健康的：You look ~ these days. 近来你气色不好。/ He has been ~ for a long time. 他病了很久了。/ She was suddenly taken ~.

她突然病了。❷坏的;邪恶的:That is ~ news to her. 对她来说,那是坏消息。/ The fellow is famous for his ~ temper. 这家伙以其坏脾气著名。Ⅱ *adv.* 坏;不利的:Don't think(speak) ~ of others. 别把他人想(说)得太坏。/ Don't ~ treat animals. 不要虐待动物。

illegal /ɪˈliːgl/ *adj.* 非法的;不合法的

illegible /ɪˈledʒɪbl/ *adj.* (字迹)难以辨认的,无法看清的,难读的:an ~ signature 难以辨认的签字/This letter is completely ~. 这封信根本没法读。

illicit /ɪˈlɪsɪt/ *adj.* ❶非法的;违法的;违禁的:the ~ drug business 非法毒品交易 ❷违反习俗的;道德不允许的;不正当的:achieve one's success through ~ means 通过不正当的手段获取成功

illiterate /ɪˈlɪtərət/ Ⅰ *adj.* 文盲的;未受教育的 Ⅱ *n.* [C]文盲

illness /ˈɪlnəs/ *n.* 病;疾病:He suffered from a serious ~ but recovered soon. 他患了重病,但很快就好了。

illogical /ɪˈlɒdʒɪkl/ *adj.* 不合逻辑的;无条理的:I cannot agree with you because you have only give me an ~ inference. 我不能同意你的观点,因为你只给了我一个不合逻辑的推论。派 illogically *adv.*

ill-treat /ˌɪlˈtriːt/ *vt.* 虐待;折磨;凌辱:Do not ~ any dumb creature. 不要虐待任何不会说话的生灵。/ They began to mock him and ~ him. 他们开始嘲弄他,凌辱他。派 ill-treatment *n.*

illuminate /ɪˈluːmɪneɪt/ *vt.* 阐明;解释;启发:Our teacher ~d the theory with ex-amples. 我们的老师用例子解释那个原理。

illuminate /ɪˈljuːmɪˌneɪt/ *vt.* ❶照明,照亮:The glow ~d her face. 光映照着她的脸。/ The sky was ~d with searchlights. 探照灯把天空照射得通亮。❷用灯装饰:The streets were ~d for the celebration. 街上张灯结彩以示庆祝。❸使易于理解;阐明;启发,启迪:~ an obscure passage 解释一段晦涩的文字 / Her book provides sufficient historical background to ~ the context. 她的书提供了丰富的历史背景以阐明其语境。

illusion /ɪˈluːʒn/ *n.* [C]幻想;错觉;假象:cast away one's ~ 丢掉幻想 / They say that safety is only an ~ in America. 他们说在美国安全只是一种幻想。

illustrate /ˈɪləstreɪt/ *vt.* (以实例、图表等)说明;加插图:Each verb in this dictionary is ~d with a sentence. 这本词典的每一个动词都用一个例句来加以说明。/ This book is well ~d. 这本书的插图配得很好。

illustration /ˌɪləˈstreɪʃn/ *n.* 说明;例证;图解;插图:Please offer more ~s to explain the problem. 请多提供一些实例来说明这个问题。/ The ~s will help you understand the article. 这些插图将帮助你理解文章的意思。

image /ˈɪmɪdʒ/ *n.* [C] ❶像;肖像;影像;图像:a TV ~ 电视图像 / We saw his ~ on the wall. 我们看到墙上挂着他的肖像。❷形象;印象:The mayor is trying hard to improve his ~ in public. 市长正努力提高他在公众中的形象。

imaginable /ɪˈmædʒɪnəbl/ *adj.* 可想象的;能想象到的:We had the greatest difficulty ~. 我们遇到了能想象到的最大困难。

imaginary /ɪˈmædʒɪnəri/ *adj.* 想象中的;不真实的;虚构的;幻想的:It's not real,— it's only ~. 那不是真的,只不

过是想象中的事情。

imagination / ɪˌmædʒɪˈneɪʃn / *n.* ❶[U]想象；想象力；创造力：have a good (poor) ~ 有(缺乏)想象力/He is a writer of rich ~. 他是一位想象力丰富的作家。❷[C]想象的事物：You didn't really see a ghost,— it was only the ~. 你并没有真正见到过鬼——那只是你想象的东西。

imaginative / ɪˈmædʒɪnətɪv / *adj.* 富于想象的；想象的；虚幻的：/ He is an ~ actor. 他是一位富于想象的演员。

imagine / ɪˈmædʒɪn / *v.* 想象；设想；认为：I ~d her as a big tall woman. 我以为她是个身材高大的女人。/ I can ~ the scene clearly in my mind. 我可以清楚地想象出那个情景。/ He never ~d this would happen. 他绝没料到会发生这种事情。

imbalance / ɪmˈbæləns / *n.* [C]不平衡，失衡；失调：correct an ~纠正不平衡的局面/a population ~人口中男女比例失调

imitate / ˈɪmɪteɪt / *vt.* 模仿；仿效：~ a diamond with crystal 用水晶仿造钻石/Young people always ~ great actors they like. 年轻人总爱模仿他们喜欢的大明星。

imitation / ˌɪmɪˈteɪʃn / *n.* 模仿，仿效；仿制品：They are mere ~s. 他们不过是仿制品而已。/ Be aware of ~. 谨防假冒。

imitative / ˈɪmɪtətɪv/ *adj.* ❶爱模仿的；喜学样的(与 of 连用)：Children are very ~ of their elders. 孩子很喜欢模仿长辈。❷模仿(性)的，模拟(性)的：the ~ behaviour of children 孩子们的模仿行为 / Portrait painting is an ~ art. 肖像画是一种模拟艺术。❸人造的；仿制的；伪造的；冒牌的：~ jewelry 假宝石 派 imitatively *adv.*；imitativeness *n.*

immaterial / ˌɪməˈtɪərɪəl / *adj.* ❶不重要的，无关紧要的，无足轻重的：His position on the board of directors is ~. 他在董事会里的地位无足轻重。❷非物质的；非实体的，无形体的；精神的：The body is material but the soul is ~. 躯体有形而灵魂无形。

immature / ˌɪməˈtjʊə(r)，ˌɪməˈtʃʊə(r) / *adj.* ❶发育未完全的；未充分成长的；未成熟的：~ fruit 没熟透的水果/for the well-being of ~ babies 为了胎儿的健康 ❷不成熟的，不够老练的；幼稚的，孩子气的：emotionally ~ adults 感情上还未成熟的成年人/It was ~ of her to do that. 她那样做太孩子气了。

immeasurable / ɪˈmeʒərəbl / *adj.* 无法度量的；无边无际的，无限的：the ~ vastness of the universe 宇宙的浩瀚无际/China is a market of ~ potential. 中国是一个具有无限潜在商机的大市场。派 immeasurably *adv.*

immediate / ɪˈmiːdɪət / *adj.* ❶立即的；即刻的：They said that they would take ~ action to settle the problem. 他们说要采取迅速行动解决这个问题。/ Please send us an ~ reply. 请立即答复我们。❷直接的；最接近的：The ~ cause of his mistake is that he was too careless. 他犯错误的直接原因是他太粗心大意。派 immediately *adv.*

immense / ɪˈmens / *adj.* 无限的；广大的；无边的：an ~ body of water 一片汪洋/ Don't be hard on me. I have made ~ improvement. 别苛求我，我已经做出巨大改进了。

immerse / ɪˈmɜːs / *v.* ❶使浸没，使浸透：~ one's feet in water 把双脚浸到水里

❷使沉浸在;使深陷于;使埋头于:Little by little she ~d herself in Moscow life. 她渐渐融入莫斯科的生活。/be ~d in work 废寝忘食地工作/~ oneself in contemplation 陷于沉思

immigrant /ˈɪmɪgrənt/ Ⅰ *n.* [C]移民;侨民:Canada has many ~s from China. 加拿大有很多中国移民。Ⅱ *adj.* 移民的;移来的:His grandfather was an ~ to the United States from India. 他祖父是美籍印度移民。

immigrate /ˈɪmɪgreɪt/ *v.* (使)移居入境;(从国外)移来:They ~d from Africa into Spain many years ago. 多年前他们从非洲移居到西班牙。

imminent /ˈɪmɪnənt/ *adj.* 临近的;附近的;就要发生的:the ~ general election 即将举行的大选/Civil war there was ~. 那儿的内战迫在眉睫。派 imminence *n.*;imminently *adv.*

immobile /ɪˈməʊbaɪl/ *adj.* ❶不活动的,固定的:keep a broken leg ~对骨折的腿进行固定/Land is ~. 土地是不能移动的。❷不在运动的,静止的;不在变化的:The dog lay at rest, its four feet stretched out, absolutely ~. 这条狗闲躺着,四脚伸开,一动不动。

immoderate /ɪˈmɒdərət/ *adj.* 不适度的;过度的;无节制的;极端的:They were dead by ~ labor and ill food. 他们因为操劳过度和饮食恶劣而死。/~ eating habits 无节制大吃的习惯

immodest /ɪˈmɒdɪst/ *adj.* ❶不正派的;不端庄的;伤风败俗的;下流的:an ~ glance 轻佻的目光/There was nothing ~ about the outfit. 这套装束没有什么不端庄的。❷不谦虚的,傲慢的;厚颜无耻的:an ~ request 厚颜无耻的要求/He has an ~ personality. 他生性傲慢。派 immodestly *adv.*

immoral /ɪˈmɒrəl/ *adj.* ❶不道德的;邪恶的;缺德的,败坏道德的:~ habits of behaviour 不道德的行为习惯/~ earnings 收受贿赂所得 ❷放荡的,浮荡的

immortal /ɪˈmɔːtl/ *adj.* 不朽的;永生的;永久的:an ~ hero 不朽的英雄

immov(e)able /ɪˈmuːvəbl/ *adj.* ❶不可移动的,固定的:an ~ friendship 不可动摇的深厚友谊 ❷不改变的;不让步的,坚定不移的:an ~ integrity 刚正不阿/heroes ~ by pain or pleasure 痛苦和享乐都无法令其屈服的英雄/He has his opinions on these subjects. He is ~. 在这些问题上他有自己的看法,决不会让步。❸不激动的;不为感情所动的;无情的:She was just as ~ as ever. 她照旧无动于衷。/an ~ heart 冷漠的心 ❹不在动的,不在变化的,静止的:He stood ~. 他一动不动地站着。/In Newton's eyes the sun stood ~ in the centre of the universe. 在牛顿看来,太阳静止不动,居于宇宙中心。

immune /ɪˈmjuːn/ *adj.* ❶免疫的;(有)免疫力的;有抵抗力的:an ~ reaction 免疫反应/The blood test shows you are not ~. 血检表明你不具免疫力。❷受到保护的;不受影响的:~ to new ideas 不受新思想的影响/The motor industry in still buoyant but cannot remain ~ from the trends in the rest of the economy. 汽车工业依然是朝阳工业,但也不可能不受其他经济部门的影响。❸免除的,豁免的(与 from 连用):~ from taxes 免税/To be ~ from error is humanly impossible. 作为人,不犯错误是不可能的。

impact /ˈɪmpækt/ *n.* ❶[C]影响;作用:The Internet makes a great ~ on our life. 因特网对我们的生活产生了巨大的影响。❷[U]冲击;碰撞:I saw the ~ of a car crashing into the pole beside the street. 我看见一辆汽车撞到路边的一根电杆上。

impair /ɪm'peə(r)/ *vt*. 损害,损伤;削弱,减少:Ozone can ~ the oxygen absorbing ability of the lungs. 臭氧会破坏肺的氧吸收功能。/ Our aim is to improve the quality of life, not ~ it. 我们的目的是要改善而不是降低生活质量。派 impair-ment *n*.

impart /ɪm'pɑːt/ *vt*. ❶告知,通知;透露:I have no news to ~. 我没有消息可以透露。❷给予(尤指抽象事物);分给;传授:The new furnishings ~ed an air of newness to the old house. 新家具给这所旧房子带来了新气象。/There is a general consensus that schools do indeed ~ values. 人们普遍认为学校确实要传授价值观念。

impartial /ɪm'pɑːʃəl/ *adj*. 不偏不倚的,中立的;公平的,无偏见的:an ~ judge 公正的法官/What I needed was totally ~ advice. 我需要的是丝毫不带偏见的建议。

impassive /ɪm'pæsɪve/ *adj*. 不动感情的;没有表情的;无动于衷的;矜持的;泰然的:a cold ~ stare 冷淡矜持的目光/Mr. Henry remained ~. 亨利先生依旧不动声色。

impatience /ɪm'peɪʃns/ *n*. [U]不耐烦;性急;急躁:His ~ made him unreasonable. 他的急躁情绪使他变得不讲道理。

impatient /ɪm'peɪʃnt/ *adj*. 不耐烦的;急躁的:We don't like teachers who are ~ with children. 我们不喜欢对孩子不耐心的老师。/ He was ~ to finish the game. 他急于结束那场比赛。

impede /ɪm'piːd/ *vt*. 阻碍,妨碍;阻止:The deep snow ~d travel. 厚厚的积雪阻碍了交通。/ Many a man is ~d in his career by a lack of belief in himself. 许多人因为缺乏自信而影响了自己事业的发展。

impel /ɪm'pel/ *vt*. (-pelled; -pelling) ❶驱策;激励;迫使:~ sb. into action 激励某人行动起来/Hunger ~led the lazy man to work. 饥饿迫使懒人干活。❷推进,推动:The wind ~led the boat toward the shore. 风把船吹处岸边。/~ developments and innovations 推动发展和革新

imperialism /ɪm'pɪərɪəlɪzəm/ *n*. [U]帝国主义

imperialist /ɪm'pɪərɪəlɪst/ Ⅰ *adj*. 帝国主义的 Ⅱ *n*. [C]帝国主义者

impermanent /ɪm'pɜːmənənt/ *adj*. 转瞬即逝的;短暂的;非永久性的:Magnetic media are notoriously ~. 磁性媒质是最不能持久的。派 impermanence (-cy)*n*.

impetus /'ɪmpɪtəs/ *n*. ❶(常用单数)推动;促进;刺激:The two trains came into collision with great ~. 两列火车猛烈相撞。/ What the economy needs is a new ~. 经济需要的是一种新的推动力。/ His prose is all ~. 他的诗给人以激励。❷[U]动量:Anything that can stop easily has little ~. 容易停下来的物体动量很小。

implant Ⅰ /ɪm'plɑːnt/ *vt*. ❶把……嵌入;埋置(与 in 连用):a ruby ~ in a gold ring 嵌在金戒指里的一颗红宝石 ❷灌输,注入;使牢固树立;使充满:~ respect for democracy in the younger generation 向青年一代灌输尊重民主的意识 ❸种植,种下:~ the seeds 播种 ❹移

植;植入:~ an artificial heart 植入人造心脏 Ⅱ /ˈɪmplɑːnt/ *n.* [C]植入物;移植片;种植体:suitable for body ~s 适合做体内植入物

implement /ˈɪmplɪmənt/ *n.* [C]工具;器材:farm ~s 农具/ kitchen ~s 厨房用具/ writing ~s 书写工具

implication /ˌɪmplɪˈkeɪʃn/ *n.* [C]含义;暗示;暗指:Mother smiled and I knew the ~ was that she wouldn't agree with me. 妈妈笑了,我知道这暗示着她并不同意我的意见。/ When reading a novel,I try to understand the cultural ~s in it. 读小说时,我尽力去理解其中的文化内涵。

implicit /ɪmˈplɪsɪt/ *adj.* ❶不言明的,暗示的;暗含的,含蓄的:an ~ answer 含蓄的回答/Her silence gave ~ consent. 她用沉默表示赞同。❷绝对的;毫无保留的;毫不怀疑的:He has ~ confidence in hi friends. 他毫无保留地信任自己的朋友。/A soldier must give ~ obedience to his officers. 士兵必须绝对服从上司。派 implicitly *adv.*

implore /ɪmˈplɔː(r)/ *vt.* 恳求;哀求;乞求:She ~d her mother to give permission for her to go on the trip. 她恳求母亲允许她去旅行。/~ aid from sb. 乞求某人援助

imply /ɪmˈplaɪ/ *vt.* 暗示;意指:Silence often implies consent. 沉默常意味着同意。/ What do you ~ by that statement? 你那句话是什么意思?

impolite /ˌɪmpəˈlaɪt/ *adj.* 不礼貌的;无礼的,失礼的;粗鲁的:grossly ~ eating habits极其粗鲁的吃相/Take care not to be ~ to customers 注意不要对顾客失礼。派 impolitely *adv.*

import Ⅰ /ɪmˈpɔːt/ *vt.* 输入;引入;进口:They ~ wool from Australia. 他们从澳大利亚进口羊毛。/ He ~ed his personal feelings into a discussion. 他把个人的感情带进讨论中。Ⅱ /ˈɪmpɔːt/ *n.* [C]输入品;进口货:~ and export trade 进出口贸易/ ~ quota 进口配额/ ~ duty (tax)进口税/ ~ license 进口许可证/ Our ~s fall short of our exports. 我们的进口商品少于出口商品。

importance /ɪmˈpɔːtəns/ *n.* [U]重要;重大:It is of no ~. 这事无关紧要。/ He hasn't realized the ~ of studying English. 他还未意识到学习英语的重要性。

important /ɪmˈpɔːtənt/ *adj.* 重要的,重大的:It is very ~ for you to study English well. 学好英语对你来讲很重要。

impose /ɪmˈpəʊz/ *vt.* 征税:We should ~ more duties on tobaccos and wines. 我们应当对烟酒多征税。

impossible /ɪmˈpɒsəbl/ *adj.* 不可能的;办不到的:It is ~ for us to accomplish that task without their help. 没有他们的帮助,我们不可能完成那项任务。/ Nothing is ~ to a willing mind. 世上无难事,只怕有心人。

impractical /ɪmˈpræktɪkəl/ *adj.* ❶不切实际的;无用的;不现实的:an ~ plan 不切实际的计划/advice of a totally ~ nature 完全脱离实际的建议 ❷不注重实际的;无动手能力的:He is intelligent but too ~ for commercial work. 他人很聪慧,但不善做实际工作,不能经商。派 impractically *adv.*

impress /ɪmˈpres/ *v.* ❶(以一物)压(另一物);印;盖记号:an ~ed stamp 盖了邮戳的邮票 ❷ 给……以深刻印象;使铭记:She repeated the words to ~ them in her memory. 她反复重述那些

词以便将它们铭记在心。/ He ~ed me favourably. 他给我的印象不错。派impressive *adj*.

impression /ɪm'preʃn/ *n*. [C]印象;感想:What are your ~s of (about) Beijing? 你对北京有何印象? / What he said makes a lasting ~ on us. 他的话给我们留下了不可磨灭的印象。

impressive /ɪm'presɪv/ *adj*. ❶给人以深刻印象的;感人的,打动人的;令人敬佩的:an ~ building 宏伟的建筑物/an ~ storm 震撼人心的风暴/ Economic development is even more ~. 经济上的发展就更令人瞩目。❷威严的;使人肃然起敬的:an ~ figure 一个令人肃然起敬的人物/an equestrian statue of ~ dignity 庄严而惹人注目的骑士雕像 派 impressively *adv*.

imprint Ⅰ/'ɪmprɪnt/ *n*. [C] ❶印记,戳记,印痕;痕迹:Your foot made an ~ in the sand. 你在沙地上留下了一个脚印。❷(常用单数)深刻的印象;影响,作用;特征,标记:The performance made a deep ~ on our minds. 那场演出给我们留下了深刻的印象。/He left the ~ of his thought on all succeeding scholars. 他的思想对所有后来的学生都产生了影响。Ⅱ/ɪm'prɪnt/ *vt*. ❶印,压印;盖(印、邮戳等)于:~ a postmark on an envelope 在信封上盖邮戳 ❷铭刻于;使牢记:try to ~ every detail on one's memory 极力想把每一个细节都刻在脑海里/a scene ~ed on sb.'s memory 深深地铭刻在某人记忆中的一幕

imprison /ɪm'prɪzn/ *vt*. 关押,监禁:The criminal was ~ed for life. 罪犯被终身监禁。派 imprisonment *n*.

improper /ɪm'prɒpə(r)/ *adj*. 不适当的;不适合的:Shouting aloud here is ~. 在这儿高声大喊是很不恰当的。

improve /ɪm'pruːv/ *v*. 改善;提高:She is improving in health. 她的健康状况正在好转。/ How much you have ~d! 你进步真大! / The government is trying to ~ the living conditions of the people. 政府正在努力改善人民的生活条件。

improvement /ɪm'pruːvmənt/ *n*. 改善;改进:Much ~ has been made in the safety construction of the factory. 工厂的安全设施有了很大的改进。

impulse /'ɪmpʌls/ *n*. [C]冲力;冲动;刺激:The new treaty has given an ~ to the trade between the two countries. 新签订的条约推动了两国之间的贸易往来。/ Our manager is a man of ~. 我们的经理是一个容易冲动的人。/ He resisted a sudden ~ to beat the stealer. 他克制了一时的冲动没有揍那小偷。

impure /ɪm'pjʊə(r)/ *adj*. 不纯洁的;不纯的;掺杂的:The water in that city is often ~. 那座城市里的水常常是不清洁的。/ This kind of salt is ~. 这种盐不纯。

impurity /ɪm'pjʊərəti/ *n*. [U]不纯;杂质;不洁:The ~ of the water made it unfit to drink. 因为水不洁净,所以不能饮用。/ They are removing the impurities in food. 他们正在清除食物中的杂质。

in /ɪn/ *prep*. ❶(表示地点、场所、部位)在……里;在……中:~ China 在中国/ ~ the world 在世界上/ ~ the village 在村子里/ ~ the sky 在空中/ ~ the factory 在工厂里/ ~ the classroom 在教室里/ ~ the corner of the room 在房子的角落里/ ~ the newspaper 在报纸上/ ~ one's mouth 在嘴里/ ~ bed 在

床上/ ~ one's hand 在某人的手里/ ~ the desk 在桌子里/ ~ the city 在城市里 / ~ the universe 在宇宙中 ❷ 进入……中：He put his hands ~ his pockets. 他把手放进口袋里。/ Please throw it ~ the fire! 把它扔进火中！❸(指时间)在：~ the 21st century 在21世纪/ ~ 1990 在1990年/ ~ the morning(afternoon, evening) 在上午(下午、晚上) /~ January 在一月/ ~ spring (summer, autumn, winter) 在春季(夏季、秋季、冬季)/ ~ the daytime 在白天/ ~ the past 过去/ ~ (the) future 将来 ❹过(若干时间)；在(若干时间)内：I'll be back ~ a moment. 我过一会儿就回来。/ Can you finish this job ~ a very short time? 你能在很短的时间内完成这项工作吗？❺ 穿着；戴着：the girl ~ red 穿红衣服的姑娘 ❻(表示所处环境)在：sitting ~ the sun(sunshine) 坐在阳光下/ ~ the open 在露天/ ~ the shade 在阴凉处/ ~ the dark 在黑夜中/ ~ the moonlight 在月光里/ ~ the rain 在雨中 ❼ (指表达的方法或使用的手段、原料等)用，以：speak ~ English 用英语说/ written ~ ink 用墨水写/ painted ~ oils 油彩画的 ❽ (表示情况或状态)处在……中：~ a troubled state 处在烦恼中/ ~ good order 整齐；情况良好/ ~ a rage 盛怒地/ ~ despair 绝望地/ ~ a hurry 匆忙/ ~ poverty 处在贫困中/ ~ debt 负债/ ~ love 恋爱中/ ~ wonder 惊奇地/ ~ secret 秘密地/ ~ a loud voice 大声地/ ~ the end 最后

inaccessible / ˌɪnæk'sesəbl / *adj.* 达不到的，难到达的；不可(或难以)进入的：an ~ butte 一座无法攀登的孤峰/The place is ~ by road. 无路通达该地。

inactive / ɪn'æktɪv / *adj.* ❶不活动的；不活跃的；缺乏活力的：an ~ volcano 不活动的火山/an ~ market 缺乏活力的市场/Nearly half the men between 55 and 65 are now economically ~ through early retirement. 由于提前退休，55至65岁的男人将近有一半现已不再活跃在经济生活中了。❷非现役的，预备役的；后备的

inadequate / ɪn'ædɪkwət / *adj.* 不足的；不够的：There are only more than 800 books in this small library and is ~ to meet the need. 小图书馆里只有800多本书，不足以满足需要。

inappropriate / ˌɪnə'prəupriət / *adj.* 不恰当的，不适合的：~ remarks 不得体的话/It is ~ that he (should) be present. 他的出席是不适宜的。

inaugural / ɪ'nɔːgjurəl/ Ⅰ *adj.* (只作定语) ❶就职的，就任的：~ celebrations 就职庆典活动 / an ~ address to the nation 向全国人民发表的就职演说 ❷首次的；开幕的；成立的，创立的：The airline made its ~ flight in October. 这条航线于10月进行了首次飞行。/ The ~ meeting was attended by men of all parties. 成立大会有各方人士参加。Ⅱ *n.* [C] 就职演说；就职典礼

inaugurate / ɪ'nɔːgjəreɪt / *vt.* 使(某人)就职(常用被动语态)：He was ~d as President. 他就任总统。

inborn / 'ɪnbɔːn / *adj.* ❶天生的，与生俱来的：an ~ sense of rhythm 天生的节奏感/Many mammals have an ~ fear of poisonous snakes. 许多哺乳动物天生就害怕毒蛇。/an ~ talent 天才 ❷先天的，遗传的：There is an ~ component in human intelligence which is genetically heritable. 人的智力中某种先天因素是可以遗传。

incapable /ɪnˈkeɪpəbl/ *adj*. 无能力的；不会的：No boss is willing to hire ~ workers. 没有老板愿意雇用无能的工人。/~ **of** 不能的；不会的；没有资格的：He is a good boy and is ~ of telling a lie. 他是个好孩子，不会撒谎。/ Is a foreigner ~ of becoming president of that country? 外国人就没有资格当那个国家的总统吗？

incense /ɪnˈsens/ *n*. [U]香；香气：the ~ of flowers 花香

incentive /ɪnˈsentɪv/ *n*. 刺激；鼓励；奖励；动机：material ~ 物质刺激/tax ~s for investing in depressed areas 鼓励向萧条地区投资的税收优惠/Competition is the strongest ~ to industry. 竞争最能激发勤奋。

incessant /ɪnˈsesənt/ *adj*. 不停的，连续的，不断的：~ rain (phone calls) 下个不停的雨(响个不停的电话铃声) / answer sb.'s ~ questions 回答某人接二连三的提问 ▧ incessantly *adv*.

inch /ɪntʃ/ *n*. [C]英寸(略作 in.)

incident /ˈɪnsɪdənt/ *n*. [C]事件(尤指不太重要的小事件)；插曲；事变：the July Seventh Incident of 1937 1937 年七七事变 / That was one of the strangest ~s in my life. 那是我一生中遇到的最奇怪的事情之一。/ There were several ~s on the frontier. 边境上发生了几起事件。

incidental /ˌɪnsɪˈdentəl/ Ⅰ *adj*. 偶然发生的：an ~ meeting of an old friend on the street 与老友的街头邂逅 / Tom insists his discoveries have been purely ~. 汤姆坚持说他所有的发现纯属偶然。Ⅱ *n*. [C] ❶偶然事件 ❷(常用 *pl*.) 杂费；杂项：a bill for tuition and ~s 学费和杂费账单

incite /ɪnˈsaɪt/ *vt*. 刺激；激起；煽动；激励：~ anger 激起愤慨/organisms that readily ~ antibody formation 容易激发抗体生成的有机物/She ~d her son to greater efforts. 她激励儿子更加发奋。

incline Ⅰ /ɪnˈklaɪn/ *v*. 使倾向；使倾斜：She was ~d to go there by ship. 她倾向于乘船去那里。/ Do you feel ~d for swimming? 你想去游泳吗？/ The man ~d toward me to hear more clearly. 那人向我俯过身来以便更清楚地听到我说的话。Ⅱ /ˈɪnklaɪn/*n*. [C]斜面；斜坡；倾斜

inclined /ɪnˈklaɪnd/ *adj*. ❶(只作表语)倾向于……的；有……意向的；喜好……的；赞成……的：a youth ~ to silence 沉默寡言的青年 / They were not ~ to help him out. 他们无意帮他的忙。❷倾斜的；斜坡的，倾面的：~ necks 歪脖子 ❸有某方面天赋的：Louise is very musically ~. 路易丝很有音乐天赋。

include /ɪnˈkluːd/ *vt*. 包括，包含：She ~s eggs in the list of things to buy. 她把鸡蛋列在购物单上。

included /ɪnˈkluːdɪd/ *adj*. (只作后置定语)包括在内的：postage ~ 内含邮费 / all charges ~ 一切费用均包括在内 / all of us, me ~我们所有的人，包括我在内

including /ɪnˈkluːdɪŋ/ *prep*. 如果包含……在内，算上……的话：There are altogether six members, ~ the chairman. 算上主席一共 6 位成员。/Your total expenses, ~ these bills, are $300. 你的总开销，包括这些账单，是 300 美元。

inclusive /ɪnˈkluːsɪv/ *adj*. 包含的；包括的；范围广的：The group consists of 12 people, ~ of the monitor. 包括班长在内，他们小组共有 12 个人。/ The rent is 450 yuan a mouth, ~ of the heating and water. 房租 450 元一个月，暖气费和水费包括在内。

income /ˈɪnkəm/ *n.* 收入；所得：an annual ~ 年收入/ a large ~ 高收入/a low ~ 低收入/a monthly ~ 月收入/ the net ~ 纯收入/ The ~ of the family was cut down one-third. 那家的收入减少了三分之一。

incomparable /ɪnˈkɒmp(ə)rəbl/ *adj.* ❶无比的，无双的：a man of ~ genius 绝顶聪明的人/the ~ beauty of Lake Garda 无与伦比的加达湖美景/a moment of ~ joy 快乐无比的时刻 ❷无从比较的；无可比性的：Censorship still exists, but now it's absolutely ~ with what is was.（新闻）审查制度依然存在，但是今日的审查制度与昔日的审查制度压根儿就没有可比性。

incompetent /ɪnˈkɒmpɪtənt/ Ⅰ *adj.* ❶无能力的；不胜任的，不称职的：~ officials 不称职的官员 / A poor manager is ~ to run a business. 蹩脚的经理没有管理企业的能力。❷无行为能力的；（证据等）不合格的，无效的：an ~ witness 法律上无资格的证人 Ⅱ *n.* [C]无能的人；不称职者；弱智者 the jealous ~s 嫉贤妒能的无能之辈 派 incompetently *adv.*

inconsiderable /ˌɪnkənˈsɪdərəbl/ *adj.* （价值、数量、尺寸等）相对较小的，小的：an ~ sum of money 一笔数目不大的款子/an ~ size 小尺寸/Her not ~ talent is dwarfed by his. 她那并不算小的才华和他一比，可就是小巫见大巫了。

inconsiderate /ˌɪnkənˈsɪdərət/ *adj.* ❶不为别人着想的，不体谅别人的：an ~ employer 一个不替别人着想的老板/She is intensely selfish, utterly ~ of others. 她为人非常自私，压根儿就不顾别人。❷考虑不周的；轻率的：~ behaviour 轻率的举动/explore the carvings on display with ~ fingers 用手随便乱摸雕刻展品

inconstant /ɪnˈkɒnstənt/ *adj.* ❶（人）反复无常的；不专一的；不坚定的，动摇的：an ~ friend 不忠实的朋友/Weak I may have been, but never ~. 我可能意志薄弱，但是我从不见异思迁。❷（事物）多变化的；无规则的：Fortune is ~. 命运无常。

inconvenience /ˌɪnkənˈviːnɪəns/ Ⅰ *n.* ❶[U]不方便；麻烦，打扰；为难，不适：We apologize for any ~ you may have been caused. 我们对可能给你们带来的任何不便表示歉意。❷[C]不方便（或让人为难）的事；麻烦事：a considerable (great) ~ 相当的（极大的）麻烦/ the ~ of living in the suburbs 住在郊区的诸多不便 Ⅱ *vt.* 给……带来不方便；麻烦，打扰；使为难：I hope I didn't ~ you. 但愿我没有给您带来麻烦。

inconvenient /ˌɪnkənˈvɪːnɪənt/ *adj.* ❶不方便的；打扰的；使人感到麻烦的；让人为难（或烦恼）的：The phone is in an ~ place. 电话放在让人感到不方便的地方。/If it is not ~ to you, I should like to meet you now. 如果你方便的话，我想现在和你见面。❷不恰当的；不适宜的；不相称的：She chose to go at a very ~ time, I must say. 应该说，她挑了个很尴尬的时间去那儿。派 conveniently *adv.*

incorporate /ɪnˈkɔːpəˌreɪt/ *vt.* ❶包含；加入；吸收：~ new insights or research findings 吸收新见解或新的研究成果/We will ~ your suggestion in this new plan. 我们将把你的建议纳入这个新计划之中。❷把……组成公司(或社团);把……吸收为公司(或社团)成员:When the businesses became large, the owners ~d it. 企业规模变大以后,老板们把它兼并了。❸使具体化;体现:~ one's thoughts in an article 把自己的思想体现在一篇文章中

incorporated /ɪnˈkɔːpəˌreɪtɪd/ *adj.* 组成公司(或社团)的;股份有限的(用于公司名称之后,略作 Inc.):an ~ company 一家股份有限公司 / Joe Bloggs Inc. 乔·布洛格斯股份有限公司

incorrect /ˌɪnkəˈrekt/ *adj.* 不正确的;错误的:This is an ~ answer. 这是一个错误答案。/ I would not support your ~ behavior. 我不会支持你的不正当行为。

increase Ⅰ /ɪnˈkriːs/ *v.* 增加;增长;增大:The town is fast increasing in population. 该镇人口迅速增加。/ He ~d the speed of the car. 他加快了汽车的速度。Ⅱ /ˈɪnkriːs/ *n.* 增加;增大;增加量:the natural ~ of population 人口自然增长/ the rate of ~ 增长率 派 increasingly *adv.*

incredible /ɪnˈkredəbl/ *adj.* 难以置信的;不可思议的:The story he told is ~. 他讲的故事令人难以置信。

incriminate /ɪnˈkrɪmɪˌneɪt/ *vt.* ❶指控,控告:He ~d the other boys to the teacher. 他向老师控告别的男孩。❷归咎于:~ cigarettes as one cause of lung cancer 把肺癌的原因之一归咎于吸烟 派 incrimination *n.*

incurable /ɪnˈkjʊərəbl/ *adj.* 治疗无效的,治不好的;不可救药的;无可矫正的:an ~ disease 不治之症/~ pessimism 不可救药的悲观情绪

incurious /ɪnˈkjʊərɪəs/ *adj.* 缺乏好奇心的,不爱刨根问底的;不感兴趣的;不关心的:an ~ student 缺乏好奇心的学生 / listless and ~ eyes 没精打采、对什么都不感兴趣的眼神

indeed /ɪnˈdiːd/ *adv.* 的确;实在;真正地:It was a wonderful travel ~. 这真是一次很奇妙的旅行。

indefinite /ɪnˈdefɪnət/ *adj.* ❶不确定的;未决定的:He said he would come to see me, but only gave me an ~ date. 他说要来看我,但只给了一个不确定的日期。❷模糊的;含糊的;不明确的:What he wants to do is rather ~. 他究竟想做什么还很不确定。❸(语法)不定的:an ~ article 不定冠词 / an ~ pronoun 不定代词

independence /ˌɪndɪˈpendəns/ *n.* [U]独立;自主:The country formally declared ~. 这个国家正式宣布独立。

independent /ˌɪndɪˈpendənt/ *adj.* 独立的:They are ~ economically. 他们在经济上是独立的。/ It is an ~ country. 这是一个独立的国家。

in-depth /ɪnˈdepθ/ *adj.* 深入的;全面的;彻底的:an ~ analysis of the problem 对问题所做的深入分析/It was given ~ coverage on television and radio. 电视台与广播电台都对此做了全面报道。

index /ˈɪndeks/ *n.* [C](*pl.* indexes 或 indices) ❶索引:a card ~ 卡片索引 / an author ~ 作者索引 / a subject ~ 分类索引 ❷指标;标志:the quality ~ 质量指标 / the profit ~ 利润指标 ❸指数:the consumer price ~ 消费品物价指数/ the stock market ~ 股票市场指数

indicate /ˈɪndɪkeɪt/ *vt.* ❶标示;表示:The arrow ~s the way to the hospital.

那个箭头符号标示到医院去的路。❷表明;暗示:The light through the window ~d that he was still in. 窗户透出的灯光表明他仍然在家。

indication /ˌɪndɪˈkeɪʃn/ *n.* ❶[U]指示;表示;指出:The teacher taught the students to use different signs for the ~ of different meanings. 老师教学生用不同的符号表示不同的意思。❷[C]迹象;暗示:Black clouds showed ~s of rain. 乌云滚滚表明有下雨的迹象。

indifference /ɪnˈdɪfrəns/ *n.* [U]漠不关心;冷淡;不感兴趣:His ~ made us angry. 他的冷漠令我们生气。

indifferent /ɪnˈdɪfrənt/ *adj.* 漠不关心的;冷淡的;不感兴趣的:He is ~ to his dress. 他对自己的衣着并不在乎。/ She is ~ of her parents. 她对父母漠不关心。

indigestion /ˌɪndɪˈdʒestʃn/ *n.* [U]消化不良,不消化:chronic ~慢性消化不良症

indignant /ɪnˈdɪgnənt/ *adj.* 愤慨的;愤愤不平的:We were ~ at his suggestion at the meeting. 对他在会上的提议我们感到愤慨。派 indignation *n.*

indignity /ɪnˈdɪgnɪti/ *n.* 轻蔑,伤害尊严;无礼举动,侮辱言行:treat sb. with ~ 侮慢地对待某人 / Spanking is an ~ to a teenager. 打屁股对十几岁的少年是一种有伤自尊心的事。/ subject (put) sb. to indignities 使某人受辱

indirect /ˌɪndɪˈrekt/ *adj.* ❶绕行的;迂回的,曲折的:an ~ course in sailing 迂回航线 / the ~ route 绕行线 ❷偶然的,意外的;非本意的:an ~ outcome 意外的结果 ❸不直截了当的;非正面的:make an ~ answer 回话时躲躲闪闪 / His methods are ~ but not dishonest. 他用的手段不那么直截了当,不过倒并非是不诚实。❹非直接的,间接的;继发的:an ~ cause 间接原因 派 indirectly *adv.*;indirectness *n.*

indispensable /ˌɪndɪˈspensəbl/ *adj.* 必需的;不可缺少的:Air, food and water are ~ to life. 空气、食物和水对于生命来说是不可缺少的。

individual /ˌɪndɪˈvɪdʒuəl/ Ⅰ *adj.* ❶个人的;个别的;独自的:~ income tax 个人收入所得税 / That is only an ~ opinion. 那只是个人意见。❷独特的;个性的:She's grown up and has an ~ style of dressing. 她已经长大了,拥有自己独特的穿着方式。Ⅱ *n.* [C]个人;个体:Many people say that he is an odd ~. 很多人都说他是一个古怪的人。

individuality /ˌɪndɪˌvɪdjʊˈælɪti/ *n.* [U]个性;个体特征:a person of marked ~ 一个极有个性的人 / This book has its own ~ that sets it apart from all others. 这本书具有区别于其他书的个体特性。

indivisible /ˌɪndɪˈvɪzɪbl/ *adj.* ❶不可分的:~ entity 不可分的统一体 ❷不能被整除的,除不尽的:8 is ~ by 3. 8 不能被 3 整除。

indolent /ˈɪndələnt/ *adj.* 懒惰的,怠惰的,好逸恶劳的;懒散的:an ~ person 懒汉/He is naturally ~ and without application to any kind of business. 他生性懒惰,做什么事都不专心。派 indolence *n.*

indoor /ˈɪndɔː(r)/ *adj.* 室内的;室内进行的:an ~ antenna 室内天线 / The boys and girls are having ~ games. 小朋友们在做室内游戏。

indoors /ˌɪnˈdɔːz/ *adv.* 在屋里;在室内:The old lady always stays ~ alone.

老太太总是一个人待在屋里。

induce / ɪn'djuːs / *vt.* ❶引诱；劝服：~ a patient to take medicines prescribed by the doctor 连哄带骗地劝病人按时服用大夫开的药/Our price is competitive enough to ~ business. 我们的价格具有足够的竞争力以招来业务。❷导致；引发：an illness ~d by overwork 工作过重而引起的疾病/The song ~d a nostalgia for Scotland in us. 这首歌引起了我们对苏格兰的怀乡之愁。

indulge / ɪn'dʌldʒ / *v.* ❶沉溺；放纵；肆意从事：He did not let himself ~ in hopeless thoughts. 他没有让自己一味地做一些无望的空想。/He ~ himself too freely with wine. 他过分贪杯。❷纵容；迁就：the daughter whom he ~d 他娇生惯养的女儿/We often ~ a sick person. 我们常常迁就病人。

industrial / ɪn'dʌstrɪəl / *adj.* 工业的；产业的；实业的：~ developing strategy 工业发展战略 / ~ production 工业生产/ ~ revolution 工业革命 / They live in an ~ city. 他们居住在一个工业城市。

industrialize(-se) / ɪn'dʌstrɪəlaɪz / *v.* (使)工业化：Japan is an ~d country. 日本是一个工业化国家。

industrious / ɪn'dʌstrɪəs / *adj.* 勤劳的；刻苦的

industry / 'ɪndəstri / *n.* ❶[U]工业；产业；生产：heavy ~ 重工业/ light ~ 轻工业/ the ~ of national defence 国防工业 ❷[C]行业：the tourist ~旅游行业 ❸[U]勤奋

inequality / ˌɪnɪ'kwɒlɪti/ *n.* ❶[U]不均等；不平等；不平衡；不等量：~ of income 收入的多寡不均 ❷[C](社会地位的)不平等事例；(等级上的)差异；(尺寸、数量等的)不相同；不规则：the ~ between the rich and the poor 贫富悬殊/~ of size 大小不等 ❸[C]不等；不等式

inevitable / ɪn'evɪtəbl / *adj.* 不可避免的；必然发生的：the ~ course of history 历史的必然进程 / The result is ~. 这个结果是必然的。派 inevitably *adv.*

inexpensive / ˌɪnɪk'spensɪv / *adj.* 花费不多的；廉价的：The student was glad that he bought an ~ computer. 那学生很高兴他买到了一台廉价的计算机。

infamous / 'ɪnfəməs / *adj.* 声名狼藉的；不名誉的：The young man is ~ in his neighborhood. 那年轻人在四邻中声名狼藉。

infant / 'ɪnfənt / *n.* [C]婴儿，幼儿；(法律用语)未成年者：The nurse held an ~ in her arms. 护士怀里抱着一个婴儿。

infantry / 'infəntri / *n.* [U]步兵：a regiment of ~步兵团

infect / ɪn'fekt / *vt.* ❶传染；感染：Her daughter was ~ed with TB. 她的女儿感染上了肺病。/ I'm afraid that you will ~ me with your bad cold. 我担心你会把重感冒传染给我。❷使受影响：It is a fact that students would be ~ed with all sorts of social ideas. 学生会受各种社会思想的影响，这是事实。

infection / ɪn'fekʃn / *n.* ❶传染；传染病：She caught eye ~ while swimming. 游泳时她染上了眼病。/ The doctors took quick action to prevent ~ in this area. 医生们采取迅速行动预防传染病在这个地区传播。❷影响；感染：The ~ of his thoughts is great. 他的思想影响是巨大的。

infectious / ɪn'fekʃəs/ *adj.* ❶(疾病)传染(性)的；感染性的：Colds are ~. 感冒会传染。❷富有感染力的；易传播的：

He has a jolly, ~ laugh. 他的笑声乐呵呵的，富有感染力。派 infectiously *adv.*; infectiousness *n.*

infer /ɪnˈfɜː(r)/ *vt.* 推断；判断：We should ~ a conclusion from facts. 我们应当根据事实来推断结论。

inference /ˈɪnfərəns/ *n.* [U]推理；推论：I got the conclusion by ~. 通过推理我得到这个结论。

inferior /ɪnˈfɪərɪə(r)/ Ⅰ *adj.* ❶(阶级、身份等)下级的；下等的；低下的：Her husband is an ~ officer. 她的丈夫是一名下级军官。/ His position is ~ to his wife. 他的地位比他妻子低。❷(质量、程度等)劣等的，低劣的，差的，次的：In order to save money, the old woman always buys ~ goods. 为了省钱，老太太总是买低档商品。Ⅱ *n.* [C] ❶下级；晚辈：An experienced worker shouldn't look down upon his ~s. 老工人不应当看不起晚辈。❷次品：I found that his TV set was a ~. 我发现他的电视机是次品。

infinite /ˈɪnfɪnət/ *adj.* 无限的，无穷的；无边无际的：The universe seems to be ~. 宇宙是广大无边的。/ Such a mistake would cause ~ damage. 这样的错误会带来极大的损害。派 infinitely *adv.*

infinitive /ɪnˈfɪnɪtɪv/ Ⅰ *n.* [C]原形(动词)；不定式 Ⅱ *adj.* 原形的；不定式的：an ~ clause 不定式短语/an ~ marker 不定式标记

infinity /ɪnˈfɪnɪti/ *n.* ❶[U]无限，无穷：The white sand beach appeared into ~. 白色的沙滩一望无垠。/ Variations on the theme of Cinderella can be developed to ~. 灰姑娘的主题可以进行无穷无尽的发挥。❷无限时空；无穷；无限量：an ~ of sea and sky 无边无际的大海和天空 ❸[C](常用单数)相当长的时间；相当大的数目：I waited an ~ for her to come back. 我等得头发都白了，她还没回来。

inflation /ɪnˈfleɪʃn/ *n.* [U]通货膨胀；物价飞涨：The government is trying to put the brakes on ~. 政府正在尽力遏制通货膨胀。

inflexible /ɪnˈfleksɪbl/ *adj.* ❶不可弯曲的；刚性的：~ plastic 刚性塑料/I felt the boots were rather narrow and ~. 我觉得这双靴子太紧，而且太硬不跟脚。❷坚定的；强硬的；不屈服的；不受影响的；不可动摇的：an ~ will to succeed 百折不挠的意志/They're so ~ with their program! 他们对自己的计划寸步不让！❸不可改变的，不容变更的：an ~ law 不可变更的法律

influence /ˈɪnfluəns/ *n.* 影响；影响力：The president has succeeded in establishing an ~ over his people. 总统在人民中成功地树立了威信。/ A teacher has great ~ over his pupils. 教师对学生有很大影响。

inform /ɪnˈfɔːm/ *vt.* 通知；告诉：Keep me ~ed of the fresh developments. 随时告诉我新的进展。/ Can you ~ me where he lives? 你能告诉我他的住处吗?

informal /ɪnˈfɔːməl/ *adj.* ❶非正式的，非正规的：an ~ talk 非正式会谈/~ education 非正规教育 ❷不拘礼节的，随便的：an ~ person 不拘礼节的人/try to make discussions more ~努力使讨论的气氛更为随意 ❸合适于日常谈话的；口语体的：~ spoken English 日常使用的英语口语

information /ˌɪnfəˈmeɪʃn/ *n.* [U]消息；

情报;信息:an ~ age 信息时代 / ~ industry 信息产业 / How did you get the ~? 你是如何得到这个消息的? / His father is working in the Information Bureau. 他的父亲在情报局工作。/ The ~ conference will be held at 3 o'clock p. m. 下午三点钟召开信息发布会。

infrared /ˌɪnfrəˈred/ Ⅰ *n.* [U]红外线 Ⅱ *adj.* 红外线的:~ rays 红外线 / ~ radiation 红外线辐射

ingredient /ɪnˈgriːdɪənt/ *n.* [C] ❶(混合物的)组成部分,成分;(烹调用的)原料:the ~s of a cocktail 鸡尾酒的调配成分/Olive oil is the classic ~ for so many fine dishes. 橄榄油是许多佳肴最重要的烹饪原料。❷(构成)要素,因素:Good management is the key ~ of success. 良好的管理是成功的关键。

inhabit /ɪnˈhæbɪt/ *vt.* 居住于;栖息于:I don't think that many people ~ the small island. 我认为很少有人住在这个小岛上。派 inhabitable *adj.*

inhabitant /ɪnˈhæbɪtənt/ *n.* [C]居民;住户:The town has about more than 900 ~s. 这个镇子大约有 900 多个居民。/ I live in a city of more than 300,000 ~s. 我住在一个有 30 多万居民的城市里。

inherent /ɪnˈhɪərənt/ *adj.* 固有的;天生的;内在的:She has ~ love of beauty. 她天生爱美。派 inherently *adv.*

inherit /ɪnˈherɪt/ *vt.* 继承:He ~ed a fortune from his uncle. 他从叔父那里继承了一笔遗产。/ The little girl ~ed her mother's kind characters. 小女孩继承了母亲善良的性格。派 inheritance *n.*

inhibit /ɪnˈhɪbɪt/ *vt.* ❶抑制;约束:Thirst ~ed the desire to eat. 口渴使他没有食欲。/ This medicine ~ed the spread of the disease. 该药物抑制了疾病的蔓延。❷禁止;阻止(与 from 连用):His presence ~s me from saying what I want to. 他的在场使我怯于说出我想说的话。

inhuman /ɪnˈhjuːmən/ *adj.* ❶无情的;野蛮的;残酷的:an ~ punishment 残酷的惩罚 / ~ words 无情的言辞 / Though there is money to be made, she found the stress ~. 虽说有钱可赚,但她发觉劳动强度太残酷。❷非人(类)的;超人的:~ perfections 非凡的造诣 / His stamina seems ~. 他似乎有着超乎凡人的精力。

inhumane /ˌɪnhjuːˈmeɪn/ *adj.* 不仁慈的;不人道的,残忍的:~ treatment of animals 对动物的虐待 / He called such a law ~. 他认为这样的法规不人道。派 inhumanely *adv.*

initial /ɪˈnɪʃl/ Ⅰ *adj.* 开始的;最初的;词首的:the ~issue 创刊号/ Headache is the ~ symptom of the disease. 头痛是这种疾病最初期的症状。/ Please capitalize the ~ letter of this word. 请大写这个词的第一个字母。Ⅱ *n.* [C] 首字母:The ~ of this word is "W". 这个词的首字母是"W"。派 initially *adv.*

inject /ɪnˈdʒekt/ *vt.* 注射;注入;插进:The nurse ~ed her with some medicine. 护士给她注射了一些药物。派 injector *n.*

injection /ɪnˈdʒekʃn/ *n.*[U]注射;注入;Some old people would have an ~ for flu in winter. 一些老人冬天会打流感预防针。

injure /ˈɪndʒə(r)/ *vt.* 伤害;损伤;损害:The driver was slightly ~d in the accident. 车祸中司机受了轻伤。/ What you said ~d her pride. 你说的话伤了她的自尊心。/ Drinking too much will ~ a man's health. 酗酒会损害人的健康。

injury /ˈɪndʒəri/ *n.* 损伤；伤害；损害：The Smiths escaped ~ in the fire. 火灾中史密斯一家幸免受伤。/ It is an ~ to his reputation. 那是对他名誉的损害。

injustice /ɪnˈdʒʌstɪs/ *n.* ❶[U]不公正，不公平；非正义：the victim of ~执法不公的牺牲品/a suffocating sense of ~一阵令人窒息的委屈 ❷[C]不公正的行为；非正义行为：It is an ~ to send an innocent man to jail. 把无辜的人投入监狱是不公正的。

ink /ɪŋk/ *n.* [U]墨水；油墨：Please write in blue ~. 请用蓝墨水写。

inland Ⅰ/ˈɪnlænd/ *adj.* 内陆的；远离海洋的；国内的：She lives in an ~ city. 她住在一个内地城市。/ I received an ~ telegraph. 我收到一封国内电报。Ⅱ/ˈɪnlænd/ *n.* [U] 内陆；内地 Ⅲ/ɪnˈlænd/*adv.* 在内陆；在内地：He often goes ~. 他常到内地去。

inlet /ˈɪnlet/ *n.* [C]进口；入口；小湾：You can see the ~ of the stream on the top of the mountain. 在山顶上你可以看到那条小溪的入口处。

inn /ɪn/ *n.* [C]客栈；小旅馆；小酒馆：We stayed in a village ~ that night. 那天晚上我们住在一家乡村客栈。

inner /ˈɪnə(r)/ *adj.* 在内的；内部的：an ~ room 内室/ an ~ part 内部

innocent /ˈɪnəsənt/ *adj.* ❶无罪的；清白的(与 of 连用)：Is he guilty or ~ of the crime? 他是无罪还是有罪？❷天真无邪的；幼稚的：as ~ as a new-born baby 像初生婴儿般天真无邪 ❸头脑简单的；无知的：He is ~ about life in a big city. 他对大城市的生活一无所知。

innovate /ˈɪnəveɪt/ *v.* 革新，改革，创新；引入新事物：The fashion industry is always desperate to ~. 时装行业总是渴望不断创新。/ ~ in products 更新产品/~ a computer operating system 改进计算机操作系统 派 innovation *n.*；innovational，innovative *adj.*

innumerable /ɪˈn(j)uːmərəbl/ *adj.* 无数的，数不清的：The sky shines with ~ stars. 天空因无数颗星星而银光闪闪。

input /ˈɪnpʊt/ Ⅰ*n.* ❶输入；投入：~ and output 输入和输出 ❷投入的资金(或物)：The project calls for more ~. 工程要求更多的投入。Ⅱ*v.* 输入；投入：~ of data into a computer 向计算机输入信息

inquire /ɪnˈkwaɪə(r)/ *v.* 询问；调查：We should ~ what he wants. 我们应该问一问他想要什么。/ ~ **after** 问候：I called at his house to ~ after his health. 我到他家去问候他。~ **about** 查问；打听；了解：This led us to ~ about his past. 这促使我们去了解他的历史。~ **for** 查找；询问：He is the person you ~ for. 他就是你要找的人。

inquiry /ɪnˈkwaɪəri/ *n.* ❶打听；询问：an ~ office 问询处 / She made an ~ of the doctor about her health. 她向大夫询问她的健康事宜。❷调查；查问：The police held an ~ into the case. 警察对那桩案件进行了调查。

insane /ɪnˈseɪn/ *adj.* ❶精神失常的，精神错乱的；疯狂的：an ~ act 疯狂的举动/You must be ~ to go out in this weather. 这种天气还要出去你真是发神经！❷蠢极的；荒唐透顶的：an ~ high-mindedness 近乎蠢极的宽宏大度/

an ~ plan for crossing the ocean in a canoe 划独木舟穿越大海的愚蠢计划

inscription /ɪnˈskrɪpʃn/ *n.* [C]铭刻;铭文;碑文;匾额;(铸币、图章、勋章等上的)刻印文字:bear an ~刻有铭文/an ~ on a monument 纪念碑上的碑文

insect /ˈɪnsekt/ *n.* [C]昆虫:a swarm of ~s 一群昆虫 / a beneficial ~ 益虫 / destructive ~s 害虫

insensible /ɪnˈsensɪbəl/ *adj.* ❶无感觉的,麻木;失去知觉的:A blind man is ~ to colors. 盲人感觉不到各种色彩。/ be ~ to suffering 对痛苦麻木 ❷无感情的,无动于衷的;冷漠的:a cold,~ man 冷漠、无同情心的人 ❸没有意识到的;不知道的;不以为然的:The boys in the boat were ~ of the dangers. 小船上的几个男孩没有意识到危险。/ It was impossible for her to be ~ of his change of manners. 他态度上的变化,她自然有所察觉。派 insensibility *n.* ;insensibly *adv.*

insert /ɪnˈsɜːt/ *vt.* 插入;嵌入:They always ~ commercials in a TV program. 他们总是在电视节目中插播广告。/ He ~ed a few words while his mother was speaking. 妈妈讲话时他插了几句。

inset Ⅰ/ˈɪnˌset/ *n.* [C] ❶(书中的额外)插页;散页:The magazine has two ~s,advertising laptop computers. 杂志中有两张散页,宣传各款便携式电脑。❷(地图幅面内的)附图;(图片内的)小型插图 Ⅱ/ɪnˈset/ *vt.* ❶插入;嵌入(与 in, into 连用):For detailed information of this section see the map ~ left. 欲了解该区详情,参见左边插图。❷饰以镶饰:a gold ring ~ with diamond 镶钻金戒 / She ~ an embroidered panel in a dress. 她将绣花饰料镶在连衣裙上。

inside /ˌɪnˈsaɪd/ Ⅰ *prep.* 在……内,在……里面:The purse is ~ the drawer. 钱包在抽屉里。Ⅱ *adv.* 在里面;在内部:There is nothing ~. 里面什么也没有。

insight /ˈɪnsaɪt/ *n.* 洞察力;眼光:The writer has a keen ~ into character. 那位作家对人物性格有敏锐的洞察力。/ The headmaster is a man of great ~. 校长是一位很有眼光的人。

insist /ɪnˈsɪst/ *v.* 坚持;坚决主张(与 on, upon 连用):The teacher ~ed on the importance of studying English. 老师强调学习英语的重要性。/ He ~ed that he had never seen the criminal. 他坚持说他从来没见过那个罪犯。

insistence /ɪnˈsɪstəns/ *n.* [U]坚持,强调;坚决要求,坚决主张:She finished the work at the boss's ~. 在老板的坚决要求下她完成了那项工作。/ The ~ in her voice made him look up. 她口气坚定,他不由得抬头望了一下。

insistent /ɪnˈsɪstənt/ *adj.* ❶坚持的;持续的(与 on 连用):the ~ buzz of the telephone 响个不停的电话铃声/ The boy was ~ that he was right. 那个男孩坚持他没错。❷急促的;急切的:the increasingly ~ demands of modernization 现代化日益迫切的要求 派 insistently *adv.*

inspect /ɪnˈspekt/ *v.* 检查;视察;检阅:The conductor was ~ing her luggage. 列车员正在检查她的行李。/ The commander will come to ~ the troops. 指挥官要来检阅部队。

inspection /ɪnˈspekʃn/ *n.* 检查;审查;检阅;视察:He undergoes a medical ~ every year. 每年他接受一次健康检查。/ The mayor made an ~ of the university yesterday. 昨天市长视察了那所大学。/ Please show the ~ report of the products. 请出示产品检验报告。/ Inspection declined. 谢绝参观。

inspector /ɪnˈspektə(r)/ *n.* [C]检查员；视察员；She is a health ~ of our class. 她是我们班的卫生检查员。

inspiration /ˌɪnspəˈreɪʃn/ *n.* ❶[U]灵感：He received his ~ in his dream. 他在梦中获得了灵感。❷[C]鼓舞人心的人或物：What an ~ she was to all around her! 她对她周围的人是一种多么大的鼓舞啊！

inspire /ɪnˈspaɪə(r)/ *vt.* 激励；鼓励；鼓舞：Success ~s us for fresh efforts. 成功激励我们去做新的努力。/ I guess you have been ~d by somebody else. 我想你一定受了别人的鼓舞。

instal(l) /ɪnˈstɔːl/ *vt.* 安装；设置：She ~ed a telephone in her bedroom. 她在卧室里装了一部电话。/ My father decided to ~ a new computer for me. 我父亲决定给我安装一台新计算机。

installation /ˌɪnstəˈleɪʃən/ *n.* ❶安装，设置：the cost for ~, maintenance and inspection 安装、维护和检修的费用 / carry out several ~s 实施几项安装工程 ❷[C]装置，设备，设施：a lighting (heating) ~ 照明(取暖)装置

installment /ɪnˈstɔːlmənt/ *n.* [C]分期付款：He bought an apartment in (by) ~s. 他以分期付款购买了一套公寓房。

instance /ˈɪnstəns/ *n.* [C]例子；实例；事例：He gave an ~ to explain the question. 他举了一个例子讲解这个问题。/ **for** ~ 例如；比如；举例说：I like animals, for ~, cats, dogs and pandas. 我喜欢动物，例如猫、狗和熊猫。

instant /ˈɪnstənt/ Ⅰ *n.* [C]即时，即刻；瞬间，刹那：He may arrive any ~. 他随时都可能到达。/ **in an** ~ 立刻，马上：He answered the teacher's questions in an ~. 他立即回答了老师的问题。Ⅱ*adj.* (食品)速溶的；方便的：I like ~ coffer. 我喜欢喝速溶咖啡。派 instantly *adv.*

instead /ɪnˈsted/ *adv.* 代替；更换：They aren't going to have a meeting this Sunday. They'll have a singing competition ~. 本星期日他们不打算开会，而是举行歌咏比赛。/ ~ **of** 代替(后接名词、代词、动名词或介词短语)：They went there on foot ~ of by bus. 他们没乘公共汽车而是步行到那里去的。/ Instead of Jane, Mary came to help me. 来帮助我的是玛丽，而不是简。

instinct /ˈɪnstɪŋkt/ *n.* 本能；直觉；天性：I trust my ~. 我相信我的直觉。/ She is only five and shows an ~ for painting. 她才五岁，却显示出绘画的天性。

institute /ˈɪnstɪtjuːt/ *n.* [C]协会；学会；学院；研究所，研究院：an art ~ 艺术学院 / an ~ of foreign languages 外国语学院 / an ~ of technology 理工学院

institution /ˌɪnstɪˈtjuːʃn/ *n.* [C]机关；社会公共机构：an educational ~ 教育机构 / a business ~ 商业机构 / a scientific ~ 科学协会 / a teaching ~ 教学机构 / a charity ~ 慈善机构

instruct /ɪnˈstrʌkt/ *vt.* ❶教；教育；指导：An old teacher ~s us in history. 一位老教师教我们历史课。/ It is my mother who first ~ed me in the correct use of dictionaries. 我妈妈最先教我正确使用字典。❷指示；命令：The doctor ~ed me to stay at home. 大夫命令我待在家里休息。❸通知；告知：He has been ~ed to start at once. 他被告知立即出发。

instruction /ɪnˈstrʌkʃn/ *n.* ❶[C](*pl.*)命令;指示;用法说明:You should follow the ~s. 你应当遵循操作指南。/ He gave me ~s to finish the work before dark. 他指示我天黑前做完工作。❷[U]教学;教训;教导:I learned how to swim through her ~. 她指导我学会了游泳。

instructive /ɪnˈstrʌktɪv/ *adj.* ❶有教育意义的;启迪性的:an ~ and entertaining essay 既有教育意义又有娱乐性的文章/Great books are the most ~. 名著最有启发性。❷增长知识的;教训开导的:The lecture on eating rituals and their cultural ramifications is ~ as well as amusing. 有关各种饮食礼仪及其文化渊源的讲座既增长知识又有趣味。

instructor /ɪnˈstrʌktə(r)/ *n.* [C]指导者;教员;讲师:a political ~ 政治指导员 / a driving ~ 汽车驾驶教练

instrument /ˈɪnstrəmənt/ *n.* [C] ❶工具;器具;仪器:medical ~s 医疗器具/ scientific ~s 科学仪器/ This factory produces all kind of teaching ~s. 这家工厂生产各种教学仪器。❷乐器:musical ~s 乐器/ orchestra ~s 管弦乐器/ a string (stringed) ~弦乐器/ a wind ~ 管乐器

insubstantial /ˌɪnsəbˈstænʃəl/ *adj.* ❶无实质的,无实体的;非实在的,虚幻的:~ plot 虚构的情节 / ~ visions 幻景 ❷不坚实的,不坚固的;脆弱的:an ~ floor 不坚固的地板 / an ~ basis for cooperation 脆弱的合作基础

insult Ⅰ/ˈɪnsʌlt/ *n.* [C]侮辱;侮辱的言行:Don't shout ~ at others even if your are angry. 即使是生气你也不要辱骂他人。Ⅱ/ɪnˈsʌlt/ *vt.* 侮辱:He ~ed me by saying that. 他说那种话来侮辱我。

insurance /ɪnˈʃʊərəns/ *n.* [U]保险;保险业;保险费:an ~ company 保险公司 / medical ~ 医疗保险 / social old age ~ 社会养老保险 / He took out ~ on his house. 他为他的房屋保了险。

insure /ɪnˈʃʊə(r)/ *vt.* 给……保险;保证;确保:He ~d his car for 100,000 yuan. 他投保了10万元车险。

intangible /ɪnˈtændʒɪbl/ *adj.* 触摸不到的;无(定)形的:~ personal property 个人的无形资产/Air is ~. 空气是触摸不到的。

integrate /ˈɪntɪgreɪt/ *v.* ❶使成一体,使合并,使结合:~ Eastern with Western art 融东西方艺术为一体 / The world economy is becoming more closely ~d. 世界经济越来越紧密地联系在一起。❷使完全融入(社会等);使获得……的成员资格:~ new buildings with their surroundings 使新建筑物与周边环境协调起来 派 integration *n.*

intellectual /ˌɪntəˈlektʃuəl/ Ⅰ*adj.* 智力的;知识的:the ~ faculties 智能 / ~ work 脑力劳动 / ~ youth 知识青年 Ⅱ*n.* [C]知识分子:young ~s 青年知识分子

intelligence /ɪnˈtelɪdʒəns/ *n.* [U] ❶智力;理解力:~ difference 智力差异 / ~ quotient 智商(IQ)/ We should care for the child who is weak in ~. 我们应该关爱弱智儿童。❷情报;谍报:He is responsible for collecting classified ~. 他负责收集保密情报。

intelligent /ɪnˈtelɪdʒənt/ *adj.* 有才智的;聪明的:an ~ child 聪明的孩子/ ~ answers 巧妙的回答

intend /ɪnˈtend/ *vt.* 想要;打算;企图:What do you ~ to do today? 你今天打算做什么? / ~ **sb. to do sth.** 要某人做

某事：We ~ them to do it. 我们打算让他们做此事。

intended / ɪnˈtendɪd / *adj*. ❶故意的；蓄意的；有预谋的：He told no one of his ~ flight but his friend Tom. 除了他的朋友汤姆，他再没把他的逃跑的事告诉别人。❷打算中的，预期中的；未来的：the ~ destination 计划的目的地/an ~ bride 准新娘

intense / ɪnˈtens / *adj*. ❶强烈的；剧烈的：~ heat 酷热 / ~ pain 剧痛 / I really can't bear the ~ sunlight here. 我真不能忍受这里的烈日暴晒。/ He has an ~ hatred of ice-cream. 他极讨厌吃冰激凌。❷热情的；热心的：In a strange place, you always want to ask an ~ person for help. 在陌生地方，你总是想找一个热心人来帮助你。派 intensely *adj*.

intensity / ɪnˈtensəti / *n*. [U] 强烈；紧张；强度：current ~ 电流强度 / labor ~ 劳动强度/ She showed the ~ of her anger. 她表示出强烈的愤怒。

intensive / ɪnˈtensɪv / *adj*. 加强的；集中的；精细的：They are having an ~ course in English. 他们正在上英语强化课程。/ I like ~ reading very much. 我非常喜欢精读。

intent / ɪnˈtent / *n*. [U] ❶意图，目的：It was not done by ~. 这件事不是故意而为的。/He declared his ~ to run in the election. 他声明自己要出马参加竞选的意向。/She approached the old man with ~ to defraud. 她怀着诈骗的目的接近那个老头儿。❷意思，含义：The ~ of the article escaped me. 我看不出那篇文章的含义。/ **to(for) all ~s and purposes** 实际上，事实上：His speech was to all ~s and purposes a declaration of love. 他这番话实际上是在表达他的爱情。

intention / ɪnˈtenʃn / *n*. 意图；目的；打算：He went to London in the ~ of Learning English. 他去伦敦就是为了学英语。/ She didn't say anything at the meeting by ~. 在会上她故意一言不发。

interact / ˌɪntərˈækt / *vi*. 相互影响；相互作用；互动：Teachers and students ~ on each other. 教学双方相辅相成。/ These two chemicals ~ to form a gas. 这两种化学物质相互作用，形成一种气体。

interest / ˈɪntrəst / Ⅰ *vt*. 使发生兴趣；引起……注意：That will certainly ~ you. 那肯定会引起你的兴趣。Ⅱ *n*. ❶[U]兴趣；关心：feel (take) a great (no, not much) ~ in 对……有很大兴趣(不感兴趣，不太感兴趣)/ He takes no ~ in English. 他对英语不感兴趣。❷[C](常用 *pl.*)利益；福利：We should put the ~s of the people before all else. 我们应把人民的利益置于其他一切之上。/ **in the ~s of** 为了……的利益：He works in the ~s of his company. 他为公司的利益干活。❸[U]利息：The bank charges low ~ on all money borrowed from it. 这家银行实行低息贷款。

interested / ˈɪntrəstɪd / *adj*. 感兴趣的；关心的：He is ~ in fishing. 他对钓鱼很感兴趣。

interesting / ˌɪntrəstɪŋ / *adj*. 有趣味的；令人感兴趣的：I don't think he is ~. 我认为他不是一个有趣的人。

interfere / ˌɪntəˈfɪə(r) / *vi*. ❶(指人)干预(他人之事)；干涉(与 in 连用)：Don't ~ in other people's business. 少管闲事。❷(指事件)妨碍；打扰(与 with 连用)：You shouldn't let pleasure ~ with business. 你不该让玩乐妨碍事业。

interference / ˌɪntəˈfɪərəns / *n.* [U] 干预;干涉;妨碍;干扰:His ~ spoiled our travel. 他的干涉破坏了我们的旅游。/ No one had the right to give ~ in the affairs of another nation. 没有人有权干涉他国内政。

interior / ɪnˈtɪərɪə(r) / Ⅰ *adj.* 内部的;里面的;内在的:My brother likes ~ design. 我哥哥喜欢室内设计。❷内地的;国内的:The delegation visited the ~ cities of the country. 代表团访问了该国的一些内地城市。Ⅱ *n.* [C] ❶内部:The ~ of the hall was beautifully decorated. 大厅内部装饰得很漂亮。❷内地:travel in the ~ 国内旅游

internal / ɪnˈtɜːnl / *adj.* 内部的;国内的;内政的:~ organs 内脏;内部器官 / ~ bleeding 内出血/ ~ trade 国内贸易 / ~ affairs 内政;内部事务

international / ˌɪntəˈnæʃnəl / *adj.* 国际的;世界的(性)的:~ trade 国际贸易/ customary ~ practice 国际惯例 / The United Nations is an ~ organization. 联合国是一个国际组织。/ The old lady knows the ~ situation very well. 老太太非常了解国际形势。

Internet / ˈɪntənet / *n.* 因特网;互联网:an ~ buff 网虫 / an ~ bar 网吧 / Our teacher taught us how to search the ~. 我们老师教我们检索因特网。/ You can find a lot of information on the ~. 你可以在互联网上查到许多资料。

interpreter / ɪnˈtɜːprɪtə(r) / *n.* [C] 口译者;译员:She wants to be an ~. 她想当一名口译员。

interrupt / ˌɪntəˈrʌpt / *vt.* 中断;打断;阻止;打扰:Traffic was ~ed by the snowstorm. 交通被暴风雪阻断。/ Don't ~ him in his work. 不要干扰他的工作。派 interruption *n.*

intersect / ˌɪntəˈsekt / *v.* 贯穿,横穿;相交,交叉:a busy stretch of road where the expressway ~s the highway 高速公路与公路交叉处的繁忙路段/The two roads ~ at the castle. 这两条路交会于那座城堡。

interval / ˈɪntəvəl / *n.* [C](两件事或两个动作的)间隔时间,间隙:There is a two hours' ~ to the next train. 下一班火车还要过两个小时才来。/ He likes to have a smoke in the ~. 幕间休息时他喜欢抽支烟。/ **at ~s** 不时,每隔……(时间或距离):There was a rain falling at ~s. 每隔一段时间就下一阵雨。/ Trees are planted at ~s of five meters. 每隔五米远种一棵树。

intervene / ˌɪntəˈviːn / *vi.* ❶干涉;调停,调解:The government can ~ to end a strike. 政府可以采取措施,制止罢工。❷(事情、情况等)介乎其间;发生于其间:We could meet more often if the sea did not ~. 若不是大海相隔,我们就更能常聚。❸干扰,阻挠;打扰:If noting else ~ s I can meet you there at 5 o'clock. 要是没有别的事打扰,我可以5点钟到那儿接你。

interview / ˈɪntəvjuː / Ⅰ *n.* [C] 接见;会见;面试;采访:The president gave an ~ on television last night. 总统昨晚在电视上接受了采访。/ Your ~ for the job is tomorrow. 你求职的面试定在明天。Ⅱ *vt.* 接见;会见;会谈:The mayor ~ed the foreign investors yesterday afternoon. 昨天下午市长会见了外国投资商。派 interviewee *n.* ;interviewer *n.*

intestine / ɪnˈtestɪn / *n.* [C](常用 *pl.*)肠

intimate / ˈɪntɪmət / *adj.* 亲密的;私人的:an ~ friend 亲密朋友 / ~ affairs 私

事 / an ~ diary 个人日记

into / ˈɪntʊ,ˈɪntə / *prep.* ❶进入……之内;向内:Come ~ the room. 进屋来。/ Don't get ~ trouble. 不要惹麻烦。❷变成(……的状况):When heated, water can be changed ~ vapor. 水加热可变成蒸气。

intonation / ˌɪntəˈneɪʃn / *n.* [U]语调,音调:The boy is good at imitating others' ~. 小男孩很擅长模仿他人的声调。

introduce / ˌɪntrəˈdjuːs / *vt.* ❶ 提出:He ~d a question for debate. 他提出一个问题进行辩论。❷ 介绍:He ~d me to your friends. 他把我介绍给你的朋友。❸引进;输入:He ~d a new theory in his report. 他在报告里引入了一种新理论。/The president ~d new ideas into education. 校长给教育引进了新的思想。

introduction / ˌɪntrəˈdʌkʃn / *n.* ❶介绍 ❷引进;传入:a letter of ~ 介绍信 / ~ of technology 技术引进 ❸导言;绪论;入门:The ~ to this book is well written. 这本书的序言写得很精彩。

intrude / ɪnˈtruːd / *vi.* 侵入;闯入:A stranger ~d into our meeting. 一个陌生人闯入了我们的会场。/ You'd better not ~ your opinions on others. 你最好不要把你的意见强加到别人头上。派 intrusion *n.*

intuition / ˌɪntjuːˈɪʃn / *n.* ❶[U]直觉;直觉力:act on one's ~凭自己的直觉行事/It is said that females have more ~ than males. 据说女性的直觉力比男性强。❷[C]直觉感知的事物;直觉知识;直觉真理:I have an ~ that my friends is ill. 我凭直觉感到朋友病了。/Our ~s may fail in moments of panic. 在紧张的瞬间我们的直觉认识或许靠不住。

invade / ɪnˈveɪd / *vt.* 侵略;侵犯;侵害:These countries were ~d in 1938. 这些国家在 1938 年都遭到了侵略。派 invader *n.*

invalid / ɪnˈvælɪd / *adj.* ❶无效果的;不得力的;无价值的:an ~ argument 站不住脚的论点/The operation was deemed ~ and valueless. 有人认为这个行动方案不得力,毫无价值。❷无效(力)的;作废的:an ~ check 无效的支票/He claimed that the referendum is legally ~. 他宣布这次公民投票没有法律效力。

invaluable / ɪnˈvæljuːəbl / *adj.* 极其宝贵的;非常贵重的;无法估价的:~ experience 宝贵的经验/Self-discipline is an ~ acquisition. 自我约束是一种无价之宝。/a book ~ for reference 很有参考价值的书

invariable / ɪnˈveərɪəbl/ Ⅰ *adj.* ❶不变的,始终如一的;恒定的:an ~ habit of getting up early 早起的老习惯 / The menu is ~ but the food is always good. 菜单千篇一律,不过饭菜一直很可口。❷不变的,固定的;常数的 Ⅱ *n.* [C]不变量;固定值;常数 派 invariably *adv.*

invasion / ɪnˈveɪʒn / *n.* [U]侵略;侵犯;侵害:They united to resist the enemy's ~. 他们团结一致抵御敌人的侵略。

invent / ɪnˈvent / *vt.* 发明;创造:Watt ~ed the steam engine. 瓦特发明了蒸汽机。/ The new machine was ~ed by a young worker. 这部新机器是一个年轻工人发明的。

invention / ɪnˈvenʃn / *n.* 发明;创造;发明物:The ~ of a space rocket took many years. 宇宙火箭的发明花了许多年时间。/ That is an ~ of Edison. 那是爱迪生的一项发明。

inverse /ɪnˈvɜːs/ Ⅰ *adj*. ❶相反的;反向的;倒转的,翻转的:an ~ order 逆序/The results are just ~ to the amount of effort put in. 结果与付出的努力正好相反。❷反的,逆的:Addition and subtraction are ~ operations. 加法与减法是逆运算。Ⅱ *n*. 相反;颠倒;反面:Dividing by three is ~ of multiplying by three. 除以3和乘以3正好互逆。

invert /ɪnˈvɜːt/ *vt*. ❶使反向;使倒置;使颠倒;使倒转:~ the glass over a fly 把杯子倒过来罩住苍蝇/Skilled farmers believe that it is never wise to ~ the topsoil. 种庄稼的老把式们认为,把土地的表土深翻从来就不是个明智的做法。❷使(词序)倒装:In this language the word order in questions is ~ed. 在这种语言中,疑问句的词序是倒装。

invest /ɪnˈvest/ *vt*. 投资;投入(资金、时间等):~ funds in stocks 投资股票/He ~ed all his savings in real estate. 他把所有的存款投资于房地产。/Our teacher ~ed a lot of time and effort in the new teaching method. 我们的老师投入许多时间和精力研究新教学法。派 investor *n*.

investigate /ɪnˈvestɪgeɪt/ *vt*. 调查;调查研究:Scientists ~d the national resources of this area. 科学家们调查了这个地区的自然资源。/The students ~d the market and learned a lot. 学生们进行了市场调查,学到了很多东西。

investigation /ɪnˌvestɪˈgeɪʃn/ *n*. 调查;审查:Let's go out to welcome the ~ group. 走,我们去欢迎考察团。/**make an ~ on (of, into) sth.** 对某事进行调查:He is making a thorough ~ on this matter. 他正对此事进行彻底调查。

investment /ɪnˈvestmənt/ *n*. ❶投资;投资物;投资的财产;值得投资的对象:open up to foreign ~对外国投资实施开放政策/They believe education is a good ~ for life. 人们认为教育是个终生值得投资的项目。❷[C](时间、精力、思考等的)投入:A happy marriage requires an ~ of time and energy. 美满的婚姻是需要付出时间和精力的。

invigorate /ɪnˈvɪg(ə)ˌreɪt/ *vt*. 使生气勃勃;使精力充沛;使活跃:They took various steps to ~ trade in the town. 他们采取各种措施来活跃镇上的商业活动。/The shower ~d her. 沐浴使她感到神清气爽。

invisible /ɪnˈvɪzəbl/ *adj*. 看不见的;无形的;不露面的:Germs are ~ to our eyes. 我们的肉眼看不见细菌。/The little girl kept herself ~ in the room. 那小姑娘躲在房里不露面。

invitation /ˌɪnvɪˈteɪʃn/ *n*. 邀请;招待;请柬:The manager accepted an ~ to attend a reception. 经理应邀出席招待会。

invite /ɪnˈvaɪt/ *vt*. 邀请;请求:He didn't ~ me in. 他没请我入内。/She is ~d out to a meal. 她应邀外出吃饭。

inviting /ɪnˈvaɪtɪŋ/ *adj*. 有吸引力的,吸引人的;诱人的:an ~ sight 吸引人的景色/give an ~ smile 妩媚地一笑/This drink smells ~ and tastes fresh. 这种饮料闻着诱人,喝着爽口。

invoice /ˈɪnvɒɪs/ *n*. [C]发票;发货清单;服务费用清单:a purchase ~购货发票/issue an ~签发货单/Please write out your ~ in quadruplicate. 发票请开一式四份。

involve /ɪnˈvɒlv/ *vt*. 包含;牵连;卷入:A foolish mistake can ~ you in a great deal of trouble. 一次愚蠢的错误可使你陷入极大的麻烦之中。

inward(s) /ˈɪnwəd(z)/ Ⅰ *adv*. ❶向内;

朝里；向中心；向家里；向国内：This end should go ~. 这一端应该向里头放。/ All the children stand in a circle facing ~, with their hands behind their backs. 所有的孩子站成一个圆圈，脸朝内，把手放在背后。❷内心里，精神上：The mind's turning ~ upon itself. 思想转向内省。Ⅱ*adj.* ❶向里面的，入内的；输入的：an ~ spiral 内旋 /~ transmission of data 数据的输入 ❷里面的，内部的；体内的：the ~ parts of the body 体内器官 ❸内心的；精神的：an ~ happiness (feelings) 内心的喜悦(感情)

ion /ˈaɪən, ˈaɪɒn/ *n.* [C]离子

IQ (=intelligence quotient)智商

iron /ˈaɪən/ Ⅰ*n.* ❶[U]铁：crude ~ 生铁 / cast ~ 铸铁 / Strike while the ~ is hot. 趁热打铁。❷[C]烙铁；熨斗：She bought a steam ~. 她买了一个蒸气熨斗。Ⅱ*v.* ❶熨；烫：~ a coat 熨烫衣服 / Mother is ~ing out her shirt. 妈妈正在熨衬衫。❷消除(困难、误解等)：After an hour's talk, they ~ed their misunderstandings. 经过一个小时的交谈，他们消除了误解。

ironic(al) /aɪˈrɒnɪk(l)/ *adj.* 冷嘲的；讽刺的；挖苦的；令人啼笑皆非的：An ~ smile indicated that she didn't agree with me. 一丝冷笑表明她并不赞同我的意见。派 ironically *adv.*

irony /ˈaɪrənɪ/ *n.* 冷嘲；反讽；反话

irrational /ɪˈræʃənəl/ *adj.* ❶不合逻辑的；不合理的；荒谬的：I felt a wave of ~ guilt and fear. 我突然产生了一阵莫名其妙的犯罪感和恐惧心。/Superstitions are ~. 迷信是荒谬的。❷没有理性的；失去理性的：~ creatures 无理性的动物/be ~ in one's attitude to one's own child 在对自己孩子的态度上不明智 ❸(数学)无理的：~ equation 无理方案

irregular /ɪˈregjələ(r)/ *adj.* 不合常规的；不规则的：~ verbs 不规则动词 / an ~ army 非正规军 / The fields are ~ in shape. 这些田地的形状很不整齐。

irrelevant /ɪˈrevləvənt/ *adj.* 不相干的；无关紧要的；不切题的：He was a man of ~ information and unasked-for good advice. 他是个爱东拉西扯又好为人师的家伙。/These references are largely ~ to the present topic. 这些参考资料与眼下的话题风马牛不相及。

irrigate /ˈɪrɪgeɪt/ *v.* 灌溉(田地、作物等)：They ~d their crops with water from this river. 他们用这条河的水浇灌庄稼。

irrigation /ˌɪrɪˈgeɪʃn/ *n.* [U]灌溉：The peasants built up an ~ channel at the foot of the mountain. 农民在山下修了一条灌溉渠。

irritate /ˈɪrɪteɪt/ *v.* 激怒；使发怒；引起恼怒：His letter ~d me a little. 他的信使我有点恼怒。

is /ɪz/ *v.*(他、她或它)是

Islam /ˈɪzlɑːm/ *n.* ❶伊斯兰教；回教 ❷(总称)伊斯兰教徒

island /ˈaɪlənd/ *n.* [C]岛，岛屿：a lonely ~ 孤岛/ an uninhabited ~ 荒岛/Taiwan is the largest ~ of China. 台湾是中国最大的岛屿。

isolate /ˈaɪsəleɪt/ *vt.* ❶隔离；孤立：Patients with the disease should be ~d. 这种病的患者应予以隔离。❷分离；分解

isolation /ˌaɪsəˈleɪʃn/ *n.* [U]隔离；分离；脱离；单独；孤立；孤独：Isolation of the infected person is necessary. 隔离受感染者很有必要。/live in ~ from other nations 闭关锁国/You can't consider one sentence in ~. 你不能孤立地考虑

一个句子。

issue /ˈɪsjuː, ˈɪʃuː/ Ⅰ *v.* ❶出来；流出：His blood ~d from the cut. 他的血从伤口流出。❷发出；发布；发表；发给：Orders were ~d from the headquarters. 命令从司令部发出。/ This magazine is ~d monthly. 这种杂志每月发行一期。/ Each student was ~d with textbook. 每个学生发了一本教科书。Ⅱ *n.* [C] ❶(引起争论的)问题，争端：Inflation is a hot ~ of the day. 通货膨胀是当今的热门问题。❷发行(物)；(报、刊的)期：I have read the latest ~ of *China Daily*. 我已读了最近一期的《中国日报》。

it /ɪt/ *pron.* ❶它(指无生命的东西，性别不明或性别不重要的动物，性别不明或性别无关紧要的婴儿)：Where is the cat? It's under the table. 猫在哪里？在桌下。❷用作句子形式上无意义的主语：①指天气状况：It's fine today. 今天天晴。②指时间：It's six o'clock now. 现在六点钟。③指距离：It's a long way from here. 距离这里很远。❸模糊地指一般情形，或指由上下文可以了解的事物：Whose turn is ~? 现在轮到谁了？❹用以强调某一句子成分：①主语：It was he who wrote this article. 是他写的这篇文章。②动词的宾语：It was John that I met in the street yesterday. 我昨天在街上碰到的是约翰。③状语：It was on Sun day that I saw him. 我看见他的那一天是星期天。❺作先行代词，指代短语或从句：①不定式短语：Is ~ difficult to learn English well? 学好英语很困难吗？It is very hard for me to do ~. 我来做这事太艰难了。②动名词短语：It's no use going to see him. 去看他无用。③从句：It doesn't matter whether we start now or later. 我们现在开始还是以后开始都没关系。

IT (=information technology)信息技术

itch /ɪtʃ/ Ⅰ *v.* ❶发痒，使人发痒：He's ~ing all over. 他浑身发痒。❷热望，渴望：I am ~ing to tell you the news. 我巴不得马上就把消息告诉你。Ⅱ *n.* [C] ❶痒：have an ~ on one's (the) back 背部发痒 ❷热望，渴望：have an ~ to go around the world 渴望周游世界

item /ˈaɪtəm/ *n.* [C]❶条；条款；项目；细目：He read the treaty ~ by ~. 他逐条阅读那份条约。/ They discussed many ~s about the design last week. 上周他们对有关设计的很多项目进行了讨论。❷(新闻等的)一条；一则：I read an interesting ~ in today's newspaper. 在今天的报上我读到一条很有趣的新闻。

iterate /ˈɪtəˌreɪt/ *vt.* 重申，重述：~ a warning 一再警告/Wise men do not ~ mistakes. 聪明的人不会重复犯错。派 iteration *n.*

its /ɪts/ *pron.* 它的(it 的所有格；形容词性物主代词)：The dog wagged ~ tail. 狗摇尾巴。

itself /ɪtˈself/ *pron.* ❶它自己，它本身(反身代词)：This novel is a history in ~. 这部小说本身就是一部历史。/ Put it by ~. 这东西单独放。❷自身，本身(表示强调)：The book ~ is worth reading. 这书本身就值得一读。/ The problem ~ is not important. 这问题本身并不重要。

ivory /ˈaɪvəri/ *n.* [U]象牙；象牙制品；象牙色：~ tower 象牙塔

J j

jack / dʒæk / *n.* [C]起重器；千斤顶：an automobile ~ 汽车千斤顶

jacket / ˈdʒækɪt / *n.* [C]短上衣；夹克：A man in ~ came in. 一个穿夹克的人走进来。

jackpot / ˈdʒækˌpɒt / *n.* [C] ❶(彩票等的)头奖；累加奖金 ❷大笔收入；巨额的奖金；意外的成功

jagged / ˈdʒægɪd / *adj.* ❶有尖突的；有锯齿状缺口的；凹凸不平的；参差不齐的：a ~ streak of lightning 锯齿状闪电/ ~ leaves 四周像锯齿似的叶片 ❷粗糙的；(声音等)刺耳的：a ~ scream 刺耳的尖叫声

jaguar / ˈdʒægjuə(r) / *n.* [C](产于南美洲的)美洲虎，美洲豹

jade / dʒeɪd / *n.* [U]玉；翡翠

jail / dʒeɪl / *n.* [C]监牢；牢狱：~-break 越狱/ ~-house 监狱；牢房/ He was sent to ~. 他被关进了监狱。

jailer(-or) / ˈdʒeɪlə(r)/ *n.* [C]监狱看守，狱卒，牢子

jam[1] / ˈdʒæm / *n.* [U]果酱：a jar of apple (peach, strawberry) ~ 一瓶苹果(桃子、草莓)酱 / She spread some apple ~ on the bread. 她在面包上涂了一些苹果酱。

jam[2] / ˈdʒæm / Ⅰ *n.* [C] ❶堵塞；阻塞；拥挤：We got in a traffic ~ on the way. 路上我们遇到堵车。❷困境；困难：He told me that he really wanted to get out of the ~ soon. 他告诉我他真想马上摆脱困境。Ⅱ *v.* (jammed; jamming) 堵塞；塞满；挤进：She ~med all her clothes into a suitcase. 她把所有的衣服塞进一个手提箱里。/ As soon as he ~med onto the bus, it started. 他一挤进公共汽车，公共汽车就开动了。

January / ˈdʒænjʊəri / *n.* 一月(略作 Jan.)

jar / dʒɑː(r) / *n.* [C]坛子；罐子；缸：a jam ~ 果酱瓶 / a ~ of water 一罐水

jasmin(e) / ˈdʒæzmɪn / *n.* [U] ❶素馨；茉莉，素方花 ❷淡黄色，素馨色

jaw / dʒɔː / *n.* [C]颚：the lower ~ 下颚 / the upper ~ 上颚

jazz / dʒæz / *n.* [U]爵士音乐；爵士舞曲：Young people like modern ~. 年轻人喜欢现代爵士乐。/ The boy is a ~ fan. 小男孩是个爵士乐迷。

jealous / ˈdʒeləs / *adj.* 羡慕的；妒忌的：She is bitterly ~ of his success. 她极妒忌他的成功。派 jealousy *n.*

jeans / dʒiːnz / *n.* 牛仔裤：He always wears ~. 他总爱穿牛仔裤。

jeep / dʒiːp / *n.* [C] 吉普车：We visited a ~ factory. 我们参观了一家吉普车生产厂。

jelly / ˈdʒeli / *n.* [U]冻；果子冻：apple

(cherry, orange) ~ 苹果(樱桃、橘子)冻

jeopardize / ˈdʒepədaɪz/ *vt.* 使处于险境;冒……的危险;损害,危及:~ one's life to do sth. 冒生命危险去做某事 / To make an exception would ~ our relations with other customers. 一次破例将有损于我们和其他客户的关系。

jeopardy / ˈdʒepədi / *n.* [U]危险,危难,危境:The spy was in constant ~ of being discovered. 该间谍处于随时都有可能暴露的危险境地。

jerk / dʒɜːk / Ⅰ *n.* [C]猛推;急拉:He gave the rope a ~ and it broke. 他猛拉绳子,绳子断了。Ⅱ *v.* 猛推;猛扯;急拉:A car ~ed to a stop in front of him. 一辆小车猛然停在了他的跟前。/ The girl ~ed her head around to see that a stranger was after her. 女孩猛地转过来看到一个陌生人跟着她。

Jesus / ˈdʒiːzəs / *n.* 耶稣

jet / dʒet / *n.* [C]喷射机;喷气客机:Have you any experience of travelling by ~? 你有过乘喷气机旅行的经历吗?

Jew / dʒuː / *n.* [C]犹太人;犹太教徒

jewel / ˈdʒuːəl / *n.* [U] ❶宝石:The ring set with a ~ is very beautiful. 那枚镶宝石的戒指真漂亮。/ She often says that her favorite ~ is a ruby. 她常说她最喜欢红宝石。❷贵重饰物;宝石饰物:

jeweler / ˈdʒuːələ(r) / *n.* [C]宝石商;珠宝商:Mr Smith is a ~. 史密斯先生是一个珠宝商。

jewelry / ˈdʒuːəlri / *n.* [U](总称)珠宝;珠宝饰物;首饰:They missed some valuable ~ in their shop last night. 昨天晚上他们商店丢失了一些贵重的珠宝。/ I don't like to wear ~ in my daily life. 在日常生活中我不喜欢佩戴珠宝饰品。

Jewish / ˈdʒuːɪʃ / *adj.* 犹太人的;犹太教的

jingle / ˈdʒɪŋgl / Ⅰ *vi.* 发出叮当声;叮当作响;响着铃铛行进:The sleigh bells ~d as we rode. 我们滑雪橇时,雪橇上的铃铛叮当直响。/ ~ the coins in one's pocket 把口袋里的硬币弄得丁零当啷直响 Ⅱ *n.* [C] 叮当声;发出叮当声的东西:The dog pricked up its ears at the ~ of its master's keys. 一听到主人钥匙的叮当声,那条狗便竖起了双耳。

job / dʒɒb / *n.* [C]职业;工作:He has done a thorough ~ of it. 他把这件事做得很彻底。/ Jim does odd ~s in his spare time. 吉姆在空余时间干些零活。/ Jobs are not easy to get. 工作不好找。/ He is out of ~. 他已失业。

jog / dʒɒg / *vi.* (jogged; jogging) ❶慢跑:My roommate goes ~ging in the park after getting up. 我的室友起床后在公园里慢跑。❷(用手、臂等)轻推;推撞:He ~ged my elbow. 他轻轻地撞了一下我的手肘。派 jogger *n.*

joggle / ˈdʒɒgl/ *v.* & *n.* [U]轻轻颠摇:The slow-moving train ~d us to sleep. 缓缓前行的列车将我们轻轻晃入梦乡。/ The ~ of the carriage put the baby to sleep. 马车轻轻颠摇,使孩子酣然入梦。

join / dʒɒɪn / *v.* ❶连接;结合:Please ~ two points by a straight line. 用直线把两点连起来。/ The new highway has ~ed our school to the city. 这条新公路把我们学校与城市连接起来了。❷参加;加入;作……的成员:~ the Party 入党/ ~ the League 入团/ ~ the army 参军/ ~ the battle 参战 ❸与……在一起;伴随(某人做某事):Will you ~ us in singing? 你和我们一块儿唱歌好吗?

joint /dʒɒɪnt/ Ⅰ*n.* [C] ❶接头;接缝;接合处;接口:The pipe was broken at the ~s. 这条管子的接口处破了。❷关节;骨节:My mother has a pain in the elbow ~. 我妈妈的肘关节痛。Ⅱ*adj.* 连接的;联合的;共同的:She said that was their ~ property. 她说那是他们的共有财产。/ Many young people want to find a job in a ~ venture enterprises. 许多年轻人想在合资企业找份工作。派 jointly *adv.*

joke /dʒəʊk/ Ⅰ*v.* 开玩笑;说笑话:I am not serious, but joking with you. 我并没有当真,只是和你开开玩笑罢了。Ⅱ*n.* [C]笑话:The table laughed at the ~. 一桌人听到这个笑话都笑了起来。

jolly /ˈdʒɒli/ *adj.* 快活的;令人高兴的:Our teacher answered our questions with a ~ laugh. 老师愉快地笑着回答了我们的问题。

jolt /dʒəʊlt/ Ⅰ*v.* ❶震动;摇动;颠簸:She ~ed his arm. 她抓住他的臂膊直摇。/The car ~ed across the rough ground. 汽车颠簸着驶过崎岖不平的道路。❷使震惊;使惊讶;惊扰,使慌忙:His sudden death ~ed us all. 他溘然去世,使我们大家大为惊愕。/The car ~ed to a halt. 汽车嘎的一震刹住了。Ⅱ*n.* [C] ❶震动,摇动;颠簸:The car gave a ~ and started. 汽车一震便启动了。❷震惊;引起震惊的事物:The news was a ~ to me. 这消息对我是一个打击。

jot /dʒɒt/ Ⅰ*vt.* (jotted; jotting)草草记下,匆匆写下:I ~ odd notes in the back of the diary. 我有时在日记的背面写些随感。/I'll just ~ that time down before I forget it. 趁现在还没有忘,我得把时间记下来。Ⅱ*n.* [C]一丁点儿,微量,丝毫:I don't care a ~ what you are going to do. 你想干什么,我才不管呢。/I haven't a ~ of sympathy for him. 我一点儿都不同情他。

journal /ˈdʒɜːnl/ *n.* [C]❶日报;杂志;期刊:a weekly (monthly) ~ 周(月)刊 / a bimonthly ~ 双月刊 / an academic ~ 学术期刊 / This is an influential ~. 这是一份很有影响的杂志。❷日志;日记:He has the habit to keep a work ~. 他习惯记工作日记。

journalism /ˈdʒɜːnəˌlɪz(ə)m/ *n.* [U] ❶新闻业;新闻工作:follow ~ as a profession 以新闻工作为职业 / Forsaking medicine, he took up ~. 他弃医投入新闻工作。❷新闻采访,新闻写作,新闻报道:That article is an example of first-class ~. 那篇文章是第一流新闻报道的范例。❸新闻学:an MA program in ~ 新闻学硕士专业

journalist /ˈdʒɜːnəlɪst/ *n.* [C]新闻工作者;报界人士:He worked as a ~ in our city after graduation. 毕业后他在我们市当了一名新闻记者。

journey /ˈdʒɜːni/ *n.* [C]旅行(尤指远距离的陆上旅行);旅程:a ~ of 3 days 三天的行程 / the ~ to success 成功之道 / a ~ on duty 出公差 / a single ~ 单程 / a pleasant ~愉快的旅程/ life's ~ 人生旅程 / a ~ on foot 徒步旅行 / He made a ~ across the country. 他做了一次横跨全国的旅行。/ Wish you a good ~. 祝你一路顺风。

joy /dʒɒɪ/ *n.* [U] 欢乐;高兴;喜悦:Success brought him ~. 成功给他带来了欢乐。/ To our great ~ we won the match at last. 使我们高兴的是我们终于赢了比赛。/ He jumped with ~. 他

高兴得跳了起来。

joyful /ˈdʒɒɪfl/ *adj*. 充满快乐的；高兴的；十分喜悦的：a ~ heart 愉快的心情 / ~ news 令人欢欣的消息 / a ~ look 高兴的样子

judge /dʒʌdʒ/ Ⅰ *n*.［C］❶审判官；法官：The ~ was very kind. 这法官很仁慈。❷仲裁人；裁判员：He acted as ~ at the race. 他在赛跑中担任裁判。❸鉴定人；鉴赏家：He is a good ~ of the fine arts. 他是一位美术鉴赏行家。Ⅱ *v*. ❶审判，审理（案件）：The man was ~d not guilty. 那人被判无罪。❷评判；评价；判断：I can't ~ whether he was right or wrong. 我不能断定他是对还是错。/ Don't ~ a person by his appearances. 不要以貌取人。

judg(e)ment /ˈdʒʌdʒmənt/ *n*. ❶ 审判；（法官或法庭的）判决：Sit in ~ on a case. 法庭听审。/ The ~ of the court is reported in all newspapers. 各报都对法院的判决做了报道。❷ 评判；判断：I let the readers form their own ~. 我让读者自己去判断。/ That is an error of ~. 那是一个判断的失误。

judicial /dʒuːˈdɪʃəl/ *adj*. ❶司法的；审判（上）的：the ~ system 司法系统/go through proper ~ procedures 履行正当的诉讼程序 ❷法官（或审判员）的；法官（或审判员）似的：~ gravity 法官（似）的威严 ❸法庭的；法院判决（或规定）的：She got a ~ separation from her husband. 她通过法院判决正式与丈夫分居。

judo /ˈdʒuːdəʊ/ *n*.［U］现代柔道（或柔术）

jug /dʒʌg/ *n*.［C］壶；大罐：a ~ of beer 一罐啤酒

juggle /ˈdʒʌgl/ *v*. 玩杂耍；变戏法；耍花招：My grandfather can ~ with three bottles. 我爷爷能用三个瓶子耍把戏。/ He ~d the little boy into telling him the truth. 他骗小男孩说出了真相。派 juggler *n*.

juice /dʒuːs/ *n*. 果汁；菜汁；肉汁：I would like a glass of vegetable ~. 我想喝一杯蔬菜汁。

July /dʒuˈlaɪ/ *n*. 七月（略作 Jul.）

jumbo /ˈdʒʌmbəʊ/ Ⅰ *n*.［C］体大而笨拙的人（或动物、物体）；庞然大物 Ⅱ *adj*. 特大（号）的；巨型的：a ~ packet of soap powder 大号袋装洗衣粉

jump /dʒʌmp/ *v*. ❶跳；跃；蹦：~ over a fence 跳过篱笆 / ~ up and down 跳上跳下 / ~ off 跳下；跳离 / ~ into a car 跳进汽车/~ onto the floor 跳到地板上 ❷（因兴奋、喜悦等）跳动，惊跳：~ for joy 高兴得跳起来 / Her heart ~ed when she heard the news. 她听到这个消息时心怦怦直跳。

junction /ˈdʒʌŋkʃn/ *n*.［C］连接点；（公路、道路等的）交叉口；（铁路）枢纽站；（河流的）汇合处：at the ~ of two hills 在两座小山的连接点/Our train waited for long time in a siding at a ~. 我们的列车在一个枢纽站的岔道上等候了好长时间。

June /dʒuːn/ *n*. 六月（略作 Jun.）

jungle /ˈdʒʌŋgl/ *n*.（常与定冠词连用，单数、复数均可）丛林，密林：I have never been to the tropical ~. 我从来没去过热带丛林。

junior /ˈdʒuːnɪə(r)/ Ⅰ *n*.［C］ ❶年少者；较年幼的人：She is your ~ by two years. 她比你小两岁。❷等级较低者；晚辈：The old worker often helps his ~. 老工人常常帮助自己的晚辈。Ⅱ *adj*. ❶年少的；较年幼的：She is ~ to you by

J

two years. (She is two years ~ to you.) 她比你小两岁。❷资历较浅的;等级较低的:a ~ class 初级班 / a ~ clerk 低级职员 / He is study-ing at a ~ high school. 他在一所初中读书。

juridic(al) /dʒʊˈrɪdɪk(əl)/ *adj.* ❶司法(上)的;审判(上)的 ❷法律(上)的;法学(上)的:a ~ association 社团法人/~ powers 法律权限

jury /ˈdʒʊəri/ *n.* [C] 陪审团;全部陪审员(或评委):The ~ decided the man was guilty. 陪审团做出决议,判定那人有罪。/ The ~ is (are) about to announce the winner. 评委即将宣布获胜者。

J

just /dʒʌst/ Ⅰ *adv.* ❶刚才;方才:They have ~ gone. 他们刚走。❷ 正好;恰好:It is ~ six o'clock. 现在正好六点。❸ 仅,只:I've come here ~ to see you. 我是专程来看你的。Ⅱ *adj.* 公平的;公正的;正义的;正直的:The teacher is ~ to us all. 老师公正地对待我们所有人。/ A judge must be ~. 法官必须公正。

justice /ˈdʒʌstɪs/ *n.* [U]公平;公正;合理:a sense of ~ 正义感 / I say, in ~ to him, that he is a good teacher of English. 公平而论,我认为他是位优秀的英语教师。

justify /ˈdʒʌstɪfaɪ/ *vt.* 证明(人的言论、行动等)为正当(或有理):He is fully justified in doing so. 他这样做是完全有道理的。

juvenile /ˈdʒuːvənaɪl/ Ⅰ *n.* [C]少年;青少年:Juveniles should be more concerned by the whole society. 青少年应当受到全社会更多的关注。Ⅱ *adj.* 青少年的;少年特有的:Her mother bought her some ~ books. 妈妈给她买了几本适合青少年读的书。

K k

kangaroo /ˌkæŋgəˈruː/ *n.* [C]大袋鼠

keen /kiːn/ *adj.* ❶热心的;渴望的:~ listeners 热心的听众 / be ~ on (doing) ...渴望(做)…… ❷激烈的;强烈的:~ competition 激烈的竞争 / ~ sense of responsibility 强烈的责任感 ❸敏锐的;敏捷的:~ sight (eye) 敏锐的眼光 ❹锋利的;刺人的:~ criticism 尖锐的批评 / ~ knife 锋利的刀

keep /kiːp/ *vt.* (kept /kept/, kept) ❶保持;保留;保存:How long may I ~ the book? 这本书我可以借多久? / ~ **in touch with** 与……保持联系:We ought to ~ in touch with him. 我们应当和他保持联系。~ **sth. in mind** 记住:Please ~ this in your mind. 请将此事牢记在心。~ **sb. in good health** 保持健康:Cold bath ~s me in good health. 冷水浴使我身体保持健康。~ **sb. (sth.) out of** 不让……进来:The cook always ~s the students out of the kitchen. 厨师总是不让学生进厨房。~ **up with** 跟上;跟……齐头并进:I can't ~ up with you. 我跟不上你。❷遵守;忠于:The Chinese people always ~ their word. 中国人民说话是算数的。/ ~ the law 遵守法律 / ~ regular hours 遵守作息时间 ❸记入,记录:~ a diary 记日记 / ~ accounts 记账 ❹(使)保持(某种状态或关系):I am sorry. I've kept you waiting. 对不起,让你久等了。/ Please ~ silent. 请保持安静。❺阻止;防止:~ **back** 阻止……向前;不告诉:The policemen had to ~ the spectators back. 警察不得不阻止群众上前围观。~ ... **from** ... 避开;阻止:He ~s nothing from me. 他什么都不瞒我。~ **sb. (sth.) from (doing) sth.** 阻止:The rain kept us from going out. 这场雨使我们不能外出。❻抑制(与 from 连用):I couldn't ~ from laughing. 我不禁大笑起来。❼继续做,不断反复做(某事)(接动名词):Why does the baby ~ crying? 为什么这婴儿不断地哭? ~ **on** 继续,持续,不停:The boy kept on talking even though the teacher asked him to stop. 虽然老师叫这男孩停止讲话,但他还是讲个不停。

keeper /ˈkiːpə(r)/ *n.* [C] ❶看护人 ❷饲养员 ❸保管员

ken /ken/ *n.* [U]认知范围;知识范围:beyond my ~在我的知识范围之外

kernel /ˈkɜːnl/ *n.* [C] ❶核,仁 ❷粒;谷粒

kerosene /ˈkerəsiːn/ *n.* [U] 煤油:a ~ lamp 煤油灯

kettle /ˈketl/ *n.* [C] 水壶;茶壶:boil a ~ 用水壶烧水 / The ~ is singing. 水烧开了。

key /kiː/ Ⅰ *n.* [C] ❶钥匙:a ~ for opening a lock 开锁的钥匙/ the ~ of a clock 给钟上发条的钥匙 / the ~ to a door (strongbox) 开门(开保险箱)的钥匙 ❷题解;答案:a ~ to the question 问题的答案 / a ~ to a puzzle 谜底/ the ~ to success 成功的窍门 ❸(琴、计算机等的)键:strike the ~s of a computer 在计算机上打字 Ⅱ *adj.* 主要的;关键的;基本的:~ factor 主要因素 / ~ point 要点 / ~ issue 关键问题

keyboard /ˈkiːbɔːd / *n.* [C]键盘

keynote /ˈkiːnəut / Ⅰ *n.* [C] ❶(音乐中的)主音;主调音 ❷(演说等的)主旨,要旨,基调;(行动、政策等的)基本方针,主导原则;(情绪等的)基本倾向;主要动向:the ~ of a speech 演说的中心意旨/Economic expansion was the ~ of the nation's foreign policy. 经济扩张是该国对外政策的主导方针。Ⅱ *vt.* 给……定基调:The governor will ~ the convention. 州长将在会上做基调演说。

kick / kɪk / *v.* 踢:The child ~ed the ball into the river. 小孩把球踢进了河里。/ The camel ~ed the poor man out. 骆驼把这可怜的人踢了出去。/ corner ~ (足球的)角球/ free ~ 任意球 / goal ~ 球门球 / spot ~ 点球 / ~ **off** 开球:John ~ed off and the football match started. 约翰开球,足球赛开始。

kickback / ˈkɪkˌbæk / *n.* [C]酬金;回扣;贿赂:He denied that he had received any ~s from contractors. 他矢口否认从承包商那里收取过佣金。

kid / kɪd / *n.* [C] ❶ 小山羊 ❷小孩:school ~s 学童

kidnap / ˈkɪdnæp / *vt.* 诱拐;绑架

kidney / ˈkɪdni / *n.* ❶[C]肾脏:transplant a ~ 移植肾脏 ❷脾气:a man of the right ~ 脾气好的人

kill / kɪl / *v.* ❶杀死,弄死:The young man was ~ed by an accident. 那位年轻人死于一次事故。/ ~ **off** 消灭,杀光:The invaders ~ed off all the people of the town. 侵略者把全城人都杀光了。❷扼杀;毁灭:~ a bill (proposal) 否决一个议案(建议) ❸消磨(时间等):~ time 打发(消磨)时光

kilogram(me) / ˈkɪləgræm / *n.* [C]千克(略作 kg)

kilometre / ˈkɪləmiːtə(r) / *n.* [C]千米;公里(略作 km)

kilowatt / ˈkɪləwɒt / *n.* [C]千瓦(略作 kw):~-hour 千瓦小时

kin / kɪn / Ⅰ *n.* [C]家族;亲属 Ⅱ *adj.* 有亲属关系的

kind / kaɪnd / Ⅰ *n.* [C]种类:another ~ of cat 另一种猫/ all ~s of books 各种书籍 / the human ~ 人类 / This ~ of thing shouldn't be allowed. 此类事是不允许的。Ⅱ *adj.* 仁慈的;友好的;和蔼的:Please give my ~ regards to her. 请代我向她问好。/ It is very ~ of you to help us. 承蒙帮助,不胜感激。/ He was ~ with his children. 他对他的孩子们很好。派 kindly *adj.* & *adv.*

kindergarten / ˈkɪndəgɑːtn / *n.* [C] 幼儿园

kindle / ˈkɪndl / *v.* ❶ 点燃;使燃烧 ❷引起,激起:~ the interest of 激起……的兴趣

kindness / ˈkaɪndnəs / *n.* [U]亲切,和蔼;仁慈;好心的行为:out of ~ 出于好心 / with (without) ~ (不)友善地 / Thank you for your ~ to me. 谢谢你对我的关心。

king / kɪŋ / *n.* [C]国王;君王:an oil ~ 石油大王 / King's English 标准英语 /

He is a ~ in name, but not in reality. 他是一位有名无实的国王。

kingdom /ˈkɪŋdəm/ *n.* [C] ❶王国：the United Kingdom 英国 ❷界，领域：the ~ of science 科学领域 / the animal ~ 动物界

kiss /kɪs/ Ⅰ *v.* 接吻（表示亲密或致意）：The two lovers ~ed passionately. 那对情侣热烈地相吻。Ⅱ *n.* [C] 接吻：~ sb. goodbye 吻别

kit /kɪt/ *n.* ❶用具包；工具箱 ❷小猫

knead /niːd/ *vt.* ❶揉，捏（湿面粉或陶土等）：~ dough on a well-floured plank 在一块撒满面粉的厚板上捏面团 ❷揉成，捏制：~ a statue of clay 捏做泥塑像/~ bread 揉做面包 ❸揉弄；按摩，推拿：She ~ed her fist into her waist. 她握起拳头揉腰。

kitchen /ˈkɪtʃɪn/ *n.* [C]厨房

kite /kaɪt/ *n.* [C]风筝：draw in a ~ 收风筝 / let up a ~ with the wind 放风筝

kitten /ˈkɪtn/ *n.* [C]小猫

knee /niː/ *n.* [C]膝盖：He was wounded in the ~ by a fall. 他跌伤了膝盖。/ **fall on one's ~s** 跪下：The children have already fallen on their ~s. 孩子们已跪下。

kneel /niːl/ *vi.* (knelt/nelt/, knelt 或 kneeled) 跪下；跪倒：~ on the ground 跪在地下 / ~ to sb. 向某人下跪/ The girl knelt down to look for a pen. 那姑娘跪下找钢笔。

knife /naɪf/ *n.* [C] (*pl.* knives /naɪvz/) 小刀；餐刀；菜刀：a butcher ~ 屠刀 / a folding ~ 折刀 / a table ~ 餐刀 / a surgeon's ~ 手术刀 / a dull ~ 钝刀 / a sharp ~ 快刀 / **get one's ~ into sb.** 欲伤害某人：Be careful with George, he wants to get his ~ into you. 注意提防乔治，他想伤害你。

knight /naɪt/ *n.* [C] ❶(中古时的)骑士 ❷(英)爵士 派 knightly *adj.* & *adv.*

knit /nɪt/ *v.* (knit 或 knitted; knitting) ❶编织(毛衣等)：~ a sweater 织毛衣 / ~ up friendship 编织友谊 ❷使接合

knitting /ˈnɪtɪŋ/ *n.* [U]编织物；针织品

knitwear /ˈnɪtweə(r)/ *n.* [U]针织品，针织物(指针织的袜子、内衣、外套等)

knob /nɒb/ *n.* [C] 门把；旋钮

knock /nɒk/ Ⅰ *vi.* 击；打；敲；碰撞，撞击：He ~ed his head against (on) the wall. 他的头撞在了墙上。/ Who is ~ing at the door? 谁在敲门？/ ~ **against (up)** 偶然遇到：Who do you think I ~ed against in the office this morning? 你猜今天早晨我在办公室碰见谁了？~ **down** 击倒，打倒：A bus ~ed her down. 一辆汽车把她撞倒了。~ **sth. out** 敲空：You should ~ the pipe out. 你的烟斗应磕干净。Ⅱ *n.* [C]敲，打(的声音)；碰撞，撞击：get a hard ~ 受到沉重打击

knot /nɒt/ *n.* [C] 结：make a ~ 打结 / ~ of a matter 问题的症结 / ~s in the mind 思想疙瘩

know /nəʊ/ *v.* (knew/njuː/, known /nəʊn/) ❶知道；懂得；理解；了解：The students ~ how to answer these questions. 学生们知道怎样回答这些问题。We don't ~ whether he is here or not. 我们不知道他是否在此。❷认识；认出；熟悉：Do you ~ Mr White? 你认识怀特先生吗？/I got to ~ him a few years ago. 几年前我认识了他。❸听说：I knew about that last week. 我上周才听说那件事。**be ~n to** 为……熟知：London is ~n to us all. 伦敦是我们大家都

熟知的。**be ~n as** 以……而著称：She was ~n as an excellent dancer. 大家公认她是一位出色的舞蹈家。**be ~n for** 称作，叫作：Guilin is ~n for its beautiful scenery. 桂林以风景优美而闻名。**~ sb.(sth.) from sb.(sth.)** 辨别，识别：~ a friend from an enemy 分清敌友 / We should ~ right from wrong. 我们应明辨是非。**make oneself ~n** 做自我介绍：You'd better make yourself ~n to the host. 你应向主人做自我介绍。

knowing /ˈnəuɪŋ/ *adj.* ❶有知识的；有见识的；消息灵通的；通晓的：a ~ scholar 知识渊博的学者/Both of them were ~ in astronomy. 他们俩在天文学方面都颇有造诣。❷心领神会的，会意的：He joined in the laugh and looked ~. 他随他人一同大笑，显出一副心领神会的样子。❸故意的，蓄意的：indiscriminate classification of innocent with ~ activity 不分青红皂白将无意和有意的活动混为一谈 派 knowingly *adv.*

knowledge /ˈnɒlɪdʒ/ *n.* [U] ❶ 了解；知道；理解：A baby has no ~ of good and evil. 婴儿不知道善恶。❷知识；学识：absorb ~ 吸收知识 / acquire ~ 获取知识 / broaden the scope of ~ 扩大知识面 / enlarge ~ 丰富知识 / build up ~ 积累知识/ My ~ of English is very poor. 我的英语很差。/ I have no ~ of London. 我对伦敦一无所知。/ Knowledge originates in practice. 认识来源于实践。

knowledg(e)able /ˈnɒlɪdʒəbl/ *adj.* 知识渊博的；见多识广的；有见识的；消息灵通的：a ~ teacher 知识渊博的教师 / a ~ critic 有见识的评论家 / according to ~ sources 据消息灵通人士说 / He is very ~ about the history of the city. 他对该城的历史了如指掌。派 knowledgeably *adv.*

knuckle /ˈnʌkl/ *n.* [C]指；指关节

kungfu /ˈkʊŋˈfuː/ *n.* [U]功夫；武术；武艺：a ~ movie 功夫(或武打)片

L l

lab /læb/ *n.* (口语)实验室(laboratory 的简写形式)

label /ˈleɪbl/ Ⅰ *n.* [C]标签;标记:There is a "poison" ~ on the box. 盒子上贴有"有毒"标记。Ⅱ *vt.* 贴标签;做记号:They ~ goods with price before they sell them. 出售前他们给商品贴上售价签。

laboratory /ləˈbɒrətri/ *n.* [C]实验室:a chemistry ~ 化学实验室/ a physics ~ 物理实验室/ a language ~ 语言实验室/ Our ~ is next to our classroom. 我们的实验室就在我们的教室隔壁。

laborious /ləˈbɔːrɪəs/ *adj.* 费力的;艰辛的;需坚持不懈的:~ and futile negotiations 艰苦而无结果的谈判/a long, ~ road 一条漫长而艰辛的道路

labo(u)r /ˈleɪbə(r)/ Ⅰ *n.* ❶[U]劳作;劳动:Labor creates the world. 劳动创造世界。/ They earn their living by manual ~. 他们靠体力劳动谋生。❷[C]工作:They have succeeded by their own ~s. 他们靠自己的艰苦工作获得了成功。Ⅱ *v.* ❶工作;劳动:They are ~ing for the happiness of the mankind. 他们正为人类的幸福工作着。❷(缓慢、吃力地)做某事:We ~ed for an hour but could not convince them. 我们花了一个小时仍未能说服他们。/ The ship ~ed through the rough seas. 船在波涛汹涌的海上艰难航行着。

labo(u)rer /ˈleɪbərə(r)/ *n.* [C](尤指非技术性的)劳动者;体力劳动者:agricultural (farm) ~s 农业工人(农场工人)

labyrinth /ˈlæbərɪnθ/ *n.* [C] ❶迷宫;曲径:a ~ of narrow, twisting alleyways 迷宫般狭窄曲折的小胡同 ❷复杂局面;(事物的)错综复杂:a ~ of rules and regulations 繁杂的规则和条例

lace /leɪs/ *n.* [U] 花边;饰带;鞋带:tie one's ~s 系鞋带 / ~ for a dress 连衣裙的花边

lack /læk/ Ⅰ *n.* [U] 缺乏;缺少;不足:The plant died for ~ of water. 那些植物因缺水而枯死了。Ⅱ *v.* 缺乏;缺少:I ~ the words with which to express my gratitude. 我无法用言语来表示我的感谢。/ Your statement ~s details. 你的叙述不够具体。/ What do you ~? 你缺什么? / **be ~ing in** 缺乏;缺少:Humour is ~ing in his speech. 他讲话缺乏幽默。

lacking /ˈlækɪŋ/ Ⅰ *adj.* (只作表语)缺少的;匮乏的;不足的;没有的:He was found ~ in stamina. 人们发现他精力不济。/ Money was badly (completely, sadly, utterly) ~ for the plan. 这项计划的经费严重不足。Ⅱ *prep.* 没有,缺乏:Lacking equipment, the scientists gave up. 因为没有设备,科学家们只好放弃了。

lad / læd / *n.* [C] 少年;小伙子

ladder / ˈlædə(r) / *n.* [C] 梯;阶梯:He who would climb the ~ must begin at the bottom. 千里之行,始于足下。/ Please place (rest) the ~ against the wall. 请把梯子靠墙放。

laden / ˈleɪdən / *adj.* 装满的,载货的:a ~ ship 满载货物的船/He returned ~ with honours. 他载誉归来。

lady / ˈleɪdi / *n.* [C] ❶贵妇;女士(对所有妇女的称呼,无论其身份或教养如何):a young ~ 未婚少女,小姐 / Ladies and Gentlemen! 女士们,先生们! ❷(*pl.*)女厕所,女盥洗室(复数形式,单数意义):Is there a Ladies nearby? 附近有女厕所吗?

lag / læg / *v.* (lagged; lagging)慢走;落后:We have ~ged behind in science and technology. 我们在科技方面已经落后了。

lair / leə(r) / *n.* [C] ❶兽窝,兽穴,兽洞:rouse the lion from out of his ~把狮子从兽洞中赶出来 ❷秘密藏身处,隐藏处,躲藏处:The police tracked him to his ~. 警方追踪至他的秘密藏身地。

lake / leɪk / *n.* [C] 湖:the West Lake 西湖

lamb / læm / *n.* 小羊,羔羊;羔羊肉

lame / leɪm / *adj.* 跛的,瘸的:The worker is ~ from a wound. 那工人因伤而跛足。

lament / ləˈment / Ⅰ *v.* ❶悲痛;恸哭;哀悼:Mothers ~ed for their missing children. 母亲们为失踪的孩子恸哭不已。❷为……感到遗憾;为……感到惋惜:We ~ the fact that this company cannot continue to make a profit. 这家公司不能继续盈利了,对此我们深感遗憾。Ⅱ *n.* [C]悲痛;哀悼;恸哭:a ~ for lost youth 对逝去的青春的哀叹/make a pathetic ~ over one's loss 惋惜自己的损失

lamp / læmp / *n.* [C] 灯:an electric ~ 电灯 / a desk (table) ~ 台灯 / turn on a ~ 开灯 / turn off a ~ 关灯 / a neon ~ 霓虹灯

land / lænd / Ⅰ *v.* 着陆;登陆;登岸:The plane ~ed safely. 飞机安全着陆。/ We ~ed in a beautiful bay. 我们在一个美丽的海湾处上了岸。Ⅱ *n.* ❶[U] 陆地(以别于水域):Some came by ~ and some by water. 一些人由陆路来,一些人从水路来。❷[U] 土地;田地:He has ~ of his own. 他有自己的土地。❸[C](*pl.*)地产:He lives on his own ~s. 他靠自己的地产过日子。❹国土;国家:China is my native ~. 中国是我的祖国。

landlord / ˈlændlɔːd/ *n.* [C] ❶地主 ❷(客栈、寄宿舍等的)房东;(酒馆等的)店主

landmark / ˈlændˌmɑːk/ *n.* [C] ❶土标,陆标;(航海或陆路上的)标志物:The post office will serve as a ~ for you to pick out on the way back. 在你回来的路上,邮局可以充当路标。❷(国界、庄园或土地等的)界标,界碑,界石 ❸(纪念碑、遗址等)历史遗存;名胜古迹;标志性建筑物 ❹(历史上的)重大事件(或事变);里程碑:The invention of computer was a ~ in science. 计算机的发明是科学史上的一座里程碑。

landscape / ˈlændskeɪp / *n.* [C]风景;景观;风景绘画

landslide / ˈlændˌslaɪd / *n.* [C] ❶山崩;滑坡;崩塌,塌方:Slight noise might set off a ~. 细微的响声也会引发崩塌。❷(竞选中政党或候选人获得的)压倒多数的选票;一边倒的(竞选)胜利

lane /leɪn/ *n.* [C] 小巷;小路;胡同

language /ˈlæŋgwɪdʒ/ *n.* ❶[U](总称)语言:The ~ we write will always differ somewhat from the ~ we speak. 我们所用的书面语与口头语总是有些差别的。❷[C](一个国家或种族的)语言:acquire (command, master) a ~ 掌握一种语言 / learn a ~ 学习(学会)一种语言 / speak (talk) a ~ 讲一种语言 / understand a ~ 懂一种语言 / a common ~ 共同语言 / the finger (gesture, hand, sign) ~ 手语 / native ~ 本族语 / A foreign ~ is a weapon in the struggle of life. 外国语是人生斗争的一种武器。

lantern /ˈlæntən/ *n.* [C]手提灯;灯笼:a signal ~ 信号灯 / light a ~ 点灯 / Lantern Festival 元宵节

lap /læp/ Ⅰ *vt.* (lapped; lapping)舔食(与 up 连用):The cat quickly ~ped up all the milk. 小猫很快将所有牛奶舔光了。Ⅱ *n.* [C]❶膝部:She held her son in her ~. 她把儿子抱在膝上。❷(跑道的)一圈:He overtook all the other runners on the last ~. 他在跑最后一圈时超过了其他的运动员。

lapse /læps/ Ⅰ *n.* [C] ❶(道德等的)沦丧;(对正道等的)背离,偏离:a ~ of principle 背离原则/a ~ in good judgement 未能做出的正确判断 ❷小错,差错,疏忽,失误:a ~ of memory 记错/a ~ of the tongue 口误 ❸(时间的)流逝,逝去,过去:a ~ of six weeks between letters 书信一来一往六个星期 ❹(地位、水平等的)降低;(状况的)恶化;(数量、来源等的)减少:a sudden ~ of morale 士气的锐减 Ⅱ *vi.* ❶(地位、水平等)降低,下降;(状况)恶化;(兴趣、信心等)减退:Their zeal upon the work ~d. 他们对这份工作的热情有所减退。❷终止,停止:We let our subscription ~. 我们终止了订单。❸进入;陷入:~ into thought 陷入沉思 ❹(时间)流逝,逝去:Years, just like the river, ~d onward day and night. 岁月就像河流一样不舍昼夜地流逝而去。❺背离正道;偏离标准:The communication satellite ~d from its orbit because it had run out of energy. 通信卫星的能量用尽,因而偏离了轨道。

large /lɑːdʒ/ *adj.* ❶庞大的;巨大的;大规模的:He has a ~ family. 他有一大家人。/ A ~ number of new teachers came to our school. 一大批新教师来到我们学校。❷广泛的;众多的:Some drugs are being used on a much larger scale than previously. 与以前相比,某些药物的使用范围更广了。派 largely *adv.*

laser /ˈleɪzə(r)/ *n.* [C]激光;激光器:a ~ disc 光盘 / a ~ printer 激光打印机 / a ~ film 激光电影 / ~ treating 激光治疗

lash[1] /læʃ/ Ⅰ *n.* [C] ❶鞭梢;鞭子 ❷鞭笞,抽打:be subject to 36 ~es 被鞭笞 36 下 ❸睫毛 Ⅱ *vt.* ❶鞭笞,抽打:The prisoners were ill-treated and sometimes they were even ~ed with electric cable. 囚犯受到虐待,有时甚至遭到电缆绳的抽打。❷猛烈抨击;严厉斥责:~ the vices of the time 鞭挞时弊 ❸猛烈冲击;拍打:The hurricane ~ed the coast. 飓风席卷海岸地区。❹(急速地)来回摆动,挥动,甩动:The cobra ~ed and hissed. 眼镜蛇快速甩动着身子,发出咝

啦的声音。

lash[2] / læʃ / *vt*. (用线、绳等)捆,系,拴:The campers ～ed their tent to a tree during the hurricane. 飓风来袭时,露营者们将帐篷拴在树上。

last[1] / lɑːst / Ⅰ *adj*. ❶最后的;末尾的(与 first 相对):the ～ month of the year 一年的最后一个月 ❷刚过去的(与 next 相对):～ night (week, month, summer, year)昨夜(上周、上个月、去年夏天、去年) / in (for) the ～ few years 在过去的几年中 Ⅱ *n*. 最后;末尾;最后的人:I want to hear the ～ of his report. 我想听到他报告的结尾部分。/ Who is the ～ out? 是谁最后离开的? /**at** ～ 最后,终于;毕竟,到底:At ～ man has reached the moon. 人类终于登上了月球。

last[2] / lɑːst / *v*. 持续,耐久:The cloth ～s well. 这布很耐穿。/The left water can ～ him for seven days. 剩下的水能够让他维持七天。

lasting / ˈlɑːstɪŋ, ˈlæstɪŋ / *adj*. 持久的,永久的;耐久的:maintain a ～ peace 维持长久的和平/have a ～ effect on 对……产生持久的效力 派 lastingness *n*.

latch / lætʃ/ Ⅰ *n*. [C] ❶闩,门闩;窗闩:close with a ～ 用门闩关上 ❷碰锁,弹簧锁 Ⅱ *vt*. 用闩闩(门、窗等);用碰锁锁(门、窗等):The cargo door had not been ～ed properly before takeoff. 货舱门在起飞前没闩好。

late / leɪt / Ⅰ *adj*. (later, latest) ❶迟的,晚的(与 early 相对):Don't be ～ for school. 上学不要迟到。/It's never too ～ to mend. 改过不嫌晚。❷(日期、季节)近末尾的,将尽的:in the ～ afternoon 在下午将尽的时候/ in ～ summer 夏末 ❸近来的:the ～ novel 新近出版的小说 Ⅱ *adv*. 迟,晚(与 early 相对):get up (go to bed, arrive home) ～ 起床很晚(睡觉很晚,到家很晚)/ It rained ～ in the afternoon. 近黄昏时下雨了。派 lately *adv*.

latent / ˈleɪtnt / *adj*. 隐藏的;潜在的;潜伏的:～ energy 潜能

later / ˈleɪtə(r) / *adv*. 后来;以后:See you ～! 再见!

lateral / ˈlætərəl / *adj*. ❶(位于)侧面的;朝侧面的;从侧面的:The lungs are ～ to the heart. 肺位于心脏的两侧。❷(新的工作或职位等与原工作)平级的;相似的:The company offered her ～ move but not a promotion. 公司给她进行了平级调动,职务没有升迁。❸边音的,旁流音的:The sound "l" is a ～ sound in English. 英语中的"l"为舌侧音。

latest / ˈleɪtɪst / *adj*. 最近的;最新的;最晚的:the ～ news 最新消息/ The old man reads the ～ newspaper everyday. 老人每天都读最新出版的报纸。

lathe / leɪð / *n*. [C]车床:a drill ～ 钻床 / operate (run) a ～ 开车床

lather / ˈlɑːðə(r), ˈlæðə(r) / *n*. ❶(肥皂水、洗涤剂等的)泡沫:soapy ～肥皂泡沫 ❷激动;愤怒;烦躁:He could easily get into a ～ when everything was a mess. 事情一乱,他就容易发急。

Latin / ˈlætɪn / Ⅰ *n*. [U]拉丁语 Ⅱ *adj*. 拉丁人的;拉丁语的:～ America 拉丁美洲

latitude / ˈlætɪtjuːd / *n*. 纬度:The city is at a ～ of 40 degrees north. 那城市位于北纬 40 度。

latter / ˈlætə(r) / *adj*. 后者的;最近的;末尾的:the ～ half of the year 下半年 /

in these ~ days 在最近这些日子里 / I agree to the ~ point. 我赞成后一个论点。

laugh / lɑːf / Ⅰ *v.* 笑；发笑：The joke made everyone ~. 那笑话使大家都笑了。/He ~s best who ~s last. 别高兴得太早。(最后笑的人笑得最好)。/ ~ **at**(因有趣而)发笑；嘲笑；取笑：What are you ~ing at? 你们在笑什么？Ⅱ *n.* [C]笑声；笑：cause (create, excite) a ~ 引人发笑 / She ~ed a hearty ~. 她纵情大笑。

laughter / ˈlɑːftə(r) / *n.* [U]笑；笑声

launch / lɔːntʃ / *vt.* ❶使(船)下水：They ~ed a ship from a shipyard. 他们让船从船坞下水。❷发射(飞弹、火箭等)；发动：~ a spaceship into space 把宇宙飞船发射到太空 / The satellite was ~ed in a rocket. 这颗卫星是装在火箭上发射的。/ They ~ed an attack on the enemy. 他们向敌人发起进攻。

launder / ˈlɔːndə(r) / *v.* ❶洗熨(衣服、亚麻布等)；(被)洗熨：He has his shirt ~ed every day. 他每天都叫人洗熨衬衫。/The cloth didn't ~ well. 这种布不经洗。❷洗(黑钱等)

laundry / ˈlɔːndri / *n.* ❶[C]洗衣店；洗衣房 ❷[U]待洗衣物；所洗衣物

lavatory / ˈlævətri / *n.* [C]厕所；洗手间；盥洗室

lavish / ˈlævɪʃ / Ⅰ *adj.* ❶丰富的；无节制的；大量的：~ gifts 丰厚的礼物/be ~ with money 花钱大手大脚 ❷非常大方的，过分慷慨的，毫不吝啬的：the ~ hospitality of the local inhabitants 当地居民的过于好客/~ display of affection 感情的过分表露 Ⅱ *vt.* 挥霍，浪费；非常慷慨地施予，滥施：~ one's love upon sb. 对某人百般爱抚/He rejects the praise that his colleagues ~ed on him with indifference. 他的同事对他滥加赞扬，但他却无动于衷。

law / lɔː / *n.* ❶[C]法律；法令：abide by the ~ 守法 / administer the ~ 执法 / break the ~ 犯法 / go to ~ 诉诸法律 / the civil ~ 民法/ the criminal ~ 刑法 / the contract ~ 合同法 / the traffic ~ 交通规则 / Does the ~ allow you to do so? 法律允许你那样做吗？/ Don't take the ~ into your hands. 不要滥用法律。❷[U]法律系统；法律学，法学：He is reading ~ at Harvard. 他在哈佛大学攻读法律。❸[C]自然法则；定律：Newton's Law 牛顿定律 / the ~s of motion 运动定律 / Ohm's Law 欧姆定律

lawful / ˈlɔːfl / *adj.* 合法的；依法的；法定的：~ rights and interests 合法权利 / ~ business operation 合法经营 / ~ property 合法财产 / He has ~ earned income in this country. 他在这个国家有合法收入。

lawn / lɔːn / *n.* [C]草地；草坪：lie on the ~ 躺在草地上/ walk over the ~ 在草坪上行走

lawsuit / ˈlɔːˌs(j)uːt / *n.* [C]诉讼：bring a ~ against sb. 对某人提起诉讼

lawyer / ˈlɔːjə(r) / *n.* [C] 律师：They hired a ~ to help them. 他们聘了一位律师来帮助他们。

lay / leɪ / *vt.* (laid /leɪd/, laid) ❶置放；搁；摆：Please ~ these glasses along, not across. 这些玻璃杯竖着放，不要横放。/He laid his hand on my shoulder. 他把手放在我肩上。❷(鸟或昆虫)产卵：Hens ~ eggs. 母鸡下蛋。❸打赌：I'll ~ you that he will not come. 我和你赌，他不会来的。❹铺，铺设；覆盖：Lay colors on the canvas. 涂颜料于画布上。/ They are going to ~ a cable under the river. 他们将在河底铺设电缆。/ ~ **aside** 放在一边;留作别用:Please ~ your book aside. 请把书搁在一边。~ **down** ①放下;使躺下:She laid herself down gently. 她轻轻地躺下来。/ He laid the box down. 他把箱子放下。②投降;放弃:Lay down your arms! 放下武器! ③牺牲:He laid down his life for truth. 他为真理而献身。~ **out** 陈列,展览;安排,布置;设计:Lay the table out for supper. 摆桌子吃晚饭。/ The hill has been laid out as a small park. 这小山被设计成了一座小公园。~ **up** 贮藏;储蓄:They are ~ing up enough money to buy a car. 他们正存钱买车。

layer /ˈleɪə(r)/ *n.* [C]层:The workers are putting a ~ of small stones on the road. 工人们在道上铺上一层小石头。

layman /ˈleɪmən/ *n.* [C]外行;门外汉:We don't need a ~ in our company. 我们公司不需要外行。

lay-off /ˈleɪɒf/ Ⅰ *n.* 解雇:The company provided several jobs for ~ workers. 这家公司为下岗工人提供了好几份工作。Ⅱ *vt.* 解雇:The boss ~ed her from her job without any reason. 老板无故把她解雇了。

layout /ˈleɪaʊt/ *n.* [C]布局;安排;设计:They are discussing the ~ of their factory. 他们正在讨论工厂的布局。

lazy /ˈleɪzi/ *adj.* 懒惰的;懒散的:Don't be so ~. 不要这样懒惰。派 laziness

lead[1] /liːd/ Ⅰ *vt.* (led/led/, led) ❶引导;指引:The servant led the visitors in. 仆人将客人领进来。/The girl led her little brother to school. 那个女孩领着她的小弟弟去上学。/ ~ **the way** 引路;带路:Our guide led us the way to the library. 我们的向导把我们带到图书馆。❷领导;率领;指挥:The Party ~s us from victory to victory. 党领导我们从胜利走向胜利。/The commander led the army against the city. 指挥官率领军队攻城。❸(使某人)过(生活):They are ~ing a happy life. 他们过着幸福的生活。❹导致(某种结果);通,达:This road ~s to wealth. 这是一条致富之路。/I don't think it will ~ to a good result. 我认为这事不会有什么好结果。Ⅱ *n.* 领导;领路;领先:They always hold the ~ in the scientific researches. 在科研中,他们总是保持领先地位。

lead[2] /led/ *n.* [C]铅

leaded /ˈledɪd/ *adj.* (汽油)含铅的

leaden /ˈledən/ *adj.* ❶(似注铅般)沉重的;缓慢的;负重的:He has ~ feet. 他走起路来脚步沉重。❷沉闷的,阴郁的;无精打采的:a ~ expression 阴郁的表情 ❸铅灰色的,暗灰色的:a ~ sky 灰蒙蒙的天空 ❹铅做的

leader /ˈliːdə(r)/ *n.* [C]领袖;领导者:They are going to interview the top ~s of the country next month. 下月他们将采访国家高层领导人。

leadership /ˈliːdəʃɪp/ *n.* [U]领导:Under the ~ of the Party, the Chinese people are becoming richer and richer. 在党的领导下,中国人民越来越富裕。

leading /ˈliːdɪŋ/ *adj.* ❶领导的;指导的:a ~ cadre 领导干部/ a ~ body 领导机关 ❷最主要的;首位的:a ~ article 社论 / He played a ~ actor in the film. 他在那部电影里担任主角。

leaf /liːf/ *n.* [C] (*pl.* leaves /liːvz/) ❶(树的)叶子:The trees come into ~ in spring. 树木在春季长叶。❷(书籍杂志

的)一张：A book of 100 pages has 50 leaves. 一本100页的书有50张。

leaflet /ˈliːflət/ *n.* [C]传单；活页：The girl is handing out some advertising ~s. 那女孩正在散发广告单。

league /liːg/ *n.* [C]同盟；联盟：the Communist League 共产主义者同盟 / the Communist Youth League 共青团 / a ~ member 团员 / the ~ between two powers 两个强国之间的联盟 / The young fellows wanted to form a football ~. 年轻小伙子们很想建立一个足球联合会。

leak /liːk/ Ⅰ *n.* [C]漏洞；裂缝：The roof has a bad ~. 屋顶有个大的裂缝。Ⅱ *v.* 漏出；泄漏：Who ~ed the news out to the public? 谁把消息泄漏给公众了？

leakage /ˈliːkɪdʒ/ *n.* 漏，泄漏；漏出物：He stopped a ~ of the secret successfully. 他成功地阻止了那个秘密的泄露。

lean /liːn/ *v.* (leaned 或 leant/lent/) ❶倚，靠：Lean a ladder against the wall. 把梯子靠在墙上。❷倾斜：It ~s to one side. 它向一边倾斜。/~ **on** 依赖于；信赖：We'll ~ on others for guidance. 我们将依靠别人的指导。~ **over** 俯身于……之上：~ over a fence 将身子探过篱笆

leap /liːp/ Ⅰ *v.* (leapt / lept /或 leaped) 跳；跃；迅速运动：The boy ~ed a ditch and ran away. 小男孩跳过一道沟跑掉了。/ You should look before you ~. 做事前你得三思而后行。Ⅱ *n.* [C]跳跃；飞跃；跃进：a big ~ forward 大跃进 / take a ~ over an obstacle 跃过障碍

learn /lɜːn/ *vt.* (learned, learned 或 learnt/lɜːnt/, learnt) ❶学习；学会：We will ~ to speak English. 我们将学讲英语。/~ **sth. by heart** 记住；背诵：You should ~ this poem by heart. 这首诗你应背诵。~ **from** 向……学习：Learn from Comrade Lei Feng. 向雷锋同志学习。❷闻知；获悉；知道：We haven't ~ed whether he arrived safely. 我们还不知道他是否安全到达了。派 learner *n.*

learned /ˈlɜːnɪd/ *adj.* 有学问的；博学的：~ periodical 学术期刊 / He is a ~ man. 他是一位学者。

learning /ˈlɜːnɪŋ/ *n.* [U]❶学习：If you want to be successful, you should be good at ~. 如果你想获得成功，你必须善于学习。❷学问；知识：a man of ~ 有学问的人 / That is only book ~. 那仅仅是书本知识。

lease /liːs/ Ⅰ *n.* [C]❶租约，租契：sign a ~签订租约 ❷租赁期限：When does the ~ of the house run out? 这房子的租约何时到期？Ⅱ *vt.* ❶租出：He ~d his apartment to a friend. 他把自己的公寓租给了一位朋友。❷租入；租得：The company ~s its cars from a local supplier. 该公司从当地的供应商那里租来汽车。

least /liːst/ (little 的最高级形式) Ⅰ *adj.* 最小的；最少的(与 most 相对)：Do you know the ~ distance between these two cities? 你知道这两座城市间的最小距离吗？Ⅱ *n.* [U]最小；最少：He was the one who did the ~ of the work. 他就是那项工作干得最少的人。/ **at (the)** ~至少：The trip will take three days at (the) ~. 这一趟旅行至少得三天。**not in the** ~ 毫不：I was not surprised in the ~. 我一点也不感到惊奇。Ⅲ *adv.* 最小；最少：He did the hardest work but was paid the ~. 他干

最苦的活，但得的报酬却最少。

leather /ˈleðə(r)/ *n.* [U]皮革；皮革制品

leave /liːv/ Ⅰ *v.* (left/left/, left) ❶离开；出发；动身：Leave the room at once. 请马上离开房间。/She is leaving for Beijing. 她即将动身去北京。❷留下，剩下；忘带：I left my books on the table. 我把书忘在桌子上了。/ ~ **sb.** (**sth.**) **alone** 不要干涉某人(某事)：Leave the cat alone. 不要动那只猫。❸交托；委托：We should ~ this problem to our monitor. 我们应当把这事交给班长处理。Ⅱ *n.* [U]离去；告别；假期：The guest took his ~ at ten. 客人十点钟告辞。/ If you want to go out, you must ask for ~ first. 如果你想出去，你得先请假。

lecture /ˈlektʃə(r)/ *n.* [C]演讲；讲课：attend a ~ 听演讲(讲课) / deliver (give) a ~ 讲演(讲课) 派 lecturer *n.*

left /left/ Ⅰ *adj.* 左边的；左侧的：There are many big buildings on the ~ side of the river. 在河的左岸有许多高楼。/ Not many people write with the ~ hand. 没有多少人用左手写字。Ⅱ *adv.* 往左；向左：Left turn (face). 向左转。Ⅲ *n.* 左边；左部：turn to the ~ 向左转 / She sat on my ~. 她坐在我的左边。/Cars in some countries keep to the ~. 在一些国家汽车靠左行驶。

leftover /ˈleftˌəʊvə(r)/ Ⅰ *n.* [C] ❶(常用 *pl.*)残羹剩饭；残渣 ❷剩余物，残留物 Ⅱ *adj.* (只作定语)剩余的；吃剩的：~ vegetables 吃剩的蔬菜

leg /leg/ *n.* [C]腿：We should learn to stand on our own ~s. 我们应当学会自立。

legacy /ˈlegəsi/ *n.* [C]遗赠物；遗产：cultural ~ 文化遗产 / intellectual ~ 精神遗产 / His father left him a ~ of a million but he refused. 他的父亲给他留下百万遗产，但是他拒绝接受。

legal /ˈliːgəl/ *adj.* 法律(上)的；合法的；法定的：~ action 法律行为 / ~ age 法定年龄 / ~ consulting 法律咨询 / ~ consultant (adviser) 法律顾问 / ~ education 法制教育 / ~ holiday 法定假日 / ~ representative 合法代表 / ~ responsibility 法律责任 / ~ sense 法律观念

legend /ˈledʒənd/ *n.* 传说；传奇文学；传奇人物

legendary /ˈledʒəndəri/ *adj.* 传奇(式)的；传奇中的；具有传奇色彩的：a ~ instead of real character 传奇而非真实的人物/a ~dragon 传说中的龙

legible /ˈledʒəbl/ *adj.* (字迹、印刷等)清晰的，容易辨认的：a book in large ,~ type 一本用易认的大号字体印刷的书籍/His cursive handwriting is hardly ~. 他那潦草的字迹几乎无法辨认。派 legibility *n.*

legislate /ˈledʒɪsˌleɪt/ *vi.* 立法，制定(或颁布)法律：~ for the abolition of apartheid 制定法律废除种族隔离政策

legislation /ˌledʒɪsˈleɪʃən/ *n.* [U]❶立法，法律的制定(或颁布)：Parliament is supposed to perform the function of ~. 议会应该履行立法职能。❷(总称)法规；法律：pass (extend) the ~ 通过法律(延长法律有效期)

legman /ˈlegmæn/ *n.* [C] ❶(到处搜集消息或跑腿等的)外勤人员 ❷驻外记者；现场采访记者

leisure /ˈleʒə(r)/ *n.* [U]空闲；闲暇；悠闲：He is busy with his business and hardly has ~ for swimming with me. 他

在忙自己的生意,没有空陪我游泳。/ The old couple are living a life of ~. 老夫妻过着悠闲的生活。

lemon / ˈlemən / *n*. ❶柠檬;柠檬树 ❷[U]柠檬色,浅黄色

lemonade / ˌleməˈneɪd / *n*. [U]柠檬水

lend / lend / *vt*. (lent/lent/,lent) 借给;租出: Will you ~ your knife to that man? 你可以将小刀借给那个人吗? / ~ **sb. a hand** 帮助: Please ~ him a hand in copying the sentences. 请帮助他抄写这些句子。

length / leŋθ / *n*. (空间的)长度;(时间的)长短,在……期间: The bridge has a ~ of about 1,000 metres. 这桥长约1000米。/ The ~ of my stay there was about two weeks. 我在那儿大约待了两周。

lengthen / ˈleŋθən / *v*. 延长;变长: She ~ed her stay in London to a month. 她把在伦敦停留的时间延长为一个月。

lens / lenz / *n*. [C](眼镜的)镜片;(相机的)镜头

leopard / ˈlepəd / *n*. [C]豹

less / les / (little 的比较级形式) Ⅰ *adj*. (与 more 相对)少量的;较少的 (与不可数名词连用): ~ food 较少的食物 / Eat ~, drink ~, sleep more. 少吃,少饮酒,多睡眠。/ The road was something ~ than smooth. 这条路不平坦。Ⅱ *adv*. 更少地;较少地: Tom is ~ clever than John. 汤姆不如约翰聪明。/ She was ~ hurt than frightened. 她没受到什么伤害,却吓坏了。

lessen / ˈlesn / *v*. 减少;减轻: They are trying hard to ~ the costs of goods. 他们正尽力降低商品的成本。

lesson / ˈlesn / *n*. [C] ❶ 课题;一课;课程: history ~s 历史课/ music ~s 音乐课 / oral ~s 口语课 / postal ~s 函授课 / I gave them a ~ in English. 我给他们上了一堂英语课。/ We have four ~s this morning. 今天早上我们有四节课。❷教训: All of us should draw a ~ from the accident. 我们都应从这次意外事故中吸取教训。

lest / lest / *conj*. 唯恐;免得: He ran away ~ he should be seen. 他唯恐别人看见而逃跑了。

let / let / *vt*. (let,let) ❶ 允许,让(其后跟不带 to 的不定式,不能用于被动句中): Will you ~ your children go to the cinema tonight? 你让你的孩子们今晚去看电影吗? / Her father won't ~ her go to dance. 她父亲不让她去跳舞。/ Let me see. 让我想想。❷让(与第一人称或第三人称的代词连用,形成间接祈使句): Let's begin to sing, shall we? 咱们开始唱歌,好吗? / Let us both have a try. 让咱们两个都试一试吧。/ Let her do it at once. 让她马上做这事。/ ~ **sb. (sth.) alone** 不理;不管: Let her alone. 别理她。~ **sb. (sth.) out** 放出;发出;说出: The woman ~ out a sigh. 那妇女叹了一口气。

L

let-down / ˈletˌdaʊn / *n*. [C] ❶失望,沮丧: The book was a bit of a ~. 这本书有些令人失望。❷减少;减弱;减退: the ~ of morale 士气的低落/I felt a terrible ~ after the party. 聚会后我感到精疲力竭。

lethal / ˈliːθəl / *adj*. 致死的;足以致命的: ate a ~ dose of amphetamine 服用足以致命的安非他明/~ weapons 杀伤性武器

letter / ˈletə(r) / *n*. [C] ❶字母: 26 ~s of the English language 英语的 26 个字母

❷信件;函件:answer (reply to) a ~ 回信 /an express ~ 快信 / a registered ~ 挂号信

lettuce /ˈletɪs/ *n.* 莴笋

level /ˈlevl/ *n.* [C]❶水平;标准:Her life has dropped to a low ~. 她的生活已降到很低的水平。❷水平面;水平线:How high are we above sea ~? 我们高出海平面多少?❸高度;平地:This has attained the world ~. 这已达到世界水平。❹级别,等级:the same educational ~ 同等学力

lever /ˈliːvə(r)/ *n.* [C]杆,杠杆:economic ~ 经济杠杆

leverage /ˈliːvərɪdʒ/ *n.* [U] ❶杠杆效率,杠杆作用 ❷手段,方法;影响:By sending more troops the country wanted to have more political ~ over this area. 该国通过增派部队试图对这一地区施加更多的政治影响力。

levy /ˈlevi/ Ⅰ *n.* [C] ❶征税 ❷征收的税款:impose 10% ~ on tobacco 对烟草征收 10%的税款 Ⅱ *vt.* 征(税等);收(罚款等):~ a heavy fine for contempt of court 对藐视法庭的行为课以高额罚款/~ a duty on imports 对进口商品征收关税

liable /ˈlaɪəbl/ *adj.*(只作表语)❶有倾向的;易于……的:Take good care of her. She is ~ to colds. 好好照看她,她很容易感冒。❷有责任的;有义务的:You should be ~ for the mistakes you made. 你应对你所犯的错误负责。

liar /ˈlaɪə(r)/ *n.* [C](惯于)说谎的人

liberal /ˈlɪbərəl/ *adj.* ❶心胸宽大的;开明的;思想开朗的:He is over sixty but he is a man of ~ views. 他虽已经六十多了,但却是一个思想开朗的人。❷慷慨的;大方的:~ donation 慷慨捐赠 ❸丰富的;富足的:~ supply 大量的供应 ❹自由主义的:They say that he has a ~ tongue. 他们说他是一个说话随便的人。

liberalism /ˈlɪbərəˌlɪz(ə)m/ *n.* [U] ❶宽容,开朗;开明的思想 ❷自由主义

liberalize /ˈlɪbərəˌlaɪz/ *vt.* 使自由化;放宽对……的限制:All the banks decided to ~ their policy of agricultural loans. 所有银行决定放宽农业贷款政策。/ That would greatly ~ the right to travel and emigrate. 这将给旅游和移民的权利以极大的自由。派 liberalization *n.*

liberate /ˈlɪbəreɪt/ *vt.* 解放;使脱离:Leaders should always think how to ~ the productive forces. 领导者应常考虑如何解放生产力。/ She is trying to ~ herself from worries. 她尽力消除自己的忧虑。

liberation /ˌlɪbəˈreɪʃn/ *n.* [U]解放:the Chinese People's Liberation Army 中国人民解放军

liberty /ˈlɪbəti/ *n.* [U]自由;自由权:gain (get) one's ~获得自由 / civil ~ 公民自由权 / Everyone is at ~ to air his view at the meeting. 每个人都可以在会上自由发表意见。

librarian /laɪˈbreəriən/ *n.* [C]图书馆馆长(或馆员)

library /ˈlaɪbrəri/ *n.* [C]图书馆

licence(-se) /ˈlaɪsns/ Ⅰ *vt.* 准许;认可:They ~d her to publish her new book. 他们批准她出版新书。Ⅱ *n.* [C]执照;许可证:a bussiness ~ 营业执照 / apply for a ~ 申请执照 / grant (issue) a ~ 颁发执照 / revoke a ~ 吊销执照 /a driving ~ 驾驶执照

lick /lɪk/ *vt.* 舔:The cat likes to ~ its

paws. 这猫老爱舔自己的爪子。

lid /lɪd/ *n.* [C] ❶盖子 ❷眼睑

lie[1] /laɪ/ *vi.* (lay/leɪ/, lain/leɪn/, lying) ❶卧,躺:~ on one's back (side) 仰卧(侧卧) / She is lying in bed. 她躺在床上。❷位于(某地):Japan ~s to the east of China. 日本位于中国以东。

lie[2] /laɪ/ Ⅰ *vi.* (lying) 说谎:He ~d to me. 他对我说谎。Ⅱ *n.* [C] 谎言;假话:Lies cannot cover up facts. 谎言掩盖不了事实。/ He never tells ~s to others. 他从不对人说假话。

life /laɪf/ *n.* [C] (*pl.* lives/laɪvz/) ❶生命;性命:~ quality 生活质量 / ~ science 生命科学 / ~ space 生活空间 / Where did ~ come from? 生命从何而来? / How many lives were lost during the war? 这场战争中有多少人丧生? / **take one's own** ~自杀:She took her own ~ by jumping from the bridge into the river. 她从桥上跳河自杀。❷一生;一辈子;终身:He has made revolution all his ~. 他干了一辈子革命。❸生活;生活方式:army ~ 军队生活 / city ~ 城市生活 / family ~ 家庭生活 / independent ~ 独立生活 / a lonely ~ 孤独的生活 / a miserable ~ 悲惨生活 / a hard ~ 艰难的生活 / We are living a happy ~. 我们过着幸福生活。

lifeblood /ˈlaɪfˌblʌd/ *n.* [U] ❶(生命赖以维持的)血液 ❷命根子,命脉;关键:Tourism is the ~ of Thailand's economy. 旅游业是泰国的支柱产业。

lifeboat /ˈlaɪfˌbəʊt/ *n.* [C] (船上或海岸的)救生艇,救生船

lifelike /ˈlaɪfˌlaɪk/ *adj.* 逼真的,栩栩如生的:a ~ computer-controlled robot 由电脑控制的像真人一样的机器人 / a ~ portrait of the queen 一幅逼真的女王肖像画

lifelong /ˈlaɪfˌlɒŋ/ *adj.* (只作定语)终身的,毕生的;持久的:a ~ habit 伴随一生的习惯 / ~ regret 终身的遗憾

lifetime /ˈlaɪfˌtaɪm/ Ⅰ *n.* [C] ❶一生,终身,一辈子:We've only been here two days, but it seems like a ~. 我们在这里待了才两天,却好像过了一辈子似的。❷长时间,很久:We waited a ~ for the doctor's report. 我们等医生的报告等了很长时间。Ⅱ *adj.* 终身的,一生的:a ~ membership 终身会员 / **of a** ~ 终身难遇的,千载难逢的:Winners of the competition will receive the tour of a ~. 这次竞争的获胜者会得到一次千载难逢的旅游机会。

lift /lɪft/ Ⅰ *v.* ❶举;抬;升高:This box is too heavy for me to ~. 这箱子太重,我抬不动。/ ~ weight 举重 / ~ up one's eyes 向上看 / ~ prices 提高价格 / The airplane ~ed from the airport. 飞机从机场起飞。❷耸立;竖起:The Monument to the People's Heroes ~s majestically above Tian'anmen Square. 人民英雄纪念碑雄伟地耸立在天安门广场上。Ⅱ *n.* [C] ❶举起;抬起 ❷电梯:She got the job to operate the ~ in the teaching building. 她得到了在教学楼里开电梯的工作。❸搭便车:**give sb. a** ~ 让某人搭车:I asked him to pull up by the side of the road to give me a ~. 我请他把车停在路边让我搭他的车。

light /laɪt/ Ⅰ *v.* (lit/lɪt/, lit 或 lighted, lighted) 点燃;照亮;使发光:~ a candle (lamp, cigarette) 点燃蜡烛(灯、烟) / ~ a fire 点火 / The streets were brightly lit up. 街上灯光明亮。/ Their houses are ~ed by the lamps. 他们的房屋用油灯照明。Ⅱ *adj.* 轻的;明亮的;淡色的:~

L

in color 颜色浅 /~ blue(green, red, brown)浅蓝(浅绿、淡红、浅褐) / The box is surprisingly ~. 这箱子轻得出奇。Ⅲ *n.* 光亮;光线;光源;发光物:The sun gives us ~. 太阳给我们带来光明。/ We want more ~ in this room. 我们这个房间需要更多的光亮。/ turn on (off) a ~ 开灯(关灯)/ The ~ goes out. 灯灭了。/ the tail ~(汽车)尾灯 / the traffic ~s 交通灯(红绿灯) / the gas ~ 煤气灯 / the head ~照明灯

lighten /ˈlaɪtn/ *vt.* 照亮;使明亮:There is a lamp on the wall to ~ the path to the toilet. 墙上有一盏灯照亮去厕所的路。

lighter /ˈlaɪtə(r)/ *n.* [C]打火机;点火器

lightning /ˈlaɪtnɪŋ/ *n.* [U] 闪电:a ~ rod 避雷针 / a ~ war 闪电战 / Lightning plays in the sky. 空中电光闪闪。

light-year /ˈlaɪtˌjɪe(r), ˈlaɪtjɜː(r)/ *n.* [C] ❶光年(指光在一年中经过的距离,约合95 000亿千米) ❷很大的差距;遥远的距离;很长的时间:Today's computers are ~s ahead of older ones in power and memory. 现在的计算机在性能和存储方面已遥遥领先于老式的计算机。

like /laɪk/ Ⅰ *v.* ❶喜欢;爱好:She ~s singing and dancing. 她喜欢唱歌跳舞。❷希望;想:I would (should) ~ the problem to be discussed in public. 我希望公开讨论这个问题。Ⅱ *adj.* 相似的;同样的;像:The two brothers are very ~. 这两弟兄长得很像。/ Like father, ~ son. 有其父必有其子。Ⅲ *prep.* 像,如:He looks ~ an artist. 他看上去像个艺术家。/ What's the weather ~ today? / 今天天气怎样? Ⅳ *n.* 相似的人或物:Like attracts ~. 物以类聚。/ Like cures ~. 以毒攻毒。/ Like knows ~. 英雄识英雄。/ Like for ~. 以牙还牙。/ We have met the ~s of you before. 我们以前碰到过像你这样的人。

likely /ˈlaɪkli/ *adj.* 有希望的;有可能的;可能发生的:It's hardly ~ to finish it within a week for me. 我不可能在一周内将这事干完。/ It is ~ that he will win. 他很可能会赢。

likeness /ˈlaɪknɪs/ *n.* ❶[C]肖像,画像;照片;相似物:This statue is a good ~ of the leader. 这座雕像非常逼真地塑造了这位领袖的形象。❷[U]相像,相似:The two sisters bear a striking ~ to each other. 这两姐妹长得一模一样。

likewise /ˈlaɪkwaɪz/ *adv.* 同样地;照样地:He fulfilled his task and I did ~. 他完成了任务,我也完成了。

lily /ˈlɪli/ Ⅰ *n.* [C] ❶百合 ❷百合花 Ⅱ *adj.* 像百合般洁白的;白嫩的,白皙的:~ hands 白嫩的手

limb /lɪm/ *n.* [C]肢(臂、腿等);(树的)主枝

limber /ˈlɪmbə(r)/ Ⅰ *adj.* ❶肢体柔韧的:a ~ athlete 身体柔韧的运动员 ❷柔软的,易弯曲的;灵巧的:~ joints 柔软的关节/She had the ~ body of a dancer. 她的身体像舞蹈演员一样柔软灵活。Ⅱ *v.* ❶柔软(与 up 连用):~ up one's fingers 松弛手指 ❷(比赛等前)热身,做准备活动(与 up 连用):He had no time to ~ up before his tennis match. 他没时间在网球比赛之前做准备活动。

lime /laɪm/ *n.* [U]石灰

limestone /ˈlaɪmstəun/ *n.* [U] 石灰石

limit /ˈlɪmɪt/ Ⅰ *vt.* 限制;限定:Try to

~ your talk within five minutes. 请尽量在五分钟之内把话说完。Ⅱ *n.* [C]限制;界限:They set a ~ of 35 to the number of passengers. 他们把乘客人数限制在35人。

limitation /ˌlɪmɪˈteɪʃən/ *n.* ❶[C]局限;限制因素;弱点;不足之处:know one's own ~s 有自知之明 / overcome the ~ 克服缺陷 ❷[U]限制:the ~ of nuclear weapons 限制核武器 / This ~ was imposed for both presidential and congressional campaigns. 在总统和国会选举中都要施行这一限制。

limited /ˈlɪmɪtɪd/ *adj.* 有限的;被限制的:We should make good use of our ~ resources. 我们应当很好地利用我们有限的资源。

limousine /ˈlɪməziːn/ *n.* [C]大型豪华轿车;高级轿车

limp /lɪmp/ *vi.* 蹒跚;跛行:The wounded soldier ~ed off the battle field. 那位负伤的战士一瘸一拐地离开了战场。

line /laɪn/ Ⅰ *n.* [C] ❶线;绳;线路:the fishing ~ 钓鱼线 / telephone ~s 电话线 / Hang the clothes on the ~. 把衣服晾在绳子上。/ The ~ is busy. Please dial later. 线路正忙,请待会儿再拨。❷线条:Draw a ~ from A to B. 从A到B画一条线。❸(人或物的)排,列:a ~ of trees (chairs,people)一排树(一排椅子,一列人)/**in ~ with** 与……一致;按照;符合:The behavior of a student should be in ~ with his school's rule. 学生的举止行为应当符合校规。Ⅱ *v.* 沿……排成行;使……成行:We ~d up to buy tickets. 我们排队买票。

linear /ˈlɪnɪə(r)/ *adj.* ❶线的;直线的;线形的:a ~ arrangement 直线排列 ❷成一直线的;在线上的 ❸长度的:a unit of ~ measure 长度度量单位

linen /ˈlɪnɪn/ *n.* [U]亚麻布;亚麻布制品

liner /ˈlaɪnə(r)/ *n.* [C]班轮;班机:Which ~ do you take to Shanghai? 你乘哪班飞机去上海?

linger /ˈlɪŋgə(r)/ *vi.* ❶(因不愿离开而)继续逗留,留恋,徘徊:The people ~ed at the door with a long good-bye. 人们在门口依依不舍,久久不肯离去。/ They ~ed over their coffee for a few minutes. 他们又喝了几分钟咖啡。❷继续存留;缓慢消失:Doubts ~ed in my mind. 我始终不能消除心中的疑团。

linguistic /lɪŋˈgwɪstɪk/ *adj.* 语言的;语言学的:a ~ science 语言科学 / Her mother thinks that she has strong ~ competence. 她母亲认为她的语言能力很强。

linguistician /ˌlɪŋgwɪsˈtɪʃn/ *n.* [C]语言学家

linguistics /lɪŋˈgwɪstɪks/ *n.* [U]语言学

link /lɪŋk/ Ⅰ *n.* [C] ❶(链条的)环,节;环状物,圈:the ~s of a chain 链条节 ❷环节;连接部分,纽带;联系,关联:The present forms a ~ with the past and the future. 现在把过去与未来联系了起来。/ There have been many ~s between America and that Continent. 美国与欧洲大陆之间存在着千丝万缕的联系。Ⅱ *v.* 串联,连接;联系(与up连用):a computer that can't be ~ed up to the other machines in the office 一台无法与办公室里其他机器连接的计算机 /The company will soon ~ up with a hotel chain. 这家公司不久将与一家旅馆连锁企业联手。

linkage /ˈlɪŋkɪdʒ/ *n.* ❶连接,连合 ❷[C]关联,联系:a ~ between cause and effect 因果关系/develop ~s with the institutes abroad 与外国学术机构建立联系

lion /ˈlaɪən/ *n.* [C] 狮子

lip /lɪp/ *n.* [C]嘴唇：bite one's ~ 咬嘴唇

lipstick /ˈlɪpstɪk/ *n.* [C]唇膏；口红

liquid /ˈlɪkwɪd/ Ⅰ *n.* 液体：The patient could only consume ~s. 那病人只能吃流质食品。Ⅱ *adj.* 液体的；流动的：I have never seen the ~ state of this material. 我从未见过这种物质的液体状态。

liquor /ˈlɪkə(r)/ *n.* [U]酒；汁

list /lɪst/ Ⅰ *n.* [C]名单；目录；一览表：a shopping ~购物单/ a name ~ 名单 / a check ~ 清单 / make a ~ 造表 / a ranking ~ 排行榜 / write out a ~ 列表 / He headed the ~ in the examination. 他考试名列第一。Ⅱ *vt.* 把……列成表；列举：Li Ming was ~ed as a candidate. 李明被列为候选人。

listen /ˈlɪsn/ *vi.* 倾听；留心听：We ~ed but heard nothing. 我们留心听，可什么也没听见。/ Listen to the teacher. 听老师讲。/ He ~s to the radio at half past six every morning. 他每天早晨六点半听收音机。/ ~ **in to** 听广播：Did you ~ in to the broadcasting programme last night? 你昨晚听广播节目了吗？派 listener *n.*

listing /ˈlɪstɪŋ/ *n.* [C] ❶一览表，明细表；目录；名册 ❷(登记表或目录等中的)一项：a ~ in the telephone directory 电话簿中的一项

literacy /ˈlɪtərəsi/ *n.* [U] ❶识字，读写能力；有文化：a national agency for adult ~国家级成人扫盲机构 ❷了解；通晓：Computer ~ is obligatory for college students. 大学生必须懂电脑。

literal /ˈlɪtərəl/ *adj.* ❶文字(上)的；字面的：There are still some ~ errors in your report. 你的报告中还有一些文字错误。❷忠实于原文的；逐字的：It is a kind of ~ translation. 这是一种直译。

literally /ˈlɪtərəli/ *adv.* 逐字地：He translated the report into English ~. 他逐字逐句地把报告译成了英语。

literary /ˈlɪtərəri/ *adj.* 文学上的；书本的：My sister likes ~ works very much. 我姐姐非常喜爱文学作品。/His speech is too ~. 他的讲话太书呆子气。

literate /ˈlɪtərət/ Ⅰ *adj.* 能读会写的；有文化的 Ⅱ *n.* [C]有文化的人

literature /ˈlɪtrətʃə(r)/ *n.* [U]文学；文学作品：Chinese ~中国文学 / classical ~ 古典文学 / contemporary ~ 当代文学 / folk ~ 民间文学 / popular ~ 通俗文学 / the Nobel Literature Prize 诺贝尔文学奖 / The girl read a great amount of ~ after class. 那个女孩在课外阅读了大量文学作品。

litre(-er) /ˈliːtə(r)/ *n.* [C]升(容量单位)

litter /ˈlɪtə(r)/ Ⅰ *n.* [U]废物；垃圾：The room is in a ~. 房间一片杂乱。Ⅱ *v.* 乱扔；乱丢；把……弄得乱七八糟：Please don't ~! 请勿乱丢杂物！

little /ˈlɪtl/ Ⅰ *adj.* (less 或 lesser, least) ❶小的(与 big 相对)：a pretty ~ house 一所漂亮的小房子 / a poor ~ girl 一个可怜的小姑娘 ❷(指时间、距离等)短的：Won't you stay a ~ while with me? 你不愿意陪我一会儿吗？❸ 少许的，少量的(修饰不可数名词)：I have very ~ time for reading. 我很少有时间读书。/ He knows ~ about Latin. 他几

乎不懂拉丁文。/ Will you have a ~ water? 你要喝点水吗? / I can speak a ~ English. 我会讲点英语。Ⅱ *n.* ❶少许;少量:She eats ~ for breakfast. 她早餐吃得很少。/ ~ **by** ~ 逐渐:He has become rich ~ by ~. 他渐渐富起来。❷短时间;短距离:After a ~ while you will feel better. 过一会儿你会觉得舒服些。Ⅲ *adv.* (less 或 lesser, least)很少;一点:He left ~ more than an hour ago. 他大约一小时前离开的。/ She slept very ~. 她睡得很少。

live¹ /lɪv/ *v.* ❶生存;活着:The patient is still living. 病人还活着。/The doctor said he could ~ to a hundred years. 医生说他可活到一百岁。/~ **on** 靠……活着:He still ~s on his parents. 他仍然靠父母生活。/ We ~ on rice, fish and vegetables. 我们以大米、鱼和蔬菜为食。❷居住(与 in, at 连用):Where do you ~? I ~ at No. 50 in this street. 你住在哪里?我住在这条街的50号。/ She ~s in London. 她住在伦敦。❸度过;过(生活):They are living a comfortable life. 他们过着舒适的生活。

live² /laɪv/ *adj.* ❶活的;有生命的:I saw some ~ fish in the basin. 我看到盆里有一些活鱼。/ Do you know the ~ issue among the young? 你知道年轻人中的热门话题是什么吗? ❷现场直播的:The game will be televised (broadcast) ~ to the public. 这场比赛将向公众作现场直播。

liv(e)able /ˈlɪvəbl/ *adj.* ❶(房屋、气候等)适于居住的:The apartment is ~ although it is far from perfect. 这套公寓虽然不是太好,但也能将就。❷(生活)过得有意义的:He found life here very ~. 他发觉这儿的生活很有意思。派 liveability *n.*

lively /ˈlaɪvli/ *adj.* ❶生动的;活泼的;有生气的:She's as ~ as a kitten. 她活泼得像只小猫。/ He has a ~ imagination. 他的想象力很丰富。❷逼真的;栩栩如生的:He can give a ~ description to what he saw. 他能把他见到的东西生动地描述出来。

liver /ˈlɪvə(r)/ *n.* [C]肝,肝脏

livestock /ˈlaɪvˌstɔk/ *n.* 牲畜;家畜:The ~ is worth a lot. 这牲畜很值钱。/ The ~ were grazing. 牲口正在吃草。

living /ˈlɪvɪŋ/ Ⅰ *n.* [U]生计;生活:the standard of ~ 生活水平 / The cost of ~ in big cities is very high. 大城市里的生活费用很高。/ He makes (gains, earns, gets) his ~ as a teacher. 他以教书为生。Ⅱ *adj.* 活着的;现存的:~ languages 现用语言 / ~ beings 生物

living-room /ˌlɪvɪŋˈruːm/ *n.* [C]起居室;客厅:He slept in the ~ last night. 昨晚他在客厅里睡觉。

lizard /ˈlɪzəd/ *n.* [C]蜥蜴

load /ləud/ Ⅰ *v.* 装载;把……装上(车、船、飞机等):The goods were ~ed upon a wagon. 这些货物被装上了车。/ The ship is ~ing for Shanghai. 这船正在上货,准备驶往上海。Ⅱ *n.* [C] 负荷量;装载量:The aeroplane is capable of carrying a ~ of ten tons. 这架飞机的载重量达十吨。

loaded /ˈləudɪd/ *adj.* ❶负载的,负重的:a ~ truck 载有货物的卡车 ❷已装好弹的:a ~ rifle 已装弹的来复枪 ❸(词语等)具隐含意义的,引起歧义的:a ~ statement 话中有话的言语/~ question 含蓄的问话

loaf /ləuf/ *n.* [C](*pl.* loaves /ləuvz/)

一条面包：a ~ of bread 一条面包 / a white ~ 白面包

loan /ləʊn/ *n.* [C]借出物；借款，贷款：government ~s 公债/ foreign ~s 外债 / domestic ~s 内债 / an agricultural ~ 农业贷款 / an interest-free ~ 无息贷款 / He came here for a ~. 他到这儿来借钱。

lobby /ˈlɒbi/ *n.* [C]（剧场、旅馆等的）前厅，大厅

lobster /ˈlɒbstə(r)/ *n.* [C]虾；龙虾

local /ˈləʊkəl/ *adj.* 地方的；当地的：the ~ doctor 当地医生 / ~ news 地方新闻 / ~ government 地方政府 / Sometimes he writes for the ~ newspaper. 有时候他也为地方报纸写稿。

L

locate /ləʊˈkeɪt/ *v.* ❶确定……的地点；使……坐落于：The office is ~d in a business centre. 办事处位于商业中心。❷探明；找出：You'd better ~ the city on a map first. 你最好先在地图上找到那个城市的位置。

location /ləʊˈkeɪʃn/ *n.* [C]位置，场所，地点；（电影的）外景拍摄地：It is a good ~ for reading. 这是一个阅读的好地方。/ You may find the director at the film ~. 你可以在电影外景拍摄地找到导演。

lock /lɒk/ Ⅰ *n.* [C]锁：Does the key fit the ~? 这把钥匙能开这锁吗？/ The ~ won't catch. 这锁锁不上。Ⅱ *v.* 锁，锁上，锁住：The door ~s automatically. 这门会自动锁上。/ The door will not ~ with his key. 他的钥匙锁不上这扇门。

locker /ˈlɒkə(r)/ *n.* [C]柜；小室；（船上的）储藏室；小舱：You can rent a ~ and put your clothes in it. 你可以租一个保管箱放衣物。

locomotive /ˌləʊkəˈməʊtɪv/ *n.* [C]机车；火车头

locust /ˈləʊkəst/ *n.* [C] 蝗虫

lodge /lɒdʒ/ *n.* [C]门房；传达室；山林小屋

loft /lɒft/ *n.* [C] ❶阁楼；顶楼 ❷（教堂或大厅的）楼厢 ❸（仓库、商业建筑物等的）顶层，天台 ❹（将仓库、商业建筑物等的顶层或天台改建而成的）天台工作室；天台房屋

lofty /ˈlɒfti/ *adj.* ❶高耸的；极高的：a ~ tower 高塔 / The Alps mountains were ~ and rugged. 阿尔卑斯山巍峨陡峭。❷高尚的；崇高的：a man with ~ expectations 胸怀大志的人 / ~ sentiments 高尚的情操 ❸高傲的；傲慢的：a ~ appearance 一脸的傲气 / a ~ butler 态度傲慢的管家 派 loftily *adv*; loftiness *n.*

log /lɒg/ *n.* [C] ❶原木；木料：The cabin is built with ~s. 小屋是用圆木建造的。❷航海（飞行）日志

logic /ˈlɒdʒɪk/ *n.* [U] 逻辑；逻辑学：What he said is of great ~. 他所说的很合逻辑。

logical /ˈlɒdʒɪkəl/ *adj.* 逻辑（上）的；符合逻辑的；合乎常理的：We have reached a ~ conclusion. 我们得出了一个符合逻辑的结论。/ What he did is ~. 他所做的是合乎常理的。

logician /ləˈdʒɪʃən/ *n.* [C]逻辑学家

logistics /ləˈdʒɪstɪks/ *n.* ❶（用作单数）后勤学；（用作复数）后勤：Logistics is a complex field. 后勤学是一个复杂的领域。/Logistics aren't going to assist you here. 在这里后勤对你没有任何帮助。❷[U]（任何行动的）细节规划，细节协调：The ~ of the office move is the problem. 问题在于转移办公场所的细

节规划。

lonely /ˈləʊnli/ *adj.* 孤单的，寂寞的；偏僻的，荒凉的：a ~ traveller 孤单的旅行者 / a ~ house 偏僻的屋子 / a ~ village 荒凉的村庄 / a ~ girl 孤寂的女孩

long[1] /lɒŋ/ Ⅰ *adj.* (空间或时间)长的：How ~ is the river? 这条河有多长？/ He hasn't been here for a ~ time. 他好久都没到这儿来了。Ⅱ *n.* [U]长时间：The work won't take ~. 这工作不会花太长时间。Ⅲ *adv.* 长久地；长时间地；很久(以前)地：Stay as ~ as you like. 你愿待多久就待多久。/I can't wait any ~er. 我不能再等了。

long[2] /lɒŋ/ *v.* 渴望：We are ~ing for peace. 我们渴望和平。/He has been ~ing to see his son. 他一直渴望见到他的儿子。

longevity /lɒnˈdʒevɪti/ *n.* [U] ❶长寿，长命：A bowl of noodles on one's birthday is a wish for ~. 过生日吃碗面条是祝愿长寿的表示。❷寿命 ❸长期供职；资深

longing /ˈlɒŋɪŋ/ Ⅰ *n.* 渴望，热望，切望：a ~ among undergraduates for knowledge 大学生中对知识的渴求 / a sudden ~ to see old friends 突然产生的想要见见老朋友的渴望 Ⅱ *adj.* 渴望的；流露出渴望之情的：a ~ look 渴望的神情 派 longingly *adv.*

longitude /ˈlɒndʒɪtjuːd/ *n.* [C]经线；经度：at a ~ of 125 degrees east 在东经125度

long-range /ˈlɒŋˌreɪndʒ/ *adj.* ❶长远的，长期的，远期的：a ~ planning 远景规划 ❷(炮弹、导弹等)远程的，远距离的：a ~ missile 远程导弹

long-term /ˈlɒŋˌtɜːm/ *adj.* 长期的；长期生效的：~ plans 长期计划/Not enough is known about the drug's ~ side effect. 有关此药的长期副作用至今所知不多。

look /lʊk/ Ⅰ *v.* 看，瞧，望：We ~ed but saw nothing. 我们看了，但什么也没看见。/ ~ **after** 照料，照管：John's mother told him to ~ after his younger brother. 约翰的母亲叫他照顾弟弟。~ **at** 看：Please ~ at the blackboard. 请看黑板。~ **back** 回顾：As he ~ed back, he felt his life was good. 他回顾过去，觉得日子过得很好。~ **down on** 轻视，不看在眼里：Mary ~ed down on her classmates. 玛丽看不起她的同班同学。~ **for** 寻找，寻求：You are ~ing for trouble. 你在自找麻烦。~ **forward to** 期待，盼望：We are ~ing forward to the vacation. 我们正盼望着假期来临。~ **into** 调查，研究，视察：I'll certainly ~ into that right away. 我一定会马上调查此事。~ **like** 好像，像：He ~s like an honest man. 他看起来像个诚实的人。~ **out** 小心，当心：Look out for the train. 小心火车。~ **over** 检查，视察；观看；研究：Would you mind ~ing over my exercises? 请你检查一下我的作业好吗？~ **through** 浏览；温习，复习：Look through your notes before the examination. 考试前温习你的笔记。~ **up** 查寻：It is a good habit to ~ up new words in the dictionary. 在字典里查生词是好习惯。~ **up to** 尊敬，敬仰：She had taught for many years, and all her students ~ed up to her. 她教了多年书，她的所有学生都尊敬她。Ⅱ *n.* [C]看，望；外表，外观：May I have a ~ at it? 让我看一看好吗？/ I don't like her ~s. 我不喜欢她的样子。

loom[1] /luːm/ Ⅰ *n.* [C]织(布)机 Ⅱ *vt.* (在

织布机上)织布

loom[2] / luːm / *vi.* ❶隐约地出现:A figure ~ed up through the mist. 一个人影在雾中隐现。/Suddenly the mountain ~ed over them. 山赫然出现在他们面前。❷(事件、前景等)不祥地逼近:Energy shortages still ~s for the human beings. 人类仍面临能源短缺。

loop / luːp / *n.* [C]圈;环;环状物:The road makes a wide ~ around the building. 那条路围着大楼绕了一大圈。

loose / luːs / Ⅰ *adj.* ❶不紧的;宽松的:~-fitting clothes 宽大的衣服 ❷不牢的;松弛的:a ~ tooth 松动的牙齿/ a ~ window 不牢的窗子 Ⅱ *v.* 松开;释放,使无约束;使松弛:Loose the screw. 把螺丝钉松开。派 loosely *adv.*

L

loosen / ˈluːsən/ *vt.* ❶使松;使松动:~ the soil 松土 / She twisted the tooth, trying to ~ it. 她把牙齿左右摇晃,想让它变松。❷松开;解开:She ~ed the bobby pins from her beret. 她松开了贝雷帽上的扁平发夹。❸放松,放宽(限制等):~ restriction on foreign trade 放宽对外贸的限制 / ~ admission standards 放宽入学(或入会等)的标准 —*vi.* 变松;松动:The tooth ~ed on its own. 牙齿自己松动了。/~ **up** 松弛;放松:His doctor told him to ~ up a bit. 医生告诉他要放松一点。

lorry / ˈlɒri / *n.* [C](英)载货卡车:The ~ is driving to the airport. 卡车正驶向机场。

lose / luːz / *vt.* (lost /lɒst/, lost) ❶失去;丧失;损失:I have lost my umbrella. 我把雨伞弄丢了。/ He has lost his job. 他失业了。/ Don't ~ your temper. 不要发怒。/ ~ **sight of** 看不见:We lost sight of him in the crowd. 我们在人群中看不见他了。❷迷失(方向);错过:She lost her way in the strange city and had to take a taxi back to the hotel. 她在那个陌生的城市里迷失了方向,不得不乘出租车回旅馆。/ I nearly lost the opportunity. 我几乎错失了良机。❸失败;输:Our school basketball team lost the match. 我们的校篮球队比赛输了。

loss / lɒs / *n.* [U]损失;遗失;输:The ~ of health would cause serious result. 失去健康会带来严重的后果。/ Can the company bear the ~ of a million dollars? 这家公司能承受100万美元的亏损吗?

lot / lɒt / *n.* ❶很多;许多 / **a ~ of (lots of)** 大量,许多:I have a ~ of new words to learn. 我有许多新词要记。/ She spent a ~ of time on her homework. 她花了很多时间做家庭作业。❷签,阄;抽签:We may draw ~s to decide who will go. 我们可以抽签决定谁去。

lotion / ˈləʊʃn / *n.* (医学上的外用)洗剂;(化妆用的)润肤剂

lottery / ˈlɒtəri / *n.* [C]博彩;抽奖:run a ~ 发行彩票 / The young man won 20 yuan in the ~. 那年轻人买彩票中了20元奖金。

lotus / ˈləʊtəs / *n.* [C]莲;荷:a ~ leaf 荷叶 / ~ flowers 荷花/ ~ roots 莲藕 / ~ seeds 莲子

loud / laʊd / Ⅰ *adj.* 大声的,高声的;喧闹的:He answered the question with ~ voice. 他大声回答问题。/ I can't bear your ~ cries. 你高声吵闹,我真受不了。Ⅱ *adv.* 大声地;高声地:Speak ~er, please. 请说大声点。派 loudly *adv.*

loudspeaker / ˌlaʊdˈspiːkə(r) / *n.* [C]扬声器

lounge /ˈlaʊndʒ/ *n.* [C](旅馆等的)休息室;休息厅:a sun ~ 日光浴廊 / a VIP ~ 贵宾休息室

lovable /ˈlʌvəbl/ *adj.* 可爱的,惹人爱的,讨人喜欢的:a ~ child 可爱的孩子/ She is really ~. 她确实讨人喜欢。

love /lʌv/ Ⅰ *vt.* ❶爱;热爱:We ~ our country. 我们爱祖国。❷喜欢;爱好:He ~s to ride a bike. 他喜欢骑自行车。/ She ~s playing the piano. 她喜欢弹钢琴。Ⅱ *n.* [U] ❶喜爱;热爱;挚爱:a mother's ~ for her children 母爱 / ~ for one's country 爱国 ❷爱情;恋爱:**be in ~ with** 与……相爱:Mary is in ~ with Tom. 玛丽与汤姆相爱了。

lovely /ˈlʌvli/ *adj.* 美丽的;动人的;可爱的:a ~ view 动人的景色 / ~ weather 好天气 / a ~ girl 可爱的小姑娘

lover /ˈlʌvə(r)/ *n.* [C] ❶恋人,爱侣 ❷爱好者:an opera ~歌剧爱好者/He is a ~ of billiards and tall stories. 他喜欢打台球,喜欢讲荒诞故事。

low /ləʊ/ *adj.* ❶低的;矮的:The moon was ~ in the sky. 月亮低挂在天空。❷(指声音)不高的,低的:He speaks in a ~ voice. 他低声说话。❸(指量、度、价值等)低的,少的:a ~ temperature 低温 / ~ prices 低价

lower /ˈləʊə(r)/ *v.* 放低;降低;减低:~ the flag 将旗降下/ ~ the rent of a house 减低房租 / ~ one's voice 降低声音/ The stocks ~ed in value. 股票跌价了。

lowercase /ˈləʊəˌkeɪs/ Ⅰ *adj.* (字母)小写体;小写字母的 Ⅱ *n.* [U]小号字体

lowly /ˈləʊli/ Ⅰ *adj.* ❶卑微的;地位低下的:a girl of ~ birth 出身卑微的姑娘/a ~ position 低卑的地位 ❷谦卑的;卑恭的;恭顺的:learn to be ~ and reverent 学会待人要谦卑恭敬 Ⅱ *adv.* 谦卑地,恭顺地

loyal /ˈlɒɪəl/ *adj.* 忠诚的;忠心的:He is ~ to his country. 他忠于祖国。/ The students are ~ to their ideals. 学生们忠于自己的理想。

loyalty /ˈlɒɪəlti/ *n.* [U]忠诚;忠心:He pledged his ~ to the company. 他发誓对公司要忠心耿耿。

lubricant /ˈluːbrɪkənt/ Ⅰ *n.* ❶润滑剂;润滑油 ❷[C]用以减少摩擦的东西:a social ~ 社交润滑剂(指在社交中能起到拉拢关系作用的东西) Ⅱ *adj.* 润滑的:a ~ additive 润滑添加剂

lubricate /ˈluːbrɪˌkeɪt/ *vt.* ❶使滑润;加润滑油于:~ the engine 给发动机上油/ The chain of my bike might need lubricating. 我的自行车链可能要加油了。❷使顺畅;缓和:~ relations between the warring factions 缓和交战双方间的关系

luck /lʌk/ *n.* [U] (好或坏的)运气,机运:try one's ~ 碰运气 / Good ~ to you! 祝你顺利(或一路平安)! / May you have better ~ next time. 祝你下次走运。/ She has bad (ill,hard) ~. 她运气不佳。

lucky /ˈlʌki/ *adj.* 幸运的;侥幸的:How ~ you are to have got the opportunity. 得到这个机会,你真幸运。/ I was ~ enough to meet him there. 我很幸运在那儿遇到了他。/ How ~ you are! 你多幸运!

luggage /ˈlʌgɪdʒ/ *n.* [U] 行李:He checked his ~ first. 他先寄存了行李。

lull /lʌl/ Ⅰ *vt.* ❶使安静;哄……入睡:~ a baby to sleep 哄婴儿入睡 ❷使缓和,减轻,消除:~ sb. 's fears (suspi-

L

cions)消解某人的恐惧感(疑惑) —*vi.* 平息,停止;减退,减弱:Conversation ~ed for an hour. 谈话暂停了一个小时。/The furious activity of the crowd finally ~ed. 这群人的愤怒行为最终平息了下来。Ⅱ *n.* [C](常用单数)(风暴、骚乱等过后的)暂停;暂时平静:a ~ storm 风暴的间歇/Following a ~ of half a decade, the country is bracing for its fifth major wave of immigration. 平静的五年过去后,该国迎来了第五次移民大潮。

lumber /ˈlʌmbə(r)/ *n.* [U](无用的)杂物;木材,木料

luminous /ˈljuːmɪnəs/ *adj.* ❶发光的,发亮的;反光的:a pair of ~ brown eyes 一双明亮的棕色眼睛/~ paint 发光漆(或涂料) ❷清楚的;易懂的:a ~ explanation 清楚的解释 派 luminously *adv.*

lump /ˈlʌmp/ *n.* [C] ❶块;团:a ~ of clay 一块黏土 ❷瘤;肿块:She has a bad ~ on the head. 她头上肿起一大块。

lunar /ˈluːnə(r)/ *adj.* 月球的;月亮的:the ~ calendar 阴历

lunch /lʌntʃ/ *n.* 午餐,午饭:We were at ~ when he called. 他来电话时,我们正在吃午饭。

luncheon /ˈlʌntʃən/ *n.* (正式的)午餐,午宴

lung /lʌŋ/ *n.* [C] 肺,肺脏

lure /ljʊə(r)/ Ⅰ *n.* [C] ❶诱惑物,引诱物;引诱力,吸引力:The ~ of art was too strong to resist. 艺术的魅力让人无法抗拒。❷(诱捕动物等的)诱饵;囮子;鱼饵:Anglers use different ~s to catch different kinds of fish. 垂钓者用不同的诱饵来钓不同的鱼。Ⅱ *vt.* 吸引,引诱,诱惑:Life in the city ~d him away from home. 城里生活诱使他离开了家乡。/Such prices ~d others into the business. 这样的价格吸引了其他一些人来购买。

luxuriant /lʌgˈʒʊərɪənt/ *adj.* ❶(草木等)茂盛的,郁郁葱葱的;(须发等)浓密的:The rain had made every growing thing fresh and ~. 雨水使一切生物都生机勃勃,葱郁茂盛。/Her ~ hair fell around her shoulders. 她那浓密的长发披散在双肩。❷(土地等)肥沃的;丰饶的;多产的:~ soil 沃土 ❸丰富的:~ imagination 丰富的想象力

luxurious /lʌgˈʒʊərɪəs/ *adj.* 奢侈的;豪华的:He stayed in a ~ hotel. 他住在一家豪华宾馆里。

luxury /ˈlʌkʃəri/ *n.* [U]奢侈;豪华:He lives in ~ but works hard. 他生活奢侈,但工作勤奋。

lymph /lɪmf/ *n.* [U]淋巴

lyric /ˈlɪrɪk/ Ⅰ *adj.* ❶(古诗)歌一般的;适于吟唱的:a ~ drama 歌剧 ❷(诗歌或歌曲等)抒情的 Ⅱ *n.* [C] ❶抒情诗 ❷歌词

lyricist /ˈlɪrɪsɪst/ *n.* [C] ❶歌词作者 ❷抒情诗人

M m

ma'am / mæm, mɑːm, məm / *n.* [C]夫人;太太;女士:A gentleman has called, ~. 有位先生打来电话,夫人。

machine / məˈʃiːn / *n.* [C]机器;机械:a washing ~ 洗衣机 / a vending ~ 自动售货机 / a video-game ~ 电子游戏机

machinery / məˈʃiːnəri / *n.* [U](总称)机器;机械:procession ~ 精密仪器 / They installed some new ~ in the lab. 他们在实验室里安装了一些新机器。

macro / ˈmækrəʊ / Ⅰ *adj.* 巨大的;极厚的;大量使用的:~ control 宏观控制 / ~ economy 宏观经济 / ~ education 宏观教育 / ~ management 宏观管理 Ⅱ *n.* [C]宏指令:~ coding 宏编码

macrocosm / ˈmækrəʊˌkɒzəm / *n.* [C] ❶整个宇宙,大宇宙;宏观世界:a cultural ~宏观文化/He desires, first, to see the spirit of the ~. 他最先渴望了解的是整个宇宙的灵魂。❷全域;大而复杂的整体:the ~ of war 错综复杂的战争过程/No population is absolutely inert in the ~ of humanity. 在人类错综复杂的整体中,没有一个种族是绝对静止不变的。

mad / mæd / *adj.* (madder, maddest) ❶疯狂的;精神错乱的:a ~ dog 疯狗 ❷非常激动的;失去理性的:They were ~ (at) missing the train. 他们没赶上火车,气得要命。派 madly *adv.*

madam / ˈmædəm / *n.* [C]夫人,太太,女士(对妇女的尊称):Madam, will you take my seat? 太太,您坐我的座位好吗? / Madam Lee is from China. 李夫人来自中国。

made-up / ˈmeɪdˌʌp / *adj.* ❶编造的,虚构的:a ~ story 虚构的故事 ❷化妆过的;化了装的:She was heavily ~. 她化了浓妆。

magazine / ˌmægəˈziːn / *n.* [C]杂志;期刊:Most ~s are published either weekly or monthly. 大多数杂志都是周刊或月刊。

magic / ˈmædʒɪk / Ⅰ *n.* [U] 魔术;戏法:He is good at performing ~. 他很会表演魔术。Ⅱ *adj.* 有魔力的:a piece of ~ cloth 魔布 / a ~ lantern 幻灯 / This kind of medicine has a ~ effect. 这种药效果神奇。

magician / məˈdʒɪʃən / *n.* [C]魔术师

magistrate / ˈmædʒɪstreɪt / *n.* [C]地方行政长官;地方法官:Her father is a ~. 她的父亲是县长。

magnet / ˈmægnət / *n.* [C]磁石,磁铁;有吸引力的人或物:~ bar codes 条形码

magnanimous / mægˈnænɪməs / *adj.* 宽厚的,气量大的;大度的,宽容的:a ~ adversary 大度的对手/be ~ toward one's enemies 对敌人宽容大度 派 magnanimously *adv.*

magnate / ˈmægneɪt, ˈmægnɪt / *n.* [C] ❶显贵，权贵；要人，大人物；企业巨头：a leading ~ in industrial circles 工业巨头/an oil ~石油大亨 ❷杰出人物，优秀人才：literary ~s 杰出的文人

magnetic / mægˈnetɪk / *adj.* 磁的；有磁性的：a ~ card 磁卡 / a ~ field 磁场 / a ~ suspension train 磁悬浮列车

magnetism / ˈmægnɪˌtɪzəm / *n.* ❶磁力，磁性：the mutual relations of the two ~ 两种磁力的相互关系/weakened ~弱化的磁性 ❷[U]魅力，吸引力：Of course any man might have rushed to save her, and reap the reward of her soft and grateful ~. 毫不奇怪，任何男人都会奋不顾身地营救她，并将她温柔、愉悦的迷人魅力当作褒赏。

magnificent / mægˈnɪfɪsənt / *adj.* 宏伟的；堂皇的：They visited the ~ Great Hall of the People when they were in Beijing. 在北京时他们参观了宏伟的人民大会堂。

magnify / ˈmægnɪfaɪ / *vt.* 放大，扩大；夸大：It can ~ the word 100 times. 它可以把字放大 100 倍。

magnitude / ˈmægnɪˌtjuːd / *n.* ❶(大小或数量的)巨大，庞大；广大：the height, strength and ~ of a building 建筑物的高大宏伟 ❷[U]伟大；重大；重要(性)；紧迫(性)：two offences of a very different nature and by no means of equal ~ 两件性质不同、轻重不等的罪名/We could not carry not a project of this ~ without assistance. 没有外援我们无法完成如此重大的项目。/ **of the first ~** (在某些方面)极出色的，一流的；头等重要的，极其重要的：an affair of the first ~头等大事/an artist of the first ~ 一流的艺术家

maid / meɪd / *n.* [C]少女；女仆

mail / meɪl / *n.* [U]邮政；邮寄；信件；邮包：send a letter by air ~ 寄一封航空信 / a ~ box 邮箱 / a ~ man 邮递员 / a ~ train 邮件火车/Is there any ~ this morning? 今上午有邮件吗?

main / meɪn / Ⅰ *adj.* 主要的；重要的：Can you grasp the ~ idea of his report? 你能抓住他报告的主要意思吗? /the ~ streets of a town 市内主要街道 / my ~ arguments 我的主要论点 Ⅱ *n.* [C]主要部分：**in the ~** 大体上；就一般而论：In the ~, the book is not interesting. 大体上说来，那本书没趣。派 mainly *adv.*

mainframe / ˈmeɪnˌfreɪm / *n.* [C](计算机的)主机，中央处理机：a time-shared ~一台分时中央处理器

mainland / ˈmenˌlænd, ˈmeɪnlænd / *n.* [C](the ~) 大陆，本土：I'll go to the ~ from the small island by a ferry. 我将乘轮渡从小岛到大陆去。

mainstream / ˈmeɪnˌstriːm / Ⅰ *n.* [C]主要倾向；主流；主流派风格：He is far from the ~ of Russian culture. 他与俄罗斯主流文化相距甚远。Ⅱ *adj.* 主流的；主要倾向的；主流派的：With its new models, the company hopes to move into the heart of the ~ market. 公司希望新的车型能够进入主流汽车市场的中心地带。

maintain / meɪnˈteɪn / *v.* 维持；保持；维修；保养：They ~ friendly relations with each other. 他们相互保持友好关系。/ The police are working hard to ~ public order. 警察努力工作以维持社会秩序。/ He is ~ing a machine. 他正在维修机器。

maize / meɪz / *n.* [U]玉米

majesty / ˈmædʒəsti / *n.* [U]崇高；尊严；

王权：We hope to pay our respects to Her Majesty. 我们希望谒见女王陛下。

major /ˈmeɪdʒə(r)/ Ⅰ *adj*. 较大的，较重要的：the ~ portion 主要部分 / Your car needs ~ repairs. 你的车需要大修。Ⅱ *n*. [C] 主修科目；某专业的学生：My sister wants to take economics as her ~. 我姐姐想专修经济学。/ He is a history ~. 他是历史专业的学生。Ⅲ *vi*. 主修；专攻：He is ~ing in business administration. 他主修工商管理课程。

majority /məˈdʒɒrəti/ *n*. 多数；大多数：His proposition was supported by the great ~ of the students. 他的提议得到大多数学生的支持。

make /meɪk/ Ⅰ *v*. (made/meɪd/, made) ❶建造；制造：Many boys like to ~ model planes. 很多男孩都喜欢制作飞机模型。❷获得；挣得；赚：He ~s a profit of 2,500 yuan a month. 他每月赚2500元利润。❸让，使；使得：Experience in the countryside made him know much. 在农村的经历使他懂得了许多。/ ~ **a dive for** 向……猛冲；冲过去拿：The owner made a dive for the rejected clothes. 店主冲向那堆挑剩的衣服。~ **a living** 谋生；度日：He ~s a living as a teacher. 他当教师谋生。~ **a mistake** 犯错误：You made a mistake in trusting him too much. 你错在过分相信他。~ **a noise** 吵闹：It made a noise like a travelling train. 它发出像火车一样的隆隆声。~ **a promise** 答应；许下诺言：He made a promise to help us, but he didn't keep his promise. 他许诺帮助我们，但不遵守诺言。~ **an apology to sb.** 向某人道歉：If you are late for class, you should ~ an apology to the teacher either at the time or after class. 你如果上课迟到，就应在当时或课后向教师道歉。**be made of (from)** 由……制成：The table cloth is made of cotton. 这桌布是棉制的。~ **faces (a face)** 做鬼脸：The sick boy swallowed the medicine and made a face. 这个生病的男孩吞下药后做了个鬼脸。~ **friends with** 与……交朋友：Within two days she made friends with everyone on the boat. 两天里她和全船的人都成了朋友。~ **fun of** 取笑：I had thought they were making fun of me. 我原以为他们在取笑我。~ **into** 制成；使转变为：Bamboo can also be made into paper. 竹子也可以造纸。~ **one's mark** 成功；出名：Shakespeare made his mark as a playwright. 莎士比亚是作为戏剧作家闻名于世的。~ **one's point** 阐明观点；证明观点：Darwin made his point by giving a lot of proofs. 达尔文以大量证据证明了他的观点。~ **one's way** 排除困难前进：As soon as he saw us, Henry made his way through the crowd to greet us. 亨利一看到我们就从人群中挤出来欢迎我们。~ **progress** 取得进步：He made such progress that before long he began to write articles in English for an American newspaper. 他进步很快，不久就开始用英文给一家美国报纸写稿。~ **repairs** 修补：The swimming pool will not be open today because some people are making repairs. 游泳池今天不开放，因为一些人正在做修补工作。~ **room for** 给……腾出地方：Can you ~ room for this guest at the dinner table? 您可以在餐桌上为这位客人腾出点地方吗？~ **sentences with** 用……造句：Please ~ sentences with these phrases after class. 请课后用这些短语造句。~ **... to one's**

measure 照某人的尺寸做：We have these suits for you to choose from, or I can ~ you one to your measure. 我们有这些衣服供你选择，或者我可以按你的尺寸给你做一件。~ **up** 组成；完成：The committee is made up of seven members. 委员会由七人组成。She had a lot of homework to ~ up yesterday. 她昨天有许多作业要完成。~ **up one's mind** 下决心：They made up their minds to sell the house. 他们下决心把房子卖掉。~ **up for** 弥补：We had to work twice as hard to ~ up for the lost time. 我们不得不加倍努力以弥补失去的时间。Ⅱ *n.* [C]制造；产品的品牌：They bought a car with the same ~ of mine. 他们买了一辆品牌和我的一样的小汽车。

M

make-up /ˈmeɪkʌp/ *n.* (*pl.* makes-up) ❶[C]补考：If you didn't pass the examination, you may take a ~ at the end of the term. 如果你考试不及格，你可以在期末参加补考。❷[U]化妆，化妆品：My sister never wears ~. 我姐姐从来不化妆。❸构造，组成：the ~ of the football team 足球队的组成 ❹性格，气质：It partly depends on your genetic ~. 这部分取决于你的遗传性格。

making /ˈmeɪkɪŋ/ *n.* ❶[U]制作，制造，生产；形成；创作：film ~电影摄制/The ~ of a violin requires great skill. 小提琴的制作需要很高的技巧。❷素质，要素；必备条件；潜力，能力：The story has all the ~ of a great movie. 这个故事具备一部优秀影片的所有条件。/**be of one's own** ~自己造成：The trouble here is of her own ~. 这里的麻烦是她自找的。**in the** ~在制造中；在形成中；在发展中；在酝酿中；即将产生的，随时出现的：The slogans and concepts are everywhere, and they add up to a new American economy in the ~. 口号与理念随处可见，这些都是正在形成的美国新经济的组成部分。

malady /ˈmælədi/ *n.* [C](身体的)不适，疾病；(慢性)病，痼病：After years of life in the tropics, he was plagued by one exhausting ~ after another. 他经年累月地待在热带丛林里，要命的疾病接踵而至。/To be ignorant of one's ignorance is the ~ of the ignorant. 无视自身的无知是无知者的通病。

malaria /məˈleərɪə/ *n.* [U]疟疾：Not many people suffer from ~ now. 现在患疟疾的人很少。

male /meɪl/ *adj.* 男的；男性的：a deep ~ voice 浑厚的男声

malfunction /mælfʌŋkʃn/ Ⅰ *n.* [C]功能失效，机能失常；故障：The pilot waited for the instruments to regain power, but the ~ continued. 飞行员等待仪器恢复运动，可故障仍旧。Ⅱ *vi.* 运转失灵，发生故障；显示功能失常：One of the motors has ~ed. 有一台发动机出了故障。

malice /ˈmælɪs/ *n.* [U]伤害欲，破坏欲；歹念，恶意；怨恨，憎恶：It was not brought about by accident, but by the ~ of Tom. 事情的发生绝非偶然，而是汤姆故意捣的鬼。/ I bear you no ~. 我对你毫无恶意。派 malicious *adj.*

malign /məˈlaɪn/ *vt.* 诬蔑，诽谤，中伤，恶毒攻击：The engineers found their motives ~ed and their conclusions impugned. 工程师们发现他们的动机被恶意中伤，他们得出的结论也受到怀疑。

mall /mɔːl/ *n.* [C]大型餐饮购物中心；购物街：People always buy their daily necessities at the shopping ~. 人们总爱在购物中心购买日用品。

malt /mɔːlt,mɔlt/ *n.* ❶[U]麦芽:~ and wheat 麦芽和小麦 ❷(一份)麦芽酒 ❸[C]麦乳精:a vanilla ~ and a chocolate ~一份香草麦乳精和一份巧克力麦乳精

mammal /ˈmæml/ *n.* [C]哺乳动物

man /mæn/ *n.* ❶[C](*pl.* men/men/)男人:a tall ~ 一个高大的男子 ❷人,人类(不加冠词):Only ~ knows how to cook. 只有人类懂得烹饪。

manage /ˈmænɪdʒ/ *v.* ❶管理;处理:~ a company 管理公司/ She ~d the problem well. 她把问题处理得很好。❷设法;对付:He ~d to accomplish his work ahead of time. 他设法提前完成了工作。

management /ˈmænɪdʒmənt/ *n.* ❶[U]管理;经营;处理:~ fees (costs)管理费 / ~ modernization 管理现代化 / closed ~ 封闭式管理 /goal ~ 目标管理 / They introduced scientific ~ in their factory. 他们公司引进了科学的管理方法。❷[C]管理部门;管理阶层;资方:The ~ held a meeting to discuss the problem. 管理方召开了一个会议讨论这个问题。

manager /ˈmænɪdʒə(r)/ *n.* [C]经理;管理人:a branch ~ 部门经理 / a general ~ 总经理 / a sales ~ 销售经理 / a service ~ 服务部经理

mango /ˈmæŋgəʊ/ *n.* [C]❶芒果 ❷芒果树

manifest /ˈmænɪˌfest/ Ⅰ *adj.* 明显的,明白的,明了的:be ~ to every man's eye 显而易见的/As will be made ~,only one answer exists to each question. 很明显,一个问题只有一个答案。/As ~ in his music, Ives's faith was real and transcendental. 正像他的音乐所明晰表达出的那样,艾夫斯的信念是真实、超脱的。Ⅱ *vt.* 明白显示,清楚表明;表露,流露(情感等):He ~ed his approval with a hearty laugh. 他用一阵发自内心的笑声清楚地表明了赞同的意思。

manipulate /məˈnɪpjʊˌleɪt/ *vt.* ❶安排;处理;利用;影响;控制:~ the plot 安排情节/It is a simple matter to ~ such a situation. 应付这样一个局面很简单。❷熟练地操作,巧妙地使用:~ the steering wheel 熟练地操作方向盘/~ a pair of scissors 巧用剪刀 派 manipulation *n.*

mankind /mænˈkaɪnd/ *n.* [U]人类;(总称)人:War is one of the greatest evils of ~. 战争是人类最大的灾祸之一。

manly /ˈmænli/ *adj.* 有男子气概的;男人的

man-made /ˈmænˌmeɪd/ *adj.* 人造的,人的;人为的:a ~ satellite 人造卫星/~ accidents 人为事故

manner /ˈmænə(r)/ *n.* [C] ❶方式;方法:Do it in this ~. 用这种方法做。❷态度,举止(用单数):I don't like his ~. 我不喜欢他的态度。She has a warm and friendly ~ to all of us. 她对我们大家的态度热情友好。❸社交行为;礼貌(常用 *pl.*):have good (bad) ~s 有(没有)礼貌 / It is bad ~s to stare at people. 瞪着眼睛看人是不礼貌的。

manpower /ˈmænpaʊə(r)/ *n.* [U]人力;劳动力:~ resources 人力资源 / ~ surplus 劳动力过剩

mansion /ˈmænʃn/ *n.* [C]❶豪宅,宅邸;大厦:the governor's ~总督的官邸 ❷公寓大厦,公寓楼;公寓楼中的套房:Sloane Avenue ~s 斯隆尼大街公寓楼/In my father's house are many ~s. 我父

亲的房子里有多套住房。

mantle /ˈmæntl/ *n.* [C] ❶斗篷，披风，氅：throw a ~ over one's shoulders 把披风披在肩上 ❷覆盖物；盖罩；幕：the ~ of darkness 夜幕 / The ground had a ~ of snow. 地上盖着一层雪。❸地幔：~ plume 地幔热柱

manual /ˈmænjʊəl/ Ⅰ *adj.* ❶用手的；人工的；体力的：~ labor 体力劳动 Ⅱ *n.* [C]手册，指南：an owner's ~ 用户指南 / You'd better first read the instruction ~ of the machine carefully. 你最好先仔细看看这台机器的使用说明书。派 manually *adv.*

manufacture /ˌmænjʊˈfæktʃə(r)/ Ⅰ *vt.* 以机器制造；加工 Ⅱ *n.* [U]制造；生产：~ industry 制造业 / ~ with order's materials 来料加工 / Have you got a ~ license? 你领到生产许可证了吗？

manufacturer /ˌmænjʊˈfæktʃərə(r)/ *n.* [C]制造者；制造商；制造厂；制造公司

manure /məˈnjʊə(r)/ *n.* [U]肥料；粪肥

manuscript /ˈmænjʊskrɪpt/ *n.* [C]手稿；原稿；底稿：a novel in ~ 小说手稿 / He sent his ~ to a publisher. 他把原稿送交出版商。

many /ˈmeni/ Ⅰ *adj.* (more/mɔː/，most /məʊst/)许多的，多的：a good ~ 很多的，相当多的 / ~ **a** 很多：Many a man would welcome the opportunity. 许多人要利用这个机会。Ⅱ *pron.* 许多：~ of them 他们中的许多人

map /mæp/ *n.* [C]地图；示意图：There is a world ~ on the wall. 墙上有一幅世界地图。

maple /ˈmeɪpl/ *n.* [C]枫树

marathon /ˈmærəθən/ *n.* [C]马拉松赛跑

marble /ˈmɑːbl/ *n.* 大理石；大理石艺术品：a ~ statue 大理石雕像

March /mɑːtʃ/ *n.* (略作 Mar.)三月

march /mɑːtʃ/ Ⅰ *v.* 前进；行军：The troops ~ed against the enemy. 部队朝着敌人方向进军。/They worked hard and ~ed from victory to victory. 他们辛勤工作，从胜利走向胜利。Ⅱ *n.* [C]前进；行军：the Long March 长征 / All of us can sing *March of the Volunteers*. 我们都会唱《义勇军进行曲》。

margin /ˈmɑːdʒɪn/ *n.* [C]页边的空白；边缘：There are some notes written in the ~. 书页边缘记有笔记。

marginal /ˈmɑːdʒɪnəl/ *adj.* ❶页边的，页边空白处的；边注的：~ notes 页边注释 ❷边缘的；边缘地区的；构成边缘的：a ~ piece of land 边缘地区的一块地 ❸最低限度的，接近承受边缘的；勉强够格的：a ~ majority 微弱(或勉强)多数/a ~ student 差生 派 marginally *adv.*

marine /məˈriːn/ Ⅰ *adj.* ❶海洋的；海里发现的；海产的：~ vegetation 海洋植物 / a ~ cable 海底电缆 /~ products 海产品 ❷航海的；海运的；海事的：~ affairs 海事 / ~ transport (transportation) 海上运输 Ⅱ *n.* [C]海军陆战队士兵(或军官)

marital /ˈmærɪtəl/ *adj.* 婚姻的；夫妻(间)的：~ vows 结婚誓言

maritime /ˈmærɪtaɪm/ *adj.* 海(上)的；海事的：Maritime Law 海洋法

mark /mɑːk/ Ⅰ *n.* [C] ❶记号；符号；标志：punctuation ~s 标点符号 / the price ~ 价目标签 / the trade ~ 商标 / While reading he always makes a ~ where he has a question. 读书时他常在有疑问的地方做记号。❷斑点；痕迹；疤

痕：There are some dirty ～s on the wall. 墙上有一些污迹。❸(考试的)分数：He got a full ～ in the English test. 英语考试他得了满分。Ⅱ *v.* 加标记，加符号；记分数：The teachers are ～ing examination papers. 老师们正在评阅考卷。

marked /mɑːkt/ *adj.* ❶相当明显的，显著的：a ～ improvement 显著的改善 /The curiously modern feeling in much of his work became more ～. 他大部分作品中奇特的现代感变得更明显了。❷受怀疑的；受仇视的：The accountant is a ～ man. 那个会计受到了怀疑。❸有记号的，打上标记的 派 markedly *adv.*

market /ˈmɑːkɪt/ *n.* [C] ❶市场；集市：～ economy 市场经济/ ～ demand 市场需求 / ～ easy 市场疲软 / ～ management 市场管理 / There are many small ～s in the town. 镇里有许多小集市。❷销售；需求：a ～ department 销售部 / ～ channel 销售渠道 / There is a very large ～ for cars in our city. 我们城市里小汽车很畅销。

marketing /ˈmɑːkɪtɪŋ/ *n.* [C] ❶销售学；市场推广：She majored in ～. 她专修市场营销。❷采购食品：Her husband did the ～ on Fridays. 她丈夫星期五负责买食物。

market-place /ˈmɑːkɪtˌpleɪs/ *n.* [C] ❶(尤指露天的)集市，市场；商业中心 ❷商界，商业圈：In a free, open ～ our goods can compete. 在自由开放的商界我们的商品才能相互竞争。❸(各种思想、观点等的)交流(或竞争)场所：a ～ for ideas 各种思想争鸣的场所

marquis /ˈmɑːkwɪs/ *n.* [C]侯爵

marriage /ˈmærɪdʒ/ *n.* 结婚；婚姻：early (late) ～ 早(晚)婚 / a ～ advertisement 征婚广告 / a ～ agent 婚姻介绍所 / Young people like group ～. 年轻人喜欢集体结婚。

married /ˈmærɪd/ *adj.* 结婚的；已婚的：Is she ～? 她结婚了吗？

marrow /ˈmærəʊ/ *n.* [U]髓，骨髓；脊髓：bone ～ transplants 骨髓移植

marry /ˈmæri/ *v.* 结婚：John is going to ～ Jane. 约翰将和简结婚。/ Tom and Alice are going to get married. 汤姆和艾丽斯要结婚了。

Mars /mɑːz/ *n.* (天文)火星

marsh /mɑːʃ/ *n.* 沼泽；湿地：～ gas 沼气

marshal /ˈmɑːʃəl/ *n.* [C](陆军)元帅

martial /ˈmɑːʃəl/ *adj.* 战争的；适合于战争的：～ array 战争布阵

martyr /ˈmɑːtə(r)/ *n.* [C]烈士；受难者：He died a ～ to his belief. 他为自己的信仰而牺牲。

marvel /ˈmɑːvəl/ *n.* [C] 奇异的事；令人惊奇的事：It is really the ～s of modern science. 这真是现代科学的奇迹。

marvel(l)ous /ˈmɑːvələs/ *adj.* 奇迹般的；惊人的；了不起的 派 marvel(l)ously *adv.*

Marxism /ˈmɑːksɪzəm/ *n.* [U]马克思主义

Marxist /ˈmɑːksɪst/ Ⅰ *adj.* 马克思主义的 Ⅱ *n.* [C]马克思主义者

masculine /ˈmæskjʊlɪn, ˈmɑːskjʊlɪn/ *adj.* ❶男子的；男性的；男性主导的：She was a woman who spoke her mind in a ～ society. 她是一个男权社会里表达自己想法的女性。❷男子气概的，男子汉的；阳刚的，强壮的：～ strength 男子汉的力量/She loved the ～ aspects of Stanley. 她爱上了斯坦利的阳刚之气。

❸阳性的 派 masculinity *n.*

mask / mɑːsk / Ⅰ *n.* [C]面具;面罩:a gas ~ 防毒面具 / She swam with a ~ on. 她戴着面罩游泳。Ⅱ *v.* 掩饰;掩盖:He talked about some other things to ~ his real purpose. 他说一些别的事情以掩盖他的真实目的。

mass / mæs / *n.* [C] 块,堆;大量;群众:The ~es are the makers of history. 人民群众是历史的创造者。/ I have got a great ~ of letters to answer. 我得回大量的信件。

massacre / ˈmæsəkə(r) / *n.* [C]大屠杀;残杀

massage / ˈmæsɑːʒ / *n.* 按摩;推拿:keep-fit ~ 保健按摩 / There is a ~ center in our town. 我们镇里有一家按摩中心。/ I am tired. Can you give me a ~? 我很疲倦,你能给我按摩一下吗? 派 massager *n.*

M

massive / ˈmæsɪv / *adj.* 粗大的;大量的;大规模的:There are four ~ pillars in the front of the hall. 大厅的前面有四根粗大的柱子。/ They made ~ efforts but failed. 他们做出了巨大的努力,但没有成功。

mast / mɑːst / *n.* [C]桅杆;旗杆

master / ˈmɑːstə(r) / Ⅰ *n.* [C] ❶主人;顾主:The ~ likes his dog. 主人很喜欢他的狗。❷名家;大师:He is a ~ in literature. 他是一个文学大师。❸硕士:a Master of Arts (Science)文科(理科)硕士 / a Master's degree 硕士学位 / a Master's thesis 硕士论文 Ⅱ *vt.* 成为……的主人;精通:Chinese is a difficult language to ~. 汉语是一门很难掌握的语言。

masterly / ˈmɑːstəli / *adj.* &*adv.* 娴熟的(地);熟练的(地);巧妙的(地);极好的(地):a ~ presentation of the budget 预算案的巧妙陈述/a ~ summing-up of the situation 对局势的精辟总结/At an obvious level, the book is simply a ~ guided tour. 显而易见,这是一本很好的导游手册。

masterpiece / ˈmɑːstəpiːs / *n.* [C]杰作,代表作;杰出的事

mat / mæt / *n.* [C]席子;垫子:She put a welcome ~ in front of her flat. 她在房门前放了一块踏脚垫。

match[1] / mætʃ / *n.* [C]火柴:a box of ~es 一盒火柴 / strike a ~ 划火柴

match[2] / mætʃ / Ⅰ *n.* [C] ❶比赛;竞赛:I like to watch a football ~. 我很喜欢看足球赛。❷婚姻,匹配:They decided to make a ~. 他们决定结婚。/ It is a high building with no ~ in the world. 这幢高楼举世无双。Ⅱ *v.* ❶比赛;竞赛:I'm ready to ~ my strength with (against) yours. 我准备跟你比力量。❷(在品质、颜色等方面)相当,相配:The carpets should ~ the curtains. 地毯应该和窗帘相配。/ You should always ~ your words with your deeds. 你应当言行一致。

matchless / ˈmætʃlɪs/ *adj.* 无与伦比的;举世无双的;无可匹敌的:a ~ art-history library 举世无双的艺术史图书馆 / ~ glory 无可匹敌的荣誉 / The lady is still in her ~ beauty. 那女子仍然是那样艳丽无比。

mate / meɪt/ Ⅰ *n.* [C] ❶(口语)(人的)配偶,伴侣,爱人;丈夫;妻子:choose one's own ~ 选择自己的伴侣 / She mourned for her dead ~. 她因丈夫的去世感到悲痛。❷(动物的)配偶:We should look for a ~ for the female panda. 我们应该给雌熊猫找个配偶。❸配

对物,(一对中的)另一个(或只、半):Find me the ~ of (to) this shoe. 把与这只鞋配对的另一只找给我。/ I've never struck the ~ to it before. 我以前从来没碰到过像这样的事儿。

material /məˈtɪərɪəl/ Ⅰ *n.* 原料;材料:dress ~s 布料 / building ~s 建筑材料 / raw ~s 原材料 / packaging ~s 包装材料 / reading ~s 阅读材料 / teaching ~s 教材 Ⅱ *adj.* 物质的(与 spiritual 相对):the ~ world 物质世界 / a ~ noun 物质名词 / ~ wealth 物质财富 / ~ benefit 物质利益

materialism /məˈtɪərɪəlɪzəm/ *n.* [U]唯物论;唯物主义:dialectical ~ 辩证唯物主义 / historical ~ 历史唯物主义

maternal /məˈtɜːnəl/ *adj.* ❶母亲的;母亲似的,慈母般的:~ love 母爱/She is very ~ towards her staff. 她对手下的职员都很慈爱。❷母系的;娘家的,母亲一方的;母亲遗传的:~ grandmother 外婆/~ aunt 姨妈/Her beautiful long hair was a ~ inheritance. 她那一头漂亮的长发是母亲的遗传。派 maternally *adv.*

mathematics /ˌmæθəˈmætɪks/ *n.* [U]数学

math(s) /mæθ(s)/ *n.* (=mathematics)数学

matter /ˈmætə(r)/ Ⅰ *n.* ❶[U]物质:She discovered a new kind of ~. 她发现了一种新的物质。❷[C] 事务;事件;问题:money ~s 金钱方面的事情 / This is a ~ I know little about. 这件事我不大清楚。/ What's the ~ with you? 你怎么啦? / No ~ what he says or does, we do not believe him. 不管他说什么,做什么,我们都不会相信他。/ **as a ~ of fact** 事实上:As a ~ of fact, he didn't know it. 事实上他并不知道此事。Ⅱ *vi.* (主要用于疑问句、否定句和条件句中)关系重大,要紧:It doesn't ~ to me what you do and where you go. 你做什么或去什么地方与我无关。

mattress /ˈmætrɪs/ *n.* [U]床垫

mature /məˈtʃʊə(r)/ *adj.* 成熟的;完全发育的;到期的:Mature fruits taste well. 成熟的水果味道好。/ After years' work, he became a ~ man. 经过多年的工作,他成熟了。

maxim /ˈmæksɪm/ *n.* [C]格言,箴言,警句;座右铭

maximize /ˈmæksɪˌmaɪz/ *vt.* ❶使达到(或增长到)最大限度:ways of maximizing profit 获取最大利润的方法 ❷充分利用:~ one's time 充分利用某人的时间 / ~ one's potential 充分挖掘某人的潜能

M

maximum /ˈmæksɪməm/ Ⅰ *n.* [C](*pl.* maxima /ˈmæksɪmə/)最大量;最高点;极点(与 minimum 相对):It is the ~ temperature recorded in London. 这是有记载的伦敦最高温度。/ The ~ load for this lorry is two ton. 这辆卡车最大载重量是两吨。Ⅱ *adj.* 最大的;最大量的:~ wage 最高工资 / to the ~ 最大限度地 / The ~ speed of this car is 80 miles per hour. 这辆车的最高时速是每小时 80 英里。

May /meɪ/ *n.* 五月:~ Day 五一国际劳动节 / the ~ 4th Movement 五四运动

may /meɪ/ *aux. v.* (might/maɪt/) ❶可能;或许:He ~ have missed the train. 或许他没赶上那班火车。/ She ~ be right in this point. 在这一点上她可能是对的。❷可以(表示许可或请求许可):May I come in? 我可以进来吗? ❸表示询问:How old ~ (might) she be? 她的年龄会有多大呢? ❹表示愿望

或希望：May they live long！祝他们长寿！/ May you succeed！祝你成功！

maybe /ˈmeɪbi/ *adv.* 大概；或许：Maybe he will come to our party tomorrow. 也许他明天会来参加我们的聚会。

mayor /meə(r)/ *n.* [C]市长

maze /meɪz/ *n.* [C] ❶迷宫：led sb. through a ~ of caves 带某人穿过迷宫般的洞穴 ❷错综复杂（的事物），盘根错节（的事物）：a ~ of interlacing water-pipes 错综复杂的水管/a ~ of disorganized facts 一大堆混乱不堪、毫无头绪的事实

me /mi/ *pron.* 我（I 的宾格）

meadow /ˈmedəʊ/ *n.* [C]草地；牧场

meal /miːl/ *n.* [C] 一餐；一顿饭；饮食：We always have three ~s a day. 我们总是一日三餐。/ Most families meet together for a big ~ on New Year's Eve. 多数家庭会在除夕夜聚在一起吃丰盛的年夜饭。

M

mean[1] /miːn/ *vt.* (meant/ment/, meant) ❶表示，意指；意欲：He ~s no harm to you. 他不想伤害你。/ What do you ~ by saying that? 说这话你什么意思？❷对……是重要的；对……有价值的：Your friendship ~s a great deal to me. 你的友谊对我极为重要。/ The word doesn't ~ anything here. 这个词用在这里毫无意义。

mean[2] /miːn/ *adj.* ❶自私的；吝啬的；小气的：The fellow is a ~ minded man. 那家伙是一个吝啬自私的人。❷卑鄙的；讨厌的：It was ~ of Jack to cheat in the exam. 杰克考试作弊是很卑鄙的。派 meanly

mean[3] /miːn/ Ⅰ *n.* [C]平均值；平均数 Ⅱ *adj.* 中间的；中等的；平均的：in the ~ time (while)在此期间 / The ~ temperature here in spring is about 12℃. 这里春季的平均温度是 12 摄氏度左右。

meaning /ˈmiːnɪŋ/ *n.* 意义；意思；含义：What's the ~ of this sentence? 这个句子的意思是什么？/ It is a word with many ~s. 这是一个多义词。

meaningful /ˈmiːnɪŋf(ʊ)l/ *adj.* ❶有意义的，意味深长的：~ names (signs) 极具含义的名字（符号）/ exchange ~ glances 意味深长地互视 ❷认真的，严肃的；重要的：She wanted a ~ relationship. 她希望有一份认真的情感。派 meaningfully *adv.*；meaningfulness *n.*

means /miːnz/ *n.* ❶[C]方式，方法；手段；工具（复数形式，常作单数使用）：A mobile-phone is a new ~ of communication that people like to use. 移动电话是人们喜欢使用的一种新的通信工具。❷财富，钱财：He has the ~ to support his family. 他有钱养活家人。/ **by ~ of** 借助；凭借；依靠：Thoughts are expressed by ~ of words. 思想用语言表达出来。**by all ~** 尽一切办法；无论如何；务必：Come to attend the meeting by all ~. 你务必要来参加会议。/ I'll finish it in two hours by all ~. 我尽力在两小时内做完这事。**by no ~** 决不；一点也不：These goods are by no ~ satisfactory. 这些货物一点也不令人满意。

meanwhile /ˈmiːnˌwaɪl/ Ⅰ *n.* [U]间隔；其间：We have to leave at seven; in the ~, let's have a drink. 我们必须在 7 点出发；走之前我们喝点东西吧。Ⅱ *adv.* ❶在此期间：Meanwhile he was only just beginning to enjoy his new life. 此间他才刚开始享受新的生活。❷与此同时；此时，那时：Meanwhile her taxes had been remitted. 与此同时，她的税款

已被汇出。

measurable /ˈmeʒ(ə)rəbl/ *adj.* ❶可测量的，可计量的：a quantifiable and ~ market share 可量化并可计量的市场份额 ❷引人注目的；重大的；具有重要意义的：~ improvements in the quality of the products 产品质量的重大提高/ have ~ impact on the lives of the people 对人们的生活产生重大影响 派 measurably *adv.*

measure /ˈmeʒə(r)/ Ⅰ *n.* ❶大小；数量；度量：give full (short) ~ 称量足(不足) / cut to one's ~量体裁衣 ❷[C]方法；步骤；措施：They took strong ~s against dangerous drivers. 他们对危害公众安全的司机采取强硬措施。Ⅱ *vt.* 量；测量：~ a piece of land 丈量一块土地 / The tailor ~d me for a suit. 裁缝给我量尺寸做套装。

measurement /ˈmeʒəmənt/ *n.* ❶[U]测定；测量；度量：Without a watch, we cannot make an accurate ~ of time. 如果没有表，我们将无法测得准确时间。❷[C](常用 *pl.*)(量得的)尺寸；大小：Do you know the ~s of your bedroom? 你知道你卧室的大小吗?

meat /miːt/ *n.* [U]肉(不包括鱼肉和禽肉)：~-eating animals 肉食动物 / cold ~ 冷盘 / fresh ~ 鲜肉 / a piece of ~ 一块肉

mechanic /məˈkænɪk/ *n.* [C]技工；机械工人

mechanical /mɪˈkænɪkəl/ *adj.* ❶机械的，机械装置的：a ~ digger 挖掘机 / He has little ~ knowledge. 他对机械了解很少。❷用机器制造的；用机器操作的：~ toys 机制玩具 ❸机械的，呆板的；缺乏思想(或感情)的；习惯性的；没有独创性的：a ~ wave (response) 机械的挥手动作(呆板的答复)/ His gratitude seemed rather ~. 他的感激看上去并无一点真心。❹机械学的；力学的：~ principles 力学原理 / ~ engineering 机械工程 派 mechanically *adv.*

mechanics /məˈkænɪks/ *n.* [U]力学；机械学：Mechanics is a very interesting subject. 力学是一门很有趣的学科。

mechanism /ˈmekəˌnɪzəm/ *n.* [C] ❶(机器等的)机械装置；连动装置：the brake ~ 制动装置 / The alarm ~ is jammed. 报警装置被卡住了。❷机构；机制：the feedback ~ 反馈机制

mechanization /ˌmekənaɪˈzeɪʃn/ *n.* [U] 机械化

medal /ˈmedl/ *n.* [C] 奖章；勋章；纪念章：He was awarded a ~ for his bravery. 因表现勇敢，他获得一枚奖章。

meddle /ˈmedl/ *vi.* 干涉，插手；好管闲事：Do not ~ in things that do not concern you. 不要插手那些与你无关的事情。

media /ˈmiːdɪə/ (medium 的复数形式) *n.* [C]媒介；传导体：mass ~ 大众传媒/ news ~ 新闻媒体 / The television is important ~ of communication. 电视是很重要的传输媒体。

median /ˈmiːdɪən/ Ⅰ *adj.* (位于)中间的，居中的：the ~ position 中间位置/a low ~ income 中等偏低的收入 Ⅱ *n.* [C] ❶中间数，平均数 ❷(三角形的)中线

mediate /ˈmiːdɪˌeɪt/ *vi.* 调解，斡旋，充当中间人(与 in 或 between 连用)：The United Nations is trying to ~ between the two warring countries. 联合国正努力调解交战两国之间的争端。/He is appointed to ~ in a legal dispute. 他被指派去调解一起法律纠纷。—*vt.* 通过调解(或斡旋等)解决(纠纷、冲突等)：

M

~ conflicts that can never be resolved 调解那些永远无法解决的争端/~ a dispute 调解纠纷 派 mediation *n.*

medical /ˈmedɪkl/ *adj.* 医学的;医疗的;内科的:a ~ school 医科学校 /~ examination 体检 / ~ insurance 医疗保险 / They pay more attention to ~ and health work now. 他们现在更加重视医疗卫生工作。

medicine /ˈmedsɪn/ *n.* ❶[U]医学;医术;内科学: study ~ and surgery 研究内科与外科 ❷药;药剂: traditional Chinese ~ 中药 / western ~ 西药/He takes too much ~. 他药吃得太多。/ This is a good (kind of) ~ for a cough. 这是(一种)治咳嗽的良药。

medieval /ˌmedɪˈiːv(ə)l/ *adj.* 中世纪的,中古(时期)的;中世纪风格的;似中世纪的;仿中世纪(风格)的:~ literature 中世纪文学

M

meditate /ˈmedɪteɪt/ *vi.* 默念,冥想: He ~s twice a day. 他每天默念两次。/ He sat on the grass meditating on his misfortunes. 他坐在草地上冥想自己的不幸。—*vt.* 计划;打算;谋划;企图:~ revenge 谋划复仇/They are meditating a reimposition of tax on electronics. 他们正计划对电子产品重新征税。

meditation /ˌmedɪˈteɪʃn/ *n.* 默念;沉思,冥思苦想:a state of ~沉思/In my ~,I came across that idea. 苦思冥想之中,我想到了那个主意。

Mediterranean /ˌmedɪtəˈreɪnɪən/ *n.* 地中海

medium /ˈmiːdɪəm/ Ⅰ*n.* [C](*pl.* mediums 或 media)媒介;传导体 Ⅱ*adj.* 中等的;适中的:He hopes to become ~ size. 他希望成为身材中等的人。

meet /miːt/ Ⅰ*v.* (met/met/,met) ❶遇见;相逢:We met by chance. 我们偶然相遇。/ ~ **with** 遭遇;偶然碰到:~ with an accident 遇到意外 / I met with an old friend in the train. 在火车上我碰到一位老朋友。❷迎接:The hotel bus ~s all the trains. 旅馆的汽车在火车站迎候各班车的旅客。❸满足(需要、要求等):Do we have enough money with us to ~ all expenses? 我们身上的钱够付全部的费用吗? Ⅱ*n.* [C]集会;会: the sports ~ 运动会

meeting /ˈmiːtɪŋ/ *n.* [C]会议;集会;聚会:a ~ room 会议室/ The manager spoke at the spot ~. 经理在现场会上发表讲话。

megaphone /ˈmegəˌfəʊn/ *n.* [C]扩音器;传声器;喇叭;话筒: address the crowd through a ~用喇叭向人群作演说

mellow /ˈmeləʊ/ Ⅰ*adj.* ❶(果实)(成)熟的;甘美多汁的:~ wine 醇香的美酒/ ~ grapes 熟透的葡萄 ❷(声音、颜色、光线等)柔和的:a sweet and ~ voice 甜美温柔的声音/~ colors of the dawn sky 拂晓时天空中柔和的色彩 ❸老练的;稳重的;成熟的:He's got ~ as he's got older. 随着年龄的增大,他变得更加成熟了。Ⅱ*v.* ❶(使)(果实)变熟 ❷(使)(声音、颜色、光线等)变得柔和: Gentle sunshine ~ed the old garden, casting an extra sheen of gold on leaves that were gold already. 温柔的阳光柔和地照在老园里,在那已金灿灿的叶子上洒上点点金辉。❸(使)(人或其性格等)变得老练(或稳重): The years have ~ed him. 这些年的日子使他变得老成了。

melody /ˈmelədi/ *n.* [C]旋律;曲调;歌曲:She played a new ~ at the party. 聚会上她演奏了一首新曲子。

melon /ˈmelən/ *n.* 瓜;甜瓜:I'd like to have a slice of ~ after supper. 晚饭后我总要吃一块瓜。

melt /melt/ *v.* (使)融化;(使)熔化:The sun soon ~ed ice. 太阳很快就使冰融化了。

member /ˈmembə(r)/ *n.* [C]分子;成员;会员:a ~ of a club 俱乐部会员 / a Party ~ 共产党员 / a League ~ 共青团员/ an honorary ~ 名誉会员

membership /ˈmembəʃɪp/ *n.* 成员(会员)资格;全体会员:Many students applied for the Party ~. 许多学生申请加入共产党。/ The club has a large ~. 这家俱乐部有很多会员。

memento /mɪˈmentəʊ/ *n.* [C]令人想起故人(或往事)的东西;纪念物,纪念品:the ~ of sb. 's time in China 那些令人想起在中国的时光的东西/a small gift as a ~ of the journey 作为此次旅行纪念的小礼品

memo /ˈmeməʊ/ *n.* (= memorandum) [C]备忘录:write a ~ about sth. 写下有关某事的备忘录

memoir /ˈmemwɑː(r)/ *n.* [C](*pl.*)回忆录;自传:The old soldier is writing war ~s. 老战士正在写战争回忆录。

memorandum /ˌmeməˈrændəm/ *n.* [C] (*pl.* memorandums 或 memoranda)备忘录

memorial /məˈmɔːrɪəl/ *n.* [C]纪念物,纪念品;纪念馆:In most English villages there is a war ~. 英国大多数村庄都有一个阵亡将士纪念碑。/ They built a ~ to the martyrs. 他们修建了一座烈士纪念碑。

memorize /ˈmeməraɪz/ *vt.* 记住;熟记:The teacher asks us to ~ new English words as many as possible. 老师要求我们尽量多记英语单词。

memory /ˈmeməri/ *n.* ❶记忆;记忆力:He has a bad ~ for dates. 他对日期的记忆很差。/ Can you tell his address from ~? 你能凭记忆说出他的住址吗? ❷(计算机)内存

menace /ˈmenəs/ *n.* ❶[C]构成威胁的人(或物):He is a ~ to society and should be locked away. 他是个社会危险分子,理应被关押起来。/Large lorries are a ~ on the narrow roads. 大型载重卡车对狭窄道路上的行人构成威胁。❷[U]威胁;恐吓:speak with a hint of ~说话时带有一种威胁的口吻

mend /mend/ *v.* ❶修补;修理:~ shoes 修补鞋子 / ~ a broken window 修理破窗户 ❷修正;改过;改善:to ~ one's ways 改过自新

mental /ˈmentəl/ *adj.* 心理的;精神的;脑力的:~ labor 脑力劳动 / ~ health 心理健康 / ~ disorder 心理障碍 / ~ outlook 精神面貌

mentality /menˈtæləti/ *n.* [C]脑力;智力;心理:normal ~ 正常心理(智力)/ try-your-luck ~ 侥幸心理/ He is studying how to develop children's ~. 他在研究如何发展儿童智力。

mention /ˈmenʃn/ Ⅰ *v.* 说到;写到;提及:Don't ~ it. 别客气(不用谢)。/ The event is ~ed in today's newspaper. 该事件在今天的报上被提及。Ⅱ *n.* [U]提到:He made no ~ of your requests. 他没提到你的请求。

menu /ˈmenjuː/ *n.* [C]菜单:the main ~ (计算机)主菜单 / He didn't look at the ~ before he ordered some fish. 他不看菜单就点了一些鱼。

merchandise /ˈmɜːtʃəndaɪz/ *n.* [U](集

M

合名词)商品;货物:They bought some general ~ in the supermarket. 他们在超市买了一些杂货。

merchant /ˈmɜːtʃənt/ *n.* [C]商人

merciful /ˈmɜːsɪfl/ *adj.* 仁慈的;宽大的:We should be ~ to the disabled. 我们对残疾人应当仁慈一些。

merciless /ˈmɜːsɪləs/ *adj.* ❶毫无同情(或怜悯)之心的,无情的;残忍的:be ~ to one's enemies 对敌人决不留情/He was ~ in his criticism of the newspapers. 他对报纸进行了无情的抨击。❷(风、雨等)强烈的,严重的;肆虐的:~ snowstorms 强暴风雪

mercury /ˈmɜːkjəri/ *n.* [U]水银;汞

mercy /ˈmɜːsi/ *n.* [U]仁慈;宽恕;慈悲心:We should learn to show ~ to others. 我们应当学会宽容他人。/ They showed little ~ to the poor. 他们对穷人毫无怜悯之意。/ **at the ~ of, at one's ~** 任由……摆布,在……掌握中:They are at the ~ of wind and waves. 他们任由风浪的摆布。

M

mere /mɪə(r)/ *adj.* 仅仅;只不过:Mere words won't help. 光说(不做)无济于事。/ Don't be hard on her. She is a ~ child. 别苛求她,她只不过是个小孩而已。

merely /ˈmɪəli/ *adv.* 仅仅;只不过:Studying in London is ~ a dream to her. 对她来说,去伦敦读书只不过是一个梦想而已。/ I ~ asked his name. 我只问了他的名字。

merge /mɜːdʒ/ *vi.* ❶合并;会合:The two firms ~d. 这两家公司合并了。/ The two roads ~ a mile ahead. 这两条路在前面一英里处会合。❷融合在一起,融为一体:The whole scheme, front and back, ~s well with the garden design. 前后部分的整个规划与庭园设计浑然天成,不露痕迹。

meridian /məˈrɪdɪən/ Ⅰ *n.* [C]❶子午线;子午圈 ❷经线:The prime ~ of 0° passes through the old observatory at Greenwich. 零度经线经过格林尼治老天文台。Ⅱ *adj.* (有关)子午线的;(有关)子午圈的:~ circle 子午环

merit /ˈmerɪt/ *n.* 价值;优点;功绩,功劳:It is an old painting of great ~. 这是一幅具有很高价值的古画。/ Frankness is one of his ~s. 直率是他的优点之一。

merry /ˈmeri/ *adj.* 愉快的;欢乐的;高兴的:Wish you a ~ Christmas! 祝你圣诞快乐!

mess /mes/ *n.* 混乱,杂乱;肮脏:Don't make a ~ of your room. 别把你的房间弄得乱七八糟。/ **in a ~** 杂乱;陷入困境:The children's room was in a ~. 孩子们的房间十分脏乱。

message /ˈmesɪdʒ/ *n.* [C](口头或书面的)通知;信息;消息:Wireless ~s told us that the ship was sinking. 无线电报传来的消息告诉我们那只船正在下沉。/ If I am out, please leave a ~. 如果我不在家,请给我留言。

messenger /ˈmesɪndʒə(r)/ *n.* [C]报信者;信差;通信员

messy /ˈmesi/ *adj.* ❶乱七八糟的;脏兮兮的;杂乱的,没有条理的:The sheets and blankets creased up into a ~ mass. 床单和毯子皱成了凌乱的一团。/He is ~ in personal habits. 他做事一向没有条理。❷难以应付的,棘手的:a ~ divorce 难办的离婚案 派 messily *adv.*; messiness *n.*

metabolism /mɪˈtæbəˌlɪzəm/ *n.* 新陈代谢,代谢作用:He has a very active ~.

他的新陈代谢功能非常强。/There elements are vital in cell ～. 这些元素在细胞新陈代谢中不可缺少。

metabolize /mɪˈtæbəˌlaɪz/ *v.* （使）发生新陈代谢：The body can ～ these proteins efficiently. 身体能够有效地将这些蛋白质代谢掉。

metal /ˈmetl/ *n.* 金属：Gold is a precious ～. 金子是一种贵重的金属。

metaphor /ˈmetəfə(r)/ *n.* 隐喻；比喻

meteor /ˈmiːtɪə(r)/ *n.* [C]流星

meteorology /ˌmiːtɪəˈrɒlədʒi/ *n.* [U]气象；气象学

meteorologist /ˌmiːtɪəˈrɒlədʒɪst/ *n.* [C]气象学家

meter[1] /ˈmiːtə(r)/ *n.* [C]计量器；计量仪表：an electric ～ 电表 / a water ～ 水表 / a gas ～ 煤气表 / a parking ～ 停车计时表

meter[2] /ˈmiːtə(r)/ *n.* （＝metre）[C]（公制长度单位）米，公尺：a cubic ～ 立方米 / a square ～ 平方

method /ˈmeθəd/ *n.* [C] 方法；办法：Our teacher adopted a new ～ to teach maths. 我们的老师用新方法教数学。

metre /ˈmiːtə/ *n.* （＝meter）[C]（公制长度单位）米，公尺

metric /ˈmetrɪk/ *adj.* 公制的；米制的：a ～ ton 一公吨

metro /ˈmetrəʊ/ *n.* 地下铁路，地铁：take the ～乘坐地铁/go to work by ～乘地铁上班

metropolis /məˈtrɒpəlɪs/ *n.* [C]大都市；主要城市

microcomputer /ˈmaɪkrəʊkəmpjuːtə(r)/ *n.* [C]微机：Her mother bought her a new ～. 她妈妈给她买了一台新的微机。

microcosm /ˈmaɪkrə(ʊ)ˌkɒz(ə)m/ *n.* [C] ❶缩影；缩图：Our city is a ～ of the whole country. 我们的城市是整个国家的缩影。❷微观世界；小宇宙

microorganism /ˌmaɪkrəʊˈɔːgəˌnɪzəm/ *n.* [C]微生物

microphone /ˈmaɪkrəfəʊn/ *n.* [C]扩音器；话筒

microprocessor /ˌmaɪkrəʊˈprəʊsesə(r)/ *n.* [C]微信息处理机；微处理器

microscope /ˈmaɪkrəskəʊp/ *n.* [C]显微镜：The researcher examined bacteria under a ～. 研究人员在显微镜下观察细菌。

microwave /ˈmaɪkrəweɪv/ *n.* [C]微波：a ～ stove 微波炉 / ～ technology 微波技术

mid /mɪd/ *adj.* （只作定语）❶（常用以构成复合词）居中的，位居中间的；在一半的：the ～ 1980s (1992, September) 20 世纪 80 年代中期（1992 年中，9 月中）/ a bouncing ball in ～-air 跳在半空中的球 / in ～-autumn 在中秋时节 ❷（位置等）中间的，中央的，中部的：a collision in ～ channel 发生于隧道中间的撞车事故

midday /ˌmɪdˈdeɪ/ *n.* [U]正午；中午：It was ～ when they arrived. 他们到达时正是正午时分。

middle /ˈmɪdl/ Ⅰ *n.* [C]中间；中部；中央：in the ～ of the century 本世纪中叶 / standing in the ～ of the street 站在街心 Ⅱ *adj.* 中间的；中部的；中央的；中等的：a ～ school 中学 / His father is a man of ～ size. 他父亲是个中等个子的人。

midland /ˈmɪdlənd/ Ⅰ *n.* [C]（the ～）（一个国家的）中部（地区）；内地，内陆

M

(地区) Ⅱ *adj*. (只作定语)中部(地区)的;内地的,内陆(地区)的:the ~ region (economy) 内地(内地经济)

midnight /ˈmɪdnaɪt/ *n*. [U]午夜;半夜:at ~ 在午夜 / The test is approaching. He had to burn the ~ oil to prepare for it. 考试临近,他不得不熬夜(开夜车)做准备。

midst /mɪdst/ *n*. [U]中部;中间;当中:There is a lodge in the ~ of the forest. 森林深处有一栋小屋。

midstream /ˈmɪdˌstriːm/ *n*. [U] ❶中流:keep the boat in ~ 使船保持在水流的中央 ❷中途,半途:in the ~ of one's career 在职业生涯途中 / She stopped in ~,coughed,then started up again. 她讲话中途停下来咳嗽,然后又继续讲。

midterm /ˈmɪdˌtɜːm/ Ⅰ *n*. ❶[U](任期等的)中期:Our next project is due at ~. 我们的下一个项目将在中期完成。❷[C](口语)期中考试 Ⅱ *adj*. 中期的,期中的:the congressional ~ election 国会中期选举/~ exams 期中考试

midtown /ˈmɪdˌtaʊn/ Ⅰ *n*. [U](介于商业区和住宅区之间的)市中心区:Most of the ~ was closed to traffic. 市中心大部分地段的交通已封闭了。Ⅱ *adj*. (位于)市中心区的:We threaded our way through the traffic in ~ Brighton. 我们穿过布赖顿市中心的车流和人流。

midway /ˌmɪdˈweɪ/ *n*. [U]中途

might[1] /maɪt/ *aux. v*. (may 的过去式形式)可能;也许;可以:I'm afraid it ~ snow tonight. 我看今晚也许会下雪。

might[2] /maɪt/ *n*. [U]力量;威力;能量:He is working with all his ~. 他正全力以赴地工作。

mighty /ˈmaɪti/ *adj*. (-ier,-iest) 伟大的;强大的;巨大的:a ~ nation 强大的国家 / the ~ ocean 浩瀚的海洋

migrant /ˈmaɪgrənt/ *n*. [C]候鸟;移居者:Swallows are ~s. 燕子是候鸟。

migrate /maɪˈgreɪt/ *vi*. 迁徙;迁移;移居 派 migration *n*.

mild /maɪld/ *adj*. 温和的;和善的;不严厉的:It is ~ today. 今天天气暖和。/ She is ~ in disposition. 她性情温和。

mile /maɪl/ *n*. [C]英里

milestone /ˈmaɪlˌstəʊn/ *n*. [C] ❶里程碑,里程标 ❷意义重大的事件,划时代的事件,里程碑:a ~ in one's life 人生中的重要转折点/The fall of Berlin was one of the ~s of the World War Ⅱ. 攻陷柏林是第二次世界大战中的重要里程碑之一。

military /ˈmɪlətəri/ *adj*. 军人的;军用的;陆军的:~ training 军事训练 / in ~ uniform 穿着军服 / ~ ranks 军衔 / He studies in a ~ academy. 他在一所军事学院读书。

milk /mɪlk/ Ⅰ *n*. [U]乳;奶(尤指牛奶):Milk is of great benefit to children. 牛奶对孩子的健康很有益。Ⅱ *v*. 挤(牛、山羊等的)奶:The girl is ~ing a cow. 姑娘正在挤牛奶。

mill /mɪl/ *n*. [C]工厂;工场:a saw (paper,silk,steel) ~ 锯厂(纸厂,丝厂,钢铁厂)

millennium /mɪˈlenɪəm/ *n*. [C](*pl*. millenniums)一千年;千年期:celebrate the ~ in the year 2000 在 2000 年庆祝千禧年

mimic /ˈmɪmɪk/ Ⅰ *vt*. (-micked; -micking) ❶ 模仿,模拟;(通过模仿他人的言行举止)取笑,戏弄:He made us all laugh by mimicking the policeman. 他学

着警察的样子，把我们大家都逗乐了。❷酷似，活像；呈现……的形象：Certain flies ~ wasps. 有些苍蝇看上去极像黄蜂。Ⅱ *n.* [C] ❶善于模仿者，精于模仿者：Chimpanzees and mocking-birds are congenital ~s. 大猩猩和嘲鸫是天生的模仿者。❷滑稽剧演员；小丑

mince /mɪns/ Ⅰ *vt.* ❶将(肉等)切碎，切细；将(肉等)绞碎：The meat has been ~d. 肉已经切碎了。❷迈着碎步扭捏走(路)：He ~d his way across the room. 他一扭扭地小步走过房间。Ⅱ *n.* [U]碎肉，肉末，肉糜

millimetre(-er) /ˈmɪlɪmiːtə(r)/ *n.* [C]毫米(略作 mm.)

million /ˈmɪljən/ *n.* [C]百万：~s of 千百万的；无数的 / She is too young to count from one to a ~. 她太小，不能从1数到100万。

millionaire /ˌmɪljəˈneə(r)/ *n.* [C]百万富翁，大富豪

mind /maɪnd/ Ⅰ *n.* ❶记忆；回忆 / **bear (keep) sth. in ~** 记住某事：You must constantly bear (keep) in ~ that haste makes waste. 你须将"欲速则不达"这句话常记在心。**go out of one's ~** 被忘记；想不起来：I'm sorry. It completely went out of my ~. 对不起，我完全忘记那件事了。❷意欲；心意；想法 / **make up one's ~** 下决心：He made up his ~ not to smoke again. 他下决心不再吸烟了。❸头脑；精神；理智：She learns physics easily. She must have a good ~. 她学物理很轻松。她一定有一个聪明的头脑。Ⅱ *v.* ❶留心；注意：Mind (out), there's a bus coming. 当心，有辆车开过来了。/ Mind your own business. 少管闲事。❷介意；反对：Do you ~ my smoking here? 你介意我在这里抽烟吗？/—Do you ~ my leaving this payment until next year? —Yes, I do ~. —这笔款项我留到明年再付，你反对吗？—当然反对。

mindless /ˈmaɪndlɪs/ *adj.* ❶不需要动脑筋的：a boring, ~ job 不用脑筋的无聊工作 ❷不注意的，不顾及的；无视的：be ~ of the dangers the workers are faced with 不顾工人们面临的危险 ❸没头脑的；愚笨的；无知的

mine[1] /maɪn/ *pron.* 我的(名词性物主代词)：She is an old friend of ~. 她是我的一位老朋友。

mine[2] /maɪn/ Ⅰ *n.* [C] ❶矿；矿山：a coal ~ 煤矿 / a gold ~ 金矿 ❷地雷；水雷：They laid a ~ in the road. 他们在公路上布雷。Ⅱ *vt.* 开采(矿物)：They live on mining coal. 他们靠采煤为生。派 miner *n.*

M

mineral /ˈmɪnərəl/ *n.* [C]矿物：~ ores 矿石 / ~ deposits 矿藏；矿床 / I prefer ~ water to tea. 我喜欢喝矿泉水，不喜欢喝茶。

mingle /ˈmɪŋgl/ *vt.* ❶相互交往，互相往来：He wandered around, trying to ~ with the guests. 他四处转悠，想跟宾客们打成一片。❷混合：His account ~d truth with exaggerations. 他的叙述中事实与夸张的东西混在一起。/She accepted the money with ~d feelings. 她怀着复杂的心情接受了这笔钱。

miniature /ˈmɪnətʃə(r)/ Ⅰ *adj.* 小型的：a ~ camera 小型照相机 Ⅱ *n.* [C]缩影；缩图；缩版；缩小的模型

minimum /ˈmɪnɪməm/ Ⅰ *n.* [C] (*pl.* minima /ˈmɪnɪmə/) 最小量；最低额(与 maximum 相对)：a ~ wage 一份最低工资 / The temperature in this room reaches a ~ of −5℃ in winter. 冬天这

房间的最低温度可达零下五摄氏度。Ⅱ*adj*. 最小的；最低的

minister /ˈmɪnɪstə(r)/ *n*. [C]部长；公使：the Prime Minister 首相；内阁总理 / The ~s are discussing how to improve their work. 部长们正讨论如何改进工作。

ministry /ˈmɪnɪstri/ *n*. [C]（政府的）部；部门：the Ministry of Foreign Affairs 外交部 / the Ministry of Education 教育部

minor /ˈmaɪnə(r)/ *adj*. 较小的；次要的：the ~ planets 小行星 / She plays a ~ part in the film. 她在电影中演配角。

minority /maɪˈnɒrəti/ *n*. [C] ❶少数；较小的一部分：They were in the ~ at the meeting. 在会上他们只占少数。❷少数民族

M

mint /mɪnt/ *n*. ❶[U]薄荷；薄荷糖 ❷[C]造币厂；制造厂

minus /ˈmaɪnəs/ Ⅰ *prep*. 减，减去：How much is twelve ~ two? 12 减 2 等于多少？Ⅱ*n*. [C]负数；负号；减号

minute[1] /ˈmɪnɪt/ *n*. [C]分钟；片刻；一会儿：There are 60 ~s in an hour. 1 小时有 60 分钟。/ I'll come back in a ~. 一会儿我就回来。/ Just a ~, please. 请稍等。

minute[2] /maɪˈnjuːt/ *adj*. 微小的；极小的：Please tell us the ~ details of the accident. 请把事故的细节告诉我们。

miracle /ˈmɪrəkl/ *n*. [C]奇迹；令人惊奇的事：work (make) ~s 创造奇迹 / ~ drugs 特效药 派 miraculous *adj*.

mirage /ˈmɪrɑːʒ, mɪˈrɑːʒ/ *n*. [C]海市蜃楼

mirror /ˈmɪrə(r)/ Ⅰ *n*. [C]镜子 Ⅱ *vt*. 反映；反射：The blue sky and white cloud are ~ed in the lake. 蓝天白云映在湖面上。

misapprehend /ˌmɪsæprɪˈhend/ *vt*. 误解，误会：~ sb.'s intentions 误会某人的意图 派 misapprehension *n*.

misbehave /ˌmɪsbɪˈheɪv/ *vi*. 行为不当，不守规矩：~ in church 在教堂不守规矩 派 misbehavio(u)r *n*.

miscalculate /ˌmɪsˈkælkjʊˌleɪt/ *v*. ❶误算，错算：~ the amount (how much) one need-ed in renovating the house 算错了翻新这幢房子所需的费用/He ~d when adding up the figures. 他在加数时算错了。❷错误地估计；对……做出错误的判断：~ the public's mood 错误地判断公众的心态

miscarry /ˌmɪsˈkæri/ *vi*. ❶流产 ❷（生意、计划）等失败，未获成功：The general's plan to depose the president has miscarried. 将军试图推翻总统的计划流产了。

mischance /mɪsˈtʃɑːns/ *n*. ❶[U]厄运；不幸；遭遇：It was (by) sheer ~ that her car ran into a tree. 她的汽车撞树纯属意外。❷[C]不幸的事情，灾难：A serious ~ prevented him from arriving. 一件非常倒霉的事情使他无法到来。

mischief /ˈmɪstʃɪf/ *n*. [C]顽皮孩子；淘气鬼：The little ~ tore my book into pieces. 那小淘气把我的书撕成了碎片。

miscount /mɪsˈkaʊnt/ Ⅰ *v*. 数错；算错：The shop assistant ~ed the customer's change. 店员算错了找给顾客的零钱。Ⅱ*n*. [C]计算错误；（尤指选票的）错点，错数：a ~ in the election results 大选结果的计票错误

miser /ˈmaɪzə(r)/ *n*. [C]守财奴；吝啬鬼

miserable /ˈmɪzrəbl/ *adj*. 痛苦的；悲惨

的:feel ~ from cold and hunger 因饥寒交迫而感到痛苦异常 / The book is about the ~ living condition of the refugees after the war. 这本书写了战后难民们悲惨的生活状况。

misery / ˈmɪzəri / *n.* [U]不幸;悲惨;痛苦;(*pl.*)不幸事件:Pollution causes great ~ to humankind. 污染带给人类巨大的痛苦。

misfortune / ˌmɪsˈfɔːtʃuːn / *n.* 不幸;灾祸:suffer ~ 遭受不幸 / companions in ~ 患难之交;患难中的伙伴

mislead / ˌmɪsˈliːd / *vt.* (misled /ˌmɪsˈled/, misled) 带错路;引(某人)入歧途:The boy was misled by bad companions. 小男孩被不良伙伴带坏了 。/ This information ~s the public. 这个消息误导公众。

Miss / mɪs / *n.* (对未婚女子的称呼)小姐:See you later, ~ Li. 李小姐再见。

miss / mɪs / *v.* ❶没赶上(火车、汽车等);未达到;未看见:The hunter fired at a tiger but ~ed (it). 猎人开枪打虎,但未打中。/ He ~ed the first train. 他没赶上早班车。/ You ~ed a word here. 你在这儿写掉了一个字。/ Wang Ying doesn't come. She ~ed the notice for the meeting. 王英没有来,她没看见开会通知。❷想念:She ~es her mother badly. 她非常想念妈妈。

missile / ˈmɪsaɪl / *n.* [C]导弹;发射物

missing / ˈmɪsɪŋ/ *adj.* ❶缺损的,缺掉的;缺少的:A definite sickness may result when something is ~ from the diet. 饮食中缺乏某种营养物质时,人体就会患一定的疾病。❷失踪的,不知去向的,下落不明的;无从查找的:They searched far and wide for the ~ children. 他们四处寻找失踪的孩子们。❸缺席的,不在场的:He's always ~ whenever there's work to be done. 每次有工作要做的时候,他总是不在。

mission / ˈmɪʃən / *n.* [C] ❶使团;代表团:Her brother is a member of a trade ~ to America. 她的哥哥是一个赴美贸易代表团的成员。❷使命;任务:The young man was sent on a diplomatic ~. 那年轻人被派去执行外交任务。

missionary / ˈmɪʃənri / *n.* [C]传教士

mist / mɪst / *n.* [U]雾:The sun rose. The ~ cleared. 太阳出来了,雾散了。

mistake / mɪˈsteɪk / Ⅰ *n.* [C]错误;过失:We all make ~s occasionally. 我们都会偶尔犯错。/ **by** ~ 错误地:I took your umbrella by ~. 我错拿了你的雨伞。Ⅱ *v.* (mistook/ mɪsˈtʊk/, mistaken/ mɪˈsteɪkən/)弄错;误解:Don't ~ my meaning. 别误解我的意思。/ He mistook the hour and so came late. 他弄错了时间,所以来晚了。

mistaken / mɪˈsteɪkən/ *adj.* ❶被误解的;弄错的:He was arrested but it later proved to be a case of ~ identity. 他被拘捕了,但后来证明这是一件张冠李戴的案子。❷(思想、观点、判断等)错误的,不正确的:~ ideas (views, impression, behavior) 错误的思想(观点,印象,行为) / She was ~ about the time of their flight. 她记错了他们航班的时间。派 mistakenly *adv.*

mister / ˈmɪstə(r) / *n.* (常缩写成 Mr.) 先生:Mr. Smith 史密斯先生

mistreat / ˌmɪsˈtriːt / *vt.* 虐待:The dog's owner ~ed it terribly. 那条狗的主人对它的虐待很严重。

mistress / ˈmɪstrəs / *n.* [C] ❶主妇;女主人 ❷情妇

mistrust / ˌmɪsˈtrʌst/ Ⅰ *n.* [U]不相信,不

M

信任：eyes full of ~ 满眼的不信任 / There is considerable ~ between labour and capital. 劳资双方之间存在着极大的不信任。Ⅱ *vt.* 不相信；不信任：The girl seems honest enough but I ~ her. 这女孩看上去很诚实，可我不相信她。派 mistrustful *adj.*

misunderstand / ˌmɪsʌndəˈstænd / *v.* (misunderstood /ˌmɪ sʌndəˈstʊd/, misunderstood) 误解，误会：You misunderstood his kindness. 你误解了他的好意。派 misunderstanding *n.*

misuse Ⅰ / ˌmɪsˈjuːs / *n.* (词语等的)误用，错用；(职权、金钱等的)滥用：~ of powers (authority)滥用职权/The machine was damaged by ~. 这台机器因操作不当而损坏了。Ⅱ / ˌmɪsˈjuːz/ *vt.* ❶误用，错用(词语等)；滥用(职权、金钱等)：The minister was accused of misusing agricultural funds. 那位部长被指控滥用农业基金。❷虐待；(不公正地)对待：The employees in this firm got ~d. 这家公司的雇员遭到了不公正对待。

M

mix / mɪks / *v.* 混合；搅和：~ flour and water 把面粉和水混合在一起 / Oil and water will not ~. 油水不相溶。

mixed / mikst/ *adj.* (只作定语) ❶混合的；掺杂的；混杂的：a ~ farming 多种经营的农场 /The past and the present world become ~ in her. 过去和现在的种种情景一起纠缠在她心中，她混淆不清了。❷由不同种族(或宗教等)混合成的；形形色色的：a ~people 种族混杂的人民 / a ~ multitude 一大群闲杂人等 ❸(情感、反应等)错综复杂的，交集的：He stared at the letter with ~ emotions. 他凝视着那封信，心中百感交集。

mixer / ˈmɪksə(r)/ *n.* [C](使食品等混合的)搅拌器，搅拌机；混合器：an electric double-duty food ~ 两用食品搅拌器

mixture / ˈmɪkstʃə(r) / *n.* 混合；混合物：~ of gases 混合气体 / The ~ is sour. 那种混合液是酸的。

moan / məʊn / Ⅰ *n.* [C] 呻吟声：We heard the ~s of the wounded under the bridge. 我们听到桥下有受伤的人在呻吟。Ⅱ *v.* 呻吟；悲叹：The old man fell down and ~ed out a plea for help. 老人跌倒在地呼唤帮助。

mob / mɒb / *n.* [C]暴徒，暴民；乌合之众

mobile / ˈməʊbaɪl / *adj.* 运动的；活动的；可移动的：a ~ phone 移动电话 / The ~ medical team often goes to the countryside. 那支流动医疗队常常下乡。

mobility / məʊˈbɪləti / *n.* [U]机动性；流动性：Personnel ~ is popular now. 现在人才流动很流行。

mobilize(-se) / ˈməʊbəlaɪz / *v.* 动员(尤指战时动员)：We ~ all people to protect our environment. 我们动员所有的人保护我们的环境。

mock / mɒk / Ⅰ *vt.* ❶嘲笑，嘲弄，讥笑：They ~ed at his idea. 他们对他的观点嗤之以鼻。❷效仿，模仿(以取笑)：His pet monkey attempted to ~ his actions. 他的宠物猴想要模仿他的举止。Ⅱ *adj.* ❶仿制的，仿造的；假(冒)的：a ~ sort of shyness 故意装出的羞涩/ one's ~ friends 虚伪的朋友 ❷模拟的；演习的：~ exam 模拟考试

modal / ˈməʊdəl / Ⅰ *adj.* ❶形式的，形态的；方式的 ❷(动词的)语气的；情态的：~ verb 情态动词 Ⅱ *n.* [C]情态动词

mode /məʊd/ *n.* [C]方法;方式;样式:Everyone has his own ~ of life. 每个人都有自己的生活方式。/ Girls always like the latest ~ of clothes. 女孩总喜欢衣物的最新款式。

model /ˈmɒdl/ *n.* [C] ❶模型;模式;原型:a ~ plane 模型飞机 / Please make sentences after the ~. 请照例子造句。❷典型;模范:a ~ worker 劳动模范 ❸模特儿

modem /ˈməʊdem/ *n.* [C](计算机)调制解调器

moderate /ˈmɒdərət/ *adj.* ❶温和的;稳健的:In discussing the problem he was trying to be a man of ~ opinions. 在讨论问题时他尽量做一个不偏激的人。❷中等的;适度地;有节制的;(价格)合理的:The old woman is over sixty and has a ~ appetite. 老太太六十多岁,食量中等。/ Prices in this supermarket are strictly ~. 这家超市里的各种价格很公道。/ She has just graduated and can only rent a ~-price room. 她刚毕业,只能租一间价格适中的房子住。派 moderately *adv.*

modern /ˈmɒdən/ *adj.* 现代的;近代的;新式的:in the ~ world 在当今世界 / ~ inventions and discoveries 现代发明与发现

modernization /ˌmɒdənaɪˈzeɪʃn/ *n.* [U] 现代化:management ~ 管理现代化

modest /ˈmɒdɪst/ *adj.* 谦虚的:He is ~ about his achievements. 他很谦虚地对待自己的成就。

modesty /ˈmɒdəsti/ *n.* [U]虚心;谦逊;端庄:Though she is excellent, she is in all ~. 尽管她很优秀,但她很谦逊。

modification /ˌmɒdɪfɪˈkeɪʃn/ *n.* ❶缓和;限制 ❷修改:Here is our report. Please make a ~ in it. 这是我们的报告,请帮助修改一下。

modify /ˈmɒdɪfaɪ/ *vt.* ❶更改;修改;改变:The manager is ~ing a production plan. 经理正在修改生产计划。❷修饰:Adjectives ~ nouns. 形容词修饰名词。

modulate /ˈmɒdjʊleɪt/ *vt.* ❶调节;修整;使适应……的需要:~ the cabinet's energy policy 调整内阁的能源政策 ❷使(声音)变得柔和;改变(说话的语调);调节(音量):When the boss entered, she ~d her voice politely. 老板进来时她有礼貌地压低了声音。

moist /mɒɪst/ *adj.* 潮湿的;多雨的;(眼睛等)湿润的:I don't like the ~ season here. 我不喜欢这里的雨季。

moisture /ˈmɒɪstʃə(r)/ *n.* [U]潮湿;湿气:~ capacity(content)湿度;含水量

molecule /ˈmɒlɪˌkjuːl/ *n.* [C] ❶分子;摩尔:hydrogen (water) ~s 氢(水)分子 / a ~ of alcohol 酒精分子 ❷微粒;一点点,些微:She has only a ~ of honesty. 她只有一点点的诚实。

moment /ˈməʊmənt/ *n.* [C]瞬间;片刻:It was done in a ~. 一会儿这事就做好了。/ **the** ~ 一……就……:I started the ~ your letter arrived. 你的信一到,我就动身了。**at the** ~ 此刻;那时:He was drawing a picture at the ~. 那时他正在画一幅画。

momentary /ˈməʊməntəri/ *adj.* ❶一刹那的,瞬间的,眨眼间的:a ~ hesitation 片刻的犹豫 ❷暂时的,临时的;短暂的,短命的:A ~ smile flicked on his features as he spoke. 他说话的当儿,脸上掠过了一个笑影儿。派 momentariness *n.*

momentous /məˈmentəs/ *adj.* 极为重

要的，重大的，具有重要意义的：a ~ occasion 重大场合/ a ~ man 举足轻重的人物/at a ~ crisis 在千钧一发的紧要关头

monarch /ˈmɒnək/ *n.* [C]君主；国王

monarchy /ˈmɒnəki/ *n.* ❶[C]君主制国家；君主制政府 ❷[U]君主政体，君主制度：the English version of bourgeois ~ 英国式的资产阶级君主制度 / abolish (overthrow) ~废除(推翻)君主制度

Monday /ˈmʌndi/ *n.* 星期一(略作 Mon.)

monetary /ˈmʌnɪtri/ *adj.* 钱的；货币的；金融的：~ crisis 金融危机 / ~ inflation 通货膨胀 / ~ circulation 货币流通 / ~ reform 货币改革 / ~ unit 货币单位 / Europe ~ market 欧洲货币市场

M

money /ˈmʌni/ *n.* [U]货币；金钱：~ in cash 现金，现款 / deposit ~ 存钱 / draw ~ 取钱/ raise ~ 筹款 / prize ~ 奖金 / make(earn) ~ 挣钱；赚钱 / Mother gives me some pocket ~ every week. 妈妈每周都给我一些零花钱。

monitor /ˈmɒnɪtə(r)/ Ⅰ *n.* [C] ❶(学校的)班长；Our ~ always helps others. 我们的班长总是帮助他人。❷监听器；检测器；监视器：a heart ~ 心脏监视器 / He used a new ~. 他使用了一种新的检测器。Ⅱ *v.* 监听；监视；监控：This instrument is used to ~ planes in the sky. 这种仪器是用来监视空中飞机的。

monk /mʌŋk/ *n.* [C]和尚；僧侣；修道士

monkey /ˈmʌŋki/ *n.* [C]猴子

monopolize /məˈnɒpəˌlaɪz/ *vt.* ❶垄断；对(商品、货物等)取得专卖权，对……实行专营；获得……的专利：~ trade 垄断交易 / A few large companies have ~d the oil industry. 几个大的公司垄断了石油工业。❷完全占据；完全吸引(注意力)：The girl ~d the attention of those present. 这个女孩吸引了在场所有人的目光。/ All her spare time was ~d by her children. 她的业余时间都被孩子们占用了。

monopoly /məˈnɒpəli/ *n.* [C] 垄断；独占；专利；专卖：break(up) a ~ 打破垄断 / grant a ~ 授予专利 / hold a ~ 拥有专利/ gain a ~ 得到独家经营权

monotonous /məˈnɒtənəs/ *adj.* 单一的，没有变化的；乏味的：a ~ piece of music 一首旋律单调的乐曲/He considered this work extremely ~. 他认为这项工作极其单调乏味。派 monotonously *adv.*；monotony *n.*

monster /ˈmɒnstə(r)/ *n.* [C]怪物；妖怪：ghosts and ~s 妖魔鬼怪

month /mʌnθ/ *n.* [C]月；月份：a baby of three ~s 三个月大的婴孩 / this ~ 本月 / last ~ 上个月 / next ~ 下个月 / He pays the workers by the ~. 他按月给工人们发工资。

monthly /ˈmʌnθli/ Ⅰ *adj.* 每月的；每月一次的：~ pay 月薪/ ~ ticket 月票 / Young people like the ~ sports magazine. 年轻人喜欢读体育月刊。Ⅱ *adv.* 每月地；每月一次地：Mother goes shopping in the supermarket ~. 妈妈每月一次去超市购物。Ⅲ *n.* 月刊

monument /ˈmɒnjʊmənt/ *n.* [C]纪念碑；纪念馆：the Monument to the People's Heroes 人民英雄纪念碑

monumental /ˌmɒnjʊˈmentəl/ *adj.* ❶纪念物的；以示纪念的：~ inscriptions 碑文 / ~ pillars 纪念性石柱 ❷(规模等)宏大的；(数量、程度、范围等)巨大

的，浩瀚的：~ respectability 威望 / a ~ task (talent) 浩大的任务(卓越的才能) / ~ statues 巨幅雕像 / a ~ traffic jam 严重的交通堵塞 ❸具有重大意义的：Einstein's ~ contributions to nuclear physics 爱因斯坦对核物理做出的巨大贡献 派 monumentally *adv.*

mood /muːd/ *n.* [C] ❶ 心情；情绪：She is a girl of ~s. 她是一个喜怒无常的女孩。/ When my grandmother is in a good ~, she would tell me interesting stories. 祖母心情好时会给我讲许多有趣的故事。❷语气：It is a subjunctive ~. 这是虚拟语气。

moody /ˈmuːdi/ *adj.* ❶情绪多变的，喜怒无常的：/ He became ~ and irritable. 他变得脾气很怪，动辄生气。❷忧郁的，情绪低落的：a ~ expression 忧伤的神情 / a ~ man 郁郁寡欢的人 / He fell into a ~ jog. 他心烦意乱地缓步走着。派 moodily *adv.* ；moodiness *n.*

moon /muːn/ *n.* (the ~) 月亮；月球

moonlight /ˈmuːnˌlaɪt/ *n.* [U]月光：He followed her out into the silver ~. 他跟着她走出屋外，来到银色的月光下。

mop /mɒp/ Ⅰ *n.* [C]拖把；拖布 Ⅱ *vt.* (mopped；mopping) 用拖把擦洗：~ the floor 拖地板

moral /ˈmɒrəl/ Ⅰ *adj.* 道德的；有道义的：~ standards 道德标准 / ~ character 道德品质 Ⅱ *n.* ❶道德，品德：professional ~s 职业道德 / public ~s 公共道德 / a man without ~s 没有道德的人 ❷[C]教训；寓意：The ~ of the story is "Knowledge is strength." 这个故事的寓意是"知识就是力量"。

morale /mɒˈrɑːl, məˈræl/ *n.* (个人或集体的)士气；精神风貌，风貌：boost one's ~增强士气/buck up a patient's ~使病人精神振作起来

morality /məˈrælɪti；mɔːˈrælɪti/ *n.* [U] ❶道德性：He wonders whether there's any ~ in politics. 他不知道搞政治是否有道德可言。❷道德，品德；美德：public ~ 公共道德 / He has a high standard of ~. 他看待道德的标准很高。❸道德标准，道德规范；道德观：a difference between ~ in America and China 中美道德标准的不同

more /mɔː(r)/ Ⅰ *adj.* (many 和 much 的比较级)(数)更多的；(量)更大的；(程度)更高的；附加的：More and ~ people have realized its importance. 越来越多的人认识到它的重要性。/ You should spend ~ time studying. 你应该花更多的时间去学习。Ⅱ *adv.* ❶ 更(与两个或两个以上音节的形容词或副词构成比较级) ❷ (much 的比较级)更多地；更大程度地：You need to sleep ~. 你需要更多睡眠。❸ 再：Once ~, please. 请再来一次。/ I shall not go there any ~ . 我再也不去那儿了。/ We saw him no ~. 我们再也没看到他了。/ ~ **and** ~ 越来越：The story gets ~ and ~ exciting. 故事越来越动人。Ⅲ *n.* 较多量；较多的人或物：More of us went to see the film. 我们中有较多的人去看了那场电影。/ **the ~..., the ~ ...** 越……，越……：The ~ he reads, the ~ he likes to read. 他书读得越多，他就越喜欢读书。

moreover /mɔːrˈəʊvə(r)/ *adv.* 并且，此外：It was dark and ~ it was raining hard. 天黑了，而且正下着大雨。

morning /ˈmɔːnɪŋ/ *n.* 早晨，上午：in the ~ 在上午 / this ~ 今天上午 / on Sunday ~ 星期天上午

mortal /ˈmɔːtəl/ Ⅰ *adj.* ❶(尤指人等生

命体)死的;注定要死的,终将死亡的:All human beings are ~. 凡人都要死的。❷极度的,极大的:the ~ hatred 深仇大恨/mortal pain 剧痛 ❸致死的,致命的:a ~ disease 致命的疾病 Ⅱ *n.* [C]凡人,普通人:the ways of ~s 芸芸众生的秉性/We are all ~s. 我们皆凡人。

mortgage /ˈmɔːɡɪdʒ/ Ⅰ *n.* [C]抵押;抵押贷款 Ⅱ *vt.* 抵押(土地、房屋等);以……作担保

mosquito /məˈskiːtəʊ/ *n.* [C] (mosquitos 或 mosquitoes) 蚊子

moss /mɒs/ *n.* 苔藓;地衣

most /məʊst/ Ⅰ *adj.* (many 和 much 的最高级)最多的;最高程度的:Those who have (the) ~ money are not always the happiest. 最有钱的人不一定最幸福。Ⅱ *n.* 最大量;最高额;大部分;大多数:The ~ I can give you is 100 *yuan*. 我能给你的最大数额是 100 元。/ Most girls like skirts. 大多数女孩爱穿裙子。/**at (the) ~** 至多:I can pay only ten yuan at the ~. 我最多只能付 10 元钱。Ⅲ *adv.* ❶最(用以构成双音节或多音节形容词和副词的最高级) ❷非常,极其,十分:This is a ~ useful book. 这是一本极其有用的书。/ I shall ~ certainly go. 我一定去。

mostly /ˈməʊstli/ *adv.* ❶大多地,大部分地;主要地:What he said was ~ true. 他说的大多是真实的。❷一般情况下,在大多数情况下,通常:Our weather is ~ warm. 我们这儿的天气一般比较温暖。/ An owl ~ hunts at night. 猫头鹰通常在夜间觅食。

motel /məʊˈtel/ *n.* [C] 汽车旅馆

mother /ˈmʌðə(r)/ *n.* [C]母亲:Mother's Day 母亲节/ step-~ 继母/ ~ tongue 本国语言

mother-in-law /ˈmʌðərɪnˌlɔː/ *n.* [C] (*pl.* mothers-in-law) 岳母,丈母娘;婆母,婆婆

motherland /ˈmʌðəlænd/ *n.* [C]祖国:We all love our ~. 我们都热爱我们的祖国。

motherly /ˈmʌðəli/ Ⅰ *adj.* ❶慈母般的,给予母爱的 ❷母亲的 Ⅱ *adv.* 慈母般地,母亲般地 派 motherliness *n.*

motion /ˈməʊʃn/ Ⅰ *n.* ❶[U]运动:~ and rest 运动与静止 ❷[C]手势;动作;姿态:make ~s with one's hand 打手势 ❸[C]提议;动议:make a ~ 提议 Ⅱ *v.* ❶打手势;示意:The chairman ~ed us (to us) to sit down. 主席做手势示意我们坐下。❷提议;动议:Our monitor ~ed to have a party on Saturday. 我们班长提议星期六聚会。派 motional *adj.*

motionless /ˈməʊʃnləs/ *adj.* 静止的,一动不动的:a ~ statue 静止的雕像 / The cat remained ~ waiting for the mouse to come out of its hole. 猫一动不动地等着老鼠出洞。派 motionlessly *adv.* ;motionlessness *n.*

motivate /ˈməʊtɪveɪt/ *vt.* 激励;驱使;促动:~sb. to take action 促使某人采取行动

motivation /ˌməʊtɪˈveɪʃn/ *n.* 刺激;动力;动机:She is good at English because she has strong ~ for learning it. 因为有很强的学习动机,她的英语学得很好。

motive /ˈməʊtɪv/ *n.* 动机;目的:The police wanted to find out his ~ for the crime. 警察想弄清楚他的犯罪动机。

motor /ˈməʊtə(r)/ *n.* [C]发动机;电动机;马达:a ~ ship 汽船 /a ~ truck 载重汽车 / the ~ industry 汽车工业

motorbike /ˈməutəbaɪk/ *n.* [C]摩托车

motorcar /ˈməutəkɑː/ *n.* [C]汽车：More and more people want to buy a ~ now. 现在越来越多的人想买汽车。

motorcycle /ˈməutəsaɪkl/ *n.* [C]摩托车

motorway /ˈməutəweɪ/ *n.* [C]汽车道；高速公路

motto /ˈmɒtəu/ *n.* [C]箴言；座右铭；格言：a school ~ 校训/ The teacher often quotes ~es to teach his students. 老师常常引用格言教育学生。

mo(u)ld /məuld/ Ⅰ *n.* [C]模子；模型；铸模：He is a person in the ~ of Lei Feng. 他是一个雷锋式的人物。Ⅱ *vt.* 使……成形；浇铸；塑造：She is trying to ~ the children into perfect people. 她正尽力把孩子们塑造成完美的人。/ He ~ed a figure out of clay. 他用模子做了一个泥像。

mount /maunt/ Ⅰ *v.* 登上(山、梯等)；增加；上升：He ~ed his horse and rode away. 他骑上马走了。/ Our living expenses are ~ing up. 我们的生活花费正在增加。Ⅱ *n.* [C]山(用于山名前，略写为 Mt.)：Mount Everest 珠穆朗玛峰

mountain /ˈmauntɪn/ Ⅰ *n.* [C] ❶山；高山，大山；(*pl.*)山区：reach the ~'s summit (peak) 抵达山巅 / They went to the ~s for their summer holiday last year. 去年他们到山区度暑假。❷(一)大批；(一)大堆；大量：a ~ of debts 一大堆债务 / The elected Prime Minister will face a ~ of (~s of) economic problems. 当选首相将面临一大堆经济问题。

mountaineer /ˌmauntɪˈnɪə(r)/ Ⅰ *n.* [C] ❶山区居民 ❷爬山者；登山运动员：He is one of the first few ~s who climbed Mount Qomolangma. 他是最早登上珠穆朗玛峰的少数几个人之一。Ⅱ *vi.* 爬山，登山：They enjoy ~ing. 他们喜欢登山。

mountainous /ˈmauntənəs/ *adj.* 有山的；多山的；巨大的：~ wave 巨浪 / He lives in a ~ district. 他住在山区。

mourn /mɔːn/ *v.* 悲伤；哀悼：The doctor ~ed for the dead child. 医生为死去的小孩感到悲伤。

mournful /ˈmɔːnful/ *adj.* ❶忧伤的，悲伤的，悲痛的：the ~ cry of the wolf 狼的哀嚎/the ~ look on one's face 脸上流露出的忧伤神情 ❷流露出悲伤之情的；令人悲痛的：~ news 令人悲痛的消息/ The music is rather ~. 这首曲子非常忧伤。派 mournfully *adv.*；mournfulness *n.*

mouse /maus/ *n.* [C] (*pl.* mice /maɪs/) ❶老鼠：All children like Mickey ~. 小孩都喜欢"米老鼠"。/ A cat catches mice. 猫会抓老鼠。❷(计算机)鼠标

moustache /məˈstɑːʃ/ *n.* [C](长在嘴唇上面的)胡子

mouth /mauθ/ *n.* [C] (*pl.* mouths /mauðz/) ❶ 嘴：The little baby hasn't any tooth in her ~. 这小婴儿嘴里还没长牙。/ Shut your ~! 闭上你的嘴！❷(袋、瓶、洞、河流等的)开口处：The town lies near the ~ of Changjiang River. 小城位于长江口附近。

mouthful /ˈmauθful/ *n.* [C]一口；满口；少量

movable /ˈmuːvəbl/ *adj.* ❶可移动的，活动的：a doll with ~ arms and legs 一个手脚可活动的洋娃娃 / The boards dividing the room into working areas are ~. 将房间隔成几个工作区的木板是活动的。❷(节日、庆祝活动等)日期不定

M

的，变更的：a ~ holiday 日期随历书变化的节日 / Thanksgiving is a ~ feast. 复活节是一个日期不定的节日。

move / muːv / *v.* ❶走动；移动；搬动：Please help me to ~ the old sofa away. 请帮我把这旧沙发搬开。/~ **in** 搬进；迁进 ~ **out** 搬出；迁出：We ~d out on Monday and the new tenants ~d in on Tuesday. 我们星期一迁出，新房客星期二就搬进来。~ **on** 继续向前；朝前走：The officer has given the order to ~ on. 军官已下达继续前进的命令。❷感动；激动：I was deeply ~d by the story. 我被故事深深地感动了。

movement / ˈmuːvmənt / *n.* 动；活动；运动：They launched a ~ against smoking in their school. 他们学校发起一场戒烟运动。

movie / ˈmuːvi / *n.* [C]影片；电影院：go to see a ~ 去看电影/ a ~ fan 影迷 / a ~ star 影星

moving / ˈmuːvɪŋ/ *adj.* ❶(只作定语)运动的；活动的；转动的：The streets of New York were brilliant with ~ men. 纽约的大街上人来人往，绚丽斑斓。/ Through the windows he could see ~ sheets of rain. 透过窗户，他可以看见那移动着的雨幕。❷感人的，打动人的：a very ~ story 非常感人的故事/ I found his recent book deeply ~. 我觉得他的新书非常感人。派 movingly *adv.*

mow /məʊ/ Ⅰ *v.* (mowed, mown/məʊn/或 mowed) ❶割，收割：~ the lawn 修剪草坪 ❷大量杀死，摧毁：The enemy gunfire ~ed down many soldiers. 敌军炮火打死许多士兵。Ⅱ *n.* [C](干草)堆；割草机；割草人

Mr.，**Mr** / ˈmɪstə(r) / *n.* (=mister)[C]先生(冠于男子姓或姓名前的称呼)：Mr. Green 格林先生

Mrs.，**Mrs** / ˈmɪsɪz / *n.* 夫人，太太(冠于已婚妇女的姓或姓名前的称呼)：Mrs. Green 格林太太

Ms.，**Ms** / mɪz / *n.* 女士，小姐(冠于已婚或未婚女子姓或姓名前的称呼)

much / mʌtʃ / Ⅰ *adj.* (more, most) 许多的；大量的：He never eats ~ for breakfast. 他早餐从来吃得不多。Ⅱ *n.* 大量；许多：He ate ~ at the dinner. 他在宴会上吃了许多东西。Ⅲ *adv.* ❶(more, most)很，非常：I shall be ~ surprised if he succeeds. 假如他成功的话，我会很惊奇的。❷很(修饰比较级或最高级)：He is ~ better today. 他今天好多了。

mud / mʌd / *n.* [U]泥；泥浆：He fell down in the ~. 他摔倒在烂泥里。

muddle / ˈmʌdl / Ⅰ *vt.* ❶将……弄乱；把……搅和在一起：~ an arrangement 打乱安排 ❷使搞混，使弄不清，使糊涂：His thoughts were ~d. 他思绪不清。/ ~ **up** 将……弄混，混淆：The man ~d up the date of arrival. 那人把抵达日期搞错了。Ⅱ *n.* ❶[C](常用单数)糊涂，混淆：He is in so much of a ~ that he is of no help. 他非常糊涂，根本帮不上忙。❷[U]混乱，凌乱；混乱的局面：the worsening ~ of the company's finances 该公司越来越糟的财政状况

muddy / ˈmʌdi/ Ⅰ *adj.* ❶泥泞的；多烂泥的：a ~ ditch 积满烂泥的阴沟 / ~ roads 泥泞的道路 ❷模糊的，不清楚的：~ colors 模糊的颜色 ❸(思想)糊涂的，思路不清的：~ thoughts 糊涂的思想 Ⅱ *vt.* ❶使沾满烂泥：The guest's boots muddied the carpet. 客人的靴子弄得地毯上全是烂泥。❷使糊涂，使弄不清，使思路不清 派 muddiness *n.*

mug /mʌg/ *n.* [C](有柄的)大杯子

mulberry /ˈmʌlbəri/ *n.* 桑树;桑葚

mule /mjuːl/ *n.* [C]骡子

multifunction /ˌmʌltɪˈfʌŋkʃn/ *n.* [C]多功能:a ~ system 多功能系统

multimedia /ˌmʌltɪˈmiːdɪə/ Ⅰ *n.* 多媒体 Ⅱ *adj.* 多种手段的;多种方式的:a ~ computer 多媒体电脑 / ~ software 多媒体软件

multiple /ˈmʌltɪpl/ Ⅰ *adj.* 多样的;多重的:a ~ choice question 多项选择题 / He is a man of ~ interests. 他是一个兴趣多样的人。Ⅱ *n.* [C]倍数

multiply /ˈmʌltɪplaɪ/ *v.* ❶乘:6 multiplied by 5 is 30. 6 乘以 5 等于 30。❷使增加;使繁殖:The teacher told the child that rabbits ~ rapidly. 老师告诉孩子兔子繁殖很快。

multitude /ˈmʌltɪtjuːd/ *n.* [C]❶大量,许多:The mass of data available in a ~ of reliable sources makes the conclusion convincing. 大量可靠来源的数据使该结论颇具说服力。❷人群,聚成一堆的人:A large ~ assembled before the auditorium for the occasion. 一大群人聚集在礼堂前等待那个重要时刻。

mum /mʌm/ *n.* [C](儿语)妈妈

mumble /ˈmʌmbl/ Ⅰ *v.* 含糊其词地说;咕哝着说:She was mumbling some indistinct words as she went. 她一面走,一面口中念念有词。Ⅱ *n.* [C]含糊的话语

mummy /ˈmʌmi/ *n.* [C] (儿语)妈妈

municipality /mjuːˌnɪsɪˈpælɪti/ *n.* ❶[C]自治市,自治镇:Small municipalities are looking for financial help from the state. 小的自治市镇正在寻求国家的财政援助。❷市政当局:The ~ has (have) closed the pleasure ground. 市政当局已关闭了那个游乐场。

murder /ˈmɜːdə(r)/ Ⅰ *n.* 谋杀;凶案:The man was declared guilty of ~. 那人被宣判犯了杀人罪。Ⅱ *vt.* 谋杀:Do you know when Lincoln was ~ed? 你知道林肯是什么时候遭谋杀的吗? 派 murderer *n.*

murmur /ˈmɜːmə(r)/ *v.* 低语;低声说:The boy came in and ~ed a secret to his mother. 小男孩走进来小声地告诉妈妈一个秘密。

muscle /ˈmʌsl/ *n.* 肌肉:He often goes into physical training to develop his ~s. 他常常进行体育锻炼以使肌肉发达。

muscular /ˈmʌskjələ(r)/ *adj.* 肌肉的;肌肉发达的;强健的:He exercises his ~s everyday and becomes a ~ man. 他每天锻炼肌肉,成为一个身体强健的人。

M

muse[1] /mjuːz/ *vi.* 沉思,深思,冥想:~ about (on) the possibility of winning the game 仔细考虑赢得比赛的可能性 / The boy lay in bed musing over what happened during daytime. 那男孩躺在床上想着白天发生的事情。

muse[2] /mjuːz/ *n.* [C](the ~)(能给予诗人、作家、艺术家创作灵感的)女神;极具创作天赋的诗人;创作灵感:waiting for the ~ 等待创作灵感的出现 / a musician whose ~ had left him 已失去创作灵感的音乐家

museum /mjʊˈziːəm/ *n.* [C]博物馆;展览馆:the Science Museum 科学博物馆/ the History Museum 历史博物馆 / the Palace Museum in Beijing 北京故宫博物院

mushroom /ˈmʌʃrʊm/ *n.* [C](食用)蘑菇

music /ˈmjuːzɪk/ *n.* [U] 音乐：a ~ cafe 音乐茶座 / a ~ hall 音乐厅 / ~ television (MTV)音乐电视 / classical ~ 古典音乐 / modern ~ 现代音乐 / I like folk ~. 我喜欢民间音乐。

musical /ˈmjuːzɪkl/ *adj.* 音乐的；悦耳的：a ~ instrument 乐器

musician /mjʊˈzɪʃən/ *n.* [C]音乐家

Muslim /ˈmʊzlɪm, ˈmʌzlɪm/ Ⅰ *n.* [C]穆斯林(即伊斯兰教的信奉者) Ⅱ *adj.* 穆斯林的；伊斯兰教的；伊斯兰文化的

must /mʌst, məst/ *aux. v.* ❶必须，应该(表示必要)：Everybody ~ obey the laws. 人人都必须遵纪守法。❷必定，必然(表示猜测)：You ~ be hungry after a long walk. 你走了那么远的路一定饿了。

M

mustache /məˈstɑːʃ/ *n.* [C](＝moustache) 髭；小胡子

mustard /ˈmʌstəd/ *n.* [U]芥末；芥子：Mustard is hot but many people like it. 芥末很辣，但很多人喜欢吃。

mute /mjuːt/ Ⅰ *adj.* 哑的；沉默的 Ⅱ *n.* ❶[C]哑巴 ❷(乐器的)弱音器

mutter /ˈmʌtə(r)/ Ⅰ *v.* 咕哝；抱怨 Ⅱ *n.* 低语；小声抱怨

mutton /ˈmʌtn/ *n.* [U] 羊肉：instant-boiled ~ 涮羊肉

mutual /ˈmjuːtʃʊəl/ *adj.* 相互的；共同的：~ benefit 互惠 / ~ help and support 互相帮助与支持

my /maɪ/ *pron.* 我的(形容词性物主代词)：It's ~ book. 那是我的书。

myself /maɪˈself/ *pron.* 我自己(反身代词)：I hurt ~. 我伤了自己。/ I can do it by ~. 我能独自做。

mysterious /mɪˈstɪərɪəs/ *adj.* 神秘的 a ~ letter 神秘信件

mystery /ˈmɪstri/ *n.* [C] 神秘：disclose a ~ 揭开奥秘 / Don't make a ~ of it. 不要让这事神秘化。

myth /mɪθ/ *n.* [C] 神话；神话式的人(或故事)：I like modern fiction as well as ~s. 我不仅喜欢神话故事，也喜欢现代小说。

mythology /mɪˈθɒlədʒi/ *n.* [U]❶神话：classical ~古典神话/~ book 神话书 ❷神话研究；神话学 ❸神话集：the mythologies of primitive races 原始民族神话集 派 mythological *adj.*

N n

nail /neɪl/ Ⅰ*n.*［C］❶钉子：draw out a ～ 拔出钉子 / drive(hammer, knock) in a ～ 把钉子敲进去 / **hit the ～ on the head** 击中要害，一针见血 ❷指甲；趾甲：cut ～s 剪指甲 / dye the ～s 染指甲 / **bite one's ～s** 咬指甲；束手无策 Ⅱ*vt.* 钉住，钉牢：～ **one's eyes on sth.** 盯住某物看，目不转睛

naive /naɪˈɪv, naɪˈiːv/ *adj.* 天真无邪的；轻信的；无经验的 派 naively *adv.*

naked /ˈneɪkɪd/ *adj.* 裸体的；无遮掩的：～ eye 肉眼 / ～ to the waist 光着上身；赤膊 / with ～ fists 赤手空拳地

name /neɪm/ Ⅰ*n.*［C］名字；姓名 Ⅱ*v.* ❶取名：We ～d the baby John. 我们给婴孩取名约翰。❷叫出名字：Can you ～ these trees? 你能叫出这些树的名字吗？❸提名，任命：Mr. Wang has been ～d for the directorship. 王先生已经被提名任董事之职。

nameless /ˈneɪmlɪs/ *adj.* ❶没有名字(或名称)的：John's son is still ～. 约翰的儿子还没有取名字。❷没有名气的；不知名的 ❸未署名的，匿名的：a ～ hero 无名英雄 / a ～ source of information 不知名的消息来源

namely /ˈneɪmli/ *adv.* 即，就是：Only one boy was absent, ～ Harry. 只有一个小孩缺席，就是哈里。

nap /næp/ *n.*［C］小睡；打盹：have (take) a ～ after lunch 午饭后小睡片刻

napkin /ˈnæpkɪn/ *n.*［C］❶餐巾 ❷小毛巾 ❸尿布

narrate /ˈnæreɪt, næˈreɪt/ *vt.* ❶叙述；讲述：Pitt ～d the desperate fight on the docks. 皮特讲述了发生在码头的激烈打斗。❷解说(电影等)；评论：～ the slide shows 充当幻灯片的解说员 派 narration *n.*

narrative /ˈnærətɪv/ Ⅰ*n.* ❶［C］记叙文；故事 ❷［U］叙述，讲述；记叙体；叙述手法：He essay has too much ～. 他的论文中叙述的成分太多。/ the use of ～ in poetry 诗歌中的叙事手法 Ⅱ*adj.* 叙述的；叙事体的；以故事形式的：a long ～ poem 一首长篇叙事诗

narrator /nəˈreɪtə(r)/ *n.*［C］叙述者

narrow /ˈnærəʊ/ Ⅰ*adj.* 窄的：The road was too ～ for cars to pass. 这条路太窄了，车辆通不过。/ ～ escape from death 幸免于难，死里逃生 Ⅱ*v.* 使变窄 派 narrowness *n.*

narrowly /ˈnærəʊli/ *adv.* 仅仅；勉强地：He ～ escaped drowning. 他差一点溺死。

nasal /ˈneɪzəl/ *adj.* ❶鼻的：the ～ cavity 鼻腔 ❷鼻音的：～ sound 鼻音

nasty /ˈnɑːsti, ˈnæsti/ *adj.* 肮脏的；卑劣的，下流的；令人厌恶的

nation /ˈneɪʃn/ *n.*［C］国家；民族：the

N

United Nations 联合国/ the Chinese ~ 中华民族

national /ˈnæʃnəl/ *adj*. 国家的;民族的:~ affairs 国家大事

nationality /ˌnæʃəˈnæləti/ *n*. 国籍;民族

nationwide /ˈneɪʃənˌwaɪd/ *adj*. 全国性的,全国范围的,遍布全国的:a ~ chain of shops 遍布全国的连锁店 / a ~ competition 全国性的比赛

native /ˈneɪtɪv/ *adj*. ❶(只作定语)出生的;出生地的:He returned to his ~ town. 他又回到了故乡。❷与生俱来的,天生的,天赋的(与 to 连用):Her ~ performing ability impressed the film director. 她那天生的表演能力给这位电影导演留下了深刻的印象。/ The swim ability is ~ to frogs. 蛙类生来就会游泳。❸本地的,当地的:The ~ guide accompanied the tourists through the whole rain forest. 当地的向导带着游客穿过了整个热带雨林。❹土生土长的;原产地的:a ~ bird 土生土长的一种鸟 / That flower is not ~ to this country. 这种花并不产于该国。

natural /ˈnætʃrəl/ *adj*. ❶自然界的;天然的:~ gas 天然气/~ science 自然科学/~ selection 自然淘汰 ❷生来的,天赋的:~gift 天赋才能/ She is a ~ leader. 她是个天生的领导者。❸常情的,通常的:It's ~ to shake hands with someone you've just met. 与初次见面的人握手是常情。派 naturalness *n*.

naturally /ˈnætʃrəli/ *adv*. ❶自然地;轻松自如地;不做作地:Catherine was too nervous to act ~. 凯瑟琳太紧张了,举止极不自然。❷天生地;天然地;非人为地:The woman is ~ kind. 那女人天生有一副好心肠。/ His hair curls ~. 他的头发是自然卷。

nature /ˈneɪtʃə(r)/ *n*. ❶[U] 自然;自然界:Is ~ at its best in spring? 自然界在春天最美吗?❷性质;本质;天性

naught /nɔːt/ *n*. 零;不存在

naughty /ˈnɔːti/ *adj*. 不听从的;顽皮的;淘气的:a ~ child 顽皮的小孩 派 naughtily *adv*.;naughtiness *n*.

nauseate /ˈnɔːzɪˌeɪt/ *vt*. ❶使呕吐,使感到恶心:The rolling of the ship ~d him. 船只一摇一晃使他感到恶心。❷使厌恶;使憎恨:His cruelty to animals ~s me. 他对动物的残暴态度令我厌恶。

naval /ˈneɪvəl/ *adj*. 海军的;军舰的

navigate /ˈnævɪˌgeɪt/ *v*. ❶航行;横渡;(飞机等)飞行,飞越:Is was a difficult passage to ~. 这是一段很难通行的航道。/In tests, the bees ~ back home after being placed in a field a mile away. 在实验中,蜜蜂被放置于一英里外的田地里后仍会飞回家。❷领航,导航;驾驭(飞机或船只等):He managed to ~ the plane through the snowstorm. 他成功地驾机穿过了暴风雪。/When traveling on fast roads at night it is impossible to drive and ~ at the same time. 夜晚在高速公路上驾车时不可能一边开车一边指路。❸穿过,走过;使挤过:It is difficult to ~ a large crowd. 很难穿过拥挤的人群。

navigation /ˌnævɪˈgeɪʃən/ *n*. [U] ❶航行;航海;航空;飞行:He demanded that that nation be open to ~ by its allies. 他要求那个国家向其盟国开放领空。/ The compass was used as the main instrument of ~. 指南针是主要的导航仪器。❷导航(术);航行学;航海术;航空术

navy /ˈneɪvi/ *n*. [C] 海军

near /nɪə(r)/ Ⅰ *adv*. (nearer, nearest)

(时间、空间等)近,邻近: He lives ~by. 他住在附近。Ⅱ *adj*. (-er,-est) 近的;接近的:Can you tell me the ~est way to the station? 你能告诉我去车站的近路吗? / The examination is ~ at hand. 考试快到了。Ⅲ *prep*. 在……附近: Don't go ~ the edge. 不要走近边沿。

nearby / ˌnɪəˈbaɪ / Ⅰ *adj*. 附近的 Ⅱ *adv*. 在附近

nearly / ˈnɪəli / *adv*. 几乎;将近: He is ~ ready. 他快准备好了。

neat / niːt / *adj*. 整洁的;整齐的;精巧的: a ~ desk 整洁的书桌 / a ~ child 爱整洁的孩子

necessarily / nesəˈserəli / *adv*. ❶必定;必然:Big men are not ~ strong. 高大的人不一定强壮。❷必要地

necessary / ˈnesəsəri / *adj*. 必要的;必需的;必然的;必定的:Sleep is ~ for health. 睡眠对保持健康是必要的。

necessity / nəˈsesəti / *n*. 必需品;急需品: bare (basic, daily, household) necessities 最低限度的(基本的、日用的、家庭的)必需品 / Food and warmth are necessities. 食物和温暖是不可缺少的东西。/ Necessity is the mother of invention. 需要是发明之母。

neck / nek / *n*. [C]颈;脖子

necklace / ˈnekləs / *n*. [C]项链;项圈

need / niːd / Ⅰ *aux. v*. 需要;必要: You ~n't talk so loud. 你不必讲得那么大声。/ Need you go yet? 你还必须去吗? Ⅱ *vt*. ❶需要:The flowers ~ rain. 这些花需要雨水。Your composition ~s rewriting. 你的文章需要重写。❷必须(通常用在疑问句和否定句中):Does he ~ to know? 他必须知道吗? / He did not ~ to be reminded about it. 不必提醒他那件事。Ⅲ *n*. 缺乏;需要;必须: A friend in ~ is a friend indeed. 患难朋友才是真正的朋友。/ **in (great) ~ of ...** (很)需要……

needle / ˈniːdl / *n*. [C]针;缝衣针;钩针

needless / ˈniːdləs / *adj*. 不必要的;多余的:~ to say 不用说,当然

negative / ˈnegətɪv / Ⅰ *adj*. ❶否定的 ❷(数学)负的:~ sign 负号 / ~ quantity 负数 ❸(电)负的;阴性的 ❹(摄影)底片的 Ⅱ *n*. [C] ❶否定;否认:Two ~s make an affirmative. 否定之否定为肯定。❷(数学)负数 ❸(摄影)底片

neglect / nɪˈglekt / Ⅰ *vt*. 忽视;忽略:He ~ed his health. 他忽视了他的健康。Ⅱ *n*. [U]怠慢,忽视:This slight ~ lech to the tragedy. 这一小小的疏忽导致了这场悲剧。派 neglectful *adj*.; neglectfully *adv*.

negligence / ˈneglɪdʒəns / *n*. [U]疏忽;玩忽职守;不留心,粗心大意:He is very concerned in case his company are sued for ~. 他小心从事,以免公司因玩忽职守遭起诉。/The fire was caused by ~. 大火是因粗心大意而引起的。

negligible / ˈneglɪdʒəbl/ *adj*. 微乎其微的,极少的;无关紧要的/ Compared with bestsellers, profits from poetry are ~. 与畅销书相比,从诗歌中获得的利润可是少之又少。

negotiate / nɪˈgəʊʃɪeɪt / *v*. 谈判;协商: They ~d a peace treaty. 他们商订和平条约。派 negotiation *n*.

Negro / ˈniːgrəʊ / *n*. [C] (*pl*. Negroes) 黑人(有轻蔑之意,现用 black, black people 或 African—American)

neighbo(u)r / ˈneɪbə(r) / Ⅰ *n*. [C]邻

N

居;邻国 Ⅱ *vi.* 相邻,紧挨着:Their farm ~s on a large stretch of woods. 他们的农场与一大片树林相邻。

neighbo(u)rhood /ˈneɪbəhʊd/ *n.* [C]邻近地区;附近地方:A house was on fire in our ~ last night. 昨晚我们附近一所房子失火了。

neighbo(u)rly /ˈneɪbəli/ *adj.* 似邻居的;友好的,和睦的:The town were ~ when we moved in. 我们搬来时镇上的人非常友好。/It's a ~ thing to help others. 帮助别人是一件善事。派 neighbo(u)r-liness *n.*

neither /ˈnaɪðə(r),ˈniːðə(r)/ Ⅰ *adj.* (与单数名词连用)(两者)都不:Neither statement is true. 两种说法都不是真的。Ⅱ *pron.* (两者)都不:I like ~ of them. 两个我都不喜欢。Ⅲ *adv.* ~ ... **nor** ... 既不……也不……:It's ~ pleasant to eat nor good for your health. 它既不好吃,也不利于你的健康。Ⅳ *conj.* (既不……)也不……,任何一个……都不……:Mary doesn't like to sing, neither does she dance. 玛丽既不喜欢唱歌,也不爱跳舞。

nephew /ˈnevjuː,ˈnefjuː/ *n.* [C]侄子;外甥

nerve /nɜːv/ *n.* ❶[C]神经 ❷[U]勇气;胆量

nerveless /ˈnɜːvlɪs/ *adj.* ❶沉着的,镇静的,冷静的:She stood ~ and unafraid. 她非常镇静地站着,面无惧色。❷缺乏勇气的,无胆量的;无生气的;无力的,虚弱的:~ limbs 软弱无力的四肢/He was ~ and weaponless. 他既没有胆量,也没有武器。派 nervelessly *adv.*

nervous /ˈnɜːvəs/ *adj.* 神经紧张的;神经过敏的:Some are ~ in the dark. 有些人在黑暗处就神经紧张。派 nervously *adv.*;nervousness *n.*

nest /nest/ Ⅰ *n.* [C]巢;窝 Ⅱ *vi.* 筑巢;做窝

net[1] /net/ *n.* ❶网;罗网:a fishing (hair, tennis) ~ 鱼(发,网球)网 ❷网络,通信网,网状系统

net[2] /net/ Ⅰ *adj.* 净的;纯的(只作定语):a ~ price 实价 / a ~ profit 纯利;净利 Ⅱ *n.* 净重;净利;实价

network /ˈnetwɜːk/ *n.* [C] ❶网状结构,网络:a ~ of sewers under the city 城市地下纵横交错的排水管道 ❷广播网;电视网;广播(或电视)联播公司:the major television ~s in the city 该市主要的几家电视网 ❸网状系统:transportation (railway) ~ 交通网(铁路网) ❹网络:send programs across a computer ~ 通过计算机网络传送程序 ❺联络网,关系网:set up a distribution ~ 建立销售网

neural /ˈnjʊrəl/ *adj.* 神经的;神经系统的

neutral /ˈnjuːtrəl/ Ⅰ *adj.* ❶中立的;公平的:be ~ on this subject 在这个问题上保持中立 ❷不明显的;不明确的;模糊的:a ~ personality 不鲜明的个性 ❸中性的;不带电的:~ particles 不带电的粒子 Ⅱ *n.* ❶[C]中立者;中立国:Switzerland was a ~ during World War Ⅱ. 第二次世界大战期间,瑞士是一个中立国。❷[U](汽车等的)空挡 派 neutrally *adv.*

never /ˈnevə(r)/ *adv.* 从未;未曾;决不:I have ~ been there. 我从未到过那里。/ ~ **mind** 不用担心:Never mind about your mistake. 别再想你犯的错了。

nevertheless /ˌnevəðəˈles/ *adv.* &.

N

conj. 然而；虽然如此；依然

new / njuː / *adj*. 新的；从未有过的；初见到的；初听到的：a ~ invention 一项新发明；/ New Year's Day 元旦 / New Year's Eve 除夕

newborn / njuːˈbɔːn，ˈnjuːbɔːn / Ⅰ *adj*. (婴儿)新出生的，刚降世的，刚出生的：~ babies 新生儿 Ⅱ *n*. [C]新生儿

newcomer / ˈnjuːˌkʌmə(r) / *n*. [C] ❶新来的人 ❷新出现的事物

newly / ˈnjuːli/ *adv*. 新近，最近(与动词的过去分词连用)：the ~ elected mayor 新当选的市长

news / njuːz / *n*. [U]新闻；消息：a piece of ~一条消息；a ~report 新闻报道

newspaper / ˈnjuːzpeɪpə(r) / *n*. [C]报纸：I read it in the ~. 我在报纸上看到的。

newsreel / ˈnjuːzriːl / *n*. [C]新闻影片

newsstand / ˈnjuː(z)stænd / *n*. [C]报摊，书报亭

next / nekst / Ⅰ *adj*. 下一个的；其次的：the ~ train 下班火车/ the ~ room 隔壁房间 / ~ Monday 下星期一 Ⅱ *adv*. 在这以后；其次；然后：What are you going to do ~? 你下一步要做什么呢? Ⅲ *prep*. 靠近；贴近：May I bring my chair ~ yours? 我可以把我的椅子搬到你的旁边吗? ~ **to** 相邻；靠近：They live ~ to the post office. 他们住在邮局隔壁。

nibble / ˈnɪbl / Ⅰ *v*. 小口地吃；一点点地咬(或吃)；啃：She was nibbling her food like a rabbit. 她像兔子一样地小口吃东西。/Inflation was nibbling away at her savings. 通货膨胀把她的积蓄一点点地吞噬掉了。Ⅱ *n*. [C] 咬下的少量食物；一小口的量；少量：There's not even a ~ left. 甚至连一口吃的都没剩下。

nice / naɪs / *adj*. 令人愉快的；优美的；宜人的；友善的：a ~ face 美丽的面孔 / ~ weather 好天气 / ~ taste 好味道 / He was ~ to us. 他对我们很友善。

nicely / ˈnaɪsli/ *adv*. ❶愉快地；高兴地；讨人喜欢地：behave ~ 表现很好 ❷恰当地；合适地：Five dollars should do quite ~ for a tip for the waiter. 给服务员 5 美元小费是很合适的。

nickel / ˈnɪkəl / *n*. [U]镍(符号 Ni)

nickname / ˈnɪkneɪm / Ⅰ *n*. [C]绰号；昵称 Ⅱ *vt*. 给(某人)取绰号；以绰号称呼

niece / niːs / *n*. [C]侄女；甥女

night / naɪt / *n*. 夜晚：They worked from morning till ~. 他们从早到晚地干活。/ **day and** ~ 夜以继日地；不断地：travel day and ~ for a week 日夜不停地旅行一个星期 **all** ~ **long** 整夜地；彻夜：We watched all ~ long. 我们彻夜看守。**at** ~ 在夜里：He came home very late at ~. 他夜里回家很晚。**by** ~ 夜间：They don't work by day but by ~. 他们白天不工作，而是夜里工作。

nightfall / ˈnaɪtˌfɔːl / *n*. [C](妇女或儿童穿着的)睡衣

nightingale / ˈnaɪtɪŋgeɪl / *n*. [C]夜莺

nightmare / ˈnaɪtmeə(r) / *n*. [C] 噩梦；梦魇般的经历

nine /naɪn / Ⅰ *num*. 九，9 Ⅱ *adj*. 九个(的)

nineteen /ˌnaɪnˈtiːn / Ⅰ *num*. 十九，19 Ⅱ *adj*. 十九个(的)

nineteenth / ˌnaɪnˈtiːnθ / Ⅰ *num*. 第十九；十九分之一 Ⅱ *adj*. 第十九的；十九分之一的

ninetieth / ˈnaɪntɪəθ / Ⅰ *num*. 第九十；九十分之一 Ⅱ *adj*. 第九十的；九十分之

一的

ninety /ˈnaɪnti/ Ⅰ *num.* 九十，90 Ⅱ *adj.* 九十个(的)

ninth /naɪnθ/ Ⅰ *num.* 第九；九分之一 Ⅱ *adj.* 第九个的；九分之一的

nip /nɪp/ Ⅰ *v.* (nipped; nipping) ❶拧，捏，掐；猛咬：The dog ~ ped at his heels. 狗咬住了他的脚后跟。/ ~ the tip off the cigar 把雪茄的头掐掉 ❷疾走，跑动：Where did you ~ off to? 你到哪里去了？Ⅱ *n.* [C]拧，捏，掐；咬：The dog gave him a few ~s on the leg. 狗在他腿上咬了几下。

nitrogen /ˈnaɪtrədʒən/ *n.* [U]氮(符号 N)

no /nəʊ/ Ⅰ *adj.* 没有的 Ⅱ *adv.* 不，并非：~ **longer** 不再：He ~ longer lived here. 他不再住这里。~ **more than** 不过，仅仅：He has ~ more than 10 dollars. 他只有十美元。/ He is ~ more than a puppet. 他只不过是一个傀儡。

N

No. /ˈnʌmbə(r)/ *n.* (=number)号码；数目：the ~ 2 Middle School 第二中学

noble /ˈnəʊbl/ Ⅰ *adj.* ❶高尚的；崇高的：a ~ deed 伟大的事迹 / a man of ~ mind 思想高尚的人 ❷贵族的；高贵的：~ birth 高贵的出身 Ⅱ *n.* [C](常用 *pl.*)贵族

nobleman /ˈnəʊblmən/ *n.* [C] (*pl.* -men) 贵族

nobody /ˈnəʊbɒdi Ⅰ *pron.* 谁都不，没人；无人：Nobody else could have done better. 其他没有人会做得更好。/ Nobody but Tony went swimming. 只有托尼一人去游泳了。Ⅱ *n.* [C]无名小卒，小人物(与 somebody 相对)：He invited virtually everybody who was anybody — but most nobodies showed up. 凡是有名气的他几乎都邀请了，但出席的大都是无名之辈。

nod /nɒd/ Ⅰ *v.* (nodded; nodding)点头(表示同意或打招呼)：I asked if he could come and he ~ded. 我问他是否能来，他点头答应了。Ⅱ *n.* [C] ❶点头；点头示意 ❷打盹；打瞌睡

noise /nɔɪz/ *n.* 噪声；嘈杂声；响声：make a big (loud) ~ 大声喧闹 / ~ pollution 噪声污染

noisy /ˈnɔɪzi/ *adj.* (-ier, -iest)吵闹的；嘈杂的：a ~ boy 吵闹的孩子

nominal /ˈnɒmɪnəl/ *adj.* ❶名义上的，徒有其名的；有名无实的：the ~ head of the state 名义上的国家首脑 ❷微不足道的，轻微的：a ~ price 极其低廉的价格 ❸名字的，列名的 ❹名词的；名词性的

nominate /ˈnɒmɪˌneɪt/ *vt.* ❶提名；推荐(与 for 连用)：~ candidates 提名候选人 / ~ sb. for president 提名某人为总统候选人 / Every movie he made was ~d for an Oscar. 他制作的每部影片都获得了奥斯卡提名。❷指定，任命：a presidential decree nominating Johnson as sports ambassador 一项任命约翰逊担任体育大使的总统令 派 nomination *n.*

nominative /ˈnɒmɪnətɪv/ Ⅰ *adj.* ❶(语法)主格的：the ~ case 主格 ❷被提名的，被推荐的；指定的 Ⅱ *n.* [C] ❶主格 ❷主格词

nonconductor /ˈnɒnkənˈdʌktə/ *n.* 非导体；绝缘体

none /nʌn/ *pron.* ❶没有一个人(或事物)：There is ~ braver than I. 没人比我更勇敢。/ I turned to bookshops and libraries seeking information and found ~. 我去书店和图书馆找资料，却什么也没找着。❷没有任何一人(或事物)：This is ~ of your business. 这不关你的事。❸一点没有，全无：I have ~ of that.

那没我的份儿。

nonsense /ˈnɒnsəns/ *n.* [U]无意义的话；废话；胡说；愚蠢的行动：That's all ~. 那全是胡说。

nonstop /nɒnˈstɒp/ Ⅰ *adj.* ❶(火车、飞机等)中途不停的，直达的：a ~ flight from Beijing to New York 从北京直飞纽约的航班 ❷不停顿的，不间断的，连续的：80 minutes of ~ music 连续演奏 80 分钟的音乐 Ⅱ *adv.* ❶直达地，不停地：They drove ~ from Los Angeles to New York. 他们从洛杉矶直驶纽约。❷不间断地：They are talking ~ for eight hours. 他们连续交谈了 8 个小时。

noodle /ˈnuːdl/ *n.* [C](常用 *pl.*)面条：Do you like ~s in chicken soup? 你喜欢吃鸡汤面吗？

noon /nuːn/ *n.* [U]中午；正午 / **at ~** 在中午：He often has a nap at ~. 他常常在中午睡一会儿。

nor /nɔː(r), nə(r)/ *conj.* ❶(与否定词 neither 连用，用以引出被否定的两项中的第二项)也不，也不是，也没有：Neither he ~ his friends came back. 他和他的朋友们都没有回来。❷(用于否定词 not, no, never 等后，表示前面否定意义的延续，用于句首时主语和谓语倒装)不，也不：There was not a cloud in the sky ~ any sun. 天空中没有云彩，也没有阳光。

norm /ˈnɔːm/ *n.* [C]❶标准；准则；规范：a universal ethical ~普遍的道德标准/ the ~ of the society 社会的行为规范 ❷规定额；平均水平；平均值

normal /ˈnɔːməl/ *adj.* 正常的；常态的；正规的：the ~ temperature of the human body 人体的正常温度 / a ~ college 师范学院

normally /ˈnɔːməli/ *adv.* ❶正常地；正规地：The radio broadcast continued ~. 电台继续正常广播。❷通常，惯常：Every summer a troupe of actors were engaged, ~ from the beginning of May to the end of October. 每年夏天都有一队演员参加，通常是从 5 月初到 10 月底。

north /nɔːθ/ Ⅰ *n.* [U]北部；北方：a room facing ~ 朝北的房子 Ⅱ *adj.* 北部的；北方的：North China 华北 Ⅲ *adv.* 在北方；向北方：I am going ~. 我要向北走。

northward /ˈnɔːθwəd/ Ⅰ *adv.* 向北，朝北：look ~ 朝北望 Ⅱ *adj.* 向北的，朝北的；北上的

northeast /ˌnɔːθ ˈiːst/ Ⅰ *n.* (the ~) 东北；东北部 Ⅱ *adj.* 东北的；向东北方的 Ⅲ *adv.* 向东北；在东北

northern /ˈnɔːðən/ *adj.* 北方的；北部的

northward /ˈnɔːθwəd/ *adv.* 向北方

northwest /ˌnɔːθˈwest/ Ⅰ *n.* (the ~) 西北；西北部 Ⅱ *adj.* 西北的；向西北的 Ⅲ *adv.* 向西北；在西北

nose /nəʊz/ *n.* [C]鼻子：eagle ~ 鹰钩鼻 / flat ~ 扁鼻子 / running ~ 流鼻涕的鼻子 / vegetable ~ 蒜头鼻子

not /nɒt/ *adv.* ❶(与 be, have 或助动词、情态动词连用，用以表示相反、否认、拒绝、禁止等)不，不是，没有：There is nothing that time will ~ cure. 时间能治愈一切。/ The same food does ~ agree with every constitution. 同一食品对各种不同体质的人不一定都合适。❷(后接 a 或 one，表示强调)没有，无：He had ~ a penny to his name. 他已一文不名。/ I'm ~ a chicken; I just don't want to offend anybody. 我绝不是胆小鬼，我只是不想得罪人。/ Not one of the students could name the president.

没有一个学生能说出总统的名字。/~ **at all** ①不用谢，别客气：—Thanks for helping. —Not at all. I enjoyed it. —谢谢你帮忙。—别客气，我乐意效劳。②一点也不：Authors are ~ mentioned at all. 压根儿就没提到作家。

notable /ˈnəutəbl/ Ⅰ *adj.* ❶值得注意的；显著的：a ~ moment in the history 历史上重要的一刻 ❷著名的，显要的：His production is ~ for its humor. 他的创作主要以其幽默而著称。Ⅱ *n.* [C]名人，显要人物

notably /ˈnəutəbli/ *adv.* ❶引人注目地，显著地：The audience was ~ small. 观众非常少。❷尤其，特别地：a ~ fine meal 特别好的一顿饭

note /nəut/ Ⅰ *n.* [C] ❶笔记；摘记：I didn't take any ~s. 我没有记笔记。❷短信；便条：write a thank-you ~ 写一张表示感谢的便条 ❸钞票 Ⅱ *v.* 注意，留心；记下：The policeman ~d down every word he said. 警察把他所说的每一个字都记了下来。

notebook /ˈnəutˌbuk/ *n.* [C] ❶笔记本 ❷笔记本电脑

noted /ˈnəutɪd/ *adj.* 著名的；闻名的

nothing /ˈnʌθɪŋ/ Ⅰ *pron.* ❶没有事情，没有东西，没有什么：He would soon have ~ left if he continued to be lavish with money. 他如果再挥金如土，将会很快破产。/ Tomorrow was far away and there was ~ to trouble about. 明天还遥远，没什么要烦闷的。❷毫无迹象：The house showed ~ of its former splendor. 这房子看不出一点儿过去的辉煌。❸无足轻重的事物；不值钱的东西：Wealth and power are ~. 财富和权力一文不值。Ⅱ *n.* [C] ❶无关紧要的事情（或东西等）；空话：Wade whispered sweet ~ into her ears. 韦德在她耳边低声地讲些毫无意义的甜言蜜语。❷无足轻重的人，小人物：It makes you feel like ~. 它使你感到自己微不足道。/ **for** ~①不花钱地，免费地：She got the painting for ~. 这幅画是她没花一分钱得来的。②没有理由地，无缘无故地：fly into a rage for ~ 无缘无故地发火 ③没有结果；徒劳：We waited for two hours and for ~ — he didn't come. 我们等了两个小时，但毫无结果，他一直没来。~ **but** 只是，仅仅：The war brought ~ but sadness, misery and tragedy. 战争只会带来悲伤、痛苦和灾难。**think ~ of** 对……不重视，不把……放在心上，小看：They think ~ of working ten hours a day. 他们觉得一天工作10个小时算不了什么。Ⅲ *adj.* 没有意义的；没有价值的：a ~ job 毫无意义的工作

notice /ˈnəutɪs/ Ⅰ *n.* 注意；布告；公告：You have to stay here till further ~. 你得留在这儿直到接到通知为止。/ **at (on) short** ~ 一接通知马上，立刻 **take no ~ of** 不注意；不理睬：Take no ~ of what they're saying about you. 别理睬他们说你什么。**take ~ of** 注意，留心 Ⅱ *v.* 注意到，留心；正式通知：I ~d a big difference. 我注意到一大差别。

noticeable /ˈnəutɪsəbl/ *adj.* 明显的，很容易看出的：The years has made a ~ change in him. 岁月在他身上留下明显的变化。/ make ~progress 取得明显的进步 派 noticeably *adv.*

notify /ˈnəutɪˌfaɪ/ *vt.* 通知，告知（与 of 连用）：We can ~ them quickly *of* our decision. 我们可以很快把我们的决定告诉他们。/ I have to ~ you that your child has failed to come to school again.

我不得不告诉你，你的孩子又没有来上学。

notion / ˈnəʊʃn / *n.* [C]观念；想法；意向

notorious / nəʊˈtɔːrɪəs/ *adj.* ❶臭名昭著的，声名狼藉的：the world's most ~ criminals 世界上最臭名昭著的罪犯 ❷众所周知的，出名的：Tokyo is ~ for its noise pollution. 东京的噪声污染是众所周知的。派 notoriously *adv.*

noun / naʊn / *n.* [C]名词：a proper ~ 专有名词

nourish / ˈnʌrɪʃ/ *vt.* ❶喂养；给……滋养，给……营养：You look ill; you should ~ yourself with healthy soups. 你的气色不好，应该喝点滋补汤补补身体。❷怀有，抱有（情感、希望等）：She has long ~ed the hope of becoming a famous actress. 她一直渴望成为名演员。❸培养（知识、情感等）；助长：~ the brain 培养智力 / The two mythologies ~ed the symbolist poets. 象征派诗人从这两种神话里受到了良好的熏陶。

nourishing / ˈnʌrɪʃɪŋ / *adj.*（尤指食物）有营养的；滋补的：This kind of food is not very ~. 这种食物营养不太丰富。/ a ~ drink 有滋养作用的饮品

nourishment / ˈnʌrɪʃmənt / *n.* [U]滋养品；营养；食物

novel[1] / ˈnɒvl / *n.* [C] 小说

novel[2] / ˈnɒvl / *adj.* 新颖的；新奇的

novelty / ˈnɒvəlti/ *n.* ❶[U]新颖（性），新奇（性）；创新（性）；原创（性）：bring ~ to the old way of doing business 旧事新办 ❷[C]新事物；新现象：The proposal is a ~ in here. 这个建议在这里尚属创举。

November / nəʊˈvembə(r) / *n.* 十一月

now / naʊ / *adv.* 现在：He is here ~. 他此刻在这儿。/ (**every**) ~ **and then** (**again**) 有时候；时常：She goes to a movie ~ and then. 她时常去看电影。~ **that** 既然：Now that you've grown up, you must stop this childish behaviour. 你既然长大了，就必须停止这种幼稚的行为。

nowadays / ˈnaʊədeɪz / *adv.* 现今；现在

nowhere / ˈnəʊˌweə(r)/ Ⅰ *adv.* 任何地方都不：This could have occurred ~ but in England. 这种事只有可能在英国发生。/ The two young men were ~ to be seen. 哪里都找不到这两个年轻人。Ⅱ *n.* [U] ❶不存在：The police appeared from ~. 警察不知是从哪里冒出来的。❷无名；默默无闻：He came out of ~ and won the nomination. 他脱颖而出获得了提名。❸不知名的地方；遥远的地方，不存在的地方：An unexpected cloud appeared from ~. 一片乌云不期而至。

nuclear / ˈnjuːklɪə(r) / *adj.* ❶核能的：~ device 核装置 / ~ explosion 核爆炸 / ~ power plant (station)核能发电站 / ~ test 核试验 ❷核的；核心的 ❸（生物）细胞核的

nucleus / ˈnjuːklɪəs / *n.* [C] (*pl.* nuclei / ˈnjuːklaɪ / 或 nucleuses) ❶核，核心 ❷（生物）细胞核 ❸原子核：the atomic ~ 原子核

nude / njuːd/ Ⅰ *adj.* 裸体的；裸露的，赤裸的：a ~ portrait 裸体画像 / Nude sunbathing is allowed on that beach. 那个海滩允许裸体日光浴。Ⅱ *n.* ❶[C]裸体画；裸像 ❷[U]裸体

nuisance / ˈnjuːsəns / *n.* [C]讨厌的人（或事）

null / nʌl / *adj.* ❶没有价值的，无意义的；无效的：It makes the previous agreement ~. 这使得原有的协议失效。/~ **and void** 无约束力的,无效的 ❷(集合)空的:a ~ set 空集合

numb /nʌm/ Ⅰ*adj.* ❶麻木的,无感觉的(与 with 连用):My fingers are ~ with cold. 我的手指冻僵了。❷无感情的,冷淡的;表情僵硬的:Nothing could rouse her from a ~ indifference. 没有什么能改变她的麻木不仁。Ⅱ*vt.* 使麻木;使失去知觉

number /ˈnʌmbə(r)/ Ⅰ*n.* ❶数:even (odd)~ 偶数(奇数) / five-digit ~ 五位数 / known (unknown)~ 已知(未知)数 / lucky ~ 吉祥数 / plural (singular) ~ 复(单)数 / winning ~ (彩票)获奖号 / wrong ~ 错电话号 / His telephone number is 6611224. 他的电话号码是6611224。❷数量;总数:They were fifteen in ~. 他们总共是 15 个。Ⅱ*v.* 编号;计数:The students of the school ~ over 2,000. 这所学校的学生人数超过 2000。

numerable /ˈn(j)uːmərəbl/ *adj.* 可数的,可计数的

numeral /ˈn(j)uːmərəl/ *n.* [C]数字:Roman ~s 罗马数字

numerous /ˈnjuːmərəs/ *adj.* 许许多多的;大批的:~ stars 许多星星

nurse /nɜːs/ Ⅰ[C] ❶护士;护理员 ❷保姆;保育员:baby ~s 奶妈 / the family ~ 家庭保姆 ❸奶妈 Ⅱ*vt.* ❶护理,照料,服侍:She ~d her father back to health. 她照料父亲,使他恢复了健康。❷治疗,调治(疾病):~ an injury 养伤 / He stayed in bed and ~d his cold. 他因感冒卧床养病。❸给……喂奶,给……哺乳:~ the baby 给孩子喂奶

nursery /ˈnɜːsəri/ *n.* [C]幼儿室;托儿所:day (night) ~ 日间(夜间)托儿所

nut /nʌt/ *n.* [C]坚果

nutrition /njuːˈtrɪʃən/ *n.* [U] ❶营养学:the science of ~ 营养学 ❷营养,滋养:food of ~ 营养食品 ❸食物;营养物,滋补品:Good ~ is essential for the recovery of patients. 良好的营养食品对病人恢复健康是很有必要的。

nutritionist /njʊˈtrɪʃənɪst/ *n.* [C]营养学家

nutritious /njʊˈtrɪʃəs/ *adj.* 有营养的:the richly ~ milk 营养丰富的牛奶

nylon /ˈnaɪlɒn/ *n.* ❶[U]尼龙 ❷[C](*pl.*)尼龙袜

N

O o

oak /əʊk/ *n.* 橡树；橡木

oar /ɔː(r)/ *n.* [C]桨；橹

oasis /əʊˈeɪsɪs/ *n.* [C](*pl.* oases) ❶(沙漠中的)绿洲 ❷令人宽慰(或愉快)的事情；安稳的地方；安定时期，平稳期：He worked six days a week and looked forward to his day off an ~ of rest and relaxation. 他每周工作六天，盼望有朝一日能够度假，尽情休息和放松。

oat /əʊt/ *n.* [C] ❶燕麦种子；燕麦谷粒；燕麦庄稼

oath /əʊθ/ *n.* [C] ❶誓言；誓约 ❷(在法庭的)宣誓

obedience /əˈbɪːdɪəns/ *n.* [U]听从，服从；顺从；遵从：A soldier must give implicit ~ to his commanding officers. 士兵必须绝对服从他的长官。/Obedience to a strict moral code is central to this society. 严格遵守道德规范是这个社会的宗旨。

obedient /əˈbiːdɪənt/ *adj.* 服从的；顺从的；听话的

obey /əˈbeɪ/ *v.* 服从；听从：Soldiers have to ~ orders. 军人须服从命令。

object Ⅰ/ˈɒbdʒɪkt/ *n.* [C] ❶物体；物品：Tell me the names of the ~s in this room. 告诉我这屋里各物的名称。❷目标；目的：an ~ of study 研究的对象 ❸(语法)宾语 Ⅱ/əbˈdʒekt/ *v.* 不赞成；反对；抗议：I ~ to doing it. 我不赞成这件事。

objection /əbˈdʒekʃn/ *n.* [C]反对；异议；反对的理由：What is your ~ to (against) my plan? 你反对我计划的理由是什么?

objective /əbˈdʒektɪv/ Ⅰ *adj.* ❶客观的；物体的；如实的 ❷(语法)宾格的 Ⅱ *n.* [C] ❶目标；宗旨 ❷(语法)宾格

obligate /ˈɒblɪgeɪt/ *vt.* ❶(在道义上或法律上)使受束缚(或制约)：I felt ~d to turn up on time. 我觉得必须准时露面。❷强迫；责成：She feels ~d to make the background of her books as factual and authentic as possible. 她觉得必须使其书中描写的背景尽量真实可信。

obligation /ˌɒblɪˈgeɪʃn/ *n.* 义务；责任

oblige /əˈblaɪdʒ/ *vt.* ❶要求：The law ~s parents to send their children to school. 法律要求父母送子女入学。❷强迫：They were ~d to sell their house in order to pay their debts. 他们被迫卖房子来还债。

oblique /əˈbliːk/ *adj.* ❶斜的，倾斜的；歪的：an ~ line 斜线 ❷不直截了当的，转弯抹角的；间接的：He took this as an ~ reference to his own affairs. 他认为这是在影射他自己的事情。

obscene /əbˈsiːn/ *adj.* ❶猥亵的；下流的；淫秽的：The press had been prosecuted for printing ~ and indecent advertising. 该出版社因印制淫秽和不健康的宣传品而受到起诉。❷(口语)很讨厌的;可恨的,可憎的:so heinous, black,~ a deed 如此凶残、邪恶、可憎的行为 派 obsceneness *n.*

obscure /əbˈskjʊə(r)/ Ⅰ *adj.* ❶晦涩的,深奥的;费解的,难懂的:The meaning of this essay is very ~; I really do not understand it. 这篇文章的意思极为深奥,我实在无法理解。❷含糊不清的;不明确的:The ~ words baffled him. 这些含糊不清的话语使他大惑不解。❸昏暗的;模糊的;不明显的:an ~ figure 隐约可见的身影 Ⅱ *vt.* ❶使变暗;使模糊,使看不清:Light rain began to fall and ~d the setting sun. 细雨开始飘落,使正在沉落的夕阳变得模糊不清了。❷使费解;使混淆不清;隐瞒,掩盖:The management deliberately ~d the real situation from federal investigators. 管理部门故意向联邦调查员隐瞒事件的真相。派 obscurely *adv.*

observation /ˌɒbzəˈveɪʃn/ *n.* [U]观察;观察力:escape one's ~ 不为某人所注意 / a man of no ~ 缺乏观察力的人

observatory /əbˈzɜːvətəri/ *n.* [C] ❶观象台,天文台:At the ~ is a big telescope through which scientists study the stars. 天文台有一架大型望远镜,科学家通过此望远镜研究恒星的活动。❷气象台,气象站;观测站,观测台 ❸(可观赏风景的)瞭望台,望楼

observe /əbˈzɜːv/ *v.* ❶看;观察:I ~d nothing queer in his behaviour. 我没发现他的行为有异常之处。❷遵守(规则等);庆祝(节日、生日、周年等):~ the laws 遵守法律 / Do they ~ Christmas Day in their country? 他们国家的人过圣诞节吗? 派 observer *n.*

observing /əbˈzɜːvɪŋ/ *adj.* 善于观察的;注意的;机警的

obsolete /ˈɒbsəliːt/ *adj.* ❶不再使用的;废弃的,作废的;淘汰的:an ~ expression 废弃的表达方式 / The aircraft speed is limited, as a result it will soon become ~. 这种飞机的速度受到了限制,因而它将很快被淘汰。❷过时的,陈旧的,老式的:~ machinery 过时的机器

obstacle /ˈɒbstəkl/ *n.* [C]障碍;妨碍:clear away ~s 排除障碍

obstinate /ˈɒbstɪnət/ *adj.* 顽固的;固执的:She was a wicked and ~ Child. 她是个淘气又执拗的孩子。

obstruct /əbˈstrʌkt/ *vt.* ❶阻塞,使堵塞:After the typhoon many roads were ~ed by collapsed trees. 台风过后,许多道路被倒塌的树木堵塞了。❷妨碍,阻碍:He got ten years in prison for ~ing the course of justice. 他因妨碍司法公正被判十年徒刑。

obtain /əbˈteɪn/ *v.* 取;获得;买:~ a prize 得奖

obvious /ˈɒbvɪəs/ *adj.* 显而易见的;清楚的;明白的:It is an ~ advantage. 那是一个明显的好处。派 obviously *adv.*

occasion /əˈkeɪʒn/ *n.* ❶[C]时机;机会:It is a favourable ~. 这是一个有利时机。/ **on** ~ 有时:I call on him on ~. 我有时拜访他。**on one** ~ 曾经;有一次:I called on him on one ~. 我曾经拜访过他一次。**take** ~ 利用机会:I took ~ to tell him about my work. 我趁机给他讲了我的工作情况。❷[U] 理由;原因:You have no ~ to be angry. 你没有理由生气。

occasional /əˈkeɪʒənəl/ *adj.* 非经常的;

偶然的：He pays me ~ visits. 他偶尔来看我。派 occasionally *adv.*

occupant / ˈɒkjʊpənt / *n.* [C] ❶占有者；占用者；居住者：There have been many distinguished ~s of the position of executive director. 已经有很多人担任过执行导演这一职位。❷房屋（或土地、办公室等）的实际占用者：The ~ is unwilling to pay rent. 那个房屋占用者不愿付房租。

occupation / ˌɒkjʊˈpeɪʃn / *n.* [U] ❶占有；占领：military ~ 军事占领 ❷职业：He has no fixed (definite) ~. 他没有固定的职业。

occupy / ˈɒkjʊpaɪ / *vt.* 占领：The building occupies an entire block. 这幢建筑物占了整整一个街区。/ **be occupied with (in)** 忙于：He has been occupied in writing his novel. 他一直忙着写小说。

occur / əˈkɜː(r) / *vi.* (occurred; occurring) ❶发生：A leap year ~s once every four years. 每四年有一次闰年。❷想起；想到：An idea ~red to me. 我想到了一个主意。❸存在：Misprints ~ on every page. 每一页都有印刷错误。

occurrence / əˌkʌrəns / *n.* [U]发生；出现：They have been studying the ~ of heart disease in various countries. 他们一直在研究心脏病在不同国家的发病率。/This word is of frequent ~s. 我们因一些突发事件而耽误了。

ocean / ˈəʊʃn / *n.* [U]海洋：~ floor 海底 / the Arctic (Atlantic, Indian, Pacific) Ocean 北冰(大西、印度、太平)洋

Oceania / ˌəʊʃɪˈeɪnɪə / *n.* 大洋洲

o'clock / əˈklɒk / *adv.* 钟点：— What time is it now? —It's five ~. —现在几点？—五点整。

October / ɒkˈtəʊbə(r) / *n.* 十月：the ~ Revolution 十月革命

odd / ɒd / *adj.* ❶奇数的：Seven is an ~ number. 7 是奇数。❷非固定的；临时的：make a living by doing ~ jobs 靠做零工维生 ❸奇异的；古怪的：an ~ person 古怪的人

odds / ɒdz / *n.* ❶机会，可能性：The ~ on the champion winning are three to two. 夺冠的可能性是三比二。/The ~ are strongly against his getting here before Saturday. 极有可能他不会在星期六前到达这儿。❷成功的可能性(或希望)

odo(u)r / ˈəʊdə(r) / *n.* [C]气味；臭气；香味：It has a pleasant ~. 它有香气。

of / ɒv, əv / *prep.* ❶表示空间距离或时间长短：five miles south ~ Chongqing 重庆以南五英里 / within a year ~ his death 他死后一年内 ❷表示来源：a man ~ humble origin 出身低微的人 / the works ~ Shakespeare 莎士比亚的著作 ❸表示原因：His father died ~ hunger. 他父亲是饿死的。❹表示材料：a dress ~ silk 绸衣 ❺表示具有某种性质：a man ~ ability 有才干的人 / How kind ~ you to help me. 你来帮助我，太感谢了。/ It was good ~ your brother to come. 你的兄弟来了，真是太好了。

off / ɔːf, ɒf / Ⅰ *prep.* 从……离开：take a book ~ the shelf 从书架上拿走一本书 Ⅱ *adv.* 在远处；离开：The town is five miles ~. 那城镇在五英里之外。

offence(-se) / əˈfens / *n.* ❶[C]犯罪；犯规；过错：minor (grave) ~ 轻(重)罪 ❷[U]冒犯；触怒；伤感情

offend / əˈfend/ *vt.* ❶伤害……的感情，得罪；使生气，惹怒：Even the hint of prejudice ~s me. 甚至连一丝偏见都会

使我大为恼火。/ She was a bit ~ed that she hadn't been invited to join them. 因为他们没请她一起去，所以她有些不快。❷使感到不舒服；使厌恶：Ashtrays on restaurant tables ~ me. 餐馆桌子上的烟灰缸令我讨厌。

offensive /əˈfensɪv/ Ⅰ *adj.* ❶冒犯的；无礼的 ❷令人不愉快的；攻击的 Ⅱ *n.* [C](the ~) 攻势；进攻

offer /ˈɒfə(r)/ Ⅰ *v.* 提供；提出；提议：She ~ed a few ideas to improve the plan. 她提出数种意见以改进那项计划。Ⅱ *n.* [C]提供；提议：an ~ of help 援助的建议

off-hour /ˈɒfˌaʊə(r)/ Ⅰ *n.* [C] ❶业余时间，非工作时间：Tom collects stamps during ~s. 汤姆在业余时间集邮。❷非高峰时间：Only one car is in service in ~. 非高峰时间只有一辆车服务。Ⅱ *adj.* ❶非工作时间的：~ diversions 业余消遣 ❷非高峰时间的

O

office /ˈɒfɪs/ *n.* [C]办公室；办事处：~ hours 营业时间；办公时间 / after ~ 在业余时间 / branch ~ 分行，分支机构 / home ~ 总部，总公司，总店，总局 / in high ~ 身居高位 / the party in ~ 执政党 / the party out of ~ 在野党

officer /ˈɒfɪsə(r)/ *n.* [C]军官；警官；高级船员

official /əˈfɪʃəl/ Ⅰ *adj.* 公务的；官方的：~ powers 职权 / ~ duties 公务 Ⅱ *n.* [C]行政人员；官员：public ~s 公务员 / bank ~s 银行职员 / He is an ~ in the Ministry of Defense. 他是国防部的官员。

offset Ⅰ /ɒfˈset/ (-set；-setting) *vt.* (用……)补偿；抵消：He ~ his travel expenses against tax. 他以旅游开销来抵税收。/Their wage increases would be ~ by higher prices. 他们工资的增加将与上扬的物价相抵消。Ⅱ /ˈɒfˌset/ *n.* 补偿；抵消

offshore /ˌɒfˈʃɔː(r)/ Ⅰ *adj.* 离岸的；近海的；(风等)向海的 Ⅱ *adv.* 离岸；近海

offspring /ˈɔːfsprɪŋ/ *n.* [C]子孙；后代

often /ˈɒfn，ˈɒftən/ *adv.* ❶(比较级和最高级形式分别为 more often，most often；口语中也可用 oftener 与 oftenest) 常常；经常：How ~ does a bus run? 公共汽车多久一班？❷通常，在大多数情况下：Women are ~ very successful in advertising. 女性在广告业通常是很成功的。

oh /əʊ/ *int.* 啊，嗬(表示惊奇、恐惧等)

oil /ɒɪl/ *n.* [U]油；石油：an ~ field(口语)油田 / an ~ lamp 油灯 / add(pour) ~ on fire 火上加油

ointment /ˈɒɪntmənt/ *n.* 药膏，软膏：The doctor gave him some ~ to stop the cut from becoming infected. 医生给他配些药膏，防止伤口感染。

OK /əʊˈkeɪ/ (= Okay)(口语) Ⅰ *adj.* 好的；可以的 Ⅱ *adv.* 好，对，可以

old /əʊld/ *adj.* (older，oldest) ❶……岁的：—How ~ are you? —I am five years ~. —你多大了？—我五岁了。❷老的；年长的：There is an ~ man in the picture. 画中有一位老人。❸旧的；古老的；过时的

olive /ˈɒlɪv/ *n.* 橄榄；橄榄树；橄榄色：~ branch 橄榄枝(和平的象征) / ~ oil 橄榄油

Olympic /əˈlɪmpɪk，əˈlɪmpɪk/ *adj.* 奥林匹克的：the ~ Games 奥林匹克运动会

omen /ˈəumən/ *n.* [C]预兆，预示：a bad (good) ~ 凶(吉)兆 / an ~ of bad luck 厄运的凶兆

omission /əˈmɪʃn/ *n.* [U] ❶省略，删除；删节：The book was shortened by the ~ of two chapters. 此书删除了两个章节，从而缩短了篇幅。❷排除，剔除：His ~ from the team cost England the match. 他的落选使英国队输掉了比赛。❸遗漏；疏漏：the ~ of his name from the list 他的名字在名单上的漏列

omit /əˈmɪt/ *vt.* (omitted; omitting) 遗漏；省略：This sentence may be ~ted. 这句可以省略。

on /ɒn/ Ⅰ *prep.* ❶在……之上(表示所处位置)：pictures ~ the wall 墙上的画 ❷在(表示时间)：~ National Day 在国庆节/ ~ Monday 在星期一 ❸关于；论及：the speech ~ international affairs 关于国际形势的演讲 ❹接近；靠近：a town ~ the coast 海边的一个城镇 / ~ my right (left)在我右(左)边 ❺进行中(表示状态的保持)：~ business 因公；有事 / ~ holiday 度假 / ~ the tour 在旅行/ ~ the way 在途中 Ⅱ *adv.* 向前；继续：Go ~ with your story. 把你的故事讲下去。The sports meet is still ~. 运动会还在进行。

once /wʌns/ Ⅰ *adv.* 一次，一度；从前：He goes to see his parents ~ a month. 他每月去看他父母一次。/ ~ **more (again)** 再一次：You should try to do it ~ more (again). 你应该再试做一次。~ **and again** 一再：He has been told ~ and again not to slam the door. 他一再被叮嘱不得将门砰的一下关上。~ **in a while** 有时；偶尔：Once in a while he goes with us to the movies on Saturday night. 他偶尔在星期六晚上同我们一道去看电影。~ **upon a time** 从前(用于故事开头)：Once upon a time there was a giant with two heads. 从前有个双头巨人。**all at** ~ 突然：All at ~ we heard a loud noise. 猛然，我们听到一声巨响。**at** ~ ①马上；立刻：She told him to leave the room at ~. 她叫他立刻离开那房间。②同时：Don't speak at ~. 不要同时说。Ⅱ *conj.* 如果；一旦；每当：Once you cross the river you are safe. 一旦渡过了河，你便安全了。

one /wʌn/ Ⅰ *num.* 一；一个 Ⅱ *pron.* 任何人；任何东西：One must love one's country. 任何人都必须爱国。Ⅲ *adj.* (任何)一个的；某一个的：They share ~ bike. 他们共用一辆自行车。

oneself /wʌnˈself/ *pron.* 自己；自身；亲自 (one 的反身代词)：She used to sit by herself and read. 她从前常常独自坐着看书。

onion /ˈʌnjən/ *n.* [C]洋葱

only /ˈəʊnli/ Ⅰ *adv.* 只，仅仅，不过：Ladies ~. 女士专用。/ We can ~ tell you what we know. 我们只能告诉你我们知道的事情。Ⅱ *adj.* 唯一的；最佳的：an ~ son 独子 / This is the ~ example John can give you. 这是约翰能给你的唯一例子。/ He is the ~ man for the position. 他是这个职位的唯一人选。

onto /ˈɒntə/ *prep.* (= on to)到……上面：The cat jumped ~ the table. 猫跳到了桌上。

open /ˈəʊpən/ Ⅰ *v.* 打开；开始：School ~s in September. 学校在 9 月开学。Ⅱ *adj.* 开着的；公共的；开放的：~ to the public 对公众开放的 / ~ to traffic 通车 / The bank is ~ at eight. 银行 8 点开门营业。/ an ~ competition (championship, scholarship) 公开赛(公开锦标赛，公开奖学金)/ The letter is torn ~. 信被撕开。派 openly *adv.*

opening /ˈəʊp(ə)nɪŋ/ *n.* ❶开始；开口：

~ ceremony 开幕式，开学典礼，通车典礼 / ~ speech 开幕词 / ~ time(营业)开始时间；开放时间 ❷洞；孔 ❸就业机会，空缺

opera / ˈɒprə / *n.* 歌剧；歌剧艺术

operable / ˈɒpərəbəl/ *adj.* ❶可操作的，可运作的：an ~ motor 可以转动的电动机 / ~ in daylight 可在日光下操作的 ❷可实施的，可行的：an ~ plan 可以实施的计划

operate /ˈɒpəreɪt / *v.* ❶(使)运转；操作：~ a machine 操作机器 ❷起作用：The medicine ~d quickly. 药很快起作用了。❸管理；经营 ❹动手术；开刀：This famous doctor has ~d on many important people. 这个著名的医生给许多重要人物动过手术。

operation / ˌɒpəˈreɪʃən/ *n.* ❶[U]操作；运作；操作方法；运行方式：maintain proper engine ~ 使发动机保持良好的工作状态 / schemes in ~ 正在实施的计划 ❷[C]外科手术：a major (minor, routine) ~一个大(小，常规)手术 ❸[C]企业，公司；营业，业务；经营活动；经营方式：a huge multinational electronics ~ 一个庞大的跨国电子公司 / a large-scale farming ~ 一大型牧场业 ❹[C]运算

operator / ˈɒpəreɪtə(r) / *n.* [C]操作人员；(电话)接线员

opinion / əˈpɪnjən / *n.* 意见；评价/ **in one's ~** 据某人看来：In my ~, you'd better wait one more day. 依我所见，你最好再多等一天。**have a good (high, low, poor) ~ of sb. (sth.)** 对某人(某事)给予好的(高的、低的、坏的)评价

opponent / əˈpəʊnənt / *n.* [C] ❶对手，敌人：a worthy ~势均力敌的对手/beat an ~ at an election 在选举中击败对手 ❷反对者：a fierce ~ of nuclear arms 核武器的强烈反对者

opportunity / ˌɒpəˈtjuːnəti / *n.* 机会；时机：have few opportunities of meeting interesting people 遇到有趣的人的机会不多 / have no (little, not much) ~ of hearing good music 没有(很少有，没有许多)机会听到好的音乐

oppose / əˈpəʊz / *vt.* 反对；拒绝：~ a new plan 反对新计划/**be ~d to** 与……相反，与……对立：I'm strongly ~d to your suggestion. 我坚决反对你的建议。

opposite / ˈɒpəzɪt / Ⅰ *adj.* ❶(位置)对面的，相对的 ❷完全不同的；相反的：~ directions 相反的方向 Ⅱ *n.* 相反的词；相对的事物：I thought quite the ~. 我想的刚好相反。/ "High" is the ~ of "low". "高"是"低"的反义词。Ⅲ *prep.* 在……对面：sit ~ each other 彼此相对而坐

opposition / ˌɒpəˈzɪʃn / *n.* ❶[U]反对，对抗：a great deal of ~ to the war 对战争的强烈反对/In spite of his ~, he respected his son's point of view. 他尽管反对，但还是尊重他儿子的观点。❷[C]对手；(政党等中的)反对派：protests from the ~反对派提出的抗议/She wanted to know the ~ before signing the contract. 她想先了解一下对手的情况再签订合同。

oppress / əˈpres / *vt.* ❶压迫；对……进行残酷统治：The dictator ~ed the conquered peoples. 独裁者对臣服的民族实行残酷统治。/ The government was accused of ~ing the workers. 政府被控压迫工人。❷使忧虑，使烦恼；使消沉：be ~ed by (with) anxiety (worry, poverty) 因焦虑(担心，贫困)而感到压抑

派 oppression *n.*

opt /ɒpt/ *vi.* 选择,挑选:I ~ed for teaching as my profession. 我选择教学为职业。/ After graduation, he ~ed to study for a master's degree. 毕业后,他选择了攻读硕士学位。/~ **out (of)** 决定不参与,决定退出:You promised to help us, so please don't ~ out (of it) now. 你答应过要帮助我们,现在可不能撒手不管啊!

optical /ˈɒptɪkl/ *adj.* ❶视觉的;视力的 ❷光的;光学的

optimism /ˈɒptɪmɪzəm/ *n.* [U]乐观;乐观主义

optimistic /ˌɒptɪˈmɪstɪk/ *adj.* 乐观的;乐观主义的;无忧无虑的

option /ˈɒpʃn/ *n.* ❶[C]选择;选择的东西:Many ~s are open to them. 他们有多种选择。/We have three ~s for this term. 这学期我们可选修三门课。❷[U]选择权;选择余地,选择自由:have little ~没有多大选择余地

optional /ˈɒpʃən(ə)l/ *adj.* 可自由选择的;非强制的;(学科)选修的 派 optionally *adv.*

or /ɔː(r), ɒr/ *conj.* ❶或者:clean ~ dirty 干净或肮脏 / **either ... or ...** 或……或……:You must either tell the truth ~ say nothing. 你须实言,不然便不要开口。❷换言之,即,也就是:twelve ~ a dozen 12 个即一打 ❸否则:Hurry up ~ (else) you'll be late. 赶快,否则你会迟到。/~ **so** 大约:I'd like twenty ~ so. 我想要 20 个左右。

oral /ˈɔːrəl/ *adj.* 口头的:an ~ test 口试

orange /ˈɒrɪndʒ/ Ⅰ *n.* ❶[C] 橙子,橘子;橘树 ❷[U]橙色,橘色 Ⅱ *adj.* ❶柑橘的 ❷橙色的;橘色的

orbit /ˈɔːbɪt/ Ⅰ *n.* (天体、人造卫星等的)轨道 Ⅱ *v.* 绕轨道运行,把(人造卫星等)送入轨道

orchard /ˈɔːtʃəd/ *n.* [C] ❶果园:a cherry ~ 樱桃园 ❷果(树)林

orchestra /ˈɔːkɪstrə/ *n.* [C]管弦乐队:The ~ was playing in the hall last week. 乐团曾于上周在这个大厅里演出。

ordeal /ɔːˈdiːl/ *n.* [C](对人格和忍耐力等的)严峻考验;磨难,折磨:an ~ such as imprisonment or illness 诸如入狱和疾病的折磨/the ~ of divorce 离婚的痛苦经历

orchard /ˈɔːtʃəd/ *n.* [C]果园:apple ~s 苹果园

order /ˈɔːdə(r)/ Ⅰ *n.* [C] ❶命令:give ~s 下命令 ❷次序;顺序:list in alphabetical ~ 按字母顺序列出/ **in ~ of ...** 照……排列:in ~ of size (importance) 依大小(重要)次序排列 ❸有规则的状况:in good (bad) ~ 整齐(不整齐);工作情况良好(不佳) ❹秩序:It is the business of the police to keep ~. 维持秩序(治安)是警察的事。❺订购;订单;订货;待交付的货:an ~ for two tons of coal 两吨煤的订单 ❻目的;意向 / **in ~ to** 为了,以便:We started early in ~ to arrive before dark. 我们很早出发,以便天黑前到达。**in ~ that** 为了,以便:In ~ that every student might understand it, the teacher explained the passage again and again. 为了使每个学生都能明白,教师一遍又一遍地讲那篇文章。Ⅱ *vt.* 命令;订购:The doctor ~ed me to (stay in) bed. 医生吩咐我卧床休息。I've ~ed lunch for 12:30. 我已经订了十二点半的午餐。

orderly /ˈɔːdəli/ *adj.* ❶井井有条的，整齐的：an ~ office 收拾得整整齐齐的办公室 / an ~ mind 条理分明的思维 ❷守纪律的；守秩序的：an ~ crowd 秩序井然的人群 / in an ~ manner 有秩序地

ordinal /ˈɔːdɪnəl/ Ⅰ *n.* [C]序数（词） Ⅱ *adj.* 序数（词）的；次序的，顺序的

ordinary /ˈɔːdnəri/ *adj.* 正常的；通常的；普通的：an ~-looking girl 相貌平常的女孩 / in ~ dress 穿着平常的衣服

ore /ɔː(r)/ *n.* 矿石；矿物

organ /ˈɔːgən/ *n.* [C] ❶（动植物的）器官 ❷机关；机构 ❸风琴

organic /ɔːˈgænɪk/ *adj.* ❶器官的 ❷有机的：~ life 有机生命/ ~ chemistry 有机化学

organism /ˈɔːgəˌnɪzəm/ *n.* [C] ❶生物体；有机体：simple ~s like corals 诸如珊瑚虫之类的简单生物体 / microscopic ~s 微生物 ❷有机组织（或机构等）：a large, complicated ~ 庞大而复杂的机体

organization /ˌɔːgənaɪˈzeɪʃn/ *n.* 组织：An army without good organization may be defeated easily. 缺乏良好组织的军队容易吃败仗。

organize /ˈɔːgənaɪz/ *vt.* 组织；创办：~ an army (a government, a political party) 组织军队（政府、政党） 派 organizer *n.*

Orient /ˈɔːrɪent/ *n.* (the ~)东方；亚洲

orient /ˈɔːrɪent/ *v.* ❶定位；定向：The explorer climbed a tree in order to ~ himself. 探险者爬上一棵树以确定自己的位置和方向。/ ~ed assignment 定向分配/market ~ed 以市场为导向 ❷使熟悉；使习惯：The freshman took a while to ~ himself. 该新生花了点时间熟悉新环境。

Oriental /ˌɔːrɪˈentl/ *adj.* 东方的；东方风格的；东方文明的

origin /ˈɒrɪdʒɪn/ *n.* 起源；开端；出身：~ of the quarrel 争吵的起源 / words of Latin ~ 源自拉丁文的词 / a man of humble ~ 出身卑微的人

original /əˈrɪdʒən(ə)l/ Ⅰ *adj.* 原先的；最初的；创举的：an ~ plan 原先的计划 / an ~ idea 创见 / an ~ design 别出心裁的设计 Ⅱ *n.* [C]原作；原文；原物

originally /əˈrɪdʒɪnəli/ *adv.* ❶最初，原先：The family ~ came from France. 那个家族最初来自法国。/ It was ~ conceived as a biography, but became a novel. 它最初被构思为一部传记，但后来又被改成了一部小说。❷独创地；崭新地：a very ~ written play 一本十分新颖独特的剧本

originate /əˈrɪdʒɪneɪt/ *vt.* ❶引起，产生：A misunderstanding ~d a quarrel. 误解引起了一场争吵。❷创设，创办；创作；发明：~ a new style of a dancing 创设一种新型的舞蹈形式 —*vi.* 起源，源自；产生：This film ~ in (from) a novel by Charles Dickens. 这部电影改编自查尔斯·狄更斯的一部小说。

ornament Ⅰ /ˈɔːnəmənt/ *n.* ❶[C]装饰品，饰物：glass ~s 玻璃饰品 ❷[C]增添光彩的人（或事物）（与 to 连用）：She has become an ~ to the company. 她已成了公司引以为荣的人。❸[U]装饰，修饰：add something by way of ~ 增添一些饰物 Ⅱ /ˈɔːnəˌment/ *vt.* ❶装饰；美化：~ the dress with lace 用饰带镶衣服 /~ a Christmas tree 装点圣诞树 ❷为……增光添彩：Several famous scientists ~d the university a great deal. 几

位知名科学家为这所大学增添了光彩。
派 ornamentation *n.*

orphan /ˈɔːfn/ *n.* [C]孤儿

other /ˈʌðə(r)/ Ⅰ *pron.* 其他的人或物;别的人或事:Thirty of them are boys. The ~s are girls. 他们中30个是男孩,其余的是女孩。/**at ~ times** 平时,在其他时候 **every ~ day** (**week,year**)每隔一天(一周、一年) **in ~ words** 换句话说 **one after the ~** (=one after another)一个接一个地,相继地:They were examined one after the ~. 他们一个一个地被检查。Ⅱ *adj.* 其他的:**on the ~ hand** 另一方面(多用在 on the one hand 之后):It's cheap, but on the ~ hand, the quality is poor. 它很便宜,但另一方面,质量很差。**the ~ day** 几天前:I saw him the ~ day. 我几天前看见过他。

otherwise /ˈʌðəwaɪz/ Ⅰ *adv.* 不同样地;除此以外 Ⅱ *conj.* 否则;不然:Put on your raincoat, ~ you will get wet. 穿上雨衣,否则你就要淋湿了。

ouch /aʊtʃ/ *int.* ❶(表示突然剧痛)哎哟 ❷(表示愤怒或不悦)哎

ought /ɔːt/ *aux. v.* (后接带 to 的不定式)应该,应当(表示责任、义务):Such things ~ not to be done. 这样的事不应该做。

ounce /aʊns/ *n.* [C] ❶(英制重量单位)盎司(=28.3495克) ❷一点,少量:He hasn't an ~ of common sense. 他一点常识都没有。

our /ˈaʊə(r)/ *pron.* 我们的(形容词性物主代词):We have done ~ share. 我们已经做了我们的那一份。

ours /ˈaʊəz/ *pron.* 我们的(名词性物主代词):The house is ~. 这房子是我们的。

ourselves /ɑːˈselvz/ *pron.* 我们自己(反身代词):We'd better go and see them ~. 我们最好亲自去见他们。

out /aʊt/ *adv.* 出;在外:go ~ for a walk 出外散步 / He walked ~ of the office. 他走出办公室。/ ~ **of breath** 上气不接下气:After he finished the long race, he was ~ of breath. 长跑过后,他累得上气不接下气了。**~-of-date** 旧式的;过时的:She will not wear ~-of-date dress. 她不会穿过时的衣服。~ **of work** 失业:When his father was ~ of work, he left school. 他父亲失业后,他就退学了。

outbreak /ˈaʊtbreɪk/ *n.* [C] ❶(情感、战争、反叛等的)突然爆发:an ~ of rioting (war, hostilities) 骚乱(战争,敌视)的突然爆发 ❷(疾病等的)突然发生(或发作):an ~ of disease 疾病的突发

outburst /ˈaʊtbɜːst/ *n.* [C] ❶(情感等的)突然爆发,迸发:an ~ of laughter 放声大笑 ❷(行动、力量等的)突然出现:~ of machine gun fire 机枪的猛射 ❸(火山的)喷发;(烟雾、蒸汽的)外冒:volcanic ~火山喷发/an ~ of steam from the pressure-cooker 高压锅中蒸汽的外冒

outcome /ˈaʊtkʌm/ *n.* [C]结果

outdated /ˌaʊtˈdeɪtɪd/ *adj.* 过时的;旧式的;不再流行的

outdo /aʊtˈduː/ *vt.* (—did /-ˈdɪd/, —done /-ˈdʌn/)在……干得更出色;优于,超过:He worked very hard as he did not want to be outdone by anyone. 他干活非常卖力,因为他不想别人超过他。/The wedding outdid any of the lavish festivities that Marcos family had hosted in the past. 婚礼远远超过马科斯家族以往举行的任何一次奢华的

宴会。

outdoor /ˈaʊtdɔː(r)/ *adj.* 户外的；野外的

outdoors /ˌaʊtˈdɔːz/ *adv.* 在户外；在野外

outer /ˈaʊtə(r)/ *adj.* 外的；外部的：a journey to ~ space 太空旅行 / the ~ walls 外墙

outgoing /ˈaʊtˌɡəʊɪŋ/ *adj.* ❶友好的；性格开朗的；善于交际的：an ~ personality 开朗的性格/an ~ hostess 一位热情好客的女主人 ❷即将退休的，即将离任的：the ~ government 任期将满的政府 ❸外出的，离去的：~ phone calls 外线电话/an ~ ship 出航的船只

outing /ˈaʊtɪŋ/ *n.* [C]外出度假；郊游

outlaw /ˈaʊtlɔː/ *n.* [C]逃犯；亡命之徒

outlet /ˈaʊtlet/ *n.* [C] ❶出口；出路 ❷发泄方法；排泄 ❸电源插座

outline /ˈaʊtlaɪn/ Ⅰ *n.* [C] ❶外形；轮廓：an ~ map of Great Britain 英国的轮廓图 ❷要点；大纲；提纲：an ~ for a lecture 一篇演讲提纲 Ⅱ *v.* 画……的轮廓；打草图；概述；概括：~ the American Civil War 略述美国的南北战争

outlook /ˈaʊtlʊk/ *n.* [C] ❶展望；远景 ❷眼界；观点；看法：broaden (narrow) one's ~ 扩大(缩小)视野 / optimistic (pessimistic) ~乐观(悲观)看法

output /ˈaʊtpʊt/ *n.* 产量：the ~ of a gold mine 金矿的产量

outright Ⅰ /aʊtˈraɪt/ *adv.* ❶完全地，彻底地：dismiss the information ~对这些消息完全不予理会 ❷公开地，公然地；毫无保留地；直截了当地：say ~ what one means 直接说出想说的话 ❸立刻，马上；当场地：Ten were killed ~. 有10人当场被杀。Ⅱ /ˈaʊtraɪt/ *adj.* ❶完全的，彻底的，十足的：~ condemnation of the film 对这部电影的全面抨击 ❷公开的，公然的；毫无保留的；直截了当的：an ~ denial 断然否认

outset /ˈaʊtset/ *n.* [C]开始，开端：at the outset(of) 在……开始时/from the ~ (of)从……起

outside /ˌaʊtˈsaɪd/ Ⅰ *n.* 外面；外部：The ~ of the house needs painting. 房子外部需要刷油漆。Ⅱ *adj.* 外面的：an ~ seat 露天座位 Ⅲ *adv.* 在外面：The car is waiting ~. 车子在外面等着。Ⅳ *prep.* 在……外面：~ the house 在屋子外面

outsider /ˌaʊtˈsaɪdə(r)/ *n.* [C]组织之外的人；局外人：The ~s see the best (most) of the game. 旁观者清。

outskirt /ˈaʊtskɜːt/ *n.* [C](常用 *pl.*)郊区；郊外；边缘

outstanding /aʊtˈstændɪŋ/ *adj.* 显著的；引人注意的：an ~ person 杰出的人

outstretch /ˈaʊtstretʃ, aʊtˈstretʃ/ *vt.* ❶前伸，向外伸出，张开(尤指手或手臂)：~ one's hand in welcome 伸手以示欢迎 ❷(范围、程度)超过：His behaviour ~ed my patience. 我已无法容忍他的行为。

outstrip /ˌaʊtˈstrɪp/ *vt.* (-stripped;-stripping) ❶比……跑得快，把……甩在后面：He far ~ped the other runners on the last lap. 他在最后一圈中把其他选手远远地甩在了身后。❷(在数量方面)比……多：Last year export growth of electronic equipment far ~ped import growth. 去年电子设备的出口增长远远高于进口。❸(在能力等方面)胜过，比……更出色：~ one's competitors in selling computers 在计算机销售方面比竞争对手干得出色

outward(s) /ˈaʊtwəd/ Ⅰ *adj.* ❶在外面的：an ~ room 外屋 ❷朝外的，向外

的:an ~ flow 外流/an ~ road 一条通向外面的道路 ❸(船只等)驶向外面(或外地)的;(旅行等)到外地的:an ~ journey 去外地的旅行 ❹外界的,外部的:Outward influences affected her deeply. 外界影响对她起了巨大的作用。❺外表的;表面的:~ appearances 外表 Ⅱ *adv.* ❶向外:This door opens ~. 这扇门向外开。❷朝着外部世界地:His country needed to look ~. 他的国家应该放眼世界。

oval /ˈəʊv(ə)l/ Ⅰ *adj.* 卵形的;椭圆形的:an ~ face 一张鸭蛋形(瓜子)脸/The mirror is ~. 镜子呈椭圆形。Ⅱ *n.* [C]卵形(物);椭圆形(物)

oven /ˈʌvn/ *n.* [C]炉,灶;烤炉,烤箱:electric (gas, microwave) ~ 电(煤气、微波)炉

over /ˈəʊvə(r)/ Ⅰ *adv.* ❶在那边;在另一边:~ there 在那边 ❷自始至终:read it ~ 通读一遍 ❸太,过分地(主要与形容词和副词构成复合词):~ anxious 太焦急的,过于忧虑的/ ~ polite 太多礼的 ❹重复地:~ **and** ~(**again**) 一再地,许多次:I've warned you ~ and ~ again not to do that. 我已一再警告你不要做那件事。Ⅱ *prep.* ❶在上方(未接触的);穿过:The sky is ~ our heads. 天空在我们的头顶上。❷在……上面:He spread his handkerchief ~ his face to keep the flies off. 他把手帕盖在脸上以避开苍蝇。❸遍及……的各部分:He is famous all ~ the world. 他是全世界闻名的人。❹超过:He spoke for ~ an hour. 他讲了一个多钟头。❺直到……过后:Can you stay ~ Sunday? 你能待在这儿过星期日吗? Ⅲ *adj.* 结束的;完的:Class is ~ 下课了。

overall /ˌəʊvərˈɔːl/ Ⅰ *adj.* 全面的;综合的 Ⅱ *n.* (*pl.*)工装裤

overcharge Ⅰ/ˌəʊvəˈtʃɑːdʒ/ *vt.* ❶向(某人)过高收费;高于正常价格收取(钱款):The taxi-driver was fined for overcharging his customers. 出租车驾驶员因宰客而被罚款。❷使(枪、炮等)装弹过多;使超重 Ⅱ/ˈəʊvəˌtʃɑːdʒ/ *n.* [C]过高的开价,超标准的收费:make an ~ on an article 对某件商品超标准收费

overcoat /ˈəʊvəkəʊt/ *n.* [C]大衣;外套

overcome /ˌəʊvəˈkʌm/ *vt.* (overcame /ˈkeɪm/, overcome) 胜过;压倒;克服:~ bad habits 改掉恶习 / ~ difficulties 克服困难 / ~ prejudices 消除成见

overdo /ˌəʊvəˈduː/ *vt.* (-did /-ˈdɪd/, -done /-ˈdʌn/;第三人称单数现在式-does /-ˈdʌz/) ❶过分做(某事);过分强调,过于夸大:~ dieting 过于节食 / He overdid the sympathy. 他的怜悯之情显得太做作了。❷过度使用:~ pepper in the soup 在汤中放入过量的胡椒 ❸将……表演得过火:~ the love scenes in the play 过火地表演剧中的爱情场面 ❹将……烤得太老(或太久);将……煮得太烂(或太久):The bread is overdone. 面包烤老了。

overflow /ˌəʊvəˈfləʊ/ *v.* 溢出;泛滥:The milk is ~ing the cup. 牛奶从杯中溢出。

overhead /ˌəʊvəˈhed/ Ⅰ *adv.* 在头顶上;在空中:the stars ~ 天上的星星 Ⅱ *adj.* 在头顶上的:an ~ bridge 天桥 / an ~ light 吊灯

overhear /ˌəʊvəˈhɪə(r)/ *vt.* (overheard /ˌəʊvəˈhɜːd/, overheard) 偶然听到;从旁听到

overlap /ˌəʊvəˈlæp/ *v.* (-lapped;-lapping)(与……)重叠;(与……)部分同时发生

overlook /ˌəʊvəˈlʊk/ *vt.* ❶俯瞰;眺望:From the house on the hillside, we can ~ the whole harbour. 我们能从山腰的房子里俯瞰港口的全景。❷忽视;漏看:~ a printer's error 看漏一个排字错误

overnight /ˌəʊvəˈnaɪt/ Ⅰ *adv.* 一夜间;一下子;整夜地 Ⅱ *adj.* 一整夜的;过一夜的

overrate /ˈəʊvəˌreɪt/ *vt.* 过高评价(或估计):He ~d his ability. 他过高地估计了自己的能力。/Her beauty is ~d. 她没有评价的那么美貌。

overseas /ˌəʊvəˈsiːz/ *adj.* 海外的:~ trade 海外贸易 / ~ Chinese 华侨

oversight /ˈəʊvəˌsaɪt/ *n.* ❶疏忽;忽视:Due to an ~, we have not paid the bill. 我们因一时疏忽,至今还未付清账单。/It was ~ that caused the accident. 正是疏忽大意造成了这次事故。❷[C]错误,失误;漏洞:My bank statement it full of ~s. 我的银行结算单中错误百出。❸[U]监督,监管;照料,照看:Under the ~ of a nurse, the patient made a remarkable recovery. 在护士的悉心照料下,病人的情况有了明显的好转。

overstep /ˌəʊvəˈstep/ *vt.* (-stepped; -stepping)超越(范围、界限等):the language that ~s the limits fo what ought to be allowed on television 超出了电视上所允许使用范畴的语言/He ~ped his authority when he ordered the prisoner to he released. 他越权下达命令将罪犯释放。

overtake /ˌəʊvəˈteɪk/ *vt.* (overtook /ˌəʊvəˈtʊk/, overtaken /ˌəʊvəˈteɪkən/) ❶追上,赶上,超过 ❷袭击;压倒

overthrow /ˌəʊvəˈθrəʊ/ Ⅰ *vt.* (overthrew /ˌəʊvəˈθruː/, overthrown /ˌəʊvəˈθrəʊn/) 推翻;颠覆:The president was ~n in a military coup. 总统在军事政变中被赶下台。Ⅱ *n.* 推翻;颠覆

overtime /ˈəʊvəˌtaɪm/ Ⅰ *n.* [U] ❶加班加点:He did four hour's ~ yesterday. 昨天他加了四小时的班。/He's on ~ tonight. 他今晚加班。❷加班费;加班时间:pay ~支付加班费 ❸加时赛(指规定时间后为决胜负而延长的时间) Ⅱ *adv.* 超时(工作)地;加班地:The staff have to work ~. 职员们必须要加班加点地工作。

overturn /ˌəʊvəˈtɜːn/ *v.* (使)颠覆;推翻:The earthquake ~ed the houses. 地震使房屋倾覆。

overwhelm /ˌəʊvəˈwelm/ *vt.* 压倒;战胜;征服:The French side was ~ed 3-0 by Italy. 意大利队以 3 比 0 轻取法国队。

overwhelming /ˌəʊvəˈwelmɪŋ/ *adj.* 压倒的;势不可挡的:an ~ majority 压倒性多数

owe /əʊ/ *v.* 欠;应归功于;应感激:We ~ a great deal to our parents and teachers. 我们得大大感激父母及师长。

owing /ˈəʊɪŋ/ *adj.* 欠着的;未付的;未给予的:~ **to** 因为;由于:Owing to the rain they could not come. 因为下雨,他们不能来。

owl /aʊl/ *n.* [C]猫头鹰

own /əʊn/ Ⅰ *adj.* 自己的(用在形容词性物主代词后):I saw it with my ~ eyes. 我亲眼看到的。Ⅱ *v.* 拥有;所有:He ~s much money. 他有许多钱。派 owner *n.*

ownership /ˈəʊnəʃɪp/ *n.* [U]所有权;物主身份:collective (individual) ~ 集体(个人)所有制 / private (public) ~ 私

有(公有)制

ox / ɒks / *n.* [C] (*pl.* oxen /ˈɒksən /) ❶(总称)牛❷公牛

oxide / ˈɒksaɪd / *n.* [C]氧化物

oxygen / ˈɒksɪdʒən / *n.* [U]氧;氧气

ozone / ˈəʊzəʊn / *n.* [U]臭氧:~ layer 臭氧层

P p

pace /peɪs/ Ⅰ *n.* [C]一步(走或跑一步的距离);(走或跑的)速度 / **keep ~ with** 与……步调一致,跟……同速前进:Scientists have to work hard to keep ~ with new development of modern science. 科学家必须努力工作以赶上现代科学的新发展。**at a good ~**快速地;相当快地:Economy of China is developing at a good ~. 中国的经济正高速发展。**set (make) the ~** 领先;树立榜样 Ⅱ *v.* 踱步:~ back and forth 来回踱步

Pacific /pəˈsɪfɪk/ *adj.* 太平洋的:the ~ Ocean 太平洋

P

pacific /pəˈsɪfɪk/ *adj.* ❶平静的,宁静的:a ~ tone of voice 平静的语调 ❷求和的,和解的;爱和平的:~ views 期望和平的主张

pacify /ˈpæsɪˌfaɪ/ *vt.* ❶安抚,使安静,使平静;平息(怒气、纷争等):~ the passengers in a railway accident 安抚火车事故中的乘客 / The babysitter tried to ~ the crying baby. 保姆想让哭闹的婴儿安静下来。❷使(国家或地区)实现和平:~ the conflicting area 使发生冲突的地区恢复安宁 派 pacification *n.*

pack /pæk/ Ⅰ *n.* [C]包;包裹:a ~ of cigarettes 一包香烟 Ⅱ *v.* 打包;包装:Have you ~ed your things? 你的东西装好了没有?

package /ˈpækɪdʒ/ *n.* [C]包;包裹

packet /ˈpækɪt/ *n.* [C]小包;小盒;小捆:a ~ of letters 一捆信件 / a ~ of 20 cigarettes 一包 20 支装的香烟

packing /ˈpækɪŋ/ *n.* [U]包装;包装用品;填料

pad /pæd/ Ⅰ *n.* [C] ❶垫;衬垫 ❷便签本 Ⅱ *vt.* (padded;padding) 填塞;填充:~ded clothes 棉衣

paddle /ˈpædl/ Ⅰ *n.* [C]桨:He rowed a boat with ~s. 他用桨划船。Ⅱ *v.* 划船运送;划桨

page /peɪdʒ/ *n.* [C]页:continue on ~ 15 下接第十五页/turn to ~ 15 翻到第十五页/ Open your books at ~8. 请打开书,翻到第八页。

pail /peɪl/ *n.* [C]桶;提桶

pain /peɪn/ *n.* ❶疼痛:Does she feel any ~? 她感到疼痛吗? ❷(*pl.*) 努力;费力;辛苦 / **No ~s, no gains.** 不劳无获。**at ~s** 尽力;用心;下苦功:He is at ~s to find out the truth. 他正尽力了解事实真相。**take ~s** 尽力;努力;下苦功:We took ~s to finish the work in time. 我们努力按时完成任务。

painful /ˈpeɪnf(ə)l/ *adj.* ❶疼痛的;痛苦的:Such a thing is ~ to him. 这样的事对他来说是很痛苦的。❷费力的;费心的;困难的:They have many ~ problems to solve. 他们有不少棘手的问题要解决。❸麻烦的;令人不快的:It is ~

to see him make mistakes. 看到他犯错误，真令人心痛。派 painfully *adv.*

painless /ˈpeɪnlɪs/ *adj.* ❶不疼的，无痛的：~ laser treatment 无痛激光治疗 ❷(口语)容易的，不麻烦的，不费力的：a ~ solution 毫不费力的解决办法 派 painlessly *adv*

painstaking /ˈpeɪnzteɪkɪŋ/ *adj.* 费力的；苦干的：He made ~ efforts to learn English. 他下苦功学英语。

paint /peɪnt/ Ⅰ *n.* [U]油漆；涂料 Ⅱ *v.* ❶漆：I'm going to ~ the desk yellow. 我打算把书桌漆成黄色。❷绘画：She ~s well. 她画得好。派 painter *n.*

painting /ˈpeɪntɪŋ/ *n.* ❶[C] 油画；水彩画 ❷[U]绘画；绘画艺术 ❸[U] 油漆

pair /peə(r)/ Ⅰ *n.* [C] ❶(一)双；(一)对；(一)副；(一)把：a ~ of shoes 一双鞋 / a ~ of trousers 一条裤子 ❷一对夫妇；一对情侣 Ⅱ *v.*(使)成对；配对

pal /pæl/ *n.* [C]朋友，伙伴，同志：my best ~我最好的朋友

palace /ˈpæləs/ *n.* [C]皇宫；宫殿；(供娱乐的)大厦：the Summer Palace 颐和园 / the Children's Palace 少年宫

pale /peɪl/ *adj.* ❶(人的脸色)苍白的，没有血色的：You are looking ~ today. 你今天脸色苍白。❷(颜色)暗淡的；浅淡的：~ blue 淡蓝色

pall /pɔːl/ *n.* [C] ❶(阴暗的)覆盖物，笼罩物：a ~ of clouds 一片乌云/A ~ of smoke hung over the site of the explosion. 一团烟雾笼罩在爆炸现场上空。❷阴郁，忧愁；神秘感：The scandal cast a deep ~ of gloom over the election. 那件丑闻为大选蒙上了一层厚厚的阴影。

palm /pɑːm/ *n.* [C] ❶手掌，(手)掌心：sweaty ~s 出汗的掌心/ **in the ~ of sb.'s hand** 完全受制于某人的，在某人手掌之中的：He's got the whole committee in the ~ of his hand. 他已完全控制了整个委员会。❷棕榈树

pamphlet /ˈpæmflət/ *n.* [C]小册子

pan /pæn/ *n.* [C]平底锅；盘子

pancake /ˈpænkeɪk/ *n.* [C]薄煎饼：a baked ~ 烙饼

panda /ˈpændə/ *n.* [C]熊猫：We like ~s very much. 我们非常喜欢熊猫。

pandemic /pænˈdemɪk/ Ⅰ *adj.* (疾病)大流行的，四处蔓延的：The disease appeared in ~ form. 这种病是以流行的方式出现的。Ⅱ *n.* [C]大流行病

panel /ˈpænəl/ *n.* [C] ❶(通常为长方形的)墙板；门板；窗格 ❷控制板；配电盘；仪表板；油画板：paint pictures on a ~在画板上画油画 ❸专家小组；讨论小组：a ~ of educators 教育家顾问小组 ❹陪审员名单；陪审团：a three-judge ~ 三人陪审团

panic /ˈpænɪk/ *n.* (常用单数)恐慌；惊慌 / **fall(get) into a ~** 陷入恐慌之中：She fell into a ~ at the news. 她一听到那个消息就惊恐起来。

pant /pænt/ Ⅰ*vi.* ❶急促地喘气：She ~ed up the stairs. 她气喘吁吁地跑上楼梯。❷想要，渴望(与 for 连用)：~ for love 渴望爱情 —*vt.* 呼吸急促地说：The policeman ~ed his apology and ran on. 那个警察气喘吁吁地说了声抱歉就又往前跑。Ⅱ *n.* [C] (急促的)喘息，喘气：breathe in rapid and shallow ~s 急速、短促地呼吸

pants /pænts/ *n.* ❶(英)男衬裤；内裤 ❷裤子，长裤；女式长裤，(女式)宽松休闲裤

paper /ˈpeɪpə(r)/ Ⅰ *n.* ❶[U]纸：a

sheet of ~ 一张纸 / a ~ bag 一个纸袋 / blank ~ 空白纸 / exam ~ 考卷 / toilet ~ 卫生纸 / waste ~ 废纸 ❷[C]报纸 ❸[C]卷：The teacher set us an English ~. 老师给我们出了一张英语试卷。❹[C]论文：a ~ on economy reform 一篇关于经济改革的论文 ❺[C]票据 Ⅱ *vt.* 用纸包装

parachute /ˈpærəʃuːt/ *n.* [C]降落伞：~ jumping 跳伞

parachutist /ˈpærəʃuːtɪst/ *n.* [C]跳伞者；伞兵

parade /pəˈreɪd/ Ⅰ *v.* 游行：The performers ~d the streets. 表演者游行于街道中。Ⅱ *n.* [C]游行：hold a ~ 举行游行

paradise /ˈpærədaɪs/ *n.* 天堂；乐土

paragon /ˈpærəgən/ *n.* [C] 杰出代表，典范，楷模：a ~ of democracy 民主的典范 / a ~ among soldiers 士兵中的杰出代表

paragraph /ˈpærəgrɑːf/ *n.* [C]段；节

parallel /ˈpærəlel/ Ⅰ *adj.* ❶平行的：Draw two ~ lines here. 在这儿画两条平行线。❷类似的；相对应的：My idea is ~ to (with) yours. 我的意见和你的相似。❸(电路)并联的：You may make a ~ connection here. 你可以在这里做电路并联。Ⅱ *n.* [C] ❶ 平行线；平行面 ❷可相比拟的事物；相似处：have (know) no ~ 举世无双；无与伦比/ without ~ in history 史无前例

parallelogram /ˌpærəˈleləʊˌgræm/ *n.* [C]平行四边形

parameter /pəˈræmɪtə(r)/ *n.* [C]❶参(变)数，参(变)量 ❷限定因素，参数；特点，特征；界限，范围：keep within the ~s of the discussion 限制在这次讨论的范围之内

paraphrase /ˈpærəˌfreɪz/ Ⅰ *n.* [C]重新阐述，意译：make a ~ of an English proverb 释译英语谚语 Ⅱ *vt.* 重新阐述，释义：~ the passage in modern Chinese 用现代汉语将这个段落重新阐述一下

parcel /ˈpɑːsl/ Ⅰ *n.* [C]包裹；小包 / **by ~** 用邮包：Mother sent me a lot of clothes by ~. 妈妈用邮包给我寄了许多衣服。Ⅱ *vt.* (-celled;-celling) ❶分；分配：~ **sth. out** 把某物分开；把某物(在几个人之间)分：The land was ~led out into small lots. 这块地被分成了若干小块。❷做成包裹

pardon /ˈpɑːdn/ Ⅰ *n.* 原谅；宽恕：I beg your ~. 请原谅。(礼貌地表示不同意别人的说法或没听清楚、没理解别人说的话，希望别人重复时的用语) Ⅱ *v.* 宽恕；原谅：Pardon my impatience, but I have to catch a train. 原谅我的性急，我必须赶上火车。

parent /ˈpeərənt/ *n.* [C]父亲；母亲

parentage /ˈpeərəntɪdʒ/ *n.* [U] ❶家系，家族，血统；出身，门第：a girl of mixed American and Chinese ~ 中美混血的女孩 ❷起源，来源：be of different ~ 来源不一

parental/pəˈrentl/ *adj.* 父母的

park /pɑːk/ Ⅰ *n.* [C] ❶公园：amusement ~ 游乐园 / zoological ~ 动物园 ❷停车场：There is a ~ near the shop. 商店附近有一个停车场。Ⅱ *v.* 停放(车辆等)：No ~ing here! 此处不准停车！

parliament /ˈpɑːləmənt/ *n.* ❶[U]英国议会；议会两院；下议院 ❷[C](其他国家的)议会；国会：dissolve ~ 解散议会

parrot /ˈpærət/ Ⅰ *n.* [C] ❶鹦鹉 ❷鹦鹉学舌者，人云亦云者；机械模仿者 Ⅱ *vt.*

(鹦鹉学舌般)机械重复(或模仿):Don't just ~ anything that she says. 别只是她说什么你说什么。

part /pɑːt/ Ⅰ*n.* [C] ❶部分:Only (a) ~ of his story is true. 他的故事只有一部分是真的。❷任务;职责;本分 ❸(剧中的)角色 ❹零件:Have you any spare ~s of this machine? 你有这台机器的备用零件吗? ❺(争论、交易等中的)一方 ❻地区;区域:They come from all ~s of the country. 他们来自全国各地。/ **act (play) a ~(in)**扮演角色;起作用:She asked to act a ~ in the TV series.. 她要求在电视剧中扮演一个角色。**do one's ~**尽本分:Whatever happens, I will do my ~. 无论发生什么事情,我都要尽我的本分。**in ~**部分地;在某种程度上 **take ~ in** 参加:He asked how many of you were going to take ~ in this maths contest. 他问你们有多少人打算参加这次数学竞赛。**take the ~ of** 与……站在一边;袒护;支持:He took the ~ of Team A. 他支持A队。Ⅱ*v.* 分离;分开:The policemen ~ed the crowd. 警察排开众人。/ **~ with** 和……分手;舍弃:He hated to ~ with his job but had to. 他不愿放弃他的工作,但又不得不放弃。派 partly *adv.*

partial /ˈpɑːʃl/ *adj.* ❶局部的;不完全的:a ~ success 部分的成功 ❷偏心的;偏袒的;不公平的:A parent should not be ~ to any of his children. 做父母的不应偏袒任何一个孩子。

participant /pɑːˈtɪsɪpənt/ *n.* [C]参加者:Each ~ will get a free ticket. 每位参加者将获得一张免费票。

participate /pɑːˈtɪsɪpeɪt/ *v.* ❶参加,参与(与 in 连用):She will ~ in our discussion tomorrow. 她将参加我们明天的讨论。❷分享,共享;分担:~ in profits 分享利润 / We'll ~ with you in your worries. 我们会与你分忧的。派 participation *n.*

particle /ˈpɑːtɪkl/ *n.* [C] ❶粒子;微粒 ❷微量:**a ~ of** 一点点;少量的:There is not a ~ of truth in what he said. 他所说的没一句实话。

particular /pəˈtɪkjələ(r)/ *adj.* 特别的;值得注意的;突出的:for no ~ reason 没有特别的理由 / **be ~ about** 对……很讲究,对……很挑剔:She is ~ about her clothes. 她对衣着很讲究。**in ~** 特别地:She loves the song in ~, because her mother used to sing it. 她特别喜欢那首歌,因为她母亲过去经常唱。

particularly /pəˈtɪkjʊləli/ *adv.* ❶尤其,特别;很,非常:be in a ~ low mood 情绪非常低落 / I like the lake, ~ in summer. 我喜欢这个湖,尤其是在夏天。❷具体地,个别地:They ~ asked for you. 他们点名要找你。❸详细地,详尽地

partisan /ˌpɑːtɪˈzæn/ *n.* [C] ❶党人;党徒 ❷游击队员

partition /pɑːˈtɪʃn/ *n.* ❶[U]划分,分开;(尤指国家或政体的)分裂,划分,分割:the ~ of profits 利润分成/the ~ of the ancient empire into several independent countries 这个古老的帝国分裂成若干独立的国家 ❷[C]隔板,隔墙;分隔物:an open-plan office with ~s between desks 办公桌用隔板隔开的敞开式办公室

partner /ˈpɑːtnə(r)/ *n.* [C] ❶合伙人;合作者 ❷(跳舞、打网球、玩纸牌等的)同伙,同伴 ❸夫;妻

partnership /ˈpɑːtnəʃɪp/ *n.* [U] 伙伴关

系;合伙关系

part-time /ˈpɑːtˌtaɪm/ *adj.* 用部分时间的;兼职的:a ~ clerk 兼职职员/I work here on a ~ basis. 我在这儿干的是兼职。

party /ˈpɑːti/ *n.* [C] ❶团体;党派,政党:the Democratic Party and the Republican Party (美国)民主党和共和党 ❷聚会;宴会:a dancing ~舞会

pascal /ˈpæskəl/ *n.* [C]帕(斯卡)(压强单位,1帕=1牛顿/米^2,略作 Pa)

pass /pɑːs/ Ⅰ *v.* ❶通过:The road was too narrow for cars to ~. 这路太窄了,车子不能通过。/ ~ **by** ①走过:He ~ed by me without greeting. 他从我身边走过而没打招呼。②忽略;不过问:I can't ~ the matter by. 我不能对此事置之不理。~ **away** 死;逝世:He ~ed away during the night. 他在晚间去世。❷度过;消磨:How shall we ~ the evening? 我们将如何消磨今晚的时间? ❸审查通过;考试及格:All of us ~ed the English examination. 我们英语考试都及格了。❹传递:Will you please ~ me that book? 请你把那本书递给我好吗? ❺(对某事或某人)表示(意见);作判决(与 upon 或 on 连用):I can't ~ an opinion on your work without seeing it. 我没看到你的作品,不能发表意见。/~ **sentence on** 判决;判刑:Before I ~ sentence on you, have you anything to say for yourself? 在我给你下判决之前,你还有什么为自己辩护的吗? Ⅱ *n.* [C] ❶考试及格:get a ~ 及格 ❷通行证;入场许可证;入场券:No one can get in the fort without a ~. 没有通行证,任何人都不能进入要塞。

passage /ˈpæsɪdʒ/ *n.* ❶[U]通过;穿过 ❷[C]通道;走道;航程 ❸[C](讲演词或文章的)一段,一节:a ~ from the Bible《圣经》中的一节

passenger /ˈpæsɪndʒə(r)/ *n.* [C]乘客

passer-by /ˌpɑːsəˈbaɪ/ *n.* [C](*pl.* passers-by)过路人

passion /ˈpæʃn/ *n.* ❶激情;热情 / **arouse (stir up) one's** ~ 激发某人的热情:A bright future aroused her ~. 美好的未来激发了她的热情。**be in a** ~在发怒;在发脾气:The boss was in a ~ then. 老板那时在发脾气。**be filled with** ~ 对……充满爱:The old man is filled with a ~ for his hometown. 老人对家乡充满了爱。❷酷爱;热爱:He tried to develop a ~ for poetry. 他努力培养对诗歌的喜爱。/ He has a ~ for football. 他酷爱足球。

passionate /ˈpæʃənət/ *adj.* 热情的;情绪激昂的

passive /ˈpæsɪv/ *adj.* ❶被动的:Your action put yourself in a ~ position. 你的行为使你自己陷入被动。❷消极的,不积极的:It is not useful to make a ~ resistance. 消极抵抗是没有用的。派 passively *adv.*

passport /ˈpɑːspɔːt/ *n.* [C]护照

password /ˈpɑːsˌwɜːd, ˈpæswɜːd/ *n.* [C]口令,密码:enter your ~输入你的口令

past /pɑːst/ Ⅰ *adj.* 过去的;已过的:for the ~ few days (weeks)过去的几天(几周) Ⅱ *n.* 过去;昔日:We cannot change the ~. 我们不能改变过去。Ⅲ *prep.*(在时间或空间上)超过;经过;在……之后:half ~ two 两点半

paste /peɪst/ Ⅰ *n.* 糨糊 Ⅱ *v.* 粘贴:~ things together 把东西贴在一起

pastime /ˈpɑːstaɪm/ *n.* [C]消遣;娱乐

pasture /ˈpɑːstʃə(r)/ *n.* [C] 牧场

P

pat /pæt/ Ⅰ *v.* (patted; patting) 轻拍，轻打：～ a dog 轻拍一条狗 / ～ **sb. on the back** 轻拍某人的背(表示赞扬或鼓励)：My brother ～ted me on the back and said, "congratulations!" 我哥哥拍着我的背说："祝贺你！" Ⅱ *n.* [C]轻拍；轻拍声

patch /pætʃ/ Ⅰ *n.* [C] ❶补片；补丁 ❷小块土地(尤指作菜地用) Ⅱ *v.* ❶ 补缀 ❷作为……的补片 ❸拼凑

patent /ˈpeɪtnt/ Ⅰ *adj.* 专利的；特许的 Ⅱ *n.* 专利；专利权：apply for a ～ 申请专利/ The factory got a ～ on (for) its products. 工厂获得了产品专利权。

paternal /pəˈtɜːnəl/ *adj.* ❶父亲的；父亲般的：～ duties 父亲的职责 ❷父亲一方的，父系的：Tom's ～ grandparents were Irish. 汤姆的祖父母是爱尔兰人。

path /pɑːθ/ *n.* [C]小路；小径 / **clear a ～ for** 为……开路；为……扫清道路：A tractor cleared the ～ for us. 一辆拖拉机为我们开路。**pave (smooth) the ～ for** 为……铺平道路：Good education will pave the ～ for you. 良好的教育将为你铺平道路。**stand in one's ～** 挡路；阻碍：Don't stand in his ～ to success. 不要阻挡他走上成功之路。**take the ～ to** 走……的道路：He took the ～ to revolution. 他走上了革命的道路。

pathetic /pəˈθetɪk/ *adj.* ❶令人同情的，可怜的；可悲的：a ～ sight 悲惨的景象 ❷可鄙的，讨厌的；差劲的：a ～ excuse 令人讨厌的借口/Sanitary conditions were ～. 卫生条件很恶劣。

patience /ˈpeɪʃns/ *n.* [U]容忍；忍耐；耐心 / **beyond one's ～** 超出某人的忍耐力 / **have ～ with (for) sb.** 对某人有耐心：The teacher has ～ with his students. 那位老师对学生很有耐心。**have the ～ to do** 有耐心做：I have the ～ to listen to your complaints. 我有耐心听你的怨言。**lose ～** 失去耐心：Don't lose ～, and you'll be successful. 不要失去信心，你会成功的。**run out of ～** 失去耐心：The conductor never runs out of ～. 那位公共汽车售票员从不失去耐心。**with ～** 耐心地：She listened to my story with ～. 她耐心地听我讲故事。

patient /ˈpeɪʃnt/ Ⅰ *adj.* 有耐心的；容忍的：Please be ～. 请耐心些。/ **be ～ in** 在……方面有耐心：She is ～ in teaching children. 她教孩子很耐心。**be ～ with sb.** 对某人有耐心：He was not ～ with the boy. 他对那男孩很不耐烦。Ⅱ *n.* [C]病人：The hospital is equipped to handle 500 ～s. 这医院的设备足以接纳 500 个病人。派 patiently *adv.*

patriot /ˈpætrɪət, ˈpeɪtrɪət/ *n.* [C]爱国者

patriotic /ˌpeɪtrɪˈɒtɪk/ *adj.* 爱国的

patriotism /ˌpætrɪətɪzəm/ *n.* [U]爱国主义

patrol /pəˈtrəʊl/ Ⅰ *n.* ❶[U]巡逻 / **on ～** 在巡逻：The policemen are out on ～. 警察在巡逻。❷[C]巡逻者，巡逻队 Ⅱ *v.* (-trolled; -trolling) 巡逻：The guards ～ the yard day and night. 卫兵在院里日夜巡逻。

patron /ˈpeɪtrən/ *n.* [C]资助人；赞助人

pattern /ˈpætn/ Ⅰ *n.* [C]模式；样式；图案：sentence ～ 句型 / new ～ of life 新的生活方式 / **after (on, upon) the ～ of** 按照……的方式；仿照…… **follow the ～** 仿效……的样式：The foreigner tried to follow the ～ of Chinese life. 那外国人试图仿效中国人的生活方式。Ⅱ *vt.* 仿制，仿造；模仿：～ **after (on, upon)** 仿造；模仿

pause /pɔːz/ Ⅰ *n.* 中止；暂停 / **without** ~ 不停地：The speaker talked on without ~. 讲演人不停地往下说。Ⅱ *vi.* 暂停；中止：He ~d for a moment. 他暂停了一会儿。

pave /peɪv/ *vt.* 铺，筑(路等)：The road in front of our classroom is ~d with bricks. 我们教室前的那条路是用砖头铺成的。/ ~ **the way for** 为……铺平道路；为……做准备：Good training ~s the way for success. 良好的训练为成功铺平道路。

pavement /ˈpeɪvmənt/ *n.* [C](英)人行道[＝(美)sidewalk]

pavilion /pəˈvɪljən/ *n.* [C] ❶凉亭；楼阁，亭子 ❷(演出或展览用的)大帐篷

paw /pɔː/ *n.* [C](动物的)爪

pawn /pɔːn/ Ⅰ *n.* ❶[U]典当；押：**in** ~ 典当：My bike was in ~. 我的自行车当掉了。❷[C]抵押物 Ⅱ *vt.* 当；抵押

pay /peɪ/ Ⅰ *v.* (paid/peɪd/, paid) ❶付给；付款 / ~ **by check** 用支票支付 ~ **by (in) installment** 分期付款 ~ **in cash** 以现金支付 ~ **in kind** 以实物支付 ~ **into one's account** 划到某人的账上 ~ **on delivery** 货到付款 ~ **off** 全部还(付)清：It took them six years to ~ off that judgment. 他们过了6年才还清所判决的债务。❷给予(注意等)/ ~ **attention to** 注意：Please ~ more attention to your work. 请更加注意你的工作。~ **a visit to** 访问，参观：We decided to ~ another visit to Mr. Smith the next day. 我们决定第二天再拜访史密斯先生。~ **back** ①偿还(借款等)：You must remember to ~ the money back to your friend. 你必须记住把钱还给朋友。②回报；报复：~ sb. back in his own coin 以其人之道，还治其人之身 / ~ sb. back blow for blow 对某人以牙还牙 ~ **for** ①付款；支付：I paid thirty-two yuan for the dictionary. 我花了32元钱买这本字典。②付出……的代价：He will have to ~ for his foolish behavior. 他得为他的愚蠢行为付出代价。Ⅱ *n.* [U]工资：base ~基本工资 / daily ~ 日工资 / fixed (regular) ~ 固定工资/ overtime ~ 加班费 / On what day does he receive his ~? 他何日领工资？

payable /ˈpeɪəbl/ *adj.* 应付的；到期的；可支付的：~ in June 6月份到期 / Interest payments are ~ monthly. 利息按月支付。

payee /ˌpeɪˈiː/ *n.* [C]收款人

payer /ˈpeɪə(r)/ *n.* [C]付款人

payment /ˈpeɪmənt/ *n.* ❶[U]支付；付款：make (a) ~ 付款/ ~ on terms 定期付款；按条件付款 ❷[C]支付的款项：We have not received the ~ for the goods. 我们还未收到货款。

PC ❶(＝personal computer) 个人电脑 ❷(＝post card) 明信片 ❸(＝post code)邮政编码

PE (＝physical education)体育(课)

pea /piː/ *n.* [C]豌豆

peace /piːs/ *n.* [U]和平；安定 / **at** ~处于和平状态：be at ~ with all countries 和所有国家和平相处 / **make** ~ (与……)讲和：The leaders of the two nations decided to make ~. 两国的领导决定讲和。

peaceful /ˈpiːsfl/ *adj.* 爱好和平的；和平的；安详的；宁静的：a ~ evening 宁静的夜晚 派 peacefully *adv.*

peacetime /ˈpiːsˌtaɪm/ *n.* [U]和平时期，和平年代：military conscription in ~ 和平时期的义务征兵

peach / piːtʃ / *n.* [C]桃子;桃树

peacock / ˈpiːkɒk / *n.* [C]孔雀

peak / piːk / Ⅰ *n.* [C] ❶山峰;山顶: climb a ~ 攀登高峰 / **at the** ~ 在顶峰: at the ~ of one's success 在成功的顶峰 ❷(物体的)尖端 Ⅱ *adj.* 最大值的;高峰的:~ hours of traffic 交通高峰期

peanut / ˈpiːnʌt / *n.* [C]花生

pear / peə(r) / *n.* [C]梨;梨树

pearl / pɜːl / *n.* [C]珍珠

peasant / ˈpez(ə)nt / *n.* [C]农民

pebble / ˈpebl / *n.* [C]鹅卵石

peck / pek / *v.* 啄食:Those sparrows are ~ing the crumbs on the ground. 那些麻雀正在啄食地上的面包屑。

peculiar / pɪˈkjuːliə(r) / *adj.* ❶奇怪的;奇特的;古怪的;不寻常的;异样的: Don't look at me in that ~ way. 别用那种异样的眼神看我。/ The old man is a bit ~ in his behaviour. 那老头儿举止有点古怪。❷特有的;独特的: a girl with ~ charm 有独特魅力的姑娘 / This kind of plant is ~ to the south. 这种植物是南方独有的。

peculiarity / pɪˌkjuːlɪˈærəti / *n.* ❶ [U]特性;独特性 ❷[C]独特之处

pedal / ˈpedəl / Ⅰ *n.* [C] ❶脚踏,踏板: The ~ has come off your bicycle. 你自行车上的一个脚踏脱落了。❷(钢琴、竖琴等的)踏板:~ bin 脚踏式垃圾桶 Ⅱ *vi.* 骑车;踩踏板:~ around on bicycles 骑自行车四处转悠

peddle / ˈpedl/ *vt.* ❶叫卖,兜售(商品): a little girl peddling flowers on a street corner 在街道拐角处叫卖鲜花的小姑娘 ❷提倡;推广,传播(主张、思想等): ~ radical ideas 鼓吹激进的思想

peddler / ˈpedlə(r) / *n.* [C]小贩

pedestrian / pɪˈdestrɪən / *n.* [C]行人: The ~ hit by a red car was dead. 红色小车撞上的那个行人死了。/No ~. 禁止行人通过。

pee / piː / Ⅰ *vi.* (口语)小便,撒尿:The bady ~d in her pants and was crying. 那个小宝宝尿了裤子,正哭呢。Ⅱ *n.* ❶小便,撒尿:go for a ~小便,解手 ❷尿(液)

peek / piːk / Ⅰ *vi.* (很快地)看一眼,瞥一眼,瞥;偷看,窥视:The man was caught while he was ~ing in through the keyhole. 那人透过钥匙孔向里面窥视时被逮个正着。/No ~ing at the present before supper. 吃晚饭之前不准偷看礼物。Ⅱ *n.* (很快的)一瞥,一看;偷看,窥视: He had a quick ~ at the answers. 他快速地扫了一眼答案。

peel / piːl / Ⅰ *v.* 剥,削(水果等的皮) Ⅱ *n.* [U]果皮

peep / piːp / Ⅰ *vi.* 窥视;偷看:~ over a wall 从墙头窥视 Ⅱ *n.* [C]窥视: **have (get, take) a ~ at** 窥视

pen / pen / Ⅰ *n.* [C] ❶钢笔 ❷围栏 Ⅱ *vt.* (penned; penning) ❶写:~ a letter 写信 ❷ 把……关在栏里 ❸关押,囚禁

penal / ˈpiːnəl / *adj.* 处罚的;刑罚的:~ laws 刑法/a ~ sum 罚金

penalty / ˈpenəlti / *n.* [C]惩罚;处罚: suffer a ~ 受处罚 / the death ~ 死刑

pencil / ˈpensl / Ⅰ *n.* [C]铅笔: ~-box 铅笔盒 Ⅱ *v.* 用铅笔写或画

pendulum / ˈpendjələm / *n.* [C](钟等的)摆

penetrate / ˈpenɪtreɪt / *v.* ❶进入;贯穿;看穿;渗透: A bullet cannot ~ a wall. 子弹不能穿透墙壁。❷了解,洞察:Can you ~ the author's symbolism?

P

你能看懂作者的象征手法吗？派 penetration *n.*

penguin /ˈpeŋgwɪn/ *n.* [C]企鹅

penicillin /ˌpenɪˈsɪlɪn/ *n.* [U]青霉素

peninsula /pəˈnɪnsjələ/ *n.* [C]半岛

penniless /ˈpenɪləs/ *adj.* 一文不名的；一贫如洗的

penny /ˈpeni/ *n.* [C](*pl.* pence/pens/或 pennies /ˈpenɪz/)便士

pension /ˈpenʃn/ *n.* [C]抚恤金；养老金；年金：The old lady lives on a ~. 老太太靠养老金生活。

pentagon /ˈpentəgən/ *n.* ❶[C]五边形；五角形 ❷(the Pentagon) 五角大楼(美国国防部所在地)

people /ˈpiːpl/ *n.* ❶(单数形式，复数意义，与复数动词连用)人；人民；人们：visit one's ~探望家里的人 ❷[C]民族：the ~s of Asia 亚洲各民族 / The Chinese ~ is a brave and hardworking ~. 中华民族是一个勤劳勇敢的民族。/ the People's Liberation Army (the PLA)人民解放军

P

pepper /ˈpepə(r)/ *n.* [U] ❶胡椒粉 ❷辣椒

per /pə(r), pɜː(r)/ *prep.* 每，每一：~ day 每天 / ~ hour 每小时

per capita /pəˈkæpɪtə/ Ⅰ *adv.* & *adj.* 按人平均地(的)：an income ~ 人均收入 Ⅱ *adj.* 人均的：What is the average ~ income in this country? 这个国家的人均收入是多少？

perceive /pəˈsiːv/ *vt.* ❶察觉；感知：Have you ~d the danger? 你察觉出危险了吗？❷认识到；意识到；理解：At once, he ~d that he was unwelcome there. 他一下子意识到了自己在那儿是不受欢迎的。

percent /pəˈsent/ *n.* [C]百分之一；百分比：Ninety-eight ~ passed the examination. 98%的人通过了考试。

percentage /pəˈsentɪdʒ/ *n.* [C]百分数；百分率

perception /pəˈsepʃn/ *n.* 感觉；悟性；洞察力

perceptive /pəˈseptɪv/ *adj.* ❶有领悟力的；有洞察力的，敏锐的：a ~ critic 颇有洞察力的评论家 ❷感知的，感觉的：~ organs 感觉器官

perch /pɜːtʃ/ Ⅰ *n.* [C](禽鸟的)栖木，栖息处 Ⅱ *vi.* 栖息；停歇

percolate /ˈpɜːkəˌleɪt/ *vi.* ❶(液体等)过滤，渗滤；渗透：The coffee was percolating. 咖啡正在过滤。❷(思想等)散布，扩散；弥漫：The news about firings began to ~ through the staff. 有关裁员的消息开始在员工中间传开。

perfect Ⅰ /ˈpɜːfɪkt/ *adj.* ❶极好的；完美的；技术精湛的：Practice makes ~. 熟能生巧。❷(语法)完成的 Ⅱ /pəˈfekt/ *vt.* 使完美；使改善：We ~ed a hand-signal system so that they could keep us informed of hazards. 我们完善了一套手势信号，这样他们就能随时告知我们有危险了。派 perfectly *adv.*

perfection /pəˈfekʃən/ *n.* ❶[U]完善，改进，提高：work on the ~ of a new drug formula 努力改进新药配方 ❷精美；精湛；造诣，成就：ancient rock paintings of amazing ~ 令人叹为观止的精美的古代岩画 / His piano playing was ~. 他钢琴弹得炉火纯青。❸[U]完全，绝对；极端，极致：Those peonies are at their full ~. 那些牡丹花开得正艳。

perform /pəˈfɔːm/ *v.* ❶执行；履行：~

one's duties 尽责任 ❷演出(戏剧);演奏(音乐);表演(戏法等):~ in the role of Romeo 扮演罗密欧的角色 派 performer *n.*

performance / pə'fɔːməns / *n.* ❶[U]执行;成果,成绩:faithful in the ~ of his duties 忠于职守/ Our team's ~ was excellent in that year. 在那年中,我们队战绩卓著。❷[C]演出,表演:The evening ~ is at 8 o'clock. 晚场在 8 点。

perfume / 'pɜːfjuːm / *n.* ❶香味;香气,芳香:a faint ~淡淡的香味 ❷香水:What French ~ are you wearing? 你用的是什么牌子的法国香水?

perhaps / pə'hæps / *adv.* 可能;也许:Perhaps I should have told the truth to him. 或许我本该对他说实话的。/— You could do it yourself. —Yeah,~. —你可以自己做。—嗯,也许吧。

peril / 'perɪl / *n.* ❶[U](尤指严重的或致命的)危险:He was in ~ of a mental collapse. 他面临精神崩溃的危险。❷[C]险事;险情,险境:survive the ~ of the expedition 经历探险过程中的艰难险阻而生存下来

period / 'pɪərɪəd / *n.* [C] ❶时代;时期:the Spring and Autumn Period 春秋时期 / the Warring States Period 战国时期 ❷学时;课时 ❸周期;一段时间 ❹结束;句号

periodic / ˌpɪərɪ'ɒdɪk / *adj.* 定期的;周期性的:the ~ motion of a planet 行星的周期性运动

periodical / ˌpɪərɪ'ɒdɪkl / *n.* [C]期刊

perish / 'perɪʃ / *vi.* ❶死亡,丧生;凋谢:Many people ~ed in the earthquake. 地震中很多人死去了。/The buds ~ed when the frost came. 霜打花蕾凋。❷被摧毁;毁灭;消亡:Buildings ~ed in flames. 一栋栋建筑在烈火中焚毁殆尽。

permanent / 'pɜːmənənt / *adj.* 长久的;持久的;永恒的:a ~ employee 长期雇员 / a ~ job 固定职业 派 permanently *adv.*

permeate / 'pɜːmɪˌeɪt/ *v.* ❶渗入;透过:The rain ~d our clothes. 雨水浸湿了我们的衣服。❷弥漫,遍布,深入;充满:The sunshine ~d the room. 阳光洒满了房间。/Fear ~d throughout the entire village. 整个村子都人心惶惶。

permissible / pə'mɪsəbəl/ *adj.* 允许的,准许的,许可的:~ dose 允许剂量 / It is not ~ to smoke in the waiting room. 等候室不准吸烟。派 permissibly *adv.*

permission / pə'mɪʃn / *n.* [U]许可;准许/ **have ~ to do sth.** 得到许可做某事:He has ~ to use this computer. 他使用这台计算机是得到许可的。**with one's ~**经某人同意:We put off the meeting with the teacher's ~. 我们经老师同意将开会日期延后。**without ~** 未经许可:No one can leave without ~. 未经许可任何人不得离开。

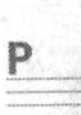

permit Ⅰ/ pə'mɪt / *v.* (-mitted;-mitting) 允许;许可:Smoking is not ~ted in this theatre. 本戏院不许吸烟。Ⅱ/'pɜːmɪt / *n.* [C]许可证;执照:export (import)~ 出口(进口)许可证

perpetual / pə'petʃʊəl / *adj.* 永久的;永恒的

perplex / pə'pleks / *vt.* 使困惑,使茫然;使费解:She behaved in a way that ~ed me. 她的行为方式令我不解。/Don't ~ a child with so many questions! 别弄这么多问题把小孩子搞得晕头转向!

perplexity / pə'pleksɪti/ *n.* ❶[U]困惑,茫然;费解:He looked at me in complete ~. 他万分困惑地看着我。❷[C]

使人困惑的事物，令人费解的事物：There were too many perplexities in such a complicated murder case. 在这样一桩错综复杂的谋杀案中有太多令人困惑不解的地方。

persecute / ˈpɜːsɪkjuːt / *vt.* 迫害；残害：They ~d those who do not conform to their ideas. 他们迫害那些不信奉他们思想的人。

perseverance / ˌpɜːsɪˈvɪərəns / *n.* [U]毅力；坚韧；不屈不挠：By ~, the lame boy learned to swim. 靠着毅力，这个跛脚儿童学会了游泳。

persevere / ˌpɜːsɪˈvɪə(r) / *vi.* 坚持（与 in 连用）：~ in one's studies 孜孜不倦地研究

persist / pəˈsɪst / *vt.* ❶坚持；执意：~ **in** (**with**)坚持：He ~s in taking cold baths in winter. 他坚持在冬天洗冷水澡。❷持续：The thick mist will ~ here. 大雾将在此持续下去。

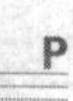

persistence / pəˈsɪstəns/ *n.* [U] ❶坚持不懈；执意：cultivate ~ in children 培养儿童的毅力 ❷持续性，持续状态；存留（状态）：have the ~ of a fever 发烧持续不退

persistent / pəˈsɪstənt/ *adj.* ❶坚持不懈的；执意的：a ~ offender 屡教不改的惯犯 / My daughter is always ~ in her questions. 我女儿总爱打破砂锅问到底。❷持续的；存留的；摆脱不掉的：a ~ drought 持续干旱 / a ~ coughing 老是不好的咳嗽 / ~ complaints 絮叨的牢骚 ❸一再的，重复的：~ questions 一再追问的问题 派 persistently *adv.*

person / ˈpɜːsn / *n.* [C] ❶（语法）人称：the first ~ (I, we), the second ~ (you), the third ~(he, she, it, they)第一人称（我，我们），第二人称（你，你们），第三人称（他，她，它，他/它们）❷人：Four ~s saw this. 有四人看见此事。/ **in** ~亲自，本人：The president appeared in ~. 总裁亲自到场。

personage /ˈpɜːsənɪdʒ / *n.* [C]人物；名士；角色：democratic ~s 民主人士

personal / ˈpɜːsənl / *adj.* ❶个人的；私人的：~ needs 个人需要/ ~ rights 个人权利 / ~ opinions 个人的意见 ❷亲自的：make a ~ call 亲自拜访 派 personally *adv.*

personality / ˌpɜːsəˈnæləti / *n.* [C]人格；个性

personification /pəˌsɒnɪfɪˈkeɪʃn / *n.* 人格化；化身；象征

personify / pəˈsɒnɪfaɪ / *vt.* 把……拟人化，把……人格化：In the poem, the oak trees are personified. 在那首诗中，橡树被拟人化了。

personnel / ˌpɜːsəˈnel / *n.* ❶（集合名词）人员，职员：The company is strict with its ~. 这家公司严格要求它的员工。❷[U]人事部门

perspective / pəˈspektɪv / *n.* [C] ❶视角；观点；想法 ❷远景；景观 ❸透视画法；透视图

persuade / pəˈsweɪd / *v.* 说服；劝导 / ~ **sb. of sth.** 使某人相信某事：I'm almost ~d of his honesty. 我几乎相信他是诚实的。~ **sb. to do sth.** 劝说某人干某事：He ~d me to go. 他劝我去。派 persuasion *n.*

persuasive / pəˈsweɪsɪv/ *adj.* ❶劝说的；劝诱的：an informative and ~ speech 内容丰富且循循善诱的演讲 ❷有说服力的；能言善道的：~ arguments 令人信服的论据 派 persuasively *adv.*

pertinent /ˈpɜːtɪnənt/ *adj.* 有关的，相关的；贴切的，切题的；合适的：I want to know all the ~ details. 我想知道所有相关的细节。/She said little at meetings but her comments were always ~. 她在会上很少发言，但她的意见总是很中肯。

pervade /pəˈveɪd/ *vt.* ❶弥漫于，渗透于：A haze ~s the park, prompting health concerns. 公园里弥漫着雾霭，引起了人们对健康的关注。/An intense poetic quality ~s her writings. 她的作品中洋溢着浓浓的诗意。❷(影响等)遍及；流行于：When the echoes had fully ceased, a light laughter at once ~d the assembly. 等回声余音寂止，聚会上顿时遍布一片轻松的欢笑声。/Uncertainty ~s the economic life. 不确定性充斥着经济生活。派 pervasion *n.*

pessimism /ˈpesɪmɪzəm/ *n.* [U] 悲观；悲观主义：Never does he show ~ in face of difficulty. 他面对困难从不悲观。

pessimist /ˈpesɪmɪst/ *n.* [C] 悲观论者；悲观主义者

pessimistic /ˌpesɪˈmɪstɪk/ *adj.* 悲观的；悲观主义的：We are never ~ about the future. 对于未来，我们从不悲观。派 pessimistically *adv.*

pest /pest/ *n.* [C] ❶讨厌的人(或物) ❷害虫，有害动物；疫病

pesticide /ˈpestɪsaɪd/ *n.* 杀虫药；杀虫剂

pet /pet/ Ⅰ *n.* [C] 宠物；宠儿：have (keep) ~s 养宠物 Ⅱ *adj.* ❶宠爱的；感兴趣的：~ name 昵称；~phrase 口头禅 ❷特别的；得意的：Snakes are my ~ hate. 蛇是我特别讨厌的动物。Ⅲ *vt.* 爱抚，抚摸，轻按

petal /ˈpetəl/ *n.* [C]花瓣

petition /pəˈtɪʃn/ *n.* & *v.* 请愿；祈求

petrol /ˈpetrəl/ *n.* [U] (英) 汽油 [＝(美)gasoline]：stop at the next ~ station 在下一个加油站停车

petroleum /pəˈtrəʊlɪəm/ *n.* [U]石油

petty /ˈpeti/ *adj.* ❶无关紧要的，微不足道的，细小琐碎的：~ expenses 微不足道的花费 /~ local news 当地的鸡毛蒜皮消息 ❷小心眼的，气量小的；可鄙的，卑劣的：It was ~ of him not to talk with her. 他不跟她讲话是心胸狭窄的表现。派 pettily *adv.*

pharmacy /ˈfɑːməsi/ *n.* ❶[U]配药业；制药业 ❷[U]配药学；药剂学；制药学 ❸[C]药店，药铺

phase /feɪz/ *n.* [C] ❶阶段；时期：The work has entered a new ~. 工作已进入了一个新阶段。❷面；方面：You should look at the other ~ of the problem. 你应当看看问题的另一方面。

phenomenon /fəˈnɒmɪnən/ *n.* [C] (*pl.* phenomena /fɪˈnɒmɪnə/) 现象：the phenomena of nature 自然现象

philatelist /fɪˈlætəlɪst/ *n.* [C]集邮家

philately /fɪˈlætəli/ *n.* [U]集邮

philosopher /fɪˈlɒsəfə(r)/ *n.* [C] ❶哲学家 ❷哲人，贤哲 ❸豁达的人；处世泰然的人：He was a ~ with a taste for what is called low life. 他为人豁达，喜欢所谓下层阶级的生活。

philosophy /fɪˈlɒsəfi/ *n.* ❶哲学：doctor of ~ 哲学博士 ❷[C]人生哲学；见解，观点：~ of life 人生哲学

phone /fəʊn/ (＝telephone) Ⅰ *n.* 电话；电话机：hang up the ~ 挂断电话 / Please answer the ~. 请接电话。Ⅱ *v.* 打电话

phonology /fəˈnɒlədʒi/ *n.* [U]语音学

photo /ˈfəʊtəʊ/ *n.* [C] (*pl.* photos) 照片;相片(photograph 的略写形式):take a ~ 拍一张照片

photograph /ˈfəʊtəɡrɑːf/ *n.* [C]照片;相片:develop a ~ 冲洗照片 / enlarge a ~ 放大照片

photographer /fəˈtɒɡrəfə(r)/ *n.* [C]摄影师

photography /fəˈtɒɡrəfi/ *n.* [U]摄影术

phrase /freɪz/ *n.* [C]片语;短语

physical /ˈfɪzɪkl/ *adj.* 物质的;物理的;体力的;肉体的;自然规律的:~ exercises 运动 / ~ education (PE)体育

physician /fɪˈzɪʃn/ *n.* [C]内科医生

physicist /ˈfɪzɪsɪst/ *n.* [C]物理学家

physics /ˈfɪzɪks/ *n.* [U]物理学

physiologist /ˌfɪzɪˈɒlədʒɪst/ *n.* [C]生理学家

physiology /ˌfɪzɪˈɒlədʒi/ *n.* [U]生理学

pianist /ˈpɪənɪst/ *n.* [C]钢琴弹奏者;钢琴家

piano /pɪˈænəʊ/ *n.* [C] (*pl.* pianos)钢琴

P

pick /pɪk/ *v.* ❶(用手)采,摘;取去:~ flowers 采花 / ~ fruits 摘果 / ~ sb.'s pocket 扒某人的口袋 ❷挑选,选择:~ words 选适当的字眼/ ~ **out** ①选择:My sister is going with me to help me ~ out a new suit. 我姐姐要陪我一起去帮我挑一套新衣服。②分辨出:~ out one's friends in a crowd 在人群中分辨出自己的朋友 ③理解:I can't ~ out the meaning of this word. 我不能理解这个词的意思。~ **up** ①捡起:~ up a stone 拾起一块石头 ②搭载;携带:The train stopped to ~ up passengers. 火车停下来搭载乘客。③学会;获得:~ up a foreign language (自然)学得一种外语

pickle /ˈpɪkl/ *n.* (常用 *pl.*)腌制食品;泡菜

picnic /ˈpɪknɪk/ *n.* [C]野餐:go on a ~ 去野餐

pictorial /pɪkˈtɔːrɪəl/ *adj.* ❶画的,绘画的:~ art 绘画艺术 ❷用图说明的,图示的;插图的:~ writings 带插图的文字作品 ❸形象化的;生动的:a ~ description of the countryside 对乡村的生动描述

picture /ˈpɪktʃə(r)/ Ⅰ *n.* [C] ❶图画;照片:~ books (尤指供儿童阅读的)图画书 / **take** (**snap**) **a** ~ 拍照:Let's have a ~ taken under the tree. 我们在树下照张相吧。❷影片;电影 ❸ 景色 Ⅱ *vt.* 描绘;想象

pie /paɪ/ *n.* (以肉或水果为馅的)烤饼;馅饼

piece /piːs/ *n.* [C] ❶块,片;部分:a ~ of paper(wood, glass, chalk, cloth)一张纸(一块木头,一块玻璃,一支粉笔,一块布) / The teapot fell and was broken to ~s. 茶壶掉下来摔成碎片。❷(艺术或音乐作品的)幅;件;首:a ~ of art work 一件艺术品 / a ~ of music 一首乐曲

pierce /pɪəs/ *v.* ❶刺入;刺穿;透入:The arrow ~d his shoulder. 箭刺入他的肩膀。/ They ~d into the heart of the forest. 他们进入了森林的中心。❷(用锐器等)在……刺孔,在……上戳洞;在……上穿孔(或打眼):the canvases ~d with jagged holes by shrapnel 被弹片刺得千疮百孔的帆布 ❸(声音)刺破;(光亮)照入;(目光)看穿:A sharp cry escaped Linda's lips, piercing the night. 一声尖叫从琳达嘴里发出,划破了夜幕。❹突破;穿过:Our forces ~d the enemy's defense. 我军突破了敌军的防线。

piercing /ˈpɪəsɪŋ/ *adj.* ❶(冷风等)刺骨的;(目光等)犀利的:a ~wind 刺骨的

风/With her ~ eyes she could drill the life out of you. 她那炯炯刺人的目光可以把你的魂挖出来。❷(声音)刺耳的，尖厉的：utter a ~ shriek 发出一声刺耳的尖叫 派 piercingly *adv.*

pig /pɪg/ *n.* [C]猪；野猪

pigeon /ˈpɪdʒɪn/ *n.* [C]鸽子

pigment /ˈpɪgmənt/ Ⅰ*n.* ❶颜料；涂料：lay on color in small strokes of pure ~ 用淡淡的纯色调涂抹颜色 ❷色素，色质：~ cell 色素细胞 Ⅱ*vt.* 给……着色；染色于

pile /paɪl/ Ⅰ*n.* [C]堆；叠：a ~ of books (wood)一堆书(木头) Ⅱ*v.* 堆起；堆积 / ~ **up** 积聚；累积：The snow is piling up. 雪正越堆越高。

pilgrim /ˈpɪlgrɪm/ *n.* [C]香客；朝圣者

pilgrimage /ˈpɪlgrɪmɪdʒ/ *n.* 朝圣：*Pilgrimage to the West*《西游记》

pill /pɪl/ *n.* [C]药丸；药片：compound ~ 合成药 / sleeping ~ 安眠药 / take a ~ 服药丸

pillar /ˈpɪlə(r)/ *n.* [C] ❶柱 ❷台柱；栋梁：Scientists are ~s of a society. 科学家是社会的栋梁。

pillow /ˈpɪləʊ/ *n.* [C]枕头

pilot /ˈpaɪlət/ Ⅰ*n.* [C]飞行员；飞行器的驾驶员 Ⅱ*vt.* 驾驶(飞机等)；为(船舶等)引航

pin /pɪn/ Ⅰ*n.* [C]❶大头针；饰针；别针 ❷(唱机的)唱针 Ⅱ*vt.* (pinned; pinning)别住；钉住 /~ **one's hopes on** 把希望寄托于：The old man ~ned his hopes on his son. 老人把希望寄托在他的儿子身上。

PIN(=personal Identification Number)个人身份证号码，个人识别码

pinch /pɪntʃ/ *v.* & *n.* [C]掐；捏；拧：She ~ed his arm as hard as she could. 她使出浑身的力气拧他的胳膊。/She gave him a little ~. 她轻轻地捏了他一下。

pine /paɪn/ Ⅰ*n.* 松树；松木 Ⅱ*adj.* 松树的

pineapple /ˈpaɪnæpl/ *n.* 凤梨；菠萝

ping-pong /ˈpɪŋpɒŋ/ Ⅰ*n.* [U]乒乓球运动 Ⅱ*v.* 被传来传去

pink /pɪŋk/ Ⅰ*n.* [U]粉红色 Ⅱ*adj.* 粉红色的

pint /paɪnt/ *n.* [C]品脱(液量或干量单位，等于1/2 加仑，或在英国等于 0.568 升，在美国等于 0.473 升)

pioneer /ˌpaɪəˈnɪə(r)/ Ⅰ*n.* [C]先锋；先驱；拓荒者：a Young Pioneer 一名少先队员 Ⅱ*v.* 当先驱；开辟(道路等)；提倡(新法等)

pipe /paɪp/ Ⅰ*n.* [C] ❶管：water ~s 水管 / gas ~ 煤气管 ❷烟斗 ❸管乐器 Ⅱ*vt.* 用管道输送

pipedream /ˈpaɪ(p)ˌdriːm/ *n.* [C]白日梦；空想，幻想：Her plans for a movie career had all been merely a ~. 她投身于电影生涯的计划仅仅是空想。

pipeline /ˈpaɪplaɪn/ *n.* [C]管道；管线

pirate /ˈpaɪrət/ *n.* [C]海盗

pistol /ˈpɪstl/ *n.* [C]手枪

pit /pɪt/ *n.* [C]坑；洼

pitch[1] /pɪtʃ/ Ⅰ*v.* ❶投，掷，扔 ❷搭；架设 Ⅱ*n.* [C] ❶投，掷，扔 ❷宿营地

pitch[2] /pɪtʃ/ *n.* [U]沥青：~-black 乌黑的

pitiful /ˈpɪtɪfəl/ *adj.* 可怜的；令人同情的

pitiless /ˈpɪtɪlɪs/ *adj.* 无同情心的；无情的；残忍的：a ~ master 铁石心肠的主人/the ~ heat of the desert 沙漠的毒

P

热

pity /ˈpɪti/ Ⅰ *n.* ❶[U]怜悯；同情 / **take (have) ~ on** 同情；可怜：Mary always takes ~ on some stray cats or dogs. 玛丽老是可怜那些迷途的猫狗。**out of** ~出于同情；出于怜悯：She gave the man some money out of ~. 出于同情，她给了那人一些钱。❷可惜；遗憾：What a ~! 多么可惜啊！It's a ~ (that) he couldn't swim. 真遗憾，他不会游泳。 Ⅱ *v.* 同情；可怜

place /pleɪs/ Ⅰ *n.* [C] ❶地方；场所：a ~ of interest 名胜 / **in** ~在合适的位置；适当的；相称的：Everything is in ~. 一切就绪。**in ~ of** 代替；取代：Jack played in ~ of Tom. 杰克上场替换了汤姆。**out of** ~ 不在合适的位置；不适当；不相称：What you said was out of ~. 你讲的话不合适。❷住所；寓所：at one's ~ 在某人家里 ❸地位；等级；名次 / **in the first** ~ 第一，首先 **take one's** ~ ①代替某人的位置 ②就座；就位 **take the ~ of** 代替；取代：I don't think TV will take the ~ of movies. 我认为电视不会取代电影。**take** ~发生；举行：Great changes have taken ~ in China. 中国发生了巨大的变化。Ⅱ *v.* ❶放置；安排 ❷发出(订单)：~ an order for books with Smith & Sons 向史密斯父子公司订购书籍

placement /ˈpleɪsmənt/ *n.* ❶[U]放置；布置；布局；部署：the ~ of furniture 家具的布置 ❷[U](人员的)安插，工作安排；(学生的)编班：a ~ office 安置办公室

plague /pleɪg/ *n.* ❶瘟疫；鼠疫 ❷(口语)天灾；灾祸

plain /pleɪn/ Ⅰ *adj.* ❶明白的；清楚的；易了解的：~ English 简明英语 ❷简单的；朴素的；平凡的：in ~ clothes 穿便衣 / ~ food 简单的食物/~ living 简朴的生活 / ~ meal 便饭 ❸(指人的思想、行为等)坦率的，直截了当的 Ⅱ *adv.* 清楚地；明白地 Ⅲ *n.* [C]平原；平地

plan /plæn/ Ⅰ *n.* [C]计划；策略：Have they made any ~s for the holidays? 他们已经制订了假期计划吗？ / **carry out a** ~执行计划：We carried out the new five-year ~. 我们执行了新的五年计划。**make ~s** 制订计划 **propose a** ~提出计划：I'll propose a new ~ at the meeting. 我要在会上提出一个新的计划。Ⅱ *v.* 设计；打算：Where do you ~ to spend your holiday? 你打算在什么地方度假？

plane[1] /pleɪn/ *n.* [C] 飞机(aeroplane 的略写形式)：**by** ~ 乘飞机：They went to London by ~. 他们乘飞机去伦敦。

plane[2] /pleɪn/ Ⅰ *n.* [C]平面；水平面 Ⅱ *adj.* ❶水平的；平坦的 ❷平面的：~ geometry 平面几何学

planet /ˈplænɪt/ *n.* [C]行星

plant /plɑːnt/ Ⅰ *n.* [C] ❶植物 ❷工厂 Ⅱ *vt.* 栽种；种植：They are ~ing trees on the hill. 他们在山上种树。

plantation /plænˈteɪʃn/ *n.* ❶[C]植物园；大农场 ❷[U]栽植；种植

plaster /ˈplɑːstə(r)/ *n.* [U] ❶灰泥 ❷膏药 ❸熟石膏

plastic /ˈplæstɪk/ Ⅰ *adj.* (物质)可塑的；(物品)由塑料做成的：~ payment 塑料货币支付(即信用卡支付) Ⅱ *n.* (常用 *pl.*)塑料；可塑物

plate /pleɪt/ *n.* [C]盘，碟

plateau /ˈplætəʊ/ *n.* [C] (*pl.* plateaus 或 plateaux /ˈplætəʊz/)高原

platform /ˈplætfɔːm/ *n.* [C](火车站的)月台；讲台；台

play /pleɪ/ Ⅰ *v.* ❶自娱;玩耍;游乐/ ~ **with** 玩;玩弄:Children were ~ing with toys. 孩子们在玩玩具。~ **truant** 逃学:Schoolboys who ~ truant should be punished. 逃学的学生应受处罚。❷踢(足球等);打(高尔夫球等) ❸扮演:Who is going to ~ Hamlet? 谁将扮演哈姆雷特? Ⅱ *n.* ❶[U]玩;游戏:The children are at ~. 孩子们在玩。❷[C]剧本;戏剧

player /ˈpleɪə(r)/ *n.* [C] ❶运动员,运动者;游戏者:seed ~ 种子选手 / star ~明星选手/ Jack is a good chess ~. 杰克是名好棋手。❷演员 ❸演奏者

playful /ˈpleɪfʊl/ *adj.* ❶爱玩耍的;嬉戏的;顽皮的:~ children 嬉戏的儿童 / as ~ as a kitten 像小猫一样顽皮 ❷开玩笑的,闹着玩的,不当真的:~ behaviour 开玩笑的举动

playground /ˈpleɪɡraʊnd/ *n.* [C](学校的)运动场,操场;游乐场:children's ~ 儿童游乐场 / The students played basketball on the ~ after class. 学生们下课后在操场上打篮球。

plaza /ˈplɑːzə/ *n.* [C] ❶(尤指西班牙城市的)广场,集市 ❷购物中心,商业区

plea /pliː/ *n.* [C]请求;恳求

plead /pliːd/ *v.* (pleaded 或 pled) ❶恳求:She ~ed with him not to go. 她恳求他不要离开。❷为……辩护;辩解

pleasant /ˈpleznt/ *adj.* 合意的;愉快的;友好的:a ~ afternoon (taste, companion)愉快的下午(合意的味道,友好的伙伴) / Whatever happens, try to make yourself ~ to the guests. 无论发生什么,都要努力做到友好地待客。/ **have a ~ time** 过得(玩得)愉快:Did you have a ~ time at the party? 你在晚会上玩得愉快吗? 派 pleasantly *adv.*; pleasantness *n.*

please /pliːz/ *v.* ❶请(用在祈使句中,表示客气地要求):Please come in. 请进来。Two coffees, ~! 请来两杯咖啡。❷使满足;取悦:Please yourself. (Do as you ~.)请随意。/ It's difficult to ~ everybody. 取悦每个人是困难的。❸喜好;想要:Take as many as you ~. 你要多少就请取多少。

pleased /pliːzd/ *adj.* (感到)愉快的;(感到)满足的/ **be ~ with (at)** 对……感到满意(be ~ at 与 be ~ with 意思相近,但 at 后常接动名词):Are you ~ with your new clothes? 你对你的新衣服感到满意吗? / I was ~ at hearing of his success. 获悉他的成功,我很高兴。

pleasing /ˈpliːzɪŋ/ *adj.* 合意的;令人喜爱的:a ~ working environment 惬意的工作环境 / a ~ sound 悦耳的声音

pleasure /ˈpleʒə(r)/ *n.* ❶[U]愉快;满足:Has he gone abroad for ~ or on business? 他出国是为娱乐还是为业务? ❷[C]乐事;乐趣:He always says that working is his ~. 他总说工作是他的乐趣。/ **have the ~ of** 有幸:I have the ~ of presenting the guests. 我很荣幸来介绍客人。**take ~ in** 从……中得到快乐:He takes great ~ in taking pictures of animals. 他从动物摄影中得到极大乐趣。/ I take little ~ in such things. 我对这类事没什么兴趣。**with ~** 愉快地;高兴地:She accepted our invitation with ~. 她高兴地接受了我们的邀请。

pledge /pledʒ/ Ⅰ *n.* [U]誓约;承诺;保证 Ⅱ *v.* 发誓;承诺;保证:be ~d to secrecy 誓守秘密

plentiful /ˈplentɪfl/ *adj.* 丰富的;充足的;富裕的:The field workers have a ~

P

supply of food. 野外作业的人员食物供应充足。

plenty /ˈplenti/ *n.* [C]许多;大量:There are ~ of eggs at home. 家里有很多蛋。/**in** ~大量;充实:They are living in ~. 他们生活富裕。

plot /plɒt/ Ⅰ*n.* [C] ❶(小的)一块地:a ~ of vegetables 一块菜地 ❷密谋:a ~ to overthrow the government 推翻政府的阴谋 ❸(小说或戏剧故事的)情节 Ⅱ*vt.* (plotted;plotting)密谋做;策划:They were ~ting to overthrow the King. 他们正在密谋要推翻国王。

plough /plaʊ/ Ⅰ*n.* [C]犁 Ⅱ*v.* 犁(田);耕(地):They are ~ing the fields. 他们正在耕地。/ The ship is ~ing the waves. 轮船破浪前进。

pluck /plʌk/ *vt.* ❶采;摘:~ some flowers 采一些花 ❷鼓起(勇气);振作:~ up courage 鼓起勇气

plug /plʌg/ Ⅰ*n.* [C] ❶塞子 ❷插头:pull out the ~ 拔出插头 Ⅱ*v.* ❶以塞子塞住 ❷插上插头:~ in the wireless set 插上收音机的插头

plum /plʌm/ *n.* [C] 李子;李子树

plunge /plʌndʒ/ *v.* (使某物)投入;(使)突入;陷入(与 into 连用):~ into action 立即投入行动 / ~ a country into a war 使一个国家陷入战争

plural /ˈplʊərəl/ Ⅰ*adj.* 复数的:The ~ form of "child" is "children". "child"的复数形式是"children"。❷多元的:Our world is indeed a plural one. 我们的世界确实是一个多元的世界。Ⅱ*n.* [C](名词或动词的)复数

plurality /plʊəˈrælɪti/ *n.* ❶[U]复数,复数形式 ❷[C]多数,大量:A text is sure to elicit a ~ of responses. 一个文本肯定会引起多种反应。

plus /plʌs/ Ⅰ*prep.* 加上:Two ~ five is seven. 二加五等于七。Ⅱ*adj.* (比所示数量)多的;正的 Ⅲ*n.* [C]正号;加号

pm, p. m. (=in the afternoon)午后;下午

pocket /ˈpɒkɪt/ Ⅰ*n.* [C]衣袋;口袋 / **have ... in one's ~** 可以操纵某人,可以任意处置某物 **keep one's hands in one's ~** 不做事,偷懒 **line one's ~**(以非法手段)中饱私囊 **pick ~** 扒窃 Ⅱ*adj.* 袖珍的;小型的:~ money 身上带的零用钱,(给小孩的)零花钱 / a ~ dictionary 袖珍字典 Ⅲ*vt.* 把……装入口袋

poem /ˈpəʊɪm/ *n.* [C]

poet /ˈpəʊɪt/ *n.* [C]诗人

poetess /ˌpəʊɪˈtes/ *n.* [C]女诗人

poetry /ˈpəʊətri/ *n.* [U](总称)诗,诗歌

point /pɒɪnt/ Ⅰ*n.* [C] ❶(针、铅笔等的)尖,尖端 ❷点:a decimal ~ 小数点 / four ~ six 4.6 ❸分数:We won by five ~s. 我们赢了 5 分。❹要点;观点;主旨:a ~ of view 观点/ **catch the ~ of** 抓住……的要点:Only a few people can catch the ~ of what he said. 只有几个人能抓住他说话的要点。**from one's ~ of view** 从某人的观点来看:From my ~ of view it would be better to be decided by himself. 从我的观点来看,这事最好由他自己决定。**off the ~** 离题的;偏离要点:Your criticism is off the ~. 你的批评离题。**to the ~** 中肯;得要领:Her answer was concise and to the ~. 她的回答简洁中肯。**on the ~ of** 即将;正要:I was on the ~ of starting when it began to rain. 我正要开始,天就下雨了。Ⅱ*v.* ❶指(方向或位置):The needle of a compass ~s to the north. 罗盘的针指向北方。❷瞄准;对着:~ a gun at sb. 以枪瞄准某人 ❸ 指出；使显著：~ out a mistake 指出错误

pointed /ˈpɒɪntɪd/ *adj.* ❶有尖头的，尖的：a ~ bullet 尖弹 / high ~ kid shoes 尖头的羊皮鞋 ❷(评论等)尖锐的；有针对性的；一针见血的：He says in a ~ voice, as if blaming her. 他话外有音，有点责怪她的味道。❸明显的，突出的：~ regard 特别的关照 ❹深刻的，敏锐的：a ~ wit 洞察一切的机智 派 pointedly *adv.* ；pointedness *n.*

pointless /ˈpɒɪntlɪs/ *adj.* ❶无尖头的，钝的：a ~ knife 一把钝刀 ❷无意义的，不得要领的；无目标的：a ~ joke 索然无味的笑话 / The statements are ~. 这些陈述不得要领。❸(比赛中)没有得分的 派 pointlessly *adv.* ；pointlessness *n.*

poison /ˈpɒɪzən/ Ⅰ *n.* 毒药；毒物 Ⅱ *vt.* 使中毒；放毒于；毒害：~ one's mind 毒害某人的思想

poisonous /ˈpɒɪzənəs/ *adj.* ❶有毒的；有害的：~ plants 有毒植物 / ~ gas 有毒气体 ❷恶毒的：She apologized for the ~ words she said. 她为自己说的那些恶毒的话而道歉。

poke /pəʊk/ *vt.* & *n.* 戳；刺

poker /ˈpəʊkə(r)/ *n.* ❶[C]火钳；火钩 ❷[U]扑克牌

polar /ˈpəʊlə(r)/ *adj.* (南、北)极的

pole /pəʊl/ *n.* [C] ❶柱；杆；竿：telegram ~ 电线杆 ❷(南、北)极：the North (South) Pole 北极(南极) ❸磁极；电极

police /pəˈliːs/ *n.* (集合名词)警察当局；警察：the ~ office 警察局 / The ~ have not made any arrests. 警察当局尚未逮捕人。

policeman /pəˈliːsmən/ *n.* [C](*pl.* policemen)警察；警员：The woman was helped by the ~. 那位妇女得到了警察的帮助。

policewoman /pəˈliːswʊmən/ *n.* [C] (*pl.* policewomen)女警察；女警员

policy /ˈpɒləsi/ *n.* [C](尤指政府、政党、商行等的)政策，方针：the foreign ~ of a country 一个国家的外交政策

polish /ˈpɒlɪʃ/ Ⅰ *v.* 磨光；擦亮；使光滑：~ furniture 擦亮家具/~ shoes 擦鞋 Ⅱ *n.* 擦亮；磨光；上光剂：You'd better give the plate a ~. 你最好把盘子擦亮。

polished /ˈpɒlɪʃt/ *adj.* ❶擦亮的，磨光的：~ wood floor 擦得锃亮的木地板 ❷光洁的，光滑的：His hair is ~. 他的头发光洁滑溜。❸完美的；精湛的；洗练的：a ~ performance of Mozart's "*Magic Flute*" 莫扎特《魔笛》的精湛表演

polite /pəˈlaɪt/ *adj.* 有礼貌的；客气的：be ~ to sb. 对某人有礼貌 / a ~ reply 有礼貌的答复 派 politely *adv.* ；politeness *n.*

political /pəˈlɪtɪkl/ *adj.* 政府的；政治的

politician /ˌpɒləˈtɪʃn/ *n.* [C]政治家；政客

politics /ˈpɒlətɪks/ *n.* [U] ❶政治学；政治；政治活动：**go in for** ~从政：He went in for ~ when he was young. 他年轻时就从政了。❷政纲；政见

poll /pəʊl/ Ⅰ *n.* [C]投票；民意调查：They conduct a ~ from time to time. 他们不时要进行民意调查。Ⅱ *vi.* 投票

pollen /ˈpɒlən/ *n.* [U]花粉

pollute /pəˈluːt/ *vt.* 使……脏；污染：The water at the bathing beach was ~d by refuse from the factory. 海滨浴水被工厂排出的垃圾污染了。派 pollution *n.*

pond /pɒnd/ *n.* [C]池塘

ponder /ˈpɒndə(r)/ *v.* 思考,考虑:He ~ed his next words thoroughly. 他仔细考虑了下一步要讲的话。/Mary ~ed over this for a time. 玛丽把这句话琢磨了一会儿。

pony /ˈpəʊni/ *n.* [C]小马

pool[1] /puːl/ *n.* [C](尤指天然的)水池,水塘:swimming ~ 游泳池 / indoor (outdoor) ~ 室内(室外)游泳池

pool[2] /puːl/ Ⅰ *n.* [C]共同资金;合伙投资:We bought a horse by the ~. 我们合资买了一匹马。Ⅱ *v.* 合并;联营:The three boys ~ed their savings and bought a boat. 这三个男孩把他们的积蓄合起来买了一条小船。

poor /pʊə(r)/ *adj.* ❶无钱的;贫穷的:the ~ 穷人 ❷可怜的:The ~ fellow lost both his legs in the war. 这个不幸的人在战争中失掉了双腿。❸ 坏的;质劣的:~ soil 瘠土 / in ~ health 健康不佳 / **be ~ in** 在……方面贫乏;在……方面很差:The country is ~ in natural resources. 这个国家自然资源贫乏。/ He is ~ in English. 他英语学得很差。

pop[1] /pɒp/ Ⅰ *n.* ❶[U]流行音乐:Carter likes ~ very much. 卡特很喜欢流行音乐。❷[C]流行歌曲:Most of the young people are fond of ~s. 多数年轻人都喜欢流行歌曲。Ⅱ *adj.* (音乐、绘画、电影等)流行的:~ music 流行音乐 / ~ singer 流行歌手

pop[2] /pɒp/ Ⅰ *n.* [C]砰的一声;啪的一声:The cork flew off with a ~. 瓶塞砰的一声飞了。Ⅱ *v.* 发出声响;突然出现;爆(玉米)

pope /pəʊp/ *n.* (常作 the Pope) (罗马天主教的)教皇

popular /ˈpɒpjələ(r)/ *adj.* ❶受欢迎的;有声望的/ **be ~ with** 受爱慕的;有名望的:He is ~ with the people. 他受到人民的爱慕和拥护。❷大众的;通俗的:~ science 大众(通俗)科学 派 popularly *adv.*

popularity /ˌpɒpjʊˈlærəti/ *n.* [U]❶名气:enjoy ~ 享有盛名 ❷普及;流行

popularize /ˈpɒpjələraɪz/ *vt.* 推广;普及:A new method was ~d in the factory. 一种新方法在工厂里得到推广。

population /ˌpɒpjʊˈleɪʃn/ *n.* 人口;人口数:a fall (rise) in ~ 人口的减少(增加) / ~ explosion 人口爆炸 / a city of one million ~ 一个拥有百万人口的城市

populous /ˈpɒpjələs/ *adj.* 人口稠密的

porcelain /ˈpɔːsəlɪn/ Ⅰ *n.* [U]瓷;瓷器 Ⅱ *adj.* 瓷的;瓷制的

porch /pɔːtʃ/ *n.* [C]有顶的门廊;(美)走廊

pore /pɔː(r)/ *n.* [C]毛孔;气孔;细孔

pork /pɔːk/ *n.* [U]猪肉

porridge /ˈpɒrɪdʒ/ *n.* [U]粥

port /pɔːt/ *n.* [C]港;港口:commercial ~商业港口 / free ~自由港

portable /ˈpɔːtəbl/ *adj.* 轻便的;便于携带的;手提的:a ~ television 便携式电视机 / a ~ radio 便携式收音机 / Do you want to buy a ~ computer? 你想买一台手提电脑吗?

porter /ˈpɔːtə(r)/ *n.* [C] 搬运工人

portion /ˈpɔːʃn/ *n.* [C] ❶部分:They bought only a small ~ of the goods. 他们只买了一小部分货物。❷(食品的)一份:distribute food in ~s 按份分发食品

portrait /ˈpɔːtreɪt/ *n.* [C] ❶(人或动物的)画像 ❷(生动的)文字描写:family ~ (picture) 全家福 / full-length ~ (picture)全身像 / group ~ (picture)团体像

portray /pɔːˈtreɪ/ *vt.* 画;描述;描写

pose /pəuz/ Ⅰ *vi.* ❶摆姿势:~ for a painter 摆姿势让画家画像 ❷假装,冒充;作态,矫揉造作,装模作样:He ~d as a plain uneducated man. 他故意装成没有受过教育的平民。—*vt.* ❶使摆好姿势;把……摆正位置:He ~d the picture on the wall. 他把墙上的那幅画扶正。❷提出(问题等):A loan boom ~s problems. 货款激增提出难题。❸造成,引起(困难等):All drugs ~ some side effects. 所有药物都会引起一定的副作用。Ⅱ *n.* [C] ❶(身体呈现的)样子,姿势:in a stiff ~身子僵直地 ❷(故意装出来的)态度,姿态,装腔作势:strike an indifferent ~ toward sth. 对某事故作不屑一顾的样子

position /pəˈzɪʃn/ *n.* ❶位置;阵地 ❷阶级;地位;职位:hold an important ~ 担任一个重要职务 ❸形势;状况:The enemy was in a difficult ~. 敌人处于困境中。❹主张;立场:What's your ~ on the problem? 在这个问题上你有什么主张?

positive /ˈpɒzətɪv/ *adj.* ❶肯定的;积极的:give a ~ (negative) reply 给予肯定的(否定的)答复 / **be ~ about (of)** 对……肯定:I am not ~ about the result. 我不能肯定结果如何。❷(数学)正的,正数的:the ~ sign 正号 ❸(电)正的,阳性的:a ~ charge 正电 ❹(语法)原级的 派 positively *adv.*

possess /pəˈzes/ *vt.* 具有;占有;拥有:This figure has long been held to ~miraculous power. 这个数字长时间以来都被认为拥有神奇的力量。

possession /pəˈzeʃn/ *n.* ❶[U]拥有,占有;所有权:lawful(unlawful)~ 合法(非法)占有 / **come into ~ of sth.** 占有某物:The young man came into ~ of a large house. 那年轻人得到了一所大房子。**take (get, have) ~ of** 占有;占领:The army took ~ of the city. 军队占领了城市。❷[C](常用 *pl.*)所有物:personal ~s 个人财产

possessive /pəˈzesɪv/ Ⅰ *adj.* 所有的 Ⅱ *n.* (语法)所有格

possessor /pəˈzesə(r)/ *n.* [C]持有者;所有者

possibility /ˌpɒsəˈbɪləti/ *n.* ❶[U]可能性:out of the bounds of ~ 在可能的范围外 / within the bounds of ~ 在可能的范围内/ Is there any ~ of your getting to London this week? 本周你有可能到伦敦吗?❷[C]可能的事;可能发生的事:I see great possibilities in this scheme. 我看这计划很可能成功。

possible /ˈpɒsəbl/ *adj.* 可能的:Is it ~ for you to come to dinner this evening? 今晚你来吃饭行吗? / **as ... as ~** 尽可能……:Come as early as ~. 尽可能早点来。**if ~**有可能的话:I'll see you off at the airport if ~. 有可能的话,我就去机场给你送行。

possibly /ˈpɒsəbli/ *adv.* 可能;或许

post /pəust/ Ⅰ *n.* ❶[U]邮政;邮件;邮局:take letters to the ~ (office)把信件送到邮局 / **by ~**邮寄:The present came by ~. 礼物是邮寄来的 ❷[C]哨所;岗位:The soldiers stood at their ~s. 士兵们各守岗位。❸[C]职位;工作:be given a ~ as general manager 被授予总经理的职务 ❹[C]柱;桩;杆:lamp ~ 灯柱 / sign ~ 标杆 Ⅱ *v.* ❶邮寄(信件等):I've come out to ~ (mail) some letters. 我出来寄几封信。❷贴出

(布告、通知等)

postage /ˈpəustɪdʒ/ *n.* [U]邮费;邮资:~ free 免付邮资 / ~ paid 邮资已付

postal /ˈpəustl/ *adj.* 邮政的;邮局的

postcard /ˈpəustkɑːd/ *n.* [C]明信片

poster /ˈpəustə(r)/ *n.* [C](张贴于公共地方的)告示;海报

postgraduate /ˌpəustˈgrædʒuət/ Ⅰ *adj.* 研究生的 Ⅱ *n.* [C]研究生

postmark /ˈpəustˌmɑːk/ *n.* [C]邮戳,日戳戳记

postpone /pəˈspəun/ *vt.* 延期;推迟:~ infinitely (temporarily) 无限(临时)延期 / The football game was ~d because of rain. 足球赛因下雨延期。

postscript /ˈpəustskrɪpt/ *n.* [C](信的)附笔;又及(略写为 P. S.)

postwar /ˌpəustˈwɔː/ *adj.* 战后的:~ problems 战后问题

pot /pɒt/ *n.* [C]罐;壶;锅

potable /ˈpəutəbl/ *adj.* 可饮的,适合饮用的:~ water 饮用水

potato /pəˈteɪtəu/ *n.* [C](*pl.* potatoes)马铃薯:baked ~es 烤马铃薯 / sweet ~es 红薯

potent /ˈpəutənt/ *adj.* ❶强有力的;有权势的;有影响的:a ~ opposition force 强大的反对派势力/a ~ figure 权势炙手可热的人物 ❷(议论等)有说服力的:Several ~ arguments were in his favour. 一些有说服力的论据对他很有利。❸(药、酒等)有效力的,有效能的;浓烈的,烈性的:a ~ coffee 浓咖啡/a ~ drink 烈酒

potential /pəˈtenʃ(ə)l/ Ⅰ *adj.* 潜在的;可能的:Try to find out the ~ demand of the market. 设法弄清市场的潜在需求。Ⅱ *n.* [U]潜力;潜能:develop one's ~ 发挥某人的潜力 / tap ~s 发掘潜力

pottery /ˈpɒtəri/ *n.* 陶器;陶器厂

poultry /ˈpəultri/ *n.* ❶家禽(谓语动词用复数):The ~ are being fed. 正在喂家禽。❷[U]家禽肉(谓语动词用单数):Poultry is expensive this Christmas. 这个圣诞节的禽肉很贵。

pound[1] /paund/ *n.* [C] ❶磅(重量单位,等于 16 盎司,也等于0.4536千克) ❷英镑(英国货币单位,等于 100 便士)

pound[2] /paund/ *vt.* ❶捣碎;舂烂:The ship was ~ed to pieces on the rock. 船在岩石上撞碎了。❷(连续)猛击,敲打:Someone is ~ing at the door with fists. 有人在用拳头打门。

pour /pɔː(r)/ *v.* ❶使流动;灌,注,倒:She ~ed the wine into the glass. 她把酒倒入一个玻璃杯。/ ~ **cold water on** 浇冷水,使沮丧 ~ **oil on the flames** 火上加油 ~ **out** 倾诉:She ~ed out her tale of misfortunes. 她倾诉自己的不幸遭遇。❷(大雨)倾盆而下:It never rains but it ~s. (谚语)不雨则已,一雨倾盆。

poverty /ˈpɒvəti/ *n.* [U]贫穷;缺乏:live in ~ 过穷日子

powder /ˈpaudə(r)/ *n.* ❶粉;细粉;粉末 ❷火药 派 powdered *adj.*

power /ˈpauə(r)/ *n.* ❶[U]力;能力;精力:water ~水力 / the natural ~s 自然力 / Knowledge is ~. 知识就是力量。❷[U]权力;势力 ❸[C]强国:the great ~s of Europe 欧洲列强 ❹[U]功率;动力:Running water produces ~ to run mills. 流水产生的动力推磨。

powerful /ˈpauəfl/ *adj.* ❶强大的;强有力的:We must build up a ~ army. 我们必须建立一支强大的军队。❷效力大的:a ~ engine 功率大的发动机 / a ~

remedy of cold 治感冒的特效药 ❸权威的;权力大的:a ~ man 有权势的人

powerless /ˈpauəlɪs/ *adj*. 无力的;无能为力的;无权力的;无效力的;无影响力的:the ~ disgust 无可奈何的厌恶 / a ~ office 没有什么权力的职位 / He wanted to do something but felt ~. 他想有所作为,但是感到无能为力。

practicable /ˈpræktɪkəbl/ *adj*. 能实行的;适用的

practical /ˈpræktɪkl/ *adj*. ❶实际的:a piece of advice with little ~ value 实际价值少的建议 ❷有实践经验的 ❸有用的;实用的:a ~ method 一种实用的方法

practically /ˈpræktɪkli/ *adv*. ❶ 实际地 ❷实事求是地 ❸(口语)几乎;差不多:We've ~ had no fine weather this month. 这个月可以说没有好天气。

practice /ˈpræktɪs/ *n*. ❶ 实施;实际;应用/ **put into** ~实践 **in** ~ 实践中;实际上:The method will not work in ~. 这个方法在实践中行不通。❷练习;实习:Piano playing needs a lot of ~. 弹钢琴需要多练习。❸习惯;常例:the ~ of closing shops on Sundays 星期日有休业的常例

practise /ˈpræktɪs/ *v*. (美国英语中也作 practice) ❶练习;实习:~ the piano 练习弹钢琴 ❷实行;习惯性地进行:~ caution 常常警惕 ❸开业当(医生,律师):My father ~s law (medicine). 我父亲开业当律师(医生)。/ ~ as a lawyer (doctor) 开业当律师(医生) 派 practised *adj*.

praise /preɪz/ Ⅰ *vt*. 称赞;赞美 / ~ **sb. for sth.** 为某事赞扬某人:They ~d the child for her courage. 他们赞扬了那孩子的勇敢。Ⅱ *n*. [U]称赞;赞扬:His heroism is worthy of great ~ (beyond ~). 他的英勇行为值得大加称赞(是赞美不尽的)。/ **in ~ of** 歌颂;表扬;称赞:The old man wrote a poem in ~ of his hometown. 老人写了一首诗歌颂他的家乡。

pray /preɪ/ *v*. ❶祈祷;祈求 / ~ **for** 请求;祈祷:The farmers are ~ing for rain. 农民们在祈雨。❷(书面语)乞求;恳求:We ~ you to show mercy. 我们恳求你发发慈悲。❸请(正式请求,相当于 please):Pray don't speak so loud. 请不要如此大声讲话。

prayer /ˈpreə(r)/ *n*. 祈祷;祈求:The sick man said his ~ for health. 这位病人祈求身体健康。

preach /priːtʃ/ *vt*. 说教;布道;鼓吹

preacher /ˈpriːtʃə(r)/ *n*. [C]传道士,牧师;说教者;鼓吹者

precaution /prɪˈkɔːʃn/ *n*. ❶[U] 预防;警惕 ❷[C]预防措施:take every possible ~ 采取一切预防措施

precede /prɪˈsiːd/ *vt*. ❶(在时间、顺序、重要性等方面)位于……之前,先于:two months preceding the flight 007 incident 007 航班事件发生的前两个月 / The solution of this problem ~s all other things. 这个问题的解决比其他事情都重要。❷走在……的前头,领先于:The usher ~d us into the theatre. 引座员在前面领我们走进了剧院。❸放在……之前,在……前加上(与 by, with 连用):~ the name by (with) Miss 在名字前加上 Miss

precedence(-cy) /ˈpresɪdəns(i)/ *n*. [U] ❶(时间、顺序或重要性上的)居前;在先,居先;领先:the order of ~ 先后顺序 ❷优先权/**take ~ over (of)** 在……之上;优先于:Quality still took ~

P

over quantity. 质量仍然优先于数量。

precedent / ˈpresɪdənt / *n.* [U]先例；惯例

preceding / prɪˈsiːdɪŋ / *adj.* 在前的；在先的：~ chapters 前面几章 / ~ years 前几年

precious / ˈpreʃəs / *adj.* 贵重的；高价的：the ~ metals 贵重金属 / ~ stones 宝石 / ~ words 金玉良言 / ~ to sb. 对某人来说很重要

precise / prɪˈsaɪs / *adj.* 准确的；正确的：~ measurements 精确的尺寸 / **at the ~ moment** 正在那时 ~ **in** 在……方面精确的：Try to be more ~ in your answers. 答案尽量要明确。

precision / prɪˈsɪʒn / *n.* [U]精确(性)；精密(度)：~ instruments 精密仪器

predecessor / ˈpriːdɪsesə(r) / *n.* [C] ❶前辈；前任者 ❷ 被取代的事物

predict / prɪˈdɪkt / *vt.* 预言；预示；预告：~ a good harvest 预示丰收

P

prediction / prɪˈdɪkʃən/ *n.* ❶预言；预测，预料，预计；预报：environmental monitoring and ~ 环境监测 / provide accurate long-term ~ 提供准确的长期预报 ❷预言的事物；预测(或预料、预计)的事物；预报的事物

predominant / prɪˈdɒmɪnənt / *adj.* ❶有势力的；重要的；占主导(或支配)地位的：a ~ member of the city council 市政厅里最有势力的成员/Fear with me became ~. 恐惧在我心里占了上风。❷(在数量等方面)占绝大多数的；显著的；普遍的：The ~ key of the opera is D minor. 这出歌剧的基调是 D 小调。/ Alice's health was her ~ worry. 艾丽丝的健康是她的一大心病。

predominate / prɪˈdɒmɪˌneɪt / *vi.* ❶占主导(或支配)地位；统治；控制：Service industries ~ for employment in the island. 服务性行业在该岛就业市场上占主导地位。❷(在数量等方面)占优势，占绝大多数：In the colder regions, pine trees ~. 在寒冷的地带，绝大多数树木是松树。

preeminent / priːˈemɪnənt / *adj.* 超群的，非凡的，卓越的，杰出的：a ~ place of industry 杰出的工业重镇/the ~ journal of applied linguistics 独树一帜的应用语言学期刊

preface / ˈprefəs / *n.* [C]序言；前言；引语：Who wrote the ~ to the book? 谁给书写的序？

prefer / prɪˈfɜː(r) / *v.* (-ferred;-ferring) 更喜爱；宁可；优先选择

preferable / ˈprefrəbl / *adj.* 更可取的；更合意的；更好的：In such hot weather, swimming is ~ to other sports. 天这样热，游泳比其他运动更好些。

preference / ˈprefrəns / *n.* 偏爱；优先；优先权 / **have a ~ for** 偏爱：Our monitor has a ~ for novels. 我们的班长特爱读小说。**in ~ to ...** 宁可……而不……：The Chinese people drink tea in ~ to coffee. 中国人爱喝茶而不爱喝咖啡。

prefix / ˈpriːfɪks / *n.* [C] 前缀(略为 pref.)

pregnancy / ˈpregnənsi / *n.* 怀孕，妊娠；怀孕期，妊娠期：She kept well throughout her ~. 整个怀孕期间她身体保养得很好。

pregnant / ˈpregnənt / *adj.* ❶怀孕的 ❷意味深长的

prehistoric / ˌpriːhɪˈstɒrɪk / *adj.* 史前的；史前时代的：the ~ period 史前期

prehistory / ˌpriːˈhɪstri / *n.* [U]史前

prejudice /ˈpredʒʊdɪs/ Ⅰ *n.* 偏见；成见 / **free from** ~毫无成见 **break down** ~ 消除成见：It is necessary to break down racial ~. 应该消除种族偏见。**have (hold) a** ~ 抱有成见(偏见)：I have no ~ against you. 我对你毫无成见。Ⅱ *vt.* 使(某人)抱有成见(偏见)：What Tom had said ~d her against her stepmother. 汤姆说的话使她对她的继母产生偏见。

preliminary /prɪˈlɪmɪnəri/ *adj.* (只作定语)预备的；初步的：a ~ examination 初试 / a ~ hearing 预审 / a ~ investigation 初步调查 / make a few ~ remarks 说几句开场白 / ~ work 前期工作

prelude /ˈprelju:d/ *n.* [C]❶序幕；前奏；先兆 ❷前奏曲

premature /ˈpremətʃə(r)/ *adj.* 过早的；早熟的：a ~ death 早死；夭折 / a ~ decision 草率的决定

premier /ˈpremɪə(r)/ Ⅰ *n.* [C]总理；首相 Ⅱ *adj.* 第一的；首位的；首席的

premium /ˈpri:mɪəm/ *n.* [C] ❶保险费；保险金：property ~s 财产保险费 ❷奖金；红利；津贴，补贴；额外费用：raise the overtime pay ~提高超时工资津贴 ❸奖品；奖励：a ~ for good conduct 品行优良奖

preparation /ˌprepəˈreɪʃn/ *n.* ❶[U]准备；预备：The meal is in ~. 饭菜正在准备中。/ **in ~ for** 为……做准备：We are doing everything in ~ for the outing. 我们正在为出游做准备。❷[C](常用 *pl.*)准备的事物：~s for war 战备 / make ~s for a voyage 做好航海的准备 / The school is making ~s for the celebration. 学校在为庆祝活动做准备。

preparatory /prɪˈpærətri/ *adj.* 预备的；初步的：~ measures 预备措施

prepare /prɪˈpeə(r)/ *v.* 准备，预备：~ a meal 预备饭菜/ **be ~d for** 为……做准备：Be ~d for bad news. 做好听到坏消息的准备。

prepay /ˌpri:ˈpeɪ/ *vt.* (prepaid /ˌpri:ˈpeɪd/, prepaid) 预付：~ the postage 预付邮费

preposition /ˌprepəˈzɪʃn/ *n.* [C]介词

prescribe /prɪˈskraɪb/ *v.* ❶开药方；开处方：The doctor ~d quinine. 医生开了奎宁。❷指示；规定：I have finished reading the ~d reference books. 我已读完了指定的参考书。

prescription /prɪˈskrɪpʃn/ *n.* 药方；处方

presence /ˈprezəns/ *n.* [U]出席；在场：Your ~ at the party is expected. 敬请光临晚会。/ **in the ~ of sb.** (**in sb.'s** ~) 在某人面前，当着某人的面：The boy was punished in the ~ of all his classmates. 那男孩在全班同学面前受惩罚。

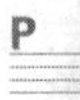

present[1] /ˈprezənt/ Ⅰ *adj.* ❶在场的；出席的：Were you ~ at the ceremony? 你出席典礼了吗？❷现存的；现在的：~ government 现政府 Ⅱ *n.* ❶[C]礼物：a birthday (Christmas) ~生日(圣诞)礼物 ❷[U]现在；目前：the past, the ~ and the future 过去、现在和将来 / **at** ~ 现在；当前：We don't need any more at ~. 现在我们不需要什么了。**up to the** ~到目前为止：She is well up to the ~. 到目前为止她身体很好。

present[2] /prɪˈzent/ *vt.* ❶呈递；提出：~ an application 呈交申请书 ❷赠；给：~ a gift 赠一份礼 ❸介绍；引见：It is my pleasure to ~ the guest to you. 我很高兴向你介绍这位客人。❹上演：The theatre will ~ *Tea House* next week. 这

家剧院下周上演《茶馆》。

presentation /ˌprəzən'teɪʃn / *n.* ❶[U]介绍;引见 ❷[C]赠品;礼物 ❸授予仪式 ❹[U]呈现 ❺上演;演出

presently /'prezəntli / *adv.* 不久;一会儿:I'll be with you ~. 我不久就可陪你。

preservation / ˌprezə'veɪʃn / *n.* [U]保存;储藏;防腐;保持;维持

preservative / prɪ'zɜːvətɪv / Ⅰ *adj.* 有保存能力的;防腐的 Ⅱ *n.* 防腐剂

preserve / prɪ'zɜːv / *vt.* 保护;使不受损失;防腐;保存;维持:Ice can help ~ food. 冰能帮助保存食物。

preside / prɪ'zaɪd / *vi.* 主持;主管/ ~ **over** 主持:The vice-chairman ~d over the meeting this time. 这次是副主席主持会议。

president / 'prezɪdənt / *n.* [C] ❶总统 ❷(公司的)董事长 ❸(学校的)院长,校长 ❹(协会的)会长

P

press / pres / Ⅰ *n.* ❶(the ~) 定期刊物;杂志;报界;新闻界:~ conference 记者招待会/ The book was favorably noticed by the ~. 这本书曾被新闻界看好。❷印刷业 ❸出版社;通讯社:the Oxford University Press 牛津大学出版社 Ⅱ *v.* ❶压,按;压平;熨平:~ the button 按按钮 / ~ a suit (with an iron) (用熨斗)熨平衣服 ❷用力推;推进;拥挤:The crowd ~ed forward to see what was happening. 群众挤向前去观看发生了什么事。❸使负重担;压迫:His responsibilities ~ heavily upon him. 他的责任沉重地压在他的身上。

pressing / 'presɪŋ / *adj.* 急迫的;迫切的

pressure / 'preʃə(r) / *n.* 压;压力;强制力;压强:atmospheric ~ 大气压/ **bring (put) ~ on** 对……施加压力:They brought (put) ~ on him to sell his land. 他们给他施加压力要他卖掉土地。**under the ~ of** 在……的压力下:Under the ~ of public opinion, he had to leave. 在舆论的压力下,他只得离开。

prestige / pre'stiːʒ / *n.* [U]威望;威信;声望:The unselfish man is of great ~. 这个无私的人有很高的威信。

prestigious / pre'stɪdʒəs/ *adj.* 有声望的,有威望的;有威信的;受尊敬的:a host of ~ awards 大量有声望的奖项 / ~ private universities 著名的私立大学 派 prestigiously *adv.* ;prestigiousness *n.*

presume / prɪ'zjuːm / *vt.* 假定;假设;揣测:From the way they talked, I ~d that they were good friends. 我从他们谈话的方式中揣测他们是好朋友。

presumption / prɪ'zʌm(p)ʃn / *n.* [C] ❶推测;推定;假设,假定:Although Government could alter the proposals, the ~ was that they would not. 按说政府是可以改变这些提案的,但是据推测他们不会这么做。❷推出推论的理由(或根据、证据):There is a strong ~ in favour of the falsehood of their story. 有一个强有力的证据足以推定他们的报道是虚假的。

pretence(-se) / prɪ'tens / *n.* ❶[U]假装;掩饰:do sth. under the ~ of friendship (religion, patriotism) 以友谊(宗教、爱国)为掩饰而做某事 ❷[C]借口;托词:It is only a ~ of friendship. 那不过是以友谊为借口罢了。

pretend / prɪ'tend / *v.* 假装(有);佯称(有):~ illness 装病 / ~ ignorance 假装不知情

pretentious / prɪ'tenʃəs / *adj.* ❶自负的,自命不凡的,狂妄的:the ~ opinions

狂妄的看法/He got called ~ for that. 就为了这件事,他被人骂成狂妄的家伙。❷炫耀的;做作的;矫饰的:The choice of title for the poem seems a little ~. 这首诗题目选得似乎有些哗众取宠。

pretext /ˈpriːtekst/ *n.* [C]借口;托词:/ **on (under) the ~ of** 以……为借口:He didn't help me on the ~ of having to see a doctor. 他以必须看病为借口不帮助我。

pretty /ˈprɪti/ Ⅰ *adj.* (-ier,-iest)悦人的;可爱的;漂亮的:What a ~ flower! 多美的一朵花! Ⅱ *adv.* 相当;颇:It's ~ cold outdoors today. 今天户外很冷。

prevail /prɪˈveɪl/ *vi.* ❶流行;盛行:The custom ~s in the area. 这种风俗在该地区很盛行。❷胜过;占优势:~ over one's enemies 战胜敌人

prevailing /prɪˈveɪlɪŋ/ *adj.* 占优势的;流行的

prevalent /ˈprevələnt/ *adj.* 流行的;盛行的

prevent /prɪˈvent/ *v.* 预防;阻止;妨碍/ ~ **sb. from doing sth.** 阻止某人做某事:The heavy rain ~ed him from coming. 大雨使他不能来。派 prevention *n.*

preventable /prɪˈventəbl/ *adj.* 可防止的,可预防的:a ~ disease 可以预防的疾病

preview /ˈpriːvjuː/ *n.* [C] ❶预观;预览;预审;预习 ❷(公开艺术展之前的)预展;(电影的)预映,试映;(戏剧等的)预演,试演:give a ~ of the director's latest film 预映该导演的最新电影 ❸预告:a ~ of next week's viewing 下星期收视节目预告

previous /ˈpriːvɪəs/ *adj.* (时间或顺序上)在前的,早先的:~ to sb.'s arrival 在某人到达之前 / ~ to departure 在出发之前 / The ~ lesson was hard. 前面的一课很难。派 previously *adv.*

prevision /ˌpriːˈvɪʒən/ *n.* [U]先见;预知

prey /preɪ/ Ⅰ *vi.* 捕获;折磨 Ⅱ *n.* [C]猎获物;(喻)牺牲品:The wolf is eating his ~. 狼在吃猎获物。

price /praɪs/ Ⅰ *n.* ❶[C] 价格;价钱:~ list 价目表 / ~ tag 价格标签/ What's the ~ of this picture? 这幅画多少钱? / **above (beyond, without)** ~ 无价的;非常贵重的 **at any** ~ 不惜任何代价:It must be done at any ~. 必须不惜任何代价把它做好。❷[U] 价值:pearls of great ~ 极贵重的珍珠 Ⅱ *vt.* 给……标价;给……定价:All goods should be clearly ~d. 所有商品都应该标明价格。

priceless /ˈpraɪsləs/ *adj.* 无价的;非常贵重的:~ paintings 极贵重的画

prick /prɪk/ Ⅰ *vt.* 刺(穿) Ⅱ *n.* [C]刺孔

pricker /ˈprɪkə(r)/ *n.* [C]针;锥子

pride /praɪd/ *n.* [U] 骄傲;傲慢;自豪;得意/ **in the ~ of** 在……的全盛(巅峰)时期:He died in the ~ of his life. 他在年富力强时期去世。**take ~ in** 对……感到自豪:She took ~ in her son's success. 她对儿子的成功感到自豪。

priest /priːst/ *n.* [C]教士;牧师;神父

primacy /ˈpraɪməsi/ *n.* [U](重要性、级别、次序等中的)首位,第一位;基础:Industrial employment took ~ over agricultural work in some countries. 在一些国家,工业就业的重要性超过了农业

primarily /praɪˈmerəli/ *adv.* 首先;最初

地；基本地；主要地：The book is ~ meant for children. 这本书主要是为小孩子写的。

primary /ˈpraɪməri/ *adj.* 主要的；最初的；基本的：a ~ school 小学

prime /praɪm/ *adj.* ❶主要的；首位的：his ~ motive 他的主要动机 ❷最佳的；第一流的：~ beef 上等牛肉

primitive /ˈprɪmətɪv/ *adj.* ❶原始的；早期的；未开化的：~ men 原始人 / ~ society 原始社会 / ~ forests 原始森林 ❷简单的；粗糙的：Some ~ weapons were found in the cave. 山洞里发现了一些简陋的武器。派 primitively *adv.*

prince /prɪns/ *n.* [C]王子；太子

princess /ˌprɪnˈses/ *n.* [C]王妃；公主

principal /ˈprɪnsəpl/ Ⅰ *adj.* 主要的；首要的；重要的 Ⅱ *n.* [C]首长；校长

principle /ˈprɪnsəpl/ *n.* ❶原则；原理：the ~s of geometry 几何学原理 ❷行为准则 / **in** ~原则上：I agree with you in ~. 我原则上同意你的意见。

P

print /prɪnt/ Ⅰ *v.* 印；印刷：These books are well ~ed. 这些书印制精良。Ⅱ *n.* ❶[U]印刷符号：in large (small) ~以大(小)字体印刷 / **in** ~ 已出版；在销售：The writer is glad to see his novel in ~. 这位作家很高兴看到他的小说出版了。**out of** ~已售完；绝版：Sorry, the book you want has been out of ~. 对不起，你要的那种书已经售完。❷[C]印迹；痕迹：a finger ~ 指纹

printer /ˈprɪntə(r)/ *n.* [C] ❶印刷工人；排版工；排字工 ❷印刷业者；印刷商 ❸印刷机；打印机

printing /ˈprɪntɪŋ/ *n.* ❶[U]印刷业；印刷术：the ~ union 印刷业联合会 ❷[C](书的)一次印数；版，版次，印刷次数：the first ~ of 3,000 copies 第一版3 000册的印数 ❸[U]印刷字体：hand ~ 手写印刷体

prior /ˈpraɪə(r)/ *adj.* 在先的；优先的：Members of the club have a ~ claim to the opportunity. 俱乐部会员对此机会享有优先权。/ ~ **to** 先于；优先于：The stadium was finished ~ to the Asian Games. 体育场在亚运会前竣工。

priority /praɪˈɒrəti/ *n.* ❶[U]在先；居前：Things should be taken up in order of ~. 办事应有个先后次序。❷[C]优先权 ❸[C]优先考虑的事：Being a parent is her finst ~. 做好母亲是她的头等大事。

prison /ˈprɪzn/ *n.* 监狱；监牢；牢房；监禁/ **put sb. in** ~把某人关进监狱：The robber was put in ~. 那盗贼被关进了监狱。

prisoner /ˈprɪznə(r)/ *n.* [C]囚犯；犯人；俘虏

privacy /ˈprɪvəsi, ˈpraɪvəsi/ *n.* [U] ❶隐居；独处，独守；不受干扰的状态：in the ~ of a living room 在静谧的客厅里 ❷隐私权；私事；私生活：He can not allow the outside world to penetrate his ~. 他不允许外界介入他的私生活。❸私下；秘密；保密：~ system 保密系统/in strict ~完全秘密地

private /ˈpraɪvət/ *adj.* 私人的；私有的；秘密的：a ~ letter 私信 / a ~ school 私立学校 / have ~ information about sth. 得到有关某事的秘密消息 派 privately *adv.*

privilege /ˈprɪvəlɪdʒ/ *n.* [C]特权；优惠：diplomatic ~s 外交特权 / enjoy the ~ in trade 享受贸易特权

privileged /ˈprɪvɪlɪdʒd/ *adj.* ❶特权的；享有特权的；优先的：a ~ job 美差/a member of a ～ class 特权阶层的一员 ❷特许的；专用的：the three ～ Bible publishers 三家特许的《圣经》出版商/a ～ parking stall 专用停车处

prize /praɪz/ Ⅰ *n.* [C]奖金；奖品：be awarded a ～ for good conducts 因表现良好而获奖 / draw a ～-winning ticket in a lottery 中彩 Ⅱ *vt.* 珍视；重视：We ～ honor above money. 我们珍视荣誉更胜于金钱。

probability /ˌprɒbəˈbɪləti/ *n.* 可能性；可能发生的事

probable /ˈprɒbəbl/ *adj.* 大概的；可能的：It is ～ that the discussion will be put off. 讨论可能会推迟。

probably /ˈprɒbəbli/ *adv.* 大概；或许

probe /prəʊb/ Ⅰ *n.* [C] ❶探索；(深入的)调查；探查：a police ～ into illegal financial dealing 警方对非法金融交易的调查 ❷探测工具；探头 ❸(医用)探针，探子 Ⅱ *v.* ❶探究；探查；探索；(深入地)调查：～ a question of morality 调查一个道德问题/The police are probing into the case. 警方正调查这一案件。❷用探针(或探测器等)探测；探查：He ascended to the edge of the snow, stopped and ～d it with his axe. 他爬上雪坡的边缘，然后停步用冰斧探一下冰层虚实。❸(用尖头工具)刺穿：The bird's bill ～d the bard crevice. 鸟喙啄入树皮裂缝。

problem /ˈprɒbləm/ *n.* [C] 问题；难题：mathematical ～s 数学题 / ～ of food and clothing 吃穿(温饱)问题

procedure /prəˈsiːdʒə(r)/ *n.* 程序；步骤；过程：follow a ～按程序办

proceed /prəˈsiːd/ *vi.* 前进；继续进行：Proceed with your story. 继续讲你的故事。派 proceeding *n.*

process /ˈprəʊses/ Ⅰ *n.* [C] ❶经过；过程：the ～es of digestion, reproduction and growth 消化、生殖和生长的过程 ❷前进；进展 / **in ～ of time** 随着时间的推进：In ～ of time, the house will be finished. 这房子迟早会建成。**in the ～ of** 在……的过程中：This theory has stood all tests in the ～ of history. 这个理论在历史进程中经受了一切考验。Ⅱ *vt.* 加工；处理：～ medical herbs 加工中草药

procession /prəˈseʃn/ *n.* ❶[C](人、车辆等的)行列，队伍：a funeral ～送葬的行列 ❷[U]列队进行：walking in ～ through the streets 列队走过街道 派 processional *adj.*

processor /ˈprəʊsesə(r)/ *n.* [C]加工者；处理者；(计算机)资料处理机(处理器)

proclaim /prə(ʊ)ˈkleɪm/ *vt.* ❶(公开或正式)宣布，公布；宣告；声明：～ war 宣战/brazenly ～ rebellion 悍然宣称要造反 ❷声称，宣称……为：The Prince ～ed King in succession to his father, who was dead. 国王驾崩，王子被宣告继承王位。

proclamation /ˌprɒkləˈmeɪʃn/ *n.* ❶[U]宣布，公布：the ～ of martial law 宣布戒严 ❷[C]公告，布告；声明：～s of independence 独立宣言

produce Ⅰ /prəˈdjuːs/ *v.* 制造；生产；产生：～ woolen goods 生产毛织品 Ⅱ /ˈprɒdjuːs/ *n.* [U]产品；(尤指)农产品：garden (farm) ～ 果园(农场)的产品

producer /prəˈdjuːsə(r)/ *n.* [C] ❶(商品或货物的)生产者；制造者；制作者：the ～ of vehicles 汽车制造商 / the world's largest ～ of natural gas 世界最

大的天然气生产商 ❷(电影或电视片等的)制片人,监制人;(广播节目的)制作人

product / ˈprɒdʌkt / *n.* [C](天然或人造的)产物;产品:industrial ~s 工业产品/ by -~ 副产品

production / prəˈdʌkʃn / *n.* ❶[U]制造;生产;产量:the ~ of crops (manufactured goods)农作物(工业品)的生产 / a fall (an increase) in ~ 产量的减少(增加) ❷[C]制造品;生产成品:his early ~s as a writer 他作为作家的早期作品

productive / prəˈdʌktɪv / *adj.* (能)生产的;丰饶的;多产的:~ forces 生产力 / a ~ writer 一位多产作家

productivity / ˌprɒdʌkˈtɪvəti / *n.* [U]生产能力;生产率

profess / ˈprəʊfes / *vt.* ❶公开声明;声称;表白:All of them ~ed an enthusiasm for the adventures. 他们所有的人都声称热衷于冒险。❷表明忠于;公开宣布(信仰):~ religion 公开表示信教

profession / prəˈfeʃn / *n.* [C]职业;(需要接受高等教育或特殊训练的)专门职业/ **by** ~ 以……为职业:He is a doctor by ~. 他的职业是医生。

professional / prəˈfeʃənl / Ⅰ *adj.* 专门的;职业的:a ~ football player 职业足球运动员 / ~ training 专业训练 Ⅱ *n.* [C] ❶职业选手 ❷专家;内行人

professor / prəˈfesə(r) / *n.* [C]教授:associate(full)~ 副(正)教授 / honourable(visiting)~ 名誉(客座)教授

proficiency / prəˈfɪʃənsi / *n.* [U] 熟练;精通(与 in 连用):He made little ~ in literary accomplishments. 他在文学方面成就不多。

proficient / prəˈfɪʃənt / *adj.* 熟练的;精通的:She was ~ in music. 她精通音乐。派 proficiently *adv.*

profile / ˈprəʊfaɪl / Ⅰ *n.* [C] ❶侧影;侧面像:a sharp ~棱角分明的侧面像/a ~ relief bust of Washington 华盛顿的侧面半身像浮雕 ❷轮廓;外貌,外观;外形:the ~ of a distant hill 远山的轮廓 ❸传略;(人物)简介,小传,素描;概貌:Hair analysis can provide a ~ of one's overall nutritional health. 分析头发可以基本上知道一个人的总的营养状况。/The magazine features celebrity ~s. 这本杂志登载名人简介。Ⅱ *vt.* ❶画……的侧面像 ❷描绘……的轮廓;显示……的轮廓:Skyscrapers are ~d against cloudless skies. 无云的天空衬托出摩天大楼的轮廓。❸写……的简介;对……做介绍;简单描述:a book profiling fourteen great cooks with a selection of their recipes 一本介绍 14 位大厨师以及他们的菜谱的书

profit / ˈprɒfɪt / Ⅰ *n.* ❶利益;益处:gain ~ from one's studies 从学习中获得好处 ❷利润:sell sth. at a ~ 有利可图地售出 / do sth. for ~为赢利做某事 Ⅱ *v.* ❶(指事物) 对……有利,对……有益:What can it ~ him? 此事对他有什么益处呢? ❷(指人)获利,获益:I have ~ed by your advice. 我从你的劝告中获益。派 profitable *adj.*

profound / prəˈfaʊnd / *adj.* 深的;深奥的;博学的;透彻的:a ~ sleep (sigh, bow)熟睡(深长的叹息,深深的鞠躬) / take a ~ interest in sth. 对某事物深感兴趣 派 profoundly *adv.*

program(me) / ˈprəʊgræm / Ⅰ*n.* [C] ❶节目单;程序表:write a ~ 列节目单 ❷计划;规划;方案;大纲;纲要:a political ~

政治纲领 / a party ~党纲 ❸(计算机)程序 ❹(学校的)教学课程：graduate (undergraduate) ~ 研究生(本科)课程 Ⅱ *v.* 编制程序；给计算机输入程序：~ a computer 给计算机编程序

progress Ⅰ / ˈprəugres / *n.* [U]进步；进展；发展/ **make** ~取得进步；取得进展：He has made great ~ in English. 他在英语方面已经取得了很大的进步。**in** ~ 在进展中：The research is in ~. 研究工作在进行之中。Ⅱ /prəˈgres / *vi.* 进步；进行：The work is ~ing steadily. 工作正在稳步进行。派 progressive *adj.*

prohibit / prəˈhɪbɪt / *vt.* 禁止；防止：~ children from smoking 禁止儿童吸烟 / Smoking is strictly ~ed here. 此地严禁吸烟。派 prohibition *n.*

project Ⅰ / ˈprɒdʒekt / *n.* [C] ❶方案；计划：The city is drawing up a ~ to develop its industries. 这座城市正在制订发展工业的方案。❷工程；项目：Project of Expectation 希望工程 / The province has carried out several capital construction ~s. 这个省实施了几个基本建设项目。Ⅱ /prəˈdʒekt/ *v.* ❶投射；放映：Please ~ the film on the screen. 请把影片放映出来。❷规划：The county has ~ed a new dam. 这个县规划要修一座新水坝。❸伸出；突出；凸出：His forehead ~ s noticeably. 他的前额明显前凸。

projection / prəˈdʒekʃən/ *n.* ❶发射；投射；抛射；投掷 ❷凸出，伸出；凸出(或伸出)物：the ~ of blood vessels 血管的突出 ❸投影；放映；影射物：the ~ room 投影室(或放映室)

projector / prəˈdʒektə(r)/ *n.* [C]放映机；幻灯机；投影仪

prolong / prəˈlɒŋ / *vt.* 延长；拖长：~ a visit 延长访问时间

prominence / ˈprɒmɪnəns / *n.* [U]显著；突出，杰出；重要：gain national ~获得突出的国内地位/achieve ~ in science 在科学界成绩斐然

prominent / ˈprɒmɪnənt / *adj.* ❶突出的；杰出的：a ~ statesman and scientist 一位杰出的政治家和科学家 ❷突起的；凸出的 ❸重要的：play a ~ part 起重要作用

promise / ˈprɒmɪs / Ⅰ *n.* ❶[C]诺言；约定：make (keep, carry out, break) a ~ 许下(信守，履行，不守)诺言 / Mother made a ~ to buy her a toy dog. 妈妈答应给她买只玩具狗。❷[U]希望；(有)前途：a writer of ~ 有前途的作家 Ⅱ *v.* ❶答应；允诺；约定：They ~d an immediate reply. 他们答应立即回答。❷有……希望；预示：The dark clouds ~ rain. 乌云预示有雨。

promising / ˈprɒmɪsɪŋ / *adj.* 有希望的：a ~ student 有前途的学生 / ~ crops 长势很好的庄稼

promote / prəˈməut / *vt.* ❶促进；发扬；使增长；使增进：~ friendships among the students 增进同学之间的友谊 / ~ economic and cultural exchanges 促进经济文化交流 /The factory is successful in promoting the sales of its products. 这家工厂促销产品很成功。❷提拔，提升：The clerk was ~d manager. 那位办事员被提升为经理。

promoter / prəˈməutə(r)/ *n.* [C](尤指体育比赛、文艺演出等的)组织者；赞助人，资助者：a boxing ~ 拳击比赛的筹划者 / Harper was an acrobatics ~ who engineered the tour. 哈珀是策划杂技巡回演出的赞助人。派 sponsor

promotion / prəˈməuʃn / *n.* [U]促进；提

升;促销:sales ~ 促销

prompt /prɒmpt/ Ⅰ *adj.* 敏捷的;迅速的;及时的:a ~ medical treatment 及时的治疗 Ⅱ *vt.* 促使;推动;激起:The good result ~ed her to new efforts. 好的结果激发她做出新的努力。

prone /prəʊn/ *adj.* ❶平卧的,俯卧的;卧倒的:a ~ position 俯卧姿势 ❷易于……的,倾向于……的;有……癖的:be ~ to fits of rage 动不动就发火/We are ~ to think of an extroverted person as a gregarious person. 我们容易把外向的人当成爱社交的人。

pronoun /ˈprəʊnaʊn/ *n.* [C]代词

pronounce /prəˈnaʊns/ *v.* ❶(尤指正式或官方)宣称,宣布:Has the judgment been ~d yet? 判决已宣布了吗? ❷发出(字母或词等)的音:Pronounce these words clearly. 把这些词读清楚。

pronounced /prə(ʊ)ˈnaʊnst/ *adj.* ❶显著的,明显的,显眼的:a whiskey of less ~ taste 味道不太浓烈的威士忌酒 ❷断然的,决然的;强硬的:a ~ opinion 强硬的观点

pronouncement /prə(ʊ)ˈnaʊnsmənt/ *n.* [C] ❶声明,公告 ❷看法,意见;决定:the ~ of literary critics on the short story 文艺批评家们对短篇小说的看法

pronunciation /prəˌnʌnsɪˈeɪʃn/ *n.* [U](一种语言的)发音;发音法

proof /pruːf/ *n.* ❶证据:Is there any ~ that the accused man was at the scene of the crime? 有什么证据证明被告在犯罪现场吗? / We finally got several ~s of her innocence. 我们最后取得数件能证实她无罪的证据。❷证明;证实:Is it capable of ~ that there exists life on the Mars? 能证实火星上有生物存在吗?

propaganda /ˌprɒpəˈgændə/ *n.* [U]宣传;传播:~ instruments 宣传工具 / carry on active ~大力宣传

propagandist /ˌprɒpəˈgændɪst/ *n.* [C]宣传员

propagate /ˈprɒpəgeɪt/ *vt.* 传播;宣传:~ one's ideas 宣传自己的观点

propel /prəˈpel/ *vt* (-pelled;-pelling)推进;推动:The ship is ~led by steam. 这船靠蒸汽动力推动。

propeller /prəˈpelə(r)/ *n.* [C]螺旋桨;推进器

proper /ˈprɒpə(r)/ *adj.* ❶正确的;正当的;适当的:Is this the tool ~ for the job? 这是做那件工作的适当工具吗? ❷专为……的;独特的(与 to 连用):the books ~ to this subject 专论此问题的一些书 派 properly *adv.*

property /ˈprɒpəti/ *n.* ❶[U]财产;资产:personal ~ 个人财产;动产 / immovable ~ 不动产 ❷[U]所有权;所有:There is no ~ in the seashore. (The seashore cannot be privately owned.)海岸不能据为私有。❸房地产:He has a small ~ in Kentucky. 他在肯塔基州有些房地产。❹[C]特性;属性;性质:herbs with healing properties 有治疗性能的草药

prophecy /ˈprɒfəsi/ *n.* [C]预言;预言能力

prophet /ˈprɒfɪt/ *n.* [C]预言家;先知

proportion /prəˈpɔːʃn/ *n.* ❶[U]比例/ **in ~ to** 与……成比例:Imports will be allowed in ~ to exports. 进口产品数量将依据出口产品数量的比例而定。**out of ~ to** 与……不成比例:The expenditure is out of ~ to the income. 支出和收入不成比例。❷[C] 部分:You have not done your ~ of the work. 你没做完你的那份工作。

proportional / prə'pɔːʃnəl / *adj.* ❶比例的；成比例的：~ distribution (reduction) 按比例分配(缩减) ❷均衡的，协调的，相称的：meet with an end ~ to one's crime 得到罪有应得的结局

proposal / prə'pəuzl / *n.* [C]建议；计划：~s of increasing trade between two countries 促进两国间贸易的计划

propose / prə'pəuz / *v.* ❶提议；建议：I ~ an early start. 我建议早些动身。❷提名；推荐：I'd like to ~ Bob for membership of our football team. 我推荐鲍勃成为我们足球队的队员。

proposition / ˌprɒpə'zɪʃn / *n.* [C] ❶命题；主题 ❷主张；建议；提议：The ~ was rejected as impractical. 因为不切实际，这个提议被否决了。

propulsion / prə'pʌlʃn / *n.* [U]推进；推进力

prose / prəuz / *n.* [U]散文：a ~ writer 散文作家

prosecute / 'prɒsɪkjuːt / *vt.* 起诉；控告：The manager was ~d for accepting bribes. 经理因受贿被起诉。

prosecution / ˌprɒsɪ'kjuːʃn / *n.* [U]起诉；控告

prosecutor / ˌprɒsɪ'kjuːtə(r) / *n.* [C]起诉者；控告人

prospect / 'prɒspekt / *n.* ❶[C]景色 ❷[C]前景；盼望的事物：The ~s for the wine harvest are poor this year. 今年的葡萄酒收成前景不好。❸[U]期望；希望：I see no ~ of his recovering. 我认为他没有痊愈的希望。

prospective / prə(ʊ)'spektɪv / *adj.* 将来的；可能发生的；即将成为的：verify the resumes of all ~ employees 查证所有雇员人选的个人简历/a ~ bride 准新娘

prosper / 'prɒspə(r) / *vi.* 繁荣；昌盛；兴旺：Our country is ~ing with each passing day. 我们的国家蒸蒸日上。

prosperity / prɒ'sperəti / *n.* [U]成功；繁荣；昌盛：a life of happiness and ~ 幸福与成功的一生

prosperous / 'prɒspərəs / *adj.* 成功的；繁荣的；昌盛的：a ~ business 兴隆的生意 / ~ years 繁荣的年代

protect / prə'tekt / *v.* 防卫；保护；防护 / ~ **from** (**against**) ... 使不受……的伤害：The army ~ed the country against attack. 军队保卫国家免遭攻击。/ She's wearing dark glasses to ~ her eyes from the sun. 她戴着墨镜，以防阳光刺眼。

protection / prə'tekʃn / *n.* ❶[U]防御；保护；警戒 ❷[C]保护者；保护物：wearing a heavy overcoat as a ~ against the cold 穿厚大衣以御寒

protective / prə'tektɪv / *adj.* 保护的；防护的：~ measures 保护措施

protein / 'prəutiːn / *n.* [U]蛋白质：animal and vegetable ~ 动物和植物蛋白质 / Milk contains much ~. 牛奶里含丰富的蛋白质。

protest Ⅰ / prə'test / *v.* 抗议；坚决反对/ ~ **against** (**about**, **at**) 对……提出抗议：Many people ~ed against the environmental pollution. 许多人都抗议环境受到污染。Ⅱ / 'prəutest / *n.* 抗议：The customer expressed his ~ against the poor quality of the goods. 顾客对商品质量低劣表示抗议。/The angry people retired in ~. 愤怒的人们为表示抗议而退场。

prototype / 'prəutətaɪp / *n.* [C]原型；典

型;范例

proud / praʊd / *adj.* ❶自尊的;自豪的 / **be ~ of ...** 对……感到自豪:They are ~ of their clever children. 他们为有聪明的孩子而感到自豪。❷傲慢的;狂妄的:He was too ~ to join our party. 他太骄傲,不屑参加我们的集会。派 proudly *adv.*

prove / pruːv / *vt.* (proved, proved 或 proven)证明;证实:Facts have ~d that practice is the sole criterion for testing truth. 事实证明实践是检验真理的唯一标准。

proverb / ˈprɒvɜːb / *n.* [C]谚语;格言

provide / prəˈvaɪd / *v.* ❶提供 / **~ for ...** 为……提供所需;为……做准备:He has a large family to ~ for. 他需要维持一个大家庭。**~ sb. with sth.** 供给某人某物:~ children with food and clothes 供给孩子们衣食 / The sun ~s us with energy. 太阳供给我们能量。❷准备;预防:~ against (for) an earthquake 做预防地震的准备 ❸规定

provided / prəˈvaɪdɪd / *conj.* 倘若;只要:Provided there is no opposition, we shall hold the meeting here. 倘若没有人反对,我们就在这儿开会。/ **~ that** 假如;若是:I'll go, ~ that you go too. 如果你去,我就去。

province / ˈprɒvɪns / *n.* [C]省;(一个国家的)大行政区:Sichuan Province (the Province of Sichuan) 四川省

provincial / prəˈvɪnʃəl / *adj.* 省的;地方的

provision / prəˈvɪʒn / *n.* ❶[U]供应:The ~ of water and gas in the city is rich. 城里水和气的供应充足。❷[U]准备;预备 ❸[C]规定;条款:They have violated the ~s of the contract. 他们违反了合同条款。❹(常用 *pl.*)给养

provisional / prəˈvɪʒənəl / *adj.* 临时的;暂时(性)的;暂定的:a ~ government 临时政府/the signing of the ~ agreement 临时协议的签署

provocative / prəˈvɒkətɪv / *adj.* 挑衅性的;挑逗的

provoke / prəˈvəʊk / *vt.* 对……进行挑衅;激发;激怒;激起:A teacher can ~ you into working harder. 老师能激励你更努力学习。/Rachel refused to be ~d. 雷切尔拒绝被激怒。

prudent / ˈpruːdənt / *adj.* ❶审慎的,慎重的,小心谨慎的:a learned and ~ man 博学而审慎的人/It would be ~ to find out more before you decide. 查问清楚再下决定是慎重的做法。❷精明的,深谋远虑的:Such caution is ~ in a business where errors of judgement can be extremely expensive. 在一个一着不慎代价惨重的行当里,这样小心从事不失为深谋远虑之举。派 prudence *n.*

pseudonym / ˈ(p)sjuːdənɪm / *n.* [C]假名,化名;笔名:Mark Twain was the ~ used by Samuel Clemens. 马克·吐温是塞缪尔·克莱门斯的笔名。

psychiatrist / saɪˈkaɪətrɪst / *n.* [C]精神病医生;精神病专家

psychiatry / saɪˈkaɪətri / *n.* [U]精神病学

psychological / ˌsaɪkəˈlɒdʒɪkl / *adj.* 心理的;心理学的

psychologist / saɪˈkɒlədʒɪst / *n.* [C]心理学家

psychology / saɪˈkɒlədʒi / *n.* [U]心理学;心理:Do you understand his ~? 你了解他的心理吗?

psychosis /saɪˈkəʊsɪs / *n.* [C](*pl.* psychoses /saɪˈkəʊsiːz/)精神病；精神错乱

pub /pʌb/ *n.* [C](英)酒吧；酒馆

public /ˈpʌblɪk/ Ⅰ *adj.* ❶公众的；公共的：a ~ library 公共图书馆 / ~ opinion 舆论 ❷国家的；政府的：a ~ enemy 国民公敌 Ⅱ *n.* 公众，民众(作主语时，谓语动词用单数或复数均可)：The ~ is (are) requested not to litter in the park. 要求公众勿在公园里丢弃废物。/ **in** ~ 公然地；公开地

publication /ˌpʌblɪˈkeɪʃn/ *n.* ❶[U]公布；出版：date of ~ 出版日期 ❷[C]出版物：Among his many ~s was a volume of light verses. 在他众多出版物中有一本消遣诗集。

publicity /pʌbˈlɪsɪti/ *n.* [U] ❶公众(或传媒等)的注意，众所周知，闻名；名声：avoid ~避免惹人注目/His latest novel received good ~. 他最近出版的小说大获好评。❷惹人注目的办法；宣传，宣扬：Her novel was published with a lot of ~. 伴随着巨大的宣传攻势，她的小说出版了。

publish /ˈpʌblɪʃ/ *v.* ❶公布；宣布：~ the news 发布消息 ❷出版：The book was ~ed last year. 这本书是去年出版的。派 publisher *n.*

pudding /ˈpʊdɪŋ/ *n.* 布丁；甜食；甜点

puff /pʌf/ Ⅰ *n.* [C]喘息；(短而快的)喷送；喷送声；一次喷出的(烟、蒸汽等的)量：~s from an engine 机车喷出的烟/ have a ~ at a pipe 吸一口烟 Ⅱ *v.* 喘息；(烟、蒸汽等)阵阵喷出：The engine ~ed out of the station. 机车喷着阵阵的烟驶出了车站。

pull /pʊl/ *v.* ❶拉；扯；拖：Pull your chair to the table. 把你的椅子拖近桌边。/ ~ **ahead (of)** 跑在前头；超过：The car soon ~ed ahead of the bus. 小汽车很快就超过了公共汽车。~ **down** ①拉下(遮帘等)：Shall I ~ down the blinds? 我可以放下百叶窗吗？②拆除；拆毁：The houses had to be ~ed down to make way for the new road. 为了让位给新路，这些房屋只有拆除。~ **on** 穿上；戴上：Help me to ~ on these boots. They are very tight. 帮我穿上靴子，它们太紧了。~ **through** ①(使)渡过难关：You will never ~ through the examination unless you work hard. 你不发奋是过不了考试这一难关的。②(使)恢复健康：He is still sick, but the doctor is sure that he will ~ through. 他的病还很重，但医生确信他会痊愈。❷(车、船等)行驶：~ **in** (车)进站：The train ~ed in at ten sharp. 火车 10 点整进站。~ **out** 离开；驶出：When he arrived at the stop, the bus had ~ed out. 他赶到车站时，公共汽车已经开出站了。~ **up** 停，使……停止：You must ~ your car up at a red light. 看到红灯时你必须得停车。

pulp /pʌlp/ *n.* [U] ❶果肉：apple ~苹果肉 ❷木浆；纸浆

pulse /pʌls/ *n.* 脉搏：feel the ~诊脉

pump /pʌmp/ Ⅰ *n.* [C]泵；抽水机；打气筒 Ⅱ *v.* 用打气筒打气；用泵抽水

pumpkin /ˈpʌmpkɪn/ *n.* [C]南瓜

punch /pʌntʃ/ Ⅰ *vt.* 打(孔)；给……穿孔；用拳猛击 Ⅱ *n.* [C]打孔器；一击，一拳

punctual /ˈpʌŋktʃʊəl/ *adj.* 准时的；守时的：He is ~ to the minute. 他严守时间。

punctuation /ˌpʌŋktʃʊˈeɪʃn/ *n.* [U]标点：~ marks 标点符号

punish /ˈpʌnɪʃ/ *v.* 处罚；惩罚：How would you ~ liars? 你如何处罚说谎

P

者? / ~ **sb. for sth.** 因某事惩罚某人:You should be ~ed for lying. 你说谎,应当受到惩罚。~ **sb. with (by)...** 用……惩罚某人:He was ~ed with a fine for spitting. 他因随地吐痰被罚款。

punishment / ˈpʌnɪʃmənt / *n.* 处罚;惩罚:The ~ for murdering is death. 对谋杀罪的惩罚是判处死刑。

pupil / ˈpjuːpl / *n.* [C] ❶学生(尤指中小学生) ❷瞳孔

puppet / ˈpʌpɪt / *n.* [C] ❶傀儡;木偶 ❷受操纵的人或组织

puppy / ˈpʌpi / *n.* [C] ❶小狗 ❷幼小的动物

purchase / ˈpɜːtʃəs / Ⅰ *n.* ❶[U]买;购买 ❷[C]购买的东西;购得物 Ⅱ *vt.* 买:~ a house 买一所房子

pure / pjʊə(r) / *adj.* ❶纯净的:~ water (milk,gold)纯水(纯牛奶、纯金) ❷纯正的;纯洁的:speak ~ English 讲纯正的英语 / ~ thoughts 纯洁的思想 派 purely *adv.*

purify / ˈpjʊərɪfaɪ / *vt.* 使纯净;提纯;精炼:~ the mind 使思想纯洁

purity / ˈpjʊərəti / *n.* [U] 纯净;纯洁;纯度

purple / ˈpɜːpl / Ⅰ *n.* [U] 紫色 Ⅱ *adj.* 紫色的

purpose / ˈpɜːpəs / *n.* 目的;计划;意向:What was the ~ of their visit? 他们来访的目的是什么? / **for (the) ~ of** 为了:He came for the ~ of training us in using computers. 他来的目的是训练我们如何使用计算机。**on** ~故意地:It is evident that someone broke his glasses on ~. 很明显有人故意摔坏了他的眼镜。派 purposely *adv.*

purse / pɜːs / *n.* [C]小钱包

pursue / pəˈsjuː / *v.* ❶追逐;追捕;追杀:~ a robber 追捕盗贼 ❷ 追求:~ pleasure 寻乐 / ~ one's ideal 追求理想

pursuit / pəˈsjuːt / *n.* [U]追赶;追求 / **in ~ of** 追求:He went here and there in ~ of truth. 他四处寻求真理。

push / pʊʃ / *v.* 推:We ~ed the boat into the water. 我们把小船推进水里。/ ~ **aside** 把……推到旁边:That rude man ~ed me aside and got on the bus ahead of me! 那个粗野的男人把我推向一边,他先上了公共汽车。~ **forward(on)** 推进;努力向前:We must ~ forward in spite of the difficulties. 尽管有困难,我们也得努力向前。/ We ~ed on through the woods until we reached an open road. 我们费力地在林中前进,直到走到一条大路上。

put / pʊt / *v.* (put,put)放;置:Where did you ~ my hat? 你把我的帽子放哪儿了? / ~ **an end to** ①结束;停止:You should ~ an end to the foolish quarrel at once. 你们应该立即结束这场愚蠢的争吵。②消灭;杀死:The dog was seriously ill, and the farmer ~ an end to it. 狗病得厉害,农夫就把它杀掉了。~ **aside** ①搁置一旁;停下:He ~ his work aside and made some coffee. 他停下工作煮咖啡。②把(钱等)存起来:She ~ aside some money for her son. 她为儿子存了一些钱。~ **away** 把……收起来;储存:He has ~ a great deal of money away. 他存了很多钱。~ **down** 控制;平息;镇压:The police are trying to ~ down violent crime in the city. 警察正在竭力控制城市里的犯罪。~ **... down** ①放下:Just as I ~ the telephone receiver down, the doorbell rang. 我刚放下电话,门铃就响了。②使(乘客等)下车:

Please ~ me down at the next corner. 请让我在下一个街角下车。③写下；记入：I ~ down her address. 我记下她的地址。④镇压；取缔：They ~ down the riot. 他们镇压了暴动。~ **forward** 提出(理论、意见等)；促进：It was Einstein who ~ forward the theory of relativity. 是爱因斯坦提出了相对论。~ **into** ①放入；输入：Put the vegetables into the pan with very little water, and heat quickly. 把这些菜放进锅里，加少许水，然后很快加热。②变成；译成：Please ~ this sentence into English. 请把这个句子译成英语。/ Every singer ~s his heart into the music, and the effect is wonderful. 每位歌手都全力投入音乐中，所以效果极佳。~ **off** ①脱掉；消除：Will you ~ off your coat, please? 请把外衣脱掉好吗？/ Her explanation ~ off my doubts. 她的解释消除了我的疑虑。②延期：Never ~ off till tomorrow what you can do today. 决不要把你今天能做的事拖到明天。~ **on** ①穿上：He ~ on his coat hurriedly and ran out of the house. 他匆匆穿上大衣，跑出了屋子。②上演：They ~ on a fine performance last Sunday. 上周日他们演出了优秀节目。~ **one's heart into** 全神贯注于：He always ~s his heart into what he is reading. 他总是全神贯注地读书。~ **out** ①伸出：It's rude to ~ out your tongue at people. 向人伸舌头是不礼貌的。②熄灭(灯或火)：Put out all fires before leaving the camping ground. 离开野营地时把所有的火灭掉。/ Please ~ the lights out before you leave the building. 你离开大楼时请关掉所有的灯。~ **...to the test** 试验；检验：We can't tell if the product will be successful until we have ~ it to the test. 直到该产品检验后我们才能知道它是否成功。~**... to use** 利用：Let's think out a way to ~ the old machine to use. 我们来想个办法利用这台旧机器。~ **up** ①举起；抬起：Put up your hand if you know the answer. 如果你知道答案就请举手。②建造；搭起：Do you know how to ~ up a tent? 你知道怎样搭帐篷吗？/ The original college buildings were ~ up in the 16th century. 原学院建筑物是 16 世纪建造的。③张贴；挂起：The examination results will be ~ up on this notice board tomorrow. 考试的结果将于明天在布告牌上张贴出来。~ **up with** 忍受：I can't ~ up with these noises any more. 我再也无法忍受这些噪声了。

puzzle /ˈpʌzl/ Ⅰ *v.* 使苦思；使迷惑：This letter ~s me. 这封信使我迷惑不解。/ ~ **over (about)...** 为……伤脑筋：We really ~d over the problem. 我们真为这个问题伤脑筋。Ⅱ *n.* [C]难题；谜：Can you solve the ~? 你能解决这个难题吗？/UFOs are still a ~ to human beings. 对于人类来说，不明飞行物仍然是一个谜。

pyramid /ˈpɪrəmɪd/ *n.* [C] ❶锥体 ❷(古埃及的)金字塔

Q q

quadrangle / ˈkwɒdˌræŋgl / *n.* [C]四边形；四方形；矩形；正方形

quake / kweɪk / *vi.* & *n.* [C] ❶(指地)震动；摇动 ❷颤抖；哆嗦

qualification / ˌkwɒlɪfɪˈkeɪʃn / *n.* [C] ❶资格；合格证明：educational ~s 学历资格 ❷限定条件：necessary ~s 必要条件

qualified / ˈkwɒlɪfaɪd / *adj.* 有资格的；合格的：a ~ engineer 一个合格的工程师

qualify / ˈkwɒlɪfaɪ / *vt.* ❶使具有资格；使合格 / ~ **sb. for sth.** (**to do sth.**) 使有资格做某事：Her education qualified her for the post. 她所受的教育使她有资格担当这个职务。~ **sb. as ...** 使有资格成为：His training qualified him as a teacher. 他所受的训练使他有资格当一名老师。❷限制；限定；修饰

qualitative / ˈkwɒlɪtətɪv / *adj.* 质的，质量的；性质的：a ~ change 质变/a ~ judgement 定性

quality / ˈkwɒləti / *n.* ❶[U]质量；品质；特质：This wool is of high ~. 这羊毛是高质量的。❷[C]特征；特性；性能：One ~ of pine wood is that it can be sawn easily. 松木的一个特性是它容易锯开。

quantitative / ˈkwɒntɪtətɪv / *adj.* 量的，数量的：a ~ change 量变/a ~ jump in agricultural production 农业生产的猛增

quantity / ˈkwɒntəti / *n.* ❶[U]量；数量：I prefer quality to ~. 我重质量胜过数量。❷[C](常用 *pl.*)大量：We've had quantities of rain this summer. 今年夏天雨多。/ **in quantities** 大量地；数量上地：buy goods in large quantities 购买大量货物

quantum / ˈkwɒntəm / Ⅰ *n.* [C](*pl.* quanta) ❶量；份额，部分：a ~ of evidence 少得不能再少的证据 ❷量子：the quanta of gravitational radiation 引力辐射的量子 Ⅱ *adj.* ❶量子的：~ physics 量子物量学 ❷大的，重大的：a ~ improvement 重大的改进

quarrel / ˈkwɒrəl / Ⅰ *vi.* (-reled 或 -relled; -reling或-relling)吵架 / ~ **with sb. about sth.** 和某人就某事发生争吵：Let us stop ~ling with them about such unimportant matters. 我们不要和他们为这些小事争吵了吧。Ⅱ *n.* [C]口角；争论：Mike had a ~ with Tom for a toy. 迈克和汤姆为了玩具而争吵。

quarrelsome / ˈkwɒrəlsəm / *adj.* 好争吵的

quart / kwɔːt / *n.* [C]夸脱(液体单位，等于 1.1365 升)

quarter / ˈkwɔːtə(r) / *n.* [C] ❶四分之一；四等份 ❷(任何一小时之前或之后

的)一刻钟：a ~ to two 差一刻两点 / a ~ past six 六点过一刻 ❸季度：the third ~ of the year 第三季度 ❹两角五分：one dollar and a ~ 一元两角五分钱 ❺(常用 *pl.*)寓所，住处：find ~s in the city 在城里找住处

quarterly /ˈkwɔːtəli/ Ⅰ*adj.* 按季度的；季度的：~ payment 按季付款 / ~ subscription 按季订阅 Ⅱ*adv.* 按季地：The committee meets ~. 委员会每季度聚会一次。Ⅲ*n.* [C]季刊

quartz /kwɔːts/ *n.* [U]石英

queen /kwiːn/ *n.* [C]女王；皇后：beauty ~ 第一美女，选美得头奖者/ campus ~ 校花/ movie ~影后

queer /kwɪə(r)/ *adj.* 奇怪的；古怪的

quench /kwent/ *vt.* ❶消除；平息；终止；满足；缓解：~ one's thirst with water 以水解渴/~ a rebellion 平息叛乱/ His thirst for knowledge will never be ~ed. 他的求知欲永无止境。❷扑灭；熄灭：The fire was ~ed by the rain. 火被雨水浇灭了。

query /ˈkwɪəri/ Ⅰ*n.* [C] ❶问题；疑问；质问；询问 The shop assistant accepted my cheque without ~. 那位商店营业员不加询问便收下了我的支票。❷问号(即"?") Ⅱ*vt.* ❶问(及)；询问：He queried whether (if) the law allowed this sort of procedure. 他询问法律是否允许这种程序。❷对……提出质疑；对……表示疑问：~ a point in sb. 's speech 就某人讲话中的一点提出质疑 He rang the water company to ~ his bill. 他给自来水公司打电话对他的水费账单提出疑问。

quest /kwest/ Ⅰ*n.* [C](历时较久或艰辛的)寻求；寻找；追求；探索：the ~ for treasure 探宝/renew the weary ~ for work 重新登上找工作的艰辛路程/ **in ~ of** 寻求；寻找：go to the south in ~ of employment 去南方寻找工作/They fanned out over the mountains in ~ of the lost child. 他们在山上成扇形展开，四处寻找那个走失的孩子。Ⅱ*vi.* ❶寻求，寻找；追求；探索：~ after truth 探求真理/~ for a cause that would give meaning to one's life 追求一种会给予自己生活意义的事业 ❷探险

question /ˈkwestʃən/ Ⅰ*n.* 问题；询问：He asked me a lot of ~s. 他问了我许多问题 / **out of ~** 毫无疑问：His sincerity is out of ~. 他的诚意是毫无疑问的。/ He is out of ~ the best student in the class. 毫无疑问，他是班上最好的学生。**out of the ~** 毫无可能，办不到：Picnic in storm is out of the ~. 在暴雨中野餐是办不到的。Ⅱ*v.* 询问；审问：He was ~ed by the police. 他被警方审问。

questionable /ˈkwestʃənəbl/ *adj.* 可疑的；不可靠的

questionnaire /ˌkwestʃəˈneə(r)/ *n.* [C]调查表；征求意见表；问卷

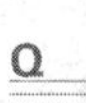

queue /kjuː/ Ⅰ*n.* [C]长队：form a ~排成一行 / jump the ~插队(不按次序抢先排到别人前面)/ stand in a ~站成一行 Ⅱ*v.* 排成长队：~ up for a bus 排长队等公共汽车 / ~ up to buy tickets for the opera 排队买歌剧票

quick /kwɪk/ Ⅰ*adj.* ❶快的；迅速的：walking at a ~ pace 快步行走 / have a ~ meal 吃一顿快餐 ❷敏捷的；机敏的：be ~ of understanding 理解力强 / The girl is ~ with her hands. 那女孩手很巧。Ⅱ*adv.* 快：Can't you run ~er? 你不能再跑快点吗？派 quickly *adv.*；quickness *n.*

quicken /ˈkwɪkən/ *vt.* ❶加快，加速：~

the pace of new-product development 加速开发新产品/They felt their breathing ~. 他们感到呼吸加快了。❷刺激,激发;使有生气;使活跃;使复活:The professor's words suddenly ~ed his own memories. 教授那番话蓦地激活了他自己的记忆。/The recent film has ~ed interest in Titanic. 最近上映的影片激起人们对"泰坦尼克号"的兴趣。

quiet /ˈkwaɪət/ *adj.* (-er,-est)静止的;安静的:the ~ sea 风平浪静的海面 / Keep ~! 保持安静! 派 quietly *adv.*; quietness *n.*

quilt /kwɪlt/ *n.* [C]被子;被褥

quit /kwɪt/ *vt.* (quit 或 quitted, quit 或 quitted; quitting) ❶离开;辞去:~ office 离职 / Bill ~ his job for advanced studies. 比尔辞职去进修。❷停止;放弃:~ school 弃学 / They ~ work when the bell rang. 铃响后他们停止工作。

quite /kwaɪt/ *adv.* ❶完全地;彻底地;十分:I ~ agree. 我完全同意。She was ~ alone. 她非常孤独。/ ~ **another (thing)** 完全是另一回事:Talking is one thing and doing is ~ another. 说是一回事,做完全是另一回事。~ **right** 很好;完全正确:—Is he from England? —Quite right. —她是英国人吗? —完全正确。❷达到某一程度:~ **a few** 相当多(用于修饰可数名词):Quite a few students like to watch the football match. 相当多的学生喜欢看足球比赛。~ **a little** 相当多(用于修饰不可数名词):He spent ~ a little money on books and newspapers. 他花了不少钱买书和报纸。~ **a lot (of)** 许多:There were ~ a lot of people at her birthday party. 很多人参加了她的生日宴会。

quiz /kwɪz/ *n.* [C](*pl.* quizzes /ˈkwɪzɪz/) 一般知识测验;小考

quota /ˈkwəutə/ *n.* [C] ❶限额;定额;(分)配额:assign an import ~制定进口配额/The removal of entry ~s encouraged young people to enter universities. 取消招生限额鼓励年轻人上大学。❷份额,(一)份;(一定)数量:have one's full ~ of love 完全拥有自己的一份爱情/His translation has the usual ~ of insidious, unnoticed Americanisms. 他的译文一如旧规,不知不觉之中掺进了一定数量的美国特色用语。

quotation /kwəuˈteɪʃn/ *n.* [C] ❶引证;引文:direct(indirect) ~ 直接(间接)引语 /~ marks 引号 / In his talk, the speaker used many ~ s from Shakespeare. 演讲者在讲话中引用了许多莎士比亚的话。❷报价;估价:~ of prices 报价

quote /kwəut/ *v.* ❶引述;引用:I can ~ what he said. 我可以引用他的话。❷报价;开价

quotient /ˈkwəuʃnt/ *n.* [C]商;商数:intelligence ~(=IQ)智商;智力商数

R r

rabbit /ˈræbɪt/ *n.* 兔；兔肉

race /reɪs/ Ⅰ *n.* [C] ❶种族；民族：the white ~s 白种人 ❷(速度上的) 比赛，竞赛：make a ~ against time 和时间赛跑 / horse ~ 赛马 / Did you run the 1,000-meter ~? 你参加了 1 000 米赛跑吗？/ **hold a ~** 举行比赛：They like swimming and often hold ~s. 他们很喜欢游泳，常常举行比赛。**lose (win) a ~** 比赛失败(获胜)：She lost the ~ last time. 上次比赛她失败了。**run a ~** 疾走；赛跑：He ran a 800-metre ~ with his classmates. 他和同学们一道进行了 800 米赛跑。Ⅱ *v.* 赛跑：Race to see what is happening. 跑去看看发生了什么事。

racial /ˈreɪʃəl/ *adj.* 种族的；人种的：~ customs 种族习俗 / ~ conflicts 种族冲突 / ~ discrimination 种族歧视

rack /ræk/ *n.* [C]搁物架；(火车、客机上的)行李架

racket /ˈrækɪt/ *n.* [C](网球等的)球拍

radar /ˈreɪdɑː(r)/ *n.* ❶[U] 雷达 ❷[C]无线电探测器

radial /ˈreɪdɪəl/ *adj.* ❶放射的；辐射状的，辐射式的：~ network 辐射(式)网络/~ avenues 呈辐射状的街道 ❷径向的，(沿)半径的，径向运动的：~ development 径向展开

radiate /ˈreɪdɪeɪt/ *vi.* ❶从中心向四周延伸；呈辐射状分布：Nerves ~ to all parts of the body from the brain. 神经从大脑呈辐射状伸向身体各个部位。❷发光；发热；发出电磁波：These wires can ~like antennas. 这些金属丝可以像天线一样发出电磁波。❸流露，洋溢，显示：All of us can see the joy that ~s from their eyes. 我们大家都能看出他们目光中流露出的快乐。

radiation /ˌreɪdɪˈeɪʃn/ *n.* ❶[U]放射；辐射 ❷[C]放射物；辐射线

radical /ˈrædɪkl/ *adj.* ❶基本的；根本的；主要的 ❷极端的；激进的 派 radicalism *n.*；radically *adv.*

radio /ˈreɪdɪəʊ/ *n.* (*pl.* radios)收音机；电台；无线电；无线电广播：He heard the news on the ~. 他从收音机里听到这则消息。/ Please tune in on Radio Beijing. 请收听北京广播电台的广播。/ We always listen to the ~ at six in the morning. 我们总是在早晨 6 点钟收听广播。/ **on (over) the ~** 通过无线电广播；在广播中：The president spoke on the ~ last Monday. 总统上周一发表了广播讲话。/ I heard the news over the ~. 我从广播里听到这则消息。**turn on (off) the ~** 开(关)收音机：He turned on the ~ and listened to the news carefully. 他打开收音机仔细地听新闻。

radioactive / ˌreɪdɪəʊˈæktɪv / *adj.* 放射性的；放射性引起的：~ dust 放射性尘埃/ ~ element 放射性元素 / ~ substances 放射性物质

radioactivity / ˌreɪdɪəʊækˈtɪvəti / *n.* [U] 放射性；放射现象

raft / rɑːft, ræft / Ⅰ *n.* [C]筏子；木筏，木排；竹筏 Ⅱ *v.* ❶用筏子运送：They ~ed the arms down the river. 他们用筏子把军火送往下游。❷划筏子：~ across (through) the river 划筏子过河

radium / ˈreɪdɪəm / *n.* [U]镭(符号 Ra)

rag / ræg / *n.* ❶碎布 ❷(*pl.*) 破旧衣服：dress in ~s 穿着破烂衣服

rage / reɪdʒ / Ⅰ *n.* 发怒：**be in a ~ with sb.** 生某人的气 **fly into a ~**勃然大怒 Ⅱ *v.* 发怒：Father ~d at (against) me for my carelessness. 由于我的粗心大意，父亲对我非常生气。

ragged / ˈrægɪd / *adj.* 衣服破烂的：a ~ old man 一个衣衫褴褛的老人

raid / reɪd / Ⅰ *n.* [C]袭击，突袭；搜捕：an air ~空袭 / **make a ~ on** 对……突然袭击：The enemy made a ~ on the oil field. 敌军突袭油田地带。Ⅱ *v.* 侵袭，袭击

R

rail / reɪl / *n.* [C] ❶栏杆；横杆；扶手 ❷铁轨；铁路

railroad / ˈreɪlrəʊd / *n.* (=railway) [C] 铁路

railway / ˈreɪlweɪ / *n.* [C] 铁路；铁道：~ station 火车站 / ~ transportation 火车运输/ We'll build many new ~s. 我们将修建许多条新铁路。/ **by ~** 通过铁路；乘火车：Will you come by ~ or by sea? 你乘火车来还是乘船来？

rain / reɪn / Ⅰ *n.* [U]雨：be caught in the ~ 淋雨 / make ~ 人工降雨 / We had plenty of ~ here last month. 上个月我们这儿雨水很多。Ⅱ *v.* 下雨：I don't know whether it will ~ or not. 我不知道是否会下雨。

rainbow / ˈreɪnbəʊ / *n.* [C]彩虹

raincoat / ˈreɪnkəʊt / *n.* [C]雨衣

rainy / ˈreɪni / *adj.* 下雨的；多雨的：~ region 多雨地区 / ~ season 多雨季节

raise / reɪz / Ⅰ *vt.* ❶提高；使升高：My wages were ~d. 我的工资提高了。❷种植(作物)；饲养(牛羊等)：She ~d chickens. 她养鸡。❸抚养：She alone ~s three children well. 她一个人把三个孩子抚养得很好。❹筹集；筹措：~ a loan 筹款 / We must ~ funds for the project. 我们得为这个项目筹集资金。❺提出：I'll ~ the question at the meeting. 我将在会上提出这个问题。Ⅱ *n.* [C]增加：get a pay ~ 获得加薪

raisin / ˈreɪzən / *n.* [C]葡萄干

rally / ˈræli / Ⅰ *v.* ❶重新聚集，重新集合；重整：The veterans rallied ten years after the war. 战后 10 年这些老兵重新聚在了一起。❷联合，团结：The president tried to ~ the people around the government. 总统试图把人民团结在政府的周围。❸重新鼓起(勇气等)；康复，恢复；振作：~ one's energy 恢复精力/ ~ from heavy disaster 从深重的灾难中恢复过来 Ⅱ *n.* [C] ❶重整旗鼓：The second ~ was defeated another time after the first defeat. 第一次失败后，重整的军队又被打败了。❷重振精神；(病后的)康复，恢复 ❸集会：at a fund-raising ~在筹款集会上/a mass ~群众集会

ramble / ˈræmbl / Ⅰ *vi.* ❶闲逛；漫步：go rambling through the fields 到田野里漫步 ❷(小路、溪流等)蜿蜒伸展；(植物)蔓生：This unknown plant ~s over the roof. 屋顶上爬满了这种不知名的植物。❸漫谈，闲聊；写随笔：Stop rambling. Let's get back to the point. 别胡扯了，咱们回到正题上来吧。Ⅱ *n.* [C] 闲逛，漫步，散步：Let's go for a ~. 我们去散步吧。

random /ˈrændəm/ Ⅰ *n.* 随意；随机/**at ~** 随意；随机：Choose any number at ~. 随便选择一个号码吧。Ⅱ *adj.* 随意的；随机的：Please make a ~ choice among these books. 请在这些书中随意选择一本。

range /reɪndʒ/ Ⅰ *v.* ❶排列；整理；把……分类 ❷(在某范围内)变动，变化：Prices range from 20 *yuan* to 100 *yuan*. 价格从 20 元到 100 元不等。Ⅱ *n.* [C] 系列：a ~ of mountains 一条山脉

rank /ræŋk/ Ⅰ *n.* ❶一列；一队；一行 ❷等级；(军队中的)官衔：officers of high ~ 高级官员 ❸阶级；社会阶层 Ⅱ *v.* 评定等级；排列：This town ~s among the famous Chinese beauty spots. 这个城市为中国著名风景点之一。

ransack /ˈrænsæk/ *vt.* ❶彻底搜索，仔细搜查：The police ~ed his house. 警方把他的房子搜了个遍。❷洗劫：The bandits ~ed the village. 匪徒将村子洗劫一空。

ransom /ˈrænsəm/ Ⅰ *n.* ❶[U]赎回；赎身 ❷[C]赎金：pay a ~ of $ 2 million 交付 200 万美元的赎金 Ⅱ *vt.* 赎，赎回：He ~ed his son for a million dollars. 他花费了 100 万美元才赎回了自己的儿子。

rap /ræp/ Ⅰ *n.* [C] 轻敲声 Ⅱ *vt.* (rapped; rapping) 敲击：The chairman ~ped the meeting to order. 主席敲桌子使会场恢复秩序。

rapid /ˈræpɪd/ *adj.* 快的；迅速的：He is making ~ progress in English study. 他在英语学习上进步很快。派 rapidly *adv.*

rare /reə(r)/ *adj.* ❶罕见的；稀有的：These flowers are very ~ in our country. 在我们国家这些花是很少见的。/ They have taken measures to protect ~ animals. 他们已经采取措施保护珍稀动物。/ It is ~ for her to go out at night. 她难得在晚间外出。❷稀薄的；稀疏的：They didn't feel well in the ~ air on the mountain top. 山顶上空气稀薄，他们感到很不舒服。派 rarely *adv.*

rarity /ˈreərəti/ *n.* ❶[U]稀有，珍贵；稀薄，稀疏 ❷[C]奇物；奇事；珍品：Such a snowstorm was a ~ in that region. 这样的雪暴在那个地区是很少见的。

rash /ræʃ/ *adj.* 匆忙的；轻率的；鲁莽的：It was ~ of her to make such a promise. 她作出如此承诺真是太轻率了。派 rashly *adv.*

rasp /rɑːsp, ræsp/ Ⅰ *vt.* ❶用锉刀锉；粗磨；刮擦：The cow ~ed her face with her tongue. 母牛用舌头舔自己的脸。❷刺激；激怒：They are always ~ing one another. 他们总是互相挑衅。Ⅱ *n.* [C] ❶锉，粗磨；刮擦 ❷粗嘎的说话声；刺耳的刮擦声：He spoke with a ~. 他说话声音嘶哑。❸粗锉刀

rat /ræt/ *n.* [C]鼠

rate /reɪt/ Ⅰ *n.* [C] ❶比率；比例：attendance ~ 出勤率 / birth ~ 出生率 / crime ~ 犯罪率 / employment ~ 就业率 / The death ~ has lowered in our country. 我国的人口死亡率已降低。❷速度：walk at the ~ of 3 miles an hour 以每小时 3 英里的速度走路 ❸等级/ **at this ~** 照此速度；照这样下去：At this ~, we'll arrive at the village only in two hours. 以这样的速度，我们在两小

时内就可以到达那个村子。**at any ~** 无论如何：You must come to our party at any ~. 你无论如何得来参加我们的聚会。Ⅱ *vt.* ❶以为：Mary was ~d as the top student in her class. 玛丽被认为是班上最优秀的学生。❷估价；评价：He was highly ~d by his teacher. 他受到老师的高度评价。

rather / ˈrɑːðə(r) / *adv.* ❶宁愿；宁可 / **had (would) rather ... than ...** 宁愿……而不……：She would ~ have the small one than the large one. 她宁愿要小的而不要大的。/ She would ~ die than surrender. 她宁死不屈。~ **than** 与其……(不如)；不是……(而是)：This kind of change is physical ~ than chemical. 这种变化是物理变化而不是化学变化。❷相当地：This book is ~ interesting. 这本书相当有趣。/He plays football ~ well. 他足球踢得很不错。

rating / ˈreɪtɪŋ / *n.* [C] ❶评级，定级；等级：pop music ~s lists 流行音乐排行榜 ❷(广播节目的)收听率；(电视节目的)收视率：~s battle 收视率大战

ratio / ˈreɪʃɪəʊ / *n.* [C] (*pl.* ratios) 比率：at a ~ of three to one 按三比一的比率 / direct (inverse) ~ 正比(反比)

R

ration / ˈræʃn, ˈreɪʃn / Ⅰ *n.* [C] ❶配给量，定量：the daily ~ of food 每天的食品配给量 ❷(配给量的)一份：a ~ of meat 一份肉/a petrol ~一份配给汽油 Ⅱ *vt.* ❶定量发放(食物等)：~ out food to an army 向部队发放食品 ❷定量供应(给养等)；向……定量供应给养：They promised to ~ us for the first six months. 他们承诺向我们提供头六个月的给养。❸限制……的使用(或发放、供应)：~ meat 限制肉类的供应

rational / ˈræʃnəl / *adj.* 合理的；理性的：~ suggestion 合理的建议 / ~ knowledge 理性知识 / Can you make a ~ explanation to this? 你能对此作出合理的解释吗？

rattle / ˈrætl / *vi.* 发出格格声；喋喋不休地讲话(与 on 连用)：He kept rattling on his ailments. 他老是唠叨自己的病情。

ravage / ˈrævɪdʒ / Ⅰ *vt.* 毁灭，毁坏：a country ~d by bloodshed and war 被战争和杀戮摧残得满目疮痍的国家 Ⅱ *n.* 毁灭；毁坏，彻底破坏：the ~s caused by the epidemic 那场传染病所造成的危害

raw / rɔː / *adj.* ❶生的；未煮过的：~ meat 生肉 ❷未加工的；自然的：~ materials 原料 ❸生疏无知的；未经训练的

ray / reɪ / *n.* [C]光线；射线；辐射线：a ~ of hope 一线希望 / X-rays are different from the ~s of the sun. X 光和太阳光是不同的。

razor / ˈreɪzə(r) / *n.* [C]剃刀

reach / riːtʃ / Ⅰ *v.* ❶到达：~ London 抵达伦敦 / It will be Christmas Day when my letter ~es. 我的信将在圣诞节到达。The city has ~ed a population of six million. 这个城市的人口已达 600 万。❷伸手取：~ **for** 伸手拿：The soldier ~ed for his gun. 战士伸手去拿枪。Ⅱ *n.* [U]能达到的范围或距离：**beyond (out of) ~** 拿不到的；达不到的：Please keep the knife out of the ~ of the children. 请把刀子放到孩子们拿不到的地方。/ The book is too difficult. It is beyond my ~ of understanding. 这书太难，我无法理解。**within ~** 可以拿到的；力所能及的：You should put your dictionary within ~. 你应该把字典放在伸手可拿的地方。

react / rɪˈækt / *vi.* ❶反应(与 to 连用)：

Have the students ~ed to the proposal? 学生们对这建议有反应吗? ❷(化学)反应(与 on 连用): How do acids ~ on metals? 酸对金属起怎样的作用? ❸反抗(与 against 连用): ~ against the old system 反对旧制度

reaction /rɪˈækʃn/ *n.* ❶反应;反作用;反作用力: action and ~ 作用与反作用 / chain ~连锁反应 / chemical ~化学反应/ organic ~有机反应 / His suggestion caused a strong ~. 他的建议引起了强烈的反应。❷反动;对抗: The forces of ~ were defeated completely. 反动势力彻底被打垮。

reactionism /rɪˈækʃənɪzəm/ *n.* [U] 反动主义;极端保守主义

reactionist /rɪˈækʃənɪst/ Ⅰ *n.* [C]反动分子 Ⅱ *adj.* 反动分子的

reactionary /rɪˈækʃənri/ Ⅰ *adj.* 反动的 Ⅱ *n.* [C]反动分子

reactor /rɪˈæktə(r)/ *n.* [C]反应器;反应堆: set up a nuclear ~ 建一个核反应堆

read /riːd/ *v.* (read/red/, read) ❶阅读;看懂: ~ a book (a letter) 读一本书(一封信)/ A driver must be able to ~ traffic signs. 驾驶员必须能看懂交通标志。❷默读;朗读: Read the text aloud, please. 请朗读课文。❸(指仪器)指示: What does the thermometer ~? 温度计指示多少度? / ~ **about** 读到……的情况: I ~ about the event in the newspaper. 我从报上获悉这件事。~ **between (the) lines** 读出字里行间的意思: When you read, you should ~ between the lines. 读书就应该读出字里行间的意思来。

readable /ˈriːdəbl/ *adj.* ❶可读的;易读的;读起来有趣味的: Rich and accurate data make essays more ~. 翔实的资料使得论文颇具可读性。/ She is very ~ to young students. 她的书很受青年学生欢迎。❷(字迹)易辨认的,清晰的: a machine-~ form 可机读的稿子 派 readability *n.*

reader /ˈriːdə(r)/ *n.* [C] ❶读者: *Reader's Digest*《读者文摘》/ My father is a fast ~. 我父亲是一个快速阅读者。❷读物;读本: basic ~s 基础读物 / English ~s 英语读物

readership /ˈriːdəʃɪp/ *n.* [C](常用单数)(报刊或作者拥有的)读者,读者群;读者人数: a decline in ~读者人数的下降 / This magazine has a ~ of thirty thousand. 这份杂志有三万读者。

readily /ˈredɪli/ *adv.* ❶不迟疑地;欣然地;乐意地: My friend ~ promised to help. 我的朋友乐意帮忙。❷容易地;无困难地: This kind of computer can ~ be bought anywhere. 这种计算机在任何地方都容易买到。

readiness /ˈredɪnəs/ *n.* [C] ❶准备好: Your muscles tense in ~ for action. 你准备行动时肌肉会紧张。❷愿意;乐意: Russia had indicated a ~ to accept his terms. 俄罗斯早已表示愿意接受他的条件。❸迅速: Quickness of hearing and ~ of speech were essential. 听得快、说得快是最重要的。

reading /ˈriːdɪŋ/ *n.* ❶[U]读;阅读: ~ lamp 台灯 / ~ room 阅览室 / intensive ~ 精读 / extensive ~ 泛读 ❷[C]读物;选读: ~s in Chinese literature 中国文学读物 / light ~s 消遣读物 ❸[C]读数;仪器指示数: What was the temperature ~ then? 那时的温度是多少?

ready /ˈredi/ *adj.* ❶(只作表语)准备好的;有准备的;自愿的: Get everything

R

~ for the journey. 为旅行做好一切准备。/ He's always ~ to help his friends. 他总是自愿帮助朋友。❷迅速的；立即的：Don't be so ~ to find faults. 不要这么急于挑剔。❸事先准备好的：buy ~ food 买煮好的食品 / **be (get) ~ to** 为……做好准备；乐于；愿意：Are you ~ to go? 你准备好走了吗？

real / ˈriːəl / *adj*. 事实上存在的；真实的：Is this ~ gold or something made to look like gold? 这是真金还是做得看起来像金子一样的假东西？

realism / ˈrɪəˌlɪzəm / *n*. [U] ❶现实主义：social ~社会现实主义 ❷写实；写实主义：artistic ~艺术写实主义

realistic / ˌrɪəˈlɪstɪk / *adj*. 现实的；现实主义的：~ novels 现实主义小说

reality / rɪˈæləti / *n*. 真实；逼真；现实：This is not imagination, but ~. 这不是想象的，而是真实的 / **in ~** 实际上；事实上：We are helping you in ~. 我们实际上是在帮助你。

realizable / ˈriːəlaɪzəbl / *adj*. 可认识的；可实现的

R

realization / ˌrɪəlaɪˈzeɪʃn / *n*. [U] ❶(计划、野心或希望的)实现：He did not live to see the~ of his dream. 他没有活到梦想成真的那一天。❷理解；认知：There is a growing ~ that changes must be made. 越来越多的人认识到改变势在必行。

realize / ˈrɪəlaɪz / *v*. ❶了解；认识到：Does he ~ his error yet? 他认识到错误没有？❷使(希望、计划等)实现：~ the plan 实现计划

really / ˈrɪəli/ Ⅰ *adv*. ❶实际上，事实上；真正地：a ~ responsible officer 一位真正负责的军官 / see things as they ~ are 看到事物的本来面目 ❷真实地，确实地：a ~ hot day 确实炎热的一天 ❸(用以强调，表示肯定)真的；没错：We were ~ glad. 我们真是感到很高兴。Ⅱ *int*. (表示疑问、惊讶、异议等)真的，当真：A: He is leaving tomorrow. B: Oh,~? 甲：他明天就要走了。乙：啊，真的吗？

realm / relm / *n*. [C] ❶王国；国度：an independent ~ 独立王国 ❷领域；范围：ideological ~ 思想领域 / the ~ of music 音乐领域 / the ~ of science 科学领域/ in the ~ of economy 在经济领域里

realty / ˈriːəlti / *n*. [U]房地产

reap / riːp / *v*. 收割；收获：~ a field of wheat 收割田中的小麦 派 reaper *n*.

rear[1] / rɪə(r) / *n*. 后部；背部：The kitchen is in the ~ of the house. 厨房在房子的后部。/ the ~ wheels (lamps) of a car 汽车的后轮(尾灯) / get down the bus by the ~ entrance 从后门下公共汽车

rear[2] / rɪə(r)/ *vt*. 抚养；饲养；培植；栽种：~ children 抚养孩子 / ~ crops 培植庄稼 / ~ cattle 养牛

rearmost / ˈrɪəˌməust / *adj*. 最后部分的，最后面的；最末端的：the ~ car 最后一辆车

reason / ˈriːzn / Ⅰ *n*. ❶理由；原因：Is there any ~ why you should not help? 你有不该帮助的理由吗？❷理智；理性：Only man has ~. 只有人类有理性。/ **by ~ of** 由于，因为：The plan failed by ~ of bad organization. 由于组织得不好，这个计划失败了。**for ~s of** 为了……的缘故：He didn't go to climb mountains with us for ~s of health. 由于健康原因，他没和我们一起去爬山。**with ~** 有理由地；合乎情理地 **without ~** 没有理由地；不合乎情理地：She

would not come late without ~. 没有理由她是不会迟到的。Ⅱ *v.* 推理；说服：The ability to ~ makes man different from animals. 推理能力使人异于禽兽。/ ~ **sb. into sth.** 说服某人做某事：He ~ed us into adopting his new method. 他说服了我们采用他的新方法。~ **sb. out of sth.** 说服某人不做某事：He ~ed his mother out of worry. 他说服母亲不要着急。

reasonable / ˈriːznəbl / *adj.* ❶合理的；有道理的：You must make a ~ excuse. 你得有个合理的解释。❷通情达理的；讲道理的：Please be ~. 请讲点道理。❸适度的；公道的：at a ~ price 售价公道

reasoning / ˈriːzənɪŋ / *n.* [U]推断，推理：His ~ on this point was quite wrong. 他在这一点上的推理大错特错。

reassure / ˌriːəˈʃʊə(r) / *vt.* 安慰，使放心，使恢复信心：Good teachers ~ their students. 优秀的教师会使他们的学生得到安慰。/She went to ~ her grandmother that she was unharmed. 她去安慰奶奶说，她没有受到伤害。

rebel Ⅰ/ ˈrebl / *n.* [C]反叛者；造反者；反抗者 Ⅱ/ rɪˈbel / *vi.* (-belled;-belling) 反叛；反抗：Some tribes ~led against the government. 一些部落武力反抗政府。

rebellion / rɪˈbeljən / *n.* 反叛；叛乱；叛变：rise in ~ 起而反叛；揭竿而起

rebellious / rɪˈbeljəs / *adj.* 造反的；叛乱的；反抗的

reborn / ˌriːˈbɔːn / *adj.* 再生的；新生的

rebuff Ⅰ/ rɪˈbʌf，ˈrɪbʌf / *n.* [C]断然拒绝，坚决回绝 Ⅱ/rɪˈbʌf/ *vt.* 断然拒绝，坚决回绝：~ the country's claims for the return of the islands 拒绝了该国提出的归还那些岛屿的要求

rebuild / riːˈbɪld / *vt.* ❶重建；改建：~ a country 重建国家 ❷重组，改组；改造：try to ~ society 试图改造社会/The president ~ his campaign staff. 总统改组了其竞选人员。

rebuke / rɪˈbjuːk / *vt.* 指责；斥责；非难

recall / rɪˈkɔːl / *vt.* (使)回忆起；(使)想起：She ~ed her childhood at the sight of that doll. 看到那个洋娃娃她便想起了自己的童年。

recede / rɪˈsiːd / *vi.* ❶退，后退：~ from the eye of 从……的视线中渐渐远去 ❷变得模糊：They went farther and the house ~d. 他们越走越远，房子已变得模糊不清。/The painful memory began to ~. 痛苦的回忆渐渐地被抹去了。❸向后倾斜，向后缩：a chin that ~s 向后缩的下巴

receipt / rɪˈsiːpt / *n.* ❶[C]收据；收条：sign a ~ 在一张收条上签字 ❷[U]收到；接到：The ~ of your letter ended my anxiety. 收到你的信才消除了我的焦虑。

receive / rɪˈsiːv / *v.* 收到；接受；得到：When did you ~ the letter? 你什么时候收到这封信的？/ He ~d a good education. 他受过良好的教育。 R

receiver / rɪˈsiːvə(r) / *n.* [C] ❶(电话)听筒：Hang up (Put down) the ~ when you finish. 打完电话就挂上(放下)听筒。❷收音机；电视机 ❸收受者；收件人；收款人；接待者：I don't know who is the ~. 我不知道谁是收件人。

recent / ˈriːsnt / *adj.* 最近的：~ news 最近的消息 派 recently *adv.*

reception / rɪˈsepʃn / *n.* ❶[U]接待；迎接：The house has a ~ room, a kitchen and three bedrooms. 这所房子有一间接待室、一间厨房和三间卧室。 ❷[C]招待会：There was a ~ after the wedding ceremony. 结婚典礼之后举行了一场招待客人的宴会。❸接收(效果)：Radio ~ is poor here in our bedroom. 我们卧室里的收听效果很差。

receptionist / rɪˈsepʃənɪst / *n.* [C]接待员

receptive / rɪˈseptɪv/ *adj.* (对知识、思想、意见、建议等)易接受的；愿意接受的：a ~ mind 善于接受新事物的头脑(或人) / be ~ to the new 愿意接受新鲜事物 / He tends to be ~ of any proposal. 他会接受任何建议。派 receptively *adv.* ；receptiveness *n.*

recession / rɪˈseʃn / *n.* ❶经济的衰退；经济的衰退期：a global ~全球性的经济衰退/get out of ~走出经济衰退期 ❷[U]后退；退回；(潮水的)退潮

recessive / rɪˈsesɪv / *adj.* ❶后退的；退回的 ❷隐性的：a ~ character 隐性性状

recipe / ˈresəpi / *n.* [C] ❶菜谱；烹饪法 ❷处方 ❸秘诀；窍门；诀窍

recite / rɪˈsaɪt / *v.* 背诵：The child can ~ many poems from memory. 这孩子能够背诵很多诗。

reckless / ˈreklɪs / *adj.* ❶不顾后果的，冒失的；鲁莽的，轻率的：a very ~ girl 放肆的姑娘/be ~ of one's life 不顾个人安危 ❷粗心的，不注意的：~ spending 无节制的消费 派 recklessly *adv.* ；recklessness *n.*

reckon / ˈrekən / *v.* / ˈrekən/ *vt.* ❶计算，算出：~ the monthly profits 计算月利润 / His expenditure was ~ed at $3,000 a month. 他每月的花销高达3 000美元。❷(常用被动语态)看作，认为：She is ~ed (to be) the most outstanding poet in her generation. 她被认为是她那一代诗人中最杰出的。

recognition / ˌrekəgˈnɪʃn / *n.* [U]认识；认出；承认 / **beyond** (**out of**) ~ 认不出：The place has changed beyond ~. 这个地方已经变得让人认不出了。**in ~ of** 承认：He said nothing more in ~ of your being right. 他没有再说什么，承认你是对的。

recognize / ˈrekəgnaɪz / *vt.* ❶认识；认出：He had changed so much that one could hardly ~ him. 他变得太多，几乎让人认不出来了。❷承认；认可：They ~d him as the lawful heir. 他们承认他是合法的继承人。

recollect / ˌrekəˈlekt / *v.* 记起；想起：~ childhood days 记起童年的日子

recommend / ˌrekəˈmend / *vt.* 推荐；介绍：Can you ~ me a good novel? 你能推荐一本好小说给我吗?

recommendation / ˌrekəmenˈdeɪʃn / *n.* ❶推荐，介绍；推荐书，推荐信：give sb. a ~ 推荐某人 / letter of ~ 推荐信 / The chairman spoke for ~ of the new method. 主席发言推荐那种新方法。❷[C]劝告；建议：make a ~ 劝告

reconcile / ˈrekənsaɪl / *vt.* 使和好；调停；调解

reconstruct / ˌriːkənˈstrʌkt / *vt.* 重建

record Ⅰ/ ˈrekɔːd / *n.* ❶[C] 纪录；记录：make (break) a ~ 创造(打破)一个纪录 / keep a ~ 保持纪录 /equal (tie) a ~ 平一项纪录 / a ~ of road accidents 车祸记录 ❷[C]唱片 ❸履历；历史：medical ~s 病历 Ⅱ/rɪˈkɔːd / *v.* 写下；记录；录音

recorder / rɪˈkɔːdə(r) / *n.* [C] ❶记录者；记录员 ❷录音机；录像机 / a video ~ 录像机：a pocket ~ 袖珍录音机

recording /rɪˈkɔːdɪŋ/ *n.* 录音：It wasn't a live performance but a BBC ~. 那不是实况转播，而是英国广播公司的录音节目。

recount /rɪˈkaʊnt/ *vt.* ❶叙述，讲述；详细说明：The novel ~s the life of a pop star. 这部长篇小说讲述了一位流行歌星的一生。/~ one's plan 详细说明某人的计划 ❷重新计数

recover /rɪˈkʌvə(r)/ *v.* ❶寻回；恢复：~ one's sight (hearing) 恢复视觉（听觉）❷复原；康复：He is slowly ~ing from his illness. 他在慢慢复原。

recovery /rɪˈkʌvəri/ *n.* ❶痊愈；复原：We wish you a speedy ~. 我们祝你早日恢复健康。❷重获；复得：~ of a lost thing 找回遗失物

recreation /ˌrekrɪˈeɪʃn/ *n.* [U]娱乐；消遣：the ~ ground 游乐场 / Reading and walking are his favorite forms of ~. 读书和散步是他最喜爱的消遣方式。派 recreational *adj.*

recrimination /rɪˌkrɪmɪˈneɪʃn/ *n.* 反责；反诉：Let's make friends, instead of wasting our time on ~. 咱们交个朋友吧，不要再浪费时间互相指责了。

recruit /rɪˈkruːt/ Ⅰ *n.* [C] ❶新兵 ❷(社团、组织等的)新成员，新会员：New ~s to our book club are always welcome. 我们的读书俱乐部随时欢迎新会员参加。Ⅱ *vt.* ❶招收……为新兵；招兵，征兵：These Africans were ~ed for military service. 这些非洲人被征召入伍。❷招募，招收：~ employees 招工

rectangle /ˈrekˌtæŋgl/ *n.* [C]长方形，矩形

rectify /ˈrektɪfaɪ/ *vt.* 纠正；调整：~ sb.'s falsehood 纠正某人的错误

recur /rɪˈkɜː(r)/ *vi.* (-curred;-curring) ❶再次发生：The mistake ~s in the second paragraph of the review. 这个错误在书评的第二段再次出现。❷(想法、念头等)重新萌生；(在头脑中)再次出现：The idea kept ~ring. 这个念头一直在脑海中出现。派 recurrence *n.*；recurrent *adj.*

recycle /ˌriːˈsaɪkl/ *vi.* 再循环；回收再用

red /red/ Ⅰ *adj.* 红色的：Red Cross 红十字(会)/ a Red Army soldier 红军战士 Ⅱ *n.* 红色：be in ~ 穿着红衣服 / bright (dark, light)~鲜(深、淡)红 / **go into the ~** 出现赤字；亏本

redeem /rɪˈdiːm/ *vt.* ❶买回；赎回：She returned to the pawnbroker's to ~ her watch. 她回到当铺赎回她的手表。❷兑现(债券、股票等)：~ bonds 将债券兑现 ❸遵守(诺言)；履行(义务、职责等)：The promise was finally ~ed. 这个诺言最终得以兑现。❹补救；弥补；补偿：These failings are ~ed. 这些失误都得到了补救。

reduce /rɪˈdjuːs/ *v.* 减少；降低：~ one's expenses 减少开支/~ one's weight 减轻体重/~ **...to** 使……成为；削减至：~ the loss of blood to a minimum 把失血减少到最低量 / Fire ~d the house to ashes. 大火使这所房屋化为灰烬。

reducible /rɪˈdjuːsəbl/ *adj.* 可减低的；可还原的

reduction /rɪˈdʌkʃən/ *n.* ❶[U] 缩减 ❷[C](图画、地图等的)缩版，缩图

redundant /rɪˈdʌndənt/ *adj.* 多余的，冗余的：remove ~ words in the sentence 删除句子中多余的词语

reed /riːd/ *n.* [C]芦苇；芦笛

reef /riːf/ *n.* [C]礁石；暗礁：strike a ~

触礁

reel /riːl/ *v.* 卷;绕;抽出:He struck, and ~ed in a good perch. 他急拉钓线,钓起好大一条河鲈。

refer /rɪˈfɜː(r)/ *v.* (-ferred;-ferring) ❶送交,提交(以处理)(与 to 连用):The dispute was ~red to the United Nations. 这一争端已提交联合国处理。❷谈及;谈到:Does that remark ~ to me? 那话是针对我说的吗? ❸参考:The speaker often ~red to his notes. 讲演者常参考他的笔记。

referee /ˌrefəˈriː/ *n.* [C](足球等的)裁判员

reference /ˈrefrəns/ *n.* ❶送交;谈到;提及;参考:You should make ~ to a dictionary. 你应该参考字典。/ **in (with) ~ to** 关于:He spoke in ~ to the project. 他就有关这项工程的问题发表了谈话。**without (any) ~ to** 与……无关;不管;无论:without ~ to age and sex 不论男女老少 ❷[C]证明书;介绍信;证明人:My ~s will prove to you that I am efficient and dependable. 我的保证人将向你证明我有能力而且可靠。❸[C]附注

R

refill /ˌriːˈfɪl/ *vt.* 再装满;再填充:~ a cigarette lighter 给打火机再充气 / The waiter ~ed my glass with beer. 侍者替我把杯子重新斟满啤酒。

refine /rɪˈfaɪn/ *v.* ❶精炼;提纯:~ crude oil into various petroleum products 将原油炼制成各种石油产品 ❷使文雅;使精美:~ one's language 使语言更文雅

refined /rɪˈfaɪnd/ *adj.* ❶优雅的,高雅的;教养的:~ manners 优雅的举止❷精炼的,提炼的;精制的:~ sugar 精制糖 ❸精确的:~ measurements 精确的尺寸

refinement /riˈfaɪnmənt/ *n.* ❶[U]优雅,高雅;有教养:invest sb. with a sense of ~ 让某人有一种高雅感 ❷[U]提炼,精炼;精制;提纯;纯度:the ~ of oil 石油的精炼 ❸[C]改进,改良:The new theory is a ~ of an earlier one. 新理论是对先前理论的一种完善。

refinery /rɪˈfaɪnəri/ *n.* [C]精炼厂;提炼厂

reflect /rɪˈflekt/ *v.* ❶(指表面)反射(光、热、声等);(指镜子)映出影像:The mirror ~s her face. 镜子映出她的脸。❷思考;考虑:She sat there, ~ing on a certain problem. 她坐在那儿思考某个问题。/ You should ~ before you do anything. 做任何事之前,你都应该考虑一下。

reflection /rɪˈflekʃn/ *n.* ❶[U]反射:~ of heat 热的反射❷[C]影像;倒影:~ in the mirror 在镜中的影像 / It is difficult to draw the ~ of trees in the water. 画树在水中的倒影是不容易做到的。❸[U]考虑;思考:She sat there, lost in ~. 她坐在那儿,陷入沉思。派 reflectional *adj.*

reflective /rɪˈflektɪv/ *adj.* ❶思考的,沉思的;反省的:a ~ expression 一副沉思的表情 / fall into a ~ mood 陷入沉思 ❷反射的;反光的:the ~ quality of the sand 沙的反射性 派 reflectively *adv.*

reform /rɪˈfɔːm/ Ⅰ *v.* ❶改革;改进;改良;改善:~ tools 改良工具 / We think it necessary to ~ the economic management system. 我们认为有必要改革经济管理体制。❷重新形成 Ⅱ *n.* 改革;改良:carry out the economic ~ 进行经济改革 / the policy of ~ and opening to the outside world 改革开放政策 派 re-

former n.

reformation / ˌrefəˈmeɪʃn / *n.* [U](社会、政治及宗教事务上的)革新

reformatory / rɪˈfɔːmətəri/ Ⅰ *adj.* 改革的;革新的;旨在改造的:~ measures 改革措施 / The object of these measures is not so much retributive as ~. 这些举措的目的是改造人而不是惩罚人。Ⅱ *n.* [C]少年管教所

refraction / rɪˈfrækʃn / *n.* [U]折射:~ of light-beam 光束折射

refrain / rɪˈfreɪn / *v.* 抑制;忍住(与 from 连用):~ from tears 忍住眼泪 / He ~ed from asking any questions. 他忍住了,没有提任何问题。

refresh / rɪˈfreʃ / *v.* 使恢复;使振作:~ oneself with a cup of tea (a warm bath) 喝杯茶(洗热水澡)以提神

refresher/rɪˈfreʃə / *n.* [C]提神物;提神饮料

refreshment / rɪˈfreʃmənt / *n.* ❶[U](精神的)恢复 ❷[C](常用 *pl.*)点心;零食

refrigerate / rɪˈfrɪdʒəreɪt / *vt.* 使冷却;冷冻;冷藏

refrigeration / rɪˌfrɪdʒəˈreɪʃn / *n.* [U]冷藏;冷冻

refrigerator / rɪˈfrɪdʒəreɪtə(r) / *n.* [C]冰箱;冷冻库

refuge / ˈrefjuːdʒ / Ⅰ *n.* 庇护;避难;避难所:seek ~ from the floods 躲避洪水 Ⅱ *vi.* 避难;逃难

refugee / ˌrefjʊˈdʒiː / *n.* [C]避难者;流亡者;难民:~ camps 难民营

refund / ˈriːfʌnd / Ⅰ *vt.* 退还;偿还:The shop ~ed the purchase price to the customer. 商店把货款退还给了顾客。Ⅱ *n.* [C]退还;偿还:demand a ~ 要求退款

refusal / rɪˈfjuːzl / *n.* 拒绝:He met with a flat ~. 他遭到断然拒绝。

refuse[1] / rɪˈfjuːz / *v.* 拒绝;不愿接受:~ a gift 拒收礼物 / Lei Feng never ~d to help others. 雷锋从不拒绝帮助别人。/ You should ~ his unreasonable request. 你应该拒绝他的不合理要求。

refuse[2] / ˈrefjuːs / *n.* [U]垃圾;废物:a heap of ~ 一堆垃圾

regain / rɪˈgeɪn / *vt.* 恢复;复得;回收:~ one's freedom 重获自由

regard / rɪˈgɑːd / Ⅰ *vt.* ❶视为;认作:~ ... **as** ... 认为……是……;把……看作……:~ sb. as a hero 视某人为英雄 / ~ sth. as a crime 把某事视为犯罪 / Abraham Lincoln is ~ed as one of the greatest presidents of America. 亚伯拉罕·林肯被人们认为是美国最伟大的总统之一。❷尊重;敬重 ❸(以某种方式)注视,凝视:Ryker ~ed him unflinchingly. 赖克毫不畏惧地看着他。Ⅱ *n.* ❶[U]注意;关心;考虑:He has very little ~ for the feelings of others. 他不大考虑别人的感受。❷尊重;尊敬;敬佩:I had great ~ for her abilities. 我非常敬佩她的能力。❸[C](*pl.*)问候;致意:Please give my kind ~s to your brother. 请代我向你的哥哥问候。/**as ~s** 关于;至于:As ~s films, we are too busy to see. 至于电影,我们太忙没时间去看。

regarding / rɪˈgɑːdɪŋ / *prep.* 关于:Do you have any suggestions ~ the new project? 对于那个新项目,你有什么建议吗?

regardless / rɪˈgɑːdləs / *adj.* 不重视的;不注意的 /**~ of** 不顾;不管:~ of expense 不考虑费用

regenerate Ⅰ / rɪˈdʒenəˌreɪt / *v.* ❶使(精神上)获得新生;使重生;使悔悟 ❷革

R

新;重建;复兴:The city was soon ~d after the earthquake. 这座城市在地震后很快就完成了重建。❸使重新产生;再生:A lizard can ~ its tail. 蜥蝎的尾巴可以再生。/Tissue ~s after skin in scratched. 皮肤划伤后组织会再生。Ⅱ / rɪˈdʒenərɪt / *adj*. ❶(精神上)新生的,重生的 ❷革新的,改造过的 派 regeneration *n*.

regime / reɪˈʒiːm / *n*. [C] ❶政体;政权;政治制度;统治;管辖:~ of centralism 中央集权统治 ❷特定的政权;特定政权的统治期

region / ˈriːdʒən / *n*. [C] ❶地方;区域:the Arctic ~s 北极地区 / the forest ~ 林区 ❷领域;界:the ~ of literature 文学领域

regional / ˈriːdʒənəl / *adj*. ❶地区性的,整个地区的:a ~ library 地区性图书馆 ❷区域的,地方的:a ~ accent 地方口音 派 regionally *adv*.

register / ˈredʒɪstə(r) / Ⅰ *n*. [C]记录;名单;登记簿 Ⅱ *v*. 记录;登记;注册:I want to ~ this letter. 我这封信寄挂号。/ ~ **with** 向……登记;向……注册:You must ~ your car with the police. 你必须向警方登记你的汽车。

R

regret / rɪˈgret / Ⅰ *v*. (-gretted;-gretting)为……感到遗憾;抱歉;悔恨;惋惜:He soon began to ~ having run away from home. 他很快就开始后悔不该从家里出走。/ I ~ being unable to help. 我不能帮忙,感到甚为抱歉。Ⅱ *n*. ❶[U]惋惜;懊悔;抱歉:Much to my ~, I am unable to accept your kind invitation. 我不能接受你的盛情邀请,深感抱歉。❷[C](*pl*.)歉意:Please accept my ~s at having to refuse. 不能奉约,谨致歉意。派 regretful *adj*.; regretfully *adv*.

regrettable / rɪˈgretəbl / *adj*. 可惜的;不幸的:~ failure 不幸的失败 派 regrettably *adv*.

regular / ˈregjələ(r) / *adj*. ❶有规律的;定期的;经常的:~ customers 老主顾 / ~ education 正规教育 / ~ income 固定收入/ ~ people 生活有规律的人们 ❷对称的 ❸(语法)(动词、名词等)变化有规则的

regularly / ˈregjʊləli/ *adv*. ❶定期地;经常地:Take the medicine ~ three times a day. 定时服药,一日三次。/ She ~ leaves work early. 她常常很早下班。❷有规律地;整齐地,匀称地

regulate / ˈregjʊleɪt / *vt*. 系统地管理;使遵守规则或标准;规范:~ one's conduct 规范某人的行为 / ~ the traffic 管制交通

regulation / ˌregjʊˈleɪʃn / *n*. ❶[U]管理;控制 ❷[C]规则;规定;法令;命令:safety ~s 安全条例 / road ~s 道路(交通)规则

rehabilitate / ˌriː(h)əˈbɪlɪˌteɪt / *vt*. ❶使康复;使恢复正常:exercises for rehabilitating damaged knees 使受伤的膝盖得到康复的活动 ❷恢复……的名誉(或职位、功能等):~ a witness 恢复证人的名誉/~ victims by the million 为上百万名受害者平反

rehearsal / rɪˈhɜːsl / *n*. 排练;排演;练习:hold a dress ~ 进行彩排

rehearse / rɪˈhɜːs / *vt*. 排练;排演;练习:When will you ~ the play again? 你们什么时候再排演这出戏?

reign / reɪn / Ⅰ *n*. [C](君主的)统治时期,在位期,执政期 Ⅱ *vi*. ❶统治,执政:The queen ~ed over her subjects for 45 years. 女王对其臣民统治了 45 年。❷当主管；主宰；权配：Let peace ~ over all. 让和平主宰一切。

rein /reɪn/ Ⅰ *n.* [C] ❶缰绳；❷(*pl.*)统治权；支配权；制约手段：hold the ~s of power 驾驭权力/the ~s of government 管理权/ **give (free) ~ to** 放任，对……完全放权：The proposals give farmers more ~ to plant what they want. 这些提议让农民更自由地去种植他们想种植的东西。**keep a tight ~ on** 对……严加约束；严格控制 Ⅱ *vt.* (用缰绳)勒住(马)

reinforce /ˌriːɪnˈfɔːs/ *vt.* 增援；增强：The lawyer ~d his argument with new facts. 律师以新的事实增强自己论点的力度。派 reinforcement *n.*

reiterate /riːˈtəˌreɪt/ *v.* 重申，重述；反复做：He ~d that this sort of behaviour was a major problem. 他一再说这种行为是主要问题。

reject /rɪˈdʒekt/ *vt.* ❶抛开；丢弃 ❷拒绝；不接受：~ an offer of help 拒绝接受帮助

rejection /rɪˈdʒekʃən/ *n.* ❶拒绝；拒绝接受；拒绝相信：Rejections of his proposal could lead to disaster. 拒绝接受他的建议可能导致灾难。❷[U]不受理；否决，驳回 ❸[U]嫌弃，厌弃 ❹[C]废弃物；淘汰品：He has nothing but ~s. 他只有一些淘汰的物件。

rejoice /rɪˈdʒɒɪs/ *vt.* 欣喜；高兴；快乐：We ~ to see that you have come back. 看到你回来，我们很高兴。

relapse Ⅰ /rɪˈlæps/ *vi.* ❶故态复萌，回到原先的状态：~ into silence 再次沉默不语/She ~d into her early failing. 她故态复萌，又步入早年的歧途。❷(病情好转后)复发，再发：~ into a coma 再度昏迷 Ⅱ /rɪˈlæps, ˈriːlæps/ *n.* [C] ❶故态复萌；回复 ❷(病情的)复发：possibility of former patients suffering ~s 已康复的患者旧病复发的可能性

relate /rɪˈleɪt/ *v.* ❶讲，说(故事等)；叙述(事实等)：He ~d to his wife some amusing stories about his employer. 他对妻子述说有关他雇主的一些趣事。❷有联系；有关系；涉及：We must ~ the conclusion with the facts. 我们必须将结论和事实联系起来。/She is a girl who notices nothing except what ~s to herself. 她是一个对一切都漠不关心而只关心自己的女孩。

related /rɪˈleɪtɪd/ *adj.* ❶有关的；关联的；相关的：The project asks a number of ~ questions. 这一计划提出了许多相关的问题。❷有族系(或血缘、姻亲)关系的：I'm ~ to the guy. 我与那个家伙是亲戚。

relation /rɪˈleɪʃn/ *n.* ❶叙述；故事 ❷联系；关系：the ~ between mother and child 母子(女)关系 / **in (with) ~ to** 关于；涉及：I have a lot to say in ~ to English study. 关于英语学习，我有很多话要说。❸[C](常用 *pl.*)(国家间)交往，关系：public ~s 公共关系 / the friendly ~s between my country and yours 贵国与我国间的友好关系 ❹[C]亲戚；亲属：He is a near ~ of mine. 他是我的一个近亲。

relationship /rɪˈleɪʃnʃɪp/ *n.* [C]关系；联系：the ~ between the two countries 两国之间的关系 / the ~ between supply and demand 供需关系 / teacher-student ~ 师生关系

relative /ˈrelətɪv/ Ⅰ *adj.* ❶比较的；相对的：They are living in ~ comfort. 他们现在生活得比较舒服。❷关于(与 to

R

连用):the facts ~ to this problem 与此问题有关的事实 ❸(语法) the ~ pronoun 关系代词 / the ~ adverb 关系副词 Ⅱ *n.* [C]亲戚;亲属:She wanted to receive letters from her ~s when she was studying abroad. 她在国外学习的时候,很想收到亲属们的来信。

relatively /ˈrelətɪvli/ *adv.* 比较而言;相对地;相当地:The accused men have been given ~ light sentences. 被告只被判以相当轻的刑罚。/ He walks ~ fast for a small child. 就一个小孩而论,他算走得相当快了。

relativity /ˌreləˈtɪvəti/ *n.* [U] ❶相互依存 ❷(物理)相对论:the general theory of ~ 广义相对论 / the special theory of ~ 狭义相对论

relax /rɪˈlæks/ *v.* (使)松弛;(使)放松;(使)松懈:~ the muscles 松弛肌肉 / ~ discipline 放松纪律

relaxation /ˌriːlækˈseɪʃn/ *n.* ❶[U]松弛 ❷消遣:Fishing and mountain-climbing are his favourite ~s. 垂钓和爬山是他最喜爱的消遣活动。

relay /rɪˈleɪ/ Ⅰ *n.* [C] ❶替班的人(或物);新补充的人(或物) ❷接力赛:a ~ race 接力赛跑 ❸转播(无线电节目) Ⅱ *vt.* (relaid /ˌriːˈleɪd/, relaid) ❶转播;传达:The satellite will be used mainly to ~ television programmes. 这颗人造卫星的主要用途是转播电视节目。❷重新铺设

release /rɪˈliːs/ *vt.* 放行;释放;免除;解开:be ~d to the press 发布给新闻界 / be ~d from debt 还清债务 / ~ a man from prison 从监狱释放某人

relevant /ˈreləvənt/ *adj.* 有关的;相应的:What he said is ~ to the question we are discussing. 他所讲的与我们正在讨论的问题有关。

reliability /rɪˌlaɪəˈbɪləti/ *n.* [U]可靠性

reliable /rɪˈlaɪəbl/ *adj.* 可靠的;可信赖的

reliance /rɪˈlaɪəns/ *n.* [U]信任,信赖;信心;依靠:We should place ~ on the strength of the masses. 我们应该依靠群众的力量。

relic /ˈrelɪk/ *n.* [C]纪念物;文物;遗俗;遗物

relief /rɪˈliːf/ *n.* [U]❶减轻;解除:The doctor's treatment gave (brought) some ~. 医生的治疗使病情有所缓解。❷帮助;救济;救济物:provide ~ for refugees 赈济难民

relieve /rɪˈliːv/ *vt.* 救济;救助;援助;减轻或解除(痛苦):~ one's feelings 发泄感情 / ~one's mind 解除某人的忧虑 / The fund is for relieving distress among the flood victims. 这基金是用于赈济水灾灾民的。/ Let me ~ you of your suitcase. 让我替你拿这个手提箱。

relieved /rɪˈliːvd/ *adj.* 宽慰的,宽心的,放心的:He was very ~ when his life recovered. 他妻子痊愈后他甚感宽慰。/We were ~ to hear the news. 听到这则消息后,我们就宽心了。

religion /rɪˈlɪdʒən/ *n.* ❶[C]宗教 ❷[U]宗教信仰

religious /rɪˈlɪdʒəs/ *adj.* ❶宗教的;宗教方面的 ❷(指人)虔诚的,敬畏神的

relinquish /rɪˈlɪŋkwɪʃ/ *vt.* ❶放弃(权利、财产、要求等):~ a claim 放弃索赔/ ~ music as a profession 放弃专业音乐工作 ❷放松,松开:He slowly ~ed his hold on the rope. 他慢慢地松开了紧拽着的绳索。

relish /ˈrelɪʃ/ Ⅰ *n.* ❶[U]喜爱,喜好,爱

R

好，兴趣，兴致：have a ~ for fast driving 喜欢开快车/eat with great ~津津有味地吃东西 ❷[C]佐料，调料，调味品：spicy ~es香料调料 Ⅱ *vt.* 对……感兴趣，喜欢，爱好：His war films were critically applauded as well as ~ed by the multitude. 他的战争影片不但为大众喜欢，还受到评论界的赞誉。

reluctant /rɪˈlʌktənt/ *adj.* 不情愿的；勉强的：He was ~ to go with me. 他不愿意跟我一道去。

rely /rɪˈlaɪ/ *vi.* 信赖；依靠（与 on 或 upon 连用）：Don't ~ on others; ~ on yourself. 别靠他人，要靠你自己。/ He can always be relied upon. 他是永远可信赖的。

remain /rɪˈmeɪn/ *vi.* ❶剩下；遗留：After the fire, very little ~ed of my house. 火烧后，寒舍所剩无几。❷ 依然存在；继续存在；保持：He ~ed silent. 他保持沉默。

remainder /rɪˈmeɪndə(r)/ *n.* ❶剩余物：Twenty people came in and the ~ stayed outside. 20 个人进来了，余者留在外面。Can the ~ of the food do for next meal? 剩下的食物还够下顿吃吗？❷[C] 余数：Take five from twenty and the ~ is fifteen. 20 减 5，余数是 15。

remains /rɪˈmeɪnz/ *n.* 残余；余额；遗体；废墟；遗迹：Here is the ~ of a temple. 这里是一座寺庙的遗迹。

remark /rɪˈmɑːk/ Ⅰ *n.* ❶[C]评论；谈话：make a few ~s 说几句话；作短评 ❷[U]注意：There was nothing worthy of ~ at the Flower Show. 花展中没有值得一看的花。Ⅱ *v.* ❶谈起；述及；评论（与 on 或 upon 连用）：~ behind sb.'s back 在背后议论 /~ on other's shortcoming 议论别人的缺点 /It would be rude to ~ upon her appearance. 谈论她的外表是不礼貌的。❷注意：Did you ~ the similarity between them? 你注意到他们之间的相似之处吗？

remarkable /rɪˈmɑːkəbl/ *adj.* 不平常的；值得注意的：a ~ event 不平常的事件 / They have made ~ achievements in their research work. 他们在研究工作中取得了显著成就。/ **be ~ for** 以……著称：The boy is ~ for his courage. 那个男孩以勇敢著称。派 remarkably *adv.*

remarry /ˌriːˈmæri/ *v.* 再婚

remedial /rɪˈmiːdɪəl/ *adj.* ❶治疗的；治疗上的：a ~ schema 治疗方案 ❷补习的：a ~ course 补习课程/a ~ class 补习班 ❸补救的，弥补性的：take ~ measures 采取补救措施

remedy /ˈremədi/ Ⅰ *n.* [C] ❶补救办法；纠正办法：Your only ~ is to go to law. 你的唯一补救办法是求助于法律。❷治疗；治疗法；药物：effective ~ 有效的药物/ This is a good ~ for colds. 这是治疗感冒的良药。Ⅱ *vt.* ❶补救；纠正：It is necessary for you to ~ the fault. 你必须纠正错误。❷治疗；医治

remember /rɪˈmembə(r)/ *vt.* ❶记得；想起/~ **doing sth.** 记得做过某事：I ~ having read the novel. 我记得曾经读过这本小说。~ **to do sth.** 记住要做某事：Please ~ to call me this afternoon. 请记住今天下午给我打电话。/ Remember to turn off the lights before you leave. 记住离开以前要关灯。❷（向某人）问候，致意（与 to 连用）：Please ~ me to your father. 请代我向您父亲问好。

remind /rɪˈmaɪnd/ *vt.* 使某人想起；提醒某人：~ **sb. of sth.** 提醒；使记起；使想起：If I forget, please ~ me of it. 如

果我忘了这事，请提醒我。/ The old lady ~s me of my grandmother. 看见那老太太，我就想起了我的祖母。~ **sb. to do sth.** 提醒某人做某事：Please ~ me to phone her on time. 请提醒我准时给她打电话。~ **sb. that ...** 提醒某人……：Remind the mayor that the visitor is waiting for him outside his office. 提醒市长，来访者正在他的办公室外面等他。派 reminder *n.*

reminiscence / ˌremɪˈnɪsəns / *n.* ❶[U]追忆；回忆；怀旧；怀念：an evening of ~ 值得怀念的夜晚 ❷[C]记起的经历；往事，旧事：a series of fragmentary ~s 一系列回忆片段 ❸[C]（常用 *pl.*）回忆录：publish sb.'s personal ~s 出版某人的个人回忆录

remiss / rɪˈmɪs / *adj.* 玩忽职守的，失职的；疏忽的：be ~ in one's duties 玩忽职守/It was ~ of you to forget to bring your textbook. 你忘带课本来上课，真是粗心。

remission / rɪˈmɪʃən/ *n.* ❶[U]汇款，寄钱 ❷（罪行等的）宽恕；赦免：the ~ of crime 免罪 ❸减刑：the ~ of sentence 减刑 ❹[C]（疾病的）缓解，好转；（疾病的）好转期：There may be ~s of tumour growth. 肿瘤的增长也许有些减缓。

remit / rɪˈmɪt / *vt.* 汇寄（钱或支票等），汇（款）：Please ~ balance due us. 请将欠我方的余款汇来。

remnant / ˈremnənt / *n.* [C] ❶剩余（物）；残余（物）；遗留物：~s of a meal 残羹剩饭/a defeat ed ~残兵败将 ❷遗存，遗迹；遗风：~s of the city's glory 这座城市昔日繁荣的遗迹

remote / rɪˈməʊt / *adj.* 遥远的；边远的；偏僻的；疏远的：~ control 遥控 / the ~ age 遥远的时代 / a ~ mountain village 边远的山村

removable / rɪˈmuːvəbl / *adj.* 可移动的；可除去的

removal / rɪˈmuːvl / *n.* [U] ❶消除；清除，去除；拆除；拆卸：the ~ of contamination 清除杂质 / the ~ of export ban 解除出口禁令 / the ~ of a tumour 肿瘤的摘除 ❷搬移，搬动；移动；调动：one's ~ abroad 移居国外 ❸罢免，免职，解职，开除：the ~ of sb. from office 免去某人的职务

remove / rɪˈmuːv / *vt.* 移动；除去：~ a boy from school for his bad health 因健康不佳让男孩休学 / ~ doubts 消除疑虑

Renaissance / ˌrenəˈsɑːns，ˈrenəˌsɑːns / Ⅰ *n.* ❶（the ~）（14—16 世纪发生在欧洲的）文艺复兴 ❷（常作 r-）复兴；复活；新生，再生：a black literary renaissance 黑人文学复兴运动 Ⅱ *adj.* 文艺复兴（时期）的；具文艺复兴风格的：a ~ artist 一位文艺复兴时期的画家

renew / rɪˈnjuː / *v.* ❶再做；再说；再给：~ a book 续借一本书/ ~ one's complaints 重新投诉 ❷更新；（使）恢复原状：~ one's youth 恢复青春

rent / rent / Ⅰ *n.*（土地、建筑物等的）定期租金；租金总额：owe three weeks' ~ for one's house 欠三个星期的房租 / collect the ~s 收租 Ⅱ *v.* 租用，出租（土地、房屋等）：Mr. Hill ~s this land to us at £500 a year. 希尔先生把这块土地租给我们，每年租金 500 英镑。

rental / ˈrentəl/ Ⅰ *n.* [C] ❶租金，租赁费：~s for housing 房租 ❷出租；租借，租用；租赁 ❸出租物；出租房；出租车 Ⅱ *adj.*（只作定语）租用的；租赁的；供出租的；可租用的：the ~ income 租金收入 / a ~ car company 出租车公司

R

repair / rɪˈpeə(r) / Ⅰ *vt.* 修补;修理:~ a watch (road) 修表(修路) Ⅱ *n.* 修理;补救:**beyond** ~ 无法修理:The TV set is broken beyond ~. 这电视机坏得无法修了。**under** ~ 在修理中:The road is under ~. 这条路正在修筑中。派 repairable *adj.*

repay / rɪˈpeɪ / *v.* (repaid /rɪˈpeɪd/, repaid) ❶付还:If you lend me £50, I'll ~ you next week. 你若借 50 英镑给我,我下星期就还你。❷报答;回报(与 for 连用):~ sb. for his kindness 报答某人的恩惠 派 repayment *n.*

repeal / rɪˈpiːl / Ⅰ *vt.* 撤销(决议等);废除(法令等):He plans to ~ a number of current policies. 他计划废除一些当前的政策。Ⅱ *n.* [U]撤销;废除

repeat / rɪˈpiːt / *v.* 重复;重说;重做:Please ~ what I said. 请复述我说的话。

repeated / rɪˈpiːtɪd/ *adj.* (只作定语)重复的,反复的,再三的:~ attempts 不断的努力 派 repeatedly *adv.*

repel / rɪˈpel / (-pelled;-pelling) *vt.* ❶击退;逐退:The foul air of the house almost ~led me. 屋子里臭气扑鼻,我差点退了回来。/The army ~led the invaders. 部队击退了入侵者。❷与……不相融:Water and oil ~ each other. 油水不相融。❸抗拒,抵御:This coat ~s rain. 这件衣服能防雨。❹排斥,相斥:Electrical charges of a similar kind ~ each other and those that are dissimilar attract. 电荷同性相斥,异性相吸。

repent / rɪˈpent/ *v.* (对……感到)后悔,懊悔:~ one's rudeness 对自己的粗暴行为感到后悔 /He ~ed his angry words. 他后悔说了那些气话。/ She ~ed shouting at her children. 她后悔对孩子们大吼大叫。

repetition / ˌrepəˈtɪʃn / *n.* 重复说;重做:Any ~ of the mistake will be punished. 再犯这种错误就会受惩罚。

replace / rɪˈpleɪs / *vt.* ❶取代;替换:I don't think television will ~ movie. 我认为电视不会取代电影。❷把……放回原处:Please ~ the books on the shelf after reading. 阅读后请把书放回书架。派 replaceable *adj.*

replacement / rɪˈpleɪsmənt/ *n.* ❶[U]接替;代替;取代:the ~ of paper and pencils with (by) computers 计算机取代纸和笔 ❷[C]取代者;接替者;代替者,代替物:~s for broken window frames 断掉窗框的替换件 / He's Mr. Brown's ~. 他是来接替布朗先生的。

replay Ⅰ / riːˈpleɪ / *vt.* ❶重放(电影、录音等) ❷重新举行(比赛) ❸重演;重奏 Ⅱ /ˈriːˌpleɪ/ *n.* [C] ❶(录音等的)重播;(电影、录像等的)重放 ❷重赛 ❸重演;重奏

replicate / ˈreplɪˌkeɪt / *v.* ❶重复做;反复做:~ a chemical experiment 重复做一个化学实验 ❷复制:The virus can ~ itself. 这种病毒可以自我复制。

R

reply / rɪˈplaɪ / Ⅰ *v.* 回答;答复:Please ~ at your earliest convenience. 请尽早答复。Ⅱ *n.* [C]回答;答复:When can you give me a ~? 你什么时候可以给我一个答复? / **in** ~ **to** 作为对……的答复:We sent her an interesting novel in ~ to her kindness. 我们送给她一本有趣的小说,作为对她的友好的答谢。

report / rɪˈpɔːt / Ⅰ *v.* ❶报道(所见或所闻):The discovery of a new planet has been ~ed. 据报道已发现一颗新行星。/ **it is** (**was**) **~ed that ...** 据报道……:It is ~ed that their experiment has succeeded. 据报道他们的实验成功

了。❷报到：You must ~ yourself to the school tomorrow. 明天你得到学校报到。Ⅱ*n.* [C]报道；报告；记事：an annual ~ 年度报告

repository /rɪˈpɒzɪtəri/ *n.* [C] ❶储藏室；存放处；仓库：a vast ~ for digital information 数字信息的巨大仓库 ❷宝库：A book is a ~ of wisdom, mystery, and truth. 书籍乃智慧、奥秘和真理的宝库。

represent /ˌreprɪˈzent/ *vt.* ❶代表：We chose a committee to ~ us. 我们选出一个委员会来代表我们。❷表示；象征；说明 ❸表现；描绘；说成

representative /ˌreprɪˈzentətɪv/ Ⅰ*adj.* 有代表性的；典型的：The exhibition is ~ of modern Chinese science. 这个展览会代表了现代中国科学。Ⅱ*n.* [C]代表；代理人：a ~ of the people 人民代表 / a diplomatic ~ 外交代表 / House of Representatives (美国)众议院

reproach /rɪˈprəʊtʃ/ Ⅰ*vt.* 责备；指摘；谴责；非难：She had not even ~ed him for breaking his promise. 她甚至对他的不守信用未加指责。Ⅱ*n.* [U]指摘；责备，责怪：He looked at her with ~. 他满眼责备地看着她。

R

reproduce /ˌriːprəˈdjuːs/ *v.* ❶繁殖；生殖：The plant ~s by seeds. 这种植物靠种子繁殖。❷复制；仿造：The painting is ~d from a magazine. 这幅画从杂志上复制而来。

reproduction /ˌriːprəˈdʌkʃn/ *n.* 再生；繁殖；复制；仿制品

reprove /rɪˈpruːv/ *vt.* 责备，责骂，指责：His father ~d him for his idleness. 他因无所事事而被其父责骂。/He was ~d by the teacher for not finishing the homework in time. 他没有及时完成家庭作业，因而受到老师责备。

reptile /ˈreptaɪl/ *n.* [C]爬行动物；(口语)两栖动物

republic /rɪˈpʌblɪk/ *n.* [C]共和国：the People's Republic of China 中华人民共和国

republican /rɪˈpʌblɪkən/ *adj.* 共和(国)的

repulse /rɪˈpʌls/ *vt.* ❶击退；驱退，赶走：~ an assault 击退进攻/The enemy was ~d. 敌人被击退了。❷拒绝，回绝：They coldly ~d our offers of friendship. 他们冷淡地拒绝了我们友好的表示。

reputation /ˌrepjʊˈteɪʃn/ *n.* [U]名誉；名声；名望：live up to one's ~ 名副其实 / have a ~ for 以……而闻名

request /rɪˈkwest/ Ⅰ*n.* ❶[U]请求：We came at your ~. 我们应你的请求而来。❷[C]所求之物：All my ~s were granted. 我所请求的事全被允许了。Ⅱ*v.* 要求，请求；邀请：Visitors are ~ed not to touch the exhibits. 请观众勿触摸展览品。

require /rɪˈkwaɪə(r)/ *vt.* ❶需要：We ~ extra help. 我们需要额外的帮助。❷命令；要求：~d courses 必修课程/They ~d me to keep silent. 他们吩咐我不要作声。派 requirement *n.*

rescue /ˈreskjuː/ Ⅰ*vt.* 援救；解救；使免于：~ a man from bandits 从土匪手中救出一个人 Ⅱ*n.* 援救；解救：come (go) to the ~ 援救 / to sb.'s ~ 救助某人 派 rescuer *n.*

research /rɪˈsɜːtʃ/ Ⅰ*n.* [U]研究；调查；探索：carry out ~es into the causes of a certain cancer 对某种癌症的起因进行研究 Ⅱ*vi.* 研究；探索；调查：So far we haven't been able to find anything, but we're still ~目前我们还没有任何发现，但是我们仍在研究。派 researcher *n.*

resemblance /rɪˈzembləns/ *n.* 相似；相似性；相似点

resemble /rɪˈzembl/ *vt.* 相似；类似：They ~ each other in shape but not in color. 它们的形状相似，但颜色不同。

resent /rɪˈzent/ *vt.* 对……不满；怨恨：I ~ the man's deeds. 我对那人的行为不满。派 resentful *adj.*；resentment *n.*

reservation /ˌrezəˈveɪʃn/ *n.* ❶[U]保留：I accept your suggestion without any ~. 我毫无保留地接受你的建议。❷预订；预约：She made a ~ with her dentist at ten tomorrow. 她跟牙医预约的时间是明天10点钟。

reserve /rɪˈzɜːv/ Ⅰ *vt.* ❶保留；留存：All rights of the book are ~d. 此书保留版权。/ The first row is ~d for our guests. 第一排座位留给我们的客人坐。❷预订：You'd better ~ some seats in the theatre. 你最好在剧院预订一些座位。Ⅱ *n.* ❶[C]储备；储备物；后备人员：~ of food 食物储备/~ of foreign exchange 外汇储备 ❷[U]保留：**with** ~ 附带条件地；有保留(顾虑)地：speak with ~ 说话谨慎 **without** ~ 无条件(保留)地；不客气地：accept the conditions without ~ 无保留地接受这些条件 ❸[C]特别保留地；保护区；禁猎区：a forest ~ 保护林 / a game ~ 禁猎区

reserved /rɪˈzɜːvd/ *adj.* ❶预备的，预留的；用作储备的；专用的：~ energy 备用能 / ~ material 专用物资 ❷矜持的；含蓄的；缄默的，寡言的：a ~ person 缄默内向的人 / His public persona was grim and ~. 他在公众场合给人的印象冷峻而矜持。派 reservedly *adv.*

reservoir /ˈrezəvwɑː(r)/ *n.* [C] ❶水库；注水池，蓄水池：the 1,200 acre ~ 1 200英亩的水库 / one's mental ~ 自己的脑子 ❷储藏所，仓库 ❸蓄积，储藏；宝库：a ~ of wisdom 智慧的宝库

reset Ⅰ /riːˈset/ *v.* (-set；-setting) ❶重新安放，重置 ❷重新设定；重调(钟、表等)：As soon as you arrive at your destination, step out of the aircraft and ~ your watch. 你一到达目的地，走出飞机就重新设置手表时间。Ⅱ /ˈriːˌset/ *n.* [C] ❶重新安放；重置 ❷复位器

reside /rɪˈzaɪd/ *vi.* 居住；驻扎

residence /ˈrezɪdəns/ *n.* 居住；驻扎；住处；住宅：country ~ 乡村住宅 / official ~ 官邸 / permanent ~ 永久性住宅 / The foreign visitors took ~ in downtown. 外国客人们在市中心下榻。

resident /ˈrezɪdənt/ *n.* [C]居民

residential /ˌrezɪˈdenʃ(ə)l/ *adj.* 居住的；住所的，住房的：locate in a ~ district 位于住宅区/multi-functional commercial and ~ complex 多功能商住区

resign /rɪˈzaɪn/ *v.* ❶放弃；辞去；辞职：Why did you ~ your right? 你为什么放弃你的权利？/ He has ~ed his position as a sales manager. 他已辞去销售经理的职位。❷听从；顺从：It will not do to ~ oneself to fate. 听天由命是不行的。

resignation /ˌrezɪgˈneɪʃn/ *n.* ❶[C]辞职，退职：one's ~ from the office 辞职 / ~ on bloc 集体辞职 ❷[C]辞呈，辞职报告：submit one's ~ 递交辞呈 ❸[U](对命运等的)屈服，屈从，顺从：~ to inevitable evils 逆来顺受

resist /rɪˈzɪst/ *v.* ❶抵抗；抵挡，抵御：~ attacks (invasions) 抵御进攻(侵略) / The good rock of the hills had ~ed the waves. 山上的这种优质石头顶住了海浪的冲击。❷抗，耐，防：~ acid 耐酸 /

~ infection 抗感染 /~ moisture 防潮 ❸抗拒(诱惑等);忍住,按捺住:Succulent peaches are hard to ~. 多汁的桃子使人忍不住想吃。

resistance /rɪˈzɪstəns/ *n.* [U] ❶抵抗;抵抗力:break down the enemy's ~ 粉碎敌人的抵抗 ❷阻力:An aircraft has to overcome the ~ of the air. 飞机必须克服空气的阻力。

resolute /ˈrezəluːt/ *adj.* 有决心的;坚决的;果敢的:We are ~ for victory. 我们决心要取得胜利。

resolution /ˌrezəˈluːʃn/ *n.* ❶[C]决定;决议:adopt (pass) a ~ 通过决议 ❷[U]决心;决意:take firm ~ to do sth. 决心做某事 ❸解决;解答

resolve /rɪˈzɒlv/ Ⅰ *v.* ❶决定;下决心:He ~d to succeed. 他下决心要成功。❷解决;解答:~ a contradiction 解决矛盾 ❸分解;溶解 Ⅱ *n.* [C] 已决定的事;决定;决心:This did not shake his firm ~. 此事未动摇他坚定的决心。

resort /rɪˈzɔːt/ Ⅰ *vi.* ❶求助;诉诸(与 to 连用):If other means fail, we shall ~ to force. 如果其他手段都失败了,我们将诉诸武力。❷常去:~ to the seaside 常去海滨 Ⅱ *n.* [C] ❶手段:as a last ~ (in the last ~) 作为最后的手段 ❷常去之处;胜地:summer ~s 避暑胜地 ❸求助:He finished the work without ~ to others. 他没有求助别人,自己完成了工作。

resource /rɪˈsɔːs/ *n.* [C](常用 *pl.*)资源:We must exploit the natural ~s of our country. 我们必须开发我国的自然资源。派 resourceful *adj.*

respect /rɪˈspekt/ Ⅰ *n.* ❶[U]尊重;敬重:Children should show ~ for their teachers. 学生应尊敬老师。❷[C](常用 *pl.*)敬意;问候:Give him my ~s. 请代我向他问好。/ **hold sb. in** ~尊敬某人:The scholar was held in ~. 那位学者很受人尊重。**have ~ for sb.** 尊敬某人:You should have ~ for her feelings. 你应当尊重她的感情。**in ~ of(to)**关于:In ~ of this problem, we don't have to discuss it here. 关于这个问题,我们没有必要在这儿讨论。**pay (show) ~ to sb.** 尊敬某人:All of us pay ~ to Professor Smith. 我们都很尊敬史密斯教授。**win one's ~** 赢得某人的尊重:His sense of responsibility for work has won our ~. 他对工作的责任感赢得了我们的尊重。**with ~ to** 关于;至于:I don't want to say anything with ~ to that problem. 关于那个问题,我什么也不想说。Ⅱ *vt.* 尊敬;敬重:I ~ your opinions. 我尊重你的意见。

respectable /rɪˈspektəbl/ *adj.* 值得尊重的;可敬的:She is poor, but quite ~. 她虽穷,但值得尊敬。派 respectably *adv.*

respectful /rɪˈspektfl/ *adj.* (只作表语)尊敬的;尊重的:The young should be ~ to the old. 年轻人应该尊重老年人。

respective /rɪˈspektɪv/ *adj.* 各自的;各个的:After the meeting we went off to our ~ classrooms. 会后我们回到各自的教室。派 respectively *adv.*

respiration /ˌrespɪˈreɪʃn/ *n.* [U]呼吸,吸气:artificial ~人工呼吸

respire /rɪˈspaɪə(r)/ *vi.* ❶呼吸,吸气:Fish ~ through gills. 鱼靠腮呼吸。❷(植物等)完成呼吸作用

respond /rɪˈspɒnd/ *vi.* 回答;答复;响应;有反应:~ to the treatment 对治疗有反应 / The class ~ed to the suggestion with applause. 全班同学对这个提议报以掌声。

R

response /rɪˈspɒns/ *n.* [C]回答；答复；响应；反应：In ~ to the call of the school, all the students threw themselves in the activities of the Civil Virtues Month. 同学们响应学校号召，投入到“文明礼貌月”的活动中。

responsibility /rɪˌspɒnsəˈbɪləti/ *n.* 责任，职责；责任心，责任感：take the ~ of education 承担教育责任 / Our monitor has a strong sense of ~. 我们班长有很强的责任感。

responsible /rɪˈspɒnsəbl/ *adj.* ❶应负责任的；有责任的 / **be ~ (to sb.) for sth.** 应对(某人)某事负责：The pilot of the plane is ~ for the passengers' safety. 飞机驾驶员对乘客的安全负有责任。❷可信赖的；可靠的：give a task to a ~ man 把工作交给可靠的人

rest[1] /rest/ Ⅰ *vi.* ❶平静；休息：We ~ed (for) an hour. 我们休息了一个小时。❷(委婉语)长眠；安息：He ~s in the churchyard. 他长眠于教堂墓地中。❸停止；暂停：They let the matter ~. 他们让这事到此为止。Ⅱ *n.* [C](常用单数)休息；宁静；睡眠 / **take (have) a ~** 休息一会儿：Let's take (have) a ~. 我们休息一会儿吧。

rest[2] /rest/ *n.* (the ~) 剩余；其余：Take what you want and throw the ~ away. 把你所要的拿去，其余的可丢弃。

restaurant /ˈrestərɒnt/ *n.* [C]饭店；餐厅

restless /ˈrestləs/ *adj.* 得不到休息的；不宁静的；静不下来的：~ night 不眠之夜 / ~ life 不平静的生活

restoration /ˌrestəˈreɪʃn/ *n.* [U]归还；恢复；复原

restore /rɪˈstɔː(r)/ *vt.* ❶归还：~ borrowed books 归还所借的书 ❷重新采用；恢复：~ old customs 恢复古老风俗 ❸使恢复(健康)；复原；痊愈

restrain /rɪˈstreɪn/ *vt.* 抑制；遏制；阻止：~ a child from doing mischief 制止小孩胡闹 / ~ oneself 克制自己 / ~ tears 忍住眼泪

restraint /rɪˈstreɪnt/ *n.* [U]抑制；遏制；克制

restrict /rɪˈstrɪkt/ *vt.* 限制；约束：He was ~ed to three cigarettes a day. 他被限制每天吸三支烟。派 restriction *n.*

restrictive /rɪˈstrɪktɪv/ *adj.* ❶限制的，约束的：The project is not able to continue because of ~ budget. 由于预算限制，该项目无法再继续下去。❷(字、词、短语等对修饰对象有)限制(或限定)性的，起限制(或限定)作用的：~ clause 限制性从句

result /rɪˈzʌlt/ Ⅰ *vi.* 发生；产生 / **~ from** 产生于；来自于：Success ~s from hard work. 成功是艰苦工作的结果。**~ in** 导致……的结果：Eating too much often ~s in sickness. 吃得太多常会惹出病来。Ⅱ *n.* 结果；效果：His limp is the ~ of an accident. 他的跛脚是一次事故的结果。/ **as a ~** 由于；因此：He has heart disease. As a ~, he cannot take part in the sports meet. 他有心脏病，因此不能参加运动会。**as a ~ of** 作为……的结果：As a ~ of the traffic jam, quite a lot of people were late. 由于交通堵塞，不少人都迟到了。**without ~** 毫无结果地：The investigation finished without ~. 调查毫无结果地结束了。

resume /rɪˈzuːm/ *v.* 重新开始；恢复；继续：~ office 官复原职 / ~ the thread of one's discourse 言归正传 / She ~d writing three years later. 三年后她又重新开始创作。

résumé / ˈrezjʊmeɪ, ˈrezəmeɪ / *n.* [C] ❶摘要;概要;文摘 ❷简历;履历

resumption / rɪˈzʌmpʃən/ *n.* [U] ❶(中断后)重新开始,继续:be ready for the ~ of negotiations 就恢复谈判已做好准备 / a ~ of peace talk 和谈的恢复 ❷重新占用,重新获得

retail / ˈriːteɪl / Ⅰ *n.* [U]零售:sell by (at) ~ 零售 Ⅱ *adj.* 零售的

retain / rɪˈteɪn / *vt.* 保持;保留;保有:Our teacher ~s the style of hard work. 我们的老师保持着努力工作的作风。

retell / ˌriːˈtel / *vt.* (retold/ˌriːˈtəʊld/,retold) 重述;复述:~ the text 复述课文 / The teacher asked him to ~ the story. 老师叫他复述故事。

retire / rɪˈtaɪə(r) / *vi.* ❶退休;退职;退役:He will ~ on a pension at 60. 他将在 60 岁退休,退休后领养老金。❷就寝:She usually ~s at 11 o'clock. 她通常在 11 点就寝。❸退下;退却;退出:He ~d hurt in the basketball match. 在篮球比赛中,他受伤退场。

R

retirement / rɪˈtaɪəmənt / *n.* 退休;退职;退役:The old professor felt busier than before after her ~. 退休后老教授感到比以前更忙了。

retort / rɪˈtɔːt / *v.* 反击;反驳

retreat / rɪˈtriːt / Ⅰ *vi.* 退却;撤退:force the enemy to ~ 迫使敌人退却 / ~ towards the capital 向首都撤退 Ⅱ *n.* 退却;撤退:The army was in full ~. 全军在大撤退。

return / rɪˈtɜːn / Ⅰ *vi.* 回来;归去:~ home 回家 —*vt.* 归还:When will you ~ the book I lent you? 你借的那本书什么时候还我? Ⅱ *n.* 返回;归还:~ key (计算机的) 回车键 / the ~ of spring 春之归来 / Many happy ~s of the day. (贺生日用语)祝你长命百岁! / **in ~ for** 报答:The boy behaved well in ~ for his mother's love. 男孩表现很好,以报答他母亲对他的爱。

reunite / ˌriːjuːˈnaɪt / *v.* 再结合;重聚:~ after many years' separation 多年分离后重聚

reuse Ⅰ /riːˈjuːz/ *vt.* 重新使用;重复使用,多次使用:Waste paper can be ~d after chemical treatment. 废纸经过化学处理之后可重新使用。Ⅱ /riːˈjuːs/ *n.* [U]二次使用;重复使用,多次使用

reveal / rɪˈviːl / *vt.* ❶揭示;揭露;泄露:He promised not to ~ the secret to anyone. 他答应不把秘密泄露给任何人。❷展现;显示:The picture ~s to us the farmers' happy life. 图画展现给我们的是农民的幸福生活。派 revelation *n.*

revenge / rɪˈvendʒ / Ⅰ *vt.* 报仇;报复:~ an injustice 对不公平对待进行报复 / ~ one's friend 为朋友报仇 Ⅱ *n.* [U]报仇;报复:He planned the murder out of ~. 他为报仇而策划了谋杀。/ **take (have) one's ~** 报仇 **take ~ on sb.** 为自己向某人报复

revenue / ˈrevəˌnjuː / *n.* ❶(国家的)岁入;税收:sources of ~ 税收来源/the total ~s of the government 政府税收总额 ❷收益;收入:business ~企业收入/~s from the sales of the trees 销售木材所得的收益

reversal / rɪˈvɜːsəl / *n.* ❶[U]反向;倒转 ❷[C](财气、运气的)逆转,恶化;背运:That's a ~of his usual position on relations with Iraq. 他在同伊拉克关系上所持的态度与平时截然不同。

reverse /rɪˈvɜːs/ Ⅰ *vt.* 颠倒;倒转;倒退:You may ~ the procedure and begin with the last item. 你可以颠倒程序,从最后一项开始。Ⅱ *n.* ❶相反;相反的情况:Don't do the ~ of what we expect. 别做与我们的期望相反的事。❷背面;反面:the ~ of a coin 钱币的反面 Ⅲ *adj.* 相反的;背面的;倒转的:in ~ order 以颠倒的顺序

review /rɪˈvjuː/ Ⅰ *v.* ❶回顾;复习:~ last week's lesson 复习上星期的功课 ❷(在报纸或期刊上)评论(作品):Mr. Hill ~s for *The Times*. 希尔先生为《泰晤士报》写评论。Ⅱ *n.* ❶回顾;复习 ❷评论文章;评论:write ~s for the monthly magazine 为月刊写书评

revise /rɪˈvaɪz/ *vt.* 修订;修改;校订:~ a plan 修改计划

revision /rɪˈvɪʒn/ *n.* ❶修改;修订;校正,勘校,审校:make extensive ~做大量修订/He made several ~s to his speech. 他多次修改自己的演讲稿。❷[C]修订本;订正版:publish a ~ of the dictionary 出版该词典的修订版

revival /rɪˈvaɪvəl/ *n.* [U] ❶复兴;再生;重新使用;再度流行:a ~ in consumer demand after a period of slow business 市场一度疲软之后消费需求的重新活跃/the ~ of old customs 旧传统的再度盛行 ❷苏醒;复活,复苏:stimulate an economic ~刺激经济复苏

revive /rɪˈvaɪv/ *v.* ❶(使)复兴;(使)再生;(使)重新使用:Her interest in piano ~d. 她又对钢琴感兴趣了。/Don't ~ those old prejudices. 不要让这些旧偏见死灰复燃。❷(使)复苏;(使)苏醒;(使)复活:The roses will ~ in water. 那些玫瑰浇了水就会活过来。/They managed to ~ the drowning man. 他们成功地把溺水者救活了。

revolt /rɪˈvəult/ Ⅰ *vi.* 反叛;叛乱;反抗;违抗 Ⅱ *n.* 叛乱,违抗

revolution /ˌrevəˈluːʃn/ *n.* [C](情况、方式等)彻底改变;革命

revolutionary /ˌrevəˈluːʃənəri/ Ⅰ *adj.* 革命的;革新的:~ cause 革命事业/~ spirit 革命精神 Ⅱ *n.* [C]革命者;革命家:A ~ would rather die on his feet than live on his knees. 一个革命者宁愿站着死,也不愿跪着生。

revolve /rɪˈvɒlv/ *v.* (使)旋转:The earth ~s on its own axis once every 24 hours. 地球每 24 小时绕自己的轴旋转一周。

revolver /rɪˈvɒlvə(r)/ *n.* [C]左轮手枪

reward /rɪˈwɔːd/ Ⅰ *n.* ❶[U]报酬;报答:get very little in ~ for one's hard work 辛苦工作得到的报酬却很少 ❷[C]酬金;赏金:offer a ~ of £100 for information about a stolen necklace 悬赏 100 英镑以求获得被盗项链的消息 Ⅱ *v.* 报答;报偿;酬谢:Is that how you ~ me for my help? 那就是你因为我的帮忙而给我的报答吗?

rewrite /ˌriːˈraɪt/ *vt.* (rewrote/ˌrɪːˈrəut/, rewritten/ˌriːˈrɪtn/)再写;重写

rhyme /raɪm/ *n.* ❶[U] 韵;押韵 ❷[C] 有韵的诗;韵文

rhythm /ˈrɪðəm/ *n.* 韵律;节奏 派 rhythmic, rhythmical *adj.*

rib /rɪb/ *n.* [C] 排骨;肋骨

ribbon /ˈrɪbən/ *n.* [C] 缎带;丝带;带状物:cut the ~ 剪彩

rice /raɪs/ *n.* [U] 稻;大米

rich /rɪtʃ/ *adj.* ❶富有的;富裕的:the ~ and the poor 富人和穷人 ❷富饶的;丰富的:China is ~ in natural resources. 中国有丰富的自然资源。/ She is ~ in love for children. 她对孩子们充满爱心。❸盛产的;肥沃的:a ~ harvest 大丰收 派 richly *adv.* ; richness *n.*

riches /ˈrɪtʃɪz/ *n.* 财产;财富;富有:a-mass great ~ 聚敛大量财富

rid /rɪd/ *vt.* (rid 或 ridded, rid 或 ridded; ridding)使获自由;解除;免除(与 of 连用):It is not easy to ~ a bad habit. 改掉恶习是不容易的。/ **get (be) ~ of** 摆脱;去掉:get ~ of fear 摆脱恐惧 / You must get ~ of the bad habit of getting up late. 你得改掉晚起的坏毛病。

riddle /ˈrɪdl/ *n.* [C]谜;谜语:guess a ~ 猜谜 / solve a ~ 解谜

ride /raɪd/ Ⅰ *v.* (rode /rəʊd/, ridden /ˈrɪdn/)骑:He jumped on his horse and rode off. 他跃上马背,疾驰而去。Ⅱ *n.* [C] 骑马;骑车:go for a ~ before breakfast 早饭前骑一会儿自行车

ridge /rɪdʒ/ *n.* [C] ❶脊;岭:~ of the roof 屋脊 ❷垄;埂

ridicule /ˈrɪdɪkjuːl/ Ⅰ *vi.* 嘲弄;戏弄 Ⅱ *n.* [U]嘲笑;挖苦

R

ridiculous /rɪˈdɪkjələs/ *adj.* 荒谬的;可笑的:~ ideas 荒谬的想法 / He looks ~ in jeans. 他穿牛仔裤的样子很可笑。派 ridiculously *adv.*

rifle /ˈraɪfl/ *n.* [C]步枪

rift /rɪft/ *n.* [C] ❶裂缝,裂纹;裂口 ❷(人际关系中的)嫌隙,裂痕,不和:After years of harmonious marriage, however, ~s began appearing. 经过多年和谐的婚姻生活之后,他们之间开始出现了裂痕。

right /raɪt/ Ⅰ *adj.* ❶正确的;对的;满意的;公正的 / **all ~** ①行了;好吧;可以 ②(病)好了;安然无恙的:Do you feel all ~? 你感觉还好吗? ③令人满意的;不错的 / **put (set) sth. ~** 使恢复正常;使恢复健康:He asked who can put the machine ~. 他问谁能修好那台机器。❷直角的 ❸右面的;右方的:In Great Britain traffic keeps to the left, not the ~ side of the road. 在英国,车辆靠左边而非靠右行驶。Ⅱ *adv.* ❶一直地;直接地:Put it ~ in the middle. 把它放在正中间。/ Go ~ on until you reach the church. 一直往前走,直到教堂。/ **~ away (now)** 马上;立即:I'll come ~ away. 我立刻就来。❷正确地;满意地;公正地:Have I guessed the answer ~ or wrong? 我猜的答案是对还是错? Ⅲ *n.* ❶[U]正确;公正:know the difference between ~ and wrong 了解是非的区别 ❷[C]权利:children's(women's) ~s 儿童(妇女)的权利 / human ~s 人权 / intellectual property ~s 知识产权 / exclusive sale ~ 专卖权 / He has a ~ to do that. 他有权做那件事。❸右边;右方:Take the first turning to the ~. 在第一个转弯处向右转。/ **on the ~** 在右边 派 rightly *adv.*

rightful /ˈraɪtf(ʊ)l/ *adj.* ❶合法的;依法享有的:the ~ heir 合法继承人/the ~ status of an independent nation 一个独立国家的合法地位 ❷正当的,正义的:a ~ act 正义的行为

rigid /ˈrɪdʒɪd/ *adj.* ❶坚硬的;刚性的 ❷严格的;僵硬的;死板的:~ discipline 严格的纪律 / They are ~ in attitude. 他们态度严厉。派 rigidly *adv.*

rigidity /rɪˈdʒɪdəti/ *n.* [U]坚硬;严格;僵硬

rigoro(u)s /ˈrɪgə(r)əs/ *adj.* ❶严格的;严厉的:a ~ critique 一篇措辞严厉的评

论 ❷精确的,准确的;严谨的:~ science attitude 严谨的科学态度 ❸(气候)恶劣的;严寒的:a ~ climate 恶劣气候

rigour /ˈrɪɡə(r)/ *n.* ❶[U]严格;严厉:be punished with the full ~ of the law 受到法律最严厉的惩处 ❷[C]艰苦,艰难;恶劣的条件:survive the ~s of winter 挨过寒冷的冬天 ❸[U]准确,精确;严密,严谨:the ~ of an argument 论证的严密性 ❹[U](肌肉的)僵硬

ring /rɪŋ/ Ⅰ *v.* (rang /ræŋ/, rung /rʌŋ/) ❶发出(清晰响亮的)声音:Start work when the bell ~s. 铃响便开始工作。❷按铃(作为召唤、警告):She rang for the waiter. 她按铃叫服务员。/ If you want something, you may ~ the bell. 如果你需要什么,可以按铃叫我。❸响着(声音等);(指耳朵)嗡嗡作响:His last words still rang in my ears. 他的遗言仍响在我耳边。/ ~ **back** 回电话:Ring me back this afternoon, please. 请今天下午给我回电话。~ **up** 打电话:He rang up Tom to tell him the good news. 他打电话给汤姆,告诉他那个好消息。/ If you see a blue car, ~ up the police at once. 如果你看到一辆蓝色的小汽车,马上给警察打电话。~ **with** 响彻着:The country is ~ing with praise. 全国上下一片赞美声。Ⅱ *n.* [C] ❶按铃;铃声 ❷电话;通话:I'll give you a ~ this evening. 今晚我给你打电话。❸戒指;环形物:diamond ~ 钻石戒指 / wedding (engagement) ~ 结婚(订婚)戒指

riot /ˈraɪət/ *n.* [C] 骚乱,暴乱;社会动荡;动乱:put down (quell, quash) an incipient ~ 平定骚乱 / a ~ sparked by rumours 由谣言引起的骚乱

ripe /raɪp/ *adj.* (指水果、谷物等)成熟的

ripen /ˈraɪpən/ *v.* 使……熟;成熟:The sun ~ed the fruits. 阳光使水果成熟了。

ripple /ˈrɪpl/ Ⅰ *n.* [C](水面上的)微波,涟漪;起伏的声音:A long ~ of laughter passed through the audience. 观众中响起一阵笑声。Ⅱ *v.* (使)起微波;(使)起伏:The wheat ~d in the breeze. 在微风吹拂下,麦浪起伏。

rise /raɪz/ Ⅰ *vi.* (rose /rəʊz/, risen /ˈrɪzən/) ❶(指太阳、月亮等)升起:The sun ~s in the east. 太阳从东方升起。❷起身;起床:He rose to welcome me. 他起身欢迎我。❸上涨;上升:The river has risen 2 feet. 河水上涨了两英尺。Prices continue to ~. 物价继续上涨。❹升级;晋升:He rose from an errand boy to the president. 他从小差使晋升为总经理。❺反叛;起义:At last the citizens rose up and defeated their cruel rulers. 最后市民们起义了,并且打败了他们残酷的统治者。Ⅱ *n.* ❶[C]进展 ❷[C]升高;增加:have a ~ in wages 提高工资 ❸[C]小山 ❹[U]起源:The river has (takes) its ~ among the hills. 这条河发源于小山中。/ **give ~ to** 引起;导致:Such a conduct might give ~ to misunderstandings. 这种行为可能会导致误解。

risk /rɪsk/ Ⅰ *n.* 风险;危险 / **at the ~ of** 冒……的危险:He was determined to get there even at the ~ of his life. 他决心到那里去,即使冒生命危险也在所不惜。**run (take) a ~ (~s)** 冒险:A businessman has to take ~s in order to make more money. 为了赚更多的钱,商人总是要冒一定风险的。Ⅱ *v.* (使)冒危险:We must ~ getting caught in a storm. 我们必须冒被暴风雨阻挡的

R

危险。

rival /ˈraɪvl/ Ⅰ *n*. [C]对手；竞争者：business ~s 商业竞争对手/ ~ in chess 棋逢对手 / ~ in love 情敌 Ⅱ *adj*. 竞争的 Ⅲ *v*. 与……竞争：~ with the visiting team for the championship 与客队争夺冠军

rivalry /ˈraɪvəlri/ *n*. 对立(状态)；敌对(状态)；竞争：an amiable ~ between the two old friends 两个老朋友之间友好的竞争关系 / a strong sense of ~ 强烈的对立感

river /ˈrɪvə(r)/ *n*. [C] 江；河：the Yellow River 黄河 / the Changjiang (Yangtze) River 长江

road /rəʊd/ *n*. [C] 路：~side 路边；路旁 / ~block 路障 / ~lamp 路灯

roam /rəʊm/ *vi*. 闲逛；漫游；流浪：He ~ed around the world for a few years. 几年来他周游列国。

roar /rɔː(r)/ Ⅰ *n*. [C]吼叫；咆哮；隆隆声，咆哮声 Ⅱ *v*. 吼叫，咆哮：The patient ~ed with pain. 那病人痛得大声喊叫。

roast /rəʊst/ Ⅰ *v*. 烤；烘 Ⅱ *adj*. 烤的；烤制的：~ beef 烤牛肉 / Beijing Roast Duck 北京烤鸭

rob /rɒb/ *v*. (robbed; robbing)抢夺；抢劫；盗窃 / ~ **sb. of sth.** 抢夺某人之物：I was ~bed of my watch. 我的手表被抢了。

robber /ˈrɒbə(r)/ *n*. [C] 抢劫者；强盗；盗贼

robbery /ˈrɒbəri/ *n*. 抢夺；剥夺

robe /rəʊb/ *n*. [C]宽松长袍；礼袍：a bath ~ 浴袍

robot /ˈrəʊbɒt/ *n*. [C]机器人：A ~ can do many things that a man can not. 机器人可以做很多人不能做的事情。

robust /rəʊˈbʌst, ˈrəʊbʌst/ *adj*. ❶健全的；充满生气的：The movie business is enjoying a ~ boom. 电影业正处于强盛时期。❷强壮的，健壮的；粗壮的：a ~ police officer 一个膀阔腰圆的警官

rock /rɒk/ Ⅰ *n*. 大石头；礁石：as firm as a ~ 坚如磐石 Ⅱ *v*. 摇晃；摇动

rocket /ˈrɒkɪt/ Ⅰ *n*. [C]火筒式烟火；火箭：~ base 火箭基地 / fire a ~ 点火发射火箭 Ⅱ *v*. ❶用火箭运载 ❷迅速增加

rocking /ˈrɒkɪŋ/ *adj*. 摇动的；摇摆的

rocky /ˈrɒki/ *adj*. ❶布满岩石的；多岩石的：a small ~ island 岩石嶙峋的小岛 / ~ landscapes 多岩石的地貌 ❷(似)岩石的 ❸坚定不移的，不动摇的：~ endurance 坚忍不拔

rod /rɒd/ *n*. [C] 棒；竿：a fishing ~钓鱼竿

role /rəʊl/ *n*. [C] ❶角色：He wants to play the ~ of Hamlet. 他想扮演哈姆雷特这个角色。❷作用；任务 / **play a ~ in** 在……中起作用：Jack played an important ~ in winning the game. 杰克为赢得比赛起了重要的作用。

roll /rəʊl/ Ⅰ *v*. (使)滚动；(使)转动：The coin fell and ~ed under the table. 硬币掉到地上，滚到桌下。/ ~ **over** (使)翻滚：The car hit a lamppost and ~ed over twice before coming to a stop. 那辆汽车碰到一根灯柱，翻滚了两次才停下来。Ⅱ *n*. [C]❶卷形的东西 ❷滚动；转动 ❸正式的表册或记录表；(尤指)名单：call the ~点名

roller /ˈrəʊlə(r)/ *n*. [C]滚柱；滚筒；滚轴

roller-coaster /ˈrəʊləˌkəʊstə(r)/ *n*. [C] ❶(游乐园等中的)过山车，云霄飞车 ❷急剧变化的局面(或事情等)：the ~

of emotions 情感的急剧变化

Roman /ˈrəʊmən/ Ⅰ *n.* [C] 古罗马人；罗马人 Ⅱ *adj.* 古罗马的；罗马的

romance /rəʊˈmæns, ˈrəʊmæns/ *n.* [C] ❶传奇文学；浪漫文学 ❷爱情故事；风流韵事

romantic /rəʊˈmæntɪk/ Ⅰ *adj.* ❶浪漫的；浪漫主义的；传奇的：Shelley was a famous English ~ poet. 雪莱是英国有名的浪漫主义诗人。❷好幻想的；不切实际的：You must get rid of all ~ ideas. 你得抛弃一切不切实际的想法。Ⅱ *n.* [C]浪漫的人；浪漫主义作家 ▒ romantically *adv.*

romanticist /rəʊˈmæntɪsɪst/ *n.* [C]浪漫主义者；浪漫主义作家

roof /ruːf/ *n.* [C]（*pl.* roofs）（建筑物、帐篷、车等的）顶，顶部

room /ruːm/ *n.* ❶[C]室；房间 ❷[U]空间：Is there ~ for me in the car? 车子里有我坐的位置吗？❸[U]机会；余地；范围：There is ~ for improvement in your work. 你的工作还有改进的余地。/ **make ~ for** 给……腾出地方：Please make a little ~ for the car to pass. 请让出点地方让汽车过去。

root /ruːt/ Ⅰ *n.* [C] ❶（植物的）根：pull up a plant by the ~s 把一株植物连根拔起 ❷（发、齿、舌）根 ❸根源；根基：~ of all evil 万恶之源 / ~ of trouble 祸根 ❹词根 Ⅱ *v.*（使）生根成长；（使）扎根

rope /rəʊp/ *n.* [C]索；绳子 / **at the end of the ~** 末尾的；末路的：The enemy has been at the end of the ~. 敌人已经日暮途穷了。

rose /rəʊz/ *n.* [C]蔷薇；玫瑰：be not all ~s 并非一切尽如人意 / There is no ~ without a thorn.（谚）没有不带刺的玫瑰。（有乐必有苦。）

rostrum /ˈrɒstrəm/ *n.* [C]（*pl.* rostrums 或 rostra /ˈrɒstrə/）讲台；讲坛

rot /rɒt/ *v.*（rotted；rotting）（使）腐烂 / **~ away** 渐渐腐烂：The wood of the stairs has ~ted away. 这梯子的木头已渐渐腐烂了。

rotate /rəʊˈteɪt/ *v.*（使）转动；（使）旋转：The moon ~s around the earth. 月球围绕地球转。

rotation /rəʊˈteɪʃn/ *n.* ❶旋转；转动：The ~ of the earth makes day and night. 地球的自转形成白昼和黑夜。❷循环；轮流：They have a ~ of duties in the office. 他们轮流值班。

rotten /ˈrɒtn/ *adj.* ❶腐烂的；变质的 ❷道德败坏的；腐化的：~ at the core 烂透了；腐败透顶

rough /rʌf/ *adj.* ❶（指表面）不平的，不光的：~ paper 粗糙的纸 / fruit with the ~ skin 粗皮水果 ❷粗暴的；浮躁的：~ behaviour 粗暴的行为 ❸粗略的；大致的：make a ~ sketch 画张草图 ▒ roughly *adv.*

round /raʊnd/ Ⅰ *adj.* 圆形的；环形的：a ~-table conference 圆桌会议 Ⅱ *prep.* ❶（表示动作）环绕：The earth moves ~ the sun. 地球绕着太阳运行。❷（表示位置）围绕：He had a scarf ~ his neck. 他颈上围有一条围巾。❸大约：Come ~ 2 o'clock. 两点左右来。Ⅲ *adv.* ❶环绕地：A crowd of people soon gathered ~. 一群人不久就围拢来了。❷循环地：Christmas will soon be ~ again. 圣诞节又快到了。/ **all the year ~** 整年；全年：They worked hard all the year ~. 他们曾一年到头辛勤劳动。**look ~ (around)** 环顾：He looked ~ (around) but didn't find the building he was looking for. 他四处张望，但是没有看到他要找的那栋楼房。**show sb. ~(around)** 带某人参观：The headmaster showed the guests ~ (around) in the school. 校长带客人们在学校参观。

roundabout /ˈraʊndəbaʊt/ *adj.* 迂回的；拐弯抹角的

rouse /raʊz/ *vt.* ❶唤醒；唤起；使惊起：The noise ~d me from sleep. 闹声把我从睡眠中吵醒。❷激起；激怒

route /ruːt/ *n.* [C]路途；路线；航线：The climbers tried to find a new ~ to the top of the mountain. 登山者试图找到一条到达山顶的新路。

routine /ruːˈtiːn/ Ⅰ *adj.* 日常的；常规的：a ~ report 例行报告/ a ~ medical examination 例行体检 Ⅱ *n.* 惯例；常规：do daily ~ 做日常工作

row /rəʊ/ Ⅰ *n.* [C]一行；一排；一列：a ~ of books 一排书 / a ~ of houses 一排房子 / a ~ of desks 一排桌子 Ⅱ *v.* 划(船等)：Let's ~ a race. 我们来比赛划船吧。

royal /ˈrɒɪəl/ *adj.* 王室的；皇家的：the Royal Air Force(英国)皇家空军 / the Royal Society (英国的)皇家学会

R

royalty /ˈrɒɪəlti/ *n.* ❶[U]王位；王权 ❷[U]王族；皇族 ❸[C] 特许使用费；版税

rub /rʌb/ *v.* (rubbed; rubbing)擦；搓：He ~bed his hands with the soap. 他给双手涂上肥皂。

rubber /ˈrʌbə(r)/ *n.* ❶[U]橡胶 ❷[C]橡皮

rubbish /ˈrʌbɪʃ/ *n.* [U]垃圾；废物

rubble /ˈrʌbl/ *n.* [U]碎石；瓦砾：The building was reduced to ~ during the war. 战争期间这幢建筑成了一片碎石乱瓦。

ruby /ˈruːbi/ *n.* ❶[C]红宝石 ❷[U]红宝石色；暗红色

rude /ruːd/ *adj.* ❶无礼的，粗鲁的：Don't be ~ to your teacher. 不许对师长无礼。/It is ~ of you to speak with your mouth full. 你满口食物说话是很不礼貌的。❷粗略的；大概的：He gave me a ~ drawing of the city. 他给了我一张城市略图。

ruffle /ˈrʌfl/ Ⅰ *vt.* ❶使变皱，弄皱；使不平，使波动：The wind began to ~ the calm surface of the sea. 平静的海面上风起浪涌。❷惹恼，使生气：be ~d from all the interruptions 因不断地被打断而大为光火 ❸草草翻阅(书页等)：He picked up a magazine and ~d the pages. 他拿起一本杂志，随便翻阅着。Ⅱ *n.* [C]皱，皱褶；皱纹；(表面的)起伏

rug /rʌg/ *n.* [C]小地毯；毛毯

rugged /ˈrʌgɪd/ *adj.* ❶(地面)高低不平，崎岖的；(地貌)多岩石的：a ~ volcanic island 岩石嶙峋的火山岛 ❷(人脸)多皱纹的；粗糙的：a ~ masculine face 男人味十足的棱角分明的脸 ❸(生活等)艰苦的：a ~ life 艰苦的生活❹(天气)恶劣的：the most ~ weather 最为恶劣的天气

ruin /ˈruːɪn/ Ⅰ *n.* ❶[U] 毁灭；严重损坏；完全丧失：the ~ of her hopes 她的希望破灭 ❷[C](*pl.*)废墟；遗迹 Ⅱ *v.* 毁灭；破坏；摧毁：The storm ~ed the crops. 暴风雨毁坏了农作物。

rule /ruːl/ Ⅰ *n.* ❶[C]法规；规则；条例：Pupils must obey the ~s of the school. 学生必须遵守校规。/ **as a ~** 通常；一般而言：As a ~, young people like beer. 年轻人通常都喜欢喝啤酒。**by ~** (=**according to ~**)按照规则：She does everything by ~. 她做任何事都照章行事。**make it a ~ to do** (＝**make a ~ of doing**) 习惯做;必做:He makes it a ~ to take a walk before breakfast. 他习惯在早餐前散散步。❷[U]管理;统治:~ under law 法治 Ⅱ *v.* 统治;管理:King Charles I ~d England for 11 years without a parliament. 查理一世在无国会的情况下统治英格兰 11 年。

ruler /ˈruːlə(r)/ *n.* [C] ❶统治者:overthrow the reactionary ~ 推翻反动统治者 ❷尺;直尺

rumble /ˈrʌmbl/ Ⅰ *vi.* ❶隆隆作响;发出隆隆声:The thunder ~d through the night. 雷声隆隆而至,划破夜空。❷隆隆行进;轰鸣着前进:A subway train ~d underneath her. 一列地铁在她脚下轰鸣着驶过。❸声音低沉地说话;嘟哝:~ about the hight price 嘟嘟哝哝地说价格太高 Ⅱ *n.* [C] 隆隆声;轰鸣声;辘辘声

rumo(u)r /ˈruːmə(r)/ *n.* [C] 谣言;传闻:start a ~ 造谣 / spread a ~ 散布谣言 / spike a ~ 辟谣

run /rʌn/ Ⅰ *v.* (ran /ræn/, run) ❶跑 ❷管理:~ a business 经营商店 / ~ a theatre 经营戏院 / ~ a bus company 经营公共汽车公司 / ~ **across** 偶然遇见:She ran across an old friend in the supermarket. 在超级市场里她偶然遇到了一位老朋友。~ **after** 追赶:The policeman ran after the thief and caught him. 警察追赶小偷并把他抓住了。~ **away** 跑掉;逃跑:Don't ~ away. I want to talk to you. 别跑,我有话跟你说。~ **errands (messages) for sb.** 为某人跑腿做信差 ~ **for** 竞选:He ran for manager of the store but failed. 他竞选商店经理,但没有成功。~ **out (of)** 用完;耗尽:I have ~ out of my oil. 我的汽油用完了。~ **over** ①溢出;超过:Her speech ran over the time limit. 她的讲话超过了规定的时限。②撞倒并碾过:The truck ran over a six-year-old child. 卡车碾倒了一个 6 岁的孩子。~ **short of sth.** 缺少某物:They said that they had ~ short of money. 他们说缺钱花。Ⅱ *n.* [C] 跑:The car makes a ~ of 120 miles an hour. 小车每小时行驶 120 英里。派 runner *n.*

runabout /ˈrʌnəbaʊt/ *n.* [C] 流浪者

runaway /ˈrʌnəweɪ/ Ⅰ *n.* [C] 逃亡者;出逃者 Ⅱ *adj.* 逃走的;私奔的

run-down /ˈrʌnˌdaʊn/ *adj.* ❶筋疲力尽的,累极的:You're looking ~. 你看起来很疲劳。❷身体虚弱的:He's severely ~ and had better see a doctor. 他看上去非常虚弱,最好去看医生。❸破败的;衰落的:a ~ neighbourhood 破败不堪的地区

running /ˈrʌnɪŋ/ Ⅰ *n.* [U] ❶奔跑,跑步;赛跑:practise ~ 练习跑步/road ~ 公路赛跑 ❷管理;照看:~ of a business 经营生意 Ⅱ *adj.* ❶(液体)流动的;流出的;流水的:~ water 流水/a ~ spring which is free of ice all winter long 整个冬天不结冰的喷泉 ❷连续的,持续不断的:a ~ battle 持续的战斗 ❸奔跑的;赛跑的:~ shoes 跑鞋 ❹(节奏、讲话等)顺畅的;流利的;顺利的:a ~ rhythm in music 音乐中流畅的节奏

rural /ˈrʊərəl/ *adj.* 农村的;农业的:~ life 农村生活 / ~ market 农村集市 / ~ policy 农业政策

rush /rʌʃ/ Ⅰ *v.* 奔;冲:The children ~ed out of the school gate. 孩子们冲出学校大门。Ⅱ *n.* ❶奔,冲;繁忙:I don't

R

like the ~ of the city life. 我不喜欢繁忙的都市生活。❷急需；抢购：the Christmas ~圣诞节的购物热 / a gold ~淘金热 / **in a** ~匆忙地：He left his office in a ~. 他匆忙地离开了办公室。Ⅲ *adj.* 急迫的；繁忙的：~ hours 交通高峰期

rust / rʌst / Ⅰ *n.* [U]铁锈：The watch doesn't gather ~ easily. 这表不易生锈。Ⅱ *v.* (使)生锈：The lock has ~ed. 那锁已经生锈了。

rustle / ˈrʌsl / Ⅰ v. (使)发出沙沙声：The leaves ~d in the wind. 树叶在风中沙沙作响。Ⅱ *n.* 沙沙声

ruthless / ˈruːθləs / *adj.* ❶无情的；冷酷的；残忍的：an invasion by a ~ totalitarian power 残忍的极权主义国家的侵略 ❷坚决的：Successfully merging two banks requires a fast and ~ attack on costs. 成功合并两家银行需要坚决快速地着手解决费用问题。

R

S s

sack /sæk/ Ⅰ *n.* [C] ❶大袋;大包:two ~s of potatoes 两袋马铃薯 ❷(the ~)解雇;革职:get the ~ 被解雇/ give sb. the ~ 解雇某人 Ⅱ *vt.* ❶把……装进袋里 ❷解雇

sacred /ˈseɪkrɪd/ *adj.* ❶神圣的;宗教的:~ music 圣乐 / ~ writings 宗教经典 ❷严肃的;郑重的:a ~ promise 郑重的诺言

sacrifice /ˈsækrɪfaɪs/ Ⅰ *n.* ❶祭品;供品 ❷献身;牺牲:He made a ~ for his country. 他为国牺牲了。Ⅱ *v.* ❶供奉;祭祀 ❷牺牲;献身:He ~d his life to save the drowning child. 他因救落水的孩子而牺牲了生命。

sad /sæd/ *adj.* 悲伤的;忧愁的:We are all ~ for his death. 我们都为他的去世感到悲伤。派 sadly *adv.* ;sadness *n.*

saddle /ˈsædl/ *n.* [C]鞍;马鞍

safe /seɪf/ Ⅰ *adj.* ❶安全的;无危险的:You'd better keep the knife in a ~ place. 你最好把刀子放在安全的地方。/ ~ **and sound** 安然无事;平安无恙:They came back ~ and sound from America. 他们平安地从美国回到家里。❷牢靠的;可靠的 Ⅱ *n.* [C]保险箱 派 safely *adv.*

safeguard /ˈseɪfˌgɑːd/ Ⅰ *n.* [C]预防措施;保障条款;保障物:a thigh ~ against fires 对火灾严密的防范措施/The new law will provide an adequate ~ for consumers. 新法律将充分保护消费者的权益。Ⅱ *v.* 保护,保卫;捍卫;维护:~ the interests of the employees 维护雇员的利益/~ against attack 防止攻击

safety /ˈseɪfti/ *n.* [U]安全;平安:~ devices 安全设施 / ~ measures 安全措施 / a ~ helmet 安全帽 / ~ in production 生产安全/ personal ~ 人身安全 / public ~ 公共安全

sail /seɪl/ Ⅰ *n.* ❶[C] 航行;帆:set ~起航;开船 ❷船(单复数同形):a fleet of twenty ~ 20 只船的船队 Ⅱ *v.* 航行:The ship ~ed from Shanghai to Hong Kong. 这船从上海驶往香港。

sailor /ˈseɪlə(r)/ *n.* [C] ❶海员;水手:~ hat 水手帽 ❷乘船者:a good (bad) ~ 不大晕(常晕)船的人

saint /seɪnt/ Ⅰ *n.* [C](基督教)圣徒 Ⅱ *adj.* 神圣的

sake /seɪk/ *n.* [C]目的;缘故;理由:**for the ~ of** 为了;由于:We must be patient for the ~ of peace. 为了和平,我们必须有耐心。

salad /ˈsæləd/ *n.* 沙拉;色拉;生菜;凉拌菜:fruit ~ 水果沙拉 / green ~ 蔬菜沙拉 / mixed ~ 什锦沙拉 / ~ oil 色拉油

salary /ˈsæləri/ *n.* 薪水;薪金:draw a~ 领薪水 / The general manager earns a ~ of $120,000 per year. 总经理年薪

12 万美元。

sale /seɪl/ *n.* 出售;卖;销售额:~s department 门市部,销售部 / ~s tax 营业税 / Is the house for ~? 这房屋出售吗? / Sales are up (down) this month. 本月销售额在增加(减少)。/ **on** ~上市;出售:This type of TV sets will be on ~ next month. 这种型号的电视机将在下个月上市。

salesgirl /ˈseɪlzɡɜːl/ *n.* [C] 女店员;女售货员

salesman /ˈseɪlzmən/ *n.* [C](*pl.* salesmen) 售货员;店员;推销员

saliva /səˈlaɪvə/ *n.* [U]唾液,涎

salivate /ˈsælɪˌveɪt/ *vi.* 分泌唾液,流涎:The dog could ~ at the sight of food. 这条狗看见食物就会流口水。派 salivation *n.*

salmon /ˈsæmən/ *n.* [C]鲑;大马哈鱼

salon /ˈsælɒn/ *n.* [C] ❶(营业性质的)厅;店;院 ❷沙龙(指定期举行的社交聚会):a literary ~ 文学沙龙

salt /sɔːlt/ Ⅰ *n.* [U]食盐:fine ~ 精盐 / a grain of ~ 一粒盐 Ⅱ *vt.* 用盐给……调味;用盐腌

salty /ˈsɔːlti,ˈsɒlti/ *adj.* ❶含盐的,咸的:I don't like the meat, it's too ~. 这肉太咸了,我不喜欢吃。❷粗俗的,猥亵的:~ humour 粗俗的幽默 派 saltiness *n.*

salute /səˈluːt/ Ⅰ *n.* [C]欢迎;致敬;举手礼:give a ~ of ten guns 鸣礼炮十响 Ⅱ *v.* 行礼;向……致敬:They ~d (each other) by raising their hats. 他们举帽(相互)致意。

salve /sælv,sɑːv/ Ⅰ *n.* 软膏;油膏;药膏:lip ~ 护唇油膏 / ~s for treating cuts 治疗创伤的各种药膏 Ⅱ *vt.* 安慰;宽慰;缓解:I felt guilty, so I tried to ~ my conscience by buying my wife a bunch of flowers. 我感到歉疚,于是就给妻子买了一束花以求得到良心上的平静。

same /seɪm/ Ⅰ *adj.* 同一的;相同的;不变的:We have lived in the ~ house for fifty years. 我们 50 年来一直住在这所房子里。/ **at the** ~ **time** ①同时:Don't sing the song at the same time. 不要同时唱那首歌。②然而:I'll forgive you, at the ~ time you must never do it again. 我会原谅你的,而你决不能再做那种事。**come (amount) to the** ~ **thing** 结果相同;无差异:You may pay in cash or check, it comes to the ~ thing. 你可付现金或支票,其结果相同。Ⅱ *pron.* 同样的事:I would do the ~ again. 我愿重做一次。/ **all (just) the** ~ ①完全一样;无所谓:Tea or coffee is all (just) the ~ for me. 对我来说,茶和咖啡都是一样的。②仍然;照样:We'll go all (just) the ~ even if it does rain. 即使下雨,我们也仍然要去。**the** ~ **as ...** 像……一样;与……相同:In Beijing the weather in summer is usually the ~ as in my hometown. 夏天,北京的天气通常和我家乡的一样。

sample /ˈsɑːmpl,ˈsæmpl/ Ⅰ *n.* [C]样品;货样;标本:provide ~s 提供样品 / random ~ 随机取样 / I want to see some ~s of your products. 我想看看你们的货样。Ⅱ *vt.* 从……取样检验

sanatorium /ˌsænəˈtɔːrɪəm/ *n.* [C](*pl.* sanatoriums 或 sanatoria/ˌsænəˈtɔːrɪə/) 疗养院;休养地

sanction /ˈsæŋkʃn/ Ⅰ *n.* ❶[U]认可,许可;准许,批准:give ~ to 允许(批准)/ with ~ of the master 主人的允许 ❷[C]约束(力);制约(因素):The best ~

against wrongdoing is that of conscience. 对不良行为的最佳约束即是良心的约束。❸[C](政治、经济等方面的)国际制裁:institute economic ~s against对……实施经济制裁 Ⅱ *vt.* ❶批准,准许,同意:The ~ed age for marriage is 22 for men. 男性的法定结婚年龄是 22 周岁。/designate Labor Day as a state-~ed day of rest 把劳动节这一天指定为国家法定休息日 ❷对……实行制裁,对……施以处罚,惩处

sand /sænd/ *n.* ❶[U]沙:a grain of ~ 一粒沙子 ❷(常用 *pl.*)沙地;沙滩 :on the ~s 在沙滩上 派 sandy *adj.*

sandal /ˈsændl/ *n.* [C] 凉鞋

sandstorm /ˈsæn(d)ˌstɔːm/ *n.* [C](沙漠上的)沙暴,沙尘暴

sandwich /ˈsænwɪdʒ/ *n.* [C](中间夹有肉等的)夹心面包片,三明治

sane /seɪn/ *adj.* ❶心智健全的,神志正常的:a ~ person 心智健全的人/be in a ~ state of mind 处于神志正常状态 ❷清醒的,明智的;合乎情理的:a ~ decision 明智的决定/keep the mind ~保护头脑清醒 派 sanely *adv.*

sanitary /ˈsænɪtəri/ *adj.* ❶卫生状况的;公共卫生的:a ~ inspector 卫生检查员 / ~ measures to combat diseases 预防疾病的卫生措施 ❷卫生的,清洁的;除菌(或尘)的:~ gloves 卫生手套

sanitation /ˌsænɪˈteɪʃn/ *n.* [U]公共卫生;卫生设备

sap /sæp/ *n.* [U](植物的)液,汁

sarcasm /ˈsɑːkæzəm/ *n.* ❶[U]讽刺,讥刺,挖苦,嘲笑:devastating ~辛辣的讽刺/Her voice dripped ~. 她的声音流露出讥讽。❷[C]讽刺话,挖苦话:a speech full of reproachful ~s 满是指摘讥讽的讲话

sardine /ˌsɑːˈdiːn/ *n.* [C]沙丁鱼

SARS, sars /sɑːs/ (=Severe Acute Respiratory Syndrome)传染性非典型性肺炎(非典)

satellite /ˈsætəlaɪt/ *n.* [C]卫星;人造卫星:a ~city (在大城市郊区兴建的)卫星城 / the manned ~ 载人卫星 / launch a weather ~ 发射一颗气象卫星

satire /ˈsætaɪə(r)/ *n.* 讽刺;讽刺作品:It is a bitter ~ on (upon) such kind of people. 这是对这种人的辛辣讽刺。

satisfaction /ˌsætɪsˈfækʃn/ *n.* [U]满意;满足:have the ~ of being successful 对成功感到满意

satisfactory /ˌsætɪsˈfæktəri/ *adj.* 令人满意的;令人满足的:The result of the experiment was ~. 实验的结果令人满意。派 satisfactorily *adv.*

satisfy /ˈsætɪsfaɪ/ *v.* 使满意;使满足:Riches do not always ~. 财富并不永远使人满足。/ **be satisfied with** 对……感到满意:I'm not satisfied with your work. You must improve it. 我不满意你的工作,你必须要改进。

saturate /ˈsætʃəˌreɪt, ˈsætjʊˌreɪt/ *vt.* ❶浸透;渗透;使湿透:The autumn rain ~d the ground. 那场秋雨浇透了大地。/It's rain-ing heavily and I was absolutely ~d. 雨下得很大,我全身被淋得湿透。❷使充满:A dreadful accident ~d local medical facilities. 一次可怕的意外事故使得当地的许多医疗机构都人满为患。

Saturday /ˈsætədɪ/ *n.* 星期六

sauce /sɔːs/ *n.* [U]调味汁;酱汁:apple ~ 苹果酱 / soy ~ 酱油 / tomato ~ 番茄酱

sauna /ˈsɔːnə, ˈsɑːnə/ *n.* [C] ❶桑拿浴，蒸汽浴；芬兰浴：have a ～洗桑拿浴 ❷桑拿浴室，蒸汽浴室

sausage /ˈsɔːsɪdʒ/ *n.* [C]香肠；腊肠

savage /ˈsævɪdʒ/ Ⅰ *adj.* ❶野蛮的；未开化的 ❷残酷的；残暴的 Ⅱ *n.* 野人；野蛮人

save /seɪv/ *v.* ❶援救；挽救 / ～ **sb.** (**sth.**) **from** 从……中挽救某人(某物)；使某人(某物)免于：Many books were ～d from the fire. 许多书得以从大火中抢救出来。❷储蓄：～ money for a holiday 存钱度假 ❸节省；省去：～ time 节约时间 / The computer ～s me much time. 计算机让我节省很多时间。❹(计算机)存储

savo(u)r /ˈseɪvə(r)/ Ⅰ *n.* [U]味道；口味，滋味；气味：food with (a) pleasant ～美味佳肴 / the ～ of soy sauce 酱油的味道 Ⅱ *vt.* ❶品尝：～ a cup of tea 品一杯茶 / ～ every mouthful 每一口都仔细品味 ❷品味；欣赏：～ the companionship of friends 品味朋友相伴左右的乐趣

saw /sɔː/ Ⅰ *n.* [C]锯：a power ～电锯 / ～-mill 锯木厂 Ⅱ *v.* (sawed, sawn /sɔːn/或sawed) 锯：He ～ed the plank in half. 他把木板锯成两截。

S

saxophone /ˈsæksəˌfəun/ *n.* [C]萨克斯管，萨克斯风

say /seɪ/ Ⅰ *v.* (said /sed/, said) 说；讲：He said nothing about his friend Tom. 关于他朋友汤姆，他什么也没说。/ ～ **hello to sb.** 向某人问好：He said hello to every teacher he met. 他向碰到的每个老师问好。**go without ～ing** 不用说；显而易见：It goes without ～ing that I'll finish the work on time. 不用说我会按时完成工作的。～ **good-bye to sb.** 向某人告别：She went to the station to ～ good-bye to her friend. 她到车站去向朋友告别。～ **sth. about** 谈谈……的情况：Please ～ something about your study in London. 请谈谈你在伦敦学习的情况。～ **to oneself** 心中暗想；思忖 **that is to** ～ 换言之；即：We'll come back three weeks tomorrow, that is to ～, the 30th of March. 我们三个星期后的明天，即3月30日回来。Ⅱ *n.* 要说的话；发言的机会；发言权/ **have a** (**no, not much**) ～ **in** 对……有(没有、没有多少)发言权：At last, he had his ～ in the matter. 最后他得到了关于此事的发言机会。

saying /ˈseɪɪŋ/ *n.* [C]谚语；格言；名言："More haste, less speed," as the ～ is. 常言道："欲速则不达。"

scab /skæb/ Ⅰ *n.* [C]痂，疤：pick the ～s 揭痂/The coarse jacket tore away the ～s that had congealed on his wounds. 粗糙夹克刮掉了结在他伤口上的痂。/ The ～ drops off. 结痂脱落。Ⅱ *vi.* (scabbed; scabbing) (伤口等)结痂，结疤

scale /skeɪl/ *n.* ❶[C]尺度；刻度：This ruler has one ～ in centimetre and another in inch. 这尺上有厘米刻度和英寸刻度。❷[C]有刻度的度量器 ❸[C]比例；比例尺：a ～ of one to a thousand 1∶1000 的比例 ❹[C]规模：**on a large** (**small**) ～ 大(小)规模：This kind of cars are being produced in their factory on a large (small) ～. 这种小汽车正在他们的工厂里大(小)规模地生产。❺[C] (*pl.*) 天平；磅秤：The workers weigh the gold in the ～s. 工人在天平上称黄金。

scan /skæn/ *vt.* (scanned; scanning)

❶细看；审视：He ~ned the horizon for any sign of land. 他仔细眺望地平线，找寻陆地的踪影。❷扫描；扫掠：The radar ~s the sky day and night. 雷达日夜扫掠天空。❸浏览：~ newspapers over breakfast 边吃早餐边浏览报纸

scandal /ˈskændəl/ *n.* [C]丑事；丑闻：uncover a ~ 揭露丑闻 / A ~ burst. 爆出丑闻。

scanner /ˈskænə(r)/ *n.* [C](计算机的)扫描器

scar /skɑː(r)/ *n.* [C]伤疤；伤痕；创伤：The soldier's right hand bore a ~. 那个士兵的右手上有一块伤疤。

scarce /skeəs/ *adj.* ❶不充足的；供不应求的：Eggs are ~ and dear this month. 本月蛋少而价高。❷稀罕的；难得的：a ~ book 珍本

scarcely /ˈskeəsli/ *adv.* ❶仅仅；几乎不；简直不：I could ~ recognize the man. 我几乎认不出那个人来。❷刚刚；才：Scarcely had we set out when it began to rain. 我们刚出发雨就开始下起来。

scarcity /ˈskeəsəti/ *n.* 缺乏；不足：The ~ of food drew much attention. 食物的不足引起了极大的关注。

scare /skeə(r)/ *vt.* 使恐惧；使受惊吓：The baby was ~d by thunder. 婴儿被雷声吓到了。/ He ~d me. 他把我吓坏了。

scarf /skɑːf/ *n.* [C](*pl.* scarves /skɑːvz/ 或 scarfs) ❶围巾；头巾 ❷领巾；领带

scarlet /ˈskɑːlɪt/ Ⅰ *n.* [U]猩红(色)，鲜红(色) Ⅱ *adj.* 猩红(色)的，鲜红(色)的：~ begonias 鲜红的秋海棠 / turn ~ with embarrassment 窘得满面通红

scatter /ˈskætə(r)/ *v.* ❶驱散；离散：The police ~ed the crowd. 警察驱散人群。/ The crowd ~ed. 人群散去了。❷撒播：~ seeds 播种

scene /siːn/ *n.* [C] ❶(实际的或想象中的)事发地点：the ~ of crime 犯罪现场 ❷(戏剧中的)一场，一景 ❸风景；景致：The boats in the harbor make a beautiful ~. 海港中的船形成很优美的风景。

scenery /ˈsiːnəri/ *n.* [U] ❶舞台布景：set up ~布景 ❷风景；景色：We enjoy the fascinating mountain ~. 我们很喜欢这迷人的山中景色。

scent /sent/ *n.* ❶[U]气味：strong ~ of hay 浓烈的干草味 ❷[U]香味：~s of flowers 各种花香 ❸[C](常用单数)(野兽的)遗臭：Hunting dogs know how to follow a ~. 猎犬知道如何追踪兽迹。

schedule /ˈʃedjuːl, ˈskedʒuːl/ Ⅰ *n.* [C]时刻表；目录表：The train arrived on ~. 火车准时到达。/ **ahead of** ~ 提前于：We labored hard to finish our job ahead of ~. 我们努力工作，以期地活儿提前干完。**behind** ~迟到；晚点：The train arrived behind ~. 火车晚点了。**on** ~ 按时间表；准时 Ⅱ *vt.* 将……列表；为……做目录；安排：The President is ~d to make a speech tomorrow. 总统定于明日发表演说。

schematic /skɪˈmætɪk/ Ⅰ *adj.* ❶图解的；草图的：It's only a ~ diagram, it doesn't show the details. 这只是个草图，没有标明细节。❷规划的；大纲的，概要的 Ⅱ *n.* [C]图解；草图，略图；(尤指)电路图

scheme /skiːm/ *n.* [C] ❶计划；规划；方案：health insurance ~ 健康保险计划 / make a ~ 制订计划 ❷诡计；阴谋：The enemy's ~ did not work. 敌人的阴谋没

有得逞。派 schemer *n.*

scholar /ˈskɒlə(r)/ *n.* [C] ❶学者 ❷学生;学习者 派 scholarly *adj.*

scholarship /ˈskɒləʃɪp/*n.* ❶[U]学问;学识 ❷[C]奖学金:apply for a ~申请奖学金 / get (receive, win) a ~ 获得奖学金 / grant a ~ 授予奖学金 / students on ~ 领奖学金的学生

school /skuːl/ *n.* ❶[C] 学校:a middle ~ 中学 ❷[U](不加定冠词)上学:attend ~ 上学 ❸ [U]上课时间;上课:School begins at 8 a.m. 八点钟开始上课。❹[C]大学;学院:law ~ 法学院 / medical ~ 医学院 ❺[C]学派;流派:poets of the Lake School 湖畔派诗人

schooling /ˈskuːlɪŋ/ *n.* [U] 教育:He has very little ~. 他受的教育很少。

schoolmate /ˈskuːlˌmeɪt/ *n.* [C]同学;学友,校友

schoolyard /ˈskuːlˌjɑːd/ *n.* [C]校园;操场

science /ˈsaɪəns/ *n.* [U]科学:social ~ 社会科学 / natural ~ 自然科学 / ~ fiction 科幻小说

scientific /ˌsaɪənˈtɪfɪk/ *adj.* 科学的;关于科学的:~ methods 科学方法 / ~ farming 科学耕作 派 scientifically *adv.*

S

scientist /ˈsaɪəntɪst/ *n.* [C]科学家

scissor /ˈsɪzə(r)/ *v.* ❶剪,剪断:~ up a paper 把纸剪开 ❷(从报纸等上)剪下:~ a photo from the magazine 从杂志上剪下一张照片。

scissors /ˈsɪzəz/ *n.* 剪刀;剪子:a pair of ~ 一把剪子

scoff /skɒf/ *vi.* 嘲笑,嘲弄,讥笑:~ at a fanciful notion 嗤笑空想念头

scold /skəʊld/ *v.* 骂;责备:~ a child for being lazy 责备孩子偷懒

scoop /skuːp/ Ⅰ *n.* [C] ❶勺子;勺形工具;舀子;戽斗:a kitchen ~厨房用勺 ❷一勺(或铲、匙等)的量:Just two ~s of mashed potato for me, please. 请给我来两勺土豆泥吧。Ⅱ *vt.* ❶(用铲等)挖,铲;(用勺等)舀:~ some sugar out on to the plate 舀一点糖放在盘子里 ❷快速地捡起,拾起,抱起:She ~ed up the wallet on the ground. 她一把捡起地上的皮夹子。

scope /skəʊp/ *n.* [U] ❶范围,视野,见识:This subject is beyond the ~ of this book. 这个主题已超越了这本书的范围。/ You should widen your ~ of knowledge. 你应拓宽你的知识视野。❷余地;机会:Give your child ~ to show his creativity. 给你的孩子展示创造力的机会。

scorch /skɔːt/ *vt.* 把……烧焦,把……烤焦;烫;炙伤:a face ~ed by tropic sun 被热带太阳饱晒过的脸/The west side of the house had been ~ed evenly free of white paint. 房子的西侧被烤得焦黑,白漆一点也没有了。

score /skɔː(r)/ Ⅰ *n.* ❶[C]得分;比分;计分:The ~ at half time was 2 to 1. 上半场的记分为二比一。❷二十个:a ~ of people 二十个人 / I've been there ~s of times. 我去那儿很多次了。Ⅱ *vt.* 得(分);记分:~ a goal 踢进一球而得分 / ~ a point 得一分

scorn /skɔːn/ Ⅰ *n.* [U]轻蔑;蔑视;藐视:express ~ for one's deeds 对某人的行为表示蔑视 Ⅱ *vt.* 轻蔑;蔑视:It is natural for people to ~ liars. 人们蔑视说谎的人是很自然的。

scout /skaʊt/ *n.* [C] ❶侦察员;侦察机 ❷发掘人才者;星探:The club sent ~s out to look for good players. 俱乐部派

出星探寻找优秀球员。

scrabble / ˈskræbl / *vi.* 乱抓,乱扒;摸索;摸索着寻找(或收集):~ through piles of photos to find the one she wanted 在成堆的照片里扒拉着找她要的照片/He ~d about (around) in the big drawer, trying to find his keys. 他在抽屉里翻找钥匙。

scrape / skreɪp / Ⅰ *v.* ❶刮;擦:~ mud from one's boots 擦去靴上的泥土 / The worker ~d the rust off the machine. 那工人擦去机器上的铁锈。❷擦伤;擦坏:The bike ~d the left side of my car. 自行车把我的小车左侧擦坏了。Ⅱ *n.* ❶[U]刮;擦;刮擦声 ❷[C]麻烦,困境:He got into ~s. 他陷入了困境。

scratch / skrætʃ/ Ⅰ *v.* ❶抓;搔:The cat ~ed me. 猫抓了我。❷发刮擦声:This pen ~es. 这钢笔写字时发出刮擦声。❸仓促地写;乱涂:~ a few lines to a friend 仓促地写几句话给一位朋友 Ⅱ *n.* [C]搔痕;抓伤;抓搔声

scream / skriːm / Ⅰ *v.* (因恐惧、痛苦等)发出尖叫声:She ~ed in anger. 她愤怒地尖声叫喊。Ⅱ *n.* 尖叫声:the ~ of a peacock 孔雀的尖叫声

screen / skriːn / *n.* [C] ❶幕;帘;帐;屏风 ❷荧光屏;银幕

screw / skruː / Ⅰ *n.* [C]螺丝;螺丝钉:I have tightened the ~s. 我已经拧紧了那些螺丝钉。Ⅱ *vt.* 拧动;拧紧:~ the cap on (off) the bottle 拧紧(拧开)瓶盖

script / skrɪpt / *n.* ❶[U](区别于印刷体的)手写体;手书,手迹:write in a tight ~字迹细密地书写 ❷书写体:italic ~斜体字 ❸书写系统:Can you read Greek ~? 你能认希腊文吗? ❹[C](戏剧、电影等的)剧本,脚本;广播稿:He deserves an Oscar for his original ~. 他应该获得奥斯卡原创电影剧本奖。

sculpture / ˈskʌlptʃə(r)/ *n.* 雕刻;雕刻作品

sea / siː / *n.* 海;洋:follow the ~ 当海员;当水手 / by ~乘船;由海路 / travel by ~ and land 经海路和陆路旅行 / **at ~** ①在海上;在航海中:The ship is at ~. 那艘船在航行中。②困惑;不知所措:He seems to be all at ~. 他似乎茫然不知所措。

seafood / ˈsiːˌfuːd/ *n.* [U]海味,海鲜,海产食品

seagull / ˈsiːˌgʌl/ *n.* (=gull)[C] 海鸥

seal[1] / siːl / Ⅰ *n.* [C]加封;封蜡;封铅;火漆;印章 Ⅱ *v.* 封住:~ a letter 封好一封信 / ~ off the area 封锁了这一地区 / ~ off from the outside world 与外界隔绝

seal[2] / siːl / *n.* [C]海豹

seam / siːm / *n.* [C] ❶缝;线缝:The bag has very strong ~s. 这包缝得很结实。❷接缝,边缝;裂缝:The ship has started at the ~s. 船板的接缝开裂了。❸(地)层;矿层;煤层:a coal ~煤层

seaman / ˈsiːmən/ *n.* [C](*pl.* seamen) ❶水手,海员;航海者:a poor ~ 不懂航海的水手 ❷(海军)水兵

seaport / ˈsiːˌpɔːt/ *n.* [C]海港;海港城市

search / sɜːtʃ / Ⅰ *v.* 搜寻;查究;探查:~ for truth 对真理追求/ ~ for the lost book (the missing child)寻找丢失的书(寻找失踪的小孩)/ The customs officers ~ed the traveller's bags for smuggled goods. 海关人员搜查旅客的行李,看是否有走私的商品。Ⅱ *n.* 搜寻;查究:make a ~ for contraband goods 搜查违禁品 / **in ~ of** 寻找:The

S

secretary looked here and there in ~ of the chairman of the meeting. 秘书到处寻找会议主席。

seashore /ˈsiːˌʃɔː(r)/ *n.* [U]海滨；海岸；海滩

seaside /ˈsiːˌsaid/ Ⅰ *n.* (常作 the ~)(常有人度假或休闲的)海边，海滨：a ~ hotel (resort) 海滨旅馆(胜地) / a holiday at the ~ 在海滨度过的假期 Ⅱ *adj.* 海边的，海滨的

season /ˈsiːz(ə)n/ Ⅰ *n.* [C] ❶季；季节：There are four ~s in a year. 一年有四季。❷时节：in ~ 旺季 / out of ~ 淡季/ The football ~ is drawing near. 足球赛季快到了。Ⅱ *vt.* 给……加味；调味：Do you want to ~ the dish with pepper? 你想给菜里加点胡椒粉吗？

seasonable /ˈsiːzənəbl/ *adj.* 当令的，应时的：snow showers far form ~ in April 与季节很不相称的 4 月降雪/Cold weather is ~ in December. 12 月份天冷是正常的。

seasonal /ˈsiːzənəl/ *adj.* 季节的；随季节变化的；季节性的：highly ~ good 季节性很强的物品/Seymour's work at the seaside resort is ~. 西摩在海滨胜地工作是季节性的。

seat /siːt/ Ⅰ *n.* [C] 座位：The back ~ of the car is wide enough for three persons. 车子的后座足够 3 个人坐。/ **take a** ~坐：Won't you take a ~? 你不坐吗？Ⅱ *vt.* ❶使坐下；使就座：Please be ~ed. 请坐下。❷有……的座位：a hall that ~s 500 有 500 个座位的大厅

seating /ˈsiːtɪŋ/ *n.* [U]座位：My car ~ for five. 我的汽车可以坐 5 个人/The symphony hall has a ~ capacity of 2,000 people. 交响音乐厅可容纳 2 000 人。

second[1] /ˈsekənd/ Ⅰ *adj.* (在地位、时间、次序、重要性等方面)第二的：February is the ~ month of the year. 二月是一年中的第二个月。/~ **to** 仅次于：She was ~ to her elder sister. 她仅次于她姐姐。**be ~ to none** 不亚于任何人(物) Ⅱ *n.* ❶第二个人或物：You are the ~ to ask me the question. 你是第二个向我问那个问题的人。❷二等货：These stockings are ~s and have some slight defects. 这些长筒袜是次等货，有瑕疵。❸(时间或角度计量单位的)秒：The winner's time was 1 minute and 5 ~s. 胜者的时间是一分零五秒。派 secondly *adv.*

second[2] /ˈsekənd/ *vt.* 支持；赞同；附议：I ~ Bill's motion. 我支持比尔的提议。

secondary /ˈsekəndri/ *adj.* ❶次要的；辅助的：It is a question of ~ importance. 那是个次要问题。❷第二位的；中级的：~ education 中等教育/ ~ school 中等学校

secret /ˈsiːkrət/ Ⅰ *adj.* 秘密的；机密的；保密的：keep sth. ~ from one's family 不把某事告诉家人 / He escaped through a ~ door. 他从暗门逃走了。Ⅱ *n.* ❶秘密：keep a ~ 保守机密 / meet in ~ 秘密会见/ state (trade)~ 国家(商业)机密 / We have no ~s from you. 我们对你不保守任何秘密。❷秘诀；诀窍：What is the ~ of his success? 他成功的秘诀是什么？派 secretly *adv.*

secretary /ˈsekrətri, ˈsekrəteri/ *n.* [C] ❶秘书 ❷书记：the Party branch ~ 党支部书记 ❸大臣；部长；国务卿：Secretary of the State Department (美)国务卿

secrete /sɪˈkriːt/ *vt.* 分泌：~s hormones 分泌激素

section /ˈsekʃn/ *n.* [C] ❶一段；一节；

部分：Have you read the second ~ of the chapter? 你读过这一章的第二节吗？❷切下的部分；切片；截面：cross ~ 横截面 ❸地域；区域

sectional /ˈsekʃənəl/ *adj.* ❶(只作定语)部分的；局部的：A special category of movies was made for a ~ audience. 专门为部分观众拍摄的一类电影。❷地区的；地方性的：~ prejudices 地域偏见

sector /ˈsektə(r)/ *n.* [C] ❶(企业、社团的)部分；部门；(尤指)经济领域：the hi-tech ~s 高科技领域/Not every ~ of the economy was hit by the recession. 并非各个经济领域都受到萧条的冲击。❷地区，区域

secure /sɪˈkjʊə(r)/ Ⅰ *adj.* 无忧的；安心的；安全的(与 from, against 连用)：feel ~ about one's future 不担心自己的前途 / Are your words really ~ from attack? 你的言辞真的无懈可击吗？ Ⅱ *v.* 使安全：By strengthening the embankments they ~d the village against (from) floods. 他们通过加固堤坝使村庄免遭洪水之灾。

security /sɪˈkjʊərəti/ *n.* ❶[U]安全：Security Council of the United Nations 联合国安理会 / sense of ~安全感 / public ~ bureau 公安局 ❷[C]提供安全之物 ❸[C](*pl.*)债券；证券：government securities 政府债券 / issue securities 发行证券

sediment /ˈsedɪmənt/ *n.* 沉淀(物)，沉积(物)；沉渣：There is (a) brownish ~ in your glass. 你的玻璃杯里有一层棕色的沉淀物。/riverine ~河流沉积物

see /siː/ *v.* (saw/sɔː/, seen /siːn/) ❶看见；看到：Seeing is believing. (谚语)眼见为实。❷了解；领会：He didn't ~ the point of the story. 他不明白那故事的寓意。/ I ~. 我明白了。❸会见；访问：Can I ~ you on business? 我因公能见你吗？ / You'd better go to ~ a doctor at once. 你最好马上去看病。❹护送；陪伴：May I ~ you home? 我可以送你回家吗？ / ~ **sb. off** 为某人送行：I was seen off by many friends. 许多朋友为我送行。~ **about** 查看；留意：I'll ~ about the notice. 我会查看一下通知的。~ **into sth.** 调查某事：Will you ~ into the matter first? 你先了解一下这件事情的情况好吗？~ **sb. through** 使某人渡过难关：Don't worry. We'll ~ you through the difficulty. 别着急，我们会帮助你克服困难的。~ **through sb. (sth.)** 看穿；识破 ~ **to it that** 一定注意，务必：See to it that all the windows are closed before you leave. 离开前一定要关好所有的窗户。

seed /siːd/ Ⅰ *n.* [C](*pl.* seed 或 seeds) 种子：spread ~s 撒种 / It is time to sow the ~. 播种的时间到了。Ⅱ *v.* 挑选……为种子选手：~ed player 种子选手 / ~ed team 种子队

seek /siːk/ *v.* (sought/sɔːt/, sought)寻找；寻求；探索：~ doctor's advice 请教医生 /His paintings are much sought after. 他的画被人争相收购。/ My sister is ~ing a job as secretary. 我姐姐正在谋求一份秘书工作。/ ~ **for (after)** 寻找；探索；追求：One shouldn't ~ only for fame and wealth. 人不能只是追名逐利。派 seeker *n.*

seem /siːm/ *vi.* 似乎；好像；仿佛：What ~s easy to some people ~s difficult to others. 对某些人似乎是容易的事可能对另一些人是困难的。/**it ~s (~ed) as if (as though)** 看样子，似乎，好像：It always ~ed as though they would marry

S

in the end. 从长远观点看来,他们最终是要结婚的。

seep /siːp/ *vi.* 渗出;渗漏:The boots allowed little water to ~ inside. 这双靴子不渗水。/Toxins had ~ed into the groundwater. 毒素渗进了地下水。

seesaw /ˈsiːˌsɔː/ *n.* [C] ❶跷跷板:play on a ~玩跷跷板 ❷一上一下的动作;此起彼伏的交替过程:a ~ of terror and delight 恐惧和兴奋的交替

segment /ˈsegmənt/ Ⅰ *n.* [C]部分;部门;片断;环节;(水果的)瓣:tangerine ~s 橘子瓣/It is an important ~ of our overall business. 这是我们整个生意中重要的一部分。Ⅱ *v.* 分割,分裂;把……分开:The pieces of an orange ~ easily. 橘子瓣很容易分开。

seize /siːz/ *v.* ❶(依照法律)扣押,查封,没收:~ sb.'s goods for payment of debt 扣押某人的货物以偿付债务 ❷强取;抓住:~ a thief by the collar 抓住小偷的衣领

seldom /ˈseldəm/ *adv.* 很少;不常:She ~ goes out. 她不常外出。

select /sɪˈlekt/ Ⅰ *v.* 选择;挑选:I want to ~ some novels for reading. 我想选几本小说读。Ⅱ *adj.* 精选的:~ passages from Shakespeare 从莎士比亚著作中精选的段落

selection /sɪˈlekʃn/ *n.* ❶[U]选择;挑选:~ committee 选拔委员会 / natural ~ 自然淘汰 / seed ~ 选种 ❷[C]挑选物;选集:We are going to read some poetic ~s. 我们要读一些诗歌选篇。

selective /sɪˈlektɪv/ *adj.* 选择的;挑选的;有选择性的:a ~ bibliography of almost 500 references 罗列了将近 500 条的精先参考节目/That wealthy lady is very ~ about clothes. 那位阔太太对衣着十分挑剔。

self /self/ Ⅰ *adj.* 自己的 Ⅱ *n.* [C](*pl.* selves /selvz/) ❶本性;特质:She was back to her old~again. 她又恢复了老样子。❷个性;自我:I want to explore and get in touch with my inner ~. 我想探寻、了解内心的自我。

self-confidence /ˌselfˈkɒnfɪdəns/ *n.* [U]自信

self-confident /ˌselfˈkɒnfɪdənt/ *adj.* 自信的

self-conscious /ˌselfˈkɒnʃəs/ *adj.* 自觉的;自我意识的

self-control /ˌselfkənˈtrəʊl/ *n.* [U]自控:lose ~ 失去自控

self-defence(-se) /ˌselfdɪˈfens/ *n.* [U]自卫:The young man said he killed the thief for ~. 那年轻人说他因自卫杀死了那个小偷。

self-examination /ˈselfɪɡˌzæmɪˈneɪʃən/ *n.* [U]自我检查;反省

self-government /ˌselfˈɡʌvənmənt/ *n.* [U]自治

self-interest /ˌselfˈɪntrɪst/ *n.* [U]自私自利

selfish /ˈselfɪʃ/ *adj.* 自私的 派 selfishly *adv.*

self-made /ˌselfˈmeɪd/ *adj.* 自制的;自己做的;白手起家的

self-respect /ˌselfreˈspekt/ *n.* [U]自尊

self-sacrifice /ˌselfˈsækrɪfaɪs/ *n.* [U]自我牺牲

self-service /ˌsefˈsɜːvɪs/ Ⅰ *adj.* (商店、餐馆、车库等)自助服务的,自助消费的 Ⅱ *n.* [U]自助服务

self-sufficient /ˌselfsəˈfɪʃənt/ *adj.* 自给自足:Japan is not ~ in raw materials. 日本在原材料方面不能自给。

S

self-supporting / ˌselfsəˈpɔːtɪŋ / *adj.* 自立的：She was ~ at the age of twelve. 她12岁就自立了。

self-taught / ˌselfˈtɔːt / *adj.* 自学(成才)的，自修(学成)的

self-willed / ˌselfˈwɪld / *adj.* 固执己见的

sell / sel / *v.* (sold /səʊld/, sold)卖；售；销：~ sth. at a good price 高价卖某物 / ~ at bargain 廉价出售；大拍卖 / ~ at a loss 亏本出售 / ~ by dozen (yard) 按打(码)出售 / ~ under the counter 私下(非法)出售 / The new book ~s well. 这本新书很畅销。/ ~ **out** 售完：This edition of the dictionary is sold out. 本版词典已售完。

seller / ˈselə(r) / *n.* [C] ❶卖主，卖方；销售者，经销者：an ice-cream ~ 卖冰激凌的人 / a carpet ~ 地毯经销商 ❷经销的商品：one of the hottest ~s in the PC market 个人电脑市场卖得最火的一款计算机

semester / sɪˈmestə(r) / *n.* [C]半年；半学年；学期：~ examination 期末考试 / The new ~ will begin next Monday. 新学期下周一开始。

semicircle / ˈsemɪsɜːkl / *n.* [C] 半圆

semicolon / ˌsemɪˈkəʊlən / *n.* [C] 分号(即";")

semicolony / ˌsemɪˈkɒlənɪ / *n.* [C] 半殖民地

semiconductor / ˌsemɪkənˈdʌktə(r) / *n.* [C] 半导体

semifinal / ˌseməɪˈfaɪnəl / *n.* [C]& *adj.* 半决赛(的)

semimonthly / ˌsemɪˈmʌnθli / *n.* [C]半月刊

seminar / ˈsemɪnɑː(r) / *n.* [C](大学的)研讨班；研讨会

senate / ˈsenət / *n.* [C]参议院

senator / ˈsenətə / *n.* [C]参议员

send / send / *v.* (sent /sent/, sent) 送；寄：~ sb. a message 送消息给某人 / I have two letters to ~. 我有两封信要寄。/ ~ **for** 派人去请；吩咐做：We had better ~ for a doctor at once. 我们最好立刻把医生找来。~ **in** ①把……请入(领入，迎入)：Send in the next person waiting, please, nurse. 护士，请把下一个等着的人领进来。②呈递；提交：Has he sent in his paper yet? 他的论文交了吗？~ **out** ①发出：The sun ~s out light and heat. 太阳发出光和热。② 生出；长出：The tree ~s out new shoots in spring. 树木在春天长出新芽。~ **up** 使升高：A piece of cake every night will ~ your weight up. 每夜吃一块饼会使你的体重增加。/ Another spaceship has been sent up recently. 最近又有一艘宇宙飞船上天。

senior / ˈsiːnɪə(r) / *adj.* 年长的；职位较高的；资深的：~ middle school 高中 / He is ten years ~ to me. 他比我年长十岁。

sensation / senˈseɪʃn / *n.* [C]感觉；知觉：a pleasant (unpleasant) ~ 愉快(不愉快)的感觉 / I felt a burning ~ on my skin. 我的皮肤有一种灼热的感觉。

sense / sens / Ⅰ *n.* [C]❶感观；感觉；知觉：have a keen ~ of hearing 听觉敏锐 ❷观念；意识：a ~ of humour 幽默感 / a ~ of duty 责任感 ❸(常用单数)判断力；判断；见识：He had a poor ~ of the worth of a thing. 他认识事物价值的能力很差。❹ 含义：a word with several ~s 有几个含义的词 / **come to one's ~s** 恢复理性；醒悟过来；(昏迷后)苏醒过

S

来 **in a** ～从某种意义上说：What he said is in a ～ true. 他说的话在某种意义上是正确的。**make** ～ 有意义；使理解：What you say does not make ～ to me. 我不理解你说的话。**out of one's ～s** 神志失常；失去理性：Why did you gamble with those persons? Are you out of your ～s? 你为什么和那些人赌博？你疯了吗？Ⅱ *v.* 感到；意识到：She fully ～d the danger of her position. 她完全感觉得到她处境危险。

senseless /ˈsensləs/ *adj.* ❶愚蠢的；无意义的：a ～ idea 愚蠢的想法 ❷无感觉的；不省人事的：fall ～ to the ground 无知觉地倒在地上

sensibility /ˌsensɪˈbɪlɪti/ *n.* ❶[U]感觉(力)，感受(力)：He has the great ～ of a stand-up comedian. 他颇有做独角喜剧演员的悟性。❷[U](情绪方面的)敏感(性)，善感(性)；感受(性)：He has a poetic ～, keen psychological insights. 他有诗人的敏感性，以及敏锐的心理洞察力。❸[C](*pl.*)感情，情绪：Her sensibilities were greatly injured. 她的感情受到极大伤害。

sensible /ˈsensəbl/ *adj.* ❶有判断力的；明智的：a ～ woman 明智的女人 ❷感知的(与 of 连用)：He is ～ of danger. 他觉察到危险。

sensitive /ˈsensətɪv/ *adj.* ❶敏感的；易受影响的(与 to 连用)：He is ～ to cold. 他极易感冒。❷灵敏的：The ears are ～ to sound. 耳朵对声音都很敏感。

sensor /ˈsensə(r)/ *n.* [C]传感器；敏感元件

sentence /ˈsentəns/ Ⅰ *n.* ❶[C]句子 / ～ **by** ～ 一句一句地；逐句地：He read the article ～ by ～. 他逐句念完了整篇文章。**make a** ～ **with** 用……造句：The teacher asked his students to make ～s with the new words. 这位老师要求他的学生用新单词造句。❷[U]判决；宣判：long (short, life) ～ 长期(短期、无期)徒刑 / death (severe) ～ 死(重)刑 Ⅱ *vt.* 判决；宣判：He was ～d to five years. 他被判刑五年。/ ～ **sb. to death** 判某人死刑：Murderers are ～d to death in some countries. 在一些国家杀人犯要被判处死刑。

sentiment /ˈsentɪmənt/ *n.* ❶[C](常用 *pl.*)意见，观点，看法：express one's own deeply felt ～s 说出自己的肺腑之言 ❷[U]感情；(文艺作品等的)情趣；感情色彩：There's no room for ～ in business. 做生意不能感情用事。/ Patriotic ～s ran high. 爱国主义感情非常高涨。

sentimental /ˌsentɪˈmentəl/ *adj.* ❶多情的，情深的；充满柔情的：～ reminiscences 深情的回忆 ❷感伤的；多愁善感的：a ～ love song 令人感怀的情歌/I felt a little ～ and lonely at times. 我时不时感到有些伤感和孤独。

separate /ˈseprət/ Ⅰ *adj.* 分离的；分开的：Cut it into three ～ parts. 把它切成三份。Ⅱ *v.* 使分离；把……隔开/ ～ ... **from** ... 把……和……分开：England is ～d from France by the Channel. 英国和法国被英吉利海峡隔开。～ **sth. into** ... 把……分成：The teacher ～d us into three study groups. 老师把我们分成三个学习小组。派 separately *adv.*

separation /ˌsepəˈreɪʃn/ *n.* [U]分离；分开：Separation from his friends made him sad. 与朋友分离使他伤心。

September /sepˈtembə(r)/ *n.* 九月

sequence /ˈsiːkwəns/ *n.* ❶连续；一连串：They have had a ～ of bumper harvests. 他们已经连续获得大丰收。❷次序;顺序:Do you know the ~ of those events? 你知道那些事件的先后次序吗?

serf /sɜːf/ *n*. [C]农奴

sergeant /ˈsɑːdʒənt/ *n*. [C] ❶士官;中士 ❷警官

serial /ˈsɪərɪəl/ Ⅰ *n*. [C] ❶连载作品;系列影片;连播节目:a television ~ 电视连续剧/appear as a ~ in a newspaper 以连载的形式刊登在报纸上 ❷期刊;(分期发表的)系列报告 Ⅱ *adj*. ❶分期连载的,分次连续播映的:a ~ publication 分期连载的出版物 ❷连续的;排成系列的;顺序排列的:Many firms mark their goods with a ~ number. 很多公司用序列号作为其商品的标记。❸系列的,连环的:~ murders 系列杀人案 派 serially *adv*.

series /ˈsɪəriːz/ *n*. [C](单复数同形) ❶系列;连续:in ~ 连续地 / TV ~ 电视连续剧 / a ~ of events 一系列事件 / The children asked me a ~ of questions. 孩子们问了我一系列问题。❷套:a ~ of coins 一套硬币 / a ~ of stamps 一套邮票 / I bought a ~ of science books yesterday. 昨天我买了一套科学图书。

serious /ˈsɪərɪəs/ *adj*. ❶严肃的;严重的:a ~ face 表情严肃 / a ~ illness 重病 ❷认真的;真诚的:Please be ~ about your work. 请认真工作。派 seriously *adv*.; seriousness *n*.

servant /ˈsɜːvənt/ *n*. [C] ❶仆人;佣人;服务员:dismiss a ~ 解雇服务员 / Do you want to employ a ~? 你要雇服务员吗? ❷(政府的)雇员,公务员

serve /sɜːv/ *v*. ❶做仆人 ❷供职;服务:~ the people 为人民服务 / He ~s as a teacher at school. 他在学校当老师。❸侍候(顾客等);供给;上(菜等);开(饭等):We are well ~d with gas (electricity) in this town. 我们这个镇的居民有足够的煤气(电)供应。/ Dinner is ~d. 饭已上好。

service /ˈsɜːvɪs/ *n*. [C] ❶服务;贡献:His ~s to the State have been immense. 他对国家的贡献很大。❷公共设施;公共设施的运转:bus (water, gas, telephone)~ 公共汽车(水、气、电话)服务设施 ❸商业性服务机构 ❹礼拜仪式:attend Sunday ~s in the church 星期天到教堂做礼拜 ❺(商品的)保养,维修,售后服务:The manufacturer provides good ~ for its products. 那家厂商提供很好的产品售后服务。

serving /ˈsɜːvɪŋ/ Ⅰ *n*. ❶[U]服务,招待,上菜 ❷[C]一份食物(或饮料),一客:a large ~ of potatoes 一大盘土豆 / There should be enough for three ~s. 这食物足够三个人享用。Ⅱ *adj*. (只作定语)上菜用的;分菜用的:A westerner doesn't put his own utensils into a ~ bowl. 西方人用餐时不把自己的餐具放进分菜用的碗里。

session /ˈseʃn/ *n*. ❶[C](议会等的)会议;一届会议:during a four-day ~ 在为期四天的会议期间 ❷[U](法庭的)开庭期;(议会等的)开会期 ❸[C]学期;(英)学年:the summer ~ of a university 大学的夏季学期 ❹[C](从事某种活动的)一段时间:a one-week training ~ 为期一周的训练时间

set /set/ Ⅰ *v*. (set, set) ❶(指太阳、月亮等天体)落下,下沉:It will be cooler when the sun has ~. 太阳落山后,天气就会凉爽些。❷置放;摆:She ~ the dishes on the table. 她把菜放在桌上。

❸树立（榜样等）；创造（纪录）：You should ~ a good example. 你应该树立好榜样。❹提出（任务等）；出（题目）：Who will ~ the questions for the examination? 试题由谁出？❺使（某人）做某事；开始从事：It's time we ~ to work. 是我们开始工作的时候了。❻嵌；镶：a gold ring ~ with gems 镶有宝石的金戒指 / ~ **about** 开始；着手：They will ~ about a new project. 我们将开始进行一项新的工程。~ **apart** 拨出；留出：They decided to ~ apart a sum of money for a new classroom building. 他们决定拨一笔钱修新教学大楼。~ **aside** ① 拨出；留出：Mother ~s aside some money each month. 妈妈每月都存一点钱。② 把……置于一旁；不理会：He ~ aside all objections and went to the mountain area. 他不顾所有人的反对而去了山区。~ **back** 推迟；延缓；阻碍：The rain ~ back our touring plan. 大雨使我们的旅游计划推迟。~ **free** 释放：Do as I tell you and you shall be ~ free. 照我吩咐的去做，你就可以获得释放。~ **off** ①出发：He ~ off for Shanghai this morning. 他今天早上动身去上海。②使爆炸：A spark will~ off fireworks. 一点火花就会使烟花爆炸。~ **out** ① 出发 ②开始（从事）：Setting out in business is not an easy job. 开创一项事业是不容易的事。③ 打算：I ~ out to make the dress by myself, but in the end I had to ask for help. 我本打算自己做这件衣服的，结果还是得求助于人。④ 说明；阐明：Be sure to ~ out the points of your argument in details. 记住一定要详细地阐明你的观点。~ **up** 建立；创立；竖立：He ~ up his tent. 他搭起了帐篷。/ They ~ up a school for children. 他们为孩子们创办了一所学校。Ⅱ *n.* [C]❶套；组；副：a ~ of silver cups 一套银质茶杯 ❷电子器械：a television ~ 电视机 Ⅲ *adj.* 不变的；固定的；规定的；约定的

setback / ˈsetˌbæk / *n.* [C]挫折；失利，失败；倒退；（旧病的）复发：a temporary ~ in one's fortunes 命运中的暂时挫折/ face up to innumerable ~s 勇敢面对无数的挫折/ an unexpected ~ in a patient's recovery 病人康复过程中意想不到的反复

setting / ˈsetɪŋ / *n.* [C] ❶安装；调整 ❷环境；背景：social ~ 社会环境 / stage ~ 舞台布景

settle / ˈsetl / *v.* ❶安家，定居（与 in，at 连用）；停留（与 on 连用）：~ in Canada 定居加拿大 / The cold has ~d on my chest. 我患了感冒。/ Isn't it time that Tom got married and ~d down? 难道汤姆结婚成家的时候还没到吗？❷解决；决定：~ an argument 结束争论 / Nothing is ~d yet. 诸事未定。❸支付；结算：~ a bill 付账 / I shall ~ (up) with you at the end of the month. 我月底和你结清账。/ ~ **down to sth.** (**to do sth.**)安下心来做某事：You should ~ down to your homework. 你应当安下心来做作业。

settlement / ˈsetlmənt/ *n.* ❶[U]安顿 ❷[U]定居，安居 ❸[C]殖民地；居留地，移居地：an Indian ~ 印第安人居留地 ❹[C]解决；和解；解决方式；和解办法；协议；契约：a peaceful ~ 和平解决方式 / No ~ of the strike is possible. 罢工的问题绝不可能解决。

set-up / ˈsetʌp / *n.* [C] ❶结构；设置；安排；组织，机构；体制：learn the ~ of a company 了解一个公司的组织情况/

We must rebuild the entire port ~. 我们必须改造整个港口的结构。❷准备,计划,方案

seven /ˈsevn/ Ⅰ *num.* 七,7 Ⅱ *adj.* 七个(的)

seventeen /ˌsevnˈtiːn/ Ⅰ *num.* 十七,17 Ⅱ *adj.* 十七个(的)

seventeenth /ˌsevnˈtiːnθ/ Ⅰ *num.* 第十七;十七分之一 Ⅱ *adj.* 第十七的;十七分之一的

seventh /ˈsevnθ/ Ⅰ *num.* 第七;七分之一 Ⅱ *adj.* 第七的;七分之一的

seventieth /ˈsevntɪəθ/ Ⅰ *num.* 第七十;七十分之一 Ⅱ *adj.* 第七十的;七十分之一的

seventy /ˈsevnti/ Ⅰ *num.* 七十,70 Ⅱ *adj.* 七十个(的)

several /ˈsevrəl/ Ⅰ *adj.* 几个的;数个的:I've read it ~ times. 我已经读过好几次了。Ⅱ *pron.* 几个;数个

severe /sɪˈvɪə(r)/ *adj.* ❶严厉的;严格的:be ~ with one's child 对孩子严厉 ❷严重的;剧烈的:~ pain 剧痛 派 severely *adv.*

sew /səʊ/ *v.* (sewed /səʊd/, sewn /səʊn/或 sewed) 缝;缝合:~ a button on 钉扣子 派 sewing *n.*

sex /seks/ *n.* [C]性别;性:equality of ~es 男女平等 / the female ~ 女性 / the male ~ 男性 / the other ~ 异性/ school for both ~es 男女生学校

shabby /ˈʃæbi/ *adj.* (-ier,-iest)破旧的;褴褛的:He looks rather ~ in those clothes. 他穿上那些衣服显得很寒碜。

shack /ʃæk/ *n.* [C]简易房屋,棚屋:The old buzzard has lived in the same ~ for 20 years. 那个老家伙在同一棚屋里住了 20 年。

shade /ʃeɪd/ Ⅰ *n.* [U] ❶阴凉处:Keep in the ~; it's cooler. 待在阴凉处吧,那儿比较凉爽。❷(图画等的)阴暗部分:There is not enough light and ~ in your drawing. 你的图画中明暗色调不够。Ⅱ *v.* 遮蔽;遮挡:He ~d his eyes with his hand. 他用手遮住眼睛。

shadow /ˈʃædəʊ/ *n.* [C]影子;阴影:The ~ gets longer when the sun sets. 太阳落山时影子会变长。/ **be afraid of one's own ~** 胆小得不得了 **catch at ~s** (=**run after a ~**)捕风捉影 **under the ~ of** ①在……的庇护之下;因……的影响 ②被置于……的危险之下

shadowy /ˈʃædəʊi/ *adj.* 有阴影的;幽暗的

shady /ˈʃeɪdi/ *adj.* (-ier,-iest)遮阳的;成荫的;背阴的:the ~ side of the street 街道阴凉的一边

shaft /ʃɑːft,ʃæft/ *n.* [C] ❶箭;箭杆;矛;矛杆:the wooden ~ of an arrow 弓箭的木制箭杆 ❷(光、闪电等的)一束;一道:A ~ of moonlight came through the open door. 一束月光从敞开的门中透射进来。

shaggy /ˈʃægi/ *adj.* ❶多粗毛的;(毛发等)粗浓的:a lion's ~ mane 狮子的粗鬃毛/His face was ~ with a black beard. 他脸上长满了粗黑的胡子。❷不修边幅的,不整洁的,凌乱的,邋遢的:a ~ woman 邋遢女人

shake /ʃeɪk/ *v.* (shook/ʃʊk/, shaken /ˈʃeɪkən/)摇动;(使)震动;(使)颤抖:~ head over 对……摇头(表不赞成) / ~ leaves from a tree 摇落树上的叶子/ ~ one's fist at sb. 向某人挥拳(表示挑战、威胁等)/ ~ one's sides with laughter 捧腹大笑 / He was shaking with cold. 他冷得发抖。/ He shook hands with me. 他和我握手。/ ~ **off** 抖落;摆脱;甩掉:~ off the cold 驱除感冒 / ~ off old ideas 抛弃旧思想

shaky /ˈʃeɪki/ *adj*. 动摇的;不可靠的;发抖的

shall /ʃæl,ʃəl/ *aux. v*. (should /ʃʊd,ʃəd/) ❶(用于构成将来时:用于第一人称肯定式、疑问式及第二人称疑问式)将,会:We ~ arrive tomorrow. 我们将于明日到达。/ Shall we go there tomorrow? 我们明天将去那儿吗? ❷(用以表示说话者的意志或意愿)一定,必定会:If you work well, you ~ have higher wages. 如果你工作好,你就可得到较高的薪水。❸(用于表示责任、命令或指示)要,应该:Shall I open the window? 要我打开窗子吗? / Shall the boy wait? 要那孩子等待吗? / You ~ not have it; it's mine. 你不可以拿它,那是我的。

shallow /ˈʃæləʊ/ *adj*. ❶浅的;不深的:~ water 浅水 / a ~ saucer 浅碟 ❷肤浅的;浅薄的

sham /ʃæm/ Ⅰ *n*. 假冒;赝品 Ⅱ *vt*. 假装:~illness 装病

shame /ʃeɪm/ Ⅰ *n*. [U] ❶羞愧,耻辱;羞耻心;羞耻感:feel ~ at having told a lie 因说谎而感到羞愧 / feel ~ at failing in an examination 因考试失败而感到羞愧 ❷(常作 a ~)不足取的事,可耻的事(口语中相当于 pity):What a ~ to deceive the girl! 欺骗那女孩是多么可耻的事啊! / That he missed the boat is a ~. 他没赶上船,太遗憾了。Ⅱ *vt*. 使感到羞愧;使丢脸

shameful /ˈʃeɪmfl/ *adj*. 可耻的;丢脸的:~ conduct 可耻的行为 派 shamefully *adv*.

shameless /ˈʃeɪmləs/ *adj*. 无耻的;厚颜的 派 shamelessly *adv*.

shampoo /ʃæmˈpuː/ Ⅰ *vt*. 用洗发剂洗(头发) Ⅱ *n*. (*pl*. shampoos) 洗发;洗发剂,洗发液

shape /ʃeɪp/ Ⅰ *n*. 样子;外形;形状:My garden is in the ~ of a square. 我的园子是长方形的。/ **in** ~ 形式上;外形上:In ~ the building looks like a ship. 这楼房在外形上像一艘轮船。**get sth. into** ~ 使成形;使有条理:I find it difficult to get my ideas into ~. 我发现很难把思路理顺。**give** ~ **to** 使成形:At last they gave ~ to the plan. 计划终于成形了。**take** ~ 成形:Bit by bit, the idea took ~ in her mind. 主意慢慢地在她的脑子里形成了。Ⅱ *v*. 成形

shapeless /ˈʃeɪplɪs/ *adj*. ❶不定型的;没有形状的:a ~ mass of dough 不成形的生面团 / ~ fears 难以名状的恐惧 ❷样子难看的,形状不美的,丑陋的;不匀称的;走了样的:a ~ dress 样子难看的连衣裙

share /ʃeə(r)/ Ⅰ *n*. [C] ❶(共有的)一份;部分:Please let me take a ~ in the expenses. 这些费用请让我出一份。/ **go ~s with sb. in sth.** 与某人分享(分担)某物:I'll go ~s with you in the expenses. 我将与你一起分担费用。**have a ~ in** 在……中参与一份:We all have a ~ in the profit of the company. 公司所赚的钱我们都有一份。❷股份:~ index 股票指数 / He holds 200 ~s in the company. 他在公司里持有 200 股。Ⅱ *v*. ❶分给;分配;分派:He would ~ his last penny with me. 他即使只有一分钱,也会分给我用。❷共有;共用;共享:He hated having to ~ the bedroom with a stranger. 他讨厌与陌生人共住这间卧室。/ ~ **sth. out among (between)** 在

……中平均分配某物：The group leader ~d the work among us. 组长把工作平均分派给我们。~ **sth. with sb.** 与某人分享(分担)某物：I ~ the book with the monitor. 我和班长共用一本书。

shark /ʃɑːk/ *n.* [C] ❶鲨鱼 ❷贪婪狡猾的人

sharp /ʃɑːp/ Ⅰ *adj.* ❶锋利的：a ~ knife 快刀 ❷尖声的；刺耳的：a ~ cry of distress 痛苦的尖叫声 ❸尖刻的；厉害的：~ words 尖刻的话 / a ~ tongue 利舌 Ⅱ *adv.* ❶准时地；整：at seven (o'clock) ~七点整 ❷突然：turn ~ to the left 突然向左转 派 sharply *adv.*；sharpness *n.*

sharpen /ˈʃɑːpən/ *v.* 使尖锐；使急剧：~ a pencil 削尖铅笔 / My razor needs ~ing. 我的剃刀需要磨了。派 sharpener *n.*

shatter /ˈʃætə(r)/ Ⅰ *vt.* ❶使粉碎，打碎，砸碎：~ a vase 打碎花瓶/ The force of the explosion ~ed the windows. 爆炸的威力把窗户玻璃震碎了。❷破坏，毁坏，损害；使(希望等)破灭：~ the world peace 破坏世界和平/Her hopes were ~ed by the news. 她的希望被那个消息粉碎了。—*vi.* 被打碎；破碎，碎裂：Glassware is liable to ~. 玻璃器皿容易破碎。Ⅱ *n.* [C]碎片：The broken vase lay in ~s. 打破的花瓶已成了碎片。

shave /ʃeɪv/ Ⅰ *v.* (shaved, shaved 或 shaven) 刮(胡子)；修面：Do you ~ yourself or go to the barber's? 你自己修面还是到理发店修面? Ⅱ *n.* [C]刮脸：My father has a ~ every morning. 我的父亲每天早晨都要刮脸。

she /强 ʃiː，弱 ʃi/ Ⅰ *pron.* ❶她：I saw you talking to a girl. Who is ~? 我看到你与一个女孩说话，她是谁? /She is the image of her father. 她长得很像她父亲。❷(用以指拟人化的国家、月亮、汽车、轮船等)她：She's a great-looking car. 这是一辆外观非常漂亮的车。/ England has done what ~ promised to do. 英国已做了她承诺要做的事情。❸女人，女性：She who listens learns. 用心听的女性就能学会。Ⅱ *n.* [C](口语)女人；女性；雌性动物：What a beautiful child! Is it a ~ or he? 这小孩多漂亮！是男孩还是女孩? /His kitten is a ~. 他的小猫是母的。

shear /ʃɪə(r)/ *vt.* ❶用剪刀剪(羊毛等)：~ wool from the sheep 剪去羊身上的毛 ❷使弯曲；使(机翼)折断；切断，剪断：The bar fell into the machinery and ~ed a connecting-bar. 那根棒掉进了机器里，把连杆给打折了。

shed[1] /ʃed/ *n.* [C]棚；小屋

shed[2] /ʃed/ *vt.* (shed, shed; shedding)脱落；流出；散发：~ tears 哭泣 / The soldiers ~ their blood for the country. 战士们为国流血牺牲。

sheep /ʃiːp/ *n.* [C](单复数同形)羊；绵羊：a black ~败家子；害群之马 / a wolf in ~'s clothing 披着羊皮的狼

sheer /ʃɪə(r)/ Ⅰ *adj.* 纯粹的；十足的，全然的；绝对的；彻底的：He won the game by ~ chance. 他全凭运气赢得了比赛。/ a ~ forgery 一件不折不扣的赝品 Ⅱ *adv.* ❶绝对地；十足地，全然地；彻底地 ❷险峻地；陡峭地；垂直地：the precipitous cliffs rising ~ form the sea 从海里笔直升出来的陡峭的绝壁

sheet /ʃiːt/ *n.* [C] ❶被单：put a clean ~ on the bed 在床上铺干净的床单 ❷一片；一张：a ~ of paper 一张纸 / as pale (white) as a ~ 脸色苍白如纸 / The book is in ~s. 这本书尚未装订。

S

shelf /ʃelf/ *n.* [C](*pl.* shelves/ʃelvz/)(食橱、书架、书柜等的)隔板,架:Please replace the books on the shelves after reading. 读完书后请放回书架。

shell /ʃel/ *n.* [C] ❶(种子、果实等的)壳;(虫的)甲,壳 ❷炮弹

shelter /ˈʃeltə(r)/ Ⅰ *n.* ❶[U]庇护;保护;遮蔽:take ~ from the rain 躲雨 ❷[C]庇护物;庇护所;避难所:a bus ~ 公共汽车候车亭 Ⅱ *v.* 庇护;保护;掩护:trees that ~ a house from cold wind 遮蔽房屋使其不受寒风侵袭的大树 / ~ an escaped prisoner 窝藏逃犯

shepherd /ˈʃepəd/ *n.* [C]牧羊人

shield /ʃiːld/ Ⅰ *n.* [C] ❶盾,盾牌 ❷防御物;保护物;保护者:protective ~ against infection 抵御感染的保护屏障 ❸盾形物:The sun showed half its ~ behind the horizon. 太阳在地平线露出半个盾形。Ⅱ *vt.* ❶(似)用盾挡住;挡护;遮挡:The ozone layer ~s all living things against harmful ultraviolet rays from the sun. 臭氧层可保护所有生物不受来自太阳有害的紫外线的辐射。❷防御;保护,防护:~ a state-owned economy from the competitive pressures of global market 保护国有经济免受全球市场的竞争压力

shift /ʃɪft/ Ⅰ *v.* 移动;变换:~ the blame (on) to sb. else 诿过于他人 / The wind has ~ed to the north. 风向转北。Ⅱ *n.* [C]❶(位置或性格的)改变,变换 ❷换班;值班:day (night) ~ 日(夜)班 / working in ~s 轮班工作

shine /ʃaɪn/ Ⅰ *v.* (shone /ʃɒn/, shone 或 shined, shined) ❶发光;照耀:His face shone with excitement. 他因兴奋而容光焕发。❷卓越;出众:He does not ~ in conversation. 他的谈吐并不出众。❸磨光;擦亮:~ shoes 擦鞋 Ⅱ *n.* [U]光亮;光泽:rain or ~无论晴雨 / Give your shoes a good ~. 把你的鞋好好擦一下。

shiny /ˈʃaɪni/ *adj.* (-ier,-iest) ❶发光的;晴朗的 ❷擦亮的;磨光的

ship /ʃɪp/ Ⅰ *n.* [C]轮船;海船:by ~ 乘船 / load (unload) a ~ 装船(卸船) / take a ~ 乘船 / The factory builds sea-going ~s. 这个工厂造海船。Ⅱ *v.* (shipped; shipping) 装上船;用船运:They ~ped the goods to Shanghai. 他们把货物用船运到上海。

shipment /ˈʃɪpmənt/ *n.* ❶[U]装运;船运:crate the car for ~ on a boat 把汽车装进板条箱供船运 ❷[C]装载(或交运)的货物(量);(一批)船货:a ~ of grain 一船谷物 / send a ~ of aid to a country 运送一批救援物资到某国

shipping /ˈʃɪpɪŋ/ *n.* [U]❶海运,船运;航运;装运;运输:cost for ~ 运(输)费 ❷(总称)(尤指一个国家、地区或航运公司的)船舶 ❸航运业;运输业

shipyard /ˈʃɪpˌjɑːd/ *n.* [C]造船厂;修船厂;船坞

shirt /ʃɜːt/ *n.* [C]男衬衣;(美)宽松的女上衣

shiver /ˈʃɪvə(r)/ Ⅰ *vi.* (尤指因寒冷或恐惧而)颤抖:~ing all over with cold 冷得全身颤抖 Ⅱ *n.* [C](常用 *pl.*)颤抖;哆嗦:get (have) the ~s 发抖/The sight sent cold ~s down my back. 那景象使我不寒而栗。

shock /ʃɒk/ Ⅰ *n.* ❶[C]击;打击 ❷[C](常用单数)震惊 ❸[U]休克 Ⅱ *vt.* 使休克;使感到震惊;使感到愤恨:I was ~ed at the news of her death. 她去世的消息使我感到震惊。

shocking /ˈʃɒkɪŋ/ *adj.* ❶使人震惊的;

骇人听闻的；触目惊心的：The massacre is ~. 这起屠杀事件令人震惊。❷极差的，极坏的；低劣的：~ luck 背运

shoe /ʃuː/ *n.* [C]鞋：put on (take off) one's ~s 穿(脱)鞋

shoelace /ˈʃuːˌleɪs/ *n.* [C]鞋带：His ~s have come loose 他的鞋带松了。

shoot /ʃuːt/ Ⅰ *v.* (shot /ʃɒt/, shot) ❶射击；开枪：They were ~ing at a target. 他们在打靶。❷发芽；生枝：Rose bushes ~ again after being cut back. 玫瑰丛在修剪后又会萌发新枝。❸拍照；摄影 ❹投(篮)；射门：~ a basket 投篮 / ~ a goal 进一球 Ⅱ *n.* ❶[C]射击 ❷芽，苗；嫩枝

shop /ʃɒp/ Ⅰ *n.* [C] 商店 Ⅱ *vi.* (shopped; shopping) 购物

shopping /ˈʃɒpɪŋ/ *n.* [U]购物：do one's ~购物 / a ~ bag 购物袋

shore /ʃɔː(r)/ *n.* [C](水域的)岸，滨

short /ʃɔːt/ *adj.* ❶短的；短暂的；矮的：a ~ stick 短棍 / a ~ man 个子矮的人 / a ~ holiday 短暂的假期 ❷不足的；缺少的：The shopkeeper was fined for giving ~ weight. 那店主因卖东西缺斤少两而被罚款。/ **be ~ of** 缺乏：They are ~ of money. 他们缺钱。**in ~**总之；简言之：In ~, we should do something for her. 总之，我们应当为她做点什么。

shortage /ˈʃɔːtɪdʒ/ *n.* [C]不足；缺少：a ~ of talented people 人才缺乏 / food ~ 食品短缺 / housing ~ 住房紧张 / labor ~ 劳动力匮乏/ teacher ~ 缺乏师资

shortcoming /ˈʃɔːˌkʌmɪŋ/ *n.* [C](常用 *pl.*)缺点，短处；缺陷：a person with many ~s 一个有许多缺点的人/reveal some serious ~s in the safety procedures 暴露安全程序中的一些严重缺陷

shortcut /ˈʃɔːtkʌt/ *n.* [C]捷径；近路：Is there a ~ we can take? 我们有近路可走吗？/ Can you find a ~ to success? 你能找到通向成功的捷径吗？

shorten /ˈʃɔːtn/ *vt.* (使)缩小；(使)减少，使不足：~ one's visit 缩短某人的访问时间 / My coat is too long; I'll have ~ed it. 我的外套太长，我得把它改短一点。

shorthand /ˈʃɔːtˌhænd/ *n.* [U] ❶速记法：The secretary took down their conversations in ~. 秘书把他们的谈话速记了下来。❷简便的表达方式：They couldn't understand the kind of ~ that we talk. 他们无法理解我们那种简略的谈话方式。

shortly /ˈʃɔːtli/ *adv.* ❶立刻；不久：I'll be back ~. 我不久就回来。/ ~ **after** 不久：The doctor came ~ after breakfast. 早饭后不久大夫就来了。❷简短地；简要地：Mr. Zhang explained the problem ~. 张先生简要地解释了这个问题。

short-sighted /ˌʃɔːtˈsaɪtɪd/ *adj.* ❶近视的：The girl is ~. 那女孩近视。❷目光短浅的：It is ~ of you to give up all efforts. 你放弃一切努力，目光太短浅了。

short-term /ˈʃɔːˌtɜːm/ *adj.* 短期的，短时间的：cope with the ~ lack of money 处理资金暂时短缺的问题/~ earnings 短期收益

shot /ʃɒt/ *n.* [C] ❶(枪、炮等的)发射，射击；枪炮声：hear ~s in the distance 听到远处的枪声 ❷射手；枪手；炮手：He's a first-class ~. 他是一流的射手。❸铅球：put a ~ 掷铅球 ❹注射：give sb. a ~ 给某人打针 ❺镜头

should /ʃʊd/ *aux. v.* ❶应当，应该(表示义务、责任)：We ~ do as he said. 我

们应该照他说的做。/ He ~ go to see a doctor earlier. 他应该早点去看医生。❷万一，一旦（表示假设）：If he ~ change his mind, let us know. 一旦他改变主意，请告知我们。❸竟然：It is strange that you ~ say so. 很奇怪，你竟然这样说。❹想，愿（表示意愿）：I ~ like to have a bath. 我想洗个澡。❺大概，可能（表示推测）：The children ~ be home by now. 孩子们现在应该到家了。

shoulder /ˈʃəʊldə(r)/ Ⅰ *n.* [C]肩/~ **to** ~ 肩并肩：The soldiers marched forward ~ to ~. 战士们肩并肩向前进。/ **have sth. on one's ~s** 肩负；承担：We young people have a heavy task on our ~s. 我们年轻人重任在肩。Ⅱ *vt.* 肩负；承担；挑起

shout /ʃaʊt/ Ⅰ *v.* 大声喊叫；大声说：He ~ed to me to go there. 他大声喊我过去。/~ **at sb.** 对某人喊叫 Ⅱ *n.* [C]大叫；呼喊：~s of joy 欢乐的喊叫

shove /ʃʌv/ Ⅰ *v.* 推，挤；猛推；用力挤过：He was ~d against the wall. 他被推到了墙边。/His mother told him to ~ along to make some room for her. 他妈妈叫他往旁边挪一挪，给她腾点地方。Ⅱ *n.* [C]推，挤，搡：Julia gave her a ~ that sent her in. 朱丽娅把她推到了里面。

shovel /ˈʃʌvl/ *n.* [C]铲；锹

show /ʃəʊ/ Ⅰ *v.* (showed, shown /ʃəʊn/或showed)❶给……看；展示：He ~ed his album to all his friends. 他把他的相册给所有的朋友看。/ ~**up** 到场；出席；露面：Nobody knew why Mr. John didn't ~ up at the evening. 没有人知道为什么约翰先生不出席晚会。❷指示；引导；带领 / ~ **around** (**round**) 带领参观：My husband will ~ you around (round) while I get the tea. 我备茶时，我丈夫会带你四周参观一下。~ **off** 卖弄；炫耀：She is always ~ing off. 她老爱炫耀自己。~ **sb. out** (**in**) 领某人出去(进来)：Don't trouble to ~ me out; I know my way. 你不必麻烦带我出去，我知道路。Ⅱ *n.* [C] ❶展览；展览会：a flower ~花展 / His plane model is still on ~. 他的飞机模型还在展出。❷表演；演出；节目：Have you seen any good ~s recently? 你最近看什么好的节目了吗?

showing /ˈʃəʊɪŋ/ *n.* [C]❶展览；展示，陈列：a ~ of some art works 一些艺术作品的展示 / visit a ~ of European movies 参观欧洲电影展 ❷表演；演出；(电影的)放映；(电视的)播放：I wasn't at my best at the ~. 演出时我不在最佳状态。

shower /ˈʃaʊə(r)/ Ⅰ n. [C]阵雨；淋浴 Ⅱ *v.* 下阵雨；洗淋浴：It ~ed last night. 昨夜里下了阵雨。

showy /ˈʃəʊi/ *adj.* (-ier,-iest)引人注目的；装饰过分的；炫耀的：a ~ dress 花哨的衣服

shred /ʃred/ Ⅰ *n.* ❶[C]碎片；细条；破布条；纸片：The violent seas ripped sails to ~s. 汹涌的大海把船帆撕成了碎征。❷少量，些许：Not a ~ of evidence has been produced in support of those accusations. 提交不出任何证据来支持那些指控。/ **tear to ~s** ①将……撕成碎片：She tore all her letters to ~s. 她将所有的信件都撕成碎片了。②彻底驳倒(论点等) Ⅱ *vt.* (shredding; shredded 或 shred)把……撕碎(或切碎)；把……弄成细条；把……放入碎纸机：This machine is used to ~ documents. 这台机器用于切碎文件。

S

shriek /ʃriːk/ Ⅰ *vi.* 尖叫 Ⅱ *n.* [C]尖叫声

shrill /ʃrɪl/ Ⅰ *adj.* 尖声的；刺耳的：a ~ whistle 刺耳的哨声 Ⅱ *v.* 尖声叫

shrimp /ʃrɪmp/ *n.* [C] ❶（小）虾 ❷矮小的人

shrine /ʃraɪn/ *n.* [C] ❶神龛；圣坛；神殿 ❷圣地，神圣的场所：The location of his grave has become a ~. 他的墓地已成了圣地。

shrink /ʃrɪŋk/ *vi.* （shrank /ʃræŋk/ 或 shrunk /ʃrʌŋk/，shrunk 或 shrunken /ˈʃrʌŋkən/） ❶皱缩；使收缩：This cloth does not ~ in the wash. 这种布料洗涤时不缩水。❷退缩；畏缩：You should not ~ before difficulties. 你不应该在困难面前退缩。

shrub /ʃrʌb/ *n.* [C]灌木

shrug /ʃrʌg/ *v.* & *n.* [C]耸肩

shut /ʃʌt/ *v.* （shut，shut）关上；关闭 / ~ **down** 停止营业；停工；关闭：They have ~ down their factory. 他们的工厂已关闭。~ **off** 切断；停止供应（煤气、水、电等）：He didn't pay for his water so the company ~ it off. 他没付水费，因此公司停止供水。~ **out** 排除；遮住；关在外面：The curtains ~ out the light. 窗帘遮光。/ Don't ~ the dog out of the room. 别把狗关在门外。~ **up**（使）闭口；（使）住嘴：Tell him to ~ up. 叫他闭口。

shutter /ˈʃʌtə(r)/ *n.* [C] ❶百叶窗 ❷（相机的）快门

shy /ʃaɪ/ *adj.* (-er 或-ier，-est 或-iest) ❶（指人）难为情的；怕羞的：John is ~ and dislikes parties. 约翰怕羞，不喜欢参加社交集会。❷（指动物等）易被惊走的，易受惊的，胆怯的：A deer is a ~ animal. 鹿是易受惊的动物。※ shyly *adv.*；shyness *n.*

sick /sɪk/ *adj.* ❶不适的；病的：He has been ~ for two weeks. 他已病了两周。❷（只用作表语）想呕吐的；恶心的：feel ~ 觉得要呕吐 ❸厌倦的；厌恶的：I am ~ of waiting. 我讨厌等待。

sicken /ˈsɪkən/ *vt.* 使恶心，使作呕；使厌恶；使厌倦：The violence in the movie ~ed me. 影片中的暴力让我恶心。/ I was ~ed at his words. 他说的这些话真让我作呕。—*vi.* 生病，显露出症状：She is ~ing for measles. 她出麻疹了。/ The baby ~ed and died shortly afterwards. 婴儿发病后很快就夭折了。

sickening /ˈsɪkənɪŋ/ *adj.* ❶令人作呕的；令人毛骨悚然的：It's ~ to see the cruel bullfight. 见到那残忍的斗牛场面真叫人毛骨悚然。❷使人厌烦的；让人生气的，恼人的；使人难受的：It's ~ that I can't go to the party. 不能去参加晚会，真叫人憋气。

sickle /ˈsɪkl/ *n.* [C] 镰刀

sickly /ˈsɪkli/ *adj.* ❶生病的；多病的：a ~ child 多病的孩子 ❷因疾病而产生的；病态的；苍白的：She was pale and ~. 她脸色苍白、满面病容。❸令人作呕的；使人厌恶的：the ~ smell of rotten fruit 使人恶心的烂水果的气味

sickness /ˈsɪknɪs/ *n.* ❶患病，生病；疾病：a pernicious ~ 致命的疾病 / A lot of workers were absent because of ~. 许多工人因病缺勤。❷[U]呕吐，作呕；恶心，反胃：Andrew entered the bedroom，which smelt of ~. 安德鲁进了卧室，那里面散发着令人作呕的味道。

side /saɪd/ Ⅰ *n.* [C] ❶（物体较平的）面：the six ~s of a cube 立方体的六个面 ❷旁边：~ effect 副作用/ ~ issue 枝

S

节问题/~ walk 人行道/ **by the ~of** 在……旁边；与……相比较：She looks small by the ~ of her companion. 她在她的同伴身旁(和她的同伴比较)显得很小。~ **by** ~ 并肩地；相互支持地：They walked ~ by ~. 他们并肩而行。**take (stand by) sb.'s** ~ 站在某人一边；支持某人：Whatever happens, I'll stand by your ~. 无论发生什么事情，我都支持你。Ⅱ *vi.* 站在……的一边；支持

side-effect /ˈsaɪdɪˌfeɪk/ *n.* [C]副作用：The ~ of the drug are loss of hair and difficulty in eating. 这种药的副作用是头发脱落和进食困难。

sideways /ˈsaɪdweɪz/ *adv.* (斜)向一边地；侧身地：You can get the large table through the door ~. 你要侧着身子才能把大桌子搬进门去。

siege /siːdʒ/ *n.* 包围；围攻；围困

sigh /saɪ/ Ⅰ *n.* [C]叹气；叹息：utter a ~ 叹一口气 Ⅱ *vi.* 叹气；叹息 /~ **at (about, over) sth.** 为某事而叹息

sight /saɪt/ *n.* ❶[U] 视力；视觉：lose one's ~ 失明；变盲 ❷看见；瞥见 / **at first** ~ 乍一看；初看起来：At first ~, she is like an actress. 初看起来她很像演员。**catch (have, get) (a)** ~ **of** 看见；看出：I caught a ~ of him. 我瞥见了他。**out of** ~ 看不见：The land is out of ~. 陆地看不见了。/ Out of ~, out of mind. (谚)眼不见，心不烦。❸[C] (*pl.*) 值得看的东西；名胜；风景：Come and see the ~s of London. 来看看伦敦的名胜吧。

sightseeing /ˈsaɪtˌsiːŋ/ Ⅰ *n.* [U]游览，观光，旅游：an afternoon of ~ and shopping 一个观光购物的下午 Ⅱ *adj.* 游览的，观光的，旅游的：a ~ expedition to Paris 一次去巴黎的观光旅行

sign /saɪn/ Ⅰ *n.* [C] ❶记号；符号：mathematical ~s 数学符号 ❷迹象；征兆：Are dark clouds a ~ of rain? 乌云是下雨的征兆吗？❸手势；示意动作：the ~ language (聋哑人用的)手语 ❹痕迹；踪迹：There is no ~ of him yet. 尚不见他的踪迹。Ⅱ *v.* ❶签字；签名：Please ~ on the dotted line. 请在虚线上签名。❷做手势：The policeman ~ed (for) them to stop. 警察做手势叫他们停下来。

signify /ˈsɪgnɪˌfaɪ/ *vt.* ❶表示……的意思；有……的意思：Nobody really knows what the marks on the ancient stones ~. 没有人真的知道这些古老石头上的符号表示什么意思。❷表明；表示；示意：We signified our agreement by raising our hands. 我们举手表示赞同。派 signification *n.*

signal /ˈsɪgnl/ Ⅰ *n.* [C]信号；暗号：traffic ~s 交通信号 / give the ~ for a retreat 发出撤退信号 Ⅱ *vi.* (向……)发信号

signature /ˈsɪgnətʃə(r)/ *n.* [C]签字：send letters to the manager for ~ 把信件送给经理签字

significance /sɪgˈnɪfɪkəns/ *n.* [U]重要性；重大意义：a matter of great ~ 重大的事

significant /sɪgˈnɪfɪkənt/ *adj.* 重要的；意义深远的：a ~ speech 重要的演说

silence /ˈsaɪləns/ *n.* [U] ❶寂静；无声：the ~ of night 夜的寂静 ❷缄默；无言：listen to sb. in ~ 默默听某人说话 / observe three minutes' ~ 默哀三分钟 / The girl sat there in ~, but she was thinking something hard. 那女孩默不作声地坐在那儿，但她在认真地思考着什么问题。/ **keep** ~ 保持沉默；保持安

静：Keep～! The baby is sleeping. 安静！宝宝正在睡觉。

silent /ˈsaɪlənt/ *adj*. ❶寂静的：～ film 无声电影 ❷寡言的；缄默的 / **be ～ about (on)** 对……保持沉默：You'd better be ～ about what happened. 你最好对发生的事保持沉默。派 silently *adv*.

silicon /ˈsɪlɪkən/ *n*. [U]硅：～ chip 硅(芯)片

silk /sɪlk/ *n*. ❶[U]丝；丝线 ❷[C] (*pl*.)绸衣

silkworm /ˈsɪlkwɜːm/ *n*. [C]蚕

silly /ˈsɪli/ *adj*. (-ier, -iest)愚蠢的；低能的：Don't be ～! 别犯傻！

silver /ˈsɪlvə(r)/ *n*. [U]银

similar /ˈsɪmələ(r)/ *adj*. 类似的；相像的：My wife and I have ～ tastes in music. 妻子和我对音乐有相似的爱好。/ **be ～ in** 在……方面相似：The two brothers are ～ in appearance. 这两弟兄相貌相似。**be ～ to** 和……相似：This specimen is ～ to that one. 这个标本与那个相似。

similarity /ˌsɪməˈlærəti/ *n*. ❶[U]类似；相似：the astonishing ～ between he and his brother 他和他弟弟的惊人相似 ❷[C]相似点

simple /ˈsɪmpl/ *adj*. ❶不复杂的；简单的：a ～ sentence 简单句 / written in ～ English 用简单的英文写出的 ❷朴素的；无装饰的：She lives a ～ life. 她过着简朴的生活。❸单纯的；直率的：She behaves as ～ as a child. 她的举止单纯得像小孩子一样。

simplicity /sɪmˈplɪsəti/ *n*. [U] ❶简单；简易：The plan is of ～ itself. 这计划很简单。❷朴素；朴实：～ in dress 衣着朴素 / speak with ～ 谈吐朴实 / The writer is famous for ～ of style. 这位作家以文风朴实著称。

simplify /ˈsɪmplɪfaɪ/ *vt*. 使单纯；使简化：The teacher asked me to ～ the sentence. 老师要我把句子简化。派 simplification *n*.

simply /ˈsɪmpli/ *adv*. ❶朴素地；朴实地：dress ～ 衣着朴素 ❷完全地；绝对地：His pronunciation is ～ terrible. 他的发音糟透了。❸仅仅；只：It is ～ a matter of working hard. 此事只需努力做就行。

simulate /ˈsɪmjuˌleɪt/ *vt*. ❶假装，伪装，冒充：He ～d insanity in order to avoid punishment for his crime. 他装疯卖傻，企图逃避对他罪行的惩罚。❷模拟：An electronic device can ～ the clicking sound. 一种电子装置可以模拟这种咔嚓声。❸仿造，仿制：～d fur 仿毛皮 / a ～d pearl 人造珍珠

simultaneous /ˌsɪməlˈteɪnɪəs/ *adj*. 同步进行(或完成的)；同时发生(或存在)的：a ～ interpreter 同声传译员/ There was a ～ broadcast of the concert on the radio and the television. 电台和电视台同步播出了这场音乐会。派 simultaneously *adv*.

since /sɪns/ Ⅰ *adv*. 自从……以来：He left home in 1950 and has not been heard of ～. 他在 1950 年离家，以后便杳无音信。Ⅱ *prep*. 自……以后；自从：She hasn't been home ～ her marriage. 她自结婚以后未曾回过家。Ⅲ *conj*. ❶自……以后；从……以来：Where have you been ～ I last saw you? 自从上次我和你见面以后，你到哪里去了？❷既然；因为：Since you can't answer the question, we'd better ask someone else. 既然你不能回答这个问

S

题，我们最好还是问别人。

sincere /sɪnˈsɪə(r)/ *adj.* 真实的；诚挚的；直率的：Are they ~ in their wish to disarm? 他们是真的希望裁军吗？派 sincerely *adv.*

sincerity /sɪnˈserəti/ *n.* [U]真诚；诚意；真实：He wrote a letter to me to show his ~. 他给我写信表示他的诚意。

sing /sɪŋ/ *v.* (sang/sæŋ/, sung /sʌŋ/) 唱：~ to the guitar 伴着吉他唱歌 / ~ in the New Year 歌迎新年 / ~ out the Old Year 唱送旧年/ ~ **high praise for (sth. or sb.)** 高度赞扬(某事或某人) 派 singing *n.*

single /ˈsɪŋgl/ *adj.* ❶唯一的；一个的：a ~ ticket 单程票 / walking in ~ file 以一路纵队行进 ❷未婚的；独身的：remain ~ 尚未成婚 派 singly *adv.*

singular /ˈsɪŋgjələ(r)/ *adj.* ❶(语法)单数的 ❷奇特的：~ clothes 奇装异服 ❸非凡的；卓越的：a man of ~ courage 非常勇敢的人

sink /sɪŋk/ *v.* (sank /sæŋk/, sunk /sʌŋk/) ❶下沉；沉没：Wood does not ~ in water. It floats. 木头在水中不沉，它漂浮着。❷使陷入；使沉浸于：He was sunk in thought. 他陷入沉思。

S

sip /sɪp/ Ⅰ (sipped; sipping) *v.* 小口地喝，抿，呷：We sat in the sun, ~ping lemonade. 我们一边坐着晒太阳，一边小口小口地喝着柠檬水。Ⅱ *n.* [C] ❶一小口的量，一啜(或一呷)之量 ❷细啜，慢饮；抿尝，浅尝：drink brandy in ~s 一口一口地饮白兰地

sir /sɜː(r)/ *n.* ❶(对男子的礼貌称呼)先生，阁下：Dinner is served, ~. 饭已备好，先生。❷(Sir)(用于有爵士称号者的名或姓名之前)爵士：Sir Edward 爱德华爵士

siren /ˈsaɪrən/ *n.* [C]汽笛；警报器

sister /ˈsɪstə(r)/ *n.* [C] ❶姐妹：elder ~ 姐姐 / younger ~ 妹妹 ❷修女

sit /sɪt/ *vi.* (sat /sæt/, sat; sitting) 坐：Let's ~ down. 我们就座吧。/ ~ **up late** 睡得晚；熬夜：He sat up late to prepare for the final examination. 他熬夜为期末考试做准备。

site /saɪt/ *n.* [C](建房的)地点，场所；遗址：conference ~会址 / construction (building) ~ 建筑工地 / test ~ 实验场 / Have you fixed the ~ for the new school? 你们选定新校址了吗？/ The museum is built on the ~ of an ancient temple. 博物馆修建在一座古庙的遗址上。

sitter /ˈsɪtə(r)/ *n.* [C]替人照看孩子的人：Can you get me a baby ~ for the vacation? 你能为我找一个在假期照看孩子的人吗？

situated /ˈsɪtʃʊeɪtɪd/ *adj.* (城镇、建筑物等)坐落于(某处)的，位于(某处)的：The village is ~ in a valley. 这个村庄坐落于山谷中。

situation /ˌsɪtʃʊˈeɪʃn/ *n.* [C] ❶(城镇、建筑物等的)位置，地点 ❷状况；事态；情势：be in an embarrassing ~ 处于窘境 / the international ~国际形势 / under the present ~在目前形势下

situp /ˈsɪtˌʌp/ *n.* [C]仰卧起坐

six /sɪks/ Ⅰ *num.* 六，6 Ⅱ *adj.* 六个(的)

sixteen /ˌsɪksˈtiːn/ Ⅰ *num.* 十六，16 Ⅱ *adj.* 十六个(的)

sixteenth /ˌsɪksˈtiːnθ/ Ⅰ *num.* 第十六；十六分之一 Ⅱ *adj.* 第十六的；十六分之一的

sixth /sɪksθ/ Ⅰ *num.* 第六；六分之一 Ⅱ

adj. 第六的；六分之一的

sixtieth /ˈsɪkstɪəθ/ Ⅰ *num*. 第六十；六十分之一 Ⅱ *adj*. 第六十的；六十分之一的

sixty /ˈsɪksti/ Ⅰ *num*. 六十，60 Ⅱ *adj*. 六十个(的)

size /saɪz/ *n*. ❶[U]大小；尺寸：a building of vast ~ 巨大的建筑物 ❷[C](衣着等的)号，码：What ~ hat do you wear? 你戴几号的帽子?

skate /skeɪt/ Ⅰ *n*. [C]溜冰鞋 Ⅱ *vi*. 溜冰：go skating 去溜冰

skeleton /ˈskelɪtən/ Ⅰ *n*. [C] ❶骨骼；骸骨；骷髅：the human ~人类的骨骼/development of ~骨骼发育 ❷骨架，框架，构架；轮廓：the bared ~ of a house 房子光秃秃的框架/the ~ of a plan 计划的纲要 Ⅱ *adj*. ❶骨骼的；像骨骼的：a pair of ~ hands 一双骨瘦如柴的手 ❷骨干的；精干的：~ staff 骨干职员

sketch /sketʃ/ *n*. [C] ❶草图；略图；素描：make a ~ of a harbor 画海港的草图 ❷简短的记载或描述；概述；大纲：He gave me a ~ of his plans for the expedition. 他对我略述了他远征的计划。

ski /skiː/ Ⅰ *n*. [C](*pl*. skis 或 ski)滑雪板；雪橇：a pair of ~s 一副滑雪板 Ⅱ *vi*. 滑雪：She went in for ~ing years ago. 数年前她很喜欢滑雪。

skill /skɪl/ *n*. 技能；技艺：The work calls for ~. 这项工作要求一定的技巧。/ He has the ~ to cope with such things. 他很善于对付这一类事情。/ She gained some ~s in handwriting. 她学会了一些书法技能。/ The pianist has great ~ with his fingers. 这位钢琴家有纯熟的指法。

skilled /skɪld/ *adj*. 经过训练的；有经验的；熟练的：~ workmen 有经验的工人；技工 / **be ~ in (at)** 在……方面灵巧：The little boy is ~ in using chopsticks. 那小男孩使用筷子很熟练。

skillful /ˈskɪlfʊl/ *adj*. 有技巧的；熟练的：He is not very ~ with chopsticks. 他用筷子不大熟练。派 skillfully *adv*.

skim /skɪm/ *v*. (skimmed; skimming) ❶撇(去)：~ (off) the cream from the milk 撇去牛奶上的奶油 ❷掠过；擦过：A bird ~med (over) the calm water of the lake. 一只鸟掠过平静的湖面。❸略读；浏览：~ (through) a novel 浏览一本小说

skin /skɪn/ *n*. [U](人或动物的)皮，皮肤

skip /skɪp/ *v*. (skipped; skipping) ❶轻快地跳：The lambs were ~ping about in the fields. 小羊在田野里跳来跳去。❷跳绳

skirt /skɜːt/ *n*. [C]女裙

sky /skaɪ/ *n*. (the ~) 天；天空：There were no clouds in the ~. 天上没有云彩。

skyjack /ˈskaɪdʒæk/ *vt*. 空中劫持(飞机) 派 skyjacker *n*.

skyscraper /ˈskaɪskreɪpə(r)/ *n*. [C]摩天大楼：Guangzhou is a modern city with ~s here and there. 广州是一座高楼林立的现代化城市。

skyward /ˈskaɪwəd/ Ⅰ *adv*. 向上地，朝天地：book ~仰望天空/The boy threw the ball ~. 男孩把球往上扔去。Ⅱ *adj*. 朝天的，向上的：a ~ direction 朝天的角度

slack /slæk/ *adj*. ❶(绳索等)松散的，松弛的，不紧的：We have to tighten these tent ropes first — they are too ~.

S

我们得先紧紧这些绑帐篷的绳子——它们太松了。❷忽视的;疏忽的,粗心的:He's been very ~ in his work lately. 近来他工作很不认真。❸(生意、市场等)萧条的,清淡的,不景气的:Travel business is always ~ at this time of year. 每年到了这个时候都是旅游淡季。

slacken /ˈslækən/ *vt.* ❶(使)松散;(使)松弛,放松:Slacken the rein, or you'll hurt the horse's mouth. 放松缰绳,不然会勒坏马嘴的。❷(使)松懈,(使)懈怠:Work ~ed a bit. 工作有点松懈了。

slam /slæm/ *vt.* (slammed; slamming) 发出砰的声音;砰地关上:The door ~med (shut). 门砰的一声关上了。

slander /ˈslɑːndə(r)/ Ⅰ *vt.* 诽谤;诋毁;造谣中伤 Ⅱ *n.* 诽谤,诋毁;诽谤性言论:spread ~ 散布诽谤性言论/ utter ~ about sb. 诽谤某人 派 slanderer *n.*

slang /slæŋ/ *n.* [U]俚语;行话;黑话

slap /slæp/ Ⅰ *v.* (slapped; slapping) 掌击;拍打:She ~ped his face. 她打了他一个耳光。Ⅱ *n.* [C]掌击;掴;拍:give sb. a ~ on the face 给某人一记耳光

slaughter /ˈslɔːtə(r)/ *vt.* & *n.* [U]屠杀;屠宰

slave /sleɪv/ Ⅰ *n.* [C]奴隶 Ⅱ *v.* 干苦活;奴役

sledge /sledʒ/ *n.* [C]雪橇;雪车:The Inuit use ~s pulled by reindeers to cross the Arctic. 因纽特人乘坐驯鹿拉的雪橇穿越北极。

slavery /ˈsleɪvəri/ *n.* [U] ❶奴役 ❷奴隶制度

sleep /sliːp/ Ⅰ *v.* (slept, slept) 睡:I slept well (badly) last night. 我昨晚睡得好(不好)。Ⅱ *n.* 睡眠;睡眠时间:have a short ~小睡一会/ He didn't get much ~. 他睡得不多。/**get to** ~ (常用于否定句)入睡,睡着:I couldn't get to ~ last night. 我昨晚睡不着。**go to** ~ 入睡,睡着:She listened to the breath so close to her and mused without being able to go to ~. 她听到这呼吸声就在身旁,不能成寐,就想着心事。

sleepy /ˈsliːpi/ *adj.* (-ier, -iest) ❶欲睡的;困乏的:feel ~ 觉得困乏 ❷(指地方)静寂的;不热闹的:a ~ little village 静寂的小村庄

sleeve /sliːv/ *n.* [C]衣袖:roll up the ~s of his shirt 卷起他衬衣的袖子 / seize sb. by the ~ 抓住某人的袖子 / **have sth. up one's** ~ 胸有成竹;暗中已有应急的打算

slender /ˈslendə(r)/ *adj.* ❶细长的;苗条的:a ~ girl 苗条的姑娘 / ~ legs 修长的双腿 ❷微薄的;微弱的;微小的:~ hope 渺茫的希望 / ~ income 微薄的收入 / You have a ~ chance of success only. 你成功的希望很小。派 slenderly *adv.* ; slenderness *n.*

slice /slaɪs/ Ⅰ *n.* [C] ❶薄片;切片:a ~ of meat 一片肉 ❷部分;一份 Ⅱ *vt.* 切(片):~ the meat 把肉切成薄片

slide /slaɪd/ Ⅰ *v.* (slid /slɪd/, slid 或 slidden /ˈslɪdən/) (使)滑动:children sliding on the ice 滑冰的孩子们 / ~ **into** ①溜进;潜入:The dog slid into the garden. 那条狗溜进花园里。②不知不觉陷入(习惯、毛病等):~ into bad habits 不知不觉地沾染上恶习/~ **over** 略过;回避;爽快地处理(问题等):He managed to ~ over the questions which were difficult for him to answer. 他设法避开了那些难回答的问题。Ⅱ *n.* [C] ❶滑;滑动 ❷滑梯;滑道;滑坡 ❸幻灯片

slight /slaɪt/ Ⅰ *adj*. ❶苗条的；细长的：a ~ figure 苗条的身材 ❷细小的；轻微的；不严重的；不重要的：a ~ error 小错误 / a ~ headache 轻微的头痛 Ⅱ *v*. 怠慢；轻视；蔑视：She felt ~ed because no one spoke to her. 她觉得受到蔑视，因为没有人和她说话。派 slightly *adv*.

slim /slɪm/ *adj*. (slimmer, slimmest) 细长的；苗条的；小的：a girl of ~ waist 一位细腰女郎

slip /slɪp/ Ⅰ *v*. (slipped; slipping) ❶失足；滑倒：He ~ped on the icy road and broke his leg. 他在结冰的路上滑倒而摔坏了腿。❷溜走；悄悄过去：She ~ped away without being seen. 她悄悄溜走而未被人看见。/ The years ~ped by. 岁月悄悄流逝。❸滑；落；滑脱：The fish ~ped out of my hand. 鱼从我手里滑脱出去。Ⅱ *n*. [C] ❶滑倒；失足 ❷小错；小失误 ❸纸条

slipper /ˈslɪpə(r)/ *n*. [C] 拖鞋；便鞋：a pair of plastic ~s 一双塑料拖鞋 / No ~s in class! 上课不准穿拖鞋！

slippery /ˈslɪpəri/ *adj*. (-ier, -iest) 滑的：be on a ~ slope 在滑坡上；在走向危险的途中 / The road is wet and ~. 路又湿又滑。

slit /slɪt/ Ⅰ *n*. [C] 狭长切口；长缝；裂缝 Ⅱ *vt*. (slitted; slitting) 切开；撕开

sliver /ˈslɪvə(r)/ *n*. [C] ❶长薄切片；狭长条，窄条：a ~ of land 一块狭长的土地 / a ~ of cake 一块蛋糕 ❷木片

slogan /ˈsləʊgən/ *n*. [C] 标语；口号：put up ~s 张贴标语 / shout ~s 呼口号

slope /sləʊp/ Ⅰ *n*. [C] 倾斜面；斜坡：mountain ~s 山坡 Ⅱ *v*. 倾斜：Our garden ~s (down) to the river. 我们的花园向河成坡形。

slow /sləʊ/ Ⅰ *adj*. ❶慢的；迟缓的：a ~ train 慢车 ❷迟钝的；呆笨的：a ~ child 迟钝的小孩 / ~ poison 慢性毒药 / **be ~ at** ...不善于……：She is ~ at calculating. 她不善于计算。Ⅱ *adv*. 低速地；缓慢地：Tell the driver to go ~er. 告诉驾驶员开慢些。Ⅲ *v*. (使)缓行；(使)减速：~ **down** (**up**) (使)放慢；减速：Has the economic growth ~ed up in that country? 那个国家的经济增长速度减慢了吗？/ Slow down before you reach the crossroads. 在你到达十字路口前你应该减速。派 slowly *adv*.；slowness *n*.

slug /slʌg/ Ⅰ *vt*. (slugged; slugging) 猛击，重击：I ~ged him on the face. 我猛击他的脸部。Ⅱ *n*. [C] 猛击，重击：He has been fined for putting the ~ on a cop. 他因殴打警察被罚了款。

slum /slʌm/ *n*. [C] 贫民窟；陋巷：live in a ~ 居于贫民窟

sly /slaɪ/ *adj*. (slyer, slyest) ❶狡猾的；狡诈的 ❷淘气的；顽皮的

smack /smæk/ Ⅰ *n*. [C] (尤指用手掌或扁平物的)拍击(声)，拍打(声)；掌掴(声)，扇击(声)：He gave the ball a bard ~. 他大力击球。Ⅱ *vt*. ❶掌击，掴，扇：I'd ~ his face. 我要扇他一记耳光。❷砰(或啪)地放下(或甩出、扔下等)：She ~ed the cup on the table. 她把杯子砰的一声放在桌子上。

small /smɔːl/ *adj*. 小的；少的：a ~ town 小镇 / a ~ audience 不多的听众 / a ~ sum of money 一小笔钱

smart /smɑːt/ *adj*. ❶鲜明的；漂亮的；整洁的；衣冠楚楚的：Go and make yourself ~ before we call on the Jonas. 在我们去拜访乔纳斯家以前，你先把自己打扮得漂漂亮亮的。❷聪明的；有技

S

巧的;有头脑的 派 smartly *adv.*; smartness *n.*

smash /smæʃ/ *v.* 捣碎;打破:The drunken man ~ed up all the furniture. 那醉汉毁坏了所有的家具。

smear /smɪə(r)/ Ⅰ *vt.* ❶(尤指油污物)弄脏,玷污:Ink ~ed my shirt. 墨水弄脏了我的衬衫。❷诽谤,诋毁:They tried to defeat him by ~ing his reputation. 他们企图玷污他的名声,以此来击败他。Ⅱ *n.* [C] ❶污迹,脏斑 ❷诽谤,诋毁

smell /smel/ Ⅰ *n.* ❶[U]嗅觉:Taste and ~ are closely connected. 味觉和嗅觉紧密相关。❷[C]气味:What a nice ~! 多好闻的气味! Ⅱ *v.* (smelt /smelt/, smelt 或 smelled, smelled) ❶嗅出:I can ~ something burning. 我闻到什么东西烧着了。/ Do (Can) fishes ~? 鱼类有嗅觉吗? ❷发出……的气味;有……的气味:The flowers ~ sweet. 花散发出香味。/ The dinner ~s good. 饭菜闻起来很香。/ The meat is beginning to ~. 这肉开始腐烂了。

smelly /'smeli/ *adj.* 味道刺鼻的,难闻的;臭的,有臭味的:The slum is horribly ~. 贫民窟里臭不可闻。/ Take your ~ shoes away. 把你那双臭鞋拿开。

smelt /smelt/ *vt.* 熔炼,精炼;从(矿石)中炼取金属,从矿石中炼取(金属):~ iron from its ores 从铁矿石中炼铁

smile /smaɪl/ Ⅰ *n.* [C]微笑:a big (broad) ~ 笑容可掬 / answer (reply) with a ~ 微笑着回答 / force a ~ 强颜欢笑 / wear a ~ 面带微笑 / There was a pleasant ~ on her face. 她的脸上露出悦人的微笑。Ⅱ *v.* 微笑;以微笑表示(愉快、兴趣、同情等):What are you smiling at? 你在笑什么? / The weather ~d on us. 天公作美(天气晴朗)。

smog /smɒg/ *n.* [U]烟雾

smoke /sməʊk/ Ⅰ *n.* ❶[U]烟:~ pouring from factory chimneys 从工厂烟囱冒出的烟 / There is no ~ without fire. (= Where there is ~, there is fire.) (谚)无风不起浪(无火不生烟)。❷[C]吸烟;香烟:Will you have a ~? 你想抽支烟吗? Ⅱ *v.* ❶冒烟;起烟雾:That oil-lamp ~s badly. 那油灯冒烟很厉害。❷吸(烟):~ a pipe 吸烟 / You mustn't ~ in this room. 你绝对不许在这房间里抽烟。派 smoker *n.*

smoking /'sməʊkɪŋ/ *n.* [U]吸烟:give up ~ 戒烟 / No ~. 禁止吸烟。

smoky /'sməʊki/ *adj.* (-ier,-iest) 多烟的;烟雾弥漫的

smooth /smuːð/ Ⅰ *adj.* 光滑的;平滑的;平静的:~ paper 光滑的纸 / a ~ road 平坦的路 / ~faced *adj.* 表面平滑的 / ~-tongued *adj.* 油嘴滑舌的;能言善辩的 Ⅱ *v.* 使(变)光滑;使(变)平静:~ down one's dress 烫平衣服 / The sea has ~ed down. 海上已风平浪静。/ ~ **away** 消除;克服:They ~ed away all kinds of difficulties and finished the task successfully. 他们克服了所有的困难,成功地完成了任务。~ **over** 掩饰;平息;排除:~ over one's faults 掩饰某人的过错 / ~ over obstacles 消除障碍 / ~ over a quarrel 平息一场争吵 派 smoothly *adv.*; smoothness *n.*

smother /'smʌðə(r)/ *vt.* ❶使窒息,使透不过气;把……闷死:The crowd ~ed me. 周围的人群挤得我透不过气来。❷把(火)闷熄:He tried to ~ the flames with a damp blanket. 他试图用湿毯子闷熄火苗。❸厚厚地覆盖:She ~ed her cake with cream. 她在饼子上涂了厚厚

一层奶油。❹掩饰;抑制;扼杀:~(up) a scandal 掩盖丑闻

smuggle /ˈsmʌgl/ *v.* 私运;偷运;走私:They ~d goods to some undeveloped countries. 他们把货物走私到一些不发达国家。

smuggling /ˈsmʌglɪŋ/ *n.* [U]走私活动

snack /snæk/ Ⅰ *n.* [C](正餐之间的)点心,小吃:I had a ~ on the train. 我在火车上吃了点心。Ⅱ *vi.* 吃快餐;吃点心:You can ~ on cake at noon. 中午你就吃点蛋糕填补一下吧。

snail /sneɪl/ *n.* [C] ❶蜗牛 ❷行动迟缓的人

snake /sneɪk/ *n.* [C]蛇

snap /snæp/ *vt.* (snapped; snapping) ❶猛咬:The dogs ~ped at our heels. 几条狗向着我们的脚后跟咬过来。❷突然折断,绷断:The wind had ~ped the tree in two. 风把树突然刮断了。

snapshot /ˈsnæpˌʃɒt/ *n.* [C] ❶快照 ❷概观,简要小结

snatch /snætʃ/ Ⅰ *v.* ❶抢;夺取:He ~ed the letter from me. 他从我手中抢去了那封信。❷迅速获得;趁机获取:~ an hour's sleep 趁机睡一小时 Ⅱ *n.* 抢;夺取;突袭

sneak /sniːk/ Ⅰ *vi.* 偷偷地走,悄悄地离开,溜,潜行:The thief took the suitcase and ~ed off. 那小偷拿起公文包,偷偷地溜走了。—*vt.* 悄悄地做;偷偷地拿(或给、吃、喝等):I ~ed a glance at Anna. 我偷偷地看了安娜一眼。Ⅱ *n.* [C]偷偷摸摸的人,鬼鬼祟祟的人

sneer /snɪə(r)/ *vi.* 嘲笑;讥笑(与 at 连用):~ at a poor girl 嘲笑一个可怜的女孩

sneeze /sniːz/ Ⅰ *n.* [C]喷嚏:Coughs and ~s spread diseases. 咳嗽和喷嚏传播疾病。Ⅱ *vi.* 打喷嚏:Use a handkerchief when you ~. 打喷嚏时应用手帕遮掩. / ~ **at** 轻视,不认为重要:John finished third in a race with thirty other runners. That is nothing to ~ at. 约翰在 30 名选手中跑第三,成绩不可小视。

sniff /snɪf/ *v.* (哧哧地)以鼻吸气:They all had colds and were ~ing and sneezing. 他们都感冒了,呼哧呼哧地吸气,并打喷嚏。

sniffle /ˈsnɪfl/ Ⅰ *v.* 抽鼻子;吸着鼻子说话 Ⅱ *n.* 抽鼻声

snob /snɒb/ *n.* [C]势利小人

snore /snɔː(r)/ *vi.* 打鼾;打呼噜

snow /snəʊ/ Ⅰ *n.* [U]雪:a heavy fall of ~下大雪 / roads deep in ~积雪很深的道路 Ⅱ *v.* [C]降雪:It ~ed all day. 雪下了一整天。

snowfall /ˈsnəʊˌfɔːl/ *n.* ❶[C]降雪:Heavy ~s this month relieved the desiccated land. 本月的几次大规模降雪使土地的旱情可以缓解。❷[U]降雪量:the average ~平均降雪量

snowflake /ˈsnəʊˌfleɪk/ *n.* [C]雪花,雪片:He watched the ~s dancing. 他看着雪花飞舞。

snowy /ˈsnəui/ *adj.* ❶雪的;下雪的;被雪覆盖的,积雪的:a ~ road 积雪的道路 ❷(天气等)多雪的:~ weather 多雪天气 ❸似雪的;雪白的,洁白的:a strand of ~ hair 一绺银发

snub /snʌb/ Ⅰ *vt.* (snubbed; snubbing)冷落,怠慢:She ~bed him by not inviting him to the party. 她故意冷落他,没有邀请他参加那个聚会。Ⅱ *n.* [C]冷落,怠慢:The move was a ~ to the government. 采取这一行动是对政

府的怠慢。

so / səʊ / Ⅰ *adv.* ❶这么,那么(表示程度):It is not ~ big as I thought it would be. 它没我想的那么大。/ Would you be ~ kind as to help me? 你能帮助我吗? / He was ~ ill that we had to send for a doctor. 他病得很厉害,我们必须去请医生。/ I'm ~ glad to see you! 见到你我真高兴! / It was ~ kind of you! 你真好! ❷像这样,像那样(表示状态):~ **far** 至此:Everything is in order ~ far. 迄今诸事顺遂。~ **long as** (=**as long as**)只要:I'll lend it to you ~ long as you return it next Sunday. 只要你下星期天还我,我就会借给你。~ **that** 为了;以便;以致;结果是:Speak clearly ~ that they may understand you. 说清楚些,以便他们能听懂你的话。~ ... **that** ... 以致:It ~ happened that I couldn't attend the meeting. 碰巧我无法参加会议。~ **as to** 以便;以致:He rose early ~ as to be in time for the first lesson. 他早起为的是赶上第一堂课。/ I will have everything ready ~ as not to keep you waiting. 我会准备好一切,不让你等候。**and** ~ **on**(**forth**)等等:She spends her day doing housework, watching television, reading, and ~ on. 她以做家务、看电视、看书等等度过一天。**or** ~ 大约:They arrived at the small town a month or ~ ago. 他们大约一个月前到达小镇的。Ⅱ *pron.* (常和动词 say, think, hope, suppose, tell 等连用,代替前文的词语和意思):—He has gone to Shanghai. —他去上海了。—I believe ~. —我想是去了。/—I went to the bookstore to look for that book and found it sold out. 我到书店去买那本书,发现已经卖完了。—I told you ~. 我早就告诉你了。Ⅲ *conj.* 因此;所以:The shops were closed ~ I couldn't get any. 商店都关门了,所以我什么也没买到。

soak / səʊk / *v.* 浸泡;(使)湿透:be ~ed to the skin 浑身湿透/ ~ in sunshine 沐浴在阳光里 / ~ in happiness 沉浸在幸福之中/ ~ oneself in the history 专心研究历史 / Soak the clothes in soapy water before washing. 洗之前把衣物放在肥皂水里泡一泡。

soap / səʊp / *n.* Ⅰ *n.* [U]肥皂;肥皂水:a bar (cake) of ~ 一块肥皂 Ⅱ *vt.* 涂肥皂于;用肥皂擦洗:He ~ed himself down and then stood under a hot shower. 他全身涂满肥皂,然后站在热水淋浴下冲洗。派 soapy *adj.*

soar / sɔː(r) / Ⅰ *vi.* ❶高飞,翱翔;升高,升腾:a wild hawk ~ing through heaven 搏击长空的鹞鹰 ❷剧增,猛增,飞涨:Banks failed; unemployment ~ed. 银行倒闭,失业率猛增。Ⅱ *n.* [C]高飞,猛增,高涨

sob / sɒb / Ⅰ *v.* (sobbed; sobbing)呜咽;啜泣;哭诉;呜咽着说:She ~bed out the story of her son's death in a traffic accident. 她呜咽着叙述她儿子死于车祸的经过。Ⅱ *n.* [C]呜咽;啜泣

so-called / ˌsəʊˈkɔːld / *adj.* 所谓的;号称的:We want no more of the ~ "help". 我们不再想要这种所谓的帮助了。

soccer / ˈsɒkə(r) / *n.* [C](美)足球

sociable / ˈsəʊʃəbl / *adj.* ❶好交际的;合群的:I was never a ~ fellow. 我本来就极不善交友。❷(场所、场合、活动等)友善的,友好的,融洽的:a ~ atmosphere 友善的氛围/~ places to work 气氛融洽的工作场所 派 sociability *n.*;sociably *adv.*

social /ˈsəʊʃl/ *adj.* ❶社会的：~ activity 社交活动 / ~ club 联谊会 / ~ customs 社会习俗 / ~ problem 社会问题 ❷群居的：~ ants 群居的蚂蚁

socialism /ˈsəʊʃəlɪzəm/ *n.* [U]社会主义

socialist /ˈsəʊʃəlɪst/ Ⅰ *adj.* 社会主义的 Ⅱ *n.* [C]社会主义者

society /səˈsaɪəti/ *n.* ❶[U]社会；社会体制 ❷[C]（为某种目的组成的）团体，会，社，协会：a ~ of engineers 工程师协会

sociology /ˌsəʊsɪˈɒlədʒi/ *n.* [U]社会学

sock /sɒk/ *n.* [C]短袜：a pair of ~s 一双袜子

socket /ˈsɒkɪt/ *n.* [C]插口；插座；管座

soda /ˈsəʊdə/ *n.* [U]❶碳酸钠；苏打 ❷苏打水：a bottle of orange ~ 一瓶橘子苏打水

sodium /ˈsəʊdɪəm/ *n.* [U]钠（符号 Na）

sofa /ˈsəʊfə/ *n.* [C]沙发

soft /sɒft/ *adj.* ❶软的；柔软的：Warm butter is ~. 温热的奶油是软的。❷（指光、颜色等）柔和的：lampshades that give a ~ light 使光线柔和的灯罩 ❸（指声音）轻柔的：~ music 轻柔的音乐/ in a ~ voice 轻声地 ❹（指空气、气候等）温和的，适合的：a ~ breeze (wind) 和风 / ~ weather 温和的气候 ❺（指饮料）软的（不含酒精的）派 softly *adv.* ；softness *n.*

softball /ˈsɒftˌbɔːl/ *n.* ❶[U]垒球运动 ❷[C]垒球

soften /ˈsɒfn/ *v.* ❶使变软，使软化；使温和；使缓和：The rain ~ed the surface. 雨水使得地表变得松软。❷使（灯光）变暗；使（声音）变轻；使（色彩）变淡：try to ~ the lighting 设法把照明弄暗

software /ˈsɒftweə(r)/ *n.* [U]（计算机的）软件；程序设备

soil /sɔɪl/ *n.* [U]土地；土壤：good (poor)~沃（瘠）土

solar /ˈsəʊlə(r)/ *adj.* 太阳的；日光的；与太阳有关的：~ calendar 太阳历 / ~ eclipse 日食 / ~ energy 太阳能 / the ~ system 太阳系

soldier /ˈsəʊldʒə(r)/ *n.* [C]（陆军）军人，士兵；战士：The children were playing at ~s. 孩子们在玩打仗的游戏。

sole /səʊl/ *adj.* 单独的；唯一的：~ agent 独家代理商 / ~ heir 唯一继承人 派 solely *adv.*

solemn /ˈsɒləm/ *adj.* ❶庄重的；郑重的：The government made a ~ statement yesterday. 政府昨天发表了一项郑重申明。❷表情严肃的；无笑容的：a ~ face 表情严肃的脸 派 solemnly *adv.* ; solemnness *n.*

solid /ˈsɒlɪd/ Ⅰ *adj.* 固体的：When water freezes and becomes ~, we call it ice. 水冻结成固体时，我们称它为冰。Ⅱ *n.* [C]固体 派 solidly *adv.*

solidarity /ˌsɒlɪˈdærəti/ *n.* [U]团结

solidify /səˈlɪdɪfaɪ/ *v.* 使团结

solitary /ˈsɒlɪtəri/ *adj.* ❶单独的，独自的：They were two ~ sufferers. 他们各人独自咀嚼自己的辛酸。❷唯一的，单一的：I can't think of a ~ example. 我一个例子也想不出来。❸独居的，隐居的：She lives a ~ life in a remote part of Ireland. 她独居于爱尔兰一个偏远的地区。❹荒凉的；僻静的；被冷落的，人迹罕至的：the ~ desert 荒凉的沙漠 派 solitariness *n.*

solo /ˈsəʊləʊ/ *n.* [C]（*pl.* solos 或 soli

S

/ˈsəʊliː/)独唱；独奏；独唱曲：sing a ~ 独唱 / violin ~ 小提琴独奏

soluble /ˈsɒljʊbl/ *adj*. ❶可溶的；可乳化的：a ~ powder 可溶性粉剂 ❷可解决的，能解除的：a ~ powder 可解决的问题

solution /səˈluːʃn/ *n*. ❶[C](问题等的)解答；(困难等的)解决办法：The ~ to (of) the problem required much time. 解决这个问题需要很多时间。❷[U]溶解：the ~ of sugar in tea 糖溶解于茶中

solve /sɒlv/ *vt*. 解答；解决：~ a problem 解决问题

some /sʌm/ Ⅰ *adj*. ❶一些(用于肯定句中，在疑问句、否定句、条件句以及有疑问、否定含义的句子中通常用 any)：There are ~ books on the table. 桌上有些书。/ Please give me ~ water. 请给我些水。❷某一个：Some Smith is waiting for you outside. 有一个叫史密斯的人在外边等你。/ ~ **day** (将来)总有一天；有朝一日 ~ **other day** 改日：We shall discuss it ~ other day. 我们改日再讨论这个问题。~ **time** 在某个时候；日后；有朝一日 Ⅱ *pron*. 一些：China has ~ of the finest scenery in the world. 中国有一些世界上最佳的风景。Ⅲ *adv*. 大约：That was ~ twenty years ago. 那大约是20年前的事。

somebody /ˈsʌmbədi/ Ⅰ *pron*. 某人；有人(在疑问句、否定句和条件句中用 anybody)：There is ~ at the door. 有人在门口。Ⅱ *n*. (只用单数)重要人物；著名人物

someday /ˈsʌmdeɪ/ *adv*. (今后)有一天；有朝一日：Someday she'll be famous. 总有一天她会成名的。

somehow /ˈsʌmhaʊ/ *adv*. ❶以某种方式；以某种手段：We must find money for the rent ~. 我们必须设法找到钱付租金。❷由于某种原因；不知为什么：Somehow I don't trust that man. 由于某种原因，我不信任那个人。

someone /ˈsʌmwʌn/ *pron*. 某人；有人

something /ˈsʌmθɪŋ/ *pron*. 某物；某事(在疑问句、否定句和条件句中用 anything)：There is ~ on the floor. 地上有一样东西。/~ **else** 另外的事；另外的东西：He said ~ else, but I didn't hear clearly. 他又说了些什么，但是我没有听清楚。~ **like** 大约；有点像：It looked ~ like a bird. 它看起来有点像一只鸟。~ **of** 在某种程度上；在某种意义上：She is ~ of a poet. 她略懂写诗。**have ~ to do with** 与……有关系：That has ~ to do with your future. 那和你的前途有关。**or ~**类似的什么；大概：He is a writer or ~. 他大概是个作家什么的。

sometime /ˈsʌmtaɪm/ *adv*. 在某一时间：I saw him ~ in May. 我在五月的某个时候见过他。

sometimes /ˈsʌmtaɪmz/ *adv*. 有时；不时；间或：Sometimes we go to the cinema and at other times we go for a walk. 有时我们去看电影，有时我们去散步。

someway(s) /ˈsʌmˌweɪ(z)/ *adv*. 以某种方式，不知怎么的

somewhat /ˈsʌmwɒt/ *adv*. 略；有点；稍：I was ~ surprised. 我有点惊讶。

somewhere /ˈsʌmweə(r)/ *adv*. ❶在某处；至某处(在疑问句、否定句和条件句中用 anywhere)：It must be ~ near here. 它一定就在附近某处。❷在(限定范围内)的某一点上；大约，左右：He was elderly, ~ in his mid-50's. 他上了年纪，有五十来岁的光景。

son /sʌn/ *n*. [C]儿子：He is the only ~

S

of the family. 他是家中的独子。

song /sɒŋ/ *n.* ❶[U]歌唱；声乐：the ~ of the birds 鸟的鸣唱 ❷[C]歌词；歌曲：a marching ~ 进行曲/ popular ~s 流行歌曲

sonic /ˈsɒnɪk/ *adj.* ❶声音的：Under water it is mostly a ~ world. 水下大多是声音的世界。❷声速的：aircraft travelling at ~ and supersonic speeds 声速的和超声速的飞行器

son-in-law /ˈsʌnɪnˌlɔː/ *n.* [C]（*pl.* sons-in-law）女婿

soon /suːn/ *adv.* ❶不久；很快：He will be here very ~. 他很快就到这里来。❷早；快：How ~ can you be ready? 你多久能准备好？/ Must you leave so ~? 你必须如此早就离开吗？/ ~ **after** 在……后不久：He arrived ~ after three. 他在三点后不久到达。**as (so) ~ as** 立即；不迟于；一……就……：He started as ~ as he received the news. 他一得到消息就立即动身了。~**er or later** 迟早；早晚：You will repent it ~er or later. 你迟早会后悔。**no ~er ... than ...** 刚……就……：I had no ~er left the house than it began to rain. 我刚离开屋子，天就下起雨来了。

soothe /suːð/ *vt.* ❶安慰，抚慰；使平静，使镇定：~ one's nerves 使自己变得心平气和/To ~ himself John read in his library. 约翰在书房读书，借以排愁解闷。❷减轻，缓解，缓和：I use it to ~ headaches. 我常常用它来缓解头疼。

sophisticated /səˈfɪstɪkeɪtɪd/ *adj.* ❶老于世故的；富有经验的 ❷复杂的；精密的；尖端的

sore /sɔː(r)/ *adj.*（指身体某部分）疼痛的

sorrow /ˈsɒrəʊ/ *n.* 悲哀；忧愁；悔恨：express ~ for having done wrong 对犯错表示悔恨 / to my great ~ 使我极为悲哀的是

sorrowful /ˈsɒrəʊfl/ *adj.*（令人）悲伤的；（令人）忧愁的

sorry /ˈsɒri/ *adj.*（只作表语）抱歉的；惭愧的；对不起的；难过的：We are very ~ to hear of your father's death. 听到你父亲去世的消息，我们甚为难过。/ I felt deeply ~ about (for) his mother's death. 他母亲过世使我深感难过。

sort /sɔːt/ Ⅰ *n.* [C]（人或物）群，类，种：Dance music is the ~ she likes most. 舞曲是她最喜欢的音乐。/ They have all ~s of goods. 他们有各种各样的货物。Ⅱ *vt.* 整理：~ (out) stamps 分类整理邮票

SOS, S. O. S. /ˌesəʊˈes/ *n.* [C]（*pl.* SOSs）❶（船只、飞机等使用的）国际无线电紧急求救信号 ❷紧急求救（或求助）

so-so /ˈsəʊsəʊ/ Ⅰ *adj.* 不好也不坏的，还过得去的 Ⅱ *adv.* 不好也不坏地，还过得去

soul /səʊl/ *n.* ❶灵魂：He eats hardly enough to keep body and ~ together. 他吃的食物几乎不够维持生命。❷热情：He put heart and ~ into the work. 他全身心投入工作。❸精髓；要旨；核心

sound[1] /saʊnd/ *adj.* ❶健全的；完好的；未受伤害的：have a ~ mind and a ~ body 有健全的身心 ❷正确的；合理的：~ advice 合理的建议 ❸彻底的；完全的：have a ~ sleep 酣睡

sound[2] /saʊnd/ Ⅰ *n.* 响声；声音：~ controller（计算机的）声卡 Ⅱ *vi.* 听起来；似乎：How sweet the music ~s! 这音乐听起来多悦耳！

soup /suːp/ *n.* [U]汤

sour / ˈsaʊə(r) / *adj.* 酸的;有酸味的

source / sɔːs / *n.* [C] ❶河的源头;水源;泉源:the ~s of the Nile 尼罗河的源头 / Where does the Rhine take its ~? 莱茵河发源于何处? ❷来源;出处:The news comes from a reliable ~. 这消息来源可靠。

south / saʊθ / Ⅰ *n.* 南部;南方:Mexico is to the ~ of the USA. 墨西哥在美国之南。Ⅱ *adj.* 南部的;南方的:the ~ entrance 南入口 Ⅲ *adv.* 在南方;在南部

southeast / ˌsaʊθˈiːst / *n.*, *adj.* & *adv.* 位于(向着、来自)东南(的)

southern / ˈsʌðən / *adj.* 在(向、来自)南方的:the ~ states of the USA 美国南方各州

southward(s) / ˈsaʊθwəd(z) / Ⅰ *adj.* 朝南的,向南的 Ⅱ *adv.* 朝南地,南向地:The ship's course lay ~. 这条船的航道向南伸展。Ⅲ *n.* [U]朝南的方向,南方;南部

southwest / ˌsaʊθˈwest / *n.*, *adj.* & *adv.* 位于(向着、来自)西南(的)

souvenir / ˌsuːvəˈnɪə(r), ˈsuːvənɪr / *n.* [C]纪念品

sovereign / ˈsɒvərɪn / Ⅰ *n.* [C]最高统治者;君主;元首;领袖;(某一领域的)掌权者;主宰:the eldest son of the ~国王的长子Ⅱ *adj.* ❶(权力、地位、级别等)最高的,至高无上的;难以超越的:the ~ body 最高权力机构/ maintain ~ power 维持至高无上的权力 ❷拥有主权的;主权独立的;自治的:~ states 主权国家

sovereignty / ˈsɒvərɪnti / *n.* [U] ❶最高权力;统治权:submit to sb. 's ~服从某人的统治 ❷主权;自治权(与 over 连用):China restored (resumed) its ~ over Hong Kong in 1997. 中国于1997年恢复对香港行使主权。

sow / səʊ / *v.* (sowed /səʊd/, sown /səʊn/或 sowed)播(种):~ a plot of land with grass seeds 在一块地里撒播青草种子

soy / sɒɪ / *n.* [U] ❶酱油 ❷大豆

soybean / ˈsɒɪbiːn / *n.* [C]大豆

space / speɪs / Ⅰ *n.* ❶[U]空间;太空 ❷空地;余地:clear a ~ on the platform for the speakers 在讲台上为演说者腾出地方 Ⅱ *vt.* 把……分隔开

spacecraft / ˈspeɪsˌkrɑːft, ˌspeɪsˈkræft / *n.* [C]航天飞行器,宇宙飞船,太空船

spacious / ˈspeɪʃəs / *adj.* 广阔的;广大的;宽敞的

spade / speɪd / *n.* [C]铲

span / spæn / Ⅰ *n.* [C] ❶一段时间:a ~ of 3 years 3 年期间 / life ~ 一生的时间;寿命 ❷跨距;跨度:The arch has a ~ of 50 meters. 这一拱跨度为 50 米。Ⅱ *vt.* (spanned; spanning)跨越:A bridge will ~ the river here. 这里将有一座大桥横跨过江。

spare / speə(r) / Ⅰ *v.* ❶匀出;挤出:We can't ~ the time for a holiday at present. 目前我们匀不出时间来度假。❷节约;节省:Some will spend and some will ~. 有人愿花钱,有人爱节约。Ⅱ *adj.* 多余的;剩余的;备用的:I have no ~ time (money). 我没有闲暇(闲钱)。

sparing / ˈspeərɪŋ / *adj.* ❶节省的,节俭的;吝惜的:The girl was ~ with her smiles. 那姑娘不苟言笑。❷有节制的;谨慎的:He advised ~ use of melodramatic tactics. 他建议夸张手法要慎用。派 sparingly *adv.*

spark / spɑːk / *n.* [C] 火星;火花:The

fireworks burst into a shower of ~s. 烟火爆发出一簇火花。

sparkle /ˈspɑːkl/ Ⅰ *vi.* 发光;闪烁;闪耀:Her diamonds ~d in the bright light. 她的钻石在亮光下闪闪发光。Ⅱ *n.* 火花;闪光

sparrow /ˈspærəʊ/ *n.* [C]麻雀

sparse /spɑːs/ *adj.* ❶稀疏的;稀少的;零散的:~ woodlands 树木稀少的林地/ ~ population 稀疏的人口 ❷(人或动物)瘦小的;(土地等)不毛的;贫弱的:~ vegetation 贫瘠的植被 派 sparsely *adv.*;sparseness *n.*

speak /spiːk/ (spoke /spəʊk/, spoken /ˈspəʊkən/) *vi.* 说话:The baby is learning to ~. 这小孩在学说话。/ ~ **highly of** 赞扬;称赞:The manager spoke highly of our success. 经理赞扬了我们的成功。~ **of** 提到;讲到:He often ~s of the old days when he was in the countryside. 他常常谈到他过去在农村的日子。**frankly ~ing** 坦白地说 **generally ~ing** 一般来说;总的来说 ~ **out** ①大声地说:The teacher told the shy boy to ~ out. 老师叫这害羞的男孩大声说。②毫不犹豫地说:Stand up and ~ out for the President's whole program. 站起来为总统的整个计划发言吧。—*vt.* 说(某种语言);说明:~ the truth 说实话/ He ~s several languages. 他说数种语言。/ Is English spoken here? 这里说英语吗?

speaker /ˈspiːkə(r)/ *n.* [C] ❶说话者;演讲者:fast ~说话快的人 / guest ~应邀演讲的人 / The ~ was loudly applauded. 演讲者赢得响亮的掌声。❷讲某种语言的人:Speakers of English like to use this word. 说英语的人都喜欢用这个词。❸扬声器;话筒

speaking /ˈspiːkɪŋ/ Ⅰ *n.* 说话;演讲:develop the skill of ~ 发展说话能力 Ⅱ *adj.* 发言的;交谈的

spear /spɪə(r)/ *n.* [C]矛;梭镖

special /ˈspeʃ(ə)l/ *adj.* 特别的;特殊的;特设的;专用的:What are your ~ interests? 你的特殊兴趣是什么? / On holidays the railways put on ~ trains. 在假日,铁路当局加派专车。派 specially *adv.*

specialist /ˈspeʃəlɪst/ *n.* [C]专家(尤指医科的):a ~ in plastic surgery 整形外科专家

specialization /ˌspeʃəlaɪˈzeɪʃn/ *n.* [U] 专门化;专业化

specialize /ˈspeʃəlaɪz/ *v.* 专门研究;专攻:~ in chemistry 专攻化学 派 specialized *adj.*

specialty /ˈspeʃəlti/ *n.* [C](企业、工厂的)拳头产品,特色产品,特种工艺:The company's ~ is the manufacture of high performance cars. 这家公司的拳头产品是高性能汽车。/They dined on the restaurant ~. 他们吃了这家餐馆的特色菜肴。

species /ˈspiːʃiːz/ *n.* [C](单复数同形)物种;种类;有共同特点的一群:many ~ of advertisement 许多种类的广告 / Wheat is a ~ of grass. 小麦是草本植物的一种。

specific /spəˈsɪfɪk/ *adj.* ❶明确的;具体的:Have you made any ~ plan? 你制订具体的计划了吗?❷特有的;特定的

specify /ˈspesɪfaɪ/ *vi.* 详细说明;明确规定:Remember to ~ your size when order-ing clothes. 订购服装时记着要详细说明你的尺码。

specimen /ˈspesɪmən/ *n.* [C]样品;标

本:collect insect ~s 采集昆虫标本 /~s of rocks and ores 岩石和矿石标本/The doctor needs a ~ of your blood. 医生需要你的血样。

spectacle /ˈspektəkl/ *n.* [C](常用 *pl.*)眼镜;护目镜

spectator /spekˈteɪtə(r)/ *n.* [C]观众;旁观者

spectrum /ˈspektəm/ *n.* [C](*pl.*-tra /-trə/或-trums) ❶光谱 ❷频谱;射频频谱 ❸电磁波谱 ❹范围;幅度;系列:A broad ~ of topological features creates a pleasant landscape. 各种各样的地貌构成了一幅宜人的风景画。

speculate /ˈspekjʊˌleɪt/ *vi.* ❶臆想;推断,猜测:They talked and ~d until after midnight. 他们一直谈论和分析到半夜。/ I wouldn't like to ~ about the price of that car. 我不想对那部汽车的价格做推断。❷思考;沉思;冥想:~ on one's future 考虑自己的前途 ❸投机:They ~ on a rise or fall. 他们利用价格上的涨跌发财。

speech /spiːtʃ/ *n.* ❶[U]说话;说话的能力:Our thoughts are expressed by ~. 我们的思想通过说话表达。❷[C]演说:make a ~ 发表演说

S

speechless /ˈspiːtʃlɪs/ *adj.* 一时语塞的:Consternation and disgust held me ~. 惊愕与厌恶使我一时语塞。/ She stood ~ with shame. 她羞得悄立无言。

speed /spiːd/ Ⅰ *n.* 迅速;快;速度 / **at a ~ of** 以……的速度:drive at a ~ of 50 miles an hour 以每小时 50 英里的速度行驶 **at full (top)~** 全(高)速行进 Ⅱ *v.* ❶(sped /sped/, sped 或 speeded, speeded) 快速行进:He sped down the street. 他沿街疾步行走。❷使加速;违章超速驾驶:The medicine ~ed her recovery. 这药加速了她的痊愈。

speedy /ˈspiːdi/ *adj.* 快的;迅速的

spell[1] /spel/ *v.* (spelled, spelled 或 spelt /spelt/, spelt) 拼(字的)字母;拼写:How do you ~ your name? 你的名字如何拼?

spell[2] /spel/ Ⅰ *n.* [C] ❶一段工作时间;轮班,轮值:He had a ~ in Congress. 他当过一段时间的国会议员。/We took ~s (with) doing the painting. 我们轮流刷漆。❷(疾病等的)发作,一阵:a dizzy ~一阵突如其来的头晕目眩/a ~ of cough-ing一阵咳嗽 ❸一段(较短的)时间;一会儿:a ~ of trench warfare 短暂的堑壕阵地战/ I lived in New York for a ~. 我在纽约住过一段时间。❹(一种天气的)一段持续期:There will be a cold ~ in a week. 一周之内将有一次寒潮。Ⅱ *vt.* 替……的班:I'd like to ~ you at doing the washing. 我想替你刷刷碗。

spelling /ˈspelɪŋ/ *n.* 拼读;拼写;拼写法:Do you use English ~(s) or American ~(s)?你用英式拼写法还是美式拼写法?

spend /spend/ *v.* (spent/spent/, spent) ❶用(钱);花费:~ a lot of care on sth. 在某事上花了许多心血 / He spent a lot of money in entertaining his friends. 他花了许多钱招待朋友。/ You should ~ more time looking after your child. 你应当多花点时间照顾孩子。/ Don't ~ too much money on clothes. 不要把太多的钱花在买衣服上。❷度过;消磨:~ a weekend in London 在伦敦度周末

sphere /sfɪə(r)/ *n.* [C] ❶球(体);地球仪:The teacher showed us China on the ~. 老师在地球仪上指出中国的位置给我们看。❷范围;领域:political ~ 政治领域 /within one's ~ 在某人的能力(活

动)范围之内

spherical / ˈsferɪkl / *adj*. 球形的;球面的

spice / spaɪs / Ⅰ *n*. ❶香料;调料品 ❷情趣;趣味;风味:The story was rather lacking in ~. 这则故事枯燥无味。Ⅱ *vt*. ❶加香料于;给……调味:The cook ~d up tuna fish by adding curry powder to it. 厨师往金枪鱼里面加了咖喱粉调味。❷使增添情趣;给……增加趣味:a book ~d with humour 一部颇有幽默情趣的书

spicy / ˈspaɪsi / *adj*. ❶加香料的;有香味的:The wood was ~ with the odour of pine and cedar. 树林里散发着松树和杉树的香味。❷辛辣的,刺激性的:Of course you do find ~ bits in Paris. 你当然会在巴黎找到一些刺激。

spider / ˈspaɪdə(r) / *n*. [C]蜘蛛

spill / spɪl / Ⅰ *n*. [C]溢出:Please clean up the soup ~s on the chair. 请把洒在椅子上的汤擦干净。Ⅱ *v*. (spilled, spilled 或 spilt/spɪlt/, spilt)(使)溢出;(使)洒落:The tea has spilt on the tea table. 茶水溢到茶几上了。

spin / spɪn / *v*. (spun/spʌn/, spun) ❶纺纱;纺线 ❷使(某物)旋转:to ~ a ball(coin, wheel)转动球(硬币,轮子)

spinach / ˈspɪnɪdʒ, ˈspɪnɪtʃ / *n*. [U] ❶菠菜 ❷(食用的)菠菜叶

spine / spaɪn / *n*. [C] ❶脊椎;脊柱 ❷突起结构;刺激 ❸精神;骨气;勇气:No one has the ~ to sound off. 没有人勇气发表意见。❹书脊

spiral / ˈspaɪrəl / *adj*. 螺旋形的;盘旋的

spirit / ˈspɪrɪt / *n*. ❶精神;心灵:be in high (low) ~s 情绪高昂(低落) / party ~ 党性 / team ~ (组或队成员的)协作(集体、团队)精神 / I shall be with you in ~. 我将从精神上支持你。❷[C]幽灵;妖怪;鬼怪

spiritual / ˈspɪrɪtʃʊəl / *adj*. 精神的;心灵的:~ civilization 精神文明 / ~ values 精神财富 / ~ outlook 精神面貌

spit / spɪt / *v*. (spat/spæt/, spat 或 spit, spit)吐(唾液);吐痰:If you ~ in the street, you may be fined. 如果你在街上吐痰,可能被处以罚款。/ ~ **out** 吐出:The baby spat out the pill. 那小孩吐出了药丸。

spite / spaɪt / *n*. [U]恶意;怨恨:do sth. out of a private ~ 出于个人怨恨做某事 / **in ~ of** 不管;不顾:I went out in ~ of the rain. 尽管下雨,我还是出去了。

splash / splæʃ / *v*. ❶溅(水等);泼湿(某人或某物):~ water on (over) the floor 把水泼到地板上 ❷(水)飞溅;溅起水花:The fountain in the park ~es all day. 这个公园中的喷泉整日飞溅。/ We ~ed (our way) across the stream. 我们蹚着水走过小溪。

splendid / ˈsplendɪd / *adj*. 壮美的;壮丽的;辉煌的:a ~ sunset 壮美的夕阳 / a ~ victory 辉煌的胜利

splendo(u)r / ˈsplendə(r) / *n*. [U]❶光彩;光辉;壮丽;壮观;豪华:the ~ of a sunset 落日的壮丽/The welcoming ceremony was conducted with modest ~. 举行的欢迎仪式虽简单但不失庄严。❷(名声等的)显赫;(业绩等的)卓著:the lofty ~ of sb.'s office 某人职位的显赫

split / splɪt / *v*. (split, split) ❶(使)裂开;(被)劈开:Some kinds of wood ~ easily. 有些木头容易劈开。❷分裂;断绝关系:He ~ with his wife several years ago. 他几年前跟他妻子离婚了。/ The party ~ up into three small groups. 该党分裂成三个小派别。

spoil / spɒɪl / *v.* (spoilt/spɒɪlt/, spoilt 或 spoiled, spoiled) ❶损害；破坏；糟蹋：fruits ~t by insects 被昆虫糟蹋的水果/ holidays ~t by bad weather 被坏天气破坏的假日 ❷宠坏；溺爱；姑息：parents who ~ their children 溺爱孩子的父母们 ❸(指食物等)变坏；腐败：Some kinds of food easily ~. 有些食物很快就腐败了。

spokesman / ˈspəʊksmən / *n.* [C] (*pl.* spokesmen) 发言人；代言人：He acts as the ~ for the company. 他是公司的代言人。

sponge / spʌndʒ / *n.* 海绵；海绵状物

sponsor / ˈspɒnsə(r) / Ⅰ *n.* [C] 发起者；主办者；担保人；赞助人：~ country 发起国 / ~ of a bill 议案的提出者 Ⅱ *vt.* ❶发起；主办：The flower show was ~ed by a park. 花展由一个公园主办。❷资助；赞助：The television program is ~ed by an oil company. 这个电视节目由一个石油公司赞助。

spontaneous / spɒnˈteɪnɪəs / *adj.* ❶自发的；非由外力诱发的：~ volunteers 自发的志愿者/ make a ~ offer of one's services 自动提供服务 ❷(动机等)无意识的，不由自主的：a ~ burst of laughter 不由自主发出的笑声 ❸(举止等)自然的，非勉强的；(人)天真率直的：a ~ display of affection 情感的自然流露 派 spontaneously *adv.*

spoon / spuːn / *n.* [C] 匙；调羹：salt ~ 盐匙 / tea ~ 茶匙 / soup ~ 汤匙 / be born with a silver ~ in one's mouth 出生在富贵人家 派 spoonful *n.* & *adj.*

sport / spɔːt / *n.* ❶[U] 娱乐；消遣；玩笑：say sth. in ~ 说着玩 ❷[C] (户外)运动；游戏：have ~s 进行体育活动 / a ~s meet 运动会 / Fishing is a popular ~ among the villagers. 钓鱼是这儿村民普遍从事的运动。

sportsman / ˈspɔːtsmən/ *n.* [C] (*pl.* sportsmen) 运动员：first-grade ~ 一级运动员

spot / spɒt / *n.* [C] ❶点；斑点；亮点：white dress material with red ~s 有红点的白色衣料 ❷地点；场所；位置：the ~ where he was murdered 他被谋杀的地点 / **on the ~** 当场；在现场

spotlight / ˈspɒtˌlaɪt / *n.* ❶[C] (舞台等的)聚光灯；聚光灯照明圈 ❷[U] 引人注意的中心；受瞩目的焦点：A young star sprang into the ~. 一位年轻的明星突然备受瞩目。

spotted / ˈspɒtɪd / *adj.* 有斑点的：the ~ furs 有斑点的毛皮/a red and yellow ~ handkerchief 有红黄两色斑点的手帕

spout / spaʊt / Ⅰ *v.* ❶喷出，喷射：Steam came ~ing out of hole. 蒸汽开始从孔中喷出来。❷不停地讲，滔滔不绝地说：Every cab-driver in town can ~ facts and gossip. 城里的出租车司机个个都特别能侃。Ⅱ *n.* [C] ❶(壶)嘴；(喷泉、水泵等的)喷口，喷嘴 ❷(喷出或流出的)水柱，水流：~s and gusts of oil 喷涌而出的石油

spray / spreɪ / Ⅰ n. [U] 水沫；水雾；浪花：sea ~ 海水浪花 Ⅱ *v.* 喷射；喷洒：~ the enemy with bullets 用子弹扫射敌人

spread / spred / Ⅰ *v.* (spread, spread) ❶展开；铺开：~ the cloth on a table 把桌布铺在桌上 / The bird ~ its wings. 鸟儿展翅。❷撒；播：~ fertilizers 施肥 / ~ butter on bread 将黄油抹在面包上 ❸(使)传播；流传：~ knowledge 传播知

识 / ~ from mouth to mouth 口口相传 / ~ through the village 传遍全村 / ~ to neighboring countries 蔓延到了邻国 / Flies ~ diseases. 苍蝇传播疾病。Ⅱ *n.* 传播；蔓延：have a broad ~ 广为传播

spring[1] / sprɪŋ / *n.* 春天；春季：in (the) ~ 在春天 / Spring Festival 春节 / Spring is the first season of the year. 春季是一年的第一个季节。

spring[2] / sprɪŋ / Ⅰ *v.* (sprang/spræŋ/, sprung /sprʌŋ/) ❶跳；跃；使……弹开：He sprang out of bed. 他从床上跳下来。❷(突然)出现：A storm sprang up. 风暴突然兴起。Ⅱ *n.* [C] ❶跳跃 ❷泉水：hot ~ 温泉 / mineral ~矿泉 ❸弹簧；发条：a watch ~ 表的发条 派 springy *adj.*

sprout / spraʊt / Ⅰ *n.* [C] (植物的)苗，芽 Ⅱ *v.* 发芽；生枝

spur / spɜː(r) / Ⅰ *n.* [C] ❶踢马刺，马靴刺 ❷激发；激励，鼓舞；鞭策：The book is a ~ to imagination. 这本书能够激发想象力。/**on the ~ of the moment** 一时冲动地；不假思索地；当场，即兴地：She could not possibly make such a decision on the ~ of the moment. 她不可能一时冲动做出这样的决定。Ⅱ *vt.* (spurred; spurring) ❶用踢马刺策(马)：He ~red the horse through the storm. 他在暴风雨中策马奔驰。❷刺激；激发(兴趣等)；鼓舞，激励；鞭策：~ on one's efforts 再接再厉/~ scientific interest 激发科学兴趣

spy / spaɪ / Ⅰ *n.* [C] ❶间谍 ❷侦探 Ⅱ *v.* 侦察：~ upon the enemy's movements 侦察敌人的动向

squad / skwɒd / *n.* [C] ❶小分队：an anti-terrorist ~反恐怖小分队 ❷(军队中的)班 ❸参赛队；球队

square / skweə(r) / Ⅰ *n.* [C] ❶正方形；方形物：a ~ of glass 一块方形的玻璃 / draw a ~ 画一个正方形 ❷平方；二次幂：Four is the ~ of two. 四是二的平方。❸直角尺；丁字尺 ❹广场：Tian'anmen Square 天安门广场 Ⅱ *vt.* 使成正方形；使方正；调整，改正 Ⅲ *adj.* ❶正方形的；成直角的：~ table 方桌 ❷平方的 ❸公正的：play a ~ game 公平比赛 派 squarely *adv.*

squash / skwɒʃ / Ⅰ *vt.* 把……压扁(或压碎)；把……挤碎；(用力)挤压：~ the cans (cartons) 压扁罐子(纸盒子) / These strawberries were at the bottom of the bag and had all got ~ed. 草莓在袋子底下，全都被挤坏了。Ⅱ *n.* 鲜果汁

squeeze / ˈskwiːz / Ⅰ *v.* ❶(尤指用手指)挤压，挤；紧握：He ~d with all his strength. 他用尽全力挤压。❷榨取；挤取：Squeeze out as much juice as you can. 尽可能多挤些汁液出来。❸榨取，压榨：Councils will want to ~ as much money out of taxpayers as they can. 各地方议会都想方设法地从纳税人那里榨取尽可能多的钱财。Ⅱ *n.* [C]挤；捏；紧握

squirrel / ˈskwɪrəl / *n.* [C]松鼠

stab / stæb / Ⅰ *v.* (stabbed; stabbing) 刺；戳：The thief ~bed the boy with a dagger. 小偷用匕首刺那男孩。Ⅱ *n.* [C]刺；戳

stability / stəˈbɪləti / *n.* [U]坚定；稳定；巩固：~ and unity 安定团结 / economic ~ 经济稳定 / political ~ 政治稳定

stabilize / ˈsteɪbɪlaɪz / *vt.* 使稳定：~ prices 稳定物价 / ~ the market 稳定市场

S

stable[1] / ˈsteɪbl / *adj*. 稳定的;不变的:~ life 稳定的生活 / ~ rate of exchange 稳定的汇率 / Prices remain ~. 物价稳定。

stable[2] / ˈsteɪbl / *n*. [C]马厩;牛棚

stack / stæk / Ⅰ *n*. [C](整齐的)堆,垛:a ~ of papers 一堆文件 Ⅱ *vt*. 把……叠成堆;使堆积:~ up books 把书堆起来

stadium / ˈsteɪdɪəm / *n*. [C](*pl*. stadiums 或 stadia)体育场;运动场:the Capital Stadium 首都体育场

staff / stɑːf / *n*. [C](集合名词)全体职员;全体工作人员:the headmaster and his ~ 校长及其教职员工们 / be on the ~ 为正式职员/ change on the ~ 人事变动 / cut down (reduce) the ~ 裁减人员

stage / steɪdʒ / *n*. [C] ❶舞台 ❷时期;阶段:at an early ~ in history of our country 在我国历史的早期 / a three-~ rocket 三级火箭

stagger / ˈstægə(r) / *v*. 蹒跚;摇晃:The man ~ed across the room. 那人蹒跚地走过房间。

staggered / ˈstægə(r)d / *adj*. ❶(感到)震惊的;迷惑的:a ~ look on her face 她脸上震惊的表情 ❷(位置或时间)交错的;错开的:a ~ row of chairs 错开排列的一排椅子/ under a ~ schedule 按错开的日程安排

stagnant / ˈstægnənt / *adj*. ❶(液体等)停滞的,不流动的:a ~ calm of air and ocean 空气和大海如凝固般的平静 ❷不发展的,停顿的;呆滞的;缺乏活力的:Measures must be taken to revive the long ~ industry. 必须采取措施搞活停滞已久的工业。

stain / steɪn / Ⅰ *v*. 玷污;染污:a tablecloth ~ed with gravy 沾有肉汁的桌布 Ⅱ *n*. [C]污渍;污点 派 stained *adj*.

stair / steə(r) / *n*. [C]楼梯;阶梯:escape ~ 安全楼梯 / screw ~ 螺旋楼梯 / I passed her on the ~s. 我在楼梯上遇见她。

stake / steɪk / *n*. ❶[C]桩;标桩:tie a horse to a ~ 把马拴在桩上 ❷[C]赌金;赌注:We play for fun, not for ~s. 我们是玩而不是赌钱。❸[C]股份:sell off one's ~ 出售股份 ❹利害关系 / **at ~** 在危险中:The child's life was then at ~. 那孩子当时有生命危险。

stale / steɪl / *adj*. ❶陈腐的;过时的:~ news 过时的消息 / ~ water 死水 / Running water never gets ~. 流水不腐。❷不新鲜的:~ fish 不新鲜的鱼 / ~ bread 陈面包 派 stalely *adv*. ;staleness *n*.

stall / stɔːl / *n*. [C] ❶货摊;书摊 ❷厩

stammer / ˈstæmə(r) / Ⅰ *vt*. 口吃;口吃地说:Five percent of children ~ at some point. 5%的儿童在某个时期会口吃。Ⅱ *n*. 口吃

stamp / stæmp / Ⅰ *n*. [C] ❶邮票;印花:cancel a ~ 用邮戳盖销邮票 / stick a ~ on a letter 给信上贴邮票 ❷章;图章 Ⅱ *v*. ❶贴邮票 ❷印(图案等)于(纸、布上等) ❸顿(足);踏:~ the ground 在地上跺脚 / The girl ~ed her feet with anger. 那女孩气得跺脚。/ **~ out** ①踏灭;踩熄:He ~ed out the fire. 他将火踏灭了。②消灭;镇压:The invaders were ~ed out at last. 入侵者终于被消灭了。

stand / stænd / Ⅰ *v*. (stood/stʊd/, stood)❶站;立:We had to ~ all the way back in the bus. 在回程的公共汽车上,我们只能站着。/ Everyone stood up when the teacher entered. 老师进来时,全体起立。❷忍受;忍耐:He can't ~

the hot weather. 他不能忍受这炎热的天气。/ ~ **at attention** 立正：You can't make the men ~ at attention for the whole afternoon. 你不能让这些人整个下午立正站着。~ **by** ①站在旁边：He stood by me at yesterday's gathering. 在昨天的集会上，他站在我旁边。②旁观：How can you ~ by so cruelly? 你怎能如此残酷地袖手旁观呢？③援助，支持；向……表示友好：I'll ~ by you whatever happens. 不论发生何事，我都支持你。~ **for** 代表；代替：P. O. ~s for Post Office or postal order. P. O. 代表 Post Office(邮局)或 postal order(邮政汇票)。~ **in the way** 妨碍；挡住去路 ~ **on end** 直立；竖立 ~ **out** 清晰地显出；引人注目：The notice ~s out clearly. 那则通知很引人注目。~**up for** 支持；维护；保卫：He is always ready to ~ up for truth. 他随时准备维护真理。~ **up to** ①勇敢地面对；抵抗 ②经得起(磨难等)；顶得住(磨难等)：~ up to any hardships (severe test)经得住任何艰难困苦(严峻考验) Ⅱ *n.* [C] ❶立足地；立场：take one's ~ at (in) 站在……立场上 / I can't see his ~. 我看不出他的立场是什么。/**take one's ~ for (against)** 表明立场支持(反对)：I hope you take your ~ for us. 我希望你表明立场支持我们。❷售货台；售货摊

standard /ˈstændəd/ Ⅰ *n.* [C]标准；规格：below the ~ 低于标准/ up to the ~ 达到标准 / The living ~ of the people has been raised greatly. 人民的生活水平极大地提高了。Ⅱ *adj.* 标准的：~ time 标准时间 / It is not so difficult to learn to speak ~ English. 学说标准英语并不难。派 standardize(-se) *vt.*

stand-by /ˈstændˌbaɪ/ Ⅰ *n.* [C] (*pl.* stand-bys) ❶忠实的支持者；坚定的追随者 ❷替补人员；备用品；代用品：Board games are a good ~ to keep the children amused if the weather is bad. 天气不好可以让孩子们下棋玩，也不失为一个好办法。Ⅱ *adj.* ❶备用的，应急的；代用的：They would have the ~ generators on in a minute or two. 他们将马上启动备用发动机。❷待命的；替补的：~ crew for firefighting 整装待命的消防队

standing /ˈstændɪŋ/ Ⅰ *n.* [C] ❶站立；站立的位置 ❷声望；地位；身份；级别：persons of considerable ~ in the academic community 学术界具有很高威望的人 ❸(成绩的)排名；(*pl.*)(体育比赛中的成绩)名次表：on top of the ~s 名列排名榜前列 Ⅱ *adj.* ❶站立的；直立的；立式的：a ~ electric fan 落地电扇 ❷长期维持的；长期有效的；常任的：She left her jobless state as a ~ burden to her parents. 她觉得自己没有工作，成了父母长期的包袱。❸停转的；停住的；停顿的：The shortage of materials put the factory in a ~ condition. 由于原材料短缺，这家工厂处于停产状态。❹(液体)不流动的，静止的

standpoint /ˈstændpɒɪnt/ *n.* [C]立场；观点：We should look at the problem from a historical ~. 我们应当从历史的角度看待这个问题。

standstill /ˈstændˌstɪl/ *n.* 停顿；停止；停滞：All train services are at a ~ today in a dispute over pay. 因为工资纠纷，今天所有的火车服务都停顿了。/The wheels sank in the mud and the car came to a ~. 车轮陷入泥里，轿车开不动了。

star /stɑː(r)/ *n.* [C] ❶星，星球 ❷明

S

星;主角;名家:Hollywood film ~s 好莱坞电影明星

stare /steə(r)/ *v.* 盯,凝视(与 at 连用):~ into the distance 凝视远方 / ~ sb. in the face 盯着某人的脸;就在某人面前 / ~ with surprise 目瞪口呆 / The little girl ~d at the toys in the window. 小女孩盯着橱窗里的玩具。

start /stɑːt/ Ⅰ *v.* ❶开始;着手:It ~ed raining (to rain). 天开始下雨了。❷出发;动身:I shall ~ for Beijing tomorrow. 我明天动身去北京。❸(因痛苦、惊愕、恐惧等)惊起,惊动:He ~ed at the sound of my voice. 他听到我的声音吓了一跳。❹发动;使开始:He can't ~ the car. 他不能启动这辆汽车。Ⅱ *n.* ❶起程;动身;着手:make an early ~早些动身(或着手) ❷(因惊愕、恐惧等)惊起:He sat up with a ~. 他一惊而起。

startle /ˈstɑːtl/ Ⅰ *vt.* 使大吃一惊:The man ~d to see that his son was jumping down from a truck. 那人吃惊地看见他儿子正从一辆卡车上往下跳。Ⅱ *n.* 吃惊

starvation /stɑːˈveɪʃn/ *n.* [U]饥饿:die of ~ 饿死 / ~ wages 不能糊口的工资 / struggle on the verge of ~ 在饥饿线上挣扎

starve /stɑːv/ *v.* ❶(使)挨饿;(使)饿死:~ to death 饿死/ The man said he would ~ rather than beg for food. 那人说他宁愿挨饿也不乞食。❷感觉饥饿:Is there anything to eat? I'm starving. 有什么吃的没有?我觉得饿了。

state /steɪt/ Ⅰ *n.* [C]❶(只用单数)情形,状态:The house was in a dirty ~. 那栋房子非常脏。❷(常用 State)国家;领土:Railways in Great Britain belong to the State. 英国的铁路属于国家所有。❸(常用 State)州;邦:How many States are there in the United States of America? 美国有多少个州?Ⅱ *vt.*(尤指仔细、详尽地)说,陈述:~ one's view 陈述观点

statement /ˈsteɪtmənt/ *n.* [C]语言表达;叙述,陈述;声明:Clearness of ~ is more important than beauty of language. 陈述清楚比语言优美更重要。/ make (issue) a ~ 发表声明 / a bank ~ 银行报告;银行结单

statesman /ˈsteɪtsmən/ *n.* [C](*pl.* statesmen)政治家;国务活动家

station /ˈsteɪʃn/ Ⅰ *n.* [C] ❶车站;办公室;站,所:gas (service) ~ 汽车加油站 / a space ~ 宇航(空间)站 / the ~ waiting room 候车室 / broadcasting ~ 广播站 / bus ~ 公共汽车站 / comfort ~ 公共厕所 / fire ~ 消防站 / police ~ 警察局/ power ~ 发电站 / radar ~ 雷达站 / railway ~ 火车站 / TV ~ 电视台 / weather ~ 气象站(台) ❷陆军或海军基地;驻扎人员 Ⅱ *v.* 驻扎;安置;配置

stationary /ˈsteɪʃənəri/ *adj.* ❶固定的;静止的;停滞的:~ shadows 静止的影子 ❷原地不动的;非移动式的,落地的:We were ~ at a set of traffic lights when a police car passed by us. 一辆警车从我们身边驶过,我们站在一组交通信号灯边一动不动。

stationery /ˈsteɪʃən(ə)ri/ *n.* [U]文具;信笺

statistical /stəˈtɪstɪkl/ *adj.* 统计的;统计学的:~ chart 统计图/ ~ data 统计资料 / ~ figure 统计数字 / ~ table 统计表 派 statistically *adv.*

statistics /stəˈtɪstɪks/ *n.* 统计;统计学;统计数字;统计资料:analyze ~ 分析统计资料

S

statue / ˈstætʃuː / *n.* [C]雕像;塑像;铸像:There is a ~ to Dr. Sun Yatsen in Nanjing. 南京有一座孙中山先生的雕像。

stature / ˈstætʃə(r) / *n.* [U] ❶身高;身材:a man of short ~身材矮小的男人/a girl who is big in ~ 大个子的姑娘 ❷(与行为、能力等相对应而具有的)声誉,名望;境界;高度,水平:sb.'s ~ in literary world 某人在文学界的声望

status / ˈsteɪtəs / *n.* [U]地位;身份;职位:economic (political) ~ 经济(政治)地位

statute / ˈstætjuːt / *n.* 立法机关通过的法令,法规,成文法:The salaries of most federal workers are ste by ~. 联邦工人的薪水有明令规定。

stay / steɪ / Ⅰ *v.* ❶停留;保持(位置或状况):~ in bed 待在床上 / I can ~ only a few minutes. 我只能停留几分钟。/ ~ **up** 不睡觉;熬夜:He ~ed up late to prepare for the final examination. 他熬夜准备期末考试。❷阻止;延缓;遏制:~ the progress of a disease 阻止疾病蔓延 Ⅱ *n.* [C] ❶停留;逗留时间 ❷延续

stead / sted / *n.* [U](职位、身份、作用等的)代替;接替:run the meeting in sb.'s ~代替某人主持会议/The publisher appointed someone unknown in his ~. 出版社指定了一位不知名的人来接替他。

steadily / ˈstedɪli / *adv.* ❶坚固地;稳定地;不变地 ❷逐步地;不断地:His health gets worse ~. 他的健康状况不断恶化。

steady / ˈstedi / *adj.* (-ier,-iest) 坚固的;不动摇的:on a ~ foundation 在牢固的基础上

steak / steɪk / *n.* (尤指)牛排;猪排;鱼排

steal / stiːl / *v.* (stole/stəʊl/, stolen /ˈstəʊlən/) ❶偷;窃取:Someone has stolen my watch. 有人偷了我的手表。❷溜进;溜走:He stole into the room. 他溜进房间。

steam / stiːm / Ⅰ *n.* [U]蒸汽;水汽:a building heated by ~ 有暖气的建筑物 Ⅱ *v.* ❶蒸发;冒蒸汽 ❷蒸煮:~ fish 蒸鱼

steel / stiːl / *n.* [U]钢

steep / stiːp / *adj.* 陡的:a ~ roof 陡斜的屋顶 / ~ rise in output 产量的激增

steer / stɪə(r) / *v.* 驾驶;操纵:~ing-wheel(船上的)舵轮;(车上的)方向盘

stem / stem / *n.* [C]茎;树干;(叶)梗

step / step / Ⅰ *v.* (stepped;stepping)走;跨步;步行:~ onto (off) the platform 走向(离开)平台 / ~ on the gas 踩油门 / ~ **aside** 让到一旁;避开:Please ~ aside to let me off the bus. 请站开点让我下车。~ **down** ①从(车厢)下来 ②辞职;让位;下台:He is not ready to ~ down yet. 他还不准备辞职。~ **in** ①走进:Step in,please. 请进来。②干涉;介入:The government may have to ~ in to settle the disagreement between the union and the employers. 政府可能不得不介入解决工会和雇主间的争论。~ **up** ①走近;向上走 ②逐步增加:Our trade with the foreign countries is ~ping up. 我们和外国的贸易正在逐步增加。Ⅱ *n.* [C] ❶脚步;一步的距离;脚步声;步态:He was walking at slow ~s. 他慢步行走。/ ~ **by** ~ 逐渐地;一步一步地:He solved the problem ~ by ~. 他逐步地解决了这个问题。❷(达到目的的)步骤,措施:take ~s to prevent the spread of influenza 采取措施阻止流行性感冒的蔓延/We should take immediate ~s to prevent air from being polluted. 我们应当立即采取措施防止空气污染。❸阶梯；台阶：Mind the ~s when you go down into the cellar. 下地窖时注意台阶。

stepbrother /ˈstepbrʌðə(r)/ *n.* [C]同父异母(或同母异父)的兄弟

stepdaughter /ˈstepdɔːtə(r)/ *n.* [C]妻子与前夫(或丈夫与前妻)所生的女儿；继女

stepfather /ˈstepfɑːðə(r)/ *n.* [C]继父

stepmother /ˈstepmʌðə(r)/ *n.* [C]继母

stepsister /ˈstepsɪstə(r)/ *n.* [C]同父异母(或同母异父)的姐妹

stepson /ˈstepsʌn/ *n.* [C]妻子与前夫(或丈夫与前妻)所生的儿子；继子

stereo /ˈsterɪəʊ/ Ⅰ *n.* 立体声 Ⅱ *adj.* 立体声的

stern /stɜːn/ *adj.* 严厉的；严格的；严肃的：a ~ master 严厉的主人/a ~ discipline 严格的纪律

stew /stjuː/ Ⅰ *vt.* 煨，炖，焖：~ a chicken gently in the pot 用罐以文火炖鸡 Ⅱ *n.* ❶煨炖的食物；炖菜：I'd like more beef ~. 我想再吃一些炖牛肉。❷(a ~)焦虑；激动；气愤：be in a ~ about the injustice received in work 为在工作中受到不公正待遇而生闷气

steward /ˈstjuːəd/ *n.* [C](轮船、飞机或火车上的)服务员

stewardess /ˌstjuːəˈdes/ *n.* [C](轮船、飞机或火车上的)女服务员

stick /stɪk/ Ⅰ *v.* (stuck/stʌk/, stuck) ❶(使)黏着；(使)附着：~ a stamp on an envelope 将邮票贴在信封上 ❷以(尖物)插入；刺；戳：~ a fork into a potato 把叉插入马铃薯 ❸(尖物)刺入；阻塞：The needle stuck in my finger. 针刺入我的手指。/~ **to** ①贴着：Wet clothes ~ to the skin. 湿衣服黏着皮肤。②坚持：If you ~ to practising the piano every day, you could become quite a good musician. 如果你每天坚持练习弹钢琴，你会成为一位优秀的音乐家。Ⅱ *n.* [C] ❶柴枝；小树枝：gather dry ~s to make a fire 拾干柴生火 ❷杖；棍；棒：The old man cannot walk without a ~. 那老人没有手杖无法走路。

sticky /ˈstɪki/ *adj.* ❶用以粘贴的：~ tape 粘胶带 ❷有黏性的，黏着的：The wall was ~ with paint. 墙上的漆发黏。❸棘手的，难对付的：answer ~ questions 回答棘手的问题/make a ~ start 出师不利

stiff /stɪf/ *adj.* 不易弯曲的；僵硬的；僵直的：be ~ in manners 态度生硬/be ~ with cold 冻僵 派 stiffly *adv.*；stiffness *n.*

still /stɪl/ Ⅰ *adj.* 不动的；静止的：Please keep ~ while I take photograph for you. 在我给你照相时，请勿动。Ⅱ *adv.* ❶仍；尚；还：He is ~ busy. 他仍很忙。❷(与比较级连用)更，愈：Tom is tall, but Mary is ~ taller. 汤姆很高，但玛丽更高。❸然而；不过：He has treated you badly; ~, he's your brother and you ought to help him. 他虽然对你不好，但他总是你的兄弟，你应该帮助他。

stimulate /ˈstɪmjʊleɪt/ *vt.* 刺激；激励；激发：The good news ~d the students' enthusiasm. 那个好消息激发了学生们的热情。

stimulation /ˌstɪmjʊˈleɪʃn/ *n.* [U]刺激作用；激励：The workers need ~ to new efforts. 工人们需要激励以做出新的

努力。

stimulus /ˈstɪmjʊləs/ *n.* [C](*pl.* stimuli)刺激物；刺激源；引发物：Parents are trying to provide constant creative, athletic and emotional ~ for their children. 家长们不断设法培养孩子们在创造性、身体和情感方面的素质。/Only money can not be the ~ to invention. 仅仅有钱是不能激发创造发明的。

sting /stɪŋ/ Ⅰ *v.* (stung/stʌŋ/, stung) ❶刺伤；蜇伤：A bee stung me on the cheek. 一只蜜蜂蜇了我的面颊。❷给……造成剧痛；伤害：He was stung by his enemy's insults. 他被敌人的辱骂伤害了。Ⅱ *n.* ❶[C](蜜蜂等的)螯针 ❷(昆虫等造成的)刺痛，刺伤：Her face was covered with ~s. 她脸上满是刺伤。❸(身体或心灵的)剧痛，刺痛：the ~ of defeat 失败的惨痛 / the ~ of a whip 鞭打的剧痛

stingy /ˈstɪŋdʒi/ *adj.* ❶吝啬的，小气的：Their employer was a ~ and idle man. 他们的雇主吝啬小气，游手好闲。❷缺乏的，不足的，极少的

stir /stɜː(r)/ *v.* (stirred; stirring) ❶动；移动：Not a leaf was ~ring. 没有一片树叶在动。❷搅和；拌：~ milk into a cake mixture 把牛奶搅和在蛋糕的混合原料中 / ~ the fire with the poker 拨火 ❸惹起；激起：The story ~red the boy's imagination. 那故事激起了孩子的想象。

stitch /stɪtʃ/ Ⅰ *n.* [C] ❶(缝纫的)一针 ❷缝线；针脚 Ⅱ *v.* 缝；缝合

stock /stɒk/ Ⅰ *n.* ❶树干的下部 ❷存货；现货：The book is in (out of) ~. 该书现有(没有)存货。❸股票；公债 Ⅱ *v.* 供应；备置；有……存货：~ a shop with goods 为商店备货

stocking /ˈstɒkɪŋ/ *n.* [C]长筒袜

stomach /ˈstʌmək/ *n.* ❶[C]胃；腹部 ❷[U]食欲；胃口：The film goes against my ~. 这电影不合我意。/ **have no ~ for** 没胃口；不对胃口；不合意：I have no ~ for sweet food. 我不喜欢吃甜食。

stomachache /ˈstʌməkˌeɪk/ *n.* [C]胃痛；肚子疼

stone /stəʊn/ *n.* 石；岩石：sand ~ 沙石 / lime ~ 石灰石

stool /stuːl/ *n.* [C]凳

stop /stɒp/ Ⅰ *v.* (stopped; stopping) ❶阻止；停下：Nothing can ~ us from going. 什么也阻止不了我们去。The train ~ped. 火车停下来了。❷逗留；住：Are you ~ping at this hotel? 你住在这家旅馆吗？/ **~ doing sth.** 停止做某事：My father is trying to ~smoking. 我父亲正努力戒烟。**~ sb. (from) doing sth.** 防止某人做某事：The trees will ~ the sand from moving towards the rich farmland in the south. 树木将阻止沙移向南方肥沃的农田。**~ to do sth.** 停下来去做某事：Now let's ~ to have a rest. 现在我们停下来休息一下。Ⅱ *n.* [C] ❶停止；中止：The train came to a sudden ~. 火车突然停下。/ **put a ~ to sth.**, **bring sth. to a ~** 使停下；使结束：The red light brought the traffic to a ~. 红灯使来往的车辆停下来。❷(公共汽车等的)车站，招呼站

storage /ˈstɔːrɪdʒ/ *n.* [U] ❶贮藏；存储；保管：~ life 储藏期限 / a room for ~ 储藏室 / ~ battery (cell) 蓄电池 ❷(计算机的)存储(方式)

store /stɔː(r)/ Ⅰ *n.* [C] ❶贮藏；储备：lay in ~s of coal for the winter 贮藏大量的煤以供冬季使用 ❷(有特殊用途的)物品，必需物：military ~s 军需品 ❸商店；百货店：a clothing ~ 服装店 /

large department ~s of London 伦敦的大百货店 ❹仓库；贮藏室：available from ~s 有存货的 Ⅱ *vt.* 贮藏；储备：Do all squirrels ~ up food for the winter? 所有的松鼠都为冬天储备食物吗？

storehouse /ˈstɔːˌhaʊs/ *n.* [C]（*pl.* storehouses）❶仓库，库房 ❷宝库：Her mind was a ~ of innocuous anecdotes. 她的脑袋里装满了无伤大雅的逸闻趣事。

storekeeper /ˈstɔːˌkiːpə(r)/ *n.* [C]店主

storey /ˈstɔːri/ *n.* [C]（房屋的）一层：a house of two ~s 两层楼的房子

storm /stɔːm/ *n.* [C] ❶风暴；暴风雨：a thunder ~ 雷雨 ❷（感情、掌声等暴风雨般的）爆发，迸发：a ~ of applause 暴风雨般的掌声

stormy /ˈstɔːmi/ *adj.* ❶暴风雨般的；激烈的，猛烈的；多风波的 spark a ~ debate 引发一场激烈的辩论 ❷（脾气、心情等）狂暴的，暴躁的：a ~ temper 暴躁的脾气 / in a ~ mood 怒容满面地 派 stormily *adv.*；storminess *n.*

story /ˈstɔːri/ *n.* [C] ❶历史；事迹；小说；传奇；故事：stories of ancient Greece 古希腊历史 / a ~ for children 儿童故事 ❷（＝storey）（房屋的）一层

stout /staʊt/ *adj.* ❶矮胖的 ❷牢固的

stove /stəʊv/ *n.* [C]火炉；电炉

straight /streɪt/ Ⅰ *adj.* 直的：a ~ line 直线 / a ~ road 笔直的公路 Ⅱ *adv.* 直地；直接地：Keep ~ on. 继续前进。派 straightness *n.*

straighten /ˈstreɪtən/ *vt.* ❶使笔直，将……弄直；使挺直；使平直：~ one's spine 挺起腰杆子/ I've ~ed the bent pin. 我已经将那枚弯的别针弄直了。❷使整洁有序，整理，清理：I stood up and ~ed my clothes. 我站起身来，整了整衣服。

straightaway /ˈstreɪtəˌweɪ/ Ⅰ *adj.* 直道的；直接的，径直的：a ~ track 直线跑道/ a ~ run of 15 miles 径直奔跑了 15 英里 Ⅱ *adv.* 立刻，马上：You have to go there ~. 你得马上到那儿去。

straightforward /ˌstreɪtˈfɔːwəd/ Ⅰ *adj.* 老实的；坦率的 Ⅱ *adv.* 正直地；坦率地

strain /streɪn/ Ⅰ *vt.* ❶尽力使用：~ one's voice 尽力提高嗓门 ❷拉紧；伸张 ❸耗损；因过分用力而损伤 Ⅱ *n.* ❶极度紧张：nervous ~ 神经紧张 / Can you stand the ~ of the life there? 你受得了那里的紧张生活吗？❷张力；拉紧：The rope broke because of ~. 因张力太大绳子断了。❸扭伤；拉伤：Jack has got a ~ in the arm. 杰克的手臂给扭伤了。

strait /streɪt/ *n.* [C] 海峡：the Taiwan Straits 台湾海峡 / the Gibraltar Straits 直布罗陀海峡 / the Magellan Strait 麦哲伦海峡

strange /streɪndʒ/ *adj.* ❶奇怪的；奇异的；不可思议的：hear a ~ sound 听到奇怪的声音 ❷（只作表语）陌生的；不习惯的（与 to 连用）：The village boy was ~ to city life. 那个村童不习惯城市生活。派 strangely *adv.*；strangeness *n.*

stranger /ˈstreɪndʒə(r)/ *n.* [C]陌生人；异乡人；异国人：The dog always barks at ~s. 狗总是向陌生人叫。

strangle /ˈstræŋgl/ *vt.* 扼杀；勒死，绞死；使窒息：This stiff collar is strangling me. 硬衣领把我卡得喘不过气。

strap /stræp/ Ⅰ *n.* [C] ❶（尤指用以捆扎或固定的）带（子），带条；皮带；铁皮条 ❷（衣服等的）背带，吊带：the camera ~相机背带 Ⅱ *vt.*（strapped; strapping）❶用带子系牢（或捆扎、固定、扣住）：

Children should be ~ped into a special car seat. 应用安全带将儿童固定在特制的汽车座位上。❷鞭打,抽打

strategic(al) /strəˈtiːdʒɪk(əl)/ *adj*. 战略的;谋略的:~ principles 战略方针 / global ~ 全球战略

strategist /ˈstrætədʒɪst/ *n*. [C]战略家;谋略家;兵法家

strategy /ˈstrætədʒi/ *n*. 战略;作战计划;对策

straw /strɔː/ *n*. [U]稻草;麦杆:a ~ mattress 草垫 / ~ man 稻草人 / ~ sandals 草鞋

strawberry /ˈstrɔːbəri/ *n*. [C]草莓

stream /striːm/ Ⅰ *n*. [C] ❶河;溪;水流:I crossed a ~. 我蹚过一条小河。❷(液体)流出;人潮:Streams of people were coming out of the railway station. 人流正从火车站涌出。Ⅱ *vi*. 流:Sweat was ~ing down his face. 汗水正从他脸上流下来。

street /striːt/ *n*. [C]街道:meet a friend in the ~ 在街上碰到一个朋友

strength /streŋθ/ *n*. [U]力量;力气:exert all one's ~ 竭尽全力 / save ~ 省力 / take great ~ to do sth. 尽力做某事

strengthen /ˈstreŋθən/ *vt*. 加强;巩固:~ discipline 加强纪律 / ~ national defense 巩固国防 / ~ unity 加强团结 / ~ up the management 加强管理

stress /stres/ Ⅰ *n*. ❶[U]压力;压迫:under the ~ of poverty 在贫困的压迫下 ❷[U]重视;强调 ❸[C]重读;重音:Stress and rhythm are important in speaking English. 说英语时轻重读和节奏很重要。Ⅱ *v*. 着重强调:He ~ed the point that everyone should respect the disabled. 他强调人人都应该尊重残疾人。

stretch /stretʃ/ Ⅰ *v*. 伸展;张开;拉长;扩大:~ a rope tight 把绳拉紧 / ~ one's neck 伸长颈子 / ~ one's arms 伸臂 / ~ oneself 伸伸懒腰 Ⅱ *n*. [C]❶伸展;张开;拉长:The cat woke and gave a ~. 猫醒后伸懒腰。❷连续;绵延:a beautiful ~ of wooded country 一大片美丽的树林覆盖的乡间 / **at a** ~ 连续地;不休息地:He worked for 12 hours at a ~. 他连续工作了12个小时。**at full** ~ 尽全力:The workers were at full ~. 工人们已尽全力了。

stretcher /ˈstretʃə(r)/ *n*. [C]担架

stricken /ˈstrɪkən/ *adj*. 患病的;受伤害的;遭不幸的;受打击的:be ~ with measles 患麻疹/ be conscience ~受良心折磨的

strict /strɪkt/ *adj*. 严厉的;严格的:a ~ father 严厉的父亲 / ~ discipline 严格的纪律/ be ~ with one's child 对孩子要求严格 派 strictly *adv*. ;strictness *n*.

stride /straɪd/ Ⅰ *n*. [C] ❶大步;步幅:He walked with long ~s. 他大步流星地走着。❷(常用 *pl*.)进展,进步:make great ~s in ...在……方面取得长足进步 Ⅱ *vi*. (strode/strəʊd/, stridden /ˈstrɪdn/)迈大步走;跨步;跨越:He strode about the room. 他在房间里大踏步踱来踱去。/ ~ over a brook 跨过小河

strike /straɪk/ Ⅰ *v*. (struck/strʌk/, struck) ❶ 打;击;敲:He struck me on the head. 他打我的头。/ ~ **at** 动手要打;向……打来:He struck at the cat, but it ran away. 他动手要打那只猫,但它跑开了。~ **in** 插嘴:Here someone struck in with a question. 这时有人插嘴发问。~ **into** 打进;刺入:It's root will ~ deep into earth in a few days. 几天后，它的根就会深深扎入土中。~ **off** 取消；删去；切除：His name was struck off the football team. 他的名字已从足球队员名单中删除。~ **out** ①用力打；猛击 ②产生；发明：~ out a new idea 产生一个新的想法 ❷打出；擦出：~ a match 擦火柴 / The matches are damp; they won't ~. 火柴潮了划不燃。❸(时钟)敲响报时：Six o'clock has already struck. 6 点已经敲过了。❹造成……印象；吸引……的注意：How does the idea ~ you? 你对那主意感觉怎么样？❺罢工：~ for higher pay 为争取较高的薪水而罢工 Ⅱ *n.* [C]罢工：a ~ of bus-drivers 公共汽车司机的罢工/ a sit-down ~ 静坐罢工 / **on** ~在罢工：Most miners have gone on ~. 大部分矿工都罢工了。

striking / ˈstraɪkɪŋ / *adj.* 引人注意的；激起兴趣的：a woman of ~ beauty 一个美貌惊人的女人

string / strɪŋ / Ⅰ *n.* 带；线；细绳：a ball of ~一圈线团 / a piece of ~ 一根线 Ⅱ *vt.* (strung /strʌŋ/, strung) ❶串起，把……连在一起：They are ~ing beads. 他们正把珠子串起来。/~ ideas together 把思想贯穿起来 ❷吊，悬，挂，绑：We strung up lanterns in the yard. 我们在院子里挂起了灯笼。❸给乐器上(调)弦：~ a violin 给小提琴装弦 ❹使紧张，使兴奋：She was highly strung for the game. 她对比赛感到非常紧张。

strip[1] / strɪp / *v.* ❶剥；脱；裸露：After he left for work I ~ped the beds and vacuumed the carpets. 他去上班后，我扯下了床罩并用吸尘器清扫了地毯。❷夺去；剥夺

strip[2] / strɪp / *n.* [C] ❶长条；狭长的一条或一片 ❷(飞机着陆时的)跑道

stripe / straɪp / *n.* [C](表面上的)条纹，线条：a white table-cloth with red ~s 有红色条纹的白桌布 派 striped *adj.*

strive / straɪv / *vi.* (strove/strəʊv/或 strived, striven /strɪvn/ 或 strived) 努力；奋斗：We are striving for further progress. 我们在为继续进步而努力。

stroke[1] / strəʊk / *n.* [C]❶击；敲 ❷中风 ❸(写字、绘画的) 一笔；笔画 ❹(报时的)钟声

stroke[2] / strəʊk / *vt.* (用手反复地)抚摸：~ **down** 平息怒气：I failed to ~ him down. 我无法平息他的怒气。

stroll / strəʊl / Ⅰ *n.* [C]漫步；闲逛：have (go for) a ~散步 Ⅱ *v.* 散步，闲逛

strong / strɒŋ / *adj.* 有抵抗力的；强大的；强壮的；坚强的：~ in English 擅长英语 / ~ in number 数量上占优势 / a ~ stick 不易折断的手杖 / a ~ will 坚强的意志 派 strongly *adv.*

structural / ˈstrʌktʃərəl / *adj.* 结构的 ~changes in society 社会结构的变化

structure / ˈstrʌktʃə(r) / Ⅰ *n.* ❶[U] 结构；构造：price ~ 价格结构 / wage ~ 工资结构 ❷[C]建筑物：build a ~ 修造建筑物 Ⅱ *vt.* 建造；建立

struggle / ˈstrʌgl / Ⅰ *v.* 抗争；奋斗；斗争；挣扎：~ against (with) difficulties 与困难作斗争/ ~ for justice 为正义而战 / The thief ~d in the policeman's arms. 那贼在警察怀中挣扎。Ⅱ *n.* [C] 抗争；奋斗；斗争；挣扎：the ~ for freedom 为争取自由而斗争 / He made many ~s to get a good education. 为了获得良好的教育，他做了很多努力。

stubborn / ˈstʌbən / *adj.* 顽固的；倔强的；顽强的；难处理或难应付的：a ~ resistance 顽强的抵抗 / ~ illness 顽疾/

He's so ~ that nobody can persuade him. 他很顽固，无人能说服他。派 stubbornly *adv.*；stubbornness *n.*

student /ˈstjuːdnt/ *n.* [C] ❶学生：medical ~s医科学生 ❷学者；研究者：a ~ of nature 研究自然的学者

studio /ˈstjuːdɪəʊ/ *n.* [C]工作室；播音室

study /ˈstʌdi/ Ⅰ n. ❶读书；研究；学习：case ~ 病历(档案、专题)研究 / make a ~ of the country's foreign trade 研究该国的国际贸易 ❷[C]书房 Ⅱ *v.* 求学；研究：~ for a degree 攻读学位/He was ~ing for the medical profession. 他在求学，准备将来当医生。/ ~ **by oneself** 自学：He studied by himself and became a lawyer. 他靠自学成为一名律师。

stuff /stʌf/ Ⅰ *n.* [U]材料；原料 Ⅱ *v.* 塞满，填塞(与 with 连用)；塞进，装入(与 into 连用)：~ a bag with feathers 用羽毛填充袋子

stuffy /ˈstʌfi/ *adj.* ❶不通风的，不透气的；(空气)混浊的，不新鲜的：a smoky ~ office 烟雾弥漫且不通风的办公室 ❷(鼻子)堵塞的，不通的：The cold made my nose ~. 我因感冒而鼻塞。❸单调乏味的，枯燥的；沉闷的：a ~ occasion 沉闷的活动场合/ Surprisingly, the magazine became rather ~. 没想到，这本杂志竟变得很乏味了。❹(人)古板守旧的；一本正经的：It would be difficult to find a stuffier man. 恐怕很难找到一个更古板守旧的人了。

stumble /ˈstʌmbl/ *vi.* ❶绊倒，绊跌；失足摔倒：~ against a stump 被树桩绊了一跤/He was drunk and ~d on the bottom step. 他喝醉了，在最后一段阶梯上摔倒了。❷跌跌撞撞地走；踉跄而行：She ~d into the bedroom. 她跌跌撞撞地走进了卧室 ❸结结巴巴地说话；断断续续地演奏：Just relax and be confident, and you won't ~ this time. 放松些，自信一点儿，这次你不会结结巴巴了。/She was nervous and ~d through a piece by Chopin. 她很紧张，断断续续地勉强演奏完了一首肖邦的曲子。

stupid /ˈstjuːpɪd/ *adj.* 笨的；愚蠢的：Don't be ~ to believe that. 不要那么蠢去相信那件事。

sturdy /ˈstɜːdi/ *adj.* (-ier，-iest) ❶强壮的；结实的：a ~ desk 结实的课桌 ❷坚定的；坚强的：~ children 坚强的孩子们

style /staɪl/ *n.* ❶方式；风格：speak in a delightful ~ 以令人喜欢的方式说话 ❷[C](衣服等的)样式，款式：the latest ~ in hats (in hair-dressing)帽子(发型)的最新式样 ❸[C](书面语)称呼；称号：Has he any right to assume the ~ of colonel? 他有权接受上校称号吗?

stylist /ˈstaɪlɪst/ *n.* [C]时装设计师；装潢设计师；发型设计师

subconscious /sʌbˈkɒnʃəs/ Ⅰ *adj.* 下意识的，潜意识的：Nail-biting is often a ~ reaction to tension. 咬指甲往往是心理紧张时的下意识动作。Ⅱ *n.* [U]下意识，潜意识：Freud's theory of the ~弗洛伊德的潜意识论/the confused thoughts of the ~下意识的杂乱念头

subdue /səbˈdjuː/ *vt.* ❶征服；制服：~ a rebel army 制服叛军/~ a forest fire 扑灭森林大火/ Rome ~d Gaul. 罗马征服了高卢。❷克制；抑制：~ one's tear 忍住泪水/ ~ one's anger 压住怒火

subject Ⅰ /ˈsʌbdʒɪkt/ *n.* [C]❶主题，题目；科目，学科：an interesting ~ for conversation 有趣的话题 / a ~ for an essay 文章的主题 ❷(语法)主语 ❸国民;臣民 ❹实验的对象 Ⅱ /ˈsʌbdʒɪkt/ *adj*. 易遭……的;受……支配的(与 to 连用):All players are ~ to the rules of the game. 所有选手都要遵守比赛规则。/ Those islands are ~ to typhoons. 那些岛屿易遭台风侵袭。Ⅲ /səbˈdʒekt/ *vt*. 使遭受;使服从

subjective /səbˈdʒektɪv/ *adj*. ❶主观(上)的;出于主观想法的:Meaning has both an objective component and a ~ component. 意义既有客观成分又有主观成分。❷个人的,私人的:~ experience 个人经验 ❸出于个人情愿的,臆想的:You're too ~ when it comes to judging her work. 当要评估她的工作时,你太感情用事了。

submarine /ˌsʌbməˈriːn, ˈsʌbməriːn/ Ⅰ *adj*. 水下的;海底的:~ plants 海底植物 Ⅱ *n*. [C]潜水艇:build a nuclear ~ 建造核潜艇

submerge /səbˈmɜːdʒ/ *vt*. ❶浸泡;浸没:Did you ~ the clothes in the sudsy water? 你把衣服泡进肥皂水里了吗? ❷淹没:The fields were ~d by the flood. 农田被洪水淹没了。❸湮灭,埋没;隐藏,隐瞒:Certain facts were ~d by the witness. 有些事实被证人隐瞒了。—*vi*. 潜入水下:The submarine ~d immediately. 潜艇很快下潜了。

submit /səbˈmɪt/ *v*. (-mitted;-mitting) (使)归顺;(使)服从;投降:~ oneself to discipline 服从纪律 / ~ to the enemy 投降敌人 / ~ a proposal to the committee 向委员会提交一项建议 / ~ to separation from one's family 忍痛与家人分离

subordinate /səˈbɔːdɪnət/ *adj*. 下级的;辅助的

subscribe /səbˈskraɪb/ *v*. ❶认捐;捐助:He ~d 500 *yuan* to the flood relief fund. 他向水灾救济基金捐款 500 元。❷订阅(报纸等):~ for books 订购书籍 ❸签(名)

subscription /səbˈskrɪpʃn/ *n*. ❶认捐;捐助 ❷订购;订阅

subsequence /ˈsʌbsɪkwəns/ *n*. 随后;后来:an affair which appeared in due ~ in the newspaper 在报纸上连载的事件

subsequent /ˈsʌbsɪkwənt/ *adj*. 随后的;后来的:~ events 后来发生的事件 派 subsequently *adv*.

substance /ˈsʌbstəns/ *n*. 物质;实质:Water, ice and snow are the same ~ in different forms. 水、冰和雪是不同形式的同种物质。

substantial /səbˈstænʃəl/ *adj*. ❶大量的,大规模的,数目可观的:a ~ majority 绝大多数/ a ~ amount of money 一大笔钱 ❷实在的,真实的,现实的 ❸坚固的,牢固的;结实的,坚实的;壮实的:a ~ physique 健壮的体形

substitute /ˈsʌbstɪtjuːt/ Ⅰ *n*. [C]代理人;代用品:She used a paper cup as a ~ in the experiment. 在实验中她用一个纸杯作为代用品。Ⅱ *v*. 用……代替,代以:They ~d plastics for glass. 他们用塑料代替玻璃。

subtitle /ˈsʌ(b)ˌtaɪtl/ Ⅰ *n*. [C] ❶副标题;小标题 ❷(尤指译制电影或电视的)对白字幕 Ⅱ *vt*. ❶给……加副标题(或小标题) ❷为……加上对白字幕

subtle /ˈsʌtl/ *adj*. ❶隐约的,依稀的;稀薄的;清淡的:~ lighting 若隐若现的灯光/This soup tastes ~. 这道汤口味清淡。❷微妙的,难以捉摸的:a ~ smile

S

不易察觉的笑容/ She is too ~ for you. 你捉摸不透她。❸诡秘的，狡诈的：Advertisements persuade us to buy things in very ~ ways. 广告总是用非常巧妙的方式诱使我们购物。

subtract /səbˈtrækt/ *vt.* 减；去掉：3 ~d from 8 gives 5. 8 减去 3 等于 5。派 subtraction *n.*

suburb /ˈsʌbɜːb/ *n.* [C]市郊；郊区：the ~s（总称）郊外；郊区

suburban /səˈbɜːbən/ *adj.* 市郊的；郊区的：~ shops 郊区商店

subway /ˈsʌbweɪ/ *n.* [C] ❶地道：You must cross the street by the ~. 你得从地道过街。❷地铁：People in the city like to take the ~. 城市居民喜欢乘地铁。

succeed /səkˈsiːd/ *vi.* ❶成功（与 in 连用）：~ in (passing) an examination 考试及格 ❷继承（与 to 连用）：~ to the throne 继承王位 / Under feudal rule only men could ~ to family property. 在封建统治下，只有男子能继承家产。—*vt.* 继续；继任；接着：Who ~ed Churchill as Prime Minister? 谁继丘吉尔出任首相的？/ The announcement was ~ed by silence. 消息宣布后，全场鸦雀无声。

success /səkˈses/ *n.* ❶[U]成功；成就：meet with ~ 获得成功 ❷[C]成功的人或物；成功例子：The plan was a great ~. 这项计划极为成功。/ **make a ~ of sth.** 做成某事：They made a ~ of their experiment. 他们的实验成功了。**win (achieve) a ~** 获得成功；赢得胜利：We have won one ~ after another in our economy. 我们在经济上已经取得了一个又一个的胜利。

successful /səkˈsesfl/ *adj.* 成功的；结果良好的：a ~ attempt 成功的尝试 派 successfully *adv.*

succession /səkˈseʃn/ *n.* ❶连续：good harvest for three years in ~ 连续三个丰收年 ❷继任；继承；接替：Who was first in ~ to the manager? 谁是经理职位的第一接任者？派 successional *adj.*

successive /səkˈsesɪv/ *adj.* 连续的；接连的：The football team won ten ~ games. 足球队连续十场比赛获胜。派 successively *adv.*

successor /səkˈsesə(r)/ *n.* [C]继承人；继任者：~s to the great cause 伟大事业的接班人

such /sʌtʃ/ Ⅰ adj. 同类的；同等的；这样的，如此的：no ~ words 没有这样的词/ ~ **as**（接名词）像，诸如：He visited several cities ~ as New York, Chicago and Boston. 他参观了几座城市，像纽约、芝加哥、波士顿等。~ **... as**（接从句）凡是；像是……的：I don't like ~ books as he recommends. 我不喜欢他推荐的那些书。~ **as to**, ~**... as to** 会到……那般的，会到……的地步：Her high blood pressure wasn't ~ as to cause anxiety. 她的高血压还未到令人担忧的地步。/ I am not ~ a fool as to believe that. 我不会傻到去相信那种事。~ **that**, ~**... that** 如此……以至于：His behaviour was ~ that we all disliked him. 他的行为不像话，以至于我们都讨厌他。/ It was ~ a cold day that there was nobody on the street. 天气非常冷，以至于街上没任何人。Ⅱ *pron.* 像这样或那样的人（或物）：I may have hurt her feelings, but ~ was certainly not my intention. 我可能伤害了她的感

情，但我的确不是故意的。Ⅲ *adv.* 如此；那么

suck /sʌk/ *v.* 用嘴吮吸(水等)；喝；自……吸取：~ the juice from an orange 吸橘子汁 / ~ poison out of a wound 吸出伤口的毒 / ~ in knowledge 吸取知识

sudden /ˈsʌdən/ Ⅰ adj. 突然的；出乎意料的；急速的：a ~ shower 骤雨 / a ~ turn in the road 路上的急弯 Ⅱ *n.* 突然：**all of a** ~ 突然地；出乎意料地：The car stopped all of a ~. 车子突然停下来。

suddenly /ˈsʌdənli/ *adv.* 突然；出乎意料地：It all happened so ~. 一切都来得那么突然。

suffer /ˈsʌfə(r)/ *v.* 遭受；蒙受：~ for one's carelessness 因粗心而食恶果 / ~ from cold and hunger 挨饿受冻 / ~ from the headache 患头痛病 / His business ~ed while he was ill. 他在生病期间生意蒙受损失。

suffering /ˈsʌfərɪŋ/ Ⅰ *n.* [U]受苦；痛苦：The medicine can ease and relieve the ~. 药能减轻和解除疼痛。/ They were bearing the ~ patiently. 他们耐心地忍受着痛苦。 Ⅱ *adj.* 受苦的；患病的

S

sufficiency /səˈfɪʃənsi/ *n.* 足量；足够(只作单数)：a ~ of fuel 足够的燃料

sufficient /səˈfɪʃənt/ *adj.* 足够的；充分的：Have we ~ food for ten people? 我们有够十个人吃的食物吗？派 sufficiently *adv.*

sugar /ˈʃʊgə(r)/ *n.* ❶[U]糖，食糖：coffee black with no ~ 不加糖的咖啡 ❷[C]一块糖；一勺糖：I'd like two ~s for my coffee. 我想在咖啡里加两勺糖。派 sugary *adj.*

suggest /səˈdʒest/ *vt.* ❶提出(意见等)；建议：I ~ a visit to the theatre. 我建议去参观戏院。❷提醒；暗示：The look on his face ~ed fear. 他的表情表明了他的恐惧。

suggestion /səˈdʒestʃn/ *n.* ❶[C]建议，提议：at the ~ of my brother 出于我兄弟的建议 ❷使人做(尤其是不好的事情的)推测的理由：There was no ~ that he was doing anything illegal. 说他在从事非法活动无任何根据。

suicide /ˈsuːɪsaɪd/ Ⅰ *n.* 自杀：commit ~ 自杀/ ~ attack 自杀性袭击 Ⅱ *v.* 自杀

suit /sjuːt/ Ⅰ *n.* [C]一套；一副：a man's ~ 男子的套装(包括外套、背心和裤子) / a woman's ~ 女子的套装(包括上衣和裙子) Ⅱ *v.* ❶使满意；适合……的要求；适应：The seven o'clock train will ~ us very well. 七点的火车很适合我们。She is ~ed for (to) teaching. 她适合教书(当老师)。❷(尤指衣服、发式等)相配；恰当；合适：It doesn't ~ you to have your hair cut short. 剪短发对你不适合。

suitable /ˈs(j)uːtəbl/ *adj.* 适合的；恰当的：clothes ~ for cold weather 适合天冷穿的衣服 / a ~ place for a picnic 适合野餐的一处地点

suite /swiːt/ *n.* [C] ❶(同一类物品的)(一)套；(一)组；(一)系列：a ~ of furniture 一套家具 ❷套房：a bridal ~结纸套房/ a hotel ~宾馆的套房 ❸成套家具：a new bathroom ~一套新的浴室家具/ a bedroom ~一套寝具

sum /sʌm/ Ⅰ *n.* [C]❶总数；总和 ❷算术题：do a ~ in one's head 心算 Ⅱ *v.* (summed；summing)总结；概括 / ~ **up** ①总计；合计：~ up the advantages 算一

算好处有多少 ②概括地说:To ~ up, she is a nice girl. 总而言之,她是一个可爱的女孩。

summarize /ˈsʌməraɪz/ *vt.* 概括;概述;总结:The monitor ~d our ideas. 班长总结了我们的想法。

summary /ˈsʌməri/ Ⅰ *adj.* 概括的 Ⅱ *n.* [C]总结;摘要;概要: give a ~ 做总结 / news ~ 新闻摘要 / **in** ~ 概括起来,总的说来

summer /ˈsʌmə(r)/ *n.* 夏季:in the ~ of 1992 1992年夏季 / the ~ holidays 暑假

summit /ˈsʌmɪt/ *n.* [C] ❶山顶,山峰: climb to the ~爬上山顶 ❷巅峰,最高点,顶点,极点:reach the ~ of sb.'s career 达到某人事业的顶峰 ❸首脑会议,最高级会议,峰会:at annual economic ~在每年一度的经济峰会上

summon /ˈsʌmən/ *vt.* 召唤;传唤:~ sb. to appear as a witness 传唤某人出席当证人

sun /sʌn/ *n.* ❶太阳: rise with the ~ 早起 / under the ~ 在地球上;在世界上 ❷阳光:bathe in ~ 做日光浴 / sit in the ~ 坐在阳光下 / draw the curtains to shut out(let in) the ~ 拉窗帘遮住(放进)阳光

Sunday /ˈsʌndi/ *n.* 星期日;礼拜日

sunken /ˈsʌŋkən/ *adj.* ❶沉没的;浸没的:~ ships 沉船 ❷低于表面的,下陷的:In this grounds there is a ~ rose garden. 他庭院里有一个凹下的玫瑰花园。❸(眼睛或双颊)凹陷的:Captain Beard had hollow eyes and ~ cheeks. 比尔德船长两眼空洞,双颊凹陷。

sunlight /ˈsʌnˌlaɪt/ *n.* [C]阳光,日光: Sunlight streamed unhindered down the slope. 阳光毫无遮拦地洒下山坡。/ The children ran outside into the white ~. 孩子们跑了出去,沐浴在灿烂的阳光之下。

sunny /ˈsʌni/ *adj.* (-ier,-iest)向阳的;阳光充足的:a ~ room 向阳的房间 /a ~ side 向阳的一面;乐观(光明)的一面

sunrise /ˈsʌnˌraɪz/ *n.* ❶日出;朝霞,晨曦:stay from ~ till darkness 从日出一直待到日落/ The sky was brilliant with the ~. 天空被旭日照得绚丽多彩。❷[U]拂晓,黎明: We found the lost child at ~. 我们在黎明时分找到了那个走失的孩子。

sunset /ˈsʌnˌset/ *n.* ❶[U]日落;傍晚,黄昏: The flower bud of a water lily opens at ~. 睡莲的花蕾在傍晚时分绽开。❷[C]晚霞,夕阳,落日余晖:a lurid ~ 绚丽的晚霞

sunshine /ˈsʌnˌʃaɪn/ *n.* [U]阳光,日光: be bathed in ~ 沐浴在阳光里

super /ˈsjuːpə(r)/ *adj.* 极好的;特级的

superb /s(j)uːˈpɜːb/ *adj.* ❶隆重的,盛大的;庄严的;豪华的,奢侈的;高贵的: a ~ site of an ancient city 一座壮观的古迹遗址/ a ~ train 豪华列车 ❷极好的,特棒的,最佳的,一流的:This chocolate cake is really ~. 这巧克力蛋糕真是太好吃了。

superficial /ˌsjuːpəˈfɪʃəl/ *adj.* 表面的;肤浅的: ~ knowledge 肤浅的知识 / ~ wound 表皮的创伤 派 superficially *adv.*

superficiality /ˌsjuːpəˌfɪʃɪˈæləti/ *n.* [U]表面性;肤浅

superior /sjuːˈpɪərɪə(r)/ Ⅰ *adj.* 优良的;优秀的: ~ **to** 优于;胜过:This cloth is ~ to that. 这种布料比那种布料好。Ⅱ *n.* [C]上司;长官;长辈;前辈:imme-

S

diate ~ 顶头上司

supermarket /ˈsjuːpəmɑːkɪt/ *n.* [C]超级市场：Many people go shopping at the ~ on weekends. 许多人周末去超级市场购物。

superstition /ˌsjuːpəˈstɪʃn/ *n.* 迷信；迷信行为

supervise /ˈsuːpəvaɪz/ *v.* 监督；主管；指导

supervision /ˌsuːpəˈvɪʒn/ *n.* [U]监督；管理；督导

supervisor /ˈsuːpəvaɪzə(r)/ *n.* [C]监督人；管理人；主管人

supper /ˈsʌpə(r)/ *n.* 晚餐：We always have ~ at half past six. 我们总是在六点半钟吃晚饭。

supplement /ˈsʌplɪmənt/ Ⅰ *n.* [C]❶增补(物)；补充(物)：She earns money as a ~ to the income of the family. 她挣钱增加家里的收入。❷(报刊等的)增刊，副刊 Ⅱ *vt.* 补充；增补

supply /səˈplaɪ/ Ⅰ *v.* 供给；供应；备办：~ food for children 供给孩子们食物 / ~ **sb. with sth. …**, ~ **sth. to sb.** 给某人提供……：They said that they would ~ us with everything(everything to us) we need. 他们说将给我们提供所需要的一切。Ⅱ *n.* ❶[U]供给；备办；贮藏：~ and demand 供与求 / **in short** ~ 供应不足：Their food is in short ~. 他们的食品供应不足。❷[C](尤指)公众必需品；生活必需品：medical supplies for the army 军需药品

support /səˈpɔːt/ Ⅰ *vt.* ❶ 支持；支撑；扶持：Is this bridge strong enough to ~ heavy lorries? 这桥承受得起载重卡车驶过吗？❷维持；赡养：He has a large family to ~. 他有很多子女要养活。❸拥护；支持；帮助：~ing troops 支援部队 / a ~ing actor 配角 Ⅱ *n.* [U]支持；支撑；扶持 / **in** ~ **of** 支持；拥护：He spoke in ~ of the proposal. 他发言支持那个建议。派 supporter *n.*

suppose /səˈpəuz/ *vt.* ❶假定：Let us ~ (that) the news is true. 让我们假定这消息是正确的。❷推测；想象：What do you ~ he wanted? 你推测他想要什么？派 supposed *adj.*

supposing /səˈpəuzɪŋ/ *conj.* 倘若；假如：Supposing it rains, what shall you do? 假如下雨，你将怎么办？

supposition /ˌsʌpəˈzɪʃn/ *n.* [U]假定；想象

suppress /səˈpres/ *vt.* ❶镇压；平定；压制：~ a rising 镇压起义 ❷扣留；查禁：~ a newspaper 查禁一家报纸 派 suppression *n.*

supreme /sjuːˈpriːm/ *adj.* ❶最高的；无上的：the Supreme Court 最高法院 ❷最重要的；极大的：make the ~ sacrifice 做最大的牺牲

sure /ʃuə(r)/ *adj.* ❶(只作表语)肯定的，必定的；确信的，有信心的：Can we be ~ of his honesty? 我们能确定他是诚实的吗？/ Do you feel ~ about it? 你对此事有把握吗？/Be ~ not to forget to bring your book with you. 一定不要忘了把书带来。/ I am ~ that the host team will win. 我确信主队要赢。/ We are not ~ whether the professor has arrived. 我们不能肯定那位教授是否已经到达。/ I am not ~ what he wants. 我不能肯定他想要什么。❷经过证实的；可靠的；稳妥的：a ~ friend 可靠的朋友/ **make** ~查明；确信：Go and make ~ of the time and place of the meeting. 去

落实一下会议的时间和地点。

surely /ˈʃʊəli/ *adv.* ❶确实，无疑：This will ~ cause problems. 这一定会带来问题。❷(用以强调推断)想必：Surely that can't be right. 想必那不可能正确。❸稳当地：The goat planted its feet ~. 那山羊稳稳地站着。❹(用作答语)当然：—May I leave now? —Surely. —我可以走了吗？—当然。

surf /sɜːf/ Ⅰ *n.* [U]激浪；碎波 Ⅱ *vi.* 进行冲浪运动：~ on the Internet (计算机)上网；网上冲浪

surface /ˈsɜːfɪs/ Ⅰ *n.* [C]表面；水面：Glass has a smooth ~. 玻璃有光滑的表面。/The submarine rose to the ~. 潜水艇升至水面。Ⅱ *adj.* 表面的；肤浅的：~ politeness 表面的礼貌

surge /sɜːdʒ/ *vi.* (浪涛)汹涌，澎湃：The floods ~d over the valley. 洪水奔腾着涌过山谷。

surgeon /ˈsɜːdʒən/ *n.* [C] 外科医师

surgery /ˈsɜːdʒəri/ *n.* ❶[U]外科；外科手术：qualified in both ~ and medicine 有资格做外科和内科医生 ❷[C]手术室；诊疗室

surgical /ˈsɜːdʒɪkl/ *adj.* 外科的

surname /ˈsɜːneɪm/ *n.* [C] 姓

surpass /səˈpɑːs/ *vt.* 超越；胜过：~ sb. in strength 在力量上胜过某人 / The beauty of the scenery ~ed my expectations. 风景的优美超出了我的预料。

surplus /ˈsɜːpləs/ *n.* 过剩；剩余物资

surprise /səˈpraɪz/ Ⅰ *n.* ❶惊奇；惊骇；惊愕：To my ~, his plan succeeded. 使我惊奇的是，他的计划成功了。/ **in** ~ 惊奇地；吃惊地：He shouted in ~. 他吃惊地大声叫喊。**take sb. by** ~ 使某人吃了一惊；冷不防捉住：The thief was taken by ~. 那贼冷不防被捉住了。/ We took the thinking boy by ~. 我们使那沉思的男孩吃了一惊。**to sb.'s** ~ 使某人惊奇的是：To my ~, the actress is over 50. 使我惊讶的是，那女演员已 50 多岁了。❷突然袭击：**take by** ~ 出奇兵攻占；突袭：The city was taken by ~. 那座城市被突然攻陷了。Ⅱ *v.* ❶使惊奇；使诧异：You ~d me! 你吓我一跳！/We were ~d at the news. 我们听到那消息很惊讶。❷不期而遇；撞见；突然袭击：~ a burglar breaking into a house 撞见闯入房子的窃贼

surprised /səˈpraɪzd/ *adj.* 吃惊的；感到惊讶的 / **be ~ at** 对……感到惊奇：We were ~ at his being late. 对于他的迟到，我们感到很惊奇。**be ~ to do** 对做某事感到吃惊：I was very ~ to learn that you had decided to go to medical school. 得知你决定上医药学校，我感到很吃惊。

surprising /səˈpraɪzɪŋ/ *adj.* 惊人的；出人意料的

surrender /səˈrendə(r)/ *v.* ❶投降；自首；投案：We shall never ~ to the enemy. 我们决不向敌人投降。❷放弃；让与：We shall never ~ our liberty. 我们永不放弃自由。

surround /səˈraʊnd/ *vt.* 包围；环绕：a house ~ed with trees 有树木环绕的一栋房子

surrounding /səˈraʊndɪŋ/ Ⅰ *adj.* 周围的：Beijing and the ~ countryside 北京及周围农村 Ⅱ *n.* [C](*pl.*) 周围的事物；环境：living in pleasant ~s 生活在美好的环境里

survey Ⅰ /səˈveɪ/ *vt.* ❶俯瞰；眺望：You can ~ the valley from the top of the hill. 你从山顶可以俯瞰山谷。❷测量；勘测：~ a railway 勘测铁路 ❸全面审视；调查 Ⅱ /ˈsɜːveɪ/ *n.* [C]俯瞰；测量；考察

survival /səˈvaɪv(ə)l/ *n.* [U]幸存；生存：the ~ of the fittest 适者生存

survive /səˈvaɪv/ *v.* 生存；幸存：~ an earthquake 在地震后仍然活着 / The old lady has ~d all her children. 那老太太的所有孩子都先她去世。

survivor /səˈvaɪvə(r)/ *n.* [C]幸存的人；生还者：send help to the ~s of the earthquake 对地震后的幸存者给予援助

suspect Ⅰ /səˈspekt/ *vt.* 怀疑；猜想：~ the truth of an account 怀疑报道的真实性 / I ~ him to be a liar. 我怀疑他是一个说谎的人。He is ~ed of telling lies. 他有说谎的嫌疑。 Ⅱ /ˈsʌspekt/ *n.* [C]嫌疑人；可疑对象

suspend /səˈspend/ *vt.* ❶悬挂，吊(与 from 连用)：lamps ~ed from the ceiling 天花板上悬吊的灯 ❷暂停；延缓；悬而未决：~ payment 延期付款 / ~ judgment 延期宣判

suspicion /səˈspɪʃn/ *n.* 怀疑；疑心；嫌疑：He was arrested on (the) ~ of having stolen the money. 他涉嫌偷钱而被捕。/ He is under the ~ of the police. 他受到警方怀疑。

suspicious /səˈspɪʃəs/ *adj.* 怀疑的：be (feel) ~ of sb. (sth.) 对某人(某事)怀疑

sustain /səˈsteɪn/ *vt.* ❶支撑；承受：The board will not ~ your weight. 这板子承受不了你的体重。❷维持；供养：which planets can ~ life? 哪些行星上可以维持生命的存在？❸遭受；经受：~ damage (an injury, a defeat) 遭受损失(受伤，失败)

swallow[1] /ˈswɒləʊ/ *v.* 吞；咽：~ one's food 吞咽食物 / ~ one's anger 强忍心中的怒火 / ~ one's words 食言

swallow[2] /ˈswɒləʊ/ *n.* [C]燕子

swamp /swɒmp/ *n.* 沼泽；湿地

swan /swɒn/ *n.* [C]天鹅

swarm /swɔːm/ *n.* [C](昆虫、鸟等的)群：a ~ of ants 一群蚂蚁

sway /sweɪ/ *v.* (使)摇摆；(使)摆动：~ between two opinions 在两种意见中摇摆不定/ ~ to the music 随着音乐节奏摇摆/ The branches of the trees are ~ing in the wind. 树枝在风中摇晃。

swear /sweə(r)/ *v.* (swore/swɔː/, sworn/swɔːn/) ❶郑重地说；发誓，宣誓：He swore to tell the truth. 他发誓要说真话。❷咒骂；辱骂：The captain swore at his crew. 船长咒骂船员。

sweat /swet/ Ⅰ *n.* [U] 汗：wipe the ~ off one's face 揩去脸上的汗 Ⅱ *v.* 出汗：The long climb made him ~. 长时间的攀登使他出汗了。

sweater /ˈswetə(r)/ *n.* [C](厚)运动衫；毛线衫

sweep /swiːp/ *v.* (swept /swept/, swept) ❶扫除；清扫：~ the floor 扫地 ❷掠过；扫过；疾驰：The wind swept along the street. 风沿街吹过。

sweet /swiːt/ Ⅰ *adj.* ❶甜的：Do you like your tea ~? 你喜欢茶里面加糖吗？❷芳香的：How ~ the roses smell! 多么芳香的玫瑰花！Ⅱ *n.* (=candy)[C] 糖果；甜食：a box of ~s 一盒糖果 派 sweeten *v.*

swell /swel/ *v.* (swelled, swelled 或 swollen /ˈswəʊlən/) 膨胀；肿胀；隆起；

增大

swift /swɪft/ *adj.* 快的；迅速的；敏捷的：a ~ revenge 迅速报复 / **be ~ to sth., be ~ to do sth.** 易于，动不动就：My boss is ~ to anger. 我的老板动不动就生气。/ My baby is ~ to fall asleep. 我的宝宝容易入睡。

swim /swɪm/ Ⅰ *v.* (swam /swæm/, swum /swʌm/) 游泳：Let's go ~ming. 我们去游泳吧。Ⅱ *n.* 游泳：have (go for) a ~去游泳

swimming /ˈswɪmɪŋ/ Ⅰ *n.* 游泳；游泳运动 Ⅱ *adj.* (只作定语)游泳(者)的；游泳(者)用的；适于(或为了)游泳(者)的：a ~ pool 游泳池

swindle /ˈswɪndl/ Ⅰ *vt.* ❶欺诈；诈骗：~ investors out of millions of pounds 诈骗投资者几百万英镑 ❷骗取；诈取：~ money out of insurers 从投保人那里骗取保金 Ⅱ *n.* [C] ❶欺诈行为，诈骗行为 ❷骗局：a tax ~逃税骗局

swing /swɪŋ/ Ⅰ *v.* (swung /swʌŋ/, swung) (使)摇摆；(使)摆动：His arms swung as he walked. 他走路的时候手臂在摆动着。Ⅱ *n.* ❶摇摆；摆动 ❷秋千；打秋千：play on the ~ 荡秋千

swirl /swɜːl/ Ⅰ *v.* (使)打转，(使)旋转：The big tree was ~ed away on the current. 那棵大树被水流卷走了。Ⅱ *n.* [C] ❶(水、大气等的)漩涡 ❷混乱：Things were in a ~ at home. 家里一片混乱。

switch /swɪtʃ/ Ⅰ *v.* ❶接通或关掉(电源等)：~ the light (radio) on (off) 开(关)灯(收音机) ❷转变；改变：~ the conversation 改变话题 Ⅱ *n.* [C] ❶开关；电闸：master ~总开关 / power ~ 电源开关 ❷转换：We had to make a ~ in our arrangement. 我们只好改变安排。

sword /sɔːd/ *n.* [C]剑

syllable /ˈsɪləbl/ Ⅰ *n.* [C] ❶音节 ❷片言只字：He did not utter a ~ at all. 他根本就一言未发。Ⅱ *vt.* 按音节读；清晰地读

syllabus /ˈsɪləbəs/ *n.* [C] (*pl.* syllabuses 或 syllabi /-ˈbaɪ/) 教学大纲；课程大纲；(论文、演说等的)提纲，摘要；考试要求简编

symbol /ˈsɪmbl/ *n.* [C] ❶象征：Rose is a ~ of beauty. 玫瑰是美丽的象征。/ Some poets regard tree as a ~ of life. 一些诗人把树当做生命的象征。❷符号；记号：chemical ~s 化学符号 派 symbolize(-se) *vt.*

symbolic(al) /sɪmˈbɒlɪk(al)/ *adj.* 象征的；象征性的：The dove is ~ of peace. 鸽子是和平的象征。派 symbolically *adv.*

symmetry /ˈsɪmɪtri/ *n.* [U] ❶对称(性)：bilateral ~ 左右对称/ His sense of ~ was satisfied. 他终于找到了对称感。❷匀称；对称美：The ~ of his face was spoiled because of great anger. 他本来匀称的脸气歪了。

sympathetic /ˌsɪmpəˈθetɪk/ *adj.* 有同情心的；表示同情心的；同情的：~ looks (words) 表示同情的样子(话语)

sympathize /ˈsɪmpəθaɪz/ *vi.* 同情，怜悯(与 with 连用)：~ with sb. in his sufferings 同情某人的痛苦

sympathy /ˈsɪmpəθi/ *n.* [U]同情；怜悯；同感：send sb. a letter of ~ 寄给某人一封慰问信 / feel ~ for sb. 对某人表示同情 / **in ~ with** 同意；赞同：We are all in ~ with your proposals. 我们都赞成

你的提议。

symphony /ˈsɪmfəni/ *n.* [C]交响乐;交响乐团

symposium /sɪmˈpəuzɪəm/ *n.* [C](*pl.* symposia)讨论会;座谈会;研讨会;专题报告会:a theoretical ~理论研讨会

synonym /ˈsɪnənɪm/ *n.* [C]同义词,近义词:"Shut" and "close" are ~s. shut 和 close 是同义词。

synthesis /ˈsɪnθəsɪs/ *n.* (*pl.* syntheses /ˈsɪnθɪsiːz/) ❶[U]合成 ❷综合;综合体:the ~ of art with everyday life 艺术与日常生活的结合

synthetic /sɪnˈθetɪk/ *adj.* 合成的;综合的;人造的:~ fiber 合成纤维 / ~ rubber 人造橡胶

system /ˈsɪstəm/ *n.* [C]❶系统:the digestive ~ 消化系统 / the nervous ~ 神经系统 / a railway~ 铁路系统 ❷(理论、原则等的)体系;制度;政体:a ~ of philosophy 哲学体系 / a ~ of government 政府制度 / under the ~ of 在……制度下

systematic /ˌsɪstəˈmætɪk/ *adj.* ❶有系统的;系统化的:make a ~ study 做系统的研究❷有计划的;有步骤的:take ~ steps 有计划地采取措施

S

T t

tab /tæb/ *n.* [C] ❶拉手;搭扣;拉环;勒带;collect metal ~s from beer cans 收集啤酒罐上的金属拉环 ❷(导卡、书册等的)检索凸舌;标签,标牌:The ~ on the card was labelled "Top Secret". 卡片的标签上标有"绝密"字样。

table /ˈteɪbl/ *n.* [C] ❶桌子:a dining ~ 餐桌 / a tea ~ 茶几/ **at** ~ 用餐:They were at ~ when we called. 我们拜访时,他们正在用餐。❷表;目录:a ~ of contents 目录 / a railway time ~ 火车时刻表

tablet /ˈtæblət/ *n.* [C] ❶药片 ❷碑匾

taboo /təˈbuː, tæˈbuː/ Ⅰ *n.* [C] (*pl.* taboos) ❶忌讳,禁忌;应避忌的事物:place sth. under (a) ~将某事定为禁忌 ❷戒条,戒律:place a ~ upon smoking in offices 禁止在办公室抽烟 Ⅱ *adj.* 被禁止的,忌讳的:~ words 忌讳的言语

tack /tæk/ Ⅰ *n.* [C] ❶小的平头钉,宽头钉 ❷(行动或思想的)方向,方法,方针,政策:Without a guide we may of course go off on the wrong ~. 没有导游我们当然会走错路。Ⅱ *vt.* 用平头钉(或图钉)钉住:He moved the table away and ~ed the carpet down. 他把桌子搬开,把地毯用平头钉钉住。

tactics /ˈtæktɪks/ *n.* 策略;战术;兵法:Tactics is subordinate to strategy. 战术从属于战略。

tag /tæg/ *n.* [C]标签;标牌:price ~ 价格标签 / shipping ~ 货运标签 / You'd better stick a name ~ to the box. 你最好在箱子上贴上标签。

tail /teɪl/ *n.* [C]尾巴

tailor /ˈteɪlə(r)/ Ⅰ *n.* [C]裁缝 Ⅱ *vt.* 裁制(衣服):He always has his suits ~ed in Paris. 他的衣服总是在巴黎做的。

take /teɪk/ *v.* (took/tʊk/, taken/ˈteɪkn/) ❶拿;握:~ one's hand 握住某人的手 / ~ sth. on one's back 背东西 / ~ **hold of** 抓住:The child took hold of my hand when he became nervous. 这孩子在紧张的时候就抓住我的手。❷捕捉;占领;(在竞赛中)获胜:~ a town 占领一城市 / ~ 500 prisoners 抓获 500 名俘虏 ❸利用;自取;偷窃:You should ~ (advantage of) this opportunity. 你应利用这个机会。/ Who has ~n my bicycle? 谁把我的自行车拿走了? ❹携带;带走:Take the luggage upstairs. 把行李拿上楼。/ ~ **away** 拿走:These books can only be read in the library, and may not be ~n away. 这些书只供在图书馆内阅读,不能带走。~ **back** 拿回;收回:I shall ~ these goods back to the shop. 我要把这些货物拿回店去。~ **down** 拿下;取下:We must ~ the curtains down for cleaning. 我们得把窗帘取下来洗一洗。~ **out** 带出;取出:

T

The building is burning; ~ the horse out quickly. 房子烧起来了,快把马牵出去。❺享有;吃;喝;接受:~ a look (a holiday, a walk, a bath, a deep breath) 看一看(休假,散步,沐浴,做深呼吸) / He asked me to ~ a seat as soon as I entered. 我一进去,他就叫我坐下。/ Will you ~ tea or coffee? 你是喝茶还是喝咖啡? ❻记录:~ notes of a lecture 记课堂笔记/~ sth. down in shorthand 用速记记下 ❼需要:It took us two hours to get there. 到那儿花了我们两小时。❽假定;推断;以为:Do you ~ me for a fool? 你把我当成傻瓜吗? / ~ ... **for granted** 认为……理所当然;认定:He spoke English so well that I took it for granted that he was an American. 他英语讲得好极了,我理所当然地认为他是美国人。❾(经询问、测量等)找出,量出/ ~ **one's temperature** 量体温:The nurse took my temperature. 护士量了我的体温。~ **after** 像,相似:He ~s after his father in mathematical ability. 他有与他父亲相似的数学才能。~ **aim** 瞄准:Before the hunter could ~ aim, the deer jumped out of sight. 在猎人瞄准前,鹿就跑掉了。~ **care of** 照顾:She stayed at home to ~ care of the baby. 她留在家里照顾孩子。~ **great trouble to do sth.** 不辞辛劳做某事:He took great trouble to finish the book. 他不辞辛劳地写完了那本书。~ **off** ①除去;脱去:~ off one's hat 脱帽 / Help me to ~ this handle off. 帮我拿掉这把手。②起飞:Three airplanes took off at the same time. 三架飞机同时起飞。③营救出:Before the ship sank, the passengers were all safely ~n off. 船沉之前,所有乘客都被安全营救出来。~ **on a new look** 呈现新面貌:After the students put up Christmas decorations, the classroom took on a new look. 同学们挂上圣诞装饰物后,教室呈现出新面貌。~ **one's place** 代替;取代(某人):Who will ~ Mr. Smith's place? 谁将代替史密斯先生? ~ **one's turn** 轮流(做):Like the other nuns, they took their turn to do household chores. 像其他尼姑一样,她们轮流做家务。~ **part in** 参加:The Swiss did not ~ part in World War Ⅱ. 瑞士人没有参加第二次世界大战。~ **place** 发生:The accident took place only a block from his home. 事故就发生在离他家一条街远的地方。~ **pride in** 以……为自豪;对……感到骄傲:The parents took pride in the boy's success. 父母为他们儿子的成功感到自豪。~ **the side of** 支持:He always ~s the side of the Republic. 他总是支持共和党一方。~ **to** ①喜欢:Tom took to the girl as soon as they met. 汤姆一见到那女孩,就喜欢上了她。②养成(习惯);染上:Don't ~ to bad habits. 别染上恶习。~ **up** 开始;从事:He recently took up gardening. 他最近开始学园艺。

tale /teɪl/ *n.* [C] 故事;传说;报告:fairy ~s 童话故事;神话故事 / ~s of adventure 冒险故事

talent /ˈtælənt/ *n.* ❶[U]天资;才气;才能:Helen has great ~ for music but not much ~ for painting. 海伦很有音乐天分,但少有绘画天分。❷[C] 人才:athletic ~s 体育人才

talented /ˈtæləntɪd/ *adj.* 有才能的;有天分的:a ~ actor 天才演员 / Mary is a ~ painter. 玛丽是天才画家。

talk /tɔːk/ Ⅰ *vi.* 说话;谈话 :~ **about** 谈到;谈论:We were ~ing about our children, and about how well they are doing at school. 我们在谈论孩子们以及他们在学校的情况。~ **of** 谈到;说到:We were just ~ing of the most interesting books that we have read recently. 我们刚才谈到我们最近读过的最有趣的书。~ **over** 商谈:Come and see me in my office and we'll ~ it over. 到我办公室来,我们商量一下这事。— *vt*. 说(一种语言);讲:~ German 说德语 / ~ business 谈正经事/~ sense (nonsense) 说有意义的话(说无聊的话) Ⅱ *n*. ❶谈话;商议:I've had several ~s with the headmaster about my boy. 我已与校长就我儿子的问题进行过数次谈话。/ There's too much ~ and not enough work. 说得太多,做得太少。❷[C](非正式的)演讲:He will give a ~ to the students on his travels in Europe. 他将对学生就他的欧洲之行进行演讲。❸[C](常用 *pl*.)正式会谈,商谈:arms ~s 军备谈判/bilateral ~s 双边会谈/notes on ~s 会谈纪要 派 talker *n*.

talkative /ˈtɔːkətɪv/ *adj*. 爱说话的,健谈的;话多的,饶舌的:a lively, ~ young man 活泼健谈的小伙子/ She isn't ~, but she is pleasant to be with. 她不爱说话,但是挺好相处。

tall /tɔːl/ *adj*. 高的:She wears high-heeled shoes to make herself look ~er. 她穿高跟鞋使自己显得高些。

tame /teɪm/ Ⅰ *adj*. ❶驯化的;驯服的:a ~ monkey 驯服的猴子/~ birds 家禽 ❷平淡的;乏味的 Ⅱ *vt*. 驯服;驯化

tan /tæn/ Ⅰ *n*. [U]棕褐色 Ⅱ *adj*. 棕褐色的;棕黄色的 Ⅲ *v*. (tanned; tanning) 晒黑:The boys were ~ned in summer. 孩子们在夏天晒黑了。

tangent /ˈtændʒənt/ Ⅰ *n*. [C]切线;切面;正切曲线 Ⅱ *adj*. 相切的;正切的:be ~ to a circle 与圆相切

tangible /ˈtændʒɪbl/ *adj*. ❶可触及的;有形的:Sculpture is a ~ art form. 雕塑是一种有形的艺术形式。❷明确的,清楚的;真实的:~ proof 确凿证据 ❸(资产等)有形的,价值易估计的:~ assets 有形资产 派 tangibility *n*. ; tangibly *adv*.

tangle /ˈtæŋgl/ Ⅰ *vt*. ❶使缠结,使纠缠:Can you help me straighten out this string? It's become ~d (up). 这条线绕成一团了,你帮我理直好么?❷缠入,使卷入,使陷入:be ~d in a controversy 被卷入争论 Ⅱ *n*. [C] ❶(一团)缠结的东西;乱七八糟的东西:Her hair was a ~. 她的头发乱蓬蓬的。❷复杂情况;混乱局面:I am in an awful ~ with my work, can you help? 我的工作一团混乱,你能帮帮忙吗?

tank /tæŋk/ *n*. [C] ❶坦克:drive a ~ 驾驶坦克 ❷槽;罐;箱:fish ~ 鱼缸/gas ~ 汽油罐(箱) / water ~ 水箱

tanker /ˈtæŋkə(r)/ *n*. [C]油船;空中加油飞机

tap[1] /tæp/ Ⅰ *n*. [C]塞子;(自来水、煤气等的)龙头:turn the ~ on (off) 打开(关掉)龙头 / Don't leave the ~s running. 别让水龙头开着。Ⅱ *vt*. (tapped; tapping) ❶打开龙头放出 ❷开发;开辟

tap[2] /tæp/ Ⅰ *v*. (tapped; tapping) 轻敲;轻拍:~ a man on the shoulder 轻拍一个人的肩膀 Ⅱ *n*. [C]轻敲;轻拍:a ~ on the window (at the door) 敲窗(门)

tape /teɪp/ *n*. [C] ❶带子;线带 ❷(录音或录像的)磁带:~ recorder 磁带录音机/ video ~录像带 ❸终点线:breast the ~ 冲过终点

tar /tɑː(r)/ *n*. [U] ❶沥青,柏油 ❷(烟

草燃烧产生的)焦油

target /ˈtɑːɡɪt/ *n.* [C] ❶靶;目标:aim at a ~ 瞄准目标 / hit the ~ 击中靶子 / miss the ~ 没有击中靶子 ❷对象;目标:the ~ of attack 进攻的目标 / The novel became the ~ of criticism. 那本小说成了批评的对象。/ The workers reached the production ~. 工人们完成了生产目标。

tariff /ˈtærɪf/ *n.* [C]关税;税率:impose a ~ on sth. 对某物征收关税 / You have to pay a ~ on the cotton. 你得为这些棉花付关税。

task /tɑːsk/ *n.* [C](尤指困难的)工作,任务:carry out (perform) a ~ 执行任务/ take up (shoulder) a ~ 承担任务 / give the boy a ~ 给这个男孩一项任务

taste /teɪst/ Ⅰ *n.* ❶味觉;味道:sweet ~ 甜味 ❷[C]爱好:He has a ~ for pop music. 他喜欢流行音乐。/ **to one's ~** 合某人的口味 Ⅱ *v.* 尝;品味:Do you ~ anything strange in this soup? 你尝出这汤有奇怪的味道吗?

tasteful /ˈteɪstful/ *adj.* 高雅的,有品位的;有吸引力的:a ~ arrangement of flowers 高雅的插花方式 / The bedroom was simple but ~. 卧室虽简朴但很雅致。派 tastefully *adv.*

tasteless /ˈteɪstlɪs/ *adj.* ❶没有味道的:The soup is ~ without salt. 汤不放盐没味道。❷不高雅的,庸俗的;没有品位的:a ~ remark 不得体的评论 / a ~ shirt 没有品位的衬衫 派 tastelessly *adv.* ;tastelessness *n.*

tasty /ˈteɪsti/ *adj.* (-ier,-iest)味美的;可口的:a ~ meal 美餐 派 tastily *adv.*

tax /tæks/ Ⅰ *n.* 税;税额:state (local) ~es 国税(地方税) / collect ~es 收税 / raise ~es 增加税收 / lower ~es 降低税收 / evade ~es 偷税 / pay ~es 纳税 / The country imposes heavy ~ on tobacco. 国家对烟草课以重税。Ⅱ *v.* 征税:~ incomes 征所得税

taxation /tækˈseɪʃn/ *n.* [U]税制;征税

taxi /ˈtæksi/ *n.* [C](*pl.* taxis 或 taxies) [=(美)cab]出租汽车;计程车

tea /tiː/ *n.* ❶[U]茶树;茶叶;茶:make ~泡茶;沏茶 / black (green)~ 红(绿)茶 ❷茶点

teach /tiːtʃ/ *v.* (taught /tɔːt/, taught) 教;授课:~ a child to swim 教小孩游泳 / ~ English 教英语 / ~ **sb. a lesson** 教训某人

teacher /ˈtiːtʃə(r)/ *n.* [C]教师;老师;先生;导师:Teachers' Day 教师节 / the ~s' office 教师办公室 / a qualified ~ 合格教师 / a practice (student) ~ 实习教师

teaching /ˈtiːtʃɪŋ/ *n.* ❶[U]教学;教导:~ assistant 助教 / ~ method 教学方法 / give up ~ for business 弃学经商 / go into ~ 投入教学工作 ❷[C]教义:follow the ~s of the Church 遵循教会的教义

team /tiːm/ Ⅰ *n.* [C]队;组:Many eyes turned to a tall, 20-year-old girl on the U. S. A. ~. 很多双眼睛都转向美国队一个 20 岁的高个儿姑娘。/He is coaching and managing a football ~. 他正训练和管理一支足球队。Ⅱ *vi.* 协作;合作

teamwork /ˈtiːmwɜːk/ *n.* [U](卓有成效的)共同行动,集体行动,合作

tear[1] /tɪə(r)/ *n.* [C]泪;眼泪:Her eyes filled with ~s. 她的眼里充满了泪水。/ ~ bomb 催泪弹 / ~ gas 催泪毒气/ **burst(break) into ~s** 突然哭起来 **in ~s**

流着泪;哭着:She was in ~s over her failure. 她为失败而流泪。**keep back one's ~s** 忍住使眼泪不流下来 派 tearful *adj*.

tear² /teə(r)/ *v*. (tore/tɔː/, torn/tɔːn/) 撕,扯;撕碎:~ a sheet of paper in two 将一张纸撕成两半/ be torn open 被撕开/ ~ **up** 拔出;连根拔起:It's a hard job ~ing up all these unwanted plants in the garden. 要把花园里不要的植物都拔起来是件艰难的工作。

tease /tiːz/ *vt*. 逗乐;戏弄;取笑:Don't ~ the dog. 别逗那条狗玩。/ ~ **sb. about sth.** 就某事取笑某人:They ~d Jack about his new hairdo. 同学们都拿杰克的新发型开玩笑。~ **sb. into ...** 逗某人做……:She ~d her sister into anger. 她把她妹妹逗生气了。

technical /ˈteknɪkl/ *adj*. 工艺的;技能的,技术的;专门的:~ terms 专门术语/ ~ difficulties 技术性困难 派 technically *adv*.

technician /tekˈnɪʃn/ *n*. [C](精通某一项专门技术的)技术员;巧匠

technique /tekˈniːk/ *n*. 技巧;技艺;(做事的)方法

technological /ˌteknəˈlɒdʒɪkl/ *adj*. 技术的;工艺(学)的

technologist /tekˈnɒlədʒɪst/ *n*. [C] 技术专家;工艺学家

technology /tekˈnɒlədʒi/ *n*. ❶[U] 技术;工艺:the Federal Institute of Technology 联邦工学院 ❷技术应用:information ~ (IT) 信息技术 ❸应用科学

tedious /ˈtiːdɪəs/ *adj*. 乏味的;沉闷的;冗长的:~ speech 乏味的演说 / ~ story 单调的故事 / The work is ~ but worthy. 那项工作单调,但值得做。派 tediously *adv*.; tediousness *n*.

teenager /ˈtiːneɪdʒə(r)/ *n*. [C](13 岁至 19 岁的)青少年:activity for ~s 青少年的活动 / The course is offered for ~s. 那门课是为青少年开的。

telecommunication /ˌtelɪkəˌmjuːnɪˈkeɪʃn/ *n*. (利用电信、电话、电视等的)长途电信,远距离通信

telegram /ˈtelɪɡræm/ *n*. [C] 电报:get (receive) a ~ from sb. 收到某人的电报/ send a ~ to 发电报给…… / They sent the invitation by ~. 他们用电报发出邀请。

telegraph /ˈtelɪɡrɑːf, ˈtelɪɡræf/ Ⅰ *n*. 电报;电报机:~ receiver 收报机 / ~ transmitter 发报机 Ⅱ *v*. 打电报;以电报传达

telegrapher /tɪˈleɡrəfə(r)/ *n*. [C]电报员;报务员

telegraphic /ˌtelɪˈɡræfɪk/ *adj*. 电报的;以电报传达的;与电报有关的

telegraphy /təˈleɡrəfi/ *n*. [U]电报术;电报学

telephone /ˈtelɪfəʊn/ Ⅰ *n*. 电话;电话机:send a message by ~ 用电话传递消息 / install a ~ 安装电话 / make (give) sb. a ~ call 给某人打电话 Ⅱ *v*. 以电话发送消息;打电话给……:I ~d the secretary that I couldn't attend the meeting. 我打电话告诉秘书说,我不能去参加会议。

telescope /ˈtelɪskəʊp/ *n*. [C]望远镜

televise /ˈtelɪvaɪz/ *vt*. 由电视播送:The Olympic Games were ~d all over the world. 奥运会通过电视向全世界播送。

television /ˈtelɪvɪʒn/ *n*. 电视;电视机:He appeared on ~ last night. 他昨晚在电视上出现。/ black-and-white(color)

~黑白(彩色)电视 / turn on (off) the ~开(关)电视

telex /ˈteleks/ *n.* 电传(系统)

tell /tel/ *v.* (told /təʊld/, told) ❶告知;告诉:~ a lie 撒谎/ ~ the truth 说实话 / He told the news to everybody in the village. 他把这消息告诉村里的每一个人。❷辨识;区别(尤与 can, could, be able to 连用) / ~... **from** ... 辨别:Can you ~ Tom from his twin brother? 你能辨别汤姆和他的孪生兄弟吗? / Every one of us should learn to ~ right from wrong. 我们每个人都应该学会明辨是非。

teller /ˈtelə(r)/ *n.* [C] ❶(银行)出纳员:a qualified bank ~合格的银行出纳 ❷(故事等的)讲述人:a fortune ~算命人/ Charlie is also a marvellous ~ of jokes. 查理的笑话讲得也很精彩。

temper /ˈtempə(r)/ Ⅰ *n.* 性情;脾气;心情:**in a good (bad)** ~ 心情好(不佳) **get (fly) into a** ~ **(about sth.)** (为某事)发脾气:At the bad news, he flew into a ~. 他一听到那坏消息就发起火来。**keep one's** ~ 忍住脾气:He kept his ~ despite the provocation. 他虽然受到挑衅,但忍着不发怒。**lose one's** ~ 发脾气:The teacher lost his ~ with my coming late. 老师因我迟到而发火。Ⅱ *vt.* 锻炼:He got ~ed in the storms of life. 他在生活的风暴中得到锻炼。

temperament /ˈtempərəmənt/ *n.* ❶气质;性情,秉性;性格 a girl with an artistic ~颇有些艺术气质的女孩/ The twins look alike, but in ~ they are different. 这对双胞胎看起来一样,但是性情却不一样。❷[U]活跃的个性:He is full of ~. 他精神饱满。

temperature /ˈtemprətʃə(r)/ *n.* ❶温度;体温:absolute (average, constant, normal) ~ 绝对(平均、恒定、正常)温度/ body (room) ~ 体(室)温 / In Hawaii there are no extremes of ~. 夏威夷的气温不特别冷也不特别热。/ The nurse took the ~s of all the patients. 护士为所有的病人量体温。❷发烧:She had a ~ last night. 昨天晚上她发烧了。

temple /ˈtempl/ *n.* [C]庙宇;寺院;神殿

tempo /ˈtempəʊ/ *n.* [C] (*pl.* -pos 或-pi /-piː/) ❶速度,节奏;拍子:play the music at a fast ~ 用快拍演奏音乐 ❷(行动或活动的)速度;步调:She has become used to the busy (fast) ~ of city life. 她已习惯了城市生活的快节奏。

temporary /ˈtemprəri/ *adj.* 暂时的;临时的:~ employment 临时的工作 派 temporarily *adv.*

tempt /tempt/ *v.* ❶劝诱,诱惑(做坏事或笨事):~ away a boy 拐走一男孩 /~ sb. off the straight path 把某人引入歧途/His bad companions ~ed him to drink heavily. 他的损友诱使他酗酒。❷吸引;引起……的兴趣:The warm weather ~ed us to go for a swim. 暖和的天气引起我们去游泳的兴趣。

temptation /tempˈteɪʃn/ *n.* ❶[U]吸引;劝诱;诱惑:face ~ 面对诱惑 / resist ~ 抵制诱惑 / yield to ~ 受诱惑 / the ~ of money金钱的诱惑 ❷[C]诱惑物;有吸引力之物:Clever advertisements are ~s for people to spend money. 巧妙的广告诱人花钱。

ten /ten/ Ⅰ *num.* 十,10:~s of thousands 好几万 / ~ **to one** 十之八九;很可能:Ten to one he will arrive late. 他很可能会迟到。Ⅱ *adj.* 十个的,十的

tenant /ˈtenənt/ *n.* [C]佃户;房客;租户

tend[1] / tend / *vt.* 护理；照料：shepherds ~ing their flocks 照料羊群的牧羊者

tend[2] / tend / *vi.* ❶走向；趋向：They ~ed to the same conclusion. 他们趋向于同一结论。❷倾向：~ to be optimistic 倾向于乐观 ❸有助于：The measure ~s to improve working conditions. 这项措施有助于改善工作环境。

tendency / ˈtendənsi / *n.* [C]趋向；趋势；倾向：resist wrong tendencies 抵制错误倾向

tender / ˈtendə(r) / *adj.* ❶脆弱的；纤弱的；易损坏的：~ blossoms 娇嫩的花 / ~ spot 痛处；弱点 / ~ wound 一触即疼的伤口 ❷(指肉)易咀嚼的，嫩的：a ~ steak 嫩牛排 ❸温和的；亲切的：a ~ smile 温和的微笑 派 tenderly *adv.*；tenderness *n.*

tennis / ˈtenɪs / *n.* [U]网球：~ court 网球场

tense / tens / Ⅰ *adj.* 拉紧的；紧张的：~ atmosphere 紧张的气氛 / The mother's face was ~ with worry. 妈妈因担忧而表情紧张。Ⅱ *n.* [C](动词的)时态：the present (past, future) ~ 现在(过去、将来)时

tension / ˈtenʃn / Ⅰ *n.* [U]紧张；紧张局势；紧张状况：ease ~ 缓和紧张状况 / heighten (increase) ~ 加剧紧张局势 / The policy caused international ~. 那项政策引起了国际局势的紧张。 Ⅱ *vt.* 使拉紧；使紧张 派 tensional *adj.*

tent / tent / *n.* [C]帐篷

tentacle / ˈtentəkl / *n.* [C](动物的)触须；触动；触手

tentative / ˈtentətɪv / *adj.* ❶试探性的，试验性的；暂行的：a ~ proposal 试探性提议 / ~ standard 试行标准 ❷犹豫不决的；不肯定的：I think we are moving to a better flat in April, but that's only ~. 我想我们4月份就能搬到一套更好的套房里去住，但是这事还不能肯定。 派 tentatively *adv.*；tentativeness *n.*

tenth / tenθ / Ⅰ *num.* 第十；十分之一 Ⅱ *adj.* 第十的；十分之一的

term / tɜːm / *n.* [C] ❶期限：a long ~ of imprisonment 长期监禁 ❷(指学校、大学等的)学期：at the end of a ~ 在期末 ❸词语；术语：technical ~s 专门术语 ❹(多用 *pl.*)条件；条款：state (accept) ~s of peace 提出(接受)和平条件 / **in ~s of** 根据；就……而言，在……方面：What does this mean in ~s of cost? 这在成本上意味着什么？ **make ~s (with sb.)** (与某人)达成协议

terminal / ˈtɜːmɪnl / Ⅰ *adj.* 末端的；终点的；极限的：~ cancer 晚期癌症 / ~ examination 期末考试 / I'll get off at the ~ station. 我在终点站下车。Ⅱ *n.* [C]末端；终端；终点(站)：airline ~ 航空终点站 / computer ~ 电脑终端 / We met at the bus ~. 我们在公共汽车终点站碰面。 派 terminally *adv.*

terminate / ˈtɜːmɪneɪt / *v.* 停止；终止

terminology / ˌtɜːmɪˈnɒlədʒi / *n.* [U]术语学；术语

terrain / təˈreɪn, ˈtereɪn, teˈreɪn / *n.* [U] 地形，地势；地域，地带：hilly ~ 山丘地带 / rocky ~ 岩石地带

terrible / ˈterəbl / *adj.* ❶可怕的；极不舒服的：a ~ war 可怕的战争 ❷极度的；厉害的：~ heat 酷热 / ~ winter 严冬 ❸很糟的；极坏的：The weather was ~ when we were there. 我们在那里时，天气糟透了。

terribly / ˈterəbli / *adv.* 可怕地；非常地；极度地：It's ~ hot. 天气非常炎热。/

T

She was ~ tired. 她累坏了。

terrific /təˈrɪfɪk/ *adj.* ❶(口语)巨大的;极度的;强力的;非常好的:We had a ~ vacation last month. 我们上个月的假期过得好极了。❷令人恐怖的;可怕的:a ~ air alarm 令人恐怖的空袭警报 派 terrifically *adv.*

terrify /ˈterɪfaɪ/ *vt.* 使感到恐惧;惊吓:The child was terrified of being left alone in the house. 那孩子因单独被留在屋里而感到惊恐。

territorial /ˌterɪˈtɔːrɪəl/ *adj.* ❶领土的:~ air 领空/~ integrity 领土完整 ❷(有)地域性的,区域性的:a ~ economy 区域经济/ These regulations are strictly ~. 这些规定完全是地区性的。

territory /ˈterətri/ *n.* ❶领土;版图:Chinese ~ 中国的领土 / They joined the army to defend the sacred ~ of their motherland. 他们参军保卫祖国的神圣领土。❷[C]领域;范围:There are many new discoveries in the ~ of physics. 物理学领域里有许多新发现。

terror /ˈterə(r)/ *n.* ❶[U]恐怖;惊骇:live in ~ 生活在恐怖之中 ❷[C]引起恐怖的人或事物:The boss was a ~ to the workers. 老板是工人们惧怕的人。

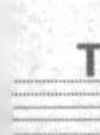

terrorism /ˈterəˌrɪzəm/ *n.* [U]恐怖主义:These measures failed to bring acts of ~ to an end. 这些措施没能结束恐怖主义行动。派 terrorist *n.* & *adj.*

test /test/ Ⅰ *n.* [C]试验;测验,考试:blood ~ 验血 /intelligence ~ 智力测验/ The theory can stand the ~ of time. 这个理论能够经受时间的考验。Ⅱ *v.* 试验;检验:have one's eyesight ~ed 检验视力 / ~ ore for gold 检验矿石以找出其中的黄金 / The machine must be ~ed before it is used. 机器在使用前必须检查一下。

testify /ˈtestɪfaɪ/ *vi.* ❶证明,证实:The open door testified to the fact that he had left in a hurry. 敞开的房门证明他离开时很匆忙。❷出庭作证:None of the onlookers would appear in court to ~ against him. 没有一个旁观者愿意出庭指证他。—*vt.* 作为……的证据,证明:Her nervous behaviour testified that she told a lie. 她行为局促不安,表明她说谎了。

testimonial /ˌtestɪˈməʊnɪəl/ n. [C] ❶(品行、资格等的)证明书;推荐信;鉴定书:All applicants for the job must come with ~. 本工作的申请人必须带有推荐信。❷馈赠物;感谢信;表扬信;奖章;奖状

testimony /ˈtestɪməmi/ *n.* ❶[U]证词,证供:take ~ from the next witness 从下一位证人那里取证词 ❷证据,证明:produce ~出示证据 /call sb. in ~ 叫某人作证

test-tube /ˈtestˌtjuːb/ *n.* [C]试管

text /tekst/ *n.* [C] ❶课文 ❷正文 ❸教科书

textbook /ˈtekstbʊk/ *n.* [C]课本;教科书

textile /ˈtekstaɪl/ Ⅰ *adj.* (只作定语)纺织的,织物的:the ~ industry 纺织工业 Ⅱ *n.* [C]织物;纺织品;纺织原料:cotton (silk, wool) ~s 棉(丝、毛)织品

texture /ˈtekstʃə(r)/ *n.* ❶质地;质感;质相:wool of a coarse ~粗羊毛/ You can't plant this crop in the soil with a loose sandy ~. 这种作物不能种在质地松散的沙质土里。❷结构,组织;纹理:The chemist is testing for the ~ of the mineral. 那位化学家正在测试该矿物的结构。

than /ðæn,ðən/ *conj.* 比(用于形容词、副词比较级之后):John is taller ~ his brother. 约翰比他兄弟高。/ **no more** ~ 仅仅;只是:I need no more ~ five people. 我只需要五个人。**no other** ~正是:The speaker was no other ~ our teacher. 演讲者不是别人,正是我们的老师。

thank /θæŋk/ Ⅰ *v.* 谢;感谢:There is no need to ~ me. 不必谢我。/ Thank you for your help. 感谢你的帮助。Ⅱ *n.* 感谢 / ~**s to** 由于,因为:Thanks to your help, we succeeded. 由于你的帮助,我们成功了。

thankful /ˈθæŋkfl/ *adj.* 感谢的;欣慰的:We are ~ to the policeman for his timely help. 我们感谢警察的及时帮助。

that /ðæt/ Ⅰ *adj.* 那(后接复数名词时用 those):Do you know ~ girl? 你认识那女孩吗? Ⅱ *pron.* ❶那,那个(指示代词):Is that your brother? 那是你兄弟吗? /That is why she cannot come here. 那就是她不能来这儿的原因。❷(关系代词):Shakespeare is the greatest poet ~ England has ever had. 莎士比亚是英国历史上最伟大的诗人。Ⅲ *conj.* ❶(引导名词从句):The trouble is ~ we are short of food. 困难是我们缺粮。❷(引导状语从句,表示目的、结果、原因或让步):Bring it nearer (so) ~ I may see it better. 把它拿近一些,好让我看得更清楚。/ He worried ~ he couldn't go to sleep. 他急得不能入睡。/ We'll let you use the room on condition (provided) ~ you keep it clean and tidy. 只要你保持房间的整洁,我们就让你使用这房间。❸(引导强调句型):It is the Party's leadership ~ makes our country rich and strong. 正是党的领导使我们国家富强。Ⅳ *adv.* (口语)如此,那样:I can't walk ~ far. 我走不了那么快。/ ~ **is to say** 即;换句话说 **in order** ~为了:He gave his life in order ~ others live happily. 为了他人能活得幸福,他牺牲了生命。**now** ~既然:Now ~ you have finished the task, you may go home. 既然已经完成任务,你们可以回家了。/ Now ~ you are well again, you can travel. 你既然恢复了健康,就可以旅行了。**That'll do.** (**That will do.**)行了,够了。

the /ðiː,ðɪ,ðə/ Ⅰ *art.* ❶作 this, these, that, those 的弱式语,用以指已经提到过或正讨论的人、物、事等 ❷与代表独一无二事物的名词连用:~ sun 太阳 / ~ moon 月亮 ❸与形容词最高级连用:~ tallest of the five 五人中的最高者 ❹用于海洋、江河、运河或其他复数地理名词前:~ Red Sea 红海 / ~ Atlantic (Ocean)大西洋 / ~ Nile 尼罗河 / ~ Alps 阿尔卑斯山脉 ❺与表示乐器的名词连用:play ~ piano (~ violin)弹钢琴(拉小提琴) ❻与形容词或分词连用表示一类人:~ rich 富人 / ~ poor 穷人 / ~ young 年轻人 / ~ old 老年人 / ~ dead 死者 / ~ dying 垂死者 Ⅱ *adv.* (用于形容词、副词比较级前)愈,更,越:The more he has, ~ more he wants. 他得到的愈多,愈想得到更多。/ Actually, ~ busier he is, ~ happier he feels. 事实上他越忙越高兴。

theater(-re) /ˈθɪətə(r)/ *n.* [C]戏院;剧场

theft /θeft/ *n.* ❶盗窃;偷窃 ❷盗窃罪

their /ðeə(r)/ *pron.* 他(她、它)们的(形容词性物主代词):They have lost ~ dog. 他们的狗丢了。

theirs /ðeəz/ *pron.* 他(她、它)们的(名词性物主代词):It's a habit of ~. 那是

他们的一种习惯。

them / ðəm / *pron.* 他(她、它)们(they的宾格)

theme / θi:m / *n.* [C](谈话或写作的)题目;主题

themselves / ðəmˈselvz / *pron.* 他(她,它)们自己(反身代词): They did the work by ~. 他们独自干了这件工作。

then / ðen / *adv.* ❶其时;当时: We were living in Chengdu ~. 当时我们住在成都。/ **by** ~到那时: I shall come back ten years from now; you'll be a big boy by ~. 我十年后才回来,到那时你将是个大孩子了。**from** ~ **on** 自那时起 **until** ~到那时 **since** ~那时以来 ❷其次;然后: We'll have fish first and ~ roast chicken. 我们先吃鱼,然后吃烤鸡。❸(通常用于句首或句尾)那么,因此: —It isn't here. —它不在这儿。—It must be in the next room, ~. —那么它一定在隔壁房间。

theoretical / θɪəˈretɪkəl / *adj.* 理论的;推理的: ~ basis 理论基础/~ knowledge 理论知识 派 theoretically *adv.*

theorist / ˈθɪərɪst / *n.* [C]理论家;空想者

theorize / ˈθɪəraɪz / *vi.* 谈理论;推理

theory / ˈθɪəri / *n.* ❶理论;原理: Your plan is excellent in ~, but would it succeed in practice? 你的计划在理论上好极了,但在实际上可行吗? It is necessary for us to combine ~ with practice. 我们必须要理论结合实际。/ **in** ~ 在理论上: In ~, the plan is feasible. 在理论上这个计划是可行的。❷学说: ~ of Marxism 马克思主义学说 ❸见解;看法

therapy / ˈθerəpi / *n.* (尤指通过锻炼、按摩等方式而非手术的)治疗(方法): shock ~休克疗法/ speech ~语言疗法

there / ðeə(r) / *adv.* ❶在那里;往那里: We shall soon be ~. 不久我们就会到那里。❷(用 there is /are)有……,……在: There is someone at the door. 有人在门口。/ There are some children playing on the street. 街上有些小孩在玩耍。/~ **and then** 当时;当场;立刻: I decided to do it ~ and then. 我决定立刻就做。**over** ~在那里: The book you want is over ~. 你要的书就在那儿。❸(there 放在句首加强语气,如句子主语不是代词,则置于动词之后)瞧,你看: There goes the last bus! 最后一辆公共汽车开走了! / There they come! 瞧,他们来了!

thereabout(s) / ˌðeərəˈbaut(s) / *adv.* ❶ 在那附近: He lives in a rented house ~. 他住在附近一栋租赁的房子里。❷大约,左右: at the age of eighteen or ~ 18 岁左右

thereby / ˌðeəˈbaɪ / *adv.* 因此;从而;由此

therefore / ˈðeəfɔ:(r) / *adv.* 因此;所以

thermal / ˈθɜ:məl / Ⅰ *adj.* ❶热的;产生热的: ~ energy 热能 ❷保暖的;隔热的: ~ underwear 保暖内衣 ❸温泉的: ~ waters 温泉水 Ⅱ *n.* ❶[C]上升暖气流: Birds and gliders circle in ~s to gain height. 鸟类和滑翔机借助上升热气流上升。❷(*pl.*)衣服,(尤指)保暖内衣

thermometer / θəˈmɒmɪtə(r) / *n.* [C]寒暑表;温度计

Thermos / ˈθɜ:məs / *n.* [C]热水瓶

these / ði:z / *adj.* & *pron.* 这些(this 的复数)

thesis / ˈθi:sɪs / *n.* (*pl.* theses/ˈθi:si:z/) [C]论题;论点;论文: He is writing a ~

on American literature. 他正在写一篇关于美国文学的论文。

they /ðeɪ/ *pron.* 他(她、它)们(he, she 和 it 的复数)

thick /θɪk/ *adj.* ❶厚的；粗大的：a ~ slice of bread 一片厚面包 / a ~ line 粗线 ❷密集的；稠密的：a ~ forest 密林 ❸浓的；稠的：~ soup 稠汤 / ~ fog 浓雾 派 thickly *adv.*；thickness *n.*

thicken /ˈθɪkən/ *v.* ❶(使)增厚；(使)变稠；(使)变浓：Thicken the sauce with a little flour. 用少许面粉将沙司弄稠一些。/ Saliva ~ed in his mouth and throat. 唾液在他的嘴里喉咙里越积越多。❷使(声音)沙哑；使哽住：Her kindness to Tom ~ed his throat as he remembered it. 一想到她的好，汤姆便哽咽起来。❸变得更复杂：The world is ~ing. 这世界变得越发纷繁。

thief /θiːf/ *n.* [C] (*pl.* thieves/θiːvz/) 贼；小偷：a common ~ 一个惯偷/ a gang of ~ 一伙贼/ The police caught a car ~. 警察抓住一个偷车贼。

thigh /θaɪ/ *n.* [C] 股；大腿

thin /θɪn/ *adj.* (thinner, thinnest) ❶薄的；细的：a ~ slice of bread 一片薄面包 / a ~ piece of string 一根细线 ❷瘦的：a ~ face 一张瘦脸 ❸稀疏的：~ audience 稀少的观众 ❹稀薄的；淡的：~ gruel 稀粥 / ~ beer 淡啤酒/ ~ mist 薄雾

thing /θɪŋ/ *n.* [C] ❶东西；事物：What are those ~s on the table? 桌上的那些东西是什么？❷事件；事情：There's another ~ I want to ask you. 还有一件事我要问问你。❸(多用 *pl.*)情况，情形；局势：That only makes ~s worse. 那只会使情况更糟。/ **above all ~s** 最重要的是；尤其 **for one ~ …, for another …** 首先……，再者…… **of all ~s** 首先

think /θɪŋk/ *v.* (thought/θɔːt/, thought) ❶思索；考虑：Are animals able to ~? 动物能思考吗？❷认为；以为：—Do you ~ it will rain? —你认为天会下雨吗？—Yes, I ~ so. —是的，我想会。/ ~ **about** ①思考：I'm sorry. I wasn't listening to you. I was ~ing about something else. 对不起，我没听你说，我在想别的事。②认为：What do you ~ about the government's latest decision? 你认为政府的最新决定如何？③考虑：We must ~ about mother's health when choosing a home. 选择住家时，我们必须考虑到母亲的健康。/ Are you still ~ing about moving to the south? 你还在考虑搬到南方去吗？~ **back to** 回想起：Every time he read the novel, he would ~ back to the days he was living in the countryside. 他每次读到那本书，就会回想起在农村生活的日子。~ **highly (well) of** 对……评价很高：We ~ highly of his action. 我们对他的行为评价很高。~ **ill of** 看不起；轻视：Don't ~ ill of him. He is something in the town. 别看不起他，他在镇里是一个重要人物。~ **nothing of** 不在乎；不考虑：Lei Feng thought nothing of himself. 雷锋从不考虑自己。~ **of** ①思考；考虑：When I said that, I was not ~ing of her feelings. 我说那事的时候，没考虑到她的感受。/ If you thought of the possible results before you acted, you wouldn't do such a foolish thing. 如果你行动之前想一想可能的后果，你就不会做出这种愚蠢的事。②想起；记住：Will you ~ of me after I've left? 我走后你能记住我吗？③提出；建议：Who ~s of the plan? 谁提出的这个计划？~

of ... as ...把……看作……：He always ~s of others' difficulties as his. 他总是把别人的困难看作自己的困难。~ **out** 想出：He thought out a solution to the problem. 他想出了一个解决问题的办法。~ **over** 仔细考虑：Think it over and let me have your decision tomorrow. 仔细考虑考虑，明天让我知道你的决定。/ I've thought the plan over and decided not to join it after all. 我仔细考虑了这个计划，最后决定不参加。派 thinker *n.*

thinking /ˈθɪŋkɪŋ/ Ⅰ *adj.* 思想的；有思考能力的：Man is a ~ animal. 人是有思维能力的动物。Ⅱ *n.* [U]思想，思考：do some hard ~ 深思 / to one's ~ 照某人的看法 / without ~ 不假思索

third /θɜːd/ Ⅰ *num.* 第三；三分之一 Ⅱ *adj.* 第三的；三分之一的 派 thirdly *adv.*

thirst /θɜːst/ *n.* [U] ❶渴：They lost their way in the desert and died of ~. 他们在沙漠中迷路而渴死了。❷热望，渴望：a ~ for knowledge 求知欲

thirsty /ˈθɜːsti/ *adj.* (-ier,-iest) ❶渴的：Do you feel ~? 你口渴吗？❷渴望的；渴求的：They are ~ for success. 他们渴望得到成功。

thirteen /ˌθɜːˈtiːn/ Ⅰ *num.* 十三，13 Ⅱ *adj.* 十三个(的)

thirteenth /ˌθɜːˈtiːnθ/ Ⅰ *num.* 第十三；十三分之一 Ⅱ *adj.* 第十三的；十三分之一的

thirtieth /ˈθɜːtiəθ/ Ⅰ *num.* 第三十；三十分之一 Ⅱ *adj.* 第三十的；三十分之一的

thirty /ˈθɜːti/ Ⅰ *num.* 三十，30 Ⅱ *adj.* 三十个的

this /ðɪs/ *adj.* & *pron.* (后接复数名词时用 these)这，这个：early ~ morning 今天一大早 / to ~ day 直到今天 / What is ~? 这是什么？

thorn /θɔːn/ *n.* [C] ❶(植物的)刺，棘：a twig covered with ~s 长满刺的细枝 ❷使人苦恼(或生气)的事(或人)：Inflation has been a constant ~ for the Premier. 通货膨胀问题一直使总理很苦恼。

thorough /ˈθʌrə/ *adj.* 完全的；彻底的；周到的；缜密的：a ~ person 一个一丝不苟的人 / give the room a ~ cleaning 把房子彻底打扫一番 / be ~ in one's work 工作认真 派 thoroughly *adv.*

those /ðəʊz/ *pron.* & *adj.* 那些(that 的复数形式)

though /ðəʊ/ Ⅰ *conj.* ❶虽然：Though they are poor, they are always neatly dressed. 他们虽然穷，衣着却总是整洁的。/ **as** ~好像；似乎：He walked as ~ he had been drunk. 他走路就好像喝醉了似的。**even** ~即使：The work must be done even ~ there is a storm. 即使有暴风雨，那工作也必须做完。❷即使：He would not give up ~ he might meet with a lot of difficulties. 即使遇到很多困难，他也不会放弃。Ⅱ *adv.* 可是；不过；然而：The vase isn't pretty, I like it ~. 这花瓶不漂亮，可是我喜欢它。

thought /θɔːt/ *n.* ❶[U]思想；思考力；思考方式；思潮：He often acts without ~. 他常鲁莽行事。/ **at first** ~乍一想：At first ~, what he said is reasonable. 乍一想，他说的有道理。**at the ~ of** 想起……：She was excited at the ~ of her success. 她一想起她的成功就激动。**on second ~(s)** 经仔细考虑后 **read sb.'s ~s** 看出某人的心思 **take ~ for** 对……挂念：The mother took ~ for her son.

母亲挂念儿子。**without a moment's** ~ 立即；当场 ❷想法；意见：He keeps his ~s to himself. 他不把自己的想法对别人说。

thoughtful /ˈθɔːtfl/ *adj.* ❶思考的；沉思的；深思的：She looked ~. 看上去她在沉思。❷体贴的；关心的；考虑周到的：It is ~ of you to remind me of the meeting. 提醒我要开会，你考虑得很周到。/ Bill is a ~ man. 比尔是一个关心别人的人。

thousand /ˈθaʊzənd/ Ⅰ *num.* 千 Ⅱ *adj.* 千个的：~s of 成千上万的 / one in a ~ 千里挑一的人物；出众的人物 / (a) ~ and one 无数的/ *The Thousand and One Nights*《一千零一夜》(《天方夜谭》)

thousandth /ˈθaʊzənθ/ Ⅰ *num.* 第一千；千分之一 Ⅱ *adj.* 第一千的；千分之一的

thread /θred/ Ⅰ *n.* ❶(一股)线：a reel of silk ~ 一卷丝线 / a needle and ~ 穿了线的针 / **hang by a** ~ 千钧一发；濒临危机 ❷[C]头绪；线索；思路：lose the ~ 抓不住论点；失去头绪 / pick up (take up) the ~ 接着讲下去 / ~s of a story 故事的线索 Ⅱ *vt.* 穿(针)

threat /θret/ *n.* ❶恐吓；威胁：**under ~ of** 在……威胁下：She obeyed his order, but only under ~ of punishment. 只是因为受到严惩的威胁，她才服从了他的命令。❷前兆；预兆：There was a ~ of rain in the dark sky. 乌云密布的天空有下雨的兆头。

threaten /ˈθretn/ *v.* ❶威胁；恐吓：~ to murder sb. 威胁要谋杀某人 ❷预示：The clouds ~ rain. 乌云预示着要下雨。

three /θriː/ Ⅰ *num.* 三，3 Ⅱ *adj.* 三个的

thrill /θrɪl/ Ⅰ *n.* [C](一阵)激动 Ⅱ *v.* 使激动：It ~ed me to hear of your success. 听说你成功了真让我激动。

thrive /θraɪv/ *vi.* (thrived 或 throve /θrəʊv/，thrived 或 thriven/ˈθrɪvɪn/)兴旺，繁荣；茁壮成长：~ on hard work 靠勤劳起家(致富)/ ~ with good management 由于管理完善而兴旺 / Markets are thriving, and prices are stable. 市场繁荣，物价稳定。

throat /θrəʊt/ *n.* [C]喉咙；咽喉：A bone has stuck in my ~. 一根骨头哽在我的喉咙里。/ clear one's ~ 清嗓子/ cut one another's ~s 相互残杀 / cut one's own ~ 自取灭亡 / have a bone in one's ~ 难以启齿 / take sb. by the ~ 掐住某人的脖子，掐死某人

throb /θrɒb/ Ⅰ *vi.* (throbbed; throbbing) ❶(急促有力地)搏动；悸动；突突跳动：My heart ~bed fast. 我的心怦怦直跳。❷(有节奏地)震动，(有规律地)颤动 Ⅱ *n.* [C] ❶(急促有力的)搏动；跳动；悸动：A ~ of pain shot through his chest. 他感到胸部一阵剧烈的抽痛。❷有规律的颤动；有节奏的抖动

throne /θrəʊn/ *n.* [C] ❶宝座；御座 ❷(the ~)王位：come to the ~ 即位 / succeed to the ~继承王位

throng /θrɒŋ/ Ⅰ *n.* [C]一大群人：a wildly cheering ~疯狂欢呼的人群/ the worldly ~芸芸众生 Ⅱ *v.* 拥入；(使)挤满；聚集：The sight of the streets were ~ed with buyers. 街道上熙来攘往的尽是购物的人们。/ The demonstrators ~ed over the bridge towards the city hall. 示威者聚集在通往市政厅的大桥上。

through /θruː/ Ⅰ *prep.* ❶穿过；越过；经过：The River Thames flows ~ London. 泰晤士河流经伦敦。❷(指时间)自始至终；从头到尾：He won't live ~ tonight. 他活不过今晚。❸(表示作用或方法)从,通过:I learnt of the position ~ a piece of newspaper advertisement. 我从一则报纸广告上获知有这个职位。Ⅱ*adv.* 从一端至另一端;自始至终;贯穿:They wouldn't let us ~. 他们不让我们过去。

throughout /θruːˈaʊt/ Ⅰ *prep.* 遍及;在各处;在整个期间:~ the country 全国各地 / ~ the war 在整个战争期间 / Qingdao is known ~ the world for its beautiful beaches. 青岛以其美丽的海滨而世界闻名。Ⅱ *adv.* 一直;各处:The wood house was rotten ~. 那座木屋已完全烂掉了。

throw /θrəʊ/ *v.* (threw /θruː/, thrown /θrəʊn/)❶投;抛;掷:He threw the ball to me. 他把球掷给我。❷摔倒:The wrestler threw his opponent. 摔跤手把对手摔倒在地。/ ~ **away** 扔掉;抛弃:Don't ~ away old newspapers; they may be of some use. 不要把旧报纸扔掉,或许还有什么用处。~ **doubt on** 怀疑:Don't ~ doubt on him. What he said is true. 别怀疑他,他说的是真的。/ Everyone was prepared to accept the statement until the chairman threw doubt on it. 在主席对这种说法产生怀疑之前,人人都准备接受它。~ **light on** 阐明;说明:Have the police been able to ~ any light on the mystery of the stolen jewels yet? 警察能解开首饰被盗之谜吗? ~ **off** ①匆匆脱掉(衣服):Throwing off his coat, he jumped into the river to save the drowning child. 他匆匆脱掉大衣就跳到河里去救那溺水的孩子。②摆脱:I wish I could ~ off these newspaper reporters who are following me everywhere. 我真希望能摆脱这些我走到哪儿就跟到哪儿的新闻记者。③扔掉;抛掉:It's very difficult to ~ off old habits of thought. 很难丢掉旧的思维习惯。~ **oneself into** 投身于……;热衷于…… ~ **sb. into prison** 把某人投入监狱:The man was thrown into prison for his robbery. 那人因抢劫而被关进监狱。

thrust /θrʌst/ Ⅰ *v.* (thrust, thrust)刺;戳;插:He ~ his hands into his pockets. 他把双手插入衣袋中。/ ~ one's way through a crowd 从人群中挤过去 / ~ sb. to death 将某人戳死 / ~ sb. to the wall 把某人逼至绝境 Ⅱ *n.* ❶[C]刺;戳 ❷[U]要点;要旨

thumb /θʌm/ *n.* [C]拇指:be all ~s 笨手笨脚 / put (turn) one's ~ up 竖起大拇指表示赞成(同意)

thunder /ˈθʌndə(r)/ Ⅰ *n.* [U]❶雷;雷声:We haven't had much ~ this summer. 今年夏天我们没听到什么雷声。❷似雷的响声:the ~ of applause 掌声如雷 Ⅱ *v.* ❶ 打雷:It was lightning and ~ing. 正在闪电打雷。❷发出如雷的声音:The train ~ed through the station. 火车轰隆隆驶过车站。

thunderous /ˈθʌndərəs/ *adj.* 打雷的;响声如雷的:~ applause 雷鸣般的掌声

thunderstruck /ˈθʌndəˌstrʌk/ *adj.* 惊呆的,吓坏了的,大吃一惊的:They seemed to be ~ at the news. 看来,这条消息让他们大吃了一惊。

Thursday /ˈθɜːzdeɪ/ *n.* 星期四

thus /ðʌs/ *adv.* 这样;因而

tick /tɪk/ *n.* [C](尤指钟表发出的)滴答声

ticket /ˈtɪkɪt/ *n.* [C] ❶票;入场券:free ~ 免费招待券 / lottery ~ 彩票 / meal

T

~ 餐券,饭票 / platform ~ 月台票/Do you want a single or a return ~? 你要单程票还是往返票? ❷罚款单: The driver was given a ~ because of driving too fast. 由于车开得太快,司机被处以罚款。

tickle /ˈtɪkl/ *v.* ❶搔痒;呵痒: I ~d him under the ears. 我在他耳后挠痒痒。❷有痒感,觉得痒: My throat had stopped tickling. 我的嗓子不痒了。❸使欢愉,逗乐: He is ~d by the idea. 这主意让他觉得开心。

ticklish /ˈtɪklɪʃ/ *adj.* ❶怕痒的;易痒的: He's ~ on the feet. 他的脚怕痒。❷棘手的,难以对付的;需小心对付的: The job is quite ~ to the ear. 这工作听起非常棘手。

tidal /ˈtaɪdəl/ *adj.* 潮(汐)的;有潮的;受潮汐影响的: a ~ basin 感潮流域/ This part of the river is ~. 这段河流受潮汐影响。

tide /taɪd/ *n.* [C] ❶潮;潮汐: at the high (low) ~ 高(低)潮时/ The ~ is rising. 涨潮了。The ~ is falling. 退潮了。❷潮流;趋势: go against the ~ 反潮流 / go with the ~ 随大流,赶潮流 / No one can turn the ~ of history. 谁也不能改变历史的潮流。/Time and ~ wait(s) for no man. 时不待我。

tidy /ˈtaɪdi/ Ⅰ *adj.* 整齐的;整洁的: a ~ room 整洁的房间 Ⅱ *vt.* 使整洁;使整齐: ~ up one's bed (desk)整理床铺(书桌)

tie /taɪ/ Ⅰ *v.* (tying /ˈtaɪɪŋ/) ❶(用带、绳等)捆,绑,拴: ~ a dog to the street railings 将狗拴在街旁的栏杆上 ❷与……得同样的分数;不分胜负: The two teams ~d. 两队打成平手。Ⅱ *n.* [C] ❶带,绳;(喻)纽带;联系;关系: the ~s of friendship 友谊的纽带 / family ~s 家庭关系 ❷(比赛)平局: The game ended in a ~. 比赛以平局结束。

tiger /ˈtaɪɡə(r)/ *n.* [C]虎: man-eating ~ 吃人虎/ paper ~ 纸老虎

tight /taɪt/ Ⅰ *adj.* ❶紧的;不松动的: These shoes are so ~ that they hurt me. 这双鞋太紧,挤得我脚痛。❷紧密的;密集的 Ⅱ *adv.* 紧紧地;牢牢地: She went upstairs, holding ~ to the banisters. 她走上楼梯,双手紧抓住扶手。派 tightly *adv.*

tighten /ˈtaɪtən/ *vt.* ❶使变紧;使绷紧;使更加牢固(与 up 连用): He ~ed his right hand into a fist. 他的右手用力握成拳头。/ ~ up a loose screw 拧紧松动的螺钉 ❷使更严格;使更有效(与 up 连用): ~ discipline 严肃纪律 / Security has been ~ed up along the border. 边境地区的安全工作得到了加强。

tile /taɪl/ *n.* [C]瓦片;瓷砖: ~ floor 瓷砖地 / Tiles are used to cover roofs. 瓦是用来盖屋顶的。

till /tɪl/ Ⅰ *prep.* 直到: I shall wait ~ ten o'clock. 我将等到十点钟。/ ~ **now** 直到现在: They have worked hard ~ now. 他们努力工作到现在。Ⅱ *conj.* 直到……之时;在……以前: Let's wait ~ the rain stops. 让我们等到雨停。

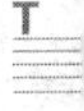

tilt /tɪlt/ Ⅰ *v.* ❶(使)倾斜,(使)倾侧: He had a way of ~ his head up when he spoke. 他讲话时总是侧仰着头。/ ~ to the left 向右倾斜 ❷(使)倾向;(使)偏向: He was ~ed towards a new economic course. 他倾向于采取新经济政策。Ⅱ *n.* [C] ❶倾斜,倾侧: She wore her hat at a ~. 她歪戴着帽子。❷倾向,偏向

timber /ˈtɪmbə(r)/ *n.* [U]木材;木料

time /taɪm/ *n.* ❶钟点;时间;时期: The

world exists in space and ~ . 世界存在于空间和时间中。/ **have a good** ~ 玩得很高兴,过得很愉快 **behind** ~ ①迟到:The train is ten minutes behind ~. 火车晚点十分钟。②落后;拖欠:He is always behind ~ with his payments. 他总是不能按时付款。**in** ~ ①及时:We were in ~ for the train. 我们及时赶上火车。②早晚;终究:You'll learn how to do it in ~. 你早晚会学会如何做此事。**on** ~ 按时,准时:The train came in on ~. 火车准时到达。**in no** ~ 立即,很快地:I'll be back in no ~. 我很快就回来。**all the** ~ 一直;始终,从头至尾:I looked all over the house for that letter, and it was in my pocket all the ~. 我在整个屋子里找那封信,而它却一直在我的口袋里。/ He's a business-man all the ~. 他一直就是个生意人。**at all ~s** 始终 **at one** ~ 曾经一个时期:At one ~ I went to mountain-climbing every summer. 曾经一个时期我每年夏天都去爬山。**at the same** ~同时:laugh and cry at the same ~又哭又笑 **at that** ~ 在那时:He was only ten years old at that ~. 那时他才十岁。**for the** ~ **being** 暂时,目前:For the ~ being you will have to share this room with another person. 你暂时得与另一个人同住这房间。**from** ~ **to** ~, **at** ~**s** 间或,有时:I saw Tom at the library from ~ to ~. 我间或会在图书馆里见到汤姆。**keep good (bad)** ~(钟表)走得准(不准):Does your watch keep good ~? 你的手表走时准确吗? **kill** ~消磨时间:I saw many passengers were killing ~ by reading at the station. 在车站我看到许多乘客以读书来打发时间。**take one's** ~不着急:Take your ~. I am waiting for you at the gate. 别着急,我在大门口等你。❷[C] 倍:Yours is ten ~s the size of mine. 你的是我的十倍大。❸[C] 次:I asked him three ~s. 我问了他三次。**many a** ~ 屡次 ~ **and again** 多次,反复地 派 timer *n.*

timely / ˈtaɪmli / *adj.* 及时的;适时的:~ treatment 及时的治疗

timetable / ˈtaɪmˌteɪbl / *n.* [C]时间表;(火车、飞机等的)时刻表;课程表:the railway ~铁路运行时刻表

timid / ˈtɪmɪd / *adj.* 胆怯的;羞怯的:That fellow is as ~ as a rabbit. 那家伙胆小如鼠。

tin / tɪn / *n.* ❶[U]锡 ❷[C] 罐头(= can):a ~ of sardines 一罐沙丁鱼

tinge / tɪndʒ / Ⅰ *vt.* ❶(轻淡地)给……着色,给……染色:hair ~d with yellow 染成略带黄色的头发 ❷稍稍影响;使……略有:His joy was ~d with sadness. 他兴奋之中还有点悲伤。Ⅱ *n.* [C](轻淡的)色调,色彩:The water has a yellowish ~. 水呈淡黄色。

tinkle / ˈtɪŋkl / Ⅰ *vi.* 发出叮当声,发出丁零声:The shop has a little bell that ~s when you open the door. 这家商店有只小铃铛,有人推门时它就叮当叮当响。Ⅱ *n.* 叮当声,丁零声

tint / tɪnt / Ⅰ *n.* [C]色彩;色调:The paint is white with a yellow ~. 这个颜料白中带黄。Ⅱ *vt.* 使带上色彩(或色调);给着色(或染色):Some fashionable boys had their hair ~ed red. 一些赶时髦的男孩把头发染成淡红色。

tiny / ˈtaɪni / *adj.* (-ier,-iest)极小的

tip[1] / tɪp / *n.* [C] ❶尖;尖端:the ~s of one's fingers 手指尖 / the ~ of one's nose 鼻尖 ❷装在末端的小物:cigarettes with filter ~s 末端装有滤嘴的香烟

tip² / tɪp / Ⅰ *n.* [C]小费；赏钱 Ⅱ *v.* (tipped; tipping)给小费：~ the driver ＄5 给司机5美元小费

tiptoe / ˈtɪpˌtəʊ/ Ⅰ *n.* [C]脚趾尖：**on ~ (~s)** 踮着脚；蹑手蹑脚：He had to stand on ~ to reach the top shelf. 他得踮着脚才能够到顶层搁板。/She led him on ~s to a small room. 她蹑手蹑脚地把他带到一个小房间。Ⅱ *vi.* 踮着脚走；蹑手蹑脚地走：The children ~d in and stared at the arrival. 孩子们蹑手蹑脚地走进来，盯着这位刚来的人看。

tiptop / ˈtɪpˌtɒp / Ⅰ *adj.* ❶头等的，第一流的：~ concerts 第一流的音乐会 ❷顶点的；极点的Ⅱ *adv.* 极其；极好地：Our research project was going along ~. 我们的研究项目进展十分顺利。

tire¹ / ˈtaɪə(r) / *v.* 使疲倦；使厌倦：The long lecture ~d the audience. 长篇演说使听众厌倦。/ ~ **out** 使筋疲力尽：I must sit down and rest. I'm ~d out. 我必须坐下歇一会，我筋疲力尽了。

tire² / ˈtaɪə / *n.* [C]轮胎[=(英)tyre]：change a ~ 换轮胎 / have a flat ~ 车胎漏气 / mount a ~ 装轮胎 / patch a ~ 补轮胎 / pump air in ~ 往车胎里打气 / spare ~ 备用轮胎

tired / ˈtaɪəd / *adj.* ❶疲乏的；累的：He is too ~ to go farther. 他太累了，再也走不动了。❷厌烦的：I'm ~ of the same kind of food every day. 我讨厌每天吃同一种食物。

tireless / ˈtaɪələs/ *adj.* 不觉得累的，不知疲倦的；不厌倦的：be ~ in teaching 诲人不倦 派 tirelessly *adv.* ；tirelessness *n.*

tiresome / ˈtaɪəsəm / *adj.* 累人的；令人厌倦的；令人讨厌的

tissue / ˈtɪsjuː / *n.* [U]薄纱；手巾纸；卫生纸：face (facial) ~ 面巾 / We have run out of toilet ~. 我们的卫生纸用完了。

titan / ˈtaɪtən / *n.* [C]巨人；庞然大物：The soft drink ~s are struggling for a bigger share of the market. 生产软饮料的巨头们正在争抢更大的市场份额。

title / ˈtaɪtl / *n.* [C] ❶名称；题目；标题：~ page 扉页 ❷称号；头衔：The school conferred the ~ of "Excellent Student" on Jack. 学校授予杰克"优秀学生"称号。❸权利；资格：Only the president has the ~ to travel by first-class. 只有校长才有资格坐头等舱旅行。/ Who gave you the ~ to enjoy free medicine? 谁给了你们享受免费医疗的权利？❹冠军：The girl won the race ~. 那姑娘赢得了短跑冠军。

to / tuː, tu, tə / *prep.* ❶(表示方向)对，至：go ~ the grocer's 前往杂货店 / fall ~ the ground 落到地上 ❷(表示时间)至，到：from beginning ~ end 自始至终 ❸(表示程度)到，至：wet ~ the skin 湿透了 ❹(表示比较)：I prefer walking ~ climbing. 我喜欢步行，不喜欢爬山。

toad / təʊd / *n.* [C]蟾蜍；癞蛤蟆

toast¹ / təʊst / Ⅰ *n.* [U]烤面包(片)；吐司：a piece of ~ 一片面包 Ⅱ *vt.* 烘；烤：~ the bread brown 把面包烤黄

toast² / təʊst / Ⅰ *n.* [C]敬酒；干杯；祝酒；祝酒词：exchange ~s 相互敬礼 / We drank a ~ to her health. 我们为她的健康干杯。Ⅱ *v.* 提议为……祝酒(干杯)：Let's ~ the friendship between the two countries. 让我们为两国之间的友谊干杯。

tobacco / təˈbækəʊ / *n.* (*pl.* tobaccos)烟

草;烟叶:This is a mixture of the best ~s. 这是由数种最好的烟叶配制成的。

today /təˈdeɪ/ Ⅰ *n.* [U]❶今天;本日:Have you read ~'s newspaper? 你看过今天的报纸吗? ❷现代;当代 Ⅱ *adv.* 今天;在当代

toe /təʊ/ *n.* [C] 脚趾;脚指头/**from top to ~** 从头到脚;完全地 **on one's ~s** ①踮着脚尖(走)的 ②提高警惕的:He carries out random spot checks to keep everyone on their ~s. 他进行现场突击检查以使每个人都保持警觉。**step on sb.'s ~s** ①踩着某人的脚尖 ②触怒(得罪)某人

together /təˈgeðə(r)/ *adv.* ❶一起;共同地:They went for a walk ~. 他们一起去散步。/ We got ~ and discussed the problem of air pollution. 我们聚在一起讨论有关空气污染的问题。/ **~ with** 和,连同:I'll send you a sample, ~ with some data. 我将连同资料一起给你寄一份样品去。❷同时:All his troubles seemed to come ~. 他的一切麻烦似乎同时来临。❸合计地:In front of the classroom building there are twenty trees all ~. 在教学大楼前总共有 20 棵树。

toil /tɒɪl/ Ⅰ *n.* [U]劳苦;辛苦 Ⅱ *v.* 辛苦工作 派 toilful *adj.*

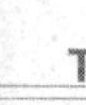

toilet /ˈtɒɪlət/ *n.* [C]卫生间;厕所:~ paper 手纸;卫生纸 / go to the ~ 上厕所

token /ˈtəʊkən/ Ⅰ *n.* [C] ❶表示;标志;象征;记号:The white flag is a ~ of surrender. 白旗是投降的标志。/**in ~ of** 作为……的标志(或象征等);表示:The visitors presented us with a banner in ~ of friendship. 客人们赠送我们一面锦旗,以示友好。❷纪念品:She kept the medals as a ~ by which to remember her dead husband. 她保存奖章以悼念她的丈夫。❸专用硬币 Ⅱ *adj.* 作为标志的;象征性的;表意的:a small ~ gift 象征性的小礼物

tolerable /ˈtɒlərəbl/ *adj.* ❶(痛苦等)可以忍受的;(错误等)可容忍的,可宽恕的:exceed ~ limits 超过可以容忍的限度 ❷还可以的,差强人意的;过得去的:The goods arrived in a ~ condition with a few cases slightly damaged. 货物到达时除有几箱稍有损坏外,总体情况还过得去。

tolerance /ˈtɒlərəns/ *n.* [U] 忍受;容忍:It is necessary for us to show ~ towards one another. 我们必须相互忍让。

tolerant /ˈtɒlərənt/ *adj.* 容忍的;有耐力的:One should be ~ of different opinions. 一个人应当容许不同意见。

tolerate /ˈtɒləreɪt/ *vt.* 容忍;忍受:I won't ~ your impudence. 我不能容忍你的无礼。

toll[1] /təʊl/ Ⅰ *n.* [C](道路、桥)通行费:~ bar 收费口 / ~ gate 收费站(处)/ ~ road(way)收费道路 Ⅱ *v.* 向……收费

toll[2] /təʊl/ Ⅰ *v.* 鸣钟,敲钟 Ⅱ *n.* (只用单数)钟声

tomato /təˈmɑːtəʊ/ *n.* [C](*pl.* tomatoes)番茄:~ juice 番茄汁

tomb /tuːm/ *n.* [C]坟墓

tomorrow /təˈmɒrəʊ/ Ⅰ *n.* [U]明天:the day after ~ 后天 Ⅱ *adv.* 在明天

ton /tʌn/ *n.* [C]吨

tone /təʊn/ *n.* ❶(只用单数)风格;气度 ❷[C]音质,音色:The piano has a wonderful ~. 那钢琴的音色好极了。❸[C]腔调;语气:You should read the sentence with a rising ~. 你应当用升调读这个句子。

tongue / tʌŋ / *n.* [C] ❶舌；舌头：The doctor asked me to put out my ~. 医生要我伸出舌头。❷语言：one's mother ~ 本国语；母语 ❸口才；说话方式：have a bitter ~ 说话刻薄 / have a ready ~ 雄辩，好口才/hold one's ~ 保持沉默

tonight / təˈnaɪt / Ⅰ*n.* [U]今晚，今夜：~'s radio news 今晚的新闻广播 Ⅱ*adv.* 在今夜

too / tuː / *adv.* ❶也；又；加之：She plays the piano, and sings, ~. 她边弹钢琴边唱歌。❷过于；太：We've had ~ much rain lately. 最近我们这儿雨下得太多。/ ~... **to** ... 太……而不能……：He is ~ old to work for his bread. 他年纪太老不能赚钱糊口了。/ The book is ~ difficult for me to understand. 这书太难，我读不懂。**cannot be** ~ ……怎么也不过分：You cannot be ~ careful. 你无论怎么小心都不过分。**only** ~非常：I am only too ready to help. 我非常乐意帮忙。

tool / tuːl / *n.* [C] ❶工具，用具；方法；手段 ❷受他人利用者；傀儡；走狗：He was a mere ~ in the hands of the dictator. 他只是独裁者手中的傀儡而已。

tooth / tuːθ / *n.* [C] (*pl.* teeth /tiːθ/) 牙齿：have a ~ out 拔牙

toothache / ˈtuːθˌeɪk/ *n.* [C]牙痛：He's got a bad ~. 他牙疼得厉害。

toothbrush / ˈtuːθˌbrʌʃ/ *n.* [C]牙刷

toothpaste / ˈtuːθˌpeɪst/ *n.* [C]牙膏

toothpick / ˈtuːθˌpɪk/ *n.* [C]牙签：use a ~ to clean the spaces between teeth 用牙签剔牙缝

top / tɒp / Ⅰ*n.* ❶顶部；顶端：at the ~ of the hill 在山顶 / at the ~ of the page 在书页的上端 / Put the red book on (the) ~ of the others. 把红皮书放在其他书上面。/**come out at the** ~ 名列前茅 **come to the** ~ 出名 **from** ~ **to bottom (toe)** 从头到脚；从上到下；全部地 **on** ~ **of the world** 感到高兴：That was all, but it sent me home feeling as if I were on ~ of the world! 我听到的就这么多，然而这几句话却使我兴高采烈地回到了家。❷最高的高度；最高地位：shout at the ~ of one's voice 高声喊叫 Ⅱ *adj.* 顶部的；首位的；最高的；头等的：~ floor 顶楼 / ~ official 高层官员 / Have you read the ~ news today? 你读了今天的头条新闻吗？ Ⅲ *vt.* (topped; topping) ❶达到……顶端：They ~ped a rise and began a slow descent. 他们爬上小山顶，然后开始慢慢下来。❷高过；超过：Losses are expected to ~ $100 million this year. 今年亏损额预计超过一亿美元。

topic / ˈtɒpɪk / *n.* [C]论题；话题；题目：What is the ~ you talked about? 你们谈的是什么话题?

topical / ˈtɒpɪkəl / *adj.* ❶有关时事的；时下关注的；成为话题的：The discussion focused on ~ issues in medicine. 讨论集中在一些人们时下关注的医学话题上。/ His wax portraits were always up to date and ~. 他做的蜡像总是当时当地的新闻人物。❷(医学)局部的：a ~ anaesthetic 局部麻醉

torch / tɔːtʃ / *n.* [C] ❶火炬；火把：hold aloft a ~ 高举火把 / hand on the ~ to 把火炬传给…… / The mayor lit the ~ for the sports meet. 市长为运动会点燃了火炬。❷手电筒：Please turn on (off) the ~. 请打开(关掉)手电筒。

torment Ⅰ /ˈtɔːment/ *n.* 痛苦;苦恼;折磨:mental ~精神折磨/ She suffered ~s. 她遭受了巨大的痛苦。Ⅱ /tɔːˈment/ *vt.* 折磨;使痛苦;使苦恼;烦扰:be ~ed with worry 忧心如焚/ I wanted to ~ her with indifference. 我曾想到要让她尝尝冷遇是什么滋味。

tornado /tɔːˈneɪdəʊ/ *n.* [C](*pl.* tornadoes 或 tornados)龙卷风:A ~ struck that area last week. 上周龙卷风袭击了那个地区。

tortoise /ˈtɔːtəs/ *n.* [C]乌龟

torture /ˈtɔːtʃə(r)/ Ⅰ *v.* 使受剧烈痛苦;折磨:~ sb. to make him confess sth. 折磨某人使他招认某事 Ⅱ *n.* [U]折磨;拷问:put a man to the ~ 折磨某人

toss /tɒs/ Ⅰ *v.* 扔;抛;掷:Jack ~ed a coin to the beggar. 杰克丢给乞丐一枚硬币。/ ~ **sb. for sth.** 掷硬币决定某事:I'll ~ you for the ticket. 我和你掷硬币,看谁赢得这张票。Ⅱ *n.* [C]扔;抛;掷:lose (win) the ~ 掷硬币时猜错(对)

total /ˈtəʊtl/ Ⅰ *adj.* 完全的;全体的:What are your ~ debts? 你的全部债务有多少1 Ⅱ *n.* [C]总数;总额:Our expenses reached a ~ of $5,000. 我们的支出总额达 5 000 美元。派 totally *adv.*

totter /ˈtɒtə(r)/ Ⅰ *vi.* ❶蹒跚,踉踉跄跄,跌跌撞撞:~ with age 因年迈而步履蹒跚 ❷变得不稳;动摇;摇摇欲坠:The government is ~ing on the edge of ruin. 该政府摇摇欲坠,已到了垮台的边缘。❸摇晃;抖动:His breast heaved, his knees ~ed. 他胸口起伏,双膝颤抖。Ⅱ *n.* [U]蹒跚的步子;踉跄;摇晃

touch /tʌtʃ/ Ⅰ *v.* ❶接触;触及:Can you ~ the top of the door? 你能摸到门顶吗? ❷触动;感动:The sad story ~ed us. 那悲惨的故事感动了我们。/ We were deeply ~ed by his efforts. 我们被他的努力感动了。❸涉及;论及 /~ **on** 谈及;提及:Do you know the topic he ~ed on at the beginning of the meeting? 你了解他在会议开始时谈到的那个话题吗? Ⅱ *n.* 接触;联系:I felt a ~ on my arm. 我觉得臂上有人碰了一下。/ **be in (out of) ~ with** 与……保持(失去)联系:The family was out of ~ with him. 家人和他失去了联系。**keep ~ with ...** 与……保持联系:He kept ~ with all his friends after graduation. 毕业后他仍然和朋友们保持着联系。**within ~ of ...** 在……能触及的地方

touching /ˈtʌtʃɪŋ/ *adj.* 动人的;感人的:a ~ story 动人的故事

tough /tʌf/ *adj.* ❶(指肉)坚韧的,咬不动的 ❷强壮的;坚强的:~ soldiers 坚强的士兵 ❸(指人)粗暴的,凶恶的:a ~ criminal 凶恶的罪犯 ❹困难的:a ~ job (problem)棘手的工作(问题)

tour /tʊə(r)/ Ⅰ *n.* ❶旅行;周游:a round-the-world ~ 环球旅行 ❷巡回演出:The company is on ~ in the countryside. 公司正在农村进行巡回演出。Ⅱ *v.* 旅行;漫游;巡回:~ western Europe 漫游西欧 / The play ~ed the rural areas. 这出剧曾在农村巡回演出。/ The delegation is on a ~ of the Asian branches. 代表团在亚洲的分支机构巡视。

tourism /ˈtʊərɪzəm/ *n.* [U]旅游;观光;旅游业:make money from ~以旅游业赚钱

tourist /ˈtʊərɪst/ Ⅰ *n.* [C]旅游者;观光者:attract ~s 吸引游客 / Jane's work is to show ~s around the city. 简的工作是带游客在城里观光。Ⅱ *adj.* 观光的;

旅行的：~ agency 旅行社；旅游公司 / ~ attraction 旅游胜地 / ~ car (coach) 观光车；游览车 / ~ guide 导游/ ~ party 观光团

tournament /ˈtuənəmənt/ *n.* [C]比赛；联赛；锦标赛；巡回赛：a friendship invitational ~友好邀请赛/a chess ~象棋锦标赛

tow /təʊ/ *v.* & *n.* 拖；牵引

toward(s) /təˈwɔːd(z)/ *prep.* ❶向；对；朝……的方向：walking ~ the sea 向海走去 ❷对于；关于：Are his feelings ~ us friendly? 他对我们友善吗？

towel /ˈtaʊəl/ *n.* [C]毛巾

tower /ˈtaʊə(r)/ Ⅰ *n.* [C]塔：control ~ (机场的)控制塔 / observation ~ 瞭望塔 / TV ~电视塔 / water ~水塔 Ⅱ *v.* 高耸：the skyscrapers that ~ over New York 高耸于纽约市的摩天大楼

towering /ˈtaʊərɪŋ/ *adj.* (只作定语) ❶高耸的，屹立的；高大的：a ~ monument 高耸的纪念碑 / At the doorway stood a ~ Othello-like figure. 门口站着一个奥赛罗式的彪形大汉。❷杰出的：a ~ figure in world literature 世界文学巨匠

town /taʊn/ *n.* [C] ❶(市)镇 ❷市内商业区；闹市区：My grandpa lives in another ~. 我爷爷住在另一座小镇。

toxic /ˈtɒksɪk/ *adj.* ❶(有)毒的；毒性的；有害的：~ chemicals 有毒化学品/ ~ gas-es毒气 ❷中毒的；由毒性引起的：~ symptoms 中毒症状/ ~ anaemia 中毒性贫血

toy /tɒɪ/ *n.* [C]玩具

trace /treɪs/ Ⅰ *n.* [C]痕迹；踪迹：They have not found any ~ of the murderer. 他们没有发现杀人犯的任何踪迹。Ⅱ *vt.* 跟踪，追踪；查找：The police ~d the thief to London. 警察追踪窃贼到了伦敦。/ ~ **sth. back to** 追溯某事到……：The custom can be ~d back to the 17th century. 这种风俗可以追溯到 17 世纪。

track /træk/ *n.* [C] ❶(车辆、行人、动物等留下的)痕迹，踪迹：~s in the snow 雪上的痕迹 ❷踏成的路；小道：a ~ through the forest 穿过森林的一条小径 ❸(火车等的)轨道：single (double) ~单(双)轨

tractor /ˈtræktə(r)/ *n.* [C]拖拉机：~ driver 拖拉机手

trade /treɪd/ Ⅰ *n.* ❶[U]买卖；交易；贸易：~ agreement 贸易协定/ border ~ 边境贸易/ export ~ 出口贸易/ international ~国际贸易 ❷职业；谋生的方式；(尤指)手艺：He's a weaver (mason, carpenter, tailor) by ~. 他是纺织工(石匠、木匠、裁缝)。 Ⅱ *v.* ❶做生意；从事贸易活动：They ~ with nearly all the countries in the world. 他们几乎和世界上所有的国家做生意。❷交换：~secrets(jokes)互换秘密 (互说笑话)

trader /ˈtreɪdə(r)/ *n.* [C] ❶商人：a retail ~ 零售商 / international ~s 国际贸易商 ❷商船，贸易船

tradition /trəˈdɪʃn/ *n.* 传统；惯例：It is still necessary to keep up the fine ~ of plain living and hard work. 保持艰苦奋斗的优良传统仍然是必要的。

traditional /trəˈdɪʃənl/ *adj.* 传统的；惯例的：~ Chinese medicine 中医；中药 / ~ friendship 传统友谊 / ~ ideas 传统观念 派 traditionally *adv.*

traffic /ˈtræfɪk/ *n.* [U] ❶交通；来往行人或车辆：~ jam 交通拥挤 / ~ lights 交通灯 / heavy (light) ~交通拥挤(畅通)/ There was not much (a lot of) ~ on the roads yesterday. 昨天路上行人

T

车辆不多(很多)。❷(火车、轮船、飞机等的)运输

tragedian /trə'dʒiːdɪən/ *n.* [C]悲剧作家;悲剧演员

tragedy /'trædʒədi/ *n.* ❶悲剧;悲剧作品:He wrote several famous tragedies. 他写了几部著名的悲剧作品。❷惨事;灾难;不幸:His carelessness caused a ~. 他的粗心大意酿成了不幸。

tragic(al) /'trædʒɪkəl/ *adj.* 悲剧的;悲惨的:a ~ drama 悲剧 / a ~ outcome 悲惨的结局 派 tragically *adv.*

trail /treɪl/ Ⅰ *n.* [C]❶踪迹;痕迹 ❷(打猎的)猎迹 ❸小径;崎岖小道 Ⅱ *vt.* 跟踪;追踪:~ along after (behind) sb. 慢吞吞地跟在某人后面走/~ from the chimney(烟)从烟囱里飘出来

trailer /'treɪlə(r)/ *n.* [C]拖车,挂车,拖斗;载货挂车

train /treɪn/ Ⅰ *n.* [C] ❶火车;列车:passenger (freight) ~s 客车(货车) / catch the ~赶上火车 / miss the ~ 没有赶上火车 / express ~ 快车 / slow ~ 慢车 / travel by ~乘火车旅行 ❷系列,一串 ❸长袍拖曳在地上的部分;拖裙 Ⅱ *v.* 训练;教养,教育:~ a horse for a race 训练马参加比赛 / They ~ed the workers to use computers. 他们训练工人使用计算机。

T

trainee /treɪ'niː/ *n.* [C]受培训者,实习者

trainer /'treɪnə(r)/ *n.* [C] ❶教员;(体育运动等的)教练(员) ❷驯马师;驯兽师

training /'treɪnɪŋ/ *n.* [U]训练;锻炼;培养:basic ~ 基本训练 / flight ~ 飞行训练 / military ~ 军事训练

trait /treɪt/ *n.* [C]特征,特点,特性,特质:Generosity is his best ~. 慷慨是他的一大特点。/One doesn't remember every feature of a face, but only its salient ~. 人们不能记住一张脸的每一特征,而只能记住其主要特征。

traitor /'treɪtə(r)/ *n.* [C]叛徒;卖国贼

tram /træm/ *n.* [C](有轨)电车:take a ~ 乘电车

tramp /træmp/ Ⅰ *vi.* ❶步履沉重地走;踏着坚实的脚步走:~ about upstairs 在楼上脚步噔噔地走来走去 ❷踩,踏:Don't let the kids play in the garden, they might ~ on my flowers. 别让这些小家伙到花园里去玩,他们会踩坏我的花。❸步行;长途跋涉;徒步旅行:~ up the hill 徒步登山 Ⅱ *n.* ❶坚实(或沉重的)脚步声 ❷[C]步行;长途跋涉;徒步旅行(者):a long day's ~一整天的长途跋涉

trample /'træmpl/ *v.* 践踏;踩坏;蹂躏:The fence had been ~d down. 树篱被踩倒了。

trance /trɑːns/ *n.* [C]恍惚;出神:fall into a ~ 精神恍惚

transact /træn'zækt/ *vt.* 办理,处理;商谈,商议;做(生意):~ private business 处理私事/~ some business 成交几笔生意

transcend /træn'send/ *vt.* ❶超越,超出(经验、理性、信念等)的范围:~ self 超越自我/The conflict between the two countries ~ed ideology. 这两个国家之间的冲突超出了意识形态的范围。❷优于,胜过,超过;克服:~ natural conditions 战胜自然条件/ ~ obstacles 扫除障碍

transect /træn'sekt/ *vt.* 横切,横断 派 transection *n.*

transfer Ⅰ /træns'fɜː(r)/ *v.* (-ferred; -ferring) ❶转移;转换:~ wasteland into rich fields 变荒地为良田 ❷调动；使……转学；转车：Jack ~red to a new school last term. 上学期杰克转到一所新学校去了。❸转让 Ⅱ /ˈtrænsfə/ *n.* 转移；转让；转车；转账：~ fee 转让费 / ~ company 转运公司 / make a ~ 转让；转账 / Do you want a ~ at the next station? 下一站你要转车吗？

transferable /trænsˈfɜːrəbl/ *adj.* 可转移的；可转让的：This ticket is not ~. 此票不可转让。

transform /trænsˈfɔːm/ *v.* ❶使转换；使变换：A steam engine ~s heat into energy. 蒸汽机使热变成能。❷改变；改造；改革：~ educational system 改革教育制度 / ~ one's world outlook 改造自己的世界观

transformation /ˌtrænsfəˈmeɪʃn/ *n.* [U]变化，转变；改造，改革：economic ~ 经济改革 / social ~ 社会改革

transistor /trænˈsɪstə(r)/ *n.* [C](电子)晶体管

transit /ˈtrænzɪt/ Ⅰ *n.* [U] ❶载运，运输：~ by rail 铁路运输/ thorough ~全程运输 ❷公共交通运输系统；公共交通设备：public ~公共运输系统 Ⅱ *vi.* 通过，经过，越过：The new large ships will be too big to ~ the canal. 这些新巨轮太大了，过不了运河。

transition /trænˈsɪʃn, trænˈzɪʃn/ *n.* 过渡；转变；变迁：the ~ from school to full-time work 从学校到全日工作的过渡

translate /trænsˈleɪt/ *v.* 翻译：~ from English into Chinese 英译汉

translation /trænsˈleɪʃn/ *n.* ❶[U] 翻译：free ~ (literal)意译(直译) / word-for-word ~逐字翻译 ❷[C]译文；译本：This is the French ~ of the contract. 这是合同的法文译本。/ Have you read the ~ of *Gone with the Wind*? 你读过《飘》的译本吗？

translator /trænsˈleɪtə(r)/ *n.* [C]翻译者

transmission /trænsˈmɪʃn/ *n.* [U]传送；传递；传导

transmit /trænsˈmɪt/ *vt.* (-mitted; -mitting)传送，传达；发射；播送：~ a disease 传播疾病 / ~ news by radio 用无线电发送消息 / ~ TV programs 传送电视节目 派 transmitter *n.*

transnational /trænsˈnæʃ(ə)nəl/ *adj.* 超国界的；跨国的：~ ideologies 超越国界的意识形态

transparency /trænsˈpærənsi/ *n.* ❶[U]透明(性)；透明度；透光度：atmospheric ~大气透明度/ market ~市场透明度 ❷[C]透明正片，幻灯片，透明物：a color ~彩色幻灯片

transparent /trænsˈpærənt/ *adj.* ❶透明的，透光的；清澈的，明净的：Those ~ curtains will never keep the light out. 那些透明窗帘根本挡不了光。/Good vinegar is clear and ~. 优质醋是晶莹剔透的。❷显而易见的，一目了然的；易识破的，易觉察的：After the war, he came to me pretending to be my nephew, but it was a ~ fraud. 战后他来到我跟前，自称是我的侄子，这显然是个骗局。❸坦诚的，坦白的，直率的：a ~ face 一张坦诚的脸

transplant /trænsˈplɑːnt/ *v.* 移植；移种

transport Ⅰ /trænˈspɔːt/ *vt.* 运送；运输：~ goods by lorry 用卡车运输货物 Ⅱ /ˈtrænspɔːt/ *n.* [U]运送；运输：lose in ~ 在运输中丢失 / ~ charges 运费 / ~ network 运输网 / ~ system 运输系统

transportation /ˌtrænspɔːˈteɪʃn/ *n.* [U]

T

运输;运送:~ company 运输公司/ ~ permit 运输许可证 / air ~ 空运 / water and land ~ 水陆运输

transverse / ˈtrænzvɜːs, ˈtrænsvɜːs / Ⅰ *adj.* 横的,横向的,横断的,横截的,横切的 Ⅱ *n.* [C]横向物,横断面

trap / træp / Ⅰ *n.* [C]捕捉机;陷阱:caught in a ~ 掉入陷阱;落入圈套/ fall into a ~ 堕入圈套 / get out of a ~ 摆脱圈套 / set a ~ 设圈套 Ⅱ *v.* (trapped; trapping)用捕捉机捕捉;设陷阱捕捉;诱捕

travel / ˈtrævl / Ⅰ *v.* (travelled 或 traveled; travelling 或 traveling)❶旅行;游历:~ round the world 环球旅行 ❷移动;行进:Light ~s faster than sound. 光比声音传播快。Ⅱ *n.* [U]旅行;游历:He is fond of ~. 他喜欢游历。派 travel(l)er *n.*

tray / treɪ / *n.* [C]盘;碟:a tea ~ 茶盘

tread /tred/ Ⅰ *v.* (trod/trɒd/, trodden /ˈtrɒdn/或 trod) ❶踏,践踏,踩碎:~ out a fire 把火踏灭/ Don't ~ on the seedlings. 别踏到幼苗。❷行走(于……) Ⅱ *n.* 踏步,脚步声

treasure / ˈtreʒə(r) / Ⅰ *n.* ❶宝物;财富:The pirates buried their ~. 海盗们把他们的财宝埋起来了。❷珍品;珍藏品:The National Gallery has many priceless art ~s. 国家艺术馆有许多无价的艺术珍品。Ⅱ *v.* ❶储藏;珍藏:~ sth. up in one's memory 铭记某事 ❷重视;珍爱:~ sb.'s friendship 珍视某人的友谊

treasury / ˈtreʒəri / *n.* [C] ❶金库,宝库;库房,珍藏室:financial ~金库 ❷国库:municipal ~市(省)库 ❸(T-)(国家)财政部;财政官员:Treasury Department (美国)财政部

treat / triːt / Ⅰ *v.* ❶对待/~ **as** 看待,视为:~ sb. as equals 平等待人,平等相处/Don't ~ me as a guest. 别把我当客人看待。❷治疗:Which doctor is ~ing her for her illness? 哪位医生在为她治病? ❸款待;招待:He ~ed me to a good dinner. 他请我吃了一顿美餐。/ I'll ~ myself to a bottle of wine. 我自己要享用一瓶酒。/ Father ~ed us to sea food last Sunday. 上星期天爸爸请我们吃海鲜。Ⅱ *n.* [C]款待;请客

treatment / ˈtriːtmənt / *n.* 对待;待遇;治疗:The wounded are under ~ in hospital. 伤员正在医院接受治疗。/ medical ~ 药物疗法/ psychological ~ 心理(精神)疗法

treaty / ˈtriːti / *n.* [C]条约;协定:a peace ~ 和约 / a non-aggression ~ 互不侵犯条约/ break a trade ~ 违反贸易条约 / conclude a ~ with 与……缔结条约 / The two countries signed a peace ~. 两国签署了和平条约。

tree / triː / *n.* [C]树木:Christmas ~ 圣诞树/ fruit ~ 果树/ in a ~ 在树上

tremble / ˈtrembl / Ⅰ *vi.* ❶(因恐惧、愤怒、寒冷等)发抖,颤抖:His voice ~d with anger. 他的声音因愤怒而发颤。❷摇曳,摇晃;微动:The bridge ~d as the heavy lorry crossed it. 那辆沉重的货车驶过桥时,桥在摇晃。Ⅱ *n.* [C]战栗;震颤;发抖:There was a ~ in his voice. 他的声音有一点发颤。

tremendous / trəˈmendəs / *adj.* 极大的;巨大的:~ differences 极大的差异 / travel at a ~ speed 高速运行 / We are making ~ efforts to learn English. 我们正作出极大的努力学好英语。派 tremendously *adv.*

trend / trend / Ⅰ *vi.* 趋向;倾向:The river ~s towards the east. 这条河向东流。/ My opinion ~s towards his. 我与

他的意见趋于一致。Ⅱ *n.* [C]倾向；趋势：~ of thought 思潮 / No one can change the ~ of history. 没有人能够改变历史趋势。

trial /ˈtraɪəl/ *n.* ❶试用；试验：by ~ and error 反复试验 / give a new typist a ~ 试用新打字员 ❷磨炼；艰苦 ❸受审：The ~ lasted a week. 审讯持续了一个星期。/**be on ~ for sth.** 因某事受审：He was on ~ for stealing. 他因偷盗而受到审判。

triangle /ˈtraɪæŋgl/ *n.* [C]三角形

tribe /traɪb/ *n.* [C]部落；宗族 派 tribal *adj.*

tribute /ˈtrɪbjuːt/ *n.* ❶(表示敬意的)礼物，献礼；颂辞，称赞：pay ~ to sb.'s achievements 赞颂某人所取得的成就/ send floral ~献花 ❷有效(或价值)的标示：His victory in the championship was a ~ to his persistence. 他夺冠成功说明他坚持不懈的努力没有白费。

trick /trɪk/ Ⅰ *n.* [C] ❶诡计；计谋；欺诈手段：He got the money from me by a ~. 他使用诡计从我这儿取得这笔钱。❷恶作剧；戏弄：play a ~ on sb. 开某人的玩笑 Ⅱ *vt.* 哄骗；欺诈：They ~ed the boy into telling them the truth. 他们哄骗那孩子说出了真相。

trickle /ˈtrɪkl/ Ⅰ *v.* (使)滴流；(使)淌：Blood ~d from the wound. 鲜血从伤口滴出。Ⅱ *n.* [C]滴；细流

trifle /ˈtraɪfl/ *n.* ❶[C]小事；琐事：Don't quarrel over ~s. 别为小事争吵。❷(a ~)有一点，稍微：His uniform made him look a ~ out of place. 他的制服让他看起来有些格格不入。

trifling /ˈtraɪflɪŋ/ *adj.* ❶不重要的，无足轻重的；微不足道的，没有多少价值：matters of ~ importance 无足轻重的事务 ❷轻浮的，轻佻的

trilateral /traɪˈlætərəl/ *adj.* ❶三边的：a ~ figure 三边形 ❷三方的；三国的：~ negotiations 三方谈判

trim /trɪm/ Ⅰ *adj.* 整齐的；整洁的：His garden was ~ and neat. 他的花园整洁美观。Ⅱ *vt.* (trimmed; trimming) 修剪；整修：~ one's hair 修剪头发/ ~ the branches off a tree 把树上的枝修掉/ ~ a dress with lace 给衣服饰花边/ The gardener ~med the trees into good shape. 花工把树修剪得很美。

trip /trɪp/ *n.* [C]旅行；(尤指)远足：a ~ to the seaside 去海滨远足 / a weekend ~ 周末旅行 / **on a ~** 在旅行：The old couple are on a ~ in France. 那对老年夫妻在法国旅行。

triple /ˈtrɪpl/ Ⅰ *adj.* ❶三倍的；三重的：take a ~ dose of the medicine 服三倍剂量的药/ The attention we received had a ~ effect. 我们所受到的关注具有三重作用。❷由三部分组成的：the ~ entrance of a cave 三叠洞口 Ⅱ *vi.* 增至三倍，增加两倍：In four years the property almost ~d in value. 四年内，财产几乎增值了两倍。

tripod /ˈtraɪpɒd/ *n.* [C]三脚架

triumph /ˈtraɪəmf/ Ⅰ *n.* 成功；胜利：return home in ~ 凯旋 Ⅱ *vi.* 获胜；成功：She ~ed over evil. 她战胜了邪恶。

triumphant /traɪˈʌmfənt/ *adj.* 成功的；胜利的

trivial /ˈtrɪvɪəl/ *adj.* 无价值的，不重要的；琐细的，轻微的：His death in 1941 was due to a ~ mishap. 他 1941 年死于一桩不幸的小事故。/ One or two of them are so ~ that really I am ashamed to mention them. 其中有一两点是不值得说的，我提到这些，实在觉得惭愧。

trolleybus / ˈtrɒlɪbʌs / *n.* [C]无轨电车

troop / truːp / Ⅰ *n.* [C]❶士兵；军队 ❷(人或动物的)一群，一队：a ~ of children 一群儿童 Ⅱ *v.* (用复数主语)成群结队而行

tropic / ˈtrɒpɪk / *n.* ❶(the ~s) 热带地区 ❷回归线

tropical / ˈtrɒpɪkl / *adj.* 热带的；炎热的：~ climate 热带气候 / ~ crops 热带作物

trot / trɒt / *vi.* & [C] *n.* (马)小跑；慢跑

trouble / ˈtrʌbl / Ⅰ *n.* ❶忧虑；苦恼；困难；麻烦 / **in** ~处于苦难中；在困境中：A person with good manners never laughs at people when they are in ~. 一个有礼貌的人决不会嘲笑处于困境中的人们。**ask (look) for** ~ 自找麻烦；自讨苦吃 **get into** ~ 陷入困境：Be careful or you'll get into ~. 仔细一点，否则你会遇到麻烦的。**get out of** ~ 摆脱困境：You may ask your teacher to help you get out of the ~. 你可以请老师帮助你摆脱困境。**make** ~ 闹事，捣乱 ❷痛苦；疾病 ❸动乱；纠纷；风潮 Ⅱ *v.* ❶使忧虑；使苦恼；使不适：be ~d by bad news 为坏消息而感到苦恼 / What ~s me is that he is often late for work. 使我感到苦恼的是他总是上班迟到。❷麻烦；使费神：May I ~ you to post the letter? 麻烦你帮我寄这封信好吗？

T

troublesome / ˈtrʌblsəm / *adj.* 令人烦恼的；讨厌的；困难的：a ~ child 使人烦恼的孩子 / a ~ problem 让人烦恼的问题

trousers / ˈtraʊzəz / *n.* (*pl.*)裤子：a pair of ~ 一条裤子

truant / ˈtruːənt / *n.* [C]逃避责任者；(尤指)逃学者：to play ~逃学

truck / trʌk / *n.* [C]货车；卡车

true / truː / *adj.* ❶真实的；真正的：be ~ in word 遵守诺言 / be ~ to life(nature) 逼真 / Is the news ~? 这消息确实吗？/ **come** ~ (希望、理想等)实现：At last, his dream came ~. 他的理想终于实现了。❷忠诚的；忠实的：a ~friend 忠实的朋友 ❸准确的：~ judgment 准确的判断

truly / ˈtruːli / *adv.* ❶(常用于信末署名前的客套语)真诚地；忠实地：yours ~ (信末署名前的客套语)您的忠实的 ❷(常用作插入语)的确，确实，真的：Truly, there could be no more delightful place in the world to visit. 确实，世上没有比这更令人愉快的地方可去了。❸真实地；真正地；如实地：The ~ educated man is not a man who knows a bit of everything. 真正有文化的人并不是一个什么都知道一点的人。❹准确地；确切地；精确地：quote sb.'s words ~ 准确地引用某人的言论

trumpet / ˈtrʌmpɪt / Ⅰ *n.* [C] ❶吹喇叭；号：blow(sound) a ~ 吹喇叭 / ~ call 集合号 / **blow one's own** ~ 自吹自擂 ❷喇叭形物；喇叭形扩音器；助听器 ❸(象等发出的)喇叭似的叫声 Ⅱ *v.* ❶吹喇叭 ❷大声宣告，到处宣扬 ❸吹嘘，自夸 派 trumpeter *n.*

trunk / trʌŋk / *n.* [C] ❶树干 ❷躯干 ❸(建筑的)主要部分 ❹象鼻子 ❺干线：~ line 铁路干线 / ~ road 干道

trust / trʌst / Ⅰ *n.* ❶信任；信赖：She doesn't place much ~ in his promises. 她不大相信他的诺言。❷责任；义务：a position of great ~ 责任重大的职位 Ⅱ *v.* 信任；相信：He is not the sort of man to be ~ed. 他不是一个可靠的人。/ ~ **in** 相信；信仰 ~ **to** 依赖；依靠：You ~ to your memory too much. 你过于依赖你的记忆了。派 trustful *adj.*

trustworthy / ˈtrʌstˌwɜːði/ *adj.* 值得信

任的；可信的；可靠的：a ～ travelling companion 可靠的旅伴 / My car is totally ～. 我的汽车笃定不会出问题。派 trustworthiness *n.*

truth /truːθ/ *n.* (*pl.* truths/truːðz, truːθs/)❶[U]真实性；真相：He didn't tell us the ～. 他没有对我们说真话。/ To tell the ～, I forgot all about your request. 说实话，我把你的要求全忘了。❷[C]真理：the ～s of science 科学的真理

truthful /ˈtruːθful/ *adj.* ❶讲真话的；诚实的：a ～ witness 诚实的证人 / To be ～ I'm not much of a drinker. 说真的，我并不经常喝酒。❷(讲话、作品等)真实的，如实的；现实主义的：a ～ account 真实的陈述 / give a ～ portrayal of life 对生活做现实主义的描绘 派 truthfully *adv.*；truthfulness *n.*

try /traɪ/ Ⅰ *v.* ❶努力：He tried to finish it, but failed. 他努力要完成它，但失败了。/ ～ **one's best** 尽某人最大努力：I'll ～ my best to finish it in time. 我要尽最大努力及时完成这事。❷试；试用：Try how far you can jump. 试试看你能跳多远。/ ～ **on** 试穿：She tried on several pairs of shoes before she found one she liked. 她试穿了好几双鞋子后才找到一双合适的。～ **out** ①试验：The scientists tried out thousands of chemicals before they found the right one. 科学家们试验了数千种化学物品才找到合适的那种。②参加选拔：Shirley will ～ out for the lead in the play. 雪莉将参加选拔主角的演出。❸审问；审判：He was tried and found guilty. 他受审判并被认定有罪。Ⅱ *n.* [C]尝试；试验；努力：Let me have another ～ at it. 让我再试一次。

tsunami /tsuːˈnɑːmi/ *n.* [C]海啸，海震

tub /tʌb/ *n.* [C]桶；盆；浴缸，浴盆

tube /tjuːb/ *n.* ❶(金属、塑料或橡皮等制的)管，筒：a ～ of toothpaste 一管牙膏 / test ～ 试管 ❷电子管；显像管 ❸地铁：Will you go to the station by ～? 你乘地铁去车站吗？/ He always takes the ～ to work. 他总是乘地铁上班。

tubular /ˈt(j)uːbjulə(r)/ *adj.* ❶管的；管状的；管式的：bamboo's ～ form 竹子的管子形状❷有管的；由管子构成的：He sat down on a ～ chair. 他坐在一张管构架椅子上。

tuck /tʌk/ *vt.* 把……夹入；把……藏入：She ～ed her hair under her cap. 她把头发拢起来塞进帽子里。

Tuesday /ˈtjuːzdi/ *n.* 星期二

tug /tʌg/ Ⅰ *v.* (tugged; tugging)用力拉，用力拖：We ～ged so hard that the rope broke. 我们用力太猛把绳子拉断了。Ⅱ *n.* [C]❶拉，扯，拖：The naughty boy gave her sister's hair a ～. 那顽皮的男孩扯了一下他姐姐的头发。❷拖船

tuition /tjuˈɪʃn/ *n.* [U] ❶教学；讲授；指导 ❷学费：pay ～ 交学费

tulip /ˈtjuːlɪp/ *n.* [C]郁金香

tumble /ˈtʌmbl/ *vi.* 摔倒；跌倒：The boy ～d off the bike. 那男孩从自行车上摔了下来。

tumo(u)r /ˈtjuːmə(r)/ *n.* [C]肿瘤：benign ～ 良性肿瘤 / malignant ～ 恶性肿瘤 / remove a ～ 切除肿瘤

tune /tjuːn/ Ⅰ *n.* [C] ❶曲，调子；语调：whistle a popular ～ 用口哨吹流行曲子 / hum a ～ 哼曲子 / **call the** ～ 发号施令，任意指挥 **change one's** ～ 改变论调(态度) **in** ～ 音调准确：This piano is in ～. 这架钢琴音调准确。**out of** ～ 音调不准确，走调：He sang out of ～. 他唱走了调。**to the** ～ **of** ...和着……的曲

调 ❷和谐；协调，一致：Bill is in ~ with his classmates. 比尔与同学们和谐相处。Ⅱ *vt*. 调谐，调音；使和谐；使一致

tunnel /ˈtʌnl/ *n*. [C]地道；隧道；坑道：dig a ~ 挖隧道(地道)

turbulence /ˈtɜːbjʊləns/ *n*. [U] ❶骚乱；动乱，动荡；混乱：a time of political ~政治动荡时期 ❷(液体或气体的)紊流，涡流；湍动(性)，紊动(性)：The plane bucked in the ~. 飞机在湍流中颤动。

turbulent /ˈtɜːbjʊlənt/ *adj*. ❶骚乱的；动乱的，动荡的；混乱的：~ political and social conditions 动荡的政治和社会状况/ in the ~ years of adolescence 处在青春活力汹涌澎湃的年代 ❷湍流的，紊流的，涡旋的：~ fluctuations 紊动

turkey /ˈtɜːki/ *n*. ❶[C]火鸡：roast a ~ 烤火鸡 ❷[U]火鸡肉

turn /tɜːn/ Ⅰ *v*. ❶(使)旋转；(使)移动 ❷(使)改变：My hair has ~ed grey. 我的头发变灰白了。/ ~ **from side to side** (把身体)转过来转过去：He ~ed from side to side and couldn't go to sleep. 他翻来覆去不能入睡。~ **against** 反对；反感：Those who were once for him have turned against him. 那些原来支持他的人现在都转而反对他。~ **down** 拒绝：He tried to join the police but was ~ed down because of poor physique. 他试图加入警察队伍，但因体格差而遭到拒绝。~ **in** ①归还：He ~ed in his badge and quit. 他归还徽章，辞掉职务。②上交，交出：You'd better ~ in the money that you found. 你最好把捡到的钱上交。~ **into** 变成，翻译成~ **off** 关上(水、气、电等)：The tap won't ~ off, and there's water all over the floor. 龙头关不上，满地都是水。~ **on** 打开(水、气、电等)：Please ~ the light on for me. It's getting dark. 请把灯给我打开，天黑了。~ **over** 翻：I heard the clock, but then I ~ed over and went back to sleep. 我听到了钟声，但我翻过身又睡着了。/ Please ~ over and read the directions on the back. 请翻页，读背后的说明。~ **to** ① 转向：Turn to me a little more. I can't see your eyes in the shadow. 向我这边转一点，在阴暗中我看不清你的眼睛。②翻到：Please ~ to page 33. 请翻到 33 页。③求助于：When he's in trouble, he always ~s to his sister. 他有麻烦时总是求助于他的姐姐。Ⅱ *n*. [C]❶旋转；转动：a few ~s of the handle 把手的数次转动 ❷时机，机会 ❸轮班，轮次：It's your ~ to read now, John. 约翰，现在该你读了。/ **in** ~ 接连地；按顺序地：The boys were summoned in ~ to see the examiner. 男孩子们依次被召去见那位考官。**by** ~**s** 轮流地：He went hot and cold by ~s. 他时而发热，时而发冷。

turnabout /ˈtɜːnəˌbaʊt/ *n*. [C]❶转向；转身；向后转：a car capable of a quick ~ 能急转弯的小汽车 ❷(政策、观点等的)突然转变，突然变化，变卦：a sudden ~ on the policy 政策的突然改变

turnaround /ˈtɜːnəˌraʊnd/ *n*. [C]❶(观点、态度等的)彻底改变，变卦：the government's ~ on interest rate policies 政府有关利率政策的改变 ❷(营业、经济等的)突然好转：It was an emphatic win and a remarkable ~ in his fortunes. 他这次获胜意义非同小可，使他时来运转，大发其财。

turning /ˈtɜːnɪŋ/ *n*. [C]转弯；转弯处；岔路口；岔道：We passed the ~. 我们经过了岔道口。/ You ought to have taken a ~ to the left. 你应该向左拐弯的。

turnip /ˈtɜːnɪp/ *n*. [C]芜菁；萝卜

turtle / ˈtɜːtl / *n.* [C]海龟;玳瑁

tusk / tʌsk / *n.* [C](象等的)长牙,尖牙

tutor / ˈtjuːtə(r) / Ⅰ *n.* [C]家庭教师;(大学)导师:Do you need a ~? 你需要请家庭教师吗? Ⅱ *vt.* 教,指导

TV / ˌtiːˈviː/ *n.* (=television)电视,电视机:~ play 电视剧 / ~ set 电视机 / ~ festival 电视节

twelfth / twelfθ / Ⅰ *num.* 第十二;十二分之一 Ⅱ *adj.* 第十二的;十二分之一的

twelve / twelv / Ⅰ *num.* 十二,12 Ⅱ *adj.* 十二个(的)

twentieth / ˈtwentɪɪθ / Ⅰ *num.* 第二十;二十分之一 Ⅱ *adj.* 第二十的;二十分之一的

twenty / ˈtwenti / Ⅰ *num.* 二十,20 Ⅱ *adj.* 二十个(的)

twice / twaɪs / *adv.* 两倍;两次:I've been there once or ~. 我去过那儿一两次。

twig / twɪɡ / *n.* [C]小枝;嫩枝

twilight / ˈtwaɪlaɪt / *n.* [U]黎明;曙光;黄昏:I like to take a walk at ~. 我喜欢在黄昏时散步。

twin / twɪn / Ⅰ *adj.* ❶成双的,成对的:They ordered a room with ~ beds. 他们订了一间有两张床的房间。❷孪生的,双胞胎的:~ brothers (sisters)孪生兄弟(姐妹) Ⅱ *n.* [C]孪生儿之一

twinkle / ˈtwɪŋkl / Ⅰ *v.* 闪烁;闪耀:stars that ~ in the sky 天上闪烁的星星 Ⅱ *n.* 闪烁;闪亮

twist / twɪst / *v.* ❶转动;旋动 ❷捻,搓:She knew how to ~ threads into a rope. 她知道怎样把线搓成绳子。❸扭伤;扭曲:I fell and ~ed my ankle. 我摔伤了脚踝。❹歪曲;曲解:Please don't ~ what I said. 请别曲解我说的话。

two / tuː / Ⅰ *num.* 二,2 Ⅱ *adj.* 两个(的)

type / taɪp / Ⅰ *n.* [C] ❶典型;模范 ❷样式;类型:It's a ~ of music I enjoy. 那是一种我喜欢的音乐。Ⅱ *v.* 打字:~ a letter 用打字机打一封信

typewrite / ˈtaɪpraɪt / *v.* (typewrote /ˈtaɪprəʊt/, typewritten/ˈtaɪpˌrɪtn/) 打字;用打字机打字

typewriter / ˈtaɪpraɪtə(r) / *n.* [C]打字机

typhoon / taɪˈfuːn / *n.* [C]台风:A ~ hit (struck) the coastal area. 台风袭击了沿海地区。

typical / ˈtɪpɪkl / *adj.* 有代表性的;典型的:~ character 典型人物 / She is ~ of her generation. 她是她这一代人的典型。派 typically *adv.*;typicality *n.*

typist / ˈtaɪpɪst / *n.* [C]打字员

tyranny / ˈtɪrənɪ / *n.* [U]暴政;专制;残暴

tyrant / ˈtaɪrəni / *n.* [C]暴君

tyre / taɪə(r) / *n.* (=tire)[C]轮胎;车胎:inflate a ~ 给轮胎充气 / spare ~ 备用轮胎

U u

UFO / ˈjuːfəʊ / *n*. (= unidentified flying object)[C]不明飞行物：find a ~ 发现不明飞行物

ugly / ˈʌgli / *adj*. (-ier,-iest) ❶难看的；丑陋的：~ furniture 难看的家具 / an ~ man 丑陋的人 ❷可怕的；讨厌的：~ smell 讨厌的气味 派 uglily *adv*. ; ugliness *n*.

ultimate / ˈʌltɪmət / *adj*. 最后的；最终的：the ~ aim 最终目的/ ~ ends of the world 天涯海角/~ strength 极限强度 派 ultimately *adv*.

ultrasonic / ˌʌltrəˈsɒnɪk / *adj*. 超声的；超音速的

ultraviolet / ˌʌltrəˈvaɪələt / Ⅰ *adj*. 紫外的 Ⅱ *n*. 紫外光；紫外辐射

umbrella / ʌmˈbrelə / *n*. [C]伞：close (shut) an ~ 收起伞/ open (put up) an ~ 撑开伞/ under the ~ of 在……的庇护下

unable / ʌnˈeɪbl / *adj*. 不能的(只作表语)：The boy is ~ to walk. 这男孩不会走路。

unacceptable / ˌʌnəkˈseptəbl / *adj*. 难以接受的；不称心的

unaccountable / ˌʌnəˈkaʊntəbl / *adj*. ❶无法理解的，难以说明的；莫名其妙的，不可捉摸的：some ~ phenomena 一些难以解释的现象/ For some ~ reason, she did not attend her daughter's wedding. 不知什么原因，她没有出席女儿的婚礼。❷不负责任的；无责任的：As a subordinate, I am surely ~ for the incident. 作为下属，此事肯定没我什么责任。

unanimous / juːˈnænɪməs / *adj*. 全体一致的；意见相同的，无异议的：the ~ demand 一致的要求/ The kids were ~ for a picnic. 孩子们一致赞成去野餐。派 unanimity *n*.

unavailing / ˌʌnəˈveɪlɪŋ / *adj*. 无效的；无用的；徒劳的：~ efforts 徒劳

unaware / ˌʌnəˈweə(r) / *adj*. 没有发觉的；不知道的

unbalanced / ˌʌnˈbælənst / *adj*. 不平衡的；不安定的

unbearable / ʌnˈbeərəbl/ adj. 难以忍受的；不能容忍的

unbelievable / ˌʌnbɪˈliːvəbl/ *adj*. 难以置信的，不可信的；惊人的：an ~ excuse 令人难以相信的借口 / streams of ~ clarity 清澈无比的河流 派 unbelievably *adv*.

unbind / ʌnˈbaɪnd / *vt*. (unbound, unbound) ❶解开；松开：Before going to bed she unbound her hair. 上床之前，她把头发松开。❷使解除束缚，使自由，解放；释放：~ the prisoners 释放囚犯

unburden / ʌnˈbɜːdən / *vt*. ❶使卸去负

担,卸去……的包袱:~ a donkey 卸去驴的驮负 ❷使消除忧愁,使解除思想负担:Talking to a psychiatrist is a good way of ~ing herself of a lot of worries. 同精神病医生交谈是让她摆脱诸多烦恼的一条有效途径。

uncertain / ʌn'sɜːtən / *adj*. ❶不肯定的;不确定的:The time of their arrival is ~. 他们到达的时间还未确定。/ I am ~ of (about, as to) his plans for the holiday. 我不确知他度假的计划如何。/ We are ~ that he will come in time. 我们不确定他能否及时来。❷易变的;无常的;靠不住的:~ weather 变化无常的天气 / Jack's father is a man with ~ temper. 杰克的父亲是个喜怒无常的人。派 uncertainly *adv*.

uncle / 'ʌŋkl / *n*. [C]伯父;姨父;叔父;舅父;姑父

unclear / ˌʌn'klɪə(r) / *adj*. 不明白的;不清楚的:It was ~ to us why they lost the game. 他们为什么输了比赛,我们不清楚。

uncomfortable / ʌn'kʌmftəbl / *adj*. 不舒服的;不自在的,不安的

uncomplaining / ˌʌnkəm'pleɪnɪŋ / *adj*. 没有怨言的;不发牢骚的;能忍受的

uncompromising / ʌn'kɒmprəˌmaɪzɪŋ / *adj*. 不妥协的,不让步的;不屈服的,坚定的;固执的:the ~ nature 坚毅的性格/ He spoke English with the most ~ French accent. 他说英语时总有改不掉的法国口音。

unconditional / ˌʌkən'diʃənəl / *adj*. 无条件的;无保留的;无限制的;绝对的,完全的:an ~ support 无条件支持/Then the real undertaking at present is the ~ freeing of the people. 那么目前真正要做的是将这些人无条件释放。

unconscious / ʌn'kɒnʃəs/ *adj*. 失去知觉的;无意识的;不知不觉的:He is still ~ after the accident. 事故后他仍然没有知觉。/ She is ~ of the danger. 她并未意识到危险。/ He is ~ that he has done wrong. 他没有意识到自己做错了事。派 unconsciousness *n*.

uncontrollable / ˌʌkən'trəʊləbl / *adj*. 难以控制的,控制不住的;无法管束的:in ~ fury 怒不可遏/ They mourned their brother with ~ grief. 兄弟之死使他们悲痛欲绝。

uncountable / ʌn'kaʊntəbl / *adj*. ❶无数的,数不清的:~ wealth 无法估量的财富/ ~ shingles devastated by white ants 被白蚁咬坏的无数屋顶板 ❷(名词)不可数的,不具数的

uncover / ʌn'kʌvə(r) / *v*. 揭开……的盖子;(喻)揭露:The police have ~ed a plot against the President. 警察局已破获一个反对总统的阴谋。

undecided / ˌʌndɪ'saɪdɪd / *adj*. ❶未定的,未决的:The whole question is still ~. 整个问题尚决定。/ The outcome of the election was left ~. 选举结果尚不明朗。❷犹豫不定的;优柔寡断的:How could he make it, being so ~? 他这样优柔寡断的,怎么能成事呢?

undeniable / ˌʌndɪ'naɪəbl / *adj*. ❶不可否认的,无可争辩的;毋庸置疑的;确凿无疑的:an ~ proof 不可否认的证据/ Mr. Jones' good intentions are ~. 琼斯先生的好意毋庸置疑。❷公认优秀的;无可挑剔的:an ~ masterpiece 一部公认的优秀作品

under / 'ʌndə(r) / *prep*. ❶(表示位置)在……下面,在……底下:~ the table 在桌子下面;私下地 / stand ~ a tree 站在树下面 ❷(表示级别、数量、标准等)

低于……,在……之下:students ~ sixteen years of age 不满 16 周岁的学生 ❸(表示条件)在……之下:~ such conditions 在这些条件下/ ~ the leadership of the Party 在党的领导下 ❹(表示过程)在……中:problem ~ decision 在考虑中的问题/ bridge ~ construction 建设中的大桥

undercover /ˌʌndəˈkʌvə(r)/ Ⅰ *adj.* 秘密从事的;隐秘的;保密的:~ enemies in disguise 伪装的暗藏敌人/ an ~ agent 卧底密探 Ⅱ *adv.* 暗中,秘密地:How do you like to disappear, I mean go ~? 你愿意潜踪吗? 我的意思是说参与秘密行为。

underdeveloped /ˌʌndədɪˈveləpt/ *adj.* 不发达的;落后的

underestimate /ˌʌndərˈestɪmeɪt/ *vt.* 低估;看轻

undergo /ˌʌndəˈgəʊ/ *vt.* (underwent, undergone) 经历;遭受;忍受:The explorers had to ~ much suffering. 探险者必须忍受许多苦难。

undergraduate /ˌʌndəˈgrædʒʊət/ *n.* [C] 大学生;尚未取得学位的大学生

underground Ⅰ /ˌʌndəˈgraʊnd/ *adv.* 在地下;秘密地:waste buried deep ~ 深埋在地下的废弃物 Ⅱ /ˈʌndəgraʊnd/ *adj.* 秘密的;地下的:the ~ activities 地下活动 Ⅲ /ˈʌndəgraʊnd/ *n.* 地面下层;地下空间:~ railway 地下铁道 / travel by ~ 乘地铁旅行

underlie /ˌʌndəˈlaɪ/ *vt.* (underlay, underlain; underlying) ❶位于……之下;置于……之下:Shale ~ the coal. 煤层底下是页岩层。❷构成……的基础;是……的潜在根源:It must ~ everything. 一切都必须以此为基础。

underline /ˌʌndəˈlaɪn/ *vt.* 在……下画线:Please ~ the important sentences while reading. 请一边阅读一边在重要的句子下画线。

undermine /ˌʌndəˈmaɪn/ *vt.* 逐渐损坏:His health was ~d by drinking. 饮酒使他的健康每况愈下。

underneath /ˌʌndəˈniːθ/ *adv.* 在下面;在底下:He went over and found a letter ~ the door. 他走过去发现门下面有一封信。

understand /ˌʌndəˈstænd/ (understood /ˌʌndəˈstʊd/, understood) *vt.* ❶懂,明白,清楚:Speech, to be effective, must first be understood. 演说要打动听众,首先要让人明白。❷理解;谅解;认识到,意识到:We don't ~ your attitude at all. 对你的态度我们完全不能理解。/ Can you ~ the position she is in? 你能体谅她的处境吗? ❸了解,熟知,通晓:Henry had perfectly understood the whole story. 亨利对整个事情了如指掌。

understanding /ˌʌndəˈstændɪŋ/ Ⅰ *n.* ❶理解力;判断力:beyond one's ~ 超过某人的理解力 ❷谅解;体谅:arrive (come to, reach) an ~ with sb. 取得某人的谅解 / mutual ~ 互相理解 Ⅱ *adj.* 了解的;善解人意的:an ~ man 善解人意的人/ He nodded with an ~ smile. 他点点头,会心地笑了。

undertake /ˌʌndəˈteɪk/ *v.* (undertook, undertaken) ❶担任;答应,许诺;担保:He undertook to finish the job by Friday. 他答应星期五之前做完那项工作。❷开始;着手;进行

undertaking /ˌʌndəˈteɪkɪŋ/ *n.* [C] ❶任务;事业;企业:finance a cultural ~资助文化事业/ charitable ~s 慈善事业 ❷担保,保证;承诺,许诺:I must have a written ~ from you. 你必须给我写一份书面保证。/ discharge one's ~履行自己的诺言

undertone / ˈʌndəˌtəun / *n*. [C] ❶低音；低声：talk in ~s 低声细气地谈话 ❷内在的性质；潜在的情感(或意思)；含义，意味：praise with an ~ of envy 带着妒忌的口气夸奖/ There was an ~ of sadness in her gaiety. 她活泼中透出丝丝忧伤。

underwater / ˌʌndəˈwɔːtə(r) / Ⅰ *adj*. (在)水下的；水下生长的；水下使用(或进行)的：an ~ camera 水下照相机/ an ~ explosion 水下爆炸 Ⅱ *adv*. 在水下；在水中：live ~生活在水中

underwear / ˈʌndəweə(r) / *n*. [U]内衣

underworld / ˈʌndəwɜːld / *n*. ❶(the ~) 阴间 ❷下层社会

undesirable / ˌʌndɪˈzaɪərəbl / *adj*. 令人不快的；讨厌的；不合意的；不受欢迎的：~ tendencies 不良倾向/ Some of these drugs have ~ side effects. 这中间有些药会产生不良副作用。派 undesirably *adv*.

undeveloped / ˌʌndɪˈveləpt / *adj*. 未(充分)开发的；未发展的；不发达的：an ~ area 未开发地区/ ~ countries 不发达国家

undistinguished / ˌʌndɪˈstɪŋgwɪʃt / *adj*. 普通的，平凡的；无特色的；平庸的：an ~ background 普通的背景/ The suspension bridge is of ~ design. 这座索桥的设计毫无特色。

undo / ʌnˈduː / *vt*. (undid, undone) ❶解开；打开；松开：~ a button 解开纽扣 / ~ a parcel 打开包裹 / ~ the string 解开绳子 ❷取消；消除；使恢复原状：What is done cannot be undone. 事已成定局，无可挽回。

undoubted / ʌnˈdaʊtɪd / *adj*. 确定的；无疑的

undoubtedly / ʌnˈdaʊtɪdli / *adv*. 无疑地；毫无疑问地

undress / ˌʌnˈdres / *v*. ❶脱去衣服；除去覆盖物 ❷揭露；暴露

uneasy / ʌnˈiːzi / *adj*. (身体)不舒服的；不安的，焦虑的：feel ~ about sb.'s future 担心某人的前途/ We grew ~ at their long absence. 对他们的长期缺席，我们渐感焦虑。

unemployed / ˌʌnɪmˈplɒɪd/ *adj*. 未被雇用的；无工作的；失业的：~ men 失业者

unemployment / ˌʌnɪmˈplɒɪmənt / *n*. [U] 失业；失业状态

unequal / ʌnˈiːkwəl / *adj*. ❶不平等的：an ~ bargain 不平等的交易/an ~ distribution of opportunity 机会的分配不均 ❷不相等的，不同的：planks of ~ length 长度不等的厚板/ classes of ~ size 不同规模的班级 ❸不合适的；不相称的；不能胜任的：We felt that he was ~ to the task. 我们觉得他不能胜任这项工作。

unexpected / ˌʌnɪkˈspektɪd / *adj*. 意料不到的；意外的：an ~ guest 不速之客/ an ~ result 意外的结果

unfair / ˌʌnˈfeə(r) / *adj*. 不公平的：~ treatment 不公平的待遇

unfamiliar / ˌʌnfəˈmɪljə(r)/ *adj*. ❶不熟悉的；陌生的：They had to adapt themselves to ~ climates. 他们只得使自己适应并不习惯的气候。❷不常见的，不一样的；非常的：an ~ treat 不一样的待遇 / This soup has an ~ taste. 这道汤别有一种风味。派 unfamiliarity *n*.

unfasten / ʌnˈfɑːsən/ *v*. 解开；松开；打

U

开;(使)脱开:~ a knot 解结 / ~ a button 解开纽扣 / The dog had learnt how to ~ the gate. 这条狗学会了打开大门。

unfavo(u)rable / ʌnˈfeɪvərəbl / *adj*. ❶不利的;不适宜的:The weather is ~ to our plans for a holiday. 这种天气对于我们安排假期颇为不利。❷相反的;反对的,不赞同的:an ~ view of the film 对影片的批评意见 ❸不讨人喜欢的;令人不愉快的:I hear he's in an ~ position with his boss. 我听说他同老板关系不妙。

unfit / ʌnˈfɪt / Ⅰ *adj*. 不适当的;不能胜任的:He is ~ to be a doctor. 他不适合当医生。Ⅱ *v*. (-fitted;-fitting) 使不适当;使不胜任

unfold / ʌnˈfəʊld / *v*. 展开;使呈现:He ~ed the letter and found it was from his mother. 他展开信一看,发现是他母亲的来信。

unforgettable / ˌʌnfəˈgetəbl / *adj*. 难忘的:It is really an ~ party. 那真是一次难忘的聚会。

unfortunate / ʌnˈfɔːtʃənət / *adj*. ❶不幸的;倒霉的:These students were ~ enough to fail in the exam. 这些学生很不幸,考试没有及格。❷遗憾的:It is ~ that they lost the game. 很遗憾他们比赛输了。派 unfortunately *adv*. ; unfortunateness *n*.

U

unfriendly / ʌnˈfrendli / *adj*. ❶不友好的;有敌意的:an ~ nation 敌对国家/ be ~ to reform 反对改革 ❷不利的;不顺利的:the ~ environment 不利的环境

ungrateful / ʌnˈgreɪtfl / *adj*. 不表示感激的;忘恩负义的

unhappy / ʌnˈhæpi / *adj*. ❶不愉快的 ❷不幸的

unidentified / ˌʌnaɪˈdentɪˌfaɪd / *adj*. 未被认出(或识别)的;来路不明的;身份不明的:an ~ flying object 不明飞行物/ The words had been spoken by an ~ Greek poet. 这些话是一位不知姓名的希腊诗人所言。

uniform / ˈjuːnɪfɔːm / Ⅰ *n*. 制服:put on (take off) the ~ 穿上(脱下)制服 / school ~(学生)校服 Ⅱ *adj*. 一样的,一致的;始终如一的:~ in size 大小相同 / The classrooms are ~ in size. 教室的大小相同。派 uniformly *adv*.

uniformity / ˌjuːnɪˈfɔːməti / *n*. [U]一样,一律;均匀

unify / ˈjuːnɪfaɪ / *vt*. 统一;使成一体;使一致:~ a country 统一国家/unified exam 统考

unimportant / ˌʌnɪmˈpɔːtənt / *adj*. 不重要的;无价值的

union / ˈjuːnɪən / *n*. ❶[U]联合;合并:the ~ of the three towns 三个镇的合并 ❷[C]同盟;协会:the Students' Union 学生会 / trade ~ 工会

unique / jʊˈniːk / *adj*. 唯一的;独一无二的:/ This stamp is ~. 这张邮票是独一无二的。/The custom is ~ to China. 这种风俗是中国特有的。

unit / ˈjuːnɪt / *n*. [C] ❶(计量的)单位:~ area 单位面积/~ price 单价 / The metre is a ~ of length. 米是长度单位。❷(指构成整体的)单位:a research ~ 科研单位 ❸(机械等的)部件,元件

unite / jʊˈnaɪt / *v*. ❶(使)联合;(使)结合:the common interests that ~ our two countries 我们两国联合的共同利益 ❷协力,团结;一致行动:Let us ~ in fighting poverty and diseases. 让我们团结起来战胜贫穷和疾病。

united /juˈnaɪtɪd/ *adj.* 联合的;团结的;统一的:the ~ front 统一战线 / the United Kingdom 联合王国,英国 / the United Nation 联合国 /the United States of America 美国

unity /ˈjuːnəti/ *n.* [U]联合,结合;统一;协调,一致:The figure on the left spoils the ~ of the painting. 左边那个人像破坏了那幅画的协调性。/ National ~ is essential in time of war. 举国一致在战争时是必要的。

universal /ˌjuːnɪˈvɜːsəl/ *adj.* ❶宇宙的;全世界的:The writer made a ~ travel. 那位作家做了环球旅行。❷普遍的;全体的:~ truth 普遍真理/ be of ~ significance 有普遍意义 ❸通用的;万能的:the ~ language 通用语

universe /ˈjuːnɪvɜːs/ *n.* 宇宙

university /ˌjuːnɪˈvɜːsəti/ *n.* [C]大学

unjust /ˌʌnˈdʒʌst/ *adj.* ❶不公正的 ❷不诚实的;不忠的

unkind /ˌʌnˈkaɪnd/ *adj.* 不亲切的;缺乏同情心的

unknown /ˌʌnˈnəʊn/ *adj.* 不为人知的;不出名的:I often receive letters from persons ~. 我常常收到一些陌生人的来信。/ a man ~ to me 我不认识的人/ ~ number 未知数/ ~ term 未知项

unlawful /ʌnˈlɔːfl/ *adj.* 非法的;不正当的

unless /ənˈles/ *conj.* 若不;除非:You will fail ~ you work hard. 如果你不努力,你就会失败。/I shall go ~ it rains. 如果不下雨我就去。

unlike /ˌʌnˈlaɪk/ Ⅰ *prep.* 不像 Ⅱ *adj.* 不同的;不像的:The two books are quite ~ . 这两本书完全不同。

unlikely /ʌnˈlaɪkli/ *adj.* 未必的;不大可能的:~ event 不大可能的事件/~ winner 不可能取胜的人/ He is ~ to succeed. 他未必会成功。/ It is ~ that he will pass the exam. 他不大可能通过考试。

unlimited /ʌnˈlɪmɪtɪd/ *adj.* 无限的;不定的

unload /ˌʌnˈləʊd/ *v.* 卸下;卸货:~ a truck 卸车/~ cargo from a ship 从船上卸货

unlock /ˌʌnˈlɒk/ *vt.* ❶开锁;开启:~ the door 打开门锁 ❷发现;揭开:The divers hoped to ~ some of the secrets of the seabed. 潜水员希望揭开海底的一些秘密。

unlucky /ʌnˈlʌki/ *adj.* 不幸的;不祥的;倒霉的

unmatched /ʌnˈmætʃt/ *adj.* ❶无比的,无与伦比的:an ~ success 空前的成功/ The research provides a model quite ~ so far. 这项研究提供了一个前所未有的模式。❷不相配的;不匹配的;不配对的:~ socks 不配对的袜子

unnatural /ʌnˈnætʃərəl/ *adj.* ❶不合乎自然规律的;违反常情的;不正常的:Her character becomes ~. 她的性格变得很反常。/ There is something ~ about this strange and sudden friendship between the two men. 这两个人之间突如其来的奇怪友谊是有些蹊跷。❷不自然的,矫揉造作的:She began to cry, and it was an ~, tearless sort of weeping. 她哭了起来,但是装模作样,没有一滴泪水。

unnecessary /ʌnˈnesəsəri/ *adj.* 不必要的;多余的

unpaid /ˌʌnˈpeɪd/ *adj.* 未付的;未偿还的

unpleasant /ʌnˈpleznt/ *adj.* 不愉快的;

令人讨厌的

unqualified /ʌnˈkwɒlɪˌfaɪd/ *adj*. ❶不合格的，不能胜任的；不够格的：She was ~ for the job. 她不能胜任这项工作。❷绝对的，完全的：an ~ denial 完全否定

unravel /ʌnˈrævəl/ *v*. ❶解开；散开；拆散：I had to ~ both sleeves since they had been knitted too small. 因为两只袖子织得太小了，我只好把它们都拆掉。/The settlement began to ~ in an embarrassingly short time. 令人尴尬的是，该协议没过多久就开始土崩瓦解了。❷(被)弄清；(被)廓清；(被)阐明；(被)解决：~ the mys-teries解开谜团/Now, if we swing back to the previous questions, the poem will begin to ~. 现在，如果我们再回过去看前面的问题，那这首诗的含义就会慢慢清楚了。

unreal /ˌʌnˈrɪəl/ *adj*. 假的；不真实的：The story is ~. 这故事不真实。

unreasonable /ʌnˈriːznəbl/ *adj*. 不讲道理的；不合理的：It is ~ to demand employees of working on weekends. 要求雇员在周末加班是不合理的。

unruly /ʌnˈruːli/ *adj*. ❶难驾驭的，不驯服的；难控制的；不服管束的：an ~ child 不服管教的孩子 ❷不守规矩(或秩序)的；不(守)法的人：the ~ people of carnival 狂欢节上无法无天的人们

U

unsatisfactory /ˌʌnˌsætɪsˈfæktəri/ *adj*. 不能令人满意的；不恰当的

unseen /ˌʌnˈsiːn/ *adj*. 未看见的；看不见的

unselfish /ʌnˈselfɪʃ/ *adj*. 无私的；慷慨的；不谋取私利的：Lei Feng was an ~ man. 雷锋是一个无私的人。派 unselfishly *adv*.；unselfishness *n*.

unsettled /ʌnˈset(ə)ld/ *adj*. ❶未解决的；未确定的；未落实的：Let's leave it ~. 咱们把问题先放一放。❷不稳定的；动荡的，动乱的：The late events in these two countries show that Africa is still ~. 这两个国家近来发生的事件说明非洲局势仍不稳定。❸未偿付的；未结算的；未付清的：an ~ account 未结清的账目 ❹不安宁的；精神失衡的：be in an ~ mood 心神不定

unshakable /ʌnˈʃeɪkəbl/ *adj*. 不可动摇的；坚定不移的：The scientist is ~ in his faith. 科学家的信仰是坚定的。

unsound /ʌnˈsaʊnd/ *adj*. ❶不正常的；不健全的，不健康的，有病的：an ~ mind 精神不健全 ❷不坚固的，不稳固的，不牢靠的；不可靠的，不安全的：an ~ business 不可靠的生意/ a bridge that is structurally ~结构不牢固的桥

unstable /ʌnˈsteɪbl/ *adj*. 不稳固的；不稳定的

unsuitable /ʌnˈsjuːtəbl/ *adj*. 不合适的；不适宜的

unthinkable /ʌnˈθɪŋkəbl/ *adj*. 难以想象的；不可思议的：At that time, he was faced with ~ difficulties. 那时他面对的是难以想象的困难。

untidy /ʌnˈtaɪdi/ *adj*. 不整洁的；凌乱的：an ~ room 凌乱的房间

untie /ʌnˈtaɪ/ *vt*. 解开；松开：~ a parcel 解开包裹 / ~ one's tie 解领带

until /ənˈtɪl，ʌnˈtɪl/ Ⅰ *prep*. ❶到……的时候，直到……为止：Payment may be deferred ~ the end of the month. 可以推迟到月底再付款。❷(用于否定句)在……之前，直到……才：Not ~ this year did he devote a single speech exclusively to the disaster. 他一直到今年才发表一篇论述灾难的讲话。Ⅱ *conj*. ❶到……为止，直到……时：I was doing just fine ~ the sound of the bell screwed me up. 我正进行得顺利的时候，铃声响了，把我搞得手忙脚乱。❷(用于否定句)直到……才：Life was dull and uninteresting ~ she returned. 在她回来之前生活枯燥乏味，没有意思。

untouched /ʌnˈtʌtʃt/ *adj*. 原样的；未动过的

unusual /ʌnˈjuːʒʊəl/ *adj*. 不常见的，不一般的；奇异的

unveil /ʌnˈveɪl/ *vt*. ❶揭去……面纱：The bridegroom ~ed the bride's face. 新郎揭开新娘脸上的面纱。❷使公开；使暴露；揭示，揭露：The government ~s the economic state of the country. 政府向公众透露了国家的经济状况。

unwilling /ʌnˈwɪlɪŋ/ *adj*. 不愿意的，不情愿的 派 unwillingly *adv*.

unworthy /ʌnˈwɜːði/ *adj*. ❶不值得的；不配得到的：The phenomenon seems ~ of our attention. 这种现象似乎不值得我们关注。❷(与……)不相配的，不相称的，不合身份的：The books have been condemned as ~ of young children. 有人指责这些书不适合小孩子们看。❸卑鄙的，卑劣的，下作的，可耻的 派 unworthiness *n*.

unwrap /ʌnˈræp/ *v*. (-wrapped; -wrapping)打开；解开：Don't ~ the box until you get home. 等你到家了才可打开这个盒子。

unzip /ʌnˈzɪp/ (-zipped; -zipping) *v*. 拉开(拉链)；拉开……的拉链：~ a jacket 拉开上衣拉链/ For about eight seconds earth's crust ~ed at more that two kilometers a second. 大约8秒钟的时间，地壳以每秒2千米以上的速度迸裂开来。

up /ʌp/ Ⅰ *adv*. ❶向上：Lift your head ~. 抬起头来。/The tide is ~. 潮水在上涨。/Prices are still going ~. 物价仍在上涨。❷起床：He's already ~. 他已起床。/She was ~ all night with a sick child. 她整夜未睡地陪伴一个病孩。❸完全；结束：We've eaten everything ~. 我们把所有食物都吃光了。/Time is ~. 时间到了。/~ **and down** 上上下下地；前后地；往返地：walking ~ and down the station platform 在车站月台上来回走动 ~ **till now** 直到现在为止 ~ **to date** 最新的；直到现在 ~ **to now** 到目前为止 Ⅱ *prep*. 向……的上端；向……的较高处：walk ~ stairs 上楼梯 / ~ **to** ①应由(某人)担任或负责：It's ~ to us to give them all the help we can. 我们理应给他们一切我们所能给予的帮助。②胜任：He is not ~ to his job. 他不能胜任工作。③正在做；正从事：What is he ~ to? 他在做什么？

update Ⅰ /ʌpˈdeɪt/ *vt*. 更新，使不落后；使现代化：The software will need to be ~d regularly. 软件必须不断地更新。/ ~ the defensive weapons 使防御武器现代化 Ⅱ /ˈʌpˌdeɪt/ *n*. ❶更新；修改 ❷[C]最新版本；最新报道；更新的内容(或数据)

upgrade Ⅰ /ʌpˈgreɪd/ *vt*. ❶提升，使升级：His job has been ~d from assistant manager to manager. 他由助理经理升任经理。❷提高；改进，改善：~d the networks 改进网络系统 Ⅱ /ˈʌpˌgreɪd/ *n*. ❶提升；升级；提高 ❷[C]改进(或更新)的设施

uphold /ʌpˈhəʊld/ *vt*. (upheld, upheld) ❶高举 ❷支持，赞成

upon /əˈpɒn/ *prep*. 在……上；……在身上：once ~ a time 从前

upper /ˈʌpə(r)/ *adj*. 较高的；上面的：

the ~ classes 上流阶层(社会)/ the ~ lip 上唇 / one of the ~ rooms 楼上的一个房间 / **get (have) the ~ hand of** 占上风;比……占优势

upright /ˈʌpraɪt/ *adj.* 垂直的;笔直的:hold oneself ~ 笔直地站着 / set the pole ~ 把杆子竖直 派 uprightly *adv.*

uprising /ˈʌpraɪzɪŋ/ *n.* [C] 起义;暴动,叛乱:put down an ~ 镇压起义

uproar /ˈʌpˌrɔː(r)/ *n.* [U] ❶骚动,骚乱:The news caused the public ~. 这条消息引发了公众骚乱。❷吵闹,喧嚣:This only increased the ~, when they heard him speak. 当人们一听到他这样说话,就更加起哄。

upset /ʌpˈset/ Ⅰ *v.* (upset, upset) ❶颠覆;推翻:Don't ~ the boat. 不要把船弄翻了。❷扰乱;使不安:~ the enemy's plan 破坏敌人的计划 / ~ one's stomach by eating too much rich food 因油腻的食物吃得太多而使胃不舒服 Ⅱ *n.* [C]颠覆;扰乱;不安:have a stomach ~ 胃不舒服 Ⅲ *adj.* 难过的;不安的

upside /ˈʌpsaɪd/ *n.* 上部;上边;上面

upside-down /ˈʌpsaɪˈdaʊn/ *adj.* 倒转的,倒置的;乱七八糟的:The house was turned ~ by the burglars. 那房子被窃贼翻得乱七八糟。

upstairs /ˌʌpˈsteəz/ Ⅰ *adv.* 向楼上;在楼上:go (walk) ~ 上楼 Ⅱ *adj.* 属于楼上的;位于楼上的:an ~ room 楼上的房间

up-to-date /ˈʌptəˈdeɪt/ *adj.* 现代的;最新的:an ~ record 最新纪录 / an ~ store 最新式的店铺

upward /ˈʌpwəd/ Ⅰ *adj.* 向上的;上升的:the ~ trend of prices 物价上升的趋势 Ⅱ *adv.* (=upwards) 向上地;上升地:The boat was on the beach, bottom ~. 那船搁置在海滩上,船底朝天。

uranium /jʊˈreɪnɪəm/ *n.* [U]铀(符号U)

urban /ˈɜːbən/ *adj.* 城市的:~ construction 城市建设 / ~ inhabitants 城市居民 / exchange between ~ and rural areas 城乡交流

urge /ɜːdʒ/ *vt.* ❶力劝;催促,敦促:The shopkeeper ~d me to buy a hat. 那店主极力劝我买一顶帽子。❷极力主张:He ~d upon his pupils the importance of hard work. 他极力向学生讲解用功的重要。❸推进;驱策

urgent /ˈɜːdʒənt/ *adj.* ❶紧急的;急迫的:It's most ~ that the patient (should) be sent to hospital. 要紧的是病人应送医院。❷催逼的;坚持要求的:They were ~ for the doctor to come. 他们急迫地催医生来。/He was ~ to have more. 他坚持要多一些。

us /ʌs/ *pron.* 我们(we 的宾格)

usage /ˈjuːzɪdʒ/ *n.* ❶使用;用法 ❷习惯;习俗

use Ⅰ /juːz/ *v.* ❶用,使用;利用 / **~ up** 消耗;用尽:He has ~d up all his strength. 他已耗尽了所有的体力。❷惯常(只用过去时,后跟不定式):You ~d to smoke a pipe, didn't you? 你过去要抽烟,是吗? Ⅱ /juːs/ *n.* ❶[U]使用;应用;利用:the ~ of electricity for lighting 利用电力照明 / **come into ~** 开始被使用:When did the word "transistor" come into ~? "transistor"一词何时开始使用的? **go (fall) out of ~** 已不再使用,废弃:The name has gone out of ~. 那名称已不再使用了。**in ~** 在使用中:The laboratory is in ~ until five o'clock. 实验室一直到 5 点钟都有人

用。**make (good, the best) ~ of** 很好地利用；充分地利用：You must make good ~ of any opportunity to practise English. 你应该好好利用一切机会练习英文。**put to ~** 投入使用：The new power station will be put to ~ next month. 这新发电厂下月投入使用。❷[C]用途；用处：a tool with many ~s 有多种用途的工具 / This big box is of good ~. 这个大箱子很有用。❸[U]价值；益处：It's no ~ complaining. 埋怨没有用。

used /juːzd/ *adj.* ❶用旧了的；二手的：a ~ car 旧汽车 ❷习惯于……的；惯常的：I'm quite ~ to speaking English. 我相当习惯讲英语。

useful /ˈjuːsfl/ *adj.* 有用的；有益的；有帮助的：a ~ tool 有用的工具 / It's ~ for one to know some English when traveling abroad. 懂点英语对在国外旅行的人是有好处的。/Dictionaries are ~ to students. 词典对学生很有用。派 usefully *adv.*；usefulness *n.*

useless /ˈjuːsləs/ *adj.* 无用的，无价值的；无益的；无效的：It is ~ to discuss the problem at present. 目前讨论这个问题没有什么价值。

user /ˈjuːzə(r)/ *n.* [C]用户；使用者

usual /ˈjuːʒʊəl/ *adj.* 通常的；惯例的：Tea is the ~ drink of Chinese. 茶是中国人通常喝的饮料。/ **as ~** 照例，照常：I went to bed at eleven as ~. 我照例11点睡觉。派 usually *adv.*

utensil /juːˈtensl/ *n.* [C]器皿；用具

utility /juːˈtɪləti/ *n.* ❶[U]效用；实用 ❷[C]有用之物 ❸[C]（常用 *pl.*）公用事业：the administration of public utilities 公共事业的管理

utilize /ˈjuːtɪˌlaɪz/ *vt.* （有效地）利用：~ the power of the wind 利用风力/ It is advantageous for employers to ~ higher paid employees for longer hours instead of hiring additional workers to increase output. 雇主给雇员加班加薪比另外雇人合算。

utmost /ˈʌtməʊst/ Ⅰ *adj.* 极度的；最大的：with the ~ pleasure 极为高兴地 Ⅱ *n.* 极限，极度；最大可能：at the ~ 至多 / do one's ~ 竭尽全力

utter[1] /ˈʌtə(r)/ *adj.* 完全的，彻底的

utter[2] /ˈʌtə(r)/ *vt.* 发出（声音）；说；讲：~ a cry of pain 发出痛苦的叫声/ He ~ed only one word or two. 他只说了一两句话。

utterance /ˈʌtərəns/ *n.* ❶[U]发声；说话；表达：Excitement deprived me of all power of ~. 我兴奋得什么话也说不出来。/ She will never give ~ to her fear. 她决不会流露出自己的恐惧。❷[C]所说的话；言语，言辞；言论：Secretaries record his every appointment and ~. 秘书们把他的每项任命、每句话都记录下来。

V v

vacancy /ˈveɪkənsi/ *n.* ❶[U]空;空白;空间:All was blackness and ~. 四下里一团漆黑,空空荡荡。❷[C]空缺;空职:His retirement caused a ~ in the office. 他退休了,办公室有个空职。/fill up the ~填补空缺 ❸[C](宾馆等待租的)空房

vacant /ˈveɪkənt/ *adj.* 空的;未占用的:a ~ room 空房间 / apply for a ~ position 申请某空缺职位

vacation /vəˈkeɪʃn/ *n.* [C]❶(大学的)假期;(法庭的)休庭期:the summer (winter) ~ 暑(寒)假 ❷休假:You can't see the manager because he is on ~. 经理在度假,你见不到他。/The old couple are going on ~ in Japan. 那对老年夫妇要去日本度假。

vaccinate /ˈvæksɪˌneɪt/ *v.* (给……)接种疫苗,(给……)打预防针:The government decided to ~ all the children against smallpox. 政府决定给所有小孩种牛痘。/~ against measles 种麻疹疫苗 派 vaccination *n.*

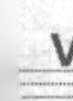

vaccine /ˈvæksiːn/ *n.* [C] ❶疫苗,菌苗:stamp out polio by using ~注射疫苗消灭小儿麻痹症 ❷抗病毒软件

vacuum /ˈvækjuəm/ Ⅰ*n.* [C] ❶真空;封闭状态;隔绝状态:Translation does not occur in a ~翻译不是在真空中进行的。❷真空;真空度:perfect ~完全真空 ❸空白;空虚;沉寂:His wife's death left a ~ in his life. 妻子的去世使他的生活变得空虚起来。❹真空吸尘器 Ⅱ*vt.* 用真空吸尘器打扫:The young lady is ~ing the carpets. 那位年轻女士正在用真空吸尘器扫地毯。

vague /veɪg/ *adj.* ❶含糊的,模糊的,不明确的:He remained ~ about when she would return to Washington. 她什么时候返回华盛顿,对此他一直含糊其词。❷没有表情的,茫然的:The poor old man looked ~, not knowing what did happened to him. 那可怜的老人一脸茫然,不知发生了什么事。派 vagueness *n.*

vain /veɪn/ *adj.* 无益的;无效的,无结果的 / **in** ~无效地,徒然:All our work was in ~. 我们的一切工作都是徒然。

valid /ˈvælɪd/ *adj.* 有效的;正当的:~ contract 有效合同 / ~ passport 有效护照 / ~ for one year (six months) 有效期一年(半年)/ One can sign up with ~ papers. 持有效证件即能报名。派 validly *adv.*

valley /ˈvæli/ *n.* [C] (*pl.* valleys) 谷;山谷;峡谷

valuable /ˈvæljuəbl/ *adj.* 有价值的;贵重的;有用的:a ~ discovery 有价值的发现

valuation /ˌvæljʊˈeɪʃn/ *n.* [U]评价;估

价:It is unwise to accept a person at his own ~. 凭一个人对自己的评价而相信他是不明智的。

value /ˈvæljuː/ Ⅰ *n.* ❶[U]重要性;有用性 ❷[U](与他物比较时某物的)价值:This book will be of great (little, some, no) ~ to him for his studies. 这本书对他的研究很有(几乎没有,有一些,没有)价值。❸[U]价格;购买力:Is the ~ of the American dollar likely to decline? 美元可能贬值吗? ❹[C](常用 *pl.*)贵重物品:You'd better keep your ~s in a safe. 你最好把你的贵重物品锁进保险柜。Ⅱ *vt.* 尊重;重视;评价:He ~d the house at half a million. 他估价这房子为 50 万。/ We ~ the teacher's advice. 我们重视老师提出的意见。

valve /vælv/ *n.* [C]阀门:safety ~ 安全阀

van /væn/ *n.* [C]大篷车;运货车:luggage ~ 行李车

vanish /ˈvænɪʃ/ *vi.* 突然不见;消失:~ from sight 从眼前消失/~ into nothing 变得无影无踪/ The moon ~ed behind the clouds. 月亮隐藏到云后面去了。

vanity /ˈvænəti/ *n.* [U]虚荣心;自负,自大

vapo(u)r /ˈveɪpə(r)/ *n.* [U](蒸)汽;雾:water ~ 水蒸气 / ~bath 蒸汽浴

variable /ˈveərɪəbl/ Ⅰ *adj.* 可变的,易变的,多变的:a specific disease in the ~ human body 人体随时变化的疾病/ His temper is ~. 他的脾气反复无常。Ⅱ *n.* [C]❶易变的事物:the major ~ in risk assessment 对风险进行评估的主要因素 ❷变量;变量符号:independent ~自变量/ dependent ~因变量

variation /ˌveərˈeɪʃn/ *n.* ❶[U]变动,变更:Date of departure is subject to ~. 启程日期可能会有变更。❷[C]变化程度;变化量:Sign languages exhibit the same types of ~ that spoken languages do. 手势语和口头语言一样,也有同样类型的变化。❸[C]变体;变化了的东西:Today, more than 1,000 computer viruses and ~ are reportedly sweeping through the world. 据报道,目前有 1 000 多种计算机病毒及其变种正席卷全球。

variety /vəˈraɪəti/ *n.* ❶[U]变化;多样:~ dish 杂烩/ ~ show 综艺节目,杂耍/ We demanded more ~ of our food. 我们要求食物品种多样化。❷[C](只用单数)种类:for a ~ of reasons 由于种种原因 / a large ~ of patterns to choose from 可供选择的多种花样

various /ˈveərɪəs/ *adj.* 不同的;各式各样的:at ~ times 在不同的时代 / a criminal who is known to the police under ~ names 为警察所知的以各种化名出现的罪犯 派 variously *adv.*

vary /ˈveəri/ *v.* (使)不同;(使)变化:~ing prices 变动的物价 / You should ~ your diet. 你应该改变饮食。/ ~ **from ... to ...**从……变化到……:The ages in our class ~ from 12 to 15. 我们班同学的年龄从 12 岁到 15 岁不等。

vase /vɑːz/ *n.* [C]花瓶

vast /vɑːst/ *adj.* 巨大的;广阔的:a ~ extension of desert 一大片沙漠 派 vastness *n.*

VCD (=video compact disc) [C]影碟;影碟机

vegetable /ˈvedʒtəbl/ *n.* [C] ❶蔬菜 ❷植物人

vegetation /ˌvedʒɪˈteɪʃn/ *n.* [U]植物;植被:~ zones 植被带/ hills covered to the top with luxuriant ~一座座被郁郁葱葱的草木覆盖的小山

vehicle /ˈvɪəkl,ˈviːəkl/ *n*.[C] ❶车辆;运载工具:heavy ~s 重型车辆 ❷传播工具;媒介:~ of propaganda 宣传工具 / Language is a ~ of human thoughts. 语言是人类思想的传播媒体。

veil /veɪl/ *n*. [C]❶面纱,面罩:put on the white ~戴上白面纱 ❷遮盖物;借口,托词:under the ~ of friendship 在友谊的幌子下/through a thin ~ of smoke in a black sky 透过黑色天空中的薄烟

vein /veɪn/ *n*.[C] ❶静脉;血管,脉 ❷趋势;气质;风格:a rich ~ of humor 颇有几分幽默/ The old man had a ~ of stubbornness. 这个老汉性格有点倔。

velocity /vəˈlɒsəti/ *n*.[C]速率;速度:at a ~ of 30 meters per second 以每秒30米的速度/ initial (terminal, uniform)~ 初(末、匀)速度

vendor /ˈvendə(r)/ *n*. [C] 小贩,摊贩:a black-market ~ 黑市小贩 / a news ~ 报贩

vengeful /ˈvendʒfʊl/ *adj*. 报复的;报仇心切的,报复心强的:But he still felt ~ even after many years. 但是即使多年以后,他报仇之心未泯。派 vengefully *adv*.

venture /ˈventʃə(r)/ Ⅰ *n*.[C]冒险;冒险事业;投机:make a ~ 冒险 / a joint ~ 合资企业 Ⅱ *v*. 冒险;大胆行事:I ~ to disagree. 我冒昧说不。/Nothing ~, nothing gain (win, have). 不入虎穴,焉得虎子。派 venturer *n*.

Venus /ˈviːnəs/ *n*. [C]❶维纳斯(爱和美的女神) ❷维纳斯雕像 ❸金星;太白星

verb /vɜːb/ *n*.[C]动词:auxiliary (link, modal) ~ 助动词(连系动词,情态动词) / regular (irregular) ~ 规则(不规则)动词 / transitive (intransitive) ~及物(不及物)动词

verbal /ˈvɜːbəl/ *adj*. ❶用言辞的,用文字的;文字上的:~ abuse 恶言,谩骂/ This is a ~ trick. 这是玩弄字眼儿。❷口头的,非书面的:erect a ~ monument 树立起口碑/ a ~ contract 口头契约 ❸动词的;源自动词的;作为动词的:~ inflexions 动词的屈折变化

verdict /ˈvɜːdɪkt/ *n*. [C] ❶裁定,裁决,决定:a ~ of guilty (not guilty) 有罪(无罪)的裁定 ❷判断,定论:wait the ~ of time 留待后人评判 / pass a final ~ on sb. 对某人下定论

verge /vɜːdʒ/ *n*.[C]边缘;边界;界限

verifiable /ˈverɪfaɪəbl/ *adj*. 可证实的;可核实的

verify /ˈverɪfaɪ/ *vt*. ❶证实;查证;证明:Truth can be verified by practice. 真理可由实践证明。❷核实:~ a report (details, figures) 核实报告(细节,数字) 派 verification *n*.

versatile /ˈvɜːsəˌtaɪl/ *adj*. ❶多才多艺的,有多种才能的:~ erudition 博学多才/ She was ~ at writing. 她是写作的多面手。❷(装置等)有多种用途的,有多种功能的:a ~ chemical 有多种用途的化学品/ A pickup is ~ in function. 轻型货车有多种功能。派 versatility *n*.

verse /vɜːs/ *n*. ❶诗体作品,诗歌;诗句,诗行,歌词:compose ~作诗/ an extempore ~即兴诗 ❷[C](诗或韵文的)节,诗节:quote a few ~s from sb. 引用某人的几句诗

version /ˈvɜːʃn/ *n*. [C]❶翻译;译本:a new ~ of the Bible《圣经》的新版本 ❷叙述,说法;说明:There were contradictory ~s of what happened. 对所发生

的事有矛盾的说法。

versus /ˈvɜːsəs/ *prep.* ❶对,以……为对手(略作 v.,vs):The match is China ~ America. 比赛是中国队对美国队。❷与……相对,与……相比:There's also something known as risk ~ benefit. 还存在权衡利弊的问题。

vertical /ˈvɜːtɪkl/ *adj.* 垂直的;竖的:~ line 垂线 / ~ plane 垂面 派 vertically *adv.*

very /ˈveri/ Ⅰ *adv.* 很;非常:~ amusing (interesting) 很好笑(有趣) / The book you lent me is ~ good. 你借给我的那本书很好。/ I like English ~ much. 我非常喜欢英语。/ Her daughter plays the violin ~ well. 她女儿的小提琴拉得非常好。Ⅱ *adj.* ❶同一的;恰好的:At that ~ moment the telephone bell rang. 就在那时,电话铃响了。❷极端的:at the ~ end (beginning) 最终(最初)

vessel /ˈvesl/ *n.* [C] ❶容器;器皿 ❷船,舰 ❸脉管;血管

vest /vest/ *n.* [C]内衣;汗衫;背心

veteran /ˈvetərən/ Ⅰ *n.* [C] ❶老手;老练的人;有经验者 ❷老兵;退役军人:disabled ~ 残疾老兵 / World War Ⅱ ~ 二战老兵 Ⅱ *adj.* 老练的;资格老的

veto /ˈviːtəʊ/ Ⅰ *n.* [C] (*pl.* vetoes) 否决;否决权:exercise (use) a ~ 行使否决权 Ⅱ *vt.* 否决:~ a bill 否决一项议案

via /ˈvaɪə/ *prep.* 经过;通过:They went to America ~ Japan. 他们途经日本去美国。/ We communicate ~ e-mail. 我们通过电子邮件交流。

vibrant /ˈvaɪbrənt/ *adj.* ❶震动的,颤动的:He was ~ with emotion. 他激动得颤抖起来。❷充满生气的,活跃的:a ~, enthusiastic person 一个活跃、热心的人/ a village ~ with life and energy 充满活力的山村

vibrate /vaɪˈbreɪt/ *v.* (使)摆动;(使)摇动;(使)震动:The house ~s whenever a heavy lorry passes. 大货车经过的时候,这屋子总要发生震动。/ The strings of piano ~ when the keys are struck. 当钢琴的琴键受击时,琴弦震动。派 vibration *n.*

vice /vaɪs/ *n.* ❶[C]缺点;毛病:You must see the ~s of modern civilization. 你得看到现代文明的缺点。❷[C]恶习:Too much drinking is a ~. 酗酒是一种恶习。❸邪恶;邪恶行为

vicious /ˈvɪʃəs/ *adj.* ❶恶毒的,狠毒的:His ~ intent is obvious to everybody. 他的恶毒用心是谁都知道的。/ It is ~ of her to make such an accusation. 她这么指责人真是恶毒。❷猛烈的,剧烈的:a ~ headache 剧烈的头痛 ❸野蛮的;残忍的:a ~ temper 残暴的性情

victim /ˈvɪktɪm/ *n.* [C]受害者;牺牲者:A fund was opened to help the ~s of the earthquake. 为了帮助地震受灾的灾民,基金会开始募捐了。

victorious /vɪkˈtɔːrɪəs/ *adj.* 胜利的;成功的;凯旋的:the ~ army 胜利之师 派 victoriously *adv.*

victory /ˈvɪktəri/ *n.* 胜利;成功:gain a ~ over the enemy 战胜敌人 / lead the troops to ~率领军队迈向胜利

video /ˈvɪdɪəʊ/ Ⅰ *n.* [C] (*pl.* videos) ❶电视;录像 ❷录像节目;录像机 Ⅱ *adj.* 电视的;录像的:~ tape 录像带 / ~ recorder 录像机

vie /vai/ *vi.* (vying) 竞争;争夺(与 with 连用):~ for the Olympic Games 申办奥林匹克运动会 / Supermarkets are vying with each other to attract customers by offering discounts. 各家超市竞相打折来招徕顾客。/ ~in beauty with Mary 与玛丽比美争艳

view / vjuː / Ⅰ *n.* ❶[U]看;视力;眼界: The speaker stood in full ~ of the crowd. 演说者站在观众完全可以看见的地方。/ After you turn round the corner, the hospital will come into ~. 你转过那个街角就看得到医院了。❷[C]景色;景物: a fine ~ in the valley 山谷中的优美景色 ❸[C]意见;观点: He holds extreme ~s. 他持极端的见解。/ **in ~ of** 鉴于,由于: In ~ of the facts, he is believable. 鉴于事实,他是可信的。Ⅱ *v.* 看;观察: They ~ed the problem in different ways. 他们以不同的方式看这个问题。

viewer / ˈvjuːə(r) / *n.* [C] ❶观看者,观众;电视观众: The film-makers kept the pace fast enough for the ~ to overlook most of the plot's absurdities. 制片人保持电影的快节奏,这样观众就看不到情节的许多荒谬之处了。❷观看器;观察镜;取镜器

viewpoint / ˈvjuːpɒɪnt / *n.* [C]观点;见解: It is necessary to look at things with a mass ~. 看问题要有群众观点。

vigilance / ˈvɪdʒɪləns / *n.* [U]警戒;警戒性

vigilant / ˈvɪdʒɪlənt / *adj.* 警戒的: A pilot must remain ~ at all times. 飞行员必须随时保持警惕。

vigorous / ˈvɪɡərəs / *adj.* 朝气蓬勃的;精力充沛的;健壮的;有力的: ~ enforcement of law 执法有力 / The football player is ~. 这足球运动员精力充沛。派 vigorously *adv.*

vigo(u)r / ˈvɪɡə(r) / *n.* [U]活力;精力: lose one's ~ 失去活力 / regain ~ 恢复活力 / He came back after the vacation, full of ~. 他度假回来后精力充沛。

village / ˈvɪlɪdʒ / *n.* [C]村庄

villager / ˈvɪlɪdʒə(r) / *n.* [C]村民

vine / vaɪn / *n.* [C]葡萄树;蔓,藤

vinegar / ˈvɪnɪɡə(r) / *n.* [U] 醋

violate / ˈvaɪəleɪt / *vt.* ❶违犯;违反;违背 ❷妨碍;扰乱 ❸玷污

violence / ˈvaɪələns / *n.* [U] ❶猛烈;凶暴: the ~ of her feelings 她强烈的情感 ❷暴行

violent / ˈvaɪələnt / *adj.* ❶暴力的;猛烈的;残暴的: a ~ attack 猛攻 / in a ~ temper 盛怒地 ❷剧烈的;厉害的 派 violently *adv.*

violet / ˈvaɪələt / Ⅰ *n.* ❶[C]紫罗兰 ❷[U]蓝紫色,紫罗兰色 Ⅱ *adj.* 紫色的

violin / ˌvaɪəˈlɪn / *n.* [C]小提琴

VIP (=very important person)要人,大人物,贵宾

viral / ˈvaɪərəl / *adj.* 病毒(性)的;病毒感染的,病毒引起的: as a result of a ~ infection 由于病毒感染

virgin / ˈvɜːdʒɪn / Ⅰ *n.* [C] ❶童男,童女 ❷处女 ❸天真的人,不谙世事的人 Ⅱ *adj.* ❶未用过的,未开发的: ~ land 生荒地 ❷纯洁的,未被玷污的: be arrayed in ~ white 打扮得一身纯白

virtual / ˈvɜːtʃʊəl / *adj.* ❶实际上的;实质上的 ❷虚拟的: ~ office 虚拟办公室/ ~ reality 虚拟现实

virtually / ˈvɜːtʃʊəli / *adv.* 实际上;事实上;几乎: They are ~ impossible to find out the secret. 事实上他们不可能发现这个秘密。

virtue / ˈvɜːtʃuː / *n.* ❶善;德行;美德;优点: Patience is a ~. 忍耐是一种美德。/ **by (in) ~ of** 由于,凭借: By ~ of his own effort he managed to finish the work. 凭自己的努力，他设法完成了工作。❷(尤指妇女的)贞操：a woman of ~ 贞洁的妇女

virtuous / ˈvɜːtjʊəs / *adj*. ❶道德高尚的，有德行的：a person who lives a ~ life 一个生活严谨道德高尚的人/ do what is ~行善 ❷贞洁的；有操守的

virus / ˈvaɪrəs / *n*. [C] ❶病毒：This ~ ruins the immune system. 这种病毒破坏人体免疫系统。❷计算机病毒

visa / ˈviːzə / *n*. [C](护照的)背签；签证：apply for a ~ 申请签证 / extend a ~ 延长签证时效 / get (receive) a ~ 获得签证/ grant (issue) a ~发放签证

visibility / ˌvɪzəˈbɪləti / *n*. [C]可见性；能见度

visible / ˈvɪzəbl / *adj*. 可见的；看得见的：The germs are not ~ to our naked eyes. 细菌是我们肉眼看不见的。

vision / ˈvɪʒən / *n*. ❶[U]视力；想象力；远见：the field of ~ 视野 / the ~ of a poet 诗人的想象力 / the ~ of a prophet 预言家的远见 ❷[C]景象；(尤指)幻想；梦想：We should not laugh at the romantic ~s of the young people. 我们不应该嘲笑年轻人浪漫的幻想。

visionary / ˈvɪʒənəri / *adj*. ❶幻觉的，幻想的：~ experiences 梦幻 ❷有眼力的，有预见的：a ~ leader 有远见卓识的领袖

visit / ˈvɪzɪt / Ⅰ *v*. 访问，拜访(某人)；游览，参观(某地)：~ a friend 访友 / ~ Rome 游览罗马 Ⅱ *n*. [C]访问；游览：pay a ~ to a friend 拜访朋友 / I paid a ~ to the writer out of my way. 我专程去拜访了那个作家。

visitor / ˈvɪzɪtə(r) / *n*. [C]访问者；来访者；宾客：summer ~s 夏季游客 / the ~s' book 来宾签字簿；游客登记簿

visual / ˈvɪzjʊəl, ˈvɪʒʊəl / *adj*. 视觉的；视力的：a ~ defect 视力缺陷/ This test was as a basis for judging his ~ acuity. 根据这个测试可判断他视觉的敏锐程度。

vital / ˈvaɪtl / *adj*. 生命力的；与生命有关的；维持生命必需的；精力充沛的：wound-ed in a ~ part 在要害处受伤

vitality / vaɪˈtæləti / *n*. [U]活力；生命力；持久力：the ~ of seeds 种子的生命力

vitamin / ˈvɪtəmɪn / *n*. [C]维生素

vivid / ˈvɪvɪd / *adj*. ❶生动的；栩栩如生的：~ in sb. 's memory 记得清清楚楚 / The novel gives a ~ description of the country life. 小说生动地描写了农村生活。❷鲜艳的：~ green 翠绿色 派 vividly *adv*.

vocabulary / vəˈkæbjələri / *n*. 词汇表；词汇

vocal / ˈvəʊkəl / *adj*. ❶嗓音的，用嗓音的；歌唱的：~ tract 声道/ The strong contrasts between them extended well beyond mere ~ quality. 他们两人强烈的对比远远超出了音质的不同。❷畅所欲言的，自由表达的：The protests are a small but ~ minority. 抗议者人数不多但敢于直言。

vocation / vəʊˈkeɪʃn / *n*. [C]职业；行业：choose (select) a ~ 挑选职业 / take up the ~ of 从事……的职业 派 vocational *adj*.

vogue / vəʊg / *n*. 时尚，流行；流行(或时髦)事物；时髦人物：Garments of this fashion have gone out of ~. 这种式样的衣服已落伍了。/ The designs are in ~. 这些图案正在流行。

voice / vɒɪs / Ⅰ *n*. ❶人声；说话声：drop (lower) one's ~ 放低声音/ lift up (raise) one's ~ 提高嗓门/ lose one's ~

嗓子哑了/ in a loud ~ 大声地 / I did not recognize her ~. 我没听出她的声音。/ **give ~ to** 说出；发表(意见)；吐露 **with one** ~ 一致地；异口同声地 ❷(语法)动词的语态：active (passive) ~ 主动(被动)语态 Ⅱ *v.* 说出来；表达；发出：The spokesman ~d the feelings of the crowd. 发言人说出了群众的心声。

volatile /ˈvɒləˌtaɪl/ *adj.* ❶易挥发的；挥发性的：~ acid 挥发酸/ Petrol is ~. 汽油易挥发。❷易变的；反复无常的；不稳定的：Demographic trends are ~ and difficult to predict. 人口统计方面的发展趋势多变，因而难以预见。派 volatility *n.*

volcano /vɒlˈkeɪnəʊ/ *n.* [C](*pl.* volcanoes) 火山：active ~活火山 / dormant ~ 休眠火山 / extinct ~ 死火山

volleyball /ˈvɒlɪbɔːl/ *n.* [U]排球运动；排球

volt /vəʊlt/ *n.* [C]伏特(电压单位)

voltage /ˈvəʊltɪdʒ/ *n.* 电压；伏特数

volume /ˈvɒljuːm/ *n.* ❶[C](尤指一部书中的)一册，一卷：an encyclopaedia in 20 ~s 有20册的一部百科全书/a hardcover (paperback) ~ 精(平)装本 / an out-of-print ~ 绝版书 ❷[U]体积；容积；容量：sails ~ 销售量/ the ~ of traffic 交通流量/ the ~ of water 水量 ❸[U](指声音)有力；响度；音量：a voice of great ~ 音量大的声音

V

voluntary /ˈvɒləntri/ *adj.* 自愿的；义务的：~ service 自愿服务(服役)

volunteer /ˌvɒlənˈtɪə(r)/ Ⅰ *n.* [C] ❶自愿者 ❷志愿兵 Ⅱ *v.* 自愿提出；自愿效劳：He ~ed for the campaign. 他自愿参加这次战役。

vomit /ˈvɒmɪt/ *vt.* ❶呕吐，吐，呕：He ~ed up the foul water he had swallowed. 他将吞下去的脏水全部吐出。❷(火山、烟囱等)喷发，喷：The volcano is ~ing volumes of black smoke. 火山正在喷出滚滚黑烟。

vote /vəʊt/ Ⅰ *n.* ❶投票(权)；表决(权)；选举(权)：Do women have the ~ in your country? 贵国的妇女有选举权吗？❷选票数：be beaten by one ~ 以一票之差落选 / pass sth. by a majority ~ 以多数票通过某事 / Will the Labor ~ increase or decrease at the next election? 在下届选举中，工党的票数将增加还是减少？Ⅱ *v.* ❶投票(与for或against连用，后接某物或某人；与on连用后接某问题)：Fifteen ~d for and twelve (~d) against it. 15票赞成，12票反对。/ Now we will ~ on this question. 现在我们来对这个问题投票解决。❷投票表决：~ a sum of money for education 投票表决一笔教育经费 派 voter *n.*

vow /vaʊ/ Ⅰ *n.* [C] 誓，誓约，誓言：break the ~ 违反诺言/ lovers' ~s 爱人的誓言 Ⅱ *vt.* 立誓给予；起誓做，发誓履行：If I do ~ a friendship, I'll perform it to the last article. 要是我发誓帮助一个朋友，我一定会帮到底。

vowel /ˈvaʊəl/ *n.* [C]元音；元音字母

voyage /ˈvɒɪɪdʒ/ Ⅰ *n.* [C](尤指长途的)航行，航海：make (go on) a ~ 航行，航海 Ⅱ *vi.* 航海；航行

vulgar /ˈvʌlgə(r)/ *adj.* 粗俗的；庸俗的

W w

wade / weɪd / *vi.* 过(河);涉(水):~ across a stream 过一条小溪

wag / wæg / Ⅰ *v.* (wagged; wagging) (使)摇摆;(使)摇动;上下移动:The dog ~ged its tail. 狗摇尾。Ⅱ *n.* 摇摆,摇动

wage[1] / weɪdʒ / *n.* [C](常用 *pl.*)工资,薪水(通常按周计算):His ~s are £80 a week. 他的工资是每周 80 英镑。

wage[2] / weɪdʒ / *vt.* 开始;进行:The Chinese people ~d a national war against the Japanese aggression in 1937. 中国人民在 1937 年开始了一场抗击日本侵略的民族战争。

wag(g)on / ˈwægən / *n.* [C] ❶四轮运货马车 ❷(铁路)敞篷货车

waist / weɪst / *n.* 腰,腰部:measure 30 inches round the ~ 腰围 30 英寸 / have no ~ 胖得看不出腰身/ let out (take in) the ~ of a dress 放大(收小)衣服的腰身

wait / weɪt / *v.* ❶等待,等候;期待:~ and see 等着瞧,观望/ Wait a moment (minute), please. 请等一等。/ ~ **for** 等候:We are ~ing for the rain to stop. 我们在等雨停。~ **in line** 排队等候:~ in line for tickets 排队等候买票 **keep sb. ~ing** 让某人一直等候:His wife never keeps him ~ing. 他妻子从不让他等候。~ **until** 等到……才:She ~ed until her daughter was asleep. 她一直等到女儿入睡。❷伺候(进餐):She couldn't get any other job except ~ing at table. 她除了端饭上菜外找不到别的工作干。/ ~ **on (upon) sb.** 服侍某人,伺候某人:They all ~ on the king. 他们都伺候国王。

waiter / ˈweɪtə(r)/ *n.* [C]男侍者,男招待,男服务员:He is not the head ~. 他并不是侍者领班。

waitress / ˈweɪtrɪs/ *n.* [C]女侍者,女招待,女服务员

wake / weɪk / *v.* (woke /wəʊk/, woken /ˈwəʊkn/ 或 waked, waked) ❶(使)醒过来:~ out of a dream 从梦中醒来/ What time do you usually ~ (up)? 你通常什么时候醒来? / The noise woke me (up). 那噪声把我吵醒了。❷认识到;激起;唤起:The event may ~ her up to the danger. 这件事可使她认识危险。

wakeful / ˈweɪkf(ʊ)l / *adj.* ❶失眠的,无法入睡的:a ~ baby 醒着没有睡的婴儿/ Old age is always ~. 上年纪的人总是难以成眠。❷不眠的:We spent a ~ night worrying about where you were. 我们不知你的去向,忧心如焚,度过了一个不眠之夜。

waken / ˈweɪkən / *v.* 醒来;唤醒:The old man ~ed (up) at 4 in the morning. 老人早上四点钟就醒了。/ Don't forget to

~ me tomorrow morning. 别忘了明天早晨叫醒我。

walk /wɔːk/ Ⅰ *v.* ❶行走；步行：/ ~ **about** (**around**) 四处走动；散步；闲逛 ~ **away** 走开 ~ **on** 继续行走，不停地走：Walk on directly for about a hundred steps and turn right, and you'll see the post-office. 继续直走大约一百步后向右转弯，你就会看到邮局了。~ **out** 走出；把（某人）带出：She ~ed the child out of the room. 她带着小孩走出房间。~ **over to** 向……走过去：The policeman ~ed over to the young man. 警察向那年轻人走过去。~ **up and down** 来回走动，走来走去：The old man ~ing up and down the path is Tom's father. 在小径上走来走去的那位老人是汤姆的父亲。~ **up to** 走近：Don't ~ up to the fire. 别走近火。❷使步行，使行走：Horses should be ~ed for a while after a race. 比赛后应让马慢走一会儿。Ⅱ *n.* ❶[C]步行；散步；徒步旅行：The station is ten minutes' ~ from my house. 从我家步行到车站需要十分钟。/ **go for a** ~ 去散步：He often goes for a ~ in the park. 他常去公园散步。**take** (**have**) **a** ~ 散步：Let's take a ~ along the river. 我们沿着河边散散步吧。❷[U]步态；步法：I recognized him at once by his ~. 从步态上我立刻认出是他。

wall /wɔːl/ Ⅰ *n.* [C]墙，壁：the Great Wall 万里长城 / She put up a beautiful picture on the ~. 她在墙上贴了一张很漂亮的画。/ There is a hole in the ~. 墙上有个洞。/ **hang** (**run**) **one's head against a** ~ 试图做不可能的事；碰壁 **drive** (**push**) **sb. to the** ~ 把某人逼到绝境 **go to the** ~ （比赛等）败北；（事业等）失败，破产 Ⅱ *vt.* 筑墙围住；用墙隔开：a ~ed city 有城墙的城市

wallet /ˈwɒlɪt/ *n.* [C]钱夹；皮夹

wallop /wɒləp/ Ⅰ *vt.* ❶痛击，犯击；袭击：~ sb. hard o the shoulder 狠捶某人的肩膀/ The hurricane ~ed the whole island last night. 昨晚飓风袭击了整个岛屿。❷（在比赛中）轻取，彻底打败：She ~ed me at badminton. 羽毛球赛中她把我打得惨败。Ⅱ *n.* [C]痛击，猛击

wallow /ˈwɒləʊ/ *vi.* ❶（动物在泥、沙、水中）打滚：Little pigs like ~ing in the mud. 小猪崽喜欢在烂泥里打滚。❷沉溺；深陷：~ in the blather 沉溺于闲聊瞎扯之中

wallpaper /ˈwɔːlˌpeɪpə(r)/ Ⅰ *n.* 墙纸，壁纸：flowery ~花墙纸 Ⅱ *vt.* 糊墙纸于：~ a room 给房间贴墙纸

walnut /ˈwɔːlnʌt/ *n.* [C]胡桃；核桃树

waltz /wɔːls, wɔːlts/ Ⅰ *n.* [C] ❶华尔兹舞❷华尔兹舞曲，圆舞曲：Strauss ~s 施特劳斯的圆舞曲 Ⅱ *vi.* ❶跳华尔兹舞 ❷轻快前进；顺利通过：The little girl ~ed into the room. 小姑娘脚步轻快地走进房间。

wander /ˈwɒndə(r)/ *v.* ❶漫游；漂泊；徘徊：~ up and down the road aimlessly 无目的地徘徊于路上 ❷走神；（精神）恍惚 ❸离题：~ from the subject 偏离主题 派 wanderer *n.*

wane /weɪn/ Ⅰ *vi.* ❶减少，缩小；衰退，衰落；减弱；消逝：The night was waning away. 夜色渐阑。/My interest in botany has ~d to extinction. 我对植物学已经毫无兴趣了。❷退潮；（月亮）亏缺 Ⅱ *n.* [C] ❶减少，缩小；衰退，衰落；减弱；消逝 ❷衰退期；尾声 ❸月亏；月亏期：**on the** ~ ①（月）亏：The moon is now at the ~. 现在正值月亏。②日益衰落，逐渐败落：The patient's health is on the ~. 病人的健康状况正每况愈下。

want /wɒnt/ Ⅰ *v.* ❶需要：These plants are drooping—they ~ water. 这些植物发蔫了——它们需要浇水。/ Will you ~ anything more, sir? 先生，你还要别的东西吗？❷想要；希望，期望：She ~s to go to Italy. 她想到意大利去。❸贫乏；缺少：~ **for** 需要；缺少：They said that they ~ed for nothing. 他们说他们什么也不缺。Ⅱ *n.* 缺少；需要：The plants died from ~ of water. 这些植物因缺水而死。/ The house is in ~ of repair. 那房子需要修理。/ If you need a waiter, you may place a ~ ad in the newspaper. 如果需要招服务员，你可以在报上登一则招聘广告。

war /wɔː(r)/ *n.* [C]战争：civil ~ 内战 / price ~ 价格战 / star ~ 星球大战/ the First (Second) World War 第一次(第二次)世界大战 / They were at ~ with three great countries. 他们同三个大国交战。/ **carry the ~ into the enemy's camp** 转为攻势；还击 **go to ~** 诉诸武力；出征

ward /wɔːd/ *n.* [C] ❶病房；病室：emergency ~ 急救病房 ❷监禁；拘留

warden /ˈwɔːdən/ *n.* [C] ❶保管人；看护人；管理人 ❷监狱长，看守长 ❸监督人；监管人；监护人；监察：a fire ~消防管员/ traffic ~s 交通管理员

wardrobe /ˈwɔːdrəʊb/ *n.* [C] 衣柜；衣橱

ware /weə(r)/ *n.* ❶(*pl.*)商品；货物：a pedlar's ~ s 高级的货物/ ~ -house 仓库，货栈 ❷(总称)物品；器皿

warfare /ˈwɔːfeə(r)/ *n.* [C]战争；战争状态；交战：ban chemical (biological, germ) ~ 禁止化学(生物、细菌)战争

warm /wɔːm/ Ⅰ *adj.* ❶暖的，温暖的；(指衣服)保暖的：Come and get ~ by the fire. 来炉火边取暖。❷热心的；热情的：give sb. a ~ welcome 热烈欢迎某人 Ⅱ *v.* 使暖和；使感到亲切 / ~ **up** ①使(变)温和；使(变)暖和：You'd better ~ up the milk before you drink it. 你喝牛奶之前最好把它热一热。②激动起来；兴奋起来；活跃起来：Having heard the good news, the children all ~ed up. 听到这个好消息，孩子们全都兴奋起来。③做热身(轻松)运动：All the players spend some minutes ~ing up before the game. 在比赛前，所有运动员都做几分钟热身运动。派 warmly *adv.*

warmth /wɔːmθ/ *n.* [U]温暖；亲切；热烈：He was pleased with the ~ of his friends' welcome. 朋友们对他的热烈欢迎使他感到很高兴。/ They welcomed the delegation with ~. 他们热烈欢迎代表团。

warn /wɔːn/ *vt.* 警告；提醒，告诫；预先通知 / ~ **sb. of sth.** 警告(惊醒)某人……：The teacher ~ed us of possible failure in the experiment. 老师提醒我们实验可能会失败。/ He was ~ed of the danger. 他被告知有危险。/~ **against** 警告；提醒；告诫(不要)：She ~ed me against eating and drinking too much. 她告诫我别暴饮暴食。/ He ~ed me against pickpockets. 他提醒我提防扒手。

warning /ˈwɔːnɪŋ/ Ⅰ *adj.* 警告的；预告的；预先通知的：He gave me a ~ look. 他向我递了一个警告的眼色。Ⅱ *n.* 警报；警告；预兆：He paid no attention to my ~s. 他忽视我的警告。

warrant /ˈwɒrənt/ *n.* ❶[C]令状；授权令；逮捕令；搜查令 ❷[U]授权；批准；

认可;担保,保证;证明:You have no ~ for signing this new contract. 你们无权签这份新的合同。/ Diligence is a sure ~ of success. 勤勉是成功的可靠保证。❸[C]准许证,许可证;委任书;委托书;证书

warranty / ˈwɒrənti, ˈwɔːrənti / *n.* ❶(对所售或所租物品的质量或所有权等的)承诺,保证,担保:Your computer will be repaired without charge because it's still under ~. 你的计算机将免费修理,因为还在保修期内。❷[C](有关商品质量的)保证书,担保书;保(修或用)单:a ~ of quality for the goods 商品质量保证书

wash / wɒʃ / Ⅰ*v.* 洗清;洗去:He never ~es (himself) in cold water. 他从不用冷水洗澡 / ~ **up** 洗餐具;洗手;洗脸:It's your turn to ~ up today. 今天轮到你洗碗碟了。Ⅱ*n.* 洗,洗涤:I must go and have a ~. 我得去洗个澡。

washable / ˈwɒʃəbl, ˈwɔːʃ- / Ⅰ*adj.* 可洗的,能洗的;耐洗的 Ⅱ*n.* [U]可洗的衣着用品

washer / ˈwɒʃə(ə), ˈwɔːʃ- / *n.* [C] ❶洗衣者 ❷洗衣机;洗涤器

wastage / ˈweɪstɪdʒ / *n.* [U] ❶浪费(量);损耗(量):cut down on ~ 降低损耗 / ~ of over 50% 超过 50%的损耗 ❷废物,废料

waste / weɪst / Ⅰ *v.* 浪费;滥用:~ time and money 浪费时间和金钱 / ~ one's words (breath) 白费唇舌 Ⅱ *n.* [U] ❶浪费;滥用 ❷废物;垃圾:lay ~ to 使……荒废 Ⅲ*adj.* ❶(指土地)未利用的,废弃的,荒芜的:~ land 荒地 ❷无用的:~ paper 废纸 / ~ products 废品

wasteful / ˈweɪstfl / *adj.* 浪费的;挥霍的;不经济的:It's ~ to use so much water to wash a bowl. 用这么多水洗一个碗是很浪费的。

watch[1] / wɒtʃ / *n.* [C]手表;挂表

watch[2] / wɒtʃ / Ⅰ*v.* 看,注视;警戒;守望;监视:She likes to ~ children play. 她喜欢看孩子们玩耍。/ Watch what I am doing. 细心看我做什么。/ The old couple usually ~es TV in the evening. 老夫妇通常在晚上看电视。/ Will you ~ over my clothes while I am swimming? 我去游泳时,你替我照看衣服好吗? / ~ **out** 当心,留神:Watch out! There's a car coming! 小心!汽车来了! ~ **out for** 密切注意;提防:~ out for the stairs 小心楼梯 Ⅱ*n.* 看;注意;警戒;守望:keep ~ 守望,放哨 / keep (maintain) a close ~ on 对……进行严密的监视 / **on** ~ 值班,值勤:Who is the man on ~ today? 今天谁值班?

watchful / ˈwɒtʃfl / *adj.* 密切注意的;警惕的 派 watchfully *adv.*

water / ˈwɔːtə(r) / Ⅰ*n.* 水;河水;湖水;海水:Water changes into steam by heat and into ice by cold. 水加热则变成蒸汽,冷却则结成冰。/ boiled ~ 开水 / fresh ~ 淡水/ mineral ~ 矿泉水/ salt ~ 盐水 / by ~ 由水路,乘船 Ⅱ*v.* 浇水;灌溉:She is ~ing the flowers. 她正在给花浇水。

waterfall / ˈwɔːtəfɔːl / *n.* [C]瀑布

watermelon / ˈwɔːtəˌmelən / *n.* 西瓜

waterproof / ˈwɔːtəpruːf / Ⅰ*adj.* 防水的:~ material 防水材料/ ~ watch 防水手表 Ⅱ*n.* [C]雨衣:Put on your ~ before you go into the rain. 下雨时穿上雨衣才出门。

watershed / ˈwɔːtəˌʃed / *n.* [C] ❶流域:the ~ of the Yellow River 黄河流域 ❷分水岭,分水线,分水界 ❸转折点;重

要关头;决定性因素:the historic ~ of war 战争的历史性转折点

waterside /ˈwɔːtəˌsaɪd/ *n.* [C]河边;湖畔;海滨:on the ~ 在水边 / stroll along the ~ 沿着湖边散步

watertight /ˈwɔːtəˌtaɪt/ *adj.* ❶防水的,不透水的,水密的:keep the submarine ~保持潜艇的不透水性 ❷(论点、计划等)严密的,无懈可击的;完美的,天衣无缝的:Their fire precautions are truly ~. 他们的火灾防范措施确实是滴水不漏。

watery /ˈwɔːtəri/ *adj.* ❶水的;含水过多的 ❷湿的;湿润的

watt /wɒt/ *n.* [C]瓦(特)(功率单位)

wave /weɪv/ Ⅰ *v.* ❶波动;飘扬;挥舞:flags waving in the wind 在风中飘扬的旗帜 ❷以挥动作为信号;挥手打招呼:~ goodbye to sb. 向某人挥手告别 / She ~d me a greeting. 她挥手给我打招呼。/ ~ **aside** 挥走;挥退;排斥:His proposal was ~d aside. 他的建议被驳回。Ⅱ *n.* [C] ❶水波;波浪:long (medium, short) ~s 长(中、短)波 / light ~s 光波/ radio ~s 无线电波/ shock ~ (爆炸的)冲击波 / sound ~s 声波 ❷挥动:with a ~ of his hand 他挥动一下手

wavelength /ˈweɪvˌleŋθ/ *n.* [C]波长:effective ~有效波长 / **on the same** ~相互协调;有相同观点(或兴趣):We seldom found ourselves on the same ~. 我们很难发现自己是琴瑟和谐的。

waver /ˈweɪvə(r)/ *vi.* ❶摇摆;摇晃;摇曳:The boy ~s a little as he walks. 这孩子走路有点摇晃。❷犹豫不决

wavy /ˈweɪvi/ *adj.* 波浪形的;波状的

wax /wæks/ Ⅰ *n.* [U]蜡:~ cloth 蜡布 / ~ doll 蜡人 / ~ work 蜡制品;蜡像 Ⅱ *vt.* 给……上蜡:It is time to ~ the furniture and the floor. 该给家具和地板上蜡了。派 waxy *adj.*

way /weɪ/ *n.* [C] ❶路,通路;道路;街:a ~ across the forest 穿过森林的路 ❷方法,方式;行动方针:the right ~ to do (of doing) a thing 做一件事情的正确方法/ Do it in your own ~ if you don't like mine. 如果你不喜欢我的方式,你可以按自己的方式做。/ **all the** ~ 一直,从头到尾;完全,全部 **by the** ~ 顺便说:By the ~, what are you doing now? 顺便问一问,你现在做什么? **by** ~ **of** 由,经过:He came by ~ of Dover. 他经多佛来此。**give** ~ 让路,让步 **in a** ~ 在某种程度上,有点,有几分 **in any** ~ 不管怎样,好歹 **in every** ~ 在各方面;以各种方式 **in no** ~ 决不,一点也不:Study can in no ~ be separated from practice. 学习决不能与实践分离。**lead the** ~ 引路,带路;示范:A young girl led the ~ for us. 一位年轻姑娘为我们带路。**make** ~ 让路;腾出地方:You should make ~ for the old. 你应当给老人让路。**make one's** ~ 前进,前往 **on one's** ~ **to** 在路上:He is on his ~ to the station. 他在去车站的路上。**under** ~ 在进行中:A new project is under ~. 一个新的项目正在进行中。

WC (=Water closet)盥洗室,厕所

we /wiː/ *pron.* 我们

weak /wiːk/ *adj.* ❶弱的,虚弱的;脆弱的;易破的:a ~ team 弱队 ❷(指感官等)功能不佳的;衰弱的:The old lady is not ~ in hearing. 那老太太听力不差。/ ~ sight 视力不佳 / a ~ heart 衰弱的心脏 ❸不精的;有欠缺的 /(be) ~ **in** 在……方面差:Jack is a little ~ in Chinese. 杰克的汉语有点差。

W

派 weakly *adv.*

weaken / ˈwiːkən / *v.* (使)变弱：The patient's heart was ~ing. 病人的心脏越来越衰弱。

weakness / ˈwiːknɪs/ *n.* ❶[U]虚弱，衰弱；软弱，懦弱；不坚定：the ~ of sb.'s health 某人身体的虚弱 / The government is accused of ~ in dealing with terrorists. 有人指责政府对恐怖分子打击不力。❷[C]弱点，缺点：a whole range of human ~es 人性的全部弱点

wealth / welθ / *n.* [U]大量财产(的拥有)；财富：a man of ~ 富人

wealthy / ˈwelθi / *adj.* (-ier, -iest)富有的；丰富的：~ in knowledge 知识丰富 / China is ~ in natural resources. 中国自然资源丰富。

weapon / ˈwepən / *n.* [C]武器，兵器：~s of mass destruction 大规模杀伤性武器 / A gun may be a ~ of offence or a ~ of defence. 枪可以是进攻武器，也可以是防卫武器。/ Are tears a woman's ~? 眼泪是女人的武器吗？

wear / weə(r) / *v.* (wore /wɔː/, worn /wɔːn/) ❶穿，戴：He was ~ing a hat (a wristwatch, a ring on his finger). 他戴着一顶帽子(戴着手表，手指上戴着戒指)。❷(面容)呈现出，显得：He ~s a troubled look. 他愁容满面。❸(使)磨损；(使)变旧；用坏：I have worn my socks into holes. 我的袜子已经穿出洞来了。/ ~ **away** 使磨损；磨平：The inscription has worn away. 那碑文已经磨平消失了。~ **out** ① 使变坏：My shoes are worn out. 我的鞋穿坏了。② 使筋疲力尽；使耗尽：I am worn out with the hard work. 这些艰苦的工作使我疲乏不堪。

wearing / ˈweərɪŋ / *adj.* ❶使人疲倦的；令人厌倦的：It's a very ~ job. 那是很令人厌倦的工作。❷消耗性的，逐渐耗损的：Reading small print can be ~ on the eyes. 看小字体耗损人的视力。

weary / ˈwɪəri / Ⅰ *adj.* 疲倦的；厌烦的：war-~ 厌战的 / **be ~ of** 对……感到厌烦：People are ~ of the war. 人们对这场战争感到厌烦。Ⅱ *vt.* 使疲乏；使厌烦 / ~ **of** 厌倦……：He wearies of living all alone. 他厌烦独居生活。~ **sb. with** 因……使某人厌烦：He wearied me with requests. 她的多次请求使我厌烦。

weather / ˈweðə(r) / *n.* [U]天气；气象：She stays indoors in wet ~. 雨天她待在家里。

weave / wiːv / *v.* (wove/wəʊv/, woven /ˈwəʊvən/)编，织(纱、线)成布；纺织：be woven by hand 手工织的/ be woven of silk 用丝织成的/~ the flowers into a wreath 把一些花编成花环 / weave a metre of cloth 织一米布 派 weaver *n.*

web / web / *n.* [C]网络；蜘蛛网

website / ˈwebsaɪt / *n.* [C](计算机)网站

wed / wed / *v.* (wedded 或 wed; wedding)结婚，嫁，娶

wedding / ˈwedɪŋ / *n.* [C]婚礼；结婚：attend a ~ 参加婚礼 / perform a ~ 主持婚礼/~ dress 结婚礼服/ ~ ring 结婚戒指

Wednesday / ˈwenzdi / *n.* 星期三(略作 Wed.)

weed / wiːd / Ⅰ *n.* [C]杂草：My garden is running to ~s. 我的花园长满了杂草。Ⅱ *v.* 除去杂草：~ the garden 除去花园里的杂草

week / wiːk / *n.* [C]周，星期：There are

a few ~s away from the final examination. 离期末考试还有几星期。

weekday /ˈwiːdeɪ/ *n.* [C]工作日：We have five ~s every week. 我们每周工作五天。

weekend /ˌwiːkˈend/ *n.* [C]周末：at (during, over) the ~ 在周末 / on ~s 每个周末 / How do you usually spend your ~? 通常你们怎样度周末？

weekly /ˈwiːkli/ Ⅰ *adj.* 每周一次的；一周的：a ~ wage of ￡150 周薪150英镑 Ⅱ *n.* [C]周刊；周报

weep /wiːp/ *v.* (wept/wept/, wept)哭泣；流泪：~ over sb.'s misfortunes 为某人的不幸而流泪 / She wept herself to sleep. 她哭着睡着了。

weigh /weɪ/ *v.* ❶称……的重量：He ~ed himself in the scales. 他在体重器上称体重。❷重(若干)：~ a ton 重一吨

weight /weɪt/ *n.* ❶[U]重量；体重；重力：lose ~ 减少体重 / put on ~ 增加体重 / The man is twice my ~. 那人的体重是我的两倍。❷[C]砝码；秤砣 ❸重压；负担

weightless /ˈweɪtlɪs/ *adj.* 失重的；无重力的：carry out experiments in the ~ conditions 在失重条件下进行实验

welcome /ˈwelkəm/ Ⅰ *adj.* ❶受欢迎的：a ~ visitor 受欢迎的来宾/~ news 佳音 ❷被允许的：You are ~ to use my bicycle. 你尽可以用我的自行车。Ⅱ *n.* [C]欢迎；接待；款待：They gave us a warm ~. 他们给予我们热情的欢迎。Ⅲ *vt.* 欢迎：We ~ criticisms. 我们欢迎批评。/ **~ sb. with open arms** 热烈欢迎某人：Come soon. We'll ~ you with open arms. 快来吧！我们会热烈欢迎你们的。

weld /weld/ Ⅰ *vt.* 焊接：~ pieces into a unit 把部件焊接成整套装置 Ⅱ *n.* 焊接

welfare /ˈwelfeə(r)/ *n.* [U]福利；幸福：work for the ~ of the people 为人民的幸福而工作 / social ~ 社会福利

well[1] /wel/ Ⅰ *adv.* (better, best) ❶好；对；满意地：They are ~ behaved children. 他们是乖孩子。/ Well done (played)! 做得好(表演得好)！❷彻底地，完全；颇，甚：Examine the account ~ before you pay it. 付款之前要仔细核对账目。/ His name is ~ up in the list. 他的名字列在前面。/ **as ~ (as)** 除……之外；也：He gave me money as ~ as advice. 他除了给我忠告外还给我钱。**be ~ in** 在……方面做得好：Tom is always ~ in playing football. 汤姆踢球总是踢得很好。**be ~ off** 生活富裕：Although she is ~ off, she lives quite simply. 虽然她很富裕，但她生活十分简朴。Ⅱ *adj.* (只作表语)(身体)健康的：be (look, feel) ~ (看来是)健康的 Ⅲ *interj.* (表示惊奇、同意等)哎呀；好；那么：Well, who would have thought it? 啊，谁想得到是这样呢？

well[2] /wel/ *n.* [C]井：drive (sink) a ~ 开(打)井 / ~ water 井水 / oil ~ 油井

well-being /ˈwelˌbiːɪŋ/ *n.* [U]健康；福利；幸福；康乐：sensation of ~幸福感/ Business executives believe that holidays are vital to their ~. 公司企业的经理们认为休假对他们的健康是至关重要的。

well-known /ˈwelˈnəʊn/ *adj.* ❶著名的；出名的：A ~ scientist will come and give us a talk. 一位知名科学家要来给我们做报告。/ The young man became ~ for this invention. 那年轻人因为这项发明而出名。❷众所周知的；熟悉的：a ~ voice 熟悉的声音/ It is a ~ fact. 那

是众所周知的事实。

wellspring /ˈwelˌsprɪŋ/ *n.* [C] ❶河源；泉源 ❷(不断的)源泉：the ~s of the creative spirit 创造精神的源泉

west /west/ Ⅰ *n.* 西方，西部：The sun sets in the ~. 太阳从西边落下。/the West 西方；西方各国(与亚洲相对而言)；(任何国家的)西部 Ⅱ *adj.* 西方的；西部的：on the ~ coast 在西海岸 / the West Lake 西湖 Ⅲ *adv.* 向西地：sail (travel) ~ 向西航行(旅行)

western /ˈwestən/ *adj.* 西方的；来自西方的：the Western Hemisphere 西半球/ the ~ nations 西方国家

westward /ˈwestwəd/ Ⅰ *adj.* 向西(的)：a ~ journey 向西的旅行 Ⅱ *adv.* 朝西地；向西地：We sailed ~. 我们向西航行。

wet /wet/ Ⅰ *adj.* (wetter, wettest) ❶湿的，潮湿的：Her cheeks were ~ with tears. 眼泪顺着她的脸颊流下。/ **be ~ through, be ~ to the skin** 全身湿透 ❷多雨的；下雨的：~ weather 雨天 Ⅱ *vt.* (wet 或 wetted, wet 或 wetted) 打(弄、淋)湿；尿湿：You should first ~ your hair before applying the shampoo. 你在抹洗发水前应先打湿头发。

whale /weɪl/ *n.* [C]鲸

what /wɒt/ Ⅰ *int.* & *adj.* (疑问形容词)什么，哪些：Tell me ~ books you have read recently. 告诉我，你近来读了些什么书。Ⅱ *pron.* ❶(疑问代词)什么，什么东西：What is he? 他是做什么的？/ ~ **about** (用于询问他人的意见或想法)……怎么样？What about going for a walk? 去散散步怎么样？~ **if** ①万一……怎么办：What if she won't answer my letter? 她要是不回我的信怎么办？②即使……又有什么关系：What if she gets angry? 即使她生气了又有什么关系？❷(关系代词)……那样的事物或人：What he says is very important. 他所说的话很重要。/ Do ~ you think right. 按照你认为正确的做法去做。

whatever /wɒtˈevə(r)/ Ⅰ *pron.* ❶无论什么；不管什么：Whatever you do, you must do it well. 无论你做什么事，一定要把它做好。/ Keep calm ~ happens. 无论发生了什么事情都要保持镇静。❷任何……的事物；凡是……的东西 Ⅱ *adj.* 不管怎样的；无论什么样的：Whatever opinion you have, tell us, please. 不管你有什么意见，都请告诉我们。

what-if /ˈwɒtˌɪf/ Ⅰ *adj.* 想象的；可能的；假定的：a ~ scenario 想象中的场景 Ⅱ *n.* [C]假定情况或事件；假定推测：a horde of ~'s 一群爱做假定推测的人

whatnot /ˈwɒtˌnɒt/ *n.* [U]诸如此类的东西：candies, crisps , cakes and ~ 糖果、薯片以及糕点之类的东西

wheat /wiːt/ *n.* [C]小麦

wheel /wiːl/ *n.* [C]轮；车轮；机轮：**at the ~** ①开车的；掌舵的②掌握着支配权的 **go on ~s** 顺利进行

when /wen/ *adv.* ❶(疑问副词)什么时候，何时：When does the train leave? 火车什么时候开？❷(关系副词)在那时：Sunday is the day ~ I am least busy. 星期天是我最不忙的日子。❸(连接副词)当……的时候，在……的时候：The pupils put up their hands ~ they know the answers. 当学生们知道答案时，他们就举手。

whenever /wenˈevə(r)/ Ⅰ *conj.* ❶无论何时：I'll talk the matter with you ~ you come. 你无论什么时候来，我都愿

意和你谈论这个问题。❷每当:Whenever I met with difficulties, he would come to help me. 每当我遇到困难的时候,他都会来帮助我。Ⅱ *adv.* (口语)究竟何时:Whenever did I tell you such a thing? 我究竟何时告诉过你这样的事情?

where /weə(r)/ *adv.* ❶(疑问副词)在哪里,在什么地方:Where are you going? 你往哪儿去? ❷(关系副词)在那里,在该处:That's the place ~ the accident happened. 那就是出事的地点。❸(连接副词)在……的地方:Where there is no rain, farming is difficult or impossible. 没有雨水的地方,很难有农业,或者根本不可能有农业。/ Where there is smoke, there is fire. (谚语)无风不起浪。

whereabouts Ⅰ /ˌweərəˈbaʊts/ *adv.* (大致)在哪里,(大概)靠近什么地方;在某地附近,在某地周围:Whereabouts did you leave my umbrella? 你把我的雨伞放哪儿了? /Whereabouts is your villa then? 您的别墅在什么地方? Ⅱ /ˈweərəˌbaʊts/ *n.* (人或物大致所在的)位置;下落;行踪:Those children's ~ are unknown. 那些孩子们的下落不明。

whereas /ˌweərˈæz/ *conj.* 但是,然而,反之:Some people like fat meat, ~ others hate it. 有人喜欢肥肉,而有人讨厌肥肉。

wherever /ˌweərˈevə(r)/ Ⅰ *conj.* 无论在哪里;无论到哪里:Sit ~ you like. 请随便坐。Ⅱ *adv.* ❶无论什么地方,任何地方:It should be available ~ you go to shop. 无论你到哪里买,这东西应该都买得到。❷(口语)究竟在哪里,究竟到哪里:Wherever can he have gone? 他究竟能去哪里呢?

whether /ˈweðə(r)/ *conj.* ❶是……还是……(常与 or 连用):I wonder ~ it will rain or snow. 我不知道天会下雨还是会下雪。/ Whether it rains or not, we'll go tonight. 无论天是否下雨,我们今晚都要去。❷是否:Could you tell me ~ it's very hot in summer in Shanghai? 你能否告诉我上海夏天天气是不是很热?

which /wɪtʃ/ Ⅰ *pron.* ❶(疑问代词)哪一个;哪一些:Which do you prefer? 你喜欢哪一个? ❷(关系代词)……的那个,……的那些:The house ~ is for sale is at the end of the street. 待售的房子在街的尽头。/ The river ~ flows through London is called the Thames. 流经伦敦的那条河称为泰晤士河。Ⅱ *adj.* 哪个;哪些:Which book would you like? 你喜欢哪一本书?

whichever /wɪtʃˈevə(r)/ Ⅰ *pron.* 无论哪个;无论哪些:Choose ~ you like best. 你最喜欢哪个就选哪个。Ⅱ *adj.* 无论哪个,无论哪些:Whichever method you use, the result is the same. 无论你用哪一种方法,结果都一样。

while /waɪl/ Ⅰ *n.* (一段)时间:Where have you been all this ~? 这一阵子你在哪儿? / **all the** ~ 始终,一直:We stayed at home all the ~ yesterday. 昨天我们一直待在家里。**in a (little)** ~ 一会儿,不久:I'll be back in a little ~. 我很快就会回来。**once in a** ~ 偶尔,间或:Once in a ~ we go to a restaurant, but usually we eat at home. 我们偶尔下馆子,但一般都在家吃饭。Ⅱ *conj.* ❶当……的时候;在……之时:He fell asleep ~ reading the grammar book. 他看语法书时睡着了。/ While there is life, there is hope. 只要有生命就有希望(留得青山在,不怕没柴烧)。❷而,然而;反之:Jane was dressed in brown ~ Mary was dressed in blue. 简穿褐色衣服,而玛丽穿蓝色衣服。❸尽管,虽然:While I admit that the problems are difficult, I don't agree that they cannot be solved. 虽然我承认这些问题很难,但我并不认为这些问题无法解决。

whip /wɪp/ Ⅰ *n.* [C]鞭子 Ⅱ *v.* (whipped; whipping)鞭笞;抽打:~ a horse 用鞭打马

whirl /wɜːl/ Ⅰ *v.* ❶(使)回旋;(使)旋转:The wind ~ed the dead leaves about. 风吹得枯叶四处飞旋。❷(指头)晕眩;(指思绪)纷乱:His head ~ed. 他的头晕了。Ⅱ *n.* (只用单数)旋转:His brain was in a ~. 他的头晕了。

whirlpool /ˈwɜːlˌpuːl/ *n.* [C]旋涡,涡流:be caught in a ~ of the river 被卷入河水旋涡之中。

whirlwind /ˈwɜːlˌwɪnd/ *n.* [C] ❶旋风,旋流,龙卷风 ❷旋风似的事物;猛烈的破坏力量:a political ~一场政治风暴

whisk /wɪsk/ Ⅰ *vt.* ❶拂去,掸掉;扫开;赶走:He tried to ~ the flies away. 他想挥手把苍蝇轰走。❷突然拿走;快速带走;急忙送走:My newspaper was ~ed away before I'd even finished it. 我的报纸还没看完就被人突然拿走了。❸搅打(奶油、蛋等) Ⅱ *n.* [C] ❶掸、拂;扫;赶:a ~ of the cow's tail 母牛尾巴的一甩 ❷掸子;刷子;小笤帚 ❸打蛋器;(奶油等的)搅拌器

whisker /ˈwɪskə(r)/ *n.* [C](*pl.*)髯;胡须

whisky /ˈwɪski/ *n.* [U]威士忌酒

whisper /ˈwɪspə(r)/ Ⅰ *v.* 低语;耳语:~ (a word) to sb. 低声对某人说;悄悄告诉某人 / It is ~ed that he is heavily in debt. 据秘密传闻他负债很多。Ⅱ *n.* [C]耳语;私语:He answered in a ~. 他低声回答。/ Whispers are going round that the firm is likely to go bankrupt. 据传闻,那家商行可能倒闭。

whistle /ˈwɪsl/ Ⅰ *n.* [C]❶哨子;汽笛:a referee's ~ 裁判的哨子 ❷口哨声;汽笛声;鸣叫声;啸叫声:We heard the ~ of a steam-engine. 我们听到蒸汽机的啸叫声。Ⅱ *v.* ❶吹口哨;鸣笛:The driver ~d before reaching the level-crossing. 司机在抵达水平交叉道之前鸣汽笛。❷用口哨发信号:He ~d his dog back. 他吹口哨唤狗回来。

white /waɪt/ Ⅰ *adj.* ❶白色的;雪白的:as ~ as a sheet 苍白如纸 / Her hair has turned ~. 她的头发变白了。❷白肤色的:~ civilization 白色人种的文明 Ⅱ *n.* ❶白色:The girl (dressed) in ~ is the famous singer. 穿白衣的女孩是著名的歌手。❷白人

white-collar /waɪtˈkɒlə(r)/ *adj.* 白领阶层的;脑力劳动的:~ workers 白领工作者

whiten /ˈwaɪtən/ *vt.* 使变白;使增白,使更白:All was well ~ed by the last night's frost. 万物被一夜的霜染成白色了。—*vi.* 渐渐变白,变苍白:My grandpa's hair had ~ed over these years. 我爷爷的头发这些年来变白了。

whitewash /ˈwaɪtwɒʃ/ *vt.* ❶粉刷;涂白:Do you want to ~ the wall? 你想把墙刷白吗? ❷粉饰;掩饰:His wife must have wanted to ~ his reputation. 他的妻子当时一定想粉饰他的臭名声。

who /huː/ *pron.* ❶(疑问代词)谁:Who are those men? 那些人是谁? / Do you know ~ broke the window? 你

W

知道窗子是谁打破的吗? ❷(关系代词)那个人:This is the man ~ wanted to see you. 这就是要见你的那个人。

whoever /huːˈevə(r)/ *pron.* ❶无论谁,不管谁:Whoever made the mistake, he must correct it. 无论是谁犯的错,都得改正。❷(口语)究竟是谁,到底是谁:Whoever did such a foolish thing? 究竟是谁做了这样一件傻事?

whole /həʊl/ Ⅰ *adj.* 整个的;完整的;全体的:I want to know the ~ truth about this matter. 我要知道这件事的全部真相。Ⅱ *n.* 完整的东西;全部,全体 / **as a** ~ 作为一个整体;整个看来 **on the** ~ 总的说来,大体上:On the ~, I'm in favour of the idea. 大体上说来,我赞成这个主意。

wholesale /ˈhəʊlseɪl/ Ⅰ *n.* [U]批发,趸售 Ⅱ *adj.* ❶批发的,成批售出的;批发价的:wholesale prices are about twenty-five per cent off retail prices. 批发价要比零售价约低25%。❷大规模的;全部的;不加区别的:the ~ application of the new method 新方法的广泛应用 Ⅲ *adv.* ❶以批发方式,成批地;以批发价:They only sell ~. 他们只搞批发销售。❷大规模地,大量地;彻底地

wholly /ˈhəʊlli/ *adv.* 完全地;完整地;整个地:I ~ agree with you. 我完全同意你的意见。

whom /huːm/ *pron.* ❶(疑问代词)谁(who的宾格):Whom did you see just now? 刚才你看到了谁? ❷(关系代词)……的那个人;……的那些人:She is the girl ~ we met at the gate. 她就是我们在大门口遇到的那个女孩。

whose /huːz/ *pron.* ❶(疑问代词)谁的(who的所有格):Whose house is that? 那是谁的房子? ❷(关系代词)那个的;那些的:The boy ~ father complained to me is very stupid. 那个男孩非常愚笨,他的父亲曾向我诉苦。

why /waɪ/ Ⅰ *adv.* ❶(疑问副词)何故,为什么;有何目的:Do you know ~ he came here? 你知道他为什么来这里吗? ❷(关系副词)……的原因:That is the reason ~ he failed. 那就是他失败的原因。Ⅱ *int.* ❶(表示惊讶):Why, it's easy! A child could do it. 哎呀,那太容易了!小孩也会做。❷(表示异议):Why, what's the harm? 嗨,难道有什么不对吗?

wicked /ˈwɪkɪd/ *adj.* ❶邪恶的 ❷淘气的;顽皮的:You ~ boy! 你这个淘气鬼! 派 wickedly *adv.*

wide /waɪd/ Ⅰ *adj.* ❶宽广的;广阔的:a ~ river 宽阔的河流 / a road twelve feet ~ 12英尺宽的道路 ❷广大的;广泛的;渊博的:a man with ~ interest 兴趣广泛的人 ❸张大的:She stared at him with ~ eyes. 她睁大眼睛注视他。Ⅱ *adv.* 宽广地;充分地;张得很大地:He was ~ awake. 他是完全清醒的。/ The window was ~ open. 那窗子是大开着的。派 widely *adv.*

widen /ˈwaɪdn/ *v.* 加宽,放宽;变宽:The workers are ~ing the road. 工人们正在加宽道路。

widespread /ˈwaɪdspred/ *adj.* 分布广的;普遍的:a ~ disease 流行病 / We cannot overlook the ~ influence of the book. 我们不能忽视该书的广泛影响。

widow /ˈwɪdəʊ/ *n.* [C]寡妇

widower /ˈwɪdəʊə(r)/ *n.* [C]鳏夫

width /wɪdθ/ *n.* 宽阔;广度:A street of great ~ goes through the city. 一条很宽的大街穿过城市。/ The boy was known for ~ of mind. 那孩子心胸开阔

是人所共知的。/ Leave a ~ of two meters here, please. 请在这里留下两米宽度。

wield / wiːld / *vt.* ❶手持(武器或工具等);使用,操纵(武器或工具等):soldiers ~ing swords 手持利剑的武士们/ ~ a new machine 操纵新机器 ❷运用,行使(权力或权威等);施加(影响等);支配,控制:You should ~ greater power in determining it. 在决定此事时,你们应该行使更大的权力。/ He ~s a lot of power in the government. 他在政府中有很大的影响力。

wife / waɪf / *n.* [C](*pl.* wives /waɪvz/)妻子

wiggle / ˈwɪgl / Ⅰ *v.* (快速地来回)摆动;晃动;扭动:He ~d his toes. 他扭动着脚趾。Ⅱ *n.* [C]摆动;晃动;扭动;波状曲线:walk with a ~ of one's hips 扭着屁股走

wild / waɪld / *adj.* ❶(指动物)野性的;(指植物)野生的:~ flowers 野花 ❷(指地方)荒凉的,无人居住的:~ mountain areas 荒凉的山区 ❸激动的;激昂的:She is ~ about music. 她酷爱音乐。/ He was ~ with anger. 他狂怒。派 wildly *adv.*

wilderness / ˈwɪldənɪs / *n.* 荒无人烟的地区;荒漠;旷野;未开垦地区:a long march through a ~经过旷无人烟地区的长征

will[1] / wɪl / *aux. v.* (would/wʊd, wəd/)

❶构成将来时(用于第二、三人称的肯定句及第三人称的疑问句):You ~ be in time if you hurry. 如果你快一点,就会及时赶到。❷表示愿意、同意、建议或应允(与第一人称连用):We said we would help him. 我们说过我们愿意帮助他。❸表示请求(用于第二人称的疑问句):Will you come in? 请进来好吗? ❹表示可能性:This ~ be the book you're looking for, I think. 我想,这可能就是你在寻找的那本书。❺表示假说、条件:They would have been killed if the car had gone over the cliff. 如果汽车当时从悬崖翻落,他们可能已丧命了。

will[2] / wɪl / *n.* ❶意志:the freedom of the ~ 意志的自由 ❷(只用单数)决心:Where there is a ~, there's a way. (谚语)有志者事竟成。❸意愿;希望:She married him against the ~ of her parents. 她违背父母意愿与他结婚。/ **at ~** 随意:You may come and go at ~. 你可以随意来去。❹[C]遗嘱:The old man's ~ is to build a school for the children. 老人的遗嘱是为孩子们修建一所学校。

wil(l)ful / ˈwɪlfʊl / *adj.* ❶有意的,故意的,存心的:~ waste makes woeful want. 肆意挥霍,家徒四壁。/ It seemed ~. 这看来是故意的。❷固执的,任性的;刚愎自用的:a ~ and difficult child 执拗而任性的孩子

willing / ˈwɪlɪŋ / *adj.* 自愿的;乐意的:He was quite ~ to pay the price I asked. 他很愿付我要的价钱。派 willingly *adv.* ;willingness *n.*

willow / ˈwɪləʊ / *n.* [C]柳树

wilt / wɪlt/ *vi.* ❶(树叶、花草等)打蔫,枯萎,凋谢:The grass ~ed under the hot sun. 草在烈日的炙烤之下打蔫了。❷(人等)无精打采,变得虚弱;支撑不住:We're all ~ing in this heat. 天气如此炎热,我们全都无精打采的。

win / wɪn / *v.* (won/wʌn/, won)赢得,获胜;战胜:~ a race 在赛跑中获胜 派 winner *n.*

wind[1] /wɪnd/ *n.* 风：the north ~ 北风 / The ~ is rising (falling). 风势增强(减弱)。派 windy *adj.*

wind[2] /waɪnd/ *v.* (wound /waʊnd/, wound) ❶迂回前进；蜿蜒：The river ~s (its way) to the sea. 那条河蜿蜒流入大海。❷给……上发条：If you forget to ~ up your clock, it will stop. 如果你忘记给钟上发条，它就会停走。

window /ˈwɪndəʊ/ *n.* [C]窗子；(计算机的)视窗

wine /waɪn/ *n.* [C]酒；(尤指)葡萄酒

wing /wɪŋ/ *n.* [C](鸟、昆虫或蝙蝠的)翅膀，翼；(飞行器的)翅膀，机翼：**on the ~** 在飞行中；在活动中 **under the ~of, under sb.'s ~** 在某人的保护之下

wink /wɪŋk/ *vi.* ❶眨眼；眨眼示意，递眼色：She ~ed at me to let me know she understood. 她对我眨眼示意她明白了。❷(灯光或信号等)闪烁；明灭；频闪发信号：I saw the car's small lights on the left hand side ~ when it turned left. 我看见那辆车往左拐的时候，左手的那些小灯频频闪烁发信号。

winter /ˈwɪntə(r)/ *n.* [C]冬季

wipe /waɪp/ *v.* 擦；抹；揩：~ the dishes 擦盘子 / ~ one's hands on a towel 在毛巾上擦手 / ~ the tears away 擦去眼泪 / ~ off the drawing from the blackboard 擦掉黑板上的图画 / ~ **out** 擦掉；除去；消灭；摧毁：The earthquake ~d out many buildings. 地震摧毁了许多建筑物。

wire /ˈwaɪə(r)/ *n.* 金属线：telephone ~(s) 电话线 / copper ~ 铜丝

wireless /ˈwaɪəlɪs/ *adj.* ❶无线的；用无线电波传送的：digital ~ phone 数字无线电话 ❷无线电报(或电话)的：my favourite ~ station 我最喜欢的无线电台

wisdom /ˈwɪzdəm/ *n.* [U]智慧；才智：words of ~ 至理名言

wise /waɪz/ *adj.* 有判断力的；聪明的；明智的：He was ~ enough not to drive when he was feeling ill. 他很明智，在感到不舒服时便不开车。

wish /wɪʃ/ Ⅰ *v.* ❶意欲；想要：They ~ed the voyage at an end. 他们期望航程结束。/ She ~ed for an opportunity to go to school. 她希望有上学的机会。/ She ~es to be alone. 她想单独待着。❷但愿：She ~ed she had passed the exam. 她但愿自己通过考试。❸祝愿：~ sb. a pleasant journey 祝某人旅途愉快 Ⅱ *n.* [C]愿望，希望；祝愿：He disregarded his father's ~es. 他把他父亲的愿望置之度外。

wishful /ˈwɪʃfʊl/ *adj.* 渴望的；向往的；热切希望的：a ~ expression 渴望的表情 / be ~ to do sth. 急切地想做某事 派 wishfully *adv.* ；wishfulness *n.*

wisp /wisp/ *n.* [C] ❶(稻草等的)小捆，小把，小束：~s of grass 几束青草 ❷(须发或烟雾等的)(一)绺；(一)缕；(一)丝，(一)根：soft ~s of baby hair 几绺柔软的婴儿头发 / A ~ of smoke curled up from the chimney. 一缕轻烟从烟囱里袅袅而上。

wit /wɪt/ *n.* [U]❶智力；才智；智能：A fall into the pit, a gain in your ~. 吃一堑，长一智。/ **at one's ~'s (~s') end** 智穷才尽；不知所措 **out of one's ~s** 失去理智；发疯 ❷风趣：He is a man of ~. 他是一个风趣的人。

with /wɪð/ *prep.* ❶有；有……的特征：a coat ~ two pockets 有两个口袋的外衣 ❷用；借助(表示使用的方法)：

write ~ a pen 用笔写字 / ~ the help of your friends 在你朋友们的帮助下 ❸与……一起(表示陪伴): to go for a walk ~ a friend 和朋友一起散步/He lives ~ his parents. 他和父母一起住。❹因为,由于(表示原因): trembling ~ fear (rage) 因恐惧(愤怒)而颤抖 ❺以……,在……的情况下(表样子、做法): do sth. ~ one's whole heart 全身心投入地做某事 / ~ ease 轻易地;毫不费劲地 / He was standing ~ his hands in his pockets. 他双手插在口袋里站着。

withdraw /wɪðˈdrɔː/ *v.* (withdrew/wɪðˈdruː/, withdrawn /wɪðˈdrɔːn/) ❶取回: ~ money from the bank 从银行取钱 ❷(使)撤退;收回: ~ troops from an exposed position 让军队从暴露的阵地上撤退

withdrawal /wɪðˈdrɔːəl/ *n.* [U]取回;收回;撤回

wither /ˈwɪðə(r)/ *v.* (使)枯萎;凋谢: The hot summer ~ed (up) the grass. 炎热的夏天使草枯萎了。

withhold /wɪðˈhəuld/ *vt.* (withheld, withheld) ❶保留,暂不给予: ~ an announcement 不予宣布 ❷压抑,抑制: I couldn't ~ my laughter. 我忍不住笑出来。❸阻挡;隐瞒: ~ the temptation of money 抵挡金钱的诱惑

within /wɪˈðɪn/ Ⅰ *prep.* 在……之内;不出: ~ an hour 在一小时内 / ~ a mile of the station 距离车站不到一英里 / live ~ one's income 量入为出 Ⅱ *adv.* 在内,在里面

without /wɪˈðaut/ *prep.* 没有,不,无: You can't buy things ~ money. 没有钱你买不到东西。

withstand /wɪðˈstænd/ *vt.* (withstood /wɪðˈstud/) 经受(住),承受(住);顶(得)住;抵住: I just couldn't ~ her taunts. 我就是受不了她的冷嘲热讽。/ Most ancient buildings have withstood the test of time. 大部分古建筑经受住了时间的考验。

witness /ˈwɪtnəs/ Ⅰ *v.* ❶亲见;目击: ~ an accident 目睹一次意外事件 ❷作证: ~ against an accused person 作不利于被告的证明 Ⅱ *n.* ❶[C]目击者;证人 ❷[U]证据;证明: give ~ on behalf of an accused person at his trial 在被告受审时替他作证

witty /ˈwɪti/ *adj.* ❶说话风趣的,谈吐诙谐的: an inventive and ~ writer 有独创性且谈吐诙谐的作家 / Poets make men ~. 读诗使人灵秀。❷(言辞等)巧妙的;诙谐的,风趣的,妙趣横生的: a ~ conversation 妙趣横生的对话 派 wittily *adv.* ; wittiness *n.*

wolf /wulf/ *n.* [C](*pl.* wolves /wulvz/)狼: **cry ~** 发虚假的警报: You've cried ~ too often. 你发虚假警报的次数太多了。

woman /ˈwumən/ *n.* [C](*pl.* women /ˈwɪ-mɪn/)妇女,女性: International Women's Day 国际妇女节 / women's room 女厕所 / Women should enjoy equal rights with men. 妇女应当与男子享有同等的权利。

womb /wuːm/ *n.* [C] ❶子宫 ❷发祥地,发源地,孕育处: the ~ of Judaism 犹太教的发祥地

wonder /ˈwʌndə(r)/ Ⅰ *n.* ❶[U]惊奇;惊叹: They were filled with ~. 他们感到惊奇。❷[C]奇事;奇迹;奇观: work ~s 创造奇迹 / It's a ~ (that) you didn't lose your way in the dark. 令人惊奇的是你在黑暗中竟未迷路。Ⅱ *v.* ❶感到惊奇;感到惊讶: I ~ at her refusing to marry him. 对她拒绝跟他结婚，我感到惊奇。❷想知道：I ~ who he is (what he wants, why he is late, whether he will come). 我不知道他是谁（他要什么，他为何迟到，他是否会来）。/ **no ~ (that ...)** 难怪……，怪不得……：No ~ he came so early; he wanted to surprise all of us. 难怪他来得这么早，他是想让我们都感到吃惊。

wonderful /ˈwʌndəfl/ *adj.* 惊人的；奇妙的，极好的；了不起的：~ weather 极好的天气 / ~ performance 精彩的演出 / ~ sight 奇妙的景象 / have a ~ time 过得非常愉快 / The girl has a ~ memory. 这女孩有惊人的记忆力。/ Edison made many ~ inventions. 爱迪生有许多了不起的发明。派 wonderfully *adv.*

wood /wʊd/ *n.* ❶[U]木，木材：Tables are usually made of ~. 桌子通常是木材做的。❷[C]（常用 *pl.*）树林：go for a walk in the ~s 在树林中散步

wooden /ˈwʊdn/ *adj.* 木制的：a ~ leg 木腿

woody /ˈwʊdi/ *adj.* (-ier, -iest) 多树木的；长满树木的：a ~ hillside 长满树木的山坡

woodpecker /ˈwʊdpekə(r)/ *n.* [C]啄木鸟

wool /wʊl/ *n.* [U]羊毛；驼毛；毛线，绒线；毛织品：wear ~ next to the skin 贴身穿羊毛衣 / the ~ trade 羊毛业

wool(l)en /ˈwʊlən/ *adj.* 羊毛制的：~ blankets 毛毯

word /wɜːd/ *n.* ❶[C]语；词；话：I have no ~s to express my gratitude. 我无法用言语来表达我的感激。/ **eat one's ~s** 收回前言；认错；道歉 **have a ~ with sb.** 和某人说句话：Mr. Smith, can I have a ~ with you? 史密斯先生，我能与你说句话吗？**get in a ~ (get a ~ in)** 插话：She spoke so fast that I couldn't get a ~ in. 她说得很快，我插不上嘴。**in a (one) ~** 总而言之 **in other ~s** 换句话说：They asked him to leave—in other ~s he was fired. 他们请他走人，也就是说，他被解雇了。❷（单数，不加定冠词）消息，音讯：Please send me ~ of your safe arrival. 请把你平安到达的消息告诉我。❸（仅用单数，常与所有格连用）诺言，保证：**break one's ~** 失信；食言：Don't break your ~. You must come on time. 别失言，你一定得准时来。**keep one's ~** 守信用，遵守诺言：You should keep your ~ and come to our meeting. 你应该遵守诺言来开会。❹文字：~ processor（计算机的）文字处理器

work /wɜːk/ Ⅰ *n.* ❶[U]工作；劳动：I always found plenty of ~ in my garden. 在花园中我总能找到许多事情做。/ **at ~** 在工作：He is at ~ now, but he'll be back at six. 他现在正在工作，不过六点钟会回来。**out of ~** 失业；（机器）出毛病：His uncle has been out of ~ for three months. 他的叔叔已经失业三个月了。/ My computer is out of ~. 我的计算机出毛病了。❷作品；著作：the ~s of Beethoven 贝多芬的作品 / new ~ on modern art 关于现代艺术的新著 ❸(*pl.*)工厂；工场：a gas ~s 煤气厂 / a brick ~s 砖厂 Ⅱ *v.* ❶工作；劳动：He's been ~ing hard all day. 他整天辛劳地工作。/ Most students ~ hard at English. 大多数学生都努力学习英语。/ **~ at** 从事；致力于：We are ~ing at a new subject. 我们正在从事新课题的研究。**~ for** 为……而工作：He is ~ing for a big company. 他在为一家大公

司工作。~ **out** 算出；制订出：The total ~s out to $5,000. 总数算出是5,000美元。❷有效；成功：Will these new methods ~? 这些新方法有效吗？❸(使)工作；(使)运动：Don't ~ your poor wife to death. 不要累死你那可怜的妻子。The machines are ~ed by electricity. 机器是电动的。❹做成；完成：~ miracles (wonders) 创造奇迹

workday /ˈwɜːkdeɪ/ *n.* [C] ❶工作日，上班日：Today is my ~. 今天我要上班。❷(一个)工时日；一天的工作时间：a 9-to-5 ~ 朝九晚五的工时日

worker /ˈwɜːkə(r)/ *n.* [C]工人；工作者

working /ˈwɜːkɪŋ/ *adj.* 工作的；劳动的：the ~ class 工人阶级

workman /ˈwɜːkmən/ *n.* [C](*pl.* workmen) ❶体力劳动者；工人：We need about 500 workmen. 我们大约需要500名劳力。❷工匠；技术工人：all-round workmen 技术全面的工匠

workmanship /ˈwɜːkmənˌʃɪp/ *n.* [U] ❶(成品的)做工，工艺；(工匠的)手艺，技艺：a bracelet of fine ~做工精细的手镯 ❷工艺品，作品：Is this teapot you ~? 这把茶壶是你做的吗？

workshop /ˈwɜːkʃɒp/ *n.* [C]车间；工场；作坊

world /wɜːld/ *n.* ❶(the ~) 地球；世界；领域：the animal (plant) ~ 动物(植物)世界/ gambling ~ 赌场/ publishing ~ 出版界 / the English-speaking ~ 讲英语的国家 ❷尘世；俗世；世事：renounce (give up) the ~ 弃绝尘世 / **in the** ~ 究竟，到底；在世界上：Who in the ~ is that fellow? 那人究竟是谁？

worldwide /ˈwɜːldwaɪd/ Ⅰ *adj.* 遍及全球的；世界范围的：The event has a ~ influence. 这事件有世界性的影响。Ⅱ *adv.* 遍及全球地：The scientist is famous ~. 那位科学家全球知名。

worm /wɜːm/ *n.* [C] ❶蠕虫；(尤指)蚯蚓 ❷(~s)寄生虫

worn /wɔːn/ *adj.* ❶用过的；用坏的：a ~ suit 一套旧衣服 ❷疲惫的；筋疲力尽的：a ~ look 面容疲惫 / You look so ~. What's wrong with you? 你看起来那么疲惫。你怎么啦？

worried /ˈwʌrɪd/ *adj.* 焦虑的；烦恼的：He looks ~. 他看起来很焦虑。

worry /ˈwʌri/ Ⅰ v. 困扰；(使)不安；(使)烦恼：Her child has a bad cough and it rather worries her. 她的小孩咳得很厉害，她极为不安。/ Don't ~ about trifles. 别为小事烦恼。Ⅱ *n.* ❶烦恼，焦虑；担忧 ❷烦恼事

worse /wɜːs/ Ⅰ *adj.* (bad 和 ill 的比较级)更坏；更差；更糟：You are making things ~. 你把事情弄得更糟。Ⅱ *n.* [U]较坏或较差的人或事：She continued to tell us the ~. 她继续告诉我们更糟的情况。Ⅲ *adv.* 更糟地；更坏地：He is behaving ~ than ever. 他的表现比任何时候都糟。/ ~ **and** ~越来越糟：He has made the matter ~ and ~. 他已经把这事弄得越来越糟了。

worship /ˈwɜːʃɪp/ Ⅰ *n.* [U] ❶崇拜；崇敬 ❷敬慕；尊敬：hero ~ 英雄崇拜 / She gazed at the film star with ~ in her eyes. 她注视着那电影明星，眼里充满着敬慕之意。Ⅱ *v.* 崇拜；尊敬

worst /wɜːst/ Ⅰ *adj.* (bad 和 ill 的最高级)最坏的；最差的：the ~ storm in the past five years 五年来最厉害的暴风雨 Ⅱ *adv.* 最差地：I played basketball ~ in the class. 在班上我的篮球打得最差。Ⅲ *n.* 最坏的人或事：at the ~ 在最

坏的情况下 / ~ of all 最坏的，最糟糕的 / You must prepare for the ~. 你必须做最坏的准备。

worth /wɜːθ/ *adj.*（只作表语）❶值……的；等于……的价值的：I paid £600 for this used car, but it's ~ much more. 我仅付 600 英镑就买了这部旧车子，但它价值更高。❷值得 / **be ~ doing sth.** 值得做某事：The novel *Song of Youth* is ~ reading. 小说《青春之歌》值得一读。/ He says life wouldn't be ~ living without friendship. 他常说无友谊的人生便没有活下去的价值。

worthless /ˈwɜːθləs/ *adj.* 无价值的；无用的

worthwhile /ˌwɜːθwaɪl/ *adj.* 值得的：It is a ~ experiment. 这是一个值得做的实验。/ It is ~ to spend more time discussing the problem. 多花点时间讨论这件事是值得的。

worthy /ˈwɜːði/ *adj.* ❶值得的：a cause ~ of support 值得支持的一项事业 ❷可敬的：a ~ gentleman 一位值得尊敬的绅士

wound /wuːnd/ Ⅰ *n.*［C］伤；创伤：a knife ~ in the arm 臂上的刀伤 / a bullet ~ 枪伤 Ⅱ *v.* 使受伤；伤害：Ten soldiers were killed and thirty ~ed. 10 名士兵阵亡，30 名受伤。

wounded /ˈwuːndɪd/ *adj.* 受伤的

wrack /ræk/ *n.*［U］毁灭；损毁；灭亡：go to ~ and ruin 毁灭；灭亡

wrangle /ˈræŋgl/ Ⅰ *n.*［C］争吵，吵架；争论，争辩：a legal ~法律纠纷 Ⅱ *vi.* 争吵，吵架；争论，争辩：~ with sb. over sth. 为某事与某人争吵

wrap /ræp/ *v.*（wrapped; wrapping）❶卷，裹（与 in 连用）：~ oneself in a blanket 把自己裹在毯子里 / The mountain top was ~ped in mist. 山顶为雾所笼罩。❷包裹；包装：Wrap it with plenty of paper. 用很多纸将它包起。

wreck /rek/ Ⅰ *n.* ❶［U］（指船只等）失事，遭难；破坏：a ship ~ 船只失事 ❷［C］失事船；残骸：Robinson Crusoe obtained food and supplies from the ~. 鲁滨孙·克鲁索从失事船上获得食物及其他物品。Ⅱ *v.* 破坏；毁灭；失事：The ship was ~ed. 那船失事了。

wreckage /ˈrekɪdʒ/ *n.*［U］❶（尤指船只、车辆或飞机等失事后的）残骸，残体：remove the ~清除残骸 ❷遇难，失事：an aerial photograph of the ~ site 从空中拍摄的失事地点的照片 ❸损毁，破坏；破灭：weep at the ~ of one's hope 因希望的破灭而哭泣

wrestle /ˈresl/ *v.* ❶摔跤 ❷斗争；搏斗 ❸奋力对付；努力处理

wretched /ˈretʃɪd/ *adj.* 可怜的；不幸的；恶劣的：lead a ~ existence in the slums 在贫民窟里可怜地过活 / ~ weather 恶劣的天气

wring /rɪŋ/ *v.*（wrung /rʌŋ/, wrung）拧，扭；绞出（与 out 连用）：~ water out of one's swimming-suit 把游泳衣上的水拧出 / ~ one's neck 拧住某人的脖子

wrinkle /ˈrɪŋkl/ Ⅰ *n.*［C］皱纹 Ⅱ *v.*（使）起皱纹；皱起：He ~d his brow in concentration. 他全神贯注地锁紧眉头。派 wrinkly *adj.*

wrist /rɪst/ *n.*［C］腕，手腕：He took me by the ~. 他握住我的手腕。

write /raɪt/ *v.*（wrote/rəʊt/, written /ˈrɪtn/）❶书写；写字：Are we to ~ in ink or in pencil? 我们用钢笔还是用铅笔书写呢？/ You'd better ~ down the address before you forget it. 你最好把

这地址写下来,以免忘了。/ Can you ~ the new words we learned yesterday? 你能写出我们昨天学的新词吗? ❷写信给(与 to 连用): He promised to ~ to me every week. 他答应每周给我写信。/ He wrote to me an account of his visit. 他写信给我讲述他的访问情况。

writer /ˈraɪtə(r)/ *n.* [C]作者,作家;书写者: a fiction ~ 小说作家 / a ghost ~ 枪手,为人作刀的作者 / a popular ~ 受欢迎的作家 / Dickens was a famous English ~. 狄更斯是著名的英国作家。/ the ~ of this letter 写这封信的人

writing /ˈraɪtɪŋ/ *n.* ❶[U]书写;写作: busy with ~ 忙于写作 ❷(*pl.*) 某专题的著述: the ~s of Swift 斯威夫特的作品

wrong /rɒŋ/ Ⅰ *adj.* ❶ 不正当的;不道德的;违法的: It is ~ to steal. 偷窃是违法的。/ It was ~ of you to use his bicycle without asking his permission. 你没得到他的允许就使用他的自行车是不对的。❷错误的: We got into the ~ train. 我们搭错了火车。❸失常的;有毛病的;状况不佳的 / **be ~ with** 有毛病: There's something ~ with my digestion. 我消化有点毛病。/ What's ~ with the machine? 机器出了什么毛病? **go ~** 发生故障,出毛病: Something has gone ~ with her washing-machine. 她的洗衣机坏了。Ⅱ *n.* [U] ❶罪;不公正的事;邪恶: do ~违法;做坏事 / know the difference between right and ~ 知道是非之别 ❷不义的行为;不公正的事: She complained of the ~s she had suffered. 她诉说她受过的委屈。/ **do sb. ~** 冤枉(委屈)某人 Ⅲ *adv.* 错误地,不正确,不对 Ⅳ *vt.* 冤枉;委屈: It's not his fault. Don't ~ him. 那不是他的错,别冤枉他。

X x

Xerox /ˈzɪərɒks/ Ⅰ *v.* 影印,(用静电法)复印(常用 xerox) Ⅱ *n.* [C]静电复印;复印件

XO (=extra old)(白兰地)特陈的(尤指法国的 XO 系列白兰地酒,贮藏年份至少在 40 年至 50 年)

Xmas (=Christmas)圣诞节

X-ray /ˈeksreɪ/ *n.* [C] & *adj.* X 射线(的),X 光(的):~ diagnosis 用 X 光诊断

Y y

yacht /jɒt/ *n.* [C]游艇;快艇

yap /jæp/ Ⅰ *n.* 犬吠;急叫 Ⅱ *vi.* 狂吠;急叫

yard[1] /jɑːd/ *n.* [C]院子;庭院

yard[2] /jɑːd/ *n.* [C]码(英美长度单位,约等于 0.9144 米)

yarn /jɑːn/ *n.* ❶[U]纱,纱线;纺线;绳索股线:cotton ~棉纱线 ❷[C]故事;奇谈:adventure ~s 探险故事

yawn /jɔːn/ Ⅰ *vi.* 打呵欠 Ⅱ *n.* [C]呵欠:John stretched himself with a ~. 约翰打着呵欠伸懒腰。

year /jɜː(r), jɪə(r)/ *n.* [C] ❶太阳年(地球环绕太阳一周所用的时间,约为 365.25 天)❷年,历年:once a ~每年一次 / He made some progress in the last two ~s. 过去两年中他取得了一些进步。/ ~ after ~ 年年,每年 / all the ~ round 一年到头 ❸岁,年龄:a boy of ten ~s 一位 10 岁的男孩

yearly /ˈjɜːli/ Ⅰ *adj.* 每年的:~ report 年报 / What is your ~ pay? 你的年薪是多少? Ⅱ *adv.* 每年

yearn /jɜːn/ *vi.* 渴望;向往;怀念;思慕:~ after letters from parents 切盼双亲的来信/~ to find a job soon 只想快快找到工作

yell /jel/ *vi.* 叫喊:~ for help 大声呼救

yellow /ˈjeləʊ/ Ⅰ *adj.* 黄色的:the Yellow River 黄河 Ⅱ *n.* 黄色:bright ~ 鲜黄色 / pale ~ 淡黄色

yes /jes/ *adv.* 是,对

yes-man /ˈjesmæn/ *n.* [C](*pl.* yes-men)(口语)唯唯诺诺的人:He'd like to be surrounded by ~. 他喜欢周围都是些俯首听命的人。

yesterday /ˈjestədeɪ/ Ⅰ *n.* 昨日:~ morning (afternoon, evening)昨天早上(下午、晚上) / Where's ~'s newspaper? 昨天的报纸在哪里? Ⅱ *adv.* 在昨天

yet /jet/ Ⅰ *adv.* ❶(用于否定句及条件句中,且通常用于句末,也可紧跟在 not 之后)到此时,至今:They are not here ~. 他们尚未来此地。/ I wonder whether they have finished the work ~. 我不知他们到此时是否已完成了工作。/ You needn't do it just ~. 至今你们无须做那事。❷(用于肯定句中)仍,尚,还:Go at once while there is ~ time. 赶快去,还来得及。Ⅱ *conj.* 然而;可是:She is vain and foolish, ~ people like her. 她自负而愚蠢,然而人们喜欢她。

yield /jiːld/ Ⅰ *v.* ❶生产;出产:trees that ~ fruit 结果的树 ❷让步;屈服;投降;放弃:~ **to** 屈服于;服从:~ to no remedy 无药可救 / ~ to none 不落人

后,不让于人 / ~ to temptation 经不住诱惑 / The disease ~ed to treatment. 疾病经过治疗而消除。Ⅱ *n.* [C]产量;收获量;收益:a good ~ of wheat 小麦的丰收 / total ~ 总产量 / yearly ~ 年产量

yielding /ˈjiːldɪŋ/ *adj.* ❶易弯曲的;有弹性的 ❷顺从的;不固执的

yoga /ˈjəʊgə/ *n.* [U]瑜伽

yogh(o)urt /ˈjəʊgət/ *n.* [U]酸乳,酸奶

yoke /jəʊk/ *n.* ❶轭,牛轭 ❷枷锁;束缚

yolk /jəʊlk/ *n.* 蛋黄:Separate the ~s from the whites. 把蛋黄和蛋清分开。

you /juː/ *pron.* ❶你;你们(人称代词主格和宾格):You are my friend. 你是我的朋友。/Does he know ~? 他认识你们吗? ❷泛指任何人:It is much easier to cycle with the wind behind ~. 顺风骑自行车容易得多。

young /jʌŋ/ Ⅰ *adj.* (-er /ˈjʌŋgə/,-est /ˈjʌŋgɪst/) 年幼的;年轻的;幼小的:a ~ man 一个年轻人 / a ~ animal 幼兽 / She is two years ~er than her sister. 她比她姐姐小两岁。Ⅱ *n.* 青年人;幼畜;幼禽:That music is popular with the ~. 那种音乐很受青年人的欢迎。/ The cat fought fiercely to defend its ~. 那猫凶狠地打斗以保护其幼仔。

youngster /ˈjʌŋstə(r)/ *n.* [C] ❶儿童;小孩 ❷小伙子;年轻人 ❸幼小动物,幼小植物

your /jɔː(r), jʊr/ *pron.* 你的;你们的(形容词性物主代词):Show me ~ hand. 把你的手伸给我看看。

yours /jɔːz, jʊrz/ *pron.* 你的;你们的(名词性物主代词):Yours was my favorite birthday present. 你送的东西是我最喜欢的生日礼物。/ That pen is ~. 那支钢笔是你的。

yourself /jɔːˈself, jʊrˈself/ *pron.* 你自己:Did you hurt ~? 你伤了自己吗?

yourselves /jɔːˈselvz, jʊrˈselvz/ *pron.* 你们自己

youth /juːθ/ *n.* ❶[U]青春;青春期;青少年时代:give one's ~ to 把青春献给…… / the friends of one's ~ 青少年时代的朋友/She lost (kept) her ~. 她青春不再(青春依旧)。❷[C](*pl.* youths /juːðz/)少年;青年:As a ~, he showed no promise of becoming a great pianist. 少年时,他未显出成为伟大的钢琴家的迹象。❸(集合名词)青年们:the ~ of the nation 全国的青年们

youthful /ˈjuːθfl/ *adj.* ❶年轻的:~ cadres 年轻干部 ❷富有青春活力的

Z z

zeal /ziːl/ *n.* [U]热心;热情:show ~ for a cause 对事业表示热心 /work with great ~ 热情洋溢地工作

zealous /ˈzeləs/ *adj.* 热心的;热情的:~ to please one's employer 热衷于讨好顾主

zebra /ˈziːbrə/ *n.* [C]斑马

zero /ˈzɪərəʊ/ *n.* ❶零 ❷零点;零位;零度:It was ten degrees below ~. 气温是零下十度。❸零分:The teacher put a ~ on his paper. 老师在他的考卷上打了零分。

zest /zest/ *n.* [U]兴趣,兴味,兴致,热情:lose one's ~ for food 食欲不振/ He had a ~ for knowledge and for the distribution of knowledge. 他有强烈的追求知识、传播知识的欲望。

zigzag /ˈzɪgˌzæg/ Ⅰ*n.* [C] ❶曲折线条;之字形道路(或壕沟);锯齿形凸出物(或图案):The mountainous areas are full of ~s. 山区尽是曲曲折折的羊肠小道。❷曲折,拐弯 Ⅱ*adj.* 之字形的,锯齿形的;弯曲的;曲折的:a ~ coastline 锯齿状的海岸线 Ⅲ(-zagged;-zagging) *vi.* 呈之字形行走;曲折前进:The little child ~ged along the road. 这个小孩子左拐右拐地在路上走过。/ The lightening ~ged through the sky. 闪电呈之字形划过天空。

zip /zɪp/ Ⅰ(zipped; zipping) *vt.* 用拉链拉开(或扣上):~one's mouth 闭嘴/ It looks like the top of one of those plastic bags that ~ shut. 这有点像那种一拉就可以封口的塑料袋子。Ⅱ*n.* [C]拉链

zinc /zɪŋk/ Ⅰ *n.* [U]锌 Ⅱ*vt.* 在……上镀锌

zone /zəʊn/ *n.* [C]❶地区;区域:the war ~ 战区 / the danger ~ 危险地带 ❷(美国的)邮区;电话分区 ❸带,地带:frigid (temperate, torrid) ~ 寒带(温带,热带)

zoo /zuː/ *n.* [C]动物园:take the children to the ~ 带孩子们去动物园 / go to the ~ 去动物园 / at the ~ 在动物园里

zoological /ˌzəʊəˈlɒdʒɪkl/ *adj.* 动物的;动物学的

zoologist /zəʊˈɒlədʒɪst/ *n.* [C]动物学家

zoology /zəʊˈɒlədʒi/ *n.* [U]动物学

English-English Dictionary

ENGLISH-ENGLISH DICTIONARY

A a

aback *adv.* backwards

abacus *n.* a frame with beads sliding on wires, for doing arithmetic

abandon Ⅰ *v.* give up; discontinue Ⅱ *n.* complete lack of control or inhibition

abase *v.* make (especially oneself) lose self-respect; make humble

abate *v.* ❶ make or become less ❷ do away with (decree, obstruction, etc.) ❸ (of winds, storms, sounds, pain, etc.) become less strong; decrease

abbreviate *v.* make shorter (usually a word or phrase)

abbreviation *n.* a short form of a word or phrase

abdicate *v.* leave an important position (usually that of a king or queen)

abdomen *n.* the part of the body containing the digestive organs

abduct *v.* carry sb. away against his will (usually by force)

abet *v.* encourage or give help to (a crime or criminal)

abhorrent *adj.* horrible or disgusting

abide *v.* keep a law, promise, etc.

abiding *adj.* lasting for a long time and unlikely to change

ability *n.* ❶ the power or capacity to do sth. ❷ cleverness; intelligence

abject *adj.* contemptible; very miserable or unhappy

ablaze *adj.* ❶ on fire ❷ very bright ❸ full of or overflowing with an emotion

able *adj.* ❶ having the power, skill or means to do sth. ❷ clever; skillful; capable

ably *adv.* in an able manner; skillfully

abnegation *n.* lack of concern for one's own wishes

abnormal *adj.* not normal; not usual

aboard *adv.* & *prep.* on or onto a ship, bus, train or an aeroplane

abolish *v.* put an end to; do away with completely

abolition *n.* the action of abolishing a system, practice, or institution

abominate *v.* hate very much; abhor

abomination *n.* a feeling of great hatred; disgust

aboriginal *adj.* of or concerning people or living things that have existed in a place from the earliest times

abort *v.* ❶ end a pregnancy too soon, so that a baby cannot live ❷ end before an expected time because of some trouble

abound *v.* be plentiful; be rich; exist in great numbers or quantities

about Ⅰ *prep.* ❶ round, near to ❷ here

A

and there ❸concerning Ⅱ *adv.* ❶near ❷nearly, almost ❸approximately; near in time, size, number, etc.

above Ⅰ *prep.* ❶(of a place or position) higher than ❷higher in rank or power than ❸too good for ❹higher or more than (a specified amount or norm) Ⅱ *adv.* ❶in or to a higher place ❷on an earlier page or higher on the same page

abridge *v.* make(sth. written or spoken) shorter by using fewer words

abroad *adv.* ❶in or to a foreign country ❷in all directions; widely

abrupt *adj.* ❶ very sudden and unexpected ❷bad tempered; unfriendly

absence *n.* ❶ the state or a period of being away or not present ❷a lack of sth. ; the fact of being without sth.

absent *adj.* not here, not present

absolute *adj.* ❶ complete; total ❷ not limited ❸definite and undoubted

absolutely *adv.* ❶ completely; totally ❷certainly

absolution *n.* release from sin, punishment or obligation

absolve *v.* declare free from sin, guilt or responsibility

absorb *v.* ❶ take or suck in ❷ attract the attention

absorbed *adj.* very interested in sth. or sb. so that you are not paying attention to anything else

absorption *n.* ❶the process or action by which one thing absorbs or is absorbed by another ❷the fact or state of being engrossed in sth.

abstain *v.* stop using sth. ; not use sth. , refrain

abstract Ⅰ *adj.* existing in thought and separated from what is real or concrete Ⅱ *n.* a shortened form of a statement, speech, etc. Ⅲ *v.* make a shortened form (of a statement, speech, etc.) by separating out what is important

abstracted *adj.* not noticing what is happening or deep in thought

abstraction *n.* ❶ an idea of a quality considered separately from any particular object or case ❷the state of not noticing what is happening

abstruse *adj.* difficult to understand

absurd *adj.* unreasonable; foolish; ridiculous

abundance *n.* a copious supply or great amount ; plenty

abundant *adj.* more than enough; plentiful

abuse Ⅰ *v.* ❶ make bad use of; use wrongly ❷ treat badly; speak very roughly to Ⅱ *n.* ❶ the improper or wrong use of sth. ; misuse ❷cruel and violent treatment; insulting and offensive language

abyss *n.* a very deep hole

academy *n.* ❶a school for higher special training ❷a society for cultivating art, literature, etc. of which membership is an honour

accede *v.* agree to; say yes to

accelerate *v.* ❶(cause to) become faster ❷(cause to) happen earlier

acceleration *n.* increase in the rate or speed of sth.

accent Ⅰ *n.* ❶ a stress given to a syllable or word in speech ❷ an individual, local or national way of

pronunciation ❸a special emphasis Ⅱ *v.* pronounce with an accent

accept *v.* ❶take or receive sth. offered ❷admit; recognize; agree to; believe

acceptable *adj.* ❶ worth accepting; pleasing or satisfactory ❷welcome

acceptance *n.* ❶the act of accepting or being accepted ❷favour; approval

access *n.* ❶a way to enter a place ❷the opportunity to use sth.

accessible *adj.* ❶easy to reach, enter, or obtain sth. ❷ easy and friendly to talk to

accessory *n.* sth. which is added to the main thing

accident *n.* sth. unfortunate and undesirable

accidental *adj.* happening or done unexpectedly or by chance

acclaim *v.* applaud loudly for

accommodate *v.* ❶ supply with lodgings, or food and lodgings ❷ have (enough) room for ❸ make suitable; adapt

accommodation *n.* ❶a place to live or work in ❷ the settling of a disagreement

accompaniment *n.* ❶sth. which is used or provided with sth. else, especially in order to improve it ❷music played at the same time as singing or to support another instrument

accompany *v.* ❶ go with sb. as a companion ❷play music while someone sings or plays on a different instrument

accomplice *n.* a person who helps sb. else to do sth. (especially sth. wrong)

accomplish *v.* carry out successfully

accomplishment *n.* achievement; attainment

accord Ⅰ *v.* ❶ give or grant sb. (welcome, praise, etc.) ❷ be harmonious or agree with sth. Ⅱ *n.* ❶ agreement or harmony ❷ a treaty or agreement(between countries)

accordingly *adv.* ❶ as the stated circumstances suggest ❷consequently; therefore

accost *v.* go and speak to a stranger (especially in a public place and in a troublesome or unpleasant way)

account Ⅰ *n.* ❶a record or statement of money(to be) paid or received ❷ an arrangement that sb. has with a bank for keeping and taking out of money, etc. ❸ a report or description of an event, person, etc. ❹reason; cause Ⅱ *v.* ❶ provide a satisfactory record, especially of money received and paid out ❷ be an explanation of ❸ consider or regard

accountable *adj.* responsible; having to give an explanation for one's actions; answerable

accountant *n.* a person whose profession is to control and examine the money accounts of businesses

accredit *v.* ❶give credit to sb. for sth. ❷ attribute an action, saying, or quality to ❸(of an official body) give authority or sanction to sb. or sth. when recognized standards have been met ❹ give official authorization

accumulate *v.* make or become greater in quantity

accumulation *n.* the acquisition or gradual gathering of sth.

A

accumulative *adj.* increasing by successive addition

accuracy *n.* the quality of being precise; exactness or correctness

accurate *adj.* exactly correct

accusation *n.* a statement saying that sb. has done sth. illegal or wrong

accuse *v.* charge (someone) with doing wrong or breaking the law

accustom *v.* make used to

accustomed *adj.* ❶in the habit of; used to ❷regular; usual

ache Ⅰ *v.* feel a continuous dull pain Ⅱ *n.* a continuous dull pain

achieve *v.* succeed in doing sth. or reaching a desired goal, level or standard

achievement *n.* ❶the process or fact of achieving sth. ❷sth. done successfully, especially by effort or skill

acid Ⅰ *adj.* ❶sour ❷(of a person's remarks) critical and severe Ⅱ *n.* sth. which has a pH value less than seven, usually a liquid, can burn or sour the thing it touches

acknowledge *v.* ❶admit or accept ❷make known that one has received ❸express thanks for

acknowledgement *n.* ❶an act of accepting that sth. exists or is true, or that sth. is there ❷an act or a statement expressing thanks to sb.; sth. that is given to sb. as thanks

acme *n.* the highest point of development, success, etc.

acoustic *adj.* of sound or the sense of hearing

acquaint *v.* make sb. familiar with or aware of sth.

acquaintance *n.* knowledge of sth.

acquire *v.* gain or come to possess sth., especially by one's own work, skill, or action, often over a long period of time

acquit *v.* ❶decide by a trial or investigation that sb. is not guilty of some crime or wrongdoing ❷do one's duty satisfactorily

acrimony *n.* bitterness, as of feelings or words

acrobat *n.* an entertainer who performs difficult gymnastic feats

across Ⅰ *prep.* ❶from one side to the other side of sth. ❷on the other side of sth. Ⅱ *adv.* from one side to the other side

act Ⅰ *v.* ❶do sth. or take action ❷have an effect; work ❸behave (like) ❹be an actor or actress; play the part of ❺pretend to be Ⅱ *n.* ❶a thing being or to be done ❷a main division of a play, an opera, etc. ❸a formal decision; a law

acting *n.* the art or profession of representing a character, especially in a play or for a film or on television

action *n.* ❶the fact or process of doing sth. ❷a legal process ❸a military engagement

activate *v.* make active; cause to work or operate

active *adj.* ❶moving or tending to move about vigorously or frequently ❷doing sth. regularly; functioning ❸having a chemical effect

activity *n.* ❶a situation in which things are happening or being done ❷a thing (to be) done in order to achieve a

particular aim

actor *n.* a man who acts in plays, films on radio or television

actress *n.* a female actor

actual *adj.* existing as a real fact

actually *adv.* (used to emphasize that sth. someone has said or done is surprising) in actual fact

actuate *v.* cause (sb.) to act; activate or motivate

acute *adj.* ❶severe or intense ❷having a perceptive understanding or insight

adapt *v.* ❶make or become suitable for new needs, different conditions, etc. ❷ change a book or play to make it become a film, TV play, etc.; rewrite

adaptable *adj.* able to change so as to be suitable for new needs, different conditions, etc.

add *v.* ❶ put sth. together so as to increase ❷ put (numbers or amounts) together to form a total

addict *n.* a person who cannot stop himself from doing sth. or using sth. harmful

addicted *adj.* ❶ dependent on sth., especially a drug and unable to stop having or taking it ❷ devoted to a particular thing or activity

addition *n.* ❶ the process or action of adding sth. to sth. else ❷ a thing or person added or joined ❸the process of calculating the total of two or more numbers

additional *adj.* beyond what is usual; added

address Ⅰ *v.* ❶ speak to or make a speech to, especially in a formal way ❷ write on an envelope the name and address of the person, company, etc. that you are sending it to by mail Ⅱ *n.* ❶ a formal speech or talk (to an audience) ❷the number of the building, name of the street and town, etc. where a person lives or to which letters, etc. may be sent

adept *adj.* having great skill in doing sth.

adequate *adj.* enough or suitable

adhere *v.* stick to sth. firmly

adherence *n.* the action of continuing to support or be loyal to sth., especially in spite of difficulties

adhesion *n.* the state or action of sticking together or to sth.

adhesive Ⅰ *n.* a substance such as glue that can stick or cause sticking Ⅱ *adj.* that can stick or cause sticking

adjacent *adj.* very close; touching or almost touching

adjective *n.* a word that describes a noun or pronoun

adjourn *v.* bring (a meeting, game, etc.) to a stop, especially for a short period or until a slightly later time

adjust *v.* make a small change in sth. to make it better

administer *v.* ❶control and manage for the running of sth. ❷apply or put into operation ❸give or provide sth.

administration *n.* ❶the management or direction of the affairs of a business, government, etc. ❷the government of a country, especially of a particular president or ruling party

admirable *adj.* deserving respect and

approval; very good

admire *v.* ❶ regard sb. or sth. with respect or approval ❷ look at sth. or sb. with pleasure, etc.

admissible *adj.* that can be accepted or considered

admit *v.* ❶ confess or agree to the truth of sth., usually unwillingly ❷ permit to enter; let in ❸ leave a chance for being possible

admittance *n.* the right or fact of entering to a place

admonish *v.* warn or speak to sb. with gentle disapproval

adolescence *n.* the period during which a young person develops from a child into an adult

adolescent *n.* a young person who is developing from a child to an adult

adopt *v.* ❶ accept or take up to use ❷ take (a child of other parents) into one's family as one's own

adorable *adj.* charming or attractive

adoration *n.* ❶ religious worship ❷ a feeling of deep love and respect

adore *v.* like, love or honour greatly

adult Ⅰ *adj.* fully grown; mature Ⅱ *n.* a fully grown person or animal, especially a person over an age stated by law

advance Ⅰ *v.* ❶ move forward in position, development, etc. ❷ put forward (an advice, idea, theory, etc.) ❸ raise (prices); promote (sb.) ❹ pay beforehand Ⅱ *n.* ❶ a forward movement; progress ❷ the payment of money before it is due

advanced *adj.* very modern or developed well in life or in progress, etc.

advancement *n.* ❶ an improvement or development ❷ the promotion of a person in rank

advantage Ⅰ *n.* ❶ sth. that may help one to be successful or to gain a favourable result ❷ a favourable condition resulting from a particular course of action Ⅱ *v.* put in a favourable or more favourable position

advantageous *adj.* helpful; profitable

advent *n.* the coming or arrival (of an important event or a person or thing)

adventure *n.* a journey, experience, etc., that is strange and exciting and often dangerous

adventurous *adj.* ❶ eager for adventure; ready to take risks; daring ❷ exciting and full of danger

adverb *n.* a word that gives information in a sentence about how, when, where, why, etc.

adversary *n.* an opponent or enemy

adverse *adj.* unfavourable; going against; opposing

adversity *n.* bad fortune; difficulties

advertise *v.* make (a product, service or event) known to the public in a public medium

advertisement *n.* a notice or an announcement in a public medium telling people about a product, service, event or job

advice *n.* an opinion given to someone about what they should do in a particular situation

advisable *adj.* sensible; wise

advise *v.* ❶ offer suggestions about the best course of action to sb. ❷

recommend(sth.) ❸ inform(sb.) about a fact or situation, typically in a formal or official way

advocate Ⅰ *v.* speak in support of sth.; recommend Ⅱ *n.* a person who supports sth. or sb.

aerial Ⅰ *n.* a wire used for receiving or sending radio wave Ⅱ *adj.* in or of the air

aeroplane *n.* a flying machine; a plane

afar *adv.* at a distance; far off

affable *adj.* friendly; easy to talk to

affair *n.* ❶ an event described in a particular way ❷ events that are of public interest and importance

affect *v.* ❶ produce a change upon; have an effect on; act on ❷ move or touch emotionally ❸ pretend to be feeling or thinking sth. ❹ attack or infect

affectation *n.* behaviour which is not one's natural manner

affected *adj.* not real, natural, or sincere; showing affectation

affection *n.* liking or loving feelings

affectionate *adj.* having or showing caring feelings and love

affirm *v.* ❶ declare strongly and publicly in answer to a question or doubt ❷ declare one's support for; uphold

afflict *v.* cause to suffer in the body or mind; trouble

afford *v.* ❶ have enough (time, money, space, etc.) or the means for ❷ be able to do sth. without risk of serious consequences ❸ provide or supply

afraid *adj.* ❶ full of fear; frightened ❷ (used to soften an unpleasant statement) filled with regret or concern

after Ⅰ *prep.* ❶ later than; following in time ❷ next in order to ❸ indicating sth. happening continuously or repeatedly ❹ as a result of; because of ❺ in pursuit or quest ❻ in the manner or style of Ⅱ *conj.* at a later time than (when)

after-effect *n.* an effect that follows after the primary action of sth.

afternoon *n.* the time between midday and evening

afterthought *n.* an idea that comes later

afterwards *adv.* at a later time

again *adv.* ❶ once more; a second time ❷ returning to a previous position or condition ❸ used to introduce a further point that contrasts with what has just been said

against *prep.* ❶ in opposition to ❷ as a contrast with

agape *adj.* gaping, open-mouthed, especially because of surprise or wonder

age Ⅰ *n.* ❶ time of life; number of years a person has lived ❷ certain time in history Ⅱ *v.* (cause to) become old or mature

aged *adj.* ❶ being of the stated number of years ❷ fully developed, especially in taste ❸ very old

agency *n.* ❶ a business or an organization that provides a particular service on behalf of others or for others ❷ a department or body providing a specific service for a government or organization ❸ action; power

agenda *n.* a list of the subjects to be dealt with or talked about at a meeting

agent *n.* ❶ one who acts on behalf of or

for another (in business, politics, etc.) ❷means; a person or thing that acts

aggression *n.* the act or tendency of starting a quarrel, fight, or war, especially without just cause

aggressive *adj.* ❶ offensive; of or for attack ❷ quarrelsome; disposed to attack ❸ pushing; not afraid of resistance

aghast *adj.* suddenly filled with great surprise, fear, and shock

agile *adj.* able to move easily and quickly

agitate *v.* ask very strongly that sth. should be changed and made better

agitation *n.* ❶a state of anxiety or worry feelings ❷a public protest or an action, unrest, etc. for or against a political or social change

ago *adv.* before the present; in the past

agony *n.* very great pain or suffering of mind or body

agree *v.* ❶say"yes"; say that one will do sth. ❷have the same opinion as sb. ❸ reach an understanding or agreement ❹ be consistent with ❺be happy together ❺be suitable (to)

agreeable *adj.* ❶ pleasant ❷ ready to agree ❸acceptable or proper

agreement *n.* ❶ the act or state of sharing the same opinion or feeling ❷a promise or contract made with sb.

agriculture *n.* the science or practice of farming

ahead *adv.* ❶ in or into a forward position; in advance; before ❷in or into the future ❸in advance; earlier

aid Ⅰ *n.* ❶help ❷a thing or person that is a source of help Ⅱ *v.* help; assist

aim Ⅰ *v.* ❶direct or point (a gun, blow, remark, etc.) at a target ❷direct one's efforts or purpose Ⅱ *n.* ❶ the act of directing sth. at a target ❷ purpose or intention

aimless *adj.* without any clear purpose or direction

air Ⅰ *n.* ❶ the mixture of gases that surrounds the earth and which we breathe ❷the sky or the space above the ground ❸that part of a piece of music that is easily recognized and remembered; tune ❹a special feeling or impression on sb. or sth. ❺ an annoyingly affected manner or attitude Ⅱ *v.* ❶ put into the open air or in a warm place ❷let air into (a room) ❸ cause others to know; show off

aircraft *n.* an aeroplane, a helicopter, or other flying machine

airline *n.* ❶ an organization that provides a regular service of air transport for the public ❷a route which forms part of a system regularly used by aircraft

airspace *n.* the air above a country and subject to its control

airtight *adj.* not allowing air to enter or escape

aisle *n.* a way between blocks of seats in a church, classroom, theatre, etc.

alarm Ⅰ *n.* ❶a loud noise or a signal that warns people of danger ❷ any device, such as a bell, noise or flag, by which a warning is given ❸a feeling of fear or danger Ⅱ *v.* ❶ worry or frighten ❷ install sth. with a device which can send warning signals

album *n.* a book with blank pages to keep photographs or stamps in, or for people to write their signatures in

alcohol *n.* the strong liquid, found in drinks such as beer, wine, etc., which used as an industrial solvent and as fuel

alcoholic *adj.* of, containing or caused by alcohol

alert Ⅰ *adj.* ❶ quick to notice any dangerous or difficult circumstances ❷ quick to see and act; perceptive Ⅱ *n.* ❶ a warning to be ready for danger ❷ a state of being ready to deal with danger, especially after a warning Ⅲ *v.* make sb. watchful and ready for possible danger

alien Ⅰ *adj.* ❶ strange or unfamiliar ❷ from another country or society; foreign Ⅱ *n.* ❶ a person who is not a native person in the country where they live ❷ being from another world

align *v.* come or bring into a straight line

alike Ⅰ *adj.* similar to each other Ⅱ *adv.* similarly; equally

alive *adj.* ❶ continuing to live ❷ full of life; lively

all Ⅰ *adj.* ❶ the whole number of; the whole extent or amount of ❷ the greatest possible amount of Ⅱ *adv.* entirely; quite Ⅲ *pron.* everybody or everything

allege *v.* claim or assert that sb. has done sth. wrong or illegal without proof

alley *n.* a narrow street between or behind buildings in a town

alliance *n.* a union, e. g. of states, groups (by treaty)

allied *adj.* ❶ joined together in agreement ❷ connected in some way

allocate *v.* give or distribute sth. to sb. or for a special purpose

allocation *n.* ❶ the act or process of allocating ❷ a share or an amount that has been allocated

allot *v.* give as a share

allow *v.* ❶ permit sb. to do sth. ❷ let sb. have sth. ❸ let sth. be done or happen ❹ set aside sth. for a special purpose

allowance *n.* a sum of money given regularly

alloy Ⅰ *n.* a substance made of two or more metals Ⅱ *v.* mix one metal with sth. in lower value

allure Ⅰ *v.* make sb. do sth. (possibly sth. bad) by offering sth. attractive Ⅱ *n.* attraction; charm

allusion *n.* an expression that is said or written about sth. indirectly, especially while speaking about sth. else

ally Ⅰ *n.* a state, person, etc. allied to another Ⅱ *v.* ❶ combine or unite by treaty, marriage, etc.

almighty *adj.* ❶ having all power; powerful beyond measure ❷ very great, enormous or serious

almost *adv.* very nearly; not quite

aloft *adv.* high up, especially in the air or among the sails of a ship

alone *adv.* ❶ without any other people ❷ (used after a noun or pronoun to emphasize one particular thing) only

along Ⅰ *prep.* towards the end of Ⅱ *adv.* ❶ onward ❷ in company; together with

aloof *adv.* & *adj.* at some distance from other people (usually in an unfriendly way)

aloud *adv.* in a voice that may be heard

alphabet *n.* ❶ a set of letters used in a language ❷ the basic elements in a system

already *adv.* ❶ before or by this (that) time ❷ (used in negative and interrogative sentences to express surprise) as soon or early as this

also *adv.* in addition; besides; too

altar *n.* a table, stone or other raised object which is the most important place in a building where a religious ceremony is held

alter *v.* change; become or make different

alteration *n.* the action or process of altering or being altered

alternate Ⅰ *adj.* (of two things) happening by turns; first one and then the other Ⅱ *v.* (cause to) follow by turns

alternative Ⅰ *adj.* providing a choice between two or more things Ⅱ *n.* a choice between two or more things; one of the things to be chosen

although *conj.* ❶ in spite of the fact that; even if ❷ and yet; nevertheless; but

altitude *n.* height above sea level

altogether *adv.* ❶ entirely; completely ❷ on the whole; with all included

always *adv.* ❶ at all times; on every occasion; forever ❷ repeatedly

amass *v.* gather together a large amount of sth.

amateur Ⅰ *n.* ❶ a person who does sth. because he enjoys doing it, and not for money or because it is not his job ❷ a person who does sth. unskillfully, because it is not his real job Ⅱ *adj.* ❶ doing sth. just for interest without payment ❷ not professional; unskilful

amaze *v.* fill with great surprise or wonder

amazement *n.* a feeling of great surprise or wonder

amazing *adj.* causing great surprise or wonder, especially because of quantity or quality; extraordinary

ambassador *n.* an important government official whose work is to live in a foreign country and conduct business with the government of that country on behalf of his own government

ambiguous *adj.* ❶ having two or more different meanings ❷ doubtful; not clear

ambition *n.* a strong desire

ambitious *adj.* having a strong desire for success, power, wealth, etc.

amble *v.* walk or move at a slow, relaxed speed

amend *v.* make or become better by getting rid of faults; improve

amendment *n.* a change that is made to improve a rule, law, statement, etc.

amiable *adj.* pleasant and well-intentioned; likable and friendly

amicable *adj.* pleasant and friendly

amid, amidst *prep.* during; in the middle

amity *n.* a friendly relationship

ammunition *n.* a supply or quantity of bullets, shells, etc.

among *prep.* ❶ surrounded by sb. ❷ being a member or members in groups of things or people

amount Ⅰ *v.* be equal to; add up to Ⅱ *n.* ❶ the total quantity or sum ❷ the quantity of sth.

amphibian *n.* an animal, such as a frog, that is able to live both on land and in water

ample *adj.* ❶ quite enough ❷ large and accommodating

amplify *v.* ❶ increase the strength of sth., especially sound coming through electrical instruments ❷ increase in size, effect, etc., especially by explaining in greater detail

amplitude *n.* ❶ the quality of being ample, especially great quantity; abundance ❷ largeness of space

amuse *v.* ❶ make someone laugh or smile ❷ make one's time pass pleasantly

amusement *n.* ❶ the state of being amused; enjoyment ❷ sth. that makes one's time pass pleasantly; diversion

amusing *adj.* making people laugh or smile; entertaining

analogous *adj.* similar in certain respects

analogue *n.* sth. that is analogous to sth. else

analogy *n.* ❶ similarity or likeness ❷ a comparison between two things

analyse(-ze) *v.* study or examine sth. in order to understand or explain it

analysis *n.* the detailed examination of sth. by dividing it into its separate parts

anatomy *n.* the dissection of a body or part of a person or animal to study the way it works or is built

ancestor *n.* ❶ a person from whom one is descended ❷ an early type of a modern animal or plant ❸ an early form of a more developed machine, system, etc.

ancestry *n.* a person's ancestors considered as a group or as a continuous line

anchor Ⅰ *n.* ❶ a piece of heavy metal, usually a hook with two arms, at the end of a chain or rope, for lowering into the water to keep a ship from moving ❷ a person or thing that provides support and a feeling of safety Ⅱ *v.* ❶ stop sailing and lower the anchor ❷ fix firmly in position

ancient Ⅰ *adj.* ❶ belonging to the very distant past ❷ very old Ⅱ *n.* an old man

anecdote *n.* a short interesting or amusing story about a person or an event

anew *adv.* again, or in a different way

angel *n.* ❶ a messenger from God, usually shown in pictures as a human being in white with wings ❷ a person who is very kind, beautiful, etc.

anger Ⅰ *n.* the fierce feeling of annoyance, displeasure or hostility Ⅱ *v.* make sb. angry

angle Ⅰ *n.* ❶ the space between two lines that meet or cross each other ❷ a point of view ❸ a particular way of considering a matter or question Ⅱ *v.* ❶ turn or move at an angle ❷ represent information, report, etc. from a particular point of view

angry *adj.* ❶ filled with anger ❷ stormy and threatening

anguish *n.* severe pain, suffering, especially of mind

animal *n.* any living thing, especially one with four legs, which can feel and

A

move about

animate Ⅰ *v.* ❶give life or excitement to ❷give the appearance of movement by showing pictures with slight difference rapidly one after one Ⅱ *adj.* having life; alive

animated *adj.* full of spirit and excitement; lively

animation *n.* ❶ excitement; spirit; liveliness ❷the making of cartoons

annals *n.* ❶a written account of events year by year in a chronological order ❷ historical records; history

anniversary *n.* a date each year on which sth. happened in the past

annotate *v.* write or give written notes adding more information or explaining sth. hard to understand

announce *v.* ❶tell people sth. officially; make known ❷ read (news) or introduce (a person or act) on the radio, television, etc. ❸ notify or inform sb. of sth.

announcement *n.* ❶a statement making publicly known sth. that has happened or will happen ❷ the act of publicly informing people about sth.

annoy *v.* make rather angry; cause trouble to

annual *adj.* happening, appearing, etc. every year or once a year

annul *v.* stop or end completely (agreement, law, rule, etc.)

anomalous *adj.* not following the usual or regular way; different from the others of a group

anonymous *adj.* without a name, or with a name that is not made known

another *adj.* & *pron.* ❶ one more; an extra thing or person ❷ different; a different person or thing

answer Ⅰ *n.* ❶ a thing that is said, written, or done as a reaction of someone asking a question, sending a letter, etc.; reply ❷ sth. which is discovered as a result especially of thinking, calculating, etc. Ⅱ *v.* ❶ say, write or do sth. as a reaction to a question or letter ❷be responsible or to blame for ❸be suitable; satisfy

answerable *adj.* ❶ able to be answered ❷ having to explain or defend one's actions; responsible; accountable

antagonist *n.* a person who is hostile to sb. or sth.; an opponent

antecedent Ⅰ *adj.* going or being before Ⅱ *n.* ❶a thing or an event, etc., that goes before ❷ the word, phrase, or sentence to which a pronoun refers ❸a person's ancestors or family and social background

antedate *v.* ❶ be earlier in history than ❷write a date earlier than the date of writing on (a letter, cheque, etc.)

anticipate *v.* ❶ think likely to happen; expect ❷do sth. before (someone else) ❸come or take place before an event or process expected for a later time

anticipation *n.* the act of anticipating

anticlockwise *adj.* & *adv.* in the direction opposite to the hands of a clock

antiquated *adj.* (usually of objects or ideas) old-fashioned or of no use

antique Ⅰ *adj.* of or connected with ancient times, especially ancient Rome or Greece Ⅱ *n.* a piece of furniture, decorative object, jewellery, etc. that was made in an earlier period and that is rare or valuable

antiquity *n.* ❶ the state of being very old; great age ❷ a building, work of art, etc., remaining from ancient times, especially before the Middle Ages

antonym *n.* a word that is opposite in meaning to another word

anxiety *n.* ❶ a state of being worried about what may happen ❷ an eager desire

anxious *adj.* feeling anxiety; worried and frightened

any Ⅰ *adj.* ❶ some; even the smallest number or amount ❷ every; (of more than two) no matter which Ⅱ *adv.* in the least; at all

anyhow *adv.* in any case; in spite of that; anyway

anyway *adv.* ❶ in spite of everything; in any case; anyhow ❷ used when going on with a story, changing a subject in conversation, etc.

apart *adv.* away from each other; to or on one side; separately

apartment *n.* a set of rooms for living in, usually on the same floor of a building

apathetic *adj.* having no interest or feeling

apathy *n.* lack of interest or feeling

ape Ⅰ *n.* a large monkey without a tail or with a very short tail, such as a gorilla or chimpanzee Ⅱ *v.* copy a person or a person's behaviour, manners, speech, etc.; imitate

apex *n.* the top or highest point of anything

apologetic *adj.* wanting to apologize for sth.; expressing regret

apologize *v.* say you are sorry for sth. you have done

apology *n.* an expression of regret for a fault, wrong, etc.

appall *v.* fill with a strong feeling of dislike and shock

appalled *adj.* feeling or showing horror or disgust at sth. unpleasant or wrong

appalling *adj.* ❶ causing fear and hatred; shocking; terrible ❷ very bad

apparatus *n.* ❶ machines, tools, materials, etc., that work together for a particular purpose ❷ an organization or a system made up of many parts

apparent *adj.* ❶ easily seen or understood ❷ seeming real or true but may not be

apparently *adv.* ❶ it seems (that); according to what you have heard ❷ it is clear (that)

appeal Ⅰ *v.* ❶ make a serious and urgent request ❷ look to (sb.) for support, help, etc. ❸ be attractive or interesting Ⅱ *n.* ❶ a serious and an urgent request ❷ the quality of being interesting or attractive

appealing *adj.* ❶ able to move the feelings ❷ attractive, pleasing or interesting

appear *v.* ❶ come into sight; become visible; show oneself publicly ❷ seem

appearance *n.* ❶ an act or fact of becoming visible or arriving ❷ outward looks or qualities

appease *v.* ❶ pacify (someone) by giving

them what is wanted ❷give a country sth. it wants to avoid war

append *v.* add or join sth. written or printed onto the end of a larger piece of written material

appendix *n.* ❶the part of the inside of the body below the stomach ❷some extra information found at the end of a book or document

appetite *n.* ❶a desire or wish to eat sth., especially food ❷a strong desire or wish

applaud *v.* ❶express approval or enjoyment by striking one's hands together ❷agree strongly with

applause *n.* approval or praise, especially shown by clapping or cheering

appliance *n.* a device or an instrument, especially one operated by electricity and designed for household use

applicable *adj.* suitable to be used

applicant *n.* a person who asks for sth. formally

application *n.* ❶an act or a way of putting to use ❷a written or spoken request ❸come into force or operation

applied *adj.* (said about a subject of study) used for a practical purpose

apply *v.* ❶put sth. into use or position to serve its purpose ❷have an effect ❸ask for; request sth. officially in writing

appoint *v.* ❶choose sb. for a position or job ❷arrange or decide (especially time or place when sth. will happen)

appointment *n.* ❶an act of choosing someone for a position or job ❷an arrangement for a meeting at an agreed time and place

appraisal *n.* a statement or an opinion based on an act of appraising

appraise *v.* assess the value or quality of

appreciable *adj.* enough to be noticed, felt or considerable

appreciate *v.* ❶estimate the worth or quality of ❷value highly; think well of; enjoy ❸be grateful for ❹rise in value

appreciation *n.* ❶understanding of the good qualities or worth of sth. ❷a judgment of the worth or facts of sth. ❸a rise in value, especially of land or possessions ❹the feeling of being grateful for ❺full understanding; recognition

apprehensive *adj.* ❶good at understanding ❷uneasy; worried

apprentice *n.* a person who is under an agreement to work for a fixed period at low wages, for a person who is skilled in a trade, in order to learn that person's skill

approach Ⅰ *v.* ❶come near to sb. or sth. in distance or time ❷ask sb. for sth. or speak to sb. about sth., typically with a request or proposal ❸be close to sth. in amount, level or quality ❹solve a problem, task, etc. Ⅱ *n.* ❶a way of dealing with sth. ❷an approximation to sth. ❸a road or other way leading to a place

approachable *adj.* (said about a person) friendly and easy to talk to

appropriate Ⅰ *adj.* suitable or correct Ⅱ *v.* ❶take sth. or one's own use without permission by stealing, by force, etc. ❷take or give money for some purpose

approval *n.* ❶ giving permission ❷ a favourable opinion or judgment

approve *v.* ❶ agree officially to ❷ consider sth. good, right, wise, etc.

approving *adj.* showing that you believe that sb. or sth. is good or acceptable

approximate Ⅰ *adj.* nearly correct but not exact Ⅱ *v.* come near to sth. in amount, nature, etc.

apt *adj.* ❶ exactly suitable; pertinent ❷ having a natural or habitual tendency to do sth.; likely

aptitude *n.* a natural ability or skill, especially in learning

arbitrate *v.* judge or settle an argument by together choosing a person, etc. to make a decision

arbitration *n.* the settling of an argument by the decision of a person or group that has been chosen by both sides

arbitrator *n.* an independent person or body officially appointed to settle an argument

arch Ⅰ *n.* ❶ a curved part of a bridge or building ❷ sth. with this shape, especially the middle of the bottom of the foot Ⅱ *v.* form an arch or make into the shape of an arch

archaeologist *n.* someone who studies archaeology

archaeology *n.* the study of ancient civilizations by digging for their physical remains and examining them

archetype *n.* ❶ the original model of sth., of which others are copies ❷ a perfectly typical example of sth.

architect *n.* ❶ one who designs buildings, etc. ❷ a person who is responsible for planning or creating an idea or project

architecture *n.* ❶ the art and science of building, including its planning, making, and decoration ❷ the style or manner of building in a particular country or period of history

archive *n.* ❶ a place in which government documents and other official or historical papers are kept ❷ documents kept in such a place

ardo(u)r *n.* great feelings of enthusiasm

arduous *adj.* needing hard and continuous effort; difficult

area *n.* ❶ a particular space or surface ❷ the extent or measurement of a surface ❸ a region part of a town, country, etc. ❹ the range or limits of a subject, activity, etc.

arguable *adj.* ❶ able to be supported with reasons ❷ doubtful in some degree; questionable

argue *v.* ❶ speak angrily to sb. because of diverging or opposite views ❷ give reasons for or against sth. ❸ show; prove ❹ persuade

argument *n.* ❶ an exchange of diverging or opposite views, especially an angry one ❷ a reason given to support or disapprove sth. ❸ the use of reason to decide sth. or persuade someone ❹ summary

arise *v.* ❶ stand up from sitting, kneeling, or lying ❷ come into being or begin to be noticed; appear

aristocrat *n.* a member of the aristocracy; a noble

aristocratic *adj.* of, belonging to, or

A

typical of the aristocracy

arm Ⅰ *n.* ❶the part of the human body between the shoulder and the hand ❷ sth. similar to an arm Ⅱ *v.* ❶ give weapons to; get weapons ❷ prepare; provide

armament *n.* ❶the process of equipping military forces for war ❷ military weapons and equipment

armchair *n.* a comfortable chair with supports for the arms

armed *adj.* having or using weapons or armour

armo(u)r *n.* ❶a covering of metal worn by soldiers in old times to protect them ❷the strong protective metal covering on modern vehicles of war

arms *n.* ❶ weapons of war ❷ a coat of arms

army *n.* ❶ a large group of soldiers organized for fighting ❷a large group

aroma *n.* a pleasant smell, usually of food or herbs

around Ⅰ *prep.* ❶ on all sides of; all round; surrounding ❷so as to avoid or get past; round ❸ near; about Ⅱ *adv.* ❶on all sides; about ❷from one place to another; to various places ❸ measured in a circle

arouse *v.* awaken from sleep; make sb. having a particular feeling

arrange *v.* ❶put sth. in order ❷plan or organize sth. in advance ❸ write or adapt a piece of music

arrangement *n.* ❶ the act, process or result of putting sth. in order ❷a plan or preparation ❸ a settlement or agreement

array Ⅰ *n.* a collection of things arranged in order Ⅱ *v.* arrange a collection of things in order

arrest Ⅰ *v.* ❶seize sb. by the authority of the law ❷put a stop to ❸catch sb.'s attention Ⅱ *n.* the act or an example of arresting

arrival *n.* ❶ an act of coming or being brought to a place ❷a person or thing that comes to a place

arrive *v.* ❶come to a place, especially to the end of a journey ❷ come to a decision, state, etc. ❸ gain success or fame

arrogant *adj.* showing very great pride; acting as though one thought that other people were much less important than oneself

arrow *n.* ❶a thin, pointed stick shot from a bow ❷a mark or sign used to show direction or position

art *n.* ❶the expression or application of human creative skill and imagination, especially in painting, drawing or sculpture ❷the skillful method of doing sth. ❸things produced by art, especially paintings and sculpture

artful *adj.* cleverly deceitful; cunning

article *n.* ❶ a piece of writing in a newspaper or magazine ❷a particular or separate item or object ❸a complete separate part in a legal agreement, constitution, etc. ❹one of the words, a, an, or the, used before nouns

artificial *adj.* ❶ made by humans, especially as a copy of sth. natural ❷lacking true feelings; insincere ❸happening as a result of human

action, not through a natural process

artillery *n.* large guns, especially on wheels or fixed in one place, e.g. on a ship or in a fort

artist *n.* ❶a person who produces works of art, especially paintings or drawings ❷ a person skilled at a particular occupation ❸ a performer such as a singer, dancer or actor

artistic *adj.* ❶of art or artists ❷having or showing skill and taste in art

artless *adj.* ❶simple; natural ❷lacking art, knowledge or skill

ascend *v.* climb, go or rise up

ascent *n.* ❶ the act of climbing or moving up; an upward journey ❷a way up; an upward slope or path

ascribe *v.* think sth. to be the cause, reason, origin, etc.

ashes *n.* ❶such powder together with the unburned remains ❷the burnt remains of a human body ❸remains of sth. that has been destroyed

ashamed *adj.* ❶ feeling shame ❷ not willing because of fearing shame

ashore *adv.* on, onto, or to the shore

aside Ⅰ *adv.* ❶to the side ❷except for Ⅱ *n.* ❶ words spoken by an actor to those watching a play, and not intended to be heard by the other characters in the play ❷a remark made or story told during a speech but which is not part of the main subject

ask *v.* ❶ say or write sth. to obtain an answer or some information ❷make a request for ❸invite

asleep *adj.* ❶sleeping ❷not being able to feel properly because the blood has not been flowing freely; numb

aspect *n.* ❶ a part or feature of a difficulty, question, subject, etc. to be particularly discussed; viewpoint ❷ appearance ❸the direction a thing faces in; the side or surface facing a given direction

aspiration *n.* ❶ a strong hope or ambition ❷the action of pronouncing a sound with an exhalation of breath

aspire *v.* direct one's hopes and efforts to some important aim

aspiring *adj.* wanting to be successful in life

assassinate *v.* murder sb. by a sudden attack usually for a political reason

assault Ⅰ *n.* a violent and sudden attack Ⅱ *v.* make a physical attack on

assemble *v.* ❶ gather or bring sth. together; collect in one place ❷ make sth. by putting pieces together

assembly *n.* ❶ a group of people, especially one gathered together for a special purpose ❷the lower chamber in various American state legislatures ❸ the process of gathering together the parts of sth. collecting

assent Ⅰ *v.* agree to; say yes to Ⅱ *n.* agreement to sth.; permission

assert *v.* ❶state or express sth. clearly and forcefully ❷ defend or maintain rights, claims, etc.

assertion *n.* a forceful statement or claim

assertive *adj.* expressing or tending to express firmly opinions or claims; showing a confident belief in one's own ability

assess *v.* ❶calculate or estimate the value

or amount of ❷evaluate or estimate the quality, importance or worth of

assessment *n.* ❶the act of assessing ❷ the value or amount at which sth. is calculated

asset *n.* ❶sth. valuable or useful which gives one an advantage ❷ property which one owns

assign *v.* ❶give as a share; allocate (a job or duty) ❷give (property, rights, etc.) to ❸appoint sb. to a job or duty ❹put forward (as a time, place, reason, etc.)

assignment *n.* ❶a duty or piece of work that is given to a particular person ❷ the act of assigning

assist Ⅰ *v.* help sb. to do sth. Ⅱ *n.* support or help

assistance *n.* help or support

assistant *n.* a person who helps another in a job or piece of work, and is under that person's direction

associate Ⅰ *v.* ❶join in a relationship based on friendship, business, or a shared purpose; combine as friends or partners ❷make a connection between people or things in thought, memory, or imagination Ⅱ *n.* ❶a person connected with another, especially in work; partner ❷a person given certain limited rights in an association

association *n.* ❶ a connection or cooperative link between things or persons ❷ a connection in mind between people or things ❸a group of persons joined together for some common purpose

assort *v.* ❶divide sth. into different sorts ❷ associate with sb. especially a bad company

assorted *adj.* of various kinds; mixed

assume *v.* ❶suppose to be the case ❷ take up; undertake ❸take upon; adopt ❹pretend

assumption *n.* ❶sth. that is taken as a fact or believed to be true without proof ❷ the act of taking or having power or responsibility

assure *v.* ❶ say sth. positively with confidence ❷cause sb. to be sure or to be certain

assured Ⅰ *adj.* ❶ having or showing certainty ❷ confident in one's own abilities Ⅱ *n.* a person whose life has been insured

astonish *v.* surprise sb. greatly

astonishment *n.* great surprise or wonder

astound *v.* shock with very great surprise

astounded *adj.* very surprised or shocked by sth.

astounding *adj.* surprisingly impressive or notable

astray *adv.* & *adj.* away from the right path or way

asymmetric(al) *adj.* having two sides or parts that are not the same in size or shape

athlete *n.* a person who practises athletics

athletic *adj.* ❶of athletes or athletics ❷ physically strong, with well-balanced proportions between the trunk and limbs

atlas *n.* a book of maps

atmosphere *n.* ❶the air surrounding the earth ❷the feeling or the mood which one receives from a place or from particular conditions

atom *n.* the smallest particle of a chemical element that can exist

atomic *adj.* of or concerning atoms, nuclear weapons, or nuclear energy

attach *v.* ❶fasten sth. in position; fix or join ❷ fasten (a related document) to another

attachment *n.* ❶the act of attaching or being attached ❷sth. that is attached or forms an extra part of sth. ❸affection or fondness

attack Ⅰ *v.* ❶use violence to hurt sb. ❷ speak or write strongly against ❸make sb. suddenly ill Ⅱ *n.* ❶an act of use violence intended to hurt sb. ❷ writings, words or actions directed forcefully against a person, plan, etc., intended to hurt or damage ❸a sudden and usually severe period of illness, especially one which tends to return

attain *v.* ❶ succeed in doing or getting sth. ❷arrive at or reach

attainment *n.* ❶ success in doing or getting sth. ❷ sth. that has been successfully gained or learned, especially a skill

attempt Ⅰ *v.* make an effort at; try Ⅱ *n.* ❶an act of trying to do sth. ❷attack

attend *v.* ❶be present at (an event or a meeting) ❷look after; care for ❸pay attention to ❹ occur with or as a result of

attendance *n.* ❶ the act or fact of attending, especially usually or regularly ❷the number of people present ❸the act of going with or being with sb.

attendant Ⅰ *n.* ❶a person employed to look after and help visitors or customers in a public place ❷a person who goes with and serves or looks after another Ⅱ *adj.* ❶happening at the same time, as or as a result of sth. else ❷on duty to help and look after someone

attention *n.* ❶the act of directing one's mind to sth. or sb. ❷ a military command to come to a straight and still standing position ❸ a person's action trying to please sb. or to show interest in sb.

attest *v.* ❶ declare sth. to be true, especially by signing sth. ❷be proof of; demonstrate

attitude *n.* ❶ a position of the body; a posture ❷a way of feeling or thinking about someone or sth., especially as this influences one's behaviour

attorney *n.* ❶ a qualified lawyer ❷ a person with legal authority to act for another in business or law

attract *v.* ❶ cause the admiration, interest, or feelings of sb. ❷ draw or pull towards oneself; cause to come near

attraction *n.* ❶ a force pulling things towards each other ❷a person or thing that attracts others

attractive *adj.* ❶pleasing or appealing to the senses ❷having good looks; pretty or handsome

attribute Ⅰ *n.* ❶ a quality of feature forming part of the nature ❷a symbol of a person or a thing Ⅱ *v.* ❶ consider sth. as being the result of or as coming from another thing ❷think of as being written or made by

auction Ⅰ *n.* a public sale in which goods are sold to the person offering the

A

highest price Ⅱ *v.* sell sth. at an auction

audacious *adj.* ❶brave and ready to take a risk ❷impudent and without any fear of authority

audience *n.* the group of people watching or listening to a performance, speech, television show, etc.

audit Ⅰ *v.* check in detail the record of money received and spent to see that the record is correct Ⅱ *n.* an examination of this kind

auditor *n.* ❶a person who conducts an audit ❷a listener

augment *v.* become or make larger by adding sth.

august *adj.* noble and grand

auspicious *adj.* giving, promising, or showing signs of future success

austere *adj.* ❶ severely and strictly moral; without comfort or enjoyment; serious ❷without decoration; plain

authentic *adj.* genuine; known to be true

author Ⅰ *n.* ❶ a writer of a book, article, play, etc. ❷a person who creates Ⅱ *v.* create or begin sth.

authoritative *adj.* having a lot of authority; reliable

authority *n.* ❶the power or right to give orders and make others obey ❷ a person with special knowledge about a subject ❸ a person or an organization having power to control a special area or region

authorize *v.* give official permission for sth. or sb. to do sth.

autocrat *n.* ❶ a ruler who has absolute power ❷ a person who expects to be obeyed by other people and does not care about their opinions or feelings

autograph *n.* a person's name in her or his own writing (signature), especially the signature of someone famous

automatic *adj.* ❶ (of a machine) working or moving by itself ❷done or occurring spontaneously without conscious thought

auxiliary Ⅰ *adj.* providing supplementary help and support Ⅱ *n.* ❶ an auxiliary verb ❷a helper or assistant

avail Ⅰ *v.* be of use, of value or of help Ⅱ *n.* use; profit; advantage

available *adj.* capable of being used; that may be obtained

avenue *n.* ❶ a road with trees on each side; a wide street in a town ❷a way or method

average Ⅰ *n.* ❶ the result of adding several quantities together and dividing the total by the number of quantities ❷ a standard or level regarded as ordinary or usual Ⅱ *adj.* ❶calculated by making an average of a number of quantities ❷ of the usual or ordinary kind

avert *v.* stop sth. from happening

aviation *n.* the flying in an aeroplane; the art or science of flying aeroplanes

avoid *v.* ❶keep or get away from doing sth. ❷contrive not to meet sb. or sth.

await *v.* ❶ (of persons) wait for ❷ (of things) be in store for; be waiting for

awake Ⅰ *v.* ❶(cause to) stop sleeping; wake ❷(cause to) become conscious or active

awaken *v.* wake up

award Ⅰ *v.* give or grant by official decision Ⅱ *n.* sth. given from the official decision, especially a prize in a competition

aware *adj.* having knowledge or realization

awareness *n.* knowing sth.; knowing that sth. exists and is important; being interested in sth.

away *adv.* ❶at a stated distance in space or time ❷so as to be gone or used up ❸all the time; continuously

awe Ⅰ*n.* a feeling of respect mixed with fear and wonder Ⅱ*v.* fill with awe

awesome *adj.* ❶extremely impressive or daunting ❷very good; excellent

awful *adj.* ❶ frightening; dreadful ❷ very great; very bad

awkward *adj.* ❶ clumsy; having little skill ❷ not well designed for use ❸ embarrassing ❹ difficult to deal with; knotty

axis *n.* ❶ a line round which a turning object spins; a political connection (not always an alliance) between two or more states ❷a line (e. g. across the middle of a circle) that divides a regular shape into two equal parts

B

B b

babble Ⅰ *n.* a foolish or childish talking Ⅱ *v.* talk foolishly or childishly

baby *n.* ❶ a very young child, especially one that cannot walk or talk yet ❷ a very young animal

babysitter *n.* a person who looks after a child in its home while its parents are out

babyhood *n.* the period of time when one is a baby

bachelor *n.* ❶ an unmarried man ❷ a person who has a bachelor's degree

back Ⅰ *n.* the part of a person's or animal's body that is the side opposite the chest, and goes from the neck to the bottom of the spine or the tail Ⅱ *adj.* toward the rear or farthest from the front Ⅲ *adv.* ❶ towards or at the back; away from the front ❷ in or into the place or position where sb. or sth. was before ❸ in return; in reply Ⅳ *v.* ❶ (cause to) go backwards; move or make sth. move backwards ❷ support and encourage, often with money; provide backing for

backbiting *n.* an unkind and unpleasant talk about someone who is absent

backbone *n.* ❶ the line of bones down the middle of the back ❷ the chief support ❸ firmness; strength

background *n.* ❶ the part of a painting or photograph that shows what is behind the main objects or people ❷ past experiences ❸ the existing condition when sth. happens

backstreet Ⅰ *n.* a small or minor street in a town Ⅱ *adj.* done secretly or illicitly

backward *adj.* ❶ towards the back or the starting-point ❷ behind; late in development

backwards *adv.* ❶ away from the front, towards the back ❷ in reverse order

bad *adj.* ❶ not good; not normal; evil ❷ severe; serious ❸ not pleasant; giving a terrible smell ❹ unfit to eat because of decay; rotten

badge *n.* ❶ a small piece of metal or plastic with a picture or words on it, worn to show a person's occupation, rank, membership of a society ❷ a mark

badly *adv.* ❶ in a bad manner ❷ to a great or serious degree; very much

baffle Ⅰ *n.* a board or other means of controlling the flow of air, water, or sound coming into or going out an enclosed space Ⅱ *v.* ❶ be too difficult to understand or solve ❷ prevent sb. from doing sth.

baggage *n.* cases, bags, boxes, etc. of a traveller; luggage

bait Ⅰ *n.* food or sth. like food used to attract fish, animals, or birds which are then caught Ⅱ *v.* put bait on a hook to catch fish, or in a trap to catch animals

bake *v.* ❶ cook in an oven ❷ make or become hard by heating

balance Ⅰ *n.* ❶ a condition of being steady ❷ an instrument for weighing things ❸ the difference between two columns of an account Ⅱ *v.* ❶ keep or put sth. in a steady state ❷ compare two contrasting things

bald *adj.* ❶ (of man) with little or no hair (on the head); (of animals) hairless; (of land) without trees or bushes ❷ without ornament; undisguised

baldly *adv.* spoken plainly, without attempting to hide unpleasant facts

ball *n.* ❶ a round object used in play; anything of this shape ❷ a big party for people gathering for dancing

ballot Ⅰ *n.* ❶ a sheet of paper used to make a secret vote ❷ the process or system of secret voting ❸ an occasion of voting or a chance to vote Ⅱ *v.* ❶ vote or decide secretly ❷ find out the views of a group by holding a vote

balmy *adj.* (especially of winds) gentle and mild

ban Ⅰ *v.* forbid sth., especially by law Ⅱ *n.* an official prohibition

band Ⅰ *n.* ❶ a thin flat strip of some material used to reinforce objects, fasten things together or as decoration ❷ a radio range of frequencies ❸ a group of persons who play music together ❹ a group of persons joined together with a common purpose Ⅱ *v.* ❶ tie with a band ❷ unite in a group

B

bandage Ⅰ *n.* a band of woven material to put round a wound or injury Ⅱ *v.* bind a wound or injury with a band of woven material

bandit *n.* an armed robber, especially who attacks travellers

bandy *v.* exchange words when arguing with sb.

bang Ⅰ *n.* a sharp blow; a sudden loud, sharp noise Ⅱ *v.* ❶ hit sharply, especially by accident; bump ❷ make a sharp loud noise or noises

banish *v.* ❶ end sb. away from a country as a punishment ❷ dismiss sth. from your mind

bank[1] *n.* the land along each side of a river or canal; the ground near a river

bank[2] Ⅰ *n.* a place in which money is kept and paid out on demand, and where related activities go on Ⅱ *v.* put or keep money in a bank

bankrupt Ⅰ *n.* a person unable to pay his debts Ⅱ *adj.* unable to pay one's debts

bankruptcy *n.* the state of being bankrupt

banner *n.* ❶ a flag ❷ a long piece of cloth on which a sign is painted, usually carried between two poles

banquet *n.* an elaborate meal, usually for a special event, at which speeches are made

bar Ⅰ *n.* ❶ a long piece of sth.; a hard, thick stick ❷ a place where people can buy and have a particular kind of food or drink Ⅱ *v.* ❶ fasten (a door, gate, etc.) with a bar or bars ❷obstruct

B

barbarian Ⅰ *n.* an uncultured or brutish person Ⅱ *adj.* uncultured; brutish

barbarous *adj.* uncivilized; cruel and savage

barbecue Ⅰ *n.* a party or feast (usually in the open air) at which the food (usually meat) is cooked over an open fire Ⅱ *v.* roast meat etc. in this way

bare Ⅰ *adj.* ❶ without clothing, covering, protection or decoration ❷ basic; not more than Ⅱ *v.* uncover; reveal

barefaced *adj.* shameless

barely *adv.* ❶ in a bare way ❷ almost not; only just; scarcely

bargain Ⅰ *n.* ❶ an agreement made between two people or groups to do sth. in return for sth. else ❷ sth. for sale or bought for less than its real value Ⅱ *v.* talk about the conditions of a sale, agreement, or contract; negotiate

bark[1] Ⅰ *n.* ❶ the cry made by dogs or foxes ❷ a sound made by people laughing or coughing Ⅱ *v.* ❶ give a bark or barks ❷say (sth.) in a sharp loud voice

bark[2] Ⅰ *n.* the strong outer covering of a tree Ⅱ *v.* ❶take the bark off ❷scrape the skin off

barren *adj.* ❶(of land) not good enough to produce crops ❷ (of women or female animals) not able to produce children or young ❸(of a tree or plant) not producing fruit or seed

barricade Ⅰ *n.* ❶ a barrier, especially one that is put up hastily across a door or street Ⅱ *v.* to block a door or street with such a barrier

barrier *n.* sth. that is used to keep people or things apart or to prevent or control their movement

barrow *n.* a small vehicle with one or two wheels used for carrying goods, usually pushed by hand

barter Ⅰ *v.* exchange goods or services for other goods or services rather than for money Ⅱ *n.* the action or system of bartering

base Ⅰ *n.* ❶the lowest part of anything, especially the part on which sth. rests or is supported; the foundation ❷ a substance into which other things are formed ❸a starting place; headquarters Ⅱ *v.* build or place sth. as the foundation or starting point for sth. Ⅲ *adj.* (of person, their behaviour, thoughts, etc.) low; dishonourable

basement *n.* a room or rooms in a house which are below street level

bash *v.* hit sb. very hard

basic *adj.* of or at the base of foundation; fundamental

basics *n.* the basic parts or principles of a subject, process, etc.

basin *n.* ❶ a round, open dish of metal, pottery, etc. for holding liquids ❷ an area of land from which water runs down into a river

basis *n.* ❶ the underlying support or foundation for an idea, argument, etc. ❷ the most important part of a mixture

basket *n.* a light container made of narrow pieces of wood, plastic, etc. woven together, and used for carrying or holding things

batch *n.* an amount or number of things or people dealt with together

bath Ⅰ *n.* an act of washing the body Ⅱ *v.* give a bath to (sb.); wash in a bath

bathe Ⅰ *v.* ❶ soak or wipe gently with liquid to clean or soothe, usually for medical reasons ❷ go into the sea, a river, a lake, etc. for sport, swimming, to get cool Ⅱ *n.* the act of swimming or spending time in the water

batter *v.* beat sth. hard and repeatedly

battle Ⅰ *n.* a fight between enemies or opposing groups; a struggle Ⅱ *v.* struggle or fight

bawl *v.* shout or cry very loudly, usually in an impolite or unpleasant way

bay *n.* a part of the land curved inwards at the edge of the sea or a lake

bazaar *n.* (in Middle Eastern countries) a market place or group of shops

beach *n.* a shore of an ocean, sea, or lake or the bank of a river covered by sand, smooth stones, or larger pieces of rock

beacon *n.* a tall object or light on or near the shore, to act as a guide or warning to sailors

bead *n.* ❶a small ball of wood, glass and other material with a hole through it for threading with others on a string or wire ❷ a drop of liquid ❸ a necklace made of such beads

beak *n.* the hard horny mouth of a bird

beaker *n.* ❶a large drinking vessel ❷an open glass vessel with a lip, often used in laboratories for chemical experiments, etc.

beam Ⅰ *n.* ❶ a long, heavy piece of square timber, ready for use in building ❷a ray of light Ⅱ *v.* ❶send out light and warmth ❷ smile happily or cheerfully

bear *v.* ❶ carry from one place to another; carry away; convey ❷produce a crop of fruit ❸ tolerate; endure ❹ support ❺give birth to ❻have; show ❼take responsibility for

bearable *adj.* that can be borne or endured

beard *n.* hair on the face below the mouth, often including the jaws, chin, and neck

bearing *n.* ❶ the way people behaves themselves; the way of standing or moving ❷relation; aspect ❸the ability to suffer sth. ❹a direction in which a place lies ❺ the part of a machine in which moving parts turn

beast *n.* ❶a four-footed animal; a large bovine farm animal ❷ a cruel or disgusting person

beat Ⅰ *v.* ❶hit repeatedly ❷defeat or do better than sb. in a game or competition ❸make a regular sound or movement Ⅱ *n.* ❶ a regular, rhythmic sound or movement ❷a main accent or rhythmic unit in music

beaten *adj.* ❶ (of metal) shaped by beating with a hammer ❷(of a path, track, etc.) given shape by the feet of those who pass along it

beating *n.* ❶ an act of giving repeated blows, usually for punishment ❷ a defeat, especially in a game or competition

beautify *v.* make sb. or sth. beautiful

B

B

beautiful *adj.* giving pleasure or delight to the mind or senses

beauty *n.* ❶ the qualities that give pleasure to the senses or lift up the mind or spirit ❷ a beautiful woman; sth. beautiful

because *conj.* for the reason that

beckon *v.* make a sign with the hand

become *v.* ❶come or grow to be; begin to be ❷happen to ❸be suitable for; look well on

bed *n.* ❶a piece of furniture to sleep on ❷the bottom of the sea, river, lake, etc.

beef *n.* the meat of farm cattle

beep Ⅰ *n.* a short high-pitched sound made by an electronic equipment or a car horn Ⅱ *v.* produce such a sound

beetle *n.* an insect with hard, shiny wing covers

befall *v.* (usually of sth. bad) happen to

befit *v.* be proper or suitable to

before Ⅰ *adv.* ❶at an earlier time; in the past ❷in advance Ⅱ *prep.* ❶in front of ❷ earlier than Ⅲ *conj.* previous to the time when

beforehand *adv.* ahead of time; in advance

befriend *v.* act as a friend to; be kind and helpful to

beg *v.* ❶ask sb. for food, money, etc. ❷ ask sb. for sth. earnestly, or with deep feeling

beget *v.* produce; be the cause of

beggar Ⅰ *n.* a person who lives by begging Ⅱ *v.* make sb. or sth. very poor

beggarly *adj.* much too little in amount; very poor

begin *v.* ❶start sth. or doing sth. ❷start to happen or exist ❸to be sth. first, before becoming sth. else ❹have sth. as the first part or the point where sth. starts

beginner *n.* a person who stats learning and without much experience

beginning *n.* the point at which sth. begins; the start; the origin

behalf *n.* (on/in ~ of, on/in sb. 's ~) for the interest of, on account of

behave *v.* ❶act or conduct oneself ❷(of machines, etc.) work or function

behavio(u)r *n.* the way of behaving; the treatment shown towards others

behead *v.* kill sb. by cutting sb. 's head off

behind *prep.* & *adv.* ❶at the back of ❷ slower in time, work, etc.

behold *v.* take notice or see sb. or sth.

being *n.* ❶existence ❷a human creature

belch *v.* ❶ send out wind from the stomach noisily through the mouth ❷ send out a large amount of smoke or flames

belief *n.* ❶sth. accepted as true or real; sth. taught as part of a religion ❷the feeling that sth. is real and true; trust; confidence

believe *v.* ❶ feel sure of the truth of sth. ; be of the opinion (that) ❷think or suppose ❸(~ in) have trust in

belittle *v.* cause to seem unimportant or of small value

bell *n.* ❶ a round, hollow metal vessel which makes a ringing sound when struck ❷the sound of a bell ❸sth. with the form of a typical bell

belly Ⅰ *n.* the part of the body containing

the stomach and bowels Ⅱ *v.* (usually of of sails) swell out when the wind blows

belong *v.* ❶ be the property of ❷ be a number of ❸ fit a certain environment

belongings *n.* a person's possessions

beloved Ⅰ *adj.* dearly loved Ⅱ *n.* a dearly loved person; darling

below Ⅰ *prep.* lower than Ⅱ *adv.* at or to a lower level

belt Ⅰ *n.* ❶ a band or strip of cloth or leather worn round the waist or over one shoulder ❷ an endless leather strap used to connect wheels and so drive machinery or carry things along ❸ an area with particular characteristics Ⅱ *v.* fasten with a belt; hit with a belt

bench *n.* ❶ a long seat of wood or stone ❷ a long worktable

bend Ⅰ *v.* ❶ cause to be out of a straight line or surface; force into a curve or angle ❷ become curved; make one's body curve forward down Ⅱ *n.* a curve or turn; a part that is not straight

beneath *adv.* & *prep.* below or lower than; in a lower place

benefaction *n.* a donation or gift

benefactor *n.* a person who does good or who gives money for a good purpose

beneficial *adj.* having good effect; favourable; helpful

benefit Ⅰ *n.* an advantage or profit gained from sth.; good done or received Ⅱ *v.* do good to; bring advantage to

benign *adj.* ❶ (of certain diseases, etc.) not very harmful ❷ kind and gentle

bent Ⅰ *adj.* ❶ made curved or crooked; not straight ❷ strongly inclined or determined ❸ dishonest; corrupt Ⅱ *n.* inclination or aptitude

bequest *n.* sth. which is bequeathed

bereave *v.* be deprived of a relative or close friend by death

bereaved *adj.* having recently suffered the death of a close relative

bereft *adj.* deprived of sth.

berth Ⅰ *n.* ❶ a place on a ship or train where one sleeps ❷ a place where a ship anchors in a harbour, etc. Ⅱ *v.* take a ship into a berth

beset *v.* surround and harass on all sides

beside *prep.* at the side of; close to

besides Ⅰ *prep.* apart from; in addition to Ⅱ *adv.* also; in addition

best Ⅰ *adj.* of the most excellent kind; very good Ⅱ *adv.* ❶ in the most excellent way ❷ most; more than all others Ⅲ *n.* the most excellent or outstanding person or thing among several

bestow *v.* give sth. to sb. as an offering

bet Ⅰ *v.* ❶ risk money on a race or on some other event of which the result is doubtful ❷ be certain Ⅱ *n.* the money that sb. risks in this way

betray *v.* ❶ be disloyal to ❷ make a secret known ❸ be or give a sign of; show

better Ⅰ *adj.* ❶ of higher quality, moral value, usefulness, etc. ❷ partly or fully recovered from illness or injury Ⅱ *adv.* in a more excellent manner Ⅲ *v.* improve; do better than Ⅳ *n.* sth. or sb. better

between *prep.* & *adv.* in or into the space or time that separates

B

beverage *n.* any sort of drink (e. g. milk, tea, beer)

bewail *v.* express deep sorrow for, especially by or as if by weeping

beware *v.* be on guard; take care

bewilder *v.* cause sb. to feel puzzled or confused

beyond Ⅰ *prep.* ❶ at, on, or to the further side of ❷ exceeding Ⅱ *adv.* further on; at or to a distance

bias Ⅰ *n.* prejudice; inclination Ⅱ *v.* make sb. come to a decision without allowing him to hear the full facts

biased *adj.* inclined to favour one side rather than another

Bible *n.* (the ~) the sacred writings of the Jews and the Christian Church

bid Ⅰ *v.* (at an auction sale) make an offer of money Ⅱ *n.* a price offered at an auction

bidding *n.* the offering of particular prices for sth., especially at an auction

bide *v.* remain or stay somewhere

big *adj.* ❶ large in size, degree, amount, etc. ❷ grown-up ❸ important; serious ❹ needing a lot of effort, money or time to succeed ❺ popular; successful

bilateral *adj.* on both sides; made by two opposing groups; having two sides

bile *n.* ❶ a bitter liquid produced by the liver to help the digestion of food ❷ anger or abomination

bilk *v.* cheat sb., especially causing them to lose money; swindle

bill *n.* ❶ a banknote ❷ a written statement of charges for goods or services ❸ a proposed law to be discussed by a parliament

billow Ⅰ *n.* ❶ a large wave ❷ a rolling mass like a large wave, typically cloud, smoke or steam Ⅱ *v.* ❶ swell out ❷ rise and move in a large mass like a large wave

bimonthly *adv.* & *adj.* ❶ appearing or happening every two months ❷ appearing or happening twice a month

bin *n.* a large container, usually with a lid

bind *v.* ❶ tie or fasten sth. with rope ❷ bandage (a wound) ❸ cause to obey, especially by a law or a solemn promise; put under an obligation

binding Ⅰ *n.* ❶ a book cover ❷ material sewn or stuck along the edge of sth., such as a dress, for strength or decoration Ⅱ *adj.* imposing a legal obligation on sb.

biography *n.* a person's life history written by an author

biology *n.* the science of life and living things

biosphere *n.* the part of the earth's surface and atmosphere in which plants and animals can live

bird *n.* a creature with wings and feathers

birth *n.* ❶ being born; coming into the world ❷ the beginning of sth. such as a new idea or situation

birthday *n.* the anniversary of the day of one's birth

bishop *n.* a clergyman of high rank who organizes the work of the Church in a city or district

bit *n.* a small amount or piece of sth.

bite Ⅰ *v.* ❶ (of a person or animal) cut into sth. with the teeth ❷ (of an animal or a person) use the teeth in order to inflict injury ❸ (of an acid) corrode a surface Ⅱ *n.* ❶ an act of cutting into sth. with the teeth ❷ a wound inflicted by an animal's or a person's teeth or by an insect or snake

biting *adj.* ❶ (of wind) so cold as to be painful ❷ harsh or cruel

bitter *adj.* ❶ having a sharp, pungent taste or smell; not sweet ❷ very sharp, causing pain or grief ❸ piercingly cold

black Ⅰ *adj.* ❶ of the very darkest colour due to the absence of or complete absorption of light; the opposite of white ❷ without light; completely dark ❸ without hope; very depressing Ⅱ *n.* ❶ the very darkest colour, like night or coal ❷ a member of a race of people who have dark skin

blacken *v.* ❶ make sth. black, or to become black ❷ damage a person's reputation

blacklist *n.* a list of people who are disapproved of

blackmail *n.* an attempt to obtain money from a person by a threat to reveal information that will disgrace him

blade *n.* ❶ the flat cutting part of a knife, sword, or other cutting tool or weapon ❷ a long flat leaf of grass or grass-like plants such as wheat

blame Ⅰ *v.* find fault with; say or think that sth. bad or wrong is caused by Ⅱ *n.* saying that sb. is responsible for sth.; responsibility for doing sth. badly

blameless *adj.* deserving no blame, innocent

bland *adj.* ❶ without anything to attract attention ❷ (of food) smooth and easily digested and usually without much taste

blank Ⅰ *adj.* ❶ with nothing written, printed or drawn on it ❷ without feeling, interest or expression Ⅱ *n.* space left empty or to be filled

blast Ⅰ *n.* ❶ a strong, sudden rush of wind ❷ a sound made by a wind-instrument ❸ an explosion Ⅱ *v.* blow up with explosives

blaze Ⅰ *n.* bright flames in a fire Ⅱ *v.* burn with bright flame; shine brightly and warmly

bleach Ⅰ *v.* cause to become white or pale, especially by means of chemicals or by the action of sunlight Ⅱ *n.* a chemical used in bleaching

bleak *adj.* ❶ exposed to cold winds ❷ with very little hope of happiness ❸ unhappy and unfriendly

bleed *v.* ❶ lose blood as a result of injury or illness ❷ feel great distress ❸ force (sb.) to pay money unjustly

blemish Ⅰ *v.* spoil the appearance of sth. Ⅱ *n.* a mark, etc., that spoils the beauty or perfection of sb. or sth.

blend Ⅰ *v.* ❶ mix two or more substances together ❷ go well together Ⅱ *n.* a mixture of different things or people

bless *v.* ask God's favour for; wish happiness or favour to

blessing *n.* ❶ prayer for God's favour; thanks to God before or after a meal ❷ anything that brings happiness or good fortune

blight Ⅰ *n.* anything which spoils one's hopes, plans, etc. Ⅱ *v.* damage or spoil

blind *adj.* ❶ without the power to see ❷

reckless; thoughtless

B

blink Ⅰ *v.* ❶ shut and open the eyes quickly ❷ (of lights) shine in an unsteady way Ⅱ *n.* ❶ an act of blinking ❷ a sudden quick gleam of light

bliss *n.* perfect happiness; great joy

blissful *adj.* ❶ extremely happy; full of joy ❷ providing perfect happiness or great joy

blithe *adj.* happy and cheerful; not anxious

blizzard *n.* a snowstorm with a strong wind

bloat *v.* ❶ cause to swell with fluid or gas ❷ become swollen with fluid or gas

block Ⅰ *n.* ❶ any large, solid piece of wood, stone, etc. ❷ a large building divided into separate parts ❸ the area or building surrounded by four streets in a town ❹ obstruction; sth. that makes movement of flow difficult or impossible Ⅱ *v.* make movement impossible on or through sth.

blockage *n.* sth. that blocks a pipe, tube, tunnel, etc.

blood *n.* ❶ the red liquid flowing throughout the body of man and the higher animals ❷ the family origin or descent

bloody *adj.* ❶ covered with blood ❷ with much bloodshed; cruel

bloom Ⅰ *n.* ❶ a flower, especially of plants admired chiefly for their flowers ❷ the greatest beauty or perfection Ⅱ *v.* be in flower; bear flowers

blossom Ⅰ *n.* ❶ flowers, especially of a fruit tree ❷ the condition or time of flowering Ⅱ *v.* ❶ produce flowers ❷ develop

blot Ⅰ *n.* a mark caused by ink spilt on paper Ⅱ *v.* ❶ make a blot or blots on (paper with ink)

blow Ⅰ *v.* ❶ (of the wind) move along; move sth. quickly and strongly in the air ❷ send air out of the mouth Ⅱ *n.* ❶ a sudden hard hit or shock ❷ a shock or disaster that is upsetting, disapproving or damaging to sb.

blue Ⅰ *adj.* ❶ having the colour of the clear sky or the deep sea ❷ sad and gloomy; depressed or depressing Ⅱ *n.* ❶ blue colour ❷ the sky or the sea

blueprint *n.* ❶ a design plan or technical drawing ❷ a detailed plan or scheme

blues *n.* ❶ a slow sad jazz song or tune, of black American folk origin ❷ (the ～) the feelings of sadness or depression bluntly

blur Ⅰ *v.* make difficult to see sth. clearly Ⅱ *n.* ❶ a dirty spot or mark; a smear of ink ❷ sth. that cannot be clearly seen

bluster *v.* complain or threaten in a noisy way

board Ⅰ *n.* ❶ a long thin flat piece of wood or other hard material, typically used for floors or other building purposes ❷ a flat piece of wood or other material used for a special purpose ❸ a group of people who control sth.; a committee; a council Ⅱ *v.* ❶ cover up with boards ❷ get on or into a ship (a plane, car, etc.)

boast Ⅰ *v.* talk too much of oneself; praise oneself too much Ⅱ *n.* talking with self-satisfaction about sth.

bodily Ⅰ *adj.* to do with the human

body or physical nature bodily Ⅱ *adv.* by moving the whole of sb.'s body; by force

body *n.* ❶ the whole material part of a man or animal; the main part of a man or animal without the head, arms and legs ❷ the dead body ❸ a group of persons who do sth. together

bog Ⅰ *n.* the land which is wet and soft Ⅱ *v.* (be ～ged down) be unable to move forward as though in a bog

boil Ⅰ *v.* ❶ (of a liquid or the vessel containing it) reach the temperature at which liquid changes into a gas ❷ cause (a liquid or the vessel containing it) to reach this temperature ❸ be very angry about sth. Ⅱ *n.* ❶ a certain temperature at which a kind of liquid is boiled ❷ the process of heating a liquid to the temperature

boiling *adj.* very hot

bold *adj.* ❶ daring; courageous; adventurous ❷ in thick strokes

bolt Ⅰ *n.* ❶ a metal fastening for a door or window ❷ a screw with no point, which fastens through a piece of metal to hold things together Ⅱ *v.* fasten with a bolt or bolts

bomb Ⅰ *n.* a hollow metal ball or shell filled with gunpowder or some other explosive Ⅱ *v.* attack with bombs

bond *n.* ❶ sth. that unites two or more people or groups, such as a shared feeling or interest ❷ an agreement or engagement that a person is bound to observe, especially one that has force in law; a document, signed and sealed, containing such an agreement ❸ a piece of printed paper issued by a government or a corporation acknowledging that money has been lent to it and will be paid back with interest

bondage *n.* slavery or captivity

bone *n.* the hard white material in the body of a person or animal

bonfire *n.* fire made in the open air

bonny *adj.* healthy looking; with a glow of health

bonus *n.* an additional payment beyond what is usual, necessary, or expected, such as a share of profits paid to those who hold shares in or work for a business or are insured with an insurance company

bony *adj.* ❶ of or like bone ❷ (a person or part of the body) so thin that the bones can be seen

book Ⅰ *n.* ❶ the printed pages attached together with a cover ❷ a number of things fastened together like a book Ⅱ *v.* buy or arrange to have tickets, rooms, etc.

boom Ⅰ *n.* ❶ a sudden increase in trade and economic activity, etc. ❷ a period when sth. such as a sport or a type of music suddenly becomes very popular and successful ❸ a loud deep sound Ⅱ *v.* ❶ make a loud deep sound ❷ become bigger, more successful, etc.

boon *n.* advantage; help

boost Ⅰ *v.* ❶ speak favourably of or advertise sth., especially in order to persuade people to buy it ❷ push forward or upwards ❸ increase the power or speed of Ⅱ *n.* ❶ acceleration or promotion ❷ increase or improvement

border Ⅰ *n.* ❶a strip around the edge of sth. ❷the line dividing two states or countries Ⅱ *v.* be near to another country or region

borderline *n.* ❶ a boundary separating two countries or areas ❷ a division between two distinct or opposite things

bore Ⅰ *v.* make sb. feel tired by being dull and uninteresting Ⅱ *n.* a person or thing that is dull and uninteresting

boredom *n.* the state of feeling bored; the quality of being very boring

boring *adj.* dull and uninteresting

born *adj.* ❶existing as a result of birth ❷destined to be

borrow *v.* ❶get or use sth. with intent to return it ❷ adopt and use sth. as one's own

bosom *n.* ❶ a woman's breast ❷ the centre or inmost part, where one feels joy or sorrow

boss Ⅰ *n.* a master; a person who controls or gives orders to workmen Ⅱ *v.* give orders to

bossy *adj.* too fond of giving orders

both *pron.* used for emphasis to refer two people or things, regarded and identified together

bother Ⅰ *v.* ❶disturb; cause trouble to ❷worry; take trouble; be anxious Ⅱ *n.* worry or trouble; sth. or sb. that carries trouble

bottle Ⅰ *n.* a container with a narrow neck Ⅱ *v.* put a liquid into a bottle

bottom *n.* ❶the lowest part of anything; the under part ❷the last part; end ❸ the part of the body on which a person sits

bottomless *adj.* without a bottom, extremely deep

bounce *v.* spring or jump back after striking sth. hard; move up and down

bound[1] *adj.* ❶intending to go(to); going (to) ❷ be certain or sure that sth. will happen

bound[2] *n.* a boundary; a limitation or restriction on feeling or action

boundary *n.* a line that marks a limit; a dividing line

boundless *adj.* without limits

bouquet *n.* ❶a bunch of flowers ❷words of praise

bout *n.* a period of exercise, work, or other activity

bow Ⅰ *v.* ❶bend the head or body ❷ submit or yield to another's wish or opinion Ⅱ *n.* an act of bending forward the head or the upper part of the body, especially to show respect

bowel *n.* ❶ the part of the alimentary canal below the stomach ❷(～s) the innermost part

bowl *n.* a deep round container for holding sth.

box[1] *n.* a container, usually with a lid, made of wood, cardboard, or metal, used for holding solids

box[2] Ⅰ *v.* give sb. a blow with the open hand on ears; fight with fists, usually with thick gloves for sport Ⅱ *n.* a blow with the open hand (on the ear)

boy *n.* a male child or a young male person

boycott Ⅰ *v.* join with others and refuse to have anything to do with or to trade with; refuse to handle Ⅱ *n.* a refusal to deal with (a firm, etc.)

boyish *adj.* like a boy

brace Ⅰ *n.* a piece of metal, wood etc. used to hold things together Ⅱ *v.* give support or strength

bracing *adj.* (especially of air) fresh and health-giving

bracket *n.* a structure of metal, wood, or plastic, often in the shape of a right angle, fixed to a wall to support sth., such as a shelf or lamp

brag *v.* talk too proudly about oneself or one's possessions, etc.; boast

braid *n.* ❶ a narrow piece of material made by twisting several strands or pieces together; pieces of hair twisted together ❷the material of this type put along the edges of clothing or used as decoration on clothing

brain *n.* ❶the part inside the head of a person or animal, which thinks and feels; the centre of the nervous system ❷ the ability to think clearly, quickly and well; intelligence

braise *v.* cook slowly in a container with a lid on, using very little water

brake Ⅰ *n.* an apparatus for slowing or lessening movement and bringing to stop Ⅱ *v.* cause to slow down by using a brake

branch Ⅰ *n.* ❶an arm-like part of a tree growing out from the trunk ❷a division or subdivision of a firm or an organization ❸a smaller part from the main part, especially from the road, river or railway Ⅱ *v.* send out; divide

brand *n.* ❶a trademark; a particular kind of goods with such a mark ❷an iron, used red-hot for burning a mark into a surface; a mark made in this way

B

brave Ⅰ *adj.* without fear; having courage; ready to face danger, pain or suffering Ⅱ *v.* have the courage to deal with some difficult things to gain sth.

bravery *n.* courage; the quality of being brave

brawl Ⅰ *n.* a noisy fight or quarrel, often in a public place Ⅱ *v.* fight or quarrel in this way

breach Ⅰ *n.* ❶an act of breaking the law or failing to do what one has promised to do ❷ a gap or opening made by breaking down part of a wall, etc. Ⅱ *v.* ❶make a gap or opening in a wall, etc. ❷not to keep an agreement or promise or fail to comply with rules, laws, etc.

break Ⅰ *v.* ❶ cause to separate into pieces by force; go or come into pieces ❷fail to observe ❸interrupt ❹beat the previous record for a particular achievement Ⅱ *n.* ❶ an opening between two or more things ❷a place where sth. especially a bone has broken ❸a short time when one stops doing sth.; a short rest from work

breakage *n.* ❶ an act of breaking ❷ a broken place or part ❸broken articles

breakdown *n.* ❶a failure in machinery, etc. ❷collapse; weakening

break-in *n.* an illegal forced entry into a building or car, typically to steal sth.

breakout *n.* a forcible escape, typically from prison

breakthrough *n.* a sudden and important discovery or development, especially in science

B

break-up *n.* ❶ an end to a relationship, typically a marriage ❷ a division of a country or organization into smaller autonomous units

breath *n.* ❶air taken into and sent out of lungs ❷life

breathe *v.* ❶take air into your lungs and send it out again ❷ send air, smoke, etc. out of your mouth ❸(of material on soil) admit or emit air or moisture

breathing *n.* the process of taking air into and expelling it from the lungs

breathless *adj.* ❶out of breath, panting ❷holding your breath with excitement

breed Ⅰ *v.* ❶ give birth to young; reproduce ❷keep(animals, etc.) for the purpose of producing young, especially in a controlled way ❸educate, bring up Ⅱ *n.* a kind or type of a thing or person

breeze *n.* a light gentle wind

brew *v.* ❶ make beer; make (tea or coffee) with hot water and prepare for drinking ❷be in preparation or ready to happen; develop

bribe Ⅰ *n.* sth. given, offered, or promised to sb. in order to get him to do sth. in favour of the giver Ⅱ *v.* offer, give a bribe to

brick Ⅰ *n.* a clay moulded and baked by fire or sun, used for building purposes Ⅱ *v.* fill in, block or seal an opening with bricks

bridge Ⅰ *n.* a structure of wood, stone, steel, concrete, etc. carrying a road across a river, canal, railway, etc. Ⅱ *v.* build or form a bridge over sth.

brief Ⅰ *adj.* lasting only for a short time Ⅱ *n.* a summary of the facts of the legal case prepared for a barrister Ⅲ *v.* give essential information

bright *adj.* ❶ giving out or reflecting much light; shining ❷ having a vivid colour ❸cheerful and happy; lit up with joy and hope ❹clever, quick-witted

brighten *v.* (cause to) grow brighter or brighter

brilliant *adj.* ❶ very bright; splendid; magnificent ❷ very clever; outstanding; remarkable

brim *n.* the edge of a cup, bowl, glass, etc.

bring *v.* ❶ come with sth. or sb. from somewhere else; cause(sb. or sth.) to be where the speaker is ❷ make sth. happen; cause to come

brisk *adj.* (of persons and movement) active; lively; quick-moving

bristle Ⅰ *n.* a short stiff coarse hair Ⅱ *v.* ❶ (of hair) stand up ❷ react in an offended or angry manner

broad *adj.* ❶ wide; having a large distance from side to side ❷including a great variety of people or things ❸ general; without detail ❹ large in area ❺clear or obvious

broadcast Ⅰ *v.* send out or give as a radio(or television) presentation Ⅱ *n.* an act of sending sound and/or pictures by radio or television

broaden *v.* make or become broad or broader

brochure *n.* a small thin book, especially one giving instructions or details of a service offered for money

broil *v.* cook meat by using direct heat

broken *adj.* ❶ violently separated into parts or pieces ❷ interrupted; disconnected ❸ damaged; not in working condition ❹ (of an agreement or promise) not kept or be breached

broker *n.* a person who acts for other people in buying and selling shares in business

bronze Ⅰ *n.* ❶alloy of copper and tin ❷ a colour of bronze Ⅱ *adj.* made of or having the colour of bronze

brook *n.* a small stream

broth *n.* soup, especially one made with meat

brotherly *adj.* ❶of or like a brother ❷ friendly; kind

brown Ⅰ *adj.* having the colour of earth Ⅱ *n.* the color of earth Ⅲ *v.* (cause sth. to) become brown

browse Ⅰ *v.* ❶(of cows, goats, etc.) feed by nibbling grass, leaves, etc. ❷ examine books in a casual, leisurely way ❸search for information on computer, typically via Internet Ⅱ *n.* ❶the act of feeding by continual nibbling grass, leaves, etc. ❷ the act of reading superficially

bruise Ⅰ *n.* ❶ an injury to the body caused by a fall or a blow which does not break the skin ❷an injury to the outside of a fruit, vegetable, or plant Ⅱ *v.* cause an injury or hurt

brush Ⅰ *n.* a tool for cleaning, smoothing or painting, made of sticks, stiff hair, nylon, etc. Ⅱ *v.* clean or smooth with a brush

brutal *adj.* cruel and violent

brutish *adj.* resembling or characteristic of a brute

bubble Ⅰ *n.* a hollow ball of liquid containing air or gas Ⅱ *v.* send up bubbles; rise in bubbles; make the sound of bubbles

bucket *n.* ❶a type of container for liquids ❷the amount of a bucket contains

bud Ⅰ *n.* a leaf, flower, or branch, at the beginning of its growth Ⅱ *v.* put out buds

budget Ⅰ *n.* an estimate of probable future income and expenditure Ⅱ *v.* plan to save money for

buffer Ⅰ *n.* a thing or person which acts in the same way Ⅱ *v.* lesson or reduce the effect of sth.

buffet[1] *n.* ❶ a meal where guests serve themselves ❷a room or counter selling light meals or snacks

buffet[2] *v.* hit or knock sth. violently

build Ⅰ *v.* ❶ make by putting parts, material, etc. together ❷ create or develop sth. Ⅱ *n.* the shape and size of the human body

building *n.* a house or other structure

built-in *adj.* ❶forming an integral part of a structure ❷ (of a characteristic) inherent; innate

bulb *n.* ❶a round root of certain plants ❷any object of this shape, especially the glass part of an electric lamp that gives out light

bulk *n.* a great size, shape, mass or quantity

bulletin *n.* an official statement of news

bullish *adj.* ❶ feeling confident and positive about the future ❷causing, or connected with an increase in the price of shares

B

bully Ⅰ *n.* a person who uses his strength or power to frighten or hurt those who are weak Ⅱ *v.* use strength, etc., in this way

bump Ⅰ *v.* hurt (one's head, etc.) by striking it against or on sth. Ⅱ *n.* ❶ a blow or knock ❷ a swelling on the body caused by such a blow

bumper Ⅰ *n.* a very full cup or glass Ⅱ *adj.* usually large or abundant

bumpy *adj.* full of bumps; causing jolts

bunch Ⅰ *n.* ❶ a number of things of the same kind fastened or growing together ❷ a group Ⅱ *v.* come or bring together into a bunch or bunches

bundle *n.* a number of articles fastened, tied, or wrapped together

bungle *v.* do sth. or make sth. very badly

buoy Ⅰ *n.* an object which floats in the water, placed there to show hidden dangers to ships Ⅱ *v.* keep afloat; keep up

buoyancy *n.* the power to float or keep things floating

buoyant *adj.* ❶ able to float ❷ cheerful and optimistic

burden Ⅰ *n.* sth. to be carried; sth. difficult to bear Ⅱ *v.* load or trouble

bureau *n.* ❶ a government or municipal department or office ❷ a chest of drawers for clothes

burglar *n.* a person who breaks into a house or building by night to steal or commit some other crime

burial *n.* the act, action, or ceremony of putting a dead body into a grave

burn Ⅰ *v.* ❶ produce light ❷ destroy, damage, or hurt by fire, heat, or the action of acid ❸ be on fire or alight; be in flames Ⅱ *n.* an injury or a mark, made by fire, heat or acid

burning *adj.* ❶ intense or extreme ❷ hotly discussed; vital

burrow Ⅰ *n.* a hole made in the ground and used as a home or shelter by rabbits, foxes, etc. Ⅱ *v.* make (a hole, etc.) by digging

bury *v.* put into the grave; hide sth. in the ground

bush *n.* a low-growing plant with several or many woody stems coming up from the root

business *n.* ❶ one's work or employment ❷ a particular money earning activity or place, such as a shop ❸ work; duty; task

bustle Ⅰ *v.* (cause to) move about quickly and noisily Ⅱ *n.* quick and noisy movement

busy Ⅰ *adj.* ❶ having a great deal to do; not free ❷ full of people or activity ❸ in use; engaged Ⅱ *v.* make oneself not free

but Ⅰ *conj.* ❶ against what might be expected; in spite of this ❷ without it being the case that Ⅱ *prep.* other than; except Ⅲ *adv.* only; no more than

butcher Ⅰ *n.* a person who kills, cuts up and sells animals for food Ⅱ *v.* kill violently, especially with a knife

buttock *n.* either side of that part of the body on which one sits

button Ⅰ *n.* ❶ a knob or round piece sewn onto clothing or other things used for fastening two parts together or decorating ❷ a button-like object used for controlling a machine, an apparatus, etc. or used as a handle or catch, either to take hold of, or to push, or to turn Ⅱ *v.* fasten with a button or buttons

buy *v.* ❶obtain sth. by paying money for it ❷ be enough to pay for sth. ❸ persuade sb. to do sth. dishonest in return for money ❹ obtain sth. by losing sth. else of great value

buzz Ⅰ *n.* the noise made by bees Ⅱ *v.* make such a noise as bees do

by Ⅰ *prep.* ❶near; at or to the side of ❷past and beyond ❸through the use or means of ❹ not later than; before ❺ during Ⅱ *adv.* ❶ near ❷ so as to go past

bypass Ⅰ *n.* a road providing a secondary passage to be used instead of the main passage Ⅱ *v.* go around

by-product *n.* ❶ sth. formed in addition to the main product ❷ a secondary result; a side effect

by-road *n.* a side road; a road that is not much used

bystander *n.* a person standing near, but not taking part in it when sth. happens

byway *n.* ❶a smaller road or path which is not much used or known ❷ less important or well-known parts of a subject

byword *n.* ❶the name of a person, place, or thing that is taken as representing some quality, often bad ❷ a common saying or expression

B

C

C c

cabin *n.* ❶ a small wooden house ❷ a room on a ship or aeroplane

cabinet *n.* ❶ a group of chosen members of a government, which is responsible for advising and deciding on government policy ❷ a cupboard

cable Ⅰ *n.* ❶ a thick heavy metal rope used on ships ❷ a set of wires that carries electricity, telephone signals, etc. ❸ a message sent by electrical signals Ⅱ *v.* send (a message) by cable

cadre *n.* ❶ a framework ❷ a highly trained and active member of political party or military force

cafe *n.* a small restaurant where light meals and drinks are served

cage *n.* ❶ a prison for animals or birds, made of wire, strong iron bars, or wood ❷ an open frame work forming the compartment in a lift

calamity *n.* great and serious misfortune or disaster (e. g. a big earthquake or flood)

calculable *adj.* able to be calculated or assessed

calculate *v.* ❶ find out by working with numbers; compute ❷ estimate

calculating *adj.* making careful plans with the intention of bringing advantage to oneself, without considering the effects on other people

calculation *n.* ❶ the act or result of calculating ❷ care in planning, especially for one's own advantage

calendar *n.* ❶ a page or series of pages showing the days, weeks, months, of a particular year ❷ a list of important dates or events

call Ⅰ *v.* ❶ speak to sb. in a loud clear voice ❷ make a short visit ❸ telephone sb. Ⅱ *n.* ❶ a shout or cry ❷ a short visit ❸ an attempt to ring someone on the telephone

calling *n.* ❶ a strong urge of feeling of duty to do a particular kind of work; vocation ❷ a person's profession or trade

callow *adj.* (of a person or behaviour) young and without experience; immature

calm Ⅰ *adj.* ❶ (of weather) not windy; (of sea) still ❷ quiet, not excited; not showing fear, etc. Ⅱ *v.* make sb. or sth. become quiet and relaxed

camp Ⅰ *n.* a place where people live for a time in tents or huts Ⅱ *v.* live in a tent

campaign Ⅰ *n.* ❶ military operations, usually in one area ❷ a planned course of action towards a special object Ⅱ *v.*

take part in or go on a campaign

can[1] *v.* ❶ be able to ❷ know how to ❸ have permission to; be allowed to

can[2] Ⅰ *n.* ❶ a round metal container for holding milk, coffee, oil, etc. ❷ contents of such a container Ⅱ *v.* preserve by putting up in airtight containers

canal *n.* a waterway dug across land for ships or small boats to go through

canard *n.* a false report or piece of news

cancel *v.* give up; call off

candid *adj.* open, honest, and sincere in manner; directly truthful, even when telling the truth is unwelcome

candidate *n.* ❶ a person who wishes, or who is put forward by others, to take an office or position ❷ a person taking an examination

canon *n.* ❶ a Church decree or law ❷ a general standard or principle by which sth. is judged

canvas *n.* ❶ a strong, coarse cloth used for tents, sails, bags, etc. and by artists for oil paintings ❷ an oil painting

canyon *n.* a deep, narrow valley with sides like cliffs

cap Ⅰ *n.* a sort of soft hat without a brim, but with a peak Ⅱ *v.* put a cap on; cover the top of

capability *n.* ❶ the power of doing things; fitness or capacity ❷ undeveloped faculties

capable *adj.* ❶ gifted; able ❷ skilful and effective, especially in practical matters ❸ open to or admitting of sth.

capacious *adj.* having a lot of space inside

capacity *n.* ❶ the ability to do things well; the power of holding knowledge and ideas ❷ the amount that a container can hold

capital Ⅰ *n.* ❶ a town or city where the government of a country, state or county is carried on ❷ a letter of the form and size that is used to begin sentences and names ❸ wealth; a valuable resource of a particular kind Ⅱ *adj.* ❶ (of a letter) written or printed in the form and size used to begin sentences and names ❷ punishable by death ❸ first-rate; excellent

capsule *n.* a tiny soluble container for a dose of medicine

captain *n.* ❶ the leader of a group of people, especially a sports team ❷ the chief person on a ship or airplane ❸ an officer of fairly high rank in the army or navy or air force

caption *n.* a short title or heading of an article in a periodical, etc.; words printed with a photograph or illustration, etc.; words on a movie film to explain the story

captious *adj.* fond of finding fault, making protests, especially about unimportant points

captivate *v.* capture the fancy of; fascinate

captive Ⅰ *n.* a person or animal that is caught Ⅱ *adj.* ❶ taken or kept as a prisoner ❷ charmed

capture Ⅰ *v.* ❶ catch, take or seize sb. or sth. by force, skill, trickery, etc. ❷ take control of sth. by force from an enemy; win; gain Ⅱ *n.* ❶ an act of seizing or taking ❷ an animal, a person or thing caught or taken

C

carcass *n.* ❶the body of a dead animal, especially one which is ready to be cut up as meat ❷the decaying remains of sth. , such as a car or a ship ❸the body of a dead or living person

card *n.* ❶a playing card ❷a piece of stiff paper or thin cardboard, as used for various purposes

cardinal *adj.* chief; most important; on which sth. depends

care Ⅰ *v.* ❶feel interest, worry, or sorry etc. ; show concern ❷be willing to ❸ look after ❹ like Ⅱ *n.* ❶ serious attention ❷ protection; charge ❸ a feeling of worry or anxiety; sth. that causes problems or anxiety

career *n.* ❶ the series of jobs that a person has in a particular area ❷ profession; occupation

carefree *adj.* free from anxiety or responsibility

careful *adj.* ❶taking care; cautious ❷ showing attention to details; thorough

careless *adj.* ❶not careful ❷free from care or worry; unconcerned

caress Ⅰ *n.* a loving touch or stroke Ⅱ *v.* touch or stroke someone lovingly

cargo *n.* sth. carried on a ship or in an aeroplane

caring *adj.* providing care and support, especially to people who need to be looked after

carnivore *n.* an animal that feeds on the flesh of other animals

carnivorous *adj.* eating meat

carriage *n.* ❶ a four-wheeled vehicle drawn by horses ❷a part of a train; a railway coach

carry *v.* ❶support the weight of sb. or sth. and take them or it from place to place ❷have sth. with you and take it wherever you go ❸contain and direct the flow of water, electricity, etc. ❹be infected with diseases ❺ support the weight of sth.

cart *n.* ❶a two-wheeled vehicle pulled by a horse, used to carry goods ❷a two-wheeled vehicle pulled or pushed by hand, used to carry goods

cartoon *n.* ❶a drawing in a newspaper or magazine that usually makes fun of a person or event ❷ a film using animation techniques to photograph a sequence of drawings

carve *v.* ❶make sth. by cutting ❷cut (cooked meat) into pieces

carving *n.* a carved object or design

case[1] *n.* ❶ an instance of a particular situation; condition ❷ an example of disease; a person having a disease ❸a special example, question to be decided in a law court

case[2] *n.* a container designed to hold or protect sth.

cash Ⅰ *n.* money in coins or notes Ⅱ *v.* exchange (a cheque or other order to pay) for the amount of money that it is worth

cashier *n.* a person employed to receive and pay out money in a bank or to receive payments in a shop or business

cast *v.* ❶throw or drop ❷assign a part to(an actor); assign an actor to(a part) ❸give a vote ❹pour(liquid metal) into a mould ❺throw off; remove; get rid of

castle *n.* a building or group of buildings

with thick walls and towers

casual Ⅰ *adj.* ❶happening by chance ❷ informal; careless ❸ not permanent Ⅱ *n.* ❶ informal shoes or clothes ❷ a worker working temporarily

casualty *n.* an accident, especially one involving loss of life

catalog(ue) Ⅰ *n.* a list of names, places, etc. in a special order Ⅱ *v.* make a systematic list of

catastrophe *n.* a sudden happening that causes great suffering, misfortune, or ruin

catch *v.* ❶stop and hold a moving object ❷take hold of sb. or sth. ❸capture a person or an animal ❹find or discover sb. doing sth. , especially sth. wrong ❺ to be in time to do sth. or for a bus, train, plane, etc. ❻happen unexpectedly

catching *adj.* ❶(of a disease) infectious ❷(of an emotion or a mood) passing quickly from one person to another

categorize *v.* put sth. in a category; classify

category *n.* a class or division of people or things with particular features in common

cater *v.* ❶supply food ❷(～ to) try to satisfy a particular need or demand

cattle *n.* cows, bulls or oxen

causal *adj.* having or showing the relationship of cause and effect

causation *n.* the relationship of cause and effect; causality

cause Ⅰ *n.* ❶ a person or thing that makes sth. happen ❷ a reason ❸ an organization or idea for which efforts are being made Ⅱ*v.* ❶make sth. happen, especially sth. bad or unpleasant ❷ lead to; be the cause of

caustic *adj.* ❶ able to burn or destroy living flesh ❷sharp; bitter; cutting

caution Ⅰ *n.* ❶ care taken to avoid danger or mistakes; paying attention ❷ warning words Ⅱ *v.* warn sb. about sth.

cautious *adj.* being careful to avoid danger or mistakes

cave Ⅰ *n.* a hollow space under the ground, especially one with an opening in the side of a hill Ⅱ *v.* (cause to) fall down and towards the centre

cavernous *adj.* large and dark, like a cavern

cavity *n.* an empty space or small hole within a solid body

cease *v.* stop happening or existing

ceaseless *adj.* not ceasing, continuing constantly

celebrate *v.* ❶do sth. to show that a day or an event is special and important ❷ praise sb. or sth.

celebrated *adj.* famous; well known

celebration *n.* a special event organized to celebrate sth.

celebrity *n.* ❶the state of being famous ❷a famous person

celestial *adj.* of the sky; of heaven

cell *n.* ❶ a very small piece of living substance, of which all plants and animals are made up ❷a small room in which a prisoner lives ❸an apparatus for making a current of electricity by chemical action

cellular *adj.* ❶ to do with cells; composed of cells ❷ (said about a fabric) woven with an open mesh that traps air and provides insulation

cement Ⅰ *n.* ❶ a powdery substance which becomes very hard when mixed with water, used for building ❷ sth. that unites people together for a common goal Ⅱ *v.* ❶ join or fill two things together with cement, glue, etc. ❷ join or fasten a relationship, an agreement, etc. firmly

censor Ⅰ *n.* an official who examines books, plays, etc. and cuts out any parts that are considered to be immoral Ⅱ *v.* examine and act upon as a censor

centenary Ⅰ *adj.* of a period of 100 years Ⅱ *n.* a period of 100 years; the 100th anniversary

central *adj.* ❶ in or at the centre or middle point; near or from the centre ❷ principal; chief

centralize *v.* concentrate power or control in one central authority

centre(-er) Ⅰ *n.* ❶ the middle point or part of sth. ❷ a place where a specified activity is concentrated Ⅱ *v.* ❶ place or be placed in the middle; bring to or come to one point ❷ have sth. as a main subject or area of concern

century *n.* a hundred years; one of the periods of 100 years before or after the birth of Jesus Christ

cereal *n.* any grain crop used as food (e.g. wheat, corn, rice)

ceremonial *adj.* formal, as used for ceremonies

ceremony *n.* ❶ an act or a series of acts that includes formal or traditional actions ❷ formal behaviour

certain *adj.* ❶ specific but not named ❷ having no doubt; sure ❸ sure to come or happen

certainly *adv.* ❶ without doubt; surely ❷ (used in answer to questions) yes; of course

certainty *n.* ❶ a thing that is certain; an assured fact ❷ the state of being certain

certificate *n.* a written official document that may be used to prove a certain fact

certify *v.* declare that sth. is true

cession *n.* the act of ceding or giving up land, property, or rights

chafe *v.* make (a part of the body) sore by rubbing against it

chain *n.* ❶ a row of metal rings joins together ❷ a series of connected things, events, etc.

chairman *n.* ❶ the person in charge of a meeting ❷ the person in charge of a committee or company

challenge Ⅰ *v.* ❶ invite sb. to enter a fight, competition, game, etc. ❷ question or dispute the truth or validity of sth. ❸ test the abilities of (a person or things) Ⅱ *n.* an invitation to a game or contest; a call to a fight

challenging *adj.* needing the full use of one's abilities and effort; difficult, but in an interesting way

chamber *n.* a room, especially a bedroom

champion Ⅰ *n.* ❶ a person or team that wins a game, a race, etc.; the best of all the players at a certain competition ❷ a person who fights for or is in support of a belief Ⅱ *v.* fight for or speak in support of a belief

chance Ⅰ *n.* ❶ a suitable time or situation when you have an opportunity to do sth. ❷ a possibility of sth. happening ❸ the unplanned and unexpected course of events regarded as a power Ⅱ *v.* ❶ take place or meet by chance ❷ take a risk

change Ⅰ *v.* ❶ become or make different ❷ give or take one thing for another; exchange ❸ leave and enter (different vehicles) in order to continue a journey Ⅱ *n.* ❶ the act or result through which sth. becomes different ❷ the money given in exchange for the same sum in larger units

changeable *adj.* ❶ able to be changed ❷ changing frequently; unpredictable

channel *n.* ❶ a narrow passage of sea, etc. ❷ a frequency band for radio ❸ a medium for communication or the passage of information

chant Ⅰ *n.* an often repeated tune to which psalms and canticles are fitted; several words to one note Ⅱ *v.* sing a chant; use a singing note (e. g. for a prayer in Church)

chaos *n.* the state of complete disorder and confusion

chaotic *adj.* in a state of complete disorder and confusion

chapter *n.* a main division of a book

character *n.* ❶ the qualities which make a person different from another ❷ a person in a book, play, etc. ❸ a letter, sign, mark, etc. used in a system of writing or printing ❹ the particular features of sth.

characteristic Ⅰ *adj.* typical of a particular person, place or thing Ⅱ *n.* a special feature or quality

characterize *v.* ❶ be characteristic of ❷ describe the character of; portray

charge Ⅰ *v.* ❶ ask a price for sth. ❷ accuse sb. of sth. Ⅱ *n.* ❶ a price asked for goods or service ❷ work given to sb. as a duty; a thing or a person given or entrusted to sb. to be taken care of ❸ an accusation that a person has done wrong, especially that he has broken a law

charitable *adj.* ❶ kind and generous, especially in giving help to the poor ❷ kind and sympathetic in judging others ❸ concerned with giving help to people who are poor or in need

charity *n.* ❶ help to the poor, the sick or anyone in need; love, kindness to others ❷ a society or organization for helping people in need

charm Ⅰ *n.* ❶ the power of pleasing or attracting people ❷ words or things that are said to be magic Ⅱ *v.* ❶ attract to get sth. or influence sb. ❷ control or get sth. by using magic or as if by magic

charming *adj.* pleasing or attractive

chart Ⅰ *n.* an outline map giving special information Ⅱ *v.* make a map

charter Ⅰ *n.* a written statement by some authority, giving sb. the power to do sth. Ⅱ *v.* hire a bus, plane, train, etc. for a special purpose

chase *v.* ❶ run after, try to catch up with ❷ drive away

chat Ⅰ *v.* have a friendly talk Ⅱ *n.* a friendly talk about unimportant things

cheap *adj.* ❶ low in price; costing little money ❷ of poor quality; worthless

cheapen *v.* ❶ make sth. cheap, or become

cheap ❷ make sth. appear to have less value

cheat Ⅰ *v.* ❶ be unfair or dishonest in order to get sth.; play tricks; act dishonestly ❷ behave in a dishonest or deceitful way in order to win an advantage, especially in a game or an exam Ⅱ *n.* a person who cheats; a dishonest person

check Ⅰ *v.* ❶ test or examine sth. in order to determine its accuracy, quality or condition ❷ hold back, cause to go slow or stop the progress of sth. Ⅱ *n.* ❶ an examination to make certain of accuracy, quality, or condition ❷ a means of control or restraint

check-in *n.* ❶ the place where you go first when you arrive at an airport, to show your ticket, etc. ❷ the act of showing your ticket, etc. when you arrive at an airport

checklist *n.* a list of items required, things to be done, or points to be considered, used as a reminder

checkout *n.* ❶ a place where customers pay for goods in a supermarket ❷ the administrative procedure followed when a guest leaves a hotel at the end of their stay

cheer Ⅰ *v.* ❶ make or become happy ❷ shout to show that you are pleased with sb. or sth. Ⅱ *n.* ❶ a shout of happiness or encouragement ❷ optimism or confidence

cheerful *adj.* ❶ full of cheer; glad ❷ bringing cheer pleasant; bright

chemical Ⅰ *adj.* of, used in, or made by chemistry Ⅱ *n.* a substance used in or made by chemical process

cherish *v.* ❶ care for sth. tenderly; love ❷ keep hope, love, or other deep feelings firmly in mind

chest *n.* ❶ the upper front part of the body, where the ribs, lungs and hearts are ❷ a large, heavy box used for storing things

chew *v.* crush and grind food into little bits in one's mouth

chief Ⅰ *n.* a leader or ruler of a people or community Ⅱ *adj.* ❶ main; most important ❷ first in rank

chiefly *adv.* ❶ mainly; mostly ❷ above all

childbirth *n.* the action of giving a birth to a baby

childhood *n.* the period of being a child

childish *adj.* of, behaving like, suitable for a child; immature

chill Ⅰ *n.* an unpleasant feeling of coldness Ⅱ *v.* make or become cold

chilly *adj.* ❶ slightly or unpleasantly cold ❷ (said about a person or manner) aloof and unfriendly

chin *n.* the part of the face below the mouth

chink *n.* (especially in a wall or door) a narrow opening or crack

chip Ⅰ *n.* ❶ a small piece cut or broken off from wood, stone, china, etc. ❷ a thin piece of a potato, fruit, etc. Ⅱ *v.* cut or break a piece off; make into small pieces

chirp Ⅰ *n.* a short, sharp sound made by some small birds and insects Ⅱ *v.* make short sounds; speak in a cheerful voice

chisel *n.* a steel-edged tool for shaping wood, stone or metal

choice Ⅰ *n.* ❶ an act of selecting or making a decision ❷ a person or thing chosen Ⅱ *adj.* carefully selected; of high quality

choke *v.* ❶ (of a person or animal) be unable to breathe because of a constricted or obstructed throat or a lack of air ❷ fill partly or completely a passage, space, etc. so that movement is difficult ❸ become speechless, especially because of strong emotion

choose *v.* ❶ pick out or select sb. or sth. ❷ prefer; decide on a course of action

chop *v.* ❶ cut sth. by hitting with an axe, knife, etc. ❷ cut sth. into small pieces

choral *adj.* composed for or sung by a choir or chorus

chord *n.* several musical notes played together

chore *n.* a routine task or job, especially in a house

chronic *adj.* (of a disease or condition) continual, lasting for a long time

chronicle Ⅰ *n.* the record of important or historical events in the order of their happening Ⅱ *v.* record events in the order of their happening

chuckle Ⅰ *n.* a quiet laugh with closed mouth Ⅱ *v.* laugh quietly; laugh to oneself

church *n.* a building where Christians go to pray and worship

circle Ⅰ *n.* ❶ a round flat figure ❷ a group of people or things arranged to form such a figure ❸ a number of people who get together and have the same interests Ⅱ *v.* ❶ surround ❷ move around; move in a circle

circuit *n.* ❶ a journey round from place to place ❷ a path of an electric current

circuitous *adj.* (said about a route) longer than the usual way, indirect

circular *adj.* round like a circle; of a circle; moving in a circle

circulate *v.* move round from place to place or from person to person

circulation *n.* ❶ movement to and fro or around sth. ❷ the number of copies of a newspaper or magazine usually sold ❸ the movement of blood around the body

circumference *n.* ❶ the outside edge around sth. ❷ the enclosing boundary round a circle

circumspect *adj.* very careful to avoid difficulty or danger

circumstance *n.* ❶ conditions connected with an event or person ❷ financial condition ❸ a fact that causes or helps to cause sth. to happen

circumstantial *adj.* ❶ giving full details ❷ (of evidence) based on or consisting of details that strongly suggest sth. but do not provide direct proof

cite *v.* ❶ call sb. to appear before a court of law ❷ refer to; mention or bring up as an example

citizen *n.* ❶ a person who belongs to a particular country and enjoys certain rights ❷ a person who is resident in a particular place

city *n.* a large and important town

civil *adj.* ❶ having sth. to do with citizens or the state ❷ not the armed forces ❸ polite and courteous

civilization *n.* the stage of human social development, especially one with a high level of art, religion, science, government, etc. and written language

C

civilize *v.* bring from a savage or ignorant condition to a higher one

claim Ⅰ *v.* ❶ask for sth. as the rightful owner or as one's right ❷say that sth. is true ❸ deserve or need Ⅱ *n.* ❶ a demand for sth. as one's own by right ❷ the right to have or do sth. ❸ a statement that sth. is true

clamber *v.* climb with some difficulty, using the hands and feet

clammy *adj.* cold and damp

clamp Ⅰ *n.* an appliance for holding things together tightly by means of screw Ⅱ *v.* put a clamp or clamps on

clan *n.* a large group of families which are all related to each other

clap Ⅰ *v.* ❶ show approval by striking the hands together ❷ hit sb. lightly with the open hand Ⅱ *n.* the sound of striking the hands together

clarify *v.* ❶become or make sth. clearer or easier to understand ❷ make sth. pure

clarity *n.* the quality being clear to see or understand

clash Ⅰ *v.* ❶(cause to) strike together suddenly ❷ happen at the same time and so interfere with each other; disagree Ⅱ *n.* ❶a loud noise by striking one metal object against another ❷ disagreement ❸a mismatch of colours

clasp Ⅰ *v.* hold sth. closely or tightly Ⅱ *n.* ❶ a tight holding or embrace ❷a metal fastener for holding two things or parts of one thing together

class *n.* ❶ a group of students taught together ❷a group people, animals or things having qualities of the same kind ❸a group of people at the same social or economical level ❹ a period of time during which pupils or students are taught together

classic Ⅰ *adj.* ❶of the highest quality; having a recognized value ❷(of art or literature) simple in style; without too much decoration ❸ remarkably and instructively typical Ⅱ *n.* a work of literature, or a writer of the highest quality

classical *adj.* regarded as representing an exemplary standard; traditional and long established in form or style

classification *n.* ❶ the process of classifying things ❷a category in which sth. is put

classified *adj.* ❶ (of advertisements) arranged according to subject matter ❷ (of information) officially secret and available only to specified people cleanser

classify *v.* ❶arrange things in classes or groups ❷ decide which group or type sb. or sth. belongs to

clatter Ⅰ *v.* (cause sth. to) make a number of rapid short knocking sounds Ⅱ *n.* ❶ a number of rapid short knocking sounds ❷the noise caused by people talking rapidly or a busy activity

clause *n.* ❶a part of a sentence with its own subject and verb ❷ a particular article in a law or contract

claw Ⅰ *n.* ❶ one of the sharp, hard points on the foot of an animal ❷ an instrument or device like a claw Ⅱ *v.* scratch, tear, seize or pull sth. with claws or nails

clay *n.* soft, sticky earth from which pots and bricks are made

clean Ⅰ *adj.* ❶free from dirt, marks or stains; not dirty ❷morally or sexually pure Ⅱ *v.* make sth. free from dirt, marks or mess especially by rubbing and often without water

cleanse *v.* make sth. thoroughly clear

clear Ⅰ *adj.* ❶ easy to perceive or understand ❷ (of a substance) transparent ❸without cloud or mist ❹ without any obstacles; having nothing in the way Ⅱ *v.* ❶take away things that are not wanted ❷ pass by or over (sth.) without touching ❸(cause to) become clear

clear-cut *adj.* distinct; having clear outlines and meaning

cleft *n.* a narrow opening, especially in the ground or in a rock

clement *adj.* ❶(of weather) mild ❷(of a person or their actions) merciful

clench *v.* ❶press or squeeze sth. tightly ❷hold sth. firmly

clerk *n.* a person who works in an office or bank to undertake administrative duties

clever *adj.* ❶ quick to learn, think or understand; intelligent ❷having ability and skill

click Ⅰ *n.* a sudden sharp sound like a light switch being turned on or off Ⅱ *v.* (of an idea, etc.) be understood suddenly

client *n.* ❶ a person who gets help or advice from a lawyer or any professional man ❷a customer (at a shop)

cliff *n.* a steep face of rock, especially by the sea

climate *n.* ❶the weather conditions in a place ❷the general feelings or opinions of a group of people at a particular time

climax Ⅰ *n.* an event or point of greatest interest or importance (e. g. in a story or drama) Ⅱ *v.* come to the most exciting or important part in sth.

climb Ⅰ *v.* ❶go up sth. towards the top ❷ move somewhere, especially with difficulty or effort ❸go higher in the sky ❹increase in value or amount Ⅱ *n.* ❶an act of climbing up a mountain, rock or large number of steps ❷an increase in value or amount ❸ progress to a higher status, standard or position

clinch Ⅰ *v.* ❶ settle sth. definitely ❷ fasten sth. firmly ❸fight or grapple at close quarters Ⅱ *n.* ❶a fight at close quarters ❷an embrace

cling *v.* stick tightly; hold firmly; keep close to; stay close to sb.

clink Ⅰ *n.* a sharp sound like that made by drinking glasses knocking together Ⅱ *v.* make sharp ringing sound

clip *v.* cut sth. with scissors or shears; make sth. short or neat

cloak *n.* ❶a loose outer garment, without sleeves ❷ sth. used to hide or keep sth. secret

clockwise *adv.* in the same direction as the hands of a clock

clog Ⅰ *n.* ❶a shoe with a wooden sole; a shoe carved out of a block of wood ❷a block of wood fastened to the leg of an animal to prevent its straying Ⅱ *v.* (cause to) be or become blocked

C

close[1] Ⅰ *v.* ❶move or cause to move so as to cover an opening ❷make the work of a shop, a store, etc. stop for a period of time ❸come to an end or bring to an end Ⅱ *n.* the end, especially of an activity or of a period of time

close[2] Ⅰ *adj.* ❶ near in relationship, friendship, or degree of connection ❷ near or not far away in space or time Ⅱ *adv.* near; not far away

closet Ⅰ *n.* ❶a small room for storing things ❷a lavatory Ⅱ *v.* shut up in a room for a private talk

clot *n.* a half-solid lump formed in the drying of certain liquids (especially blood)

cloth *n.* a material made by weaving threads together

clothe *v.* put clothes on; supply clothes for

clothes *n.* the things covering a person's body

cloud Ⅰ *n.* ❶grey or white mist in the sky ❷ a mass of smoke, dust or anything like a cloud ❸mass things in the air moving together ❹ sth. that causes unhappiness or fear Ⅱ *v.* ❶grow or become cloudy ❷ (of sb.'s face) show worry, sorrow or anger

cloudy *adj.* ❶ full of or covered with clouds ❷not clear or transparent

clown Ⅰ *n.* a person (usually with a painted face and strange clothes) whose work is to do foolish things to amuse people (especially in a circus)

club *n.* ❶a society of persons who meet together for a common purpose; the building or house used by such a society ❷a heavy stick of wood; a stick used in games

clue *n.* a thing that helps to find the answer to a problem

clump *n.* a number of things close together (usually trees or plants)

clumsy *adj.* likely to drop things or move in an awkward way

cluster Ⅰ *n.* a number of things of the same kind growing or being close together in a group Ⅱ *v.* gather or grow in one group or more groups

clutch Ⅰ *v.* take hold of sth. very tightly Ⅱ *n.* a tight hold

clutter Ⅰ *v.* make untidy Ⅱ *n.* an untidy condition

cluttered *adj.* covered with or full of a lot of things or people, in a way that is untidy

coalition *n.* an alliance of a number of groups, especially the joining of a number of political parties in order to form a government

coarse *adj.* ❶not smooth or soft; rough; of poor quality ❷not polite; rude

coast *n.* the land along the sea or ocean

coat *n.* ❶a piece of clothing with sleeves and an opening in the front, which one can wear outside ❷ an outer garment with long sleeves, often fastened at the front with buttons and usually covering the body down to the knees, worn especially to keep warm or for protection

coating *n.* a thin layer or covering

coax *v.* get sb. or sth. to do sth. by kindness or patience

cobble Ⅰ *n.* a stone worn round and

smooth by water and used for paving Ⅱ *v.* pave with these stones

cock *n.* ❶ an adult male chicken; a male bird ❷ a tap or valve controlling the flow of a liquid or gas in a pipe

cocky *adj.* slightly over confident or arrogant

code *n.* ❶ a system of words, letters, figures, or symbols used to represent others, especially for the purposes of secrecy ❷ a set of moral principles or rules of behavior ❸ a systematic collection of laws or statutes

codify *v.* arrange laws, rules, etc. into a system

coexist *v.* exist at the same time

coexistence *n.* peaceful existence side by side of states with opposed political systems

coffer *n.* ❶ a large strong box used to hold money or other valuable things in safety ❷ (～s) the funds or financial reserves of a group or institution

coffin *n.* a box in which a dead body is put

cogent *adj.* logical and convincing

cognate *adj.* ❶ having the same source of origin ❷ related; having much in common

cognition *n.* the mental action or process of acquiring knowledge and understanding through thought, experience, and the senses

cognizance *n.* knowledge; awareness

cognizant *adj.* having knowledge or information; aware

cohere *v.* stick together; be or remain united; be consistent

coherent *adj.* ❶ united as or forming a whole ❷ (especially of speech, thought, ideas, reasoning) logical and clear, easy to understand

cohesion *n.* tendency to stick together; force with which molecules cohere

coil Ⅰ *n.* sth. arranged in a series of circles Ⅱ *v.* arrange sth. in the form of a coil

coin Ⅰ *n.* a round piece of metal money Ⅱ *v.* ❶ make metal into coins ❷ invent (especially a new word)

coincide *v.* ❶ happen at the same time ❷ (of ideas or opinions, etc.) be in agreement

coincidence *n.* ❶ the fact or process of happening at the same time or being in the same place ❷ a remarkable occurrence of similar or corresponding events at the same time by chance

cold Ⅰ *adj.* ❶ having a low temperature; not hot ❷ not friendly or cheerful Ⅱ *n.* ❶ relative absence of heat; a low temperature ❷ a common illness that affects the nose and throat

cold-blooded *adj.* ❶ having blood that varies with the temperature (e. g. fish, reptiles) ❷ (of persons, their actions) without feeling; pitiless

collaborate *v.* ❶ work together with others especially in literature ❷ work treasonably, especially with enemy forces

collapse Ⅰ *v.* ❶ fall down or inwards suddenly; come or break into pieces ❷ fall down and become unconscious Ⅱ *n.* ❶ the act of collapsing ❷ the sudden and complete loss of strength or will

C

collar Ⅰ *n.* the part of clothes that fits round the neck Ⅱ *v.* ❶ seize (sb.) tightly; take hold of roughly ❷ take sth. without permission

collate *v.* examine and compare(copies of books, notes, etc.) carefully in order to find the differences between them

colleague *n.* persons working together and (usually) having similar ranks and duties

collect *v.* ❶come or bring together in one place so as to form a group or mass; gather ❷ask for or obtain payment of (money, taxes, rent, etc.)

collection *n.* ❶things collected systematically ❷a number of things that have come together or been placed together ❸money collected for a charity or at a church service

collective Ⅰ *adj.* to do with a group taken as a whole Ⅱ *n.* a cooperative enterprise

college *n.* a name given to various types of places of learning and also the staff and students of these institutions

collide *v.* ❶come together violently; meet and strike; be in conflict ❷ disagree with sb. over sth. strongly such as ideas, opinions, etc.

collision *n.* ❶an instance of one moving object or person striking violently against another ❷an instance of conflict between opposing ideas, interests, or factions

colony *n.* a country or territory that has been developed by people from another country

colo(u)r Ⅰ *n.* ❶the quality that makes things look green, yellow, red, etc. ❷ redness of the face ❸a substance(e. g. paint or dye) used to give colour to sth. Ⅱ *v.* ❶give colour to; put colour on ❷ take on colour or change colour

colo(u)rful *adj.* ❶ full of colour ❷ lively or exciting, with plenty of detail

column *n.* ❶a tall pillar supporting part of a building, or standing alone ❷ a section of a newspaper or magazine regularly devoted to a particular subject or written by a particular person ❸ a large number of rows of people, vehicles, etc., following one behind the other

coma *n.* a condition like a deep sleep, caused by injury, disease or poison

comb Ⅰ *n.* an object used for tidying, arranging, or straightening the hair usually consisting of a piece of plastic, metal, bone, etc. with a row of thin teeth Ⅱ *v.* ❶tidy, arrange, or straighten (especially the hair) with a comb ❷ search (a place) thoroughly

combat *n.* & v. fight; struggle

combatant *n.* a person taking a direct part in fighting

combination *n.* ❶ the state of being joined or put together ❷a number of people or things that combined or united in a common purpose

combine Ⅰ *v.* ❶ unite; merge; form a group ❷ put two or more different things, features or qualities together ❸ do two or more things at the same time ❹come together to work or act together Ⅱ *n.* a group of people or companies acting together for a commercial purpose

combustible Ⅰ *adj.* catching fire and burning easily Ⅱ *n.* a flammable substance

come *v.* ❶ move towards or near to the speaker or a particular place ❷ extend; arrive ❸ happen; take place; become seen; appear ❹ become

comedian *n.* ❶ an actor who plays comic parts in plays, broadcast and TV ❷ a comedy writer

comedy *n.* ❶ a branch of drama that deals with everyday life and humorous events ❷ an amusing activity or incident in real life

comfort Ⅰ *n.* ❶ the state of being free from suffering, pain, etc. ❷ help or kindness to sb. who is suffering sth. Ⅱ *v.* give hope to

comfortable *adj.* ❶ having or providing comfort ❷ with no pain or worry

comic Ⅰ *adj.* ❶ funny; humorous; having to do with comedy ❷ of comedy Ⅱ *n.* a person who is funny or amusing, especially a professional comedian

coming Ⅰ *n.* arrival; approach Ⅱ *adj.* approaching; next

command Ⅰ *v.* ❶ give an authoritative order ❷ control or restrain ❸ have authority over; be in charge of Ⅱ *n.* ❶ an order; a direction ❷ the power to control; mastery

commander *n.* a person who commands

commanding *adj.* ❶ having a position of authority ❷ possessing or giving superior strength ❸ indicating or expressing authority; imposing

commemorate *v.* keep or honour the memory of a person or event; be in memory of (things)

commemoration *n.* a ceremony or celebration in memory of a person or event

commence *v.* begin; start

commencement *n.* ❶ beginning ❷ a ceremony at which degrees are conferred

commend *v.* ❶ entrust sth. for safekeeping to ❷ praise, speak favourably of ❸ recommend

commendation *n.* ❶ praise ❷ an award involving the giving of special praise

comment Ⅰ *n.* a written or spoken opinion, explanation, or judgment made about an event, person, situation, etc. Ⅱ *v.* make a comment; give an opinion

commentary *n.* a description spoken during a special event, match, etc.

commentate *v.* report on an event as it occurs, especially for a news or sports broadcast; provide a commentary

commentator *n.* a person who gives a commentary on the radio or television

commerce *n.* the buying and selling of goods and services; trade

commercial *adj.* of or for commerce

commission *n.* ❶ the act of giving authority to sb. to act for another ❷ money paid to a salesman for his services ❸ a group of people specially appointed to perform certain duties

commit *v.* ❶ do sth. bad or wrong ❷ send; entrust ❸ make oneself responsible; undertake; bind (oneself)

commitment *n.* a promise; a pledge or undertaking

committee *n.* a group of people chosen to

C

do a job

commodity *n.* a product or a raw material that can be bought and sold

C

common *adj.* ❶ usual and ordinary; happening or found often in many places ❷belonging to or shared equally by two or more

commonplace Ⅰ *adj.* ordinary or usual Ⅱ *n.* sth. that happens very often and not unusual

commonwealth *n.* ❶ an independent state or community, especially a democratic republic ❷ a community or organization of shared interests in a non-political field

communicate *v.* ❶ pass on ideas, feelings, thoughts, etc. ❷ share or exchange information, news, ideas, etc. with sb. ❸pass an illness

communication *n.* ❶ the act of communicating ❷ the means of communicating ❸ a letter, message or call

communicative *adj.* willing to talk and give information

community *n.* a group of people having the same religion, race, occupation, etc. or with common interests

commute *v.* ❶ exchange; change ❷ reduce a judical sentence

compact Ⅰ *adj.* ❶ smaller than that is usual ❷ using or filling only a small amount of space ❸ closely and firmly packed together Ⅱ *n.* ❶ a small car ❷ an agreement between two or more people or countries Ⅲ *v.* press sth. together firmly

companion *n.* ❶ a person who goes somewhere with or spends time with another, either because of friendship or by chance ❷ either of a pair or set of things; one thing that matches another

company *n.* ❶ the presence of another person; companionship ❷ an organization made up of people who work together for purposes of business or trade ❸ a number of persons working together

comparable *adj.* that can be compared

comparative *adj.* ❶ having to do with comparison or comparing ❷ measured or judged by comparing; relative

compare *v.* ❶examine or judge one thing in relation to another in order to show the points of similarity or difference ❷ describe as being alike

comparison *n.* ❶ a consideration or estimate of the similarities or dissimilarities between two things or people ❷ the quality of being similar or equivalent

compartment *n.* a division in a train; any of the separate parts into which an enclosed space is divided

compass *n.* ❶ an instrument with a needle that always points north ❷ an instrument for drawing circles, measuring distance on a map, etc.

compassion *n.* sympathetic pity and concern for the suffering of others

compassionate *adj.* feeling or showing sympathy for people who are suffering

compel *v.* force sb. to do sth.

compensate *v.* make a suitable payment; give sth. that makes up for a loss

compete *v.* try to win sth. by defeating

sb. else who is trying to do the same thing

competence *n.* ❶ the ability to do sth. successfully ❷ (of a court, a magistrate) legal capacity

competent *adj.* having the ability or skill to do sth.

competition *n.* ❶ an event in which people compete with each other to find out who is the best at sth. ❷a situation of striving to gain or win sth. by defeating others engaged in the same attempt

competitive *adj.* in or for which there is competition

competitor *n.* a person who competes with another or others

compile *v.* collect information and arrange(in a book list, etc.)

complacent *adj.* smug or self-satisfied

complain *v.* ❶ express displeasure ❷ state the presence of pain, illness etc.

complaint *n.* ❶the act of complaining ❷ a reason or cause for complaining

complement Ⅰ *n.* ❶ that which makes sth. complete ❷ the full number or quantity needed Ⅱ *v.* add to or make complete

complete Ⅰ *adj.* ❶having all necessary, usual, or wanted parts; lacking nothing ❷finished; ended ❸ total; thorough Ⅱ *v.* finish; bring to an end (especially sth. that takes a long time); make perfect

completion *n.* an act of completing; the state of being completed

complex *adj.* made up of closely connected parts; difficult to understand or explain

complexion *n.* ❶ a natural colour, appearance of the skin, especially of the face ❷a general character or aspect of conduct, affair, etc.

complexity *n.* ❶ the state of being formed of many parts; the state of being difficult to understand ❷(~s) a factor involved in a complicated process or situation

compliant *adj.* ❶willing to comply or obey ❷ meeting a standard or requirement

complicate *v.* make(sth.) complex; make (sth.) more difficult to do or understand

complicated *adj.* difficult; not easy to do or understand

complication *n.* ❶ the state of being complex, confused, difficult ❷sth. that adds new difficulties

compliment Ⅰ *n.* ❶ an expression of praise, admiration or approval ❷(~s) polite greetings Ⅱ *v.* express admiration or approval

comply *v.* act in accordance with a demand, order, rule, etc.

component *n.* one of the parts of which sth. is made up

compose *v.* ❶write or create a work of art, especially a piece of music or poem ❷make up ❸calm or settle

composed *adj.* having one's feelings and expression under control; calm

composite Ⅰ *adj.* made up of a number of different parts or styles Ⅱ *n.* sth. made by putting together different parts or materials

composition *n.* ❶ the act of composing

music, poetry, etc. ❷a piece of music or writing ❸the various parts from which sth. is made up

C

composure *n.* complete control over one's feelings; calmness

compound Ⅰ *adj.* made up of different materials; having more combined parts Ⅱ *n.* a substance formed by the chemical combination of two or more elements

comprehend *v.* ❶ understand sth. fully ❷include

comprehension *n.* the action or capability of understanding sth.

comprehensive *adj.* of broad scope; including nearly all

compress *v.* press together; force into a narrower space

comprise *v.* include; be made up of

compromise Ⅰ *n.* a settlement of a dispute by which each side gives up sth. it has asked for and neither side gets all it has asked for Ⅱ *v.* ❶ settle a dispute, etc. by giving up some of your demands when you disagree with sb. to make an agreement ❷ bring (sb. or sth.) under suspicion by unwise behaviour, etc.

compulsive *adj.* ❶ acting from a compulsion ❷ extremely exciting or interesting

compulsory *adj.* that must be done because of a law or a rule

comrade *n.* ❶ a friend ❷ a fellow member of a union, political party, etc.

concave *adj.* (especially of lenses) curving inwards; having the shape of the inside of a circle or sphere

concavity *n.* the state or quality of being concave

conceal *v.* hide; keep secret

concede *v.* admit or agree that sth. is true or valid

conceit *n.* too much pride in one's own power, ability, value, etc.

concentrate *v.* ❶ (cause to) come together in or around one place ❷direct (one's thoughts, efforts, attention, etc.) towards a particular activity or purpose

concentration *n.* ❶ the process of concentrating ❷ the ability to concentrate on sth. ❸ the mass or amount of a substance contained in a specified amount of a solvent or in a mixture

concept *n.* an idea of sth.; a general notion

conception *n.* ❶ a general understanding; an idea ❷ the act of forming an idea, plan, etc.

concern Ⅰ *v.* ❶have to do with sth. ❷ worry; make anxious Ⅱ *n.* ❶the thing of interest or important to sb. ❷ anxiety; worry

concerned *adj.* ❶ worried or anxious about sth. ❷ involved or interested in sth.

concerning *prep.* about; to do with

concert *n.* an entertainment at which a number of pieces of music are played or sung

concise *adj.* saying a lot in few words

conclude *v.* ❶come to an end ❷come to believe after thinking of known facts ❸ establish an agreement with sb. formally and finally

conclusion *n.* ❶an end or finish of an event ❷ the summing-up of an argument or text ❸the arrangement or settling of sth.

conclusive *adj.* putting an end to all doubt or uncertainty; decisive or convincing

concord *n.* ❶ agreement or harmony between people or groups ❷a treaty

concordance *n.* ❶ agreement ❷ an alphabetical list of the words of a book with references to the passages in which they occur

concordant *adj.* in agreement; harmonious

concrete Ⅰ *adj.* real or solid Ⅱ *n.* a building material made by mixing sand, very small stones, cement and water

concur *v.* ❶agree ❷happen or occur at the same time

concurrent *adj.* happening or occuring at the same time

condemn *v.* ❶ express very strong disapproval of sb. or sth. ❷ judge (a person) guilty

condense *v.* ❶ (of a liquid) (cause to) increase in density or strength to become thicker ❷put (a piece of writing or speech) into fewer words

condition *n.* ❶ a state of being or existence ❷sth. on which another thing depends ❸(～s) circumstances

conditional *adj.* depending upon, containing a certain condition or conditions

condole *v.* express sympathy or regret at a loss, misfortune, etc.

condolence *n.* an expression of sympathy or regret

condone *v.* forgive; allow some wrong action to go unpunished or be forgotten

conduct *v.* ❶ direct or lead ❷ allow (heat, electric current, etc.) to pass through ❸control; direct

conductor *n.* ❶ a thing that conducts heat or electricity ❷ a person who collects fares and sells tickets on a public vehicle ❸a person who directs a group of musicians

confederation *n.* a group of nations, societies, business firms, etc. that have joined together because of some interest or purpose which they share

confer *v.* ❶give or grant (a degree, right, favour) ❷consult or discuss

conference *n.* a meeting for exchanging opinions and ideas

confess *v.* say or admit (that one has done wrong); acknowledge

confession *n.* an admission of a crime or fault

confidant *n.* a person you confide in

confide *v.* ❶tell (a secret, etc.) to sb. ❷ have trust or faith in

confidence *n.* ❶ a belief in oneself or others or in what is said, reported, etc.; a belief that one is right or that one is able to do sth. ❷the belief that one can have faith in sb. or sth.

confident *adj.* sure about oneself or about sth.

confidential *adj.* ❶ meant to be kept secret; said or written in confidence ❷ entrusted with private information

configuration *n.* a shape or outline

configure *v.* ❶shape or put together in

a particular form or configuration ❷ arrange or order (a computer system or an element of it) so as to fit it for a designated task

C

confine *v.* ❶keep sth. within limits ❷ shut or keep in a small space

confirm *v.* ❶make certain; give proof of ❷approve; make sth. effective formally

conflict *n.* ❶a prolonged armed fight or struggle ❷ opposition; difference; argument

conform *v.* be in agreement with or comply with (generally accepted rules, standards, etc.)

conformation *n.* the structure or form of a thing

conformity *n.* conforming to accepted rules or standards

confound *v.* ❶ cause surprise or confusion ❷ mix up or confuse (ideas, etc.)

confront *v.* ❶ face and challenge an opponent or enemy ❷ be present as sth. you have to deal with ❸face up to a problem and deal with it ❹ bring opponents face to face

confuse *v.* ❶make sb. become unclear or perplexed about sth. ❷mix up

confusion *n.* ❶ the act of confusing or mixing up ❷ the state of being bewildered or unclear in one's mind about sth.

congeal *v.* change from liquid to solid (especially because of cold)

congenial *adj.* ❶ having the same interests and ideas, and therefore friendly ❷ pleasant and suitable for oneself

congenital *adj.* existing in a person from birth

congratulate *v.* express pleasure at a person's success, good fortune, etc.

congratulation *n.* (～s) words of joy and praise to sb. who has done well

congress *n.* ❶ the elected law-making body of certain countries ❷a series of meetings of representatives of societies, etc. for discussion

conjecture Ⅰ *v.* guess; come to an opinion about some facts without having enough information Ⅱ *n.* an opinion or conclusion formed on the basis of incomplete information

conjunction *n.* ❶a word that joins other words, clauses, etc. ❷ the state of being joined

connect *v.* ❶ be joined together ❷join sth. to the main supply of electricity, gas, water, etc. or to another piece of equipment ❸ have a link with sb. or sth. ❹arrive just before another leaves so that passengers can change from one to the other ❺form a good relationship with sb. so that you can understand each other

connection *n.* ❶the act of connecting or the state of being connected; a point where two things are connected; a thing which connects ❷ (～s) a person connected to others by a family relationship

conquer *v.* ❶ beat an enemy and take control of a country ❷ defeat or overcome problems, bad habits, etc.

conscience *n.* the feeling inside one's mind; the moral sense of right and wrong

conscientious *adj*. taking care to do one's work or duty as well as possible

conscious *adj*. ❶having all one's senses working and able to understand what is happening; not in a sleeplike state ❷ knowing, understanding or recognizing sth. ; aware ❸intentional

consecutive *adj*. following one after another continuously

consensus *n*. a general agreement or feeling of a number of people

consent Ⅰ *v*. agree Ⅱ *n*. an agreement or permission

consequence *n*. ❶sth. that follows from an action or set of conditions; a result ❷importance

consequential *adj*. ❶ happening as a result or an effect of sth. ❷ important; significant

consequently *adv*. as a result; therefore

conservative *adj*. ❶opposed to great or sudden changes ❷careful or cautious

conserve *v*. save sth. from loss or damage; keep sth. to be used when needed

consider *v*. ❶think carefully about sth. or about what to do ❷regard as; think that sth. is true

considerable *adj*. notably large in amount, size, or extent

considerate *adj*. thoughtful of others

consideration *n*. ❶ careful thought; thoughtful attention ❷ thoughtful attention to or care for the wishes, needs, or feelings of others ❸a fact to be considered when making a decision ❹a payment for a service; reward

considering *prep*. taking sth. into consideration

consign *v*. ❶ send (goods, etc.) for delivery ❷hand over; put into the care of sb. else

consist *v*. ❶ (~ of) be composed or made up of ❷ (~ in) have as an essential feature

consistent *adj*. ❶ in agreement or accordance ❷continually keeping to the same principles or course of action; having a regular pattern

console *v*. try to make sb. happier when he has suffered some loss or misfortune

consolidate *v*. become or make stronger or firmer

consonance *n*. agreement or compatibility between opinions or actions

consonant Ⅰ *n*. ❶a sound which is not a vowel; a sound in which the breath is stopped in the mouth or throat in some way ❷ a letter or symbol for such a sound Ⅱ *adj*. in agreement

conspicuous *adj*. standing out so as to be clearly visible

constancy *n*. the quality of being constant or loyal

constant *adj*. ❶ fixed or unchanging; invariable ❷ continually happening or repeated; regular ❸loyal; faithful

constituent Ⅰ *adj*. ❶forming or helping to make a whole ❷having the right to make or alter a political constitution Ⅱ *n*. ❶a person who has a parliamentary vote ❷a component part

constitute *v*. make up; form

constitution *n*. ❶a general structure of a thing; the act or manner of constituting

❷a set of laws governing a country ❸a general physical structure and condition of a person's body

C

constrain *v.* ❶make sb. do sth. by force ❷restrict or limit sth. or sb.

constrict *v.* fasten tightly so as to make smaller or prevent free movement

construct *v.* ❶ build; make by putting together or combining parts ❷ form sth. by bringing various conceptual elements together

construction *n.* ❶the act of constructing ❷a building or other structure

constructive *adj.* helping to construct; giving helpful suggestions

consulate *n.* the office or building where a consul works

consult *v.* ❶ seek information or advice from a person ❷ discuss with ❸ refer for information or suggestion to (a book, diary or watch) in order to ascertain sth.

consume *v.* ❶eat, drink or ingest ❷use up ❸buy (goods or services)

consumer *n.* a person who buys goods or uses services

consumption *n.* using up or consuming of food, energy, materials, etc.; the quantity consumed

contact Ⅰ *n.* ❶the state or condition of physical touching ❷ the act of communicating with sb., especially regularly Ⅱ *v.* communicate with sb. by telephone, mail, etc.

contain *v.* ❶hold or have within itself or as a part ❷ hold back; keep under control or within limits

contemplative *adj.* ❶ fond of contemplating things, thoughtful ❷ devoted to religious contemplation

contemporary Ⅰ *adj.* ❶ modern; belonging to the present time ❷of or belonging to the same time Ⅱ *n.* a person living at the same time or of the same age as another

contempt *n.* ❶ a lack of respect or admiration ❷ a condition of being looked down upon or despised ❸ disregard or disrespect; total disregard

contemptuous *adj.* feeling or showing contempt

contend *v.* compete as in a race or against difficulties

content[1] Ⅰ *adj.* satisfied; happy; not wanting more than one has Ⅱ *n.* a state of satis- faction Ⅲ *v.* make happy or satisfied

content[2] *n.* ❶ (～s) those that are contained ❷(～s) a list of chapters in a book ❸ the substance (of a book, speech, etc., as opposed to its form)

contention *n.* ❶the act of quarrelling or arguing ❷an assertion made in arguing

contest Ⅰ *n.* a struggle or fight to gain control or advantage Ⅱ *v.* take part in competition, etc. to win

context *n.* ❶ the words around a particular word or phrase, helping understanding ❷ the background or environment of sth.

continent *n.* one of the big land masses of the world

contingency *n.* uncertainty of occurrence; an event that happens by chance

continual *adj.* repeated; frequent;

uninterrupted

continue *v.* ❶ keep existing, doing or happening without stopping ❷ go or move further in the same direction ❸ remain in a particular job or condition ❹ recommence or resume after interruption

continuity *n.* ❶ the state of being continuous ❷ the uninterrupted existence of sth. or succession of events

continuous *adj.* going on without stopping

contort *v.* bend sth. so that it loses its proper shape

contract Ⅰ *v.* ❶make an agreement ❷ become liable for ❸ make or become smaller or shorter Ⅱ *n.* ❶ a formal agreement; an agreement to supply goods(at a fixed price) ❷a signed paper on which the conditions of such an agreement are written

contraction *n.* ❶ contracting or being contracted ❷a short form of a word

contradict *v.* ❶ be opposite to; be contrary to ❷declare sth. or sb. to be wrong; deny

contradiction *n.* a combination of statements, ideas, or features of a situation which are opposed to one another

contrary Ⅰ *adj.* completely different or wholly opposed Ⅱ *n.* the opposite

contrast Ⅰ *n.* ❶ the comparison of objects or situations that are dissimilar, especially to show differences ❷ the difference between people or things that are compared Ⅱ *v.* ❶ compare (two things or people) so that differences are made clear ❷ show a difference when compared

contribute *v.* ❶ help to cause or bring about sth. ❷join with others in giving help, money, etc. ❸write(articles, etc.) and send in

contribution *n.* ❶sth. done to help make another thing successful; any one of a number of individual efforts in a common endeavor ❷ money, things, etc. contributed ❸ an article or other piece of writing submitted for publication in a collection

contributory *adj.* contributing to a result

contrive *v.* cleverly manage to do sth.

control Ⅰ *v.* ❶rule; have power over ❷ hold down; keep in check Ⅱ *n.* ❶ the power or authority to rule ❷the act of controlling ❸ (～s) a device used to control a machine

convenience *n.* ❶ the quality of being convenient ❷an apparatus, service, etc. which gives advantage to its user

convenient *adj.* ❶useful or suitable; not causing problems ❷near; easy to reach

convention *n.* ❶a conference of members of a society, political party, etc. , devoted to a particular purpose ❷ formal agreements ❸ a general consent (especially about forms of behaviour); practice or custom based on general consent

conventional *adj.* ❶ done or doing things in the accepted way; traditional ❷(of weapons) not nuclear

converge *v.* move together and meet; tend to meet at a point

conversation *n.* a talk between two or

more people

converse Ⅰ *v.* talk with sb. Ⅱ *adj.* opposite or reverse Ⅲ *n.* the opposite of another

C

conversion *n.* the process or action of changing or causing sth. to change from one form to another

convert Ⅰ *v.* ❶change sth. into sth. else ❷cause a person to change his belief, etc. Ⅱ *n.* a person who has been converted, especially to a different religion

convex *adj.* (especially of lenses) curving outwards, having the shape of the outside of a circle or sphere

convey *v.* ❶carry or take sth. from one place to another; transport ❷make (ideas, views, feelings, etc.) known to another person

convict Ⅰ *v.* (of a judge, jury, lawyer, etc.) say or prove that sb. is guilty of a crime Ⅱ *n.* a person in prison after being found guilty of a crime

conviction *n.* ❶an act of convicting ❷a strong belief

convince *v.* ❶make sb. feel sure about sth.; persuade sb. to believe sth. ❷persuade sb. to do sth.

convincing *adj.* capable of causing someone to believe that sth. is true or real

cook Ⅰ *v.* ❶make food ready to eat ❷(of food) be heated so that the state or condition required for eating is reached Ⅱ *n.* a person who cooks

cool Ⅰ *adj.* ❶pleasantly cold ❷calm; not excited ❸not showing interest or enthusiasm Ⅱ *v.* ❶make sth. less hot or become less hot ❷keep calm; calm down

cooperate *v.* ❶work together for a particular purpose ❷give help to sb. that needs help

cooperative *adj.* ❶willing to work helpfully with another person ❷providing cooperation

coordinate Ⅰ *adj.* equal in importance Ⅱ *v.* make coordinate; put into proper relation

cope *v.* deal with sth. successfully

copy Ⅰ *n.* ❶sth. made to be like another ❷an example of a book, newspaper, etc. of which many have been made Ⅱ *v.* ❶make sth. like another exactly ❷follow (sb. or sth.) as a standard or pattern; imitate ❸cheat by writing (exactly the same thing) as someone else

cord *n.* ❶a thick string or thin rope ❷a piece of electrical wire with a protective covering

cordial *adj.* warm and sincere

core Ⅰ *n.* ❶the central part of certain fruits, containing seeds ❷the central or the most important part of anything Ⅱ *adj.* main or essential

corn *n.* any plant that is grown for its grain; the grain of these plants

corner Ⅰ *n.* ❶a point or an area where two or more edges, sides or surfaces of sth. join ❷the area inside a room, box or similar space where its edges or walls meet ❸a part of the world, especially a distant one Ⅱ *v.* ❶put into a difficult position ❷(of a vehicle, etc.) turn a corner

corporal *adj.* of the body

corporate *adj.* ❶shared by members of a group ❷forming a corporation

corporation *n.* ❶ a group of persons authorised to act as an individual (e.g. for business purpose) ❷ a large company

corporeal *adj.* ❶ that can be touched; physical rather than spiritual ❷ of or for the body

corps *n.* one of the technical branches of an army

corpse *n.* a dead body of a human being

correct Ⅰ *adj.* true; right; proper Ⅱ *v.* ❶ make right; take out mistakes from ❷point out the faults of

correction *n.* ❶the process of correcting sth. or of being corrected ❷ an alteration made to sth. to make it correct

correlate *v.* have or show a mutual relation or connection

correspond *v.* ❶be in agreement with; suit ❷ be equal to; be similar ❸ exchange letters

correspondence *n.* ❶ agreement or similarity ❷ the act of exchanging letters or the letters exchanged

correspondent *n.* a journalist employed to provide news for newspapers or broadcast media

corridor *n.* a long narrow passage in a building or train

corrode *v.* wear away or damage by chemical changes

corrosive Ⅰ *adj.* tending to cause corrosion Ⅱ *n.* a substance having the tendency to cause corrosion

corrupt Ⅰ *adj.* ❶ immoral; wicked; bad ❷dishonest; open to bribery Ⅱ *v.* make or become morally depraved

cosmic *adj.* of the whole universe or cosmos

cost Ⅰ *v.* ❶be obtainable at the price of; be worth; require the payment of ❷ result in the loss or injury of Ⅱ *n.* ❶ the price or the money to be paid when buying sth. ❷ that which is used, needed or given to obtain sth.

costly *adj.* ❶ of great value; costing much ❷gained or won at a great loss

costume *n.* the style of dress

cottage *n.* a small house in the country

couch Ⅰ *n.* a long seat on which one can sit or lie Ⅱ *v.* ❶(of animals) lie flat ❷ express a thought, etc. in words

cough Ⅰ *v.* send out air from the lungs violently and noisily Ⅱ *n.* an act or sound of coughing

council *n.* ❶ a meeting held for consultation or advice ❷ a group of people appointed or elected to make laws, rules, or decisions, or to give advice

counsel Ⅰ *n.* ❶ advice; opinions; suggestions ❷ a lawyer or lawyers giving legal advice Ⅱ *v.* advice; recommend

counsel(l)or *n.* a person who has been trained to advise people with problems, especially personal problems

count Ⅰ *v.* ❶ say or name number in order ❷consider (sth. or sb.) to be Ⅱ *n.* an act of counting; number got by counting

countdown *n.* the process of counting numbers backwards to zero before a precisely timed event, e. g. when launching a space rocket

countenance Ⅰ *n.* a person's face, or the expression on it Ⅱ *v.* allow sth. as acceptable or possible

counter *n.* ❶ a table or flat surface on which goods are shown, customers served, in a shop or bank ❷ a device for keeping count (in machinery, etc.)

counteract *v.* act against and make (action, force, poison) of less effect

counterfeit Ⅰ *adj.* made in imitation of another thing in order to deceive Ⅱ *v.* copy (coins, handwriting, etc.) in order to deceive Ⅲ *n.* a forgery

country *n.* ❶ an area of land with clear borders in which people of one nation live ❷ the land which is not the town or city

countryside *n.* land outside towns and cities, used for farming or left unused; country areas

county *n.* a major division of a country or state

couple *n.* ❶ two people or things of the same kind that are together ❷ two people who are married, engaged, or otherwise closely associated romantically or sexually ❸ several people or things

courage *n.* the ability to do sth. dangerous or to face pain without showing fear

course *n.* ❶ the way in which sth. progresses or develops ❷ a set of lessons or studies

court *n.* ❶ a place where judges and lawyers listen to law cases ❷ a place where a king or queen and the followers meet ❸ a piece of ground marked for a sport

courteous *adj.* having good manners; polite

courtesy *n.* courteous behaviour; politeness

cover Ⅰ *v.* ❶ place (one substance or thing) over or in front of another ❷ travel (a certain distance) ❸ have as a size ❹ include; comprise; extend over ❺ protect Ⅱ *n.* ❶ sth. made to be put over, on or in front of sth. ❷ the outside of a book ❸ a thing which lies on, over or around sth. in order to protect or conceal it ❹ a shelter or protection sought by people

covering *n.* sth. that covers

coverlet *n.* a bedspread

covert Ⅰ *adj.* secret or hidden; not openly shown or admitted Ⅱ *n.* a thick growth of bushes and small trees in which animals can hide

covet *v.* desire eagerly especially sth. belonging to another person

covetous *adj.* too eager for wealth or property for someone else's possessions

coward *n.* a man who lacks courage; one who escapes from danger, difficulty or pain

crack Ⅰ *n.* ❶ a thin line where sth. is broken ❷ a sharp noise Ⅱ *v.* ❶ break, but not into separate parts ❷ make a sharp noise, like gun Ⅲ *adj.* first-rate

cradle *n.* ❶ a kind of small bed for a baby ❷ a place where sth. starts

craft *n.* ❶ a trade needing special skill with one's hands ❷ an art or skill ❸ the skill in deceiving; cunning

craftsman *n.* a male worker skilled in a particular craft

craftsmanship *n.* ❶ the level of skill shown by sb. in making sth. beautiful with their hands ❷ the quality of design and work shown by sth. that has been made by hand

crafty *adj.* ❶ cunning or deceitful ❷ ingenious

cram *v.* fill with too many things; push into sth. so that it becomes too full

cramp Ⅰ *n.* sudden pain and tightening of the muscles, caused by cold or overuse of the muscles Ⅱ *v.* prevent easy movement; keep in a small space

crash Ⅰ *v.* fall down or strike sth. violently Ⅱ *n.* ❶ a violent collision, typically of one vehicle with another or with an object ❷ a sudden loud noise as made by a violent blow, fall, break, etc. ❸ ruin or collapse (e. g. in trade, finance)

crave *v.* ask earnestly for; have a strong desire for

craving *n.* a strong wish or desire for sth.

crawl *v.* ❶ move slowly by dragging the body along the ground or on hands or knees ❷ move slowly

crayon *n.* a soft coloured pencil, wax or chalk

craze *n.* sth. in which people have an interest, which is great but is not likely to last for a long time

crazy *adj.* ❶ mad, foolish ❷ wildly excited or enthusiastic

create *v.* ❶ make sth. happen or exist ❷ cause sth. to happen as a result of one's actions

creation *n.* ❶ the act or process of creating sth. ❷ sth. which has been made or invented

creative *adj.* having the power of creating new things

creature *n.* a living thing, person or animal

credibility *n.* ❶ the quality of being believable or convincing ❷ the quality of being trusted and believed in

credible *adj.* that can be believed; trust worthy

credit Ⅰ *n.* ❶ belief in the truth of sth.; confidence ❷ good name; reputation ❸ honour or approval that comes to a person, because of what he is or does ❹ the money in a person's bank account Ⅱ *v.* believe; trust

creek *n.* a small river

creep *v.* move quietly, often with the body close to the ground

crew *n.* all the persons working on a ship, aircraft, train, etc.

crime *n.* ❶ a bad act that is against the law ❷ a foolish or useless action

criminal Ⅰ *adj.* ❶ of or being a crime ❷ concerned with crime Ⅱ *n.* a person who commits a crime or crimes

crimp *v.* ❶ press material into small folds or ridges ❷ make waves in hair with a hot iron

cripple Ⅰ *n.* one who is lame or physically or emotionally disabled Ⅱ *v.* ❶ cause sb. not to walk normally any longer ❷ damage; weaken

crisis *n.* ❶ a time of difficulty or danger

❷a turning point

crisp *adj.* ❶hard, dry and easily broken ❷fresh ❸(of one's manners of speech, etc.) quick, clear, not hesitating ❹(of air, etc.) cool, dry and refreshing

criterion *n.* a standard by which one can judge sth.

critic *n.* ❶a person who says whether a book, film, play, piece of music, etc. is good or not, and gives reasons for his decision (usually in a newspaper or magazine) ❷ a person who always notices the bad points and mistakes about anything

criticism *n.* ❶an unfavourable judgment or expression of disapproval ❷ the forming and expressing of judgments about the good or bad qualities of anything, especially artistic work

criticize *v.* ❶ judge with disapproval; point out the faults of ❷ make judgments about the good and bad points of

crook *n.* ❶ a long stick with a bent end used by a bishop or a shepherd ❷any bent or curved thing or part

crooked *adj.* ❶ not straight; twisted; bent ❷dishonest

crop *n.* ❶agricultural plants in the field ❷yearly or season's products of grain, grass, fruit, etc.

cross *v.* ❶go from one side to the other; pass over ❷put or lie across

crossing *n.* ❶an act of going across ❷a place where sth. as a street, river, etc. may be crossed ❸ a place where two lines, roads, etc. cross

crossroads *n.* ❶ a place where two or more roads cross one another ❷a point at which a crucial decision must be made which will have far-reaching consequences

crosswise *adj.* & *adv.* in the form of a cross, with one thing crossing another

crowd Ⅰ *n.* a large mass of people Ⅱ *v.* come together in a large mass; fill (a space) with people

crown Ⅰ *n.* ❶a circle worn on the head by a king or a queen ❷a championship title Ⅱ *v.* ❶put a crown on a king or queen ❷be or have at the top of ❸put a happy finishing touch to

crucial *adj.* very important, and coming at a time of great danger or difficulty

crude *adj.* ❶not mature ❷rough ❸in a natural state; unrefined ❹ giving a general information of sth. simply

cruel *adj.* ❶ liking to cause pain and suffering ❷painful; causing suffering

cruelty *n.* ❶ callous indifference to or pleasure in causing pain and suffering ❷ behaviour which causes pain or suffering to a person or animal

cruise Ⅰ *v.* sail from place to place Ⅱ *n.* a sea voyage

crumble *v.* break or fall into small pieces; come to nothing; pass away

crumple *v.* (cause to) be pressed or crushed into folds or creases

crush Ⅰ *v.* ❶press hard or be pressed, so that there is breaking or injury ❷ (cause to) become full of folds ❸ conquer; defeat ❹press; come crowding into Ⅱ *n.* ❶ a crowd of people pressed closely together, especially in an enclosed space ❷a drink made of juice of crushed fruit

crust Ⅰ *n.* the hard outer covering Ⅱ *v.* cover or become covered with a hard outer layer

cry Ⅰ *v.* ❶(of persons, animals, birds) make sounds that express feelings ❷(of persons) weep; shed tears Ⅱ *n.* ❶a loud sound of fear, pain, grief, etc.; a loud excited utterance of words ❷watchwords or phrases used for a principle or cause

cube Ⅰ *n.* ❶a solid figure with six equal square faces ❷the number got by multiplying itself twice Ⅱ *v.* calculate the cube of

cubic *adj.* ❶cube-shaped ❷denoting a unit of measurement equal to the volume of a cube whose side is one of the linear unit specified

cuddle Ⅰ *v.* hold close and lovingly in one's arms Ⅱ *n.* the act of cuddling; a hug

cue *n.* a signal or sign to sb. that he should begin to do sth.

cultivate *v.* ❶prepare land for growing crops ❷plant; grow ❸develop

cultivated *adj.* well-educated and well-mannered

culture *n.* ❶a nation's or a group of people's beliefs, accomplishments, behaviour patterns, customs, art and science in general ❷improvement of the body and mind through education and training

cumulative *adj.* getting larger by being added to

cunning Ⅰ *adj.* clever in deceiving Ⅱ *n.* cleverness in deceiving

cup *n.* ❶a small bowl with a handle for drinking ❷the amount that a cup will hold ❸a gold or silver bowl as a prize

curb Ⅰ *n.* anything which acts as a control in this way Ⅱ *v.* keep(feelings, etc.)under control

cure Ⅰ *n.* ❶restoration to health ❷sth. that will end a problem or an illness Ⅱ *v.* ❶eliminate a disease or an injury with medical treatment ❷solve a problem

curiosity *n.* ❶a strong desire to know or learn sth. ❷a strange or unusual object or fact

curious *adj.* ❶wanting to know about sth. ❷strange; unusual

curl Ⅰ *n.* ❶a small mass of hair twisting upwards ❷the state of having the shape of curl Ⅱ *v.* cause (hair) to form a curl or curls

currency *n.* a system of money used in a country

current Ⅰ *adj.* ❶of the present time ❷in common or general use Ⅱ *n.* ❶a continuous flow of water, air or any liquid ❷the flow of electricity through a wire, etc. ❸a general course or movement

curriculum *n.* courses of study in a school, college, etc.

curse Ⅰ *n.* words, phrases or sentences calling for the punishment, injury or destruction of sth. or sb. Ⅱ *v.* use bad language against

curve Ⅰ *n.* a bent line having no angles; a rounded bend Ⅱ *v.* (cause to) have the form of a curve; move in the course of a curve

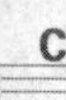

custodian *n.* a guardian or keeper, especially of a public building

custody *n.* duty or work of protecting sth. or keeping sth. safe

custom *n.* ❶ usually and generally accepted behaviour among members of a social group ❷ (～s) import duties; a government department which collects these taxes

customer *n.* a person who buys things, especially one who gives his custom to a shop

cut Ⅰ *v.* ❶ divide, separate, wound, or make an opening with a sharp tool ❷ make short; make smaller in quantity, price, length, etc.; reduce Ⅱ *n.* ❶ an act of cutting; a piece of sth. that has been cut off ❷ becoming shorter, less, lower, etc.

cute *adj.* ❶ quick and clever ❷ (of children or young women) pretty

cycle *n.* ❶ a series of events taking place in a regularly repeated order ❷ the short form for bicycle or motorcycle

D d

D

dab Ⅰ *n.* ❶a slight or light touch ❷a small quantity, especially of a soft or liquid substance Ⅱ *v.* ❶touch lightly or gently, usually several times ❷cover with light quick strokes and usually carelessly and incompletely

dabble *v.* ❶work at or study sth. without serious intentions ❷move one's hands, feet, etc. playfully around in water

daft *adj.* foolish; stupid

dagger *n.* a short knife used as a weapon

daily Ⅰ *adv.* & *adj.* happening, appearing every day(or every weekday) Ⅱ *n.* a newspaper published every day

dainty *adj.* small, pretty and delicate in appearance

dally *v.* be slow to do sth. or waste time

damage Ⅰ *n.* physical harm caused loss of value or usefulness Ⅱ *v.* harm or spoil sb. or sth.

damn *v.* ❶criticize(sth.)severely ❷used when swearing at sb. or sth. to show that you are angry

damp *adj.* slightly wet; wet on the surface

dampen *v.* ❶make sth. wet ❷reduce the strength of (feelings, especially of happiness or keenness)

damper *n.* an influence that makes people feel sad or discouraged

dance Ⅰ *v.* move the feet and body in a way that matches the speed or movements of music Ⅱ *n.* ❶an act of dancing ❷a social meeting or party for dancing

danger *n.* ❶the possibility of suffering loss or harm ❷sth. or sb. that causes harm or injury

dangerous *adj.* able or likely to cause danger; harmful

dangle *v.* hang loosely

dare Ⅰ *v.* ❶be bold or brave enough to do ❷challenge: The other boys ~d him to dive from the bridge. Ⅱ *n.* sth. bold that you do because another person asks you

daring *adj.* ❶courageous ❷bold in a new way

dark Ⅰ *adj.* ❶partly or completely without light ❷tending towards black Ⅱ *n.* the absence of light; darkness

darken *v.* ❶make or become dark or darker ❷make or become angry or unhappy

darling Ⅰ *n.* dear or loved person Ⅱ *adj.* greatly loved; dear

dash Ⅰ *v.* rush quickly; run suddenly and quickly Ⅱ *n.* a short race run at full speed

data *n.* information, details, facts, or figures about sth.

date Ⅰ *n.* ❶ the time, shown by the day of the month and sometimes the year ❷ a meeting that you have planned with sb. Ⅱ *v.* ❶ write the date on; determine the time when sth. took place ❷ go on or have an appointment (with sb. or each other)

daub *v.* ❶ paint in an unskilled way ❷ cover (sth. or somewhere) with sth. dirty or sticky

daunt *v.* make someone afraid or discouraged

dawdle *v.* waste time; move or do sth. very slowly

dawn Ⅰ *n.* ❶ the time when the sun rises ❷ the beginning Ⅱ *v.* ❶ grow light in the east in the morning ❷ come out; appear ❸ begin to be understood or realized ❹ begin; start

day *n.* ❶ the period of twenty-four hours that begins at midnight ❷ the time when it is light; the opposite of night ❸ time or period

daybreak *n.* dawn; the first light of day

daydream *n.* a pleasant dreamlike set of thoughts while one is awake

daylight *n.* ❶ the natural light of the sun ❷ dawn; daybreak

daze *v.* make confused or unable to think clearly

dazzle Ⅰ *v.* ❶ make a person unable to see because the light is too strong ❷ cause to feel stupid or make unable to think clearly Ⅱ *n.* brightness that stops you from seeing clearly

dead Ⅰ *adj.* ❶ not living ❷ not active; not working; unable to feel anything ❸ without movement or activity ❹ complete; exact Ⅱ *adv.* completely; exactly Ⅲ *n.* (the ～) those who have died

deaden *v.* make pain or noise, etc. weaker

deadline *n.* the latest time or date by which sth. should be completed

deadlock *n.* a situation in which no progress can be made

deadly Ⅰ *adj.* ❶ likely to kill; causing or able to cause death ❷ extremely accurate or effective Ⅱ *adv.* ❶ as if dead ❷ extremely

deaf *adj.* ❶ unable to hear anything or hear very well ❷ unwilling to listen

deafen *v.* make so much noise that it is difficult or impossible to hear the sounds for sb.

deal[1] *n.* (a good/great ～) ❶ much; a lot ❷ to a considerable extent

deal[2] Ⅰ *n.* an agreement or arrangement in business or politics, especially one that is to the advantage of both sides Ⅱ *v.* ❶ give out ❷ buy and sell ❸ do business or trade with ❹ solve or cope with (affairs)

dear *adj.* ❶ loved or cherished by sb. ❷ lovable; sweet ❸ used in speech as a way of addressing a person in a polite way ❹ used as the polite introduction to a letter ❺ greatly valued

dearly *adv.* ❶ very much ❷ at great cost

death *n.* dying; ending of life

debate Ⅰ *n.* a formal argument or discussion of a question, e. g. at a public meeting or in parliament Ⅱ *v.* have a discussion about

debase *v.* ❶reduce the quality or value of sth. ❷make sb. less respected

debilitate *v.* make sb. very weak and infirm

debt *n.* ❶the money that one must pay to sb. else ❷a feeling that sb. has to the person who has helped or been kind to the body

decade *n.* a period of ten years; a group or series of ten

decay Ⅰ *v.* (cause to) go bad Ⅱ *n.* the destroyed parts of teeth

deceit *n.* an act of deceiving; a dishonest act

deceive *v.* make sb. believe what is not true

decelerate *v.* become or make sth. become slower

decent *adj.* ❶right and suitable; fit and proper; respectable ❷satisfactory; fairly good ❸kind

decide *v.* ❶reach a decision; make up one's mind ❷settle; give a judgement

decided *adj.* ❶noticeable; definite ❷having clear and definite opinions; determined

decision *n.* ❶a conclusion or resolution reached after consideration ❷the action or process of deciding sth. or of resolving a question

decisive *adj.* ❶showing determination and firmness; resolute ❷leading to a clear result; putting an end to a doubt ❸unquestionable

declaim *v.* ❶make a speech; read aloud ❷forcefully protest against or criticize sth.

declaration *n.* ❶the act of making a formal statement; a formal statement representing sth. ❷a statement giving official information

D

declare *v.* ❶make sth. known publicly and clearly ❷say sth. openly or firmly

decline Ⅰ *v.* ❶slope downwards ❷go from a better to a worse position, or from higher to lower ❸refuse a request or offer, usually politely; express unwillingness Ⅱ *n.* a period or process of declining; the movement to a lower or worse position

decompose *v.* (cause to) go bad or rotten and undergo chemical changes

decorate *v.* provide with sth. that is added because it is attractive or beautiful(not because it is necessary)

decrease Ⅰ *v.* become less in size, amount, strength, or quality; reduce Ⅱ *n.* the process of reducing sth. in size, amount, strength, or quality; the amount reduced

decree Ⅰ *n.* an official command or decision Ⅱ *v.* order sth. officially, with the force of law

decry *v.* speak disapprovingly of; say bad things about

dedicate *v.* give a lot of time and effort to a particular task or purpose

deduce *v.* determine or decide(sth.) from general principle

deduct *v.* take away (an amount, a part) from a total; subtract

deduction *n.* ❶an amount that is deducted from sth.; the act or action of deducting ❷the inference of particular instances by reference to a general law

deed *n.* ❶ an action that is performed intentionally ❷action or performance

deep Ⅰ *adj.* ❶going far down; reaching far from the surface or the outside edge ❷strong in colour ❸strong in voice ❹ (of sleep) profound ❺felt strongly Ⅱ *adv.* far down or in

deepen *v.* make or become deep or deeper

deface *v.* damage or spoil the appearance of

defame *v.* damage the good name of, usually by unfair means

default Ⅰ *v.* fail to pay a loan, perform a duty, or appear in a law court when required Ⅱ *n.* failure to pay a loan, perform a duty or appear in a law court

defeat Ⅰ *v.* win a victory over; overcome Ⅱ *n.* losing a game, fight, war, etc.

defect *n.* a fault

defense *n.* ❶the action of fighting against attack ❷ sth. that keeps away dangerous things or people ❸ arguments used in favour of an accused person; a lawyer acting for such a person

defend *v.* ❶protect sb. or sth. from harm or damage ❷ speak or write in support of

defensive *adj.* used or intended to defend

defer *v.* wait until later before doing sth.

deficiency *n.* the quality of having none or not enough; alack

deficient *adj.* ❶ having none or not enough(of); lacking(in); inadequate ❷ having some defects

defile *v.* destroy the pureness of sth.

define *v.* ❶state or show the meaning of words or phrases clearly ❷explain the exact qualities, limits, duties, etc. of sth.

definite *adj.* clearly known, seen, or stated; without any uncertainty

definition *n.* the statement of the meaning of a word

deflect *v.* cause sth. to turn away from a direction

deform *v.* change or spoil the shape or form of sth.

deformation *n.* the process or result of changing and spoiling the normal shape of sth.

deformity *n.* a deformed part of the body

deft *adj.* light, quick and clever (especially in using the hands in a job which needs skill)

defy *v.* ❶ resist openly ❷ be ready to fight against; challenge sb. to do sth.

degenerate Ⅰ *v.* become worse in physical, mental or moral qualities Ⅱ *adj.* having become worse in character, quality, etc. in comparison with a former state

degrade *v.* ❶bring down in the opinion of others, in self-respect, or in behaviour ❷reduce in rank or status

degree *n.* ❶a step or stage in a scale or process ❷ a unit of measurement for temperature or angle ❸a title given by a university

dejected *adj.* unhappy and upset

delay Ⅰ *v.* ❶cause sb. to be slow or late ❷put off or postpone Ⅱ *n.* ❶the act of delaying or the state of being delayed ❷ the time during which sth. or sb. is delayed

delegate Ⅰ *n.* a person to whom sth. is delegated Ⅱ *v.* appoint as a representative

delegation *n.* a group of delegates

delete *v.* strike or take out sth. written or printed

deliberate Ⅰ *adj.* ❶ carefully considered; thoroughly planned; done on purpose; intentional ❷ done or acting in a careful and unhurried way Ⅱ *v.* consider sth. carefully

deliberation *n.* ❶ long and careful consideration or discussion ❷ careful movement or thought

delicacy *n.* ❶ the state or the quality of being delicate ❷ sth. pleasing to eat that is considered rare or costly

delicate *adj.* ❶ fine; tender ❷ easily broken or becoming ill

delicious *adj.* pleasing in taste or smell; very satisfying

delight Ⅰ *v.* ❶ please greatly ❷ take great pleasure in doing sth. Ⅱ *n.* great pleasure; joy

delightful *adj.* very pleasant

delinquency *n.* wrong-doing; neglect of duty

delinquent *adj.* & *n.* (a person) doing wrong or failing to perform a duty

deliver *v.* ❶ bring hand over ❷ give a speech, talk, etc. or other official statement ❸ give birth to a baby

delivery *n.* ❶ the action of delivering letters, parcels or ordered goods ❷ the manner of speaking ❸ the process of giving birth to a child

delude *v.* make sb. believe sth. that is not true

demand Ⅰ *v.* ❶ ask for sth. firmly ❷ need urgently Ⅱ *n.* the act of demanding; the claim and desire of people for particular goods or services

demean *v.* lower oneself in dignity, reputation, etc.

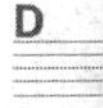

demeanour *n.* the way of behaving

demerit *n.* a fault or defect

democracy *n.* ❶ a system of government by the people, or by elected representatives of the people ❷ a country governed by its people or their representatives

democratic *adj.* ❶ of or favouring democracy ❷ believing in or practising the principle of equality

demolish *v.* ❶ destroy (especially a large structure); pull or tear down ❷ prove an idea, concept or theory completely wrong

demon *n.* ❶ an evil spirit ❷ a person with excellent strength, skill, etc.

demonstrate *v.* ❶ prove or make clear (a fact), especially by reasoning or providing examples ❷ take part in a public show of strong feelings or opinions, often with marching, big signs, etc.

demonstration *n.* ❶ the showing of existence or truth of sth. by giving proof or evidence ❷ the outward showing of feelings ❸ a practical exhibition and explanation of how sth. works or is performed ❹ a public meeting or march protesting against sth. or expressing views on a political issue

demonstrative *adj.* ❶ showing or proving sth. ❷ expressing your feelings openly

demoralize *v.* take away sb.'s courage, confidence, self-control, etc.

denial *n.* ❶the action of declaring sth. to be untrue ❷a statement that a thing is not true ❸a refusal of a request or wish

denomination *n.* ❶ any branch of the Christian churches ❷ a type of unit measuring height, weight, money, etc.

denote *v.* be a name of; mean

denounce *v.* ❶publicly declare sth. to be wrong ❷ tell the police, etc. about a crime committed by someone

dense *adj.* ❶crowded together in great numbers ❷(of liquids or vapour) not easily seen through

density *n.* ❶ the quality of being dense ❷the relation of weight to volume

dent Ⅰ *n.* a small hollow place in the surface of sth. which is the result of pressure or of being hit Ⅱ *v.* make a hollow in

dental *adj.* of or related to the teeth

deny *v.* ❶ say that sth. is not true ❷ refuse a request

depart *v.* ❶ leave, typically to start a journey ❷leave one's job or position

department *n.* any of the important divisions or branches of a government, business, college, etc.

departure *n.* ❶the action of leaving and going to another place ❷ a deviation from an accepted or traditional course of action or thought

depend *v.* ❶rely; trust ❷have confidence in

dependence *n.* ❶ the state of being dependent; inability to exist or operate without the help or support of sb. or sth. else ❷trust; reliance

dependent *adj.* ❶ needing the help or support of sb. or sth. else ❷that will be decided by

depict *v.* represent or show in or as if in a picture

deplete *v.* use sth. by a large amount so that little or none is left

deplore *v.* feel or express strong disapproval of sth.

deploy *v.* make soldiers move into a line ready for a battle

depose *v.* make a king or other ruler leave his position

deposit Ⅰ *v.* ❶put or set down; place ❷ put sth. into a bank, store or entrust for safe keeping Ⅱ *n.* ❶ a sum of money stored in a bank account ❷ a sum of money that is given as the first part of a larger payment

depreciate *v.* ❶make or become less in value ❷say that sth. has little value

depress *v.* ❶press down ❷cause to feel sad and without hope; discourage ❸ cause (prices) to be lower; make less active

depressed *adj.* ❶(of a person) in a state of general unhappiness or despondency ❷(of a place or economic activity) suffering the damaging effects of a lack of demand or employment

depressing *adj.* making you feel very sad and without enthusiasm

depression *n.* ❶the state of sadness and low spirits ❷ period when business is depressed

deprivation *n.* ❶ the lack of the basic

benefits that most people have, such as a home and enough food ❷ the lack of sth. that you need

deprive *v.* take away from; prevent from using or having sth.

depth *n.* ❶ the degree of deepness; the distance from the top down ❷ complexity and profundity of thought

depute *v.* appoint (someone) to do sth. instead of oneself

deputy *n.* a person appointed to act on behalf of or represent another

derive *v.* ❶ get; obtain ❷ come from or originate

descend *v.* come, fall, or sink from a higher to a lower level; go down

descendant *n.* a person who is descended from another

descent *n.* ❶ an action of coming or going down ❷ family origins ❸ a sudden attack

describe *v.* ❶ give an account of what sth. or sb. is like ❷ mark out or draw

description *n.* a statement or account that describes sth. or sb.

desert[1] *n.* a large sandy piece of land where there is very little rain and not much plant life

desert[2] *v.* ❶ leave sb. without help or support ❷ leave military service without permission

deserve *v.* have earned by one's actions or character; be worthy of

design Ⅰ *n.* ❶ a drawing or plan of sth. which is to be made ❷ a general arrangement or planning of a picture, book, building, machine, etc. ❸ a decorative pattern ❹ a plan or an intention Ⅱ *v.* ❶ make designs for ❷ do or plan sth. with a specific purpose or intention in mind

designate *v.* ❶ point out or call by a special name ❷ choose or name for a particular job or purpose

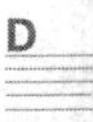

desirable *adj.* (of a thing or an object) worth having, doing, or desiring

desire Ⅰ *v.* wish earnestly; long for strongly Ⅱ *n.* a strong wish

desolate Ⅰ *adj.* ❶ empty and without people in ❷ lonely and unhappy Ⅱ *v.* make sb. feel lonely or sad

despair Ⅰ *v.* lose all hope or confidence Ⅱ *n.* complete loss of hope or confidence

desperate *adj.* ❶ ready for any wild act and not caring about danger, especially because of loss of hope; reckless ❷ (of a situation) extremely difficult and dangerous

despise *v.* look down upon; consider worthless

despite *prep.* in spite of

despondent *adj.* completely without hope and courage; feeling that no improvement is possible

destination *n.* the place you are going to or sth. is sent to

destiny *n.* what is determined to happen; fate

destroy *v.* break to pieces; put an end to

destruction *n.* the act or state of destroying or being destroyed

detach *v.* take apart; separate

detached *adj.* ❶ (said about a house) not joined to another ❷ free from emotion or bias; objective

D

detail Ⅰ *n.* an individual feature, fact, or item Ⅱ *v.* describe fully; give full details of

detain *v.* keep back; keep under arrest

detect *v.* discover or investigate

deteriorate *v.* make or become worse

determination *n.* ❶ firmness or purpose ❷ the act of finding out or calculating

determine *v.* ❶ firmly decide; make up one's mind ❷ be the decisive factor in ❸ discover the facts about sth.; calculate sth. exactly

detest *v.* hate sb. or sth. strongly

detour *n.* a road which is used when the usual road cannot be used; a journey made on such a road

detract *v.* take sth. of value away from; cause to be or seem less valuable

develop *v.* ❶ (cause to) grow, increase or become larger or more complete ❷ (cause to) become noticeable, visible or active ❸ bring out the economic possibilities of sth., especially land or natural substances

development *n.* ❶ the process of developing or being developed ❷ a new event or stage which is the result of developing

device *n.* ❶ a thing made or adapted for a special purpose ❷ a scheme; a trick

devil *n.* an evil spirit; the enemy of God

devise *v.* think out; plan; invent

devote *v.* give all or most of one's time, energy, attention, etc. to sb. or sth.

devoted *adj.* very loving or loyal

devotion *n.* ❶ the act of devoting; loyalty ❷ deep, strong love

devour *v.* ❶ eat very hungrily and greedily ❷ destroy ❸ read or look at sth. with great interest

devout *adj.* (of people) seriously concerned with religion; sincere

diagnose *v.* discover the nature of (a disease or fault) by making a careful examination

diagnosis *n.* a statement of the nature of a disease or other condition made after observing its signs and symptoms

diagram *n.* a plan drawn to explain an idea, or how sth. works

dialect *n.* a spoken form of a language, found in a particular area of a country

dialogue *n.* a conversation, especially in a book or play

diameter *n.* the line going through the centre of a circle

diary *n.* a book for daily record of events, thoughts, etc.

dictator *n.* ❶ a ruler who has unlimited power, especially one who has taken control by force ❷ a domineering person

diction *n.* ❶ the choice of words and phrases to express meaning ❷ the way in which a person pronounces words

die *v.* ❶ stop living ❷ cease to exist; disappear ❸ have a great wish for or to

diet *n.* ❶ the food you eat ❷ special food eaten by people who want to get thinner, or for medical

differ *v.* ❶ be different ❷ disagree

difference *n.* ❶ the way a person or a thing differs from another ❷ the amount by which one number is greater than another ❸ disagreement; quarrel

different *adj.* ❶ not the same ❷ separate and individual

differential Ⅰ *adj.* of, showing, or depending on a difference Ⅱ *n.* a difference between amounts of things

differentiate *v.* recognize or ascertain a difference between sth. or sb.; distinguish or discriminate

difficult *adj.* ❶not easy; needing effort or skill to do or to understand sth. ❷(of people) not easy to please or deal with

difficulty *n.* ❶the state or quality of being hard to do or to understand sth. ❷sth. hard to do or understand

diffuse Ⅰ *v.* spread out freely in all directions; disperse Ⅱ *adj.* ❶spread out over a large area ❷using too many words and not keeping to the point

dig *v.* make a hole in the ground; move earth

digest Ⅰ *v.* ❶change food in the stomach into the substances of a form that the body can use ❷understand or assimilate sth. Ⅱ *n.* a short account(of a piece of writing) which gives the most important facts

digit *n.* ❶any of the numbers from 0 to 9 ❷a finger or a toe

digital *adj.* ❶of or based on a system in which information is represented in the form of changing electrical signals ❷showing information in the form of numbers, rather than as a point on a scale, etc. ❸of the fingers and toes

dignified *adj.* having or showing dignity

dignify *v.* give respect or importance to (especially sth. that does not deserve it)

dignity *n.* ❶the state or quality of being worthy of honour or being noble ❷a high office or position

digress *v.* turn aside from the subject which one is speaking or writing about, and deal with sth. else

dilemma *n.* a position in which one has to choose between two unpleasant things

diligence *n.* careful hard work or effort

diligent *adj.* hard-working; putting care and effort into what you do

dilute Ⅰ *v.* make (a liquid) weaker and thinner by mixing another liquid with it Ⅱ *adj.* that has been diluted

dim Ⅰ *adj.* ❶not shining brightly ❷not clear to be seen Ⅱ *v.* make or become less bright or clear

dimension *n.* ❶a measurement in any one direction especially as used for establishing the position of sth. in space ❷the stated number of the size; the range of sth.

diminish *v.* make or become less or smaller

dip Ⅰ *v.* ❶put sth. into a liquid and then take it out again ❷go below a surface or level; slope downward Ⅱ *n.* the act of dipping or being dipped; a quick swim or bathe; a downward slope

diplomacy *n.* the art and practice of establishing and continuing relations between nations

dire *adj.* very serious or bad

direct Ⅰ *adj.* ❶straight; not turning ❷going straight to the point; plain Ⅱ *adv.* not stopping; not going a long way round Ⅲ *v.* ❶show sb. the way; be in charge of sth. or sb. ❷order; command

direction *n.* ❶a course taken by a moving person or thing; a way that a person or thing looks or faces ❷ guidance; order; command ❸ (~s) information or instructions about what to do, where to go, how to do, etc.

D

directly *adv.* in a direct manner; without delay; exactly in a specified position

director *n.* ❶one of senior managers who run a company ❷ a person who tells actors and actresses what to do in a play or a film ❸a controlling machine

directory *n.* ❶a book containing a list of telephone subscribers, inhabitants of a district, members of a profession, business firms, etc. ❷a file containing a group of other files in a computer

dirty *adj.* ❶having dirt on it; not clean ❷concerned with sex in thought or talk

disable *v.* make unable to do sth., especially take away power of action; wound

disability *n.* ❶ a physical or mental condition that limits a person's movements or senses ❷a handicap

disadvantage *n.* an unfavourable condition

disagree *v.* ❶ have a different opinion, fail to agree ❷ (of food, climate) have bad effects on

disagreeable *adj.* ❶ unpleasant or unenjoyable ❷ unfriendly and bad-tempered

disappear *v.* ❶go out of sight ❷be lost; become extinct

disappoint *v.* fail to fulfil the hopes of sb.

disapprove *v.* express an unfavourable opinion

disarm *v.* ❶ take away weapons from; reduce the size or give up the use of armed forces ❷ make sb. less suspicious, angry, hostile, etc.

disaster *n.* a great or sudden misfortune; a terrible accident

disastrous *adj.* ❶causing great damage ❷resulting in a complete failure

disbelieve *v.* refuse to believe; be unable or unwilling to believe (in)

discard *v.* throw away; give up (sth. useless, and unwanted)

discharge Ⅰ *v.* ❶allow (a liquid, gas, or other substance) to flow out ❷ send (sb.) away; allow (sb.) to leave; dismiss ❸pay (a debt); perform (a duty) Ⅱ *n.* ❶the action of allowing a liquid, gas, or other substance to flow out ❷the act of allowing sb. to leave somewhere, especially sb. in a hospital or the army ❸the act of performing a duty or paying a debt

discipline Ⅰ *v.* ❶ train or develop, especially in obedience and self-control ❷punish Ⅱ *n.* ❶a method of training to produce obedience and self-control ❷a state of order and control gained as a result of this training ❸punishment

disclaim *v.* a state that one does not have or accept; deny

disclose *v.* make sth. known; allow sth. to be seen

discomfort *n.* lack of comfort

discompose *v.* make (someone) lose control and become worried

disconnect *v.* break the connection of or between sth.

disconsolate *adj.* unhappy at the loss of sth.

discontent Ⅰ *adj.* disgruntled; dissatisfied Ⅱ *n.* lack of satisfaction; unhappiness

discontinue *v.* stop doing or providing sth.

discord *n.* disagreement between people

discount Ⅰ *n.* the amount taken off a price Ⅱ *v.* take out a certain amount from a price; do not believe sth. or sb. completely

discourage *v.* ❶take away the courage or confidence of ❷ persuade sb. not to do sth.

discourse Ⅰ *n.* ❶ a serious speech or piece of writing about a particular subject ❷ a serious conversation ❸ a connected language in a speech or writing Ⅱ *v.* make a long formal speech about

discourteous *adj.* not polite; showing bad manners; rude

discourtesy *n.* an act of not being polite

discover *v.* find out sth. for the first time; come to know or realize (sth.)

discovery *n.* the action or process of discovering or being discovered; sth. or sb. discovered

discredit Ⅰ *v.* cause people to lack faith in; stop people believing in or having respect for Ⅱ *n.* ❶loss of belief, trust, or the good opinion of others ❷sb. or sth. that brings shame or loss of respect; a disgrace

discreet *adj.* careful and tactful in what one says and does; prudent

discrete *adj.* separate; distinct

discriminate *v.* ❶ see or make a difference between things or people; distinguish ❷ recognize the difference between people or things

discuss *v.* talk together about; argue about

disease *n.* an illness or unhealthy condition caused by infection, a disorder, etc., but not by an accident

disengage *v.* ❶come loose and separate ❷loosen and separate

disfigure *v.* spoil or damage the appearance of

disgrace Ⅰ *n.* shame or loss of honour and respect Ⅱ *v.* bring shame and dishonour on; be a shame to

disguise Ⅰ *v.* change one's clothes or appearance in order not to be recognized Ⅱ *n.* the art of changing appearance to make others not recognize you

disgust Ⅰ *n.* a strong feeling of dislike or profound disapproval Ⅱ *v.* cause to feel dislike or profound disapproval

disgusting *adj.* extremely unpleasant

dish *n.* ❶a little flat plate for food ❷ food which is prepared and ready to eat

dishearten *v.* discourage; make less sure of success

dishonour Ⅰ *n.* a state of disgrace or shame; a person or thing that brings shame Ⅱ *v.* bring shame upon

disinfect *v.* make sth. clean by destroying bacteria that may cause disease

disinterested *adj.* ❶willing or able to act fairly because one is not influenced by personal advantage; objective ❷ not caring; uninterested

disjointed *adj.* not well connected; not following in reasonable order

dislike Ⅰ *v.* not like; hate Ⅱ *n.* a feeling

of not liking

dislocate *v.* ❶put a bone in the body out of its proper position ❷ disturb; disarrange; put sth. out of order

dismal *adj.* causing or showing sadness

dismiss *v.* ❶discharge from employment or office ❷send away or allow to leave

disobey *v.* fail to obey (rules, a command or sb. in authority)

disorder *n.* lack of order; confusion

dispassionate *adj.* calm and impartial, not considering one's personal feelings and so able to decide what is right

dispatch Ⅰ *v.* send off Ⅱ *n.* ❶the act of sending off or being sent off ❷a quick message, especially an official message or news report

dispel *v.* drive away

disperse *v.* scatter in different directions; disappear

dispirited *adj.* unhappy and without hope

displace *v.* ❶ take the place of sth. by pushing out ❷ force out of the usual place

display Ⅰ *v.* ❶place or spread out sth. so that there is no difficulty in seeing ❷ show signs of sth. , especially a quality or feeling Ⅱ *n.* showing; performance

displease *v.* cause displeasure to; annoy

disposal *n.* ❶an action of getting rid of sth. ❷ arrangement ❸ the power or right to use sth. freely

dispose *v.* ❶place in good order; arrange ❷(～ of) finish with; get rid of; deal with ❸(～ to) give a tendency to

disposition *n.* ❶ a person's inherent qualities of mind or character ❷ an inclination or tendency ❸the action of arranging people or things in a particular way

disprove *v.* show that sth. is not true

dispute Ⅰ *v.* argue or debate (with or agaist sb. on or about sth.); disagree about or question the truth or correctness of Ⅱ *n.* a disagreement, argument or debate quarrel

disqualify *v.* make or declare sb. unfit, unsuitable, or unable to do sth.

disregard Ⅰ *v.* pay no attention to; treat as unimportant or unworthy of notice Ⅱ *n.* lack of proper attention to or respect for sb. or sth.

disrepute *n.* loss or lack of people's good fame; bad repute

disrespect *n.* lack of respect or politeness

disrupt *v.* bring or throw (an event, activity or process) into disorder

dissatisfy *v.* fail to satisfy; displease

dissemble *v.* conceal your true feelings

dissent Ⅰ *v.* (～ from) have or express opinions which are opposed to official views, religious teaching, etc. Ⅱ *n.* the holding or expression of opinions

dissident Ⅰ *adj.* not agreeing with others; refusing to accept the beliefs or leadership of others Ⅱ *n.* a person who does not agree with others

dissolute *adj.* unrestrained by convention or morality

dissolution *n.* ❶ putting an end to a marriage or partnership ❷ formally ending a parliament or assembly

dissolve *v.* ❶(cause to) become liquid as the result of being taken into a liquid; melt ❷ disappear; bring or come to an end

dissuade *v.* persuade sb. not to do sth. ; make sb. agree not to do sth. by talking to him

distance *n.* a measure of space between two points, places, etc. ; the state of being far off

distant *adj.* separate in space or time; far off

distend *v.* (cause to) swell out by pressure from inside

distil *v.* make(a liquid) into gas and then make the gas into liquid

distinct *adj.* ❶ easily heard, seen or understood ❷separate; different

distinction *n.* ❶a difference or contrast ❷excellence that sets sb. or sth. better than many others ❸ a special mark, grade or award that is given to sb.

distinctive *adj.* that distinguishes one thing from others

distinguish *v.* ❶recognize the difference between two things or people ❷ see, hear, or notice as being separate or distinct; recognize clearly ❸ be a characteristics that makes two things or people different

distinguished *adj.* ❶ having a high reputation ❷ noble and dignified in appearance or behaviour

distort *v.* twist out of the shape; give a false account of; twist out of the truth

distract *v.* take (persons or their attention) off sth. , especially for a short time

distressed *adj.* suffering from extreme anxiety, sorrow, or pain

distribute *v.* ❶ divide and give out ❷ spread out over an area

distribution *n.* the action of sharing sth. out among a number of recipients

district *n.* a fixed division of a country, a city, etc. , made for various official purposes

distrust Ⅰ *v.* lack trust or confidence in; have little faith in Ⅱ *n.* a feeling of not being able to trust sb. or sth.

disturb *v.* ❶break the quiet, calm, peace, or order of ❷ change the usual or natural condition of ❸ make (sb.) anxiously dissatisfied; worry

ditch *n.* a long narrow channel dug in the fields or at the side of the road to carry off water

dive *v.* ❶ jump into water with the head and arms going in first ❷ go under water using breathing equipment ❸ go quickly to a lower level; go down or out of sight suddenly

diverse *adj.* different; various

diversify *v.* make or become different in forms, qualities, aims, or activities; vary

divert *v.* ❶cause to turn aside or change from one use or direction to another ❷ entertain or amuse

divide *v.* ❶separate or be separated into parts; keep apart or set apart ❷ separate and give out or share ❸ find out how many times one number contains another

dividend *n.* ❶a benefit from an action ❷ a number that is to be divided by another

division *n.* ❶ the action of separating sth. into parts ❷the distribution of sth. separated into parts ❸a major unit or section of an organization

divorce Ⅰ *n.* the official ending of a marriage, especially as declared by a court of law Ⅱ *v.* ❶ officially end a marriage between(a husband and wife) or to(a husband or a wife) ❷separate

dizzy *adj.* having an uncomfortable feeling in the head, as though things were moving

dock Ⅰ *n.* a place where ships are loaded, unloaded, or repaired Ⅱ *v.* (of a ship) come into dock

doctor *n.* ❶ a person who has been trained in medical science ❷ a person who has received the highest degree given by a university

doctrine *n.* beliefs and teachings (of a church, political party, school of scientists, etc.)

document *n.* sth. written or printed to be used as a record or in evidence

dodge Ⅰ *v.* ❶avoid sth. by moving suddenly aside ❷ avoid (a responsibility, duty, etc.) by a trick or in some dishonest way; evade Ⅱ *n.* ❶ a quick movement to avoid sth. ❷ a dishonest trick

dole Ⅰ *v.* (～ out) give out in small amounts Ⅱ *n.* ❶ money given every week by the government to people without work ❷sth. distributed

domain *n.* ❶ lands owned or controlled by one person, a government, etc. ❷ an area of activity, interest, or knowledge

domestic *adj.* ❶ of the home, family, household ❷ not foreign, native ❸ (of animals, etc.) kept by man

dominance *n.* the fact of position of dominating; power or controlling influence

dominant *adj.* ❶ most noticeable or important ❷ high and easily seen ❸ having control or authority; dominating

dominate *v.* ❶ have a commanding influence on ❷have the most important place or position (in); be the most obvious thing in a place

donate *v.* give money of goods, especially to a charity; contribute

doodle *v.* make a drawing or pattern while thinking about sth. else

dormitory *n.* a room for sleeping, with several beds

dose Ⅰ *n.* an amount of medicine to be taken at one time Ⅱ *v.* give medicine to

dot Ⅰ *n.* a small spot Ⅱ *v.* ❶mark with a small spot or spots ❷ be scattered over

dote *v.* (～ on) show much or too much fondness

double Ⅰ *adj.* ❶ twice as much as ❷ made for two persons or things ❸ having two like things or parts ❹ having two different uses or qualities; dual Ⅱ *n.* ❶ a number or amount twice as much ❷ a person or thing like another Ⅲ *v.* ❶ make or become twice as great ❷ fold over

doubt Ⅰ *n.* a feeling of uncertainty; a reason for being unsure about Ⅱ *v.* feel doubt about; be unsure of sth.; not believe

down Ⅰ *adv.* ❶from a higher place to a lower place ❷in or towards the south ❸ to a lower degree Ⅱ *prep.* from a higher to a lower level; along

downfall *n.* a fall from prosperity or power

download *v.* transfer data from one system to another or to a disk

downright Ⅰ *adj.* frank, direct Ⅱ *adv.* completely

downstairs Ⅰ *adv.* to, on a lower floor; down the stairs Ⅱ *adj.* on a lower floor, especially the ground floor

downwards *adv.* towards what is lower

doze Ⅰ *v.* sleep lightly Ⅱ *n.* a short, light sleep

dozen *n.* a group or set of twelve

dozy *adj.* ❶ feeling sleepy or lazy ❷ stupid; slow in understanding

draft Ⅰ *n.* ❶a plan, design, or outline of sth. to be done ❷ a written order for payment of money by a bank Ⅱ *v.* make a draft of; prepare the outline or design of

drag *v.* ❶pull along ❷move or go slowly

drain Ⅰ *v.* make water flow away; flow away Ⅱ *n.* a means of draining, such as a ditch or underground pipe that carries waste water away

drama *n.* stories that can be acted; plays

dramatic *adj.* ❶ of or to do with drama ❷ exciting and impressive

draw Ⅰ *v.* ❶ move by pulling after or behind ❷ make a picture, especially with a pen or pencil ❸ attract; extract ❹ come to or arrive at a point in time ❺ obtain from a source Ⅱ *n.* ❶ a result with neither side winning ❷ a person or thing that attracts especially the public

drawer *n.* ❶ a sliding box-like compartment in a piece of furniture ❷a person who draws or designs sth. ❸the person who writes out a cheque

drawing *n.* ❶ a picture made with a pencil, pen, or crayon rather than paint ❷the art or skill of making drawings

dread Ⅰ *n.* great fear and anxiety; terror Ⅱ *v.* fear greatly; look forward to sth. with great fear

dreadful *adj.* ❶ causing great fear ❷ very bad; very unpleasant

dream Ⅰ *n.* ❶sth. that one seems to see or experience during sleep ❷ sth. imagined while awake; daydream Ⅱ *v.* see, hear, think in sleep; have a picture or idea in one's mind while sleeping

drench *v.* make very wet

dress Ⅰ *n.* ❶ clothing in general, especially outer garments ❷ an outer garment worn by a woman or girl, gown or frock Ⅱ *v.* ❶put on clothes ❷wear clothes in a particular way

dressing *n.* ❶ a bandage, plaster, ointment, etc. for a wound ❷ a sauce of oil, vinegar, herbs, etc. for a salad ❸ the act of putting on clothes

dribble *v.* ❶let saliva or liquid fall from the mouth ❷ (of liquid) fall in small drops

drift Ⅰ *v.* ❶(cause to) be carried slowly by wind or water ❷(of people) move casually or aimlessly ❸(cause to) pile up under the force of the wind or water Ⅱ *n.* ❶a continuous slow movement ❷ a mass of matter blown up by wind

drill¹ Ⅰ *n.* training in military exercises Ⅱ *v.* train (soldiers) in military movements

drill² Ⅰ *n.* a tool or pointed instrument for

making holes in or through hard substances Ⅱ *v.* make a hole in sth. with a special fool or machine

drink Ⅰ *v.* ❶take(liquid)into the mouth and swallow ❷have an alcoholic drink Ⅱ *n.* a liquid for drinking; alcoholic liquid

drip Ⅰ *v.* fall down in drops Ⅱ *n.* the action or sound of falling in drops

drive Ⅰ *v.* ❶operate a motor-vehicle ❷ take (someone) in a vehicle ❸force to go ❹force a nail, etc. into sth. ❺force sb. to be (in a certain state); cause sb. to do sth. Ⅱ *n.* ❶a journey in a vehicle (especially for pleasure) ❷energy

drizzle *v.* rain in very small drops

droop *v.* bend or hang downwards through tiredness or weakness

drop Ⅰ *n.* ❶ a small round or pear-shaped mass of liquid ❷a small amount of any liquid ❸the act of going down; a sudden fall Ⅱ *v.* ❶let sth. fall; fall or let fall in drops ❷ become lower or weaker ❸ allow (sb.) to get out of a vehicle

drought *n.* a period of dry weather, causing a shortage of water

drown *v.* ❶(cause to) die in water ❷ make (a sound) inaudible by making a loud noise

drowsy *adj.* sleepy; half asleep; making a person feel sleepy

drug *n.* ❶a medicine for curing a disease ❷a chemical substance that affects the nervous system, especially a narcotic

drunk Ⅰ *adj.* unable to think or behave properly, through having had too much alcoholic drink Ⅱ *n.* a person who is drunk

dry Ⅰ *adj.* ❶ not wet; free from moisture ❷emptied of water ❸dull and uninteresting Ⅱ *v.* remove water from; make or become dry

dual *adj.* of two; having two parts

due Ⅰ *adj.* ❶owed or owing as a debt or right; requiring immediate payment ❷ expected or supposed to happen, arrive, etc. ❸proper, correct, or suitable Ⅱ *n.* sth. that rightfully belongs or is owed to someone, especially sth. non-material

duel *n.* ❶ a formal fight between two people with swords or guns ❷any two-sided contest

dull *adj.* ❶ not bright or light; (of colour) lacking brightness ❷ slow in understanding; not sharp ❸ uninteresting or not exciting; boring

duly *adv.* punctually; properly

dumb *adj.* ❶ not able to speak ❷ unwilling to speak; silent

dump Ⅰ *v.* ❶ drop or unload (sth.) heavily or carelessly, in a rough pile ❷ sell goods abroad at low prices Ⅱ *n.* a place for dumping waste materials

duplicate Ⅰ *v.* copy exactly Ⅱ *n.* sth. that is exactly like another Ⅲ *adj.* exactly like another made as a copy of sth.

durable *adj.* able to last a long time and not become damaged or broken

duration *n.* the time during which sth. lasts

during *prep.* ❶ throughout; all through ❷ at some time while sth. else is happening

dusk *n.* the time just before it gets

quite dark

dutiful *adj.* having a responsibility to; showing respect and obedience

duty *n.* ❶sth. that one ought to do in his job, by law, by morality, etc. ❷money you pay at the customs on goods when they are brought into a country

dwarf Ⅰ *n.* a person, animal, or plant that is much smaller than the usual one Ⅱ *v.* ❶ stunt the growth or development of ❷cause to look smaller than the usual one

dwell *v.* live; make one's home

dwindle *v.* become steadily fewer, smaller or weaker

dye Ⅰ *n.* the matter used in dyeing; colour produced by dyeing Ⅱ *v.* give colour to sth. or change the colour

dying *adj.* ❶ approaching death ❷ at death

dynamic *adj.* ❶ of power and forces producing motion ❷ (of a person) having great energy

dynasty *n.* a succession of rulers belonging to one family; a period during which a particular dynasty rules

E e

each *adj.* & *pron.* every person or thing in a group separately; every

eager *adj.* full of strong interest or desire

ear *n.* ❶an organ that you hear with ❷ an ability to recognize, appreciate sounds, especially in music and languages

early Ⅰ*adv.* at or near to the beginning of a period of time; sooner than usual or than others Ⅱ*adj.* coming or happening at the beginning of a period of time

earn *v.* ❶ get money by working ❷ receive sth. for doing sth. good; get sth. that you deserve ❸get money as profit or interest on money you lend, or you have in a bank, etc.

earnest Ⅰ*adj.* very serious and sincere Ⅱ*n.* a thing intended or regarded as a sign or promise of what is to come

earth *n.* ❶ the planet where we live ❷ soil

earthly *adj.* ❶to do with the earth, or human life on it ❷ used to emphasize sth.

ease Ⅰ*n.* the state of being comfortable and without worries or problems Ⅱ*v.* become less serious or severe; relax one's efforts

easy Ⅰ*adj.* ❶ not difficult ❷ comfortable and not worried ❸lacking anxiety or awkwardness; not embarrassed Ⅱ*adv.* ❶ in an easy manner ❷at ease; without effort

eat *v.* ❶ take food into the mouth and swallow it; have a meal ❷ destroy gradually

ebb Ⅰ*v.* ❶(of the tide) flow back from the land to the sea ❷grow less; become gradually weaker or fainter Ⅱ*n.* ❶the flowing out of the tide ❷ low state; decline or decay

eccentric *adj.* ❶strange; unusual ❷(of circles) not having the same point

echo Ⅰ*n.* ❶ a sound reflected or sent back ❷ a person who repeated the words or opinions of another Ⅱ*v.* ❶(of places) reflect back a sound ❷(of sounds) be sent back or repeated after the original sound has stopped ❸agree or repeat an idea or opinion

economic *adj.* connected with trade, industry and wealth; of economics

economical *adj.* not wasteful; saving; thrifty

economize *v.* avoid waste; reduce one's expenses

economy *n.* ❶ the control and management of money, goods and other resources ❷ careful management of available resources; freedom from waste

ecstasy *n.* a state of very strong feeling, especially of joy and happiness

ecstatic *adj.* causing or experiencing great joy and happiness

edge Ⅰ *n.* ❶the part or place where sth. ends or begins or that is farthest from its centre ❷the thin sharp cutting part of a blade, tool, etc. Ⅱ *v.* provide with an edge or border

edging *n.* sth. that forms an edge or border

edible *adj.* suitable for eating

edict *n.* an official command by a person in authority

edit *v.* prepare (another person's writing) for printing, broadcasting, etc., by deciding what shall be included or left out

edition *n.* ❶ the form in which sth. is published ❷all the copies of a book or newspaper issued at the same time ❸a particular version or broadcast of a regular radio or television programme

educate *v.* give intellectual, moral and social instruction to; train

education *n.* the process of teaching and learning

effect Ⅰ *n.* ❶ a result or condition produced by a cause; sth. that happens when one thing acts on another ❷ an impression produced in the mind of a person Ⅱ *v.* cause; bring about; accomplish

effective *adj.* ❶successful in producing a desired result ❷actual or existing

effectively *adv.* ❶in an effective way ❷ in fact; in effect

effectual *adj.* (of an action) successful in producing the intended effect; effective

efficiency *n.* the ability to work well and quickly

efficient *adj.* working well and getting a lot of things done

effort *n.* ❶the strength and energy to do sth. ❷an energetic attempt; struggle

ego *n.* a person's sense of self-esteem or self-importance

either Ⅰ *adj.* & *pron.* one or the other of two Ⅱ *adv.* (with negative) used to indicate a similarity or link with a statement just made Ⅲ *conj.* (~ ... or...) used to show a choice of two things

elaborate Ⅰ *adj.* involving many arranged parts or details carefully worked out and with a large number of parts and details Ⅱ *v.* work out, explain or describe sth. in details

elapse *v.* (of time) go by; pass

elastic *adj.* ❶(of an object or material) able to return to its original size or shape after being pulled or pressed ❷ (especially of plans or arrangements) able to be changed if the situation changes; not fixed

elasticity *n.* the quality that sth. has of being able to stretch and return to its original size and shape

elderly *adj.* rather old; ageing

elect Ⅰ *v.* ❶ choose sb. for an official position by voting ❷ choose or decide (to do sth.) Ⅱ *adj.* ❶ chosen or singled out ❷chosen for a position but not yet in office

election *n.* the choosing of representatives

by voting

elective *adj*. for which the holder is chosen by election

electric *adj*. ❶of, worked by, carrying or producing electricity ❷very exciting

electrify *v*. ❶ make sth. to a system using electric power ❷charge sth. with electricity ❸ cause sb. to feel excited and surprised greatly; shock sb.

elegant *adj*. having the qualities of grace and beauty; stylish

element *n*. ❶a substance which has not so far been separated into simpler one by ordinary chemical methods ❷one of the parts which sth. is made up of; a necessary or typical part of sth.

elementary *adj*. simple and easy; basic; of the beginning stage

elevate *v*. lift up or raise sth. to a higher position

elevation *n*. ❶the act of elevating or the state of being elevated ❷height above sea level

eliminate *v*. get rid of; remove

elite *n*. a group of people considered to be the best in a particular society or group

eloquent *adj*. fluently and expressively in speaking or writing

else *adv*. ❶ besides; in addition ❷ otherwise; if not

elude *v*. escape from sb. or sth., especially by means of a trick

emanate *v*. produce or show sth.

emancipate *v*. set someone free from slavery or some form of restraint

embargo *n*. an official order to stop trade, especially with another country

embark *v*. get onto a ship; put sth. onto a ship

embarrass *v*. cause to be ashamed or uncomfortable

embarrassment *n*. ❶ the act of embarrassing or the state of being embarrassed ❷ a person or thing causing problems for sb.

embassy *n*. a group of officials led by an embassador who represent their government in a foreign country

embed *v*. fix sth. into a substance very firmly

embellish *v*. make sth. more beautiful by adding decorations to it

embezzle *v*. use (money placed in one's care) in a wrong way for one's own benefit

emblem *n*. an object which is the sign of sth.

embody *v*. ❶ give a tangible or visible form to an idea, feeling, etc. ❷ include; collect

embrace Ⅰ *v*. ❶take and hold (someone or each other) in the arms as a sign of affection ❷accept or support (a theory or belief) willingly and eagerly Ⅱ *n*. an act of embracing

embroider *v*. sew a pattern or picture onto cloth

embroidery *n*. the art or activity of embroidering

emend *v*. alter sth. written in order to remove mistakes

emerge *v*. come out or appear from inside or from being hidden

emergency *n*. an unusual and dangerous situation in which one has to act quickly

emigrate *v*. go away from one's own

country to another to settle there

eminent *adj.* ❶ (of people) well-known and respected ❷greater than usual

emit *v.* produce and discharge

emotion *n.* any of the strong feelings of the human spirit

emphasis *n.* special importance given to sth.

emphasize *v.* ❶ place emphasis on; stress ❷ give extra force to a word or phrase

empire *n.* a group of states or countries under one ruler, usually an emperor or empress

employ *v.* ❶ give work to sb. and pay them for working for you ❷make use of sb. or sth.

employee *n.* the person who is employed

employer *n.* the person who employs people

emptiness *n.* ❶ a feeling of being sad because nothing seems to have any value ❷the fact that there is nothing or nobody in a place

empty Ⅰ *adj.* ❶containing nothing ❷ without meaning or value Ⅱ *v.* ❶make sth. empty ❷remove (the contents of) sth. and put them somewhere else

enable *v.* make (sb.) able to do sth.; make (sth.) possible; give power or means to do sth.

enact *v.* make or pass a law

enactment *n.* a law or a single provision of a law which has been made officially

enchant *v.* ❶be very pleasant to sb.; be liked very much by sb. ❷use magic on

encircle *v.* surround; form a circle round

enclose *v.* ❶ put a wall, fence, etc. to surround or close off on all sides ❷put (sth.) in an envelope together with a letter

encompass *v.* include or be concerned with (a wide range of activities, subjects, ideas, etc.)

encounter Ⅰ *v.* meet or have to deal with (sth. bad, especially a danger or a difficulty); be faced with Ⅱ *n.* a sudden meeting, usually either unexpected or dangerous

encourage *v.* give hope, courage, support, etc. to (sb.)

encumber *v.* make free action or movement difficult for; weigh down

encyclopedia *n.* a book or set of books dealing with every branch of knowledge, or with one particular branch, usually in alphabetical order

end Ⅰ *n.* ❶the farthest or last part or point ❷a small piece that remains after sth. has been used ❸ a finish or termination of a state or situation ❹ death ❺an aim or a goal Ⅱ *v.* (cause to) come to an end; finish

endanger *v.* put (sb. or sth.) in danger; make it possible that harm or damage will be caused

endear *v.* cause to be loved or liked

endeavour Ⅰ *v.* try hard to do or achieve sth. Ⅱ *n.* ❶ an attempt to achieve a goal ❷earnest and industrious effort, especially when sustained over a period of time ❸ an enterprise or undertaking

endless *adj.* never finishing; having no end

endorse *v.* declare one's approval

or support

endurance *n.* the state or power to last

endure *v.* bear (pain, suffering, etc.) patiently or for a long time

enemy *n.* ❶ a person who is hated or opposed to someone ❷ (the ～) armed forces of a hostile nation

E

energetic *adj.* full of energy; full of force

energy *n.* ❶ the strength and vitality to sustain physical or mental activity ❷ the ability of matter to work ❸ a source of power used for driving machines, providing light and heat, etc.

enforce *v.* ❶ compel observance of sth., especially a law, rule or obligation ❷ give force or strength to

engage *v.* ❶ be busy with; work at; take part in ❷ promise or enter into a contract to do sth. ❸ employ ❹ agree to marry

engaged *adj.* ❶ busy; occupied ❷ having formally agreed to marry

engagement *n.* ❶ an agreement to marry ❷ a promise to meet or go out with sb.; appointment; date ❸ a formal promise

engine *n.* ❶ a piece of machinery which converts power into motion ❷ the part of a train that pulls the rest

engrave *v.* cut or carve (words, designs, etc.) on the surface of a hard object

engross *v.* ❶ absorb completely the interest and attention of ❷ produce (a legal document) in its final or definitive form

engulf *v.* (of a natural force) surround and swallow up

enhance *v.* increase or further improve the value, quality, status or beauty of

enjoy *v.* get pleasure from (things and experiences); like

enjoyable *adj.* giving enjoyment, pleasant

enjoyment *n.* ❶ the pleasure, joy or satisfaction given by what is enjoyed ❷ the fact of having and using sth. ❸ sth. enjoyed; sth. that gives joy and pleasure

enlarge *v.* (cause to) grow larger or wider

enlighten *v.* cause to understand deeply and clearly, especially by making free from false beliefs

enlist *v.* ❶ (cause to) join the armed forces ❷ get help or support

enliven *v.* make more active, cheerful, or interesting

enmity *n.* a feeling of hatred towards each other by enemies

enormous *adj.* extremely large

enough *adj.* & *adv.* as much or as many as may be necessary

enquire *v.* ask for information from someone

enrich *v.* make sb. or sth. rich or richer; improve by adding sth.

enroll *v.* make (oneself or another person) officially a member of a group

enslave *v.* ❶ make a slave of ❷ make sb. or sth. completely depend on sth.

ensure *v.* make (sth.) certain to happen

entail *v.* involve (sth.) as a necessary or result

enter *v.* ❶ go or come into (a place) ❷ join; become a member of; cause sb. to be admitted

enterprise *n.* ❶ an organization, especially a business firm ❷ willingness and initiative to take risks and do things that are difficult, new, or daring

enterprising *adj.* showing initiative; adventurous

entertain *v.* ❶ provide (sb.) with food and drink ❷ provide (sb.) with amusement or enjoyment

entertainment *n.* a public performance or activity (at a theatre, circus, etc.) designed to entertain others

enthusiasm *n.* ❶ a feeling of eager; liking for sth. or interest in sth. ❷sth. you are interested in

enthusiastic *adj.* having or showing intense and eager enjoyment, interest, or approval

entire *adj.* whole; complete

entitle *v.* ❶ give a title or name to (a book, etc.) ❷give a right to

entity *n.* anything which exists independently

entrance[1] *v.* overcome, carry away (someone) as in a dream, with wonder and delight

entrance[2] *n.* ❶ an opening that allows access to a place ❷the act of coming or going in ❸ the right or opportunity of entering somewhere or being a member of an institution or society

entrap *v.* arrest; make sb. or sth. into a trap; trick or deceive sb.

entreat *v.* ask sb. earnestly

entreaty *n.* an earnest humble request

entrust *v.* assign the responsibility for doing sth. to sb.

entry *n.* ❶the act of coming or going in ❷a door, gate, or passage by which one enters ❸ the right of entering ❹ sth. written in a list, a book, etc.

envelope *n.* a flat paper cover for a letter; any covering which contains sth.

envious *adj.* feeling or showing envy

environment *n.* ❶ the natural world in which people, animals and plants live ❷ surroundings, or conditions, etc. affecting people's lives

envy Ⅰ *v.* wish for that belonging to someone else Ⅱ *n.* the feeling of disappointment and ill will at someone else's possessions, qualities or luck

epic Ⅰ *n.* a long poem of the deeds of heroes, or of a nation's past history Ⅱ *adj.* having the features of an epic

epidemic Ⅰ *n.* ❶a disease occurring in a large number at the same time ❷ a widespread occurrence of an infectious disease Ⅱ *adj.* of, relating to, or of the nature of an epidemic

episode *n.* an event, a situation, or a period of time in a chain of events, sb.'s life, a novel, etc.

epoch *n.* a period of time in history, life, etc. marked by special events

equable *adj.* ❶(of a person) of even calm temper; not easily annoyed ❷ (of temperature) without great changes; even and regular

equal Ⅰ *adj.* (of two or more) same in size, number, value, rank, etc. Ⅱ *n.* a person or thing considered to be the same as another Ⅲ *v.* (of a size or number) to be the same as

equality *n.* the state of being equal

equally *adv.* ❶in the same manner; to an equal degree ❷in equal shares ❸(used to introduce a further comment on a topic) at the same time and having the same importance

equate *v.* consider or make equal

equip *v.* supply with what is needed; fit out; furnish

equipment *n.* the set of things needed for a particular activity, especially an activity of a practical or technical kind

equitable *adj.* fair and just

equity *n.* fairness; the process of not treating sb. better than sb. else

equivalent Ⅰ *adj.* equal in value, amount, meaning, etc. Ⅱ *n.* a person, thing or amount that is equal to or corresponds with another

era *n.* a set of years which is counted from a particular point in time

eradicate *v.* destroy, remove completely; tear out by the roots

erase *v.* rub out or remove sth., especially a pencil mark

erect Ⅰ *adj.* upright or straight; standing on end Ⅱ *v.* ❶ set into an upright position ❷ build sth. ❸ create or establish sth.; set up

erode *v.* wear away gradually; destroy by taking away small pieces

err *v.* make a mistake; do sth. wrong

errand *n.* a short journey made to carry a message, or to do or get sth.

errant *adj.* wandering away from the accepted course and behaving in a bad or irresponsible way

error *n.* ❶ a mistake ❷ the condition of being wrong in belief or conduct

erupt *v.* ❶ (especially of a volcano) burst out ❷ break out suddenly and violently

escalate *v.* increase in intensity or extent

escape Ⅰ *v.* get free from Ⅱ *n.* an act of getting free from sth. or somewhere

escort Ⅰ *n.* a person or group of people or vehicles going with another or others to give protection or as a sign of honour Ⅱ *v.* go with (sb.) as an escort

especial *adj.* ❶ special or outstanding ❷ mainly suitable for one person or thing

especially *adv.* ❶ to a great degree; in particular ❷ most of all

essay Ⅰ *n.* a piece of writing, usually short and in prose, on a particular subject Ⅱ *v.* try or attempt

essence *n.* ❶ the most important feature or quality of sth. which makes a thing what it is ❷ the best part of a substance, taken out and reduced to a jelly, liquid, etc.

essential *adj.* completely necessary for the existence, success, etc. of sth.

establish *v.* ❶ set up; found ❷ settle or place (a person, oneself) in a position, place, etc. ❸ achieve permanent acceptance for (a belief, claim, custom, etc.)

establishment *n.* ❶ the process of establishing sth. ❷ a business organization, public institution, or household

esteem Ⅰ *v.* ❶ respect and admire (especially a person) greatly ❷ consider Ⅱ *n.* the respect and admiration for a person

estimate Ⅰ *v.* judge or calculate the extent, value, size, quantity, etc. of sth. roughly; form an opinion about Ⅱ *n.* a calculation or judgment of the extent, value, size, quantity, etc., of sth.

estimation *n.* ❶ a judgment or opinion about the value or quality of sb. or sth. ❷esteem ❸a judgement about the size, extent or quantity of sth.

eternal *adj.* ❶ lasting or existing forever; having no end ❷ happening often and seeming never to stop

ethical *adj.* ❶connected with ethics ❷ morally good or right

ethics *n.* ❶the science of moral principles ❷ moral principles that control or influence a person's behaviours

evacuate *v.* remove people from a place of danger to a safer place

evade *v.* get out of the way of or escape from

evaluate *v.* form an opinion of the value, amount or quality of sth. ; give an opinion of; estimate

evaporate *v.* (of a liquid) change or cause to change into vapour

evasive *adj.* ❶not willing to give a clear answer; not frank or straightforward ❷ seeking to avoid or prevent sth.

eve *n.* the day or evening before an event, especially a religious festival or holiday

even Ⅰ *adv.* ❶ (used just before the surprising part of a statement, to add to its strength) which is more than might be expected ❷ (used for making comparisons stronger) Ⅱ *adj.* ❶flat, level, and smooth; forming a straight line ❷(of things that can be measured and compared) equal

evening *n.* ❶the end of the day and early part of the night(between about 6 p. m. and bedtime) ❷a party, performance, etc. happening in the early parts of the night ❸the last period, as of life

evenly *adv.* ❶ in a smooth, regular or equal way ❷ with equal amounts for each person or in each place

event *n.* a thing that happens or takes place, especially an important, or unusual one

eventful *adj.* full of interesting or exciting events

eventual *adj.* (of an event) happening at last as a result

eventually *adv.* at last; in the end

eventuate *v.* result in; happen as a result

ever *adv.* ❶at any time up to the present ❷ used after a comparative or superlative for emphasis ❸ used in questions expressing astonishment or outrage for emphasis

everlasting *adj.* ❶ lasting for ever; without an end ❷ unceasing; repeated too often

every *adj.* ❶(preceding a singular noun) used to refer to all the individual members of a set without exception ❷ all possible

everywhere Ⅰ *adv.* in or to every place Ⅱ *conj.* wherever

evict *v.* make a person leave a house or land by law

evidence *n.* sth. such as facts, signs, or objects that give proof or reasons to make you believe or agree with sth.

evident *adj.* clear; obvious

evidently *adv.* that can be seen or understood clearly; plainly or obviously

evil Ⅰ *adj.* morally bad or cruel; wicked; harmful Ⅱ *n.* ❶ sin; wrong-doing ❷ sth. which is harmful or undesirable

evoke *v.* produce or call up

evolution *n.* ❶ the development of plants, animals, etc. from very simple forms of life ❷ the process of change and development

evolve *v.* ❶ develop gradually by a long continuous process ❷ develop over successive generations as a result of natural selection

exact *adj.* correct in every detail; completely according to fact; precise

exacting *adj.* demanding much care, effort, and attention

exactly *adv.* ❶ in an exact manner; to an exact degree ❷ used to express agreement with what someone has said or emphasizing that it is right

exaggerate *v.* represent sth. as being larger, greater, better, or worse than it really is

exalt *v.* give a higher rank or position to (sb.)

examination *n.* ❶ the process of examining sb. or sth. ❷ a formal test of a person's knowledge or ability by means of oral or written questions ❸ a formal questioning of a witness or an accused person in a law court

examine *v.* ❶ inspect (sb. or sth.) in detail in order to test their nature or condition ❷ give sb. a test to see how much knowledge they get about a subject

example *n.* ❶ a particular event or thing to show the meaning of a statement or rule; instance ❷ a person or a person's behaviour that is worthy of being copied

excavate *v.* dig; make by digging; uncover by digging

exceed *v.* ❶ go beyond what is necessary or allowed ❷ be more than

excel *v.* be or do better than (others); be very good at

excellence *n.* the quality of being outstanding or extremely good

excellent *adj.* very good; of high quality

except Ⅰ *prep.* other than; not including Ⅱ *v.* take out; exclude

exception *n.* a person or thing that is not included

excerpt Ⅰ *n.* sth. selected; a short extract taken out of a film, broadcast, film or book Ⅱ *v.* select (a short extract) from a book, etc.

excess Ⅰ *n.* sth. which is greater in amount than what is normal or proper Ⅱ *adj.* extra or additional (to the usual or permitted amount)

excessive *adj.* more or greater than what is normal or necessary

exchange Ⅰ *v.* give sth. and receive sth. (of the same type or equal value) in return Ⅱ *n.* the act of exchanging

excite *v.* ❶ cause to lose calmness and have strong feelings, especially of expectation and happiness ❷ bring out or give rise to (a feeling or reaction)

excited *adj.* feeling or showing expectation, happiness; not calm

excitement *n.* ❶ the state of being excited ❷ an exciting event

exciting *adj.* causing excitement or interest

exclaim *v.* speak or say loudly and suddenly, because of surprise or other strong feelings

exclamation *n.* yelling; speaking with sudden strong feelings

exclude *v.* ❶ prevent sb. or sth. from entering a place or taking part in sth. ❷ not include sth. in what you are doing or considering

excluding *prep.* except; apart from

excursion *n.* a short journey for pleasure

excuse Ⅰ *v.* ❶ forgive sb. for a small fault or offence ❷ free sb. from a duty or requirement Ⅱ *n.* a reason given to explain or defend one's conduct

execute *v.* ❶ carry out or put sth. into action ❷ administer; put into effect ❸ kill sb. as a legal punishment

executive Ⅰ *n.* ❶ a senior person or group of people with authority to manage a business organization ❷ the branch of a government with responsibility for putting laws and decisions into effect Ⅱ *adj.* having the powers to put laws or decisions into effect

exemplify *v.* be or make an example

exercise Ⅰ *n.* ❶ activity set to practise or a skill ❷ physical or mental activity carried out to stay healthy or become stronger Ⅱ *v.* (cause to) take exercise

exert *v.* try one's best; put into use; use one's strength of body or mind

exertion *n.* ❶ the process of exerting ❷ a great effort

exhale *v.* breathe out the air or smoke

exhaust Ⅰ *v.* ❶ use up completely ❷ expel (gas or steam) from or into a particular place Ⅱ *n.* the pipe which allows unwanted gas, steam, etc., to escape from an engine or machine

exhausted *adj.* ❶ drained of one's physical or mental resources; very tired ❷ (of resources or reserves) completely used up

exhibit Ⅰ *n.* an object or a work of art on public display Ⅱ *v.* ❶ show in public ❷ show clearly a particular feeling, quality or ability

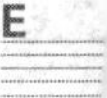

exhibition *n.* ❶ a public display of works of art or other items in a museum or gallery ❷ a display or show of feeling

exile *v.* force someone to leave their native country

exist *v.* be real or actual; have being; continue to live

existence *n.* ❶ the state of being or being real ❷ a way of living

exit Ⅰ *n.* ❶ a way out ❷ departure of an actor from the stage Ⅱ *v.* go out; (of an actor) leave (the stage)

expand *v.* ❶ make or become larger or more extensive; spread out ❷ become less reserved in character or behaviour ❸ give more details to what you are talking

expanse *n.* a wide area of open land, sea, or space

expansion *n.* the process of expanding; an increase or extension

expansive *adj.* ❶ covering a wide area in terms of space or scope; extensive or wide-ranging ❷ (of a person or their manner) generous and communicative because feeling at ease ❸ tending towards economic or political expansion

expect *v.* think or believe that sth. will happen

expectancy *n.* the state of thinking or

hoping that sth., especially sth. pleasant, will happen or be the case

expectant *adj.* expecting sth. to happen; hopeful

expectation *n.* ❶a strong belief that sth. will happen ❷a belief that someone will or should achieve sth.

E

expedite *v.* make(a plan or arrangement) happen sooner or go faster

expedition *n.* ❶ a journey done for a purpose, especially that of exploration or scientific research ❷the people who make such a journey

expel *v.* ❶send away from a school or an organization as a punishment ❷ send out with force

expend *v.* spend or use up(money, time, energy, etc.)

expenditure *n.* ❶the spending of money or other resources ❷the amount spent

expense *n.* ❶spending of money; cost ❷ (~s) money needed or used for sth. or in doing sth.

expensive *adj.* costing a lot of money

experience Ⅰ *n.* ❶ knowledge or skill which comes from practice in an activity or doing sth. for a long time, rather than from books ❷ sth. that happens to one and has an effect on the mind and feelings Ⅱ*v.* feel, suffer, or learn by (an) experience

experiment Ⅰ *n.* a scientific test made in order to learn sth. or prove the truth of an idea Ⅱ *v.* do a scientific test

expert *n.* a person with special skill or knowledge which comes from experience or training

expertise *n.* the expert knowledge or skill in a particular field

expire *v.* ❶die ❷send out; breath from the lung ❸(of a period of time)come to an end

explain *v.* ❶ show or tell sb. about sth. in a way that makes it easy to understand ❷ give a reason why sth. happens

explanation *n.* a statement, fact, circumstance, etc. that tells you why sth. happened

explicit *adj.* clearly stated in detail

explode *v.* ❶(cause sth. to) burst with a loud voice; blow up ❷ (of a person) show sudden and violent emotion

exploit[1] *n.* a brave and exciting act

exploit[2] *v.* ❶ make full use of and get benefit from (a resource) ❷ benefit unfairly from sb. by making them overwork and not giving them much in return

explore *v.* ❶ travel into or through (a place) for the purpose of discovery ❷ examine (especially a subject or question) carefully in order to find out more

explosion *n.* ❶a violent and destructive shattering or blowing apart of sth., as is caused by a bomb ❷a sudden outburst of sth. such as noise, light, or violent emotion, especially anger ❸ a sudden great increase

export Ⅰ *v.* send sth. out of the country to another country for sale Ⅱ *n.* (~s) sales of goods or services to other countries

exposc *v.* ❶ uncover; leave (sth.) unprotect-ed; lay open to(danger) ❷ show for sale; display ❸make known or public ❹ allow light to reach (film, etc.)

expound *v.* explain by giving details

express Ⅰ *v.* ❶show or make known a feeling, opinion, or fact by words, looks or actions ❷ press or squeeze out (especially juices or oil) ❸ send (a letter, parcel, etc.) fast by special delivery Ⅱ *n.* ❶a fast train that stops at few stations ❷a service provided by the post office, railways, road services, etc. for carrying goods quickly Ⅲ *adj.* ❶clearly and definitely stated; explicit ❷travelling or operating at high speed

expression *n.* ❶ the appearance of the face, showing one's feelings ❷ the process of showing feelings or thoughts in some way ❸ a word or group of words used to convey an idea

expressive *adj.* ❶ expressing a lot of feelings or thoughts ❷communicating the specified thought or feeling

exquisite *adj.* very finely made or done; extremely beautiful or skillful

extend *v.* ❶ (of land, time) spread to cover a wider area or last longer ❷ spread out the body at full length ❸ give sth.; offer

extension *n.* ❶the process or action of extending ❷a part that is added to sth. to enlarge or prolong it

extensive *adj.* ❶occupying a large area ❷large in amount or scale

extent *n.* the size, scale or range of sth.

exterior Ⅰ *adj.* relating to or coming from the outside Ⅱ *n.* the outside; the outer appearance or surface

external *adj.* ❶connected with, coming from or located on the outside ❷ relating to foreign countries

extinct *adj.* ❶no longer existing ❷no longer active or alight

extinction *n.* ❶the state or process of making sth. extinct or becoming extinct ❷ the state or process of extinguishing sth.

extinguish *v.* ❶put out (a light or fire) ❷ destroy sth.

extra Ⅰ *adj.* additional; beyond what is usual or necessary Ⅱ *n.* sth. added, for which an extra charge is made

extract Ⅰ *v.* pull or take out, especially with effort or difficulty Ⅱ *n.* a short passage taken from a book, film or a piece of music

extraction *n.* ❶the action of taking out sth., especially using effort or force ❷ the ethnic origin of someone's family

extraordinary *adj.* more than what is ordinary; peculiar; strange

extravagance *n.* ❶lack of restraint in spending money or use of resources ❷a thing on which too much money has been spent or which has used up too many resources ❸ excessive elaborateness of style, speech, or action

extreme Ⅰ *adj.* ❶ as far away as possible; remote ❷at the furthest point Ⅱ *n.* the greatest degree

exude *v.* (of moisture or a smell) come out, allow to come out, in small (from somewhere) slowly and steadily

eyesight *n.* the ability to see

F f

F

fable *n.* ❶a story which teaches a moral lesson ❷a story incorporating elements of legend and myth

fabric *n.* ❶ the basic structure of a building; the essential structure of a society, an organization, etc. ❷ woven material made by wool, cotton silk, etc.

fabulous *adj.* ❶very good; very big ❷ strange; unusual and interesting; amazing

face Ⅰ *n.* ❶the front part of the head ❷ the expression on the face ❸dignity; reputation Ⅱ *v.* ❶ be opposite sb. or sth.; have the face or front pointing towards sb. or sth. ❷confront and deal with or accept

facet *n.* ❶one of the sides of a precious stone which has been cut into shape ❷a part of sth.

facile *adj.* easily done or achieved; not requiring much effort or skill (and often of a poor quality)

facilitate *v.* make an action easier

facility *n.* ❶ a quality which makes learning or doing things easy or simple ❷ anything which makes doing sth. easier and more convenient

fact *n.* ❶sth. that has actually happened or is happening; sth. known to be or accepted as being true ❷things that are true rather than things that have been invented ❸a thing that is believed or claimed to be true

faction *n.* a small group of people within a political party

factor *n.* any of the forces, conditions, influences, etc., that acts with others to bring about a result

factory *n.* a place or building where goods are manufactured or assembled chiefly by machine

faculty *n.* ❶a power of mind; a power of doing things ❷a group of departments concerned with a major division of knowledge in a university ❸ the teaching or research staff in a university (of U. S.)

fade *v.* ❶ (cause to) lose brightness, colour, strength, freshness, etc. ❷ disappear or die gradually

fail Ⅰ *v.* ❶be unable to do sth. or do not succeed in doing sth. ❷be not enough ❸lose strength; become weaker Ⅱ *n.* (without ～) emphasize that sth. always happens or an order or a promise

failing Ⅰ *n.* a flaw or weak point Ⅱ *prep.* if a thing is not the case or does not happen

failure *n.* ❶lack of success ❷a person or

thing that fails

faint Ⅰ *adj.* ❶ lacking strength; weak and dizzy ❷ not clear, dim Ⅱ *v.* lose consciousness

fair[1] *n.* ❶ a very large show of goods, advertising, etc. ❷ a market, especially one held at a particular place at regular periods for selling farm produce

fair[2] *adj.* ❶ free from injustice, dishonesty, or self-interest ❷ moderately good; average ❸ (of weather) good ❹ (of the skin or hair) light in colour; not dark; blond

fairly *adv.* ❶ to a moderately sufficient extent or degree ❷ in a way that is honest or just

fairy *n.* a tiny, graceful, imaginary being with magic powers

faith *n.* ❶ a strong belief; unquestioning confidence ❷ a system of religious belief

faithful *adj.* keeping faith, loyal and true (to sb., to a cause, to a promise, etc.)

fake Ⅰ *v.* ❶ make sth. false or a copy of sth. with the intent to deceive ❷ pretend Ⅱ *n.* a person who makes deceitful pretenses; sth. that is a counterfeit Ⅲ *adj.* artificial; false

fall Ⅰ *v.* ❶ go down freely from a higher to a lower position or level, e. g. by losing balance or as a result of gravity ❷ become lower in level, degree, or quantity ❸ come or happen, as if by descending ❹ hang loosely ❺ die in a battle ❻ become Ⅱ *n.* ❶ an act of falling ❷ autumn ❸ a waterfall

fallible *adj.* likely to make a mistake

false *adj.* ❶ not true or correct ❷ not natural

falsify *v.* ❶ alter a document dishonestly ❷ misrepresent facts

fame *n.* the condition of being well known

familiar *adj.* ❶ well known to; often seen or heard ❷ friendly and informal

family *n.* ❶ a group of parents and children living together as a unit ❷ a group of related animals, plants, languages

famine *n.* ❶ extreme scarcity of food in a region ❷ a particular shortage

famous *adj.* ❶ known by a lot of people ❷ excellent; magnificent

fan[1] Ⅰ *n.* a thing that you hold in the hand and wave to make a current of air for cooling Ⅱ *v.* make a current of air by waving sth.

fan[2] *n.* a fanatical supporter of sth.

fanciful *adj.* ❶ produced by the imagination; not based on reason of good sense ❷ full of strange decorative details, decorated in an unusual style

fancy Ⅰ *n.* ❶ imagination, especially in a free and undirected form ❷ a hobby, especially one that is transient Ⅱ *adj.* decorative or brightly coloured; not ordinary; elaborate Ⅲ *v.* ❶ form a picture of; imagine ❷ have a liking for; wish for

fantastic *adj.* ❶ imaginative or fanciful ❷ wild and strange; bizarre or exotic ❸ (of ideas, plans) impossible to carry out; remote from reality ❹ very good; wonderful

fantasy *n.* fancy or imagination, especially when extravagant

far Ⅰ *adv.* ❶ from, at, to or by a great

distance ❷ very much; by a great deal Ⅱ *adj.* ❶ distant; remote ❷ more distant than another object of the same kind

fare Ⅰ *n.* ❶ the money charged for a journey (by bus, ship, taxi, etc.) ❷ food, especially as provided at a meal Ⅱ *v.* perform or get on with sth.

farewell Ⅰ *int.* goodbye Ⅱ *n.* an act of parting; words said at departure

farm Ⅰ *n.* an area of land and buildings for growing crops, raising animals, etc. Ⅱ *v.* use land for growing crops, raising pigs, etc.

far-sighted *adj.* able to see the future effects of present actions

farther Ⅰ *adj.* more distant Ⅱ *adv.* at or to a greater distance

fascinate *v.* ❶ charm or attract sb. greatly ❷ take away power of movement by a fixed look

fascination *n.* ❶ a very strong attraction that makes sth. very interesting ❷ the state of being attracted to and interested in sb. or sth.

fashion *n.* ❶ a popular trend (of clothes, ornament, manners of behaviour, etc.) which is most popular ❷ a manner or way of doing sth.

fashionable *adj.* in fashion; popular

fast Ⅰ *adj.* ❶ moving or able to move quickly ❷ (of a clock) showing a time in advance of the correct time ❸ firmly fixed and unlikely to move or change ❹ loyal; close ❺ unfading Ⅱ *adv.* ❶ firmly; tightly ❷ at a high speed

fasten *v.* ❶ make fast; fix firmly; tie or join together ❷ direct one's eyes, thoughts, attention, etc. upon sb.

fat Ⅰ *n.* any oily materials found in animal bodies, especially when deposited as a layer under the skin or around certain organs Ⅱ *adj.* ❶ covered with fat ❷ thick and well-filled ❸ rich; fertile

fatal *adj.* ❶ causing or resulting in death ❷ bringing danger or ruin, or having unpleasant results

fate *n.* ❶ the unknown cause beyond a person control, regarded as predetermined by a supernatural power ❷ a person's ultimate condition or the outcome of a particular situation for sb. or sth.

fated *adj.* destined by fate; doomed

fateful *adj.* showing an around certain organs important and decisive effect on future events

father *n.* ❶ a man in relation to his natural child or children ❷ (a title of address) priest ❸ an ancestor ❹ the founder or first of sth. or doing sth.

fatigue Ⅰ *n.* great tiredness; exhaustion Ⅱ *v.* make tired

fault *n.* ❶ a bad or weak point, but not of a serious moral kind, in someone's character ❷ a mistake or imperfection; sth. wrong or incorrect

faultless *adj.* without a fault; perfect

faulty *adj.* having faults; not working or made correctly

favour Ⅰ *n.* ❶ an attitude of liking or approval ❷ an act of kindness Ⅱ *v.* ❶ feel or show approval or preference for ❷ give more help, kindness, etc. to one person than to others

favourable *adj.* ❶ making people have a

good opinion of sb. or sth. ❷expressing approval ❸ to the advantage of sb. or sth.

favourite Ⅰ *adj.* liked more than others of the same kind; most loved Ⅱ *n.* sth. or sb. that is liked or loved above all others

fear Ⅰ *n.* ❶ an unpleasant and usually strong feeling caused by the presence or expectation of danger ❷anxiety for the safety (of sb. or sth.) Ⅱ *v.* ❶be afraid of ❷ feel anxiety or apprehension (for sb. or sth.)

fearful *adj.* ❶causing fear; horrifying ❷ feeling afraid; showing fear or anxiety

fearless *adj.* without fear

feasible *adj.* possible or able to be done or carried out

feast Ⅰ *n.* a meal with a lot of good food especially in celebration of sth. Ⅱ *v.* ❶ enjoy a big dinner ❷ take part in or make a large meal

feat *n.* a successful completion of sth. needing skill, strength or courage

feature Ⅰ *n.* ❶the face as a whole ❷a characteristic or striking aspect of sth. ❸ a main film in a cinema programme Ⅱ *v.* ❶have as a prominent aspect ❷ include as a leading performer

federal *adj.* of or being a federation

federation *n.* a group of states, united with one government which decides foreign affairs, defence, etc., but in which each state can have its own government to decide its own affairs

fee *n.* a payment made to someone or public body for professional advice or service

feeble *adj.* ❶lacking physical strength; weak; frail ❷ failing to convince or impress; not showing determination

feed Ⅰ *v.* ❶ give food to; provide a supply of food for ❷ supply with material; supply sth. to sb. or sth. ❸(of an animal) eat sth. Ⅱ *n.* ❶an act of giving food, especially to animals and babies ❷a meal

feedback *n.* information about a product, etc. that a user gives back to its supplier, maker, etc.

feel *v.* ❶touch; examine by touching; try to find by touching ❷give a sense of being; be conscious ❸have a particular opinion or attitude

feeling *n.* ❶the ability to feel things ❷ mental awareness or emotion ❸an idea or belief not wholly based on reason ❹ sensitivity; readiness to feel sympathy ❺an opinion or attitude ❻ (～s) the emotional side of a person's nature, as distinct from the intellectual side

fell *v.* ❶knock down ❷cut down

fellow Ⅰ *n.* ❶ a man or boy ❷(～s) a person in the same position or activity Ⅱ *adj.* of the same class, kind, etc.

fellowship *n.* ❶friendly association with other people; companionship ❷a society or group of people meeting to pursue a shared interest or aim

female Ⅰ *adj.* ❶of the sex that can bear offspring or produce eggs ❷of women Ⅱ *n.* a female person, animal or plant

feminine *adj.* ❶ of or having the qualities suitable for a woman ❷for or belonging to the class of words that usually includes most of the words

F

for females

fence Ⅰ *n.* a barrier of wood or wire used to keep people and animals out of a place Ⅱ *v.* ❶put a fence around ❷fight with sword as a sport

ferment Ⅰ *n.* ❶a substance capable of bringing about fermentation ❷ excitement and unrest (especially political or social) Ⅱ *v.* ❶ undergo fermentation, giving off a gas ❷excite; stir up

ferocious *adj.* very angry and violent

fertile *adj.* ❶(of land) which produces or can produce good crops ❷ (of a person's mind) inventive; full of suggestions, ideas, etc. ❸ (of living things) able to produce young or fruit

fertilize *v.* ❶ make soil fertile or productive, especially by adding substances to it ❷introduce pollen into a plant or sperm into an egg or female animal so that it develops seed or young

festival Ⅰ *n.* a day or time of religious or other celebration Ⅱ *adj.* of or suitable for a festival

fetch *v.* ❶ go for and bring back ❷ be sold for

feud *n.* a quarrel between two people or two groups, families, etc. lasting a long time

feudalism *n.* the system in which people were given land and protection by people of higher rank and worked and fought for them in return

fever *n.* ❶ a body temperature that is higher than usual ❷ a disease marked by high temperature ❸ a state of agitation or great excitement

few Ⅰ *adj.* ❶(a ~) a small number (of) ❷ not many Ⅱ *pron.* not many; not enough

fib *n.* a small and not very important lie

fibre(-er) *n.* any of the thin thread-like parts that together from many animal and plant growths such as wool, wood, or muscle

fiction *n.* ❶sth. imagined or invented ❷ literature in the form of prose, especially novels that describes imaginary events and people

fictional *adj.* belonging to fiction; told as a story

fictitious *adj.* untrue; or not real; being fabricated

fiddle Ⅰ *n.* ❶ a violin ❷ an act of defrauding or cheating Ⅱ *v.* ❶play the violin ❷move things aimlessly in one's fingers

fidelity *n.* ❶ faithfulness; willingness to give support and help to sb. whatever the danger or difficulties ❷ accuracy; the ability to produce the same sound, shape, colour, etc. as an original

field *n.* ❶ an area of land for growing crops or feeding animals ❷ a piece of land for some special use ❸a particular brand of study or sphere of activity

fierce *adj.* ❶cruel; violent ❷intense

fight Ⅰ *v.* struggle with the hands or with weapons; use physical force (as in war) Ⅱ *n.* an act of fighting

figment *n.* sth. imagined and untrue

figurative *adj.* using or containing a figure of speech; metaphorical, not literal

figure Ⅰ *n.* ❶ any of the number signs

from 0 to 9 ❷ the human shape considered from the point of view of being attractively thin ❸ an often numbered drawing or diagram used in a book to explain sth. ❹ an important person Ⅱ *v.* ❶ imagine; picture mentally ❷ calculate or work out ❸ consider; believe

file Ⅰ *n.* ❶ a box, folder, etc. for storing papers in an ordered way, especially in an office ❷ a steel tool with a rough surface, used for rubbing down, making smooth, or cutting through hard surfaces ❸ a line of people one behind the other Ⅱ *v.* ❶ place on or in a particular order ❷ rub or cut sth. with a file ❸ march in an orderly manner

fill Ⅰ *v.* make sth. full of; become full of sth. Ⅱ *n.* an amount of sth. as much as one can eat or drink

filter Ⅰ *n.* a coloured glass which allows light of certain wave lengths to pass through Ⅱ *v.* (cause to) flow through a filter; purify (a liquid) by using a filter

filth *n.* foul, disgusting dirt

filthy *adj.* ❶ disgustingly dirty ❷ obscene; immorally foul

final Ⅰ *adj.* ❶ last; coming at the end ❷ (of a decision, offer, etc.) that cannot be changed Ⅱ *n.* (~s) ❶ the last and most important examinations in a college course ❷ the last and most important in a set of matches

finale *n.* the last division of a piece of music or a musical show

finally *adv.* ❶ at last ❷ as the last of a number of things; lastly ❸ so as not to allow further change

finance Ⅰ *n.* the commercial or government activity of providing funds and capital Ⅱ *v.* provide money for

financial *adj.* relating to or involving money

find Ⅰ *v.* ❶ discover sth. by searching; get sb. or sth. that was hidden, lost, or not known ❷ discover (sb. or sth.) to be, by chance or experience ❸ obtain by effort ❹ become aware of by chance or experience Ⅱ *n.* sth. good or valuable that is found

fine Ⅰ *adj.* ❶ clear; bright; not raining ❷ of superior grade or quality ❸ very thin or delicate ❹ in good health or reasonably happy Ⅱ *adv.* ❶ very well ❷ in a delicate way Ⅲ *n.* a sum of money that must be paid as a punishment for breaking a law or rule

fineness *n.* ❶ the quality of being made of thin threads or lines very close together; the state or quality of being fine ❷ the quality of sth.

finish Ⅰ *v.* ❶ end; complete ❷ eat, drink or use what is left of sth. ❸ complete sth. or make sth. perfect ❹ destroy sb. or sth. Ⅱ *n.* the end of sth. or the last part of sth.

finished *adj.* ❶ properly made and perfected ❷ ended or brought to an end ❸ no longer existing or happening

finite *adj.* having limits or bounds

fire Ⅰ *n.* ❶ the hot, bright flames produced by things that are burning ❷ a mass of burning material, heat, etc. ❸ the shooting by weapons, especially by guns; firing Ⅱ *v.* ❶ shoot off bullets ❷ set fire to

firm Ⅰ *adj.* ❶ solidly fixed in a place; not soft or yielding to pressure ❷ not shakable or unlikely to change Ⅱ *n.* an organization which sells or produces sth. or provides a service which people pay for

first Ⅰ *num.* the one that happens or comes before all the others of the same kind Ⅱ *adv.* for the initial time Ⅲ *n.* ❶ the beginning ❷ the first person or thing

fist *n.* a tightly closed hand

fit[1] Ⅰ *adj.* ❶ meeting adequate standards for a purpose ❷ strong and healthy Ⅱ *v.* ❶ be the right measure, shape and size for sb. or sth. ❷ put into place

fit[2] *n.* ❶ a sudden(usually short)attack of illness ❷ a sudden display of anger, etc.; outburst

fitness *n.* ❶ the state of being physically fit ❷ the quality of being suitable

fix Ⅰ *v.* ❶ fasten firmly in position ❷ repair ❸ arrange and establish(an exact time, place, price, etc.), especially through agreement Ⅱ *n.* an awkward or difficult position

fixed *adj.* fastened; not movable or changeable

flabby *adj.* fat with loose flesh

flag Ⅰ *n.* a coloured piece of cloth which is used as a sign Ⅱ *v.* ❶ decorate with flags ❷ signal to(sb.)or stop(a train, etc.)by waving a flag

flagrant *adj.* (of sth. dishonest or bad) not hidden

flake Ⅰ *n.* a small thin piece of sth., especially one that has broken off a larger piece Ⅱ *v.* come off in small thin pieces

flame Ⅰ *n.* a hot bright stream of burning gas of a fire Ⅱ *v.* ❶ be aflame or in flames ❷ become red, bright, etc. by or as if by burning

flaming *adj.* very hot or bright

flammable *adj.* easily set on fire

flank Ⅰ *n.* the side of a building or mountain Ⅱ *v.* be placed beside sth.

flare Ⅰ *n.* a bright but unsteady light or flame Ⅱ *v.* ❶ burn brightly, but with an unsteady flame or for a short time ❷ suddenly become angry

flash Ⅰ *n.* ❶ a sudden quick bright light ❷ instant; a short time Ⅱ *v.* ❶ shine very brightly for a short time; make a flash in this way ❷ move very fast

flashy *adj.* unpleasantly big, bright, decorated, etc., and perhaps not of good quality

flat Ⅰ *adj.* ❶ smooth and level; even ❷ having a broad level surface but little height or depth ❸ complete; with no more argument Ⅱ *n.* a group of living rooms on one floor

flatter *v.* ❶ praise (sb.) too much or insincerely, especially in order to gain advantage ❷ give pleasure to

flavo(u)r *n.* ❶ the quality of a particular food or drinks as perceived by the taste buds ❷ a particular quality or characteristic

flaw *n.* ❶ a fault or a defect ❷ a crack

flee *v.* run away from

fleece *v.* swindle sb. or deprive sb. of sth. by trickery

fleet *n.* ❶ a group of warships, naval

aircraft, etc. under one command ❷ a group of buses, aircraft, etc. under one control

flesh Ⅰ *n.* the soft part consisting of muscle and fat between the skin and bones of animal or human Ⅱ *v.* add more details or information to sth.

flexible *adj.* ❶ easily bent without breaking ❷ able to change to suit new conditions or situations

flicker Ⅰ *v.* burn unsteadily; shine with an unsteady light Ⅱ *n.* light shining in an unsteady way

flight *n.* ❶ the act of flying ❷ a plane making a particular journey ❸ a series of stairs between two floors or landings

flit *v.* move quickly and lightly from place to place

float Ⅰ *v.* be held on the surface of a liquid, or up in air move with moving liquid Ⅱ *n.* ❶ the act or process of floating ❷ sth. that floats, especially a piece of wood or other light object used on a fishing line or to support the edge of a fishing net

flock Ⅰ *n.* ❶ a group of animals or birds that stay together ❷ a group of people; crowd Ⅱ *v.* gather in large numbers; come or go in large numbers

flood Ⅰ *n.* ❶ the covering with water of a place that is usually dry; a great overflow of water ❷ a large quantity or flow Ⅱ *v.* become so full that it spreads out

floor Ⅰ *n.* ❶ the surface on which one stands indoors; the surface nearest the ground ❷ all the rooms that are on the same level of a building Ⅱ *v.* make sb. fall down by hitting them

flourish Ⅰ *n.* an impressive act or way of doing sth. Ⅱ *v.* ❶ grow vigorously ❷ wave about sth. to make people look at it

flow Ⅰ *n.* ❶ the action or fact of moving along in a steady continuous stream ❷ the rise of the tide Ⅱ *v.* ❶ (of a liquid) move along steadily and continuously in a current or stream ❷ (of the tide) rise

flower Ⅰ *n.* ❶ the part of a plant that produces seeds or fruits ❷ the finest or best part of sth. Ⅱ *v.* produce flowers; bloom

fluctuate *v.* frequently change from higher to lower; rise and fall irregularly in number or amount

fluent *adj.* able to speak easily and articulately

fluid Ⅰ *adj.* ❶ having the quality of flowing、❷ unsettled; not fixed Ⅱ *n.* a liquid or a gas substance

flush Ⅰ *v.* ❶ become red in face; make face turn red ❷ flow or rush suddenly ❸ clean or wash with a flush of water ❹ (cause to) become excited Ⅱ *n.* ❶ a rush of blood to the face, reddening caused by this ❷ a sudden feeling of anger, excitement, etc. Ⅲ *adj.* ❶ exactly on a level (with); even in surface ❷ having plenty of money

fluster Ⅰ *v.* make sb. too excited or worried to be able to do sth. properly Ⅱ *n.* a condition of being flustered

flutter Ⅰ *v.* ❶ move the wings lightly and quickly ❷ wave back and forth, quickly and lightly ❸ (cause to) move about in an excited, confused way Ⅱ *n.*

❶a quick, light movement ❷a state of nervous or confused excitement

fly Ⅰ *n.* a small flying insect with two wings Ⅱ *v.* ❶ move or be moved through the air by means of wings ❷ travel by aircraft ❸pass rapidly; hurry; move at speed

F

foam Ⅰ *n.* a mass of very small bubbles on the surface of a liquid, on skin, etc. Ⅱ *v.* produce a mass of small bubbles

focus Ⅰ *n.* ❶ the thing or person that people are most interested in ❷ a meeting-point of rays of light, heat, etc.; a point or distance at which an object is most clearly seen by the eye or through lens Ⅱ *v.* ❶ pay particular attention to ❷arrange the lens in (an instrument) so as to obtain a clear picture (of)

fodder *n.* food for cows, horses, sheep, etc. which has been stored

fog Ⅰ *n.* a thick cloud of tiny drops of water in the air which obscures or restricts visibility Ⅱ *v.* cover or be covered with fog or steam

foggy *adj.* ❶full of or covered with fog ❷not clear; confused; puzzled

foil[1] *n.* ❶ metal hammered into a thin sheet like paper ❷a person or a thing which makes another seem better, more beautiful, more clever, etc. in contrast

foil[2] *v.* prevent sb. from doing sth. (especially sth. wrong)

fold Ⅰ *n.* a line made in material, paper, etc., by folding Ⅱ *v.* ❶ turn or press back one part of (sth., especially paper or cloth) and lay it on the remaining part; bend into two or more parts ❷ press (a pair of limbs) together ❸ wrap; cover

foliage *n.* leaves of a plant

folk Ⅰ *n.* people in general Ⅱ *adj.* of the common people of a country; of a tribe

follow *v.* ❶go or come after (in space, time or order); pursue steadily ❷ go along ❸understand clearly ❹take as a guide, a leader or an example

follower *n.* ❶a person who supports or believes in a person or cause ❷a person who moves or travels behind sb. or sth.

following Ⅰ *n.* a body of believers or supporters Ⅱ *adj.* about to be mentioned Ⅲ *prep.* after or as a result of

folly *n.* foolish words or behaviours

fond *adj.* ❶loving; tender ❷(～ of) having an affection or liking for

fondle *v.* touch in a loving way

food *n.* sth. that living creature or plants take into their bodies to give them strength and help them to develop and to live

fool Ⅰ *n.* a person who behaves or speaks in a way that lacks intelligence or good judgement Ⅱ *v.* trick or deceive

foolish *adj.* lacking good sense or judgement unwise; silly; like a fool

foot *n.* ❶the part of your leg that you stand on or walk ❷the bottom of sth. ❸ a measure of length equal to twelve inches

foothold *n.* ❶ a place wide enough to put a foot when climbing ❷ a secure position from which further progress can be made

footmark *n.* a mark made by a foot

footstep *n.* ❶the distance covered by one step ❷ a footprint ❸ the sound of a person's step

forbear *v.* refrain; restrain an impulse to do sth.

forbearance *n.* patience; self-control

forbearing *adj.* patient and restrained

forbid *v.* ❶command sb. not to do sth. ❷make sth. difficult or impossible

forbidden *adj.* not allowed; prohibited

forbidding *adj.* having a fierce, unfriendly or dangerous appearance

force Ⅰ *n.* ❶ a power, person or thing that has strong influences ❷ fierce or uncontrolled use of strength or violence ❸ an organized body of armed or disciplined men ❹ (of a rule, order, law, etc.) the state of being in effect, use, or operation Ⅱ *v.* ❶ use power to get or do sth.; oblige sb. to do sth. ❷ make a way through or into by physical strength

forced *adj.* made or driven by force; done by unusual effort

forceful *adj.* strong and powerful

forcible *adj.* ❶ using physical force ❷ strong and effective; powerful

fore Ⅰ *adj.* situated in the front Ⅱ *adv.* in or towards the front part of a ship or aircraft

forebear *n.* a person from whom one is descended; ancestor

forecast Ⅰ *n.* a statement of future events, based on some kind of knowledge or judgment Ⅱ *v.* predict or estimate what is going to happen at some future time especially with the help of some kind of knowledge

forefather *n.* ❶ a member of the past generations of one's family or people; an ancestor ❷ a precursor of a particular movement

foregoing *adj.* mentioned or stated earlier

foreign *adj.* ❶to, from, of, or concerning a country or language that is not one's own or not the one being talked about or considered ❷ coming or introduced from outside; having no relation (to)

foreigner *n.* a person from another country

foremost *adj.* the most prominent in rank, position or importance

foresee *v.* see or know sth. in advance

foreshadow *v.* be a sign that sth. dangerous or unpleasant is coming

foresight *n.* an ability to know or guess what will happen in the future

forest *n.* a large area of land covered with trees and undergrowth

forestall *v.* do sth. with the aim of preventing another person from doing it

foretell *v.* tell sth. beforehand

forethought *n.* wise planning for future needs; consideration of what is to come

forever *adv.* ❶ for all future time ❷continually

forewarn *v.* tell sb. of some danger etc. which is coming

forget *v.* ❶lose from the memory; fail to remember or recall ❷ put out of the mind; stop thinking about

forgetful *adj.* ❶tending to forget things

forgive *v.* stop feeling angry or resentful towards sb.; no longer have the wish to punish sb. for (an offence, a sin, etc.);

pardon or show mercy

forgiving *adj.* willing or able to forgive

fork Ⅰ *n.* ❶an implement with two or more points, used for lifting food to the mouth ❷a place where a road, river or tree branch, etc. divides into two parts Ⅱ *v.* ❶lift, move, carry sth. with a fork ❷(of a road, river, etc.) divide into two directions

F

forked *adj.* having one end divided into two or more points

form Ⅰ *n.* ❶ the shape or outward appearance ❷ a general plan or arrangement that sth. shows or expresses itself; kind or sort ❸a printed document with blank spaces in which to answer questions and give other information Ⅱ *v.* ❶ make up or produce, especially by combining parts ❷ come or bring gradually into existence; develop ❸ bring together parts or combine to create (sth.)

formal *adj.* ❶ according to accepted rules or custom ❷of the outward shape or appearance (not the content or matter)

formality *n.* ❶ the rigid obedience of rules and accepted forms of behaviour ❷a thing that you must do as a formal or official part of a legal process ❸sth. that is done as a matter of course and has lost its real meaning

format *n.* the way in which sth. is arranged or set out

formation *n.* ❶the action of forming or making ❷ an arrangement of people, ships, aircrafts, etc.

formative *adj.* causing sb. or sth. to have a certain type of nature

former *adj.* ❶ of an earlier period ❷ denoting the first of two people or things just mentioned

formerly *adv.* in earlier times

formless *adj.* ❶without shape ❷lacking order or arrangement

formulate *v.* ❶ express in an exact or systematic way ❷ create or devise a plan, suggestion, etc.

forsake *v.* give up; break away from; desert

forswear *v.* make a solemn promise to give up or to stop doing (sth.)

forth *adv.* ❶from that time ❷towards a place; forwards

forthcoming *adj.* ❶ happening or appearing soon ❷ ready or made available when needed

fortitude *n.* courage, endurance and self-control in facing pain, danger of difficulty

fortnight *n.* two weeks

fortress *n.* a place built with walls and defences

fortunate *adj.* favoured by fortune; lucky; prosperous; having, bringing, brought by good fortune

fortune *n.* ❶chance; luck; fate ❷a great deal of money; wealth

forum *n.* any place for public discussion

forward Ⅰ *adj.* ❶at or directed towards the front, the end, or the future ❷ advanced or early in development Ⅱ *adv.* ❶onward so as to make progress ❷ towards the future; onward in time Ⅲ *v.* ❶help advance the development of ❷send or pass on(letters, parcels, etc.)

to a new address

forwards *adv.* towards the front of a place; in advance; ahead

fossil *n.* remains of a very old plant, animal etc., which has been kept from destruction in hard rock

foster *v.* ❶ care for or bring up sb.; develop(a feeling or idea in oneself) ❷ encourage or promote the development of sth.

foul *adj.* ❶very dirty; with bad smell ❷ obscene or profane ❸ wicked or immoral ❹done contrary to the rules of a sport ❺(of weather) rough; stormy

found *v.* start the building of; lay the base of; establish

foundation *n.* ❶founding or establishing ❷ the lowest load-bearing part of a building ❸a principle, an idea or a fact that sth. is based on

founder Ⅰ *n.* the person who founds or establishes an organization, institution, etc. Ⅱ *v.* (of a ship) fill with water and sink

fountain *n.* ❶ a natural or man-made spring of water ❷ a source origin of sth.

fowl *n.* any bird that is kept for its meat and eggs

fraction *n.* ❶ a very small piece ❷ a small part or amount ❸a division of a whole number

fracture Ⅰ *n.* the breaking of a bone Ⅱ *v.* break or cause to break

fragile *adj.* easily broken; delicate

fragment Ⅰ *n.* a part broken off Ⅱ *v.* divide or break into pieces

fragmentary *adj.* consisting of fragments

fragrance *n.* a pleasant smell

fragrant *adj.* having a pleasant smell

frame Ⅰ *n.* ❶ the form or shape of a human or animal body ❷ the support structure of a building, vehicle, etc. ❸ the general ideas or system that forms the background to sth. Ⅱ *v.* ❶put or build a frame around sth. ❷ express sth. in words; compose or formulate

framework *n.* the part of a structure that gives shape and support

frank *adj.* expressing clearly one's thoughts and feelings

frankly *adv.* ❶ in an open and honest manner ❷speaking honestly and plainly

fraud *n.* ❶ the crime of making sb. believe sth. which is not true, in order to get sth. from him ❷a person or thing intended to deceive others not true

freak Ⅰ *n.* a plant, animal, person etc. that is unusual and unnatural in form Ⅱ *adj.* strange and unusual

free Ⅰ *adj.* ❶ not in the power of another person; not in prison; having personal rights ❷not busy; not working ❸ without payment; costing nothing; having no duty or charge ❹ ready to give; generous Ⅱ *v.* make free

freedom *n.* ❶the state of being free ❷ the power to do, say, think, or write as one pleases

freeway *n.* a divided highway for fast travelling on which usually no tolls are charged; expressway

freeze *v.* ❶become hard and often turn to ice ❷be or feel very cold ❸not allow (money or assets) to be used or

F

exchanged for a period of time

freezing *adj*. very cold; chilling

freight Ⅰ *n*. goods carried by truck, ship, train, or aircraft Ⅱ *v*. send or carry goods by truck, train, ship or aircraft

frequency *n*. ❶ the state of happening often ❷ the rate at which sth. happens or is repeated

F

frequent Ⅰ *adj*. found or happening often; habitual Ⅱ *v*. visit a place often or habitually

fresh *adj*. ❶ newly made, produced, gathered grown, etc. ; not tinned, frozen or preserved ❷ new or different; no previously known or used ❸ (of the air, wind, weather) cool, refreshing ❹ bright and attractive

freshman *n*. a student in the first year at a high school, college, or university

freshwater *adj*. of, living in, or being a river or inland lake; not belonging to the sea

friction *n*. ❶ the rubbing of one thing against another ❷ the force that slows the motion of things that touch ❸ conflict or difference caused by a clash of wills, temperaments or opinions

friend *n*. ❶ a person that you know well and like ❷ a person who supports an organization, a country or a cause by giving financial or other help; a person who supports a particular idea, etc.

friendly *adj*. of a friend; having the attitude of a friend; kind and willing to make friends

friendship *n*. a relationship of being friends

fright *n*. a feeling or experience of fear

frighten *v*. fill with fright or terror; alarm suddenly

frightful *adj*. dreadful; terrible; shocking

frigid *adj*. ❶ very cold ❷ very unfriendly; showing no emotions

frill *n*. ❶ a piece of cloth used as a decoration on a dress, etc. ❷ anything unnecessary and used only as a decoration

frolic Ⅰ *n*. any noisy and happy action Ⅱ *v*. behave noisily and happily

front Ⅰ *adj*. of or at the front Ⅱ *n*. ❶ the most forward part of sth. ❷ the place where fighting takes place in a war Ⅲ *v*. (of a building or piece of land) have the front facing towards

frontier *n*. a boundary between countries

frost Ⅰ *n*. ❶ a weather condition at a temperature below the freezing point of water ❷ a deposit of white ice crystals forms on the ground or other surfaces when the temperature drops below 0℃ Ⅱ *v*. cover sth. or become covered with frost

frosty *adj*. ❶ covered with frost ❷ very cold ❸ unfriendly and cold in manner

frown Ⅰ *v*. draw the eyebrows down over the nose, as you do when you are angry or thinking Ⅱ *n*. a facial expression or look characterized by such a furrowing of one's brows

frugal *adj*. careful, economical of food, money or expenditure; costing little

fruit *n*. ❶ a part of a plant or tree that contains the seeds and is used as food ❷ (the ～) the profit, result, or reward of labour, industry, study, etc.

fruitful *adj.* ❶bearing plenty of fruit ❷successful; producing good results

fruitless *adj.* ❶producing no fruit ❷(of an effort) useless, unsuccessful, not bringing the desired result

frustrate *v.* defeat sb. or sb.'s effort

frustrated *adj.* ❶ feeling annoyed and impatient because you cannot do or achieve what you want ❷ prevented from progressing, succeeding, or being fulfilled

frustration *n.* defeat or disappointment

fry *v.* cook sth. or be cooked in hot fat or oil

fuel Ⅰ *n.* any material that is used for producing heat or power by burning Ⅱ *v.* supply sth. with material that can be burnt to produce heat or power

fulfil *v.* do or perform what is required or necessary

full Ⅰ *adj.* ❶ containing or holding as much or as many as possible; having a lot of a particular quality ❷ complete with nothing missing ❸ reaching the highest or greatest possible ❹ (of a shape or sb.'s body) plump or rounded; fleshy

fully *adv.* completely; entirely

fume Ⅰ *n.* ❶ (~s) smoke or gas that smells strongly or is dangerous to breathe in ❷rage or fury Ⅱ *v.* ❶give off smoke ❷be very angry and restless

fun Ⅰ *n.* amusement; pleasure Ⅱ *adj.* amusing or enjoyable; providing pleasure

function Ⅰ *n.* a special duty (of a person) or purpose (of a thing) Ⅱ *v.* work or act in the correct way

fund Ⅰ *n.* ❶a large stock or supply of sth. ❷a sum of money available for a purpose Ⅱ *v.* provide money for an activity, organization, etc.

fundamental Ⅰ *n.* a central or primary rule, law, etc. on which a system is based Ⅱ *adj.* being at the base or from which all else develops

funeral *n.* a burial or ceremony for a dead person

funnel *n.* ❶a type of tube with a wide mouth and a narrow bottom, used for pouring liquid, etc. into a container ❷ the part of a steamship or steam engine where smoke comes out

funny *adj.* ❶ amusing or causing laughter ❷ strange or curious; hard to explain

furnish *v.* ❶supply what is necessary for a special purpose ❷put furniture in; supply with furniture

furniture *n.* movable articles of a building or room, such as tables and beds

further Ⅰ *adv.* ❶ at or to a greater distance or more distant point; farther ❷ more; to a greater degree or extent ❸over a greater expanse of time Ⅱ *v.* help (sth.) advance or succeed

furthermore *adv.* in addition; moreover; besides

furthermost *adj.* located at the greatest distance from sth.

furthest Ⅰ *adj.* ❶located at the greatest distance from sth. ❷extremely remote Ⅱ *adv.* at or by the greatest distance

fury *n.* great anger

fuse Ⅰ *n.* a small container with a short thin piece of wire, placed in an electric apparatus or system Ⅱ *v.* ❶ melt or cause metal to melt in great heat ❷join or become joined by melting ❸ (cause to) stop working owing to the melting of a fuse

fusion *n.* the process of mixing or joining

fuss Ⅰ *n.* ❶an unnecessary or excessive expression of excitement, anger, impatience, etc. ❷ an anxious nervous condition Ⅱ *v.* disturb or bother

fussy *adj.* ❶full of or showing nervous excitement; worrying about little things ❷ over ornamented; having too many unimportant details, etc.

future Ⅰ *n.* ❶ the time or a period of time coming after the present ❷ the possibility of being successful or surviving at a later time Ⅱ *adj.* coming after the present

G g

gab *v.* talk continuously and without thought

gabble Ⅰ *v.* speak quickly and indistinctly Ⅱ *n.* words or word-like sounds spoken so quickly that they cannot be heard clearly

gain Ⅰ *v.* ❶ obtain sth. useful, advantageous, wanted, profitable, etc. ❷ have an increase in ❸ reach (somewhere), especially with effort or difficulty Ⅱ *n.* ❶(the act of making) a profit ❷an increase in amount

gainful *adj.* paid or profitable

galaxy *n.* ❶ huge mass of millions of stars ❷ (Galaxy) the extremely large group of stars and planets to which the Earth belongs and which is seen at night as a faint band of light across the sky

gale *n.* ❶ a strong wind ❷ a noisy outburst

gall *n.* ❶bitter liquid made by the liver ❷ anything bitter; a bitter feeling ❸ rudeness; bad manners

gallery *n.* a room or building used to show collections of pictures, statues, or other works of art

gallop Ⅰ *n.* a fast gait of a horse Ⅱ *v.* do sth. in a hurry

gamble Ⅰ *v.* play games for chance of money; take risks of the chance for making a profit Ⅱ *n.* a risky matter or act

game *n.* ❶a form of play or sport ❷(～s) athletic contests ❸a single part of a set into which a match is divided, e. g. in tennis, bridge, etc. ❹ a trick or secret plan

gang *n.* ❶ an organized group of people working together ❷ a group of criminals

gap *n.* ❶ an empty space between two objects or two parts of an object ❷a big difference between two groups of people, things, or sets of ideas

gape *v.* ❶look at sb. or sth. in surprise or wonder, especially with the mouth open ❷come apart or open widely

garage *n.* ❶ a building in which motor vehicles can be kept ❷ a place where motor vehicles are repaired and petrol and oil may also be sold

garbage *n.* waste food put out as worthless, or for pigs, etc.; rubbish, refuse of any kind

garden Ⅰ *n.* a piece of land, often around or at the side of a house, which may be covered with grass or planted with flowers, fruit and vegetables Ⅱ *v.* work in a park, keeping it tidy, making plants grow, etc.

garland *n.* a woven circle of flowers or leaves used as a sign of victory

garment *n.* an article of dress

gas *n.* ❶a substance like air, which is not solid or liquid and usually cannot be seen ❷ a substance of this type, especially natural gas, which is burnt in the home for heating and cooking and formerly also for light

gash Ⅰ *n.* a long, deep cut in the skin or in the surface of sth. Ⅱ *v.* wound with a large deep cut

gasp *v.* ❶take one's breath suddenly and in a way that can be heard, especially because of surprise, shock, etc. ❷ breathe quickly, especially with difficulty, making a noise

gateway *n.* ❶an opening in a fence, wall, etc., across which a gate may be put ❷ a way of reaching or gaining (especially sth. desirable)

gather *v.* ❶get or assemble together ❷ pick up and arrange together; collect ❸ introduce information that you have found out, especially when you have found it out in an indirect way

gathering *n.* a group of persons to gather in one place

gaudy *adj.* bright and showy

gauge Ⅰ *n.* ❶ an instrument for measuring ❷ accepted or approved instance or example of a quantity or quality against which others are judged or measured or compared standard measure; extent Ⅱ *v.* ❶ measure by means of a gauge ❷ estimate; judge; guess

gay *adj.* ❶cheerful; happy; full of fun ❷ bright or attractive, so that one feels happy to see it, hear it, etc.

gaze Ⅰ *v.* look steadily, especially for a long time and often without being conscious of what one is doing Ⅱ *n.* a steady fixed look

gear *n.* ❶ an apparatus, especially one consisting of a set of toothed wheels, that allows power to be passed from one part of a machine to another so as to control the power, speed, or direction of movement ❷ clothing equipment, etc. for a particular purpose

gem *n.* ❶ a jewel; a precious stone ❷ anything of great value

gender *n.* a person's sex

general Ⅰ *adj.* ❶ common; universal ❷ applying to all or most members of a category or group ❸ not specialized or limited to the main things only Ⅱ *n.* a senior army officer of very high rank

generate *v.* produce; bring into; bring about

generation *n.* a period of time in which a human being can grow up and have a family (about 25 or 30 years)

generosity *n.* ❶ the quality of being generous ❷a generous act

generous *adj.* ❶ showing readiness to give money, help, kindness, etc. ❷plentiful

genial *adj.* cheerful and cheering; kindly; pleasant

genius *n.* ❶ great ability or skill in a particular subject ❷ someone who has exceptional intellectual ability and originality

gentle *adj.* ❶mild, calm and kind ❷not rough or severe; soft and mild

gentleman *n.* ❶ a man who is kind, polite, and honest ❷a polite word for any man

gently *adv.* ❶ in a gentle manner; with little weight or force ❷ in a gradual manner

genuine *adj.* ❶not fake or counterfeit ❷ honest or frank; sincerely felt or expressed

germ *n.* ❶ a disease-producing bacterium; microbe ❷ the portion of a living organism capable of becoming a new organism

germinate *v.* (of a seed) begin to grow and put out shoots; cause (a seed) to sprout in such a way

gesture *n.* a movement of the hand or other part of the body to indicate or illustrate an idea, feeling, etc.

get *v.* ❶come into the possession of sth. ❷buy ❸fetch ❹receive ❺catch (an illness) ❻ understand ❼ become ❽ arrive at or reach a place or point

ghost *n.* the spirit of a dead person who appeared again

giant Ⅰ *n.* (in fairy tales) an imaginary person of very great size and strength Ⅱ *adj.* much larger than most others

gibe *n.* an aggressive remark directed at a person and intended to have a telling effect

gift *n.* ❶sth. which is given willingly; a present ❷ a natural ability to do sth.; talent

gifted *adj.* having great natural ability

gigantic *adj.* exceedingly large or extensive

giggle Ⅰ *n.* a silly laugh Ⅱ *v.* laugh in a silly way

gild *v.* cover thinly with gold or gold paint

gird *v.* ❶ prepare oneself for a military confrontation ❷encircle or surround

gist *n.* the central meaning or theme of a speech or literary work

give *v.* ❶ cause someone to have, hold, receive, or own ❷pay in order to buy; pay in exchange (for sth.) ❸ cause to experience ❹ provide or supply ❺ perform or carry out (an action) ❻ allow to have ❼ set aside (time, thought, strength, etc.) for a purpose

glacial *adj.* ❶of ice or glaciers ❷of an ice age ❸very cold

glacier *n.* a big mass of ice that moves slowly down a mountain

glad *adj.* ❶pleased and happy about sth. ❷causing happiness

gladden *v.* make glad or happy

glamour *n.* an attractive and exciting quality that sth. has, often because it involves famous and successful people

glance Ⅰ *v.* ❶take a quick look ❷flash Ⅱ *n.* a quick or hurried look

glare Ⅰ *v.* ❶shine with a strong light or in a way that hurts the eyes ❷look in an angry way Ⅱ *n.* ❶a hard unpleasant effect given by a strong light ❷ an angry look or stare

glaring *adj.* ❶ very bright; dazzling ❷ very easily seen

gleam Ⅰ *v.* give out a gentle light; shine softly Ⅱ *n.* ❶ a gentle light, especially one that is small or shines for a short time ❷a sudden showing of a feeling or quality for a short time

glee *n.* a feeling of joy caused by success or triumph

glide Ⅰ *v.* move along smoothly and continuously Ⅱ *n.* the act of moving smoothly along a surface while remaining in contact with its movement

glimpse Ⅰ *n.* a very quick sight Ⅱ *v.* see very quickly

glitter Ⅰ *v.* shine with a bright sparkling light Ⅱ *n.* a brilliant light

glittering *adj.* ❶ shining with a shimmering or sparkling light ❷ impressively successful or elaborate

global *adj.* ❶of or concerning the whole world ❷taking account of or including (almost) all possible considerations

globe *n.* ❶the planet we live on; an object shaped like a ball; the earth ❷an object shaped like a ball with a map of the earth on it

gloom *n.* ❶darkness ❷a feeling of deep sadness or hopelessness

gloomy *adj.* ❶dark, poorly lit ❷sad and without hope ❸without much hope of success or happiness in the future

glorify *v.* ❶praise or make sth. seem better than it is; worship ❷give fame to

glorious *adj.* ❶splendid and impressive ❷ having great fame or success; honourable

glory *n.* ❶the fame and honour won by great achievements ❷ the quality of being beautiful or magnificent

gloss[1] *n.* a bright shine on the surface of sth.

gloss[2] Ⅰ *n.* an explanation or definition of a word in a text Ⅱ *v.* provide explanations for words or phrases

glossary *n.* a list of glosses; a list of words needing special explanation

glossy *adj.* shiny and smooth

glove *n.* a covering for the hand and wrist (usually with a separate place for each finger)

glow Ⅰ *v.* ❶give out heat and soft light without flames or smoke ❷ show redness and heat, especially in the face, e. g. after hard work or because of strong feelings Ⅱ *n.* ❶ a dull, steady light from sth. burning without flames or smoke ❷a strong feeling

glower *v.* look angrily at

glue Ⅰ *n.* a sticky substance which is used for joining things together Ⅱ *v.* join or stick sth. with glue

glum *adj.* in low spirits; gloomy

gnaw *v.* ❶ bite sth. repeatedly ❷ torment; cause to keep worrying

go Ⅰ *v.* ❶leave a place (so as to reach another) ❷pass into a different state, either by a natural change or by changing on purpose; become ❸ be placed where sth. is usually placed ❹become weak, damaged, or worn out ❺(of a machine, etc.) work (properly) ❻happen in a certain way Ⅱ *n.* ❶one's turn (especially in a game) ❷an attempt to do sth.

goad Ⅰ *n.* sth. driving a person to do sth. Ⅱ *v.* urge; drive forward

goal *n.* ❶the posts between which the ball has to pass in football and other games ❷the point made by doing this

❸one's aim or purpose

gobble *v.* eat in lumps, quickly and noisily

god *n.* ❶one of the spirits or beings that are believed to have power over the world or nature ❷ the supernatural being conceived as the perfect originator and the ruler of the universe of the universe

goddess *n.* a female god, especially in Greek and Latin mythology

godless *adj.* ❶not having belief in God; not recognizing God ❷wicked

godly *adj.* showing great reverence or obedience to God

gold Ⅰ *n.* ❶ a shining, bright-yellow valuable metal ❷a bright, yellow colour ❸money or wealth ❹a gold medal Ⅱ *adj.* bright yellow in colour; like gold

golden *adj.* ❶ of gold or like gold in value or colour ❷ precious; excellent; important

good Ⅰ *adj.* ❶of a high quality, level ❷ happy and enjoyable ❸strong; healthy ❹ having the ability to do sth. ❺ thorough; complete Ⅱ *n.* that which is pleasing or valuable or useful

goodness *n.* ❶the quality of being good; virtue ❷the best part of sth.

goods *n.* ❶things which you can buy or sell ❷possessions which can be moved, as opposed to houses, land, etc.

goodwill *n.* ❶a friendly attitude toward others ❷ good reputation which increases the value of the business

gorgeous *adj.* richly coloured; magnificent

gossip Ⅰ *n.* ❶idle talk about the affairs of others ❷a person fond of idle talk Ⅱ *v.* talk about the affairs of others and reveal their secrets

govern *v.* ❶ be officially in charge of a country or a place and have responsibility for making laws, managing the economy and controlling public services ❷ direct or strongly influence the behaviour of

government *n.* ❶the ruling of a country, etc. ❷the method or system by which a community or other political unit is governed ❸the organization that is the governing authority of a political unit

grab Ⅰ *v.* take hold of sth. suddenly; snatch Ⅱ *n.* a sudden snatch

grace Ⅰ *n.* ❶ elegance and beauty of movement or manner ❷ the ways of behaving and doing things which are considered polite and well-mannered Ⅱ *v.* give grace or honour to

graceful *adj.* having or showing grace

gracious *adj.* pleasant and kind; polite

grade Ⅰ *n.* ❶ the degree of rank or quality ❷a group of classes in which all the students are of a similar age ❸the mark Ⅱ *v.* sort things into sizes, kinds, etc.

gradual *adj.* happening a little at a time rather than suddenly

graduate Ⅰ *v.* get a university degree, complete a course at an educational institution Ⅱ *n.* a person who has a university degree

graft Ⅰ *v.* transfer a part of one living thing to another Ⅱ *n.* the act of grafting sth. onto sth. else

grain *n.* ❶ a small, hard seed of food plants such as wheat and rice ❷a tiny piece of sand, sugar or salt, etc.

grammar *n.* ❶a study of the right way to put words together when we speak and write ❷ the way in which someone obeys the rules of language when they write or speak

grand *adj.* ❶very big, or impressive in size or appearance ❷of most or greatest importance ❸very enjoyable

G

grandeur *n.* greatness; magnificence

grange *n.* a large country house with farm buildings

grant Ⅰ *n.* an amount of money given by a state or other institution for a particular purpose Ⅱ *v.* ❶agree to fulfil or allow to be fulfilled ❷ admit that sth. is true

graph *n.* a diagram which shows the relationship between two or more sets of numbers or measurements

graphic *adj.* ❶of writing or drawing ❷ clear and vivid

grasp Ⅰ *v.* ❶hold tightly in the hand; take a firm hold of; seize ❷understand Ⅱ *n.* ❶a firm hold of the hand ❷the understanding of the nature or meaning or quality or magnitude of sth.

grasping *adj.* eager for more, especially more money, and often ready to use unfair or dishonest methods

grassy *adj.* covered with growing grass

grate Ⅰ *n.* a metal frame work where a fire is lit Ⅱ *v.* rub into small thin pieces with a special instrument

grateful *adj.* ❶ feeling or showing gratitude ❷ affording comfort or pleasure

gratify *v.* make happy or satisfied

gratitude *n.* a feeling of thankfulness and appreciation

grave[1] *adj.* ❶ requiring careful consideration; important ❷serious

grave[2] *n.* the place in the ground where a dead person is buried

gravel *n.* a mixture of sand and small stones, often used for making garden paths

graveyard *n.* a piece of ground, sometimes around a church, where people are buried; a cemetery

gravitate *v.* move or tend to move under the influence of gravitational force; be strongly attracted

gravitation *n.* the force of mutual attraction between all masses in the universe, especially the attraction of the earth's mass for bodies near its surface

gravity *n.* ❶ the quality of being serious ❷ the force which attracts objects towards the centre of the earth

grease Ⅰ *n.* ❶animal fat; that has been made softer by heating ❷any thick, oily substance Ⅱ *v.* put grease or fat on

greasy *adj.* ❶covered with or containing grease ❷ slippery ❸ insincerely polite; smarmy

great *adj.* ❶ of excellent quality or importance ❷ unusually good; very enjoyable

greed *n.* a strong desire to have a lot of sth., especially food, money, or power, often in a way that is selfish or unfair to other people

green Ⅰ *adj.* ❶of the colour between yellow and blue, which is the colour of leaves or grasses ❷ not ripe; not completely grown ❸ not trained or experienced Ⅱ *n.* ❶ the colour of grass or many other plants ❷ (～s) green vegetables

greenhouse *n.* a building with sides and roof of glass, used for growing plants that need protection from the weather

greet *v.* ❶ say hello to sb. or to welcome them; say words of welcome to ❷ receive or acknowledge sth. in a specified way

greeting *n.* the words or actions used to welcome or address sb.

grey *adj.* ❶ of black mixed white ❷ (of the skin of the face) of pale colour because of sudden fear or illness ❸ half dark; cloudy

grief *n.* ❶ great sadness caused by trouble or loss; heavy sorrow ❷ a cause of sorrow or sadness

grievance *n.* sth. that you think is unfair and that you complain or protest about

grieve *v.* ❶ feel sorrow or sadness ❷ cause grief to; make very unhappy

grievous *adj.* extremely serious

grill Ⅰ *v.* cook sth. under or over strong heat Ⅱ *n.* an arrangement of a metal shelf under a gas flame or electric heat, used to cook food quickly

grim *adj.* ❶ unpleasant and depressing ❷ looking or sounding very serious ❸ determined in spite of fear or great difficulty

grind *v.* ❶ crush or make into small pieces or powder ❷ polish or sharpen by rubbing on a hard surface ❸ rub harshly together

grip Ⅰ *v.* ❶ seize or hold firmly in hand; grasp ❷ attract the attention of sb. Ⅱ *n.* a very tight forceful hold

grocery *n.* ❶ things sold by a grocer ❷ the shop or trade of a grocer

groove *n.* a long narrow hollow cut in the wood, etc.

grope *v.* ❶ feel or search about as one does in the dark ❷ search with uncertainty of success for an idea or fact

gross *adj.* ❶ visible to the naked eye ❷ rough, impolite, and offensive ❹ (of income, profit, or interest) without deduction of tax or other contributions; total

ground Ⅰ *n.* ❶ soil; on the surface of the earth ❷ the solid surface of the earth ❸ a piece of land for a special purpose ❹ a large garden or small park around a building ❺ (～s) a good or true reason for sth. ❻ background Ⅱ *v.* ❶ lay on place(sth.) on the ground ❷ base

groundless *adj.* not based on any good reason

groundwork *n.* the work that lays the basis for sth.

group Ⅰ *n.* ❶ a number of people, things, or organizations gathered, placed together or connected in a particular way ❷ a number of people that work together or share certain beliefs Ⅱ *v.* form into, gather in a group or groups

grove *n.* a small group of trees; a small wood

grow *v.* ❶ live and develop naturally in a certain place ❷ raise by planting seeds and caring for ❸ become gradually

grown-up Ⅰ *adj.* mature; arrived at full growth Ⅱ *n.* a grown man; an adult

growth *n.* ❶ development; the process of growing ❷ sth. that has grown

grub *v.* ❶turn over the soil, especially by digging with the hands or paws ❷dig up by the roots

grudge Ⅰ *v.* feel resentful that someone has achieved (sth.) Ⅱ *n.* a feeling of ill-will or resentment

grudging *adj.* unwilling; reluctant

grumble Ⅰ *v.* express discontent or dissatisfaction; complain in a quiet but bad-tempered way Ⅱ *n.* a complaint or expression of dissatisfaction

G

guarantee Ⅰ *v.* ❶promise to do sth. or sth. will happen ❷give a promise to replace or repair a product free if it goes wrong Ⅱ *n.* a promise that certain conditions will be fulfilled

guard Ⅰ *n.* ❶ a person, especially a soldier, policeman, or prison officer, who watches over people or places to prevent escape, danger, attack, etc. ❷the act or duty of protecting property, places or people from danger or attack Ⅱ *v.* ❶ watch over in order to control or, protect ❷take precautions against

guess Ⅰ *v.* ❶ give an answer that you feel may be right ❷suppose; consider Ⅱ *n.* an attempt to guess

guest *n.* a person who is invited to visit the home of another or to a particular event

guidance *n.* advice or information aimed at resolving a problem or difficulty

guide Ⅰ *n.* ❶a person who shows others the way ❷a thing that helps someone to form an opinion or make a decision ❸ a book, document or display of information Ⅱ *v.* ❶show (sb.) the way by leading ❷direct or have an influence on the course of action of

guideline *n.* a general rule, principle, or piece of advice

guilt *n.* ❶a feeling of shame for having done wrong or failed in an obligation ❷ the fact of having committed an implied offence or crime

guilty *adj.* ❶ having broken a law ❷ conscious of or affected by a feeling of guilt

guise *n.* an external form or appearance, typically concealing the true nature of sth.

gulf *n.* a deep inlet of the sea with land on three sides of it

gulp Ⅰ *v.* ❶swallow down food or drink quickly in large amounts ❷ make a sudden swallowing movement as if surprised or nervous Ⅱ *n.* the amount swallowed at a single time; a large mouthful

gurgle *n.* a sound like water flowing quickly through a narrow space

gush Ⅰ *v.* ❶pour or flow suddenly and quickly ❷ talk continuously Ⅱ *n.* ❶a sudden flow (of a liquid, words, etc.) ❷ a sudden strong expression of feeling

gushing *adj.* expressing admiration, pleasure, etc. too strongly and perhaps without true feelings

gust *n.* ❶a sudden strong rush of wind ❷ a burst of anger or other strong feelings

gut *n.* ❶the stomach or belly ❷courage and determination

guy *n.* a man or fellow

gymnastics *n.* exercises that develop and show the body's strength and ability to move and bend easily, often does as a sport in competitions

H h

habit *n.* ❶ a tendency to behave in a particular way or do particular things, especially regularly and repeatedly over a long period ❷ general shape or mode of growth, especially of a plant

habitable *adj.* able to be lived in

habitat *n.* the natural home or surroundings of animals and plants

habitation *n.* ❶ the state or process of living in a place ❷ a house or home

habitual *adj.* ❶ regular; usual ❷ having a regular habit

hacker *n.* someone who is able to use or change the information in other people's computer systems without their permission

haggle *v.* bargain over the price of sth.

hail Ⅰ *n.* ❶ frozen rain drops which fall as little hard balls of ice ❷ a number of things which strike at sb. with violence, causing pain or damage Ⅱ *v.* small balls of ice fall like rain from the sky

hairdresser *n.* a person whose job is to cut and arrange other's hair

hale *adj.* (especially of an old person) very healthy and active

half Ⅰ *n.* either of the two equal parts into which sth. is or could be divided Ⅱ *pron.* an amount equal to a half Ⅲ *adv.* partly; not completely

halfway *adv.* ❶ at a point between and equally distant from two others ❷ to some extent

hall *n.* ❶ a big room or building for meetings, concerts, etc. ❷ the room or space (inside the front entrance) of a house, with doors of other rooms

halt Ⅰ *v.* (cause to) stop abruptly Ⅱ *n.* a stop or pause

halting *adj.* stopping and starting especially through lack of confidence

halve *v.* ❶ divide sth. into two equal parts ❷ lessen or reduce by half

hamper *v.* hinder; get in the way of

hand Ⅰ *n.* ❶ the part of the body of the end of the arm, including the fingers ❷ a person who is employed to do manual work ❸ a pointer on a clock, watch, instrument, etc. ❹ side or direction ❺ (a ～) help in doing sth. Ⅱ *v.* ❶ give; pass ❷ hold the hands of sb. in order to help them move

handcuff *n.* (～s) a pair of linked metal rings for fastening a prisoner's wrists together

handful *n.* ❶ a quantity as much as can be held in one hand ❷ a small number of amount

handicap Ⅰ *n.* ❶ a condition that markedly restricts a person's ability to function physically, mentally or socially ❷a circumstance that make it difficult for sb. to do sth. Ⅱ *v.* ❶(of a quality or situation) cause (sb.) to have a disadvantage ❷(of a physical or mental disability) prevent (sb.) from acting and living as most people do

handicraft *n.* a skill which needs careful use of the hands

H

handiwork *n.* sth. made by hand

handle Ⅰ *n.* a part of a tool or instrument that you hold in the hand Ⅱ *v.* ❶touch or move by hand ❷deal with; control ❸buy and sell

handover *n.* an act or instance of handing sth. over

handsome *adj.* ❶(of men) good-looking; of attractive appearance ❷(especially of women) strong-looking; attractive with a firm, large appearance rather than a delicate one ❸ generous; plentiful

handwriting *n.* ❶writing done by hand with a pen or pencil ❷a person's style of writing

handy *adj.* ❶(of things) convenient to handle; used easily ❷skilled with the hands ❸(of places) located near to sb. or sth. or in a convenient place

hang *v.* ❶fix sth. at the top so that the lower part is free : Hang your coat (up) on the hook. ❷stick (wallpaper) to a wall ❸ (cause to) kill sb. as a punishment for a crime, by dropping with a rope around the neck

hanging *n.* the practice in which death is caused by hanging a person from a rope round the neck as a form of punishment

hangout *n.* a place that a person lives in or often visits

hanker *v.* have a strong desire for; want very much

haphazard *adj.* by chance; without design

happen *v.* ❶take place; occur ❷have the luck or chance (to do sth.) ❸find or meet by chance

happy *adj.* ❶full of joy; feeling pleasure ❷(of behaviour, thoughts, etc.) suitable and appropriate ❸ willing or glad to do sth.

harass *v.* ❶ trouble; worry ❷ make repeated attacks on

hard Ⅰ *adj.* ❶ firm; solid; not easily broken, bent or cut ❷difficult to do or understand ❸needing a great deal of physical or mental effort ❹ full of difficulty and trouble ❺strict; not kind; unfeeling Ⅱ *adv.* ❶with great effort; with strength ❷ with a great deal of force; violently

harden *v.* (cause to) become hard

hardly *adv.* ❶ almost not; scarcely ❷ only a very short time before ❸not at all; not reasonably ❹severely

hardship *n.* ❶a circumstance that causes discomfort or suffering ❷ severe suffering

hardy *adj.* robust; able to endure hardship

harm Ⅰ *n.* damage; injury Ⅱ *v.* hurt; damage

harmful *adj.* causing or likely to cause harm

harmless *adj.* unable or unlikely to cause harm

harmonious *adj.* ❶ combining together in a pleasant and attractive way ❷ free from disagreement or ill feeling

harmonize *v.* make consistent

harmony *n.* ❶ a state of complete agreement (in feelings, ideas, etc.) ❷ the combination of simultaneously sounded music notes to produce chords in a pleasant sounding way

harry *v.* ❶ raid and ravage; attack frequently ❷ harass (sb.) frequently

harsh *adj.* ❶ rough and unpleasant to the senses ❷ stern or cruel

harvest Ⅰ *n.* ❶ the act or time of gathering the crops ❷ the amount of the crops gathered ❸ the result of past work or action Ⅱ *v.* ❶ gather a crop ❷ receive the result of past work or action

haste *n.* hurry; quickness of movement

hasten *v.* ❶ move or act quickly ❷ cause (sb.) to hurry; cause (sth.) to be done or to happen quickly or earlier

hasty *adj.* ❶ done in a hurry ❷ too quick in acting or deciding, often with bad or unwanted results; rash

hatch Ⅰ *v.* ❶ (cause to) break out of an egg ❷ think out and produce (a plot, etc.) Ⅱ *n.* an opening in a wall, floor, etc., through which people or things can pass

hate Ⅰ *v.* ❶ feel hatred towards (sb. or sth.); dislike very strongly ❷ regret; be reluctant Ⅱ *n.* the feeling of extreme or violent dislike or ill-will

hateful *adj.* arousing or evoking hatred

hatred *n.* the emotion of extreme dislike or hate

haul Ⅰ *v.* pull with effort or force Ⅱ *n.* ❶ the act of pulling sth. with effort or force ❷ the amount of fish caught when fishing with a net

have *v.* ❶ possess, own; hold; keep ❷ take; receive; get; drink ❸ experience; enjoy ❹ suffer from an illness or a disease ❺ want; wish; make; let ❻ allow; permit

haven *n.* harbour; a place of safety

hawk *v.* ❶ sell (goods) on the street or at the doors of houses, especially while moving from place to place ❷ spread (information, ideas, etc.) around, especially by speech

hazard Ⅰ *n.* sth. likely to cause damage or loss; a danger or risk Ⅱ *v.* ❶ risk; put in danger ❷ offer (a suggestion, a guess, etc.) when there is a risk of being wrong or unwelcome

hazardous *adj.* risky or dangerous

haze *n.* light mist; air that is not clear

hazy *adj.* ❶ filled or abounding with fog or mist ❷ vague or indistinct in outline ❸ feeling confused or uncertain

head Ⅰ *n.* ❶ the top part of your body, where eyes, ears, nose and mouth are ❷ the unit of a herd or flock ❸ a ruler or leader ❹ the mind or brain; mental abilities ❹ the top part of some plants, as when several leaves or flowers grow together ❺ the top of a page ❻ the front of people, vehicles, etc. Ⅱ *v.* ❶ lead; be at the front of ❷ be in charge of ❸ be at the top of; provide a heading for ❹ go or come toward

heading *n.* a word or words put at the

top of a section of printing or writing as a title

headmaster *n.* the principle master of a school

headquarters *n.* the place that serves as the administrative center of an enterprise

headstrong *adj.* determined to have one's own way

heal *v.* ❶ (usually of injuries and wounds) become well ❷ cure; restore to health

H

healing *n.* the process of becoming or making sb. or sth. healthy again; the process of getting better after an emotional shock

health *n.* ❶the condition of body or mind ❷the state of being well in the body and mind, and free from disease

healthy *adj.* ❶physically strong and not suffering from illness; usually in good health ❷good for mind or character ❸ showing good health

heap Ⅰ *n.* ❶a pole of things arranged in a rather messy way ❷a lot Ⅱ *v.* ❶put things in a large pile ❷ load or place sth. in a pile

hear *v.* ❶take in sound through the ears; listen to (music, a lecture, etc.) ❷ be told and get to know, usually accidentally

hearing *n.* ❶ the sense which makes it possible for them to be aware of by sounds ❷the distance within which one can hear

heart *n.* ❶ the organ inside the chest, which controls the flow of blood by pushing it round the body ❷ deep feelings and beliefs ❸courage; strength of mind ❹ the most central and important part of sth. ❺ a beloved person ❻the mood

heartache *n.* deep sorrow or grief

heartbreak *n.* overwhelming sorrow caused by loss of a loved one

heartbroken *adj.* suffering from overwhelming sorrow

hearten *v.* make a person feel cheerful or encouraged

heartless *adj.* not feeling any pity or sympathy

hearty *adj.* ❶ friendly and sincere; warmhearted ❷ (of a person) strong and healthy; full of vigour ❸(of meals) large and very satisfying ❹loud and too cheerful

heat Ⅰ *n.* ❶ the quality or quantity of being warm or cold; the degree of hotness; temperature of sth. ❷the very hot weather ❸ the intense feeling, especially of anger or excitement Ⅱ *v.* make or become hot

heating *n.* the system and equipment used to provide heat to a building

heave *v.* ❶lift or pull sth. with difficulty ❷rise and fall regularly; move up and down ❸throw with great effort

heaven *n.* ❶the place where God or the angels are said to live, and where good people are believed to go after they die ❷(~s) the sky ❸a place or state of complete bliss and happiness

heavy *adj.* ❶hard to lift or carry; having great weight or density ❷ of greater than usual; great in amount or force ❸ clumsy; slow

hedge Ⅰ *n.* a fence of bushes or low trees, heels usually along the edge of a lawn, garden, or field Ⅱ *v.* ❶put fence around ❷ avoid answering questions directly

heed Ⅰ *v.* pay attention to Ⅱ *n.* attention; notice

heel Ⅰ *n.* ❶the back part of the foot ❷ the back part of the bottom of a shoe, sock, etc. Ⅱ *v.* move along at the heels of someone

height *n.* ❶ distance from the base of sth. to the top or from a person's head to foot ❷ the highest degree ❸ a high place

heir *n.* a person who has the legal right to get money or goods when someone dies

hell Ⅰ *n.* ❶(in some religions) a place where the souls of bad people are said to be punished after death ❷a place or condition of pain and turmoil Ⅱ *int.* a swear word, used in anger or to give force to an expression

helm *n.* a long handle or wheel, used for turning the rudder of a ship

helmet *n.* a covering to protect the head

help Ⅰ *v.* ❶do sth. or part of sth. for sb. ❷ encourage, improve, or produce favourable conditions for(sth.) Ⅱ *n.* ❶ the act of helping ❷a person or thing that helps

helpful *adj.* giving help

helpless *adj.* without help; unable to help oneself

hem Ⅰ *n.* a lap made by folding over cloth; the border on a shirt, etc. Ⅱ *v.* fold over and sew down the edge

hemisphere *n.* one half of the earth

hence *adv.* ❶from here; from now ❷for this reason

henceforth *adv.* from this time on

herd Ⅰ *n.* ❶a group of animals of the same kind ❷a large number of people; mob Ⅱ *v.* drive animals as a herd

here *adv.* ❶at, in or to this place ❷used for drawing attention to sth. or sb.

hereafter *adv.* from now on, in the future

hereby *adv.* by this means

hereditary *adj.* passed from one generation to another

herein *adv.* in or into this place, thing, document, etc.

herewith *adv.* with this letter

heritage *n.* any attribute or immaterial possession which has been or may be inherited from ancestors

hermit *n.* a person who lives alone (often in order to lead a religious life)

hero *n.* ❶a man who does sth. great or brave ❷the chief man in a poem, story, play, etc.

heroic *adj.* ❶showing the qualities of a hero; extremely courageous ❷ of or concerning heroes

heroine *n.* ❶a woman who is admired for her brave or noble deeds ❷the chief female character in a story, play, or poem

heroism *n.* very great courage

hesitate *v.* ❶ stop for a moment before speaking or acting; be slow in deciding ❷be unwilling

hiccup Ⅰ *n.* ❶ a high gulping sound made when your breath is briefly interrupted ❷a brief hitch or setback Ⅱ *v.* make the sound of a hiccup

hidden *adj.* difficult to see or find

hide *v.* ❶ put or keep out of sight; prevent from being seen or found; conceal ❷ keep (facts, feelings, etc.) from being known ❸ place oneself or be placed so as to be unseen

high Ⅰ *adj.* ❶ having a long way from the bottom to the top when it is upright ❷ close to the top of a particular range of notes ❸ costing a lot of money ❹ morally good ❺ senior; important ❻ (of time) far advanced Ⅱ *adv.* in or to a high point, place, amount or degree

highland *n.* mountainous land

highlight Ⅰ *n.* ❶ the most interesting or outstanding feature of sth. ❷ a light or bright area in a painting, picture etc. Ⅱ *v.* draw special attention to sth.

highly *adv.* ❶ to a high degree ❷ very

highway *n.* ❶ a public road ❷ a main route by land, sea, or air

hijack *v.* ❶ take control of (a vehicle or aircraft) by force of arms ❷ stop and rob

hike Ⅰ *v.* ❶ go on a hike ❷ increase suddenly and steeply Ⅱ *n.* a long walk in the country, especially over rough ground, and taken for pleasure

hill *n.* ❶ an area of land that is higher than the land that surrounds it ❷ a small heap (of earth)

hinder Ⅰ *v.* keep back; delay; be an obstacle Ⅱ *adj.* located at or of the back part

hindmost *adj.* furthest back; last

hinge Ⅰ *n.* the joint on which a lid, door, etc. turns and swings Ⅱ *v.* attach with a hinge; turn or depend on

hint Ⅰ *n.* ❶ a statement or action that gives a small or indirect suggestion ❷ a slight indication Ⅱ *v.* suggest or mention indirectly

hip *n.* the fleshy part of either side of the human body above the legs

hire Ⅰ *v.* ❶ pay for the use of; rent ❷ employ sb. or pay them for working Ⅱ *n.* the act of hiring sth. or sb.

hiss Ⅰ *v.* ❶ make a sound like a long "s" ❷ show disapproval and dislike of Ⅱ *n.* a hissing sound

historic *adj.* important in history

history *n.* ❶ (the study of) events in the past, especially events concerning the rulers and government of a country, social and trade conditions, etc. ❷ a written account of history ❸ series of past events or experiences connected with an object, a person or a place

hit Ⅰ *v.* ❶ give a blow to; strike ❷ come against sth. with force ❸ reach ❹ find sth. by accident or after searching Ⅱ *n.* ❶ a blow; a stroke ❷ a successful attempt or performance; a conspicuous success

hitchhike *v.* go on a journey by getting rides in other people's cars

hitherto *adv.* until this time

hive *n.* ❶ a box (of wood, straw, etc.) for bees to live in ❷ a swarm of bees ❸ a place where there is a lot of activities or people are busy working

hoarse *adj.* (of sound) rough and harsh sounding

hoax Ⅰ *n.* a trick, intended to deceive; a deliberate trickery Ⅱ *v.* play a trick on (someone)

hobby *n.* sth. you do for pleasure in your spare time

hoist Ⅰ *v.* lift up and put in a higher position Ⅱ *n.* an upward push

hold Ⅰ *v.* ❶grasp and keep; take in the hands or arms ❷ put or keep in a certain position ❸ bear the weight of; support ❹ keep back or control ❺ contain; have room for ❻ possess (money, land or a position) ❼ arrange and take part in ❽ have a belief or an opinion about sb. or sth. ❾ have a particular job or position; own or have sth. Ⅱ *n.* ❶the act of grasping ❷sth. which can be held, especially in climbing ❸the part of a ship(below deck) where goods are stored

hole *n.* ❶ a hollow place in sth. ❷ a burrow of an animal

holiday *n.* ❶ a day of festival or recreation ❷(～s) a period of rest from work or study

hollow Ⅰ *adj.* ❶having an empty space inside ❷(of parts of the body) lacking flesh so that the skin sinks inwards ❸ (of sounds) having a ringing sound like the note when an empty container is struck ❹(of feelings, words) not real; empty of real meaning Ⅱ *v.* make a hollow or hollows in

holy *adj.* ❶ connected with God and religion; sacred ❷devoted to the service of God or religion

home Ⅰ *n.* ❶the place where one lives with one's family ❷the place where one was born ❸a place where people who are homeless, poor, old or sick may live ❹a place where sth. originates or where an animal or plant is native or exists Ⅱ *adv.* ❶to or at one's home ❷at, in, or to one's native country Ⅲ *adj.* ❶of or connected with one's home ❷in one's native country; inside the country; domestic ❸(of a game) playing in one's own ground

homeland *n.* a person's native land

homely *adj.* ❶ simple and plain ❷ not good-looking; unattractive

homesick *adj.* upset because you are away from home

hometown *n.* the place where you were born or lived as a child

honest *adj.* ❶ not lying or deceiving; truthful ❷ (of actions, appearance, etc.) typical of an honest person ❸(of actions, etc.) sincere but undistinguished

honesty *n.* the quality of being honest

honeymoon *n.* the holiday taken by a husband and wife immediately after their marriage

honour Ⅰ *n.* ❶good name; fame; glory ❷great respect, often publicly expressed ❸a person or thing that brings honour ❹ a title to some judges or people of importance Ⅱ *v.* ❶show respect for; give public praise and distinction to sb. ❷accept and pay when due

honourable *adj.* deserving or satisfying honour

hood *n.* ❶a piece of clothing that covers the head and neck, often fastened to a coat ❷the covering of an open car

hook Ⅰ *n.* ❶ a bent piece of metal or plastic, for catching hold of sth. or for hanging sth. on ❷ a curved tool for cutting Ⅱ *v.* ❶attach sth. with a hook ❷fasten with a hook

hooked *adj.* ❶ shaped like a hook ❷ addicted to sth.

hoop *n.* a thin ring of metal, wood, plastic etc.

hoot Ⅰ *n.* ❶ a loud high-pitched noise showing anger, disapproval, amusement etc. ❷ noise made by the horn of a motorcar, factory whistle etc. Ⅱ *v.* ❶ make a loud noise

H

hope Ⅰ *v.* wish for and expect Ⅱ *n.* ❶ the feeling that one desires and expects ❷ a person, thing, on which hope is based on

hopeful *adj.* ❶ (of people) having or feeling hope ❷giving cause for hope of success; promising

hopeless *adj.* ❶feeling no hope; giving or promising no hope ❷incurable

horizon *n.* ❶ the limit of one's view across the surface of the earth, where the sky seems to meet the earth or sea ❷ the limit of one's ideas, knowledge, or experience

horizontal *adj.* parallel to the horizon

horn *n.* ❶the hard, curved outgrowths on the head of cattle, deer, and some other animals ❷a substance made of this ❸a musical wind instrument that makes a loud noise when you blow through it ❹ the device on a car, bus, etc. which makes a noise as a signal

horrible *adj.* ❶causing great shock, fear and disgust ❷ very unkind or unpleasant; awful

horrid *adj.* very unpleasant; disgusting

horrific *adj.* causing or intended to cause horror; horrifying

horrify *v.* fill someone with horror, or shock someone

horror *n.* ❶a feeling of extreme fear or dislike ❷a naughty child

hose Ⅰ *n.* a long, flexible pipe made of rubber, canvas, or plastic for directing water on to fires, watering gardens, etc. Ⅱ *v.* water or wash with a hose

hospitable *adj.* friendly, generous and kind to guests

hospital *n.* a place where people are treated for illness or injuries

hospitality *n.* friendly and generous reception and entertainment towards guests

host Ⅰ *n.* ❶the person who invited the guests and entertains them; a country city or organization provides the facilities for an event to take place ❷ the keeper of a hotel ❸a large number (of) ❹ a compere of a television program, etc. Ⅱ *v.* act as a host or hostess of an activity or to a person

hostage *n.* a person who is kept as a prisoner by an enemy so that the other side will meet what the enemy demands

hostile *adj.* ❶showing extreme dislike or disapproval; unfriendly ❷ belonging to an enemy

hot *adj.* ❶having a lot of heat; not cold ❷having a strong, burning taste ❸(of news) fresh, very recent and usually sensational ❹full of strong feeling; easy and quick to get angry

hotel *n.* a building where meals and rooms are provided

hour *n.* ❶ a period of 60 minutes ❷ a

time of day when a new hour starts ❸ (~s) a fixed point or period of time, especially one that is set aside for a particular purpose or activity ❹ an important moment or period: in the ~ of danger

hourly Ⅰ *adj.* ❶done or occurring every hour ❷continual Ⅱ *adv.* ❶every hour; once every hour ❷at any hour

house Ⅰ *n.* ❶ a building where people live ❷all the people who live together in such a building ❸ a building for animals or goods ❹ a business firm, controlled by a family or one in the business of publishing ❺assembly ❻a theatre or audience in a theatre Ⅱ *v.* ❶ provide with a house ❷store(goods)

household *n.* all the people living together in a house

housewife *n.* a married woman whose main occupation is looking after the household

housing *n.* ❶ houses and flats; accommodation ❷ a rigid cover enclosing a piece of machinery

however Ⅰ *adv.* ❶in whatever degree ❷in spite of this; nevertheless Ⅱ *conj.* in whatever way

howl Ⅰ *n.* a long, loud cry of dogs, wolves, etc. Ⅱ *v.* ❶give a long, loud crying sound ❷ give a long loud cry expressing pain, anger or unhappiness ❸utter in a very loud voice

huddle Ⅰ *v.* (cause to) crowd together, in a group or in a pile Ⅱ *n.* a crowd of people or things, close together and not in any ordered arrangement

hue *n.* ❶ a colour ❷ the quality of a colour as determined by its dominant wavelength

hug Ⅰ *v.* ❶ hold (sb.) tightly in the arms, especially as a sign of love ❷hold on to(an idea) with a feeling of pleasure or safety ❸go along while staying near Ⅱ *n.* a tight embrace

huge *adj.* very large; very big; very great

hugely *adv.* very much; extremely

hum Ⅰ *v.* ❶ make a low continuous sound as bees do ❷utter with the lips closed; not using words ❸ (of work being carried out) be active; move fast Ⅱ *n.* the sound of humming

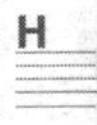

human Ⅰ *adj.* ❶ of or concerning people, especially as opposed to animals, plants, or machines ❷ showing the feelings, especially those of kindness, which people are supposed to have Ⅱ *n.* any living or extinct member characterized by superior intelligence, articulate speech, and erect carriage

humane *adj.* compassionate or merciful

humanity *n.* ❶ the quality of being humane or human ❷ human beings generally ❸ (humanities) learning or literature concerned with human culture, especially literature, history, art, music and philosophy

humankind *n.* human beings collectively

humble Ⅰ *adj.* ❶having or showing a modest opinion of oneself, one's position, etc. ❷low in rank or position; unimportant Ⅱ *v.* cause to feel shame; lower the rank or self importance of

humdrum *adj.* dull, ordinary or boring

humid *adj.* (usually of an atmosphere or climate) damp and usually very hot

humiliate *v.* make ashamed; hurt the pride of

humility *n.* being humble or modest

humo(u)r Ⅰ *n.* ❶ an ability to cause to feel amusement ; a quality in sth. that makes you laugh ❷ temper or mood Ⅱ *v.* make sb. happy by doing what he wants

hunger Ⅰ *n.* ❶ the feeling of being hungry ❷ a strong desire ❸ a lack of food Ⅱ *v.* ❶ have a strong desire or craving for ❷ starve

H

hungry *adj.* ❶ having an uncomfortable or painful feeling in stomach and wanting to eat food ❷ having a strong desire

hunt *v.* ❶ go after wild animals for food or as a sport ❷ search for someone in order to catch or harm them ❸ search carefully ❹ drive away

hunter *n.* ❶ a person who hunts wild animals for food or as a sport ❷ the animal such as a dog, a horse, etc. that is used by people who hunt

hurl *v.* ❶ throw with great force ❷ utter sth. with force; shout; yell

hurricane *n.* a storm with a violent wind, especially a tropical cyclone

hurry Ⅰ *v.* ❶ (cause to) move or do sth. quickly ❷ send or bring quickly Ⅱ *n.* a condition of urgency making it necessary to hurry

hurt Ⅰ *v.* ❶ cause physical pain or damage to (especially a part of the body) ❷ cause (a person) to suffer pain of the mind upset Ⅱ *n.* harm or damage especially to feelings

husband *n.* a man to whom a woman is married

hush Ⅰ *v.* ❶ make or become silent or quiet ❷ prevent sth. from becoming generally known, especially sth. shameful Ⅱ *n.* tranquil silence

hut *n.* a small wooden or stone house with one room

hygiene *n.* conditions or practices conducive to maintaining health and preventing disease, especially through cleanliness

hypothesis *n.* sth. which is assumed in order to argue or explain

hypothetical *adj.* based only on a suggestion that has not been proved or shown to be real; imaginary

hysteria *n.* ❶ nervous excitement causing feelings and behaviour that cannot be controlled ❷ an extremely excited and exaggerated way of behaving

hysterical *adj.* ❶ in a state of hysteria ❷ extremely funny

I i

I *pron.* the person who is speaking or writing

ice Ⅰ *n.* frozen water Ⅱ *v.* make very cold

iceberg *n.* a huge mass of ice floating in the sea with the greater part under water

ice cream *n.* a soft frozen food made with sweetened and flavored milk fat

iced *adj.* ❶ (of drink or other liquid) cooled in or mixed with pieces of ice ❷ (of a surface or object) covered or coated with ice

icon *n.* ❶ an important person or thing who or which is a symbol of a particular thing ❷ a picture on a computer screen which represents a special function

icy *adj.* ❶ extremely cold ❷ covered with ice ❸ very cold and unfriendly in manner

idea *n.* ❶ an opinion or a belief about sth. ❷ a plan or suggestion, especially about what to do ❸ a thought in the mind ❹ the aim or purpose of sth.

ideal Ⅰ *adj.* perfect in every aspect Ⅱ *n.* (a belief in) high principles or perfect standards

idealism *n.* ❶ the practice of forming or pursuing ideals, especially sth. unrealistic ❷ the representation of things in ideal or idealized form

idealize *v.* regard or represent a person or thing as perfect, or as better than they are

identification *n.* ❶ the process of showing who or what sb. or sth. is ❷ sth. used to identify a person or thing

identify *v.* ❶ say, show, prove who or what sb. or sth. is ❷ consider to be the same

identity *n.* ❶ sameness; exact likeness ❷ who or what a particular person or thing is

idiom *n.* ❶ a phrase which means sth. different from the meanings of the separate words from which it is formed ❷ the way of expression typical of a person or people in their use of language

idol *n.* ❶ an image in wood, stone, etc. of a god ❷ a person or thing greatly loved

idolize *v.* treat as an idol; admire or love sb. deeply

if *conj.* ❶ on condition that; supposing that ❷ used with a past tense for imaginary situations ❸ accepting that; although ❹ whether ❺ when; whenever ❻ used like that after words expressing surprise, sorrow, or pleasure ❼ expressing a wish

ignite *v.* catch fire; set on fire

ignoble *adj.* dishonorable; shameful

ignorance *n.* the lack of knowledge, information, or consciousness, especially of sth. one ought to know about

ignorant *adj.* ❶ (of persons) knowing little or nothing; not aware ❷ caused by or showing ignorance ❸ rude or impolite, especially because of lack of social training

ignore *v.* pay no attention to; not notice

ill Ⅰ *adj.* ❶ sick; in bad health; not well ❷ bad; harmful; evil Ⅱ *adv.* ❶ badly ❷ scarcely Ⅲ *n.* ❶ (usually *pl.*) difficulty; trouble; misfortune ❷ evil; harm

illegal *adj.* forbidden by law; unlawful

illness *n.* (a) disease; unhealthy state of the body or mind

illogical *adj.* ❶ contrary to the principles of sound reasoning; not logical ❷ not reasonable

illuminate *v.* ❶ give light to; fill (especially a room) with light ❷ decorate (buildings, streets, etc.) with lights for a special occasion ❸ cause to understand; explain; make clear

illumination *n.* ❶ the lighting or light ❷ (*pl.*) lights used in decorating a building or other structures ❸ the spiritual or intellectual enlightenment ❹ clarification

illusion *n.* ❶ sth. that a person wrongly believes to exist ❷ false idea or belief

illustrate *v.* ❶ make the meaning of sth. clearer by giving related examples ❷ add pictures to (sth. written) ❸ show that sth. is true or a situation exists

image *n.* ❶ a picture formed of an object in front of a mirror or lens, such as the picture formed on the film inside a camera or one's reflection in a mirror ❷ the general opinion about a person, an organization, etc. that has been formed or intentionally created in people's minds ❸ a copy; a similar people or thing ❹ an object made to represent a god or a person to be worshipped

imaginable *adj.* that can be imagined possibly

imaginary *adj.* not real, but produced from pictures or ideas in someone's mind; existing only in imagination

imagination *n.* ❶ the ability to imagine ❷ sth. that is imagined

imaginative *adj.* ❶ having or showing the imagination ❷ good at inventing imaginary things or artistic forms, or at producing new ideas

imagine *v.* ❶ form a picture in the mind; think of (sth.) as possible ❷ suppose or have an idea about (sth. that is false or does not exist) ❸ think that sth. is possibly true

imaginings *n.* thoughts or fantasies

imbalance *n.* a situation in which two or more things are lack of balance or proportion

imitate *v.* ❶ copy the behavior of; take as an example ❷ be like; make a likeness of

imitation *n.* ❶ the act or an action of copying sb. or sth. ❷ a copy of the quality goods

immature *adj.* not yet fully grown or developed

immeasurable *adj.* too big or great to be measured

immediately Ⅰ *adv.* at once, without any

delay Ⅱ conj. as soon as

immense *adj.* very large or great

immensity *n.* unusual largeness in size, extent or number

immerse *v.* ❶ put deep under water ❷ cause(oneself) to enter deeply into an activity; absorb

immigrant *n.* a person who comes into a foreign country or region to live

immigration *n.* the process of coming to live in a foreign country forever

immodest *adj.* not decent; rude and not socially acceptable

immoral *adj.* wrong; evil; not conforming to accepted standards of morality

immortal *adj.* living and lasting forever; having fame for all time

immovable *adj.* impossible to or cannot move

impact *n.* ❶ the force of one object hitting another ❷ a strong or powerful influence or effect, especially caused or produced by an idea, invention, event, etc.

impair *v.* weaken; damage

impart *v.* give, pass on qualities, knowledge, etc. to other people

impartial *adj.* just; fair to both sides

impassioned *adj.* full of passion or strong feelings

impassive *adj.* showing no sign of feelings; unmoved

impatience *n.* lack of patience

impatient *adj.* ❶ not patient; irritated ❷ eager; expecting sth. to happen soon

impede *v.* get in the way of or slow down the movement or development of; hinder

impel *v* drive, force, urge

imperative *adj.* ❶ very urgent or important and needing actions right now; necessary ❷ not to be disobeyed ❸ of the verb form that expresses a command

imperfect *adj.* ❶ not perfect; not complete; faulty ❷ tense of the verb expressing an action not yet completed

imperialism *n.* (a belief in the) policy of extending a country's power and influence in the world through diplomacy or military force, and especially by acquiring colonies

imperil *v.* endanger sb. or sth.

impersonal *adj.* ❶ not influenced by personal feeling; showing no emotion ❷ not referring to a particular person ❸ having no existence as a person

implant *v.* fix in deeply usually into the body or mind

implement Ⅰ *n.* tool; instrument Ⅱ *v.* complete; perform; carry out

implore *v.* ask (for) in a begging manner; entreat

impolite *adj.* not polite

import Ⅰ *v.* bring in from a foreign country Ⅱ *n.* sth. that is imported

important *adj.* ❶ of great effect or value; very serious and significant ❷ (of people) powerful; having influence

importation *n.* ❶ the act or business of importing ❷ sth. brought in from another place or country, especially an object or way of behavior typical of another place

importer *n.* a person, company, etc. that buys goods from another country to sell them in their own country

impose *v.* ❶ lay or place (a tax, duty, etc.) on ❷ force sth. on ❸ take advantage of

imposing *adj.* grand in appearance or large in size; impressive

impossible *adj.* ❶ not possible ❷ that cannot be endured or dealt with

impractical *adj.* not practical; unwise; not realistic

imprecise *adj.* not precise; not clear

impress *v.* ❶ press (one thing on another); make a mark, etc. by doing this ❷ have a strong influence on; fill (sb.) with admiration ❸ make the importance of (sth.) clear to (sb.)

impression *n.* ❶ a mark left by pressure ❷ an effect produced in the mind; feelings ❸ all the copies of sth. (such as a book) made at one time

impressive *adj.* causing admiration, especially by giving sb. a feeling of size, importance, or great skill; making a strong or good impression

imprint *v.* fix firmly in the mind

imprison *v.* put or keep in prison; shut up closely

impromptu *adj.* & *adv.* without preparation

improper *adj.* ❶ not suitable for morality or honesty ❷ not correct

improve *v.* ❶ make better ❷ become better ❸ increase the value of (land or property) by farming, building, etc.

improvement *n.* ❶ the act of making sth. better ❷ sth. which improves, which adds to beauty, usefulness, value, etc.

impudent *adj.* rude; insolent; disrespectful

impulse *n.* ❶ an impetus; a driving force ❷ a sudden wish to do sth.; sudden urge

impure *adj.* ❶ not pure, but mixed with sth. else ❷ morally bad, especially with regard to sexual behaviour

impurity *n.* ❶ the state of being not pure ❷ an impure thing or element

in Ⅰ *prep.* ❶ contained by (sth. with depth, length, and height) ❷ showing direction of movement ❸ at some time; during; at the time of ❹ during not more than (the space of) ❺ showing the condition of a person or thing ❻ indicating occupation, activity, etc. ❼ (of dress) wearing ❽ indicating the method (tool, medium, material, etc.) ❾ indicating surroundings ❿ (showing division and arrangement) so as to be Ⅱ *adv.* ❶ used with many verbs in different meanings ❷ (used with verb be) present, especially at home ❸ from a number of people, or from all directions to a central point ❹ fashionably Ⅲ *adj.* ❶ used for sending sth. to one ❷ fashionable

inability *n.* the state of being unable to do sth.

inaccessible *adj.* not accessible to reach or get

inaccurate *adj.* not accurate or exact

inactive *adj.* ❶ not active; idle ❷ no longer working

inadequacy *n.* ❶ the quality of being not enough or qualified ❷ an example of incompleteness or poor quality; shortcoming

inapt *adj.* not suitable or fitting

inattention *n.* the lack of attention to sb. or sth.

inattentive *adj*. not attentive; not paying attention to sb. or sth.

inaugural *adj*. of or for the beginning of sth. important

inaugurate *v*. ❶ introduce (a new official, professor, etc.) at a special ceremony ❷ open with a ceremony ❸ open; begin

inbuilt *adj*. existing as an original or essential part of sth. or sb.

incalculable *adj*. too great to be measured or counted

incapable *adj*. not capable

incessant *adj*. continual; never stopping

incidence *n*. ❶ the rate at which sth. happens or exists ❷ a way or scope in which sth. affects things

incident Ⅰ *n*. ❶ an event (especially in a story) ❷ a political event (that includes violence, such as fighting or explosions) Ⅱ *adj*. forming a natural or expected part of; naturally connected with

incidental *adj*. happening or existing in connection with sth. else that is more important

incite *v*. urge sb. to do sth. (usually sth. wrong)

inclination *n*. ❶ a natural tendency to act in a certain way ❷ an interest or a liking for sth. ❸ a slope or slant ❹ a leaning or bending movement, usually of a head

incline Ⅰ *v*. ❶ (cause to) slope ❷ cause to move downwards Ⅱ *n*. a slope or a sloping surface

inclined *adj*. ❶ wanting to do; feeling a wish (to) ❷ likely; tending (to)

include *v*. ❶ have as a part of the whole; contain ❷ regard as a member of a group; take into account

including *prep*. containing as part of the whole

inclusive *adj*. ❶ including; taking in; counting in ❷ including everything concerned

incoherent *adj*. (especially with reference to speeches, thoughts, ideas and explanations, etc.) not fitting together; not easy to understand

income *n*. money which is regularly received for work done, from trade, etc.

incoming *adj*. ❶ coming in ❷ about to take over from someone else

incomparable *adj*. ❶ without an equal; matchless ❷ not able to be compared; unsuitable for comparison

incompatible *adj*. not able or suitable to go together

incomplete *adj*. not complete; not having all the necessary parts

incomprehensible *adj*. not able to be understood

inconceivable *adj*. difficult to believe; that cannot be thought of or imagined

inconsiderate *adj*. not thinking of other people's feelings; thoughtless

inconsistent *adj*. ❶ (of ideas, opinions, etc.) not in agreement with each other or with sth. else ❷ tending to change

inconvenience Ⅰ *n*. discomfort or trouble Ⅱ *v*. cause inconvenience to

inconvenient *adj*. causing difficulty or trouble

incorrect *adj*. not correct or true; wrong

increase Ⅰ *v*. make or become large in amount or number Ⅱ *n*. a rise in amount, numbers, etc.

incredible *adj.* ❶ too strange to be believed; unbelievable or very hard to believe ❷ wonderful; unbelievably good

incur *v.* bring upon oneself

incurable *adj.* that cannot be cured

indecisive *adj.* ❶ giving an uncertain result; inconclusive ❷ having or showing inability to make decisions

indeed *adv.* ❶ truly, really, certainly ❷ used to intensify ❸ used as a comment to show interest or surprise, etc.

indefinite *adj.* ❶ not clear or exact ❷ lasting for an uncertain time

indelicate *adj.* (with reference to speech or behaviour) rude; coarse

independent Ⅰ *adj.* ❶ not governed by another country; self-governing ❷ not dependent on (other persons or things) Ⅱ *n.* a person who does not belong to the same political party

index Ⅰ *n.* ❶ a thing that is a sign of sth. else. ❷ a list of names, subjects, etc. in ABC order, at the end of a book, etc. ❸ the system of numbers by which prices, costs, etc. can be compared to a former level Ⅱ *v.* provide with or include in an index

Indian *adj.* & *n.* ❶ (someone) belonging to or connected with India ❷ (someone) belonging to or connected with any of the original peoples of North, Central, or South America except the Eskimos

indicate *v.* ❶ state or show briefly ❷ show (the direction in which one is turning in a vehicle) with hand signals, lights, etc. ❸ show a need for; suggest ❹ make a sign (for)

indication *n.* ❶ the act or sign that shows sth. is happening ❷ a thing that indicates; a sign

indicative *adj.* ❶ showing or suggesting sth. ❷ stating a fact

indicator *n.* ❶ a needle or pointer on a machine showing a measurement, e. g. of temperature, pressure, amount of petrol, etc. ❷ the lights on a car which flash to show which way it is turning

indifferent *adj.* ❶ not interested in; not caring about or noticing ❷ not very good; mediocre

indirect *adj.* not straight; not directly connected

indiscreet *adj.* careless in behaviour; telling secrets to other people; going beyond the limits of what is proper or sensible

indistinct *adj.* not clearly seen, heard, etc.

individual Ⅰ *adj.* ❶ of or for one person ❷ (often with each) single; particular; separate ❸ (of a manner, style, or way of doing things) particular to the person, thing, etc. concerned (and different from others); distinctive Ⅱ *n.* ❶ a single person or thing, considered separately from the class or group to which he, she, or it belongs to ❷ a person

indoors *adv.* in a house or building; not in the open air; into a house

induce *v.* ❶ persuade or influence sb. to do sth. ❷ bring about

induction *n.* ❶ the act of inducting sb. to a new job, party, etc. ❷ the act of inducing a pregnant woman ❸ a ceremony in which a person is inducted into a position or organization ❹ (an) introduction into a new job, company, etc. ❺ the production of electricity in one object by another which already has electrical (or magnetic) power ❻ (an example or result of) a process of reasoning using known facts to produce general rules or principles

inductive *adj.* using induction; reasoning from known facts to produce general principles

indulge *v.* ❶ allow (oneself or someone else) to have or do what they want, especially sth. bad ❷ let oneself or someone else have (their wish to do or have sth., etc.) ❸ satisfy (a perhaps unwarranted or illicit desire)

indulgent *adj.* ❶ allowing someone to have whatever they want, often in a way that is not good for them ❷ tolerant or lenient

industrial *adj.* ❶ connected with industry; used by industries ❷ having highly developed industries

industrialize *v.* (cause to) become industrially developed

industry *n.* ❶a particular branch of trade or manufacture which produces goods from raw material ❷a particular sort of work, usually employing lots of people and using machinery and (or) modern methods ❸ a quality of being hard-working; being always employed usefully

inedible *adj.* not suitable for eating

ineffective *adj.* ❶that does not produce any result; of little use ❷(of a person) unfit for work; incapable

inefficient *adj.* not able to work well and produce good results

inelegant *adj.* ❶ not having very good manners; not graceful ❷not beautiful in appearance or not well-made

inequality *n.* the state of not being equal

inert *adj.* ❶ without active chemical properties ❷not moving; slow

inexact *adj.* not correct in every way; having mistakes

inexpensive *adj.* not expensive; cheap

inexperience *n.* the lack of experience

inexplicable *adj.* that cannot be explained and understood

infamous *adj.* well known for wicked behaviour

infancy *n.* ❶ a period when one is an infant; early childhood ❷an early stage of development or growth

infant *n.* ❶a child during the first few years of his life ❷a person under the age of 18

infect *v.* cause to get a disease; cause to have a certain feelings

infection *n.* the act or result of causing a disease; a disease spread by infecting

inference *n.* ❶the process of inferring ❷ sth. which is inferred; a conclusion

inferior Ⅰ *adj.* ❶lower in position ❷not good or less good in quality or value Ⅱ *n.* a person who has a lower rank or position

infinite *adj.* ❶without limits or end ❷ very great; not able to measure

inflame *v.* make red or angry

inflate *v.* ❶cause to swell with air or gas ❷cause prices to increase by increasing the amount of money in use

inflation *n.* ❶the act of swelling or state

of being inflated ❷ a rise in prices caused by the expansion of the supply of money, etc.

inflexible *adj.* ❶ firm; unyielding; steadfast ❷ that cannot be changed ❸ not easily bent; stiff

influence Ⅰ *n.* ❶ the power to affect a person's character or actions ❷ the power to shape policy or ensure favourable treatment from sb. ❸ a person who has power or effect on others Ⅱ *v.* have an effect on; affect

influential *adj.* having great influence on sb. or sth.

inform *v.* ❶ give information to ❷ give evidence or make an accusation against sb. (to the police) ❸ give sth. its essential feature or character; pervade ❹ find out information about sb. or sth. ❺ have effect on

informal *adj.* not formal; without ceremony

information *n.* (sth. which gives) knowledge in the form of facts, news, etc.

informed *adj.* ❶ having or showing knowledge; having information ❷ using one's knowledge of a situation

informer *n.* a person who informs against someone else

infraction *n.* the breaking of a rule or law

infrequent *adj.* not happening often

infringe *v.* ❶ break a law or rule ❷ go beyond what is right; violate; interfere with

infusion *n.* ❶ the act of soaking ❷ a liquid made by infusing, often for medical use ❸ the act of mixing or filling with sth. new

ingenious *adj.* showing cleverness at making or inventing things

ingredient *n.* ❶ one of the parts of a mixture ❷ a component or element of sth.

inhabit *v.* live in

inhabitant *n.* a person or an animal that lives in a certain place

inhere *v.* (with reference to qualities) naturally belong to or exist in

inherit *v.* ❶ receive property, a title, etc. as heir ❷ derive (qualities, etc.) from ancestors

inhibit *v.* ❶ hinder, restrain ❷ make sb. nervous and embarrassed

inhuman *adj.* not human; cruel

inhumane *adj.* without pity for suffering; not humane

inhumanity *n.* extremely cruel and brutal behaviours

initial Ⅰ *adj.* that is (at) the beginning Ⅱ *n.* a capital letter at the beginning of a name, especially when used alone to represent a person's first name(s) and last name Ⅲ *v.* write one's initials on (a piece of writing), usually to show approval or agreement

initiate Ⅰ *v.* ❶ be the first one to start; begin ❷ admit (a person) by special forms or ceremonies into a group or society ❸ explain sth. to sb. and help to get a first understanding Ⅱ *n.* a person who is or has been initiated

initiation *n.* the act of starting sth.; being made acquainted with the rules of a society, etc.

inject *v.* put (liquid) into (someone) with a special needle (syringe)

injection *n.* an act of injecting sb. with a drug, etc.

injure *v.* ❶ hurt sb., especially in an accident ❷ damage sb.'s feelings, reputation, etc.

injury *n.* ❶ a harm or damage (to sb.'s feeling, reputation, etc.) ❷ a place (in the body) that is hurt or wounded; an act that hurts

injustice *n.* ❶ the lack of justice ❷ an unjust act or thing

ink[1] *n.* a coloured liquid used for writing, printing, or drawing

ink[2] *v.* put ink on

inkstand *n.* a stand for pens, ink bottles, etc., usually kept on a desk

inkwell *n.* an ink container which fits into a hole in a desk

inky *adj.* ❶ marked with ink ❷ very dark

inlaid *adj.* ❶ decoratively set into another substance ❷ having another substance set in it

inland Ⅰ *adj.* away from the border or the coast; carried on within a country Ⅱ *adv.* towards or in the heart of the country

inlet *n.* ❶ a strip of water extending into the land from a large body of water (the sea, a lake), or between islands ❷ sth. let in or inserted ❸ a way in for (water, liquid, etc.)

inn *n.* a small hotel

inner *adj.* ❶ towards or close to the middle ❷ close to the centre of a place or sth.

innocence *n.* the quality or state of being naive

innocent *adj.* ❶ not guilty (of wrongdoing) ❷ harmless ❸ knowing nothing of evil or unpleasant things

innovate *v.* change by bringing in sth. new

innovation *n.* the act of bringing in sth. new

innumerable *adj.* too many to be counted

input *n.* ❶ an action of putting sth. in ❷ things or an amount of things put in or supplied

inquire *v.* ❶ ask for information ❷ look into

insane *adj.* (of people and their acts) not sane; mad; senseless

inscribe *v.* write or cut words in or on sth.

inscription *n.* sth. inscribed; words on a coin, monument, etc.

insect *n.* a small creature with no bones, six legs, a body divided into three parts (the head, thorax, and abdomen) and usually two pairs of wings, such as an ant or a fly

insecure *adj.* not properly fastened; not safe

insensible *adj.* ❶ not able to feel or notice ❷ not aware of; without knowledge of ❸ unconscious ❹ not easily felt; too slow to be noticed

insensitive *adj.* ❶ not sensitive; without feeling ❷ slow to feel or notice

inseparable *adj.* that cannot be separated

insert Ⅰ *v.* put, fit, place (sth. in, into, between, etc.) others Ⅱ *n.* sth. added or put into sth. else

insertion *n.* ❶ the action of putting sth.

inside sth. else ❷a thing that is inserted

inset Ⅰ *v.* decorate sth. with sth. set into its surface Ⅱ *n.* ❶sth. set into a larger thing ❷a small map printed within the frame of a larger one

inside Ⅰ *n.* ❶the inner side or surface; the part(s) within ❷belly; stomach and bowels Ⅱ *adj.* ❶forming the inner part of sth.; not on the outer side ❷told or performed by sb. who is in a building, a group or an organization Ⅲ *adv.* ❶on or to the inside ❷in prison Ⅳ *prep.* on the inner side of

insight *n.* ❶the power of using one's mind to see or understand the true nature of a situation ❷an example or the understanding of this

insignificant *adj.* not of value and importance

insincere *adj.* not sincere

insist *v.* ❶declare or maintain a statement firmly ❷demand or order sth. strongly

insistence *n.* the act of demanding or saying sth. firmly

insistent *adj.* ❶repeatedly insisting one's demand or idea ❷needing to be done, answered, or dealt with; urgent

inspect *v.* examine the details of sth.; make an official visit to judge the quality of; review (troops)

inspection *n.* an act of looking closely at sb. or sth.; an official visit to a place

inspiration *n.* ❶sth. or sb. which gives a person the urge or the ability to do sth., especially to produce works of the imagination ❷a person or thing that inspires ❸a sudden good idea

inspire *v.* ❶give sb. the desire or ability to act, especially with a good result ❷be the force which produces (usually a good result)

inspired *adj.* so clever or good as to seem to show inspiration, especially from God

inspiring *adj.* that inspires sb. to do sth.

install *v.* ❶set (an apparatus) up, ready for use ❷settle in a place ❸settle (someone) in an official position, especially with ceremony

installation *n.* ❶a formal entry into an organization, position or office ❷the act of installing sth.; sth. that is installed

instance Ⅰ *n.* an example Ⅱ *v.* give as an example

instant Ⅰ *adj.* ❶happening or working at once ❷urgent; pressing ❸(of food) that can be made ready for use quickly Ⅱ *n.* a precise point of time

instantly *adv.* at once; immediately

instead *adv.* ❶in place of or as an alternative to ❷on the contrary

instill *v.* put (ideas, feelings, etc.) into someone's mind by a continuous effort; train sb. to behave in a particular way gradually

instinct Ⅰ *n.* a natural way of doing things; an ability that seems to come naturally Ⅱ *adj.* filled with

instinctive *adj.* based on instinct, not coming from training or teaching

institute Ⅰ *n.* a society or an organization formed to do special work or for a special purpose Ⅱ *v.* set up (a society, rules, actions in law, etc.) for the first time

institution *n.* ❶the act of instituting or

setting up sth. ❷ a large society or organization, usually set up to do sth. for others

instruct *v.* ❶ teach; train; educate ❷ order; command; direct ❸ tell; inform

instruction *n.* ❶ teaching; education ❷ directions; orders ❸ detailed information which tells you how to use or operate sth.

instructive *adj.* giving useful information that increases knowledge or understanding

instrument *n.* ❶ an object used to help in work ❷ an object, such as a piano, horn, drum, etc., played to give musical sounds

instrumental *adj.* ❶ helpful (in); being (part of) the cause of ❷ (of music) for instruments, not voices

insubstantial *adj.* ❶ not existing in reality; imaginary ❷ lacking strength or force

insult Ⅰ *n.* words or action that hurt another's feelings Ⅱ *v.* speak or behave rudely to sb.; speak or act in a way that hurts sb.'s feelings

insurance *n.* ❶ an agreement by contract to pay money, especially in case of a misfortune, such as illness, death, or an accident ❷ money paid to an insurance company in order to make or keep such a contract ❸ sth. you do to protect against future loss ❹ the business of providing people with insurance

insure *v.* ❶ make a contract that promises to pay a sum of money in case of accident, loss, death, etc. ❷ be careful or certain to do sth.

intact *adj.* not having been touched; not damaged; complete

intake *n.* the quantity, number, etc. entering or taken in

intangible *adj.* that cannot be touched; that cannot be clearly understood

integrate *v.* ❶ combine two or more things together ❷ bring sb. into a group from other groups

integrity *n.* ❶ a state of being whole and undivided; completeness ❷ honesty; trustworthiness

intellect *n.* ❶ the ability to use the power of reasoning and understanding (rather than to feel or take action) ❷ a person of high intelligence and reasoning power

intellectual Ⅰ *n.* a person who works and lives by his mind, and who is interested in activities which includes thinking and understanding rather than feeling and laboring Ⅱ *adj.* ❶ of, using, or needing the use of the intellect ❷ having a high intellect; well educated

intelligence *n.* ❶ a good ability to learn and understand ❷ information gathered, especially about an enemy country

intelligent *adj.* ❶ clever; wise ❷ able to take action in response to different situation

intend *v.* ❶ plan or mean (to do sth.) ❷ mean to be

intended *adj.* that you are planning or meaning to do or have

intense *adj.* ❶ very great; strong; extreme ❷ ardent; showing strong feelings

intensify *v.* make or become more intense

intensive *adj.* ❶concentrating all one's efforts on a specific area ❷giving force and emphasis ❸extremely thorough

intent Ⅰ *adj.* ❶(of looks) eager; earnest ❷showing fixed attention (in doing or wishing to do) Ⅱ *n.* purpose; intention

intention *n.* plan; aim; purpose

intentional *adj.* done on purpose, deliberate and not accidental

interact *v.* ❶act upon, have effect on each other ❷(of people) act together or cooperatively ❸ communicate with others; exchange ideas with each other

intercede *v.* try to settle an affair; ask a favor for sb.

intercept *v.* stop or catch (sb. or sth.) between the starting-point and the destination

interchange Ⅰ *v.* ❶ put each of two things in the other's place ❷make an exchange ❸(cause sth. to) alternate Ⅱ *n.* ❶(an example of) the act or action of interchanging or exchanging ❷(on a motorway) a system of smaller roads by which two main roads are connected

intercourse *n.* communication between people, businesses, schools, or governments, such as exchange of thoughts, services, or feelings

interdependent *adj.* dependent on each other

interest Ⅰ *n.* ❶the condition of wanting to know or learn about sth. or sb. ❷sth. with which one concern oneself ❸(*pl.*) advantage or profit for sb. ❹money paid for the use of money Ⅱ *v.* ❶cause (someone) to have a feeling of interest ❷ make (someone) want to buy, eat, or do sth.

interested *adj.* ❶ concerned; having or showing interest ❷ in a position to obtain an advantage (from sth.); not impartial

interesting *adj.* causing interest; catching the attention

interfere *v.* ❶concern oneself with other person's affairs without invitation or being interfered with ❷touch or move (sth.) in a way that is annoying or not allowed ❸ obstruct sth. wholly or partially; prevent sth. from being done or carried out properly

interference *n.* ❶ the act or fact of interfering or being interfered with ❷ (radio and television, etc.) the signals interfering

interlink *v.* join or connect (two or more things) together

interlock *v.* lock or join firmly together

interlude *n.* a period of time between two events during which sth. else happens or is done (e. g. between two acts of a play)

intermarry *v.* become connected by marriage

intermediate *adj.* being between two things(in time, space, degree, etc.)

intermission *n.* interval; pause; rest

internal *adj.* ❶ of or in the inside, especially of the body ❷ inside of a country; of the home affairs of a country; domestic

international *adj.* having to do with more than one nation

Internet *n.* an international computer network that allows users throughout the world to communicate and exchange information with one another

interpersonal *adj.* being, relating to, or involving relations between persons

interplay *n.* the action or effect of (two) things on each other

interpret *v.* ❶ put sth. spoken in one language into the words of another language ❷ understand the likely meaning of (statement, action, etc.); consider to be the meaning of ❸ show, make clear ideas of the meaning of either in words or by artistic performance

interrelate *v.* connect with each other

interrogate *v.* question sb. thoroughly for a long time to get some information

interrupt *v.* ❶ break the flow of (sth. continuous) for a short time ❷ break the flow of speech or action of (someone) by saying or doing sth.

intersect *v.* cross one another; divide by cutting across

interval *n.* ❶ a period of time (between two events or two parts of an action); the time between two acts of a play, two parts of a concert, etc. ❷ a space between two objects or points

intervene *v.* ❶ occur between other events or between certain points of time ❷ come between persons or groups to help settle a dispute; act as intermediary

interview Ⅰ *n.* ❶ a meeting with sb. for discussion or conference ❷ a meeting at which a reporter, etc. asks sb. questions in order to find out his views ❸ a meeting at which someone is asked questions to find out if they are suitable for a job or school Ⅱ *v.* ❶ conduct an interview in television, newspaper, and radio reporting ❷ ask someone questions to find out if they are suitable for a job, etc.

intimate[1] Ⅰ *adj.* ❶ having an extremely close relationship ❷ personal; private ❸ detailed and thorough; resulting from a close study ❹ having a sexual relationship with sb. Ⅱ *n.* a very close friend

intimate[2] *v.* make known indirectly; suggest

intimidate *v.* make sb. do, or not do sth. by frightening him

into *prep.* ❶ to the inside of ❷ so as to be in ❸ expressing the change of state ❹ used when dividing one number by another

intolerable *adj.* that cannot be tolerated

intonation *n.* the rise and fall of the voice in speaking

intone *v.* say (a poem, prayer, etc.) in an almost level voice

intoxicant *n.* sth. which intoxicates, especially an alcoholic drink

intoxicate *v.* make drunk; make very excited, as if one were drunk

intricate *adj.* complicated; puzzling; difficult to follow or understand

introduce *v.* ❶ make known for the first time to each other or someone else, especially by telling two people each other's names ❷ bring (sth.) into use or operation for the first time ❸ be a sign that sth. is about to happen ❹ carry out or put forward a plan, an order, etc. for the first time

introduction *n.* ❶the act of bringing in sth. or the fact of being introduced ❷an occasion of telling people each others' names ❸ a written or spoken explanation at the beginning of a book or speech

introductory *adj.* serving as an introduction to a subject

introspect *v.* examine or be concerned with one's own thoughts and feelings

intrude *v.* ❶introduce without initiation ❷enter a place where sb. is unwanted or unasked

intuition *n.* ❶the ability to understand sth. quickly without having to think about it carefully ❷ the knowledge gained by this ability

intuitive *adj.* using knowledge, etc. that is believed to be true

invade *v.* ❶ enter (a country) with armed forces in order to attack ❷crowd into a place in large numbers ❸attack or affect (body, etc.) in an unpleasant way

invalid[1] *adj.* not correct or correctly expressed, especially in law; not (any longer) suitable for use

invalidate *v.* make (sth.) invalid; show that (sth.) is not correct

invalidity *n.* ❶ the state of being not legally acceptable ❷the state of being an invalid because of illness

invaluable *adj.* of value too high to be measured

invariable *adj.* never changing; always the same

invariant *adj.* never changing

invasion *n.* an act of entering another country, especially an attack in war when the enemy spreads into and tries to control a country, city, etc.

invent *v.* ❶make or produce sth. which did not exist before ❷make up

invention *n.* ❶the process of inventing sth. ❷sth. that has been invented

inventive *adj.* skilled at inventing things, especially ideas

inventory *n.* (usually with reference to the contents of a house, shop, store, etc.) complete list

inverse Ⅰ *adj.* exactly opposite; reversed in position, direction, or tendency Ⅱ *n.* the exact opposite of sth.

inversion *n.* ❶the process of inverting or reversing ❷sth. that is inverted ❸a form of a chord in which the root is not the lowest note

invert Ⅰ *v.* put upside down or in the opposite order, position or arrangement Ⅱ *n.* sth. inverted

invest *v.* ❶put money (in) ❷spend a lot of time or energy on sth. that you think it will be useful ❸buy (sth. considered useful) ❹ decorate; surround with qualities

investigate *v.* try to find out more information about; examine the reasons for (sth.), the character of (someone), etc.

investigation *n.* ❶ the action of investigating sth. or sb.; a formal or systematic examination or research ❷a formal inquiry or systematic study

investigative *adj.* involving investigation or making inquiries, especially as distinct from merely reporting what is known

investment *n.* ❶ the process of investing money in sth. ❷ an amount of money invested ❸ sth. worthwhile in which money, time, or effort is invested

invigorate *v.* make vigorous; give strength or courage to

inviolate *adj.* not violated, attacked or destroyed; secure; pure

invisible *adj.* that cannot be seen; hidden from sight

invitation *n.* ❶ a written or spoken request made to someone, asking them to come to an event, such as a meal or a meeting, or take part in an activity, etc. ❷ a paper or sth. else used to invite sb. ❸ sth. tempt sb. to do sth., especially sth. bad

invite Ⅰ *v.* ❶ ask sb. politely to come somewhere or to take part in sth. ❷ ask for Ⅱ *n.* a colloquial expression for invitation

inviting *adj.* attracting you to do sth. pleasant and tempting

invoice Ⅰ *n.* a bill for goods received Ⅱ *v.* make an invoice for (foods)

involuntary *adj.* not controlled by the will; done without intention

involve *v.* cause (someone) to become connected or concerned

involved *adj.* ❶ complicated and difficult to understand ❷ concerned or sharing in sth.

invulnerable *adj.* that cannot be wounded or harmed

inward *adj.* ❶ on the inside ❷ moving towards the inside

iron Ⅰ *n.* ❶ a hard and heavy metal from which steel is made ❷ a tool made of iron, heated and used for smoothing clothes ❸ (*pl.*) chains for a prisoner's hands or feet Ⅱ *v.* make (clothes) smooth with an iron

ironic(al) *adj.* expressing your meaning is the opposite of what you have said

irony *n.* ❶ a way of speaking or writing in which the ordinary meaning of the words is the opposite of the thought in the speaker's mind ❷ an event which is the opposite of what would naturally be expected

irradiate *v.* ❶ make bright by throwing light on ❷ treat with X-rays, etc. ❸ treat (food) with X-rays to kill bacteria and preserve it

irrational *adj.* not controlled by reason

irregular *adj.* ❶ not inflect in the normal way ❷ not belonging to the regular armed forces ❸ uneven; not regular in shape, arrangement, etc.

irrelevant *adj.* having nothing to do with the subject

irreparable *adj.* that cannot be repaired or put right

irrepressible *adj.* not able to be controlled

irresolute *adj.* not able to decide what to do; hesitating

irrespective *adj.* without regard for; without paying attention to

irresponsible *adj.* ❶ (of persons) not responsible for their actions ❷ not having a proper sense of responsibility

irreversible *adj.* not reversible; unable to be altered or revoked

irrigate *v.* ❶ supply water to land in order to help crops grow ❷ wash (a wound) with a flow of liquid

irritate *v.* ❶ make angry or annoyed ❷ make sore or inflamed; cause discomfort to part of the body

is *aux.* & *v.* the singular form of the present tense of "be" and used with "he, she or it"

island *n.* ❶ a piece of land surrounded by water ❷ sth. resembling an island, because it is isolated

isle *n.* an island (usually used in poetry except in the names of places e. g. the British Isles)

isolate *v.* ❶ separate, put, or keep apart from others ❷ separate (a substance, germ, etc.) from its combinations or surroundings

isolated *adj.* ❶ far away from other places, buildings, or people; remote and difficult to reach ❷ having little contact or little in common with others ❸ single; exceptional

issue Ⅰ *v.* ❶ come, go or flow out ❷ give out or provide officially Ⅱ *n.* ❶ the act of coming out or being produced ❷ publication; sending out ❸ sth. which is produced so as to be publicly sold or given out ❹ a question that arises for discussion

it *pron.* ❶ used to refer to lifeless things or animals ❷ used to identify a person or thing ❸ used as the subject of "be" to say what the time, day, or date is ❹ used to emphasize one part of a sentence

italic Ⅰ *adj.* (of printed letters) sloping Ⅱ *n.* (usually *pl.*) italic letters

itch Ⅰ *n.* ❶ the feeling of irritation on the skin, causing a desire to scratch ❷ a strong desire or longing Ⅱ *v.* ❶ have an itch ❷ long for

item Ⅰ *n.* ❶ a single thing among a set or on a list ❷ a piece or paragraph (of news) Ⅱ *adv.* (used when listing or enumerating items) also

its *pron.* of it; belonging to it

itself *pron.* ❶ (the reflexive form of "it") the same thing, animal or baby as the one that the sentence is about ❷ used to emphasize an animal or a thing

ivory *n.* ❶ a hard, creamy-white substance of which an elephant's tusks are made ❷ the colour of this substance; a creamy-white colour

ivy *n.* a climbing plant, with shiny three-or-five-pointed leaves

J j

jab Ⅰ *v.* ❶push, usually with sth. sharp ❷give short, quick blow with the fist Ⅱ *n.* a sudden, rough thrust or blow

jack *n.* ❶an apparatus for lifting off the ground anything of heavy weight, such as a car, etc. ❷a playing card bearing a representation of a soldier, page, or knave, normally ranking next below a queen

jackboot *n.* ❶ a military boot which covers the leg up to the knee ❷the cruel rule of military men

jacket *n.* ❶a short coat with sleeves ❷ paper wrapper; record sleeve ❸the skin of potatoes

jackpot *n.* the biggest amount of money to be won in a game of cards or in any competition decided by chance

jade *n.* a type of hard, green stone used to make ornaments, etc.

jaded *adj.* tired and unhappy

jag Ⅰ *v.* cut or tear roughly Ⅱ *n.* sth. rough and sharp which jags; a cut caused by this

jagged *adj.* rough and sharp; with sharp edges

jail Ⅰ *n.* a prison Ⅱ *v.* put in jail

jailbreak *n.* an escape from prison, especially by more than one person

jam[1] Ⅰ *v.* ❶ push (things) tightly together ❷get stuck; become unable to work because the moving parts have got stuck ❸ block (radio or telephone signals) by broadcasting noise Ⅱ *n.* ❶a number of things or people crowded together, preventing movement ❷ an awkward position; a difficult situation

jam[2] *n.* a food made by boiling fruit with sugar to a thick mixture

jamb *n.* a side post of a door or window

jammed *adj.* ❶not able to move ❷very full; crowded

jammy *adj.* ❶easy ❷lucky, especially in a way that makes other people annoyed

jangle *v.* (cause to) make an unpleasant noise like pieces of metal striking one another

January *n.* the first month of the year

jar[1] *n.* a tall vessel with a wide mouth made of glass, stone, clay, etc.

jar[2] *v.* ❶have an unpleasant effect ❷be out of harmony

jasmine *n.* a shrub plant with sweet-smelling, white or yellow flowers

jaunty *adj.* ❶(showing that one feels) satisfied with oneself and pleased with life ❷lively

javelin *n.* a light spear for throwing, now

used mostly in sport

jaw Ⅰ *n.* the lower part of the face Ⅱ *v.* ❶talk in a boring way; gossip ❷scold or lecture (a person)

jawbone *n.* either of the big bones of the jaws, especially the lower jaw

jazz Ⅰ *n.* a popular music, originally created by African American musicians Ⅱ *v.* ❶ play or dance jazz ❷ play (music) as jazz ❸make lively

jazzy *adj.* ❶attracting attention, as with (too) bright colours ❷like jazz music

jealous *adj.* ❶ envious; feeling unhappiness because of the better fortune, etc. of others ❷wanting to keep what one has; possessive

jean *n.* ❶a strong, cotton cloth ❷(*pl.*) overalls or trousers made of this cloth

jeep *n.* a type of small car, suitable for travelling over rough ground

jeer Ⅰ *v.* laugh rudely (at); make fun of Ⅱ *n.* sarcastic remarks

jell *v.* ❶(of a liquid) become firmer, like jell ❷(of ideas, thoughts, etc.) take a clear shape

jellied *adj.* cooked and served in jelly

jelly *n.* ❶a soft food made from gelatine, fruit juice and sugar ❷any almost solid substance like this

jellyfish *n.* a sea animal with a jelly-like body and stinging tentacles

jemmy *n.* a type of iron bar used by thieves to open doors and windows

jerk Ⅰ *n.* a sudden pull, push, start, stop, twist, lift, or throw Ⅱ *v.* move with a jerk or jerks

jerry-built *adj.* built quickly, cheaply, and badly

jersey *n.* a tight-fitting garment with sleeves and few or no buttons in front (usually made from wool or cotton)

jest Ⅰ *n.* a thing said or done to cause amusement; a joke Ⅱ *v.* speak without serious intention; joke

jet *n.* ❶a fast, narrow stream of liquid, gas, etc., coming out of a small hole ❷ an aircraft with a jet engine

jetsam *n.* ❶goods thrown from a ship in order to lighten it in distress ❷goods of this kind washed on the shore

jetty *n.* a long, narrow structure, built into the sea for getting into or out of a boat, or to protect a harbour

jewel *n.* ❶ a precious stone such as a diamond, etc. ❷ an important or valuable person or thing

jewel(l)ed *adj.* decorated or fitted with jewels

jewel(l)er *n.* businessmen who buy and sell jewel or watches

jibe Ⅰ *n.* an insulting or mocking remark Ⅱ *v.* say sth. rude or sth. that is intended to make another person look foolish

jig *n.* a lively dance; the music for it

jigger *n.* ❶a small measure for alcoholic drinks ❷any small piece of apparatus

jiggered *adj.* ❶ very surprised ❷ very tired

jiggle *v.* (cause to) move from side to side with short, quick and light jerks

jigsaw *n.* ❶a type of narrow saw driven by a machine ❷a picture on cardboard or wood and cut in irregularly shaped pieces to be fitted together again

jilt *v.* refuse to marry sb. after having

promised to do so; end a relationship with a lover

jingle Ⅰ *n.* a metallic clinking or ringing sound (as of coins, keys or small bells) Ⅱ *v.* make a light ringing sound

jitters *n.* (*pl.*) feeling of being anxious and nervous, especially before an important event

job *n.* ❶a piece of work or task that you have to do ❷a paid position of regular employment ❸a duty or responsibility

jobbing *adj.* doing separate small jobs for various people

jobless *adj.* without a job; unemployed

jockey *n.* the professional rider in horse-race

jockstrap *n.* a tight-fitting undergarment for supporting the male sex organs, worn while doing sports

jog *v.* ❶push or knock slightly with the arm, hand, etc. ❷ move slowly, also shake up and down or from side to side ❸ run slowly and steadily, especially for exercise

joggle *v.* (cause to) shake or move slightly

join *v.* ❶ take part in ❷ fasten or bring together; connect; unite

joiner *n.* a skilled workman who makes the inside woodwork of buildings, etc.

joint Ⅰ *n.* ❶ the place at which two things or parts are connected ❷a large piece of meat ❸ a place or part where two bones or corresponding structures are connected Ⅱ *adj.* shared and done by two or more persons Ⅲ *v.* fasten together by a joint or joints; give a joint or joints

jointed *adj.* having joints, especially movable ones

joke Ⅰ *n.* ❶ sth. said or done to cause amusement, laughter, etc. ❷a person or thing that is ridiculous or annoying Ⅱ *v.* make jokes; not speak seriously, or not seriously enough

joker *n.* ❶ a person who likes to make jokes ❷ a person who is not serious or who should not be taken seriously ❸ an additional card with no fixed value, used in certain games

jolly Ⅰ *adj.* full of high spirits; cheerful Ⅱ *v.* (informal) encourage sb. in a cheerful way; try to keep someone cheerful

jolt Ⅰ *v.* shake while moving; shake suddenly; give a shock to Ⅱ *n.* a sudden shake or shock

joss *n.* a Chinese god worshiped in the form of an idol

jostle *v.* push roughly against (usually where there is little room e. g. in a crowd)

jot Ⅰ *n.* a very small amount; a bit Ⅱ *v.* write down quickly, especially without preparation

jotter *n.* a number of pieces of paper joined together, used for writing notes on

journal *n.* ❶ a newspaper or periodical which deals with a particular subject ❷a daily record of sth. you do, see, etc.

journalese *n.* the language considered to be typical of newspapers, especially that full of hackneyed expressions

journalism *n.* the profession of writing for newspapers and magazines

journalist *n.* a person whose occupation is journalism; a reporter; a news editor, etc.

journey *n.* a trip from one place to another, especially by land over quite a long distance

journeyman *n.* ❶ a trained workman who works for another person and is often paid by day ❷ an experienced person whose work is good, but not the very best

jovial *adj.* cheerful; friendly

jowl *n.* the lower part of the side of the face, especially loose skin and flesh near the lower jaw

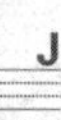

joy *n.* ❶ great pleasure; happiness; gladness ❷ a thing that cause you to feel happy or pleasant

joyful *adj.* full of joy; causing great pleasure or happiness

joyless *adj.* without joy; unhappy

joyous *adj.* full of or causing joy

joyride *n.* a ride for pleasure in a vehicle, especially a stolen car, often with careless driving

jubilant *adj.* filled with or expressing great joy, especially at a success

jubilee *n.* (a special occasion marking) the return of the date of some important events

judder *v.* shake violently

judge Ⅰ *v.* ❶ act as a judge in a court ❷ decide the results of a competition ❸ form an opinion or conclusion about sth. Ⅱ *n.* ❶ an officer appointed to hear and try cases in a court of law ❷ a person who decides the winner in a sport contest or competition

judgement *n.* ❶ the ability to judge wisely; a good sense ❷ an opinion or conclusion ❸ the decision of a judge or law court ❹ judging, or being judged

judicial *adj.* of or by a court of law; of a judge or judgement

judiciary *n.* the judges and system of law courts in a country; judicial departments

judicious *adj.* having or showing the ability to form sensible opinions; making sensible decisions, etc.

judo *n.* a sport of wrestling and self-defence between two people who try to throw each other to the ground

jug Ⅰ *n.* a deep vessel with a handle and a lip for holding and pouring liquids Ⅱ *v.* stew or boil in a jug or jar

juggle *v.* keep (several objects) in the air at the same time by throwing them up quickly and catching them again

juggler *n.* a person who juggles, especially an entertainer

juice *n.* ❶ the liquid from fruits, vegetables, and meat ❷ (*pl.*) the liquid in a certain part of the body, especially the stomach, that helps people and animals to digest food

juicy *adj.* ❶ containing a lot of juice ❷ interesting, especially that providing information about bad behaviours ❸ desirable, especially that is likely to produce a lot of money

July *n.* the seventh month of the year

jumble Ⅰ *v.* be mixed or mix in an untidy way Ⅱ *n.* a confused mixture of sth.

jumbo *adj.* unusually big

jump Ⅰ *v.* ❶ spring from the ground; bound ❷ (especially of prices or quantities) rise suddenly and sharply ❸ move suddenly and quickly Ⅱ *n.* an act of jumping

jumper *n.* ❶ a person or animal that springs ❷a woollen garment for the top half of the body ❸ a dress without sleeves, usually worn over a blouse

jumpy *adj.* nervously excited, often before sth. bad happens

junction *n.* ❶the act or process of joining ❷a place or point of joining or crossing, as of highways or railroads

juncture *n.* a particular point in time or in a course of events

June *n.* the sixth month of the year

jungle *n.* ❶a tropical forest which is too thick to walk through easily ❷ any confused and disordered mass of things

junior Ⅰ *adj.* ❶(of a person) younger ❷ lower in rank than another ❸connected with young people below a particular age ❹of or for students in the third year of a course which last for four years in college or high school Ⅱ *n.* the younger

junk *n.* ❶old things of no value ❷a flat-bottomed Chinese sailing ship ❸ things that are thought useless or of little value

juridical *adj.* of or related to the law or judges

jurisdiction *n.* the right to use the power of an official body, especially in order to make decisions on questions of law

jurist *n.* a person with a thorough knowledge of law; a legal expert

juror *n.* a member of a jury

jury *n.* the persons (usually twelve) chosen to sit in a court of law and decide whether the accused person is guilty or not

just Ⅰ *adj.* ❶morally right and proper; fair ❷ deserved or appropriate in a particular situation Ⅱ *adv.* ❶exactly ❷ only; no more than ❸only a short time ago; only now and not sooner ❹at this (that) very moment ❺really; absolutely

justice *n.* ❶the quality of being fair and just ❷the administration or authority of the law ❸judge of the Supreme Courts

justifiable *adj.* able to be shown to be right or reasonable; defensible

justification *n.* a good reason why sth. exists or is done

justified *adj.* ❶ having, done for, or marked by a good or legitimate reason ❷having been adjusted so that the print fills a space evenly or forms a straight line at the margin

justify *v.* show that sth. is right or reasonable

juvenile Ⅰ *n.* a young person who is not yet an adult Ⅱ *adj.* of, connected with or for young people

K k

kaleidoscope *n.* the tube containing mirrors and small pieces of coloured glass, turned to produce changing patterns

kangaroo *n.* an Australian animal that jumps along on its powerful hind legs (the female has a pouch in which its young are carried)

karaoke *n.* a form of entertainment in which people sing well-known songs over a prerecorded backing tracks

karat *n.* a unit of measurement of the purity of gold, pure gold being 24 karats

keel Ⅰ *n.* a long piece of wood or steel along the bottom of a ship, to which the sides of the ship are fixed Ⅱ *v.* turn over; fall over

keen *adj.* ❶ eager; desiring; very fond of ❷ sharp; with a fine cutting edge ❸ very clever and aware of what is happening

keep *v.* ❶ have for some time or more time ❷ cause to remain or continue in a particular state or situation ❸ take care of and provide with food, money, etc. ❹ fulfill what you have promised to do ❺ write down details of sth. so that they can be referred to later ❻ not let others know, not make known ❼ prevent ❽ continue (doing sth.), do sth. continuously, frequently or repeatedly ❾ own and manage

keeper *n.* ❶ a person who keeps or looks after sth. ❷ a goalkeeper or wicket keeper ❸ a gamekeeper ❹ a person in charge of animals in a zoo

keeping *n.* the act of caring and protecting sth.

keepsake *n.* sth. kept in memory of the giver

kennel *n.* a small hut in which a dog is kept

kerb *n.* the stone edge of a pavement

kernel *n.* ❶ the inner, softer part of a nut, or seed ❷ the central or most important part of sth.; core; essence

ketchup *n.* a type of sauce, usually made from tomatoes

kettle *n.* a metal pot with a lid, a handle and a long curved mouth for boiling water

key Ⅰ *n.* ❶ a metal instrument used to fasten or unfasten a lock ❷ a set of answers to questions; explanations on a map ❸ sth. that controls the entrance to a place ❹ one of a set of parts pressed in playing a piano, in typewriting, etc. ❺ a set of musical notes based on a particular note Ⅱ *adj.* essential; basic; chief; crucial

keyboard[1] *n.* a row or several rows of keys on a musical instrument or a machine

keyboard[2] *v.* ❶ work the keyboard of (especially a computer) ❷ provide a machine with (information) by working a keyboard

keyhole *n.* a hole for the key in a (door) lock, a clock, etc.

keynote *n.* ❶ the central theme of a speech, book, etc. ❷ the particular note on which a musical key is based

keypad *n.* a small keyboard, which is of numbered buttons

keystone *n.* ❶ the stone in the top of an arch, which keeps the other stones in position ❷ an idea, belief, etc., on which everything else depends

kick Ⅰ *v.* ❶ strike or hit with the foot ❷ score (a goal) by a kick ❸ strike out with the foot Ⅱ *n.* a blow or forceful thrust with the foot

kickback *n.* ❶ a sudden forceful recoil ❷ (informal) a payment made to someone for help they have given, especially in doing sth. dishonest

kicker *n.* ❶ a person or animal that kicks ❷ an extra clause in a contract

kid *n.* ❶ a young goat ❷ a child or a young person ❸ the leather made from skin of a kid

kidnap *v.* take sb. away and ask for money in return for bringing them back safely

kidney *n.* ❶ one of the pair of organs in the body of animals, birds, etc. that separate waste from the blood ❷ the kidney of an animal, cooked for food ❸ (of a person) nature; disposition; temperament

kill *v.* put to death; cause the death of

killer *n.* a person, animal, or thing that kills

kilo *n.* kilogram

kilobyte *n.* a unit of memory or data, equal to 1,024 bytes

kilogram(me) *n.* a measure of weight, equal to 1,000 grams

kilometer *n.* a measure of length, equal to 1,000 metres

kilowatt *n.* a unit of electrical power, equal to 1,000 watts

kilter *n.* the good working order

kin Ⅰ *n.* family; relations Ⅱ *adj.* related by blood

kind Ⅰ *n.* a group of people or things which share similar type Ⅱ *adj.* in a gentle, caring and helpful way toward other people

kindergarten *n.* the school for very young children, who is below the age of compulsory education

kindle *v.* ❶ (cause to) start to burn; make sth. burn ❷ rouse or stimulate (strong feelings, interest, etc.)

kindling *n.* materials for lighting a fire, especially dry wood, leaves, grass, etc.

kindly Ⅰ *adj.* friendly; good-natured Ⅱ *adv.* ❶ in a kind or friendly way ❷ naturally

kindness *n.* ❶ the quality or habit of being friendly ❷ the kind act or treatment

kindred Ⅰ *n.* ❶ the relationship by blood ❷ one's relatives or family Ⅱ *adj.* ❶ related; having a common source

❷similar

kinetic *adj.* connected with, or caused by motion

king *n.* ❶the male ruler of a country ❷a person of great influence ❸a principal in the game of chess; a court card with a picture of a king

kingdom *n.* ❶a country headed by a king or queen ❷ a realm regarded as being under the control of sb. or sth.

kingfisher *n.* a small bird that feeds on fish in rivers, lakes, etc.

kingly *adj.* belonging to or suitable to a king

kingpin *n.* the most important person in a group, upon whom the success of the group depends

kingship *n.* the condition or official position of a king

kink *n.* ❶an (unwanted) sharp turn or twist in hair, a rope, a chain, a pipe, etc. ❷a peculiarity of the mind or character

kinship *n.* ❶ a family relationship ❷ a close feeling between people who have similar attitudes or origins

kinsman *n.* a male relative

kinswoman *n.* a female relative

kiss Ⅰ *v.* touch with the lips to show affection or as a greeting Ⅱ *n.* an act of kissing

kit *n.* ❶a set of articles or tools needed for a particular purpose ❷ a set of clothes and other articles needed for daily life, especially by soldiers, sailors, etc. or for playing a particular sport

kitchen *n.* the room used for cooking

kitchenware *n.* the utensils used in a kitchen

kite *n.* ❶a toy with a light frame covered with paper or cloth which flies in the air on the end of a long string ❷a bird of prey of the hawk family

kith and kin *n.* friends and relations

kitten *n.* a very young cat

kitty *n.* ❶money which is gambled for in various games ❷a kitten

knack *n.* a special skill or ability, usually as the result of practice

knacker *n.* a person who buys and slaughters useless horses, for the purpose of selling the meat and hides

knapsack *n.* a small bag with straps, carried on the back (especially by soldiers and travellers)

knee *n.* the middle joint of the leg, where it bends

kneel *v.* go down or remain on one's knees

knell *n.* ❶ the sound of a bell rung slowly after a death or at a funeral ❷ signs of the end or death of sth.

knickers *n.* (*pl.*) pants, undergarment worn by women and girls

knife *n.* a blade fixed in a handle, used for cutting as a tool or weapon

knight Ⅰ *n.* ❶a noble soldier who has a duty to fight for his king ❷a man who is given a title by the Queen of England, and whose name has "Sir" in front of it ❸a person who represented a shire or country in Parliament ❹ a piece in the game of chess, usually made with a horse's head Ⅱ *v.* make (sb.) a knight

knightly *adj.* consisting of knights; typical of a knight

knit *v.* make (thing to wear) by joining

woolen threads into a close network with long needles (knitting needles)

knitting *n.* the action or process of knitting; sth. being knitted

knitwear *n.* knitted garments

knob *n.* ❶ a handle, usually round, or control button of a door, drawer, etc. ❷ an isolated, rounded hill or mountain ❸ a round-shaped swelling or mass on the surface of sth. (e. g. a tree trunk)

knobbly *adj.* having round, knob-like lumps

knock Ⅰ *v.* ❶ strike or hit a surface, especially when waiting to be let in through a door ❷ collide with sb. or sth. with a hard blow ❸ make (a hole or dent) in sth. by striking it forcefully ❹ injure by striking Ⅱ *n.* a blow; a short and sharp sound of a blow

knockabout *adj.* ❶ suitable for rough use ❷ boisterous

knocker *n.* ❶ a hinged metal flap for knocking against a door to summon a person ❷ (informal) a person who continually criticizes

knockout Ⅰ *adj.* ❶ (about a competition) in which the loser in the next stage has to drop out ❷ that knocks a boxer out Ⅱ *n.* ❶ a blow that knocks a boxer out ❷ a competition in which the loser in each round is eliminated ❸ (informal) an extremely attractive or outstanding person or thing

knoll *n.* a small hill or mound

knot Ⅰ *n.* a join made by tying a piece or pieces of rope, string, cord, etc. Ⅱ *v.* form a knot in (rope, etc.); tie with knots

knotty *adj.* ❶ (of wood) containing knots ❷ full of difficulties

know *v.* ❶ have sth. clearly in the mind or memory; have knowledge or information ❷ be acquainted with ❸ recognize or distinguish sb. or sth. ❹ have personal experience with

knowing *adj.* ❶ showing that you know or are aware of sth. ❷ done in full awareness or consciousness

know-it-all *n.* one who claims to know everything

knowledge *n.* ❶ the state of understanding sth. ❷ what a person knows; the facts, information, skills, and understanding that one has gained, especially through learning or experience ❸ familiarity with; information about

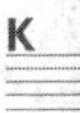

known *adj.* generally recognized by a lot of people

knuckle *n.* the finger joint

koala *n.* an Australian tree-climbing animal with thick grey fur and large ears, feeding on eucalyptus leaves

kowtow *v.* touch the ground with the forehead (as a sign of respect, submission, etc.); obey without question; be too humble

kumquat *n.* ❶ an orange-like fruit related to the citruses, with an edible sweet rind and acid pulp. It is eaten raw or used in preserves ❷ the East Asian shrub or small tree which yields this fruit, and which hybridizes with citrus trees

kung fu *n.* a primarily unarmed Chinese martial art, resembling karate

L l

label Ⅰ *n.* ❶a small piece of paper, cloth, etc. fixed on sth. to show what it is or where sth. is to go ❷a word or phrase applied to describe a person, group, etc. Ⅱ *v.* ❶ put a label on ❷ describe or classify sb. or sth.

labial *n.* & *adj.* (a speech sound) made with one or both lips

laboratory *n.* a room or building used for scientific experiment or test, especially on chemistry

laborious *adj.* requiring hard work; not easy

labo(u)r Ⅰ *n.* ❶ work, especially physical work ❷ workers, especially manual workers ❸ the British Labour Party Ⅱ *v.* work, especially work hardly

labo(u)red *adj.* showing signs of effort and difficulty

labo(u)rer *n.* a worker whose job needs strength rather than skill, especially one who works outdoors

labo(u)ring *n.* a hard physical work needs strength rather than skill

labyrinth *n.* a network of winding paths, roads, etc. through which it is difficult to find one's way without help; entangled state of affairs

lace *n.* ❶ a string or cord put through small holes in shoes to draw edges together ❷ a net-like decorative cloth made of fine thread

lack *v.* ❶be without; not have ❷have less than enough of need Ⅱ *n.* the state of being without or not having enough of sth.

lacking *adj.* ❶ having not enough of sth.; missing ❷ not present or not available

lactate *v.* (said of a female mammal) produce milk

lactation *n.* ❶the production of milk for babies by a human or animal mother ❷ the time that this lasts

lactic *adj.* of or obtained from milk

lactose *n.* a sugary substance found in milk, sometimes used as a food for babies and sick people

lad *n.* a boy or a young man

ladder Ⅰ *n.* ❶two lengths of wood, metal or rope, with cross pieces, used in climbing up and down walls, a ship's side, etc. ❷ the fault in a stocking caused by stitches becoming undone so that there is a vertical ladder-like flaw Ⅱ *v.* (of stockings, etc.) develop ladders

laden *adj.* carrying sth. heavy; loaded

lady *n.* ❶a polite word for any woman ❷

a woman of good manners or education or of good social position ❸ (Lady) a title for the wife and daughter of some noblemen ❹ (ladies) a women's public lavatory

ladybird *n.* a small flying beetle, usually red with black spots

ladylike *adj.* suitable for a lady; well-mannered and refined

lag *v.* walk or move too slowly; stay or fall behind

lagging *n.* a material used to lag a water pipe or container

lair *n.* a place where a wild animal lives

lake *n.* a large area of water, surrounded by land

lam[1] *v.* beat; thrash; flog

lam[2] Ⅰ *n.* a sudden flight or escape Ⅱ *v.* escape or flee

lamb Ⅰ *n.* ❶a young sheep ❷meat from a young sheep Ⅱ *v.* give birth to lambs

lambast(e) *v.* beat or attack fiercely, usually with words or blows

lambskin *n.* leather made from the skin of a lamb, especially with the wool on it

lame *adj.* ❶not able to walk properly because one's leg or foot is hurt or has some sort of weakness ❷ not easily believed; weak

lamely *adv.* in a way that does not sound very confident; that does not persuade other people

lament *v.* express or feel great sorrow; weep

lamented *adj.* ❶mourned or grieved for ❷regretted

lamp *n.* Ⅰ a device for giving light Ⅱ ❶ supply with lamps; illuminate ❷hit sb. or sth. hard

lampoon[1] *n.* a piece of writing fiercely attacking a person, government, etc., by making them seem foolish

lampoon[2] *v.* attack in an amusing way

lamp post *n.* a tall post for a lamp which lights a street or other public area

lampshade *n.* a usually decorative cover placed over a lamp, especially to soften or screen its light

lancet *n.* ❶ a pointed two-edged knife used by surgeons ❷ a tall, narrow pointed arch or window

land Ⅰ *n.* ❶the ground used for a special purpose ❷ the solid, dry part of the earth's surface ❸a county or nation Ⅱ *v.* ❶come or put on land (from a ship, an aircraft, etc.) ❷ bring to, reach a position or situation

landform *n.* a natural feature of the earth's surface

landing *n.* ❶ the act of coming or bringing to ground ❷ a place where persons or goods are landed ❸ a platform between flights of stairs

landlord *n.* ❶a person who lets land or a house or room, etc. to tenants ❷ a person who runs a public house

landmark *n.* ❶a conspicuous and easily recognized object in or feature of a landscape ❷ an event that marks an important stage or development in the history of sth. ❸a building or a place that is important for its history

landmine *n.* an explosive mine laid on or just under the surface of the ground

landscape Ⅰ *n.* ❶a picture showing view of the countryside ❷the art of painting such scenes ❸ all the visible features of an area of land Ⅱ *v.* make (land) more pleasant to look at by arranging trees, flowers, etc.

landslide *n.* ❶ the sliding down of a mass of earth or rock from a mountain or cliff ❷ an overwhelming majority of votes for one side in an election

landward Ⅰ *adv.* towards the land Ⅱ *adj.* facing towards land as opposed to sea

lane *n.* ❶ a narrow country road ❷ a narrow street ❸ a route regularly used by ships or aircraft ❹ a marked division of a road, running track, etc.

language *n.* ❶ words that are spoken or written ❷ a form of speech used by a certain nation or race ❸ special words and terms used in a certain field ❹ any way of expression

languor *n.* ❶ the state of tiredness of mind or body; the state of lack of strength or will ❷ the pleasant or heavy stillness ❸ a feeling or state of mind of tender sadness and desire

lank *adj.* (with reference to hair) straight and soft

lanky *adj.* (with reference to persons) tall, thin and rather clumsy

lantern *n.* a light in a transparent case which will stay bright in wind or rain

lap Ⅰ *v.* ❶ drink by taking up with the tongue, as a cat does ❷ (of water) move or hit with little waves and soft sounds Ⅱ *n.* ❶ one circuit of a track ❷ a piece of or a section of sth.

lapdog *n.* ❶ a small pet dog ❷ a person completely under the control of another (usually important) person

lapel *n.* the part of the front of a coat or jacket folded back and joined to the collar

lapse Ⅰ *n.* ❶ a slight error in speech or behaviour ❷ a failure in correct behaviour, belief, duty, etc. ❸ (of time) passing away Ⅱ *v.* ❶ (of time) pass ❷ fail to keep one's position; fall from good ways into bad ways

laptop *n.* a portable computer for use while traveling

larch *n.* a tall, upright tree with bright green, needle-like leaves and hard-skinned fruit (cones)

lard Ⅰ *n.* the fat of pigs or hogs prepared for use in cooking Ⅱ *v.* ❶ put pieces of fat on or in ❷ insert strips of fat or bacon in (meat) before cooking ❸ polish (speech or writing) with sth.

larder *n.* a place where food is kept; pantry

large *adj.* ❶ of considerable size, extent or capacity ❷ of greater size than the ordinary, especially with reference to size of clothes ❸ of wide range or scope

largely *adv.* ❶ to a great extent; mainly ❷ much; in great quantity

lark *n.* a small songbird, especially the skylark

laryngitis *n.* a painful, swollen condition of the larynx

larynx *n.* (*pl.* larynges) the hollow boxlike part at the upper end of the throat in which the sounds of the voice are produced by the vocal cords

laser *n.* ❶ a narrow and very intense beam of light that can be used to cut metal, help medical operation, etc. ❷ an instrument that produces this kind of light

lash Ⅰ *v.* ❶ strike with or as if with a whip ❷ tie firmly, especially with rope Ⅱ *n.* ❶ the flexible part of a whip ❷ a blow given with or as with a whip, etc. ❸ an eyelash

lashing(s) *n.* a large amount, especially of food and drink

lass *n.* a girl; a sweetheart

last Ⅰ *adj.* ❶ final; the only remaining ❷ coming immediately before the present ❸ the lowest in importance or rank ❹ the least likely or suitable Ⅱ *adv.* ❶ on the occasion nearest in the past; most recently ❷ after anything else; after the others Ⅲ *n.* the person, thing, or group after all others Ⅳ *v.* continue for the stated length of time; go on

lasting *adj.* able to last for a long time

lastly *adv.* in the last place; finally

latch *n.* ❶ a small piece of wood or iron used to fasten a door ❷ a type of simple door lock opened by a latch key

latchkey *n.* a key for opening a lock on an outside door of a house or flat

late Ⅰ *adj.* ❶ after the right, fixed or usual time ❷ former (and now dead) ❸ former (and still living) Ⅱ *adv.* ❶ after the usual, right, fixed or expected time ❷ toward the end of a period ❸ at a time in the near future

lately *adv.* not long ago; in the recent past; recently

latent *adj.* present but not yet noticeable, active, or fully developed

later Ⅰ *adj.* the comparative degree of the word late Ⅱ *adv.* after that time you are talking about

lateral *adj.* relating to the sides of sth.; sideways

latest *n.* the most recent news, fashion, or example

latex *n.* ❶ a milky fluid produced by certain plants, e. g. the rubber tree ❷ a synthetic product resembling this, used to make paints and coatings

Latin Ⅰ *n.* the language of ancient Rome and its empire Ⅱ *adj.* of the Latin language; of peoples speaking language descended from Latin

latitude *n.* the angular distance in degrees from the equator

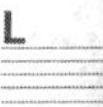

latter *adj.* nearer to the end or to the present time

laud *v.* praise sb. or sth.

laudable *adj.* worthy of high praise

laudatory *adj.* expressing praise or admiration

laugh *v.* show pleasure, amusement or contempt by expressions and sounds

laughter *n.* an act or a sound of laughing

launch Ⅰ *v.* ❶ send (a rocket) into the air ❷ send into the water ❸ start or set up an activity, or enterprise, etc. Ⅱ *n.* ❶ an act of launching ❷ an open motorboat used for pleasure

launcher *n.* a structure that holds a rocket or missile during launching

launder *v.* ❶ wash, or wash and iron (clothes, sheets, etc.) ❷ give (sth., especially money obtained illegally) the appearance of being legal

laundry *n.* ❶ a place or business where clothes, sheets, etc. are washed and ironed ❷ clothes, sheets, etc. needing washing or that have just been washed (or washed and ironed)

laureate *n.* someone who has won a particular high honour

laurel *n.* a type of small tree with evergreen leaves, used in ancient times as a sign of honour or victory; bay tree

lava *n.* the melted rock coming out of a volcano and becoming hard when cool

lavatory *n.* ❶ a toilet ❷ a room for washing the hands and face in

lavender *n.* ❶a type of plant with small, sweet-smelling, pale purple flowers which can be dried and used as a scent ❷the colour of lavender flowers

lavish Ⅰ *adj.* giving or producing freely, liberally, or generously Ⅱ *v.* give abundantly and generously

law *n.* a rule made by the government for all the people of a country; a rule in science, art or a game

lawful *adj.* allowed by law; according to law; recognized by law

lawless *adj.* ❶ (of a country or place) not governed by laws ❷ uncontrolled; wild

lawn *n.* an area of grass kept closely cut and smooth; such an area of grass used for a game

lawsuit *n.* a claim or complaint against sb. in a court of law

lawyer *n.* a person who is trained and qualified in legal matters, especially a solicitor

lay *v.* ❶put sth. carefully in a particular position; place ❷(of a bird, insect, etc.) produce eggs ❸put down sth. and set it in position ❹ put forward an idea or suggestion, etc.

layer Ⅰ *n.* ❶ a quantity or thickness of some material laid over a surface ❷ a person or thing that lays sth. ❸a bird, especially a hen, that lays eggs ❹a plant stem that has been fastened partly under the ground, in order to grow roots and so become a separate plant Ⅱ *v.* fasten a stem down(and cover with soil)

layman *n.* a person who does not have specialized knowledge of a subject

layout *n.* ❶the planned arrangement of a town, garden, building, etc., especially as shown in a drawing ❷ the way in which printed matter is set out on paper

laze *v.* do nothing; be lazy; rest lazily

lazy *adj.* not wanting to work; doing little work; not diligent; idle

lead Ⅰ *v.* ❶guide a person by the hand, etc. ❷ act as chief; direct ❸ influence; have sth. as a result ❹ have a certain kind of life ❺ show the way, especially by going in front ❻ be a way to a particular place Ⅱ *n.* ❶ the position ahead of all others ❷a length of rope, leather, chain, etc., fastened to an animal, usually a dog, to control it

leaded *adj.* ❶ covered or framed with lead ❷ (said about petrol) containing a lead compound

leaden *adj.* ❶of the colour of lead; dull grey ❷ without cheerfulness or excitement

leader *n.* ❶ a person who guides or directs a group, team, organization, etc. ❷a person or thing that is ahead of others ❸ the chief violin player of an orchestra ❹ the strongest stem or branch of a tree

leadership *n.* ❶ the position of leader ❷ the ability to lead

lead-in *n.* remarks made by someone to introduce a radio or television show

leading *adj.* ❶ most important; chief; principal ❷ guiding; directing ❸ playing the main part

leading light *n.* a person of importance or influence

leading question *n.* a question formed in such a way that it suggests the expected answer

leaf *n.* ❶ one of the green flat parts on trees or plants ❷ a single piece of paper in a book forming two pages

leaflet *n.* ❶ a small young leaf ❷ a small sheet, often folded, of printed matter, usually given free to the public

leafy *adj.* covered with leaves; having many leaves

league *n.* ❶ an agreement made between persons, groups or nations for their common welfare, e. g. to work for peace; the parties that make such an agreement ❷ a group of sports clubs or players that play matches between themselves ❸ a class or category of quality or ability

leak Ⅰ *n.* a hole, crack, etc., caused by wear, injury, etc., may wrongly get in or out Ⅱ *v.* let (a liquid, gas, etc.) in or out of a hole or crack

leakage *n.* ❶ the act and process of fluid or gas escaping through a hole or crack ❷ an instance of this; sth. which leaks in or out; the amount of such a leak

leaky *adj.* having a leak

lean[1] *v.* ❶ slope or bend from an upright position ❷ support or rest oneself in a bent or sloping position

lean[2] *adj.* producing or having little value

leaning *n.* a tendency to prefer sth. or believe in sth.

leap Ⅰ *v.* ❶ (cause to) jump over ❷ seize a chance eagerly Ⅱ *n.* a forceful jump or quick movement

learn *v.* ❶ gain knowledge of (a subject) or skill in (an activity), especially through experience or through being taught ❷ become informed (of)

learned *adj.* ❶ having or showing much knowledge, especially of the humanities ❷ of, for, or concerning advanced study

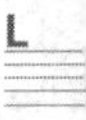

learning *n.* ❶ the process of learning ❷ the advanced knowledge gained by careful study

lease Ⅰ *n.* a written legal agreement by which the use of a building or piece of land is given by its owner to someone for a certain time in return for rent Ⅱ *v.* give or take the use of (land or buildings) on a lease

leaseback *n.* an arrangement by which one sells or gives sth. to sb., but he continues to have the use of it in return for rent

leaseholder *n.* someone who lives in a leasehold house, flat, etc.

leash *n.* a string or strip of leather for holding a dog (usually fastened to a collar)

least Ⅰ *adj.* smallest in size, amount, or degree; fewest in number Ⅱ *adv.* in the smallest degree Ⅲ *n.* the smallest number or amount

leather *n.* treated animal skin used for making shoes, bags, etc.

leatherette *n.* a cheap material made to look like leather

leave Ⅰ *v.* ❶go away(from) ❷cause to remain or to be in a certain place or condition ❸abandon your wife, husband or partner ❹ entrust sth. to be kept, collected, etc. Ⅱ *n.* the permission (to be absent from duty or work); a period of such absence

leaven[1] *n.* ❶a substance that is added to flour and water mixture to make it swell and make bread ❷ an influence that causes a gradual change in character

leaven[2] *v.* ❶ add leaven to (a cooking mixture, especially flour and water); cause to puff up with a leaven ❷ influence or change gradually

leavings *n.* things that are left or unwanted, especially food after a meal

lecture Ⅰ *n.* ❶a talk to a group of people for the purpose of teaching ❷ a long angry talk, especially one given as a reprimand Ⅱ *v.* ❶ give a lecture (course) ❷scold; reprove

lecturer *n.* ❶ a person who gives lectures, especially at a university or college ❷a person who holds the lowest teaching rank at a British or American university or college

ledger *n.* a book in which accounts of money are written

lee *n.* a place on the side away from the wind, which gives shelter

leech *n.* a type of worm which fastens itself to the skin and sucks blood

leeward Ⅰ *adj.* in the direction towards which the wind blows Ⅱ *n.* the side or direction towards which the wind blows

leeway *n.* ❶the amount of freedom that is available to move or act ❷a ship's sideways drift to leeward of its proper course

left Ⅰ *adj.* & *adv.* of, in, on the side of the body that usually contains the heart Ⅱ *n.* the location near or the direction toward the side to the north when a person or object faces east

leftover Ⅰ *n.* the food not finished at a meal Ⅱ *adj.* remaining after the rest has been used or finished

leg *n.* ❶one of the parts of an animal's or a person's body used for walking; the part of body from hip to ankle ❷ the support of a chair, table, etc.

legacy *n.* ❶the money or property left by sb. on his death to sb. else ❷ anything left from the past

legal *adj.* of or connected with the law; permitted by the law; required by the law

legalistic *adj.* placing great importance on keeping exactly to what the law says, rather than trying to understand and act in accordance with its true meaning and intention

legality *n.* the condition of being allowed by law

legalize *v.* make sth. legal

legend *n.* ❶ an old story about great deeds and men of ancient times having slight possible base in truth ❷ the literature of such stories ❸ the inscription on a coin or medal; words on a map, below a picture, etc.

legendary *adj.* ❶ of, like, or told in a legend ❷ very famous

leggings *n.* coverings, usually made of wool or of strong cloth, leather, etc., worn to keep the lower legs warm, or to protect them

legible *adj.* (with reference to handwriting, print, etc.) that can be read easily; clear

legislate *v.* make laws

legislation *n.* the act of making laws; the laws made

legislature *n.* a body of people who have the power to make and change laws

legit *adj.* legitimate; legal

legitimate *adj.* correct or allowable according to the law

legroom *n.* the room enough to position one's legs comfortably when seated

legwork *n.* the work that needs much walking or tiring effort

leisure *n.* the time when you are not working and can do what you want

leisured *adj.* having plenty of free time to do what you enjoy

leisurely[1] *adj.* moving, acting, or done at leisure

leisurely[2] *adv.* without haste or hurry

lemon *n.* ❶ a fruit with a light yellow skin and sour juice ❷ the colour of this fruit; the light bright yellow

lemonade *n.* a soft drink with a lemon flavour

lend *v.* ❶ give sth. to sb. for a limited time ❷ add or give sth., especially a quality ❸ provide sb. with help, support, etc.

length *n.* the measurement from end to end (in space or time)

lengthen *v.* make or become longer

lengthways *adv.* from end to end; along the longest part

lengthy *adj.* very long in time and size

lenient *adj.* not severe in judgment or punishment; gentle

lens *n.* a piece of glass or substance like glass, with one or both sides curved (used in binoculars, cameras, glasses or telescopes, etc.)

lentil *n.* ❶ a type of plant with a small bean ❷ the seed of this plant

leopard *n.* a large animal of the cat family which has a yellowish coat with many black spots

less Ⅰ *adj.* not so much; to a smaller quantity of Ⅱ *adv.* to a smaller extent; not so much

lessen *v.* ❶ make or become less, weaker, etc. ❷ cause (sth.) to appear smaller, less important

lesser *adj.* & *adv.* (not used with than) not so great or so much as the other (of two) in worth, degree, size, etc.

lesson *n.* ❶ sth. to be learnt or taught; a period of time given to learning or teaching; a unit of teaching; a part of a subject to be taught or studied at one time ❷ sth. learnt from experience

lessor *n.* a person who gives the use of a house, building, or land by a lease to someone else (the lessee) for a certain time, in return for payment

lest *conj.* ❶ for fear that; in order that... not ❷ that (used after fear, be afraid, be anxious

let[1] *v.* ❶ allow (to do or happen) ❷ used with first and third person pronouns to supply an indirect imperative

let[2] *v.* give the use of (a room, a building, land, etc.) in return for rent

let-down *n.* sth. that is disappointing

lethal *adj.* causing, able to cause death

letter *n.* ❶ a written or printed message sent usually in an envelope ❷ any of the signs in writing or printing that represent a speech sound

lettering *n.* ❶ the act of writing or drawing letters or words ❷ written or drawn letters, especially of the stated style

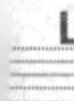

letters *n.* literature in general literary knowledge, ability or leaning

letting *n.* a house or flat that is (to be) rented

lettuce *n.* a type of vegetable with green leaves (usually eaten uncooked)

let-up *n.* (a) stopping or lessening of activity

levee *n.* ❶ an embankment alongside a river constructed to prevent flooding ❷ a quay

level Ⅰ *adj.* ❶ flat; smooth; even ❷ equal in height, degree, value, etc. Ⅱ *v.* make or become level or flat Ⅲ *n.* ❶ the line or surface parallel to the horizon, especially with reference to its height ❷ a relative position in rank, class or authority ❸ a particular standard

lever Ⅰ *n.* a bar or other tool turned on a fulcrum to lift sth. or to force sth. open, e. g. a window or drawer Ⅱ *v.* move (sth. up, along into, out of position, etc.) with a lever

leverage *n.* ❶ the action, power, or use of a lever ❷ influence; power

levy Ⅰ *v.* demand and collect officially Ⅱ *n.* an official demand and collection, especially of a tax

lexical *adj.* ❶ to do with the words of a language ❷ to do with a lexicon or dictionary

lexicography *n.* the writing of dictionaries

lexicon *n.* ❶ the vocabulary of a person, language, or branch of knowledge ❷ a dictionary

liability *n.* ❶ the state of being responsible for sth. ❷ a debt or obligation ❸ a handicap or disadvantage

liable *adj.* ❶ obliged by law to pay for ❷ be subject to

liaison *n.* the process of keeping the different parts of a large organization (especially an army or armies) in touch with each other

liar *n.* a person who tells lies

lib *n.* (the abbreviation for liberation) (a movement for) social equality and the removal of disadvantages suffered by particular social groups

libel Ⅰ *n.* sth. printed or written, etc., which accuses sb. wrongly and so harms him; anything that harms sb. wrongly Ⅱ *v.* publish a libel about sb.

liberal Ⅰ *adj.* ❶ favouring some change, as in political or religious affairs ❷ willing to understand and respect the ideas and feeling of others ❸ willing to give; generous Ⅱ *n.* a person with wide understanding, who is in favour of change

liberalism *n.* liberal opinions and beliefs, especially in politics

liberality *n.* ❶ the respect for political, religious or moral views, even if you do not agree with them ❷ the quality of being generous

liberalize *v.* make sth. less strict

liberate *v.* set free (from control, prison, etc.)

liberation *n.* the state of setting free or being set free

liberty *n.* the state of being free from conditions that limit one's actions, so that one can do what one likes without the permission of others; the right or power to do as one chooses

librarian *n.* a person who is in charge of or helps to run a library

library *n.* (a room or building for) collection of books for reading or borrowing

license Ⅰ *n.* ❶ an official document showing that permission has been given to own, use or do sth. ❷ formal or official permission to do sth. ❸ the wrong use of freedom Ⅱ *v.* give official permission to or for

licensed *adj.* ❶ having an official license ❷ (of places) having a license for the sale of alcoholic liquor

lick Ⅰ *v.* ❶ pass the tongue over or under ❷ (especially of flames or waves) pass lightly or with rapid movements over or against (a surface) ❸ defeat sb.; exceed; surpass Ⅱ *n.* ❶ an act of licking with the tongue ❷ speed ❸ a slight use (of paint, etc.)

licking *n.* ❶ a severe beating ❷ a heavy defeat

lid *n.* ❶ a top or cover for closing the opening of a box, pot, jar, etc. ❷ an eyelid

lie[1] *v.* ❶ have or put one's body in a flat or resting position on a horizontal surface ❷ (of things) be at rest on a surface ❸ be situated ❹ extend or spread out in a particular place ❺ be found; exist

lie[2] Ⅰ *v.* make an untrue statement in order to deceive Ⅱ *n.* an untrue statement purposely made to deceive

life *n.* ❶ the quality that people, animals or plants have when they are not dead ❷ activities and experiences that are typical of a way of living ❸ living things ❹ spirit; liveliness; cheerfulness

lifeblood *n.* ❶ a person's or animal's blood which is necessary to life ❷ an influence or force that gives strength and vitality to sth.

lifeboat *n.* ❶ a boat specially constructed for going to help people in danger at sea along a coast ❷ a small boat carried on a ship for use if the ship has to be abandoned at sea

lifeless *adj.* ❶ without life; not living ❷ unconscious ❸ lacking vitality or excitement

lifelike *adj.* looking exactly like a real person or thing

lifestyle *n.* a person's way of living

lifetime *n.* ❶ the duration of a person's life ❷ of a thing's existence or usefulness ❸ a very long time

lift Ⅰ *v.* raise to a higher level or position Ⅱ *n.* ❶ a movement in which sth. is lifted up ❷ a boxlike apparatus in a building for taking people up or down to another floor

light Ⅰ *n.* ❶ the energy from the sun, lamp, etc. that makes things visible ❷ sth. that gives light; the source of light, especially an electric lamp Ⅱ *adj.* ❶ having light ❷ not deep or dark in colour; pale ❸ not heavy ❹ gentle ❺ not serious; for amusement Ⅲ *v.* ❶ (cause to) start to burn ❷ give light to

lighten *v.* ❶ make or become less heavy; reduce the weight of ❷ make light or bright ❸ become light or bright ❹ send out lightning

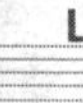

lighter *n.* a device for lighting cigarettes or cigars; a person or thing that lights

lighting *n.* ❶ an equipment for providing light to a room, building or street, etc. ❷ the effect of lights

lightly *adv.* ❶ with little weight or force; gently ❷ to a slight or little degree; not much ❸ with little effort; easily ❹ without careful thought or reasoning

lightning *n.* a flash of bright light produced by natural electricity between clouds in the sky and clouds on the ground, often with thunder

light year *n.* ❶ a unit of distance equivalent to the distance that light travels in one year, 9.46 trillion kilometers ❷ great difference; a long distance

like[1] *v.* ❶ regard with pleasure or fondness; have good feelings about; enjoy ❷ be willing (to)

like[2] Ⅰ *prep.* with the same qualities as Ⅱ *adj.* similar to another person or thing

likelihood *n.* probability; the chance of sth. happening

likely *adj.* ❶ that is expected; probable ❷ seeming suitable

liken *v.* show or say that sth. is like sth. else; compare one to another

likeness *n.* ❶ the fact of being like; resemblance ❷ an instance of being like; a point of resemblance ❸ a portrait, picture or photograph of sb.

likes *n.* ❶ things that one likes ❷ people of the stated type

likewise *adv.* ❶ in the same way; similarly; the same ❷ also; in addition

liking *n.* a feeling of regard or fondness

lily *n.* a plant growing from a bulb, with large white or reddish flowers

limb *n.* ❶ a leg, an arm, or a wing ❷ a large branch (of a tree)

limber *adj.* flexible or supple

limbo *n.* the state of uncertainty

lime Ⅰ *n.* a white substance used in making cement and mortar Ⅱ *v.* add or put lime on (fields, etc.)

limelight *n.* ❶ the centre of public attention ❷ a bright white light produced by heating lime in a strong flame, which was formerly used in theatres to light the stage

limerick *n.* an amusing poem of five lines and having a special rhythm

limit Ⅰ *n.* a line or point that may not be passed Ⅱ *v.* keep below or at a certain point or amount

limitation *n.* ❶ the condition of limiting and being limited ❷ (*pl.*) the condition, fact, or circumstance that limits; disability or inability

limited *adj.* small in amount, power, etc. , and not able to increase; restricted; narrow

limousine *n.* a large, luxurious motorcar (usually with a separate compartment for the driver)

limp Ⅰ *adj.* not stiff or firm; lacking strength Ⅱ *v.* walk lamely or unevenly when one leg or foot is hurt or stiff

line Ⅰ *n.* ❶a long, narrow mark made by a pen, pencil, etc. ❷ a long piece of rope, cord or wire ❸a row of persons or things ❹a system of railroads, buses or airplanes that carries passengers Ⅱ *v.* ❶ mark with line; draw a line on ❷form a line along (sth.)

lineage *n.* the line of descendants from an ancestor

lineal *adj.* in a direct line of descent or ancestry

linear *adj.* ❶of or in a line or lines ❷ of length

linen[1] *n.* a type of cloth made from flax ❷ tablecloths, shirts, sheets, handkerchiefs, etc. made from linen or some other cloth

liner[1] *n.* ❶ a large passenger ship of a steamship company ❷ an aircraft of a line ❸ a pencil, brush or material used around the eyes to give a usually dark line

liner[2] *n.* sth. used for lining; a piece of material used inside another to protect it

lines *n.* ❶the words learnt by an actor to be said in a play ❷ a usually stated number of written lines to be copied by a pupil as a punishment ❸a poem

lineup *n.* ❶ an arrangement of people, especially side by side in a line looking forward ❷ a line of this sort organized by the police, containing a person thought to be guilty of a crime and looked at by a witness who tries to recognize the criminal ❸ the (arrangement of) players or competitors at the beginning of a race or game ❹ a set of events, following one after another

linger *v.* stay for a long time; be late or slow in going away

linguist *n.* ❶ a person skilled in languages ❷ a person who makes a scientific study of language(s)

linguistic *adj.* of (the study of) languages

lining *n.* (a piece of) material covering the inner surface of a garment, box, etc.

link Ⅰ *n.* ❶a person or thing that unites or connects to others ❷ one ring of a chain ❸ the relationship between two countries, organizations, etc. ❹a means of travelling between two place Ⅱ *v.* join or connect

linkage *n.* ❶ a system of links or connections ❷ a connecting relationship (between things or ideas)

linkman *n.* a person whose job is to introduce all the separate parts of a television or radio broadcast

links *n.* a piece of ground on which golf is played

linoleum *n.* a covering for a floor made of canvas, cork and oil

linseed *n.* the seed of flax

lint *n.* a linen fabric with the nap raised

on one side, used for covering cuts and wounds

lion *n.* a sort of big, wild animal of the cat family found in Africa and parts of Southern Asia, and also is called the king of beasts

lip *n.* either of the two fleshy edges of the opening of the mouth

lipstick *n.* a small stick of cosmetic paste, which is set in a case for colouring the lip

liquefy *v.* become or make liquid

liquid Ⅰ *n.* ❶one of the three main forms of matter; a substance that is neither a solid nor a gas Ⅱ *adj.* ❶in the form of a liquid; not gaseous or solid ❷clear and clean; like water ❸(of sounds) clear, pure and flowing ❹easily converted into cash ❺not fixed

liquidate *v.* settle the affairs of a bankrupt business company by selling its property to pay its debts; (with reference to the business) be settled in this way

liquidity *n.* ❶the state of having money in one's possession, or goods that can easily be sold for money ❷the state of being liquid

liquidize *v.* crush (especially fruit or vegetables) into a liquid-like form

liquor *n.* ❶(an) alcoholic drink ❷liquid produced by boiling or fermenting a food substance

list Ⅰ *n.* a set of names of things written one after the other, so as to remember them or keep them in order that they can be found Ⅱ *v.* make a list of; put on a list

listen *v.* ❶try to hear; pay attention to ❷tell sb. to notice what you are saying

listener *n.* a person who listens

listing *n.* a list or catalogue

listless *adj.* not having enough energy or interest to do sth.

literacy *n.* the ability to read and write

literal Ⅰ *adj.* ❶corresponding exactly to the original ❷taking words in their usual and obvious sense Ⅱ *n.* a mistake in printed matter

literally *adv.* in a literal manner or sense; exactly

literary *adj.* of literature or authors

literate *adj.* able to read and write

literature *n.* a written works which are of artistic value; all the writings of a country or a period

litter Ⅰ *n.* ❶things (to be) thrown away, especially paper scattered untidily ❷a group of young animals born at the same time to one mother ❸straw, etc. used as bedding for animals. Ⅱ *v.* ❶scatter; spread; cover untidily ❷supply straw, etc. as bedding for animals ❸bring forth young

litterbin *n.* a container for objects to be thrown away, especially in a public place

little Ⅰ *adj.* ❶young ❷short (in time, distance, stature) ❸small Ⅱ *adv.* ❶not at all; not much ❷rarely Ⅲ *n.* a small amount or duration

live¹ *v.* ❶be alive ❷have one's home at a place ❸spend or experience sth. in a particular way

live² *adj.* ❶alive; living; full of energy ❷(of a broadcast) transmitted while actually happening, not recorded or edited

liveable *adj.* ❶ worth living ❷ suitable for living in

livelihood *n.* a means of living; a way in which one earns money

lively *adj.* ❶gay; full of life and spirit ❷ (of colour) bright and strong ❸lifelike; realistic; as if real; vivid

liven *v.* become or make lively

liver *n.* ❶a large organ of the body near the stomach ❷animal's liver as food

livestock *n.* farm animals; domestic animals kept as a source of food and other products

livid *adj.* ❶of the colour of lead, blue-grey ❷ (of a person or his looks) furiously angry

living Ⅰ *adj.* ❶alive ❷of or for life; for living in ❸existing in use Ⅱ *n.* ❶a way of life ❷a means of keeping alive

lizard *n.* a type of small, four-legged reptile with a long tail and dry scaly skin

load Ⅰ *n.* ❶an amount which a cart, etc. can take ❷ sth. which is carried or supported; a feeling of care, responsibility, etc. Ⅱ *v.* ❶put (a load) on or in (a vehicle, structure, etc.) ❷ put bullets, etc. into (a gun) or film into (a camera)

loaded *adj.* ❶unfairly; favouring one side ❷(of a question) put in such a way as to suggest a particular answer ❸having lots of money ❹drunk

loadstar *n.* ❶the star used as a guide in navigation, especially the polar star ❷a guiding principle

loadstone *n.* a kind of iron ore that is magnetic

loaf[1] *n.* (*pl.* loaves) a bread shaped and baked in one piece, usually fairly large

loaf[2] *v.* spend time idly; waste time, especially by not working when one should

loam *n.* a good-quality soil made of sand, clay, and decayed plant material

loan Ⅰ *n.* ❶sth. which is lent, especially money ❷ the act of lending Ⅱ *v.* give (sb.) the use of (sth.); lend

loathsome *adj.* causing or able to cause nausea; highly offensive

lobster *n.* ❶ a shellfish with eight legs and two claws, bluish-black before and scarlet after being boiled ❷ its flesh as food

local *adj.* of or in a certain place or area, especially the place one lives in

locality *n.* ❶the position or site of sth. ❷a district or neighbourhood

localize *v.* ❶restrict sth. to a particular area ❷ assign (sth.) to a particular place

locate *v.* ❶find the place of ❷place in a certain place; situate

location *n.* ❶ the act of finding the position of or state of being located ❷a place or position ❸a place away from a film studio, where one or more scenes are made for a cinema picture

lock Ⅰ *n.* an apparatus for closing and fastening sth., usually by means of a key Ⅱ *v.* fasten with a lock

locker *n.* a box with a lid which can be locked (usually fixed to a wall and used in places where there are many people each of whom can have his own for his clothes, books, etc.)

lodge *v.* ❶give or find (someone) a home for a time, usually for payment ❷stay, usually for a short time in return for paying rent

lodgings *n.* one or more rented furnished rooms

loft *n.* the room at the top of a building just under the roof

lofty *adj.* ❶very high and impressive ❷ noble; grand; very proud

log *n.* ❶a long piece of the trunk that has been cut down ❷a daily record of what happens during a ship's voyage ❸ an instrument telling the speed of a ship

logic *n.* the science and methods of reasoning

L

logical *adj.* ❶according to the rules of logic ❷ having or showing good clear reasoning; sensible

logically *adv.* ❶ in a logical way ❷ according to what is reasonable or logical

logician *n.* a person who studies or is skilled in logic

logistics *n.* ❶ the planning and organization that is needed to carry out any large and difficult operation ❷ the study or skill of moving soldiers, supplying them with food, etc.

logo *n.* a symbol or other small design adopted by a company or an organization to identify its products, uniform, vehicles, etc.

loin *n.* ❶ the lower part of the back between the hipbones and the ribs ❷the front part of the hindquarters of beef, lamb, veal, etc.

lollipop *n.* a type of sweet at the end of a stick

lone *adj.* ❶ without other person or things ❷without a husband or wife

lonely *adj.* ❶ by oneself; by itself; without others near ❷ (of places) not often visited; far from inhabited places

long[1] Ⅰ *adj.* ❶ (of extent in space) measuring much from end to end ❷ having a great or specified duration or extent in time Ⅱ *adv.* a long time Ⅲ *n.* a long time

long[2] *v.* want sth. very much

longevity *n.* long life

longing Ⅰ *n.* a feeling of wanting sth.; a strong wish Ⅱ *adj.* showing a strong wish

longitude *n.* the position on the earth east or west of a meridian, usually measured in degrees, from Greenwich

longlived *adj.* living or lasting a long time

longsighted *adj.* able to see objects or read things clearly only when they are far from the eyes

longstanding *adj.* having existed in the same form for a long time

longwinded *adj.* (of a person, speech, piece of writing, etc.) going on too long and using too many words

look Ⅰ *v.* ❶turn or fix one's eyes in order to see; try to see ❷appear to be; seem ❸ search for; try to find ❹pay attention to Ⅱ *n.* ❶ an act of looking ❷ the appearance of sb. or sth.; an expression on the face

lookout *n.* ❶a place from which you can keep watch ❷a person whose job is to keep watch ❸ looking out or watching for sth. ❹ a future prospect ❺ (informal) a person's own concern

loom Ⅰ *n.* a machine for weaving cloth Ⅱ *v.* appear indistinctly or in a threatening way

loophole *n.* the way of escaping from a law, restriction, etc.

loose *adj.* ❶ free; not held, tied up, fastened, packed, or contained in sth. ❷ moving more freely than usual ❸ (of clothes) not tight

loosely *adv.* ❶in a way that is not firm or tight ❷in a way that is not exact

loosen *v.* ❶become or make loose ❷make sth. weaker

lord *n.* ❶a peer; a nobleman ❷a supreme male ruler ❸(Lord) God; Christ

lorry *n.* a large motor vehicle for carrying big goods

lose *v.* ❶ have sth. or sb. taken away from one by accident, misfortune, old age, death, etc. ❷ fail to win ❸ be or become worse off

loser *n.* ❶a person or thing that loses or has lost sth., especially a game or contest ❷a person or thing that is put at a disadvantage by a particular situation or course of action.

loss *n.* ❶ the act or fact of losing possession (of sth.) ❷a person, thing, or amount that is lost or taken away ❸ the money that has lost by a business

lost *adj.* ❶ no longer possessed; that cannot be found ❷not used, obtained, or won ❸ destroyed; ruined; killed; drowned, etc. ❹having gone astray

lot[1] *n.* a great quantity, number, or amount

lot[2] *n.* any of a set used for making a choice or decision by chance

lotion *n.* a type of liquid rubbed on the skin or hair to cure a disease or improve one's appearance

lottery *n.* an arrangement to give prizes to holders of numbered tickets previously bought by them and drawn by lot

lotus *n.* any of several water lilies of tropical Africa and Asia

loud *adj.* having or producing great strength of sound; not quiet or soft; easily heard

loudspeaker *n.* a device that converts electrical signals into audible sound, especially one used as part of a public address system

louse *n.* (*pl.* lice) any of several types of small insect that live on the skin and in the hair of people and animals, especially when they are dirty

love Ⅰ *v.* ❶have a strong affection for ❷ like very much; take pleasure in Ⅱ *n.* ❶ a strong emotion of regard and affection ❷ a person or thing that you like very much

lov(e)able *adj.* deserving, causing, or worthy of love; pleasant; attractive

lovely *adj.* ❶ beautiful; attractive; pleasant ❷enjoyable; amusing

lover *n.* ❶ a person who is fond of or devoted to (sth.) ❷man and woman in love ❸ a man in love with or having a sexual relationship with a woman outside of marriage

lovesick *adj.* sad or ill because of

unreturned love

loving *adj.* showing or expressing love

low Ⅰ *adj.* ❶not high; not extending far upwards ❷(of sounds) not loud; not high in pitch ❸below others in status, etc. ❹weak and depressed Ⅱ *adv.* in or to a low position, point, degree, manner, etc.

lower *v.* ❶(cause to) become less high; bring down ❷make less or lower

lowly *adj.* low in social position; not proud; simple

loyal *adj.* true and faithful (to)

loyalty *n.* the quality or conduct of being loyal; loyal conduct

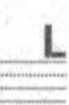

luck *n.* chance; fortune (good or bad); sth. that is considered to come by chance

lucky *adj.* ❶ having a good luck ❷ bringing good luck

lug *v.* pull with force; drag roughly or with effort

luggage *n.* boxes, bags, etc. for travelling; baggage

lull Ⅰ *v.* (cause to) become quiet slowly Ⅱ *n.* a period of quietness in a storm or when there is noise and activity

lumber Ⅰ *n.* ❶ useless or unwanted articles stored away or taking up space (e. g. old furniture) ❷roughly prepared wood; wood that has been sawn into planks, boards, etc. Ⅱ *v.* cut trees or wood into timber

luminous *adj.* giving light; shining; clear

lump Ⅰ *n.* ❶a piece of hard or solid mass ❷a hard swelling in part of the body Ⅱ *v.* ❶form into a lump ❷walk or move along in a heavy way

lunar *adj.* of, for, or to the moon

lunatic Ⅰ *adj.* mad, crazy or stupid Ⅱ *n.* a person who is mad

lunch *n.* a meal between breakfast and supper; midday meal

lung *n.* one of the two organs of breathing in animals and humans

lure Ⅰ *v.* attract or tempt, especially away from what one should do into sth. one should not Ⅱ *n.* a piece of equipment, such as a plastic bird or fish, to attract animals into a place where they can be caught; decoy

lush *adj.* ❶(of plants, especially grass) growing very well; thick and healthy ❷ luxurious and making you feel comfortable

lust Ⅰ *n.* ❶strong sexual desire ❷intense desire for sth. or enjoyment of sth. Ⅱ *v.* feel a strong desire for sb. or sth.

luster *n.* the shining quality of sth. (e. g. of polished metal, smooth cloth, etc.)

lustrous *adj.* shining; brilliant

lusty *adj.* strong; vigorous

luxuriant *adj.* growing thickly in great quantity

luxurious *adj.* supplied with luxuries; very comfortable

luxury *n.* ❶ the great comfort, as provided by wealth ❷ a pleasant and often expensive thing that is not necessary

lymph *n.* an almost colourless fluid, containing chiefly white blood cells, that is collected from the tissues of the body

lyric *adj.* like a song or expressing strong personal feelings

M m

ma *n.* a short form for mamma; mother

machine *n.* ❶ instrument with many parts that move together to do work ❷ persons organized to control (part of) an organization, a group, etc.

machinery *n.* ❶ machines collectively ❷ moving parts of a machine ❸ methods; the organization of sth.

machinist *n.* a person who operates a machine, especially a machine tool

macrocosm *n.* the universe that contains smaller structure

macroeconomics *n.* (*pl.*) the part of economics concerned with large-scale or general economic factors, such as interest rates and national productivity

mad *adj.* ❶ crazy; sick in mind ❷ very angry

madam *n.* the polite word that you say when you speak to a woman who is a stranger or when you write a business letter to a woman

made *adj.* ❶ formed with sth. particular ❷ assured of success ❸ fictitious or imaginary

made-up *adj.* ❶ wearing make-up ❷ invented; not true

magazine *n.* ❶ a paper book with different articles, which appears usually every week or month ❷ a store for arms, ammunition, explosives, etc.

magic Ⅰ *n.* ❶ strange powers that make wonderful or unusual things happen ❷ an art or skills of getting mysterious results by tricks Ⅱ *adj.* having or apparently having supernatural powers

magical *adj.* ❶ containing magic; used in magic ❷ resembling magic; produced or working as if by magic

magician *n.* ❶ a person who can do magic tricks ❷ a person with magical powers

magma *n.* hot melted rock found below the solid surface of the earth

magnanimous *adj.* generous and noble

magnate *n.* sb. who is rich or important (especially in business)

magnet *n.* a piece of iron, often shaped like a horseshoe, which is able to attract iron

magnetic *adj.* ❶ having the properties of magnet ❷ attractive to sb. or sth.

magnetism *n.* ❶ the quality of strong personal charm; the power to attract, etc. ❷ the physical property of being magnetic

magnificent *adj.* extremely splendid or grand; noble; greatly nice

magnifier *n.* a piece of equipment that is used to make things look larger

magnify *v.* ❶ make (sth.) appear larger

than in reality ❷ make sth. seem more important, etc. that it really is

magnitude *n.* ❶ greatness of size or importance ❷ size ❸ the degree of brightness of a star

magpie *n.* a black and white bird of the crow family, which sometimes is thought to steal small bright objects

maid *n.* ❶ a girl or (young) woman who is not married ❷ a woman servant

maiden Ⅰ *n.* a girl or unmarried woman Ⅱ *adj.* ❶ of a girl or woman ❷ first or earliest ❸ not used before; fresh

maidenly *adj.* ❶ like or suitable to a young unmarried girl ❷ in a gentle or modest manner

mail Ⅰ *n.* ❶ the postal system of carrying and delivering letters and parcels ❷ letters and anything else sent or received by post, especially those travelling or arriving together Ⅱ *v.* post

mailbox *n.* a letter box

main Ⅰ *n.* ❶ principal pipe bringing water or gas, wire transmitting electricity into a building ❷ sea, especially a wide expanse of sea Ⅱ *adj.* most important; chief

mainframe *n.* ❶ a large high-speed computer, especially one supporting numerous workstations or peripherals ❷ the central processing unit and primary memory of a computer

mainland *n.* the main area of land of a country, without its islands

mainline *v.* take an illegal drug into one of the chief veins of the body, either for pleasure or because one is dependent on it, not for medical reasons

mainly *adv.* for the most part; mostly

mainmast *n.* the largest or most important of the masts which hold up the sails on a ship

mains *n.* a supply of electricity produced centrally and brought to houses, etc. by wires

mainstay *n.* sb. or sth. which provides the chief means of support

mainstream *n.* the main or most widely accepted way of thinking or acting in relation to a subject

maintain *v.* ❶ keep up; continue ❷ support ❸ claim to be true ❹ keep in safety and protect from harm, etc. ❺ keep sth. in good condition by regularly checking and repairing it

maintenance *n.* ❶ the act of maintaining or being maintained ❷ what is needed to support life

maize *n.* a kind of grain plant

majestic *adj.* having or showing majesty

majesty *n.* ❶ sth. that is magnificent; nobility ❷ supreme power of authority ❸ (Majesty) a title used to refer to the king or queen

major Ⅰ *adj.* greater or more important of two (parts, etc.); older of two brothers Ⅱ *n.* ❶ a chief or special subject at a university ❷ an army officer between a captain and a colonel Ⅲ *v.* study as the chief subject(s) when doing a university degree

majority *n.* ❶ the greater number or part (of) ❷ the number by which votes for one side exceed those for the other side ❸ a legal age of reaching manhood or womanhood

make Ⅰ *v.* ❶ produce by work or action ❷ used with a large number of nouns in various special senses ❸ cause to be or cause to do sth. ❹ force or cause (a person to do sth. or a thing to happen) ❺ earn or gain money; win ❻ arrive at or reach a place ❼ reckon or consider ❽ have the qualities of (especially sth. good) ❾ travel (a distance) or at a speed ❿ turn out to be; result in ⓫ equal with or add up to; amount to; come to ⓬ establish (a law) ⓭ be about (to) ⓮ eat or have (a meal) ⓯ write, compose or prepare with Ⅱ *n.* a type of product, especially as produced by a particular maker; a method or style of manufacture

make-believe *n.* the act of imagining that sth. is real; pretence

makeover *n.* a complete transformation or remodeling of sth., especially a person's hairstyle, make-up, or clothes

male Ⅰ *adj.* of the sex that does not give birth to young ❷ (of a flower or plant) not producing fruit Ⅱ *n.* a person or animal, etc. who or which belongs to the sex that can't have babies

malformation *n.* ❶ the condition of being formed or shaped wrongly ❷ a shape, structure, or part (especially of the body) that is formed badly or wrongly

malformed *adj.* made or shaped badly

malfunction *n.* a fault in operation

malignancy *n.* ❶ the state of being malignant ❷ a dangerous growth of cells; tumour of a malignant kind

malignant *adj.* ❶ (of persons or their actions) filled with or showing a desire to hurt ❷ (of diseases) harmful to life; violent

mallet *n.* a hammer with a wooden head

malnourished *adj.* suffering from malnutrition

malnutrition *n.* (of persons) the poor state of health caused by the lack of enough food or the right kind of food

malpractice *n.* a careless, improper or illegal behaviour while in a professional job

malt *n.* grain (e. g. barley, oats) specially treated in making beer or spirits

maltreat *v.* behave cruelly towards someone

mammal *n.* an animal of a class that give birth to live babies and feeds its young on milk

mammy *n.* (a child's word for) mother

man Ⅰ *n.* ❶ an adult male human ❷ a human being ❸ the human race ❹ a husband, lover, or other adult male with whom a woman lives ❺ an adult male under the authority of another or in employment ❻ used for addressing an adult male, especially when the speaker is excited or angry Ⅱ *v.* ❶ strengthen one's spirits or courage ❷ provide with men for operation

manage *v.* ❶ control or guide (especially a business) ❷ succeed in dealing with (a problem) ❸ succeed in taking or using

management *n.* ❶ the act of managing, especially a business or other organizations ❷ delicate contrivance; skillful treatment ❸ the people who are in charge of a firm, industry, etc., considered as one body

manager *n.* ❶ a person who controls a business ❷ a person who conducts business or manages household affairs ❸ a person dealing with the business of an entertainer, a sportsman, etc.

mandarin *n.* ❶ (in former times) important Chinese official ❷ a small kind of orange

mandate *n.* ❶ an instruction or a permission (especially from a superior official) ❷ the right and power given to a government, or any body of people chosen to represent others or to act according to the wishes of those who voted for it

mandatory Ⅰ *adj.* of, containing a command which must be obeyed; compulsory, obligatory Ⅱ *n.* a person or state to whom a mandate has been given

mandible *n.* ❶ a jaw which moves, especially the lower jaw of an animal or fish, or a jawbone ❷ the upper or lower part of a bird's beak ❸ either of the two biting or holding parts in insects and crabs

mane *n.* long hair on the back of the neck of some animals (e. g. horse, lion)

manger *n.* a long open box that cattle and horses feed from

mango *n.* ❶ a kind of tropical fruit which has yellow skin when ripe ❷ a tree bearing this fruit

manhandle *v.* ❶ move (sth. heavy or awkward) by using the strength of men, not machines ❷ treat sb. or sth. roughly

manhole *n.* a hole, with a cover, through which a man can go down to look at or repair pipes, sewers, etc. under the ground

manhood *n.* ❶ the condition or period of time of being a man ❷ the good qualities of a man, such as courage, strong will, etc. ❸ all the men of a nation, considered together as one body

manhunt *n.* a search for a wanted person, especially a criminal

maniac *n.* ❶ a person (thought to be) suffering from mania ❷ a wild thoughtless person

manic *adj.* ❶ of or suffering from mania ❷ very excited; wild in behaviour

manifest Ⅰ *adj.* plain to see or clear to the mind Ⅱ *v.* ❶ show (sth.) plainly ❷ give signs of

manipulate *v.* ❶ handle or control (a tool, mechanism, etc.), typically in a skilful manner ❷ control or influence (a person or situation) cleverly, unfairly, or unscrupulously ❸ examine or treat (a part of the body) by feeling or moving it with the hand

mankind *n.* the human race

manly *adj.* ❶ having the qualities suitable to a man ❷ (of things, qualities, etc.) right for a man ❸ (of a woman) having a man's qualities

manner *n.* ❶ the way in which sth. is done or happens ❷ (only singular) person's way of behaving toward others ❸ (*pl.*) the habits and customs of a particular group of people ❹ (*pl.*) social behaviour that is considered to be polite ❺ a style in literature or art ❻ a kind or sort

mannered *adj.* having an unnatural way of behaving

mannish *adj.* (of a woman) like a man in character, behaviour, or appearance

manpower *n.* the number of people working or available for work

mansion *n.* ❶ a large and stately house ❷

(*pl.*)(in proper names) block of flats

mantle Ⅰ *n.* a loose sleeveless cloak; a layer of sth. that covers a surface Ⅱ *v.* ❶cover in or as in a mantle ❷flow into the blood vessels of; (of the face) flush

manual Ⅰ *adj.* of or using hands Ⅱ *n.* ❶a handbook or textbook ❷a keyboard of an organ, played with the hands

manufacture Ⅰ *v.* ❶make (goods, etc.) on a large-scale by machinery ❷invent (evidence, an excuse, etc.), make up Ⅱ *n.* the act of making

manuscript *n.* a book or article in handwriting or typewritten form

many Ⅰ *adj.* (more, most) a large number(of) Ⅱ *n.* the majority of people

map Ⅰ *n.* a flat drawing of a large surface Ⅱ *v.* show in the form of a map; make a map of

maple *n.* ❶trees with five-pointed leaves grown for wood or shade ❷wood of this tree

mar *v.* damage or spoil sth. good

marathon Ⅰ *n.* ❶(in athletics) running race of 26 miles ❷any long race, journey or activity Ⅱ *adj.* very long

marble *n.* ❶a hard sort of limestone used for building, sculpture, gravestones, etc. when cut and polished, and usually showing an irregular pattern of colours ❷a small ball of glass, clay, or stone used in games

march Ⅰ *v.* ❶walk with regular steps ❷make sb. walk quickly Ⅱ *n.* ❶way of walking with regular steps ❷a piece of music to which soldiers march

March *n.* the third month of the year

mare *n.* a female horse or donkey

margin *n.* ❶the extreme edge or limit of a place ❷the space at each edge of a page without writing or printing ❸an amount beyond the minimum necessary ❹the condition near the limit or borderline below or beyond which sth. is impossible ❺the difference between the cost and the selling price of a product

marginal *adj.* ❶written in a margin ❷of or at an edge ❸very slight in amount ❹(said about a parliamentary seat) having a very small majority in the previous election

marine Ⅰ *adj.* ❶of, by, found in or produced by the sea ❷of ships, sea trade, the navy, etc Ⅱ *n.* ❶(only the merchant marine, all the merchant) ships of a country ❷a soldier who serve for a naval ship

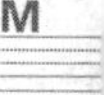

mariner *n.* a sailor, especially one who assists in navigating a ship

marital *adj.* of a husband; of marriage

maritime *adj.* ❶of the sea or navigation ❷near the sea

mark Ⅰ *n.* ❶line, scratch, cut, stain, etc., that spoils the appearance of sth. ❷a noticeable spot on the body by which a person or animal may be recognized ❸a figure or printed or written sign which shows sth. ❹a figure, letter, or sign which represents a judgment of the quality of someone's work, behaviour, performance in a competition, etc. ❺the object or place one aims at ❻an acceptable level of quality Ⅱ *v.* ❶make a mark or marks on appearance ❷give marks to ❸pay attention (to); watch or listen to carefully

marked *adj.* clearly noticeable

marker *n.* ❶ sth. that serves to mark a position ❷ a pen with a broad felt tip ❸ a person who records the score in games

market Ⅰ *n.* ❶ a place where people can bring goods to sell ❷ trade in a certain class of goods ❸ the state of trade as shown by prices or the rate at which things are bought and sold ❹ the demand to purchase goods and services Ⅱ *v.* buy or sell in a market

marketer *n.* a person who works in a certain sort of market

marketer *n.* a person or firm that sells a product

marketing *n.* the commercial process involved in promoting, selling and distributing a product or service

marketplace *n.* ❶ an open area, especially a square, where a market is held ❷ the area of business activity in which buying and selling are done

marking *n.* (any of a set of) coloured marks on an animal's skin, fur, or on a bird's feathers

marksman *n.* a person who can shoot well with a gun

marksmanship *n.* the quality of ability of a marksman; skill in shooting

markup *n.* the amount by which a price is raised by a seller to pay for costs and allow for profit

marmot *n.* a small European plant-eating animal that lives in holes in the ground

maroon[1] *v.* leave (someone) alone in a place where no one lives, with no means of getting away

maroon[2] *adj.* a small rocket that explodes high in the air, used as a signal, especially at sea

marriage *n.* a legal union of a man and woman as husband and wife; the state of being married

married *adj.* ❶ having a husband or wife ❷ of the state of marriage

marry *v.* ❶ take sb. as a husband or wife ❷ (of a priest or official) perform the ceremony of marriage for (two people)

marshal Ⅰ *n.* ❶ an officer of the highest rank in certain army and air force ❷ an official responsible for important public events or ceremonies ❸ an official with the functions of a sheriff Ⅱ *v.* ❶ arrange in good or correct order ❷ lead (a person) to the correct place, especially on a ceremonial or important occasion

martial *adj.* having to do with war

martyr Ⅰ *n.* one who dies because of his religion or who is badly treated because of his beliefs Ⅱ *v.* put sb. to death; cause to suffer as a martyr

marvel Ⅰ *n.* sth. that is wonderful and surprises people Ⅱ *v.* be greatly surprised at

marvel(l)ous *adj.* wonderful; surprisingly good

Marxism *n.* the political and economic theories of Karl Marx and Friedrich Engels, later developed by their followers to form the basis for the theory and practice of communism

mascara *n.* a substance used to make the eyelashes darker

mascot *n.* sth. or sb. that is supposed to bring good luck

mash Ⅰ *n.* any kind of soft mixture Ⅱ *v.* compress (food) with violence so that it forms a soft mass

mask Ⅰ *n.* ❶a covering for the face to hide or protect it ❷a false face worn by an actor or actress ❸the head of a fox Ⅱ *v.* ❶conceal ❷cover (the face) with a mask

masked *adj.* wearing a mask

mass Ⅰ *n.* ❶ a lump or quantity of matter, without regular shape ❷a large number ❸the amount of a material in a body measured by its resistance to change of motion ❹ the mass of the majority of (people) Ⅱ *v.* gather together in large numbers

massacre Ⅰ *n.* the killing of a large number of (usually defenseless) people Ⅱ *v.* kill in this way

massage Ⅰ *v.* take away stiffness or pain by rubbing and pressing parts of the body Ⅱ *n.* the action of rubbing and pressing parts of the body

masses *n.* the body of common people in society

massive *adj.* of great size, especially strong, solid, and heavy

mast *n.* ❶a long, upright pole of wood or metal that supports the sails on a ship ❷a tall pole for a flag ❸a tall steel structure for the aerials of a radio or television transmitter ❹ the fruit of beech, oak, and other forest trees (as food for pigs)

master Ⅰ *n.* ❶a chief person; the person who controls sb. or sth. ❷the captain of a merchant ship ❸the master of a house ❹a male teacher in a school ❺a person that is extremely skilled at a particular activity Ⅱ *v.* ❶become the master of ❷control; become skilled in

masterful *adj.* ❶(said about a person) powerful or domineering ❷very skilful

masterly having or revealing supreme skills

mastermind Ⅰ *n.* a person with superior brain Ⅱ *v.* plan or direct a scheme

masterpiece *n.* a very good piece of work or art

mastery *n.* ❶complete control over sb. or sth. ❷thorough knowledge or skill

mat Ⅰ *n.* ❶ a floor covering made of woven straw, wood, etc. ❷a small piece of material placed under objects on a table ❸ anything thickly tangled or twisted together Ⅱ *v.* (cause to) become thickly tangled or knotted

match Ⅰ *n.* ❶ a game or contest ❷ a person equal in strength, ability, etc. ❸ marriage ❹a person or thing combining well with another Ⅱ *v.* ❶ put in competition ❷find an equal for; be equal to ❸ correspond with (quality, colour, etc.)

matching *adj.* having the same colour, pattern, style, etc. and therefore looking attractive together

matchless *adj.* so good that nothing can be compared with it

material Ⅰ *n.* ❶ anything from which sth. is or can be made ❷knowledge of facts from which a (written) work is produced Ⅱ *adj.* ❶made or connected with matter or substance ❷of the body; of physical needs ❸important; essential

materialism *n.* ❶ the theory that everything in the world is made up of matter or depends on matter ❷ the tendency to value, valuation of material things too much and spiritual and intellectual things (wealth, bodily comforts, etc.) too little

materialist Ⅰ *n.* a believer in materialism Ⅱ *adj.* of materialism

materialistic *adj.* of materialism or materialists

materialize *v.* ❶appear or become visible ❷become a fact or happen

maternal *adj.* ❶of or like a mother ❷ related through the mother's part of the family

maternity *n.* being a mother

mathematician *n.* a person who is skilled in mathematics

mathematics *n.* the study or science of numbers

matriarchy *n.* a social system in which the oldest woman is the head of the family, and passes power and possessions on to her daughters

M

matron *n.* ❶ a woman in charge of nurses in a hospital ❷ a woman in charge of the feeding, medical care, etc. in a school

matter Ⅰ *n.* ❶ the physical material of which everything that we can see or touch is made, as opposed to thought or mind ❷ sth. printed or written ❸ a subject to which one gives attention; situation or affair ❹ used to emphasize how small an amount is or how short a period of time is ❺ importance ❻ a trouble or a cause of pain, illness, etc. Ⅱ *v.* be important or have an important effect on sb. or sth.

matting *n.* a rough material used for covering floors, etc.

mattress *n.* a large flat bag full of soft material on which we sleep

mature Ⅰ *adj.* ❶ fully grown and developed ❷ careful; perfected Ⅱ *v.* (cause to) become mature

max Ⅰ *n.* a maximum amount or degree Ⅱ *adv.* at the most Ⅲ *v.* reach or cause to reach the limit of capacity or ability

maxi- *pref.* large; long

maxim *n.* a widely accepted rule of conduct or general truth which is briefly expressed

maximal *adj.* greatest or largest possible; being a maximum

maximum Ⅰ *n.* the largest amount, number, or size Ⅱ *adj.* as large, fast, etc. as possible

May *n.* the fifth month of the year

may *aux. v.* ❶(used to show possibility) be likely to ❷ used to express or to indicate permission or request for permission ❸ used to indicate the purpose

maybe *adv.* perhaps; possibly

mayor *n.* the head of a town or city government

maze *n.* ❶a complex system of paths or tunnels in which it is easy to get lost; labyrinth ❷ sth. jumbled or confused; the state of being confused

me *pron.* the object form of I

meadow *n.* ❶grassland on which cattle, sheep, etc. may feed ❷a low land by the bank of a river, lake or stream

meager *adj.* ❶ thin; lacking flesh ❷ not enough in quantity, quality, strength, etc.

meal *n.* ❶ the food taken at one time ❷ food that is eaten

mean[1] *v.* ❶ represent or express (a meaning) ❷ have sth. as a purpose or intention ❸ be determined about; act on

❹be a sign of ❺be of importance or value to

mean² *adj.* ❶(especially of a place) poor or poor-looking ❷unwilling to give or share what one has; ungenerous ❸(of behaviour) unkind; nasty ❹(of the understanding, the natural powers) inferior; poor

mean³ Ⅰ *adj.* of an average amount, figure, or value Ⅱ *n.* a state or way of behaviour or course of action which is not too strong or too weak, too much or too little, but in between or in the middle position

meaning Ⅰ *n.* sth. that is meant or intended Ⅱ *adj.* rich in significance or implication

meaningful *adj.* significant; full of meaning

means *n.* ❶the method, process or way by which a result may be obtained ❷money, income, or wealth, especially large enough for comfort

meantime Ⅰ *adv.* in the time that sth. else is happening Ⅱ *n.* the period of time between two events; at the same time

meanwhile Ⅰ *n.* the period of time before sth. happens or while sth. else is happening Ⅱ *adv.* during this time; in the same period of time

measurable *adj.* able to be measured, or large enough to be measured

measure Ⅰ *n.* ❶the size, quantity, degree, weight, etc. as found by a standard or unit ❷an unit, standard, or system used in stating size, quantity, or degree ❸sth. with which to test size, quantity, etc. ❹a sign of the size or the strength of sth. Ⅱ *v.* ❶find the size, extent, volume, degree, etc. of sth. or sb. ❷assess; gauge

meat *n.* ❶the flesh of animals, apart from fish and birds, which is eaten ❷(of fruits, eggs, nut, etc.) the part that can be eaten ❸valuable matter, ideas, etc.

meatball *n.* a small round ball of finely cut-up meat

meaty *adj.* ❶full of meat ❷full of valuable ideas

mechanic *n.* a person who has been trained to work with machines

mechanical *adj.* ❶of, connected with machinery or produced by machinery ❷(of people or their acts) as if moved by machinery or habit, not by will

mechanics *n.* ❶the science of motion and force; the science of machinery ❷the ways in which sth. works, produces results, etc.

mechanism *n.* ❶working parts of a machine, etc. ❷parts of an organism or system which work together ❸the way in which sth. works or is constructed

medal *n.* a piece of metal with a design or words on it given to sb. to show that he has done sth. special

medallion *n.* a round medal like a large coin, usually worn round the neck for decoration

medallist *n.* a person who has won a medal, especially in sport

meddle *v.* take too much interest in, or take action about other people's private affairs; interfere (with)

media *n.* a means or instrumentality which convey information to the public

medial *adj.* ❶situated in the middle ❷of average size

median Ⅰ *adj.* situated in or passing through the middle Ⅱ *n.* ❶ a middle point or line ❷a medial number or point in a series

mediate *v.* act as a peacemaker between opposing sides

medical *adj.* ❶of the art of medicine; of curing disease ❷ of the treatment of disease by medicine than by operation

medicated *adj.* containing a medicinal substance

medication *n.* a medical substance, especially a drug; medicine

medicinal *adj.* used to treat and cure illnesses

medicine *n.* ❶the science of treating and understanding illnesses ❷ things which we drink or eat when we are ill to help us to get better

medieval *adj.* relating to or belonging to the Middle Ages (about A. D. 476—1500)

mediocre *adj.* not very good; neither very good nor very bad; second rate

Mediterranean *adj.* of the sea surrounded by Europe, Asia Minor and Africa

medium Ⅰ *n.* ❶means by which sth. is expressed or communicated ❷sth. that is in the middle between two extremes ❸a substance or surroundings in which sth. exists or moves or is transmitted Ⅱ *adj.* in the middle between two amounts, extremes, etc. ; average

meet Ⅰ *v.* ❶come face to face with; come across by chance ❷ go to a place and await the arrival of ❸ make the acquaintance of ❹ satisfy (a demand, etc.) ❺ pay sth. ❻ undergo or experience Ⅱ *n.* coming together of a number of people for a purpose

meeting *n.* ❶the coming together of two or more people by chance or arrangement ❷a gathering of people for a purpose

mega *adj.* ❶very large; huge ❷excellent

megalithic *adj.* ❶of megaliths ❷of the time when these stones were put up

megaphone *n.* a metal horn for speaking through to make the voice sound louder

melancholy Ⅰ *adj.* sad; depressed; low-spirited Ⅱ *n.* feeling of sadness

melodrama *n.* a play in which there are a lot of exciting and emotional events and in which people's emotions are very exaggerated

melody *n.* ❶the arrangement of music in a tuneful way; melodiousness ❷ a song or tune ❸the part which forms a clearly recognizable tune in a larger arrangement of notes

melon *n.* any of a few kinds of fruit which are large and rounded, with very juicy flesh inside and a firm skin

melt *v.* ❶ reduce or cause to be reduced from a solid to a liquid state usually by heating ❷(of a solid in a liquid) (cause to) dissolve ❸ (of a person, heart, feelings) soften or be softened ❹ gradually disappear

melting *adj.* (especially of a voice) gentle, soft, and pleasant

member *n.* a person belonging to a group, club, society, etc.

memento *n.* sth. which one keeps to remember a person or a special occasion

memo *n.* a short form of memorandum

memorable *adj.* worthy to be

remembered

memorandum *n.* ❶a note or record for future use; a brief informal note or report ❷ an informal business communication, usually unsigned

memorial Ⅰ *n.* sth. made to remind people of an event, person, etc. Ⅱ *adj.* in honour of someone who has died so that they will be remembered

memorize *v.* learn by heart; commit to memory

memory *n.* ❶ the ability to remember things ❷ the time during which things happened which someone can remember ❸sth. that you remember from the past

mend Ⅰ *v.* ❶ repair; make sth. torn or broken good again ❷be free from faults or errors ❸recover or heal Ⅱ *n.* the part mended after breaking; a patch or darn

mental *adj.* ❶ of or in the mind ❷ concerning illness of the mind

mention Ⅰ *v.* speak or write about sth. briefly Ⅱ *n.* brief reference to sb. or sth.

menu *n.* ❶a list of different kinds of food that can be obtained in a hotel, restaurant, etc. ❷a list of options from which a user can choose which is displayed on a computer screen

merchandise *n.* products that are bought, sold or traded

merchant *n.* a person who buys and sells goods, especially in large amount in foreign countries

merciful *adj.* having or showing mercy

merciless *adj.* cruel; without mercy

mercury *n.* a silver-coloured metal, usually liquid

Mercury *n.* a small planet that is the closest to the sun in the solar system, sometimes visible to the naked eye just after sunset

mercy *n.* willingness to forgive, not to punish; kindness and pity

mere *adj.* not more than; no better than; only

merely *adv.* only; simply

merge *v.* combine or cause (two or more things) to combine, especially gradually, so as to become a single thing

merit Ⅰ *n.* ❶sth. that is good in sth. or sb.; excellence; good quality ❷ the quality or fact of deserving reward Ⅱ *v.* be worthy of; deserve; have a right to

meritorious *adj.* having merit; deserving praise

mermaid *n.* an imaginary creature supposed to live in the sea, with a woman's body but a fish's tail instead of legs

merrily *adv.* ❶in a cheerful way ❷in a brisk and lively way

merriment *n.* laughter and sounds of fun and enjoyment

merry *adj.* cheerful; full of lively happiness, fun, etc.

mesh Ⅰ *n.* ❶a piece of material woven in a fine network with small holes between the threads ❷ the threads in such a network Ⅱ *v.* connect; be held together

mess Ⅰ *n.* a state of disorder or untidiness Ⅱ *v.* put (sth.) into an untidy state

message *n.* a spoken or written piece of information passed from one person to another

messenger *n.* a person who takes message

metal Ⅰ *n.* ❶ a hard substance such as iron, tin, gold, etc. ❷ small broken stones for making roads Ⅱ *v.* cover (a road) with small broken stones

metaphysics *n.* a branch of philosophy dealing with the nature of existence, truth and knowledge

meteor *n.* a piece of rock or metal travelling through space which glows with heat when it enters the earth's atmosphere

meteoric *adj.* ❶ to do with meteors ❷ like a meteor in brilliance or sudden appearance

meteorite *n.* a piece of rock or metal that has fallen to earth as a meteor

meter Ⅰ *n.* a device that measures and indicates the quantity or rate of sth., such as the amount of electricity used or the distance travelled Ⅱ *v.* measure the use of sth. by means of a meter

M

method *n.* ❶ a way or manner of doing sth. ❷ the order or system in doing things or thinking

methodical *adj.* doing things carefully, using an ordered system

methodology *n.* the set of methods used for study or action in a particular subject, as in science or education

metre *n.* ❶ a unit for measuring length, equal to 100 centimeters ❷ any arrangement of words in poetry into strong and weak beats

metric *adj.* ❶ based on the metric system ❷ made or measured using the metric system

metricize *v.* change to the metric system

metro *n.* an underground railway system in cities in France and various other countries

metropolis *n.* ❶ a chief city or the capital city of a country ❷ an important center of a particular activity

metropolitan *adj.* to do with or belonging to a metropolis

mew Ⅰ *n.* the sound made by a cat Ⅱ *v.* make the sound as a cat makes

microbe *n.* a living thing that is so small that it cannot be seen without a microscope, and that may cause disease; bacterium

microcosm *n.* sth. small and self-contained that represents all the qualities, activities, etc., of sth. larger; miniature represen-tation (of)

microphone *n.* an instrument which can change sound waves into electric waves, and can therefore be used in recording people's voices, etc.

microprocessor *n.* a small electronic device containing a silicon chip and used in calculators, computers, etc.

microscope *n.* an instrument with lenses which makes very small things appear bigger

microscopic *adj.* ❶ to do with a microscope ❷ too small to be visible without the aid of a microscope ❸ extremely small

mid *adj.* in the middle of; middle

midday *n.* 12 o'clock of the day; in the middle of the day

middle Ⅰ *adj.* ❶ of the same distance from each end or side ❷ in the middle; intermediate Ⅱ *n.* ❶ a point or part which is at the same distance from each side or end ❷ waist

middleman *n.* ❶ a person who buys from producers of goods and sells to consumers ❷ a go-between or intermediary

middling Ⅰ *adj.* ❶ moderate or average in size or quality ❷ neither very good nor very bad Ⅱ *adv.* fairly or moderately

midfield *n.* ❶ the central part of a football pitch away from the goals ❷ the players on a team who play in a central position between attack and defense

midnight *n.* the middle of the night; 12 o'clock at night

midst *n.* the middle part

midterm *n.* the middle of a period of office, an academic term, or a pregnancy

might *n.* great power, strength or force

mightily *adv.* ❶ with power or strength ❷ to a great extent or degree

mighty Ⅰ *adj.* ❶ having great power or strength ❷ very great Ⅱ *adv.* very

migrant *n.* a person or animal, especially bird that migrates

migrate *v.* ❶ move from one place to another to live there ❷ (of birds and fishes) come and go with the seasons

mild *adj.* ❶ gentle; not violent ❷ (of food, drink, etc.) not strong or bitter in taste

mildew Ⅰ *n.* (usually destructive) growth of tiny fungi forming on plants, leather, food, etc. in warm and damp conditions Ⅱ *v.* affect or become affected with mildew

mile *n.* ❶ a unit of distance, equal to approximately 1.6 kilometers ❷ a race over this distance

milestone *n.* ❶ a stone set beside a road to mark the distance between places ❷ an important event or stage in life or history

militant *adj.* (especially of a person or a political group) ready to fight or use force; taking an active part in a struggle

military *adj.* having to do with the army or war

milk Ⅰ *n.* white liquid produced by female mammals as food for their young Ⅱ *v.* ❶ take milk from e. g. a cow ❷ take away the poison from (a snake) ❸ get money, knowledge, etc. from sb. or sth. by clever or dishonest means

milky *adj.* ❶ of or like milk; mixed with milk ❷ (of a jewel or a liquid) not clear; cloudy

mill Ⅰ *n.* ❶ a building or place where grain is made into flour ❷ a factory where things are made by machinery ❸ a small machinery for grinding grain into flour Ⅱ *v.* put through a machine for grinding

millennium *n.* ❶ a period of 1,000 years ❷ the point at which one period of a thousand years ends and another begins ❸ a period of great happiness and prosperity

miller *n.* a man who owns or works a mill that produces flour

millet *n.* a cereal crop bearing grain in the form of very small seeds; the seeds (as food)

millimeter *n.* one thousandth of a meter

million *num.* & *n.* one thousand thousand

millionaire *n.* a person who has a million dollars, pounds, etc.; an extremely rich man

mime Ⅰ *n.* actions done without words, often as an entertainment Ⅱ *v.* do actions of this kind

mimic Ⅰ *adj.* imitated or pretended; done in play Ⅱ *v.* ❶ copy sb.'s speech or actions to make people laugh ❷ (of

M

things) resemble closely

mince Ⅰ *v.* ❶cut meat or other food into very small pieces ❷ walk with short steps in a manner that is meant to be elegant but only looks foolish Ⅱ *n.* meat which has been cut into very small pieces

mind Ⅰ *n.* ❶ an ability to remember; a person's memory ❷ a person's way of thinking or feeling; thoughts; opinion; intention ❸ the ability to think and reason Ⅱ *v.* ❶take care of sb. or sth. ❷ dislike; object to ❸be willing to do sth. ❹used to tell sb. to be careful about sth. or warn them about danger

minded *adj.* ❶having a mind of a certain kind ❷having certain interests

mine[1] *pron.* that or those belonging to me

M

mine[2] Ⅰ *n.* ❶a big hole in the ground that people make when they are looking for coal, metal, etc. ❷ a rich source of knowledge ❸ explosive device that explodes on contact Ⅱ *v.* dig out sth. from a mine

mineral Ⅰ *n.* any of various especially solid substances that are formed naturally in the earth, such as stone, coal, and salt, especially that obtained from the ground for human use Ⅱ *adj.* of the class of minerals; containing or mixed with minerals

mingle *v.* bring or combine together or with sth. else

mini- *pref.* of small size, length, etc.

miniature Ⅰ *adj.* copied on a small scale Ⅱ *n.* ❶a very small picture of someone ❷any very small thing

minibus *n.* a small bus with seats for between six and twelve people

minicab *n.* a taxi that can be called by telephone, but not stopped in the street

minimize *v.* ❶ reduce to the least possible amount or degree ❷ put the value, importance, effect, etc. of sth. at the lower possible amount

minimum Ⅰ *n.* the smallest amount of sth. that is possible or has actually been recorded Ⅱ *adj.* the smallest or lowest that is possible or recorded

mining *n.* the action or industry of getting minerals out of the earth by digging

minister Ⅰ *n.* ❶a person who is in charge of a particular government department ❷a person who is sent to a foreign country to represent his own government ❸ a person who performs the services in a church Ⅱ *v.* perform duties to help sb.

ministry *n.* ❶a government department led by a minister ❷a building where such a department works ❸the office, duties or position of a minister

minor Ⅰ *adj.* smaller or less; less important Ⅱ *n.* a person under the legal age

minority *n.* ❶ the smaller number or part; less than half a total ❷a group of people who are different from a larger group in race, religion, etc. ❸ any age prior to the legal age

mint Ⅰ *n.* a place where money is made Ⅱ *v.* ❶make (a coin) ❷invent (a new word, phrase, etc.)

minus Ⅰ *prep.* being subtracted from another by (the stated quantity) Ⅱ *adj.* (of a number or quantity) less than zero Ⅲ *n.* a sign(—) used for showing that a number is less than zero, or that the second number is to be taken away from the first

minute[1] *n.* ❶one of the sixty parts of an hour ❷a short length of time ❸(*pl.*) the written records of the things that are discussed or decided at a meeting

minute[2] *adj.* ❶ very small ❷ very detailed; careful and exact

miracle *n.* ❶a surprising and wonderful event; wonder; a remarkable example ❷ a wonderful or amazing affair

miraculous *adj.* wonderful; surprising; like a miracle

mire Ⅰ *n.* a soft wet area of low-lying land that sinks underfoot Ⅱ *v.* cover with mud; cause to be fast in deep mud

mirror[1] *n.* ❶ a piece of glass, or other shiny or polished surface, that reflects images ❷ an exact or close representation (of sth.)

mirror[2] *v.* reflect as in a mirror

misapprehension *n.* an understanding of sth. that is not correct

misappropriate *v.* take sth. and use it for a wrong purpose; use what belongs to another for one's own purposes

misbehave *v.* behave badly

miscalculate *v.* ❶ calculate sth. incorrectly ❷ assess (a situation) wrongly

miscarriage *n.* ❶mistake in judgement or in punishment; failure ❷an untimely delivery (of woman); abortion

miscarry *v.* ❶(of a woman) have a miscarriage ❷(of an intention, plan, etc.) be unsuccessful; fail to have the intended result

miscast *v.* ❶give an unsuitable part in a play, film, etc. ❷put an unsuitable actor or actors into (a part, play, etc.)

mischance *n.* bad luck

mischief *n.* ❶damage or harm, especially on purpose ❷ behaviour, especially of children that causes trouble and possible damage, but no serious harm

mischievous *adj.* ❶ (said about a person) behaving badly in a troublesome way ❷ (said about an action) causing trouble or harm

misconceive *v.* understand wrongly; have a wrong conception (of)

misconception *n.* failure to understand; a wrong idea

misconduct Ⅰ *v.* ❶ behave badly or improperly ❷manage badly Ⅱ *n.* ❶bad behaviour, especially improper sexual behaviour ❷bad management

miscount Ⅰ *v.* count wrongly Ⅱ *n.* a wrong reckoning of the total number of sth.

misdeed *n.* a wicked or illegal act

misdiagnose *v.* make an incorrect diagnosis of (a particular illness)

miser *n.* a person who loves money for its own sake and spends or gives away as little as possible

miserable *adj.* ❶very unpleasant ❷poor in quality ❸making people unpleasant

misfire *v.* ❶(of a gun, etc.) fail to fire properly ❷ fail to have the intended result

misfit *n.* someone who is unsuitable for a position or for his surroundings

misfortune *n.* ❶bad luck ❷an unlucky accident, or event

misgiving *n.* (usually *pl.*) feelings of fear, doubt and distrust

misguided *adj.* having or showing faulty judgement or reasoning

mishap *n.* an unfortunate accident or event(usually not serious)

mishear *v.* hear sb.'s words wrongly or mistakenly

misinterpret *v.* explain wrongly; not understand correctly

misjudge *v.* ❶ form a wrong opinion of sb. or sth. ❷ estimate an amount or distance incorrectly

mislay *v.* put a thing somewhere and be unable to find it later

mislead *v.* ❶ lead or guide wrongly ❷ cause to be or do wrong; give a wrong idea to

mismanage *v.* manage or deal with (sth.) badly, unskillfully, etc.

mismatch *v.* match wrongly or unsuitably, especially in marriage

misplace *v.* ❶(of love, trust, etc.)give to an undeserving person or thing ❷ put sth. in the wrong place and unable to find it temporarily ❸ put sth. in an unsuitable or wrong place

misread *v.* read or understand sth. wrongly

misrepresent *v.* give a wrong idea of

miss[1] *n.* (Miss) used before the first and family name of a woman who is not married

miss[2] *v.* ❶ fail to hit, hold, catch , see, etc. ❷ feel sadness or regret at the absence of sb. or sth. ❸fail to put in or say ❹keep away from; escape

misshapen *adj.* not having the normal or natural shape or form

missile *n.* any object or weapon that is thrown or projected

missing *adj.* out of its usual place; not to be found; lost; gone

mission *n.* ❶ a number of people sent abroad with special work ❷an important assignment that a person or group of people is given to do, especially when they are sent abroad ❸one's duty in life

missionary *n.* a person who is sent to another country to spread a religious faith

misspent *adj.* spend time or money in a careless rather than a useful way; used foolishly

misstate *v.* state wrongly; give a false account of

misstep *n.* ❶a wrong step ❷a mistake in judgement or action

mist *n.* a cloud of tiny drops suspended in the air just above the ground, that makes it difficult to see

mistake Ⅰ *n.* a wrong opinion, judgement or action Ⅱ *v.* ❶ be wrong or have a wrong idea about ❷fail to recognize

mistaken *adj.* wrong; incorrect

mistreat *v.* treat sb. or sth. badly

mistress *n.* ❶ a woman as the head of a household or family ❷a woman teacher ❸a woman with a good knowledge or control of sth.

mistrust *v.* feel no confidence in

misunderstand *v.* understand wrongly; put a wrong meaning on

misunderstanding *n.* ❶ a failure to understand sth. correctly ❷ a disagreement or quarrel

misuse *v.* ❶use (sth.) in a wrong way or for a wrong purpose ❷ treat (sb. or sth.) badly Ⅱ *n.* (an example of) bad, wrong, or unsuitable use

mix Ⅰ *v.* ❶ put different things together to make sth. new; join together ❷ (of persons) come or be together in society Ⅱ *n.* the combination of different substances, prepared to be ready, or nearly ready, for the stated use

mixed *adj.* ❶ consisting of different kinds of things or people ❷ involving people from different races or social classes ❸ for people of both sexes

mixer *n.* ❶ a machine or device for mixing or blending things ❷ a person who gets on in a certain way with others ❸ a soft drink for mixing with an alcoholic drink

mixture *n.* ❶ sth. made by mixing ❷ (a mixture of) a combination of different qualities, things or emotions

moan Ⅰ *n.* a low sound of pain or sorrow Ⅱ *v.* make a low sound of pain or sorrow

mob Ⅰ *n.* ❶ a disorderly crowd of people ❷ a criminal gang Ⅱ *v.* (of people) crowd round in great numbers, either to attack or to admire

mobile *adj.* ❶ movable; not fixed in one position ❷ changing quickly, as of a person's face that quickly shows changes in his feelings or thoughts

mobilize *v.* ❶ organize troops for active service in war ❷ bring people or resources together for a particular purpose

mock Ⅰ *v.* ❶ mimic to laugh at sb. or sth. ❷ laugh at; make fun of ❸ cause to become useless Ⅱ *adj.* not real; false Ⅲ *n.* mockery

mode *n.* ❶ a way in which sth. is done ❷ a fashion or style of dress; most usual fashion or custom

model Ⅰ *n.* ❶ a small copy of sth. ❷ a person or thing used as an example ❸ a person who takes up a certain position for a painter, etc. Ⅱ *v.* ❶ fashion or shape a figure in a malleable material ❷ make from a model; take as a copy or an example ❸ work as a fashion model

moderate *adj.* average in degree, amount, quality, etc. Ⅱ *n.* a person who holds moderate opinions Ⅲ *v.* make or become less in force, degree, rate, etc.

modern *adj.* ❶ of the present or recent times ❷ new and up-to-date

modernize *v.* make modern; bring up to the present ways or standards

modest *adj.* ❶ not making oneself noticed or talking too much about one's own abilities or possessions ❷ moderate; not large in size, degree or amount

modesty *n.* the state of being modest

modification *n.* ❶ the action of modifying sth. ❷ a change made

modifier *n.* a word or a group of words that give additional information about another word

modify *v.* ❶ make partial or minor changes to sth. in order to improve it ❷ make sth. less severe or extreme ❸ qualify the sense of (another word)

modular *adj.* consisting of independent units or modules

modulate *v.* ❶ adjust or regulate sth. ❷ vary the tone or pitch of your voice ❸ change from one key to another ❹ alter the amplitude, frequency, or phase of a carrier wave so as to convey a particular signal

module *n.* ❶each of a set of standardized parts or units used to make sth. more complex ❷a section of a course of study ❸ a self-contained unit attached to a spacecraft

moist *adj.* slightly wet; damp or humid

moisture *n.* condensed vapour on a surface; liquid in the form of vapour

molecule *n.* a smallest unit into which a substance could be divided without a change in its chemical nature

moment *n.* ❶ a very short time; a brief period of time ❷importance

momentous *adj.* very important or significant

momentum *n.* the quantity of motion of a moving body

monarchy *n.* a form of government rule by a king or queen

Monday *n.* the day of the week after Sunday

money *n.* coins or paper notes

monitor Ⅰ *n.* ❶a pupil given disciplinary or other duties over his fellows ❷ a person whose job is to check that sth. is done fairly, especially in a foreign country ❸ an apparatus for testing transmissions by radio or TV, for detecting radioactivity, for tracing the flight of missiles, etc. Ⅱ *v.* ❶keep under systematic review ❷listen to and report on (a foreign radio broadcast)

monk *n.* one of a religious community of men living under vows of poverty, chastity and obedience

monkey Ⅰ *n.* ❶ a tree-climbing animal with a long tail and with paws that look like human hands ❷a child who is fond of mischief Ⅱ *v.* behave in a foolish way

mono- *pref.* one ; single

monologue *n.* a long talk or speech by one person

monopolize *v.* ❶ control or use sth. so that other people are excluded ❷get or keep exclusively to oneself

monopoly *n.* ❶ the exclusive possession or control of trade, talk, etc. ❷the sole right to supply or trade in some commodity or service ❸a commodity or service controlled in this way

monotonous *adj.* not varying; unchanging

monsoon *n.* ❶a seasonal wind (mainly in Southeast Asia) blowing from the South-west for part of the year and from the northeast for another part ❷a rainy season caused by the south-west monsoon

monster *n.* ❶a large imaginary creature that looks very ugly and has a strange or unusual shape, often very big ❷ an animal, plant, that is abnormal in form ❸a person who is remarkable for some bad or evil quality

month *n.* one of the twelve periods of time which make a year

monthly Ⅰ *adj.* done every month; once a month Ⅱ *adv.* every month; once a month Ⅲ *n.* a magazine issued once a month

monument *n.* a building, statue, etc. in memory of a person or event

mood *n.* ❶the state of mind or spirits ❷ one of the groups of forms that a verb may take to show whether things are regarded as certain, possible or doubtful

moody *adj.* ❶having moods that change often and quickly ❷sad; gloomy

moon *n.* the object which goes around the earth and can be seen at night ❷ the satellite of other planets

mop Ⅰ *n.* a piece of cleaning implement for washing floors or dishes Ⅱ *v.* clean with, or as if with a mop

moral Ⅰ *adj.* ❶ concerning principles of right and wrong ❷ good and virtuous ❸ teaching good behaviour ❹ based on the sense of what is right or just rather than on what the law says should be done ❺ psychological rather than physical or tangible in effect Ⅱ *n.* (*pl.*) moral habits; standards of behaviour

morale *n.* the state of discipline and spirit in an army, a nation, etc.; the temper state of mind, as expressed in action

moralist *n.* ❶ a teacher of moral principles ❷ a person who tries to control other people's morals

moralistic *adj.* having convention and narrow ideas about right and wrong behaviour

morality *n.* rightness or pureness of behaviour or an action

moralize *v.* express one's thoughts on the rightness or, more usually, the wrongness of behaviour

morally *adv.* ❶ with regard to moral principles ❷ in a moral way ❸ most probably

morbid *adj.* ❶ connected with disease ❷ (of sb.'s mind or ideas) unhealthy

more Ⅰ *adj.* greater in number, size, amount, degree, etc. Ⅱ *adv.* ❶ in a greater quantity; to a greater degree ❷ again Ⅲ *n.* a greater amount of sth. than before or than sth. else or than average

moreover *adv.* in addition; besides

morning *n.* an early part of the day; the time between sunrise and noon

mortal Ⅰ *adj.* ❶ which must die; which cannot live for ever ❷ causing death; fatal ❸ lasting until death; marked by great hatred ❹ accompanying death ❺ extreme or intense Ⅱ *n.* an ordinary person

mortar[1] *n.* a mixture of lime or cement or both with sand and water, used in building to hold bricks, stones, etc. in place

mortar[2] *n.* a short gun which fires shells high into the air

mortgage Ⅰ *n.* the conditional conveyance of property as security for the payment of a loan Ⅱ *v.* give a person a claim on one's house, etc. as a security for payment of a loan

mortify *v.* hurt the feelings of; make sb. feel ashamed or embarrassed

mosquito *n.* small flying insects that sucks blood and can carry malaria from one person to another

moss *n.* a green or yellow plant growing in thick masses on the wet surface

most Ⅰ *adj.* greatest in number, amount, etc. Ⅱ *n.* the biggest number, amount, part, etc. Ⅲ *adv.* ❶ used to form the superlative of adjective's and adverb's of two or more syllables ❷ very much ❸ almost

mostly *adv.* mainly or chiefly; in large part

motel *n.* a hotel which makes special arrangements for customers who have cars

moth *n.* ❶ a winged insect, similar to the butterfly flying chiefly at night ❷ a type of moth whose larva feed on cloth, fur, etc., and make holes

mother Ⅰ *n.* a woman who has given birth to a child or a term of address to her Ⅱ *v.* care for as a mother does

motherland *n.* one's own or one's ancestors' native country

motion Ⅰ *n.* ❶ a natural event that involves a change in the position or location of sth. ❷ a particular movement, especially of the hands to communicate ❸ a proposal to be discussed at a meeting Ⅱ *v.* direct by a motion or gesture

motivate *v.* ❶provide sb. with a (strong) reason for doing sth. ❷ be the reason why sth. is or was done

motivation *n.* the state of being motivated; need or purpose

motive Ⅰ *n.* the cause of or reason for action; that which urges a person to act in a certain way Ⅱ *adj.* causing or able to cause motion

motor Ⅰ *n.* a machine that changes power into movement; engine Ⅱ *adj.* driven by a motor

motorcar *n.* a vehicle on wheels, driven by an engine, that you can travel in car

motorcycle *n.* a bicycle worked by an engine

motto *n.* a saying, phrase, or word used as a rule or guide of life

mo(u)ld Ⅰ *n.* ❶loose soil rich in organic matter ❷ a hollow container which shapes whatever was poured into Ⅱ *v.* ❶become covered with a greenish-white substance which grows on food and clothes if they are left in warm wet air ❷make sth. into the shape you want it to be ❸shape or influence sb. or sth.

mound *n.* a large, rounded pile of earth; a small hill

mount Ⅰ *n.* (abbr. Mt.) mountain, used before proper names Ⅱ *v.* ❶ climb up sth.; get on a horse or bicycle ❷become greater in amount; rise ❸put and fix in position ❹prepare or begin (an attack) ❺put (a play) on the stage

mountain *n.* ❶a very high hill, usually of bare or snow-covered rock ❷ a very large amount; sth. immense

mountaineer *n.* a person who climbs mountains or who is skilful at climbing mountains

mountaineering *n.* the sport or activity of climbing mountains

mountainous *adj.* ❶ having many mountains ❷huge; rising like mountains

mourn *v.* feel or show sorrow or regret for the loss of sth. or sb.

mournful *adj.* causing a sad feeling or expressing sorrow

mourning *n.* ❶(the expression of) grief, especially for a death ❷ the clothes, black in some countries, worn to show grief at the death of someone

mouse *n.* a small furry animal with a long tail that lives in houses and in fields, related to but smaller than a rat

mouth Ⅰ *n.* ❶the opening through which people and animals take in food ❷ opening or outlet ❸ the place where a river flows into the sea Ⅱ *v.* speak (words) with too much movements of the jaws

mouthful *n.* ❶a quantity of food or drink that fills the mouth ❷ a long or awkward word or phrase that is difficult to say

mouthy *adj.* inclined to talk a lot, especially in a cheeky way

movable *adj.* ❶ that can be moved ❷ varying in date from year to year

move Ⅰ *v.* ❶ (cause to) change place or position ❷ arouse the feeling of ❸ (cause to) be in motion; go, walk, run, etc., especially in a particular way ❹ cause sb. to do sth. ❺ put forward sth. for discussion and decision (at a meeting) ❻ change residence Ⅱ *n.* ❶ the act of going from one place to another; a change of position ❷ (in games such as chess) an act of taking a piece from one square and putting it on another ❸ an action that you do or need to do to achieve sth.

movement *n.* ❶ moving or being moved ❷ the act of changing position ❸ united actions and efforts of a group of people for a special purpose ❹ the whole of the activities of a person, especially when he is at a distance

mover *n.* ❶ a person or thing in motion, especially an animal ❷ a person whose job is to remove and transport furniture from one house to another ❸ a person undertaking or undergoing a move or change in a particular aspect of their life

movie *n.* a cinema picture; a film

moving *adj.* ❶ in motion ❷ arousing strong emotions, especially of sorrow or sympathy

mow Ⅰ *v.* cut grass short Ⅱ *n.* a place in a barn where hay, grain, etc. is piled

Mr. *n.* a title used before a man's name

Mrs. *n.* a title used before a married woman's name

Ms. *n.* a title for any woman, instead of "Miss" or "Mrs."

much Ⅰ *adj.* great in quantity, amount, etc. Ⅱ *n.* a great quantity; a great deal Ⅲ *adv.* ❶ to a great degree; greatly ❷ almost; nearly

mud *n.* the soft, wet earth

muddle Ⅰ *v.* put into disorder; mix up; confuse Ⅱ *n.* a state of confusion and disorder

muddling *adj.* causing confusion; difficult to understand

muddy Ⅰ *adj.* ❶ full of mud ❷ mud-coloured Ⅱ *v.* make sth. dirty with mud

muffle *v.* ❶ wrap or cover for warmth or protection ❷ make the sound less easily heard, especially with a material

mugger *n.* a person who attacks someone violently in a street in order to rob them of their money

muggy *adj.* (of weather) oppressively warm and damp

mulberry *n.* ❶ a tree whose leaves are used for feeding silkworms ❷ the fruit of this kind of tree ❸ purplish red colour

mule *n.* ❶ an animal whose parents are a donkey and a horse ❷ a stubborn person

mull *v.* think carefully about sth.

multi- *pref.* more than one; many

multicultural *adj.* made up of people of different races and cultures

multilateral *adj.* ❶ having many sides ❷ involving many groups, countries, etc.

multiple *adj.* including many different parts, types, etc.

multiply *v.* ❶ combine by multiplication ❷ greatly increase in number or amount ❸ reproduce in large numbers

multitude *n.* ❶ a great number (especially of people gathered together) ❷ greatness of number ❸ the masses; the common people

mum[1] Ⅰ *n.* silence Ⅱ *adj.* silent

mum[2] *n.* mummy

mummy[1] *n.* a dead body treated in a special way so that it does not decay

mummy[2] *n.* (used by and to children) mother

municipal *adj.* concerning or belonging to a town or city, under its own government

munitions *n.* military weapons, ammunition, equipment and stores

murder Ⅰ *n.* the crime of killing a human being intentionally Ⅱ *v.* kill (sb.) unlawfully and on purpose

M

murmur Ⅰ *n.* a low continuous sound as that of a stream, wind or talk Ⅱ *v.* make a low continuous sound; speak or say in a low voice

muscle *n.* ❶ a band or bundle of fibrous tissue in a human or animal body that can be tightened or loosened to produce movement ❷ the bodily strength

muscular *adj.* ❶ of or affecting the muscles ❷ having well-developed muscles

muse *v.* think deeply, ignoring what is happening around

museum *n.* a building in which objects of art, history, science, etc. are kept and shown

mushroom Ⅰ *n.* ❶ fungus of which some kinds can be eaten ❷ anything that grows and develops rapidly Ⅱ *v.* grow and spread rapidly

music *n.* ❶ the art of making pleasing combinations of sounds in rhythm and harmony ❷ the sounds and composition so made ❸ written or printed signs representing these sounds

musical Ⅰ *adj.* ❶ of or relating to music ❷ fond of music; skilled in music Ⅱ *n.* a play or film with songs and dances

musician *n.* a person skilled in the art of music; a performer or composer of music

must Ⅰ *aux. v.* ❶ have to ❷ be likely or certain to ❸ be necessary ❹ should or ought to ❺ indicating insistence ❻ indicating the occurrence of sth. perverse or sth. contrary to what was wanted Ⅱ *n.* sth. which it is necessary or very important to have or experience

mustard *n.* ❶ a plant with yellow flowers and seeds ❷ a hot-tasting yellow or brown paste made from the crushed seeds of this plant ❸ a dark yellow colour

muster[1] *v.* ❶ assemble (troops, etc.), especially for battle; collect ❷ summon up (a feeling, attitude or response)

muster[2] *n.* ❶ assembling of troops for inspection ❷ persons or things assembled ❸ commercial samples

musty *adj.* ❶ with an unpleasant smell as if old

mute Ⅰ *adj.* ❶ not speaking; making no sound ❷ (of a letter) not pronounced Ⅱ *n.* a dumb person

mutinous *adj.* rebellious or disobedient

mutter Ⅰ *v.* speak in a low voice Ⅱ *n.* a quiet sound or words that are difficult to hear

mutton *n.* meat from a sheep as food

mutual *adj.* ❶ (of a situation, feeling or

action) experienced, felt or done by both of two people mentioned ❷ (of love, respect, etc.) shared

muzzle Ⅰ *n.* ❶ the front part of an animal's face, with the nose and mouth ❷ a covering round an animal's mouth to prevent it from biting ❸ the open end or mouth of a firearm Ⅱ *v.* ❶ put a muzzle on ❷ prevent (a person, society, newspaper, etc.) from expressing opinions freely

my *pron.* ❶ belonging to the speaker ❷ as a part of a form of address ❸ used in various expresses of surprise

myopic *adj.* unable to see clearly things which are far away; short-sighted

myself *pron.* ❶ (the reflexive form of I) used when the speaker or writer is also the person affected by an action ❷ I or me personally (used to emphasize the speaker)

mysterious *adj.* difficult to understand or explain; full of mystery

mystery *n.* ❶ sth. which cannot be explained or understood ❷ a strange secret nature or quality

mystic *adj.* of hidden meaning or spiritual power; causing a feeling of wonder

myth *n.* ❶ a story, handed down from old times, especially one that was told to explain some natural or social phenomenon and typically involving supernatural beings or events ❷ such stories collectively ❸ a person, thing, etc., that is imaginary, fictitious, or invented

mythological *adj.* connected with ancient myths

mythology *n.* ❶ a collection of myths, especially one belonging to a particular religious or cultural tradition ❷ a set of stories or beliefs about a particular person, institution, or situation, especially when exaggerated or fictitious ❸ the study of myths

N n

nab *v.* ❶catch (someone) in an act of wrongdoing ❷get or catch quickly

nag *v.* ❶criticize continuously; annoy by scolding ❷worry or annoy

nagging *adj.* ❶ continuing for a long time and difficult to cure or remove ❷complaining

nail Ⅰ *n.* ❶a layer of hard substance over the outer tip of a finger or toe ❷a thin piece of metal with a sharp point at one end and a flat head at the other for hammering into a piece of wood, usually to fasten the wood to sth. else Ⅱ *v.* make secure with a nail or nails

naive *adj.* simple and innocent in what one says and does because of lack of experience or ability

naked *adj.* ❶ without clothes on ❷ without the usual covering or protection ❸ not hidden, especially by false statements

name Ⅰ *n.* ❶a word or words by which a person, animal, place, thing, etc. is called or known by ❷ (only singular) reputation; the opinion that people have about sb. or sth. Ⅱ *v.* ❶give a name to ❷ tell the name(s) of ❸ choose or appoint

nameless *adj.* ❶having no name or no known name ❷ whose name is kept secret; anonymous ❸difficult or too bad to describe

namely *adv.* that is to say; specifically

namesake *n.* a person or thing with the same name as another

nap Ⅰ *n.* a short sleep, especially during the day Ⅱ *v.* sleep for a short time, especially during the day

napkin *n.* a piece of cloth used at meals for protecting one's clothes and for cleaning one's hands and lips

nappy *n.* a piece of cloth or soft paper folded round a baby's bottom to absorb urine, etc.

narrate *v.* tell (a story); give an account of

narrow Ⅰ *adj.* ❶of small width from one side to the other ❷ limited in extent, amount or scope ❸almost not enough or only just successful ❹ having little sympathy for the ideas, etc. of others Ⅱ *v.* make or become narrow

narrowly *adv.* ❶ only just; hardly ❷ closely; carefully

nation *n.* people associated with a particular country under one government

national Ⅰ *adj.* ❶typical of the people or customs of a particular country or nation ❷ owned or controlled by the central government of a country Ⅱ *n.* citizens of a particular nation

nationalism *n.* a feeling of love for and pride in one's own nation

nationality *n.* ❶ being a member of a nation ❷ a large group of people with the same race, origin, language, etc.

nationalize *v.* put an industry or business under the state ownership or control

native Ⅰ *adj.* ❶ of the place of one's birth ❷ of one's native country (land) ❸ belonging to someone from birth without having to learn ❹ growing, living, produced, found, etc., in a place, not brought in from another place Ⅱ *n.* ❶ a person born in a place, country, etc. ❷ an animal or plant natural to a certain area

natural *adj.* ❶ existing in or caused by nature ❷ born with certain qualities or powers ❸ occurring as a matter of course and without debate; inevitable

naturalism *n.* (in art and literature) the theory or practice of drawing, painting, or describing things as they are in nature

naturalist *n.* someone who studies natural history

naturalize *v.* ❶ give a person of foreign birth the right of citizenship of a country ❷ adopt a foreign word or custom, often adapting it so that it fits local practice ❸ cause a plant or animal to grow or live naturally in a country where it is not native

naturally *adv.* ❶ by nature ❷ of course

naturalness *n.* ❶ the state or quality of being like real life ❷ the quality of behaving in a normal, relaxed or innocent way ❸ the style or quality of happening in a normal way that you would expect

nature *n.* ❶ the world including plants, animals, the landscape, and other features and products of the earth ❷ qualities naturally belonging to a person or thing ❸ force (s) controlling the physical world

naught Ⅰ *n.* the number 0 Ⅱ *pron.* nothing

naughty *adj.* ❶ (of children) disobedient; causing trouble ❷ immorally, especially because related to sex

naval *adj.* of a navy; of warships

navigable *adj.* ❶ (of a body of water) deep and wide enough to allow ships to travel ❷ (of a ship, aircraft, etc.) able to be guided; steerable

navigate *v.* ❶ (cause to) sail or travel on the water or in the air ❷ direct the course of (a ship, plane, etc.)

navy *n.* the organization, including ships, people, buildings, etc., which makes up the power of a country for war at sea

near Ⅰ *adv.* to or at a short distance Ⅱ *prep.* close to (in space, time, etc.) Ⅲ *adj.* ❶ not far (in time or space) ❷ close in relation Ⅳ *v.* come closer (to) in space or time

nearby Ⅰ *adv.* close by Ⅱ *adj.* near; not far away Ⅲ *prep.* at a short distance from

nearly *adv.* ❶ almost; not quite ❷ closely

neat *adj.* ❶ tidy and clean; in good order

❷ cleverly said or done ❸ (of alcoholic drinks) without ice or water or other liquid

necessary Ⅰ *adj.* ❶ that is needed or essential ❷ which cannot be avoided; which must be; determined or fixed by the nature of things Ⅱ *n.* (usually *pl.*) the basic requirements for living

necessitate *v.* cause a need for; make necessary

neck *n.* ❶ the part of the body between the head and shoulders ❷ the part of a garment for this part of the human body ❸ a narrow part of sth. like a neck in shape or position

necklace *n.* an ornamental string of beads or precious stones worn round the neck

need Ⅰ *n.* ❶ the condition in which sth. is necessary ❷ (*pl.*) a thing that is wanted or required ❸ the state of poverty or misfortune Ⅱ *v.* want or require sth. Ⅲ *aux. v.* (with negative or in questions) have to; be necessary

N

needle Ⅰ *n.* ❶ a thin, pointed piece of metal used in sewing, knitting, etc. ❷ a thin (usually metal) pointer on a dial, e. g. of a compass, meter, etc. ❸ a very thin hollow pointed tube, at the end of a hypodermic syringe, which is pushed into someone's skin to put a liquid (especially medicine) into the body Ⅱ *v.* push through sth. with or as if with a needle

needless *adj.* unnecessary; not needed

needlewoman *n.* a woman or girl who has sewing skills or who sews for a living

needlework *n.* sewing and embroidery work, especially fancy work, done with needle and thread

needs *adv.* in a way that cannot be avoided

needy *adj.* not having enough money, food, clothing, etc.

negate *v.* ❶ cause to have no effect ❷ disapprove the truth or fact of; deny

negation *n.* the contradiction or denial of sth.

negative Ⅰ *adj.* ❶ (of words and answers) showing no or not ❷ without any positive character ❸ less than zero ❹ (of electricity) of the type that is carried by electrons Ⅱ *n.* ❶ a word or statement that denies ❷ a number less than zero ❸ a film with lights and shades reversed Ⅲ *v.* refuse to accept; say no to

neglect Ⅰ *v.* ❶ give no or too little attention or care to ❷ fail or forget to do sth. that should be done Ⅱ *n.* the state or fact of being neglected or not receiving enough attention

neglectful *adj.* forgetful or careless

negligence *n.* the failure to give sb. or sth. enough care or attention

negligent *adj.* not taking or showing enough care

negligible *adj.* so small or insignificant as to be not worth taking into account

negotiable *adj.* ❶ able to be changed after being discussed ❷ (said about a cheque) able to be converted into cash or transferred to another person

negotiate *v.* ❶ discuss in order to come to an agreement ❷ arrange by discussion ❸ succeed in dealing with or getting past (sth. difficult)

negotiation *n.* an act of negotiating

neigh Ⅰ *n.* a long loud cry that a horse makes Ⅱ *v.* (of a horse) make such a sound

neighbo(u)r Ⅰ *n.* a person, thing or country that is near another Ⅱ *v.* be near or next to

neighbo(u)rhood *n.* ❶a group of people and their homes forming a small area within a larger place such as a town ❷ the area around a point or place ❸ a district especially one forming a community

neighbourly *adj.* kind and friendly to the people living near you

neither Ⅰ *pron.* not one and not the other of two Ⅱ *adv.* also not Ⅲ *conj.* used to show that a negative statement is true of two things

nephew *n.* the son of one's brother or sister

nerve *n.* ❶ threadlike parts in the body which carry feelings and messages to and from the brain ❷(*pl.*) the state of being easily excited or anxious

nerveless *adj.* ❶ lacking strength or feeling ❷not nervous and confident

nervous *adj.* ❶of the nerves ❷tense and anxious; easily excited or worried

nest Ⅰ *n.* ❶a place or structure built or chosen by a bird for its eggs ❷the home thought of as the safe place Ⅱ *v.* build or make a nest

nestle *v.* ❶ settle comfortably and warmly ❷press (oneself) closely to

net[1] Ⅰ *n.* material of strings, wires, threads, etc. twisted, tied, or woven together for a special purpose Ⅱ *v.* catch (fish, bird, etc.) with a net

net[2] Ⅰ *adj.* remaining when nothing further is to be subtracted Ⅱ *v.* gain (sth.) as a net profit

network *n.* ❶an arrangement or pattern of intersecting lines or parts ❷a chain of interconnected people or operations ❸a group of radio or television stations which broadcast the same programmes ❹a set of computers which are linked to one another

neural *adj.* to do with a nerve or the nervous system

neuron *n.* a cell that is part of the nervous system and sends impulses to and from the brain

neutral Ⅰ *adj.* ❶taking neither side in a quarrel or a war ❷ belonging to an impartial party, state or group Ⅱ *n.* an impartial person or country

neutralize *v.* ❶make sth. ineffective by applying an opposite force or effect ❷ make a substance chemically neutral

never *adv.* ❶not ever; at no time ❷not at all

nevertheless *adv.* however; in spite of that; all the same

new *adj.* ❶never known or used before; invented or discovered recently; seen or heard of for the first time ❷ only recently found or known ❸ unfamiliar with ❹first picked of a crop

newly *adv.* ❶recently ❷in a new way

news *n.* new information; report of a recent event or events

newspaper *n.* ❶ a daily or weekly publica-tion printed on large sheets of paper, containing news reports, articles and features, advertisements, etc. ❷ the sheets of paper from old newspapers

next Ⅰ *adj.* ❶ coming immediately after, in order or space ❷ (of a day of the week) following; nearest Ⅱ *adv.* just afterwards; after this or that Ⅲ *prep.* beside; at the side of

nice *adj.* ❶ good, fine, pleasant or agreeable ❷ needing care and exactness; fine or subtle ❸ kind; friendly ❹ hard to please or showing delicate tastes

nickname Ⅰ *n.* a name used informally instead of sb.'s own name Ⅱ *v.* give sb. a nickname

niece *n.* the daughter of one's brother or sister

niggle *v.* ❶ cause slight but persistent annoyance, discomfort, or anxiety ❷ find fault with (someone) in a petty way

night *n.* ❶ the time of darkness between evening and morning ❷ a sad period or experience

nightfall *n.* the beginning of darkness at the end of the day

nightingale *n.* a small bird known for its beautiful singing, heard mostly at night

nightly *adj.* ❶ happening or done in the night ❷ happening or done every night

nimble *adj.* ❶ able to move quickly and easily ❷ sharp; quick to understand

nine *num.* the number 9

nineteen *num.* the number 19

ninety *num.* the number 90

ninth *num.* ❶ next after eighth ❷ one of nine equal parts of a thing

nip[1] Ⅰ *v.* ❶ give sb. or sth. a quick painful bite or pinch ❷ go quickly or go for a short time Ⅱ *n.* ❶ the act of nipping; pinch ❷ coldness

nip[2] *n.* a small amount of a strong alcoholic drink, (not beer or wine)

no Ⅰ *adj.* not a; not any Ⅱ *int.* as a short reply, expressing refusal or disagreement, opposite to "Yes" Ⅲ *adv.* (with comparatives) Ⅳ *n.* ❶ an answer or decision of no ❷ a vote or voter against a question to be decided, especially in a parliament

nobility *n.* the quality of being noble; the noble birth or rank; the noble as a class

noble Ⅰ *adj.* ❶ (of character and quality) good; fine ❷ of high rank or title, usually by birth ❸ grand, great or excellent in size or quality Ⅱ *n.* a person of noble birth

nobleman *n.* a person of noble birth or rank

nobody *pron.* ❶ no one; no person; not anybody ❷ an unimportant person

nod Ⅰ *v.* ❶ bend (one's head) slightly to express agreement or greet to sb. ❷ let one's head drop forward when sleepy or asleep, while sitting Ⅱ *n.* the act of nodding to express agreement or greet to sb.

noise Ⅰ *n.* a loud and unpleasant sound Ⅱ *v.* make much noise

noisy *adj.* ❶ making much noise ❷ full of noise

nomad *n.* members of a tribe which wanders from one place to another seeking pasture, etc.

nominate *v.* suggest for election to a position

nomination *n.* an instance of nominating

nominative Ⅰ *n.* the case used for the

subject of a verb, etc. Ⅱ *adj.* ❶ relating to or denoting a case of nouns, pronouns, and adjectives in Latin, Greek, and other inflected languages, used for the subject of a verb ❷ of or appointed by nomination as distinct from election

none Ⅰ *pron.* not any, not one Ⅱ *adv.* by no means; not at all

nonsense *n.* meaningless words; foolish statements or ideas

noodle *n.* (usually *pl.*) paste of flour and eggs prepared in long, narrow strips and used in soups, etc.

noon *n.* the middle of the day

nor *conj.* ❶ and not ❷ (used at the beginning of an expression just before a verb) and also not

norm *n.* ❶ a standard, model or pattern considered as typical ❷ an amount of work required or expected in a working day in a factory, etc.

normal Ⅰ *adj.* usual; regular; ordinary Ⅱ *n.* sth. regarded as a normative example

normalize *v.* make sth. normal, or to become normal

normally *adv.* under normal or usual conditions; as a rule

north Ⅰ *n.* the direction which is on your left when you face the rising sun Ⅱ *adv.* in towards the north

northern *adj.* of, in or from the north part of world, a country, etc.

nose Ⅰ *n.* ❶ the part of the face above the mouth for breathing and smelling ❷ the sense of smell ❸ sth. like a nose in shape or position Ⅱ *v.* ❶ smell; discover by smelling ❷ push sth. with the nose

nostalgia *n.* homesickness; a desire for sth. that has known in the past

nostril *n.* each of the two openings in the nose through which air is admitted

not *adv.* ❶ used to make a negative ❷ used in front of word referring to a distance, length of time, or other amount to say that the actual distance, time or amount is less than the one mentioned ❸ used to represent the negative of a word, group or clause that has just been used

notable Ⅰ *adj.* worthy of notice; remarkable; eminent Ⅱ *n.* notable person

notation *n.* a set of signs or symbols representing numbers, musical notes, etc.

note Ⅰ *n.* ❶ a written record or reminder ❷ a short letter ❸ a remark added to a piece of writing and placed outside the main part of the writing, e. g. at the side or bottom of a page, especially to give more information ❹ a formal letter between governments ❺ a piece of paper money ❻ a single musical sound of a particular length and degree of highness or lowness ❼ a stated quality or feeling ❽ fame or importance ❾ notice; attention Ⅱ *v.* ❶ notice or pay careful attention to sth. ❷ call attention to; remark

noted *adj.* famous or well-known

noteworthy *adj.* worth noting; remarkable

nothing Ⅰ *n.* ❶ not anything; no things ❷ sb. or sth. of no importance Ⅱ *adv.* in no way; not at all

notice Ⅰ *n.* ❶ information; news about

sth. to happen ❷warning or information about sth. that to happen ❸a statement of opinion, especially in a newspaper, about a new book, play, etc. ❹the act of noticing or paying attention Ⅱ *v.* pay attention to

noticeable *adj.* easily seen or noticed

notify *v.* inform (sb.) about sth. officially

notion *n.* ❶ an idea, opinion or belief about sth. ❷a desire or intention

notorious *adj.* well-known for sth. bad

nought *n.* ❶(the figure) 0; zero ❷used in particular phrases to mean nothing

noun *n.* a word that is the name of a person, thing, place, etc.

nourish *v.* ❶keep alive, well or strong by giving food, water, etc. ❷have (certain feelings)

novel Ⅰ *n.* a long written story in prose printed as a book Ⅱ *adj.* new; strange

novelty *n.* ❶ the quality of being new, different and interesting ❷sth. new and strange ❸a small toy, decoration, etc. of low value

November *n.* the 11th month of the year

now Ⅰ *adv.* ❶at the present time; at this moment ❷at once; without delay ❸used by the speaker to continue a narrative, request, warning, etc. Ⅱ *conj.* since Ⅲ *n.* the present time or moment Ⅳ *adj.* at this time

nowadays *adv.* at the present time

nowhere Ⅰ *adv.* in, at or to no place Ⅱ *n.* no place; an insignificant or unexpected place

nuclear *adj.* ❶of a nucleus ❷of, concerning, or using atomic energy

nucleus *n.* ❶ a central part, around which other parts are grouped or collected ❷ the central part of an atom ❸the central part of a living cell

nude Ⅰ *adj.* not wearing any clothes, especially of a human figure in art Ⅱ *n.* ❶a person not wearing any clothes ❷a painting of a naked human figure (especially in art)

null *adj.* having no effect or force

nullify *v.* ❶make sth. null and void ❷ cancel or neutralize the effect of sth.

numb Ⅰ *adj.* unable to feel or move Ⅱ *v.* make numb

number Ⅰ *n.* ❶a word or sign that shows how many ❷a number used to show the position of sth. in an ordered set or list ❸ a series of numbers that you dial when you are making a telephone call ❹ issue of a periodical, newspaper ❺ a quantity or amount ❻ a change in the form of words, especially nouns and verbs, depending on whether one or more than one thing is talking about Ⅱ *v.* ❶reach as a total; be in number ❷ give a number to ❸ include or be included as one of a particular group

numberless *adj.* too many to count

numeral Ⅰ *adj.* of number Ⅱ *n.* a sign that represents a number

numerator *n.* ❶ the number above the line in a vulgar fraction ❷a person or thing that numbers

numerical *adj.* of a number; having sth. to do with numbers

numerous *adj.* ❶many; large in number ❷made up of a large number

nurse Ⅰ *n.* ❶a woman who takes care of the sick, the old, babies or small children, etc. as a job ❷ a person, typically a woman, who is trained to take care of sick, hurt, or old people, especially as directed by a doctor in a hospital Ⅱ *v.* ❶take care of as or like a nurse ❷ (of a woman) feed (a baby) with milk from the breast ❸give special care to

nurture Ⅰ *v.* care for and educate; nourish; encourage the growth of Ⅱ *n.* education, training, and development

nut *n.* ❶ the fruit with a hard shell enclosing a kernel that can be eaten ❷a small piece of metal with a threaded hole for screwing on to the end of a bolt

nutrition *n.* the process of providing or being provided with nourishment; nourishing food

nutritious *adj.* valuable to the body as food; nourishing

nutritive *adj.* of or providing nourishment

nylon *n.* a strong light synthetic fibre or fabric

O o

oaf *n.* a stupid or clumsy fellow

oak *n.* a large tree with hard wood; the wood of this sort of tree

oar *n.* a long pole with a flat blade, used for rowing a boat

oasis *n.* ❶ a place with water and trees in a desert ❷ a place or situation that is different from its surroundings usually in a pleasant or comforting way

oath *n.* a solemn promise

oatmeal *n.* crushed oats used for making cakes and porridge

obedient *adj.* willing to do what one is told to do

obey *v.* do what one is asked or ordered to do

object[1] *n.* ❶ a thing that can be seen or touched ❷ an aim or a purpose ❸ the word(s) towards which the action of the verb is directed or to which a preposition shows some relation

object[2] *v.* be opposed (to)

objection *n.* ❶ the action or feeling of disliking, opposing or disapproving ❷ the reason of protesting

objective Ⅰ *adj.* not influenced by personal feelings or opinions; fair Ⅱ *n.* an aim, especially one that must be worked towards over a long period; goal

obligate *v.* make (sb.) feel it necessary (to do sth.), especially because of a sense of duty

obligation *n.* promise, duty, or condition that indicates what action ought to be taken

obligatory *adj.* that is necessary, required by rule, law or custom; compulsory

oblige *v.* ❶ make sb. do sth. ❷ do (sb.) a favour

oblivious *adj.* completely unaware of what is happening around you

oblong Ⅰ *n.* a shape which has two long sides and two short sides and two short sides and in which all the angles are right angles Ⅱ *adj.* shaped like an oblong

obscene *adj.* connected with sex in a way that most people find offensive

obscure *adj.* dark, not clear; hard to understand

observable *adj.* that can be seen or noticed

observance *n.* ❶ the practice of acting in accordance with a law, ceremony, or custom ❷ performed as a part of a religious ceremony

observant *adj.* ❶ quick at noticing

things ❷ acting in accordance with especially religious law or custom

observation *n.* ❶ observing or being observed ❷ power of noticing things ❸ report on things observed

observatory *n.* a place from which the stars and other heavenly bodies may be observed

observe *v.* ❶ see and notice; watch carefully ❷ obey; pay attention to (rules, etc.) ❸ say; make a remark

observer *n.* ❶ one who observes ❷ a person who attends a conference, etc. only to listen, not to speak

obsess *v.* fill (someone's) mind continuously

obsessional *adj.* thinking too much about a particular person or thing, in a way that is not normal

obsessive *adj.* causing or showing obsession

obstacle *n.* sth. in the way that prevents action or progress

obstruct *v.* get in the way of; block

obstruction *n.* ❶ obstructing or being obstructed ❷ a thing that obstructs

obstructive *adj.* causing or intended to cause obstruction

obtain *v.* get sth., especially by making an effort

obtainable *adj.* that can be obtained

obtrude *v.* ❶ (cause to) stick out ❷ (cause to) be noticed especially when unwanted

obtrusive *adj.* ❶ sticking out very much ❷ fond of pushing oneself, or one's ideas, etc. forward

obvious *adj.* clear; easy to see or understand

occasion Ⅰ *n.* ❶ the time when sth. (usually special) happens ❷ a suitable time for sth. ❸ a reason or need Ⅱ *v.* cause sth.

occasional *adj.* ❶ fortuitous; not regular ❷ written or intended for a special event, purpose, etc.

Occident *n.* (the countries of) the West Europe and America, contrasted with the Orient

occupancy *n.* the action or fact of occupying a place

occupant *n.* a person who resides or is present in a house, vehicle, seat, place, etc. at a given time

occupation *n.* ❶ a person's job or profession ❷ a way of spending time ❸ capturing a country or region by military force

occupational *adj.* to do with or caused by your occupation

occupy *v.* ❶ capture; hold possession of ❷ fill (a position, space or time) ❸ keep oneself busy doing sth. or with sth. ❹ live in

occur *v.* ❶ happen; take place ❷ come into (sb.'s mind) ❸ exist or be found somewhere

occurrence *n.* ❶ sth. that happens or exists ❷ fact or process of occurring

ocean *n.* ❶ a great mass of water that surrounds the landmass ❷ one of the main divisions of this mass

o'clock *adv.* (used in telling time) exactly the hour

octagon *n.* a plane figure with eight sides and eight angles

October *n.* the tenth month of the year

oculist *n.* an eye doctor

odd *adj.* ❶ not even; that cannot be divided exactly by two ❷ strange, peculiar or unusual ❸ not regular; occasional

odds *n.* (*pl.*) the chances in favour of or against

odo(u)r *n.* ❶ pleasant or unpleasant smell ❷ reputation

odourless *adj.* without a smell

of *prep.* ❶ belonging to sb. or sth. ❷ containing ❸ showing a part in relation to a whole ❹ made from ❺ about; having as a subject ❻ coming from ❼ by; through ❽ from among

off Ⅰ *prep.* ❶ not on; away from; down from ❷ branching from (a larger one) ❸ in the near Ⅱ *adv.* ❶ not being used ❷ away from a place ❸ indicating completion ❹ (of food) no longer fresh

offense *n.* ❶ sth. unpleasant ❷ a wrong or crime ❸ the hurting of sb.'s feeling; the state of being hurt in feelings ❹ the act of attacking

offend *v.* ❶ hurt the feelings of; make unhappy or angry; annoy ❷ do wrong; commit an offense ❸ cause unhappiness or annoyance to (sb. or sth.)

offender *n.* someone who offends, especially a criminal

offending *adj.* causing displeasure, discomfort, or inconvenience

offensive[1] *adj.* ❶ causing offense to the mind or senses; unpleasant ❷ of or for attacking

offensive[2] *n.* a continued military attack

offer Ⅰ *v.* ❶ make sth. available or provide the opportunity for sth. ❷ express willingness (to do sth.) ❸ put forward Ⅱ *n.* ❶ a statement offering (to do) sth. ❷ an amount of money offered

offering *n.* sth. offered, especially to God

offhand Ⅰ *adv.* at once; without preparation Ⅱ *adj.* without preparation

office *n.* ❶ the room where business is done ❷ a government department ❸ important position

officer *n.* ❶ a person in command in the armed forces, police force, etc. ❷ a person with authority

official Ⅰ *n.* a person holding public office or working in government Ⅱ *adj.* of or from the government; of a position of trust or authority

officious *adj.* too anxious to help; interfering; too eager to show one's authority

offing *n.* (with reference to an event) about to happen

offload *v.* ❶ unload goods ❷ get rid of sth. that you don't need or want

offset *v.* (offset) balance; make up for

offshoot *n.* ❶ a side shoot on a plant ❷ sth. that develops from sth. else

offshore *adj.* ❶ at sea not far from the land ❷ blowing seawards from the land

offside *adj.* ❶ (in certain sports) in a position in which play is not allowed ❷ on the right-hand side, especially of an animal, a car or a road

offspring *n.* child; children; descendants of animals

offstage *adv.* & *adj.* not on the open stage; out of sight of those watching a play

often *adv.* many times; in a large proportion of the instances

oh *int.* an exclamation of surprise, fear, etc.

oil *n.* a fatty liquid used for burning, for making machines work smoothly, or for cooking

oily *adj.* ❶containing, covered, or soaked in oil ❷ like oil ❸ behaving in an insincerely polite and smooth way; trying to win favour by flattery

ointment *n.* a substance (often medicinal) with oil or fat to be rubbed on the skin

OK Ⅰ*adv.* & *adj.* all right; correct Ⅱ *n.* agreement Ⅲ *v.* agree to

old *adj.* ❶having lived a long time; not young ❷ of age ❸ belonging to past times; in use for a long time; not new ❹ known for a long time or familiar

old-fashioned *adj.* ❶ old in style ❷ keeping to old ways, ideas, customs, etc.

olive *n.* ❶(tree of Europe with a) small oval fruit, green when unripe and black when ripe, used for food and for oil ❷a yellowish-green colour of an unripe olive

Olympic *adj.* of Olympia

ominous *adj.* being an omen, especially of sth. bad

omission *n.* ❶the act of omitting; neglect ❷sth. omitted or neglected

omit *v.* ❶ fail to do; leave undone ❷ leave out

omnibus *n.* ❶ a large book containing several works ❷a former name for bus

on Ⅰ *prep.* ❶ (showing position) in relation to a surface or supported by a surface ❷ during; at the time of ❸ with regard to; about ❹ to; towards; in the direction of ❺directly after (and often as a result of) ❻in a state or process of Ⅱ *adv.* ❶ further in space or time; forward ❷continuously; not stopping ❸ (especially of a machine or electrical apparatus) working; operating

once Ⅰ *adv.* ❶one time ❷at a time in the past; formerly Ⅱ *conj.* when; as soon as

one *num.* & *pron.* ❶ the number ❷ a certain ❸ any person ❹ a particular example or type (of) ❺ the same ❻ (the) only necessary and desirable

oneself *pron.* one's own self

ongoing *adj.* continuing; still in progress

onion *n.* a round white vegetable with a strong smell, which is made up of one skin inside another

online *adj.* directly connected to and or controlled by a computer

onlooker *n.* a person who watches sth. that is happening; spectator

only Ⅰ *adj.* single and isolated from Ⅱ *adv.* ❶nothing more than; with no one or nothing else added or included ❷ no more interesting, serious, etc. than; merely Ⅲ *conj.* but; except that

onrush *n.* a strong movement forward

onset *n.* the beginning

onshore *adj.* moving towards the shore; on the land

on-stream *adv.* & *adj.* (of an industrial process, a piece of equipment, etc.) in operation or ready to go into operation

onto *prep.* to a position on

onus *n.* the burden or responsibility

for sth.

onward(s) *adj.* & *adv.* forward; on from here

oops *int.* a word said when someone has fallen, dropped sth., or made a mistake

opaque *adj.* ❶not allowing light to pass through; that cannot be seen through ❷ hard to understand

open Ⅰ*adj.* ❶not closed or shut ❷ready for business ❸ sincere; frank ❹ not covered ❺ not enclosed, fenced in, barred, or blocked Ⅱ*v.* ❶(cause to) become open ❷cause to start

opener *n.* ❶a device for opening tins or bottles ❷ a person or thing that opens sth.

opening Ⅰ*n.* ❶a clear space or gap ❷an opportunity; a position in a firm that is to be filled ❸the start or beginning Ⅱ *adj.* first; beginning

O

openly *adv.* without secret; frankly or honestly

openness *n.* ❶the quality of being honest and not hiding information or feelings ❷ the quality of not being confined or covered

opera *n.* a musical play, in which the words are sung

operable *adj.* (of a disease or medical condition) able to be treated by means of an operation

operate *v.* ❶ produce effects ❷ cut the body in order to set right or remove a diseased part ❸ have or produce an effect

operation *n.* ❶ working; the way sth. works ❷a cutting into the body to cure a certain disease ❸ the state in which effects can be produced

operational *adj.* ❶ready to be used ❷of or about operations

operative *adj.* ❶(of plans, laws, etc.) in operation; producing effects ❷ most suitable

operator *n.* ❶ a person who works a machine, apparatus, etc. ❷ a person who works a telephone switchboard

opinion *n.* a view or idea one holds about sth.

opium *n.* a substance prepared from poppy seeds, used as a drug

opponent *n.* a person who takes the opposite side in a game, a fight, an argument, etc.

opportune *adj.* ❶ (of time) suitable, favourable; good for a purpose ❷(of an action or event) done, coming at the right time

opportunist *n.* a person who is quick to take advantage of opportunities, often in an unprincipled way

opportunity *n.* a favourable time or chance for sth.

oppose *v.* be against; act against

opposed *adj.* ❶in opposition to (a policy or an attitude, etc.) ❷ against (a person, activity, plan, etc.)

opposing *adj.* ❶ in conflict or competition with a specified or implied subject ❷facing; opposite

opposite Ⅰ *adj.* ❶ facing ❷ contrary; different Ⅱ prep. on the other side of a space from sth. Ⅲ*n.* a person or thing that is entirely different from another

opposition *n.* ❶ the state of being opposite or opposed ❷ political parties opposing the government

oppress *v.* ❶rule in a hard and cruel way ❷cause to feel troubled, uncomfortable

optic *adj.* of or belonging to the eyes or the sense of sight

optical *adj.* ❶of the sense of sight ❷for looking through; to help eyesight

optimism *n.* the belief that everything will come right or end well

optimist *n.* a person who always expects good things to happen or things to be successful

optimistic *adj.* showing optimism; hopeful

optimum *adj.* best; most profitable

option *n.* ❶the freedom to choose ❷the thing that is or may be chosen; choices

or *conj.* ❶(used before the last of a set of possibilities) ❷if not; otherwise

oral *adj.* ❶spoken rather than written ❷ of or by the mouth

orange *n.* ❶ a round, juicy fruit with thick, yellow-red skin ❷ the colour of an orange

oration *n.* a formal public speech

orator *n.* a person who makes a speech (especially a good speaker)

orb *n.* ❶ a ball standing for the sun or another heavenly body, especially one carried by a king or queen on formal occasions as a sign of power and justice ❷ an eye, especially the eye of a beautiful lady

orbit Ⅰ *n.* the path of one heavenly body round another Ⅱ *v.* move in an orbit

orbital *adj.* ❶ (said about a road) passing round the outside of a city ❷to do with an orbit

orchard *n.* the field where fruit trees grow

orchestra *n.* a group of people who play musical instruments together

orchid *n.* a type of plant with flowers, many of which have bright colours and unique but beautiful shapes

order Ⅰ *n.* ❶the way in which people or things are placed or arranged in relation to one another ❷a condition in which things are carefully and neatly arranged ❸a command ❹ a request to supply goods Ⅱ *v.* ❶ use your position of authority to tell sb. to do sth. or say that sth. must happen ❷ give an order for

orderly *adj.* ❶ well arranged, tidy ❷ methodical ❸well-behaved and obedient

ordinarily *adv.* ❶ usually ❷ in a normal way

ordinary *adj.* normal; not unusual or different in any way

ore *n.* a kind of rock or earth in which metal is found

organ *n.* ❶a part of an animal or plant that serves a special purpose ❷ an official organization ❸ a musical instrument made of many pipes through which air is forced

organism *n.* living being with parts which work together; individual animal or plant; any system with parts dependent upon each other

organization *n.* ❶ the arrangement of parts so as to form an effective whole ❷ a group of people with a special purpose

organize *v.* form into a whole; arrange

organized *adj.* having good and effective

organization

orient Ⅰ*n.* Asia; the (Far) East Ⅱ*adj.* ❶eastern ❷(of the sun) rising Ⅲ*v.* ❶ make a building, etc. face a direction ❷ find out one's position in relation to sth. else ❸get oneself used to unfamiliar surroundings, conditions, etc.

oriental Ⅰ*n.* a person or thing of or from the Orient Ⅱ*adj.* of or from the Orient

orientate *v.* ❶ arrange or direct with a particular purpose ❷ establish the position of (oneself or sth. else) especially in relation to a map or compass

orientation *n.* ❶ an act or the state of orienting or being oriented ❷ the position relative to surroundings ❸ the direction of a person's attitude or interest, especially sexual or political

origin *n.* ❶ the country, race or living conditions of one's parents or ancestors ❷a starting point

original Ⅰ*adj.* ❶ existing at the beginning of a particular period, process or activity ❷new; not copied ❸able to produce new ideas; creative Ⅱ*n.* ❶the earliest form of sth. (from which copies can be made) ❷a document, a work of art or a piece of writing that was first written

originality *n.* ❶ the ability to think independently and creatively ❷ the quality of being novel or unusual

originally *adv.* ❶ from or in the beginning; at first ❷ in a novel and inventive way

originate *v.* (cause to) begin; bring about; create

ornament Ⅰ*n.* ❶things which is added to make sth. richer in style or more beautiful ❷an object possessed beautiful rather than useful ❸a thing or a person that adds honour, importance, or beauty to sth. Ⅱ*v.* add ornament to

ornamental Ⅰ*adj.* serving or intended as an ornament; decorative Ⅱ*n.* a plant grown for its attractive appearance

ornamentation *n.* ❶things added to sth. to provide decoration ❷ the action of decorating sth. or making it more elaborate

ornate *adj.* ❶ richly ornamented ❷ not simple in style or vocabulary

orphan *n.* a child whose parents are dead

ostrich *n.* a very large African bird with a long neck, unable to fly, but run fast

other Ⅰ*adj.* remaining; more as well Ⅱ*adv.* (otherwise) in a different way

otherwise Ⅰ*adv.* ❶ differently; in another way ❷ in other respects or conditions Ⅱ*conj.* if not; or else

ouch *int.* an exclamation of pain

ought *aux. v.* ❶(usually indicate duty or obligation) used to say what is the right thing to do ❷will probably

our *pron.* of or belonging to us

ours *pron.* the one or ones belonging to us

ourselves *pron.* ❶used instead of us as the object of a verb or preposition for emphasis ❷(used for referring to the people rather than anyone else) ❸our usual state of mind or body

out *adv.* ❶not at home or at a place of work ❷to or at an end ❸(of a fire or light) not burning ❹clearly and loudly so that people can hear ❺ away from a place, the usual condition, etc. ❻ on strike ❼ far away ❽ so as to be clearly seen, shown, understood, etc.

outback Ⅰ *adj.* of the back country Ⅱ *adv.* to the back country Ⅲ *n.* the back country

outboard *adj.* an engine which can be attached to the outside of a boat

outbreak *n.* ❶ the sudden start of sth. unpleasant, especially violence or disease ❷ an uprising

outburst *n.* a burst of steam, energy, laughter, anger, etc.

outcast *n.* a person without a home or friends

outclass *v.* be much better than

outcome *n.* an effect or result

outcry *n.* ❶ a loud shouting or crying ❷ a public show of anger

outdated *adj.* old-fashioned; not modern

outdistance *v.* go further or faster than (especially in a race)

outdo *v.* do better than

outdoor *adj.* done, existing, happening, or used outside

outdoors *adv.* outside; in the open air

outer *adj.* of the outside; farther from the centre

outermost *adj.* furthest outside or furthest from the middle

outface *v.* ❶ meet and deal with bravely ❷ cause (someone) to look away by looking at steadily

outfall *n.* ❶ an outlet of a river, drain, etc.; river mouth

outfit *n.* all the clothes or tools that are needed for a certain job or occasion

outflow *n.* ❶ an outward flow ❷ an amount of liquid, money or people that flows out

outgo Ⅰ *v.* go beyond or faster than; excel Ⅱ *n.* money paid out; expenditure

outgoing *adj.* ❶ sociable and friendly ❷ leaving an office or position, especially after an election or term of office

outgrow *v.* ❶ grow too big for clothes, etc. ❷ become older to stop doing sth.

outing *n.* a short pleasure trip

outlaw Ⅰ *n.* a criminal; a person punished by being placed outside the protection of the law Ⅱ *v.* declare sth. unlawful; ban

outlet *n.* ❶ an opening that permits escape or release for water, etc. ❷ a way of expressing or releasing sth.

outline Ⅰ *n.* ❶ lines showing shape ❷ main facts; chief points; a general idea Ⅱ *v.* draw in outline; give an outline of

outlook *n.* ❶ a view from a particular place; future probabilities ❷ a way of thinking ❸ the future probabilities; a prospect

outlying *adj.* far from the centre (of a town, etc.); distant

outmoded *adj.* old-fashioned; not modern

outnumber *v.* be more in number than

outpatient *n.* a person who gets treatment at a hospital but does not live there during treatment

outpost *n.* ❶ (soldiers in an) observation post at a distance from the main body of troops ❷ any distant settlement

output *n.* the amount of goods etc. produced

outrage Ⅰ *n.* (an act of) extreme violence or cruelty Ⅱ *v.* do sth. which shocks people; act cruelly towards someone

outside Ⅰ *n.* the outer part of sth. Ⅱ *adv.* on or to the outside Ⅲ *prep.* at or on the outer side of

outsider *n.* ❶ a person who is not accepted as a member of a particular social group ❷ a person or animal not expected to win a race or competition

outsize *adj.* larger than the usual size

outskirts *n.* (*pl.*) the outer parts of a town, etc.

outspoken *adj.* saying openly what one thinks

outstanding *adj.* ❶ excellent; easily seen ❷ still to be done

outstretched *adj.* stretched out to full length

outward Ⅰ *adj.* of or towards the outside Ⅱ *adv.* (also ～s) towards the outside

outweigh *v.* be more in weight, value, importance, etc. than

oval Ⅰ *adj.* egg-shaped; elliptic Ⅱ *n.* a shape like an egg

oven *n.* a device that is like a box with a door heated for baking, roasting, etc.

over Ⅰ *prep.* ❶ directly above; in or to a position higher than but not touching ❷ resting on and covering ❸ to the other side of ❹ more than ❺ in or on all or most parts of sth. Ⅱ *adv.* ❶ across (a distance, etc.) ❷ down ❸ finished; ended ❹ through; again ❺ remaining; more ❻ in all parts of; everywhere ❼ too ❽ upwards and downwards ❾ more; in addition

overact *v.* act a part in a play in an unnatural or exaggerated fashion

overall[1] *adj.* & *adv.* ❶ including everything ❷ on the whole; generally

overall[2] *n.* a loose-fitting coat-like garment worn over other clothes to protect them

overbalance *v.* fall over; (cause to) lose balance

overbearing *adj.* forcing others to obey one's will

overboard *adv.* over the side of a ship or boat into the water

overcast *adj.* cloudy; full of dark clouds

overcharge *v.* charge too much

overcoat *n.* a long coat worn over other clothes in cold weather

overcome *v.* ❶ fight successfully (against); defeat ❷ be victorious; triumph

overdo *v.* do too much; cook (meat, etc.) too much

overdose *n.* too much of a drug taken at one time

overdraft *n.* a deficit in a bank account caused by drawing more money than the account holds

overdraw *v.* ❶ draw more money (from a bank account) than the amount that is in it ❷ exaggerate

overdue *adj.* later than the arranged time (for payment, arrival, etc.)

overestimate *v.* ❶ have too high an opinion of ❷ give too high a value for (an amount)

overgrown *adj.* ❶ covered ❷ having grown fast

overhaul Ⅰ *v.* ❶ examine thoroughly and perhaps repair if necessary ❷ come up to from behind and pass; overtake Ⅱ *n.* a complete examination followed by any necessary repairs

overhead *adv.* & *adj.* above one's head

overhear *v.* ❶ hear what one is not intended to hear; hear by chance ❷ hear without the knowledge of the speaker(s)

overjoyed *adj.* very glad; delighted

overlap *v.* partly cover and extend beyond one edge (of sth.)

overload *v.* ❶ load too heavily ❷ cause to produce too much electricity

overlook *v.* ❶ have or give a view of from a higher position ❷ fail to notice; miss

overnight *adj.* & *adv.* ❶ sudden(ly) ❷ on the night before

overrate *v.* value sth. or sb. too highly

overseas *adj.* & *adv.* to, from or situated in places across the sea

oversee *v.* look after, control (e. g. work or workers); supervise

overshadow *v.* cause to seem less important

oversight *n.* failure to notice or do sth.

oversleep *v.* sleep too long or too late

overstate *v.* say sth. in a way that makes it seem more important than it really is

overtake *v.* ❶ catch up with and pass (e. g. in a vehicle) ❷ come to suddenly and unexpectedly

overthrow *v.* put an end to; defeat; destroy

overtime Ⅰ *n.* the time beyond the usual time, especially working time Ⅱ *adv.* beyond the regular time

overturn *v.* turn over; cause sth. to turn over

overweight *adj.* weighing too much

overwhelm *v.* ❶ (of water) cover completely and suddenly ❷ defeat sb. completely ❸ (of feeling) overcome completely; greatly affect the emotion of

ovum *n.* a female cell or egg from which animals develop

owe *v.* ❶ have to pay ❷ feel grateful ❸ be indebted to as the source of

owing *adj.* still to be paid

owl *n.* a bird with large eyes which hunts mice and small birds (usually at night)

own Ⅰ *adj.* belonging to oneself Ⅱ *v.* ❶ possess ❷ admit that sth. is true

owner *n.* a person who owns sth.

ownership *n.* the fact of owning sth.

ox *n.* an animal of the cattle family kept for milk or meat; a cow or bull

oxidize *v.* ❶ combine or cause a substance to combine with oxygen ❷ form or make sth. form a layer of metal oxide, as when sth. becomes rusty

oxygen *n.* a chemical element or a gas present in the air, without colour, taste, or smell, but necessary for all forms of life on earth

oyster *n.* a flat shell-fish used for food

ozone *n.* ❶ a colourless gas which is a form of oxygen ❷ the invigorating air at the seaside

P p

pace Ⅰ *n.* ❶a step in walking or running ❷ the rate or speed in walking or running Ⅱ *v.* ❶walk with slow regular steps ❷measure by taking steps of an equal and known length

pacific *adj.* ❶making or loving peace; peace-loving ❷ showing calmness ❸ of the Pacific Ocean

pacify *v.* ❶calm or quieten ❷bring the state of peace to sth.

pack Ⅰ *v.* ❶put (things) into (a case, box, etc.) ❷crowd together into a place Ⅱ *n.* ❶ a bundle of things tied or wrapped together for carrying ❷a group of wild animals that hunt together ❸ a group of similar people or things

P

package Ⅰ *n.* a parcel, bale or bundle of things which are packed together Ⅱ *v.* make into or tie up as a package

packed *adj.* (of a room, building, etc.) full of people; crowded

packet *n.* a paper or cardboard container in which goods are packed for selling

packing *n.* the action or process of putting clothes, possessions, etc. into bags or boxes

pact *n.* a formal agreement between individuals or parties

pad Ⅰ *v.* ❶fill with soft material in order to protect, shape, or make more comfortable ❷ make (a sentence, speech, story, etc.) longer by adding unnecessary words or sentences Ⅱ *n.* ❶ anything filled with a soft material used to protect, give comfort or improve the shape of sth. ❷sheets or paper fastened together, used for writing letters

page *n.* ❶one or both sides of a sheet of paper in a book, newspaper, etc. ❷ an event written in history book

pagoda *n.* a tower built with several floors or levels, often with an ornamental roof at each level

paid *adj.* ❶(of work or leave) for or during which one receives pay ❷(of a person in a specified occupation) in receipt of pay

pain Ⅰ *n.* ❶feelings of suffering of the body or mind; a feeling of hurting ❷ (*pl.*) great trouble; careful effort Ⅱ *v.* make sb. unhappy; cause pain to

painful *adj.* causing pain or distress

painless *adj.* ❶ causing no pain ❷ needing no effort or hard work

paint Ⅰ *n.* a liquid coloring matter which can be spread on a surface to make it a certain color Ⅱ *v.* ❶put paint on ❷make a picture using paint ❸describe vividly in words ❹(*pl.*) a set of small tubes or cakes of paint of different colors, usually in a box (paint box), used for making pictures

painter *n.* a person whose job is painting, either pictures or things like houses

painting *n.* ❶the process of using paint; the occupation of a painter ❷ a painted picture

pair Ⅰ *n.* ❶a single article with two parts always joined ❷two things of the same kind used together or regarded as a unit ❸two people closely connected or doing sth. together Ⅱ *v.* form a pair or pairs

pal *n.* a friend

palace *n.* ❶a very large, grand house of king or other rulers ❷ any large and splendid building (for entertainment)

pale *adj.* ❶with little colour in the face; having skin that is rather white ❷ (of colours) not bright or vivid ❸(of light) dim, faint

palm *n.* the inner surface of the hand

pamphlet *n.* a small paper book that collects information about a particular subject

pan *n.* ❶a metal plate used for cooking ❷ sth. shaped like a pan

panda *n.* a large black and white animal like a bear

pandemic Ⅰ *adj.* (of a disease) occurring over a whole country or the whole world Ⅱ *n.* an outbreak of such a disease

pander *v.* do what sb. wants, or try to please them, especially when this is not acceptable or reasonable

pang *n.* a sharp, sudden pain or feeling

panic Ⅰ *n.* a sudden, uncontrollable fear or terror Ⅱ *adj.* resulting from a sudden terror

pant Ⅰ *n.* the acting of gasping Ⅱ *v.* ❶ take short, quick breaths ❷ have a strong wish for sth.

pantry *n.* a small room in which food is kept

pants *n.* ❶ a piece of clothing worn under other clothes from the middle of the body to the top of legs ❷trousers

papa *n.* an informal term for children to address their father

paper *n.* ❶the material made in the form of sheets from very thin threads of wood, used for writing, printing, etc. ❷ a newspaper ❸official documents; documents establishing the identity of the bearer ❹ a set of printed examination questions

par *n.* ❶an average or normal amount or condition ❷the value of a bond, share, etc., that is printed on it ❸ (golf) the score which is considered as a standard for a particular golf course

parade Ⅰ *v.* ❶ gather together for a formal display; march through or around ❷ display; show off Ⅱ *n.* ❶ a ceremonial review of troops ❷an act of showing one's skill, knowledge, feelings, etc., with the intention of attracting people's attention or gaining admiration

paradise *n.* a place of complete happiness; heaven

paragraph Ⅰ *n.* ❶a piece of writing that begins on a new line ❷a small item of news in a newspaper Ⅱ *v.* divide into paragraphs

parallel Ⅰ *adj.* ❶ being the same

distance apart at every point ❷ very familiar ❸ marking a circuit connected in parallel Ⅱ *n.* ❶ similar features ❷ a person, situation, event, etc. that is exactly similar to another Ⅲ *v.* ❶ be parallel to ❷ be similar to ❸ be compared with

paralysis *n.* a loss of feeling in, and loss of control of all or some of the body muscles

parameter *n.* ❶ a quantity that is constant in the case in question but varies in different cases ❷ a numerical or other measurable factor forming one of a set that defines a system or sets the conditions of its operation ❸ a limit that defines the scope of sth.

paramount *adj.* most important; most powerful

paraphrase Ⅰ *n.* a re-expression of sth. written or said in different words, especially the words that are easier to understand Ⅱ *v.* make or give an explanation of (sth. written or said)

parasite *n.* ❶ an animal or plant living on or in another and getting its food from it ❷ a useless person who is supported by the wealth or efforts of others

parcel Ⅰ *n.* things wrapped and tied up for carrying Ⅱ *v.* wrap sth. up and make it into a parcel for carrying

pardon Ⅰ *v.* excuse; forgive Ⅱ *n.* the act of forgiving sb.

parent Ⅰ *n.* ❶ a person's father or mother ❷ an organism that produces another Ⅱ *adj.* referring to a progenitor

parish *n.* an area looked after by one christian priest or served by one church

park Ⅰ *n.* a large, usually grassy, enclosed piece of land in a town, used by the public for pleasure and rest Ⅱ *v.* put or place (a car or other vehicle) in a particular place for a time

parking *n.* ❶ the act of stopping a vehicle at a place and leaving it there for a period of time ❷ a space or an area for leaving vehicles

parliament *n.* (in some countries) the main law-making body, made up of members wholly or partly elected by the people of the country

parlo(u)r *n.* a sitting room in a house

parrot Ⅰ *n.* ❶ a sort of birds with a hooked beak and usually brightly-coloured feathers that can be taught to imitate human speech ❷ a person repeating, often without understanding the words or action of another Ⅱ *v.* repeat the words or actions of someone else without thinking or understanding

part Ⅰ *n.* ❶ one of the pieces into which a thing is divided ❷ a person's duty ❸ a character in a play ❹ a component of a machine ❺ a general area or division of a country, without fixed limits Ⅱ *v.* separate; make people leave each other

partial *adj.* ❶ not complete; not all; in part ❷ favoring one side over another; biased ❸ having a particular liking for sth.

participant *n.* a person who participates in an activity or event

participate *v.* have a share; take part in

particle *n.* ❶ a very small piece of matter ❷ a very small amount or degree

particular *adj.* ❶ different from others;

special; unusual ❷hard to satisfy

particularly *adv.* ❶ to a higher degree than usual or average ❷ used to single out a subject to which a statement is especially applicable ❸ so as to give special emphasis to a point; specifically

parting *n.* ❶ the action of leaving or being separated from someone ❷ a line where hair is combed away in different directions

partly *adv.* to some degree; not completely

partner *n.* ❶a person who takes part in an undertaking with another or others, especially in a business with shared risks and profits ❷the person that you are married ❸ an organization or a country which shares an agreement with another

partnership *n.* ❶ the state of being a partner, especially in business ❷ a business owned by two or more partners

part-time *adj.* for only part of the usual working day or week

party *n.* ❶ a group of people who have the same political ideas ❷ a group of people travelling or working together ❸ a social gathering attended by the people invited

pass Ⅰ *v.* ❶go by (a person or place); go through ❷give (especially by hand) ❸ succeed in an examination ❹ (of time) go by; spend time Ⅱ *n.* ❶a narrow way through mountains ❷ a ticket or a written permission to pass

passage *n.* ❶an act of passing movement from one place to another ❷a voyage ❸a narrow way in a building that leads to other rooms; a corridor ❹ a piece of a speech or writing ❺the passing of a bill

passenger *n.* a person travelling in a train, bus, plane, etc. or in a car in addition to the driver

passer-by *n.* a person who (by chance) is walking, driving, etc. past a place

passing Ⅰ *adj.* moving by; not lasting very long; going by Ⅱ *n.* the act of going by

passion *n.* ❶ a very strong feeling of love, anger, etc. ❷ an activity, sports, etc. that you like very much

passive *adj.* acted upon but not acting

passport *n.* a document to be carried when visiting foreign countries, with details concerning oneself and showing that one has the protection of one's government

password *n.* ❶ a secret word or phrase used to distinguish friends from enemies ❷ a word you need to gain access to certain computer files

past Ⅰ *n.* ❶the time gone by ❷the life in earlier time or history Ⅱ *adj.* passed; gone by Ⅲ *prep.* beyond in time (space, number, degree)

pasta *n.* an Italian food consisting of a dried paste made with flour and produced in various shapes

paste Ⅰ *n.* ❶a mixture used for sticking two things together ❷any soft, smooth mixture Ⅱ *v.* stick with paste

pastime *n.* anything done to pass time pleasantly

pastor *n.* a minister in charge of a church

pasture Ⅰ *n.* ❶ the grass considered or

used as food for cattle ❷ grassland for cattle Ⅱ *v.* put (farm animals) to graze

pat Ⅰ *v.* touch gently with the hand several times; tap lightly with the open hand Ⅱ *n.* a gentle blow with the open hand

patent Ⅰ *n.* ❶ an authority from the government to manufacture sth. and also to prevent it from being imitated ❷ sth. that is protected by a patent Ⅱ *v.* get a patent for Ⅲ *adj.* ❶ plain; easily seen ❷ protected by a patent

paternal *adj.* ❶ of (like) father ❷ related through the father's side

path *n.* ❶ a narrow way made by the passing of people or animals ❷ a way along which an object moves

patience *n.* the capacity to accept or tolerate delay, trouble, or suffering without getting angry or upset

patient Ⅰ *n.* a sick person who is being treated by a doctor Ⅱ *adj.* having or showing patience

P

patriot *n.* a person who loves and loyally defends his country

patron *n.* ❶ a person who supports a person with money or encouragement ❷ a famous or important person who takes an honorary position in a charity ❸ a regular customer of a restaurant, hotel, shop, etc.

patronage *n.* ❶ the support, encouragement from sb. ❷ a customer's support ❸ the manner of treating sb. as if he were an inferior person

pattern *n.* ❶ an excellent example ❷ a model, style or design ❸ a regular decorative design on cloth, material, carpets, etc.

pause Ⅰ *n.* a short period of stopping doing sth. Ⅱ *v.* stop for a time

pave *v.* cover (street, sidewalk) with stones, bricks, etc.

pavement *n.* a path at the side of a road for people to walk on

pavilion *n.* ❶ a building at the side of a sports ground for the use of players and spectators ❷ a decorated building for concerts, dancing, etc.

pay Ⅰ *v.* ❶ give money to sb. in exchange for goods that one has bought, services that have been provided, or work that has been done ❷ distribute wages ❸ give (money that is owed); settle (a bill, debt, etc.) Ⅱ *n.* the money received in exchange for work

payable *adj.* ❶ needing to be paid ❷ able to be paid

payment *n.* ❶ the action or process of paying sb. for sth. or of being paid ❷ the money given in return for work, goods, or services

pea *n.* a plant with seeds in pods, used for food

peace *n.* the state of freedom from war and disturbance

peaceful *adj.* ❶ calm and quiet ❷ liking peace

peacemaker *n.* a person who restores friendly relations

peach *n.* ❶ a round fruit with yellowish-red skin and a rough stone-like seed ❷ the color of the skin of this fruit; yellowish-red

peacock *n.* a large bird with beautiful green, blue and gold feathers

peak Ⅰ *n.* ❶ the top of a hill or a mountain ❷ the pointed front part of a cap ❸ the highest point or level of an amount, rate, etc. Ⅱ *v.* come to the highest point

peanut *n.* a nut that grows underground in a thin shell

pear *n.* a sweet juicy fruit, narrow at the stem end and wide at the other

pearl *n.* ❶ a smooth, round, hard ball formed inside some oysters ❷ the color of this; silvery-white ❸ sth. or sb. very precious

peasant *n.* a farmer who owns and lives on a small piece of land

peck *v.* strike sth. with the beak

peculiar *adj.* odd, strange or unusual, especially in a way that is unpleasant

peddle *v.* go from house to house trying to sell small articles

peddler *n.* ❶ a person who sells dangerous or illegal drugs ❷ a pedlar

pedestrian Ⅰ *n.* a person who goes on foot along roads or streets; a walker Ⅱ *adj.* ❶ connected with walking; for pedestrians ❷ dull; without imagination; uninspired

peek Ⅰ *n.* a quick or secret look Ⅱ *v.* look quickly or secretly

peel Ⅰ *n.* the skin of fruits or vegetables Ⅱ *v.* take the skin off

peep Ⅰ *v.* ❶ look at secretly and quickly; look through a crack ❷ come gradually into view; appear partly

peer Ⅰ *v.* look at carefully; stare at Ⅱ *n.* ❶ a person of the same age, social status, ability as another person ❷ a member of the nobility in Britain or Ireland, comprising the ranks of duke, marquess, earl, viscount, and baron

peerless *adj.* without an equal; better than any other

pen[1] *n.* a tool used for writing with ink

pen[2] *n.* a small yard or enclosure for cattle, etc.

penalty *n.* ❶ a punishment for breaking a rule or a law; sth. that is ordered as a punishment ❷ a disadvantage suffered by a player for breaking a rule

pencil Ⅰ *n.* a writing instrument made of wood with graphite in it which marks the paper Ⅱ *v.* write or draw with a pencil

penetrate *v.* make a way into or through sth.

penetrating *adj.* ❶ able to make a way into or through sth. ❷ (of a voice or sound) loud, clearly heard above or through other sounds

penguin *n.* a seabird of the Antarctic with wings used for swimming

peninsula *n.* an area of land almost surrounded on three sides by water

pension *n.* an amount of money paid to an officer or a worker who has completed his service, from the time he gives up work to his death

pensive *adj.* deep in thought; anxious

people *n.* ❶ persons in general; the citizens of a country, especially when considered in relation to those who govern them ❷ all the persons in a society, especially those common ones ❸ race; nation ❹ one's family; one's near relations

pepper Ⅰ *n.* a powder made from the

crushed seeds of certain plants and used to give food a hot taste Ⅱ *v.* put pepper on food

per *prep.* for each

per capita *adv.* & *adj.* for each person; in relation to people taken individually

perceive *v.* have or come to have knowledge of sth. through one of the senses or through the mind

per cent *n.* one part in every hundred

percentage *n.* ❶ an amount or rate in each hundred ❷ proportion

perceptible *adj.* that can be perceived or noticed

perception *n.* ❶ the ability to perceive ❷ an act of being aware of sth.

perch Ⅰ *n.* a bar, branch or anything on which a bird can rest Ⅱ *v.* fly down and rest on sth.

perfect Ⅰ *adj.* excellent; having no faults; completely correct Ⅱ *v.* make perfect

perfection *n.* ❶ the best possible state ❷ being perfected ❸ a perfect example

perfectly *adv.* ❶ extremely well ❷ totally

perform *v.* ❶ act, play, sing or dance, etc. before the audience ❷ do; carry out; accomplish ❸ work well or badly

performance *n.* ❶ the action or process of carrying out an action, task or function ❷ result; score ❸ (of machines) the ability to do sth. ❹ an act of presenting a play, concert, etc.

performer *n.* a person who performs, especially an actor, musician, etc.

perfume Ⅰ *n.* ❶ a sweet smell ❷ a liquid having the sweet or pleasant smell of flowers Ⅱ *v.* ❶ (of flowers, etc.) give a fragrant smell to (sth.) ❷ put perfume on (sb. or sth.)

perhaps *adv.* probably; possibly

peril *n.* ❶ serious danger ❷ sth. that causes danger

period *n.* ❶ a length of time with a beginning and an end ❷ one of the set divisions of the day in a school allocated to a lesson or other activities

periodic *adj.* occurring or appearing at regular intervals

periodical Ⅰ *adj.* ❶ happening, appearing again and again at regular times ❷ published at regular times Ⅱ *n.* a magazine, newspaper, etc. published at regular times

perish *v.* ❶ destroy completely ❷ die, especially in a sudden violent way

permanent *adj.* never changing; lasting for a long time

permissible *adj.* allowable or permitted according to laws or rules

permission *n.* the right to do sth., given by someone in authority

permit Ⅰ *v.* allow sb. to do sth. Ⅱ *n.* a formal written order giving permission to do sth.; a license

perpetual *adj.* ❶ lasting forever or for a long time ❷ happening often or uninterruptedly

perplex *v.* puzzle; cause to feel confused

persecute *v.* ❶ cause to suffer, usually for religious or political beliefs ❷ annoy sb. persistently

perseverance *n.* the quality of doing constant effort to achieve sth.

persevere *v.* continue firmly in spite of difficulties

persist *v.* continue firmly; refuse to stop or be changed

persistence *n.* the state of continuing firm or obstinate attempt in a course of action in spite of difficulty or opposition

persistent *adj.* continuing firmly or obstinately in a course of action in spite of difficulty or opposition

person *n.* ❶ a human regarded as an individual ❷ a human, especially one who is not identified

personal *adj.* ❶ private; of a single person ❷ done in person; directly by oneself ❸ of the body or appearance ❹ (of remarks) directed against a particular person ❺ showing the person

personality *n.* a famous person, especially in sport or entertainment ❷ the qualities of a person which make him different from others

personally *adv.* ❶ in person, not through someone else ❷ as a person; in a personal capacity ❸ from one's personal standpoint or according to their particular nature; in a subjective way ❹ as regards yourself

personify *v.* ❶ represent an idea in human form or a thing as having human characteristics ❷ embody a quality in your life or behaviour

personnel *n.* ❶ staff; all the people employed in any business service or public institution ❷ the department in a company that deals with (the complaints and difficulties of) these people

perspective *n.* ❶ the art of picturing objects on a flat surface so as to give the appearance of their relative height, width, depth, distance, etc. ❷ a picture in perspective ❸ a view ❹ a point of view

perspiration *n.* ❶ the process of sweating ❷ drops of sweat

persuade *v.* cause to do sth. by reasoning, arguing, etc.

pertain *v.* belong to; have connection with

pertinent *adj.* having to do directly with what is being discussed, etc.; very suitable

perverse *adj.* ❶ refusing to do what is right or what one is told ❷ deliberately wrong; unnatural

pervert Ⅰ *v.* ❶ turn sb. or sth. away from what is right and normal ❷ use sth. for a bad purpose Ⅱ *n.* a perverted person (especially one with a sexual perversion)

pessimism *n.* ❶ a tendency to believe that the worse thing is most likely to happen ❷ a belief that evil will always triumph over good

pessimist *n.* a person subject to pessimism

pessimistic *adj.* showing pessimism; gloomy

pest *n.* ❶ an insect or animal that eats or damages crop ❷ a person or thing that causes trouble, harm or destruction

pesticide *n.* a substance for killing harmful insects and other pests

pet Ⅰ *n.* ❶ an animal kept at home as a companion ❷ a delightful or lovely person Ⅱ *adj.* favorite; lovely Ⅲ *v.* fondle; treat with affection

petal *n.* a coloured leaf-like part of

a flower

petitioner *n.* ❶ someone who makes or signs a petition ❷ someone asking for the ending of their marriage

petrochemical Ⅰ *n.* a chemical substance derived from petroleum oil or natural gas Ⅱ *adj.* of or having to do with petrochemicals or petrochemistry

petrol *n.* a liquid used as a fuel for motor vehicles

petroleum *n.* mineral oil found under the surface of the earth or under the sea bed

petty *adj.* ❶ unimportant; on a small scale ❷ having or showing a narrow mind; mean

pharmacist *n.* a person who is trained to prepare and sell medicines

pharmacology *n.* the scientific study of medicinal drugs and their effects on the body

pharmacy *n.* ❶ the study of how to prepare drugs and medicines ❷ a place where drugs and medicines are sold

P

phase *n.* ❶ a stage of development ❷ an aspect; a side ❸ (of the moon) amount of bright surface visible from the earth (new moon, full moon, etc.) Ⅱ *v.* plan or carry out sth. in stages

phenomenon *n.* ❶ sth. that happen or exist in nature or society ❷ an outstanding person or impressive thing

philanthropy *n.* ❶ love of mankind ❷ the help given to people, especially those who are unfortunate in some way

philately *n.* the collecting of postage stamps as a hobby

philosopher *n.* ❶ a person studying or teaching philosophy ❷ a person governed by reason and calmness, especially in times of difficulty

philosophy *n.* ❶ the study or creation of theories about basic things such as the nature of existence or how people should live ❷ calmness and quiet courage, especially in spite of difficulty or unhappiness

phobia *n.* a strong, unnatural, and usually unreasonable fear and dislike of sth.

phoenix *n.* a magic bird of the Arabian desert, said to live for hundreds of years and then burn itself on a funeral pyre, rising from its ashes young again to live for another cycle

phone Ⅰ *n.* a machine used for talking to people over a long distance Ⅱ *v.* make a call to sb.

phonetic *adj.* ❶ of or concerning the sounds of human speech ❷ using signs to represent the actual sounds of speech

phonetics *n.* the study and science of speech sounds

photo Ⅰ *n.* a short, informal form of photograph Ⅱ *v.* take a photo of

photogenic *adj.* having an appearance that would make a good photograph

photograph Ⅰ *n.* a picture made with a camera Ⅱ *v.* take a photo (picture) of

photographer *n.* a person who takes photographs

photography *n.* the art or process of taking photographs

photosynthesis *n.* the process by which green plants use sunlight to turn carbon dioxide, which is taken from the air, and water into complex substances, giving off oxygen

phrase *n.* ❶a group of words that gives a particular idea ❷ an idiomatic expression

phrase book *n.* a book giving and explaining phrases of a particular (foreign) language, for people to use when they go abroad

physical *adj.* ❶of the body rather than the mind ❷of matter, material; of the laws of nature ❸ connected with physics, studying mechanics, heat, light, etc.

physically *adv.* ❶ in a way that is connected with a person's body rather than their mind ❷according to the laws of nature or what is probable

physician *n.* a doctor, especially one who treats diseases with medicines

physicist *n.* a person who studies physics

physics *n.* the science dealing with the study of matter and natural forces

physiology *n.* the study of the way in which the body of a living thing works under normal conditions

physique *n.* the way in which the body is formed or developed

pianist *n.* a person who plays the piano

piano *n.* a large musical instrument played by striking keys

pick Ⅰ *n.* ❶an act of choosing sth. ❷sb. or sth. that has been chosen Ⅱ *v.* ❶take (what one likes or considers best or most suitable) from a group or number of sb. or sth.; choose ❷take (part of a plant) from a tree or plant; gather ❸ steal or take from, especially in small amounts

pickings *n.* additional money or profits taken dishonestly

pickle Ⅰ *v.* put meat, vegetables, etc. in salt water or vinegar, etc. Ⅱ *n.* vegetables which have been pickled

pickpocket *n.* a person who steals things from people's pockets or handbags in public places

pickup *n.* ❶a small open truck or van ❷ the part of a record player that holds the stylus

picky *adj.* choosy; difficult to please

picnic *n.* a pleasure trip with a meal in the open air

picture Ⅰ *n.* ❶ a drawing, painting or photograph ❷ a movie or film ❸ an image on a television screen ❹a portrait Ⅱ *v.* paint or draw; imagine

picturesque *adj.* ❶charming; having the quality of being like a picture ❷ (of language) unusually clear, vivid and descriptive

pie *n.* meat, fruit or vegetables baked in a dish with pastry

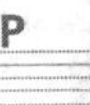

piece *n.* ❶ a portion of an object or of material, produced by cutting, tearing or breaking the whole ❷ a single item ❸ parts of sth. that has broken up ❹ an article of a magazine, news, etc.

pier *n.* ❶ a landing place for ships that extends over the water ❷ a pillar supporting a span of a bridge ❸ a brickwork between windows

piercing *adj.* ❶ (of wind) very strong and cold ❷ (of sound) very sharp and clear, especially in an unpleasant way ❸ going straight to the center or the main point

pig *n.* a fat, short-legged animal with a

usually curly tail and thick skin with short stiff hairs, often kept for its meat

pigeon *n.* a fat bird with a small head, short legs. and cooing voice, typically having gray and white plumage

piggery *n.* a place where pigs are bred or kept

piggy Ⅰ *n.* a pig or piglet Ⅱ *adj.* like a pig

pile Ⅰ *n.* a mass of sth. lying one upon another Ⅱ *v.* make into a pile; heap up

piles *n.* an illness in which there is a painful swelling around the anus

pilgrim *n.* a person who travels to a sacred place as an act of religious devotion

pill *n.* a small ball or tablet of medicine for swallowing whole

pillar *n.* ❶ a tall vertical structure, usually made of stone, used as a support or ornament ❷ sth. resembling this in shape ❸ a person or thing regarded as one of the chief support of sth.

P

pillion *n.* the pad or seat behind the driver's on which a passenger can sit

pillow Ⅰ *n.* a cloth bag filled with soft material, used for supporting head in bed Ⅱ *v.* rest or support (sth.) on or as if on a pillow

pilot *n.* ❶ a person who flies an airplane ❷ a person who steers a big ship into (out of) a harbor

pimp *n.* a man who finds customers for prostitutes

pimple *n.* a small, inflamed spot on the skin

pin Ⅰ *n.* a short thin piece of metal that looks like a small nail, used for fastening together pieces of cloth, paper, etc., used e. g. when making clothes Ⅱ *v.* fasten or join with a pin or pins

pincer *n.* (*pl.*) a tool for gripping things and holding them tight (e. g. to take nails out of wood, etc.)

pinch Ⅰ *v.* ❶ squeeze between the thumb and forefinger ❷ hurt being too tight ❸ steal sth. that is not valuable Ⅱ *n.* ❶ an act of pinching ❷ a very small amount

pine Ⅰ *v.* ❶ waste away with hunger, pain or deep sorrow ❷ have a desire to do sth. Ⅱ *n.* one of several kinds of (mostly) evergreen trees with needle-shaped leaves and cones

pineapple *n.* a large oval fruit that grows in tropical area; a plant which bears this fruit

ping-pong *n.* table tennis

pink Ⅰ *n.* ❶ light or pale red ❷ a garden plant with sweet-smelling white, pink, crimson flowers Ⅱ *adj.* of pale red color

pinnacle *n.* ❶ a pointed rock or high peak ❷ the highest point (e. g. of someone's career, achievements, etc.)

pioneer Ⅰ *n.* ❶ one who is first or among the first to explore or settle a region ❷ one who is first or among the first to open up or develop an area of thought, inquiry or endeavor Ⅱ *v.* explore or develop sth. new

pioneering *adj.* involving new ideas or methods

pip *n.* ❶ a small seed in an apple, orange, etc. ❷ a note of the time signal on the telephone or radio

pipe Ⅰ *n.* ❶ a tube through which liquids or gases can flow ❷ a small bowl attached to a hollow stem, used for smoking ❸ a musical instrument in the shape of a pipe Ⅱ *v.* ❶ carry sth. by means of pipes; supply with pipes ❷ play on a pipe

pipeline *n.* ❶ a pipe for carrying oil, gas, water, etc. over long distances ❷ a channel of supplying goods or information

pirate Ⅰ *n.* ❶ a sea robber ❷ one who appropriates the work, invention, or ideas of another without permission or authorization Ⅱ *v.* use or reproduce a book, a recording, another's work, etc. without authorization

pistol *n.* a small gun held in one hand

pit Ⅰ *n.* ❶ a hole in the ground ❷ a coal mine ❸ a covered hole as a trap for wild animals, etc. Ⅱ *v.* match against in a fight

pitch Ⅰ *n.* ❶ (in sport) a special marked-out area of ground on which football, hockey, netball, etc., are played ❷ a degree of highness or lowness of tone ❸ the highest point of sth. Ⅱ *v.* ❶ set up; fix firmly in the ground ❷ (cause to) fall heavily or suddenly forwards or outwards ❸ throw sb. or sth. with force

pitcher *n.* ❶ (in baseball) a player who throws the ball towards the person who is batting ❷ a large container for holding liquids with a handle and a lip for pouring; a jug

pith *n.* ❶ a soft substance inside the stem, etc. of some plants ❷ the most necessary, essential part of sth.

pitiless *adj.* showing no pity

pity Ⅰ *n.* a feeling for the sorrow of others Ⅱ *v.* feel sorrow for

pizza *n.* an Italian dish consisting of a layer of dough baked with meat, vegetables, etc. on top

place Ⅰ *n.* ❶ a particular position, point, or area ❷ a particular city, town, etc. ❸ a building or area used for a specified purpose or activity ❹ a person's home ❺ a portion of space occupied by sb. ❻ a person's rank or status ❼ the role played by or the importance to (sb. or sth.) ❽ a position in a sequence, especially in sporting contest Ⅱ *v.* ❶ put in a particular position ❷ cause to be in a particular situation ❸ find a home or employment for ❹ dispose of sth. ❺ give instructions about sth. or make a request for sth. to happen ❻ achieve a specified position in a race

placed *adj.* ❶ in the stated situation ❷ be placed (especially of a horse) to be one of the first three to finish a race

placement *n.* the act or an example of placing sb. or sth. in position

placid *adj.* peaceful; not easily made angry

plague Ⅰ *n.* ❶ a very dangerous infectious disease ❷ a disaster ❸ annoyance; trouble Ⅱ *v.* annoy with repeated requests or questions

plain Ⅰ *adj.* ❶ clear; easy to understand; easily seen or heard ❷ simple; ordinary ❸ honest; sincere; frank Ⅱ *n.* a flat stretch of land

plainly *adv.* ❶ in a plain way; easily seen or heard ❷ in a clear and obvious way

plainspoken *adj.* speaking in a direct and honest way, sometimes in a rude way

plaint *n.* an expression of great sorrow

plaintiff *n.* a person who brings a charge against sb. in court

plan Ⅰ *n.* ❶an arrangement for carrying out some future activities; a design; a scheme ❷an outline drawing of a house, machine, etc. Ⅱ *v.* ❶ make an arrangement for ❷design sth.

plane Ⅰ *n.* ❶an airplane ❷a flat or level surface ❸a carpenter's tool for making a wood surface smooth Ⅱ *v.* use a plane on sth. Ⅲ *adj.* flat or level

planet *n.* ❶ one of the heavenly bodies which move round a star, such as the sun ❷the earth

planner *n.* a person who plans, especially one who plans the way in which towns develop

planning *n.* the process of making plans for sth.

plant Ⅰ *n.* ❶ living things that have leaves and roots, and grow from the ground, especially the kind smaller than trees ❷a factory ❸the large equipment for industrial purposes Ⅱ *v.* put in the ground to grow

P

plantation *n.* ❶a large piece of land on which crops such as tea, sugar and rubber are grown ❷ a large group of growing trees planted especially to produce wood

plaster Ⅰ *n.* ❶ a soft mixture of lime, sand, water, etc. used for coating walls and ceilings ❷ a similar quick drying substance used for supporting broken limbs, making models, etc. ❸a kind of sticky material used for covering small cuts or sores Ⅱ *v.* ❶cover a wall, etc. with plaster ❷cause to adhere or lay flat

plasterer *n.* a person whose job is to plaster walls

plastic Ⅰ *n.* substances made of the light material that are produced chemically from oil or coal, and then are manufactured into various articles, especially synthetic resinous substances Ⅱ *adj.* ❶(of goods) made of plastic ❷(of materials) easily shaped or moulded

plate Ⅰ *n.* ❶ a flat round dish ❷ the amount of food that this will hold ❸ metal articles made of gold or silver; a common metal with a thin covering of gold or silver ❹ a colored picture in a book, printed on different paper from the written part ❺a large piece of metal or glass Ⅱ *v.* ❶coat thinly with gold, silver or other metal ❷ cover with metal plate

plateau *n.* a large area of high and fairly flat land

plateful *n.* the amount that a plate will hold

platform *n.* ❶ a raised level surface on which people or things can stand; a raised floor of boards for speakers, performers, etc. ❷ a raised flat surface built along the side of the track at a railway station ❸ a statement of main ideas and plans set forth by a party or group

plating *n.* a thin coating of gold, silver, or other metal

platinum *n.* a soft, white, valuable metal

platitude *n.* a statement of sth. obvious or of sth. which has often been said before, but now used by a speaker as if it were sth. new

platonic *adj.* (of a relationship between a man and woman) just friendly, not sexual

platoon *n.* a small number of soldiers organized as a single unit

plausible *adj.* ❶ appearing to be true or reasonable ❷ good at making up sounding honest and sincere excuses, etc.

play Ⅰ *n.* ❶ sth. done for amusement ❷ a work written to be acted on the stage ❸ the influence of sth. on sb. or sth. else Ⅱ *v.* ❶ do sth. for pleasure, especially using toys; have fun ❷ take part in a sport or game ❸ perform (musical instruments); produce or give out music ❹ perform or act ❺ make; carry out

player *n.* ❶ a person who takes part in a sport or game ❷ an actor; a person playing a musical instrument

playful *adj.* ❶ fond of fun and amusement ❷ done in fun; not meant seriously

playground *n.* a piece of ground for children to play on

playing card *n.* one of the 52 cards used for various games and for telling fortunes

playing field *n.* a field used for outdoor team games

plaything *n.* ❶ a toy ❷ a person who is treated without seriousness or consideration by another

playtime *n.* a (short) period of time, especially at a school, when children can go out to play

plaza *n.* ❶ a public square or marketplace, especially in towns in Spanish-speaking countries ❷ a group of public buildings in a town

plea *n.* ❶ a statement by a person in a court of law, saying whether or not he is guilty of a charge ❷ an earnest request ❸ an excuse; a reason offered for wrongdoing

plead *v.* ❶ offer reasons for ❷ beg or request earnestly ❸ offer as an excuse

pleasant *adj.* ❶ giving pleasure; agreeable ❷ friendly and polite

please *v.* ❶ be used when asking politely for sth. ❷ give pleasure or happiness to; satisfy ❸ like sth. or be willing to do sth.

pleasing *adj.* that gives you pleasure or satisfaction

pleased *adj.* glad; feeling or showing satisfaction

pleasure *n.* ❶ a state of being delighted and satisfied ❷ sth. that pleases you

pleat Ⅰ *n.* a fold made by doubling cloth on itself Ⅱ *v.* make pleats in

pledge Ⅰ *n.* ❶ a solemn promise ❷ sth. given as a sign of love, approval, etc. ❸ sth. valuable left with someone else as proof that one will fulfill an agreement or pay back money you owe Ⅱ *v.* ❶ promise solemnly or formally ❷ give as security

plenary *adj.* ❶ (of a meeting) attended by everyone who has the right to attend ❷ complete; without limit

plentiful *adj.* in large amounts or numbers

plenty Ⅰ *n.* a large number or quantity of sth. Ⅱ *adv.* quite; very

plight *n.* a bad or sorrowful situation or condition

plod *v.* ❶ walk slowly and heavily ❷ work slowly but without resting

plodder *n.* a person who works slowly and steadily but without imagination

plot Ⅰ *n.* ❶ a small piece of ground ❷ an outline of the events of a story or drama ❸ a secret plan Ⅱ *v.* ❶ make a secret plan ❷ write the plot of

plough Ⅰ *n.* a tool used in farming for turning up soil Ⅱ *v.* use a plough upon to dig and turn over a field or other area of land

ploy *n.* an idea or action which is often used to gain some advantages

pluck Ⅰ *v.* ❶ pick ❷ show bravery in spite of fear Ⅱ *n.* courage and will

plug Ⅰ *n.* ❶ a small, usually round, piece of rubber, wood, metal, etc., used for blocking a hole, especially in sth. that contains liquid ❷ a small plastic object with two or three metal pins that are pushed into an electric socket to connect an apparatus with the electricity supply Ⅱ *v.* ❶ block, close, or fill with a plug ❷ connect to a supply of electricity with a plug

P

plum *n.* a round, juicy fruit with a large seed in it which grows in cool dry areas

plumber *n.* a person who fits and repairs pipes for water, gas, etc. in buildings

plume Ⅰ *n.* ❶ feather especially a large one used as a decoration ❷ ornament of feathers ❸ a thing that rises into the air in the shape of a feather Ⅱ *v.* (of a bird) smooth (its feathers)

plump *adj.* rather fat; fat in a pleasant-looking way

plural Ⅰ *adj.* ❶ more than one in number ❷ (of a word or form) denoting more than one Ⅱ *n.* ❶ a plural word or form ❷ the plural number

plus Ⅰ *prep.* with the addition of Ⅱ *adj.* positive Ⅲ *n.* ❶ the sign "+" ❷ a positive quality

p. m., P. M. *abbr.* after midday

pock *n.* a mark on the skin caused by smallpox

pocked *adj.* having holes or hollow marks on the surface

pocket *n.* a small bag sewn in clothing for carrying things

pod *n.* a long seed vessel containing the seeds of some plants, e. g. peas or beans

poem *n.* a piece of writing in verse

poet *n.* a writer of poems

poetic *adj.* of, like, or connected with poetry

poetry *n.* ❶ the art of a poem; poems in general ❷ the quality of beauty, grace, and deep feeling

point Ⅰ *v.* direct to; show the position of Ⅱ *n.* ❶ a tip; a sharp end ❷ a position (real or imagined) in space or time ❸ a score; a mark or unit on a scale of measurement ❹ the main idea in sth. that is said or done ❺ the purpose or aim of sth.

pointed *adj.* ❶ having a sharp end ❷ directed clearly against a particular person or his behaviour

pointless *adj.* ❶ having no meaning or purpose ❷ not having scored any points

poise Ⅰ *v.* keep balanced; hold lightly in a position of being steady Ⅱ *n.* ❶ balance

❷the way of holding one's head or body ❸good self-control and self-possession

poison Ⅰ *n.* ❶a drug or other substance very dangerous to life and health ❷ harmful thoughts, feelings, etc. Ⅱ *v.* harm or kill with poison; put poison into (onto)

poisonous *adj.* ❶ containing poison; having the effect of poison ❷ morally injurious

poke *v.* push (a pointed thing) into sth. (sb.)

poker[1] *n.* a long, metal rod for stirring up the coals, wood, etc. in a fire

poker[2] *n.* a card game which is usually played for money

polar *adj.* ❶ of or near the North or South Pole ❷directly opposite

polarity *n.* the property of having poles or being polar

pole *n.* ❶ a tall, slender piece of wood, etc. that stands on the ground to hold sth. up ❷either the north or south end of the earth's axis ❸either of the two ends of a magnet; either of the two points of an electric battery

police Ⅰ *n.* (*pl.*) (the ～) the civil force of a state, responsible for the prevention and detection of crime and the maintenance of public order Ⅱ *v.* keep order in a place with police or as with police; control

policy *n.* ❶ a general plan of a political party, government, business company ❷ a wise and sensible conduct; the art of government ❸ terms of a contract of insurance

polish Ⅰ *v.* ❶ make or become smooth and shiny by rubbing ❷improve sth. by making changes, modifying, etc. Ⅱ *n.* a substance used to give smoothness or shine

polished *adj.* ❶ elegant or refined ❷ accomplished and skillful

polite *adj.* having or showing good manners; courteous

political *adj.* ❶ relating to politics ❷ connected with different parties

politician *n.* a person taking part in politics or much interested in politics; one who is skilled in maneuvering

politics *n.* the science of political affairs

poll Ⅰ *n.* ❶ the giving of votes at an election ❷the number of votes recorded at an election Ⅱ *v.* vote at an election

polling *n.* the act of voting

pollutant *n.* a substance, especially a waste product of an industrial process, that pollutes sth.

pollute *v.* make dirty or impure

pollution *n.* ❶ the act or process of making air, water, etc. dirty or being polluted ❷ a substance that pollutes water, air, or atmosphere

pond *n.* a small area of water that is smaller than a lake

ponder *v.* consider; think over

pool Ⅰ *n.* ❶a small area of still water ❷a small amount of any liquid on a surface ❸ the total of money staked by a number of gamblers ❹ an arrangement by business firms to share business and divide profits, to avoid competition and agree on prices ❺ a common fund or service provided by or shared among many contributors ❻a game on a billiard table with six pockets Ⅱ *v.* put money or other assets into a common fund

poor *adj.* ❶having little or no money ❷ unfortunate; needing pity or sympathy ❸bad in quantity

poorly Ⅰ *adj.* unwell Ⅱ *adv.* in a way or at a level which is considered inadequate

poorness *n.* lowness of quality; lack of a desired quality

pop[1] *n.* a modern popular music of a simple kind with a strong beat and not of lasting interest, liked especially by younger people

pop[2] Ⅰ *n.* a sound like that of a slight explosion Ⅱ *v.* ❶(cause to) make a short sharp explosive sound ❷ go or come quickly

pope *n.* (often the Pope) the head of the Roman Catholic Church

popular *adj.* ❶ liked or enjoyed by the general public ❷suited to the understanding or needs of the general ❸ of the ordinary people

P

popularity *n.* the quality of being liked, favoured, or admired by the ordinary people

popularize *v.* ❶cause to be well known and generally liked or used ❷make (a difficult subject or idea) easily understood to ordinary people

popularly *adv.* generally; by most people

population *n.* ❶people living in a place, country, etc. ❷ the total number of people who live there

porcelain *n.* a hard, shiny substance made by heating clay and used for making delicate cups and decorative objects; objects that are made of this

pore *n.* a tiny opening (especially in the skin) through which fluids (especially sweat) may pass

pork *n.* meat from a pig (usually fresh and not smoked or salted)

porridge *n.* a thick, sticky food made from oats cooked in water or milk

port *n.* ❶ a harbour ❷ a town or a city with a harbour

portable *adj.* able to be easily carried

porter *n.* ❶a doorkeeper; a gatekeeper ❷ a person whose job is to carry things

portfolio *n.* ❶ a flat, portable case for carrying papers, etc. ❷the position and duties of a minister of state or a member of a cabinet

portion Ⅰ *n.* ❶ a part; a share ❷ the amount of food given to one person at a meal Ⅱ *v.* divide into parts or shares

portrait *n.* ❶ a picture of a person ❷ a very clear description in words of a person's appearance and character

pose *v.* ❶ (cause to) sit or stand in a particular position, especially in order to be photographed, painted, etc. ❷ask (a question that is difficult or needs to be carefully thought about)

position *n.* ❶ a place where a thing or person is ❷ a certain way of holding body; a posture ❸a condition; a situation

positive *adj.* ❶ definite and clear ❷ practical and constructive ❸ showing pleasing progress

positively *adv.* ❶ in a positive way ❷ with certainty; so as to leave no room for doubt

possess *v.* ❶ own or have sth. ❷ have influence on sb.'s feelings

possession *n.* ❶ the state of holding or having sth. ❷ (usually *pl.*) sth. possessed; personal property

possessive *adj.* ❶ of possession or ownership ❷ showing that sth. belongs to sb. or sth.

possibility *n.* ❶ sth. that is possible ❷ the state of being possible; (degree of) likelihood

possible *adj.* ❶ that can exist, happen, or be done ❷ that can be reasonable or acceptable

possibly *adv.* ❶ used to emphasize that someone has or will put all their effort into sth. ❷ perhaps

post[1] Ⅰ *n.* a strong thick upright pole or bar made of wood, metal, etc. , fixed into the ground or some other base, especially as a support Ⅱ *v.* display (a notice) in a public place

post[2] Ⅰ *n.* ❶ the official system for carrying letters, parcels, etc. , from the sender to the receiver ❷ letters and parcels delivered Ⅱ *v.* send (a letter, parcel, etc.) by post

postage *n.* the money charged for carrying a letter, parcel, etc. by post

postal *adj.* ❶ connected with the public letter service ❷ sent by post

postbag *n.* ❶ a postman's bag for carrying letters ❷ all the letters received by someone at one particular time

postcard *n.* ❶ a card of a fixed size for sending messages by post without an envelope ❷ a card like this with a picture or photograph on one side

postdate *v.* ❶ write a date later than the actual date of writing on (a letter, cheque, etc.) ❷ occur or come at a later date

poster *n.* a large notice or picture stuck on a wall or notice board for advertisement

postgraduate Ⅰ *adj.* (of studies, etc.) done after taking a first academic degree Ⅱ *n.* a person engaged in postgraduate studies

postpone *v.* put off to a later time

postscript *n.* sth. added at the end of a letter, after the signature (usually introduced by the letters P. S.)

posture Ⅰ *n.* ❶ the position of the body; a way of holding the body ❷ a particular way of dealing with or considering sth. ; an approach or attitude Ⅱ *v.* ❶ put in a certain position; pose ❷ behave in a way that is intended to impress or mislead others

post-war *adj.* existing after a war, especially the Second World War

pot Ⅰ *n.* a round vessel of earthenware, metal or glass for holding liquids or solids, for cooking things in Ⅱ *v.* put into a pot

potato *n.* a roundish root plant with white flesh, commonly used as a vegetable

potent *adj.* ❶ having a strong and rapid effect on the body or mind ❷ strongly persuasive; convincing ❸ (of a male) able to have sexual relations ❹ having great power, especially politically

potential Ⅰ *adj.* existing in possibility; that may come into action Ⅱ *n.* ❶ the possibility for developing or being developed ❷ electromotive force expressed in volts

potted *adj.* ❶(of a piece of writing) shortened or abridged from a longer version ❷(of food) preserved in a pot

pottery *n.* ❶ vessels and other objects made of baked clay ❷ the craft or profession of making pottery, or the place where it is made

pouch *n.* ❶a small bag ❷a part of the body coming out to form a bag on the stomach for carrying their young, or in the cheeks for storing food

poultry *n.* (*pl.*) any domestic fowl as chickens, turkeys, geese, and ducks, usually raised for their meat or eggs

pour *v.* ❶(cause to) flow from a container ❷ express one's ideas, etc. freely ❸(of rain) fall heavily

poverty *n.* the condition of being poor

powder Ⅰ *n.* ❶a dry mass of very small fine pieces or grains ❷gunpowder Ⅱ *v.* ❶crush or grind into powder ❷ cover with powder; use powder on the face

P

power Ⅰ *n.* ❶the ability to do or act ❷(*pl.*) the faculty of the body or mind ❸ energy of force that can do work, especially electrical energy ❹ the right or authority ❺the right to act, given by law, rule, or official position ❻strength or influence in a particular area of activity ❼the number of times that an amount is to be multiplied by itself; the result of this multiplying Ⅱ *v.* provide with power

powerful *adj.* having or producing great power

practical Ⅰ *adj.* ❶ having to do with action or practice rather than thought or theory ❷ engaged in actual work; experienced ❸ fit for actual practice; workable Ⅱ *n.* an exam or a lesson in which theories are applied to do sth. or make things

practically *adv.* ❶in a practical way ❷ nearly; almost

practice Ⅰ *n.* ❶actual use; actual doing of sth. ❷repeated exercise or training of doing sth. ❸the business of a doctor or a lawyer Ⅱ *v.* =practise

practise *v.* ❶ do sth. repeatedly or regularly in order to become skilful; do sth. actively ❷do the work of a doctor or a lawyer, etc.

practised *adj.* expert and skillful, typically as the result of much experience

prairie *n.* a very large area of flat, grassy land, especially in North America

praise Ⅰ *v.* speak well of; express admiration of; applaud Ⅱ *n.* an expression of admiration

pray *v.* ❶ speak to God with love and worship ❷ask earnestly ❸please

prayer *n.* ❶the act of praying to god; a form of church worship ❷a fixed form of words used in praying

preach *v.* ❶give religious talk (sermon) especially as a part of service in church ❷ advise or urge others to accept or believe sth.

precedent Ⅰ *n.* a previous action or decision that is taken as an example to be followed in other cases of the same kind Ⅱ *adj.* preceding in time, order, or importance

precious *adj.* ❶ having great value ❷ highly valued; dear ❸ (of language, style, etc.) overrefined; unnatural ❹considerable

precise *adj.* ❶ strictly accurate; definite ❷ strictly observant, as of rules or standards ❸particular; exact; very

precisely *adv.* ❶ in a precise manner; exactly ❷ used to express agreement with what someone has said

predestine *v.* (usually with reference to fate or God) decide in advance

predetermine *v.* decide before an event occurs

predicate Ⅰ *n.* the part of a sentence which makes a statement about the subject Ⅱ *v.* declare to be true or real

predict *v.* tell or declare beforehand

prediction *n.* ❶ sth. predicted ❷ the action of predicting sth.

predominant *adj.* most powerful, noticeable, or important

preface Ⅰ *n.* a note written at the beginning of a book; foreword Ⅱ *v.* provide with a preface

prefer *v.* choose one thing rather than another; like better

preferable *adj.* worthy of being chosen; more desirable

preference *n.* ❶ a desire for one thing rather than another ❷ the thing preferred ❸ a special favour or consideration shown to a person, group, etc.

prefix Ⅰ *n.* ❶ syllable(s) put at the beginning of a word to change its meaning ❷ a word used before a person's name (e. g. Mr. Dr. , etc.) Ⅱ *v.* add a prefix to; add at the beginning of sth.

pregnant *adj.* ❶ (of woman) having a child in the womb ❷full of meaning

prejudice *n.* an opinion formed before looking at the facts

prelude Ⅰ *n.* ❶sth. that comes before and acts as introduction to sth. more important ❷a short piece of music that introduces a large musical work Ⅱ *v.* serve as a prelude to

premier Ⅰ *n.* the head of the government in certain countries Ⅱ *adj.* first in position, importance, etc.

premise *n.* ❶a statement which is taken to be true and from which certain conclusions are drawn ❷ (*pl.*) a house or building, including the lands, etc. belonging to it

preparation *n.* ❶things or work done to get ready for sth. ❷ the act of getting (making) ready ❸ the act of preparing school lessons ❹ a kind of medicine which is specially prepared

prepare *v.* ❶make ready for use, work or a purpose ❷make food ready to be eaten

preposition *n.* a word used with a noun or pronoun to show its relation to another (e. g. to, by, with, from, etc. can be used as prepositions)

presence *n.* ❶ the state of being present in a place ❷the fact of being present ❸a person's impressive appearance and manner

present[1] Ⅰ *adj.* ❶ being in the place ❷ existing or being considered now Ⅱ *n.* the time now

present[2] Ⅰ *v.* ❶ give (sth.) away, especially at a ceremonial occasion ❷ introduce sb. to someone else formally;

take part in (a television or radio show) Ⅱ *n.* a gift

presentation *n.* ❶ the process of presenting sth. ❷ sth. that is presented ❸ an exhibition or performance

presently *adv.* ❶ after a short time; soon ❷ at the present time; now

preservation *n.* the act of preserving sth.

preserve *v.* keep safe; keep from harm; maintain

preside *v.* be in charge or lead a meeting, etc.

president *n.* ❶ the head of government in many modern states ❷ the head of a club, society, etc.

press Ⅰ *v.* ❶ push, use force on (sth.) with the hand or finger ❷ smooth with an iron ❸ urge; keep asking earnestly Ⅱ *n.* ❶ an act of pressing or pushing ❷ a business of printing; printing machines ❸ (the ~) a business for publishing and selling books, magazines, etc.; a collection of newspapers and magazines

P

pressing Ⅰ *adj.* (of a problem, need, or situation) requiring quick or immediate action or attention Ⅱ *n.* a thing made by the application of force or weight, especially a record

pressure *n.* an action of weight or the force; the force per unit of area

prestige *n.* respect that results from the good reputation (of a person, nation, etc.)

presume *v.* ❶ take for granted; suppose ❷ dare to do sth.

pretend *v.* show a false appearance of; claim falsely

pretty Ⅰ *adj.* ❶ (especially of a woman, a child) charming and attractive without being very beautiful or good-looking ❷ pleasing to look at, listen to, etc. Ⅱ *adv.* to some extent; rather

prevail *v.* ❶ gain control or victory; win a fight ❷ (continue to) exist or be widespread

prevent *v.* keep from happening

previous *adj.* existing or occurring before a particular time

price *n.* ❶ the amount of money for sth. that is sold; the cost in money ❷ the unpleasant thing that you must experience as a result of what you have gotten

priceless *adj.* too valuable to be priced; invaluable

pride Ⅰ *n.* ❶ a feeling of deep pleasure or satisfaction that you get when you or people who are connected with you have done sth. well or own sth. that other people admire ❷ a feeling of confidence in your ability, etc. ❸ a person or thing that gives people a feeling of pleasure or satisfaction Ⅱ *v.* be proud of sth.

primary *adj.* ❶ earliest in time or order of development; elementary ❷ original

prime Ⅰ *adj.* ❶ first in rank; chief ❷ of the best quality; first-rate ❸ primary Ⅱ *n.* ❶ the earliest or first part ❷ the best part; the state of greatest perfection Ⅲ v. ❶ get ready for ❷ fill (a person) with food or drink

primitive *adj.* ❶ of the earliest time; of an early stage of social development ❷ simple; having undergone little development

prince *n.* ❶ a son or other near male

relation of a king or queen ❷ a ruler, usually of a small country or of a state protected by a bigger country ❸ a very great, successful, or powerful man of some stated kind

princess *n.* a daughter or other near female relation of a king or queen; the wife of a prince

principal Ⅰ *adj.* chief; most important Ⅱ *n.* ❶ heads of colleges and of some other organizations ❷ a person directly responsible for a crime ❸ money lent or invested on which interest is paid

principle *n.* ❶ a moral rule or belief that influences your action ❷ a law, rule or theory that sth. is based on ❸ a belief that is accepted as a reason for acting or thinking in a particular way ❹ a general or scientific law that explains how sth. works or why sth. happens, especially that applied across a wild field

print Ⅰ *v.* ❶ produce books, newspapers, etc. by printing them in large quantities ❷ publish text or picture in such a way ❸ produce a paper copy of (information stored on a computer) ❹ produce a photograph from a film ❺ write (text) clearly without joining the letters together Ⅱ *n.* ❶ the business of producing newspapers, magazines and books ❷ letters, words, numbers, etc. that have been printed onto paper ❸ a mark left by your finger, foot, etc. on the surface of sth. ❹ a photograph produced from film

printer *n.* ❶ a person employed in the trade of printing ❷ an owner of a printing business ❸ a machine for making copies, especially one printing text

prior *adj.* ❶ earlier in time, order, etc. ❷ existing already and therefore more significant ❸ before a period of time

priority *n.* ❶ the right or need to receive attention before other people or things ❷ a person or thing given priority

prison *n.* a place where people who break the law are locked up

prisoner *n.* ❶ a person who is put into prison ❷ a person who is not free to move

privacy *n.* a state of being private and not disturbed by other people

private *adj.* ❶ personal ❷ that you don't want other people to know about ❸ owned or managed by an individual person or an independent company rather than by the state ❹ not likely to be disturbed; quiet

privilege *n.* a special right, advantage, or immunity granted or available only to a particular person or group

privileged *adj.* having privileges or advantages over other people

prize Ⅰ *n.* ❶ sth. won in a contest; an award ❷ anything struggled for or worth struggling for ❸ sth. (a ship or its cargo) captured at sea during a war Ⅱ *adj.* ❶ given as an award ❷ worthy of a prize ❸ having won a prize Ⅲ *v.* ❶ value or treasure sth. highly ❷ use force to get (a box, lid, etc.) open or up

probability *n.* ❶ the quality or state of being probable; likelihood ❷ a probable event or result

probable *adj.* most likely to happen or exist, etc.

probably *adv.* most likely; almost certainly

probe Ⅰ *n.* ❶ a slender surgical instrument for exploring a body cavity, wound, or similar probing ❷ a thorough investigation or examination Ⅱ *v.* investigate, examine, explore thoroughly; examine with a surgical probe

problem *n.* a question to be worked out; sth. that is difficult to be solved

procedure *n.* ❶ an established or official way of doing sth. ❷ a series of actions conducted in a certain order or manner

proceed *v.* move forward; go on after having stopped

proceeding *n.* ❶ a course of actions ❷ sth. done; a piece of conduct

process Ⅰ *n.* a connected series of actions, changes, etc. Ⅱ *v.* treat or prepare by some special methods

procure *v.* ❶ obtain, especially with care or effort ❷ bring about; cause

P

produce Ⅰ *v.* ❶ make or manufacture things to be sold ❷ take out; bring out ❸ give birth to; lay (eggs) ❹ bring about, cause to happen Ⅱ *n.* things that have been produced or grown, especially by farming

producer *n.* ❶ a person or company that produces goods, foods, or materials ❷ a person in charge of producing a play, film, or similar entertainment

product *n.* ❶ anything that is produced ❷ the result or consequence of actions, etc. ❸ a number or algebraic expression obtained by multiplication

production *n.* ❶ the act or process of producing ❷ the amount produced

productive *adj.* ❶ producing a large number of goods, crops, etc. ❷ tending to produce

profess *v.* ❶ claim (sth.) often falsely ❷ state openly ❸ publicly declare one's faith in (a religion)

profession *n.* ❶ an occupation that requires special education and training, as law, medicine, etc. ❷ a declaration (of one's belief, opinion or feeling) ❸ the whole people in a particular occupation

professional Ⅰ *adj.* ❶ of a profession ❷ doing sth. as a profession rather than as a hobby Ⅱ *n.* a person who does sth. for payment rather than pleasure

professor *n.* ❶ a teacher of the highest rank in a college, university, or other institution of higher education ❷ any teacher in a university

proficient *adj.* highly skilled; expert

profile *n.* ❶ a side view (e. g. of someone's face) ❷ the edge or outline of sth. seen against a background ❸ a summary of a person's character and career in a newspaper or on television

profit *n.* the advantage or money obtained from doing sth.

profitable *adj.* bringing profit; beneficial

profound *adj.* ❶ deep, far-reaching ❷ having great knowledge; showing deep understanding ❸ very strongly or deeply felt

profuse *adj.* ❶ in large amounts; abundant ❷ expressing or giving sth. freely or generously, lavishing with sth.

program(me) Ⅰ *n.* ❶ a list of items, events, etc. as for a concert, or to be broadcast for radio or TV, or for a sports meeting ❷ a plan of what to be done ❸ a coded collection of information, data, etc. fed into an electronic computer ❹ sth. that people watch on TV or listen to on the radio Ⅱ *v.* make a programme of or for; supply (a computer) with a program(me); plan

progress Ⅰ *n.* the process of advancing or developing Ⅱ *v.* move forward; make progress

prohibit *v.* forbid formally sth. by law, rule, or sth. else

project Ⅰ *n.* ❶ a plan or scheme that to be carried out ❷ an individual or collaborative enterprise that is carefully planned and designed to achieve a purpose Ⅱ *v.* ❶ make plans for ❷ cause a shadow (an outline, a picture from a film or slide) to fall on a surface, etc. ❸ stick out

prologue *n.* an introductory part of a poem or play

prolong *v.* make longer

prominent *adj.* easily seen; important; famous

promise Ⅰ *v.* ❶ tell sb. that one will certainly do sth. ❷ give reason to expect; give hope of Ⅱ *n.* a written or spoken undertaking to do, or not to do sth.

promising *adj.* showing signs of future success

promote *v.* ❶ help in the growth of; help the progress of ❷ raise in rank or position

promotion *n.* ❶ an advancement on rank, position, honor or grade ❷ the action to help sth. develop or succeed ❸ a set of advertisements of a product or commercial enterprise

prompt Ⅰ *adj.* quick in action; done without delay; on time Ⅱ *adv.* punctually Ⅲ *v.* cause sb. to do sth.

promptly *adv.* ❶ without delay ❷ exactly at the correct time or at the time mentioned ❸ immediately

prone *adj.* ❶ lying flat with face downwards ❷ inclined to do sth.; likely to suffer sth.

pronoun *n.* a word used in place of a noun or a noun phrase

pronounce *v.* ❶ make the sound of ❷ declare formally

proof Ⅰ *n.* ❶ an evidence that is sufficient to show, or helps to show, that sth. is a fact ❷ the process of testing whether sth. is true ❸ a test, trial or an examination Ⅱ *adj.* able to resist or withstand Ⅲ *v.* make sth. waterproof

propagate *v.* increase the number of plants or animals by reproduction

propel *v.* ❶ drive forward ❷ force sb. to move or take actions

proper *adj.* ❶ suitable; fitting; right ❷ belonging particularly; relating distinctively ❸ strictly so called; according to the exact meaning of ❹ thorough; complete

properly *adv.* ❶ correctly or satisfactorily ❷ in a way that is socially or morally acceptable ❸ in the strict sense; exactly

property *n.* ❶ things owned; possessions ❷ a special quality that belongs to sth.

prophecy *n.* the power of telling what is

going to happen; a statement about the future

proportion *n.* ❶ a part or share, especially when measured and compared with the whole ❷ the compared relationship between two things in regard to size, amount, importance, etc.

proposal *n.* ❶ sth. proposed; a plan or scheme ❷ an offer of marriage

propose *v.* ❶ put forward; suggest ❷ make an offer of marriage to sb.

proposition *n.* ❶ a proposal or a suggestion ❷ a question with the answer or without the solution; a statement in which a judgment is expressed

propound *v.* put forward an idea, problem, etc. for consideration

prose *n.* writing that is not in verse form

prosecutor *n.* a law officer conducting prosecutions on behalf of the state or in the public interest

P

prospect *n.* sth. expected, hoped for or looked forward to

prosper *v.* cause to prosper or do well; be successful; develop well

prosperity *n.* the state of being successful

prosperous *adj.* financially successful

protect *v.* keep safe; make sure sb. or sth. is not harmed, etc.

protection *n.* ❶ the action of protecting sb. or sth. or the state of being protected ❷ a person or thing that protects

protective *adj.* giving or showing a desire of protection

protein *n.* a body-building substance essential to good health in food, such as milk, eggs, meat

protest Ⅰ *v.* object to; say sth. against Ⅱ *n.* a statement of objection or disapproval

protrude *v.* stick out; stand out

proud *adj.* ❶ arrogant; having or showing too much pride ❷ having or showing a proper pride or dignity

prove *v.* ❶ show that sth. is true; supply proof of ❷ test the validity of sth. by an example or experiment ❸ turn out to be; be found to be

proverb *n.* a short, pithy saying expressing popular wisdom

provide *v.* ❶ make ready; supply; furnish ❷ stipulate in a will or other legal document

provided *conj.* on the condition that

province *n.* any of the main divisions of some countries, and formerly of some empires that forms a separate whole for purposes of government control

provision *n.* ❶ an amount or sth. provided ❷ the action of providing sth. ❸ food (stored) or food supplies ❹ a condition or regulation (in an agreement or law)

provoke *v.* make angry; cause or arouse anger

proximity *n.* nearness in space, time, or relationship

pry *v.* look into; investigate (especially other people's affairs)

psychological *adj.* ❶ do with or affecting the mind and its working ❷ to do with psychology

psychology *n.* ❶ the science of the mind and its processes ❷ the mental nature, processes, etc. of a person

pub *n.* a place where people go to drink and meet friends

public Ⅰ *adj.* ❶ of, for, connected with, or owned by people in general ❷ known to people in general ❸ provided, especially by the government for people in general ❹ where there are lots of people Ⅱ *n.* people in general

publication *n.* ❶ anything that is published (e. g. book, newspaper, magazine) ❷ the act of publishing sth.

publicity *n.* ❶ the public attention directed upon a person or thing ❷ the process of drawing public attention to a person or thing; the spoken, written, or other material by which this is done

publicize *v.* make publicly known; advertise sth.

publish *v.* ❶ make known to the public ❷ print and offer for sale; issue

pudding *n.* (dish of) food, usually a soft, sweet mixture, served as part of a meal, generally eaten after the meat course

puff Ⅰ *v.* ❶ breathe rapidly and with effort, usually during or after hurried movement ❷ breathe in and out while smoking a cigarette, pipe, etc. Ⅱ *n.* ❶ a short, explosive burst of breath or wind ❷ breath ❸ a hollow piece of light pastry filled with cream, etc.

pull *v.* ❶ draw (sth.) along behind one while moving ❷ remove sth. from a place by pulling ❸ damage a muscle, etc. by using too much force ❹ open or close curtains, etc. ❺ attract sb. sexually

pulse Ⅰ *n.* ❶ the regular beating of blood in the main blood vessels carrying blood from the heart ❷ regular or rhythmical beating ❸ transient amplification or intensification of a wave characteristic Ⅱ *v.* beat or throb with regular movements

pump Ⅰ *n.* a machine for forcing liquids or gas into or out of things Ⅱ *v.* ❶ remove or raise by a pump; use a pump on ❷ tire out; put out of breath ❸ keep on questioning

pumpkin *n.* a large, round, orange-coloured vegetable with a thick skin

pun Ⅰ *n.* a type of joke in which words have more than one meaning or in which two expressions sound the same Ⅱ *v.* make such a joke

punctual *adj.* neither early nor late; be on time

punctuation *n.* the marks used in writing that divide sentences and phrases; the art or practice of punctuating

punish *v.* ❶ cause pain, loss or trouble to a person for wrongdoing ❷ blame sb., especially oneself

punishment *n.* ❶ an act or a way of punishing sb. ❷ the penalty inflicted for wrongdoing

pupil *n.* ❶ a young person who is learning in school or from a private teacher ❷ a circular opening in the center of the iris of the eye, regulating the passage of light

puppet *n.* ❶ a toy-like jointed wooden or cloth figure of a person or animal, that is made to move by someone pulling wires or strings that are fixed to it ❷ a person or group whose actions are not independent, but controlled by someone else

puppy *n.* a young dog

purchase Ⅰ *v.* buy sth. Ⅱ *n.* an act of buying

pure *adj.* ❶ unmixed with any other substance ❷ without evil or sin ❸ complete, thorough

purely *adv.* ❶ in a pure way ❷ entirely; only

purify *v.* make sth. pure or cleanse it of impurities

purity *n.* the quality or condition of being pure

purple Ⅰ *n.* a color of red and blue mixed together Ⅱ *adj.* ❶of such a color ❷over written

purpose *n.* ❶the reason for which sth. is done or created or for which sth. exists ❷the function of sth. ❸determination; the power of forming plans and keeping to them

purse Ⅰ *n.* ❶ a small bag for money ❷ money; funds Ⅱ *v.* draw together

P

pursue *v.* ❶go after in order to catch up with; capture ❷ try to achieve sth. in a particular time

pursuit *n.* ❶ the act of pursuing sb. or sth. ❷ an activity to which you devote time

push Ⅰ *v.* ❶use force on (sth. or sb.) to cause forward movement ❷ compel or urge sb. to do sth. , especially to work hard Ⅱ *n.* an act of pushing

put *v.* ❶ lay or place sth. in a particular place ❷bring into a certain condition ❸ express in words; say ❹ mark or write sth. on sth.

puzzle Ⅰ *v.* confuse; cause uncertainty Ⅱ *n.* ❶a problem to be solved ❷a toy or problem for testing cleverness, skill, or ingenuity

pyramid *n.* ❶ a solid having triangular sides meeting in a point ❷ a large building with a square or triangular base and sloping sides that meet in a point at the top

Q q

quadruple Ⅰ *adj*. made up of four parts; including four people Ⅱ *v*. make or become four times greater

quake Ⅰ *v*. (of the earth) shake Ⅱ *n*. an earthquake

qualification *n*. ❶ any quality, skill knowledge, experience, etc. that fits a person for a position, office, profession, etc. ❷ limitation to sth.

qualified *adj*. ❶ having the necessary or desirable qualities; fit or competent for sth. ❷ limited in some way

qualify *v*. give the necessary qualities to; make fit; obtain the knowledge, skill to perform certain acts

quality *n*. ❶ the standard of sth. as measured against other things of a similar kind; the degree of excellence of sth. ❷ a distinctive attribute or characteristic possessed by sb. or sth.

quantity *n*. ❶ an amount or a number of sth. ❷ the measurement of sth. by saying how much of it there is

quarrel Ⅰ *v*. have or take part in a quarrel; disagree by using angry words Ⅱ *n*. ❶ an angry argument; a violent disagreement ❷ the cause of a quarrel

quarter Ⅰ *n*. ❶ one of four equal parts; one fourth ❷ a period of 15 minutes before or after any hour ❸ one fourth of a year; one of four terms into which a school or university year may be divided ❹ a special part of a town; a section; a district ❺ (*pl*.) a place where one lives ❻ a source of supply, help, information, etc. Ⅱ *v*. ❶ divide into four parts ❷ provide quarters for soldiers

quarterly Ⅰ *adj*. (happening, appearing, etc.) every three months Ⅱ *adv*. once a quarter of a year

queen *n*. ❶ the wife of a king; a woman ruler in her own right ❷ any of the four playing cards with a picture of a queen ❸ the large leading female insect of a group

queer *adj*. ❶ strange; odd; peculiar ❷ unwell; faint

quest *n*. a long search for sth.

question Ⅰ *n*. ❶ a sentence that asks sth.; a request for information, which demands an answer ❷ a matter or topic that need to be settled or dealt with ❸ a doubt Ⅱ *v*. ❶ ask a question or questions of; examine ❷ express or feel doubt about

questionnaire *n*. a list of questions seeking information from people for use in a survey or statistical study

queue Ⅰ *n*. a line of people, vehicles, etc.

waiting for sth. or to do sth. Ⅱ *v.* wait in a line of people, vehicles, etc. for sth. or to do sth.

quick *adj.* ❶moving fast; done in a short time ❷keenly perceptive; alert

quicken Ⅰ *v.* ❶make or become quicker; increase the speed of ❷make or become more lively, vigorous or active

quickly *adv.* ❶ fast ❷ soon; after a short time

quiet Ⅰ *adj.* ❶ with little or no movement or sound ❷ calm, free from trouble or anxiety ❸ secret Ⅱ *n.* quietness; calmness Ⅲ *v.* make or become calmer

quilt Ⅰ *n.* a bed covering made of two pieces of clothes with soft material kept in Ⅱ *v.* make such a cloth cover for a bed

quit *v.* ❶go away from; leave; give up ❷ stop doing sth.

quite *adv.* ❶ to the greatest possible degree ❷to some degree ❸really

quiver Ⅰ *v.* shiver, shake or tremble slightly Ⅱ *n.* a light, quick, trembling motion

quotation *n.* ❶ a passage or group of words from a book or speech that is repeated by someone other than the original writer or speaker ❷the process of quoting or being quoted ❸a statement or estimation of a price

quote *v.* ❶repeat (in speech or writing) the words of ❷mention an example of sth. to give force to one's argument ❸ give a price

R r

rabbit *n.* ❶ a common small long-eared animal of the hare family that lives in holes ❷ the fur or meat of this animal

race[1] Ⅰ *n.* a competition in speed Ⅱ *v.* compete against sb. or sth. to see who can go faster or fastest, and who can do sth. first, etc.; take prat in a race or races

race[2] *n.* a group of people descended, or believed to be descended, from the same ancestors; a section of mankind different from others in colour, etc.

racial *adj.* relating to race

racially *adv.* from the point of view of race

racing Ⅰ *n.* ❶ the sport of racing horses ❷ any sport that involves competing in races Ⅱ *adj.* designed or bred for racing

racket *n.* ❶ a light bat used for hitting the ball in tennis, badminton, etc. ❷ an uproarious, loud noise ❸ a dishonest way of getting money, e. g. by threatening or cheating people

radar *n.* an instrument for determining the distance and direction of unseen objects by the reflection of radio waves

radiant *adj.* ❶ sending out rays of light; shining ❷ (of a person or his appearance) showing love and happiness

radiation *n.* ❶ the emission of energy as electromagnetic waves or as moving subatomic particles, especially high-energy particles which cause ionization ❷ the energy transmitted in this way

radio *n.* ❶ use of a wireless telegraph or telephone ❷ an apparatus for receiving programmes

radioactive *adj.* having the quality of giving off rays which pass through the solids

raft *n.* a flat boat made from large pieces of wood which is bound together

rag *n.* ❶ a piece of old cloth ❷ (*pl.*) old and torn clothes

rage Ⅰ *n.* a feeling of furiousness and wild anger Ⅱ *v.* ❶ be violently angry ❷ (of illness, disaster, etc.) spread quickly

ragged *adj.* ❶ (with clothes) badly torn ❷ having rough or irregular outlines or surfaces ❸ lacking uniformity or smoothness; imperfect

rail *n.* ❶ a bar of wood or metal placed level between two posts ❷ a steel line laid on the ground as one side of a track for trains or trams

railroad *n.* a track for trains

railway *n.* a track with rails on which

trains run

rain Ⅰ *n.* ❶ water falling in drops from the sky ❷ (*pl.*) the season in tropical countries when rain falls continually Ⅱ *v.* fall in drops of water; fall or pour down rain

rainbow *n.* an arch of different colours that sometimes appears in the sky opposite the sun, especially after rain

raincoat *n.* a light coat of waterproof

rainproof *adj.* able to keep rain out

rainy *adj.* having much rain

raise *v.* ❶ lift up; hold up ❷ cause to rise or appear ❸ bring forward for consideration; present; offer ❹ bring up (a child); breed or grow (animals or plants)

raiser *n.* ❶ a person who raises especially money or animals ❷ a person who causes sth.

rally Ⅰ *v.* ❶ come or bring together (again) for a shared purpose or effort ❷ return to a former good state, e. g. after illness or difficulty Ⅱ *n.* a large, especially political public meeting

R

rampage Ⅰ *v.* rush about wildly or angrily Ⅱ *n.* a period of violent and uncontrollable behaviour

ranch *n.* ❶ a very large farm ❷ any kind of farm

random Ⅰ *n.* the state of being aimless Ⅱ *adj.* done, made, etc. aimlessly; without purpose

range Ⅰ *n.* ❶ a row or line; a continuous series ❷ the distance between certain limits ❸ an area where shooting is practised ❹ extent; the distance between two things Ⅱ *v.* ❶ put in order; arrange ❷ stretch; extend ❸ vary or extend between specified limits

rank Ⅰ *n.* ❶ a line (row) of persons or things ❷ a position in the hierarchy of the armed forces ❸ (*pl.*) the stated class or group Ⅱ *v.* ❶ hold a certain grade or position ❷ take precedence over

ranking *n.* a position in a scale of achievement or status; a classification

ransack *v.* ❶ search thoroughly (often causing great untidiness or disorder) ❷ steal everything from

ransom *n.* an amount of money that has to be paid to set sb. free

rape Ⅰ *v.* ❶ have sex with sb. against one's will ❷ seize and carry off by force Ⅱ *n.* the act of raping

rapid *adj.* quick, fast; moving or occurring with great speed

rapids *n.* (*pl.*) a part of a river where the water flows very fast, usually over rocks

rapture *n.* a feeling of great joy and delight

rare *adj.* not often seen or happening

rarely *adv.* seldom; not often

rash *adj.* overbold; not thinking enough of the results

rat Ⅰ *n.* ❶ a big mouse ❷ a low, worthless or dishonest person Ⅱ *v.* ❶ trap rats ❷ act in a disloyal way; break a promise

rate Ⅰ *n.* ❶ the speed with which sth. moves, etc. ❷ a price which is paid for sth. ❸ a rank or class in an organization, a country, etc. Ⅱ *v.* regard as

rather *adv.* ❶ more willingly; by preference or choice ❷ in or to some degree; somewhat ❸ more truly, accurately or precisely

rating *n.* a class to which sth. (e. g. a ship) belongs

ratio *n.* the relation in degree or number between two similar things

ration Ⅰ *n.* a fixed allowance served out to, e. g. members of the armed forces; the fixed quantity, especially of food allowed to one person Ⅱ *v.* limit (sb.) to a fixed ration

rational *adj.* (of ideas and behaviour, etc.) sensible; according to reason

rattle Ⅰ *v.* make a number of short sounds when shaken Ⅱ *n.* (a toy or an instrument that makes) a rattling noise

ravage *v.* ❶rob or plunder with violence ❷destroy sth. badly

ravishing *adj.* very beautiful; causing great delight

raw *adj.* ❶ uncooked ❷ in the natural state; not yet treated for use ❸ (of persons) untrained, unskilled

ray *n.* ❶a thin light or narrow beam of radiant light, heat or energy ❷ any one of a number of lines coming out from a center

razor *n.* a sharp tool for cutting hair from the skin

reach *v.* ❶ get to; arrive at (in) ❷ hold out (one's hand)

reachable *adj.* that is possible to reach

react *v.* ❶ act as a result of another happening ❷act in chemical way

reaction *n.* ❶ an action performed in response to a situation or event ❷ an action set up by one substance in another; a change within the nucleus of an atom ❸ opposition to political or social progress

reactor *n.* ❶ a large machine for the controlled production of atomic energy ❷a container for a chemical reaction

read *v.* ❶look at and get the meaning of; repeat with the voice ❷ understand (a foreign language) when it is written; understand the nature of sth. by observation ❸ understand sth. in a particular way ❹ show a particular weight, pressure, etc.

readable *adj.* ❶easy or enjoyable to read ❷able to be read

readdress *v.* write a different address on (a letter that has been delivered to one's own address)

reader *n.* ❶ a person who reads, especially one who spends much time in reading ❷ a textbook for reading in class; a book with selections for reading by students of a language

readiness *n.* ❶ willingness to do sth. ❷ the state of being ready ❸ immediacy, quickness, or promptness

reading *n.* ❶ an act of one who reads ❷knowledge, especially of books ❸selections or materials for reading ❹a figure of measurement, etc., as shown on a dial, scale, etc.

readjust *v.* get or put back into the proper state or position

ready *adj.* ❶ prepared ❷ willing to do sth. ❸in need of ❹likely to do sth. ❺ quick or prompt

reaffirm *v.* declare again; in answer to a question or doubt

real *adj.* ❶ not false; genuine ❷ actually

existing; not imagined or supposed ❸ true or actual ❹ complete

realism *n.* (art and literature) showing of real life, facts, etc. in a true way

realist *n.* a person whose social, political, and artistic ideas are based on realism

realistic *adj.* ❶ showing realism ❷ (of art or literature) lifelike ❸ having or showing a sensible and practical idea of what can be achieved or expected

reality *n.* ❶ the state of being real or true ❷ the true state of affairs; the true nature; a real thing

realization *n.* ❶ the process of becoming aware of sth. ❷ the achievement of sth. desired

realize *v.* ❶ see clearly; understand ❷ bring into actual existence; make real; accomplish

really *adv.* ❶ truly; in fact; actually ❷ used to express surprise or interest, etc.

reap *v.* ❶ cut (grain); gather (crops) ❷ obtain as a result of effort

reaper *n.* a person or machine that harvests crops

R

rear[1] Ⅰ *n.* the back Ⅱ *adj.* in or at the back

rear[2] *v.* ❶ help to grow; bring up ❷ (of a horse or other animals) raise itself upright on its hind legs ❸ breed and raise

rearing *n.* ❶ the process of caring for children as they grow up, teaching them how to behave as members of society ❷ the process of breeding animals or birds and caring for them as they grow

rearrange *v.* put into a different order

reason Ⅰ *n.* an explanation; a cause Ⅱ *v.* ❶ say by way of argument (that) ❷ make use of one's reason ❸ persuade (someone) to do or not to do

reasonable *adj.* ❶ fair, practical and sensible ❷ not too expensive

reasonably *adv.* ❶ sensibly ❷ quite; fairly

reasoned *adj.* (of a statement, an argument, etc.) clearly thought out; based on reason

reasoning *n.* the use of one's reason

rebel Ⅰ *v.* fight against and refuse to obey Ⅱ *n.* a person who fights against authority instead of obeying

rebellion *n.* ❶ an act or the state of rebelling ❷ a refusal to obey orders or accept rules, etc.

rebirth *n.* a renewal of life or existence

reborn *adj.* as if born again

rebuild *v.* ❶ build again or build new parts to ❷ make sb. or sth. recover again

recall Ⅰ *v.* ❶ bring back to the mind ❷ call back ❸ take back Ⅱ *n.* the power of remembering

recapture *v.* ❶ get into one's power again ❷ bring back into the mind; cause to be experienced again

receipt Ⅰ *n.* ❶ the action of receiving sth. or the fact of its being received ❷ (*pl.*) money received during a particular period by a firm, etc. ❸ a written statement that sth. has been received Ⅱ *v.* write out and sign or stamp a receipt

receivable *adj.* ❶ able or fit to be received ❷ (of a bill or debt) for which money is to be received

receive *v.* ❶ come into possession of (sth. that is given or sent to one); get

❷suffer, experience, or be subject to ❸welcome or entertain

receiver *n.* ❶the person who receives ❷ the part of a radio or TV set that produces sound and pictures ❸the part of a telephone through which one hears ❹the person officially appointed to take charge of the property and affairs of a bankrupt

recent *adj.* done or made not long ago; fresh

reception *n.* ❶ the way of receiving or being received ❷a party or gathering to entertain visitors ❸ people in a hotel whose job is to receive guests, etc.; the place where such people work

recess *n.* ❶a period of time during which work stops ❷a hollow space in a wall for a bed, cupboard, etc. ❸a remote or secret place

recipe *n.* a set of instructions on how to prepare a certain kind of food

recipient *n.* a person who receives sth.

reckless *adj.* not caring about danger; very careless

reckon *v.* ❶calculate sth. approximately ❷guess or have an opinion about sth.

reclaim *v.* ❶make (land) fit for use ❷ ask for the return of

recognition *n.* ❶the action or process of recognizing or being recognized ❷ the state of being acknowledged

recognize *v.* ❶ know again (sb. or sth. one has seen, heard, or experienced before) ❷accept as being legal or real, or as having value

recollection *n.* ❶ an act or power of recollecting or recalling ❷ sth. recollected or remembered; a memory

recommend *v.* ❶advise; suggest ❷speak in favour of ❸make sb. or sth. attractive

recommendation *n.* ❶ the act of suggesting sb. or sth. should be used, etc. ❷a statement that recommends sb. or sth. ❸a suggestion

reconcile *v.* ❶ cause to become friends after having an argument or a disagreement ❷ bring into harmony with; cause to agree with

reconsider *v.* think again and change one's mind about (a subject)

reconstruct *v.* ❶rebuild after damage ❷ build up a complete description or picture of (sth. only partly known)

record Ⅰ *v.* ❶write down (a description or piece of information) so that it will be known in the future ❷ preserve (sound or a television broadcast) so that it can be heard and/or seen again Ⅱ *n.* ❶ a written statement of facts, events, etc. ❷ the best yet done, especially in sport; the highest (lowest) figure ever reached

recorder *n.* ❶ a person who makes or keeps records ❷ a device for recording sounds

recover *v.* get back (sth. lost); get back the use of

recreation *n.* a way of occupying free time pleasantly

recruit Ⅰ *n.* a new member of an organization; a person newly joined in the armed forces Ⅱ *v.* get (recruits) for the armed forces

recur *v.* ❶happen again; be repeated ❷go back (to sth.) in words or thought ❸ (of passed events) come back

recycle *v.* treat (waste material) so that it can be used again

red Ⅰ *n.* the colour of blood Ⅱ *adj.* of the colour of blood

redeem *v.* ❶ buy back; get back by payment or doing sth. ❷ perform (a promise or pledge) ❸ compensate; make up for

redo *v.* ❶ do sth. again or differently ❷ redecorate a room, etc.

redouble *v.* increase greatly

reduce *v.* make less or smaller

reduction *n.* ❶ the act of making sth. less or smaller; the state of being made less or smaller ❷ sth. on a smaller scale (e. g. a map or price) ❸ the amount reduced ❹ (in mathematics) the cancelling of common factors in the numerator and denominator of a fraction

reef *n.* a line of sharp rocks or bank of sand, at or near the surface of the sea

refer *v.* ❶ concern, mention; speak about or of ❷ make reference

R

referee *n.* ❶ a judge to keep the rules of a game ❷ a person who is asked to settle disagreement

reference *n.* ❶ the use for help or information ❷ a note in a publication referring the reader to another source ❸ the action of mentioning or alluding to sth. ❹ a submission of a case to sb. ❺ a statement about a person's character or ability

refill Ⅰ *v.* fill again Ⅱ *n.* (a container holding) a quantity of ink, petrol, etc. to fill sth.

refine *v.* purify; make or become pure

refined *adj.* ❶ made pure ❷ elegant and cultured

refit Ⅰ *v.* (especially of a ship) be made ready for further use Ⅱ *n.* the process of being refitted

reflect *v.* ❶ throw back (light or sound); send back an image of ❷ show the nature of sth. ❸ bring back as a result ❹ think deeply

reflection *n.* ❶ the throwing back by a body or surface of light, heat, or sound without absorbing it ❷ deep and careful thought ❸ sth. reflected

reform Ⅰ *v.* make or become better; improve the condition, character, etc. Ⅱ *n.* the action or process of reforming an institution or practice

reformation *n.* improvement; the act of reforming or state of being reformed

refrain *v.* hold oneself back

refresh *v.* make fresh again; give new strength to

refreshing *adj.* ❶ restoring strength and energy ❷ welcome and interesting because it is new or different

refreshment *n.* ❶ the state of refreshing or being refreshed ❷ (usually *pl.*) light food and drinks

refrigerator *n.* a fridge; an ice box; a machine which keeps food or drink at a low temperature

refuel *v.* (especially with reference to an aeroplane) get or provide with more fuel

refuge *n.* (a place that provides) protection or shelter from danger

refugee *n.* a person who has been forced to flee from danger, e. g. from floods, war, political persecution

refund Ⅰ *v.* pay back money Ⅱ *n.* the paying back of money; the money paid back

refuse *v.* turn down; say no to; decline to accept

regain *v.* ❶get back again ❷reach again; get back to

regard *v.* ❶consider; think of ❷gaze at steadily in a specified fashion

regarding *prep.* with reference to; concerning

regardless *adv.* without paying attention to the present situation; despite the prevailing circumstances

regenerate *v.* ❶give new life or strength to sth. ❷reform someone spiritually or morally ❸grow new tissues or organs to replace damaged ones

region *n.* ❶ a division or area with or without definite boundaries ❷a field of interest or activity ❸a part of the body

register Ⅰ *v.* ❶ write down in a list; record officially ❷ make sth. known publicly, especially your opinion Ⅱ *n.* ❶ a list or record of names, facts, etc. ❶(a book containing) an official record or list

regret Ⅰ *v.* be sorry for the loss of Ⅱ *n.* ❶ a feeling of sadness at the loss of sth.; a feeling of sorrow ❷a feeling of annoyance because of sth. done; a polite reply to refuse an invitation

regrettable *adj.* that is to be regretted that you are sorry about

regular *adj.* coming, happening or done again and again at even intervals every time

regularity *n.* the state or quality of being regular

regularly *adv.* at regular times

regulate *v.* keep at some standard; adjust; control by rule, principle or system

regulation *n.* ❶ the act of controlling sth. by rule, principle or system of affairs ❷an official rule or order

rehearsal *n.* ❶ the action or process of rehearsing ❷ a trial performance of a play

rehearse *v.* practise for public performance

reign Ⅰ *v.* hold office as a monarch Ⅱ *n.* the period of dominance

rein *n.* a long narrow band usually of leather, by which a horse, or sometimes a young child, is controlled and guided

reinforce *v.* ❶make stronger by adding or supplying more men or materials ❷ increase the amount, size or the thickness of sth. so that it supports more weight

reinforcement *n.* ❶ the act of making sth. stronger ❷(*pl.*) more men sent to strengthen an army

reject *v.* ❶ refuse to take, accept or believe ❷ throw away, cast aside as useless

rejection *n.* the act of refusing to accept

rejoin[1] *v.* ❶ join sth. together again ❷ return to sth.; join sb. or sth. again after leaving it

rejoin[2] *v.* answer; reply

relate *v.* ❶tell; give an account of ❷show or make a connection between two or more things

R

related *adj.* ❶connected with sb. or sth. ❷connected by birth or marriage

relation *n.* ❶the connection between two or more people, etc. ❷a person who is connected to another by blood or marriage; relative; kinship ❸the action of telling a story; sth. narrated

relationship *n.* ❶ the state of being related ❷a family connection

relative Ⅰ *adj.* ❶ having relation with each other ❷ referring to an earlier noun, clause or sentence ❸comparative; compared with another Ⅱ *n.* a person connected by blood or marriage

relatively *adv.* quite; compared to other people or thing

relativity *n.* ❶ the state or quality of being relative ❷ the relationship between time, size and mass, which is said to change with increased speed

relax *v.* make tenser; cause to become tighter

relaxation *n.* ❶ the act of resting and enjoying oneself ❷sth. done for rest and amusement

R

relaxed *adj.* ❶ free from tension and anxiety easy in manner ❷(especially of a group, situation or surroundings) comfortable and informal; restful

relaxing *adj.* making one feel relaxed

release Ⅰ *v.* set free; liberate Ⅱ *n.* the state of releasing or being released

relevant *adj.* connected with what is being discussed

reliable *adj.* that can be trusted or relied on

relief *n.* ❶the feeling of happiness that you have when sth. unpleasant has stopped and will not happen again ❷ money or food given to people in need of them ❸a person appointed to go on duty ❹a method of carving or moulding in which a design stands out from a flat surface

relieve *v.* ❶ lessen(pain or trouble) ❷ bring aid to; help ❸ take one's turn on duty

relieved *adj.* feeling relief; no longer worried

religion *n.* ❶ the belief in one or more gods ❷a particular system of belief and the worship, behaviour, etc.

religious *adj.* ❶of or concerning religion ❷much interested in religion; devoted to the worship of god or gods

religiously *adv.* ❶ in a careful and thorough way ❷connected with religion in a way

relish Ⅰ *n.* great enjoyment, especially of food; pleasure and satisfaction Ⅱ *v.* enjoy; be pleased and satisfied with

relive *v.* experience again, especially in the imagination

reload *v.* load (a gun) again

relocate *v.* move to or establish in a new place

reluctant *adj.* unwilling; offering resistance

rely *v.* ❶ depend on; look to (sb.) for help ❷trust sb. or sth.

remain *v.* ❶ be left after sth. has been removed, taken, etc. ❷stay; last without changing; continue

remains *n.* ❶the part or parts that is/are left ❷ a dead body ❸ historical or archaeological relics

remake Ⅰ *v.* make (especially a film) again Ⅱ *n.* a thing remade

remark Ⅰ *v.* ❶explicit notice or observe ❷say sth. by way of comment; give view Ⅱ *n.* ❶explicit notice or observation ❷ comment or sth. that you say about sth.

remarkable *adj.* worth mentioning, especially because unusual or noticeable

remarry *v.* marry again

remedy Ⅰ *n.* a treatment or sth. else to cure a disease, etc. such as medicine Ⅱ *v.* ❶ cure a disease or relieve pain ❷ correct or improve sth.

remember *v.* ❶ keep in mind ❷ bring back to mind; recall

remind *v.* ❶bring sth. to the attention of sb. ❷cause sb. to remember

reminder *n.* sth. that makes one remember

remit *v.* ❶ send (money, etc.) to a person or place, especially by post ❷free sb. from

remote *adj.* ❶far off in distance or time ❷ being distantly related by blood or marriage ❸cold and unfriendly; aloof ❸ slight ; not very great

removal *n.* ❶ the state of removing, or being removed ❷ the transfer of furniture, etc. when moving house

remove *v.* take away; take off

rename *v.* give a new name to

render *v.* ❶ give sb. sth. in return or exchange ❷offer sb. sth. ❸send in (an account for payment) ❹ give a performance of ❺ express in another language ❻ cause to be; make ❼ melt down (fat), typically in order to clarify it

renew *v.* ❶make new or fresh again ❷ begin again ❸obtain a further period of lending for sth.

renown *n.* fame and respect

rent Ⅰ *v.* ❶pay a sum of money for the use of property or goods ❷allow the use of property or goods in return for a sum of money Ⅱ *n.* a regular payment for the use of property

reorganize *v.* organize again or in a new way

repair Ⅰ *v.* ❶return (restore) to good condition; fix or mend ❷put right again; make up for Ⅱ *n.* the action of mending sth.

repay *v.* ❶pay back (money) ❷make a return for sth. or to sb. ; give in return

repayment *n.* the act of paying back money that you have borrowed from a bank, etc.

repeat *v.* ❶ say, do, make or perform again ❷say over from memory; recite

repeatedly *adv.* again and again

repel *v.* ❶drive away (as if) by force ❷ cause strong feelings of dislike

repetition *n.* ❶the fact of doing or saying the same thing many times ❷ sth. repeated ❸a copy; an imitation

replace *v.* ❶ put back in its former or proper place again ❷take the place of; fill the place with another

replacement *n.* ❶the action or process of replacing sb. or sth. ❷sb. or sth. that takes the place of another

replay *v.* play again

reply Ⅰ *v.* give an answer; answer Ⅱ *n.* an act of replying

report *v.* give a spoken or written account

of (sth. seen, heard, done, etc.)

reportedly *adv.* according to what is said

reporter *n.* a person who reports for a newspaper, for radio or TV

represent *v.* ❶ act or speak for ❷ stand for; symbolize

representation *n.* ❶ the act or condition of representing or being represented ❷ sth. that represents ❸ (usually *pl.*) a strong appeal; arguments or protest

representative Ⅰ *adj.* ❶ being an example; typical ❷ carried out by elected people Ⅱ *n.* a person who represents others

repress *v.* ❶ bring under control ❷ put down

reproach Ⅰ *v.* find fault with sb. Ⅱ *n.* ❶ the expression of disapproval or disappointment ❷ the state of disgrace or discredit

reproduce *v.* ❶ bring about a natural increase; give birth to ❷ cause to be heard, seen, etc. again

reproduction *n.* ❶ the process of reproducing ❷ sth. reproduced; a copy of sth.

reproof *n.* blame; words of blame

reprove *v.* blame; find fault with; rebuke

republic *n.* a country that is governed by a president and politicians elected by the people and where there is no king or queen

republican *adj.* belonging to a republic

reputation *n.* ❶ the beliefs of opinions that are generally held about sb. or sth. ❷ the state of being held in high repute

request Ⅰ *v.* ❶ politely or formally ask for ❷ politely ask sb. to do sth. Ⅱ *n.* ❶ an act of asking politely or formally for sth. ❷ a thing that is asked for ❸ an instruction to a computer to provide information or to perform another function

require *v.* ❶ need; want; call for ❷ demand; order

requirement *n.* sth. that is needed or that is demanded as necessary

rescue Ⅰ *v.* save from danger or harm Ⅱ *n.* an act of saving or being saved from danger or distress

research Ⅰ *n.* a careful study or investigation Ⅱ *v.* do study or investigation

resemblance *n.* the fact of being similar

resemble *v.* be like; be similar to

resent *v.* feel angry or bitter at

resentful *adj.* feeling bitter and indignant about sth.

reservation *n.* ❶ the act of reserving sth.; a limiting condition ❷ a room, etc. in a hotel to be kept for you ❸ an area of land reserved for a special purpose

reserve Ⅰ *v.* ❶ store; keep back unused, but available if needed ❷ have or keep for sb. (or sth.) ❸ order; book Ⅱ *n.* ❶ sth. that has been stored for later use ❷ a feeling that you do not want to accept or agree to sth.

reservoir *n.* ❶ a natural or artificial lake for keeping water ❷ a large supply (of facts or knowledge)

resident Ⅰ *n.* a person who resides in a place Ⅱ *adj.* living in a particular place

resign *v.* ❶ give up (a job or claim) ❷ submit oneself passively; accept as inevitable

resist *v.* ❶ fight back when attacked ❷refuse to accept sth. and try to stop it from happening

resistance *v.* ❶the act of opposing sb. or sth. ❷the force that stops sth. moving or makes it move more slowly ❸ the power or ability not to be affected by sth.

resistant Ⅰ *adj.* not affected by sth. ; able to resist sth. Ⅱ *n.* a person who resists

resolute *adj.* fixed in determination or purpose

resolution *n.* ❶ the quality of being resolute or determined ❷ a formal decision made by a group vote ❸the act of solving or settling a doubt, question, discord, etc.

resort Ⅰ *v.* ❶make use of sth. as a means of achieving sth. ❷go (to a place, etc.) often Ⅱ *n.* ❶ the act of using sth. ❷ a place which people often go to for rest or pleasure

resource *n.* ❶ any of the possessions or qualities of a person, an organization, or a country ❷cleverness in finding a way to avoid difficulties; the practical ability

respect Ⅰ *v.* ❶ honour or admire sb. or sth. ❷ agree to recognize and abide by Ⅱ *n.* ❶the feeling of admiration for sb. or sth. ❷(*pl.*) regards; polite greetings

respectable *adj.* ❶ deserving respect; that should be respected ❷ of good character and good social position; having the qualities associated with such positions

respecting *prep.* concerning; with respect to

respective *adj.* belonging separately to each one mentioned

respectively *adj.* separately or in turn, and in the order mentioned

respond *v.* act in answer to the action of another; reply

response *n.* an answer and a reaction to sth. that has been said, etc.

responsibility *n.* ❶the condition of being responsible ❷sth. for which a person is responsible; duty

responsible *adj.* (of a person) legally or morally liable for carrying out a duty; in charge of

rest[1] *n.* what is left; the ones that still remain

rest[2] Ⅰ *n.* (a period of) freedom from activity or from sth. tiring or worrying Ⅱ *v.* relax, sleep or do nothing after a period of activity or illness

restaurant *n.* a place where meals can be bought and eaten

restful *adj.* ❶peaceful; giving a feeling of rest ❷(of colour, music, etc.) causing a person to feel calm or pleasant

restless *adj.* ❶ without rest or sleep ❷ never quite; unwilling or unable to stay still

restore *v.* ❶ give back; return ❷ bring back to a former condition or place ❸ repair or reconstruct

restrain *v.* prevent sb. from doing sth.

restrict *v.* put a limit on sb. or sth.

restriction *n.* the act of limiting or controlling sb. or sth.

result Ⅰ *n.* ❶a consequence, an effect, or an outcome of sth. ❷ sth. found by calculation; answer to a mathematical problem, etc. Ⅱ *v.* ❶be a result of; have as a result (from, in) ❷ bring about; have as a consequence

resume *v.* ❶ go on after stopping for a time; begin again ❷ take or occupy again

retail Ⅰ *v.* ❶ sell goods in small quantities ❷ repeat to others in turn Ⅱ *n.* the sale of goods to customers in small quantities Ⅲ *adv.* being sold in such a way

retain *v.* ❶ keep; continue to have or hold ❷ employ (especially a lawyer or adviser) to act for one by paying in advance

retell *v.* tell again; tell in a different way or in a different language

retire *v.* ❶ give up or cause to leave one's work or position ❷ go to bed ❸ (of an army) retreat from an enemy or an attacking position

retired *adj.* having stopped working, usually because of old age

retirement *n.* ❶ a case or the act of retiring ❷ the period of the life after a person has stopped work at a particular age

R

retort Ⅰ *v.* reply quickly and sharply Ⅱ *n.* a sharp reply

retrace *v.* go back over

retract *v.* ❶ pull sth. or be pulled back or in ❷ withdraw a statement or accusation ❸ go back on an agreement or promise

return Ⅰ *v.* ❶ come or go back to a former place ❷ give or send back; repay Ⅱ n ❶ the act or an example of coming back ❷ the act of giving, putting, or sending sth. back

reunion *n.* ❶ a gathering of old friends, former colleagues, etc. after separation ❷ the state of being brought together again

reunite *v.* bring or come together again

reveal *v.* ❶ allow to be seen; display ❷ make known

revenue *n.* money coming in (especially to the government from taxes, etc.)

reversal *n.* ❶ a change to an opposite direction, position, or course of action ❷ an adverse change of fortune

reverse Ⅰ *n.* a complete change of direction or action Ⅱ *v.* ❶ move backwards ❷ change sth. completely so that it is the opposite Ⅲ *adj.* opposite

review Ⅰ *v.* ❶ look again at sth. you have studied ❷ think about past events Ⅱ *n.* an act of thinking about past events

revise *v.* ❶ read carefully in order to correct errors ❷ change opinions or plans

revive *v.* ❶ come and bring back to life ❷ come or bring back to a fresh condition

revolt Ⅰ *v.* ❶ rebel; rise in rebellion ❷ fill with disgust or horror Ⅱ *n.* a protest against authority, etc.; the state of being revolted

revolution *n.* ❶ an overthrow of an established government or political system ❷ a movement around some point in a circle ❸ a complete change

revolutionary Ⅰ *adj.* ❶ of a revolution; connected with a revolution ❷ bringing or causing great changes Ⅱ *n.* a person who works for or engages in political revolution

revolve *v.* ❶ (cause to) go round in a circle ❷ turn over in the mind; think about all sides of (a problem) ❸ recur at periodic intervals

reward Ⅰ *n.* a return made for sth. done; payment offered Ⅱ *v.* give sth. to sb. for services, efforts, or successes

rhyme Ⅰ *n.* ❶ a short poem where lines end in the same sounds ❷ a word that has the same sound as another ❸ correspondence of sound between words or the endings of words Ⅱ *v.* put together to form a rhyme; be in rhyme

rhythm *n.* the movement with regular repetition of a beat, accent, rise and fall; repetition of musical beats; the arrangement of syllables or cadences in a line of poetry

ribbon *n.* a long narrow strip of silk material used in decorating clothes, tying hair, etc.

rice *n.* a plant growing in water as a source of food ; the grains of this plant

rich *adj.* ❶ having much money, land, goods, etc. ; wealthy ❷ containing and producing much; abundant ❸ fine; splendid; costly ❹ (of food) containing a large proportion of fat, spices, sugar, etc. ❺ (of colours, sounds, etc.) full; deep; mellow ❻ highly entertaining; giving opportunities for humor

rid *v.* make free from

ride Ⅰ *v.* ❶ sit on and control the movement of an animal (especially a horse) or a bicycle, or motor cycle ❷ take part in as a passenger Ⅱ *n.* a journey on horseback, a bicycle, etc. , or in public conveyance

rider *n.* a person who rides

right Ⅰ *adj.* ❶ morally good, justified, or acceptable ❷ true or correct as a fact ❸ according to what is correct for a particular situation or thing ❹ in a satisfactory or normal state ❺ of, on or towards the side of the body that is towards the east when a person faces north Ⅱ *n.* ❶ the right side ❷ sth. that is good, just, etc. Ⅲ *adv.* ❶ completely ❷ correctly ❸ on or to the right ❹ properly; satisfactorily

rightly *adv.* ❶ correctly or properly ❷ in accordance with justice or what is morally right

rigid *adj.* ❶ stiff, unbending ❷ strict; not to be changed

ring[1] Ⅰ *v.* ❶ cause (a bell) to sound ❷ be filled with sound ❸ telephone (someone) Ⅱ *n.* ❶ the sound of a bell or a bell-like sound ❷ a certain quality that words, sounds, etc. have

ring[2] *n.* ❶ a small circular band worn on a finger as an ornament or a token of marriage or authority ❷ a circular band of any material

rip Ⅰ *v.* divide or make a hole in (sth.) by pulling sharply Ⅱ *n.* an uneven or ragged tear or cut

ripe *adj.* ❶ full-grown and ready to be gathered or eaten; mature ❷ ready or suitable for sth. to happen ❸ (of cheese or wine) full matured or developed

ripen *v.* become ripe; make ripe

ripple Ⅰ *n.* a very little wave on the surface of liquid Ⅱ *v.* cause to move in small waves

rise Ⅰ *v.* ❶ appear above the horizon; move upward; go (come) up ❷ increase; go higher in price, quality, sound, degree, etc. ❸ get up from a lying, sitting, kneeling position ❹ get out of bed Ⅱ *n.* an upward movement; increase

risen *adj.* having moved to a higher position

risk Ⅰ *v.* expose in a dangerous situation Ⅱ *n.* the possibility of loss, harm or danger

risky *adj.* full of risk; dangerous

rite Ⅰ *n.* a ceremony, especially a religious ceremony Ⅱ *adj.* connected with rites

ritual Ⅰ *n.* ❶ a series of actions used in a religious or other ceremony; a particular form of this ❷ a procedure that is regularly followed ritual Ⅱ *adj.* to do with or done as a ritual

rival Ⅰ *n.* a person who competes with another Ⅱ *adj.* of competitor or competition Ⅲ *v.* compete with

river *n.* a large stream of water

road *n.* a way between places; highway; a specially prepared way, publicly or privately owned

roam *v.* go about with no special plan or aim; wander

R

roar Ⅰ *v.* make or utter a loud deep and prolonged sound Ⅱ *n.* a loud, deep and prolonged sound

roast Ⅰ *v.* ❶ cook with dry heat, as in an oven or near hot coals ❷ dry by exposing to heat Ⅱ *n.* ❶ a joint of meat roasted ❷ an outdoor picnic at which food is roasted

rob *v.* ❶ take away by force; steal ❷ deprive a person of (what is legally due to him)

robber *n.* a person who commits robbery

robbery *n.* the act of stealing money or goods from a person, shop, etc.

robot *n.* a machine made in imitation of a human being; a mechanical device that does routine work in response of commands

rock Ⅰ *n.* (a type of) stone forming part of the Earth's surface Ⅱ *v.* (cause to) move regularly backwards and forwards or from side to side

rocket Ⅰ *n.* ❶ an engine with long round sides that pushes a spacecraft up into the space ❷ fireworks for aerial display Ⅱ *v.* increase very rapidly

rocky *adj.* ❶ of, like or made of rock ❷ full of rocks

rod *n.* ❶ a thin, straight piece of wood or metal ❷ (the ～) a stick used for punishing

role *n.* ❶ a character in a play ❷ the part played in activities; a task or duty in an undertaking

roll Ⅰ *v.* ❶ move along by turning over and over ❷ wrap or rotate sth. around and around upon itself, or around sth. else Ⅱ *n.* ❶ a rolling movement, over and over or to and for sideways ❷ a list of names

romance Ⅰ *n.* ❶ an exciting and adventurous story ❷ a love story; a love affair Ⅱ *v.* carry on a love affair

romantic *adj.* ❶ showing a strong feeling of love ❷ dealing with or suggesting adventure or love ❸ fanciful; not practical

roof Ⅰ *n.* the top covering of a building or vehicle Ⅱ *v.* cover with a roof

room Ⅰ *n.* ❶ a division of a building, with its own walls, floor and ceiling ❷ space that could be filled, or that's enough for any purpose Ⅱ *v.* occupy a room or rooms of other persons' house; lodge

roost Ⅰ *n.* a bar, pole on which birds rest Ⅱ *v.* sleep or rest on a roost

root Ⅰ *n.* ❶the part of a plant that grows beneath the ground ❷ the part from which sth. grows and develops; the basic cause of a thing Ⅱ *v.* cause to send out roots and begin to grow

rooted *adj.* ❶developing from or being strongly influenced by sth. ❷fixed in a place; not moving or changing

rope Ⅰ *n.* ❶a thick, strong cord made by twisting finer cords or wires together ❷ (the ～) the cord used in hanging; punishment by hanging ❸a number of things strung together Ⅱ *v.* tie or fasten with a rope

rose Ⅰ *n.* a kind of brightly-coloured, usually sweet-scented flower Ⅱ *adj.* pinkish-red; pink in colour

rosy *adj.* ❶rose-coloured, deep pink ❷ promising or hopeful

rot Ⅰ *v.* (cause to) decay, go bad or spoil Ⅱ *n.* the process or condition of decaying

rotate *v.* ❶move round a central point ❷ take turns or come in succession

rotten *adj.* ❶decayed; having gone bad ❷very bad; very unpleasant

rough Ⅰ *adj.* ❶not smooth; not level ❷ not gentle; rude Ⅱ *n.* a violent, noisy man Ⅲ *v.* make untidy or uneven

round Ⅰ *prep.* so as to enclose, surround, etc. Ⅱ *adv.* on all sides; in circular motion Ⅲ *adj.* shaped like a ball, circle or ring Ⅳ *v.* make round

rouse *v.* ❶ wake up; cause to be more active, interested or excited ❷stop being inactive and start doing sth.

route Ⅰ *n.* a way or course to travel from one place to another Ⅱ *v.* plan a route for

routine Ⅰ *n.* a fixed regular way of doing sth. Ⅱ *adj.* usual; ordinary

row[1] *n.* a number of things or people arranged a line

row[2] Ⅰ *v.* ❶move (a boat) using oars ❷ carry in a rowboat Ⅱ *n.* (a ～) a trip in a rowing boat

royal *adj.* ❶of or concerning a king or queen ❷magnificent; splendid

rub Ⅰ *v.* ❶ move one thing back and forth against another, or on the surface; make clean or dry by doing this ❷cause irritation by rubbing Ⅱ *n.* ❶the act of rubbing a surface ❷difficulty; a point at which doubt arises

rubber *n.* ❶ a strong elastic substance made from the juice of certain plants ❷a piece of rubber used to remove pencil marks, etc.

rubbish *n.* ❶waste stuff of no use ❷silly words or thoughts; nonsense

ruby *n.* ❶a clear, hard and red precious stone ❷the colour of this stone; a deep red colour

ruddy *adj.* looking red and healthy

rude *adj.* ❶rough; impolite ❷primitive; roughly made; simple; in the nature state

rudiment *n.* (usually *pl.*) first things to be learnt in a subject

rug *n.* ❶a piece of covering for a floor (usually made of wool or animal skin) ❷a thick, warm piece of material which can be put over the legs when travelling, etc.

ruin Ⅰ *v.* destroy or damage sth. that it loses its value, etc. Ⅱ *n.* an extreme damage; the state of being decayed, destroyed or collapsed

rule Ⅰ *n.* ❶ a law or statement which guides or controls behavior or action ❷ the government or control of a country or a group of people, etc. Ⅱ *v.* ❶ control; govern; have authority (over) ❷ (especially in law) give an official decision (on)

ruler *n.* ❶ a person who governs ❷ a straight strip of wood or metal, etc. used for measuring or for drawing straight lines

ruling Ⅰ *adj.* ❶ exercising control or authority ❷ predominant Ⅱ *n.* an official decision

rumble Ⅰ *v.* (cause to) make rumbling sounds Ⅱ *n.* a rumbling sound

rumo(u)r Ⅰ *n.* a story which people are repeating, which may not be true Ⅱ *v.* (usually passive) be reported as a rumour

run Ⅰ *v.* ❶ go on with quick steps ❷ go away in a hurry; escape ❸ (of a car, train, ship, etc.) be moved or driven ❹ be in charge of or organize a business or an activity Ⅱ *n.* ❶ an act or period of running on foot ❷ the instance or period of travelling by car, train, etc. ❸ a space for domestic animals, fowls ❹ a point scored in the game of cricket or baseball

runaway *n.* a person, horse, etc. that runs away

running Ⅰ *n.* an act of sb. or sth. that runs Ⅱ *adj.* ❶ done while running ❷ without a break; continuous ❸ flowing

runway *n.* an area of hard surface in an airfield on which planes land and take off

rural *adj.* connected with the country

rush Ⅰ *v.* ❶ move suddenly and hastily in the stated direction ❷ do (sth.) as soon as possible ❸ take sb. or sth. to a place quickly Ⅱ *n.* ❶ a rapid, headlong movement; a sudden swift advance ❷ a situation in which you need to go somewhere or do sth. very quickly Ⅲ *adj.* hasty or busy

rust Ⅰ *n.* reddish-brown coating formed on iron by the action of water and air; the colour of this Ⅱ *v.* become covered with rust

rustle Ⅰ *n.* a soft sound, like the sound leaves make in the wind Ⅱ *v.* ❶ make this sound ❷ cause sth. to make this sound

rusty *adj.* ❶ affected with rust ❷ rust-coloured ❸ weakened by lack of use or practice ❹ (of a voice) croaking

ruthless *adj.* without mercy or kind feelings; having no pity

S s

sacred *adj.* ❶ of God; connected with religion ❷solemn

sacrifice Ⅰ *n.* the offering of sth. precious to a god or the thing offered Ⅱ *v.* give up sth. that is important to you for another person

sad *adj.* unhappy; causing unhappy feelings

sadness *n.* the feeling of being sad

safe Ⅰ *adj.* ❶free from or protected from danger ❷ of very little risk of loss or failure Ⅱ *n.* a strong box in which money and other valuables are kept

safeguard Ⅰ *n.* anything that serves as a protection from harm, risk or danger Ⅱ *v.* protect; keep safe; guard against hurt, danger or attack

safety *n.* the state of being safe; the state of freeing from danger

sage Ⅰ *n.* a very wise man Ⅱ *adj.* having or showing wisdom or good judgement

sail Ⅰ *n.* ❶a sheet of large cloth used to catch the wind and move a boat ❷ a sailing ship ❸a voyage by ship Ⅱ *v.* ❶ move over the sea, a lake, etc. ❷direct a boat with sails

sailing *n.* ❶ the skill of directing the course of a ship ❷the sport of riding in or directing a small boat with sails ❸an occasion of a ship leaving a port

sailor *n.* a member of a ship's crew; seaman

saint *n.* a person acknowledged as holy or virtuous, because of the way they have lived and died

sake *n.* cause; aim; purpose

salad *n.* a dish usually consisting of raw green vegetables tossed with a dressing

salary *n.* a fixed payment for regular work

sale *n.* ❶ the act of selling things ❷ the act of selling at lower prices

saliva *n.* a liquid that comes into the mouth to help chewing, etc.

salmon *n.* ❶a large silver-coloured fish, valued for food ❷the colour of its flesh; orange-pink

salon *n.* ❶an elegant drawing room ❷an assemblage of persons, usually of social or intellectual distinction, who frequent the home of a particular person

salt Ⅰ *n.* ❶a kind of white powder which has the taste of sea water ❷a chemical compound of a metal and an acid ❸ an experienced sailor Ⅱ *v.* give salt to; preserved with salt Ⅲ *adj.* containing, full of or tasting of salt; salty

saltwater *adj.* of or living in salty water

or the sea

salty *adj.* ❶ of, containing, or tasting of salt ❷ (of talk, stories, etc.) slightly improper in an amusing or exciting way; racy

salute Ⅰ *n.* a formal greeting of respect Ⅱ *v.* ❶ greet in a friendly way ❷ show or state the admiration for sb. or their achievements

salvage Ⅰ *n.* ❶ the act of saving things from damage or danger ❷ the property be saved ❸ waste material that can be used again after being processed Ⅱ *v.* save a sick or wounded person, etc.

salvation *n.* ❶ the act of saving; the state of having been saved from sin and its consequences ❷ the state of being saved or preserved from harm, loss, disaster, etc.

samba *n.* (a piece of music for) a quick dance of Brazilian origin

same Ⅰ *adj.* being one person or thing; alike in every way Ⅱ *pron.* the same thing

sameness *n.* ❶ the state of being the same; very close likeness; similarity ❷ the quality of wearisome constancy, routine, and lack of variety

sample Ⅰ *n.* a part to show what the whole is like Ⅱ *v.* take a sample (samples) of; taste a small amount of food or drink

sampling *n.* ❶ the taking of a sample or samples ❷ a sample

sanctuary *n.* ❶ a holy or sacred place, especially a church or temple ❷ a place of refuge ❸ an area where birds are protected by law

sand Ⅰ *n.* ❶ tiny grains of crushed or worn-down rock ❷ (*pl.*) a wide area of sand Ⅱ *v.* cover or sprinkle with sand

sandwich Ⅰ *n.* two slices of bread with meat, cheese, etc. between them Ⅱ *v.* put sth. between two others

sandy *adj.* ❶ containing sand; filled or covered with sand ❷ yellowish red

sane *adj.* ❶ healthy in mind; not mad ❷ reasonable and sensible

sanitary *adj.* ❶ clean ❷ of, concerned with the protection of health

sanitation *n.* arrangements to protect health

sanity *n.* the state of being sane

Santa Claus *n.* a person who, small children are told, puts toys in their stockings by night at Christmas

sardine *n.* a type of small sea fish (often preserved in oil in a tin and eaten as food)

satellite *n.* ❶ a smaller body that revolves around a planet ❷ a man-made object fired into space round the Earth ❸ a state controlled by a more powerful neighbouring ❹ a follower or attendant upon a person of importance

satire *n.* ❶ (a work of) literature, theatre, etc. intended to show the foolishness or evil of some person, organization, or practice in an amusing way ❷ a piece of writing that does this

satisfaction *n.* ❶ the act of satisfying or the state of being satisfied ❷ pleasure or contentment

satisfactory *adj.* good enough for a purpose; giving satisfaction

satisfied *adj.* contented or pleased

because you have got or achieved sth.

satisfy *v.* make contented; give sb. what he wants or needs

Saturday *n.* the day after Friday and before Sunday in a week

sauce Ⅰ *n.* ❶ liquid preparation served with food to give flavor ❷ talk or behaviour that is annoying or impudent Ⅱ *v.* be impudent to

sauna *n.* ❶a small room used as a hot air or steam bath for cleaning and refreshing the body ❷ a steam bath in such a room

sausage *n.* chopped meat cooked in a tube of thin skin

savage[1] Ⅰ *adj.* ❶in an uncivilized state ❷ fierce; cruel ❸ out of temper Ⅱ *n.* ❶ a person who belongs to a tribe that is simple and not developed; a cruel person ❷ a member of a people regarded as primitive and uncivilized

save Ⅰ *v.* ❶make or keep safe from loss, injury, etc. ❷ store up; keep for future use ❸avoid wasting or using more than necessary Ⅱ *prep.* except

saving *n.* ❶ an act or way of using less money, time, etc. ❷ the amount of money saved up

savo(u)r Ⅰ *n.* a taste or smell; a flavor Ⅱ *v.* taste or smell with pleasure

saw Ⅰ *n.* a type of tool with toothed edge, used for cutting wood, metal, etc. Ⅱ *v.* use a saw to cut sth.

say Ⅰ *v.* ❶ pronounce; speak; utter ❷ express in words; tell; state; declare ❸ indicate; show ❹suppose; assume

saying *n.* ❶a well-known statement that most people believe is wise; a proverb ❷ the act of making a statement

scalar[1] Ⅰ *adj.* ❶in, on or of a scale ❷ designating or of a quantity that has magnitude but no direction in space Ⅱ *n.* a scalar quantity

scald Ⅰ *v.* ❶ burn with hot liquid or stream ❷ heat (a liquid, e. g. milk) almost to the point of boiling Ⅱ *n.* a burn from hot liquid or steam

scale *n.* ❶a set of regularly spaced marks made on sth. for use as a measure; a system of measurement ❷ a set of numbers or standards for measuring or comparing ❸a group of notes going up or down in order ❹ the size of measurements on a map, etc. compared with the real size of sth. shown by it ❺ the size of an activity

scan *v.* ❶look at closely; examine with care ❷look at quickly without careful reading ❸ fit into a particular rhythm or meter

scandal *n.* ❶an unkind talk about sb. ❷ an event or action that is thought morally or legally wrong and causes general public outrage ❸the outrage or anger caused by such an event or action

scanner *n.* a device for examining, reading or monitoring sth. using beams of light sound

scant *adj.* hardly any; not very much

scar Ⅰ *n.* a mark left by a healed cut, wound, burn, or sore Ⅱ *v.* ❶mark with a scar ❷form a scar

scarce *adj.* ❶not enough; not plentiful ❷ rare; seldom

scare Ⅰ *v.* frighten; be frightened; cause to do sth. by frightening Ⅱ *n.* a (sudden) fright; a frightened condition

scarf *n.* a piece of cloth, worn about the neck, shoulders, or head

scarlet Ⅰ *n.* a very bright red colour Ⅱ *adj.* very bright red

scatter *v.* ❶ throw here and there ❷ send, drive in different directions ❸ go in different directions

scattered *adj.* situated at various points apart from each other

scene *n.* ❶ the setting or place of an incident ❷ view, landscape

scenery *n.* ❶ landscape; general natural features of a district ❷ the printed backdrop on a theatrical stage

scenic *adj.* having fine natural scenery

schedule Ⅰ *n.* ❶ a planned list or order of things to be done, dealt with, etc. ❷ a formal list of prices, details, etc. Ⅱ *v.* plan or arrange sth. for a definite time or date

scheme Ⅰ *n.* ❶ a plan or arrangement ❷ a secret and dishonest plan Ⅱ *v.* make dishonest plans

scholar *n.* ❶ a person with much knowledge ❷ a university student holding a scholarship

S

scholarly *adj.* ❶ involving or relating to serious academic study ❷ having or showing knowledge and learning; devoting to academic pursuits

scholarship *n.* ❶ a grant of money to pay for a person's education, usually awarded on the basis of academic achievement ❷ the work of scholars, advanced academic work

school *n.* ❶ an institution for educating children ❷ lessons; the time when teaching is given ❸ a group of people who share the same or similar ideas in their works, etc. ❹ a department in college or university that teach a particular subject

science *n.* knowledge learned from research and arranged in an ordered system

scientific *adj.* ❶ of science ❷ following the rules of science

scientist *n.* a person who has expert knowledge of some branch of science

scissors *n.* a cutting instrument with two blades and two handles fastened together

scoop Ⅰ *n.* a kitchen tool like a small shovel Ⅱ *v.* take up or hollow up with a scoop

scope *n.* ❶ the range of action or observation ❷ the opportunity or possibility to do or achieve sth.

score Ⅰ *n.* ❶ a record of points made in a game or test, etc. ❷ a cut, scratch or mark made on a surface Ⅱ *v.* gain (a point) in a game

scorn Ⅰ *n.* a feeling that sb. or sth. deserves no respect Ⅱ *v.* feel or show contempt for

scrap Ⅰ *n.* ❶ a small piece of sth., especially cloth, paper, etc. ❷ bits of uneaten food ❸ a picture or paragraph cut from a periodical, etc. for a collection ❹ any waste articles or material Ⅱ *v.* throw away or discard sth. that is no longer practical or useful

scratch Ⅰ *v.* ❶ make lines on or in a surface; hurt with sth. pointed or sharp ❷ rub to relieve itching ❸ withdraw from a game, competition, etc. ❹ score or mark the surface of sth. with a sharp or pointed object Ⅱ *n.* a mark, injury or sound made by scratching

scream Ⅰ *v.* cry out loudly and shrilly, as from pain or fear Ⅱ *n.* a loud, shrill cry or noise

screen Ⅰ *n.* ❶ the white or silver surface on which a picture is projected for viewing ❷ sth. that serves to divide, conceal, or protect, as a movable room partition Ⅱ *v.* conceal or protect sth. from view

script *n.* ❶ a handwriting as distinguished from a print ❷ a writing done by hand, especially as in English with the letters of words joined

scripture *n.* ❶ sacred writings that are regarded as holy in a religion ❷ the Bible

sculpture Ⅰ *n.* ❶ the making of three-dimensional works of art in stone, clay, metal, wood, etc. ❷ works created in this manner Ⅱ *v.* make or represent (a form) by carving, casting, or other shaping techniques

sea *n.* ❶ the continuous body of salt water that covers most of the surface of the earth ❷ a vast number, expanse or extent

seal[1] Ⅰ *v.* close or fasten sth. tightly Ⅱ *n.* a piece of wax, soft metal or paper that is placed across the opening of sth. to stop people from opening it without permission

seal[2] *n.* a large animal with a rounded body and flat legs called flippers, living in and near the sea

search Ⅰ *v.* make a thorough examination in order to find sth. Ⅱ *n.* an act of looking for sth.

seashore *n.* an area of sandy, stony, or rocky land bordering and level with the sea

season Ⅰ *n.* ❶ one of the four equal divisions of the year according to the weather ❷ a special time of the year suitable or normal for sth. Ⅱ *v.* ❶ improve the flavour of food (with salt, pepper, etc.) ❷ soften; moderate ❸ make more acceptable or suitable by adding sth. else

seasonal *adj.* ❶ happening or needed during a particular season; varying with the seasons ❷ typical of or suitable for the time of year, especially Christmas

seasoned *adj.* experienced and competent because of training and practice

seasoning *n.* a substance used to season food

seat Ⅰ *n.* ❶ sth. that may be sat on as a chair ❷ an official position as a member of a committee, organization, etc. Ⅱ *v.* sit down in a place

second Ⅰ *adj.* next after the first Ⅱ *n.* ❶ a person or thing that comes next to the first ❷ a length of time equal to 1/60 of a minute Ⅲ *v.* give support or one's approval to

secondary Ⅰ *adj.* ❶ immediately derived from what is primary ❷ inferior; less important than Ⅱ *n.* a person that acts in an auxiliary or subordinate capacity

second-hand *adj.* ❶ not new, already owned by someone else ❷ obtained from others, not based on personal observation, etc.

secret Ⅰ *adj.* kept or hidden from the knowledge of others Ⅱ *n.* sth. known by few persons or hidden

secretary *n.* ❶ a person employed to handle correspondence and do clerical work ❷ an officer of an organization ❸ the minister in charge of a government office

sect *n.* a group of people united by beliefs or opinions that differ from those more generally accepted

section Ⅰ *n.* ❶ a part, division or slice that result from cutting a solid along a plane ❷ one of a number of parts that can be put together as a whole ❸ a distinct part of a community, country, etc. Ⅱ *v.* separate or divide into parts

sector *n.* ❶ the part connected with that specified type of industry of a country's economy ❷ an area or portion that is distinct from others

secure Ⅰ *adj.* ❶free from danger; feeling confident and safe ❷certain and sure (to happen or succeed) Ⅱ *v.* cause to be firmly attached

S

security *n.* sth. that provides to protect sb. from danger or anxiety; measures or actions that take to make secure

sediment *n.* a matter that settles to bottom of a liquid

seduce *v.* ❶ persuade a person to have sexual intercourse with ❷ persuade sb. to do sth. wrong

see *v.* ❶ perceive with the eye; have the power of sight ❷ understand sth. ❸ receive (a person); call on; visit sb.

seed *n.* the small, hard part of a plant from which another plant can grow

seek *v.* ❶ look for or try to find ❷ ask for; go to request ❸ try; attempt

seem *v.* have or give the impression or appearance of being or doing

seeming *adj.* apparent but perhaps not real or genuine

seemingly *adv.* ❶ so as to give the impression of having a certain quality; apparently ❷ according to the facts as one knows them; as far as one knows

seemly *adj.* ❶ proper or suitable for a particular social situation ❷ of pleasing appearance; decent

seesaw Ⅰ *n.* a plank balanced on support at its center Ⅱ *v.* move up and down or to and from

segregate *v.* keep separate from others

seize *v.* ❶ take hold of sth. or sb. suddenly and forcibly ❷ take possession of (property, etc.) by law ❸ see cleverly and use ❹ have a sudden effect upon; overwhelm

seldom *adv.* not often, rarely

select *v.* choose from among a group of people or things; pick out

selection *n.* ❶ the act of choosing; a choice ❷ sth. to choose from ❸ a collection of things that have been selected

selective *adj.* ❶ chosen or choosing carefully ❷ involving or allowing a choice

self *n.* ❶ the total being of one person; the individual ❷ one's own interests, welfare, or advantage

self-control *n.* the ability to control oneself, in particular one's emotions and desires or the expression of them in one's behaviour, especially in difficult situations

selfish *adj.* caring too much for oneself and too little for others

sell *v.* ❶give in exchange for money ❷be on sale

seller *n.* ❶a person who sells sth. ❷sth. that is sold

semester *n.* a half of a school or university year

semifinal *n.* a match or round immediately preceding the final, as in a series of competitions

seminar *n.* a small group of advanced students engaged in special study

send *v.* ❶cause sth. to be carried to a place ❷tell sb. to do sth. or to go to a place ❸cause to become or behave in a particular way

senior Ⅰ *adj.* older; higher in rank or status Ⅱ *n.* a student in the final year in a university or high school

seniority *n.* ❶the fact of being older or of a higher rank than others ❷the rank that you have in a company because of the length of time you have worked there

sensation *n.* ❶a physical feeling that you have when sth. happens to your body ❷a feeling of deep interest and excitement

sensational *adj.* ❶causing excitement ❷of or relating to sensation

sense Ⅰ *n.* ❶ any of the functions of hearing, sight, smell, touch, and taste ❷the ability to understand and appreciate ❸ a consciousness to the presence or importance of sth. ❹the ability to judge external conditions Ⅱ *v.* feel sth. or be aware of sth.

sensibility *n.* ❶ the ability to feel or perceive ❷ (usually *pl.*) a person's feelings, especially delicate feelings

sensible *adj.* ❶showing reason or sound judgement ❷able to feel or perceive ❸ reasonable; practical

sensitive *adj.* ❶ quick to receive impressions ❷ (of photographic film, paper, etc.) affected by light ❸ easily hurt in the spirit; easily offended ❹able to respond to a very slight change

sensitivity *n.* the quality or degree of being sensitive

sensor *n.* a device that detects and responds to a signal or stimulus

sensory *adj.* of the senses or sensation

sentence Ⅰ *n.* ❶ a grammatical unit comprising a word or group of words that usually consists of at least one subject and a finite verb or verb phrase ❷the statement of a judicial decision to punish; the penalty which forms a part of such a statement Ⅱ *v.* state the penalty to be paid

sentiment *n.* ❶an attitude which is based on thoughts and feelings ❷ (usually *pl.*) an opinion about a specific matter; view ❸ thought or attitude based on emotion rather than reason

separate Ⅰ *adj.* not joined to sth. else Ⅱ *v.* move apart; (cause to) become disconnected physically or in the mind

separation *n.* ❶ the process of separating, or of being separated ❷ a legal arrangement by which a couple live apart while remaining married

September *n.* the ninth month of the year

serial *n.* a story appearing in parts once weekly, monthly, etc.

series *n.* ❶ a group of events related by order of occurrence ❷ a group of related books stamps, etc.

serious *adj.* ❶ causing fear or anxiety by threatening great harm ❷ concerned with work or important matters rather than play or trivialities

servant *n.* ❶ a person paid to wait on another or others, especially to do work in or around a house ❷ a person employed in the service of government or a company ❸ a person devoted to sb. or sth.

serve *v.* ❶ be a servant to; work for ❷ perform duties ❸ provide people with sth. that they need ❹ be satisfactory for a need or purpose

service *n.* ❶ sth. done to help or benefit another or others ❷ benefit or advantage ❸ sth. that the public needs, such as hospitals, parks, etc. which is supplied in an organized way ❹ an examination, test, etc. of sth. to make sure it keeps working or operating

S

session *n.* ❶ a formal meeting of an organization, especially a law-making body or court ❷ the part of a year or of a day during which a school holds classes ❸ a meeting or period of time used especially by a group for a particular purpose

set Ⅰ *v.* ❶ bring into or cause to be in a special state or relation ❷ disappear below the horizon, as the sun, etc. ❸ put, place or lay sth. in a particular place ❹ cause (sb.) to do sth. Ⅱ *n.* a number of things that belong together or that are thought of as a group

setback *n.* sth. that stops or slows progress

settle *v.* ❶ place (sb. or oneself) so as to be comfortable ❷ make an agreement about; decide ❸ make or become calm or untroubled ❹ pay ❺ make one's home in a place permanently

settlement *n.* ❶ the act of settling a dispute, debt, etc. ❷ the property given ❸ a place where people have come to live and have built homes

set-up *n.* ❶ a way of organizing sth.; a system ❷ a set of equipment needed for a particular activity or purpose

seven *num.* the number 7

seventeen *num.* one more than sixteen, or seven more than ten

seventeenth *num.* being number 17 in a series; being one of the 17 equal parts of anything

seventh *num.* being number 7 in a series; being one of the 7 equal parts of anything

seventieth *num.* being number 70 in a series; being one of the 70 equal parts of anything

seventy *num.* the number equivalent to the product of seven and ten; ten less than eighty

several Ⅰ *adj.* ❶ three or more; some ❷ separate; individual Ⅱ pron. a few; some

severe *adj.* ❶ intensely or extremely bad or unpleasant in degree or quality ❷ stern; strict

sew *v.* work with a needle and thread

sewing *n.* the activity of making, repairing or decorating things made of cloth using a needle and thread

sex *n.* ❶being male or female ❷males or females as a group

sexual *adj.* of sex or sexes

shabby *adj.* ❶ poorly dressed; looking badly worn ❷ mean or shameful in a petty way

shadow Ⅰ *n.* ❶ the region of relative darkness caused by the interception of the light ❷ sth. unsubstantial or unreal ❸ darkness in a place or on sth. ❹ a slight trace Ⅱ *v.* ❶ darken; cover sth. with a shadow ❷ follow after, especially in secret

shady *adj.* ❶ sheltered from bright sunlight by trees or buildings ❷ questionable; of doubtful honesty

shake Ⅰ *v.* ❶move or cause to move up and down and to and from with short jerky movements ❷ shock or quiver ❸ weaken(belief or confidence) Ⅱ *n.* ❶an act of shaking ❷ a moment

shall *aux. v.* ❶ sometimes used with I and we to express the future tense ❷ used to show a promise, command, or obligation, etc.

shallow Ⅰ *adj.* ❶of little depth ❷lacking depth of intellect or knowledge; concerned only with what is obvious Ⅱ *n.* ashallow part of a body of water Ⅲ *v.* become shallow

shamble *v.* walk in an unsteady way

shame Ⅰ *n.* ❶a painful emotion resulting from the loss of self-respect caused by doing sth. wrong ❸a state of dishonour ❹sth. that make you feel ashamed Ⅱ *v.* cause to be ashamed

shameful *adj.* causing shame; disgraceful

shameless *adj.* having or showing no feeling of shame

shampoo Ⅰ *n.* ❶a special kind of soap, liquid, powder, etc. for washing the hair ❷an act of washing the hair Ⅱ *v.* wash the hair

shape Ⅰ *n.* ❶an outer form; a total effect produced by a thing's outlines ❷ the physical condition of sb. or sth. Ⅱ *v.* give a shape or form to

share *n.* a part or division

shark *n.* ❶ a large fish that eats other fish and sometimes attacks people ❷ a person clever at getting money from others in dishonest ways

sharp Ⅰ *adj.* ❶having a fine point or a thin edge for cutting; pointed ❷ quick aware of things; acute ❸severe or harsh ❹ changing direction suddenly Ⅱ *adv.* punctually

sharpen *v.* ❶ make or become sharp ❷ become better at noticing sth. , thinking or doing sth.

she Ⅰ *pron.* ❶ a female person already referred to ❷a female animal or thing, such as a ship, the moon, nation, etc. Ⅱ *n.* a female

shear Ⅰ *v.* ❶ remove (the wool, hair, etc.) by cutting or clipping with a sharp instrument ❷ deprive or divest Ⅱ *n.* a pair of large sized scissors

shed[1] *n.* a small structure for storage or shelter

shed[2] *v.* ❶ pour forth or cause to pour forth ❷loose by a natural process ❸give off

sheep *n.* ❶ a farmed animal with heavy wool ❷a person who is gentle or timid

sheer *adj.* ❶ complete; thorough; absolute ❷ straight up and down; very steep

sheet *n.* ❶a large piece of cloth used on a bed ❷ a broad, flat piece of some thin material ❸wide expanse

shelf *n.* ❶a flat piece of wood or metal used for holding books or dishes, etc. ❷ sth. like a shelf

shell *n.* ❶ the hard outside covering of sth. , such as a fruit, seed, egg, etc. ❷a metal case, filled with explosive, to be fired from a large gun

shelter Ⅰ *n.* ❶ sth. that gives safety or protection ❷the condition of being kept safe Ⅱ *v.* give protection to

shepherd Ⅰ *n.* a person who takes care of sheep Ⅱ *v.* take care of; guide or direct (people) like sheep

shift Ⅰ *n.* ❶ a change of position, direction, condition, etc. ❷one of two or more recurring periods in which different groups of workers do the same jobs in relay Ⅱ *v.* change opinion, attitude, etc. to another

S

shine Ⅰ *v.* ❶give out or reflect light; be bright ❷be brilliant or excellent at sth. Ⅱ *n.* high polish or sheen; luster

shiny *adj.* polished or rubbed bright

ship Ⅰ *n.* a seagoing vessel of considerable size Ⅱ *v.* transport (goods or people) on a ship

shipment *n.* ❶ the act of sending goods from one place to another ❷ the goods sent at one time to a person or a company

shirt *n.* a garment for the upper part of a man's body (usually of thin cloth)

shiver Ⅰ *v.* tremble, especially from cold or fear Ⅱ *n.* a trembling that cannot be controlled

shock Ⅰ *n.* ❶a violent force from a hard blow, crash, explosion, etc. ❷a state or feeling caused by a sudden, unexpected, and usually very unpleasant event or situation that severely upsets the mind and feelings Ⅱ *v.* surprise and upset sb.

shoe Ⅰ *n.* a covering of leather, rubber, etc. that you wear on your foot Ⅱ *v.* ❶ be wearing shoes of a specified kind ❷fit (a horse) with a shoe or shoes ❸protect sth. with a metal shoe

shoot *v.* ❶hurt or kill a person or animal with a bullet or arrow ❷pass quickly by or along ❸photograph (a scene)

shop Ⅰ *n.* a building or part of a building where goods are shown and sold Ⅱ *v.* visit one or more shops in order to buy things

shore *n.* the land along the edge of a sea, lake, etc.

short Ⅰ *adj.* ❶ not long ❷ not having enough of sth. ❸ small in height ❹ lasting a small amount of time Ⅱ *adv.* abruptly; suddenly

shortage *n.* the condition of having not enough

shortcoming *n.* fault; failure to reach a required standard

shorten *v.* make or become shorter

shorthand *n.* a system of rapid writing using special signs

shortly *adv.* ❶in a short time; soon ❷in a few words ❸ in an impolite or curt manner

shorts *n.* trousers which stop above

the knees

should *aux. v.* ❶ ought to ❷ probably happen ❸ used in conditional sentences ❹ used in that clauses after adjectives and verbs like anxious, intend, desire, demand, etc.

shoulder Ⅰ *n.* the part of the body at each side of the neck where the arms are connected Ⅱ *v.* push sb. or sth. with the shoulder

shout Ⅰ *n.* a loud call or cry Ⅱ *v.* say or utter in a loud voice

shovel Ⅰ *n.* a tool for lifting and moving loose material Ⅱ *v.* take up and throw with a shovel

show Ⅰ *n.* ❶ sth. that is shown; exhibition ❷ an act of showing Ⅱ *v.* ❶ allow to look at; permit sb. to see ❷ display; exhibit ❸ point out; guide

shower Ⅰ *n.* ❶ a brief fall of rain ❷ a bath in which water pours down on the body from above in small jets Ⅱ *v.* ❶ wash oneself in a shower ❷ fall or be thrown in a shower

showing *n.* ❶ the presentation of a cinema film or television programme ❷ the evidence or quality that someone shows

shred Ⅰ *n.* ❶ a small piece of sth.; fragment ❷ a small amount; particle Ⅱ *v.* tear or scrape into small pieces

shrill Ⅰ *adj.* (of sounds) sharp, piercing Ⅱ *v.* make a loud, usually unpleasant noise

shrimp Ⅰ *n.* a small shellfish Ⅱ *v.* catch shrimps

shrine *n.* a holy place

shrink *v.* ❶ draw together; contract ❷ draw back; turn away ❸ become or make smaller in size or amount

shrub *n.* a small low plant that have several woody stems

shrug Ⅰ *v.* lift and drop the shoulders to show that you do not know or do not care Ⅱ *n.* a movement involving raising one's shoulders

shut *v.* keep from entering or leaving; enclose

shutdown *n.* ❶ the closing of a factory or business ❷ the turning off of a computer or other device

shuttle Ⅰ *n.* ❶ a device used in weaving to carry the thread back and forth ❷ the regular service to and from by air, bus, etc. between two places Ⅱ *v.* move back and forth by or as if by a shuttle

shy *adj.* not at ease in front of strangers; easily frightened

sick *adj.* ❶ ready to throw up food ❷ suffering from disease; ill; not well

sickbed *n.* the bed on which a sick person is lying

sickly *adj.* ❶ often ill or in poor health ❷ causing poor health ❸ causing sickness or nausea

sickness *n.* ❶ the state of being ill ❷ the act of vomiting

side Ⅰ *n.* ❶ one of the parts of sth. that is not the top, bottom, back, or front ❷ the right or left half of the body ❸ an area separated from another by some intervening line, barrier, or other feature ❹ a part to be considered, usually in opposition to another; an aspect Ⅱ *v.* support on a person or group in a quarrel, fight, etc. against another

sideways Ⅰ *adv.* to, towards or from the side; with the side or edge first Ⅱ *adj.* toward one side

sigh Ⅰ *v.* let out a very long, deep breath because one is sad, tired, or relieved Ⅱ *n.* the act or sound of sighing

sight Ⅰ *n.* ❶ the power of seeing ❷ the action or fact of seeing sb. or sth. ❸ sth. seen; a remarkable view Ⅱ *v.* see sth. suddenly, especially sth. you have been looking for

sightseeing *n.* the act of visiting interesting places in a town, etc.

sign Ⅰ *n.* a mark, symbol or word which has a message for the person who sees it or them Ⅱ *v.* write one's name on

signal Ⅰ *n.* any kind of mark, light, sound, movement, etc. which gives an idea to someone, or controls his actions in some way Ⅱ *v.* make a signal or signals

signature *n.* the writer's name at the end of a letter

significance *n.* the meaning or importance of sth.

significant *adj.* having a special meaning; important

signify *v.* ❶ mean; be a sign of ❷ be matter; be of importance

signing *n.* ❶ the action of writing one's signature on an official document ❷ the action of recruiting someone, especially to a professional sports team or record company

silence Ⅰ *n.* ❶ the absence of sound; stillness ❷ the state of being or keeping silent Ⅱ *v.* make silent and quiet

silent *adj.* ❶ with no sound; quiet ❷ saying nothing; giving no answer

silk *n.* (smooth soft cloth made from) fine thread which is produced by a silkworm

silky *adj.* soft, fine, or smooth like silk

silly Ⅰ *adj.* absurd and foolish Ⅱ *n.* (chiefly used to or by children) a foolish person

silver *n.* ❶ a soft whitish precious metal that is a simple substance (element), carries electricity very well, can be brightly polished, and is used in jewellery, coins, and knives, forks, etc. ❷ a shiny grayish-white colour

similar *adj.* like or alike; of the same kind; almost but not exactly the same in nature or appearance

similarity *n.* the state or fact of being like

simple *adj.* ❶ easy to understand; not complicated ❷ basic and plain without anything extra ❸ ordinary; not special

simplify *v.* make sth. simple or simpler

simply *adv.* ❶ in a simple manner ❷ absolutely; completely ❸ merely; only

simulate *v.* pretend to be or to have

simultaneous *adj.* happening or done at the same time (with)

since Ⅰ *adv.* before now; ago Ⅱ *conj.* (used with the present perfect or past perfect tenses) from an event in the past until a later past event, or until now

sincere *adj.* (of a person, feelings, or behaviour) without any deceit or falseness; real, true, or honest; genuine

sing *v.* ❶ make music with the voice ❷ (of a bird) make characteristic melodious whistling and twittering sounds ❸ make or be filled with a ringing sound ❹celebrate in verse

singer *n.* a person who sings, or whose job is singing, especially in public

single Ⅰ *adj.* ❶ one only; one and no more ❷ not married Ⅱ *n.* (tennis and golf) a game with one person on each side Ⅲ *v.* pick out; select

singly *adv.* ❶one by one ❷alone

singular *adj.* ❶very unusual or strange; out of the ordinary ❷of or being a word or form representing exactly one

sink Ⅰ *v.* ❶ go down, especially below the horizon or the surface of water or other liquid ❷ make by digging Ⅱ *n.* a basin fixed to a wall or floor and having a drainpipe and a piped water supply

Sino- *pref.* Chinese (e. g. Sino-Japanese trade)

sir *n.* ❶a respectful form of address to a man ❷a prefix to the name of a knight or baronet

sister *n.* ❶ a female relative with the same parents ❷ (a title for) a nurse (usually a female) in charge of a department (WARD) of a hospital

sit *v.* ❶rest on the bottom of the back ❷ (of bird) settle; rest ❸ cause to take a seat

site Ⅰ *n.* ❶a place where sth. of special interest existed or happened ❷the place where there is a building or where one may be placed Ⅱ *v.* place in a position; locate

sitting-room *n.* a room in a house where we can sit during the day; a lounge

situate *v.* place in a certain stop; locate

situation *n.* ❶the position or condition at the moment ❷ a job; a position of employment

six *num.* the number 6

sixteen *num.* six more than ten

sixteenth *num.* next after the fifteenth; one of sixteen equal parts

sixth *num.* next after the fifth; one of six equal parts

sixtieth *num.* next after the fifty-ninth; one of sixty equal parts

sixty *num.* the number 60

size *n.* ❶ the degree of largeness or smallness ❷each of the classes, typically numbered, into which garments or other articles are divided according how large they are

skate Ⅰ *n.* a sharp-edged steel blade fastened to a boot for moving over ice Ⅱ *v.* move on skates

skeleton *n.* the framework of all the bones in a human or animal body

sketch Ⅰ *n.* ❶ a rough, quickly-made drawing ❷ a short account or description; a rough draft or general outline ❸ a short, humorous play or piece of writing Ⅱ *v.* make a rough drawing or brief description of

ski Ⅰ *n.* (*pl.* ski or ～s) one of a pair of long, narrow strips of wood, strapped under the feet for moving over snow Ⅱ *v.* move over snow on ski(s)

skill *n.* ❶the ability to do sth. well ❷a particular kind of ability

skilled *adj.* ❶ having or showing the knowledge, ability, or training to perform a certain activity or task well ❷ based on such training or experience;

S

showing expertise

skil(l)ful *adj.* ❶having or showing skill ❷done with skill

skin *n.* ❶the outer covering of a person, animal or plant ❷ an outer layer or covering

skip *v.* ❶jump (over) lightly ❷pass over or omit what you should do, read, etc. next

skirt Ⅰ *n.* ❶ a garment for a woman or girl that hangs from the waist ❷the part of a dress or other garment that hangs below the waist ❸ (*pl.*) border; extreme parts ❹a (young) woman Ⅱ *v.* ❶go along the border (edge) of ❷avoid

skull *n.* the bones of the head

sky *n.* the upper air; the space above the Earth where clouds and the sun, moon, and stars appear

slam *v.* shut with a bang; bang

slander Ⅰ *n.* a false statement that damages a person's reputation Ⅱ *v.* talk falsely about

slang Ⅰ *n.* words, phrases, etc. often used in conversation but not suitable for formal occasions Ⅱ *v.* use violent language to; abuse

slap *v.* strike with the open hand or with sth. flat

slash Ⅰ *v.* ❶cut with a violent, sweeping movement ❷ cut down or reduce severely Ⅱ *n.* a cut or wound made by sharp movement with a knife, etc.

slaughter Ⅰ *v.* ❶ kill (especially many people) cruelly or wrongly; massacre ❷ kill (animals) for food ❸defeat severely in a game Ⅱ *n.* ❶ killing of animals (especially for food) ❷killing of many people at once

slave *n.* a person who is legally owned by someone else; a servant without personal freedom

sledge Ⅰ *n.* ❶a vehicle on long runners, used for transporting loads across snow and ice ❷a heavy hammer with a long handle, used by black smith Ⅱ *v.* travel or carry on a sledge

sleep Ⅰ *n.* the natural resting state of unconsciousness of the body Ⅱ *v.* rest in the condition of sleep; be or fall asleep

sleepless *adj.* ❶ characterized by or experiencing lack of sleep ❷ unable to sleep

sleepwalk *v.* walk around while you are asleep

Sleepy *adj.* ❶needing or ready for sleep ❷quiet; inactive

sleet *n.* rain which is frozen or partly frozen

sleeve *n.* a part of a garment for covering (part of) an arm

slender *adj.* ❶(of a person or the body) thin in an attractive and graceful way ❷ slight; scanty; inadequate

slice Ⅰ *n.* ❶a thin, flat piece cut off sth., especially bread or meat ❷ a part or share of sth. ❸a knife with a broad, thin and flexible blade Ⅱ *v.* cut into slices

slick Ⅰ *adj.* smooth; clever (perhaps too clever) Ⅱ *n.* an amount of oil, etc. on the surface of the sea

slide Ⅰ *n.* an act of sliding Ⅱ *v.* move smoothly over a surface

slightly *adv.* ❶ slenderly ❷ to a slight degree; somewhat

slim *adj.* ❶ attractively thin; not fat ❷ (of chance, etc.) very small

slip Ⅰ *v.* fall or almost fall as the result of losing one's balance Ⅱ *n.* an act of shipping

slipper *n.* (usually *pl.*) a loose-fitting shoe worn in the house

slippery *adj.* ❶ (of a surface) smooth, wet, difficult to hold or move on ❷ (of person) unreliable; unscrupulous

slit Ⅰ *v.* cut or tear in a straight line Ⅱ *n.* a narrow cut, tear or opening

slogan *n.* a word, phrase or sentence used to advertise sth. or to make clear the aim(s)

slop Ⅰ *v.* spill over the edge; flow over Ⅱ *n.* dirty waste water from kitchen, etc.

slope Ⅰ *v.* go up or down at an angle Ⅱ *n.* ❶ a surface that slopes; a piece of ground going up or down ❷ a degree of sloping

slow Ⅰ *adj.* ❶ not fast; taking a long time ❷ dull; not quick to learn Ⅱ *v.* (cause to) go at a slower speed

slum Ⅰ *n.* a street of dirty and crowded houses, especially in an area of a city that is very poor Ⅱ *v.* live very cheaply

slump Ⅰ *v.* ❶ sit down heavily ❷ go down in number or strength Ⅱ *n.* a sudden depression in prices, value, etc.

sly *adj.* having or showing a deceitful nature

small *adj.* ❶ not large in degree, size, etc. ❷ young ❸ not important ❹ little; not much

smart *adj.* ❶ bright; new-looking; clean and well-dressed ❷ intelligent; clever; quick in mind ❸ beautiful and fashionable

smear Ⅰ *v.* ❶ cover or spread with sth. sticky or greasy ❷ make dirty marks on sth. ❸ damage sb. or sb.'s reputation Ⅱ *n.* ❶ a mark made by smearing ❷ a suggestion or accusation that damages sb.'s reputation ❸ a specimen of a substance spread on a slide to be examined under a microscope

smell Ⅰ *v.* get the odor or scent of sth. through the nose; sniff at Ⅱ *n.* ❶ the sense of smelling ❷ an odor or scent

smile Ⅰ *n.* a pleased, happy, or amused expression on the face Ⅱ *v.* give a smile; have a smile on the face

smirk Ⅰ *v.* smile in a silly or self-satisfied way Ⅱ *n.* this type of smile

smith *n.* a worker in iron or other metals

smog *n.* fog or haze intensified by smoke or other atmospheric pollutants

smoke Ⅰ *n.* the cloud of gas and tiny solid particles that rise from anything burning Ⅱ *v.* ❶ give out smoke ❷ draw in and let out the smoke of burning tobacco or other substance

smooth Ⅰ *adj.* ❶ having a surface like that of glass; free from roughness ❷ having an even or gentle motion Ⅱ *v.* make smooth

snack Ⅰ *n.* a light meal (of sandwiches, etc.), usually eaten between meals Ⅱ *v.* eat snacks between or instead of main meals

snail *n.* a soft creature without bones or legs, but with a round shell on its back, which eats plants

snake Ⅰ *n.* ❶ any of various kinds of long legless crawling reptile, some of which are poisonous ❷ a treacherous person who pretends to be a friend Ⅱ *v.* move in a snake-like manner

sneak Ⅰ *v.* ❶ go quietly and secretly ❷ give information, especially to a teacher about the wrongdoings of others Ⅱ *n.* (used by schoolchildren) someone who gives information

sneer Ⅰ *v.* express dislike and disrespect by a kind of unpleasant smile Ⅱ *n.* scornful expressions, words, etc. that express contempt

sneeze Ⅰ *n.* a sudden, uncontrollable outburst of air through the nose and mouth Ⅱ *v.* make a sneeze at

snigger Ⅰ *n.* a type of quiet laugh, often showing disrespect Ⅱ *v.* laugh in this way

snob *n.* a person who cares only for people who are rich or of high birth

snobbish *adj.* of, characteristic of, or like a snob

snore Ⅰ *v.* breathe roughly and noisily when sleeping Ⅱ *n.* the sound of snoring

snow Ⅰ *n.* frozen water falling in soft white flakes Ⅱ *v.* snow from the sky

snowfall *n.* a fall of snow; the amount of snow that falls

snowflake *n.* a flake of snow

snowy *adj.* ❶ full of snow ❷ of or like snow

so Ⅰ *adv.* ❶ to such a great degree ❷ in this way; in that way ❸ extremely; very much ❹ that is the case ❺ the truth ❻ similarly ❼ expressing agreement Ⅱ *conj.* with the result that

soak Ⅰ *v.* ❶ (let) stay in water or other liquid ❷ penetrate; enter or pass ❸ absorb, take up (liquid) ❹ extract money from charging or taxing too much Ⅱ *n.* an act of soaking

soap Ⅰ *n.* a substance people use for washing Ⅱ *v.* wash with soap

soar *v.* ❶ (of birds) fly or go up high in the air ❷ rise high

sob Ⅰ *v.* ❶ weep or sigh with short quick breaths ❷ tell while doing this Ⅱ *n.* the act or sound of sobbing

sober *adj.* ❶ not drunk; in control of oneself ❷ thoughtful, serious or solemn ❸ plain and rather dull

so-called *adj.* ❶ used to show that sth. or sb. is commonly designated by the name or term specified ❷ used to express one's view that such a name or term is inappropriate

soccer *n.* a type of football in which the ball may not normally be touched by the hands, except by the goalkeeper

sociable *adj.* friendly; fond of meeting other people

social *adj.* ❶ having to do with human beings in a group where people meet each other for pleasure ❷ relating to the society

society *n.* ❶ the system by which people live together in an organized community ❷ people in general, considered with regard to the structure of laws, organizations, etc. that makes it possible for them to live together

sociology *n.* the science of the nature and growth of society

sock *n.* ❶ a piece of clothing covering for the foot, inside the shoe ❷ a loose sole used inside a shoe

soda *n.* ❶a substance used to make soap, glass, etc. ❷water containing a gas to make it bubble

sofa *n.* a long seat with raised ends and back, on which several persons can sit

soft *adj.* ❶ not hard; not firm ❷ mild; gentle ❸ smooth and pleasant to touch ❹(of sound or voice) quiet and gentle

soften *v.* cause to become soft, gentle, less stiff, or less severe

software *n.* programs for databases, word processing, and other tasks a computer performs, as distinct from the machinery in which these are loaded (called hardware)

soil[1] *n.* ❶ the top layer of the earth in which plants, trees, etc. grow ❷ a country; an area of land

soil[2] *v.* make or become dirty

solar *adj.* concerning the sun

soldier *n.* ❶ a member of an army ❷ a person who works for a cause

sole Ⅰ *adj.* one and only; single Ⅱ *n.* the bottom of the foot or shoe

solemn *adj.* ❶(of a person) not happy or smiling ❷ formal and dignified; characterized by deep sincerity

solid Ⅰ *adj.* ❶ not liquid or gas ❷ that can be depended on Ⅱ *n.* a solid object; sth. that does not flow

solidify *v.* make or become solid; make or be made into a hard mass

solitary *adj.* ❶ habitually done or existing alone ❷ (of a place) alone or isolated

solitude *n.* ❶being without companions; a solitary state ❷a solitary place

solo Ⅰ *n.* a piece of music performed by one person; any musical performance by one person Ⅱ *adj.* of a musical solo

solution *n.* ❶a way of solving problems or difficulties ❷the process of dissolving a solid in liquid ❸ a liquid or mixture formed by dissolving

solve *v.* find the answer to (a problem); find a way out of (a difficulty)

solvent Ⅰ *n.* a substance that can dissolve another substance Ⅱ *adj.* ❶ able to dissolve ❷able to pay all one's debts

some Ⅰ det. ❶an unspecified amount or number of ❷used to refer to sb. or sth. that is unknown or specified ❸ approximately ❹ a large number or amount of sth. ❺ a small number or amount of sth. Ⅱ *pron.* ❶an unspecified number or amount of people or things ❷a part of the whole number or amount being considered Ⅲ *adv.* to some extent; quite a lot

somebody Ⅰ *pron.* some person; someone Ⅱ *n.* a person of some importance

someday *adv.* at some future time

somehow *adv.* ❶by some means; in some way not yet known or stated ❷for some reason that is not clear

someone *pron.* ❶ an unknown or unspecified person; some person ❷ a person of importance or authority

somersault Ⅰ *n.* the act of jumping and turning over completely and landing on the feet again Ⅱ *v.* turn a somersault

something Ⅰ *pron.* ❶a thing not named or known; some thing ❷ an amount or description, etc. that is not exact Ⅱ *adv.* sth. like; somewhat

sometime *adv.* &*adj.* ❶at some time ❷

former(ly)

sometimes *adv.* at times; now and then

somewhat *adv.* rather; in some degree

somewhere *adv.* ❶ in some place ❷ at some point in amount, degree, time, etc.

son *n.* ❶a male child of a person ❷a male descendant

song *n.* a piece of music with words for singing

sonic *adj.* ❶of or concerning sound or sound waves ❷ denoting or having a speed equal to that of sound

soon *adv.* ❶ in a short time ❷ quickly; early

soothe *v.* ❶ quiet, calm or comfort sb. who is upset or anxious ❷ make less painful; relieve

sophisticated *adj.* ❶wise in the ways of the world; cultured; elegant ❷advanced; developed to a high degree

sore Ⅰ *adj.* (of a part of one's body) painful Ⅱ *n.* a painful or injured place

sort Ⅰ *n.* a kind or a group of people or things that are the same Ⅱ *v.* arrange in groups; separate things of one kind from things of other kinds

S

so-so *adj.* neither very good nor very bad

soul *n.* ❶ the spiritual part of a person that thinks, feels and makes the body act ❷a central, most important or most active part

sound Ⅰ *adj.* ❶ healthy; not damaged, hurt, etc. ❷reliable; wise; reasonable ❸ thorough and good Ⅱ *n.* a thing that can be heard; noise; voice; tone Ⅲ v. ❶ convey a specified impression when heard ❷(cause to) make a voice

soup *n.* a liquid food made by cooking meat, vegetables, etc. in water

sour Ⅰ *adj.* ❶having a sharp taste (like that of vinegar, lemon, etc.) ❷ made sour by fermentation ❸ bad-tempered and unpleasant Ⅱ *v.* become sour

source *n.* ❶ the beginning of a river; a place of origin ❷ a place from which sth. comes or is got

south Ⅰ *n.* ❶one of the four main points of the compass, the direction which is on the right of a person facing the rising sun ❷the southern part of a country or continent, etc. Ⅱ *adj.* lying towards or situated in the south; facing south Ⅲ *adv.* towards the south

southwest Ⅰ *n.* the direction halfway between south and west; a district in that direction Ⅱ *adj.* ❶ lying in or directed towards the southwest ❷ blowing from the southwest Ⅲ *adv.* towards the southwest

souvenir *n.* sth. that reminds one of a person or place

sow *v.* put (seed) on or in soil; plant (a piece of land) with seed

soya *n.* protein derived from the beans of an Asian plant, used as a replacement for animal protein in certain foods

spa *n.* ❶a spring, the water of which can be used as a medicine ❷a place where there is a spring like this

space *n.* ❶the physical universe beyond the earth's atmosphere ❷the interval or distance between two or more objects ❸ a period of time

spacious *adj.* having much space; roomy

spade Ⅰ *n.* ❶a tool for digging ❷(one of a) suit of playing cards Ⅱ *v.* dig with a spade

span Ⅰ *n.* ❶the distance or part between the supports of an arch ❷the length in time, from beginning to end Ⅱ *v.* extend across (from side to side)

Spanish Ⅰ *adj.* of or belonging to Spain, its people, or language Ⅱ *n.* ❶ the people of Spain ❷the language of Spain

spanner *n.* a tool for loosening and tightening nuts on screws and bolts

spare Ⅰ *adj.* ❶ additional to what is usually needed ❷ (of time) not occupied, available to do sth. you want rather than work Ⅱ *v.* be able to give (time, money, etc.)

spark Ⅰ *n.* a tiny particle of fire Ⅱ *v.* send out little sparks or flashes

sparkle Ⅰ *n.* a shiny flash of light Ⅱ *v.* ❶ shine in small flashes ❷ send out little sparks

sparrow *n.* a small, gray-brown bird

sparse *adj.* spread widely and in small numbers

spawn Ⅰ *n.* eggs of fish, frogs, etc. Ⅱ *v.* produce eggs

speak *v.* ❶ say words with your own voice ❷ be able to use a particular language ❸talk to sb. about sth. ❹give a speech to sb.

spear Ⅰ *n.* a weapon with a long stem and a sharp-pointed head Ⅱ *v.* pierce, wound, make (a hole) in sth. with a spear

special *adj.* ❶ unusual; out of the ordinary; not common; different from others ❷ designed or organized for a particular person, purpose, or occasion

specialist *n.* a person who is very skillful on a particular subject; an expert

speciality *n.* ❶a special field of work or study ❷a type of food or product that a restaurant or place is famous for

specialize *v.* ❶ study a subject with special intensity; become a specialist ❷ have a product, etc. to which you devote special attention

species *n.* a group of animals or plants having similar characteristics

specific *adj.* ❶ connected with one particular or fixed thing only ❷detailed and exact; clear in meaning or explanation

specify *v.* mention or name clearly; tell or state in detail

specimen *n.* ❶a single typical thing or example ❷a piece or amount of sth. to be shown, tested, etc. ❸ an odd or peculiar kind of person

speckle Ⅰ *n.* a small spot; a speck Ⅱ *v.* mark or cover with or as if with speckles

spectacular Ⅰ *adj.* striking or impressive Ⅱ *n.* an event or performance produced on a large scale and with striking effects

spectator *n.* a person who watches, especially an event or sport without taking part in

speech *n.* ❶ a talk or address given in public ❷ the power, act or manner of speaking

speed Ⅰ *n.* ❶ the rate of movement ❷ quickness of movement Ⅱ *v.* (cause to) move along, go quickly

speedy *adj.* ❶moving quickly ❷done or coming without delay

spell Ⅰ *v.* name or write the letters (of a

word) in their proper order Ⅱ *n.* a short period

spend *v.* ❶ pay money for sth. ❷ give time, energy, etc. to sth.

sperm *n.* ❶ a cell that is produced by the male sex organs and that can combine with a female egg to produce young ❷ the liquid that is produced by the male sex organs that contains these cells

sphere *n.* ❶ globe; ball ❷ one of the heavenly bodies; star or planet ❸ range; field; extent

spicy *adj.* flavored with spice

spider *n.* a kind of small animal with eight legs, which makes webs to catch insects for food

spinach *n.* a plant with dark green leaves, used as a vegetable

spine *n.* ❶ the backbone of an animal or person ❷ hard, sharp-pointed parts like needles on some plants and animals

spiral Ⅰ *adj.* circling about a center; winding Ⅱ *n.* a spiral curve Ⅲ *v.* move in continuous circles

spirit *n.* ❶ the part of a person that includes their soul or mind ❷ courage, determination or energy ❸ feelings; the state of mind

spirited *adj.* ❶ full of liveliness and courage ❷ having a character or mood of a specified kind

spiritless *adj.* lacking courage or vigour

spiritual Ⅰ *adj.* ❶ of the spirit or soul; not of material things; of God ❷ of spirits ❸ caring much for things of the spirit ❹ connected with the religion Ⅱ *n.* a religious song sung originally by the black slaves of the US

splendid *adj.* ❶ glorious; brilliant; grand ❷ worthy of honour or fame; distinguished ❸ very good; fine; excellent

splendo(u)r *n.* ❶ magnificence; brightness ❷ glory

split *v.* break into two or more parts, especially from end to end

spoil *v.* ❶ make useless or unsatisfactory ❷ harm the character of (children) by lack of discipline

spoken *adj.* speaking in a certain way

spokesman *n.* a person who speaks on behalf of a group or an organization

sponge Ⅰ *n.* ❶ a type of sea animal with a body full of holes to allow water to enter ❷ a substance full of holes used for cleaning and wiping ❸ a type of very soft and light cake Ⅱ *v.* clean or wipe with a sponge

sponsor Ⅰ *n.* ❶ a person who promises to be responsible for another person ❷ a person or business company that gives financial support to a radio or television programme, a concert, an exhibition, etc. (usually in return for publicity and the right to advertise goods) Ⅱ *v.* be sponsor for

spoon Ⅰ *n.* a utensil with a shallow bowl on a handle, used for taking up food Ⅱ *v.* take (up, out) with a spoon

sport *n.* ❶ an athletic game or outdoor amusement ❷ amusement or plaything

spot Ⅰ *n.* ❶ a particular place or area ❷ a personal fault or defect ❸ a small dirty mark or stain on sth. Ⅱ *v.* make dirty

spotlight Ⅰ *n.* ❶ a beam of light directed on to a small area, or a lamp giving this

❷ public attention Ⅱ *v.* ❶ direct a spotlight on sth. ❷ draw attention to sth.

spouse *n.* a husband or wife

sprawl Ⅰ *v.* ❶ stretch out (oneself or one's limbs) awkwardly in lying or sitting ❷ spread ungracefully Ⅱ *n.* ❶ a sprawling position or movement ❷ a widespread untidy area, especially covered with buildings

spray Ⅰ *n.* ❶ water in very small drops blown from sea, a waterfall, etc. ❷ kinds of liquid preparation, such as perfume, disinfectant or insecticide, etc. ❸ an atomizer, etc. used for applying such a liquid Ⅱ *v.* scatter or be scattered in small drops under pressure

spread Ⅰ *v.* ❶ open sth. so as to show an extended surface ❷ make sth. be known by more people Ⅱ *n.* ❶ a variety or range of sb. or sth. ❷ an increase in amount, number or area

spring Ⅰ *n.* ❶ the first season of the year ❷ leap; jump ❸ a flow of water from the ground; fountain Ⅱ *v.* leap; jump; bound

sprout Ⅰ *v.* start to grow Ⅱ *n.* a newly sprouted part of a plant

spur Ⅰ *n.* ❶ sth. that urges a person on to greater activity ❷ a sharp-toothed instrument attached to a rider's heels used to urge the horse forward Ⅱ *v.* ❶ ride fast or hard ❷ urge on with, or as with spurs

spy Ⅰ *n.* a person who tries to get secret information about the enemy or another country Ⅱ *v.* act as a spy (upon); watch secretly

square Ⅰ *adj.* ❶ having the shape of a square ❷ of or being quantity multiplied by itself Ⅱ *n.* a figure having four equal straight sides and a right angle at each corner ❷ an open area in a place

squeeze *v.* ❶ press on from the opposite side or from all sides; change the shape, size, etc. of sth. by doing this ❷ get or force out by squeezing

squirrel *n.* ❶ a small gray, or brown animal with a big furry tail, which lives in trees ❷ the fur of squirrel

stable Ⅰ *adj.* firmly fixed; steady Ⅱ *n.* a building in which horses are kept

stack Ⅰ *n.* ❶ a pile of hay or straw ❷ an orderly pile ❸ a large amount or number ❹ a chimney Ⅱ *v.* make into a neat pile; arrange in a stack

stadium *n.* an enclosed area of land for games, sports, etc. usually with stands

staff *n.* ❶ a group of assistants working together under a manager ❷ a strong stick used as a support when walking

stage Ⅰ *n.* ❶ a raised floor in a hall where the actors or performers stand ❷ time or step in a long event Ⅱ *v.* put on the stage; put before the public

staggered *adj.* very surprised and shocked at sth. you are told or at sth. that happens

stagnant *adj.* ❶ (with reference to water) not moving, therefore dirty ❷ (with reference to business, work, etc.) not changing, growing or developing

stainless *adj.* ❶ without stains; not liable to stains ❷ resisting rust

stair *n.* ❶ a set of steps one above the other on which one can go up or down in a building ❷ one of these steps

stairway *n.* a set of steps or stairs and its surrounding walls or structure

stale *adj.* ❶not fresh; tasting old and dry ❷ uninteresting because sth. that has been spoken or talked about many times before

stalk *n.* the main upright part of a plant that is not a tree; the long part that supports leaves or flowers

stall *n.* ❶a compartment for an animal in a stable ❷a small open shop, especially one in a market

stammer Ⅰ *v.* speak with difficulty, repeating the same sounds Ⅱ *n.* a tendency to stammer

stamp Ⅰ *v.* ❶put (one's foot) down with force ❷put a stamp on Ⅱ *n.* ❶a small piece of paper stuck on a letter or parcel to show how much money has to be paid to send it ❷an act of putting the foot down hard

stand Ⅰ *n.* ❶ stopping of motion or progress ❷a small article of furniture, support on or in which things are placed Ⅱ *v.* ❶be on one's feet or legs ❷be in a certain place condition or state ❸ go through; bear; endure

standard *n.* a level or degree of quality that is considered proper or acceptable

standing Ⅰ *adj.* without change; permanent Ⅱ *n.* ❶a period of time ❷the position in society; rank

staple Ⅰ *n.* ❶ a chief sort of article or goods produced or traded in ❷ a chief material or element (of sth.) ❸fibre Ⅱ *adj.* forming the chief element or material

star *n.* ❶a very large mass of burning gas in space, especially one that can be seen as a small bright point of light in a clear sky at night ❷ a famous or very skillful performer

stare *v.* look fixedly with wide open eyes, as in wonder, fear, or deep thought

start Ⅰ *v.* ❶begin a journey, activity, etc. ❷begin to move or travel ❸(cause to) come into existence ❹make sth. begin to exist Ⅱ *n.* an act of setting out or leaving on a journey

startle *v.* surprise; give shock to

startling *adj.* surprising or alarming

starve *v.* not have enough to eat; suffer or die from hunger

state Ⅰ *n.* ❶the condition of a person or thing ❷the body of people living under a single independent government; a nation ❸ an organized political community forming part of a country Ⅱ *v.* express in words, especially carefully, fully, and clearly

statement Ⅰ *n.* stating orally or on paper Ⅱ *v.* ❶sth. stated; a single declaration or remark ❷ a summary of a financial account

statesman *n.* a person taking an important part in the management of state affairs

station Ⅰ *n.* a building or place used for a certain purpose Ⅱ *v.* place in a certain spot

stationer *n.* a dealer in writing materials, etc.

statistics *n.* ❶ numbers that give information about a subject ❷ the science that deals with collecting and using such facts

statue *n.* a figure of a person or animal carved in wood, stone, metal or other material

stature *n.* ❶the height of the body ❷the quality or position gained by proved worth

status *n.* ❶the rank or social position in relation to others ❷ a superior social position ❸ the situation at a particular time

stay Ⅰ *v.* ❶remain in a place ❷remain in a certain condition Ⅱ *n.* an act of staying; the time spent in one place as a guest

steady Ⅰ *adj.* ❶ firm in position; not shaking; balanced ❷ regular in movement, speed, direction, etc. ❸regular in behavior, habits, etc. ❹constant; unchanging Ⅱ *v.* make or become stable, regular, or less changing

steak *n.* ❶ a slice of meat or fish for cooking ❷beef steak

steal *v.* ❶ take away unlawfully or without permission ❷ move secretly or quietly

steam Ⅰ *n.* water in the form of vapor Ⅱ *v.* give out (off) steam

steamer *n.* ❶ a boat or ship driven by steam ❷ a type of saucepan in which food can be steamed

steel Ⅰ *n.* ❶ iron mixed with carbon so that it is very hard, strong and rough ❷ sword; a steel weapon Ⅱ *v.* harden

steep *adj.* ❶(of a slope) rising or falling sharply ❷unreasonable; excessive

steer *v.* direct the course of (a ship, car, etc.)

stem Ⅰ *n.* the part of a plant coming up from the roots; the part of a leaf, flower or fruit that joins it to the main stalk or twig Ⅱ *v.* ❶arise (from) ❷remove the stems from sth. ❸(of a boat) make headway against the tide or current

step Ⅰ *v.* lift one's foot and move it in a particular direction; walk into Ⅱ *n.* ❶ one movement forwards and backwards when you walk, dance, etc.; the sound of walking, etc. ❷one in a list of things that you must do ❸a place for the foot in going up or coming down; stair

stereotype Ⅰ *n.* ❶ an over-simplified image or idea of a type of person or thing that has become fixed through being widely held ❷ a relief printing plate cast from a mould Ⅱ *v.* represent or view sth. as a stereotype

stew Ⅰ *v.* cook or be cooked slowly and gently in liquid Ⅱ *n.* a dish consisting usually of meat and vegetables cooked together in liquid

stick Ⅰ *n.* ❶a thin piece of wood; sth. like this ❷such a piece of wood shaped for a special use Ⅱ *v.* ❶ fasten or fix with glue, paste, etc. ❷push a pointed thing into; prick

sticker *n.* ❶an adhesive label or notice, which is generally printed or illustrated ❷a determined or persistent person

sticky *adj.* ❶able or tending to stick to things ❷(said about weather) hot and humid ❸difficult or awkward

stiff *adj.* ❶not easily bent; hard to move ❷difficult or strict ❸not friendly; rigid

still Ⅰ *adj.* without motion; motionless Ⅱ *adv.* ❶ continuing until a particular time ❷even; more

stimulate *v.* encourage by exciting the

mind or interest

stimulus *n.* ❶ sth. that produces a reaction in an organ or tissue of the body ❷ sth. that rouses a person or thing to activity or energy

sting Ⅰ *n.* a sharp, often poisonous, pointed organ of some insects Ⅱ *v.* prick or stab with the sharp, pointed organ of some insects and other animals

stingy *adj.* not generous; unwilling to spend or give

stir *v.* ❶ mix by moving round with a stick or spoon ❷ excite; be roused ❸ be moving; cause to move

stock Ⅰ *n.* ❶ a supply or store of goods that is available for sale ❷ the capital of a company divided into shares Ⅱ *v.* supply or equip with; keep in stock

stocking *n.* a covering of wool, cotton, silk, nylon, etc. which fits the leg and foot tightly and reaches to the knee or to the top of the leg

stomach *n.* ❶ a bag-like organ in the body where food is digested ❷ the front part of the body below the chest; abdomen ❸ (usually negative) appetite; an inclination or liking for things

S

stop Ⅰ *n.* ❶ an act or the state of stopping or being stopped ❷ a place where a bus or tram stopped regularly Ⅱ *v.* ❶ (cause to) cease ❷ prevent from

storage *n.* ❶ the act of storing; the state of being stored ❷ a place for storing goods

store Ⅰ *n.* ❶ a place where goods are kept ❷ the quantity or supply of sth. kept for use as needed Ⅱ *v.* keep goods for later use

storm Ⅰ *n.* ❶ the bad weather with strong wind, heavy rain, thunder, lightning, etc. ❷ a violent outburst of feelings Ⅱ *v.* capture (a place) by sudden and violent attack

story *n.* ❶ a description of events and people telling people sth. that are true or untrue ❷ an account of past events ❸ an untrue statement

stove *n.* a structure or device used for cooking or heating

straight Ⅰ *adj.* ❶ not bent or curved ❷ honest, frank and upright Ⅱ *adv.* directly

strain Ⅰ *n.* ❶ a condition of being stretched ❷ exhaustion Ⅱ *v.* draw or stretch

strait Ⅰ *n.* ❶ a narrow passage of water connecting two large bodies of water ❷ (usually *pl.*) difficult position Ⅱ *adj.* narrow

strange *adj.* ❶ unusual; peculiar ❷ unknown or not familiar

stranger *n.* ❶ a person not known, seen or heard before ❷ a person in an unfamiliar place ❸ a person without experience

strategic *adj.* ❶ relating to the identification of long-term or overall aims and interests and the means of achieving them ❷ carefully designed or planned to serve a particular purpose or advantage

strategy *n.* the art of planning operations in war, etc.

straw *n.* dry, cut stalks of wheat, barley, etc.

strawberry *n.* a plant having a juicy red

fruit with tiny seeds on its surface

stream Ⅰ *n.* ❶running water, as a small river, or brook ❷anything flowing forth like a stream Ⅱ *v.* flow freely; move continuously and smoothly in one direction

street *n.* a town or village road with houses on one side or both

strength *n.* the quality of being strong in body or mind

stress Ⅰ *n.* ❶ the condition causing depression, mental illness, etc. ❷ an extra force used in speaking, on a particular word or syllable Ⅱ *v.* put extra force to a word or syllable when speaking or emphasis on

stretch *v.* ❶ make wider, longer or tighter by pulling; be or become wider, etc. when pulled ❷extend or spread over an area of land

strict *adj.* stern; demanding obedience or exact observance

stride Ⅰ *v.* walk with long steps Ⅱ *n.* (distance covered in) one long step

strike Ⅰ *n.* the act of stopping working for more money or sth. else Ⅱ *v.* ❶hit; give a blow or blows to; aim a blow (at) ❷stop working because of disagreement

striking *adj.* ❶that draws the attention ❷on strike

string Ⅰ *n.* ❶a thick thread or very thin cord ❷ the thin cord or wire of some musical instruments ❸ a number of things in a line or row Ⅱ *v.* put strings on

strive *v.* ❶struggle with or against sb. or sth. ❷make great efforts (for sth. or to do sth.)

stroke Ⅰ *n.* ❶an act of hitting or blowing ❷a line made by a single movement of a pen or brush in writing or painting Ⅱ *v.* rub gently with the hand

strong *adj.* ❶not weak; powerful ❷(of a drink, drug, etc.) having a lot of material which gives taste, produces effects, etc. ❸ having great power of body or mind ❹ hard to break or knock down

structure *n.* ❶the way in which parts are formed into a whole ❷ sth. built; a building

struggle Ⅰ *v.* fight; make great efforts Ⅱ *n.* a strong effort; a hard attempt

student *n.* ❶a person who is studying, especially at college or university; anyone who is at school ❷anyone who studies or who is devoted to learning knowledge

studio *n.* ❶a workroom of a painter or photographer ❷ a place where cinema films or recordings are made or from there television or radio programmes are made or produced

studious *adj.* ❶ having or showing the habit of learning ❷ painstaking ❸deliberate

study Ⅰ *n.* ❶ the activity of learning or gaining knowledge, either from books or by examining things in the world ❷ room (in one's home) used for reading, writing, etc. Ⅱ *v.* spend time in learning; examine

stun *v.* ❶make senseless or unconscious ❷shock deeply; astonish

stunning *adj.* extremely good and attractive

stupid *adj.* foolish; slow-thinking

style *n.* ❶the manner, method or way of speaking, writing, doing or building ❷a general manner of doing sth. which is typical or representative of a person or group, a time in history, etc. ❸fashion

stylist *n.* ❶ a designer of fashionable styles of clothing ❷a hairdresser

subconscious Ⅰ *adj.* to do with mental processes of which we are not fully aware but which influence our actions Ⅱ *n.* the part of the mind in which these processes take place

subcontract *v.* hire a company or person outside your company to do a particular part of your work

subdue *v.* ❶ conquer; overcome ❷ make milder; soften

subdued *adj.* ❶ (said about a person) quiet, shy, or slightly depressed ❷ not loud, harsh, or bright

subject Ⅰ *n.* ❶ an area of knowledge discussed or studied in school, college, etc. ❷individual that experiences sth. or is subjected to sth. Ⅱ *adj.* under the authority of sb. or sth.

subjective *adj.* giving the thoughts or feelings of one particular person

submarine Ⅰ *n.* a ship that can go under water Ⅱ *adj.* existing or living underwater

submerge *v.* ❶ put under water; cover with liquid ❷sink out of sight; go down under the surface

submissive *adj.* gentle and willing to obey orders

submit *v.* ❶ put (oneself) under the control of another ❷ put forward for opinion, discussion, decision, etc. ❸ suggest; argue

subnormal *adj.* below normal

subscribe *v.* ❶ contribute ❷ order in advance and pay ❸ agree; approve ❹ write (one's name, etc.) at the foot of a document

subscription *n.* ❶an act of subscribing ❷ a payment to subscribe to sth. ❸a fee for membership of a society, etc.

subsequent *adj.* following or coming after

subside *v.* ❶fall or sink lower ❷become quieter; grow less

subsidy *n.* money paid (especially by a government) to help an industry or another country to keep prices up or down etc.

subsist *v.* exist; be kept in existence

substance *n.* ❶material of which a thing is made; matter ❷ the real element or part of a thing ❸ money; property ❹ firmness; solidity

substandard *adj.* less good than usual or than the average

substantial *adj.* ❶ made of good substance; strong; solid; firm ❷ having real existence; actual ❸large in amount or value; important ❹ possessing considerable property; well-to-do

substitute Ⅰ *n.* a person or thing act or used in place of another Ⅱ *v.* act as a substitute; be used instead of sth.

subtitle Ⅰ *n.* ❶ a secondary title ❷ the translation of a foreign language film, printed on the film Ⅱ *v.* give a subtitle or subtitles to (sth.)

subtle *adj.* ❶delicate; hardly noticeable

❷ingenious; complex ❸quick and clever at seeing or making delicate differences; sensitive

subtract *v.* take (a number, quantity) away from (another number, etc.)

subtropical *adj.* near the tropics; almost tropical

suburb *n.* an outlying district of a town or city

subversive *adj.* trying or likely to destroy or damage a government or political system by attacking it secretly or indirectly

subway *n.* ❶an underground passage or tunnel ❷an underground railway in a town

succeed *v.* ❶turn out well; do well ❷follow another; come next in order ❸take place of another; become the successor ❹take the place of; follow

success *n.* the achievement of one's aim

successful *adj.* ❶accomplishing an aim or purpose ❷having achieved popularity, profit, or fruit

succession *n.* ❶the coming of one thing after another in time or order ❷the act, right, or process of succeeding to an office, property, or rank; a person who has this right

successive *adj.* coming one after the other

successor *n.* a person who succeeds another

such Ⅰ *adj.* of that sort Ⅱ *adv.* of that kind; of the same kind; like that Ⅲ *pron.* such person(s) or thing(s)

suck *v.* ❶draw (liquid) into the mouth by the action of lips and breathing ❷take liquid, etc. out of

sudden *adj.* happening or done quickly or unexpectedly

suffer *v.* feel or have pain, loss, etc.

suffering *n.* ❶pain of body or mind ❷(usually *pl.*) misery; distress

sufficient *adj.* enough for a particular purpose

suffix Ⅰ *n.* an addition made to the end of a word Ⅱ *v.* add as a suffix

sugar Ⅰ *n.* a sweet substance made from sugarcane or sugar beets Ⅱ *v.* make sweet with sugar

suggest *v.* ❶put forward for consideration; propose ❷bring (an idea, possibility) into the mind

suggestible *adj.* easily influenced by people's suggestions

suggestion *n.* ❶an act of suggesting, or being suggested ❷sth. suggested ❸a slight trace

suggestive *adj.* ❶tending to suggest an idea ❷indicative or evocative

suicide *n.* ❶the action of killing oneself ❷a person who commits suicide ❸an action destructive to one's interests or welfare

suit Ⅰ *n.* ❶a set of clothes ❷a lawsuit Ⅱ *v.* look well; be appropriate

suitable *adj.* right for the purpose or occasion; fitting; proper

suite *n.* ❶a set of rooms or furniture ❷a company of followers ❸an orchestral composition made up of three or more related parts

sum Ⅰ *n.* the total obtained by adding Ⅱ *v.* add up; give the total of

summary Ⅰ *n.* a short account giving the

main points Ⅱ *adj*. brief; giving the main points only

summer *n*. the warmest season of the year coming between spring and autumn

summit *n*. the highest point; the top, especially of mountain

summon *v*. ❶ demand the presence of; call or send for ❷ gather together; make a great effort to have a particular quality in yourself

sun *n*. the burning star in the sky around which the Earth moves and from which it receives light and heat

Sunday *n*. the day of the week before Monday and after Saturday

sunflower *n*. a very tall plant with large yellow flowers, grown in gardens for its seeds and oil that are used in cooking

sunny *adj*. ❶ having much sunshine ❷ cheerful and happy

super Ⅰ *adj*. excellent; splendid; wonderful Ⅱ *n*. an article of superior quality

superb *adj*. of the finest quality; excellent; grand

superficial *adj*. ❶ of or on the surface only ❷ not thorough or profound

superhighway *n*. a divided highway for high-speed traffic

superhuman *adj*. having much greater power, knowledge, etc. than is normal

superior *adj*. ❶ better or greater in quality ❷ higher in rank, class or position ❸ showing confidence that you are better than others

supermarket *n*. a big shop where you collect things in a basket and pay when you leave

supernatural *adj*. of that which is not controlled or explained by physical laws

superpower *n*. a powerful and influential nation

supersonic *adj*. faster than the speed of sound

superstition *n*. a belief resulting from ignorance of what really exists

supervise *v*. watch over and direct (work, workers)

supper *n*. the evening meal

supple *adj*. easy to bend or move

supplement Ⅰ *n*. sth. added to a book or newspaper to give further information Ⅱ *v*. make an addition or additions to

supply Ⅰ *v*. furnish; provide; satisfy the needs of Ⅱ *n*. an act of supplying

support Ⅰ *v*. ❶ hold up or keep in place; bear the weight of ❷ take the side of; help ❸ provide everything necessary, especially money, so that sb. or sth. can live or exist Ⅱ *n*. the state of supporting or being supported

supporting *adj*. ❶ a supporting actor in a play or film (movie) has an important part but not the leading one ❷ carrying the weight of sth.

suppose *v*. ❶ take it a fact that ❷ guess; think

supposedly *adv*. according to what is generally assumed or believed (often used to indicate that the speaker doubts the truth of the statement)

suppress *v*. put an end by force; put down

surcharge Ⅰ *n*. an extra charge Ⅱ *v*. take an extra charge

sure Ⅰ *adj*. certain to do sth. or confident that sth. will happen Ⅱ *adv*. certainly

surely *adv.* ❶ with certainty ❷ express strongly one's hope or belief ❸ (in answers) certainly; of course

surf Ⅰ *n.* waves of the sea breaking on the shore Ⅱ *v.* engage in surfing

surface *n.* the outside of any objects

surge Ⅰ *v.* ❶move forward, roll on, in or like waves ❷ (of a feeling) arise powerfully Ⅱ *n.* ❶ forward or upward movement ❷ an onrush of a strong feeling

surgeon *n.* a doctor who treats patients by operations

surgery *n.* ❶the science and practice of treating injuries and disease by manual and instrumental operations ❷a doctor's or dentist's room where patients come to consult him

surname *n.* a family name; a last name

surpass *v.* rise above; go beyond

surplus *n.* the amount of money that remains after needs have been supplied

surprise Ⅰ *n.* ❶a feeling caused by sth. unexpected ❷an event or sth. else that is unexpected Ⅱ *v.* give a feeling of surprise; astonish

surrender *v.* give up or yield to the power (especially of an enemy), as a sign of defeat

surround Ⅰ *v.* be all around on every side Ⅱ *n.* a usually decorative edge or border

surrounding Ⅰ *adj.* encircling; around and nearby Ⅱ *n.* (*pl.*) everything around and about a place; conditions that may affect a person

survey Ⅰ *v.* ❶take a general view of ❷ examine the general condition of Ⅱ *n.* a piece of study, examination, etc. of a particular group; a map or record of this

survival *n.* ❶the fact or likelihood of continuing to live ❷ sth. which has continued to exist from an earlier time, especially when similar ones have disappeared

survive *v.* remain alive; live longer than

suspect *v.* feel doubt about

suspend *v.* ❶hang sth. from above ❷stop for a time; delay; keep in an undecided state for a time

suspicion *n.* ❶ a feeling that a person has when he suspects; the state of suspecting or being suspected ❷a small amount of; a little; a slight

suspicious *adj.* having, showing or causing suspicion; not trusting

sustain *v.* ❶ hold up; support ❷ (enable to) keep up; maintain ❸suffer; undergo ❹uphold; give a decision in favour of

sustainable *adj.* ❶able to be maintained at a certain rate or level ❷(especially of development, exploitation, or agriculture) conserving an ecological balance by avoiding depletion of natural resources

swagger *v.* walk in a proud way; behave in this way

swallow Ⅰ *v.* ❶ cause or allow to go down the throat ❷take back; retract ❸ believe without question ❹ suffer or experience ❺take in; exhaust; cause to disappear; use up Ⅱ *n.* ❶ an act of swallowing; the amount swallowed at one time ❷a kind of small swift-flying insect-eating bird with a forked tail

swan *n.* a large, long-necked bird that is usually white

swarm Ⅰ *v.* move, be present in large numbers Ⅱ *n.* a large number of insects, etc.

swear *v.* say solemnly or emphatically

sweat Ⅰ *n.* moisture that is given off by the body through the skin Ⅱ *v.* (cause to) give out sweat

sweater *n.* a woollen jersey or jacket

sweep Ⅰ *v.* clear away (dust, dirt, etc.) with a brush or broom; clean by doing this; push away Ⅱ *n.* an act of cleaning

sweeping *adj.* ❶ wide-ranging ❷ (said about a statement) making no exceptions or limitations; too general

sweet Ⅰ *adj.* ❶ tasting like sugar or honey ❷ pleasing to the senses Ⅱ *n.* candy; dessert

swell *v.* (cause to) become great in volume, thickness, or force

swift *adj.* fast; rapid

swim Ⅰ *v.* ❶ move the body through water by using arms, legs, fins, the tail, etc. ❷have a dizzy feeling

swing *v.* move back and forth regularly

switch Ⅰ *n.* a device for turning on or off an electrical equipment Ⅱ *v.* ❶turn on or turn off ❷change

swollen *adj.* larger than normal, especially as a result of disease or an injury

sword *n.* a weapon with a long sharp blade

symbol *n.* ❶ a sign, mark, object, etc. representing sth. ❷a sign, number, etc. that has a fixed meaning

symbolism *n.* the use of symbols to represent things

symbolize *v.* ❶be a symbol of sth. ❷ represent sth. by means of symbols

sympathize *v.* ❶ feel or express sympathy (with) ❷ agree; share or understand another's feeling

sympathy *n.* ❶having the same feeling as another ❷agreement with or approval of an opinion or aim

symptom *n.* ❶a sign of illness, etc. ❷a sign of the existence of sth. bad

synonym *n.* word that means the same or nearly the same as another word

synthesis *n.* the combining of separate things ideas, etc., into a complete whole

system *n.* a set of things or parts forming a whole

systemic *adj.* affecting or connected with the whole of sth., especially the human body

T t

table *n.* ❶a piece of furniture consisting of a flat top ❷a list (of facts or figures)

tablecloth *n.* a cloth for covering a table, especially during a meal

table mat *n.* a small mat made of material that will not let heat pass, placed under hot dishes to protect a table's surface

tablet *n.* ❶a pill; a small piece of medicine ❷ a lump of hard soap, etc. ❸ a flat piece of stone or metal that has words written on it ❹ a flat sheet of wood, stone, etc. for cutting words on

taboo Ⅰ *n.* sth. which is forbidden by religious belief or custom Ⅱ *adj.* strongly forbidden by social custom, especially because offensive or likely to cause social discomfort

tacit *adj.* accepted or understood without anything being said

tackle Ⅰ *v.* try to deal with or solve Ⅱ *n.* the equipment used in sports

tact *n.* the ability to do or to say the right thing at the right time; the skill in handling people without causing offence

tactful *adj.* having or showing the ability to deal with difficult situation without annoying others

tactical *adj.* ❶ to do with tactics, especially as distinct from strategy ❷ (said about weapons) intended to support the immediate needs of a military operation ❸ (of a person or their actions) showing adroit planning; aiming at an end beyond the immediate action

tactics *n.* ❶(usually singular) the art of arranging military forces for battle and moving them during battle ❷the art of handling a situation, of gaining advantage or success

tadpole *n.* a young frog after it has left its egg and before it is fully grown

tag *n.* ❶a label attached to sb. or sth. for the purpose of identification or to give other information ❷ a nickname or description popularly given to someone or sth. ❸ a character or a set of characters appended to an item of data in order to identify it ❹a small piece or part that is attached to a main body

tail Ⅰ *n.* a movable rear end of an animal's body Ⅱ *v.* follow closely behind

tailor Ⅰ *n.* a person whose business is making clothes Ⅱ *v.* cut out and sew

taint Ⅰ *v.* make or become infected Ⅱ *n.* a trace of some bad quality, decay or infection

take *v.* ❶get into one's hand ❷carry to a

place; go carrying ❸ avail oneself of; use; use or borrow without permission; steal ❹ spend; use up; need

takeover *n.* the act of taking control of sth., especially of one business company by another

tale *n.* ❶ a story, especially ones involving magic or exciting events ❷ a report or account; a trivial lie

talent *n.* a natural ability to do sth. well

talented *adj.* having a natural talent or skill

talk Ⅰ *n.* a conversation Ⅱ *v.* say things; speak to give information

talkative *adj.* talking a lot; full of trivial conversation

talker *n.* ❶ a person who talks, especially one who talks a lot or in a persuasive way ❷ a bird that can copy human speech

talkie *n.* a cinema film with sounds and words, rather than a silent film

talks *n.* a formal exchange of opinions and views

tall *adj.* ❶ having a greater height than is normal or average ❷ hard to believe; excessive

T

tame Ⅰ *adj.* ❶ not wild; accustomed to living with human beings ❷ (of a person) spiritless; submissive ❸ dull or not exciting Ⅱ *v.* make sth. tame

tamper *v.* interfere; change; damage

tan Ⅰ *n.* the yellowish brown colour Ⅱ *adj.* yellowish brown Ⅲ v. ❶ make (skin of an animal) into leather ❷ (cause sth. to) become brown by exposure to the sun

tangible *adj.* able to be touched; real

tango[1] *n.* (a piece of music for) a lively dance originated in South America

tango[2] *v.* dance the tango

tank *n.* ❶ a large container for liquid or gas ❷ an enclosed heavily armed and armored vehicle that moves on two endless metal belts

tap Ⅰ *n.* ❶ a sort of handle that you turn to let water, gas, etc., come out of a pipe ❷ a quick, light blow ❸ a sound made by a light blow Ⅱ *v.* ❶ strike lightly ❷ make a hole in sth. so as to let out or draw off a liquid ❸ furnish (a cask, etc.) with a tap ❹ extract or obtain

tape Ⅰ *n.* ❶ a length of narrow material, used for tying up parcels, packets, etc. ❷ a string stretched between the winning posts on a race track ❸ (a length of) narrow plastic material covered with a special magnetic substance on which sounds or pictures can be recorded Ⅱ *v.* ❶ record (sounds, pictures, etc.) on tape ❷ fasten or tie (a parcel, packet, etc.) with tape

target Ⅰ *n.* ❶ an object to be aimed at in shooting ❷ an objective to be achieved Ⅱ *v.* aim sth.

tariff *n.* ❶ a list of rates or fees; a price list ❷ a list or system of duties imposed on imported or exported goods

task *n.* a piece of work which has to be done

taskmaster *n.* a person who gives sb. tasks to do and keeps him busy

taste[1] *v.* ❶ have a particular flavour in the mouth ❷ feel or try the flavour of sth. in the mouth ❸have experience of; meet

taste[2] *n.* ❶(with a or the) a sense or feeling given by sth. in the mouth ❷(with a) small quantity for sample ❸a liking (or preference) for sth. ❹the choice or judgment in the things ❺appreciation

tasteless *adj.* ❶without taste in the mouth having no or little flavour ❷having or showing bad taste

tasty *adj.* having a pleasant taste in the mouth

tax Ⅰ *n.* money which has to be paid to the government of a country by those who live in it Ⅱ *v.* ❶put a tax on; make sb. pay a tax ❷test severely

taxation *n.* ❶money taken by taxes; an act of taxing ❷the imposition or payment of tax

taxi Ⅰ *n.* a motorcar, especially one with a meter, which maybe hired for journeys Ⅱ *v.* ❶ride in a taxi ❷move on wheels along the ground slowly

taximeter *n.* a small machine fitted in taxis to calculate the charge for each journey

taxing *adj.* needing great effort; physically or mentally demanding

taxpayer *n.* any person or organization that has a legal duty to pay tax

tea *n.* ❶the leaves of a small low bush which are dried and prepared for use as a drink ❷a drink made by adding boiling water to tea leaves or tea bags

teach *v.* instruct or give lessons to sb. to show how to do sth.

teacher *n.* a person who teaches, especially as a profession

teaching *n.* ❶the work of a teacher ❷sth. that is taught

tea house *n.* a restaurant in China or Japan where tea is served

team Ⅰ *n.* a group of people who play sports together on one side Ⅱ *v.* work together (with sb.), especially for a common purpose

teamwork *n.* the ability of a group of people to work together effectively; the work done through combined effort

teapot *n.* a container with a handle and a spout, in which tea is made and served

tear[1] *n.* a drop of salty water coming from the eyes

tear[2] Ⅰ *v.* ❶pull sharply apart or to pieces; make a rough hole in sth. by pulling sharply ❷remove sth. from sth. else by pulling it roughly or violently

tearful *adj.* ❶crying or inclined to cry ❷causing tears; sad or emotional

tease *v.* make fun of (a person)

teaspoon *n.* a small spoon for stirring tea

technical *adj.* ❶of special, practical knowledge ❷of or connected with a particular craft science

technician *n.* a skilled worker or expert, especially a scientific or industrial subject

technique *n.* the technical or mechanical skill in art, music, science, etc.

technological *adj.* of or related to technology

technologist *n.* a specialist in technology

technology *n.* the science of the mechanical and industrial arts

teenager *n.* a person in his or her teens

teens *n.* the period of one's life from the age of 13 to 19

telecast Ⅰ *n.* a television broadcast or programme Ⅱ *v.* broadcast by television

telecommunications *n.* the process or business of receiving or sending messages by telephone, radio, television, or telegraph

telegram *n.* (a piece of paper with) a message sent by telegraph

telegraph Ⅰ *n.* an apparatus for sending messages by the use of electric current along wires or by wireless Ⅱ *v.* send a telegram to

telephone Ⅰ *n.* a system for sending the human voice by electric current through wires or by radio; a machine used for this Ⅱ *v.* send (a message to sb.), speak (to sb.) by telephone

telephoto Ⅰ *adj.* having pictures taken in a distance Ⅱ *n.* ❶ a camera lens that help you to take a picture of a distant object ❷ a picture sent from one place to another by radio, etc.

telescope *n.* a tube-like instrument with special glass that makes distant objects appear bigger and nearer

television *n.* the sending of pictures from a distance and their reproduction on a screen by means of radio waves

telex Ⅰ *n.* ❶ a telegraphic method of sending printed messages ❷ a message received or sent in this way Ⅱ *v.* send a message to a person or a place by telex

tell *v.* ❶ make known; give information to sb. by speaking or writing ❷ distinguish one thing from another

teller *n.* ❶ a person employed to receive and pay out money in a bank ❷ a person who counts votes

telling *adj.* having a great or important effect; significant

temper *n.* the condition of the mind and emotions

temperate *adj.* ❶ showing or behaving with temperance ❷ (of climate) free from extremes of heat or cold

temperature *n.* ❶ the degree of heat or coldness ❷ a body temperature above the normal

temple *n.* ❶ a building for the worship of a god or gods ❷ the flat area on either side of the forehead

temporary *adj.* lasting only for a short time; not permanent

tempt *v.* try to make sb. do sth. wrong or foolish

temptation *n.* the act or state of tempting or being tempted

ten *num.* the number 10

tenant Ⅰ *n.* a person who pays rent for the use of a house or land Ⅱ *v.* (usually passive) occupy as a tenant

tend *v.* ❶ move or turn in a certain direction ❷ take care of; look after; attend to

tendency *n.* a trend or inclination towards a particular action, etc.

tender Ⅰ *adj.* ❶ easily hurt or damaged; quickly feeling pain ❷ showing kindness or gentleness Ⅱ *n.* ❶ a small boat for carrying passengers, supplies, etc. between the shore and a larger boat ❷ a vehicle carrying coal or water, pulled behind a railway engine

tenderhearted *adj*. easily made to have feelings of love, pity, or sorrow

tennis *n*. a game played between two people (singles) or two pairs of people (doubles) who use rackets to hit a small ball backwards and forwards across a low net on a specially marked area

tension *n*. ❶ the state of being stretched tight ❷ a feeling of nervous anxiety, worry, or pressure

tent Ⅰ *n*. a shelter of cloth over poles, which can be put up and taken down quickly Ⅱ *v*. stay or live in a tent

tentative *adj*. made or done to find out what may happen; experimental; not yet decided

term *n*. ❶ a period of time when schools, universities, etc. hold classes ❷ a word or phrase used as the same of sth., especially connected with a particular type of language

terminal Ⅰ *adj*. ❶ of or taking place each term ❷ of the end Ⅱ *n*. ❶ the end of a railway line, bus route, etc.; the center (in a town) for passengers using an airport ❷ a connection in an electric circuit

terminate *v*. bring or come to an end

termination *n*. ❶ an act of ending sth. ❷ the last part or last letter of a word

terminus *n*. the last stop where a journey by air, bus or railway, etc. ends

termly *adj*. happening each term

terms *n*. ❶ the conditions of an agreement, contract, etc. ❷ the stated conditions concerning payment, prices, etc. ❸ a relationship of the stated quality ❹ a way of expressing yourself or of saying sth.

terrace Ⅰ *n*. ❶ a porch or balcony ❷ a raised bank of earth with vertical or sloping sides and a flat top Ⅱ *v*. form into a terrace

terrible *adj*. ❶ causing great fear or horror ❷ very bad or of very poor quality

terribly *adv*. ❶ very; extremely ❷ in a terrible manner

terrific *adj*. ❶ very good; enjoyable; excellent ❷ very great in amount, value, etc. ❸ causing terror; terrifying

terrify *v*. fill with fear

territory *n*. ❶ an area of land under the control of a ruler or state ❷ an area for which a person has responsibility or in which a person conducts an activity ❸ a special sphere of thought or experience ❹ an area which an animal defends against others of the same species

terror *n*. ❶ a great fear ❷ sth. or sb. that causes great fear ❸ a troublesome person (usually a child)

terrorist *n*. a person who is in favour of the practice of using violence to obtain political demands

test *n*. an examination or trial (of sth.) to find its quality, value, composition, etc.

testament *n*. ❶ (often in last will and ～) the most recent will that sb. has made, especially the last will that is made previous to sb.'s death ❷ one of the two main parts of the Bible

testify *v*. ❶ say as a witness; give testimony in a court of law ❷ give evidence of; serve as evidence of

text *n.* ❶ the main body of writing in a book ❷ the words written by the author; the original words of a writer

textbook *n.* a standard printed book for the study of a subject, especially used in schools

textile Ⅰ *n.* any material made by weaving Ⅱ *adj.* ❶ woven or capable of being woven ❷ of or having sth. to do with textile

texture *n.* ❶ the way that a substance feels when touching it ❷ the structure of (food or soil, etc.)

than *conj.* ❶ introducing the second part of a comparison ❷ (of number, quantity, etc.) above or below another

thank Ⅰ *v.* express gratitude to Ⅱ *n.* a grateful feeling; an expression of this

thankful *adj.* feeling or expressing thanks; grateful

thankless *adj.* unpleasant or difficult to do and unlikely to bring you any rewards or thanks from anyone

thanks Ⅰ *int.* used to show that you are grateful to sb. for sth. they have done thanksgiving Ⅱ *n.* ❶ an expression of gratefulness, especially to God ❷ a festival for giving thanks to God (in USA, the fourth Thursday in November; in Canada, the second Monday in October)

T

that Ⅰ *pron.* ❶ referring to a person or thing that is not near the speaker ❷ used to identify a specific person or thing observed or heard by the speaker ❸ used as a relative pronoun used to introduce a defining clause, especially one essential to identification ❹ instead of "which" "who" or "whom" Ⅱ *conj.* used after some verbs, adjectives and nouns to introduce a new part of the sentence Ⅲ *adv.* to such a degree; so

thaw Ⅰ *n.* a period of warmer weather when snow and ice melt, usually at the end of winter Ⅱ *v.* become or cause to become soft or liquid

the Ⅰ *art.* ❶ used for mentioning a particular thing, either because you already know which one is being talked about or because only one exists ❷ used with an adjective to make it into a noun meaning all members of a group or class Ⅱ *adv.* ❶ used with the superlative ❷ used in comparisons, to show that two things happen together

theater *n.* ❶ a building for the performance of plays, for dramatic spectacles, etc. ❷ a hall or room with seats in rows rising one behind another ❸ a scene of important events

theft *n.* ❶ the act of stealing ❷ an instance of this ❸ sth. stolen

their *adj.* of or belonging to them

theirs *pron.* sth. belonging to them

them *pron.* the object form of they

theme *n.* ❶ the subject of a talk, book, etc. ❷ repeated melody in a symphony, etc.

themselves *pron.* ❶ a reflexive form of they ❷ a strong form of they ❸ their real selves

then *adv.* ❶ at that time (in the past or future) ❷ next; after that; afterwards ❸ if that so; in that case ❹ besides; also

theoretically *adv.* ❶ in a theoretical way; not practically ❷ according to theory but not really

theorist *n.* a person who forms or studies the theory of a subject

theorize *v.* form a theory or theories; speculate

theory *n.* general principles, put forward to explain certain facts

there Ⅰ *adv.* ❶ in, at, or to that place or position ❷ existing or available ❸ in that respect; on that issue Ⅱ *int.* ❶ used to call attention, usually stressed ❷ used to praise or encourage small children

thereabouts *adv.* ❶ near that place ❷ somewhere near that number or quantity or time, etc.

thereby *adv.* by that means; because of that

therefore *adv.* for this or that reason; on this or that account

thereof *adv.* of that; from that source

thereon *adv.* on that or it

thereupon *adv.* ❶ as a result of that; about that matter ❷ without delay after that; happening immediately after sth. else has happened

thermometer *n.* an instrument used for measuring and showing temperature

thesis *n.* ❶ an opinion or statement that is supported by reasoned argument to prove it is true ❷ a long piece of writing done for a higher university degree

they *pron.* the subject form or plural of he, she, it

thick *adj.* ❶ of great depth from one surface to the opposite ❷ growing closely together in small area ❸ relatively dense in consistency

thicken *v.* ❶ make or become thick or thicker ❷ become more closely grouped together or more solid than it was before

thickness *n.* ❶ the state or degree of being thick ❷ a layer of sth.

thief *n.* a person who steals or robs secretly and without violence

thieve *v.* steal things; rob people; act as a thief

thin *adj.* ❶ with little space from one side to the opposite side; not thick ❷ not having much flesh ❸ (especially of sth. said or written) not having the necessary qualities of the intended result; unsatisfactory

thing *n.* ❶ any material object ❷ sth. that is non-material ❸ a circumstance or an event; the course of an action

think *v.* ❶ form in the mind; have in the mind as an idea ❷ consider; be of the opinion

thinker *n.* a person who thinks

thinking Ⅰ *adj.* thoughtful; reasoning Ⅱ *n.* ❶ thought; reasoning ❷ opinion; judgement

third *num.* ❶ next after the second ❷ one of three equal parts

thirdly *adv.* in the third place

thirst *n.* the feeling caused by a desire or need to drink; suffering caused by this

thirteen *num.* the number 13

thirty *num.* the number 30

this Ⅰ *pron.* ❶ used to refer to a person or thing that is near you ❷ used to introduce sb. or sth. that you are going to talk about Ⅱ *adv.* to this extent; so

thorn *n.* ❶ a sharp pointed part on the stem of a plant ❷ sth. that causes irritation and annoyance

thorny *adj.* ❶ prickly; having thorns ❷ difficult to deal with; causing worry or trouble

thorough *adj.* complete in every way

those *pron.* & *adj.* plural of that

though Ⅰ *conj.* in spite of the fact that Ⅱ *adv.* however

thought *n.* ❶ the process of thinking ❷ an idea, opinion, or intention formed by thinking

thoughtful *adj.* ❶ full of thought; showing thought ❷ considerate; thinking of or showing thought for the needs of others

thoughtless *adj.* ❶ careless; unthinking; showing lack of thought ❷ selfish; inconsiderate (of others)

thousand *adj.* & *num.* & *n.* (of) the number 1000

thread Ⅰ *n.* ❶ a line, thin piece of cotton, wool, etc. for sewing or weaving ❷ sth. very thin, suggesting a thread ❸ a chain or line ❹ a spiral ridge round a screw Ⅱ *v.* ❶ pass one end of a thread through ❷ make (one's way) through

threat *n.* ❶ an expression of an intention to inflict pain, injury, or evil ❷ the possibility of trouble, danger or disaster

threaten *v.* ❶ utter threats against ❷ give signs or warning of; be a menacing indication of sth. ❸ give the danger or threat to; likely to harm, spoil, ruin, etc.

threatening *adj.* ❶ having a hostile or deliberately frightening quality or manner ❷ (of a person or situation) causing someone to feel vulnerable or at risk ❸ (of the sky, clouds, etc.) showing that bad weather is likely

three *num.* the number

threshold *n.* ❶ a piece of wood or stone fixed beneath the door into a house ❷ the point just before a new start or beginning

thrift *n.* the quality and practice of being careful in the use of money or goods

thriller *n.* a book, play, or film that tells a very exciting story, especially of crime and violence

thrilling *adj.* exciting and enjoyable

thrive *v.* prosper; succeed; grow strong and healthy

throat *n.* ❶ the front part of the neck ❷ the passage in the neck through which food passes to the stomach and air to the lungs

throb *v.* ❶ (with reference to the heart) beat more strongly ❷ beat or work regularly like the heart

throng Ⅰ *n.* a large crowd of people Ⅱ *v.* go (as if) in a crowd

through *prep.* ❶ from one end or side of sth. to the other (opening, channel, or location) ❷ so as to make a hole or opening in (a physical object) ❸ continuing in time towards completion of a process (or period) ❹ from the beginning to the end of (an experience or activity, typically a tedious or stressful one) ❺ by means of; because of

throughout Ⅰ *adv.* in every part; in, into or during every part Ⅱ *prep.* during the whole period of time

throw *v.* go through the air, usually with

a force, by a movement of the arm or by mechanical means

thrust Ⅰ *v.* push suddenly or violently Ⅱ *n.* the act of pushing suddenly or violently

thumb Ⅰ *n.* the short thick finger at the side of the hand, slightly apart from the other four Ⅱ *v.* ❶ turn over pages with or as if with one's thumb

thunder Ⅰ *n.* ❶ the loud noise which usually follows a flash of lightning ❷ a loud sound like a thunder Ⅱ *v.* make a noise like thunder

thunderstorm *n.* a storm with thunder and lightening, usually with heavy rain

Thursday *n.* the day of the week after Wednesday and before Friday

thus *adv.* ❶ in this way ❷ consequently; hence ❸ to a stated degree or extent

tick Ⅰ *n.* ❶ a light and regularly repeated sound, especially of a clock or watch ❷ a mark (√) used to show that sth. is correct ❸ a moment; a second Ⅱ *v.* ❶ (of a clock, watch, etc.) make a regularly repeated short sound ❷ mark with a tick

ticket *n.* a written or printed piece of card or paper, giving the holder right to do sth.

tide *n.* ❶ a rise and fall of the level of the sea, caused by the attraction of the moon ❷ a flow or tendency

tidemark *n.* ❶ a mark round the inside of an emptied bath that shows the level to which the bath had been filled ❷ a dirty mark on the skin left by incomplete washing

tidewater *n.* ❶ water that flows onto the land when the tide is very high ❷ the water in the tidal parts of rivers and streams

tidings *n.* news; information

tidy Ⅰ *adj.* ❶ in good order; arranged neatly ❷ considerable; fairly large Ⅱ *v.* make (a place) neat

tie Ⅰ *v.* ❶ fasten or bind ❷ be equal in points, marks, etc. Ⅱ *n.* ❶ a long, narrow piece of cloth that a man wears round the neck of his skirt ❷ a piece of string or wire used for tying sth.

tiepin *n.* a small decorative clip, often of silver or gold, for holding a tie in place

tiger *n.* a type of very large, fierce, wild animal that has yellowish fur with black lines across and lives in Asia

tight *adj.* fastened, fixed, or held firmly

tighten *v.* make or become tight or tighter

tigress *n.* a female tiger

till Ⅰ *conj.* up to the time when; up to; down to Ⅱ *prep.* until

tilt *v.* lean, cause to lean, so as to be no longer level or upright

timber *n.* ❶ wood used for building and making things ❷ a large piece of shaped wood or beam, forming a support

time *n.* ❶ all the days of the past, present and future ❷ the point of time stated in hours and minutes of the day ❸ an occasion when sb. do sth. or when sth. happens

timeless *adj.* not affected by the passage of time or by changes of taste or fashion

timely *adj.* occurring at a suitable or useful time

timer *n.* ❶a device for timing things ❷a device for activating sth. at a preset time

timetable Ⅰ *n.* a list showing the time at which certain events will happen, e. g. when buses or trains leave and arrive, or when lessons take place in a school Ⅱ *v.* organize events in a timetable

timid *adj.* easily frightened; nervous

timing *n.* the choosing of exactly the right moment to do sth. so as to get the best effect

tin Ⅰ *n.* ❶ a type of soft metal ❷ a container (usually airtight) made of tinplate Ⅱ *v.* put food, etc. in an airtight tin Ⅲ *adj.* like tin; making a sound like tin when struck

ting Ⅰ *v.* (cause to) make a high clear ringing sound Ⅱ *n.* a high clear sound such as that made by a small bell

tiny *adj.* very small in size or amount

tip Ⅰ *n.* ❶the pointed or thin end of sth. ❷a gift or money to a porter, waiter, etc. for personal services Ⅱ *v.* ❶ touch or strike slightly

tiptoe Ⅰ *n.* the tip of the toe Ⅱ *v.* walk on the front parts of your foot

T

tired *adj.* ❶needing to rest or sleep ❷no longer interested in; annoyed with

tireless *adj.* not tiring easily; having a lot of energy

tiresome *adj.* troublesome; making you feel annoyed; causing to be tired

tiring *adj.* making tired; causing fatigue

tissue *n.* ❶(any kind of) woven fabric ❷ a collection of cells that from different parts of humans, animals and plants ❸a piece of soft absorbent paper

title *n.* ❶an identifying name given to a book, painting, etc. ❷a claim or right, especially a legal right to ownership ❸a name that describes the rank or office ❹ championship

to Ⅰ *prep.* ❶in the direction of; toward ❷ (indicating comparison, ratio and reference) ❸(of time) before ❹so as to cause (especially a feeling) Ⅱ *adv.* into a shut position

toast Ⅰ *n.* ❶ sliced bread heated and browned ❷the act of drinking in honor of sb. or sth. Ⅱ *v.* wish happiness, success, etc. to sb. (or sth.) while raising a glass of wine

toaster *n.* an electrical device for toasting bread

tobacco *n.* a plant or its large leaves, prepared for smoking in cigarettes, pipes, etc.

today *n.* ❶on this day ❷at the present time; nowadays

toe *n.* each of the five divisions of the front part of the foot; the similar part of an animal's foot

together *adv.* in company; with or near each other

toilet *n.* ❶ the process of dressing, arranging the hair, etc. ❷a room with receptacle for waste matter from the body

tolerable *adj.* fairly good or acceptable; that can be tolerated

tolerance *n.* the ability to suffer pain, hardship, etc., without being damaged

tolerant *adj.* having or showing tolerance

tolerate *v.* allow or endure with protest

toleration *n.* the quality of allowing people to behave in a way that may not please one, without becoming annoyed

toll[1] *n.* ❶ money paid to use a bridge, ferry, road, etc. ❷ damage; loss

toll[2] *v.* (with reference to a bell) ring slowly and deeply

tomato *n.* ❶ a soft red fruit eaten as a vegetable ❷ the plant on which this fruit grows

tomb *n.* a grave, especially a large decorated one

tombstone *n.* a memorial stone set up over a grave

tomorrow Ⅰ *n.* ❶ the day after today ❷ the future Ⅱ *adv.* during or on the day after today

ton *n.* ❶ a measure of weight, or the internal capacity of a ship ❷ a large weight, quantity, or number

tone Ⅰ *n.* ❶ the quality of a sound, especially with reference to its quality, feeling, etc. ❷ the shade of colour; the degree of light ❸ (only singular) the general spirit, character, morale of a community, etc. ❹ a proper and normal condition of the body Ⅱ *v.* give a particular tone of sound or colour to

tongue *n.* ❶ the movable part in the mouth, used in talking, tasting, licking, etc. ❷ a particular language

tonic Ⅰ *n.* ❶ a medicine giving strength and energy ❷ anything which increases health or strength ❸ the keynote; the first note of a musical scale Ⅱ *adj.* ❶ giving strength or energy ❷ of or based on the keynote

tonight Ⅰ *adv.* on this present night Ⅱ *n.* the night of today

too *adv.* ❶ also; as well; in addition ❷ in a higher degree that is allowable, required, etc.

tool *n.* ❶ any instrument used in doing work, especially with the hands ❷ means ❸ a person used by another for dishonest purposes

tooth *n.* one of the white bony objects which grow in the mouth

toothpaste *n.* a paste for cleaning the teeth

toothpick *n.* a small pointed piece of wood, etc. for removing bits of food from between the teeth

top *n.* ❶ the highest part of sth. ❷ the highest or most important rank or position

topic *n.* a subject for conversation, talk, writing, etc.

topical *adj.* ❶ (of a subject) of immediate relevance, interest, or importance owing to its relation to current events ❷ relating to a particular subject; classified according to subject

torch *n.* a piece of wood, twisted flax, etc., treated with oil, soaked in tallow, etc., for carrying or using as a flaming light

torment Ⅰ *n.* the severe bodily or mental pain or suffering Ⅱ *v.* cause severe suffering to; annoy

tornado *n.* a violent wind which goes round and round

torrent *n.* ❶ a violently rushing stream ❷ a violent outpouring

toss *v.* ❶ throw into or through the air ❷ (cause to) move about violently and rapidly ❸ mix lightly ❹ produce quickly with little effort

total Ⅰ *adj.* complete; entire Ⅱ *v.* find the total; reach the total of; amount to Ⅲ *n.* the whole amount

totality *n.* the whole of sth.

totally *adv.* completely; absolutely

totter *v.* move or walk as if about to fall

touch Ⅰ *v.* ❶ bring a part of the body (especially the hand) into contact with ❷ tap or nudge lightly Ⅱ *n.* the act or fact of putting your hands or fingers onto sb. or sth.

touched *adj.* caused to feel sympathy or gratitude

touching *adj.* rousing kind feelings, sympathy or pity

touchy *adj.* ❶ (of a person) oversensitive and irritable ❷ (of an issue or situation) requiring to be dealt with carefully

tough *adj.* ❶ (of meat) hard to cut or to get one's teeth into ❷ difficult; demanding effort

toughen *v.* become or make tough

tour Ⅰ *n.* a journey made for pleasure during which several places are visited Ⅱ *v.* travel around a place

tourism *n.* the business of providing entertainment, hotels, etc. for tourists

tourist Ⅰ *n.* a person travelling for pleasure Ⅱ *adj.* of or for a tour

tournament *n.* a number of contests

tout *n.* a person who offers tickets that are in short supply for sale at a price higher than usual

toward(s) *prep.* ❶ in the direction of ❷ near in time

towel Ⅰ *n.* a piece of cloth for drying sth. wet Ⅱ *v.* dry or rub (oneself) with a towel

tower *n.* a tall building, either standing alone or forming part of a church, castle or other large building

towering *adj.* ❶ very tall ❷ of great importance; outstanding ❸ very great; intense

town *n.* a center of population, larger than a village but smaller than a city

toxic *adj.* poisonous or caused by poisonous substances

toy Ⅰ *n.* sth. for amusement; an object for children to play with Ⅱ *v.* amuse oneself

trace Ⅰ *n.* a mark, sign, etc. of the former presence or passage of some person, thing, or event Ⅱ *v.* mark out; outline

track *n.* ❶ a line or route along which sth. travels or moves ❷ a railway line ❸ marks left on sth.

traction *n.* ❶ the act of drawing or pulling a heavy load over a surface ❷ the form or type of power used for this ❸ the force that prevents a wheel from slipping over the surface on which it runs ❹ the process of being pulled by a special medical apparatus in order to cure a broken bone or similar injury

tractor *n.* a vehicle for pulling heavy loads

trade Ⅰ *n.* ❶ buying and selling of goods; an exchange of goods for money or other goods; a particular branch of this ❷ occupation; a way of making a living; employment of any kind; handicraft Ⅱ *v.* buy and sell

trademark *n.* a company's legally registered name or emblem, used to identify its products or services

tradition *n.* a custom, habit and belief handed down from generation to generation

traffic Ⅰ *n.* ❶ (the movement of) people, vehicles, etc. along a street, road, etc. ❷ the business done by a railway line, steamship line or airline ❸ trading; commerce Ⅱ *v.* trade (in) (especially illegal)

tragedian *n.* a person who writes tragedies

tragedy *n.* a play for the theater, a film play of a serious or solemn kind, with a sad ending

tragic *adj.* ❶of or related to tragedy ❷ very sad, unfortunate, etc.

tragicomedy *n.* ❶ a play that is both funny and sad ❷ an event that is both funny and sad

trail *n.* a line, a mark or series of marks, drawn or left behind by sb. or sth. that has passed by

train Ⅰ *n.* ❶ a line of railway carriages pulled by an engine ❷ a series or chain of sth. Ⅱ *v.* teach; drill; bring up

trainee *n.* a person who is being trained for a particular job or profession

trainer *n.* ❶ a person who trains people or animals ❷ an aircraft used to train pilots, or a machine simulating an aircraft

training *n.* the act or process of learning the skills

trait *n.* a special feature (especially of sb.'s character)

tram *n.* a public vehicle, driven by electricity, that runs along metal lines set in the road

tramp Ⅰ *v.* walk with heavy steps Ⅱ *n.* ❶ a long walk ❷a person with no home or job, who wanders from place to place and usually begs for food or money

tranquil *adj.* quiet and peaceful

transact *v.* conduct, carry through (business, etc. with sb.)

transaction *n.* ❶ the process of doing sth. ❷a piece of business carried out ❸a published report of the proceedings of a learned society

transcend *v.* go or be beyond or outside the range of

transcribe *v.* (especially with reference to writing out in full notes taken in shorthand) write out again

transcript *n.* a written or printed version of sth. originally in a different medium

transfer Ⅰ *v.* change position; move from a thing or a place to another thing or place Ⅱ *n.* an act of moving from a place, etc. to another one

transform *v.* change the shape, appearance, quality, or nature of sth.

transformation *n.* the act or state of changing shape, etc.

transfuse *v.* take blood from one person and put it into another

transfusion *n.* the process of putting new blood into a person or an animal

transistor *n.* ❶ a small electrical apparatus, especially used in radios, televisions, etc. ❷a radio that has these instead of valves

transit *n.* an act of moving or being moved across or through

transition *n.* an act of changing or passing from one state, subject, or place to another

translate *v.* give the meaning of words of one language in another language

translation *n.* ❶ translating ❷ sth. translated

translator *n.* a person who translates (especially sth. written)

transmission *n.* the act of transmitting or state of being transmitted

transmit *v.* ❶ pass or hand on; send on ❷ allow through or along

transmitter *n.* a device or set of equipment for transmitting radio or television signals

transparency *n.* ❶ a state of being transparent ❷ a positive photograph printed on film or glass; a slide

transparent *adj.* ❶ clear and capable of being seen through ❷ easily discovered or found out ❸ clear; easily understood

transplant Ⅰ *v.* ❶ plant sth. again in a different place ❷ transfer (tissue or an organ) from one body to another ❸ (of people) move from one place to another Ⅱ *n.* ❶ sth. transplanted ❷ an act or operation of transplanting

transport Ⅰ *v.* carry from one place to another Ⅱ *n.* conveying or being conveyed; means of conveyance

transverse Ⅰ *adj.* lying or passing across; placed crosswise; crossing from side to side Ⅱ *n.* ❶ a transverse part, beam, etc. ❷ horizontal axis; the longer axis of an ellipse ❸ muscle which is transverse to other part of the body

trap Ⅰ *n.* a device used to capture animals Ⅱ *v.* set a trap; catch with trap

trapper *n.* a person who traps wild animals, especially for their fur

trappings *n.* ornaments; signs of a rank or military rank

trash *n.* ❶ useless things; rubbish ❷ a worthless material, writing, or person

trashcan *n.* a dustbin or a public litter-bin

travel *v.* ❶ make (especially long) journeys ❷ move or run along

travel(l)er *n.* a person on a journey

travel(l)ing *adj.* ❶ performing in different places around an area or a country ❷ carried by or used by a traveler ❸ of or connected with travel

traverse *v.* pass across

tray *n.* a flat piece of wood or metal with raised edges, used for carrying small articles

tread *v.* put the foot down while walking

treasure Ⅰ *n.* ❶ valuable things as gold, silver, jewels, etc.; wealth ❷ a highly valued object or person Ⅱ *v.* keep sth. or care for sth. carefully

treat *v.* ❶ act or behave towards ❷ try to cure by medical means ❸ regard or consider

treatment *n.* ❶ (a particular way of) dealing with sb. or sth.; what is done to obtain a desired result ❷ sth. that is done to relieve or cure an illness or a defect, etc.

treaty *n.* ❶ an agreement made and signed between nations ❷ the agreement or negotiation between persons

tree *n.* a tall plant with a wooden trunk and branches, that lives for many years

tremble Ⅰ *v.* ❶ shake because of fear, cold, etc. ❷ move and shake slightly ❸ be in a state of agitation Ⅱ *n.* shudder; uncontrollable shaking

tremendous *adj.* ❶ very great in size, amount, or degree ❷ wonderful; extremely good

trend Ⅰ *n.* the general direction; tendency Ⅱ *v.* have a certain trend

trendy[1] *adj.* very fashionable; deeply influenced by the latest fashions

trendy[2] *n.* a trendy person

trial *n.* ❶ a process of testing or proving ❷ examination in a law court before a judge

triangle *n.* ❶ a flat shape with three straight sides and three angles ❷ a thing shaped like this ❸ the situation involving three people, ideas, opinions, etc.

tribe *n.* a group of people of the same race, language, customs, etc.

trick Ⅰ *n.* ❶ sth. done to deceive, outwit, or outdo sb.; sth. done to make a person appear ridiculous ❷ a mischievous act; a practical joke Ⅱ *v.* make sb. believe that sth. is true

tricycle *n.* a cycle with three wheels (often used by young children instead of a bicycle)

trifling *adj.* trivial or unimportant

trilogy *n.* a group of three books or plays about the same subject

trip Ⅰ *n.* a journey, especially a pleasure excursion Ⅱ *v.* walk, run, or dance with quick, light steps

triple Ⅰ *adj.* made up of three parts or parties Ⅱ *v.* make, become or be three times bigger

triumph Ⅰ *n.* a complete victory or success Ⅱ *v.* gain victory or success, especially in dealing with a very difficult situation or opponent

trivial *adj.* ❶ of small value or importance ❷ ordinary; commonplace

troop *n.* ❶ a group of soldiers ❷ a large group of persons or animals

tropic *n.* one of the two circles round the earth about 23°26′ north or south of the equator

tropical *adj.* ❶ to do with or located in the tropics ❷ (said about the climate) hot and humid

trouble Ⅰ *v.* cause worry, discomfort or anxiety to Ⅱ *n.* ❶ a mental disturbance, worry, problem, etc. ❷ (political or social) disorder or violent situation

troublemaker *n.* someone who constantly causes trouble

troublesome *adj.* ❶ causing trouble or anxiety ❷ difficult to deal with

trousers *n.* a two-legged outer garment, reaching from the waist to the ankles

truck Ⅰ *n.* ❶ an open cart used on a railway for carrying heavy goods ❷ a motor lorry ❸ a railway porter's barrow Ⅱ *v.* carry on a truck

true *adj.* ❶ real; in agreement with the fact ❷ behaving loyal and faithful as promised

truelove *n.* the person one loves; a sweetheart

truly *adv.* ❶ exactly; in accordance with the truth ❷ really ❸ sincerely ❹ (Yours ~) used at the end of a formal letter, just before the signature, when addressing someone as Sir, Madam, etc.

trust Ⅰ *v.* believe sb. is sincere, etc. and that they will not try to harm you Ⅱ *n.* a confidence, strong belief in the goddess, strength, reliability of sth. or sb.

trustworthy *adj.* worthy of trust; dependable

truth *n.* ❶ sth. that is true; the true facts ❷ the quality or state of being true ❸ a fact, belief, principle, etc. accepted as true

truthful *adj.* ❶ (said about a person) always telling the truth ❷ true or accurate

try Ⅰ *v.* ❶ make an effort to do; attempt to do ❷ use sth. or do sth. as an experiment or test, to see whether it is effective Ⅱ *n.* an attempt or effort

tube *n.* ❶ a long pipe of metal, glass, rubber, etc. used to carry liquid or gas ❷ a soft metal container with a screw-cap, used for pastes, paints, etc. ❸ (in London) underground railway ❹ electron tube or vacuum tube

Tuesday *n.* the third day of the week, after Monday

tune *n.* the succession of notes forming a melody (of a song, hymn, etc.)

tunnel Ⅰ *n.* a large hole dug for a road or railway through a hill or under a river, town, or mountain Ⅱ *v.* make a tunnel (through or into)

turkey *n.* a large bird with a red featherless head and big flaps under the chin

turn Ⅰ *v.* ❶ (cause to) move around a point; (cause to) move so as to face in a different direction ❷ (cause to) change in nature, quality, condition, etc. Ⅱ *n.* ❶ a turning; a change in direction or condition ❷ an occasion or opportunity for doing sth., especially in one's proper order among others

turnabout *n.* a sudden and complete change or reversal of policy, opinion, or situation

turning *n.* a place where one road meets another, forming a corner

turnover *n.* ❶ the amount of money a business takes in a particular period ❷ the rate at which goods are sold ❸ the rate at which workers leave and are replaced

twice *adv.* two times

twin Ⅰ *n.* one of two children born at the same time to the same mother Ⅱ *adj.* ❶ used to describe one of a pair of twins ❷ used to describe two things that are used as a pair

twist Ⅰ *v.* ❶ wind or turn one around the other ❷ turn and curve in different directions; change position or direction Ⅱ *n.* the action of twisting or being twisted

two *num.* the number 2

tycoon *n.* a very rich and powerful businessman

type Ⅰ *n.* ❶ a particular kind, class, or group; a group or class of people or things that share certain qualities and are different from those outside the group or class ❷ a person or thing that has all the characteristics of a particular group or class; a standard example Ⅱ *v.* write with a typewriter or using a word processor

typewriter *n.* a typing machine with keys for printing letters on a piece of paper

typhoon *n.* a violent tropical storm with very strong winds

typical *adj.* ❶ having or showing the usual qualities of a people, thing, etc. ❷ behaving in the way that sb. expected

typically *adv.* ❶ used to say that sth. usually happens in the way that you are stating ❷ in a way that shows the usual qualities or features of a particular type of person, thing or group

typify *v.* be a representative specimen of sb. or sth.

typist *n.* a person whose job is to type or who uses a typewriter

tyre *n.* a band of solid rubber on the rim of a wheel, especially the kind on bicycle and motorcar wheels

T

U u

ugly *adj.* unpleasant to look at

ultimately *adv.* ❶in the end; finally ❷at the most basic and important level

umbrella *n.* a cover with a handle used to shelter one from rain or sun

unable *adj.* not able to do sth.

unacceptable *adj.* that you cannot accept, allow or approve of

unaccustomed *adj.* ❶ not accustomed; not used to sth. ❷not familiar; unusual or strange

unaffected *adj.* ❶ not affected; not influenced; unchanged ❷ natural; without affectation

unavailable *adj.* not able to be used or obtained; not at someone's disposal

unavoidable *adj.* not able to be avoided

unaware *adj.* not having knowledge or consciousness (of sth.)

U

unbalanced *adj.* not keeping or showing an even balance

unbelievable *adj.* very surprising; difficult to believe

uncertain *adj.* ❶ not known with certainty; unable to decide; not certain ❷changeable; not reliable

uncertainty *n.* ❶ the state of being uncertain ❷the state of being uncertain

uncle *n.* ❶the brother of one's father or mother ❷the husband of one's aunt

unclean *adj.* not clean

uncomfortable *adj.* not comfortable; uneasy

uncommon *adj.* unusual; remarkable

uncountable *adj.* that cannot be counted or used with a or an

undecided *adj.* ❶ not having made a decision ❷not settled or resolved

under *prep.* ❶in or to a lower position than ❷ less than ❸ used to express dominance or control

underclothes *n.* underwear

underestimate *v.* guess too low a value for (an amount)

undergo *v.* have an unpleasant experience; suffer from

undergraduate *n.* a student who is doing a university course for a first degree

underground Ⅰ *adj.* ❶under the ground ❷secret Ⅱ *adv.* ❶under the surface of ground ❷secretly

underline *v.* draw a line under; emphasize sth.

understand *v.* ❶get the meaning (of) ❷ know or believe sth. because you have been told ❸assume to be the case; take for granted

understanding Ⅰ *adj.* good at knowing

how other people feel; sympathetic Ⅱ *n.* ❶the power of abstract thought ❷the capacity for sympathizing ❸ an informal agreement

understate *v.* not state strongly or fully enough

undertake *v.* ❶ start sth. or be responsible for sth. ❷promise; agree

underwater Ⅰ *adj.* situated, used, or done beneath the surface of water Ⅱ *adv.* beneath the surface of water

underwear *n.* clothes worn under outer garments, especially next to the skin

underworld *n.* ❶ the place of departed spirits of the dead ❷the criminal world

undesirable Ⅰ *adj.* not wanted, not welcomed; unpleasant Ⅱ *n.* an unwanted person, especially someone regarded as immoral, criminal, or socially unacceptable

undeveloped *adj.* not developed; (usually of a place) in its natural state

undo *v.* ❶untie or unfasten ❷remove the effects of

undoubted *adj.* certain; accepted as true

undress *v.* ❶take the clothes off ❷take one's clothes off

unearth *v.* dig up

uneasy *adj.* not easy in body or mind; anxious

uneducated *adj.* showing a lack of (good) education

unemployed *adj.* not having a job

unemployment *n.* ❶ the state of being unemployed ❷ the number of unemployed workers

unequal *adj.* not equal or balanced

uneven *adj.* ❶not level or smooth ❷not regular or uniform ❸ not equally balanced

unexpected *adj.* not expected or anticipated; not planned

unfair *adj.* not just, reasonable, or honest

unfaithful *adj.* not true to a promise; not faithful to marriage vows

unfavo(u)rable *adj.* ❶ expressing or showing a lack of approval or support ❷ adverse; inauspicious

unfortunate *adj.* ❶ having bad luck; unlucky ❷unsuitable or regrettable

unhappy *adj.* not happy; sad and depressed

unhealthy *adj.* not in good health; likely to cause poor health

uniform Ⅰ *adj.* the same; not changing Ⅱ *n.* clothes worn by all members of a group

unify *v.* make parts into one whole

uninformed *adj.* showing a lack of knowledge or enough information

uninterested *adj.* having or showing no interest in sb. or sth.

uninteresting *adj.* not interesting

union *n.* ❶the act or state of uniting or joining ❷ an association for a group of people

unique *adj.* ❶having no equal; being the only one ❷ often considered nonstandard; unusual

unit *n.* ❶ an individual thing or person regarded as single and complete, especially for purposes of calculation ❷ an amount or quantity used as a standard of measurement

unite *v.* ❶ join together into one ❷ act together for a purpose

U

unity *n.* ❶concord between two or more persons; harmony ❷ the state of being one, or the condition of being united

universal *adj.* ❶of the whole world ❷ affecting all; general; of or for all

universe *n.* everything that exists everywhere; the whole of space and all the stars, planets and other forms of matter

university *n.* an educational institution that provides instruction and facilities for research in many branches of advanced learning, and which awards degrees

unjust *adj.* not right or fair, not just

unkind *adj.* not kind; cruel

unknown *adj.* ❶ not known; not familiar; strange ❷ not famous; not well known

unless *conj.* ❶ if not; except; if it were not that ❷except when...

unlike Ⅰ *prep.* not like; different from Ⅱ *adj.* different; not the same

unlikely *adj.* improbable; not likely to happen or be true

unlock *v.* use a key to open the lock of

unmoved *adj.* showing no pity or sympathy

unnatural *adj.* not natural; unusual

unnecessary *adj.* not necessary or wanted

unpack *v.* remove (possessions) from (a container)

unpleasant *adj.* causing dislike; not enjoyable; disagreeable

unqualified *adj.* not having suitable knowledge or qualifications

unquiet *adj.* not calm or at rest

unreal *adj.* seeming more like a dream than reality

unreasonable *adj.* unfair in demands; not sensible

unsound *adj.* not in good condition

untidy *adj.* in disorder; not tidy

untie *v.* ❶loosen or unfasten a knot, etc. ❷make free; release

until *prep* & *conj.* ❶up to a certain time or event ❷(in negative) before a certain time or event

untold *adj.* ❶not told or expressed ❷too great to be counted or measured; limitless

untrue *adj.* false; not true

unusual *adj.* not usual; rare; strange

unusually *adv.* very; more than is usual

unveil *v.* remove a covering from; show sth. to the public

up Ⅰ *prep.* ❶to or in a higher position ❷ along Ⅱ *adv.* ❶to or in a higher place or position ❷to the place where sb. or sth. is ❸at or in a higher position; above ❹so as to be completely finished ❺ at or towards a higher level, e. g. in price or quantity; from a smaller to a larger amount ❻ at or to a higher level of intensity

upbringing *n.* the care, training, and education that someone receives, especially from their parents, when they are growing up

upcoming *adj.* about to happen

update Ⅰ *v.* ❶make more modern or up-to-date ❷ supply with the latest information Ⅱ *n.* an act of modernizing and providing with the most recent information

upgrade *v.* put in a higher grade

upon *prep.* =on

upper *adj.* higher in rank; situated above

upright Ⅰ *adv.* in or into a vertical position Ⅱ *adj.* ❶ vertical; erect ❷ just; honest

uproar *n.* (usually with an) a loud and impassioned noise and shouting

upset Ⅰ *v.* ❶ knock (sth.) over; be turned over ❷ make sb. unhappy or worried or make sth. go wrong Ⅱ *adj.* worried; anxious; feeling unhappy about sth.

upside *n.* the upper side; the top part; the top surface

upstairs Ⅰ *adv.* to or on the upper floor Ⅱ *adj.* situated on or of upper floors of a building

up-to-date *adj.* of the latest kind; right up to the present

upward Ⅰ *adj.* moving or directed up Ⅱ *adv.* (also upwards) towards what is higher

upwards *adv.* ❶ towards a higher level, position ❷ towards a higher amount or price

urban *adj.* of a town or city

urge Ⅰ *v.* force or push forward sb. to do sth. Ⅱ *n.* a strong desire

urgent *adj.* that must be dealt with immediately

usable *adj.* ❶ that can be used; capable of use ❷ suitable for use

use Ⅰ *v.* ❶ cause to act or serve a purpose ❷ consume; finish ❸ treat in the stated manner Ⅱ *n.* ❶ the action of using or being used ❷ a purpose for which sth. is used

useful *adj.* ❶ effective in use; bringing help or advantage ❷ satisfactory

useless *adj.* having no use; worthless; having no effect

user *n.* a person who uses or operates sth.

usual *adj.* in common use; that happens in most cases; ordinary

utility *n.* ❶ the degree of usefulness ❷ a useful service for the public, such as supplies of water to the home, the bus service, etc.

utmost *adj.* & *n.* of the greatest degree; most extreme

V v

vacant *adj.* ❶ empty; not occupied or filled ❷(of a job) not filled at present ❸ empty of thought

vacation *n.* a holiday; a period of rest from work, school or court

vacuum *n.* a space completely empty of substance or gas; a space from which air or other gas has been removed

vague *adj.* not clear in shape or not definite in form, meaning; unable to express oneself clearly

vain *adj.* ❶without value, use or result ❷thinking too highly of oneself

valid *adj.* well based; effective according to law

valley *n.* ❶an area of lowland between hills or mountains and usually having a river or stream flowing along its bottom ❷a wide region of flat, low country drained by a great river system

valuable[1] *adj.* ❶worth a lot of money ❷ having great usefulness or importance

valuable[2] *n.* sth., especially sth. small such as a piece of jewellery, that is worth a lot of money

value Ⅰ *n.* ❶ the material or monetary worth of sth. ❷ the importance or preciousness of sth. ❸the usefulness of sth. Ⅱ *v.* ❶think highly of ❷estimate the value, price or worth of

vanish *v.* ❶disappear; become invisible ❷ stop existing

variety *n.* ❶the quality or state of being different ❷kind or sort

various *adj.* ❶ differing from one another; different in kind ❷ several; many

vary *v.* (cause to) be different; change

vase *n.* a holder or container used chiefly for ornament or for holding flowers

vast *adj.* large and wide; great in number or amount

vastly *adv.* very greatly

vegetable *n.* plants grown for food

vehicle *n.* ❶ sth. that can carry people and things ❷ means of conveying thoughts, and feelings

veil Ⅰ *n.* a covering of light, thin cloth or net for a woman's face Ⅱ *v.* put a veil over; hide

verb *n.* a word or group of words that is used in describing an action, experience, or state

verbal *adj.* ❶spoken; not written ❷of or in words ❸word for word ❹of verbs

verify *v.* test or prove the truth of

verse *n.* ❶a writing in regular lines and with rhythm ❷a group of lines of this kind forming a unit in rhyme scheme ❸ any of the numbered (groups of) sentences that together form one numbered division (chapter) of a holy book, especially

version *n.* ❶ a form of a written or musical work that exists in more than one form ❷ an interpretation of a matter from a particular viewpoint

versus *prep.* against

very Ⅰ *adv.* in a high degree; extremely Ⅱ *adj.* exact; this and no other

vessel *n.* ❶ a container for holding liquids ❷ a ship or large boat ❸ a tube, such as a vein, that carries blood or other liquid through the body, or plant juice through a plant

vet Ⅰ *n.* a trained animal doctor Ⅱ *v.* treat (an animal) medically

via *prep.* ❶ by way of ❷ by means of; using

vice *n.* (an example of) badness of character

vicious *adj.* ❶ full of bad habits or behaviour ❷ cruel; having or showing the desire to hurt

victim *n.* a person who suffering pain, death, loss, injury, destruction, etc.

victor *n.* a person who defeats an enemy in battle; a person who wins

victory *n.* a success in a struggle, war or competition

video *adj.* ❶ connected with or used in the showing of pictures by television ❷ using videotape

view Ⅰ *n.* ❶ the ability to see or be seen from a particular place ❷ sth. seen from a particular place, especially a stretch of pleasant country; a scene ❸ a personal opinion, belief, idea, etc., about sth. Ⅱ *v.* ❶ examine; look at thoroughly ❷ consider, regard; think about

villa *n.* a pleasant country house in its own garden, often used for only part of the year for holidays, especially in southern Europe

village *n.* ❶ a group of houses in a country area, smaller than a town ❷ people of a village

violent *adj.* ❶ forceful; fierce, severe ❷ caused by damaging force

violet *n.* ❶ a type of very small flower, usually blue or purple ❷ the blue or purple colour

violin *n.* a musical instrument with four strings played with a bow

VIP *abbr.* a very important person

virtual *adj.* being actual or nearly sth.

virtue *n.* ❶ a good quality of a person's character ❷ an advantage

virus *n.* a living thing even smaller than bacteria which causes infectious disease in the bodies, plants, etc.

visible *adj.* able to be seen; noticeable, obvious (to the eye)

vision *n.* ❶ the ability to see; the visual faculty ❷ a vivid mental dream; sth. imagined

visit Ⅰ *v.* go to see (sb.); go to (a place) for a time Ⅱ *n.* the act of going to (a place, etc.)

visiting *adj.* ❶ (of a person) on a visit to a person or place ❷ (of an academic) working for a fixed period of time at another institution

visitor *n.* ❶ a person who visits or is

visiting; a guest ❷ a bird that frequents certain areas at regular seasons

visual *adj.* ❶ connected with or having an effect on the sense of sight ❷ able to be seen; gained by seeing

vital *adj.* necessary (for life); very important

vitamin *n.* any of a group of substances necessary for healthy life, different ones occurring in different natural things such as raw fruit, dairy products, fish, meat, etc.

vivid *adj.* ❶ strong and very bright ❷ full of life; lively; active

vocabulary *n.* ❶ all the words of a language ❷ a list of words in alphabetical order with meaning

vocal *adj.* using or connected with the voice

vocation *n.* ❶ occupation; employment ❷ a particular fitness or ability for a certain kind of work, especially of a worthy kind

voice Ⅰ *n.* ❶ the sound produced when speaking or singing ❷ the opinion on a particular topic Ⅱ *v.* put into words

void *adj.* completely empty; that can't be used any longer

volcano *n.* a hill or mountain with an opening through which melting rock, ashes, gases, steam, etc. come out

volleyball *n.* a game in which a large ball is struck by hand backwards and forwards across a net without being allowed to touch the ground

volume *n.* ❶ a book, especially one of a set of books ❷ the amount of space filled by sth. ❸ the degree of loudness of sound ❹ the amount produced by some kind of activity

volunteer Ⅰ *n.* ❶ a person who offers his service or help, etc. without payment ❷ a person who offers to enter the armed services Ⅱ *v.* do sth. as a volunteer

vote Ⅰ *v.* pass or determine by marking a piece of paper or holding up hands Ⅱ *n.* a choice made by voting

vow Ⅰ *v.* make a serious promise or decision that you will do it Ⅱ *n.* a serious promise or decision to do sth.

vowel *n.* ❶ any one of the human speech sounds, in which the breath is let out without any stop or any closing of the air passage in the mouth or throat that can be heard ❷ a letter that stands for such a sound

voyage Ⅰ *n.* a long journey, often by sea Ⅱ *v.* make a long journey by sea

W w

wade *v.* walk with an effort (through water, mud, etc.)

wage *n.* the payment received for labour or service

waist *n.* ❶ the part of a person's body between the ribs and the hips ❷ the part of an article of clothing which goes round one's waist

wait *v.* ❶ stay in a place until sb. comes or sth. happens ❷ serve meals, especially as a regular job

wake *v.* (cause to) stop sleeping

waken *v.* (cause to) wake

walk Ⅰ *v.* move along on foot in a natural way, in such a way that one foot is always touching the ground Ⅱ *n.* ❶ a natural way of moving on foot in which a person's feet are lifted one at a time, in such a way that one foot is always touching the ground ❷ a place, path, or course for walking

walker *n.* ❶ a person who walks, especially for pleasure or exercise ❷ an apparatus for helping sb. to walk, especially a frame used by babies or people who cannot walk properly

walking *adj.* ❶ used in the process of moving on foot ❷ consisting of or done by travelling on foot ❸ used to describe a human or living example of the thing mentioned

wall *n.* a side of a house or room; a vertical solid structure made of stone or brick enclosing a piece of land

wallet *n.* a small flat leather case which can be folded for holding papers and paper money

wander *v.* go from place to place without special purpose

want Ⅰ *v.* ❶ have a desire to or for; wish for ❷ say that sth. needs to be done ❸ a lack of sth. Ⅱ *n.* need; sth. needed

war *n.* an armed conflict (between countries)

ward *n.* a separate room in a hospital

wardrobe *n.* a room, closet, or piece of furniture for holding clothes

warm Ⅰ *adj.* ❶ neither hot nor cold; of medium heat (between hot and cool) ❷ friendly; hearty Ⅱ *v.* make or become warm

warn *v.* tell in advance (of sth. bad or dangerous)

warning Ⅰ *n.* a statement or an event that indicates sth. bad or dangerous Ⅱ *adj.* giving a warning

warrior *n.* a soldier who fights in a battle

warship *n.* a naval ship used for war

wash Ⅰ *v.* ❶ make sth. clean with water or other liquid ❷ carry away in the moving water or liquid Ⅱ *n.* ❶ an act of washing or being washed ❷ clothes to be washed or being washed

waste Ⅰ *v.* use wrongly; make no use of Ⅱ *n.* ❶ the act of using sth. wrongly or carelessly ❷ waste material or sth. else that is not needed Ⅲ *adj.* (of land) that cannot be used; ruined

watch Ⅰ *v.* ❶ look at sb. or sth. continuously; observe carefully; keep the eyes on ❷ look after ❸ be careful of sb. or sth. Ⅱ *n.* the act of watching sb. or sth. in case of possible danger or problems

water Ⅰ *n.* a liquid without colour, smell or taste that forms the seas, lakes, rivers and rain Ⅱ *v.* ❶ put water on ❷ (of the eyes or mouth) fill with water; have mouth liquid

watt *n.* a unit of electrical power

wave Ⅰ *v.* ❶ (cause to) move the hand or arm from side to side or up and down ❷ move freely and gently while remaining fixed to one point Ⅱ *n.* ❶ curving lines of water, especially on the sea, which rise and fall ❷ the act of waving, especially of sth., as a signal ❸ a form in which some types of energy move, such as light and sound

wax *n.* a solid material made of fats or oils which changes to a thick liquid when melted by heat

way *n.* ❶ a road, path or street ❷ a route or road you take to some place ❸ the distance from one place to another ❹ a method or manner of doing sth. ❺ an aspect of sth.

we *pron.* the plural form of I

weak *adj.* ❶ lacking in strength ❷ not good at ❸ containing a lot of water

wealth *n.* ❶ many valuable possessions; much money or property; riches ❷ a large quantity; abundance

wealthy *adj.* (especially of a person, family, or country) rich

weapon *n.* ❶ a tool used for fighting or attacking sb. ❷ means of attack or defense

wear Ⅰ *v.* ❶ have sth. on one's body, especially as clothing, but sometimes also for protection, decoration or other purposes ❷ have (a particular expression) on the face ❸ be reduced, weakened, or damaged by continued use, rubbing, etc. ❹ have one's hair or beard arranged in a specific style Ⅱ *n.* ❶ the act of wearing, especially clothes ❷ clothes of the stated type, or for the stated purpose

weary Ⅰ *adj.* feeling or showing tiredness Ⅱ *v.* cause to become tired

weather *n.* the condition of rain, wind, sunshine, etc. in a particular area and at a specific time

weave *v.* (wove, woven) ❶ make (threads, etc.) into cloth, etc. ❷ put together; compose (a story, etc.)

weaver *n.* a person whose job is to weave cloth

web *n.* ❶ a thin net woven by a spider ❷ a system of interconnected elements

wedding *n.* a marriage ceremony

Wednesday *n.* the day of the week after Tuesday and before Thursday

weed Ⅰ *n.* the unwanted wild plant,

especially one which prevents crops or garden flowers from growing properly Ⅱ *v.* remove weeds from (a place where crops or flowers grow)

weedy *adj.* ❶thin and physically weak ❷ weak in character ❸full of weeds

week *n.* a period of seven days (and nights), from Sunday to Saturday or from Monday to Sunday

weekday *n.* any day except Saturday and Sunday

weekend *n.* Saturday and Sunday

weekly Ⅰ *adv.* once a week Ⅱ *adj.* of, for a week Ⅲ *n.* a newspaper or magazine that is published once a week

weep *v.* cry; let tears fall from the eyes

weigh *v.* ❶measure how heavy sth. is ❷ have a weight of ❸ consider the importance of sth., especially before a decision or action

weight *n.* ❶the heaviness of a person or thing ❷ the ability to influence sb.'s actions and decisions ❸ the great responsibility

welcome Ⅰ *v.* ❶greet in a friendly way; show pleasure at the arrival of ❷accept or receive sth. happily Ⅱ *adj.* that one is glad to have, receive, see, etc. Ⅲ *n.* an instance or manner of greeting sb.

welfare *n.* the condition of being well or doing well; health, happiness and prosperity

well Ⅰ *adj.* ❶in good health Ⅱ *adv.* ❶in a good way; satisfactorily, kindly, successfully, etc. ❷ much; quite ❸ thoroughly and completely Ⅲ *int.* used for introducing an expression of surprise, doubt, acceptance, etc.

well-dressed *adj.* fashionably dressed

well-known *adj.* famous; widely known

west *n.* ❶the direction in which the sun goes down ❷ the western part of a country, region, etc.

western *adj.* toward the west; from the west; of or in the west

westerner[1] *n.* ❶someone who lives in or comes from the west ❷ someone who lives in or comes from the west of America

westward Ⅰ *adj.* that towards the west Ⅱ *adv.* towards the west

wet Ⅰ *adj.* covered or soaked with liquid; rainy Ⅱ *v.* cause sth. to be wet

whale *n.* a very large animal living in the sea and looking like a fish

what *pron.* ❶used in questions about an unknown thing or person, or kind of thing or person ❷ the thing or things that Ⅱ *int.* used in exclamations to emphasize sth. surprising or remarkable

whatever Ⅰ *pron.* ❶anything that ❷no matter what Ⅱ *adj.* any that; no matter what

wheat *n.* a plant producing grain from which flour is made

wheel *n.* a circular object with an outer frame which turns round an inner part the hub to which it is joined, used for turning machinery, making vehicles move, etc.

wheelchair *n.* a chair with large wheels which can be turned by the user, used especially by people who are unable to walk

when Ⅰ *adv.* at what time Ⅱ *conj.* ❶at or during the time that ❷although ❸just after which

whenever *adv.* & *conj*. when; at whatever time; at any time that

where *adv.* at, to, or from what place, position, or situation; at or to the place that

whereabouts Ⅰ *adv.* where; near what place Ⅱ *n.* the place where a person or thing is

whereas *conj.* ❶ on the contrary; but; while ❷ (especially in legal preambles) considering that; since

whereby *adv.* by which; by what

wherever Ⅰ *adv.* used in questions to mean where, expressing surprise Ⅱ *conj*. to or in any place; no matter where

whether *conj.* ❶ expressing a doubt or choice (often used in indirect questions) ❷ used to show that sth. is true in either of two cases

which *pron.* ❶ (used in questions, when a choice is to be made) what particular one or ones ❷ used to refer to sth. previously mentioned when introducing a clause

while Ⅰ *conj*. ❶ during the time that sth. is happening ❷ although ❸ whereas; however Ⅱ *n.* a short period of time

whip Ⅰ *n.* a long piece of leather or rope fastened to handle, used for urging a horse on or for punishing Ⅱ *v.* hit or drive with a whip

whirl Ⅰ *v.* (cause to) move fast round and round Ⅱ *n.* the act or sensation of whirling

whisper Ⅰ *v.* speak or say in a soft and low voice Ⅱ *n.* a soft or low voice or sound; sth. said secretly

white Ⅰ *adj.* ❶ of the colour of milk, salt, and snow ❷ morally pure; innocent ❸ very pale ❹ (coffee or tea) added with milk or cream Ⅱ *n.* white colour; white clothes or material

who *pron.* ❶ (used in questions) what or which person or people ❷ used to show what person or people is(are) meant

whoever *pron.* any person that; no matter who

whole Ⅰ *adj.* complete; total Ⅱ *n.* a complete amount of sth.; all of sth. Ⅲ *adv.* completely different or new

wholesale Ⅰ *n.* the selling of goods in large quantities to shopkeepers and traders who then sell them to the public Ⅱ *adj.* of wholesale as a method of trade Ⅲ *adv.* on a large scale; including almost everybody, everything

wholesome *adj.* be good for health; healthy

whom *pron.* the object form of who

whose *pron.* belonging to or associated with which person

why Ⅰ *adv.* for what reason Ⅱ *int.* expressing surprise, protest, approval, hesitation, etc.

wicked *adj.* ❶ very bad; evil; morally wrong ❷ behaving badly; mischievous

wide Ⅰ *adj.* ❶ of great width from side to side or edge to edge ❷ fully open ❸ including a great variety of sb. or sth. Ⅱ *adv.* ❶ to a great distance from side to side ❷ (in sport) far away from the right point

widow Ⅰ *n.* a woman whose husband is dead Ⅱ *v.* cause to become a widow or widower

wife *n.* a married woman considered in relation to her husband

wild *adj.* ❶living or growing in natural conditions; untamed; uncultivated ❷(scenery or region) in its natural state ❸very angry, excited, passionate, etc.

will[1] *v.* ❶used for expressing the simple future tense ❷be willing to; be ready to ❸used when asking someone to do sth. ❹shows what always happens ❺used like can to show what is likely

will[2] *n.* ❶the power of the mind to make decisions and acts in accordance with them, sometimes in spite of difficulty or opposition ❷what is wished or intended (by the stated person) ❸an official statement of the way someone wants his property to be shared out after his death

willow *n.* a tree with long, thin branches

win *v.* ❶get or gain (victory, a stated place, prize, etc.) in competition, etc. ❷gain or receive as a result of victory or success in any kind of competition

wind[1] *n.* moving air; a current of air, especially one moving strongly or quickly

wind[2] *v.* ❶follow a twisting course, with many changes of direction ❷turn or twist (sth.) repeatedly, especially round an object ❸tighten the working parts of sth. by turning round and round

window *n.* an opening in the wall, etc. to let in light or air

wine *n.* an alcoholic drink made from grapes, fruit, etc.

wing *n.* a movable limb which a bird, insect, etc. uses for flying

winner *n.* a person, animal, or thing that wins

winning *adj.* ❶very pleasing or attractive; charming ❷that wins or has won sth. in a race or competition

winter *n.* a season between autumn and spring when it is cold

wipe *v.* ❶make clean or dry by rubbing with a cloth, etc.

wire *n.* a thin, flexible thread of metal

wireless Ⅰ *adj.* having or requiring no wires Ⅱ *n.* broadcasting or telegraphy using radio signals

wisdom *n.* ❶the quality of being wise; a good sense and judgment ❷knowledge gained through learning or experience

wise *adj.* having or showing good sense and judgment, and the ability to understand and decide on the right action

wish Ⅰ *v.* ❶want to do sth.; express a desire to do sth. ❷have a desire that is impossible to be satisfied at present ❸hope that (sb.) has (sth.) Ⅱ *n.* ❶a desire or hope for sth. to happen; sth. wished for ❷an invocation or recitation of a hope or desire ❸an attempt to make a particular desired thing or situation expressed in a special way or silently; an act of wishing

wit *n.* ❶keen intelligence; quickness of the mind ❷the ability to express ideas in a clever and humorous manner

with *prep.* ❶in the presence or company of; near, beside, or among ❷having or possessing ❸by means of; using ❹because of or considering the fact of ❺concerning; in regard to or in the case of ❻indicating the manner ❼in support of; in favour of ❽ against ❾ at the same time and rate as ❿ in spite of ⓫ indicating separation

withdraw *v.* ❶ (cause to) move away or back ❷ go away ❸ take away or back

within Ⅰ *prep.* ❶ inside sb. or sth. ❷ during a particular period of time ❸ not further than a particular distance ❹ inside the range of sth. Ⅱ *adv.* inside; inwardly

without Ⅰ *prep.* ❶ in the absence of ❷ not doing sth. mentioned Ⅱ *adv.* outside

withstand *v.* resist; continue in good condition in spite of

witless *adj.* (as if) lacking in ability to think; silly

witness Ⅰ *n.* ❶ a person who was present at an event, especially sth. bad ❷ a person giving sworn testimony to a court of law or the police Ⅱ *v.* ❶ see an event, especially sth. bad take place ❷ give evidence of

witty *adj.* full of wit; clever and amusing

woe *n.* great sorrow

wolf *n.* a wild animal of the dog family which hunts other animals in a group

woman *n.* a fully grown human female

womb *n.* an organ of a woman or female animal inside which a baby grows before it is born

wonder Ⅰ *n.* ❶ a feeling of strangeness, surprise, etc., usually combined with admiration that is produced by sth. unusually fine or beautiful, or by sth. unexpected or new to one's experience ❷ sth. that causes this feeling, especially a wonderfully made object Ⅱ *v.* ❶ be surprised and want to know (why) ❷ express a wish to know, in words or silently

wonderful *adj.* causing wonder; surprising ❷ very good; excellent

wood *n.* ❶ the substance of which the trunks and branches of trees are made, which is cut and used for various purposes, such as burning, making paper or furniture, etc. ❷ a place where trees grow thickly, smaller than a forest

wooden *adj.* ❶ made of wood ❷ stiff, clumsy

woodpecker *n.* a bird that can make holes in the wood of trees and pull out insects

word *n.* ❶ a written, printed or spoken unit of a language ❷ a short remark or statement ❸ a promise ❹ a message; a piece of news

wordless *adj.* without words; unable to speak; speechless

work Ⅰ *n.* ❶ an activity which uses bodily or mental powers ❷ employment or occupation ❸ a task or tasks to be undertaken ❹ what is produced by work, especially of the hands ❺ the product of an artist, composer, writer, etc. Ⅱ *v.* ❶ do work; do physical or mental activity ❷ do work; engage in physical or mental activity ❸ make (a machine) operate ❹ produce a particular effect or result

workable *adj.* that can be worked or operated; that will work

worker *n.* a person who works

workman *n.* a man who works, especially with his hands

workshop *n.* a room or place where things are made or repaired

world *n.* ❶the body in space on which we live; the earth ❷ all the people on the earth ❸a part or an aspect of human life or of the natural features of the Earth ❹ a large number or amount

worm Ⅰ *n.* a small, thin creature with no bones or limbs, like a round tube of flesh, especially an earthworm Ⅱ *v.* move gradually by twisting or wriggling

worn *adj.* ❶used until no longer fit for use ❷physically exhausted; very tired

worry Ⅰ *v.* (cause to) feel anxious or troubled Ⅱ *n.* ❶ a feeling or state of anxiety ❶a source of anxiety

worse Ⅰ *adj.* ❶less good or desirable ❷ more serious or severe ❸becoming more ill or sick Ⅱ *adv.* less well or more seriously Ⅲ *n.* a more serious or unpleasant event or condition

worst Ⅰ *adj.* & *adv.* most bad or ill; most badly Ⅱ *n.* the worst thing or condition

worth Ⅰ *adj.* ❶ deserving; valuable or useful for sb. ❷ having a value in money, etc. Ⅱ *n.* price or value

worthy Ⅰ *adj.* ❶ having worth ❷ deserving Ⅱ *n.* a person of importance

would *v.* ❶ used instead of will to describe what someone has said, asked, etc. ❷if only ❸shows that sth. always happens or is typical ❹ expressing a polite request

wound Ⅰ *v.* ❶ deliberately damage the body by cutting, striking, shooting at it, etc. ❷ cause a person to have an unpleasant feelings Ⅱ *n.* ❶a deliberate damage done to the body ❷ a painful feeling

wrap *v.* cover sth. in a material folded around

wreck Ⅰ *v.* destroy; cause to be destroyed Ⅱ *n.* a ship, car, building, etc. which has been destroyed

wreckage *n.* the broken parts of a destroyed thing

wrinkle Ⅰ *n.* a small fold or line in the skin (especially of the kind produced by age) or on the surface of sth. Ⅱ *v.* have wrinkles; become full of wrinkles

wrist *n.* the joint between the hand and the arm

write *v.* ❶make letters or words by using a pen, a pencil, etc. ❷ put down in words ❸make up (a book, story, etc.) for publication ❹ produce and send a letter (to)

wrong Ⅰ *adj.* ❶ not correct; not in accordance with the facts or the truth ❷ evil; against moral standards ❸not good or normal in condition, health, results, work, etc. ❹not suitable Ⅱ *adv.* with an incorrect result Ⅲ *n.* ❶ an action or behaviour that is not morally right or correct ❷ a seriously bad or unjust action Ⅳ *v.* act unjustly or dishonestly towards (sb.)

X x

x *n.* ❶a quantity that is unknown until a calculation has been made ❷ an unknown person, value, etc.

x-ray Ⅰ *n.* a powerful, unseen beam of light that can penetrate solids and makes it possible to see into or through them; photograph taken using this Ⅱ *v.* examine, treat, photograph with X-rays

Y y

yacht *n.* a boat for pleasure trips or racing, equipped with sails or engines, or both of them

yard *n.* ❶ an area outside a building, usually with a hard surface and a surrounding wall ❷ a unit of length equal to ❸ feet

yawn *v.* open the mouth wide and take a breath when tired or bored

year *n.* the period of time of about 365 days from January 1 to December 31

yearly *adj.* & *adv.* once a year; every year

yearn *v.* have a strong or intense desire for sth.

yell Ⅰ *n.* a strong, loud outcry Ⅱ *v.* cry out with a strong and loud sound

yellow Ⅰ *adj.* having the color like lemon or butter Ⅱ *n.* the color like lemon or butter

yes Ⅰ *adv.* ❶used to express agreement, affirmation, etc. ❷ used to show that one has heard a call or command Ⅱ *n.* an affirmative answer or decision

yesterday Ⅰ *n.* ❶the day before today ❷ the time just past Ⅱ *adv.* ❶on the day preceding today ❷ in the recent past; only a short time ago

yet Ⅰ *adv.* up until now or then; by a particular time; already Ⅱ *conj.* in spite of that; but

yield *v.* ❶ produce, bear, or provide, especially as a result of work or effort ❷give up control (of)

yoga *n.* a religious way of life (originally followed mainly by some Hindus) which includes prayer, deep breathing, physical exercise and fasting

yogh(o)urt *n.* a thick, liquid food made from sour milk

you *pron.* ❶ the person or people being spoken to ❷a person; anyone; one

young Ⅰ *adj.* in a early stage of life, growth, development, etc.; recently born or begun Ⅱ *n.* young people considered as a group; any immature animal

youngster *n.* a young person; a child, especially a boy

your *pron.* of or belonging to you

yours *pron.* sth. belonging to you

yourself *pron.* ❶ used to emphasize the person that you are referring to ❷refer to the person that a speaker or writer is talking or writing to ❸ your real or true condition

youth *n.* ❶the state of being young; the period of life between childhood and maturity ❷young people

youthful *adj.* young; having the qualities of youth

Z z

zeal *n.* eagerness or enthusiasm in pursuit of sth.

zealous *adj.* full of zeal; actively enthusiastic

zebra *n.* a wild mammal of southern and eastern Africa, related to the horse and donkey but striped with dark or white bands

zero Ⅰ *num.* ❶ the figure 0 Ⅱ *n.* ❶ a freezing point on the centigrade and Celsius scale ❷ the quantity that registers a reading of zero on a scale

zone *n.* ❶one of the five divisions of the earth's surface, marked by imaginary lines parallel to the equator ❷an area or a region with particular qualities

zoo *n.* a place where animals are kept and shown for the public to see

zoology *n.* the science of animals; the study of animals and animal life

zoom Ⅰ *n.* the low, deep humming sound of the sudden upward flight of an aircraft Ⅱ *v.* (of an aircraft) move upwards at high speed

Chinese-English Dictionary

CHINESE-ENGLISH DICTIONARY

A a

a

阿(ā)(a prefix used before pet names, monosyllabic surnames, or numbers denoting order of seniority in a family, to form terms of endearment)

另见 970 页 ē

【阿尔卑斯山】 Alps

【阿基米德原理】 Archimedes Principle

【阿拉伯数字】 Arabic numerals

【阿门】 amen(用于祈祷或圣歌结束时,表示诚心所愿)

【阿司匹林】 aspirin

【阿姨】 ❶ one's mother's sister; aunt; auntie ❷ a nurse in a family or in a nursery school or kindergarten

ai

哎(āi) exclamation of surprise or regret

【哎呀】 ah;Oh,my!

【哎哟】 ouch;ow;hey

哀(āi) ❶grief;sorrow ❷mourning ❸pity

【哀愁】 sad;sorrowful

【哀悼】 grieve over sb. 's death: 深切~ profound condolence

【哀歌】 a mournful song;dirge

【哀号】 cry;wail

【哀怜】 feel compassion for

【哀鸣】 whine plaintively

【哀求】 weep plaintively;implore

【哀伤】 distressed;grieved;sad

【哀思】 grief; sad memories (of the deceased)

【哀叹】 bewail;lament

【哀痛】 deep sorrow;grief

【哀乐】 funeral music;dirge

挨(āi) ❶get close to; be next to ❷in sequence;by turns

另见本页 ái

【挨次】 in turn;in order;one after another;one by one;by turns: ~入场 file in

【挨近】 get close to;be near to;draw on 我们家~商业区。Our house is close to the shopping center.

【挨门挨户】 from door to door; from house to house

唉(āi)(used to respond) right; yes; (expressing disappointment or regret) alas

【唉声叹气】 moan and groan; heave deep sighs;sigh in despair

挨(ái) suffer; endure; drag out; delay; play for time;stall

另见本页 āi

【挨打】 be beaten; get a beating; get a thrashing;come under attack

【挨饿】 starve; go hungry; suffer from

A

hunger

【挨骂】be scolded

【挨批评】be criticized

皑 (ái) pure white; snow white

【皑皑】pure white

癌 (ái) cancer; carcinoma: 肺～lung cancer; 肝～cancer of the liver

【癌变】canceration

【癌细胞】cancer cell

【癌症】cancer

矮 (ǎi) ❶short (of stature) ❷low

【矮凳】a low stool

【矮胖】short and stout; dumpy; roly-poly

【矮小】short and small; low and small; undersized: 身材～ short and slight in figure; ～的帐篷 a small, low tent

【矮子】dwarf; a short person

艾 (ài) ❶Chinese mugwort (Artemisia argyi) ❷end; stop

【艾滋病】AIDS (Acquired Immune Deficiency Syndrome)

爱 (ài) ❶love; affection: 母～maternal love ❷like; be fond of ❸take good care of; treasure; hold dear; cherish ❹be apt to; be in the habit of: 她～晕车。She's apt to get carsick.

【爱称】pet name

【爱戴】love and esteem

【爱抚】pet; show tender care for

【爱国】love one's country; be patriotic

【爱国心】patriotic feeling; patriotism

【爱国者】patriot

【爱国主义】patriotism

【爱好】❶fancy; hobby; interest ❷like; love; be fond of; be interested in; go in for; be keen on

【爱好者】amateur; lover (of art, sports, etc.); fan: 音乐～music lover; 体育～sports enthusiast; sports fan

【爱护】cherish; take good care of; treasure

【爱怜】show tender affection for; show love or fondness for; love and pity

【爱恋】be in love with; feed deeply attached to

【爱侣】lovers; sweethearts

【爱美】set great store by one's appearance; love to make up and wear beautiful clothes

【爱面子】be sensitive about one's reputation

【爱莫能助】be willing but unable to help

【爱慕】❶admire; adore ❷admiration

【爱情】love; affection

【爱情故事】love story; romance

【爱人】❶lover; sweetheart ❷one's wife (or husband)

【爱神】god of love; Cupid

【爱惜】cherish; treasure

【爱憎分明】be clear about what to love and what to hate

隘 (ài) narrow; pass

【隘口】(mountain) pass

碍 (ài) stand (or be) in the way; hinder; obstruct

【碍口】be too embarrassing to mention: 这事有点～,不好说。It's rather embarrassing; I don't know how to bring it up.

【碍事】stand (or be) in the way; be a hindrance; 不～ it doesn't matter

【碍眼】be unpleasant to look at; be an eyesore; offend the eye

【碍于情面】just to spare sb.'s feelings; for fear of hurting sb.'s feelings

暧 (ài) (of daylight) dim

【暖昧】❶ambiguous ❷dubious

an

安（ān）❶ safety; security; stability ❷fit; fix; install; put ❸ set（sb.'s mind) at ease; calm ❹secure; peaceful; quiet; tranquil; stable; satisfied ❺safe; in good health ❻place in a suitable position; find a place for ❼bring (a charge against sb.); give（sb. a nickname）❽ampere

【安插】place in a certain position; assign to a job; plant

【安定】❶ stability ❷ stabilize; maintain ❸stable; quiet; settled

【安定人心】reassure the public

【安定团结】stability and unity

【安顿】❶ find a place for; help settle down; arrange for ❷undisturbed; peaceful

【安放】lay; place; put in a proper place

【安分】❶ be law-abiding ❷ know one's place

【安抚】console; appease; pacify

【安好】safe and sound; well

【安家】settle down; set up a home

【安静】quiet; calm; peaceful: 保持～keep quiet

【安居乐业】live and work happily

【安乐】❶ peace and happiness; ease ❷comfortable

【安乐死】euthanasia; mercy killing

【安理会】the Security Council

【安谧】(of a place) tranquil; quiet; peaceful

【安眠】sleep peacefully

【安眠药】sleeping tablet (or pill)

【安宁】❶peaceful; tranquil: 世界不～的根源 the causes for the unpeaceful world ❷calm; composed; free from worry

【安排】arrange; plan; fix up

【安全】safety; security; secure; safe

【安全措施】safety measures

【安全带】safety strap; seat（or safety）belt

【安全感】sense of security

【安全规则】safety regulations

【安全帽】safety helmet

【安全设备】safety devices

【安全通道】safe passage

【安然】❶safe ❷easy; peaceful

【安然无恙】safe and sound

【安危】safety; safety and danger: 不顾个人～ be regardless of one's personal safety

【安慰】comfort; console

【安稳】smooth and steady; safe and secure

【安息】rest in peace (used to mourn)

【安闲】enjoying leisure

【安详】calm and serene; composed; unruffled

【安心】❶ feel at ease; be relieved; set one's mind at ease ❷keep one's mind on sth.: ～学习 keep one's mind on one's study

【安逸】easeful; easy; easy and comfortable; leisurely: 贪图～ love comfort

【安营扎寨】camp; pitch a camp

【安葬】bury; burial

【安置】arrange for; find a place for; help settle down; place（a person）in certain post

【安装】install; erect; fix; set up

鞍（ān) saddle

【鞍马】pommelled horse; side horse

岸（àn）❶bank; shore; coast ❷lofty

A【岸然】in a solemn manner

按 (àn) ❶note;comment ❷press;push down ❸restrain;control ❹keepone's hand on ❺ according to;in accordance with;in the light of;on the basis of;by

【按比例】in proportion;pro rata

【按部就班】in an orderly and logical way

【按成】according to percentage; proportionately:~计算 reckon in terms of percentages;~分配红利 distribute the bonuses proportionately

【按次】in due order;in sequence:~发言 speak in due order

【按……规定】according to

【按件计工】reckon by the piece

【按键】button

【按揭】mortgage

【按劳分配】distribute to each according to one's work

【按理】according to reason (or principle)

【按摩】massage

【按钮】push button

【按期】on time;on schedule

【按时】on time;on schedule:~完成 meet the deadline;finish... in time

【按需分配】distribute to each according to one's need

【按语】note;comment

【按照】as;according to;by

案 (àn) ❶an old-fashioned long, narrow table or desk ❷ records; files ❸proposal ❹law case;case:办~handle a case;破~ clear up (or solve) a criminal case;a plan submitted for consideration;proposal

【案板】kitchen chopping board

【案件】law case; legal case:民事~a civil case;刑事~a criminal case

【案情】details of a case; facts of a legal case

暗 (àn) ❶dark;dim;dull ❷hidden;secret;unclear

【暗暗】secretly;inwardly

【暗藏】conceal;hide

【暗处】❶a dark place ❷a secret place;a covert place;cover

【暗淡】dim;dismal;faint;gloomy

【暗地里】secretly

【暗沟】underground drainage ditch; underground drain

【暗害】❶kill secretly ❷stab in the back

【暗河】underground river

【暗箭】an arrow shot from hiding;attack by a hidden enemy

【暗井】blind shaft;winze

【暗礁】submerged rock

【暗流】undercurrent

【暗码】secret code;private mark

【暗杀】kill secretly;assassinate

【暗伤】❶ internal (or invisible) injury ❷indiscernible damage

【暗示】drop a hint;suggest;hint

【暗事】clandestine or illicit action:明人不做~。An honest man does nothing underhand.

【暗锁】built-in lock

【暗探】detective;spy;secret agent

【暗想】muse;ponder;turn over in mind

【暗笑】laugh in one's sleeve;sneer at

【暗中】in secret;secretly

ang

肮 (āng)

【肮脏】❶dirty;filthy:~的阴沟 a filthy sewer ❷foul;squalid

【肮脏勾当】dirty work;foul deed

昂 (áng) ❶ hold one's head high ❷high;soaring

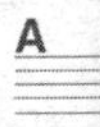

【昂贵】(price) high; expensive; costly

【昂首】lift up the head; hold one's head high

【昂扬】in high spirits; high-spirited: 斗志~ have high morale; be full of fight; be militant

盎 (àng) brimming; abundant

【盎然】abundantly; exuberantly; overflowing; full: 趣味~ full of interest; 生机~ overflowing with vigor; 春意~ Spring is in the air.

【盎司】ounce

ao

凹 (āo) dented; concave

【凹透镜】concave lens

【凹凸不平】uneven; bumpy

遨 (áo) stroll; saunter

【遨游】travel; roam; stroll

熬 (áo) ❶ boil; cook in water ❷ endure; bear; stand; hold out

【熬煎】suffering; torture

【熬夜】stay up late; sit up late (or all night); burn the midnight oil

鏖 (áo) engage in fierce battle

【鏖战】fight hard; engage in fierce battle

袄 (ǎo) coat; jacket: 棉~a cotton-padded jacket; 皮~a fur coat

傲 (ào) ❶ defy; refuse to yield to; brave ❷proud; haughty

【傲骨】lofty and unyielding character; self-esteem

【傲慢】arrogant; insolent: 态度~ put on airs

【傲气】❶ air of arrogance; haughtiness ❷arrogant; haughty

【傲视】turn up one's nose; look down on (or upon); show disdain for; regard superciliously

奥 (ào) profound and difficult to understand; abstruse

【奥林匹克运动会】the Olympic Games; the Olympics

【奥秘】profound mystery

【奥妙】mystery; mysterious; subtle; wonderful; ❷mystic

【奥委会】the Olympic Committee

澳 (ào)

【澳大利亚】Australia

【澳门】Aomen; Macao

懊 (ào) ❶regret ❷regretful ❸annoyed

【懊悔】regret; repent; feel remorse; regret: 我~没听他的忠告。I regretted having failed to take his advice.

【懊恼】annoyed; upset; displeased; annoyed; vexed: 这门课没学完他心里很~。He was quite upset at not having completed the course.

B

B b

ba

八 (bā) eight：第～ eighth；十～ eighteen

【八宝粥】eight-treasure rice porridge

【八成】❶eighty percent ❷most probably; most likely

【八方】all directions

【八哥】myna

【八九不离十】pretty close; very near; about right

【八一建军节】Army Day (August 1, anniversary of the founding of the Chinese People's Liberation Army)

【八月】❶ August ❷ the eighth month of the lunar year

【八折】twenty percent discount; twenty percent off

巴 (bā) ❶ stick to; cling to ❷ hope earn-estly; wait anxiously

【巴不得】be eager to; be anxious to; earnestly wish; eagerly look forward to

【巴结】curry favor with; fawn on; make up to

【巴掌】palm; hand

扒 (bā) ❶ cling to; hold on to; catch hold of ❷take off; strip off ❸dig up; pull down ❹push aside

另见 1123 页 pá

【扒车】climb onto a slow-going train, etc.

芭 (bā)

【芭蕉】Chinese banana

【芭蕾舞】ballet

疤 (bā) scar

拔 (bá) ❶ pull out (or up) ❷ draw; suck out ❸ choose; pick; select ❹raise; lift ❺capture; seize ❻surpass

【拔草】pull up weeds

【拔除】pull out; remove; wipe out; tear up; uproot

【拔河】tug-of-war

【拔尖儿】❶ tiptop; top-notch ❷ push oneself to the front

【拔牙】pull out a tooth

把 (bǎ) ❶ handle ❷ grasp; hold; take hold of ❸control ❹watch; guard

【把柄】❶handle ❷mistake; fault

【把舵】hold the rudder; hold (or take, be at) the helm; steer

【把关】❶guard a pass ❷check on

【把手】handle; grip; knob

【把守】guard

【把握】❶ grasp; hold ❷ be sure ❸ assurance; certainty

【把戏】trick; game：耍～ play tricks; acrobatics; jugglery

靶 (bǎ) target：打～shoot at the target

【靶场】shooting range

【靶心】bull's-eye；center of a target

【靶子】target

坝 (bà) ❶ dam；embankment ❷ dyke (or dike) ❸sandbar

爸 (bà) father；dad

罢 (bà) ❶stop；cease ❷dismiss ❸finish

【罢工】strike；go on strike；down tools

【罢课】❶ strike of students ❷ boycott a class

【罢了】(bàle) (used at the end of a declarative sentence) that's all；nothing else

【罢了】(bàiliǎo) let it pass；be done with it

【罢免】recall；dismiss；remove sb. from office

【罢手】give up

【罢赛】boycott a game

【罢休】give up；let the matter drop：不达目的，绝不～。We'll not stop until we reach our goal.

霸 (bà) ❶ tyrant；bully ❷ dictator ❸hegemony ❹dominate；occupy (or seize) by force；lord it over

【霸道】❶ tyranny ❷ high-handed；overbearing

【霸权】hegemony；supremacy

【霸王条款】imparity clause

【霸占】seize (or occupy) by force；forcibly occupy：～土地 forcibly occupy the land

【霸主】overlord

bai

掰 (bāi) break off with fingers

白 (bái) ❶ white ❷ clear：真相大～ everything is clear now ❸ pure；plain；blank：一穷二～ poor and blank ❹free of charge

B

【白案】flour and rice cooking

【白班】day shift

【白菜】Chinese cabbage

【白搭】no use；no good

【白费力气】waste one's energy；in vain

【白宫】the White House

【白果】ginkgo；gingko

【白鹤】white crane

【白酒】liquor；white spirit；alcohol

【白卷】blank examination paper

【白兰地】brandy

【白领】white collar

【白皮书】white paper；white book

【白人】white man (or woman)

【白日梦】daydream

【白手起家】build up from nothing

【白糖】(refined) white sugar

【白天】daylight；daytime：在～in the daytime

【白天黑夜】day and night

【白皙】(of skin) fair and clear

【白细胞】white blood cell；leucocyte

【白血病】leukaemia

【白杨】white poplar

【白蚁】termite；white ant

【白银】silver

【白纸黑字】(be) written in black and white；commit sth. to paper

百 (bǎi) hundred：数以～计 hundreds of；by hundreds

【百宝箱】treasure box

【百倍】a hundredfold；a hundred times

【百读不厌】be worth reading a hundred times

B

【百分比】percentage
【百分之百】❶a hundred percent ❷absolutely
【百分制】hundred-mark system
【百合】lily
【百货】general merchandise
【百货商店】 general store; department store
【百科全书】encyclopedia
【百忙之中】while fully engaged
【百年】❶a hundred years; a century ❷lifetime
【百听不厌】 worth hearing a hundred times
【百万】million
【百万富翁】millionaire
【百姓】common people
【百折不挠】keep on fighting in spite of all setbacks

摆（bǎi）❶put; lay; place; arrange; set ❷swing; wave ❸put on airs; assume ❹state clearly; lay bare ❺pendulum
【摆布】order about; manipulate
【摆动】swing; sway
【摆渡】ferry
【摆渡车】shuttle bus; ferry push car
【摆放】put; place; lay
【摆架子】put on airs
【摆阔】parade one's wealth
【摆弄】❶move back and forth; fiddle with ❷order about; manipulate
【摆平】be fair to; be impartial to
【摆设】❶furnish and decorate ❷decoration
【摆手】❶shake one's hand in admonition or disapproval ❷beckon; wave
【摆摊儿】set up a stall
【摆脱】rid off; get rid of; throw off; break away from

败（bài）❶lose; be defeated ❷defeat; beat ❸fail ❹failure ❺spoil ❻counteract ❼decay; wither
【败笔】❶a faulty stroke in calligraphy or painting; ❷a faulty expression in writing
【败坏】ruin; corrupt
【败家子】squanderer; spendthrift
【败露】be exposed: 阴谋～the conspiracy was brought to light
【败落】decline (in wealth and position)
【败诉】lose a lawsuit
【败兴】 have one's spirits dampened; feel disappointed
【败仗】lost battle; defeat: 打～suffer a defeat; be defeated in a battle

拜（bài）❶worship ❷make a courtesy call ❸ acknowledge sb. as one's master, godfather, etc. ❹do obeisance
【拜读】have the honor to read
【拜访】call on; call at; pay a visit: 顺便～drop in
【拜见】pay a formal call; call to pay respects
【拜年】wish sb. a Happy New Year; pay a New Year call
【拜票】canvass
【拜师】formally acknowledge sb. as one's master; take sb. as one's teacher
【拜寿】congratulate an elderly person on his/her birthday; offer birthday felicitations
【拜托】request sb. to do sth.; entrust sth. to sb.

ban

扳（bān）pull; turn; switch; shift gears
【扳倒】pull down

【扳机】trigger
【扳平】draw; equalize
【扳手】spanner, wrench

班 (bān) ❶class; grade; team ❷shift; duty: 上~go to work; go on duty; 上夜~be on night shift; 下~get off duty ❸a measure word (e.g. number of flight or bus)

【班车】regular bus
【班次】❶order of classes or grades at school ❷number of runs or flights
【班级】classes and grades in school
【班轮】regular passenger or cargo ship; re-gular steamship service
【班委会】class committee
【班长】❶class leader; monitor ❷team (or squad) leader
【班主任】head teacher; a teacher in charge of a class; the director of the class

般 (bān) ❶sort; kind; way ❷same as; just like

【般配】well matched (in marriage, etc.); well suited

颁 (bān) issue; promulgate

【颁布】publish; issue; promulgate
【颁发】award; issue

斑 (bān) ❶ stripe; speckle; speck; spot: 锈~ rusty spot ❷ spotted; striped

【斑白】grey; grizzled
【斑点】spot; stain
【斑斓】bright-colored
【斑马】zebra
【斑纹】stripe; streak
【斑竹】mottled bamboo

搬 (bān) ❶take away; remove ❷move ❸ copy mechanically; apply indiscriminately

【搬家】❶move; remove ❷removal
【搬弄】❶fiddle with ❷show off; display
【搬弄是非】gossip; tell tales; spread discord
【搬运】carry; transport; convey

板 (bǎn) ❶ shutter ❷ board; plank; plate ❸bat ❹look serious; stop smiling ❺ stiff ❻ unnatural ❼ an accented beat

【板凳】stool; wooden bench
【板房】prefabricated house
【板栗】Chinese chestnut
【板球】cricket
【板刷】scrubbing brush
【板着脸】keep a straight face
【板子】board; plank

版 (bǎn) ❶edition: 绝~ out of print; 普及~ popular edition; 修订~ revised edition; 原~original edition ❷page (of a newspaper); ❸printing plate (or block)

【版本】edition; version
【版画】woodblock; woodcut; engraving
【版面】space of a whole page; layout of a printed sheet
【版权】copyright
【版税】royalty (on books); copyright royalty
【版图】territory; domain

办 (bàn) ❶ do; handle; manage; deal with; attend to; cope with; tackle ❷set up; run ❸buy a fair amount of; ❹ get sth. ready ❺punish; bring to justice

【办案】handle a legal case
【办法】way; means; method; measure
【办公】handle official business; attend the office; work (usually in an office)
【办公室】office

【办理】deal; handle; manage; conduct
【办事】work; handle affairs: 按原则~act according to principles
【办事处】office; agency
【办事员】clerk; office worker
【办学】run a school

半 (bàn) ❶half: 一个~小时 one and a half hours ❷the least bit ❸very little ❹partly ❺in the middle of; halfway ❻semi-
【半辈子】half a lifetime
【半边】half of sth. ; one side of sth.
【半边天】❶half of the sky ❷women of the new society
【半场】❶half court ❷half of a game or contest: 上~ the first half (of a game)
【半成品】semi-finished products
【半导体】semiconductor; transistor
【半岛】peninsula
【半点】the least bit: 没有~慌张 not the least bit flurried
【半工半读】part work, part study
【半饥半饱】half-starving
【半价】half price
【半斤八两】six of one and half a dozen of the other
【半径】radius; semidiameter
【半决赛】semi-finals
【半路】halfway; midway; on the way
【半票】half-price ticket; half fare
【半球】hemisphere
【半天】❶half a day ❷a long time; quite a while
【半透明】semi-transparent; translucent
【半途而废】give up halfway; leave sth. unfinished
【半信半疑】half-believing; half-doubting
【半夜】in the middle of the night; midnight
【半圆】semicircle
【半月刊】semimonthly; fortnightly

扮 (bàn) ❶be dressed up as; play the part of; disguise oneself as ❷put on an expression
【扮鬼脸】make a face; make faces
【扮相】the appearance of an actor or actress in costume and makeup
【扮演】act; play the role (or part) of

伴 (bàn) ❶company; companion; partner: 做~ keep sb. company ❷accompany
【伴郎】groomsman; best man
【伴侣】company; companion; partner; mate
【伴娘】bridesmaid
【伴随】accompany; follow
【伴奏】accompany; accompaniment: 钢琴~piano accompaniment

拌 (bàn) mix; mix and stir
【拌嘴】quarrel; squabble

绊 (bàn) stumble; trip
【绊脚石】obstacle; stumbling block
【绊手绊脚】be in the way

bang

邦 (bāng) nation; country; state
【邦交】relations between two countries; diplomatic relations: 建立~establish diplomatic relations

帮 (bāng) ❶help; assistance; favour; aid ❷band; gang
【帮补】subsidize
【帮扶】help; assist; aid
【帮忙】help; lend aid to; do a favour; give a hand; do a good turn

【帮派】clique; faction

【帮腔】speak in support of sb.; echo sb.; chime in with sb.

【帮手】helper; assistant

【帮凶】accomplice; accessory

【帮助】help; assistance; aid: 在……的～下 with the help of; 在……方面～某人 help sb. with; 对……～很大 a great help to; 没多大～ be of little help

绑 (bǎng) tie; bind; fasten

【绑带】bandage

【绑匪】kidnapper

【绑架】kidnap; abduct

【绑票】kidnap (for ransom)

【绑扎】wrap up; bind up; tie up; bundle up; pack

榜 (bǎng) ❶notice; announcement ❷a list of names posted up: 发～publish the list of successful candidates; a list of names posted up

【榜样】pattern; example; model: 树立～set an example

膀 (bǎng) ❶arm; upper arm ❷shoulder ❸wing (of a bird)

棒 (bàng) ❶stick; club; cane ❷good; fine; excellent ❸strong

【棒冰】ice lolly; frozen sucker

【棒球】baseball

【棒子】stick; cane; club; cudgel

傍 (bàng) be close to; draw near by

【傍大款】find a sugar daddy; lean on a money bag

【傍晚】evening; at dusk; at nightfall; toward evening

磅 (bàng) ❶pound ❷scales ❸weigh 另见 1125 页 páng

【磅秤】platform scales; platform balance

bao

包 (bāo) ❶bag; sack: 手提～handbag; 书～school bag ❷bundle; package; pack; packet; parcel: 邮～postal parcel ❸wrap; cover ❹surround; encircle ❺include; contain ❻assure; guarantee ❼hire; charter

【包办】take care of everything; take sole charge of; do things or make decisions without consulting others

【包庇】shield; cover up; harbour

【包车】charter a bus (or car)

【包船】charter a boat

【包袱】❶cloth-wrapper ❷load; weight; burden: 思想～ a load on one's neck; a weight on one's mind

【包工】❶contractor ❷undertake to perform work within a time limit and according to specifications

【包裹】❶wrap up; bind up ❷bundle; package; parcel: 解开～ undo a parcel

【包含】contain; include

【包间】booth cabin; small room in a restaurant

【包括】consist of; cover; include

【包容】pardon; forgive; tolerate

【包围】surround; encircle; be close in (or around)

【包销】undertake exclusive sales

【包月】make monthly payment

【包扎】wrap up: ～伤口 bind up; dress the wound

【包装】packing; package; pack

【包子】steamed stuffed bun

剥 (bāo) strip; peel; shell; skin 另见 902 页 bō

【剥光】strip bare

【剥皮】skin; peel off the skin

褒(bāo)commend;honour;praise

【褒贬】❶appraise ❷speak ill of;cry down

【褒奖】praise and honour;commend and award

【褒义】commendatory

雹(báo)hail

【雹灾】a hail disaster

薄(báo) ❶ thin; flimsy ❷ weak; light ❸ cold; lacking in warmth ❹ infertile;poor

另见 903 页 bó;bò

【薄板】sheet;sheet metal

【薄饼】thin pancake

【薄片】flake;slice

饱(bǎo) ❶have eaten one's fill;be full ❷satisfy ❸full;plump ❹fully;to the full

【饱餐】eat to one's heart's content

【饱读】be well-read

【饱和】saturation

【饱满】❶full:精神~ full of vigor;energetic ❷plump:谷粒很~。The grains are quite plump.

宝(bǎo) ❶ treasure ❷ treasured; precious

【宝贝】❶treasure ❷darling;baby

【宝典】a treasured book;a revered book

【宝贵】valuable;precious

【宝库】treasure-house:知识~ treasure-house of ideas

【宝石】diamond;precious stone;gem

【宝塔】pagoda

【宝藏】treasury;hidden treasure;precious deposits

保(bǎo) ❶ protect; defend ❷ keep; maintain ❸ ensure; guarantee ❹stand guarantor for sb. ❺guarantor

【保安】❶ensure public security ❷security servant

【保镖】bodyguard;escort

【保持】keep; maintain; remain; preserve; keep up:~安静 keep silence;keep quiet ~警惕 maintain vigilance; be on the alert ~联系 keep in touch with;~中立 remain neutral

【保存】preserve;keep;conserve

【保管】preserve;keep in custody

【保护】❶ protect; preserve; safeguard ❷protection:~环境 protect the environment against pollution;~区 conservation area; reserve; ~视力 preserve eyesight;~主义 protectionism

【保健】health care (or protection):~操 fitness (or setting-up) exercises;~食品 health-care food;functional food

【保洁】keep a public place clean;do sanitation work:~公司 sanitation (or cleaning) company

【保龄球】bowling;tenpins

【保留】❶ retain; continue to have; keep ❷hold (or keep) back;reserve

【保密】keep sth. secret;maintain secrecy

【保命】save one's life;survive

【保姆】❶(children's) nurse; baby-sitter ❷housekeeper

【保全】❶ save from damage; preserve ❷maintain;keep in good repair

【保湿】keep moisture

【保释】bail;release on bail

【保守】❶conserve ❷conservative

【保卫】❶defend;safeguard ❷defence

【保温瓶】thermos;vacuum bottle

【保鲜袋】fresh keeping package

【保险】❶insurance:~单 insurance policy;~费 insurance premium;~公司 insurance company ❷safe:~柜 safe;strong box ❸be sure; be bound to

【保修】guarantee to keep sth. in good repair

【保养】❶ take care of one's health ❷maintain; keep in good repair

【保佑】bless

【保证】❶ guarantee; assure; ensure: 向……~ promise ❷security; assurance

【保证金】earnest money; cash deposit

【保重】take care; take care of oneself

堡 (bǎo) fort; fortress

【堡垒】fort; stronghold; fortress

报 (bào) ❶newspaper: 日~daily; 晚~evening paper ❷ report; bulletin ❸periodical ❹telegram; cable ❺report; announce; declare ❻reply; respond

【报案】report a case to the security authorities

【报表】report forms

【报仇】revenge; avenge

【报酬】reward; remuneration; pay: 不计~ not concerned about pay

【报答】repay; reward: 作为~ in return

【报单】taxation form; declaration form

【报到】check in; register; report on duty

【报道】report; cover: 据~it is reported that...; 新闻~ news report; story

【报恩】pay a debt of gratitude

【报废】reject; report sth. as worthless

【报复】retaliate; get even with sb.

【报告】❶ make known; report; inform ❷report; speech; talk; address; lecture: 时事~report on current events (or affairs); 总结~summing-up report; 作~give a talk (or lecture)

【报关】declare (at customs)

【报价】❶make an offer; quote ❷quoted price

【报警】❶report (an incident) to the police ❷give an alarm

【报刊】newspapers and periodicals

【报考】enter oneself for an examination

【报名】enroll; enlist; sign up

【报幕】announce the programme

【报数】number off: ~! Count off!

【报摊】news stand; news stall

【报信】notify; inform

【报应】❶due punishment ❷retribution

【报账】render an account

刨 (bào) plane; plane sth. down 另见 1125 页 páo

【刨冰】flake ice; shavings of ice

【刨花】wood shavings

【刨子】plane (a carpenter's tool)

抱 (bào) ❶ hold (or carry) in the arms; embrace; hug ❷ adopt (a child) ❸ cherish: 不~幻想 cherish no illusions

【抱不平】feel angry at injustice; be outraged by an injustice (done to sb. else)

【抱负】ideal; ambition; aspiration

【抱歉】be sorry; feel apologetic; apology; regret

【抱怨】complain; grumble

豹 (bào) leopard; panther

暴 (bào) ❶sudden and violent ❷cruel; fierce; savage ❸ short-tempered; hot-tempered

【暴病】sudden illness; sudden attack of a serious illness

【暴跌】steep fall (in price); slump: 股票~ a slump in the stocks

【暴动】uprising; rebellion; revolt; riot; insurrection

【暴发】❶ break out ❷ suddenly become rich (or important); get rich quick

B

【暴发户】upstart; new rich; jumped-up people

【暴风】❶storm wind ❷storm (or force11 wind)

【暴力】violence; force: 采用~ resort to violence

【暴利】extortionate profits; sudden huge profits

【暴露】disclose; discover; expose; reveal; lay bare; exposed to the open air

【暴乱】riot; rebellion; revolt

【暴怒】violent rage; fury

【暴晒】be exposed to the sun (for a long time)

【暴行】savage act; outrage; atrocity

【暴雨】shower; torrential rain; rainstorm

【暴躁】irritable; irascible: 性格~的 hot-tempered

【暴涨】(of floods, prices etc.) rise suddenly and sharply: 物价~prices soared (or skyrocketed)

【暴政】tyranny

爆 (bào) ❶explode; burst ❷quick-fry; quick-boil

【爆发】❶ burst; burst out (or forth); break out ❷outburst

【爆裂】pop; crack; blow

【爆满】❶(of a stadium, etc.) be filled to capacity ❷(of a theatre, cinema, etc.) have a full house; house full

【爆炸】explode; blow up; burst

【爆竹】firecracker: 放~let off firecrackers

bei

杯 (bēi) cup; glass; tumbler; mug: 奖~ prize cup; trophy 茶~tea cup; 啤酒~ mug

卑 (bēi) ❶ low ❷ inferior ❸humble; modest

【卑鄙】mean; base; despicable; contemptible

【卑贱】low; humble

【卑微】petty and low

背 (bēi) ❶carry on the back ❷bear; shoulder

另见 893 页 bèi

【背包】knapsack; rucksack; infantry pack; field pack

【背包袱】have a load on one's mind

【背包客】backpacker

【背负】bear; carry on the back

【背黑锅】be made a scapegoat

【背债】be in debt; be saddled with debts

悲 (bēi) ❶compassion ❷sad; sorrowful

【悲哀】❶sad; grieved ❷sadness; sorrow

【悲惨】miserable; tragic

【悲从中来】feel sadness welling up

【悲歌】sad melody

【悲观】pessimistic

【悲剧】tragedy

【悲苦】grief; sorrow

【悲凉】sad and dreary; forlorn; desolate

【悲伤】sadness; sorrow

【悲痛】sorrow; grief

【悲喜交集】mixed feelings of grief and joy

碑 (bēi) an upright stone tablet; stele: 墓~tombstone; 人民英雄纪念~the Monument to the People's Heroes

【碑记】a record of events inscribed on a tablet

【碑文】an inscription on a tablet

北 (běi) north

【北半球】the Northern Hemisphere

【北冰洋】the Arctic (Ocean)

【北方】❶ north ❷ the northern part of the country

【北风】north wind
【北回归线】Tropic of Cancer
【北极】the North Pole; the Arctic
【北极星】Polaris; the North Star
【北极熊】polar bear
【北美洲】North America
【北漂】North Drift people (people who live and work in Beijing, while without Beijing registered residence and change their houses from time to time)

贝 (bèi) shellfish

【贝雕】shell carving
【贝壳】shell

备 (bèi) ❶ equipment ❷ have; be equipped with ❸ prepare; get ready ❹ provide (or prepare) against ❺ in every possible way; fully

【备案】put on record (or file); keep on record; enter (a case) in the records
【备查】for future reference
【备份】backup; copy
【备件】spare parts
【备课】prepare lessons
【备忘录】memorandum
【备用】spare; reserve; alternate
【备注】remarks; notes

背 (bèi) ❶ the back of the body ❷ the back of an object ❸ turn away ❹ hide sth. from; do sth. behind sb.'s back ❺ learn by heart; recite; memorize ❻ hard of hearing ❼ out-of-the-way

另见 892 页 bēi

【背道而驰】run in the opposite direction
【背地里】behind sb.'s back; privately
【背后】❶ behind; at the back ❷ behind sb.'s back
【背景】background
【背井离乡】leave one's native land (or place)
【背靠背】back to back
【背面】the back; the reverse side
【背弃】abandon; desert
【背诵】learn by heart; recite; repeat from memory
【背心】a sleeveless garment; vest
【背信弃义】be perfidious; break faith with sb.; betray a trust

倍 (bèi) ❶ times; -fold: 五~five times; fivefold ❷ double

【倍数】multiple
【倍增】double; redouble

悖 (bèi) go against; run contrary to

【悖论】antinomy; paradox

被 (bèi) ❶ quilt ❷ by

【被捕】be arrested; be under arrest
【被单】bed sheet
【被动】passive
【被告】defendant; the accused
【被害人】the injured party; the victim
【被迫】be compelled to do sth.; be forced to do sth.; be constrained
【被褥】bed clothes and mattress; bedding
【被套】❶ bedding bag ❷ quilt cover

辈 (bèi) ❶ generation ❷ lifetime ❸ the like; people of a certain kind

【辈出】come forth in large numbers
【辈分】seniority in a family or clan; position in the family hierarchy

ben

奔 (bēn) ❶ run quickly ❷ rush; hurry; hasten ❸ flee; run away

另见 894 页 bèn

【奔波】be busy running about; rush about
【奔驰】❶ run quickly; speed ❷ Benz (世界

著名汽车品牌）

B

【奔放】bold and unrestrained

【奔赴】hurry to;rush to

【奔流而入】pour (or flow) into

【奔忙】be busy rushing about; bustle about

【奔腾】❶gallop ❷surge forward; roll on in waves

【奔走相告】run around spreading the news

本（běn）❶the root or stem of a plant ❷book;copy ❸edition:精装～ hardback edition; 平装～ paperback ❹foundation;basis;origin ❺one's own; native ❻according to

【本部】headquarter

【本地】❶this locality ❷local;native

【本分】❶one's duty;obligation: 尽～do one's bit (or duty) ❷honest;decent

【本国】home;homeland;one's own country

【本行】one's line;one's own profession

【本届】current;this year's

【本金】principal;capital

【本科】undergraduate course;regular college course

【本来】❶original; proper ❷originally; at first ❸of course;it goes without saying: ～面目 true features;true colors

【本领】skill;ability;capability;faculty

【本末倒置】take the branch for the root; put the incidental before the fundamental

【本能】❶instinct ❷by instinct

【本年度】this year;the current year

【本人】❶I(or me);myself ❷in person

【本色】❶true (or inherent) qualities;distinctive character ❷natural color

【本事】skill;ability;capability

【本性】nature;natural instinct (or character);inherent quality

【本义】original meaning;literal sense

【本意】original idea;real intention

【本质】nature;essence

【本子】book; notebook: 账 ～ account book;日记～diary

奔（bèn）❶go straight towards; head for ❷approach;be getting on for 另见 893 页 bēn

【奔头儿】sth. to strive for;prospect

笨（bèn）❶stupid; foolish; silly ❷clumsy;awkward ❸cumbersome; unwieldy

【笨蛋】fool;idiot

【笨手笨脚】❶clumsy; ❷awkward

【笨头笨脑】slow-minded;dull-minded

【笨重】heavy;cumbersome

【笨拙】clumsy;awkward;stupid

beng

崩（bēng）❶burst ❷collapse: 山～ landslip; landslide; bursting ❸ execute by shooting;shoot

【崩溃】collapse;ruin;crumble;fall apart

【崩裂】burst apart;break apart;crack

【崩陷】fall in;cave in

绷（bēng）❶stretch (or draw) tight ❷pin;tack

【绷带】bandage

泵（bèng）pump:水～water pump

迸（bèng）burst forth; gush; spout; spurt

【迸发】burst out (or forth);break out

【迸裂】split;burst (open)

蹦（bèng）skip;leap;jump;spring

【蹦床】trampoline

【蹦极】bungee (jumping)

bi

逼 (bī) ❶press upon; compel ❷drive; press for; extort ❸ press on towards; close in on

【逼供】extort a confession

【逼近】approach; close in; draw near

【逼人太甚】drive sb. too hard; put too much pressure on sb.

【逼问】❶ force sb. to answer ❷ question closely

【逼债】press for payment of debts; dun

【逼真】lifelike; true to life

鼻 (bí) nose: 牵着～子走 lead by the nose; 抠～子 pick one's nose

【鼻孔】nostril

【鼻腔】nasal cavity

【鼻涕】nasal mucus: 流～ have a running nose

【鼻祖】the earliest (first) ancestor; founder; forefather; originator

比 (bǐ) ❶ proportion ❷ comparison ❸compare; contrast ❹match; compete ❺draw an analogy ❻be like; liken to; compare to

【比不上】not to be compared with

【比方】for example (or instance); such as

【比分】score

【比……更】more ...than

【比价】❶ price relations; parity; rate of exchange: 工农业产品～ the price parities between industrial and agricultural products ❷compare bids or prices

【比肩】shoulder to shoulder

【比较】❶ compare; contrast ❷ relative; comparative ❸relatively; fairly

【比例】proportion; scale

【比邻】❶next-door; neighbour ❷next to; near

【比率】ratio; rate

【比如】for example; for instance; such as

【比赛】❶match; game; race; competition: 进行～ have (or hold) a match; ❷play; contest; compete

【比试】❶ have a competition ❷ measure with one's hand or arm ❸make gestures

【比喻】metaphor; figure of speech; analogy

【比照】❶ contrast ❷ according to; in the light of

【比重】❶proportion ❷specific gravity

彼 (bǐ) that; those; the other; another: 由此及～ proceed from one to the other

【彼岸】❶ Faramita ❷the other shore

【彼此】each other; one another

笔 (bǐ) ❶pen; pencil: 钢～pen; 圆珠～ ballpoint; 毛～brush ❷write ❸technique of writing, calligraphy or drawing ❹stroke

【笔调】(of writing) tone; style

【笔锋】❶ the tip of a writing brush; ❷vigour of style in writing; stroke; touch

【笔杆】penholder

【笔画】strokes of a Chinese character

【笔记】notes: 记～take notes; ～本 notebook

【笔记本电脑】laptop; notebook computer

【笔迹】handwriting; hand

【笔名】pen name: 用～写作 write under a pen name

【笔墨】❶words; writing ❷pen and ink

【笔试】written test (or examination)

【笔顺】order of strokes observed in calligraphy

【笔算】do a sum in writing

【笔挺】very straight; bolt upright; well-

ironed
【笔误】a slip of the pen
B
【笔芯】refill; pencil lead
【笔者】the author; the writer
【笔直】perfectly straight; bolt upright

鄙 (bǐ) ❶low; mean ❷despise; disdain
【鄙薄】scorn; despise
【鄙弃】disdain; loathe
【鄙视】look down on (or upon)

币 (bì) money; currency; banknote; coin
【币值】currency value
【币制】monetary standard; currency (or monetary) system

必 (bì) ❶ must; have to ❷ certainly; surely; necessarily
【必不可少】essential; absolutely necessary; indispensable
【必定】be bound to; be sure to
【必然】necessary; inevitable; certain ～性 necessity; certainty
【必修课】required course
【必须】must; have to: 对……是～的 be a must for
【必要】necessary; essential; need: 如有～ if necessary; in case of necessity

毕 (bì) ❶ finish; conclude; accomplish ❷fully; completely
【毕竟】after all; all in all; at all; in the final analysis
【毕生】all one's life; the whole life; lifetime
【毕业】❶graduate; finish school ❷graduation
【毕业典礼】graduation ceremony
【毕业论文】graduation thesis
【毕业生】graduate
【毕业证】diploma; graduation certificate

闭 (bì) shut; close; stop up; obstruct
【闭关政策】closed-door policy
【闭会】close (or end) a meeting
【闭口】shut up; shut one's mouth
【闭门羹】usu. used in 飨以～ shut the door in sb.'s face—refuse to receive sb.
【闭幕】❶ lower the curtain; the curtain falls ❷close; conclude
【闭幕词】closing address; closing speech
【闭幕式】closing ceremony
【闭塞】❶stop (or close) up ❷hard to get to; out-of-the-way
【闭嘴】hold one's tongue; shut up

庇 (bì) shelter; protect; shield
【庇护】shelter; protect; take under one's wing
【庇佑】bless; prosper

毙 (bì) ❶die; get killed ❷ kill or execute by shooting; shoot
【毙命】meet a violent death

敝 (bì) ❶ worn out; declining ❷ my; our; this
【敝帚自珍】value one's own old broom—cherish sth. of little value simply because it is one's own

弊 (bì) ❶ fraud; abuse; malpractice ❷disadvantage; harm
【弊病】❶illness; malady ❷drawback
【弊端】malpractice; abuse

碧 (bì) ❶ green jade ❷ bluish green; blue
【碧蓝】dark blue
【碧绿】dark green
【碧玉】jasper

壁 (bì) ❶wall ❷cliff
【壁报】wall newspaper

【壁橱】closet; cupboard; built-in wardrobe
【壁虎】gecko; house lizard
【壁画】mural (painting); fresco
【壁垒】barrier; rampart: 关税～tariff barrier
【壁炉】fireplace

避 (bì) ❶avoid ❷prevent; keep away; shun; prevent

【避风】❶take shelter from the wind ❷lie low
【避讳】❶a word or phrase to be avoided as taboo; taboo ❷evade
【避开】avoid; flee; keep off; keep away from; evade
【避雷针】lightning rod
【避免】avoid; refrain (or prevent) from; get rid of; keep away from
【避难】take refuge
【避暑】❶be away for the summer holidays; spend a holiday at a summer resort ❷prevent sunstroke
【避雨】take shelter from rain
【避孕】birth control; contraception; contracept; prevent pregnancy

臂 (bì) arm; upper arm: 助一～之力 give sb. a hand

【臂章】❶armband; armlet ❷shoulder patch

bian

边 (biān) ❶side: 右～right side; right; 左～left side; left ❷margin; edge: 在……～上 at the edge of ❸boundary; frontier; border ❹bound; limit ❺close by

【边防】frontier (or border) defence
【边际】boundary; bound; limit: 不着～not to the point
【边疆】border area
【边界】border; boundary
【边境】border; frontier
【边框】frame; rim
【边缘】rim; edge; border

编 (biān) ❶weave; plait ❷organize; group; arrange ❸edit; compile ❹write; compose ❺make up; cook up; invent

【编凑】fabricate; invent; make up; cook up
【编导】❶write and direct ❷director (of a play or a film); scenarist
【编订】compile and edit
【编号】❶number ❷serial number
【编辑】❶edit; compile ❷editor; compiler: 总～ editor-in-chief; ～部 editorial department
【编剧】❶write a play ❷screenwriter; scenarist
【编码】coding
【编目】catalogue; make a catalogue
【编年史】annals; chronicle
【编排】arrange; lay out
【编审】❶read and edit ❷senior editor
【编译】translate and edit; compile
【编造】❶compile; draw up; work out ❷invent; make up
【编者】editor; compiler
【编织】weave; knit; plait; braid
【编制】❶work out; draw up ❷organization; establishment
【编著】compile; write

蝙 (biān)

【蝙蝠】bat

鞭 (biān) ❶whip; lash ❷flog

【鞭策】spur (or urge) on; encourage
【鞭长莫及】❶too far away for sb. to be able to help; ❷beyond the reach of

one's power
【鞭打】whip; lash; flog
【鞭炮】firecrackers

贬 (biǎn) ❶reduce; devalue ❷belittle; depreciate ❸demote
【贬低】play down; belittle
【贬损】disparage; defame; preach down
【贬值】devalue; devaluate

扁 (biǎn) flat
【扁担】carrying (or shoulder) pole
【扁平】flat
【扁桃体】tonsil

变 (biàn) ❶change; change (or turn) into ❷become different; transform; alter
【变白】go white
【变成】change (or turn) into; become; go; get: 由……~change from ...into ...
【变动】❶change; alteration ❷change
【变革】transform; change; convert; reform
【变故】accident; unexpected event
【变卦】go back on one's word
【变幻】change irregularly; fluctuate: ~莫测 changeable
【变节】turn one's coat; betray; defect
【变脸】❶ change facial expression ❷turn hostile
【变凉】cool
【变卖】sell off (one's property)
【变迁】changes; vicissitudes; change of fortunes; fluctuation: 时世~the changes of the times
【变速】speed change; gearshift
【变态】❶ metamorphosis ❷ abnormal; anomalous
【变通】be flexible; accommodate (or adapt) sth. to circumstances
【变相】in disguised form; covert
【变心】break faith; change loyalties; cease to be faithful
【变形】❶ be out of shape; become deformed ❷ deformation; shape change; variant ❸ anamorphosis
【变异】variation; variety; variant
【变质】go bad; deteriorate
【变种】mutation
【变奏】variation: ~曲 variations (on a theme)

便 (biàn) ❶informal; plain; ordinary ❷ convenient; handy ❸ relieve oneself ❹urine or excrement
另见 1129 页 pián
【便当】❶ convenient; handy; easy ❷ fast food in box
【便饭】a simple meal
【便服】casual (or everyday) clothes
【便笺】notepaper; memo
【便利】❶convenient; easy ❷facilitate
【便秘】astriction; constipation
【便民】for the convenience of the people: ~措施 facilities for the convenience of the people
【便携式】portable
【便衣】civilian clothes; plain clothes
【便于】easy to; convenient for

遍 (biàn) ❶ time ❷ all over; everywhere
【遍地】everywhere; all around
【遍及】❶ throughout; over; all over ❷spread all over
【遍体鳞伤】be beaten black and blue; be black and blue all over

辨 (biàn) distinguish; differentiate; tell
【辨别】distinguish; differentiate; tell ... from ...
【辨明】make a clear distinction; distin-

guish

【辨认】identify; recognize

辩 (biàn) argue; dispute; debate

【辩白】offer an explanation; plead innocence; try to defend oneself

【辩护】❶defend; plead ❷speak in defence of; argue in favour of

【辩解】excuse; justify

【辩论】debate; argue

【辩证】dialectical

【辩证唯物主义】dialectical materialism

biao

标 (biāo) ❶mark; sign ❷label; put a mark ❸prize; award ❹tender; bid

【标榜】❶flaunt; parade; advertise ❷boost; excessively praise

【标本】specimen; sample

【标的】❶target ❷purpose; object

【标点符号】punctuation; punctuation mark

【标记】mark; sign; flag; label; symbol

【标价】❶mark a price ❷marked price

【标明】mark; indicate

【标签】label; tag: 贴上~stick on a label

【标识】logo

【标题】heading; headline; title: 小~ sub-heading; crosshead

【标语】slogan; poster

【标志】❶mark; sign; symbol ❷indicate; mark; signify

【标致】❶pretty; beautiful; handsome ❷Peugeot (法国汽车品牌)

【标准】❶standard; criterion ❷level ❸normal

【标准化】❶standardization ❷standardize

飙 (biāo) violent wind

【飙升】skyrocket; rise quickly

表 (biǎo) ❶table; list; form: 填~ fill in a form ❷watch ❸meter: 体温~clinic thermometer ❹surface; external; outside ❺show; express

【表白】show; assert; vindicate

【表达】express; show; convey; voice

【表格】form; table; list

【表决】decide by vote: 唱名~ roll-call vote; 交付~ put to a vote; take a vote; 举手~vote by a show of hands; 口头~ voice vote

【表里不一】❶double faced ❷think in one way and behave in another

【表面】face; surface; outside; appearance

【表明】make known; indicate; make clear; show; prove; state clearly

【表情】❶expression ❷express one's feelings

【表示】express; show; indicate

【表述】explain; state

【表率】example; model

【表态】take a stand; clarify one's position

【表现】❶show; display; express; behave ❷behaviour; conduct

【表演】❶perform; act; play ❷performance; acting: 体育~ sports exhibition

【表演节目】give a performance; put on a show

【表扬】praise; commend

【表彰】commend; honour; cite

bie

憋 (biē) ❶suppress; hold back ❷suffocate; feel oppressed

【憋闷】be depressed; be dejected

【憋气】❶feel suffocated ❷feel injured

别 (bié) ❶difference; distinction: 天渊之~ a world of differences ❷leave;

part ❸distinguish; differentiate ❹fasten with a pin ❺others; another ❻(used in giving commands or advice) don't; had better not

另见本页 biè

【别处】elsewhere; another place

【别管】no matter

【别管闲事】don't put your finger in the pie; mind your own business

【别见怪】don't be offended

【别紧张】take it easy

【别客气】don't mention it

【别离】take leave of; leave; depart

【别名】another name; alternative name

【别人】others; other people

【别墅】villa

【别说】to say nothing of; not to mention; let alone

【别无他法】have no other way out

【别样】❶ other; different ❷ a different style

【别针】pin; safety pin; brooch

【别致】novel; unique

别 (biè) persuade sb. to change his opinion or give up his idea

另见本页 bié

【别扭】❶not smooth; awkward ❷difficult to deal with; troublesome ❸not get along well ❹cannot see eye to eye: 闹～ be at odds

bin

宾 (bīn) guest

【宾馆】guesthouse; hotel

【宾客】guest; visitor

【宾朋】friends and guests; guests

【宾语】object

【宾至如归】guests feeling as at home

滨 (bīn) shore; bank

【滨海】by the sea

濒 (bīn) ❶border on; close to ❷be on the point of; be on the brink of

【濒临】approach; be close to; border on; be on the verge of

【濒危】be in imminent danger

【濒于】be on the point; be on the brink of; be on the verge of

摈 (bìn) discard; get rid of

【摈除】discard; get rid of; dispense with

【摈弃】abandon; discard; cast away

殡 (bìn) ❶ lay a coffin in a memorial hall ❷ carry a coffin to the burial place

【殡殓】encoffin a corpse

【殡仪馆】the undertaker's; mortuary house

【殡葬】funeral and interment

bing

冰 (bīng) ❶ice ❷put on ice ❸feel cold

【冰雹】hail; hailstone

【冰川】glacier

【冰点】freezing point

【冰雕】ice carving; carved ice; ice sculpture

【冰冻】freeze

【冰棍儿】ice lolly; frozen sucker; ice sucker

【冰激凌】ice cream

【冰凉】ice-cold

【冰球】ice hockey

【冰山】iceberg

【冰糖】crystal sugar; rock candy

【冰天雪地】a world of ice and snow

【冰箱】refrigerator; icebox; fridge

【冰鞋】skating boots
【冰镇】iced

兵 (bīng) ❶soldier; fighter ❷troops; army ❸weapons; arms

【兵变】mutiny
【兵法】warcraft; art of war; military strategy and tactics
【兵力】military strength; armed forces; troops
【兵马】troops and horses; military forces
【兵器】weapons; arms
【兵团】corps; army
【兵役】military service

秉 (bǐng) grasp; hold

【秉持】adhere to (principles, etc.); hold onto
【秉公】justly; impartially
【秉性】nature

饼 (bǐng) round flat cake

【饼干】biscuit; cracker
【饼子】pancake

屏 (bǐng) ❶hold (one's breath) ❷get rid of; reject

另见 1133 页 píng

【屏除】get rid of; dismiss; brush aside
【屏气】hold one's breath
【屏弃】discard; reject; throw away; abandon
【屏声】hold one's breath and keep quiet: ~倾听 listen in rapt silence

禀 (bǐng) ❶report; petition ❷receive; be endowed with

【禀赋】natural endowment; gift
【禀性】natural disposition

并 (bìng) ❶combine; merge; incorporate ❷moreover; and; besides ❸side by side

【并不】not at all; by no means; in no sense
【并存】exist side by side
【并发症】complication
【并非】not
【并肩】shoulder to shoulder; side by side
【并进】advance side by side
【并立】exist side by side; exist simultaneously
【并联】parallel connection
【并列】stand side by side; put close together
【并排】side by side; abreast
【并且】❶and; also; and... as well; in addition ❷besides; moreover; furthermore
【并入】merge into; incorporate into
【并行】❶walk abreast; run side by side ❷carry on (two things) at the same time
【并用】use two things simultaneously: 手脚~ use both hands and feet
【并重】lay equal stress on; pay equal attention to

病 (bìng) ❶disease; illness; sickness: 传染~infection disease; 急性~acute disease; 慢性~chronic disease; 重~serious disease ❷fall ill; be ill

【病变】pathological changes
【病床】sick bed
【病倒】fall ill; be down with an illness
【病毒】virus
【病房】ward; sickroom: 内科~medical ward; 外科~surgical ward; 查~make ward rounds
【病根】❶an incompletely cured illness; an old complaint ❷the root cause of trouble
【病故】die of an illness
【病假】sick leave: 请~ ask for sick leave
【病句】a faulty sentence

B

【病菌】germs;pathogenic bacteria;

【病历】case history;medical record

【病例】medical case

【病魔】serious illness

【病情】patient's condition;state of an illness

【病人】patient:急诊~ emergency case;门诊~ out-patient

【病入膏肓】be past (or beyond) cure (or remedy)

【病态】morbid state

【病痛】slight illness;ailment

【病危】be critically ill

【病因】cause of disease

【病友】a friend made in hospital or people who become friends in hospital; wardmate

【病愈】recover (from an illness)

【病员】sick personnel;person on the sick list;patient

【病状】symptom

bo

拨(bō) ❶stir; turn; poke ❷set aside; allocate;appropriate

【拨号码】dial (telephone) number

【拨开】push aside

【拨快】set ahead

【拨款】❶allocate funds ❷appropriation

【拨慢】set (or put) back

【拨弄是非】stir up troubles by gossip; gossip

【拨弦】pluck a string

【拨正】set right;correct

【拨钟】set a clock

波(bō) ❶wave ❷an unexpected turn of events

【波长】wavelength

【波动】rise and fall;wave;fluctuate

【波段】wave band

【波及】spread to;involve;affect

【波兰语】Polish

【波浪】wave

【波涛】great waves

【波涛汹涌】surging waves

【波纹】❶ripple ❷corrugation

【波折】twists and turns;setbacks

玻(bō)

【玻璃】glass

【玻璃杯】glass;tumbler

【玻璃钢】glass fibre reinforced plastic

【玻璃管】glass tube

剥(bō)
另见 889 页 bāo

【剥夺】deprive;strip

【剥离】(of tissue, skin, covering, etc.) come off;peel off;be stripped

【剥削】exploit;exploitation

播(bō) ❶ spread; broadcast ❷sow; seed

【播放】❶broadcast ❷broadcast a TV programme

【播撒】spread;scatter;sprinkle

【播送】transmit;send out;broadcast

【播音】transmit; broadcast:开始~go on the air;停止~go off the air

【播音室】broadcasting studio

【播音员】announcer

【播种】sow (seeds);seed

伯(bó)father's elder brother;uncle

【伯父】uncle;a term of address for a man of one's father's generation who is older than one's father

【伯乐】❶a legendary connoisseur of horses ❷a good judge of talent

【伯爵】earl; count

【伯母】aunt; auntie; wife of father's elder brother

驳（bó）refute; argue: 不值一～ not worth arguing

【驳斥】refute; denounce; deny; disprove

【驳倒】demolish sb.'s argument; refute; prove to be false; outargue

【驳回】turn down; reject; overrule; refute

泊（bó）anchor; berth

勃（bó）exuberant; vigorous

【勃发】❶thrive; prosper ❷break out

【勃然】❶agitatedly ❷vigorously

脖（bó）neck

博（bó）❶win; gain ❷gamble ❸wide; rich; abundant

【博爱】universal love

【博彩】gamble

【博大】broad; extensive

【博得】win; gain; get

【博古】❶ conversant with things of the past ❷paintings of ancient objects

【博客】❶blog ❷blogger

【博览会】fair; exposition

【博览群书】❶well-read ❷read extensively

【博士】doctor; learned scholar: 给某人授予～学位 confer a doctor's degree on sb.

【博士后】postdoctoral student; postdoctoral study

【博物】natural science

【博物馆】museum: 中国革命～ the Museum of the Chinese Revolution

【博学】❶learned; erudite ❷great learning

【博弈】play chess; have a game of chess

搏（bó）❶ combat; struggle; fight ❷beat

【搏斗】wrestle; struggle; fight

【搏击】strike; fight with hand

【搏杀】❶fight with a weapon ❷(in chess games) be locked in

薄（bó）❶ look down upon; despise ❷slight; small; thin

另见 890 页 báo; 本页 bò

【薄瘠之地】unfertile land

【薄礼】slight gift; modest present

【薄利多销】small profits but quick turnover

【薄膜】film; membrane

【薄暮】dusk; twilight

【薄片】thin slice (or section)

【薄情】inconstant in love; fickle

【薄弱】weak; feeble: 意志～ weak-willed

【薄雾】mist; haze

跛（bǒ）lame: 一颠一～ walk with a limp

【跛行】limp; walk lamely

薄（bò）

另见 890 页 báo; 本页 bó

【薄荷】field mint; peppermint

bu

补（bǔ）❶help; benefit ❷mend; patch; repair ❸fill; make up for; supply

【补报】❶make a report after the event; make a supplementary report: 调查结果以后～。Findings will be reported later. ❷repay a kindness

【补偿】make up; make up for; compensate

【补充】❶replenish; add; supplement; complement ❷ supply ❸ additional; supplementary

【补丁】patch: 打～patch up

【补给】supply

B

【补救】remedy; make up for
【补考】make up examination
【补课】make up a missed lesson
【补品】tonic
【补缺】fill a vacancy; supply a deficiency
【补贴】❶subsidize ❷allowance
【补习】take lessons after school (or work); take a remedial course
【补选】by-election
【补牙】fill a tooth; have a tooth stopped
【补养】take a tonic or nourishing food to build up one's health
【补药】tonic
【补衣服】patch (or mend) clothes
【补益】❶ benefit; help ❷ be of help (or benefit)
【补助】❶ subsidize ❷ allowance; subsidy: 生活～extra expenses
【补缀】mend; patch; patch up
【补足】make up for; fill

捕 (bǔ) catch; seize; arrest: 被～be arrested

【捕获】capture; seize; catch: 当场～ catch sb. red handed
【捕捞】fish for (aquatic animals and plants); catch
【捕猎】hunt; trap
【捕食】catch and feed on; prey on
【捕捉】catch; seize

哺 (bǔ) feed; nurse

【哺乳】breast-feed; nurse; suckle
【哺育】nurture; foster

不 (bù) ❶no; not so ❷can not; not able to; unable to ❸ don't; needn't ❹without

【不安】❶discomfort; uneasiness ❷upset; uneasy; intranquil ❸sorry
【不安定】unsettled; unstable; insecure
【不安分】discontented with one's lot
【不安心】not settle down to
【不必】❶needless; unnecessary ❷no need ❸need not; not have to
【不必说】it goes without saying; needless to say
【不变】❶invariable ❷fixedly
【不便】❶ inconvenient; discomfortable ❷have no money at hand; be short of cash
【不测】accident; mishap; contingency; unexpectedness
【不曾】never; not yet
【不成】❶won't do: 只说不做，那是～的。Mere talk and no action won't do. ❷(used at the end of a rhetorical question beginning with 难道 or 莫非): 难道就这样算了～? How can we let it go at that?
【不成文】unwritten
【不称职】unfit for job
【不承认】❶ nonrecognition ❷ ignore; refuse to recognize
【不出所料】as expected
【不辞而别】leave (or go away) without saying goodbye; take a French leave
【不辞辛劳】take pains; spare no effort
【不错】❶correct; right ❷not bad ❸exactly: 很～nice; pretty good; 对……～ be good to sb.
【不但】not only
【不惮】not fear; not be afraid of: ～其烦 not mind taking the trouble; take great pains; be very patient
【不当】improper; unsuitable: 处理～ be handled not properly; 措辞～wrong choice of words
【不倒翁】self-righting doll; tumbler
【不道德】immoral

【不得】❶cannot ❷should not; may not; must not; be not allowed

【不得不】have to do; be obliged to do; cannot help doing; cannot but; have no choice but to do

【不得了】❶desperately serious; disastrous ❷extremely

【不得已】have no choice; act against one's will; have no alternative but to

【不定】❶indefinite; indeterminate ❷hard to say

【不定期】irregular; non scheduled

【不懂事】ignorant; badly behaved

【不动】still; motionless

【不动产】immovable property; real estate (or property)

【不断】❶constant; continuous; unceasing ❷all the time

【不对】incorrect; wrong; amiss; abnormal

【不对称】asymmetry

【不法行为】unlawful practice; an illegal act

【不凡】out of the ordinary; out of the common run

【不妨】there is no harm in

【不放心】be anxious about; feel worried about

【不分彼此】share everything

【不分胜负】come out even; draw

【不服】disobey; refuse to obey

【不负责任】❶be ignorant of duty ❷irresponsible

【不甘】unreconciled to; not resigned to

【不敢】dare not; not dare

【不敢当】I really don't deserve this; you flatter me

【不感兴趣】lose interest in

【不公平】unfair; unjust

【不辜负】live up to; be worthy of

【不顾】❶ignore; disregard ❷despite; in spite of

【不关……的事】none of one's business

【不关心】be indifferent to; not concern oneself with

【不管】in spite of; regardless of

【不管怎样】anyway; however; in any case; whatever happens; no matter how; come what may

【不光】❶not the only one ❷not only

【不光彩】dishonourable; disgraceful

【不规则】irregular

【不过】❶only; just; merely; nothing but; no more than ❷but; however

【不好】poor; bad

【不好意思】shy; too shy to; embarrassed

【不合】❶not agree with; be unsuited to; be out of keeping with ❷not fit ❸disagreement

【不合标准】not up to the standard

【不合法】illegal

【不合格】❶disqualified; unqualified ❷disqualification

【不合理】unreasonable

【不合时宜】behind the time; out of times

【不合适】improper; out of place

【不和】discord; be on bad terms

【不慌不忙】in no hurry; leisurely

【不会】❶be unlikely ❷be unable to; can't; will not (act, happen, etc.) ❸have not learned to; be unable to

【不及】not as good as; inferior to

【不及格】fail

【不计报酬】regardless of pay

【不计其数】countless; innumerable

【不简单】not simple; unusual; remarkable

【不见不散】hot leave without seeing each other; be sure to wait

【不见得】not necessarily; not likely

B

【不禁】cannot help doing; cannot refrain from

【不仅】❶not only; not merely ❷not the only one

【不经意】carelessly; by accident

【不景气】depression; hard time; recession

【不久】soon; shortly; by and by; before long; in a short while: 前～ not long ago (or before)

【不拘小节】❶regardless of small matters ❷not bother about small matters

【不可】must not; should not; can not

【不可避免】be inevitable

【不可或缺】indispensible

【不可救药】❶hopeless; incurable ❷past (or beyond) cure

【不可抗拒】irresistible

【不可逆转】irreversible

【不可收拾】unmanageable; out of control

【不可思议】❶unimaginable; unthinkable ❷mysterious

【不客气】❶frank; straight forward ❷don't mention it; you are welcome; not at all ❸rude; impolite

【不愧】be worthy of; deserve to be called; prove oneself to be

【不劳而获】reap without sowing

【不劳无获】no pains, no gains

【不理】refuse to acknowledge; pay no attention to; take no notice of; ignore

【不理睬】ignore; neglect; turn a deaf ear to; pay no attention to

【不力】not do one's best; not exert oneself

【不利】❶disadvantage ❷harmful; bad; unsuccessful; unfavourable

【不良风气】unhealthy custom and practice

【不料】to one's surprise; unexpectedly

【不灵】not work; be ineffective

【不露声色】not show one's feelings (or intentions)

【不伦不类】neither fish nor foul

【不论】❶no matter; whether ...or ... ❷regardless of; despite

【不论……还是……】either ... or ...; whether ...or ...

【不满】dissatisfied; discontented; resentful

【不忙】there is no hurry; take one's time

【不毛之地】desert; barren land

【不明】❶not clear; unknown ❷fail to understand

【不明是非】confuse right and wrong

【不能】❶unable ❷must not; cannot; should not; fail to

【不怕】❶be not afraid of; not fear ❷fearless

【不平】❶injustice; unfairness; wrong; grievance ❷indignant; resentful

【不平等】❶unfair ❷unfairness

【不平衡】disequilibria; out of balance

【不期而遇】have a chance encounter; meet by chance; come upon; come across; run into

【不巧】unfortunately; as luck would have it

【不切实际】unrealistic; impracticable

【不求上进】have no desire for progress; not seek to make progress

【不求甚解】not seek to understand things thoroughly; be content with superficial understanding

【不屈】unbending; inflexible; unyielding: 坚强～ iron-willed and unyielding

【不然】otherwise; or else; if not

【不人道】inhuman; inhumane

【不忍】cannot bear to

【不忍坐视】cannot bear to stand idly by

【不容】not tolerate; not allow

【不容置疑】beyond doubt
【不如】❶had better; would rather ❷not as good as
【不三不四】dubious
【不善】❶not good at ❷a bad hand at
【不少于】no less than
【不失时机】lose no time; seize the opportunity
【不时】❶often; from time to time; now and then ❷at times
【不适】unwell; indisposed; out of sorts
【不适应】not accustomed (or suited, adapted) to; not fit to
【不守信用】not keep one's word; break one's word (or promise); go back on one's word
【不停】continuous
【不通】be obstructed; be blocked up; be impassable; not make sense; be illogical; be ungrammatical
【不同】❶difference ❷not alike; not proper; unlike
【不透明】opaque
【不透气】airtight
【不透水】waterproof
【不妥】not proper; inappropriate
【不畏艰险】be regardless of hardship and danger
【不闻不问】be indifferent; take no notice of
【不稳】unstable; unsteady; not firm
【不惜】❶stint no effort; not spare ❷not hesitate (to do sth.)
【不惜一切代价】at any cost; at all costs
【不相干】have no business with; have nothing to do with
【不相容】incompatible
【不详】❶not in detail ❷not quite clear
【不祥】ominous
【不像】unlike
【不像话】unreasonable
【不孝】not in accordance with filial piety
【不协调】out of tune
【不屑】disdain to do sth.; think sth. not worth doing
【不屑一顾】not worth a single glance
【不懈】untiring; unremitting; indefatigable
【不信任】distrust; not believe in; have no confidence in
【不行】❶will not do ❷be not allowed ❸not work ❹be not good; be poor
【不幸】❶misfortune; ill luck ❷unhappy; unlucky; sad; unfortunate
【不朽】immortal; eternal; undying
【不锈钢】stainless steel
【不许】not allow (or permit); forbid; must not
【不学无术】have neither learning nor skill
【不寻常】unusual; uncommon; extraordinary
【不言而喻】it goes without saying; it is self-evident; as a matter of course
【不要紧】it doesn't matter; never mind; it's nothing serious; unimportant
【不要脸】have no sense of shame; shameless
【不一定】not sure; uncertain; not necessarily so
【不一会儿】in a moment; in a little while; after a while; a few moments later
【不依】❶not comply; not go along with ❷not let off
【不宜】not suitable; inadvisable
【不用】need not
【不约而同】happen to coincide
【不再】no longer (or more); not any longer (or more)
【不在】❶absence ❷absent; be out; not

be in

【不在乎】❶ regardless of ❷ not mind; not care

【不在话下】be nothing difficult

【不争气】be disappointing; fail to live up to expectations

【不正常】abnormal; irregular; unusual

【不正当】❶improper ❷dishonest

【不正之风】unhealthy tendency; immoral trends

【不知】not know; have no idea of; be ignorant of

【不知不觉】unconsciously

【不知所措】be at a loss; be at one's wits' end

【不值】not worth

【不止】❶without end; incessantly ❷more than; not limited to

【不至于】cannot go so far as to; be unlikely to

【不中用】useless; good for nothing; not good for use

【不准】not allow; forbid; prohibit

【不自量力】go beyond one's strength

【不自在】ill at ease; uncomfortable; uneasy

【不足】❶ shortage ❷ scarce; not enough; insufficient

【不足挂齿】not worth mentioning

【不足为奇】nothing surprising; no wonder

布 (bù) ❶ cloth; textiles; fabric: 棉~ cotton ❷ declare; announce; publish ❸spread ❹arrange; dispose

【布帛】cloth and silk; cotton and silk textiles

【布达拉宫】the Potala (in Lhasa, Tibet)

【布丁】pudding

【布告】notice; bulletin: 张贴~ paste up a notice

【布谷鸟】cuckoo

【布景】setting; scenery; scenes

【布局】layout; pattern; composition

【布料】cloth

【布匹】cloth; piece goods

【布衣】❶cotton dress ❷commoner

【布置】❶ fix up; arrange; furnish ❷ arrange; make arrangements for

【布置工作】give instructions about work; assign work

步 (bù) ❶step; pace ❷stage ❸walk; go on foot; move

【步兵】infantry; foot soldier

【步步】step by step; at every step

【步步登高】ascend step by step; rise steadily in one's career

【步调】pace; step

【步调一致】keep in step; keep pace; march in step; act in unison

【步伐】pace; step: 跟上时代的~ keep pace with the times

【步枪】rifle

【步人后尘】follow sb. 's footsteps; step into sb. 's shoes

【步入】step in

【步行】walk; go on foot

【步骤】step; move; procedure; measure

部 (bù) ❶part; section ❷unit; department; ministry ❸troops; forces

【部队】troops; force; army

【部分】part; section; division; portion; in part; partly

【部件】part; unit; component

【部落】tribe; clan

【部门】department; branch; section

【部首】radicals by which characters are arranged in traditional Chinese dictionaries; radicals in Chinese characters

【部署】dispose; arrange; deploy; lay out

【部委】ministries and commissions
【部位】position; place; region
【部下】subordinate
【部长】minister; head of a department

簿 (bù) book: 登记～ register

【簿册】books for taking notes or keeping accounts
【簿籍】account books, registers, records, etc.

C

C c

ca

擦 (cā) ❶clean ❷brush ❸wipe ❹shine ❺rub; scrub

【擦边球】❶edge ball; touch ball ❷borderline practice

【擦车】wax a car

【擦地板】mop the floor

【擦掉】wipe away (or out); erase

【擦干净】clean

【擦汗】wipe the sweat away

【擦亮】polish; shine; scour

【擦去】wipe off

【擦伤】abrade; bruise

【擦身而过】pass each other so close that they almost rubbed each other

【擦洗】scrub; clean

【擦子】eraser:橡皮～ rubber

cai

猜 (cāi) ❶guess; conjecture; speculate ❷suspect

【猜测】guess; surmise

【猜度】surmise; conjecture:他心里在～,这位老人家是谁? He was wondering who that old man could be.

【猜谜】guess (or solve) a riddle; guess

【猜拳】a finger-guessing game; mora

【猜疑】mistrust; suspect; be suspicious

【猜中】guess correctly; solve

才 (cái) ❶ability; talent; gift ❷just; a moment ago ❸only ❹a capable person ❺not until

【才干】ability; capability

【才华】talent; gift; brilliance; literary or artistic talent

【才华横溢】brim with talent; have superb talent

【才略】ability and sagacity

【才能】ability; talent

【才气】literary talent

【才疏学浅】have little talent and less learning

【才思敏捷】have a facile imagination

【才学】talent and learning; scholarship

【才艺】talent and skill

【才智】ability and wisdom

材 (cái) ❶ timber ❷ material ❸ ability; talent

【材料】material; findings; infomation; data 原～raw material data; 参考～reference material; 第一手～ first hand information; 调查～ findings; 学习～ material for study; 搜集～ collect data; gather material

财 (cái) wealth; money: 发～ get rich

【财宝】money and valuables; treasure

【财产】wealth; property; possessions

【财大气粗】he who has wealth speaks louder than others
【财富】treasure;wealth;riches
【财经】finance and economics
【财会】finance and accounting
【财贸】finance and trade; finance and commerce
【财务】financial affairs
【财物】property;belongings
【财源】financial resources;source of revenue;finances
【财运】luck in making money
【财政】finance
【财政拨款】financial allocation
【财政赤字】financial deficits

裁 (cái) ❶cut (paper, cloth, etc.) into parts ❷reduce; cut down; dismiss ❸judge; decide
【裁并】cut down and merge (organizations):这个科已～到总务处。This section has been merged into the general affairs department.
【裁处】make arrangement after due consideration;make a decision after consideration and then deal with
【裁定】judge;decide;decree
【裁缝】tailor;dressmaker
【裁减】reduce;cut down
【裁剪】tailor;cut out
【裁决】adjudicate ruling;adjudication
【裁军】❶disarmament ❷disarm
【裁判】❶judge;umpire; ❷referee ❸judge
【裁员】cut (or reduce) the staff; lay off the staff;cut down the number of persons employed

采 (cǎi) ❶adopt; select ❷pick; pluck; gather ❸mine;extract
【采编】gather and edit
【采伐】lumber;cut timber;log
【采访】report;interview
【采购】buy;purchase
【采花】pick flowers
【采集】gather;collect
【采矿】mining
【采纳】accept;adopt
【采取】adopt;take;resort to
【采样】take a sample;sample
【采药】gather herbs
【采用】put to use; adopt; use; introduce; employ;make use of
【采摘】pluck; pick (fruit, flowers, leaves, etc.)

彩 (cǎi) ❶ color ❷ prize ❸ variety; splendour ❹cheer;applause
【彩笔】color pencil;crayon
【彩车】decorated vehicles; float in a parade
【彩带】colored streamer;colored ribbon
【彩灯】colored lights
【彩虹】rainbow
【彩礼】betrothal gifts
【彩民】lottery buyer;lottery holder
【彩排】dress rehearsal
【彩票】lottery ticket
【彩旗】colored flag (or banner)

睬 (cǎi) pay attention to; take notice of:理～pay attention to; show interest in

踩 (cǎi) step on;trample;tread
【踩线】foot fault

菜 (cài) ❶ vegetable; greens:卷心～cabbage; 青～greens; 甜～sugar beet;咸～pickles ❷ course; dish:荤～meat dish;素～vegetable dish;做～do the cooking;prepare the dishes
【菜板】chopping board
【菜单】menu;bill of fare

【菜刀】kitchen knife

【菜花】❶cauliflower ❷canola flower; rape flower

【菜鸟】rookie; newbie; green hand

【菜谱】recipe

【菜市】food market; vegetable market

【菜油】rapeseed oil; canola oil

【菜园】vegetable garden; vegetable farm

can

参 (cān) ❶ enter; join; take part in ❷refer

另见 915 页 cēn

【参拜】pay respect (or homage) to; formally call on; pay a courtesy call

【参观】visit; tour; look around; look into; go over; pay a visit to: 带领某人～ show sb. round (or around)

【参加】join; attend; go in for; join in; take part in: 积极 ～ take an active part in

【参见】see; refer to

【参军】join the army; join up; enlist

【参考】❶consult; refer to ❷reference

【参考书目】a list of reference books

【参赛】participate in a match or contest

【参数】parameter

【参透】thoroughly understand

【参议员】senator

【参与】take part in; participate in; have a hand in

【参展】be put on show; participate in an exhibition

【参战】enter a war

【参照】refer to; consult

餐 (cān) ❶food; meal: 快～quick meal; fast food; snack; 正～dinner ❷eat

【餐馆】restaurant

【餐巾】table napkin

【餐具】tableware; dinner set

【餐厅】❶ restaurant ❷ dining room; dining hall

【餐桌】dining table

残 (cán) ❶ incomplete; deficient ❷ injure; damage ❸ remaining; remnant ❹broken; imperfect ❺savage

【残存】remnant; remaining; surviving

【残废】crippled; disabled

【残羹剩饭】remains of a meal; leftovers

【残骸】remains; wreckage

【残害】cruelly injure (or kill)

【残疾】deformity; disability

【残疾人】a handicapped person

【残疾人奥运会】the Paralympics; the Special Olympics

【残局】❶ the final phase of a game of chess ❷the situation after the failure of an undertaking or after social unrest

【残酷】cruel; brutal; savage

【残留】remain; be left over

【残年】the last days of the year; the evening of life

【残缺】incomplete; fragmentary

【残杀】murder; slaughter

【残阳】the setting sun

【残余】remains; remainder

【残渣】residual; residue; slag

蚕 (cán) silkworm

【蚕豆】broad bean

【蚕茧】silkworm cocoon

【蚕食】nibble; encroach on

【蚕丝】natural silk; silk

惭 (cán) feel ashamed

【惭愧】❶shame ❷shameful; ashamed

惨 (cǎn) ❶ miserable; pitiful; sad ❷cruel

【惨案】❶ tragedy; murder case; tragic case; ❷massacre
【惨白】deathly pale: 脸色～look deathly pale
【惨败】crushing defeat; disastrous defeat
【惨变】a tragic turn of fortune
【惨不忍睹】too horrible for the eye
【惨淡经营】keep (an enterprise, etc.) going by painstaking effort; take great pains to carry on one's work under difficult circumstances
【惨绝人寰】tragic beyond compare in this human world; extremely tragic
【惨痛】deeply grieved; bitter; excruciatingly painful
【惨无人道】brutal; cruel; inhuman
【惨重】heavy; grievous: 损失～suffer heavy losses
【惨状】a miserable condition; a pitiful or horrible sight

灿 (càn)

【灿烂】splendid; brilliant; bright; magnificent

cang

仓 (cāng) storehouse; warehouse: 谷～barn

【仓促】hurriedly; hastily; in a hurry
【仓皇失措】be scared out of one's wits; be panic-stricken
【仓皇逃窜】flee in confusion
【仓库】warehouse; storehouse: 清理～take stock

苍 (cāng) ❶dark green (or blue) ❷grey; ashy; ashen

【苍白】pale; pallid: 脸色～ look pale
【苍翠】dark green; verdant
【苍劲】❶old and strong ❷vigorous; bold
【苍老】❶old (in appearance); hoary; (of an old man's voice) hoarse ❷(of calligraphy or painting) vigorous
【苍茫】vast; boundless; indistinct
【苍天】the blue sky; Heaven
【苍鹰】goshawk
【苍蝇】fly

沧 (cāng) dark blue

【沧海】the deep blue sea; the sea
【沧海桑田】from seas into mulberry fields and from mulberry fields into seas—time brings great changes to the world
【沧海一粟】a drop in the ocean

舱 (cāng) cabin; module: 客～ cabin

【舱口】hatchway; hatch
【舱门】hatch door; cabin door
【舱室】cabin
【舱位】❶ cabin seat; berth ❷ shipping place

藏 (cáng) ❶ hide; conceal ❷ store; lay by

另见 1300 页 zàng

【藏污纳垢】shelter evil people and countenance evil practices
【藏龙卧虎】(used esp. in) ～之地 a place where dragons and tigers are hiding—a place where people of unusual ability are to be found
【藏匿】conceal; hide; go into hiding
【藏书】❶ collect books ❷ a collection of books; library

cao

操 (cāo) ❶conduct; behaviour ❷exercise ❸ drill ❹ grasp; hold ❺ do; act; operate

【操办】manage affairs; make preparations

or arrangements for

【操场】playground; sports ground; schoolyard; drill ground

【操持】manage; handle attend to

【操劳】❶work hard ❷take care; look after

【操练】drill; practice

【操心】worry (or trouble) about

【操纵】operate; control; manipulate

【操作】❶operate ❷operation

【操作程序】operation sequence

嘈 (cáo) noise; dim

【嘈杂】noisy

草 (cǎo) ❶grass ❷straw ❸careless; hasty; rough

【草案】draft: 决议～ a draft resolution

【草草了事】get a job done any old way

【草场】meadow; pasture; grassland

【草地】lawn; grass; grassland; meadow: 别踩～ keep off the grass

【草稿】rough draft; draft

【草根】❶ grass-root ❷ people of lower classes

【草绿】grass green

【草帽】straw hat

【草莓】strawberry

【草拟】draft; draw up

【草皮】sod

【草坪】lawn

【草食动物】plant-eating animal; herbivore

【草率】careless; rash

【草率从事】act rashly; take hasty action

【草堂】cottage; thatched hut

【草图】draft; rough map; sketch

【草药】herbal medicine

【草鱼】grass carp

【草原】grasslands; prairie

ce

册 (cè) ❶volume; book ❷copy

【册子】book; volume: 小～ booklet; pamphlet

厕 (cè) lavatory; toilet; washroom; water closet (or W. C.): 公～ public lavatory; (英) convenience; (美) comfort station; 男～ men's room; 女～ women's room

【厕所】lavatory; toilet; W. C.

侧 (cè) ❶side: 左～ the left side; 右～ the right side ❷incline; lean

【侧门】side door

【侧面】side; aspect; side face

【侧目而视】look askance at sb. (with fear or indignation)

【侧身】lean to one side; on one's side; sideways

【侧卧】lie on one's side

【侧影】silhouette; profile

【侧重】lay particular emphasis on; stress

测 (cè) ❶ measure; survey ❷ conjecture; infer

【测绘】mapping; survey and drawing

【测量】survey; measure

【测试】❶test (a machine, meter or apparatus) ❷test (a student's proficiency)

【测算】measure and calculate

【测验】test: 进行～ have (or give) a test; 小～ quiz; 智力～ intelligence test

恻 (cè) sorrowful; sad

【恻隐之心】compassion; pity

策 (cè) plan; scheme: 决～ policy making; 失～ take a false step

【策划】scheme; engineer; plan; plot

【策略】tactics; policy

【策源地】source;place of origin

cen

参 (cēn)
另见 912 页 cān

【参差】uneven;irregular

【参差不齐】uneven;not uniform;irregular

ceng

层 (céng) ❶storey (or story);floor ❷layer;coat ❸one on top of another;overlapping

【层层】layer upon layer

【层出不穷】emerge in an endless stream

【层次】level;gradation

【层峦叠嶂】peaks rising one higher than another

曾 (céng) already;yet

【曾几何时】before long;not long after

【曾经】ever;once

【曾经沧海】have sailed the seven seas—have much experience of life;have seen much of the world

叉 (chā) ❶fork ❷crisscross;intersect

【叉车】forklift;fork truck;forklift truck

【叉腰】akimbo

【叉子】fork

cha

差 (chā) ❶difference ❷mistake;error ❸weak;inferior
另见 916 页 chà;917 页 chāi

【差别】difference;disparity

【差错】mistake;error:出~make a mistake

【差额】difference;balance

【差价】price difference:地区~regional price differences

【差距】disparity

【差强人意】just passable;barely satisfactory;fair

【差异】difference;divergence;discrepancy;diversity

插 (chā) insert;thrust;stick in

【插班】join a class in the middle of the course

【插队】jump the queue;cut in a line

【插话】interpose;interrupt;chip (or put) in;get in a word

【插曲】❶interlude ❷episode;incident ❸songs in a film or play

【插手】take part in;lend a hand

【插头】plug:接上~通电 plug in

【插图】❶illustration;plate ❷illustrate

【插秧】transplant rice seedlings (or rice shoots)

【插足】❶put one's foot in ❷participate

【插嘴】interrupt;chip in

【插座】outlet;socket

茶 (chá) tea:淡~weak tea;浓~strong tea;绿~green tea;花~jasmine tea;沏~make tea

【茶杯】teacup

【茶匙】❶teaspoon ❷teaspoonful

【茶道】tea ceremony

【茶点】refreshments

【茶缸子】mug

【茶馆】teahouse

【茶壶】teapot;tea kettle

【茶花】camellia

【茶几】teapoy;tea table;side table

【茶具】tea set;tea-things;tea service

【茶楼】a teahouse with two or more storeys

【茶盘】tea tray;tea-board

C

【茶树】tea tree
【茶亭】tea-booth; tea-stall; tea-kiosk
【茶叶】tea; tea leaves
【茶余饭后】over a cup of tea or after a meal

查 (chá) ❶ examine; check ❷ investigate; look into; find out ❸ look up

【查案】investigate a case
【查抄】make an inventory of a criminal's possessions and confiscate them
【查出】find out
【查处】investigate and prosecute
【查房】make the rounds of the wards
【查访】investigate; go around and make inquiries
【查封】close down; seal up
【查户口】check residence cards; check on household occupants
【查看】see; look over; examine
【查明】prove through investigation; ascertain
【查票】examine (or check) tickets
【查清】check up on; make a thorough investigation of
【查实】check and verify
【查收】❶ find sth. enclosed ❷ check and accept
【查无实据】investigation reveals no evidence (against the suspect)
【查血】have a blood test
【查询】inquire about
【查验】check; examine
【查阅】consult; look up; refer to
【查找】seek
【查证】verify
【查资料】consult data
【查字典】look up a word in the dictionary; consult a dictionary

察 (chá) examine; look into

【察访】go about to find out; make an investigation trip
【察觉】get aware of; find; discover; sense
【察言观色】carefully weigh up a person's words and closely watch his expression

岔 (chà) ❶ accident; trouble ❷ branch off; forked; turn off the main road

【岔开】❶ branch off; diverge ❷ diverge to (another topic) ❸ stagger
【岔口】fork (in a road)
【岔路】forked (or branch) road; byroad; side road
【岔子】accident; trouble; something wrong; fault

诧 (chà) be surprised

【诧异】❶ be surprised; be amazed; be astonished ❷ surprise; amazement

差 (chà) ❶ differ from; fall short of ❷ wrong; short of; wanting; missing ❸ poor; bad

另见 915 页 chā; 917 页 chāi

【差不多】❶ almost; nearly; just about; about the same; similar ❷ not bad; just about right (or enough); not far off
【差得多】entirely (or very) different
【差点儿】❶ not quite up to the mark; not good enough ❷ nearly; almost

姹 (chà) beautiful

【姹紫嫣红】brilliant purples and reds; beautiful flowers; gaily dressed maidens

chai

拆 (chāi) ❶ tear open; take apart ❷ pull down; dismantle

【拆除】pull down; remove; demolish; dismantle
【拆封】unseal; open up a seal

【拆毁】pull down; tear down; demolish
【拆开】take apart; open; separate
【拆迁】pull down the old houses and its occupants move else where
【拆散】(chāi sǎn) break (a set)
【拆散】(chāi sàn) break up (a marriage, family, etc.)
【拆洗】wash after removing the padding or lining; take apart and clean
【拆下】take down
【拆卸】dismantle; dismount

差 (chāi) ❶ job; mission ❷ send on an errand; dispatch errand

另见 915 页 chā; 916 页 chà

【差旅费】allowances for a business trip
【差遣】send sb. on business; send sb. on an errand or mission; dispatch; send; assign
【差使】send; assign; appoint; official post
【差事】errand; mission; assignment; official post

柴 (chái) firewood

【柴火】firewood; faggot
【柴油】diesel oil
【柴油机】diesel engine

豺 (chái) jackal

【豺狼】jackals and wolves
【豺狼当道】jackals and wolves hold sway—the cruel and the wicked are in power

chan

掺 (chān) mix; blend

【掺和】mix; mingle
【掺假】adulterate
【掺水】fill with half truth

搀 (chān) ❶ support sb. with one's hand; help by the arm ❷ mix; mingle

【搀扶】support sb. with one's hand

谗 (chán) slander; speak ill of sb.; backbite

【谗言】slanderous talk; calumny

馋 (chán) ❶ ravenous; voracious ❷ be greedy for; gluttonous

【馋涎欲滴】mouth drooling with greed
【馋嘴】❶ gluttonous ❷ glutton; a greedy eater

缠 (chán) ❶ wrap; wind; twine ❷ tie up; tangle; pester

【缠绕】twist; bind; wind; pester
【缠手】troublesome; hard to deal with

蝉 (chán) cicada

【蝉联】continue to hold a post (or title)
【蝉翼】cicada's wings

潺 (chán)

【潺潺】murmur; babble; purl

蟾 (chán) toad

【蟾蜍】❶ toad ❷ the fabled toad in the moon ❸ the moon

产 (chǎn) ❶ product ❷ property; estate ❸ bear; give birth to ❹ produce; yield

【产地】place of production; place of origin
【产房】delivery room
【产妇】confined woman; lying-in woman
【产假】maternity leave
【产量】production; output; yield
【产卵】lay eggs; spawn; oviposit
【产品】product; produce: 农～ farm produce
【产前检查】antenatal (or prenatal) examination
【产权】property right

C

【产物】output;result
【产销】production and marketing
【产业】industry; property; estate 劳动密集型～ labor intensive industry;夕阳～ sunset industry;支柱～ pillar industry
【产业链】industry chain
【产值】output value
谄 (chǎn) fawn on;curry favour with; toady to
【谄媚】flatter; fawn on; toady; curry favour with
铲 (chǎn) ❶ shovel ❷ lift (or move) with a shovel
【铲除】uproot;root out;eradicate
【铲子】spade;shovel
阐 (chǎn) explain;illustrate
【阐明】expound;clarify
【阐述】elaborate;set forth (or out)
忏 (chàn) repent
【忏悔】❶ repent; be penitent ❷ confess (one's sins)
颤 (chàn) quiver; tremble; shiver; shudder
另见 1304 页 zhàn
【颤动】quiver;vibrate
【颤抖】quiver;shake;shiver;tremble

chang

昌 (chāng) flourishing;prosperous
【昌盛】prosperous
猖 (chāng) ferocious
【猖獗】❶running wild ❷rampant
【猖狂】furious;savage
娼 (chāng) prostitute
【娼妓】prostitute;streetwalker
长 (cháng) ❶ length ❷ strong point ❸ lasting ❹ long ❺ be good at; strong in;be proficient in
另见 1305 页 zhǎng
【长臂猿】gibbon
【长波】long wave
【长城】the Great Wall
【长处】merit; good qualities; strong (or good) points
【长此以往】if things go on like this; if things continue this way
【长度】length
【长短】❶length ❷strong and weak points ❸accident;mishap
【长方体】cuboid; rectangular parallelepiped
【长方形】rectangle;oblong
【长江】the Changjiang (or Yangtze) River
【长江三峡】Three Gorges of the Yangtze River
【长颈鹿】giraffe
【长久之计】a long term plan;a permanent solution
【长裤】trousers;pants
【长廊】a covered corridor;gallery
【长眠】have an eternal sleep;be dead
【长年累月】over the years; year in year out
【长跑】long distance race (or running)
【长篇大论】a lengthy speech or article
【长期】long-term; over a long period of time
【长驱直入】drive straight in
【长生不老】live forever and never grow old
【长寿】❶ long-lived; longevous ❷ a long life
【长叹】deep sigh

【长途】long-distance
【长途跋涉】make a long, arduous journey; trudge a long distance; trek a long way
【长途汽车】long-distance bus; coach
【长远】long-term; long-range
【长征】❶ expedition; long march ❷ the Long March
【长治久安】a long period of peace and order; lasting political stability
【长足进步】make great strides; make rapid progress

肠 (cháng) intestines; bowels

【肠胃】intestines and stomach; belly
【肠胃病】stomach disease
【肠炎】enteritis

尝 (cháng) ❶taste ❷experience; come to know

【尝试】try; attempt; have a try; make an attempt to do sth.
【尝鲜】have a taste of a delicacy; have a taste of what is just in season

常 (cháng) ❶ common; ordinary; normal: 习以为～ be used to sth. ❷often; usually

【常常】usually; often; frequently
【常规】rule; convention; common practice; routine
【常见】common
【常客】frequent visitor; regular guest
【常理】general rule; what is normal
【常绿植物】evergreen plant; evergreen
【常年】❶ throughout the year; year in year out; ❷an average year
【常青】evergreen
【常人】ordinary person
【常任】permanent; standing
【常胜将军】an ever-victorious general
【常识】common (or general) knowledge; common sense; elementary knowledge
【常态】normality; normal behaviours or conditions
【常委会】standing committee
【常温】normal atmospheric temperature
【常务委员】member of the standing committee
【常言】common (or popular) saying; proverb
【常用】in common use
【常驻】resident; permanent

偿 (cháng) ❶ repay; compensate ❷ meet; fulfill

【偿还】repay; pay back; pay (or answer) for
【偿命】repay with one's life; a life for a life
【偿清】clear off; pay back in full

嫦 (cháng)

【嫦娥】the goddess of the moon (the lady in the legend who swallowed elixir stolen from her husband and flew to the moon)

厂 (chǎng) plant; works; mill; factory

【厂房】factory building
【厂矿】factories and mines
【厂长】director (of a factory); factory manager

场 (chǎng) ❶place; ground; field: 溜冰～rink; 体育～stadium; sports field ❷stage; spot; scene: 当～抓获 be caught on the spot; 在～be present at the scene ❸round

【场地】place; site; space: 比赛～ground; court; 施工～construction site
【场合】occasion; situation

【场面】scene; occasion; spectacle; appearance; front; facade

【场所】spot; site; place; arena

C

敞 (chǎng) ❶spacious; roomy ❷open; uncovered

【敞开】open wide

【敞篷车】open car; convertible car

怅 (chàng) disappointed; sorry

【怅恨】feel bitter at one's frustration; feel disappointed and resentful

【怅然】upset

畅 (chàng) ❶ smooth: 流~ easy and smooth ❷free; uninhibited

【畅快】delightful; carefree; free from inhibitions

【畅所欲言】speak without any inhibitions; speak one's mind freely; speak out freely

【畅谈】speak glowingly of; have a delightful talk; talk freely and to one's heart's content

【畅通】unblocked; unimpeded

【畅销】sell well; have a ready market; be in great demand

【畅销书】best seller

【畅游】have a good swim; enjoy a sightseeing tour

倡 (chàng) initiate; advocate

【倡导】propose; initiate: 在某人的~下 on the initiative of sb.

【倡议】propose; sponsor: 在某人的~下 at one's suggestion

唱 (chàng) ❶sing ❷call; cry

【唱段】aria

【唱反调】sing a different tune; speak or act contrary to

【唱高调】mouth high-sounding words; say fine-sounding things; affect a high moral tone

【唱歌】❶sing ❷singing

【唱票】call out the names of those voted for while counting ballot-slips

【唱戏】act in an opera

chao

抄 (chāo) ❶copy; transcribe ❷lift ❸ grab; take up ❹fold one's arms

【抄本】copy; hand-copied book; transcript

【抄家】search sb.'s house and confiscate his (or her) property

【抄近路】take a shortcut

【抄送】make a copy for; send a duplicate to

【抄袭】borrow aimlessly from other people's experience; lift; plagiarize

【抄写】copy; transcribe

钞 (chāo) bank note; paper money: 现~cash

【钞票】bank note; paper money; note; bill

超 (chāo) exceed; surpass; overtake; go beyond

【超编】overstaff

【超标】exceed the set standard

【超常】above average; extraordinary

【超车】overtake other cars

【超出】❶ overstep; go beyond; exceed ❷over; above; out of

【超短裙】miniskirt

【超额】above quota

【超负荷】overload; overburden

【超过】❶outstrip; surpass; exceed; run over ❷above; over; beyond ❸more than

【超过限度】go beyond the limit

【超级】super

【超前教育】superior education

【超然】aloof; detached

【超人】❶be out of the common run ❷superman

【超声波】supersonic wave

【超市】supermarket

【超脱】❶ unconventional ❷ be detached; stand aloof

【超越】transcend; surpass; overstep

【超载】overload;

【超支】overspend

【超重】overload; overweight

巢 (cháo) nest: 鸟～ bird's nest

【巢穴】lair; nest; hideout

朝 (cháo) ❶dynasty ❷government; an emperor's reign ❸have an audience with (a king, an emperor, etc.); royal court ❹make a pilgrimage to ❺face; towards

另见 1306 页 zhāo

【朝拜】worship; pay religious homage to; pay respects to (a sovereign)

【朝北】northward

【朝代】dynasty

【朝东】eastward

【朝南】southward

【朝前看】look straight ahead

【朝前走】march ahead

【朝圣】make a pilgrimage to a sacred place; pilgrimage

【朝西】westward

【朝鲜半岛】the Korean Peninsula

嘲 (cháo) ridicule: 冷～热讽 freezing irony and burning satire

【嘲讽】sneer at

【嘲笑】laugh at; jeer at; make fun of; scorn

潮 (cháo) ❶tide: 涨～ the tide is flowing; 落～ the tide is ebbing ❷ current; trend: 思～ trend of thought; (social) upsurge ❸damp; moist

【潮流】❶tide ❷tidal current; trend: 革命～ revolutionary trend; 历史～ historical trend

【潮湿】damp; moist

【潮水】tidewater; tide

【潮汐】morning and evening tides; tide

吵 (chǎo) ❶make a noise ❷quarrel

【吵架】quarrel: 同某人～ have a quarrel (or row) with sb.

【吵闹】❶brawl ❷kick up a row ❸noisy; wrangle: ～不休 quarrel on and on ❹ din; hubbub

炒 (chǎo) ❶fry; stir-fry ❷speculate

【炒菜】❶stir-fry; sauté ❷a fried dish

【炒饭】❶fry rice ❷fried rice

【炒股票】stock trading

【炒买炒卖】 buy quick and sell quick; speculate

【炒面】❶ chow mein; fried noodles ❷ parched flour

【炒鱿鱼】give sb. the sack; sack; fire a person

【炒作】speculate; sensationalize

che

车 (chē) ❶vehicle: 机～engine; 吉普～ jeep; 轿～sedan; saloon; 救护～ambulance; 卡～lorry; truck; 客～coach; car; 缆～cable car; 旅游～sightseeing bus; 马～carriage; 面包～minibus; 小卧～automobile; car; 手推～push-cart; 消防～fire engine; 运货～wagon ❷wheeled machine or instrument ❸ machine ❹lathe

【车把】handlebar (of a bicycle); shaft (of

a wheelbarrow)

【车次】train number; coach number (indicating order of departure)

C

【车贷】auto loan

【车道】(traffic) lane; roadway

【车灯】general name for lights on a vehicle (e. g. headlights, bicycle lamp, etc.)

【车费】fare

【车祸】traffic (or road) accident

【车间】workshop; shop

【车库】garage

【车辆】vehicle; car: 来往～ traffic

【车票】(train, bus) ticket

【车水马龙】incessant stream of horses and carriages; heavy traffic

【车速】speed of a motor vehicle

【车胎】tyre

【车位】parking place; parking spot; parking space

【车险】auto insurance

【车厢】carriage; compartment; railroad car

【车站】station; stop

扯 (chě) ❶ pull; drag; haul ❷ tear ❸ chat; gossip

【扯淡】talk nonsense; nonsense

【扯后腿】hold (or pull) sb. back; be a drag on sb.

【扯谎】tell a lie; lie

【扯开】tear away (or apart); pull apart

【扯皮】argue back and forth

【扯下】tear off (or down)

彻 (chè) thorough; penetrating: 响～云霄 resound through the skies

【彻底】❶ thorough; complete ❷ thoroughly; entirely; completely: 不～halfway

【彻头彻尾】throughout; out and out; through and through; downright

【彻悟】fully recognize the truth; come to understand thoroughly

【彻夜】all through the night; all night

撤 (chè) ❶ withdraw; retreat ❷ take (or clear) away; remove; evacuate

【撤除】remove; dismantle

【撤换】dismiss; recall; replace

【撤军】withdraw troops

【撤离】withdraw from; evacuate

【撤退】withdraw; retreat; pull out

【撤销】do away with; cancel; revoke; rescind

【撤职】dismiss sb. from his post; remove sb. from office

【撤走】withdraw

chen

尘 (chén) dust; dirt: 一～不染 spotless

【尘埃】dust

【尘世】the mortal world

【尘土】dust; dirt

【尘缘】the bonds of this world; destiny; the fate of the world: ～未断 have not broken free the bonds of this world

沉 (chén) ❶ sink ❷ heavy ❸ keep down; lower ❹ deep; profound

【沉船】wreck; sunken ship

【沉淀】settlings; sediment; precipitate

【沉浮】❶ sink and rise; bob on water ❷ ups and downs of fortune; vicissitudes

【沉寂】quiet; still

【沉静】quiet; calm; still; serene; placid

【沉闷】❶ dull; depressed ❷ in low spirits; oppressive; depressing ❸ not outgoing; withdrawn

【沉迷】indulge; wallow

【沉湎】be given to; be in the habit of; indulge in

【沉没】sink; submerge

【沉默】❶reticent; taciturn; uncommunicative ❷ silent ❸ in silence: 保持～ remain silent

【沉思】be lost in thought; think deeply; meditate

【沉痛】deep sorrow; deep feeling of grief or remorse

【沉稳】❶ steady; staid; sedate ❷ untroubled; sound

【沉重打击】a heavy blow

【沉住气】keep calm (or cool); be steady

【沉着】calm; composed; steady; cool-headed: ～应战 meet an attack calmly; 勇敢～ brave and steady

【沉醉】get drunk; become intoxicated

陈 (chén) ❶ state; explain ❷ lay out; put on display ❸old

【陈腐】old and decayed; outworn

【陈规陋习】bad old customs and habits

【陈旧】old; out-of-date; outmoded; obsolete; old-fashioned

【陈列】display (or show); set out; exhibit

【陈述】❶statement ❷state; declare

晨 (chén) morning

【晨风】morning breeze; matinal

【晨练】morning exercise

【晨曦】the first rays of the morning sun

衬 (chèn) ❶ line; place sth. underneath ❷ lining; liner ❸ provide a background for; set off; serve as a foil to

【衬衫】shirt: 女～ blouse; shirt

【衬托】set off; serve as a foil to

称 (chèn) fit; match; suit
另见本页 chēng

【称心如意】after one's own heart; very gratifying and satisfactory

【称职】be competent; be qualified; fill a post with credit

趁 (chèn) take advantage of (time, opportunity, etc.); avail oneself of

【趁机】take advantage of the occasion; seize the chance: ～溜走 seize the chance and sneak away

【趁热打铁】strike while the iron is hot

【趁势】take advantage of a favourable situation

【趁早】as early as possible; before it is too late; at the first opportunity

cheng

称 (chēng) ❶name ❷call ❸ say; state ❹praise ❺weigh
另见本页 chèn

【称病】plead illness

【称道】speak approvingly of; praise; acclaim

【称号】title; name

【称颂】praise; extol; eulogize

【称谢】thank; express one's thanks

【称兄道弟】call each other brothers; be on intimate terms

【称赞】praise; commend

撑 (chēng) ❶ support; brace; prop up ❷push or move with a pole ❸maintain; keep up ❹unfurl ❺fill to the point of bursting ❻ brace; stay

【撑竿】vaulting pole

【撑竿跳高】pole-vault; pole jump

【撑腰】support sb.; stand by sb.; be at sb.'s back; back up

成 (chéng) ❶achievement; result ❷accomplish; succeed ❸ become; turn into; change into ❹ fully developed (or grown) ❺established; ready-made ❻all right; O. K. ❼able; capable ❽one tenth

【成本】cost

【成比例】be proportionate to

【成才】become a talented (or useful) person
【成对】in pairs
【成分】part; component; element; ingredient; composition
【成功】❶succeed ❷success
【成规】set rules; convention: 墨守～stick to conventions
【成果】result; fruit; gain; product; achievement
【成活】survive
【成绩单】school report; report card
【成见】preconceived idea
【成交】close a deal; strike a bargain; conclude a transaction; clinch a deal
【成就】❶ accomplishment; achievement; success ❷achieve
【成立】❶come (or bring) into being ❷ found; establish; set up
【成名】make a name; become famous
【成年累月】year in year out; for years on end
【成品】finished product; end product
【成器】grow up to be a useful person
【成千上万】thousands upon thousands; thousands and tens of thousands of
【成全】help sb. to achieve his (or her) aim
【成群结队】in crowds
【成人】❶grow up; become full-grown ❷ adult; grown-up
【成人教育】adult (or further) education; continuing education
【成人之美】help sb. to fulfil his (or her) wish; aid sb. in doing a good deed
【成熟】mature; ripe
【成天】all day long; all the time
【成为】become; turn into; get; come to be
【成效】effect; result
【成心】intentionally; on purpose; with deliberate intent
【成形】take shape; shaping; forming
【成语】idiom; set phrase
【成员】member
【成长】develop; grow up; grow to maturity

呈 (chéng) ❶ assume ❷ submit or present (a report, etc.) to a superior
【呈报】submit a report; report a matter (to a superior)
【呈现】appear; present; take on

诚 (chéng) ❶ sincere; honest ❷ really; actually
【诚服】submit oneself willingly
【诚惶诚恐】with reverence and awe; in fear and trepidation
【诚恳】❶ sincere; cordial ❷ sincerely; heartily
【诚然】❶truly; really ❷used correlatively with no doubt; to be sure; it is true
【诚心】sincere desire; wholeheartedness
【诚心诚意】earnestly and sincerely
【诚信】honesty; good faith
【诚挚】sincere; cordial

承 (chéng) ❶bear; hold; carry ❷undertake; contract (to do a job) ❸be indebted (to sb. for a kindness); be granted a favour ❹continue; carry on
【承办】undertake
【承包】undertake; contract
【承保】accept insurance; under writing acceptance
【承担】undertake; charge; bear; assume
【承接】❶continue ❷contract to accept; undertake the task of
【承诺】promise to undertake; undertake to do sth.
【承认】admit; accept; acknowledge; recog-

nize 不~ deny

【承受】bear；endure；suffer

【承先启后】inherit the past and usher in the future；serve as a link between past and future

【承袭】adopt；follow；inherit

【承重】load-bearing；bearing

城 (chéng) city；town；city wall

【城堡】castle

【城郊】suburb；outskirts (of a town)

【城里】inside the city；in town

【城门失火，殃及池鱼】in a disturbance innocent bystanders get into trouble

【城墙】city wall

【城市】city；town；metropolis

【城市改造】urban renewal

【城市规划】city planning

【城市建设】urban construction

【城乡】town and country；city and countryside；urban and rural

【城乡结合】integration of town and country

【城镇】cities and towns：~居民 urban dwellers

乘 (chéng) ❶ times ❷ ride ❸ bear ❹ multiply ❺ carry ❻ take advantage of

【乘车】ride；take

【乘船】by boat；by ship

【乘方】involution；power

【乘飞机】by plane (or air)

【乘风破浪】brave the wind and the waves

【乘火车】by train

【乘机】seize the opportunity

【乘客】passenger

【乘凉】enjoy the cool

【乘兴而来】arrive in high spirits；set out cheerfully

【乘虚而入】break through at a weak point；act when one's opponent is off guard；exploit one's opponent's weakness

程 (chéng) ❶ rule；regulation ❷ order ❸ journey ❹ distance

【程度】degree；level；extent：在很大~上 to a great extent；在一定~上 in a way；to a certain extent

【程式】form；pattern；formula

【程序】program；procedure；order；course：法律~legal procedure

惩 (chéng) punish；penalize

【惩办】punish；chastise

【惩罚】punish

【惩戒】punish sb. to teach him a lesson；discipline sb. as a warning；take disciplinary action against

澄 (chéng) clear；pure

【澄清】clarify；clear up

橙 (chéng) orange

【橙黄】orange color

【橙汁】orange juice

【橙子】orange (the fruit)

逞 (chěng) ❶ show off：得~get one's own way；succeed in one's scheme；flaunt ❷ carry out (an evil design)；succeed (in a scheme) ❸ indulge；give free rein to

【逞能】show off one's skill (or ability)；parade one's ability

【逞强】flaunt one's superiority

秤 (chèng) balance；steelyard；scales：杆~ steelyard；台~ platform balance；弹簧~ spring balance

chi

C

吃 (chī) ❶eat; take; have one's meals ❷live on

【吃饱】 eat one's fill

【吃不消】 be unable to stand

【吃穿】 food and clothing

【吃醋】 be jealous of

【吃得开】 be popular; be much sought after

【吃饭】 eat; have (or take) a meal: 靠工资~live on one's wages; make a living

【吃光】 eat up

【吃喝玩乐】 eat, drink and be merry; idle away one's time in pleasure-seeking

【吃惊】 be surprised (or astonished, taken aback, amazed, shocked, startled)

【吃苦耐劳】 bear hardships and stand hard work; work hard and endure hardships

【吃亏】 ❶suffer losses; come to grief; get the worst of it; take (or get) a beating ❷at a disadvantage; in an unfavourable situation

【吃老本】 live off one's past gains

【吃里爬外】 live off one person while secretly helping another

【吃力】 entail strenuous effort; be a strain

【吃零食】 eat snacks

【吃奶】 suck the breast

【吃透】 have a thorough understanding of

【吃香】 be popular; be cherished; be much sought after; be well-liked

【吃药】 take medicine

嗤 (chī) sneer

【嗤笑】 laugh at

【嗤之以鼻】 give a snort of contempt; despise

痴 (chī) idiotic; silly; stupid; foolish; crazy about

【痴呆】 stupid

【痴狂】 irrational; crazy

【痴情】 ❶ unreasoning passion; infatuation; ❷be infatuated

【痴人说梦】 idiotic nonsense; lunatic ravings

【痴心妄想】 wishful thinking; fond dream

池 (chí) ❶pool; pond: 游泳~swimming pool; 浴~bathing pool ❷an enclosed space with raised sides ❸ stalls (in a theatre)

【池塘】 pool; pond

【池鱼之殃】 a disaster for the fish in the moat—trouble not of one's own making

迟 (chí) slow; late; tardy

【迟到】 be late for; come (or arrive) late

【迟钝】 slow; dull: 反应~be slow in reacting; respond slowly

【迟缓】 slow; tardy; sluggish: 进度~make slow progress

【迟疑不决】 hesitate to make a decision; be irresolute; be undecided

【迟早】 sooner or later; in time

持 (chí) ❶hold; grasp ❷support; maintain ❸manage; run; handle

【持久】 lasting; enduring; keep on

【持平】 unbiased; fair

【持枪】 ❶hold a gun ❷port arms

【持续】 ❶last; continue ❷sustained

【持有】 hold

【持之以恒】 persevere (in doing sth.)

尺 (chǐ) ❶rule; ruler ❷ chi, a unit of length (1 chi = 1/3 meter): 三角~ triangle; 千分~ micrometer

【尺寸】 size; measurement; dimension: 照某人的~去做 make sth. to one's measurements

【尺码】size;measures

【尺子】ruler

齿 (chǐ) ❶tooth ❷a tooth-like part of anything; mention: 不足挂～ not worth mentioning

【齿轮】gear wheel;gear

耻 (chǐ) ❶shame;disgrace ❷shameful

【耻辱】shame;disgrace;humiliation

【耻笑】sneer at;mock;hold sb. to ridicule

叱 (chì) loudly rebuke;shout at

【叱喝】shout at;bawl at

【叱咤风云】commanding the wind and the clouds; shaking heaven and earth; all-powerful

斥 (chì) scold; blame; upbraid; repel; exclude

【斥骂】reproach

【斥责】scold;rebuke;excoriate

赤 (chì) ❶red ❷bare ❸loyal;sincere

【赤膊】 half-naked; barebacked; be stripped to the waist

【赤诚】absolute sincerity

【赤道】the equator

【赤脚】barefoot

【赤金】pure gold

【赤裸裸】❶bare;naked ❷out-and-out

【赤手空拳】bare-handed;unarmed

【赤子之心】the heart of a newborn baby—utter innocence

炽 (chì)flaming;ablaze

【炽烈】burning fiercely;blazing

【炽热】❶red-hot;blazing ❷passionate

翅 (chì) ❶wing ❷shark's fin

【翅膀】wing

chong

冲 (chōng) ❶pour boiling water on ❷ charge; rush; dash; clash ❸ important place ❹rinse;flush ❺ develop

【冲茶】make tea

【冲出去】rush (or dash) out

【冲刺】spurt;sprint

【冲淡】❶dilute ❷water down

【冲动】❶get excited ❷impulse

【冲锋】charge;assault

【冲毁】 destroy by rush of water (or floods,rain)

【冲击】lash;impact;charge

【冲进】rush into

【冲口而出】say sth. unthinkingly; blurt out

【冲破】break through;breach

【冲天】towering;soaring

【冲突】clash;conflict

充 (chōng) ❶serve (or act) as ❷pretend to be;pose as ❸full;sufficient

【充斥】flood;congest

【充当】act (or serve) as;play the part of

【充电】charge (a battery);charge up

【充电器】charger

【充耳不闻】turn a deaf ear to

【充分】❶full;ample;abundant;sufficient; thorough; good ❷ well; enough ❸ to the full

【充满】❶full of; crowded with ❷fill; fill with; brimming with; permeated with; imbued with

【充沛】plentiful; abundant: 精力～ energetic

【充实】❶ rich; substantial ❷ enrich; replenish

【充足】enough;sufficient;ample;adequate

憧(chōng)

【憧憬】long for; look forward to

虫(chóng) insect; worm; bug: 甲~ beetle

【虫害】insect pest

【虫子】insect; worm

重(chóng) ❶ repeat; duplicate ❷ again; once more

【重播】rebroadcast; replay; resow (the same field)

【重操旧业】return to one's old trade

【重唱】an ensemble of two or more singers, each singing one part

【重重】layer upon layer; ring upon ring

【重蹈覆辙】follow the track of the overturned cart; follow the same old road to ruin

【重叠】overlap; one on top of another

【重返】return

【重逢】meet again; have a reunion: 久别~ meet again after a long separation

【重复】❶ repeat; duplicate ❷ repetition; duplication

【重建】rebuild; reconstruct; reestablish; rehabilitate

【重申】restate

【重孙】great-grandson

【重提】bring up again: 旧事~ recall past events

【重温旧梦】revive an old dream; relive an old experience

【重现】reappear

【重新】again; anew; afresh

【重新做人】start one's life afresh; turn over a new leaf

【重修旧好】renew cordial relations; become reconciled; bury the hatchet

【重阳节】the Double Ninth Festival (the 9th day of the 9th lunar month)

【重整旗鼓】rally one's forces (after a defeat)

【重组】restructure; reorganize: 资产~ reorganization of assets

崇(chóng) ❶ esteem; worship ❷ high; lofty; sublime

【崇拜】adore; worship: 盲目~ worship blindly

【崇高】high; noble; lofty

【崇敬】esteem; respect; revere

【崇山峻岭】lofty ridges and towering mountains

【崇尚】advocate; uphold

【崇信】believe in; trust

宠(chǒng) dote on; spoil; bestow favour on

【宠爱】make a pet of sb.; dote on

【宠儿】pet; favourite

【宠物】pet

chou

抽(chōu) ❶ pull; take out (from in between) ❷ take (a part from a whole) ❸ put forth ❹ whip; lash; thrash

【抽查】spot-check; selective examinations; spot test

【抽打】whip; lash; thrash

【抽奖】draw for a prize; draw a lottery

【抽筋】❶ pull out a tendon ❷ cramp

【抽空】manage to find time

【抽签】draw lots; cast lots

【抽水机】water pump

【抽屉】drawer

【抽象】abstract

【抽血】draw blood

【抽样调查】sample survey; sampling

【抽油烟机】range hood; kitchen ventilator

仇(chóu) ❶ enemy; foe ❷ hatred; enmity

【仇恨】❶hatred;enmity;hostility ❷hate

【仇人】personal enemy;foe;enemy

【仇怨】grudge;hatred;spite

惆 (chóu)

【惆怅】sad;disconsolate;melancholy

绸 (chóu) silk;silk fabric

【绸缎】silks and satins

【绸子】silk fabric

酬 (chóu) reward;payment

【酬金】monetary reward;remuneration

【酬劳】reward;thank sb. with a gift

【酬谢】thank sb. with a gift

稠 (chóu) ❶thick ❷dense

【稠密】dense

愁 (chóu) worry;be anxious

【愁苦】anxiety;distress

【愁眉不展】with a worried frown; with knitted brows

【愁眉苦脸】have a worried look; pull a long face

【愁闷】feel gloomy;be depressed

筹 (chóu) ❶prepare;plan:统~overall planning ❷chip;counter

【筹办】make preparations;make arrangements

【筹备】arrange;prepare

【筹划】plan and prepare;design

【筹集】accumulate;raise (money)

【筹建】prepare to establish (or construct) sth.

【筹款】raise money (or funds)

踌 (chóu)

【踌躇】hesitate;shilly-shally

【踌躇不前】hesitate to move forward; hesitate to make a move

【踌躇满志】enormously proud of one's success;smug;complacent

丑 (chǒu) ❶ugly;unsightly;hideous ❷disgraceful;shameful;scandalous

【丑恶】ugly;hideous

【丑化】uglify;defame;smear

【丑陋】ugly

【丑态百出】act like a buffoon;cut a contemptible figure

【丑闻】scandal

臭 (chòu) foul;bad;smelly

【臭虫】bedbug

【臭名昭著】notorious; of ill repute; ill famed

【臭气】bad smell;stink;offensive odour

【臭味相投】people of the same ilk like each other

【臭氧】ozone

chu

出 (chū) ❶go (or come) out ❷exceed; go beyond ❸put up;give;offer;issue ❹produce;turn out ❺arise;happen;occur;take place ❻pay out;expend ❼put forth;vent ❽rise well (with cooking) ❾a dramatic piece

【出版】publish;print;come off the press; come out

【出版社】publishing house;press

【出版业】publishing;publishing business

【出殡】hold a funeral procession

【出岔子】go wrong;get into trouble

【出差】be on a business trip;go away on official duty

【出产】produce;turn out;manufacture

【出场】appear on the scene; come upon

the stage; enter the playing ground; enter the arena
【出丑】make a fool of sb. or oneself; bring shame on oneself
C
【出处】source
【出错】make mistakes
【出点子】offer advice; make suggestions
【出动】set (or turn, start, call, send) out
【出尔反尔】go back on one's word; contradict oneself
【出发】❶ set out; start off ❷ leave for; head for ❸ start from
【出格】❶ be out of the ordinary ❷ overstep the bounds; exceed what is proper
【出轨】❶ go off the rails ❷ overstep the bounds
【出国】go abroad
【出汗】sweat
【出乎意料】exceeding one's expectations; beyond one's expectations; unexpectedly
【出击】attack; hit out
【出家】become a monk or nun
【出价】offer a price
【出境】leave the country
【出口】❶ export ❷ speak; utter ❸ exit; way out
【出口成章】words flow from the mouth as from the pen of a master; talk in literature; have an outstanding eloquence
【出口贸易】export trade
【出类拔萃】stand out from one's fellows
【出力】make great efforts; exert oneself
【出路】outlet; way out
【出毛病】go (or be) out of order; go wrong; break down
【出门】go on a journey; go out; leave home
【出名】well-known; famous
【出谋划策】offer advice; give counsel; mastermind
【出纳】cashier; teller
【出品】produce; manufacture; make product
【出奇制胜】defeat one's opponent by a surprise move
【出勤】❶ turn out for work; be out on duty ❷ attendance
【出糗】make an ass of oneself
【出去】go (or get, turn) out
【出人头地】stand out among one's fellows
【出入】❶ go out and come in ❷ discrepancy; divergence; inconsistency
【出色】splendid; remarkable; outstanding; excellent
【出身】❶ class origin ❷ family background ❸ one's previous experience or occupation
【出神】be lost in thought; mind wandering
【出生】❶ birth ❷ be born
【出生入死】go through fire and water; risk one's life
【出示】show; produce
【出事】meet with a mishap; have an accident
【出售】sell; sale; on sale
【出台】❶ appear on the stage ❷ come out; come into force
【出逃】flee; escape; run away
【出头露面】appear in public; be in the limelight: ~的人物 a public figure
【出土】❶ be unearthed ❷ come up out of the ground
【出息】prospects; a bright future
【出席】be present; attend; show up
【出现】appear; arise; emerge; turn up;

come before (or along); come into being (or view); be seen by

【出血】bleeding; bleed

【出言不逊】make impertinent remarks; speak insolently

【出于无奈】as it cannot be helped; there being no alternative

【出于自愿】of one's own accord (or choice)

【出狱】be released from prison

【出院】leave hospital after recovery

【出众】outstanding

【出主意】make suggestions; offer advice

【出走】leave one's home or country under compulsion; run away; flee

【出租】let; hire (or rent) out; hire

【出租车】taxi; cab

初 (chū) ❶first ❷original ❸elementary ❹at the beginning of; for the first time ❺in the early part of ❻elementary; rudimentary

【初版】first edition

【初步】❶first step ❷initial; preliminary; tentative

【初出茅庐】just come out of one's thatched cottage—at the beginning of one's career; young and inexperienced

【初次】the first time

【初等】elementary; primary

【初等教育】elementary education

【初稿】first draft

【初级】elementary; primary

【初恋】first love; calf love

【初露锋芒】display one's talent for the first time

【初期】initial stage; early days

【初试】❶first try ❷preliminary examination

【初选】primary election

【初学】begin to learn; be a beginner

【初中】junior middle school

【初衷】original intention

除 (chú) ❶remove; get rid of ❷divide ❸except; except for; but ❹in addition to; besides

【除暴安良】get rid of bullies and bring peace to good people

【除草】weed

【除尘】dust; remove dust

【除臭剂】deodorant

【除此之外】moreover; in addition; besides

【除非】only if; only when; unless

【除根】❶dig up the roots; root out; grub; stub ❷cure once and for all; eradicate

【除旧布新】get rid of the old to make way for the new; do away with the old and set up the new

【除了】❶ except; except for; but ❷ besides; in addition to

【除夕】New Year's Eve

【除……之外】❶ except ❷ besides; apart from

厨 (chú) kitchen

【厨房】kitchen

【厨师】cook; chef

锄 (chú) ❶hoe ❷do hoeing ❸uproot; eliminate; wipe out

【锄草】hoe up weeds

【锄地】hoe the fields

【锄头】hoe

雏 (chú) ❶young bird ❷young

【雏菊】daisy

【雏鸟】squab; nestling; fledgling

【雏形】miniature; embryo

橱 (chú) closet; cabinet: 衣～ wardrobe; 书～ book case

C

【橱窗】❶shopwindow; show (or display) window; showcase ❷glass-fronted billboard

【橱柜】cupboard

处 (chǔ) ❶get along with ❷manage; handle; deal with; ❸ punish; sentence ❹ be situated in; be in a certain condition

另见本页 chù

【处罚】punish

【处方】prescription

【处分】take disciplinary action against; punish

【处境】unfavourable situation; plight

【处理】handle; take care of; do with; treat; deal with; manage; settle; dispose of; treat by a special process

【处世】conduct oneself in society

【处心积虑】deliberately plan (to achieve evil ends); incessantly scheme

【处于困境】be in trouble; be in difficulty

【处之泰然】take things calmly; remain unruffled

【处置】manage; deal with; dispose of; handle

储 (chǔ) keep (or have) in reserve; store up; save

【储备】❶store; reserve ❷lay in; lay up

【储藏】store; store up; save and preserve

【储户】depositor

【储量】reserves

【储蓄】❶ save; deposit savings: 定期～ fixed deposit; 活期～ current deposit

处 (chù) ❶place: 住～ quarters; dwelling place ❷department; section; office; bureau ❸part; point

另见本页 chǔ

【处处】everywhere; up and down; in all respects

【处所】location; place

【处长】section chief; director; the head of a department

畜 (chù) domestic animal; livestock

【畜生】❶domestic animals ❷beast

触 (chù) ❶ contact; keep in touch with; touch ❷hit; strike ❸move (or touch) sb.; stir up sb.'s feelings

【触电】get an electric shock

【触动】❶touch sth. ❷move sb.; stir up sb.'s feeling

【触犯】offend; violate; go against

【触及】touch

【触角】feeler; antenna; tentacle

【触景生情】the sight strikes a chord in one's heart

【触觉】sense of touch; tactile sensation; tactual sensation

【触类旁通】grasp a typical example and you will grasp the whole category; comprehend by analogy

【触目惊心】shocking; startling

矗 (chù) stand tall and upright

【矗立】stand tall and upright; tower over sth.

揣 (chuǎi) estimate; speculate; surmise; conjecture

【揣测】guess; figure; reckon

【揣摩】try to fathom; try to figure out

chuan

川 (chuān) ❶river ❷plain

【川菜】Sichuan Dish

【川流不息】in a continuous flow; never-ending

穿 (chuān) ❶wear; put on; be dressed in; have ... on ❷ pass (or go)

through; cross ❸ penetrate; pierce through ❹string together

【穿插】❶ alternate; do in turn ❷ interweave; weave in; insert

【穿戴】dress; wear

【穿过】cross; go across; pass (or go) through

【穿孔】❶bore a hole; punch a hole ❷ perforation

【穿透】pierce through; run through; penetrate

【穿衣】dress; wear; have (or put) on clothes

【穿越】across; pass through

【穿凿附会】give strained interpretations and draw farfetched analogies

【穿针引线】act as a go-between; do sewing work; thread a needle

【穿着】dress; attire; apparel; what one wears

传(chuán) ❶ pass; pass on ❷ hand down ❸ spread ❹ conduct; transmit ❺ express; convey ❻ infect; be contagious

另见 1326 页 zhuàn

【传遍】spread throughout (or around, about, all over)

【传播】spread; propagate

【传承】import and inherit

【传单】leaflet; handbill

【传导】transmit; conduct

【传递】pass; hand; pass on; deliver; transmit; transfer

【传动】transmission; drive

【传话】pass on a message

【传唤】summon to court

【传教士】missionary; preacher

【传开】spread; get round

【传媒】media

【传奇】legend; romance

【传球】pass ball

【传染病】infectious disease ~医院 hospital for infectious diseases; isolation hospital

【传人】❶pass on a skill or craft to others ❷ successor; exponent ❸summon sb.

【传神】vivid; lifelike

【传授】pass on; impart; teach; instruct

【传说】❶it is said that ...; they say ❷legend; tale

【传送】❶ communicate; transmit; send over ❷deliver; convey

【传统】tradition

【传闻】hearsay; rumour; it is said; they say

【传阅】pass round for perusal

【传真】facsimile; fax

船(chuán) ship; boat; vessel

【船舶】shipping; boats and ships

【船舱】cabin; ship's hold

【船队】fleet

【船费】fare

【船员】seaman; crew; sailor

【船闸】(ship) lock

【船长】shipmaster; captain; skipper

【船只】shipping; vessels

喘(chuǎn) breathe heavily; gasp for breath; pant asthma

【喘气】❶ gasp; breathe deeply; pant ❷ take a breather

【喘息未定】before catching one's breath; before one has a chance to catch one's breath

串(chuàn) ❶string together ❷collaborate ❸ move about; conspire; go from place to place; run about; rove ❹ play a part (in a play) ❺ string; bunch;

cluster

【串联】❶ establish ties; contact ❷ series connection

C

【串门】call on sb.; drop in on sb.

【串通】gang up; collaborate; work hand in glove; collude

【串戏】(of an amateur actor) play a part in a professional performance

chuang

创 (chuāng) wound
另见本页 chuàng

【创痕】scar

【创口】cut; wound

【创伤】wound; trauma

疮 (chuāng) sore; skin ulcer

【疮疤】scar

【疮痍满目】everywhere a scene of devastation meets the eye

窗 (chuāng) window: 百叶~ shutter; 纱~ screen window; 天~ skylight

【窗户】window; casement

【窗花】paper-cut for window decoration

【窗口】window; wicket: 坐在~边 sit at the window

【窗帘】window curtain: 拉开~draw the window curtain apart

【窗台】windowsill

床 (chuáng) bed; sth. shaped like a bed: 单人~single bed; 双人~double bed; 上~ go to bed; 铺~ make the bed; 卧病在~ be laid up

【床单】sheet

【床垫】mattress

【床头】the head of a bed; bedside

【床罩】bedspread

闯 (chuǎng) rush; dash; break through; charge

【闯荡】roam about to make a living

【闯红灯】race (or jump) a red light

【闯祸】get into trouble; bring disaster

【闯路】blaze a trail; open a way; break a path

【闯入】break (or run, burst) into; intrude

创 (chuàng) start doing sth.; establish; create; achieve (sth. for the first time)
另见本页 chuāng

【创办】establish; set up; found

【创汇】earn foreign exchange (or income)

【创纪录】set a record

【创见】original idea (view); creative idea; brand-new idea

【创建】found; establish; set up

【创举】pioneering work

【创刊】start publication

【创立】set up; originate; found

【创奇迹】work miracles; work wonders

【创始】initiate; originate

【创新】create sth. new; bring forth new ideas

【创业】start (or build) a business; break new ground

【创意】original concept (or idea)

【创造】produce; invent; create; bring about

【创造力】creative ability (or power)

【创作】❶ create; write; compose; produce ❷creation

chui

吹 (chuī) ❶blow; puff ❷boast ❸break off (or up); fall through

【吹吹打打】beating drums and blowing trumpets; piping and drumming

【吹笛】play the flute

【吹风】❶be in a draught; catch a chill ❷

let sb. in on sth. in advance ❸give a cue ❹hairdryer

【吹拂】sway;stir

【吹灰之力】the effort needed to blow away a speck of dust;just a small effort

【吹口哨】blow a whistle;whistle

【吹喇叭】wind a trumpet

【吹落】blow off

【吹毛求疵】find fault;pick holes in sth.

【吹牛】boast;talk big

【吹嘘】boast of;boast about

【吹奏】play

炊 (chuī) cook a meal

【炊具】cooking utensils;kitchenware

【炊事员】a cook or a kitchen staff

【炊烟】smoke from kitchen chimneys

垂 (chuí) ❶ hang down; let fall ❷ go (or hand) down;droop

【垂钓】fish

【垂泪】shed tears;weep

【垂柳】weeping willow

【垂头丧气】in low spirits;downcast

【垂危】at death's door;at one's last gasp:生命～ dying

【垂涎】slaver over sth.

【垂直】perpendicular;vertical

捶 (chuí) beat;pound

【捶打】beat

【捶门】bang on the door

【捶胸顿足】beat (or thump) one's breast and stamp one's feet (in deep sorrow, etc.)

锤 (chuí) ❶hammer into shape;knock with a hammer ❷hammer;weight

【锤炼】hammer into shape;temper;steel;try to perfect one's skill or technique by strenuous effort;hammer out;polish

chun

春 (chūn) ❶spring ❷life;vitality

【春播】spring sowing;spring seeding

【春风】spring breeze

【春风得意】ride on the crest of success

【春耕】spring ploughing

【春光明媚】with spring in all its brightness and charm

【春节】the Spring Festival

【春雷】spring thunder

【春联】Spring Festival couplets

【春秋】❶ spring and autumn; year ❷ chronicle;annals

【春色】spring scenery:满园～a garden full of the beauty of spring

【春笋】bamboo shoots in spring

【春晚】Spring Festival Gala

【春意盎然】spring is in the air

【春游】spring outing

【春运】transport during the Spring Festival

纯 (chún) ❶pure;unmixed ❷simple ❸ pure and simple ❹skillful;practiced

【纯粹】❶pure;purely ❷only;simply;

【纯度】degree of purity

【纯洁】❶clean and honest;pure ❷purity:心地～(of a person) above any ultra intentions

【纯净】❶pure;clean ❷purity

【纯利】net profit

【纯美】pure and beautiful

【纯朴】honest;simple

【纯熟】skillful;practiced

【纯真】innocent; unsophisticated; pure and sincere

【纯正】pure;unadulterated

唇 (chún) lip：上～ upper lip；下～ lower lip

【唇膏】lipstick

【唇枪舌剑】a battle of words

C

淳 (chún) pure；honest

【淳厚】pure and honest；simple and kind；devoted

【淳朴】honest；simple；unsophisticated

蠢 (chǔn) stupid；clumsy；foolish；dull；silly

【蠢笨】clumsy；awkward；stupid

【蠢蠢欲动】ready to make trouble；ready to start wriggling

【蠢人】fool；blockhead

【蠢事】a stupid thing；folly

chuo

戳 (chuō) thrust；stab；poke；jab stamp；seal

【戳穿】❶ puncture；pierce through ❷ lay bare；expose

啜 (chuò) ❶sip；suck ❷sob

【啜泣】sob

绰 (chuò) ample；spacious

【绰绰有余】enough and to spare；more than enough

【绰号】nickname

辍 (chuò) stop；cease

【辍笔】stop in the middle of writing or painting

【辍学】drop out of school；quit school

ci

词 (cí) ❶ word；❷ term statement；speech；❸开幕～ opening speech；台～ line of an opera ❹ a Chinese poetic genre

【词不达意】the language fails to express the meaning

【词典】dictionary：简明～ concise dictionary；袖珍～ pocket dictionary

【词根】root；etyma

【词汇】vocabulary；words and phrases

【词库】lexicon；word bank

【词类】parts of speech；word class

【词语】words and expressions

【词组】phrase；expression；word group

瓷 (cí) china；porcelain：细～ fine china

【瓷器】chinaware；porcelain

【瓷土】china clay

辞 (cí) ❶diction；phraseology ❷a type of classical Chinese literature ❸ballad ❹a form of classical poetry ❺take leave；depart：不～而别 leave without saying goodbye；告～take one's leave ❻ dismiss；discharge ❼decline；resign

【辞别】say goodbye；bid farewell；take one's leave

【辞典】dictionary

【辞书】dictionary；lexicographical work

【辞退】dismiss；discharge；sack；fire

【辞行】say goodbye before setting out on a journey

【辞职】resign；quit

慈 (cí) kind；loving

【慈爱】kindness；love；affection

【慈悲】mercy；benevolence；pity：大发～ have pity；show mercy

【慈母】loving mother

【慈善】charitable；benevolent

【慈祥】kindly；benign

磁 (cí) magnetism;magnet

【磁场】magnetic field

【磁化】❶magnetization ❷magnetize

【磁力】magnetic force

【磁铁】magnet

【磁性】❶ magnetism; ❷ magnetic; magnetic performance

【磁悬浮列车】maglev train (magnetic-levitation train)

雌 (cí) female

【雌花】female (or pistillate) flower

【雌雄】❶male and female ❷victory and defeat:决~ see who's master

糍 (cí)

【糍粑】cooked glutinous rice pounded into paste;glutinous rice cake

此 (cǐ) ❶ now; here: 从~以后 from now on ❷this

【此处】this place;here

【此后】hereafter; after that (or this); afterwards;henceforth

【此刻】now;at this moment;at present

【此起彼伏】rise one after another;as one falls,another rises

【此时】now;right now;at this moment;at present

【此外】moreover;besides;in addition

次 (cì) ❶position in a series;place in a sequence; order: 依~in due order; one by one;one after another ❷second; next time; ❸second-rate ❹occurrence; time

【次第】❶order; sequence ❷one after another

【次品】substandard goods (or products); defective goods

【次日】the next day

【次数】number of times

【次序】order;sequence

【次要】secondary; minor; less important; subordinate

【次于】next to

【次之】take second place

伺 (cì)
另见 1197 页 sì

【伺候】wait upon;serve

刺 (cì) ❶thorn ❷sting; stab; thrust ❸ excite; stimulate; irritate ❹ spy; detect

【刺鼻】pungent;acrid

【刺穿】pierce;cut through

【刺刀】bayonet

【刺耳】harsh;ear piercing;grating on the ear;jarring

【刺激】excite;stimulate

【刺身】sashimi

【刺痛】sting

【刺猬】hedgehog

【刺绣】❶embroider ❷embroidery

【刺眼】dazzling;glaring

赐 (cì) ❶bestow; confer ❷gift; grant; favour

【赐福】blessing

【赐教】condescend to teach;grant instruction

【赐予】grant

cong

匆 (cōng) hastily;hurriedly

【匆匆】hurriedly; in a hurry (or rush); in haste

【匆忙】❶ hurried; hasty ❷ in a hurry; hastily;in haste

葱 (cōng) onion

【葱白】❶very light blue ❷scallion stalk

【葱绿】light green; pale yellowish green; verdant

【葱头】onion

【葱郁】verdant; luxuriantly green

聪 (cōng) ❶faculty of hearing ❷acute hearing: 右耳失～ become deaf in the right ear

【聪慧】bright; intelligent

【聪明】clever; intelligent; bright; wise; smart

从 (cóng) ❶follower; attendant ❷follow; obey ❸join; take part in; be engaged in ❹in a certain manner ❺according to a certain principle ❻ from; through; since ❼secondary; subordinate

【从不】never

【从此】hence; from this time on; from now on

【从而】thus; therefore; thereby

【从来】ever; always; at all times; all along

【从前】before; formerly; once upon a time; in the past; once

【从容】❶calm; unhurried ❷plentiful; sufficient; enough

【从上到下】from top to bottom

【从事】be engaged in; go in for; undertake

【从属】subordinate

【从头】from the beginning

【从头再来】start all over again

【从头至尾】from top to bottom; from beginning to end

【从未见过】have never seen before

【从无到有】grow out of nothing

【从现在起】from now on

【从小】from childhood; as a child

【从远处】from far away

【从早到晚】from dawn to dusk; from morning till night

【从中】from among; out of

丛 (cóng) ❶clump; thicket ❷crowd; collection ❸crowd together

【丛林】forest; jungle: 热带～ tropical forest

【丛书】collection; a series of books: 自学～self-study series

COU

凑 (còu) ❶gather; collect ❷move close

【凑份子】club together

【凑合】❶ make do ❷ gather together ❸passable

【凑巧】luckily; fortunately

【凑热闹】❶join in the fun ❷add trouble to

【凑数】make up the number

CU

粗 (cū) ❶wide; thick ❷coarse; crude; rough ❸careless; negligent ❹unrefined; vulgar; rude ❺ gruff; husky ❻roughly

【粗暴】rough; rude; brutal; tough; crude

【粗糙】❶coarse; rough ❷crude ❸roughly

【粗犷】rough; rude

【粗话】vulgar (or obscene) language

【粗活】heavy manual labor; unskilled work

【粗劣】of poor quality

【粗陋】coarse and crude

【粗鲁】rough; rude

【粗略】roughly; slightly

【粗浅】simple; shallow; superficial

【粗俗】vulgar; coarse

【粗细】❶(degree of) thickness ❷crude-ness or fineness; degree of finish; quality of work

【粗心】careless; thoughtless

【粗枝大叶】crude and careless

【粗壮】strong; thickset

促 (cù) ❶ urge; promote ❷ (of time) short; hurried; urgent ❸ close to; near

【促成】help to bring about; facilitate

【促进】 advance; promote; stimulate; help; accelerate

【促使】impel; urge; make; cause; hasten

【促销】promote the sale

猝 (cù) suddenly; unexpectedly

【猝不及防】be taken by surprise

【猝死】sudden death

醋 (cù) ❶ vinegar ❷ jealousy (as in a love affair)

簇 (cù) ❶ form a cluster; pile up ❷ cluster; bunch

【簇新】brand new

【簇拥】cluster round

cuan

窜 (cuàn) ❶ run about; flee ❷ expel ❸ change (the wording in a text, manuscript, etc.); alter

【窜改】alter; tamper with; falsify

【窜逃】flee in disorder; falsify

篡 (cuàn) usurp; seize

【篡夺】usurp; seize

【篡改】distort; misrepresent

【篡位】usurp the throne

cui

催 (cuī) urge; speed up; press; hasten; hurry

【催办】urge to do

【催促】urge; hasten; press

【催化剂】factors promoting the development of a thing; catalyst

【催眠曲】cradlesong; lullaby

摧 (cuī) break; destroy; ruin

【摧残】destroy; wreck

【摧毁】blast; wreck; destroy; smash; shatter: 猛烈的炮火～了敌人的阵地。Intense fire destroyed the enemy ramparts.

璀 (cuǐ)

【璀璨】bright; resplendent

脆 (cuì) ❶ fragile; brittle ❷ crisp ❸ ringing; clear and sharp

【脆骨】gristle (as food)

【脆弱】weak: 感情～ be easily upset

【脆性】brittleness; shortness

翠 (cuì) ❶ emerald green ❷ kingfisher ❸ jadeite

【翠绿】emerald green

【翠鸟】kingfisher

cun

村 (cūn) ❶ village; hamlet ❷ rustic; boorish

【村民】villager; village people

【村野】❶ villages; countryside ❷ rustic; countrified

【村镇】villages and small towns

【村庄】village; hamlet

存 (cún) ❶ exist; live ❷ store; keep ❸ accumulate; deposit; save ❹ leave with; check ❺ remain on balance; be in stock ❻ cherish; harbour

【存储】store; deposit; memory; storage

【存档】place on file; file; keep in the archives

【存放】deposit; leave in sb.'s care; check

【存活】survive; remain alive

【存货】goods in stock; existing stock

【存款】deposit; bank savings

【存心】on purpose; intentionally

【存在】❶ exist; be; lie; remain ❷ existence; being

【存折】deposit book

忖 (cǔn) turn over in one's mind; ponder; speculate

【忖度】speculate; conjecture; surmise

寸 (cùn) ❶ a traditional unit of length (1 cun = 1/3 decimeter) ❷ very little; very short; small

【寸步不离】keep close to; follow sb. closely

【寸步难行】difficult to move even one step; cannot move a single step

【寸草不生】not even a blade of grass grows

cuo

搓 (cuō) ❶ rub with hands; scrub ❷ roll; twist

【搓手顿脚】wring one's hands and stamp one's feet—get anxious and impatient

【搓衣板】washboard

【搓澡】give sb. a rubdown with a damp towel

磋 (cuō) consult

【磋商】consult; exchange views; confer

撮 (cuō) ❶ gather; bring together ❷ scoop up (with a dustpan or shovel) ❸ pick up or hold (dust, powder, etc.) between the thumb and the first finger

【撮合】make a match; act as go-between

蹉 (cuō)

【蹉跎】waste time

【蹉跎岁月】let time slip by accomplishing nothing; idle away one's time

挫 (cuò) defeat; frustrate; subdue; lower

【挫败】defeat; frustrate

【挫伤】❶ dampen; discourage ❷ bruise

【挫折】reverse; setback: 遭受～ suffer setbacks

措 (cuò) ❶ arrange; manage; handle ❷ make plans

【措辞】wording; diction

【措施】measure; step: 采取～ take a measure (or steps)

【措手不及】be caught unprepared; be caught unawares

【措置得当】handle properly

锉 (cuò) ❶ file ❷ make smooth with a file; file

错 (cuò) ❶ fault; mistake; error: 认～ admit one's mistake ❷ wrong; mistaken ❸ complex interlocked and jagged; intricate; stagger ❹ uneven

【错案】misjudged case

【错别字】wrongly written or mispronounced characters

【错车】one vehicle gives another the right of way

【错怪】blame sb. wrongly

【错过】miss; cross; let slip

【错觉】illusion; misconception; wrong impression

【错开】stagger

【错乱】in disorder (or confusion): 精神～ mentally disturbed; in mental disorder; deranged

【错落不齐】disorderly and uneven

【错落有致】in picturesque disorder

【错事】wrong

【错误】❶ wrong; mistaken; erroneous: ～思想 wrong thinking; mistaken idea ❷ mistake; error; fault: ❸改正～ correct a mistake 犯～ make a mistake; commit an error

【错综复杂】intricate; complex; complicated

D d

da

搭 (dā) ❶put up; build ❷take; travel (or go) by ❸put over ❹come into contact; join ❺throw in more (people, money, etc.) ❻add ❼lift sth. together

【搭伴】join sb. on trip; travel together

【搭便车】hitchhike; ask sb. for a lift

【搭档】❶cooperate; work together ❷partner

【搭伙】❶join as partner ❷eat regularly in (a mess, canteen, etc.)

【搭救】save; rescue; go to the rescue of

【搭理】respond; answer; reply

【搭配】❶arrange in proper proportions; match; collocate ❷collocation

【搭起】set (or put) up

【搭桥】put up a bridge

答 (dā)
另见本页 dá

【答应】❶make a promise; accept ❷answer; reply; respond

打 (dá) dozen: 半~half a dozen
另见本页 dǎ

达 (dá) ❶reach; amount to ❷understand thoroughly ❸extend; lead to ❹express; communicate

【达标】meet the standard

【达成】come to; arrive at; reach

【达到目的】achieve the goal

【达观】take things philosophically; philosophical; having broad perspective

【达人】talent; intelligent; expert

【达人秀】talent show

答 (dá) ❶answer; reply; respond ❷return; reciprocate
另见本页 dā

【答案】answer; solution; key: 练习~key to an exercise

【答辩】defend; reply (to a charge, query or an argument)

【答复】answer; write back; reply

【答谢】return one's thanks for; express appreciation (for sb.'s kindness or hospitality); acknowledge

打 (dǎ) ❶ strike; hit; beat; knock ❷break; smash ❸ make; forge ❹mix; stir ❺knit; weave ❻tie up; pack ❼open; dig ❽hunt; catch ❾play
另见本页 dá

【打靶】shooting practice

【打败】❶defeat; beat ❷suffer a defeat; lose

【打扮】dress (or make) up

【打包】pack

【打抱不平】defend sb. against an injustice; take up the cudgels for the injured party; be the champion of the oppressed

【打草惊蛇】beat the grass and startle the

snake;act rashly and alert the enemy
【打岔】cut in;interrupt
【打打闹闹】have boisterous fun; horse-play
【打得火热】be very thick with each other;be as thick as thieves
【打电话】phone; call (or ring) up; telephone;make a phone call;call;give sb. a ring
【打动】strike;touch;move
【打赌】bet;make a bet;wager
【打断】❶ interrupt; break in ❷ break; cut short
【打发】❶dismiss;send away ❷kill time
【打躬作揖】bow and raise one's clasped hands in salute; fold the hands and make deep bows;bow and scrape
【打工】do work for others; hire out for work;do manual work for sb.
【打官司】go to court;go to law;engage in a lawsuit
【打滚】roll about
【打哈欠】yawn
【打鼾】snore
【打火机】lighter
【打击】strike;hit;shock;attack
【打假】crack down on producers of counterfeit products; crack down on fake products
【打架】come to blows;fight;scuffle
【打交道】come into contact with; have dealings with
【打搅】trouble;disturb;bother
【打劫】commit robbery;loot;plunder
【打开】❶open;unfold;unwrap ❷turn on; switch on ❸open up;spread
【打瞌睡】doze off;nod
【打垮】beat; break (or strike) down; defeat
【打篮球】play basketball
【打捞】get out of water;salvage
【打雷】thunder
【打量】measure;size up;look sb. up and down;reckon
【打猎】hunt;go hunting
【打乱】mess up;disrupt
【打骂】beat and scold;maltreat
【打拍子】beat time
【打牌】play cards
【打喷嚏】sneeze
【打破常规】break free from old rules and conventions
【打破纪录】break a record
【打起精神】pluck up courage;cheer up
【打气】❶pump up ❷encourage;cheer up
【打拳】boxing;shadowboxing
【打扰】interrupt;disturb;bother;break in
【打伞】hold up an umbrella
【打扫】sweep;clean;dust
【打死】beat to death
【打算】❶ plan; mean; intend ❷ consideration;calculation
【打算盘】❶calculate on an abacus ❷calculate;scheme
【打碎】smash;break up;break into pieces
【打听】ask (or inquire) about
【打消】give up;cancel;dispel
【打印】print
【打印机】printer
【打赢】win
【打鱼】❶catch fish ❷fishing
【打杂】do odd jobs;do odds and ends
【打仗】fight;go to war
【打招呼】greet sb.; nod; say hello; let sb. know
【打折扣】give a discount;sell at discount
【打针】inject;give an injection
【打中】hit the mark (or target)

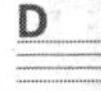

【打主意】seek; try to win sth. ; scheme for
【打转】revolve; spin; move about
【打字】type; typewrite

大 (dà) ❶size ❷age ❸bigness ❹great; enormous; big ❺heavy; strong; loud ❻general; main; major ❼old ❽much; quite ❾fully; largely; greatly; extremely

【大巴】bus; coach
【大白菜】Chinese cabbage
【大败】utterly be defeated; suffer a crushing defeat
【大半】❶ great part; more than half; most; largely ❷very likely; most probably
【大本营】❶ supreme headquarters ❷ base camp
【大便】❶stool ❷defecate; empty the bowels
【大饼】large flat bread; pancake
【大伯】uncle; one's father's elder brother
【大部分】mostly; the greater part
【大步流星】at great strides; with big strides
【大材小用】large material put to small use; one's talent wasted on a petty job; not do justice to sb. 's talents
【大车】cart; trolley
【大吃大喝】eat and drink extravagantly
【大吃一惊】be greatly surprised; be quite taken aback; be startled (or astounded)
【大葱】Chinese green onion
【大慈大悲】infinitely compassionate and merciful
【大错特错】completely mistaken; absolutely wrong
【大大地】greatly; widely; enormously
【大大咧咧】careless; casual: 别看他～的，什么事他都很在心。He seems unconcerned, but nothing escapes his attention.
【大胆】bold; daring; bravery
【大刀阔斧】bold and resolute; be drastic
【大地】mother earth; the world; earth
【大动干戈】go to war; get into a fight
【大豆】soybean; soya
【大都市】metropolis
【大度】broad-minded; magnanimous
【大度包容】regard with kindly tolerance; be magnanimous and tolerant; be magnanimous
【大队】❶ brigade; army; group ❷ a large body of
【大多数】majority; mass
【大而无当】large but impractical; unwieldy
【大发雷霆】be furious; fly into a rage; bawl at sb. angrily
【大法官】the grand justice
【大方】❶generous; liberal ❷natural
【大风】gale; high (or strong) wind
【大风大浪】strong storms; wind and waves
【大概】general idea; outline; approximate; probably; perhaps; possibly; maybe; most likely
【大纲】outline; synopsis
【大哥】eldest brother; elder brother
【大公无私】unselfish; selfless; impartial
【大功告成】accomplish (a project; work) successfully; be crowned with success
【大规模】❶large scale; mass ❷massive
【大海捞针】fish for a needle in the ocean; look for a needle in a haystack
【大好河山】one's beloved motherland; beautiful rivers and mountains
【大合唱】chorus
【大话】big talk; boast: 说～talk big

【大会】congress; session; general membership meeting; conference

【大祸临头】disaster is imminent; disaster is hanging over one

【大惑不解】be extremely puzzled; be unable to make head or tail of sth.

【大吉大利】good luck and great prosperity (an expression of good wishes)

【大计】matters of vital importance

【大家】all; everyone; everybody; great master; authority

【大家闺秀】a girl from a good family; a well-bred girl; lady

【大减价】bargain sale

【大江】great river

【大将】senior general

【大街】avenue; main street

【大街小巷】streets and lanes:～彩旗飘扬。The streets and lanes are decked with bunting.

【大捷】great success; victory

【大惊小怪】be surprised at sth. quite normal; make a fuss

【大局】general (or overall) situation:顾全～take the whole situation into account

【大考】final exam; end-of-term examination

【大可不必】not at all necessary:其实这种担心～。As a matter of fact there's no need to worry about it at all.

【大快人心】affording general satisfaction; most gratifying to the people; to the immense satisfaction of the people

【大款】rich people; moneybags

【大理石】marble

【大礼堂】great hall; auditorium

【大量】a great deal of; a lot of; lots (or plenty) of; large quantities of

【大楼】tall building; multi-storied building

【大陆】continent; mainland

【大路】main road

【大麦】barley

【大门】gate; front door; entrance door

【大米】rice

【大名鼎鼎】famous; well-known; celebrated

【大拇指】thumb

【大脑】cerebrum; brain

【大炮】gun; cannon

【大批】a large (or great) number of; large quantities of

【大气】atmosphere; air

【大器晚成】great vessels take years to produce; great minds mature slowly

【大千世界】the kaleidoscopic world; the boundless universe

【大人物】great man; big shot; very important person (or VIP)

【大扫除】general cleaning; thorough cleanup

【大厦】mansion

【大声】loud; aloud

【大失所望】greatly disappointed; to one's great disappointment

【大师】great master

【大使】ambassador

【大使馆】embassy

【大事】great event; important matter:关心国家～concern oneself with affairs of state; 头等～a matter of prime importance

【大势】general trend; prevailing tendency of events

【大是大非】major issues of principle; wrong or right

【大手大脚】be wasteful; be extravagant

【大蒜】garlic

【大体】❶ on the whole; in the main ❷

more or less
【大厅】hall;lobby
【大庭广众】before a big crowd;on a public occasion
【大同小异】very much the same;alike except for slight differences; much the same but with minor differences
【大腿】thigh
【大西洋】the Atlantic (Ocean)
【大喜过望】be overjoyed that things are better than one expected
【大虾】prawn
【大显神通】give full play to one's remarkable skill (or abilities)
【大相径庭】totally different;entirely contrary
【大象】elephant
【大小】size
【大笑一场】have a good laugh
【大写】capital letter; capital form of a Chinese numeral
【大猩猩】gorilla
【大型】large-scale;large
【大熊猫】giant panda
【大选】general election
【大学】university; college:上～go to college (or university);在～ in (or at) college;广播电视～radio and television university;科技～university of science and technol-ogy
【大学生】university (or college) student
【大学校长】president
【大雪】snowstorm;heavy snow
【大言不惭】brag unblushingly;talk big
【大雁】wild goose
【大洋】ocean
【大洋洲】Oceania
【大衣】coat;overcoat:棉～ cotton-padded overcoat
【大意】❶general idea;main points ❷carelessness
【大义灭亲】place righteousness above loyalty to one's family; sacrifice ties of blood to righteousness
【大有可为】be well worth doing; have bright prospects
【大有作为】have full scope for one's talents;be able to develop one's ability to the full;have great possibilities
【大雨】downpour;heavy rain
【大元帅】generalissimo
【大约】❶about; generally; or so ❷some; approximately;
【大丈夫】true man;man
【大志】lofty ambition;high aim
【大致】in the main; for the most part; roughly;more or less
【大智若愚】a man of great wisdom often seems slow-witted
【大众】the masses;the public;the people
【大专院校】universities and colleges; institutions of higher education
【大洲】continent
【大自然】nature

dai

呆 (dāi) foolish; silly; stupid; slow-witted;dull
【呆板】stiff;rigid;not natural;inflexible
【呆账】bad debts
【呆子】idiot;simpleton;blockhead
待 (dāi) stay
另见 947 页 dài
【待会儿】after a moment
歹 (dǎi) bad;evil;vicious
【歹徒】outlaw;gangster;ruffian
【歹意】malice;malicious intent;evil inten-

tion

逮 (dǎi) catch; arrest; seize; capture; reach

【逮捕】arrest;take into custody

【逮住】catch;seize

代 (dài) ❶dynasty;era;historical period:古～ ancient times;近～modern times;现～contemporary times ❷generation ❸take the place of;be in place of;substitute

【代办】do sth. for sb. ;be on sb. 's behalf

【代表】❶deputy; representative; delegate ❷present;stand for ❸in the name of;on behalf of

【代表大会】congress; representative assembly or conference

【代表团】delegation;mission

【代沟】generation gap

【代价】price;cost:付……的～pay for;不惜任何～ at any (or all) cost

【代驾司机】designated driver

【代理】❶agent ❷act for

【代码】code

【代售】be commissioned to sell sth.

【代替】replace; substitute; take the place of;instead of;in place of

【代言人】spokesman;mouthpiece

带 (dài) ❶ belt; ribbon; band; cord; strap;tape;girdle:领～necktie;皮～leather belt; 鞋 ～ shoelaces; shoestrings ❷zone;area ❸take;bring;carry ❹lead;head ❺look after;bring up;raise

【带到】take to

【带电】charged;electrified

【带动】drive;spur on;bring along

【带回】bring back

【带来】fetch;bring;bring over

【带劲】❶ energetic; forceful ❷ interesting;exciting

【带领】lead;guide;take;show

【带路】show (or lead) the way

【带头】take the lead;be the first:起～作用 play a leading role

【带鱼】hairtail

【带子】string;belt;band;tape

【带走】take away

贷 (dài) ❶ loan ❷ borrow or lend ❸ shift (responsibility); shirk ❹ pardon;forgive

【贷方】credit side;credit

【贷款】❶provide (or grant) a loan;extend credit to;make loans ❷loan;credit

待 (dài) ❶ treat; deal with ❷ await; wait for ❸entertain

另见 946 页 dāi

【待人接物】the way one gets along with people

【待业】wait to be employed;job-waiting

【待遇】❶treatment ❷pay;wages;salary

怠 (dài) lazy;idle;remiss;slack

【怠慢】snub; show indifference to sb. ; cold-shoulder;slight

袋 (dài) bag;pocket:口～pocket;bag

【袋鼠】kangaroo

【袋子】sack;bag

戴 (dài) wear; have on; put on respect;honour

【戴帽子】wear a hat

【戴上】put on

【戴手套】put on gloves

【戴眼镜】wear spectacles (or glasses)

dan

丹 (dān) ❶red ❷pellet or power

【丹顶鹤】red-crowned crane

D

【丹田】the pubic region

【丹心】loyal heart;loyalty

担 (dān) ❶ carry on the shoulder ❷ take on;undertake;bear

另见 948 页 dàn

D

【担保】assure;guarantee;vouch for

【担当】take on; assume the responsibility;undertake;bear the burden

【担风险】take risks;face the risk of

【担架】stretcher

【担惊受怕】feel alarmed; be in a state of anxiety

【担任】hold the post of; take charge of; assume the office of

【担心】fear;feel anxious;worry;concern; be in fear of

【担忧】fear;be anxious;be afraid of;worry

单 (dān) ❶one;single ❷bill;list:名～ name list ❸ simple;plain ❹ odd ❺ alone;only;singly

【单薄】❶ (of clothing) thin ❷ thin and weak;frail:力量～ weak in strength ❸flimsy

【单程】one way;single trip

【单纯】❶ simple;pure ❷ alone;purely; merely;simply

【单词】individual word;word

【单打】singles

【单调】dull;monotonous;drab

【单独】alone;by oneself;on one's own

【单方面】one-sided;unilateral

【单杠】horizontal bar

【单个】individual;single

【单价】unit price

【单句】simple sentence

【单据】receipts;bills

【单枪匹马】single-handed;all by oneself; alone

【单亲家庭】single parent family

【单人床】single bed

【单身】single;unmarried

【单数】❶ singular ❷ singular (or odd) number

【单位】unit:基层～ basic unit

【单项】individual event

【单行道】one-way road

【单眼皮】single-fold eyelid;single-edged eyelid

【单一】single;unitary

【单元】unit;cell;location;element;section

【单子】bill;form;list:填写～ fill in a form

耽 (dān)delay

【耽搁】❶stop over;stay ❷delay

【耽误】hold up;delay

【耽于】addict;indulge in

殚 (dān) use up;exhaust

【殚精竭虑】do one's utmost;go all out; use every ounce of one's energy

胆 (dǎn) ❶ courage;bravery ❷ gall bladder;guts

【胆大】bold;brave;daring

【胆敢】dare;have the audacity to

【胆量】courage;pluck;spunk

【胆略】courage and resourcefulness

【胆怯】timid;cowardly;faint-hearted

【胆识】courage and insight

【胆小】timid;cowardly

【胆小如鼠】as timid as a mouse;chicken-hearted

【胆子】courage;nerve:放开～ pluck up courage

旦 (dàn) ❶ dawn;daybreak ❷day ❸ the female character type in Beijing Opera,etc.

【旦夕】this morning or evening;in a short

while

但 (dàn) ❶but; yet; still; nevertheless ❷only; merely

【但凡】 without exception; as long as; in every case

【但是】 but; however; yet; though; on the other hand

【但愿】 ❶if only ❷I wish

担 (dàn) ❶dan, a unit of weight (1 dan=50 kilograms) ❷a carrying (or shoulder) pole and the loads on it; load; burden

另见 949 页 dān

【担子】 ❶load; burden ❷responsibility

诞 (dàn) ❶birth ❷absurd; fantastic

【诞辰】 birthday

【诞生】 birth; be born; come into being; emerge

淡 (dàn) ❶tasteless; weak; without enough salt ❷thin; light ❸light; pale

【淡泊】 not to seek fame and wealth; seek neither fame nor wealth

【淡淡】 slight; light

【淡而无味】 tasteless; insipid

【淡化】 ❶desalinate ❷desalination

【淡季】 dull season; off season

【淡漠】 indifferent; nonchalant; dim; hazy

【淡然处之】 treat coolly; take it easy

【淡水】 fresh water

【淡忘】 fade from one's memory

【淡雅】 simple and elegant; quietly elegant

【淡妆浓抹】 (of a woman) whether lightly or heavily made up

弹 (dàn) ❶bullet; bomb: 氢～H-bomb; hydrogen bomb; 原子～atom bomb ❷ball; pellet

另见 1204 页 tán

【弹弓】 catapult

【弹壳】 shell case

【弹头】 bullet; warhead

【弹丸之地】 a tiny area; a small bit of land

【弹药】 ammunition

蛋 (dàn) egg; an egg-shaped thing: 下～lay eggs

【蛋白质】 protein

【蛋糕】 cake

【蛋黄】 yolk

【蛋壳】 eggshell

【蛋清】 egg white

dang

当 (dāng) ❶ought; should; must ❷work (or serve, act) as; be ❸bear; accept; deserve ❹manage; be in charge of; direct ❺equal ❻when; as; while in sb.'s presence; to sb.'s face ❼just at (a time or place) ❽the sound of a gong or a bell

另见 950 页 dàng

【当班】 be on duty

【当兵】 serve in the army; be a soldier

【当场】 on the spot; then and there

【当初】 at the beginning; in the first place; at that time; originally

【当代】 the present age; contemporary; the contemporary era

【当地】 at the place in question; in the locality; local

【当红】 be in the height of one's popularity

【当机立断】 decide quickly; make a prompt decision

【当家】 manage household affairs

【当家做主】 be master in one's own house; be the master of one's own affairs (or destiny)

【当今】 nowadays; now; at present

【当面】 to sb.'s face; in sb.'s presence

【当年】in those years; in those days; the prime of life

【当前】❶ current; present ❷ before one; facing one

【当然】❶ natural ❷ naturally; surely; certainly; of course; without doubt ❸ to be sure; as it should be

【当仁不让】not decline to shoulder a responsibility; not leave to others what one ought to do oneself; not pass on to others what one is called upon to do

【当日】the same day

【当时】then; meantime; at that time

【当事人】person (or party) concerned

【当头一棒】a head-on blow

【当务之急】urgent matter; the most pressing matter of the moment; a top priority task

【当心】mind; take care; be careful; look out

【当选】be elected

【当政】be in power; be in office

【当之无愧】fully deserve (a title, an honour, etc.); be worthy of

【当之有愧】not deserve (a title, an honour, etc.); not be worthy of

【当中】among; in the middle of; in the midst of; in the centre of

【当众】in public; in the presence of all

裆 (dāng) ❶ crotch (of trousers) ❷ crotch

挡 (dǎng) ❶ block; resist; get in the way of ❷ keep off; ward off ❸ fender; gear (of a car)

【挡风】shelter sth. from the wind; keep out the wind

【挡路】stand (or get, be) in the way

党 (dǎng) party; political party; clique; gang

【党费】party membership dues

【党风】a party's work style; party conduct

【党籍】party membership

【党纪】party discipline

【党派】political parties and groups; party groupings

【党旗】party flag

【党委】Party Committee

【党员】party member

【党章】constitution of the party

【党支部】party branch

【党中央】the Central Committee of the Party

当 (dàng) ❶ match; equal to ❷ treat as; regard as; take as (or for) ❸ think ❹ pawn ❺ proper; right

另见 949 页 dāng

【当成】regard as; treat as; take for

【当年】the same year; that very year

【当铺】pawnshop

【当时】right away; immediately; at once

【当天】the same day; that very day

【当真】❶ take seriously ❷ in earnest; (really) true ❸ really; sure enough

荡 (dàng) ❶ swing; sway; wave ❷ loaf about ❸ rinse ❹ clear away; sweep off

【荡气回肠】very touching; pathetic

【荡秋千】have a swing

【荡然无存】all gone; nothing left

【荡漾】ripple; undulate

档 (dàng) ❶ shelves (for files); pigeonholes ❷ files; archives ❸ grade

【档案】files; archives; record; dossier

【档次】grade

dao

刀 (dāo) ❶ knife; sword ❷ sth. shaped like a knife: 卷笔~pencil sharpener;

剃须～ razor ❸one hundred sheets (of paper)

【刀叉】knife and fork

【刀光剑影】the glint and flash of daggers and swords

【刀具】cutting tool

【刀口】blade; knife edge; the crucial point

【刀片】razor blade

【刀山火海】a mountain of swords and a sea of flames—most dangerous places; most severe trials

【刀削面】shaved noodles

导 (dǎo) ❶ lead; guide ❷ conduct; transmit ❸ give guidance to; teach; instruct

【导弹】guided missile

【导电】conduct (or transmit) electricity; electric conduction

【导管】pipe; duct

【导航】pilot; navigate

【导火线】❶fuse; (blasting) fuse ❷a small incident that touches off a big one

【导师】teacher; tutor

【导体】conductor

【导线】(conducting) wire; conductor; traverse; harness

【导向】lead; guide; direct; show the way

【导演】❶director ❷direct (a film, play, etc.)

【导游】❶ guide; tour guide ❷ conduct a sightseeing

【导致】cause; bring about; lead to; result in

岛 (dǎo) island

【岛国】island country

【岛屿】islands; islands and islets

捣 (dǎo) pound with a pestle, etc.; beat with stick; smash harass; disturb

【捣蛋】make trouble

【捣鬼】play tricks; do mischief

【捣毁】smash up; destroy; demolish

【捣碎】pound to pieces; stamp breaking; stamp crushing

倒 (dǎo) ❶ fall down ❷ topple ❸ collapse ❹ fail ❺ close down; go bankrupt ❻change; exchange ❼move around

另见 952 页 dào

【倒班】change shifts; work by turns; work in shifts

【倒闭】go bankrupt; close down

【倒霉】unlucky; have bad luck; be out of luck; meet with reverses

【倒塌】fall; collapse; topple down

【倒台】collapse; downfall; fall from power

【倒胃口】spoil one's appetite

祷 (dǎo) ❶pray ❷ask earnestly; ❸beg

【祷告】say one's prayers

到 (dào) ❶arrive; reach ❷go to; leave for ❸ by; until; up to ❹ thoughtful; considerate

【到场】be present; show (or turn) up

【到处】everywhere; about; throughout; around; here and there; up and down; at all places; on all sides

【到处碰壁】run into snags everywhere

【到达】get to (or in); arrive at (or in); reach

【到底】❶ ever; indeed; after all ❷ to the end; to the finish

【到……尽头】at the end of

【到来】❶arrival; advent ❷arrive

【到目前为止】up to now; so far; by now

【到那时】by that time

【到期】become due; mature; expire

【到任】take office; assume a post

D

【到……时为止】by; until; till
【到手】come to hand; in one's hands (or possession)
【到头】throughout; to (or at) the end
【到位】put sth. in place; attain a predetermined position
【到现在】by now

倒 (dào) ❶ pour; tip ❷ turn upside down; move backward ❸inverted on the contrary
另见 951 页 dǎo

【倒背如流】know sth. thoroughly by heart
【倒不如】it's better to do; no better than
【倒车】back a car
【倒挂】hang upside down
【倒计时】countdown: ~钟 countdown clock
【倒垃圾】dump (or tip) rubbish
【倒立】❶stand upside down ❷handstand
【倒退】reverse; fall back; go backwards
【倒影】inverted image; inverted reflection in water
【倒装】❶inversion ❷upside down mounting; upside-down charging

盗 (dào) ❶thief; robber ❷steal; rob

【盗版】piracy; illegal copy
【盗匪】bandits; robbers
【盗窃】steal; rob
【盗用】usurp; embezzle
【盗贼】robber; bandit

悼 (dào) mourn; grieve

【悼词】memorial speech
【悼念】mourn; grieve over

道 (dào) ❶ road; way ❷ channel; course: 快车~ freeway; 人行~ (英) pavement; (美) sidewalk; 小~path ❸ way; method ❹ Taoism ❺ Taoist ❻ say; talk; speak

【道德】morals; morality; ethics
【道贺】congratulate
【道教】Taoism
【道具】prop; stage property
【道理】❶ reason; argument ❷ hows and whys; principle; truth
【道路】way; road; path
【道歉】apologize: 向某人~ make an apology to sb.; say sorry to sb.
【道听途说】hearsay; gossip; rumour: 这是~,不足为信。This is only hearsay, and is not to be taken seriously.
【道喜】congratulate sb. on a happy occasion
【道谢】express one's thanks; thank
【道义】morality and justice

稻 (dào) rice; paddy

【稻草】rice straw
【稻草人】scarecrow; jackstraw
【稻米】rice
【稻田】rice (or paddy) field

de

得 (dé) ❶ get; gain; obtain ❷ result in ❸be finished; be ready ❹ indicating agreement or disagreement
另见 953 页 děi

【得病】get (or fall) ill; become sick
【得不偿失】the loss outweighs the gain
【得逞】prevail; succeed; have one's way: 阴谋未能~。The plot fell through.
【得宠】find favour with sb.
【得出】come to (or reach, arrive at) a conclusion
【得寸进尺】reach for a yard after getting an inch; give him an inch and he'll take a yard (or a mile, an ell); be insatiable

【得当】proper; suitable: 措辞～ aptly word-ed; appropriate wording
【得到】get; gain; obtain; receive
【得分】score; goal
【得奖】be awarded a prize; win a prize
【得力】❶benefit from; get help from ❷capable; competent
【得力助手】right-hand man
【得人心】be loved and supported by the people
【得胜】win; triumph
【得失】gain and loss; success and failure
【得体】proper; appropriate
【得天独厚】be richly endowed by nature; enjoy exceptional advantages
【得心应手】❶with facility; with high proficiency ❷serviceable; handy
【得意】❶proud of oneself; pleased with oneself ❷proudly
【得意扬扬】be immensely proud; look triumphant
【得志】achieve one's ambition; have a successful career
【得罪】offend; displease

德 (dé) ❶virtue; morals: 品～ moral character ❷kindness; favour: 以～报怨 return good for evil
【德才兼备】have both talent and virtue; have both ability and political integrity; combine ability with character
【德高望重】be of noble character and high prestige
【德行】moral integrity; moral conduct
【德育】moral education; moral culture

dei

得 (děi) ❶need 这个项目～两个月才能完成。This project will take two months to complete. ❷must; have to 有问题就～解决。Wherever problems exist, they must be solved.

另见 952 页 dé

deng

灯 (dēng) lamp; light; lantern: 交通～ traffic lights; 路～ street lamp; 台～ desk (or reading) lamp
【灯光】lamplight
【灯会】lantern festival
【灯火辉煌】brilliantly illuminated; blaze with lights
【灯笼】lantern
【灯谜】riddles; lantern riddles
【灯泡】bulb; light bulb
【灯塔】lighthouse; beacon
【灯罩】lampshade

登 (dēng) ❶ascend; mount ❷publish; record; enter ❸press with the foot ❹step on; tread
【登岸】go ashore; land
【登报】publish in the newspaper
【登场】appear on the stage
【登高】climb up; ascend a height
【登广告】advertise
【登机】board a plane
【登记】register; check in; enter one's name
【登陆】❶land ❷landing; disembark
【登录】❶log in ❷register
【登门拜访】pay sb. a visit; call at sb.'s house
【登山】mountain climbing; climb a mountain; mountaineering
【登台】mount a platform; go upon the stage
【登堂入室】pass through the hall into the inner chamber — reach a higher level in one's studies or become more proficient

in one's profession

等 (děng) ❶class; grade: 特～ special class ❷wait; await ❸equal; be equal to ❹when; till ❺and so on; and so forth

【等边】equilateral

D

【等待】await; wait for

【等到】wait until; when; by the time

【等等】❶and so on; so on and so forth ❷wait a minute

【等候】wait; expect

【等级】❶class; grade; rank ❷degree; rate ❸social estate; social stratum

【等价】of equal value; equal in value

【等距离】equidistance

【等式】equality; equation

【等同】equate; be equal

【等闲视之】regard sth. as unimportant; treat sth. lightly (or casually)

【等一下】just a moment; just a minute

【等于】equal to; a mount to; tantamount to

凳 (dèng) stool: 方～square stool; 长～ bench

【凳子】stool; small seat

瞪 (dèng) open (one's eyes) wide; stare; glare

【瞪眼】open one's eyes wide; glare (or stare) at; glower and glare at sb.; get angry with sb.

di

低 (dī) ❶ let droop; hang down ❷ low; short

【低潮】low tide; low ebb

【低成本】low cost

【低调】❶low-keyed ❷play a low profile

【低估】underestimate; underrate

【低级】❶elementary; lower ❷vulgar; low

【低劣】❶mean; low-grade; inferior ❷poor in quality

【低落】low; low-spirited; downcast

【低能】of low ability; mental deficiency; feeble-mindedness

【低人一等】inferior to others

【低三下四】abject; servile; subservient; obsequious

【低烧】low fever; slight fever

【低声】under one's breath; in a low voice; with bated breath

【低声下气】speak humbly and under one's breath; be meek and subservient; be obsequious

【低碳生活】low-carbon lifestyle

【低头】❶ bow (or lower) one's head ❷yield

堤 (dī) dyke; dam

【堤岸】bank

【堤防】embankment

【堤坝】dykes and dams

提 (dī) carry (in one's hand with the arm down): ～溜 carry

另见 1207 页 tí

【提防】be on guard against; be watchful; beware of; take precautions against

滴 (dī) ❶drop ❷drip

【滴答】tick; ticktack

【滴水不进】not take even a drop of water—unable to eat or drink

【滴水不漏】❶watertight ❷tightly packed or completely enclosed

【滴水成冰】(so cold that) the water freezes as it drips; freezing cold

迪 (dí) enlighten; guide

【迪斯科】disco

的 (dí) true; really

【的确】indeed;really

敌 (dí) ❶enemy;foe ❷fight;resist;oppose ❸match;equal

【敌对】hostile;oppose;antagonistic

【敌情】the enemy's situation;the state of the enemy

【敌人】enemy;foe

【敌视】be hostile to (or toward);regard with hostility

【敌我矛盾】contradictions between ourselves and the enemy

【敌意】hostility;enmity

笛 (dí) flute;whistle

【笛子】flute;bamboo flute

的 (dí) true;really

【的确】indeed;really;for certain

嫡 (dí) ❶of or by the wife (as distinguished from a concubine under the feudal-patriarchal system) ❷ of lineal descent;closely related

【嫡传】be handed down in a direct line from the master

诋 (dǐ) slander;defame

【诋毁】vilify;defame;calumniate

抵 (dǐ) ❶support ❷resist;withstand ❸ balance;set off ❹reach;arrive at

【抵偿】make good;compensate for

【抵触】conflict;contradict

【抵达】arrive in (or at);reach

【抵挡】resist;keep out;ward off;check

【抵抗】resist;stand up to;withstand

【抵赖】deny;disclaim;disavow

【抵消】offset;cancel out

【抵押】mortgage

【抵制】boycott;resist

底 (dǐ) ❶bottom;base ❷end ❸ground ❹ins and outs; ❺background;foundation ❻a copy kept as a record

【底层】❶(英) ground floor;(美) first floor ❷bottom

【底稿】draft;manuscript

【底色】bottom;ground color

【底下】below;under;beneath;underneath

【底线】bottom line;base line;end line

【底薪】basic wage

【底子】❶ foundation; base; bottom ❷ sketch ❸a copy

砥 (dǐ) whetstone

【砥柱】baffle

地 (dì) ❶earth; land; soil ❷ fields ❸ ground; floor ❹place; locality ❺position; situation ❻ background; ground ❼distance

【地板】floor

【地步】❶ condition; plight ❷ extent ❸ room for action

【地产】land estate;real estate

【地大物博】vast territory and abundant resources

【地道】❶tunnel;subway ❷genuine;true;pure;typical

【地点】place;spot;location;point;site

【地段】sector of an area

【地方】position;locality;space;place

【地广人稀】a vast but thinly populated area;a vast territory with a sparse population

【地基】foundation

【地窖】cellar;basement

【地理】geography:经济～economic geography;自然～ physical geography

【地灵人杰】a remarkable place produces outstanding people

【地面】the earth's surface;ground;floor

【地平线】horizon:在～上 on the horizon

【地球】the earth; the globe
【地球仪】globe
【地球引力】gravity
【地区】part; area; region; district
【地毯】carpet; rug
D 【地铁】metro; tube; underground; subway
【地图】map; atlas
【地位】position; standing; ranking place; status
【地下】❶underground; subterranean ❷secret (activities)
【地下室】basement; cellar
【地震】earthquake; seism
【地址】address: 回信~return address
【地中海】the Mediterranean (Sea)
【地主】landlord

弟 (dì) younger (or little) brother

【弟妹】❶ younger brother and sister ❷ one's younger brother's wife; sister-in-law
【弟兄】brothers
【弟子】follower; pupil; disciple; student

帝 (dì) ❶god ❷emperor ❸imperialism

【帝国】empire
【帝王】emperor; king

递 (dì) hand over; send to; pass; give

【递加】 progressive increase; increase gradually
【递减】decrease gradually; reduce
【递送】send; deliver
【递增】increase by degree

第 (dì) ❶the first ❷the residence of a high official

【第二】second
【第三】third
【第三产业】tertiary industry; the service industry
【第三世界】the third world
【第一】❶first of all ❷first; primary; foremost
【第一把手】first in command; number one man; a person holding primary responsibility
【第一流】first-class; first-rate
【第一名】❶ first ❷ first place: 得 ~win first place (or a championship); get a first
【第一手】firsthand
【第一线】forefront; front line; first line

缔 (dì) form (a friendship); conclude (a treaty)

【缔交】❶establish diplomatic relations ❷ contract a friendship
【缔结】conclude; establish
【缔造】found; create

dian

掂 (diān) weigh in the hand

【掂量】 ❶weigh in the hand ❷think over; weigh up

颠 (diān) ❶ top; summit ❷ jolt; bump ❸ fall; turn over; topple down ❹ run; go away

【颠簸】jolt; bump; rock; toss
【颠倒】reverse; turn (or put) upside-down
【颠倒是非】confound right and wrong
【颠覆】❶overturn; subvert ❷subversion
【颠来倒去】over and over: 就那么点事，他却~说个没完。It was only a small matter but he kept harping on it.
【颠沛流离】homeless and miserable, drift from place to place
【颠三倒四】disorderly

癫 (diān) mentally deranged; insane

【癫狂】❶demented;mad ❷frivolous

典 (diǎn) ❶standard;law ❷ceremony; allusion; literary quotation ❸ be in charge of ❹mortgage

【典范】model;example

【典故】allusion

【典礼】ceremony;celebration

【典型】❶type;model ❷typical

【典雅】refined;elegant

点 (diǎn) ❶point:起 starting ~;终~ destination;end ❷dot;speck;spot ❸ aspect;feature ❹a little;a bit ❺o'clock ❻light;burn;kindle ❼point out;hint ❽ check ❾drip ❿choose

【点菜】order dishes; choose dishes from a menu

【点灯】light a lamp

【点滴】❶drop ❷a bit

【点火】light a fire;ignition;stir up trouble

【点击】click;hit

【点名】call the roll;mention sb. by name

【点明】point out;put one's finger on

【点球】penalty kick

【点燃】kindle;light;light up

【点数】check the number;count

【点头】nod

【点头之交】nodding (or bowing) acquaintance:我和他只是~。I have only a nodding acquaintance with him. (He and I are only nodding acquaintances.)

【点心】light refreshments;pastry;dessert

【点缀】adorn;ornament;embellish

【点字】Braille(盲文)

【点子】❶spot;dot ❷idea ❸key point ❹to the point;

碘 (diǎn) iodine (I)

【碘酊】tincture of iodine

踮 (diǎn) stand on tiptoe

【踮起脚】stand on tiptoe

电 (diàn) electricity:负~ negative electricity;正~ positive electricity

【电表】electric meter; electricity measuring meter;kilowatt-hour meter

【电冰箱】fridge; freezer; refrigerator; icebox

【电波】electric wave;radio wave

【电车】tram;trolley;streetcar;trolleybus

【电池】battery;cell:太阳能 ~ solar cell

【电磁波】electromagnetic wave

【电灯】electric lamp;electric light

【电工】electrician

【电话】phone;phone call;telephone:挂上~hang up;回~call back;长途~long distance call;市内~local call

【电话簿】telephone directory (or book)

【电话占线】the line is busy; number engaged

【电缆】cable

【电力】electricity;electric power

【电铃】electric bell

【电流】electric current

【电炉】electric stove

【电路】electric circuit

【电脑】computer

【电脑病毒】computer virus

【电脑黑客】computer hacker

【电瓶车】electromobile; storage battery car

【电器】electric device;electric appliance

【电扇】electric fan

【电视】television (or TV):看~ watch television

【电视机】television set

【电视剧】TV play

【电视台】TV station;television station

【电梯】lift;elevator

【电筒】torch;flashlight

【电线】(electric) wire

【电信】telecommunications

【电影】film;movie;motion picture:彩色～color film

【电影演员】film (or movie) actor (or actress)

D

【电影院】cinema;movie house;movie theatre

【电源】power supply (or source);mains

【电子计算机】electronic computer

【电子商务】e-business;e-commerce

【电子图书】electronic books;e-book

【电子网络】electrical network

【电子邮件】e-mail

店 (diàn) ❶ shop; store: 书～bookshop; bookstore; 水果～fruit stall; 食品～food provision store ❷inn: 住～stop at an inn

【店铺】shop;store

【店员】clerk;shop assistant;salesman

【店主】shopkeeper;storekeeper

玷 (diàn) ❶a flaw in a piece of jade ❷ blemish;disgrace

【玷污】stain;sully;tarnish

垫 (diàn) ❶mat;pad:椅～chair cushion ❷fill up;pad;put under

【垫板】❶ base plate; underboarding ❷ make ready overlay

【垫付】pay for sb. and expect to be repaid later

【垫平】level up

【垫子】mat;pad;cushion

淀 (diàn) ❶form sediment;settle;precipitate ❷(usu. used as part of a place name) shallow lake: 白洋～ Baiyangdian Lake (in Hebei Province)

【淀粉】starch;amylum

惦 (diàn) remember with concern; be concerned about

【惦记】remember with concern; be concerned about;keep thinking about

【惦念】keep thinking about; be anxious about

奠 (diàn) ❶ establish; settle ❷ make offerings to the spirits of the dead

【奠定】establish;settle

【奠基】lay a foundation (or cornerstone)

殿 (diàn) ❶ hall; palace; temple ❷ at the rear

【殿军】rearguard a person who comes last in a contest or last among the winners; the last of the successful candidates

【殿堂】palace or temple buildings (or halls)

diao

刁 (diāo) tricky;sly

【刁悍】cunning and fierce

【刁难】create difficulties;make things difficult

【刁钻】artful;wily

叼 (diāo)hold in the mouth

凋 (diāo)wither

【凋零】withered, fallen and scattered about

【凋落】wither and fall

【凋谢】wither and fall

貂 (diāo)marten

【貂皮】fur of pelt of a marten;marten

碉 (diāo)

【碉堡】stronghold;blockhouse;pillbox

【碉楼】watch tower

雕 (diāo) ❶carve;engrave ❷ vulture

【雕虫小技】insignificant skill (esp. in writing); the trifling skill of a scribe; literary skill of no high order

【雕刻】carve; engrave

【雕梁画栋】carved beams and painted rafters—a richly ornamented building

【雕塑】sculpture

【雕像】statue

【雕琢】❶cut and polish (jade) ❷write in an ornate style

吊 (diào) ❶hang; suspend ❷lift up or let down with a rope, etc. ❸condole; mourn ❹put in a fur lining ❺revoke; withdraw ❻crane

【吊车】crane; hoist

【吊床】hammock

【吊灯】pendent lamp

【吊桥】suspension bridge

【吊扇】ceiling fan

【吊销】revoke; withdraw

【吊唁】condole

钓 (diào) fish with a hook and line; angle

【钓饵】bait

【钓竿】fishing pole; fishing rod; angling rod

【钓钩】fishhook; hook

【钓具】fishing tackle

【钓鱼】angle; go fishing

调 (diào) ❶tone; tune; melody; air ❷transfer; move; shift

另见 1211 页 tiáo

【调查】investigate; examine; look into; inquire into; survey

【调查问卷】questionnaire: 发出～ distribute questionnaires

【调动】❶arouse; bring into play; mobilize ❷shift; transfer; move

【调度】arrange; dispatch; control

【调虎离山】lure the tiger out of the mountains; lure the enemy away from his base

【调换】change; exchange

【调配】allocate; deploy

【调遣】assign; dispatch: 听从～ (be ready to) accept an assignment

【调研】investigate and study

【调运】allocate and transport

【调职】be transferred to another post

【调子】❶tune; melody ❷tone (of speech)

掉 (diào) ❶fall; drop; come off ❷reduce ❸fall behind ❹turn ❺change; exchange ❻(used after certain verbs indicate removal)

【掉队】fall (or lag) behind; drop out (or off)

【掉泪】come to tears; tears falling

【掉色】lose color; fade

【掉头】turn away (or round, about); turn one's head

【掉眼泪】shed tears; come to tears

die

爹 (diē) father; dad; daddy; pa

【爹爹】father; dad; daddy; pa

跌 (diē) fall; drop; tumble; stumble

【跌打损伤】injuries from falls and knocks

【跌倒】tumble; fall

【跌价】❶fall (or drop) in price ❷price reduction

【跌跤】fall

【跌伤】fall and get hurt

迭 (dié) ❶alternate; change ❷repeatedly; again and again ❸in time for

【迭起】occur repeatedly; happen frequently

D

谍 (dié) ❶ espionage ❷ intelligence agent; spy

【谍报】❶ information obtained through espionage ❷ intelligence report; intelligence

喋 (dié)

【喋喋不休】chatter away; talk endlessly

叠 (dié) ❶pile up ❷repeat ❸fold

【叠起】pile up; fold up

【叠字】reduplicated word; reduplication

碟 (dié) small plate; small dish

【碟子】small plate (or dish)

蝶 (dié) butterfly

【蝶泳】butterfly stroke

ding

丁 (dīng) ❶man ❷members of a family; population ❸a person engaged in a certain occupation ❹ small cubes of meat or vegetable ❺ the fourth of the ten Heavenly Stems

【丁克族】DINKS (a short term for "dual income, no kids")

【丁香】❶lilac ❷clove

叮 (dīng) sting; bite

【叮嘱】urge again and again; warn; exhort

盯 (dīng) stare; stare (or gaze) at

【盯住】keep close watch on; fix one's eyes on

钉 (dīng) ❶ nail; tack ❷ urge; press ❸ follow closely

另见 961 页 dìng

【钉锤】nail hammer

【钉鞋】spiked shoes; spikes

【钉子】nail; snag

顶 (dǐng) ❶ peak; top ❷ go against ❸carryon the head ❹take the place of ❺most ❻best ❼retort; turn down ❽ cope with; stand up to ❾take the place of; substitute; replace ❿very; most; extremely

【顶部】top; roof

【顶点】summit; peak; zenith; pinnacle; vertex; apex

【顶多】at the most; at best

【顶风冒雨】brave wind and rain; be undeterred by wind and rain; in spite of wind and rain

【顶尖】❶tip ❷top; first rate; topnotch

【顶梁柱】backbone; pillar

【顶替】take the place of; substitute; replace; instead

【顶天立地】indomitable; gigantic

【顶头上司】one's direct superior; immediate superior

【顶用】be of use; serve the purpose

【顶针】thimble

【顶撞】contradict (one's elder or superior)

【顶嘴】talk (or answer) back; reply defiantly

鼎 (dǐng) ❶ an ancient cooking vessel with two loop handles and three or four legs ❷pot ❸enter upon a period of

【鼎沸】like a seething cauldron; noisy and confused

【鼎盛时期】prime; heyday; in a period of great prosperity; at the height of power and splendour

【鼎足之势】tripartite balance of forces; triangular balance of power

订 (dìng) ❶ conclude; draw up; agree on ❷ subscribe to (a newspaper, etc.); book (seats, tickets, etc.); order ❸revise; ❹make corrections ❺staple together

【订单】order for goods

【订合同】make (or enter into) a contract

【订婚】be engaged (to be married); be betrothed

【订货】place an order for goods

【订立】conclude (a treaty or an agreement); make (a contract, etc.)

【订阅】subscribe to (a newspaper, periodical, etc.)

【订正】make corrections; revise; emend

钉 (dìng) nail; sew on
另见 960 页 dīng

定 (dìng) ❶decide ❷fix; set ❸fixed; settled; established ❹stable; calm ❺subscribe to; book (seats, tickets, etc.) ❻surely; certainly; definitely

【定夺】make a final decision; decide

【定额】quota; norm

【定稿】❶final draft; final version or text ❷finalize a manuscript

【定购】a system of fixed quotas for purchasing

【定价】❶fix a price ❷fixed price; price

【定见】definite opinion; set view: 这事儿请你们讨论，我没有～。Please discuss the matter among yourselves. I have no definite opinion about it.

【定金】earnest; deposit; down payment

【定居】settle down

【定律】law

【定论】final decision

【定期】❶regular; periodical ❷regularly; at a fixed time; at regular intervals ❸fix a date

【定期存款】fixed deposit; time deposit

【定然】definitely; certainly

【定神】❶collect oneself; compose oneself; pull oneself together ❷concentrate one's attention

【定时炸弹】time bomb

【定数】❶fix a number or amount ❷a fixed number or amount

【定位】❶fixed position; location; orientation ❷orientate; position

【定限】❶a fixed limit (to quantity, or degree) ❷a fixed time limit

【定义】definition

【定罪】declare sb. guilty; convict sb. of a crime

【定做】have sth. made to order (or measure)

diu

丢 (diū) ❶lose; mislay ❷throw; cast ❸put (or lay) aside

【丢丑】lose face

【丢掉】❶lose ❷discard; throw away; cast away

【丢饭碗】lose one's job

【丢面子】lose face

【丢弃】abandon; give up; discard

【丢人现眼】make a fool of oneself; make a spectacle of oneself

【丢三落四】forgetful; scatterbrained

【丢失】lose

【丢卒保车】give up a pawn to save a chariot—sacrifice minor things to save major ones

dong

东 (dōng) ❶east: 中～Middle East; 远～Far East ❷owner; master ❸host

【东半球】the Eastern Hemisphere

【东北】northeast; northeast of China; the Northeast

【东奔西跑】run around here and there
【东窗事发】be exposed; come to the light
【东倒西歪】leaning; unsteady; tottering: 三间~的屋子 three tumbledown rooms
【东道主】host
D 【东方】❶the east ❷the East; the Orient
【东海】the East China Sea
【东拉西扯】drag in irrelevant matters; talk at random; ramble
【东南】southeast; southeast China; the Southeast
【东南亚】Southeast Asia
【东跑西颠】rush here and hurry there; rush about
【东拼西凑】scrape together
【东山再起】stage a comeback; bob up like a cork
【东西】❶ thing ❷ creature ❸ from east to west
【东亚】East Asia
【东张西望】gaze around; peer around

冬 (dōng) ❶ winter ❷ dub-a-dub; rat tat
【冬瓜】wax gourd; white gourd
【冬季】winter
【冬眠】winter sleep; hibernation
【冬泳】winter outdoor swimming

董 (dǒng) ❶direct; superintend; supervise ❷director; trustee
【董事】director; trustee
【董事会】board of directors
【董事长】chairman of the board

懂 (dǒng) understand; know
【懂礼貌】have good manners
【懂事】❶sensible ❷intelligent

动 (dòng) ❶action ❷move; stir; shake ❸ act ❹ touch; move; arouse ❺change
【动不动】easily; frequently
【动产】movable property; movables; personal property
【动车】bullet train
【动工】start building
【动画片】cartoon; animated drawing
【动机】motive; intention
【动静】movement; activity; the sound of sth. astir
【动力】❶motive (or driving) power ❷motive (or driving) force
【动乱】disturbance; turbulence
【动脉】artery
【动脑筋】think hard
【动人】charming; pleasing; touching; attractive; moving; exciting
【动身】leave for (for a distant place); set out on a journey; start; start (or set) off
【动手】❶start work; get to work ❷touch; handle ❸raise a hand to strike; hit out
【动手动脚】get fresh with sb.: 别~的。Keep your hands to yourself.
【动手术】operate; perform an operation
【动态】trends; developments
【动听】interesting (or pleasant) to listen to; pleasing to the ear
【动武】start a fight; come to blows
【动物】creature; animal
【动物园】zoo; zoological garden
【动心】one's mind is perturbed; one's desire, enthusiasm is aroused
【动摇】shake; waver
【动用】employ; use; draw on
【动作】movement; motion; action

冻 (dòng) ❶freeze ❷feel very cold; be frostbitten ❸jelly
【冻疮】chilblain
【冻结】❶freeze ❷freezing
【冻伤】frostbite

【冻死】freeze to death; die of frost

栋 (dòng) ❶ ridgepole ❷ (for buildings)

【栋梁】ridgepole and beam—pillar of the state

【栋梁之材】one with the makings of a statesman

洞 (dòng) ❶ cave; hole; opening ❷ penetratingly; thoroughly

【洞察】have an insight into; see (or understand) clearly

【洞察力】insight; perception

【洞穿】pierce through; penetrate

【洞房】bridal (or nuptial) chamber

【洞见症结】see clearly the crux of the matter; get to the heart of the problem

【洞悉】know clearly; understand thoroughly

【洞晓】have a clear knowledge of

【洞穴】cave; cavern

胴 (dòng) ❶ trunk; body ❷ large intestine

【胴体】trunk (esp. of a slaughtered animal); carcass

dou

都 (dōu) all; both; even already
另见 964 页 dū

【都不】neither …nor …; none of

兜 (dōu) ❶ pocket; bag ❷ wrap up in a piece of cloth, etc. ❸ move round ❹ take upon oneself; take responsibility for sth.

【兜风】❶ catch the wind ❷ go for a ride or drive, ride or sail

【兜圈子】❶ go around in circles; circle ❷ beat about the bush

篼 (dōu) container made of bamboo, wicker, ratten, etc.

【篼子】a bamboo chair for one person carried on two poles by two men

斗 (dǒu) ❶ dou (=1 decalitre), a unit of dry measure for grain ❷ a dou measure ❸ an object shaped like a cup or dipper
另见本页 dòu

【斗胆】make bold; venture

【斗笠】bamboo hat

抖 (dǒu) ❶ tremble; shiver; quiver ❷ shake; jerk rouse; stir up ❸ get on in the world: 冷得发～shiver with cold

【抖动】shake; tremble; vibrate

【抖擞】enliven; rouse

陡 (dǒu) ❶ steep; precipitous ❷ suddenly; abruptly

【陡立】rise steeply

【陡坡】steep slope

【陡然】suddenly

斗 (dòu) ❶ contest (or contend) with ❷ struggle against ❸ fight
另见本页 dǒu

【斗牛】bullfight

【斗殴】fight; exchange blows

【斗争】❶ struggle; fight; battle; combat ❷ accuse and denounce at a meeting ❸ strive for; fight for

【斗志】will to fight; fighting will

【斗嘴】quarrel

豆 (dòu) bean; pea; anything in the form of a bean or pea: 豌～ peas

【豆瓣酱】thick broad-bean sauce

【豆腐】bean curd; tofu

【豆浆】soy bean milk

【豆蔻年华】a blooming girl; an adolescent girl; marriageable age

【豆沙】sweetened bean paste

【豆芽儿】bean sprouts

逗 (dòu) ❶ stay; stop ❷ amuse tease; play with ❸ provoke (laughter, etc.)

【逗号】comma(,)

【逗乐】tickle;amuse

【逗留】stay;remain;stop

【逗引】tease

痘 (dòu) ❶smallpox ❷smallpox pustule ❸(bovine) vaccine

【痘苗】(bovine) vaccine

du

都 (dū) ❶capital (of a country) ❷big city;metropolis

另见 963 页 dōu

【都市】a big city;metropolis

【都市化】urbanization

督 (dū)superintend and direct

【督办】supervise and manage

【督促】supervise and urge:已经布置了的工作,应当认真~检查。We must supervise and accelerate fulfilment of the assignments.

毒 (dú) ❶poison;toxin ❷narcotics ❸poisonous;noxious;poisoned ❹malicious; ❺cruel;fierce ❻kill with poison

【毒打】beat up;beat cruelly

【毒贩】drug dealer;drug trafficker

【毒害】❶murder by poisoning ❷poison (sb.'s mind)

【毒辣】cruel;fierce;vicious;sinister;diabolic

【毒品】narcotic drugs

【毒杀】kill with poison

【毒蛇】poisonous snake

【毒手】murderous scheme

【毒素】toxin;toxicant

【毒物】poison

【毒药】poison;toxicant

【毒液】venom

【毒瘾】drug addiction

独 (dú) ❶single;only ❷alone;by oneself;in solitude ❸old people without offspring;the childless

【独霸】dominate exclusively;monopolize

【独白】soliloquy;monologue

【独裁】dictatorship;autocratic rule

【独出心裁】show originality;by original

【独创】original creation

【独当一面】take charge of a department or locality; assume responsibility for a certain sector

【独到之处】distinctive qualities; specific characteristics

【独具匠心】show ingenuity; have originality

【独具一格】be original in style

【独来独往】coming and going all alone—unsociable; aloof:她老是~的。She kept pretty much to herself.

【独立】❶independence ❷independent;by oneself;on one's own ❸separate

【独立思考】independent thinking

【独立性】independence

【独立自主】stand on one's own;maintain independence and keep the initiative in one's own hands

【独身】❶singleness ❷unmarried;single;separated from one's family

【独生子女】only child

【独树一帜】fly one's own colors—develop a school of one's own

【独特】unique;peculiar;distinctive

【独一无二】unmatched; unique; matchless;unparalleled

【独占鳌头】come out first;head the list of successful candidates;be the champion

【独自】alone;by oneself

【独奏】solo;play a solo:钢琴~ piano solo

读 (dú) ❶read; read aloud ❷attend (or go to) school

【读书】❶ read ❷ study ❸ attend (or go to) school

【读书笔记】reading notes

【读物】reading material: 科普～popular science readings; 课外～books for outside reading

【读音】pronunciation

【读者】reader

渎 (dú) ❶show disrespect or contempt ❷ditch; drain

【渎职】malfeasance; dereliction of duty

笃 (dǔ) ❶ sincere; earnest ❷ serious; critical

【笃信】sincerely believe in; be a devout believer in

堵 (dǔ) ❶stop up; block up ❷stifled; suffocated ❸ wall

【堵车】traffic jam; traffic congestion

【堵塞】stop up; block up: 交通～traffic jam

赌 (dǔ) gamble; bet

【赌博】gamble

【赌场】gambling house

【赌气】feel wronged and act rashly

【赌徒】gambler

【赌注】stake

睹 (dǔ) see

【睹物思人】seeing the thing one thinks of the person—the thing reminds one of its owner

杜 (dù) shut out; stop; prevent

【杜鹃】❶cuckoo ❷azalea

【杜绝】stop; put an end to

【杜撰】make up; fabricate

肚 (dù) belly; stomach; abdomen

【肚量】tolerance

【肚脐】navel; belly button

【肚子】belly; stomach

妒 (dù) envy; be jealous of; be envious of

【妒忌】be jealous of; envy

【妒贤嫉能】be jealous of the worthy and the able

度 (dù) ❶measure; degree ❷limit; extend ❸ time; occasion ❹ spend; pass ❺ a unit of measurement for angles, temperature, etc.; degree kilowatt-hour (kwh) ❻ tolerance; magnanimity ❼ consideration ❽ occasion; time ❾ spend; pass

【度过】spend; pass

【度假】have (or spend) one's holidays

【度量】tolerance; magnanimity

【度量衡】length, capacity and weight; weights and measures

【度蜜月】spend one's honeymoon

渡 (dù) ❶ cross ❷ tide over; pull through

【渡船】ferryboat

【渡过难关】pull through; get (or tide) over difficulties: 帮助某人～ see sb. through

【渡河】cross a river

【渡口】ferry crossing

镀 (dù) plate

【镀金】❶gold-plating ❷get gilded

【镀铜】copper facing; copper plating

【镀银】silver-plating; silvering

duan

端 (duān) ❶end; beginning ❷hold sth. level with both hands; carry ❸ ex-

tremity
【端口】port
【端午节】the Dragon Boat Festival
【端详】❶details ❷look sb. up and down
【端正】❶ upright; regular ❷ proper; correct
【端庄】dignified; sedate

短 (duǎn) ❶lack ❷weak point; fault ❸ short; brief
【短波】short-wave
【短处】shortcoming; fault; weakness; failing
【短见】❶shortsighted view ❷suicide
【短裤】shorts
【短路】short circuit
【短跑】dash; sprint
【短篇小说】short story
【短评】brief comment
【短期】short-term:在～内 in a short (or brief) time
【短浅】narrow and shallow:目光～short-sighted
【短缺】shortage; be short of; deficient
【短途旅行】brief trip
【短袜】socks
【短小精悍】❶not of imposing stature but strong and capable ❷short and pithy
【短信息】short message
【短语】phrase
【短暂】of short duration; brief

段 (duàn) ❶ part; passage section ❷ paragraph; ; piece
【段落】passage; paragraph

断 (duàn) ❶break (or cut) off; stop; snap; give up; abstain from decide; judge:当机立～ make a prompt decision ❷ absolutely; decidedly
【断定】judge; conclude; decide; claim
【断断续续】now and then; off and on
【断交】break off the friendship (or diplomatic relations); break off diplomatic ties
【断裂】break; crack
【断然】flatly; absolutely; positively
【断线】disconnect; break off
【断线风筝】a kite with a broken string—gone beyond recall
【断言】affirm; say with certainty; assert categorically
【断章取义】quote or interpret out of context
【断肢再植】replantation of a severed limb

缎 (duàn) satin
【缎纹】satin weave

煅 (duàn) ❶forge ❷calcine
【煅烧】calcine

锻 (duàn) forge
【锻炼】❶ have physical training; take exercise ❷temper; steel
【锻造】forging; smithing

dui

堆 (duī) ❶ heap; pile; stack ❷ pile (or heap) up
【堆放】pile (or heap) up; stack
【堆积】pile up; heap up

队 (duì) team; group: 客～visiting team; 主～home team
【队伍】procession; ranks; troops: 游行～procession; parade
【队形】formation
【队友】teammate; fellow player
【队员】team member: 替补～ substitute
【队长】team leader

对 (duì) ❶pair; couple ❷answer; reply ❸treat; cope with ❹ face ❺ check;

compare ❻right; correct ❼opposite; opposing ❽be directed at ❾at; to; toward

【对岸】the opposite bank; the other side of the river

【对半】half-and-half; fifty-fifty

【对比】contrast: 鲜明～ a sharp contrast

【对不起】❶excuse me; sorry; pardon me; I beg your pardon ❷let sb. down; be unworthy of; do a disservice to; be unfair to

【对策】countermeasure; countermove

【对称】symmetry

【对答如流】answer fluently; answer questions without hesitation

【对待】treat; handle; regard:

【对等】equity; reciprocity

【对方】the opposite side; the other party

【对付】manage; do (or deal, cope) with; tackle

【对号】❶check the number ❷tally; fit; match ❸check mark (√); tick

【对号入座】sit in the right seat

【对话】dialogue

【对接】link up

【对抗】❶antagonism; confrontation ❷oppose; confront ❸against

【对立】opposite; oppose; set sth. against; be antagonistic to

【对联】antithetical couplet

【对面】❶opposite ❷face to face; right in front

【对牛弹琴】play the lute to a cow—choose the wrong audience

【对手】opponent; adversary; enemy match; equal

【对外】external; foreign

【对外开放】opening to the outside world

【对外贸易】foreign trade

【对象】❶target; object ❷boy (or girl) friend

【对应】correspond

【对于】toward; about; for; over; in relation to; as to; with regard to

【对照】contrast; compare

【对症下药】suit the medicine to the illness

【对峙】stand facing each other; confront each other

【对准】aim at

兑 (duì) exchange

【兑换】change; exchange

【兑奖】cash in a lottery ticket

【兑现】❶cash; get cash for ❷fulfil; make good: 政策～materialize a policy

dun

吨 (dūn) ton; metric ton

【吨位】tonnage

蹲 (dūn) ❶squat on the heels; crouch ❷stay

【蹲点】work at a selected spot

【蹲下】squat down

炖 (dùn) ❶stew ❷warm sth. by putting the container in hot water

钝 (dùn) ❶dull ❷stupid; slow

【钝刀】dull knife

【钝角】obtuse angle

顿 (dùn) ❶pause ❷settle ❸suddenly; immediately

【顿号】slight pause mark

【顿开茅塞】suddenly see the light; be suddenly enlightened: 闻兄大教，～。Your excellent advice has opened my eyes.

【顿时】at once; immediately

遁 (dùn) escape; flee; fly

【遁迹】live in seclusion

【遁入空门】become a monk or nun

duo

D

多 (duō) ❶ many; much; more ❷ have (a specified amount) more or too much ❸ (used in questions) to what extent ❹ (used in exclamations) to what an extent ❺ to an unspecified extent: 很~a great deal; a good many; plenty of

【多半】❶most; most likely ❷mostly

【多边】multilateral

【多变】varied; changeable; changeful

【多才多艺】versatile; gifted in many ways

【多愁善感】be sentimental; emotional; sensitive

【多此一举】make an unnecessary move

【多次】many times; again and again; time and again

【多多少少】more or less

【多方面】many-sided; in many ways

【多功能】multi-functional; multi-purpose

【多管闲事】poke one's nose into others' business

【多亏】thanks to

【多劳多得】more pay for more work

【多么】how; what

【多媒体】multimedia

【多面手】a many-sided person; a versatile person; an all-rounder

【多面体】polyhedron

【多谋善断】resourceful and decisive; sagacious and resolute

【多瑙河】the Danube

【多少】number; amount; more or less; to some extent; some what; as much as

【多事之秋】an eventful period or year; troubled times

【多数】majority; most

【多退少补】refund for any overpayment or a supplemental payment for any deficiency

【多样化】diversification

【多疑】suspicious

【多余】surplus; unnecessary; spare

【多雨】rainy

【多元化】be pluralistic; pluralise

【多云】cloudy

【多种多样】varied; manifold

【多嘴】speak out of turn; long-tongued; shoot off one's mouth

哆 (duō)

【哆嗦】tremble; shiver: 气得直~tremble with rage

夺 (duó) ❶ seize; take by force; wrest ❷contend (or compete, strive) for ❸force one's way; deprive ❹decide

【夺标】❶win the first prize; win the trophy (or championship) ❷ win the contract

【夺得】get; win; obtain

【夺回】recapture; retake; seize back

【夺取】capture; strive for; seize

【夺去】take away from

【夺走】take away from

垛 (duǒ) ❶buttress ❷battlements

【垛口】crenel

踱 (duǒ) pace; stroll

【踱来踱去】pace up and down; pace to and fro

躲 (duǒ) hide; conceal

【躲藏】hide (or conceal) oneself; go

into hiding

【躲开】hide; avoid; withdraw; keep out of

【躲懒】shy away from work

【躲雨】take shelter from the rain

【躲债】avoid a creditor

舵 (duò) rudder; helm: 掌～ take the helm

【舵手】helmsman; steersman

堕 (duò) fall; sink; descend

【堕落】sink low; degenerate

惰 (duò) lazy; idle

【惰性】inertia

跺 (duò) stamp (one's foot)

E

E e

e

阿 (ē) play up to; pander to
另见 879 页 ā

【阿弥陀佛】❶ Amitabha Buddha (who presides over the Western Paradise and whose name is used as an incantation repeated by the faithful) ❷(used as an exclamation) may Buddha preserve us; Buddha be praised

【阿谀奉承】flatter; toady to; fawn upon

婀 (ē)

【婀娜】(of a woman's bearing) graceful

讹 (é) ❶ erroneous; mistaken ❷ extort; blackmail

【讹传】false rumour

俄 (é) ❶very soon; presently; suddenly ❷Russian

【俄罗斯人】Russian

【俄语】Russian

鹅 (é) goose

【鹅蛋】goose egg

【鹅卵石】cobblestone; cobble

额 (é) ❶forehead ❷a horizontal tablet ❸specified number (or amount)

【额度】quota; limit

【额头】forehead

【额外】extra; additional; added

恶 (ě)
另见本页 è; 1235 页 wù

【恶心】feel sick

厄 (è) ❶a strategic point ❷adversity; disaster; hardship

【厄运】misfortune

扼 (è) ❶clutch; grip ❷guard; control

【扼杀】strangle; throttle

【扼要】brief and to the point

恶 (è) ❶evil; wickedness ❷fierce; ferocious ❸wicked; bad
另见本页 ě; 1235 页 wù

【恶毒】evil; vicious; malicious; venomous

【恶狠狠】fierce; ferocious

【恶化】take a turn for the worse; worsen; deteriorate

【恶劣】disgusting; bad

【恶人】wicked fellow; evil person

【恶习】bad habit

【恶性】malignant; vicious

【恶性循环】vicious cycle

【恶意】ill will; evil intentions; malice

【恶作剧】trick; mischief

饿 (è) ❶hunger ❷hungry

【饿虎扑食】like a hungry tiger pouncing on its prey

【饿死】be starved to death

颚 (è) jaw：上～upper jaw；下～lower jaw

遏 (è)check；hold back

【遏制】keep within limits；contain

噩 (è) shocking；upsetting

【噩耗】bad news；grievous news

【噩梦】horrible dream；nightmare

鳄 (è)

【鳄鱼】crocodile；alligator

en

恩 (ēn) kindness；favour；grace

【恩爱】❶be deeply in love with each other；affectionate ❷conjugal love

【恩惠】grace；kindness；favour：给某人以～do someone a favour

【恩情】loving-kindness

【恩人】benefactor

er

儿 (ér)youngster；youth；son；child

【儿歌】children's song

【儿科】pediatrics

【儿女】sons and daughters；children

【儿孙】children and grandchildren；descendants；posterity

【儿童】children；kids

【儿童读物】children's books

【儿童节】Children's Day

【儿媳】daughter-in-law

【儿戏】trifling matter

而 (ér)but；yet；and；while

【而后】after that；then

【而且】besides；moreover；and also；but also

【而已】that is all；nothing more

耳 (ěr) ear；ear of a utensil：内～the inner ear；外～the outer ear

【耳垂】earlobe

【耳朵】ear

【耳光】a slap on the face；a box on the ear：打某人～box sb.'s ear；slap sb.'s face

【耳环】earring

【耳机】earphone

【耳聋】deaf

【耳目一新】find everything fresh and new

【耳闻目睹】what one sees and hears

【耳语】whisper；whisper in sb.'s ear；

饵 (ěr) bait；lure cakes；pastry

二 (èr) ❶two ❷different

【二百五】❶ stupid person ❷smatterer

【二分之一】half

【二胡】erhu fiddle，a two-stringed bowed instrument

【二郎腿】cross-legged

【二楼】(英)first floor；(美)second floor

【二手】secondhand

【二手房】second-hand house；resold apartment

【二手烟】passive smoking；second hand smoking

【二氧化碳】carbon dioxide

【二月】February

F f

F

fa

发 (fā) ❶send out; deliver; distribute; issue ❷ discharge; shoot; emit ❸come (or bring) into existence ❹start; set out ❺ swell; expand ❻ (of foodstuffs) rise or expand when fermented or soaked ❼prosper ❽open up; discover ❾get into a certain state; become ❿showone's feeling

另见 973 页 fà

【发表】 publish; announce; bring out; issue

【发表演说】 make a speech

【发表意见】 express an opinion

【发布命令】 give an order; issue orders

【发财】 make a fortune; get rich

【发车】 depart; dispatch a car (truck, bus, etc.)

【发出】 send off (or out); let out; give off; issue

【发达】 ❶ develop; prosper ❷ developed; flourishing

【发达国家】 developed country

【发呆】 be in a trance; stare blankly; be in a daze

【发电】 ❶generate electricity ❷power generation ❸furnish power

【发动】 start; launch

【发抖】 shiver; tremble; shake

【发放】 issue; grant; distribute

【发奋】 work energetically (hard); exert oneself; rouse oneself

【发疯】 go mad; be out of one's mind

【发工资】 pay out wages

【发光】 give out light; shine; beam; glow

【发慌】 feel nervous; feel alarmed

【发挥】 give play to; bring into play

【发火】 get angry; flare up

【发货】 send out goods; deliver goods

【发奖】 award a prize

【发觉】 discover; find out; detect

【发掘】 excavate; unearth

【发狂】 go crazy (or mad)

【发牢骚】 complain; grumble

【发亮】 shine

【发霉】 go mouldy; become mildewed

【发明】 ❶invent ❷invention

【发明家】 inventor

【发票】 bill; receipt; invoice

【发起】 ❶initiate ❷launch; start

【发人深思】 set people thinking; call for deep thought

【发烧】 fever; have a fever; run a temperature

【发射】 shoot; send; launch; let fly; fire

【发生】 happen; occur; take place; go on; bring (or come) about; break out

【发誓】 swear; pledge; vow

【发通知】issue a notice
【发现】❶discover；find out；come across；catch sight of ❷realize；notice
【发笑】laugh
【发泄】vent；let off
【发行】distribute；issue；publish；put out
【发芽】sprout；come up
【发言】❶speech ❷take the floor；speak；make a speech
【发炎】get inflamed
【发扬】develop；carry on
【发音】❶pronounce ❷pronunciation
【发育】grow；develop
【发源地】birthplace；fountainhead；source
【发展】❶develop；grow；expand ❷development
【发展中国家】developing country
【发作】❶break out；burst out ❷flare up

乏 (fá) ❶lack ❷tired；weary

【乏味】dull；tasteless

伐 (fá) chop；fell；cut down

【伐木】lumbering；felling；cutting

罚 (fá) punish

【罚金】fine；forfeit
【罚款】fine；penalty：处以～fine sb.；impose a fine on sb.
【罚球】penalty shot；penalty kick

阀 (fá) valve

【阀门】valve

筏 (fá) raft

【筏道】log chute；logway
【筏子】raft

法 (fǎ) ❶law；rule：守～observe the law；违～break the law ❷way；method；mode ❸follow；model after：效～take as model ❹religious doctrine

【法宝】a magic weapon
【法典】code
【法定】legal
【法官】judge；justice
【法规】statutes；laws and regulations
【法纪】law and discipline
【法律】law；statute：制定～make laws
【法人】legal person；juridical person；corporation
【法庭】court；tribunal
【法学】the science of law
【法医】forensic doctor
【法语】French
【法院】court；law court；court of justice
【法则】law；rule：自然～law of nature
【法制】legal system；legality
【法治】rule by law；government by law；governed by law

发 (fà) hair：理～have one's hair cut；染～have one's hair dyed；烫～have a permanent wave；洗～have one's hair shampooed (or washed)

另见 972 页 fā

【发际】hairline
【发夹】hairpin；hair clip；bobby pin
【发式】hairstyle；hairdo；coiffure

fan

帆 (fān) sail

【帆板】windsurfer；sailboard
【帆布】canvas；duck
【帆船】sailing boat；junk；sailboat

番 (fān) ❶aborigines ❷foreign；barbarian ❸(used in names for certain plants originally introduced from abroad)

【番号】the designation of a military unit

【番茄】tomato

【番薯】sweet potato

翻 (fān) ❶ turn over; ❷ turn upside down or inside out ❸ reverse ❹cross; get over ❺ search ❻ multiply ❼translate ❽fall out; break up

F

【翻案】reverse a verdict

【翻版】reproduction; copy; reprint

【翻番】increase by a specified number of times

【翻跟头】turn somersaults (or handsprings)

【翻滚】tumble; roll over; toss

【翻来覆去】❶ toss and turn ❷ again and again; repeatedly

【翻录】pirate recordings

【翻身】❶free oneself; stand up ❷turn (or roll) over

【翻天覆地】earth-shaking; world-shaking

【翻译】❶translate; interpret ❷translation

【翻印】reprint

凡 (fán) ❶ ordinary ❷ this mortal world; the earth ❸ every; any; all ❹altogether

【凡例】notes on the use of a book etc.; guide to the use of a book, etc.

【凡人】❶ordinary person ❷mortal

【凡事】everything

【凡是】every; any; all

【凡响】common music; ordinary music: 非同~ out of the ordinary

烦 (fán) ❶be annoyed ❷be tired of; be fed up with ❸be vexed; be irritated ❹superfluous and confusing ❺trouble

【烦闷】unhappy; annoyed; moody

【烦恼】worry; be vexed; trouble: 令人~ troublesome

【烦扰】bother; feel disturbed

【烦人】annoying; vexing; troubling

【烦躁】agitated

繁 (fán) ❶numerous; in great numbers ❷propagate

【繁多】❶various ❷plenty ❸in great numbers

【繁花】❶ full-blown flowers ❷ flowers of different colors

【繁华】flourishing; bustling; busy

【繁忙】busy

【繁茂】lush; luxuriant

【繁荣】flourishing; prosperous; booming

【繁殖】breed; reproduce

【繁重】heavy

反 (fǎn) ❶ turn over ❷oppose; combat ❸rebel; revolt ❹ in an opposite direction; in reverse; inside out ❺ on the contrary; instead ❻ return; counter ❼ oppose; combat

【反败为胜】turn defeat into victory; turn the tide

【反比】inverse relation; inverse proportion

【反比例】inverse ratio; inverse proportion

【反驳】rebut; refute; disprove

【反差】contrast

【反常】unusual; strange; abnormal

【反动】❶reaction ❷reactionary

【反对】oppose; object to; combat; fight; combat opposed to

【反复】❶repeatedly; again and again; over and over ❷reversal; relapse ❸repetition ❹repeated

【反复无常】❶ changeable; inconstant ❷ chop and change

【反感】dislike; be disgusted with

【反光】❶reflect light ❷reflection of light

【反悔】go back on one's word (or one's promise)
【反抗】resist;revolt;resist
【反恐】anti-terrorism
【反馈】feedback
【反面】wrong (or negative) side; contrary;opposite
【反射】❶reflect;reflex ❷reflection
【反弹】rebound
【反问】❶rhetorical question ❷ask a question in reply
【反响】echo;reflection
【反省】self-examination conscience; introspection reflect on oneself; examine one's own
【反义词】antonym
【反应】❶respond ❷reaction;response;repercussion
【反映】❶reflect;mirror ❷reflection;make known
【反语】irony
【反正】anyway;anyhow;in any case;after all
【反之】on the contrary;on the other hand
【反作用】counteraction;reaction

返 (fǎn) return;come or go back

【返潮】get damp
【返程】return journey
【返工】redo;do poorly done work over again
【返还】return;repay;pay back
【返回】return;go (or come) back

犯 (fàn) ❶criminal;offender ❷violate; offend ❸attack;work against ❹have a recurrence of (an old illness) ❺commit (a mistake, crime, etc.)

【犯病】have an attack of one's old illness: 她妈又~了。Her mother is ill again.
【犯愁】worry;be anxious
【犯错误】make a mistake
【犯法】break the law
【犯规】❶break the rules ❷foul
【犯难】feel embarrassed;feel awkward
【犯人】prisoner;criminal;convict
【犯傻】❶pretend to be naive, ignorant, or stupid ❷do a foolish thing ❸be in a daze;stare blankly
【犯疑】become suspicious
【犯罪】commit a crime;do wrong
【犯罪嫌疑人】criminal suspect
【犯罪现场】crime scene

饭 (fàn) rice;meal;food;cooked rice or other cereals

【饭菜】meal:做~ prepare (or cook) a meal
【饭店】restaurant;hotel
【饭锅】❶pot for cooking rice;rice cooker ❷means of living;livelihood
【饭盒】lunch-box;dinner pail
【饭量】appetite
【饭厅】dining hall (or room)
【饭碗】❶rice bowl ❷job
【饭桌】dinner table

泛 (fàn) ❶float;overflow; be suffused with ❷flood ❸extensive;general

【泛读】extensive reading
【泛泛而谈】speak in generally; talk in generalities
【泛滥】overflow;flood
【泛滥成灾】flood;run rampant;run wild
【泛论】a general survey or discussion
【泛指】make a general reference

范 (fàn) pattern;example;model;limits:示~demonstrate

【范畴】category

F

【范例】example;model

【范围】sphere;scope;range;limits

【范文】model essay

贩 (fàn) ❶ trader; pedlar ❷ buy to resell;traffic

【贩毒】drug trafficking; traffic in narcotics

【贩卖】traffic;peddle;sell

F 【贩卖人口】traffic in human beings; human traffic; (specifically) traffic in women

【贩运】transport goods for sale;traffic

fang

方 (fāng) ❶square ❷involution;power ❸ short for square metre or cubic metre ❹ upright; honest ❺ direction:四面八～in all directions ❻side;party ❼ method;way

【方案】scheme; program; plan:制订～draw up (or make) a plan

【方便】convenient;handy

【方便面】instant noodles

【方才】just now

【方程】equation

【方法】way; means; method:用各种～in all sorts of ways;by every means

【方根】root

【方框】square frame

【方面】direction; respect; side; aspect; field:次要～secondary aspect;另一～ on the other hand;主要～ principle aspect

【方式】pattern;manner;mode;way:生活～way of life;life-style

【方位】direction and position; bearing; placement

【方向】direction;way;orientation

【方兴未艾】be fast unfolding; be in the ascendant

【方形】square

【方言】dialect

【方圆】❶ neighbourhood; vicinity ❷ circumference

【方正】❶ upright and foursquare ❷ straightforward;upright;righteous

【方桌】a square table

芳 (fāng) ❶sweet-smelling;fragrant ❷ good reputation;virtuous

【芳草】fragrant grass

【芳香】❶ fragrant; aromatic ❷ perfume; fragrance;aroma

防 (fáng) ❶defense (or defence);embankment ❷ defend; guard against; provide against

【防爆】anti-explosion

【防备】make preparation against; guard against; provide against; take precautions

【防病】prevent disease

【防不胜防】very hard to guard against

【防潮】dampproof;moistureproof protection against the tide

【防尘】dustproof

【防磁】antimagnetic

【防弹】bulletproof;shellproof

【防弹玻璃】bulletproof glass

【防盗】guard against theft; take precautions against burglars

【防盗门】anti-theft door

【防毒】protect against poison gas;gas defense

【防范】be on guard;keep a lookout

【防风林带】windbreak belt

【防腐】antiseptic;anticorrosive

【防旱】take precautions against drought

【防洪】prevent (or control) flood

【防护】protect; shelter
【防护林】shelter-forest
【防火】fireproof; fire prevention
【防晒霜】sun cream
【防守】defend; guard
【防水】waterproof
【防御】defend
【防止】prevent from; avoid; guard against
【防治】provide prevention and cure

妨 (fáng) hinder; hamper; impede; obstruct

【妨碍】prevent from; be (or stand) in the way of; hinder; hamper; impede; obstruct
【妨害】impair; jeopardize; be harmful to

房 (fáng) ❶room; house ❷chamber

【房产权】house property right
【房车】motor home
【房贷】housing loan; home mortgage lending
【房地产】real estate
【房顶】roof
【房东】landlord; landlady; the owner of the house one lives in
【房基】foundations (of a building)
【房间】room
【房卡】room card
【房奴】house slave; mortgage slave
【房屋】house; building
【房檐】eaves
【房主】house-owner
【房子】❶house; building ❷room
【房租】rent (for a house, flat)

仿 (fǎng) ❶imitate; copy ❷resemble; be like

【仿佛】❶seem ❷as if (or though) ❸be more or less the same
【仿冒】pretend to be authentic; forge; counterfeit
【仿生学】bionics
【仿效】imitate; follow the example of
【仿照】imitate; follow: 这个办法很好,各地可以~办理。This is a good method. It might well be adopted by other localities.
【仿真】simulation; emulation
【仿制品】imitation; copy

访 (fǎng) ❶visit; call on (or at) ❷try to get; seek by inquiry or search

【访谈】interview and discuss
【访问】❶visit; call on; pay a visit to ❷visit: 国事~a state visit
【访问团】visiting delegation

纺 (fǎng) ❶spin ❷a thin silk cloth

【纺车】spinning wheel
【纺纱】spin; spinning; yarn manufacture
【纺织】spinning and weaving
【纺织品】textile; fabric

放 (fàng) ❶put; place; lay ❷set free; let go; release ❸put in; add ❹give way to ❺lend (money) for interest ❻let out; expand ❼blossom ❽open ❾send away

【放出】send (or let) out; emit
【放大】enlarge; amplify
【放大镜】magnifier
【放胆】act boldly and with confidence: 你尽管~去干! Don't hesitate to forge ahead!
【放风】❶let in fresh air ❷let prisoners out for exercise ❸leak certain information
【放风筝】fly a kite
【放火】❶set fire to; set on fire; commit

F

arson ❷create disturbances

【放假】have a holiday or vacation; have a day off

【放进】put in (or into); let in

【放宽】widen; relax restrictions; liberalize; be more flexible

【放款】make loans; loan

【放牧】put out to pasture; herd; graze

F 【放炮】❶fire a gun ❷set off firecrackers ❸blast ❹(of a tyre, etc.) blow out; burst ❺shoot off one's mouth

【放屁】❶break wind; fart ❷ What crap! Shit!

【放弃】surrender; give up; abandon

【放任】not interfere; let alone; let things drift; noninterference

【放哨】stand sentry; be (or go) on sentry

【放声大哭】burst into tears; utter a stifled cry of agony

【放声歌唱】lift up one's voice and sing

【放水】❶ turn on the water ❷ draw off some water (from a reservoir, etc.)

【放肆】unbridled; wanton: ~的行为 unbridled behaviour

【放松】ease; relax

【放下】lay (or put, set) down

【放心】feel relieved; be at ease; set one's mind at rest; rest assured; feel relieved

【放学】classes are over; school is over (for the day); leave school

【放眼】take a broad view; scan widely: ~未来 look toward the future

【放映】show; project

【放置】place; put; lay up; lay aside

【放纵】indulge; connive at; let sb. have his own way; undisciplined

【放走】let go; set free; release

fei

飞 (fēi) ❶flight ❷fly; flit ❸hover (or flutter) in the air swiftly ❹ unexpected; accidental

【飞奔】dash; fly; gallop

【飞驰】speed along

【飞船】airship; spaceship

【飞碟】❶ skeet shooting; skeet; trapshooting ❷flying saucer; UFO (Unidentified Flying Object)

【飞机】airplane; aircraft; plane

【飞机场】airport; airfield

【飞机票】plane ticket

【飞溅】splash

【飞快】at top speed; very fast; at lightning speed

【飞来横祸】unexpected disaster

【飞逝】(of time, etc.) slip by (or past); fly; elapse

【飞速】at full speed

【飞腾】fly swiftly upward

【飞艇】airship; dirigible

【飞舞】dance in the air

【飞翔】circle in the air; hover

【飞行】flight; flying

【飞行员】pilot; flyer; aviator

【飞扬】fly upward; rise

【飞跃】leap

妃 (fēi) ❶ imperial concubine ❷ the wife of a prince

【妃子】imperial concubine

非 (fēi) ❶wrong; evildoing: 为~作歹 do evil ❷not conform to; run counter to; not; no ❸blame; censure ❹ have got to; simply must

【非常】❶ extraordinary; unusual; special ❷much; most ❸greatly; extremely; very;

so; highly ❹badly ❺a lot

【非法】illegal; unlawful; illicit

【非凡】uncommon; extraordinary; outstanding

【非分之想】inordinate ambitions

【非金属】nonmetal

【非礼】❶ assault; violate ❷ indecent assault

【非卖品】not for sale

【非难】blame; censure; reproach

【非亲非故】be neither kith nor kin

【非同小可】be no trivial (trifling) matter; be not usual

【非议】blame; reproach: 无可～beyond reproach

【非政府组织】NGO (non-governmental organization)

【非正式】informal; unofficial

【非洲】Africa

菲 (fēi) ❶(of flowers and grass) luxuriant and rich with fragrance ❷phenanthrene ❸short for 菲律宾(the Philippines)

另见本页 fěi

【菲林】dial a roll of film; film

绯 (fēi) red

【绯红】bright red; crimson

【绯闻】scandal; pink news

扉 (fēi) door leaf

【扉页】title page

霏 (fēi) ❶(of rain or snow) fall thick and fast ❷thin, floating clouds; mist

【霏霏】(of rain, snow, mist, cloud, etc.) thick and fast; heavy

肥 (féi) ❶ fertilizer; manure ❷ fat ❸ fertile; rich ❹ loose-fitting; loose; large

【肥大】loose; stout; fat; large; plump; corpulent

【肥美】❶fertile; rich ❷luxuriant; plump; fleshy; fat

【肥料】fertilizer; manure

【肥胖】fat; fleshy; corpulent

【肥瘦】❶ the girth of a garment ❷ the proportion of fat and lean

【肥沃】fertile; rich

【肥皂】soap

【肥壮】stout and strong

匪 (fěi) ❶bandit; robber ❷ not

【匪帮】bandit gang; a felonious political gang

【匪徒】gangster

诽 (fěi) slander

【诽谤】slander; defame; calumniate; libel

菲 (fěi) poor; humble

另见本页 fēi

【菲薄】❶poor; humble ❷belittle

悱 (fěi) be at a loss for words

【悱恻】laden with sorrow; sad at heart: 缠绵～ lingering sorrow

斐 (fěi) (of literary talent) striking; brilliant

【斐然】striking; brilliant; splendid

翡 (fěi)

【翡翠】❶ halcyon (a bird) ❷jadeite (a mineral)

吠 (fèi) bark; yap; yelp

【吠叫】(of a dog) bark; yap; yelp

肺 (fèi) lung

【肺癌】lung cancer
【肺腑之言】words from the bottom of one's heart
【肺活量】vital capacity
【肺结核】pulmonary tuberculosis (TB)
【肺炎】pneumonia

废 (fèi) ❶give up; abandon; abolish ❷waste; useless ❸disabled; maimed

F

【废除】abolish; do away with
【废话】nonsense; rubbish; superfluous words
【废旧】(of things) old and useless
【废料】waste; waste material
【废品】waste product; reject
【废弃】discard; abandon; cast aside
【废寝忘食】be so absorbed (or occupied) as to forget food and sleep; lose sleep and forget to eat from anxiety, etc.
【废铁】scrap iron
【废物】❶rubbish; waste material; trash ❷good-for-nothing
【废物利用】make use of waste material
【废墟】ruins
【废止】abolish; put an end to
【废纸】broke; wastepaper

沸 (fèi) boil

【沸点】boiling point
【沸水】boiling water
【沸腾】❶ boiling; ❷ seethe with excitement; boil over

费 (fèi) ❶charge; expenses; dues; fee: 学~tuition; fee; 免~free of charge; 生活~living expenditure ❷spend; cost

【费工夫】❶take time and energy ❷painstaking
【费话】take a lot of talking or explaining
【费解】difficult (or hard) to understand; obscure; unintelligible
【费尽心血】exert one's utmost; spare no pains
【费劲】need (or use) great effort; be strenuous
【费钱】cost a lot; be costly
【费时】take time; be time-consuming
【费事】give or take a lot of trouble
【费心】❶take a lot of care (or trouble) ❷(used in making a request or giving thanks) may I trouble you (to do sth.); would you mind (doing sth.)
【费用】expenses; cost

疿 (fèi)

【疿子】prickly heat
【疿子粉】prickly heat powder

fen

分 (fēn) ❶ minute ❷ point; mark ❸ branch ❹fraction ❺divide; separate; part ❻distinguish ❼distribute; assign ❽ one tenth (of certain units of the metric system)

另见 982 页 fèn

【分贝】decibel
【分辨】distinguish; tell apart; differentiate
【分辩】defend oneself (against a charge); offer an explanation
【分别】❶part; separate; leave each other ❷distinguish; differentiate ❸ difference ❹respectively; separately
【分布】❶distribute; disperse ❷be distributed; be scattered; be dispersed
【分成】divide into tenths; share
【分寸】proper limits for speech or action; sense of propriety; sense of proportion
【分担】share
【分道扬镳】go different ways; part com-

pany
【分店】branch of a shop
【分发】distribute; deliver; hand out; issue
【分隔】divide; separate
【分工】share the work; divide the work
【分管】be assigned personal responsibility for; be put in charge of
【分行】branch of a bank
【分红】share bonus; draw extra profits
【分家】❶ divide up family property and live apart; break up the family and live apart ❷separate; break up
【分级】grade; classify
【分解】decompose; break down; resolve; disintegrate; split up; explain (used in traditional novels)
【分界线】boundary
【分开】part; split; separate
【分类】classify; assort
【分离】❶part; separate ❷apart
【分流】by-pass; distributary; split-flow
【分门别类】put into different categories; classify
【分娩】child birth
【分秒】every minute and second; instant
【分秒必争】not a second is to be lost; every second counts; seize every minute and se-cond
【分明】❶ be distinct; be clear: 爱憎～be clear about what to love and what to hate ❷clearly; plainly; evidently
【分配】❶distribute; assign ❷distribution
【分期】by stages; by installments
【分歧】difference; divergence
【分清】distinguish; draw a clear line of demarcation between
【分散】disperse; scatter
【分手】part company
【分数】❶mark; point; grade: ～线 minimum passing score ❷fraction
【分析】analyse
【分享】share
【分忧】share sb. 's cares and burdens; help sb. to get over a difficulty
【分支】branch; subfield; offtake
【分子】❶molecule ❷numerator
【分组】❶ divide into groups ❷ grouping; subgroup; block sort; curtate

芬 (fēn) fragrance; sweet smell

【芬芳】❶ fragrance ❷ fragrant; sweet-smelling

吩 (fēn)

【吩咐】tell; instruct; order instructions

纷 (fēn) ❶confused; tangled; disorderly ❷many and various; profuse; numerous

【纷繁】numerous and complicated
【纷纷】❶one after another; in succession ❷numerous and confused
【纷纷扬扬】(of snowflakes, flowers, leaves, etc.) flying or fluttering in profusion
【纷乱】numerous and disorderly
【纷扰】confusion; turmoil
【纷纭】diverse and confused: 众说～opinions are widely divided
【纷争】dispute; wrangle

氛 (fēn)

【氛围】atmosphere

坟 (fén) grave; tomb

【坟地】graveyard; cemetery
【坟墓】grave; tomb

【坟头】grave mound

焚 (fén) burn

【焚化】incinerate; cremate

【焚烧】burn; set on fire

粉 (fěn) ❶powder ❷cosmetics in powder form ❸ noodles or vermicelli made from bean, etc. ❹ whitewash ❺pink

F

【粉笔】chalk

【粉尘】dust

【粉刺】acne

【粉红色】pink

【粉末】powder

【粉饰太平】present a false picture of peace and prosperity

【粉刷】whitewash

【粉丝】❶ vermicelli made from bean starch, etc. ❷fans

【粉碎】smash; break to pieces; crush

【粉条】noodles made from bean or sweet potato starch

分 (fèn) ❶component ❷what is within one's rights or duty

另见 980 页 fēn

【分量】weight; quantity

【分内】one's job

【分外】❶ particularly; especially ❷ not one's job

份 (fèn) part; share; portion:

【份儿】degree extent: 到这～上你该死心了。You should give up when things have come to this.

【份额】share; portion

【份子】❶ one's share of expenses for a joint undertaking as in buying a gift for a mutual friend ❷a gift of money

奋 (fèn) ❶act vigorously; exert oneself ❷raise; lift

【奋斗】fight; strive; struggle

【奋发图强】make efforts; go all out to make the country strong

【奋力】spare no effort; do all one can; go all out

【奋起】rise up

【奋勇前进】advance bravely

【奋战】fight bravely

粪 (fèn) ❶ excrement; faeces; dung; droppings ❷ apply manure ❸ clear away; wipe out

【粪便】excrement and urine; night soil

【粪土】dung and dirt; muck

愤 (fèn) anger; indignation; resentment

【愤恨】detest

【愤慨】(righteous) indignation

【愤怒】anger; wrath

【愤青】young cynic; angry youth

feng

丰 (fēng) ❶ abundant; rich; plentiful ❷great

【丰碑】monument; monumental work

【丰富】❶plentiful; rich; abundant ❷enrich

【丰富多彩】rich and colorful

【丰功伟绩】great achievements

【丰满】❶full and round; well-developed ❷ plentiful; ❸ chubby (cheeks, face); plump (figure)

【丰年】a bumper harvest year; a good year

【丰润】plump and smooth-skinned

【丰盛】lavish; abundant; rich

【丰收】bumper harvest

【丰衣足食】be well-fed and well-clothed; have ample food and clothing

风（fēng）❶wind ❷put out to dry or air; winnow ❸ custom; practice ❹ style ❺scene; view ❻news; information

【风暴】❶storm; windstorm ❷tempest

【风波】disturbance

【风采】mien; elegant bearing

【风餐露宿】eat in the wind and sleep in the dew—endure the hardships of an arduous journey

【风车】❶windmill ❷winnower ❸pinwheel (a child's toy)

【风尘仆仆】have endured the hardships of a long journey; be travel-stained; be travel-worn and weary

【风吹草动】❶the rustle of leaves in the wind ❷a sign of disturbance or trouble

【风吹雨打】be exposed to the weather; be buffeted by wind and rain; to stand a severe test

【风度】bearing; appearance; demeanor

【风风火火】hustling and bustling

【风风雨雨】❶difficulties and hardships ❷ groundless gossip

【风干】air-dry：木材经过～可以防止腐烂。Air-drying can prevent wood rotting away.

【风格】style; manner

【风光】scene; view; sight

【风和日丽】a bright sun and a gentle breeze; warm and sunny weather

【风化】air-slake; weathering; morals and manners; decency

【风景】landscape; scenery

【风景区】scenic spot

【风凉话】irresponsible and sarcastic remarks

【风流】❶distinguished and admirable ❷ talented and romantic; ❸romantic; amorous ❹dissolute; loose

【风流人物】❶a man of untrammeled spirit; a romantic person; ❷great men

【风貌】❶style and features ❷view; scene ❸elegant appearance and bearing

【风靡】fashionable

【风气】general mood; atmosphere; common (or established) practice：社会～ tendencies of society

【风趣】❶humour; wit ❷funny

【风扇】fan; electric fan

【风势】❶the force or speed of the wind ❷ situation ❸circumstances

【风霜】wind and frost：饱经～ weather-beaten

【风俗】custom

【风味】special flavour; local color (or flavour)

【风险】risk：冒～take risks

【风雪】snowdrift

【风衣】windbreaker

【风雨】wind and rain

【风云人物】man of the day; influential figure

【风筝】kite

封（fēng）❶seal; wrapper; envelope ❷ for sth. envelope ❸confer (a little, territory, etc.) upon

【封闭】❶seal off (or up) ❷close

【封底】back cover

【封冻】(of a river, the ground, etc.) freeze

【封口】seal; heal

【封面】front cover

【封皮】paper wrapping

【封锁】blockade; seal off; block：经济～ economic blockade

【封条】paper strip seal

【封装】seal and package

疯 (fēng) mad; crazy; insane

【疯狗】mad dog; rabid dog

【疯话】mad talk; ravings; nonsense

【疯狂】mad; crazy; insane; frenzied; unbridled

峰 (fēng) ❶ peak; summit; crest ❷ hump: 山~mountain peak

【峰回路转】the path winds through high peaks

【峰会】summit (or conference)

【峰峦】ridges and peaks

烽 (fēng) beacon

【烽火】❶beacon-fire (used to give border alarm in ancient times); beacon ❷ flames of war

【烽烟】beacon-fire; beacon

锋 (fēng) ❶ a sharp point or acting edge (of a knife, sword, etc.) ❷vanguard ❸front

【锋快】❶(of a knife, sword, etc.) sharp; keen ❷penetrating; incisive

【锋利】❶ sharp; keen; incisive ❷ sharp; poignant

【锋芒】❶cutting edge; spearhead ❷talent displayed; abilities

【锋芒毕露】make a showy display of one's talent

蜂 (fēng) bee; wasp in swarms: 蜜~ honeybee

【蜂巢】honeycomb

【蜂蜜】honey

【蜂鸟】hummingbird

【蜂王】queen bee

【蜂箱】beehive; hive

【蜂拥而至】come swarming; swarm forward

逢 (féng) meet; come upon

【逢年过节】on New Year's Day or other festivals

【逢凶化吉】turn calamities into blessings; turn ill luck into good

缝 (féng) sew; stitch
另见 985 页 fèng

【缝补】sew and patch; sew and mend

【缝合】suture, sew up (a wound, an incision)

【缝纫机】sewing machine

【缝制】❶ sew ❷ sewing make (clothes, bedding, etc.)

讽 (fěng) ❶ mock; satirize ❷ irony: 冷嘲热~burning satire and freezing irony

【讽嘲】satirize; mock

【讽刺】mock; ridicule; satirize

【讽刺画】caricature

凤 (fèng) phoenix

【凤凰】phoenix

【凤梨】pineapple (the plant and its fruit)

【凤毛麟角】rarity of rarities

奉 (fèng) ❶ give or present with respect ❷ receive (orders, etc.) ❸ believe in ❹ esteem ❺ wait upon; attend to

【奉承】flatter

【奉告】let sb. know; inform

【奉公守法】be law-abiding

【奉还】return sth. with thanks

【奉陪】keep sb. company

【奉送】offer as a gift

【奉献】offer as a tribute; present with all respect; devote

【奉献精神】spirit of devotion

缝 (fèng) seam; crack; crevice 无~seamless

另见 984 页 féng

【缝隙】gap; slit; chink; crack; crevice

fo

佛 (fó) ❶Buddha ❷Buddhism ❸image of Buddha: 拜~worship Buddha; 信~believe in Buddhism

【佛法】❶Buddha dharma; Buddhist doctrine ❷power of Buddha

【佛教】Buddhism

【佛塔】pagoda

【佛像】statue of Buddha

【佛学】Buddhist philosophy

fou

否 (fǒu) negate; deny

【否定】❶deny; negate ❷negative

【否决】vote down; reject

【否认】deny; renounce: 不可~undeniable

【否则】otherwise; or else; if not

fu

夫 (fū) ❶husband ❷man ❸a manual worker ❹person pressed into service

【夫妇】husband and wife; married couple

【夫人】wife; lady; madame

肤 (fū) skin

【肤浅】shallow; superficial

【肤色】complexion; color of skin

孵 (fū) hatch; brood; incubate

【孵化】hatch

【孵育】hatch; incubate

敷 (fū) ❶apply (powder, ointment, etc.) ❷spread; layout ❸be sufficient for

【敷贴】apply ointment or plaster (to an affected part of the body)

【敷衍】act in a perfunctory manner; go through the motions

伏 (fú) ❶lean over; bend over ❷lie prostrate ❸subside; go down ❹hide ❺admit ❻the hottest days of the year

【伏笔】a hint foreshadowing later developments in a story essay, etc.; foreshadowing

【伏兵】(troops in) ambush

【伏法】be executed

【伏天】the hottest summer days

【伏贴】fit perfectly

扶 (fú) ❶support with the hand; place a hand on sb. (or sth.) for support ❷help sb. up ❸support; help

【扶持】give aid to; support

【扶老携幼】holding the old by the arm and the young by the hand; bringing along the old and the young

【扶贫】poverty relief; poverty alleviation

【扶手】handrail; rail; banisters; armrest

【扶梯】staircase

【扶助】help; assist; support

芙 (fú)

【芙蓉】❶cottonrose hibiscus ❷another name for lotus

拂 (fú) ❶stroke ❷whisk; flick

【拂拭】whisk or wipe off

【拂晓】dawn; daybreak

【拂袖而去】go off in a huff; leave with a flick of one's sleeve

服 (fú) ❶clothes; dress ❷take medicine ❸obey; be convinced

【服从】submit (or yield, bend) to; obey; be subject to; be subordinated to

【服法】submit to the law

【服气】be convinced; be persuaded

【服饰】dress and personal adornment; dress

【服输】admit defeat; acknowledge defeat

【服帖】❶obedient; docile; submissive ❷be convinced ❸fitting; appropriate; well arranged

【服务】❶serve; give service to; submissive: 为人民～serve the people ❷service

【服务员】attendant; waiter; waitress

【服药】take medicine

【服役】serve; be on service in the army; be on active service

【服装】dress; clothing; garment; costume

俘（fú）capture; take prisoner: 战～prisoner of war; captive

【俘获】capture; seize

【俘虏】❶capture; take prisoner ❷captive; prisoner of war

浮（fú）❶float ❷swim ❸on the surface; superficial ❹shallow and frivolous; superficial ❺hollow; inflated ❻excessive; surplus

【浮标】buoy; float

【浮尘】floating dust; surface dust

【浮沉】now sink, now emerge; drift along

【浮雕】relief (sculpture)

【浮动】❶float; drift ❷unsteady; fluctuate

【浮华】showy; ostentatious; flashy

【浮力】buoyancy

【浮生若梦】this fleeting life of ours is like an empty dream

【浮现】present itself; rise (or appear) before one's eyes; come back to one's mind

【浮想】❶thoughts flashing across one's mind ❷recollections

【浮云】floating clouds

符（fú）❶symbol ❷accord with; tally with ❸a tally issued by a ruler to generals, envoys, etc., as credentials in ancient China

【符号】symbol; sign; mark; insignia

【符合】accord (or correspond) with; suit; fit; conform to; be in keeping with: ～事实 tally with the reality

幅（fú）width; size: 大～照片 a large-sized photo

【幅度】range; scope; extent

【幅员辽阔】(a country) with a vast expanse; (a country) with a vast territory

辐（fú）spoke (of a wheel)

【辐射】❶radiate ❷radiation

福（fú）good fortune; blessing; happiness

【福分】good luck; good fortune; a happy lot: 有～ fortunate; lucky

【福利】welfare; material benefits; well-being

【福气】happy lot; good fortune

【福星】lucky star; mascot

抚（fǔ）❶comfort; console ❷nurture; foster ❸stroke

【抚爱】caress; fondle

【抚摩】pat; stroke

【抚慰】comfort; console; soothe

【抚恤】comfort and compensate a bereaved family

【抚恤金】pension

【抚养】raise; bring up; foster

【抚育】bring up; nurture; tend

斧 (fǔ) axe; hatchet

【斧头】hatchet; axe

【斧正】(please) make corrections

【斧子】axe; hatchet

俯 (fǔ) bow (one's head); bend down

【俯冲】dive

【俯瞰】look down at; overlook

【俯身】bend over; bend down

【俯视】look down at; overlook

【俯卧】lie prostrate; lie face down (on the ground)

辅 (fǔ) assist; complement; supplement: 相~相成 complement each other

【辅导】coach; give guidance in study

【辅导员】coach; assistant; instructor

【辅助】❶ assist; aid ❷ supplementary; auxiliary

腐 (fǔ) ❶rotten; stale; decayed ❷bean curd

【腐败】❶ bad; decayed; putrid (food) ❷ corrupt; rotten

【腐化】corrupt; rot; decay

【腐烂】❶rot away ❷rotten; decayed; corrupt

【腐蚀】corrode

父 (fù) ❶father ❷male relative of a senior generation

【父辈】people of father's generation; elder generation

【父老】elders (of a country or district)

【父老乡亲】fellow countrymen

【父母】parents; father and mother

【父亲】father; dad

【父亲节】Father's Day

【父子】father and son

付 (fù) ❶pay ❷give; hand (or turn) over to

【付出】pay out (or for); expend

【付方】credit side; credit

【付款】pay; make a payment

【付清】pay off; pay in full; clear a bill

【付税】pay taxes

【付诸东流】all one's efforts wasted

【付诸行动】put into practice

负 (fù) ❶carry on the back or shoulder ❷ shoulder; bear ❸ have at one's back; rely on ❹ suffer ❺ betray; fail in one's duty, obligation, etc. ❻ lose (a battle, game, etc.); be defeated: 不分胜~end in a draw (or tie) ❼ minus; negative ❽ negative

【负担】❶burden; load: 精神~mental burden; load on one's mind ❷bear; shoulder

【负荷】❶work load; load ❷shoulder; bear

【负面】negative side

【负伤】be injured; be wounded; be hurt

【负数】negative number

【负心】ungrateful (esp. in love); untrue; heartless

【负责】be responsible for; be in charge of

【负债】❶be in debt; incur debts ❷liabilities

【负重致远】bear a heavy burden and go a long way—shoulder heavy responsibilities

妇 (fù) woman; wife; married woman

【妇道】female virtues

【妇女】woman; lady

【妇女节】 Women's Day; International Work-ing Women's Day

【妇人】married woman

【妇幼】women and children

附 (fù) ❶ add; attach; enclose ❷ get close to; be near ❸agree to

【附带】❶attached ❷in passing ❸subsidiary; supplementary

【附和】echo; follow; chime in with

【附加】add; attach additional; attached; appended

【附加费】extra charge

F

【附件】❶annex; appendix ❷enclosure ❸ accessories; attachment ❹fitting; modification kit ❺adnexa ❻adnexal

【附近】❶nearby; neighbouring ❷close to; in the vicinity of ❸neighbourhood

【附录】appendix

【附属】❶attach; belong to ❷attached ❸ subsidiary; auxiliary

【附注】notes appended to a book, etc.; annotations

【附着】adhere to; stick to

赴 (fù) attend; go to

【赴会】attend a meeting; keep an appointment (to meet sb.)

【赴任】go to one's post; be on the way to one's post

【赴宴】go to a feast; attend a banquet

【赴约】keep an appointment

复 (fù) ❶answer; reply ❷recover; resume ❸duplicate ❹complex; compound ❺again

【复本】duplicate

【复查】recheck; reexamine

【复仇】revenge; avenge

【复读机】repeat recorder; repeater

【复电】❶send a telegram in reply ❷a telegram in reply

【复发】have a relapse: 旧病~have an attack of an old illness

【复返】return

【复古】restore ancient ways

【复合】complex; composite; compound

【复合型人才】interdisciplinary talent

【复活】come (or bring) back to life; revive

【复审】❶review a case ❷reexamine

【复试】reexamination; final examination

【复述】retell; repeat

【复苏】❶come back to life (or consciousness) ❷recovery

【复习】review; revise; go over

【复现】reappear

【复兴】revive; rejuvenate

【复印】duplicate; copy; xerox

【复印机】duplicator; duplicating machine; copying machine

【复原】❶heal; recover; get well ❷restore

【复员】demobilize

【复杂】complex; complicated

【复制】reproduce; make a copy of; duplicate

副 (fù) ❶deputy; assistant; vice ❷auxiliary; subsidiary; secondary ❸correspond to; fit

【副本】copy; duplicate; transcript

【副标题】subheading; subtitle

【副产品】by-product

【副词】adverb

【副教授】associate professor

【副经理】deputy manager

【副刊】supplement

【副食品】non-staple food

【副手】assistant

【副职】deputy post

【副主席】vice-chairman

【副总理】vice-premier

【副总统】vice-president

【副作用】side effect; by-effect

富 (fù) rich; wealthy; abundant

【富国利民】enrich the country and benefit the people

【富国强兵】make the country rich and its military force efficient

【富丽堂皇】splendid

【富强】prosperous and strong

【富饶】rich; fertile; abundant

【富人】the rich; rich people

【富翁】 moneybags; rich man; man of wealth

【富有】rich; wealthy

【富于】be full of; be rich in; abound in

【富余】 redundant; have enough and to spare

【富裕】wealthy; well-off; rich; well-to-do

【富足】plentiful; rich

腹 (fù) belly; stomach; abdomen

【腹部】stomach

【腹地】hinterland

【腹稿】a draft worked out in one's mind

【腹痛】bellyache; stomachache

覆 (fù) ❶cover ❷overturn; upset

【覆盖】cover

【覆没】❶turn over and sink ❷capsize and sink ❸be overwhelmed; be wiped out

缚 (fù) tie up; bind

馥 (fù) fragrance

【馥郁】 strongly fragrant; sweet-scented; sweet-smelling

G g

ga

旮 (gā)

【旮旯儿】❶ nook; corner ❷ out-of-the-way place

嘎 (gā) ❶ a loud, high-pitched ❷ sound

【嘎嘎】the quacking sound made by a duck; quack

gai

该 (gāi) ❶should; ought to ❷be one's turn to do sth. ❸deserve

【该当】deserve

改 (gǎi) ❶ change; transform ❷ correct; put right ❸revise; alter

【改编】❶adapt; rearrange; revise ❷reorganize

【改变】change; transform; shift

【改道】❶ change one's route ❷ change its course

【改掉】give up; drop

【改动】change; modify; revise

【改革】reform

【改革开放】reform and opening up to the outside world

【改观】get (or take on) a new look

【改过】correct one's mistakes

【改行】change one's occupation

【改换】change; change over to

【改悔】repent and mend one's ways

【改建】reconstruct; rebuild

【改进】❶ improve; make better ❷ improvement

【改良】❶reform ❷improve; ameliorate

【改期】postpone; put off; change the date

【改善】improve; better

【改邪归正】give up vice and return to virtue; turn over a new leaf

【改写】rewrite; adapt

【改造】reform; remould; transform; remake

【改正】correct; amend; put right

【改制】ownership reform; structural reform

【改装】❶change one's costume or dress ❷ repack; repackage ❸ modify; refit; reequip

【改组】reorganize

钙 (gài) calcium

【钙化】calcify

盖 (gài) ❶lid; cover ❷build ❸top ❹affix

【盖世无双】unparalleled anywhere on earth; matchless throughout the world; peerless; unrivalled

【盖章】seal; stamp

【盖子】cover; lid; cap; top

概 (gài) ❶general idea; broad outline ❷generally; approximately ❸without exception ❹the manner of carrying oneself; deportment

【概而论之】generally speaking

【概况】survey; general situation

【概括】❶generalize; summarize; epitomize ❷briefly; in broad outline

【概论】introduction; outline

【概率】chance; probability

【概貌】general view (or picture)

【概念】idea; concept; conception; notion

【概述】give a brief account of

【概要】summary; essentials; outline

gan

干 (gān) ❶dried food ❷have sth. to do with ❸dry; be concerned with; be implicated in ❹empty; hollow ❺take into nominal kinship ❻dried food

另见 992 页 gàn

【干杯】bottom up; drink a toast

【干瘪】❶dry ❷shrivelled; wizened ❸(of writing) dull; drab; dryasdust

【干菜】dried vegetable

【干草】hay

【干脆】❶clear-cut; straight forward ❷simply; altogether

【干儿子】adoptive son

【干饭】cooked rice

【干戈】weapons of war; war

【干旱】dry

【干涸】dry up; run dry

【干净】❶clean; neat and tidy ❷completely; totally

【干枯】withered; dried-up; dry; wizened

【干冷】dry and cold (weather)

【干粮】solid food (prepared for journey); rations for journey

【干扰】❶disturb; trouble; bother; interfere; obstruct ❷interference; jam

【干涉】interfere; intervene; meddle

【干洗】dry-clean; dry cleaning

【干预】intervene; interpose; meddle

【干燥】dry; arid

【干燥剂】drier; drying agent; desiccant

【干着急】be anxious but unable to do anything

甘 (gān) ❶sweet; pleasant ❷willing ❸willingly; of one's own accord

【甘拜下风】candidly admit defeat (in friendly competition, etc.)

【甘苦】❶hardships and difficulties ❷joys and sorrows; sweetness and bitterness

【甘露】❶sweet dew ❷manna

【甘薯】sweet potato

【甘甜】sweet

【甘心】❶willing ❷willingly; readily

【甘愿】do sth. willingly

【甘愿效劳】be glad to do sth. for sb.

【甘蔗】cane; sugarcane

杆 (gān) pole; stick; staff; bar: 旗～flagpole

肝 (gān) liver

【肝癌】liver cancer

【肝胆】❶open-heartedness; sincerity ❷heroic spirit; courage

【肝胆相照】(of friends) treat each other with all sincerity; be devoted to each other heart and soul

【肝功能】liver function

【肝炎】hepatitis

柑 (gān)mandarin orange

【柑橘】❶oranges and tangerines ❷citrus

竿 (gān) pole; rod

【竿子】bamboo pole

尴（gān）

【尴尬】awkward；embarrassed

杆（gǎn）❶the shaft or arm of sth. ❷（for a long and thin cylindrical object）

【杆秤】steelyard

秆（gǎn）stalk

G

赶（gǎn）❶catch up with；overtake ❷rush for；pursue ❸make a dash for；try to catch ❹rush（or hurry）through ❺drive ❻drive away；expel ❼happen to；find oneself in；avail oneself of

【赶不上】lag behind；miss；be unable to catch up with

【赶场】go to the village fair or market

【赶超】catch up with and surpass

【赶潮流】follow the fashion；follow the trend

【赶工】hurry through；speed up work

【赶紧】hastily；at once；quickly；without losing time

【赶快】at once；quickly

【赶上】overtake；catch up with；keep pace with

【赶往】rush to

【赶早】do sth. as early as possible

【赶走】drive off

敢（gǎn）❶dare ❷courageous；daring；bold

【敢作敢为】bold and decisive in action

感（gǎn）❶sense；feeling：安全～sense of security；责任～sense of responsibility；荣誉～feeling of honor ❷feel；sense ❸affect；move；touch ❹grateful；obliged

【感触】thoughts and feelings

【感到】feel；sense

【感动】move；strike；affect；touch；impress

【感恩】be grateful（or thankful）

【感恩节】Thanksgiving Day

【感官】sense organ；sensory organ

【感激】be grateful（or thankful）；feel indebted

【感觉】❶feel；perceive；become aware of ❷sense；perception；sensation；feeling

【感慨】sigh with emotion

【感慨万分】all sorts of feelings well up in one's mind

【感冒】❶cold ❷catch cold；have a cold：流行性～influenza ❸be interested in；enthusiastic about

【感情】emotion；feeling；sentiment；affection

【感情用事】give oneself over to blind emotions

【感染】❶get；catch；infect：细菌～bacterial infection ❷affect；influence

【感染力】appeal；power of influence

【感人】moving；touching

【感受】feel；experience

【感叹】sigh

【感同身受】sympathetic visage；empathizing with others

【感悟】come to realize

【感想】thoughts；impressions；reflections

【感谢】thank；be grateful to；be thankful for；appreciate

【感兴趣】be interested in

【感应】❶interact；respond ❷response；induction

橄（gǎn）

【橄榄】olive；the fruit of the canary tree

【橄榄球】rugby；American football

干（gàn）❶main part；trunk；stem ❷do；work ❸capable；able

另见 991 页 gān
【干部】cadre
【干掉】kill;get rid of
【干活】work;work on a job
【干劲】drive;enthusiasm;vigour;energy
【干练】capable and experienced
【干流】trunk stream;main stream
【干什么】❶why on earth;whatever for ❷ what to do
【干线】main line;trunk line

gang

刚 (gāng) ❶firm;strong ❷just;exactly ❸barely;only
【刚愎自用】headstrong; self-willed; opinionated
【刚才】just now; a short time (or moment) ago
【刚刚】a moment ago;just now;just;only;exactly
【刚好】❶just;exactly ❷happen to;it so happened that
【刚劲有力】powerful and vigorous
【刚烈】fiery and forthright; upright and unyielding
【刚强】tough;firm
【刚毅】resolute and steadfast
【刚正不阿】upright and above flattery
【刚直】upright and outspoken

肛 (gāng)anus
【肛门】anus

纲 (gāng) ❶ outline; program ❷ the head-rope of a fishing net ❸ key link;guiding principle ❹ class
【纲领】program;guiding principle
【纲要】outline;sketch

钢 (gāng) steel: 不锈~stainless steel
【钢笔】pen;fountain pen
【钢材】steel products;steels;rolled steel
【钢管】steel tube (or pipe)
【钢轨】rail
【钢筋】reinforcing bar
【钢盔】(steel) helmet
【钢琴】piano
【钢琴家】pianist
【钢丝】steel wire:走 ~ walk the wire
【钢铁】iron and steel;steel

缸 (gāng) ❶jar; crock; vat; bowl ❷a compound of sand, clay, etc. for making earthenware ❸a jar-shaped vessel
【缸盆】glazed earthen basin
【缸子】mug;bowl

岗 (gǎng) ❶hillock;mound ❷sentry; guard: 站~be on sentry ridge
【岗楼】watchtower
【岗哨】❶lookout post ❷sentry
【岗亭】police (or sentry) box
【岗位】post; station: 坚守 ~ hold out one's post

港 (gǎng)port;harbour
【港澳同胞】Hong Kong and Macao compatriots
【港币】Hong Kong currency (or dollar)
【港口】harbour;port
【港湾】harbour

杠 (gàng) ❶a thick stick ❷bar ❸cross out;delete
【杠杆】lever
【杠铃】barbell

gao

高 (gāo) ❶tall;high ❷of a high level or degree;above the average ❸high priced;expensive;dear ❹loud

【高矮】height

【高昂】❶hold high (one's head, etc.) ❷ high; elated; exalted ❸ dear; expensive; exorbitant

【高不可攀】too high to reach; unattainable

【高才生】a brilliant (or an outstanding, a top) student

【高超】superb; excellent; magnificent

【高潮】❶climax ❷high tide; high water ❸ upsurge

【高大】❶ tall and big; tall: 身材～be of great stature ❷lofty

【高档】high grade

【高等教育】higher education

【高等院校】colleges and universities; institutions

【高低杠】uneven (parallel) bars

【高度】❶height ❷high degree ❸highly

【高度评价】think highly of; hold sth. in high regard

【高尔夫球】golf

【高峰】peak; summit; height

【高歌】sing heartily

【高管】senior executive; top manager

【高贵】❶high; magnificent; noble; gallant ❷nobility

【高喊】shout (or cry) loudly; call out loudly

【高级教师】senior teacher

【高级职称】title of senior academic (or professional) rank

【高级中学】senior middle school

【高价】high price

【高架路】elevated road

【高考】college entrance examination

【高科技】high-level science and technology; high technology (or high-tech, hi-tech)

【高空】high altitude; upper air

【高粱】Chinese sorghum

【高楼】high-rise building

【高妙】ingenious; masterly

【高明】excellent; clever; wise

【高尚】noble; lofty

【高深莫测】too profound to be understood

【高声说话】speak out loud

【高手】master-hand; expert

【高速】high speed

【高速发展】develop at top speed; develop by leaps and bounds

【高速公路】speedway; expressway; freeway

【高铁】high-speed rail

【高位】a high position

【高温】high temperature

【高下】relative superiority or inferiority

【高效】high efficiency

【高新技术】advanced high technology; new and high-tech

【高兴】❶ happy; glad; cheerful; joyful; pleased ❷rejoice; be glad to do ❸happily; gladly

【高性能】high performance

【高血压】high blood pressure; hypertension

【高雅】elegant; tasteful

【高原】highland; plateau

【高原反应】altitude reaction

【高瞻远瞩】stand high and see far

【高涨】rise; upsurge; run high

【高质量】high quality

【高中】short for 高级中学(senior middle school); high school

羔 (gāo) lamb; kid; fawn

【羔羊】lamb—an innocent and helpless

person or a scapegoat

睾 (gāo)

【睾丸】testis;testicle

膏 (gāo) ❶ fat; grease; oil ❷ paste; cream;ointment

糕 (gāo) cake;pudding

【糕点】cake;pastry

搞 (gǎo) ❶do;carry on;be engaged in ❷make; produce; work out ❸ get; get hold of

【搞错】mistake

【搞鬼】play tricks

【搞好】do well;make a good job of

【搞活】vitalize;enliven

【搞乱】make a mess of;confuse;mess up

稿 (gǎo) ❶draft;sketch ❷manuscript

【稿本】manuscript (of a book, etc.)

【稿费】payment (or reward) for an article (or book)

【稿子】❶draft;sketch:写~ draft an article ❷manuscript

告 (gào) ❶ tell; inform; announce; declare ❷ accuse; go to law against; bring an action against;charge ❸ask for ❹make known

【告白】a public notice or announcement

【告别】say goodbye to; leave; part from: 挥手~wave farewell

【告辞】take leave (of one's host)

【告假】ask for leave

【告捷】❶win ❷report a victory

【告诫】 warn; admonish: 再三~ repeated exhortation

【告密】tip off;inform against (or on)

【告示】❶ official notice; bulletin ❷ notify;announce

【告诉】tell;let know;inform

【告慰】❶comfort;console ❷feel relieved

【告知】inform;acquaint;notify

【告状】❶ bring a lawsuit against sb.; accuse ❷complain

ge

戈 (gē) dagger-axe

【戈壁】❶gobi ❷the Gobi Desert

疙 (gē)

【疙瘩】❶pimple;lump ❷knot ❸a knot in one's heart

哥 (gē) ❶ elder brother ❷ a friendly term of address for male older acquaintances

【哥特式】Gothic

胳 (gē)arm

【胳膊】arm

鸽 (gē)dove;pigeon:信~ carrier pigeon

【鸽哨】a whistle tied to a pigeon

搁 (gē) ❶ put ❷ put aside; leave over;shelve

【搁浅】be (or go,run) ashore;be grounded

【搁置】shelve;put aside

割 (gē) cut;sever

【割爱】give up what one treasures

【割草】cut grass;mow

【割断】cut off

【割麦】cut wheat

【割舍】give up;part with

歌 (gē) ❶song ❷sing

【歌唱】sing

【歌词】lyrics;words of a song
【歌喉】(singer's) voice;singing voice
【歌剧】opera
【歌谱】music score of a song; music of a song
【歌曲】song
【歌声】sound of singing;singing
【歌手】singer;vocalist
【歌颂】sing the praises of
【歌舞】song and dance
【歌星】a singing star;accomplished vocalist
【歌谣】ballad;folk song;nursery rhyme

革 (gé) ❶ leather; hide: 人造~imitation leather ❷ change; transform ❸ dismiss;remove sb. from office

【革除】❶abolish;get rid of: ~陋习 eliminate irrational practices ❷ expel; dismiss;remove sb. from office
【革新】❶innovate ❷innovation
【革职】remove sb. from office;cashier
【革制品】leather goods

阁 (gé) ❶pavilion ❷cabinet ❸old boudoir ❹ shelf

【阁楼】attic;garret

格 (gé) ❶ squares formed by crossed lines; check ❷ division ❸ standard; style; pattern ❹ character; quality; demeanor ❺fight

【格调】❶ (literary or artistic) style ❷ one's style of work as well as one's moral quality
【格格不入】incompatible with; out of tune with
【格局】pattern;setup
【格式】pattern;form
【格外】especially;all the more
【格言】proverb;maxim;motto
【格子】check;chequer;lattice

隔 (gé) ❶ separate; cut off; partition; stand (or lie) between ❷ be apart from;at a distance from

【隔壁】next door;neighbour
【隔行】of different trades or professions
【隔阂】misunderstanding: 消除~remove the misunderstanding
【隔绝】cut off;insulate
【隔离】isolate;keep apart
【隔膜】❶lack of mutual understanding ❷ be unfamiliar with
【隔墙有耳】someone may be listening on the other side of the wall
【隔日】every other day
【隔夜】of the previous night
【隔音】give sound insulation

个 (gè)individual

【个别】❶single; individual; specific ❷separately ❸very few;one or two
【个人】❶individual ❷personal: 以~名义 in one's own name
【个人所得税】personal income tax
【个体】individual
【个性】personality;individuality
【个子】height;build;stature

各 (gè)each;every;different;various

【各持己见】each sticks to his own view
【各处】everywhere;here and there
【各得其所】each is in his proper place; each is properly provided for;each has a role to play
【各方面】all sides
【各行各业】various walks of life; every walk of life
【各级】all (or different) levels
【各界】all walks of life;all circles
【各取所需】each takes what he needs

【各抒己见】each airs his own views
【各位】everybody
【各有千秋】each has something to recommend him; each has his strong points
【各有所长】each has his own strong points
【各有所好】each has his likes and dislikes
【各种】all kinds (or sorts) of
【各自】each; respective
【各族人民】people of all nationalities

gei

给 (gěi) ❶give; grant; hand ❷let; allow ❸for
另见 1037 页 jǐ
【给以】give; grant

gen

根 (gēn) ❶root ❷foot; base ❸cause; origin; source ❹thoroughly; completely
【根本】❶base; origin ❷basic; essential
【根除】root out; eliminate; eradicate
【根基】❶foundation; basis ❷property accumulated over a long time; resources
【根据】❶basis; ground ❷according to; on the basis of; in the light of; in line with; by
【根据地】base
【根深蒂固】be deeply rooted; be firmly established; ingrained; inveterate
【根源】source; origin; root
【根治】effect a radical cure; cure once and for all; fundamental solution
跟 (gēn) ❶heel ❷follow ❸with ❹and
【跟前】in front of; close to
【跟上】catch up with; keep pace with
【跟随】follow; go after
【跟头】❶fall ❷somersault
【跟踪】trail; track; follow the tracks of; follow along behind sb.

geng

更 (gēng) change; replace
另见本页 gèng
【更改】change; alter
【更名】change one's name
【更替】replace
【更新】renew; replace: 万象～everything takes on a new look
【更衣】change one's clothes; change dresses
【更衣室】locker room; changing room
【更正】correct; make corrections
耕 (gēng) plough; cultivate
【耕地】❶plough; till ❷arable land
【耕牛】farm cattle
【耕耘】ploughing and weeding; cultivation
【耕种】cultivate; till
羹 (gēng) a thick soup
【羹匙】soup spoon; tablespoon
耿 (gěng) ❶honest and just; upright ❷bright ❸dedicated
【耿直】upright; frank and fair; honest and frank; straight forward
哽 (gěng) choke (with emotion); feel a lump in one's throat
【哽咽】choke with sobs
梗 (gěng) ❶stem; stalk ❷block; obstruct
【梗概】broad outline; gist; main idea
【梗阻】❶block; obstruct; hamper ❷obstruction
更 (gèng) more; further
另见本页 gēng

【更差】worse
【更多】more
【更好】better
【更加】still;more;still (or far,even) more
【更少】fewer;less
【更远】farther;further

gong

工 (gōng) ❶ workman; worker ❷ labor; work ❸ project ❹ industry ❺ skill;craftsmanship ❻exquisite

G

【工厂】works;plant;mill;factory
【工程】engineering;project
【工程师】engineer
【工地】building (or construction) site
【工段】workshop section
【工蜂】worker (bee)
【工夫】❶time ❷workmanship;skill;art ❸ work;labor;effort
【工会】trade (or labor) union
【工匠】craftsman;artisan
【工具】tool;instrument
【工具书】reference book
【工龄】length of service;working years
【工钱】❶money paid for odd jobs;charge for a service ❷ wages;pay
【工人】worker;workman
【工伤】injury suffered on the job; injury incurred while working;industrial injury
【工商界】industrial and commercial circles;business circles
【工商业】industry and commerce
【工头】boss;foreman
【工薪阶层】salaried workers; wage-earners
【工序】process;working procedure
【工业】industry:轻～light industry;手～handicraft;重～heavy industry
【工业化】❶ industrialize ❷ industrialization
【工业品】industrial product
【工业污染】industrial pollution
【工艺品】handicraft article
【工艺水平】technological level
【工整】carefully and neatly done
【工资】pay;wages
【工作】❶work;job;task ❷work
【工作量】amount of work;work load
【工作日】workday

弓 (gōng) ❶bow ❷bend;arch;bow

【弓箭】bow and arrow
【弓弦】bowstring
【弓腰】bend over;bend down

公 (gōng) ❶male animal ❷public (or official) business ❸make public ❹ public; collective; state-owned ❺ common; general ❻ equitable; impartial; fair;just ❼(a respectful address for an elderly man) ❽metric ❾duke ❿father-in-law;husband's father

【公安】public security
【公安局】public security bureau
【公布】publish;announce;make public
【公差】(gōng chā) ❶ common difference ❷ tolerance
【公差】(gōng chāi) public errand; noncombatant duty
【公道】❶justice ❷ fair; just; reasonable; impartial:办事～be evenhanded;主持～uphold justice
【公德】public morality;social ethics
【公断】❶arbitrate ❷consider and decide impartially
【公费】public expense
【公愤】public indignation;popular anger
【公告】❶ bulletin; announcement ❷ de-

clare;make known
【公共】common;public;communal
【公共财产】public property
【公共关系】public relations
【公共汽车】bus
【公关】❶public relations ❷to use connections
【公海】open sea;high seas
【公害】public hazard;social effects of pollution
【公鸡】cock
【公开】❶ public; open ❷ in public ❸ make public
【公款】public money
【公里】kilometer (or km.)
【公理】❶ generally acknowledged truth ❷axiom
【公路】road;highway
【公民】citizen
【公民权】civil rights
【公平】fair;just
【公平交易】fair deal
【公婆】husband's father and mother;parents-in-law
【公然】openly;undisguisedly;brazenly
【公认】(universally, generally) accepted; established
【公式】formula
【公事】public affairs;official business
【公司】company;corporation
【公文】official document
【公务】official business;public affairs
【公务员】civil servant
【公益】public good;public welfare
【公益事业】cause of public good
【公用】public;for public use
【公寓】flat;apartment;block of flats
【公元】the Christian era:~2015 年 A. D. 2015
【公园】park
【公约】❶convention;pact ❷joint pledge
【公债】(government) bonds
【公章】official seal
【公正】just;fair;impartial
【公之于众】make known to the public (or world);make public
【公职】public office
【公众】the public:~利益 public interest
【公主】princess

功 (gōng) ❶ merit; achievement ❷ result ❸skill ❹work

【功臣】meritorious statesman; a person who has rendered outstanding service
【功成名就】achieve success and win recognition
【功夫】❶skill;workmanship ❷kungfu
【功绩】achievements; contributions; merits
【功课】❶ schoolwork; homework ❷ a school subject
【功劳】merit;credit;contribution
【功率】power
【功能】function
【功效】effect;efficacy
【功勋】exploit;meritorious service

攻 (gōng) ❶ accuse; charge ❷ attack; take the offensive ❸study;specialize in

【攻打】attack;assault
【攻读】make a study of
【攻关】❶storm a strategic pass ❷tackle key problems
【攻击】❶attack;assault;launch an offensive ❷accuse;charge;vilify
【攻克】capture;overcome;take
【攻势】offensive
【攻无不克】all-conquering;ever-victorious
【攻占】attack and occupy;seize;take

G

供 (gōng) ❶provide ❷supply; feed for 另见本页 gòng

【供不应求】supply falls short of demand

【供电】❶power supply; current supply ❷ supply electricity

【供过于求】supply exceeds demand

【供给】supply; provide; afford; furnish

【供暖】heating

【供求】supply and demand

【供应】supply; provide

宫 (gōng) ❶ palace; temple ❷ a place for cultural activities and recreation ❸womb; uterus

【宫殿】palace

【宫廷】court; palace

恭 (gōng) respectful; reverent

【恭贺】congratulate

【恭候】await respectfully

【恭敬】respectful

【恭维】compliment; flatter

【恭喜】❶congratulate ❷congratulations

躬 (gōng) ❶ personally ❷ bend forward; bow

【躬亲】attend to personally

巩 (gǒng) consolidate; make firm; strengthen

【巩固】 ❶ make firm; consolidate; strengthen; secure ❷ firm; strong; solid; stable

汞 (gǒng) mercury; hydrargyrum (Hg)

拱 (gǒng) surround; arch

【拱桥】arch bridge

【拱形】arch

共 (gòng) ❶share ❷common; general ❸all; whole ❹ altogether; in all ❺ short for 共产党 (the Communist Party)

【共产党】the Communist Party; Communist

【共产党员】Party member

【共存】coexist

【共度】spend (an occasion) together

【共和国】republic

【共计】❶come (or amount) to; total; add (or sum) up to ❷in all

【共鸣】❶sympathy; sympathetic response ❷resonance

【共青团】the Communist Youth League

【共事】work together; be fellow workers

【共同】 ❶ common ❷ together; jointly in common

【共享】share; enjoy together

【共性】general character; generality

【共振】resonance

贡 (gòng) tribute

【贡献】contribute; offer; devote; dedicate

供 (gòng) ❶supply; feed ❷provide to ❸lay (offerings) ❹offerings ❺confess ❻confession

另见本页 gōng

【供奉】❶make offerings to ❷supply and serve ❸ enshrine and worship; consecrate

【供品】offerings

【供认】confess; make a confession

【供养】make offerings to

【供职】hold office

【供桌】altar table

gou

勾 (gōu) ❶cross (or strike) out ❷cancel ❸delineate; draw; tick off ❹induce; evoke; call to mind

另见 1001 页 gòu

【勾画】draw the outline of; sketch

【勾勒】❶draw the outline of; sketch the contours of ❷ give a brief account of; outline

【勾引】tempt; lure; seduce

沟 (gōu) ❶ ditch; channel; trench ❷ groove; rut; furrow ❸gully; ravine

【沟坎】ditch; trench

【沟渠】canals and ditches

【沟通】link up; connect

钩 (gōu) ❶ hook ❷ hook stroke (in Chinese characters) ❸check mark; tick ❹secure with a hook; hook ❺cro-chet ❻sew with large stitches

【钩虫】hookworm

【钩心斗角】plot against each other

【钩住】catch; hook

【钩子】❶hook ❷a hook-like thing

篝 (gōu) cage

【篝火】bonfire; campfire

苟 (gǒu) ❶careless; negligent; indiffer-ent (to right or wrong) ❷if

【苟全】aimlessly preserve (one's own life):~性命 barely manage to survive

【苟同】(usu. used in the negative) agree without giving serious thought; readily subscribe to (sb.'s view)

狗 (gǒu) dog: 猎~hunting dog; hound

【狗窝】kennel; doghouse

【狗熊】❶black bear ❷coward

【狗仗人势】like a dog bullying on its master's strength

勾 (gòu)
另见 1000 页 gōu

【勾当】(dirty) deal

构 (gòu) ❶construct; form; compose ❷ fabricate; make up

【构成】form; constitute; compose; make up

【构思】(of writers or artists) work out the plot; conceive conception; design

【构图】composition (of a picture)

【构想】an idea; a conception; a plan; a scheme

【构造】❶ build; construct ❷ structure; construction

购 (gòu) buy; purchase

【购买】buy; purchase

【购买力】purchasing power

够 (gòu) ❶reach; be up to: 伸手去~ reach for ❷enough; sufficient

【够本】make enough money to cover the cost; break even

【够得着】within one's reach

【够格】be qualified; be up to standard

【够条件】reach the standard; be qualified

gu

估 (gū) estimate; appraise

【估计】appraise; estimate; figure

【估价】appraise; evaluate

咕 (gū) the clucking of a hen; the coo-ing of a pigeon

【咕嘟】bubble; gurgle

【咕咕叫】coo

孤 (gū) ❶orphaned; parentless ❷isola-ted; alone ❸lonely

【孤傲】proud and aloof

【孤单】❶alone ❷lonely; friendless

【孤独】lonely; solitary

【孤儿】orphan

【孤寡】orphans and widows

【孤苦伶仃】orphaned and helpless

【孤立】❶alone; isolated ❷isolate

【孤陋寡闻】ignorant and ill-informed
【孤僻】unsociable and eccentric
【孤注一掷】stake everything on a single throw

姑 (gū) ❶ aunt; father's sister ❷ husband's sister; sister-in-law ❸ nun ❹ tentatively; for the time being
【姑父】uncle; the husband of one's father's sister
【姑妈】father's (married) sister; aunt
G 【姑娘】girl; maid
【姑婆】❶ husband's aunt ❷ paternal grandaunt
【姑且】tentatively; for the moment
【姑嫂】a woman and her brother's wife; sisters-in-law
【姑息】appease; tolerate

轱 (gū)
【轱辘】❶ wheel ❷ roll

辜 (gū) guilt; crime
【辜负】let down; disappoint

古 (gǔ) ancient; age-old
【古板】old-fashioned and inflexible
【古代】❶ ancient times; antiquity ❷ ancient
【古典】classical
【古董】❶ antique; curio ❷ old fogey
【古迹】historic site
【古今中外】ancient and modern, Chinese and foreign; at all times and in all lands
【古老】age-old; ancient
【古朴】(of art, architecture, etc.) simple and unsophisticated; of primitive simplicity
【古人】the ancients; our forefathers
【古往今来】since time immemorial; of all ages; through the ages
【古为今用】make the past serve the present
【古文】ancient Chinese prose
【古装】ancient costume

谷 (gǔ) ❶ valley; gorge ❷ grain; millet ❸ unhusked rice
【谷仓】granary; barn
【谷草】❶ millet straw ❷ rice straw
【谷物】grain; corn; cereal

汩 (gǔ) (of running water) gurgle
【汩汩】gurgle

股 (gǔ) ❶ thigh ❷ section (of an office; enterprise, etc.) ❸ strand ❹ share in a company or one of several equal parts of property
【股东】shareholder; stockholder
【股份】share; stock
【股民】investor; share holder
【股票】share; stock

骨 (gǔ) ❶ bone ❷ skeleton ❸ framework ❹ character; spirit
【骨干】❶ diaphysis ❷ backbone; mainstay; core member; key member
【骨骼】skeleton
【骨牌】dominoes
【骨气】strength of character; moral integrity; backbone
【骨瘦如柴】thin as a lath; worn to a shadow; a mere skeleton; a bag of bones
【骨髓】marrow
【骨折】fracture

蛊 (gǔ) a legendary venomous insect
【蛊惑】poison and bewitch
【蛊惑人心】confuse and poison people's minds; resort to demagogy

鼓 (gǔ) ❶ drum ❷ beat; strike ❸ stir up; rouse ❹ swell; agitate; pluck up

❺bulge；swell

【鼓动】instigate；agitate；arouse；stir；incite

【鼓励】encourage；urge；inspire

【鼓舞】❶inspire；hearten；encourage ❷encouragement

【鼓掌】clap one's hands；applaud

【鼓足干劲】go all out

固 (gù) ❶ consolidate；make firm；strengthen ❷ firm；solid；strengthen ❸ firmly；resolutely ❹ originally；in the first place；as a matter of course

【固定】❶fix ❷fixed；regular

【固定收入】fixed (or regular) income

【固定资产】capital (or fixed) assets

【固然】surely；no doubt；of course；admittedly；it is true

【固态】solid state

【固体】solid

【固执】❶stubborn ❷hold to；persist in

【固执己见】stubbornly stick to one's opinions

故 (gù) ❶ incident；accident ❷ cause；reason ❸ die ❹ hence；therefore；so；for this reason ❺ former；old ❻ friend；acquaintance ❼ (of people) die；dead

【故步自封】stand still and refuse to make progress；be complacent and conservative

【故都】onetime capital；former capital

【故宫】the Imperial Palace

【故居】former residence (or home)

【故弄玄虚】purposely make a mystery of simple things；be deliberately mystifying

【故去】die；pass away

【故事】story；tale：民间～folktale

【故乡】native place；hometown；birthplace

【故意】on purpose；intentionally；willfully

【故障】breakdown；trouble

顾 (gù) ❶ look round (or back)；look at ❷ attend to；take care of ❸ take into consideration ❹ visit；call on (or at)

【顾此失彼】cannot attend to one thing without neglecting the other；have too many things to take care of at the same time

【顾及】take into account；attend to；give consideration to

【顾客】customer；shopper；client

【顾虑】worry；misgiving；apprehension

【顾面子】❶ save face；keep up appearances ❷spare sb.'s feelings

【顾名思义】as implied by the name；as the term suggests

【顾全大局】take the whole into account

【顾问】consultant；adviser

雇 (gù) hire；employ

【雇车】hire a car

【雇用】hire；employ；take on

【雇员】employee

【雇主】employer

gua

瓜 (guā) melon：冬～white gourd；黄～cucumber；南～pumpkin 西～watermelon

【瓜分】divide (or carve) up

【瓜葛】connection；association

【瓜子】melon seeds

刮 (guā) ❶scrape；smear with (paste, etc.)；scratch ❷ extort；plunder ❸ blow；sweep

【刮脸】shave (the face)

【刮目相看】see sb. in a new light

寡 (guǎ) ❶ widowed ❷ few；scant ❸ tasteless ❹few；scant

【寡不敌众】be hopelessly outnumbered; fight against hopeless odds

【寡妇】widow

【寡言】silent; mute; of few words; close-mouthed

挂 (guà) ❶ hang; put up ❷ hitch; get caught ❸ ring off ❹ call (or ring) up; put sb. through to ❺ keep in mind; be concerned about ❻ register

【挂车】trailer

G

【挂号】❶ register (at a hospital, etc.) ❷ send by registered mail

【挂历】hanging (or wall) calendar

【挂名】titular; nominal

【挂念】miss; be concerned (or worried) about

【挂失】report (or declare) the loss

【挂图】wall map; hanging chart

褂 (guà) a Chinese-style unlined garment; gown

【褂子】a Chinese-style unlined upper garment; short gown

guai

乖 (guāi) ❶ well-behaved (child); good ❷ clever; shrewd; alert

【乖乖】❶ well-behaved; obedient ❷ (to a child) little dear; darling ❸ good gracious

【乖巧】lovely; cute

【乖张】eccentric and unreasonable

拐 (guǎi) ❶ turn: 往右~ turn to the right ❷ abduct; kidnap ❸ swindle; make off with ❹ limp ❺ crutch ❻ walking stick ❼ corner

【拐角】corner; turning: 在街道~ at a street corner

【拐卖人口】kidnap and sell people

【拐骗】abduct; swindle

【拐弯】❶ turning; bend ❷ turn a corner ❸ turn round; pursue a new course

【拐弯抹角】beat about the bush

【拐杖】cane; stick

怪 (guài) ❶ monster; demon; evil being ❷ blame ❸ find sth. strange; wonder at ❹ strange; odd ❺ quite; rather

【怪不得】❶ no wonder; so that's why; that explains why ❷ not to blame

【怪话】cynical remark; grumble; complaint

【怪僻】eccentric; odd

【怪事】strange thing

【怪物】monster; freak

【怪异】❶ monstrous; strange; unusual ❷ strange phenomenon; portent; prodigy

【怪罪】blame sb.

guan

关 (guān) ❶ customs ❷ critical moment ❸ barrier ❹ close; shut ❺ lock up; shut in ❻ turn off ❼ close down ❽ concern; involve

【关闭】❶ close; shut ❷ close down; shut down

【关电灯】turn off the light

【关掉】shut (or turn) off

【关怀】show care for; concern; care

【关键】❶ key ❷ crucial

【关键词】keyword

【关键时刻】a crucial moment

【关节】❶ joint ❷ a key (or crucial) link

【关节炎】arthritis

【关联】be related; be connected

【关门】❶ shut (or close) a door ❷ (of a business) close down ❸ refuse discussion or consideration

【关切】❶ considerate; thoughtful ❷ be deeply concerned; show concern over

【关税】customs duty; tariff
【关头】juncture; key moment
【关系】❶ relations; relationship: 与……有~have sth. to do with sb. bearing; impact; significance ❷ concern; have to do with
【关心】❶ care; concern ❷ care for (or about); think of; be concerned with; show solicitude for
【关于】about; on; over; concerning; with regard (or respect) to; regarding
【关照】❶look after; keep an eye on ❷inform; notify
【关注】follow with interest; pay close attention to; show solicitude for

观 (guān) ❶ sight; view ❷ outlook: 人生~outlook on life ❸ look at; observe; watch
【观测】observe; view
【观察】observe; watch; view
【观点】view; viewpoint; standpoint; point of view: 从……~来看 in the eye of; from the point of view of
【观光】go sightseeing; visit; tour
【观看】see; watch; view; look on
【观摩】inspect and learn from each other's work; view and emulate
【观念】sense; idea; concept
【观赏】view and admire; enjoy the sight of
【观望】wait and see; look on
【观象台】observatory
【观众】spectator; viewer; audience

官 (guān) official; officer
【官兵】❶ officers and men ❷ government troops
【官邸】official residence
【官方】of or by the government; official
【官司】lawsuit
【官员】official: 外交~ diplomatic official
【官职】government post; official position

冠 (guān) ❶ hat ❷ corona; crown: 王~ crown
另见 1006 页 guàn
【冠冕】royal crown; offcial hat
【冠冕堂皇】high-sounding

棺 (guān)
【棺材】coffin

鳏 (guān) wifeless; widowered
【鳏夫】an old wifeless man; bachelor or widower

馆 (guǎn) hall; shop: 咖啡~cafe; coffee house; 美术~ art gallery; 体育~ gymnasium; 图书~library; 展览~exhibition hall
【馆藏】❶(of a library or a museum) have a collection of ❷collection
【馆子】restaurant

管 (guǎn) ❶ tube; pipe: 试~test tube ❷ manage; run; be in charge of ❸ control ❹bother about; mind
【管道】pipe; pipeline
【管教】subject sb. to discipline
【管理】❶ govern; rule; manage; run; handle; direct ❷management; direction
【管辖】have jurisdiction over
【管弦乐】orchestral music
【管线】pipes and power lines
【管制】control; govern: 交通~ traffic control

贯 (guàn) ❶pass (or go) through ❷be linked together ❸in procession
【贯穿】penetrate; run (or go, pass) through
【贯通】have a thorough knowledge of; be well versed in

【贯注】concentrate on; be absorbed in

冠 (guàn) ❶put on a hat ❷precede; crown with ❸first place; the best
另见 1005 页 guān

【冠词】article

【冠军】champion: 全能~all-round champion

惯 (guàn) ❶be used to; used to do; be in the habit of ❷spoil

【惯犯】habitual offender; repeater; old offender

G

【惯例】rule; custom; usual practice: 打破~break away from usual practices (or customs)

【惯性】inertia

盥 (guàn) wash

【盥洗室】washroom; closet

灌 (guàn) ❶irrigate ❷fill; pour

【灌溉】❶water; irrigate ❷irrigation

【灌木】bush; shrub

【灌输】instill into; implant

鹳 (guàn) stork

罐 (guàn) jar; pot; tin

【罐头】tin; can

【罐子】pot; jar; pitcher; jug

guang

光 (guāng) ❶honour; glory ❷brightness ❸light; ray ❹glorify ❺bare; naked ❻bright ❼smooth ❽used up; nothing left ❾scenery ❿only; merely

【光标】cursor

【光彩夺目】with dazzling brightness; brilliant; resplendent

【光棍】bachelor

【光华】brilliance; splendour

【光滑】smooth; polished; glossy; sleek; not rough: 皮肤~ smooth skin

【光辉】❶glowing; brilliant; sparkling; glorious ❷brilliance

【光洁】bright and clean

【光亮】❶light; shine ❷bright; shiny ❸brightly

【光临】presence (of a guest; etc.)

【光芒】rays of light; brilliant rays

【光明】❶brightness ❷light; bright

【光明磊落】frank and open hearted

【光年】light-year

【光盘】laser disc; optical disc; compact disc (or CD)

【光荣】❶glory; honour ❷glorious; honourable: 为……感到~ be proud of; take pride in

【光头】bareheaded

【光线】light; ray

【光阴】time

【光阴似箭】time flies like an arrow

广 (guǎng) ❶expand; spread ❷wide; broad; vast; extensive ❸many; numerous ❹expand; spread

【广播电台】radio station; broadcasting station

【广博】(of a person's knowledge) extensive; wide

【广场】square; public square

【广大】broad; wide; vast; extensive

【广度】scope; range

【广泛】widespread; wide; extensive

【广告】advertisement

【广告牌】billboard

【广阔】wide; broad; vast

【广厦】a spacious mansion

【广义】❶broad sense ❷generalized

逛 (guàng) stroll; ramble; roam

【逛荡】loiter; loaf about

gui

归 (guī) ❶go back to; return ❷return sth. to; give back to ❸belong to ❹converge; come together ❺turn over to; put in sb.'s charge

【归并】❶incorporate into; merge into ❷lump together; add up

【归根结底】in the final analysis

【归功于】owe to

【归国】return to one's country

【归国华侨】returned overseas Chinese

【归还】return; give (or send) back

【归结】❶come to a conclusion; sum up; put in a nutshell ❷end (of a story, etc.)

【归来】get back; return

【归类】classify; sort out

【归纳】induce; conclude; sum up

【归期】date of return

【归属】belong to

【归途】homeward journey; one's way home

【归心似箭】anxious to return

【归于】❶belong to; be attributed to ❷result in; end in

龟 (guī) tortoise; turtle

【龟甲】tortoise-shell

规 (guī) ❶compasses; dividers ❷rule; regulation ❸admonish; advise ❹plan; map out

【规避】evade; dodge; avoid

【规定】❶rule ❷provide for; formulate; stipulate ❸fix; set

【规范】standard; pattern; model; norm; code

【规格】standards; specifications; norms

【规划】plan; program: 长远～ long-term program

【规矩】❶rule; custom; established practice ❷well-behaved; well-disciplined: 没～ have no manners

【规律】law; rule; regular pattern

【规模】size; scale; scope; dimensions

【规劝】exhort; admonish

【规则】❶rule; regulation ❷regular

【规章制度】rules and regulations

皈 (guī)

【皈依】❶the ceremony of proclaiming sb. a Buddhist ❷be converted to Buddhism or some other religion

闺 (guī) ❶a small door ❷lady's chamber; boudoir

【闺女】❶girl; maiden ❷daughter

瑰 (guī) rare; marvellous

【瑰宝】rarity; treasure; gem

【瑰丽】surpassingly beautiful; magnificent

硅 (guī) silicon

【硅谷】silicon valley

轨 (guǐ) track; rail: 双～ double track; 单～ single track

【轨道】❶track; rail ❷orbit; course; path

【轨道交通】rail transit; track traffic

【轨迹】❶locus ❷orbit

诡 (guǐ) ❶pretend ❷deceitful; tricky; cunning

【诡计】trick; a crafty plot; a cunning scheme; ruse

【诡诈】cunning; crafty; treacherous

鬼 (guǐ) ❶ghost; spirit; apparition ❷stealthy; surreptitious ❸terrible; damnable ❹clever; smart; quick

【鬼聪明】clever in a shallow way

【鬼鬼祟祟】sneaking; furtive; stealthy

【鬼魂】ghost; spirit; apparition

【鬼脸】❶funny face; grimace ❷mask used as a toy: 做~ make faces; make a face

【鬼神】ghosts and gods; spirits; supernatural beings

柜 (guì) chest; case; cupboard; cabinet: 碗~ kitchen cupboard; 书~ bookcase; 衣~ wardrobe

【柜台】counter; bar

【柜子】cupboard; cabinet; case

刽 (guì) cut off; chop off

【刽子手】❶ executioner; headsman ❷ slaughterer; butcher

贵 (guì) ❶ dear; costly; expensive ❷ valuable; precious ❸ of high rank; noble; distinguished

【贵宾】distinguished (or honoured) guest; VIP

【贵贱】❶the eminent and the humble ❷ the expensive and the cheap: 管它~,只要看中了,就买了来。Whatever the price is, if it caught my eyes, I would buy it.

【贵重】valuable; precious

桂 (guì) ❶cassia ❷laurel; bay tree ❸ sweet-scented osmanthus

【桂冠】laurel (as an emblem of victory or distinction)

【桂花】sweet-scented osmanthus

【桂圆】longan

跪 (guì) kneel; go down on one's knees

【跪拜】worship on bended knees; kowtow

【跪下】kneel down; go down on one's knees

gun

滚 (gǔn) ❶roll ❷get away

【滚动】roll over; rotate

【滚瓜烂熟】(recite; etc.) fluently; (know sth.) off pat

【滚开】get away; get out

【滚热】piping hot; burning hot; boiling hot

【滚圆】round as a ball

棍 (gùn) ❶ cane; rod; stick ❷ scoundrel; rascal

【棍棒】stick; club; cudgel; bludgeon

guo

锅 (guō) pan; pot: 平底煎~ frying pan; 蒸~ steamer

【锅巴】rice crust; crust of cooked rice

【锅铲】spatula; turner

【锅盖】the lid of a cooking pot

蝈 (guō)

【蝈蝈儿】katydid; long-horned grasshopper

国 (guó) ❶ country; state; nation ❷ of the state; national ❸of our country

【国宝】national treasure

【国宾】state guest

【国策】national policy

【国产】domestic; made in our country; made in China

【国耻】national humiliation

【国粹】the quintessence of Chinese culture

【国法】(national) law

【国防】national defence

【国歌】national anthem

【国花】national flower

【国画】traditional Chinese painting
【国徽】national emblem
【国会】parliament;Congress
【国籍】citizenship;nationality
【国计民生】the national economy and the people's livelihood
【国际】international
【国际地位】international status
【国际关系】international relations
【国际贸易】international trade
【国家】country;state;nation
【国界】national boundaries
【国库】national treasury
【国民】a member of a nation; the people of a nation;national
【国内】civil;internal;domestic;home
【国内生产总值】gross domestic product (or GDP)
【国旗】national flag
【国企】state-owned enterprise
【国情】the condition of a country
【国庆】National Day
【国色天香】ethereal color and celestial fragrance(said of the peony or a beautiful woman)
【国泰民安】The country is prosperous and the people are at peace.
【国土】land;territory
【国外】external;overseas;abroad
【国王】king
【国务院】the State Council
【国语】national language
【国债】national debt;government loan

果 (guǒ) ❶fruit: 干~ dry fruit;鲜~ fresh fruit ❷ firm; resolute; determined ❸result;consequence ❹really;as expected;sure enough ❺if indeed;if really

【果冻】jelly
【果断】resolute;decisive
【果脯】preserved fruit;candied fruit
【果敢】courageous and resolute; resolute and daring
【果酱】jam
【果品】fruit
【果然】really; just as expected; sure enough indeed
【果肉】pulp
【果实】fruit;gains: 劳动~ fruits of labor
【果树】fruit tree
【果园】orchard
【果汁】fruit juice

裹 (guǒ) wrap;bind

【裹足不前】hesitate to move forward

过 (guò) ❶ fault; mistake ❷ cross ❸ pass;spend ❹go through (or over) ❺ go beyond ❻ too ❼ across; past; through;over ❽after;past

【过程】process;course
【过秤】weigh (on the steelyard)
【过错】mistake;fault
【过道】passageway;corridor
【过冬】pass the winter;winter
【过度】❶excessive ❷too;undue;over
【过渡时期】transitional period
【过分】❶excessive ❷too:做得太~go too far;overdo sth.
【过关】❶pass a barrier;go through an ordeal ❷pass a test;reach a standard
【过后】afterwards;later
【过活】live; make a living: 靠……~ live on
【过火】overdo;go too far;go to extremes
【过节】celebrate a festival
【过境】pass through the territory of a country;be in transit
【过来】❶come over (or up) ❷come round

【过劳死】death from overwork
【过路】pass by on one's way
【过路人】passerby
【过滤】filtrate; filter
【过敏】❶ hypersensitive; allergic ❷ allergy: 皮肤～ skin allergy
【过年】celebrate (or spend) the Spring Festival
【过期】be overdue
【过去】❶past ❷in (or of) the past; in the old days ❸go by; go over; pass by
【过日子】live; get along
【过剩】excess; surplus
【过失】fault; mistake; error; slip
【过时】out-of-date; out of fashion
【过问】take an interest in; concern oneself with
【过眼云烟】like floating smoke and passing clouds
【过夜】❶put up for the night ❷stay overnight
【过瘾】satisfy a craving; enjoy oneself to the full; do sth. to one's heart's content
【过犹不及】going too far is as bad as not going far enough
【过于】too; unduly; excessively

H h

ha

哈 (hā) ❶ blow one's breath; breathe out (with the mouth open) ❷ ha; aha

另见本页 hǎ

【哈哈大笑】 laugh heartily; roar with laughter

【哈哈镜】 distorting mirror

【哈欠】 yawn

蛤 (há)

【蛤蟆】 ❶ frog ❷ toad

哈 (hǎ) scold

另见本页 hā

【哈达】 hada, a piece of silk (usu. white in color) used as a greeting gift among the Zang and Mongol nationalities

hai

还 (hái) ❶ still; yet ❷ also; too; as well; in addition ❸ fairly ❹ even

另见 1026 页 huán

【还好】 ❶ not bad; passable ❷ fortunately

【还是】 ❶ or ❷ still; yet ❸ expressing a preference for an alternative ❹ no matter what, how

【还有】 besides; moreover; in addition

孩 (hái) child

【孩童】 child

【孩子】 ❶ child; kid ❷ son or daughter

【孩子气】 ❶ childish ❷ childishness

骸 (hái) ❶ bones of the body; skeleton ❷ body

【骸骨】 bones of the dead

海 (hǎi) ❶ sea; big lake ❷ a great number of people or things coming together ❸ extra large; of great capacity

【海岸】 seacoast; seashore

【海拔】 elevation; altitude

【海报】 poster; bill

【海豹】 seal

【海滨】 seaside; beach

【海产】 marine products

【海带】 kelp

【海岛】 island

【海盗】 pirate

【海底】 seabed; sea (or ocean) floor

【海防】 coast defence

【海风】 sea breeze; sea wind

【海港】 harbour; seaport

【海关】 customs; customhouse

【海归】 returned overseas students

【海龟】 sea turtle

【海军】 navy

【海阔天空】 as boundless as the sea and sky; unrestrained and far-ranging

【海量】 ❶ magnanimity ❷ great capacity for liquor

【海洛因】heroin
【海绵】❶sponge ❷foam rubber or plastic
【海面】sea surface
【海难】perils of the sea; marine disaster
【海鸥】sea gull
【海平面】sea level
【海市蜃楼】mirage
【海滩】beach; sea beach
【海豚】dolphin
【海外】overseas; abroad
【海湾】gulf; bay
【海味】seafood

【海峡】strait; channel: 台湾～ the Taiwan Straits; 英吉利～ the English Channel
【海啸】tsunami
【海燕】storm petrel
【海洋】seas and oceans; ocean
【海员】seaman; sailor
【海运】sea transportation
【海藻】marine alga; seaweed
【海蜇】jellyfish

骇 (hài) be astonished; be shocked

【骇人听闻】shocking; appalling

害 (hài) ❶evil; harm ❷do harm to; impair; injure; hurt ❸ suffer from ❹ kill; murder ❺harmful; destructive

【害病】get (or fall, be) ill: 害了一场大病 have been seriously ill
【害虫】injurious insect; pest
【害处】harm: 吸烟过多对身体有～。Excessive smoking is harmful to one's health.
【害怕】fear; be afraid; be frightened; be scared
【害群之马】black sheep
【害人害己】do harm to both others and oneself
【害臊】feel ashamed
【害羞】shy; bashful

han

酣 (hān) (drink, etc.) to one's heart's content

【酣畅】❶merry and lively (with drinking) ❷ sound (sleep) ❸ with ease and verve; fully
【酣畅淋漓】heartily; to one's heart's content
【酣然】❶ merrily (drunk) ❷ sound (asleep)
【酣睡】be fast asleep

憨 (hān) ❶ foolish; silly ❷ straightforward; naive

【憨痴】idiotic
【憨厚】simple and honest
【憨笑】smile fatuously; simper; smirk

鼾 (hān) snore

【鼾声】sound of snoring
【鼾声如雷】snore thunderously

含 (hán) ❶ contain; bear ❷ keep in mouth ❸nurse; cherish; harbour

【含苞待放】❶ still in bud; the buds are getting ready to burst (指花卉) ❷ Just budding, not yet open in early puberty (指青春期)
【含糊】ambiguous; vague
【含糊其词】talk ambiguously; equivocate
【含混】indistinct
【含泪】with tears in one's eyes
【含量】content: 牛奶的乳糖～ the lactose content of the milk
【含情脉脉】(soft eyes) exuding tenderness and love
【含沙射影】attack by innuendo
【含笑】with a smile
【含辛茹苦】endure suffering; bear hard-

ships

【含羞】bashfully; with a shy look

【含蓄】❶ implied; contain; embody ❷ implicit; veiled ❸ reserved: 她是一个非常~的人。She is a very reserved person.

【含义】meaning; implication

【含有】have; contain

【含冤】bear (or suffer) a wrong

函 (hán) ❶ case; envelope ❷ letter

【函电】letters and telegrams; correspondence

【函件】letters; correspondence

涵 (hán) ❶ contain ❷ culvert

【涵养】❶ ability to control oneself; self restraint ❷ conserve

寒 (hán) ❶ cold; chilly ❷ poor; needy

【寒潮】cold wave

【寒窗】poor condition for learning; a cold window—the difficulties of a poor student

【寒带】frigid zone

【寒风】cold wind: ~凛冽 a piercing wind

【寒假】winter vacation (or holidays)

【寒冷】cold; chilly; icy; frigid

【寒流】cold current

【寒舍】my humble home

【寒暑表】thermometer

【寒暄】❶ greeting words ❷ exchange of conventional greeting words

【寒意】a nip (or chill) in the air

【寒战】shiver (with cold or fear); chill

罕 (hǎn) rarely; seldom

【罕见】seldom seen; rare

【罕物】a rare thing

【罕有】very rare

喊 (hǎn) cry; shout; yell; call

【喊话】❶ propaganda directed to the enemy at the front line ❷ communicate by tele-equipment

【喊叫】shout; cry out; call

【喊冤叫屈】cry out about one's grievances; complain loudly about an alleged injustice

汉 (hàn) ❶ the Han Dynasty ❷ the Han nationality ❸ Chinese ❹ man: 好~ man of courage; hero

【汉白玉】white marble

【汉堡包】hamburger

【汉语】Chinese

【汉字】Chinese character: 简化~ simplified Chinese characters

【汉族】the Han nationality; China's main nationality

汗 (hàn) sweat

【汗脚】feet that sweat easily; sweaty feet

【汗孔】pore of a sweat gland

【汗流浃背】sweat streaming down and drenching one's back; soaked with sweat

【汗马功劳】❶ distinctions won in battle; war exploits ❷ one's contributions in work; render great services

【汗毛】fine hair on the human body

【汗如雨下】dripping with sweat

【汗衫】undershirt; T-shirt

【汗水】sweat

【汗腺】sweat gland

【汗液】sweat; perspiration

【汗渍】❶ sweat stain ❷ be soaked with sweat

旱 (hàn) ❶ dry spell; drought dryland ❷ on land ❸ dryland ❹ dry; arid

【旱冰】roller-skating
【旱冰场】roller rink
【旱季】dry season
【旱情】damage to crops by drought; ravages of a drought
【旱灾】drought

捍 (hàn) defend; guard

【捍卫】defend; protect; guard

悍 (hàn) ❶ brave; bold ❷ fierce; ferocious

【悍然】outrageously; brazenly; flagrantly

H

焊 (hàn) weld; solder

【焊工】❶ welding; soldering ❷ welder; solderer
【焊接】welding

撼 (hàn) shake

【撼动】shake; vibrate
【撼天动地】shake heaven and earth

翰 (hàn) ❶writing brush ❷writing

【翰林】member of the Imperial Academy

憾 (hàn) regret

【憾事】a matter for regret

瀚 (hàn) vast

【瀚海】big desert

hang

夯 (hāng) ❶ rammer; tamper ❷ ram; tamp; pound ❸strike heavily ❹carry sth. heavy on one's shoulder

行 (háng) ❶ line; row ❷ seniority among brothers and sisters ❸ trade; profession; line of business ❹ business firm

另见 1254 页 xíng

【行辈】seniority in the family or clan; position in the family hierarchy
【行当】line of business; profession
【行家】expert; connoisseur
【行距】row spacing
【行列】lines; ranks
【行情】market prices; market conditions
【行业】trade; occupation; profession; industry

航 (háng) sail; navigate

【航班】flight; flight number
【航海】navigation
【航空】aviation
【航天飞机】space shuttle
【航线】marine (or air) route; line; course
【航行】sail; navigate by water; fly; navigate by air
【航运】shipping

hao

号 (háo) ❶howl; yell ❷wail
另见 1015 页 hào

【号叫】howl; yell

毫 (háo) ❶fine hair ❷writing brush ❸ at all ❹milli-

【毫不】not at all
【毫发不爽】not deviating a hair's breadth; without the slightest error
【毫克】milligram (mg.)
【毫毛】soft hair on the body
【毫米】millimetre (mm.)
【毫升】millilitre (ml.)
【毫无道理】completely unreasonable
【毫无例外】without exception
【毫无用处】completely useless; of no use

豪 (háo) ❶talented person ❷bold and unconstrained; forthright; unrestrained ❸despotic; bullying

【豪放】bold and unrestrained

【豪华】magnificent; luxurious

【豪杰】hero

【豪迈】bold and generous; heroic

【豪门】rich and powerful family; wealthy and influential clan

【豪情】lofty sentiments

【豪爽】straightforward

【豪言壮语】brave words

好 (hǎo) ❶get (or be) well; be in good health ❷good; fine; nice ❸friendly; kind ❹OK ❺well; all right ❻how ❼so as to; so that; in order that

另见本页 hào

【好比】can be compared to; may be likened to; be just like

【好处】advantage; benefit; good

【好歹】❶good and bad ❷what's good and what's bad ❸mishap; disaster ❹in any case; anyhow

【好感】favourable impression; good impression

【好汉】brave man; true man; hero

【好话】❶a good word; words of praise ❷fine words

【好看】❶lovely; good-looking; nice ❷interesting ❸honoured; proud ❹on the spot

【好莱坞】Hollywood

【好人】❶a good (or fine) person ❷a healthy person ❸a soft person who tries to get along with everyone (often at the expense of principle)

【好事多磨】❶the road to happiness is strewn with setbacks ❷the course of true love never did run smooth

【好手】good hand; past master

【好似】seem; be like

【好听】pleasant to hear

【好玩】funny; interesting; amusing

【好戏】good play

【好像】❶seem; be like ❷as if (or though)

【好笑】funny; laughable

【好心】kind-hearted

【好意】kindness

【好运】luck

【好在】fortunately; luckily

【好转】take a turn for the better; take a favourable turn; improve: 局势逐渐～。The situation took a favourable turn gradually.

【好自为之】look out for yourself; conduct oneself well

号 (hào) ❶name ❷assumed name; alternative name ❸sign; mark; signal ❹number ❺size ❻date ❼order ❽bugle; bugle call

另见 1014 页 háo

【号称】❶be known as ❷claim to be

【号角】horn; bugle

【号码】number

【号脉】feel the pulse

【号手】trumpeter; bugler

【号召】call; appeal: 响应～ answer the call; respond to the call

好 (hào) ❶like; be fond of; love ❷be likely to; be liable to

另见本页 hǎo

【好客】be hospitable; keep open house

【好奇】curious; full of curiosity

【好强】eager to do well in everything

【好胜】seek to do others down

【好学】eager to learn; fond of learning

【好逸恶劳】love ease and hate work

耗 (hào) ❶consume; cost ❷waste time; dawdle ❸bad news

【耗费】expend; consume; cost

【耗损】consume; waste; lose: ～精神 take up one's energy

【耗资】cost (a large sum of money)

【耗子】mouse; rat

浩 (hào) great; vast; grand

【浩大】vast; huge; great

【浩荡】vast and mighty

【浩瀚】vast

【浩劫】catastrophe

【浩气】noble spirit

皓 (hào) ❶white ❷bright; luminous

H

【皓白】white; pure white

he

呵 (hē) ❶ breathe out (or with the mouth open) ❷scold

【呵斥】berate; excoriate

【呵护】take good care of

喝 (hē) ❶drink ❷drink alcoholic liquor 另见 1018 页 hè

【喝茶】take (or have, drink) tea

【喝酒】drink wine

【喝汤】take soup; eat soup

【喝醉】get drunk

禾 (hé) standing grain (esp. rice)

【禾苗】seedlings of cereal crops

合 (hé) ❶combine; unite; join ❷agree; suit ❸ close; shut ❹ add up to; amount to

【合办】operate or run jointly

【合编】❶compile in collaboration with ❷ merge and reorganize (army units, etc.)

【合并】combine; merge

【合唱】chorus

【合成】❶compound; synthesize ❷synthesis ❸synthetic

【合法】legal; lawful; rightful

【合格】qualified; up to standard

【合乎】conform with; correspond to; accord with; tally with

【合伙】form a partnership

【合计】(hé jì) total; amount to; add up to

【合计】(hé ji) think over; figure out

【合家欢乐】❶ family happiness ❷ The whole family is happy.

【合理】reasonable: 合情～fair and reasonable

【合流】❶ flowing together; confluence ❷ collaborate; work hand in glove with sb. ❸ different schools (of thought, art, etc.) merge into one

【合拍】in harmony

【合群】❶get on well with others; be sociable ❷be gregarious

【合身】fit

【合适】suit; fit

【合算】❶paying; worthwhile ❷reckon up

【合同】contract: 签订～ sign a contract

【合意】suit; be to one's liking

【合营】jointly owned; jointly operated

【合影】have a group photo taken

【合用】❶share ❷of use

【合资】joint stock

【合奏】instrumental ensemble

【合作】❶cooperate; collaborate ❷cooperation ❸cooperatively

何 (hé) what; which; how; why

【何必】there is no need; why

【何不】why not

【何等】❶what kind ❷(used in exclamations) what; how

【何苦】why bother; is it worth the trouble

【何况】much less; let alone

【何许】what kind of;what

【何以】❶how ❷why

【何止】far more than

河 (hé)river:小~ creek;stream;brook

【河岸】river bank;riverside

【河川】rivers and creeks

【河床】river bed

【河道】river course

【河堤】dike

【河谷】river valley

【河马】hippopotamus;hippo;river horse

【河渠】rivers and canals;waterways

【河山】rivers and mountains; land; territory

【河运】river transport

和 (hé) ❶peace ❷draw; tie ❸gentle; mild;kind ❹and; as well as ❺with; together with ❻indicating relationship, comparison, etc. ❼and ❽sum

【和蔼】amiable;kind;gentle

【和蔼可亲】friendly;amiable;kindly;affable

【和风】soft breeze

【和好】become reconciled

【和缓】❶gentle;mild ❷ease up;relax

【和解】become reconciled

【和美】harmonious

【和睦】harmony;amity

【和暖】pleasantly warm;genial

【和盘托出】reveal everything; hold nothing back

【和平】❶peace ❷peaceful

【和气】❶ gentle; kind; polite; amiable; friendly ❷ in a friendly way; good-natured

【和善】kind and gentle;genial

【和尚】monk

【和谈】peace talks

【和谐】harmony;concord

【和煦】pleasantly warm;genial

【和颜悦色】a (pleasant) benign countenance

【和约】peace treaty

【和悦】kindly;affable;amiable

荷 (hé) lotus

【荷尔蒙】hormone

【荷花】lotus

【荷叶】lotus leaf

核 (hé) ❶pit; stone; kernel ❷nucleus: 原子~ atomic nucleus ❸ examine; check ❹nuclear

【核爆炸】nuclear explosion; nuclear burst; atomic blast

【核弹】nuclear bomb

【核导弹】nuclear missile

【核电站】nuclear power station

【核定】check and ratify; appraise and decide

【核对】check

【核反应】nuclear reaction

【核辐射】nuclear radiation

【核能】nuclear energy

【核潜艇】nuclear-powered submarine

【核燃料】nuclear fuel

【核仁】kernel (of a fruit-stone)

【核实】verify;check

【核算】examine and calculate;assess

【核桃】walnut

【核心】nucleus;core;kernel

【核准】examine and approve; check and approve

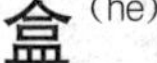

盒 (hé)box;case

【盒饭】box meal

贺 (hè) congratulate;celebrate

【贺词】congratulations;greetings
【贺卡】greeting card
【贺礼】congratulatory gift
【贺年】extend New Year greetings;pay a New Year call
【贺岁片】New Year's film
【贺喜】congratulate sb. on a happy occasion

喝 (hè)shout loudly
另见 1016 页 hē

【喝彩】acclaim;cheer
【喝问】shout a question to

赫 (hè) ❶conspicuous;grand ❷ hertz

【赫赫有名】distinguished;illustrious
【赫然】❶impressively;awesomely ❷terribly (angry)

褐 (hè) ❶ coarse cloth or clothing ❷brown

【褐色】brown

鹤 (hè)crane

【鹤发童颜】white hair and ruddy complexion;healthy in old age

hei

黑 (hēi) ❶darkness ❷black ❸dark

【黑暗】❶dark ❷darkness
【黑白】❶ black and white ❷ right and wrong
【黑白分明】with black and white sharply contrasted;in sharp contrast
【黑板】blackboard
【黑沉沉】(of the sky) gloomy;overcast
【黑点】stain;blemish;smirch
【黑客】hacker
【黑名单】blacklist
【黑幕】the inside story of a plot
【黑色幽默】black humor
【黑社会】criminal underground organization
【黑匣子】black box
【黑心】black heart;evil mind
【黑夜】night

hen

痕 (hén) mark; trace: 泪～tear stains; 伤～ scar

【痕迹】mark;trace;trail;track

很 (hěn) very;quite;much;awfully

【很好】quite well;very good

狠 (hěn) ❶ ruthless; relentless ❷ suppress (one's feelings); harden (the heart) ❸firm;resolute

【狠毒】vicious; brutal; venomous; malicious
【狠心】cruel-hearted;heartless

恨 (hèn) ❶hatred ❷hate ❸regret

【恨不得】have a strong desire to
【恨之入骨】hate sb. to the marrow of one's bones; bear a bitter hatred for sb.;bitterly hate

heng

亨 (hēng)go smoothly

【亨通】go smoothly;be prosperous

哼 (hēng) ❶groan;snort ❷hum;croon

【哼哧】puff hard

恒 (héng) ❶permanent; lasting ❷perseverance ❸ usual; common; constant

【恒等】identically equal;identical
【恒定】constant

【恒久】permanent
【恒温】constant temperature
【恒心】constancy of purpose
【恒星】(fixed) star

横 (héng) ❶ horizontal ❷ violently; fiercely ❸ across
另见本页 hèng

【横穿】cross
【横笛】bamboo flute
【横渡】sail across; cross a river
【横断面】cross section
【横幅】banner; streamer
【横祸】unexpected calamity; sudden misfortune
【横跨】stretch across (or over)
【横七竖八】in disorder; at sixes and sevens
【横扫】sweep away; make a clean sweep
【横向】crosswise; horizontal
【横行霸道】tyrannize

衡 (héng) ❶ the graduated arm of a steelyard ❷ weighing apparatus ❸ weigh; measure; judge

【衡量】weigh; measure; judge

横 (hèng) ❶ harsh and unreasonable; perverse ❷ unexpected
另见本页 héng

【横暴】perverse and violent
【横财】ill-gotten wealth (or gains): 发~ get rich by foul means; have a windfall
【横蛮】rude and unreasonable

hong

轰 (hōng) ❶ boom; bang ❷ drive off; shoo away ❸ rumble

【轰动】make a stir; cause a sensation
【轰轰烈烈】vigorous; dynamic
【轰隆】rumble; roll
【轰鸣】thunder; roar
【轰炸】bomb

哄 (hōng) ❶ roars of laughter ❷ hubbub
另见 1020 页 hǒng

【哄传】(of rumours) circulate widely
【哄闹】(of a crowd of people) make a lot of noise; make a racket
【哄抬】drive up (prices)
【哄堂大笑】the whole room rocking with laughter

烘 (hōng) ❶ dry (or warm) by fire ❷ bake ❸ set off

【烘干】❶ dry over heat ❷ stoving
【烘烤】toast; bake
【烘托】❶ set off by contrast; throw into sharp relief ❷ (in Chinese painting) add shading around an object to make it stand out

弘 (hóng) ❶ great; grand; magnificent ❷ enlarge; expand

【弘扬】develop and expand; enhance

红 (hóng) ❶ success: 开门~ get off to a good start ❷ dividend; bonus ❸ red ❹ symbol of success

【红榜】honour roll (or board)
【红宝石】ruby
【红茶】black tea
【红光满面】one's face glowing with health; in the pink
【红火】flourishing; prosperous
【红军】❶ the Red Army ❷ the Red Army man
【红利】bonus; extra dividend
【红脸】❶ blush ❷ flush with anger; get angry ❸ red face, face painting in Beijing opera, etc., traditionally for the heroic or the honest
【红领巾】❶ red scarf ❷ Young Pioneer
【红绿灯】traffic lights (or signal)

【红娘】go-between; matchmaker
【红扑扑】flushed
【红旗】red flag (or banner)
【红润】ruddy; rosy
【红色】red
【红色旅游】Red Tour (travel to historical sites of the Chinese Revolution)
【红烧】braise in soy sauce
【红十字会】the Red Cross
【红薯】sweet potato
【红糖】brown sugar
【红外线】infrared ray
【红眼】❶become infuriated; see red ❷ be envious; be jealous of
【红运】good luck
【红肿】red and swollen

宏 (hóng) huge; great; grand; magnificent
【宏大】grand; great; vast
【宏观】macroscopic
【宏论】informed opinion; intelligent view
【宏图】great plan; grand prospect
【宏伟】grand; magnificent
【宏愿】great aspirations; noble ambition

洪 (hóng) ❶flood ❷big; vast
【洪恩】great kindness; great favour
【洪福】great blessing
【洪亮】loud and clear
【洪水】flood; floodwater
【洪灾】a big flood; inundation

虹 (hóng) rainbow

鸿 (hóng) ❶swan goose ❷letter
【鸿沟】gulf; wide gap
【鸿毛】a goose feather-something very light or insignificant
【鸿雁】wild (or swan) goose

哄 (hǒng) ❶fool; humbug ❷coax; humour
另见 1019 页 hōng
【哄逗】keep (esp. a child) in good humour; coax
【哄骗】cheat
【哄劝】coax

hou

喉 (hóu) throat; larynx
【喉结】Adam's apple
【喉咙】throat
【喉痛】have a sore throat

猴 (hóu) ❶ monkey ❷ clever boy; smart chap
【猴戏】monkey show; a show by a performing monkey
【猴子】monkey

吼 (hǒu) roar; howl: 狮～the roar of a lion
【吼叫】roar; howl

后 (hòu) ❶back; rear ❷offspring ❸afterwards; later: 不久以～ before long; soon later
【后备】reserve; backup
【后备军】❶reserves ❷reserve force
【后辈】❶younger generation ❷posterity
【后代】future (or later) generations; offspring
【后盾】backing; backup force
【后方】rear; behind
【后跟】heel
【后顾之忧】cares at home; family considerations that cause delay in decision; fear of an attack from the rear
【后果】consequence: 前因～ cause and effect
【后患】future trouble

【后悔】regret
【后悔莫及】too late to regret
【后继有人】there is no lack of successors; have qualified successors
【后劲】❶delayed effect; aftereffect ❷reserved strength
【后来】afterwards; later
【后来居上】the latecomers surpass the formers
【后门】back door
【后面】behind; at the back; in the rear
【后年】the year after next
【后排】back row
【后勤】logistics
【后人】future generations; posterity; descendants
【后生】❶young man; lad ❷having a youthful appearance
【后天】the day after tomorrow
【后退】draw (or fall) back; retreat
【后卫】❶rear guard ❷football full back; defender ❸basketball guard
【后裔】descendant
【后遗症】❶sequelae ❷aftereffect; hangover
【后援】reinforcements; backup force; backing
【后者】the latter

厚 (hòu) ❶thick ❷deep; profound ❸kind; magnanimous ❹large; generous ❺rich or strong in flavour ❻favor; stress

【厚爱】your kind thought; your kindness
【厚道】kind and honest
【厚度】thickness
【厚礼】generous gifts
【厚实】thick and solid
【厚望】great expectations
【厚颜无耻】shameless
【厚重】❶thick and heavy ❷rich and generous ❸kind and dignified

候 (hòu) ❶season; time ❷symptom ❸wait; await

【候补】alternate; candidate
【候车室】waiting room (in a railway or a bus station)
【候鸟】migrant; migratory bird
【候审】await trial
【候选人】candidate
【候诊】wait to see the doctor
【候诊室】waiting room (in a hospital)

H

hu

呼 (hū) ❶call ❷shout; cry out ❸breathe out

【呼喊】shout; exclaim; cry (or call) out
【呼唤】❶call; shout ❷summon
【呼叫】❶call out; shout ❷call
【呼叫转移】call forwarding; call divert
【呼救】call for help
【呼声】cry; voice
【呼吸】❶breath ❷breathe; respire
【呼吸器】respirator
【呼啸】whistle; scream; whizz
【呼应】echo; work in concert
【呼吁】appeal; call on

忽 (hū) ❶neglect; overlook; ignore ❷suddenly

【忽略】ignore; overlook; neglect
【忽然】suddenly; all of a sudden
【忽视】ignore; neglect
【忽悠】flicker; jerk sb. around

囫 (hú)

【囫囵】whole
【囫囵吞枣】swallow dates whole; read without understanding

狐 (hú) fox

【狐臭】body odour;bromhidrosis
【狐狸】fox
【狐朋狗友】evil associates

弧 (hú)arc

【弧度】radian
【弧线】arc
【弧形】arc;curve

胡 (hú) ❶non-Han nationalities living in the north and west in ancient times ❷ introduced from the northern and western nationalities or from abroad ❸ recklessly; wantonly; outrageously ❹ why ❺ moustache, beard or whiskers

【胡扯】(talk) nonsense
【胡话】ravings;wild talk
【胡椒】pepper
【胡乱】carelessly;casually
【胡萝卜】carrot
【胡闹】run wild;make trouble
【胡说】❶talk nonsense ❷sheer nonsense
【胡思乱想】go off into wild fancies
【胡同】lane; alley: 死～ blind alley; dead end
【胡子】beard;moustache
【胡作非为】do all kinds of evils

壶 (hú)pot;kettle bottle;flask

葫 (hú)

【葫芦】bottle gourd;calabash

湖 (hú)lake

【湖滨】lakeside;lakeshore

蝴 (hú)

【蝴蝶】butterfly
【蝴蝶花】fringed iris
【蝴蝶结】bowknot;bow

糊 (hú) ❶paste;gruel ❷stick;paste

【糊口】keep body and soul together;make a living
【糊里糊涂】muddle-headed;mixed up
【糊涂】muddled;confused;bewildered

虎 (hǔ) ❶tiger ❷brave

【虎将】a brave general
【虎口】tiger's mouth—jaws of death
【虎口余生】survive a disaster;have a narrow escape
【虎视眈眈】glare like a tiger eyeing its prey;eye with hostility
【虎头虎脑】(usu. of a boy) looking strong and good-natured
【虎穴】tiger's den—a danger spot

琥 (hǔ)

【琥珀】amber

互 (hù) mutually;each other

【互补】mutually complementary
【互动】interact
【互换】exchange
【互惠】mutually beneficial;reciprocal
【互敬互爱】mutually respect and love
【互利】 mutually beneficial; of mutual benefit
【互联网】Internet
【互让】yield to each other;give in to each other
【互相】each other;one another;mutually
【互助】help each other

户 (hù) ❶door ❷household; family ❸ account ❹ family status: 挨家挨～ from door (or house) to door (or house)

【户籍】❶census register; household register ❷registered permanent residence
【户均】per household; per family
【户口】registered permanent residence; number of households and total population
【户内】indoor
【户头】(bank) account
【户外】outdoor
【户主】head of a household

护 (hù) ❶ protect; guard; shield ❷ be partial to; shield from censure
【护城河】city moat
【护发素】hair conditioner
【护工】nursing worker; care worker
【护航】convoy
【护理】❶tend; nurse ❷nursing
【护士】nurse
【护送】escort
【护卫】❶protect; guard ❷bodyguard
【护膝】kneepad
【护养】❶cultivate; nurse; rear ❷maintain
【护照】passport

hua

花 (huā) ❶flower; bloom; blossom: 百合～ lily; 茶～ camellia; 茉莉～ jasmine; 兰～ orchid; 玫瑰～ rose; 梅～ plum blossom ❷spend; expend
【花白】grey
【花瓣】petal
【花苞】bud
【花边】❶ decorative border; floral border ❷lace
【花草】flowers and plants
【花车】festooned vehicle
【花得起】afford
【花朵】flower
【花费】❶spend; expend; cost ❷expense
【花粉】pollen: ～管 pollen tube
【花好月圆】 blooming flowers and full moon; perfect conjugal bliss
【花花公子】dandy; coxcomb; playboy; a loose fish; a sad dog
【花花绿绿】brightly colored; colorful: 穿得～的 be colorfully dressed; ～的招贴画 poster in color
【花环】garland
【花卉】❶flowers and plants ❷traditional Chinese Painting of flowers and plants
【花会】flower fair
【花季】bloom of youth; youthful time
【花甲】a cycle of sixty years
【花椒】Sichuan pepper
【花轿】bridal sedan chair
【花篮】flower basket
【花露水】toilet water; perfumed toilet water
【花苗】flower seedling
【花名册】register; membership roster
【花木】flowers and trees
【花农】flower grower
【花盆】flowerpot
【花瓶】vase
【花圈】wreath
【花容月貌】 flower-like features and moon-like face—a great beauty
【花色】design and color
【花哨】garish; showy
【花生】peanut
【花束】bouquet; a bunch of flowers
【花坛】flower bed
【花团锦簇】bouquets of flowers and piles of silks rich multicolored decorations
【花纹】decorative pattern; figure: 各种～的地毯 carpets of different patterns
【花鞋】embroidered shoes
【花絮】titbits (of news); interesting side-

lights

【花言巧语】sweet words

【花样】❶ decorative pattern; variety ❷trick

【花样游泳】water ballet; synchronized swim-ming

【花园】garden：屋顶～roof garden

【花招】trick

【花枝招展】(of women) be gorgeously dressed

划 (huá) ❶row; paddle ❷cut; scratch 另见本页 huà

H

【划不来】be not worth it; do not pay：为这点儿小事跑那么远的路～。It doesn't pay to walk such a long way for a trifle.

【划船】❶boating; rowing ❷row (or paddle) a boat

【划得来】it's worthwhile; it pays

【划破】scratch

【划算】❶ calculate; weigh ❷ be to one's profit; pay

【划艇】canoe：～运动 canoeing

华 (huá) ❶China ❷best part; cream ❸ Chinese ❹prosperous; flourishing ❺ splendid; magnificent

【华灯】colorfully decorated lantern; light

【华而不实】flashy and without substance; superficially clever

【华尔兹舞】waltz

【华发】grey hair

【华贵】luxurious; costly

【华丽】magnificent

【华侨】overseas Chinese：归国～ returned overseas Chinese

【华人】Chinese：美籍～ an American Chinese

【华盛顿】Washington

【华裔】foreign citizen of Chinese origin

【华语】Chinese (language)

哗 (huá) noise; clamour

【哗然】in an uproar; in commotion

滑 (huá) ❶ slip; slide ❷ slippery; smooth ❸cunning

【滑冰】❶skate ❷skating

【滑倒】slip

【滑动】slide; slip; glide

【滑竿】a kind of litter

【滑稽】funny; amusing; comical

【滑坡】landslide

【滑水】water skiing

【滑梯】slide

【滑翔】glide

【滑雪】❶ski ❷skiing

化 (huà) ❶change; turn; transform ❷ convert; influence ❸melt; dissolve ❹ digest ❺ burn up ❻(动词后缀)-ize; -ify：电气～ electrify; 工业～ industrialize; 自动～ automatize; 现代～ modernize

【化除】eliminate; dispel; remove：～成见 dispel prejudices

【化肥】chemical fertilizer

【化工】chemical industry

【化合】chemical combination

【化合物】compound

【化身】incarnation; embodiment

【化石】fossil

【化食】help (or aid) digestion

【化痰】reduce phlegm：～止咳 reduce phlegm and relieve coughing

【化险为夷】turn danger into safety; head off a disaster

【化学】chemistry

【化妆】make up; put on makeup

【化装】disguise; dress up

划 (huà) ❶plan ❷stroke ❸divide; delimit ❹draw; mark; delineate

另见本页 huá

【划分】❶divide ❷differentiate

【划清界限】make a clear distinction

【划清是非】make a clear distinction between right and wrong

话（huà）❶ word; talk; saying: 留～ leave a message (or word) ❷ talk (or speak) about

【话别】say goodbye

【话剧】modern drama; stage play: 演出～ put on (or perform) a play

【话题】topic; subject of a talk

【话筒】❶ microphone ❷ telephone transmitter

【话音】one's voice in speech

【话语】words; speech; utterance

画（huà）❶drawing; painting; picture: 漫～ caricature; cartoon; 水彩～ water color; 油～ oil painting ❷draw; paint

【画板】drawing board

【画笔】painting brush; brush

【画饼充饥】draw cakes to allay hunger; feed on illusions

【画册】picture album

【画家】painter; artist

【画廊】gallery

【画眉】blacken eyebrows; draw eyebrows: ～鸟 thrush

【画图】❶draw designs, maps, etc. ❷picture

【画线】draw a line; underline; delineate

【画像】❶portrait ❷portray

【画展】art exhibition

huai

怀（huái）❶ bosom ❷ mind ❸ cherish; keep in mind ❹think of; miss ❺conceive (a child)

【怀抱】❶bosom ❷embrace

【怀旧】remember past times or old or old acquaintances

【怀念】miss; cherish the memory of; think of

【怀疑】distrust; doubt; suspect

【怀孕】be pregnant; conception

踝（huái）ankle

【踝骨】anklebone

坏（huài）❶go bad; spoil; ruin ❷bad; awful ❸badly; awfully

【坏处】harm

【坏蛋】bad egg; bastard

【坏话】malicious remarks; unpleasant words; vicious talk: 说～ speak ill of

【坏人】bad person; evildoer; bastard

【坏事】❶ evil deed; bad thing: 做～ do wrong ❷ruin sth. ; make things worse

【坏习惯】bad habit

huan

欢（huān）glad; joyous; merry

【欢蹦乱跳】healthy-looking and vivacious

【欢唱】sing merrily

【欢度】spend (an occasion) joyfully

【欢呼】cheer; applaud; hail

【欢聚】happy reunion; happy get-together

【欢乐】merry; happy; joyous; gay; cheerful

【欢庆】celebrate joyously

【欢声笑语】cheers and laughters

【欢送】set (or send) off; bid farewell

【欢天喜地】wild with joy; overjoyed

【欢喜】delighted; pleased; happy; joyful

【欢笑】laugh heartily

【欢心】favour; liking; love

【欢欣】joyous; elated

【欢迎】welcome; greet

【欢跃】jump for joy

还 (huán) ❶go (or come) back ❷give back; return; repay

另见 1011 页 hái

【还击】fight back; return fire; counterattack

【还价】counter-offer; bargain; counter-bid; abate a price

【还礼】❶return a salute ❷send a present in return; present a gift in return

【还清】pay off

【还手】strike (or hit) back

【还乡】return to one's native place

【还债】pay one's debt; repay a debt

【还嘴】answer (or talk) back; retort

环 (huán) ❶ ring; hoop ❷ link: 耳～earring ❸surround; encircle

【环保产品】environment-friendly product

【环抱】surround; encircle

【环城】around the city: ～赛跑 round-the-city race; ～公路 ring road; belt highway; beltway

【环顾】look about; look round

【环节】link: 主要～a key link

【环境】surroundings; environment; circumstances

【环境保护】environmental protection

【环境污染】environment pollution

【环球】❶round the world ❷the earth; the whole world

【环绕】surround; encircle

【环形】annular; ringlike

【环游】tour around (a place): ～世界 take a round-the-world tour

缓 (huǎn) ❶delay; put off; postpone ❷ slow; unhurried ❸relaxed

【缓步】walk unhurriedly

【缓冲】buffer; cushion

【缓和】❶relaxed ❷ease up; relax

【缓急】❶pressing or otherwise; of greater or lesser urgency ❷emergency

【缓解】alleviate; relieve; lessen

【缓慢】slow: 行动～ slow in action

【缓期】postpone a deadline; suspend

幻 (huàn) ❶unreal; imaginary; illusory ❷changeable; magical

【幻灯】❶slide show ❷slide projector

【幻觉】hallucination

【幻灭】vanish into thin air

【幻听】phonism

【幻想】illusion; fancy; fantasy

【幻影】unreal image; mirage; phantom

换 (huàn) ❶change ❷exchange; trade

【换班】❶change shifts ❷relieve a person on duty ❸changing of the guard

【换车】change trains or buses

【换代】replace; regenerate: 产品更新～ replace the older generations of products by new ones

【换挡】shift gears

【换货】exchange goods; barter: ～和付款协定 goods exchange and payments agreement

【换届】change a leader at the end of a fixed term

【换句话说】in other words

【换气】take a breath (in swimming)

【换钱】❶change money (or bills) ❷sell

【换取】exchange sth. for

【换药】change bandage; use fresh dressing for a wound

【换衣服】change clothes

唤 (huàn) call out

【唤起】❶arouse ❷call

【唤醒】awaken; wake up

涣 (huàn) melt; vanish

【涣然】(of misgivings, doubts, etc.) melt away; disappear; vanish
【涣散】❶demoralize ❷lax; slack
患 (huàn) ❶trouble; disaster ❷anxiety; worry ❸contract; suffer from
【患病】fall ill; suffer from a disease
【患处】affected part of a patient's body
【患得患失】worry about personal gains and losses
【患难与共】go through thick and thin together; share weal and woe
【患难之交】a friend indeed (or in need); tested friends
【患者】patient; sufferer
焕 (huàn) shining; glowing
【焕发】shine; glow; irradiate
【焕然一新】take on an entirely new look (or aspect); look brand new

huang

荒 (huāng) ❶wasteland ❷famine ❸waste ❹desolate
【荒草】weeds
【荒诞】fantastic; absurd
【荒岛】a desert (or uninhabited) island
【荒地】wasteland
【荒废学业】neglect one's studies (or lessons)
【荒凉】desolate; deserted; wild
【荒谬】absurd; preposterous
【荒漠】❶desolate and boundless: ~的草原 desolate and boundless grasslands ❷bleak and boundless desert; wilderness
【荒唐】❶absurd; fantastic; preposterous ❷dissipated; loose; interoperate
【荒无人烟】desolate and uninhabited
【荒野】wasteland; wilderness; the wilds
【荒淫无耻】shamelessly dissipated: 过着~的生活 lead a life of shameless dissipation
慌 (huāng) ❶nervous; flustered; confused ❷awfully; unbearably
【慌乱】alarmed and bewildered
【慌忙】hurriedly; in a great rush (or haste)
【慌手慌脚】in a rush; in a flurry
皇 (huáng) ❶grand; magnificent ❷emperor; sovereign
【皇宫】imperial palace
【皇冠】imperial crown
【皇后】empress
【皇权】imperial power (or authority)
【皇上】❶the emperor; the throne; the reigning sovereign ❷Your Majesty; His Majesty
黄 (huáng) ❶yellow; sallow ❷short for the Huanghe River ❸fizzle out; fall through
【黄灿灿】bright yellow; golden: ~的稻子 golden rice
【黄豆】soybean
【黄瓜】cucumber
【黄河】the Yellow River; the Huanghe River
【黄昏】dusk
【黄金】gold
【黄金时代】golden age
【黄金周】golden week
【黄牛】❶ox; cattle ❷scalper of tickets, etc.
【黄泉】the world of the dead; the underworld; the nether world
【黄雀】siskin
【黄色】❶yellow ❷decadent; obscene; pornographic
【黄色书】obscene book
【黄油】butter

H

【黄种人】the yellow race;xanthoderm

惶 (huáng) fear;anxiety;trepidation

【惶惶】in a state of anxiety; on tenterhooks;alarmed

【惶恐不安】in a state of alarm (or trepidation)

蝗 (huáng) locust

【蝗虫】locust

【蝗灾】plague of locusts

恍 (huǎng) ❶ seem; appear ❷ suddenly; all of a sudden ❸ as if (or though)

【恍惚】❶in a trance ❷dimly

【恍然大悟】suddenly realize;suddenly see the light

晃 (huǎng) ❶dazzle ❷flash past 另见本页 huàng

【晃眼】❶dazzle ❷twinkling

谎 (huǎng)lie;falsehood

【谎报】lie about sth. ;give false information;start a canard

【谎话】falsehood;lie:说~lie;tell a lie

【谎骗】deceive;cheat;dupe

【谎言】lie;falsehood:戳穿~ expose a lie

幌 (huǎng) heavy curtain

【幌子】❶shop sign;signboard ❷pretence;cover;front

晃 (huàng)shake;sway 另见本页 huǎng

【晃荡】rock;shake

【晃悠】wobble; stagger; shake from side to side

hui

灰 (huī) ❶grey ❷ash ❸lime;mortar ❹dust ❺disheartened;discouraged

【灰白】greyish white;ashen;pale:~的鬓发 greying temples

【灰尘】dust;dirt

【灰沉沉】gloomy; leaden: 天空~的 a gloomy sky;a leaden sky

【灰姑娘】Cinderella

【灰烬】ashes: 化为~ be reduced to ashes

【灰蒙蒙】dusky; overcast: ~的夜色 a dusky night scene

【灰色】❶grey;ashy ❷pessimistic;gloomy ❸obscure;ambiguous

【灰心】lose heart (or hope); be discouraged;be disheartened

诙 (huī)

【诙谐】humorous

挥 (huī) ❶wipe off ❷command (an army) ❸wave;shake;move ❹scatter;disperse

【挥动】wave;shake

【挥汗如雨】dripping with sweat

【挥霍】spend freely;squander

【挥金如土】spend money like water

【挥洒】❶ sprinkle (water); shed (tears) ❷write or paint freely and easily

【挥手告别】wave farewell;wave goodbye

【挥舞】wave;wield

恢 (huī) extensive;vast

【恢复】recover (one's health, consciousness, etc.); renew; restore; resume (diplomatic relation, etc.)

【恢恢】extensive 法网~。Justice has long arms.

辉 (huī) ❶ splendour; brightness ❷ shine ❸bright

【辉煌】glorious;splendid;brilliant

【辉映】shine;reflect

徽 (huī) ❶ emblem; badge; insignia ❷ fine;glorious

【徽记】sign;mark

【徽章】badge;insignia

回 (huí) ❶chapter ❷return;go back ❸circle;wind ❹turn round ❺reply;answer ❻decline;refuse;cancel;dismiss ❼time;occasion

【回报】repay;give (or do) sth. in return

【回避】avoid;evade

【回车键】return key

【回程】❶ return trip ❷ return (or back) stroke

【回答】answer;reply;respond;response

【回到】get back to;return to

【回访】pay a return visit

【回顾】look back;recall;review

【回锅】❶heat up (a cooked dish) ❷cook again ～肉 double cooked pork slices

【回击】fight back;return fire;counterattack

【回绝】refuse;decline:一口～ flatly refuse

【回扣】sales commission;kickback;rebate

【回来】return;come (or get,be) back

【回去】❶(used after a verb to indicate returning to where sth. came from) back ❷return;go back;be back

【回升】rise again;pick up

【回声】echo

【回收利用】recycle

【回首】❶ turn one's head;turn round ❷ look back;call to mind

【回头见】see you later

【回头是岸】repent and be saved

【回味】❶ aftertaste ❷ call sth. to mind and ponder over it

【回响】reverberate;echo;resound

【回想】recall;think back;recollect

【回心转意】change one's views; come around

【回信】write back;write in reply;answer a letter

【回味】❶after taste ❷enjoy in retrospect

【回忆】❶ call to mind;recall;recollect ❷memories

【回音】❶echo ❷reply:立候～ hoping for an immediate reply ❸turn

【回应】answer;respond

【回赠】send a present in return;present a gift in return

悔 (huǐ) regret;repent

【悔改】repent and mend one's ways

【悔过自新】repent and turn over a new leaf;repent and make a fresh start

【悔恨】regret deeply

【悔悟】realize one's error and show repentance

毁 (huǐ) ❶ destroy;ruin;damage ❷ burn up ❸slander

【毁坏】destroy;damage

【毁灭】destroy;ruin

【毁容】disfigure one's face

【毁于一旦】be destroyed in a moment

【毁誉】praise or blame;praise or condemnation

【毁约】break one's promise;scrap a contracted treaty

汇 (huì) ❶collection ❷gather together ❸mail;send;remit ❹converge

【汇报】report;give an account of

【汇编】collection;compilation

【汇合】join;unite;meet;converge

【汇集】gather;collect;compile

【汇款】❶remit money;make a remittance ❷remittance

【汇流】converge;flow together

【汇率】exchange rate

【汇总】gather;collect;pool

H

会 (huì) ❶ meeting; gathering; get-together; party; conference ❷ society; association; union ❸ chief city; capital ❹ chance ❺ meet; see ❻ assemble; get together ❼ be good at; be skillful in ❽ be able to; can ❾ be likely to; be sure to ❿ understand

另见 1076 页 kuài

【会场】meeting-place
【会费】membership dues
【会话】❶ converse ❷ conversation
【会徽】emblem of a sports meet, etc.
【会见】meet with
【会聚】assemble; flock together
【会客】receive visitors (or guests)
【会面】meet; come together
【会师】join forces
【会说】have the gift of the gab; be a glib talker
【会谈】talk; conversation
【会堂】hall; assembly hall
【会晤】meet
【会心】understanding; knowing: ～的微笑 an understanding smile
【会议】meeting; session; conference
【会议室】meeting room
【会员】member: 正式～ full member
【会战】meet for a decisive battle

讳 (huì) ❶ avoid as taboo ❷ forbidden word; taboo

【讳言】dare not or would not speak up: 毫不～ make no attempt to conceal the truth; confess freely

荟 (huì) luxuriant growth (of plants)

【荟萃】(of distinguished people or exquisite objects) gather together; assemble

绘 (huì) paint; draw

【绘画】painting; drawing
【绘声绘色】vivid; lively
【绘图】mapping

贿 (huì) ❶ wealth ❷ bribe

【贿赂】❶ bribe ❷ bribery

彗 (huì) broom

【彗星】comet

晦 (huì) ❶ the last day of a lunar month ❷ dark; obscure; gloomy ❸ night

【晦暗】dark and gloomy
【晦涩】hard to understand; obscure

秽 (huì) ❶ dirty ❷ ugly; abominable

【秽迹】dirty business; scandalous affair

惠 (huì) ❶ favour; kindness; benefit ❷ kind; gracious

【惠存】please keep; to so-and-so
【惠顾】your patronage

慧 (huì) intelligent; bright

【慧心】wisdom
【慧眼】mental discernment (or perception); insight; acumen

hun

昏 (hūn) ❶ dusk ❷ lose consciousness; faint ❸ confused; muddled ❹ dark; dim

【昏暗】dim; dusky
【昏过去】pass out; lose consciousness
【昏花】dim-sighted
【昏厥】faint; faint away
【昏乱】dazed and confused
【昏迷】unconscious coma
【昏眩】dizzy

荤 (hūn) ❶ meat or fish ❷ strong-smelling vegetables forbidden to

Buddhist vegetarians, such as onions, leeks, garlic, etc.

【荤菜】meat dish

【荤油】lard

婚 (hūn) ❶marriage; wedding ❷marry

【婚假】marriage leave

【婚礼】wedding ceremony; wedding

【婚期】wedding day

【婚事】marriage; wedding: 操办~prepare a wedding

【婚姻】marriage

【婚姻法】marriage law

浑 (hún) ❶muddy ❷foolish; stupid ❸simple and natural ❹whole; all over

【浑厚】❶simple and honest ❷(of writing, painting, etc.) simple and vigorous

【浑然一体】one integrated mass; a unified entity; an integral whole

【浑身】from head to foot; all over the body

【浑水摸鱼】fish in troubled waters

【浑浊】muddy; turbid

混 (hún) ❶muddy; turbid ❷foolish; stupid ❸simple and natural; unsophisticated ❹whole; all over

另见本页 hùn

【混蛋】blackguard; wretch; scoundrel; bastard; skunk

魂 (hún) ❶soul ❷spirit

【魂不守舍】❶absent-minded ❷lose one's mind

【魂飞魄散】be frightened out of one's wits

【魂魄】soul

混 (hùn) ❶mix; confuse ❷get along with sb. ❸pass for; pass off as ❹drift on (or along)

另见本页 hún

【混合】mix; blend

【混合物】mixture

【混乱】❶confused; chaotic ❷confusion; chaos

【混凝土】concrete

【混日子】drift along aimlessly

【混为一谈】confuse sth. with sth. else

【混淆】confuse; mix up

【混淆是非】confuse right and wrong

【混血儿】half-breed

【混浊】muddy; turbid

huo

豁 (huō) ❶slit; break; crack ❷give up; sacrifice

另见 1033 页 huò

【豁出去】go ahead regardless; be ready to risk everything

【豁嘴】❶harelip ❷a harelipped person

活 (huó) ❶work: 零~odd jobs ❷product ❸live ❹alive; living ❺vivid; lively ❻moving; movable

【活靶】manoeuvring target

【活宝】a bit of a clown; a funny fellow

【活动】❶move about ❷activity ❸action ❹movable; flexible ❺shaky; unsteady

【活该】serve sb. right; get what one deserves

【活话】indefinite words; vague promise

【活活】while still alive

【活计】❶handicraft work; manual labor ❷handiwork; work

【活力】vigour; vitality; energy

【活路】❶means of subsistence; way out ❷workable method

【活命】❶earn a bare living; scrape along; eke out an existence ❷save sb.'s life ❸life

【活泼】lively；vivacious；vivid

【活期存款】current deposit；current account

【活生生】❶in real life ❷actual；real；living

【活水】flowing water；running water

【活下来】survive

【活跃】❶ active；brisk；dynamic ❷ enliven；animate

【活着】alive

【活捉】capture alive

【活罪】❶living hell；untold suffering ❷ living punishment

H

火 （huǒ）❶fire：生～ make a fire；着～ be on fire ❷firearms；ammunition ❸ flaming；fiery ❹ urgent；pressing ❺ angry

【火把】torch

【火柴】match

【火车】train

【火车站】railway station

【火锅】chafing dish；hotpot

【火海】a sea of fire

【火红】red as fire；flaming；fiery

【火花】spark

【火化】cremation

【火鸡】turkey

【火箭】rocket：发射～ fire（or launch）a rocket

【火警】fire alarm

【火炬】torch

【火坑】fiery pit；pit of hell；abyss of suffering

【火力】firepower；fire

【火炉】stove

【火冒三丈】fly into a rage

【火苗】a tongue of flame；flame

【火气】❶ internal heat（as a cause of illness）❷anger；temper

【火山】volcano

【火势】the intensity of a fire

【火腿】ham

【火线】❶battle（or firing，front）line ❷ live wire

【火焰】flame

【火药】gunpowder；powder

【火灾】fire（as a disaster）；conflagration

【火葬】cremation

【火种】❶kindling material；kindling；tinder ❷ live cinders kept for starting a new fire

伙 （huǒ）❶partner；mate ❷company；partnership ❸mess；board；meals ❹ group；gang；band ❺combine；join

【伙伴】partner；companion

【伙食】food；mess；meals

或 （huò）❶ maybe；or else；perhaps ❷or

【或然】probable

【或许】maybe；perhaps

【或者】❶maybe；perhaps ❷or；either ... or ...

货 （huò）❶goods；commodity ❷money

【货币】money；currency

【货币贬值】currency devaluation

【货车】freight car（or train）

【货船】freighter；cargo ship

【货机】cargo aircraft（or plane）；air freighter

【货款】payment for goods

【货摊】stall；stand

【货物】goods；merchandise

【货箱】packing box

【货源充足】an ample supply of goods

【货运】freight transport；shipment of commodities

【货真价实】❶ genuine goods at a fair

price ❷ supply honest goods at a honest price

获（huò）❶ capture; catch ❷ obtain; win; reap ❸harvest; gather in

【获得】 obtain; gain; get; acquire; win; achieve

【获奖】 win a prize; be awarded a prize

【获救】 be rescued

【获利】 make a profit; reap profits

【获胜者】 winner

【获释】 be released; be set free

【获悉】 learn (of an event)

【获准】 get permission; be approved

祸（huò）❶misfortune; disaster; calamity ❷bring disaster upon; ruin: 车～ traffic accident

【祸从天降】 a disaster comes from sky

【祸害】 ❶disaster; course; scourge ❷damage; destroy

【祸事】 disaster; calamity; mishap

惑（huò）❶ be puzzled; be bewildered ❷delude; mislead

【惑乱】 delude and confuse

霍（huò）suddenly; quickly

【霍地】 suddenly

【霍乱】 ❶cholera ❷ acute gastroenteritis

豁（huò）❶ clear; open; open-minded; generous ❷exempt; remit

另见 1031 页 huō

【豁达】 sanguine; optimistic

【豁亮】 ❶ roomy and bright ❷ sonorous; resonant

【豁免】 exempt; remit

藿（huò）leaves of pulse plants

【藿香】 wrinkled giant hyssop (Agastache rugosa)

J j

jī

几 (jī) ❶a small table ❷nearly; almost 另见 1037 页 jǐ

【几乎】 nearly; almost

讥 (jī) ridicule; mock; satirize

【讥讽】 ridicule; satirize

【讥笑】 ridicule; jeer

击 (jī) ❶ beat; hit; strike ❷ attack; assault ❸ come in contact with; bump into

【击败】 defeat; beat

【击穿】 puncture; breakdown

【击毁】 destroy; smash

【击落】 shoot down

【击退】 beat back

【击中】 hit

饥 (jī) ❶ famine; crop failure ❷ hungry; starve; famish

【饥不择食】 a hungry person is not choosy about food

【饥饿】 ❶hungry ❷hunger; starvation

【饥寒交迫】 suffer from hunger and cold

【饥荒】 ❶famine; crop failure ❷be short of money

【饥民】 famine refugee; famine victim

机 (jī) ❶ machine; engine; motor ❷ plane ❸opportunity; chance ❹crucial point

【机不可失】 cannot lose the opportunity

【机场】 airport; airfield

【机电产品】 mechanical and electrical product

【机动】 ❶ motor-driven ❷ kept in reserve ❸flexible

【机构】 organization; office

【机关】 ❶office; organ; body ❷scheme

【机会】 chance; opportunity: 借此~take this opportunity

【机警】 alert; sharp-witted

【机灵】 clever; smart

【机密】 secret; confidential

【机器】 machine

【机械】 ❶machinery ❷mechanical

【机遇】 chance; opportunity

【机智】 resourceful; quick-witted; sharp-witted

【机组】 ❶aircrew; flight crew ❷ unit; set

肌 (jī) muscle; flesh

【肌肤】 skin

【肌腱】 tendon

【肌肉】 muscle

鸡 (jī) chicken: 小~chick; 公~cock; 母~ hen

【鸡蛋】 egg

【鸡蛋碰石头】 hit an egg on a rock

【鸡冠】 cockscomb

【鸡毛蒜皮】trifles; trivial matters

【鸡犬不宁】even fowls and dogs are not left in peace

【鸡肉】chicken

【鸡汤】chicken broth

【鸡尾酒】cocktail

奇 (jī) ❶odd (number) ❷ a fractional amount (over that mentioned in a round number); odd lots

另见 1137 页 qí

【奇数】odd number

积 (jī) ❶ collect; store up; accumulate ❷accumulated ❸age-old

【积存】store up; lay up; stockpile

【积德】accumulate virtue

【积分】integral

【积极】❶active; energetic; vigorous ❷positive

【积累】accumulate; store up

【积少成多】many a little makes a mickle

【积习】old habit

【积蓄】❶savings ❷save; accumulate

【积雪】accumulated snow

基 (jī) ❶base; foundation; basis ❷basic; key; primary; cardinal ❸ radical; base; group

【基本】❶base; basis ❷basic; main ❸basically; in the main; on the whole

【基本功】basic training; basic skill; essential technique

【基层】basic level; primary level; grassroots unit

【基础】foundation; basis; base: 打～ lay the foundation of

【基地】base

【基点】basic point

【基督教】Christianity

【基价】base price

【基金】fund

【基因】gene

【基因工程】genetic engineering

【基于】on the basis of; because of; in view of

缉 (jī) seize; catch; arrest

【缉捕】seize; arrest

【缉私】seize smugglers

畸 (jī) ❶lopsided; unbalanced ❷irregular; abnormal

【畸变】distortion

【畸形】❶deformity; abnormality ❷abnormal

稽 (jī)

【稽查】❶ check (to prevent smuggling, tax evasion, etc.) ❷an official engaged in such work; customs officer

【稽核】check; examine

激 (jī) ❶ arouse; stimulate; stir; excite ❷ violent; fierce ❸ swash; surge; dash ❹excitement; stimulation

【激动】❶stir; heat; excite; agitate; inspire ❷excitement; emotion ❸excitedly

【激发】set off; stir up; stimulate; arouse

【激光】laser

【激化】sharpen; intensify; become acute

【激活】activate; stimulate

【激将法】prodding sb. into action

【激励】urge; encourage

【激怒】enrage

【激起】stir up; arouse

【激情】passion; enthusiasm

【激素】hormone

及 (jí) ❶ reach ❷ timely ❸ and; as well as

【及格】pass a test or exam; get through

【及时】timely; in time; seasonable; at the right time promptly; without delay

【及早】as soon as possible

吉 (jí) lucky; auspicious; propitious

【吉利】lucky; auspicious; propitious

【吉他】guitar

【吉祥】lucky; auspicious; propitious

【吉祥如意】as lucky as one wishes

【吉祥物】mascot

【吉兆】good omen; propitious sign

汲 (jí) draw (water)

【汲取】draw; absorb

级 (jí) ❶ grade; class ❷ stage; step ❸ degree

J

【级别】rank; level

极 (jí) ❶ end; limit ❷ pole ❸ exert (or use) to the utmost ❹ extreme ❺ extremely; exceedingly

【极大】maximum

【极地】polar region: ~航行 arctic navigation; polar air navigation

【极度】extremely; to the utmost

【极端】end; limit; extreme: 走~go to extremes

【极光】aurora; polar lights

【极力】do one's utmost; spare no effort

【极品】best quality; highest grade

【极其】most; extremely; exceedingly

【极限】the limit; the maximum

即 (jí) ❶ reach ❷ be ❸ present ❹ namely ❺ even ❻ at once ❼ in immediate future ❽ prompted by the occasion

【即便】even; even though; even if

【即将】be about to; be in the point of

【即日】this very day; that very day; within a few days

【即使】even; even though; even if

【即兴】impromptu; extemporaneous

急 (jí) ❶ urgency; emergency ❷ worry ❸ be eager to ❹ anxious; impatient ❺ irritable ❻ urgent; pressing ❼ violent; fast ❽ in haste; in a hurry

【急病】acute disease

【急不可待】be too impatient (or anxious) to wait

【急救】first aid; emergency treatment

【急剧】sharp; drastic; rapid; sudden

【急流】❶ torrent; rapids ❷ jet stream

【急忙】in haste; in a hurry

【急迫】urgent; pressing; imperative

【急切】❶ in a hurry; in haste ❷ eager; impatient; urgent; imperative; anxious

【急速】❶ fast; rapid; swift ❷ rapidly; swiftly; fast; quickly

【急弯】sharp turn: 拐了个~made a sharp turn

【急需】❶ be badly in need of ❷ urgent need

【急用】urgent need

【急于】be eager (or impatient, anxious)

【急躁】❶ irritable ❷ impatient; rash

【急诊】emergency case; emergency call; emergency treatment

【急症】sudden attack (of illness); acute disease; emergency case

【急中生智】have quick wits in emergency

疾 (jí) ❶ illness; disease; sickness ❷ suffering ❸ hate ❹ swift; fast; rapid quick ❺ vigorous; strong

【疾病】illness; sickness; disease

【疾步】walking quickly; at a fast pace: ~上前 go forward quickly

【疾患】illness; disease

【疾苦】sufferings; hardships

棘 (jí) ❶ sour jujube ❷ thorn bushes; brambles ❸ spine; spina

【棘手】troublesome; thorny; knotty

集 (jí) ❶ market; fair ❷ collection ❸ volume; part ❹ collect; gather

【集合】❶gather up;assemble;muster;call together ❷Fall in!(word of command)

【集会】rally;gathering

【集结】gather together

【集市】market;fair

【集思广益】draw on collective wisdom and absorb all useful ideas

【集团】group; bloc; clique; community; circle; an organization; a body of people;a faction

【集训】assemble for training

【集邮】collect stamps

【集中】concentrate; put together; centre; centralize;focus;amass:精神～ concentrate one's mind

【集中营】concentration camp

【集资】raise funds

嫉 (jí) ❶be jealous;be envious ❷hate

【嫉恨】hate out of jealousy

瘠 (jí) ❶lean;thin and weak ❷barren; poor;lean

【瘠田】infertile land

籍 (jí) ❶ book ❷ native place; home town; birthplace ❸ membership:党～party membership

【籍贯】native place

几 (jǐ) ❶how many ❷several; some; a few;odd

另见 1034 页 jī

【几多】how many;how much

【几个】several;some;a few

【几何】❶how much (or many) ❷geometry

【几经】several times;time and again

【几时】when;at what time

【几天前】the other day;several days ago; a couple of days ago

己 (jǐ) ❶oneself; one's own; personal ❷ the sixth of the ten Heavenly Stems

【己方】one's own side

【己任】one's duty

挤 (jǐ) ❶crowd ❷squeeze;push (or elbow, shoulder) one's way in (or out) ❸squeeze;press

【挤兑】a run on a bank

【挤奶】milk

【挤压】extrude;press

【挤眼】wink

【挤占】encroach

济 (jǐ)

另见 1039 页 jì

【济济】(of people) many;numerous

【济济一堂】gather together under the same roof

给 (jǐ) ❶supply;provide ❷ample;well provided for

另见 997 页 gěi

【给水】❶ watersupply:～工程 watersupply engineering ❷ feed water: 锅炉～ boiler feed water

【给养】provisions

【给予】give;render

脊 (jǐ) ❶backbone;spine ❷ridge

【脊背】back (of a human being)

【脊髓】spinal cord

【脊柱】spinal column;backbone

【脊椎】vertebra

计 (jì) ❶ meter; gauge ❷ idea; plan; trick: 中～fall into a trap ❸calculate;count

【计策】stratagem;plan;trick

【计程表】taximeter

【计程车】taxi;cab

【计划】❶plan;program ❷planned

【计划经济】planned economy

【计价】valuate

J

【计较】❶care about; mind ❷argue ❸think over
【计时】reckon by the hour
【计算】❶calculate; count ❷consider; plan
【计算机】computer
【计算器】calculator

记 (jì) ❶notes; record ❷mark; sign ❸remember; bear in mind; keep in mind; memorize ❹record; write (or take) down
【记笔记】take notes
【记得】remember; keep (or bear) in mind
【记分】keep the score
【记功】record a great service (or a merit)
【记挂】be concerned about; keep thinking about; miss
【记号】mark; sign; symbol
【记录】record; minutes; notes: 保持～ keep a record; 创～ set a record; 打破～ break a record
【记名】sign: 无～投票 secret ballot
【记起】call back to mind; recall; remember; recollect
【记事】❶keep a record of events; make a memorandum ❷account; record of events; chronicles
【记事本】notebook
【记述】record and narrate
【记性】memory
【记叙】narrate
【记忆】❶memory ❷recall; remember
【记忆犹新】remain fresh in one's memory
【记载】❶record; write down ❷account
【记者】reporter; correspondent
【记住】remember; learn by heart; bear in mind

伎 (jì) ❶skill; ability; trick ❷a professional female dancer or singer in ancient China
【伎俩】trick; intrigue; manoeuvre

纪 (jì) ❶discipline ❷age
【纪录片】documentary film
【纪律】discipline: 违反～ break discipline; 遵守～ keep discipline
【纪念】❶commemorate ❷keepsake; souvenir ❸anniversary
【纪念碑】monument: 人民英雄～ the Monument to the People's Heroes
【纪念馆】museum in memory of sb.; memorial hall
【纪念品】keepsake; souvenir
【纪念日】commemoration day; red-letter day
【纪要】summary
【纪传体】history presented in a series of biographies

技 (jì) skill; ability; trick: 绝～consummate skill
【技能】skill; ability
【技巧】skill; technique; craftsmanship
【技术】skill; technology; technique
【技术知识】technological know-how; technical knowledge

忌 (jì) ❶be jealous of; envy ❷fear ❸avoid; shun; abstain from ❹quit; give up
【忌妒】be jealous of; envy
【忌讳】❶taboo ❷abstain from
【忌酒】give up drink (or alcohol); abstain from wine
【忌烟】quit (or give up) smoking

际 (jì) ❶border; edge ❷time; moment ❸lot; fortune ❹between; among ❺on the occasion of one's lot; circumstances
【际遇】favourable turns in life; spells of good or bad fortune

季 (jì) season：淡～dull season；旺～busy season

【季度】quarter (of a year)

【季节】season：旅游～ tourist season；农忙～a busy farming season

【季军】the third prize winner

剂 (jì) medicament

【剂量】dose；dosage

迹 (jì) ❶ remains；ruins；vestige ❷ an outward sign；indication ❸ mark；trace；stain；print；sign

【迹象】sign；indication

济 (jì) ❶ cross a river ❷ aid；relieve；help ❸ be of help；benefit

另见 1037 页 jǐ

【济贫】aid the poor；relieve the poor

【济世】benefit mankind；do good to society

既 (jì) ❶ already ❷ since；as；now that ❸ both ...and ...；as well as

【既定】set；fixed

【既然】since；as；because；now that

【既往不咎】forgive one's past misdeeds

继 (jì) ❶ continue；follow；succeed ❷ then；afterwards

【继承】❶ carry on ❷ inherit ❸ succeed

【继父】stepfather

【继母】stepmother

【继任】succeed sb. as ...

【继续】❶ go on；continue；keep on；proceed ❷ continuation

祭 (jì) ❶ hold a memorial ceremony for ❷ offer a sacrifice to ❸ wield

【祭奠】hold a memorial ceremony for

【祭品】sacrificial offerings；oblation

【祭扫】offer sacrifices at and sweep (the tomb)

【祭祀】offer sacrifices to gods or ancestors

寄 (jì) ❶ send；post；mail ❷ entrust；deposit；check ❸ attach to

【寄出】send off

【寄存】leave with；check；deposit：行李～处 checkroom；left-luggage office

【寄费】postage

【寄居】live in the house of sb.

【寄人篱下】live under sb.'s roof

【寄宿】❶ lodge；put up ❷ board

【寄托】❶ entrust to the care of sb.；place on；leave with sb. ❷ place (hope, etc.) on；pin one's hopes on；find sustenance in；repose

【寄信】send a letter；post a letter

【寄信人】sender；addresser

【寄意】send one's regards

【寄予】❶ place (hope, etc.) on ❷ show；give；express

寂 (jì) ❶ silent；quiet；still ❷ lonely；lonesome；solitary

【寂静】quiet；silent；still

【寂寞】lonely；lonesome

【寂然】silent；still：～无声 quiet and still

jia

加 (jiā) ❶ add ❷ increase ❸ plus；augment ❹ put in；append

【加班】work overtime

【加倍】double；redouble

【加大】increase；enlarge

【加法】addition

【加工】❶ process ❷ machining；working

【加固】reinforce；strengthen；consolidate

【加号】plus sign (+)

【加紧】speed up

【加劲】put more energy into；make a greater effort

【加剧】aggravate；become more serious

【加宽】broaden; widen

【加气】❶gas filling ❷air entrainment: ~水泥 air entraining cement

【加强】strengthen; enhance; argument; reinforce

【加热】heating

【加入】❶add; mix; put in ❷join; accede to

【加上】❶add; give ❷moreover; in addition

【加深】deepen

【加速】quicken; speed up; accelerate

【加油】❶ oil; refuel ❷ make greater efforts; make an extra effort: ~干 work with added vigour ❸come along (or on)

【加重】❶ make or become heavier ❷ increase the weight of ❸make or become more serious; aggravate ❹ aggravation; exacerbation; weighting; bodiness

夹 (jiā) ❶ carry sth. under one's arm ❷hold tightly; pinch ❸mix ❹clip

另见 1041 页 jiá

【夹板】❶boards for pressing sth. or holding things together ❷splint

【夹层】double layer

【夹带】❶ carry secretly; smuggle ❷ notes smuggled into an examination hall

【夹缝】a narrow space between two adjacent things; crack; crevice

【夹克】jacket

【夹杂】be mixed up with; be mingled with

【夹子】clip; wallet; folder

佳 (jiā) beautiful; fine; good

【佳话】a story on everybody's lips; a deed praised far and wide; a much-told tale

【佳节】festival; happy festival time

【佳句】beautiful line (in a poem); well-turned phrase

【佳肴】delicacies

【佳音】good news; good tidings; favourable reply

【佳作】a fine piece of writing; an excellent work; masterpieces

枷 (jiā) cangue

【枷锁】fetters; shackles; chains

家 (jiā) ❶family; household ❷home ❸ a person or family engaged in a certain trade ❹a specialist in a certain field ❺a school of thought; school ❻domestic

【家蚕】silkworm

【家常】the daily life of a family; domestic trivia

【家常便饭】❶simple meal; homely food ❷ usual practice

【家丑】family scandal; the skeleton in the cupboard (or closet)

【家畜】livestock; domestic animal

【家传】handed down from the older generations of the family

【家伙】❶fellow ❷weapon; tool

【家教】family education; upbringing

【家境】family financial situation

【家具】furniture

【家谱】family tree; genealogical tree; genealogy

【家人】family members

【家属】family members

【家庭暴力】family violence

【家庭作业】homework

【家务】house work; household duties: ~劳动 household chores

【家乡】hometown; homeplace; native place; homeland

【家业】family property; property

【家用电器】household appliances

【家喻户晓】known to every family; widely known

【家园】homeplace; homeland; home

【家长】❶head of a family; parents; patriarch ❷the parent or guardian of a child
【家政服务】household management service
【家族】family; clan
嘉 (jiā) ❶good; fine ❷praise; commend
【嘉宾】honoured (or distinguished) guest
【嘉奖】commend; cite; praise
【嘉年华】Carnival
夹 (jiá) double-layered; lined
另见 1040 页 jiā
【夹衣】lined coat (or jacket)
颊 (jiǎ) cheek: 面 ~ cheek
甲 (jiǎ) ❶shell ❷nail: 手指~ fingernail ❸first
【甲板】deck
【甲虫】beetle
【甲级】first grade (or class, rate)
【甲鱼】soft-shelled turtle
假 (jiǎ) ❶make use of ❷false; unreal ❸ if; suppose; assume; grant; presume ❹borrow; avail oneself as
另见本页 jià
【假扮】disguise as; dress up as
【假钞票】forged note; counterfeit money
【假定】❶suppose; assume ❷hypothesis
【假发】wig: 戴~ wear a wig
【假公济私】seek personal gain in the name of public service
【假话】lie; falsehood: 说~ tell a lie
【假冒】pass oneself off as; counterfeit; imitate
【假面具】mask
【假如】if; supposing; in case; in the event that
【假山】rockery
【假设】❶ suppose; assume; grant ❷ hypothesis
【假使】if; in case; in the event that
【假想】imagination; hypothesis; supposition; fiction
【假象】false appearance
【假意】❶hypocrisy; unction; insincerity ❷ pretend; put on
【假装】pretend; make believe
价 (jià) price; cost; value
【价格】price
【价值】value; worth: 毫无~worthless; 有~ valuable
驾 (jià) drive; pilot; sail; harness
【驾轻就熟】do a familiar job with ease
【驾驶】drive; pilot; sail
【驾驭】❶ control; master; dominate ❷drive
架 (jià) ❶ frame; rack; shelf; stand ❷put (or set, build) up ❸ kidnap ❹quarrel; fight
【架构】frame work
【架设】put (or set, build) up; erect; construct
【架子】❶rack; shelf; stand; frame ❷airs: 摆~put on airs
假 (jià) ❶holiday; vacation ❷leave: 请病~ ask for a sick leave
另见本页 jiǎ
【假期】vacation; period of leave
【假日】holiday
【假日经济】holiday economy
【假条】❶application for leave ❷leave permit
嫁 (jià) ❶ marry; get married ❷ shift; transfer
【嫁祸于人】shift the blame (or on) to sb. else

【嫁接】grafting

【嫁妆】dowry

jian

尖 (jiān) ❶point; tip; top: 针～pinpoint ❷pointed; sharp; acute; shrill; piercing ❸the best of its kind; the pick of the bunch; the cream of the crop

【尖刀】sharp knife; dagger

【尖端】❶pointed end; peak ❷advanced; sophisticated

【尖叫】scream

【尖利】sharp; keen; cutting; shrill; piercing

J

【尖锐】❶sharp-pointed ❷intense; sharp; acute

【尖酸刻薄】tart and mean; bitterly sarcastic

奸 (jiān) ❶traitor ❷wicked; evil; treacherous; crafty

【奸猾】deceitful; cunning; crafty

【奸计】an evil plot

【奸污】rape; seduce

【奸细】spy; traitor; enemy agent

【奸笑】sinister smile

【奸贼】traitor

【奸诈】crafty; treacherous; fraudulent

歼 (jiān) annihilate; wipe out; destroy

【歼击机】fighter plane; fighter; pursuit plane

【歼灭】wipe out; annihilate; destroy

坚 (jiān) ❶hard; strong; firm; solid ❷firmly; resolutely

【坚不可摧】indestructible

【坚持】insist on; uphold; stick (or adhere) to; persist in; hold to

【坚持不懈】consistently; unremitting; persistent

【坚持不渝】persistent; persevering

【坚定不移】firm and unshakable; unswerving; unflinching

【坚固】sturdy; firm; solid; strong

【坚决】firm; resolute; determined

【坚强】firm; strong

【坚韧】tough and tensile

【坚韧不拔】firm and indomitable; stubborn and unyielding

【坚如磐石】as solid as a rock; rock-firm

【坚实】solid

【坚守】stick to; hold fast to

【坚信】firmly believe; hold a firm belief in (or that)

【坚毅】firm and persistent; with unswerving determination; with inflexible will

【坚硬】hard; solid

【坚贞不屈】remain faithful and unyielding

间 (jiān) ❶between; among ❷within a definite time or space ❸room

另见 1045 页 jiàn

【间冰期】interglacial stage; interglacial

【间不容发】not a hair's breadth apart or away—extremely critical

肩 (jiān) ❶shoulder ❷undertake; bear; shoulder; take on

【肩膀】shoulder

【肩负】take on; undertake; shoulder; bear

【肩章】❶shoulder loop; shoulder strap ❷epaulet

艰 (jiān) difficult; hard

【艰巨】difficult; arduous

【艰苦奋斗】hard struggle

【艰苦朴素】hard work and plain living

【艰难】hard; difficult; arduous

【艰难困苦】difficulties and hardships

【艰深】difficult to understand; abstruse

【艰险】hardships and dangers

【艰辛】hardships

监 (jiān) ❶prison; jail ❷watch; supervise; oversee

【监测】monitor

【监察】supervise

【监督】❶ supervise; superintend; control ❷supervisor

【监工】❶supervise work; oversee ❷overseer; supervisor

【监禁】take into custody

【监考】invigilate; monitor examinations

【监牢】prison; jail

【监视】keep watch on; oversee; watch

【监听】monitor

【监狱】prison; jail: 关进～ put in jail; throw into prison

兼 (jiān) ❶double; twice; both ❷simultaneously; concurrently

【兼备】have both ...and ...

【兼并】annex (territory, property, etc.)

【兼而有之】have both at the same time

【兼顾】give consideration to two or more things

【兼容】compatible

【兼职】❶hold two or more posts at the same time ❷ concurrent post; part-time job

缄 (jiān) seal; close

【缄口】keep one's mouth shut; hold one's tongue; say nothing

【缄默】keep silent; be reticent

煎 (jiān) fry

【煎熬】suffering; torture

【煎饼】pancake

【煎锅】frying pan

拣 (jiǎn) ❶ pick; choose; select ❷ pick up

【拣便宜】get a bargain; gain a small advantage

茧 (jiǎn) ❶cocoon: 蚕～ silkworm cocoon ❷callus: 老～ thick callus

柬 (jiǎn) card; note; letter: 请～ invitation card

俭 (jiǎn) thrifty; frugal

【俭朴】frugal; simple; thrifty and simple; economical

【俭省】thrifty; economical

捡 (jiǎn) pick up; collect; gather

【捡漏】repair the leaky part of a roof; plug a leak in the roof

检 (jiǎn) ❶ check; examine ❷ restrain oneself; control; be careful in one's conduct

【检测】test; examine; check up

【检查】❶go over; check; inspect; examine ❷self-criticism: 作～ criticize oneself

【检点】❶ check; examine ❷ be cautious (about what one says or does)

【检讨】❶ self-criticism ❷ make self-criticism

【检修】examine and repair; overhaul

【检验】examine; check on; test

【检疫】quarantine

【检阅】❶review; inspect ❷inspection

减 (jiǎn) subtract; reduce; decrease; cut

【减产】❶ drop in production ❷ reduction of output

【减低】cut; bring down; reduce; lower; decrease

【减肥】reduce (or lose) weight; slim

【减负】lighten (or alleviate) burdens; ease the pressure on

【减缓】slow down; retard

【减价】reduce the price; mark down

【减免】reduce; remit

【减排】emission reduction

【减轻】lighten; ease; mitigate

【减去】❶minus ❷subtract

【减弱】weaken; abate

【减少】reduce; decrease; lessen; cut down

【减税】❶tax reduction ❷reduce taxes

【减速带】speed bump; deceleration strip

【减缩】reduce; cut down; retrench: ~开支 reduce expenditure

【减退】go down; come down; decrease; drop

【减压】reduce pressure; decompress: ~器 pressure reducer; decompressor

【减灾】reduce natural disasters

剪 (jiǎn) ❶scissors; shears; clippers ❷cut (with scissors); clip ❸wipe out

【剪报】newspaper cutting (or clipping)

【剪裁】cut out; tailor

【剪彩】cut the ribbon at an opening ceremony

【剪刀】scissors; shears: 一把~ a pair of scissors

【剪发】haircut

【剪贴】clip and paste

【剪影】❶paper-cut silhouette ❷outline; sketch

【剪纸】paper-cut

睑 (jiǎn) eyelid

简 (jiǎn) ❶letter ❷simple; brief ❸bamboo slips (used for writing on in ancient times) ❹letter ❺select; choose

【简报】bulletin; brief report

【简便】handy; simple and convenient

【简称】❶short form; abbreviation ❷be called sth. for short

【简单】❶simple; brief; uncomplicated ❷oversimplified; casual ❸simply

【简短】brief; short

【简而言之】to make a long story short; in short

【简化】simplify

【简洁】terse; concise

【简介】brief introduction; synopsis

【简历】resume

【简练】terse; succinct; pithy: 内容丰富，文字~ rich in content and succinct in style

【简陋】❶shabby; crude ❷simple and crude

【简明】simple and clear; concise

【简朴】simple; plain

【简要】concise; brief

【简易】simple and easy

【简直】simply; at all

见 (jiàn) ❶view; opinion ❷see; catch sight of ❸meet with; meet; call on ❹refer to

【见报】appear in the newspaper

【见长】be good at; be expert at (or in)

【见多识广】with rich experience and extensive knowledge

【见鬼】go to hell

【见机】according to circumstances; as the opportunity arises; as befits the occasion

【见解】understanding; view; opinion

【见面】meet; see

【见识】❶experience; knowledge ❷widen (or enrich) one's knowledge

【见世面】see the world

【见外】take sb. as an outsider

【见闻】what one sees and hears; knowledge

【见效】work; take effect

【见义勇为】act bravely for a just cause

【见证】witness; testimony
【见证人】witness
件 (jiàn) ❶(for matters in general) ❷ (for clothing, furniture, luggage, etc.) ❸single item ❹letter; correspondence; paper; document
间 (jiàn) ❶space in between; opening ❷sow discord ❸separate
另见 1042 页 jiān
【间谍】spy
【间断】interrupt
【间隔】interval
【间或】sometimes; occasionally
【间接】indirect; secondhand
【间隙】space; gap; interval
饯 (jiàn) ❶give a farewell dinner ❷ preserve (fruits)
【饯行】give a farewell dinner
建 (jiàn) ❶build; construct; erect ❷establish; set up; found
【建材】construction materials
【建国】❶found (or establish) a state ❷ build up a country
【建交】establish diplomatic relations
【建军节】Army Day (August 1)
【建立】build; form; set up; found; establish
【建设】build; construct
【建议】❶suggest; propose ❷suggestion; proposal; advice
【建筑】❶build; construct; erect ❷building; construction architecture
荐 (jiàn) recommend: 毛遂自～ volunteer one's services
【荐引】recommend; introduce
贱 (jiàn) ❶low-priced; inexpensive; cheap ❷lowly; humble ❸low-down; base; despicable ❹my
【贱货】❶cheap goods ❷ miserable (or contemptible) wretch
剑 (jiàn) sword; sabre
【剑客】chivalrous swordsman (in old novels)
【剑麻】sisal hemp
【剑眉】straight eyebrows slanting upwards and outwards; dashing eyebrows
【剑术】swordsmanship; art of fencing; fencing skill
舰 (jiàn) warship
【舰队】fleet
健 (jiàn) ❶strengthen; build up ❷be strong in; be good at ❸healthy; strong
【健步】walk with vigorous strides: ～登上主席台 mount the rostrum in vigorous strides
【健将】master sportsman; topnotch player
【健康】❶health ❷healthy; fit; well
【健康食品】health food
【健美】strong and handsome; vigorous and graceful
【健全】❶perfect ❷improve; strengthen
【健身】improve one's health; keep fit; build up one's body
【健身操】bodybuilding exercises
【健身房】gymnasium
【健谈】❶talkative ❷be a good talker; be an eloquent talker; be a brilliant conversationalist
【健忘】forgetful; liable to forget; have a poor memory
【健在】be still living and in good health
【健壮】healthy and strong; robust
舰 (jiàn) warship; naval vessel; man-of-war
【舰队】fleet; naval force

【舰艇】naval ships and boats; naval vessels

【舰长】captain (of a warship)

渐 (jiàn) gradually; step by step; little by little; by degrees

【渐渐】gradually; little by little; by degree; bit by bit

【渐进】inch; advance step by step

践 (jiàn) ❶ trample; tread on ❷ carry out; put into effect; perform; do

【践踏】tread on; trample underfoot

【践约】keep a promise (or appointment)

溅 (jiàn) splash; spatter

J

【溅落】(of a space vehicle; etc.) splash down

毽 (jiàn) shuttlecock

【毽子】shuttlecock

鉴 (jiàn) ❶ reflect; mirror ❷ inspect; examine

【鉴别】distinguish; discern

【鉴定】❶ appraise ❷ appraisal: 毕业～ graduation appraisal

【鉴赏】appreciate

【鉴于】❶in view of; in consideration of ❷ since; as

键 (jiàn) key: 钢琴～ piano key

【键盘】keyboard; fingerboard

箭 (jiàn) arrow: 射～ shoot an arrow

【箭步】a sudden big stride forward

【箭头】❶arrowhead ❷arrow (as a sign)

jiang

江 (jiāng) river

【江岸】river bank

【江湖】❶rivers and lakes ❷all corners of the country: 跑～travel from place to place to make a living

【江畔】river bank; beside the river

【江山】country; state power

将 (jiāng) ❶be going to; be about to; shall; will ❷challenge

另见 1047 页 jiàng

【将错就错】make use of a mistake

【将功补过】make amends for one's mistakes by giving good services

【将计就计】turn sb.'s own trick against him; beat sb. at his own game

【将近】close to; almost; nearly

【将就】make the best of; make do with

【将军】❶ general ❷ put sb. on the spot; embarrass

【将来】future; in the future

【将心比心】put oneself in sb.'s shoes

【将信将疑】half believing

【将要】be going to; will; be about to; shall

姜 (jiāng) ginger

僵 (jiāng) ❶stiff; numb: 冻～stiff with cold ❷deadlocked

【僵持】reach (or come to) a deadlock (of both parties) refuse to budge

【僵化】become rigid; ossify

【僵局】deadlock; impasse; stalemate

【僵死】dead; ossified

【僵硬】stiff; rigid; inflexible

缰 (jiāng) reins; halter

【缰绳】reins; halter

疆 (jiāng) boundary; border

【疆场】battlefield

【疆域】territory; domain

讲(jiǎng) ❶speak; say; tell ❷explain; make clear; interpret

【讲故事】tell stories

【讲和】make peace; settle a dispute; become reconciled

【讲话】 speak; talk; address; make a speech

【讲价】bargain; haggle over the price

【讲解】explain; interpret

【讲究】❶ pay attention to; stress; strive for; be particular about ❷ tasteful; elegant; exquisite

【讲课】teach; lecture

【讲理】reason with sb.; argue; be sensible; be reasonable

【讲评】comment on and appraise: ~学生的作业 comment on the students' work

【讲情】intercede; plead for sb.: 为他~ plead for him

【讲求】be particular about; pay attention to; stress; strive for: ~效率 strive for efficiency

【讲授】lecture; teach; give a lecture

【讲台】platform; rostrum

【讲习】lecture and study

【讲学】give lectures

【讲义】teaching materials

【讲座】a course of lectures

奖(jiǎng) ❶award; prize; reward ❷encourage; praise; reward

【奖杯】cup

【奖惩】rewards and punishments; rewards and penalties

【奖金】bonus; money award; prize; premium

【奖励】 award; reward; encourage; commend

【奖牌】medal

【奖品】prize; award; trophy

【奖券】lottery ticket

【奖学金】scholarship

【奖章】medal; decoration

【奖状】certificate of merit; certificate of award; honorary credential

桨(jiǎng) oar; scull; paddle

匠(jiàng) craftsman; artisan

【匠心】craftsmanship; ingenuity; originality

【匠心独运】consummate craftsmanship

降(jiàng) ❶ fall; drop ❷ lower; cut down; reduce

另见 1245 页 xiáng

【降低】reduce; decrease; drop; lower; cut down

【降级】downgrade; demote

【降价】reduce (or lower) the prices

【降落】fall; descend; touch down; land

【降落伞】parachute

【降旗】lower a flag

【降生】be born

【降温】reduce (or lower) the temperature; drop in temperature

【降下】drop; fall down

【降雨】rainfall

【降雨量】rainfall: 年~ annual rainfall

将(jiàng) ❶ general; commander in chief ❷ the chief piece in Chinese chess ❸command; lead

另见 1046 页 jiāng

【将领】general

【将门】the family of a general

【将士】commanders and fighters; officers and men

【将帅】commander-in-chief

酱(jiàng) ❶a thick sauce; jam; sauce; paste ❷ cooked or pickled in soy sauce

【酱菜】pickles

【酱肉】pork cooked in soy sauce

【酱油】soy sauce; soy

犟 (jiàng) stubborn; self-willed

【犟嘴】reply defiantly; answer back; talk back

jiao

交 (jiāo) ❶ friend ❷ friendship; relation; relationship: 患难之～ tested friend ❸deal; bargain: 成～make a deal ❹hand in; give up; turn (hand) over; deliver ❺meet; join ❻cross ❼make friends ❽reach ❾together

【交班】hand over to the next shift

【交叉】❶ cross; intersect; crisscross ❷ overlapping ❸alternate; stagger

【交差】report to the leadership after accomplishing a task

【交代】❶ hand (or turn) over; transfer; make clear; brief; tell; explain (policy, etc.) ❷account for; justify oneself ❸tell ❹confess

【交锋】cross swords; engage in a battle or contest

【交付】pay turn (or hand) over; deliver; consign

【交互】interact

【交还】give back; return

【交换】exchange; interchange

【交货】delivery

【交际】social intercourse; communication

【交接】❶ join; connect ❷ hand over and take over

【交界】have a common border; have a common boundary; border on

【交警】traffic police

【交卷】hand in an examination paper

【交流】❶ interchange; exchange; interflow; communication ❷ alternating

【交配】❶mate; copulate ❷mating; copulation

【交强险】compulsory insurance for traffic accident of motor-driven vehicle

【交融】blend; mingle

【交涉】negotiate; take up with; make representations

【交谈】talk with each other; have a conversation; chat

【交替】❶ replace; give place to ❷ alternately; take place by turn; in turn

【交通】traffic; communications

【交通规则】traffic regulations

【交通事故】traffic accident

【交通阻塞】traffic jam; traffic block

【交往】❶ associate with ❷ association; contact

【交响乐】symphony; symphonic music

【交心】open one's heart to

【交易】business; trade; deal

【交友】make friends

【交织】mingle; interweave; intertwine

郊 (jiāo) suburbs; outskirts

【郊区】suburbs; outskirts

【郊外】the countryside around a city; outskirts

【郊游】outing; excursion

浇 (jiāo) pour liquid on; water; sprinkle water on; irrigate

【浇灌】water; irrigate

【浇花】water flowers

【浇水】water

【浇铸】casting; mould

娇 (jiāo) ❶spoil ❷lovely; charming ❸ fragile; delicate

【娇惯】spoil;pamper

【娇嫩】tender and lovely;delicate;fragile

【娇妻】a beloved wife;a pretty young wife

【娇气】delicate;finicky

【娇生惯养】spoiled;pampered

【娇小玲珑】delicate and exquisite; petite and dainty

骄 (jiāo) proud;arrogant;conceited

【骄傲】❶proud;conceited ❷take pride in; be proud

【骄傲自满】conceited and self-satisfied; arrogant and complacent

【骄横】arrogant and imperious

【骄阳】blazing sun

胶 (jiāo) ❶ glue; gum ❷ stick with glue; glue ❸ gluey; sticky; gummy ❹rubber

【胶版】offset plate

【胶囊】capsule

【胶水】glue

【胶着】deadlocked; stalemated: ～状态 deadlock;stalemate;impasse

教 (jiāo) teach;instruct
另见 1050 页 jiào

【教书】teach

【教书育人】impart knowledge and educate people

焦 (jiāo) ❶coke:炼～coking ❷burnt; scorched;charred ❸worried;anxious

【焦点】❶focus ❷point at issue;central issue

【焦急】anxious;worried

【焦距】focal length

【焦渴】terribly thirsty;parched

【焦虑】feel anxious; have worries and misgivings

【焦炭】coke

【焦头烂额】battered; in a difficult situation

【焦躁】restless;impatient

礁 (jiāo) reef:触～ strike a reef

【礁石】reef;rock

嚼 (jiáo) chew

【嚼舌】wag one's tongue;gossip

角 (jiǎo) ❶horn ❷bugle;horn ❸corner ❹angle
另见 1066 页 jué

【角度】❶angle ❷point of view;angle

【角落】corner

侥 (jiǎo)

【侥幸】by luck;by a fluke;lucky

【侥幸心理】trusting to luck; the idea of leaving things to chance

佼 (jiǎo) handsome;beautiful

【佼佼】above average;outstanding

狡 (jiǎo) foxy;cunning

【狡辩】quibble

【狡猾】foxy;crafty;cunning;tricky;sly

【狡诈】deceitful;crafty;sly

饺 (jiǎo)

【饺子】dumpling (with meat and vegetable stuffing)

绞 (jiǎo) twist;wring;hang

【绞尽脑汁】rack one's brains

【绞痛】angina

【绞刑】death by hanging

矫 (jiǎo) ❶ rectify; correct ❷ strong ❸brave

【矫健】strong and vigorous

【矫揉造作】affected; pretentious; artificial; unnatural;

【矫正】correct; put right; rectify

皎 (jiǎo) clear and bright

【皎洁】(of moonlight) bright and clear

脚 (jiǎo) ❶foot ❷base

【脚本】script; scenario

【脚步】step

【脚跟】heel: 站稳～stand firm

【脚尖】tiptoe

【脚踏实地】❶down-to-earth ❷in a down-to-earth way

【脚印】footprint; footmark

【脚趾】toe

【脚趾甲】toenail

【脚注】footnote

搅 (jiǎo) ❶stir; mix ❷disturb; annoy

【搅拌】stir; mix

【搅动】mix; stir: 拿棍子～灰浆 stir the plaster with a stick

【搅乱】confuse; throw into disorder; mess up

【搅匀】mix up

缴 (jiǎo) ❶pay; hand over (or in) ❷capture; surrender

【缴获】capture; seize

【缴销】hand in for cancellation: ～营业执照 hand in the business licence for cancellation

叫 (jiào) ❶cry; shout ❷hire; order ❸name; call ❹ask; order

【叫喊】shout; yell; cry

【叫好】applause

【叫苦】complain of hardship of suffering; moan and groan

【叫骂】shout curses

【叫卖】peddle

【叫屈】complain of being wronged

【叫嚷】shout; cry

【叫醒】wake up; awaken

【叫座】appeal to the audience; draw well

觉 (jiào) sleep

校 (jiào) check; proofread; collate
另见 1248 页 xiào

【校订】check against the authoritative text

【校对】❶proofread ❷proofreader

【校勘】collate ～学 textual criticism

【校正】proofread and correct; rectify

【校准】calibration: 方位～ bearing calibration

轿 (jiào) sedan (chair)

【轿车】car; sedan

较 (jiào) ❶ compare; as compared with; in comparison with ❷comparatively; relatively; fairly; quite; rather ❸ clear; obvious; marked

【较劲】match strength

【较量】❶ have a contest; have a test of strength ❷argue; dispute

教 (jiào) ❶religion ❷teaching ❸teach; instruct
另见 1049 页 jiāo

【教案】teaching plan

【教本】textbook

【教材】textbook; teaching material

【教程】❶ course of study ❷ (published) lectures

【教导】❶instruct; teach ❷teaching; guidance

【教父】godfather

【教官】instructor; drillmaster

【教会】church

【教诲】teaching; instruction

【教具】teaching aid
【教科书】textbook
【教练】❶train;drill ❷coach
【教师】teacher
【教师节】Teacher's Day
【教室】classroom
【教授】❶professor ❷teach;instruct
【教唆】instigate;abet
【教堂】church;cathedral
【教学】education;teaching
【教学相长】teaching benefits teacher and student alike;teaching benefits teachers as well as students
【教训】❶teach (or give) sb. a lesson ❷lesson;moral
【教研组】teaching and research group
【教养】❶educate;bring up;train ❷breeding;education;upbringing;culture
【教育】❶educate;teach ❷education
【教员】teacher;instructor
【教长】religion imam;dean

窖 (jiào) ❶ cellar or pit for storing things:菜～vegetable cellar ❷ store sth. in a cellar or pit

【窖藏】store sth. in a cellar or pit

酵 (jiào)ferment

【酵母】yeast

jie

阶 (jiē) ❶steps;stairs ❷rank

【阶层】social stratum
【阶段】stage;period
【阶级矛盾】class contradictions
【阶梯】a flight of steps;ladder
【阶下囚】prisoner;captive

皆 (jiē)all;each and every

【皆大欢喜】everybody is happy; to the satisfaction of all

结 (jiē)bear;form
另见 1052 页 jié

【结巴】❶stammer ❷stammerer
【结果】bear fruit;fructify
【结实】❶ solid; sturdy; durable ❷ robust; strong;tough

接 (jiē) ❶ connect; join ❷ receive ❸ meet;welcome ❹take over

【接触】get in touch with;contact
【接待】receive
【接二连三】one after another; in quick succession
【接风】give a dinner of welcome (to a visitor from afar)
【接管】take over;control
【接轨】join track;integrate
【接济】give financial help to
【接见】receive;meet
【接近】be close to;approach;near
【接连】in succession;in a row
【接纳】admit;take in
【接洽】discuss (or consult) with
【接壤】border on
【接收】take over;admit;receive
【接受】accept;take
【接替】replace; take the place of; take over
【接通】put through
【接吻】kiss
【接应】❶come to sb.'s aid ❷supply
【接着】❶follow; carry on; go on (with); proceed ❷then;after that ❸catch
【接种】inoculate;have an inoculation
【接住】catch

秸 (jiē)stalks;straw:麦～ wheat straw

揭 (jiē) ❶tear (or take) off ❷uncover ❸expose; reveal; bring to light

【揭穿】expose; lay bare; show up

【揭短】find fault with; disclose sb.'s faults

【揭盖子】take the lid off sth.; bring sth. into the open

【揭开】disclose; uncover; open; reveal: ~宇宙的奥秘 reveal the secrets of the universe

【揭露】lay bare; uncover; expose; bring to light; unmask; show up

【揭幕】unveil; inaugurate

【揭晓】make known; announce

J

街 (jiē) street

【街道】❶ street ❷ residential district; neighbourhood

【街坊四邻】neighbours; neighbourhood

【街区】block

【街头巷尾】streets and lanes

孑 (jié) lonely; all alone

【孑然】solitary; lonely; alone

【孑然一身】all alone in the world

节 (jié) ❶joint; knot ❷part; division; section ❸ festival; holiday ❹ moral integrity ❺ detail; story ❻ economize; save

【节假日】festivals and holidays

【节俭】thrifty; frugal; economical

【节目】program; item

【节能】save energy

【节日】festival; holiday

【节省】economize; save; cut down on

【节食】be moderate in eating and drinking; be (or go) on a diet

【节外生枝】raise side issues

【节余】surplus (as a result of economizing)

【节约】economize; save; practise thrift

【节制】❶control; check; be moderate in ❷ temperance

【节奏】rhythm; tempo

劫 (jié) ❶ disaster; misfortune ❷ rob; plunder; raid

【劫持】kidnap; hijack

【劫机】hijack a plane

杰 (jié) ❶ outstanding person; genius ❷outstanding

【杰出】remarkable; brilliant; outstanding; prominent; distinguished

【杰作】masterpiece

拮 (jié)

【拮据】be hard up; be short of money

洁 (jié) clean

【洁白】pure (spotlessly) white

【洁净】clean

【洁具】toilet utensils

结 (jié) ❶ knot ❷ tie; knit; weave ❸ congeal; form; forge; cement ❹ conclude; settle

另见 1051 页 jiē

【结疤】become scarred

【结伴而行】go (or travel) in a group

【结冰】freeze; ice up

【结彩】adorn (or decorate) with festoons

【结成】form: ~同盟 form an alliance; become allies

【结构】structure; composition; Construction

【结果】❶kill ❷finally; at last; as a result

【结合】combine; link; unite: 劳逸~ combine work with rest

【结婚】marry; get married

【结集】❶concentrate; mass ❷collect articles, etc. into a volume: ～付印 compile a collection of writings and send it to the press

【结交】make friends with; associate with

【结晶】❶crystallize ❷crystal ❸crystallization: 智慧的～ a crystallization of wisdom

【结局】outcome; ending; final result

【结论】conclusion: 得出～ come to a conclusion

【结盟】form an alliance; ally

【结识】get to know sb.; acquaint with; make the acquaintance of

【结束】end; finish; bring (or come) to an end; wind up

【结尾】ending; winding-up stage

【结余】cash surplus; surplus; balance

捷 (jié) ❶victory; triumph ❷prompt; quick; nimble

【捷报频传】news of victory keeps pouring in

【捷径】shortcut

【捷足先登】the swift footed arrive first; the early bird catches the worm

睫 (jié) eyelash; lash

【睫毛】eyelash; lash

截 (jié) ❶section; chunk; length ❷cut ❸stop; check; intercept ❹up to

【截断】cut off (or short); block; interrupt

【截流】dam a river; locking of the river

【截取】cut off a section of sth.

【截肢】amputation

【截然】sharply; entirely; completely

【截止】end; close

【截至】up to; by (a specified time)

竭 (jié) use up; run out; exhaust

【竭诚】wholeheartedly; with all one's heart; with heart and soul

【竭尽全力】spare no effort; do one's utmost; do all one can

【竭力】do one's utmost; spare no effort: 尽心～ try one's best

姐 (jiě) elder sister

【姐夫】elder sister's husband; brother-in-law

【姐姐】elder sister; sister

【姐妹】sisters

解 (jiě) ❶solution ❷explain; interpret ❸understand ❹remove ❺separate; divide ❻untie; undo ❼relieve

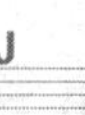

【解馋】satisfy a craving for good food

【解除】get rid of; relieve; remove

【解答】answer; explain

【解冻】thaw; unfreeze

【解毒】detoxify; detoxicate

【解乏】get refreshed; refresh

【解放军】liberation army

【解雇】dismiss; fire; sack; discharge

【解恨】have one's hatred vented; find satisfaction in venting out one's hate

【解惑】resolve (or remove, dispel) doubts

【解禁】lift a ban

【解救】save; rescue; deliver

【解决】❶solve; settle ❷finish off

【解开】untie; undo; unfasten

【解渴】relieve one's thirst

【解闷】divert oneself

【解聘】dismiss

【解剖】dissect

【解热】allay a fever

【解散】❶dismiss ❷dissolve; disband (an organization, etc.)

【解释】explain; interpret

【解手】relieve oneself; go to the lavatory (or toilet); wash one's hands

【解说】explain orally; comment

【解题】solve a (mathematical, etc.) problem

【解脱】❶free oneself from; extricate oneself (from a predicament, etc.) ❷absolve; exonerate

【解围】❶rescue sb. from a siege ❷get sb. out of a predicament

【解约】cancel a contract; terminate an agreement

介 (jiè) ❶lie between ❷take to heart; mind

【介词】preposition

J

【介入】get involved; intervene

【介绍】❶introduce; present ❷let know; brief ❸recommend; suggest

【介意】mind; care about

戒 (jiè) ❶ring ❷Buddhist monastic discipline ❸guard against ❹warn ❺drop; stop; give up ❻(finger) ring

【戒备】be on guard; be on the alert; guard

【戒除】drop; stop; give up; get rid of

【戒忌】❶taboos; don'ts ❷be wary of violating a taboo

【戒骄戒躁】guard against arrogance and haste

【戒烟】give up smoking

【戒指】ring

届 (jiè) fall due; expire

【届满】at the expiration of one's term of office

【届期】when the day comes; on the appointed date

【届时】at the appointed time; on the occasion

界 (jiè) ❶boundary; border ❷range; scope; extent ❸circle; world

【界碑】boundary marker (or tablet)

【界定】define; delimit

【界河】boundary river

【界面】interface

【界限】dividing line; limits; bounds

【界线】boundary line

诫 (jiè) ❶warn; admonish ❷commandment: 十～ the Ten Commandments

借 (jiè) ❶borrow: 向……～东西 borrow sth. from ❷lend: 把东西～给某人 lend sth. to sb. ❸make use of ❹use as a pretext

【借出】lend

【借贷】❶borrow (or lend) money ❷debit and credit sides

【借调】temporarily transfer; loan

【借读】study at a school on a temporary basis

【借方】debtor

【借古讽今】use the past to disparage the present

【借故】find an excuse

【借火】ask for a light

【借鉴】use for reference; draw lessons from

【借口】❶use as an excuse (or a pretext) ❷excuse; pretext

【借款】offer a loan; ask for a loan; borrow (or lend) money

【借题发挥】make use of the subject under discussion to put over one's own ideas—seize on an incident to exaggerate matters

【借条】receipt for a loan

【借用】borrow

【借助】with the help of

【借住】stay at sb. else's place

jin

巾 (jīn) a piece of cloth: 毛～towel; 围～scarf

【巾帼】❶ ancient woman's headdress ❷ heroine ❸ woman

【巾帼英雄】a heroic woman; heroine

斤 (jīn) ❶ Chinese weight measurement ❷ used as weight

【斤斤计较】care much about petty gain or loss; haggle over every ounce

【斤两】weight

今 (jīn) ❶ today ❷ now: 至～up to now; to date; 从～以后 from now on ❸ modern; present ❹ this (year); of this year

【今非昔比】the past cannot be compared with the present; no comparison between past and present

【今后】from now on; in the days to come; henceforth; hereafter; in future

【今年】this year

【今日】❶ today; this day ❷ present; now

【今世】❶ this life ❷ this age

【今昔】the present and the past; today and yesterday

【今昔对比】contrast the past with the present

【今夜】tonight; this evening

金 (jīn) ❶ metal ❷ money ❸ gold ❹ golden ❺ highly respected; precious

【金杯】gold cup

【金额】amount; sum

【金刚石】diamond

【金黄色】golden

【金库】treasury; national (state) treasury

【金矿】goldmine

【金牌】gold medal

【金融】finance; banking

【金色】golden: ～的朝阳 golden rays of the morning sun; golden dawn

【金属】metal

【金条】gold bar

【金字塔】pyramid

津 (jīn) ❶ saliva ❷ sweat ❸ ferry crossing; ford

【津津乐道】talk with great relish; take delight in talking about

【津津有味】with keen interest; with gusto; with relish

【津贴】subsidy; allowance

筋 (jīn) ❶ muscle ❷ sinew ❸ vein

【筋斗】somersault

【筋骨】bones and muscles-physique

【筋疲力尽】worn (or tired) out; exhausted

禁 (jīn) ❶ contain; restrain ❷ bear; stand; endure

另见 1057 页 jìn

【禁不起】be unable to stand (tests, trials, etc.)

【禁不住】❶ be unable to bear (or endure) ❷ can't help doing; cannot refrain from

【禁受】bear; stand; endure

襟 (jīn) front of a garment

【襟怀】heart; mind; bosom

仅 (jǐn) only; merely; barely; just

【仅供参考】just for reference; for reference only

【仅仅】only; merely; just; barely

尽 (jǐn) ❶ extremely; to the greatest extent ❷ within the limits of; no more than ❸ at the furthest end of

另见 1056 页 jìn

【尽管】though; although; even though (or

if); despite; in spite of

【尽可能】as far as possible; to the best of one's ability; as best as one can

【尽快】as soon (or quickly) as possible

【尽量】to the best of one's ability; as far as possible: ～采用先进技术 make the widest possible use of advanced technology

紧 (jǐn) ❶tight; close ❷strict ❸fast ❹urgent ❺tighten

【紧巴巴】❶tight ❷hard up; short of money: 日子过得～的 be in financial straits

【紧逼】press hard; close in on: 步步～ press on at every stage

【紧跟】follow closely (on sb.'s heels); keep in step with; keep up with

【紧急】urgent; critical; pressing; emergent

【紧接】next

【紧密】❶close together; inseparable: ～团结 be closely united ❷rapid and intense

【紧张】❶nervous ❷tense; strained

锦 (jǐn) ❶brocade ❷bright and beautiful

【锦标赛】Championships

【锦旗】silk banner

【锦绣】as beautiful as brocade; beautiful; splendid

谨 (jǐn) ❶ careful; cautious; circumspect ❷solemnly; sincerely

【谨防】beware of; be cautious of; guard against

【谨慎】careful; cautious; prudent

【谨严】careful and precise: 治学～ careful and exact scholarship

尽 (jìn) ❶exhausted; finished ❷to the utmost; to the limit ❸ use up; exhaust; run out ❹try (or do) one's best ❺exhaustive ❻all; completely

另见 1055 页 jǐn

【尽力】try (or do) one's best; do all one can

【尽量】as far as possible; to the best of one's ability; as best as one can

【尽情】as much as one likes; to one's heart's content

【尽然】(usu. used in the negative) entirely so: 也不～ not exactly so; not exactly the case

【尽善尽美】perfect

【尽是】full of; all; without exception

【尽头】end; limit

【尽孝】fulfil one's duty to one's parents; display filial piety towards one's parents

【尽心】with all one's heart

【尽兴】to one's heart's content; enjoy oneself to the full

【尽义务】do one's duty; fulfil one's obligation

【尽责】do one's duty; discharge one's responsibility

进 (jìn) ❶advance; move forward ❷enter; come (or go) in ❸receive

【进步】❶ progress; advance; improve ❷progressive

【进城】❶go into town; go to town ❷enter the big cities (to live and work)

【进程】course; process

【进出】❶get in and out ❷receipt and payment ❸(business) turnover

【进出口】❶ imports and exports ❷ exit and entrance; exit

【进度】❶rate of progress ❷schedule; timetable

【进化】❶evolve ❷evolution

【进货】stock (a shop) with goods; lay in a stock of merchandise; replenish one's stock

【进军】march; advance

【进口】❶enter port ❷import ❸entrance
【进来】come in; enter
【进取】be eager to make progress; be enterprising
【进入】get into; enter
【进食】take food; have one's meal
【进退两难】find it difficult to advance or to retreat—be in a dilemma
【进行】❶carry on ❷be underway; go on
【进修】❶ advanced studies ❷ take a refresher course; pursue further studies
【进言】offer a piece of advice or an opinion: 大胆～ make so bold as to offer an opinion
【进展】make progress; make headway
【进站】get into (or draw into, pull into) a station
【进账】income; receipts

近 (jìn) ❶ near; close ❷ approaching; approximately; close to ❸ intimate; closely related ❹easy to understand
【近处】vicinity; neighbourhood
【近代】modern times
【近海】coastal waters; inshore; offshore
【近乎】close (or next) to; near
【近郊】outskirts of a city; suburbs; environs
【近况】present condition; recent developments; how things stand
【近来】recently; of late; lately
【近邻】near neighbour
【近路】shortcut: 走～ take a shortcut
【近年】recent years: ～来 in recent years
【近期】in the near future
【近亲】close relative
【近视】❶ myopia; nearsighted ness ❷nearsighted
【近水楼台】waterside pavilion—a favourable position
【近似】approximate; similar
【近义词】near synonym

劲 (jìn) ❶ strength ❷ vigour; spirit; drive; zeal ❸interest; attraction

另见 1060 页 jìng

【劲头】❶strength ❷spirit

晋 (jìn) ❶enter; advance ❷promote
【晋级】be promoted; rise in rank
【晋升】promote

浸 (jìn) soak; steep
【浸泡】soak; immerse
【浸染】❶ steep; tincture ❷ be contaminated; be gradually influenced

禁 (jìn) ❶ prohibit; forbid; ban ❷ imprison

另见 1055 页 jīn

【禁毒】prevent drug abuse; curb drug trade
【禁忌】❶avoid; abstain from ❷taboo
【禁令】prohibition; ban
【禁区】forbidden zone
【禁书】banned book
【禁止】forbid; ban; prohibit

jing

茎 (jīng) stem; stalk

京 (jīng) ❶capital ❷Beijing
【京都】capital
【京剧】Beijing opera
【京腔】Beijing accent: 撇～ affect a Beijing accent

经 (jīng) ❶longitude ❷scripture; classic ❸ pass through; undergo ❹ engage in ❺stand; bear; endure ❻constant ❼by way of ❽after; through

【经办】handle;deal with
【经常】always;constantly
【经典】❶classic ❷classical
【经度】longitude
【经费】funds
【经管】be in charge of
【经过】❶pass; go through; undergo ❷go by; pass by ❸course; process ❹after; through
【经济】❶economy ❷economic ❸financial ❹economical;thrifty
【经济适用房】 economically affordable housing
【经济头脑】commercially minded
【经久】prolonged;enduring;durable
【经理】manager
【经历】❶experience;undergo;go through ❷experience
【经商】 be in business; be engaged in trade;go into business
【经受】experience; stand; undergo; withstand;stand;weather
【经书】❶Confucian classics ❷Scripture
【经心】careful;mindful;conscientious
【经验】experience
【经营】manage;run;operate;engage in

荆 (jīng) chaste tree; vitex: 负~请罪 bearing the rod and willingly taking the punishment—to offer a humble apology
【荆棘】thistles and thorns;brambles

旌 (jīng) an ancient type of banner hoisted on a feather-decked mast
【旌旗】banners and flags

惊 (jīng) ❶ start; be frightened ❷ shock;alarm;surprise
【惊动】❶alarm;shock ❷disturb
【惊愕】stunned;stupefied
【惊弓之鸟】a bird that starts at the mere twang of a bow-string—a badly frightened person
【惊呼】cry out in alarm
【惊慌失措】frightened out of one's wits; seized with panic;panic-stricken
【惊魂】the state of being frightened:~稍定 barely recovered from a fright
【惊叫】exclaim;scream
【惊恐】frightened;seized with terror
【惊奇】be surprised;wonder
【惊人】 astonishing; amazing; striking; wonderful;alarming
【惊叹】wonder at;exclaim
【惊天动地】shaking heaven and earth; earth-shaking;world-shaking
【惊喜】be pleasantly surprised
【惊吓】frighten;scare
【惊险】thrilling;breathtaking
【惊心动魄】soul-stirring;breath-taking
【惊醒】❶awaken suddenly; wake up with a start ❷ sleep lightly; easily rouse from sleep
【惊讶】surprised;astonished

晶 (jīng) ❶ brilliant; glittering ❷ quartz;(rock) crystal ❸any crystalline substance
【晶体】crystal
【晶莹】sparkling and crystal-clear

睛 (jīng)eyeball

兢 (jīng)
【兢兢业业】cautious and conscientious

精 (jīng) ❶energy ❷spirit ❸essence ❹ refined; picked ❺ perfect; excellent ❻smart;clever;skilled;conversant;proficient ❼meticulous;fine
【精兵简政】better troops and simpler administration; better staff and simpler

administration; streamlined administration

【精彩】brilliant; splendid; wonderful

【精诚】absolute sincerity; good faith

【精打细算】careful calculation and strict budgeting

【精雕细刻】work at sth. with the care and precision of a sculptor; work at sth. with great care

【精干】intelligent and capable

【精耕细作】intensive and meticulous farming; intensive cultivation

【精光】❶ with nothing left ❷ bright and clean; shiny

【精华】essence; cream; soul 去其糟粕，取其～ discard the dross and select the essence

【精简】simplify; reduce; cut; retrench

【精力】energy; vigour

【精力充沛】full of vim and vigour; vigorous; energetic

【精练】concise; succinct; terse: 语言～ succinct language

【精美】fine; exquisite; delicate; elegant

【精密】precise; accurate

【精妙】exquisite: 书法～ write a beautiful hand

【精明】shrewd; astute

【精疲力竭】tired (or worn) out; exhausted

【精辟】penetrating

【精品】❶fine works ❷quality goods

【精确】exact; precise; accurate

【精深】profound

【精神】spirit; mind

【精神病】mental disease; mental disorder; psychosis

【精神抖擞】full of energy (or vitality); vigorous: ～地迈着大步 walk with long, vigorous strides

【精神文明】cultural and ideological progress

【精神污染】spiritual contamination; cultural contamination; ideological pollution

【精髓】marrow; essense

【精通】have a good command of; be expert at (or in)

【精细】meticulous; fine; careful: 手工十分～ show fine workmanship

【精心】painstakingly

【精益求精】constantly improve

【精致】fine; exquisite

【精装】❶ clothbound ❷ hardback; hardcover

【精子】sperm; spermatozoon

鲸 (jīng) whale

【鲸须】baleen; whalebone

【鲸鱼】whale

井 (jǐng) ❶well: 油～oil well; 矿～mine ❷sth. in the shape of a well ❸neat; orderly

【井底之蛙】a frog in a well; a person with a limited outlook

【井井有条】well-arranged; in good order

【井然有序】in good order; orderly; methodical

【井水】well water

颈 (jǐng) neck

【颈动脉】carotid

【颈椎】cervical vertebra

景 (jǐng) ❶view; scenery; scene ❷situation; condition

【景点】scenic spot

【景观】natural landscape (or scenery)

【景色】view; scene; scenery; landscape;

outlook

【景仰】respect and admire; hold in deep respect

【景致】view; scenery; scene

警 (jǐng) ❶alarm; warning ❷police ❸warn; alarm ❹alert

【警报】alarm; warning; alert

【警察】police; policeman

【警车】police car; police van

【警笛】police whistle; siren

【警服】police uniform

【警告】❶warning ❷warn; caution

【警棍】policeman's baton; truncheon

【警戒】❶guard against; keep a watch on ❷warn

【警觉】vigilance; alertness

【警犬】police dog

【警卫】guard

【警钟】alarm bell

劲 (jìng) strong; powerful; sturdy 另见 1057 页 jìn

【劲敌】formidable adversary; strong opponent (or contender)

【劲风】a strong wind

径 (jìng) ❶ path; footpath ❷ way; means ❸diameter ❹directly

【径赛】track

【径直】straight; directly; straightaway

净 (jìng) ❶clean ❷make clean ❸net ❹completely ❺all the time; all ❻only; merely; nothing but

【净额】net amount

【净化】purify

【净价】net price

【净收入】net income

【净增】net increase; net growth: 人口～率 net growth rate of population

【净重】net weight

竞 (jìng) contest; vie

【竞标】competitive bidding; competitive tender

【竞猜】guessing game

【竞聘】compete for a post

【竞赛】contest; competition; race

【竞选】campaign (or run) for

【竞争】compete; vie

【竞走】heel-and-toe walking race

竟 (jìng) ❶finish; complete ❷go so far as to ❸in the end; after all; eventually ❹unexpectedly

【竟敢】actually dare; have the audacity; have the impertinence

【竟然】❶unexpectedly; to one's surprise; actually ❷go to the length of; have the impudence to

敬 (jìng) ❶respect; honour ❷respectfully

【敬爱】respect and love

【敬酒】propose a toast; toast

【敬老爱幼】respect the aged and cherish the young

【敬老院】home of respect for the aged; old folks' home

【敬老尊贤】respect the aged and honour the worthy

【敬礼】❶salute ❷with best wishes

【敬佩】admire; hold in esteem

【敬业】be devoted to one's work

【敬意】respect; tribute; regards

【敬重】highly esteem; look up to with great respect; deeply respect; revere; honor

静 (jìng) still; calm; quiet

【静电】static electricity

【静观】watch quietly

【静脉】vein

【静默】❶mourn in silence ❷become silent ❸observe silence

【静悄悄】quiet

【静态】static state

【静养】rest quietly to recuperate; convalesce

【静止】still; motionless

【静坐】❶sit quietly ❷sit-in

境 (jìng) ❶border; boundary ❷condition; situation; circumstances ❸area; territory

【境界】❶boundary ❷extent; state; realm

【境况】condition; circumstances; situation

【境遇】one's lot; circumstances

镜 (jìng) ❶mirror ❷lens ❸glass

【镜框】❶picture frame ❷spectacles frame

【镜片】lens

【镜头】❶camera lens ❷shot; scene: 特写~close-up shot

【镜子】mirror; looking glass

jiong

迥 (jiǒng) ❶far away ❷widely different

【迥然不同】utterly different; not in the least alike

【迥异】totally different

炯 (jiǒng) bright; shining

【炯炯】bright

【炯炯有神】(of eyes) bright and piercing

窘 (jiǒng) embarrassed; ill at ease

【窘境】awkward situation; plight; predicament: 摆脱~ extricate oneself from a predicament

【窘迫】❶very poor; hard up; poverty-stricken ❷embarrassed; in a predicament

【窘态】embarrassment

jiu

纠 (jiū) ❶correct; make (or put, set) right ❷assemble ❸entangle ❹gather together

【纠察】❶keep the peace; maintain order ❷picket

【纠缠不清】too tangled up to unravel

【纠纷】dispute; quarrel; trouble

【纠结】❶be entangled with; be intertwined with ❷entanglement

【纠正】make (or put, set) right; correct

究 (jiū) ❶study; make a study of; go into; investigate ❷really; after all

【究竟】❶outcome; result ❷after all; in the end ❸exactly; actually; in fact (or reality)

阄 (jiū) lot: 抓~ draw lots; decide by lot

揪 (jiū) ❶take (or keep) hold of; seize ❷pull; tug; drag; give a hard tug

【揪出】uncover; dig up

【揪心】❶worried; anxious ❷heartrending; agonizing; gnawing

九 (jiǔ) nine: 第~ ninth

【九九表】multiplication table

【九九归一】when all is said and done; in the last analysis; after all

【九牛二虎之力】tremendous effort

【九牛一毛】a drop in the ocean

【九泉之下】down in the Nine Springs in the nether regions; after death

【九十】ninety

【九死一生】a narrow escape from death

【九月】September

【九折】ten percent discount

【九州】❶the nine divisions of China in remote antiquity ❷a poetic name for China

久 (jiǔ) long

【久别重逢】meet after a long separation

【久病成医】prolonged illness makes a doctor of a patient

【久等】wait for a long time

【久而久之】after a long time; as time passes; in the long run

【久经考验】long-tested; seasoned

【久留】stay long

【久违】have not met for a long time

【久远】far back; remote

韭 (jiǔ) ❶ fragrant ❷ flowered garlic; (Chinese) chives

【韭菜】fragrant-flowered garlic; (Chinese) chives

【韭黄】hotbed chives

酒 (jiǔ) ❶ alcoholic ❷ drink; wine; liquor; spirits: 啤~ beer; 葡萄~ wine

【酒杯】wine glass

【酒店】❶wineshop; pub ❷hotel

【酒鬼】drunkard

【酒驾】drunk driving; driving while intoxicated

【酒精】alcohol

【酒量】capacity for liquor; one's drinking capacity

【酒窝】dimple

【酒席】feast; banquet

旧 (jiù) ❶old ❷old-fashioned ❸ used; worn

【旧病复发】fall back into illness (or evil); have a relapse

【旧地重游】revisit a once familiar place

【旧好】❶old friendship ❷an old friend

【旧交】an old acquaintance; an old friend

【旧居】former residence; old home

【旧情】old or former friendship; former affection

疚 (jiù) remorse: 内~have a guilty conscience; be filled with remorse

救 (jiù) ❶save; rescue ❷help; relieve

【救兵】relief troops

【救出】rescue; help out

【救护】relieve the sick (or injured); give first aid; rescue

【救护车】ambulance

【救火】put out a fire

【救济】give relief; relieve the distress of

【救命】save sb.'s life

【救生】❶ lifesaving ❷ save life (esp. through the prevention of drowning)

【救援】rescue; aid; help; come to sb.'s rescue (or help)

【救灾】❶provide disaster relief ❷help to overcome disaster

【救治】treat and cure

【救助】help sb. in danger (or difficulty)

就 (jiù) ❶ begin; enter into ❷ come near; move towards ❸ go to; take up; undertake; engage in; enter upon ❹ accomplish; make; achieve ❺go with ❻ suit; fit ❼let ❽right away; at once ❾as soon as ❿already ⓫only; just

【就餐】have a meal; eat; dine

【就地】on the spot

【就地取材】draw on local resources

【就近】nearby

【就擒】be seized; be captured

【就寝】go to bed

【就任】take up one's post; take office

【就事论事】consider sth. in isolation or out of context; deal with a matter on its merits

【就是】quite right; exactly; precisely

【就绪】be completed; be in order; be ready

【就业】❶obtain employment; get a job ❷ be provided with employment

【就医】go to (or see) a doctor

【就职】assume (or take) office

【就座】be seated; take one's seat

舅 (jiù) ❶ mother's brother; uncle ❷ wife's brother; brother-in-law

【舅舅】uncle; mother's brother

【舅母】aunt; wife of mother's brother

【舅子】wife's brother; brother-in-law

ju

拘 (jū) ❶ arrest ❷ restrain; restrict ❸ inflexible; rigid

【拘谨】overcautious; reserved

【拘礼】be punctilious; stand on ceremony

【拘留】detain; hold in custody; intern; detention; provisional apprehension

【拘泥】be a stickler for; rigidly adhere to

【拘束】❶ restrain; restrict ❷ timid; ill at ease

居 (jū) ❶residence; house ❷live ❸occupy ❹claim to be

【居安思危】think of possible danger in peace time; be vigilant in peace time

【居高临下】in a commanding position

【居功自傲】become arrogant because of one's achievements; claim credit and put on airs

【居家】live at home; run a household: ~过日子 keep house (economically and efficiently)

【居留证】residence permit

【居民】resident; inhabitant

【居民身份证】ID card; resident identification card

【居然】❶unexpectedly ❷go so far as to; go to the length of

【居心不良】harbour evil intentions

【居中】❶(mediate) between two parties ❷be placed in the middle

【居住】live; reside; dwell

驹 (jū) colt; foal

鞠 (jū) rear; bring up

【鞠躬】bow

【鞠躬尽瘁】exert oneself to the utmost

局 (jú) ❶office; bureau: 邮~post office ❷set; game ❸part; portion

【局部】part

【局促不安】ill at ease

【局面】aspect; phase; situation

【局势】situation

【局外人】outsider; a person not in the know

【局限】limit; confine

菊 (jú)

【菊花】chrysanthemum

【菊石】ammonite

橘 (jú) orange; tangerine

【橘汁】orange juice

咀 (jǔ) chew

【咀嚼】❶ masticate ❷ mull over; ruminate; chew the cud

沮 (jǔ) stop; prevent

【沮丧】depressed; dispirited; discouraged

举 (jǔ) ❶act; deed ❷lift; raise; hold up ❸choose; elect ❹cite; list ❺start ❻ whole; entire

【举办】hold; run; conduct

【举报】report an offence to authorities; turn sb. in

【举动】act; movement

【举国】❶the whole (or entire) nation ❷throughout (or all over) the country

【举荐】recommend

【举例】give an example; cite an instance

【举棋不定】be unable to make up one's mind

【举世瞩目】attract worldwide attention; become the focus of world attention

【举手】raise (or put up) one's hand

【举行】hold; stage

【举一反三】get to know more by inferences; draw inferences about other cases from one instance

【举止】behaviour; bearing; manner

【举止大方】have an easy manner

【举重】weight lifting

【举足轻重】hold the balance; play a decisive role; carry big weight on

矩 (jǔ) ❶carpenter's square; square ❷rules; regulations ❸moment

【矩形】rectangle

巨 (jù) huge; tremendous; gigantic

【巨变】great change

【巨大】huge; tremendous; enormous

【巨额】a huge sum

【巨款】a huge sum of money

【巨人】giant

【巨头】tycoon; magnate

【巨型】giant; colossal

【巨著】great work; monumental work

句 (jù) sentence

【句号】full stop; period

【句型】sentence pattern

【句子】sentence

拒 (jù) ❶refuse ❷resist ❸repel

【拒捕】resist arrest

【拒绝】refuse; reject; decline; turn down

具 (jù) ❶tool; instrument ❷possess; have

【具备】possess; have

【具体】concrete; specific; particular

炬 (jù) ❶torch ❷fire

俱 (jù) ❶entire; complete; all ❷completely; entirely

【俱乐部】club

剧 (jù) ❶drama; play; opera: 悲～tragedy; 喜～comedy ❷violent; intense; acute

【剧本】drama; play script

【剧场】theatre

【剧烈】violent; fierce; acute

【剧目】a list of plays or operas

【剧情】plot; story

【剧照】stage photo

【剧作家】playwright; dramatist

惧 (jù) fear; dread

【惧怕】fear; dread

据 (jù) ❶occupy; seize; take possession of; lay hold of ❷rely on; depend on ❸according to; on the grounds of ❹evidence; proof; grounds

【据称】it is said; they say; allegedly

【据实】according to the facts; according to the actual situation

【据说】it is said that...; they say

【据为己有】take forcible possession of; appropriate

【据悉】it is reported that...

距 (jù) ❶distance ❷in between; remote from

【距离】❶distance ❷be apart (or away) from; be at a distance from

飓 (jù)

【飓风】hurricane

锯 (jù) saw

【锯齿】sawtooth

【锯末】sawdust

聚 (jù) assemble; gather; get together

【聚餐】dine together; have a dinner party

【聚会】❶meet; get together ❷get-together

【聚积】accumulate; collect; build up

【聚集】gather; assemble; collect

【聚精会神】concentrate one's attention on; be concentrated; be intent on; attentively

【聚居】live together; inhabit a region (as an ethnic group); live in a compact community

踞 (jù) ❶crouch; squat ❷sit ❸occupy

juan

捐 (juān) ❶tax ❷donate ❸give up

【捐款】contribute money

【捐躯】sacrifice one's life; lay down one's life (for one's country)

【捐献】contribute (to an organization); donate; present

【捐赠】contribute (as a gift); donate; present

【捐助】offer (financial or material assistance); contribute; donate

涓 (juān) a tiny stream

【涓涓】trickling sluggishly

娟 (juān) beautiful; graceful

【娟秀】beautiful; graceful

镌 (juān) engrave

【镌刻】engrave

卷 (juǎn) ❶roll ❷roll up; coil ❸sweep off; carry along

另见本页 juàn

【卷笔刀】pencil sharpener

【卷尺】tape measure

【卷发】curly (or wavy) hair

【卷曲】curl

【卷入】be drawn into; be involved in

【卷心菜】cabbage

【卷轴】reel

卷 (juàn) ❶book ❷volume ❸examination paper ❹file; dossier

另见本页 juǎn

【卷子】examination paper

【卷宗】❶folder ❷file; dossier

倦 (juàn) weary; tired

【倦容】a tired look

【倦意】a feeling of tiredness

绢 (juàn) thin, tough silk

【绢花】silk flower

圈 (juàn) pen; fold; sty

另见 1153 页 quān

【圈肥】barnyard manure

眷 (juàn) ❶family dependant ❷have tender feeling for

【眷爱】regard with affection; love

【眷恋】be sentimentally attached to

【眷属】family dependants

J

jue

撅 (juē) stick up; pout

【撅嘴】pout one's lips

决 (jué) ❶decide; determine ❷burst ❸ definitely; certainly; surely; under any circumstances ❹execute a person ❺ be breached; burst

【决策】❶make policy ❷policy-making

【决出】contest (prizes); fight for

【决堤】breach a dyke

【决定】❶determine; decide; make up one's mind ❷decision

J

【决断】❶ make a decision ❷ determination; resolve; decisiveness; resolution

【决计】❶ have decided; have made up one's mind ❷definitely; certainly

【决裂】split; break with

【决赛】finals: 半~semifinals

【决胜】decide the issue of the battle; determine the victory

【决算】final accounts; final accounting of revenue and expenditure

【决心】determination: 下~make up one's mind

【决一雌雄】fight it out; fight to see who is the stronger

【决议】resolution

【决意】have one's mind made up; be determined

【决战】decisive battle

诀 (jué) ❶ formula ❷ knack; tricks of the trade ❸part; bid farewell

【诀别】bid farewell; part

【诀窍】secret of success; knack; tricks of the trade;

抉 (jué) pick (or single) out

【抉择】choose; pick; make a choice

角 (jué) ❶ role; part; character ❷ contend; compete

另见 1049 页 jiǎo

【角斗】wrestle

【角色】role; part: 扮演~play a role

觉 (jué) ❶ sense; feel ❷ awake; wake up ❸ become aware; become awakened

【觉察】become conscious (or aware) of; sense; read; find; perceive

【觉悟】❶ consciousness; understanding; awareness ❷ become awakened; come to understand

【觉醒】awake; awaken; rouse

绝 (jué) ❶ stop; cut off ❷ unique; superb; matchless ❸ hopeless; desperate ❹exhausted; used up; finished ❺extremely; most ❻absolutely; in the least; by any means; on any account ❼leaving no leeway; making no allowance; uncompromising

【绝笔】❶the last work ❷last words written before one's death

【绝壁】precipice

【绝处逢生】be unexpectedly rescued from a desperate situation

【绝顶】❶extremely; utterly ❷ peak; summit

【绝对】❶absolute ❷absolutely; perfectly; definitely

【绝技】unique skill

【绝迹】disappear; vanish; become extinct; be stamped out

【绝交】break off relations

【绝境】hopeless situation; blind alley

【绝路】❶blind alley; dead end; impasse ❷ block the way out; leave no way out

【绝密】top-secret; most confidential

【绝情】heartless;cruel
【绝食】go on a hunger strike;fast
【绝望】despair;give up all hope
【绝无仅有】 unique; the only one of its kind
【绝缘】❶ insulation ❷ be cut off from the world
【绝症】incurable disease;fatal illness

倔 (jué) gruff;surly
另见本页 juè

【倔强】stubborn;unbending;unyielding

掘 (jué)dig

【掘土机】excavator

崛 (jué)rise abruptly

【崛起】❶ rise abruptly; rise sharply ❷ spring up;rise

爵 (jué) an ancient wine vessel with three legs and a loop handle

【爵士乐】jazz

矍 (jué)

【矍铄】hale and hearty

攫 (jué)seize;grab

【攫取】seize;grab

倔 (juè)gruff;surly
另见本页 jué

【倔头】❶a stubborn and surly person ❷a difficult customer

jun

军 (jūn) ❶army;troops ❷corps ❸military

【军备】armament;arms
【军车】military vehicle
【军队】armed forces;army;troops
【军法】military law
【军服】uniform
【军港】naval port
【军功】military exploit
【军官】officer
【军徽】army emblem
【军机】❶military plan ❷military secret
【军纪】military discipline
【军舰】warship;naval vessel
【军旗】army flag
【军情】military (or war) situation
【军区】military region;military area command
【军人】soldier;armyman;serviceman
【军事】military affairs
【军事演习】military exercise
【军团】army group
【军委】(中央军事委员会的简称) the Central Military Commission
【军衔】military rank
【军校】military school;military academy
【军训】military training
【军装】military uniform;uniform

均 (jūn) ❶ equal; even ❷ without exception;all;completely;entirely

【均等】equal;fair
【均衡】balance;even
【均摊】share equally;share alike
【均匀】even;well-distributed;uniform

君 (jūn) ❶gentleman ❷monarch; sovereign;supreme ruler ❸(used as a title) Mr. ❹(used in direct address) you;sir

【君王】monarch;sovereign;emperor
【君主】monarch;sovereign
【君主制】monarchy
【君子】gentleman

菌 (jūn) ❶fungus ❷bacterium
另见 1068 页 jùn

俊 (jùn) pretty; handsome

【俊杰】 a person of outstanding talent; hero

【俊美】 pretty; handsome

【俊秀】 pretty; of delicate beauty

【俊雅】 refined and elegant

峻 (jùn) ❶ high; steep ❷ harsh; severe; stern

【峻峭】 high and steep

骏 (jùn) fine horse; steed

【骏马】 fine horse; steed

菌 (jùn) mushroom
另见 1067 页 jūn

竣 (jùn) complete; finish

【竣工】 (of a project) be completed

K k

ka

咖（kā）

【咖啡】coffee

【咖啡因】caffeine

卡（kǎ）❶card ❷block; check

【卡车】truck; lorry

【卡拉 OK】karaoke

【卡通】cartoon; caricature

kai

开（kāi）❶ open ❷ turn on ❸ begin; start ❹set up; run; operate ❺drive; pilot ❻hold ❼write out ❽pay ❾boil ❿ come loose ⓫off; away

【开办】open; set up; run; start

【开场白】opening remarks

【开车】drive; start

【开除】dismiss; fire; sack; discharge

【开创】start; initiate

【开导】enlighten; bring sb. to reason

【开端】beginning; start

【开发】develop; open up

【开发商】developer

【开放】❶come into bloom ❷open to the outside world ❸lift a ban, restriction, etc.

【开关】switch; button

【开户】open an account

【开花】bloom; blossom

【开会】hold (or have, attend, go to) a meeting

【开卷考试】an open-book exam

【开垦】open up (or reclaim) wasteland

【开阔】open; wide

【开朗】optimistic

【开门见山】come straight to the point

【开枪】shoot; fire a shot

【开设】open; set up

【开始】❶ begin; start; open; come to; go (or set) about ❷beginning; outset ❸at the beginning of; at first

【开水】❶boiling water ❷boiled water

【开锁】unlock

【开拓】pioneer; open up; explore

【开玩笑】joke; make fun of

【开小差】be absent-minded

【开心】❶ feel happy; joyous; elated ❷ amuse oneself at sb.'s expense; make fun of sb.

【开学】school opens; term begins

【开药方】write out a prescription

【开业】start business; open for business

【开展】❶ develop; carry out; launch; unfold ❷open-minded; politically progressive

【开张】❶ open a business; begin doing

business ❷conduct the first transaction of a day's business ❸(of certain activities) begin; start

【开支】❶expense; expenditure ❷pay

揩 (kāi) wipe

【揩汗】wipe off sweat

【揩眼泪】wipe off tears

凯 (kǎi) triumphant; victorious

【凯歌】a song of triumph; paean

【凯旋】triumphant return

铠 (kǎi)

【铠甲】armour

慨 (kǎi) ❶indignant ❷deeply touched ❸generous

【慨叹】sigh with regret

楷 (kǎi) pattern; model

【楷模】model; pattern

【楷书】regular script

kan

刊 (kān) ❶periodical; issue: 半月～fortnightly; 季～quarterly; 年～annual; 期～periodical; 双月～bimonthly; 月～monthly; 周～weekly ❷publish; print

【刊登】carry; publish in a newspaper (or magazine)

【刊物】publication; periodical

【刊印】compose and print

【刊载】publish; carry

看 (kān) ❶look after; take care of; tend ❷guard; keep watch on

另见本页 kàn

【看管】❶look after; attend to ❷guard; watch

【看护】nurse; look after; take care of; tend; attend to

【看家】❶look after the house; mind the house ❷outstanding (ability)

【看守】❶watch; guard; keep watch on ❷jailer; warder

勘 (kān) ❶read and correct the text of; collate ❷investigate; survey

【勘测】survey; explore

【勘误】correct errors in printing

坎 (kǎn) ❶bank; ridge ❷pit; hole

【坎坷】❶bumpy; rough ❷full of frustrations

砍 (kǎn) cut; chop; fell

【砍刀】chopper

【砍倒】cut (or chop) down; fell

【砍伐】fell; cut down

【砍价】bargain down; knock down prices

看 (kàn) ❶see; look at; watch ❷read ❸think; consider; view; observe ❹call on; visit ❺look after ❻depend on ❼treat

另见本页 kān

【看报】read newspapers

【看病】❶see a doctor ❷treat a patient

【看不见】❶invisible; unseen ❷be out of sight; lose sight of

【看成】regard (or consider, treat, think of, see, look upon) as

【看穿】understand thoroughly; see through

【看待】treat; regard; look on

【看到】catch sight of; see

【看电影】see a film; go to the movies

【看法】view; opinion; attitude

【看见】see; catch sight of

【看来】it seems; it looks as if

【看轻】to look down upon

【看清】see clearly; see through; understand

【看书】read books

【看台】stands

【看望】call on (or at); visit; see; look up (or in)

kang

康 (kāng) well-being; health

【康复】restored to health; recovered

【康乃馨】carnation

慷 (kāng) generous; free-handed

【慷慨】❶generous ❷liberal ❸vehement; fervent

糠 (kāng) ❶chaff; bran; husk ❷(usu. of a radish) spongy

【糠油】oil extracted from rice husks

扛 (káng) carry on the shoulder; shoulder

【扛活】work as a farm laborer

亢 (kàng) ❶ high; haughty ❷ excessive; extreme

【亢奋】stimulated; excited

伉 (kàng)

【伉俪】married couple; husband and wife

抗 (kàng) ❶resist; combat; fight ❷refuse; defy ❸be a match for; contend with

【抗癌】anticancer

【抗病毒】anti-virus

【抗衡】contend with

【抗洪】combat a flood; fight a flood

【抗拒】resist; defy

【抗生素】antibiotic

【抗体】antibody

【抗议】protest

【抗灾】fight (or combat) natural calamities

【抗争】make a stand against; resist

炕 (kàng) ❶kang, a heatable brick bed ❷bake or dry by the heat of a fire

【炕席】a kang mat

kao

考 (kǎo) ❶ examine; test; give (or take) an examination ❷ check; inspect ❸investigate; study; go into

【考查】test; check

【考察】❶ inspect; investigate ❷ observe and study; search into

【考场】examination hall (or room)

【考分】mark; score

【考核】examine; check

【考卷】examination paper

【考虑】consider; take into account; think about (or over)

【考勤】cheek on attendance

【考试】❶examine ❷examination; test: 期中～mid-term examination; 期终～end-of-term (or final) examination

【考验】trial; test

拷 (kǎo) ❶torture ❷beat; torture

【拷贝】copy

烤 (kǎo) roast; bake; toast

【烤火】warm oneself by a fire

【烤炉】oven

【烤鸭】roast duck

犒 (kào) reward with food and drink

【犒劳】reward with food and drink

靠 (kào) ❶lean on (or against); rest against ❷ depend (or rely) on ❸ trust ❹keep to; get near; come up to ❺ near; by

【靠岸】pull in to shore

【靠背】back (of a chair)

【靠近】❶draw near; approach ❷near; by

【靠自己】❶rely on oneself ❷by oneself

ke

苛 (kē) harsh; severe; demanding

【苛刻】harsh

【苛求】be overcritical

科 (kē) ❶ section; department ❷ subject ❸family

【科幻小说】science fiction

【科技】science and technology

【科教兴国】national rejuvenation through science and education

【科目】subject; course; headings in an account book

【科学】❶science ❷scientific

【科学家】scientist

【科研】scientific research

【科长】section chief

棵 (kē) (usu. for plants): 一～树 a tree

颗 (kē) (usu. for anything small and roundish)

【颗粒】❶grain ❷pellet

磕 (kē) ❶knock ❷rap

【磕打】knock out

【磕碰】❶ collide with; bump against ❷ clash; squabble

【磕头】kowtow

瞌 (kē)

【瞌睡】sleepy; drowsy

蝌 (kē)

【蝌蚪】tadpole

壳 (ké) shell; casing

咳 (ké) cough

【咳嗽】cough

可 (kě) ❶may; can ❷need; be worth ❸ approve ❹ but; yet; however ❺ fit; suit

【可爱】lovely; likeable; charming; delightful; lovable

【可悲】sad; miserable

【可持续发展】sustainable development

【可耻】shameful; disgraceful

【可观】considered

【可好】as luck would have it; by a happy coincidence

【可恨】hateful

【可见】it is thus clear or evident, obvious that

【可敬】respected

【可靠】reliable; dependable; trustworthy

【可口】tasty; good to eat

【可口可乐】Coca-Cola

【可怜】❶ wretched; pitiful; poor ❷ have pity on; pity ❸meagre; wretched; miserable

【可能】❶ possible; probable ❷ would; might; will; may; can ❸ possibly; maybe; perhaps

【可怕】frightful; fearful; awful; terrible

【可取】desirable; advisable

【可是】but; though; yet; however

【可视电话】videophone; picture-phone

【可惜】unfortunately

【可喜】gratifying; heartening

【可笑】funny; laughable; ridiculous; ludicrous

【可行】practicable; workable

【可行性】feasibility

【可疑】suspicious

【可以】❶may; might; can; could ❷passable; pretty good; not bad ❸terrible; awful

渴 (kě) ❶thirst ❷thirsty

【渴求】ask earnestly

【渴望】thirst (or long, yearn) for

克 (kè) ❶ gramme (or g.) ❷ overcome; capture ❸restrain

【克服】❶overcome; conquer ❷put up with (hardships, inconveniences, etc.)

【克隆】❶clone ❷duplicate

【克制】restrain; hold back

刻 (kè) ❶ quarter ❷ moment ❸ cut; carve ❹unkind; harsh ❺in the highest degree

【刻板】❶ stiff; inflexible ❷ cut blocks for printing

【刻版】cut blocks for printing; carve printing blocks

【刻本】block-printed edition

【刻不容缓】be of great urgency; admit no delay

【刻骨铭心】be engraved on one's bones and heart—be remembered with deep gratitude

【刻画】depict; portray

【刻苦】hardworking; assiduous; painstaking

恪 (kè) scrupulously and respectfully

【恪守】scrupulously abide by (a treaty, promise, etc.)

客 (kè) ❶guest; visitor: 贵～a distinguished guest ❷traveller; passenger ❸customer ❹objective

【客车】coach; passenger train

【客船】passenger ship; passenger boat

【客店】inn

【客服】customer service

【客观】❶objective ❷objectivity

【客观规律】objective law

【客户】client; customer

【客机】passenger plane; airliner

【客气】❶polite; courteous ❷modest: 您太～了。You are being too modest. ❸ make polite remarks or act politely; be polite; be courteous: 别～。(to a guest) Make yourself at home. (to a host) Please don't bother.

【客人】guest; visitor

【客厅】sitting room; lounge

【客源】source of tourists; potential customers or tourists

课 (kè) ❶class; lesson: 讲～give a lecture; 上～go to class; 听～attend a lecture; 下～finish class; get out of class; 补～make up missed lessons ❷ subject; course: 必修～required courses; 选修～optional courses

【课本】textbook

【课表】school timetable

【课程】course; curriculum

【课时】class hour; period

【课堂】classroom

【课桌】desk

ken

肯 (kěn) ❶agree ❷be willing (or ready) to

【肯定】❶affirm; confirm; approve ❷positive ❸definite; sure ❹certainly; definitely

垦 (kěn) cultivate

【垦殖】reclaim and cultivate wasteland

恳 (kěn) ❶ request ❷ earnestly; sincerely

【恳切】sincere; earnest

【恳请】earnestly request

【恳求】beg; implore

啃 (kěn) bite; nibble

【啃老族】boomerang children; the NEET (Not in Education, Employment or Training) group

keng

坑 (kēng) ❶hole; pit; hollow: 泥～mud puddle ❷tunnel

【坑道】tunnel

K 【坑人】❶ cheat; entrap ❷ be upset (by a heavy loss)

铿 (kēng) the sound of clanging or clattering

【铿锵】(of sound produced by the gong, piano, cymbals, etc.) rhythmic and sonorous

kong

空 (kōng) ❶sky; air ❷empty; hollow; void ❸for nothing; in vain

另见本页 kòng

【空洞】empty; hollow

【空话】empty talk (or words); idle talk

【空间】space; room

【空军】air force

【空旷】open and spacious

【空名】❶ empty title; empty name ❷ undeserved reputation

【空难】air crash (or disaster)

【空气】air; atmosphere

【空前】unprecedented

【空调】air conditioner

【空想】fancy; dream; fantasy

【空虚】empty; void

【空运】airlift; air transport (or freight)

【空中小姐】stewardess

孔 (kǒng) hole; opening

【孔雀】peacock

【孔穴】hole; cavity

【孔子】Confucius

恐 (kǒng) ❶ fear; dread ❷ terrify; frighten ❸afraid

【恐怖】fright; terror; horror

【恐怖分子】terrorist

【恐吓】frighten; threaten: ～信 threatening letter

【恐惧】fear; dread: ～不安 be frightened and restless

【恐龙】dinosaur

【恐怕】❶ fear; be afraid of ❷ perhaps; maybe; probably

空 (kòng) ❶empty space; room ❷free (or spare) time ❸empty ❹unoccupied; vacant

另见本页 kōng

【空白】margin; blank; gap

【空格】blank space

【空缺】vacancy

【空隙】gap; interval: 填补～ fill up a gap

【空闲】❶spare; free ❷leisure

控 (kòng) ❶ accuse; charge ❷ control; dominate

【控股公司】holding company

【控诉】make a complaint against

【控制】control; dominate; command

kou

口 (kǒu) ❶mouth ❷opening; entrance; inlet; outlet; exit: 出～exit; outlet; 入～entrance ❸cut; hole ❹edge

【口岸】port

【口才】eloquence

【口吃】stammer

【口袋】pocket;bag;sack

【口服药】oral medicine

【口福】gourmet's luck; the luck to get sth. very nice to eat

【口红】lipstick

【口角】quarrel;bicker;wrangle

【口渴】❶thirst ❷thirsty

【口令】password;watchword

【口哨】whistle

【口是心非】say yes and mean no

【口水】saliva

【口算】do a sum orally

【口味】taste

【口香糖】chewing gum

【口译】interpret

【口音】accent;voice

【口语】spoken language

叩 (kòu) ❶ knock ❷ kowtow ❸ inquire;ask

【叩拜】kowtow

【叩见】visit (one's superior);call on

扣 (kòu) ❶buckle; button; knot ❷fasten;button up ❸take off;deduct ❹ detain;arrest ❺press;pull ❻smash or spike (a ball)

【扣除】take off;deduct

【扣人心弦】thrilling;exciting

【扣押】detain;hold in custody

【扣子】knot;button

ku

枯 (kū) ❶withered ❷dull ❸dried

【枯竭】dried up

【枯萎】wither

【枯燥】dull and dry;uninteresting

哭 (kū)cry;weep;sob

【哭泣】weep;sob;cry

【哭诉】complain tearfully

窟 (kū) ❶hole;cave ❷den;lair

苦 (kǔ) ❶hardship;suffering;pain;bitterness ❷cause sb. suffering;give sb. a hard time ❸suffer from;be troubled by ❹take pains to;be at pains ❺ bitter ❻bitterly ❼with great pains

【苦处】suffering;hardship;difficulty

【苦瓜】balsam pear;bitter gourd

【苦尽甘来】after suffering comes happiness

【苦难】misery;suffering;distress

【苦恼】distressed

【苦笑】a forced (or wry) smile

【苦衷】difficulties that one is reluctant to mention

库 (kù) storehouse; warehouse; depository;depot

【库存】stock;reserve

裤 (kù) trousers; pants: 长~trousers; 短~shorts;牛仔~jeans;工作~work pants;内衣~underwear

【裤腿】trouser legs

【裤腰】waist of trousers

酷 (kù) ❶ cruel; brutal; oppressive ❷ cool ❸very;extremely;exceedingly

【酷爱】be very fond of;ardently love

【酷热】extremely hot

【酷似】resemble closely

kua

夸 (kuā) ❶boast;overstate;exaggerate ❷praise:自~sing one's own praises

【夸大】overstate;exaggerate;magnify

【夸奖】praise;commend

【夸耀】show off;boast of

【夸张】exaggerate;overstate

垮 (kuǎ) fall; break down; collapse

【垮台】collapse; fall down

跨 (kuà) ❶ step; stride ❷ go beyond; span; cross ❸ cover ❹ ride

【跨度】span

【跨国公司】transnational corporation (TNC)

【跨过】stride over; cross; span; step over

【跨栏】hurdle race

【跨越】stride across; leap over; cut across

kuai

会 (kuài)
另见 1030 页 huì

【会计】❶ accounting ❷ bookkeeper; accountant

【会计师】accountant; treasurer

快 (kuài) ❶ hurry up; make haste ❷ be about to ❸ quick; rapid; swift; speedy ❹ keen; sharp ❺ quick-witted ❻ pleased; happy ❼ fast ❽ soon; before long

【快步】trot; quick step

【快餐】quick lunch (or meal); fast food; snack

【快递】express delivery; fast mail

【快活】happy; gay; cheerful; lively

【快乐】❶ delight; joy; pleasure ❷ gay; happy; joyful ❸ happily

【快速】fast; quick; speedy; rapid

【快照】snapshot

块 (kuài) ❶ block; cake; piece; mass; lump ❷ (for gold or silver dollars, Renminbi, and certain paper money)

【块头】(physical) build

脍 (kuài) ❶ meat chopped into small pieces; minced meat ❷ chop meat or fish into small pieces

【脍炙人口】(of a piece of good writing, etc.) win universal praise; enjoy great popularity

筷 (kuài) chopsticks

【筷子】chopsticks

kuan

宽 (kuān) ❶ breadth; width ❷ relax; relieve ❸ extend ❹ wide; broad ❺ generous; merciful ❻ well-off

【宽敞】spacious

【宽大】❶ spacious; roomy ❷ liberal ❸ lenient; merciful

【宽带】wideband; broadband

【宽度】width; breadth

【宽阔】broad; wide; vast

【宽容】tolerant; lenient

【宽恕】excuse; pardon

【宽限】extend a time limit

【宽心】feel relieved (or relaxed); be at ease

款 (kuǎn) ❶ article; section; item ❷ sum; fund; money ❸ entertain ❹ leisurely; slow

【款待】entertain

【款式】style; design

【款项】fund; a sum of money

kuang

狂 (kuáng) ❶ mad; crazy: 发～go (or become, run) mad ❷ violent; wild

【狂暴】violent; wild; frantic; frenzied; furious; outrageous; ungoverned

【狂风】whole gale; fierce wind

【狂欢节】carnival

【狂热】fanatical; feverish

【狂妄自大】arrogant and conceited

【狂喜】be wild with joy

旷 (kuàng) ❶neglect ❷waste ❸vast; spacious ❹large-minded: 心～神怡 carefree and happy

【旷课】 cut school (or classes)

【旷野】 wilderness

矿 (kuàng) ❶mine ❷mineral deposit ❸ore

【矿藏】 mineral resources

【矿产】 mineral products

【矿工】 miner; mine worker; pitman

【矿井】 mine

【矿区】 ore district

【矿泉】 mineral spring

【矿山】 mine

【矿物】 mineral

况 (kuàng) condition; situation

【况且】 besides; moreover

框 (kuàng) ❶frame; case ❷draw a frame round ❸restrict; restrain; bind

【框架】 framework; frame; setting

kui

亏 (kuī) ❶lose ❷suffer: 吃～suffer losses ❸short; deficient ❹luckily; fortunately ❺treat unfairly

【亏本】 lose money in business

【亏待】 treat unfairly; treat shabbily; be unfair to

【亏损】 ❶lose ❷loss

【亏心】 have a guilty conscience

盔 (kuī) helmet

【盔甲】 suit of armour

窥 (kuī) peep; spy

【窥见】 catch a glimpse of

【窥视】 peep at; look into; spy on

【窥探】 spy on; poke one's nose into; pry about

葵 (kuí) certain herbaceous plants with big flowers

【葵花】 sunflower

魁 (kuí) ❶chief; head ❷of stalwart build

【魁伟】 big and tall; majestic; strongly-built

【魁梧】 big and tall

睽 (kuí) go against; run counter to

【睽睽】 stare; gaze

匮 (kuì) deficient

【匮乏】 be deficient in; be short of

馈 (kuì) make a present

【馈赠】 present; make a present of sth.

溃 (kuì) ❶break through ❷be defeated ❸burst

【溃败】 be defeated

【溃烂】 fester; ulcerate

【溃逃】 escape in disorder; flee

愧 (kuì) ❶ashamed; conscience-stricken ❷embarrassed; uneasy

【愧色】 ashamed look; sign of shame

kun

昆 (kūn) ❶elder brother ❷offspring

【昆虫】 insect; bug

【昆曲】 Kunqu opera

捆 (kǔn) ❶bundle ❷bind; tie; bundle up; wrap

【捆绑】 bind; tie up; fasten

困 (kùn) ❶surround; encircle; besiege ❷tired; weary

【困乏】 sleepy; tired

【困惑】❶puzzled ❷at a loss

【困境】difficult position：陷入～get in a tight corner

【困苦】deep poverty

【困难】❶difficulty ❷hard；difficult

【困扰】puzzle；perplex

kuo

扩（kuò）❶ expand；enlarge ❷ extend；lengthen

【扩充】expand；enlarge

【扩大】enlarge；expand；extend

【扩建】extend（factory，mine，etc.）

【扩展】expand；spread；develop

括（kuò）❶ draw together（muscles，etc.）；contract ❷include

【括号】brackets

阔（kuò）❶ wide；broad；vast ❷ rich；wealthy

【阔别】long separated；long parted

【阔步】take big steps：昂首～ stride proudly ahead

廓（kuò）❶wide；extensive ❷outline

L l

la

垃 (lā)

【垃圾】rubbish; trash; refuse; waste

【垃圾车】garbage truck; dust cart

【垃圾食品】junk food

【垃圾箱】dustbin; trash can; garbage can; ash can

拉 (lā) ❶ pull; draw; drag ❷ transport ❸ play ❹ give (or lend) a helping hand; help ❺ drag in; implicate ❻ draw in; win over; canvass ❼ empty the bowels

【拉扯】❶ drag; pull ❷ take great pains to bring up ❸ drag in; implicate ❹ chat

【拉丁文】Latin

【拉肚子】suffer from diarrhea; have loose bowels

【拉家常】talk about everyday matters; engage in small talk; chitchat

【拉开】pull open; draw back

【拉链】zipper: 拉上～zip up

【拉拢】draw sb. over to one's side

喇 (lǎ)

【喇叭】❶ trumpet: 吹～blow a trumpet ❷ loudspeaker

【喇嘛】lama

腊 (là) ❶ an ancient sacrifice which took place each (or lunar) year ❷ shortly after the winter solstice ❸ the twelfth lunar month ❹ cured

【腊肠】sausage

【腊梅】wintersweet

【腊肉】bacon

蜡 (là) ❶ wax ❷ candle

【蜡笔】wax crayon

【蜡黄】wax yellow; waxen; sallow

【蜡烛】candle

辣 (là) ❶ hot; peppery ❷ ruthless; cruel; heartless; cold-blooded

【辣酱】chilli sauce

【辣椒】hot pepper; chilli

【辣手】thorny; troublesome

lai

来 (lái) ❶ come; arrive ❷ happen; take place ❸ coming; next ❹ since

【来宾】guest; visitor

【来得及】have time to do; be able to do sth. in time

【来电显示】call display; call ID display

【来访】come to visit; call in (or at, on); visit

【来回】❶ back and forth; to and fro ❷ make a round trip

【来历】origin; source

【来日方长】there is a long time ahead

【来往】❶come and go ❷contact

【来源】source; origin

【来之不易】hard-earned

赖 (lài) ❶rely (or depend) on ❷hang on in a place; hold on to a place ❸deny one's fault (or responsibility); go back on one's word ❹blame sb. wrongly; put the blame on sb. else ❺blame ❻poor

【赖床】be feeling too lazy to get out of bed

【赖账】❶refuse to pay a debt; repudiate a debt ❷go back on one's words

lan

L

兰 (lán) orchid; lily magnolia

【兰草】fragrant thoroughwort (Eupatorium fortunei)

【兰花】cymbidium; orchid

拦 (lán) block; hold back; hinder; stop

【拦劫】hold up; stop and rob

【拦路】block (or bar) the way

【拦网】block

【拦住】stop; check; hold up; keep away

栏 (lán) ❶ bar; fence; railing ❷ pen; shed: 牛～cowshed; 羊～sheep pen ❸ column: 备注～remarks column; 布告～bulletin board; notice board

【栏杆】fence; railing; banisters

【栏目】the heading or title of a column (in a magazine, etc.)

蓝 (lán) blue

【蓝宝石】sapphire

【蓝天】blue sky

【蓝图】blueprint

篮 (lán) ❶basket ❷goal; basket: 投～shoot; shoot a basket; shooting

【篮球】basketball: 打～play basketball

【篮球场】basketball court

【篮球队】basketball team

览 (lǎn) see; look at

【览胜】visit scenic spot

揽 (lǎn) ❶grasp ❷attract ❸pull in to one's arms ❹ fasten with a rope, etc. ❺take on; take upon oneself; canvass ❻grasp; monopolize

【揽活】take on work

缆 (lǎn) ❶cable; thick rope ❷hawser; mooring rope

【缆车】cable car

【缆绳】thick rope; cable

懒 (lǎn) ❶lazy ❷sluggish

【懒惰】lazy

【懒汉】lazybones

【懒散】idle; sluggish

烂 (làn) ❶ rot; decay ❷ broken; worn-out ❸messy ❹soft; mashed

【烂漫】❶ bright-colored ❷ unaffected: 天真～naive; innocent

【烂泥】mud; slush

【烂醉】dead drunk

滥 (làn) ❶overflow; flood ❷excessive; indiscriminate

【滥用】abuse; make wrong use of; misuse

【滥竽充数】be present just to make up the number

lang

郎 (láng) ❶an official title in imperial times ❷used in forming nouns designating certain classes of persons: 令郎

your son ❸(used by a woman in addressing her husband or lover) my darling

【郎中】a physician trained in herbal medicine; doctor

狼 (láng) wolf

【狼狈】in a difficult (or awkward) position; in a tight corner

【狼吞虎咽】wolf down

【狼牙棒】wolf-teeth club (a club with spikes on one end and a long handle on the other, formerly used as a weapon)

琅 (láng)

【琅琅】a tinkling or jingling sound; the sound of reading aloud

廊 (láng) porch; corridor

朗 (lǎng) ❶bright ❷loud and clear

【朗读】read loudly and clearly

【朗诵】recite

浪 (làng) ❶ wave; billow; breaker ❷ loose ❸ unrestrained; dissolute ❹ stroll; roam

【浪潮】tide; wave: 改革的～ tide of reform

【浪费】waste; run through; squander

【浪花】❶ spray; the foam of breaking waves ❷episodes in one's life

【浪漫】❶romantic ❷romance

lao

捞 (lāo) ❶fish for; drag for; dredge up ❷gain; get by unfair means; get by improper means

【捞取】fish for

牢 (láo) ❶jail; prison ❷firm; fast; tight

【牢不可破】unbreakable

【牢固】firm; fast; tight

【牢记】keep (or bear) firmly in mind

【牢靠】❶firm; strong; sturdy ❷ dependable; reliable

【牢笼】❶cage ❷bonds

【牢骚】complaint

劳 (láo) ❶tiredness; fatigue: 积～成疾 break down from endless overwork ❷work; labor ❸ trouble; bother ❹ express one's regards (or appreciation)

【劳保】labor insurance; labor safety

【劳动】work; labor

【劳动节】International Labor Day

【劳动人民】working people

【劳动日】workday

【劳驾】excuse me; may I trouble you (to do sth.)

【劳累】tired; overworked; worn-out

【劳力】❶ labor force; manpower ❷ able-bodied person

【劳务】labor services

【劳逸】labor and rest

老 (lǎo) ❶old; aged ❷outdated ❸overdone; tough ❹always; constantly

【老百姓】common people

【老板】boss

【老伴】(of an old married couple) husband or wife

【老辈】one's elders; old folks

【老当益壮】be old but vigorous

【老虎】tiger

【老交情】❶ long-standing relationship ❷ old friend

【老练】experienced; expert

【老龄化】ageing

【老人】old man (or woman); the aged; the old

【老师】teacher

【老实】❶honest; frank: 忠诚 ~ loyal and honest ❷ well-behaved; good ❸ simple-minded
【老式】old-fashioned
【老天爷】God; Heavens
【老眼光】old views: 拿~看人 judge sb. by old standards
【老鹰】hawk; eagle
【老字号】time-honoured brand
【老祖宗】forefather

姥 (lǎo)

【姥姥】grandmother; grandma

烙 (lào) ❶iron ❷bake in a pan

【烙饼】pancake
【烙印】❶brand; stamp ❷indelible mark

L

涝 (lào) water logging; waterlogged

【涝灾】damage or crop failure caused by water logging

le

乐 (lè) ❶ happy; cheerful; joyful: 助人为~ find pleasure in helping others ❷ be glad to; enjoy; find pleasure in ❸laugh

另见 1296 页 yuè

【乐观】❶optimistic ❷optimism
【乐趣】delight; pleasure; joy
【乐天】carefree; happy-go-lucky
【乐意】❶ be willing (or ready, happy, glad) to ❷with pleasure ❸pleased; happy
【乐于助人】be happy to help others
【乐园】❶paradise ❷playground; amusement park

勒 (lè) ❶rein in ❷force
另见本页 lēi

【勒令】order; force
【勒索】extort; blackmail

lei

勒 (lēi) tie (or strap) sth. tight; fasten
另见本页 lè

【勒紧】tighten

累 (léi)
另见本页 lěi; lèi

【累赘】❶burdensome ❷burden

雷 (léi) ❶thunder ❷mine

【雷达】radar
【雷电】thunder and lightning
【雷厉风行】vigorously and speedily
【雷鸣】thunderous
【雷同】be identical; be duplicate
【雷雨】thunderstorm

镭 (léi) radium

垒 (lěi) ❶rampart; fort ❷pile up

【垒球】softball

累 (lěi) ❶pile (or keep, store) up; accumulate ❷involve ❸continuous; repeated
另见本页 léi; lèi

【累积】accumulate
【累计】add up

肋 (lèi) rib

【肋窝】armpit

泪 (lèi) tear; teardrop: 流 ~ shed tears

【泪花】tears in one's eye
【泪水】tear; teardrop
【泪眼】tearful eyes

类 (lèi) ❶ kind; type; class; sort; category ❷resemble; be similar to

【类比】❶analogize ❷analogy
【类别】sort; kind; type; class
【类似】similar
【类型】type; model

累 (lèi) ❶tire; wear out ❷work hard; toil ❸tired; weary; fatigued
另见 951 页 léi; 951 页 lěi

【累死累活】tire oneself out with back-breaking toil; work oneself to death

擂 (lèi) beat (a drum)

【擂台】ring (for martial contests); arena

leng

棱 (léng) ❶edge ❷corrugation; ridge

【棱角】❶edges and corners ❷edge; pointedness
【棱镜】prism

冷 (lěng) ❶ cold ❷ empty; deserted; unfrequented

【冷暴力】emotional abuse; tacit violence; cold violence
【冷不防】suddenly; by surprise
【冷餐】buffet
【冷藏】refrigeration
【冷场】awkward situation
【冷淡】❶ cold; indifferent ❷ cheerless; desolate
【冷冻】freeze
【冷静】calm; cool-minded; cool-headed: 保持～ keep calm
【冷落】❶treat coldly; leave out in the cold ❷desolate
【冷门】❶ an unexpected winner; dark horse ❷a profession, trade or branch of learning that receives little attention
【冷却】cool off
【冷若冰霜】frosty in manner
【冷笑】sneer
【冷饮】cold drink
【冷遇】cold treatment (or reception)

愣 (lèng) ❶stupefied ❷rash

li

厘 (lí) ❶centi- ❷a unit of Chinese currency ❸a very small amount; a fraction, the least ❹regulate; rectify

【厘米】centimetre (or cm.)

离 (lí) ❶ leave; part from; be away from ❷away from ❸without

【离别】leave; part; depart; farewell
【离婚】divorce
【离境】leave a country; leave a place
【离开】leave; depart from; go off
【离奇】odd; fantastic
【离任】leave office; leave one's post
【离题】stray away from the point

梨 (lí) pear

犁 (lí) plough

【犁头】❶ploughshare ❷plough

黎 (lí) multitude; host

【黎明】dawn; daybreak

篱 (lí) fence; hedge

【篱笆】twig fence; bamboo fence

礼 (lǐ) ❶ceremony: 婚～wedding ceremony; 丧～funeral ❷courtesy ❸gift; present

【礼拜】❶ religious service: 做～ go to church ❷week ❸Sunday
【礼服】full dress: 晚～ evening dress
【礼节】courtesy
【礼貌】❶courtesy; manners ❷politeness;

L

有～have good manners; be polite; 无～ be impolite; have no manners

【礼品】gift; present: 互赠～ exchange presents

【礼堂】assembly hall; auditorium

【礼仪】ceremony and propriety

李 (lǐ) plum

【李代桃僵】❶substitute one thing for another; substitute oneself for another person ❷ bear the blame for another person's mistake

里 (lǐ) ❶lining; inside ❷neighbour ❸ hometown ❹inner ❺in; inside

【里边】inside; in; within

【里程碑】milestone

【里程表】mileage meter; odometer

L 【里里外外】inside and outside

理 (lǐ) ❶reason ❷natural science: 数～化 mathematics, physics and chemistry ❸manage; run ❹put in order; tidy up ❺pay attention to

【理财】manage money matters

【理睬】pay attention to; take interest in: 不予～turn a blind eye to; turn a deaf ear to

【理发】haircut; have one's hair cut

【理发师】barber; hairdresser

【理解】understand: 加深～ deepen one's understanding

【理论】theory

【理念】idea; concept

【理所当然】of course; naturally; certainly

【理想】ideal; dream

【理性】❶ reason; rational faculty ❷ rational: 恢复～ come to one's sense; 失去～lose one's reason

【理由】ground; cause; reason

鲤 (lǐ) carp

【鲤鱼】carp

力 (lì) ❶power; strength; force; ability: 兵～military strength; 电～electric power ❷do all one can; exert oneself; make every effort

【力度】❶strength ❷intensity

【力量】strength; power; force

【力求】make every effort to; try hard to; strive to

【力所能及】in one's power

【力挺】back up strongly; strongly support

【力争】❶work hard for; strive to; do all one can to ❷argue strongly

历 (lì) ❶calendar: 阴～lunar calendar ❷ go through; undergo; experience ❸all previous ❹covering all; one by one

【历程】course

【历次】all previous

【历法】calendar

【历来】always; all through the ages

【历年】over the years; in the past years

【历时】last; take

【历史】❶history ❷historical

厉 (lì) ❶strict ❷stern; severe

【厉害】❶severe; sharp ❷terrible

【厉行】make great efforts to carry out

立 (lì) ❶stand ❷found; establish; set up ❸live on one's own ❹upright ❺ immediately; at once

【立碑】erect a monument

【立场】standpoint; stand; position

【立春】Beginning of Spring

【立定跳远】standing long jump

【立法】make laws; legislate

【立方】cube

【立竿见影】get instant results

【立功】perform praiseworthy service; make contributions; win honor

【立即】at once; immediately; promptly
【立交桥】flyover; overpass
【立刻】immediately; right away; at once
【立业】establish a business
【立正】stand at attention
【立志】make up one's mind
【立足】❶have (or get) a foothold; gain a footing ❷base oneself on

丽 (lì) beautiful; pretty

【丽人】beauty; beautiful woman

利 (lì) ❶advantage; benefit; gain ❷interest ❸do good to; benefit ❹sharp ❺favourable ❻smooth

【利弊】advantages and disadvantages; pros and cons
【利国利民】benefit both the nation and the people
【利害】advantages and disadvantages; gains and losses; interests
【利率】interest rate
【利落】❶ agile; nimble ❷ neat ❸ settled; finished
【利润】profit
【利益】interest; benefit
【利用】❶use; make use of ❷take advantage of; exploit

例 (lì) ❶example; instance: 举~give an example ❷precedent ❸rule; regulation ❹regular; routine

【例会】regular meeting
【例假】❶official holiday ❷menstrual period
【例句】model sentence
【例如】for example (or instance); such as
【例外】exception: 毫无~ without exception

隶 (lì) be subordinate to; be under a person in servitude

【隶属】be subordinate to; be under the command of

荔 (lì)

【荔枝】litchi; lichee

俪 (lì) ❶paired; parallel ❷husband and wife; married couple: 伉~ husband and wife; married couple

砾 (lì) gravel; shingle

【砾石】gravel whetstone

栗 (lì) ❶chestnut ❷tremble

粒 (lì) ❶grain ❷pill

痢 (lì) dysentery

【痢疾】dysentery

lian

连 (lián) ❶company ❷join; link; connect ❸ repeatedly; in succession ❹including

【连词】conjunction
【连贯】❶link up; connect; piece together; hang together ❷coherent; consistent
【连环画】picture story book
【连接】join; link; connect
【连累】get sb. into trouble; involve
【连绵】continuous
【连任】be reappointed (or reelected) continuously; renew one's term of office
【连日】for days on end; day after day
【连锁店】chain stores
【连锁反应】chain reaction
【连同】together with; including; plus
【连续】continuous; successive; running: 电视~剧 TV play series
【连衣裙】dress

怜 (lián) ❶pity; sympathize with; pity ❷love

【怜爱】love tenderly; have tender affection for

【怜惜】have pity for; pity

帘 (lián) ❶ flag as a shop sign ❷ (hanging) screen; curtain

【帘子】screen; curtain

莲 (lián) lotus

【莲花】lotus flower; lotus

【莲藕】lotus root

【莲子】lotus seed

涟 (lián) ❶ ripples ❷ continuous flow (of tears)

【涟漪】wavelet; ripples

联 (lián) ❶ antithetical couplet: 春～ Spring Festival couplet ❷ unite; join; relate; connect; link

【联邦】federation; commonwealth

【联播】radio hookup: 新闻～news hookup

【联合】❶ unite; ally ❷ alliance; union ❸joint

【联合国】the United Nations (UN)

【联欢】have a get-together

【联结】join; connect; link

【联络】contact; get in touch with; come into contact with

【联赛】league matches

【联系】❶contact; get in touch with: 保持～keep in contact with ❷integrate; relate; link: 理论～实际 integrate theory with practice

【联想】associate with

廉 (lián) ❶ honest and clean ❷ cheap; inexpensive

【廉价】cheap

【廉洁】honest and clean

【廉明】upright and incorruptible

【廉政】construction of a clean and honest government

【廉租房】low-rent housing; tenement house

镰 (lián) sickle

【镰刀】sickle

敛 (liǎn) ❶hold back; restrain ❷collect

【敛财】accumulate wealth by unfair means

脸 (liǎn) ❶ face: 丢～ lose face ❷ the front part

【脸红】blush

【脸颊】cheeks

【脸面】face; self-respect; sb.'s feelings

【脸盆】washbasin; washbowl

【脸谱】facial makeup in operas

【脸色】❶ complexion; look ❷ facial expression

练 (liàn) ❶ practise; train; drill ❷ skilled; experienced

【练功】do exercises in gymnastics, acrobatics, etc.; practise one's skill

【练习】practise: 做～do exercises

【练字】practise handwriting

炼 (liàn) ❶ smelt; refine ❷ temper with fire

【炼钢】steel-making

【炼乳】condensed milk; evaporated milk

【炼油】❶oil refining ❷extract oil by heat ❸heat edible oil

恋 (liàn) ❶ love ❷ feel attached to; cling to ❸fall in love with

【恋爱】love; love affair: 谈～be in love; have a love affair

【恋恋不舍】be reluctant to part with; hate to tear oneself away; hate to see sb. go

【恋人】sweetheart; lover

链 (liàn) chain

【链锯】chain saw

【链条】❶chain ❷roller chain (of a bicycle)

liang

良 (liáng) ❶good; fine ❷good people ❸very; very much

【良策】good plan (or policy); sound strategy

【良机】good opportunity

【良久】a good while; a long time: 沉思～ ponder for a long time

【良师益友】good teacher and helpful friend

【良田】good field; fertile farmland

【良心】conscience

【良心不安】have an uneasy conscience

【良性】❶favourable ❷benign

【良性循环】virtuous cycle

【良药苦口】good medicine tastes bitter but helps

【良友】good friend; mentor

凉 (liáng) ❶cool ❷cold: 着～catch a cold ❸discouraged; disappointed; disheartened

【凉菜】cold dish

【凉快】❶nice and cool ❷cool oneself; cool off

【凉爽】pleasantly cool; nice and cool

【凉水】❶cold water ❷unboiled water

【凉席】summer sleeping mat

【凉鞋】sandals

梁 (liáng) ❶bridge ❷roof beam

【梁桥】beam bridge

【梁上君子】thief; burglar

量 (liáng) ❶measure ❷appraise; evaluate; estimate

另见本页 liàng

【量尺寸】take sb.'s measurements

【量体温】take sb.'s temperature

粮 (liáng) grain: 粗～coarse grain; 细～refined grain

【粮仓】granary; barn

【粮店】grain shop

【粮食】grain; cereals; food

两 (liǎng) ❶both ❷some; a few ❸two

【两半】❶two halves ❷in half

【两倍】❶twice ❷double; twofold

【两边】both sides

【两面】❶both (or two) sides; two aspects ❷dual; double

【两面派】double-dealer

【两难】be in a dilemma

【两栖】amphibious

【两全其美】satisfy both sides

【两用】dual-purpose

【两者】both

亮 (liàng) ❶shine ❷show ❸bright; shining; light ❹loud and clear ❺enlightened

【亮点】❶bright spot ❷focus of attentions

【亮度】brightness; brilliance

【亮晶晶】sparkling; glittering

【亮相】❶strike a pose on the stage ❷make one's position (or view) known; appear in public

谅 (liàng) forgive; excuse; pardon; understand

【谅解】understand; come to an agreement: 达成～reach (or come to) an understanding

量 (liàng) ❶capacity: 酒～capacity for drinking ❷quantity; amount ❸estimate; measure

另见本页 liáng

【量变】quantitative change

【量才录用】give sb. work according to his (or her) abilities

【量化】quantify

【量力而行】do what one is capable of; act according to one's ability

【量体裁衣】act according to actual circumstances

晾(liàng) ❶dry in the sun; sun; dry in the air; air ❷neglect sb.

【晾干】dry by airing; dry in the air

【晾衣服】sun clothes

liao

辽(liáo) distant; faraway

【辽阔】vast; boundless: 幅员～ vast territory

疗(liáo) treat; cure: 治～ treat a patient; give medical care to

【疗程】course (or period) of treatment

【疗效】curative effect

【疗养】recuperate

聊(liáo) ❶ chat ❷ merely; just ❸slightly

【聊表谢意】just a token of gratitude; just to show my appreciation

【聊天】chat

寥(liáo) ❶few; scanty ❷silent; deserted

【寥寥无几】very few

嘹(liáo)

【嘹亮】loud and clear

缭(liáo) ❶ entangled ❷ sew with slanting stitches

【缭乱】confused: 心绪～ in a confused state of mind; 眼花～ be dazzled

【缭绕】wind around; curl up

潦(liáo)

【潦草】illegible: ～的字迹 careless handwriting

【潦倒】be dispirited (or disappointed); be down on one's luck

燎(liáo) burn

【燎原】set the prairie ablaze: 星星之火，可以～ a single spark can start a prairie fire

了(liǎo) ❶know; understand: 明～ understand ❷end; finish; settle; solve: 没完没～endless

【了不起】remarkable; terrific; great; extraordinary

【了解】❶ know; understand; grasp ❷ inquire; go into

【了却】settle; solve

【了然】be clear; understand: 一目～ be clear at a glance

【了如指掌】know sth. like the palm of one's hand

【了愿】fulfill a wish

料(liào) ❶material: 燃～fuel; 原材～ raw material ❷makings ❸grain feed ❹expect; anticipate

【料酒】cooking wine

【料理】❶ arrange; take charge of; manage; take care of ❷cuisine; food

【料想】expect; presume

瞭(liào) watch from a height or a distance

【瞭望】❶look far into the distance ❷keep a lookout

【瞭望台】observation tower; lookout tower

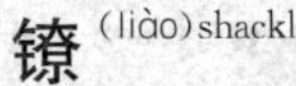

镣(liào) shackles

【镣铐】handcuffs; chains; shackles

lie

咧 (liě)

【咧嘴】draw back the corners of the mouth; grin

列 (liè) ❶row; rank ❷line up ❸list

【列表】make a list

【列车】train

【列举】enumerate; list: ~事实 cite facts

劣 (liè) inferior; of low quality; poor

【劣等】poor; low-grade; inferior

【劣根性】deep-rooted bad habits

【劣迹】misdeed; evil doing; wrongdoing

【劣势】inferior position or strength

【劣质】❶poor; bad; inferior ❷of low quality

烈 (liè) ❶strong; violent; intense ❷fiery ❸sacrificing

【烈火】raging flames

【烈日】burning (or scorching) sun

【烈士】martyr

【烈性】strong; fierce; violent

猎 (liè) hunt

【猎枪】hunting rifle; shotgun

【猎取】seek; hunt for; pursue

【猎犬】hunting dog

【猎人】hunter

【猎物】prey; game

裂 (liè) split; break; crack: 分~ split; break up

【裂变】fission

【裂缝】crack

【裂口】❶breach; gap; split ❷vent

【裂纹】crackle

趔 (liè)

【趔趄】stagger; reel

lin

拎 (līn) carry; lift

【拎包】handbag; shopping bag; bag

邻 (lín) ❶ neighbour ❷ neighbouring; near

【邻国】neighbouring country

【邻近】near; close to

【邻居】neighbour

林 (lín) ❶forest; woods ❷forestry ❸a group of persons or things

【林场】forestry centre; tree farm

【林地】forest land; woodland

【林立】stand in great numbers like trees in a forest

【林业】forestry

临 (lín) ❶face; overlook ❷arrive; come near ❸ copy ❹ on the point of; just before

【临场】❶on the spot ❷when attending an exam

【临床】clinical

【临到】❶on the point of; just before ❷befall; happen to

【临近】close to

【临时】temporary; interim; provisional

【临危不惧】show no fear before danger; face danger fearlessly

【临行】on leaving (or parting)

【临终】❶dying ❷just before one's death; on one's deathbed; at the last moment

淋 (lín) pour; sprinkle: 日晒雨~ sun-scorched and rain-drenched

【淋巴】lymph

【淋漓】❶ dripping wet: 鲜血 ~dripping

with blood ❷大汗～ dripping with sweat;sweating all over ❸have ease of mind;be carefree

【淋漓尽致】thoroughly

【淋雨】get wet in the rain;be caught in the rain

【淋浴】shower bath;shower:洗～take a shower bath

琳 (lín)beautiful jade

【琳琅满目】full of beautiful things in eyes;an eyeful of goodies

鳞 (lín) scale(of fish,etc.)

【鳞甲】scale and shell

【鳞片】scale

凛 (lǐn) ❶cold ❷strict;stern;severe ❸afraid;apprehensive

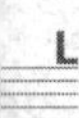

【凛冽】freezing cold

吝 (lìn)stingy;closefisted;tightfisted

【吝啬】stingy;tightfisted;miserly;mean

【吝惜】grudge

ling

伶 (líng) actor or actress

【伶仃】 lonely:孤苦～ alone and uncared for

【伶俐】clever;quick-witted;smart;bright

灵 (líng) ❶spirit:心～soul;mind ❷quick;sharp;clever ❸effective

【灵便】❶easy to handle;handy ❷nimble;quick;agile

【灵感】inspiration

【灵魂】soul;spirit

【灵活】❶nimble;quick;agile:脑子～be quick-witted ❷flexible

【灵敏】quick;keen;sensitive

【灵巧】nimble;clever;skillful

【灵堂】mourning hall

【灵通】well-informed:消息～人士 well-informed sources

玲 (líng)

【玲珑】 ❶ ingeniously and delicately wrought;exquisite ❷clever and nimble

铃 (líng) ❶bell:门～door bell ❷anything in the shape of a bell:哑～dumbbell

【铃铛】small bell

【铃声】the tinkle of bells:～震耳 the sound of the bell shakes the ears

凌 (líng) ❶insult ❷rise high;tower aloft

【凌晨】early hours in the morning;early morning

【凌乱】messy;disorderly

陵 (líng) ❶ hill;mound ❷ imperial tomb;mausoleum

【陵墓】tomb

【陵园】cemetery;graveyard

聆 (líng)listen;hear

【聆听】listen(respectfully)

菱 (líng) ling;water chestnut;water caltrop

【菱形】diamond;rhombus;lozenge

羚 (líng)antelope

【羚羊】antelope;gazelle

零 (líng) ❶nought;zero;nil ❷part ❸fragmentary;odd

【零分】zero;scoreless

【零工】❶odd job:打～do odd jobs ❷odd-job man;odd jobber

【零件】spare parts

【零乱】in a mess

【零钱】❶small change ❷pocket money
【零散】scattered
【零食】snacks:吃~ nibble between meals
【零售】retail;sell retail

龄 (líng) age; year:工~length of service;党 ~Party standing

领 (lǐng) ❶neck ❷neckband; collar ❸ main point ❹lead; guide ❺receive; draw; get ❻understand; grasp

【领班】boss; foreman; headwaiter
【领唱】❶lead a chorus ❷leading singer
【领带】necktie; tie
【领导】❶ lead; guide; exercise leadership ❷leader
【领地】territory
【领队】❶lead a group ❷team leader
【领工资】take one's wages
【领海】territorial waters; territorial sea
【领航】navigate; pilot
【领奖】receive a prize
【领巾】scarf; neckerchief
【领空】territorial sky
【领口】collar; neckband
【领路】lead the way
【领略】taste; experience; have a taste of
【领情】feel grateful to sb.
【领取】draw; receive
【领事】consul:总~consul general
【领事馆】consulate
【领头】❶take the lead ❷be the first; at the head of
【领土】territory
【领悟】understand; grasp; comprehend
【领先】be in the lead; lead:遥遥~be far ahead
【领衔】head the list of; lead the cast
【领袖】leader
【领养】adopt
【领域】❶territory ❷field

另 (lìng) ❶separate; another; other ❷ in addition; besides

【另打主意】make some other plans
【另谋生路】find a new (or another) way of living
【另起炉灶】make a fresh start
【另请高明】find someone better
【另外】in addition; moreover; besides
【另行】separately
【另有企图】have other intentions

令 (lìng) ❶order; command ❷season ❸your ❹make; cause

【令人吃惊】shocking; surprising
【令人垂涎】make one's mouth watering
【令人鼓舞】inspiring
【令人满意】satisfactory
【令人钦佩】admirable
【令人信服】convincing
【令人厌烦】boring
【令人遗憾】regrettable
【令堂】your mother
【令尊】your father

liu

溜 (liū) ❶ slide; glide ❷ slip away; steal; sneak off ❸smooth; slippery

【溜冰】skate:去~go skating
【溜达】stroll; take a walk; go for a walk
【溜走】slip (or steal) away; leave stealthily

浏 (liú) glance over; skim through

【浏览】take a glance at

留 (liú) ❶stay; remain ❷ask sb. to stay ❸reserve; keep ❹let grow ❺leave

【留步】don't bother to see me out
【留存】keep; remain
【留级】fail to go up to the higher grade
【留恋】can't bear to leave; hate to tear

oneself away; be unwilling to part

【留念】accept (or keep) as a souvenir

【留情】show mercy (or forgiveness)

【留声机】phonograph

【留守】stay behind to take care of things

【留宿】stay over (or put up for) the night

【留心】be attentive; pay attention; take care; keep one's eyes open

【留学】study abroad

【留学生】student studying abroad; overseas student

【留言】leave a message; leave one's comments

【留一手】hold back a trick or two

【留意】keep one's eyes open; be careful; look out; take care

【留影】have a picture taken as a souvenir

流 (liú) ❶stream; current: 电～electric current ❷class; rate; grade: 第一～ first-class; first-rate ❸ flow; run ❹ spread widely; pass from hand to hand ❺worsen; change for the worse ❻send into exile ❼wondering; drifting; moving

【流产】❶fall through; miscarry; abort: 计划～了 the plan fell flat ❷abortion; miscarriage

【流畅】easy and smooth; fluent

【流程】technological process

【流传】spread widely; circulate; hand down

【流传后世】hand down to later generations

【流动】❶go from place to place ❷flow ❸ on the move

【流芳百世】leave a good name for a hundred generations

【流放】banish; exile; send into exile

【流感】flu

【流汗】sweat

【流浪】roam about; wander about

【流浪汉】vagrant; tramp

【流泪】shed tears

【流利】fluent; smooth

【流连忘返】enjoy oneself so much as to forget to return; linger on

【流露】reveal; show signs of; betray

【流落他乡】wander away from home in misery

【流氓】hooligan; hoodlum; rogue: 耍～behave like a hoodlum; take liberties with women

【流派】school; sect: 学术～schools of thought

【流失】❶be washed away ❷flow away; drain

【流逝】pass: 光阴～time flows away

【流水】running water

【流体】fluid

【流通】circulate

【流亡】be forced to leave one's native land; go into exile

【流行】fashionable; popular

【流行歌曲】popular song

【流行性】epidemic: ～感冒 influenza; flu ～腮腺炎 mumps

【流血】bleed; shed blood

【流言蜚语】rumours and slanders

【流域】drainage area; valley

硫 (liú) sulphur (S)

【硫酸】sulphuric acid

榴 (liú) pomegranate

【榴弹】high explosive shell

【榴莲】durian

瘤 (liú) tumor: 毒～ malignant tumor 良性～ benign tumor

柳 (liǔ) willow: 垂～weeping willow

【柳条】willow twig

【柳絮】catkin

六 (liù) six

【六畜兴旺】the domestic animals are all thriving

【六根清净】free from human desires and passions

【六亲】one's kin; the six relations ～不认 refuse to have anything to do with all one's relatives and friends

【六一国际儿童节】International Children's Day

【六月】June

long

龙 (lóng) ❶dragon ❷imperial

【龙船】dragon boat

【龙灯】dragon lantern

【龙飞凤舞】like dragons flying and phoenixes dancing; lively and vigorous flourishes in calligraphy

【龙井】Dragon Well tea

【龙卷风】tornado

【龙头】❶faucet; tap; cock: 打开～turn on the tap; 关上～turn off the tap ❷handlebar

【龙王】the Dragon King

【龙虾】lobster

【龙眼】longan

【龙舟】dragon boat

聋 (lóng) deaf; hard of hearing

【聋哑】deaf-mute; deaf and dumb

笼 (lóng) ❶cage: 鸡～chicken coop; 鸟～bird cage ❷steamer; steam box: 蒸～food steamer

另见本页 lǒng

【笼屉】food steamer

隆 (lóng) ❶swell; bulge ❷rise ❸grand ❹prosperous; thriving

【隆冬】the depth of winter; midwinter

【隆隆】rumble: 雷声～the rumble of thunder; 炮声～the rumble of gunfire

【隆重】grand; solemn; ceremonious ～开幕 open ceremoniously

垄 (lǒng) ❶ridge (in a field) ❷raised path between fields ❸a thing like a ridge

【垄断】❶monopoly ❷monopolize

笼 (lǒng) ❶envelop; cover ❷a large box or chest; trunk

另见本页 lóng

【笼络人心】try to win popular favour

【笼统】general

【笼罩】envelop; cover

lou

楼 (lóu) ❶building: 办公～office building; 教学～classroom building ❷storey; floor: 一～(英) ground floor; (美) first floor; 二～(英) first floor; (美) second floor ❸tower: 城～city gate tower; 鼓～drum-tower; 钟～bell tower

【楼层】floor; storey

【楼道】corridor; passageway

【楼房】a building of two or more stories

【楼上】upstairs

【楼梯】stairs; staircase

【楼下】downstairs

搂 (lǒu) hold in one's arms; embrace; hug

【搂抱】cuddle; embrace; hug

陋 (lòu) ❶humble; mean ❷vulgar; corrupt ❸ugly

L

【陋规】objectionable practices
【陋习】bad habits; corrupt custom

漏 (lòu) ❶leak: 走~消息 leak information ❷miss; leave out

【漏电】leakage of electricity
【漏洞】❶leak ❷flaw
【漏斗】funnel
【漏网】❶ escape unpunished ❷ slip through the net: ~之鱼 fish that has escape the net
【漏子】❶funnel ❷flaw; trouble

露 (lòu) reveal; show; expose
另见 1095 页 lù

【露丑】make a fool of oneself in public
【露风】divulge a secret; leak out information
【露面】appear in public; make public appearance; show up
【露馅儿】let the cat out of the bag; give the game (or show) away
【露一手】show off

L

lu

芦 (lú) reed

【芦苇】reed
【芦席】reed mat

炉 (lú) ❶ stove; furnace: 壁~fireplace ❷heat: 一~钢水 a heat of steel

【炉灶】kitchen (or cooking) range: 另起~ make a fresh start

颅 (lú) cranium; skull

【颅骨】skull
【颅腔】cranial cavity

鲁 (lǔ) ❶ stupid; dull ❷ rash; rough; rude

【鲁莽】rash; reckless

陆 (lù) land

【陆地】dry land; land
【陆路】land route: 走~travel by land
【陆续】one after another; in succession; one by one

录 (lù) ❶ record; collection: 回忆~ memories ❷write down; copy ❸employ ❹record

【录取】enroll; admit
【录像机】video recorder
【录音电话机】telegraphone; answering machine
【录音机】recorder
【录用】employ: 量才~give sb. work according to his abilities

鹿 (lù) deer: 公~stag; buck; 母~doe; 小~fawn

【鹿角】deerhorn; antler
【鹿死谁手】who will win the prize; who will gain supremacy

碌 (lù) ❶commonplace ❷busy

【碌碌】❶busy with miscellaneous work ❷ mediocre; commonplace

路 (lù) ❶ road; path; way: 公~highway; 迷~ lose one's way ❷ line ❸ route ❹class

【路标】road sign
【路程】distance travelled; journey: 三天~ three days' journey
【路灯】street (or road) lamp
【路费】travelling expenses
【路过】pass by
【路径】❶route; way ❷method; means: 成功的~ way to success
【路口】crossing: 三岔~fork; 十字~crossroads
【路况】road conditions
【路人】stranger
【路人皆知】know by everybody

【路上】❶on the road ❷on the way:在回家的~on the way home
【路途】❶road;path;way ❷journey
【路障】roadblock;barrier;bar
露 (lù) ❶ dew ❷ beverage ❸ distilled from flowers, fruit or leaves; syrup:果子~fruit syrup ❹show;reveal
另见 1094 页 lòu
【露出】show;reveal
【露水】dew
【露宿】sleep in the open
【露天】in the open;outdoors
【露营】camp;encamp

lü

驴 (lǘ)donkey;ass
侣 (lǚ)companion;associate
旅 (lǚ) ❶ troops; force ❷ brigade ❸travel
【旅伴】 travelling companion; fellow traveller
【旅店】inn;hotel
【旅费】travelling expenses
【旅客】hotel guest;traveller;passenger
【旅途】 journey; trip: 踏 上 ~ start one's journey
【旅行】travel;tour;journey
【旅行社】travel service (or agency)
【旅游者】tourist
铝 (lǚ) aluminium
【铝合金】aluminium alloy
屡 (lǚ) time and again;repeatedly
【屡次】time and again;repeatedly
【屡教不改】 refuse to mend one's ways despite repeated education
履 (lǚ) ❶caterpillar belt ❷shoe ❸footstep ❹tread (or walk) on:步~艰难 walk with difficulty ❺carry out;fulfill
【履历】resume
【履行】perform;carry out;fulfill
【履约】keep an appointment
律 (lǜ) ❶law; rule ❷keep under control; discipline: 严于~己 be strict with oneself
【律师】lawyer
虑 (lǜ) ❶consider; ponder; think over ❷worry:无忧无~carefree
率 (lǜ)rate;proportion;ratio
另见 1192 页 shuài
绿 (lǜ)green
【绿茶】green tea
【绿豆】green gram;mung bean
【绿化】 afforest; make a place green by planting trees
【绿卡】green card; permit of permanent residence
【绿色食品】 green food; pollution-free food
【绿洲】oasis
氯 (lǜ) chlorine
【氯化钾】potassium chloride
【氯化钠】sodium chloride
滤 (lǜ)filter;strain
【滤液】filtrate
【滤纸】filter paper

luan

孪 (luán) twin
【孪生】twin
卵 (luǎn)ovum;egg

【卵巢】ovary

【卵石】pebble

乱 (luàn) ❶disorder; unrest; turmoil ❷confuse; upset ❸confused; disturbed ❹disorderly; in disorder; in confusion ❺random

【乱码】error codes

【乱纷纷】disorderly; chaotic

【乱七八糟】at sixes and sevens; in a mess; in great disorder (or confusion)

【乱说】gossip; speak carelessly

【乱糟糟】messy; disorderly

【乱子】disturbance

lüe

掠 (lüè) ❶rob; plunder; sack ❷skim over; brush past; sweep

【掠夺】rob; plunder; sack; loot

【掠过】sweep past; skim over

略 (lüè) ❶summary; brief account; outline ❷plan; strategy ❸omit; leave out ❹seize ❺simple; brief ❻slightly

【略去】omit; leave out

【略胜一筹】a little better; slightly better

【略图】sketch map

【略微】a little

【略知一二】know a little; know sth. about

lun

伦 (lún) ❶human relations ❷logic; order ❸peer; match

【伦理】ethics; moral principles

沦 (lún) ❶sink ❷fall

【沦落】fall low; be reduced to poverty

【沦陷】❶be occupied by the enemy; fall into enemy's hands ❷submerge; inundate; flood; drown

轮 (lún) ❶wheel ❷steamboat; steamer ❸round ❹take turns ❺in turn; by turns

【轮班】in shifts; by turns

【轮船】ship; steamboat; steamship; steamer

【轮渡】ferry

【轮番】by turns

【轮廓】outline; rough sketch

【轮流】❶take turns ❷in turn; by turns; alternatively

【轮胎】tyre

【轮休】have holidays by turns

【轮椅】wheelchair

论 (lùn) ❶view; opinion: 舆~public opinion ❷theory ❸discuss; discourse; talk about ❹mention ❺consider ❻decide; determine ❼on ❽by

【论点】argument; point of view

【论及】touch on (or upon); speak (or write) about

【论据】argument

【论理】❶reason ❷as things should be

【论述】discuss

【论坛】forum

【论题】proposition

【论文】thesis; article; paper: 毕业~graduation thesis; 学术~ research paper

【论证】❶demonstrate; prove ❷proof; demonstration

【论著】work; book

【论罪】decide on the nature of the guilt

luo

啰 (luō)

【啰唆】❶talkative; long-winded; wordy ❷fussy ❸overelaborate; troublesome

罗 (luó) ❶net ❷a kind of silk gauze ❸collect; gather ❹display; list

【罗列】spread out; list; display
【罗马】Rome
【罗盘】compass
【罗网】net; trap: 布下～ spread (or lay, set) a trap; 自投～ walk straight into the trap

萝 (luó) trailing plants

【萝卜】radish; turnip

逻 (luó) patrol

【逻辑】❶logic ❷logical: 不合～ illogical

锣 (luó) gong: 敲～strike a gong

【锣鼓】gong and drum

箩 (luó) a square-bottomed bamboo basket

【箩筐】bamboo (or wicker) basket

骡 (luó) mule

【骡马店】an inn with sheds for carts and animals

螺 (luó) snail: 田～ field snail

【螺母】nut
【螺丝】screw
【螺旋】spiral
【螺旋桨】propeller

裸 (luǒ) bare; naked; exposed

【裸婚】naked marriage
【裸体】naked; nude

骆 (luò) a white horse with a black mane (mentioned in ancient texts)

【骆驼】camel

落 (luò) ❶ settlement ❷ whereabouts ❸fall; drop ❹ go down; set: 太阳～山了 the sun has set ❺lower ❻decline; sink; go down ❼lag (or fall) behind: 名～孙山 fail in an exam

【落榜】fail in an entrance examination
【落差】❶ drop in elevation; head drop ❷gap
【落成】be completed
【落地签证】landing visa; visa on arrival
【落后】❶fall (or lag) behind ❷backward
【落户】settle: 安家～ settle down
【落脚】stay; put up
【落空】come to nothing; end up in nothing: 希望～fail to attain one's hope
【落泪】shed tears; weep
【落落大方】graceful
【落难】meet with misfortune; be in a tight corner
【落日】the setting sun
【落实】❶make sure ❷put into effect
【落汤鸡】like a drenched chicken; soaked through
【落网】fall into the trap (or net); be captured; be caught
【落伍】drop behind (or out); be out of date
【落选】lose an election
【落叶归根】fallen leaves return to the roots—a person residing elsewhere finally returns to his ancestral home

M m

ma

妈 (mā) ❶ ma; mum; mummy; mother ❷ aunt: 大～aunt; 姑～aunt; 舅～aunt; 姨～aunt

M

【妈妈】ma; mum; mummy; mother

抹 (mā) ❶ wipe ❷ rub sth. down (or off)

另见 1110 页 mǒ; mò

【抹布】rag; dishcloth; duster cloth

麻 (má) ❶ hemp; flax; jute ❷ sesame ❸ anaesthesia ❹ tingle; have pins and needles ❺ numb; tingling

【麻布】sackcloth; linen

【麻烦】❶ trouble; bother: 自找～ask for trouble ❷ troublesome; inconvenient

【麻花】fried dough twists

【麻利】quick and neat; nimble; deft

【麻木】numb

【麻雀】sparrow

【麻醉】❶ anaesthesia ❷ anaesthetize ❸ poison

马 (mǎ) horse: 公～ stallion; 母～mare; 小～pony

【马鞍】saddle

【马车】carriage; cart

【马达】motor

【马大哈】❶ a careless person ❷ careless

【马到成功】gain an immediate victory; win instant success

【马后炮】belated effort (or advice)

【马脚】sth. that gives the game away

【马克思主义】Marxism

【马拉松】marathon

【马铃薯】potato

【马路】road; street; avenue

【马马虎虎】❶ careless ❷ not so bad; so-so

【马球】polo

【马上】soon; immediately; straight (or right) away; at once

【马戏团】circus troupe

吗 (mǎ)

【吗啡】morphine

码 (mǎ) ❶ size ❷ yard ❸ pile up; stack

【码头】wharf; dock; quay; pier

蚂 (mǎ)

【蚂蟥】leech

【蚂蚁】ant

骂 (mà) abuse; scold; call sb. names; curse

【骂名】bad name; infamy

mai

埋 (mái) bury; cover up

另见 1099 页 mán

【埋藏】bury; hide

【埋伏】ambush；lie (or wait) in ambush：设～lay an ambush
【埋没】❶bury；cover up ❷neglect；stifle
【埋头苦干】immerse oneself in hard work
【埋葬】bury

买 (mǎi) buy；purchase

【买单】pay the bill
【买价】buying price
【买卖】business；trade
【买一赠一】buy one，get one free
【买主】customer；buyer；purchaser

迈 (mài) ❶ step；stride ❷ old；advanced；aged

【迈步】step forward；take a step
【迈进】stride forward

麦 (mài) wheat；barley，etc.：大～barley；小～wheat；燕～oats

【麦秆】straw
【麦克风】microphone
【麦苗】wheat seedling
【麦片】oatmeal；wheat flakes
【麦穗】ear of wheat；wheat head
【麦子】wheat

卖 (mài) ❶ sell ❷ betray ❸ exert all one's strength ❹show off

【卖场】market place
【卖点】selling point
【卖掉】sell off
【卖方】the selling party (of a contract，etc.)
【卖光】sell out
【卖光】sell out
【卖老】flaunt one's seniority；put on the airs of a veteran
【卖力】spare no effort；do all one can；exert all one's strength
【卖弄】show off
【卖完】sell out
【卖主】seller
【卖座】draw large audiences

脉 (mài) ❶pulse：号～feel one's pulse ❷arteries and veins ❸vein

【脉搏】pulse
【脉络】❶ veins ❷ train of thought；sequence of ideas

man

埋 (mán)
另见 1098 页 mái

【埋怨】blame；complain；grumble

蛮 (mán) rough；wild；savage

【蛮不讲理】persist in being wild and unreasonable
【蛮横】wild and unreasonable

馒 (mán)

【馒头】steamed bun；steamed bread

瞒 (mán) hide the truth from

【瞒哄】deceive；cheat

满 (mǎn) ❶fill ❷full；filled ❸content；satisfied ❹ conceited ❺ completely；entirely

【满不在乎】not worry at all；not care in the least
【满额】fulfill the (enrolment，etc.) quota
【满腹牢骚】be full of complaints
【满贯】❶reach the limit ❷(in mahjong，card games，etc.)perfect score；slam
【满怀】be full of；have one's heart filled with；be imbued with
【满怀信心】be full of confidence
【满口答应】readily promise (or agree)
【满面笑容】smile from ear to ear；be all smiles
【满目】see nothing but；get an exclusive

view of
【满腔】be filled with
【满腔热情】full of enthusiasm
【满天】all over the sky
【满心欢喜】filled with joy
【满意】satisfied; pleased; contented
【满载而归】return with fruitful results
【满足】❶ satisfied; contented ❷ satisfy; meet

曼 (màn) ❶graceful ❷prolonged; long-drawn-out
【曼妙】(of dancing) lithe and graceful
【曼陀罗】datura: ~卡 Datura card

谩 (màn) disrespectful; rude
【谩骂】abuse at

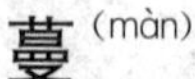

蔓 (màn)
【蔓延】stretch; spread

幔 (màn) curtain; screen
【幔帷】heavy curtain

漫 (màn) ❶overflow; brim over; flood ❷free; unrestrained; casual ❸everywhere
【漫不经心】careless; casual
【漫步】stroll
【漫长】very long; endless
【漫画】cartoon; caricature
【漫骂】use bad language against sb.; fling abuse
【漫山遍野】all over the wilderness; all over the mountains and plains
【漫谈】have an informal discussion
【漫无边际】❶boundless; limitless ❷rambling
【漫无目的】aimless
【漫游】wander; roam

慢 (màn) slow down
【慢车道】slow traffic lane
【慢慢】slowly; gradually
【慢跑】jog
【慢条斯理】leisurely; unhurriedly
【慢性】chronic

mang

芒 (máng) awn; beard; arista
【芒果】mango

忙 (máng) ❶hurry; make haste ❷busy
【忙活】be busy with sth.
【忙乱】be in a messy rush; tackle a job in a hasty and disorderly manner

盲 (máng) ❶blind; sightless: 色~color blindness; 夜~night blindness ❷illiterate
【盲从】follow blindly
【盲点】blind spot; blackspot; scotoma
【盲干】act aimlessly or rashly
【盲目】blind
【盲人】blind person
【盲文】braille

茫 (máng) ❶ boundless and indistinct ❷ignorant; in the dark
【茫茫】boundless and indistinct
【茫然】at a loss: 感到~be at a loss

莽 (mǎng) ❶rank grass ❷rash
【莽汉】a boorish fellow; boor
【莽撞】crude and impetuous; rash

mao

猫 (māo) cat
【猫眼】❶ cat's eye; cat eye ❷ peephole (fixed in a door)
【猫头鹰】owl

毛 (máo) ❶hair; down; feather ❷wool ❸mildew ❹semifinished ❺gross ❻little; small ❼careless

【毛笔】writing brush

【毛病】❶trouble ❷shortcoming; fault ❸illness; disease

【毛虫】caterpillar

【毛发】hair

【毛巾】towel

【毛毛雨】drizzle

【毛遂自荐】offer one's services like Mao Sui (of the Warring States Period) did—volunteer one's services

【毛毯】woolen blanket

【毛线】knitting wool

【毛衣】woollen sweater

【毛躁】❶short-tempered ❷rash and careless

矛 (máo) spear

【矛盾】❶contradict ❷contradiction ❸contradictory: 自相~self-contradictory

【矛头】spearhead

茅 (máo) cogongrass

【茅厕】latrine

【茅塞顿开】be suddenly enlightened

【茅屋】thatched cottage

锚 (máo) anchor: 抛~drop (or cast) anchor; 起~weigh anchor

茂 (mào) ❶luxuriant ❷rich and splendid

【茂密】dense; thick

【茂盛】luxuriant

冒 (mào) ❶emit; give off; send out ❷risk; brave ❸rashly ❹falsely

【冒充】pretend to be; pass oneself off as

【冒犯】offend; give offence to

【冒汗】perspire; sweat

【冒号】colon

【冒火】be enraged; flare up; fly into a rage

【冒进】advance rashly

【冒名】go under sb. else's name

【冒牌】counterfeit; imitation; fake

【冒失】rash: 说话 ~speak rashly

【冒险】take (or run) a risk; take chances

【冒险家】adventurer

【冒烟】smoke

贸 (mào) trade; commerce: 外 ~ foreign trade

【贸然】rashly; hastily

【贸易】trade: 对外~foreign trade; 国际~ international trade; 国内 ~ domestic trade

帽 (mào) hat; cap: 草~straw hat; 螺丝 ~screw cap

【帽子】❶hat; cap ❷label; brand: 扣~put a label on sb.

貌 (mào) looks; appearance: 美~good looks; 新 ~ new look; 人不可 ~ 相 never judge people by their appearance

【貌不惊人】look mediocre

【貌似】seem (or appear) to be; look like

mei

没 (méi) ❶no ❷not ❸without

另见 1110 页 mò

【没把握】be not sure (or certain)

【没办法】❶can do nothing about; cannot help it ❷helpless

【没出路】❶have no way out ❷hopeless

【没出息】good for nothing; not promising

【没错儿】❶cannot go wrong ❷I am sure

【没赶上】miss

【没关系】it doesn't matter; that's all right; never mind

【没规矩】have bad manners; be improper

【没精打采】in low spirits; spiritless

【没脸】feel ashamed; feel embarrassed

【没良心】❶ ungrateful ❷ without conscience

【没门儿】have no way out

【没趣】❶feel put out; feel snubbed: 自讨～ask for a snub ❷dull; boring

【没什么】it doesn't matter; that's all right; never mind; not at all

【没完没了】❶endless ❷endlessly

【没有结果】come to nothing

【没主意】cannot make up one's mind; have no idea; be at a loss

玫 (méi) rose

【玫瑰】rose

M

眉 (méi) eyebrow; brow

【眉开眼笑】beam with joy; be all smiles

【眉目】❶features; looks ❷logic ❸shape

【眉批】notes made at the top of a page

【眉梢】brow tip: 喜上～look very happy

【眉头】brows: 皱～frown; knit the brows

梅 (méi) plum

【梅花】plum blossom

【梅花鹿】sika deer

媒 (méi) ❶ match maker; go-between ❷intermediary

【媒介】medium

【媒人】matchmaker; go-between

【媒体】media

煤 (méi) coal

【煤矿】coal mine

【煤气】gas

【煤炭】coal

【煤油】kerosene

酶 (méi) ferment; enzyme

霉 (méi) ❶ mold; mildew ❷ become mildewy; go moldy: 这块饼～了。The cake is moldy.

【霉菌】mold

【霉烂】mildewed and rotten

每 (měi) ❶ every; each ❷ often ❸ on each occasion ❹per

【每当】every time; each time; whenever

【每个人】everybody; everyone

【每人】each one; every one

【每时每刻】all the time; at all times

【每天】❶everyday ❷every day

【每月】monthly; every month

【每周】every week; weekly

美 (měi) ❶ be pleased with oneself ❷ beautify ❸ beautiful; pretty ❹ good; fine

【美餐】❶tasty food; table delicacies ❷eat and drink one's fill

【美德】virtue; goodness

【美发】hair care

【美发师】hair dresser; hair stylist

【美工】❶art designing ❷art designer

【美观】beautiful; artistic; pleasing to the eye

【美好】fine; nice; lovely

【美化】beautify; prettify

【美籍华人】Chinese American; American citizen of Chinese origin

【美甲】manicure

【美景】beautiful scenery

【美丽】beautiful; pretty

【美满】perfect; satisfactory

【美梦】fond dream

【美妙】splendid; wonderful

【美人】beauty

【美容院】beauty salon

【美术】❶fine arts ❷painting

【美味】❶delicious food ❷delicious; tasty

【美学】aesthetics
【美言】put in a good word for sb.
【美育】art (or aesthetic) education
【美元】American (or US) dollar

妹 (mèi) younger sister; sister

【妹夫】brother-in-law
【妹妹】younger sister; sister

媚 (mèi) ❶fawn on; favor with; toady to ❷charming; fascinating; enchanting

【媚态】coquetry; subservience

昧 (mèi) ❶be ignorant ❷hide: 拾金不～not pocket the money one happens to pick up

【昧心】against one's conscience

魅 (mèi) evil spirit

【魅力】charm; enchantment; fascination

men

闷 (mēn) ❶shut indoors ❷stifling ❸stuffy; close ❹cover tightly ❺(of a sound) muffled

另见本页 mèn

【闷气】stifling; close; stuffy
【闷热】stiflingly hot; muggy

门 (mén) ❶door; gate: 前～front door; 后～back door ❷valve ❸way ❹family ❺sect; school ❻field; branch

【门道】❶gateway ❷way to do sth.; social connections
【门岗】gate sentry
【门户】❶door; gate ❷gateway ❸faction; sect
【门槛】threshold
【门口】doorway
【门类】class; kind
【门帘】door curtain
【门铃】doorbell
【门面】❶shop front ❷appearance: 装点～keep up appearance
【门牌】house number
【门票】entrance ticket
【门庭若市】the house is as crowded with visitors as a marketplace
【门外汉】layman
【门卫】gate guard
【门诊】outpatient service

闷 (mèn) ❶bored ❷tightly closed; stifling

另见本页 mēn

【闷闷不乐】in low spirits
【闷气】❶stuffy ❷the sulks: 生～be in a fit of sulks

meng

蒙 (mēng) ❶cheat; deceive ❷make a wild guess ❸unconscious; senseless

另见本页 méng; 1104 页 Měng

【蒙蒙亮】first glimmer of dawn; daybreak
【蒙骗】cheat; deceive

萌 (méng) sprout; shoot forth; bud

【萌发】bud; shoot forth; sprout
【萌芽】❶sprout; germinate; shoot; bud ❷rudiments; seed; germ

蒙 (méng) ❶cover ❷receive; suffer ❸ignorant

另见本页 mēng; 1104 页 Měng

【蒙蔽】hide the truth from; deceive
【蒙昧】❶uncivilized; uncultured ❷ignorant; benighted
【蒙难】be killed; be murdered
【蒙冤】be wronged; suffer an injustice

盟 (méng) ❶alliance: 结～form an alliance ❷league

【盟友】ally

【盟约】a treaty of alliance

朦 (méng)

【朦胧】❶ dim moonlight ❷ obscure; dim; hazy

猛 (měng) ❶fierce; violent; vigorous ❷ suddenly; quickly

【猛冲】dash; dive: 向……~dash at; make a dive for

【猛攻】❶fierce attack ❷make a fierce attack on

【猛烈】vigorous; violent; fierce

【猛然】suddenly

【猛兽】beast of prey

【猛醒】❶ suddenly wake up ❷ suddenly realize

M

【猛涨】increase drastically; soar

蒙 (Měng) Mongolian
另见 1103 页 mēng; méng

【蒙古人】Mongolian

【蒙古语】Mongol

【蒙古族】the Mongolian nationality; the Mongolians

梦 (mèng) dream: 做~dream

【梦幻】dream; illusion

【梦见】dream about (or of)

【梦境】dreamland

【梦寐以求】long for sth. day and night

【梦想】dream of

【梦语】sleeptalking

mi

弥 (mí) fill; cover

【弥补】make up; remedy

【弥合】bridge; close

【弥留】be dying

【弥漫】❶be filled up with ❷fill the air; spread all over the place

【弥天大罪】serious crime

迷 (mí) ❶ fan; enthusiast: 足球~a football fan ❷be lost ❸be crazy about; be absorbed in ❹ confuse; perplex; fascinate

【迷彩】camouflage colors

【迷宫】maze

【迷航】lose one's course; get lost

【迷糊】❶ misted; blurred; dimmed ❷ dazed; confused

【迷惑】puzzle; confuse

【迷恋】cling to; feel attached to; fall in love with

【迷路】lose one's way; get lost

【迷人】charming

【迷失】lose

【迷途】❶wrong way: 误入~go astray ❷ lose one's way

【迷雾】dense fog

【迷信】❶ superstition; blind faith ❷ have blind faith in

谜 (mí) ❶ riddle: 猜~guess a riddle ❷puzzle

【谜底】answer to a riddle

【谜团】doubts and suspicions; mystery

【谜语】riddle

米 (mǐ) ❶rice ❷seed ❸metre

【米饭】rice

【米粉】rice noodles

【米酒】rice wine

【米色】cream-colored

【米粥】congee; rice gruel; porridge

觅 (mì) look for; hunt for; seek

【觅取】look for; hunt for; seek

秘 (mì) secret

【秘方】secret recipe：祖传～a secret family recipe

【秘密】secret：保守～keep sth. secret；泄露～ disclose a secret

【秘书】secretary：私人～private secretary

密 (mì) ❶secret：绝～top-secret ❷intimate ❸dense；thick ❹careful

【密闭】airtight

【密布】densely covered：阴云～ dark clouds cover the sky

【密度】density；thickness

【密封】seal up

【密码】cipher；secret code

【密密麻麻】close and numerous

【密切】❶close ❷closely；carefully

【密如蛛网】as fine as a spider's web

【密谈】❶ secret talk ❷ talk behind closed doors

【密友】close (or bosom) friend

蜜 (mì) ❶honey ❷sweet；honeyed

【蜜蜂】honeybee；bee

【蜜饯】candied fruit

【蜜月】honeymoon

mian

眠 (mián) ❶sleep ❷dormancy

绵 (mián) ❶soft ❷continuous

【绵延】stretch long and unbroken；be continuous

【绵羊】sheep

棉 (mián) cotton：皮～ginned cotton；原～raw cotton

【棉袄】cotton-padded jacket

【棉被】wadded-quilt

【棉布】cotton cloth

【棉大衣】cotton-padded overcoat

【棉毛衫】cotton jersey

【棉桃】cotton boll

【棉絮】cotton wadding

免 (miǎn) ❶excuse (or exempt) sb. from sth. ❷avoid ❸remove；dismiss ❹forbidden；not allowed

【免不了】be unavoidable；be bound to

【免除】❶avoid ❷remove sb. from office ❸remit；excuse；exempt；relieve：～债务 remit a debt

【免得】❶so as not to ❷so as to avoid

【免费】free of charge；cost-free

【免票】free ticket

【免试】be excused from an examination

【免提电话】hand-free phone

【免疫】be immune to

【免职】remove sb. from office

勉 (miǎn) ❶make efforts；exert oneself ❷encourage；urge ❸try to manage (or handle)

【勉励】encourage；urge

【勉强】❶try to manage ❷force sb. to do sth. ❸unwillingly；reluctantly ❹forced

缅 (miǎn) remote；far back

【缅怀】recall；cherish the memory of

腼 (miǎn)

【腼腆】shy；bashful

面 (miàn) ❶face ❷surface ❸cover ❹side：左～left side ❺range：知识～range of knowledge ❻powder ❼flour ❽noodles ❾personally；directly

【面包】bread

【面不改色】remain calm

【面带笑容】wear a smile

【面对】face；confront

【面对面】face to face

【面额】face value；denomination

【面粉】wheat flour;flour
【面积】area:建筑~built-up area 居住~floor space
【面颊】cheek
【面具】mask:防毒~gas mask
【面临】be faced with
【面貌】appearance;look
【面膜】beauty mask
【面目全非】be changed beyond recognition
【面目一新】take on a new look
【面前】in front of;before
【面试】interview
【面授】❶instruct somebody in person ❷classroom teaching
【面熟】look familiar
【面条】noodles
【面子】❶face;self-respect:爱~care much about self-respect;不讲~show no consideration for sb.'s self-respect;丢~lose face;给~show respect to sb.'s feelings;顾~save face ❷show consideration for sb.'s feelings

miao

苗 (miáo) sprout; seedling; young plant
【苗圃】nursery (of young plants); seed plot
【苗条】slender;slim
【苗子】❶young plant; seedling ❷young successor ❸symptom of a trend; suggestion of a new development

描 (miáo) ❶touch up;retouch ❷trace; copy
【描红】trace in black ink over characters printed in red (in learning to write with a brush)
【描绘】draw;paint;describe
【描述】describe:详细~describe in detail
【描图】trace
【描写】describe

瞄 (miáo) aim;concentrate one's gaze on
【瞄准】take aim;aim at

秒 (miǎo) second
【秒表】stopwatch
【秒针】second hand

渺 (miǎo) ❶far and hazy ❷tiny
【渺茫】❶distant and indistinct; far and hazy;vague ❷uncertain:音信~haven't heard from sb. for ages
【渺小】tiny

藐 (miǎo) ❶slight; despise ❷tiny; small
【藐视】belittle;look down upon
【藐小】tiny; negligible; insignificant; paltry

妙 (miào) wonderful;fine
【妙不可言】too wonderful for words
【妙计】excellent scheme
【妙龄】young;youthful;tender age
【妙趣横生】full of wit and humour
【妙语】witty remark

庙 (miào) temple
【庙会】temple fair;fair

mie

灭 (miè) ❶go out;put out:火~了 the fire went out ❷destroy;wipe out
【灭火】❶put out a fire ❷cut out an engine
【灭绝】wipe out;become extinct
【灭亡】perish; die out; be destroyed; be-

come extinct

蔑（miè）❶ slight；belittle ❷ slander；smear

【蔑视】look down upon；despise；scorn

min

民（mín）❶ people ❷ person；man；woman：牧～herdsman；渔～fisherman ❸folk ❹civilian

【民办】run by people；run by community；privately-run

【民办大学】private university

【民法】civil law

【民愤】public（or popular）indignation（or rage）

【民风】folkways

【民歌】folk song

【民航】civil aviation

【民间】❶ among the people；❷ popular；folk ❸nongovernmental

【民间传说】folk legend

【民间艺术】folk art

【民警】people's police

【民情】❶ public feeling ❷ condition of the people

【民权】civil rights

【民事案件】civil case

【民俗】folk custom；folkways

【民心】popular feelings：深得～enjoy the wide support of the people

【民谣】ballad

【民意】will（or opinion）of the people

【民营企业】private enterprise

【民用】for civil use

【民乐】❶folk music ❷traditional musical instruments

【民众】the common people；the masses；the public

【民主】❶democracy ❷democratic

【民主党派】democratic parties

【民主协商】democratic consultation

【民族】nation；nationality：中华～the Chinese nation；少数～Chinese national minority；national minority of China

泯（mǐn）vanish；die out

【泯灭】die out；vanish

悯（mǐn）❶commiserate；pity ❷sorrow

【悯惜】take pity on；have pity on

敏（mǐn）quick；nimble

【敏感】sensitive：政治～political sensitivity

【敏捷】quick；nimble

【敏锐】sharp；acute；keen：目光～have sharp eyes（or sight）；be sharp-eyed；听觉～have good（or fine）ears；嗅觉～have a keen sense of smell

ming

名（míng）❶name；title ❷fame；reputation：不为～，不为利 seek neither fame nor wealth ❸give name；name ❹famous；well-known

【名不虚传】enjoy a well-deserved reputation；live up to one's reputation

【名城】a famous city

【名垂青史】leave a name in history

【名存实亡】exist only in name

【名单】list；roll

【名额】the number of people assigned

【名副其实】be worthy of the name；the name matches the reality

【名贵】famous and rare

【名列前茅】be among the best；come out at the top；come out in the front

【名落孙山】fail in an exam

【名目】❶ names of things; items ❷ excuse: 巧立～invent all kinds of names (or stories)

【名气】reputation; fame; good name: 有～be well-known; be of great (or high) repute

【名人】famous person; celebrity

【名人效应】celebrity effect

【名声】reputation; repute

【名胜古迹】scenic spots and historical sites

【名望】fame and prestige

【名言】famous quotation; well-known saying

【名扬四海】be well-known (or famous) all over the world

【名义】❶ name: 假借……的～under the pretence of; make use of the name of; 盗用……的～unlawfully use the name of ❷in name

【名誉】❶fame; reputation ❷honorary

【名正言顺】❶ with good reasons ❷ perfectly justifiable

【名著】masterpiece; famous book (or work); classic

明 (míng) ❶ sight ❷ understand; know ❸ bright ❹ clear ❺ open ❻ clear-sighted ❼aboveboard; honest ❽next

【明白】❶clear; plain ❷see; know; realize; understand ❸frankly; explicitly ❹sensible; reasonable

【明辨是非】make a dear distinction between right and wrong

【明澈】bright and limpid; transparent

【明处】in the open; in public

【明灯】bright lamp; beacon

【明断】pass (fair) judgement

【明镜】bright mirror

【明朗】❶ bright and clear ❷ obvious ❸ forthright and cheerful; bright and gay

【明亮】❶bright; shining ❷clear

【明了】❶ be clear about; understand ❷ clear; plain: 简单～simple and clear

【明媚】bright and beautiful

【明目张胆】openly and abruptly

【明年】next year

【明确】clear and definite; clear-cut

【明天】tomorrow

【明显】clear; obvious

【明信片】postcard

【明星】star: 电影～movie (or film) star

【明喻】simile

【明知故犯】do sth. which one knows is wrong; do wrong knowingly

【明智】sensible; wise

鸣 (míng) ❶cry of birds, animals or insects: 鸟～chirping; 鸡～crowing of a cock ❷ring; sound ❸express; voice; air

【鸣不平】complain of unfairness; cry out against injustice

【鸣笛】whistle: 禁止～! No tooting!

【鸣礼炮】fire a salute

【鸣枪】fire a shot

【鸣谢】express one's thanks formally; express gratitude

冥 (míng) ❶dark; obscure ❷deep; profound ❸ dull; stupid ❹ underworld; the nether world

【冥思苦想】rack one's brains; think long and hard; meditate

【冥想】deep thought; meditation

铭 (míng) ❶inscription ❷engrave

【铭记】engrave on one's mind; engrave on memory

【铭刻】❶ inscription ❷ engrave on one's mind; always remember

【铭心】be engraved on one's heart—be

remembered with gratitude：刻骨～deeply engraved in one's heart

瞑（míng）

【瞑目】close one's eyes in death；die content

命（mìng）❶life：逃～run for one's life；救～！Help！❷lot；fate；destiny ❸command ❹order ❺assign

【命案】homicide case

【命定】be determined by fate；be predestined

【命根子】lifeblood

【命令】order；command；decree：服从～obey orders

【命名】name

【命运】destiny；fate；lot

【命中注定】be predestined

【命中】hit the target

miu

谬（miù）wrong；false；mistaken

【谬论】fallacy

【谬误】falsehood；error；mistake

mo

摸（mō）❶touch；feel ❷feel（or grope）for ❸get to know；try to find out

【摸索】❶grope；fumble；feel about：在黑暗中～而行 feel one's way in the dark ❷try to find out

【摸透】get to know sb. or sth. very well

摹（mó）copy；trace

【摹本】facsimile

【摹刻】❶carve a reproduction of an inscription or painting ❷a carved reproduction of an inscription or painting

模（mó）❶model；pattern：楷～model；劳～ model worker ❷imitate；copy

另见 1111 页 mú

【模本】calligraphy or painting

【模范】model；fine example：劳动～model worker

【模仿】imitate；copy；model oneself on

【模糊】❶dim；vague ❷blur；confuse；mix up

【模拟】imitate；simulate

【模特儿】model

【模型】❶model ❷mould

膜（mó）❶membrance ❷thin-coating；film

【膜拜】prostrate oneself；worship

摩（mó）❶rub；scrape；touch ❷think over；consider：揣～try to fathom

【摩擦】❶rub ❷friction ❸clash：与某人发生～have a brush with sb.

【摩拳擦掌】itch to have a go；be eager for fighting

【摩天】skyscraping

【摩托车】motorcycle；motorbike

磨（mó）❶rub ❷grind ❸sharpen ❹wear down（or out）❺trouble；worry ❻dawdle

另见 1111 页 mò

【磨蹭】move slowly；dawdle；dawdle away

【磨杵成针】grind a rod into a needle

【磨刀】sharpen a knife

【磨合】❶grind in；wear in ❷adapt to each other

【磨合期】run-in time

【磨炼】temper（or steel）oneself

【磨难】hardship；suffering

【磨损】wear out；wear and tear

蘑（mó）mushroom

【蘑菇】mushroom

魔 (mó) devil;demon;evil spirit magic

【魔法】witchcraft;sorcery

【魔鬼】devil

【魔力】charm;magic power

【魔术】magic;sorcery

抹 (mǒ) ❶dab; paint; daub ❷wipe off ❸strike (or rub) out;cancel ❹apply

另见 1098 页 mā;本页 mò

【抹杀】write off;blot out

【抹眼泪】wipe one's eyes

末 (mò) ❶tip; end ❷powder; dust ❸trifle:本~倒置 put the cart before the horse ❹last

【末班车】last bus

【末路】dead end;blind alley:穷途~come to the dead end

【末期】last stage;final period:20 年代~in the late twenties

【末梢】tip;end

没 (mò) ❶sink ❷disappear ❸seize by authority; confiscate; take possession of ❹till the end

另见 1101 页 méi

【没齿难忘】will never forget to the end of one's life

【没奈何】be helpless

【没收】confiscate; expropriate; seize by authority

抹 (mò) ❶daub;plaster ❷skirt;bypass

另见 1098 页 mā;本页 mǒ

【抹灰】plastering: ~工 plasterer

茉 (mò)

【茉莉花】jasmine

沫 (mò) foam 肥皂~ soapsuds;lather

【沫子】foam;froth

陌 (mò) path; road; a path between fields

【陌路】stranger

【陌生】strange;unfamiliar

莫 (mò) ❶no;not ❷don't

【莫非】can it be that;is it possible that

【莫过于】nothing is more...than...

【莫名其妙】without rhyme (or reason)

【莫须有】groundless

蓦 (mò)suddenly

【蓦地】unexpectedly;all of a sudden

漠 (mò) ❶desert ❷indifferent:冷~ cold and indifferent

【漠不关心】cold;indifferent

【漠视】ignore;overlook

墨 (mò) ❶China ink;ink stick:研~rub an ink stick on an inkstone ❷handwriting;painting ❸black;dark

【墨迹】❶ink marks ❷painting;handwriting

【墨家】Mohist School

【墨镜】sunglasses

【墨守成规】stick to convention; stay in a rut

【墨水】❶Chinese ink ❷ink ❸book learning

【墨鱼】cuttle fish

默 (mò) silent

【默哀】stand in silent tribute

【默不作声】keep silent

【默读】read silently;silent reading:~课文 read a text silently

【默默】quietly;silently

【默默无闻】unknown to the public

【默契】tacit understanding (or agreement):达成~reach a tacit agreement

【默认】tacitly accept;tacitly approve;give tacit consent to

【默写】write from memory;dictation
【默许】give tacit consent to
磨 (mò) ❶mill; millstones: 推～turn a millstone ❷grind ❸turn round
另见 1109 页 mó
【磨坊】mill
【磨子】mill;millstones

mou

牟 (móu) try to gain;seek;obtain
【牟利】seek profit
【牟取】obtain;hunt for
谋 (móu) ❶plan; scheme; trick ❷work for; seek; plot
【谋反】conspire against the state; plot a rebellion
【谋福利】work for the well-being of
【谋利】seek profit
【谋略】strategy;tactics
【谋求】seek;strive for
【谋杀】murder
【谋生】make a living
某 (mǒu) certain;some: 在～种意义上 in a sense
【某地】some place
【某某】so-and-so
【某人】a certain person

mu

模 (mú) mould;pattern
另见 1109 页 mó
【模板】formwork;pattern plate;template
【模具】mould;pattern
【模样】appearance; look: 讨人喜欢的～a pleasant look
母 (mǔ) ❶mother ❷female
【母爱】mother (or maternal) love
【母鸡】hen
【母老虎】❶tigress ❷vixen shrew
【母牛】cow
【母亲】mother
【母亲节】Mother's Day
【母校】one's old school;Alma Mater
【母语】mother tongue
牡 (mǔ) male (of some birds and animals)
【牡丹】tree peony;peony
拇 (mǔ)
【拇指】thumb
木 (mù) ❶tree: 果～fruit tree; 伐～fell trees ❷timber; wood; log ❸wooden ❹numb
【木板】plank;board
【木柴】firewood
【木耳】an edible fungus
【木匠】carpenter
【木刻】woodcut;wood engraving
【木兰】lily magnolia
【木料】timber
【木偶】❶ puppet; marionette ❷ wooden image;carved figure
【木炭】charcoal
【木星】Jupiter
【木已成舟】the wood is already made into a boat;what is done is done
目 (mù) ❶ eye: 历历在～distinct in one's mind ❷item ❸list; catalogue: 书～book list ❹look;regard
【目标】target; aim; goal; objective: 命中～ hit the target
【目不暇接】the eye cannot take it all in
【目不转睛】look fixedly;gaze;stare
【目的】purpose; objective; goal; aim; end: 达到～achieve one's aim; achieve one's goal;最终～ultimate aim (or goal)

【目光】❶sight; vision; view ❷gaze; look
【目击者】eyewitness; witness
【目录】catalogue; list
【目前】at present; at the moment; right now: 到～为止 so far; up to now
【目送】follow with one's eyes; watch sb. go; gaze after
【目眩】dizzy; dazzled
【目中无人】look down on everyone

沐 (mù) wash one's hair

【沐浴】❶have a bath; bathe ❷immerse

牧 (mù) herd; tend

【牧草】herbage; forage grass
【牧场】grazing land; pasture
【牧笛】reed pipe
【牧民】herdsman
【牧童】shepherd; buffalo boy
【牧羊犬】shepherd dog

募 (mù) ❶collect; raise ❷enlist; recruit

【募集】raise; collect
【募捐】collect donations

墓 (mù) grave; tomb: 烈士～tombs of revolutionary martyrs

【墓碑】tombstone; gravestone
【墓地】graveyard; cemetery
【墓志铭】epitaph

幕 (mù) ❶curtain; screen: 启(落)～the curtain rises (or falls) ❷act: 第三～ the third act; Act Ⅲ

【幕后】backstage: 退居～retire backstage

慕 (mù) admire; adore: 爱～adore; 仰～ adore; look up to with admiration

【慕名而来】come to sb. because of his reputation

暮 (mù) ❶sunset; evening; dusk ❷towards the end; late

【暮年】old age; late life
【暮色】dusk; twilight; gloaming

穆 (mù) solemn; reverent

【穆斯林】Moslem; Muslim

N n

na

拿 (ná) ❶ hold; take; bring; get ❷ seize; capture ❸ hold command of ❹with

【拿出】❶take out; show ❷afford

【拿架子】put on airs

【拿开】take away

【拿手好戏】a game one is good at one's speciality

【拿稳】hold steadily; keep hold of

【拿主意】decide; make up one's mind

哪 (nǎ) ❶which; what ❷any

【哪个】❶which ❷who

【哪里】wherever; where

【哪能】how can

【哪年】what year

【哪怕】even if (or though); even; no matter how

【哪些】which; who; what

【哪知】who would have thought

那 (nà) that

【那边】over there; there

【那里】there; that place

【那么】❶like that; in that way ❷about; or so: 再有~两三天就够了 another two or three days will probably be enough ❸then; in that case

【那时】at that time; then; in those days: 从~以来 since then

【那些】those

【那样】like that; so; that way

呐 (nà)

【呐喊】shout loudly; cry out

纳 (nà) ❶receive; admit ❷accept; take in; adopt ❸enjoy ❹pay ❺bring into

【纳闷儿】feel puzzled; wonder

【纳米】nanometer

【纳入】bring (or fit) into

【纳入正轨】get into the right course; set something on the right track

【纳税】pay taxes

钠 (nà) sodium

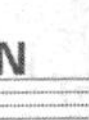

nai

奶 (nǎi) ❶ breasts ❷ milk ❸ suckle; breast-feed

【奶粉】milk powder; powdered milk

【奶酪】cheese

【奶奶】grandmother; grandma; granny

【奶牛】milk cow; cow

【奶瓶】feeding (or nursing) bottle; milk bottle

【奶糖】toffee

【奶油】cream; butter

【奶制品】dairy product

奈 (nài) ❶what; how; but ❷bear; endure

【奈何】❶(used in a rhetorical question) what alternative is there; what's to be done ❷how; why ❸do sth. to (a person); cope with; deal with

耐 (nài) be able to bear (or endure); stand

【耐穿】durable; stand wear and tear

【耐烦】patient: 不～ impatient

【耐寒】cold-resistant

【耐火】fire-resistant

【耐久】durable; lasting long

【耐力】endurance; stamina

【耐磨】wearproof; wear-resisting

【耐热】heat-resisting; heatproof

【耐人寻味】thought-provoking

【耐心】patient

【耐用】durable

nan

男 (nán) ❶man; male ❷son; boy

【男厕所】men's lavatory

【男方】the bridegroom's or husband's side

【男孩】boy

【男女】men and women

【男女平等】equality of men and women

【男朋友】boyfriend

【男人】❶man ❷menfolk ❸husband

【男生】boy student; schoolboy

【男声】male voice

【男性】male

【男演员】actor

【男主角】leading actor; leading man; hero

南 (nán) south: 华～ South China

【南北】❶north and south ❷from north to south

【南边】south; the southern side

【南部】south; southern part

【南瓜】pumpkin

【南国】the southern part of the country; the South

【南海】the Nanhai Sea; the South China Sea

【南极】the South Pole; the Antarctic Pole

【南极洲】Antarctica; the Antarctic Continent

【南美洲】South America

【南腔北调】speak with a mixed accent

【南辕北辙】act contrary to one's purpose; move in the opposite direction

难 (nán) ❶put sb. into a difficult position ❷difficult; hard ❸unpleasant ❹hardly

另见 1115 页 nàn

【难办】hard to do

【难保】❶there is no guarantee; one cannot say for sure; it's hard to say ❷difficult to preserve, protect, defend, etc.

【难辨是非】difficult to tell right from wrong

【难处】(nán chǔ) disagreeable; hard to get along with

【难处】(nán chù) difficulties, troubles; disaster, predicament

【难得】❶rare ❷hard to come by ❸seldom; rarely

【难点】a difficult point; difficulty

【难懂】hard (or difficult) to understand

【难度】degree of difficulty

【难关】difficulty; crisis

【难过】❶have a hard time; live a hard life ❷feel sorry (or bad)

【难堪】❶embarrassed ❷unbearable

【难看】❶ugly ❷shameful
【难免】hard to avoid; unavoidable
【难受】❶ feel unwell (or uncomfortable, ill) ❷feel unhappy (or sorry, bad)
【难说】it's hard to say
【难题】a difficult problem (or question): 出～set difficult questions
【难忘】unforgettable; memorable
【难为情】shy; embarrassed
【难闻】smell bad
【难以】difficult to
【难以想象】unimaginable
【难以捉摸】unfathomable; mysterious
【难于启齿】❶have a bone in the throat ❷ difficult to speak out

难 (nàn) ❶catastrophe; disaster: 逃～ flee from disaster ❷blame
另见 1114 页 nán

【难民】refugee
【难兄难弟】fellow sufferers

nang

囊 (náng) ❶bag; pocket ❷bladder

【囊括】include all; embrace
【囊中羞涩】be short of money

nao

挠 (náo) scratch

【挠头】❶ scratch one's head ❷ difficult to tackle

恼 (nǎo) ❶irritate; annoy ❷vexed; angry

【恼火】annoyed; irritated; angry
【恼怒】be in a rage; be angry
【恼羞成怒】be shamed into a rage; fly into a rage from shame

脑 (nǎo) ❶brain; head ❷mind

【脑袋】❶head ❷brains; mind
【脑海】brain; mind
【脑筋】❶ brains; mind: 动～ use one's brains (or head); beat one's brains ❷idea; belief: 旧～outdated idea
【脑力】mental power; intelligence
【脑力劳动】mental work
【脑震荡】cerebral concussion
【脑汁】brains: 绞尽～ beat (or rack) one's brains
【脑子】❶brain ❷brains; mind; head: 没～ have no brains ～灵活 quick-witted

闹 (nào) ❶make a noise ❷stir up (or make) trouble: 大～一场 raise an uproar; make a great trouble ❸go after; seek; hunt for ❹ give vent to; vent ❺ suffer from; be troubled by ❻go in for ❼noisy

【闹别扭】❶be at odds with sb. ❷be hard on sb.
【闹肚子】have loose bowels
【闹鬼】❶be haunted ❷play tricks behind sb.'s back; use underhand means
【闹哄哄】noisy
【闹饥荒】suffer from famine
【闹脾气】lose one's temper
【闹情绪】fall into a mood; become moody
【闹市】downtown; shopping centre; busy streets
【闹事】make trouble
【闹笑话】make a fool of oneself
【闹意见】be at odds with sb.
【闹钟】alarm clock

nei

内 (nèi) ❶inner; inside ❷within: 三天之～within three days

【内部】inside
【内存】internal memory; RAM

【内地】inland
【内涵】intention;connotation
【内行】expert:冒充~pose as an expert
【内河】inland river (or waterway)
【内疚】guilty conscience:感到~feel guilty
【内科医生】physician
【内裤】briefs;pants;knickers
【内陆】inland
【内幕】inside story
【内勤】❶office work;inside job ❷desk-man
【内情】true picture;inside story
【内容提要】synopsis
【内务】internal affairs
【内伤】internal injury
【内详】name and address of sender enclosed
【内向】introverted
【内心】heart;innermost being:发自~from the bottom of one's heart
N
【内心世界】one's inner world
【内需】domestic demand
【内衣】underclothes;underwear
【内因】internal cause
【内脏】internal organs
【内政】internal (or domestic) affairs

nen

嫩 (nèn) ❶ tender;delicate ❷ under-done;tender ❸ light ❹ inexperienced;green
【嫩绿】pale (or light) green

neng

能 (néng) ❶ ability;capability ❷ skill ❸energy:太阳~solar energy;原子~atomic energy ❹can;be able to;be capable of ❺able;capable
【能动】active;dynamic;vigorous
【能干】able;capable;competent
【能歌善舞】good at both singing and dancing
【能够】can;be able to;be capable of
【能见度】visibility
【能力】ability;capability:生产~production capacity;阅读~ reading ability
【能量】energy
【能手】expert;good hand;adept
【能言善辩】eloquent
【能源】sources of energy;energy resources
【能源危机】energy crisis

ni

尼 (ní) Buddhist nun
【尼姑】nun;Buddhist nun
【尼古丁】nicotine
【尼龙】nylon
【尼罗河】the Nile
呢 (ní) wool;woolen cloth;heavy woolen cloth
【呢喃】twittering (of swallows)
【呢绒】woollen goods
泥 (ní) ❶mud ❷mashed vegetable or fruit:蒜~mashed garlic
【泥泞】muddy
【泥鳅】loach
【泥人】clay figurine
【泥沙】silt
【泥石流】mud-rock flow
【泥塑】clay sculpture
【泥土】❶earth;soil ❷clay
霓 (nǐ) secondary rainbow
【霓虹灯】neon;neon light (or lame)
拟 (nǐ) ❶draw up;draft ❷plan ❸imitate;copy

【拟订】work out; draw up; draft

【拟稿】make a draft; draft

【拟人】personification

你 (nǐ) you

【你好】how do you do; how are you; hello

【你追我赶】vie with one another; be unwilling to lag behind

逆 (nì) ❶go against; defy; rebel ❷contrary; counter ❸traitorous

【逆耳】❶unpleasant to the ear ❷jar on the ear: 忠言～good advice jars on the ear

【逆光】against the light

【逆境】adversity; adverse circumstances

【逆流】countercurrent

【逆时针】anticlockwise

【逆水】against the current

【逆水行舟】sail against the current

【逆转】turn in the opposite direction; take a turn for the worse; reverse; deteriorate

匿 (nì) hide; conceal

【匿迹】go into hiding; be in hiding: 销声～lie low; disappear from view; be in hiding

【匿名】anonymous

腻 (nì) ❶fatly; greasy ❷fine and smooth ❸be bored of; be fed up with

溺 (nì) ❶drown ❷be addicted to ❸excessively

【溺爱】be excessively fond of; dote on

【溺水】be drowned

nian

年 (nián) ❶year: 今～this year; 明～next year; 去～last year; 学～school year ❷age ❸New Year: 拜～pay a New Year visit; pay a New Year call ❹harvest: 丰～good harvest ❺annual; yearly

【年报】annual report

【年产量】annual output

【年初】the beginning of the year

【年代】❶age; years; time: 战争～during the war years ❷decade

【年底】the end of the year

【年度】year: 财政～ financial year

【年复一年】year after year; year in and year out

【年富力强】in the prime of life; in one's prime

【年糕】New Year cake; New Year pudding (made of glutinous rice flour)

【年华】time; years: 虚度～idle away one's time; waste one's life

【年画】New Year picture

【年会】annual meeting

【年货】special shopping for the Spring Festival

【年级】grade; year

【年纪】age: 你多大～? How old are you?

【年假】annual leave

【年鉴】yearbook; almanac

【年景】the year's harvest: 好～ year of good harvest

【年龄】age: 入学～ school age

【年轮】annual ring; growth ring

【年轻】young

【年息】annual interest

【年限】fixed number of years: 使用～service life

【年薪】annual salary

【年幼】young; under age

【年终】the end of the year; year end

鲇 (nián) catfish

【鲇鱼】catfish

黏 (nián) sticky; glutinous

【黏合】adhere; bond; bind

【黏土】clay

捻 (niǎn) twist with fingers

碾 (niǎn) ❶grind; husk ❷roller

【碾碎】pulverize

撵 (niǎn) drive out; oust

念 (niàn) ❶ thought; idea: 私心杂～ selfish thoughts ❷ read ❸ study ❹ think of; miss

【念叨】talk about repeatedly; harp on

【念佛】chant the name of Buddha; pray to Buddha

【念念不忘】always keep in mind; always bear in mind

N

【念书】go to school; study

【念诵】read aloud; chant

【念头】thought; idea

niang

娘 (niáng) ❶ mother; mum ❷ aunt ❸girl

【娘家】a married woman's parents' home

酿 (niàng) ❶wine: 佳～good wine ❷ make wine; brew beer ❸make honey ❹develop into; result in

【酿成大祸】bring about a great disaster

【酿酒】make wine; brew beer

niao

鸟 (niǎo) bird

【鸟巢】bird's nest

【鸟瞰】❶a bird's-eye view ❷get a bird's-eye view

【鸟笼】birdcage

【鸟枪】air gun

【鸟嘴】beak; bill

尿 (niào) ❶ urine ❷ make (or pass) water; piss

【尿布】diaper; nappy

【尿床】bed-wetting

nie

捏 (niē) ❶pinch ❷mould with fingers ❸make up; invent

【捏把汗】be breathless with anxiety or tension; be keyed up; be on edge

【捏造】concoct; fabricate; invent

镊 (niè) ❶ tweezers ❷ pick up sth. with tweezers

【镊子】tweezers

镍 (niè) nickel

蹑 (niè) ❶lighten one's step; walk on tiptoe ❷step on; walk with

【蹑手蹑脚】sneak; tiptoe

孽 (niè) ❶monster; sin ❷unfaithful

【孽障】evil creature

ning

宁 (níng) peaceful; quiet; tranquil 另见 1119 页 nìng

【宁静】peaceful; tranquil; quiet

【宁日】peaceful day

狞 (níng) (of facial expression) ferocious; hideous

【狞笑】grin hideously

柠 (níng)

【柠檬】lemon

凝 (níng) ❶congeal ❷concentrate; focus

【凝固】solidify
【凝结】condense;congeal
【凝聚力】cohesion;cohesive force
【凝神】with fixed attention;concentrate:~思索 be deep in contemplation
【凝视】gaze;stare

拧 (nǐng) ❶ wrench; screw; twist ❷wrong

【拧紧】tighten up
【拧开】screw off

宁 (nìng) peaceful;tranquil 另见 1118 页 níng

【宁肯】would rather (or sooner);prefer...to;prefer to...rather than
【宁缺毋滥】rather go without than have something poor;better fewer but good

niu

牛 (niú) ox;cattle:公~bull;母~ cow;水~water buffalo;小~ calf

【牛车】ox cart
【牛痘】cowpox
【牛顿】newton (the standard metre-kilogram-second unit of force, named after Sir Isaac Newton)
【牛犊】calf
【牛角尖】❶tip of a horn ❷unimportant (or insoluble) problem:钻~take pains over an insoluble problem;split hairs
【牛马】oxen and horses—beasts of burden;slave
【牛奶】milk
【牛排】beefsteak
【牛皮】❶brag;boast:吹~talk big (or brag;boast) ❷cowhide,oxhide
【牛皮纸】kraft (paper)
【牛肉】beef
【牛仔】cowboy
【牛仔裤】jeans

扭 (niǔ) ❶turn round ❷sprain;wrench ❸ twist; screw ❹ grab; seize ❺ roll;swing

【扭打】wrestle;grapple
【扭过头】turn about (or round)
【扭亏为盈】turn losses into profits
【扭力】twisting force
【扭曲】distort;twist
【扭伤】sprain;wrench
【扭转】❶turn round (or about) ❷ turn back;reverse

纽 (niǔ) ❶button ❷bond;tie ❸knob

【纽带】link;tie;bond
【纽扣】button
【纽约】New York

拗 (niù) stubborn;obstinate

【拗不过】unable to dissuade sb.; fail to talk sb. out of doing sth.

N

nong

农 (nóng) ❶agriculture;farming:务~do farm work;go farming ❷peasant;farmer:棉~cotton grower

【农产品】agricultural products; farm products
【农场】farm
【农村】rural area;country;countryside
【农副产品】subsidiary agricultural products
【农活】farm work
【农机】agricultural machinery
【农具】farm tools
【农历】the traditional Chinese calender;the lunar calender
【农忙】busy farming season
【农民】farmer;peasant
【农民工】peasant-worker; migrant work-

ers
【农田】farmland;cropland
【农闲】slack farming season
【农业】agriculture;farming
【农作物】crops
浓 (nóng) ❶dense;thick ❷strong;rich ❸great;keen:兴趣~take great interest
【浓度】density
【浓厚】❶dense;thick ❷deep;strong
【浓眉】heavy (or thick) eyebrows
【浓密】thick;dense
【浓缩】condense
弄 (nòng) ❶play with;fool with ❷do;make;handle ❸manage to get
【弄错】make a mistake;misunderstand
【弄好】do well;get sth. done:把事情~do a good job
【弄坏】ruin;spoil:把事情~make a mess of things
【弄假成真】 the make-believe comes out true
【弄巧成拙】outsmart oneself; try to be clever only to end up with a blunder
【弄清】straighten out;make clear
【弄通】gain a clear understanding of;straighten out
【弄虚作假】practise fraud;play tricks
【弄脏】stain;pollute;make sth. dirty

nu

奴 (nú) ❶slave ❷enslave
【奴隶】slave
【奴仆】servant
努 (nǔ) ❶put forth;exert ❷jut out
【努力】❶hard ❷try (or work) hard;exert oneself;make great efforts;take pains:尽最大~ do one's utmost (or best)
【努嘴】pout one's lips as a signal
弩 (nú) crossbow
怒 (nù) ❶ anger; rage; fury ❷ be (or get) angry;fly into a rage (or fury) ❸burst:心花~放 be highly delighted ❹ angry ❺angrily
【怒不可遏】be beside oneself with anger;be in wild anger
【怒冲冲】in a great rage
【怒放】in full bloom:百花~flowers are blooming in profusion
【怒吼】roar;howl
【怒火】rage;fury
【怒目而视】glare (or stare) at
【怒气冲冲】❶in great rage ❷flaming with anger

nü

女 (nǚ) ❶ woman; female ❷ girl;daughter:独生~only daughter;子~children
【女儿】daughter;girl
【女方】the bride's side;the wife's side
【女服务员】waitress
【女皇】empress
【女教师】woman teacher
【女警察】policewoman
【女朋友】girlfriend
【女强人】a woman of exceptional talent and ability;a strong woman
【女人】women;womenfolk
【女神】goddess
【女生】schoolgirl
【女声】female voice
【女士】lady
【女王】queen
【女性】female;woman

【女婿】son-in-law
【女演员】actress
【女英雄】heroine
【女主人】hostess
【女装】women's clothing

nuan

暖 (nuǎn) ❶ warmth ❷ warm up ❸warm
【暖房】greenhouse; hothouse
【暖和】❶warm ❷warm up
【暖气】heating; warm air
【暖色】warm color
【暖水瓶】thermos (flask)

nüe

虐 (nüè) cruel
【虐待】maltreat; ill-treat

nuo

挪 (nuó) move; shift
【挪动】move; shift
【挪开】move away
【挪用】❶embezzle ❷divert: 把钱~到别处 divert money to other purposes
诺 (nuò) ❶promise ❷make a promise; say yes ❸yes
【诺贝尔奖】the Nobel Prize
【诺言】promise: 遵守~keep one's word
懦 (nuò) weak; cowardly; faint-hearted
【懦夫】coward
【懦弱】weak; cowardly; faint-hearted

O o

ou

讴（ōu）❶sing ❷folk songs；ballads

【讴歌】sing the praises of；celebrate in song

欧（ōu）short for Europe

【欧美】Europe and America；Western；the west

【欧盟】European Union

【欧姆定律】Ohm's Law

【欧元】Euro

【欧洲】Europe

殴（ōu）beat；strike

【殴打】beat；strike：相互～come to blows；exchange blows

鸥（ōu）gull：海～seagull

呕（ǒu）vomit

【呕吐】vomit

【呕心沥血】take great pains；work one's heart out

偶（ǒu）❶image；idol：木～puppet ❷spouse ❸occasional ❹by chance；occasionally

【偶尔】once in a while；occasionally

【偶感】❶random thoughts（often used in titles of articles）❷suddenly feel；occasionally feel

【偶合】coincidence

【偶然】❶accidental ❷accidentally

【偶数】even number

【偶像】image；idol

藕（ǒu）lotus root

【藕断丝连】the lotus root snaps but its fibres stay joined—（of lovers，etc.）still in contact though apparently separated；separated but still in each other's thoughts

【藕粉】lotus root starch

怄（òu）❶sulk；be sulky ❷irritate；upset；annoy

【怄气】sulk；be sulky

P p

pa

趴 (pā) ❶ lie on one's stomach; lie prone ❷ bend over; lean over; lean on

扒 (pá) ❶rake ❷stew ❸steal 另见 884 页 bā

【扒手】 pickpocket

爬 (pá) ❶crawl; creep ❷climb

【爬竿】 pole-climbing

【爬山】 climb a mountain (or hill)

【爬树】 climb a tree

【爬行】 crawl; creep

【爬行动物】 reptile

耙 (pá) ❶ rake ❷ make smooth with a rake

【耙子】 rake

帕 (pà) handkerchief

怕 (pà) ❶ fear; be afraid of ❷ for fear of; in case ❸ for fear that I suppose; perhaps

【怕生】 (of young child) be shy with strangers

【怕事】 be afraid of getting into trouble; overcautious: 胆小～timid and overcautious

【怕死】 fear (or be afraid of) death

【怕羞】 coy; shy; bashful

pai

拍 (pāi) ❶bat; racket: 乒乓球～ping-pong bat ❷ beat; time ❸ clap; pat; beat ❹take a picture ❺shoot (or make) a film ❻send a telegram ❼flatter; fawn on (or upon)

【拍板】 have the final say

【拍打】 pat; beat

【拍电影】 shoot a film

【拍马屁】 lick one's boots; fawn on; soft-soap; flatter

【拍卖】 auction

【拍摄】 take (a picture); shoot

【拍手】 clap one's hands; applaud

【拍照】 have a picture taken; take a picture

【拍子】 ❶ bat; racket ❷ beat; time: 打～beat time

排 (pái) ❶row; line; rank ❷raft: 木～timber raft ❸platoon ❹arrange; put in order; line up ❺rehearse ❻discharge; exclude ❼drain ❽reject

【排版】 composing; typesetting

【排比】 parallelism

【排查】 investigate all concerned

【排斥】 reject; repel; exclude

【排除】 remove; get rid of

【排挡】 food stall; snack stall

【排毒养颜】 eject toxins from inside the

body and nourish the face
【排队】queue up;line up
【排放】discharge
【排风扇】ventilator;ventilating fan
【排骨】ribs,spareribs
【排行榜】ranking list
【排解】❶reconcile; mediate ❷divert oneself from a bad mood, etc.
【排练】rehearse
【排列】❶ arrange; range; put in order ❷ permutation
【排名】ranking
【排球】volleyball
【排水管】drain pipe
【排尾】the last person in row; the person at the end of a row
【排污】discharge waste water;emit pollutants
【排戏】rehearse a play
【排险】remove dangers
【排忧解难】remove worries and difficulties

徘 (pái)

【徘徊】❶walk up and down (or to and fro, back and forth); wander about ❷ hesitate;waver;hover

牌 (pái) ❶plate; board; table: 布告~ notice board; 门~ doorplate; 招~ shop sign; signboard ❷ brand; trade mark ❸cards: 扑克~ playing cards; 桥~bridge
【牌坊】memorial archway
【牌价】posted price; list price; market quotation:零售~ retail sales price;批发~ wholesale price
【牌照】license plate;license

派 (pài) ❶group; school ❷faction ❸ style;manner;bearing ❹send
【派别】group;school
【派出所】local police station
【派遣】send;dispatch
【派驻】accredit to;dispatch sb. to stay at

pan

攀 (pān) ❶climb:高不可~too high to reach ❷ seek connections in high places ❸try to engage a talk
【攀比】vie with others;compare unrealistically with sb. better than oneself:互相~ make unrealistic comparison with each other
【攀登】climb;scale:~科学高峰 scale new heights of science
【攀升】climb up
【攀谈】have a chat;engage in small talk
【攀岩】❶rock-climbing ❷climb a rock
【攀折】pull down and break off (twigs, etc.); break off: 请勿~花木! Please don't pick the flowers or break off the branches!

盘 (pán) ❶tray;plate;sth. shaped like or used as a tray, plate, etc.;dish: 棋~chessboard ❷coil;wind ❸check;examine
【盘存】take inventory
【盘点】check;make an inventory of:~库存 take stock
【盘活】revitalize;realize
【盘绕】wind;coil
【盘算】calculate;plan
【盘腿】cross one's legs
【盘问】interrogate;examine
【盘旋】spiral;circle

蹒 (pán)

【蹒跚】stagger;limp;walk haltingly

判 (pàn) ❶distinguish; set (or tell) apart ❷mark;grade:~卷子 grade examination papers ❸judge; decide ❹sentence

【判案】decide a case

【判处】sentence: ~ 死刑 be sentenced to death

【判断】judge; decide

【判决】give judgment; sentence; judge

【判明】distinguish; set apart; tell apart

【判明是非】distinguish between right and wrong

【判明真相】ascertain the facts

【判若两人】not be one's old self at all

【判刑】pass a sentence on (a convict); sentence (a convict) to (death, imprisonment, etc.)

盼 (pàn) hope (or long) for; expect; look forward to

【盼头】prospects; expectations; hope

【盼望】hope (or long) for; look forward to; expect

叛 (pàn) betray; rebel; revolt

【叛变】betray; turn traitor

【叛乱】rebellion

【叛逆】❶rebel (or revolt) against ❷rebel

【叛徒】traitor

pang

滂 (pāng) rushing; gushing; pouring

【滂沱】torrential

庞 (páng) ❶face ❷big; huge

【庞大】tremendous; enormous; huge

【庞杂】numerous and jumbled

旁 (páng) ❶side: 路~roadside ❷other; else

【旁白】aside (in a play)

【旁边】❶side ❷at the side of; beside

【旁观】look on: 袖手~look on with folded arms

【旁观者】onlooker

【旁人】other people

【旁若无人】act as if there were no one else present

【旁听席】public gallery; visitor's seat

【旁系亲属】collateral relatives

磅 (páng)
另见 889 页 bàng

【磅礴】boundless; majestic

螃 (páng)

【螃蟹】crab

胖 (pàng) plump; fatty; fat: 长 ~ get fat; put on weight

【胖墩儿】(esp. referring to children) roly-poly; fatty

【胖子】fatty; plump (or fat) person

pao

抛 (pāo) ❶ throw; cast; toss; fling ❷ leave behind; abandon

【抛锚】❶cast anchor ❷break down

【抛弃】throw away (or off); abandon; desert

【抛砖引玉】cast a brick to attract out jade; use the little to get the big

刨 (páo) ❶ dig; excavate ❷ excluding; not counting
另见 891 页 bào

【刨根问底】get to the root (or bottom) of things

咆 (páo)(of beast of prey) roar; howl

【咆哮】roar; thunder: ~如雷 in a thundering rage

炮 (páo) prepare herbal medicine by roasting or parching (in a pan)

另见 1126 页 pào

【炮制】❶the process of preparing Chinese medicine, as by parching, roasting, baking, steaming, etc. ❷ concoct; cook up

跑 (pǎo) ❶run; race: 长～long-distance race; 短～dash ❷run away; escape; flee ❸run about ❹away; off

【跑遍】go around; travel all over

【跑表】stopwatch

【跑步】run; jog

【跑步机】walking machine

【跑车】❶racing bike ❷roadster

【跑道】❶ runway ❷ racing track; skating rink

【跑题】(of talk, writing, etc.) irrelevant; beside the point

泡 (pào) ❶ bubble ❷ dawdle ❸ soak; bathe

【泡菜】pickled vegetables; pickles

【泡茶】make tea

【泡沫】foam; bubble

【泡泡糖】bubble gum

【泡影】❶bubble ❷vain hope

炮 (pào) ❶ gun; cannon; artillery ❷ bombard ❸firecracker ❹a blasthole filled with dynamite

另见 1125 页 páo

【炮兵】artillery; artilleryman

【炮弹】shell

【炮火】gunfire; artillery fire

【炮声】thunder of guns; report of artillery; roar of guns

【炮手】gunner

【炮台】fort; battery

疱 (pào)

【疱疹】❶bleb ❷herpes

pei

陪 (péi) accompany; keep company

【陪伴】keep company; accompany

【陪衬】❶ serve as a contrast; set off ❷ foil; setoff; contrast

【陪读】accompany on in one's study

【陪酒】drink with an honored guest

【陪审团】jury

【陪审员】juror; juryman

【陪同】accompany; go along with

培 (péi) ❶ earth up; bank up with earth ❷train; foster; develop

【培土】earth up; bank up with earth

【培训】train

【培训班】training class

【培训费】training costs (or expenses)

【培养】❶ train; develop; educate ❷ training; education

【培育】cultivate; breed; foster

【培植】cultivate; train; develop

赔 (péi) ❶compensate; pay for ❷stand a loss; lose

【赔本】run a business at a loss; sustain losses in business; lose

【赔偿】pay for; compensate

【赔偿费】compensation

【赔礼】apologize; make an apology

【赔钱】❶lose money in business ❷pay for a loss

【赔笑】smile an apologetic smile; smile obsequiously, apologetically or appealingly

沛 (pèi) copious; abundant

佩 (pèi) ❶ wear: ～刀 wear a sword ❷admire

【佩带】wear; bear; carry

【佩戴】wear (a badge, insignia, etc.) on the chest, arm, or shoulder

【佩服】admire; have admiration for

配 (pèi) ❶ compound ❷ deserve; be worthy of; be qualified for ❸ fit; complete; make up ❹ apportion ❺ match

【配备】❶ provide; equip ❷ outfit; equipment

【配对】❶ pair ❷ (of animals) mate

【配额】quota

【配方】❶ formula ❷ make up (or fill) a prescription

【配合】❶ cooperate ❷ cooperation

【配件】❶ fittings (of a machine, etc) ❷ a replacement

【配角】supporting role

【配偶】spouse

【配乐】select passages to serve as background music

【配制】make up

pen

喷 (pēn) ❶ spurt; spout ❷ spray; sprinkle

另见本页 pèn

【喷壶】sprinkling can

【喷绘】spraying painting

【喷泉】fountain

【喷洒】sprinkle; spray: ～农药 spray insecticide

【喷水池】fountain

【喷嚏】sneeze: 打～sneeze

【喷头】❶ shower nozzle ❷ sprinkler head

【喷雾器】sprayer

盆 (pén) basin; tub: 脸～washbasin

【盆地】basin; plain area skirted by mountains or highland

【盆景】potted landscape

【盆浴】bath in a tub

【盆栽植物】pot plant

喷 (pèn)

另见本页 pēn

【喷香】fragrant; delicious

peng

抨 (pēng) attack (in speech or writing); assail; lash out at

【抨击】attack

烹 (pēng) ❶ cook; boil ❷ fry quickly

【烹饪】cooking

朋 (péng) friend

【朋友】friend: 交～make friends with; befriend

棚 (péng) shed; shack: 车～bicycle shed

【棚户区】shantytown

【棚屋】hut; shed

蓬 (péng) fluffy

【蓬荜增辉】lustre lent to a humble house (said in thanks for a visit or a gift such as a scroll)

【蓬勃】vigorous

【蓬松】fluffy

【蓬头垢面】with messy hair and a dirty face; unkempt

鹏 (péng) roc

【鹏程万里】(make) a roc's flight of 10,000 li—have a bright future

澎 (péng) splash; spatter

【澎湃】surge

膨 (péng) swell; expand

P

【膨胀】❶ swell; expand ❷ inflate: 通货~inflation

捧 (pěng) ❶ hold in both hands ❷ boost; flatter ❸a double handful

【捧场】boost; flatter; praise

【捧腹大笑】be convulsed with laughter; split one's sides with laughter

【捧上天】praise one into the sky

碰 (pèng) ❶ touch ❷ hit; bump ❸ meet; come across; run into ❹ take one's chance

【碰壁】run up against a stone wall; be rebuffed

【碰瓷】finding fault with sb.; racketeering

【碰钉子】meet with a rebuff

【碰见】meet; run into; hit on; come across

【碰碰车】bumper (or dodgem) car

【碰巧】❶ by chance ❷ happen (or chance) to

【碰头】meet and discuss

【碰硬】stand up against adversary

【碰运气】try one's luck; take a (or one's) chance

【碰撞】run into; knock against; hit

pi

批 (pī) ❶batch; group; lot ❷wholesale ❸ write comments on ❹ criticize ❺slap

【批驳】refute; criticize; rebut

【批发】wholesale

【批发商】distributor; wholesaler

【批复】give an official, written reply to a subordinate body

【批改】correct

【批量】in batches

【批判】❶criticize ❷critique

【批评】❶criticize ❷criticism

【批语】written comments; written remarks

【批准】approve; authorize; ratify

纰 (pī) ❶become unwoven or untwisted ❷be spoilt

【纰漏】small accident; make a slip

坯 (pī) ❶base; semifinished product ❷ unburned brick; earthen brick

【坯模】mold

披 (pī) put (or throw) on

【披风】cloak

【披肩】cape; shawl

【披荆斩棘】break (or beat) a path in woods; hack one's way through difficulties

【披露】❶publish ❷disclose; expose

【披头散发】wear long untidy hair

【披星戴月】travel (or work) day and night

砒 (pī) arsenic

【砒霜】(white) arsenic

劈 (pī) ❶ split; chop; cut ❷ strike ❸ right against

另见 1129 页 pǐ

【劈开】split; cut open (or apart)

霹 (pī)

【霹雳】thunderbolt; thunderclap

皮 (pí) ❶skin: 树~bark ❷fur ❸leather; hide ❹cover; wrapper ❺sheet ❻ naughty ❼not crisp ❽indifferent

【皮包骨】skinny

【皮鞭】leather-thonged whip

【皮草】leather and fur; leather and fur products

【皮带】leather belt; strap

【皮肤】skin

【皮革】leather; hide
【皮具】leatherwear; leather articles
【皮球】rubber ball; ball
【皮箱】leather suitcase
【皮鞋】leather shoes
【皮影戏】shadow play

毗 (pí) adjoin; be adjacent to

【毗邻】join; border on; be adjacent to

疲 (pí) tired; weary; exhausted: 精~力尽 exhausted (or tired) out

【疲惫】tired out; exhausted
【疲倦】tired; weary
【疲劳】tired; weary; fatigued
【疲软】sluggish; weaken
【疲于奔命】be kept endlessly on the go; be tired from running about

啤 (pí)

【啤酒】beer
【啤酒节】beer festival

脾 (pí) spleen

【脾气】temper: 发~ lose one's temper
【脾性】temperament; disposition; nature

匹 (pǐ) match; equal; be equal to; be a match for

【匹敌】be equal to; be well matched
【匹夫】❶an ordinary man: 国家兴亡，~有责 every man has a share of responsibility for the fate of his country ❷an ignorant person
【匹配】match

劈 (pǐ) ❶divide; split ❷break off; strip off ❸injure one's legs or fingers by opening them too wide

另见 1128 页 pī

【劈叉】do the splits

癖 (pǐ) addiction; weakness for

【癖好】favourite hobby

屁 (pì) wind; fart: 放~break wind

【屁股】buttocks; bottom

辟 (pì) ❶ open up (territory, land etc.); break (ground) ❷ penetrating; incisive ❸refute; repudiate

【辟谣】refute a rumor

媲 (pì)

【媲美】compare favourably with; rival

僻 (pì) ❶ out-of-the-way; secluded ❷ eccentric ❸rare

【僻静】secluded; lonely

pian

偏 (piān) ❶inclined; slant; lean ❷partial; biased

【偏爱】favour; have partiality for
【偏护】be partial to and side with; be biased and shield
【偏激】extreme
【偏见】prejudice; bias
【偏离】deviate; go out of the way
【偏僻】remote; out-of-the-way
【偏袒】favour; be partial to
【偏题】tricky question
【偏远】remote; faraway

篇 (piān) sheet; piece

【篇目】contents
【篇章】sections and chapters

翩 (piān)

【翩翩】❶dance lightly ❷elegant ❸smart
【翩然】lightly; trippingly

便 (pián)
另见 898 页 biàn

【便便】bulging; swelling: 大腹~ bulging;

swelling
【便宜】❶cheap; inexpensive ❷petty (or easy) gains: 贪小~covet small gains ❸ let sb. off easily

片 (piàn) ❶piece; sheet; slice; tablet: 雪~snowflakes ❷area; district
【片刻】a moment; a second; an instant
【片面】one-sided; unilateral
【片区】area; section

骗 (piàn) cheat; deceive; fool: 受~be taken in; be deceived
【骗保】insurance fraud
【骗钱】swindle money
【骗人】deceive people
【骗术】deceitful trick; ruse; hoax
【骗子】swindler; cheat

piao

剽 (piāo) rob
【剽窃】lift; copy; plagiarize

漂 (piāo) float; drift
另见本页 piǎo; piào
【漂泊】drift; lead a wandering life
【漂浮】float

缥 (piāo)
【缥缈】dimly dissemble; misty

飘 (piāo) float; wave
【飘带】streamer; ribbon
【飘动】float (in the air or upon the waves); flutter; drift
【飘忽】❶float (of wind, cloud, etc.) ❷ swing; sway; rock: 情绪~不定 in uncertain mood
【飘落】drift and fall slowly
【飘飘然】walk on air
【飘扬】flutter; wave; fly: 随风~flying in the wind
【飘摇】sway in the wind

瓢 (piáo) gourd ladle; wooden dipper
【瓢虫】ladybug; ladybird
【瓢泼大雨】downpour

漂 (piǎo) ❶bleach ❷rinse
另见本页 piāo; piào
【漂白】bleach; whiten
【漂洗】rinse: ~衣裳 rinse clothes

瞟 (piǎo) look sidelong at; glance sideways at

票 (piào) ❶ticket: 来回~return ticket ❷vote; ballot: 反对~negative vote; 赞成~affirmative vote; 投~ vote for ❸ bill; bank note; note: 钞~bill
【票房】box office; booking office
【票价】fare; admission fee; the price of a ticket
【票据】❶bill; note ❷voucher; receipt
【票箱】ballot box
【票子】bank note; money; bill

漂 (piào) float; drift
另见本页 piāo; piǎo
【漂亮】❶ beautiful; pretty; handsome; good-looking ❷brilliant; splendid

pie

撇 (piē) ❶cast aside; throw overboard ❷skim
【撇开】leave aside; bypass

瞥 (piē) ❶ glimpse; glance ❷ take a glance
【瞥见】catch a glimpse of; glimpse

pin

拼 (pīn) ❶put (piece) together ❷go all out; risk one's life
【拼搏】fight; struggle hard; exert oneself

P

to the utmost;go all out

【拼车】car sharing;car pooling

【拼客】partaker

【拼写】spell;transliterate

【拼音】spell

【拼音字母】phonetic alphabet (or letter)

【拼装】fit together;assemble

贫 (pín) ❶poor ❷be poor in; be deficient in

【贫乏】poor; wanting; lacking; meagre: 知识~be lacking in knowledge

【贫富悬殊】wide gap between the rich and the poor

【贫寒】poverty-stricken; poor: 家境~of a poor family

【贫瘠】barren

【贫苦】poor;poverty-stricken

【贫困】poor;in straitened circumstances

【贫穷】poor;needy;impoverished

频 (pín) ❶ frequent ❷ frequently; repeatedly

【频道】channel

【频繁】❶frequent ❷frequently; repeatedly;often

【频率】frequency

品 (pǐn) ❶article; product; 商~goods; commodity; merchandise; 生活必需~ daily necessities; 产~ product ❷ grade; class; rank: 上等~top grade ❸ character; quality: 人~character; moral quality ❹taste; savour

【品茶】sample tea

【品尝】taste;sample;savour

【品德】moral character

【品格】one's character and morals

【品貌】looks;appearance

【品牌效应】brand effect

【品牌意识】brand awareness

【品头论足】find fault with

【品位】❶ grade ❷ quality (of products, literary works, etc.)

【品味】taste;savour

【品行】behaviour

【品行端正】behave oneself well

【品性】moral character

【品学兼优】of good character and fine scholarship

【品质】❶character: 道德~moral character ❷quality: 优良~fine quality

【品种】kind;breed;variety;strain

聘 (pìn) engage;employ

【聘期】period of employment (or engagement)

【聘请】engage;invite;hire;employ

【聘任】engage sb. as

【聘书】letter of appointment;contract

【聘用】employ

【聘用制】system of employment under contract

ping

乒 (pīng) table tennis;ping-pong

【乒乓球】ping-pong;table tennis: 打~play ping-pong

【乒赛】table tennis match or tournament

平 (píng) ❶equal; be at the same level ❷suppress; put down ❸level; even; smooth ❹calm; calm down ❺flat; level; even; smooth ❻fair ❼quiet; peaceful: 心~气和 even-tempered ❽ average; common; ordinary; usual

【平安】safe and sound; without mishap; well: 一路~! Have a good trip!

【平安无事】all is well

【平安险】free of particular average

【平安夜】Christmas Eve

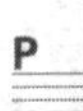

【平板电视】flat panel TV;plate TV

【平辈】of the same generation

【平常】❶ordinary;common;usual ❷generally;ordinarily;usually

【平川】level land;plain:一马~ wide expanse of flat land

【平淡】flat;dull;tasteless

【平等】❶equal ❷equality:男女~equality between men and women;sex equality

【平等互利】equality and mutual benefit

【平等竞争】❶ equal competition ❷ compete on equal footing

【平定】❶calm down;calm ❷suppress;put down

【平凡】ordinary;common:在~的岗位上 at an ordinary post

【平方米】square metre (or sq. m.)

【平分】divide equally

【平跟鞋】flat-heeled shoes

【平和】moderate;gentle;mild

【平衡】balance:失去~lose one's balance;保持~keep one's balance;收支~balance between income and expenditure

【平缓】❶gentle ❷gently ❸mild

【平角】straight angle

【平静】calm;quiet;peaceful;still

【平局】draw;tie:球赛踢成~。The football game ended in a draw.

【平均】average

【平均寿命】average life span;life expectancy

【平面几何】plane geometry

【平面镜】plane mirror

【平面图】plane figure

【平平】average;indifferent:成绩~。The results are about up to the average.

【平起平坐】be on an equal footing;sit as equals at the same table

【平时】ordinarily;usually;in peacetime

【平台】platform;活动~ platform for activity

【平坦】level;flat:~的道路 smooth road

【平稳】stable;steady:物价~。Prices are stable.

【平稳过渡】smooth transition

【平息】❶ calm (or quiet) down ❷ put down;suppress

【平心而论】in all fairness

【平心静气】❶calm;cool-headed ❷calmly

【平行】parallel

【平抑物价】stabilize prices

【平易近人】 amiable and easy of approach;folksy and friendly

【平原】plain

【平整】level;neat;smooth

【平装】paperback

评 (píng) ❶comment;review;note:书~book review;短~brief comment ❷criticize ❸judge;appraise;evaluate

【评比】compare;appraise

【评断】judge;arbitrate:~是非 judge between right and wrong

【评分】grade;mark

【评估】appraise;evaluate

【评级】grade

【评价】appraise;evaluate:高度~set a high value on;speak highly of

【评奖】decide on awards through appraisal

【评论】❶comment on ❷comment;review

【评判】judge

【评说】comment on;appraise;evaluate:~古人 comment on the ancients

【评委】member of a selection committee

【评选】choose through appraisal

【评语】comment;remark

苹 (píng)

【苹果】apple

凭 (píng) ❶evidence; proof ❷lean on (or against) ❸rely (or depend) on; be based on ❹by; according to

【凭借】rely on; depend on

【凭据】evidence; proof

【凭空】groundlessly

【凭证】evidence; proof; receipt; certificate

屏 (píng) screen
另见 901 页 bǐng

【屏蔽门】shielded gate; shielding barrier

【屏幕】screen

【屏障】protective screen

瓶 (píng) ❶bottle; vase ❷a bottle of

【瓶颈】bottleneck

【瓶装】bottled

po

坡 (pō) slope: 山～ hillside; 陡～ steep slope

【坡度】slope

泼 (pō) ❶ pour; splash ❷ shrewish; rude and unreasonable

【泼辣】❶shrewish ❷pungent ❸bold; daring: 工作大胆～be bold and vigorous in one's work

【泼冷水】pour cold water on; discourage; dampen the enthusiasm (or spirits) of

【泼洒】spill (liquid); splash

【泼水节】the Water-Pouring Festival; the Water-Splashing Festival

颇 (pō) rather; quite

婆 (pó) ❶old woman ❷a woman in a certain occupation ❸ husband's mother; mother-in-law

【婆家】husband's family

【婆婆】❶mother-in-law ❷grandmother

迫 (pò) ❶compel; force; press; make ❷approach; go near; get close to ❸urgent; pressing

【迫不得已】have to; have no alternative (but to); be forced (or compelled) to

【迫不及待】too eager to hold (or keep) oneself back; too impatient to wait; unable to hold

【迫害】persecute

【迫近】approach; get close to; draw (or come, go, move) near

【迫切】urgent; pressing

【迫使】force; oblige; compel; press

破 (pò) ❶break; split ❷get rid of; do away with; abolish ❸defeat; capture ❹expose; lay bare; find out the truth about ❺poor; shabby ❻broken; torn

【破案】clear (or solve) a case

【破败】❶ruined; dilapidated; run down ❷ decline; wane; be at the wane: ～的家庭 family on the decline

【破产】❶bankrupt; go bankrupt ❷bankruptcy ❸fall through

【破费】put sb. to expense; go to the expense of; spend money: 让你～了。You really shouldn't have spent all this money (said when receiving a gift or a treat).

【破釜沉舟】make up one's mind to fight to the bitter end

【破格】break a rule; make an exception

【破坏】destroy; damage; undermine; break; violate

【破纪录】break a record

【破解】decode; solve

【破旧】shabby; worn-out

【破烂】ragged; shabby

【破裂】break; split; burst

【破落】decline

【破灭】vanish; be shattered; fall through

【破碎】❶crush; break into pieces ❷broken

【破天荒】for the very first time

【破土动工】break ground for construction

【破晓】dawn; daybreak

【破绽】flaw; defect

魄（pò）❶ soul ❷ vigour; daring; spirit; boldness

【魄力】daring resolution; boldness: 工作有～be bold and daring in one's work

pou

剖（pōu）❶cut open; rip open ❷analyse; examine

【剖腹产】Caesarean birth: ～术 Caesarean section (or operation)

【剖解】analyse (reasons, etc.): ～细密 make a minute analysis

【剖面】section

pu

扑（pū）❶throw (or hurl, fling) oneself on ❷devote oneself to ❸rush at ❹flap

【扑鼻】(of strong scent) assail the nostrils: 香气～. A sweet smell greeted us.

【扑救】put out a fire to save life and property

【扑克牌】❶playing cards: 打～play cards ❷poker

【扑空】fail in one's efforts

【扑面】blow (or drift) on one's face

【扑灭】stamp (or put) out; destroy

铺（pū）❶spread ❷pave; lay
另见 1135 页 pù

【铺床】make the bed

【铺垫】bedding; foreshadowing

【铺盖】bedding

【铺路】pave a (or the) way

【铺平】❶level ❷smooth out

【铺天盖地】overwhelmingly

【铺展】unfold and spread

【铺张】extravagant

【铺张浪费】extravagant and wasteful

仆（pú）servant: 公～public servant; 男～manservant; 女～maidservant; servant girl

【仆人】servant

菩（pú）

【菩萨】❶Bodhisattva ❷Buddha

【菩提】bodhi, supreme wisdom or enlightenment, necessary to the attainment of Buddhahood

葡（pú）grape

【葡萄酒】grape wine; wine

朴（pǔ）simple; plain

【朴实】❶simple; plain ❷down to earth ❸naive and honest: 言行～ sincere and honest in words and deeds

【朴素】simple; plain; modest: 生活～ plain living

【朴质】simple and unadorned; natural

普（pǔ）general; universal

【普遍】universal; general

【普法教育】popularize law education

【普及】popularize

【普九】（普及九年制义务教育的简称）popularize the Nine Year Compulsory Education

【普天下】all over the world

【普通】ordinary; common; average; general

【普通话】standard Chinese (or pronunciation);Mandarin Chinese

【普选权】universal suffrage

谱 (pǔ) ❶a register or record for easy reference (in the form of charts, tables, lists, etc.) ❷manual; guidebook ❸music score; music ❹set to music; compose (music)

【谱曲】set (words) to music; compose music for

铺 (pù) ❶shop; store ❷plank bed 另见 1134 页 pū

【铺位】bunk; berth: 上~upper berth; 下~lower berth

瀑 (pù) waterfall

【瀑布】waterfall; falls

Q q

qi

七 (qī) seven

【七颠八倒】at sixes and sevens; all upside down; topsy-turvy

【七零八落】❶scattered here and there ❷ in broken pieces

【七拼八凑】disorderly piece together

【七巧板】seven-piece puzzle; tangram

【七情】❶ the seven human emotions, namely, joy, anger, sorrow, fear, love, hate and desire ❷the seven emotional factors (joy, anger, melancholy, brooding, sorrow, fear and shock, considered to be the internal factors causing diseases)

【七上八下】in confused uncertainty

【七月】July

【七嘴八舌】all talking in chorus

沏 (qī) infuse (with boiling water)

【沏茶】infuse tea; make tea

妻 (qī) wife: 夫~husband and wife

【妻儿老小】parents, wife and children—a married man's entire family

栖 (qī) ❶perch ❷dwell; stay

【栖身】stay; sojourn

【栖息】perch; rest

凄 (qī) ❶ cold; chilly ❷ lonely; bleak; de-solate ❸sad; miserable

【凄惨】miserable; tragic

【凄凉】desolate

【凄婉】❶doleful ❷(of sound) plaintively melodious: ~的笛声 heartrending notes of a flute

期 (qī) ❶ stage; term; period ❷ deadline; set time ❸number; issue ❹expect; hope

【期待】expect; hope; look forward to

【期间】time; period: 在……~ during; in the course of

【期刊】periodical; journal

【期满】expire; come to an end

【期末考试】term (or final) examination

【期盼】expect; await; look forward to

【期望】hope; expect; long for

【期限】set time; deadline; time limit

【期许】ardently hope or expect (usu. used of one's juniors)

【期中考试】midterm examination

欺 (qī) ❶deceive; cheat; fool ❷bully

【欺负】bully; treat sb. high-handedly; insult

【欺瞒】hoodwink; dupe; pull the wool over sb.'s eyes

【欺骗】deceive; cheat; fool

【欺辱】humiliate; insult: 受尽～ have one's fill of insult

【欺软怕硬】bully the weak but fear the strong

【欺侮】bully; insult; treat sb. high-handedly

漆 (qī) paint; lacquer

【漆工】painter

【漆匠】❶ lacquerware worker ❷ lacquerer; lacquer man; painter

齐 (qí) ❶ reach the level of ❷ neat; even; tidy ❸ alike ❹ all ready (or present) ❹ together ❺ along; at; in good order

【齐备】complete; all ready (or arranged): 货色～ commodities of complete specifications

【齐唱】chorus; group singing; sing in unison

【齐名】enjoy equal fame

【齐全】❶complete ❷perfect

【齐头并进】❶ go forward side by side ❷ do things at the same time

【齐心协力】work as one

【齐整】❶even; neat; uniform orderly ❷in good order

其 (qí) ❶ his; her; its; their ❷ he; she; it; they ❸that ❹such

【其次】❶secondly ❷then ❸next

【其间】in the meantime; meanwhile

【其实】in fact (or reality); as a matter of fact; really; truly; actually

【其他】❶other; else ❷the rest; others

【其中】among them; of them; in it

奇 (qí) ❶ surprise; wonder: 令人惊～ surprising ❷strange; queer; rare; unusual ❸ unexpected ❹ be surprised; be astonished ❺extremely; unusually

另见 1035 页 jī

【奇才】a rare talent; genius

【奇怪】strange; peculiar; queer; odd

【奇观】wonder; wonderful view

【奇幻】❶ fantastic; visionary: ～的遐想 fantastic imagination ❷dreamlike; kaleidoscopic

【奇迹】miracle; wonder: 创造～ perform (or work) wonder (or miracles)

【奇妙】wonderful; marvelous

【奇特】peculiar; queer; singular

【奇文共赏】share the pleasure of reading a rare piece of writing

【奇闻】an unheard (or fantastic) story

【奇异】strange; peculiar; queer; odd; unusual

【奇遇】adventure

【奇珍异宝】rare treasures

歧 (qí) ❶fork; branch ❷different

【歧途】wrong way: 误入～take the wrong way

【歧义】different meanings; various interpretations

祈 (qí) ❶pray; beg ❷entreat: 敬～指导。We respectfully request your guidance.

【祈祷】pray; say one's prayers

【祈求】earnestly hope; pray for: ～上帝 pray to God ～和平 pray for peace

骑 (qí) ❶ horseman ❷ riding horse ❸ride

【骑车】❶go by bike ❷by bicycle

【骑虎难下】be on a tiger's back and unable to get off; unable to extricate oneself from a difficult situation

【骑马】❶ride; ride a horse ❷on horseback

【骑士】horseman

【骑术】horsemanship; equestrian skill

棋 (qí) chess: 下～ play chess; 象～ Chinese chess; international chess

【棋逢对手】be a match for; be well-matched in a contest

【棋盘】chessboard; checkerboard

【棋手】chess player

【棋子】piece; chessman

旗 (qí) flag; banner: 国～national flag; 锦～brocade banner; 升～raise a flag

【旗杆】flagpole; flag post

【旗鼓相当】be a match for; be well-matched

【旗舰产品】flagship product

【旗开得胜】win the first battle; win speedy success

【旗袍】chi-pao: cheongsam

【旗帜】❶ stand ❷ flag; banner ❸ model; example

乞 (qǐ) beg

【乞丐】beggar

【乞讨】beg; go begging: 沿街～go begging from door to door

岂 (qǐ) used to ask a rhetorical question

【岂敢】how dare

【岂有此理】preposterous; outrageous; absurd

企 (qǐ) anxiously expect; hope for

【企鹅】penguin

【企及】hope to attain: 难以～ unattainable

【企盼】hope for; yearn for: ～合家欢聚 yearn for a happy family reunion

【企求】seek; seek for

【企事业单位】enterprises and institutions

【企图】try; seek; attempt

【企望】hope for

【企业】business; enterprise

【企业改制】enterprise restructuring

【企业管理】business management (or administration)

【企业精神】enterprise spirit

【企业竞争】enterprise competition

【企业文化】enterprise (or business) culture

【企业自主权】decision-making power of the enterprise

启 (qǐ) ❶ open ❷ start ❸ awaken; enlighten

【启程】start; start on a journey; set (or start) out

【启迪】enlighten; awaken

【启动】start; switch on

【启动键】start (or boot) key

【启动资金】start-up fund

【启发】arouse; inspire; enlighten: 有～instructive

【启蒙】❶ enlighten ❷ teach the ABC to beginners

【启蒙老师】the first teacher; abecedarian

【启示】enlightenment; inspiration; revelation

起 (qǐ) ❶case; instance ❷batch; group ❸get up; stand up ❹rise ❺appear ❻ remove ❼draft ❽build; set up ❾start ❿ since; from

【起步】start; begin

【起步价】starting fare of a taxi

【起草】make a draft; draw up; draft

【起初】at first; at the beginning

【起床】rise; get up; get out of bed

【起点】start; starting point

【起点站】starting station; jumping-off place

【起飞】take off: 经济～economic take-off

【起伏】❶rise and fall ❷ups and downs

Q

【起航】set sail; weigh anchor
【起火】❶break out ❷flare up; catch fire ❸cook meals
【起居】daily life
【起来】❶stand (or sit, get) up; rise ❷be aroused
【起立】rise; stand up; rise to one's feet
【起码】❶minimum ❷at least
【起锚】weigh anchor; set sail
【起跑线】starting line
【起身】❶get up ❷leave; set (or start) out
【起诉书】bill of prosecution (or complaint)
【起先】at first; in the beginning
【起因】cause; origin
【起源】❶origin ❷originate; come from; begin with
【起止】beginning and end: ~日期 dates of beginning and end
【起作用】❶play a part (or role) ❷work; take effect

绮 (qǐ) ❶figured woven silk material; damask ❷beautiful; gorgeous
【绮丽】beautiful; gorgeous

气 (qì) ❶gas: 煤~gas ❷air ❸breath: 呼~breathe out; 吸~breathe in ❹smell ❺spirit: 垂头丧~ in low spirits ❻manner ❼bully: 受~be bullied ❽irritate; make angry ❾get angry
【气冲冲】furious; beside oneself with rage
【气垫】air-cushion
【气度】deportment; spirit: ~不凡 of unusual verve
【气氛】atmosphere
【气愤】indignant; furious
【气概】lofty quality; spirit: 英雄~heroic spirit
【气功】qigong, a system of deep breathing exercises; breathing exercises
【气候】❶climate ❷situation
【气量】tolerance
【气流】airstream; air current; airflow
【气恼】get angry
【气馁】feel discouraged
【气派】dignified air; imposing manner
【气泡】bubble
【气球】balloon
【气色】complexion; color; spirit
【气势】imposing manner; momentum
【气态】gas state; gaseity
【气体】gas
【气味】❶smell; odour; flavour ❷taste
【气味相投】be two of a kind; be birds of a feather; be like-minded
【气温】temperature
【气息】❶breath ❷scent; flavour
【气象】❶meteorological phenomena ❷atmosphere; scene
【气象卫星】meteorological (or weather) satellite
【气象预报】weather forecast
【气压】atmospheric pressure
【气宇轩昂】have an impressive bearing
【气质】❶temperament; disposition ❷qualities
【气壮如牛】fierce as a bull

迄 (qì) ❶up to; till ❷so far; all along
【迄今】up to now; so far; until now

弃 (qì) give up; throw away; discard; abandon
【弃儿】abandoned child; foundling
【弃旧图新】turn over a new leaf
【弃权】waive the right

汽 (qì) steam; vapour
【汽车】automobile; car: 公共~ bus
【汽车保险】auto (or motor vehicle) insur-

ance

【汽车排放】motor vehicle emission

【汽笛】horn; siren; whistle: 鸣～ sound a siren

【汽水】soda; soda water; soft drink

【汽艇】motorboat; steamboat

【汽油】petrol; gas; gasoline

泣 (qì) weep; sob

【泣不成声】choke with sobs

【泣诉】give a tearful account: 呜咽～ tell what has happened between sobs

契 (qì) contract; agreement: 默～ tacit agreement(or understanding)

【契合】agree with; correspond to

【契约】contract; agreement

砌 (qì) build by laying bricks or stones

【砌墙】build a wall (with bricks, stones, etc.)

器 (qì) ❶utensil; ware ❷organ ❸capacity

【器材】equipment

【器官】organ

【器官移植】organ transplant

【器量】open-mindedness; tolerance

【器皿】household utensils; containers esp. for use in the house

【器械】apparatus; instrument: 体育～ sports apparatus

【器重】have a high opinion of; think highly of

qia

掐 (qiā) ❶pinch; nip ❷clutch

【掐断】nip off; cut off

洽 (qià) ❶be in harmony ❷touch; arrange (or consult) with

【洽谈】consult with; talk over with

恰 (qià) ❶proper ❷just; exactly

【恰当】proper; appropriate

【恰到好处】just right

【恰巧】❶by chance; fortunately ❷happen to; chance to

【恰如其分】apt; appropriate; proper

qian

千 (qiān) ❶many ❷thousand

【千变万化】ever-changing

【千差万别】be different in thousands of ways

【千锤百炼】❶tempered and steeled; toughened ❷repeatedly refined

【千方百计】in a thousand and one ways; by every possible means

【千古】through the ages

【千回百转】full of twists and turns

【千家万户】countless families; every family

【千金】❶daughter ❷lots of money

【千钧一发】a hundredweight hanging by a hair

【千克】kilogram (or kg.)

【千里迢迢】from a thousand li away; from afar

【千里之行，始于足下】a thousand-li journey starts by taking the first step

【千米】kilometre (or km)

【千篇一律】stereotyped; following the same pattern

【千奇百怪】all sorts (kinds) of strange things; exceedingly strange

【千秋万代】for all ages; forever

【千瓦】kilowatt (or KW)

【千万】❶ten million; millions upon millions of ❷by all means ❸be sure

【千辛万苦】countless hardships; innumerable trials and tribulations

【千言万语】thousands and thousands of words

【千载难逢】❶once in a blue moon ❷very rare ❸occurring only once in a thousand years

【千真万确】absolutely true; really and truly

迁 (qiān) ❶ move; transfer; shift ❷change

【迁就】adapt oneself to; yield to

【迁移】move; migrate

牵 (qiān) ❶ pull; draw; lead by the hand; lead along ❷involve

【牵肠挂肚】feel deep anxiety; be very worried; be on tenterhooks

【牵扯】involve

【牵动】affect; influence: ~全局 have an impact on the overall situation

【牵挂】worry; care: 没有~carefree; free from care

【牵连】involve; tie up with; implicate

【牵强】forced; farfetched; unnatural

【牵涉】involve; concern; relate

【牵头】take the lead; be the first to do sth.

【牵线】❶ act as a go-between ❷ pull strings; control from behind the scenes

【牵线搭桥】act as a go-between (or middleman)

【牵引】pull; draw; drag; lead

铅 (qiān) lead

【铅笔】pencil

【铅笔刀】pencil-sharpener; pen-knife

【铅笔盒】pencil-case; pencil-box

【铅球】shot: 掷~put the shot

谦 (qiān) modest

【谦恭】modest and courteous

【谦和】modest and amiable: 为人~ be amiable towards people

【谦让】give way to others; modestly decline

【谦虚谨慎】modest and prudent

【谦逊】modest; unassuming

签 (qiān) ❶a slender pointed piece of bamboo: 牙~toothpick ❷label; tag: 书~bookmarker sign

【签到】sign in; register one's attendance at a meeting or at an office

【签发】sign and issue: ~文件 sign and issue a document

【签名】sign one's name; sign

【签收】sign after receiving sth.; sign to acknowledge the receipt of sth.

【签证】visa: 入境~entry visa; 出境~exit visa

【签字】sign; affix one's signature

【签字仪式】signing ceremony

前 (qián) ❶ front ❷ former ❸ first ❹ ago; before ❺forward; ahead

【前辈】the older generation

【前边】in the front; ahead

【前车之鉴】lessons drawn from others' mistakes

【前程】future

【前方】❶front; ahead ❷front lines

【前赴后继】advance wave upon wave

【前后】❶from beginning to end ❷about; around ❸in front and behind

【前几年】in the past years

【前进】advance; go (or march) forward

【前景】prospect; future

【前列】front rank; forefront

【前面】❶in the front; ahead; at the head

❷above ❸foregoing

【前年】the year before last

【前期】earlier stage; early days

【前人】forefathers; predecessors

【前任】predecessor

【前思后想】think over again and again

【前所未有】unprecedented; never existed before; hitherto unknown

【前台】❶front desk ❷stage

【前提】premise; prerequisite

【前天】the day before yesterday

【前途】future; prospect

【前往】go to; leave for; proceed to

【前线】front; frontline

【前言】preface; foreword; introduction

【前因后果】cause and effect

【前瞻性】foresight; far-sightedness

【前兆】omen; forewarning; premonition: 这次地震很突然,没有任何~。The earthquake was very sudden. There'd been no warning signs whatsoever.

【前者】the former

虔 (qián) pious; sincere

【虔诚】pious; devout

Q

【虔心】❶pious; sincere; devout: 一片~ a pious heart ❷ devout; sincere; pious; reverent: ~忏悔 repent sincerely

钱 (qián) money: 挣~make (or earn) money

【钱包】pocketbook; wallet; money-bag; purse

【钱币】coin

【钱财】money; wealth

钳 (qián) ❶pincers ❷grip

【钳子】pincers; pliers

乾 (qián)

【乾坤】heaven and earth; the universe

潜 (qián) ❶hide ❷hidden; latent ❸secretly; stealthily

【潜藏】hide; go into hiding

【潜规则】latent rule; unspoken rule; hidden rule; potential rule

【潜力】potential

【潜能】latent (or potential) energy

【潜入】slip (sneak) into; steal in

【潜水艇】submarine

【潜台词】❶unspoken words ❷implication

【潜逃】abscond; steal off; slip away; flee

【潜移默化】influence unknowingly

【潜意识】subconsciousness; the subconscious

【潜在】latent; potential

浅 (qiǎn) ❶ shallow ❷ simple; easy ❸ superficial ❹ not close; not intimate ❺light

【浅薄】shallow; superficial

【浅色】light color

【浅显】plain; easy

遣 (qiǎn) ❶send ❷dispel

【遣词造句】choice of words and building of sentences; wording and phrasing

【遣散】send away; dismiss

【遣送】send back; repatriate

谴 (qiǎn) condemn; denounce; censure

【谴责】condemn; denounce

欠 (qiàn) ❶ yawn ❷ owe ❸ short of; lacking in

【欠发达地区】underdeveloped (or less developed) region

【欠发达国家】underdeveloped (or less developed) country

【欠缺】❶ be lacking in; be short of ❷shortcoming

【欠条】bill of debt;IOU

【欠妥】improper;not proper

【欠债】be in debt;owe a debt

纤 (qiàn) a rope for towing a boat; towline

另见 1241 页 xiān

【纤夫】boat tracker

倩 (qiàn) beautiful; pretty; attractive; handsome

【倩影】(usu. of a woman) beautiful figure

堑 (qiàn) moat; ditch; chasm; trench that cuts off a road

【堑壕】trench;entrenchment

歉 (qiàn) ❶ apology: 道～ offer (or make) an apology ❷apologize ❸sorry ❹lean; poor

【歉收】have a poor harvest

【歉意】apology;regret

qiang

枪 (qiāng) gun; rifle; pistol: 机～machine gun;开～open fire

【枪击】shoot with a gun: 遭～身亡 be shot dead

【枪林弹雨】hail of bullets

【枪炮】arms;guns

【枪声】shot;report of a gun

【枪手】marksman;gunner

腔 (qiāng) ❶cavity ❷accent:南～北调 mixed accent ❸speech ❹tune

【腔调】❶tune ❷accent;intonation;tone

强 (qiáng) ❶strong; powerful ❷better than;more than

另见 1144 页 qiǎng

【强大】powerful;formidable

【强盗】robber;bandit

【强调】❶stress;emphasize ❷emphasis

【强度】intensity

【强化】strengthen;intensify;consolidate

【强化训练】intensive training

【强加于人】impose (one's views, etc.) on others

【强奸】rape;violate

【强健】strong and healthy

【强劲】powerful;forceful

【强力】❶ great force: ～夺取 seize by great force ❷ power of resistance; strength

【强烈】❶strong;intense;violent ❷strongly;violently

【强身】keep fit by physical exercise or taking tonics:～术 way to keep fit

【强盛】powerful and prosperous

【强项】strong point (or suit);advantage

【强行】by force

【强硬措施】firm measures

【强有力】strong;forceful;vigorous

【强者】the strong

【强制措施】coercive measures

【强壮】❶strong;sturdy;robust:～的体魄 of strong build; of robust construction ❷strengthen;build up

墙 (qiáng) wall:隔～有耳 walls have ears

【墙报】wall newspaper

【墙脚】❶the foot of a wall ❷base;foundation:挖～undermine the foundation of

【墙头草】❶grass at the top of a wall ❷ person who follows the crowd

【墙纸】wallpaper

蔷 (qiáng)

【蔷薇】rose

抢 (qiǎng) ❶ snatch ❷ rob ❸ vie for ❹rush

【抢答】vie to answer a question

【抢夺】grab;seize;take by force

Q

【抢饭碗】vie for a job; snatch another's job

【抢购】rush to purchase

【抢劫】rob; loot

【抢救】rescue; save

【抢时间】seize the hour; race against time

【抢收】rush to harvest

【抢手货】goods in great demand

【抢险】rush to deal with an emergency

【抢险救灾】rescue in emergency and disaster and give relief

【抢修】rush to repair

【抢眼】eye-catching; noticeable

强 (qiǎng) make an effort; force; compel

另见 1143 页 qiáng

【强辩】defend against reason

【强词夺理】reason fallaciously

【强记】strain to memorize

【强加于人】impose sth. on others

【强迫】force; compel

【强人所难】make one do what he does not want to

qiao

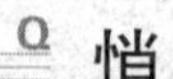

悄 (qiāo)

【悄悄】❶ quietly; stealthily; on the quiet ❷without being noticed

跷 (qiāo) ❶lift up; hold up ❷on tiptoe ❸stilts

【跷蹊】fishy; dubious

敲 (qiāo) knock; beat; sound; strike

【敲打】beat; strike; rap; tap; knock

【敲定】settle; decide finally; make a final decision

【敲警钟】sound the alarm; sound (or give) a warning

【敲锣打鼓】beat drums and strike gongs

【敲门】knock at the door

【敲诈】❶blackmail; extort ❷extortion

乔 (qiáo) ❶disguise ❷tall

【乔木】arbor; tree

【乔迁】❶move house ❷get a promotion

【乔迁之喜】congratulations on your new home

【乔装打扮】disguise oneself; masquerade

侨 (qiáo) person living abroad: 华～ overseas Chinese

【侨胞】countrymen residing abroad

【侨民】nationals living abroad

【侨务】affairs concerning nationals living abroad

桥 (qiáo) bridge

【桥墩】pier

【桥拱】bridge arch

【桥孔】bridge opening

【桥梁】bridge

【桥牌】bridge

翘 (qiáo) raise or lift up (one's head): ～首 raise or lift up one's head and look

另见 1145 页 qiào

【翘首以待】be on the tiptoe of expectation

憔 (qiáo)

【憔悴】wan and sallow; thin and pallid

瞧 (qiáo) look; see; glance at

【瞧不起】look down upon

【瞧得起】think highly of; value; prize

巧 (qiǎo) ❶happen (or chance) to ❷ clever; skillful; deft ❸cunning; artful: 花言～语 honeyed words ❹ by chance; coincidentally

【巧夺天工】wonderful workmanship (or superb craftsmanship) excelling nature

【巧合】coincidence

【巧计】clever device (or plan, trick)

【巧匠】clever artisan; skilled workman; crafts-man

【巧克力】chocolate

【巧妙】clever; skillful; ingenious; deft

【巧遇】❶chance encounter (or meeting) ❷meet by chance

俏 (qiào) ❶ pretty; smart-looking; handsome ❷sell well; be in great demand

【俏丽】pretty

【俏皮】witty

峭 (qiào) steep

【峭壁】cliff; steep

窍 (qiào) key: 诀~knack

【窍门】key; knack

翘 (qiào) stick (or stand) up in one end; cock

另见 1144 页 qiáo

【翘尾巴】be cocky

qie

切 (qiē) ❶cut; slice ❷tangency

另见本页 qiè

【切除】excise; resect

【切磋】exchange experiences; compare notes; learn from each other by exchanging views

【切片】❶section ❷slice; cut into slices

【切入点】penetration (or break through) point

【切碎】cut up

【切削】cut; cutting

茄 (qié) eggplant; aborigine

【茄子】eggplant; aborigine

且 (qiě) ❶even ❷both...and...

【且慢】wait a moment; not so soon; not so fast

切 (qiè) ❶match; suit; fit in with; correspond to ❷ be sure to ❸ eager; anxious ❹faithfully

另见本页 qiē

【切肤之痛】pain of cutting one's body; a deep sorrow; an acute pain

【切合实际】in agreement with the reality; fit in with the reality; be practical

【切记】be sure to keep in mind; always remember

【切忌】avoid earnestly; be sure to keep away from; avoid by all means

【切身利益】immediate (or personal) interests

【切身体会】personal experiences

【切实】❶ practical; realistic ❷ earnestly; seriously; faithfully

【切题】keep to the point; stick to the topic

【切中要害】❶to the point ❷strike home

怯 (qiè) timid; cowardly; nervous; fearful

【怯场】have stage fright

【怯弱】faint-hearted; timid and weak-willed

窃 (qiè) ❶steal: 盗~steal ❷secretly

【窃取】steal; usurp; grab

【窃听】eavesdrop; bug; tap

【窃贼】thief; burglar

惬 (qiè) be satisfied

【惬意】be pleased; be satisfied

qin

钦 (qīn) ❶ admire; respect ❷ by the emperor himself

【钦慕】admire and respect; hold in esteem

【钦佩】admire; esteem

侵 (qīn) invade; intrude into (or upon)

【侵犯】intrude; invade; violate; infringe

【侵害】invade and damage; encroach on

【侵略】invade

【侵权】tort; infringement

【侵入】invade; intrude into; make incursions into

【侵蚀】corrode; erode

【侵占】invade and occupy; seize

亲 (qīn) ❶ parent ❷ marriage ❸ blood relation ❹ relative ❺ bride ❻ kiss ❼ close; dear; intimate ❽ personally

【亲爱】dear; beloved

【亲笔】❶ in one's own handwriting ❷ one's own handwriting

【亲骨肉】one's own flesh and blood (i. e. parents and children, brothers and sisters)

Q

【亲近】be close to; be on intimate terms with

【亲口】say sth. personally

【亲密】close; intimate

【亲戚】relative

【亲切】warmhearted; cordial

【亲情】affection between family members; emotional attachment among family members

【亲人】one's family members; kin; kinsfolk

【亲如一家】as dear as one's family

【亲善大使】goodwill ambassador

【亲身】personally; in person

【亲生】one's own (children, parents)

【亲事】marriage

【亲手】with one's own hands; personally; oneself

【亲属】kin; kinsfolk; relatives

【亲吻】kiss

【亲兄弟】blood brother

【亲眼】with one's own eyes

【亲友】relatives and friends; kith and kin

【亲子鉴定】paternity test; child identification

【亲缘】affinity; blood relations

【亲自】❶personally; in person ❷oneself

芹 (qín)

【芹菜】celery: 药～ medicinal celery

琴 (qín) musical instrument: 胡～ fiddle; 钢～piano

【琴键】key

【琴棋书画】lute-playing, chess, calligraphy, and painting—accomplishments of a scholar of the old school

【琴弦】string (of a musical instrument)

禽 (qín) birds; fowls: 家～ domestic fowls; poultry

【禽流感】bird flu; avian flu

【禽兽】birds and beasts: 衣冠～ beast in human clothing

勤 (qín) ❶duty; attendance: 值～be on duty ❷ hardworking; diligent ❸ frequently; often

【勤奋】diligent; hardworking; industrious

【勤工俭学】part-work and part-study system

【勤俭持家】be industrious and thrifty in running a household

【勤恳】diligent and conscientious

【勤劳】diligent; hardworking; industrious

【勤勉】diligent

【勤杂】odd-job

【勤政廉洁】diligent administration and clean government

擒 (qín) catch; seize; capture

【擒获】catch; capture; arrest: ～歹徒 capture a scoundrel

【擒拿】catch; arrest

寝 (qǐn) ❶bedroom ❷sleep: 就～go to bed (or sleep); 废～忘食 forget to eat and sleep

【寝具】bedding

【寝室】bedroom; dormitory

沁 (qìn) ❶ooze; seep; exude ❷let one's head droop downward; hang ❸ put sth. into water

【沁人心脾】gladdening the heart and refreshing the mind; mentally refreshing; refreshing

【沁润】(of liquid, aroma, etc.) soak into; permeate through; penetrate to

qing

青 (qīng) ❶ blue; green ❷ black ❸young

【青菜】greens; green vegetables

【青出于蓝而胜于蓝】the pupil who learns from the master outdoes the master

【青春】youth; youthfulness

【青春痘】pimple

【青春期】youth; adolescence; puberty

【青黄不接】green and yellow have not joined; a new crop has not yet come

【青睐】favour: 受到～be in one's good graces (or favour); be in favour with

【青霉素】penicillin

【青年】youth; young people

【青年节】Youth Day

【青山绿水】blue mountains and green waters—beautiful scenery

【青少年】teenagers; young boys and girls; youngsters

【青少年犯罪】juvenile delinquency

【青蛙】frog

轻 (qīng) ❶make light of; belittle; take lightly ❷light ❸young ❹not serious (or important) ❺ easy; relaxed ❻ gently; softly; lightly

【轻便】light; portable

【轻薄】frivolous; flirtatious: 态度～ frivolous attitude

【轻而易举】easy to do (or accomplish)

【轻放】put down gently

【轻浮】light-minded; not serious; frivolous

【轻工业】light industry

【轻轨】light rail

【轻快】❶brisk; smart; lively ❷lighthearted

【轻慢】treat sb. without proper respect; slight: ～失礼 act impolitely by slighting sb.

【轻描淡写】mention casually

【轻蔑】scorn

【轻柔】soft; gentle

【轻伤】slight wound; flesh wound

【轻视】look down upon; despise; scorn; make light of; underestimate

【轻率】❶ rash; hasty; reckless ❷ rashly; recklessly

【轻松】light; relaxed

【轻微】slightly

【轻信】be credulous; readily believe

【轻易】❶easily; readily ❷lightly; rashly

【轻音乐】light music

【轻盈】quick and graceful in movement

【轻重】❶ weight ❷ seriousness; importance ❸propriety

【轻重缓急】order of priority (or importance and urgency)

【轻装】with light packs

氢 (qīng) hydrogen

【氢弹】hydrogen bomb; H-bomb

【氢气球】hydrogen balloon

倾 (qīng) ❶deviation; tendency ❷lean; incline ❸pour out; empty ❹collapse ❺do one's utmost (or best); do all one can

【倾巢出动】turn out in full force (or strength)

【倾倒】❶topple; fall; collapse ❷pour out; dump; empty

【倾家荡产】lose all family fortunes

【倾力】go all out; do one's utmost

【倾慕】adore

【倾盆大雨】❶heavy downpour ❷rain cats and dogs

【倾诉衷肠】pour out one's heart, reveal one's innermost feelings

【倾听】listen carefully to; lend an attentive ear to

【倾向】❶tendency; trend ❷tend to; be inclined to

【倾销】dump; sell goods at a very low price

【倾斜】❶tilt; incline; slope; slant; lean ❷be preferential (or favorable; partial)

【倾心】❶admire; fall in love with ❷sincere; heart-to-heart

清 (qīng) ❶settle; clear up ❷count; check ❸distinct ❹clean; clear; pure ❺quiet ❻just and honest ❼completely

【清白】clean; pure; innocent; unblemished; unsullied; sinless; clean-handed; blameless: 历史~have a clean record

【清查】❶check ❷uncover; comb out

【清晨】early morning

【清除】clear away (or out); clear; get rid of; remove

【清楚】❶clear; plain; distinct ❷be clear about; understand ❸clear-headed

【清纯】❶pretty and pure: ~秀丽 pretty and innocent ❷fresh and pure: 泉水~ fresh spring water

【清单】detailed list; list of items; checklist; stock list; bill; databook; muster: 开~ make an inventory

【清淡】❶light; weak; delicate ❷not greasy or strongly flavored; light ~的食物 light food

【清点】check; make an inventory of; sort through and check: ~物资 make an inventory of materials

【清风】cool breeze

【清高】❶noble-minded and aloof ❷stand aloof

【清还】clean up and pay off; discharge (a debt)

【清洁】clean

【清净】❶peace and quiet: 图~seek peace and quiet ❷quiet and peaceful

【清冷】❶chilly: ~的秋夜 chilly autumn night ❷desolate ❸deserted; empty

【清理】put in order; sort out

【清廉】honest and upright

【清凉】cool and refreshing

【清亮】clear and sonorous; resonant; ringing: 嗓音~ have a resonant voice

【清明节】Qingming Festival; Tomb-sweeping Day

【清贫】poor

【清爽】❶cool and fresh ❷relaxed; relieved

【清水衙门】place of little funds and material benefits

【清晰】distinct;clear-cut;clear

【清洗】❶purge; comb out ❷wash; clean; launder; rinse

【清闲】❶leisurely; at leisure ❷idle; free

【清香】delicate fragrance; refreshing fragrance

【清新】pure and fresh

【清醒】❶clear-headed:头脑～clear-headed; cool-minded ❷regain (or recover) consciousness; come to (or round)

【清秀】delicate and pretty; handsome

【清一色】all of the same color; uniform

【清幽】secluded and beautiful

【清真】Islamic; Muslim

【清正】honest and upright:为官～ be an honest and upright official

【清正廉洁】be honest and clean

蜻 (qīng)

【蜻蜓】dragonfly

【蜻蜓点水】❶touch lightly ❷in a skimming manner

情 (qíng) ❶ feeling; emotion; sentiment:热～enthusiasm ❷love; affection ❸kindness; favour:求～ask for a favour ❹ condition; situation:病～ patient's condition

【情爱】❶(esp. between a man and a woman) love; affection ❷caring love

【情报】information; intelligence

【情操】sentiment

【情场】arena of love; love affair; love relationship:～失意 be frustrated in love; be a failure in love

【情敌】rival in a love triangle

【情调】❶sentiment ❷emotional appeal

【情窦初开】(of a young girl) first awakening (or dawning) of love

【情感】emotion; feeling

【情感教育】affective education

【情感需要】emotional need

【情歌】love song

【情怀】emotions; sentiments; feelings:抒发～ express one's feelings and thoughts

【情急智生】hit on an idea in a moment of desperation

【情节】❶plot; story ❷circumstances

【情结】 emotional ties; complex; love knot:浓重的思乡～ strong nostalgia

【情景】scene; sight; circumstances

【情况】things; condition; way; case; situation; state of affairs

【情理】reason; sense:合乎～be reasonable

【情侣】sweethearts; lovers

【情侣表】his-and-hers watches

【情面】feelings:留～spare one's feelings 不顾～ have no consideration for sb.'s feelings

【情趣】❶temperament ❷interest; appeal; delight

【情人】sweetheart; lover

【情人节】Valentine's Day; lover's day

【情商】emotion quotient (EQ)

【情书】love letter

【情丝】affection; tender feelings:～万缕 a wealth of tender love

【情态】spirit; mood

【情同手足】like brothers; with brotherly love for each other

【情投意合】agree in opinion; be closely allied in opinion and feelings; be (work) hand in glove with

【情网】love net (or snare):坠入～ fall in love; be caught in the snares of love

【情文并茂】(of writing) excellent in both content and language

【情形】state of affairs; condition; situation

【情谊】friendly feelings; friendly sentiments

【情意】tender regards; affection; goodwill: 深厚的～ deep friendship

【情有可原】pardonable; excusable

【情愿】❶ be willing to ❷ prefer; would rather

【情致】interest; taste: 别有～ of special appeal

晴（qíng）fine; clear

【晴空万里】a clear and boundless sky; the vast clear skies

【晴朗】fine; sunny; clear; bright

【晴天霹雳】a bolt from the blue sky

擎（qíng）prop (or hold, lift) up

【擎天柱】a man in a responsible position; mainstay

顷（qǐng）❶hectare ❷moment

【顷刻】in an instant; instantly; in a moment (or while) ～瓦解 collapse instantly

请（qǐng）❶ ask; beg ❷ please ❸ invite; engage

【请安】pay respects to; wish sb. good health

【请便】do as you wish; please yourself

【请功】ask a superior to record a merit for sb.

【请假】ask for leave

【请柬】invitation card

【请教】ask for advice; consult

【请客】stand treat; entertain guests; give a dinner party; invite sb. to dinner

【请求】ask for; pray; beg

【请示】ask for instructions

庆（qìng）❶ celebration ❷ celebrate; congratulate

【庆典】celebration

【庆幸】rejoice

【庆祝】❶celebrate ❷celebration

qiong

穷（qióng）❶limit; end: 无～无尽 endless ❷ poor; poverty-stricken ❸ extremely; thoroughly

【穷光蛋】pauper; poor wretch

【穷家富路】one should be frugal at home but well equipped for a journey

【穷尽】limit; end

【穷困】poverty-stricken; poor

【穷年累月】for years on end; year after year

【穷人】the poor; poor people

【穷日子】days of poverty

【穷途末路】have no way out; come to a dead end; be in an impasse

【穷乡僻壤】a remote and barren place

【穷则思变】poverty gives rise to a desire for change

琼（qióng）fine jade

【琼浆】good wine

qiu

丘（qiū）❶mound; hillock; hill ❷grave

【丘陵】hills

【丘疹】papule; pimple

秋（qiū）❶ autumn; fall ❷ year ❸ time; period

【秋高气爽】the autumn sky is clear and the air is bracing (a set phrase for describing fine autumn weather)

【秋耕】autumn ploughing

【秋毫之末】the tip of an autumn hair a minute, almost indiscernible particle

【秋季】(英)autumn;(美)fall
【秋千】swing: 打 ~have a swing; go on a swing
【秋色】autumn scenery
【秋收】autumn harvest
【秋游】autumn outing
【秋装】autumn clothes (or dress)

蚯 (qiū)

【蚯蚓】earthworm

囚 (qiú) ❶ prisoner; captive ❷ imprison; shut up

【囚犯】prisoner; captive; convict
【囚禁】imprison; put in jail; shut up; throw into jail
【囚牢】jail; prison

求 (qiú) ❶ demand: 供不应~ supply falls short of demand ❷ ask; beg ❸ seek; look for; pursue: 实事~是 seek truth from facts

【求才】seek (or look for, woo) talents
【求和】sue for peace
【求婚】propose
【求见】ask to see; ask for an interview
【求教】ask for advice: 登门~ call on sb. for advice
【求解】find the solution (of a mathematical problem); solve a problem
【求救】cry (or ask) for help
【求饶】beg for mercy; ask for pardon
【求人】ask sb. for help; seek help from others
【求生】seek to live on; seek to survive
【求实】be realistic (or practical minded)
【求实精神】realistic (or matter-of-fact, down-to-earth) attitude
【求索】explore; seek; grope for; search for
【求学】pursue one's studies; seek knowledge; go to school
【求真务实】seek truth and be realistic
【求证】seek to prove; seek evidence or verification
【求知欲】thirst for knowledge
【求职】look (or hunt, apply) for a job
【求治】seek medical treatment
【求助】turn (or look) to sb. for help; seek help

球 (qiú) ❶ sphere; globe ❷ ball: 传~ pass a ball; 篮~ basketball; 排~ volleyball; 足~ football; 高尔夫~ golf; 保龄~ bowling ❸ globe; sphere

【球场】court; field
【球队】team
【球门】goal
【球迷】(ball game) fan: 足~ football fan
【球拍】racket; bat
【球赛】ball game; match
【球网】net (for ball games)
【球鞋】tennis shoes; sneakers
【球星】ball-game star
【球形】❶ round; spherical ❷ sphere

qu

区 (qū) ❶ area; district; region; division: 商业~shopping (or business) area ❷ divide; distinguish

【区别】❶ distinguish; tell apart (or from) ❷ difference
【区间】interval
【区域】area; region; district
【区域合作】inter-regional cooperation

曲 (qū) ❶ curve ❷ yeast ❸ wrong; injustice ❹ bend ❺ wrong ❻ crooked; bent; curved; twisted

【曲棍球】❶ hockey ❷ hockey ball
【曲解】twist; distort; misinterpret
【曲径通幽】a winding path leads to quiet seclusion

【曲奇】cookie

【曲线】curve

【曲折】❶tortuous; winding; zigzag ❷complicated ❸complications

驱 (qū) ❶drive; run ❷expel; dismiss; run: 并驾齐~ run neck and neck; 长~直入 drive straight in (or into)

【驱车】drive a vehicle

【驱除】drive out (or away); get rid of

【驱赶】drive away

【驱使】❶drive; urge; spur; cause ❷order about (or around)

【驱逐】drive out; expel; banish

屈 (qū) ❶ wrong; injustice ❷ bend; bow; curve ❸yield; submit: 宁死不~ would rather die than yield ❹wrong; unjustifiable

【屈从】submit to; yield to; knuckle under to

【屈服】give in; yield to; bow to; submit to

【屈辱】insult; disgrace; humiliation

【屈指可数】can be counted (or numbered) on one's fingers—very few

祛 (qū) dispel; remove; drive away

【祛除】dispel; get rid of; drive out

【祛暑】drive away summer heat

【祛痰】make expectoration easy

躯 (qū) the human body: 捐~lay down one's life

【躯干】trunk

【躯体】body

趋 (qū) ❶tend ❷hasten; hurry

【趋势】trend; tendency

【趋向】❶ trend; tendency ❷ tend (or incline) to

渠 (qú) channel; canal; ditch

【渠道】ditch; canal; channel

曲 (qǔ) ❶song; melody; tune ❷music: 作~ compose (or write) music: 进行~ march

【曲调】tune; melody

【曲目】items of song or performance; repertoire

【曲子】melody; tune; song

取 (qǔ) ❶take; get; fetch ❷look for; seek ❸adopt; choose

【取材】draw materials

【取长补短】learn from others' strong points to make up for one's own weaknesses

【取代】replace; take the place of

【取得】get; gain; obtain; achieve; acquire

【取而代之】replace sb.; supersede sb.

【取经】learn from others' experience

【取决于】depend on; be up to; be decided by

【取款】draw money

【取款机】cashomat: 自动~ autonomous teller machine (ATM)

【取名】name; give (or take) a name

【取暖】warm oneself (by a fire, etc.)

【取暖器】heater; warmer

【取舍】make one's choice

【取胜】win victory; win success

【取消】cancel; call off; abolish

【取笑】ridicule; make fun of

【取信于民】win the public's confidence (or trust)

【取悦】try to please; ingratiate oneself with sb.

娶 (qǔ) marry (a woman); take to wife

【娶亲】(of a man) get married

龋 (qǔ)

【龋齿】❶dental caries ❷decayed tooth

去 (qù) ❶go; leave for: 你~过欧洲吗? Have you ever been to Europe? ❷ remove; get rid of; cancel

【去火】reduce internal heat; relieve inflammation or fever

【去掉】get rid of; remove; cancel

【去路】outlet; way

【去年】last year

【去世】die; pass away

【去向】❶whereabouts; direction ❷the direction in which sb. or sth. has gone

趣 (qù) interest; delight: 有~ interesting

【趣事】amusement; fun; joke; funny thing: 逸闻~ anecdotes; episodes; jokes

【趣味】interest; taste: 低级~ vulgar taste

【趣闻】interesting story; interesting news

quan

圈 (quān) ❶circle; ring ❷enclose; encircle ❸draw a circle

另见 1065 页 juàn

【圈掉】cancel (or cross out) with a circle

【圈定】circle the name of someone as one's choice

【圈内人士】insider

【圈套】trap: 设~ lay a trap

【圈外人士】outsider

【圈子】circle; ring

权 (quán) ❶right: 公民~ civil right; 选举~ right to vote ❷ authority; power: 当~ in power ❸ advantageous position

【权贵】influential officials; bigwigs

【权衡】balance; weigh

【权力】power; authority

【权利】right

【权威】❶ authority; authoritativeness ❷ a person of authority; authority

【权限】limits of authority (or power)

【权宜之计】an expedient measure; makeshift (device); stopgap

【权益】rights and interests

全 (quán) ❶complete; make perfect ❷ full; whole; entire; total ❸completely; entirely

【全部】❶all; total; complete; ❷whole; entire ❸ totally; wholly; entirely; completely

【全称】full name; unabbreviated form

【全程】whole course (or journey)

【全方位】all-inclusive; comprehensive; overall

【全国】the whole (or entire) nation (or country); nationwide; countrywide; throughout the country

【全国人民代表大会】the National People's Congress (NPC)

【全家福】family photo (or picture)

【全景】panorama

【全局】the overall situation

【全局利益】overall interest

【全军】the whole (or entire) army

【全力以赴】go all out

【全力支持】give all-out support

【全貌】a full view; complete picture

【全面】full-scale; overall; all-round; comprehensive

【全面发展】all-round (or overall) development

【全面改革】comprehensive reform

【全民教育】education for the entire people

【全能】all-round

【全能冠军】an all-round champion

【全年】❶the whole year ❷annual; yearly

【全盘】overall; comprehensive

【全盘否定】totally repudiate
【全球】❶all over the world; the world over ❷the whole world
【全球变暖】global warming
【全球化】globalize
【全球经济】global economy
【全球通】global system for mobile communications (GSM)
【全球战略】global strategy
【全日制】full-time; full-day
【全日制教育】full-time schooling
【全神贯注】concentrate; be absorbed in; apply the whole mind to
【全胜】❶ complete victory ❷ win every match; be all-victorious
【全世界】❶the whole world ❷all over the world; the world over
【全体】all; whole; entire; total
【全脱产】be fully off duty; be fully released from work
【全文】full text
【全心全意】whole-heartedly; heart and soul
【全新包装】wrap in a completely new package
Q
【全休】be off duty completely; be on full sick leave
【全员】all members; the whole personnel (or staff)
【全责】all responsibility
【全职】full-time job
【全职妈妈】stay-at-home mom; full-time mother
【全自动】❶full automatic ❷full automation

泉 (quán) spring: 喷~fountain; 温~hot spring
【泉水】spring; spring water
【泉源】❶ springhead ❷ source (of wisdom, strength, etc.)

拳 (quán) ❶fist ❷boxing
【拳击】boxing
【拳术】Chinese boxing
【拳头】fist

痊 (quán) recover from an illness
【痊愈】fully recover from an illness; be fully recovered

蜷 (quán) curl (or huddle) up
【蜷伏】curl (or huddle) up
【蜷缩】roll up; curl up

颧 (quán)
【颧骨】cheekbone

犬 (quǎn) dog: 猎~hunting dog; 警~police dog; 效~马之劳 serve faithfully

劝 (quàn) ❶ advise; persuade; convince; try to persuade ❷encourage
【劝导】induce; talk sb. round
【劝和】try to persuade two parties to become reconciled; mediate
【劝架】try to reconcile parties to a quarrel or to stop people from fighting each other; mediate
【劝解】try to persuade sb. out of worrying; make peace between
【劝勉】admonish and encourage: 互相~encourage each other
【劝说】persuade; convince

券 (quàn) ticket; coupon: 国库~ treasury bond; 公债~ government bond; 入场~admission ticket
【券商】broker; securities trader (or dealer; broker)

que

缺 (quē) lack; be lacking in; be short of

【缺德】mean; wicked

【缺点】shortcoming

【缺乏】lack; be lacking in; be short of

【缺乏活力】lack vitality

【缺货】be in short supply; be out of stock

【缺课】miss a class (or lesson); be absent from school

【缺口】gap; shortage

【缺勤】be absent from duty (or work)

【缺少】lack; be short of

【缺席】be absent

【缺陷】defect; flaw; weak point

瘸 (qué) limp; be lame

【瘸腿】lame

【瘸子】lame person

却 (què) ❶ fall (or draw, go, get) back; go backwards; retreat; withdraw ❷ refuse; decline ❸ drive back ❹ but; yet

【却步】step (or hang) back

雀 (què) sparrow

【雀跃】jump with joy

确 (què) ❶true; real; correct ❷firmly; really

【确保】ensure; guarantee

【确定】❶ fix; determine; decide on ❷ certain; definite

【确立】establish; build up; set up

【确切】definite; accurate; precise; exact

【确认】affirm; confirm

【确实】❶ true; real; certain ❷ really; indeed; exactly; surely

【确信】firmly believe; be deeply convinced; be sure (or certain)

【确诊】make a definite diagnosis; diagnose

【确证】❶ prove conclusively or positively ❷ proof positive; conclusive or irrefutable evidence

qun

裙 (qún) skirt: 围～apron

【裙带】❶belt (as a decoration for a skirt or dress) ❷connected through one's female relatives

【裙裤】culottes

【裙子】skirt

群 (qún) ❶crowd; group ❷herd; flock; group ❸collective

【群策群力】pool the wisdom and efforts of the masses

【群芳】❶beautiful and fragrant flowers ❷ a group of beauties or artists

【群峰】connected mountain peaks

【群集】get together; assemble; mass; congregate; throng; troop together; swarm

【群龙无首】a host of dragons without a head—a group without a leader

【群体】group

【群体行为】group (or mass) behaviour

【群体意识】group consciousness (or awareness)

【群众】the masses

【群众监督】supervision by the masses

【群租客】tenant groups

R r

ran

然 (rán) ❶right;correct ❷so;like that ❸but;nevertheless

【然而】yet; but; however; though; while; nevertheless

【然后】afterwards;then;after that

燃 (rán) burn;light

【燃料】fuel

【燃煤】fuel coal

【燃眉之急】pressing need;matter of great urgency

【燃烧】burn

冉 (rǎn)slowly

【冉冉】❶(of hair, twigs, etc.) hang down softly ❷slowly;gradually ～上升 rise slowly

染 (rǎn) ❶dye ❷be affected by; acquire

【染发】dye the hair

【染色】dyeing;coloring

rang

嚷 (rāng) shout;yell
另见本页 rǎng

嚷 (rǎng) ❶shout; yell; make an uproar ❷make widely known
另见本页 rāng

【嚷叫】shout;yell;make an uproar

壤 (rǎng) ❶soil ❷earth ❸area

让 (ràng) ❶give in (or up); give way (or ground) ❷invite;offer ❸let; allow

【让步】yield; give ground (or way); give in;back down;make a concession

【让价】price concession

【让开】make way (or room); get out of the way;step aside

【让利】reduce (or cut) price

【让路】make way (or room) for;give way

【让座】❶offer one's seat to sb. ❷invite a guest to get seated

rao

饶 (ráo) ❶forgive; pardon; show mercy: 求～ beg for mercy; ask pardon ❷rich;plentiful

【饶命】spare one's life

【饶恕】forgive; pardon; spare sb. punishment

扰 (rǎo) trouble

【扰乱】cause confusion;cause trouble

绕 (rào) ❶wind; coil ❷circle; move around ❸bypass; take a roundabout way;go round

【绕道】take a roundabout way; go by a roundabout way
【绕口令】tongue twister
【绕圈子】circle; go round and round; beat around the bush
【绕行】❶make a detour; bypass ❷move round; circle

re

惹 (rě) ❶invite; ask for ❷offend ❸attract; cause
【惹祸】court disaster; stir up trouble
【惹麻烦】ask for (or invite) trouble
【惹是生非】stir up (or cause) trouble

热 (rè) ❶fever: 发～have a fever (or temperature) ❷strong interest; rush; craze ❸heat; warm up ❹hot; warm ❺ardent ❻popular ❼envious
【热爱】have deep love for; love
【热播剧】hot TV serials (or dramas)
【热潮】upsurge
【热忱】zeal; enthusiasm: 满腔～ full of enthusiasm
【热带】the tropics; the torrid zone
【热岛效应】tropical island effect
【热点问题】a hot issue
【热狗】hot dog; sausage roll; red-hot
【热火朝天】buzzing (or bustling) with activity; in full swing
【热浪】heat (or hot) wave
【热泪盈眶】eyes brimming with tears
【热恋】be passionately in love
【热烈】enthusiastic; warm; ardent; heated
【热流】❶thermal current ❷warm current
【热门话题】a topical subject
【热闹】❶lively ❷have a jolly time
【热气球】hot air (or fire) balloon
【热切】❶fervent; eager ❷eagerly
【热情】❶enthusiasm; zeal; warmth ❷enthusiastic; warmhearted ❸warmly
【热情洋溢】full of enthusiasm; glowing (or filled) with enthusiasm
【热身】warm-up
【热水瓶】thermos flask (or bottle); thermos
【热水器】water heater
【热线电话】hot line
【热销】sell well; be in great demand
【热心】enthusiastic; warmhearted
【热胀冷缩】expand with heat and contract with cold
【热衷】❶long (or crave) for ❷be keen on

ren

人 (rén) ❶human being; man; person; people: 成年～ adult; grown-up ❷others; other people ❸personality; character ❹everybody
【人才】❶a talented (or trained) person; qualified personnel ❷handsome appearance
【人才储备】personnel (or talent) reserve
【人才短缺】shortage of qualified personnel (or talent)
【人才交流】exchange of talent (or qualified people)
【人才竞争】talent competition; headhunt
【人才流动】mobility of trained personnel; flow of competent people (or talent)
【人才培养】talent (or personnel) training
【人才外流】brain drain
【人才需求】demand for talent (or qualified people)
【人才引进】talent (or qualified people) introduction
【人才招聘】personnel recruitment
【人才中心】centre for talent (or qualified people) exchange

【人潮】stream of people; large crowds
【人次】person-time
【人大】(人民代表大会的简称) the National People's Congress
【人道主义】humanitarianism
【人地生疏】be unfamiliar with the place and the people; be a complete stranger
【人丁兴旺】have a growing family; have a flourishing population
【人贩子】people trafficker; trader in human beings
【人非木石】man is not made of wood or stone—man is not feelingless
【人格】personality; character
【人格高尚】have a noble character
【人工】❶ man-made ❷ manual work ❸ manpower; ❹man-day
【人工成本】labor cost
【人工处理】human treatment
【人工呼吸】artificial respiration
【人工智能】artificial intelligence (or AI)
【人际沟通】human (or interpersonal) communication
【人际关系】social intercourses; human relations; interpersonal relationship
【人迹罕至】without human trace; uninhabited; untraversed
R
【人杰地灵】the greatness of a man lends glory to a place
【人尽其才】let everyone bring his ability into full play; make the best possible use of men
【人均】per capita
【人均国内生产总值】per capita gross domestic product (or per capita GDP)
【人均可支配收入】per capita dispensable income
【人均收入】per capita income
【人均消费】per capita consumption
【人口】population
【人口调查】population survey
【人口过剩】over population
【人口老龄化】aging of population; population aging
【人口普查】population census
【人口素质】population quality
【人口压力】population pressure
【人类】mankind; man
【人类基因组】human genome; human genome map
【人类居住环境】human living environment
【人力资源】human resource (HR)
【人脉】social network
【人面桃花】a charming face among peach blossoms
【人民】people
【人民币汇率】China yuan (or RMB) exchange rate
【人民公仆】people's public servant
【人命关天】a case involving human life is one of supreme importance
【人品】personal character; moral quality
【人气】popularity; popular enthusiasm
【人情】❶feelings ❷favour: 做~ do sb. a favour ❸gift; present
【人情冷暖】social snobbery
【人穷志不短】poor but proud; poor but ambitious
【人权】human right
【人群】crowd
【人人自危】everyone finds himself in danger; everyone feels insecure
【人山人海】large crowds of people
【人身安全】personal (or life) safety
【人生】life
【人生观】outlook on life
【人生价值】value of life

【人世】this world; the world
【人世沧桑】tremendous changes in this world of ours
【人事】❶ personnel matters ❷ consciousness: 不醒~ lose consciousness
【人事管理】personnel management
【人手】manpower
【人寿保险】life insurance
【人体】human body: ~模型 manikin
【人体彩绘】human body painting
【人微言轻】the words of the lowly carry little weight
【人为】artificial; man-made
【人为污染】man-made pollution
【人为因素】human factor
【人文关怀】humanistic care (or concern)
【人文环境】humanistic environment
【人文景观】cultural scenery (or landscape)
【人物】personage; figure
【人像】portrait; image
【人心惶惶】popular anxiety
【人心所向】popular sentiment; the feelings of the people
【人行道】pavement; sidewalk
【人行横道】zebra crossing; pedestrian crosswalk
【人性】human nature; humanity
【人性化管理】human-based management
【人员】personnel; staff
【人员素质】personnel quality
【人云亦云】repeat word for word what others say; echo the views of others; follow another's lead in voicing opinions
【人缘】relations with others; popularity
【人造】man-made; artificial
【人造卫星】man-made satellite
【人证】testimony of a witness
【人之常情】what is natural and normal (in human relationships)
【人质】hostage
【人种】ethnic group; the human species; race

仁 (rén) ❶ kindheartedness; benevolence; humanity ❷ kernel

【仁爱】kindheartedness; benevolence
【仁慈】kind; benevolent; merciful
【仁厚】kind-hearted and tolerant: ~待人 treat people with generosity
【仁义】amiable; kind; reasonable
【仁义道德】humanity, justice and virtue; virtue and morality
【仁至义尽】show extreme goodwill

忍 (rěn) ❶ endure; bear; forbear; tolerate ❷ be hardhearted enough to

【忍不住】unable to bear; can't help (or avoid, refrain from)
【忍俊不禁】cannot help laughing
【忍耐】endure; bear; tolerate
【忍让】❶ forbear ❷ forbearance; be forbearing and conciliatory: 互相~ be mutually accommodating
【忍受】bear; endure; tolerate; put up with
【忍痛割爱】part reluctantly with what one treasures
【忍无可忍】past all bearing; beyond endurance
【忍心】be hardhearted enough to; have the heart to
【忍住】repress; refrain; control

认 (rèn) ❶ know; recognize ❷ admit; acknowledge; own

【认出】recognize; make out; identify
【认错】admit one's mistake (or fault); acknowledge a mistake
【认定】hold; be deeply convinced; firmly believe
【认可】approve; confirm; accept

【认领】❶claim ❷adopt
【认清】see clearly; make out; clearly understand
【认识】❶know; recognize; understand; get to know ❷knowledge; understanding
【认输】admit defeat; throw in the towel
【认同】agree; identify with; approve of; recognize
【认为】believe; consider; regard; think; feel
【认养】undertake the responsibility of raising
【认账】admit what one has said or done; acknowledge a debt
【认真】❶serious; earnest ❷take seriously; take to heart
【认字】learn to read
【认罪】admit one's guilt

任 (rèn) ❶post; office: 上～ take office ❷appoint ❸take up; work as ❹let; allow ❺undertake; bear
【任何】whatever
【任何人】anybody; anyone
【任何事物】anything
【任教】take up teaching; teach; be a teacher
【任劳任怨】work hard and be upset by no complaints
【任免】appoint and dismiss
【任命书】commission; letter of appointment; term of office
【任凭】❶at one's convenience ❷as one likes ❸be up to despite; no matter (what, how, etc.)
【任期】term of office; a tour of duty
【任人唯贤】appoint people on their merits
【任务】task; mission
【任性】wilful; self-willed
【任意】❶wilfully; at will ❷wanton; arbitrary; willful
【任用】appoint; assign sb. to a post
【任重道远】the burden is heavy and the road is long—shoulder (or take, bear) heavy responsibilities

韧 (rèn) pliable but strong; tenacious; tough
【韧带】ligament
【韧性】toughness; tenacity

妊 (rèn) be pregnant
【妊娠】gestation; pregnancy

reng

扔 (rēng) ❶throw; cast; toss; fling ❷throw away (or out)
【扔掉】throw off (or away, out)
【扔下】drop; abandon

仍 (réng) still; yet
【仍旧】❶remain the same ❷still; yet
【仍然】❶still; yet ❷all (or just) the same

ri

日 (rì) ❶sun ❷day; daytime: 生～ birthday ❸daily; every day; with each passing day ❹time
【日报】daily paper; daily
【日常】day-to-day; daily; everyday
【日常开支】daily expense
【日程】schedule; timetable
【日出】sunrise
【日工资】daily wage (or salary)
【日光】sunlight; sunshine
【日光浴】sun bath
【日积月累】accumulate (or collect, gather) over a long period
【日记】diary: 记～ keep a diary
【日渐】day by day; with each passing day

【日久见人心】it takes time to know a person; time reveals a person's heart
【日均】average per day
【日历】calendar
【日落】sunset; sundown
【日期】date
【日趋】gradually; change with each passing day; day by day: ～繁荣 become prosperous on a daily basis
【日新月异】change rapidly; alter from day to day; bring about new changes
【日以继夜】 day and night; round-the-clock
【日益】day by day; increasingly
【日用品】articles of everyday use
【日月星辰】the sun, the moon and the stars; the heavenly bodies
【日子】❶day; date ❷time ❸life

rong

荣（róng）❶ honour; glory; fame ❷ thrive; flourish
【荣获】have the honour to get (or win, receive); win as an honour; be awarded
【荣辱与共】(of friends) share honour or disgrace, weal or woe
【荣幸】be honoured (or lucky, fortunate)
【荣誉】honour; glory: 给……带来～ do honour to
【荣誉证书】certificate of honour

绒（róng）❶ fine hair; down ❷ cloth with a soft nap
【绒毛】fine hair; down

容（róng）❶looks; expression; appearance ❷hold; contain ❸tolerate ❹allow; permit
【容光焕发】glow with health
【容量】capacity
【容貌】looks; appearance
【容纳】hold; contain
【容器】container; vessel
【容忍】put up with; tolerate
【容许】permit; allow; let
【容颜】looks; appearance
【容易】❶easy ❷easily ❸likely; liable; apt

溶（róng）dissolve
【溶化】dissolve
【溶液】solution

熔（róng）melt
【熔点】melting point
【熔化】melt

融（róng）❶ melt ❷ blend; fuse; mix: 水乳交～ blend as well as milk and water do
【融合】fuse; mix together; merge: 文化～ cultural ferment
【融化】melt
【融洽】❶harmonious; on friendly terms: 关系～ congenial relations ❷in harmony
【融入社会】integrate into society
【融资】❶finance; raise funds ❷financing; funds-raising

冗（rǒng）❶superfluous; redundant ❷ full of trivial details ❸busyness
【冗长】tediously long; lengthy

rou

柔（róu）❶soft; flexible ❷gentle; mild
【柔道】judo
【柔和】❶soft; gentle; mild ❷softly; gently
【柔美】soft and graceful
【柔情】tender feeling
【柔情似水】tender feelings like water be deeply attached; be passionately devoted
【柔韧】pliable and tough

【柔软】soft
【柔弱】weak;delicate
【柔顺】gentle and agreeable;meek

揉 (róu) rub;knead

【揉搓】rub;knead

肉 (ròu) ❶meat;flesh: 牛~ beef;羊~ mutton;猪~ pork ❷pulp of fruit

【肉店】butcher's (shop)
【肉末】ground meat
【肉片】sliced meat
【肉食】carnivorous: ~动物 carnivorous animal;carnivore
【肉松】dried meat floss
【肉汤】broth
【肉馅】meat stuffing
【肉眼】naked eye

ru

如 (rú) ❶like;such as ❷according to ❸ for example (or instance) ❹as;as if

【如出一辙】be exactly the same
【如此等等】and so on;and so forth
【如此这般】thus and thus;thus and so
【如果】❶if ❷in case;in the event of
【如何】how;what
【如虎添翼】like adding wings to a tiger; with might redoubled
【如火如荼】like raging fire
【如获至宝】as if finding a precious treasure
【如饥似渴】❶eager ❷eagerly ❸thirst for
【如今】❶ now; nowadays; at present ❷ these days
【如临大敌】as if faced with a formidable enemy
【如履薄冰】as if treading on the thin ice
【如梦初醒】 as if awakening from a dream;beginning to see the light
【如期】 as scheduled; on schedule (or time): ~抵达目的地 arrive on time
【如上】as above
【如实】❶as things actually are ❷according to the very fact
【如释重负】as if relieved of a heavy load
【如同】❶like ❷as;as if
【如意算盘】wishful plan (or thinking)
【如有可能】if (or when) possible
【如鱼得水】feel just like fish in water;be in one's element
【如愿以偿】achieve one's goal (or purpose);fulfil one's wish

儒 (rú) ❶scholar ❷Confucianism;Confucianist

【儒家】the Confucian

蠕 (rú) wriggle;squirm

【蠕虫】worm;helminth

乳 (rǔ) ❶breast ❷milk ❸newborn

【乳白】milky white
【乳房】breast
【乳酪】cheese
【乳名】pet name
【乳牛】dairy cattle;milk cow
【乳臭未干】be very young and inexperienced;be wet behind the ears
【乳牙】 deciduous teeth; primary teeth; milk teeth
【乳汁】milk

辱 (rǔ) ❶ shame; disgrace; dishonour; insult; humiliation ❷ insult; humiliate;bring disgrace to

【辱骂】call sb. names;abuse

入 (rù) ❶income ❷enter;join ❸agree with ❹into

【入不敷出】be unable to make both ends meet;run behind one's expenses

【入场】❶enter ❷entrance; admission
【入场费】price of admission; admission fee
【入场券】admission ticket
【入党】join the party; become a party member
【入耳】pleasant to the ear: 不堪～ offensive to the ear
【入伙】join a gang (or group, partnership)
【入境】enter a country
【入口】entrance; gateway
【入门】❶learn the ABC of a subject ❷elementary course; ABC
【入迷】be fascinated (or absorbed)
【入侵】invade
【入神】be entranced (or absorbed)
【入时】fashionable
【入世】❶enter the WTO ❷entry into the WTO; WTO entry (or access)
【入手】start (or begin) with
【入睡】fall asleep
【入托】start going to a nursery
【入围】be included for further competition
【入伍】join the army; enlist
【入乡随俗】do as the Romans do
【入选】be chosen; be selected
【入学考试】entrance examination
【入学年龄】school age
【入狱】be put in prison (or jail)
【入院】be admitted to hospital; be hospitalized

褥 (rù) cotton-padded mattress: 被～ bedding; bedclothes; quilt
【褥单】bed sheet
【褥套】quilt cover; mattress cover

ruan

软 (ruǎn) ❶soft; flexible ❷mild; gentle ❸ weak; feeble ❹ poor ❺ easily moved (or touched)
【软包装】soft package (or packing)
【软化】❶soften; change from steadfast to wavering; from being stiff to being compliant: 态度逐渐～ softening attitude ❷ soften: ～血管 soften the blood vessels
【软件】software
【软件工程师】software engineer
【软件开发】software development
【软件维护】software maintenance
【软木】cork
【软弱】weak; powerless; feeble
【软卧】soft berth; sleeping carriage with soft berths
【软硬兼施】resort to both soft and hard tactics
【软指标】soft target
【软着陆】soft landing

rui

蕊 (ruǐ) stamen; pistil: 雄～ stamen; 雌～ pistil
锐 (ruì) ❶fighting spirit ❷sharp; keen ❸sharply
【锐不可当】be irresistible
【锐角】acute angle
【锐利】sharp; keen: 目光～ sharp-eyed
【锐气】spirit; drive
【锐意】be bent on; be determined

瑞 (ruì) lucky
【瑞雪】timely snow: ～兆丰年。A timely snow bodes well for a year of abundance.

run

闰 (rùn) intercalation
【闰年】leap year

【闰月】leap month

润 (rùn) ❶profit ❷lubricate ❸moisten ❹moist; smooth

【润唇膏】lip gloss

【润发露】hair lotion

【润肤露】skin lotion

【润喉片】throat lozenge

【润滑油】lubricating oil

【润色】polish; touch up

【润泽】❶moist; smooth; sleek ❷moisten; lubricate

ruo

若 (ruò)❶seem ❷like ❸if; as if

【若非】❶if not; if it had not been for ❷without

【若干】❶a certain number (or amount) ❷some

【若隐若现】dimly visible

【若有所思】❶seem lost in thought ❷as if deep in thought

弱 (ruò) ❶weak; feeble ❷inferior; poor ❸young

【弱点】weakness; weak point

【弱化】weaken

【弱势】❶downward trend ❷underprivileged; disadvantaged

【弱势群体】disadvantaged group

【弱视】❶poor eyesight ❷poor eye-sighted

【弱项】weak point

【弱小】small and weak

S s

sa

撒 (sā) cast; let go
另见本页 sǎ

【撒谎】tell a lie
【撒娇】act like a spoiled child
【撒泼】be unreasonable and make a scene: ~放刁 act in a rascally manner
【撒手】❶let go ❷die
【撒野】run wild; act wildly

洒 (sǎ) sprinkle; spray

【洒泪】shed tears
【洒水车】spraying car; watering car
【洒脱】free and easy in manner

撒 (sǎ) ❶spread; scatter ❷spill; drop
另见本页 sā

【撒种】sow seeds

飒 (sà)

【飒爽】of martial bearing; valiant

sai

腮 (sāi) cheek

【腮腺炎】parotitis; mumps

塞 (sāi) ❶ plug; cork; stopper ❷ fill in; stuff
另见本页 sài

【塞车】❶traffic jam ❷be jammed in traffic
【塞子】stopper; plug; spigot; cork

塞 (sài) fort; fortress
另见本页 sāi

【塞翁失马】the old frontiersman losing his horse—a blessing in disguise

赛 (sài) ❶match; game ❷contest; compete ❸ surpass; be as good as; can compare with

【赛车】❶racing vehicle (or bicycle) ❷cycle (or motorcycle, automobile race)
【赛马】horse racing
【赛跑】race
【赛区】playing (or competition) zone (or area)
【赛事】competition; competition event; game; match; contest
【赛艇】❶rowing ❷racing boat; shell

san

三 (sān) ❶several; many ❷three

【三八妇女节】International Women's Day
【三部曲】trilogy
【三长两短】unexpected misfortune; ill luck; mishap
【三等奖】the third prize (or place)
【三番五次】time and again
【三伏天】dog days; the three hottest peri-

ods of the year

【三个臭皮匠,赛过诸葛亮】the wisdom of the masses exceeds that of the wisest individual

【三角板】set square

【三角形】triangle

【三轮车】tricycle;trike

【三三两两】in (or by) twos and threes

【三生有幸】very fortunate; consider oneself most fortunate (to make sb.'s acquaintance, etc.)

【三思而行】think thrice before you act; look before you jump

【三维空间】three-dimensional space

【三无产品】brandless and dateless product by a nameless maker; three-no-product

【三五成群】in threes and fours

【三心二意】be of (or in) two minds; be half-hearted

【三月】March

伞 (sǎn) ❶ umbrella ❷ umbrella-like: 降落~ parachute

散 (sǎn) ❶come lose; fall apart; loosen ❷scattered

另见本页 sàn

【散漫】undisciplined; scattered

【散文】prose

S

【散装】unpackaged; loose packed; in bulk

散 (sàn) ❶ break up; disperse ❷ distribute; give out ❸ get rid of; dispatch

另见本页 sǎn

【散播】spread

【散步】take a walk; take a stroll; go for a walk

【散发】❶sent out (or forth); diffuse; emit ❷give (or hand) out; distribute

【散开】spread out (or apart); scatter

【散落】❶fall scattered ❷be scattered

【散热】❶dissipate heat ❷radiate heat

【散心】drive away one's cares (or worries); relieve boredom

sang

丧 (sāng) funeral; mourning

另见本页 sàng

【丧事】funeral arrangements

【丧葬】funeral: ~费 funeral expenses

桑 (sāng) mulberry

【桑拿浴】sauna bath

【桑蚕】silkworm

【桑葚】mulberry

嗓 (sǎng) throat; voice

【嗓音】voice

【嗓子】❶ throat ❷ voice: 清一清~ clear one's voice

丧 (sàng) lose

另见本页 sāng

【丧魂落魄】be frightened out of one's life

【丧家之犬】a homeless dog; a homeless stray

【丧命】lose one's life

【丧生】lose one's life; get killed

【丧失】lose

【丧失时机】miss the opportunity

【丧志】dispirited; demoralized; dejected: 玩物~ sap one's aspiration by seeking pleasure

sao

搔 (sāo) scratch

【搔痒】scratch where it itches

骚 (sāo) disturb

【骚乱】disturbance; restlessness: 引起～ cause a disturbance
【骚扰】harass; raid; disturb
【骚扰电话】nuisance (or obscene, harassing) phone call

扫 (sǎo) sweep
另见本页 sào

【扫地】❶sweep the floor ❷be dragged in the dust
【扫黑】crime sweep; crack down on underground crimes
【扫黄】anti-porn campaign
【扫盲】wipe out illiteracy
【扫描仪】scanner
【扫墓】sweep a grave—pay respects to a dead person at his tomb
【扫清】clear away
【扫视】(of eyes) glance
【扫兴】feel disappointed; have one's spirits dampened

嫂 (sǎo) elder brother's wife; sister-in-law

【嫂嫂】sister-in-law

扫 (sào)
另见本页 sǎo

【扫帚】broom

se

色 (sè) ❶color ❷kind: 各～各样 of all kinds; all kinds of ❸scenery; scene: 夜～ scenery at night ❹quality

【色彩】color; shade; tint; hue
【色彩鲜明】in bright (or gay) color
【色拉油】salad oil
【色狼】sex maniac; lecher; lecherous man
【色盲】color blindness; achromatopsia
【色香味美】good in color, smell and taste
【色泽】color; luster: ～鲜明 bright and lustrous

涩 (sè) ❶ puckery; astringent ❷ unsmooth; hard-going ❸hard to understand; obscure

【涩滞】(of style of writing) not smooth

sen

森 (sēn) ❶full of trees ❷dark; gloomy

【森林】forest
【森林火灾】forest fire
【森林资源】forest reserves (or resources)
【森罗万象】all-embracing; all-inclusive

seng

僧 (sēng) monk

【僧多粥少】there is too little gruel for too many monks; not enough to go round

sha

杀 (shā) ❶weaken ❷fight ❸kill

【杀虫剂】insecticide
【杀敌】fight the enemy
【杀毒软件】virus killer; virus-killing software
【杀害】murder; kill
【杀鸡取卵】kill the hen to get the eggs
【杀鸡吓猴】kill the chicken to frighten the monkey; punish sb. as a warning to others
【杀价】❶beat down the price; beat a seller down ❷sell at a reduced price
【杀人】kill a person; murder
【杀伤】kill and wound; inflict casualties on: ～力 antipersonnel capacity
【杀头】put to death; behead
【杀一儆百】kill one man to warn a hundred

沙 (shā) ❶ sand ❷ powder ❸ hoarse; husky

【沙包】❶sand dune ❷sandbag

【沙暴】sandstorm

【沙尘暴】sand duststorm

【沙发】sofa; settee; couch

【沙化】desertification

【沙坑】jumping pit

【沙拉】salad

【沙龙】salon

【沙漠】desert

【沙沙】rustle：风吹得树叶～响。The leaves rustled in the wind.

【沙滩】beach; sand beach

【沙哑】hoarse; husky

纱 (shā) ❶yarn ❷gauze

【纱布】gauze

【纱窗】screen window

刹 (shā) stop; put on the brakes; brake

【刹车】❶brake ❷put on the brakes; brake ❸put a check on; stop

砂 (shā)

【砂布】emery cloth; abrasive cloth

【砂土】sandy soil; sand

傻 (shǎ) ❶ foolish; stupid ❷ mechanical; tactless

【傻瓜】fool; blockhead

【傻乎乎】simple-minded; silly; foolish

【傻笑】laugh (or grin) foolishly

【傻样】a foolish look

厦 (shà) a tall building

煞 (shà) ❶evil spirit ❷very

【煞有介事】pretend to be serious

霎 (shà) ❶moment ❷instant ❸a very short time

【霎时间】in a twinkling; in a split second

shai

筛 (shāi) ❶sieve ❷sieve; sift

【筛选】❶screen ❷select

【筛子】sieve, sifter screen

晒 (shài) ❶ shine upon ❷ dry in the sun ❸bask

【晒场】sunning ground (for drying grain, etc.)

【晒太阳】bask in the sunshine

shan

山 (shān) hill; mountain

【山崩地裂】mountains collapsing and the earth cracking up

【山城】mountain city

【山川】landscape; mountains and rivers; land

【山村】mountain village

【山顶】mountain top (or summit); hilltop

【山洞】cave

【山峰】peak

【山高水远】the mountains are high and the rivers are far away—a long distance

【山沟】gully

【山谷】valley

【山河】mountains and rivers; the land of a country

【山脚】the foot of a hill (or mountain)

【山林】❶ wooded mountain (or hill) ❷ woods on the mountain (or hill)

【山麓】the foot of a mountain

【山峦】a chain of mountains; multipeaked mountain

S

【山脉】mountain range; mountains
【山坡】hillside; mountain slope
【山穷水尽】at the end of one's rope; in a tight corner
【山泉】mountain spring
【山水】❶mountains and waters ❷scenery with mountains and rivers
【山水画】landscape painting
【山外有山】there's always a mountain beyond a mountain—there's always something better; nothing can be perfect
【山崖】cliff
【山羊】goat
【山寨版】cheap copy
【山珍海味】delicacies from land and sea; all kinds of costly foods
【山庄】mountain villa (or village)

删 (shān) delete; leave (or cut) out; cancel
【删除】delete; leave (or cut) out; cancel
【删繁就简】simplify a complicated thing
【删节】abridge; abbreviate
【删改】revise; delete and change

姗 (shān)
【姗姗来迟】be slow in coming; be late

珊 (shān)
【珊瑚】coral
【珊瑚岛】coral island

扇 (shān) ❶fan ❷slap ❸incite; instigate; fan up; stir up
另见本页 shàn
【扇风耳】protruding ears; flappy ears

煽 (shān)
【煽动】stir up; flap; instigate; excite; incite; whip
【煽情】❶stir up emotions (or enthusiasm; excitement) ❷emotion-stirring

闪 (shǎn) ❶flash; sparkle ❷dodge; get out of the way ❸suddenly twist; sprain
【闪电】lightning
【闪躲】dodge; evade: ～不开 too late or slow to dodge
【闪光灯】❶flash lamp; flashlight; photoflash ❷flashlight (used for signals)
【闪婚】lightning marriage; flash marriage
【闪亮登场】mount the stage brilliantly; come to the scene in glory
【闪念】an idea which flashes through one's mind
【闪射】glitter; shine; radiate
【闪失】mishap; accident
【闪烁】❶twinkle; glisten ❷evasive
【闪现】flash before one: 英雄的形象～在我的眼前。The image of the hero flashed before my eyes.
【闪耀】glitter

扇 (shàn) fan
另见本页 shān
【扇贝】scallop; fan shell
【扇形】❶fan-shaped ❷sector
【扇子】fan

善 (shàn) ❶kindness; kind action ❷make a success (or good job) of ❸be good at ❹be likely (or apt) to ❺kind ❻good ❼properly
【善变】be apt to change; be changeable
【善待】treat friendly (or well)
【善待生命】cherish life
【善恶分明】be clear about what is good and what is bad
【善后】properly cope with the aftermath of sth.
【善举】philanthropic act
【善良】kind; kind-hearted

【善始善终】start well and end well
【善意】goodwill;good intention
【善有善报,恶有恶报】good will be rewarded with good,and evil with evil
【善于】be skilled (or expert) in; be good at
缮 (shàn) ❶repair; mend: 修~ repair ❷copy; write
擅 (shàn) ❶ arrogate to oneself; do sth. on one's own authority ❷ be good at;be expert in
【擅长】be good at; be expert (or skilled) in
【擅自】do sth. without authorization
膳 (shàn) meals;board
【膳食】meals;board;food
【膳宿】board and lodging
赡 (shàn) ❶support; provide for ❷sufficient;abundant
【赡养费】alimony;payment for support of one's parents

shang

伤 (shāng) ❶ wound; injury: 致命~ mortal wound; fatal wound ❷ hurt; wound; injure ❸be sick of ❹be harmful to ❺sad;sorrowful;grieved
【伤疤】scar
【伤残人】disabled (or handicapped) person
【伤感】be sick at heart;sentimental
【伤害】harm;injure;hurt
【伤怀】sad;grieved;brokenhearted
【伤口】wound;cut
【伤脑筋】troublesome
【伤神】overtax the mind; overtax one's nerves;be nerve-racking
【伤势】the condition of an injury (or wound)
【伤痛】❶grieved;distressed ❷the pain of an injury or wound
【伤亡】casualties
【伤心】heart-broken;sad;grieved
【伤员】the wounded
商 (shāng) ❶ commerce; business; trade ❷ merchant; businessman; trader;dealer discuss;consult
【商标】trade mark;brand
【商场】market;shopping place
【商城】❶shopping centre ❷plaza;mall
【商店】shop;store
【商定】decide through discussion;agree
【商贩】small retailer;pedlar
【商机】business opportunity
【商量】discuss;consult;talk over
【商品】commodity;goods
【商品包装】commodity package
【商品房】commercial housing (or house, residence)
【商品化】❶ commercialize ❷ commercialization
【商品交易会】commodities fair
【商品经济】commodity economy
【商榷】discuss;deliberate
【商人】merchant; businessman; trader; dealer
【商厦】department store; shopping centre;plaza;mall
【商讨】discuss;deliberate over
【商务】business (or commercial) affairs
【商务英语】business (or commercial) English
【商业】commerce;trade;business
【商业公司】business (or commercial) company
【商业广告】business (or commercial) advertisement

【商业机密】business (or commercial) secret

【商业区】business (or commercial) district (or quarter)

【商业网站】commercial web site

【商议】discuss; confer

【商战】commercial (or business, trade) war

晌 (shǎng) ❶part of the day ❷noon

【晌午】midday; noon

赏 (shǎng) ❶award; reward ❷award; reward ❸appreciate; enjoy

【赏赐】award

【赏罚】reward and punishments

【赏金】money reward

【赏脸】honour me with your presence

【赏识】appreciate

【赏雪】enjoy a beautiful snow scene

上 (shàng) ❶go up; get on ❷go to; leave for ❸go ahead ❹submit; present ❺come on the stage; enter the court and play ❻fill; replenish ❼fix; set ❽apply; color ❾wind; screw; tighten ❿be carried; be put on record ⓫amount to upper higher ⓬first ⓭upward

【上岸】land; go ashore

【上班】go to work; be on duty

【上半场】first half (of a game, concert, etc.)

【上榜】be (or get) on the list

【上报】❶report to the leadership ❷appear in the newspaper

【上苍】Heaven; God

【上策】the best way (or plan, tactic)

【上场】appear (or come) on the stage; enter the court and play

【上传】upload

【上床】go to bed

【上当】be fooled (or taken in)

【上当受骗】be taken in

【上等】first-class; first-rate; superior

【上帝】God

【上吊】hang oneself

【上访】appeal to higher authorities for help

【上风】advantage: 占～get the upper hand; have the advantage over

【上岗】start to work; take on a job; take up a post

【上岗证】work (or job) license

【上工】go to work; start work

【上供】❶offer up a sacrifice; lay offerings on the altar ❷give presents to the higher-ups expecting favours in return

【上级】higher authorities; higher level

【上缴】turn over to the higher authorities

【上街】go into the street; go shopping

【上进】make progress

【上进心】desire to do (or get) better

【上镜】❶appear in a film (or TV program) ❷make a good image in film (or TV)

【上课】go to class; be in class; have a class

【上来】come up

【上路】set out; start off

【上面】❶higher authorities ❷in the above ❸above; over; on; on top of

【上年纪】❶get on in years ❷aging; aged

【上铺】upper berth

【上任】take office

【上上下下】❶high and low ❷old and young; everybody

【上升】rise; go up

【上市】❶appear in the market ❷be listed

【上市公司】listed company

【上手】❶left-hand seat; seat of honour ❷start; begin

【上述】above-mentioned; aforesaid
【上司】superior; boss
【上诉人】appellor; appellant
【上吐下泻】throw up on top and purge down below; suffer from vomiting and diarrhoea; have loose bowels and vomit
【上网】go on-line; link (or get on) the Internet; surf the Internet
【上网手机】web-connected cell phone
【上新台阶】reach a new level (or new stage)
【上下】❶about; or so ❷from top to foot ❸seniors and juniors in all
【上行下效】subordinates follow the example of their superiors; those below follow the (usu. bad) example of those above; if a leader sets a bad example, it will be followed by his subordinates
【上学】attend school; go to school
【上演】put on the stage; perform
【上瘾】be addicted to; get into the habit of
【上映】show; be on
【上游】❶ upstream; upper reaches ❷ advanced position
【上涨】rise; go up
【上肢】upper limb
【上座】❶seat of honour ❷be a draw

尚 (shàng) ❶ esteem; value; set great store by ❷still; yet

【尚书】❶a high official in ancient China ❷minister (in the Ming and Qing Dynasties)

shao

捎 (shāo) take along sth. to (or for) sb.; bring to sb.

【捎带】in passing

烧 (shāo) ❶fever ❷burn ❸cook; heat ❹have a fever (or temperature)

【烧化】❶cremate ❷burn (paper, etc. as an offering to the dead)
【烧火】make (or light) a fire
【烧伤】burn (an injury)
【烧纸】❶burn paper money for the dead ❷paper money burnt as an offering to the dead

稍 (shāo) slightly; a little (or bit)
另见 1173 页 shào

【稍微】slightly
【稍息】stand at ease

勺 (sháo) ladle; spoon

少 (shǎo) ❶ be short of; lack ❷ be missing; lose ❸ stop ❹ few; little; less
另见本页 shào

【少而精】smaller quantity, better quality; fewer but better
【少量】❶a small amount ❷a little; a few
【少数】a small number; few; minority
【少数民族】minority nationality; ethnic minority
【少许】a little; a few

少 (shào) young
另见本页 shǎo

【少妇】young married woman
【少男少女】inexperienced young men and women; unmarried young men and young women
【少年】young person (or teenager); juvenile
【少年宫】Children's Palace
【少女】young girl
【少壮不努力，老大徒伤悲】If one does not exert oneself when young, one will regret it in old age

哨 (shào) ❶ whistle: 吹～ blow a whistle ❷ sentry post: 放～ stand sentry (or guard)

【哨岗】sentry post

【哨子】whistle

稍 (shào)
另见 1172 页 shāo

【稍息】stand at ease

she

奢 (shē) ❶ luxurious; extravagant ❷ excessive; inordinate

【奢侈】luxurious; wasteful

【奢望】wild wishes; extravagant hopes

赊 (shē) buy or sell on credit

【赊欠】give or get credit

【赊账】on credit

舌 (shé) ❶ tongue ❷ sth. shaped like a tongue

【舌苔】coating on the tongue

【舌战】❶argue; dispute ❷a hot dispute; a verbal battle

折 (shé) ❶break ❷lose money in business
另见 1307 页 zhē; zhé

【折本】lose money in business

【折耗】damage and loss (to goods during transit, storage, etc.)

蛇 (shé) snake

【蛇形】snakelike; S-shaped

舍 (shě) ❶ give up; abandon ❷ give alms
另见 1174 页 shè

【舍不得】hate to part with or use; grudge

【舍得】be willing to do sth.; not grudge

【舍己救人】sacrifice oneself to save sb. else

【舍近求远】seek from afar what is close at hand

【舍命】risk one's life

【舍弃】give up; abandon

【舍生取义】lay down one's life for a just cause

设 (shè) ❶ set up; establish ❷ work out; try to find ❸suppose

【设备】equipment

【设计】plan; design

【设立】set up; establish; found; bring into being

【设身处地】put oneself in the position of sb.

【设施】facilities; installation

【设想】❶imagine; conceive; assume ❷consider; give a thought to

【设置】set (or put) up; establish

社 (shè) society; body; agency

【社保】social security

【社会安定】social stability

【社会办学】run schools by non-governmental forces (or sectors)

【社会保险】social insurance

【社会保障】social security

【社会保障体系】social security system

【社会弊端】social sickness

【社会分工】division of labor in society

【社会风气】social morals

【社会福利】social welfare

【社会福利院】social welfare institute

【社会服务】social service

【社会公德】social morals (or morality, ethics)

【社会公平】social equality

【社会公益事业】work for the public's good; cause for the good of the society

【社会关系】❶human relations in society; social relations ❷ one's social connections; relatives and friends

【社会环境】social environment
【社会救助】social help and relief
【社会认可】social acceptance
【社会团体】social group (or organization)
【社会稳定】social stability
【社会养老保险】social old-age insurance
【社会舆论】public opinion
【社会责任】social responsibility (or duty)
【社会秩序】public (or social) order
【社会主义法制】socialist legal system
【社会主义精神文明】socialist spiritual civilization
【社会主义物质文明】socialist material civilization
【社会转型】social transformation
【社交】social life; social intercourse
【社区】community
【社区服务】community service
【社区医院】community hospital

舍 (shè) house; shed; hut: 校～ school building
另见 1173 页 shě

【舍利子】Buddhism relics left after the cremation of Buddhas or saintly monks (deposited in stupas for worship)

射 (shè) ❶ shoot; fire ❷ discharge ❸ send out ❹allude to sth. or sb.

【射击】shoot; fire
【射门】goal shooting
【射手】❶shooter; marksman ❷goal getter
【射线】ray

涉 (shè) ❶wade; ford ❷involve

【涉及】involve; relate to; have sth. to do with
【涉世】gain life experience
【涉外】❶foreign-related ❷concerning foreign affairs or foreign nationals
【涉外工作】work concerning foreign affairs and nationals
【涉外经济】foreign-related economy
【涉外企业】enterprise related with foreign investment or trade
【涉险】go through dangers
【涉足】set foot in

赦 (shè) remit; pardon

【赦免】remit; pardon
【赦罪】pardon sb.; absolve sb. from guilt

摄 (shè) ❶take a picture (or photo) ❷ absorb

【摄像】make a video recording (with a video camera or TV camera)
【摄影】❶shoot a film ❷take a picture (or photo)
【摄制】produce
【摄制组】production team

慑 (shè) fear; be awed

【慑服】❶ submit in fear; succumb ❷ cow sb. into submission

shen

申 (shēn) state

【申奥成功】be successful in bidding for hosting the Olympic Games
【申办】bid to host (or for hosting): ～下届运动会 bid for the next sports meet
【申办城市】bidding city
【申报】❶report to a higher body ❷declare sth. (to the customs)
【申领】apply for
【申明】declare; state
【申请】apply for; file an application
【申请入学】❶ apply for admission to a school ❷application
【申述】state; explain in detail

【申诉】appeal
【申冤】❶appeal for putting right a wrong ❷right a wrong appeal for redress of a wrong

伸 (shēn) stretch; extend; reach out

【伸手】❶stretch out one's hand ❷ask for
【伸缩】❶ stretch out and draw back; lengthen and shorten; expand and contract ❷flexible; elastic; adjustable
【伸腰】straighten oneself up; straighten one's back
【伸展】stretch; spread; expand; extend
【伸张正义】uphold justice

身 (shēn) ❶body ❷life ❸oneself; personally ❹one's moral character and conduct ❺the main part of a structure

【身不由己】involuntarily; in spite of oneself
【身材】figure; stature
【身残志坚】be broken in body but firm in spirit
【身份证】identity card; identification card
【身高】height of a person
【身临其境】be personally on the scene
【身躯】body
【身手】skill; talent: 好～ good skill
【身受】experience personally: 感同～ feel as if one experiences sth. personally
【身体力行】practice what one advocates
【身体素质】physique; constitution
【身心】body and spirit; body and mind
【身心健康】sound in body and mind; physically and mentally healthy
【身孕】pregnancy

深 (shēn) ❶deep ❷profound; close ❸dark ❹late ❺greatly; deeply; very

【深奥】profound; abstruse
【深层】❶depth; deeper layers ❷deep-going; thorough; incisive: ～原因 deep-seated cause
【深长】profound; lingering
【深沉】❶reserved ❷dark ❸deep
【深度】depth
【深更半夜】in the depth of night; in the dead of night; in the small hours
【深广】deep and broad
【深厚】deep; deep-seated; profound
【深化】deepen
【深化改革】deepen the reform
【深刻】deep; thorough; profound
【深明大义】have a good understanding of good and wrong
【深谋远虑】be careful and far-sighted
【深情】deep feeling (or love)
【深入浅出】explain what is profound in plain language
【深入人心】take root in the hearts of the people
【深思熟虑】carefully consider
【深信】be deeply convinced; firmly believe
【深夜】late at night
【深渊】abyss
【深远】far-reaching; profound and lasting
【深造】take up advanced studies; take a more advanced course of study or training

什 (shén)
另见 1181 页 shí

【什么】what; whatever; something; anything

神 (shén) ❶god ❷spirit; mind; soul ❸look; expression ❹magic; supernatural ❺clever

【神不知鬼不觉】in secret; secretly
【神话】mythology; fairy tale; myth
【神经】nerve
【神秘】mysterious

S

【神妙】wonderful; marvellous; ingenious: ～莫测 wonderful; marvellous
【神奇】magical
【神气活现】very cocky; high and mighty
【神情】look; expression
【神情自若】with an easy expression
【神色】look; expression
【神色紧张】look nervous
【神圣】sacred; holy: ～的使命 sacred mission
【神速】at amazing speed
【神态】expression; manner
【神态自若】in easy manner (or attitude)
【神往】be carried away; be rapt; be charmed: 心驰～ yearn after as if one's mind were already there
【神仙】supernatural being; immortal
【神志】mind; senses: ～不清 be unconscious

审 (shěn) ❶examine; go over ❷try ❸careful; close

【审查】examine
【审定】examine and approve
【审度】study and weigh
【审核】verify; check
【审计】audit
【审理】try; hear: 依法～ try a case according to law
【审美】appreciation of the beautiful
【审美标准】aesthetic criteria
【审美能力】aesthetic ability (or judgment)
【审判】try; bring sb. to a trial
【审判长】presiding judge
【审批】examine and approve
【审慎】careful; cautious
【审时度势】judge the hour and size up the situation
【审视】look closely
【审阅】examine carefully and critically

婶 (shěn) aunt; auntie

【婶娘】wife of father's younger brother; aunt

肾 (shèn) kidney

【肾结石】kidney stone; renal calculus
【肾移植】kidney transplant; renal transplant
【肾脏】kidney

甚 (shèn) ❶ very; extremely ❷ more than

【甚为】very; extremely: ～痛快 find it most satisfying
【甚至】❶even ❷go so far as to; so much so that

渗 (shèn) ooze; seep into

【渗入】penetrate; seep into
【渗透】seep; penetrate

慎 (shèn) careful; cautious

【慎言慎行】be cautious in speech and conduct
【慎重】careful; cautious

sheng

升 (shēng) ❶rise; go up ❷promote

【升高】rise; go up
【升级】❶ upgrade; promote ❷ upgrading; promotion
【升级换代】upgrade and update
【升降】go up and down
【升旗】raise (or hoist) a flag
【升温】rise (or go up) in temperature
【升学考试】entrance examination
【升学率】rate of promotion into higher

schools

【升值】revalue; appreciate

生（shēng）❶ student; pupil ❷ livelihood ❸ life ❹ give birth to; bear ❺ grow ❻ live ❼ take place ❽ light; kindle ❾ cause ❿ living ⓫ raw; uncooked ⓬ unripe ⓭ unrefined; unprocessed ⓮ unfamiliar; strange ⓯ stiff ⓰ very

【生搬硬套】copy mechanically

【生病】fall (or be) ill

【生产】❶ give birth to a child ❷ produce

【生产厂家】factory; producer; maker

【生产责任制】production responsibility system; system of production responsibility

【生成】come or bring into being

【生词】new words

【生存】❶ exist; live ❷ living; existence ❸ survive

【生存竞争】struggle for life (or existence)

【生动】lively; vivid

【生发剂】hair-restorer; hair regrowth liniment

【生活】❶ live ❷ life: 日常～ daily life ❸ livelihood

【生活补贴】living (or living-cost) allowance

【生活费】living expenses (or cost)

【生活救济】relief

【生活设施】living facilities

【生活质量】quality of life; life quality

【生火】make (or light, kindle) a fire

【生机】❶ vitality ❷ opportunity of living: ～勃勃 vibrate with life; imbued with vitality

【生计】livelihood; means of livelihood: 另谋～ try to find some other means of livelihood

【生老病死】birth and old age, sickness and death—the lot of man

【生离死别】part for ever

【生龙活虎】full of vigour like a dragon or a tiger

【生路】❶ means of livelihood ❷ solution; way out

【生命科学】life science

【生命力】vitality

【生命线】lifeline

【生怕】be afraid of; fear

【生平事迹】life; life story

【生气】❶ get angry ❷ vitality; life

【生前】before one's death

【生人】stranger

【生日】birthday

【生日贺词】birthday greetings

【生日礼物】birthday present

【生身】give birth to: ～父母 biological parents

【生事】make trouble

【生手】sb. new to a job; greenhand; novice

【生疏】❶ not familiar: 人地～ be a complete stranger ❷ out of practice; rusty: 技艺～ be impaired in skill by inaction or neglect ❸ getting distant: 感情～ feel not as close as before

【生死】life and death

【生态保护】ecological protection

【生态环境】ecological environment

【生态建设】ecological construction

【生态旅游】ecological tourism; ecotourism

【生态平衡】ecological balance

【生态破坏】ecocide

【生态危机】ecological crisis

【生态系统】ecological system; ecosystem

【生态效应】ecological effect

【生态循环】ecological cycle
【生物】living things (or beings); organisms
【生物技术】biotech; biological technology
【生物链】biological chain
【生物学】biology
【生物钟】biological clock
【生效】come (or go) into effect
【生效日期】go-into-effect date; effective date
【生意】business; trade: 做~ do business
【生育】give birth to; bear
【生源】source (or supply) of students
【生长】grow; grow up
【生殖】reproduction

声 (shēng) sound; voice

【声辩】argue; explain away; defend
【声道】sound channel
【声调】tone; note
【声明】❶ declare; state ❷ declaration; statement: 发表~ make a statement
【声情并茂】(of a singer) be remarkable for both voice and expression
【声势】momentum; impetus
【声望】prestige; reputation; popularity
【声威】❶ renown; prestige: ~大震 gain great fame and high prestige ❷ power; strength; momentum
【声像】❶ sound and picture ❷ audio-visual
【声音】sound; voice
【声誉】good name; fame; reputation: ~卓著 be famous; enjoy high reputation
【声张】make public; disclose

牲 (shēng) ❶ domestic animal ❷ animal sacrifice

【牲畜】livestock; domestic animals

甥 (shēng) sister's son; nephew

【甥女】niece; sister's daughter

绳 (shéng) ❶ rope; string; cord ❷ restrict; restrain

【绳索】rope
【绳之以法】restrain by law

省 (shěng) ❶ province ❷ save; economize ❸ leave out; omit
另见 1254 页 xǐng

【省吃俭用】skimp and save; live frugally
【省会】provincial capital
【省力】save labor (or effort)
【省略】❶ leave out; omit ❷ ellipsis
【省钱】save money; be economical; economize
【省事】save trouble; simplify matters
【省委】provincial Party committee
【省心】be carefree; save worry

圣 (shèng) ❶ king; emperor ❷ sage; saint ❸ holy; sacred

【圣诞】the birthday of Jesus Christ
【圣诞节】Christmas Day; Christmas
【圣诞老人】Santa Claus
【圣诞礼物】Christmas present (or gift)
【圣地】sacred place
【圣洁】holy and pure
【圣经】the Bible; the Holy Bible
【圣贤】sage and man of virtue

胜 (shèng) ❶ victory ❷ win ❸ surpass; be better than; get the better hand of ❹ be qualified for; be equal to ❺ victorious ❻ wonderful; lovely

【胜败】victory or defeat
【胜出】outplay other opponents
【胜地】a famous scenic spot: 避暑~ a famous summer resort
【胜境】wonderful scenery; beautiful place
【胜利】❶ victory; triumph; win ❷ successful
【胜任】be qualified (or competent); be e-

qual to
【胜似】surpass;be better than
【胜诉】win a lawsuit
【胜仗】victory
盛 (shèng) ❶ thrive; flourish ❷ grand ❸ vigorous ❹ plentiful ❺ fashionable ❻ greatly
【盛传】be circulated extensively; be widely known; be widely rumoured
【盛大】grand;magnificent
【盛会】grand meeting; distinguished gathering
【盛况空前】an exceptionally (or unprecedentedly) grand occasion
【盛名】great fame;great reputation
【盛气凌人】overbearing; domineering; arrogant
【盛情难却】the invitation is too kind to decline; it would be ungracious not to accept your kindness
【盛世】times of prosperity; flourishing age: 太平～ times of peace; times of peace and prosperity
【盛夏】midsummer; the height of summer
【盛行】be fashionable; be current; be in vogue
【盛宴】a grand banquet (or dinner)
【盛装】splendid attire; rich dress
剩 (shèng) ❶ leave; leave over; remain ❷ leftover; remnant; surplus
【剩下】leave; leave over; remain; be left (or leftover)
【剩余】❶ surplus; leftover; remaining ❷ remainder

shi

尸 (shī) dead body; corpse; remains
【尸骨】bones of the dead
【尸体】corpse; dead body; remains
失 (shī) ❶ loss ❷ fault; slip ❸ lose ❹ let slip ❺ fall short of ❻ fail to keep
【失败】❶ lose; fail ❷ failure
【失策】❶ be unwise; err in planning (or calculation) ❷ wrong stratagem
【失常】out of order (or the usual); not normal
【失当】improper; inappropriate: 处理～ not properly handled
【失掉】❶ lose ❷ miss; fail to get hold of; let slip
【失衡】lose balance; unbalance; out-of-balance: 比例～ unbalanced proportions
【失魂落魄】be out of one's wits
【失火】catch fire; be on fire
【失控】❶ out of control ❷ runaway: 物价～ runaway prices
【失利】suffer a setback
【失恋】be disappointed in love; be jilted
【失灵】fail to work; be out of order; be ineffective
【失落感】feeling of being neglected
【失眠】suffer from insomnia
【失窃】have sth. stolen
【失去】lose
【失散】be separated from and lose touch with each other; become scattered
【失事】have an accident; meet with a disaster or misfortune: 飞机～ plane crash; aviation accident
【失手】❶ drop sth. accidentally ❷ suffer defeat
【失算】misjudge; miscalculate
【失态】lose control of oneself; forget oneself; be not one's usual self: 酒后～ forget oneself in drink
【失调】❶ imbalance; lose balance; dislocation: 供求～ imbalance of supply and de-

mand ❷lack of proper care and rest
【失望】lose hope;get disappointed
【失误】fault;muff;error
【失效期】expiring date
【失信】go back on one's word; break one's promise
【失修】be in bad repair
【失学】discontinue one's schooling;be unable to go to school
【失学儿童】young school dropout
【失言】make a slip of the tongue
【失业】❶lose one's job; be out of work ❷unemployment
【失业保险】unemployment insurance
【失业人员】the unemployed (or jobless); unemployed person
【失约】fail to keep an appointment;stand sb. up
【失之交臂】just miss the person or opportunity
【失职】fail in (or neglect) one's duty; neglect one's duty
【失主】owner of lost property

师

(shī) ❶teacher;master ❷model;example ❸division ❹army
【师道尊严】dignity of the teaching profession
【师范】❶ teacher-training ❷ teachers training university (or college)

S

【师傅】master
【师生关系】teacher-student relationship
【师长】teacher;division commander
【师资】teachers:培养～ cultivate teachers

诗

(shī) poem;verse;poetry
【诗歌】poem;poetry
【诗经】the Book of Songs
【诗礼之家】a highly cultured household;a family of scholars
【诗人】poet:女～poetess
【诗意】poetry;poetic quality or flavour

虱

(shī) louse
【虱子】louse

狮

(shī) lion
【狮身人面像】sphinx
【狮子】lion
【狮子座】Leo

施

(shī) ❶carry out ❷bestow;give ❸apply;use ❹exert
【施暴】❶take violent action ❷rape; violate
【施肥】spread manure;apply fertilizer
【施工】❶construct ❷construction
【施礼】salute
【施行】❶put in force;put in effect ❷do; perform;carry out
【施展】give full play to;bring into play; put to good use

湿

(shī) wet
【湿地】wetland
【湿度】humidity
【湿润】moist
【湿透】wet through;drenched

十

(shí) ten
【十二月】December
【十分】fully;very;completely
【十佳】ten best;top ten
【十拿九稳】90 percent sure; quite certain;practically certain
【十万八千里】a distance of one hundred and eight thousand li;poles apart
【十一月】November
【十月】October
【十之八九】very likely;almost

【十字路口】crossroads

【十足】❶ plentiful; full of ❷ downright ❸percent

什 (shí) ❶assorted; varied ❷ ten 另见 1175 页 shén

【什锦】assorted; mixed

石 (shí) ❶stone; rock ❷stone inscription

【石碑】stone tablet

【石雕】❶stone carving ❷carved stone

【石膏】gypsum; plaster stone

【石拱桥】stone arch bridge

【石灰】lime

【石匠】mason

【石窟】grotto; rock cave

【石榴】pomegranate

【石磨】❶stone mill ❷grinding stone

【石器】❶stone artifact ❷stone vessel

【石头】stone; rock

【石英钟】quartz clock

【石油】oil; petroleum

【石子】cobble; pebble

时 (shí) ❶ hour ❷ time ❸ times ❹ opportunity ❺ now and then; sometimes

【时不我待】time and tide wait for no man

【时差】time difference

【时常】often; frequently

【时代】times; age; era; epoch

【时代精神】zeitgeist; the spirit of the age

【时而】❶now and then; from time to time ❷ now... now...; sometimes... sometimes...

【时光】❶time ❷days; years

【时过境迁】things change as time passes; things have changed with the lapse of time

【时机】opportunity; chance

【时间】time; hour

【时局】the current political situation

【时刻】❶hour; time; moment ❷always; all the time

【时刻表】timetable; schedule

【时空】time and space

【时来运转】time has moved in one's favour; fortune favours sb.

【时髦】❶in vogue ❷fashionable

【时期】period

【时区】time zone

【时尚】fad; fashion: 不合～ out of fashion

【时事】current affairs; current events

【时限】time limit

【时效】❶ effectiveness for a given period of time ❷prescription ❸ageing

【时宜】what is appropriate to the occasion; what suits the occasion: 不合～ be not appropriate for the occasion; be inappropriate

【时运】luck; fortune

【时针】❶hands of a clock (or watch) ❷ hour hand

【时钟】clock

【时装】fashionable dress; fashion

【时装表演】fashion show

【时装设计】fashion design

识 (shí) ❶knowledge ❷know

【识别】distinguish; discern; spot

【识大体，顾大局】keep (or have) the whole situation in mind

【识破】see through; penetrate

【识时务】understand the times; be sensible

【识羞】feel ashamed; have a sense of shame: 好不～ so shameless

【识字】learn to read; become literate: 读书～ read and write

实 (shí) ❶fruit ❷reality; fact ❸true; real ❹solid

S

【实报实销】reimburse the amount actually spent; be reimbursed for what one spends
【实处】right place (or spot) where it really matters
【实弹】❶be loaded:荷枪～ carry a loaded rifle ❷live shell; live ammunition
【实地】on the spot
【实感】true or genuine feelings; real sentiments:真情～ true feelings
【实干精神】down-to-earth spirit
【实话实说】tell the plain truth; speak frankly
【实惠】❶substantial benefit; tangible (or material) benefit ❷substantial
【实际能力】actual ability
【实际效果】actual result (or effect)
【实践】❶practice ❷put into practice; live up to; carry out
【实景】actual setting
【实况转播】live broadcast
【实例】living example; example
【实名制】real-name system
【实情】truth; the actual situation
【实情实理】the actual situation and the real reason
【实施】put into effect; carry out; give effect to

S

【实施方案】execution plan
【实事求是】seek truth from facts
【实物】actual thing
【实习】practice; fieldwork
【实习生】trainee
【实效】actual effect; substantial results; practical results
【实心眼ル】❶honest and serious-minded ❷an honest and serious-minded person
【实行】practise; put into practice; carry out
【实验】❶experiment ❷test
【实业家】industrialist
【实用】practical
【实用价值】utility value
【实在】❶true; real; honest ❷really; honestly ❸indeed; in fact
【实质】essence

拾 (shí) ❶pick up ❷ten

【拾金不昧】pocket nothing picked up
【拾取】pick up; collect
【拾物】(lost) articles found:～招领处 lost and found (bureau); lost-property office

食 (shí) ❶food; meal ❷feed; fodder ❸eat ❹edible; feed ❺for cooking

【食不甘味】eat without relish
【食而不化】eat without digesting; read without understanding
【食量】appetite; capacity for eating
【食疗】food (or dietetic) therapy
【食品】food; foodstuff:罐头～ tinned or canned food
【食品安全】food safety
【食品包装】food packaging
【食品添加剂】food addictive
【食品卫生】food hygiene
【食谱】recipes; cookbook
【食堂】dining room (or hall); canteen
【食物】food; eatables; edibles
【食物中毒】food poisoning
【食油】edible oil; cooking oil
【食欲】appetite
【食指】index finger; forefinger

蚀 (shí) ❶lose ❷erode; corrode

【蚀本】lose one's capital

史 (shǐ) ❶history ❷official historian in ancient China

【史册】history; annals

【史籍】historical records; history
【史迹】historical site or relics
【史前】prehistoric: ~时代 prehistoric age
【史诗】epic; heroic poetry
【史实】historical facts
【史无前例】unprecedented

矢 (shǐ) ❶arrow ❷swear; vow

【矢口否认】deny by oath; deny positively
【矢志不移】swear not to change

使 (shǐ) ❶messenger; envoy ❷send ❸use; employ ❹make; cause

【使馆】embassy
【使坏】play a trick; make mischief (or trouble)
【使唤】❶order about ❷use
【使劲】use strength; exert strength
【使命】mission; task
【使命感】sense of mission (or calling)
【使团】diplomatic mission
【使用】use; employ; apply; make use of
【使用费】utilization fee; fee of utilization
【使用说明书】operation (or user's) manual; operation instructions
【使者】envoy; messenger

始 (shǐ) beginning; start

【始发站】starting station
【始末】the whole story; all the facts of a matter
【始终】from beginning (or start) to end; all along; throughout
【始终不渝】unswerving; consistent; steadfast
【始祖】first ancestor

驶 (shǐ) ❶sail; drive ❷speed

屎 (shǐ) ❶ excrement; faeces; stool; dung; droppings: 拉~ shit; empty the bowels ❷secretion (from the eye, ear, etc.): 眼~ eye discharge; gum in the eyes; 耳~ earwax

士 (shì) ❶scholar ❷noncommissioned officer (NCO) ❸a person trained in a certain field ❹commendable person ❺bodyguard, one of the pieces in Chinese chess

【士兵】soldier
【士气】morale

氏 (shì) ❶family; clan ❷(used after a married woman's maiden name) ❸(used after the surname of a famous person)

【氏族】clan

示 (shì) ❶show ❷instruct

【示范】demonstrate; set an example
【示例】give typical examples; give a demonstration
【示威】❶ demonstration ❷ demonstrate; display one's strength
【示意】hint; give a hint
【示众】put before the public; expose to the public

世 (shì) ❶ world ❷era; age ❸generation ❹life; lifetime

【世代】for generations
【世代相传】pass on from generation to generation
【世道】the manners and morals of the time; social conditions
【世故】❶worldly wisdom ❷worldly wise
【世纪】century
【世交】❶friendship lasting through generations ❷old family friends
【世界杯】the World Cup
【世界观】world outlook
【世界贸易组织】World Trade Organiza-

tion (WTO)

【世面】society; world; life

【世人】common people

【世上】in the world; on earth

【世上无难事,只怕有心人】nothing in the world is difficult if one gives his mind to it

【世态】❶ways of the world ❷attitude of the public

【世外桃源】the Land of Peach Blossoms—a fictitious land of peace, away from the turmoil of the world; a haven of peace

仕 (shì) ❶be an official ❷bodyguard, one of the pieces in Chinese chess

【仕女】❶a maid in an imperial palace; maid of honour ❷traditional Chinese painting of beautiful women

【仕途】official career

市 (shì) ❶market ❷city

【市场】market; marketplace

【市场导向】❶market-oriented ❷market orientation

【市场竞争】market competition

【市场调节】market regulation; regulation by the market

【市场需求】market demand

S

【市话】local telephone service (or call)

【市郊】suburb; outskirts

【市容】appearance of a city; city appearance

【市委】municipal Party committee

【市长】mayor

【市政】municipal administration

式 (shì) ❶model; pattern ❷type; style ❸ceremony

【式样】type; style; model; pattern

【式子】❶posture ❷formula

势 (shì) ❶power ❷tendency ❸situation ❹gesture; posture

【势必】certainly; possibly; surely

【势不可挡】irresistible

【势均力敌】match each other in strength; be equal to each other

【势力】momentum; trend; power; influence

【势态】position; situation: ~严重 in a serious situation

【势在必行】be imperative (under the circumstances)

事 (shì) ❶matter; business; thing; affair ❷trouble; accident ❸job; work ❹attend upon ❺be engaged in; engage in

【事半功倍】get twice the result with half the effort

【事变】incident; the course of events; events

【事不宜迟】the matter will bear no delay; admit of no delay

【事出有因】there is good reason for it; it is by no means accidental

【事故】accident; mishap

【事过境迁】things change when the matter is over

【事后】after the event; afterwards; later

【事件】incident; event

【事例】example; instance

【事情】matter; business; thing; affair

【事实胜于雄辩】facts speak louder than words

【事先】beforehand; in advance; before the event

【事业】❶cause; undertaking ❷facilities

【事业心】devotion to one's work; aspiration; will for achievements

【事由】the origin of an incident; particulars of a matter

【事在人为】it is up to man to settle a matter; it is the man who disposes

侍 (shì) wait (or attend) upon

【侍候】wait upon

【侍者】attendant; waiter; servant

饰 (shì) ❶decoration ❷decorate ❸play (or act) the part of

【饰物】articles for personal adornment; jewelry; ornaments; decorations

【饰演】play the role of

试 (shì) ❶exam; examination; test; experiment ❷test; try

【试唱】try out a song

【试穿】try on

【试管婴儿】test-tube baby

【试金石】touchstone

【试卷】examination paper

【试题】examination questions

【试想】just think

【试销】❶trial sale (or marketing) ❷put on trial sale

【试验】❶trial; test; experiment ❷try out

【试用】❶try out ❷be on trial (or probation)

【试用期】probation period

视 (shì) ❶look; look at ❷look upon as; regard ❸inspect

【视察】inspect; visitation; inspection; visit

【视而不见】turn a blind eye to; take no notice of

【视力】sight; eyesight

【视频】video frequency

【视听材料】audio-visual materials

【视同路人】regard as a stranger; treat like a stranger

【视线】view

【视野】field of vision

拭 (shì) wipe; wipe away; clean

【拭目以待】wait and see; be watchful (or on the watch)

柿 (shì) persimmon

【柿饼】dried persimmon

是 (shì) ❶be ❷exist ❸correct; right ❹yes

【是非】❶right and wrong: 明辨～ tell right clearly from wrong ❷dispute; gossip: 搬弄～ tell tales; talk gossip

【是非颠倒】confuse right and wrong

【是非之地】place of trouble

【是否】whether; if

适 (shì) ❶fit; suitable ❷right ❸comfortable; well

【适当】suitable; proper; appropriate; adequacy: 措辞～ appropriately worded

【适度】❶proper; moderate ❷moderate degree: 繁简～ neither too simple nor too elaborate

【适合】suit; fit; suit with; part to; be suited to; frame

【适可而止】know when and where to stop; stop when necessary; stop before going too far

【适量】an appropriate amount or quantity

【适龄】of right age

【适时】at the right time; timely; in good time

【适销】salable

【适宜】fit; suitable; appropriate

【适应】suit; fit; adapt to

【适应能力】adaptive capacity; adaptability

【适用】suit; apply to

【适者生存】survival of the fittest

【适中】❶moderate ❷well situated

恃 (shì) depend on; rely on

S

【恃强凌弱】use one's power to bully the weak

室 (shì) room

【室内】indoor

【室内设计】indoor design

【室外】outdoor

逝 (shì) ❶pass ❷die; pass away

【逝世】die; pass away

释 (shì) ❶explain ❷clear up ❸relieve; let go ❹release; set free; free

【释放】set free; release

【释然】feel relieved; feel at ease

嗜 (shì) have a liking for; be fond of

【嗜好】have a liking for; be fond of

誓 (shì) ❶oath; vow ❷swear; pledge; vow

【誓不罢休】swear not to give up (or stop); swear not to rest

【誓词】oath; pledge

【誓言】pledge; oath: 立下～ swear an oath

shou

收 (shōu) ❶income; revenue ❷receive; accept ❸collect ❹gather in ❺close ❻bring to an end; stop ❼control ❽put in jail ❾money received; receipts ❿harvest; gather in

S

【收藏】collect; store

【收场】❶end ❷end (or wind, round) up; stop; bring (or come) to an end

【收成】harvest; yield

【收发】❶dispatcher ❷receive and send off

【收费】charge; collect fees

【收费站】toll (or tolling) gate

【收复】recover; recapture

【收购】buy; purchase

【收回】❶take (or get) back; call in; recall ❷withdraw

【收获】❶result; gains ❷harvest; gather in

【收集】collect; gather

【收据】receipt

【收款机】cash register

【收款人】payee

【收录机】radio recorder

【收录】❶receive and record ❷employ

【收罗】collect; gather; recruit; enlist: ～人才 recruit qualified personnel

【收纳】receive; take in: 如数～ accept a sum of money as indicated

【收取】get payment; receive; collect: ～手续费 collect service (or handling) charges

【收容】❶take in; house ❷detention

【收入】income; revenue

【收拾】❶put in order; tidy ❷pack ❸repair; mend ❹settle with; punish

【收视率】viewing (or audience) rate (or rating); rating

【收缩】draw back contract; shrink

【收听】listen in; listen to (the radio): ～天气预报 listen to a weather forecast

【收效】yield results; bear fruit; produce effects: ～显著 bring notable results

【收养】adopt

【收益】income; gains; profit; earnings

【收银机】cash register

【收银员】cashier

【收支】income and expenses

手 (shǒu) ❶hand ❷skilled person; craftsman ❸hold; hold in one's hand ❹handy ❺by hand

【手臂】❶arm ❷ reliable helper

【手表】watch

【手柄】arm; handle

【手不释卷】always have a book in one's

hand; be a diligent reader

【手册】handbook; manual

【手到擒来】just stretch the hand and bring it back very easy

【手电筒】flashlight; torch

【手法】❶skill; technique ❷trick

【手风琴】accordion

【手稿】manuscript

【手工】❶handwork ❷manual ❸by hand

【手工艺品】handicrafts

【手机】cellphone; cellular; mobile (or cellular) telephone

【手疾眼快】quick of eye and deft of hand

【手脚利落】be nimble

【手巾】handkerchief; towel

【手铐】handcuffs

【手枪】pistol

【手巧】deft; skillful with one's hands; nimble-fingered: 心灵～ clever and deft

【手软】be softhearted

【手势】gesture: 打～ make a gesture

【手术】operation: 动～ undergo (or perform) an operation

【手套】gloves; mittens

【手提包】handbag; bag

【手推车】handcart; wheelbarrow

【手舞足蹈】dance for joy

【手下】❶under sb. ❷at the hands of ❸on (or at) hand

【手心】❶centre of the palm ❷control

【手续】formalities; procedures

【手续费】service (or handling) charges

【手艺】❶ trade; handicraft ❷ craftsmanship; workmanship

【手语】sign language

【手掌】palm

【手指】finger

【手纸】toilet paper

【手镯】bracelet; bangle

【手足】❶movement ❷brothers

守 (shǒu) ❶ guard; defend ❷ keep watch ❸observe ❹close to; near

【守法】keep (or observe) the law

【守恒】conservation: 能量～ conservation of energy

【守候】❶keep watch ❷wait for

【守门】❶ be a doorkeeper; be on duty at the gate ❷keep goal

【守门员】goalkeeper

【守岁】stay up late on New Year's Eve

【守卫】guard; defend

【守信】keep one's word; keep one's promise

【守则】rules; regulations

【守职】stand fast at one's post; be faithful in the discharge of one's duties: ～尽责 be committed to one's duties

首 (shǒu) ❶head ❷leader; head; chief ❸bring a charge against; accuse sb. of ❹first

【首创】initiate; pioneer

【首次】for the first time

【首都】capital (of a country)

【首付】down payment

【首富】top rich person; the richest person

【首届】the first time

【首脑】head: 政府～head of government

【首饰】jewelry; ornaments

【首尾】❶head and tail; beginning and end ❷from beginning to end

【首位】the first place

【首席】❶seat of honour ❷chief

【首先】first; first of all

【首相】prime minister

【首选】first choice

【首要】first; chief; of the first important

【首映】premiere (show)

【首长】senior officer; leading cadre; leader

寿（shòu）❶ life；age ❷ birthday ❸ long-lived

【寿辰】birthday（of an elderly person）：八十～ the 80th birthday

【寿礼】birthday present

【寿命】life；lifespan

【寿司】sushi

【寿桃】❶ peaches offered as a birthday person ❷peach-shaped birthday cake

【寿星】❶the god of longevity ❷a person whose birthday is being celebrated

【寿终正寝】die in one's bed；die a natural death；die in bed of old age

受（shòu）❶ receive；accept ❷ bear；stand ❸suffer ❹be agreeable to

【受潮】become damp；be affected with damp

【受罚】be punished

【受害不浅】suffer not a little；suffer a lot

【受话人】receiver

【受贿罪】crime of accepting bribes

【受惊】be frightened；be startled

【受苦受难】live in misery；have one's fill of sufferings

【受理】❶ accept and handle ❷（of the court）accept and hear（a case）

【受凉】catch cold；get a cold

【受命】receive instructions or assignments

S

【受骗】be taken in；be deceived

【受聘】accept an appointment（to a post）

【受辱】be insulted；be disgraced；be humiliated：当场～ be insulted on the spot

【受伤】be wounded；be injured

【受托】be entrusted

【受刑】be tortured；be put to torture

【受益】benefit from（or by）；be benefited；profit by

【受益人】beneficiary

【受灾】be hit by a natural disaster：～地区 disaster area；stricken（or affected）area

【受之无愧】deserve；merit

【受之有愧】feel ill at ease to receive sth.；receive it with shame

【受罪】have a hard time；be on the rack；endure hardship，torture，etc.；have an unpleasant experience

狩（shòu）hunting

【狩猎】hunting

授（shòu）❶ give；award；confer ❷ teach；instruct

【授奖】award a prize

【授课】teach；give lessons；give instruction

【授权】authorize；empower

【授学位】grant degrees

【授予】give；award；confer；endow

售（shòu）sell：出～ put on sale

【售后服务】after-sale service

【售货机】vending machine

【售价】price

【售楼处】ready houses（or flats）selling store（or shop）

【售票处】ticket（or booking，box）office

【售票口】wicket

【售票员】ticket seller；conductor；booking-office clerk

兽（shòu）❶animal；beast ❷beastly

【兽性】brutish nature

【兽医】vet；veterinarian

瘦（shòu）❶thin ❷lean ❸tight

【瘦长】tall and thin；lanky：～脸 thin face

【瘦肉】lean meat

【瘦弱】thin and weak

【瘦小】thin and small

shu

书 (shū) ❶book ❷letter ❸document ❹write

【书包】schoolbag

【书橱】bookcase

【书呆子】bookworm

【书店】bookshop; bookstore

【书法】calligraphy; penmanship

【书房】study

【书稿】manuscript

【书号】book number: 国际标准~International Standard Book Number (or ISBN)

【书架】bookshelf

【书刊】books and periodicals

【书眉】top of a page; top margin

【书面语】written language; literary language

【书名】title

【书目】booklist

【书评】book review

【书签】bookmark

【书商】book seller (or dealer, distributor)

【书生】scholar

【书摊】bookstand; bookstall

【书写】write

【书信】letter

【书展】book exhibition

【书桌】desk; writing desk

抒 (shū) express

【抒发】express; give expression (or vent) to

【抒情】express one's emotion

【抒写】describe; express in writing; write of

枢 (shū) centre; pivot

【枢纽】pivot; hub; centre; axis; key position

叔 (shū) uncle; father's younger brother

【叔父】uncle

【叔叔】❶father's younger brother; uncle ❷(a child's form of address for any young man whose generation is senior) uncle

殊 (shū) ❶ different ❷ outstanding; special; unusual

【殊荣】special honours

【殊途同归】get to the same place by different ways

梳 (shū) comb

【梳理】carding comb out (one's hair)

【梳头】comb one's hair

【梳妆】dress and make up

【梳子】comb

淑 (shū) kind and gentle, fair

【淑女】a fair maiden; a virtuous maiden; a noble lady

舒 (shū) ❶stretch; ease ❷leisurely

【舒畅】free from care and worry: 心情~ have a mind of ease; have ease of mind

【舒服】❶comfortable ❷well

【舒缓】❶slow and unhurried; leisurely: 节拍~的歌声 singing in a slow tempo ❷ relaxed; mild: 语调~ in a mild tone

【舒散】❶ stretch and flex ❷ shake off one's fatigue or cares: ~心中的郁闷 shake off a gloomy mood

【舒适】cosy; comfortable

【舒心】comfortable; happy

【舒展】❶outspread ❷comfortable

疏 (shū) ❶ neglect ❷ dredge ❸ scatter ❹ unfamiliar ❺ thin; sparse ❻ void

❼distant

【疏导】dredge

【疏忽】❶ignore；neglect；overlook ❷carelessness；negligence

【疏解】❶mediate ❷ease up；mitigate

【疏落】sparse；scattered：～的晨星 sparse morning stars

【疏散】❶disperse；evacuate ❷scattered；sparse

【疏松】❶loosen ❷loose

【疏通】❶dredge ❷act as a peacemaker；mediate between two parties

【疏远】become alienated；estrange；drift apart

输 (shū) ❶transport ❷lose；be defeated

【输出】❶send out ❷export ❸exportation

【输入】❶bring in ❷import ❸importation

【输送】❶transport ❷convey；carry；infuse；wheel；send；feed；provide

【输血】blood transfusion

【输赢】❶victory or defeat ❷winnings and losses in gambling

蔬 (shū) vegetable

【蔬菜】vegetables；greens；greenstuffs

孰 (shú) ❶who；which：～是～非？Which is right and which is wrong? ❷what

赎 (shú) ❶redeem；ransom ❷atone for

【赎金】ransom money；ransom

【赎身】(of slaves，prostitutes) redeem oneself；buy back one's freedom

【赎罪】atone for one's crime

熟 (shú) ❶ripe ❷cooked ❸refined ❹familiar ❺skilled；experienced；practised ❻deeply；thoroughly

【熟练】skilled；skillful；practised；proficient

【熟门熟路】a familiar road and a familiar door things that one knows well

【熟能生巧】practice makes perfect；skills come from practice；practice develops skills

【熟人】acquaintance

【熟食】cooked food

【熟视无睹】turn a blind eye to；overlook；take no notice of

【熟手】old hand；practised hand

【熟睡】sleep soundly；be fast asleep；sleep like a log

【熟悉】know well；be familiar with

暑 (shǔ) ❶hot weather ❷summer ❸hot

【暑假】summer vacation (or holidays)

【暑热】hot summer weather：～难耐 intolerably hot summer weather

【暑天】hot summer days；dog days

属 (shǔ) ❶family member ❷class；kind ❸belong to ❹be category ❺genus ❻be under；be subordinate to

【属下】subordinate

【属相】popular name for 生肖：any one of the names of symbolic animals associated with a 12-year cycle，often used to denote the year of a person's birth

【属性】attribute；property

【属于】belong to；be one part of

署 (shǔ) ❶government office ❷make arrangement for；arrange ❸handle by proxy；act as deputy ❹put one's signature to；sign

【署名】sign；put one's signature to

鼠 (shǔ) mouse；rat

【鼠辈】mean persons；scoundrel；nobody：无名～ a nobody

【鼠标】mouse

【鼠目寸光】be shortsighted like mice

数 (shǔ) ❶count ❷be reckoned as exceptionally (or good, bad, etc.) ❸ enumerate; list

另见本页 shù

【数不清】countless

【数不胜数】❶beyond count ❷too many to count; countless; innumerable; incalculable

【数九寒天】coldest days of the year

【数一数二】count as one of the very best; rank very high

薯 (shǔ) potato; yam

曙 (shǔ) daybreak; dawn

【曙光】dawn; the first light of morning

束 (shù) ❶bundle; bunch ❷tie; bind ❸ control; restrain; limit

【束缚】tie; bind

【束之高阁】put (lay) on the shelf; have (sth.) shelved and forgotten; brush sth. aside

述 (shù) state; relate; narrate

【述说】state; recount; narrate

【述职】report on one's work

树 (shù) ❶tree ❷set up; establish ❸ grow ❹bring up

【树丛】grove; thicket

【树大根深】a big tree with deep roots (said of an influential person or a huge organization)

【树干】tree trunk; trunk

【树根】tree stump, root

【树冠】crown (of a tree)

【树立】set up; establish

【树苗】sapling

【树木】trees

【树皮】bark

【树荫】the shade of a tree

【树枝】branch; twig

竖 (shù) ❶set upright; erect; stand ❷ upright; vertical

【竖立】set upright; erect; stand

【竖起】erect; stand; hold up

恕 (shù) forgive; pardon; excuse

【恕不奉陪】excuse me for not keeping you company

数 (shù) ❶number; figure: 人~ number of people; 整~ integer; 小~ decimal; 分~ fraction ❷several; a few

另见本页 shǔ

【数额】a fixed number; a definite amount

【数据】data

【数据库】databank; database

【数理化】mathematics, physics and chemistry

【数量】amount; quantity

【数码】❶numeral ❷digit ❸digital

【数码摄像机】digital video (DV)

【数目】number; amount

【数学】math; mathematics

【数字化】❶digitalize ❷digitalization

【数字图书馆】digital library

漱 (shù) rinse (the mouth); gargle

【漱口】rinse the mouth; gargle

【漱口剂】gargle

shua

刷 (shuā) ❶brush; scrub ❷swish; rustle ❸daub ❹brush off; remove

【刷卡】swipe (or stump, punch) a card

【刷新】renew

【刷牙】brush one's teeth

【刷子】brush; scrub

耍 (shuǎ) ❶play ❷play with

【耍把戏】❶play acrobatics ❷play tricks

【耍弄】make fun of; make a fool of; fool

【耍脾气】go into a huff; get into a temper

【耍手腕】play tricks

shuai

衰 (shuāi) ❶ weaken; decline ❷ week; feeble

【衰减】weaken; fail; diminish: 功能~ weaken function

【衰竭】failure; exhaustion: 心力~ heart failure

【衰弱】❶weaken ❷week; feeble

摔 (shuāi) ❶ throw; cast ❷ fall; tumble; lose one's balance ❸ hurtle down; plunge ❹cause to fall and break

【摔跤】❶ tumble and fall ❷ suffer a setback ❸come a cropper ❹ wrestling

甩 (shuǎi) ❶ swing; wave ❷ throw; cast; fling; toss ❸ leave behind; throw off

【甩卖】clearance sale; reduction sale; disposal of goods at reduced prices

帅 (shuài) ❶ commander-in-chief ❷ graceful; handsome

【帅哥】handsome boy; dashing guy

【帅旗】the flag of a commander in chief

率 (shuài) ❶ lead; command ❷ rash; hasty ❸ frank; straightforward ❹ generally; usually

另见 1095 页 lǜ

【率领】lead; head; command: ~队伍 command a troop

【率直】straightforward; unreserved: 说话~ speak frankly

shuan

闩 (shuān) ❶bolt; latch ❷bolt

拴 (shuān) tie; fasten

【拴绑】tie up; bind up

涮 (shuàn) rinse

【涮羊肉】instant-boiled mutton; mutton fondue

shuang

双 (shuāng) ❶ pair ❷ even ❸ both ❹ double ❺two

【双胞胎】twins

【双边贸易】bilateral trade

【双层】double deck

【双程票】round (or return) ticket

【双重】double; twofold

【双方】both sides; two parties

【双飞】round-trip flight

【双杠】parallel bars

【双关】having a double meaning: ~语 pun

【双规】require to report one's problems within a prescribed period and in a prescribed place

【双亲】father and mother; parents

【双全】complete in both respects; possessing both: 文武~ be well versed in both literary and martial arts

【双刃剑】double-edge sword

【双数】even number

【双双】❶in pairs ❷both

【双喜临门】a double blessing has descended upon the house

【双向选择】two-way choice

【双休日】two-day weekend

【双学位】double degree

【双赢】win-win; victory for both sides
【双语教学】bilingual teaching

霜 (shuāng) ❶frost ❷white

【霜冻】frost
【霜叶】frosty leaves—autumn maple leaves

孀 (shuāng) widow

爽 (shuǎng) ❶ clear; bright ❷ open-hearted; frank; straight forward ❸well

【爽口】tasty and refreshing
【爽快】❶ delightful ❷ frank; straightforward
【爽朗】❶ bright; clear; fine ❷ frank; straightforward
【爽直】frank; straightforward: 性情～ straightforward disposition

shui

谁 (shuí)(又读 shéi) ❶who ❷anyone ❸everyone ❹someone

【谁知】who knows; who would have thought

水 (shuǐ) ❶water ❷liquid ❸juice

【水坝】dam
【水泵】pump; water pump
【水表】water meter
【水彩画】watercolor
【水产】aquatic products
【水车】❶waterwheel ❷water wagon
【水到渠成】when water flows, a channel is formed
【水稻】paddy; rice
【水滴石穿】dripping water wears through a stone
【水电费】water and electricity charges
【水电站】hydropower station
【水短缺】shortage of water
【水分】❶moisture ❷exaggeration; untrue content
【水管】water pipe; pipe
【水果】fruit
【水花】spray
【水火不容】be incompatible as fire and water
【水货】smuggled goods
【水饺】dumpling
【水晶】crystal
【水井】well
【水库】reservoir
【水利】❶water conservancy ❷water conservancy project
【水流】current
【水龙头】tap; faucet; bibcock
【水落石出】when the water falls, rocks will come to light; the whole thing comes to light
【水面】surface of water
【水泥】cement; concrete
【水牛】water buffalo
【水平】level; standard; horizontal
【水平测试】proficiency test
【水渠】channel; ditch; canal
【水乳交融】as well blended as milk and water—in complete harmony
【水手】sailor; seaman
【水塔】water tower
【水塘】pond
【水天一色】the water and the sky blended in one color (said of a vast body of water)
【水田】paddy field
【水土】water and soil; natural environment and climate
【水土保持】water and soil conservation

【水土不服】be not used to the climate
【水土流失】soil erosion
【水污染】water pollution
【水污染防治】prevention and control of water pollution
【水仙】narcissus
【水泄不通】even water can not trickle through;be watertight
【水星】Mercury
【水银】mercury;quicksilver
【水域】waters;water area;body of water
【水源】❶ the source of a river ❷ source of water
【水灾】floods
【水蒸气】steam;water vapour
【水质】water quality
【水准】level;standard
【水资源】water resources
【水资源保护】water resources protection

税 (shuì) tax;duty:课~ levy a tax on;纳~ pay taxes;收~ collect taxes;偷~ evade taxes
【税法】tax law
【税费改革】tax-for-charge reform
【税后利润】after-tax profit
【税率】tax rate; rate of taxation; tariff rate
【税收】tax revenue

S

睡 (shuì) sleep
【睡袋】sleeping bag
【睡裤】pyjama trousers
【睡眠】sleep
【睡醒】wake up
【睡衣】pyjamas

shun

顺 (shùn) ❶obey;yield to ❷bring into line ❸ take the opportunity to ❹ smooth ❺agreeable ❻along
【顺便】in passing;by the way
【顺畅】smooth and easy;unhindered
【顺次】in order; in succession; in proper sequence
【顺从】be obedient to;yield to
【顺耳】pleasing to the ear
【顺口】❶read smoothly ❷speak thoughtlessly ❸be agreeable to the taste
【顺口溜】jingle
【顺理成章】in line with the rules (or logic);logical
【顺利】smoothly;without trouble
【顺路】not out of the way;on the way;directly
【顺势】❶ take advantage of ❷ in the wake of
【顺手】❶ smoothly ❷ conveniently ❸ at one's convenience
【顺水推舟】push the boat along with the current—make use of an opportunity to gain one's end
【顺心】agreeable;satisfactory:诸事~all is well
【顺序】❶ order ❷ in order (or turn);by turns
【顺意】satisfactory;as one wishes
【顺应】act in line with;go in line with

瞬 (shùn)wink;twinkling
【瞬息】twinkling
【瞬息万变】undergoing a myriad changes in the twinkling of an eye;fast changing

shuo

说 (shuō) ❶ theory ❷ speak; say; talk ❸explain ❹blame;scold
【说不定】perhaps;maybe
【说不过去】groundless;unjustifiable

【说长道短】gossip
【说唱】rap;talking and singing
【说大话】talk big;boast
【说到做到】do what one says; live up to one's word; match one's deed to one's words
【说得过去】justifiable;passable
【说定】agree on;get sth. settled;settle
【说法】❶ statement ❷ wording; formulation
【说服】prevail on;persuade;convince
【说话】speak;say;talk
【说话算数】mean what one says;stand by one's word
【说谎】lie;tell a lie
【说空话】use fine words;talk nonsense
【说理】❶argue;reason things out ❷listen to reason;be reasonable
【说明】❶ explanation ❷ explain; make clear
【说明书】directions;manual
【说情】plead for mercy for sb. ;intercede for sb.
【说一不二】mean what one says

烁 (shuò)shining;bright

【烁烁】glitter;sparkle

硕 (shuò) large

【硕果累累】countless achievements
【硕士】master:理学~ Master of Science (or MS.);文学~ Master of Arts (or MA.);~学位 master's degree

sī

司 (sī) ❶department ❷take (or be in) charge of

【司法】administration of justice; judicature
【司法部】Ministry of Justice
【司法公正】justice;judicial fairness
【司法鉴定】judicial testimony
【司法人员】judicial functionaries
【司机】driver
【司空见惯】a common occurrence
【司令】 commander: 总 ~ commander in chief
【司令部】headquarters
【司仪】master of ceremonies

丝 (sī) ❶silk ❷a threadlike thing ❸a tiny bit

【丝绸】silk;silk cloth
【丝带】silk ribbon
【丝瓜】towel gourd;dishcloth gourd
【丝毫不差】fit to a hair;be just the same
【丝巾】silk scarf
【丝丝入扣】(mostly of a writing or artistic performance) (done) with meticulous care and flawless artistry
【丝袜】silk stockings

私 (sī) ❶ personal; private ❷ selfish ❸illegal

【私产】private property
【私房钱】personal savings
【私家车】private car;privately-owned car
【私交】personal friendship
【私立学校】private school (or college, university)
【私利】personal interests
【私了】settle privately (out of the court)
【私企】private enterprise
【私人】personal;private
【私生活】personal (or private) life
【私事】personal affairs
【私下】in private (or secret);privately
【私心】selfishness
【私营】private;privately owned
【私语】whisper

【私自】privately; secretly; illegally; without permission

思 (sī) ❶ thought; thinking ❷ think; consider; deliberate ❸ think of; long for ❹ miss

【思潮】❶ thoughts ❷ trend of thought

【思考】think; think about; think deeply; ponder over; reflect on

【思路】train of thought; thinking

【思念】think of (or about); miss; long for

【思维】thinking; thought

【思想】thought; thinking; idea

【思想家】thinker

【思想解放】ideological emancipation

【思想素质】quality of thought

【思想压力】pressure on mind

【思绪】❶ train of thought ❷ feeling: ~万千 myriad of thoughts well up in one's mind; ~不宁 feel perturbed

斯 (sī) ❶ this ❷ then; thus

【斯文】gentle; refined

厮 (sī) together

【厮打】fight together

【厮杀】fight at close quarters (with weapons)

撕 (sī) tear

S

【撕成两半】tear in two

【撕成碎片】tear into pieces

【撕下】tear off

嘶 (sī) ❶ neigh ❷ hiss ❸ hoarse

【嘶哑】hoarse

死 (sǐ) ❶ die ❷ deadly rigid; fixed ❸ dead ❹ end ❺ closed ❻ extremely ❼ to the death

【死板】stiff; rigid; fixed

【死党】diehard followers

【死对头】deadly enemy

【死而后已】until one's dying day; to the end of one's days

【死胡同】blind alley; dead end

【死活】❶ life or death; fate ❷ anyway

【死火山】extinct volcano

【死机】system halt (or crash)

【死结】fast knot

【死里逃生】escape from the jaws of death

【死路】❶ blind alley ❷ road to ruin

【死皮赖脸】thick-skinned and shameless

【死去活来】faint away and come to in great pain (or grief); hovering between life and death; extremely sad and painful

【死伤】the dead and the wounded; casualties: ~惨重 suffer heavy casualties

【死水】stagnant water

【死亡】death; doom: ~率 death rate; mortality; ~线 verge of death

【死心塌地】be dead set; be hellbent

【死心眼儿】❶ person of a one-track mind ❷ stubborn

【死刑】death sentence; death penalty; capital punishment

【死账】bad loan (or debt)

【死罪】capital crime

四 (sì) four

【四边】❶ four sides ❷ all around; on all sides

【四边形】quadrilateral

【四处】all around; everywhere

【四海】all over the country (or world)

【四海为家】make one's home wherever one is

【四合院】a courtyard; quadrangle

【四季】❶ the four seasons ❷ all the

year round

【四邻】one's near neighbours: 街坊～ neighbours

【四面八方】in all directions; far and near

【四平八稳】steady; running no risk; balanced

【四通八达】easy of access in all directions

【四项基本原则】the Four Cardinal Principles

【四月】April

【四肢】the four limbs; arms and legs

寺 (sì) temple

【寺庙】temple

【寺院】temple; monastery

似 (sì) ❶seem; appear ❷like ❸as if (or though); as

【似曾相识】seem to have met before

【似乎】❶ it seems ❷ as if (or though) ❸seemingly

【似水流年】time passes swiftly like flowing water

伺 (sì) ❶watch ❷wait for 另见 937 页 cì

【伺机】watch out for a chance; wait for an opportunity to

饲 (sì) raise; rear

【饲料】feed; fodder

【饲养】raise; rear

肆 (sì) ❶shop; store ❷four ❸wantonly

【肆无忌惮】be unbridled

【肆意】wilfully; wantonly

song

松 (sōng) ❶pine ❷loosen; relax ❸unfasten; untie; undo ❹ loose ❺ not hard up ❻soft

【松绑】❶ untie a person ❷ relax control (or restriction)

【松弛】❶limp; flabby; slack: 肌肉～ flaccid muscles ❷lax: 纪律～ lax discipline

【松紧】❶degree of tightness ❷elasticity

【松口】soften; become less rigid

【松软】soft; loose

【松散】relax; loose

【松手】let go; loosen one's grip

【松鼠】squirrel

【松树】pine tree

【松土】loosen the soil

【松懈】slacken; relax

【松脂】rosin

【松子】pine nut

怂 (sǒng)

【怂恿】incite; egg sb. on; abet

耸 (sǒng) ❶ towering; lofty ❷ alarm; shock

【耸动】❶shrug (one's shoulders) ❷create a sensation

【耸肩】shrug one's shoulders

【耸立】tower high

【耸人听闻】make a sensation by high-sounding talk

悚 (sǒng)

【悚然】terrified; horrified

送 (sòng) ❶give as a present; ❷deliver ❸see sb. off or out; accompany; escort ❹take sb. (or sth.) to

【送报】deliver newspaper

【送别】see sb. off

【送还】return; give back

【送货上门】deliver goods to the customer's home

【送交】deliver; hand over

【送旧迎新】see off the old and welcome

the new; ring out the Old Year and ring in the New Year
【送客】see a visitor out
【送礼】give sb. a present
【送人情】do sb. a favour
【送温暖】visit to offer help
【送信】❶deliver letters ❷deliver a message; send a word
【送行】❶see sb. off ❷give a send-off party
【送葬】take part in a funeral procession

诵 (sòng) ❶read aloud; chant ❷recite
【诵读】read aloud; chant

颂 (sòng) ❶song; ode ❷praise; extol; eulogize; laud ❸express good wishes in letters
【颂扬】sing sb.'s praises; praise; laud; extol

sou

搜 (sōu) search
【搜捕】track down and arrest
【搜查】ransack; rummage
【搜集】collect; gather
【搜缴】search for and capture: ~凶器 search for and capture a lethal weapon
【搜救】search and rescue
【搜索】search (or hunt) for; scout around
【搜索引擎】search engine
【搜寻】search for; look for

嗖 (sōu) whiz

馊 (sōu) sour; spoiled
【馊主意】a stupid suggestion; a lousy idea

su

苏 (sū) revive; come to
【苏丹】❶sultan ❷the Sudan
【苏醒】revive; regain consciousness; come to (oneself); come to one's senses

酥 (sū) ❶crisp; short ❷short pastry; shortbread ❸limp; weak
【酥脆】crisp
【酥软】limp; weak; soft
【酥油】butter

俗 (sú) ❶custom ❷layman ❸popular; common ❹vulgar ❺secular
【俗称】commonly called
【俗话】proverb; common saying
【俗气】vulgar; in poor taste
【俗套】convention; conventional pattern

夙 (sù) long-standing; ever-lasting; old
【夙敌】long-time enemy
【夙愿】long-cherished wish

诉 (sù) ❶tell; relate ❷vent ❸complain; accuse
【诉苦】air one's suffering; vent (or pour out) one's grievances
【诉说】tell; relate
【诉讼】suit; lawsuit; legal action

肃 (sù) ❶wipe out ❷solemn; serious; grave ❸respectful ❹eliminate; clean up; mop up
【肃静】in solemn silence
【肃立】stand in respect and solemnity
【肃然起敬】be filled with deep respect

素 (sù) ❶vegetable ❷element ❸white ❹plain ❺native ❻usually
【素不相识】be strangers to each other
【素材】material
【素菜】vegetable dish

【素餐】❶vegetarian meal; be a vegetarian ❷not work for one's living

【素净】plain and neat; quiet: 衣着~ be plainly and neatly dressed

【素来】always; usually

【素昧平生】be strangers to each other; have never met before

【素描】❶sketch ❷literary sketch

【素雅】simple but elegant; plain and in good taste: 衣着~ be tastefully dressed in a simple style

【素质教育】quality-oriented education; education aimed at all-round development; character development education

速 (sù) ❶ speed; velocity ❷ speedy; quick; fast; swift

【速成班】crash course; accelerated course

【速冻食品】fast-frozen food

【速度】speed; velocity

【速决】make a quick decision; bring to a quick end

【速溶咖啡】instant coffee

【速写】sketch; literary sketch

宿 (sù) ❶lodge; put up; stay ❷veteran ❸old; long-standing

【宿舍】dormitory; living quarters

【宿营】camp

粟 (sù) foxtail millet; millet

【粟米】maize; Indian corn; corn

塑 (sù) model; mould: 泥~ clay sculpture

【塑料】plastics

【塑料袋】plastic bag

【塑身】shape one's body

【塑像】❶mold a statue ❷statue

【塑造】❶ model; mould ❷ portray; describe; create

溯 (sù) ❶go against the stream ❷trace back; recall

【溯源】trace to the source

簌 (sù)

【簌簌】❶ rustle ❷ (of tears) streaming down

suan

酸 (suān) ❶acid ❷sour ❸pedantic ❹sad ❺ aching ❻ sick at heart; grieved; distressed

【酸菜】pickled Chinese cabbage; Chinese sauerkraut

【酸楚】grieved; miserable; distressed

【酸溜溜】❶sour ❷aching ❸sad ❹bitter; biting ❺pedantic

【酸奶】yoghurt

【酸涩】❶ (of smell, taste, feeling) sour and bitter ❷sad; sick at heart

【酸甜苦辣】joys and sorrows

【酸痛】ache

蒜 (suàn) garlic

【蒜泥】mashed garlic

算 (suàn) ❶calculate ❷include ❸plan ❹reckon ❺count

【算计】❶calculate ❷plan; consider ❸reckon ❹ plot: 被人~ be plotted against by others

【算盘】abacus

【算术】arithmetic

【算数】count; hold; stand: 他们说话是~的。They mean what they say.

sui

虽 (suī) though; although

【虽然】though; although

绥 (suí) ❶peaceful ❷pacify

【绥靖】pacify; appease

随 (suí) ❶follow ❷obey ❸do as one likes ❹along with

【随笔】informal essay; jottings

【随便】❶do as one likes ❷at one's convenience ❸free; casual; careless ❹wilful

【随处】everywhere; anywhere

【随大流】follow the trend; go with the tide

【随地】anywhere; everywhere: 随时～ at any time and in any place

【随风转舵】tack with the wind

【随和】amiable

【随后】later; afterwards

【随机】❶act in line with circumstances ❷at random

【随机应变】act according to the state of affairs; do as the changing circumstances demand

【随身】along with one; with one

【随身携带】take along with

【随声附和】echo; echo to what others say; chime in with others

【随时随地】❶at all times and places ❷at any time

【随手】at one's convenience; conveniently

S

【随心所欲】do as one likes; do as one pleases

【随意】at will; as one pleases; to one's liking: ～出入 come in and out at will

岁 (suì) year

【岁寒三友】the three plant friends who thrive in cold weather—the pine, the bamboo and the plum

【岁数】age; years: 上～ get on in years; get old

【岁月】years: ～不饶人 time and tide wait for no man; ～如流 time passes like fleeting water

遂 (suì) ❶succeed; be successful ❷satisfy; fulfil

【遂意】to one's liking; suit one's expectations

【遂愿】have one's wish fulfilled: 称心～ perfectly satisfied; be highly satisfied

碎 (suì) ❶break into pieces ❷broken ❸garrulous

【碎石】crushed stones; broken stones

【碎纸机】paper shredder

隧 (suì)

【隧道】tunnel

穗 (suì) ❶ear ❷tassel

sun

孙 (sūn) ❶grandson ❷generations below that of the grandchild

【孙女】granddaughter

损 (sǔn) ❶decrease; lose ❷harm; damage ❸injure ❹mean; harsh

【损害】harm; damage; injure

【损耗】❶loss; wear and tear ❷wastage

【损坏】damage; injure

【损人利己】benefit oneself at others' expense

【损失】❶loss ❷lose

笋 (sǔn) bamboo shoot

【笋尖】tender tips of bamboo shoots

suo

唆 (suō) instigate; abet

【唆使】instigate

梭 (suō) shuttle

【梭子】❶weaver's shuttle ❷a clip (of bullets)

缩 (suō) ❶ contract; shrink ❷ draw back; withdraw

【缩短】shorten; cut down; reduce

【缩减】cut; reduce

【缩手缩脚】❶be timid; be overcautious ❷ shrink with cold

【缩水】shrink

【缩小差距】narrow the gap

【缩印】reprint books in a reduced format

【缩影】miniature

所 (suǒ) place

【所得】income; earnings; gains

【所得税】income tax

【所见所闻】what one sees and hears

【所谓】❶what is called ❷so-called

【所以】so; therefore; as a result

【所以然】the reason why; the whys and wherefores

【所有】❶possessions ❷everything ❸possess; own

【所有权】ownership; proprietary rights

【所在】❶place; location ❷where

【所作所为】one's behaviour or conduct

索 (suǒ) ❶ rope ❷ search; seek ❸ demand; ask

【索道】cableway; ropeway

【索价】ask a price; charge: ~过高 demand an exorbitant price

【索赔】claim damages (or an indemnity); claim for damages; make a claim; claim

【索取】claim; demand; ask for; exact; extort

【索引】index

琐 (suǒ) trivial; petty

【琐事】trifles

【琐碎】trifling; trivial

【琐细】trifling; trivial

锁 (suǒ) ❶ lock ❷ lock up ❸ lock and chains; chains

【锁定】lock; lock in

【锁骨】collarbone; clavicle

【锁链】chains

T t

ta

他 (tā) ❶he; him ❷other; another

【他的】his

【他们】they; them

【他们自己】themselves

【他人】others; other people

【他日】some day

【他乡】strange land; place away from home

【他自己】himself

它 (tā) it

【它的】its

【它们】they; them

【它们的】❶their ❷theirs

【它们自己】themselves

她 (tā) she; her

【她的】❶her ❷hers

【她们】they; them

【她们的】❶their ❷theirs

【她自己】herself

塌 (tā) ❶collapse; fall down ❷sink ❸feel at ease; calm down

【塌方】❶cave in; collapse ❷landslide

【塌陷】sink; cave in; subside

踏 (tā)

【踏实】❶earnest free from anxiety ❷feel at ease ❸free from anxiety

塔 (tǎ) ❶pagoda ❷tower: 灯～ lighthouse; beacon; 纪念～ memorial tower

【塔钟】tower clock; turret clock

榻 (tà) couch; bed: 下～ stay at

【榻榻米】tatami

踏 (tà) ❶tread; stamp; step on ❷go to the spot

【踏板】treadle; footboard; footrest

【踏勘】make an on-the-spot survey

【踏青】go for an outing in spring

tai

胎 (tāi) ❶padding ❷tire: 轮～ tire ❸birth

【胎动】movement of the foetus which can be felt by the mother

【胎儿】fetus

【胎教】antenatal instruction

台 (tái) ❶platform; stage; terrace: 月～ railway platform; 讲～ platform ❷stand; support ❸desk; table ❹broadcasting station ❺special telephone service

【台布】table cloth

【台词】actor's lines
【台灯】desk (or table, reading) lamp
【台风】typhoon
【台阶】a flight of steps; step
【台历】desk calendar
【台球】billiard ball; billiards
【台湾海峡两岸】both sides of the Taiwan Straits

抬 (tái) ❶raise; lift up ❷carry

【抬杠】argue for the sake of arguing; bicker; wrangle
【抬举】praise; promote; favour
【抬起】raise; lift
【抬头】raise one's head; look up; rise

太 (tài) ❶extreme ❷too ❸extremely ❹very; quite

【太极拳】Taijiquan; shadow boxing
【太空】space; outer space
【太空船】spaceship
【太空服】space coat (or clothes)
【太空垃圾】space trash (or rubbish, garbage)
【太平】peace
【太平盛世】the piping times of peace
【太平洋】the Pacific Ocean
【太太】❶Mrs. ❷madame; lady ❸wife
【太阳】sun
【太阳镜】sunglasses
【太阳能】solar energy
【太阳能热水器】solar energy water heater
【太阳穴】temple

态 (tài) form; condition

【态度】❶manner; bearing: 耍～ lose one's temper ❷attitude: 工作～ attitude towards work
【态势】state; posture

泰 (tài) ❶safe; peaceful ❷extreme ❸most

【泰斗】a leading authority; an eminent scholar, musician, artist, etc.
【泰然处之】take sth. calmly
【泰然自若】behave with perfect composure; be self-possessed

tan

坍 (tān) collapse; fall

【坍塌】cave in; collapse

贪 (tān) ❶seek; covet ❷greedy ❸embezzle; practise graft; corrupt ❹have an insatiably desire for

【贪财】be greedy for money
【贪官污吏】corrupt officials; venal officials
【贪婪】greedy; avaricious; rapacious
【贪图】seek; hanker after; covet
【贪污】❶gain money dishonestly ❷corruption; graft
【贪污受贿】embezzle public funds and accept bribes
【贪心】❶greed ❷greedy
【贪嘴】be greedy for food; gluttonous

摊 (tān) ❶stand; stall: 水果～ fruit stall; 报～ news-stand ❷unfold; spread out ❸take a share in

【摊点】stand; booth
【摊贩】pedlar
【摊开】unfold; spread out
【摊牌】lay one's cards on the table; show one's hand; have a showdown
【摊派】share out; apportion
【摊位】stand; stall; booth: 固定～ fixed vendors' stands

滩 (tān) ❶beach; sands ❷shoal: 险～ dangerous shoal

瘫 (tān) paralysis

【瘫痪】❶paralysis ❷be paralysed

坛 (tán) ❶jar ❷altar:天～ the Temple of Heaven ❸circles;world

【坛子】jar;jug

昙 (tán) cloudy;overcast

【昙花一现】flower briefly as the broad-leaved epiphyllum;last briefly

谈 (tán) ❶talk ❷talk;chat;discuss

【谈到】speak (or talk) of

【谈得来】get along well (with sb.)

【谈何容易】by no means easy

【谈话】conversation;talk;chat;statement

【谈恋爱】fall in love with each other; be lovers

【谈论】discuss;talk about

【谈判】negotiation;talk:举行～ hold talks

【谈天】chat;make conversation

【谈笑风生】 talk cheerfully with wit and humour

【谈心】heart-to-heart talk

弹 (tán) ❶shoot;send forth ❷spring;leap ❸play ❹attack;impeach ❺elastic

另见 949 页 dàn

【弹唱】sing while playing a stringed instrument

T 【弹钢琴】play the piano

【弹劾】impeach

【弹簧】spring

【弹力】elastic force;elasticity;spring

【弹跳】bounce;spring

【弹奏】play;pluck

潭 (tán) deep pool (or pond):龙～虎穴 dragon's pool and tiger's den; a danger spot

坦 (tǎn) ❶level;smooth ❷open;candid ❸calm;composed

【坦白】❶ frank and straightforward ❷ confess;make a confession;own up

【坦诚】frank and sincere:心地～ open-hearted;相见～ treat sb. with sincerity

【坦荡】❶broad and level ❷broadminded

【坦克】tank

【坦然】calm;unperturbed

【坦率】❶frank;straightforward ❷frankly

袒 (tǎn) ❶ leave uncovered ❷ shield;protect

【袒护】shield; protect; be partial to; take under one's wing

【袒露】❶bare;naked ❷expose

毯 (tǎn) blanket; rug; carpet: 地～ carpet

【毯子】blanket

叹 (tàn) ❶ sigh ❷ exclaim in admiration (or praise)

【叹服】voice one's admiration;gasp in admiration

【叹为观止】acclaim (a work of art, etc.) as the acme of perfection

【叹息】sigh

炭 (tàn) charcoal

【炭窑】charcoal kiln

探 (tàn) ❶try to find out;explore:试～ sound out ❷visit;call on ❸scout;spy ❹stretch (or reach) out

【探测】survey;sound;probe

【探察】observe; look carefully at:～地形 survey the terrain

【探监】visit a prisoner

【探秘】explore the mysteries; probe the secrets:宇宙～ probe the secrets of the universe

【探亲】go home to visit one's family

【探求】pursue; search for: ~真理 seek truth

【探索】❶search; seek; explore; probe; investigate ❷exploration; investigation

【探望】❶visit; call on; pay a visit to ❷look about

【探问】inquire after; make inquiries about

【探险】explore: ~队 exploring team

【探险家】explorer

【探寻】seek; search; look for: ~真理 search for truth

【探询】inquire cautiously

碳 (tàn) carbon

tang

汤 (tāng) ❶soup; broth ❷hot (or boiling) water

【汤匙】soup spoon

【汤圆】sweetly-stuffed dumpling

唐 (táng)

【唐人街】Chinatown; Chinese quarters

【唐装】Tang suit

堂 (táng) hall: 食~ dining hall; dining room; 人民大会~ the Great Hall of the People

【堂皇】grand; stately

【堂堂正正】impressive or dignified open and above-board

【堂兄弟】cousins

塘 (táng) ❶dike ❷pool; pond: 池~ pond

搪 (táng) ❶keep out ❷evade

【搪塞】evade; give vague answers

膛 (táng) chest: 胸~ chest

糖 (táng) ❶candy; sweets ❷sugar

【糖果】sweets; candy

【糖葫芦】sugarcoated haws on a stick

【糖衣】sugarcoating

螳 (táng) mantis

【螳臂当车】a mantis trying to stop a chariot; overrate oneself and try to hold back an overwhelmingly superior force

倘 (tǎng) if; supposing

【倘若】supposing; in case; if

淌 (tǎng) shed; drip; trickle

【淌眼泪】shed tears

躺 (tǎng) lie

【躺下】lie down

【躺椅】deck (or sling) chair; lounge

烫 (tàng) ❶burn ❷warm; heat ❸iron; press ❹very (or boiling, burning) hot

【烫发】perm

【烫伤】scald

【烫手】troublesome; sticky; knotty

tao

掏 (tāo) ❶draw (or pull, fish) out ❷dig ❸pick people's pockets

【掏出】take (or pull) out

【掏腰包】❶pay out of one's pocket; foot a bill ❷pick one's pocket

滔 (tāo) inundate; flood

【滔滔不绝】pouring out words in a steady flow

逃 (táo) ❶run away; escape; flee ❷evade; shirk

【逃避】shirk; escape; evade

【逃窜】run away; flee in disorder

【逃犯】runaway criminal; escaped criminal
【逃命】run for one's life
【逃难】flee from a disaster; be a refugee
【逃跑】escape; run away; flee
【逃票】❶stow away; jump the bus ❷fare-dodging; fare evasion
【逃生】flee for one's life: 死里～ have a narrow escape
【逃税】❶evade a tax ❷tax evasion
【逃学】cut class; play truant
【逃走】take to one's heels; flee; run away

桃 (táo) peach

【桃花】peach blossom
【桃李】❶peaches and plums ❷one's pupils
【桃李满天下】have pupils everywhere

陶 (táo) ❶ pottery; earthenware ❷ make pottery ❸educate; train

【陶瓷】pottery and porcelain; ceramics
【陶器】earthenware; pottery
【陶艺】ceramics
【陶醉】be intoxicated

淘 (táo) ❶wash ❷clean out

【淘气】naughty; mischievous
【淘汰】❶eliminate ❷die out
【淘汰制】elimination system

讨 (tǎo) ❶make a punitive expedition against ❷demand; ask (or beg) for ❸invite ❹discuss; study

T

【讨好】find (or curry) favour with sb.; fawn on; toady to
【讨价】ask a price
【讨论】❶discuss; talk over ❷discussion
【讨饶】ask (or beg) for mercy (or forgiveness)
【讨厌】❶disgusting; disagreeable; ❷troublesome ❸dislike; disgust
【讨债】demand the payment of a loan

套 (tào) ❶case; cover ❷set; suit; suite ❸cover; slip on ❹ fasten ❺ model on; copy

【套餐】❶ set meal ❷ package goods (or service)
【套间】suite; apartment
【套衫】pullover: 男～ man's pullover
【套用】apply mechanically
【套装】suit

te

特 (tè) ❶spy; secret agent ❷special; particular; unusual; exceptional ❸ for a special purpose; specially

【特别】❶special; out of the ordinary ❷especially
【特别行政区】special administrative region (SAR)
【特产】special local product; speciality
【特长】special skill; strong point; specialty; what one is skilled in
【特此】hereby
【特地】specially
【特点】feature; characteristic
【特定】❶ specially designated (or appointed): ～的人选 person specially designated for a post ❷specific; specified; given: ～环境 specific environment; specific surroundings
【特护病房】intensive care unit (ICU)
【特级】special grade
【特级教师】special-class teacher
【特技表演】stunt show
【特价】special (or bargain) price: ～出售 sell at a bargain price
【特价商品】specials; red-tag goods
【特价书】discount book
【特价书店】discount bookstore

【特警】special police (or force)

【特快】❶express train ❷express mail delivery

【特困】destitute; extremely poor

【特困生】destitute (or extremely poor) student; most needy student

【特例】special case

【特区】special zone; special administrative region (SAR)

【特色】characteristic; distinguishing feature

【特使】special envoy

【特殊】special; peculiar; particular; exceptional

【特殊化】be privileged

【特殊教育】education for the disabled (or mentally retarded)

【特务】special (or secret) agent; spy

【特效】special effect: ~药 specific drug; specific; effective cure

【特性】characteristic; special property: 民族~ national characteristic

【特许】special permit

【特邀】specially invite

【特邀嘉宾】specially-invited guest in honour

【特异功能】extraordinary powers; super-function

【特意】specially

【特有】peculiar; characteristic

【特约】engage by special arrangement

【特征】feature; characteristic

【特种】special type; particular kind

【特种部队】special force (or troops)

teng

疼 (téng) ❶ache; pain; sore ❷be fond of; love dearly

【疼爱】be fond of; love dearly

【疼痛】❶ache; pain; sore; soreness ❷painful

腾 (téng) ❶jump: 欢~jump for joy ❷rise ❸set aside; make room; spare

【腾飞】❶fly swiftly upward; soar ❷make rapid advance; develop rapidly: 经济~ rapid economic development

【腾挪】❶ transfer (funds, etc.) to other use ❷move sth. to make room

【腾越】jump over

【腾云驾雾】❶ fly by clouds ❷ feel dizzy (or giddy, confused)

誊 (téng) transcribe (by hand); copy out

【誊写】copy out

藤 (téng) ❶cane; rattan ❷vine

【藤椅】cane chair

ti

剔 (tī) ❶clean with a pointed instrument; pick ❷remove: 挑~ pick holes in; find fault with

【剔除】remove; get rid of

梯 (tī) stairs; ladder; steps: 电~lift; elevator; 电动扶~ escalator

【梯田】terraced fields

【梯形】trapezoid

踢 (tī) kick

【踢皮球】❶kick the ball ❷kick (or pass) the buck

【踢足球】play football

提 (tí) ❶carry ❷promote; raise; lift ❸raise; put forward; bring forth ❹draw out ❺mention; refer to; bring up

另见 954 页 dī

【提拔】promote

【提包】bag; handbag

T

【提倡】advocate; encourage; promote; recommend

【提成】take a proportion

【提出】raise; put forward; bring forth

【提纯】purify; refine

【提纲】outline: 写发言～ make an outline for a speech

【提高】raise; heighten; enhance; increase; improve

【提高竞争力】sharpen the competitive edge; enhance competitiveness

【提高人口素质】improve (or raise) the population quality

【提高生活质量】improve (or raise) the quality of life

【提高效率】promote (or increase) efficiency

【提供】offer; supply; furnish; provide

【提货】pick up goods; take delivery of goods

【提及】mention; speak of

【提价】raise the price

【提交】hand over; submit to

【提款】draw money; withdraw deposit

【提炼】refine; extract and purify; abstract

【提名】name; nominate

【提前】❶advance ❷ahead of time; in advance

【提琴】violin: 大～ violoncello; cello; 小～ violin

T 【提请】submit sth. to

【提取】❶draw; pick up ❷extract

【提神】refresh oneself; give oneself a lift

【提升】❶ promote; advance ❷ hoist; elevate

【提示】prompt; point out

【提速】speed up; raise the speed

【提问】question; put questions to

【提醒】warn; remind; call attention to

【提选】select; choose

【提议】❶ propose; suggest; move ❷ proposal; motion; suggestion

啼 (tí) ❶cry ❷crow

【啼笑皆非】not know whether to laugh or cry; find sth. both funny and annoying

题 (tí) ❶ topic; subject ❷ title ❸ question; problem: 考～ examination questions ❹inscribe

【题材】theme; subject matter

【题词】❶ inscription ❷ write an inscription; inscribe

【题库】question bank

【题目】❶title ❷topic; subject

蹄 (tí) hoof

【蹄筋】tendons of beef, mutton or pork

体 (tǐ) ❶body ❷substance: 固～ solid; 气～ gas; 液～ liquid ❸style; form: 文～ literary style ❹experience

【体裁】types or forms of literature

【体操】gymnastics

【体察】experience and observe: ～民情 be aware of the condition of the people

【体改】structural reform; restructure

【体格】physique; build

【体会】❶ realise; experience; understand ❷knowledge ❸understanding

【体积】volume

【体力】physical strength: 增强～ build up one's strength

【体例】stylistic rules and layout; style

【体谅】take into consideration; make allowances for

【体貌】❶one's figure and features; general physical appearance: ～特征 ❷characteristics of one's figure and appearance

【体面】❶dignity; face ❷honourable

【体能】physical strength
【体魄】physique:锻炼~ go in for physical training
【体态语】body language
【体贴】be thoughtful of others' feelings; be considerate of
【体温】temperature:量~ take one's temperature
【体温计】thermometer
【体系】system
【体现】embody;give expression to
【体恤】be considerate about
【体验】experience
【体育】physical culture; sports; physical training:进行~运动 have sports
【体育彩票】sports lottery (or ticket)
【体育场】stadium;sports field
【体育馆】gym
【体育课】physical education (or PE)
【体制改革】structural reform; system reform
【体质】physique;constitution:增强人民~ build up the people's health
【体重】weight:增加~ put on (or gain) weight;减轻~ lose weight

屉 (tì) ❶steamer tray ❷drawer

剃 (tì) shave

【剃胡子】shave
【剃须刀】shaving razor

涕 (tì) ❶tear:痛哭流~ shed bitter tears ❷snivel

替 (tì) ❶replace;take the place of ❷in place of ❸for;on behalf of

【替补】substitute for
【替补队员】reserve;bench player
【替代】replace;take the place of
【替身】substitute
【替罪羊】scapegoat

tian

天 (tiān) ❶sky;heaven ❷day:今~ today;后~ the day after tomorrow;明~ tomorrow;前~ the day before yesterday;昨~ yesterday ❸season:春~ spring;夏~ summer;秋~(英)autumn;(美)fall;冬~ winter ❹weather ❺God; Heaven ❻nature

【天安门广场】Tian'anmen Square
【天才】genius;talent;gift
【天窗】skylight
【天从人愿】Heaven grants man's wish; by the grace of God
【天敌】natural enemy
【天底下】in the world;on earth
【天地】❶heaven and earth;world ❷field
【天地良心】can say in all honesty; must point out in all fairness
【天鹅】swan
【天翻地覆】earthshaking
【天府之国】a land of plenty; a land of abundance
【天赋】inborn (or innate) gift; talent; endowments
【天高气爽】the sky is clear and the air is crisp—fine autumn weather
【天花板】ceiling
【天花乱坠】as if it were raining flowers
【天价】sky-high price
【天经地义】(be regarded) as unalterable principles
【天井】❶small yard;courtyard ❷skylight
【天空】air; sky; heaven:仰望~ look up into the sky
【天蓝】sky blue;azure
【天良】conscience:丧尽~ conscienceless; heartless

【天亮】dawn; daybreak
【天伦之乐】family happiness
【天罗地网】tight dragnet
【天命】God's will; fate
【天南海北】❶all over the country ❷discursive; rambling
【天平】balance; scales
【天气】weather
【天气条件】weather conditions
【天气预报】weather forecast
【天桥】overline bridge; platform bridge
【天然】natural
【天然气】natural gas
【天壤之别】❶ poles apart ❷ a world of difference
【天色】time of the day
【天生】born; inborn; inherent; innate:~丽质 born beautiful; naturally beautiful
【天使】angel
【天堂】paradise; heaven
【天文】astronomy
【天文台】observatory
【天无绝人之路】there is always a way out
【天下】❶the world:~无难事,只怕有心人 Nothing in the world is difficult for one who sets his mind on it. ❷ state power: 打~ fight for state power
【天下太平】peace reigns under heaven; the world (or the country) is at peace
【天仙】❶goddess ❷beauty
T 【天线】aerial; antenna
【天性】nature; natural instincts: ~善良 be good and kind by nature
【天旋地转】(feel as if) the sky and earth were spinning round; dizzy
【天涯】the ends of the earth
【天衣无缝】flawless
【天灾人祸】natural and man-made calamities
【天造地设】created by nature; heavenly; ideal
【天真】innocent; naive
【天真烂漫】innocent and artless; simple and unaffected
【天职】bounden duty; vocation
【天资】natural gift; talent

添 (tiān) add; increase

【添补】replenish; add; get more
【添加】add; increase
【添加剂】addictive
【添置】add; buy; add to one's possessions
【添砖加瓦】do one's bit

田 (tián) ❶field; farmland ❷an open area abounding in same natural product; field

【田地】❶field; farmland ❷plight; wretched situation: 他怎么落到这步~? How did he get into such a plight?
【田间】❶field; farm ❷countryside
【田径】track and field
【田径运动】track and field sports
【田野】field; open country
【田园】rural area; countryside
【田园生活】idyllic life

恬 (tián) ❶quiet; tranquil; calm ❷not care at all; remain unperturbed

【恬淡】❶indifferent to fame or gain: 心怀~ remain indifferent ❷quiet; tranquil; peaceful
【恬静】quiet; peaceful
【恬然】unperturbed; calm; nonchalant

甜 (tián) ❶sweet; honeyed ❷sound: 睡得香~ have a sound sleep; sleep soundly

【甜菜】beet; beetroot
【甜点】sweets; dessert
【甜瓜】muskmelon

【甜美】❶ sweet; luscious ❷ pleasant; refreshing
【甜头】❶ sweet taste ❷ benefit: 尝到～ draw benefit from sth.

填 (tián) ❶fill up; stuff ❷write; fill in

【填报】fill in a form and submit it to the leadership
【填充】fill in the blanks; fill up; stuff
【填词】compose a poem
【填满】fill up
【填写】write; fill in (or out)
【填鸭】❶ force-feed a duck ❷ a force-fed duck: ～式教学法 forced-feeding method of teaching

舔 (tiǎn) lick; lap

tiao

挑 (tiāo) ❶ choose; select; pick ❷ carry; shoulder

另见本页 tiǎo

【挑错】find fault; pick holes
【挑肥拣瘦】choose whatever is to one's personal advantage
【挑食】be very choosy about what one eats
【挑选】choose; pick; select

条 (tiáo) ❶ twig ❷ strip; slip ❸ item; article: 逐～ item by item ❹ order: 有～不紊 in good order

【条件】❶ condition; term ❷ requirement; qualification
【条款】item; clause; article
【条理】order; proper arrangement or presentation: ～分明 well-organized
【条码】bar code; universal product code (or UPC)
【条文】article; clause

迢 (tiáo) far; remote:

【迢迢】far away; remote: 千里～ from a thousand li away; from afar

调 (tiáo) ❶mix ❷adjust ❸suit well ❹ mediate ❺tease

另见 959 页 diào

【调羹】spoon
【调工资】readjust (or raise) the wage (or salary)
【调和】❶be in harmonious proportion ❷ mediate; reconcile
【调和油】mixed oil
【调剂】❶ adjust; regulate ❷ make up a prescription
【调价】❶ readjust the price ❷ readjustment of prices
【调节】❶adjust; regulate ❷adjustment
【调解】make peace; mediate
【调酒师】bartender
【调控】regulate and control
【调理】nurse one's health; recuperate; take care of; subject sb. to discipline
【调料】condiment; seasoning; flavouring
【调皮】❶naughty; mischievous ❷unruly; tricky; play tricks
【调色板】palette
【调试】debug; adjust and test
【调停】make peace; mediate
【调味】flavor; season
【调味品】seasoning
【调匀】mix well
【调整】adjust; readjust

挑 (tiǎo) ❶raise with a pole (or stick) ❷poke ❸stir up; instigate

另见本页 tiāo

【挑大梁】play the leading role; shoulder the major responsibility
【挑动】stir up; incite

【挑明】no longer keep it back; let it all out; bring it out into the open
【挑衅】provoke
【挑战】challenge to battle
【挑战极限】challenge the limitations of human capacity

眺 (tiào) look into the distance from a high place
【眺望】look into the distance from a high place

跳 (tiào) ❶jump; leap; spring ❷beat; move up and down ❸jump over
【跳板】gangplank; springboard; diving board
【跳槽】❶ change one's job ❷ job-hop; job-hopping
【跳级】skip a grade
【跳楼价】end-of-world sale price
【跳高】high jump: 撑竿~ pole jump
【跳马】vaulting horse
【跳棋】Chinese checkers
【跳伞】parachute
【跳绳】❶rope skipping ❷jump rope
【跳水】diving
【跳台】diving tower (or platform)
【跳舞】dance
【跳远】long (or broad) jump: 三级~ hop, step and jump
【跳蚤】flea

tie

T

贴 (tiē) ❶ allowance ❷ paste; stick; glue ❸keep close to ❹subsidize
【贴补】❶subsidize ❷subsidy
【贴近】keep (or press) close to
【贴切】apt; suitable; appropriate; proper
【贴心】intimate; close

帖 (tiě) ❶invitation ❷note
【帖子】note

铁 (tiě) ❶iron ❷arms; weapon: 手无寸~ unarmed; bare-handed ❸ hard (or strong) as iron
【铁饼】discus: 掷~ throw discus
【铁锤】hammer
【铁道】railway; railroad: 地下~tube; subway; underground railway
【铁匠】blacksmith; ironsmith
【铁链】iron chain
【铁路】railway; railroad
【铁面无私】impartial and upright
【铁锹】spade; shovel
【铁丝】iron wire
【铁索】cable; iron chain
【铁腕】iron hand
【铁锈】rust
【铁证】ironclad evidence

ting

厅 (tīng) ❶hall: 餐~ dining hall; restaurant ❷office ❸a government department at the provincial: 教育~ the Education Department

听 (tīng) ❶tin; can ❷listen; hear ❸obey ❹allow; let
【听从】obey; listen to; comply
【听到】hear of (or about)
【听候】wait for
【听话】obedient; willing to obey
【听见】hear
【听讲】listen to a talk (or lecture)
【听觉】sense of hearing; hearing
【听课】attend (or go to) a class
【听力】❶hearing ❷aural comprehension
【听命】take orders from
【听任】allow; let
【听说】❶it is said that ❷hear of; be told
【听筒】❶receiver ❷headphone; earphone

【听写】have (or take, give) dictation
【听信】believe what one hears; believe
【听证会】public hearing (or meeting)

亭 (tíng) pavilion

【亭亭玉立】❶ stand graceful ❷ gracefully slim

庭 (tíng) ❶yard; court ❷law court

【庭外和解】❶ settle out of the court ❷ out-of-court settlement
【庭院】yard; court

停 (tíng) ❶ stop; cease; pause ❷ stay; stop over ❸park; anchor

【停办】close down
【停泊】anchor
【停车】❶stop ❷park ❸parking a car
【停车场】parking lot
【停车费】parking fee
【停车站】stop
【停电】❶power cut (or failure) ❷stop (or cut) the supply of electricity
【停顿】pause; break
【停放】park; place
【停火】ceasefire
【停刊】stop publication
【停课】suspend classes
【停留】stay; stop; pause
【停水】cut off water supply
【停息】stop; cease
【停业】close down; stop business
【停职】suspend sb. from his duties
【停职处分】job-suspension
【停止】stop; cease; halt

挺 (tǐng) ❶stand; hold out ❷straighten up ❸straight ❹very; quite

【挺拔】❶tall and straight ❷forceful
【挺立】❶stand upright ❷stand firm
【挺起胸膛】throw (or stick) out one's chest
【挺身】❶stand forward ❷straighten one's back
【挺直】straight; upright

艇 (tǐng) light boat: 救生~lifeboat; 汽~ steamboat; 游~ yacht

tong

通 (tōng) ❶expert ❷open up ❸lead to ❹connect ❺notify; tell ❻know; understand ❼ thorough ❽ logical ❾ common; general ❿all; whole

【通报】❶ circulate a notice ❷ circular ❸journal
【通病】common mistake; common fault; common failing
【通才】all-rounder; versatile person; universal genius
【通常】❶general; usual ❷as a rule; generally; usually
【通畅】❶ easy and smooth; fluent ❷ unobstructed; clear
【通称】❶ be generally called ❷ common name
【通达】understand things; be sensible or be reasonable: ~人情 be understanding and considerate
【通道】passage; passageway; thoroughfare
【通读】read over
【通风】❶ventilate ❷tip off; leak out ❸airy
【通关】clear the custom
【通观】viewed overall; viewed in an overall way; take an overall view: ~全局 take the whole situation into consideration
【通过】❶pass (or go) through ❷pass; adopt ❸by; through; by means of
【通红】very red; red through
【通话费】telephone call charge

【通货膨胀】inflation
【通缉令】order for arrest
【通奸】commit adultery
【通力】concerted effort
【通亮】well-illuminated; brightly lit
【通令嘉奖】issue an order of commendation
【通路】thoroughfare; highway; route; passage across
【通盘】overall; all-round; comprehensive: ~筹划 overall planning
【通气】ventilate; be in touch with each other; have communication with
【通情达理】understanding reasonable
【通融】make an exception in one's favour; get around regulations
【通史】comprehensive history; general his-tory
【通顺】clear and smooth
【通俗】simple and easy; popular; common
【通俗音乐】pop music
【通向】lead to
【通宵】all night; the whole night
【通晓】know well; thoroughly understand; be proficient in
【通信服务】communication service
【通行】❶pass (or go) through ❷current ❸in general use
【通行费】passage fee (or charge); toll
【通行证】pass; permit
【通信簿】address book
【通用】❶ in common use; current ❷ in general use ❸interchangeable
【通用语言】universal language
【通则】general rule; general provision
【通知】❶notice ❷notify; inform
【通知书】letter of notice

同 (tóng) ❶ same; alike ❷ together ❸ with ❹and ❺together; in common

【同班】be in the same class: ~同学 classmate
【同伴】companion; fellow
【同胞】born of the same parents; fellow countryman; compatriot
【同辈】of the same generation
【同比】compared with the same period of the previous year
【同病相怜】fellow sufferers sympathize with one another
【同步】synchronize; go at the same speed (or pace)
【同窗】❶ schoolmate ❷ study at the same school
【同等学力】the same educational level; comparable schooling
【同甘共苦】share bitter and sweet
【同感】the same feeling
【同归于尽】perish (or die) together
【同行】❶of the same trade or occupation ❷people of the same trade or occupation
【同伙】❶partner ❷be in partnership; collude with; associate; confederate
【同类】of the same kind; similar
【同龄人】contemporary; people of the same age
【同路】go the same way
【同盟】league; union; alliance
【同年】❶ in the same year ❷ of the same age
【同期】the corresponding period; the same term; the same year
【同情】pity; show sympathy for
【同仁】colleague
【同时】❶ at the same time; meantime; meanwhile ❷moreover; besides
【同事】co-worker; workmate; colleague
【同乡】a person from the same place

【同心协力】work with one heart

【同行】travel together:一路~ travel together all the way

【同姓】of the same surname

【同学】schoolmate;classmate;fellow student

【同样】❶same;similar;alike ❷similarly

【同意】agree;approve:不~ disagree

【同舟共济】sail (or cross a river) in the same boat

铜 (tóng) copper

【铜牌】bronze prize (or medal); third place

【铜像】bronze statue

童 (tóng) child

【童话】fairy tale

【童年】childhood

【童声】child's voice

【童心】childlike innocence:~未泯 retain a childlike heart

【童谣】children's folk rhyme or song

【童装】children's clothes (or wear)

瞳 (tóng) pupil

【瞳孔】pupil

统 (tǒng) ❶unite;gather into one ❷unified ❸completely

【统称】❶general name ❷be called by a joint name

【统筹】plan as a whole

【统筹兼顾】make overall plans and take all factors into consideration

【统计】❶statistics ❷add up;count

【统计数字】statistical figures

【统考】unified examination (or test):全国~ nationwide unified examinations

【统帅】commander;commander in chief

【统率】command; lead:~全军 command or lead the whole army

【统一】❶unite;unify;integrate ❷uniform;centralized

【统一认识】seek (or achieve) unity of understanding

捅 (tǒng) ❶poke ❷disclose

【捅娄子】make (or get into) trouble

桶 (tǒng) tub;pail;barrel;bucket

筒 (tǒng) a section of thick bamboo; tube:邮~ mailbox

【筒裙】straight skirt

恸 (tòng) deep sorrow;grief

【恸哭】wail;cry one's heart out

痛 (tòng) ❶ache; pain:头~ headache ❷sadness ❸ache; pain; be sore ❹painful ❺bitterly;heavily;heartily

【痛楚】pain; anguish; suffering; distress:内心~万分 be overwhelmed by grief; be greatly grieved

【痛打】beat soundly (or heavily)

【痛哭】cry one's heart out;cry bitterly

【痛苦】❶misery; suffering; pain ❷painful;miserable

【痛快】❶delighted; very happy ❷simple and direct ❸heartily to one's heart's content;to one's great satisfaction

【痛骂】scold severely;curse severely

【痛惜】deeply regret;deplore

【痛痒】❶important matter ❷sufferings

tou

偷 (tōu) ❶steal ❷secretly;stealthily

【偷渡】❶illegal immigration ❷immigrate (or steal) into a country illegally

【偷看】peep; peek
【偷空】snatch a moment; take time off
【偷懒】be lazy; loaf on job
【偷拍】❶ shoot pictures secretly ❷ secret shooting
【偷税漏税】❶ evade taxes ❷ evasion of taxes
【偷听】eavesdrop; listen secretly; overhear
【偷偷】stealthily; secretly

头 (tóu) ❶ head: 点～ nod; 摇～ shake one's head ❷ top ❸ end ❹ beginning ❺ head; chief; boss ❻ first
【头版】front page
【头等】first-class; first-rate
【头等大事】matter of prime importance; major event
【头顶】top of the head
【头发】hair
【头昏】dizzy; giddy
【头巾】scarf; kerchief
【头盔】helmet
【头脑】brains; mind
【头脑简单】simple-minded
【头脑清醒】clear-headed
【头饰】head ornaments
【头条新闻】top (or headline) news
【头痛】❶ headache ❷ have a headache
【头头是道】❶ clear and logical ❷ in good order
【头衔】title
T【头屑】dandruff; scurf
【头绪】main threads
【头重脚轻】top-heavy and unsteady

投 (tóu) ❶ throw; cast ❷ put in; drop ❸ throw oneself into ❹ send; post; deliver ❺ fit in with; appeal (or cater) to
【投保】insure
【投保人】applicant; policy holder
【投标】enter a bid; bid; tender; bid (or tender) for
【投产】go (or put) into production
【投递】deliver
【投递员】postman; mailman
【投放】❶ put on the market ❷ throw in; put in
【投机】❶ speculate ❷ be opportunistic ❸ congenial; agreeable: 话不～ disagreeable conversation ❹ speculate; be a profiteer
【投篮】shoot a basket
【投票】vote; cast a vote
【投入产出】input and output; investment and production
【投入市场】put into the market for sale
【投射】throw; cast; project
【投诉】complain
【投诉中心】complaining (or complaint) centre
【投医】seek (or go to) a doctor; seek medical treatment
【投影仪】projector
【投缘】agreeable; congenial
【投资】❶ invest ❷ investment
【投资项目】investment item
【投资效益】investment returns (or result, profit)

透 (tòu) ❶ penetrate; pass (or seep) through ❷ fully; thoroughly: 湿～ wet through
【透彻】penetrating; thorough; deep-going
【透风】❶ let in air; ventilate ❷ leak
【透亮】❶ bright; transparent ❷ obvious; (perfectly) clear
【透露】leak; disclose; reveal
【透明】transparent
【透气】❶ ventilate ❷ breathe freely ❸ leak information
【透支】❶ overdraft ❷ make an overdraft;

overdraw

tu

凸 (tū) sticking out; protruding

【凸凹不平】rough and uneven

【凸面镜】convex mirror

【凸透镜】convex lens

秃 (tū) ❶bald; bare ❷blunt; without a point ❸incomplete; unsatisfactory

【秃头】❶bald head ❷bald-headed

突 (tū) ❶dash; charge ❷sticking out ❸ suddenly

【突变】sudden change

【突出重点】highlight the priority

【突发事件】eventuality; contingency; emergency

【突击检查】surprise inspection (or check, test)

【突破难关】overcome a difficulty

【突破口】❶breakthrough; point of breakthrough ❷breach

【突然】❶sudden; unexpected ❷suddenly; unexpectedly; all of a sudden

【突如其来】arise suddenly (or all of a sudden)

图 (tú) ❶ picture; drawing; map ❷ intention ❸plan ❹seek

【图案】pattern; design

【图表】chart; table; figure; diagram; graph

【图钉】thumbtack; drawing pin

【图画】drawing; painting; picture

【图景】view; prospect

【图例】legend (of a map, etc.)

【图片】picture

【图书馆】library

【图腾】totem

【图像】picture; image

【图形】graph; figure

【图样】pattern; design; draft; drawing; mold

【图章】seal; stamp

荼 (tú) ❶ a bitter edible plant ❷ the white flower of reeds, etc.

【荼毒生灵】plunge the people into the depths of suffering

徒 (tú) ❶apprentice: 学~ apprentice ❷ in vain ❸on foot

【徒步】on foot: ~旅行 hike; travel on foot

【徒然】in vain; for nothing

【徒手】bare-handed; unarmed

【徒有其名】❶in name only ❷nominal

途 (tú) way; road; journey: 半~而废 give up halfway; 沿~ along the way

【途经】by way of; via

【途径】way; channel

涂 (tú) ❶spread on; apply ❷blot out ❸ scribble; scrawl

【涂改】alter

【涂料】coating; paint

【涂写】scribble; scrawl; doodle

【涂鸦】graffiti; scribble; scratch; poor handwriting

屠 (tú) ❶slaughter ❷massacre

【屠杀】massacre; slaughter: 大~ mass massacre

土 (tǔ) ❶ soil; earth ❷ land; ground ❸ local; native ❹ indigenous ❺ unrefined

【土产】local product

【土地】land; soil; ground; territory

【土地开发】land development (or exploitation)

【土地利用】land use (or utility)

【土地买卖】land sale

【土地使用证】certificate (or permit) of land use

【土地征用】land acquisition (or expropriation)

【土地转让】land transfer (or remising)

【土地租赁】land lease

【土豆】potato

【土话】slang;dialect

【土建】civil engineering

【土木】building; construction:大兴～ go in for large-scale construction

【土木工程】civil engineering

【土壤】soil

【土特产】local and special product

吐 (tǔ) ❶spit ❷say;tell
另见本页 tù

【吐露真情】tell the truth; unbosom oneself

【吐痰】spit

吐 (tù) vomit;spit
另见本页 tǔ

【吐血】spit out blood

【吐泻】vomiting and diarrhoea

兔 (tù) hare; rabbit:家～ rabbit;野～ hare

【兔唇】harelip;cleft lip

tuan

湍 (tuān)

【湍急】rapid;torrential

【湍流】❶swift current;rushing waters ❷ turbulent flow;turbulence

团 (tuán) ❶ group; society; organization ❷regiment ❸ball;mass ❹unite ❺roll ❻round

【团队】group;team;corps;collective with some property:体育～ sports team

【团购】group (or organization) purchase

【团结】❶unite;rally ❷unity

【团结就是力量】unity is strength

【团聚】gather (or get) together;reunite

【团体旅游】group tour

【团员】League member

【团圆】reunion

tui

推 (tuī) ❶push ❷push forward; promote ❸infer; deduce ❹push away; shirk; shift ❺ put off; postpone ❻ choose;elect

【推测】guess;infer

【推陈出新】weed through the old to bring forth the new

【推迟】postpone;put off;delay

【推出】offer to the public

【推辞】decline (an appointment; invitation)

【推倒】overturn;push over

【推动】promote;push on

【推断】infer;conclude

【推翻】overthrow;overturn

【推广】popularize;spread;extend

【推荐】recommend

【推举】elect;choose press

【推开】push away

【推理】❶reasoning ❷reason

【推论】inference;deduction

【推拿】massage

【推让】decline

【推算】calculate;reckon;work out

【推脱】evade;shirk

【推销】sell;market;promote sales

【推卸】shirk;push away:～职责 shirk or evade one's duty

【推行】carry out;practise:～新方案 carry out a new work plan

【推选】elect;choose:～代表 choose representatives

【推移】elapse; pass: 日月～ as time passes

颓 (tuí) ❶ruined ❷declining ❸dispirited

【颓废】decadent; dispirited

【颓唐】declining fortune

腿 (tuǐ) leg: 后～ hind legs; 前～ foreleg; 小～ calf; shank; 大～ thigh

【腿脚】ability to walk

退 (tuì) ❶return; give back ❷retreat; move back ❸withdraw ❹quit ❺cancel

【退步】go backward; lag (or fall) behind

【退潮】ebb; ebb tide

【退出】withdraw from; secede; quit

【退耕还林】return farmland to forest

【退化】degenerate

【退还】return

【退换】exchange

【退回】return; send (or give) back

【退货】❶return of goods ❷return goods; return goods for money

【退路】❶route of retreat ❷room for manoeuver; leeway: 留个～ leave some leeway

【退让】yield; give in; make a concession

【退烧】bring down a fever

【退缩】shrink back; flinch

【退休金】pension; retirement pay

【退休者】retiree

蜕 (tuì) ❶ slough off; exuviate; moult ❷exuviate

【蜕化】❶degenerate ❷slough off

褪 (tuì) ❶take off (clothes); shed (feathers) ❷(of color) fade

【褪色】color fading

tun

吞 (tūn) ❶ take possession of ❷ swallow

【吞服】swallow; take

【吞吐量】handling capacity

【吞咽】swallow; gulp down

屯 (tún) ❶ village ❷ collect; store up ❸station

【屯集】assemble; collect

囤 (tún) store up; hoard

【囤积】stock up; hoard for speculation

tuo

托 (tuō) ❶support ❷hold in the palm; support with the hand ❸serve as a foil; set off ❹ entrust ❺ ask ❻ make an excuse

【托词】excuse; pretext

【托儿所】child-care center; nursery

【托福】TOEFL(Test of English as a Foreign Language)

【托付】entrust

【托管】trusteeship

【托架】bracket

【托盘】tray

【托运】consign for shipment; check

拖 (tuō) ❶pull; drag ❷delay

【拖把】mop

【拖车】trailer

【拖后腿】be a drag on sb.; hold sb. back

【拖拉】slow; dilatory

【拖欠】fail to pay one's debt

【拖鞋】slipper

【拖延】delay; put off

脱 (tuō) ❶ shed; peel; come off ❷ take off ❸ escape from; get out of ❹ miss out

【脱产】be released from production or one's regular work to take on other duties：~学习一年 be released from work for one year's study

【脱掉】remove；take off

【脱轨】be derailed

【脱节】come apart；be disjointed；be out of line with

【脱口而出】say sth. unwittingly；blurt out；let slip

【脱口秀】talk show

【脱离】separate oneself from；break away from；be divorced from

【脱落】❶drop；fall (or come) off：毛发~ lose one's hair ❷omit：字句~ omission of words and sentences (in an article)

【脱贫致富】get rid of poverty and become well-off (or prosperous)

【脱身】get away (or free)；extricate oneself；slip away

【脱俗】be cleansed of vulgarity；refined：超凡~ stand out from the general run of people

【脱险】be out of danger；escape danger：虎口~ escape mortal danger

【脱销】out of stock；sold out

【脱衣服】undress；take off

【脱脂奶粉】defatted (or skim，skimmed，nonfat) milk powder

【脱脂牛奶】skim (or skimmed，nonfat) milk

陀 (tuó)

【陀螺】top (a toy)

驮 (tuó) carry on the back

驼 (tuó) ❶camel：骆~ camel ❷hunchbacked

【驼背】hunchback

【驼铃】camel bell

妥 (tuǒ) ❶ proper；appropriate ❷ finished；settled；ready

【妥当】proper；appropriate

【妥善】proper；appropriate；well-arranged

【妥帖】appropriate；proper；fitting

【妥协】compromise；come to terms：达成~ reach a compromise

拓 (tuò) open up；develop

【拓宽】extend；broaden：~视野 broaden one's view

【拓展】❶expand ❷extend；develop

唾 (tuò) ❶saliva；spittle ❷spit

【唾弃】cast aside

【唾液】saliva

T

W w

wa

挖 (wā) dig

【挖掘】 unearth; dig

【挖掘潜力】 tap the potential

【挖苦】 speak sarcastically; make biting remarks

洼 (wā) ❶low-lying area ❷hollow

【洼地】 depression; low-lying land

蛙 (wā) frog

【蛙泳】 breaststroke

娃 (wá) baby; child; kid

【娃娃鱼】 giant salamander

瓦 (wǎ) ❶tile ❷clay

【瓦房】 tile-roofed house

【瓦解】 disintegrate; fall to pieces

【瓦砾】 rubble; debris

【瓦特】 watt

袜 (wà) socks; stockings: 长～ stocking; 短～ sock

【袜裤】 panty hose

wai

歪 (wāi) crooked; slanting

【歪打正着】 hit the mark by a fluke; but harvest exactly what one wishes; do sth. unintentionally

【歪点子】 bad idea; devil's advice

【歪理】 false reasoning

【歪门邪道】 crook (or honest) ways

【歪扭】 twisted; awry

【歪曲】 distort; misrepresent

【歪斜】 crooked; slanting

外 (wài) ❶other ❷foreign; external ❸besides ❹outside; outward

【外包装】 outer package

【外币】 foreign currency

【外边】 ❶ outside; out; exterior ❷ a place other than where one lives or works

【外表】 appearance; exterior; surface

【外宾】 foreign guest (or visitor)

【外部】 outside; outer

【外出】 go out

【外传】 ❶spread; leak ❷it is said; they say

【外观】 appearance; exterior

【外观设计】 external design

【外国】 foreign country

【外国人】 foreigner

【外行】 layman; nonprofessional

【外号】 nickname

【外汇】 foreign exchange

【外汇储备】 foreign exchange reserve

【外籍】 foreign nationality

【外籍华人】 Chinese of foreign nationality

【外加】more; extra; additional

【外交】❶ diplomatic ❷ diplomacy; foreign affairs

【外交部】the Ministry of Foreign Affairs; the Foreign Ministry

【外交部部长】foreign minister; minister of foreign affairs

【外交官】diplomat; diplomatist

【外交关系】diplomatic relations

【外界】the external (or outside) world

【外景】outdoor scene

【外科】surgery; surgical department

【外壳】outer covering; shell; case

【外来人口】from-other-parts population; nonnative

【外流】outflow; drain: 人才～ brain drain

【外卖】takeout; takeout; takeout service

【外贸】foreign trade

【外貌】appearance; exterior; looks

【外面】❶ outward ❷ surface ❸ outside; outer

【外人】stranger; outside

【外伤】injury; wound

【外商】foreign businessman (or merchant)

【外商独资企业】enterprises with sole foreign capital

【外事】foreign affairs

【外孙】grandson

【外孙女】granddaughter

【外套】overcoat; garment

【外向型经济】export-oriented economy

【外星人】❶extraterritorial being (or ET) ❷person out of touch with the society

【外形】shape; form

【外延】denotation; extension

【外溢】❶outflow; drain: 资金～ drain of fund ❷spill; overflow

【外因】external cause

【外用】for external use

【外语】foreign language

【外遇】❶extramarital love affair ❷extramarital lover

【外援】foreign aid; brought-in foreign player (or sportsman)

【外在】external; extrinsic: ～因素 external factor

【外债】foreign debt

【外资】foreign capital (or funds, investment)

【外资企业】foreign company; foreign-funded (or foreign-invested, foreign-owned) enterprise

【外祖父】grandfather

【外祖母】grandmother

wan

弯 (wān) ❶bend; curve ❷bent; curved

【弯路】zigzag path; detour

【弯曲】❶bend; bow; curve ❷winding; meandering; zigzag; crooked; curved

【弯腰】stoop; bend down

湾 (wān) ❶ a bend in a stream ❷ gulf; bay

剜 (wān) cut out; scoop out

【剜肉补疮】cut out a piece of flesh to cure a boil—resort to a remedy worse than the ailment; resort to a stopgap measure detrimental to long-term interests

湾 (wān) ❶a bend in a stream: 河～ river bend ❷gulf; bay: 渤海～ Bohai Bay ❸moor

蜿 (wān) wind; zigzag

【蜿蜒】❶wriggle ❷zigzag; wind

丸 (wán) ball; pill

完 (wán) ❶ use up; run out ❷ finish; complete; be over ❸ pay ❹ intact; whole

【完备】complete; perfect

【完毕】complete; come to an end; finish; end

【完璧归赵】return the jade intact to the State of Zhao—return sth. to its owner in perfect condition

【完成】complete; achieve; fulfil

【完蛋】be done for; be finished

【完好】in good condition; intact; whole

【完婚】get married

【完满】perfect; satisfactory

【完美】❶perfect; flawless ❷perfectly

【完全】❶ perfect; complete; entire; whole ❷fully; entirely; completely; wholly

【完善】perfect

【完胜】❶win a complete victory ❷complete victory

【完事】be settled; finish doing sth.

【完整】complete; whole; intact; entire

玩 (wán) ❶ play ❷ use; employ ❸ enjoy; appreciate

【玩得快活】have a wonderful time

【玩忽职守】ignore one's duty

【玩花招】play tricks

【玩具】toy

【玩弄】play with; employ; use

【玩偶】doll

【玩耍】play; amuse oneself

【玩味】ponder; ruminate

【玩笑】joke; jest; fun: 开～ play a joke on

顽 (wán) ❶ stupid ❷ stubborn; obstinate ❸naughty; mischievous

【顽固】headstrong; stubborn

【顽劣】stubborn and stupid: ～异常 be unusually obstinate

【顽皮】naughty; mischievous

【顽强】indomitable; unyielding

【顽童】naughty child; urchin

宛 (wǎn) ❶winding; tortuous ❷as if

【宛如】❶as if (or though) ❷just like

挽 (wǎn) ❶ draw; pull ❷ roll up ❸ lament

【挽回】retrieve; redeem

【挽救】save; remedy; rescue

【挽留】urge sb. to stay; persuade sb. to stay

晚 (wǎn) ❶ evening; night ❷ late ❸ younger

【晚安】good night

【晚班】night shift

【晚辈】younger generation

【晚餐】supper; dinner

【晚点】❶late ❷behind schedule

【晚饭】supper; dinner

【晚会】evening party: 联欢～ get-together party

【晚婚晚育】late marriage and late birth

【晚间新闻】evening (or night) news

【晚礼服】night wear; night dress

【晚年】old age; late years: 度过幸福的～ lead a happy life in old age

【晚期】❶late ❷later period

【晚秋】late autumn

【晚上】evening; night

【晚霞】sunset glow

【晚育】late childbirth

惋 (wǎn) sigh

【惋惜】regret; feel sorry for (or about)

婉 (wǎn) ❶gentle ❷tactful; artful

【婉拒】decline politely

【婉言谢绝】politely refuse (or decline)

【婉转】❶ tactful ❷ in a round-about way

❸sweet and agreeable：歌声～ sweet and melodious notes of a song

碗 (wǎn) bowl

【碗橱】cupboard

万 (wàn) ❶by no means；by all means ❷ten thousand

【万般】all the different kinds；utterly；extremely

【万般无奈】have no alternative

【万端】(of moods) multifarious：感慨～ a turmoil of feelings wells up in one's mind

【万恶】extremely evil (or vicious)

【万分】extremely；very much

【万古长青】remain fresh forever；be everlasting

【万家灯火】a myriad twinkling lights (of a city)

【万籁俱寂】all is quiet and still

【万里长城】the Great Wall

【万马奔腾】ten thousand horses galloping ahead—all going full steam ahead

【万难】all kinds of difficulties

【万能】❶almighty；all-powerful ❷all-purpose

【万年历】perpetual calendar (or almanac)

【万念俱灰】all thoughts (or ambitions) are blasted；all hopes dashed to pieces

【万千】❶ countless；innumerous；myriad ❷multifarious：变化～ constant changes

【万全之计】a completely safe plan

【万人空巷】the whole town turns out (to celebrate or to welcome sb.)

【万事如意】may all your heart's wishes be fulfilled

【万水千山】ten thousand mountains and rivers on the way

【万岁】❶ long live ❷ the emperor；Your Majesty

【万无一失】❶ no risk at all ❷ perfectly safe

【万物】all things on the earth

【万象更新】all things take on a new aspect；everything looks new and fresh

【万幸】very lucky (or fortunate)

【万一】❶in case ❷accident

【万有引力】gravitation

【万众一心】millions of people all of one mind

腕 (wàn) wrist

【腕儿】big shot

wang

汪 (wāng) ❶(of a body of water) deep and vast ❷(of liquid) collect；accumulate ❸pond；pool

【汪洋】vast；boundless：一片～ a vast stretch of water

亡 (wáng) ❶ die ❷ flee；run away ❸ lose；be gone ❹conquer

【亡故】die；pass away

【亡魂】soul；ghost

王 (wáng) ❶ king；prince ❷ grand；great

【王朝】imperial court；dynasty

【王宫】imperial palace

【王冠】crown

【王国】kingdom

【王后】queen

【王牌】trump card

【王子】prince

网 (wǎng) ❶net ❷network；web：广播～ broadcasting network；因特～ Internet ❸catch with a net

【网吧】Internet bar (or cafe)；net bar；cyber cafe

【网虫】cyber cult; netter; Internet buff (or geek, worm, potato)
【网购】online shopping; E-commerce
【网恋】online (or Internet, cyber) love affair; cyber romance
【网聊】❶network chatting ❷chat online
【网罗】❶trap ❷enlist: ～人才 enlist talented people
【网络】network; web; Internet
【网络安全】network safety (or security)
【网络犯罪】cyber crime
【网络公司】Internet (or network) company
【网络会议】net-meeting
【网络技术】network technology
【网络教学】network (or net-based) teaching
【网络文化】network culture
【网络小说】network fiction (or novel)
【网络新闻】network (or net, cyber, Internet) news
【网络营销】network (or online) marketing (or sale, selling)
【网迷】net (or Internet) addict; cyber cult (head, addict)
【网球】tennis
【网球场】tennis court
【网球拍】tennis racket
【网上书店】online book store
【网上游戏】online games
【网上招聘】online recruitment
【网上征婚】seek a spouse online (or on the Internet)
【网页】web page
【网瘾】web addiction
【网友】cyber acquaintance; net (or web, cyber) friend (or partner)
【网站】website; cyber station; network station
【网址】website web address; Internet site

枉 (wǎng) ❶ wrong; treat unjustly ❷ twist ❸vainly
【枉费】❶waste; try in vain ❷vainly
【枉费心机】rack one's brains in vain
【枉然】❶futile ❷in vain; to no purpose

往 (wǎng) ❶ go ❷ previous; former; past ❸to; toward; in the direction of
【往常】in the past
【往返】move to and fro; go there and back
【往返票】return (or round-trip) ticket
【往后】from now on; here after; afterwards
【往来】❶contact ❷come and go ❸to and fro ❹visit each other
【往年】in past years; former years
【往事】past events; the past
【往往】often

惘 (wǎng) feel frustrated; feel disappointed
【惘然】frustrated; disappointed

妄 (wàng) ❶absurd ❷presumptuous
【妄动】rash action: 轻举～ act rashly
【妄加评论】make rash comments
【妄说】talk irresponsibly; talk nonsense: 无知～ ignorance and absurdity
【妄想】❶ vain hope; wishful thinking ❷ vainly hope
【妄自尊大】be self-important

忘 (wàng) ❶forget ❷neglect; overlook

【忘恩负义】ungrateful; unthankful
【忘记】❶forget ❷overlook; neglect
【忘却】forget
【忘我】❶selfless ❷selflessness: ～的精神 spirit of selflessness

旺 (wàng) flourishing; prosperous

【旺季】high (or busy, rush, peak) season
【旺盛】vigorous; exuberant
【旺销】❶sell well ❷well-selling; fast-selling: ~商品 commodities in big demand

望 (wàng) ❶reputation ❷look; look at ❸visit; call on ❹hope; expect; look forward to

【望尘莫及】be too far behind to catch up
【望眼欲穿】look forward to with great eagerness
【望远镜】telescope; binoculars

wei

危 (wēi) ❶danger; peril ❷endanger; imperil ❸dying

【危害】harm; jeopardize; endanger
【危机】crisis
【危机感】sense (or awareness) of crisis
【危及】endanger; compromise: ~生命 endanger life
【危急】critical
【危急关头】critical moment
【危难】danger and disaster
【危亡】in peril; at stake: 民族~的时刻 when the nation's existence is in peril
【危险】❶danger ❷dangerous
【危在旦夕】in imminent danger
【危重】mortally ill: 抢救~病人 rescue the critically ill

威 (wēi) strength; power: 示~ demonstrate

【威风】power and prestige
【威吓】threaten; bully
【威力】power; might
【威名】mighty reputation: ~远扬 the fame of sb. spreads far and wide
【威尼斯】Venice
【威士忌】whisky
【威望】prestige
【威武】might; force; power
【威胁】❶threat ❷threaten
【威严】awe-inspiring; majestic

微 (wēi) minute; tiny

【微波】microwave
【微波炉】microwave stove
【微博】microblog; twitter
【微不足道】too trivial to be worth mentioning; insignificant
【微处理器】microprocessor
【微风】gentle breeze
【微观】microcosmic
【微观调控】microeconomic readjustment and control
【微利】small profit; low profit: 蝇头~ petty benefit
【微量元素】trace element
【微妙】delicate; subtle
【微软公司】Microsoft Corporation
【微生物】microorganism
【微小】small; little; tiny; slight
【微笑】with a smile
【微笑服务】❶serve with smiles ❷smiling service
【微型】miniature
【微型照相机】miniature camera; minicam

巍 (wēi) towering; lofty

【巍然】towering; majestic; lofty

为 (wéi) ❶do; act ❷serve (or act) as ❸be; become ❹mean
另见 1228 页 wèi

【为难】❶make things difficult for ❷feel at a loss; feel embarrassed
【为期】for a certain period of time; by a definite date: ~不远 be drawing near
【为人】behave; conduct oneself: ~忠厚 honest and tolerant; sincerely and kind-

ly

【为首】❶led by; headed by ❷be the leader ❸head

【为所欲为】do whatever one likes; do as one pleases

【为限】within the limit of

【为止】up to; till

违 (wéi) ❶disobey; violate ❷be separated: 久～了！ I haven't seen you for ages!

【违背】go against; disobey; violate

【违法】❶illegal ❷break the law

【违法乱纪】violate the law and discipline

【违反】violate; go against; break

【违规操作】operate against rules and regulations

【违纪】violate (or breech) the discipline

【违纪行为】act of discipline-violating

【违禁品】contraband goods; contraband

【违抗】disobey; defy

【违心】against one's will (or intention)

【违约】❶violate (or break) a contract; violate a treaty ❷break one's promise; break off an engagement

围 (wéi) ❶enclose; surround; encircle ❷all round; around

【围捕】surround and seize; round up: ～逃犯 hunt down a fugitive

【围观】surround and watch (or look on)

【围巾】scarf; shawl; muffler

【围困】besiege; hem in; pin down

【围棋】go; I-go; weiqi, a game played with black and white pieces on a board of 361 crosses

【围墙】enclosure; enclosing wall

【围裙】apron

【围绕】❶ round; around ❷ surround; go round

桅 (wéi) mast

【桅杆】mast

唯 (wéi) ❶only; alone ❷but
另见 1228 页 wěi

【唯物辩证法】materialist dialectics

【唯一】only; sole

【唯有】only; alone

帷 (wéi) bed-curtain

【帷幕】heavy curtain

惟 (wéi) ❶only; alone ❷but

【惟妙惟肖】true to life; absolutely lifelike

维 (wéi) ❶thinking; thought ❷dimension ❸ link; hold together ❹ maintain; safeguard

【维持】keep up; maintain; preserve

【维持稳定】maintain stability

【维持秩序】keep order

【维和部队】peacekeeping force

【维护】safeguard; defend; uphold; protect

【维护大局】safeguard the interests of the whole

【维权】protect (or safeguard) one's right

【维生素】vitamin

【维修】repair; maintain

伟 (wěi) big; great

【伟岸】tall and sturdy; stalwart: 身材～ of tall and sturdy stature

【伟大】great; grand; mighty

【伟人】great man

【伟业】great cause

伪 (wěi) ❶puppet ❷false; fake

【伪钞】forged bank note

【伪劣产品】fake and inferior products

【伪造】❶forge; falsify ❷forgery; falsification

【伪装】❶pretend; feign ❷disguise; mask

苇 (wěi) reed

【苇席】reed mat

纬 (wěi) ❶weft; woof ❷latitude

【纬度】latitude

尾 (wěi) ❶tail ❷end

【尾灯】tail light

【尾气】tail gas (or exhaust)

【尾声】❶epilogue ❷end

【尾数】number after a decimal point; last number of a multidigit figure

【尾随】tail behind; follow at one's heels; tag along after

纬 (wěi) ❶weft; woof ❷latitude

【纬度】latitude

【纬线】❶parallel ❷weft

委 (wěi) ❶end ❷committee member ❸entrust ❹appoint ❺shift ❻indirect; roundabout ❼listless; spiritless ❽certainly

【委屈】❶feel wronged; nurse a grievance ❷put sb. to great inconvenience

【委托】entrust; trust

【委婉】❶tactfully ❷tactful; mild and roundabout

【委员】committee member

萎 (wěi) wither

【萎靡】❶listless; spiritless: 神志～ look spiritless ❷in low spirits

【萎缩】shrink; shrivel; wither

唯 (wěi)

另见 1227 页 wéi

【唯唯诺诺】be a yesman; be submissive

猥 (wěi) ❶numerous; multifarious ❷base; obscene; salacious; indecent

【猥亵】❶obscene; salacious ❷act indecently towards (a woman)

卫 (wèi) defend; guard; protect

【卫生】hygiene; health

【卫生城市】hygienic (or sanitary) city

【卫生防疫站】sanitation and antiepidemic station

【卫生间】toilet

【卫生设施】sanitary facilities

【卫生纸】toilet paper

【卫视】satellite television

【卫星】satellite: 人造～ man-made satellite

【卫星电视】satellite television

【卫星定位系统】global position system (GPS)

为 (wèi) ❶for; in the interests of ❷for; for the sake of ❸because; on account of

另见 1226 页 wéi

【为此】for this reason; for this purpose

【为何】❶why ❷for what reason

【为了】❶for; for the sake (or interest) of; in order to; so as to ❷so that; in order that

【为什么】why; what for

未 (wèi) ❶no ❷not; not yet

【未必】❶may not ❷not necessarily

【未卜先知】foresee; have foresight

【未曾】have not; did not

【未成年人】juvenile; adolescent

【未成年人保护】protection of juveniles

【未婚】unmarried

【未来】❶future; tomorrow ❷in the future

【未免】rather; a bit too

【未能】haven't been able to; fail to; cannot

【未完】unfinished

【未知】unknown
【未知数】unknown number
位 (wèi) ❶place; location; site ❷position ❸figure ❹throne
【位移】displacement; difference between the later position and the original position
【位于】lie; be located (or situated) in
【位置】seat; place; location; site; position
味 (wèi) ❶ taste; flavour ❷ smell; odour ❸interest; delight
【味道】taste
【味觉】sense of taste
畏 (wèi) ❶ fear: 无～ fearless ❷ respect; awe
【畏惧】fear: 无所～ be fearless
【畏罪潜逃】flee from justice
胃 (wèi) stomach
【胃口】❶ appetite ❷ liking: 合～ to one's liking
【胃口好】have a good appetite
【胃痛】❶stomachache ❷have a stomachache
谓 (wèi) ❶ say ❷ call; name: 所～ so-called
【谓语】predicate
喂 (wèi) ❶feed ❷hello; hey
【喂奶】breastfeed; nurse
【喂养】❶feed ❷raise; keep
蔚 (wèi) ❶luxuriant; grand ❷colorful
【蔚蓝】sky blue; azure
慰 (wèi) ❶ console; comfort ❷ be relieved
【慰劳】bring gifts and regards to
【慰问】give regards to

wen

温 (wēn) ❶ temperature ❷ warm (or heat) up ❸warm ❹review; revise
【温饱】have enough to eat and wear
【温差】difference in temperature
【温存】❶be attentive to ❷gentle; kind
【温带】temperate zone
【温度计】thermometer
【温和】❶temperate ❷gentle; a mild: 语气～ in mild tone
【温良】gentle and kindhearted
【温暖】❶warmth; kindness ❷warm
【温泉】hot spring
【温柔】❶gentle; soft; tender ❷gently
【温室效应】greenhouse (or hothouse) effect
【温顺】docile; meek
【温文尔雅】refined and cultivated
【温习】review
【温馨】cosy; warm: ～的家 warm and sweet home
【温煦】❶warm ❷kind and cordial
瘟 (wēn) ❶acute communicable diseases ❷ (of traditional opera) dull and insipid
【瘟疫】pestilence
文 (wén) ❶ character; script ❷ language ❸writing ❹civil
【文本】text; version
【文本编辑】text editing
【文笔】style of writing
【文采】❶rich and bright colors ❷literary grace; literary talent
【文档】file
【文房四宝】the four treasures of the study (writing brush, ink, paper and inkstone)
【文风】style of writing

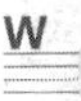

【文稿】manuscript; draft
【文过饰非】conceal faults and wrongs
【文豪】great writer; literary giant
【文化】❶ culture; civilization ❷ education; schooling
【文化背景】cultural background
【文化冲突】cultural clash (or conflict)
【文化宫】cultural palace
【文化素质】cultural quality
【文化遗产】cultural heritage
【文集】collected works
【文件】document; paper
【文件夹】folder
【文静】gentle and quiet
【文具】stationery
【文科】liberal arts
【文秘】clerk and secretary; clerical worker
【文庙】Confucius temple
【文明】civilization; culture: 精神~ spiritual civilization; 物质~ material civilization
【文凭】diploma
【文人】scholar; man of letters; literati
【文坛】literary world
【文武】❶civil and military skills ❷ statecraft and military exploits: ~双全 be well versed in both polite letters and martial arts
【文物】cultural (or historical) relics: 出土~ unearthed cultural relics
【文献检索】document (or literature) retrieval

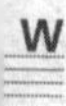

【文胸】bra; brassiere
【文学】literature
【文学作品】literary works
【文雅】elegant; refined
【文艺】literature and art
【文娱活动】recreational activities
【文摘】abstract; digest
【文章】❶ essay; article ❷ literary works; writings ❸ hidden meanings; implied meaning
【文质彬彬】gentle
【文字】❶character ❷writing
【文字处理】word processing (or procession)

纹 (wén) lines; veins; grain: 皱~ lines; wrinkles

【纹理】veins; grain

闻 (wén) ❶news; story ❷hear ❸smell

【闻风而动】go into action at the news
【闻名】renowned; famous; well-known

蚊 (wén) mosquito

【蚊帐】mosquito net

刎 (wěn) cut the throat: 自~ cut one's own throat

吻 (wěn) ❶ lips ❷ kiss ❸ an animal's mouth

【吻合】be in agreement; coincide

紊 (wěn) disorderly; confused

【紊乱】❶disorder; chaos; confusion ❷disorderly; confused

稳 (wěn) ❶steady; stable; firm; secure ❷sure; certain

【稳步增长】grow (or increase) steadily
【稳当】reliable; safe; secure
【稳定大局】stabilize the situation as a whole
【稳定人心】set the people's mind at easy
【稳定物价】stabilize commodity prices
【稳固】firm; stable
【稳健】❶firm; steady ❷steady; sure; reliable; not rash; not reckless

【稳妥】safe;reliable

【稳重】steady;calm and measured

问 (wèn) ❶ask; require ❷ask (or require) after ❸interrogate ❹hold responsible

【问安】pay one's respects

【问答】questions and answers:~题 problems to be answered

【问寒问暖】ask after one's health with deep concern

【问好】say hello to

【问号】question mark

【问候】❶greetings ❷greet; extend greetings to

【问卷调查】questionnaire survey

【问世】be published; come out

【问责制】accountability system

weng

翁 (wēng) old man

瓮 (wèng) urn; earthen jar

【瓮中之鳖】❶a turtle in a jar ❷be bottled up; be caught in a trap

wo

涡 (wō) whirlpool; eddy: 旋~ eddy

【涡流】the circular movement of a whirling fluid; eddy

窝 (wō) ❶ nest; den ❷ harbour; hide; shelter

【窝点】lair; den; hideout

【窝囊】❶feel vexed; be annoyed ❷good-for-nothing; hopelessly stupid

【窝头】steamed bread of corn, sorghum, etc.

蜗 (wō) snail

【蜗牛】snail

我 (wǒ) ❶I; me ❷self

【我的】❶my ❷mine

【我们】we; us

【我们的】❶our ❷ours

【我行我素】stick to one's own way

【我自己】myself

沃 (wò) rich; fertile: 肥~的土地 fertile (or rich) soil

卧 (wò) ❶lie: 仰~ lie on one's back ❷sleeping

【卧床】lie in bed:~不起 become bed-ridden

【卧倒】❶drop to the ground ❷lie down

【卧铺】sleeper; sleeping berth

【卧室】bedroom

【卧薪尝胆】volunteer to suffer long hardships to strengthen one's will

握 (wò) hold; grasp; get hold of

【握别】shake hands at parting

【握力】grip; the power of gripping

【握手】shake hands with

wu

乌 (wū) ❶crow ❷black; dark

【乌龟】tortoise

【乌黑】pitch-black; jet-black

【乌七八糟】in a horrible mess

【乌鸦】crow

【乌烟瘴气】pestilential atmosphere; foul atmosphere

【乌云】dark clouds

【乌贼】cuttlefish; inkfish

污 (wū) ❶dirt; filth ❷stain; smear; defile ❸dirty; filthy ❹corrupt

【污垢】dirt; filth

【污染】❶pollute ❷pollution
【污染防治】pollution prevention and control
【污染物】pollutant
【污染源】pollution source
【污染治理】pollution abatement
【污辱】insult;humiliate
【污水处理】waste water (or sewage) treatment (or disposal)
【污浊】dirty;filthy;foul

巫
(wū) witch

【巫婆】witch
【巫师】wizard;sorcerer

呜
(wū) toot;hoot

【呜呼】❶ alas;alack ❷die ❸all is lost
【呜咽】sob;whimper

诬
(wū) falsely accuse

【诬赖】falsely incriminate:~好人 incriminate innocent people
【诬陷】frame sb.

屋
(wū) house;room

【屋顶】roof;housetop
【屋脊】roof ridge:世界~ roof of the world
【屋檐】eaves

无
(wú) ❶nothing ❷not ❸without

【无比】matchless;incomparable
【无边无际】limitless;vast;boundless
【无常】changeable
【无偿使用】gratuitous (or free) use
【无偿献血】voluntary blood donation
【无耻】shameless
【无处】nowhere
【无从】have no way;not be in a position to
【无的放矢】shoot an arrow without a target
【无动于衷】unmoved;untouched;unconcerned
【无端】for no reason;for nothing
【无法形容】beyond description
【无非】❶nothing but;no more than;only ❷simply
【无风不起浪】there are no waves without wind
【无干】have nothing to do with
【无公害】pollution-free; environment-friendly
【无辜】innocent
【无关】have nothing to do with
【无害】harmless
【无济于事】❶won't help ❷of no use
【无家可归】homeless
【无价之宝】priceless treasure
【无尽】endless
【无精打采】❶ listless; spiritless ❷ in low spirit
【无可救药】❶beyond (or past) cure ❷incurable;hopeless
【无可挽回】irretrievable
【无孔不入】seize every opportunity
【无礼】rudeness
【无力】❶feel weak;lack strength ❷unable;incapable;powerless
【无利可图】profitless
【无论】regardless of
【无论如何】❶in any case;at any rate;at all events ❷whatever happens
【无名】❶unknown ❷nameless
【无奈】cannot help but;have no choice
【无能为力】helpless
【无期徒刑】life imprisonment
【无情】ruthless;heartless;cruel

【无穷】infinite; boundless; endless
【无人售票】self-service ticket
【无人问津】no one shows any interest in it
【无声】noiseless; silent
【无时无刻】all the time
【无视】ignore; disregard; defy; overlook
【无事生非】make trouble out of nothing
【无数】countless; innumerable
【无双】unparalleled; matchless
【无私】unselfish; selfless
【无所畏惧】fearless; dauntless
【无条件】unconditional; without preconditions
【无望】hopeless
【无味】tasteless; dull; uninteresting
【无畏】fearless
【无暇】have no time; be too busy
【无限】infinite; limitless; boundless; immeasurable
【无线】wireless
【无线上网服务】wireless Internet system
【无线通信】radio (or wireless) communication
【无效】of no avail; to no avail; invalid; null and void
【无懈可击】invulnerable
【无形】invisible
【无须】need not; not have to
【无烟工业】smokeless (or smoke-free) industry
【无烟区】no-smoking area
【无恙】❶well; safe ❷in good health: 安然～ safe and sound
【无疑】❶ beyond doubt; certainly; undoubtedly ❷no doubt
【无益】❶ useless; unprofitable ❷ of no good
【无意识】unconscious
【无垠】vast; boundless
【无用】❶futile; useless ❷of no use
【无与伦比】❶without equal ❷incomparable matchless
【无缘无故】without cause (or reason); for no reason at all
【无知】ignorant
【无止境】have no limits; know no end
【无足轻重】of little importance; insignificant
【无罪】innocent

五

(wǔ) five

【五彩】colorful; five colors of blue, yellow, red, white and black
【五官】❶the five sense organs ❷features
【五官端正】have regular features
【五湖四海】all corners of the land
【五花八门】of a wide variety
【五角星】five-pointed star
【五连冠】❶five successive championships ❷win five successive championships
【五四青年节】Youth Day (or May 4)
【五四运动】the May 4th Movement
【五味】all kinds of tastes
【五线谱】staff; stave
【五星红旗】the Five-Starred Red Flag
【五星级宾馆】five-star hotel
【五颜六色】of various colors; colorful
【五一劳动节】International labor Day; May Day
【五月】May

午

(wǔ) noon; midday

【午饭】lunch
【午间新闻】mid-day (or noon-break, lunch-hour) news
【午睡】❶ afternoon nap ❷ take a nap after lunch

【午休】noon break;noontime rest

【午夜】midnight

伍 (wǔ) ❶army:入~ join the army;退~ leave the army ❷company

武 (wǔ) ❶force ❷military ❸connected with boxing skill;sword play ❹valiant;fierce

【武功】martial art;Kung fu;military accomplishments

【武警】armed police (or policeman)

【武力】force;military force

【武林高手】martial art master

【武器】weapon;arms:核~ nuclear weapons

【武术】martial arts

【武侠小说】swordsman (or knight) fiction

【武装】❶military equipment;arms;battle outfit ❷arm;provide troops with arms ❸army;armed forces

侮 (wǔ) insult;bully

【侮辱】insult

舞 (wǔ) ❶dance ❷move about as in a dance ❸dance with sth. in one's hands ❹flourish;wield;brandish:手~足蹈 dance for joy ❺wield

【舞弊】fraudulent practices;irregularities;embezzlement

【舞步】dancing step:~轻盈 graceful dancing steps

【舞蹈】dance

【舞动】wave;brandish

W

【舞会】dance;ball;dancing party:举行~ hold a ball

【舞龙灯】perform a dragon lantern dance

【舞曲】dance music

【舞台】stage

兀 (wù) ❶rising to a height;towering ❷bald

【兀立】stand upright

务 (wù) ❶affair;business ❷be engaged in ❸must;be sure to

【务必】must;be sure to

【务实】be practical

【务实作风】practical style of work;practical working style

物 (wù) ❶ thing; matter ❷ content;substance

【物产】product;produce

【物归原主】return sth. to its rightful owner

【物价】price

【物价调整】price adjustment

【物理学】❶innate laws of things ❷physics

【物流】flow (or distribution) of goods and materials;logistics;material distribution

【物美价廉】good quality and fair price

【物品】article;goods:贵重~ valuables

【物色】select;look for

【物业】property;real estate;realty

【物业管理】property (or realty) management

【物以类聚】birds of a feather flock together

【物以稀为贵】a thing is valued if it is rare

【物质】matter;substance;material

【物质财富】material wealth

【物质文明】material civilization

【物种灭绝】species extinction

【物主】owner;proprietor

【物资】goods and materials

误 (wù) ❶mistake;error ❷miss ❸by mistake (or accident)

【误差】error

【误导】❶mislead;misguide ❷misleading

【误点】❶late;overdue ❷behind schedule

【误解】❶ misunderstand; misread ❷ misunderstanding

【误期】exceed the time limit; be behind schedule

【误伤】accidentally injure

【误诊】❶make a wrong diagnosis ❷miss the chance for diagnosis and treatment

恶（wù） dislike; hate: 好～ likes and dislikes

另见 970 页 ě;è

悟（wù） realize; awaken

【悟性】power of understanding; comprehension

晤（wù） meet; interview; see

雾（wù） fog: 有～ be foggy

【雾茫茫】misty; foggy

【雾气】fog; mist

X x

xi

 (xī) sunset; evening; night

【夕阳】setting sun

【夕阳西下】the sun is setting

【夕照】the glow of the setting sun; evening glow

西 (xī) ❶west ❷western

【西半球】the Western Hemisphere

【西北】northwest

【西部大开发】West China Development

【西部地区】western region of China; west China

【西餐】western-style food

【西方】❶the west; westward ❷the West: ~国家 the Western countries

【西风】❶ west wind; westerly wind ❷ Western social mores and culture

【西瓜】watermelon

【西红柿】tomato

【西南】southwest

【西式】Western style: ~糕点 Western pastry

【西药】Western medicine

【西医】❶ Western medicine (as distinguished from traditional Chinese medicine) ❷ a doctor trained in Western medicine

【西装】western-style clothes

吸 (xī) ❶breathe in; draw; inhale ❷absorb; suck ❸attract

【吸尘器】dust catcher; vacuum cleaner

【吸毒贩毒】drug abuse and trafficking

【吸毒者】drug addict

【吸附】absorb

【吸管】straw

【吸力】suction; attraction

【吸取】draw; absorb

【吸取教训】learn (or draw) a lesson

【吸取养分】absorb nutriment

【吸收】❶suck; draw; take in; absorb ❷admit

【吸吮】suck; absorb

【吸水纸】absorbent paper

【吸烟】smoke

【吸引】attract; draw

【吸引人才】attract talents

【吸引外资】absorb (or attract) foreign investment

【吸引眼球】❶attract eye ❷eye-catching

希 (xī) hope

【希求】❶hope for ❷wish; desire

【希望】hope; wish; expect: 没~ hopeless; 有~ hopeful

【希望工程】Hope Project

【希望小学】Hope Project Primary School

昔 (xī) past; former

【昔日】in former times; in the past (or old) days

析 (xī) ❶ divide; separate; fall to pieces; come apart ❷analyse

牺 (xī) sacrifice

【牺牲】❶sacrifice oneself; lay down one's life ❷ sacrifice; give up; do sth. at the expense of

【牺牲品】victim

息 (xī) ❶breath ❷news; message ❸interest ❹stop ❺rest

【息息相关】be closely related

奚 (xī)

【奚落】scoff at; taunt; gibe

悉 (xī) ❶know; learn: 惊～ be shocked to learn; 熟～ know very well ❷ all; entire

【悉数】❶all; every ❷entirely; completely

【悉心】whole-heartedly; heart and soul

淅 (xī) wash rice

【淅沥】the sound of a light rain, a breeze, falling leaves, etc.: 雨声～。The rain went pitter-pattering.

惜 (xī) ❶cherish; care for; treasure ❷ grudge ❸feel sorry for

【惜别】hate to part

稀 (xī) ❶ rare; uncommon ❷ sparse; scattered ❸thin; watery

【稀薄】thin

【稀饭】porridge; rice gruel

【稀罕】❶ scarce; uncommon ❷ value as a rarity; cherish; treasure

【稀客】rare visitor

【稀奇】rare; curious: ～古怪 eccentric

【稀少】few; rare

【稀世】rare on earth: ～珍宝 rare treasure

【稀释】dilute

【稀有】rare; unusual

锡 (xī) tin

【锡婚】tin wedding

溪 (xī) brook; small stream

【溪涧】mountain stream

【溪流】brook; rivulet

熄 (xī) put out; go out

【熄灯】put out the light

【熄灭】❶go (or die) out; extinct ❷extinction

嬉 (xī) play

【嬉戏】play

【嬉笑】be laughing and play

习 (xí) ❶habit; custom ❷review; practise; do exercises ❸be used to; be familiar with

【习惯】habit; custom: 养成～ get the habit of

【习俗】custom

【习题】exercises (in school work)

【习性】character; nature

【习以为常】get used to; fall into the habit of

【习作】❶do exercises in composition ❷an exercise in composition, drawing, etc.

席 (xí) ❶ seat; place: 入～ take one's seat ❷feast; banquet; dinner ❸mat

【席地】on the ground

【席位】seat; place

袭 (xí) make a sudden attack on; raid

【袭击】❶make a sudden (or surprise) attack on; raid ❷a sudden attack

媳 (xí) daughter-in-law

【媳妇】❶ son's wife; daughter-in-law ❷wife

洗 (xǐ) ❶wash; bathe ❷loot; sack

【洗车】car washing; vehicle cleaning

【洗车处】car wash

【洗尘】give a dinner of welcome

【洗涤】wash

【洗耳恭听】listen with great attention

【洗发剂】shampoo

【洗礼】baptism a severe test

【洗脸】wash one's face

【洗脸盆】washbasin; washbowl

【洗面奶】face cleansing cream

【洗手】❶wash one's hands ❷quit a job

【洗漱】wash one's face and rinse one's mouth

【洗刷】❶ wash and brush; scrub ❷ clear oneself of; wash off

【洗碗机】dish washer

【洗衣粉】washing powder

【洗衣机】washer; washing machine

【洗澡】have (or take) a bath; bathe

喜 (xǐ) ❶ happy event: 双～临门 be blessed with double happiness ❷ like; be fond of ❸happy; pleased

【喜爱】enjoy; love; like; be fond of

【喜报】bulletin of glad tidings

【喜从天降】a heaven-sent fortune; a heavenly blessing—an unexpected piece of good fortune; a gift from the gods

【喜欢】❶ enjoy; like; love; be fond of ❷ happy; delighted

【喜酒】wedding feast; drinks offered to guests at a wedding

【喜剧】comedy

【喜乐】happiness

【喜马拉雅山】the Himalayas

【喜怒无常】moody

【喜气洋洋】full of joy

【喜庆】joyous; jubilant

【喜糖】wedding sweets or candies

【喜帖】wedding invitation card

【喜闻乐见】love to see and hear

【喜笑颜开】light up with pleasure; brighten up

【喜讯】happy (or good) news

【喜悦】happy; delightful; joyful; cheerful

【喜滋滋】feeling greatly pleased; filled with joy

戏 (xì) ❶ play; show; drama; opera: 京～ Beijing opera; 马～ circus show ❷ play ❸joke; make fun of

【戏剧】drama; theatre

【戏剧家】dramatist; playwright

【戏迷】theatre fan

【戏曲】traditional opera

【戏台】stage

【戏言】❶joke; joking remarks: 一句～ a joking remark ❷jest; banter: ～身后事 jest

about arrangements after one's death

【戏院】theatre

【戏装】theatrical costume; stage costume

系 (xì) ❶system ❷department ❸tie; fasten ❹be concerned ❺be

【系列】set; series

【系列产品】serial (or line of) products

【系列片】serial; serialized film

【系统】system

【系统工程】system engineering (or project)

【系统化】❶systematize ❷systematization

【系统维护】system maintenance

细 (xì) ❶thin; slender ❷in small particles; fine; delicate ❸careful; detailed

❹minute; trifling

【细胞】cell

【细长】slim; slender

【细节】details; particulars

【细菌】germ; bacterium

【细腻】❶ fine and smooth ❷ minute; exquisite

【细水长流】economize to avoid running short; go about sth. little by little without a letup

【细谈】talk in details

【细微】slight; fine; minute

【细心】❶careful; attentive ❷carefully

【细雨】drizzle; fine rain

【细致】careful

xia

虾 (xiā) shrimp: 对~ prawn

瞎 (xiā) ❶ blind ❷ groundlessly; aimlessly; blindly

【瞎猜】make a wild guess

【瞎说】talk nonsense

【瞎指挥】give blind orders

匣 (xiá) a small box; a small case; casket

【匣子】small box or case with a lid; casket

侠 (xiá) ❶ a person adept in martial arts and given to chivalrous conduct (in olden times) ❷ having a strong sense of justice and ready to help the weak; chivalrous

【侠义】having a high sense of justice and ready to help the down and under: ~心肠 chivalrous temperament

峡 (xiá) gorge: 海~ strait; 长江三~ the Three Gorges on the Changjiang River

【峡谷】gorge

狭 (xiá) narrow

【狭隘】❶narrow ❷narrow-minded

【狭长】long and narrow: ~的山谷 long and narrow valley

【狭小】narrow and small; narrow: 气量~ be narrow-minded

【狭义】narrow sense

【狭窄】❶ contracted; cramped; narrow ❷ (of mind, knowledge, etc.) narrow; limited: 心地~ intolerant; narrow-minded

遐 (xiá) ❶far; distant ❷lasting; long

【遐迩】far and near: 闻名~ be well-known far and near

【遐想】❶think imaginatively ❷reverie

瑕 (xiá) ❶ flaw in a piece of jade ❷ flaw; defect; shortcoming

【瑕疵】flaw; blemish

辖 (xiá) have jurisdiction over; administer; govern

【辖区】area under one's jurisdiction

霞 (xiá) morning or evening glow

【霞光】rays of morning or evening sunlight

下 (xià) ❶ fall ❷ get down (or off) ❸ form; make ❹ give in ❺ finish ❻ put in ❼ issue ❽ exit ❾ take away (or off) ❿ go to ⓫ give birth to; lay lower; inferior next; second ⓬ less than ⓭ below; down; under downward

【下巴】chin; jaw

【下班】go off work (or duty)

【下笔】put pen to paper; begin to write or paint: ~千言 finish writing a thousand words at one go

【下不为例】not to be repeated

【下层】❶lower levels ❷grass roots
【下车】get off a car (or bus)
【下船】go ashore; disembark
【下次】❶next time ❷next
【下达】make known (or transmit) to subordinates
【下蛋】lay eggs
【下跌】(of water level, price, etc.) fall; drop; plunge
【下颚】the lower jaw
【下放】transfer to a lower level
【下浮】lower; go down; drop; fall
【下岗】❶lay off ❷laid off
【下岗人员】laid-off worker; laid-offs
【下功夫】take pains; make efforts
【下滑】slip (or glide) down; fall; drop; decline
【下降】drop; fall; decline: 气温～ drop in the temperature
【下结论】draw a conclusion
【下决心】make up one's mind
【下课】get out of class; finish class
【下列】following
【下令】give (or issue) orders; order
【下楼】go downstairs
【下落】❶whereabouts ❷fall; drop
【下面】❶ below; under ❷ next; following ❸lower level ❹subordinate
【下坡】downward; downhill
【下铺】lower berth
【下棋】play chess
【下属】subordinate
【下台】❶ step down from the stage ❷ leave office
【下午】❶afternoon ❷in the afternoon
【下限】lower (or floor) limit
【下陷】sunken; hollow: 眼眶～ sunken eyes
【下线】❶log off the line; log off ❷off-line
【下乡】go to the countryside
【下雪】snow
【下药】❶ prescribe medicine: 对症～ suit the medicine to the illness ❷put poison on or into sth.
【下游】❶ downstream; downriver ❷ backward position: 不可甘居～. Don't resign yourself to backwardness.
【下载】download
【下肢】lower limbs

吓 (xià) frighten; scare

【吓唬】frighten; scare
【吓一跳】be startled; give sb. a start

夏 (xià) summer

【夏季】summer
【夏令营】summer camp
【夏收】summer harvest
【夏装】summer clothing; summer wear

xian

仙 (xiān) celestial being; immortal

【仙鹤】white crane
【仙境】fairyland; wonderland; paradise
【仙女】fairy maiden; female celestial
【仙人】celestial being; immortal
【仙人球】ball cactus
【仙人掌】cactus

先 (xiān) ❶ancestor ❷first; earlier ❸ earlier; before ❹before; in advance

【先辈】predecessor; elder generation
【先导】guide; forerunner
【先锋】vanguard; van; pioneer: 起～作用 play a vanguard role
【先后】❶ early or late ❷ order ❸ successively; one after another
【先见之明】foresight

【先进】❶ advanced：～工作者 advanced worker ❷ advanced individual or unit：后进赶～ those behind trying to catch up with those ahead

【先进工作者】advanced worker

【先进集体】advanced group

【先决】prerequisite：～条件 prerequisite；precondition

【先例】precedent；former example

【先前】before；previously

【先驱】pioneer；forerunner

【先人】❶ ancestor；forefather ❷ my late father

【先生】❶teacher ❷Mr.；gentleman；sir

【先头】ahead；in front；in advance

【先行】go ahead of the rest；start off before the others ❷beforehand；in advance

【先兆】omen：不祥的～ ill omen

【先知】❶a person of foresight ❷prophet

纤 (xiān) fine；minute

另见 1143 页 qiàn

【纤巧】dainty；delicate

【纤体】slim figure

【纤维】fiber；staple：人造～ synthetic fiber

【纤细】fine；thin

掀 (xiān) lift (a cover, etc.)

【掀翻】throw over

【掀起】❶ surge ❷ set off；start on a large scale

锨 (xiān) shovel

鲜 (xiān) ❶ fresh ❷ bright-colored；bright ❸tasty ❹delicacy

另见 1242 页 xiǎn

【鲜红】bright red；scarlet

【鲜花】(fresh) flowers

【鲜美】delicious；tasty

【鲜明】❶bright：色彩～ colorful；in bright colors ❷distinct；clear-cut；sharp；striking

【鲜嫩】fresh and tender：～的藕 fresh and tender lotus roots

【鲜艳】bright-colored；colorful

闲 (xián) ❶spare (or free) time；leisure ❷idle；free

【闲工夫】spare (or free) time；leisure

【闲逛】stroll

【闲话】❶chat ❷complaint；gossip

【闲聊】chat

【闲情逸致】leisurely and carefree mood

【闲人】❶ loafer；idler ❷ person not concerned

【闲散资金】idle capital (or fund, money)

【闲事】other people's business：少管～！Mind your own business！

【闲暇】leisure

【闲心】leisurely mood

【闲置】let sth. lie idle；set aside

贤 (xián) ❶a virtuous person ❷virtuous and talented

【贤德】❶ virtue and kindheartedness ❷ virtuous：～女子 virtuous and kindhearted woman

【贤惠】virtuous

【贤内助】a virtuous wife

【贤能】❶virtuous and able：～之士 virtuous and talented person ❷virtuous and talented person

【贤妻良母】a good wife and loving mother；a virtuous wife and caring mother

【贤哲】good and wise man

弦 (xián) ❶chord ❷string

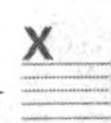

【弦外之音】overtones；under tone；implication

【弦乐器】stringed instrument

咸 (xián) salted；salty

【咸菜】pickles; salted vegetables
【咸肉】bacon

娴 (xián) ❶skilled ❷refined

【娴静】gentle and refined
【娴熟】adept; skilled

衔 (xián) ❶ rank; title ❷ hold in the mouth

【衔接】link up; join; connect

舷 (xián) side of a ship

【舷梯】❶gangway ladder ❷ramp

嫌 (xián) ❶ suspicion ❷ grudge ❸ dislike

【嫌弃】dislike and avoid
【嫌疑】❶ suspicion ❷ suspicious: 不避～ unafraid of other people's suspicion
【嫌疑人】suspect

显 (xiǎn) ❶ show; display ❷ obvious; noticeable; outstanding

【显得】look; seem; appear
【显而易见】❶plain; obvious ❷obviously
【显贵】❶occupying a distinguished position; of high position; illustrious: ～人物 ❷illustrious person of high position ❸ high officials (in former times)
【显赫】renowned; celebrated
【显露】become visible; appear; come to light
【显然】obviously; clearly; evidently
【显示】show; display
【显示器】monitor
【显微镜】microscope
【显现】appear; show
【显形】show one's (true) colors; betray oneself
【显眼】showy; obvious
【显著】marked; noticeable; remarkable; notable

险 (xiǎn) ❶danger ❷risk: 脱～ get out of danger ❸narrow pass ❹sinister; vicious ❺dangerous ❻nearly; by a hair's breadth

【险恶】❶ sinister ❷ perilous; dangerous: 处境～ be in a perilous position
【险峰】steep peak
【险境】dangerous situation
【险峻】dangerously steep; precipitous
【险情】dangerous state or situation
【险胜】❶win by a narrow margin; win a narrow victory ❷narrow victory
【险些】narrowly; nearly

鲜 (xiǎn) little; rare
另见 1241 页 xiān

【鲜见】rarely seen; seldom met with

县 (xiàn) county

【县城】county town
【县委】county Party committee
【县长】county magistrate

现 (xiàn) ❶ show; appear; visible ❷ present ❸now

【现场】❶scene ❷site; spot
【现场调查】on-the-spot investigation
【现场指导】on-the-spot guidance
【现钞】cash
【现成】ready-made
【现出】appear; come in view
【现存】❶in stock ❷existing; living
【现代化】❶modernize ❷modernization
【现代人】modern man; man of the modern age
【现代文明】modern civilization
【现货】merchandise on hand; spots
【现金】cash; ready money
【现金支付】❶cash payment ❷pay in cash
【现年】present age
【现任】at present hold the office of; cur-

rent in office

【现实】❶ reality; actuality ❷ realistic; practical; real; actual

【现世】this life: ～报 retribution in this life

【现象】phenomenon; appearance

【现形】reveal one's true features; betray oneself

【现有】now available; existing

【现在】now; right now; at present: 到～为止 up to now

【现状】present situation; existing state of affairs; current situation

限 (xiàn) ❶limit; bounds ❷set a limit; restrict: 期～ time limit

【限定】set a limit to; restrict

【限度】limit; limitation: 超过～ go beyond the limit

【限价】❶fix the price; set a limit to the price ❷the (officially) fixed price

【限量】put a limit to; set bound to

【限期】❶time limit; deadline ❷set a time deadline (or limit)

【限时抢购】flash sale

【限行】traffic controls

【限于】be limited to

【限制】restrict; limit: 年龄～ age limit; 时间～ time limit

线 (xiàn) ❶thread; wire; line: 穿针引～ thread a needle ❷route; line

【线路】line; route; circuit: 电话～ telephone line

【线索】clue; thread

【线头】❶end of a thread ❷an odd piece of thread

【线装书】thread-bound Chinese book

宪 (xiàn) ❶statute ❷constitution

【宪法】constitution; charter

【宪章】charter

陷 (xiàn) ❶trap ❷flaw; defect ❸sink ❹frame up ❺fall; be captured (or occupied)

【陷害】frame; frame up

【陷阱】pit; snare; trap; pitfall: 设～ lay a trap

【陷入】❶sink (or fall) into ❷be lost (or deep) in

馅 (xiàn) filling; stuffing

【馅饼】meat pie

羡 (xiàn) admire; envy

【羡慕】admire; envy

献 (xiàn) ❶ show; display ❷ offer; present

【献爱心】show (or display) loving heart (or good will)

【献策】offer advice; make suggestions

【献出】offer; sacrifice

【献给】dedicate to

【献计献策】offer ideas and schemes

【献礼】present a gift

【献身】❶devote (or dedicate) oneself to; give one's life to ❷devotion

【献血】❶donate blood ❷blood donation

xiang

乡 (xiāng) ❶country; countryside; rural area ❷native (or home) place; home town ❸township

【乡愁】homesickness

【乡村】village; countryside; rural area

【乡村音乐】country music

【乡亲】villagers; folks

【乡土风味】local flavour

【乡音】local accent

【乡镇】town; villages and towns

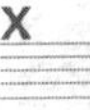

【乡镇企业】village and township enterprises

相

(xiāng) each other; one another; mutually

【相安】get along in peace: ~无事 live in peace with each other

【相比】compare (with)

【相差】❶differ ❷difference

【相称】suit; be worthy of; match

【相处】get along (with)

【相当】❶ match; balance; be equal to ❷ proper; suitable ❸rather; quite

【相等】be equal to

【相对】❶ opposite ❷ face to face ❸ comparatively; relatively

【相对论】the theory of relativity; relativity

【相反】❶opposite; contrary ❷on the contrary

【相逢】meet (by chance); come across

【相辅相成】complement each other; supplement each other

【相隔】be at a distance; be separated (or apart)

【相关】be related; be interrelated

【相互】❶mutual ❷each other; one another

【相间】alternate with

【相交】❶intersect ❷make friends with

【相距】apart; away from; at a distance of

【相连】be linked together; be joined

【相配】be suited to each other; be well-matched; be a good match

【相亲】size up a prospective mate in an arranged meeting

【相让】❶ exercise forbearance; give in; make concessions ❷ defer to each other politely

【相识】❶be acquainted with each other ❷ acquaintance

【相似】resemble; be similar; be alike

【相提并论】mention in the same breath

【相同】same; alike

【相向】❶in opposite directions: ~而行 go in opposite directions ❷face to face; facing each other

【相信】❶have faith in; be convinced of ❷ believe; trust

【相依】depend on each other: 唇齿~ be as close as lips and teeth; be closely related and mutually dependent

【相映】reflect each other; set each other off; form a contrast: ~生辉 set each other off wonderfully

【相助】come to sb.'s help; aid: 彼此~ help each other

香

(xiāng) ❶ incense ❷ spice; perfume ❸ sweet-smelling ❹ delicious ❺ soundly: 睡得~ sleep soundly

【香槟酒】champagne

【香波】shampoo

【香肠】sausage

【香格里拉】Shangrila

【香菇】mushroom

【香花】fragrant flowers

【香蕉】banana

【香蕉人】Banana person (yellow outside, white inside); American Born Chinese

【香料】perfume; spice

【香水】perfume; scent

【香甜】❶fragrant and sweet ❷soundly

【香味】fragrance; perfume; sweet smell

【香油】sesame oil

厢

(xiāng) box; carriage

【厢式货车】delivery van

箱

(xiāng) box; case; trunk

【箱子】box; case; trunk; chest; suitcase

镶 (xiāng) ❶set; inlay ❷edge; frame

【镶嵌】inlay; set

详 (xiáng) ❶detail ❷detailed; minute

【详尽】detailed

【详情】details

【详细】❶detailed ❷in detail

降 (xiáng) ❶surrender ❷tame
另见 1047 页 jiàng

【降服】yield; surrender and acknowledge allegiance

享 (xiǎng) enjoy

【享福】enjoy a happy life

【享乐】live in comfort and pleasure; enjoy oneself

【享年】die at the age of

【享受】❶enjoy ❷enjoyment: 贪图～ seek ease and comfort; seek to enjoy oneself in life

【享有】enjoy (rights, prestige, etc.)

【享誉】enjoy good fame (or reputation)

响 (xiǎng) ❶ sound; noise ❷ sound; ring ❸loud; noisy

【响动】sound of movement; sound of sth. astir

【响亮】loud and clear

【响应】❶ echo; answer; response ❷ respond; answer

想 (xiǎng) ❶think; feel; believe ❷suppose; consider ❸would like to; want to ❹miss

【想不到】be unexpected

【想到】think of (or about)

【想得开】not take to heart

【想方设法】❶ try one's best; try every means ❷by every means

【想念】miss; think about

【想起】remember; call to mind; think of

【想入非非】indulge in fantasy

【想象】❶imagine; fancy: 不可～ unimaginable; 难以～ hard to imagine; unthinkable ❷imagination

【想要】wish; want

向 (xiàng) ❶direction ❷face; turn towards ❸side with; take the part of; be partial to ❹to; toward

【向导】guide

【向后】backward

【向来】always; all along

【向前】forward; ahead; along; forth: 努力～ push on

【向前看】look forward

【向日葵】sunflower

【向上】❶make progress ❷up; upward

【向外】outwards

【向往】look forward to; yearn for

【向阳】be exposed to the sun; have a southern exposure

项 (xiàng) ❶nape of the neck ❷sum item

【项链】necklace

【项目】item; event: 田径～ track and field events

【项目开发】project development

巷 (xiàng) lane; alley

相 (xiàng) ❶looks; appearance ❷photo ❸bearing; manner ❹examine

【相册】photo album

【相机】camera

【相貌】looks; appearance

【相片】photograph; photo; picture

【相声】cross talk

象 (xiàng) ❶ elephant ❷ appearance; shape; image ❸ resemble ❹ look as

if; seem ❺such as; like

【象棋】chess: 下～ play chess

【象形文字】pictograph

【象牙】ivory

【象征】❶ symbol; sign ❷ symbolize; stand for

像 (xiàng) ❶ picture; portrait: 画～ portrait; 铜～ bronze statue ❷seem; look as if (or as though); appear ❸ be like; resemble ❹imitate ❺like; as

【像模像样】up to the mark; presentable; decent

【像素】pixel

橡 (xiàng) oak

【橡皮擦】rubber; eraser

【橡树】rubber tree

xiao

削 (xiāo) peel; cut; chop

枭 (xiāo) ❶ owl ❷ brave; valiant ❸smuggler

【枭雄】a fierce and ambitious person; a formidable man

骁 (xiāo) valiant; brave; spirited

【骁勇】brave; valiant

逍 (xiāo)

【逍遥】carefree; free and unfettered

消 (xiāo) ❶disappear; vanish ❷remove ❸cause to disappear; eliminate; dispel remove ❹ pass time in a pleasant way

X

【消沉】low-spirited; cause to disappear; eliminate; dispel remove

【消除】remove; clear up

【消除误解】patch up misunderstanding

【消除隐患】remove hidden dangers (or troubles)

【消毒】sterilize

【消毒柜】disinfecting cabinet; sterilizer

【消防】fire control; fire fighting

【消防车】fire engine (or truck)

【消防队】fire brigade

【消防设备】fire-fighting equipment (or facilities)

【消费】❶consumption ❷consume

【消费观念】consuming concept

【消费者权益保护法】law on the protection of consumer's rights and interests

【消耗】❶ consumption ❷ consume; use up; expend

【消化】digest

【消化不良】indigestion

【消极】passive; negative; inactive

【消灭】❶ eliminate; abolish; wipe out ❷ perish; pass away; become extinct; die out

【消磨时间】kill time; while away time

【消气】calm one's anger; cool down; be mollified

【消遣】❶amuse oneself ❷pastime

【消失】❶disappear; die away (or out) ❷ out of sight

【消食】help digestion

【消逝】fade away; elapse

【消退】abate; subside; decrease

【消息】news; information: 头版～ front-page story

【消息灵通】well-informed

【消夏】spend summer in a leisurely way

【消闲】❶ while away one's leisure time; fill one's spare time ❷easy; at leisure

【消炎】diminish inflammation; reduce inflammation; dephlogisticate

宵 (xiāo) night

【宵禁】curfew:实行～ impose a curfew

萧 (xiāo)

【萧条】❶bleak; desolate ❷depression: 经济～ economic depression

【萧萧】❶sound of a neighing horse or a whistling wind, etc. ❷ grizzled and sparse

硝 (xiāo) nitre; saltpetre

【硝酸】nitric acid

【硝烟】smoke of gunpowder

销 (xiāo) ❶melt ❷cancel; write off ❸ sell; market ❹spend

【销毁】destroy by melting or burning

【销路】sale; market

【销路好】have a good sale; be much in demand

【销声匿迹】disappear from the scene

【销售】❶sell; market ❷sale

【销售渠道】channel of distribution

【销账】cancel or remove from an account; write off

潇 (xiāo) ❶(of water) deep and clear ❷ Xiao River, a tributary of the Xiang River

【潇洒】free and easy; natural and unrestrained

【潇潇】❶ (of wind and rain) driving; whistling and pattering ❷drizzling; drizzly

霄 (xiāo) ❶clouds ❷sky; heaven: 高入云～ towering into the sky

嚣 (xiāo) clamour; hubbub; din

【嚣张】rampant; arrogant; aggressive

淆 (xiáo) confuse; mix up: 混～ confuse; mix up

小 (xiǎo) ❶small; little ❷young ❸for a while; for a short time

【小百货】small articles of daily use

【小半】less than half; the lesser (or smaller) half

【小报】small-sized newspaper; tabloid

【小辈】junior members of a family

【小便】❶ urine ❷ (of humans) urinate; piss; void; pass (or make) water

【小册子】pamphlet; booklet

【小丑】clown; buffoon

【小刀】pocket knife

【小道】path

【小道理】minor (or lesser) reason

【小道消息】hearsay

【小动作】petty trick

【小恩小惠】small favors

【小贩】pedlar; vendor

【小费】tip

【小规模】small-scale

【小孩】kid; child

【小河】brook; stream

【小环境】micro environment

【小伙子】lad; young fellow

【小轿车】car; sedan

【小节】small matter: 不拘～ not care (or bother) about small matters

【小姐】❶Miss ❷young lady; girl

【小看】belittle; look down upon

【小康】well-off; well-to-do relatively comfortable life

【小麦】wheat

【小卖部】small shop; canteen

【小米】millet

【小朋友】❶child; children ❷little friend; little boy or girl

【小便宜】small gain

【小品】essay; sketch

【小气】❶mean; stingy; miserly ❷narrow-minded; petty

【小巧】small and delicate: 身体～(of the body) be small and delicately shaped

【小区】residential quarters (or area, district)

【小圈子】a small social circle

【小声】in a low voice

【小时】hour

【小事】trifle; minor matter

【小瞧】look down upon; under estimate; slight

【小睡】nap; short sleep

【小说】novel; story

【小提琴】violin

【小偷】thief; pilferer

【小写】small letter

【小心】❶careful ❷take care; be careful

【小型】 small-sized; small-scale; miniature: ～会议 small-scale meeting

【小学】primary (or elementary) school

【小学生】pupil

【小学校长】principal

【小传】brief biography

【小组】group

【小坐】sit for a short while: ～片刻 sit for a short while

晓 (xiǎo) ❶ dawn; daybreak ❷ know: 家喻户～ known to all ❸tell

【晓得】know

孝 (xiào) filial piety

【孝敬】give presents (to one's elders or superiors)

X

【孝顺】showing filial piety

【孝心】filial sentiments; filial devotion: 一片～ one's filial devotion

肖 (xiào) resemble; be like: 惟妙惟～ lifelike

【肖像】portrait

【肖像权】portraiture right

校 (xiào) school; college; university 另见 1050 页 jiào

【校报】campus (or school) newspaper

【校风】school spirit (or practice)

【校服】school uniform

【校规】school rules

【校花】school beauty; campus belle

【校刊】school magazine; college journal

【校庆】 anniversary of the founding of a school or college; school-founding anniversary

【校舍】schoolhouse; school building

【校训】school motto

【校友】alumnus; alumna

【校园】schoolyard; campus

【校长】❶ headmaster; principal ❷ president; chancellor

哮 (xiào) ❶heavy breathing; wheeze ❷ roar; howl

【哮喘】asthma

笑 (xiào) ❶ laughter; smile; laugh ❷ laugh; smile: 哈哈大～ roar with laughter ❸laugh at

【笑哈哈】with a laugh; laughingly

【笑话】❶joke: 说～ make a joke ❷laugh at; ridicule

【笑话百出】make many funny mistakes

【笑脸】smiling face

【笑脸相迎】greet sb. with a smile

【笑料】laughing stock; joke; sth. funny or laughable

【笑眯眯】smilingly; with a smile

【笑容】smile; smiling expression

【笑容满面】be all smiles

【笑声】laugh; laughter

【笑星】comic star; comedian

【笑逐颜开】be wreathed in smiles

效 (xiào) ❶effect: 生～ take effect ❷ imitate; follow ❸devote to

【效仿】imitate; follow the example of
【效果】effect; result
【效劳】do service to; work in the service; work for
【效力】❶render a service ❷effect
【效率】efficiency: 提高～ promote efficiency
【效益】beneficial result; benefit: 经济～ economic results
【效用】usefulness

啸 (xiào) ❶whistle ❷howl; roar

xie

些 (xiē) some

【些许】a little; a few: ～小利 some small benefits

歇 (xiē) ❶rest; have (or take) a rest ❷ stop

【歇脚】stop on the way for a rest
【歇息】❶have (or take) a rest; rest ❷put up for the night; go to bed

协 (xié) ❶aid; help; assist ❷joint

【协办】cosponsor
【协和】coordinate; harmonize
【协会】association; society
【协商】❶consult; talk things over ❷consultation
【协调】coordinate; harmonize; bring into line
【协议】agreement: 达成～reach an agreement; 撕毁～ tear up an agreement
【协助】aid; help; assist
【协奏曲】concerto
【协作】❶cooperation ❷cooperate
【协作精神】team spirit

邪 (xié) ❶evil; wickedness ❷evil ❸un usual; abnormal

【邪恶】❶evil; wicked ❷wickedness
【邪念】evil thought; wicked idea

胁 (xié) ❶upper side of the body ❷threaten; coerce; force

挟 (xié) ❶hold sth. under the arm ❷ coerce; force sb. to submit to one's will ❸harbor

【挟持】❶ seize sb. on both sides by the arms ❷hold sb. under duress

偕 (xié) together with; in the company of

【偕同】in the company by; along with

斜 (xié) slanting; sloping; tilted; inclined

【斜度】degree of inclination; gradient
【斜坡】slope
【斜射】cast oblique rays (or beams) on an object
【斜眼】wall-eye; cross-eye
【斜阳】setting sun

谐 (xié) ❶ in harmony; in accord ❷ come to an agreement ❸humorous

【谐趣】wit and humour
【谐音】❶homophony ❷ partials

携 (xié) ❶take; carry; bring ❷take sb. by the hand; hold sb. by the hand

【携带】take; carry; bring; take with (or along)
【携手】hand in hand

鞋 (xié) shoe: 凉～ sandals; 拖～ slippers

【鞋带】shoelace; shoestring
【鞋垫】shoe-pad; insole
【鞋跟】heel
【鞋油】shoepolish

写 (xiě) write; describe

【写景】describe scenery
【写生】paint or sketch from life; draw (or

paint, sketch) from nature: 静物～ still-life painting

【写信】write a letter

【写真】portrayal of a person portrait

【写字楼】office building

【写作】writing

血 (xiě) blood: 流～ bleed
另见 1260 页 xuè

【血淋淋】bloody

泄 (xiè) ❶let out; discharge ❷leak; let out ❸vent; give vent to

【泄洪】discharge floods

【泄漏】leak; let out; give away

【泄气】lose heart; feel discouraged; be disheartening

泻 (xiè) ❶flow (or rush) swiftly; pour ❷have loose bowels

【泻药】laxative; evacuant; cathartics

卸 (xiè) ❶ unload ❷ remove; strip ❸shirk

【卸货】unload

【卸任】leave office

【卸载】❶unload the cargo from a vehicle or a ship ❷uninstall

【卸妆】remove ornaments and formal dress

亵 (xiè) ❶ treat with irreverence; be disrespectful ❷obscene; indecent

【亵渎】blaspheme; profane; pollute

屑 (xiè) crumbs; scraps; bits

械 (xiè) ❶ tool; instrument; machine ❷weapon

【械斗】fight with weapons

谢 (xiè) ❶thank ❷wither ❸decline

【谢恩】express gratitude for a favour

【谢绝】refuse; decline: 婉言～ politely refuse; decline politely

【谢幕】❶curtain call ❷respond to a curtain call

【谢谢】thank: 不用谢 don't mention it; you're welcome; not at all

【谢意】thankfulness; gratitude

懈 (xiè) ❶slack; lax ❷slacken; relax

【懈怠】slack; slacken

蟹 (xiè) crab

xin

心 (xīn) ❶heart ❷feeling; mind ❸centre; core

【心爱】❶love; treasure ❷beloved

【心不在焉】absent-minded

【心裁】idea: 别出～ be original

【心潮】tidal surge of emotion; surging thoughts and emotions: ～澎湃 feel an upsurge of emotion

【心慈手软】softhearted

【心得】understanding; experience

【心底】❶the bottom of one's heart ❷ intention

【心地善良】kindhearted; good-natured

【心烦】be upset; be vexed; go hot and cold; be perturbed

【心扉】the door of one's heart

【心甘情愿】be willing to; be happy (or ready) to

【心狠】cruel; merciless

【心花怒放】burst with joy; be wild with joy

【心慌】be nervous (or alarmed)

【心计】calculation; trick; planning

【心焦】anxious; worried

【心惊胆战】tremble with fear

【心境】mood; state of mind

【心口如一】mean what one says; say what

one thinks
【心宽】broad-minded;tolerant of anything undesirable
【心旷神怡】carefree and joyous
【心里】at heart; in mind; in the heart; in the mind:记在～ keep (or bear) in mind
【心理健康】❶ psychological (or mental) health ❷psychologically healthy
【心理平衡】psychological balance
【心理压力】psychological pressure
【心理障碍】psychological barrier
【心力】mental and physical efforts
【心连心】be of one mind with
【心灵】❶intelligent;clever ❷heart;soul
【心灵手巧】clever and deft
【心领神会】 understand tacitly; readily take a hint
【心满意足】❶be fully satisfied ❷to one's heart's content
【心目】mind; view: 在某人的～中 in one's eyes
【心平气和】❶even-tempered ❷calmly
【心切】eager; impatient; anxious: 求胜～ be anxious to gain victory
【心情】feeling;mind;mood
【心情舒畅】have ease of mind
【心软】be softhearted;be tenderhearted
【心神】mind;state of mind
【心声】words from heart
【心思】 ❶ thought; idea ❷ thinking; thoughts
【心酸】be grieved;feel sad
【心态】state of mind;mentality
【心细】careful; cautious: 胆大 ～ bold but cautious
【心胸开阔】broad-minded
【心胸狭窄】narrow-minded
【心虚】❶ be afraid of being found out; with a guilty conscience ❷ lack in self-confidence
【心血】thoughts and energies;painstaking care (or effort);painstaking labor:花费～ expend one's thoughts and energies
【心意】❶regards;kindly feelings ❷mind; will;intention
【心愿】wish;desire
【心脏】heart
【心直口快】frank and outspoken
【心中有数】feel certain;feel assured

芯
(xīn) lamp pith

【芯片】chip

辛
(xīn) ❶hard ❷hot ❸painful

【辛苦】hard; laborious; hardworking; undergo;go to great troubles
【辛辣】pungent; hot; bitter sharp, bitter or pungent language:～的讽刺 bitter irony;biting sarcasm
【辛劳】pains;toil:不辞～ spare no pains
【辛勤】diligent;industrious;hardworking
【辛酸】sad; bitter; miserable: ～泪 sad tears;hot and bitter tears

欣
(xīn) joyful;happy;glad

【欣然】with pleasure;joyful
【欣赏】enjoy;appreciate;admire
【欣慰】feel happy;be grateful
【欣喜】❶joy;delight ❷glad;happy;joyful
【欣欣向荣】thriving;flourishing

新
(xīn) ❶ new; fresh ❷ up-to-date ❸ newly;freshly ❹recently

【新版】new edition
【新潮】❶new trend (or tide); new fashion:文艺～ new trends in literature and art ❷ fashionable; modish: ～发型 new hair style;modish hairdo
【新陈代谢】❶metabolism ❷the new su-

perseding the old

【新高】a new high：创～ hit a new high

【新观念】new concept (or idea)

【新婚夫妇】newlyweds; newly married couple

【新纪元】new era (or epoch)：开创～ open a new era

【新阶段】new stage (or phase)

【新近】❶recent; latest ❷in recent times; freshly; recently; newly; lately

【新居】new home; new house; new residence

【新举措】new move (or measure, action)

【新郎】bridegroom

【新能源】new energy

【新年】❶New Year ❷New Year's Day：～礼物 New Year's gift

【新娘】bride

【新奇】new and strange

【新任】newly appointed：～局长 newly appointed bureau director

【新生】newly born; newborn

【新生代】new generation

【新生力量】new force

【新式】new-type; new-style

【新手】green hand; newcomer; new hand

【新思维】fresh (or new) thinking

【新闻】news：国际～ world news; 国内～ home news; 简明～ news in brief

【新闻记者】reporter; journalist; newsman

【新闻热点】hot issue in media; hot news

【新闻人物】newsmaker; news figure

【新鲜】fresh; novel

【新新人类】New Human Being; X-generation

【新兴产业】new (or rising) industry

【新兴科学】new (or rising) branch of science

【新型】❶new type; new pattern ❷new

【新秀】new talent; new (or rising) star; new excellent person

【新颖】new and original; novel：题材～ original in choice of subject (or theme)

【新作】new literary or art work：新人～ new work by a new author

薪 (xīn) ❶firewood ❷salary：发～ pay out the salary

【薪水】pay; salary; wage：加～ give sb. a rise (or raise)

信 (xìn) ❶letter ❷message; word; information ❸sign ❹trust; faith; confidence ❺believe ❻have faith in; believe in ❼at will

【信贷】credit

【信访】letters and visits to lodge complaints

【信访部门】unit to handle letters and visits of complaints

【信封】envelope

【信服】be convinced; completely accept

【信鸽】homing pigeon; carrier pigeon

【信号】signal

【信笺】letter paper; writing paper

【信口开河】talk nonsense

【信赖】trust; have faith in; depend on

【信念】faith; belief; conviction

【信任】trust; have trust (or confidence) in; believe in

【信使】courier; messenger

【信守】abide by; stand by

【信徒】believer; disciple; follower

【信托】trust; entrust

【信息】news; message; information

【信息安全】information safety (or security)

【信息传播】information communication

【信息发布会】information release conference

【信息反馈】information feedback

【信息共享】❶information sharing ❷share information

【信息管理】information management

【信息化】informationize

【信息库】information bank (or base)

【信息流通】information flow (or circulation)

【信息社会】informationized society; information-based society

【信箱】❶letter box; mailbox ❷(邮局里供人租用的)post-office box (P. O. B.)

【信心】confidence; faith: 满怀~ full of confidence; 丧失~ despair; lose one's confidence; 有~ be confident

【信仰】faith; belief; conviction

【信用】credit; trustworthiness: 讲~ keep one's word; 丧失~ lose one's credit

【信用等级】credit rating

【信用卡】credit card

【信用危机】credit crisis

【信誉】credit; reputation

xing

兴 (xīng) ❶become popular ❷encourage ❸start; begin ❹permit; allow 另见 1225 页 xìng

【兴办】set up; initiate

【兴奋】❶be excited ❷excitement ❸excited; exciting ❹excitedly

【兴奋剂】dope; excitant; analeptic

【兴建】build; construct

【兴隆】prosperous; thriving; flourishing; brisk: 生意~ business is brisk

【兴盛】prosperous; in the ascendant

【兴师动众】move troops about and stir up the people; drag in many people (to do sth.)

【兴旺】prosperous; thriving; blossoming

【兴许】perhaps; maybe

星 (xīng) ❶star: 行~ planet; 卫~ satellite ❷bit; particle ❸star: 歌~ star singer; 球~ star player; 影~ film star; movie star

【星光】starlight

【星火】spark: ~燎原 a single spark can start a prairie fire

【星际】interplanetary; interstellar: ~空间 interplanetary space

【星空】starry sky; star-studded sky; starlit sky

【星期】❶week ❷day of the week

【星球】heavenly body; star

【星系】galaxy

【星星】tiny spot; speck: ~点点 tiny spots; bits; pieces

【星夜】starlit (or starry) night

猩 (xīng) orangutan

【猩红】scarlet; bloodred

惺 (xīng)

【惺惺】❶ clear-headed; awake ❷wise; intelligent

腥 (xīng) ❶raw meat or fish ❷having the smell of fish, seafood, etc.

【腥气】❶offensive smell of fish, seafood, etc. ❷stinking; fishy

刑 (xíng) ❶ punishment; sentence: 狱中服~ serve one's term in prison; 判~sentence; pass sentence ❷torture

【刑罚】punishment; penalty

【刑法】criminal law

【刑警】criminal police

【刑期】term of imprisonment

【刑事案件】criminal case

【刑事犯罪】criminal offence (or act)

【刑事责任】criminal responsibility

【刑种】categories of punishment

行 (xíng) ❶act; action; deed; behaviour ❷go; walk ❸travel ❹be current ❺do; carry out ❻capable; competent ❼all right; OK ❽certainly

另见 1014 页 háng

【行不通】won't do (or work)

【行程】journey; distance course: 历史发展～ course of historical development

【行船】sail; navigate

【行动】❶act; take action ❷action; deed: 采取～ take action

【行动小组】action (or group, squad) team

【行好】act charitably; be merciful; be charitable

【行贿】bribe; offer a bribe; resort to bribery

【行进】march forward; advance: ～路线 march route

【行径】act; action

【行礼】salute (bow, raise hand, etc.)

【行李】luggage; baggage: 随身～ personal luggage

【行囊】travelling bag carried for a trip

【行骗】cheat; swindle

【行人】pedestrian

【行善】do good works; do good turns

【行使】exercise; perform

【行驶】run; go; travel

【行书】running hand

【行为规范】behaviour (or conduct) norms (or code)

【行为准则】code (or norms) of behaviour (or conduct)

X

【行星】planet

【行医】practise medicine: 挂牌～ practise medicine with a license

【行政部门】administrative department

【行政处罚】administrative penalty (or punishment)

【行政干预】administrative intervention

【行政审批】administrative sanction (or examination and approval)

【行政长官】chief executive

【行之有效】effective

【行装】luggage

【行踪】whereabouts; track

【行走】go on foot; walk

形 (xíng) ❶form; shape ❷body ❸be expressed in ❹compare ❺appear

【形成】form; take shape; bring into being; become

【形而上学】metaphysics

【形迹】❶person's movements and expression: ～可疑 of suspicious appearance; suspicious-looking ❷trace; mark; sign: 不留～ betray nothing in one's expression and movements ❸manners; formality; etiquette: 不拘～ without formality; not standing on ceremony

【形容】describe; modify: 难以～difficult to describe; beyond description

【形式】form; shape

【形势】situation; circumstance

【形态】form; shape

【形同虚设】exist in name only

【形象】image

【形象代言人】image spokesperson

【形象工程】image-making project

【形形色色】of all shades (or forms, kinds)

【形状】form; shape: 呈……的～ take the shape of

型 (xíng) model; type; pattern

【型号】model; type

省 (xǐng) ❶examine oneself ❷visit ❸be aware (or conscious)

另见 1178 页 shěng
【省亲】pay a visit to one's parents (or elders)
【省悟】realize (or wake up to) the truth
醒 (xǐng) ❶ wake up ❷ come to ❸ be clear-headed
【醒来】wake up
【醒目】eye-catching; striking
【醒悟】wake up to reality
兴 (xìng) interest; excitement; mood
另见 1253 页 xīng
【兴冲冲】with interest; excitedly; with joy
【兴高采烈】in high spirits
【兴趣】interest: 感~be interested in; take interest in
【兴致勃勃】with great interest
杏 (xìng) apricot
【杏仁】apricot kernel; almond
幸 (xìng) ❶ feel joy in ❷ hope ❸ lucky ❹ fortunately; luckily
【幸存】❶ survive ❷ survival
【幸存者】survivor
【幸而】luckily; fortunately
【幸福】❶ happy ❷ happiness ❸ happily
【幸福指数】happiness index
【幸好】luckily; fortunately
【幸亏】❶ luckily; fortunately ❷ thanks to
【幸免】have a narrow escape; escape by luck
【幸运】fortunate; lucky
性 (xìng) ❶ nature; character; disposition: 本~ true nature ❷ sex: 男~ male sex; 女~ female sex ❸ property
【性别】sex; sexual distinction
【性感】❶ sexual appeal ❷ sexy
【性格】character
【性急】impatient; short-tempered
【性价比】performance-to-price ratio
【性教育】sex education
【性命】life
【性能】function; property; quality; performance
【性能可靠】reliable performance
【性情】temper; disposition; temperament
【性骚扰】sex harassment; sexual assault (or disturbance)
【性质】nature; quality
姓 (xìng) family name; last name; surname
【姓名】name; surname and personal name; full name
【姓氏】surname

xiong

凶 (xiōng) ❶ violence; murder ❷ fierce ❸ terrible; fearful ❹ disastrous
【凶残】ruthless
【凶犯】murderer
【凶狠】fierce and cruel
【凶猛】violent; fierce
【凶器】a tool or weapon for criminal purposes; a lethal weapon
【凶手】murderer
【凶险】dangerous and dreadful
【凶相】ferocious features; fierce look
兄 (xiōng) elder brother
【兄弟】❶ brother ❷ younger brother
【兄长】respectful form of address for one's male friend
汹 (xiōng) surging
【汹涌】surging; turbulent; tempestuous
胸 (xiōng) ❶ chest; bosom ❷ mind; heart
【胸部】chest; bosom
【胸花】chest ornament

【胸怀坦荡】open-hearted
【胸襟】mind;heart
【胸膛】bosom; chest: 挺起～ throw out one's chest
【胸有成竹】have a ready idea
【胸罩】brassiere;bra
【胸针】brooch
【胸中有数】know what's what

雄 (xióng) ❶male ❷grand ❸powerful

【雄辩】❶ convincing argument ❷ forcible speech:事实胜于～ facts speak louder than words
【雄风】❶ strong wind ❷ awe-inspiring bearing;stately appearance
【雄厚】rich;abundant
【雄浑】vigorous and firm;forceful
【雄鸡】cock
【雄健】powerful;vigorous
【雄劲】vigorous;robust;powerful
【雄师】powerful army
【雄伟】grand;imposing
【雄心】great ideas;great ambitions
【雄心壮志】great ambitions and lofty aspirations
【雄壮】magnificent;majestic
【雄姿】majestic appearance; heroic posture

熊 (xióng) bear

【熊猫】panda: 大～ giant panda; 小～ lesser panda
【熊熊烈火】raging flames;blazing fire
【熊掌】bear's paw

xiu

休 (xiū) ❶ stop; cease; end ❷ rest; pause

【休会】adjourn
【休假】❶holiday ❷have a holiday; be on leave (or holiday)
【休克】shock
【休戚与共】share joys and sorrows
【休息】❶ rest ❷ take a rest; have a break;rest
【休闲】❶leisure ❷be at leisure
【休闲服】leisure wear (or suit, clothes, dress,coat,jacket)
【休闲生活】leisure life;life of leisure
【休止】stop;cease;end

修 (xiū) ❶ repair; mend ❷ build; construct ❸ decorate ❹ trim ❺ write ❻ study ❼long;slender

【修补】patch up; repair; mend; make repairs
【修长】slender;tall and thin
【修辞】rhetoric
【修订版】revised edition
【修复】repair;restore
【修改】revise; correct; alter; makeover; modify
【修剪】trim
【修建】build;construct
【修理】repair;mend;fix
【修身】cultivate one's moral character
【修饰】❶decorate ❷polish ❸make up and dress up ❹modify
【修行】❶practice Buddhism or Taoism ❷ cultivate oneself according to religious doctrine
【修养】❶ accomplishment; training; mastery ❷self-cultivation

羞 (xiū) ❶ shame; disgrace ❷ blush; feel ashamed ❸shy; ashamed; bashful

【羞耻】shame;sense of shame
【羞答答】shy;bashful
【羞人】feel embarrassed or ashamed

【羞辱】❶ disgrace; dishonor; shame ❷ bring disgrace on; put sb. to shame
【羞涩】shy; bashful; embarrassed

朽 (xiǔ) ❶ decay; rot ❷ rotten; decayed ❸ aged

【朽烂】rotten; decayed
【朽木】❶ rotten wood (or tree) ❷ a hopeless case; a good-for-nothing

秀 (xiù) beautiful; graceful; fair

【秀才】scholar; intellectual; skillful writer
【秀发】beautiful hair
【秀美】graceful; elegant
【秀气】delicate; graceful; refined
【秀雅】tasteful and refined; graceful; elegant

袖 (xiù) sleeve

【袖口】cuff
【袖珍】pocket-size
【袖子】sleeve

绣 (xiù) ❶ embroidery ❷ embroider

【绣花】embroider; do embroidery
【绣花鞋】embroidered shoes

锈 (xiù) ❶ rust ❷ become rusty; rust

【锈蚀】spoilt by rust; corroded by rust

嗅 (xiù) smell; sniff

【嗅觉】sense of smell

xu

须 (xū) ❶ beard; mustache ❷ must; have to

【须发】beard and hair
【须眉】beard and eyebrows
【须知】points for attention; notice

虚 (xū) ❶ emptiness ❷ empty; unoccupied ❸ false ❹ timid ❺ modest ❻ weak ❼ in vain

【虚度】waste time; spend time in vain
【虚构】❶ make up ❷ fictitious
【虚幻】unreal; illusory
【虚假】false; sham
【虚空】hollow; void
【虚名】undeserved reputation; false reputation
【虚拟空间】virtual space; cyberspace
【虚荣】vanity
【虚实】false or true; the actual situation (as of the opposing side)
【虚伪】hypocritical; false; two-faced
【虚心】open-minded; modest
【虚张声势】bluff

需 (xū) ❶ necessaries; needs ❷ need; want

【需求】demand; requirement
【需要】❶ need; want ❷ demand; be in need of

徐 (xú) slowly; gently

【徐徐】slowly; gently

许 (xǔ) ❶ allow; permit ❷ promise ❸ praise ❹ maybe; perhaps

【许多】❶ many; much ❷ lots of; a lot of; plenty of; a great many of
【许久】for a long time; for ages
【许可】❶ permission ❷ permit; allow
【许可证】licence; permit
【许诺】promise; make a promise
【许愿】❶ promise sb. a reward ❷ make a vow

栩 (xǔ)

【栩栩】vivid; lively
【栩栩如生】lifelike

旭 (xù) brilliance of the rising sun

【旭日】the rising sun

序 (xù) ❶order ❷preface; introduction ❸introductory

【序列】❶alignment ❷ sequence

【序幕】prelude

【序数】ordinal number

【序言】preface; foreword; introduction

叙 (xù) ❶chat; talk ❷narrate; relate

【叙旧】talk about the old days

【叙述】❶narrate; relate ❷account; narration

【叙谈】chat; chitchat

畜 (xù) raise (domestic animals)

【畜牧业】animal husbandry; livestock husbandry; livestock farming

【畜养】raise (domestic animals)

绪 (xù) ❶thread ❷mood; state of mind ❸ mental or emotional state ❹ task; cause

【绪论】preface; foreword; introduction

续 (xù) ❶ add ❷ continue; extend ❸ continuous; successive

【续集】continuation

【续借】renew

【续聘】❶ renew contract ❷ further employment

蓄 (xù) ❶ store up; save ❷ keep in mind; harbour

【蓄电池】storage battery

【蓄积】store (or save) up

【蓄水】store water

【蓄水池】reservoir; water tank

【蓄意】premeditated; deliberate

xuan

宣 (xuān) ❶declare ❷drain; lead off

【宣布】declare; announce; make known

【宣传】❶propagate ❷propaganda

【宣传品】publicity (or promotion) material

【宣读】read out in public

【宣判】pronounce judgment; declare sentence

【宣誓】make a vow; take an oath; swear; make a pledge

【宣扬】propagate; publicize; advocate

喧 (xuān) noisy

【喧闹】noisy; bustle; racket

【喧腾】noise and excitement; hubbub

玄 (xuán) ❶black; dark ❷profound ❸ unreliable; incredible

【玄奥】profound

【玄妙】mysterious; abstruse

【玄虚】deceitful trick

悬 (xuán) ❶ hang; suspend ❷ keep thinking about; feel anxious ❸ suspended; unsettled ❹far apart

【悬垂】overhang

【悬而未决】suspended; unsettled

【悬挂】hang; hang up

【悬空】hang in the air

【悬念】suspension

【悬赏】offer a reward

【悬殊】a wide gap; a great disparity

【悬崖】cliff

旋 (xuán) ❶circle; spin; revolve ❷return; come back

【旋律】melody

【旋绕】curl up; wind around

【旋涡】whirlpool; eddy

【旋舞】whirling dance

【旋转】spin; rotate; revolve; whirl

选 (xuǎn) ❶selection ❷choose; pick; select ❸elect

【选拔】❶select;choose ❷selection
【选材】select suitable material
【选出】pick out
【选答题】alternative question
【选购】select and buy
【选举】❶elect;vote ❷election
【选录】select
【选民】voter;elector
【选派】select;detail;appoint
【选取】select;choose
【选手】player;(selected) contestant
【选修课】elective (or optional) course
【选用】select and use;choose and apply
【选择】❶ make a choice; select; choose ❷alternative
【选中】pick on;decide on;settle on

炫 (xuàn) ❶dazzle ❷show off;display

【炫目】dazzling
【炫耀】show off;make a display of

绚 (xuàn) magnificent;colorful

【绚烂】splendid;gorgeous
【绚丽多彩】bright and colorful

旋 (xuàn) ❶whirling ❷at the last moment

【旋风】whirlwind

xue

削 (xuē) cut;pare;peel

【削价】cut (or lower) the price
【削减】cut down;reduce
【削弱】weaken
【削足适履】cut the feet to fit the shoes

靴 (xuē) boots

穴 (xué) cave;den;hole;opening

【穴位】acupuncture point

学 (xué) ❶learning;knowledge ❷subject ❸college;school ❹study;learn ❺imitate;mimic

【学报】journal
【学费】tuition fee;tuition;school fee
【学风】style of study
【学府】institution of higher learning;seat of learning
【学富五车】have read five cartloads of books—be very learned
【学会】❶ learn; master ❷ academy; institute; association; society; learning society
【学科】subject;branch of learning
【学历证书】academic certificate
【学龄】school age
【学年】school year;academic year
【学派】school of thought;school
【学期】quarter;semester;term
【学生】pupil;student
【学生票】student ticket
【学生证】student's identity card
【学识】knowledge; learning; scholarly attainments
【学术】systematic learning; academic research
【学术交流】academic exchange
【学说】doctrine;theory;teaching
【学徒】apprentice;trainee
【学位】academic degree; degree: 博士～ doctor's degree; 硕士～ master's degree;学士～ bachelor's degree
【学位证】academic degree
【学问】scholarship;knowledge;learning
【学习】study;learn:向……～ learn from
【学习成绩】academic score (or achievement)
【学习能力】learning capability

【学校】school
【学业】school work; studies
【学员】student; trainee
【学院】college; institute
【学杂费】tuition and fees
【学者】scholar: 青年～ young scholar
【学子】student

雪 (xuě) ❶snow ❷wipe out; avenge

【雪白】snow-white; snowy white: ～的墙壁 snow-white wall
【雪崩】snowslide
【雪糕】ice cream
【雪花】snowflake
【雪亮】bright as snow; shiny
【雪片】flying snowflakes
【雪橇】sled; sleigh
【雪人】snowman; snow piled up in the shape of a human being
【雪山】snow capped mountain
【雪中送炭】give timely help

血 (xuè) blood: 流～ shed blood; bleed 另见 1250 页 xiě

【血管】blood vessel
【血汗】blood and sweat; hard toil
【血迹】bloodstain
【血泪】shed tears of blood when one cries with grief
【血亲】relatives by blood; blood relations
【血肉】flesh and blood
【血统】blood relationship
【血腥】bloody; reeking of blood
【血型】blood type
【血压】blood pressure
【血液】❶blood ❷lifeblood; lifeline
【血缘】blood relationship; ties of blood

xun

勋 (xūn) merit; worthy service; achievement

【勋章】medal; decoration

熏 (xūn) smoke

【熏染】affect
【熏陶】influence
【熏制】smoke; cure (meat, etc.) by smoking

旬 (xún) ❶a period of ten days ❷a period of ten years in a person's age (applied only to old persons)

【旬刊】a publication appearing once every ten days
【旬日】ten days

寻 (xún) seek; search; look for

【寻常】usual; common
【寻根】get to the bottom of sth.; investigate deeply into
【寻开心】joke; make fun of
【寻觅】seek; look for
【寻味】chew sth. over; ruminate
【寻找】seek; look (or search) for; be after
【寻找商机】seek (or look for) a business opportunity
【寻租】seek renting

巡 (xún) patrol; make one's rounds

【巡查】go on a tour of inspection; make one's rounds
【巡航】cruise
【巡回演出】❶performance tour (or itinerary) ❷go on a performance tour
【巡警】patrol police; patrolman; patrolwoman
【巡逻】go on patrol; patrol
【巡视】make an inspection tour

询 (xún) ask; inquire

【询查】enquire about; demand; make enquiries

【询问】❶ask; ask about; inquire; enquire ❷inquiry

循 (xún) follow

【循环】❶cycle ❷move in cycles

【循环经济】cycle economy

【循序渐进】go in order; go step by step

【循循善诱】teach skillfully and patiently

训 (xùn) ❶ model; example; standard ❷instruct; admonish; give sb. a lecture ❸ instructions ❹ train; teach; lecture

【训斥】rebuke; dress down

【训话】❶ give a dressing ❷ down to one's subordinates

【训练】❶train; drill ❷training

【训练基地】training base

讯 (xùn) ❶message; dispatch ❷ interrogate ❸news; message; dispatch

【讯问】❶ask about; enquire ❷interrogate

汛 (xùn) seasonal flood

【汛期】flood season; high-water season

迅 (xùn) fast; swift

【迅即】immediately; at once

【迅猛】swift and violent

【迅速】❶quick; swift; rapid; speedy ❷rapidly; fast; quickly

驯 (xùn) ❶tame ❷

【驯服】❶tame; bring under control ❷docile; obedient

【驯化】domestication; taming

【驯养】domesticate; raise and train

徇 (xùn) comply with; yield to

【徇私舞弊】do wrong to profit oneself

逊 (xùn) ❶modest ❷inferior; secondary

【逊色】inferior; secondary

殉 (xùn) ❶ be buried alive with the dead ❷lay down one's life

【殉国】give one's life for one's country

【殉难】die for a just cause

【殉职】die at one's post

Y y

ya

丫 (yā) bifurcation; fork

【丫头】❶ girl ❷slave girl

压 (yā) ❶ pressure ❷ press; weigh down ❸keep under control; control ❹suppress ❺come near; approach ❻pigeonhole

【压倒】overpower; overwhelm; prevail over

【压低】bring down; lower; reduce

【压服】bring under control with force; force down the price

【压价】force prices down; demand a lower price

【压力】❶pressure ❷overwhelming force

【压迫】❶oppress; repress ❷constrict

【压岁钱】lunar New Year money gift (to children)

【压缩】compress; reduce; cut down; condense

【压弯】bend with pressure

【压抑】❶constrain; depress; hold back: 精神～ feel depressed ❷ oppressive; stifling ❸depression; gloominess

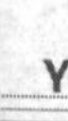

【压榨】❶squeeze; press ❷exploit; extort

【压制】suppress; inhibit; stifle

【压轴戏】the last item but one

押 (yā) ❶signature ❷deposit; give as security ❸take into custody ❹escort

【押金】cash pledge; security

【押送】send (a prisoner or captive) under escort; escort

【押韵】rhyme

鸦 (yā) crow

【鸦片】opium

【鸦片战争】the Opium War

【鸦雀无声】soundless; completely silent

鸭 (yā) duck: 公～ drake; 母～ duck

【鸭蛋】❶duck's egg ❷zero (as a score or mark)

【鸭绒】duck's down

【鸭嘴兽】duckbill; duckmole

牙 (yá) ❶tooth ❷ivory

【牙雕】ivory carving

【牙膏】toothpaste

【牙签】toothpick

【牙刷】toothbrush

【牙痛】❶toothache ❷have a toothache

芽 (yá) sprout; shoot; bud

【芽豆】sprouted broad bean

崖 (yá) precipice; cliff

【崖画】cliff painting

【崖刻】cliff inscription

哑 (yǎ) ❶dumb; mute ❷hoarse; husky

【哑巴】dumb person; mute

【哑铃】dumbbell

【哑谜】puzzling remark

【哑语】sign language; dactylology

雅 (yǎ) ❶refined; graceful ❷appropriate

【雅观】❶graceful; refined ❷in good taste

【雅虎】Yahoo

【雅量】❶broad-mindedness; generosity ❷great capacity for liquor

【雅趣】refined taste

【雅俗共赏】appeal to both refined and popular tastes

【雅致】❶refined; tasteful ❷in good taste

轧 (yà) ❶roll; run over ❷oust; squeeze out; push out

【轧伤】run over and injure

【轧碎】roll to pieces

亚 (yà) second; inferior

【亚健康】sub-healthy; sub-health level

【亚麻】flax

【亚热带】subtropical zone; subtropics

【亚运会】the Asian Games

【亚洲】Asia

【亚洲人】Asian

揠 (yà) pull up

【揠苗助长】help the shoots grow by pulling them upward

yan

咽 (yān) pharynx

【咽喉】❶pharynx and larynx; throat ❷bottleneck ❸key point; strategic passage

【咽炎】pharyngitis

胭 (yān)

【胭脂】rouge

烟 (yān) ❶smoke ❷mist ❸tobacco; cigarette ❹be irritated by smoke

【烟草】tobacco

【烟尘】smoke and dust

【烟斗】(tobacco) pipe

【烟灰】tobacco (or cigarette) ash

【烟灰缸】ashtray

【烟头】cigarette end

【烟雾】❶smoke; mist; vapour; a mixture of smoke and vapour ❷smog

【烟消云散】disappear like smoke and mist

【烟瘾】craving for tobacco; crave for smoking

【烟云】smoke, mists and clouds

淹 (yān) flood; drown

【淹没】flood; submerge; drown

【淹死】be drowned

腌 (yān) preserve in salt, sugar, etc.; pickle; salt

【腌肉】salted meat

【腌制】make by pickling or salting

嫣 (yān) handsome; beautiful

【嫣然】beautiful; sweet: ~一笑 give a winsome smile

延 (yán) ❶extend; prolong; lengthen; protract ❷put off; delay

【延长】lengthen; prolong; extend

【延缓】put off; delay; postpone

【延年益寿】prolong life

【延伸】extend; stretch; elongate

【延续】continue; last; go on

【延展】extend; stretch

严 (yán) ❶tight ❷strict; stern; severe

【严惩】punish severely
【严词】in strong terms; in stern words
【严打】❶crash down on crimes ❷crash-down campaign
【严冬】severe winter; cold winter; hard winter
【严格】strict; rigorous; rigid; stringent
【严加管教】keep under rigorous discipline
【严谨】❶exact and careful; careful and precise ❷well-knit
【严酷】❶cruel; ruthless ❷harsh; bitter; grim
【严厉】harsh; stern; severe
【严令】give strict orders
【严密】tight; close
【严师诤友】a strict teacher and a friend who will give unpalatable advice
【严实】❶tight; close ❷in safe hiding
【严守】keep secret; strictly observe
【严守纪律】observe strict discipline
【严肃】serious in manner; grave; serious; earnest
【严刑】❶cruel torture ❷severe punishment
【严于律己】be strict with oneself
【严阵以待】be fully ready for fighting; in combat readiness
【严重】grave; serious
【严重亏损】heavy loss
【严重损失】great loss

言 (yán) ❶character ❷word; speech ❸say; talk; speak

【言不及义】beat about the bush; talk off the point
【言不由衷】speak insincerely; have one's tongue in one's cheek
【言出必行】suit the action to the word
【言传身教】teach by both instruction and personal example
【言辞】one's words; what one says
【言归于好】make it up with sb.; become friends again
【言过其实】overstate sth.; exaggerate
【言和】make peace; become reconciled; bury the hatchet
【言简意赅】concise and comprehensive; compendious
【言论】opinion on public affairs; expression of one's political view; speech
【言情小说】love (or romantic) novel
【言说】put into words; say
【言谈举止】speech and deportment
【言外之意】hidden meaning; implication
【言行】words and actions
【言行不一】fail to match one's actions with one's words; the deeds do not match the words
【言行一致】be as good as one's word; suit the act to the word
【言语】speech; spoken language
【言者无心,听者有意】a careless word may reveal much to an attentive listener; a casual remark sounds significant to a suspicious listener
【言之成理】sound reasonable; make sense
【言之无物】talk without sense; not make sense
【言之有物】make (or speak, talk) sense

岩 (yán) ❶rock ❷cliff; crag

【岩洞】grotto; cave
【岩画】rock painting
【岩石】rock

炎 (yán) ❶inflammation ❷burning hot

【炎热】burning hot

【炎夏】torrid or scorching summer
【炎症】inflammation

沿 (yán) ❶edge ❷follow ❸along

【沿岸】along the bank; along the coast
【沿海】❶along the coast ❷coastal
【沿街叫卖】peddle sth. in the streets
【沿路】on the way; along the road
【沿线】along the line
【沿用】continue to use

研 (yán) ❶study ❷grind

【研读】delve into; study carefully
【研发】research and develop
【研究】❶study; make a study of; research ❷discuss; consider
【研究生】graduate student; postgraduate
【研究院】research institute
【研讨】study and discuss; deliberate
【研讨会】seminar; symposium
【研修】study; do research work

盐 (yán) salt

【盐分】salt content
【盐湖】salt lake
【盐矿】salt mine
【盐水】salt water; brine
【盐业】salt industry

阎 (yán) the entrance to a lane

【阎王】❶King of Hell; god of the underworld; Yama ❷cruel person; monster

颜 (yán) face

【颜面】face; prestige: 顾全～ save face
【颜色】❶facial expression ❷color

奄 (yǎn) ❶ cover; include ❷ all of a sudden ❸suddenly

【奄然】suddenly; quickly
【奄奄一息】❶ breathe feebly ❷ dying; on the verge of death

俨 (yǎn) majestic; solemn; dignified

【俨然】❶ solemn; dignified ❷ neatly arranged ❸just like

衍 (yǎn) ❶spread out; develop; amplify ❷ redundant; superfluous ❸ low-lying ❹flatland ❺marsh; swamp; bog

【衍变】develop; evolve

掩 (yǎn) ❶cover; hide ❷close; shut

【掩鼻而过】pass by holding the nose
【掩藏】hide; conceal; cover
【掩耳盗铃】plug one's ears to steal a bell; deceive oneself
【掩护】shield; cover
【掩口而笑】laugh in secret; hide one's smile
【掩埋】bury
【掩饰】cover up; gloss over; put a good face on; conceal

眼 (yǎn) ❶eye ❷hole ❸key point

【眼不见心不烦】out of sight, out of mind
【眼馋】eye sth. covetously
【眼福】❶good luck of seeing sth. rare ❷ lucky to see sth. rare
【眼高手低】ambitious but incompetent
【眼光】❶insight; foresight; sight ❷view
【眼光远大】farsighted
【眼花缭乱】be dazzled
【眼尖】❶have sharp eyes ❷sharp-eyed
【眼睫毛】eyelash
【眼界】field of vision; vision; horizon; outlook
【眼镜】spectacles; glasses
【眼泪】tears
【眼力】❶eyesight ❷vision ❸judgment

【眼明手快】quick of eye and deft of hand; sharp-eyed and deft-handed

【眼皮】eyelid:上~the upper eyelid;下~the lower eyelid

【眼球】eyeball

【眼色】❶meaningful glance ❷wink:使~wink at sb.

【眼神】❶eye expression ❷eyesight

【眼熟】look familiar

【眼纹】eye print

【眼下】at present;at the moment;now

【眼药】eye ointment;eyedrops

【眼睁睁】looking on helplessly

演 (yǎn) ❶evolve;develop ❷deduce ❸practice; drill ❹ act; play; put on;stage

【演变】❶evolve; develop ❷development; evolution

【演播室】studio

【演唱】sing (in a performance)

【演出】❶perform; put on a show ❷performance;show

【演化】evolution

【演技】acting

【演讲】❶make a speech;give a lecture ❷speech;lecture

【演示】demonstrate

【演算】❶calculate ❷calculation

【演戏】❶put on a play;put on a show;act ❷playact;pretend

【演艺界】performing art circles

【演绎】deduction

【演员】actor;performer;actress

【演奏】play

厌 (yàn) ❶be disgusted with ❷be fed up with;be tired (or sick) of

【厌倦】be tired of

【厌弃】spurn;turn one's nose up at

【厌食】be tired of eating

【厌世】be world-weary;be pessimistic

【厌恶】be disgusted with; detest; abominate

【厌学】be tired of (or fed up with) schooling (or one's lessons)

砚 (yàn)inkstone;ink slab

【砚台】inkstone;brick ink slab

咽 (yàn) swallow

【咽气】die;breathe one's last

艳 (yàn) colorful

【艳丽】bright-colored and beautiful

【艳阳天】bright spring day;bright sunny sky

宴 (yàn) ❶ banquet ❷ entertain at a banquet

【宴会】banquet:欢迎~ welcoming banquet

【宴席】banquet;feast

唁 (yàn) extend condolences

【唁电】telegram of condolence

验 (yàn) ❶ check; examine ❷ prove ❸work

【验钞机】counterfeit currency detector

【验光】optometry

【验货】examine goods

【验收】check and accept;check upon delivery

【验算】checking computations

【验血】blood test

【验证】test and verify

雁 (yàn) wild goose

焰 (yàn) flame

【焰火】fireworks

燕 (yàn) swallow

【燕麦】oats

【燕窝】edible bird's nest

【燕子】swallow

赝 (yàn) spurious; fake; counterfeit

【赝币】counterfeit currency

【赝品】art forgery

yang

央 (yāng) ❶center ❷entreat

【央行】central bank

【央求】beg; plead

【央视】China Central Television (CCTV)

殃 (yāng) ❶disaster; calamity ❷bring disaster to

【殃及无辜】bring trouble to innocent people

秧 (yāng) ❶seedling ❷rice seedling

【秧歌】yangge (dance) —a popular rural folk dance

【秧田】rice seedling bed

扬 (yáng) ❶raise ❷winnow ❸spread

【扬长避短】show one's strong points and hide one's weaknesses

【扬帆】hoist the sails; set sail

【扬眉吐气】feel proud and elated

【扬声器】loudspeaker

【扬言】threaten (that one is going to take action)

羊 (yáng) sheep: 绵～ sheep; 母～ ewe; 公～ ram; 山～ goat

【羊羔】lamb

【羊毛】wool

【羊毛衫】woolen sweater

【羊皮】sheepskin: 披着～的狼 a wolf in sheep's clothing

【羊肉串】barbecue mutton

阳 (yáng) ❶sun ❷open ❸positive

【阳春】spring

【阳春白雪】highbrow art and literature

【阳光】sunlight; sunshine

【阳极】positive pole

【阳历】solar calendar

【阳台】balcony

【阳性】positive

杨 (yáng) poplar

【杨柳】willow

【杨树】poplar

佯 (yáng) pretend; feign

【佯装】pretend; feign

洋 (yáng) ❶ocean ❷foreign ❸modern

【洋插队】to study, work or live in a foreign country; stay abroad

【洋葱】onion

【洋快餐】foreign fast (or snack) food

【洋娃娃】doll

【洋为中用】make foreign things serve China

【洋相】silly sight (or show)

【洋洋得意】proud and happy

【洋溢】brim with; be filled with; be permeated with

仰 (yǎng) ❶admire; respect; look up to ❷rely (or depend) on ❸face upward

【仰角】angle of elevation

【仰慕】admire; respect; look up to

【仰头】raise one's head

【仰望】❶look up at ❷look up to

【仰卧】lie on one's back; lie supine

【仰泳】backstroke

养 (yǎng) ❶ support; provide for ❷ raise; grow; rear; keep ❸ give birth to ❹ foster; adopt ❺ form ❻ take rest to recover health ❼ maintain; keep in good repair

【养兵千日,用兵一时】maintain an army for a thousand days in order to use it for an hour

【养病】take rest to recover health

【养蚕】❶ breed silkworms ❷ silkworm breeding

【养成习惯】form (or develop, fall into) a habit

【养父】foster father

【养护】maintain; conserve

【养花】grow flowers

【养活】support; provide for; keep

【养家】support (or keep) a family

【养老】❶ provide for the aged ❷ live out one's life in retirement

【养老保险】retirement insurance

【养老院】rest home; nursing home for the aged

【养路】maintain a highway (or railway)

【养母】foster mother

【养伤】rest to get a wound (or an injury) healed; nurse one's injuries or wounds

【养身】health promotion

【养神】take rest to refresh oneself

【养颜】face care

【养育】bring up; rear; educate

【养殖业】animal husbandry

【养尊处优】enjoy high position and live in ease and comfort

氧 (yǎng) oxygen

【氧化】oxidize

【氧化物】oxide

痒 (yǎng) itch; tickle

样 (yàng) ❶ form; shape; appearance ❷ sample; pattern; model ❸ kind

【样板房】model house; sample house; show apartment

【样本】sample

【样稿】sample manuscript

【样品】sample; specimen

【样式】pattern; style; model

夭 (yāo) ❶ die young ❷ tender and luxuriant

【夭折】❶ die young ❷ end halfway

妖 (yāo) ❶ demon; monster; evil spirit ❷ evil ❸ coquettish; bewitching

【妖怪】demon; monster

【妖精】❶ evil spirit ❷ alluring woman

【妖魔鬼怪】demons and ghosts

【妖娆】pretty and charming; enchanting; fascinating; bewitching

要 (yāo) ❶ ask; demand; require ❷ force

【要求】ask; demand; require; claim

腰 (yāo) ❶ waist ❷ middle

【腰包】pocket; purse; wallet

【腰鼓】waist drum

【腰围】waistline

【腰椎】lumbar vertebra

邀 (yāo) ❶ invite; ask ❷ solicit; seek ❸ intercept

【邀请】give an invitation to; invite

【邀请书】invitation

【邀约】invite; send an invitation to

窑 (yáo) ❶ kiln: 砖～ brickkiln ❷ pit: 煤～ coal pit

【窑洞】cave dwelling

谣 (yáo) ❶ ballad; rhyme: 童～ children's rhyme ❷ rumor: 造～cook up (or invent) a story;start a rumor

【谣传】rumor

【谣言】rumor:戳穿~ give the lie to the rumor;散布~ spread rumor

摇 (yáo) shake;wave;rock

【摇荡】rock;sway;swing

【摇动】wave;rock;sway;shake;swing

【摇滚乐】rock and roll

【摇号】license-plate lottery

【摇奖】hold a lottery

【摇来摇去】swing to and fro; wave back and forth

【摇篮曲】lullaby;cradle-song

【摇钱树】a legendary tree that sheds coins when shaken; a ready source of money

【摇头】shake one's head

【摇头晃脑】shake the head in pleasure

【摇摇晃晃】staggering

【摇摇欲坠】about to fall

【摇椅】rocking chair

遥 (yáo) distant

【遥控】❶ remote control; telecontrol ❷ control at a distance

【遥控器】remote controller;zapper

【遥望】look into the distance

【遥相呼应】echo each other at a distance

【遥遥领先】be far ahead;get a good lead

【遥遥相对】face each other at a distance

【遥远】distant;faraway;remote:路途~ a long journey;a long way to go

瑶 (yáo) precious jade;jasper

【瑶族】the Yao ethnic group

杳 (yǎo) distant and out of sight

【杳无音信】there has been no news whatsoever about sb. ;have never been heard of since

咬 (yǎo) ❶bite ❷pronounce ❸incriminate;cause to seem guilty:反~一口 countercharge the accuser ❹bark ❺be exact about the wording

【咬定】assert emphatically;insist:一口~ assert positively;state categorically

【咬紧牙关】grit the teeth; clench the teeth

【咬伤】bite

【咬文嚼字】mince words in speech or writing

【咬牙切齿】grind the teeth

舀 (yǎo) ladle out;spoon up (or out); scoop up

【舀子】dipper;ladle;scoop

药 (yào) ❶ medicine; drug: 服~ take medicine;感冒~medicine for colds; 预防~preventive medicine;抓~ have a prescription filled ❷chemical ❸poison

【药店】chemist's shop;drugstore

【药方】prescription:开~write out a prescription

【药房】❶chemist's shop;drugstore ❷dispensary;pharmacy

【药费】charges for medicine

【药膏】ointment

【药片】tablet

【药铺】herbal medicine shop

【药水】medicinal liquid;liquid medicine

【药丸】pill

【药物】medicine

【药效】efficacy of a drug

【药皂】medicated soap

要 (yào) ❶desire; wish; want; ask (or demand) for ❷must;should ❸shall; will;be going (or about) to ❹take;need ❺important ❻if

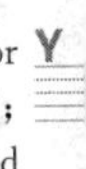

【要隘】strategic pass
【要不是】if it were not for; but for
【要道】thoroughfare; important passage (or line)
【要点】❶main point; essentials ❷key ❸strongpoint
【要害】❶vital part; crucial point: 击中~ hit home ❷strategic point
【要好】❶be on good terms; be close friends ❷be eager to make progress
【要紧】❶vital; important; essential ❷be critical; be serious; matter
【要领】❶main point (or idea); gist ❷essentials of doing sth.
【要强】eager to outdo (or excel); be anxious to outdo others
【要事】important matter
【要素】essential factor; key element
【要闻】important news; front page story
【要职】important post: 身居~ hold an important post

钥 (yào)

【钥匙】key: 房门的~key to the door

耀 (yào) ❶glory; honour ❷shine ❸boast of

【耀眼】dazzling

ye

耶 (yē)

【耶稣】Jesus

椰 (yē) coconut palm; coconut

【椰子】❶coconut ❷coconut palm; coconut tree
【椰子油】coconut oil (or butter)

噎 (yē) choke

爷 (yé) ❶grandfather ❷uncle ❸lord; master; sir ❹god

【爷爷】grandfather; grandpa

也 (yě) ❶also; too; as well; either ❷even ❸as well as; in addition to

【也许】perhaps; maybe; probably

冶 (yě) smelt (metal)

【冶炼】smelt

野 (yě) ❶open country; wilderness ❷limit ❸wild; untamed; ❹uncultivated; undomesticated ❺rough; rude ❻unruly ❼out of office; not in power

【野菜】edible wild herbs
【野餐】picnic
【野草丛生】be choked with weeds
【野炊】cook in the open air
【野火】prairie (or bush) fire
【野鸡】(ring-necked) pheasant
【野蛮】❶barbarous; cruel ❷uncivilized; savage
【野生】wild; uncultivated
【野生动物园】wildlife park
【野兽】wild animal (or beast)
【野兔】hare
【野外】open country; the open; field
【野心】wild ambition; strong desire
【野性】wild nature; wildness
【野营】❶camp ❷camping: 出外~ go camping

业 (yè) ❶line of business; trade: 各行各~ all walks of life; all trades and professions ❷occupation; profession; job: 失~ be out of job ❸course of study ❹cause ❺property ❻already

【业绩】achievement
【业内人士】insider of a trade
【业外人士】outsider
【业务】professional work; business

【业务范围】business scope
【业务能力】professional ability
【业务素质】business competence (or qualification)
【业务学习】professional study
【业余】❶ spare time; after-hours ❷ amateur
【业余爱好】hobby
【业主】owner; proprietor

叶 (yè) ❶ leaf: 长新～ put forth new leaves ❷ leaf-like thing ❸ part of a period: 初～ early part; 中～ middle part; 末～ latter part
【叶公好龙】Lord Ye's love of dragons—professed love of what one really fears
【叶脉】leaf vein
【叶枝】leafy branch
【叶子】foliage

页 (yè) ❶page ❷leaf; sheet
【页码】page number
【页面】page

夜 (yè) night; evening
【夜班】night shift: 上～ go on the night shift; 值～ be on night duty
【夜餐】night snack
【夜长梦多】a long night brings many dreams; a delay causes many mishaps
【夜空】the night sky
【夜间】❶at night ❷night
【夜景】night scene
【夜阑人静】in the dead of night; in the still (or quiet) of the night
【夜盲】night blindness
【夜幕】curtain of night; night screen
【夜色】dim light of night; moonlight; starlight
【夜晚】night
【夜以继日】❶ day and night; the clock round ❷round the clock
【夜总会】nightclub

液 (yè) liquid; juice
【液化气】liquid gas
【液晶】liquid crystal
【液晶电视】liquid crystal TV; LCD television set
【液态】liquid state
【液体】liquid

腋 (yè) ❶axilla; armpit ❷axil
【腋臭】underarm odour
【腋窝】armpit; junction of the arm and shoulder

yi

一 (yī) ❶ same ❷ all; whole ❸ every; each ❹whole-hearted ❺one ❻also ❼ throughout ❽per ❾as soon as; once
【一把手】❶ member; partner; hand ❷ chief; head
【一把抓】❶ take everything into one's own hands ❷deal with all things at once
【一般】❶ general; common; ordinary ❷ same as
【一般规律】general rule (or law)
【一般见识】(lower oneself to) the same level as sb.
【一般情况】general condition
【一般人】common people
【一半】one half
【一报还一报】❶return like for like; pay sb. back in his own coin ❷measure for measure
【一辈子】❶ throughout one's life ❷ all one's life; a lifetime
【一本正经】in dead earnest; in all serious-

Y

ness

【一笔勾销】write off at one stroke; cancel once for all

【一臂之力】a helping hand: 助我～ lend me a hand

【一边】❶one side ❷beside ❸by the side of ❹at the same time ❺while; as

【一表人才】with a striking appearance

【一波三折】full of ups and downs

【一不做，二不休】carry sth. through once it is started

【一步一个脚印】every step leaves its print; do solid and honest work

【一刹那】in a moment; in a second

【一唱百和】one sings, all follow; when one starts singing, the others join in

【一唱一和】echo each other; when one sings, another joins in

【一尘不染】not dirtied by any dust

【一成不变】invariable; unalterable

【一传十，十传百】pass quickly from mouth to mouth

【一锤定音】give the final word

【一次付清】❶pay off at one time ❷lump sum payment

【一寸光阴一寸金】time is gold

【一打】a dozen

【一旦】❶in a single day; in a very short time; overnight ❷suddenly ❸once

【一道】together; alongside; side by side

【一等】first-class; first-rate; top-grade

【一等奖】first prize (or place)

【一点一滴】little by little; bit by bit

【一定】❶fixed; specified ❷constant ❸certain; given ❹must ❺surely; certainly

【一而再，再而三】again and again; time and again

【一发千钧】a hundredweight hanging by a hair —in imminent peril

【一帆风顺】plain sailing; smooth sailing

【一方】❶one side; a party ❷an area (or region)

【一方面】for one thing; on one side (or hand)

【一概而论】treat as the same

【一干二净】thoroughly; completely

【一共】altogether; in all

【一鼓作气】get sth. done in one sustained effort

【一国两制】one nation, two systems

【一呼百应】hundreds responding to a call

【一伙】a gang (or band) of

【一级教师】first-grade teacher

【一技之长】a professional skill

【一家之言】a distinctive doctrine or theory; an original system of thought

【一见如故】feel like old friends at the first meeting

【一见钟情】fall in love at first sight

【一箭双雕】kill two birds with one stone

【一经】as soon as; once

【一举】with one action; at one stroke

【一举成名】become famous overnight

【一举两得】kill two birds with one stone

【一举一动】any move; any action

【一卡通】universal card

【一刻】a short while; an instant

【一孔之见】narrow view; limited view

【一口气】❶one breath ❷in one breath; without a break; at one go; at a stretch

【一块儿】together; at the same place

【一来二去】in the course of frequent contact; in the course of time

【一览无余】take in everything at a glance

【一连】❶in a row ❷running

【一连串】a string (or chain, series) of

【一了百了】all troubles end when the main trouble ends

【一流服务】first-class (or tip-top) service

【一流设备】first-class equipment

【一流质量】first-class (or top) quality

【一路】❶all the way ❷go the same way; go together of the same kind

【一路平安】have a good trip; have a pleasant journey

【一律】❶same; alike ❷without exception

【一马当先】take the lead; be in the forefront

【一面】❶ side ❷ aspect ❸ while ❹ at the same time

【一面之交】have met only once

【一鸣惊人】surprise the world with a single act

【一模一样】exactly alike; as like as two peas

【一目了然】be clear at a glance

【一目十行】take in ten lines at a glance

【一年半载】a year or so; in about a year

【一年四季】all the year round; throughout the year

【一年一度】once a year

【一念之差】a wrong decision made in a moment of weakness

【一诺千金】a promise that must be kept; a promise worth a thousand pieces of gold—a promise that can be counted on

【一瞥】❶a quick glance ❷a glimpse

【一贫如洗】as poor as a church mouse; penniless

【一曝十寒】have one day's sun and then ten day's cold—work by fits and starts

【一起】❶in the same place ❷together

【一钱不值】❶not worth a penny ❷mere trash ❸utterly worthless

【一窍不通】know nothing about; have no knowledge of

【一切】❶all; everything ❷every

【一切就绪】all in order

【一清二楚】very clear; as clear as daylight; perfectly clear

【一清早】early in the morning

【一去不复返】gone for ever

【一群】a group (or crowd)

【一日千里】❶ a thousand li a day—at a tremendous pace; with giant strides ❷at high speed

【一如既往】just as before (or in the past); as always (or usual)

【一扫而光】make a clean sweep of; clear off; finish off

【一色】❶ of the same color ❷ of the same kind

【一生】all one's life; throughout one's life

【一声不响】keep silent; be silent; not say a word

【一失足成千古恨】a single slip, the regret of a life

【一时】❶ for a short time (or while) ❷momentary

【一视同仁】treat all people alike; treat equally without discrimination

【一事无成】achieve nothing

【一手】❶skill: 露 ~ show off one's skill ❷trick ❸single-handed ❹all by oneself; all alone

【一瞬】the twinkling of an eye; a moment; an instant

【一丝不苟】not be the least bit negligent; be scrupulous about every detail; be conscientious and meticulous

【一丝不挂】be naked; not have a stitch on

【一丝一毫】a tiny bit; a trace

【一套】❶a set; a suit; a suite ❷a set way of doing things: 他做事有~。He has his own set way of doing things. ❸ the same stuff: 老~ the same old stuff

【一天到晚】from morning to night; all day long

【一条心】be of one mind

【一同】together; at the same time and place

【一统天下】unify the whole country

【一吐为快】cannot rest until one has one's say

【一团和气】keep on good terms with everyone

【一往情深】be head over heels in love

【一望无际】spread as far as the eye can see; stretch as far as the eye can see

【一味】blindly

【一文不值】❶not worth a cent ❷worthless ❸of no use

【一无是处】❶ lacking in any merit ❷ without any merit

【一无所获】make no gain; have gained nothing

【一无所有】not own a thing in the world; not have a thing to one's name; have nothing at all

【一无所知】know nothing about; have no idea of

【一五一十】completely and clearly

【一息尚存】so long as one still has a breath left

【一系列】a series (or string, train) of

【一线希望】a ray of hope

【一厢情愿】one's own wishful thinking

【一向】❶all along; always; usually ❷lately; in the past

【一笑置之】laugh out of court; laugh off

【一些】some; a number of

【一心一意】❶ heart and soul; wholeheartedly ❷of one mind

【一言不发】keep silent; not say a word; keep one's mouth shut

【一言为定】that is settled then

【一眼】at a glance: 看～take (or give) a glance at

【一样】❶same; alike ❷equally ❸as ... as

【一夜成名】become famous overnight

【一意孤行】act wilfully; be bent on having one's own way

【一应俱全】complete in every line; everything needed being there

【一语道破】drive a point home; lay bare the truth with one remark

【一语中的】hit the mark with one remark

【一月】January

【一再】again and again; time and again

【一早】early in the morning

【一张一弛】tension alternating with relaxation

【一朝被蛇咬,十年怕井绳】once bitten, twice shy

【一朝一夕】in one morning or evening; in a short time

【一阵】a burst; a fit; a peal

【一直】straight; always; all the way; all along

【一致】unanimously; in agreement (or line) with

【一致同意】agree unanimously

【一掷千金】spend gold on one throw; throw away money like dirt

【一准】surely; certainly

【一字之差】the difference of one word

伊 (yī) she; he

【伊甸园】the Garden of Eden; paradise

【伊斯兰教】Islam; Islamism

【伊始】beginning

衣 (yī) ❶ clothes; clothing: 单～ unlined coat; 夹～ lined coat ❷coating; covering: 糖～药片 sugar-coated pills

【衣不遮体】wear rags; wear shabby clothes
【衣橱】wardrobe;clothes press
【衣服】clothes;clothing
【衣冠不整】be carelessly dressed
【衣柜】wardrobe
【衣架】❶clothes stand (or tree) ❷hanger;clothes-rack
【衣领】collar
【衣衫褴褛】be dressed in rags; shabbily dressed;out at elbows
【衣食住行】❶food, clothing, shelter and transportation ❷daily necessities of life
【衣物】clothing and other articles of daily use
【衣箱】suitcase;trunk
【衣着】clothing, headgear and footwear

医 (yī) ❶ doctor ❷ medicine; medical science ❸ medical service ❹ treat; cure;heal

【医保】health insurance
【医改】medical innovation
【医科大学】medical university
【医疗】❶medical treatment ❷treat
【医疗保健】medical care;health care
【医疗保险】medical insurance
【医疗设备】medical equipment
【医生】doctor: 外科～ surgeon; 内科～ physician
【医术】medical skill;art of healing
【医务人员】medical staff
【医学】medicine;medical science
【医药费】medical expenses
【医院】hospital
【医治】heal;cure;treat
【医嘱】doctor's advice

依 (yī) ❶depend (or rely) on ❷listen to ❸according to; in line ❹with; in the light of;by

【依此类推】and so on and so forth
【依次】in order;in turn
【依从】listen to;yield to;comply with
【依存】depend on sb. or sth. of existence
【依法办事】handle official affairs in accordance with the law
【依法查处】investigate and handle according to the law
【依法逮捕】arrest in the name of the law
【依附】depend on;attach oneself to
【依据】❶according to; in the light of; in line with; on the basis of; by ❷ evidence;basis:没有～groundless;baseless
【依靠】❶rely (or depend) on ❷support; backing
【依恋】find it hard to tear oneself away from;be reluctant to leave
【依然】as before (or usual);still
【依然如故】remain as before (or unchanged)
【依托】❶rely (or depend) on ❷support; backing
【依偎】snuggle up to;lean close to
【依依不舍】be reluctant to part
【依照】according to;in the light of;by

仪 (yí) ❶ appearance ❷ ceremony ❸ present;gift ❹apparatus

【仪表】❶appearance;bearing ❷meter
【仪表堂堂】look noble and dignified impressive-looking
【仪器】apparatus;instrument
【仪容】looks;appearance
【仪式】ceremony:发奖～ prize-giving ceremony;举行～ hold a ceremony
【仪态】bearing;manner
【仪仗队】guard of honour;honour guard: 三军～ guard of honour of the three services

怡 (yí) happy;joyful;cheerful

【怡然】happy;delightful

【怡然自得】happy and pleased with oneself;feel a glow of happiness

宜 (yí) ❶should; ought to ❷suitable; fitting;fit

【宜人】pleasant;delightful

贻 (yí) ❶make a gift of sth. ;present ❷ bequeath; leave behind; hand down

【贻害无穷】cause lasting (or endless) troubles

【贻误】affect adversely

【贻笑大方】make a laughing- stock of oneself before experts

姨 (yí) ❶mother's sister;aunt ❷wife's sister;sister-in-law

【姨父】uncle;husband of mother's sister

【姨母】aunt

【姨奶奶】sister of one's paternal grandmother;great-aunt

胰 (yí) pancreas

【胰岛素】insulin

【胰腺】pancreas

移 (yí) ❶ move; remove; shift ❷ change;alter

【移动】move;shift

【移动通信】mobile telecommunication

【移风易俗】change the habits and customs;change the style of life

【移交】turn (or hand) over;transfer

【移居】migrate

【移民】❶immigrant;emigrant ❷migrate; emigrate;immigrate

【移植】transplant

遗 (yí) ❶lost article (or property) ❷ lose;miss ❸leave out;slip over;omit ❹leave behind; keep back ❺leave behind at one's death;hand down

【遗产】legacy

【遗传】inheritance;heredity

【遗传工程】genetic engineering

【遗风】traditions and customs handed down from a certain age

【遗孤】orphan

【遗憾】regret;pity:终身~ lifelong regret

【遗迹】historical remains;traces

【遗留】leave over;hand down

【遗漏】leave out;slip over;omit

【遗弃】abandon;cast off

【遗容】❶remains:瞻仰~ pay one's respects to the remains of sb. ❷portrait of a dead person

【遗失】lose

【遗书】❶posthumous papers ❷a letter of note left by one immediately before death

【遗孀】widow;relict

【遗体】remains:向~告别 pay one's last respects to the remains of sb.

【遗忘】forget

【遗物】things left behind by a dead person

【遗训】teachings of the deceased

【遗愿】unfulfilled wish;last wish

【遗址】site

【遗志】unfulfilled wish

【遗嘱】will;dying words:立~ make a will

【遗著】writings of a dead author;posthumous work (of an author)

颐 (yí) ❶cheek;chin ❷keep fit

【颐和园】the Summer Palace

【颐养天年】take good care of oneself so as to fulfil one's allotted life span

疑 (yí) ❶doubt; feel uncertain; disbelieve ❷doubtful; uncertain; disbelieving

【疑点】doubtful point

【疑惑】feel uncertain
【疑虑】doubt; misgivings
【疑难】difficulty; knotty
【疑神疑鬼】be even afraid of one's own shadow
【疑似】doubtful
【疑问】doubt; question: 毫无～ doubtless; without a doubt; out of question; without question
【疑心】be suspicious; suspect

已 (yǐ) ❶ stop; end ❷ already ❸ thereafter; afterwards ❹ too

【已故】late; deceased
【已经】already
【已往】before; in the past

以 (yǐ) ❶ by; according to ❷ because of ❸ in order to; so as to

【以备不虞】be prepared for any contingency
【以便】❶ in order to; so as to ❷ with the aim of; for the purpose of ❸ so that
【以德报怨】return good for evil
【以点带面】fan out from point to area; use the experience of selected units to promote work in the entire area
【以毒攻毒】fight poison with poison
【以防万一】be ready for any possible event
【以寡敌众】pit few against many
【以后】after; afterwards; later; hereafter: 从今～ from now on
【以及】as well as; and; along with
【以假乱真】mix the false with the true; mix the spurious with the genuine
【以旧换新】❶ old for new service ❷ trade in
【以来】since: 长期～ for a long time past; 五年～ in the past five years
【以礼相待】treat sb. with due respect
【以理服人】convince people by reasoning
【以貌取人】judge people by their appearance
【以免】lest; in case
【以内】within; less than; inside of
【以偏概全】take a part for the whole
【以前】before; ago
【以权谋私】abusing power for personal gains
【以人为本】people oriented
【以上】❶ the above ❷ in the above ❸ more than; over; above
【以身作则】set an example
【以史为鉴】draw lessons from history
【以外】beyond; outside; other than; except
【以往】before; in the past; formerly
【以为】think; believe; consider
【以……为依托】❶ on the basis of ❷ based on
【以小人之心，度君子之腹】gauge the heart of a gentleman with one's own mean measure
【以一当十】pit one against ten
【以逸待劳】wait at one's ease for a tired enemy
【以怨报德】return evil for good; repay good with evil; bite the hand that feeds one
【以至】❶ up to; down to ❷ so that; so ... that ...; to such a degree that ❸ to such a degree as to
【以致】so that; as a result; with the result that; consequently

倚 (yǐ) ❶ lean (or rest) against (or on) ❷ rely (or count) on

【倚靠】lean (or rest) against
【倚仗】rely on; count on
【倚重】rely on; rely heavily on somebody's service

椅 (yǐ) chair：安乐～easy chair；扶手～ armchair

旖 (yǐ)

【旖旎】charming；enchanting

亿 (yì) a hundred million

【亿万】millions upon millions；hundreds of millions

【亿万富翁】billionaire

义 (yì) ❶ justice；righteousness ❷ meaning ❸ friendly feeling ❹ just ❺ adopted；adoptive ❻ meaning；significance

【义不容辞】be duty-bound；have an unshirkable duty

【义愤填膺】filled with righteous anger

【义工】volunteer

【义举】a magnanimous act undertaken for the public good

【义卖】sale of goods for charity

【义士】high-minded person

【义无反顾】be duty-bound and not to turn back

【义务】❶ duty；obligation ❷ compulsory ❸voluntary

【义务教育】compulsory education

【义务劳动】voluntary labor

【义演】benefit (or charitable) performance

【义诊】volunteer medical consultation (or diagnosis)

艺 (yì) ❶skill ❷art

【艺名】stage name

【艺人】❶actor；artist ❷handicraftsman

【艺术】❶skill；art：领导～art of leadership ❷tasteful；artistic

【艺术家】artist

【艺术节】art festival

【艺术品】work of art

【艺术天才】gift for art

【艺术院校】academies of arts

忆 (yì) recall

【忆苦】recall past suffering

【忆想】recall；recollect；call to mind

议 (yì) ❶ opinion；view ❷ discuss；exchange views on；talk over

【议程】agenda

【议和】negotiate peace

【议价】❶ negotiate a price ❷ negotiated price

【议论】discuss；talk

【议题】topic for discussion；item on the agenda

【议院】parliament；congress

【议政】deliberate state (or government) affairs

屹 (yì) towering like a mountain peak

【屹立】stand towering like a giant；stand erect

【屹然】towering；majestic

异 (yì) ❶ different ❷ unusual；strange ❸other；another

【异常】❶unusual ❷unusually；extremely

【异端】heterodoxy；heresy：～邪说 heresies；heretical beliefs

【异国】foreign country (or land)

【异乎寻常】unusual；extraordinary

【异口同声】with one voice

【异曲同工】achieve (or get) the same result by different methods

【异同】similarities and differences

【异味】❶a rare delicacy ❷a peculiar smell

【异乡】foreign (or strange) land

【异想天开】have fanciful ideas；expect

wonders；have wild hopes

【异性】❶ the opposite sex ❷ different in nature

【异样】❶difference ❷unusual

【异域】❶ a foreign country ❷ an alien land；a strange land

抑（yì）❶repress；suppress ❷but ❸or

【抑扬】（of sound）rise and fall；modulate

【抑郁】depressed；gloomy；disheartened

【抑制】restrain；check；control

译（yì）translate；interpret：笔～written translation；口～ interpretation；意～ free translation

【译文】translation；translated text

【译员】interpreter；translator

【译注】translate and annotate：～古籍 translate and annotate ancient books

【译作】translations

易（yì）❶change ❷exchange ❸easy ❹ amiable

【易燃】inflammable

【易如反掌】as easy as turning one's hand over

【易碎】breakable

【易于】be easy to

驿（yì）post

【驿站】（in former times）post station

疫（yì）epidemic disease；pestilence

【疫病】epidemic disease

【疫苗】vaccine

【疫区】an epidemic-stricken area

益（yì）❶ advantage；profit；benefit；good ❷increase

【益处】benefit；profit；good

【益寿】lengthen one's life

【益友】helpful friend

逸（yì）❶toil ❷escape；flee ❸be lost ❹ excel all others

【逸事】anecdote

意（yì）❶meaning；idea ❷wish；desire；intention ❸expectation ❹expect

【意会】perceive by intuition；sense：只可～，不可言传 can be sensed，but not explained in words

【意见】❶opinion；view；idea ❷complaint

【意见分歧】be of different opinions；disagree

【意见一致】be of the same opinion；agree

【意料】expect

【意料之外】unexpected

【意念】idea；thought

【意气风发】in high spirits

【意识】❶consciousness ❷be conscious（or aware）of；awake to；realize

【意识形态】ideology

【意思】❶ idea；meaning ❷ wish；desire ❸ fun；interest

【意图】intention

【意外】❶ unexpected；unforeseen ❷ mishap；accident

【意味】❶meaning ❷interest

【意味深长】full of meaning；having deep meaning；of profound significance

【意向】intention；purpose

【意向性协议】agreement of intention

【意义】❶meaning；sense：在某种～上 in a sense ❷ importance：具有重大～be of great importance

【意译】free translation

【意愿】wish；desire；aspiration

【意在言外】the meaning is implied

【意志】will；determination；willpower

【意志坚强】strong-willed

【意中人】the beloved one；the person one is in love with；the person of one's heart

溢 (yì) ❶overflow; spill ❷too much

【溢出】overflow; spill over

【溢于言表】(of feelings) show clearly in one's words and manner

毅 (yì) firm

【毅力】willpower; will

【毅然决然】resolutely; determinedly

臆 (yì) ❶chest ❷subjectively

【臆测】conjecture; surmise

【臆想】a wishful imagination

【臆造】fabricate (a story, reason, etc.); make up

翼 (yì) wing: 机～ wings of a plane

【翼翅】wing

【翼护】shield sb. with one's own body

yin

因 (yīn) ❶cause; reason ❷because of; as a result of ❸ because; for; as; since

【因材施教】 teach according to the student's aptitude

【因此】therefore; for this reason; so; consequently

【因地制宜】use methods suitable to local conditions

【因而】❶as a result ❷with the result that

【因公】on duty (or business)

【因果】cause and effect

【因祸得福】profit from a misfortune

【因时制宜】use methods suitable to the time

Y

【因素】factor; element

【因特网】Internet

【因为】❶because of; on account of ❷because; for; as; since

【因小失大】lose a lot for the sake of a little

阴 (yīn) ❶shade ❷cloudy; overcast ❸hidden; secret ❹negative

【阴暗】dark; gloomy

【阴干】be placed in the shade to dry

【阴沟】sewer; drain

【阴间】netherworld

【阴冷】❶gloomy and cold ❷sombre

【阴历】lunar calendar

【阴凉】shady and cool

【阴面】shady side; back side

【阴盛阳衰】women doing better than men

【阴天】❶cloudy day ❷overcast sky

【阴险】sinister; insidious; treacherous

【阴影】shadow

【阴云】dark clouds

音 (yīn) ❶sound ❷news

【音调】tone; the pitch of a sound

【音符】note

【音量】volume

【音频】audio frequency

【音容】voice and facial expression ～宛在 the same voice and face seem still there (usu. inscribed on a funeral banner)

【音色】tone color; timbre

【音响】sound; acoustics

【音像制品】 audiovisual product; audio-video product

【音信】message; news: 互通～ communicate with each other; 杳无～ have not been heard from (sb.) since

【音乐】music: 古典～classical music; 民间～ folk music; 轻～ light music

【音乐电视】music TV(MTV)

【音乐会】concert

【音乐家】musician

【音乐节】music festival
【音乐厅】concert hall
【音质】tone quality

姻 (yīn) ❶marriage ❷relation by marriage
【姻亲关系】relationship by marriage
【姻缘】the fate that brings lovers together:美满～ happy marriage

殷 (yīn) ❶ abundant; rich ❷ eager; ardent ❸hospitable
【殷富】wealthy; well-off: 家道～ wealthy family
【殷切】eager: ～的期望 ardent expectations
【殷勤】eagerly attentive

吟 (yín) ❶ chant; recite ❷ song ❸ the cry of certain animals
【吟诗】recite poems
【吟诵】recite; chant

银 (yín) ❶ silver ❷ silvery; silver-colored
【银杯】silver cup
【银币】silver coin
【银发】silver hair:满头～ silver-haired
【银行】bank:中国人民～People's Bank of China;中国～ Bank of China
【银行利率】bank rate
【银行信用卡】bank credit card
【银河】the Milky Way
【银灰】silver grey
【银幕】screen
【银牌】silver medal

淫 (yín) ❶ excessive ❷ obscene; lewd; pornographic
【淫秽】obscene; salacious; bawdy ～书刊 pornographic literature
【淫乱】(sexually) promiscuous; licentious

引 (yǐn) ❶draw ❷guide; lead ❸cause; make ❹quote; cite ❺lure; attract
【引爆】ignite; detonate
【引导】guide; lead
【引渡】❶extradite ❷extradition
【引吭高歌】sing heartily; sing joyfully in a loud voice
【引号】quotation marks (“”)
【引火烧身】bring fire against oneself; bring trouble on oneself
【引见】introduce; present
【引荐】recommend
【引进】introduce from elsewhere; import
【引进外资】absorb foreign investment; solicit foreign funds
【引经据典】quote the classics
【引咎辞职】take the blame and resign
【引狼入室】invite a wolf into the house; open the door to an enemy
【引领】lead; guide
【引路】lead the way
【引起】give rise to; lead to; set (or touch) off
【引起公愤】arouse public indignant
【引起共鸣】arouse sympathy; evoke sympathy
【引桥】approach (or access) to a bridge
【引人入胜】absorbing; fascinating; enchanting
【引人注目】noticeable; conspicuous; spectacular
【引入歧途】lead sb. onto a wrong path
【引申】extend (the meaning of a word, etc.)
【引退】retire; fade out; resign
【引文】quotation
【引线】❶ wire-like fuse ❷ go-between ❸ sewing needle
【引言】foreword; introduction; preface
【引以为戒】learn a lesson; take warning
【引用】quote; cite

Y

【引诱】lure;seduce

【引资】❶bring in foreign investment (or capital,funds) ❷capital inviting

饮 (yǐn) ❶drink: 冷～ cold drinks ❷keep in the heart;nurse

【饮料】drink;beverage

【饮泣】weep in silence

【饮食】food and drink

【饮水机】water dispenser

【饮水思源】when you drink water, think of its source; never forget where one's happiness comes from

【饮用水】drinking water;potable water

【饮鸩止渴】drink poison to quench thirst

隐 (yǐn) hidden;concealed

【隐蔽】conceal;hide;take cover

【隐藏】hide;conceal;remain under cover

【隐患】hidden danger;hidden trouble

【隐居】live in seclusion;be a hermit

【隐瞒】conceal;hide;hold back;cover up

【隐秘】secret

【隐情】facts one wishes to hide

【隐士】hermit;recluse

【隐私】private (or personal) matters; one's secrets

【隐私权】right of privacy

【隐退】retire from society;retire from political life

【隐形眼镜】contact lens

【隐喻】metaphor

【隐隐约约】faintly

印 (yìn) ❶seal ❷mark;print

【印第安人】Indian

Y

【印度洋】the Indian Ocean

【印发】print and distribute

【印花】printing

【印迹】trace;mark;vestige

【印刷】printing

【印象】impression:深刻的～ deep impression

【印章】seal;signet;stamp

【印证】confirm;verify;corroborate

ying

应 (yīng) ❶ should; ought to ❷ answer; respond ❸ agree; promise; accept

另见 1284 页 yìng

【应该】should;ought to

【应届毕业生】graduating students

【应许】❶agree (to do sth.); promise ❷permit;allow

【应有尽有】have everything that one expects to find

【应允】agree to;consent

英 (yīng) ❶flower ❷hero;outstanding person ❸Britain ❹English

【英镑】pound sterling

【英才】person of outstanding ability

【英尺】foot

【英寸】inch

【英豪】hero;outstanding figure

【英俊】❶ talented ❷ smart; handsome and spirited

【英里】mile

【英烈】❶heroic and fiery; valiant ❷martyr

【英明】wise:～果断 wise and determined

【英气】heroic spirit

【英雄】hero:女～ heroine

【英雄气概】heroic spirit

【英勇】heroic;valiant;brave;gallant

【英勇善战】brave and skillful in fighting

【英语】English;the English language

【英语水平考试】English Proficiency Test

【英姿】heroic bearing; heroic posture;

bright and valiant look

婴 (yīng) baby;infant

【婴儿】baby;infant

罂 (yīng) small-mouthed jar

【罂粟】opium poppy

樱 (yīng) ❶cherry ❷oriental cherry

【樱花】oriental cherry

【樱桃】cherry

鹦 (yīng)

【鹦鹉】parrot

鹰 (yīng) hawk;eagle

【鹰犬】falcons and hounds—lackeys; hired thugs

迎 (yíng) ❶meet; greet; welcome; receive ❷face;move towards

【迎宾小姐】usherette

【迎宾员】usher;doorman

【迎风】❶facing the wind; against the wind ❷down (or with,in) the wind

【迎合】cater to;aim to satisfy

【迎接】meet;greet;welcome

【迎面】❶in one's face ❷head-on

【迎娶】(of a man) get married

【迎头赶上】catch up with

【迎新】❶see the New Year in ❷welcome new arrivals (or comers)

【迎战】meet to fight

【迎着】in face of;towards

盈 (yíng) ❶have a surplus ❷plentiful; filled;full

【盈亏】profit and loss

【盈利】profit;gain

【盈盈】❶clear;limpid:春水～ clear spring water ❷(of one's manner) delicate; dainty

【盈余】surplus;profit

营 (yíng) ❶camp ❷battalion ❸seek ❹ run;manage;operate

【营火】campfire

【营建】construct; build: ～宿舍楼 construct a dormitory building

【营救】rescue; manage to save; come to one's rescue: ～遇险船员 rescue the sailors in danger

【营利】seek profits;make money

【营私舞弊】engage in fraud for selfish ends

【营销】marketing

【营销路线】marketing strategy

【营养】nutrition;nourishment

【营养品】nutriment;nourishment

【营业额】turnover;volume of business

【营业范围】scope of business

【营业执照】business license (or permit)

【营运权】operation right

【营造】build;construct;build up

萦 (yíng) entangle;encompass

【萦回】hover;linger

【萦绕】linger on

蝇 (yíng) fly;housefly

【蝇头小利】a fly's head of profit; a petty profit

赢 (yíng) ❶win;beat ❷gain

【赢得】win; gain; obtain; attain: ～信任与支持 obtain trust and support

【赢家】winner

【赢利】profit;gain

影 (yǐng) ❶shadow ❷photo;picture ❸ film;movie;motion picture

【影碟】video disc; video disk; video com-

pact disc (VCD)
【影集】photo album
【影迷】movie fan
【影片】film; movie; motion picture
【影评】film review
【影视】movie and television
【影视文化】video culture
【影坛】movie circles
【影响】❶affect; influence ❷effect; impact
【影星】movie (or film) star
【影院】cinema; movie theatre
【影子】❶shadow; reflection ❷trace; sign; vague impression

应 (yìng) ❶ answer; respond; echo ❷ deal with; cope with
另见 1282 页 yīng

【应变】meet an emergency; cope with an emergency(or contingency): 随机～ act according to circumstances
【应变能力】emergency-meeting capacity
【应酬】engage in social activities; have special intercourse with; treat with courtesy
【应答如流】reply readily and fluently
【应付】❶ meet; handle; deal with ❷ do sth. after a fashion ❸make do with
【应和】echo each other: 同声～ echo simultaneously
【应急措施】emergency measure (or policy)
【应急灯】emergency light (or lamp)
【应考】take an exam
【应聘】❶accept a job offer ❷apply for an offered job
【应试教育】examination-oriented education; education for examinations

【应试能力】capability to pass examinations
【应验】come true; be fulfilled; be confirmed
【应邀】at the invitation of; on invitation
【应用】apply; use: 把理论～于实践 apply theory to practice
【应用文】practical writing
【应用型人才】application-oriented person (or people, talent)
【应征】❶enlist ❷be recruited

映 (yìng) reflect; mirror; shine

【映射】shine upon; cast light upon
【映像】image
【映照】shine upon; cast light upon: 晚霞～ glory of the dusk shines upon (sth.)

硬 (yìng) ❶force oneself to do; manage to do sth. with difficulty ❷ firm; strong ❸hard; stiff; tough

【硬笔书法】hard pen calligraphy
【硬币】coin
【硬撑】hold on in spite of difficulties
【硬道理】absolute (or infallible) principle (or truth)
【硬度】hardness; rigidity
【硬汉子】a man of iron
【硬环境】hard environment
【硬件】hardware
【硬朗】hale and hearty
【硬盘】hard disk
【硬卧】hard berth; hard sleeper (on a train)
【硬性规定】hard and fast rules; rigid rules
【硬着头皮】force oneself to do sth.
【硬指标】hard quota

yong

佣 (yōng) ❶hire ❷servant
另见 1286 页 yòng

【佣工】hired laborer; servant
【佣人】servant

拥（yōng）❶ embrace; hold in one's arms ❷ gather around; go around ❸ crowd ❹ support ❺ have; own; possess

【拥抱】embrace; hold in one's arms; hug

【拥戴】support

【拥堵】traffic jam

【拥护】support; uphold; endorse

【拥挤】❶ crowded ❷ push and squeeze

【拥有】have; own; possess

庸（yōng）❶ commonplace; mediocre ❷ inferior; second-rate

【庸人】a mediocre person

【庸人自扰】worry about imaginary troubles

【庸俗】vulgar; low

永（yǒng）perpetually; forever; always

【永别】part never to meet again; pass away; part forever; die

【永不】never

【永恒】eternal; perpetual

【永久】everlasting; permanent; perpetual; forever

【永世】forever; for life

【永世难忘】never forget in one's life

【永远】always; forever

咏（yǒng）❶ sing of; chant; intone ❷ express in poetic form

【咏唱】chant; sing

泳（yǒng）swim

【泳道】lane (in a swimming race)

勇（yǒng）brave; courageous

【勇敢】brave; courageous

【勇气】courage; bravery

【勇往直前】march forward bravely

【勇于】be brave (or bold) in; have the courage to

【勇于创新】dare to innovate; be bold to innovate

【勇于负责】be brave in shouldering responsibilities

【勇于改过】be bold enough to correct one's mistakes

涌（yǒng）spring (or well) up; rise; emerge

【涌动】surge

【涌现】spring (or well) up; come to light; emerge in large numbers

踊（yǒng）jump (or leap) up

【踊跃】❶ jump; leap ❷ vie with one another ❸ eagerly

用（yòng）❶ expense ❷ use; usefulness ❸ employ; apply ❹ need ❺ eat; drink; take ❻ by; with

【用处】use

【用法】use; usage

【用工】❶ employment; recruitment ❷ work allocation (or assignment)

【用功】❶ study hard ❷ diligent; studious

【用户】customer; user; subscriber; client

【用户名】user's name

【用尽心机】exhaust one's wits

【用尽一切办法】use every possible means

【用劲】exert strength; put forth one's strength; try hard

【用具】utensil; apparatus; appliance

【用品】article: 生活～ articles for daily use

【用钱】spend money

【用人制度】❶ system of personnel allocation ❷ system of employment (or recruitment)

【用途】use

【用武】❶ use force ❷ by force: 有～之地 there's ample scope for one's abilities

【用心】❶fix one's mind on ❷attentively; with concentrated attention: 学习～ concentrate on one's studies; study diligently

【用意】intention; purpose

佣 (yòng) commission
另见 1285 页 yōng

【佣金】commission; brokerage; middleman's fee

you

优 (yōu) excellent

【优待】give preferential treatment to

【优待券】complimentary ticket (or coupon); rebate coupon

【优等】first-class; first-rate; excellent; high-class

【优等生】top student

【优点】strong point; merit; advantage; virtue

【优厚】favourable; munificent; liberal

【优化】❶optimize ❷optimization: ～组合 optimization grouping or regrouping

【优化资源配置】optimize the allocation (or distribution) of resources

【优惠】favourable; preferential

【优惠券】complimentary ticket (or coupon); rebate coupon

【优惠政策】preferential policy

【优良】fine; good

【优良作风】fine style; good manners

【优美】graceful; fine; exquisite

【优缺点】merits and demerits; strong and weak points

【优生】give birth to healthy babies

【优胜劣汰】survival of the fittest; select the superior while eliminate the inferior

【优胜者】winner

【优势】superiority; preponderance

【优势互补】complement with each other's advantage

【优先发展】give priority to the development of

【优先权】preferential right

【优秀】excellent; splendid

【优选】select the best

【优雅】❶ graceful; exquisite; elegant; in good taste ❷beautiful and elegant

【优异】outstanding; excellent

【优越】superior; advantageous; favourable

【优质产品】high (or top, good) quality product

【优质服务】high (or top, good) quality ser vice

忧 (yōu) worry; care; anxiety; sorrow: 无～无虑 carefree

【忧愁】sad; heavyhearted; worried

【忧国忧民】be concerned about one's country and one's people

【忧患意识】sense (or awareness, consideration) of mishaps

【忧虑】worried; anxious; concerned

【忧伤】weighed down with sorrow; sad; sorrowful

【忧郁】heavyhearted; melancholy

幽 (yōu) ❶ imprison ❷ deep and remote; profound ❸ secret ❹ quiet; tranquil ❺of the nether world

【幽暗】dim; gloomy

【幽浮】UFO (unidentified flying object)

【幽静】quiet and peaceful

【幽灵】ghost; spirit

【幽美】secluded and beautiful: 景色～ secluded and beautiful sights

【幽默】❶humor ❷humorous

【幽默感】sense of humor

【幽香】delicate (or faint) fragrance: ～四

溢 give out a delicate fragrance; delicate fragrance permeate the air

【幽雅】quiet and tasteful

悠 (yōu) ❶ remote in time or space ❷leisurely

【悠长】long; long-drawn-out

【悠久】long; long-standing; age-old: 历史～ have a long history

【悠然】light-hearted; carefree and leisurely

【悠闲】carefree and leisurely

尤 (yóu) ❶outstanding ❷especially

【尤其】especially; particularly

由 (yóu) ❶ cause; reason ❷ obey ❸ be up to sb. ❹ because of; due to; owing to ❺from ❻by; through; by way of

【由表及里】from the outside to the inside

【由不得】❶ be beyond the control of ❷ cannot help (or avoid)

【由此可见】❶judging from this ❷thus it can be seen; this shows; that proves

【由简到繁】from the simple to the complex

【由近及远】from the near to the distant

【由浅入深】from the easy to the difficult; from the elementary to the profound

【由于】because of; due to; owing to; thanks to

【由衷】❶from the bottom of one's heart ❷sincere; heartfelt

邮 (yóu) mail; post

【邮戳】postmark

【邮递员】postman; mailman

【邮电局】post and telecommunications office

【邮购】mail-order

【邮购服务】mail-order service

【邮寄】mail; post

【邮件】post; mail; postal matter

【邮局】post office

【邮票】(postage) stamp

【邮筒】pillar box; postbox; mailbox

【邮箱】postbox; mailbox

【邮展】philatelic exhibition

【邮政编码】zip code; postcode

【邮政特快专递】express mail service (EMS)

犹 (yóu) ❶just; just as before ❷still

【犹然】still; just as before

【犹如】❶as; like ❷as if (or though)

【犹豫】hesitate; be irresolute

油 (yóu) ❶oil; fat ❷oil; paint ❸oily

【油泵】oil pump

【油饼】oil cake

【油灯】oil lamp

【油罐】oil tank

【油光】glossy; shiny; varnished

【油画】oil painting: 画～ paint in oils

【油库】oil depot

【油轮】oil tanker

【油漆】❶paint ❷cover with paint; paint

【油田】oil field

【油箱】oil box; fuel tank

【油纸】oilpaper

【油渍】grease stains on clothes, etc.

【油嘴滑舌】❶ glib-tongued ❷ have a glib tongue

铀 (yóu) uranium

游 (yóu) ❶reach: 上～ upper reaches; 下～ lower reaches ❷swim ❸travel; tour ❹wander ❺moving; wandering

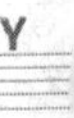

【游船】pleasure boat; yacht

【游荡】wander; roam; loaf about

【游动】move about; go here and there

【游逛】wander here and there; go sightseeing
【游击队】guerrilla forces
【游记】travel notes; travels
【游客】visitor; sightseer; tourist; excursionist
【游览】tour; go sightseeing; visit
【游览车】tourist coach
【游览区】tourist area (or resort)
【游乐园】amusement park
【游历】travel; tour; travel for pleasure
【游民】vagrant; vagabond
【游人】visitor; sightseer; tourist
【游山玩水】make a sightseeing tour; visit various scenic spots
【游说】go about selling an idea; go canvassing
【游艇】yacht; pleasure-boat
【游玩】❶play ❷stroll about; go sightseeing
【游戏】❶recreation; game ❷play
【游行】march; parade
【游泳池】swimming pool
【游泳帽】swimming cap; bathing cap
【游泳衣】swimsuit
【游园】visit a garden or parkyóu

友 (yǒu) ❶friend ❷friendly

【友爱】friendly love; friendly affection; fraternal love: 团结～ fraternal unity
【友好】friendly; amicable
【友情】friendship
【友人】friend: 国际～ foreign friend
【友善】friendly; good-willed
【友谊】friendship: 建立～ build up ties of friendship

Y

有 (yǒu) ❶have; possess; own ❷exist; be ❸some ❹certain

【有把握】be certain (or sure) of
【有备无患】preparedness prevents dangers
【有偿】with compensation; compensated; paid
【有出息】be promising
【有待】remain (to be done); await
【有底】feel assured; feel sure how things are
【有的放矢】shoot the arrow at the target
【有福同享,有祸同当】share joys and sorrows
【有根据】be well-founded; be well-grounded
【有关】❶have sth. to do with; be related to ❷related; concerned
【有关部门】departments concerned
【有害物质】hazardous (or harmful) substance
【有机可乘】there is an opportunity to take advantage of
【有计划】❶ according to a plan; in a planned way ❷be organized about
【有奖促销】premium promotion
【有口皆碑】be praised by all
【有口难辩】find it hard to justify oneself
【有口难言】find it hard to speak one's mind
【有口无心】have a sharp tongue but not an ill will
【有理】reasonable
【有力】powerful; forceful; strong; energetic; vigorous: 领导～ strong leadership
【有利】favourable; advantageous; beneficial
【有利条件】favourable condition
【有名】well-known; famous; celebrated
【有名无实】in name but not in reality
【有目共睹】clear enough for all to see

【有凭有据】 fully substantiated; well-documented

【有钱】 rich; wealthy

【有趣】 interesting; fascinating; amusing

【有生以来】 since one's birth

【有声读物】 audio book

【有声有色】 full of sound and color—vivid and dramatic

【有时】 now and then; at times; from time to time; sometimes

【有识之士】 sensible man; man of insight

【有史以来】 since the beginning of history; throughout history

【有始有终】 carry everything started through to the end

【有数】 ❶know how things are (or stand) ❷not many; only a few

【有条不紊】 in good order; systematically

【有为】 promising

【有喜】 be pregnant; be expecting; be in a family way

【有限责任公司】 limited liability company

【有效】 effective; valid

【有效期】 term (or period) of validity

【有些】 ❶some ❷somewhat; rather

【有心】 ❶on purpose ❷set one's mind to sth.; give one's soul to

【有幸】 be lucky to; have the good fortune to

【有言在先】 make clear beforehand; forewarn; warn beforehand

【有氧运动】 aerobic exercise; aerobics

【有益】 useful; profitable; beneficial

【有意】 ❶on purpose; purposely ❷have a mind to do sth.

【有意识】 knowingly; consciously; purposely; in a planned way

【有余】 ❶have enough and to spare; have a surplus ❷odd: 三十～ thirty odd

【有缘】 be predetermined by fate; be predestined; have a bond; have an affinity

【有则改之，无则加勉】 correct mistakes if you have made any and guard against them if you have not

【有责任】 be duty-bound

【有志者事竟成】 where there is a will there is a way

【有志之士】 person with lofty ideals

【有助于】 help; contribute to

【有资格】 qualified

又

(yòu) ❶again ❷and

右

(yòu) right

【右边】 right side

【右手】 right hand

幼

(yòu) ❶ the young; children ❷young

【幼儿】 infant; child

【幼儿教师】 kindergarten teacher

【幼儿教育】 preschool education

【幼儿园】 kindergarten

【幼苗】 seedling

【幼小】 young; immature

【幼稚】 ❶young ❷childish

柚

(yòu) pomelo

【柚子】 shaddock; pomelo; grapefruit

诱

(yòu) ❶guide; lead ❷lure; seduce

【诱导】 guide; lead

【诱饵】 bait

【诱拐】 abduct; kidnap

【诱惑】 ❶attract ❷lure

【诱奸】 entice into unlawful sexual intercourse; seduce

【诱骗】 trick into; lure; coax

【诱因】 cause

yu

迂 (yū) ❶winding; roundabout ❷bookish; pedantic

【迂腐】pedantic; bookish

【迂回】winding; roundabout

淤 (yū) ❶become silted up ❷silt

【淤泥】sludge; silt; ooze

【淤血】extravasated blood

于 (yú) ❶in; at; on ❷to; for ❸than

【于是】then; as a result; thereupon; hence; consequently

余 (yú) surplus; spare

【余波】repercussions

【余地】room; leeway: 留有～ leave some leeway

【余额】❶vacancies yet to be filled ❷remaining sum ❸balance

【余晖】evening glow

【余力】strength to spare; surplus energy or strength

【余年】one's remaining years

【余热】❶surplus energy ❷retiree's service to the society

【余生】❶remainder of one's life; evening years; one's remaining years ❷survival

【余数】remainder

【余味无穷】leave enduring impression

【余暇】spare time; leisure time

【余下】❶remain; leave over ❷remaining; leftover

【余音】lingering sound

【余震】aftershock

鱼 (yú) fish

【鱼刺】fishbone

【鱼饵】bait

【鱼缸】fish jar (or bowl)

【鱼钩】fishhook

【鱼贯而入】file in; enter in a single file

【鱼龙混杂】good and bad people mixed up

【鱼米之乡】rich land that produces much fish and rice

【鱼群】shoal of fish

【鱼肉】❶flesh of fish; fish ❷oppress

【鱼水情深】as close as fish and water

娱 (yú) ❶joy; pleasure ❷delight; entertain; amuse

【娱乐】entertainment; amusement

【娱乐活动】recreational activities

【娱乐设施】entertainment facilities

【娱乐业】entertainment industry

渔 (yú) ❶fishing ❷profit without the right

【渔船】fishing boat

【渔夫】fisherman

【渔竿】fishing rod

【渔港】fishing harbor; fishing port

【渔歌】fisherman's song

【渔家】fisherman's family

【渔利】❶reap unfair gains; profit when one does not have the right ❷unfair gains (or profit)

【渔民】fisherman; fisherfolk

【渔网】fishnet; fishing net

【渔业】fishery

逾 (yú) ❶go beyond ❷even more

【逾期】go beyond the time limit; be overdue

【逾越】go beyond

愉 (yú) cheerful; joyful; happy; pleased; merry

【愉快】happy; joyful; cheerful; pleased; merry: 过得～ have a good time

【愉悦】joyful; cheerful; delighted

榆 (yú)

【榆树】elm

愚 (yú) ❶fool; make a fool of ❷foolish; stupid; silly

【愚蠢】foolish; stupid; silly

【愚昧无知】benighted; ignorant; unenlightened

【愚弄】fool; make a fool of

【愚人节】All Fools' Day; April Fool's Day

与 (yǔ) ❶give; offer ❷with; against ❸and; together with

另见 1292 页 yù

【与其……不如……】would rather...than...

【与人为善】help others with good will

【与日俱增】grow with each passing day

【与时俱进】advance (or keep pace) with the times

【与世长辞】pass away; depart from the world

【与世无争】stand aloof from the world

【与众不同】outstanding; unusual

宇 (yǔ) ❶eaves ❷house ❸space; universe

【宇航服】spacesuit

【宇航员】astronaut; spaceman

【宇宙】space; universe

【宇宙飞船】spaceship

羽 (yǔ) feather

【羽毛丰满】full-fledged

【羽毛球】❶badminton ❷shuttlecock

【羽绒被】down (or eiderdown) quilt

【羽绒服】down (or eiderdown) coat (jacket)

雨 (yǔ) rain

【雨点】raindrop

【雨后春笋】mushrooming bamboo shoots after a spring rain

【雨季】rainy season

【雨林】rain forest

【雨露】❶rain and dew ❷favour; grace: ~之恩 favour and kindness

【雨披】waterproof cape; rain cape

【雨伞】umbrella

【雨水】rainfall; rainwater

【雨鞋】rubbers

【雨靴】rubber or plastic boots; rain boots; waterproof boots

【雨衣】raincoat; waterproof

语 (yǔ) ❶language; tongue ❷sign; signal: 手~ sign language ❸speak

【语调】intonation

【语法】grammar

【语句】sentence: ~不通 incoherent sentence

【语库】language data bank

【语气】❶tone; manner of speaking ❷mood

【语文】❶ language and literature ❷ language ❸Chinese

【语无伦次】speak without order

【语序】word order

【语言】language

【语言能力】language competence

【语言艺术】language art

【语义双关】have a double meaning

【语音】speech sounds; pronunciation; voice

【语重心长】speak sincerely and meaningfully

与 (yù) take part in

另见 1291 页 yǔ

【与会】attend a meeting

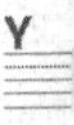

玉 (yù) ❶jade ❷pure

【玉雕】jade carving

【玉米】corn;maize

【玉器】jade article; jadeware; jade artworks

郁 (yù) ❶strongly fragrant ❷luxuriant;lush ❸gloomy;depressed

【郁结】smouldering; pent-up; unable to vent what's building up in one's heart

【郁闷】depressed;gloomy;oppressive

育 (yù) ❶give birth to; bear ❷raise; rear;breed;bring up ❸educate

【育才】cultivate talent;train people

【育龄】childbearing age

【育人】educate (or cultivate, foster) people:教书~ impart knowledge and educate people

【育种】breeding

狱 (yù) prison;jail:入~ be put in prison

【狱警】prison guard;jailer

浴 (yù) ❶bath ❷bathe

【浴场】outdoor bathing place

【浴巾】bathing towel

【浴帽】bathing (or shower) cap

【浴盆】bathtub

【浴室】bathroom; shower room; bathhouse

【浴液】liquid bathing soap

【浴衣】bathrobe

预 (yù) beforehand;in advance

【预报】forecast

【预备】❶get ready;prepare ❷reserve

【预测】calculate;forecast

【预订】book;subscribe;order

【预定】fix in advance; predetermine; schedule

【预防】prevent;guard against

【预付款】❶advance payment (or charge) ❷pay in advance

【预感】have a premonition;premonition

【预告】❶ advance notice ❷ announce in advance

【预计】estimate;calculate in advance

【预见】❶foresee ❷foresight

【预警】early warning;forewarning

【预考】preliminary examination; preliminary

【预料】expect;predict as expected

【预期】expect;anticipate

【预赛】trial match;preliminary contest

【预示】betoken;be a sign of

【预算】budget

【预习】prepare lessons before class; preview

【预先】beforehand;in advance

【预选】forward selection; preliminary selection (or election)

【预约】❶order;place an order for ❷make an appointment

【预兆】❶omen;sign ❷be a sign of

【预祝】congratulate beforehand

域 (yù) territory;region

【域名】domain name

欲 (yù) ❶desire; longing ❷wish; want ❸be about to;be on the point of

【欲罢不能】desire to stop but cannot

【欲盖弥彰】the more one tries to hide, the more one is exposed

【欲速则不达】more haste, less speed

【欲望】desire;longing

遇 (yù) ❶chance ❷meet; meet with; come across;run into

【遇到】meet; run into; come across; encounter

【遇害】be murdered

【遇见】meet;come across

【遇救】be saved; be rescued: ～脱险 be rescued out of danger
【遇难】be murdered; die in an accident
御 (yù) ❶drive (a carriage) ❷manage; control ❸of an emperor; imperial
【御寒】keep out the cold
【御医】imperial physician; court physician
寓 (yù) ❶ residence; house ❷ reside; live ❸imply
【寓教于乐】instruct by pleasing
【寓所】residence; dwelling place; abode
【寓言】fable; allegory; parable
【寓意】implied meaning; moral; message
愈 (yù) ❶recover ❷more and more
【愈合】heal
【愈加】even more; all the more; increasingly

yuan

冤 (yuān) ❶ wrong; injustice ❷ bitter feeling; hatred ❸not worthwhile
【冤案】case of injustice
【冤家】❶lover; sweetheart ❷enemy
【冤屈】wrong; injustice
【冤枉】❶ wrong; treat unjustly ❷ not worthwhile
渊 (yuān) ❶deep water ❷deep
【渊博】broad and profound
【渊源】origin; source
元 (yuán) ❶unit ❷first ❸chief ❹basic
【元旦】New Year's Day
【元老】senior statesman; founding member
【元气】vitality
【元帅】❶marshal ❷supreme commander
【元素】element
【元宵】❶the night of the 15th of the first lunar month ❷sweet dumplings made of glutinous rice flour
【元宵节】the Lantern Festival
【元凶】prime culprit
【元勋】founding father
【元月】January; first month of the lunar calendar
园 (yuán) ❶ plot for growing plants; garden ❷place for public recreation
【园地】❶field ❷garden; plot
【园丁】gardener
【园林】gardens; park
【园艺】gardening; horticulture
员 (yuán) member
【员工】staff; personnel
原 (yuán) ❶plain; open country ❷excuse; pardon ❸ primary; original ❹raw
【原班人马】the old cast
【原版】❶ original version ❷ original-versioned
【原本】❶original manuscript; master copy ❷originally
【原材料】raw material
【原产地】country of origin; place of origin
【原稿】manuscript; master copy
【原价】original price; former price
【原件】original manuscript
【原来】❶original ❷so ❸it turns out to be
【原理】principle
【原谅】forgive; pardon; excuse
【原料】raw material
【原貌】original appearance
【原始】❶original ❷primitive
【原始森林】primitive (or virgin) forest
【原委】whole story; all the details
【原文】the original; original text

【原先】former;original
【原形】❶original shape ❷true nature
【原型】model;prototype
【原样】original appearance or state; same old way
【原野】open country;champaign
【原意】real meaning; real intention; original intention
【原因】cause;reason
【原油】crude oil
【原原本本】❶the whole story ❷from beginning to end
【原则】principle
【原址】former address
【原著】original work;original
【原装】❶ factory-assembled; factory-packed ❷original packing
【原装进口】imported in the original package

圆 (yuán) ❶circle ❷round ❸tactful; sly ❹satisfactory ❺make plausible; justify

【圆场】mediate; help to effect a compromise
【圆规】compasses
【圆滑】❶smooth ❷sly
【圆满】satisfactory
【圆梦】oneiromancy;divination by dreams
【圆圈】circle;ring
【圆润】❶mellow and full ❷fluid;smooth
【圆通】flexible; accommodating: 她为人~。She's a very flexible person.
【圆心】center of a circle
【圆形】round
【圆周】circumference;boundary of a circle
【圆珠笔】ballpoint;ball pen
【圆柱】cylinder
【圆锥】circular cone;taper
【圆桌】round table

援 (yuán) ❶quote;cite ❷aid;help

【援兵】relief troops;reinforcements
【援救】save;rescue
【援手】❶lend a hand ❷helping hand
【援外】❶ foreign aid ❷ in aid of a foreign country
【援引】quote;cite
【援助】help;aid;support

缘 (yuán) ❶edge; brink ❷reason ❸along

【缘分】lot;luck
【缘起】❶ cause; origin ❷ account of the reasons for sponsoring sth.
【缘由】reason;cause

猿 (yuán) ape

【猿猴】apes and monkeys
【猿人】ape-man:北京~ Peking Man

源 (yuán) source

【源流】source and course
【源泉】source;fountainhead;wellspring
【源远流长】with a distant source and a long development (or stream)

远 (yuǎn) distant;far

【远程】long-distance;long-range
【远大】long-range;long and broad:前途~ have a bright future; 眼光~ have a broad vision
【远道而来】come a long way; come from afar
【远东】the Far East
【远航】take a long voyage
【远见】foresight;vision
【远郊】outer suburbs;outskirts;exurbs
【远近】far and near;distance
【远景规划】long-term planning

【远距离】long-distance; remote; long-range

【远离】far away from

【远虑】long view;foresight

【远水解不了近渴】water far away cannot quench present thirst; the aid is too slow in coming to be of any help

【远扬】spread far and wide:声名～ One's fame spreads far and wide. 臭名～ be notorious

【远洋】ocean;sea waters that are far away from the continent

【远走高飞】fly far and high

【远足】pleasure trip on foot;walking tour

怨 (yuàn) ❶resentment ❷blame

【怨不得】cannot blame (or complain about)

【怨恨】❶grudge ❷have a grudge against

【怨声载道】complaints are heard everywhere

【怨天怨地】blame both heaven and earth

【怨言】complaint:毫无～without a word of complaint

院 (yuàn) ❶yard; courtyard ❷college ❸hospital

【院士】academician

【院子】yard;courtyard

愿 (yuàn) ❶hope; wish; desire ❷be willing (or ready) ❸vow (made before Buddha or a god)

【愿望】desire; wish; aspiration: 主观～ wishful thinking;subjective desire

【愿意】be willing (or ready)

yue

约 (yuē) ❶appointment; agreement ❷limit; restrict ❸invite; ask ❹make an appointment ❺economical ❻about; around

【约定】agree on; arrange; appoint; make an appointment

【约会】❶make an appointment ❷appointment

【约见】make an appointment of interview

【约束】bind;keep within bounds;restrain

【约束力】binding force

月 (yuè) ❶moon ❷month ❸monthly

【月报】❶monthly report ❷monthly

【月饼】moon cake

【月度】monthly: ～计划 a monthly plan

【月份】month

【月光】moonlight;moonbeam

【月光族】moonlight clan;moonlite

【月季】Chinese rose

【月经】menses; menstruation; period: ～周期 menstrual cycle

【月刊】monthly;monthly magazine

【月历】monthly calendar

【月嫂】confinement-care woman; maternity matron

【月色】moonlight; moonshine; moonbeam: 荷塘～ the moon over a lotus pond

【月食】lunar eclipse

【月台】railway platform;platform

【月息】monthly interest

【月薪】monthly salary (or pay)

【月夜】moonlit night

【月租费】monthly rent (or rental fee)

【月子】month of confinement after giving birth to a child

乐 (yuè) music
另见 1082 页 lè

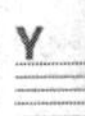

【乐队】band;orchestra

【乐谱】music score;music

【乐器】musical instrument

【乐坛】music circles

【乐团】philharmonic society or orchestra

阅 (yuè) ❶read; go over ❷review; inspect ❸experience; pass through

【阅兵】review troops

【阅兵式】military review

【阅读】read

【阅读理解】reading comprehension

【阅卷】grade examination papers; read and mark examination papers

【阅览室】reading-room

【阅历】experience

悦 (yuè) ❶ please; delight ❷ happy; pleased; delighted

【悦耳】pleasing to the ear; sweet-sounding

【悦服】admire from the bottom of one's heart; heartily admire

【悦目】pleasing to the eye; good-looking

跃 (yuè) leap; jump

【跃进】leap forward; make a leap

【跃跃欲试】be eager to have a try

越 (yuè) ❶go (or jump, leap) over ❷ go beyond; surpass ❸more and more

【越发】all the more; even more

【越轨】transgress; go beyond the norms; violate the rule; go beyond the bound

【越过】cross; get over; go beyond

【越界】overstep the boundary; cross the border

【越境】cross the boundary illegally; sneak in or out of a county

【越来越……】more and more

【越南】Vietnam

Y 【越南人】Vietnamese

【越南语】Vietnamese

【越权】exceed one's power; overstep one's authority

【越位】offside

【越洋电话】cross-ocean (or transocean) telephone call

【越野】cross-country

【越野汽车】cross-country (or off-road) vehicle (or car)

【越野赛】cross-country (road-off) race

【越狱】❶break jail ❷jailbreak

【越俎代庖】take sb. else's job into one's own hands

晕 (yūn) ❶dizzy; giddy ❷faint 另见 1297 页 yùn

【晕场】stage fright; dizziness at performance (or examination)

【晕倒】faint; fall in a faint

【晕头转向】be confused

云 (yún) ❶cloud ❷say

【云层】cloud layer

【云朵】fluffy cloud; mass of cloud; cloud

【云海】sea of clouds

【云集】come together from all directions; gather

【云雀】skylark

【云雾】cloud and mist

【云霞】rosy clouds

匀 (yún) ❶ even up; divide ❷ spare ❸ even; smooth

【匀称】proportional; well-balanced; well-proportioned; symmetrical: 身材～ of proportional build

【匀净】even; uniform

允 (yǔn) ❶allow; permit ❷fair; just

【允诺】promise; agree

【允许】allow; permit

陨 (yǔn) fall from the sky of outer space

【陨石】aerolite; stony meteorite

殒 (yǔn) perish; die

【殒命】meet one's death; perish

孕 (yùn) ❶pregnant ❷pregnancy

【孕妇】pregnant woman

【孕期】pregnancy; gestation

【孕育】be pregnant with; breed

运 (yùn) ❶motion; movement ❷luck; fortune ❸use ❹transport; carry

【运动】❶ motion; movement ❷ drive ❸ sports; athletics; exercise

【运动场】sports venue; athletic ground; playground; stadium

【运动会】sports meet; games

【运动衫】sports shirt

【运动项目】sports item

【运动鞋】sports (or exercise; athletic) shoes

【运动员】sportsman; player

【运费】transportation expenses; freight; carriage

【运河】canal

【运气】luck; fortune

【运输】❶transport ❷transportation

【运算】❶operate ❷operation

【运行】❶move ❷operate

【运营成本】operating cost

【运用】apply; put to use; use; employ

【运载】carry

【运转】❶turn ❷work; operate

【运作】❶operate; function ❷operation

晕 (yùn) dizzy; giddy
另见 1296 页 yūn

【晕场】have stage fright; feel dizzy due to excessive nervousness or other reasons

【晕车】carsickness

【晕船】seasickness

【晕机】airsickness

韵 (yùn) ❶ rhyme ❷ charm ❸ sweet sound ❹pleasant sound

【韵脚】rhyme

【韵律】rhyming rule; rhyme scheme

【韵律操】rhythmic gymnastics

【韵文】verse

蕴 (yùn) accumulate; contain

【蕴藏】hold in store; store; contain

【蕴涵】implication

熨 (yùn) iron

【熨斗】iron

Z z

za

扎 (zā) tie; bind
另见 1302 页 zhā

【扎彩】hang up festoons

杂 (zá) mixed

【杂草】rank grass; weeds

【杂费】❶ incidental expenses; incidentals ❷sundry fees

【杂活儿】odd jobs

【杂货】groceries; sundry goods

【杂货店】grocery

【杂记】❶literature of random thoughts ❷ notes; random notes

【杂技】acrobatics

【杂交】hybridize; cross

【杂乱无章】disorderly; in disorder; in a mess

【杂念】distracting thoughts

【杂食】omnivorous; eating different kinds of both meat and plants

【杂七杂八】mixed; assorted

【杂文】essay

【杂务】odd jobs; sundry duties; chore

【杂志】magazine

【杂质】impurity

砸 (zá) ❶strike ❷break ❸fail

【砸饭碗】get the sack; be fired; lose one's work

【砸碎】break into pieces

zai

灾 (zāi) ❶disaster; calamity ❷misfortune

【灾害】disaster; calamity

【灾后重建】post-disaster rehabilitation

【灾难】disaster; calamity; suffering

【灾情】the condition of a disaster

【灾区】disaster area

栽 (zāi) ❶ grow; cultivate; plant ❷ tumble; fall ❸force sth. on sb.

【栽跟头】❶ fall; tumble ❷ fail; suffer a setback

【栽培】❶grow ❷educate; train; foster ❸ help advance one's career; promote

【栽种】grow; plant

载 (zǎi) ❶record ❷year
另见 1299 页 zài

【载入史册】record in the history

宰 (zǎi) ❶kill; butcher ❷govern; rule

【宰客】overcharge the customer

【宰杀】kill; butcher

【宰相】prime minister; chancellor

崽 (zǎi) ❶son ❷young animal; whelp

再 (zài) ❶return; come back again ❷ still ❸once more; again

【再版】second edition;reprint

【再度】once more;a second time

【再会】goodbye;see you again

【再婚】❶remarriage ❷remarry ❸remarried

【再见】goodbye;see you again

【再接再厉】make continuous efforts

【再就业】❶ re-employment ❷ re-employed;be re-employed

【再三】again and again;over and over again;time and again

【再生资源】renewable resources;recycled (or renewed) resources

【再现】represent;reappear;reproduce

【再循环】recycling

在 (zài) ❶exist;be;there be ❷depend on;be up to;rest with ❸in;at;on

【在案】be recorded in archives;be on record

【在编人员】employed worker;worker on the payroll;personnel

【在读】studying at school

【在岗】be on job (or one's post,duty)

【在岗工人】on-the-job worker

【在行】be expert (or good) at;know well;be a professional

【在乎】❶lie in;rest with ❷mind;take to heart;care about

【在即】very soon;in the near future:毕业～ will soon be graduating

【在建项目】project under construction

【在理】right;reasonable;sensible

【在内】included

【在所不辞】will not refuse (or hesitate)

【在所难免】can hardly be avoided;be unavoidable

【在望】❶be visible;be in sight (or view) ❷be expected

【在位】❶ be on the throne;reign;be a monarch ❷ hold an official post;be a leader

【在线】❶on-line ❷be on line

【在线服务】❶ on-line service ❷ service on line

【在意】mind;care about;take to heart

【在于】❶lie in;rest with ❷depend on;be determined by ❸lie in;consist in

【在职】on the job;at one's post;in office

【在职培训】on-job (or in-service) training

【在职研究生】on-job (or in-service) graduate student

【在座】❶be present ❷present

载 (zài) ❶carry;be loaded with ❷at the same time ❸and;as well as

另见 1298 页 zǎi

【载歌载舞】sing and dance at the same time

【载人航天飞船】manned spaceship

【载誉归来】return home in glory

【载运】convey by vehicles, ship, etc.

【载重】load;carrying capacity

zan

咱 (zán) ❶we;us ❷I

【咱们】we;us

攒 (zǎn) save

【攒钱】save money

暂 (zàn) for the time being;for the moment

【暂定】arranged (or fixed) for the time being

【暂缓】put off

【暂时】❶for the moment;for the time being ❷temporary

【暂停】suspend;time-out:要求～ ask for time-out

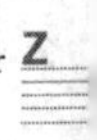

【暂停键】pause button (or key)
【暂行】provisional; temporary; interim: ~规定 temporary (or interim) provisions
【暂住人口】temporary resident
赞 (zàn) ❶support ❷praise
【赞不绝口】not stop praising; be full of praise
【赞成】approve of; agree with
【赞美】praise
【赞赏】appreciate
【赞叹】highly praise; gasp in admiration
【赞同】agree with; approve of; endorse; consent
【赞许】speak favourably of; praise; commend
【赞扬】speak highly of; praise
【赞助】support; assistance

zang

赃 (zāng) ❶stolen goods; booty; spoils ❷bribes
【赃款】illicit money; embezzled money; accepted bribes; stolen money
【赃物】stolen goods; booty; spoils; bribes
脏 (zāng) dirty; soiled
【脏话】dirty words; obscenities
【脏乱】dirty and messy
葬 (zàng) bury; lay in the grave
【葬礼】funeral
【葬送】ruin; bring to an end; put an end to
藏 (zàng) ❶ storing place; depository ❷Buddhist or Taoist scriptures
另见 913 页 cáng
【藏传佛教】Tibetan Buddhism
【藏药】Tibetan medicine

zao

遭 (zāo) meet with
【遭到】meet with; suffer; encounter
【遭殃】suffer; suffer disaster
【遭遇】❶ meet with; run up against; encounter ❷bitter experience; fate
【遭罪】have a difficult time
糟 (zāo) ❶ terrible ❷ rotten ❸ poor ❹ distillers ❺ in the terrible state; in a mess
【糟糕】terrible; too bad
【糟粕】thing of no value; waste matter; dregs
【糟蹋】❶ waste; ruin ❷ insult; ravage ❸ rape; violate
凿 (záo) ❶chisel ❷dig; chisel
【凿井】dig a well
早 (zǎo) ❶ morning ❷ early ❸ long ago; for a long time
【早安】good morning
【早班】morning shift
【早餐】breakfast
【早操】morning exercises
【早晨】morning; early morning
【早春】early spring
【早婚】early marriage
【早恋】early love (or love affair)
【早年】one's early years; many years ago; in the past
【早期】early stage; early period; early days
【早衰】early ageing
【早退】leave early
【早晚】❶ sooner or later ❷ some day ❸ morning and evening
枣 (zǎo) jujube; (Chinese) date

【枣红】purplish red;claret
【枣树】jujube tree

澡 (zǎo) bath: 洗~ take a bath;bathe

【澡盆】bathtub

皂 (zào) ❶soap: 肥~ soap ❷香~ toilet soap ❸black

灶 (zào) ❶ kitchen range; cooking stove

【灶神】kitchen god
【灶台】the top of a kitchen range

造 (zào) ❶attainments ❷make;create ❸build ❹ invent; cook up ❺ train; educate ❻go to

【造成】cause;bring about;give rise to;result in;make
【造访】pay a visit to;call on (or at);visit
【造福】bring benefit to;benefit
【造化】❶the Creator ❷luck;fortune
【造就】❶ bring up; train; educate ❷ achievements
【造句】❶sentence-making ❷make a sentence
【造林】❶afforest ❷afforestation
【造血机能】blood-making function
【造谣】start a rumour
【造诣】attainment or accomplishment
【造纸】paper making
【造作】affected;artificial

噪 (zào) ❶ (of birds, insects, etc.) chirp ❷confusion of voices

【噪声治理】noise abatement
【噪声污染】noise pollution

燥 (zào)dry

【燥热】hot and dry

躁 (zào)rash;impetuous;restless

【躁动】move restlessly

ze

责 (zé) ❶ responsibility; duty ❷ require;demand ❸blame

【责备】blame;reproach
【责罚】punish;fine
【责怪】blame
【责骂】scold
【责难】blame
【责任】responsibility;duty
【责任感】sense of responsibility
【责无旁贷】be duty-bound

择 (zé) choose;pick;select

【择期】select a day or time
【择校】select a school
【择业观念】attitude toward employment (or job-taking)
【择优录取】enroll (or accept) the outstanding ones;admit (or enroll) the superior ones
【择优上岗】choose the superior ones for the post

zei

贼 (zéi) ❶thief ❷traitor ❸evil;wicked ❹sly;cunning

【贼船】pirate ship: 上~ board the pirate ship
【贼心】evil design;evil intention

zen

怎 (zěn) why;how

【怎么样】❶how ❷quite
【怎样】❶how ❷how things are (or were)

zeng

增 (zēng) increase;gain;add

【增白剂】whitener
【增补】make additions to; supplement
【增产】increase production
【增高】❶ get higher; rise; increase ❷ improve; elevate; heighten; increase
【增光】do credit to; win honours for
【增加】increase; grow in number (or quantity); add
【增进】promote; improve
【增强】strengthen; build up; heighten
【增收】increase income (or revenue)
【增援】reinforce
【增长】increase; grow; rise

憎 (zēng) hate; detest; abhor

【憎恨】hate

赠 (zèng) give as a present

【赠别】present a friend with gifts, poems, etc. at parting
【赠品】gift; giveaway
【赠券】complimentary ticket; gift coupon
【赠言】parting words of advice (or encouragement); words of advice
【赠阅】given free by publisher

zha

扎 (zhā) ❶prick ❷plunge (or get) into 另见 1298 页 zā

【扎根】take root
【扎实】❶ strong ❷ solid: 工作～ do a solid job
【扎手】❶ prick the hand ❷ troublesome; thorny; difficult
【扎眼】❶dazzle ❷unpleasantly noticeable

轧 (zhá) roll

【轧钢】❶steel rolling ❷rolled steel
【轧伤】run over and injure

闸 (zhá) ❶ floodgate; water gate ❷ brake: 手～ hand brake

【闸门】water gate

炸 (zhá) fry in deep oil; deep-fry; fry

【炸鸡】fried chicken
【炸薯条】French fries

眨 (zhǎ) wink; blink

【眨眼】❶ wink; blink ❷ in a wink; very short time

乍 (zhà) for the first time

【乍一听】at first hearing; on hearing

诈 (zhà) ❶cheat ❷pretend

【诈骗】cheat; swindle

炸 (zhà) ❶ burst; explode ❷ blow up; bomb

【炸弹】bomb
【炸药】explosive (charges); dynamite

榨 (zhà) ❶press; extract ❷a press for extracting oil, juice, etc.

【榨菜】hot pickled mustard tuber; a kind of preserved vegetable
【榨汁机】juice extractor (or press, squeezer); juicer

zhai

摘 (zhāi) ❶pluck; pick ❷select; make extracts from

【摘编】extract and compile
【摘录】❶make extracts ❷extracts
【摘要】❶summary ❷make a summary
【摘引】quote

宅 (zhái) residence; house

【宅急送】❶ express delivery company ❷ home delivery ❸ZJS Express

【宅男】indoorsman;Otaku
【宅女】indoorswoman;Otaku girl
【宅院】a house with a courtyard;house

窄 (zhǎi) ❶ narrow-minded; petty ❷ narrow ❸badly off
【窄道】narrow path

债 (zhài) debt:欠～ be in debt;get into debt
【债款】loan
【债权】creditor's rights
【债券】bond
【债务】debt
【债务人】debtor

zhan

沾 (zhān) ❶ wet; soak ❷ be stained with ❸touch ❹profit
【沾边】❶have something to do ❷touch on only lightly;be related
【沾光】get a share of advantage; benefit from association with sb. or sth.
【沾染】be tainted with
【沾沾自喜】be pleased with oneself

粘 (zhān)glue;stick;paste
【粘贴】paste;stick
【粘住】stick;adhere

瞻 (zhān) look forward (or up)
【瞻前顾后】look ahead and behind in great caution; be over-cautious and indecisive
【瞻仰】look at with great respect; pay one's respects to

斩 (zhǎn) slay;cut
【斩草除根】cut the weeds and get rid of the roots
【斩钉截铁】be resolute and decisive; be firm

展 (zhǎn) ❶ exhibition; show; display ❷ open up; spread out ❸ give full play to; bring into play ❹ extend; prolong ❺show;display;exhibit
【展翅】spread the wings
【展出】be on show;put on display;exhibit
【展馆】exhibition hall (or centre)
【展开】❶open up; spread out; unfold ❷ carry out on a large scale
【展览】❶exhibition; show:花卉～flower show ❷put on display;exhibit
【展览馆】exhibition centre
【展品】exhibit;item on display
【展示】show;lay bare
【展厅】exhibition hall (or room)
【展望】look forward;look into the future
【展现】unfold before one's eyes;emerge;show;appear
【展销】exhibit and sell
【展销会】trade (or commodity) fair

崭 (zhǎn) ❶ towering (over) ❷ fine;swell
【崭露头角】begin to show one's brilliant talents;become outstanding
【崭新】completely new;brand-new

辗 (zhǎn)
【辗转】pass through many hands or places
【辗转反侧】toss about (or in bed)

占 (zhàn) ❶ take up ❷ occupy ❸ hold;take
【占据】occupy;hold
【占领】❶occupy; seize ❷occupation; seizure
【占便宜】take advantage of; profit at others' expense
【占线】❶busy line ❷the line is busy

【占用】take hold of for one's own use; occupy and use
【占有】❶ own; possess; have ❷ occupy; hold

栈 (zhàn) ❶ warehouse ❷ inn; hostel ❸ shed; pen
【栈道】a plank roadway built along perpendicular rock-faces by means of wooden brackets fixed into the cliff

战 (zhàn) ❶ war; fight; battle ❷ fight ❸ shiver; tremble
【战败】defeat; be defeated (or beaten); lose a war (or battle); beat
【战场】battlefield; battleground: 上~go to the front
【战抖】shiver; tremble: 全身~ tremble all over
【战斗】fight; battle
【战犯】war criminal
【战歌】battle (or fighting) song
【战功】battle achievement
【战果】❶ results of battle ❷ victory
【战况】battle situation
【战乱】chaos caused by war; war turmoil
【战略目标】strategic goal
【战胜】overcome; defeat; win
【战时】wartime
【战士】soldier; fighter; man
【战术】tactics
【战役】campaign; battle
【战友】comrade-in-arms; battle companion
【战战兢兢】❶ be careful ❷ trembling all over with fear
【战争】war; warfare

站 (zhàn) ❶ station; stop; center ❷ stand; be on one's feet; take a stand
【站得高,看得远】stand high and see far
【站队】stand in line; fall in; line up
【站岗】stand guard
【站立】stand; rise; be on one's feet
【站票】standing ticket
【站台】platform
【站稳】stand firm; take a firm stand
【站住】❶ stop; halt ❷ stand one's ground

绽 (zhàn) split; burst
【绽放】(of flowers) burst forth; burst into bloom

湛 (zhàn) ❶ profound; deep ❷ crystal clear
【湛蓝】(of the sky, the sea, a lake, etc.) azure blue; azure

颤 (zhàn) quiver; tremble
另见 918 页 chàn

蘸 (zhàn) dip in

zhang

张 (zhāng) ❶ piece; sheet ❷ stretch; spread; open ❸ look
【张榜】put up a notice; post a notice; put up a proclamation
【张皇】alarmed; scared
【张皇失措】lose one's head in alarm; get into a panic
【张口结舌】be tongue-tied; stare with the mouth open; be at a loss for words
【张罗】❶ take care of; make arrangements ❷ look after; attend to ❸ manage to raise money
【张望】peep; look around
【张扬】make public; make known; publicize
【张嘴】❶ open one's mouth ❷ ask for a loan or a favour

章 (zhāng) ❶ seal: 私~ personal seal; 公~ official seal ❷ badge; medal: 臂

~arm band；领~collar badge ❸chapter ❹order ❺rule

【章程】rules；regulations；constitution

【章节】chapters and sections

长 (zhǎng) ❶ head；chief ❷ increase；grow ❸develop ❹older；elder；senior 另见 918 页 cháng

【长辈】elder；senior

【长大】grow up；be brought up

【长见识】gain experiences；increase one's knowledge

【长进】❶make progress ❷progress

【长相】looks；appearance；features

【长者】elder；senior

【长子】eldest son

涨 (zhǎng) rise；go up 另见 1305 页 zhàng

【涨潮】❶rising (or flood) tide ❷the tide rises

【涨价】rise in price

【涨落】(of water，prices，etc.) rise and fall；fluctuate

掌 (zhǎng) ❶palm ❷sole ❸slap；strike with open hand ❹be in charge of

【掌厨】chef；be the head cooker

【掌舵】be at the helm；steer a ship

【掌故】anecdotes

【掌权】be in power；wield power

【掌声】applause；clapping

【掌纹】friction ridge；palm print

【掌握】control；master；grasp；know well

丈 (zhàng) ❶a unit of length (＝3.13 metres) ❷senior；elder

【丈夫】husband

【丈量】measure

【丈母娘】mother-in-law

【丈人】father-in-law

仗 (zhàng) ❶ battle；war；fight ❷ rely on；rest on；depend on

【仗势欺人】bully others on the strength of one's (or sb. else's) power

【仗义】❶ uphold justice ❷ be loyal to (one's friends)

【仗义执言】speak out from a sense of justice

帐 (zhàng) ❶ curtain；canopy ❷ account ❸account book ❹debt；credit

【帐篷】tent：搭~ pitch a tent

账 (zhàng) ❶account ❷account book ❸debt

【账簿】account book

【账单】bill；check

【账户】account

【账目】❶ accounts：清理~ square accounts ❷items of an account

胀 (zhàng) expand；swell

涨 (zhàng) swell 另见 1305 页 zhǎng

障 (zhàng) ❶ barrier ❷ hinder；obstruct

【障碍】barrier：制造~ set up barriers

zhao

招 (zhāo) ❶ trick；move ❷ beckon ❸ enroll；enlist ❹ bring upon oneself；invite ❺ own up；confess ❻ provoke；tease

【招标】❶invite bids (or tenders，to bid) ❷bid invitation；invitation for bid

【招兵买马】recruit followers

【招待】entertain；receive；serve；treat sb. to

【招待会】reception：记者~ press conference；举行~ give a reception

【招待员】receiver；receptionist

【招工】recruit workers

【招工启事】Workers Wanted

【招呼】❶call ❷greet ❸tell ❹take care of; look after

【招考】give (or hold) public entrance examination

【招徕顾客】solicit customers

【招揽生意】drum up trade; tout for business; solicit customers

【招领】announce the finding of lost property:拾物~处 Lost and Found Office

【招牌】signboard; shop sign

【招聘】advertise for workers; invite applications for a job

【招聘广告】workers wanted ads; recruiting advertisement

【招聘会】job fair

【招认】confess one's crime (s); plead guilty

【招商】invite (or solicit, attract) business (or investment, business people)

【招商引资】attract (or solicit, invite) investment

【招生】recruit students; enroll new students

【招生办公室】admission office

【招生考试】admission examination

【招收】recruit

【招手】beckon; wave

【招数】trick; device; move

【招贴画】poster

【招贤】summon people of worth to serve their country

【招摇撞骗】deceive

【招引】attract

【招致】bring about; lead to; result in

昭 (zhāo) clear

【昭然若揭】abundantly clear

【昭雪】exonerate

【昭著】clear; evident

着 (zhāo) ❶a move in chess ❷trick; device; move ❸put in; add ❹all right; OK

另见 1366 页 zháo; 1328 页 zhuó

【着数】❶a move in chess ❷a movement in wushu ❸trick; device

朝 (zhāo) early morning

另见 921 页 cháo

【朝晖】morning sunlight

【朝露】morning dew—ephemeral; transitory

【朝气蓬勃】full of youthful spirit (vitality)

【朝思暮想】long day and night

【朝夕】❶day and night ❷moment: 只争~ seize the day, seize the hour; seize every minute

【朝霞】rosy clouds of dawn; rosy dawn

【朝阳产业】sunrise industry

着 (zháo) ❶touch ❷be affected by ❸light; burn

另见 1306 页 zhāo; 1328 页 zhuó

【着火】catch fire; be on fire

【着急】worry; feel anxious

【着凉】catch cold

【着迷】be charmed; be fascinated

【着魔】be bewitched; be possessed; be entranced

【着色】coloration

爪 (zhǎo) claw

【爪牙】talons and fangs—lackeys; underlings

找 (zhǎo) ❶look for; seek; try to find ❷ask for; invite ❸give change ❹call on; want to see

【找补】make up a deficiency

【找麻烦】look for (or court, invite, ask for) trouble; cause sb. trouble

【找钱】give changes

【找事】❶look for a job ❷find fault with sb. ❸ cause trouble; court (or look for) trouble

【找寻】look for; search; seek

沼 (zhǎo) natural pond

【沼气】marsh gas

【沼泽】marsh; swamp

召 (zhào) call together

【召唤】call; summon

【召集】call together; convene

【召开】hold; convene

兆 (zhào) ❶sign ❷billion; million

【兆头】sign; omen; portent

照 (zhào) ❶ picture; photo ❷ shine; light up ❸take a picture ❹mirror ❺ look after; take care of ❻understand; be aware ❼according to; by

【照办】act accordingly; act upon; follow

【照常】as usual

【照发】❶ approved for distribution ❷ be paid as usual

【照顾】❶ give consideration to; have regard for; take ... into account ❷ look after; care for ❸take special care of ❹in consideration of

【照旧】as before (or usual); as of old

【照看】look after; keep an eye on; watch over

【照例】as a rule; as usual

【照料】take care of; tend; look after: ~病人 look after patients

【照明】lighting; illumination

【照排】imaging

【照片】picture; photo

【照射】shine; illuminate; light up

【照相】❶ take a picture ❷ have a picture taken

【照样】❶as before; in the same way; all the same ❷after a model

【照应】❶look after; take care of ❷coordinate: 互相~ be well coordinated

【照章办事】act according to rules; act by rules

罩 (zhào) ❶cover; wrap ❷shade; casing; hood

【罩袍】overall; dust-robe

【罩衣】dustcoat

肇 (zhào) cause

【肇事】cause trouble

zhe

折 (zhē) turn (or roll) over
另见 1173 页 shé; 本页 zhé

【折腾】❶ turn (or roll) over; turn from side to side ❷do over and over again ❸ cause suffering

遮 (zhē) hide; cover; block

【遮蔽】hide from view; cover; block

【遮挡】shelter from; keep out

【遮盖】cover; hide

【遮拦】block; obstruct; impede

【遮羞】hide one's shame; cover up one's embarrassment; conceal one's disgrace

【遮阳】sunshade

折 (zhé) ❶folder; bankbook ❷discount ❸fold ❹break; snap ❺ bend ❻ turn ❼ lose ❽ convert to; amount to ❾ discount; rebate ❿ turning stroke in Chinese Characters

另见 1173 页 shé; 本页 zhē

【折叠】fold

【折服】❶be convinced; be filled with admiration：令人～ compel (or command) admiration ❷subdue；bring into submission；convince

【折光】❶refract light ❷refracted light

【折回】turn back (halfway)

【折价】convert into money

【折旧费】depreciation charge

【折扣】discount；rebate：打～出售 sell at a discount

【折磨】cause suffering；torture；cause to suffer

【折算】convert

【折中】compromise

哲 (zhé) ❶ wise；sagacious ❷ wise man；sage

【哲理】philosophy：人生～ philosophy of life

【哲人】sage；philosopher

【哲学】philosophy

【哲学家】philosopher

这 (zhè) ❶this ❷now

【这般】like this：如此～ thus and thus；thus and so

【这次】❶this time ❷present

【这儿】❶here ❷now；then

【这个】❶this ❷this one

【这会儿】at the moment；now

【这么】this way；like this

【这些】these

【这样】so；like this；this way

zhen

贞 (zhēn) ❶loyal；faithful ❷chastity or virginity

【贞操】❶ chastity or virginity ❷ loyalty；moral integrity

【贞洁】chaste and undefiled

针 (zhēn) ❶needle；pin ❷stitch ❸injection：打～give (or have) an injection

【针对】❶be directed against；be aimed at；aim at ❷in view of

【针锋相对】give tit for tat

【针灸】acupuncture and moxibustion

【针线】needlework

【针眼】❶ eye of a needle；needle's eye ❷pinprick

【针织】knitting

侦 (zhēn) detect；investigate；go into

【侦查】investigate；go into

【侦破】investigate and uncover

【侦探】❶detect ❷detective

【侦探小说】detective novel

珍 (zhēn) ❶treasure ❷value ❸valuable

【珍爱】be very fond of；treasure；love dearly

【珍宝】treasure；jewellery

【珍本】rare edition；rare book

【珍藏】collect (art treasures，rare books，etc.)

【珍品】treasure

【珍视】value；prize；cherish；treasure

【珍惜】treasure；value；cherish

【珍稀】rare and precious

【珍重】❶take good care of yourself ❷value highly；treasure

【珍珠】pearl

真 (zhēn) ❶true；real ❷indeed；really；truly；in fact

【真才实学】real talent and learning；real ability and learning；genuine talent

【真诚】sincere；true

【真谛】true essence；true meaning

【真假难辨】not to know the real from the false

【真金不怕火炼】true gold fears no fire；a

person of integrity can stand severe tests

【真空】vacuum

【真理】truth：坚持~ uphold the truth；寻求~ seek truth

【真面目】true colors (or features)：认清~ see sb. in his true colors

【真凭实据】hard evidence

【真切】❶clear；distinct；graphic ❷sincere；genuine

【真情】❶real or true situation；facts；actual state of affairs；truth ❷true feelings；real sentiments

【真人真事】people and event from life

【真善美】the true，the good and the beautiful

【真实】true；real；actual；authentic

【真率】sincere；candid；unaffected；straightforward

【真相大白】the whole truth has come out (or to light)

【真心】❶sincere；wholehearted；heartfelt ❷sincerely ❸sincerity

【真正】true；real

【真知灼见】real knowledge and deep insight

【真挚】cordial；sincere

砧

(zhēn) anvil

【砧子】anvil

诊

(zhěn) examine

【诊断】❶diagnose ❷diagnosis

【诊脉】feel the pulse

【诊所】clinic

【诊治】diagnose and treat

枕

(zhěn) ❶pillow ❷rest the head on

【枕巾】towel used to cover a pillow

【枕木】sleeper；tie

阵

(zhèn) ❶front；position ❷a period of time

【阵地】position

【阵势】situation；position

【阵痛】❶labor pains；throes (of childbirth) ❷growing pains

【阵线】front；ranks；alignment：统一~ united front

【阵营】camp；group of people who pursue a common interest

【阵雨】shower

振

(zhèn) brace (or pluck) up

【振臂】raise one's arm

【振动】vibration

【振奋】inspire (or excite) sb.；rise with courage and spirit

【振奋精神】inspirit；activate the spirit

【振奋人心】❶inspire people ❷inspiring；exciting

【振兴经济】invigorate (or revitalize) the economy

【振振有词】speak plausibly and volubly

【振作】brace (or pluck) up；bestir oneself

赈

(zhèn) relieve；aid

【赈灾】aid (or relieve) people stricken by disasters

【赈灾义演】benefit performance for disaster-hit victims

震

(zhèn) ❶earthquake ❷shake；shock；vibrate ❸shocked ❹greatly excited；deeply astonished

【震颤】tremble；quiver

【震动】shake；shock；vibrate；quake

【震耳欲聋】deafening

【震撼】shock；shake；vibrate

【震惊】shock；amaze；astonish：~世界

shock the world
【震源】focus of an earthquake
【震中】epicentre

镇 (zhèn) ❶ town ❷ garrison post ❸ keep down; press ❹ garrison; guard ❺calm; ease ❻cool with ice (or water)
【镇定自若】be perfectly calm and collected
【镇静】calm; cool; composed; unruffled
【镇守】garrison; guard
【镇痛】ease pain

zheng

争 (zhēng) ❶ argue; dispute ❷ strive (or fight, struggle) for
【争辩】argue; debate; contend: 真理不怕~。Truth does not fear contention.
【争吵】quarrel; squabble
【争端】dispute: 解决~settle a dispute
【争夺】fight for; vie with sb. for sth.
【争光】win honour for
【争论】❶argument; controversy; dispute; debate ❷argue
【争气】try to make a good name; win credit for
【争取】strive (or fight) for; try to win over
【争胜】compete for first place
【争先恐后】try to be the first and fear falling behind
【争议】dispute
【争战】fight; war: 两军~ war between two armies

征 (zhēng) ❶sign ❷proof ❸go a long way to fight ❹go on an expedition ❺recruit; draft ❻levy; collect ❼ask for; solicit
【征兵】recruit; draft
【征程】journey
【征服】conquer
【征稿】solicit contributions
【征婚】❶spouse-seeking ❷seek a spouse
【征集】collect; draft; recruit
【征聘】invite applications for a job
【征求】ask for; solicit; seek
【征收】levy; collect; impose
【征途】expedition; journey
【征文】solicit articles
【征象】sign; symptom; indication
【征询意见】call for (or solicit) comments (or opinion)
【征引】quote; cite
【征用】take over for use; requisition; commandeer
【征战】go on an expedition (or a campaign)
【征兆】sign; omen; portent

挣 (zhēng) struggle to get free; try to throw off
另见 1312 页 zhèng
【挣扎】struggle

睁 (zhēng) open the eyes
【睁着眼睛说瞎话】tell a plain lie
【睁只眼,闭只眼】wink at; pretend not to see; turn a blind eye to

蒸 (zhēng) ❶evaporate ❷steam
【蒸发】evaporate
【蒸饺】steamed dumpling
【蒸笼】food steamer
【蒸气】vapor
【蒸汽机】steam engine
【蒸腾】rising
【蒸蒸日上】❶thriving ❷thrive with each passing day

拯 (zhěng) save; rescue; deliver

【拯救】save; rescue

整 (zhěng) ❶put in order ❷cause to suffer; punish ❸do; make ❹whole; complete; entire: 八点～ eight o'clock sharp ❺tidy; neat

【整队】get (or bring) the ranks into orderly alignment; line up

【整顿】put in good order; reorganize; rectify; consolidate

【整改】rectify and reform

【整个】whole; entire

【整合】❶integrate ❷integration

【整洁】clean and tidy; neat

【整理】sort out; arrange; put in order

【整齐】❶tidy; neat; even ❷in good order

【整容】face-lifting

【整体】whole; entirely

【整体实力】overall strength

【整天】all day long

【整形】❶ impair and restore deformed body ❷reshaping; shaping; plastic

【整修】rebuild; renovate; repair

【整治】❶get in good order (or condition) ❷make sb. suffer; fix sb.

【整装待发】get (or be) ready to set out

正 (zhèng) ❶set right; correct ❷main ❸straight; upright ❹sharp: 九点～ nine o'clock sharp ❺right ❻honest; ❼ pure ❽chief ❽regular ❾just

【正版】original (or copyrighted) edition

【正本】❶original ❷reserved copy

【正比】direct proportion

【正常】normal; regular: 恢复～ return to the normal

【正大光明】upright; open and aboveboard

【正当】(zhèng dāng) just when; just the time for

【正当】(zhèng dàng) proper; rightful

【正当理由】good cause

【正当权益】rightful (or lawful) interests

【正当要求】just demand

【正道】❶right way; correct path ❷correct principle; correct way

【正点】on time (or schedule); punctually

【正反】positive and negative

【正规】regular; standard

【正规学校】former (or accredited) school

【正轨】the right path

【正好】❶just in time ❷as it happens ❸ happen to; chance to

【正路】right way (or course); correct path

【正门】front door

【正面】❶front ❷the right side ❸frontal ❹positive ❺directly

【正面引导】positive guidance

【正南】due south

【正能量】positive energy

【正牌货】brand name goods (or commodity)

【正品】quality products; quality goods

【正气】healthy atmosphere

【正巧】❶happen (or chance) to ❷as it happens; just in time; at the right time

【正确】correct; right

【正如】just (or exactly) as

【正式】formal; official

【正式文件】authentic document

【正事】one's proper business

【正视】face; face up to

【正题】subject

【正厅】main hall

【正统】orthodox

【正文】text

【正义感】sense of justice

【正在】in process of; in course of

【正直】honest; upright

【正中下怀】be just what one hopes for

【正宗】❶orthodox school ❷genuine

证 (zhèng) ❶proof; evidence ❷certificate: 身份～ identification card (ID Card) ❸prove

【证词】testimony

【证婚】witness a wedding

【证件】papers; certificate; credentials

【证据】proof; evidence; testimony

【证据不足】lacking in evidence

【证明】❶ prove; testify; certify ❷ certificate; identification; testimonial

【证券交易】securities exchange

【证券投资】securities (or portfolio) investment

【证人】witness

【证实】affirm; confirm; verify

【证书】certificate; credential

【证物】exhibit

【证言】testimony

政 (zhèng) ❶ politics; political affairs ❷administration ❸affairs

【政策】policy

【政策扶持】policy-supporting

【政党】political party

【政法机关】judicial affair organs

【政风】work style of the government

【政府】government

【政府补贴】❶government subsidy ❷subsidized by the government

【政府职能】function of the government

【政府资助】❶government funding ❷subsidized by the government

【政改】reform of political structure

【政绩】achievement by an official; achievements in one's official career

【政见】political view (or opinion)

【政界】political circles

【政局】political scene (or situation)

【政论】political comment

【政企分开】separate the functions of the government from that of the enterprise

【政权】state power

【政务公开】open government affairs to the public

【政协】the Chinese People's Political Consultative Conference

【政治】politics

【政治经济学】political economy

【政治局面】political situation

【政治前途】political prospects

【政治素质】political quality (or caliber)

【政治稳定】political stability

挣 (zhèng) ❶struggle to get free; try to throw off ❷earn; make
另见 1310 页 zhēng

【挣钱】earn money

症 (zhèng) illness; disease

【症状】symptom

zhi

之 (zhī)

【之后】after that; later; afterwards; after

【之间】between; among

【之内】in; within

【之上】on; above; over

【之外】besides; beyond; except

【之下】under

【之中】in; during; among; in the middle of

支 (zhī) ❶ branch ❷ prop ❸ support; bear; back ❹ send away; put off ❺ pay; draw money

【支边】❶go to work in the border region ❷support the border area

【支撑】support; prop up

【支持】❶ support; back up; stand by ❷ keep up; hold out

【支出】❶pay ❷payment; expenses

Z

【支点】❶fulcrum;pivot about which a lever turns ❷strongpoint;fortified point;stronghold
【支队】detachment
【支付】pay
【支付能力】paying ability; payment capacity
【支架】stand;prop;support
【支教】go to support education in backward area
【支流】❶ tributary; affluent ❷ minor aspects;nonessentials
【支农】❶support agriculture ❷go to help in farm work
【支配】❶ arrange; allocate; budget ❷ control;determine
【支票】check; cheque: 空白～ blank check;空头～ rubber check;开～write (or draw) a check
【支取】draw
【支援灾区】support the disaster-hit area
【支柱】prop;post
【支柱产业】pillar (or mainstay) industry

只 (zhī) single
另见 1315 页 zhǐ

【只身】alone;by oneself
【只言片语】a word or two

汁 (zhī) juice

枝 (zhī) branch;twig

【枝节】❶side issue ❷minor matters
【枝条】branch;twig
【枝叶】❶branches and leaves ❷nonessentials;minor details

知 (zhī) ❶ knowledge ❷ know; be aware of

【知道】know;be aware of
【知底】know the inside story; know the background;be in the know
【知己】bosom friend
【知觉】consciousness:恢复～recover consciousness; come to; 失去～lose consciousness
【知名】well-known;noted;famous
【知名度】degree of popularity (or publicity)
【知名企业】well-known (or famous) enterprise
【知名商标】 well-known (or famous) trademark
【知难而进】press forward in face of difficulties
【知情】be in the know
【知情权】right to be informed;right to information
【知趣】be sensible; know how to behave oneself
【知人知面不知心】know a person's face but not his heart
【知识】knowledge
【知识产权】intellectual property rights
【知识更新】upgrade (or renew) knowledge
【知识结构】structure of knowledge
【知识经济】knowledge economy
【知识面广】have a broad spectrum of knowledge
【知悉】know;be aware of;understand
【知晓】know;understand;be aware of
【知心朋友】intimate friend;bosom friend
【知音】bosom friend
【知足】be content with one's lot

肢 (zhī)limb

【肢体】❶limbs ❷limbs and trunk

织 (zhī) ❶weave ❷knit

【织补】darning;invisible mending

【织布】weaving cotton cloth;weaving

【织毛衣】knit a sweater

脂 (zhī)

【脂肪】fat

蜘 (zhī)

【蜘蛛】spider

【蜘蛛网】spider web

执 (zhí) ❶take charge of ❷hold ❸carry out ❹stick to

【执笔】write;do the actual writing

【执导】be a director;direct

【执法】enforce the law

【执法部门】law-enforcing department

【执法力度】law-enforcement efforts

【执法人员】law enforcer (or executor); law-enforcing personnel

【执迷不悟】refuse to come to one's senses

【执勤】be on duty

【执行】carry out;perform;implement

【执业律师】certified lawyer

【执意】be bent on

【执掌】be in control of;be in charge of

【执照】license;permit

【执着】persistent; persevering; inflexible; rigid;work unflaggingly

直 (zhí) ❶ straighten ❷ frank; outspoken ❸ straight ❹ honest; upright ❺ directly ❻continuously

【直播】live broadcast

【直尺】straightedge

【直达】nonstop;through

【直达航班】direct (or straight, nonstop) flight

【直到】until;up to

【直飞】❶fly direct (or straight) ❷direct (or straight, non-stop) flight

【直观】direct perception

【直角】right angle

【直接】direct;immediate

【直接责任】direct responsibility

【直截了当】direct; straightforward; point-blank

【直径】diameter

【直觉】intuition

【直升机】helicopter

【直抒己见】be plainspoken; state one's views frankly;speak one's mind frankly

【直属】directly under; directly subordinate to;affiliated to

【直率】frank;straightforward

【直爽】straightforward;forthright

【直辖市】municipality directly under the central government

【直线】❶straight line ❷steep;sharp

【直性子】 straightforward; forthright; downright

【直言不讳】speak without reservation (or fear);speak one's mind fearlessly

侄 (zhí) nephew

【侄女】niece

【侄子】nephew

值 (zhí) ❶value ❷be worth:不~一提 be not worth mentioning ❸ happen (or chance) to ❹be on duty

【值班】be on duty

【值得】be worthy of; be worth; deserve; merit

【值钱】valuable; costly: 不~ worthless; valueless

【值勤】be on duty

【值日】be on duty;be on duty for the day

职 (zhí) ❶duty ❷office;post

【职称】the title of a technical or profes-

sional post
【职称评定】professional title appraisal
【职工素质】quality (or caliber) of employees (or personnel)
【职能转换】transformation of function
【职前培训】pre-job training
【职权】power; authority
【职权范围】scope of power and function
【职守】duty; post: 忠于~ be faithful on doing one's duties; 擅离~ be away without leave
【职位】position
【职务津贴】post-related allowance
【职业】trade; occupation; profession; vocation
【职业病】occupational disease
【职业道德】professional ethics
【职业技能】job skill
【职业培训】professional (or job, vocational) training
【职业选择】job selection
【职业演员】professional actor (or actress)
【职业指导】career (or job) guidance
【职业资格证书】job qualification certificate
【职员】office worker; staff member; clerk
【职责】duty; responsibility

植 (zhí) plant; grow

【植被】vegetation
【植树】❶plant trees ❷tree planting
【植树节】National Treeplanting Day
【植树造林】❶afforestation; tree planting ❷afforest
【植物】plant
【植物人】(human) vegetable

殖 (zhí) breed; multiply

【殖民】establish a colony; colonize

止 (zhǐ) ❶stop; cease; discontinue ❷only ❸to ❹till

【止境】end; limit
【止咳】relieve a cough
【止渴】quench one's thirst
【止痛药】painkiller
【止血】stop bleeding
【止痒】relieve itching
【止住】stop; halt

只 (zhǐ) only; merely; just
另见 1313 页 zhī

【只得】have to; cannot but
【只顾】❶be absorbed in; fix one's mind on ❷care only for ❸only; merely; simply
【只好】have to; be forced to
【只怕】be afraid of
【只是】❶only; merely ❷simply ❸but; however
【只要】so long as; if only; provided

旨 (zhǐ) ❶purpose; aim ❷decree

【旨意】decree; order

纸 (zhǐ) paper

【纸板】paperboard
【纸包不住火】paper cannot wrap fire in; truth will out
【纸币】note; paper money; banknote
【纸巾】tissue; tissue paper; napkin
【纸尿布】paper diaper
【纸扇】paper fan
【纸上谈兵】fight only on paper
【纸条】❶slip of paper ❷note
【纸烟】cigarette

指 (zhǐ) ❶finger ❷point to (or at) ❸indicate; point out; refer to

【指标】target; quota; index

【指出】point out
【指导】❶guidance ❷guide; direct
【指点】show how; give directions; guide
【指定】appoint; assign
【指定教材】appointed textbook
【指挥】❶command; direct; conduct ❷commander; director
【指挥官】commander
【指挥中心】command centre
【指甲】nail
【指甲刀】nail clippers
【指教】❶give directions or guidance; instruct; teach; indoctrinate; coach ❷used to ask sb. to give advice or comments
【指路】show the way (to)
【指路牌】signpost; fingerpost
【指明】show clearly; point out
【指南】guide; guidebook
【指派】appoint; name
【指使】instigate
【指示】❶point out ❷instruct ❸instruction; directive
【指手画脚】❶make gestures ❷make rash remarks
【指望】❶look to; count on; look forward to ❷hope
【指纹】fingerprint
【指引】guide; show the way; lead; direct
【指责】censure; criticize
【指正】❶point out the mistakes ❷used to invite sb. to make comments or critical remarks

咫 (zhǐ)

【咫尺】very close: 近在～ close at hand

趾 (zhǐ) toe; foot

【趾高气扬】strut in a cocky way

Z

至 (zhì) ❶extremely; most ❷to ❸till; until

【至诚】❶complete sincerity ❷sincere; straight forward
【至此】❶here and now; at this point; up to here; hereto ❷unto; thus far ❸until now; up to this time; be now
【至关紧要】of utmost importance
【至今】up to now; so far
【至理名言】maxim; golden saying
【至上】supreme; the highest
【至少】at least
【至于】❶go as far as to ❷as for (or to)

志 (zhì) ❶will ❷records ❸sign; mark ❹keep in mind

【志气】aspiration; ambition: 有～ have high aspirations
【志趣】bent; aspiration and interest; inclination
【志同道合】have a common goal; cherish the same ideals
【志向】ideal: 远大的～ lofty ideals
【志愿】❶ideal ❷do sth. of one's own will; volunteer

制 (zhì) ❶system ❷make; manufacture ❸work out ❹control; restrict

【制裁】punish; sanction
【制订】work out
【制度创新】system (or institutional) innovation
【制服】❶bring under control; conquer ❷uniform
【制剂】preparation
【制冷】❶refrigerate ❷refrigeration
【制片人】producer; film producer
【制约】restrict
【制约因素】restraining factor
【制造假象】put up a false front
【制止】check; stop; prevent
【制造商】manufacturer
【制作】manufacture; produce; make

质 (zhì) ❶nature ❷quality ❸matter ❹ simple; plain ❺question

【质变】qualitative change

【质量】quality: 检查~ test quality

【质量管理】quality control (or management)

【质量监督】quality supervision (or monitoring)

【质量认证】quality authentication

【质朴】simple; plain; unaffected

【质问】question

【质疑】raise a doubt about; query; call in question

【质优价廉】high quality but low price

治 (zhì) ❶ manage; govern; rule ❷ treat; cure ❸ wipe out; control ❹punish

【治安】peace; public security

【治病救人】cure the sickness to save the patient

【治国】run a country; manage state affairs

【治理】❶bring under control ❷govern; rule

【治理污染】curb (or abate) pollution

【治疗】treat; cure; heal

【治水】❶flood control ❷regulate rivers; dredge a watercourse to prevent floods

【治学】pursue one's studies: ~严谨 be a rigorous scholar; seek precision in one's studies

挚 (zhì) sincere; earnest

【挚诚】sincere; earnest

【挚友】intimate (or bosom) friend

致 (zhì) ❶ send; extend; deliver ❷ devote ❸cause; result in; bring upon

【致癌物】carcinogen; cancer-producing substance

【致富】become rich

【致敬】salute; pay one's respects to

【致力】devote oneself to; give one's mind to

【致使】cause; result in

【致意】give one's regards; greet: 点头~ nod a greeting; 挥手~ wave a greeting

秩 (zhì) ❶order; rank ❷decade

【秩序】order: 维持~ keep order

【秩序井然】in good order

痔 (zhì) haemorrhoids; piles

【痔疮】haemorrhoids; piles

窒 (zhì) stop up; obstruct; block

【窒息】stifle; suffocate

智 (zhì) wisdom; wit

【智多星】mastermind

【智慧】wisdom

【智力】intelligence

【智力发展】intellectual development

【智力竞赛】quiz show (or program)

【智力开发】❶intellectual development ❷ tap intellectual resources

【智谋】wisdom; resourcefulness

【智能】intelligence; aptitude; brainpower; capacity

【智取】take by strategy

【智商】intelligence quotient (IQ)

【智勇双全】be both brave and resourceful

【智障儿童】mentally retarded child

滞 (zhì) stagnant; sluggish

【滞后】lag (or fall) behind

【滞纳金】fine for delayed payment; overdue-payment fine

置 (zhì) ❶ buy ❷ place; put ❸ set up; establish

【置办】buy；purchase
【置换】displacement
【置身】place oneself；place oneself in；stay
【置业】❶house (or property) purchasing ❷purchase a house；purchase property
【置疑】doubt
【置之度外】give no thought to

稚 (zhì) young；childish
【稚嫩】❶young and tender ❷immature
【稚气】childishness

zhong

中 (zhōng) ❶center；middle ❷China ❸ medium ❹ mean；moderate ❺ in；among；during

另见 1320 页 zhòng

【中巴】minibus；van；medium-sized bus
【中部崛起】the rise of central China
【中餐】Chinese food
【中草药】Chinese herbal medicine
【中场休息】half-time break (or interval)
【中档】of middling quality or price
【中等】❶ secondary ❷ medium；moderate；middling
【中低收入阶层】people with low and medium income
【中断】suspend；break off；be (or put...) on hold
【中共中央】the Central Committee of the Communist Party of China
【中国】China
【中国工程院】China Engineering Academy (CEA)
【中国共产党】the Communist Party of China
【中国国情】China's actual conditions
【中国结】Chinese knot (or knotting)
【中国科学院】Chinese Academy of Sciences (CAS)
【中国人】Chinese
【中国人民解放军】the Chinese People's Liberation Army
【中国特色社会主义】socialism with Chinese characteristics
【中华】China
【中级】intermediate
【中纪委】Central Commission for Discipline Inspection of the CPC
【中间】❶ among；between ❷ middle；central
【中间人】middleman；go-between
【中介】intermediary；intermediary agent
【中介服务】intermediate service
【中看】be pleasant to the eye
【中考】entrance examination for senior middle and specialized secondary school
【中老年人】middle-aged and old people
【中立】neutrality：保持～ remain neutral
【中流砥柱】firm rock in midstream；main stay
【中年人】middle-aged person
【中期】mid-term；medium-term
【中式】Chinese style
【中式快餐】Chinese fast food
【中听】be pleasant to the ear；agreeable
【中途】halfway；midway
【中外】❶China and foreign countries ❷ Chinese and foreign ❸at home and abroad
【中外合资企业】Chinese-foreign joint venture
【中文】Chinese；the Chinese language
【中文字幕】Chinese subtitle (or caption)
【中午】noon；midday
【中小企业】small-and-medium sized enterprises (SME)
【中心】center：商业～ business center

【中心思想】central idea
【中型】medium-sized;middle-sized
【中性】neutral
【中性打扮】unisex look
【中学】middle school
【中学毕业证书】senior middle school diploma
【中学校长】principal
【中央】❶center;middle ❷central authorities
【中央处理器】central processing unit (CPU)
【中央军委】the Central Military Commission
【中央空调】central air-conditioning
【中央人民政府】Central People's Government
【中央委员】member of the central committee
【中央银行】central bank
【中药】traditional Chinese medicine
【中医】❶traditional Chinese medical science ❷doctor of Chinese medicine
【中医学院】college of traditional Chinese medicine
【中用】be of use;be useful
【中游】middle reaches (of a river)
【中原】Central Plains
【中正】equity;impartiality;justice
【中止】suspend;break off;discontinue
【中指】middle finger;medius;long finger
【中转站】transfer (or relay) station
【中子】neutron

忠 (zhōng) loyal; faithful; devoted; honest
【忠诚】loyal;faithful
【忠告】❶sincerely advise ❷sincere advice
【忠厚】honest and tolerant; honest and sincere
【忠实】true;faithful;honest;devoted
【忠心耿耿】most faithful and true; loyal and devoted
【治本】effect a permanent cure
【忠言逆耳】good advice jars on the ear
【忠于职守】be devoted to one's duty
【忠贞不渝】be loyal forever

终 (zhōng) ❶death ❷end;finish ❸all; whole;entire ❹after all;in the end
【终点】❶terminal point ❷finish
【终端用户】end user
【终归】in the end;after all;finally:~无效 eventually prove useless
【终极】final; ultimate: ~目的 ultimate aim
【终结】end;conclusion;final stage
【终究】in the end;after all;finally
【终年】❶all the year round ❷the age at which one dies
【终身】❶lifelong ❷all one's life
【终身伴侣】lifelong companion
【终身保修】lifelong guaranteed service
【终身大事】a great event in one's life (usu. referring to marriage)
【终身学习】lifelong learning
【终审】❶last instance;final judgement:~判决 final judgement ❷final censoring
【终生】throughout one's life;all one's life
【终于】at last;in the end;finally
【终止】stop;end;terminate

钟 (zhōng) ❶clock:挂~ wall clock ❷bell:撞~ ring a bell ❸hour;time
【钟爱】dote on;cherish
【钟表】timepiece;clocks and watches
【钟点工】❶hourly-paid work ❷hourly worker
【钟情】fall in love with;be deeply in love

衷 (zhōng) inner feelings;heart
【衷肠】words from one's heart: 倾吐~

pour out one's feelings

【衷心】heartfelt; wholehearted

肿 (zhǒng) ❶swell ❷swelling ❸swollen

【肿瘤】tumor

【肿胀】swelling; tumescence

种 (zhǒng) ❶seed ❷kind; sort; type ❸race ❹species ❺bravery

另见 1320 页 zhòng

【种类】kind; sort; type

【种子】seed

【种族】race

【种族平等】racial equality

中 (zhòng) ❶hit: 击~要害 hit home ❷suffer

另见 1318 页 zhōng

【中标】win a bid

【中彩】win a prize in lottery; win the lot

【中毒】be poisoned

【中计】be trapped; fall into a trap

【中奖】win a prize in lottery; win the lot

【中奖号码】winning (or prizewinning) number

【中奖者】lottery (or lot) winner

【中暑】❶ suffer sunstroke ❷ sunstroke; heatstroke

【中选】be chosen (or elected)

【中意】be to one's liking; catch one's fancy

仲 (zhòng) ❶ the second mouth of a season ❷the second among brothers ❸middle; intermediate

【仲裁】❶arbitration ❷arbitrate

众 (zhòng) ❶ crowd; masses ❷ many; much

【众多】❶numerous ❷in large quantities (or numbers)

【众口难调】hard to cater to all tastes

【众目睽睽】❶all the eyes of the masses are fixed on sb. ❷in the public eye (or gaze)

【众叛亲离】with the masses rising in revolt and associates deserting

【众人】everybody

【众矢之的】target of public criticism

【众说纷纭】opinions vary

【众所周知】as all know; as is known to all of people's expectations

【众望所归】enjoy popular confidence

【众志成城】unity of will makes a stronghold

种 (zhòng) grow; plant

另见 1320 页 zhǒng

【种花】grow flowers

【种植】grow; plant

【种庄稼】❶plant crops ❷do farming

重 (zhòng) ❶weight: 净~ net weight; 毛~ gross weight ❷ stress; lay stress on; think highly of ❸ heavy; weighty ❹important ❺serious; deep ❻attach importance to

【重彩】strong colors (used in painting): 浓墨~(paint in) dark ink and rich colors

【重大】important; weighty; great; heavy

【重大决策】important policy-making

【重大事故】major accident

【重大突破】major breakthrough

【重大新闻】important news

【重担】heavy burden; difficult task

【重地】important location: 工程~ construction site

【重点】focal point; stress; emphasis

【重点保护】❶intensive protection ❷protect with intensive efforts

【重点大学】key university

【重点工程】major project

【重点中学】key (or major) middle school

【重负】heavy load; heavy burden
【重活】heavy work
【重工业】heavy industry
【重奖】❶big (or ample) award ❷give ample award
【重力】gravity; gravitational force
【重利】❶heavy interest; high rate of interest; usury ❷great profit; huge profit ❸ value material gains: ～轻义 put material gains above justice
【重量】weight
【重任】heavy responsibility; important task
【重视】value; lay stress on; think highly of
【重托】great trust
【重心】centre of gravity; centre of mass heart; core
【重型】heavy-duty; heavy: ～汽车 heavy vehicle
【重要】important; significant; major: ～问题 big issue; major problem
【重用】put sb. in an important position
【重责】❶ heavy responsibility: 身负～ bear heavy responsibilities ❷ severely reprimand or punish
【重症监护室】intensive care unit (or ICU)

zhou

周 (zhōu) ❶week ❷circle ❸thoughtful
【周边环境】peripheral (neighboring) environment
【周长】girth; circumference; perimeter
【周到】thoughtful; attentive: 服务～ offer good service
【周刊】weekly; weekly publication
【周六】Saturday
【周密】careful; thorough
【周末】weekend
【周年】anniversary
【周期】period; cycle
【周全】❶thorough; comprehensive ❷help sb. to reach his goal
【周围】❶ round; around; about ❷ surroundings
【周游】travel round; journey round
【周折】twists and turns; setbacks
【周转】possibility to meet the need

洲 (zhōu) continent
【洲际】intercontinental

粥 (zhōu) porridge; gruel
【粥少僧多】the gruel is meager and the monks are many; not enough to go round

轴 (zhóu) axle; shaft
【轴线】spool thread; spool cotton
【轴心】axis

肘 (zhǒu) elbow

咒 (zhòu) ❶incantation ❷curse; damn
【咒语】incantation

昼 (zhòu) daytime; daylight; day
【昼夜】❶round the clock ❷day and night

皱 (zhòu) ❶wrinkle; line ❷wrinkled
【皱眉头】frown; knit one's brows
【皱纹】wrinkles; lines
【皱褶】fold

骤 (zhòu) sudden; abrupt
【骤然】suddenly; abruptly

zhu

珠 (zhū) ❶pearl ❷bead

【珠宝】pearls and jewels;jewellery

【珠算】calculation with an abacus

【珠子】❶pearl ❷bead

株 (zhū) ❶ trunk of a tree; stem of a plant ❷individual plant

【株连】involve;get sb. into trouble

诸 (zhū) all;various

【诸多】a lot of;a good deal;lots of

【诸如此类】and the like;and so on;and so forth

【诸位】ladies and gentlemen

猪 (zhū) pig;swine:养~ raise pigs

【猪圈】pigsty;pigpen

【猪肉】pork

蛛 (zhū) spider

【蛛丝马迹】clue;trace

【蛛网】spider web;cobweb

竹 (zhú) bamboo

【竹编】bamboo basketry

【竹林】bamboo forest

【竹竿】bamboo pole

【竹器】bamboo ware; articles made of bamboo

【竹席】bamboo mat

逐 (zhú) ❶ pursue; chase ❷ expel; drive out

【逐步】step by step;progressively

【逐步取消】phase out;cancel by stages

【逐渐】gradually;bit by bit;by degrees

【逐年】year by year;year after year

【逐日】day by day;every day

【逐字逐句】word for word

烛 (zhú) candle

【烛光】candlelight

【烛花】snuff

【烛台】candlestick

主 (zhǔ) ❶ owner ❷ host; hostess ❸ master ❹ person (or party) concerned ❺God;Lord ❻stand for;uphold; advocate ❼main;major;chief

【主板】mainboard

【主办】sponsor;direct

【主办单位】sponsor;sponsoring (or host) unit

【主编】chief editor

【主菜单】main menu

【主场比赛】home match

【主唱】❶ be the leading singer ❷ leading singer

【主持】❶ uphold; stand for ❷ preside over;chair

【主持正义】uphold justice

【主厨】❶do the cooking ❷be the chief (or chief cook) ❸chef

【主创】be the chief writer

【主次】primary and secondary

【主打商品】flagship;major commodity

【主导】leading;guiding;dominating

【主动】initiative;active

【主妇】housewife;hostess

【主干】❶trunk ❷backbone;mainstay

【主干道】trunk road

【主顾】customer;client

【主管】❶ be in charge of; be responsible for ❷person in charge

【主航道】main waterway

【主见】one's own ideas; one's own judgment

【主角】leading role;lead:女~ leading lady

【主考】chief examiner
【主课】major subject; major course
【主力】main force; main strength of an army
【主力军】main force
【主流】main current (or trend; mainstream)
【主渠道】main (or major) channel
【主权】sovereignty; sovereign rights
【主人】❶owner ❷master ❸host; hostess
【主人公】leading character in a novel, etc.; hero; heroine; protagonist
【主人翁】❶master ❷hero; heroine
【主任】head; chief; director: 办公室～ office director
【主食】staple food; principal food
【主题】theme; subject
【主题歌】theme song
【主题音乐】theme music
【主体】❶main body (or part) ❷subject
【主体工程】main project; principal part of a project
【主席】chairman; president
【主心骨】❶one's own judgment (or idea); definite view ❷mainstay; backbone
【主修课】major course
【主旋律】main melody; theme
【主演】❶act the leading role; star ❷starred by
【主要】main; major; chief
【主要成分】main ingredient
【主页】home page
【主意】❶idea; plan ❷definite view
【主张】❶advocate; stand for; hold; maintain ❷position; stand; view
【主政】preside over government work

煮
(zhǔ) cook; boil

【煮饭】cook rice
【煮鸡蛋】boil eggs

嘱
(zhǔ) enjoin; advise; urge

【嘱咐】tell; enjoin; exhort
【嘱托】entrust

瞩
(zhǔ) gaze; look steadily

【瞩目】fix one's eyes upon; focus one's attention upon

助
(zhù) assist; help; aid

【助残】help (or aid) the handicapped (or disabled)
【助教】teaching assistant
【助理】assistant
【助人为乐】take pleasure (or delight) in helping others
【助手】assistant; aide; helper
【助学金】stipend; grant-in-aid
【助一臂之力】lend sb. a helping hand
【助长】encourage

住
(zhù) ❶live; stay ❷stop; cease

【住处】residence; dwelling place
【住读生】resident student
【住房】housing; lodgings
【住房制度改革】reform of housing system
【住户】household; resident
【住家】❶live; reside in ❷household; resident
【住手】stop; stay one's hand
【住宿】❶stay; put up ❷accommodation
【住所】residence; dwelling place
【住院部】inpatient department
【住宅】residence; house
【住址】address

贮
(zhù) store; save; lay aside

【贮藏】store up;lay in keep

【贮存】stock;store;keep in storage

注（zhù）❶ note ❷ add notes ❸ keep one's mind on ❹ pour ❺ record;register

【注册会计师】registered（or chartered）accountant;Certified Public Accountant（CPA）

【注册商标】registered trademark

【注解】❶explanatory note ❷add notes

【注入活力】inject vigor（or life）;invigorate

【注入资金】invest;inject money（or capital）;channel capital into

【注射】❶inject ❷injection

【注视】gaze at;look at attentively;watch

【注销】write off;cancel

【注意】pay attention to;take note of

【注意事项】matters（or points）for attention

驻（zhù）❶stop;stay ❷station

【驻港部队】PLA garrison in Hong Kong

【驻守】garrison;guard

【驻足】halt;stop;go no further

柱（zhù）post

【柱子】post;pillar

祝（zhù）express good wishes;wish

【祝词】speech of good wishes;congratulations

【祝福】blessing;benediction

【祝贺】congratulate

【祝酒】toast;drink a toast:致～辞 propose a toast;向来宾～ toast the guests

【祝寿】offer birthday congratulations

【祝愿】wish:谨致良好的～ with best wishes

著（zhù）❶ work;book ❷ write ❸ marked;outstanding

【著称】celebrated;famous

【著名】well-known;famous

【著者】author;writer

【著作权】copyright

【著作权保护法】copyright protection law

筑（zhù）build;construct

【筑巢引凤】❶ make a nest to attract phoenixes ❷create a good environment to attract investors

【筑路】construct a road

zhua

抓（zhuā）❶grab;seize ❷arrest;catch ❸attract ❹stress ❺be in charge of

【抓捕】catch;capture

【抓紧时机】seize the opportunity

【抓紧时间】make the best use of one's time

【抓紧】firmly grasp;pay close attention to

【抓拍】take a snapshot

【抓住机遇】seize（or take hole of）the opportunity

爪（zhuǎ）claw;talon;paw

【爪子】claw;paw

zhuan

专（zhuān）❶ keep one's mind on;be absorbed in;concentrate on ❷ monopolize ❸expert ❹special ❺specialized

【专长】special skill;specialized knowledge

【专车】special bus（or car,train）

【专程】special trip:～看望 make a special trip to visit sb.

【专访】exclusive interview

【专攻】specialize（or major）in

【专机】special (or private) plane
【专辑】album
【专家】expert;specialist
【专家组】specialist (or expert) group
【专刊】special issue;monograph
【专科】speciality; special field of study; specialized subject
【专科学校】college for professional training;training school
【专科医生】medical specialist
【专款】special fund;fund earmarked for a special purpose:教育～ education fund
【专利产品】patent product
【专利证书】letter (or certificate) of、patent
【专列】special train
【专卖店】❶ specialty shop ❷ franchise shop;exclusive shop
【专卖商品】monopolized commodities
【专门人才】specialized talent
【专区】prefecture
【专升本】upgrade (or promote) from a junior college to a university
【专题】special topic;special subject
【专题节目】feature program
【专题讨论】seminar
【专线】❶special railway line ❷special telephone line
【专线旅游】special route tour
【专项基金】special-purpose fund
【专项治理】wage a special-target campaign
【专心】be absorbed in;concentrate on
【专修】specialize (or major) in
【专业】❶branch of learning;field of study;major ❷profession
【专业服务】professional service
【专业化】❶ specialization ❷ specialized;professional
【专业技能】professional skill
【专业课】major subject;specialty course
【专业训练】specialized training
【专业知识】professional knowledge;specialized knowledge
【专一】single-minded;concentrated
【专用】special use;special purpose
【专用设备】special-purpose equipments (or facilities)
【专职教师】full-time teacher
【专制】autocratic
【专注】concentrate on;be absorbed in;devote one's mind to

砖 (zhuān) brick;tile:瓷～ ceramic tile

【砖厂】brick field
【砖头】fragment of a brick

转 (zhuǎn) ❶ turn; change; shift ❷ pass on
另见 1326 页 zhuàn

【转败为胜】turn failure (or defeat) into victory (or success)
【转变】change;transform
【转变观念】change (or transform) one's concept
【转达】pass on
【转发】❶transmit ❷republish ❸relay
【转告】pass sth. on (or to)
【转行】change one's occupation (or job)
【转换】change;transform
【转换方向】change direction
【转机】favourable turn of events; turn a corner
【转基因】❶transgene ❷transgenic
【转基因食物】genetically-modified food; GM food;transgenic food
【转嫁】shift;transfer
【转交】pass sth. on (or to)
【转借】❶lend a borrowed thing to someone else ❷lend one's personal certificate

Z

to sb. else

【转脸】❶turn one's face ❷in no time; in the twinkling of an eye

【转让】transfer

【转世】❶reincarnation ❷reincarnate

【转手】❶pass on ❷resell

【转售】resell

【转弯】make a turn

【转弯抹角】beat about the bush; speak in a roundabout way

【转危为安】pass (or get, go) through danger into safety

【转型】reshape; restructure; transform

【转学】transfer (or move) to another school

【转眼】in the twinkling of an eye; in a twinkle; in a moment

【转移】shift; change

【转移视线】divert one's attention

【转载】reprint

【转账】transfer account

【转折】turn

【转正】become a regular worker (or member); become a full worker (or member)

【转制】reshape; restructure; transform

传 (zhuàn) ❶ biography; life story ❷ story; novel

另见 933 页 chuán

【传记】biography; life story

转 (zhuàn) turn; revolve; rotate

另见 1325 页 zhuǎn

【转动】turn; revolve

【转圈】circle; go round and round

【转椅】revolving (or swivel) chair

【转悠】❶turn; move from side to side ❷ stroll; take a leisurely walk

赚 (zhuàn) ❶ profit; make a profit ❷earn

【赚钱】make (or earn) money; make a profit

撰 (zhuàn) write; compose

【撰述】❶write; compile: ~文章 write articles ❷book; work: ~甚多 have written many books

【撰写】write; compose: ~碑文 write an inscription for a tablet

zhuang

庄 (zhuāng) ❶village ❷manor ❸banker

【庄稼】crops: 种~ grow crops

【庄严】solemn; stately

【庄重】grave; solemn

桩 (zhuāng) stake; pile

装 (zhuāng) ❶clothing ❷stage make-up and costume ❸dress up; decorate ❹ pretend ❺ load; pack ❻ contain ❼ fix; install

【装扮】❶dress up ❷disguise

【装备】❶equip ❷equipment

【装裱】mount

【装船】shipment

【装点】decorate; dress; deck: ~门面 put on a facade; keep up appearances

【装糊涂】pretend not to know

【装潢公司】decorating company

【装货】❶load ❷loading

【装假】pretend; make believe

【装门面】put up a front; keep up appearances

【装模作样】put on an act

【装配】assemble

【装饰】❶decorate; ornament ❷decoration

【装饰艺术】art of decoration

【装蒜】 feign ignorance; pretend not

to know

【装卸】load and unload

【装修】fit up

【装运】shipment; loading

【装置】❶install ❷installation

壮 (zhuàng) ❶ strengthen ❷ strong ❸magnificent

【壮胆】boost one's courage; embolden; build up sb.'s courage

【壮观】❶grand ❷grand sight

【壮阔】vast; grand; magnificent: 波澜～ surging forward with grand momentum; unfolding on a magnificent scale ❷ great; grand: 规模～ grand in scale

【壮丽】magnificent; majestic

【壮实】robust; sturdy

【壮士】brave man; heroic man; hero; warrior

【壮志】lofty ideal; great ambition

状 (zhuàng) ❶shape; form; appearance ❷state; condition ❸certificate

【状态】condition; state

【状元】Number One Scholar

撞 (zhuàng) ❶strike; collide ❷run into; meet with ❸dash

【撞车】❶ collide ❷ conflict; clash ❸ conflicting

【撞击】strike; dash against

【撞墙】run up against a wall; be rebuffed

【撞线】breast the tape

zhui

追 (zhuī) ❶chase; run after ❷seek; go after ❸ look into; try to find out ❹recall

【追本溯源】trace to its source

【追捕】pursue and capture

【追查】investigate; look into; trace; find out

【追悼】mourn over one's death

【追赶】try to catch up; run after

【追怀】call to mind; recall; reminisce: ～往事 reminisce about the old days

【追悔】regret; repent

【追加】add to

【追究】look into; try to find out

【追究责任】find who is to blame

【追名逐利】seek fame and gain

【追求】seek; pursue

【追思】recall; reminisce: ～往事 recall the past

【追溯】trace back to

【追随】follow

【追尾】❶rear-end ❷rear-ending; tailgate

【追问】question closely

【追想】recall; reminisce

【追星族】star fan

【追寻】seek; search

【追忆】recall; call to mind

【追逐】seek; pursue

【追踪】trace; track; trail

【追踪调查】follow-up investigation

坠 (zhuì) ❶fall; drop ❷weigh down

【坠毁】crash

【坠落】fall; drop

【坠子】weight; plummet; pendant; eardrop

赘 (zhuì) superfluous; redundant

【赘述】give unnecessary details; say more than is needed

zhun

谆 (zhūn)

【谆谆】earnestly and tirelessly

准 (zhǔn) ❶ standard ❷ allow; permit ❸ exact; accurate ❹ certainly; defi-

nitely

【准备】❶plan;intend ❷get ready;prepare

【准考证】examination permit

【准妈妈】will-be mother;mother-to-be

【准确】precise;accurate;exact

【准生证】birth permit

【准时】❶punctual ❷on time

【准许】permit;allow

【准予】grant;approve;permit

【准则】standard

zhuo

拙 (zhuō) clumsy;awkward;dull

【拙劣】clumsy;inferior:文笔～ poor writing

捉 (zhuō) ❶ catch ❷ hold in hand;grasp

【捉襟见肘】have too many problems to tackle

【捉迷藏】❶ hide-and-seek ❷ play hide-and-seek

【捉拿】catch;arrest

【捉弄】tease;make fun of

桌 (zhuō) table

【桌布】table cover;tablecloth

【桌面】desktop

【桌子】table;desk

灼 (zhuó) ❶burn;scorch ❷bright;luminous

【灼见】profound view;penetrating insight:真知～ profound knowledge and penetrating insight

【灼热】scorching hot

茁 (zhuó) thriving

【茁壮】healthy and strong;sturdy

卓 (zhuó) ❶ tall and upright ❷ outstanding

【卓绝】extreme:艰苦～ extremely difficult;英勇～ extremely brave

【卓识】outstanding insight

【卓有成效】remarkably successful

【卓越】outstanding;brilliant

【卓著】outstanding

浊 (zhuó) ❶turbid muddy ❷deep and thick ❸chaotic;confused

【浊音】voiced sound;sound articulated by vibrating the vocal chords

酌 (zhuó) ❶pour out ❷drink ❸consider;weigh

【酌情】consider the circumstances

着 (zhuó) ❶ whereabouts ❷ wear ❸ send ❹touch;apply;bring into contact with

另见 1306 页 zhāo;zháo

【着笔】set pen to paper;begin to write or paint

【着陆】land;touch down

【着落】❶possible source ❷whereabouts

【着色】color;put color on

【着手】set about;begin;start

【着想】consider

【着眼点】starting point

【着意】❶give one's mind to;take pains;spare no pains;exert oneself ❷take seriously;mind

【着重】stress;emphasize

琢 (zhuó) chisel;carve

【琢磨】❶carve and polish ❷improve (literary works);polish;refine

zi

孜 (zī)

【孜孜以求】seek diligently

咨 (zī) consult;take counsel

【咨询】consult; seek advice from; take counsel
【咨询电话】inquiry telephone
【咨询费】consulting fee
【咨询热线】information hotline
【咨询台】information desk
【咨询中心】consultation centre

姿 (zī) ❶looks ❷gesture; posture

【姿容】looks; appearance: ～秀美 good-looking; pretty
【姿势】posture; carriage; gesture
【姿态】❶posture; carriage ❷attitude

资 (zī) ❶money; capital ❷gift ❸qualification ❹ subsidize; supply with money ❺provide; supply

【资本】capital
【资本家】capitalist
【资不抵债】be unable to pay debts with all assets
【资产】❶property ❷capital
【资产重组】assets reorganization
【资产管理】assets management
【资产管理公司】assets management company
【资产评估】assets appraisal
【资产运作】assets operation
【资格】qualification
【资格考试】qualification examination
【资格审查】qualification check
【资格证书】credentials
【资金】❶fund ❷capital
【资金到位】fully-funded
【资金流动】flow of funds (or capital, money)
【资金周转】turnover of capital
【资历】qualifications; seniority; record of service: ～浅 have little previous experience
【资料】data; material
【资信】credit
【资讯】data; information
【资源】resources: 人力～manpower resources
【资源保护】resources protection
【资源共享】resources sharing
【资源开发】development (or exploitation) of resources
【资源利用】resources use (or utility)
【资源配置】resources allocation (or distribution)
【资源再生】resources regeneration (or recovery)
【资质】quality (caliber)

滋 (zī) ❶ grow; multiply ❷ more ❸ spurt; burst

【滋补】nourish
【滋润】❶moist ❷moisten
【滋生】❶breed ❷create; cause
【滋味】taste; flavour
【滋养】❶nourish; supplying ❷nutriment: ～品 nutriment; nourishment; nourishing food ❸nutriment; nourishment
【滋长】develop; grow

子 (zǐ) ❶person ❷child; son

【子菜单】submenu
【子弹】bullet
【子弟】❶ younger generation; children; juniors: ～兵 army made up of the sons of the people; people's own army ❷ younger brothers, sons, nephews, etc.: 职工～ children of the workers and staff (of a factory, etc.)
【子公司】subsidiary
【子目录】subcatalogue
【子女】children
【子孙】children and grandchildren; de-

scendants

【子夜】midnight

仔 (zǐ)(of domestic animals of fowls) young

【仔细】❶careful ❷be careful; look out

姊 (zǐ) elder sister

【姊妹】elder and younger sister; sisters

紫 (zǐ) purple; violet

【紫丁香】lilac

【紫禁城】the Forbidden City

【紫荆花】bauhinia

自 (zì) ❶ self; oneself ❷ naturally ❸ from; since ❹since

【自爱】self-respect

【自拔】free oneself (from pain or evil-doing); extricate oneself

【自卑】feel oneself inferior (or humble); be self-abased: ~感 sense of inferiority; inferiority complex

【自便】as one pleases

【自不量力】have too high an opinion of one's ability

【自残】injure oneself; kill each other (in the same group); autotomy

【自惭形秽】be ashamed of oneself being inferior

【自测】❶self-test ❷test oneself

【自称】❶claim to be ❷self-styled

【自吹自擂】blow one's own trumpet

【自从】from; since

【自得】self-satisfied; contented; self-complacent

【自动】❶of one's own accord; voluntarily ❷automatic

【自动报警】automatic alarm; auto-alarm

【自动化】automation

【自动门】automatic door

【自动取款机】automatic teller machine (or ATM)

【自动售货机】vending machine; slot machine

【自费】❶ at one's own expense ❷ self-funded; self-financed; self-paid; self-funding; self-financing

【自费留学】study abroad at one's own expense

【自费生】self-funded (or self-financed) student

【自封】❶self-styled ❷call by oneself

【自负】❶be responsible for one's own action ❷have too high an opinion of oneself; think highly of oneself

【自负盈亏】responsibility for the profits and losses

【自告奋勇】volunteer; offer to undertake

【自古】since ancient times; since antiquity; from time immemorial

【自豪】be proud of; take pride in

【自己】oneself

【自给自足】❶ self-sufficient ❷ self-sufficiency

【自驾游】self-driving travel

【自救】save oneself; support oneself; provide for and help oneself: ~生产 support oneself by engaging in production

【自居】consider oneself to be; pose as

【自觉】conscious; aware

【自觉自愿】willingly; voluntarily

【自绝】alienate oneself

【自夸】crack oneself up; sing one's own praise

【自来水】running water; tap water

【自理】take care of sth. oneself

【自力更生】❶self-reliance ❷rely on oneself

【自立】stand on one's own feet; earn one's

own living

【自律】self-discipline

【自命不凡】have too high an opinion of oneself

【自谋出路】find one's own means of livelihood

【自欺欺人】deceive oneself as well as others

【自强不息】never relax one's effort to become stronger

【自然】❶ nature ❷ naturally; of course ❸natural

【自然保护区】natural reserve; natural preserve

【自然博物馆】museum of natural history

【自然规律】natural law

【自然灾害】natural calamities

【自如】freely;with great ease

【自杀】commit suicide;take one's own life

【自上而下】from top to bottom; from above to below

【自食其果】reap what one has sown

【自食其力】earn one's own living; live on one's own labor;earn one's own bread

【自始至终】from beginning (or start) to end (or finish)

【自首】❶(of a criminal) voluntarily surrender oneself;confess one's crime;give oneself up (to law) ❷make a political recantation;surrender to the enemy

【自私】selfish

【自讨苦吃】ask for trouble

【自卫】❶self-defense ❷defend oneself

【自问】❶ask oneself;examine oneself:反躬～ examine oneself; examine one's conscience ❷ reach a conclusion after weighing a matter

【自我】self;oneself

【自我保护意识】sense of self-protection

【自我发展】self-development

【自我激励】self-stimulating; self-encouraging

【自我教育】self-education

【自我批评】self-criticism

【自我完善】❶ self-perfection ❷ perfect oneself

【自习】study by oneself in free time

【自相矛盾】❶contradict oneself ❷inconsistent

【自新】turn over a new leaf; make a fresh start

【自信】be self-confident

【自行车】bicycle;bike

【自修】study by oneself; study on one's own

【自学】study independently; study on one's own;teach oneself

【自学成才】become talented through self-study

【自言自语】talk to oneself;think aloud

【自用】❶ obstinately holding to one's own views ❷for private use;personal

【自由】❶freedom;liberty ❷free

【自由贸易】free trade

【自由自在】free and at ease

【自圆其说】justify oneself; make one's words consistent

【自愿】❶voluntary ❷of one's own accord (or will)

【自在】free;unrestrained;comfortable;at ease

【自找】ask (look) for;court;invite

【自制】❶make by oneself ❷self-control ❷ dead-weight;dead load

【自主】act on one's own; decide for oneself

【自主经营】independent management

【自主权】right to independent decision-making

【自助餐】buffet

【自助餐厅】cafeteria; self-service restaurant

【自助游】self-service tour

【自传】autobiography

【自尊】 self-respect; self-esteem; proper pride

【自作聪明】think oneself clever

【自作主张】act on one's own

字 (zì) word; character

【字典】dictionary: 查～consult a dictionary; look up a word in a dictionary

【字画】calligraphy and painting

【字迹】handwriting; writing

【字句】words and expressions; writing

【字库】word bank

【字里行间】between the lines

【字谜】riddle about a word

【字面意思】literal meaning

【字母】letter

【字母表】alphabet

【字幕】captions

【字体】font; word style

【字条儿】note; brief note

【字义】meaning of a word: 解释～ interpret or explain the meaning of a word

恣 (zì) willful

【恣意】be willful

zong

宗 (zōng) ❶ ancestor ❷ clan ❸ sect; faction; school ❹ purpose; principal aim

【宗教】religion

【宗旨】aim; purpose

综 (zōng) sum up

【综观】make a comprehensive survey: ～全局 take a broad view of the whole situation

【综合】❶comprehensive ❷synthesize

【综合测试】integrated test (or testing)

【综合防治】comprehensive protection and control

【综合改革】overall (or comprehensive) reform

【综合国力】overall national strength

【综合经济效益】overall economic returns

【综合评价】overall (or general) evaluation

【综合素质】overall quality (or caliber)

【综合治理】overall (or comprehensive) control and improvement

【综述】❶ summarize; sum up ❷ summary survey

【综艺大观】variety show; vaudeville

【综艺节目】item (or program) of variety show (or vaudeville)

棕 (zōng) palm

【棕榈】palm

【棕毛】palm fibre

【棕色】brown

踪 (zōng) footprint; trace; track; trail: 跟～ follow the tracks of

【踪影】trace; sign

总 (zǒng) ❶put together; add up; sum up ❷chief ❸general; total; overall ❹ after all

【总部】headquarters

【总裁】chief executive

【总产值】gross output value

【总导演】director in chief

【总额】 total; total amount: 存款～ total deposits

【总而言之】in a word; in short (or brief);

all in all;to make a long story short
【总方针】general policy
【总公司】parent company;company headquarters
【总共】altogether;in all
【总和】sum;total
【总计】total;add up to;amount to
【总结】❶sum up;summarize ❷summary
【总结发言】summary speech
【总经理】general manger
【总括】sum up:~起来说 to sum up;to state succinctly
【总揽】take on everything
【总理】premier;prime minister
【总领事】consul general
【总评】overall appraisal;general comment
【总趋势】general trend
【总设计师】chief designer
【总数】sum;total
【总思路】overall guideline
【总算】at last;finally;on the whole
【总体】overall;total
【总体布局】general layout (or arrangement)
【总统】president
【总投资】total investment
【总则】general rules;general principles
【总账】general ledger;general account
【总之】in a word;in short (or brief)
【总值】total value
【总指挥】general director; commander in chief

纵 (zòng) ❶set free;release ❷let loose ❸from north to south
【纵步】❶stride;jump:~向前走去 stride forward ❷jump;bound
【纵横驰骋】(of an army) move about freely and quickly; sweep through the length and breadth of
【纵火】set fire to;set on fire
【纵酒】drink to excess
【纵览】look far and wide; scan:~四周 look all round
【纵目远望】look into the distance
【纵情】heartily;to one's heart's content; as much as one likes:~快乐 indulge in unbridled joy
【纵然】even if (or though)
【纵容】wink at;pretend to overlook
【纵使】even if;even though
【纵向】❶ vertical; longitudinal; lengthwise:~比较 vertical comparison ❷from north to south

ZOU

走 (zǒu) ❶ walk; go ❷ run; move ❸ leave;go away ❹visit;call on;pay a visit to ❺change
【走出低谷】get out of the trough (or valley)
【走出困境】get out of (or free oneself from) the dire straits (or tight corner)
【走出误区】get out (or get rid) of misconceptions
【走调】out of tune
【走动】❶walk about;stretch one's legs ❷ visit each other (or one another)
【走访】pay a visit to; have an interview with;call on (or at)
【走钢丝】walk on a tightrope
【走高】go up;rise
【走好】go on (or proceed) well
【走红】become popular;enjoy popularity; make a hit:凭借独一无二的嗓音,他迅速~。He made a hit with his incomparable voice.
【走火】❶discharge ❷overstate
【走廊】corridor;passage;passageway

【走路】❶walk; go on foot ❷leave; go away

【走马观花】look at flowers while riding a horse; gain a shallow understanding from a fleeting glance

【走马上任】take up office; go to one's post

【走南闯北】go north and south; go all over the country

【走俏】sell well; get to sell well; be in great demand

【走热】become popular

【走神儿】wander; be absent-minded

【走失】wander away; be lost

【走私】smuggle

【走私货】smuggled goods

【走投无路】have no way out; be hopeless

【走向世界】go to the world; join the trend of the world; get on the stage of the world

【走运】have good luck; be lucky

【走着瞧】wait and see

奏 (zòu) ❶play; perform; strike up ❷achieve

【奏效】prove effective; be successful; work

【奏乐】play music; strike up a tune

zu

租 (zū) ❶rent ❷hire; rent ❸let out; lease

【租借】rent; hire; lease; charter

【租金】rent; rental

【租用】rent; hire; take on lease

足 (zú) ❶foot; leg ❷enough

【足够】enough

【足迹】track; footmark; footprint

【足球】(英)football; (英)soccer

【足以】enough to

【足智多谋】be resourceful

卒 (zú) ❶soldier ❷finish; end ❸finally; at last ❹die

族 (zú) ❶clan ❷race ❸family ❹nationality

【族谱】family tree; genealogical tree

【族人】clansman; members of the same clan or family

诅 (zǔ)

【诅咒】curse; swear; wish sb. evil; imprecate

阻 (zǔ) block; hinder

【阻碍】block; hinder

【阻挡】stop; hinder

【阻截】stop; obstruct; bar the way

【阻拦】stop; bar the way

【阻力】resistance

【阻塞】block: 交通～ traffic jam

【阻止】prevent; hold back; stop

组 (zǔ) ❶group ❷group; organize; form

【组办】organize

【组成】form; make up

【组队】form (or organize) a team

【组稿】commission authors to write on given topics; contributions

【组合】❶make up; compose; constitute ❷association; solicit combination

【组建】organize; establish; set up

【组团】organize a delegation

【组织】❶organize; form ❷organization

【组织协调】organize and coordinate

【组装】put together; assemble; kludge

祖 (zǔ) ❶grandfather ❷ancestor ❸founder

【祖辈】ancestors; forefathers; ancestry

【祖传】handed down from one's ancestors

【祖父】grandfather
【祖国】one's country; homeland; motherland
【祖籍】original family home; ancestral home
【祖母】grandmother
【祖先】ancestry; ancestors; forbears; forefathers
【祖宗】ancestor
【祖祖辈辈】from generation to generation; for generations

zuan

钻 (zuān) ❶get into ❷drill; bore ❸dig into; make a deep study of
另见 1176 页 zuàn
【钻空子】take advantage of loopholes
【钻探】❶drill ❷drilling: ~机 drilling machine
【钻研】dig into; make a deep study; study intensively: 刻苦~ study hard; ~理论 dig into theories

纂 (zuǎn) compile; edit

钻 (zuàn) ❶drill ❷diamond
另见 1175 页 zuān
【钻戒】diamond ring
【钻石】diamond jewel
【钻台】drilling platform

zui

嘴 (zuǐ) mouth
【嘴巴】mouth: 打~ box one's ears; slap sb. in the face
【嘴馋】fond of good food
【嘴唇】lip
【嘴乖】clever and pleasant when speaking to elders
【嘴甜】pleasing in speech; honey-mouthed; honey-tongued
【嘴严】tight-lipped

最 (zuì) most
【最初】initial; first
【最大】greatest; biggest; maximum
【最低成本】minimum cost
【最低费用】minimum expense
【最低工资】minimum wage
【最低生活保障制度】system of ensuring minimum standard of living
【最低生活标准】minimum standard of living
【最低收入】minimum income
【最多】❶maximum ❷at most
【最高】the highest; summit
【最高法院】supreme court
【最好】❶first-class; best; first-rate ❷had better (or best)
【最后】❶final; last ❷finally; at last
【最佳方案】best plan
【最佳组合】best lineup
【最近】❶the nearest ❷of late; lately; recently; soon; in the near future
【最少】least; at the least; minimum
【最先】the first (or earliest)
【最新消息】the latest news
【最终】❶final ❷finally

罪 (zuì) ❶crime; guilt; sin: 无~ innocent; 有~guilty ❷fault; blame: 归~于人 put the blame on others ❸suffering; hardship; pain: 受~ suffer; have a bad time
【罪恶】crime; evil
【罪犯】criminal; offender
【罪过】fault; guilt; sin
【罪名】charge; accusation
【罪人】guilty person; sinner

【罪行】crime;guilt

【罪有应得】deserve the punishment

【罪证确凿】evidences of the crime are beyond doubt

醉（zuì）drunk;drunken

【醉汉】drunkard;drunken man

【醉人】❶intoxicate;make drunk ❷intoxicating; enchanting; fascinating: 春意～ enchanting springtime

【醉翁之意不在酒】the drinker's heart is not in the cup; have other things in mind

【醉心】be bent on

【醉意】signs or feeling of getting drunk

zun

尊（zūn）❶respect ❷senior

【尊称】❶ respectful address ❷ address sb. respectfully

【尊贵】honourable;respectable;respected

【尊敬】respect;honour

【尊师重教】respect teachers and attach importance to education

【尊严】dignity;honor

【尊长】seniors;elders:尊重～ respect the elders and betters

【尊重】respect;value;esteem

【尊重人才】respect talents

遵（zūn）abide by;observe;obey;keep

【遵从】obey;follow;defer to

【遵法守纪】observe discipline and the law

【遵守诺言】keep one's word; honour one's promise

【遵守时间】be on time;be punctual

【遵循】follow;adhere to

zuo

作（zuō）workshop
另见 1177 页 zuò

【作坊】workshop

昨（zuó）yesterday

【昨天】yesterday

左（zuǒ）❶left side ❷left ❸wrong ❹different;opposite

【左边】the left;left side;left-hand side

【左顾右盼】look here and there; glance right and left

【左击】left click

【左手】left hand

【左思右想】❶ turn sth. over in one's mind ❷think from different angles

【左右】❶ left and right ❷ about; or so; thereabouts ❸influence;control

【左右为难】be in a dilemma

佐（zuó）❶assistant ❷assist

【佐餐】be eaten（or go）with rice（or bread）: ～之佳品 go well with rice or bread

【佐证】evidence;proof

作（zuò）❶work ❷write ❸do;make ❹pretend ❺act as ❻regard（or take）...as
另见 1177 页 zuō

【作案】commit a crime (or an offense)

【作保】be sb.'s guarantor;vouch for

【作弊】cheat

【作答】answer;reply

【作对】❶set oneself against;oppose ❷in opposition of

【作恶多端】do all kinds of evil

【作法】way of doing things;method;practice

【作风】style;way;style of work

【作家】writer

【作家协会】the Writers' Union

【作假】❶falsify ❷cheat

【作茧自缚】get caught in a net of one's own spinning

【作乐】enjoy oneself;have a good time:寻欢～ seek pleasure and make merry

【作料】condiments;seasoning

【作呕】❶disgusting ❷feel sick

【作品】works

【作曲】compose;write music

【作势】assume a posture;attitudinize:装腔～ be pretentious;strike a posture

【作数】count;be valid

【作为】❶action ❷accomplish:无所～accomplish (or achieve) nothing ❸regard...as;take...as (or for);look on (or upon) as ❹as

【作文】❶write a composition ❷composition

【作息】work and rest

【作秀】show;do a show

【作业】homework;work

【作用】❶effect:副～side effect;起～ take effect ❷act on ❸action

【作者】writer;author

【作证】bear witness;give evidence

坐 (zuò) ❶sit;take a seat ❷ride;go by;take a bus (or taxi) ❸put;place

【坐标】coordinate

【坐待】sit back and wait:～胜利 sit and wait for victory

【坐等】sit back and wait

【坐垫】cushion

【坐井观天】look at the sky from the bottom of a well;have a very narrow view

【坐牢】be imprisoned;be in jail

【坐立不安】feel uneasy;be ill at ease

【坐落】be situated (or located) in

【坐失良机】let slip a golden chance

【坐卧不安】❶feel restless;be ill at ease ❷unable to sit or sleep at ease

【坐席】❶take one's seat at a banquet table;attend a banquet ❷seat

【坐享其成】sit idle and enjoy the fruits of others' work;reap where one has not sown

【坐以待毙】sit waiting for death (or one's doom)

【坐镇】assume personal command

座 (zuò) ❶seat;place ❷base;stand

【座次】seating arrangements;order of seats:～表 seating chart

【座上客】guest of honour

【座谈会】discussion;forum

【座位】seat;place

【座无虚席】all seats are occupied

【座右铭】motto;maxim

做 (zuò) ❶make;produce ❷do;engage in ❸write ❹be used as ❺be;become;act (or serve) as ❻cook

【做伴】keep sb. company

【做操】do exercises

【做到】achieve;manage to:说到～ be as good as one's words;abide by one's promise

【做法】way;method

【做饭】do the cooking;cook

【做工】❶work ❷workmanship

【做广告】advertise

【做鬼脸】make faces

【做假账】doctor (or salt) accounts

【做客】be a guest

【做买卖】do business;carry on trade:～的 businessman;trader;merchant

【做媒】be a matchmaker (or go-between)

【做梦】have (or dream) a dream; dream; daydream

【做人】❶behave (or conduct) oneself ❷be a good man

【做声】make a sound:别～! Keep quiet!

【做实事】do real deeds

【做事】❶work; do a deed; handle affairs ❷work; have a job

【做寿】celebrate the birthday

【做头发】do (or up) one's hair

【做戏】❶act ❷put on a show

【做学问】engage in scholarship; do research

【做文章】❶write a composition ❷make an issue of; make use of

【做义工】do voluntary work

【做贼心虚】have a guilty conscience like a thief; have sth. on one's conscience

【做主】❶decide ❷back up; support

新版国际音标发音表

	发 音	例 词
单元音	[iː]	tea three piece receive
	[ɪ]	six picture decide
	[e]	any lesson head bread
	[æ]	hand happy
	[ʌ]	bus come blood trouble
	[ɜː]	girl turn work learn
	[ə]	China today teacher doctor dollar
	[uː]	do food room blue
	[ʊ]	put look foot should
	[ɔː]	small autumn short warm four
	[ɒ]	hot watch
	[ɑː]	car garden class plant
双元音	[eɪ]	name play great rain they
	[aɪ]	bike night my
	[ɔɪ]	boy soil voice
	[əʊ]	go know boat
	[aʊ]	house flower
	[ɪə]	beer near here fierce idea
	[eə]	bear chair there care
	[ʊə]	tour poor sure
半元音	[w]	when window
	[j]	your yellow
舌侧音	[l]	long world